Contemporary Authors

# Contemporary Authors

A BIO-BIBLIOGRAPHICAL GUIDE TO
CURRENT AUTHORS AND THEIR WORKS

**ANN EVORY**

Editor

*volumes* **37-40**

first revision

GALE RESEARCH COMPANY • BOOK TOWER • DETROIT, MICHIGAN 48226

*CONTEMPORARY AUTHORS*

Published by
Gale Research Company, Book Tower, Detroit, Michigan 48226
*Each Year's Volumes Are Revised About Five Years Later*

Frederick G. Ruffner, *Publisher*          James M. Ethridge, *Editorial Director*

Christine Nasso, *General Editor, Contemporary Authors*

Ann Evory, *Editor, Revision Volumes*
Linda Metzger, *Associate Editor*
Peter M. Gareffa, Penelope S. Gordon, Victoria France Hutchinson,
Margaret Mazurkiewicz, Ed McKenna, Catherine Stadelman,
Deborah Straub, and Thomas Wiloch, *Assistant Editors*
Ellen Koral, *Editorial Assistant*

Michaeline Nowinski, *Production Manager*

# Preface

This volume represents a complete revision of bio-bibliographical material which originally appeared in *Contemporary Authors,* Volumes 37-40, published in 1973. The material is up-to-date, in most cases, through late 1978.

### Questions and Answers About Revised Volumes
### of
### *Contemporary Authors*

**How much change is undertaken when past volumes of *Contemporary Authors* are revised?** Every part of every sketch is changed, if necessary. Present production techniques provide for fast, economical typesetting of all material used in revised volumes, and no attempt is made to minimize changes.

About 80-85% of all sketches in revised volumes have one or more changes from the original volume. The nature and extent of the revisions can be seen by comparing the original listings for Julie Andrews, Adelle Davis, Paul Joseph Schrader, Erich von Daeniken, Gillian Paton Walsh, Don Widener, Kate Wilhelm, and Helen Yglesias with revised sketches in this volume.

**How are revised volumes prepared?** Clippings of previously published sketches are sent to authors at their last-known addresses. Authors mark material to be deleted or changed, and insert any new personal data, new affiliations, new books, new work in progress, new sidelights, and new biographical/critical sources. Gale makes great efforts to encourage responses from all authors, and has a toll-free telephone number so authors can conveniently reply by phone without personal expense.

**How do you revise previously published sketches if the authors do not return marked clippings?** First, every attempt is made to reach authors through previous home addresses, business affiliations, publishers, organizations, or other practicable means either by mail or telephone. When necessary, searches are made to determine whether the authors have died. A number of sources are checked for obituaries, including newspaper and magazine indexes.

If living authors fail to reply, or if authors are now deceased, work proceeds on verifying and updating the previously published information. Biographical dictionaries are checked (a task made easier through the use of Gale's *Biographical Dictionaries Master Index* and *Author Biographies Master Index*), as are bibliographical sources, such as *Cumulative Book Index, The National Union Catalog,* etc. In other words, all steps are taken which can reasonably be expected to confirm or invalidate previous information, or to provide additional information. Sketches not personally verified by the authors are marked as follows:

    † Research has yielded new information which has been added to the sketch
  † † Research has yielded no new information

**Do all sketches in a revised volume undergo some change?** No, they do not. In a sense, however, *all* sketches in a revised volume are "revised" sketches, in that the authors have examined them and indicated that the information they furnished for the previous edition is currently correct, or a revision editor has checked as many facts as possible and made the same determination. Obviously, previously published information which is verified as still accurate is just as helpful to the reference user as information newly added.

**How much revision takes place in an average volume?** It is difficult to measure. Revised Volumes 1-4, for example, showed a net increase of about 70 pages, and Revised Volumes 5-8 an increase of

200 pages. These increases represented only the *net* change in the number of pages, however; they did not measure the total amount of change, since things like new addresses do not affect sketch length, and deletions of memberships or transfers of items from "Work in Progress" to the bibliography of published works usually result in decreases in space used. Even when a substantial number of sketches were transferred from volumes 9-36 to the *Contemporary Authors—Permanent Series,* the resulting revised volumes were larger than the corresponding original volumes.

**What is the *Contemporary Authors—Permanent Series*?** The two *Permanent Series* volumes contain entries of deceased authors and authors past normal retirement age who were either known or presumed to be no longer actively writing. These sketches were removed from volumes 9-36 during the revision cycle. Because this practice had unsuspected disadvantages, the *Permanent Series* was discontinued with the publication of Volume 2. Now, all entries appearing in original volumes of *Contemporary Authors* remain in those volumes when they are revised. The *Permanent Series* volumes are, of course, an integral part of the entire *Contemporary Authors* series, and they will be kept in print along with all other volumes.

**Can any volumes of *Contemporary Authors* safely be discarded because they are obsolete?** Users who have all the revised volumes through 33-36 *and* the two *Permanent Series* volumes can discard the superseded volumes. Beginning with Volume 37-40, each original volume may be discarded after a corresponding revised volume is published.

**An unusual number of biographical publications have been appearing recently, and the question is now often asked whether a charge is made for listings in such publications. Do authors listed in *Contemporary Authors* make any payment or incur any other obligation for their listings?** Some publishers charge for listings or require purchase of a book by biographees. There is, however, absolutely no charge or obligation of any kind attached to being included in *CA*. Copies of the volumes in which their sketches appear are offered at courtesy discounts to persons listed, but less than five percent of the biographees purchase copies.

## Cumulative Index Should Always Be Consulted

Since *CA* is a multi-volume series which does not repeat author entries from volume to volume, the cumulative index published in alternate new volumes of *CA* will continue to be the user's guide to the location of an individual author's listing. Authors transferred to the *Contemporary Authors—Permanent Series* are indicated in the cumulative index as having appeared in specific original volumes of *CA* (for the benefit of those who do not hold *Permanent Series* volumes), *and* as having their finally revised sketches listed in a specific *Permanent Series* volume.

For the convenience of *CA* users, the *CA* cumulative index also includes references to all entries in two related Gale series—*Contemporary Literary Criticism,* which is devoted entirely to current criticism of major authors, poets, and playwrights, and *Something About the Author,* a series of heavily illustrated sketches on juvenile authors and illustrators.

As always, suggestions from users about any aspect of *CA* will be welcomed.

# CONTEMPORARY AUTHORS

† Research has yielded new information which has been added to the sketch, but the author has not personally verified the entry in this edition.

† † Research has yielded no new information, but the author has not personally verified the entry in this edition.

# A

**ABEL, Reuben 1911-**

*PERSONAL:* Born November 25, 1911, in New York, N.Y.; son of Louis and Dora (Friedsell) Abel; married Marion Buchman, July 30, 1937; children: Richard L., Elizabeth F. *Education:* Columbia University, A.B., 1929; New York University, J.D., 1934; New School for Social Research, M.S.Sc., 1941, Ph.D. (magna cum laude), 1952. *Home:* 17 Monroe Ave., Larchmont, N.Y. 10538. *Office:* Graduate Faculty of Political and Social Science, New School for Social Research, 66 West 12th St., New York, N.Y. 10011.

*CAREER:* New School for Social Research, New York, N.Y., lecturer, 1952-55, assistant professor, 1955-59, adjunct associate professor, 1959-67, adjunct professor of philosophy in Graduate Faculty, 1967—, chairman of Humanities Division, 1965—, associate dean of New School, 1972-74. *Member:* American Philosophical Association, Conference on Methods in Philosophy and the Sciences (secretary-treasurer, 1950-53; member of executive committee, 1953—; chairman, 1966-68), Philosophy of Science Association, International Association for Philosophy of Law and Social Philosophy, American Society for Aesthetics, American Arbitration Association, American Association of University Professors.

*WRITINGS: The Pragmatic Humanism of F.C.S. Schiller,* Columbia University Press, 1955; (editor and author of introduction) *Humanistic Pragmatism,* Macmillan, 1966; (author of foreword) Kenneth Winetrout, *F.C.S. Schiller and the Dimensions of Pragmatism,* Ohio State University Press, 1967; (contributor) Sidney Hook, editor, *Language and Philosophy,* New York University Press, 1969; (contributor) Ervin Pollock, editor, *Human Rights,* Jay Stewart, 1971; *Man Is the Measure: A Cordial Invitation to the Central Problems of Philosophy,* Free Press, 1976. Contributor to *Encyclopedia of Philosophy;* contributor of about twenty articles and reviews to *Saturday Review* and to philosophy journals.

\* \* \*

**ADAMS, Georgia Sachs 1913-**
**(Georgia Sachs)**

*PERSONAL:* Born May 23, 1913, in Ortonville, Minn.; daughter of John Frederick (owner of a boat line) and Ella (Merry) Wein; married Clair A. Sachs, July, 1933; married

second husband, Joseph John Adams, September 7, 1947; children: Margaret (Mrs. Lawrence Cross), Jo-Ann, Joe, Mary. *Education:* University of Southern California, A.B., 1933, M.S., 1935, Ph.D., 1941; postdoctoral study at University of Chicago, summer, 1941, and Claremont College (now Claremont Graduate School), 1951-52. *Home:* 2772 North Lake Ave., Altadena, Calif. 91001. *Office:* Department of Education, California State University, 5151 State College Dr., Los Angeles, Calif. 90032.

*CAREER:* Pasadena City Schools, Pasadena, Calif., research assistant, 1936-39, research director, 1939-51; Muir College, Pasadena, instructor in mathematics and English, 1951-52, 1953-54; California State University, Los Angeles, assistant professor, 1954-58, associate professor, 1958-62, professor of education, 1962—. Lecturer, Claremont Graduate School, 1953—; visiting professor, University of Hawaii, summer, 1959. *Member:* American Psychological Association (fellow), Pi Lambda Theta (national president, 1970-73).

*WRITINGS:* (Under name Georgia Sachs; with Guy V. Bennett) *Exploring the World of Work,* Society for Occupational Research, 1937; *Evaluation of Group Guidance Work in Secondary Schools,* University of Southern California Press, 1945; (with Theodore L. Torgerson) *Measurement and Evaluation for the Elementary-School Teacher,* Dryden, 1954; (with Torgerson) *Measurement and Evaluation for the Secondary-School Teacher,* Dryden 1956; *Measurement and Evaluation in Education, Psychology and Guidance,* Holt, 1964. Also author of numerous monographs and tests.

*WORK IN PROGRESS:* A revision of *Measurement and Evaluation in Education, Psychology and Guidance.*

\* \* \*

**ADAMSON, Ed(ward Joseph) 1915(?)-1972**

1915(?)—October 1, 1972; American film and television producer and writer of scripts for films, radio, and television. Obituaries: *New York Times,* October 3, 1972.

\* \* \*

**AGAR, William (Macdonough) 1894-1972**

February 14, 1894—June 10, 1972; American geologist, educator, United Nations official, and author of books on geology and other topics. Obituaries: *New York Times,* June 12, 1972; *Current Biography,* July, 1972.

## AGRANOFF, Robert 1936-

*PERSONAL:* Born May 25, 1936, in Minneapolis, Minn.; son of Phillip Paul and Rose (Stern) Agranoff; married Zola O. Besco, December 29, 1959; children: Karen. *Education:* Wisconsin State University, River Falls (now University of Wisconsin—River Falls), B.A., 1962; University of Pittsburgh, M.A., 1963, Ph.D., 1967. *Politics:* Democratic. *Home:* 1315 Stafford St., De Kalb, Ill. 60115. *Office:* Center for Governmental Studies, Northern Illinois University, De Kalb, Ill. 60115.

*CAREER:* Northern Illinois University, De Kalb, assistant professor, 1966-72, associate professor of political science, 1972—, coordinator of mental health and human services program, Center for Governmental Studies, 1972-77, director of Center for Governmental Studies, 1977—. Campaign director, Minnesota Democratic-Farmer-Labor Party, 1968-69. U.S. member, comparative study group on social planning and human resource administration, International Institute of Administrative Sciences. Consultant in public administration, mental health, and human services to numerous institutions and governmental boards, including Illinois Department of Mental Health, Institute of Politics and Government in Arkansas, and National Science Foundation. *Military service:* U.S. Navy, 1955-57. *Member:* American Political Science Association, American Association for Public Opinion Research, American Society for Public Administration (member of executive committee, 1974-77; chairperson of Section on Human Resources Administration, 1975-76), Association of Mental Health Administrators (chairperson of executive committee, 1973-75), Policy Studies Organization, Academy of Health Administration, Midwest Political Science Association (public relations director, 1972-74; membership chairperson, 1973-74). *Awards, honors:* Mellon fellow, University of Pittsburgh, 1962-64; Falk Foundation grant, 1963; National Science Foundation award, University of Michigan, 1965; National Institute of Mental Health award, 1973.

*WRITINGS:* (Contributor) P. Allen Dionisopoulis, editor, *Racism in America,* Northern Illinois University Press, 1971; (contributor) Ray Hiebert and others, editors, *The Political Image Merchants: Strategy in New Politics,* Acropolis, 1971; *The New Style in Election Campaigns,* Holbrook, 1972; (contributor) Thomas J. Mikulecky, editor, *Human Services Integration,* American Society for Public Administration, 1974; (editor with Arthur Dykstra, Jr.) *Mental Health Administration in Transition,* Association of Mental Health Administrators, 1975; (editor with Walter Fisher, Joseph Mehr, and Philip Truckenbrod, and contributor) *Explorations in Competency Module Development: Relinking Higher Education and the Human Services,* Center for Governmental Studies, Northern Illinois University, 1975; *The Management of Election Campaigns,* Holbrook, 1976; (editor) *Coping with the Demands for Change within Human Services Administration,* American Society for Public Administration, 1977; (contributor) H. George Frederickson and Charles Wise, editors, *Public Administration and Public Policy,* Heath, 1977.

Principle author of script and technical consultant for film, "Political Parties in America: Getting the People Together," Encyclopaedia Britannica Films, 1976. Contributor to professional journals, including *American Political Science Review, American Behavioral Scientist,* and *Policy Studies Journal.* Member of editorial advisory board, *Journal of Mental Health Administrators,* 1975—; advisory editor, *Human Services Policy and Administration,* 1976—. Editorial consultant to numerous professional journals.

*WORK IN PROGRESS:* A study on state departments of human resources for Health Resources Administration, U.S. Department of Health, Education, and Welfare; a study on the dimensions of human services integration.

*BIOGRAPHICAL/CRITICAL SOURCES: Campaign Insight,* March, 1972.

\*      \*      \*

## AGUILERA, Donna Conant

*PERSONAL:* Born in Kinmundy, Ill.; daughter of Charles E. and Daisy (Frost) Conant; married George L. Aguilera (a club manager), February 17, 1948; children: Bruce Allen, Craig Steven. *Education:* Gordon Keller School of Nursing, R.N., 1947; Los Angeles Valley College, A.A., 1960; University of California, Los Angeles, B.S., 1963, M.S., 1965; University of Southern California, Ph.D., 1974. *Politics:* Republican. *Religion:* Roman Catholic. *Home:* 3924 Dixie Canyon Ave., Sherman Oaks, Calif. 91423. *Office:* California State University, 5151 State University Dr., Los Angeles, Calif. 90032.

*CAREER:* California State University, Los Angeles, associate professor of psychiatric nursing, 1966—. Consultant to Benjamin Rush Centers, 1966—. *Member:* American Academy of Nursing (president, 1977-78), American Association of University Professors, University of California (Los Angeles) Alumnae Association.

*WRITINGS:* (With Janice Messick) *Psychiatric Nursing: Where? What? How?* (monograph), Stuart James, 1969; (with Messick) *Crisis Intervention: Theory and Methodology,* Mosby, 1970, 3rd edition, 1978; (with Mary Topalis) *Psychiatric Nursing,* Mosby, 1978; (with Messick) *Crisis: Paradigm of Intervention,* Mosby, in press. Contributor of about a dozen articles to psychiatric nursing journals. Member of editorial board, *Journal of Psychiatric Nursing and Mental Health Services,* 1972—.

*WORK IN PROGRESS:* Research on problem-solving abilities in college students and crisis intervention.

*AVOCATIONAL INTERESTS:* Travel.

\*      \*      \*

## AIDENOFF, Abraham 1913-1976

*PERSONAL:* Born June 14, 1913, in Cleveland, Ohio; son of Louis and Esther (Weiner) Aidenoff; married Layle Silbert (a free-lance editor), May, 1945. *Education:* University of Chicago, B.A., 1934; George Washington University, graduate study, 1948-49. *Home:* 17 West 82nd St., New York, N.Y. 10024. *Office:* United Nations, New York, N.Y. 10017.

*CAREER:* Public Assistance Agency, Chicago, Ill., casework supervisor, 1934-40; Illinois Division of Placement and Unemployment Compensation, Chicago, chief of research and statistics, 1940-46; United Nations Relief and Rehabilitation Administration, Shanghai, China, chief statistician, 1946-47; U.S. Bureau of the Census, Washington, D.C., chief economic statistician, 1947-49; Statistical Office of the United Nations, New York, N.Y., chief statistician for industrial and national accounts, 1949-63, deputy director, 1963-75, senior technical adviser, 1975-76. Chief statistician, Provost Marshal General's Office of the Army, 1943-44. Statistical consultant to governments of Burma, Thailand, Pakistan, Colombia, and Peru, 1949-57. *Military service:* U.S. Army, 1942-43. *Member:* American Economic Association, American Statistical Association (fellow), International Association for Research in Income and Wealth, Association for Research in Income and Wealth, American Academy of Political and Social Science, Econometric Society, Phi Beta Kappa.

*WRITINGS: Basic Statistics for the Use of Developing Countries in Economic and Social Development,* United Nations Publications, 1958; *The Growth of World Industry, 1938-61,* two volumes, United Nations Publications, 1965; (with Richard Stone) *A System of National Accounts,* United Nations Publications, 1968.

*WORK IN PROGRESS:* Formulation of a system of demographics and social statistics, a system of price and quantity statistics, and a system of environmental statistics.†

(Died January 9, 1976)

\*      \*      \*

## ALBAUM, Gerald (Sherwin) 1933-

*PERSONAL:* Born November 2, 1933, in Los Angeles, Calif.; son of Leslie and Edith (Elster) Albaum; married Carol Weinstein, October 10, 1954; children: Marc, Lisa, Daniel. *Education:* University of Washington, Seattle, B.A., 1954, M.B.A., 1958; University of Wisconsin, Ph.D., 1962. *Religion:* Jewish. *Home:* 554 Pinto Way, Eugene, Ore. 97401. *Office:* College of Business Administration, University of Oregon, Eugene, Ore. 97403.

*CAREER:* University of Wisconsin—Madison, instructor in marketing, 1960-62; University of Pittsburgh, Pittsburgh, Pa., assistant professor of marketing, 1962-64; University of Arizona, Tucson, associate professor of marketing, 1964-67; University of Massachusetts—Amherst, associate professor of marketing, 1967-69; University of Oregon, Eugene, associate professor, 1969-72, professor of marketing, 1972—. University of Hawaii, visiting associate professor of marketing, 1968-69, visiting professor of marketing, 1971; visiting professor of marketing, Arizona State University, 1976. *Military service:* U.S. Army, 1954-56. *Member:* American Marketing Association, American Institute for Decision Sciences, Academy of International Business, Association for Consumer Research.

*WRITINGS:* (Editor with J. H. Westing) *Modern Marketing Thought,* Macmillan, 1964, 3rd edition, 1975; *Price Formulation,* Division of Economics and Business Research, University of Arizona, 1965; (with F.L.W. Richardson) *Human Interaction and Sales Success,* Division of Economics and Business Research, University of Arizona, 1967; (with Gordon E. Miracle) *International Marketing Management,* Irwin, 1970; (editor with M. Venkatesan) *Scientific Marketing Research,* Free Press, 1971; (with Donald S. Tull) *Survey Research: A Decisional Approach,* Intext, 1973. Contributor of articles to marketing and management journals.

*WORK IN PROGRESS:* Studying research methodology; a book on measurement and scaling in research.

\*      \*      \*

## ALBERT, A(braham) Adrian 1905-1972

November 9, 1905—June 6, 1972; American mathematician, educator, editor, consultant to government and business, and author of books on higher mathematics. Obituaries: *New York Times,* June 7, 1972; *Washington Post,* June 8, 1972; *L'Express,* June 12-18, 1972.

\*      \*      \*

## ALDERFER, Clayton P. 1940-

*PERSONAL:* Born September 1, 1940, in Sellersville, Pa.;

son of J. Paul (a company manager) and Ruth (Buck) Alderfer; married Charleen Frankenfield (a nurse), July 14, 1962; children: Kate Elizabeth, Benjamin Paul. *Education:* Yale University, B.S. (with high honors), 1962, Ph.D., 1966. *Home:* Ann Dr., Bethany, Conn. 06525. *Office:* School of Organization and Management, Yale University, 56 Hillhouse Ave., New Haven, Conn. 06520.

*CAREER:* Cornell University, Graduate School of Business and Public Administration, Ithaca, N.Y., assistant professor of administration, 1966-68; Yale University, New Haven, Conn., assistant professor, 1968-70, associate professor of administrative sciences, 1970—. Lecturer at University of the West Indies, 1968, and Cornell University, 1968-71. *Member:* American Psychological Association (fellow), American Sociological Association, Society for Applied Anthropology, National Training Laboratories Institute for Applied Behavioral Science (adjunct fellow), International Association of Applied Social Scientists (charter member), Sigma Xi, Tau Beta Pi.

*WRITINGS: Existence, Relatedness, and Growth: Human Needs in Organizational Settings,* Free Press, 1972; (contributor) Harvey Hornstein and Warner Burke, editors, *The Social Technology of Organizational Development,* National Training Laboratories Learning Resources Inc., 1972; (with L. Dave Brown) *Learning from Changing: Organizational Diagnosis and Development,* Sage Publications, 1975; (contributor) M. D. Dunnette, editor, *Handbook of Industrial and Organizational Psychology,* Rand McNally, 1976. Contributor to psychology and behavioral science journals.

*WORK IN PROGRESS: Group Relations and Organizational Diagnosis; Intergroup Relations and Organizational Behavior.*

\*      \*      \*

## ALFORD, Norman (William) 1929-

*PERSONAL:* Born September 2, 1929, in Croydon, England; son of William James (a hotel clerk) and Alice E. (Wooding) Alford; married Mary Rose Symington (a teacher), May 16, 1967. *Education:* University of London, B.A. (honors), 1963; University of Texas, Ph.D., 1966. *Politics:* "Indefinite." *Religion:* "Indefinite." *Home:* 965 Trans-Canada Highway, Victoria, British Columbia, Canada. *Office:* Department of English, University of Victoria, Victoria, British Columbia, Canada.

*CAREER:* Teacher in England, Ceylon, and Southern Rhodesia, 1951-63; University of Victoria, Victoria, British Columbia, assistant professor of English, 1966—. *Military service:* British Army, gunner, 1947-49.

*WRITINGS: The Rhymers' Club,* Charles Skilton, 1973. Also author of a novel, *In Pursuit of Any Ass.* Contributor of short stories to literary journals, including *Malahat Review, Journal of Canadian Fiction, Nantucket Review,* and *Fiddlehead,* and to Canadian Broadcasting Corp. (CBC) Radio.

*WORK IN PROGRESS:* A biography of Mary Chavelita Golding Bright (George Egerton), for the Eighteen Nineties Society's "Makers of the 'Nineties" series; *Living and Partly Living,* a novel; short stories.

\*      \*      \*

## ALINSKY, Saul (David) 1909-1972

January 30, 1909—June 12, 1972; American social reformer and author of books on social activism. Obituaries: *New York Times,* June 12, 1972; *Washington Post,* June 14, 1972;

*Antiquarian Bookman,* June 26, 1972; *Newsweek,* June 26, 1972; *Time,* June 26, 1972; *Current Biography,* July, 1972.

\* \* \*

## ALISOV, Boris P. 1892-1972

1892—November 27, 1972; Russian scientist and author of books on climatology. Obituaries: *New York Times,* November 29, 1972.

\* \* \*

## ALLIS, Oswald T(hompson) 1880-1973

September 9, 1880—January 12, 1973; American theologian, Old Testament scholar, and editor. Obituaries: *New York Times,* January 13, 1973.

\* \* \*

## ALPHONSO-KARKALA, John B. 1923-

*PERSONAL:* Surname legally changed; born May 30, 1923, in South Kanara, Mysore State, India; son of Anthony (a teacher) and Theresa (Pinto) Alphonso; married Leena Anneli Hakalehto (an assistant professor of German), December 20, 1964; children: Siita Karoliina, Juho Krishna. *Education:* Bombay University, B.A. (honors), 1950, M.A., 1953; University of London, graduate study, 1954-55; Columbia University, Ph.D., 1964. *Politics:* Liberal. *Religion:* "Hindu/Buddhist/Christian (one-third each)." *Home:* 20 Millrock Rd., New Paltz, N.Y. 12561. *Office:* Department of Literature, State University of New York College, New Paltz, N.Y. 12561.

*CAREER:* State University of New York College at New Paltz, assistant professor, 1964-65, associate professor, 1965-68, professor of literature, 1969—. Visiting lecturer, City College of the City University of New York, 1963; visiting professor, Columbia University, 1969-70. Worked with Indian Foreign Missions in Geneva, Switzerland, London, England, and United Nations, New York, N.Y., 1953-60. *Member:* Modern Language Association of America (group chairman, 1970), American Oriental Society, International Congress of Orientalists, International Congress of Comparative Literature. *Awards, honors:* State University of New York faculty research fellowships, 1966-67, 1969-70.

*WRITINGS: Indo-English Literature in the Nineteenth Century,* Mysore University, 1970; (editor) *Anthology of Indian Literature,* Penguin, 1971; *Jawaharlal Nehru: A Literary Portrait,* Twayne, 1972; *Nightless Nights,* Hind (New Delhi), 1974; (with wife, Leena Karkala) *Bibliography of Indo-English Literature, 1800-1966,* Nirmal (Bombay), 1974; *Comparative World Literature: Seven Essays,* Nirmal, 1974. Contributor of articles to numerous journals.

*WORK IN PROGRESS: Introduction to Comparative South Asian Literature; Indian Classic Novel,* with wife, Leena Karkala.

\* \* \*

## AMELIO, Ralph J. 1939-

*PERSONAL:* Born January 26, 1939, in Chicago, Ill.; son of Ernest F. (a shoemaker) and Carmella (Pullano) Amelio; married Dorothy Dabrowski (a teacher), June 28, 1964; children: Ralph Christopher, Victoria Ann. *Education:* Loyola University, Chicago, Ill., B.S., 1961, M.A., 1964; graduate study at University of Chicago, 1967-68, Columbia College, Chicago, 1969, Hampshire College, summer, 1971, and University of Illinois American Film Institute, summer, 1972.

*Home:* 8338 West Summerdale, Chicago, Ill. 60656. *Office:* Willowbrook High School, 1250 South Ardmore, Villa Park, Ill. 60181.

*CAREER:* Willowbrook High School, Villa Park, Ill., instructor in English and film study, 1961—. Instructor in film, Wright College, Chicago, Ill., 1971-74, and National College of Education, Evanston, Ill., 1974—. Film consultant and lecturer, 1968—; has conducted film study workshops at Boston University, New School for Social Research, University of Wisconsin—Madison, Northwestern University, University of Illinois at Chicago Circle, and other colleges; film consultant to Center for Understanding Media, New York, N.Y., to Chicago Board of Education, 1971, and to annual Chicago International Film Festival. *Member:* Screen Educators' Society (member of executive board), American Film Institute. *Awards, honors:* National Endowment for the Humanities grant, Northwestern University, 1977.

*WRITINGS*—All published by Pflaum Standard: (With Anita Owen and Susan Schafer) *Willowbrook Cinema Study Project,* 1969; *Film in the Classroom,* 1971; *Hal in the Classroom: Science Fiction Films,* 1974; *The Filmic Moment,* 1975. Contributor to journals. Media editor, *See Magazine,* 1970—.

*BIOGRAPHICAL/CRITICAL SOURCES: See Magazine,* March, 1972.

\* \* \*

## AMPRIMOZ, Alexandre 1948-

*PERSONAL:* Surname is accented on last syllable which rhymes with "rose"; born August 14, 1948, in Rome, Italy; son of Louis (a French army officer and chemist) and Carmelina (Vitale) Amprimoz; married Jeannette Deslippe (a high school French teacher), July 10, 1971. *Education:* University of Marseille, Bac. Math., 1966, D.U.E.S.P.C., 1967; Prytanee Militaire, Math. Sup. and Math. Spe., 1968; University of Toronto, additional study, 1969; University of Ottawa, L.F.I. teaching certificate, 1969; University of Windsor, M.A., 1970; University of Western Ontario, Ph.D., 1978. *Religion:* Roman Catholic. *Home address:* Box 7186, Sandwich P.O., Windsor, Ontario, Canada N9C 3Z1. *Office:* French Programs, St. Clair College, Windsor, Ontario, Canada.

*CAREER:* Assumption College High School, Windsor, Ontario, teacher of French, 1968-73; St. Clair College, Windsor, administrator of French programs, 1977—.

*WRITINGS: Jiva and Other Poems,* CSA Press, 1971; (translator) *Initiation a Menke Katz,* Les Presses Libres, 1972; *Re and Other Poems,* Vantage, 1972; *Visions,* Tarnhelm, 1973; *An Island in the Heart and Other Dialogues,* Tarnhelm, 1973; *Against the Cold,* Fiddlehead, 1978; *Chant Solaire,* Naaman, 1978. Contributor of poems and short stories to literary magazines, including *Orion, Poetry Australia, International Poetry Review, Prism International,* and *Bitteroot.*

\* \* \*

## AMUNDSEN, Kirsten 1932-

*PERSONAL:* Born March 4, 1932, in Hammerfest, Norway; daughter of Aasmund and Gully (Bang) Amundsen; married Kjell Steinmo (a mechanical engineer), 1952 (divorced); children: Sven, Erik. *Education:* Attended University of Oslo, 1950-52; University of California, Berkeley, M.A., 1965; University of California, Davis, Ph.D., 1971.

*Home:* 1207 Cypress Lane, Davis, Calif. 95616. *Office:* Department of Political Science, California State University, Sacramento, Calif. 95819.

*CAREER: Hoeyres Pressekontor,* Oslo, Norway, reporter, 1951-52; *Adresseavisen,* Trondheim, Norway, reporter, 1952-53; California State University, Sacramento, assistant professor of political science, 1969—. *Member:* American Political Science Association, National Organization for Women, Women's Caucus, Western Political Science Association.

*WRITINGS: The Silenced Majority: Women and American Democracy,* Prentice-Hall, 1971; *Sexist Ideology and Its Victims,* North American Publishing, 1972; *A New Look at the Silenced Majority,* Prentice-Hall, 1977. Former Mideast war correspondent, *Arbeiderbladet* (Norwegian newspaper).

*WORK IN PROGRESS: Feminism and the UN: New Worlds in Collision.*

*SIDELIGHTS:* Kirsten Amundsen told *CA:* "My major vocational interest is comparative politics and I have traveled widely—both for professional and personal reasons. Two summers were recently spent in Brazil in the hope of gathering material for a book on the Brazilian Revolution. I was sidetracked, however, into writing on 'the woman question'—a subject so complex, vast and yet neglected, that it doesn't look like I can get off it for quite a while yet!"

\* \* \*

## ANASTAPLO, George 1925-

*PERSONAL:* Born November 7, 1925, in St. Louis, Mo.; son of Theodore and Margaret (Syriopoulou) Anastaplo; married Sara J. Prince, January 28, 1949; children: Helen Margaret, George Malcom Davidson, Sara Maria, Theodora McShan. *Education:* University of Chicago, A.B., 1948, J.D., 1951, Ph.D., 1964. *Home:* 5731 Harper Ave., Chicago, Ill. 60637. *Office:* University of Chicago, 1307 East 60th St., Chicago, Ill. 60637.

*CAREER:* University of Chicago, Chicago, Ill., lecturer in liberal arts, 1956—; Rosary College, River Forest, Ill., professor of political science and philosophy, 1964—. Research director, Governor's Commission on Personal Privacy, State of Illinois, 1974-75. *Military service:* U.S. Army Air Forces, 1943-47; became second lieutenant. *Member:* Phi Beta Kappa.

*WRITINGS: The Constitutionalist: Notes on the First Amendment,* Southern Methodist University Press, 1971; *Human Being and Citizen: Essays on Virtue, Freedom, and the Common Good,* Swallow Press, 1975; *American Constitutionalism and the Virtue of Prudence,* University of Dallas Press, 1976; *The Artist as Thinker,* Swallow Press, 1979. Contributor to journals, anthologies, and newspapers.

*WORK IN PROGRESS: American Constitutionalism: Documents and Commentary.*

\* \* \*

## ANDERSEN, Kenneth E(ldon) 1933-

*PERSONAL:* Born December 28, 1933, in Harlan, Iowa; son of Edward and Anna (Christiansen) Andersen; married Mary Klaaren, August 20, 1964; children: Erik. *Education:* University of Northern Iowa, B.A., 1954, M.A., 1955; University of Wisconsin, Ph.D., 1961. *Home:* 2002 Galen Dr., Champaign, Ill. 61820. *Office:* Department of Speech Communication, University of Illinois, Urbana, Ill. 61801.

*CAREER:* University of Colorado, Boulder, instructor in speech, 1955-56; New Mexico State University, Las Cruces, instructor in speech, 1957-58; University of Michigan, Ann Arbor, instructor, 1961-63, assistant professor, 1963-67, associate professor of speech, 1967-70; University of Illinois at Urbana-Champaign, associate professor, 1970-72, professor of speech communication, 1972—, associate head of department, 1971—. Visiting lecturer, University of Illinois at Chicago Circle, 1966; visiting associate professor, University of Southern California, 1968. *Military service:* U.S. Army, 1956-58. *Member:* Speech Communication Association (member of administrative committee and finance board, 1974-76), American Forensic Association (member of national council, 1968-70), American Association of University Professors, American Association for Public Opinion Research, International Communication Association, Central States Speech Association (executive secretary, 1969-72; vice-president, 1972-73; president, 1974-75). *Awards, honors:* Central States Speech Association award, 1962.

*WRITINGS:* (With Edward Stasheff) *A Study of Current Developments in the Teaching of Preaching in America and in the United Kingdom,* Indianapolis Area Methodist Church, 1963; (with Howard Martin) *Speech Communication: Analysis and Readings,* Allyn & Bacon, 1968; *Persuasion Theory and Practice,* Allyn & Bacon, 1971, 2nd edition, 1978; *Introduction to Communication Theory and Practice,* Cummings, 1972. Contributor to speech journals. Editor, *Journal of the American Forensic Association,* 1968-70, *Speaker and Gavel,* 1975-78.

*WORK IN PROGRESS:* Research on effects of persuasion on the source; *Ethics, Values, and Communication.*

\* \* \*

## ANDERSON, Donald K(ennedy), Jr. 1922-

*PERSONAL:* Born March 18, 1922, in Evanston, Ill.; son of Donald K. (a broker) and Kathryn (Shields) Anderson; married Kathleen E. Hughes, September 11, 1949; children: David J., Lawrence W. *Education:* Yale University, A.B., 1943; Northwestern University, M.A., 1947; Duke University, Ph.D., 1957. *Politics:* Democrat. *Religion:* Methodist. *Home:* 1309 Ridge Rd., Columbia, Mo. 65201. *Office:* Department of English, University of Missouri, Columbia, Mo. 65201.

*CAREER:* Geneva College, Beaver Falls, Pa., instructor in English, 1947-49; Rose Polytechnic Institute (now Rose-Hulman Institute of Technology), Terre Haute, Ind., instructor, 1952-53, assistant professor, 1953-57, associate professor of English, 1957-58; Butler University, Indianapolis, Ind., assistant professor, 1958-62, associate professor of English, 1962-65; University of Missouri—Columbia, associate professor, 1965-67, professor of English, 1967—, associate dean of Graduate School, 1970-74. *Military service:* U.S. Navy, Intelligence, 1943-46; served in Pacific; became lieutenant junior grade. *Member:* Modern Language Association of America. *Awards, honors:* Folger Shakespeare Library fellow, summer, 1965.

*WRITINGS:* (Editor) John Ford, *Perkin Warbeck,* University of Nebraska Press, 1965; (editor) John Ford, *The Broken Heart,* University of Nebraska Press, 1968; *John Ford,* Twayne, 1972. Contributor of articles to scholarly journals.

*WORK IN PROGRESS:* Research on Tudor and Stuart drama.

## ANDERSON, J(ohn) E(dward)   1903-

*PERSONAL:* Born May 5, 1903, in Bordighera, Imperia, Italy; son of John Coussmaker (a barrister) and Minnie (Storr) Anderson; married Muriel Caroline Bradford (a music teacher and composer); children: John F., Evelyn Margaret Anderson Saunders-Robin, Michael H. *Education:* University College, Oxford, honours degree, 1924, teaching certificate in French and German, 1925. *Home:* Kingsfold, Chepbourne Rd., Bexhill-on-Sea, Sussex, England. *Agent:* John Farquharson Ltd., 15 Red Lion Sq., London WC1R 4QW, England.

*CAREER:* Clerk in holy orders, Church of England; Charterhouse School, Godalming, England, chaplain and assistant master, 1925-44; rector of Lamport, Northamptonshire, England, 1945-53; Aldenham School, Elstree, England, chaplain and assistant master, 1955-59; Beehive School, Bexhill, England, chaplain, 1959-64; free-lance translator from French and German, 1963-70. *Member:* Society of Authors. *Awards, honors:* Ford Foundation grant from National Translation Center, 1967-69, for translation of Alain's *Propos.*

*WRITINGS: 36 Outline Sermons for Country Parishes,* Mowbray, 1951; *40 Outline Sermons for Country Parishes,* Mowbray, 1961; *The Missing Word* (vocabulary practice), Cassell, 1965; *La France vers l'An 2000,* Cassell, 1966.

Translator: Leviticus, *A Commentary,* S.C.M. Press, 1965; *Stages of Experience: The Year in the Church,* Darton, Longman & Todd, 1965; Jean E. Charon, *Man in Search of Himself,* Walker & Co., 1967; Marc L. B. Bloch, *Land and Work in Mediaeval Europe,* University of California Press, 1967; Francois Bordes, *The Old Stone Age,* McGraw, 1968; Lefebre, *Napoleon,* Volume II, Routledge & Kegan Paul, 1968; Marc L. B. Bloch, *Ile-de-France: The Country around Paris,* Cornell University Press, 1971; Meinecke, *Historism,* Routledge & Kegan Paul, 1972.

*AVOCATIONAL INTERESTS:* Conservation of the countryside and national resources, organic soil culture and food reform, railways, walking, reading—especially biographies, travel, the teaching of English.

\*   \*   \*

## ANDERSON, Lee   1896-1972

July 19, 1896—July 25, 1972; American poet and lecturer. Obituaries: *New York Times,* July 26, 1972; *Antiquarian Bookman,* September 25, 1972. (See index for *CA* sketch)

\*   \*   \*

## ANDERSON, Richard Lloyd   1926-

*PERSONAL:* Born May 9, 1926, in Salt Lake City, Utah; son of Lloyd Ernest (a newspaper publisher) and Agnes (a teacher; maiden name Ricks) Anderson; married Carma Rose de Jong, 1951; children: Roselle, Nathan Richard, Gerrit Lloyd, Chandelle. *Education:* Brigham Young University, B.A., 1951, M.A., 1957; Harvard University, J.D., 1954; University of California, Berkeley, Ph.D., 1962. *Religion:* Church of Jesus Christ of Latter-day Saints (Mormon). *Home:* 1857 North 500 E., Provo, Utah 84601. *Office:* Brigham Young University, 132 Joseph Smith Building, Provo, Utah 84602.

*CAREER:* Brigham Young University, Provo, Utah, instructor, 1955-56, assistant professor of religion, 1956-58; University of California, Berkeley, lecturer in classical and medieval rhetoric, 1960-61; Brigham Young University, associate professor, 1961-62, professor of history and religion,

1962—. Private law counselor, 1955-65. *Military service:* U.S. Naval Reserve, aviation radioman, 1944-46. *Member:* Association of Ancient Historians, Society of Biblical Literature, Mormon History Association, Phi Kappa Phi. *Awards, honors:* Danforth fellow, 1958-59; Woodrow Wilson fellow, 1959-60; Mormon History Association prize for best articles on Mormon history, 1969-70; Latter-day Saints Education Commissioner's research fellow, 1974-75.

*WRITINGS: Joseph Smith's New England Heritage,* Deseret, 1971; (contributor) Hugh Nibley and others, *To the Glory of God,* Deseret, 1972. Contributor of over fifty articles to history and religion journals. Senior editor, "Brigham Young University Studies"; member of board of editors, *Journal of Mormon History.*

*WORK IN PROGRESS: The Letters of Emma and Joseph Smith;* a new edition and commentary of Lucy Smith's history of Joseph Smith; research on the Gospels and other New Testament subjects.

\*   \*   \*

## ANDREWS, J. Cutler   1908-1972

September 9, 1908—June 2, 1972; American historian and educator. Obituaries: *New York Times,* June 5, 1972.

\*   \*   \*

## ANDREWS, Julie   1935-
### (Julie Edwards)

*PERSONAL:* Name originally Julia Elizabeth Wells, took the surname of her stepfather when her mother married music hall singer, Edward Andrews; born October 1, 1935, in Walton-on-Thames, Surrey, England; daughter of Edward C. Wells (a schoolteacher known as Ted Wells) and Barbara (a pianist; maiden name, Ward) Wells Andrews; married Tony Walton (a theatrical designer), May 10, 1959; married second husband, Blake Edwards (a producer and director), November 12, 1969; children: (first marriage) Emma Kate Walton; adopted children: Amy Leigh, Joanna Lynne; stepchildren: Jennifer Edwards, Geoff Edwards. *Education:* Educated privately by tutors; studied voice with Madame Stiles-Allen. *Office:* c/o Trellis Enterprises, Inc., 1888 Century Park East, Los Angeles, Calif. 90067. *Agent:* (Theatrical) Creative Artists Agency, Inc., 1888 Century Park East, Los Angeles, Calif. 90067.

*CAREER:* Her singing in a bomb shelter at the age of eight led to professional training and a debut at twelve at the Hippodrome in London in the revue, "Starlight Roof"; had the title role in "Humpty Dumpty," 1948, "Red Riding Hood," 1950, and "Cinderella," 1953, and played in other revues and pantomimes in England before making a Broadway debut at the Royale Theatre in "The Boy Friend," September, 1954; played Eliza in the Broadway production of "My Fair Lady," 1956-60, and Guinevere in "Camelot," 1960-62. Appeared opposite Bing Crosby in the television version of "High Tor," 1956, and in the television remake of Rodgers and Hammerstein's "Cinderella," 1957. Television specials include: "Julie and Carol at Carnegie Hall," 1961, "The Julie Andrews Show," 1966, "An Evening with Julie Andrews and Harry Belafonte," 1969, "The World of Walt Disney," 1971, "Julie and Carol at Lincoln Center," 1971, and the television series, "The Julie Andrews Hour," 1972-73. Her first screen role was in the Academy Award-winning "Mary Poppins," 1964, followed by "The Americanization of Emily," 1964, "Torn Curtain," 1966, "The Sound of Music," 1966, "Hawaii," 1966, "Thoroughly Modern Millie," 1967, "Star!," 1968, "Darling Lili," 1971, "The Tamarind Seed," 1974, and "The Return of the Pink Panther," 1975. Recordings include the original cast records of "My Fair Lady" and "Camelot," "Julie Andrews and Carol Burnett at Carnegie Hall," and other albums.

*AWARDS, HONORS:* New York Drama Critics Award for "My Fair Lady," 1956; Oscar Award from Academy of Motion Picture Arts and Sciences, as best actress for "Mary Poppins," 1964; Woman of the Year award from *Los Angeles Times*, 1965; named best actress of the year and world's favorite actress by Hollywood foreign press, 1967; Star of the Year award from Theatre Owners of America, 1967; honorary D.F.A. from University of Maryland, 1970; Emmy Award from National Academy of Television Arts and Sciences, as star of outstanding variety musical series, 1972-73, and Silver Rose Montreaux, 1973, both for "The Julie Andrews Hour." Also received three Golden Globe Awards.

*WRITINGS*—Under name Julie Edwards; all for children: *Mandy*, Harper, 1971; *The Last of the Really Great Whangdoodles*, Harper, 1974.

*WORK IN PROGRESS:* A novel.

*SIDELIGHTS:* Speaking of herself as a writer, Julie Andrews commented in *Publishers Weekly:* "I don't think I count as a professional. To me it's just such a joy to write, to watch the pages grow. Creating something, making a whole new world, is such a pleasure. [It] has been very much a family affair. 'Mandy,' my first book, was written for my stepdaughter Jenny, and the little girl in [*The Last of the Really Great Whangdoodles*] is very much like my own daughter Emma, when she was younger."

While looking up a word in the dictionary, Julie Andrews came across the word "Whangdoodle," and decided immediately to use it in the title of her second book. The Professor, one of the characters in *The Last of the Really Great Whangdoodles*, is based on author T. H. White, whose novel *The Once and Future King* served as a source for the musical "Camelot," in which Andrews starred.

*AVOCATIONAL INTERESTS:* Boating, skiing, horseback riding.

*BIOGRAPHICAL/CRITICAL SOURCES: Christian Science Monitor*, November 11, 1971; Lee Bennett Hopkins, *More Books by More People*, Citation, 1974; *Publishers Weekly*, July 22, 1974; *People*, March 14, 1977.

\* \* \*

## ANDRUS, Hyrum L(eslie) 1924-

*PERSONAL:* Born March 12, 1924, in Lewisville, Idaho; son of Newton Leslie (a businessman) and Zina Alberta (Allen) Andrus; married Helen Mae Hillman, March 31, 1949; children: John Leslie, Richard Milo, David Hyrum. *Education:* Ricks College, B.S., 1951; Brigham Young University, M.S., 1952; Syracuse University, Ph.D., 1955. *Religion:* Church of Jesus Christ of Latter-day Saints (Mormon). *Home:* 530 East 1980 N., Provo, Utah 84601. *Office:* College of Religious Instruction, Brigham Young University, Provo, Utah 84601.

*CAREER:* Ricks College, Rexburg, Idaho, director of religious studies, 1955-56; Brigham Young University, Provo, Utah, assistant professor, 1957-60, associate professor, 1960-64, professor of religion and social science, 1964—. *Military service:* U.S. Army, 1945-46; became technical sergeant.

*WRITINGS: Helps for Missionaries*, Ricks College, 1949;

*Joseph Smith and World Government*, Deseret, 1958; *Joseph Smith the Man and the Seer*, Deseret, 1960; *Liberalism, Conservatism, and Mormonism*, Deseret, 1965; *Doctrinal Commentary on the Pearl of Great Price*, Deseret, 1967; *God, Man, and the Universe*, Bookcraft, 1968; *Principles of Perfection*, Bookcraft, 1970; *Doctrines of the Kingdom*, Bookcraft, 1973; *They Knew the Prophet*, Bookcraft, 1974; *Mormon Manuscripts to 1846*, Brigham Young University Press, 1977. Contributor of articles to journals and pamphlets in his field.

*WORK IN PROGRESS:* A book, tentatively entitled *Prophecy and Judgment*.

\* \* \*

## ANGELL, Ernest 1889-1973

June 1, 1889—January 11, 1973; American lawyer, consultant to government and business and professional organizations, and author of works on American and international law. Obituaries: *New York Times*, January 12, 1973; *Time*, January 22, 1973.

\* \* \*

## ANGLIN, Douglas G(eorge) 1923-

*PERSONAL:* Born December 16, 1923, in Toronto, Ontario, Canada; son of George Chambers (a physician) and Ruth Cecilia (Cale) Anglin; married Mary Elizabeth Watson, June 26, 1948; children: Margaret Alice, Deirdre Ruth. *Education:* University of Toronto, B.A. (honors), 1948; Oxford University, B.A., 1950, M.A., 1954, D.Phil., 1956. *Religion:* United Church of Canada. *Home:* 2691 Basswood Crescent, Ottawa, Ontario, Canada K1V 8K2. *Office:* Department of Political Science, Carleton University, Ottawa, Ontario, Canada K1S 5B6.

*CAREER:* University of Manitoba, Winnipeg, assistant professor, 1951-57, associate professor of political science and international relations, 1957-58; Carleton University, Ottawa, Ontario, associate professor, 1958-65, professor of political science, 1965—. Vice-chancellor, University of Zambia, 1965-69. *Military service:* Royal Canadian Naval Volunteer Reserve, active duty, 1943-45; became lieutenant. *Member:* International Studies Association, Canadian Political Science Association, African Studies Association, Canadian Association of African Studies (president, 1973-74). *Awards, honors:* Rhodes scholar, 1948.

*WRITINGS:* (Editor with Millar MacLure) *Africa: The Political Pattern*, University of Toronto Press, 1961; *The St. Pierre and Miquelon Affaire of 1941*, University of Toronto Press, 1966, revised edition, 1970. Contributor of chapters to several books; contributor to professional journals.

*WORK IN PROGRESS:* Zambia and confrontation with Southern Africa.

*BIOGRAPHICAL/CRITICAL SOURCES: Horizon*, November, 1966; *Canadian Journal of Economics and Political Science*, August, 1967.

\* \* \*

## ANGRESS, R(uth) K(lueger) 1931-

*PERSONAL:* Born October 30, 1931, in Vienna, Austria; U.S. citizen; daughter of Viktor (a physician) and Alma (a physiotherapist; maiden name, Gredinger) Klueger; married Werner Thomas Angress (a historian), March, 1953 (divorced, 1962); children: Percy, Dan. *Education:* Hunter College (now Hunter College of the City University of New

York), B.A., 1950; University of California, Berkeley, M.A., 1964, Ph.D., 1967. *Religion:* Jewish. *Office:* Department of German, University of California, Irvine, Calif. 92717.

*CAREER:* California State College at Hayward (now California State University, Hayward), assistant professor of German, 1965-66; Case Western Reserve University, Cleveland, Ohio, 1966-70, began as assistant professor, became associate professor; University of Kansas, Lawrence, associate professor of German, 1970-73; University of Virginia, Charlottesville, associate professor of German, 1973-76, chairman of department, 1974-76; University of California, Irvine, member of faculty of department of German, 1976—. Visiting professor at University of Cincinnati, 1972-73. *Member:* American Association of University Professors, Modern Language Association of America.

*WRITINGS:* (Translator) Alfred Neumeyer, *The Search for Meaning in Modern Art,* Prentice-Hall, 1964; *The Early German Epigram,* University Press of Kentucky, 1971. Contributor of articles and reviews to scholarly journals.

\*        \*        \*

## ANTONICK, Robert J.  1939-
### (Nick Kamin)

*PERSONAL:* Born October 9, 1939, in Chicago, Ill.; son of Nicholas (an engineer) and Anne (Kaminski) Antonick; married Martha Hunter, June 19, 1965. *Education:* University of Dayton, B.F.A., 1961. *Politics:* "Conscientious radical." *Religion:* "Fallen." *Home:* 470 Blue Ridge Dr., Dayton, Ohio 45415.

*CAREER:* School of the Dayton Art Institute, Dayton, Ohio, instructor in graphic communications, 1965-68; Sabatino Advertising, Dayton, creative director, 1968-72; Darqram (imports), Dayton, partner, 1970-72; affiliated with Bergen Advertising Art, Dayton, 1972-75. Product and graphic design consultant. *Awards, honors:* Several national and a number of local awards, primarily in graphics.

*WRITINGS*—Novels under pseudonym Nick Kamin: *Earthrim* (bound with *Phoenix Ship* by Walt Richmond), Ace Books, 1969; *The Herod Men* (bound with *Dark Planet* by John Rackham), Ace Books, 1971. Associate editor, *Exponent,* 1959-64, and *Rap,* 1970-71.

*SIDELIGHTS:* Robert J. Antonick says that "being born in Chicago, having Canadian parents, being raised in a small midwestern American town, and living each summer in Manitoba may have had a dichotomous effect. On one hand, my grandparents' house never had electricity, running water, or indoor conveniences; for me a perfectly acceptable way of life in the middle of the 20th century. On the other hand, I argued in favor of atomic transmutation, in grade school, before the term filtered down to the textbooks and the faculty. In short, 'generation gap' has never struck me as understandable."†

\*        \*        \*

## APPLETON, Sarah  1930-
### (Sarah Appleton Weber)

*PERSONAL:* Born April 14, 1930, in New York, N.Y.; daughter of William Channing (an executive in textile business) and Ellen (Sherman) Appleton; married Joseph Gardner Weber (a professor of French literature), March 13, 1965; children: Elizabeth Gardner, David Appleton. *Education:* Vassar College, B.A., 1952; Ohio State University, M.A., 1957, Ph.D., 1961. *Residence:* Syracuse, N.Y.

*CAREER:* Smith College, Northampton, Mass., instructor in English literature and poetry, 1962-65; Radcliffe Institute, Cambridge, Mass., fellow, 1970-72. Has given poetry readings and conducted poetry workshops. *Member:* Mediaeval Academy of America, Society of Radcliffe Fellows, Teilhard de Chardin Association. *Awards, honors:* Creative Artists Public Service Program grant, 1975-76.

*WRITINGS:* (Under name Sarah Appleton Weber) *Theology and Poetry in the Middle English Lyric: A Study of Sacred History and Aesthetic Form,* Ohio State University Press, 1969; *The Plenitude We Cry For: A Poem,* Doubleday, 1972; *Ladder of the World's Joy: Poems,* Doubleday, 1977. Contributor of poetry to periodicals, including *Commonweal, Midwest Review, Forum, America,* and *Catholic Worker.* Poetry editor, *Literature East & West,* 1967-68.

*WORK IN PROGRESS: Book of Hunger/Book of the Earth.*

\*        \*        \*

## ARMSTRONG, (Raymond) Paul  1912-

*PERSONAL:* Born January 15, 1912, in Mingo, Iowa; son of Aldus Raymond (a railroad station agent and house painter) and Edna Marie (Lint) Armstrong; married Jean Weber (a producer and director for educational television), February 4, 1946; children: Raymond Paul, Jr. *Education:* Chico State College (now California State University, Chico), B.A., 1946; University of Oregon, M.A., 1948. *Politics:* Republican. *Religion:* Episcopalian. *Home:* 2227 Agate St., Eugene, Ore. 97403.

*CAREER:* Has worked as a migrant fruit harvester, cannery worker, and house painter; Grays Harbor College, Aberdeen, Wash., instructor in English, 1948-50; teacher of English and journalism in high school in Lebanon, Ore., 1950-52; Stanford University, Stanford, Calif., receiving clerk, 1959-65; Lane Community College, Eugene, Ore., assistant professor of English, 1965-77. *Military service:* U.S. Army, 1941-46; received presidential citation with two oak leaf clusters.

*WRITINGS: Somewhere Is Dawn,* Grays Harbor Post, 1950; (editor) *Lebanon Expressions* (anthology), Lebanon Express, 1952; *The Flip Side of Paul Armstrong,* Lane Community College Press, 1971. Author of documentary scripts for television and radio. Contributor of articles and poems to national periodicals, including *Good Housekeeping, Christian Science Monitor,* and *McCalls,* to literary, agriculture, and religious magazines, and to newspapers.

*WORK IN PROGRESS:* Short poems.

*SIDELIGHTS:* Paul Armstrong told *CA:* "Poets editorialize existence. They interpret what they see, hear, feel, and sense in the broadest use of the word. I find life and people interesting and amusing and want to share that interest and amusement. I can't remember when I was so young that my thoughts and feelings were not important. My elders often disagreed; I went on expressing how I felt anyway.

"Having things to say which I want understood generally, I tend to avoid the esoteric approach to poetry. I have never written for an 'in' group, nor have I tended to slant toward what I thought some publisher wanted. I have written what pleased me and trusted that I might find a publisher who would agree that my product had merit. I have never equated length with quality in poetry. I have felt that if I couldn't get it said in fourteen lines or less, that I probably couldn't get it said at all.

"These are strictly personal views and I am quick to add that I recognize that there are as many approaches to poetry as there are people with something to be expressed." He sums up his overall view by stating, "If you have something to say, say it effectively; if you have nothing to say, say it beautifully."

*AVOCATIONAL INTERESTS:* Gardening, bowling, golfing.

*BIOGRAPHICAL/CRITICAL SOURCES: Pace,* May, 1969.

\*      \*      \*

## ARNOLD, Herbert 1935-

*PERSONAL:* Born June 23, 1935, in Buchau, Czechoslovakia; son of Joseph (a manager) and Maria (Rothberger) Arnold; married Annemarie Stuck, February 11, 1961; children: Bettina, Corinna Maria, Christiane Vivien. *Education:* Attended University of Freiburg, 1956-58; University of Wuerzburg, Staatsexamen, 1962, Dr.phil., 1966. *Residence:* Portland, Conn. *Office:* College of Letters, Wesleyan University, Middletown, Conn. 06457.

*CAREER:* Has taught in Germany and England; Wesleyan University, Middletown, Conn., instructor, 1963-66, assistant professor, 1966-67, associate professor of German, 1967—, director of programs in Bonn, Germany, 1967-69, and 1972-73, coordinator of Intensive Language Program, 1970-71, co-director of College of Letters, 1970-71, and 1973-76. Member of board of trustees, American Field Service International Scholarships, 1972-74. *Member:* Modern Language Association of America, American Association of Teachers of German (Connecticut chapter; vice-president, 1974-75; president, 1975-76), American Historical Association, North East Modern Language Association. *Awards, honors:* Bavarian State grant for study abroad, 1961; Wesleyan University, summer research grants, 1968, 1969, and 1970, fellow of East College and Center for Humanities, 1971-72; National Endowment for the Humanities program grant, 1974-78.

*WRITINGS—Translator:* Bode Scheurig, *Free Germany,* Wesleyan University Press, 1969; Eberhard Jackel, *Hitler's Weltanschauung,* Wesleyan University Press, 1972. Contributor of translations, articles and reviews to *American Historical Review, Historische Zeitschrift, Zeitschrift fuer deutsche Philologie, History and Theory, Reprint Bulletin, Perspective, Monatschefte,* and *Choice.*

*WORK IN PROGRESS: Ideology of Hitler's SS;* translations.

\*      \*      \*

## ARNOUX, Alexandre (Paul) 1884-1973

February 27, 1884—January 5, 1973; French novelist, short story writer, and screenwriter. Obituaries: *L'Express,* January 15-21, 1973.

\*      \*      \*

## ARUEGO, Jose

*PERSONAL:* Born in Manila, Philippines; son of Jose M. (a lawyer) and Constancia (Espiritu) Aruego. *Education:* University of the Philippines, B.A., 1953, LL.B., 1955; Parsons School of Design, Certificate in Graphic Arts and Advertising, 1959. *Residence:* New York, N.Y.

*CAREER:* Village Display Co., New York City, apprentice, 1959-60; Hayden Publishing Co., New York City, de-signer, 1960-62; Mervin & Jesse Levine (fashion advertising agency), New York City, mechanical boardman, 1963-64; Norman Associates (studio), New York City, mechanical boardman, 1964-65; Ashton B. Collins, Inc. (advertising agency), New York City, assistant art director, 1965-68; writer and illustrator of books for children. *Awards, honors:* Outstanding picture book of the year awards from the *New York Times,* for *Juan and the Asuangs,* 1970, for *The Day They Parachuted Cats on Borneo,* 1971, for *Look What I Can Do,* 1972; *Whose Mouse Are You?* and *Milton the Early Riser* were American Library Association Notable Book selections, 1970, 1972; *Look What I Can Do, The Chick and the Duckling,* and *A Crocodile's Tale* were included in Children's Book Council Showcase, 1972, 1973; *A Crocodile's Tale* was included in the American Institute of Graphic Arts' list of Children's Books of the year, 1972; Brooklyn Art Books for Children citation, 1974, and Society of Illustrators citation, 1976, both for *Milton the Early Riser.*

*WRITINGS—Self-illustrated children's books: The King and His Friends,* Scribner, 1969; *Juan and the Asuangs: A Tale of Philippine Ghosts and Spirits,* Scribner, 1970; *Symbiosis: A Book of Unusual Friendships,* Scribner, 1970; *Pilyo the Piranha,* Macmillan, 1971; *Look What I Can Do,* Scribner, 1971; (with Ariane Aruego) *A Crocodile's Tale,* Scribner, 1972.

Illustrator: Robert Kraus, *Whose Mouse Are You?,* Macmillan, 1970; Kay Smith, *Parakeets and Peach Pies,* Parents' Magazine Press, 1970; Jack Prelutsky, *Toucans Two and Other Poems,* Macmillan, 1970; Charlotte Pomerantz, *The Day They Parachuted Cats on Borneo: A Drama of Ecology* (play), Young Scott Books, 1971; Christina Rossetti, *What Is Pink?,* Macmillan, 1971; Kraus, *Leo the Late Bloomer,* Windmill Books, 1971; Elizabeth Coatsworth, *Good Night,* Macmillan, 1972; (with Ariane Aruego) Vladimir G. Suteyev, *The Chick and the Duckling,* translation by Mirra Ginsburg, Macmillan, 1972; (with Ariane Aruego) Kraus, *Milton the Early Riser,* Windmill Books, 1972.

Illustrator with Ariane Dewey: Natalie Savage Carlson, *Marie Louise and Christophe,* Scribner, 1974; Suteyev, *Mushroom in the Rain,* adapted by Ginsburg, Macmillan, 1974; Kraus, *Herman the Helper,* Windmill Books, 1974; Kraus, *Owliver,* Windmill Books, 1974; Ginsburg, *How the Sun Was Brought Back to the Sky: Adapted from a Slovenian Folktale,* Macmillan, 1975; Kraus, *Three Friends,* Windmill Books, 1975; Carlson, *Marie Louise's Heyday,* Scribner, 1975; Ginsburg, *Two Greedy Bears: Adapted from a Hungarian Folk Tale,* Macmillan, 1976; Kraus, *Noel the Coward,* Windmill Books, 1977; David Kherdian, editor, *If Dragon Flies Made Honey: Poems,* Morrow, 1977. Contributor of cartoons to *New Yorker, Look, Saturday Review,* and other magazines.

*WORK IN PROGRESS:* Illustrations for a story about camouflage, starring a hippopotamus; writing and illustrating three stories.

*SIDELIGHTS:* "Most of my books have what you would call a humorous atmosphere," Jose Aruego told an interviewer. "Before I accept a manuscript, I look for humor. That has been—and is—the basis of my characters, because I think that a humorous character is easy to love and I want that emotional response from children. I want them to make the characters their own." Susan Stark says: "Aruego's world is a happy one, dominated by clean line and considerable detail, a world in which spontaneity and color play a great part. His animals are fanciful, simplified versions of their real-life counterparts, but their feelings and predicaments—expressed through subtle changes in expression and posture—have immediacy.'' Stark added: ''His impact on the field of picture books in less than a decade has been nothing short of phenomenal. Without question he, along with Tomie de Paola . . . are the most in-demand—and prolific—children's book illustrators working today.''

Although he has travelled extensively in the United States as a member ambassador for a friendship program, and has toured around the world, Jose Aruego's favorite city is New York. His mural of New York City hangs at the International House on Riverside Drive. *Look What I Can Do* has been published in French.

*BIOGRAPHICAL/CRITICAL SOURCES: New York Times Book Review*, April 26, 1970, May 2, 1971, May 7, 1972, November 12, 1972; *National Observer*, April 27, 1970; *Christian Science Monitor*, November 11, 1971; *Washington Post*, November 5, 1972; *Detroit Free Press*, November 3, 1978.

\*      \*      \*

## ASHBROOK, James B(arbour)   1925-

*PERSONAL:* Born November 1, 1925, in Adrian, Mich.; son of Milan Forest (a minister) and Elizabeth (Barbour) Ashbrook; married Patricia Cober (director of a day-care center), August 14, 1948; children: Peter, Susan, Martha, Karen. *Education:* Denison University, B.A. (with honors), 1947; Colgate Rochester Divinity School, B.D., 1950; Union Theological Seminary and William Alason White Institute of Psychiatry, graduate fellow, 1954-55; Ohio State University, M.A., 1962, Ph.D., 1964. *Politics:* Democrat. *Home:* 359 Rockingham St., Rochester, N.Y. 14620. *Office:* Bexley Hall, Colgate Rochester Divinity School, 1100 South Goodman St., Rochester, N.Y. 14620.

*CAREER:* Clergyman of Baptist Church; pastor in Rochester, N.Y., 1950-54, Granville, Ohio, 1955-60; Colgate Rochester Divinity School, Rochester, N.Y., associate professor, 1960-65, professor of pastoral theology, 1965-69, professor of psychology and theology, 1969—. Visiting lecturer at Denison University, 1958-60, and Princeton Theological Seminary, 1970-71. Summer clinical pastoral training at Rochester State Hospital, 1949, Bellevue General Hospital, 1950, Illinois State Training School for Boys, 1951. Consultant and supervisor, Counseling Center, University of Rochester, 1969—, and Genesee Ecumenical Pastoral Counseling Center, 1975—; consultant to Chief of U.S. Air Force Chaplains, 1969, to Rochester Board of Education, 1969-73, to Family Court of Monroe County (N.Y.), 1972-74, and to St. Ann's Home for the Elderly, 1972—.

*MEMBER:* American Association of Pastoral Counselors (diplomate; chairman of centers and teaching committee, 1970-71), American Psychological Association, American Board of Professional Psychology, Phi Beta Kappa. *Awards, honors:* American Association of Theology Schools faculty fellowships, 1963-64, 1971-72; postdoctoral fellowship at University of Rochester Center for Community Studies, 1971-73; alumni citation, Denison University, 1972; LL.D., Denison University, 1976.

*WRITINGS:* (Contributor) Simon Doniger, editor, *The Minister's Consultation Clinic*, Channel Press, 1955; (contributor) Hans Hoffman, editor, *Religion and Mental Health*, Harper, 1961; (contributor) David Belgum, editor, *Religion and Medicine*, Iowa State University Press, 1967; (contributor) William Bier, editor, *Psychological Testing for Ministerial Selection*, Fordham University Press, 1970; *Be/Come Community*, Judson, 1971; *In Human Presence:*

*Hope*, Judson, 1971; *Humanitas: Human Becoming and Being Human*, Abingdon, 1973; *The Old Me and a New i: An Exploration of Personal Identity*, Judson, 1974; *Responding to Human Pain*, Judson, 1975; (with Paul W. Walaskay) *Christianity for Pious Skeptics*, Abingdon, 1977. Contributor to psychology and religion journals. Member of editorial board, ''Ministry Monograph Series,'' 1965-70; member of editorial advisory board, *Journal of Pastoral Care*, 1965—; consulting editor, *Journal of Counseling Psychology*, 1968-74.

*WORK IN PROGRESS:* A *Theology of Consciousness; Probing the Psyche.*

\*      \*      \*

## ASLANAPA, Oktay   1914-

*PERSONAL:* Surname is pronounced *As*-lan-a-pa; born December 17, 1914, in Kuetahya, Turkey; son of Celal and Hacer Aslanapa; married Selma Gunseli Pamukcu, April 20, 1956; children: Cigdem, Banu (daughters). *Education:* Studied at Istanbul University and University of Vienna; University of Vienna, Ph.D., 1943. *Religion:* Muslim. *Residence:* Aksaray, Istanbul, Turkey. *Office:* Edebiyat Fakueltesi, Istanbul Universitesi, Istanbul, Turkey.

*CAREER:* Istanbul University, Istanbul, Turkey, assistant professor, 1943-49, associate professor, 1949-60, professor of Turkish and Islamic art history, 1960—, chairman of Institute for History of Art, 1977. *Military service:* Turkish Army, 1940-42, 1945; became lieutenant.

*WRITINGS:* (Translator) Ernst Diez, *Tuerk Sanati* (title means ''Turkish Art''), Ueniversite Matbaasi, 1949, revised edition (co-author with Diez), V. Edebiyat Fakueltesi, 1955; *Osmanlilar Devrinde Kuetahya Cinileri* (title means ''Kuetahya Faience in the Ottoman Period''), Ucler Basimevi, 1949; *Edirnede Osmanli Devri Abideleri* (title means ''Ottoman Monuments of Edirne''), Ucler Basimevi, 1949; (with Diez and M. M. Koman) *Karaman Devri Sanati* (title means ''Art of the Karaman Period''), [Istanbul], 1950; *Turkish Arts: Seljuk and Ottoman Carpets, Tiles and Miniature Paintings* (manuscript translated by Herman Kreider and revised by Sheila O'Callaghan), Dogan Kardes (Istanbul), 1961; (editor) *Beitrage zur Kunstgeschichte asiens in memoriam Ernst Diez*, Baha Matbaasi, 1963; *Anadoluda Tuerk Cini ve Keramik Sanati* (title means ''Turkish Ceramic and Tile Art of Anatolia''), Baha Matbaasi, 1965; (editor with Rudolf Naumann) *Forschungen zur Kunst asiens in memoriam Kurt Erdmann*, I. V. Edebiyat Fakueltesi, 1969.

*Turkish Art and Architecture*, Faber, 1971, Praeger, 1972; (with Yusuf Durul) *Selcuklu Halilari* (title means ''Seljuk Carpets''), Ak Yahinlari, 1973; (editor and contributor) *Tuerk Sanati* (title means ''Turkish Art''), Volume I: *Baslangicindan Bueyuek Selcuklularin sonuna kadar* (title means ''From the Beginning to the Great Seljuks''), 1972, Volume II: *Anadolu'da Tuerk Mimarisi* (title means ''Turkish Art and Architecture in Anatolia''), 1973, Volume III: *Yuezyillar boyunca Tuerk Sanati* (title means ''Turkish Art during the Fourteenth Century''), 1977, Volume IV, in press. Also author of published works on archaeological excavations at Iznik, Diyarbakir, Kalehisar, Yenisehir, Kayseri, Konya, and Van, 1961-72. Contributor of articles in Turkish, German and English to journals and encyclopedias.

\*      \*      \*

## ATHERTON, Alexine   1930-

*PERSONAL:* Born April 28, 1930, in Philadelphia, Pa.;

daughter of Thomas Homer and Eloise (Wicks) Atherton. *Education:* Bryn Mawr College, A.B. (cum laude), 1952; University of Pennsylvania, M.S., 1957, Ph.D., 1962. *Religion:* Society of Friends (Quaker). *Home:* Apt. C-26, Oxhaven Apartments, Oxford, Pa. 19363. *Office:* Department of Political Science, Lincoln University, Lincoln University, Pa. 19352.

*CAREER:* Young World Federalists, Amsterdam, Holland, executive secretary, 1952; American Friends Service Committee, co-leader of team working in refugee camps in Germany, 1953-54; Chestnut Hill Academy, Philadelphia, Pa., teacher, 1954-58; Drexel Institute of Technology (now Drexel University), Philadelphia, lecturer in political science, 1963; University of Pennsylvania, Philadelphia, assistant professor of political science, 1963-69; Lincoln University, Lincoln University, Pa., associate professor of political science, 1969—. Lecturer, Swarthmore College, 1965; chairman of social sciences, Community College of Philadelphia, 1965-66. Member of Experiment in International Living, summers, 1955-58, 1965-66; member of board of directors and president's advisory committee, World Affairs Council of Philadelphia.

*MEMBER:* American Society of International Law, American Political Science Association, American Association of University Professors, International Studies Association. *Awards, honors:* Fulbright fellow and Penfield fellow, University of Vienna, 1960-62.

*WRITINGS: The Dynamics of International Organization,* Dorsey, 1965, revised edition, 1972; *Decision: An International Simulation,* World Affairs Council of Philadelphia, 1972; (editor) *International Organizations: A Guide to Information Sources,* Gale, 1976. Contributor to law, history, and political science journals.†

\* \* \*

### ATIYAH, P(atrick) S(elim) 1931-

*PERSONAL:* Born March 5, 1931, in London, England; son of Edward Selim (a writer and public official) and Jean (Levens) Atiyah; married Christine Best, October 20, 1951; children: Julian P., Andrew M., Simon W., Jeremy F. *Education:* Magdalen College, Oxford, B.A., 1953, B.C.L., 1954, M.A., 1957, D.C.L., 1974, F.B.A., 1978. *Home:* The Old Rectory, Middleton Stoney, Oxfordshire, England. *Office:* St. John's College, Oxford University, Oxford, England.

*CAREER:* Called to the Bar, London, England, 1956; London School of Economics and Political Science, University of London, London, England, assistant lecturer, 1954-55; University of Khartoum, Khartoum, Sudan, lecturer, 1955-59; legal assistant at Board of Trade, London, England, 1961-64; Oxford University, Oxford, England, lecturer in law, 1964-69; Australian National University, Canberra, Australian Capital Territory, professor of law, 1969-73; University of Warwick, Coventry, England, professor of law, 1973-77; Oxford University, professor of English law, 1977—. Member, Law Reform Commission, Australian Capital Territory, 1971-73.

*WRITINGS: The Sale of Goods,* Pitman, 1957, 5th edition, 1975; *An Introduction to the Law of Contract,* Oxford University Press, 1961, 2nd edition, 1971; *Vicarious Liability in the Law of Tort,* Butterworth & Co., 1967; *Accidents, Compensation and the Law,* Fred B. Rothman, 1970, 2nd edition, Weidenfeld & Nicolson, 1975; *Consideration in Contracts: A Fundamental Restatement,* Australian National University Press, 1971; *A Review of Insurance in Relation to Road

Safety,* Australian Government Publications Service, 1973; *The Rise and Fall of Freedom of Contract,* Oxford, in press. Contributor of articles to legal journals.

*WORK IN PROGRESS:* Research on law relating to road accidents, contracts, and modern legal history.

\* \* \*

### AUBERY, Pierre 1920-

*PERSONAL:* Born August 8, 1920, in Mt. St. Aignan, France; son of E. and Y. Aubery; married Eve Lukacs, 1950; children: Eric. *Education:* University of Toulouse, Licence es Lettres, 1944; Duke University, M.A., 1952; Sorbonne, University of Paris, Doctorate, 1954. *Office:* Department of Modern Languages, State University of New York, Buffalo, N.Y. 14260.

*CAREER:* Duke University, Durham, N.C., instructor in Romance languages, 1952-57; Mount Holyoke College, South Hadley, Mass., assistant professor of French, 1957-61; University of Alberta, Edmonton, assistant professor of French literature, 1961-62; State University of New York at Buffalo, associate professor, 1962-67, professor of French, 1967—. Paris correspondent, 1947-52. *Member:* Modern Language Association of America, American Association of Teachers of French, International Association of Sociologists, Society for Eighteenth Century Studies, Society for Twentieth Century Studies. *Awards, honors:* Guggenheim fellow, 1964-65.

*WRITINGS: Milieux Juifs,* Plon (France), 1957; *Pour une lecture ouvriere,* Editions Syndicalistes (Paris), 1971; *Meicislas Goldberg: An Intellectual Biography,* Minard, in press. Civilization editor of *The French Review,* 1967-75; associate editor, *Contemporary French Civilization,* 1976—.

\* \* \*

### AUVERT-EASON, Elizabeth 1917-

*PERSONAL:* Born June 12, 1917, in Maracaibo, Venezuela; daughter of Rodolfo Augusto (a newspaper publisher and merchant) and Albertina (Silva) Auvert; divorced; children: Annabelle, Melissa, Bettina. *Education:* University of Arkansas, Ph.D., 1967. *Politics:* Christian Democrat. *Religion:* Roman Catholic. *Home and office:* Aptdo. Correos, No. 120, Maracaibo, Venezuela.

*CAREER:* Centenary College, Shreveport, La., associate professor, beginning 1969.

*WRITINGS:* (Editor) Lope de Vega, *El Duque de Viseo,* Ediciones Albatros, 1969; *Comparative Historical Chronology of Spain: Twelfth Century B.C. to Twelfth Century A.D.,* Ediciones Albatros, 1972.

*WORK IN PROGRESS:* Editing *Manual de las Comedias de la primera manera,* by Lope de Vega.††

\* \* \*

### AXFORD, H. William 1925-

*PERSONAL:* Born April 7, 1925, in Butte, Mont.; son of Harold F. (a newspaperman) and Della (Albert) Axford; married Lavonne Brady (a librarian), November 11, 1956; children: Victoria Leigh, Katharine Anne. *Education:* Reed College, A.B., 1950; University of Denver, M.A., 1958, Ph.D., 1969. *Home:* 2250 Lawrence, Eugene, Ore. 97405. *Office:* University Library, University of Oregon, Eugene, Ore. 97403.

*CAREER:* University of Denver, Graduate School of Librarianship, Denver, Colo., adjunct member of faculty,

1959-67, assistant director, 1960-65, director of libraries, 1965-67; Florida Atlantic University, Boca Raton, director of libraries, 1967-70; Arizona State University, Tempe, university librarian, 1970-73; University of Oregon, University Library, Eugene, dean and university librarian, 1973—. Visiting faculty member, Graduate School of Library Science, University of Illinois, 1969. New Mexico representative, National Foundation for Infantile Paralysis, 1955-57; head librarian, *Denver Post,* 1958-60; consultant to vice-chancellor for academic affairs, State University System of Florida, 1969-70. *Military service:* U.S. Army, 1943-46. *Member:* American Library Association, National Microfilm Association, Library Automation, Research and Consulting Association (president, 1971; member of board of directors, 1972—). *Awards, honors:* Fulbright lectureship, University of the Punjab, Lahore, West Pakistan, 1963-64.

*WRITINGS: Gilpin County Gold,* Swallow Press, 1977. Editor, *Proceedings of LARC Institutes* series, 1972—.

*     *     *

## AYAL, Igal   1942-

*PERSONAL:* Surname (pronounced Ay-*al*) has been legally changed; born December 1, 1942, in Tel Aviv, Israel; son of Yehoshua (a businessman) and Sara (Walfish) Altstock; married Haviva Wigman (a psychologist), February 6, 1964; children: Ayran, Adi, Guy. *Education:* Hebrew University of Jerusalem, B.S., 1963, Graduate Diploma in Business Administration, 1967; Tel Aviv University, M.B.A. (with distinction), 1968; Harvard University, D.B.A., 1972. *Religion:* Jewish. *Home:* 95 University St., Ramat Aviv, Tel Aviv, Israel. *Office:* Faculty of Management, Tel Aviv University, Ramat Aviv, Tel Aviv, Israel.

*CAREER:* High school teacher of mathematics and physics, in Israel, 1962-63; Israel Ministry of Housing, Jerusalem, consultant to Department of Socio-Economic Research, 1966-68; Creative Studies, Inc., Boston, Mass., senior consultant, 1969-72; University of Connecticut, Storrs, assistant professor of marketing, 1970-74; Tel Aviv University, Ramat Aviv, Tel Aviv, Israel, senior lecturer in marketing, 1974—. *Military service:* Israel Defence Forces, 1963-68; became captain. *Member:* American Marketing Association, Operations Research Society of Israel.

*WRITINGS:* (With wife, Haviva Ayal and A. Berler) *Israeli Towns: A Comparative Study,* Israel Ministry of Housing, 1969; (with J. J. Ziff and E. Orbach) *Marketing a New Product* (Player's Manual and Instructor's Guide), Macmillan, 1971; (with Ziff, Orbach and W. T. Archey) *Sales Strategy and Management* (Player's Manual and Instructor's Guide), Macmillan, 1971; (with Ziff and Orbach) *Supermarket Strategy* (Player's Manual and Instructor's Guide), Macmillan, 1971; (with Ziff) *Sales Forecasting for Field Sales Managers,* American Management Association, 1973.

*WORK IN PROGRESS:* Model-based information systems for marketing new products; models of housing and durable goods markets; experience-based learning.

# B

**BACKUS, Oswald P(rentiss) III 1921-1972**

March 11, 1921—July 9, 1972; American historian and writer on Russian and Slavic subjects. Obituaries: *New York Times*, July 11, 1972. (See index for *CA* sketch)

\*   \*   \*

**BADASH, Lawrence 1934-**

*PERSONAL:* Surname is pronounced *Bay*-dash; born May 8, 1934, in Brooklyn, N.Y.; son of Joseph (a statistician) and Dorothy (Langa) Badash; children: Lisa, Bruce. *Education:* Rensselaer Polytechnic Institute, B.S., 1956; Yale University, Ph.D., 1964. *Home:* 489 Paso Robles Dr., Santa Barbara, Calif. 93108. *Office:* Department of History, University of California, Santa Barbara, Calif. 93106.

*CAREER:* Yale University, New Haven, Conn., instructor, 1964-65; Cambridge University, Cambridge, England, NATO postdoctoral fellow, 1965-66; University of California, Santa Barbara, assistant professor, 1966-73, associate professor of history, 1973—. President of Channel Cities Memorial Society, 1968-69 and 1971-72; member of board of directors, Santa Barbara Chapter of American Civil Liberties Union, 1971-72; member of national board of directors, Sane, 1972—. *Military service:* U.S. Navy, naval aviator, 1956-59; became lieutenant. *Member:* American Association for the Advancement of Science, History of Science Society (member of council, 1974-77), West Coast History of Science Society (co-founder, 1971).

*WRITINGS:* (Editor) *Rutherford and Boltwood: Letters on Radioactivity*, Yale University Press, 1969. Also author of *Rutherford, Kapitza, and the Kremlin*, Yale University Press. Contributor to *Encyclopaedia Britannica, Encyclopedia Americana, Dictionary of Scientific Biography, Dictionary of American History*, and of articles and reviews to academic journals.

*WORK IN PROGRESS:* Research on the history of radioactivity; a biography of Ernest Rutherford; a history of applications of nuclear energy.

\*   \*   \*

**BADGLEY, John 1930-**

*PERSONAL:* Born September 24, 1930, in Missoula, Mont.; son of E. Kirk and Nell (Shepard) Badgley; married Patricia McMeekin (an artist), December 13, 1952; children:

Lya, John Christopher. *Education:* Montana State University (now University of Montana), B.A., 1952; Johns Hopkins School of Advanced International Studies, M.A., 1957; University of California, Berkeley, Ph.D., 1962. *Office:* Institute of the Rockies, 622 Evans, Missoula, Mont. 59801.

*CAREER:* Rangoon University, Rangoon, Burma, acting director of Rangoon-Hopkins Center, 1958; Miami University, Oxford, Ohio, assistant professor of political science and director of non-Western civilizations program, 1962-67; Johns Hopkins University, School of Advanced International Studies, Washington, D.C., associate professor of political science and director of Asian studies, 1967-73; Institute of the Rockies, Missoula, Mont., president, 1973—. Visiting professor, Kyoto University, 1964-65; U.S. State Department lecturer in Asia, Australia, and New Zealand, 1970; adviser on social science program in Thailand, Rockefeller Foundation, 1965. Member of Bitterroot Resource Conservation and Development District, Missoula. Consultant to U.S. Agency for International Development (AID). *Military service:* U.S. Army, 1953-55; became first lieutenant; served in Japan. *Member:* American Political Science Association, Association for Asian Studies (member of board of directors, 1970-73), Asia Society, Burma Research Society. *Awards, honors:* Fulbright scholar in Burma, 1957-58; Ford Foundation foreign area fellow, 1960-62; Danforth associate, 1966-72.

*WRITINGS: A Survey of Burma's Foreign Economic Relations* (monograph), Rangoon University, 1959; (with Robert Osgood and George Packard) *Japan and the United States in Asia*, Johns Hopkins Press, 1969; *Politics among Burmans: A Study of Intermediary Leadership*, Ohio University Press, 1970; *Asian Development: Problems and Prognosis*, Free Press, 1971.

Contributor: Masamichi Inoki, editor, *Japan's Future in Southeast Asia*, Kyoto University Press, 1965; A. M. Halpern, editor, *Policies toward China*, McGraw, 1966; C. W. McWilliams, editor, *Garrisons and Governments*, Chandler Publishing, 1967; Robert Scalapino, editor, *The Communist Revolution in Asia*, Prentice-Hall, 1968; J. Cantori and C. Spiegel, editors, *Comparative Regional International Politics*, Prentice-Hall, 1971; Charles Leslie, editor, *Films and Popular Culture in Asia*, Praeger, 1972. Writer of monographs; contributor of fifteen articles to *Asian Survey, Pacific Affairs, Asian Film, Challenge, Government and Op-*

*position,* and *SAIS Review.* Member of editorial board, *Asian Survey.*

\*     \*     \*

## BADIAN, Ernst 1925-

*PERSONAL:* Born August 8, 1925; son of Joseph and Sally Badian; married Nathlie Anne Wimsett; children: Hugh I., Rosemary J. *Education:* University of New Zealand, B.A., 1944, M.A., 1945; Oxford University, B.A., 1950, M.A., 1954, D.Phil., 1956; Victoria University, Lit.D., 1962. *Office:* Department of History, Harvard University, Cambridge, Mass. 02138.

*CAREER:* University of Sheffield, Sheffield, England, assistant lecturer in classics, 1952-54; University of Durham, Durham, England, lecturer in classics, 1954-64; University of Leeds, Leeds, England, professor of ancient history, 1965-68; State University of New York at Buffalo, professor of classics and history, 1969-71; Harvard University, Cambridge, Mass., professor of history, 1971—. Committee member, Austrian Academy of Sciences, 1975. *Member:* Society for Roman Studies (London), Society for Hellenic Studies (London), Classical Association (England), Virgil Society (London), British Institute of Persian Studies, Classical Association of Canada, American Philological Association, American Numismatic Society, Association of Ancient Historians. *Awards, honors:* Conington Prize, Oxford University, 1959, for *Foreign Clientelae;* British Academy fellow, 1965; American Academy of Arts and Sciences fellow, 1974.

*WRITINGS: Foreign Clientelae (264-70 B.C.),* Clarendon Press, 1958; *Studies in Greek and Roman History,* Barnes & Noble, 1964; (editor and author of introduction) *Polybius,* Pocket Books, 1966; (editor) *Ancient Society and Institutions,* Barnes & Noble, 1967; *Roman Imperialism in the Late Republic,* University of South Africa, 1967, Cornell University Press, 1968; *Publicans and Sinners,* Cornell University Press, 1972. Contributor of numerous articles to journals around the world, and to *Encyclopaedia Britannica, Oxford Classical Dictionary, Artemis Lexikon der Alten Welt.* Editor, *American Journal of Ancient History.*

*WORK IN PROGRESS:* Two books, *Roman Provincial Administration under the Republic* and *The Freedom of the Greeks;* articles on Greek and Roman history and on the history of classical scholarship.

\*     \*     \*

## BADURA-SKODA, Eva 1929-

*PERSONAL:* Born January 15, 1929, in Munich, Germany; daughter of Karl (a doctor of laws) and Elisabeth (Goette) Halfar; married Paul Badura-Skoda (a concert pianist), September 19, 1951; children: Ludwig, Christina, Elisabeth, Michael. *Education:* Studied at University of Heidelberg, 1949, Academy of Music, Vienna, 1949-51, and University of Vienna, 1949-52; University of Innsbruck, Ph.D., 1953. *Religion:* Roman Catholic. *Office:* Zuckerkandlgasse 14, Vienna A-1190, Austria.

*CAREER:* International Summer Academy Mozart, Salzburg, Austria, professor of musicology, 1962-63; University of Wisconsin—Madison, Brittingham Guest Professor, 1964, professor of musicology, 1966-74; Council on Intercultural Relations, Vienna, Austria, faculty member, 1973-75; musicologist, writer. Guest lecturer at Mozart Conference at Stanford University, at University of Amsterdam, and for music academies and societies in the United States, Canada,

England, Denmark, Holland, Germany, Austria, Hungary, Israel, Russia, and Japan. *Member:* International Musicological Society, American Musicological Society, Music Library Association, and a number of other international and national professional societies.

*WRITINGS:* (With husband, Paul Badura-Skoda) *Mozart–Interpretation,* Wancura (Vienna), 1957, translation by Leo Black published as *Interpreting Mozart on the Keyboard,* St. Martin's, 1962, 2nd edition, 1965; (editor) *Musik alter Meister,* Volume VII, Akademie Graz, 1959; *Mozart's Klavierkonzert in c-moll,* Fink Verlag (Munich), 1972. Also editor of piano trios by Franz Schubert and of three concertos by W. A. Mozart. Contributor to *Musik in Geschichte und Gegenwart, Mozart-Jahrbuch, Grove's Dictionary of Music and Musicians* (6th edition), and music journals.

*WORK IN PROGRESS:* A history of the Viennese singspiel before Mozart; an edition of Mozart's piano sonatas; a book on Schubert.

*SIDELIGHTS:* In addition to the English translation, the Badura-Skodas' *Mozart–Interpretation* has been published in French, Italian, Japanese, and Russian. *Avocational interests:* Chess, skiing.

\*     \*     \*

## BAENSCH, Willy E(dward) 1893-1972

February 5, 1893—November 1, 1972; German-born physician, radiologist, and educator. Obituaries: *New York Times,* November 3, 1972.

\*     \*     \*

## BAILEY, Joe A(llen) 1929-

*PERSONAL:* Born April 25, 1929, in Amarillo, Tex.; son of James William and Jewel (Cox) Bailey. *Education:* Amarillo College, A.S., 1948; West Texas State College (now University), B.S., 1950, M.A., 1951; University of Texas, Ph.D., 1960. *Politics:* Democrat. *Home:* 120 Dorking Rd., Rochester, N.Y. 14610. *Office:* Marketing Education Center, Eastman Kodak Co., 343 State St., Rochester, N.Y. 14650.

*CAREER:* Teacher in secondary schools of Amarillo, Tex., 1950-52; West Texas State College (now University), Canyon, instructor in speech and coordinator of department of public services, 1952-54; University of Texas at Austin, assistant professor of speech, 1960-68; Eastman Kodak Co., Marketing Education Center, Rochester, N.Y., coordinator of educational design and manager of marketing fundamentals, 1968—, coordinator of validation services, 1976—; State University of New York College at Brockport, associate professor of communication, 1971—. Communication consultant, U.S. Office of Economic Opportunity, 1967-68; lecturer, School of Business, Rochester Institute of Technology, 1976—. *Military service:* U.S. Army, 4th Armored Division, information and education officer, 1953-56; became first lieutenant.

*MEMBER:* Speech Association of America, University Film Producers, National Society for the Study of Communication, Southern Speech Association, New York State Speech Association, Phi Delta Kappa. *Awards, honors:* National Association of Broadcasters grant, 1966.

*WRITINGS:* (Contributor) R. Wayne Pace, editor, *Teaching Business and Professional Speaking,* University of Montana, 1967; (with Kelton C. Lahue) *Glass, Brass, and Chrome,* University of Oklahoma Press, 1972; (with Lahue) *Collecting Vintage Cameras,* Amphoto, Volume I, 1972;

*Peterson's Guide to Architectural Photography,* Peterson's Guides, 1973; *Peterson's Guide to Photography Equipment Restoration,* Peterson's Guides, 1973.

Films: (Author, director, and photographer) "A Present to Your Future," West Texas State College, 1954; (editor and photographer) "Dedicated Hands," Holy Cross Films, 1963; (editor and photographer) "They Can't Stay Home," Franciscan Films, 1964. Photographs have been used in brochures and displays for universities and other organizations. Contributor to speech and photography journals. Editor, *Photographic Historical Society Newsletter.*

*WORK IN PROGRESS:* Volume II and III of *Collecting Vintage Cameras.*

*AVOCATIONAL INTERESTS:* Woodworking, electronics, business history.

* * *

## BAILEY, John A(medee) 1929-

*PERSONAL:* Born November 26, 1929, in Rochester, N.Y.; son of George Olney (a manufacturer) and Dorothy (Cerf) Bailey; married Marjean Linn, May 22, 1954; children: Amadea Cerf, Adam Olney, Saskia, Aaron. *Education:* Harvard University, A.B. (with high honors), 1951; Union Theological Seminary, New York, N.Y., B.D. (with honors), 1955; University of Goettingen, graduate study, 1956-57; University of Basel, D.Theol. (with high honors), 1959. *Politics:* Democrat. *Home:* 1931 Lorraine Pl., Ann Arbor, Mich. 48104. *Office:* Department of Near Eastern Languages and Literature, University of Michigan, Ann Arbor, Mich. 48104.

*CAREER:* Clergyman of Protestant Episcopal Church, ordained in 1960; Colorado College, Colorado Springs, instructor, 1959-61, assistant professor of religion and acting chairman of department, 1961-62; St. Paul's United Theological College, Limuru, Kenya, tutor, 1962-66; University of Michigan, Ann Arbor, assistant professor, 1966-71, associate professor in department of Near Eastern languages and literatures, 1971—, director of studies in religion program, 1969-71. Lecturer, Mindolo Ecumenical Center, Kitwe, Zambia, 1963. Co-chairman, Ann Arbor Interfaith Council for Peace. *Member:* Society of Biblical Literature, American Academy of Religion, American Schools of Oriental Research. *Awards, honors:* University of Michigan Distinguished Service Award for outstanding teaching, 1971.

*WRITINGS: The Traditions Common to the Gospels of Luke and John,* E. J. Brill, 1963; *The Ministry of the Church in the World,* Oxford University Press, 1967. Contributor to religion journals.

*WORK IN PROGRESS:* A study in biblical theology.

*AVOCATIONAL INTERESTS:* Art, music, travel.

* * *

## BAKKE, Mary S(terling) 1904-

*PERSONAL:* Surname is pronounced *Bach*-key; born March 3, 1904, in Sioux City, Iowa; daughter of Howard H. (a contractor) and May L. (Ralya) Sterling; married E. Wight Bakke (Sterling Professor of Economics at Yale University), September 1, 1926 (died, November, 1971); children: Karl Edward, Carolyn Sterling (Mrs. Albert S. Bacdayan), William Wight. *Education:* Morningside College, Diploma in Education, 1923; further study at University of Nebraska, 1924, Yale University, 1928, and Northwestern University, 1929. *Politics:* Independent. *Religion:* Society

of Friends (Quaker). *Office:* Sterling Heights, Sterling Hill Rd., Lyme, Conn. 06371.

*CAREER:* High school teacher in Emerson, Neb., 1923-26; Quinnipiac College, New Haven, Conn., teacher of English and business letters, 1930-53, dean of women and director of remedial services, 1947-53 (college has since been relocated in Hamden, Conn.). Research assistant at Yale University. Former secretary, Woodbridge Recreation Commission; chairman, Future Planning Committee; chairman, Cooperative Community Nursery School. *Member:* American Association of University Women (member of executive board, New Haven branch), New Haven Colony Historical Society, Lyme Historical Society, Yale Club of New York City.

*WRITINGS:* (With late husband, E. Wight Bakke) *Campus Challenge: Student Activism in Perspective,* Archon Books, 1971. Also author of *A Sampler of Lifestyles: Womanhood and Youth in Colonial Lyme,* 1976. Assisted her husband in research and editing of four books published under his name.

*WORK IN PROGRESS:* With Bessie L. Gambrill, a book on Japanese children; children's stories on frontier life; history of Sterling City area in Connecticut.

*SIDELIGHTS:* Mary S. Bakke told *CA:* "Discovery of a lot of local history and primary source materials, while doing research for *A Sampler of Lifestyles,* but not appropriate for that because [it was] not of [the] colonial period, has given me a new project. Encouraged by interest and excellent sale of the previous book, I feel that the story of how people lived and played in the years since the colonial period will also be well received. Moreover, the new friendships of informants are enjoyable."

*BIOGRAPHICAL/CRITICAL SOURCES: New Haven Register,* June 25, 1972.

* * *

## BANDY, W(illiam) T(homas) 1903-

*PERSONAL:* Born May 11, 1903, in Nashville, Tenn.; son of William Thomas and Margaret (Villines) Bandy; married Alice Scudder Burghardt, November 5, 1929; married second wife, Carol Dieckman, October 19, 1970; children: (first marriage) Jane (Mrs. Burr McWilliams), William Thomas III, Peter Burghardt, Helen Margaret (Mrs. George B. Spiegelman), Carol Villines (Mrs. Michael Oberdorfer), Cynthia Palmer (Mrs. Thomas J. O'Brien). *Education:* Vanderbilt University, B.A., 1923, M.A., 1926; George Peabody College for Teachers, Ph.D., 1931; also attended University of Grenoble, 1924, University of Paris, 1925, 1926-27, University of Illinois, 1927-28, and University of Strasbourg, 1928. *Home:* 3415 West End Ave., Nashville, Tenn. 37203. *Office:* Department of French, Vanderbilt University, Nashville, Tenn. 37203.

*CAREER:* Stephens College, Columbia, Mo., head of department of modern languages, 1931-36; University of Wisconsin—Madison, assistant professor, 1936-44, associate professor, 1944-49, professor of French, 1949-68, chairman of department of French and Italian, 1959-68; Vanderbilt University, Nashville, Tenn., distinguished professor of French and director of Center for Baudelaire Studies, 1968-73, professor emeritus, 1973—. *Military service:* U.S. Naval Reserve, active duty, 1942-46; became commander.

*MEMBER:* Modern Language Association of America (member of executive council, 1966-70), American Association of Teachers of French, Association internationale des Etudes francaises, Societe d'Histoire litteraire de la France.

*Awards, honors:* American Field Service fellow, 1928-30; Fulbright research scholar, 1955-56; Prix Racine of Societe Racinienne (Paris), 1956.

*WRITINGS:* (Translator) Paul Valery, *Stendhal,* Black Manikin Press (Paris), 1930; (compiler) *A Word-Index of Baudelaire's Poems,* privately printed, 1939; (with Jules Mouquet, author of introduction and notes) *Baudelaire en 1848* (extracts from *Tribune Nationale*), Emile-Paul (Paris), 1946; *Repertoire des ecrits sur Baudelaire,* privately printed, 1953; *Index des mots d'Athalie* (booklet), Klincksieck (Paris), 1955; (with Claude Pichois) *Baudelaire devant ses contemporains* (based on *Baudelaire Judged by His Contemporaries,* 1933), Editions du Rocher (Monaco), 1957, new edition, UGE (Paris), 1967; *Baudelaire: An Exhibition Commemorating the Centennial of "Les Fleurs du mal"* (booklet), Memorial Library, University of Wisconsin, 1957; (with Henri Peyre and others) *The Centennial Celebration of Baudelaire's "Les Fleurs du mal,"* edited by Paul Engle, University of Texas Press, 1958; *The Influence and Reputation of Edgar Allan Poe in Europe* (Edgar Allan Poe Society lecture, 1959), privately printed, 1962; *Baudelaire and Poe* (exhibition catalog), Center for Baudelaire Studies, Vanderbilt University, 1969; (with Richard Switzer and others) *Pensee et Litterature francaise* (anthology), McGraw, 1971; (with Pichois) *Etudes Baudelairiennes II,* Editions de la Baconniere (Neuchatel), 1971; (translator and editor) Baudelaire, *Seven Tales by Poe,* Schocken, 1971; (editor) Baudelaire, *E. A. Poe: Sa vie et ses ouvrages,* University of Toronto Press, 1973.

Contributor to more than thirty journals. Editor, *Bulletin Baudelairien;* member of editorial advisory board, *Essays in French Literature* and *L'Esprit createur.*

*WORK IN PROGRESS:* Editing Baudelaire's translation of George Croly's *The Young Enchanter;* a comprehensive bibliography of writings by and about Baudelaire.

*AVOCATIONAL INTERESTS:* Cryptography, bass fishing, carpentry and tinkering, photography, tennis.

*      *      *

## BANGS, Robert B(abbitt)   1914-
### (Robert Babbitt)

*PERSONAL:* Born February 18, 1914, in Paullina, Iowa; son of Cecil Warren (a school administrator) and Madge (Babbitt) Bangs; married Lucretia Lillie (a treasurer), September 9, 1937; children: Stephen J., Geoffrey E. *Education:* Coe College, B.A., 1935; Tufts University, M.A., 1937; Brown University, Ph.D., 1941. *Politics:* Democrat. *Religion:* Congregational.

*CAREER:* U.S. Department of Commerce, Washington, D.C., economist, 1941-43; Indiana University at Bloomington, assistant professor of economics, 1945-46; National Housing Agency, Washington, D.C., economist, 1946-47; U.S. Treasury Department, Washington, D.C., economist, 1947-51; U.S. Department of Commerce, deputy director of program planning, 1951-53; consultant in economic development to governments of Egypt and Burma, 1953-56; Federal Reserve System, Board of Governors, Washington, D.C., senior economist in government finance, 1956-62; U.S. Department of Commerce, Washington, D.C., senior economist, 1962-72. Researcher, Patent, Trademark, and Copyright Research Institute, George Washington University, 1956-71. Consultant Central Bank of Costa Rica, 1961, and to governments of Iran, 1964, and Ethiopia, 1965. *Military service:* U.S. Army Air Forces, 1943-45; became first lieu-

tenant. *Member:* American Economic Association, National Economists Club, Tax Institute of America.

*WRITINGS: Financing Economic Development: Fiscal Policy for Emerging Countries,* University of Chicago Press, 1968; *Men, Money, and Markets: An Introduction to Economic Reasoning,* Boxwood Press, 1972; (under name Robert Babbitt) *The Adventures of Bumpy,* Exposition Press, 1973. Contributor of over fifty articles to professional journals.†

*      *      *

## BARASCH, Frances K.   1928-

*PERSONAL:* Born April 10, 1928, in New York, N.Y.; daughter of Jacob Michael (a merchant) and Eva (Hochberg) Karten; married Seymour Barasch (a college administrator), June 8, 1952; children: Jerry, Elihu M., Daniel. *Education:* Brooklyn College (now Brooklyn College of the City University of New York), B.A., 1949; New York University, M.A., 1952, Ph.D., 1964. *Home:* 93-26 86th Ave., Woodhaven, N.Y. 11421. *Office:* Department of English, Bernard M. Baruch College of the City University of New York, New York, N.Y. 10010.

*CAREER:* Worked on *Brooklyn Eagle,* Brooklyn, N.Y., after finishing high school, and taught dance professionally while an undergraduate at Brooklyn College and graduate student at New York University; New York University, New York City, administrative assistant, 1957-60, instructor in English, 1959-61; Pace College (now University), New York City, assistant professor of English, 1961-64; Long Island University, New York City, assistant professor of English, 1964-65; Bernard M. Baruch College of the City University of New York, New York City, assistant professor, 1965-72, associate professor, 1972-77, professor of English, 1977—. *Member:* Modern Language Association of America, American Association of University Professors, Education Writers Association, Northeast Modern Language Association, New York University Graduate Alumni Association (president, 1977), Medieval Club of New York.

*WRITINGS: Review Notes and Study Guide to Shakespeare's "Henry IV, Part II,"* Monarch, 1964; (editor and revisor) Grover Cronin, Jr., *The Romantic Poets,* Monarch, 1966; (bibliographer) Ruth Z. Temple, editor, *Modern British Literature,* Ungar, Volume III, 1966; (editor and author of introduction) Thomas Wright, *A History of Caricature and the Grotesque in Literature and Art,* Ungar, 1968; (editor) Martin Tucker, general editor, *The Critical Temper,* Volume II: *The Romantic Period,* Ungar, 1969; *The Grotesque: A Study in Meanings,* Gruyter, 1971; (editor and revisor) Dorothy Rabinowitz and Yedida Nielsen, *Home Life,* Macmillan, 1971; *Academic Women and Unions,* Modern Language Association, 1974; (contributor) Barry R. Gross, editor, *Reverse Discrimination,* Prometheus, 1977. Also editor and revisor of other Monarch study guides to literature. Writer of column, "Women in a Corner," for *Action,* 1971-72. Contributor to professional journals on higher education and public issues. Editor, *PSC Clarion,* 1972—.

*WORK IN PROGRESS: New Essays on the Grotesque,* with Robert E. Helbling.

*SIDELIGHTS:* Frances Barasch writes: "Whether I do 'academic journalism' or scholarly work, I write to keep my own head straight about what there is to know and how to organize knowledge that I want others to learn, not only the ivory-tower subjects of language and literature, but also those that concern the larger world. It seems to me that a writing-educator is the best kind of educator to be."

*BIOGRAPHICAL/CRITICAL SOURCES:* New York Times, November 16, 1966; Romanic Review, May, 1974.

\* \* \*

## BARBARA, Dominick A. 1914-

*PERSONAL:* Born August 24, 1914, in New York, N.Y.; son of Anthony (a tailor) and Josephine Barbara; married Virginia Bambara (a nurse); children: Dominick, Jr., Joanne, Paul. *Education:* University of Alabama, A.B., 1936; University of Bologna, M.D., 1940; American Institute of Psychoanalysis, Psychoanalyst, 1949. *Religion:* Roman Catholic.

*CAREER:* Psychoanalyst in private practice in Hewlett, N.Y. *Member:* American Psychiatric Association, International Platform Association, Queens County Medical Society. *Awards, honors:* American Medical Writers Association award in communication, 1966.

*WRITINGS*—Published by C. C Thomas, except as indicated: *Stuttering,* Julian Press, 1954; *Your Speech Reveals Your Personality,* 1958; *The Art of Listening,* 1960; *Psychological and Psychiatric Aspects of Speech and Hearing Problems,* 1962; *New Directions in Stuttering,* 1964; *The Psychotherapy of Stuttering,* 1966; (with Robert T. Oliver) *The Healthy Mind in Communion and Communication,* 1966; *Questions and Answers on Stuttering,* 1967; *How to Make People Listen to You,* 1972; *Loving and Making Love,* Farnsworth Publishing, 1975. Editor of "American Lecture Series in Communication."†

\* \* \*

## BARKIN, David Peter 1942-

*PERSONAL:* Born February 3, 1942, in New York, N.Y. *Education:* Columbia University, A.B., 1962; Yale University, M.A., 1963, Ph.D., 1966. *Home:* 789 West End Ave., Apt. 2C, New York, N.Y. 10025. *Office:* Department of Economics, Herbert H. Lehman College of the City University of New York, Bronx, N.Y. 10468.

*CAREER:* Washington University, St. Louis, Mo., assistant professor of economics, 1966-68; New York University, New York, N.Y., assistant professor of economics, 1968-71; Herbert H. Lehman College of the City University of New York, Bronx, N.Y., associate professor of economics, 1971—. Visiting professor, Collegio de Mexico, 1967, 1969, 1970, 1971. *Awards, honors:* American Philosophical Society grant, South America, 1970; Social Science Research Council fellow, Mexico, 1970-71; Foreign Area Fellowship Program fellow, Chile, 1972-73.

*WRITINGS:* (With Timothy King) *Regional Economic Development: The River Basin Approach in Mexico,* Cambridge University Press, 1970; (with Nita R. Manitzas) *Cuba: Camino Abierto,* Siglo XXI Editores, S.A. (Mexico), 1972; (editor with Manitzas) *Cuba: The Logic of the Revolution,* Warner Modular Publications, 1973; *Mexico's Albatross: The United States Economy,* Institute of Latin American Studies, University of Texas at Austin, 1973. Also author of numerous economic research reports. Contributor to professional journals.

*WORK IN PROGRESS:* Research on economic growth, political manipulation and social stagnation in Mexico; Cuba's development; *Education: The Maintenance of the Status Quo.*†

\* \* \*

## BARRETT, Gerald Van 1936-

*PERSONAL:* Born August 3, 1936, in Bellefontaine, Ohio; son of Charles L. (a physician) and Evelyn (Snap) Barrett; married C. Patricia Gregory, September 9, 1960; children: Chas, Jera, Gregory. *Education:* Wittenberg University, B.A., 1958; Western Reserve University (now Case Western Reserve University), M.S., 1959, Ph.D., 1962. *Home:* 3088 Highland Dr., Silver Lake, Ohio 44224. *Office:* Department of Psychology, University of Akron, Akron, Ohio 44325.

*CAREER:* Western Reserve University (now Case Western Reserve University), Cleveland, Ohio, research associate, 1959-62; Cleveland State College (now University), Cleveland, instructor, 1962; Goodyear Aerospace Corp., Akron, Ohio, research associate, 1962-64, director of human factors laboratory, 1964-67; University of Pittsburgh, Pittsburgh, Pa., assistant director of management research center, 1967-68; University of Rochester, Rochester, N.Y., associate professor in Graduate School of Management and department of psychology and associate director of Management Research Center, 1968-73; University of Akron, Akron, Ohio, professor of psychology and head of department, 1973—. Diplomate in industrial and organizational psychology, American Board of Professional Psychology. Consultant to numerous organizations, including Goodyear Aerospace Corp., Canada Council, Squire, Sanders & Dempsey, Singer, Sybron, and Bausch & Lomb. *Member:* American Psychological Association (fellow), American Association for the Advancement of Science, Human Factors Society.

*WRITINGS: Motivation in Industry,* Howard Allen, 1966; (with B. M. Bass) *Man, Work, and Organization: An Introduction to Industrial and Organizational Psychology,* Allyn & Bacon, 1972, 2nd edition, in press.

Contributor: John B. Blood, Jr., editor, *Management Science in Planning,* Technical Association of the Pulp and Paper Industry, 1969; Jean Boddewyn, editor, *Comparative Management: Teaching, Training and Research,* New York University Press, 1970; B. M. Bass, R. C. Cooper, and J. A. Haas, editors, *Managing for Task Accomplishment,* Heath, 1970; L. E. Abt and B. F. Riess, editors, *Progress in Clinical Psychology: Industrial Applications,* Grune, 1971; Samuel S. Dubin, editor, *Professional Obsolescence,* English Universities Press, 1971; K.N. Wexley and G. A. Yukl, editors, *Organizational Behavior and Industrial Psychology,* Oxford University Press, 1975; M. D. Dunnette, editor, *Handbook of Industrial and Organizational Psychology,* Rand McNally, 1976; Anant R. Negandhi and Bernhard Wilpert, editors, *Work Organization Research: European and American Perspectives,* Kent State University Press, 1978.

Author or co-author of a number of research reports for U.S. Department of Health, Education and Welfare and Goodyear Aerospace Corp. Contributor of over sixty articles to professional journals.

\* \* \*

## BARRETT, J(ohn) Edward 1932-

*PERSONAL:* Born December 18, 1932, in Philadelphia, Pa.; son of John Edward (a transportation company general manager) and Edna Mae (Borlase) Barrett; married Suzanne Lehr, March 7, 1959; children: Jeanne Heather, Elizabeth Sue. *Education:* Susquehanna University, A.B., 1955; Princeton University, B.D., 1958, Th.M., 1960; University of St. Andrews, Scotland, Ph.D., 1965. *Religion:* Presbyterian. *Home address:* Route 1, New Concord, Ohio 43762. *Office:* Department of Religion and Philosophy, Muskingum College, New Concord, Ohio 43762.

*CAREER:* Minister of Presbyterian Church, ordained in 1958; First Presbyterian Church, Glassboro, N.J., minister, 1958-62; Muskingum College, New Concord, Ohio, associate professor, 1964-75, professor of religion and philosophy, 1975—. *Member:* American Association of University Professors, American Academy of Religion.

*WRITINGS: How Are You Programmed?*, John Knox, 1971. Contributor of articles to *Zygon, Christian Century, Presbyterian Life,* and *Christian Ministry.*

*WORK IN PROGRESS:* Writings on the nature of religious experience and on comparative theories of human nature.

\*　　\*　　\*

### BARRETT, Nancy Smith 1942-

*PERSONAL:* Born September 12, 1942, in Baltimore, Md.; daughter of James Brady (a physician) and Katherine (Pollard) Smith; married Harold Clark Barrett (a stockbroker), April 16, 1966; children: Harold Clark, Jr., Christopher. *Education:* Goucher College, A.B. (summa cum laude), 1963; Harvard University, M.A., 1965, Ph.D., 1968. *Home:* 2034 Hillyer Pl. N.W., Washington, D.C. 20009. *Office:* Department of Economics, American University, Washington, D.C. 20016.

*CAREER:* American University, Washington, D.C., instructor, 1966-67, assistant professor, 1967-70, associate professor, beginning 1970, currently professor of economics. Consultant, Department of Commerce of the Economic Development Administration, 1969, and International—American Development Bank, 1969—. Member of regional advisory panel, Woodrow Wilson Foundation, 1971—. *Member:* American Economic Association, Phi Beta Kappa. *Awards, honors:* Woodrow Wilson fellowship, 1963-64; American University award, 1970-71, as outstanding woman faculty member; U.S. Department of Labor Manpower Administration research grant, American University, 1972-73; honorary Fulbright fellow, University of Gothenburg, Sweden, 1973.

*WRITINGS: The Theory of Macroeconomic Policy,* Prentice-Hall, 1972, 2nd edition, 1975; (with G. Bocchieri and T. Hart) *Prices and Wages in U.S. Manufacturing: A Factor Analysis,* Heath, 1973; *The Theory of Microeconomic Policy,* Heath, 1974; (contributor) Jane R. Chapman and Margaret Gates, editors, *Economic Independence for Women: The Foundation for Equal Rights,* Volume I, Sage Publications, 1976; (contributor) Juanita M. Kreps, editor, *Women and the American Economy: A Look to the 1980s,* Prentice-Hall, 1976. Contributor of articles to *Journal of Political Economy, American Economic Review, Swedish Journal of Economics, Journal of Human Resources, Quarterly Journal of Economics,* and other economics journals.

\*　　\*　　\*

### BARRY, Herbert III 1930-

*PERSONAL:* Born June 2, 1930, in New York, N.Y.; son of Herbert, Jr. (a psychiatrist) and Lucy (Brown) Barry. *Education:* Harvard University, B.A., 1952; Yale University, M.S., 1953, Ph.D., 1957. *Politics:* Democrat. *Home:* 123 University Pl., Pittsburgh, Pa. 15213. *Office:* School of Pharmacy, University of Pittsburgh, Pittsburgh, Pa. 15213.

*CAREER:* Yale University, New Haven, Conn., assistant professor of psychology, 1960-61; University of Connecticut, Storrs, assistant professor of psychology, 1961-63; University of Pittsburgh, School of Pharmacy, Pittsburgh, Pa., associate professor, 1963-70, professor of pharmacology,

1970—. Member of alcohol research review committee, National Institute on Alcohol Abuse and Alcoholism, 1972-76. *Military service:* U.S. Army Reserve, 1951-57; became sergeant. *Member:* Society for Cross-Cultural Research (president, 1973-74), Phi Beta Kappa, Sigma Xi. *Awards, honors:* Research Scientist Development Award from National Institute of Mental Health, 1967-77.

*WRITINGS:* (With Henrik Wallgren) *Actions of Alcohol,* two volumes, Elsevier, 1970. Contributor of more than a hundred articles to scientific journals. Managing editor, *Psychopharmacology,* 1974—; consulting editor to several journals on alcohol and pharmacology research, and on cross-cultural comparisons.

*WORK IN PROGRESS: Bio-Medical Statistics,* a textbook; research on effects of drugs, including alcohol and marijuana, on behavior of rats; cross-cultural research comparing child training with other customs; studying birth order and first name as determinants of adult personality and behavior.

*SIDELIGHTS:* Herbert Barry told *CA:* "I believe that the key to successful writing is a chronic obsession with the project. With this prerequisite, the brain continually creates both the general ideas and the specific phrases, even at times when the conscious thoughts and efforts are elsewhere. Two techniques, which are helpful for most writers, are . . . thorough revisions of what has been written, . . . [and] a regular schedule of several consecutive hours at the same time of day devoted to the writing."

\*　　\*　　\*

### BARRY, James P(otvin) 1918-

*PERSONAL:* Born October 23, 1918, in Alton, Ill.; son of Paul A. (a U.S. army officer) and Elder (Potvin) Barry; married Anne Jackson (an education librarian), April 16, 1966. *Education:* Ohio State University, B.A. (cum laude), 1940; U.S. Army Command and General Staff College, honor graduate, 1959. *Home:* 353 Fairway Blvd., Columbus, Ohio 43213. *Office:* Ohioana Library Association, 1105 Ohio Departments Buildings, 65 South Front St., Columbus, Ohio 43215.

*CAREER:* U.S. Army, Artillery, 1940-66, with worldwide assignments ranging from adviser to Turkish Army to staff and editorial work in the Pentagon; became colonel; Capital University, Columbus, Ohio, administrator, 1967-71; freelance writer and editor, 1971—. Director, Ohioana Library Association, 1977—. *Member:* Marine Historical Society, Great Lakes Historical Society, Ohio Historical Society, Phi Beta Kappa, World Ship Society, Royal Canadian Yacht Club. *Awards, honors:* Award from American Society for State and Local History, 1974, for *Ships of the Great Lakes.*

*WRITINGS: Georgian Bay: The Sixth Great Lake,* Clarke, Irwin, 1968, revised and enlarged edition, 1978; *The Battle of Lake Erie* (young adult), F. Watts, 1970; *Bloody Kansas* (young adult), F. Watts, 1972; *The Noble Experiment* (young adult), F. Watts, 1972; (illustrated with photographs by author) *The Fate of the Lakes,* Baker Book, 1972; *The Louisiana Purchase* (young adult), F. Watts, 1973; *Henry Ford and Mass Production* (young adult), F. Watts, 1973; *Ships of the Great Lakes,* Howell-North Books, 1973; *The Berlin Olympics* (young adult), F. Watts, 1975; *The Great Lakes* (children), F. Watts, 1976; *Old Forts of the Great Lakes,* Trans-Anglo, 1978. Contributor of articles and reviews to journals and magazines. Former editor of military publications. Editor, *Ohioana Quarterly,* 1977—.

*WORK IN PROGRESS:* A photo book on Lake Erie.

*SIDELIGHTS:* James P. Barry has been interested in writing since high school and two articles by him were published in *Yachting* while he was in college. Afterward, he wrote "technical military publications until [his] retirement from the army in 1966." Since then, he has returned to historical and regional writing.

A reviewer for *Financial Post* (Toronto) says of *Ships of the Great Lakes,* "Few documentations could prove as moving as this vivid, technically superior picture book." In *Yachting,* a reviewer writes of the same book: "A project of this enormous scope requires of its narrator not only an intimate knowledge of a dozen subjects touching upon these large and famous bodies of water, but a style that will make the layman follow attentively in the author's footsteps. Mr. Barry happily possesses both these qualities and more."

*AVOCATIONAL INTERESTS:* Photography, beagling, sailing, theater, travel.

*BIOGRAPHICAL/CRITICAL SOURCES: Financial Post,* June 23, 1973; *Yachting,* August, 1973.

\* \* \*

## BARTEK, E(dward) J(ohn) 1921-

*PERSONAL:* Surname legally changed, January, 1945; born November 25, 1921, in Hartford, Conn.; son of Michael and Anna (Zabiecka) Bartosiewicz; married Eugenia Redekas, November 19, 1949; children: Alexander, Thomas. *Education:* Attended University of Connecticut; Hillyer College (now University of Hartford), B.A., 1953, M.Ed., 1954. *Home:* 68 Walnut St., East Hartford, Conn. 06108.

*CAREER:* Has worked as legal investigator and claims examiner; A. I. Prince School, Hartford, Conn., teacher of English literature, grammar, and social studies, 1954-74, head of department of general education, 1955-74. Instructor at University of Connecticut, 1957-58, Howell-Cheney School, Manchester, Conn., 1969, Manchester Community College, 1970-78, Experimental College, 1971-72, Young Men's Christian Association (YMCA), Hartford, 1971-74, and Middlesex Community College, 1976-78. Consultant in philosophical guidance and psychology, 1970-78. *Military service:* U.S. Navy, 1939-45. *Member:* American Philosophical Association, American Society for Value Inquiry, International Society for Comparative Study of Civilizations.

*WRITINGS*—All published by Trinity College Press, except as indicated: *A Treasury of Parables,* Philosophical Library, 1959; *Truth and Wisdom* (poetry), four volumes, 1964-69; *To Go to Sleep,* 1964; *The Mind of Future Man,* 1965; *Unifying Principles of the Mind,* 1965; *To Relax Tensions,* 1965; *The Ultimate Philosophy: Trinityism,* 1968; *Unifying Principles of Philosophy,* 1971; *The Philosophy of Trinityism,* 1972, revised edition, 1974; *The Trinitarian Philosophy: An Abstract,* 1972; *Trinitarian Philosophical Psychology,* 1974; *Trinitarian Philosophy-Psychology Poems,* 1975.

*WORK IN PROGRESS: Dream-Analysis for Self-Analysis; Three Lives for One,* a novel; *Rational Unifying Principles of the Soul and Time/Motion/Space.*

*SIDELIGHTS:* E. J. Bartek writes: "I have taken a lifetime to find the ultimate philosophy based on the ultimate principles of the Ultimate Creation, to which all knowledge is coherently unified, and from which all knowledge may be rationally deduced. This philosophy may explain all knowledge by 33 principles and one structure that are common to all the divinities, humanities and sciences. . . . It easily elimi-

nates bigotry, without cost, as billions of dollars [have] not done. There is something wrong when this advance in the mind of man remains unknown though it has never been denied."

\* \* \*

## BARTLEY, William Warren III 1934-

*PERSONAL:* Born October 2, 1934, in Pittsburgh, Pa.; son of William Warren, Jr. and Elvina (Henry) Bartley. *Education:* Harvard University, A.B., 1956, A.M., 1958; London School of Economics and Political Science, Ph.D., 1962. *Office:* Department of Philosophy, California State University, Hayward, Calif. 94542.

*CAREER:* University of London, London, England, London School of Economics and Political Science, lecturer in logic, 1960-63, Warburg Institute, lecturer in history of the philosophy of science, 1961-63; University of California, Berkeley, and University of California, San Diego, associate professor of philosophy, 1963-67; University of Pittsburgh, Pittsburgh, Pa., professor of philosophy and history, and philosophy of science, 1967-73, associate director of Philosophy of Science Center, 1971-73; California State University, Hayward, professor of philosophy, 1970—. Member of governing panel, Werner Erhard Charitable Foundation, 1976—; member of board of advisors, est (educational company), London, 1977—. *Member:* American Philosophical Association, Mind Association, Aristotelian Society, Royal Institute of Philosophy, British Society for Philosophy of Science, Pacific Coast Theological Society, Lewis Carroll Society. *Awards, honors:* Fulbright award, 1958-60; Danforth Foundation award, 1956-60, 1966-67; Cambridge University fellow, 1966-67; American Council of Learned Societies award, 1972-73, for study in China.

*WRITINGS: The Retreat to Commitment,* Knopf, 1962; *Flucht ins Engagement,* Szczesny (Munich), 1964; *Morality and Religion,* St. Martin's, 1971; *Wittgenstein,* Lippincott, 1973; *Lewis Carroll's Symbolic Logic,* C. N. Potter, 1977; *Werner Erhard: The Transformation of a Man: The Founding of est,* C. N. Potter, 1978. Contributor of articles to *New York Review of Books, Harper's, New Republic, New Statesman, Commentary, Times Literary Supplement, Encounter,* and professional journals. Associate editor, *History and Theory,* 1958-65; member of editorial board, *Soundings,* 1967-69, *Philosophical Forum,* 1967—.

*WORK IN PROGRESS:* A critical study of the philosophy of Sir Karl Popper; a work on the theory of rationality and the ecology of consciousness.

*SIDELIGHTS:* William Warren Bartley III told *CA* that he is recognized for his "theory of rationality" and for his "solution to Goodman's paradox of grue emeralds." He discovered "the long-lost second volume of Lewis Carroll's symbolic logic" and "unearthed a mass of new information about the life of philosopher Ludwig Wittgenstein." A reviewer in *New Yorker* called Bartley's *Wittgenstein* "the pioneer work on this topic." In *British Journal for the Philosophy of Science,* it was described as "more interesting and provocative than anything else written about Wittgenstein."

Bartley can read German, Dutch, French, and Chinese, and he has some knowledge of Greek and Latin. He is a collector of Chinese art and an expert in Chinese painting and textiles. He lived and taught in England for six years, and has lived, taught, and done research in Germany, Austria, and Asia.

*BIOGRAPHICAL/CRITICAL SOURCES: Journal of

*Religion*, January, 1973; *Book World*, May 27, 1973; *New Yorker*, July 23, 1973; *Times Literary Supplement*, August 17, 1973; *National Review*, October 26, 1973; *Choice*, November, 1973; *Christian Century*, November 21, 1973, December 19, 1973; *New Statesman*, March 22, 1974; *Observer*, April 7, 1974; *British Journal for the Philosophy of Science*, June, 1974.

\*    \*    \*

## BASKIN, Esther Tane 1926(?)-1973

1926(?)—January 4, 1973; American author of nature books. Obituaries: *New York Times*, January 5, 1973.

\*    \*    \*

## BASTIAS, Constantine 1901(?)-1972

1901(?)—December 26, 1972; Greek journalist, historian, and government official. *New York Times*, December 27, 1972.

\*    \*    \*

## BASTICO, Ettore 1876-1972

1876—December 1, 1972; Italian field marshal and historian. *New York Times*, December 2, 1972.

\*    \*    \*

## BATBEDAT, Jean 1926-
### (Michel Larneuil)

*PERSONAL:* Born February 15, 1926, in Paris, France; son of Gerard (a theatrical director) and Jeanne (Laborde) Batbedat; married Suzanne Magnier (a civil servant in French Ministry of Foreign Affairs), December 8, 1956; children: Jeanne, Gerard. *Education:* College of Dax, Dax, Landes, Baccalaureat, 1943; University of Paris, Licence en Droit, 1950; National School of Oriental Languages, Paris, diplomas in Chinese and Indian languages. *Religion:* Roman Catholic. *Home:* 15 rue des Beaux-Arts, 75006 Paris, France. *Office:* 37 Quai D'Orsay, 75007 Paris, France.

*CAREER:* French Ministry of External Affairs, Paris, civil servant, 1950—, with posts at various times in Bombay, New Delhi, and Calcutta, India, Tunisia, and the Soviet Union, in Paris since 1969, under-director, 1973-75, joint director of personnel and general administration, 1975—, chief of cultural exchange section, 1976—. *Awards, honors:* Chevalier of Legion of Honor; Chevalier of national order of merit.

*WRITINGS*—Novels under pseudonym Michel Larneuil: *La Petite marche du Telengana*, Albin Michel, 1968, translation by June P. Wilson and Walter B. Michaels published as *The Short March in Telengana*, Morrow, 1970; *Le Vautour et l'enfant*, Albin Michel, 1971; *Le Dieu assassine*, Albin Michel, 1974.

*WORK IN PROGRESS:* More novels.

*SIDELIGHTS:* Jean Batbedat's *The Short March in Telengana* is a novel about India seen through the eyes of a British journalist. A *New York Times Book Review* critic says the author "accumulates metaphysical and political subtleties without delaying the headlong pursuit that gives the novel its exciting momentum."

Batbedat is fluent in Hindi and English and has "some competence" in Chinese and Russian.

*BIOGRAPHICAL/CRITICAL SOURCES: New York Times Book Review*, January 11, 1970; *America*, May 23, 1970.

## BATES, Paul A(llen) 1920-

*PERSONAL:* Born June 22, 1920, in Sioux City, Iowa; son of Merritt DeVore (an engineer) and Pearl (Luther) Bates; married Mary Fagan (an artist), February 7, 1941; children: Rebecca, Daniel, Paul Patrick, Pearl. *Education:* State University of Iowa, B.A., 1941; University of Michigan, M.A., 1949; University of Kansas, Ph.D., 1955. *Religion:* Unitarian-Universalist. *Home:* 609 Duke Lane, Fort Collins, Colo. 80521. *Office:* Department of English, Colorado State University, Fort Collins, Colo.

*CAREER:* Teacher in high school in Flint, Mich., 1945-47; University of Kansas, Lawrence, instructor in English, 1949-55; Colorado State University, Fort Collins, assistant professor, 1955-61, associate professor, 1961-66, professor of Shakespeare and Renaissance poetry, 1966—. Visiting professor, University of Kansas, summer, 1966; chairman of the humanities, Pershing College, 1968-70. Vice-president, Colorado AFL-CIO, 1975—. *Military service:* U.S. Army, Ordnance, 1941-43. U.S. Army Air Forces, radio operator, 1943-45. *Member:* American Association of University Professors (president of local chapter, 1965), American Federation of Teachers (president of local chapter, 1972-75). *Awards, honors:* Reader at Henry L. Huntington Library, 1954; Amherst College grant, Folger Library, 1956; Colorado State University Research Foundation grants, 1958, 1964; Colorado State University Faculty grant, 1971-72.

*WRITINGS: Faust: Sources, Works, and Criticism*, Harcourt, 1968. Contributor to literature journals.

*WORK IN PROGRESS:* Research on the Christian characters in *Merchant of Venice*.

*SIDELIGHTS:* Paul A. Bates told *CA* that he is writing his first novel. He added: "I believe that literature should engage the great issues of the time. And maybe my novel will. But mainly it just flows up from the subconscious."

\*    \*    \*

## BATTISTI, Eugenio 1924-
### (Angiolo Rinaldini)

*PERSONAL:* Born December 14, 1924, in Turin, Italy; son of Luigi and Maria (Castagna) Battisti; married Giuseppa Saccaro Guardavora Rocchetti del Buffa, 1948; children: Francesco. *Education:* Attended University of Turin, Laurea, 1947; University of Rome, Diploma in Art History, 1953. *Office:* 227 Arts II, Pennsylvania State University, University Park, Pa. 16802.

*CAREER:* University of Rome, Rome, Italy, assistant professor of art history, 1951-60; University of Genoa, Genoa, Italy, associate professor of art history, 1963-65; Pennsylvania State University, University Park, professor of art history, 1965—. Visiting professor, University of North Carolina, 1968. *Member:* Association Internationale des Critiques d'Art, Istituto per la Storia dell'Arte Lombarda, Associasione Italiana per l'Archeologia Industriale (president), Associazione Stampa Italiana, Institute for the Arts and the Humanistic Studies.

*WRITINGS: Giotto*, Skira, 1960, translation by James Emmons, Zwemmer, 1960; (with Lionello Venturi and Amedeo Majuri) *Pittura italiana del Medioevo*, Skira, 1960; *Rinascimento e Barocco*, Einaudi, 1960; *Per una Indagine sociologica sui librettisti napoletani buffi del Settecento*, De Luca, 1960; *Guido La Regina*, translation by Robert Enggass, De Luca, 1961; *L'Antirinascimento*, Feltrinelli, 1962; *Hogarth Incisore*, Romero, 1962; *Velazquez*, Ricordi, 1962, translation by Bryn Brooks, Ricordi, 1964; *Cimabue*, Istituto Editoriale Italiano, 1963, enlarged edition, with translation by Robert Enggass and Catherine Enggass, Pennsylvania State University Press, 1967; (with wife, Giuseppa Battisti) *La Civilta delle streghe,* Lerici, 1964; (with G. C. Argan, R. J. Clements, F. Negri Arnoldi, and Silvano Casartelli) *Michelangelo scultore,* Curcio, 1964; *Michelangelo: A Modern Interpretation* (lectures), Pennsylvania State University, Department of Art History, 1965; (with Luciano Berti and Bianca Bellardoni) *L'Angelico a San Marco,* Curcio, 1966; (with Enrico Crispolti) *L'Arte Oggi,* Curcio, 1966; (author of text) *Il Crocifisso di Cimabue* (booklet), Istituto Editoriale Italiano, 1967; (with group of students at University of Genoa) *Bellori, Le Vite,* University of Genoa Press, 1967; *L'Arte come Invenzione,* Bompiani, 1969; *Hoch Renaissance und Manierismus,* Holle Verlag, 1970; (with G. Battisti) *Guarna: Scimmia,* De Luca, 1970; (with group of students at Pennsylvania State University) *Seminar One,* Pennsylvania State University, Department of Art History, 1971; *Piero della Francesca,* two volumes, Istituto Editoriale Italiano, 1971; *L'Albero Solitario,* Guaraldi, 1973; *Il Rinascimento in Italia,* Mondadori, 1974; *Brunelleschi,* Electa, 1975.

Co-editor, *Enciclopedia Universale dell'Arte.* Contributor to *Mondo* (weekly), at times under pseudonym Angiolo Rinaldini. Editor, *Marcatre,* 1963—; co-editor, *Arte,* 1966—.

*WORK IN PROGRESS:* A book on the historical fortune of Michelangelo, for Penguin; a book on the critical problems of the major works of Michelangelo, also for Penguin; *Simbolismi per il barocco,* for Einaudi; an illustrated history of utopian cities.

*SIDELIGHTS:* Eugenio Battisti writes: "I am especially interested in the history of ideas, and in the changing of civilisations. I try to understand, according to the method of the structuralism, the process of an artist or of a writer, to evaluate the impact of his activity on the public, to study the survival of his ideas and the reaction of the critics. The big styles, Renaissance, Mannerism, [and] Baroque, interest me because of the interdisciplinary work which is their origin."

\*    \*    \*

## BAUM, Bernard H(elmut) 1926-

*PERSONAL:* Born April 18, 1926, in Giessen, Germany; came to United States in 1933, naturalized citizen in 1934; son of Theodor (a dental surgeon) and Beatrice (Klee) Baum; married Barbara B. Eisendrath, June 13, 1953; children: David M., Jonathan K., Victoria L., Lisa B. *Education:* University of Chicago, Ph.B., 1948, M.A., 1953, Ph.D., 1959. *Home:* 1405 Lincoln St., Evanston, Ill. 60201. *Office address:* School of Public Health, University of Illinois at the Medical Center, Box 6998, Chicago, Ill. 60680.

*CAREER:* U.S. Civil Service Commission, Chicago, Ill., qualifications rating examiner and board adviser, 1952-54; Roosevelt University, Chicago, professorial lecturer in sociology, 1955-66; Continental Casualty and Continental Assurance Companies (CNA Insurance), Chicago, director of organizational analysis, 1960-66; University of Illinois at Chicago Circle, associate professor and associate dean, College of Business Administration, 1966-69, professor of management and sociology, 1969—; University of Illinois at the Medical Center, School of Public Health, professor of health and resource management, 1973—, director, 1977—. Lecturer, University of Chicago, 1961-68, and Illinois Institute of Technology, 1966; visiting professor, Northwestern University, 1970. Member of grievance panel, Department of Personnel, State of Illinois, 1968—; member of board of

directors, Selfhelp Home for the Aged, 1959-68. *Military service:* U.S. Army, 1943-46. National Guard, 1948-53. U.S. Army Reserve, 1953—; present rank, colonel.

*MEMBER:* American Sociological Association, Academy of Management, American Academy of Political and Social Science, American Association for the Advancement of Science, Midwest Business Administration Association, Industrial Relations Association of Chicago (member of executive committee, 1966-70). *Awards, honors:* Winner of Ford Foundation Business Administration and Social Science Doctoral Dissertation Competition, 1960.

*WRITINGS: Decentralization of Authority in a Bureaucracy,* Prentice-Hall, 1961; (with Robert W. French) *Basics for Business,* Whitehall, 1968.

Contributor: D. E. McFarland, editor, *Current Issues and Emerging Concepts in Management,* Houghton, 1966; A. S. Tannenbaum, editor, *Control in Organizations,* McGraw, 1968; R. T. Golembiewski and Michael Cohen, editors, *People in Public Service: A Reader in Public Administration,* F. E. Peacock, 1970; McFarland, editor, *Personnel Management,* Penguin, 1971; R. J. Coleman and M. J. Riley, editors, *MIS: Management Dimensions,* Holden-Day, 1972; P. M. Whisenand and R. G. Ferguson, editors, *The Managing of Police Organizations,* Prentice-Hall, 1973; B. H. Baum, P. F. Sorensen, and others, editors, *Dimensions in Organization Behavior: Influence, Authority and Power,* Stipes, 1975. Contributor of articles and reviews to behavioral sciences and business journals.

*WORK IN PROGRESS: Dignity and Organizations.*

\*    \*    \*

## BAYLEY, Barrington J(ohn) 1937-
## (Alan Aumbry, P. F. Woods)

*PERSONAL:* Born April 9, 1937, in Birmingham, England; son of John (a toolmaker) and Clarissa (Love) Bayley; married Joan Lucy Clarke, October 30, 1969; children: Sean, Heather. *Education:* Attended school in Shropshire, England. *Politics:* None. *Religion:* None. *Home:* 48 Turreff Ave., Donnington TF2 8HE, Telford, Shropshire, England. *Agent:* Scott Meredith Literary Agency, 845 Third Ave., New York, N.Y. 10022.

*CAREER:* Writer. Has worked in the civil service, in the Australian public service in London, and as a coal miner. *Military service:* Royal Air Force, 1955-57.

*WRITINGS—Science fiction: Star Virus,* Ace Books, 1970; *Annihilation Factor,* Ace Books, 1972; *Empire of Two Worlds,* Ace Books, 1972; *Collision Course,* Daw Books, 1973; *The Fall of Chronopolis,* Daw Books, 1974; *The Soul of the Robot,* Doubleday, 1974; *The Garments of Caean,* Doubleday, 1976; *The Grand Wheel,* Daw Books, 1977. Stories included in anthology, *The Knights of the Limits,* Allison & Busby, 1977. Contributor of articles and stories, some under pseudonyms Alan Aumbry and P. F. Woods, to British science fiction journals and popular periodicals.

*WORK IN PROGRESS: A One-Shot Universe; Galactic Alchemist,* for Daw Books; *The Rod of Light* (sequel to *The Soul of the Robot),* for Allison & Busby; *Dark Fables,* an anthology; *The Creation of Wealth,* a study in economics,

*SIDELIGHTS:* "My primary ambition as a science fiction writer has been to be able to inspire others as I have been inspired," Barrington Bayley told *CA.* "A good story is one you carry on thinking about long after you have read it."

## BEALS, Alan R(obin) 1928-

*PERSONAL:* Born January 24, 1928, in Oakland, Calif.; son of Ralph Leon (a college professor) and Dorothy (Manchester) Beals; married Constance Mayfield, December 15, 1957 (divorced May 6, 1975); married Kathleen Truman, March 23, 1977; children: (first marriage) Jeannie, Cassie, Michelle, Robert. *Education:* University of California, Los Angeles, B.A., 1948; University of California, Berkeley, Ph.D., 1954. *Residence:* Riverside, Calif. *Office:* Department of Anthropology, University of California, Riverside, Calif. 92521.

*CAREER:* U.S. Department of Army, Washington, D.C., research assistant in psychology, 1954-56; Stanford University, Stanford, Calif., acting assistant professor, 1956-58, assistant professor, 1958-63, associate professor of anthropology, 1963-68; University of California, Riverside, professor of anthropology, 1968—, chairman of department, 1968-72, 1975-78. *Military service:* U.S. Army, 1952-54. *Member:* American Anthropological Association, Society for Applied Anthropology, American Ethnological Society, Association for Asian Studies, American Association for the Advancement of Science, American Sociological Association, Kroeber Anthropological Society (founding member; vice-president, 1950), Peace Research Society, Ethnographic and Folk Culture Society (life member), Southwestern Anthropological Association (president, 1964-65; member of advisory board, 1965-73), Sigma Xi. *Awards, honors:* Social Science Research Council fellow in India, 1952-53; National Science Foundation fellow, 1958-61; American Institute of Indian Studies grant, 1965-66.

*WRITINGS:* (Contributor) M. Marriott, editor, *Village India: Studies in the Little Community,* University of Chicago Press, 1955; (with Victor B. Cline and Dennis Seidman) *Evaluation of a Four-week and Eight-week Basic Training for Men of Various Intelligence Levels,* Human Resources Research Office, George Washington University, 1956; (contributor) Richard Leonard Park and Irene Tinker, editors, *Leadership and Political Institutions in India,* Princeton University Press, 1959; (with John T. Hitchcock) *Field Guide to India,* National Academy of Sciences-National Research Council, 1960; *Gopalpur, a South Indian Village,* Holt, 1962; (contributor) Muzafer Sherif, editor, *Inter-group Relations and Leadership,* Wiley, 1962; (contributor) Edward B. Harper, editor, *Religion in South Asia,* University of Washington Press, 1964; (with Bernard J. Siegel) *Divisiveness and Social Conflict,* Stanford University Press, 1966; (with George Spindler and Louise Spindler) *Culture in Process,* Holt, 1967, revised edition, 1973; (editor with Bernard J. Siegel) *Biennial Review of Anthropology,* Stanford University Press, 1967.

(Contributor) George Spindler, editor, *Being an Anthropologist: Fieldwork in Eleven Cultures,* Holt, 1970; (contributor) K. Shivapur Ishwaran, editor, *Change and Continuity in India's Villages,* Columbia University Press, 1970; (contributor) Andree F. Sjoberg, editor, *Symposium on Dravidian Civilization,* Jenkins Publishing Co., 1971; (contributor) Mary C. Curkin, editor, *People in States,* Addison-Wesley, 1972; (editor with Bernard J. Siegel and Stephan A. Tyler) *Annual Review of Anthropology,* six volumes, Annual Reviews, Inc., 1972-77; *Village Life in South India,* Aldine, 1974; (contributor) Charles Leslie, editor, *Asian Medical Systems: A Comparative Study,* University of California Press, 1976; (with father, Ralph L. Beals and Harry Hoijer) *Introduction to Anthropology,* 5th edition (Alan Beals was not associated with earlier editions), Macmillan, 1977.

Contributor to anthropology journals. Special publications editor, *American Anthropologist,* 1963-65; associate editor and member of editorial committee, *Annual Review of Anthropology,* 1971-78.

*WORK IN PROGRESS: South Indian Village Quarrels; Cultural Change in South India;* population and marriage patterns in South India.

\* \* \*

## BEARDSLEE, John W(alter) III 1914-

*PERSONAL:* Born March 9, 1914, in Holland, Mich.; son of John Walter, Jr. (a teacher) and Frances (Davis) Beardslee; married Edith Brown, June 18, 1943; children: Nancy Eunice. *Education:* Yale University, A.B., 1935, Ph.D., 1957; Princeton Theological Seminary, B.D., 1941. *Home:* 8 Bishop Pl., New Brunswick, N.J. 08901. *Office:* New Brunswick Theological Seminary, 17 Seminary Pl., New Brunswick, N.J. 08901.

*CAREER:* American School for Boys, Basrah, Iraq, English teacher, 1935-38; acting pastor of a Reformed Church in America congregation in Tarrytown, N.Y., 1941-43; Annville Institute (secondary school), Annville, Ky., dean of boys, 1943-44; George Washington University, Washington, D.C., assistant professor of religion, 1948-51; Central College (now University), Pella, Iowa, visiting professor, 1951-53, associate professor, 1953-63, professor of religion, 1963-64; New Brunswick Theological Seminary, New Brunswick, N.J., professor of church history, 1964—. *Member:* American Society of Church History, American Academy of Religion, American Association of University Professors, American Civil Liberties Union, Clergy and Laymen Concerned.

*WRITINGS:* (Editor and translator) *Reformed Dogmatics,* Oxford University Press, 1965; (contributor) Jean Meyendorff, *The New Man,* Agora Books, 1973. Contributor of articles and reviews to religious periodicals.

*WORK IN PROGRESS:* Translating and editing, *F. Turretin on Scripture.*

*BIOGRAPHICAL/CRITICAL SOURCES: Christian Century,* March 1, 1967.

\* \* \*

## BEARE, (M. A.) Nikki 1928-

*PERSONAL:* Born March 7, 1928, in Detroit, Mich.; daughter of Elbert Stanley (in chemical sales) and Dorothy M. (Welch) Brink; married Richard A. Beare (a financial adviser), June 15, 1946; children: Sandra Lee. *Education:* Attended Northwestern Michigan Community College and Miami Dade Junior College. *Politics:* Democrat. *Religion:* Methodist. *Home:* 14301 Southwest 87th Ave., Miami, Fla. 33158. *Office:* Nikki Beare & Associates, Inc., 5900 Southwest 73rd St., South Miami, Fla. 33143.

*CAREER:* Free-lance writer; *Miami News,* Miami, Fla., reporter, 1966-67; Project HOPE, southeastern area director, representing hospital ship HOPE, fund raising and public relations, 1967-69; assistant vice-president, I/D Associates, Inc. (corporate identity firm), 1969-70; Nikki Beare & Associates, Inc. (public relations), South Miami, Fla., president, 1970—. Owner, South Miami Travel Service. President, Florida Feminist Credit Union. Member of national policy council, National Women's Political Caucus; consultant, PACE Services Co. *Member:* Public Relations Society of America, National Organization for Women (member of national board), Florida Public Relations Association, Historical Association of South Florida (vice-president), Dade County National Organization for Women (past president). *Awards, honors:* Silver Image Award of Florida Public Relations Association.

*WRITINGS: Pirates, Pineapples, and People,* Atlantic Printers & Lithographers, 1961; *From Turtle Soup to Coconuts,* Atlantic Printers & Lithographers, 1963; *Bottle Bronze,* Hurricane House, 1965. Also editor of *National Feminist Directory,* 1976. Writer of columns, "On the Go," for *Miami News,* and "Write On," for Syndicate Bonanza. Contributing editor, *Source,* 1977.

*WORK IN PROGRESS:* Two books, *The Political Facts of Life* and *Mark Catesby: Early America's Audubon.*

\* \* \*

## BEASLEY, Jerry C(arr) 1940-

*PERSONAL:* Born September 15, 1940, in Nashville, Tenn.; son of Guy E. (a salesman) and Gaynelle (Rucker) Beasley; married Rita M. Shontz, April 6, 1966; children: Amy, Pamela. *Education:* George Peabody College for Teachers, B.A., 1963; University of Kansas, M.A., 1967; Northwestern University, Ph.D., 1971. *Politics:* Democrat. *Home:* Grove Neck Rd., Earleville, Md. 21919. *Office:* Department of English, University of Delaware, Newark, Del. 19711.

*CAREER:* Alfred I. DuPont School District, Wilmington, Del., English teacher, 1963-64; Nashville City Schools, Nashville, Tenn., English teacher, 1964-65; University of Delaware, Newark, assistant professor, 1969-74, associate professor of English, 1974—. *Member:* Modern Language Association of America, American Society for Eighteenth Century Studies.

*WRITINGS: A Check List of Prose Fiction Published in England, 1740-1749,* University Press of Virginia, 1972; (editor) *English Fiction, 1660-1800: A Guide to Information Sources,* Gale, 1978.

*WORK IN PROGRESS: Novels of the 1740's,* a critical study of the decade's fiction; *Early Theories of Fiction.*

*SIDELIGHTS:* Jerry Beasley writes: "A high-school teacher, Frances Bowen, first inspired me to take the study of literature seriously; later, my love of history and my exciting discovery of Fielding's *Tom Jones* joined to propel me into study of early fiction. I now teach and write about eighteenth- and nineteenth-century English fiction, which (incidentally) has much to teach us about the confusion and disorder of our twentieth-century existence."

*AVOCATIONAL INTERESTS:* Organic gardening.

\* \* \*

## BEATTIE, John (Hugh Marshall) 1915-

*PERSONAL:* Born May 8, 1915, in Liverpool, England; son of John Crawford (a civil servant) and Jean M. (Jones) Beattie; married Honor M. Davy, December 27, 1946; children: Hugh, Frances. *Education:* Trinity College, Dublin, B.A., 1937; Oxford University, B.Litt., 1951, D.Phil., 1956. *Home:* The Cottage, Headington Hill, Oxford OX3 0BT, England. *Office:* Linacre College, Oxford University, Oxford OX1 2JD, England.

*CAREER:* Worked in administrative service in Tanganyika Territory (now Tanzania), 1940-49; Oxford University, Oxford, England, lecturer in social anthropology, 1953-71; University of Leiden, Leiden, Netherlands, professor of African studies (cultural anthropology and sociology), 1971-

75; Oxford University, Linacre College, supernumary fellow, 1976—. Fellow, Center for Advanced Study in the Behavioral Sciences, Stanford, Calif., 1959-60; Malinowski Lecturer, London School of Economics and Political Science, University of London, 1965. Did field research for a period of almost two years in Bunyoro, Uganda, between 1950-55. *Member:* Royal Anthropological Institute of Great Britain and Ireland, African Studies Association (United Kingdom), Association of Social Anthropologists of the Commonwealth.

*WRITINGS: Nyoro Kinship, Marriage and Affinity* (booklet; articles originally published in *Africa*), Oxford University Press, 1958; *Bunyoro: An African Kingdom,* Holt, 1960; *Other Cultures: Aims, Methods and Achievements in Social Anthropology,* Free Press, 1964; *Understanding an African Kingdom: Bunyoro,* Holt, 1965; (editor with John Middleton, and contributor) *Spirit Mediumship and Society in Africa,* Africana Publishing, 1969; *The Nyoro State,* Clarendon Press, 1971; (editor with R. G. Lienhardt, and contributor) *Studies in Social Anthropology: Essays in Memory of E. E. Evans-Pritchard by His Former Oxford Colleagues,* Clarendon Press, 1975. Contributor of articles and reviews to sociology and anthropology journals.

*WORK IN PROGRESS:* Two additional books on Bunyoro, *The Nyoro Community* and *Myoro Ritual;* another book on ritual.

\* \* \*

## BECKER, Marion Rombauer 1903-1976

*PERSONAL:* Born January 2, 1903, in St. Louis, Mo.; daughter of Edgar Roderick (a lawyer) and Irma (original author of *Joy of Cooking;* maiden name, von Starkloff) Rombauer; married John William Becker (an architect), June 18, 1932 (deceased); children: Mark, Ethan. *Education:* Attended Mary Institute, St. Louis, 1921, Vassar College, 1922-23, and Washington University, St. Louis, 1924; Vassar College, A.B., 1925. *Residence:* Cincinnati, Ohio.

*CAREER: Women's Wear,* New York, N.Y., representative in St. Louis, Mo., 1927-28; art director at John Burroughs School, Clayton, Mo., 1928-32, and Hillsdale School, Cincinnati, Ohio, 1932, 1935, 1936; assisted her mother, Irma S. Rombauer, in testing recipes, and as illustrator and producer, for the first privately-printed edition of *Joy of Cooking,* 1931, and has been associated with the book since, as co-author, 1951-62, and sole reviser, beginning 1962. President, Regional Planning Council of Greater Cincinnati, 1934-36; member of board, Better Housing League, Cincinnati, 1935-63; Cincinnati Modern Art Society, member of board of directors, 1942-47, secretary of board, director, and program chairman, 1947-54; Cincinnati Nature Center, secretary of board, beginning 1966, and horticulture chairman.

*MEMBER:* Herb Society of America, Wilderness Society, Nature Conservancy, Sierra Club, National Association for the Advancement of Colored People, American Civil Liberties Union, Americans for Democratic Action, Planned Parenthood-World Population, Garden Club of America (member of board of directors, beginning 1970), Garden Center of Greater Cincinnati, Town and Country Garden Club (member of board of directors), Noonday Club (president, 1935-36), Cincinnati Vassar Club (president, 1951-52). *Awards, honors:* Amy Angell Collier Montague Civic Achievement Award of Garden Club of America, 1961.

*WRITINGS:* (With her mother, Irma S. Rombauer) *Joy of Cooking,* privately printed, 1931, Bobbs-Merrill, 1936, 12th edition, 1964 (Irma Rombauer's name still appears on the book although her daughter has been sole reviser since the 10th edition, 1962); *Little Acorn: The Story Behind the 'Joy of Cooking,' 1931-1966,* Bobbs-Merrill, 1969; (with Paul B. Sears and Frances Jones Poetker) *Wild Wealth,* illustrations by Janice Rebert Forberg, Bobbs-Merrill, 1971. Editor, Better Housing League reports, 1938-50, catalogues of Cincinnati Modern Art Society, 1947-54, and Garden Center bulletins, 1952-53.

*SIDELIGHTS:* There have been more than thirty-five printings of *Joy of Cooking* since 1962, with sales exceeding five million copies. In dedicating the twelfth edition to her mother, who died in 1962, Marion Rombauer Becker mentioned that her husband, John, also "contributed verve to this undertaking. . . . We look forward," she continued, "to a time when our two boys—and their wives—will continue to keep 'The Joy' a family affair." Mimi Sheraton reported in *New York Times* that Becker's younger son, who has studied at Le Cordon Bleu cooking school in Paris, will indeed assume the writing of the next edition of *Joy of Cooking* which will probably be published in 1985.

*BIOGRAPHICAL/CRITICAL SOURCES:* Riesman, Glazer, and Denny, *The Lonely Crowd,* Yale University Press, 1953; Smalzried, *The Everlasting Pleasure,* Appleton, 1956; Danzig and Schorr, *Rhetoric of the Essay,* Wadsworth, 1969; *Vogue,* February 1, 1972; *New York Times,* December 30, 1976.†

(Died December 28, 1976)

\* \* \*

## BECKER, Russell J(ames) 1923-

*PERSONAL:* Born July 1, 1923, in Rochester, N.Y.; son of William Henry (a baker) and Alcey (Cole) Becker; married Dorothy Kiefth, July 1, 1945; children: Jonathan, Carl, Kurt. *Education:* Kalamazoo College, B.A., 1944; Colgate Rochester Divinity School, B.D., 1946; University of Chicago, Ph.D., 1950. *Home:* 229 Park Ave., Glencoe, Ill. 60022. *Office:* Glencoe Union Church, 263 Park Ave., Glencoe, Ill. 60022.

*CAREER:* Ordained minister of the United Church of Christ, 1945; University of Chicago, Chicago, Ill., instructor in religion and personality, 1951-52; Kalamazoo College, Kalamazoo, Mich., assistant professor of psychology and dean of men, 1952-53; College of Wooster, Wooster, Ohio, assistant professor, 1953-56, associate professor of psychology, 1956-57; Glenview Community Church, Glenview, Ill., minister of pastoral care, 1957-60; Yale University, New Haven, Conn., associate professor of pastoral theology, 1960-69; Glencoe Union Church, Glencoe, Ill., minister, 1969—. *Member:* American Psychological Association, American Academy of Psychotherapists, Association for Humanistic Psychology.

*WRITINGS: Family Pastoral Care,* Prentice-Hall, 1965; *When Marriage Ends,* Fortress, 1971; (contributor) Mervin Strommen, editor, *Research in Religion and Personality Development,* Meredith, 1971.

*WORK IN PROGRESS: Jung as Radical Theologian.*

\* \* \*

## BECKMANN, Martin J(osef) 1924-

*PERSONAL:* Born July 5, 1924, in Ratingen, Germany; son of Josef (a civil servant) and Katharina (Linnartz) Beckmann; married Gloria Gronna Rice (a musician), December 31, 1956; children: Sybilla, Carl-Josef, Chantal, Gwendolyn.

*Education:* University of Goettingen, Diplom (mathematics), 1948; University of Freiburg, Diplom (economics), 1949, Dr. rer. pol. (summa cum laude), 1950. *Religion:* Roman Catholic. *Home:* 77 Arlington Ave., Providence, R.I. 02906; and Lochhamerstrasse 38, 8032 Lochham, Germany. *Office:* Department of Economics, Brown University, Providence, R.I. 02912; and Institute of Applied Mathematics, Technical University Munich, Munich, Germany.

*CAREER:* University of Chicago, Chicago, Ill., fellow in political economy, 1950-51, research associate, Cowles Commission for Economic Research, 1951-55; Yale University, New Haven, Conn., assistant professor of economics, 1955-59; Brown University, Providence, R.I., associate professor, 1959-61, professor of economics, 1961—; University of Bonn, Bonn, Germany, professor of econometrics, operations research, and economics, 1962-69; Technical University Munich, Institute of Applied Mathematics, Munich, Germany, professor of applied mathematics, 1969—. Member of committee on theory of traffic flow, U.S. Highway Research Board, 1957—; consultant to Transportation Science Division, General Motors Research Laboratories, 1968—. *Military service:* German Army, 1942-45.

*MEMBER:* Econometric Society (fellow), International Institute of Statistics, American Economic Association, Regional Science Association (founding member), Operations Research Society of America, Institute of Management Sciences, List Gesellschaft. *Awards, honors:* Center for Advanced Study in the Behavioral Sciences fellow, 1955-56.

*WRITINGS:* (With C. B. McGuire and Christopher B. Winsten) *Studies in the Economics of Transportation,* RAND Corp., 1955, Yale University Press, for Cowles Commission for Research in Economics, 1956; *Linear Programming,* Fachverlag fuer Oekonometrie (Ludwigshafen), 1959; *Location Theory,* Random House, 1968; *Dynamic Programming of Economic Decisions,* Springer-Verlag (New York and Berlin), 1968; (with Hans P. Kuenzi) *Mathematik fuer Oekonomen,* Springer-Verlag, 1969, revised edition, 1973; (editor) *Scientific Papers of Tjalling Koopmans,* Springer-Verlag, 1970. Also editor with Kuenzi of *Lecture Notes in Operations Research.*

*WORK IN PROGRESS:* Research on mathematical models of location and regional science, transportation planning, dynamic programming, economics of stability and growth, and on mathematical approaches to social science.

*AVOCATIONAL INTERESTS:* Collecting books, scholars' autobiographies, and travel memoirs (he commutes between professorships in Germany and America).

\* \* \*

## BECKWITH, Charles E(milio) 1917-

*PERSONAL:* Born June 8, 1917, in Oberlin, Ohio; son of Charles Clifton (an auditor) and Anna (Wilkinson) Beckwith; married Elizabeth M. Ungar, September 8, 1951 (divorced, 1967); married Joanne Kay Glossop (an administrative assistant), December 19, 1971; children: (first marriage) Constance Anne, James Allan, Margaret Andrea. *Education:* University of California, Berkeley, A.B., 1948, M.A., 1950; Yale University, Ph.D., 1956. *Politics:* Democrat. *Religion:* Unitarian. *Office:* Department of English, California State University, 5151 State University Dr., Los Angeles, Calif. 90032.

*CAREER:* Cornell University, Ithaca, N.Y., instructor in English, 1956-57; California State University, Los Angeles, assistant professor, 1957-62, associate professor, 1962-64, professor of English, 1964—, chairman of department, 1964-67, 1977—. *Military service:* U.S. Army, Medical Administrative Corps, 1942-46; became second lieutenant. *Member:* American Studies Association.

*WRITINGS:* (Editor) *Twentieth Century Interpretations of "A Tale of Two Cities,"* Prentice-Hall, 1972; (with Vinton A. Dearing) *John Gay's Poetry and Prose,* Oxford University Press, 1972.

\* \* \*

## BEDDOES, Richard H(erbert) 1926-

*PERSONAL:* Born March 26, 1926, in Sheep Tracks, Alberta, Canada; son of Herbert (a farmer) and Olive (Perkins) Beddoes; married Margaret E. Carson (a nurse), July 20, 1954; children: Myfanway Jean, Kimberly Olivia. *Education:* Attended University of Alberta, 1946-51. *Politics:* "Maverick." *Religion:* "Nominal Protestant." *Home:* 15 St. George's Rd., Islington, Ontario, Canada. *Office: Toronto Globe and Mail,* 140 King W., Toronto, Ontario, Canada.

*CAREER:* Has worked as a farmer in Sheep Tracks, Alberta, and a free-lance broadcaster in Toronto, Ontario; *Toronto Globe and Mail,* Toronto, Ontario, sports columnist, 1964—. Alderman, Ward 2, Borough of Etobicoke. *Military service:* Canadian Army, 1944-45. *Awards, honors:* Canadian Newspaper Award for sports writing, 1960; Bill Corum Award, for horse race writing, 1969.

*WRITINGS: Countdown to Grey Cup,* McClelland & Stewart, 1965; (with Stan Fischler and Ira Gitler) *Hockey!: The Story of the World's Fastest Sport,* Macmillan, 1968, 3rd revised edition, 1973. Author of column appearing weekly in *North Shore Citizen* (North Vancouver, British Columbia).

*WORK IN PROGRESS:* A biography of Conn Smythe, who was responsible for Toronto Maple Leaf hockey franchise; a book on the Russia-Canada hockey series.†

\* \* \*

## BEER, Lawrence W(ard) 1932-

*PERSONAL:* Born May 11, 1932, in Portland, Ore.; son of Norman Henry (an international businessman) and Lucile (Hodges) Beer; married Keiko Harada, July 18, 1961; children: David, Christopher, Kimberley, Lawrence, Jr. *Education:* Gonzaga University, A.B., 1956, M.A., 1957; graduate study at Fordham University, summer, 1957, and Sophia University, Tokyo, Japan, 1958-60; University of Washington, Seattle, Ph.D., 1966. *Politics:* "Progressive Democrat." *Religion:* Roman Catholic. *Home:* 639 Mapleton Ave., Boulder, Colo. 80302. *Office:* Department of Political Science, University of Colorado, Boulder, Colo. 80302.

*CAREER:* Sophia University, Tokyo, Japan, instructor in English and philosophy, autumns, 1957, 1960-61; California Credit Union League, Pomona and Oakland, director of training, autumns, 1961-62; University of Colorado, Boulder, assistant professor, 1966-69, associate professor, 1969-74, professor of political science, 1974—, director of Center for East Asian Studies, 1971—. Visiting professor at University of Denver, fall, 1968, Tokyo University, 1969-71, Sophia University, summer, 1970, University of Kansas, 1973, and Semester-at-Sea Program, 1977. Founder and director, Credit Union Information Center (Japan), 1960-61; sponsor, Court of Man Foundation. *Member:* American Political Science Association, Association for Asian Studies (chairman of committee on Asian law, 1973-77), Law Association for

Asia and the Western Pacific, Public Law Association of Japan, Japanese-American Society for Legal Studies (auditor, 1976—). *Awards, honors:* University of Colorado faculty fellowship, 1968-70; Japan Foundation fellowship, 1973; World Academy of Scholars fellowship, 1976—.

*WRITINGS:* (Editor with Colin Chilton, and contributor) *Credit Union Family Financial Counseling,* California Credit Union League, 1962; (contributor) Dan F. Henderson, editor, *The Constitution of Japan: Its First Twenty Years, 1947-1967,* University of Washington Press, 1969; (translator) John M. Maki, *We, the Japanese,* Praeger, 1972; (contributor) King Chen, editor, *The Foreign Policy of China,* East-West Who Press, 1972; (contributor) Richard Claude, editor, *Comparative Human Rights,* Johns Hopkins University Press, 1976; (with Hiroshi Itoh) *The Constitutional Case Law of Japan: Selected Supreme Court Decisions, 1961-1970,* University of Washington Press, 1977; (co-author) *Asian Views of the American Constitutional Influence: A Symposium in Comparative Law,* in press.

Member of editorial advisory board, "Occasional Papers in Contemporary Asian Studies" reprint series, 1976—. Contributor of articles and reviews to law and political science journals in the United States and Japan. Co-editor, *Law in Japan: An Annual.*

*WORK IN PROGRESS: Freedom of Expression in Japan; The Constitution of Japan, 1947-1980: Cases and Commentary,* with Hiroshi Itoh; research on East Asian politics and public law, on the inter-relationships of the United States, Japan, China, and Korea, and on the quality of education in the United States concerning Asia.

*SIDELIGHTS:* Lawrence W. Beer told *CA:* "From railroad gang to philosophy and poetry to cooperativism and anthropology to East Asian politics and law, that has been the interesting road I have traveled. As a specialist on East Asia, I am most concerned that Americans, through education on all levels, achieve to some degree the capacity to see East Asians as slightly different, but very ordinary people." Beer spent over six and a half years in East Asia, and has a knowledge of Japanese, Latin, classical Greek, French, Spanish, and a little Chinese. He says: "I value God, practical kindness and silence, on the philosophical level. [I] also enjoy family, classical and folk music, books, most sports, good weather, and friendly conversation. I am rooted in the American Northwest and East Asia."

\* \* \*

## BEHRENS, John C. 1933-

*PERSONAL:* Born February 7, 1933, in Lancaster, Ohio; son of Charles H. and Dorothy M. Behrens; married Patricia Ann Beaty (a therapeutic dietitian), June, 1956; children: Cynthia Sue, Mark Andrew. *Education:* Bowling Green State University, B.S. (journalism), 1955; Pennsylvania State University, M.A., 1956. *Home:* 57 Stebbins Dr., Clinton, N.Y. 13323. *Office:* Department of Journalism, Utica College, Syracuse University, Burrstone Rd., Utica, N.Y. 13502.

*CAREER: Lancaster Eagle-Gazette,* Lancaster, Ohio, sports editor, 1958-62; Ohio Wesleyan University, Delaware, instructor in journalism, 1962-63; Marshall University, Huntington, W.Va., assistant professor of journalism and member of university public relations staff, 1963-65; Syracuse University, Utica College, Utica, N.Y., 1965—, began as associate professor, currently professor of journalism and coordinator of journalism studies. Summer or part-time editorial employee of *Columbus Dispatch, Co-*

*lumbus Citizen,* and other newspapers. Curator, Student Press in America Archives, 1968—; publications consultant, Utica School of Commerce, 1970—; correspondent, *Financial Weekly,* 1973-75. Treasurer, Mohawk Valley Council of Churches, 1969-72. *Military service:* U.S. Army, 1956-58; served in Far East; staff writer, *Pacific Stars and Stripes.* *Member:* American Society of Journalists and Authors, Authors Guild, Association for Education in Journalism, National Council of College Publications Advisers, American Association of University Professors, American College Public Relations Association, Sigma Delta Chi, Pi Delta Epsilon, Kappa Tau Alpha. *Awards, honors:* National Council of College Publications Advisers distinguished service award, 1975.

*WRITINGS: Magazine Writer's Workbook,* Dodrill Press, 1968, 2nd edition, Grid Publishing, 1972; (editor) *Wood and Stone: Landmarks of the Upper Mohawk,* Central New York Community Arts Council, 1972; *Reporter's Worktext,* Grid Publishing, 1974; *The Typewriter Guerrillas: Closeups of Twenty Top Investigative Reporters,* Nelson-Hall, 1977. Author of business column, *Elks,* 1976—. Contributor of more than 600 articles to periodicals, including *Writer's Digest, Mankind, National Enquirer, Editor & Publisher, Library Journal, Quill, Radio and TV Weekly, Nieman Reports,* and *Accent on Living.* Department editor, *College Press Review,* 1973—.

*WORK IN PROGRESS: Survey of New York Dailies, 1978-1980;* third edition of *Magazine Writer's Workbook;* a book on the future of small business; investigations into famous news leaks.

*SIDELIGHTS:* John Behrens told *CA:* "The more I write and the longer I teach the subject, the more convinced I become that writing is a craft. Like a doctor who becomes a skillful surgeon or specialist because of the experiences he acquires in the operating room or in treating an illness, a writer grows with each publishing experience. He shapes his stories from his experiences in selecting words and 'crafting' a prose that excites and interests.

"Alex Haley is the person responsible for turning me around mid-career. I spent two years exchanging thoughts on writing for tips about classroom techniques during his stay in the Mohawk Valley. Alex had never taught and I had not written a best-seller so we helped one another reach for new goals. It was Alex's anguished early years—hundreds of stories and no sales—that impressed me. My writing career had started with such a conspicuous success—I sold the very first thing I put on paper—I couldn't understand why I wasn't selling everything several years later. Alex offered me a glimpse of the patience, persistence and commitment it takes to be a successful writer. I've never forgotten it ... and I don't let students forget it either."

\* \* \*

## BEIGEL, Hugo George 1897-

*PERSONAL:* Born February 17, 1897, in Vienna, Austria; naturalized U.S. citizen; son of Peter Maximilian and Clara Katherine (Kreuzig) Beigel; married Grete Ujhely, August, 1931; children: Uli Joan (Mrs. Donald Monaco). *Education:* University of Vienna, Ph.D., 1924. *Home and office:* 138 East 94th St., New York, N.Y. 10028.

*CAREER:* Private practice in hypnotherapy and counseling, 1926—; director of marriage and family guidance center in Berlin, Germany, 1929-35; A. G. fuer Anlagewerte, Berlin, director of personnel department, 1935-37; Grove School, Madison, Conn., mental hygiene therapist, 1943-44; Key-

stone Junior College, La Plume, Pa., instructor in psychology, 1946-47; Long Island University, Brooklyn, N.Y., assistant professor, 1947-50, associate professor of psychology, 1950-62; *Journal of Sex Research,* New York, N.Y., editor-in-chief, 1965-77. Consultant, Educational Cooperative of America. *Member:* American Psychological Association, Society for Experimental and Clinical Hypnosis (cofounder; treasurer, 1958-61; fellow), Society for the Scientific Study of Sex (co-founder; secretary, 1958-70; member of executive board; fellow), American Association of Sex Educators, Counsellors and Therapists (fellow), Deutsche Gesellschaft fuer Sexual Forschung (fellow).

*WRITINGS: Architectural Beauty in Europe,* Part I: *Germany,* Ungar, 1946; *Art Appreciation,* Stephen Daye, 1950; *Encyclopaedia of Sex Education,* Stephen Daye, 1952; *Sex from A to Z,* Stephen Daye, 1961; (editor and contributor) *Advances in Sex Research,* Hoeber, 1963; (contributor) H. L. Silverman, editor, *Marital Counseling,* C. C Thomas, 1967; *German-English Psychological Dictionary,* Ungar, 1971; *Application of Hypnosis to Sexual Problems,* C. C Thomas, 1978. Contributor to *Journal for Psychosomatic Dentistry and Medicine, Osteopathic Physician, Sociological Review, Ciba Review,* and *Rational Living.*

\* \* \*

## BELL, Charles G. 1929-

*PERSONAL:* Born April 8, 1929, in Los Angeles, Calif.; son of John Allison (a teacher) and Katherine (Titus) Bell; married Claudi E. Myers, October, 1965; children: Shannon E. *Education:* Pomona College, B.A., 1952; University of Southern California, M.A., 1958, Ph.D., 1966. *Politics:* Democrat. *Religion:* None. *Home:* 18751 DeVille Dr., Yorba Linda, Calif. 92686. *Office:* Department of Political Science, California State University, Fullerton, Calif. 92631.

*CAREER:* California State College, San Diego (now San Diego State University), assistant professor of political science, 1963-64; California State University, Fullerton, assistant professor, 1964-67, associate professor, 1967-72, professor of political science, 1972—, chairman of department, 1969-72. *Member:* American Political Science Association, Western Political Science Association.

*WRITINGS: Growth and Change,* Dickenson, 1973; *The Legislative Process in California,* American Political Science Association, 1973; *The First Term,* Sage Publications, 1975. *Western Political Quarterly,* associate editor, 1970-72, 1977—, editor of special edition, "Politics in the West," 1975.

*WORK IN PROGRESS: California Government and Politics,* for Dorsey.

\* \* \*

## BELL, Robert E(ugene) 1914-

*PERSONAL:* Born June 16, 1914, in Marion, Ohio; married Emily Virginia Merz (a high school teacher), August 31, 1938; children: David Eugene, Patricia Bell Lindsay. *Education:* Attended Ohio State University, 1936-38; University of New Mexico, B.A., 1940; University of Chicago, M.A., 1943, Ph.D., 1947. *Home:* 1625 South Berry Rd., Norman, Okla. 73069. *Office:* Department of Anthropology, University of Oklahoma, 455 West Lindsey, Norman, Okla. 73069.

*CAREER:* University of Chicago, Chicago, Ill., laboratory assistant, 1940-43, director of dendrochronology laboratory, 1946-47; University of Oklahoma, Norman, assistant professor, 1947-51, associate professor, 1951-55, professor of anthropology, 1955-68, George L. Cross Research Professor, 1968—, curator of Stovall Museum, 1955—. *Military service:* U.S. Army, Medical Corps, 1943-46. *Member:* American Anthropological Association, Society for American Archaeology (former chairman of executive board), American Association for the Advancement of Science, Oklahoma Anthropological Society. *Awards, honors:* University of Oklahoma Excellent Teaching Award, 1955; Fulbright research fellow, New Zealand, 1955-56, Ecuador, 1960, 1961.

*WRITINGS:* (Editor) *Guide to the Identification of Certain American Indian Projectile Points,* Oklahoma Anthropological Society, Volume I, 1958, Volume II, 1960; *Archaeological Investigations at the Site of El Inga, Ecuador,* Department of Anthropology, University of Oklahoma, 1965; (with Edward B. Jelks and W. W. Newcomb) *A Pilot Study of Wichita Indian Archaeology and Ethnohistory,* Southern Methodist University Press, 1967; *Oklahoma Archaeology: An Annotated Bibliography,* University of Oklahoma Press, 1969; *The Harlan Site: A Prehistoric Mound Center in Cherokee County, Eastern Oklahoma,* Oklahoma Anthropological Society, 1972; (with Jelks and Newcomb) *Wichita Indian Archaeology and Ethnology,* Garland Publishing, 1974. Book review editor, *American Antiquity,* 1961-65, editor-elect, 1965-66, editor, 1966-70; editor and manager, newsletter, special bulletins, and memoirs, Oklahoma Anthropological Society, 1952-66, 1970—.

*       *       *

## BELLI, Angela 1935-

*PERSONAL:* Born October 8, 1935, in Brooklyn, N.Y.; daughter of Albert (a musician) and Anna (Miraglia) Belli. *Education:* Brooklyn College (now Brooklyn College of the City University of New York), B.A., 1957; University of Connecticut, M.A., 1959; New York University, Ph.D., 1965. *Residence:* Brooklyn, N.Y. *Office:* English Department, St. John's University, Grand Central & Utopia Pkwys., Jamaica, N.Y. 11439.

*CAREER:* University of Connecticut, Storrs, instructor in English, 1957-59; Brooklyn College of the City University of New York, New York, N.Y., instructor in English, 1959-66; St. John's University, Jamaica, N.Y., assistant professor, 1966-69, associate professor of English, 1969—, director of independent studies program, 1968-70. *Member:* Modern Language Association of America, Society for Health and Human Values.

*WRITINGS: Ancient Greek Myths and Modern Drama: A Study in Continuity,* New York University Press, 1969. Contributor to *Modern Drama, Comparative Literature,* and *Comparative Literature Studies.*

*BIOGRAPHICAL/CRITICAL SOURCES: Journal of Modern Literature,* Volume I, issue 3, 1970.

*       *       *

## BELOZERSKY, Andrei (Nicolaevich) 1905-1972

August 24, 1905—December 31, 1972; Russian biochemist and educator. Obituaries: *New York Times,* January 3, 1973.

*       *       *

## BENJAMIN, Roger W. 1942-

*PERSONAL:* Born April 18, 1942, in Lansing, Mich.; son of C. Wayne and Evelyn (Leazier) Benjamin; married Gail Rhian (an anthropological linguist), September 8, 1962; chil-

dren: Christopher. *Education:* Michigan State University, B.A., 1963; Washington University, St. Louis, Ph.D., 1967. *Home:* 5125 Dupont Ave. S., Minneapolis, Minn. 55419. *Office:* Department of Political Science, University of Minnesota, Minneapolis, Minn. 55455.

*CAREER:* University of Minnesota, Minneapolis, assistant professor, 1966-70, associate professor of political science, 1970—. Fulbright research professor, Tokyo University, Tokyo, Japan, 1969-70. *Member:* International Peace Research Society, American Political Science Association, Japanese Political Science Association, American Association for the Advancement of Science, Asian Studies Association, International Studies Association, Law and Society Association, Phi Beta Kappa. *Awards, honors:* Midwestern University Consortium on International Activities grant, 1971-73.

*WRITINGS: Political Development,* Little, Brown, 1972; (with Alan Arian, Richard Blue, and Steve Coleman) *Patterns of Political Development: Japan, India, Israel,* McKay, 1972. Also author, with Theodore B. Pedeliski, of two reports for the Minnesota Public Defender's Office, 1968. Contributor of articles to professional journals, including *Journal of Conflict Resolution, American Political Science Review, Midwest Journal of Political Science,* and *Law and Society Review.*

*WORK IN PROGRESS: Tradition and the Politics of Change in Japan.†*

*       *       *

## BENNETTS, Pamela 1922-

*PERSONAL:* Born July 23, 1922, in Hampstead, London, England; daughter of William Courtenay and Margaret (Broadbridge) James; married William George Bennetts (a planning engineer), April 5, 1942; children: Felicity Margaret (Mrs. David Hill). *Education:* Attended schools in London, England. *Politics:* None. *Religion:* Church of England. *Home:* 104 Salusbury Rd., London NW6 6PB, England.

*CAREER:* Church of England, London, member of staff of London Diocesan Fund, 1938—; novelist, 1967—.

*WRITINGS*—All fiction; all published by R. Hale except as indicated: *The Borgia Prince,* 1968, St. Martin's, 1975; *The Borgia Bull,* 1968; *The Venetian,* 1968; *The Suzerain,* 1968; *The Adversaries,* 1969; *The Black Plantagenet,* 1969; *Envoy from Elizabeth,* 1970, St. Martin's, 1973; *Richard and the Knights of God,* 1970, St. Martin's, 1973; *The Tudor Ghosts,* 1970; *Royal Sword at Agincourt,* St. Martin's, 1971; *A Crown for Normandy,* 1971; *Bright Sun of York,* 1971; *The Third Richard,* 1972; *The Angevin King,* 1972; *The de Montfort Legacy,* St. Martin's, 1973; *The Lords of Lancaster,* St. Martin's, 1973; *The Barons of Runnymede,* St. Martin's, 1974; *A Dragon for Edward,* St. Martin's, 1975; *The She-Wolf,* 1975, St. Martin's, 1976; *My Dear Lover England,* St. Martin's, 1975; *Death of the Red King,* St. Martin's, 1976; *Stephen and the Sleeping Saints,* St. Martin's, 1977; *The House in Candle Square,* 1977; *Don Pedro's Captain,* St. Martin's, in press.

*WORK IN PROGRESS: A Voice in the Darkness; Ring the Bell Softly; One Dark Night; The Quick and the Dead.*

*SIDELIGHTS:* Pamela Bennetts holds a full-time job, so her research and writing has to be done on week-ends, early in the morning, late at night, and on holidays. She writes historical novels because she finds "the modern world unsatisfactory and vastly unromantic." She adds, "I know that I shall never write the kind of novel which critics would applaud or would make people think deeply.... What I try to do is to help people escape for a few hours from their present surroundings."

*BIOGRAPHICAL/CRITICAL SOURCES: Time and Tide,* March 6, 1969.

\* \* \*

## BENOFF, Mac   1915(?)-1972

1915(?)—November 16, 1972; American writer for radio, television, and motion pictures. Obituaries: *New York Times,* November 18, 1972.

\* \* \*

## BENSON, Dennis C(arroll)   1936-

*PERSONAL:* Born June 8, 1936, in Detroit, Mich.; son of Dennis C. (an advertising man) and Dolores (Hill) Benson; married Marilyn J. Workman, August 13, 1960; children: Amy, Jill. *Education:* Attended University of Detroit, 1954-55; University of Michigan, B.A., 1958; McCormick Theological Seminary, M.Div., 1962; University of Chicago, postgraduate study, 1962-65. *Address:* P.O. Box 12811, Pittsburgh, Pa. 15241.

*CAREER:* Ordained United Presbyterian minister; Children's Memorial chaplain, 1961-62; McCormick Theological Seminary, Chicago, Ill., lecturer in New Testament, 1965-66; Waynesburg College, Waynesburg, Pa., chaplain, 1966—. WDVE-Radio, radio personality, 1968—. Director of youth ministry, Pittsburgh Council of Churches, 1967-68; director of communications, Christian Association of Southwestern Pennsylvania, 1968-71; full-time writer, 1971—. Associate producer, SCAN syndicated radio program, 1975—. *Member:* American Federation of Television and Radio Artists. *Awards, honors:* Golden Mike Award, from American Legion Auxiliary, 1971, for best youth program in Pennsylvania.

*WRITINGS: The Now Generation,* John Knox, 1969; *Let It Run,* John Knox, 1971; *Gaming,* Abingdon, 1971; *Electric Liturgy,* Abingdon, 1972; *Electric Evangelism,* Abingdon, 1973; *Electric Love,* John Knox, 1973; *My Brother Dennis,* Word, 1975; *The Recycle Catalogue,* Abingdon, 1975; *The Rock Generation,* Abingdon, 1976; *The Recycle Catalogue II,* Abingdon, 1977; (with wife, Marilyn Benson) *Promises to Keep,* Friendship, 1978; (with Stan Stuart) *The Ministry of Children,* Abingdon, in press. Editor, *Recycle* and *Scan;* co-founder, associate editor, *Treking* (Australia).

*WORK IN PROGRESS:* Research on relationships among media, learning, culture, and life; a book of meditations on running, for Abingdon.

\* \* \*

## BENSON, Larry D(ean)   1929-

*PERSONAL:* Born June 20, 1929, in Sioux Falls, S.D.; son of Joseph Robert and Elsie (Ellis) Benson; married Margaret Owens, January 5, 1951; children: Cassandra, Gavin, Amanda, Geoffrey. *Education:* Attended Arizona State College at Tempe (now Arizona State University), 1948-50; University of California, Berkeley, A.B., 1954, M.A., 1956, Ph.D., 1959. *Politics:* Democrat. *Religion:* Lutheran. *Home:* 24 Woodland Rd., Lexington, Mass. 02173. *Office:* 271 Widener Library, Harvard University, Cambridge, Mass. 02138.

*CAREER:* Harvard University, Cambridge, Mass., instructor, 1959-62, assistant professor, 1962-65, associate professor, 1966-69, professor of English, 1969—, Allston Burr Senior Tutor, Quincy House, 1963-65. *Military service:* U.S. Marine Corps, 1946-48, 1950-51. *Member:* Modern Language Association of America, Mediaeval Academy of America (fellow; associate executive secretary), Academy of Literary Studies, International Arthurian Association. *Awards, honors:* Guggenheim fellow, 1964-65; M.A., Harvard University.

*WRITINGS: Art and Tradition in "Sir Gawain and the Green Knight,"* Rutgers University Press, 1965; (editor and translator with T. M. Andersson) *The Literary Context of Chaucer's "Fabliaux,"* Bobbs-Merrill, 1971; *King Arthur's Death: The Alliterative "Morte Arthure" and the Stanzaic "Morte Arthur,"* Bobbs-Merrill, 1974; (editor) *The Learned and the Lowed,* Harvard University Press, 1975; *Malory's "Morte Darthur,"* Harvard University Press, 1976. Assistant editor, *Speculum,* 1965—. Contributor to professional journals.

*WORK IN PROGRESS: A History of the Ring Tournament.*

\* \* \*

## BENSON, Sally   1900-1972
### (Esther Evarts)

September 3, 1900—July 19, 1972; American author of short stories, plays, screenplays, and reviews. Obituaries: *New York Times,* July 22, 1972; *Washington Post,* July 22, 1972; *Newsweek,* July 31, 1972; *Current Biography,* September, 1972. (See index for *CA* sketch)

\* \* \*

## BENZIE, William   1930-

*PERSONAL:* Born July 10, 1930, in Aberdeen, Scotland; son of James (an engineer) and Agnes (Beddie) Benzie. *Education:* Aberdeen University, M.A., 1953, M.A. (honors English), 1955, M.Ed., 1957, Ph.D., 1967. *Religion:* Protestant. *Office:* Department of English, Victoria University, Victoria, British Columbia, Canada.

*CAREER:* Victoria University, Victoria, British Columbia, 1958—, began as lecturer, associate professor of English, 1972—. *Military service:* Royal Air Force, 1948-50.

*WRITINGS: The Dublin Orator: Thomas Sheridan's Influence on Eighteenth-Century Rhetoric and Belles Lettres,* Scolar Press (England), 1972. Contributor to *Leeds Studies in English.*

*WORK IN PROGRESS:* Research on contribution of F. J. Furnivall, editor and scholar, to English scholarship in the nineteenth century.†

\* \* \*

## BERG, Fred Anderson   1948-

*PERSONAL:* Born July 19, 1948, in Macon, Ga.; son of Bernard (a tour guide) and Winifred (Hartung) Berg. *Education:* Oxford College of Emory University and Emory College of Emory University, B.A., 1970; University of Georgia, additional study. *Politics:* "Indefinite." *Religion:* Christian. *Home:* 1714 Foster Pl., Macon, Ga. 31201.

*CAREER:* Southeast Archaeological Center, Macon, Ga., archaeological assistant, summer, 1967; University of Georgia, Athens, teaching assistant in anthropology, 1971-73. *Member:* Company of Military Historians.

*WRITINGS: Encyclopedia of Continental Army Units:*

*Battalions, Regiments, and Independent Corps,* Stackpole, 1972.

*WORK IN PROGRESS:* Research on clothing supply to rebel forces in the American Revolution; research on pre-Columbian population migrations in the Southeast; translating Khotel and Sieg, *Handbuch der Uniformkunde.*

*AVOCATIONAL INTERESTS:* American travel, farming, gardening.†

\* \* \*

## BERG, Louis 1901-1972

June 19, 1901—October 1, 1972; English-born American psychiatrist, physician, and author of books on prison life, sexuality, and human personality. Obituaries: *New York Times,* October 2, 1972.

\* \* \*

## BERGER, Evelyn Miller 1896-

*PERSONAL:* Born November 7, 1896, in Hanford, Calif.; daughter of George Amos (a Methodist bishop) and Margaret (Ross) Miller; married Jesse Arthur Berger, June 16, 1939 (deceased); married C. Maxwell Brown, November 20, 1972. *Education:* Stanford University, A.B., 1921, M.A., 1930; Columbia University, Ph.D., 1932. *Home:* 34 La Salle Ave., Piedmont, Calif. 94611. *Office:* East Bay Psychological Center, 315 14th St., Oakland, Calif. 94612.

*CAREER:* Teacher in Panama and at high schools in California; Allegheny College, Meadville, Pa., associate professor of Spanish and dean of women, 1932-36; University of Idaho, Moscow, dean of women, 1936-37; San Diego State College (now University), San Diego, Calif., dean of women, 1937-38; East Bay Psychological Center, Oakland, Calif., administrative director, 1941—. Teacher and director of Casa Espanola, University of the Pacific, summer sessions, 1929-30. Diplomate in counseling, American Board of Examiners in Professional Psychology; licensed psychologist and marriage and family counselor, State of California; corporate member, American Institute of Family Relations. Conductor of television programs, "Crosswinds" and "It's a Family Affair," KRON-TV, San Francisco. Has also done social service and field work with youth in Chile and Argentina for the Methodist Church. Member of board of directors, Fred Finch Children's Home; trustee, Scarritt College.

*MEMBER:* American Psychological Association (fellow), American Association of Marriage Counselors (fellow), International Council of Psychologists, National Council on Family Relations, National Vocational Guidance Association, Academy of Religion and Mental Health, American Association of University Women, Western Psychological Association, California State Marriage Counseling Association, California State Psychological Association, Family Relations Council of Northern California, California Writers' Club, Phi Beta Kappa, Kappa Delta Pi, Phi Sigma Iota, Pi Lambda Theta. *Awards, honors:* D.Ph., University of the Pacific, 1960.

*WRITINGS: Triangle: The Betrayed Wife,* Nelson-Hall, 1971. Also author of books written in Spanish, all published by Methodist Press, Santiago, Chile: *La Joven, El Hogar social, La Huerfana.* Writer of methods booklet on high school extracurricular activities, and pamphlets and articles on youth and family problems.

## BERGER, Rainer 1930-

*PERSONAL:* Born July 3, 1930, in Graz, Austria; U.S. citizen; son of Anton (a physician) and Marie (Schnoor) Berger; married Christine Perry, 1959; married Ildiko Viola Martha Borbely, 1973; children: W. Chris, G. Marie. *Education:* Studied at Cambridge University, 1951-53, and University of Kiel, 1953-55; University of Illinois, Ph.D., 1960. *Home:* 20556 Little Rock Way, Malibu, Calif. 90265. *Office:* Institute of Geophysics, University of California, Los Angeles, Calif. 90024.

*CAREER:* Convair Science Research Department, San Diego, Calif., staff scientist, geochemistry, 1960-62; Lockheed Aircraft Corp., Los Angeles, Calif., senior research scientist, 1962-63; University of California, Los Angeles, assistant professor, 1963-68, associate professor, 1968-72, professor of anthropology, geography, and geophysics, 1972—. Consultant to National Aeronautics and Space Administration, 1964-65. Member of board of directors, Chamber of Commerce and Junior Chamber of Commerce. *Military service:* 1944-45. *Member:* American Association for the Advancement of Science, American Chemical Society, American Anthropological Association, Geophysical Society, Geochemical Society, New York Academy of Sciences. *Awards, honors:* Fulbright fellow, 1955-57; National Aeronautics and Space Administration fellow, 1966-67; National Science Foundation fellow, 1966-68; Distinguished Service Award, University of California, Los Angeles, 1968; Guggenheim fellow, 1968-69.

*WRITINGS: Scientific Methods in Medieval Archaeology,* University of California Press, 1970. Contributor of about ninety scientific articles to journals in his field.

*WORK IN PROGRESS:* Research on past and present environment and man's interaction with it; research on geo- and cosmo-chemistry.

\* \* \*

## BERGER, Terry 1933-

*PERSONAL:* Born August 11, 1933, in New York, N.Y.; daughter of Morris A. (a dress manufacturer) and Belle (Otchet) Wapner; married Jerome Berger (director of King Features, Heart Metrotone News), December 21, 1952; children: David, Susan. *Education:* Attended Vassar College, 1950-52; Brooklyn College (now Brooklyn College of the City University of New York), B.A., 1954; Hunter College (now Hunter College of the City University of New York), teaching degree, 1962. *Politics:* Liberal. *Religion:* Jewish.

*CAREER:* Elementary school teacher in New York, N.Y., 1963-68; free-lance writer, 1968—.

*WRITINGS—All juveniles: Black Fairy Tales,* illustrated by David Omar White, Atheneum, 1969; *I Have Feelings,* illustrated with photographs by I. Howard Spivak, Behavioral Publications, 1971; *Lucky,* J. Philip O'Hara, 1974; *How Does It Feel When Your Parents Get Divorced,* Messner, 1977.

All published by Advanced Learning Concepts; illustrated with photographs by Heinz Kluetmeier: *Being Alone, Being Together,* 1974; *A Friend Can Help,* 1974; *Big Sister, Little Brother,* 1974; *A New Baby,* 1974.

*WORK IN PROGRESS: Not Everything Changes,* for Union of American Hebrew Congregations; *I'm Not Good, I'm Not Bad,* for Windmill Books.

*SIDELIGHTS: Black Fairy Tales* is in the Kerlan Collection and was recorded by Caedmon. *I Have Feelings* has been made into a film by Jam Handy.

*BIOGRAPHICAL/CRITICAL SOURCES: Time,* October 18, 1971.

\*      \*      \*

## BERMAN, Sanford    1933-

*PERSONAL:* Born October 6, 1933, in Chicago, Ill.; son of Samuel (a retail clerk) and Dorothy (Feinman) Berman; married Lorraine Oliver, May 31, 1968; children: Marlise Jill, Paul. *Education:* University of California, Los Angeles, B.A. (with highest honors), 1955; Catholic University of America, M.S. in L.S., 1961. *Politics:* Libertarian socialist. *Religion:* None. *Home:* 2225 Irving Ave. S., Minneapolis, Minn. 55405.

*CAREER:* District of Columbia Public Library, Washington, assistant chief of acquisitions department, 1957-62; U.S. Army Special Services Libraries, administrative librarian in Karlsruhe, Worms, and Mannheim-Sandhofen, West Germany, 1962-66; Schiller College, Kleiningersheim, West Germany, librarian, 1966-67; University of California, Los Angeles, periodicals librarian in Research Library, 1967-68; University of Zambia Library, Lusaka, Zambia, assistant librarian in charge of periodicals section, 1968-70; Makerere University, Kampala, Uganda, librarian at Makerere Institute of Social Research, 1971-72; Hennepin County Library, Edina, Minn., head cataloger, 1973—. *Military service:* U.S. Army, 1955-57. U.S. Army Reserve, 1957-63. *Member:* American Library Association (member of Social Responsibilities Round Table, Task Force on Alternatives in Print), Jewish Librarians Caucus, African Studies Association (member of subcommittee on cataloging and classification), American Civil Liberties Union, Minnesota Library Association, Council on Interracial Books for Children, Phi Beta Kappa, Beta Phi Mu. *Awards, honors:* California State Seal of Merit, 1950; H. W. Wilson Library Periodical Award, 1976, for *HCL Cataloging Bulletin;* Minnesota Librarian of the Year, 1977.

*WRITINGS: Spanish Guinea: An Annotated Bibliography,* Catholic University of America Libraries, 1961; (contributor) Helen Kitchen, editor, *Educated African,* Praeger, 1962; (consultant/contributor) Bill Katz, editor, *Magazines for Libraries,* Bowker, 1969, 2nd edition, 1972, supplement, 1975; (contributor) Eric Moon, editor, *Book Selection and Censorship in the Sixties,* Bowker, 1969; *Prejudices and Antipathies: A Tract on the LC Subject Heads Concerning People,* Scarecrow, 1971; (contributor) *Readings in Development,* Canadian University Services Overseas, 1971; (contributor) Celeste West and Elizabeth Katz, editors, *Revolting Librarians,* Booklegger Press, 1972; (contributor) Katz, editor, *Library Lit.2: The Best of 1971,* Scarecrow, 1972; (compiler) *African Liberation Movements and Support Groups: A Directory,* Makerere Institute of Social Research Library, 1972; (compiler) *Subject Headings Employed at the Makerere Institute of Social Research Library,* MISR Library, 1972; (contributor) Katz, editor, *Library Lit.5: The Best of 1974,* Scarecrow, 1975; (contributor) Deirdre Boyle, editor, *Expanding Media,* Oryx Press, 1977; (contributor) Joan K. Marshall, *On Equal Terms: A Thesaurus for Non-Sexist Indexing and Cataloging,* Neal-Schuman, 1977; (compiler) *Alternative Library Publications,* Task Force on Alternative Library Publications, 1977; (contributor) *Requiem for the Card Catalog: Proceedings of the ACM Conference on Management Issues in Automated Cataloging,* Greenwood Press, 1978. Compiled indices for E. J. Josey

and Kenneth E. Peeples, editors, *Opportunities for Minorities in Librarianship,* Scarecrow, 1977, and for Josey and Ann A. Shockley, *Handbook of Black Librarianship,* Libraries Unlimited, 1977; also compiled subject index for *Sources,* Gaylord, 1977. Also compiler or editor of other publications at University of Zambia Library and Makerere Institute of Social Research Library.

Contributor of articles, poems, letters, and reviews to *African Affairs, Wilson Library Bulletin, Junior Natural History Magazine, Library Journal, Ufahamu, Newsletter on Intellectual Freedom, Phylon, Assistant Librarian, Jewel of Africa,* Zambia Library Association *Journal, Ugandan Libraries, Times Literary Supplement, Africa Report, Unabashed Librarian, School Library Journal,* and other periodicals. Editor, *HCL Cataloging Bulletin,* 1973—, *ALA/SRRT Newsletter,* 1973-75; editorial advisor, *New Periodicals Index, African Books in Print.*

*SIDELIGHTS:* Sanford Berman writes: "My purpose in writing, editing and indexing is two-fold: first, to help make librarianship the dynamic, responsive, and creative profession it should be; second, to expand and invigorate library resources, as well as simplifying and promoting user-access to those resources."

\*      \*      \*

## BERNARD, Jean-Jacques    1888-1972

July 30, 1888—September 12, 1972; French playwright. Obituaries: *L'Express,* September 18-24, 1972.

\*      \*      \*

## BERNSTEIN, Barton J(annen)    1936-

*PERSONAL:* Born September 8, 1936, in New York, N.Y.; son of Norman (a businessman) and Lillian (Jannen) Bernstein; married Meredith Marsh (a writer and painter), August 9, 1967. *Education:* Queens College (now Queens College of the City University of New York), B.A., 1957; Washington University, St. Louis, Mo., graduate study, 1957-58; Harvard University, Ph.D., 1963. *Home:* 2300 Hanover, Palo Alto, Calif. 94308. *Office:* Department of History, Stanford University, Stanford, Calif. 94305.

*CAREER:* Queens College of the City University of New York, Flushing, N.Y., summer lecturer in history, 1960-62; Bennington College, Bennington, Vt., member of faculty of social science, 1963-65; Stanford University, Stanford, Calif., assistant professor, 1965-68, associate professor of history, 1968—. Member of executive board, Conference on Peace Research in History, 1973—. *Member:* American Historical Association, Organization of American Historians, Southern Historical Association. *Awards, honors:* Grants from American Philosophical Society, summer, 1964, American Council of Learned Societies, 1964-65; Rabinowitz Foundation fellow, summer, 1965; Charles Warren fellow at Harvard University, 1967-68; Harry S Truman Institute fellow, 1967-68; Center for Advanced Study (Illinois), fellow, 1970-71; Hoover Institute fellow at Stanford University, 1974-75; National Endowment for the Humanities fellow, 1977-78; Dean's teaching award, Stanford University, 1977.

*WRITINGS:* (Editor with A. J. Matusow) *The Truman Administration: A Documentary History,* Harper, 1966; (editor) *Towards a New Past: Dissenting Essays in American History,* Pantheon, 1968; (editor with Matusow) *Twentieth-Century America: Recent Interpretations,* Harcourt, 1969, 2nd edition, 1972; (editor) *Politics and Policies of the*

*Truman Administration,* Quadrangle, 1970; (editor with J. Banner and S. Hackney) *Understanding the American Experience: Recent Interpretations,* Harcourt, 1973; (editor) *The Atomic Bomb: The Critical Issues,* Little, Brown, 1976; *The Atomic Bombings of Japan and the Origins of the Cold War, 1941-1945,* General Learning, 1975. Contributor to historical journals.

*WORK IN PROGRESS:* Studies of the Cold War, of the atomic bomb, of the Truman administration, and of the 1952 election, and epilogue on the Eisenhower years.

*BIOGRAPHICAL/CRITICAL SOURCES: Newsweek,* April 22, 1968; *New York Times Book Review,* May 12, 1968; *New York Review,* August 1, 1968; *Nation,* August 26, 1968; *Commonweal,* November 15, 1968; *Partisan Review,* Number 2, 1969; *Times Literary Supplement,* October 23, 1970.

\* \* \*

## BERRIAN, Albert H. 1925-

*PERSONAL:* Born July 8, 1925, in Miami, Fla.; son of Neal (a contractor) and Florence (Peake) Berrian; married Mary Miles, April 7, 1945; children: Brenda, Antoinette (Mrs. Herbert Mabry), Albert, Jr., Derek. *Education:* New York University, B.A., 1948, M.A., 1949, Ph.D., 1954; Sorbonne, University of Paris, summer study, 1956. *Religion:* Baptist. *Home:* 57 Astor Pl., Jersey City, N.J. 07304. *Office:* State Department of Education, 99 Washington Ave., Albany, N.Y. 12224.

*CAREER:* Clark College, Atlanta, Ga., chairman of department of foreign languages, 1949-52; Texas Southern University, Houston, associate professor of French and German, 1954-56; Central State College (now University), Wilberforce, Ohio, chairman of department of foreign languages and director of humanities, 1956-58; North Carolina College at Durham (now North Carolina Central University), chairman of department of foreign languages, 1958-60; U.S. Department of State, Agency for International Development (AID), English Language Services, Leopoldville, Congo, director of English language teaching, 1960-62; State University of New York College at Plattsburgh, professor of French, 1962-64; Hampton Institute, Hampton, Va., professor of French and dean of faculty, 1964-69; State University of New York at Buffalo, associate vice-president for academic affairs, 1969-70; New York State Department of Education, Albany, associate commissioner for higher education, 1970—. Member of boards of directors, Southern Fellowship Fund, 1967—, and Hampton Community Action Agency; member of Panel on Alternate Approaches to Higher Education, 1971—. Consultant in linguistics, International Business Machines Corp. (IBM), 1965-67; consultant, Southern Association of Colleges and Schools, 1967—.

*MEMBER:* Modern Language Association of America, College Language Association, American Association of University Administrators (vice-president, 1973—), Association for Higher Education, American Conference of Academic Deans. *Awards, honors:* Centennial Medal, Hampton Institute, 1968; L.H.D., Canisius College, 1973.

*WRITINGS: Education for Life in a Multi-cultural Society,* Hampton Institute Press, 1967; (editor with Richard A. Long) *Negritude: Essays and Studies,* Hampton Institute Press, 1967; *Black Spiral,* Black Academy Press, 1972. Member of editorial board of *Black Academy Review* and *Journal of Human Relations,* 1956—.

*WORK IN PROGRESS: Relevant Education,* for Black Academy Press.†

## BERRY, Jack 1918-

*PERSONAL:* Born December 13, 1918, in Leeds, England; son of Harry (an engineer) and Nellie (Butterfield) Berry; married Winifred Mary Ingle, April 24, 1942; children: Mark Adrian. *Education:* University of Leeds, B.A., 1939; University of London, Ph.D., 1952. *Home:* 2119 Lincoln, Evanston, Ill. 60201. *Office:* Department of Linguistics, Northwestern University, Evanston, Ill. 60201.

*CAREER:* University of London, London, England, lecturer, 1946-55, reader, 1955-60, professor of African studies, 1960-63; Michigan State University, Lansing, professor of African studies, 1963-64; Northwestern University, Evanston, Ill., professor of linguistics, 1964—. *Military service:* British Army, 1939-46; became captain. *Member:* Linguistic Society of America, Philological Society of Great Britain, Linguistic Society of New York.

*WRITINGS: English, Twi, Asante, Fante Dictionary,* Macmillan, 1960; (editor with Joseph H. Greenberg) *Current Trends in Linguistics,* Volume VII, Mouton & Co., 1971. Editor, *Journal of African Languages,* 1962-64.

*WORK IN PROGRESS: Folklore of West Africa.*

\* \* \*

## BESSETTE, Gerard 1920-

*PERSONAL:* Born February 25, 1920, in Sabrevois, Quebec, Canada; son of Jean-Baptiste and Victoria (Bertrand) Bessette; married Irene Bakowski (an attorney, law librarian, and professor), September 3, 1971. *Education:* Externat Classique Sainte-Croix, B.A., 1941; University of Montreal, licence es lettres and M.A., 1946, D.Litt., 1950. *Home:* 270 Frontenac St., Kingston, Ontario, Canada. *Office:* Department of French, Queen's University, Kingston, Ontario, Canada.

*CAREER:* University of Saskatchewan, Saskatoon, instructor, 1946-49, assistant professor of French, 1949-51; Duquesne University, Pittsburgh, Pa., assistant professor of French, 1952-58; Royal Military College, Kingston, Ontario, associate professor of French, 1958-60; Queen's University, Kingston, professor of French, 1960—. *Member:* Royal Society of Canada, Societe des Ecrivains Canadiens. *Awards, honors:* Olympic Games, 1948, bronze medal; Literary Prize of Quebec, 1965, for *L'Incubation;* Governor General's Award, 1966, for *L'Incubation,* and 1972, for *Le Cycle.*

*WRITINGS: Poemes temporels,* Regain, 1954; *La Bagarre,* Cercle du Livre, 1958; *Le Libraire,* Rene Julliard, 1960, translation by Glen Shortliffe published as *Not for Every Eye,* Macmillan (Toronto), 1962; *Les Images en poesie canadienne-francaise,* Beauchemin, 1960; *Les Pedagogues,* Cercle du Livre, 1960; *L'Incubation,* Librairie Deom, 1965, translation by Glen Shortliffe published as *Incubation,* Macmillan (Toronto), 1967; *Une Litterature en ebullition,* Editions du Jour, 1968; *Le Cycle,* Editions du Jour, 1971; *Trois Romanciers quebecois,* Editions du Jour, 1973; *La Commensale,* Editions Quinze, 1975; *Les Anthropoides,* Editions La Presse, 1977.

*WORK IN PROGRESS:* Research on French Canadian literature.

*BIOGRAPHICAL/CRITICAL SOURCES:* Patricia Smart, editor, *Litterature canadienne-francaise,* University Press of Montreal, 1969; Rejean Robidoux, *Livres et auteurs quebecois,* Editions Jumonville, 1971.

## BEST, James J(oseph) 1938-

*PERSONAL:* Born December 14, 1938, in Chicago, Ill.; son of James J. (a policeman) and Valerie (Pahlke) Best; married Lynda Weaver, August 26, 1961; children: Bryan Sean, Brett Jameson. *Education:* University of Chicago, B.A., 1960; Tufts University, M.A., 1962; University of North Carolina, Ph.D., 1965. *Politics:* Democrat. *Home:* 608 Fairchild, Kent, Ohio 44240. *Office:* Department of Political Science, Kent State University, Kent, Ohio 44240.

*CAREER:* University of Vermont, Burlington, assistant professor, 1964-66; University of Washington, Seattle, assistant professor of political science, 1966-73; Kent State University, Kent, Ohio, assistant professor of political science, 1973—. Exchange professor, Catholic University of Louvain, Belgium, 1975. *Member:* American Political Science Association. *Awards, honors:* Ford Foundation Legislative Service Project fellowship, 1970-72.

*WRITINGS: Public Opinion: Micro and Macro,* Dorsey, 1973; (contributor) James A. Robinson, editor, *State Legislative Innovation: Case Studies of Washington, Ohio, Florida, Illinois, Wisconsin, and California,* Praeger, 1973; (contributor) Thomas Hensley and Jerry Lewis, editors, *May 4, 1970: A Social Science Perspective,* Kendall/Hunt, 1978; (contributor) Josephine Milburn, editor, *Government and Politics in New England,* Schenkman, 1978. Contributor of articles to *Western Political Quarterly, Midwest Journal of Political Science,* and *Experiments in the Study of Politics.*

*WORK IN PROGRESS:* Extensive study of the political and governmental impact of industrial relocation.

*AVOCATIONAL INTERESTS:* Photography, collecting illustrated books.

\*     \*     \*

## BEST, Michael R(obert) 1939-

*PERSONAL:* Born May 26, 1939, in Adelaide, South Australia; son of Rupert J. (a virologist) and Effie (an environmentalist; maiden name, Deland) Best; married Terilyn J. McKenzie, May 11, 1968; children: Jacqueline M., Kirsten E. *Education:* University of Adelaide, B.A. (honors), 1961, Ph.D., 1966. *Office:* Department of English, University of Victoria, Victoria, British Columbia, Canada V8W 2Y2.

*CAREER:* High school teacher in England and Australia, 1964-67; University of Victoria, Victoria, British Columbia, assistant professor, 1967-72, associate professor of English, 1972—, chairman of department, 1976—. *Member:* Modern Language Association of America, Association of University Teachers of English, Canadian Society for Renaissance Studies.

*WRITINGS:* (Editor with Frank H. Brightman) *The Book of Secrets of Albertus Magnus,* Clarendon Press, 1972. Contributor of articles to journals in his field.

*WORK IN PROGRESS:* An edition of Gervase Markham's *The English Housewife (1615),* completion expected in 1978; a study of Shakespeare and the man's-eye view of women.

*SIDELIGHTS:* Michael Best told *CA* he has "a general interest in the popular culture of Renaissance England, focusing on drama and the popular press." *Avocational interests:* Playing oboe, oboe d'amore, and English horn.

\*     \*     \*

## BEYLE, Thad L. 1934-

*PERSONAL:* Born May 11, 1934, in Syracuse, N.Y.; son of Herman Carey (a teacher) and Madelon (McCulloch) Beyle; married Patricia Cain (a teacher), April 13, 1957; children: Carey, Jeffrey Lewis, Jonathan West, Aimee Maurene. *Education:* Syracuse University, A.B., 1956, A.M., 1960; University of Illinois, Ph.D., 1963. *Politics:* Democrat. *Religion:* Protestant. *Home:* 503 Landerwood Lane, Chapel Hill, N.C. 27514. *Office:* Department of Political Science, University of North Carolina, Chapel Hill, N.C. 27514.

*CAREER:* Merchants National Bank and Trust Co., Syracuse, N.Y., mortgage officer, 1958-60; Denison University, Granville, Ohio, assistant professor of government, 1963-64; National Center for Education in Politics faculty fellow in office of Governor of North Carolina, 1964-65; Duke University, Durham, N.C., research associate of Terry Sanford in "A Study of American States," 1965-67; University of North Carolina at Chapel Hill, assistant professor, 1967-69, associate professor, 1969-76, professor of political science, 1976—, director of graduate studies in political science, 1969-71, associate chairman, 1978—. Southern Growth Policies Board, acting executive director, 1971-72, consultant. Director of Center for Policy Research and Analysis, National Governors' Conference, 1974-76.

*WRITINGS:* (Contributor) Douglas M. Knight and E. Shepley Nourse, editors, *Libraries at Large,* Bowker, 1969; (author of introduction in reprint) Herman C. Beyle, *Identification and Analysis of Attribute-Cluster-Blocs* (first published by University of Chicago Press, 1931), Johnson Reprint, 1970; (editor with George T. Lathrop, Jr., and contributor) *Planning and Politics,* Odyssey, 1970; (editor with J. Oliver Williams, and contributor) *The American Governor in Behavioral Perspective,* Harper, 1972; (editor with Merle Black, and contributor) *Politics and Policy in North Carolina,* Mss Information, 1975; (with others) *Integration and Coordination of State Environmental Programs,* Council of State Governments, 1975. Contributor of about twenty-five articles to journals of political affairs. Book review editor, *Public Administration Review,* 1974-77.

*WORK IN PROGRESS:* Research on state government reorganization, governors, and cities in the South.

\*     \*     \*

## BICKET, Zenas J(ohan) 1932-

*PERSONAL:* Born October 14, 1932, in Hartford, Ill.; son of Paul James (a clergyman) and Marie (Johansen) Bicket; married Rhoda Price, August 28, 1954; children: Deborah, Daniel, David. *Education:* Wisconsin State University, Ed.B., 1954; Central Bible College, Springfield, Mo., Th.B., 1957; University of Arkansas, M.A., 1963, Ph.D., 1965. *Home:* 2257 Claiborne, Springfield, Mo. 65804. *Office:* Office of Academic Dean, Evangel College, 1111 North Glenstone, Springfield, Mo. 65802.

*CAREER:* Licensed clergyman, Assemblies of God Church. Central Bible College, Springfield, Mo., assistant professor of English, 1957-61, head of department, 1959-61; Evangel College, Springfield, associate professor, 1964-70, professor of English, 1970—, academic dean, 1966-70, 1973—, head of languages, literature, and communications department, 1970-73. Director of Southwest Missouri Consortium, 1966-72. *Member:* National Council of Teachers of English, Phi Delta Kappa.

*WRITINGS*—All published by Gospel Publishing House, except as indicated: (Editor) *Gospel Publishing House Style Manual,* 1958, 2nd edition, 1968; (editor) *Key 73 Congregational Resource Book,* Concordia, 1972; (editor) *The Effective Pastor,* 1973; *Walking in the Spirit,* 1977; *We Hold*

*These Truths: A Survey of the Cardinal Doctrines and Their Presentation in the Classroom,* 1978. Contributor of articles to *Abstracts of English Studies* and other journals.

*WORK IN PROGRESS:* Editing *And He Gave Pastors: A Handbook of Pastoral Theology,* for Gospel Publishing House.

\* \* \*

## BIDDLE, Phillips R. 1933-

*PERSONAL:* Born December 17, 1933, in Sioux City, Iowa; son of Durward Randolph and Madeline (Phillips) Biddle; married Jerry L. Allen (divorced, 1971); children: Haven Anne, Randolph Lee. *Education:* Portland State University, A.B., 1961; University of Illinois, M.A., 1963, Ph.D., 1966. *Home address:* P.O. Box 768, Pine Grove, Calif. 95665. *Office:* Department of Communication Studies, California State University, Sacramento, Calif. 95819.

*CAREER:* University of Massachusetts—Amherst, instructor in rhetoric, 1963-65; California State University, Sacramento, associate professor, 1966-76, professor of interpersonal communication, 1976—. *Military service:* U.S. Army, 1953-55. *Member:* International Society for General Semantics, American Schizophrenia Association.

*WRITINGS:* (With Halbert E. Gulley) *Essentials of Discussion,* Holt, 1970; (with Gulley) *Essentials of Debate,* Holt, 1972.

*WORK IN PROGRESS: I Am I: The Integrated Self,* completion expected in 1978.

*SIDELIGHTS:* Phillips Biddle wrote *CA,* "Communication is the means for attaining self wholeness, interpersonal oneness, and universal attunement." *Avocational interests:* Music, painting, wood-working.

\* \* \*

## BIEHLER, Robert F(rederick) 1927-

*PERSONAL:* Born January 14, 1927, in Summit, N.J.; son of August C. (an accountant) and Margaret (Janssen) Biehler; married Judith Carlson (an artist), July 1, 1961. *Education:* Syracuse University, B.A., 1950; University of Minnesota, M.A., 1951, Ph.D., 1953. *Home:* 1536 Manchester Rd., Chico, Calif. 95926.

*CAREER:* University of Massachusetts—Amherst, instructor in psychology, 1953-54; California State University, Chico, instructor, 1954-56, assistant professor, 1956-59, associate professor, 1959-64, professor of psychology, 1964-77; writer, 1977—. *Military service:* U.S. Army, 1945-47; became sergeant. *Member:* American Psychological Association, American Educational Research Association, Phi Beta Kappa, Phi Kappa Phi.

*WRITINGS: Psychology Applied to Teaching,* Houghton, 1971, 3rd edition, 1978; (editor) *Psychology Applied to Teaching: Selected Readings,* Houghton, 1972; *Child Development: An Introduction,* Houghton, 1976.

\* \* \*

## BIEMILLER, Ruth Cobbett 1914-

*PERSONAL:* Surname is pronounced *Bee*-miller; born June 5, 1914, in Morristown, N.J.; daughter of Frederick Burford (a lawyer and local historian) and Margaret (a teacher; maiden name, Dickison) Cobbett; married Reynard Biemiller (a graphics designer and calligrapher), November 5, 1938; children: Christopher Cobbett. *Education:* College of William and Mary, B.A., 1935; workshop study at New York University and New School for Social Research. *Politics:* "Fairly radical." *Home:* 3 Peter Cooper Rd., New York, N.Y. 10010.

*CAREER:* Mutual Benefit Life Insurance Co., Newark, N.J., member of editorial staff, 1937-41; Brooklyn Navy Yard, Brooklyn, N.Y., editor, *The Shipworker,* 1942-44; *New York Herald Tribune,* New York City, crossword puzzle editor and feature writer, 1952-66; free-lance writer and editor, 1966—; *National Star,* New York City, pun, anagram and crossword puzzle editor, 1974; Cornell University-New York Hospital, New York City, public relations officer, 1975-76. *Military service:* U.S. Naval Reserve, Women's Reserve, 1942-44; became lieutenant junior grade. *Member:* Overseas Press Club (member of board of governors and committee chairman, 1972—), Newswomen's Club of New York.

*WRITINGS:* (With Ferdi Backer) *Nat Fein's Animals,* Gilbert Press, 1955; *Dance: The Story of Katherine Dunham,* Doubleday, 1969; *Next Stop . . . Paris,* Symphonette Press, 1974. Also author of four purse-size crossword puzzle books, Bonomo, 1977. Contributor of articles to popular journals, including *New York* and *Saturday Review.* Contributing editor, *The Family Bible Encyclopedia,* Curtis Books, 1972.

*WORK IN PROGRESS:* Two novels, *German Adventure* and *Horizontal/Vertical.*

\* \* \*

## BIJOU, Sidney W(illiam) 1908-

*PERSONAL:* Born November 12, 1908, in Baltimore, Md.; married Janet R. Robias, August 31, 1934; children: Robert Keneth, Judith Ann. *Education:* Attended Lehigh University, 1928-30; University of Florida, B.S., 1933; Columbia University, M.A., 1937; University of Iowa, Ph.D., 1941. *Politics:* Democrat. *Home:* 5131 North Soledad Primera, Tucson, Ariz. 84718. *Office:* Department of Psychology, University of Arizona, Tucson, Ariz. 84721.

*CAREER:* Board of Education, New York, N.Y., psychologist, 1936-37; State Mental Hygiene Clinic and Hospital, Farnhurst, Del., psychologist, 1937-39; Wayne County Training School, Northville, Mich., research associate, 1941-42, 1946-47; Indiana University at Bloomington, assistant professor of psychology and director of graduate training clinic, 1946-48; University of Washington, Seattle, associate professor, 1948-51, professor of psychology, 1951-65, director, Gatzert Institute for Child Development, 1948-65; University of Illinois at Urbana-Champaign, professor of psychology, director of Child Behavior Laboratory, and member of Institute for Research on the Exceptional Child, 1965-75; University of Arizona, Tucson, adjunct professor of psychology, 1975—. Associate, Center for Advanced Study, University of Illinois, 1972. Member of mental health study section, National Institutes of Health, 1959-63; member of National Science Advisory Board and National Program on Early Childhood Education. Consultant to American Institute of Research. *Military service:* U.S. Army Air Forces, Office of Air Surgeon, 1942-46; became captain.

*MEMBER:* American Psychological Association (president of Division of Development Psychology, 1965-66), Psychonomic Society, Society for Research in Child Development, Society for Behavior Therapy and Experimental Psychiatry, National Association for Retarded Children, American Association of University Professors, International Society for the Study of Behavior Development, Midwestern Psychological Association (member of council, 1976-78), Association of Behavior Analysts (president, 1978). *Awards, honors:* National Institutes of Mental Health senior research fellow, 1961-62; American Association on Mental Deficiency research award, 1974; University of Veracruz (Mexico) certificate of merit, 1974; Fulbright-Hays fellowship at Universidad Central de Venezuela.

*WRITINGS:* (With D. M. Baer) *Child Development: A Systematic and Empirical Theory,* Appleton, Volume I, 1961, Volume II, 1965; (editor with Baer) *Readings in Experimental Analysis,* Appleton, 1967; (editor with Emilio Ribes-Inesta) *Behavior Modification: Issues and Extensions,* Academic Press, 1972; *Child Development: The Basic Stage of Early Childhood,* Prentice-Hall, 1976. Contributor of articles to psychology journals. Editor, *Journal of Experimental Child Psychology,* 1963-72; member of editorial board, *International Review of Research in Mental Retardation, Journal of Behavior Therapy and Experimental Psychiatry, Review of Early Childhood Education, Journal of Applied Behavior Analysis, Psychological Record,* and *Journal of Abnormal Psychology.*

*WORK IN PROGRESS: Analisis de la conducta applicade a ensenanza,* with E. Rayek-Zaga; *Teaching Young Handicapped Children,* for Prentice-Hall.

\*        \*        \*

## BILBO, Queenie    ?-1972

?—December 3, 1972; American editor and author of books on Africa and the Middle East. Obituaries: *New York Times,* December 5, 1972.

\*        \*        \*

## BIRNBAUM, Eleazar    1929-

*PERSONAL:* Born November 23, 1929, in Hamburg, Germany; son of Solomon Asher (a Hebrew palaeographer and philologist of Jewish languages) and Irene (Grunwald) Birnbaum; married Rebecca Pardes (a teacher), May 30, 1962; children: Nathan J., Samuel M., Abraham U., Sarah M., Miriam D. *Education:* School of Oriental and African Studies, London, Diploma in Oriental and African Studies (Hebrew palaeography), 1949, B.A. Hons. (Arabic), 1950, B.A. Hons. (Turkish), 1953. *Religion:* Jewish. *Home:* 132 Invermay Ave., Downsview, Ontario, Canada M3H 1Z8. *Office:* Department of Middle East and Islamic Studies, University of Toronto, Toronto, Ontario, Canada M5S 1A1.

*CAREER:* University of Durham, Durham, England, oriental librarian, 1953-60; University of Michigan, Ann Arbor, Near East bibliographer, 1960-64; University of Toronto, Toronto, Ontario, associate professor, 1964-70, professor of Turkish studies, 1970—. *Member:* American Oriental Society, Middle East Studies Association, American Research Institute in Turkey, Turkish Studies Association, Middle East Librarians Association, Oriental Club of Toronto (president, 1977-78). *Awards, honors:* Canada Council grants, 1968, 1970, 1973.

*WRITINGS:* (Compiler) *Books on Asia from the Near East to the Far East: A Guide for the General Reader,* University of Toronto Press, 1971; (compiler) *The Islamic Middle East: A Short Annotated Bibliography,* Department of Islamic Studies, University of Toronto, 1975; (editor with R. M. Savory, and contributor) *Introduction to Islamic Civilisation,* Cambridge University Press, 1976. Contributor to *Encyclopaedia of Islam* and to Middle East, orientalist, and historical journals. Chairman of publications committee, American Research Institute in Turkey, 1970-73.

*WORK IN PROGRESS: The 'Kabusname' in Turkish: The Earliest Old Ottoman Translation,* to be published by Sources of Oriental Languages and Literature; a critical edition of the *Divan* of Lufti, a fifteenth-century Chagatay Turkish poet; other studies in Turkish literature and history and in the history of Jews in the Middle East and the Orient.

\*        \*        \*

## BITTINGER, Desmond W(right)    1905-

*PERSONAL:* Born December 16, 1905, in Eglon, W.Va.; son of Jonas H. (a farmer) and Etta (Fike) Bittinger; married Irene Frantz, June 15, 1927; children: Stanley, Pattie (Mrs. Irven Stern), Richard, Mary (Mrs. Harlan Francis). *Education:* Elizabethtown College, B.A., 1927; University of Pennsylvania, M.A., 1933, Ph.D., 1940. *Religion:* Protestant. *Home and office:* 2203 Bayview Heights Dr., No. 170, San Diego, Calif. 92105.

*CAREER:* McPherson College, McPherson, Kan., professor of anthropology, 1940-44, president of college, 1950-65; Chapman College, Orange, Calif., chancellor of college, 1966-67, dean of World Campus afloat, 1967-76, dean emeritus, 1976—. Lecturer at Bethany Biblical Seminary, 1948-49, and Elgin Community College, 1949-50. *Member:* Association of Kansas Colleges (past president), Pi Kappa Delta, Rotary Club. *Awards, honors:* Litt.D., Elizabethtown College, 1962; L.H.D., Bridgewater College, 1970.

*WRITINGS: Black and White in the Sudan,* Elgin Press, 1940; *Wu Feng: Companion of Head Hunters,* Tunghai University Press, 1962; *Studia Missionalia,* University Gregoriana (Rome), 1970; *The Church of the Brethren,* Brethren Press, 1971; *The Song of the Drums,* Vantage, 1978. Contributor to *Annals of American Academy of Political and Social Science* and other journals. Editor of *The Messenger,* Church of the Brethren, 1944-50.

*SIDELIGHTS:* Desmond Bittinger told *CA:* "My writings have grown from years spent as an anthropologist and a teacher among aboriginal peoples in Taiwan, Africa, New Guinea, and Australia. I have tried to reach a 'soul tie' with them and really let them write of their own lives and beliefs. It is enlightening to me; it is real fun!"

\*        \*        \*

## BITTINGER, Emmert F(oster)    1925-

*PERSONAL:* Born September 22, 1925, in Petersburg, W.Va.; son of Foster Melvin (a clergyman) and Esther (Beir) Bittinger; married Esther Landis (a teacher), June 8, 1947; children: Marion (Mrs. Carl Bowman), Mildred (Mrs. Ronald Arnett), Lorraine (Mrs. David Lineweaver). *Education:* Bridgewater College, B.A., 1945; Bethany Theological Seminary, B.D., 1952; University of Maryland, M.A., 1951, Ph.D., 1964. *Politics:* Democrat. *Home:* Route 1, Bridgewater, Va. 22812. *Office:* Department of Sociology, Bridgewater College, Bridgewater, Va. 22812.

*CAREER:* Pastor of churches of the Brethren, 1948-58, 1960-63; Bridgewater College, Bridgewater, Va., assistant professor, 1963-66, associate professor, 1966-70, professor of sociology, 1970—. *Member:* American Sociological Association, Southern Sociological Association, Virginia Social Science Society, Virginia Archaeological Society, Alpha Kappa Delta.

*WRITINGS: Heritage and Promise: Perspectives on the Church of the Brethren,* Brethren Press, 1971. Contributor to religious periodicals.

*AVOCATIONAL INTERESTS:* American incunabula from Saur and Ephrata presses.

## BLACK, Hugh C(leon) 1920-

*PERSONAL:* Born February 22, 1920, in Wellington, Tex.; son of Hugh Shannon and Ethel (Forbis) Black; married Shirley Mae Costlow, July 2, 1944; children: Mrs. Gregory Fitzgerald, Vicki Hugh, Sarah Benita. *Education:* Rice Institute (now Rice University), B.A. (with distinction), 1941; University of Texas, Main University (now University of Texas at Austin), M.Ed., 1947, Ph.D., 1949. *Politics:* Liberal Democrat. *Religion:* Methodist. *Home:* 934 K St., Davis, Calif. 95616. *Office:* Department of Education, University of California, Davis, Calif. 95616.

*CAREER:* Rice Institute (now Rice University), Houston, Tex., assistant professor, 1949-54, associate professor of philosophy and education, 1955-60, associate professor of education, 1961-62; University of California, Davis, associate professor, 1962-67, professor of education, 1967—, head of department, 1962-67. Visiting professor at summer sessions, University of Houston, 1952, University of Texas, 1954, University of Illinois, 1961, University of Nebraska, 1955, 1956, 1957, 1958, 1959, 1960, 1962, 1969. *Military service:* U.S. Army, 1942-46; became captain. *Member:* Philosophy of Education Society (fellow), History of Education Society, American Educational Studies Association, National Educational Association, Far Western Philosophy of Education Society, Comparative and International Education Society, California Teachers Association, Phi Delta Kappa, Delta Tau Kappa.

*WRITINGS:* (Editor with Kenneth V. Lottich and Donald S. Seckinger) *The Great Educators: Readings for Leaders in Education,* Nelson-Hall, 1972. Contributor of articles to *Educational Forum, Educational Theory,* and *Progressive Education.*

*WORK IN PROGRESS:* Articles for various professional journals.

\* \* \*

## BLACK, Irma Simonton 1906-1972

June 5, 1906—June 18(?), 1972; American author of books for children and advice for parents. Obituaries: *New York Times,* June 19, 1972; *Antiquarian Bookman,* July 17-31, 1972. (See index for *CA* sketch)

\* \* \*

## BLACKWELL, (Annie) Louise 1919-1977

*PERSONAL:* Born May 7, 1919, in Benmore, Miss. *Education:* Attended Twentieth Century Business College, 1937-39, and Tulane University, 1948-49; University of Houston, B.A., 1951; graduate study at Johns Hopkins University, 1952-54, Vanderbilt University, 1957-58, and University of Tennessee, 1962-63; Florida State University, M.A., 1964, Ph.D., 1966. *Office:* Department of English, Florida Agricultural and Mechanical University, Tallahassee, Fla. 32307.

*CAREER:* Secretary, 1939-43; legal secretary in Mobile, Ala., 1946-48; Johns Hopkins University, Baltimore, Md., technical assistant, department of biostatistics, 1951-52; Camp Cherryfield for Adults (a summer program in adult education), Brevard, N.C., director, 1956-62; Florida Agricultural and Mechanical University, Tallahassee, associate professor of English, 1966-77. Instructor in creative writing, Watkins Institute, 1959-60; Fulbright lecturer in American literature, University of Sao Paulo, 1972-73. Staff director, Knoxville Area Human Relations Council, 1961-62; member of Florida Governor's Commission on the Status of Women,

1967-69; Danforth associate, beginning 1970; member of National Council on the Humanities, 1971-76. *Military service:* U.S. Army Air Forces, Ninth Air Force, Bombardment Division, court reporter, 1943-45; received Bronze Star Medal. *Member:* Modern Language Association of America, College English Association, Society for the Study of Southern Literature, Authors Guild of America, South Atlantic Modern Language Association, Lambda Iota Tau.

*WRITINGS: The Men around Hurley,* Vanguard, 1957; (with Frances Clay) *Lillian Smith,* Twayne, 1971. Contributor of articles and short stories to literary journals.

*WORK IN PROGRESS: My Web and My Place,* a novel; *Bienville and the Governor's Daughter* and *Somewhere in England,* three-act plays.†

(Died December 25, 1977)

\* \* \*

## BLAISDELL, Donald C. 1899-

*PERSONAL:* Born August 12, 1899, in Chautauqua, N.Y.; son of Thomas Charles (a teacher) and Kate (Christy) Blaisdell; married Dorothea Nesbitt Chambers, August 14, 1926; children: Nesbitt Chambers, Ann Lang (Mrs. R. Allen Irvine). *Education:* Pennsylvania State College (now University), B.S., 1920; Columbia University, M.A., 1926, Ph.D., 1929. *Politics:* Democrat. *Religion:* Protestant. *Home and office:* R.F.D. 1, Box 278, 11148 Harding Rd., Laurel, Md. 20810.

*CAREER:* Lycoming Rubber Co., Lycoming, Pa., manufacturing accountant, 1920-22; Robert College, Istanbul, Turkey, teacher of engineering, 1922-25; Columbia University, New York City, instructor in political science, 1928-30; Williams College, Williamstown, Mass., assistant professor of political science, 1930-35; employee of U.S. Department of Agriculture, Washington, D.C., 1936-40, and of U.S. Congress, 1940-41; U.S. Department of State, Washington, D.C., assistant and associate division chief, 1941-47, representative in Geneva, Switzerland, 1951-53; College of the City of New York (now City College of the City University of New York), New York City, professor of political science, 1955-67, chairman of department, 1955-57; owner and operator, with wife, Dorothea Blaisdell, of Well House Certified Tree Farm. Washington representative of Committee to Defend America by Aiding the Allies, 1940-41. Visiting professor at University of Wisconsin, 1935-36, University of Illinois, 1949, and University of Florida, 1953-54; lecturer at Armed Forces Strategic Intelligence School, 1949-50; Mary Whiton Calkins Visiting Professor of Political Science at Wellesley College, 1954-55. Fulbright student selection committee, European section, member, 1956, chairman, 1957; board member and trustee, Overseas Education Fund of League of Women Voters, 1957-69. United States delegation to the United Nations, adviser, 1946-47, principal executive officer, 1948. *Member:* American Political Science Association, American Association for the Advancement of Science (fellow), Authors Club, Sigma Tau, Phi Delta Theta, Cosmos Club (Washington).

*WRITINGS: European Financial Control in the Ottoman Empire,* Columbia University Press, 1929; *The Farmer's Stake in World Peace,* Carnegie Endowment for International Peace, 1935, 2nd revised edition, 1937; *Government and Agriculture: The Growth of Federal Farm Aid,* Farrar & Rinehart, 1940, reprinted, Da Capo, 1974; *Economic Power and Political Pressures,* U.S. Government Printing Office, 1941; *Government under Pressure,* Public Affairs Committee, 1942, 2nd revised edition, 1946; *Arming the*

*United Nations*, U.S. Government Printing Office, 1947; *American Democracy under Pressure*, Ronald, 1957; *Unofficial Government: Pressure Groups and Lobbies*, American Academy of Political and Social Science, 1958; (editor and contributor) *The Riverside Democrats*, McGraw, 1960; *International Organization*, Ronald, 1966; *Technology—The Key to Better Environment: Values, Profits, and Growth in Post-Industrial Society*, Exposition Press, 1973.

\*     \*     \*

## BLAKELY, R(obert) J(ohn) 1915-

*PERSONAL:* Born February 24, 1915, in Springview, Neb.; son of Percy Lee (a farmer) and Mary (Watson) Blakely; married Eleanor W. White, December 26, 1938; married Alta Eckhoff (a high school English teacher), September 5, 1964; children: (first marriage) Susan (Mrs. Paul Shurin), Craig Baird, Stephen Bush. *Education:* State University of Iowa, B.A. (with highest distinction), 1937; Harvard University, further study, 1937-38. *Politics:* Independent. *Religion:* Protestant. *Home and office:* 5418 South Blackstone Ave., Chicago, Ill. 60615.

*CAREER:* Newspaper man for *Des Moines Register*, Des Moines, Iowa, 1939-48, *St. Louis Star Times*, St. Louis, Mo., 1948-51, and *Chicago Daily News*, Chicago, Ill., 1964-68; executive, Fund for Adult Education, 1951-61; State University of Iowa, Iowa City, member of faculty and dean, 1961-64; free-lance writer, 1968—. *Military service:* U.S. Marine Corps, 1943-46; became first lieutenant; received Purple Heart. *Member:* Adult Education Association of the United States of America, National Association of Educational Broadcasters.

*WRITINGS: Adult Education in a Free Society*, Guardian Bird, 1958; *How to Read a Newspaper*, Chicago Daily News, 1968; *The People's Instrument: A Philosophy of Programming for Public Television*, Public Affairs Press, 1971; *Fostering the Need to Learn: Monographs and Annotated Bibliography on Continuing Education for Health Manpower*, U.S. Government Printing Office, 1974; *A History of Educational Broadcasting in the United States*, Syracuse University Press, 1978. Contributor of articles to professional journals.

\*     \*     \*

## BLATT, Sidney J(ules) 1928-

*PERSONAL:* Born October 15, 1928, in Philadelphia, Pa.; son of Harry (a merchant) and Fannie (Feld) Blatt; married Ethel Shames, February 1, 1951; children: Susan, Judith, David. *Education:* Pennsylvania State University, B.S., 1950, M.S., 1952; University of Chicago, Ph.D., 1957; study at Western New England Institute for Psychoanalysis, 1972. *Home:* 28 Mulberry Rd., Woodbridge, Conn. 06525. *Office:* Departments of Psychology and Psychiatry, Yale University, 25 Park St., New Haven, Conn. 06510.

*CAREER:* Michael Reese Hospital, Chicago, Ill., psychologist, 1957-59; Yale University, New Haven, Conn., assistant professor, 1960-65, associate professor, 1965-73, professor of psychology, 1973—. *Member:* Psi Chi, Sigma Xi. *Awards, honors:* Foundation Fund fellow, 1961-64; National Institute of Mental Health postdoctoral fellow.

*WRITINGS:* (With Joel Allison and Carl N. Zimet) *The Interpretation of Psychological Tests*, Harper, 1968; (with Cynthia M. Wild) *Schizophrenia: A Developmental Analysis*, Academic Press, 1976.

## BLEICHER, Michael N(athaniel) 1935-

*PERSONAL:* Surname rhymes with "teacher"; born October 2, 1935, in Cleveland, Ohio; son of David B. and Rachel (Faigin) Bleicher; married Betty Isack, June 4, 1957; children: Helene, Laurence, Benjamin. *Education:* California Institute of Technology, B.S., 1957; Tulane University, M.S., 1959, Ph.D., 1961; University of Warsaw, Doctorate, 1961. *Politics:* Democratic. *Religion:* Jewish. *Home:* 1930 Regent St., Madison, Wis. 53705. *Office:* Department of Mathematics, University of Wisconsin, Madison, Wis. 53706.

*CAREER:* University of Wisconsin—Madison, assistant professor, 1962-66, associate professor, 1966-70, professor of mathematics, 1970—, chairman of department, 1972-74. Democratic National Convention, delegate and member of credentials committee, 1968, 1972, 1976, member of rules committee, 1976; chairman, Democratic Party of Wisconsin, 1976—. *Member:* American Mathematical Society, Mathematics Association of America, American Federation of Teachers, American Association of University Professors, Sigma Xi.

*WRITINGS: Excursions into Mathematics*, Worth Publishers, 1969. Contributor of articles to technical journals.

*WORK IN PROGRESS:* Mathematical papers on geometry and number theory.

\*     \*     \*

## BLENKINSOPP, Joseph 1927-

*PERSONAL:* Born March 4, 1927, in Bishop Auckland, England; son of Joseph and Mary (Lyons) Blenkinsopp; married Irene Cunningham, March 30, 1968; children: David. *Education:* University of London, B.A. (honours), 1951; Istituto Biblico, Rome, Italy, L.S.S., 1958; Oxford University, D.Phil., 1967. *Religion:* Catholic Christian. *Home:* 409 East Napoleon Blvd., South Bend, Ind. 46617. *Office:* Department of Theology, University of Notre Dame, Notre Dame, Ind. 46556.

*CAREER:* Chicago Theological Seminary, Chicago, Ill., teacher of Biblical studies, 1968-69; Hartford Seminary Foundation, Hartford, Conn., associate professor, 1969-70; University of Notre Dame, Notre Dame, Ind., associate professor of theology, 1970—. Visiting lecturer, Vanderbilt University, 1968. *Member:* American Academy of Religion, American Association of University Professors, Society of Biblical Literature, Society of Old Testament Studies (British), Catholic Biblical Association.

*WRITINGS: The Corinthian Mirror*, Sheed, 1964; *The Promise to David*, Darton, Longman, Todd, 1964; *From Adam to Abraham*, Darton, Longman, Todd, 1965; *Paul's Life in Christ*, Darton, Longman, Todd, 1965; *Jesus Is Lord*, Paulist Press, 1967; *A Sketchbook of Biblical Theology*, Herder & Herder, 1968; *Sexuality and the Christian Tradition*, Pflaum, 1968; *Celibacy, Ministry, Church*, Herder & Herder, 1968; *The Men Who Spoke Out*, Darton, Longman, Todd, 1969; (with John Challenor) *Pentateuch* (commentary), ACTA Foundation, 1971; *Gibeon and Israel*, Cambridge University Press, 1972. Contributor of articles to *Journal of Biblical Literature*, *Biblica*, and *Commonweal;* translator from German, French, and Italian.

*WORK IN PROGRESS:* Research on post-biblical Jewish history during the intertestamental period; a study of the symbolism in the novels of Hesse.

*SIDELIGHTS:* Joseph Blenkinsopp has traveled extensively in Europe and the Middle East, spent a year (1963-64) of travel, teaching, and research in Guatemala, and done archaeological work in Palestine.

*BIOGRAPHICAL/CRITICAL SOURCES: Commonweal,* October 10, 1969.

\* \* \*

## BLIVEN, Bruce 1889-1977

*PERSONAL:* Born July 27, 1889, in Emmetsburg, Iowa; son of Charles Franklin (a farmer) and Lilla Cordelia (Ormsby) Bliven; married Rose Frances Emery, May 17, 1913; children: Bruce, Jr. *Education:* Stanford University, A.B., 1911. *Politics:* Independent. *Home:* 21 Kingscote Gardens, Stanford, Calif. 94305.

*CAREER: San Francisco Bulletin,* San Francisco, Calif., member of editorial staff, 1909-12; advertisement writer and free-lance writer, 1912-14; University of Southern California, Los Angeles, director of department of journalism, 1914-16; *Printer's Ink,* New York City, member of editorial staff, 1917-19; *New York Globe,* New York City, member of editorial board, 1919-23; *New Republic,* New York City, managing editor, 1923-30, editor, 1930-55, member of editorial board, 1923-55; Stanford University, Stanford, Calif., lecturer in communication and journalism, 1956-77. New York correspondent, *Manchester Guardian,* 1927-47. Member of board of directors of Foreign Policy Association of the United States, 1923-45, and Twentieth Century Fund, 1923-56. *Member:* National Association of Science Writers.

*WRITINGS: The Men Who Make the Future,* Duell, Sloan & Pearce, 1942; (editor) *What the Informed Citizen Needs to Know,* Duell, Sloan & Pearce, 1945; (editor) *Twentieth Century Unlimited,* Lippincott, 1950; *Preview for Tomorrow: The Unfinished Business of Science,* Knopf, 1953; *The World Changers,* John Day, 1965; *Five Million Words Later* (autobiography), John Day, 1970; *A Mirror for Greatness: Six Americans,* McGraw, 1976. Contributor of articles to national magazines, including *New Republic, Reader's Digest, Harper's, Saturday Evening Post, Atlantic, Ladies' Home Journal, McCall's, Redbook, American Heritage,* and *New York Times Magazine.*

*WORK IN PROGRESS:* A history of the last part of the nineteenth century in the United States, in the form of biographical sketches.

*SIDELIGHTS:* Bruce Bliven, called by the *New York Times* a "champion of liberalism," was best known for his editorship of the *New Republic.* "The editor's chair of that small but very influential weekly was an ideal vantage point for witnessing the history of our times," said the *New Yorker.* Helen Fuller writes, "Bruce Bliven stood steadfastly behind his senior editors, his publishers, dozens of Good Causes, and always in support of colleagues striving for technical excellence in the publishing trade." Bliven told a *New York Times* interviewer, "The essence of liberalism is a desire to have an open mind, a desire to have an open society, a desire to know the fundamental truth, a desire that as many people as possible should have a better life."

*AVOCATIONAL INTERESTS:* Reading, music, theatre, walking.

*BIOGRAPHICAL/CRITICAL SOURCES: New York Times,* July 27, 1969, May 29, 1977; *Five Million Words Later* (autobiography), John Day, 1970; *New Republic,* January 9, 1971; *New Yorker,* January 23, 1971; *Washington Post,* May 29, 1977; *Time,* June 13, 1977; *AB Bookman's Weekly,* June 27, 1977.†

(Died May 27, 1977)

## BLOESSER, Robert 1930-

*PERSONAL:* Born February 11, 1930, in Stotesbury, Mo.; son of Henry Lawrence (a farmer) and Kittie (Martin) Bloesser. *Education:* University of Missouri, B.A., 1958, M.A., 1961. *Politics:* Democratic. *Religion:* Methodist. *Home:* 563 Heathertree Lane, San Jose, Calif. 95129. *Office:* Department of English, Foothill College, 12345 El Monte, Los Altos Hills, Calif. 94022.

*CAREER:* Foothill College, Los Altos Hills, Calif., 1967—, began as assistant professor, professor of English, 1970—. President, Foothill Academic Senate, 1977-78. *Military service:* U.S. Navy, 1951-55.

*WRITINGS: Making It as a Writer,* Holbrook, 1972; *Kittie and Other Fine Dishes,* privately printed, 1974; *The Martins: They Speak for Themselves,* Intercollegiate Press, 1976.

*WORK IN PROGRESS:* A history of Stotesbury, Mo., and the Bloesser family; *College Rhetoric: A Prescription.*

\* \* \*

## BLUEFARB, Samuel 1919-

*PERSONAL:* Born April 21, 1919, in London, England; son of Lewis (a master tailor) and Millie (Engel) Bluefarb; married Eva Martinez (a social welfare worker), May 23, 1955. *Education:* Los Angeles City College, A.A., 1949; University of California, Los Angeles, B.A., 1951; University of Southern California, M.S. (library science), 1954, M.A. (English), 1961; University of New Mexico, Ph.D., 1967. *Politics:* Republican. *Religion:* Jewish. *Residence:* Torrance, Calif. *Office:* Department of English, Los Angeles Harbor College, Wilmington, Calif. 90744.

*CAREER:* California State Library, Sacramento, librarian, 1954-55; San Bernardino (Calif.) Public Library, librarian, 1955-57; high school teacher of English in San Pedro, Calif., 1957-62; Los Angeles Harbor College, Wilmington, Calif., teacher in evening courses, 1958-62, instructor, 1962-65, assistant professor, 1965-67, associate professor of English, 1967—. *Military service:* U.S. Army, Combat Engineers, 1941-45; received European Theater medal with four campaign stars. *Member:* American Association of University Professors, University Centers for Rational Alternatives, Los Angeles College Teachers Association, Jewish War Veterans.

*WRITINGS:* (Contributor) Leslie Field and Joyce Field, editors, *Bernard Malamud and the Critics,* New York University Press, 1970; (contributor) J. K. Bowen and R. Van Der Beets, editors, *American Short Fiction,* Bobbs-Merrill, 1970; *The Escape Motif in the American Novel,* Ohio State University Press, 1972; (contributor) Leslie Field and Joyce Field, editors, *Bernard Malamud: A Collection of Critical Essays,* Prentice-Hall, 1975; (contributor) Therman B. O'Daniel, editor, *James Baldwin: A Critical Evaluation,* Howard University Press, 1977. Contributor of about twenty-five articles and reviews to *New Orleans Review, Texas Quarterly, Trace, Los Angeles Times, Modern British Literature,* and other publications.

*WORK IN PROGRESS:* A novel, *Another Fall.*

*SIDELIGHTS:* "My first love has always been the writing of fiction," Samuel Bluefarb told *CA,* "yet I seem to hit it off better with critical writing.... Maybe (literary) criticism is as much the child of intuition as it is of the cooler analytical faculty." *Avocational interests:* Travel, especially in high desert country.

## BLYN, George 1919-

*PERSONAL:* Born May 2, 1919, in New York, N.Y.; son of Philip E. (a businessman) and Rose (Faiby) Blyn; married Charlotte Lilly (a physician), June 22, 1952; children: Stefany, Roslyn, Corliann. *Education:* University of Pennsylvania, B.A., 1951, M.A., 1953, Ph.D., 1961. *Home:* 511 Winding Way, Merion Station, Pa. 19066. *Office:* Department of Economics, Rutgers University, Camden, N.J. 08102.

*CAREER:* Villanova University, Villanova, Pa., assistant professor of economics, 1954-62; Rutgers University, Camden College of Arts and Sciences, Camden, N.J., assistant professor, 1961-62, associate professor, 1962-67, professor of economics, 1967—. Research associate, Institute for Economic Development and Cultural Change, 1957-58. *Military service:* U.S. Army, 1943-46. *Member:* American Economic Association, Association of Asian Studies, Association of American Geographers. *Awards, honors:* Faculty research fellow, American Institute of Indian Scholars, 1965-66.

*WRITINGS: Agricultural Trends in India, 1891-1947: Output, Availability, and Productivity,* University of Pennsylvania, 1966. Contributor to economics and geography journals.

*WORK IN PROGRESS: Nutritional Adequacy among Cultivator Families in Northwestern India.*

\* \* \*

## BOASE, Paul H(enshaw) 1915-

*PERSONAL:* Surname is pronounced Bowes; born July 13, 1915, in Topeka, Ind.; son of Herbert (a minister) and Mary H. (McLaughlin) Boase; married Marjorie Brigham, September 18, 1947; children: Catherine Sue (Mrs. Tom Ehrhardt), Terri Lee (Mrs. Daniel Rosser), Brian Paul. *Education:* Manchester College, A.B., 1937; University of Wisconsin, M.S., 1947, Ph.D., 1952. *Politics:* Democrat. *Religion:* Methodist. *Home:* 2 Canterbury Dr., Athens, Ohio 45701. *Office:* School of Interpersonal Communication, Ohio University, Athens, Ohio 45701.

*CAREER:* Teacher in public schools in Indiana, 1937-41; Oberlin College, Oberlin, Ohio, instructor, 1948-50, assistant professor, 1950-53, associate professor of speech, 1953-64; Ohio University, Athens, professor of speech and director of School of Interpersonal Communication, 1964—. *Military service:* U.S. Army Air Forces, 1941-46; became captain. *Member:* Speech Communication Association of America, American Association of University Professors, Central States Speech Association (president, 1968-69).

*WRITINGS: Basic Speech,* Macmillan, 1964, 3rd edition, 1975; *The Rhetoric of Christian Socialism,* Random House, 1969. Contributor of about fifty articles and reviews to journals in his field. Associate editor, *Quarterly Journal of Speech,* 1966-68.

*WORK IN PROGRESS:* Editing *The Rhetoric of Protest and Reform: 1878-1900.*

\* \* \*

## BOCKELMAN, Wilfred 1920-

*PERSONAL:* Born November 15, 1920, in Napoleon, Ohio; son of Carl H. (a farmer) and Sophia (Helberg) Bockelman; married A. Eleanor Lehman (a writer), May 26, 1946; children: Karen Gaye, Marla Joy. *Education:* Capital University, B.A., 1942; Evangelical Lutheran Theological Seminary, B.D., 1945; Columbia University, M.S., 1956. *Politics:* Republican. *Home:* 6013 Kellogg Ave., Minneapolis, Minn. 55424. *Agent:* Author's and Publisher's Service, 146-47 29th Ave., Flushing, N.Y. 11354. *Office:* American Lutheran Church, 422 South Fifth St., Minneapolis, Minn. 55415.

*CAREER:* Lutheran minister; *Lutheran Standard,* Minneapolis, Minn., associate editor, 1947-65; American Lutheran Church, Minneapolis, assistant director of public relations, 1966—.

*WRITINGS:* "It Will Be Your Duty," Augsburg, 1956; *On Good Soil,* Friendship, 1958; *You Can Help Make It Happen,* Augsburg, 1971; (with wife, A. Eleanor Bockelman) *An Exercise in Compassion: The Church in South Africa,* Augsburg, 1972; (with A. E. Bockelman) *Ethiopia: Where Lutheran Is Spelled "Mekane Yesus,"* Augsburg, 1972; *Gothard: The Man and His Ministry—An Evaluation,* Quill, 1976; *Politics with Integrity—Al Quie of Minnesota,* Eye of the Needle, 1978. Also author of *Eye of the Needle,* a monthly newsletter for corporation executives and church leaders.

*WORK IN PROGRESS:* Several books; a series of columns intended to give current and relevant interpretations of religion.

\* \* \*

## BOESEN, Victor 1908-
### (Jesse Hall, Eric Harald)

*PERSONAL:* Surname is pronounced *Bo*-sun; born September 7, 1908, in Plainfield, Ind.; son of Jens Eugene and Helene (Petersen) Boesen; married Nancy Hagedorn, October 2, 1940. *Education:* Attended University of Missouri, 1928-30. *Politics:* Democrat. *Religion:* "No affiliation." *Home:* 971 Chattanooga Ave., Pacific Palisades, Calif. 90272.

*CAREER:* Writer. *Wichita Beacon,* Wichita, Kan., reporter, 1930; City News Bureau, Chicago, Ill., reporter, rewriter, and editor, 1931-35; WBBM-CBS Radio, Chicago, news and commentary writer, 1935-38; KNX-CBS Radio, Los Angeles, Calif., news writer, 1940; *Skyways* (magazine), New York City, roving correspondent, 1942-44; *Liberty* (magazine), New York City, Pacific and Near East correspondent, 1945-46. *Member:* Overseas Press Club of America.

*WRITINGS:* (With Joseph Karneke) *Navy Diver,* Putnam, 1962; *They Said It Couldn't Be Done: The Incredible Story of Bill Lear,* Doubleday, 1971; *William P. Lear: From High School Dropout to Space Age Inventor* (juvenile), Hawthorn, 1974; *Doing Something about the Weather* (juvenile), Putnam, 1975; *Edward Sheriff Curtis: Visions of a Vanishing Race,* Crowell, 1976; *Edward S. Curtis: Photographer of the North American Indian* (juvenile), Dodd, 1977; *Irving Krick vs the US Weather Bureaucracy,* Putnam, 1978. Contributor of articles to approximately thirty-five national magazines, including *Saturday Evening Post, Collier's, Coronet, Esquire, Nation's Business,* and *Look;* and, under pseudonyms Jesse Hall and Eric Harald, to *Skyways* and *West.*

*WORK IN PROGRESS:* Books on weather control; a book on retirement living.

\* \* \*

## BOGUE, Lucile Maxfield 1911-
### (Max Bogue, Lucy Max)

*PERSONAL:* Born April 21, 1911, in Salt Lake City, Utah;

daughter of Roy Douglas (a rancher) and Maude (Callicotte) Maxfield; married Arthur E. Bogue (a manager of a federal land bank), December 25, 1935 (died December 19, 1976); children: Sharon Kay (Mrs. Thomas Young), Bonnie Gale Cebulski. *Education:* Colorado College, A.A. (with honors), 1932; University of Northern Colorado, B.A., 1934; University of California, Berkeley, additional study, 1966; California State University, San Francisco (now San Francisco State University), M.A. (with distinction), 1972. *Politics:* Democrat. *Religion:* Unitarian Universalist. *Home:* 2611 Brooks, El Cerrito, Calif. 94530.

*CAREER:* Teacher in elementary schools and high schools in Colorado, 1934-62; Yampa Valley College (now United States International University, Colorado Alpine Campus), Steamboat Springs, Colo., founder and president, 1962-66; American School in Japan, Tokyo, director of guidance, 1966-68; Anna Head School, Oakland, Calif., dean, 1968-71. Registrar and librarian, Perry-Mansfield School of Theatre, 1951-57; has also taught in San Miguel de Allende, Mexico, Managua, Nicaragua, Guayaquil, Ecuador; guidance consultant, Foreign School in Japan. *Member:* World Citizens, World Association of World Federalists, California Writers Club (vice-president), California Federation of Chaparral Poets, Ina Coolbrith Poetry Circle. *Awards, honors:* Named Colorado's poet by Colorado Women's Club, 1941; Governor's Award of Colorado Centennial for "Freedom Trail," 1959; Browning Society of San Francisco Award for "Blood across the Bay," 1966; Bogue Library and Lucy Bogue Hall of United States International University (Colorado Alpine Campus) have been named for Lucile Bogue; nominated for Colorado's Woman of Achievement award, 1967; awarded grand prize, World of Poetry Contest, 1976; awarded gold medal, All Nations Poetry Contest, 1976, for poem, "Blood of Malinche"; National Writers Club poetry award, 1977.

*WRITINGS: Typhoon! Typhoon!: An Illustrated Haiku Sequence,* Tuttle, 1970; *Eye of the Condor,* Casa del Cultura, 1975, revised edition, 1976.

Plays: "Whatever Heaven," first produced at Steamboat Springs, Colo., 1954; "The Lucky Ones," first produced at Steamboat Springs, Colo., 1956; "Freedom Trail," first produced in Denver, Colo., 1959; "Citizen Number One"; "Drums Carry a Far Distance"; "The Supper"; "Make a Joyful Noise"; "Private Moments"; "Paradise Lost"; "Fedra."

*WORK IN PROGRESS: Dancers on Horseback; Journey to Yeats Country; Bluffer's Cookbook.*

*SIDELIGHTS:* Lucile Maxfield Bogue told *CA:* "Writing became a habit with me at age seven when I wrote my first poem. I have been writing ever since—with great joy and satisfaction—and little fame or fortune. Writing is something I do as some people eat peanuts—I can't stop. I love it. My thoughts seem to cling to paper in various forms, in poetry, drama, historical novels, juvenile books, nonfiction, and music. Although I don't consider myself a poet, that is the field in which I have earned international recognition, publication, and monetary rewards. But I find my greatest pleasure in writing serious drama—and my greatest sorrow in my failure to convince a New York producer that it can be a Broadway hit. My output has been tremendous and unceasing, but my publication spotty. Editors tell me my writing is 'sparkling,' 'well-crafted,' 'powerful.' But the 'subject is not quite right for today's market.' Ah well, I shall go on writing forever—and leave my children trunk's full of 'sparkling' unpublished manuscripts. I can not stop now."

## BOHLANDER, Jill 1936-

*PERSONAL:* Born December 17, 1936, in Evanston, Ill.; daughter of Frank Wesley (an insurance representative) and Helen Montgomery (Davenport) Rorabach; married Benny L. Bohlander, June, 1958 (divorced, 1965); married Raymond Wilson Keller (a sculptor), July, 1971; children: (first marriage) Eric Douglas. *Education:* Attended MacMurray College for Women, 1954; Illinois Wesleyan University, B.A., 1958; Illinois State University, additional study, summers, 1960, 1961; University of Illinois, M.A., 1959; additional study at University of California, Los Angeles, 1965-66, 1967-68, and University of Wuerzburg, 1966-67. *Politics:* "Feminist." *Address:* P.O. Box 723, Topanga, Calif. 90290. *Office:* Department of English, Los Angeles Pierce College, 6201 Winnetka Ave., Woodland Hills, Calif.

*CAREER:* Has worked as a horse trainer, free-lance editor and writer, waitress, director of educational films, and illustrator of children's books; English teacher in high school in Danvers, Ill., 1959-60; Illinois State University, Normal, instructor in English, 1960-63; University of Maryland, Overseas Extension, Schwerinfurt and Wuerzburg, Germany, instructor in English, 1963-65, 1966-67; University of California, Los Angeles, research assistant, 1965-66, teaching assistant, 1967-68; Santa Monica City College, Santa Monica, Calif., instructor in English, 1968-69; Los Angeles Pierce College, Woodland Hills, Calif., instructor in English, 1969—. *Member:* American Federation of Teachers, American Association of University Professors, American Civil Liberties Union, California Humanities Association, California Confederation of the Arts, California Federation of Teachers, California Junior College Association.

*WRITINGS: The Scope of Recognition,* Holt, 1972. Contributor to *Los Angeles Free Press, Akeweswance Notes, Nishwabe News, Lesbian Tide, Topanga Messanger, Amnesty International,* and other periodicals.

*WORK IN PROGRESS: Alphabet,* a self-illustrated children's book; a book of poems and lithographs, with Ray Keller; a film on William Blake's engravings; "To God's Children," an animated film for children; poems; a novel; a play.

*SIDELIGHTS:* Jill Bohlander told *CA:* "I write for love and hate, from hope and despair. If one poem can make one reader naked when he was clothed, I have been a success. I am an exhibitionist and a doctor. I believe art must make man better rather than worse by undressing him or his world. I love words, animals, stones and people. I hate greed and power. I hope for a world of haves. I despair at the millions of havenots we have created. I write. I live."

\*       \*       \*

## BOKUM, Fanny Butcher 1888-
## (Fanny Butcher)

*PERSONAL:* Born February 13, 1888, in Fredonia, Kan.; daughter of L. Oliver (an artist) and Hattie May (Young) Butcher; married Richard Drummond Bokum, February 13, 1935 (died, 1963). *Education:* Lewis Institute (now Illinois Institute of Technology), A.A., 1908; University of Chicago, B.A., 1910. *Politics:* Republican. *Home:* 1209 Astor St., Chicago, Ill. 60610.

*CAREER: Chicago Tribune,* Chicago, Ill., feature writer, social-travel columnist, music critic, and literary editor, 1913-63. Owner, Fanny Butcher Books (bookstore), 1919-1927. *Member:* P.E.N. International (former president of

Chicago chapter), Society of Midland Authors (director), Arts Club of Chicago (director), Fortnightly of Chicago (honorary member), Scribblers, Chicago Press Club, Children's Reading Round Table (honorary member), Alliance of Business and Professional Women (honorary member), Friends of American Writers (honorary member), Kappa Phi Delta. *Awards, honors:* Constance Lindsay Skimmer Award, 1955; Communicator of the Year, University of Chicago Award, 1964; Chicago Foundation of Literature Award, 1972; Patron Saints Award, Society of Midland Authors, 1973.

*WRITINGS:* (Under name Fanny Butcher) *Many Lives—One Love* (autobiography), Harper, 1972. Contributor of numerous book reviews to *Chicago Tribune.*

\*      \*      \*

## BOLES, John B.   1943-

*PERSONAL:* Born October 20, 1943, in Houston, Tex.; son of B. B. (a farmer) and Mary (McDaniel) Boles; married Nancy Gaebler, September 2, 1967: children: David Christopher. *Education:* Rice University, B.A., 1965; University of Virginia, Ph.D., 1969. *Politics:* Democrat. *Religion:* "Baptist/Lutheran." *Home:* 1217 Melody Dr., Metairie, La. 70002. *Office:* Department of History, Tulane University, New Orleans, La. 70118.

*CAREER:* Towson State University, Baltimore, Md., assistant professor, 1969-72, associate professor, 1972-75, professor of history, 1975-77; Rice University, Houston, Tex., visiting associate professor of history, 1977-78; Tulane University, New Orleans, La., associate professor of history, 1978—. National Endowment for the Humanities fellow in anthropology, 1976-77. *Member:* Organization of American Historians, Southern Historical Association, Maryland Historical Society.

*WRITINGS: Guide to the Papers of William Wirt* (pamphlet), Maryland Historical Society, 1971; *The Great Revival, 1787-1805: The Origins of the Southern Evangelical Mind,* University Press of Kentucky, 1972; *Guide to the Papers of John Pendleton Kennedy* (pamphlet), Maryland Historical Society, 1972; (editor) *America: The Middle Period: Essays in Honor of Bernard Mayo,* University Press of Virginia, 1973; (editor) *Maryland Heritage: Five Baltimore Institutions Celebrate the American Bicentennial,* Maryland Historical Society, 1976; *Religion in Antebellum Kentucky,* University Press of Kentucky, 1976. Contributor of articles and reviews to historical journals. Editor, *Maryland Historical Magazine,* 1974-77. Acting editor, *Journal of Southern History,* 1977-78.

*WORK IN PROGRESS:* Researching slave culture and religion in the Antebellum South.

\*      \*      \*

## BOLL, Theophilus E(rnest) M(artin)   1902-
## (Ernest Boll, Theo Boll)

*PERSONAL:* Born January 6, 1902, in New York, N.Y.; son of Henry Paul and Caroline (Panton) Boll. *Education:* University of Pennsylvania, A.B., 1922, A.M., 1924, Ph.D., 1930. *Home:* 16565 Chattanooga Pl., Pacific Palisades, Calif. 90272. *Office:* Department of English, 119 Bennett Hall, University of Pennsylvania, Philadelphia, Pa. 19104.

*CAREER:* University of Pennsylvania, Philadelphia, instructor, 1922-36, assistant professor, 1936-46, associate professor, 1946-72, professor emeritus of English, 1972—, secretary of college faculty, 1946-60. *Member:* International

Association of University Professors of English, Modern Humanities Research Association, Dickens Fellowship, Phi Beta Kappa.

*WRITINGS: The Works of Edwin Pugh (1874-1930),* Lyon & Armor, 1934; (author of biographical and critical introduction) Stephen Hudson, *Richard, Myrtle, and I,* edited by Violet Schiff, University of Pennsylvania, 1962; *Miss May Sinclair: Novelist,* Fairleigh Dickinson University, 1973. Contributor of articles to *Modern Philology, Studies in Philology, Modern Language Quarterly, Psychoanalytic Review, Psychiatry, English Literature in Transition,* and other journals.

*WORK IN PROGRESS:* A critical biography of Morley C. Roberts; *A Taxonomy of the Twentieth Century English Novel.*

\*      \*      \*

## BOLTEN, Steven E.   1941-

*PERSONAL:* Born November 14, 1941, in Bayonne, N.J.; son of Paul (a stockbroker) and Hortense (Horowitz) Bolten; married Marjorie O'Farrell, June 5, 1967. *Education:* University of Pennsylvania, B.S., 1963; New York University, M.B.A., Ph.D. *Office:* Department of Finance, School of Business, University of South Florida, Tampa, Fla. 33620.

*CAREER:* Faculty member, University of Houston, Houston, Tex.; currently associate professor, department of finance, School of Business, University of South Florida, Tampa. Investment counselor. *Member:* American Finance Association.

*WRITINGS: Security Analysis and Portfolio Management: An Analytical Approach to Investment,* Holt, 1972; *Cases in Security Analysis and Portfolio Management,* Holt, 1973; *Managerial Finance: Principles and Practice,* Houghton, 1976. Contributor of articles to *Journal of Finance, Mississippi Valley Journal of Economics and Business.*†

\*      \*      \*

## BOND, Horace Mann   1904-1972

November 8, 1904—December 21, 1972; American educator, researcher, and social scientist. Obituaries: *New York Times,* December 22, 1972; *Washington Post,* December 23, 1972; *Newsweek,* January 1, 1973. (See index for *CA* sketch)

\*      \*      \*

## BONE, Robert C(larke)   1917-

*PERSONAL:* Born March 18, 1917, in Coatesville, Pa.; son of Robert C. and Emma C. Bone; divorced; children: Rita (Mrs. James Whittington), Martha. *Education:* Haverford College, B.S., 1937; Yale University, additional study, 1950-51; Cornell University, Ph.D., 1957. *Politics:* Independent. *Home:* 2057 Florida Ave., Tallahassee, Fla. 32303. *Office:* Department of Government, Florida State University, Tallahassee, Fla. 32306.

*CAREER:* National Archives, Washington, D.C., junior archivist, 1946-47; foreign service officer, U.S. State Department, 1947-53; Tulane University, New Orleans, La., assistant professor of political science, 1957-61; Florida State University, Tallahassee, associate professor, 1961-65, professor of government, 1965—. *Military service:* U.S. Army, 1941-46; became first lieutenant. *Member:* American Political Science Association, Southern Political Science Association.

*WRITINGS: Contemporary Southeast Asia*, Random House, 1962; *Origin and Development of the Irian Problem*, Cornell University Press, 1963; *Action and Organization*, Harper, 1972; *American Government*, Barnes & Noble, 1977. Contributor of articles to *American Political Science Review, Journal of Politics, Journal of International Affairs, Pacific Affairs*, and *Far Eastern Survey*.

*WORK IN PROGRESS: From Democracy to Oligarchy.*

\* \* \*

## BONESS, A. James 1928-

*PERSONAL:* Born April 18, 1928, in Milwaukee, Wis.; son of Arthur James, Sr. and Minnie (Wachs) Boness; married Ann Entenberg, August, 1973. *Education:* University of Wisconsin, B.A., 1949, M.A., 1950; University of Chicago, Ph.D., 1962; also attended University of Minnesota, 1950-51, 1955, and Marquette University, 1955-58. *Home:* 311 Old Meadow Rd., East Amherst, N.Y. 14051. *Office:* School of Management, State University of New York, Buffalo, N.Y. 14214.

*CAREER:* University of Pittsburgh, Pittsburgh, Pa., assistant professor of finance and economics, 1962-64; Institute for Defense Analysis, Arlington, Va., economist and editor, 1964-65; Center for Naval Analyses, Arlington, economist, 1965-68; State University of New York at Buffalo, associate professor of finance, 1968—. *Military service:* U.S. Army, 1952-54. *Member:* American Economic Association, American Finance Association, Econometric Society.

*WRITINGS: Capital Budgeting: The Private and Public Sectors*, Praeger, 1972. Contributor of articles to *Journal of Finance, Journal of Business, Naval Research Logistics Quarterly*, and other journals.

*WORK IN PROGRESS:* Research on capital market organization and convertible security valuations.

*AVOCATIONAL INTERESTS:* Chess.

\* \* \*

## BORCHERT, Gerald L(eo) 1932-

*PERSONAL:* Born March 20, 1932, in Edmonton, Alberta, Canada; son of Leo F. and Lillian (Bucholz) Borchert; married Doris Ann Cox (an instructor), May 23, 1959; children: Mark Gerald Leo, Timothy Walter. *Education:* Attended University of Calgary, 1951-52; University of Alberta, B.A., 1955, LL.B., 1956; Eastern Baptist Theological Seminary, M.Div. (summa cum laude), 1959; Princeton Theological Seminary, Th.M. (first class), 1961, Ph.D. (cum laude), 1967. *Home:* 452 Heatherton Dr., Naperville, Ill. 60540. *Office:* Northern Baptist Theological Seminary, 660 East Butterfield Rd., Lombard, Ill. 60148.

*CAREER:* Ordained clergyman by Baptist Union of Western Canada, 1959. Princeton Theological Seminary, Princeton, N.J., teaching fellow and lecturer in Greek, 1960-62; North American Baptist Seminary, Sioux Falls, S.D., associate professor, 1963-68, professor of New Testament, 1968-77, academic vice-president and dean, 1970-77; Northern Baptist Theological Seminary, Lombard, Ill., professor of New Testament and dean, 1977—. Treasurer, Sioux Empire Drug Education Committee and Awareness House, Sioux Falls, S.D., 1970-77; secretary, Baptist Joint Committee on Public Affairs for the United States and Canada, 1972-74. *Wartime service:* Civilian retreat master for U.S. Army, 1968-69. *Member:* Studiorum Novi Testamente Societas, American Academy of Religion, Society of Biblical Literature and Exegesis, American Schools of Oriental

Research, American Institute of Holy Land Studies in Jerusalem (director, 1971-74), Commission on Cooperative Christianity of the Baptist World Alliance (secretary, 1968-75; vice-chairman, 1975-76), Sioux Falls Kiwanis Club (director, 1970-72; president, 1974-75).

*WRITINGS: Great Themes from John*, Baptist Life Association Press, 1966; *The Dynamics of Pauline Evangelism*, Roger Williams Press, 1969; *Today's Model Church*, Roger Williams Press, 1971; (contributor) R. Longnecker and M. Tenny, editors, *New Dimensions in New Testament Study*, Judson, 1974; (contributor) J. L. Garrett, editor, *Baptist Relations with Other Christians*, Judson, 1974; *Dynamics of Evangelism*, Word Books, 1976. Author of column, "Forum," in *The Baptist Herald*. Contributor of articles to *Foundations, Report from the Capital, Christianity Today, Evangelical Quarterly, International Standard Bible Encyclopedia, The Watchman Examiner*, and *Dictionary of Christian Ethics*.

*WORK IN PROGRESS:* Coptic Gnostic translation and reading for the international translation committee of the Nag Hamadi documents; *The Bible and Sexuality;* preparation of television series of a thirteen week bible study entitled, "The Gospel of John."

\* \* \*

## BOROVSKI, Conrad 1930-

*PERSONAL:* Born December 4, 1930, in Prettin, East Germany; U.S. citizen; son of Joseph L. (a physician) and Anna (Truszis) Borovski; married Catherine Perrot (a librarian), April 10, 1962; children: Julia Madeleine. *Education:* University of California, Berkeley, B.A., 1957, M.A., 1958; Universite de Strasbourg, Doctorate, 1960. *Home:* 2173 Santa Cruz Ave., Menlo Park, Calif. 94025. *Office:* Department of Foreign Languages, San Jose State University, San Jose, Calif. 95192.

*CAREER:* University of Maryland Overseas Program, instructor in German, 1961-62; San Jose State University, San Jose, Calif., assistant professor, 1962-67, associate professor of German, 1967—. *Military service:* U.S. Army, 1952-54; became sergeant; received Bronze Star. *Member:* Medievalist Association of the Pacific.

*WRITINGS: Active German Idioms*, Hueber Verlag, 1972. Contributor of poems and of articles on higher education to journals.

*WORK IN PROGRESS: The Lady: Romantic Image and Social Reality; Introduction to Critical Readings in Comparative Literature.*

*AVOCATIONAL INTERESTS:* All forms of art, travel.

\* \* \*

## BORUS, Michael E(liot) 1938-

*PERSONAL:* Born May 12, 1938, in Washington, D.C.; son of Joseph B. (an economist) and Rosalie (Bierman) Borus; married Judith F. Weinstein (an audiologist), February 19, 1961; children: Emily Anne, Jamie Ruth, Joseph Nathan. *Education:* Trinity College, Hartford, Conn., B.A., 1959; Yale University, M.A., 1960, Ph.D., 1964. *Home:* 270 Halligan Ave., Worthington, Ohio 43085. *Office:* Center for Human Resource Research, Ohio State University, Columbus, Ohio 43201.

*CAREER:* Yale University, New Haven, Conn., acting instructor in economics, 1963-64; Michigan State University, School of Labor and Industrial Relations, East Lansing, research associate, 1964-65, assistant professor, 1965-67, associate professor, 1967-72, professor of economics, 1972-77; Ohio State University, Faculty of Labor and Human Resources, Columbus, professor and director of the Center for Human Resource Research, 1977—. Brookings economic policy fellow, U.S. Department of Labor, 1968-69. Visiting associate professor, Ohio State University, 1970-71. *Member:* American Economic Association, Industrial Relations Research Association, Phi Beta Kappa, Pi Gamma Mu.

*WRITINGS: The Economic Effectiveness of Retraining the Unemployed,* Federal Reserve Bank of Boston, 1966; (with William Tash) *Measuring the Impact of Manpower Programs: A Primer,* Institute of Labor and Industrial Relations, University of Michigan-Wayne State University, 1970; (with Einar Hardin) *The Economic Benefits and Costs of Retraining,* Heath, 1971; (editor and author of introduction) *Evaluating the Impact of Manpower Programs,* Heath, 1972. Contributor to industrial relations, labor, and statistical journals.

*          *          *

**BOUCHER, John G(regory)    1930-**

*PERSONAL:* Born June 4, 1930, in Cambridge, Mass.; son of Edmond and Gabrielle (Gregoire) Boucher; married Norma J. Gorton, June 16, 1956; children: Robert, Peter. *Education:* Attended College de Ste. Anne de la Pocatiere, Quebec, 1947-51; Seminaire St. Joseph, Trois-Rivieres, Quebec, B.A., 1954; Boston University, M.Ed., 1967. *Home:* 95 Warren St., Concord, N.H. 03301. *Office:* Concord Senior High School, Warren St., Concord, N.H. 03301.

*CAREER:* Robert B. Pitcher, General Agent, Boston, Mass., insurance agent, 1954-56; John Hancock Mutual Life Insurance Company, Boston, underwriter, 1956-61; Newmarket, N.H., Whitefield, N.H. school districts, teacher of French, 1961-65; The Derryfield School, Manchester, N.H., teacher of French, 1965; state supervisor of foreign language education, New Hampshire State Department of Education, 1965-67; St. Anselm's College, Manchester, assistant professor of French, 1967-74; Concord High School, Concord, N.H., chairman of foreign language department, 1974—. *Member:* American Association of Teachers of French, American Council of the Teaching of Foreign Languages, New Hampshire Association for the Teaching of Foreign Languages.

*WRITINGS:* (With Robert L. Paris) *Contrastes,* Allyn & Bacon, 1972; (with Paris) *Debuts,* Allyn & Bacon, 1975; (with Andre O. Hurtgen and Paris) *Reprise,* Allyn & Bacon, 1976; (with Hurtgen) *Encore,* Allyn & Bacon, 1976; (with Hurtgen) *La Famille Martin,* Holt, 1977; (with Hurtgen) *En Visite Chez les Martin,* Holt, 1977.

*          *          *

**BOULARAN, Jacques    1890-1972**
   **(Jacques Deval)**

June 27, 1890—December 19, 1972; French playwright. Obituaries: *New York Times,* December 21, 1972.

*          *          *

**BOULBY, Mark    1929-**

*PERSONAL:* Born March 7, 1929, in Leeds, England; son of Mark (an accountant) and Jane (Morgan) Boulby; married Jean Saxby, March 31, 1956; children: Marion Jane, Sarah Margaret. *Education:* Cambridge University, B.A., 1949, M.A., 1953; University of Leeds, Ph.D., 1952. *Home:* 4219 Doncaster Way, Vancouver, British Columbia, Canada. *Office:* Department of German, University of British Columbia, Vancouver, British Columbia, Canada.

*CAREER:* University of Leeds, Leeds, England, lecturer in German, 1955-61; University of Hull, Hull, England, lecturer in German, 1961-63; City College of the City University of New York, New York, N.Y., lecturer in German, 1963-64; Case Western Reserve University, Cleveland, Ohio, associate professor, 1964-67, professor of German, 1967-70, head of department, 1968-70; University of British Columbia, Vancouver, professor of German, 1970—. *Military service:* Royal Air Force, 1951-54; became flight lieutenant. *Member:* Modern Language Association of America, American Society for Eighteenth Century Studies, American Lessing Society, Canadian Association of University Teachers of German.

*WRITINGS:* (Editor) *Gerhart Hauptmann Die Weber,* Harrap, 1962; *Hermann Hesse: His Mind and Art,* Cornell University Press, 1967; (editor) *H. & J. Hart: Kritische Waffengaenge,* Johnson Reprint, 1969; *Uwe Johnson,* Ungar, 1974; *Moritz: The Fringe of Genius,* Toronto University Press, 1978. Contributor of articles to *PMLA Review, Modern Language Review* and other journals.

*WORK IN PROGRESS:* A book tentatively entitled, *Autobiography and the Novel.*

*AVOCATIONAL INTERESTS:* Mysticism and the mystical tradition.

*          *          *

**BOURDON, David    1934-**

*PERSONAL:* Born October 15, 1934, in Glendale, Calif.; son of David and Marilyn (Casale) Bourdon. *Education:* Columbia University, B.S., 1961. *Home:* 30 Fifth Ave., New York, N.Y. 10011. *Office:* Arts Magazine, 23 East 26th St., New York, N.Y. 10010.

*CAREER: Life,* New York City, assistant editor, 1966-71; *Saturday Review,* New York City, associate editor, 1972; *Smithsonian Magazine,* Washington, D.C., associate editor, 1972-74; *Arts Magazine,* New York City, associate editor, 1973—.

*WRITINGS: Christo,* Abrams, 1971. Contributor of articles to *Art News, Art in America, Art International* and *New York* magazine. Art critic, *Village Voice,* 1974-77.

*          *          *

**BOUVARD, Marguerite Anne    1937-**

*PERSONAL:* Born January 10, 1937, in Trieste, Italy; married Jacques Bouvard (a systems analyst), November 25, 1959; children: Pierre, Laurie Anne. *Education:* Northwestern University, B.A., 1958; Radcliffe College, M.A., 1960; Harvard University, Ph.D., 1965; Boston University, M.A. (creative writing), 1977. *Politics:* Democrat. *Religion:* Roman Catholic. *Home:* 6 Brookfield Cir., Wellesley, Mass. 02181. *Office:* Department of Political Science, Regis College, Weston, Mass. 02193.

*CAREER:* Regis College, Weston, Mass., assistant professor, 1966-73, associate professor of political science, 1973—, director of European Studies, 1969—, chairwoman, department of political science. Fellow, Radcliffe Institute, Harvard, 1971-72. *Member:* American Political Science Association (women's caucus), American Association of

University Professors, United Nations Association of the United States, New England Political Science Association.

*WRITINGS: Growth of a European Pressure Group: Labor Movements in the European Communities,* Praeger, 1972; *The Search for Community: Building a New Moral World,* Kennikat, 1975; (contributor) Roland Warren, editor, *New Perspectives on the American Community,* Rand McNally, 1977. Contributor of articles to *European Studies/I and II, European Community,* and *Society.* Also contributor of poems to literary magazines including *Southwest Review.*

*WORK IN PROGRESS:* A book of poems, *Learning the Scales of Touch.*

*SIDELIGHTS:* Marguerite Bouvard told *CA* that her writings in both political science and poetry "are inspired by my love affair with the world; the world of ideas and of society on the one hand, and the very private world of things and individuals on the other. For me, poetry is vision, a way of coming closer and closer to reality."

\* \* \*

## BOUVIER, Emile 1906-

*PERSONAL:* Born March 29, 1906, in Montreal, Quebec, Canada; son of Joseph Ephrem and Charlotte Marion Bouvier. *Education:* Boston College, A.B., 1928, A.M., 1930; Georgetown University, Ph.D., 1932. *Home:* 2625 Portland St., Apt. 5, Sherbrooke, Quebec, Canada. *Office:* Department of Economics, Sherbrooke University, Sherbrooke, Quebec, Canada.

*CAREER:* Roman Catholic priest of Society of Jesus (Jesuits); University of Montreal, Montreal, Quebec, director of industrial relations section, 1945-51, director of Industrial Research Center, 1946-51; University Iberoamericana of Mexico, Mexico City, instructor in industrial relations, 1952-55; Georgetown University, Washington, D.C., professor of labor economics and industrial relations, 1954-60, acting chairman of department of economics, 1954-60; Laurentian University, Sudbury, Ontario, president, 1960-62; University of Sherbrooke, Sherbrooke, Quebec, professor of labor economics, 1962—. Director, Centre International de Recherches et d'Information sur l'Economie Collective, 1969-76. *Member:* American Economic Association, Industrial Relations Research Association, Association of Social Economics (past president). *Awards, honors:* Medal of Union Amerique latine, 1949.

*WRITINGS: Neither Right nor Left in Labor Relations,* University of Montreal, 1951; *Labor Problems,* Georgetown University, 1958; *Les Rouages de l'Economie,* Guerin, 1970, 2nd edition, 1978; *L'Education Cooperative,* C.C.C., 1970; *Les Cooperatives devant les progres modernes,* Caraquet, 1970; *How to Control Inflation,* Quebec Metal Mining Association, 1970; *Exercices et problemes sur les Rouages de l'Economie,* Guerin, 1971; *Le Maniel du maitre a propos des Rouages de l'Economie,* Guerin, 1971; *L'Economique et la Coexistence du secteur public et du secteur prive,* Guerin, 1971; *La Solution des conflits de Travail,* University of Sherbrooke, 1973.

*WORK IN PROGRESS: Relations Industrielles au Quebec.*

\* \* \*

## BOWEN, Barbara C(herry) 1937-

*PERSONAL:* Born May 4, 1937, in Newcastle, England; daughter of Harold E. (a teacher) and Hilda (Meech) Can-

nings; married Vincent E. Bowen (a professor), January 12, 1963; children: Sarah Lyn, Tessa Jane. *Education:* Oxford University, B.A., 1958, M.A., 1962; University of Paris, Doctorat d'Universite, 1962. *Politics:* Democrat. *Religion:* Episcopalian. *Office:* Department of French, University of Illinois, Urbana, Ill. 61801.

*CAREER:* University of Illinois at Urbana–Champaign, instructor, 1962-63, assistant professor, 1963-66, associate professor, 1966-72, professor of French, 1973—. *Member:* Modern Language Association of America, Renaissance Society of America.

*WRITINGS: Les Caracteristiques essentielles de la farce francaise, et leur survivance dans les annees 1550-1620,* University of Illinois Press, 1964; *Four Farces,* Basil Blackwell, 1967; *The Art of Bluff: Paradox and Ambiguity in Rabelais and Montaigne,* University of Illinois Press, 1972; (editor) *The French Renaissance Mind: Studies Presented to W. G. Moore,* L'Esprit Createur, 1976. Contributor of articles to *Modern Language Review, L'Esprit Createur, Studies in Philology, Bibliotheque d'Humanisme et Renaissance, French Studies, Comparative Drama, Kwartalnik Neofilologiczny,* and other periodicals.

*WORK IN PROGRESS:* Research in attitudes to language in French Renaissance literature.

*AVOCATIONAL INTERESTS:* Theatre, walking in the mountains, travel.

\* \* \*

## BOWEN, James Keith 1932-

*PERSONAL:* Born April 18, 1932, in Chicago, Ill.; son of Keith (a taxi driver) and Jean (Gassan) Bowen; married Charlotte LeMaire, February 13, 1958; children: Keith Charles, Gregory Dale. *Education:* Attended University of Illinois, 1954-56; University of Nevada, B.A., 1963, M.A., 1965; University of the Pacific, additional study, 1967-68. *Politics:* "Open." *Religion:* "Open." *Office:* Department of English, Southern Oregon College, Ashland, Ore. 97520.

*CAREER:* Southern Oregon College, Ashland, instructor, 1965, assistant professor, 1968-70, associate professor of English, 1970—. Lecturer, University of the Pacific, summer, 1968. Editorial consultant, Harper & Row. *Military service:* U.S. Army, 1952-54; became captain. *Member:* Modern Language Association of America, College English Association, Melville Society. *Awards, honors:* Dunbar Carpender research fellow, 1967-68.

*WRITINGS:* (Compiler) *Confrontations: Readings for Composition.* Scott, Foresman, 1969; (editor with Richard Van DerBeets) *American Short Fiction: Readings and Criticism,* Bobbs-Merrill, 1970; (editor with Van DerBeets) Mark Twain, *The Adventures of Huckleberry Finn* (critical edition), Scott, Foresman, 1970; (with Van DerBeets) *Critical Guide to Herman Melville,* Scott, Foresman, 1970; (editor with Van DerBeets) *Drama: A Critical Introduction,* Harper, 1971; (editor with Van DerBeets) *Classic Short Fiction: An International Collection,* Bobbs-Merrill, 1972. Also editor, with Van DerBeets, *American Gothic Literature,* Everett/Edwards. Co-editor, *American Literature Abstracts,* 1967—. Contributor of articles to professional journals and poems to literary quarterlies.

*WORK IN PROGRESS: Infinite Possibilities: A Prelude to a Life-Style of the Future;* and *Rhythm and Other Poems.*†

\* \* \*

## BOWER, David A(llan) 1945-

*PERSONAL:* Born December 21, 1945, in Weymouth,

Mass.; son of Wendell Thayer and Dorothy (Little) Bower. *Education:* Eastern Nazarene College, A.B. (cum laude), 1967; Rutgers University, M.L.S., 1968. *Politics:* Independent. *Religion:* Congregationalist. *Home:* 433 Pleasant St., South Weymouth, Mass. 02190.

*CAREER:* Curry College, Milton, Mass., assistant librarian, 1968-71; Aspinall Jr. High School, St. Thomas, V.I., school librarian, 1972-73; Morse Institute, Natick, Mass., cataloger, 1974—. *Member:* Alden Kindred of America (member of executive board, 1971).

*WRITINGS:* (With Carol Campbell Strempek) *Index to "Evergreen Review,"* Scarecrow, 1972. Contributor of book reviews to *Library Journal.*

\* \* \*

**BOWYER, John W(alter) 1921-**

*PERSONAL:* Born April 29, 1921, in Onward, Ind.; son of John Walter (a farmer) and Cecil (Metzger) Bowyer; married Ingeborg Becker, July 4, 1948; children: Karen, Linda. *Education:* Indiana University, B.S., 1942, M.S., 1943, D.B.A., 1950. *Religion:* Lutheran. *Home:* 782 Elmwood Ave., Kirkwood, Mo. 63122. *Office:* Washington University, St. Louis, Mo. 63130.

*CAREER:* Washington University, St. Louis, Mo., assistant professor, 1952-56, associate professor, 1956-60, professor of finance, 1960—. *Military service:* U.S. Army, Quartermaster Corps, 1943-46, 1950-51; became captain. *Member:* American Finance Association.

*WRITINGS: Investment Analysis and Management,* Irwin, 1955, 4th edition, 1972.

*WORK IN PROGRESS:* Research on comparative banking systems.

\* \* \*

**BOWYER, Mathew J(ustice) 1926-**

*PERSONAL:* Born February 9, 1926, in Covington, Va.; son of Mathew Wilson and Gertrude (Tolley) Bowyer; married Virginia A. Austin (a bookkeeper), June 28, 1952; children: Kevin Wilson, Karen Lucille. *Home:* 5397 Summit Dr., Fairfax, Va. 22030.

*CAREER:* Postal supervisor, Washington, D.C. *Military service:* U.S. Army, 1944-46.

*WRITINGS*—All published by A. S. Barnes, except as indicated: *They Carried the Mail: A Survey of Postal History and Hobbies,* Luce, 1972; *Collecting Americana,* 1977; *Dictionary of Mystical Terminology,* 1978; *Premiers of the Posts,* 1978.

*SIDELIGHTS:* Mathew Bowyer told *CA:* "Communication is the tour de force of life. We are alive to the extent we communicate, dead to the depth we are silent. He who speaks from behind the hidden curtain gives life to the living. That is why I write; it is a search for my soul."

\* \* \*

**BOYER, Sophia Ames 1907(?)-1972**

1907(?)—December 10, 1972; American author of books for children. Obituaries: *New York Times,* December 11, 1972.

\* \* \*

**BRACKEN, Joseph Andrew 1930-**

*PERSONAL:* Born March 22, 1930, in Chicago, Ill.; son of Andrew Joseph (a real estate agent) and Agnes (Ryan)

Bracken. *Education:* Xavier University, Litt.B., 1953; Loyola University, M.A., 1960; University of Freiburg, Ph.D., 1968. *Religion:* Roman Catholic. *Home and office:* Marquette University, Milwaukee, Wis. 53233.

*CAREER:* St. Mary of the Lake Seminary, Mundelein, Ill., assistant professor of systematic theology, 1969-74, associate dean of studies, 1970-74; Marquette University, Milwaukee, Wis., associate professor of theology, 1974—. *Member:* American Catholic Theological Society, American Academy of Religion, American Theological Society (Midwest Division).

*WRITINGS: Freiheit und Kausalitat bei Schelling,* Verlag Karl Alber (Freiburg), 1972. Contributor of articles to *American Ecclesiastical Review, Chicago Studies, Theological Studies, Review for Religious, Heythrop Journal,* and *Journal of the History of Philosophy.*

*WORK IN PROGRESS: A Philosophy and Theology of Community; What Are They Saying about the Trinity?*

\* \* \*

**BRADBURN, Norman M. 1933-**

*PERSONAL:* Born July 21, 1933, in Lincoln, Ill.; married Wendy McAneny, December 15, 1956; children: Isabel, Andrew, Laura. *Education:* University of Chicago, B.A. (with honors), 1952; Oxford University, B.A., 1955; Harvard University, M.A., 1958, Ph.D., 1960. *Home:* 5326 South University, Chicago, Ill. 60615. *Office:* University of Chicago, G-101, 5848 South University Ave., Chicago, Ill. 60637.

*CAREER:* University of Chicago, Chicago, Ill., assistant professor, 1960-65, associate professor, 1965-68, professor of social psychology, 1968-77, Tiffany and Margaret Blake Distinguished Service Professor, 1977—, director of National Opinion Research Center, 1967-71, senior study director, 1971—, associate dean, Division Social Science, 1971-73, chairman, department of behavior science, 1974—. *Member:* American Sociological Association, American Statistical Association. *Awards, honors:* Ford Foundation traveling fellow, 1958-59; Alexander von Humboldt-Stiftung (Humboldt Foundation) fellowship for research in Germany, 1970-71.

*WRITINGS:* (With D. Caplovitz) *Reports on Happiness,* Aldine, 1965; *The Structure of Psychological Well-Being,* Aldine, 1970; (with S. Sudman and G. Gockel) *Side by Side,* Quadrangle, 1972; (with Sudman) *Response Effects in Surveys,* Aldine, 1974.

National Opinion Research Center reports: (With J. A. Davis) *Great Aspirations: Career Plans of America's June, 1961 College Graduates,* 1961; *In Pursuit of "Happiness": A Pilot Study of Behavior Related to Mental Health,* 1963; *Inter-plant Transfer: The Sioux City Experience,* 1964; *Social Class and Psychological Adjustment: A Preliminary Report,* c. 1966; (with Sudman) *Social Psychological Factors in Inter-group Housing,* 1966; *Racial Integration in American Neighborhoods: A Comparative Survey,* 1970.

\* \* \*

**BRADLEY, Brigitte L(ooke) 1924-**

*PERSONAL:* Born September 17, 1924, in Siemianowice, Poland; daughter of Herbert and Hedwig (Pollok) Looke; married Warren F. Bradley, May 9, 1947 (died, 1966); children: Marita, Beatrice. *Education:* College of William and Mary, B.A., 1957; Universite de Strasbourg, Docteur d'Univ., 1960; Columbia University, Ph.D., 1965. *Resi-*

dence: New York, N.Y. *Office:* Department of German, Barnard College, 606 120th St., New York, N.Y. 10027.

*CAREER:* Barnard College, New York, N.Y., instructor, 1962-65, assistant professor, 1965-68, associate professor, 1968-74, professor of German, 1974—, head of department, 1968—. *Member:* Modern Language Association of America, American Association of Teachers of German, American Association of University Professors, Phi Beta Kappa.

*WRITINGS: R. M. Rilkes "Neue Gedichte": Ihr zyklisches Gefüge,* A. Francke (Bern and Munich), 1967; *R. M. Rilkes "Der neuen Gedichte anderer Teil": Entwicklungsstufen seiner Pariser Lyrik,* A. Francke, 1976. Contributor of essays to various books on Rilke and Frisch. Also contributor of articles to *Germanic Review, German Quarterly, Monatshefte, Modern Language Notes,* and *Colloquia Germanica.* Member of editor board, *Germanic Review.*

*AVOCATIONAL INTERESTS:* Travel, opera, art, film, theater, the sociological aspects of literature and culture.

\* \* \*

## BRADLEY, James V(andiver) 1924-

*PERSONAL:* Born January 6, 1924, in Anderson, S.C.; son of Robert Foster (a professor) and Rhoda (Vandiver) Bradley. *Education:* Washington and Lee University, B.A., 1947; University of Virginia, M.A., 1949; Purdue University, Ph.D., 1962. *Home address:* Route 3, Box 170P, Las Cruces, N.M. 88001. *Office:* Department of Psychology, New Mexico State University, Las Cruces, N.M. 88003.

*CAREER:* National Advisory Committee on Aeronautics, Langley Field, Va., physical science aide, 1951-52; Aerospace Medical Research Laboratories, Wright Field, Ohio, research psychologist, 1952-66; Department of Health, Education and Welfare, Washington, D.C., mathematical statistician, 1966-67; Antioch College, Yellow Springs, Ohio, research associate of Behavior Research Laboratory, 1967-68; New Mexico State University, Las Cruces, associate professor, 1968-73, professor of psychology, 1973—. *Military service:* U.S. Army, 1943-46. *Member:* American Statistical Association, Psychonomic Society. *Awards, honors:* Human Factors Society, Jerome H. Ely award, 1971, for the outstanding journal article in *Human Factors.*

*WRITINGS: Distribution-Free Statistical Tests,* Prentice-Hall, 1968; *Probability, Decision, Statistics,* Prentice-Hall, 1976.

\* \* \*

## BRADLEY, Van Allen 1913-

*PERSONAL:* Born August 24, 1913, in Albertville, Ala.; son of Van A. (a teacher) and Lula (Montgomery) Bradley; married Patricia Elaine Thompson, November 5, 1939 (divorced, 1966); married Sharon Lee Luedke, December 3, 1966; children: (first marriage) Van Allen III, Pamela (Mrs. Victor Michael), Susan (Mrs. Stuart Robertson); (second marriage) Gremlyn Angelica. *Education:* Attended Harding College, 1930-32; University of Missouri, B.J., 1933. *Home:* 623 Border Lane, Barrington, Ill. 60010. *Office:* Van Allen Bradley, Inc., Box 578, Lake Zurich, Ill. 60047.

*CAREER:* Finished college in the depression and spent a year in the Alabama hills doing some writing, 1933-34; *Nashville Tennessean,* Nashville, Tenn., reporter, 1934-35; *Omaha Bee-News,* Omaha, Neb., 1935-37, started as reporter, became copy chief; *Chicago Herald and Examiner,* Chicago, Ill., copy editor, 1937-38; *Chicago Tribune,* Chi-

cago, 1938-42, began as copy editor, became assistant picture editor; *Chicago Sun,* Chicago, 1942-48, began as copy editor, became copy chief; *Chicago Daily News,* Chicago, literary editor, 1948-71, editorial writer, 1953-60, writer of syndicated column, "Gold in Your Attic"; left newspaper work in 1971 to write and head his own rare book company, Van Allen Bradley, Inc. Teacher of newspaper writing courses and lecturer, Northwestern University, Medill School of Journalism, 1942-54. President, Lincolnwood (Ill.) Board of Education, 1952-60. *Member:* Chicago Press Veterans Association, Tavern Club (Chicago). *Awards, honors:* Chicago Foundation for Literature Award for services to literature, 1956; Page One Award, Chicago Newspaper Guild, 1960, for the best all-around performance by a Chicago newspaper editor.

*WRITINGS: Music for the Millions* (centenary history of W. W. Kimball Co.), Regnery, 1957; *Gold in Your Attic,* Fleet, 1958, revised edition published as *The New Gold in Your Attic,* 1968; *More Gold in Your Attic,* Fleet, 1960, revised edition, 1972; *The Book Collector's Handbook of Values,* Putnam, 1972, 3rd edition, 1978. Ghost-writer of another book. Contributor to *World Book Encyclopedia, World Book Yearbook,* and national magazines.

*WORK IN PROGRESS: Price Guide to Western Americana,* completion expected in 1979; *A Chicago Anthology: The City as Seen by Visitors and Stay-at-Homes,* 1980.

*SIDELIGHTS:* Van Allen Bradley began collecting books as a boy, was a Faulkner fan in his high school days, and has Faulkner and Nelson Algren collections in his library of more than 15,000 volumes.

At one time Bradley had the largest collection of signed Jack London books outside the Huntingdon Library collection. He then sold the collection, bought them back at double the price, and then sold them again. "Much," Bradley adds, "to my regret." He also owned some rare Hemingway materials, but sold them.

*BIOGRAPHICAL/CRITICAL SOURCES:* Roy Newquist, *Conversations,* Rand McNally, 1967.

\* \* \*

## BRANCAFORTE, Benito 1934-

*PERSONAL:* Born November 15, 1934, in Noto, Italy; son of Rosario and Maria (Valvo) Brancaforte; married Charlotte Lang (an associate professor of German), November 11, 1961; children: Elio, Daniela, Stefania. *Education:* Brooklyn College (now Brooklyn College of the City University of New York), B.A. (magna cum laude), 1959; University of Colorado, M.A., 1961; University of Illinois, Ph.D., 1965. *Home:* 1727 Summit, Madison, Wis. *Office:* Department of Spanish, University of Wisconsin, Madison, Wis. 53706.

*CAREER:* University of Illinois at Urbana-Champaign, began as instructor, became assistant professor of Spanish; University of Wisconsin—Madison, assistant professor, 1966-69, associate professor, 1969-74, professor of Spanish, 1974—. Visiting professor at University of Washington, 1970, University of California, 1972, and Sweet Briar College, 1976. *Military service:* U.S. Army, 1960-61. *Member:* Modern Language Association of America, Renaissance Society of America, American Association of Teachers of Italian, Phi Beta Kappa.

*WRITINGS: Benedetto Croce y su critica de la literatura espanola,* Gredos (Madrid), 1972; (author of introduction and notes) Francisco de Cascales, *Tablas poeticas,* Espasa-

Calpe, 1975; (author of introduction and notes) *Deffensa de la Poesia: An Anonymous 17th Century Spanish Translation of Philip Sidney's 'Defense of Poesie'*, University of North Carolina Press, 1977; (with wife, Charlotte Lang Brancaforte) *La primera traduccion italiana del 'Lazarillo de Tormes' por Giulio Strozzi*, Ravenna, 1977. Contributor of articles to *Italica, Symposium, Hispanic Review, Bulletin of Hispanic Studies*, and other journals.

*WORK IN PROGRESS:* An edition of Francisco Cascales, *Tablas Poeticas (1617)*, for publication by Clasicos Castellanos; author of introduction and notes with Mateo Aleman, *Guzman de Alfarache*.

\* \* \*

## BRAND, Myles 1942-

*PERSONAL:* Born May 17, 1942, in New York, N.Y.; son of Irving (an engineer) and Shirley (Berger) Brand; married Peg Zeglin (an artist), January 27, 1978; children: (previous marriage) Joshua. *Education:* Rensselaer Polytechnic Institute, B.S., 1964; University of Rochester, Ph.D., 1967. *Office:* Department of Philosophy, University of Illinois, Chicago, Ill. 60680.

*CAREER:* University of Pittsburgh, Pittsburgh, Pa., assistant professor of philosophy, 1967-72; University of Illinois at Chicago Circle, Chicago, associate professor, 1972-76, professor of philosophy, 1976—, chairman of department, 1972—. *Member:* American Philosophical Association, Philosophy of Science Association.

*WRITINGS:* (Editor) *The Nature of Human Action*, Scott, Foresman, 1970; (editor) *The Nature of Causation*, University of Illinois Press, 1976; (co-editor) *Action Theory*, D. Reidel, 1976. Contributor of articles to journals in his field.

*WORK IN PROGRESS:* Articles for professional journals.

\* \* \*

## BRANDT, Vincent S. R. 1924-

*PERSONAL:* Born June 11, 1924, in Boston, Mass.; son of Edmund Selden Randolph Brandt (a naval officer); married Hi Kyung Chung, September 25, 1958; children: Lisbeth Kim, Richard, Maea Van Wyck. *Education:* Harvard University, A.B., 1948, A.M., 1962, Ph.D., 1968. *Home address:* R.F.D. 3, Putney, Vt. 05346.

*CAREER:* Social anthropologist. *Military service:* U.S. Army, Mountain Infantry, 1943-46; served in Italy. *Member:* American Anthropological Association, Association of Asian Studies, Royal Ocean Racing Club, Eastern Amateur Ski Association, New England Lawn Tennis Association.

*WRITINGS: A Korean Village: Between Farm and Sea*, Harvard University Press, 1972.

*WORK IN PROGRESS:* A book on rural urban migration and Korean migrant city slums.

*AVOCATIONAL INTERESTS:* Sailing, skiing, tennis.

\* \* \*

## BRAUDY, Leo 1941-

*PERSONAL:* Born June 11, 1941, in Philadelphia, Pa.; son of Edward and Zelda (Smith) Braudy; married Susan Orr (an editor), August 27, 1964 (divorced December 13, 1973); married Dorothy McGahee (a painter), December 24, 1974. *Education:* Swarthmore College, B.A., 1963; Yale University, M.A., 1964, Ph.D., 1967. *Home:* 207 Woodlawn Rd., Baltimore, Md. 21210. *Agent:* Maxine Groffsky, 2 Fifth

Ave., New York, N.Y. 10011. *Office:* Department of English, Johns Hopkins University, Baltimore, Md. 21218.

*CAREER:* Yale University, New Haven, Conn., instructor in English, 1966-68; Columbia University, New York, N.Y., assistant professor, 1968-70, associate professor, 1970-73, professor of English, 1973-76; Johns Hopkins University, Baltimore, Md., professor of English, 1977—. *Member:* Modern Language Association of America, American Society for Eighteenth-Century Studies. *Awards, honors:* Guggenheim fellow, 1971-72; American Council of Learned Societies grant-in-aid, 1971.

*WRITINGS: Narrative Form in History and Fiction: Hume, Fielding, and Gibbon*, Princeton University Press, 1970; *Jean Renoir: The World of His Films*, Doubleday, 1972; (editor and author of introduction) *Norman Mailer: A Collection of Critical Essays*, Prentice-Hall, 1972; (editor and author of introduction) *Focus on Shoot the Piano Player*, Prentice-Hall, 1972; *The World in a Frame*, Doubleday, 1976; (editor with Morris Dickstein, and author of introduction) *Great Film Directors: A Critical Anthology*, Oxford Book Co., 1978.

*WORK IN PROGRESS: The Frenzy of Renown*, a book on the history of fame as a cultural idea; research on the evolution of modern definitions of character.

*BIOGRAPHICAL/CRITICAL SOURCES: Yale Review*, winter, 1971.

\* \* \*

## BRAUN, J(oachim) Werner 1914-1972

November 16, 1914—November 19, 1972; German-born American geneticist and educator. Obituaries: *New York Times*, November 21, 1972.

\* \* \*

## BRAWER, Florence B(lum) 1922-

*PERSONAL:* Born September 29, 1922, in Brooklyn, N.Y.; daughter of Henry Jacob (a merchant) and Sali (Wintner) Blum; children: Anne Blair, Michael Kenneth. *Education:* University of Michigan, B.A., 1944; University of California, Los Angeles, M.A., 1962, Ed.D., 1967. *Politics:* Democrat. *Religion:* Jewish. *Home:* 1749 Mandeville Lane, Los Angeles, Calif. 90049. *Office:* Department of Education, University of California, Los Angeles, Calif. 90024.

*CAREER:* University of Illinois, Champaign, psychometrist, 1944-45; Glendale College, Glendale, Calif., psychometrist and counselor, 1946-49; University of California, Los Angeles, assistant research educationist, 1968-72, associate research educationist, 1972-77, research educationist, 1978—. *Member:* American Psychological Association, Society for Personality Assessment.

*WRITINGS:* (Editor with Bruno Klopfer and Mortimer M. Meyer) *Developments in the Rorschach Technique*, Volume III, Harcourt, 1970; (contributor) Arthur M. Cohen, editor, *A Constant Variable*, Jossey-Bass, 1971; (with Cohen) *Confronting Identity*, Prentice-Hall, 1972; *New Perspectives on Personality Development in College Freshmen*, Jossey-Bass, 1973; (with Cohen and others) *College Responses to Community Demands*, Jossey-Bass, 1975; (with Cohen) *The Two-Year College Instructor Today*, Praeger, 1977. Contributor of monographs and articles to professional journals.

\* \* \*

## BREARLEY, Denis 1940-

*PERSONAL:* Born November 8, 1940, in Chatham, Ontario, Canada; son of George H. (a merchant) and Madeleine (Glazier) Brearley. *Education:* University of Western Ontario, B.A. (honors), 1963, M.A., 1964; University of Toronto, Ph.D., 1967. *Office:* Department of Classical Studies, University of Ottawa, Ottawa, Ontario, Canada.

*CAREER:* University of Ottawa, Ottawa, Ontario, assistant professor, 1967-72, associate professor of classical studies, 1972—, chairman of department, 1975—. *Member:* Classical Association of Canada (treasurer, 1969-72), American Philological Association, Classical Association (England), Mediaeval Academy of America, Society for the Promotion of Roman Studies, Societe des Etudes Latines.

*WRITINGS:* (Editor) *Commentum Sedulii Scotti in Maiorem Donatum Grammaticum,* Pontifical Institute of Mediaeval Studies (Toronto), 1975.

*WORK IN PROGRESS:* Late Latin and palaeography; an edition of Sedulius Scottus' *Collectaneum,* completion expected in 1979.

\* \* \*

## BRENNAN, Neil F(rancis) 1923-

*PERSONAL:* Born March 1, 1923, in Savannah, Ga.; son of Francis Michael (an army officer) and Mary (Devine) Brennan; married Maxine Lindem (a librarian), December 11, 1948; children: Julia, Michael, Bernadette, Margaret. *Education:* Attended Rice University, 1940-42; University of Chicago, M.A., 1949; Sorbonne, University of Paris, additional study, 1949-50; University of Illinois, Ph.D., 1959. *Religion:* Roman Catholic. *Home:* 122 Buckingham Dr., Rosemont, Pa. 19010. *Agent:* Ann Watkins, Inc., 77 Park Ave., New York, N.Y. 10016. *Office:* Department of English, 201 Vasey Hall, Villanova University, Villanova, Pa. 19085.

*CAREER:* Auburn University, Auburn, Ala., instructor, 1950-53; University of Illinois at Urbana–Champaign, instructor, 1953-57; Cornell University, Ithaca, N.Y., instructor, 1957-60; Villanova University, Villanova, Pa., assistant professor, 1960-63, associate professor of English literature and composition, 1963—. *Military service:* U.S. Army, 1943-46, became captain; received Distinguished Service Cross, 1944, Silver Star, 1945. *Member:* American Association of University Professors, Modern Language Association of America, Phi Kappa Phi.

*WRITINGS:* (With Robert O. Evans and others) *Graham Greene: Some Critical Considerations,* University of Kentucky Press, 1963; *Anthony Powell,* Twayne, 1972. Contributor of articles and reviews to *Commonweal, Thought, English Literature in Transition, Accent, Epoch,* and *Modern British Literature.*

*WORK IN PROGRESS:* A study of the literary development of the English novelist, Graham Greene.

\* \* \*

## BRENNAN, Ray 1908(?)-1972

1908(?)—August 8, 1972; American journalist. Obituaries: *Washington Post,* August 9, 1972.

\* \* \*

## BRENNECKE, John H(enry) 1934-

*PERSONAL:* Born November 6, 1934, in Willowbrook, Calif.; son of Henry Joseph and Chrystell (Franks) Brennecke; married Jean Arlene Snyder, June 2, 1956 (divorced, 1967); married Bernadette Leilani Soares (a psychiatric so-cial worker), June 14, 1969; children: (first marriage) James Andrew, Jeffrey Douglas; (second marriage) Jason Keoni, Kisha Nahunoni. *Education:* Long Beach City College, A.A., 1954; LaVerne College, B.A., 1956; Bethany Theological Seminary, Oak Brook, Ill., Master of Divinity, 1959; additional study at DePaul University, 1959-60, Los Angeles State College of Applied Arts and Sciences (now California State University, Los Angeles), 1961-63, and Claremont Graduate School and University Center (now Claremont Graduate School), 1963-64. *Politics:* Democrat. *Religion:* Humanist. *Home:* 1174 Nashport St., La Verne, Calif. 91750. *Office:* Department of Psychology, Mount San Antonio College, Walnut, Calif. 91789.

*CAREER:* Ordained minister, Church of the Brethren, 1959. Bethany Hospital, Chicago, Ill., chaplain, 1958-61, director of hospital development, 1959-61; Chaffey College, Alta Loma, Calif., instructor in psychology, 1963; Fullerton Junior College, Fullerton, Calif., instructor in psychology, 1963-64; Edgewood Family Counseling Agency, West Covina, Calif., psychotherapist, 1964-67; Tri-City Mental Health Authority, Pomona, Calif., psychotherapist, 1964-69; Pioneer Foundation, Pomona, psychotherapist, 1968; Mount San Antonio College, Walnut, Calif., instructor in psychology, 1964—. *Member:* Association for Humanistic Psychology, National Education Association, California Teachers Association.

*WRITINGS*—All published by Glencoe Press: (With Robert Amick) *The Struggle for Significance,* 1971, 2nd edition, 1975; *Significance: The Struggle We Share,* 1971, 2nd edition, 1975; (editor with Amick) *Psychology and Human Experience,* with reader and workbook, 1974, 2nd edition, 1978. Contributor to *Youth Magazine.*

*WORK IN PROGRESS:* A trade book on "wholistic selfhood."

*SIDELIGHTS:* John H. Brennecke told *CA* that his major goals of his writings are "to enable readers to think for themselves about key issues of relevance to their own individuation (in Jungian terms)." *Avocational interests:* Sailing, volleyball, travel, music, transpersonal psychology, wholistic medicine and health.

\* \* \*

## BRIGGS, R(obert) C(ook) 1915-

*PERSONAL:* Born September 8, 1915, in Granite, Okla.; son of Robert Cook (a farmer) and Nora (McGehee) Briggs; married Elizabeth Flint, July 14, 1934; children: Robert C. III, Clyde Ray, Elizabeth Anne (Mrs. Walter Barnes), John William. *Education:* Southwestern State College, A.B., 1937; Southern Baptist Theological Seminary, Th.M., 1943, Th.D., 1946; additional study at University of Edinburgh, University of Zurich, University of Tuebingen, and University of Marburg. *Home:* 1328 Chalmette Dr. N.E., Atlanta, Ga. 30306. *Office:* Interdenominational Theological Center, Atlanta, Ga. 30314.

*CAREER:* Union University, Jackson, Tenn., assistant professor, 1947-49, associate professor, 1949-50, professor of religion and philosophy, 1950-57; Southeastern Baptist Seminary, Wake Forest, N.C., professor of New Testament, 1957-64; Vanderbilt University, Nashville, Tenn., visiting professor of New Testament interpretation, 1964-66; Interdenominational Theological Center, Atlanta, Ga., professor of New Testament interpretation, 1966—. *Member:* Society of Biblical Literature, Theta Phi, Lion's Club.

*WRITINGS*—Published by Abingdon: *Interpreting the Gospels,* 1969; *Interpreting the New Testament,* 1973.

*AVOCATIONAL INTERESTS:* Fishing, sports.

\* \* \*

## BRITTAIN, Joan Tucker 1928-

*PERSONAL:* Born December 13, 1928, in Manchester, Ga.; daughter of Walter R. and Blanche (LaGrone) Tucker; married William A. Brittain (an announcer), August 30, 1947; children: Sally Marie, William Roger, Robert Ashley, Timothy Blake. *Education:* Attended LaGrange College, 1945-47; Kentucky Southern College (now University of Louisville), B.A., 1965; University of Louisville, M.A., 1966, Ph.D., 1970. *Politics:* Democrat. *Religion:* Methodist. *Home:* 709 South Third St., Louisville, Ky. 40202. *Office:* Department of English, Bellarmine College, 2000 Norris Pl., Louisville, Ky. 40205.

*CAREER:* Bellarmine College, Louisville, Ky., instructor, 1967-69, assistant professor, 1969-71, associate professor, 1971-76, professor of English, 1976—. *Member:* English-Speaking Union, South Atlantic Modern Language Association, Kentucky Historical Society, Phi Kappa Phi. *Awards, honors:* National Endowment for the Humanities fellow, 1972-73.

*WRITINGS:* (With Leon V. Driskell) *The Eternal Crossroads: The Art of Flannery O'Connor,* University Press of Kentucky, 1971; *Laurence Stallings,* G. K. Hall, 1975. Contributor to *Renascence, Georgia Review, Bulletin of Bibliography,* and *Explicator.*

\* \* \*

## BROADUS, Catherine 1929-

*PERSONAL:* Born October 26, 1929, in Jacksonville, Fla.; daughter of Rossie Ellis and Nettie (Goodbread) Yonge; married Loren Arthur Broadus, Jr. (a professor), July 24, 1951; children: Mark Stephen, Barry Andrew, Philip Allen. *Education:* Florida State University, B.S.H.E., 1951; further study at University of Florida, 1952, and Lexington Theological Seminary, 1958-60. *Politics:* Democrat. *Religion:* Christian Church (Disciples of Christ). *Home:* 1928 Beacon Hill, Lexington, Ky. 40504.

*CAREER:* Teacher of family life and child development in high schools in Jacksonville Beach, Fla., 1951-52, and Jacksonville, Fla., 1952-56. International Christian Women's Fellowship, representative from Kentucky, and publicity coordinator for United States and Canada, 1974-78. *Member:* Church Women United (chairman, Women in Community Service), Phi Mu.

*WRITINGS:* (With husband, Loren Broadus) *Laughing and Crying with Little League,* Harper, 1972; (with Loren Broadus) *From Loneliness to Intimacy,* John Knox, 1976. Also author of six plays for International Christian Women's Fellowship, 1964 and 1968, and of four monographs, 1978.

*WORK IN PROGRESS: To Laugh at Oneself Is to Survive.*

\* \* \*

## BROADUS, Loren, Jr. 1928-

*PERSONAL:* Born February 5, 1928, in Providence, Ky.; son of Loren Arthur (a commercial artist) and Mescal (Langston) Broadus; married Catherine Yonge, July 24, 1951; children: Mark, Barry, Philip. *Education:* University of Florida, B.Sc., 1951; Lexington Theological Seminary, B.D., 1960. *Politics:* Democratic. *Home:* 1928 Beacon Hill Rd., Lexington, Ky. 40504. *Office:* Lexington Theological Seminary, 631 Limestone St., Lexington, Ky. 40508.

*CAREER:* Clergyman of Christian Church (Disciples of Christ); high school teacher and coach in Florida, 1951-52; Foremost International Dairies, Jacksonville, Fla., worked in sales department, 1952-56, became district sales manager; Lexington Theological Seminary, Lexington, Ky., co-director of development, 1960-64; minister in Mayfield, Ky., 1964-68; Lexington Theological Seminary, associate professor, 1968-70, professor of ministerial practice, 1970—, director of field education, supervisor of supervised professional practice in doctor of ministry program. Sponsor, Youth Council of Graves County, 1965-68. *Military service:* National Guard and U.S. Army Reserve, 1948-62.

*WRITINGS:* (With wife, Catherine Broadus) *Laughing and Crying with Little League,* Harper, 1972; (with C. Broadus) *From Loneliness to Intimacy,* John Knox, 1976. Contributor to religion journals.

*WORK IN PROGRESS: Procrastination: Causes and Cures; To Laugh at Oneself Is to Survive; Three Speeds.*

*SIDELIGHTS:* Loren Broadus told *CA:* "I write for three reasons . . . to think through specific people's problems (interpersonal and intrapersonal) . . . to express an aesthetic need—this is a goal that has not been reached. Thus, in addition to writing everyday I 'study' writing almost everyday . . . to feel good about me. I like to see and create clever clauses and humorous incidents. After I complete a manuscript, it no longer interests me."

\* \* \*

## BROCKWAY, Wallace 1905-1972

1905—November 4, 1972; American editor and music historian. Obituaries: *New York Times,* November 11, 1972; *Publishers Weekly,* November 20, 1972; *Antiquarian Bookman,* December 4, 1972.

\* \* \*

## BRODY, Elaine 1923-

*PERSONAL:* Born April 21, 1923, in New York, N.Y.; daughter of S. Lawrence (a businessman) and Helen (Golding) Brody; married Paul Shapiro, December 19, 1943; married second husband, David Silverberg (a businessman), July 4, 1966; children: (first marriage) Sue Shapiro. *Education:* Attended Vassar College, 1940-41; New York University, A.B., 1944, Ph.D., 1964; Columbia University, A.M., 1960. *Politics:* Democrat. *Religion:* Jewish. *Home:* 35 East 84th St., New York, N.Y. 10028. *Agent:* Marie Rodell—Frances Collin Literary Agency, 141 East 55th St., New York, N.Y. 10022. *Office:* Music Department, New York University, 268 Waverley Bldg., Washington Sq., New York, N.Y. 10003.

*CAREER:* New York University, New York, N.Y., instructor at Washington Square College, 1963-65, assistant professor at University College of Arts and Science, 1965-67, associate professor, 1967-69, professor of music, 1969—, chairman of department, 1966—. Concert pianist. Member of education committee, Metropolitan Opera Guild. Consultant, National Endowment for the Humanities, and New York University Press. *Member:* International Musicological Society, International Music Library Association, American Musicological Society, Music Library Association, Goethe House, French Institute, Colloquim of Comparativists, Phi Beta Kappa. *Awards, honors:* William Randolph Hearst Foundation grant, 1972-77.

*WRITINGS: Music in Opera: A Historical Anthology,* Prentice-Hall, 1970; (with Robert A. Fowkes) *The German*

*Lied and Its Poetry*, New York University Press, 1971; *Music in the Romantic Era*, Macmillan, in press. Author with Claire Brook, "Music Guide" series, 1973—. Also editor of eleven books on musical performance practices. Contributor to *Grove's Dictionary of Music and Musicians, Notable American Women Supplement*, and contributor of many articles to musicological and scholarly journals.

*WORK IN PROGRESS:* The French Revival: French Music from 1870 and 1925, for Harper.

\* \* \*

## BROF, Janet 1929-

*PERSONAL:* Born January 28, 1929, in New York, N.Y.; daughter of Leon L. (a lawyer) and Sophie (a musician; maiden name, Moltz) Brof. *Education:* Pembroke College, B.A., 1950; Bank Street College of Education, graduate, 1956. *Home:* Perugino, 35-3, Mexico 19, D. F. Mexico.

*CAREER:* Former mathematics teacher; writer, translator, and educational therapist.

*WRITINGS:* (Editor and translator with Hortense Carpentier) *Doors and Mirrors: Fiction and Poetry from Spanish America, 1920-1970*, Grossman, 1972.

*WORK IN PROGRESS:* A novel, tentatively entitled *Perugino, 35.*

*AVOCATIONAL INTERESTS:* Dance.

\* \* \*

## BROGLIE, Marguerite de 1897-1973

April 20, 1897—January 9, 1973; French poet and artist. Obituaries: *Washington Post*, January 10, 1973.

\* \* \*

## BRONSEN, David 1926-

*PERSONAL:* Born June 4, 1926, in Columbus, Ohio; son of Samuel and Rebecca Bronsen. *Education:* Ohio State University, B.A. (summa cum laude), 1951; Mexico City College, additional study, 1947-48; University of Vienna, Ph.D., 1956; University of Paris, Certificates, 1957; Harvard University, Ph.D., 1975. *Religion:* Jewish. *Home:* 7120 Cambridge Ave., St. Louis, Mo. 63130. *Office:* Department of German, Washington University, St. Louis, Mo. 63130.

*CAREER:* University of Lille, Lille, France, lecturer in German, 1956-57; Harvard University, Cambridge, Mass., instructor in German, Extension Division, 1959-60; Kent State University, Kent, Ohio, visiting assistant professor of German, 1961-62; Washington University, St. Louis, Mo., assistant professor, 1962-66, associate professor, 1966-70, professor of German and comparative literature, 1970—. Visiting professor, University of Haifa, 1969-70 and University of Tel Aviv, 1969-70. *Military service:* U.S. Navy, 1945-47. *Member:* Modern Language Association of America, American Association of Teachers of German, American Association of University Professors, American Council for the Study of Austrian Literature, Leo Baeck Institute, Association for Jewish Studies, Phi Beta Kappa. *Awards, honors:* Sinclair Kennedy and Jens Aubrey Westerngard fellowship, Harvard University, 1960-61; Alexander von Humboldt grant, 1968-69; National Endowment for the Humanities senior fellowship, 1973-74.

*WRITINGS: Joseph Roth: Eine Biographie*, Kiepenheuer & Witsch Verlag (Cologne), 1974; *Joseph Roth und die Tradition*, Athenaeum Verlag (Frankfurt), 1975; Carl Winter, editor, *Jews and Germans from 1860 to 1933: The Problem-*

*atic Symbiosis*, Universitats Verlag (Heidelberg), 1978. Contributor of more than fifty articles to various journals in his field.

*WORK IN PROGRESS: Jewish Ambition in the Old World and the New.*

\* \* \*

## BROSS, Irwin D(udley) J(ackson) 1921-

*PERSONAL:* Born November 31, 1921, in Halloway, Ohio; son of Samuel (a medical doctor) and Mina (Jackson) Bross; married Rida Singer, August 6, 1949; children: Dean, Valerie, Neal. *Education:* University of California, Los Angeles, B.A., 1942; North Carolina College of Agriculture and Mechanic Arts (now North Carolina State University at Raleigh), M.A., 1948; University of North Carolina, Ph.D., 1949. *Home:* 109 Maynard Dr., Eggertsville, N.Y. 14226. *Office:* Roswell Park Memorial Institute, 666 Elm Street, Buffalo, N.Y. 14263.

*CAREER:* Johns Hopkins University, Baltimore, Md., resident associate biostatist, 1949-52; Cornell University, New York City, statistic consultant in public health and preventive medicine for medical college, 1952-59; Sloan-Kettering Institute, New York City, head of research design and analysis service, 1955-59; Roswell Park Memorial Institute, Buffalo, N.Y., director of biostatistics, 1959—, acting chief of epidemiology, 1966-73. *Military service:* U.S. Army, Signal Corps, 1941-45. *Member:* American Association for Advancement of Science, American Association for Cancer Research, American Statistical Association, Biometric Society, New York Academy of Science, Sigma Xi.

*WRITINGS: Design for Decision*, Macmillan, 1953; (contributor) Wilson G. Smillie, editor, *Preventive Medicine and Public Health*, Macmillan, 1963; (contributor) Charles R. B. Joyce, editor, *Psychopharmacology*, Lippincott, 1968; (contributor) Vadambe P. Godambe, editor, *Foundations of Statistical Inference*, Holt (Canada), 1971; *Scientific Strategies in Human Affairs: To Tell the Truth*, Exposition Press, 1975.

\* \* \*

## BROWN, Dale W. 1926-

*PERSONAL:* Born January 12, 1926, in Wichita, Kan.; son of Harlow J. (a grocer) and Cora (Weaver) Brown; married Lois D. Kauffman (a piano teacher), August 17, 1947; children: Deanna, Dennis, Kevin. *Education:* McPherson College, A.B., 1946; Bethany Biblical Seminary, B.D., 1949; graduate study at Drake University, 1954-56, and Garrett Biblical Institute, 1956-58; Northwestern University, Ph.D., 1962. *Politics:* Independent. *Home:* 18 West 709 22nd St., Lombard, Ill. 60148. *Office:* Bethany Theological Seminary, Butterfield and Meyers Rds., P.O. Box 408, Oak Brook, Ill. 60521.

*CAREER:* Clergyman of Church of the Brethren, ordained in 1946; pastor in Enders, Neb., summer, 1946, Des Moines, Iowa, 1949-56, and Wichita, Kan., summer, 1958; Bethany Biblical Seminary and Training School, Oak Brook, Ill., field worker and part-time instructor, 1956-58; McPherson College, McPherson, Kan., director of religious life and assistant professor of philosophy and religion, 1958-62; Bethany Theological Seminary, Oak Brook, Ill., associate professor, 1962-70, professor of Christian theology, 1970—. Visiting Lilly Professor, Berea College, 1977-78.

*WRITINGS: In Christ Jesus: The Significance of Jesus as the Christ*, Brethren Press, 1965; *Four Words for World,*

Brethren Press, 1968; *So Send I You,* Faith & Life, 1969; *Brethren and Pacifism,* Brethren Press, 1970; *The Christian Revolutionary,* Eerdmans, 1971; *Understanding Pietism,* Eerdmans, 1978; *Biblical Definitions of the Holy Spirit,* Brethren Press, 1978. Contributor to religious journals.

*WORK IN PROGRESS:* Brethren historical theology; mysticism and the Holy Spirit; radical and revolutionary theology.

*AVOCATIONAL INTERESTS:* Travel.

*BIOGRAPHICAL/CRITICAL SOURCES: Christian Century,* December 15, 1971; *Messenger,* January 1, 1972.

\*       \*       \*

## BROWN, Morris Cecil    1943-
### (Marianne Goslovich)

*PERSONAL:* Born July 3, 1943, in Bolton, N.C.; son of Cecil Culphert (a farmer) and Dorothy (Waddell) Brown. *Education:* Columbia University, B.A.; University of Chicago, M.A. *Politics:* "Anti-Slavery Party." *Agent:* Sterling Lord Agency, 660 Madison Ave., New York, N.Y. 10021.

*CAREER:* Instructor in English, University of Illinois at Urbana-Champaign and Merrit College, Oakland, Calif.; currently instructor in English at University of California, Berkeley.

*WRITINGS: The Life and Loves of Mr. Jiveass Nigger,* Farrar, Straus, 1969. Editor, *Yardbird Reader.*†

\*       \*       \*

## BROWN, Murray   1929-

*PERSONAL:* Born July 4, 1929, in Alden, N.Y.; son of Leo (a businessman) and Sarah (Katz) Brown; married Barbara Kingon, June 3, 1954; children: Erica. *Education:* University of Buffalo (now State University of New York at Buffalo), A.B., 1952; graduate study at Columbia University, 1953-55, and New York University; New School for Social Research, Ph.D., 1956. *Home:* 80 Fairlawn Dr., Eggertsville, N.Y. 14226. *Office:* Department of Economics, State University of New York at Buffalo, Amherst Campus, 714 O'Brian Hall, Amherst, N.Y. 14260.

*CAREER:* National Bureau of Economic Research, New York City, research assistant, 1955-56; University of Pennsylvania, Wharton School of Finance and Commerce, Philadelphia, assistant professor of economics, 1956-62; George Washington University, Washington, D.C., professor of econometrics, 1964-67; State University of New York at Buffalo, professor of economics, 1967-72, Goodyear Professor of Economics, 1972—, currently at Amherst Campus. Lecturer, College of the City of New York (now City College of the City University of New York), New York City, 1955-56; visiting scholar in Stockholm, 1958, and at Econometric Institute, Rotterdam, 1961-62; guest lecturer at University of Basle, 1962, and University of Rome, 1971; research associate, Center of Economic Studies and Plans, Rome, 1966. Consultant to U.S. Department of Commerce, 1962-65, Organization of American States, 1965, and U.S. Department of Justice, 1965.

*MEMBER:* American Statistical Association, Econometric Society, American Economic Association. *Awards, honors:* Special award for effective teaching, University of Pennsylvania, 1960; Ford Foundation faculty fellowship, 1961-62; Guggenheim fellowship, 1965-66; grants from American Philosophical Society, 1960, Social Science Research Council, 1963, and National Science Foundation, 1963-64, 1967-68.

*WRITINGS: On the Theory and Measurement of Technological Change,* Cambridge University Press, 1966; (editor and author of introduction) *The Theory and Empirical Analysis of Production,* National Bureau of Economic Research, 1967; (editor with Kozuo Sato and Paul Zarembka) *Essays in Modern Capital Theory,* North-Holland Publishing, 1976. Contributor to statistical and economics journals.

\*       \*       \*

## BROWNE, Robert S(pan)    1924-

*PERSONAL:* Born August 17, 1924, in Chicago, Ill.; son of William H., Jr. (a civil servant) and Julia (Barksdale) Browne; married Huoi Nguyen, April 6, 1956; children: Mai, Alexi, Marshall. *Education:* University of Illinois, B.A., 1944; University of Chicago, M.B.A., 1947; City University of New York, graduate study, 1963-66. *Home:* 214 Tryon Ave., Teaneck, N.J. 07666. *Office:* Black Economic Research Center, 112 West 120th St., New York, N.Y. 10027.

*CAREER:* U.S. Foreign Aid Program, Cambodia and Vietnam, economist, 1955-61; Phelps Stokes Fund, New York City, project director, 1963-64; Fairleigh Dickinson University, Teaneck, N.J., assistant professor of economics, 1965—; Black Economic Research Center, New York City, director, 1969—. Member of board of directors, Emergency Land Fund, Twenty First Century Foundation, National Sharecroppers Fund, American Committee on Africa, Saxon Industries, National Rural Center, and Harlem Commonwealth Council; member of advisory committee, Congressional Budget Office, Office of Technology Assessment. *Military service:* U.S. Army Air Forces, 1944-46; became sergeant. *Member:* American Economic Association, Caucus of Black Economists.

*WRITINGS: Race Relations in International Affairs,* Public Affairs Press, 1961; (editor with Charles V. Hamilton, Howard E. Freeman, Jerome Kagan, and A. Kimball Romney) *The Social Scene,* Winthrop, 1972. Contributor of articles to academic journals and popular magazines, including *Esquire, Ramparts, New Republic, Ebony, Business and Society Review,* and *New York Times Magazine,* and to newspapers. Editor, *Review of Black Political Economy;* editorial consultant, *Africa Today;* reader, *Social Science Quarterly.*

\*       \*       \*

## BROWNE, Walter A(nderson)    1895-

*PERSONAL:* Born February 15, 1895, in Houston, Mo.; son of Jack (an agriculturist) and Fannie (Tolbert) Browne; married Nellie May Budd, May 16, 1926; children: Jack. *Education:* Southwest Missouri State College (now University), A.B., 1924; George Peabody College for Teachers, A.M., 1927, Ph.D., 1935; also attended University of Wisconsin, 1928-29. *Residence:* Kirksville, Mo.

*CAREER:* Stephen F. Austin State College (now University), Nacogdoches, Tex., assistant professor, 1927-35, associate professor of geography, 1935-37; East Carolina College (now University), Greenville, N.C., professor of geography, 1937-47; Northeast Missouri State College (now University), Kirksville, professor of geography, 1947-66. Teacher at George Peabody College for Teachers, summers, 1936-41. *Military service:* U.S. Navy, 1917-18. *Member:* Association of American Geographers, National Council of Geographic Education, Pi Gamma Mu, Phi Delta Kappa, Rotary International.

*WRITINGS:* (With George T. Renner and others) *Global Geography,* Crowell, 1944; *Missouri Geography,* Harlow Publishing, 1956; *The American Development,* Simpson Printing & Publishing, 1964, revised edition, 1966. Author, with Harris Harvill, of ''Missouri: Its Geography and Resources,'' a series of filmstrips. Contributor of articles to scholarly journals.

\*    \*    \*

## BROWNING, David (George) 1938-

*PERSONAL:* Born May 21, 1938, in London, England; son of George Henry and Winifred (Strevens) Browning; married Greta Francies (a physiotherapist), 1961; children: Ralph, Guy, Pippa. *Education:* Reading University, B.A., 1961; Oxford University, M.A., D. Phil., 1968. *Home:* 63 Yarnells Hill, Oxford, England. *Office:* School of Geography, Oxford University, Oxford, England.

*CAREER:* Ditchley Foundation, England, research secretary, 1962-65; Her Majesty's Diplomatic Service, El Salvador, second secretary, 1965-67; Oxford University, Oxford, England, university lecturer in geography, 1968—, fellow, St. Cross College, 1968—. *Military service:* Royal Navy, 1956-58.

*WRITINGS: El Salvador: Landscape and Society,* Clarendon Press, 1971.

*WORK IN PROGRESS: Regional Integration in the Third World; Population Atlas of Colonial America.*

\*    \*    \*

## BROWNING, Gordon 1938-

*PERSONAL:* Born March 31, 1938, in Little Rock, Ark.; son of William Leslie and Kathryn (Egan) Browning. *Education:* Louisiana Polytechnic Institute (now Louisiana Tech University), B.A., 1960; Louisiana State University, M.A., 1961, Ph.D., 1966. *Politics:* Republican. *Religion:* Presbyterian. *Home:* Route 6, Richmond, Ky. 40475. *Office:* Department of English, Eastern Kentucky University, Richmond, Ky. 40475.

*CAREER:* Oklahoma State University, Stillwater, instructor, 1963-65, assistant professor of English, 1965-66; Eastern Kentucky University, Richmond, associate professor, 1966-70, professor of English, 1970—. *Member:* Popular Culture Association.

*WRITINGS:* (With Bert C. Bach) *Fiction for Composition,* Scott, Foresman, 1968; (with Bach) *Drama for Composition,* Scott, Foresman, 1973. Editor, *Help Yourself,* 1974—.

\*    \*    \*

## BRUFFEE, Kenneth A. 1934-

*PERSONAL:* Born September 1, 1934; son of James H. and Bessie (Blakeslee) Bruffee. *Education:* Wesleyan University, B.A., 1956; Northwestern University, M.A., 1957, Ph.D., 1964. *Residence:* Brooklyn, N.Y. *Office:* Department of English, Brooklyn College of the City University of New York, Brooklyn, N.Y. 11210.

*CAREER:* University of Virginia, Charlottesville, instructor in English, 1962-65; Columbia University, New York City, instructor in English, 1965-66; Cooper Union College, New York City, instructor in the humanities, 1966-67; Brooklyn College of the City University of New York, Brooklyn, N.Y., began as assistant professor, currently professor of English. *Military service:* U.S. Army, 1957-59. *Member:* Modern Language Association of America, Na-

tional Council of Teachers of English, College English Association.

*WRITINGS: A Short Course in Writing,* Winthrop, 1972. Contributor to a Norton critical edition of Joseph Conrad's *Heart of Darkness.*

*WORK IN PROGRESS:* Studying the elegiac romance; research on problems of teaching in higher education.

\*    \*    \*

## BRUNNER, James A(lbertus) 1923-

*PERSONAL:* Born June 28, 1923, in Bexley, Ohio; son of Charles A. (a manufacturer) and Frances (Langloh) Brunner; married Eleanor M. Floyd, August 8, 1947; children: James Mark, John Floyd, Richard Allan. *Education:* Ohio State University, B.S., 1946, B.A., 1946, M.B.A., 1947, Ph.D., 1955. *Politics:* Republican. *Religion:* Methodist. *Home:* 3312 Corey Rd., Toledo, Ohio 43615. *Office:* Department of Marketing, University of Toledo, 2801 West Bancroft, Toledo, Ohio 43606.

*CAREER:* Otterbein College, Westerville, Ohio, assistant professor of marketing, 1947-51; University of Toledo, Toledo, Ohio, assistant professor, 1951-55, associate professor, 1955-59, professor of marketing, 1959—. Member of board of directors and treasurer, Scholarship Fund Inc., 1969—; member of board of directors, Great Lakes Marketing Associates, 1972—; member of board of trustees, Crestview Corp., 1972—. *Member:* American Marketing Association (chapter president, 1958), Phi Eta Sigma, Phi Kappa Phi, Alpha Kappa Psi, Beta Gamma Sigma, Rotary Club of Toledo.

*WRITINGS: Administrative Research,* University of Toledo Press, 1971; *Marketing Information Systems: Readings and Cases,* University of Toledo Press, 1972, revised edition, 1978; *Administrative Research Reports,* University of Toledo Press, 1972; *Business Research Center,* University of Toledo Press, 1972. Contributor of articles to *Journal of Marketing, Journal of Marketing Research, Baylor Business Review,* and *Journal of Environmental Systems.*

*WORK IN PROGRESS:* Research in marketing information systems, marketing health care, and the senior citizen market.

\*    \*    \*

## BRUNS, William J(ohn), Jr. 1935-

*PERSONAL:* Born July 13, 1935, in Pasadena, Calif.; son of William John (a business executive) and Carol Jane (Stalder) Bruns; married Barbara Jean Dodge, April 12, 1957; children: Robert, John, David, Michael. *Education:* University of Redlands, A.B., 1957; Harvard University, M.B.A., 1959; University of California, Berkeley, Ph.D., 1963. *Politics:* Independent. *Religion:* Protestant. *Home:* 9 Jericho Lane, Wayland, Mass. 01778. *Office:* Graduate School of Business Administration, Harvard University, Boston, Mass. 02163.

*CAREER:* Yale University, New Haven, Conn., assistant professor of economics and industrial administration, 1962-66; University of Washington, Seattle, associate professor, 1966-71, professor of accounting, 1971-72; Harvard University, Graduate School of Business Administration, Boston, Mass., professor of business administration, 1972—. Advisory editor, Addison-Wesley Publishing Co., 1967—. *Member:* American Economic Association, American Accounting Association. *Awards, honors:* Danforth fellow, 1957-63; D.B.A., University of the Redlands, 1976.

*WRITINGS: Accounting for Decisions: A Business Game,* Macmillan, 1966; (editor with Don T. DeCoster) *Accounting and Its Behavioral Implications,* McGraw, 1969; *Introduction to Accounting: Economic Measurement for Decisions,* Addison-Wesley, 1971; (with Richard F. Vaneil) *A Primer on Replacement Cost Accounting,* Thomas Horton, 1976. *Accounting Review,* book review editor, 1967-69, member of editorial board, 1969-77.

*WORK IN PROGRESS: Case Problems in Management Accounting and Control.*

\*　　\*　　\*

## BRUTTEN, Gene J. 1928-

*PERSONAL:* Born May 28, 1928, in New York, N.Y.; son of Samuel (a horologist) and Sonia (Yontef) Brutten; married Sheila Ruth Rosenbaum (a teacher), April 3, 1955; children: Lori Beth, Mark Andrew. *Education:* Kent State University, B.A., 1950; Brooklyn College (now Brooklyn College of the City University of New York), M.A., 1952; University of Illinois, Ph.D., 1957. *Home:* 28 Pinewood, Carbondale, Ill. 62901. *Office:* Department of Speech Pathology and Audiology, Southern Illinois University, Carbondale, Ill. 62901.

*CAREER:* Adelphi College (now University), Garden City, N.Y., instructor in speech and hearing pathology, 1953-54; Cortland State Teachers College (now State University of New York College at Cortland), assistant professor of speech and hearing pathology, 1954-56; Southern Illinois University at Carbondale, assistant professor, 1957-61, associate professor, 1962-64, professor of speech and hearing pathology, 1965; Hunter College of the City University of New York, New York, N.Y., visiting professor and director of speech and hearing pathology, 1966-67; Southern Illinois University, research professor in department of speech pathology and audiology, 1967—. Visiting professor, University of Minnesota, summer, 1964; lecturer or consultant at more than forty other universities or colleges. Consultant, U.S. Federal Prison, Marion, 1969-71.

*MEMBER:* American Speech and Hearing Association (fellow), American Psychological Association, Association for Advancement of Behavior Therapy, Psi Chi, Phi Kappa Delta. *Awards, honors:* Fulbright-Hays research grant at University of Utrecht, 1971-72.

*WRITINGS:* (With D. J. Shoemaker) *The Modification of Stuttering,* Prentice-Hall, 1967.

Contributor: R. R. Reiber and R. S. Brubaker, editors, *Progress in Speech Pathology,* North-Holland Publishing, 1966; B. N. Gray and G. England, editors, *Stuttering and the Conditioning Therapies,* Monterey Institute for Speech and Hearing, 1969; M. Fraser, editor, Conditioning in *Stuttering Therapy,* Speech Foundation of America, 1970; L. E. Travis, editor, *Handbook of Speech Pathology and Audiology,* Appleton, 1971; S. Dickson, editor, *Communication Disorders,* Scott, Foresman, 1974; J. Eisenson, editor, *Stuttering; A Second Symposium,* Harper, 1975. Contributor to professional journals.

\*　　\*　　\*

## BUCHANAN, George Wesley 1921-

*PERSONAL:* Born December 25, 1921, in Denison, Iowa; son of George (a laborer) and Helen (Kral) Buchanan; married Gladyce Dyer, February 14, 1947; married second wife, Harlene Bower (a high school history teacher), January 10, 1970; children: (first marriage) George Wesley, Jr., Mary Colleen. *Education:* Attended Tabor College, 1940-42; Simpson College, B.A., 1947; Garrett Theological Seminary, M.Div., 1951; Northwestern University, M.A., 1952; Hebrew Union College, postgraduate study, 1957-60; Drew University, Ph.D., 1959. *Home:* 114 Newport Mills Rd., Silver Springs, Md. 20902. *Office:* Wesley Theological Seminary, Washington, D.C. 20016.

*CAREER:* Farmer in Denison, Iowa, 1942-44; high school English and science teacher in Kiron, Iowa, 1943-44; clergyman of United Methodist Church and pastor in Iowa, Illinois, Wisconsin, New Jersey, and Ohio, 1944-59; Wesley Theological Seminary, Washington, D.C., professor of New Testament, 1959—. Researcher in Goettingen, Germany, summer, 1968. *Member:* Society of Biblical Literature, Studiorum Novi Testamenti Societas, American Association of University Professors, International Platform Association, Middle Atlantic States Society for Biblical Literature (president, 1965-66). *Awards, honors:* Bollingen grant to participate in archaeological excavation at Shecham, Jordan, summer, 1957; American Association of Theological Schools grant for research in Lebanon, Syria, and Jordan, summer, 1966; Hebrew Union College Biblical and Archaeological Schools fellowship for research in Israel, 1966-67; Litt. D., Simpson College, 1973.

*WRITINGS:* (Author of introduction) R. H. Charles, *Eschatology: The Doctrine of a Future Life in Israel, Judaism and Christianity,* Schocken, 1963; *The Consequences of the Covenant,* E. J. Brill, 1970; (translator and author of introduction) H. S. Reimarus, *The Goal of Jesus and His Disciples,* E. J. Brill, 1970; (author of commentary) *To the Hebrews,* Doubleday, 1972; *Revelation and Redemption,* Western North Carolina Press, in press. Contributor to *International Standard Biblical Encyclopedia;* contributor of more than fifty articles and reviews to *Christian Home, Christian Century, Catholic Biblical Quarterly,* and other religious and scholarly journals. Member of editorial board, *Biblical Archaeology Review.*

*WORK IN PROGRESS: The Historical Jesus,* distinguishing his teachings from those of the Church; commentary on *Book of Revelation.*

*SIDELIGHTS:* George Buchanan told *CA:* "Research and writing for me is not easy, but necessary. I would not do it if there were not important questions to answer which others are not even asking or are not answering adequately. I only offer the answers that are obvious, and only then after it is clear that these are correct and that no one else is going to give them. Most of my research deals with ancient history that has important implications for twentieth century ethics. My research begins by assuming ancient texts mean just what they seem to say against their own background, deprived of complex European and American philosophical, sociological, psychological, and theological interpretations. To find the correct analysis, I constantly study ancient languages, literature, archaeology, and geography. I publish mostly for scholars but also for clergy and lay reading publics as well. My strongest concerns and motivating ideals are involved with the church and world peace. Although I frequently grow weary, it is no easier for me to leave an important research project than for a good hound dog to leave a hot trail. It is unlikely, however, that I will live long enough to complete the many projects in which I am now engaged."

Buchanan works "with different degrees of facility" in German, French, Spanish, Latin, Hebrew, Greek, Aramaic, Syriac, Ethiopic, and Arabic.

## BUCHER, Bradley 1932-

*PERSONAL:* Born July 16, 1932, in Astoria, Ill.; son of Ezra G. (a carpenter) and Irma (Onion) Bucher. *Education:* Knox College, B.A., 1953; Princeton University, Ph.D. (mathematics), 1957; University of Pennsylvania, Ph.D. (psychology), 1965. *Home:* 688 Fanshawe Park Rd. E., London, Ontario, Canada. *Office:* Department of Psychology, University of Western Ontario, London, Ontario, Canada.

*CAREER:* University of California, Los Angeles, assistant professor, 1965-70; University of Western Ontario, London, associate professor of psychology, 1970—. Consultant to Children's Psychiatric Research Institute, London, Ontario. *Member:* American Psychological Association, Association for the Advancement of Behavior Therapy, Behavior Therapy and Research Society.

*WRITINGS:* (Compiler with Ivar Lovaas) *Readings in Behavior Modification with Deviant Children,* Prentice-Hall, 1973.

Contributor: *Miami Symposium on the Prediction of Behavior: Aversive Stimulation,* University of Miami Press, 1968; *Advances in Behavior Therapy, 1969,* Academic Press, 1970; *Learning Approaches to Behavior Change,* Aldine, 1970; *Advances in Behavior Therapy, 1971,* Academic Press, 1972; *Handbook of Child Psychopathology,* McGraw, 1972. Contributor to *Behavior Therapy, Behavior Research and Therapy, American Journal of Occupational Therapy,* and *Journal of Experimental Child Psychology.*

\* \* \*

## BUCK, Vernon E(llis) 1934-

*PERSONAL:* Born April 7, 1934, in Kansas City, Mo.; son of W. Ellis Buck (a tool and die maker) and Artie Lee Roller; married Judith Brooks Taylor (a teacher of child development), March 23, 1957; children: Nancy Elise, Laurie Brooks. *Education:* Yale University, B.A., 1956; Cornell University, M.S., 1960, Ph.D., 1963. *Home:* 4212 43rd Ave. N.E., Seattle, Wash. 98105. *Office:* Graduate School of Business Administration, University of Washington, Seattle, Wash. 98195.

*CAREER:* General Mills, Inc., Minneapolis, Minn. and Chicago, Ill., personnel administrator, 1956-58; Yale University, New Haven, Conn., 1961-68, began as lecturer, became assistant professor; University of Washington, Seattle, associate professor of business administration, 1968—, director of the doctoral program, 1971-74. *Member:* American Psychological Association, American Sociological Association, Academy of Management.

*WRITINGS: Working under Pressure,* Crane, Russak, 1972. Contributor to *Business Horizons.*

\* \* \*

## BUDZIK, Janet K. Sims 1942-

*PERSONAL:* Born December 1, 1942, in Princeton, Ind.; daughter of Clarence A. (a teacher) and Dorothy (Bachman) Sims; married Richard S. Budzik (a vocational instructor and author of sixteen books on sheet metal work), June 4, 1964. *Education:* Northern Illinois University, B.S., 1965; DePaul University, M.B.A., 1971. *Home:* 176 Riverside Rd., Riverside, Ill. 60546.

*CAREER:* Morton West High School, Berwyn, Ill., business teacher, 1965-72. *Member:* Illinois Business Education Association, Pi Omega Pi.

*WRITINGS:* (With father, Clarence A. Sims) *Basic Data Processing Text and Workbook,* Addison-Wesley, 1972; (with husband, Richard S. Budzik) *Today's Practical Guide to Increasing Profits for Contractors with Easy-to-Use Suggestions and Aids,* Practical Publications, 1974.

\* \* \*

## BUEHRIG, Edward H(enry) 1910-

*PERSONAL:* Born October 4, 1910, in Minier, Ill.; son of Edward S. (a merchant) and Emma (Kuhfuss) Buehrig; married Margaret Masters, June 18, 1935; children: Edward Masters, Robert Masters. *Education:* University of Chicago, Ph.B., 1932, M.A., 1934, Ph.D., 1942. *Home:* 1301 Maxwell Lane, Bloomington, Ind. 47401. *Office:* Department of Political Science, Indiana University, Bloomington, Ind. 47401.

*CAREER:* Indiana University at Bloomington, instructor, 1934-42, assistant professor, 1942-46, associate professor, 1946-53, professor of political science, 1953-63, University professor, 1963—. Member of faculty, National War College, 1950; Smith-Mundt Lecturer, American University in Beirut, 1957-58. Visiting member, Institute for Advanced Studies, Princeton, N.J., 1948; member of Brookings Institution, 1951-52. Officer of U.S. Department of State, Division of International Security Affairs, 1944-46; technical adviser to U.S. delegations at San Francisco Conference, 1945, and United Nations session (London), 1946; secretary-general, Italo-Yugoslav Boundary Commission, 1946; consultant to United Nations Secretariat, 1947. *Member:* American Society of International Law, American Political Science Association, International Studies Association, Middle East Institute. *Awards, honors:* Social Science Research Council fellow, 1948-49, 1965-66.

*WRITINGS: Woodrow Wilson and the Balance of Power,* Indiana University Press, 1956; (editor and contributor) *Wilson's Foreign Policy in Perspective,* Indiana University Press, 1957; (editor) *Essays in Political Science,* Indiana University Press, 1965; *The UN and the Palestinian Refugees,* Indiana University Press, 1971; (editor with Albert Lepawsky and Harold D. Lasswell, and contributor) *The Search for World Order,* Appleton, 1971. Contributor of articles to political science journals.

\* \* \*

## BUELER, William Merwin 1934-

*PERSONAL:* Born March 29, 1934, in New Orleans, La.; son of Eugene Lee (a doctor) and Gladys Lou (Ray) Bueler; married Lois West Eaton (a professor of English), June 7, 1962; children: Katherine, Edward. *Education:* University of Colorado, B.A., 1956, M.A., 1970. *Home:* 522 East Sarnia St., Winona, Minn. 55987.

*CAREER:* Central Intelligence Agency, Washington, D.C., intelligence officer, 1962-69. *Military service:* U.S. Army, 1956-60. *Member:* Phi Kappa Phi. *Awards, honors:* U.S. China Policy included on list of outstanding academic books, 1972, by *Choice* magazine.

*WRITINGS: Mountains of the World: A Handbook for Climbers and Hikers,* Tuttle, 1970; *U.S. China Policy and the Problem of Taiwan,* Colorado Associated University Press, 1971; *Chinese Sayings,* Tuttle, 1972; *Roof of the Rockies: A History of Mountaineering in Colorado,* Pruett, 1974; (contributor) Michael Tobias and Harold Drasdo, editors, *A Mountain Aesthetic,* Overlook Press, 1978. Contributor of articles to numerous periodicals, including *Colorado Quarterly, World Today, Worldview,* and *Summit.*

*WORK IN PROGRESS:* A political fantasy set in the future.

*SIDELIGHTS:* William Bueler's interest in mountaineering has taken him climbing in the U.S., Taiwan, Japan, Borneo, Switzerland, Venezuela, Mexico, Tanzania, and Korea. He is professionally proficient in the Chinese language.

\* \* \*

## BUERGENTHAL, Thomas 1934-

*PERSONAL:* Born May 11, 1934, in Lubochna, Czechoslovakia; son of Mundek (a banker) and Gerda (Silbergleit) Buergenthal; married Dorothy Anne Coleman, June 6, 1959; children: Robert, John, Alan. *Education:* Bethany College, Bethany, W.Va., B.A., 1957; New York University, J.D., 1960; Harvard University, LL.M., 1961, S.J.D., 1968. *Politics:* Democrat. *Religion:* Jewish. *Home:* 6103 Highland Hills Dr., Austin, Tex. 78731. *Office:* School of Law, University of Texas, 2500 Red River, Austin, Tex. 78705.

*CAREER:* University of Pennsylvania Law School, Philadelphia, instructor, 1961-62; State University of New York at Buffalo, School of Law, assistant professor, 1962-64, associate professor, 1964-67, professor of law, 1967-75; University of Texas at Austin, School of Law, visiting professor, 1975-76, professor, 1976-77, Fulbright and Jaworski Professor of Law, 1977—. Director of International Institute of Human Rights (France) and U.S. Institute of Human Rights; chairman of human rights committee, U.S. National Commission for UNESCO; U.S. representative at various UNESCO intergovernmental meetings. *Member:* American Society of International Law (member of executive council), American Law Institute, International Law Association, Harvard Law School Association.

*WRITINGS:* (Translator with G. O. W. Mueller) *The German Penal Code,* Sweet & Maxwell, 1961; *Law-Making in the International Civil Aviation Organization,* Syracuse University Press, 1969; (with Louis B. Sohn) *International Protection of Human Rights,* Bobbs-Merrill, 1973; (with Sohn) *Documents on International Protection of Human Rights,* Bobbs-Merrill, 1973; (with Judith V. Torney) *International Human Rights and International Education,* U.S. National Commission for UNESCO, 1976; (editor) *Human Rights, International Law, and the Helsinki Accord,* Allonheld, Osman & Co., 1977. Contributor of articles to law journals in the United States and Europe. Member of board of editors, *American Journal of Comparative Law,* 1968-76, *Revue des Droits de l'Homme, Cahiers de Droits Europeen, American Journal of International Law,* and *Europaeische Grundrechte Zeitschrift.*

*WORK IN PROGRESS:* Second edition of *International Protection of Human Rights.*

*BIOGRAPHICAL/CRITICAL SOURCES:* Odd Nansen, *Tommy,* Gyldendal Norsk Forlag, 1970.

\* \* \*

## BUNKER, Gerald Edward 1938-

*PERSONAL:* Born January 25, 1938, in Chicago, Ill.; son of George Maverick (an executive) and Virginia (Saunders) Bunker; married Elaine Ford (a writer), October 18, 1958; children: Mark, Geoffrey, Lisa, Andrew, Anne Elizabeth. *Education:* Harvard University, B.A., 1959, M.A., 1964, Ph.D., 1970; additional graduate study at Yale University and Columbia University. *Office:* Department of Far Eastern Languages and Literatures, Harvard University, Cambridge, Mass. 02138.

*CAREER:* St. John's College, Annapolis, Md., tutor, 1968-70; Associated Press, Boston, Mass., newsman, 1970; *Washington Post,* Washington, D.C., newsman, 1970; Harvard University, Cambridge, Mass., research fellow and lecturer in Far Eastern languages, 1971—.

*WRITINGS: The Peace Conspiracy: Wang Ching-Wei and the China War, 1937-1941,* Harvard University Press, 1972.

*WORK IN PROGRESS: Life of Sir Robert Hart: 1834-1911.*

*SIDELIGHTS:* Bunker speaks Chinese, Russian, Japanese, French, and Greek.†

\* \* \*

## BUNN, John T(homas) 1924-

*PERSONAL:* Born February 10, 1924, in Mount Gilead, N.C.; son of John H. (a minister) and Fannie (Finch) Bunn; married Lois Webb, August 8, 1951; children: David, Stephen, George. *Education:* Wake Forest University, B.A., 1948; Southern Baptist Theological Seminary, B.D., 1951, Th.D., 1955; postdoctoral study at American Schools of Oriental Research, 1956, Hebrew University, 1965, and Union Theological Seminary, 1971. *Politics:* Democrat. *Home:* 100 Powell, Buies Creek, N.C. 27506. *Office:* Department of Religion, Campbell College, Buies Creek, N.C. 27506.

*CAREER:* Minister in Baptist churches in Midway, Ky., 1953-55, and Durham, N.C., 1956-61; Campbell College, Buies Creek, N.C., assistant professor, 1961-62, associate professor, 1963-64, professor of Old Testament and archaeology, 1965-69, Tyner Chair of Religion, 1969—, chairman of department of religion, 1965, assistant to president, 1963-65, director of seminary extension, 1972. Lecturer at Rollins College and Wake Forest University, 1966. Educational director, Institute of Mediterranean Studies, 1966; researcher, British Museum and Near Eastern Museum, 1968. Has participated in archaeological excavations at Dhiban, Jordan, 1956, and Tell Arab, Israel, 1965. Member of board of trustees, Good Hope Hospital and Baptist Hospital; member of board of directors, Wright's Refuge. *Member:* American Academy of Religion, American Schools of Oriental Research, Society of Biblical Literature, Association of Baptist Professors of Religion (vice-president, 1970-71, president, 1971-72), North Carolina Teachers of Religion.

*WRITINGS: Commentary on the Song of Solomon,* Broadman, 1972; *Commentary on the Book of Ezekiel,* Broadman, 1972. Contributor to medical and religious publications. Book review editor, *Journal of Religious Studies.*

*WORK IN PROGRESS: Introducing Old Testament Archaeology; The Concept of the Messiah in the Inter-Biblical Period;* articles on Jean Astruc, physician extraordinaire, and on origins of Codified Law.†

\* \* \*

## BURACK, Elmer H(oward) 1927-

*PERSONAL:* Born October 21, 1927, in Chicago, Ill.; son of Charles and Rose (Taerbaum) Burack; married Ruth Goldsmith; children: Charles M., Robert J., Alan J. *Education:* University of Illinois, B.S., 1950; Illinois Institute of Technology, M.S., 1956; Northwestern University, Ph.D., 1964. *Home:* 2755 Marl Oak Dr., Highland Park, Ill. 60035. *Office:* Stuart School of Management, Illinois Institute of Technology, 31st and State St., Chicago, Ill. 60616.

*CAREER:* Chicago Molded Products, Chicago, Ill., production supervisor, 1950-53; The Richardson Company, Melrose Park, Ill., production superintendent, 1953-55; Federal Tool Corporation, Lincolnwood, Ill., production manager, 1955-59; Booz, Allen & Hamilton, Chicago, consultant, 1959-60; Illinois Institute of Technology, Chicago, lecturer, 1960-64, associate professor, 1964-68, professor of management, 1968—, head of department, 1969-71. *Military service:* U.S. Army Air Forces, 1945-47. *Member:* Academy of Management (chairperson, Personnel Division and Health Care Division), The Institute of Management Sciences, Industrial Relations Associates of Chicago (president, 1974-75), Association for Computing Machinery, American Institute of Decision Sciences, Midwest Academy of Management (president, 1971-72).

*WRITINGS:* (With James Walker) *Manpower Planning and Programming,* Allyn & Bacon, 1972; *Strategies for Manpower Planning and Programming,* General Learning, 1972; *Organization Analysis,* Dryden, 1975; (with R. D. Smith) *Personnel Management: A Human Resources Approach,* West Publishing, 1977; (with A. Negandhi) *Organization Design: Theoretical Perspectives and Empirical Findings,* Kent State University Press, 1978; *Personnel Management: Cases and Exercises,* West Publishing, 1978. Also author of *Human Resource Planning,* 1978. Contributor of papers to a variety of journals; contributor of reviews to *Academy of Management Journal,* 1969—, and to *Business Perspectives,* 1970—. Consulting editor for two series, "Human Resource Management," and "Management of Health Services," 1972. Member of editorial review board, *Organization and Administrative Sciences.*

\* \* \*

## BURGER, Albert E. 1941-

*PERSONAL:* Born September 6, 1941, in Ponca City, Okla.; married. *Education:* Oklahoma State University, B.A., 1962, M.S., 1963; Purdue University, Ph.D., 1968. *Home:* 210 Quindaro Dr., R.R. 2, Florissant, Mo. 63034. *Office address:* Federal Reserve Bank, P.O. Box 442, St. Louis, Mo. 63166.

*CAREER:* Federal Reserve Bank, St. Louis, Mo., financial economist, 1967-71, senior economist, 1972-73, assistant vice-president, 1974—.

*WRITINGS: The Money Supply Process,* Wadsworth, 1972. Contributor of numerous articles on monetary theory and financial conditions to professional journals.

\* \* \*

## BURKE, J(ohn) Bruce 1933-

*PERSONAL:* Born September 23, 1933, in Akron, Ohio; son of Charles Mayhew (a salesman) and Esther (Plum) Burke; married Nancy Adrich Dobson, July 30, 1955; children: Anne, Abigail, Sarah. *Education:* Colgate University, A.B., 1955; Union Theological Seminary, New York, N.Y., B.D., 1958; Syracuse University, Ph.D., 1963. *Politics:* Independent. *Home:* 430 West Jefferson, Grand Lodge, Mich. 48837. *Office:* College of Education, Michigan State University, East Lansing, Mich. 48823.

*CAREER:* Pulteney Presbyterian Church, Pulteney, N.Y., minister, 1958-59; Syracuse University, Syracuse, N.Y., instructor in religion, 1961-64; Michigan State University, East Lansing, professor of humanities, 1964-68, professor of education, 1975—, director of Humanities Teaching Institute, 1968-75. Consultant to U.S. Office of Education. *Member:* National Association for Humanities Education

(director, 1969-73), American Association of University Professors, Presbytery of Grand River. *Awards, honors:* Fulbright-Hays research grant to the United Arab Republic, 1965.

*WRITINGS:* (With James B. Wiggins) *Foundations of Christianity,* Ronald, 1971; (contributor) W. Robert Houston and Robert Howsam, editors, *Competency Based on Teacher Education,* S.R.A. Associates, 1972. Also author, with N. Kagan, of *Influencing Human Interaction in Public Schools,* 1976. Editor, *Bulletin on Research in Humanities Education,* 1970-71.

*WORK IN PROGRESS:* Research and writings on affective education, creativity, and visual literacy; films on concept development for teachers.

\* \* \*

## BURKE, John Emmett 1908-

*PERSONAL:* Born August 22, 1908, in Chicago, Ill.; son of James Joseph (an electrician) and Susan (Haughey) Burke; married Evelyn Perkins, March 11, 1950; children: James Joseph, Daniel Redmond, Suzanne Maureen, Sean. *Education:* De Paul University, B.A., 1930, B.S., 1931, M.A., 1936; University of Chicago, B.L.S., 1947; University of Denver, Ed.D., 1957. *Politics:* Democrat. *Religion:* Roman Catholic. *Home:* 1201 Earl St., Commerce, Tex. 75428. *Office:* Library, East Texas State University, Commerce, Tex. 75428.

*CAREER:* St. Mary's College, Winona, Minn., dean and assistant librarian, 1936-40; Christian Brothers College, St. Louis, Mo., head librarian, 1943-49; George Peabody College for Teachers, Nashville, Tenn., assistant professor, 1949, associate professor, 1950, head librarian, 1949-53; East Texas State University, Commerce, professor of library science and director of library, 1953—. *Member:* American Library Association, Association of College and Research Libraries, American Association of Colleges of Teacher Education, National Education Association.

*WRITINGS: School Librarian at Work,* East Texas State University Press, 1954; *Guideposts to Improved Library Service,* East Texas State University Press, 1958; *Planning the Modern Functional College Library,* East Texas State University Press, 1961; *Specifications for Library Furniture,* East Texas State University Press, 1963; *The Rising Tide: Research Libraries,* East Texas State University Press, 1966. Contributor of articles to library and education journals.

*WORK IN PROGRESS:* Research on educational accountability, on the role of new media in American society, and a bibliography of doctoral dissertations in library science, 1960-70.

\* \* \*

## BURKE, W. Warner 1935-

*PERSONAL:* Born May 12, 1935; son of Alfred Vernard (a sales manager) and Ruby Inez (Gilbert) Burke; married Roberta Luchetti, October 5, 1974; children: Donovan, Courtney. *Education:* Furman University, B.A., 1957; University of Texas, M.A., 1961, Ph.D., 1963. *Home:* 52 Meadowbrook Cir., Sudbury, Mass. 01776. *Office:* Department of Management, Clark University, Worcester, Mass. 01610.

*CAREER:* University of Texas, Main University (now University of Texas at Austin), instructor in psychology, 1962-63; University of Richmond, Richmond, Va., assistant professor of psychology, 1963-66; National Training Laboratories Institute, Center for Organization Studies, Washington, D.C., director, 1966-74; free-lance consultant in organization and management, 1974-76; Clark University, Worcester, Mass., chairperson of department of management, 1976—. Executive director, Organization Development Network. *Military service:* U.S. Army Reserve, 1953-64. *Member:* International Organization for Applied Social Scientists, American Psychological Association, Academy of Management, Institute of Management Sciences.

*WRITINGS:* (With W. B. Eddy, V. A. Dupre, and O. P. South) *Behavioral Science and the Manager's Role,* N.T.L. Learning Resources Corp., 1969; (editor with R. Beckhard) *Conference Planning,* N.T.L. Learning Resources Corp., 1970; (with H. A. Hornstein, B. A. Bunker, M. G. Gindes, and R. J. Lewicki) *Social Intervention: A Behavioral Science Approach,* Free Press, 1971; (editor with Hornstein) *Social Technology of Organization Development,* N.T.L. Learning Resources Corp., 1972; (editor) *Contemporary Organization Development: Approaches and Interventions,* N.T.L. Learning Resources Corp., 1972; (editor) *Current Issues and Strategies in Organization Development,* Human Sciences Press, 1977; (editor) *Current Theory and Practice in Organization Development,* University Associates, 1978. Contributor to journals, including *Journal of the American Psychological Association.* Member of editorial board and book review editor, *Journal of Applied Behavioral Science.*

*WORK IN PROGRESS:* A textbook, *Organization Development,* for Little, Brown; editing *Readings in Organization Development.*

\*    \*    \*

## BURKET, Harriet   1908-

*PERSONAL:* Born June 14, 1908; daughter of John Franklin and Betty (Hoege) Burket; married Maurice C. Reinecke, September 26, 1935 (deceased); married Francis Brewster Taussig (a publisher), October 7, 1960 (deceased); children: (first marriage) Rosalind (Mrs. Gordon Eggum). *Education:* Vassar College, B.A., 1931. *Politics:* "Varies ..." *Religion:* Episcopalian. *Home:* 14 Sutton Pl. S., New York, N.Y. 10022.

*CAREER: Arts and Decoration,* New York City, associate editor, 1933-36; *Creative Design,* New York City, associate editor, 1935-37; *House and Garden,* New York City, associate editor, 1936-44; *Woman's Home Companion,* New York City, interior design editor, 1944-52; *House and Garden,* executive editor, 1952-58, editor-in-chief, 1958-70. *Member:* International Fashion Group (member of board of governors, 1953-55; vice-president, 1955-58), National Home Fashion League (charter member), American Institute of Interior Designers, National Trust for Historic Preservation, Decorators Club, International Platform Association, Municipal Art Society (New York), Cosmopolitan Club. *Awards, honors:* Dallas Market Award for distinguished service in home furnishing, 1962.

*WRITINGS: House and Garden's Complete Guide to Interior Decorations,* Simon & Schuster, 1970; *House and Garden's Complete Guide to Creative Entertaining,* McGraw, 1971; (with Francis Heard and JoAnn Francis Gray) *Founders Guide to Modern Decorating,* Popular Library, 1974.

*WORK IN PROGRESS:* A book on fifty years of decorating.

*AVOCATIONAL INTERESTS:* International travel, collecting rare shells, contemporary paintings, aboriginal bark paintings, Lowestoft cottages, needlepoint.

## BURR, Wesley R(ay)   1936-

*PERSONAL:* Born August 19, 1936, in Bingham, Utah; son of Clifton Ray (a carpenter) and Emily Mazel (Bryan) Burr; married Ruth Joy Darton (a music teacher), November 14, 1958; children: Kenneth Ray, Steven Lynn, Robert Glen, Nicole. *Education:* Attended University of Utah, 1954-56; Brigham Young University, B.S., 1960, M.S., 1961; University of Minnesota, Ph.D., 1967. *Office:* Department of Child Development and Family Relations, Brigham Young University, Provo, Utah 84601.

*CAREER:* University of Minnesota, Minneapolis, instructor in child development and family relations, 1963-66; Portland State University, Portland, Ore., assistant professor of sociology, 1966-69; Brigham Young University, Provo, Utah, associate professor of child development and family relations, 1969—. *Member:* American Sociological Association, Pacific Sociological Association, National Council on Family Relations, Utah Council on Family Relations.

*WRITINGS: Supplementary Readings for Family Relationships,* Brigham Young University Press, 1970; *Theory Construction and the Sociology of the Family,* Wiley, 1973; *Successful Marriage: A Principles Approach,* Dorsey, 1976; (senior editor) *Contemporary Theories about the Family,* Free Press, Volume I, 1978, Volume II, 1979. Contributor of articles to journals in his field.

\*    \*    \*

## BURTON, Robert H(enderson)   1934-

*PERSONAL:* Born March 20, 1934, in New Orleans, La.; son of Robert H. (a lawyer) and Winnifred Lee (Cambias) Burton; married Carmen Smith, December 16, 1964; children: Cynthia, Robert, Robin, Ray, Joseph, Janet. *Education:* Tulane University, B.B.A., 1954, M.B.A., 1955; Louisiana State University, Ph.D., 1967. *Office:* Department of Economics, University of South Florida, Tampa, Fla. 33620.

*CAREER:* University of South Florida, Tampa, 1963—, currently associate professor of economics. *Military service:* U.S. Air Force; became captain. *Member:* American Economic Association, Southern Economic Association, Southeastern Conference on Latin American Studies.

*WRITINGS:* (With Warren Shows) *Microeconomics,* Heath, 1972; (with Gordon Brunhild) *Macroeconomics,* Prentice-Hall, 1973; (with George Petrello) *Personal Finance,* Macmillan, 1978.

\*    \*    \*

## BUSH, (John Nash) Douglas   1896-

*PERSONAL:* Born March 21, 1896, in Morrisburg, Ontario, Canada; became U.S. citizen in 1940; son of Dexter Calvin (a businessman) and Mary (Nash) Bush; married Hazel Cleaver, September 3, 1927; children: Geoffrey Douglas. *Education:* University of Toronto, B.A., 1920, M.A., 1921; Harvard University, Ph.D., 1923. *Politics:* Democrat. *Home:* 3 Clement Circle, Cambridge, Mass. 02138.

*CAREER:* Harvard University, Cambridge, Mass., instructor in English, 1924-27; University of Minnesota, Minneapolis, assistant professor, 1927-28, associate professor, 1928-31, professor of English, 1931-36; Harvard University, associate professor, 1936-37, professor, 1937-57, Gurney Professor of English, 1957-66. *Member:* Modern Language Association of America, Modern Humanities Research Association (president, 1955), American Philosophical Society, British Academy (corresponding fellow), Cambridge Scientific Club, Signet Society, Phi Beta Kappa. *Awards, honors:* Sheldon fellowship, Harvard University, 1923-24; Guggenheim fellow, 1934-35; Society for Libraries Medal, from New York University, 1947; American Council of Learned Societies humanities award, 1957. Litt.D., Tufts University, 1952, Princeton University, 1958, University of Toronto, 1958, Oberlin College, 1959, Harvard University, 1959, Swarthmore College, 1960, Boston College, 1965, Michigan State University, 1968, Merrimack College, 1969; L.H.D., Southern Illinois University, 1962, Marlboro College, 1966.

*WRITINGS: Mythology and the Renaissance Tradition in English Poetry,* University of Minnesota Press, 1932, revised edition, Norton, 1963; *Mythology and the Romantic Tradition in English Poetry,* Harvard University Press, 1937; *The Renaissance and English Humanism,* University of Toronto Press, 1939, revised edition, 1956; *"Paradise Lost" in Our Time,* Oxford University Press, 1945; *English Literature in the Earlier Seventeenth Century,* Clarendon Press, 1945, 3rd edition, 1966; (editor) John Milton, *The Portable Milton,* Viking, 1949; *Science and English Poetry,* Oxford University Press, 1950; (editor) Alfred Tennyson, *Tennyson: Selected Poetry,* Random House, 1951; *Classical Influences in Renaissance Literature,* Harvard University Press, 1952; *English Poetry: The Main Currents from Chaucer to the Present,* Oxford University Press, 1952; (editor) John Keats, *John Keats: Selected Poems and Letters,* Houghton, 1959.

(Editor with Alfred Harbage) William Shakespeare, *Shakespeare's Sonnets,* Penguin, 1961; *John Milton,* Macmillan, 1964; *Prefaces to Renaissance Literature,* Harvard University Press, 1965; (editor) John Milton, *Milton: Complete Poetical Works,* Houghton, 1965; *John Keats,* Macmillan, 1966; *Engaged and Disengaged,* Harvard University Press, 1966; *Pagan Myth and Christian Tradition in English Poetry,* American Philosophical Society, 1968; (editor) *Variorum Commentary on the Poems of Milton,* Columbia University Press, Volume I (with J. E. Shaw and A. B. Giametti): *Latin and Greek Poems,* 1970, Volume II (with A.S.P. Woodhouse and Edward Weismiller): *Minor English Poems,* 1972; *Matthew Arnold,* Macmillan, 1971; *Jane Austen,* Macmillan, 1975; (contributor) *Milton Encyclopedia,* Bucknell University Press, 1978. Contributor to *Encyclopaedia Britannica.* Contributor of articles to literary journals, including *Kenyon Review, Sewanee Review,* and *American Scholar.*

*BIOGRAPHICAL/CRITICAL SOURCES: Times Literary Supplement,* February 2, 1967; *Virginia Quarterly Review,* spring, 1969.

\*     \*     \*

## BUSH, William (Shirley, Jr.) 1929-

*PERSONAL:* Born July 21, 1929, in Plant City, Fla.; son of William Shirley (an auto dealer) and Vera (Crews) Bush; married Mary Sutcliffe (a teacher of French), April 2, 1959; children: Anastasia, James, John, Andrew. *Education:* Stetson University, A.B., 1950; University of South Dakota, M.A., 1953; Universite de Paris, Docteur de l'Universite de Paris, 1959. *Religion:* Greek Orthodox. *Home:* 81 Wychwood Park, London, Ontario, Canada N6G 1R4. *Office:* Department of French, University of Western Ontario, London, Ontario, Canada N6A 3K7.

*CAREER:* Duke University, Durham, N.C., instructor, 1959-62, assistant professor, 1962-65, associate professor of

Romance languages, 1965-66; University of Western Ontario, London, associate professor of Romance languages, 1966-67, professor of French, 1967—. *Member:* American Association of Teachers of French, Amitie Charles Peguy, Fellowship of S. Alban and S. Sergius (president, 1967-69; secretary, 1971-72, 1973-77), Amis de Crisy-la-Salle. *Awards, honors:* Fulbright Awards, 1956-57 and 1957-58; Duke University summer fellowships, 1963, 1966; Canada Council leave fellowship, 1972-73.

*WRITINGS: Souffrance et expiation dans la pensee de Bernanos,* Lettres Modernes (Paris), 1962; *L'Angoisse du mystere,* Minard (Paris), 1966; *Georges Bernanos,* Twayne, 1970; (editor) *Regards sur Baudelaire,* Lettres Modernes, 1974. Contributor to *A Critical Bibliography of French Literature.* Contributor of articles to *Etudes Bernanosiennes, Prism, Concern.*

*WORK IN PROGRESS:* A novel, *The Seventh Summer; Morality and Poetic Structure: Essay on "Les Fleurs du mal"; The Evolution of Bernanos' Creative Vision.*

\*     \*     \*

## BUTTIMER, Anne 1938-
### (Sister Mary Annette)

*PERSONAL:* Born October 31, 1938, in County Cork, Ireland; daughter of Jeremiah (a farmer) and Eileen (Kelleher) Buttimer. *Education:* National University of Ireland, B.A. (first honors), 1957, M.A. (first honors), 1959; Seattle University, Teaching Certificate, 1961; University of Washington, Seattle, Ph.D., 1965; Catholic University of Louvain, postdoctoral study, 1965-66. *Permanent address:* Glenville, County Cork, Ireland. *Office:* Graduate School of Geography, Clark University, Worcester, Mass. 01610.

*CAREER:* Roman Catholic nun of Dominican Order; religious name, Sister Mary Annette; Seattle University, Seattle, Wash., lecturer in social science, 1963-64, assistant professor of geography, 1966-68; University of Glasgow, Glasgow, Scotland, lecturer in urban studies, 1968-70; Clark University, Worcester, Mass., assistant professor, 1970-73, associate professor of geography, 1973—. University of Lund, Sweden, visiting research scholar, 1973, Fulbright-Hays Visiting Professor of Social Ecology, 1976; visiting research professor, Stadens Rad foer Samhoellsforskning, Stockholm, Sweden, 1977-79. International Geographical Union, member of Commission on the History of Geographic Ideas, 1969-72, member of U.S. national committee, 1973-76.

*MEMBER:* Association of American Geographers (national councillor-at-large), American Geographical Society, Royal Society of Health (England), American Institute of Planners, Economie et Humanisme. *Awards, honors:* Belgian-American Educational Foundation postdoctoral fellow at Catholic University of Louvain, 1965-66; Social Science Research Council grant for critical evaluation of planning standards at University of Glasgow, 1968-70; postdoctoral fellow at Clark University, 1970-71.

*WRITINGS: Society and Milieu in the French Geographic Tradition,* Rand McNally, for Association of American Geographers, 1971; (with J. Forbes and others) *Social Science and Planning,* Scottish Academic Press, 1973; *Values in Geography,* Commission on College Geography, 1974; (with Torsten Haegerstrand) *Dwelling,* University of Lund, in press. Contributor to *International Encyclopedia of the Social Sciences* and to sociology and geography journals. Member of editorial committee, *Urban Studies Journal,* 1968-70; editorial correspondent, *l'Espace Geographique.*

*WORK IN PROGRESS:* Research in the philosophy of science and the history of ideas; developing a critical approach to the problems of communication between disciplines emphasizing the implications of scientific theory and its practical applications in everyday life in Sweden.

*SIDELIGHTS:* Anne Buttimer told *CA:* "The games people play in the academic world tend to result in a kind of functional specialization which fragments knowledge and life. Many of the 'issues' on which the political economy of research is often based, are those which we create and maintain via our ideas and praxis. One of the most urgent vocations for the academic writer, it seems to me, is to reflect critically on his/her own taken-for-granted world and then share the homework with society as a whole. We should become provokers of awareness rather than indoctrinators of theory, and our writing should call forth creativity and centeredness not only in our own lives but also in those whose lives are influenced in any way by our ideas and practice. I long for the gift of communication but the medium of print is opaque and abstract: in many ways we have perhaps abused it because we have allowed it to become the only medium of academic exchange."

*BIOGRAPHICAL/CRITICAL SOURCES:* J. O. Jackle, *Annotated Bibliography on Urban Social Geography,* Council of Planning Librarians, 1969.

\*       \*       \*

## BUZZOTTA, V. R(alph)  1931-

*PERSONAL:* Born March 18, 1931, in St. Louis, Mo.; son of Joseph and Antonia (Morella) Buzzotta; married Merle Lee Brock, August 29, 1953; children: Ann Nina, Robert Joseph. *Education:* Washington University, St. Louis, Mo., A.B., 1952, Ph.D., 1956. *Home:* 9466 Bonhomme Woods, St. Louis, Mo. 63132. *Office:* Psychological Associates, Inc., 8201 Maryland Ave., St. Louis, Mo. 63105.

*CAREER:* Veterans Administration Hospital, St. Louis, Mo., clinical psychologist, 1953-56; Jefferson Barracks Hospital, St. Louis, research clinical psychologist, 1956-57; research clinical psychologist in St. Louis, 1957-58; Psychological Associates, Inc., St. Louis, Mo., staff director, 1958—. Lecturer, Washington University, St. Louis, 1956-65. Member of president's council, St. Louis University, 1968-70. *Member:* American Psychological Association, Missouri Psychological Association.

*WRITINGS:* (With R. E. Lefton and M. Sherberg) *Dimensional Management Strategies,* Behavioral Science Press, 1970; (with Lefton and Sherberg) *Effective Selling through Psychology,* Wiley, 1972; (with Lefton, Sherberg, and Karraker) *Effective Motivation through Performance Appraisal,* Wiley, 1977. Contributor of articles to management journals.

*WORK IN PROGRESS:* Research on organizational development.

\*       \*       \*

## BYNUM, David E(liab)  1936-

*PERSONAL:* Born January 26, 1936, in Louisville, Ky.; son of Robert Lee (a businessman) and Virginia (Boll) Bynum; married Grace Mugar, 1966; children: Trevor Lee, Evan Hewer. *Education:* Harvard University, A.B., 1958, A.M., 1962, Ph.D., 1964; University of Belgrade, Yugoslavia, graduate study, 1960-61. *Office:* Widener Library 791, Harvard University, Cambridge, Mass. 02138.

*CAREER:* Harvard University, Cambridge, Mass., instructor, 1964-67; assistant professor of Slavic languages and literatures, 1967-72; curator of The Milman Parry Collection in Harvard College Library, 1972—, chairman of board of tutors in folklore and mythology, 1968—, member of standing committee on degrees in folklore and mythology, 1968—, lecturer on oral literature, 1973-74, executive officer of Center for the Study of Oral Traditions, 1974—, member of standing committee on African studies, 1974—. Member of Advisory Committee on Library Needs, Subcommittee on East-Central and Southeast European Studies, American Council of Learned Societies, 1968-69. *Member:* International Society for Folk-Narrative Research, Modern Language Association of America (associate bibliographer, 1968—), Comparative Literature Association, American Folklore Society. *Awards, honors:* Grant from Yugoslav Government, 1960-61; National Defense Language fellow, 1962-64; American Council of Learned Societies grant, 1965-66; Clark Foundation grant, 1967-68; Canaday Humanties Foundation grant, 1969; National Endowment for the Humanities research grant, 1972-73; Ella Lyman Cabot Trust grant, 1973-74.

*WRITINGS:* (Editor and compiler with A. B. Lord) *A Bulgarian Literary Reader,* Mouton (The Hague), 1968; (contributor with Lord) Charles Jelavich, editor, *Language and Area Studies, East Central and Southeastern Europe: A Survey,* University of Chicago Press, 1969; (contributor) Paul L. Horecky, editor, *Southeastern Europe: A Guide to Basic Publications,* University of Chicago Press, 1970; *Four Generations of Oral Literary Studies at Harvard University,* Center for the Study of Oral Literature, Harvard University, 1974; (editor and translator with Lord) Avdo Mededovic, *The Wedding of Smailagic Meho,* Harvard University Press, 1975. Managing editor of publications of the Milman Parry Collection, 1973—.

*WORK IN PROGRESS:* *Laertes' Orchard: A Study of Oral Narrative; Serbo Croatian Heroic Songs,* Volumes 5 and 6.†

# C

## CAHILL, Susan Neunzig 1940-

*PERSONAL:* Born September 12, 1940, in New York, N.Y.; daughter of Frank (a sales engineer) and Florence (Splain) Neunzig; married Thomas Quinn Cahill (a writer and teacher), November 4, 1966. *Education:* College of New Rochelle, B.A., 1962; New York University, M.A., 1965.

*CAREER:* Teacher since 1964 in New York, N.Y. pre-schools, grammar and high schools, and colleges; taught writing courses at Queens College for "Operation See," a program of City University of New York for high school graduates with college potential from poverty areas. Part-time faculty member of "Excel" program, Fordham University at Lincoln Center.

*WRITINGS:* (Editor with Michele F. Cooper) *The Urban Reader,* Prentice-Hall, 1971; (editor with husband, Thomas Cahill) *Big City Stories,* Bantam, 1971; (with T. Cahill) *A Literary Guide to Ireland,* Scribner, 1973; (editor) *Women and Fiction: Short Stories by and about Women,* New American Library, Volume I, 1975, Volume II, 1978; *Earth Angels: Portraits from Childhood and Youth,* Harper, 1976. With her husband, designed, edited, and published "A Literary Calendar 1973."

*WORK IN PROGRESS:* Short stories.

*SIDELIGHTS:* The Cahills spent a year in Dublin and traveling through Ireland.†

\* \* \*

## CAIRNS, (Thomas) Dorian 1901-1973

July 4, 1901—January 4, 1973; American educator and student of phenomenology. Obituaries: *New York Times,* January 7, 1973.

\* \* \*

## CALAMARI, John D(aniel) 1921-

*PERSONAL:* Born June 22, 1921, in New York, N.Y.; son of Agostino (a bridge operator) and Margaret (Cassella) Calamari; married Louise Marzano, June 18, 1955; children: Paul, Cynthia. *Education:* Fordham University, A.B. (cum laude), 1942, L.L.B., 1947; New York University, L.L.M., 1950. *Home:* 50 Rockledge Dr., Pelham Manor, New York, N.Y. 10803. *Office:* School of Law, Fordham University, 140 West 62nd St., New York, N.Y. 10023.

*CAREER:* United States Trucking Corp., New York City, assistant to general counsel, 1947-51; Fordham University, School of Law, New York City, lecturer, 1952-54, assistant professor, 1954-57, associate professor, 1957-59, professor of law, 1959—. *Military service:* U.S. Army, 1943-46, 1951-52; became lieutenant colonel. *Member:* American Bar Association, Fordham Law Review Association, Columbus Alliance, Columbian Lawyers.

*WRITINGS:* (With Joseph Perillo) *Contracts,* West Publishing, 1970, 2nd edition, 1977; (with Perillo) *Casebook on Contracts,* West Publishing, in press.

*AVOCATIONAL INTERESTS:* Sports.

\* \* \*

## CALDWELL, Harry B(oynton) 1935-

*PERSONAL:* Born September 11, 1935, in St. Louis, Mo.; son of Harry Boynton and Bernice Alberta (Hilkeman) Caldwell; married Christina Marie Griffes, March 26, 1960; children: Charis Marie, Heather Bernice. *Education:* Westminster College, Fulton, Mo., B.A.,1957; Vanderbilt University, M.A., 1961, Ph.D., 1968; University of London, certificate, 1962; also attended National University of Mexico. *Politics:* Democrat. *Religion:* Protestant. *Home:* 141 Cloverleaf Ave., San Antonio, Tex. 78209. *Office:* Trinity University, 715 Stadium, San Antonio, Tex. 78284.

*CAREER:* Domestic Engineering Publications, Chicago, Ill., assistant to sales promotion manager, 1959-60; University of Cincinnati, Cincinnati, Ohio, instructor in English, 1961-63; Colorado State University, Fort Collins, instructor in English, 1965-66; Westminster College, Fulton, Mo., assistant professor of English, 1966-68; Trinity University, San Antonio, Tex., 1968—, began as associate professor, currently professor of English. Fulbright-Hays lecturer, Al. I. Cuza University, Iasi, Romania, 1973-75. Affiliated with AMSPEC, United States Information Agency, 1976. *Member:* Modern Language Association of America, South Central Modern Language Association.

*WRITINGS:* (Editor with David L. Middleton) *English Tragedy, 1370-1600: Fifty Years of Criticism,* Trinity University Press, 1971; (editor) *Folk-Play and Related Forms,* Trinity University Press, 1972; *Good Morning, Children,* Editura didactica si pedagogica (Bucharest), 1976. General editor, "Checklists in the Humanities and Education." Contributor to literature journals.

*AVOCATIONAL INTERESTS:* Travel.

## CALDWELL, Oliver Johnson 1904-

*PERSONAL:* Born November 16, 1904, in Foochow, China; son of Harry Russell (a Methodist minister) and Mary Belle (Cope) Caldwell; married Eda Joslin Holcombe, June 29, 1935; children: Joslyn (Mrs. Edmund F. Becker, Jr.), Gail (Mrs. Warren Robinson). *Education:* Oberlin College, B.A., 1926, M.A., 1927; attended De Rezke Skagle School of Music, 1927-29. *Politics:* Independent liberal. *Religion:* Methodist. *Home address:* Route 2, Box 177, Cobden, Ill. 62920.

*CAREER:* Teacher at Harvey School, Hawthorne (now at Katonah), N.Y., 1929-35; University of Amoy, Amoy, China, associate professor of English, 1935-36; University of Nanking, Nanking, China, professor, 1936-38; executive secretary of Christian colleges in China, New York, N.Y., 1938-43; U.S. Department of State, Washington, D.C., variously employed, 1946-52; U.S. Department of Health, Education and Welfare, Office of Education, Washington, D.C., assistant commissioner, 1952-66; Southern Illinois University at Carbondale, dean and professor, 1966-74; currently a farmer. Chairman of U.S. delegation, UNESCO-International Bureau of Education Annual Conference on Public Education, 1964, 1965. Visiting professor, University of Maryland, 1965-66. Negotiator in Moscow of continuing exchange of U.S.-Soviet educators under the Lacey-Zaroubin Agreement, 1958. Education consultant to various institutions and organizations, 1946—. Vice-chairman of school board, Falls Church, Va., 1966-72. Clement Stone Chairman, Bridge-International Education Foundation. *Military service:* U.S. Army, 1943-45; served in China; became major. *Member:* American Association for the Advancement of Science, American Academy of Arts and Sciences, American Society for Cybernetics (founding member), Phi Delta Kappa, Rotary International. *Awards, honors:* LL.D. from Ithaca College and Albright College; L.H.D. from Baldwin-Wallace College.

*WRITINGS:* (Contributor) Pearl S. Buck, editor, *Asian Heritage in American Life,* John Day, 1945; (editor) *Education and Information Development,* U.S. Government Printing Office, 1957; (with Loren Graham) *Moscow in May, 1963,* U.S. Government Printing Office, 1964; (contributor) Stephen Kertesz, editor, *The Task of Universities in a Changing World,* University of Notre Dame Press, 1971; *A Secret War: Americans in China, 1944-1945,* Southern Illinois University Press, 1972. Also author of ten papers on education in Russia. Contributor of about one hundred articles and essays to journals.

*WORK IN PROGRESS: Bird of Heaven: An American Family in China during the Last Years of the Dragon Throne; The Merchants of Light: Education as a Tool of National Policy; A Dictionary of Selected Chinese Place Names; The Meaning of Wen: The Chinese Concept of Literature and Civilization; A Voice from the Ice: Growing Old in America.*

*SIDELIGHTS:* Oliver Johnson Caldwell spoke Chinese before he spoke English; he spent nearly twenty-five years in Asia and has traveled in more than eighty countries. He told *CA* that he is now raising daffodils, Christmas trees, and black walnuts. His farm ''has been designated by the American Forest Institute as a member of the American Tree Farm System.''

\* \* \*

## CALHOUN, Calfrey C. 1928-

*PERSONAL:* Born June 29, 1928, in Tarrytown, Ga.; son of Vance Omer (a farmer) and Mary (Anderson) Calhoun; married Marjorie Rogers (a teacher), December 4, 1960; children: Maria Ellen, Ronald Alan. *Education:* University of Georgia, B.S., 1949; Georgia State College (now University), B.B.A., 1956; George Peabody College for Teachers, M.A., 1956; Ohio State University, Ph.D., 1960. *Politics:* Democrat. *Religion:* Baptist. *Home:* 190 Pendleton Dr., Athens, Ga. 30601. *Office:* College of Education, University of Georgia, Athens, Ga. 30601.

*CAREER:* High school teacher in Georgia, 1952-53, 1954-55; Ford Motor Co., Hapeville, Ga., accountant, 1953-54; instructor in business education at George Peabody College for Teachers, Nashville, Tenn., 1956, and Ohio State University, Columbus, 1957-59; Georgia State College (now University), Atlanta, assistant professor of business education, 1959-62; University of Georgia, Athens, associate professor, 1962-66, professor of business education, 1966—, chairman of department, 1962—. Research specialist and program advisor on vocational education, U.S. Office of Education, 1966-67. Visiting summer professor at University of Illinois, 1969, and University of South Florida, 1970. Member of Policies Commission for Business and Economic Education; member of advisory committee for Center for Research and Leadership Development in Vocational-Technical Education and for Consumers Union; field reader and vocational education consultant, U.S. Office of Education. *Military service:* U.S. Army, 1950-52.

*MEMBER:* National Association for Business Teacher Education (member of executive board, 1967-69, 1977-79), American Vocational Association, American Educational Research Association, National Business Education Association, Commission for Business School Accreditation, Southern Business Education Association, Eastern Business Teachers Association, Georgia Business Education Association (president, 1966), Georgia Vocational Association, Delta Pi Epsilon, Kappa Delta Pi, Phi Delta Kappa. *Awards, honors:* Foundation for Economic Education postdoctoral fellow, 1962; Distinguished Service Award in vocational-technical education, Ohio State University, 1970.

*WRITINGS:* (With Alton V. Finch) *Human Relations for Office Workers,* C. E. Merrill, 1972; *Vocational and Career Education: Operations and Concepts,* Wadsworth, 1976. Co-editor and contributor, *Contributions of Research to Business Education* (yearbook), National Business Education Association, 1971. Contributor to symposia, business journals, and other yearbooks. National Business Education Association, editor in Research Division, 1967-69, and of *Research in Business Education,* 1976; editor for the National Association for Business Teacher Education, 1977—.

*WORK IN PROGRESS: Managing the Learning Process in Business Education,* a textbook.

\* \* \*

## CALLIS, Robert 1920-

*PERSONAL:* Born June 1, 1920, in Grand Tower, Ill.; son of Marion Jasper and Edith (Todd) Callis; married Thelma M. Lewis, October 23, 1942; married second wife, Sharon K. Pope (a psychologist), September 4, 1971; children: (first marriage) Ronald W., Steven M. *Education:* Southern Illinois University, B.Ed., 1942; University of Minnesota, M.A., 1946, Ph.D., 1948. *Home address:* Route 4, Columbia, Mo. 65201. *Office:* 3 Hill Hall, University of Missouri, Columbia, Mo. 65201.

*CAREER:* University of Missouri, Columbia, assistant professor, 1945-50, associate professor of psychology, 1950-55, professor of education, 1955—, associate director of testing and counseling service, 1948-53, director, 1953-64, dean of extra-divisional administration, 1964-69, consulting psychologist in Student Health Service, 1969—. Visiting summer professor, University of Illinois, 1954; Syracuse University, 1958. Consulting psychologist, William, Lynde and Williams, 1955-64. *Military service:* U.S. Naval Reserve, 1942-46; became lieutenant. *Member:* American Psychological Association (fellow), American Personnel and Guidance Association (member of senate, 1970-71), American College Personnel Association (president, 1959), Missouri Personnel and Guidance Association (president, 1970), Sigma Xi, Phi Delta Kappa.

*WRITINGS:* (With W. W. Cook and C. H. Leeds) *Minnesota Teacher Attitude Inventory,* Psychological Corp., 1951; (contributor) R. F. Berdie, editor, *Counseling and the College Program,* University of Minnesota Press, 1954; (with P. C. Polmantier and E. C. Roeber) *A Casebook of Counseling,* Appleton, 1955; (with G. A. Renzaglia and D. K. Ottman) *The University of Missouri English Placement Test, 1956 Edition,* University of Missouri Testing and Counseling Service, 1956; (with D. N. West and E. L. Ricksecker) *The Counselor's Handbook: Profile Interpretation of the Strong Vocational Interest Blanks,* R. W. Parkinson & Associates, 1964; (with W. H. Johnson) *Missouri College English Test,* Harcourt, 1965; (with E. F. Gardner, Jack Merwin, and R. M. Madden) *Stanford Achievement Test: High School Level,* Harcourt, 1966; (with Gardner, Merwin, and Madden) *Stanford Test of Academic Skills,* Harcourt, 1972. Contributor of about forty articles to counseling journals. Editor of *Journal of College Student Personnel,* 1963-69.

\* \* \*

## CALVERT, Laura D. 1922-

*PERSONAL:* Born June 29, 1922, in Port Clinton, Ohio; daughter of Floyd Silas (a professor) and Adda (Harbarger) DeLashmutt; married Edward H. Calvert (a government employee), February 12, 1942; children: Anne Elizabeth (Mrs. Jack Cully, Jr.). *Education:* University of New Mexico, B.A., 1955, M.A., 1956; Ohio State University, Ph.D., 1966. *Home:* 422 Ridge Pl. NE, Albuquerque, N.M. 87106.

*CAREER:* University of New Mexico, Albuquerque, instructor, 1957-58, 1961-66, assistant professor of Spanish, 1966-67; University of Massachusetts—Amherst, assistant professor of Spanish, 1967-68; University of Maryland Baltimore County, Baltimore, associate professor of Spanish, beginning 1968, coordinator of Spanish, 1969-71, member of graduate council, 1971-73. Director of Spanish training, University of New Mexico, Peace Corps Training Center, 1963-64; assistant director, National Defense Education Act (NDEA) Institute, Quito, Ecuador. *Member:* Modern Language Association of America, American Society of Teachers of Spanish and Portuguese, American Council on Teaching Foreign Languages, American Association of University Professors, Washington Linguistics Club, Phi Sigma Iota, Phi Kappa Phi.

*WRITINGS:* (Contributor) John Bailey, editor, *Post Scripts* (poems), [Philadelphia], 1952; *Francisco de Osuna and the Spirit of the Letter,* Department of Romance Languages, University of North Carolina, 1973. Also author, with Elizabeth DeLashmutt and M. M. Hobson, of a radio drama produced by WOSU, 1942. Contributor of articles and poems to literature journals, including *Journal of Medieval and Renaissance Studies.*

*AVOCATIONAL INTERESTS:* Theater, music.†

## CAMERON, William Bruce 1920-

*PERSONAL:* Born December 17, 1920, in Fairfax, Okla.; son of Emory C. (a clergyman and teacher) and Regina May Cameron; married C'Mari de Schipper (a teacher), June 30, 1946; children: Katherine (Mrs. Charles Gulley), David Bruce. *Education:* Butler University, B.A., 1943, M.A., 1943; Fordham University, postgraduate study, 1943-44; University of Wisconsin, Ph.D., 1952. *Religion:* Protestant. *Office:* Department of Sociology, University of South Florida, Tampa, Fla. 33620.

*CAREER:* Butler University, Indianapolis, Ind., 1948-50, began as instructor, became assistant professor of sociology; University of Cincinnati, Cincinnati, Ohio, assistant professor of sociology, 1950-55; Bradley University, Peoria, Ill., 1955-64, began as associate professor, became professor of sociology and chairman of department; University of South Florida, Tampa, director of social sciences and professor of sociology, 1964—. *Military service:* U.S. Army, 1943-46. *Member:* American Sociological Association, American Association of University Professors, Southern Sociological Society.

*WRITINGS: Informal Sociology,* Random House, 1963; *Modern Social Movements,* Random House, 1966. Contributor of articles to professional journals and to radio magazines.

*WORK IN PROGRESS: From a Sociologist's Window; The Complete Beginner's Book of Golf;* research on electronics.

*SIDELIGHTS:* William Bruce Cameron is also a jazz musician and a ham radio operator.

\* \* \*

## CAMPBELL, Elizabeth McClure 1891-

*PERSONAL:* Born November 29, 1891, in Jefferson City, Mo.; daughter of Walter Tennant (a clergyman) and Dora (Cottey) McClure; married Arthur Morrow Campbell (a clergyman), October 12, 1918 (died, 1922); children: Walter McClure, Arthur Morrow, Jr. *Education:* University of Missouri, A.B., 1914; University of Colorado, M.A., 1928; University of Chicago, graduate study, 1933-35. *Politics:* "Democrat generally." *Religion:* Presbyterian. *Home and office:* 831 Main St., Parkville, Mo. 64152.

*CAREER:* Cottey Junior College, Nevada, Mo., member of faculty and chairman of English department, 1927-33; Park College, Parkville, Mo., assistant professor, 1935-36, associate professor of English, 1936-57, professor emerita, 1957—; National College, Kansas City, Mo., associate professor of English, 1957-59. *Member:* American Association of University Women (president of local chapter, 1955-57), National Council of Teachers of English, American Association of University Professors, National Retired Teachers Association, PEO Sisterhood, United Presbyterian Women (president of local chapter, 1963), Associate in National Christian Education (honorary life member), Phi Mu.

*WRITINGS:* (With T. A. Perry) *Orientation English,* Park College Press, 1939; (with B. F. Fuson) *Communications Handbook,* Burgess, 1953, revised edition, 1955; *The Cottey Sisters of Missouri,* Park College Press, 1970. Contributor of articles to literature journals.

*WORK IN PROGRESS:* Research on people of Missouri Ozark region during and after the Civil War.

## CAMPBELL, Ernest Q(ueener)   1926-

*PERSONAL:* Born September 15, 1926, in Stephens, Ga.; son of George McLaughlin (a farmer) and Margaret (Queener) Campbell; married Berdelle Taylor (administrator of a family planning program), August 28, 1949; children: John McLaughlin, Ernest Paul, Alison Leigh, Wallace Scott. *Education:* Furman University, B.A., 1945; University of Pennsylvania, M.A., 1946; graduate study at Yale University, summer, 1948, University of North Carolina, 1949-50, and Harvard University, 1957-58; Vanderbilt University, Ph.D., 1956. *Home:* 4407 Howell Pl., Nashville, Tenn. 37205. *Office:* 322A Garland Hall, Vanderbilt University, Nashville, Tenn. 37235.

*CAREER:* Mississippi Southern College (now University of Southern Mississippi), Hattiesburg, instructor, 1947-48, assistant professor of sociology, 1948-51; College of Wooster, Wooster, Ohio, instructor in sociology, 1951-54; Florida State University, Tallahassee, assistant professor of sociology, 1956-57; University of North Carolina at Chapel Hill, assistant professor, 1958-61, associate professor of sociology, 1961-63; Vanderbilt University, Nashville, Tenn., professor of sociology, 1963—, chairman of department of sociology and anthropology, 1963-71, chairman of faculty senate, 1972-73, dean of Graduate School, 1973—. Visiting professor and chairman of department of sociology at University College, University of East Africa, 1968-69; external examiner, University of Ibadan, 1970-72. Member of advisory panel, National Science Foundation, 1966-68; member of developmental behavioral sciences study section, National Institutes of Health, 1972-75.

*MEMBER:* American Sociological Association (chairman of committee on training and professional standards, 1964-67; member of council, 1977-80), Sociological Research Association (president, 1975-76), Southern Sociological Society (president, 1967-68; member of graduate record examination board). *Awards, honors:* Social Science Research Council fellow at Harvard University, 1957-58; Rockefeller Foundation grant in Kenya, 1968-69.

*WRITINGS:* (With Thomas F. Pettigrew) *Christians in Racial Crisis: A Study of Little Rock's Ministers,* Public Affairs Press, 1959; *When a City Closes Its Schools,* University of North Carolina, Institute for Research in Social Science, 1960; (with James S. Coleman and others) *Equality of Educational Opportunity,* U.S. Government Printing Office, 1966; (editor and author of introduction) *Racial Tensions and National Identity,* Vanderbilt University Press, 1972; *Socialization: Culture and Personality,* W. C. Brown, 1975.

Contributor: Bartlett H. Stoodley, editor, *Society and Self: A Reader in Social Psychology,* Free Press of Glencoe, 1962; R. M. Pavalko, editor, *Sociology of Education: A Book of Readings,* F. E. Peacock, 1968; B. C. Rosen, H. J. Crockett, and C. Z. Nunn, editors, *Achievement in American Society,* Schenkman, 1969; David A. Goslin, editor, *Handbook of Socialization Theory and Research,* Rand McNally, 1969; Liston O. Mills, editor, *Perspectives on Death,* Abingdon, 1969; Mark Abrahamson, editor, *Readings on Sociological Concepts, Methods, and Data,* Van Nostrand, 1969; George L. Maddox, editor, *The Domesticated Drug: Drinking among Collegians,* College & University Press, 1970. Contributor of about thirty articles to sociology journals. Associate editor, *Social Forces,* 1958-63, *Sociological Inquiry,* 1964-67, 1967-70, and *American Sociological Review,* 1971-74; *Sociometry,* member of editorial board, 1966-72, associate editor, 1972-74; member of editorial advisory board, *Southern Education Report,* 1966-68.

## CAMPS, Francis Edward   1905-1972

*PERSONAL:* Born June 28, 1905, in Teddington, England; son of Percy William (a medical practitioner) and Alice (Redfern) Camps; married Mary Winifred Ross Mackenzie, 1940 (deceased); children: Elizabeth Ann, Peter, Jeremy, Jennyer. *Education:* Attended Marlborough College; Guy's Hospital Medical School, University of London, M.B. and B.S., M.D., F.R.C.P.; School of Tropical Medicine, University of Liverpool, D.T.M. and H.; also studied at University of Neuchatel. *Home:* 190 Andrewes House, Barbican, London, England; and Limes, Purleigh, Essex, England. *Agent:* Curtis Brown Ltd., 1 Craven Hill, London W2 3EW, England.

*CAREER:* Guy's Hospital, London, England, house physician; University of London, London Hospital Medical College, London, reader, 1954-63, professor of forensic medicine, 1963-70, professor emeritus, 1970-72, director of department. Former pathologist at Chelmsford and Essex Hospital; consultant pathologist to Essex County Council and to Emergency Medical Service. Former examiner in forensic medicine at Universities of St. Andrews, London, Sheffield, Durham, and Bristol. Member of British Medical Association Special Committee on the Recognition of Intoxication and the Relation of Alcohol to Road Accidents, 1951, Coroners Rules Committee, British Home Office, 1953, and Mortuaries Committee, Ministry of Housing and Local Government, 1955; consultant on forensic medicine to British Army; scientific adviser for the television programs, "The Strange Report" and "The Hidden Truth."

*MEMBER:* Royal Society of Medicine, British Medical Association, British Academy of Forensic Medicine (past secretary-general), American Academy of Forensic Sciences, Royal College of Pathology, Royal Society of Arts, Society for the Study of Addiction (president), Association for the Prevention of Addiction (president), Harvard Associates in Police Science (honorary member), Worshipful Company of Blacksmiths, Savile Club, Savage Club. *Awards, honors:* Kellogg Foundation traveling fellow; Officer of Order of St. John of Jerusalem; Swiney Prize for Medical Jurisprudence of Royal Society of Arts, 1969.

*WRITINGS: Medical and Scientific Investigations in the Christie Case,* Medical Publications, 1953, Macmillan, 1954; (with W. Bentley Purchase) *Practical Forensic Medicine,* Hutchinson's Medical Publications, 1956, Macmillan, 1957, 2nd revised edition (with J. M. Cameron and David Lanham), Hutchinson's Medical Publications, 1971; (editor) *Medicine, Science and Law,* Sweet & Maxwell, 1964; (with Richard Barber) *The Investigation of Murder,* M. Joseph, 1966; (editor and reviser) Rutherford B. H. Gradwohl, *Gradwohl's Legal Medicine,* Williams & Wilkins, 1968, 3rd edition, Year Book Medical Publishers, 1976; (editor) *Recent Advances in Forensic Pathology,* J. & A. Churchill, 1969, Williams & Wilkins, 1970; (contributor) Edward Shatter, editor, *Matters of Life and Death,* Darton, Longman & Todd, 1970; (editor) *Sudden and Unexpected Deaths in Infancy (Cot Deaths),* J. Wright, 1972; *Camps on Crime,* David & Charles, 1973. Contributor to pathological and medico-legal journals.†

(Died July 8, 1972)

\*    \*    \*

## CANFIELD, John A(lan)   1941-

*PERSONAL:* Born June 2, 1941, in Pittsburgh, Pa.; son of James Willard Canfield and Clydetta Ann Conlon Walker; married June Louise Smith, July 22, 1961; children: John,

Christopher, Susan. *Education:* Potomac State College, A.A., 1959-61; West Virginia University, B.S., 1963. *Politics:* Democrat. *Religion:* Roman Catholic. *Home:* 5411 Staunton Ave. S.E., Charleston, W.Va. 25311. *Office:* Office of the Governor, State Capitol, Charleston, W.Va. 25305.

*CAREER:* Press secretary to Governor Hulett C. Smith, 1964-69; WSAZ-TV and WXIT radio, Charleston, W.Va., newsman, 1969-71; press secretary to John D. Rockefeller IV, Charleston, 1971-73; member of West Virginia legislature, 1974-77; partner in public relations firm, 1974-77; special assistant to Governor John D. Rockefeller IV, 1977—. Delegate to Democratic National Convention, 1968. *Member:* Sigma Delta Chi.

*WRITINGS:* (Editor) *The Papers and Public Addresses of Governor Hulett C. Smith*, State of West Virginia, 1970.

*WORK IN PROGRESS:* Handbook for broadcast journalists.

\* \* \*

## CAPONIGRI, A(loysius) Robert 1915-

*PERSONAL:* Born November 16, 1915, in Chicago, Ill.; son of Nicola (a journalist) and Lucia (Sorrocco) Caponigri; married Winifred France (a professor), October 6, 1946; children: Victoria (Mrs. John Stephan), Robert John, Lisa Marie. *Education:* Loyola University, Chicago, Ill., A.B., 1935, M.A., 1936; Harvard University, postgraduate study, 1937-39; University of Chicago, Ph.D., 1942. *Religion:* Roman Catholic. *Home:* 317 East Napoleon Blvd., South Bend, Ind. 46617. *Office:* Department of Philosophy, University of Notre Dame, Notre Dame, Ind. 46556.

*CAREER:* University of Iowa, Iowa City, instructor in humanities, 1943-46; University of Notre Dame, Notre Dame, Ind., assistant professor, 1946-52, associate professor, 1952-56, professor of philosophy, 1956—, chairman of committee on humanities, 1967—. Fulbright visiting professor, University of Madrid, 1964-66; visiting scholar, Center for Study of Democratic Institutions, spring, 1975, and Harvard Center for Italian Renaissance Studies in Florence, Italy, summer, 1975. *Member:* American Philosophical Society, American Catholic Philosophical Society (member of executive board), Mediaeval Academy of America, Metaphysical Society of America. *Awards, honors:* Italian Institute for Historical Studies, Fulbright research professor, 1950-51, Rockefeller Foundation fellow, 1952-53, 1974-75; research fellowships from American Philosophical Society, 1958, 1969, Grace Foundation, 1959, American Council of Learned Societies, 1969; research grants from Italian Institute of Culture, New York, 1961, Marquette Foundation, 1961, 1964, 1969, Instituto de Cultura Hispanica, Madrid, 1970; Fulbright lectureship in Italy, 1971; Folger Library fellow, spring, 1976.

*WRITINGS: Time and Idea: The Theory of History in Giambattista Vico*, Regnery, 1953, new edition, University of Notre Dame Press, 1968; *History and Liberty: The Historical Writings of Benedetto Croce*, Regnery, 1955; (translator) Pico della Mirandola, *Oration on the Dignity of Man*, Regnery, 1956; *Modern Catholic Thinkers*, Harper, 1960, new edition in two volumes, 1964; (translator, contributor, and author of introduction) Machiavelli, *The Prince*, Regnery, 1963; *History of Western Philosophy*, five volumes, University of Notre Dame Press, 1963-70; (associate editor) *Masterpieces of Catholic Literature*, two volumes, Salem Press, 1965; (translator) *Major Trends in Mexican Philosophy*, University of Notre Dame Press, 1966; (translator and

editor) *Contemporary Spanish Philosophy*, University of Notre Dame Press, 1967; (translator, selector, and author of introduction) Diogenes Laertius, *Lives of the Philosophers*, Regnery, 1969.

Contributor: *Studi in onore di M. F. Sciacca*, Marzorati, 1959; *La Philosophie et ses problemes: Recueil d'etudes offert a Msgr. R. Jolivet*, Lyon Emmanuel Vitte, 1960; (author of introduction) Luigi Sturzo, *Church and State*, University of Notre Dame Press, 1962; (author of introduction) Yves Simon, *A General Theory of Authority*, University of Notre Dame Press, 1962; Ernan McMullin, editor, *The Concept of Matter*, University of Notre Dame Press, 1963; *Les Grands courants de la pensee mondiale contemporaine*, Marzorati, Volumes IV, V, and VI, 1964; *New Themes in Christian Philosophy*, University of Notre Dame Press, 1968; *Michele F. Sciacca: Saggi in Onore*, Marzorati, 1968. Contributor of more than fifty articles to philosophy journals in the United States and Europe.

*WORK IN PROGRESS:* Translating from the Spanish, Xavier Zubiri, *On Essence;* research for *Intellectual History of Modern Catholicism*.

\* \* \*

## CAPORALE, Rocco 1927-

*PERSONAL:* Born August 21, 1927; son of Francis (an engineer) and Frances (Badolato) Caporale. *Education:* Aloisianum College, B.A., 1950; De Nobili College, S.Th.L., 1957; Tata University, M.S.W., 1959; Columbia University, Ph.D., 1965. *Politics:* Democrat. *Religion:* Roman Catholic. *Home:* 184-56 Hovenden Rd., Jamaica Estates, N.Y. 11432. *Office:* Department of Sociology, St. John's University, Jamaica, N.Y. 11439.

*CAREER:* Manhattanville College, Purchase, N.Y., assistant professor, 1963-66; University of California, Berkeley, research associate, 1966-68; St. John's University, Jamaica, N.Y., associate professor, 1968-69; Claremont Colleges, Claremont, Calif., director of research, 1969-72; St. John's University, professor of sociology, 1972—. Consultant to Vatican Secretariat for Non-Believers and to Agnelli Foundation (Turin, Italy). Trustee of Sophia Research Center (Greenbrook, N.J.) and Louis Lomax Foundation. *Member:* American Sociological Association, American Academy of Social and Political Science, Society for the Scientific Study of Religion, Society of Priests for a Free Ministry.

*WRITINGS: Vatican II: Last of the Councils*, Helicon, 1964; *Les Hommes du Concile*, Editions du Cerf, 1965; *El ultimo de los concilios*, Edition Terra Nova, 1965; (editor with A. Grumelli) *The Culture of Unbelief*, University of California Press, 1971; *Nuovi e Vecchi Dei*, Valentino Press, 1975.

*WORK IN PROGRESS:* Research on systems of inheritance, on emerging forms of religious consciousness, and on patterns of safety in the United States.

*SIDELIGHTS:* Rocco Caporale speaks Italian, French, German, Spanish, Sinhalese, and Latin; he has traveled and lived in Asia, Africa, South America, and Europe.

\* \* \*

## CAPPELLUTI, Frank Joseph 1935-1972

*PERSONAL:* Born November 12, 1935, in Newark, N.J.; son of Cosmo and Rose (DeTaranto) Cappelluti; married Dorothy Giglio, July 1, 1962; children: Erika. *Education:* Rutgers University, Newark, N.J., B.A., 1958, New Brunswick, N.J., M.A., 1959, Ph.D., 1967. *Home:* 45 Magnolia St., Belleville, N.J. 07109. *Office:* Department of History, St. Peter's College, Kennedy Blvd., Jersey City, N.J.

*CAREER:* Rutgers University, Rutgers, N.J., instructor in evening school; St. Peter's College, Jersey City, N.J., associate professor of history, 1963-72, head of department, 1970-72.

*WRITINGS:* (With Ruth Grossman) *The Human Adventure,* Field Educational Publications, 1970, 3rd edition, 1976.†

(Died August 17, 1972)

\*    \*    \*

## CAPPS, Clifford Lucille Sheats   1902-1976

*PERSONAL:* Born September 30, 1902, in Carrolton, Ga.; daughter of Thomas George (a physician) and Elizabeth (Kelly) Sheats; married James Penn Capps, December 24, 1920 (died, 1933); children: James, Beverly, Elizabeth (Mrs. Garland Perdue). *Education:* West Georgia College, Normal diploma, 1935; Oglethorpe University, B.S., 1953. *Politics:* Democrat. *Religion:* Baptist.

*CAREER:* Fulton County Board of Education, Atlanta, Ga., elementary teacher, 1935-60; script writer, WABE-Radio. *Member:* Georgia Writers Association, Atlanta Writers Club, Manuscript Club (president, 1954-56), Alpha Kappa Delta, Alpha Delta Kappa.

*WRITINGS:* (With Eugenia Burney) *Colonial History of Georgia,* Thomas Nelson, 1972; *John Wesley in Georgia: Minister, Missionary, Medicine Man,* Martin Johnson, 1972. Contributor of biographical story to *South Carolina Magazine.*†

(Died October 10, 1976)

\*    \*    \*

## CARLSON, Arthur E(ugene)   1923-

*PERSONAL:* Born May 10, 1923, in Whitewater, Wis.; son of Paul A. (a professor emeritus) and Dorothy (Cooper) Carlson; married Lorraine Bronson, August 19, 1944; children: George Arthur. *Education:* University of Wisconsin, Ed.B., 1943; Harvard University, M.B.A., 1947; Northwestern University, Ph.D., 1954. *Politics:* Republican. *Religion:* Episcopal. *Home:* 8023 Gannon Ave., St. Louis, Mo. 63130. *Office:* Department of Accounting, Washington University, St. Louis, Mo. 63130.

*CAREER:* Ohio University, Athens, instructor in accounting, 1947-50; Northwestern University, Evanston, Ill., lecturer in management, 1950-52; Washington University, St. Louis, Mo., assistant professor of management, 1952-56, associate professor, 1956-61, professor of accounting, 1961—. Visiting professor in accounting, University of Hawaii, Honolulu, 1963-64. Consultant to Jewish Hospital, St. Louis, 1957, Monsanto Co., St. Louis, 1958, Doane's Agricultural Service, St. Louis, 1967. *Military service:* U.S. Navy, 1942-46; became lieutenant commander. *Member:* National Association of Accountants (president, St. Louis chapter, 1961-62), Association for Systems Management (president, St. Louis chapter, 1971-72), American Accounting Association, American Association of University Professors, University City Kiwanis Club (president, 1970-71). *Awards, honors:* University of Wisconsin Distinguished Alumni Award, 1970.

*WRITINGS:* (With Ben Carson and Clem Boling) *College Accounting,* 8th edition (Carlson was not associated with

earlier editions), South-Western, 1967, 10th edition, 1977; (with Jerry Howe) *Accounting Principles Workbook,* South-Western, 1969, 3rd edition, 1977. Contributor to *Accounting Review, Management Accounting, Business Viewpoints, Journal of Systems Management,* and other periodicals.

*WORK IN PROGRESS:* Research on current costs in financial reporting and on inflation accounting.

*AVOCATIONAL INTERESTS:* Gardening and photography.

\*    \*    \*

## CARLSON, Loraine   1923-

*PERSONAL:* Born May 6, 1923, in Los Angeles, Calif.; daughter of Leon W. (a finance corporation administrator) and Belle (Fowles) Cumings; married Cecil Spencer, November 2, 1946 (divorced, 1951); married Neil Carlson (a graphic artist), December 18, 1958. *Education:* University of Redlands, B.A., 1944; University of Southern California, graduate study, 1950-53.

*CAREER:* Hughes Aircraft Co., Culver City, Calif., technical writer and publications supervisor, 1953-58; TRW Systems, Redondo Beach, Calif., technical writer in Research Division, 1964-66; has also worked as elementary school teacher, journalist, and travel agent.

*WRITINGS: Mexico: An Extraordinary Guide,* maps and illustrations by husband, Neil Carlson, Rand McNally, 1971.††

\*    \*    \*

## CARMICHAEL, William Edward   1922-
### (Adam Best)

*PERSONAL:* Born March 27, 1922, in Birmingham, Ala.; son of Robert Edward and Annie Louise (Noyes) Carmichael. *Education:* University of Alabama, B.A., 1942; Princeton University, graduate study, 1944. *Politics:* Independent. *Religion:* Roman Catholic. *Home and office address:* Turtle Hill Farm, Box 1, Great Falls, Va. 22066. *Agent:* Curtis Brown Ltd., 575 Madison Ave., New York, N.Y. 10022; (lectures) Wide World Lecture Bureau, 18 East 48th St., New York, N.Y.

*CAREER: Tricolor Magazine,* New York City, associate editor, 1944-46; *Fascination Magazine,* New York City, editor, 1946-48; *Holiday Magazine,* Mexico City, Mexico, Latin-American correspondent, 1948-49; National Symphony Orchestra, Washington, D.C., director of advertising and public relations, 1950-53; director of advertising and public relations for Philadelphia and Boston Symphony Orchestras on tour in Washington, D.C., 1953-55; professional lecturer on collecting and collectors, and free-lance writer. Publicity director, Wolf Trap Farm Park for the Performing Arts, Vienna, Va. *Member:* Authors Guild, National Press Club, Arts Club of Washington.

*WRITINGS: Spaniel in the Lion's Den* (juvenile), Hyperion Press, 1947; *The Best Years* (poems), New Athenaeum, 1960; *Incredible Collectors, Weird Antiques, and Odd Hobbies,* Prentice-Hall, 1971. Former feature writer for *Washington Post, Washington Sunday Star,* and *Newsday;* writer of syndicated column on antiques, "A Din of Antiquity."

*WORK IN PROGRESS: Hop O' My Thumb,* a biography of Charles Stratton, known to theatrical history as Tom Thumb; *The Artifacts of Life* (sequel to *Incredible Collectors, Weird Antiques and Odd Hobbies*).

## CARNEY, Richard Edward 1929-

*PERSONAL:* Born February 5, 1929, in Miami, Fla.; son of Clifford R. (a chemist and inventor) and Johnnie Ora (Des Roches) Carney; married Jane Rima Wallace (a teacher-director of a preschool, and instructor at Grossmont College), June 20, 1953; children: Cathleen Jane, Daniel Richard, Bonnie Ann. *Education:* Attended Florida State University, 1947-48; University of Washington, Seattle, B.S., 1954, M.S., 1956; University of Michigan, Ph.D., 1961. *Politics:* Democrat (independent). *Religion:* Unitarian Universalist. *Home and office:* 2130 Balboa Ave., San Diego, Calif. 92109.

*CAREER:* National Security Agency, Washington, D.C., analytical research specialist, 1952-53; Pinel Foundation, Seattle, Wash., part-time psychiatric aide, 1953; Drake University, Des Moines, Iowa, assistant professor of psychology, 1958-62; Indiana University Northwest, Gary, assistant professor of psychology, 1962-64; United States International University, San Diego, associate professor of psychology, 1964-70, chairman of department, 1964-67; Eastern Kentucky University, Richmond, professor of psychology, 1970-72; California School of Professional Psychology, San Diego, member of faculty, 1972—, chairman, 1976-77. Psychologist, licensed in California, 1975—. President, Carney Enterprises, Inc. (consulting and management firm), San Diego; consultant on development of automated teaching equipment, Non-Linear Systems, Inc., Del Mar, 1967-69; consultant on drug abuse prevention, Educators Assistance Institute, Los Angeles, 1972-75; president, TIMAO Foundation for Research and Development, San Diego, 1976—; consultant to Resources for Non-Sexist Education, San Diego, 1977—; co-director, Carney, Weedman & Associates. *Military service:* U.S. Army, 1948-52, mainly as Russian language interpreter; became sergeant.

*MEMBER:* American Psychological Association, American Association for the Advancement of Science, American Association of University Professors, Western Psychological Association, California Psychological Association, Sigma Xi, Psi Chi.

*WRITINGS: Toward a Better Technology of Teaching and Testing,* Non-Linear Systems, 1968; (editor and contributor) *Risk-Taking Behavior,* C. C Thomas, 1971; *Manual for the Risk-Taking Attitude-Values Inventory,* Pennant Educational Materials, 1975. Writer of a series of technical reports on salmon behavior, and on evaluation of drug abuse, delinquency treatment, and prevention programs. Contributor of articles and reviews to professional journals.

*WORK IN PROGRESS: The Drug Solution,* a book on drug abuse and means of prevention; two science fiction books.

*AVOCATIONAL INTERESTS:* Music (singing solo and in groups), tennis, swimming, basketball, acting in little theater productions.

\*     \*     \*

## CARPENTER, Frances 1890-1972

April 30, 1890—November 2, 1972; American author of children's books. Obituaries: *New York Times,* November 9, 1972; *Publishers Weekly,* December 4, 1972; *Antiquarian Bookman,* December 4, 1972. (See index for *CA* sketch)

\*     \*     \*

## CARPENTER, James A. 1928-

*PERSONAL:* Born April 2, 1928, in Kings Mountain, N.C.; son of Clarence Edward and Elizabeth (Webb) Carpenter; married Mary Louise Dunbar, February 22, 1954; children: James A., Jr., Mark D. *Education:* Wofford College, B.A., 1948; Duke University, B.D., 1951; Cambridge University, Ph.D., 1959. *Politics:* Democrat. *Home:* 3 Chelsea Square, New York, N.Y. 10011. *Office:* General Theological Seminary, 175 Ninth Ave., New York, N.Y. 10011.

*CAREER:* Rector of Episcopal church in Pittsboro, N.C., 1952-53; vicar of Episcopal church in Alexandria, La., 1959-63; General Theological Seminary, New York, N.Y., assistant professor, 1963-65, professor of theology, 1965—, sub-dean, 1974—. Member of staff, St. Luke's Parish (Cambridge), 1957-59. Visiting professor, University of the South, summer, 1965. Program director, "The Church and the World" (a television series), 1961-63. Member of review board, Psychiatric Institute of New York, 1975—. *Military service:* U.S. Army chaplain, 1953-56; became first lieutenant. *Member:* Academy of Religion and Mental Health, American Theological Society, Society for Arts, Religion and Culture. *Awards, honors:* Fulbright scholar, University of St. Andrews (Scotland), 1956-57; American Philosophical Society grant for research on Coleridge's prose works, 1968.

*WRITINGS: Gore: A Study in Liberal Catholicism,* Faith Press, 1960; *Charles Gore and Christian Socialism,* Crucible, 1961; *The New Theology and the Old Religion,* Witness, 1965. Contributor to *Encyclopedia Americana;* contributor of articles to *Anglican Theological Review, St. Luke's Journal,* and other theology journals.

*WORK IN PROGRESS:* Research on Augustine of Hippo; the phenomenology of love, and grace in world religions.

\*     \*     \*

## CARR, Arthur C(harles) 1918-

*PERSONAL:* Born November 27, 1918, in Buffalo, N.Y.; son of John Edward and Katherine (Haas) Carr. *Education:* New York State College for Teachers (now State University of New York at Buffalo), B.S., 1941; Columbia University, M.A., 1946; University of Chicago, Ph.D., 1952; postdoctoral study at William A. White Institute, 1953-54, New York Society of Clinical Psychologists, 1954, 1960, and Institute of Group Therapy, 1957-58. *Office:* Psychiatric Institute, 722 West 168th St., New York, N.Y. 10032.

*CAREER:* Veterans Administration trainee in clinical psychology, Hines, Ill., 1947-52; Creedmoor State Hospital, Queens Village, N.Y., psychologist, 1952-56; Adelphi College (now University), Garden City, N.Y., assistant professor of psychology, 1952-56; Columbia University, College of Physicians and Surgeons, New York, N.Y., associate professor in department of psychiatry, 1956-70, professor of medical psychology, 1970—, associate clinical psychologist at Psychiatric Institute, 1956-68, principal psychologist, 1968—. Certification of American Board of Examiners in Professional Psychology, 1956. Lecturer, Queens College (now Queens College of the City University of New York), 1956. *Military service:* U.S. Army, 1941-46; became major. *Member:* American Psychological Association (fellow), Society for Personality Assessment (president, 1971-72), Eastern Psychological Association, New York State Psychological Association, New York Society of Clinical Psychologists.

*WRITINGS:* (Contributor) Daniel Brower and Lawrence E. Abt, editors, *Progress in Clinical Psychology,* Volume III, Grune & Stratton, 1958; (with others) *The Prediction of Overt Behavior through the Use of Projective Techniques,* C. C Thomas, 1960; (with Showert H. Frazier) *Introduction* to *Psychopathology*, Macmillan, 1964; (contributor) Lawrence C. Kolb, Franz Kallman, and Philip Polatin, editors, *Schizophrenia*, Little, Brown, 1965; (with Herbert Hendin and Willard Gaylin) *Psychoanalysis and Social Research*, Doubleday, 1965; (contributor) Alfred Freedman and Harold Kaplan, editors, *Comprehensive Textbook of Psychiatry*, Williams & Wilkins, 1967; (contributor) Charles Spielberger, Robert Fox, and Bruce Masterton, editors, *Contributions to General Psychology*, Ronald, 1968; (editor with Bernard Schoenberg and Helen Pettit, and contributor) *Teaching Psychosocial Aspects of Patient Care*, Columbia University Press, 1968; (contributor) Austin Kutscher, editor, *But Not to Lose*, Fell, 1969; (author of appendix) Hendin, *Black Suicide*, Basic Books, 1969.

(Editor with Schoenberg, Kutscher, and David Peretz, and contributor) *Loss and Grief: Its Management in General Medical Practice*, Columbia University Press, 1970; (editor with Schoenberg, Peretz, and Kutscher, and contributor) *Psychosocial Aspects of Terminal Care*, Columbia University Press, 1972; (editor with Kutscher and Schoenberg, and contributor) *The Dying Patient: Oral Management*, Health Sciences, 1972; (editor with Schoenberg and others, and contributor) *Anticipatory Grief*, Columbia University Press, 1974; (contributor) Freedman, Kaplan, and Benjamin Sadock, editors, *Comprehensive Textbook of Psychiatry*, Williams & Wilkins, 1975; (editor with Schoenberg and others, and contributor) *Bereavement: Its Psychological Aspects*, Columbia University Press, 1975. Contributor of about thirty articles to professional journals. Consulting editor and member of editorial board, *Journal of Personality Assessment*, 1967-73; associate editor, *Journal of Abnormal Psychology*, 1965-70, and *Journal of Thanatology*, 1971—; editor-in-chief, *Man and Medicine*, 1975—.

\*    \*    \*

## CARR, David William    1911-

*PERSONAL:* Born December 9, 1911, in Leney, Saskatchewan, Canada; son of Samuel Henry and Lillian (Moore) Carr; married Frances Close, November 10, 1939; children: Glenna Lea, Candace Gail, Gertrude Lillian, Frances Lynn. *Education:* University of Saskatchewan, B.A. and B.S.A., 1948; University of Wisconsin, M.Sc., 1949; Harvard University, Ph.D., 1953.

*CAREER:* McGill University, Macdonald College, Montreal, Quebec, lecturer in economics, 1951-53; economic adviser, Royal Commission on Newfoundland Agriculture, 1953-55; chief of economics research, Canadian Department of Fisheries, 1955-58; D. William Carr and Associates Ltd., Ottawa, Ontario, president, 1959—; Carr Publishing Company, Ottawa, president, 1971—. Consultant, Resources Tomorrow Conference, 1960, Royal Commission on Transportation, 1960-61, Royal Commission on Banking and Finance, 1962-63, Emergency Measures Organization, 1963-72, International Joint Commission, 1964-65, Resource Ministers Council, 1966-67, Atlantic Development Board, 1966-68, U.S. Embassy, 1967, government of Canada, 1967-68, government of Yukon Territory, 1967-68 and 1972, Federal Ministry of Transportation, Ottawa, 1971-72, and National Capital Commission, 1972; special consultant, African Development Bank, 1969, and St. Lawrence Seaway Authority, 1969; director of a study on the St. Lawrence Seaway for Canadian Department of Transportation, 1969-71. *Military service:* Royal Canadian Air Force, 1940-45; became flying officer. *Member:* American Economic Association, American Men of Science, Canadian Economic Association, Canadian Political Science Association.

*WRITINGS:* (With F. W. Anderson) *The Yukon Economy, Its Potential for Growth and Continuity*, Queen's Printer, 1968; *The Seaway in Canada's Transportation: An Economic Analysis*, Queen's Printer, 1970; *Recovering Canada's Nationhood*, Carr Publishing Company, 1971.†

\*    \*    \*

## CARRISON, Daniel J.    1917-

*PERSONAL:* Born January 20, 1917, in Camden, S.C.; son of Henry George (a banker) and Phyllis (Hickson) Carrison; married Aurela Wisniewski, August 4, 1941; children: Lore (Mrs. Fred Sachs), Daniel J., Jr., Everest. *Education:* U.S. Naval Academy, B.S., 1939; Stanford University, M.A., 1950; National War College, Graduate, 1959. *Politics:* Republican. *Religion:* Episcopal. *Home:* 210 Briarcliffe, Myrtle Beach, S.C. 29577. *Office:* Federal Consultants, Inc., 1627 Eye St. N.W., Washington, D.C. 20006.

*CAREER:* U.S. Navy, 1939-66; became captain. Planning Research Corp., Washington, D.C., director of Marine Systems Division, 1966-68; Westwood Research, Inc., Washington, D.C., director of Washington operations, 1968-69; Office of U.S. Senator Strom Thurmond, Washington, D.C., administrative assistant, 1970-74; Federal Consultants, Inc., Washington, D.C., president, 1974—. *Member:* American Society of Naval Engineers, International Oceanographic Foundation, U.S. Navy League, U.S. Naval Institute. *Awards, honors*—Military: Two Bronze Stars, Presidential Unit Commendation, World War II Pacific campaign ribbons, Korea campaign ribbons.

*WRITINGS: The Navy from Wood to Steel*, F. Watts, 1965; *Christopher Columbus*, F. Watts, 1967; *Captain James Cook*, F. Watts, 1967; *George Washington*, F. Watts, 1968; *The U.S. Navy*, Praeger, 1968. Contributor of about twenty articles to *Parent's Magazine*, *Outdoor Life*, *American Mercury*, *Outdoor West*, and naval journals.

*WORK IN PROGRESS:* An historical account of a rice planter (author's great-grandfather) in the low country of South Carolina.

\*    \*    \*

## CARROLL, John M(elvin)    1928-

*PERSONAL:* Born March 4, 1928, in Bryan, Tex.; son of Lester N. (a regular officer, U.S. Army) and Mary (Leonard) Carroll. *Education:* University of Texas, B.A., 1951. *Residence:* Bryan, Tex.

*MEMBER:* Western History Association, Westerners.

*WRITINGS: American Indian Posters*, Class National Publishing, 1970; (editor) *The American Indian* (reprint of an old magazine), Liveright, 1970; *Buffalo Soldiers West*, Old Army Press, 1971; (editor) *The Black Military Experience in the American West*, Liveright, 1971; (editor) *Grand Duke Alexis in the U.S.A.*, Interland, 1972; (editor) *American Indian Treaty Book*, Interland, 1972; *Harold Von Schmidt, the Complete Illustrator*, Old Army Press, 1973; *Roll Call on the Little Big Horn*, Old Army Press, 1974; *Custer in Periodicals: A Bibliographic Checklist*, Old Army Press, 1974; *The Benteen-Goldin Letters on Custer and His Last Battle*, Liveright, 1974; *The Two Battles of the Little Big Horn*, Liveright, 1974; *Eggenhofer: The Pulp Years*, Old Army Press, 1975; *Custer in Texas*, Liveright, 1975; (editor) *Custer in the Civil War: His Unfinished Memoirs*, Presidio Press, 1978; (editor) *General Custer and the Battle of the Little Big Horn: The Federal View*, Presidio Press, 1978.

Also author of *The Papers of the Order of Indian Wars*, Old Army Press, *Four on Custer*, Guidon Press, and *The Life and Death of Crazy Horse: The Hinman Interviews*, Garry Owen Press. Editor of *The Indian Removals*, five volumes, AMS Press, *Annual Reports of the Bureau of Indian Affairs, 1824-1848*, twelve volumes, AMS Press, and *The Red Man Magazine*, eight volumes, Johnson Reprint. Editor of numerous reprints for Sol Lewis Books.

*WORK IN PROGRESS:* Editing, for Presidio Press, *Military Record of Civilian Appointments in U.S. Army*, two volumes, *Notes Illustrating the Military Geography of the U.S.*, *Four Brothers in Blue*, *Custer Genealogies*, *Fort Reno*, and *The Old Sergeant's Story*.

\* \* \*

## CARROLL, Kenneth Lane 1924-

*PERSONAL:* Born 1924, in Easton, Md.; son of Albert Raymond and M. Ethel (Lane) Carroll. *Education:* Duke University, A.B., 1946, B.D., 1949, Ph.D., 1953. *Politics:* Independent. *Religion:* Society of Friends (Quaker). *Office:* Department of Religious Studies, Southern Methodist University, Box 202, Dallas, Tex. 75222.

*CAREER:* Southern Methodist University, Dallas, Tex., instructor, 1952-53, assistant professor, 1953-56, associate professor, 1956-60, professor of religious studies, 1960—. Lecturer, Pendle Hill, 1956; T. Wistar Brown fellow, Haverford College, 1969-70. Member of regional executive committee, American Friends Service Committee, 1961-70; member of Friends World Committee and Friends General Conference. Has attended International New Testament Conference and Anglo-American Historical Conference. *Member:* Society of Biblical Literature (life member), Friends Historical Association, Friends Historical Society (England), Maryland Historical Society, Blue Key, Phi Beta Kappa.

*WRITINGS: Joseph Nichols and the Nicholites*, Easton Publishing, 1962; (editor) *Creative Center of Quakerism*, Friends World Committee (England), 1965; *Quakerism on the Eastern Shore*, Maryland Historical Society, 1970; *John Perrot: Early Quaker Schismatic*, Friends Historical Society (London), 1971. Contributor of more than fifty articles to history and religion journals.

*WORK IN PROGRESS:* Several books and monographs on early Quaker history and on New Testament studies.

*SIDELIGHTS:* Kenneth Carroll has traveled in Europe, Asia, Africa, Australia, New Zealand, and the South Pacific.

\* \* \*

## CARTER, Frances Monet 1923-
### (Frances Monet Carter Evans)

*PERSONAL:* Born August 6, 1923, in Mayfield, Ky.; daughter of Orlando Lee and Hattie Lois (Buckingham) Carter; married Carl Gwin Baker, January 26, 1946; married second husband, Donald Louis Matthies, July 24, 1954; married third husband, Henry Herman Evans, June 7, 1963 (divorced, 1972). *Education:* Louisville General Hospital School of Nursing, R.N., 1944; University of Minnesota, certificate in advanced psychiatric nursing instruction, 1945; University of California, Los Angeles, B.S., 1948; San Francisco State College (now University), M.A., 1957. *Home:* 55 Conrad St., San Francisco, Calif. 94131. *Office:* School of Nursing, University of San Francisco, San Francisco, Calif. 94117.

*CAREER:* Teacher of psychiatric nursing in service agencies; University of San Francisco, School of Nursing, San Francisco, Calif., professor of psychiatric nursing, 1957—. Consultant to School of Nursing at Gustavus Adolphus College and Indiana University; member of advisory board, Community Mental Health Services of the City and County of San Francisco. *Member:* American Nurses Association, American Association of University Professors, National Association for Mental Health, International Association of Social Psychiatry, National League for Nursing, American Red Cross, American Association for Social Psychiatry, San Francisco Museum of Art, San Francisco Symphony Association, Louisville General Hospital School of Nursing Alumni, University of California, Los Angeles School of Nursing Alumni, Sigma Theta Tau. *Awards, honors:* World Health Organization fellow, 1961-62, 1970; distinguished teaching award, University of San Francisco, 1972.

*WRITINGS:* (Under name Frances Monet Carter Evans) *The Role of the Nurse in Community Mental Health*, Macmillan, 1968; (under name Frances Monet Carter Evans) *Psychosocial Nursing: Theory and Practice in Community Mental Health*, Macmillan, 1971, 2nd edition, 1976. Contributor to nursing journals.

*AVOCATIONAL INTERESTS:* Opera, chamber music, cats, sculpture, painting, plants.

\* \* \*

## CARTER, Frances Tunnell

*PERSONAL:* Born in Springville, Miss.; daughter of David Atmond and Mary Annie (McCutcheon) Tunnell; married John T. Carter (a professor), March 16, 1946; children: John Wayne, Frankye Nell. *Education:* Wood Junior College, A.A., 1942; attended Blue Mountain College, 1942; University of Southern Mississippi, B.S., 1946; University of Tennessee, M.S., 1948; University of Illinois, Ed.D., 1954; postdoctoral study at Ursuline College, 1961, Dayton University, 1963, Samford University, 1975-76, and University of Alabama in Birmingham, 1976-77. *Politics:* Republican. *Religion:* Baptist. *Home:* 2561 Rocky Ridge Rd., Birmingham, Ala. 35243. *Office:* School of Education, Samford University, Birmingham, Ala. 35209.

*CAREER:* Elementary school teacher in Thaxton, Miss., 1942-43, and Cumberland, Miss., 1943-44; home economics teacher in high schools in Randolph, Miss., 1944-45, and Maben, Miss., 1946-47; Wood Junior College, Mathison, Miss., professor of home economics, 1948; East Central Junior College, Decatur, Miss., professor of home economics and chairman of department, 1948-49; Clarke Memorial College, Newton, Miss., professor of home economics, 1950-56; Samford University, Birmingham, Ala., assistant professor, 1956-57, associate professor, 1957-63, professor of education, 1963—. Visiting professor, Hong Kong Baptist College, 1966. Member of Governor's Committee on Status of Women, 1964-68; member of advisory board, National Dairy Council of Greater Birmingham, 1966-72. Civil Air Patrol, lieutenant colonel, director of senior member training for State of Alabama, and Information Officer of Alabama Wing, 1975—.

*MEMBER:* American Association of University Women (second vice-president), National League of American Penwomen (local president, 1968-69, 1976-78), Association for Childhood Education International (local advisor, 1965—; state president, 1970-72), International Council on Education for Teachers, Daughters of the American Revolution (corresponding secretary, 1976-78), Kappa Delta Epsilon (national vice-president, 1966-70), Alpha Delta Kappa (local president; state historian), Kappa Delta Pi (local co-sponsor). *Awards, honors:* American Red Cross special service award, 1963; visiting professor award, Hong Kong Baptist College, 1966; honored guest at Honors Convocation, University of Alabama in Birmingham, 1977; selected as Birmingham's Woman of the Year, 1977, for civic activities.

*WRITINGS*—Juvenile, except as indicated: *Sammy in the Country,* Baptist Home Mission Board, 1959; *'Tween-Age Ambassador,* Convention Press, 1970; (with husband, John T. Carter) *Sharing Times Seven,* Baptist Home Mission Board, 1971; *Ching Fu and Jim,* Women's Missionary Union, 1977; *Principles of Early Childhood Education* (textbook), Workshops, Inc., 1977. Also author of six curriculum units and a song. Contributor of about twenty poems and forty-five articles to magazines.

*WORK IN PROGRESS:* A high school textbook, *Psychology in Today's World,* with husband John T. Carter; revision and expansion of *Principles of Early Childhood Education.*

*SIDELIGHTS:* Frances Tunnell Carter writes: "What a joy it is to write and to be published! Having never written before the ordeal of writing a dissertation in 1954, I have learned *much* since that time! Most of my writing has been by consignment and has been to promote my Baptist denominations' teachings for preschoolers and school-age youth. Likewise, four of my five books were for age-groups. I have been able to write several articles and one book for adults that have been quite a challenging opportunity—an opportunity as a Christian for which I am most thankful. Additionally, I realize the *responsibility* of writing for the large number of readers in the Baptist denomination."

\* \* \*

## CARTER, Hugh  1895-

*PERSONAL:* Born April 5, 1895, in San Antonio, Tex.; son of David Wendel and Cornelia (Keith) Carter; married Isabel Gordon (a consultant in social research), June 22, 1925; children: Eleanor Jean (Mrs. Charles W. Brome), Janet Gordon (Mrs. Frank Hannigan). *Education:* Southwestern University, Georgetown, Tex., A.B., 1916; University of Minnesota, M.A., 1922; Columbia University, Ph.D., 1927. *Politics:* Liberal Democrat. *Religion:* Humanist. *Home and office:* 2039 New Hampshire Ave. N.W., Washington, D.C. 20009.

*CAREER:* University of Pennsylvania, Philadelphia, instructor, 1924-31, assistant professor of sociology, 1932-45; Immigration and Naturalization Service, Washington, D.C., statistician, 1945-52; U.S. Department of Health, Education and Welfare, Washington, D.C., chief of marriage and divorce statistics, 1952-65; writer and consultant, 1966—. Visiting professor, Purdue University, 1966. *Military service:* U.S. Army, 1917-19; became second lieutenant. *Member:* American Sociological Association, Population Association (secretary-treasurer, 1953-56; vice-president, 1957), International Population Union, Society for Study of Social Biology, District of Columbia Sociological Society (president, 1959-60).

*WRITINGS: Social Theories of L. T. Hobhouse,* University of North Carolina Press, 1927, reprinted, 1968; (with Paul C. Glick) *Marriage and Divorce: A Social and Economic Study,* Harvard University Press, 1970, revised edition, 1976. Contributor of articles to *New York Times Magazine* and professional journals.

*WORK IN PROGRESS:* Research in marriage, family and divorce.

\* \* \*

## CASMIR, Fred L.  1928-

*PERSONAL:* Born December 30, 1928, in Berlin, Germany; naturalized U.S. citizen; son of Arthur and Gertrude (Wolter) Casmir; married Marjorie M. Rogers, 1952; children: Karen-Anne, Fred Otis. *Education:* David Lipscomb College, B.A., 1950; Ohio State University, M.A., 1955, Ph.D., 1961. *Office:* Division of Communication, Pepperdine University, Malibu Campus, 24255 Pacific Coast Hwy., Malibu, Calif. 90265.

*CAREER:* Minister, Church of Christ; ministerial work in Heppenheim, Germany, 1950-54, Columbus, Ohio, 1954-56, West Los Angeles, Calif., 1956-61, Crescenta-Canada, Calif., 1965-68, and Monrovia, Calif., 1969—; Pepperdine University, Los Angeles, Calif., assistant professor, 1957-62, associate professor, 1962-70, professor of communication at Malibu Campus, 1970—, university marshall, 1958—. Part-time faculty member at California State University, Northridge, 1961-73, and East Los Angeles College, 1973-74. Lecturer in adult education programs in Germany, 1965-66, and at University of Heidelberg, 1966, University of Tuebingen, University of Cologne, and University of Landau, 1976. Thirty-first Congressional District of California, Republican nominee for U.S. House of Representatives, 1970, Republican Central Committee, chairman, 1970-72, treasurer, 1971-72. National Education Institute, president, 1972, consultant, 1972-74; management consultant, 1975—.

*MEMBER:* Speech Communication Association, International Society of Phonetics, American Association of University Professors (president of Pepperdine University chapter, 1961-62), Western Speech Communication Association, Deutsche Gesellschaft fuer Sprechkunde, Communication Association of the Pacific (honorary director), California Speech Association, California College and University Faculty Association, Southern California Council on Literature for Children and Young People, Pi Kappa Delta. *Awards, honors:* Outstanding Teacher Award, Pepperdine University, Malibu Campus, 1973.

*WRITINGS:* (With others) *Sprache und Sprechen,* Deutsche Gesellschaft fuer Sprechkunde, Volume II, 1965, Volume III, 1972; (editor with L. S. Harms) *International Studies of National Speech Education Systems,* Burgess, Volume I, 1970; *Interaction: An Introduction to Speech Communication,* C. E. Merrill, 1974. Contributor to speech and religion journals. Founding editor, *International and Intercultural Communication Annual,* 1973-76.

\* \* \*

## CASPER, Henry W.  1909-

*PERSONAL:* Born August 3, 1909, in Milwaukee, Wis.; son of John Bernard and Elinor (Weber) Casper. *Education:* Attended St. Stanislaus Seminary, 1927-31; St. Louis University, A.B., 1932, M.A., 1935; St. Mary's College, St. Marys, Kan., S.T.L., 1941; Catholic University of America, Ph.D., 1945. *Politics:* Independent. *Home:* 1404 West Wisconsin Ave., Milwaukee, Wis. 53233.

*CAREER:* Entered Society of Jesus (Jesuits), 1927, ordained Roman Catholic priest, 1940; Regis College, Denver, Colo., instructor in history, 1935-37; Creighton University, Omaha, Neb., assistant professor, 1945-53, associate professor, 1953-62, professor of history, 1962-63, dean of graduate school, 1946-54; Marquette University, Milwaukee, Wis., professor of history, 1964-74, professor emeritus, 1974—. Archivist, Omaha Archdiocese, Omaha, Neb., 1954-63. *Member:* American Historical Association, Catholic Historical Association, Wisconsin State Historical Society, Alpha Sigma Nu, Pi Gamma Mu.

*WRITINGS: American Attitudes toward the Rise of Napoleon III,* Catholic University of America Press, 1947; *The Church on the Northern Plains,* Bruce, 1960; *The Church on the Fading Frontier,* Bruce, 1967; *Catholic Chapters in Nebraska Immigration,* Bruce, 1967.

*WORK IN PROGRESS:* A book on the Hungarian revolution, 1848.

\* \* \*

## CASSEL, Russell N. 1911-

*PERSONAL:* Born December 18, 1911, in Harrisburg, Pa.; son of Herman I. (a contractor) and Sallie A. (Hummer) Cassel; married, 1951; married second wife, Lan Mieu Dam (a psychologist), October 5, 1964; children: (first marriage) Louis A., Angelica V. (Mrs. Anthony Fazio), Gary R., Lynn M., Gail J.; (second marriage) Sallie M., Susie L. *Education:* State Teachers College (now Millersville State College), B.S., 1937; Pennsylvania State University, M.Ed., 1939; University of Southern California, Ed.D., 1949. *Politics:* Republican. *Religion:* Lutheran. *Home:* 1362 Santa Cruz Ct., Chula Vista, Calif. 92010. *Office:* Office of the Vice-President, Soares University, San Diego, Calif.

*CAREER:* Teacher and psychologist in junior high school in Dauphin Borough, Pa., 1935-40; San Diego State College (now University), San Diego, Calif., associate professor of educational psychology, 1949-51; Lompoc Unified Schools, Lompoc, Calif., director of pupil personnel services, 1957-61; U.S. Department of State, research psychologist in psychological measurement in Vietnam and Liberia, 1961-67; University of Wisconsin—Milwaukee, professor of educational psychology, 1967-74; Project Innovation, Chula Vista, Calif., editor, 1974-77; Soares University, San Diego, Calif., vice-president, 1977—. *Military service:* U.S. Army, overseas research psychologist, 1940-46. U.S. Air Force, research psychologist, 1951-57. U.S. Air Force Reserve, 1957-68; became colonel.

*MEMBER:* American Psychological Association (fellow), American Educational Research Association, American Association of Correctional Psychologists (vice-president, 1954-55; president, 1955-56), American Association for the Advancement of Science, National Commission for Measurement in Education.

*WRITINGS: The Psychology of Child Discipline,* C. A. Gregory Co., 1955; *The Psychology of Instruction,* Christopher, 1957; *UWM FORTRAN Measurements Programs,* Psychologists and Educators Press, 1970; *Drug Abuse Education,* Christopher, 1971. Also author of about twenty-five psychological tests. Contributor of more than three hundred articles to professional journals. Editor, *Air Force Instructors Journal,* 1952-55, *Education,* 1969, *College Student Journal,* 1969—, and "Air Force Counselor Notes on Space Age Education."

\* \* \*

## CASSELL, Frank Hyde 1916-

*PERSONAL:* Born October 12, 1916, in Chicago, Ill.; son of Frank V. (an actor) and Alicia (Robinson) Seymour; married Marguerite Ellen Fletcher, April 24, 1940; children:

Frank Allan, Thomas W., Christopher B. *Education:* Wabash College, A.B., 1939; University of Chicago, graduate study, 1947-48. *Politics:* Democrat. *Religion:* Protestant. *Home:* 128 Church Rd., Winnetka, Ill. 60093. *Office:* Department of Industrial Relations, Northwestern University, 2001 Sheridan Rd., Evanston, Ill. 60201.

*CAREER:* Inland Steel, Chicago, Ill., assistant vice-president, 1948-68, vice-president of Inland-Ryerson Foundation, 1964-68; Northwestern University, Evanston, Ill., professor of industrial relations policy, 1968—. Chairman, Governor's Commission on Unemployment, 1961-63; director, U.S. Employment Service, 1966-68; president, Community Renewal Society (Chicago), 1968-69. Member of board of directors, Chicago Urban League; member of Mayor's Committee on Manpower and Economic Development (Chicago); consultant to government and business. *Military service:* U.S. Army, 1941-43. *Member:* Industrial Relations Research Association (member of board of directors, 1966-70), American Economic Association, National Assembly for Social Policy (member of board of directors), Lincoln Academy (Illinois; rector, 1968—). *Awards, honors:* Distinguished Achievement Award, U.S. Department of Labor, 1967, 1975.

*WRITINGS: The Employment Service,* University of Michigan Press, 1968; (with Arnold Weber and Woodrow Ginsburg) *Public-Private Manpower Policies,* Industrial Relations Research Association, University of Wisconsin, 1969; *Collective Bargaining in the Public Sector,* Grid Publishing, 1976; (contributor) *The Social Welfare Forum, 1977,* Columbia University Press, 1978. Contributor of articles to professional journals.

*WORK IN PROGRESS: International Labor Markets,* for Basic Books.

*SIDELIGHTS:* Frank Cassell writes: "Writing, for me, is the means for expressing my concerns about the human condition. It provides the discipline needed to give form and substance to masses of data and information and to shape the ideas and concepts which emerge into usable means for effective change."

\* \* \*

## CASTELLAN, N(orman) John, Jr. 1939-

*PERSONAL:* Born January 21, 1939, in Denver, Colo.; son of Norman John (a professor) and Mary (Biebl) Castellan; married Diane C. Swift, July 18, 1964; children: Caryn Lynn, Norman John III, Tanya Cecile. *Education:* Stanford University, A.B., 1961; University of Colorado, Ph.D., 1965. *Religion:* Roman Catholic. *Home:* 703 Ravencrest, Bloomington, Ind. 47401. *Office:* Department of Psychology, Indiana University, Bloomington, Ind. 47401.

*CAREER:* Indiana University at Bloomington, assistant professor, 1965-68, associate professor, 1968-74, professor of psychology, 1974—. *Member:* American Psychological Association, American Statistical Association, Association for Computing Machinery, Sigma Xi.

*WRITINGS:* (With K. R. Hammond and J. E. Householder) *Introduction to the Statistical Method,* 2nd edition (Castellan was not associated with first edition) with workbook, Knopf, 1970-71; (co-editor) *Cognitive Theory,* Erlbaum Associates, Volume I, 1975, Volume II, 1977, Volume III, 1978. Contributor of articles to psychology, nursing, statistics, and education journals.

*WORK IN PROGRESS: Human Judgment and Decision Making;* research on human judgment.

## CASTRO, Americo 1885-1972

May 4, 1885—July 26, 1972; Spanish-born American hispanist. Obituaries: *New York Times,* July 27, 1972.

\*      \*      \*

## CATANIA, A(nthony) Charles 1936-

*PERSONAL:* Born June 22, 1936, in New York, N.Y.; son of Charles J. (a pharmacist) and Elizabeth (Lattarulo) Catania; married Constance J. Britt, February 10, 1962; children: William John, Kenneth Charles. *Education:* Columbia College, B.A., 1957; Columbia University, M.A., 1958; Harvard University, Ph.D., 1961. *Home:* 10545 Rivulet Row, Columbia, Md. 21044. *Office:* Department of Psychology, University of Maryland Baltimore County, 5401 Wilkens Ave., Catonsville, Md. 21228.

*CAREER:* Harvard University, Cambridge, Mass., postdoctoral research fellow, 1960-62; Smith, Kline & French, Philadelphia, Pa., senior pharmacologist, 1962-64; New York University, University College of Arts and Science, New York, N.Y., assistant professor, 1964-66, associate professor, 1966-69, professor of psychology, and chair of department, 1969-73; University of Maryland Baltimore County, Catonsville, professor of psychology, 1973—. *Member:* American Association for the Advancement of Science (fellow), American Psychological Association (fellow of divisions 25 and 28; president of division 25, 1976-79). *Awards, honors:* Research grants from National Science Foundation and National Institute of Mental Health.

*WRITINGS:* (Editor) *Contemporary Research in Operant Behavior,* Scott, Foresman, 1968; (editor with T. A. Brigham) *Handbook of Applied Behavior Analysis,* Irvington, 1978; *Learning,* Prentice-Hall, in press. Contributor of chapters to books on psychology and of articles to professional journals. *Journal of the Experimental Analysis of Behavior,* editor, 1966-69, review editor, 1969-76; member of board of editors, *Behaviorism.*

\*      \*      \*

## CAVA, Esther Laden 1916-

*PERSONAL:* Born April 3, 1916, in Duluth, Minn.; daughter of Jacob (a salesman) and Sarah (Sukov) Laden; married Michael P. Cava (a professor of chemistry), June 11, 1951; children: John Michael. *Education:* St. Luke's Hospital School of Nursing, Duluth, R.N., 1937; University of Michigan, B.A. (with distinction), 1951; Boston University, M.A., 1952; Ohio State University, Ph.D., 1967. *Home:* 312 Penn Rd., Wynnewood, Pa. 19096. *Office:* PATH, Inc., 8001 Roosevelt Blvd., Philadelphia, Pa. 19152.

*CAREER:* University of Michigan Hospital, Ann Arbor, staff nurse, 1939-42; worked as secretary in Detroit, Mich., 1945-46, and office nurse in Ypsilanti, Mich., 1947-48; lecturer in child development at Lynn General Hospital, Lynn, Mass., and psychological technician at Massachusetts General Hospital, Boston, 1952-53; owner of book store in Columbus, Ohio, 1955-57; Northeast Guidance Center, Detroit, staff psychologist, 1967-69; Harcum Junior College, Bryn Mawr, Pa., assistant professor of psychology, 1969-70; St. Joseph's College, Philadelphia, Pa., lecturer in psychology, 1970-71; Temple University, Philadelphia, assistant professor of psychology, 1970-71, 1972—; St. Christopher's Hospital for Children, Philadelphia, staff psychologist, 1971—; PATH, Inc., Philadelphia, clinical psychologist, 1974—. Clinical psychologist in private practice. *Military service:* U.S. Army Nurse Corps, 1942-45; became first lieu-

tenant; received battle stars for service in European theater. *Member:* American Psychological Association, Pennsylvania Psychological Association, Phi Beta Kappa, Phi Kappa Phi.

*WRITINGS: The Complete Question-and-Answer Book of Child Training,* Hawthorn, 1972; (contributor) *Textbook of Pediatrics,* 10th edition, Saunders, 1975. Contributor to psychology journals.

*AVOCATIONAL INTERESTS:* Music, drama, literature, civil rights, disarmament, consumer protection, "real attempts at rehabilitating the poor and lawbreakers."

\*      \*      \*

## CAVE, Alfred A. 1935-

*PERSONAL:* Born February 8, 1935, in Albuquerque, N.M.; son of Robert L. (a building contractor) and Jane (Harscher) Cave; married Harriett J. Bennett, 1960 (divorced, 1976); children: Ruth, Larry, Elizabeth, Rachel. *Education:* Linfield College, B.A., 1957; University of Florida, M.A., 1959, Ph.D., 1961. *Politics:* Democrat. *Office:* College of Arts and Sciences, Gilham Hall, University of Toledo, Toledo, Ohio 43606.

*CAREER:* University of Florida, Gainesville, instructor in social science, 1959-61; City College of the City University of New York, New York, N.Y., instructor in history, 1961-62; University of Utah, Salt Lake City, assistant professor, 1962-66, associate professor, 1966-68, professor of history, 1968-73, dean of College of Humanities, 1969-73; University of Toledo, Toledo, Ohio, dean of College of Arts and Sciences, 1973—. *Member:* Phi Beta Kappa, Phi Alpha Phi. *Awards, honors:* National Endowment for the Humanities fellow, summer, 1969.

*WRITINGS: Jacksonian Democracy and the Historians,* University of Florida Press, 1964; *American Civilization: A Documentary History,* W. C. Brown, 1966; *An American Conservative in the Age of Jackson,* Texas Christian University Press, 1969.

*WORK IN PROGRESS:* Research on the image of the Indian in American historical writing.

\*      \*      \*

## CAVERT, Samuel McCrea 1888-1976

*PERSONAL:* Born September 9, 1888, in Charlton, N.Y.; son of Walter I. (a farmer) and Elizabeth (Brann) Cavert; married Ruth Miller, November 14, 1918 (died February 10, 1920); married Twila Lytton, June 28, 1927; children: (first marriage) Mary Ruth (Mrs. Harold A. Ramsey). *Education:* Union College, Schenectady, N.Y., B.A. (summa cum laude), 1910; Columbia University, M.A., 1914; Union Theological Seminary, New York, N.Y., B.D. (summa cum laude), 1915. *Home:* 161 Boulder Trail, Bronxville, N.Y. 10708.

*CAREER:* Ordained Presbyterian minister, 1915; Federal Council of Churches of Christ in America, New York City, associate secretary, 1920, general secretary, 1921-50; National Council of Churches of Christ in the U.S.A., New York City, general secretary, 1951-54; World Council of Churches, New York City, executive secretary, 1954-57. Liaison official between German Evangelical Churches and American Military Government (U.S. Zone, Germany), 1946; member of President Roosevelt's advisory committee on political refugees; World Council of Churches, member of assemblies in Amsterdam, 1948, Evanston, Ill., 1954, New Delhi, India, 1961, and Uppsala, Sweden, 1968; executive director, Interchurch Center (New York City), 1963-64; guest of Vatican Council II, 1964. Honorary trustee, Christian Century Foundation; trustee, Union College, 1938-72; Union Theological Seminary, director, 1937-67, vice-chairman of board, 1948-67. *Military service:* U.S. Army, chaplain, 1918-19; became first lieutenant.

*MEMBER:* Century Club (New York City), Phi Beta Kappa. *Awards, honors:* D.D., Union College, New York City, 1935; LL.D., Ohio Wesleyan University, 1942; D. Theol., University of Goettingen, 1948; D.D., Yale University, 1948; D.D., Princeton University, 1951; L.H.D., American University, 1951; Litt.D., Park College, 1952; D.D., Kalamazoo College, 1956.

*WRITINGS: Securing Christian Leaders for Tomorrow,* George H. Doran Co., 1926; *The Adventure of the Church,* Missionary Education Movement, 1927; (with Henry P. Van Dusen) *The Church Through Half a Century,* Scribner, 1936; (editor) *The Church Faces the World,* Round Table Press, 1939; *On the Road to Christian Unity,* Harper, 1961; (contributor) Edwin T. Dahlberg, editor, *Herald of the Evangel* (festschrift to Jesse Moren Bader), Bethany Press, 1965; *The American Churches in the Ecumenical Movement, 1900-1968,* Association Press, 1968; *Church Cooperation and Unity in America: 1900-1970,* Association Press, 1970. Also editor of *The Church and Industrial Reconstruction,* 1920, *Christian Unity: Its Principles and Possibilities,* 1921, and *The Teaching Work of the Church,* 1923. Contributor of articles to religious journals. Senior editor, *Pulpit Digest,* 1958-68; member of editorial board, *Religion in Life,* beginning 1934.

*WORK IN PROGRESS:* A book on current trends in religious life.

*SIDELIGHTS:* Samuel McCrea Cavert was a lifelong leader of the Protestant ecumenical movement. His books on the history of the movement in America (*The American Churches in the Ecumenical Movement, 1900-1968* and *Church Cooperation and Unity in America, 1900-1970*) are regarded as standard in the field of ecumenical history. In a review in *Christian Century,* Harold E. Fey wrote, "exceptional importance, deriving both from significance of subject matter and from authority of authorship, attaches to this examination . . . of the growing pattern of cooperation . . . of the North American churches." Cavert was a member of the Provisional Committee that brought the World Council of Churches into existence in 1948, and was chairman of the committee on arrangements for its first assembly, in Amsterdam in 1948. He was an invited guest at Vatican Council II in 1964.

*BIOGRAPHICAL/CRITICAL SOURCES: Christian Century,* November 20, 1968, March 3, 1971; *Catholic World,* February, 1969; *Ecumenical Review,* July, 1969; *Church History,* June, 1970; *Theology Today,* October, 1971.†

(Died December 21, 1976)

\*        \*        \*

## CAZDEN, Norman 1914-

*PERSONAL:* Born September 23, 1914, in New York, N.Y.; son of Charles and Elizabeth Cazden; married Courtney Borden, 1946 (divorced, 1972); children: Elizabeth, Joanna. *Education:* Juilliard School of Music, Piano Diploma, 1930, Postgraduate Piano Diploma, 1931, Teacher's Diploma (with honors), 1932, graduate study, 1932-39, Diploma in Composition, 1939; City College (now City Col-

lege of the City University of New York), B.S. (cum laude), 1943; Harvard University, A.M., 1944, Ph.D., 1948. *Home:* 3A Webster Rd., Orono, Me. 04473. *Office:* Department of Music, University of Maine, Orono, Me. 04473.

*CAREER:* Private teacher of piano and theory in New York City, 1928-43, Bridgeport, Conn., 1953-61, and Lexington, Mass., 1961-69; Juilliard School of Music, New York City, instructor in piano, 1934-39; Vassar College, Poughkeepsie, N.Y., assistant professor of music, 1947-48; Peabody Conservatory, Baltimore, Md., teacher of theory, 1948-49; University of Michigan, Ann Arbor, assistant professor of music, 1949-50; University of Illinois at Urbana-Champaign, assistant professor of music, 1950-53; University of Maine, Orono, associate professor, 1969-72, professor of music, 1973—. Lecturer at Vassar College, 1956, and New School for Social Research, 1956-58. Appeared as pianist, 1924-43, with debut recital at Town Hall, New York City, at age of twelve. Music director for Station WLIB, 1942, Humphrey-Weidman Repertory Company, 1942-43, Camp Woodland and Folk Festivals of the Catskill Mountains, 1943-48, 1954-60.

*MEMBER:* American Musicological Society, American Society for Aesthetics, American Society of Composers, Authors and Publishers, College Music Society, Society for Ethnomusicology, Phi Beta Kappa, Pi Kappa Lambda. *Awards, honors:* MacDowell Colony, resident fellow, 1964, 1966, 1969, 1971, 1972, 1974, 1975; Ninth Pedro Paz Award in Musical Composition from Olivet College, 1971.

*WRITINGS: Dances from Woodland,* 2nd edition, privately printed, 1955; *The Abelard Folksong Book,* Abelard, 1958; *A Book of Nonsense Songs,* Crown, 1961; *Merry Ditties,* Bonanza Books, 1973; *A Catskill Songbook,* Purple Mountain Press, 1978.

Co-author of musical portions: Katherine Miller, *Five Plays from Shakespeare,* Houghton, 1964; Edward D. Ives, *Folksongs from Maine,* Northeast Folklore, 1966; Edith Fowke, *Lumbering Songs from the Northern Woods,* University of Texas Press, 1970; Bruce Jackson, *Wake Up, Dead Man,* Harvard University Press, 1972. Composer, with published compositions numbering more than one hundred, including piano solo works, orchestra and stage works, chamber music, and records. Contributor of articles to music and folklore journals.

*WORK IN PROGRESS: The Psychology of Musical Perception;* systemic reference of musical consonance response; a concerto for viola and orchestra.

\*        \*        \*

## CEGIELKA, Francis A(nthony) 1908-

*PERSONAL:* Born March 16, 1908, in Grabow, Poznan, Poland; came to United States in 1948, naturalized in 1954; son of Martin (an exporter) and Maryann (Nieszczesna) Cegielka. *Education:* Finished college and philosophy studies in Wadowice, Poland, 1927; Pontifical Gregorian University, Rome, Italy, Th.B., 1928, B.C.L. (canon law), 1929, Th.L., 1929, Th.D., 1931. *Home:* 303 Goundry St., North Tonawanda, N.Y. 14120.

*CAREER:* Entered Society of the Catholic Apostolate (Pallottines), 1926, ordained Roman Catholic priest, 1931; chaplain of Polish Catholic Mission, Caen, France, 1931-32; Minor Seminary, Society of the Catholic Apostolate, Chelmno, Poland, teacher, 1932-34; Major Seminary, Society of the Catholic Apostolate, Wadowice, Poland, instructor, 1934-36; director of Polish Catholic Mission in

Paris, France, 1937-47 (spent part of this period as German prisoner in concentration camps at Sachsenhausen and Dachau; returned to France after liberation by U.S. 7th Army); lecturer and retreat master in United States, Europe, and Africa, 1948-67; Felician College, Lodi, N.J., professor of theology and chairman of department, 1967-71; Holy Family College, Philadelphia, Pa., professor of theology and chairman of religious studies department, 1971-76. Conductor of workshops and retreats. *Member:* American Association of University Professors, Polish Institute of Arts and Sciences in America. *Awards, honors:* Legion d'Honneur for wartime work in France, 1946; Outstanding Educator of America Award, Holy Family College, 1972, 1974-1975.

*WRITINGS: Wynagrodzicielska Mistyka Nazaretu*, Sisters of the Holy Family of Nazareth (Philadelphia), 1951, translation published as *Reparatory Mysticism of Nazareth*, Sisters of the Holy Family of Nazareth, 1951; *The Pierced Heart: The Life of Mother Mary Angela Truszkowska, Foundress of the Congregation of the Sisters of St. Felix*, Bruce, 1955; *Life on the Rocks: Among the Natives of the Union of South Africa*, Pallottinum, 1957; *In the Service of Redemption: Religious Life a Living Mass*, Pallottinum, 1959; *Spiritual Theology for Novices*, Immaculate Conception College, 1961; *Segregavit nos Dominus*, Bruce, 1963; *Duchowosc 'Nazaretu,'* Sisters of the Holy Family of Nazareth (Rome), 1963, translation by Sister Mary Theophame and Mother Mary Laurence published as *"Nazareth" Spirituality*, Bruce, 1966; *Three Hearts: Felician Meditations*, Bruce, Volume I, 1963, Volume II, 1964; *All Things New: Radical Reform and the Religious Life*, Sheed, 1969; *Handbook of Ecclesiology and Christology*, Alba, 1971. Also author of *Toward a New Spring of Humankind*.

Books published only in Polish: *Szlakiem Tulaczy*, Dom Prasy (Warsaw), 1934; *Pallotyni w Polsce*, Wydawnictwo Ksiezy Pallotynow, 1935; *Dobra Matka*, Dom Prasy, 1939; *Mistyka Ojczyzny*, Wydanictwo Gimnazjum Polskiego w Chevilly (France), 1946; *Apel Milosci* (translation of *Un Appel a l'amour*), Felicjana (Buffalo), 1949; *Oblubienica Chrystusa w slubzie Odkupienia*, Felicjana, 1951; *Msza swieta szkola zycia zakonnego*, Felicjana, 1953; *Zycie Ukryte 'Nazaretu,'* Sisters of the Holy Family of Nazareth, 1954; *Siostra Faustyna, Szafarka Milosierdzia Bozego*, Pallottinum, 1954, 2nd edition, 1958.

*SIDELIGHTS:* Francis Cegielka is competent in six languages—Polish, German, French, Italian, English, and Latin. He conducted retreats in Africa, 1955-56, 1960-61, visited Palestine, 1956, 1970, and Pakistan, India, Thailand, and Japan, 1970.

\*　　\*　　\*

## CHANDOLA, Anoop C. 1937-

*PERSONAL:* Born December 24, 1937, in Rawatgaon, Pauri, India; son of Satya Prasad and Kishori (Ghildiyal) Chandola; married July 14, 1963; wife's name Sudha; children: Manjul (son). *Education:* Allahabad University, B.A., 1954; Lucknow University, M.A. (Hindi literature), 1956; University of California, Berkeley, M.A. (linguistics), 1961; University of Chicago, Ph.D., 1966. *Politics:* "Philosophy of Mahatma Gandhi." *Religion:* Hindu. *Home:* 50 South Padilla Pl., Tucson, Ariz. 85705. *Office:* Department of Oriental Studies, University of Arizona, Tucson, Ariz. 85721.

*CAREER:* Sardar Vallabh Bhai Vidyapeeth University, Vallabh Vidyanagar, India, tutor, 1956-57, lecturer in Hindi, 1957-58; Maharaja Sayajirao University of Baroda, Baroda, India, lecturer in Hindi literature, 1958-59; University of

Arizona, Tucson, assistant professor, 1963-66, associate professor, 1967-71, professor of linguistics, Hindi, and Sanskrit, 1971—. Visiting summer assistant or associate professor at University of Wisconsin, 1965, University of California, Berkeley, 1967, 1968, and University of Washington, Seattle, 1969, 1970. *Member:* Linguistic Society of America, Linguistic Society of India, Association for Asian Studies (member of literature and language development committee of South Asia Regional Council, 1972—).

*WRITINGS:* (With Norman Zide, Collins Masica, and K. C. Bahl) *A Premchand Reader*, East-West Center, 1965; (contributor) F. Robert Paulsen, editor, *Changing Dimensions in International Education*, University of Arizona Press, 1969; *A Systematic Translation of Hindi-Urdu into English*, University of Arizona Press, 1970; *Folk Drumming in the Himalayas: A Linguistic Approach to Music*, AMS Press, 1977. Contributor of short stories, articles, and reviews in English and Hindi to journals in the United States and India.

*WORK IN PROGRESS: Situation to Sentence*, for AMS Press; *Mystic and Love poetry of Medieval Hindi*, for Today's and Tomorrow's Publishers (New Delhi).

\*　　\*　　\*

## CHAPIN, June Roediger 1931-

*PERSONAL:* Born May 19, 1931, in Chicago, Ill.; daughter of Henry W. and Stephanie (Palke) Roediger; married Ned Chapin (an author and a consultant), June 12, 1954; children: Suzanne, Elaine. *Education:* University of Chicago, B.A., 1952, M.A., 1954; Stanford University, Ed.D., 1963. *Home:* 1190 Bellair Way, Menlo Park, Calif. 94025. *Office:* Education Department, College of Notre Dame, Belmont, Calif. 94002.

*CAREER:* San Francisco State College (now University), San Francisco, Calif., part-time instructor, 1963-65; University of Santa Clara, Santa Clara, Calif., assistant professor, 1965-67; College of Notre Dame, Belmont, Calif., associate professor of education, 1967—. *Member:* National Council for the Social Studies, American Sociological Association, American Educational Research Association, American Association of University Professors, Pi Lambda Theta.

*WRITINGS:* (With Richard Gross and Raymond McHugh) *Quest for Liberty*, Field Educational Publications, 1971; (with Jan Allerman) *Voices of a Nation*, Field Educational Publications, 1972; (with Gross and Margaret S. Branson) *Teaching Social Studies Skills*, Little, Brown, 1973; (with Branson) *Women: The Majority-Minority*, Houghton, 1973.

*AVOCATIONAL INTERESTS:* Stamp collecting.

\*　　\*　　\*

## CHAPIN, William 1918-

*PERSONAL:* Born December 17, 1918, in Proctor, Vt.; son of Edward Eaton (a sugar refiner) and Miriam (Hitchcock) Chapin; married Eleanor O'Hara, June 18, 1941; children: Mark, Pennell Chapin Eakle. *Education:* Dartmouth College, B.A., 1940; additional study at Massachusetts Institute of Technology, 1942. *Politics:* Independent radical. *Home:* 16 Cazneau Ave., Sausalito, Calif. 94965. *Agent:* Joan Daves, 515 Madison Ave., New York, N.Y. 10022. *Office:* Journalism Department, San Francisco State University, San Francisco, Calif. 94132.

*CAREER: San Francisco Chronicle*, San Francisco, Calif., editor, 1952-65, reporter, 1965-69; San Francisco State University, San Francisco, 1970—, began as assistant professor, currently associate professor of journalism. *Military service:* U.S. Army Air Forces, 1942-46; served as meteorologist and bomber pilot in World War II, flying thirty-four missions in Europe; retired on disability as a captain. *Member:* Sigma Delta Chi.

*WRITINGS:* (With Alvin Hyman and Jon Carroll) *The Suburbs of San Francisco,* Chronicle Books, 1969; *Wasted,* McGraw-Hill, 1972. Also author of guidebook on newspaper editing and reporting. Wrote a daily sports column for *San Francisco Chronicle,* 1965 and 1966.

*AVOCATIONAL INTERESTS:* Carpentry, chess.

\* \* \*

## CHAPMAN, Elwood N. 1916-

*PERSONAL:* Born July 21, 1916, in Butte, Mont.; son of Archiebald and Laura (Shovel) Chapman; married Martha T. Tiller, August 14, 1941; children: William Norman, Thomas Knight. *Education:* University of California, Berkeley, B.S., 1939; Claremont College (now Claremont Graduate School), M.A., 1950. *Politics:* Republican. *Home:* 210 West Sixth St., Ontario, Calif. *Office:* Department of Business, Chaffey College, Alta Loma, Calif. 91761.

*CAREER:* Chaffey College, Alta Loma, Calif., instructor, 1950-51, assistant professor, 1952-54, associate professor, 1954-55, professor of business, 1955—. Management consultant and lecturer; has given talk, "Your Attitude Is Showing" more than eight hundred times. *Military service:* U.S. Army, 1940-45; became major; received Legion of Merit.

*WRITINGS: Your Attitude Is Showing,* Science Research Associates, 1964, 3rd edition, 1977; *Your Attitude Is Changing,* Science Research Associates, 1966; *So You're a College Freshman?,* Science Research Associates, 1968; *Supervisor's Survival Kit,* Science Research Associates, 1969; *Career Games,* Educational Development Corp., 1970; *Big Business: A Positive View,* Prentice-Hall, 1972; *College Survival,* Science Research Associates, 1974; *Career Search,* Science Research Associates, 1976.

*WORK IN PROGRESS: Career Success,* for Science Research Associates.

\* \* \*

## CHARANIS, Peter 1908-

*PERSONAL:* Born August 15, 1908, in Lemnos, Greece; son of George and Chrysanthe (Stroutmtsus) Charanis; married Madeline Schiltz, August 5, 1939; children: Alexandra, Anthony G. *Education:* Rutgers University, B.A., 1931; University of Wisconsin, Ph.D., 1935; University of Brussels, postdoctoral study, 1936-38. *Politics:* Democrat. *Religion:* Greek Orthodox. *Home:* 105 North Seventh Ave., Highland Park, N.J. 08904. *Office:* Bishop House, Rutgers University, New Brunswick, N.J. 08903.

*CAREER:* Rutgers University, New Brunswick, N.J., instructor, 1938-41, assistant professor, 1941-46, associate professor, 1946-49, professor, 1949-63, Voorhees Professor of History, 1963-76, professor emeritus, 1976—. Visiting professor, University of Wisconsin, 1950-51; Dumbarton Oaks, visiting scholar, 1956-57, honorary associate of Dumbarton Oaks Research Library and Collection; former member of New Jersey Regional Committee for Prevention of Heart Disease. *Member:* Mediaeval Academy of America, American Historical Association, Society of Church History, Phi Beta Kappa. *Awards, honors:* Guggenheim fellow, 1956-57; Royal Order of the Phoenix bestowed by King of Greece, 1969; Doctorate honoris causa, University of Thessalonica, 1972.

*WRITINGS: Church and State in the Later Roman Empire: The Religious Policy of Anastasius the First,* University of Wisconsin Press, 1939; *Studies on the Demography of the Byzantine Empire: A Collection,* Variorum Reprints, 1972; *Social, Economic, and Political Life in the Byzantine Empire: Collected Studies,* Variorum Reprints, 1973. Contributor of articles and reviews to scholarly journals.

*WORK IN PROGRESS:* A book on the social structure of the Byzantine Empire.

*AVOCATIONAL INTERESTS:* Gardening.

\* \* \*

## CHARLES, Sascha 1896(?)-1972

1896(?)—August 28, 1972; Russian-born American author, playwright, and translator. Obituaries: *New York Times,* August 28, 1972.

\* \* \*

## CHARLIER, Patricia (Mary) Simonet 1923-

*PERSONAL:* Born July 12, 1923, in Enderlin, N.D.; daughter of John Jerome (a vice-president of Soo Railroad) and Sophia Cecelia (Krueger) Simonet; married Roger Henri Charlier (a professor of geology, geography, and oceanography at Northeastern Illinois University), June 17, 1958; children: Constance Cecelia-Paula, Jean-Armand Leonard. *Education:* University of Minnesota, B.S., 1944, M.A., 1958, Ph.D., 1960; University of Bordeaux, D.Psy., 1973; also attended College of St. Scholastica, 1941-43, University of Aix-Marseilles, summer, 1958, University of Paris, 1958-59, and University of Bordeaux, 1971-73. *Home:* 4055 North Keystone Ave., Chicago, Ill. 60641. *Agent:* Daniel S. Mead, 915 Broadway, New York, N.Y. 10010. *Office:* College of Education, University of Illinois at Chicago Circle, P.O. Box 4348, Chicago, Ill. 60680.

*CAREER:* High school teacher and librarian in Minnesota, 1944-47, and high school principal, 1949-56; University of Minnesota, Minneapolis, instructor and assistant principal, University High School, 1956-58, 1959-60; Parsons College, Fairfield, Iowa, associate professor of education and psychology and chairman of department of secondary education, 1960-61; Chicago Teachers College (now Chicago State University), Chicago, Ill., associate professor of education and psychology, 1961-64; Loyola University, Chicago, visiting professor, 1964-65; University of Illinois at Chicago Circle, associate professor of education and psychology, 1965—, head of department of curriculum, instruction, and evaluation, 1974-77. Visiting summer professor at Western New Mexico University, 1963-66, National Center for Marine Research, Constantza, Rumania, 1970, and University of Bordeaux, 1971-73. Director, Educational Travel Projects, 1954—. Lecturer, U.S. Information Service, 1971—.

*MEMBER:* National Education Association, National Council of Teachers of English, Association for the Education of Teachers of Science, Association for Supervision and Curriculum Development, American Association for Higher Education (charter member), National Association of Secondary School Principals, American Association of University Professors, Comparative Education Society, American Association for the Advancement of Science, Association Francophone pour l'Education Comparee, Chicago Psychological Association, Phi Kappa Phi. *Awards, honors:* International Research and Exchange Committee grant, 1970; Silver Medal of Arts, Sciences, Letters (France), 1972;

Chevalier de l'Ordre des Palmes Academiques, 1972; French Government grant, 1972-73; Pro Mundi Beneficio, Brazil, 1975.

*WRITINGS:* (Co-author) *American Academe, Educational Travel, and Study Abroad,* Chicago Teachers College North, 1964; (contributor) Roger H. Charlier, editor, *Geography of the USSR,* Northeastern Illinois University, 1967; (editor with husband, Roger H. Charlier, and John J. Karpeck) *The World around Us: A Book of Readings,* MSS Educational Publishing, 1970; *Matching Curriculum, Instruction, and Evaluation,* College of Education, University of Illinois, 1977. Contributor of more than forty articles to professional journals.

*WORK IN PROGRESS:* A book on contemporary French psychologists, with emphasis on Alain, Chateau, Wallon, and others; second edition of *Matching Curriculum, Instruction, and Evaluation.*

*SIDELIGHTS:* Patricia Simonet Charlier has travelled to all the continents over the last twenty-five years. She has presented scholarly papers to international meetings in England, France, USSR, and Senegal.

\*     \*     \*

# CHARLIER, Roger H(enri)  1921-
## (Henri Rochard)

*PERSONAL:* Born November 10, 1921, in Antwerp, Belgium; naturalized American citizen; son of Armand A. J. (chief of Legal Affairs Division, City of Antwerp) and Pauline B. (a teacher; maiden name, Uyterhoeven) Charlier; married Patricia Mary Simonet (an associate professor of education and psychology at University of Illinois at Chicago Circle), June 17, 1958; children: Constance Cecelia-Paula, Jean-Armand Leonard. *Education:* Royal Athenaeum of Antwerp, A.A. (summa cum laude), 1939; Free University of Brussels, M.Pol.Sc., 1941, M.S., 1945; State University of Liege, B.S. (geography; cum laude), 1942, B.S. (geology), 1943; University of Erlangen, Ph.D. (magna cum laude), 1947; Industrial College of the Armed Forces, Diploma, 1952; University of Paris, Litt.D. (magna cum laude), 1957, Sc.D. (summa cum laude), 1958. *Home:* 4055 North Keystone Ave., Chicago, Ill. 60641. *Office:* Northeastern Illinois University, Bryn Mawr at St. Louis Ave., Chicago, Ill. 60625.

*CAREER:* Teacher at secondary school in Belgium, 1941-42; United Nations Relief and Rehabilitation Administration, deputy director of various assembly centers in Germany, 1946-48; Polycultural University, Washington, D.C., associate professor of geography and chairman of department, 1950-52; teacher at Berlitz School, Newark, N.J., 1951-52; Finch College, New York, N.Y., professor and chairman of department of physical sciences, and mathematics, 1952-55; Hofstra University, Hempstead, N.Y., professor and chairman of department of geology and geography, 1955-58; University of Paris, Faculty of Sciences, Paris, France, adjunct professor of geology, 1958-59; University of Minnesota, Minneapolis, visiting professor of education, 1959-60; Parsons College, Fairfield, Iowa, professor of earth sciences, 1960-61; Northeastern Illinois University, Chicago, Ill., professor of geology, geography, and oceanography, 1961—, coordinator of earth sciences, 1961-65, research scholar, 1962-64. Visiting professor at University of Western New Mexico, summers, 1963-66, DePaul University, 1965-67, University of Baja California, summer, 1967, University of Bordeaux, 1970-73, and Free University of Brussels, 1971—. Newspaper correspondent in Europe,

1945-50; travel project director for various agencies, 1948-71, and director, Division of Educational Travel, University Travel, Inc., Chicago, 1963-67; professional lecturer on travel and foreign affairs, 1949—; lecturer, U.S. Information Service, 1971—. *Military service:* Belgian Army, 1940-44; became major (joined underground after King Leopold's surrender and was imprisoned by Germans for work with Allies).

*MEMBER:* Centre International d'Histoire de l'Oceanographie, Geological Society of America (fellow), American Association for the Quaternary, Association of American Geographers, American Association for the Advancement of Science, National Education Association, American Association of University Professors, Academie Nationale des Sciences, Arts, et Belles-Lettres, Societe belge d'etudes geographiques, Societe royale belge de Geographie, Societe royale de Zoologie d'Anvers, Societe belge de geologie, hydrologie et paleontologie, New Jersey Academy of Science (fellow; president, 1954-57), Chi Beta Phi.

*AWARDS, HONORS:* Carnegie Corp. fellow, 1953; special fellow, French Government, 1958; Chevalier, Ordre des Palmes Academiques (France), 1969; Medaille du Merite Touristique (Belgium), 1969; Cravate et Medaille de Vermeil des Arts, Sciences et Lettres (France), 1971; Knight of Order of Leopold (Belgium), 1973. Grants from the governments of South Africa, Zambia, and Rhodesia, 1968, Israel, 1969, Romania, 1970, and Belgium, 1976, and 1978; other grants from National Science Foundation, International Research and Exchange Committee, North Atlantic Treaty Organization, and other organizations.

*WRITINGS: Cours d'analyse infinitesimale,* five volumes, G. Schreiber (Brussels), 1940; *The Gifted, A National Resource,* University of Minnesota Bureau of Educational Research, 1950; *Introductory Earth Science,* Burgess, 1960; *Introduction to Oceanography,* Maplegrove-Montgrove Books, 1964; *The Physical Environment: A Short Outline,* W. C. Brown, 1966; (editor) *Geography of the USSR,* Northeastern Illinois University, 1967; *Harnessing the Energies of the Ocean* (booklet), Marine Technology Society (Washington, D.C.) and Northeastern Illinois State College, 1970; (editor with wife, Patricia S. Charlier, and John J. Karpeck) *The World around Us: A Book of Readings,* MSS Educational Publishing, 1970; (editor) *A Digest of Master's Theses in Geography at Northeastern Illinois University,* Northeastern Illinois University, 1972; (contributor) B. L. Gordon, editor, *Marine Resources,* Book and Tackle Publications, 1972; *Esquisse d'un cours d'oceanographie regionale,* Institute Geologie du Bassin d'Aquitaine (Bordeaux), 1973; (contributor) J. B. Ray, editor, *The Oceans and Man,* Kendall-Hunt, 1975; (contributor) Gordon, editor, *Energy from the Sea,* Book and Tackle Publications, 1977; *Economic Oceanography,* Flemish Free University (Brussels), 1977; (contributor) N. Ginsburg and E. M. Bergese, editors, *Ocean Yearbook,* University of Chicago Press, 1978.

Under pseudonym Henri Rochard: *I Was a Male War Bride,* Montgrove Press, 1947; *Pensees,* Montgrove Press, 1962; *For the Love of Kate,* Exposition Press, 1963.

Contributor of about six hundred articles to periodicals and newspapers, over one hundred of them to scientific and other scholarly journals in United States and abroad. Translation editor, *Newsletter* of International Geographic Union, 1954-56; contributing editor, *Oceanic Index,* 1955—; consulting editor, *Foreign Language Quarterly,* 1956-61, and *Hexagon,* 1961-63.

*WORK IN PROGRESS: Tidal Power,* for Van Nostrand;

editing *Proceedings* of fifth and sixth convocations of Pacem in Maribus, with E. M. Borgese.

*SIDELIGHTS:* "I Was a Male War Bride" was filmed by Twentieth Century-Fox, 1949. In addition to his native French and English, Charlier is fluent in German, Italian, Flemish, Dutch, and Swahili; he has a working knowledge of other languages, including Spanish, Afrikaans, and the Scandinavian languages. He and his professor-wife visit Europe, South America, and Central America annually and have made multiple trips to Asia, Africa, and the Pacific area.

\* \* \*

## CHASINS, Abram 1903-

*PERSONAL:* Surname rhymes with "patience"; born August 17, 1903, in New York, N.Y.; son of Saul and Elizabeth (Hochstein) Chasins; married Julia Haberman, 1935 (divorced, 1946); married Constance Keene (a concert pianist and teacher), April 22, 1949. *Education:* Attended Ethical Culture School, 1914-18, Columbia University, 1919-21, Juilliard School, 1918-25, and Curtis Institute of Music, 1926-28. *Home:* 200 East 78th St., New York, N.Y. 10021; and 10501 Wilshire Blvd., Los Angeles, Calif. 90024.

*CAREER:* Composer and concert pianist; WQXR-Radio (radio network of *New York Times*), New York, N.Y., music director, 1942-65; University of Southern California, Los Angeles, musician-in-residence, 1972—, artistic director of KUSC-Radio (radio station of University of Southern California), 1972-77. Member of Faculty of Curtis Institute of Music, 1926-35, and Tanglewood, 1940-41; lecturer at American universities. Consultant to governments of Canada and Israel; music expert in court cases involving copyright infringements. *Awards, honors:* U.S. Treasury Department awards, 1944, 1945, for meritorious and patriotic services; Mahler Society Award, 1958; String Teachers' Guild award, 1959; Peabody Award for radio projects on behalf of musical education, 1960.

*WRITINGS: Speaking of Pianists,* Knopf, 1957, revised edition, 1962; *The Van Cliburn Legend,* Doubleday, 1959; *The Appreciation of Music,* Crown, 1965; *Music at the Crossroads,* Macmillan, 1972. Composer of "Three Chinese Pieces," "Two Piano Concertos," "Period Suite for Orchestra," "Twenty-four Preludes for Piano," and many works for two pianos. Contributor of articles to national magazines, including *Saturday Review, Saturday Evening Post, McCall's, Ladies' Home Journal,* and *Hi-Fidelity,* and to *New York Times.*

*WORK IN PROGRESS: Stoki, the Ageless Apollo,* a biography of Leopold Stokowski, for Hawthorn; musical research.

*SIDELIGHTS:* Abram Chasins told *CA:* "I write books because it is as necessary a form of expression to me as the need to compose, perform, teach, and broadcast music. Words also enable me to pass on to others some of the fruits of my unusual opportunities to associate and study with truly great people." *Avocational interests:* Bridge, chess.

\* \* \*

## CHATFIELD, (Earl) Charles (Jr.) 1934-

*PERSONAL:* Born March 11, 1934, in Philadelphia, Pa.; son of Earl Charles (a sales manager) and Virgie (McGee) Chatfield; married Mary F. Poffenberger, June 16, 1957; children: David, Carol Anne. *Education:* Monmouth College, Monmouth, Ill., A.B., 1956; Vanderbilt University, M.A., 1958, Ph.D., 1965; also attended University of Chi-

cago, 1965-66. *Religion:* United Church of Christ. *Residence:* Springfield, Ohio. *Office:* Department of History, Wittenberg University, Springfield, Ohio 45501.

*CAREER:* Wittenberg University, Springfield, Ohio, instructor, 1961-65, assistant professor, 1965-69, associate professor, 1969-74, professor of history, 1974—, director of international education, 1975—. *Member:* American Historical Association, Organization of American Historians, Conference for Peace Research in History (president). *Awards, honors:* Publication Award, from Ohio Academy of History, 1972, for *For Peace and Justice.*

*WRITINGS*—Published by Garland Publishing, except as indicated: *For Peace and Justice: Pacifism in America, 1914-1941,* University of Tennessee, 1971; (editor) *American Peace Movements,* Schocken, 1973; *The Radical "NO": Correspondence and Writings of Evan Thomas on War,* 1974; *International War Resistance through 1945,* 1975; *The Americanization of Gandhi,* 1976; *Devere Allen: Life and Writings,* 1976; *Kirby Page and the Social Gospel,* 1977. Co-editor, "Garland Library of War and Peace," 1972. Contributor to *Dictionary of Southern History,* and *Dictionary of the History of American Foreign Policy;* contributor of articles to periodicals. Guest editor, *American Studies,* spring, 1972.

*WORK IN PROGRESS:* Research on history of peace and war and its expression as social reform.

\* \* \*

## CHATMAN, Seymour B(enjamin) 1928-

*PERSONAL:* Born August 30, 1928, in Detroit, Mich.; son of William B. and Betty (Davis) Chatman; divorced; children: Emily, Jennifer. *Education:* Wayne University (now Wayne State University), B.A., 1949, M.A., 1950; University of Michigan, Ph.D., 1956. *Home:* 9 Fairlawn, Berkeley, Calif. *Office:* Department of Rhetoric, University of California, Berkeley, Calif.

*CAREER:* Cornell University, Ithaca, N.Y., research associate, 1951-52; Wayne State University, Detroit, Mich., instructor in English, 1954-56; University of Pennsylvania, Philadelphia, assistant professor, 1956-60; University of California, Berkeley, 1960—, began as assistant professor of speech, currently professor of rhetoric. Consultant, Systems Development Corp., 1962. *Member:* Modern Language Association of America, Linguistic Society of America. *Awards, honors:* Fulbright research grant, 1963-64; Guggenheim fellowship, 1969-70.

*WRITINGS:* (With Morse Peckham) *Word, Meaning, Poem,* Crowell, 1959; *Theory of Meter,* Mouton, 1965; *Introduction to the Language of Poetry,* Houghton, 1968; (with Samuel Levin) *Essays on the Language of Literature,* Houghton, 1968; (editor) *Literary Style: A Symposium,* Oxford University Press, 1971; *The Later Style of Henry James,* Basil Blackwell, 1972.

*WORK IN PROGRESS:* A book on narrative structure.

\* \* \*

## CHATTERTON, Wayne 1921-

*PERSONAL:* Born July 14, 1921, in Franklin, Idaho; son of Jesse R. (a barber) and Josephine (Hill) Chatterton; married Ardath Louise Lefler, July 19, 1945. *Education:* Albion State Normal School, normal certificate, 1942; Brigham Young University, B.S., 1945, M.A., 1946; University of Utah, Ph.D., 1963. *Residence:* Boise, Idaho. *Office:* Department of English, Boise State University, Boise, Idaho 83725.

CAREER: Carbon Junior College, Price, Utah, chairman of department of English and speech, 1946-47; Southern Idaho College of Education, Albion, instructor in English and drama, 1947-48; College of Idaho, Caldwell, associate professor, 1949-63, professor of English, 1963-68; Boise State University, Boise, Idaho, professor of English, 1968—. *Military service:* U.S. Marine Corps, 1942-44. *Member:* National Council of Teachers of English (member of board of directors, 1967-69), English Education Association, Modern Language Association of America, American Studies Association, Conference on College Composition and Communication, Western Literature Association, Rocky Mountain Modern Language Association, Idaho Council of Teachers of English (liaison officer, 1966-69).

WRITINGS: *Vardis Fisher: The Frontier and Regional Works,* Boise State College, 1972; (with Martha Heasley Cox) *Nelson Algren,* Twayne, 1975; *Nathaniel West's " The Day of the Locust,"* Monarch, 1977; *Alexander Woollcott,* Twayne, 1978. Co-editor, Boise State College "Western Writers Series." Contributor to literature journals.

WORK IN PROGRESS: *Irvin S. Cobb, The Novel of the American Frontier, 1790-1890, The Novel of the American West, 1890-1980, Eugene Field, Snake River,* and *The Irish Players in America,* all for Twayne; *A Reader's Guide to the Works of Nathaniel West.*

\* \* \*

## CHAUFFARD, Rene-Jacques 1920(?)-1972

1920(?)—October 30, 1972; French actor and playwright. Obituaries: *L'Express,* November 13-19, 1972.

\* \* \*

## CHELF, Carl P. 1937-

PERSONAL: Born September 16, 1937, in Pike View, Ky.; son of Ralph (a farmer) and Nellie (Ard) Chelf; married Earlene Niday, June 30, 1962; children: Jennifer Sue, David Andrew. *Education:* Western Kentucky University, B.A., 1959; University of Nebraska, M.A., 1961, Ph.D., 1968. *Politics:* Democrat. *Religion:* Baptist. *Home:* 498 Lansdale Ave., Bowling Green, Ky. 42101. *Office:* Western Kentucky University, College Heights, Bowling Green, Ky. 42101.

CAREER: Western Kentucky University, Bowling Green, instructor, 1963-64, assistant professor, 1964-68, associate professor of political science, 1968-73, professor of government, 1973—, associate dean for instruction, 1970-72. Dean of Bowling Green Community College, 1973—. Treasurer, Warren County Democrats for Better Government, 1967-68; delegate, Democratic State Convention, 1972. *Member:* American Political Science Association, Center for the Study of Democratic Institutions, Center for the Study of the Presidency, Kentucky Conference of Political Scientists, Pi Sigma Alpha. *Awards, honors:* American Political Science Association Congressional fellow, 1962-63; American Council on Education intern and fellow, 1969-70; American Political Science Association legislative service fellow, 1972-73.

WRITINGS: (With Patton Wheeler) *100 Questions about a Constitutional Convention,* Kentucky Constitutional Revision Committee, 1960; (with Mary Santopolo) *Planning and Zoning Law in Kentucky,* Kentucky Legislative Research Commission, 1961; *A Manual for Members of the Kentucky General Assembly,* American Political Science Association, 1973; (with Thomas W. Madron) *Political Parties in the*

United States: A Systems Analysis, Holbrook, 1973; *Congress in the American System,* Nelson-Hall, 1977.

WORK IN PROGRESS: A basic text in the national policy process, tentatively entitled *Under the Political Big Top: Policy Making in the U.S.A.;* research for a book on the impact of science and technology on American political parties and politics.

\* \* \*

## CHEN, Joseph Tao 1925-

PERSONAL: Born January 30, 1925, in Shanghai, China; son of Hung-chun (a businessman) and Wei-tseng (Sze) Chen; married Marjorie Wong (an airline officer), October 28, 1940; children: Barbara Joanne, Cynthia Anne. *Education:* College of Emporia, B.A., 1953; University of California, Berkeley, M.A., 1958, Ph.D., 1964. *Home:* 640 North June St., Los Angeles, Calif. 90004. *Office:* Department of History, California State University, Northridge, Calif. 91324.

CAREER: University of California, Center for Chinese Studies, Berkeley, head librarian, 1963-64; California State University, Northridge, assistant professor, 1964-68, associate professor, 1968-71, professor of history, 1971—. Guest lecturer, University of California, Santa Barbara, 1970-72. *Member:* Association for Asian Studies. *Awards, honors:* Social Science Research Council grant, 1965; Danforth Foundation associateship, 1968—; American Philosophical Society grant, 1974.

WRITINGS: *The May Fourth Movement in Shanghai,* E. J. Brill, 1971. Contributor to *Journal of Asian History* and *Journal of Modern Asian Studies.*

WORK IN PROGRESS: *The May 30 Movement in Shanghai; Grass Roots Revolutionary Education and Political Education in China.*

\* \* \*

## CHEN, Tony 1929-

PERSONAL: Born January 3, 1929, in West Indies; son of Arthur (a merchant) and Marie (Ho Pow) Chen; married Pura DeCastro, March 2, 1956; children: Richard, David. *Education:* Attended Art Career School, 1949-51; Pratt Institute, B.F.A. (cum laude), 1955. *Religion:* Roman Catholic. *Home:* 53-31 96th St., Corona, N.Y. 11368.

CAREER: *Newsweek,* New York, N.Y., art director, 1961-72; Nassau Community College, Garden City, N.Y., instructor in art, 1972-73. Painter and sculptor, with one-man shows in New York; writer and illustrator of books for children. *Awards, honors:* Awards from Society of Illustrators and from Creativity '71; American Institute of Graphic Arts book award, 1972; Society of Illustrators Award of Excellence, 1972; Creativity Award from *Art Direction* magazine, 1972; *Honshi* was selected as a Children's Book Showcase title, 1973.

WRITINGS—Self-illustrated children's book: *Run, Zebra Run,* Lothrop, 1972.

Illustrator: Helen E. Buckley, *Too Many Crackers,* Lothrop, 1962; Isabelle Chang, *Tales From Old China,* Random House, 1969; Herbert H. Wong and Matthew F. Vessel, *Pond Life: Watching Animals Find Food,* Addison-Wesley, 1970; Hannah Johnson, *Hello, Small Sparrow,* Lothrop, 1971; Edith Hurd, *The White Horse,* Harper, 1971; Ruth Dale, *Do You Know a Cat?,* Singer, 1971; Doris Evans, *Breakfast with the Birds,* Putnam, 1972; Aline Glasgow,

*Honshi,* Parents' Magazine Press, 1972; *Dakota Sons,* Harper, 1972; Seymour Simon, *The Rockhound Book,* Viking, 1973; Laurence Pringle, *Follow a Fisher,* Crowell, 1973; Applebaum and Cox, *A Not so Ugly Friend,* Holt, 1973; Charlotte Pomerantz, *The Princess and the Admiral,* Addison-Wesley, 1974.

*WORK IN PROGRESS: Little Koala,* a children's book.

*SIDELIGHTS:* Much of Chen's painting and sculpture is in private collections. *Avocational interests:* Collecting art, especially animal sculpture from diverse cultures.

*BIOGRAPHICAL/CRITICAL SOURCES: American Artist,* May, 1972; *New York Times Book Review,* May 7, 1972; *Publishers Weekly,* May 22, 1972.

\*    \*    \*

## CHEN, Vincent 1917-

*PERSONAL:* Born June 23, 1917, in Ningpo, China; came to United States, 1948; naturalized, 1961; son of R. F. (a farmer) and M. C. (Lin) Chen; married Ellen M. Chang (a professor), June 11, 1960; children: Lucian, Michele. *Education:* National Chung Cheng University, China, LL.B., 1944; University of Chicago, M.A., 1951; Yale University, Ph.D., 1957. *Home:* 88-30 195th St., Hollis, N.Y. 11423. *Office:* Department of Political Science, St. John's University, Jamaica, N.Y. 11432.

*CAREER:* Albertus Magnus College, New Haven, Conn., assistant professor, 1957-61, associate professor of political science, 1961-64, head of department, 1957-64; St. John's University, Jamaica, N.Y., associate professor, 1964-68, professor of political science, 1968—. State visiting professor of political science, National Taiwan University, 1971. *Member:* American Political Science Association, American International Law Society, International Studies Association, Association for Asian Studies.

*WRITINGS: Sino-Russian Relations in the Seventeenth Century,* Nijhoff, 1966; (contributor) James Hsiung, editor, *The Logic of "Maoism": Critiques and Explication,* Praeger, 1974.

\*    \*    \*

## CHERNISS, Michael D(avid) 1940-

*PERSONAL:* Born April 7, 1940, in Los Angeles, Calif.; son of Edward H. (an executive) and Blanche (Cohen) Cherniss; married Elizabeth Whitmore, 1961 (divorced, 1965); married Susan Kelso, September 2, 1967 (divorced, 1975); children: (stepchild) Bonnie Brooks Cullum. *Education:* University of California, Berkeley, A.B., 1962, M.A., 1963, Ph.D., 1966. *Home:* 1104-A Cynthia, Lawrence, Kan. 66044. *Office:* Department of English, University of Kansas, Lawrence, Kan. 66044.

*CAREER:* University of Kansas, Lawrence, assistant professor, 1966-70, associate professor, 1970-76, professor of English, 1976—. *Member:* Modern Language Association of America, Mediaeval Academy of America, Midwest Modern Language Association.

*WRITINGS: Ingeld and Christ: Heroic Concepts and Ideals in Old English Poetry,* Mouton (The Hague), 1972.

*WORK IN PROGRESS:* A book on middle English vision poems.

\*    \*    \*

## CHESEN, Eli S. 1944-

*PERSONAL:* Born May 18, 1944, in Sioux City, Iowa; son of Louie E. (owner of a broom-importation company) and Edith (Skalowsky) Chesen; married Peggy Ann Blue (a mathematics teacher), December 23, 1967; children: Chelsea Lynn. *Education:* University of Nebraska, B.S., 1965, M.D., 1969. *Politics:* "Too complex to define in this space." *Religion:* Jewish.

*CAREER:* Good Samaritan Hospital, Phoenix, Ariz., intern, 1969-70, resident, beginning 1970. Formerly chief of mental health, Nellis Air Force Base, Nevada.

*WRITINGS: Religion May Be Hazardous to Your Health,* Peter H. Wyden, 1972; *President Nixon's Psychiatric Profile: A Psychodynamic–genetic Interpretation,* Peter H. Wyden, 1973.

*WORK IN PROGRESS:* A book of science fiction; a follow-up book to *Religion May Be Hazardous to Your Health.*

*AVOCATIONAL INTERESTS:* Classical music, electronics, auto mechanics, painting.

*BIOGRAPHICAL/CRITICAL SOURCES: New York Times Magazine,* March 19, 1972.†

\*    \*    \*

## CHI, Richard Hu See-Yee 1918-
## (Chuan-Chin, Ernest Moncrieff)

*PERSONAL:* Born August 3, 1918, in Peking, China; son of Mi Kang and Pao (Ten) Chi. *Education:* Nankai University, B.Sc., 1937; Oxford University, M.A., 1962, D.Phil., 1964; Cambridge University, Ph.D., 1964. *Religion:* Buddhism. *Home:* 3650 Gast Will Sowders Rd., Bloomington, Ind. 47401. *Office:* Department of East Asian Languages and Literatures, Indiana University, Bloomington, Ind. 47401.

*CAREER:* Cambridge University, Cambridge, England, lecturer in Chinese, 1960-62; Oxford University, Oxford, England, university lecturer in Sinology, 1962-65; City of Bristol, England, city curator of Oriental art, 1965; Indiana University at Bloomington, associate professor, 1965-71, professor of Chinese language and literature, 1971—. Summer lecturer, University of London, 1961; visiting summer professor, University of Michigan, 1968. Consultant on translation of Buddhist texts, Buddhist Association of the United States; associate adviser, Centro Superiore di Logica e Scienze Comparate; adviser for film, "Buddhism in China," 1972.

*MEMBER:* Society for Asian and Comparative Philosophy (member of board), Royal Asiatic Society, China Academy (fellow), Asian Studies Institute (member of advisory board), Oriental Art Society (founding member), Association for Symbolic Logic, Mind Association, Linguistic Society of America, Association for Asian Studies, Cambridge University Buddhist Society (vice-president, 1961-64), King's College Association (life member), Indianapolis Museum of Art (voting member).

*WRITINGS: A New Interpretation of the Nyayapravesa,* [Tientsin], 1937; (under pseudonym Chuan-Chin; in Chinese) *On Fallacies,* [Peking], 1947; *Buddhist Logic and Its Consequences,* Indiana University Press, 1967; *A General Theory of Operators,* Indiana University Press, 1967; *Buddhist Formal Logic,* (revision and enlargement of *Buddhist Logic and Its Consequences* and *A General Theory of Operators*), Royal Asiatic Society, 1969. Contributor to philosophy journals and journals of Asian studies in the United States and Europe, at least one contribution under the pseudonym Ernest Moncrieff.

*WORK IN PROGRESS: The Last of the Patriarchs,* recorded sayings of Shen-hui, the seventh patriarch of Zen, with an introduction by Thomas Merton; *The Importance of Being Intuitive,* recorded sayings of Bodhidharma, the first patriarch of Zen; *Introduction to the Middle Path: The Madhyamakavatara by Candrakirti,* an interpretation of Nagarjuna's critical philosophy.

*SIDELIGHTS:* Chi told *CA* that he proposes four steps in the study of Buddhist thought: "[first] This unfamiliar school of thought should be intrepreted accurately and objectively in a language comprehensible to western philosophers. [second] East-West Parallels, whether genuine or spurious, whether whole or partial, should be critically compared and evaluated. [third] The insights and theories of Buddhist thought should be integrated into the corpus of philosophy, not unlike those of any other school of thought. [fourth] The study of this ancient thought should be aimed at finding the consequences of the integration mentioned above on the discipline of philosophy itself; i.e. what Buddhist thought should mean to *our* thought. Otherwise, Buddhist philosophy would remain forever an exotic subject alien and inconsequential to world philosophy."

\*     \*     \*

## CHICHESTER, Francis (Charles)   1901-1972

September 17, 1901—August 26, 1972; British air and sea pioneer, and author of books on his travels and on other subjects. Obituaries: *Chicago Tribune,* August 27, 1972; *New York Times,* August 27, 1972; *Newsweek,* September 4, 1972; *Publishers Weekly,* September 4, 1972; *L'Express,* September 4-10, 1972; *Current Biography,* October, 1972. (See index for *CA* sketch)

\*     \*     \*

## CHILDERS, Thomas (Allen)   1940-

*PERSONAL:* Born July 2, 1940, in Chillicothe, Ohio; son of William Allen (a prison director) and Jeannette Marie (Kohlrush) Childers. *Education:* University of Maryland, B.A., 1962; Rutgers University, M.L.S., 1963, Ph.D., 1970. *Home:* 4628 Hazel Ave., Philadelphia, Pa. 19143. *Office:* Graduate School of Library Science, Drexel University, Philadelphia, Pa. 19104.

*CAREER:* Baltimore County Public Library, Baltimore, Md., adult and young adult librarian, 1965-67; Rutgers University, Graduate School of Library Services, New Brunswick, N.J., research fellow, 1967-70; Drexel University, Graduate School of Library Science, Philadelphia, Pa., assistant professor, 1970-74, associate professor, 1974—. Visiting faculty member, Syracuse University School of Library Science, summer, 1970. *Military service:* U.S. Army, 1963-65. *Member:* American Library Association (councilor), American Society for Information Science, American Association of University Professors, American Civil Liberties Union.

*WRITINGS:* (With Terence Crowley) *Information Service in Public Libraries: Two Studies,* Scarecrow, 1971; *The Information-Poor in America,* Scarecrow, 1975; (contributor) Manfred Kochen and Joseph C. Donahue, editors, *Information for the Community,* American Library Association, 1976. Contributor to library journals.

*WORK IN PROGRESS:* Research on information and referral service in public libraries; planning for inter-type library cooperation; testing reference performance.

## CHILDS, David (Haslam)   1933-

*PERSONAL:* Born September 25, 1933, in Bolton, England; son of John Arthur (an industrial worker; mayor of Bolton) and Ellen (Haslam) Childs; married Monir Pishdad, June, 1964; children: Martin, Julian. *Education:* London School of Economics and Political Science, B.Sc., 1956, Ph.D., 1962; University of Hamburg, graduate study, 1956-57. *Office:* Department of Politics, University of Nottingham, Nottingham NG7 2RD, England.

*CAREER:* School teacher in London, England until 1961; television scriptwriter on documentary films, 1961-64; school teacher and teacher in further education courses, 1964-66; University of Nottingham, Nottingham, England, lecturer then senior lecturer, 1966-76, reader in politics, 1976—. Candidate for Parliament, 1964. *Member:* Association of University Teachers, University Association for Contemporary European Studies, European Movement.

*WRITINGS: From Schumacher to Brandt: The Story of German Socialism, 1945-1964,* Pergamon, 1966; *East Germany,* Praeger, 1969; *Germany Since 1918,* Harper, 1971; *Marx and the Marxists: An Outline of Practice and Theory,* Benn, 1973; (contributor) Roger Tilford, editor, *The Ostpolitik and Political Change in Germany,* Lexington Books, 1975; (contributor) James Riordan, editor, *Sport under Communism,* Hurst & Co., in press. Also author of *Britain since 1945,* Benn. Contributor to *Times Literary Supplement, Guardian, Contemporary Review, World Today,* and other general and political affairs journals.

\*     \*     \*

## CHILDS, Harwood   1898-1972

May 1, 1898—June 8, 1972; American political scientist and educator. Obituaries: *New York Times,* June 9, 1972. (See index for *CA* sketch)

\*     \*     \*

## CHING, James C(hristopher)   1926-

*PERSONAL:* Born October 12, 1926, in Honolulu, Hawaii; son of James I. and Elsie (Ching) Motoyama; married Won May Lee, December 15, 1950; children: James Michael. *Education:* Wabash College, B.A., 1951; University of Hawaii, M.A., 1953; University of Missouri, Ph.D., 1962. *Home:* 1641 Eleanor Ave., St. Paul, Minn. 55116. *Office:* Department of Speech and Theatre Arts, Hamline University, St. Paul, Minn. 55104.

*CAREER:* University of Missouri—Columbia, instructor in speech, 1953-56; University of Hawaii, Honolulu, member of faculty, 1956-58; *Voice of East Oahu,* Honolulu, Hawaii, managing editor, 1958-60; Wabash College, Crawfordsville, Ind., assistant professor of speech, 1960; Tulane University, New Orleans, La., assistant professor, 1960-63, associate professor of speech and drama, 1963-67; Illinois State University, Normal, professor of speech, 1967-68; University of Bridgeport, Bridgeport, Conn., professor of speech and dramatic arts and chairman of department, 1968-69; University of Missouri—Columbia, visiting professor of speech, 1969-70; Hamline University, St. Paul, Minn., professor of speech and theatre, chairman of department of speech and theatre arts, 1970—. *Military service:* U.S. Army, 1944-46. *Member:* American Theatre Association, Speech Communication Association, American Association of University Professors, Southern Speech Association, Phi Kappa Phi, Tau Kappa Alpha, Phi Kappa Psi, Blue Key.

*WRITINGS:* (With Edward Rogge) *Advanced Public*

*Speaking,* Holt, 1966. Also author of *Confrontation: A Rhetoric of Crisis.* Contributor of articles to *Journalism Quarterly, Comparative Education Review, Speech Monographs, Quarterly Journal of Speech.*†

\* \* \*

## CHIPMAN, Bruce L(ewis) 1946-

*PERSONAL:* Born June 1, 1946, in Philadelphia, Pa.; son of I. Lewis (a physician) and Janet (Ingerson) Chipman; married Pamela Leary (a teacher), June 15, 1968; children: Zachary. *Education:* University of Virginia, B.A., 1968; Tufts University, M.A., 1970, doctoral candidate, 1970—. *Home:* 26 Westover Circle, Wilmington, Del. 19807. *Agent:* Perry Knowlton, 60 East 56th St., New York, N.Y. 10022. *Office:* Department of English, Tatnall School, 1501 Barley Mill Rd., Wilmington, Del. 19807.

*CAREER:* Worked as a hod-carrier in Wilmington, Del., summers, 1966, 1967; Tufts University, Medford, Mass., instructor in American literature, 1969-73, faculty adviser in dormitory, 1970-73; Tatnall School, Wilmington, teacher of literature and creative writing, 1973—. Part-time lecturer, University of Delaware. *Member:* Modern Language Association of America.

*WRITINGS: Hardening Rock: An Organic Anthology of the Adolescence of Rock and Roll,* Little, Brown, 1972. Contributor to *Rapier* and *Delawarean Magazine.*

*WORK IN PROGRESS:* Research on the vision of Hollywood in the novel.

*AVOCATIONAL INTERESTS:* Film, cooking, music, travel.

*BIOGRAPHICAL/CRITICAL SOURCES: Wilmington Evening Journal,* April 22, 1972; *Wilmington Morning News,* April 24, 1972; *Rock Magazine,* July 1972.

\* \* \*

## CHISHOLM, Hugh J., Jr. 1913-1972

1913—November 13, 1972; American poet and translator. Obituaries: *New York Times,* November 16, 1972.

\* \* \*

## CHISHOLM, Mary K(athleen) 1924-

*PERSONAL:* Born April 28, 1924, in Edinburgh, Scotland; son of William and Mary D. Chisholm. *Education:* Attended Trinity Academy, Edinburgh; Leith General Hospital, R.G.N.; Western General Hospital, S.C.M. *Religion:* Church of Scotland. *Home:* 28 Comely Bank Pl., Edinburgh EH4 1EP, Scotland.

*CAREER:* Registered nurse practicing in Edinburgh, Scotland; state certified midwife and health visitor. *Member:* Royal College of Nursing. *Awards, honors:* Essay prizes of the British Medical Association; first annual Ballier Prize for nursing studies, 1973.

*WRITINGS: An Insight into Health Visiting,* Williams & Wilkins, 1970. Contributor of articles and reviews to *Nursing Mirror, Midwife and Health Visitor, Nursing Times, District Nursing,* and to newspapers and magazines.

*WORK IN PROGRESS:* Articles for nursing journals.

\* \* \*

## CHISHOLM, Michael (Donald Inglis) 1931-

*PERSONAL:* Born June 10, 1931, in London, England; children: two daughters, one son. *Education:* St. Catharine's

College, Cambridge, M.A., 1957; Oxford University, M.A. (by incorporation), 1957. *Office:* Department of Geography, Cambridge University, Cambridge, England.

*CAREER:* Oxford University, Oxford, England, departmental demonstrator in Institute for Research in Agricultural Economics (now Institute for Agricultural Economics), 1954-59; University of London, Bedford College, London, England, assistant lecturer in geography, 1960-62, lecturer in geography, 1962-64; University of Ibadan, Ibadan, Nigeria, visiting senior lecturer in geography, 1964-65; University of Bristol, Bristol, England, lecturer, 1965-67, reader in economic geography, 1967-72, professor of economic and social geography, 1972-76; Cambridge University, Cambridge, England, professor of geography and head of department, 1976—. Associate, Economic Associates Ltd. (consultants), London, England, 1965-77. Social Science Research Council, member, 1967-72, chairman of human geography committee and of joint committee for human geography and planning, 1967-72; member, Local Government Boundary Commission for England, 1971—. External examiner in geography, University of Reading, 1971-73, and University of Nottingham, 1976—. *Military service:* British Army, Royal Engineers, 1950-51. *Member:* Royal Geographical Society. *Awards, honors:* Gill Memorial Prize of Royal Geographical Society, 1969; grants from Social Science Research Council, 1968-71, and Nuffield Foundation, 1971-72.

*WRITINGS: Rural Settlement and Land Use: An Essay in Location,* Hutchinson, 1962, Wiley, 1967, 2nd revised edition, Aldine, 1970, 3rd revised edition, Hutchinson, in press; *Geography and Economics,* Praeger, 1966, revised edition, G. Bell, 1970; (editor with A. E. Frey and P. Haggett, and contributor) *Regional Forecasting,* Shoe String, 1971; (editor with G. Manners, and contributor) *Spatial Policy Problems of the British Economy,* Cambridge University Press, 1971; *Research in Human Geography,* Heinemann, for Social Science Research Council, 1971; (contributor) J. A. Steers, editor, *Applied Coastal Geomorphology,* M.I.T. Press, 1971; (editor and contributor) *Resources for Britain's Future* (collection of articles published in *Geographical Magazine,* 1969), Penguin, 1972; (editor with B. Rodgers) *Studies in Human Geography,* Heinemann for Social Science Research Council, 1973; (with P. O'Sullivan) *Freight Flows and the Spatial Aspects of British Economy,* Cambridge University Press, 1973; (with J. Oeppen) *The Changing Pattern of Employment: Regional Specialisation and Industrial Localisation in Britain,* Croom Helm, 1973; *Human Geography: Evolution or Revolution?,* Penguin, 1975; (editor with R. Peel and Huggett, and contributor) *Processes in Physical and Human Geography,* Heinemann, 1975.

Contributor to other symposia, and to planning, geography, and economics journals. Editor, ''Focal Problems in Geography'' series, Macmillan, 1967-72; geography advisory editor, Hutchinson University Library, 1973—. Member of editorial board, *Regional and Urban Economics: Operational Methods,* 1970-74; member of editorial board, *Regional Studies,* 1976—.

*SIDELIGHTS: Geography and Economics* has been published in Japanese and Spanish translations, and *Rural Settlement* and *Land Use* in Japanese.

\* \* \*

## CHITTUM, Ida 1918-

*PERSONAL:* Born April 6, 1918, in Canton, Ohio; daughter of Harry A. (a farmer) and Ida (Klingaman) Hoover; married James R. Chittum (a tool designer), August 26, 1936; children: Rosalind (Mrs. Thomas Lawrence), James H., Thomas W., Edith Irene, Samme R. *Education:* Attended school through eighth grade in Illinois and Missouri. *Residence:* Findlay, Ill. *Agent:* Ruth Cantor, 156 Fifth Ave., New York, N.Y. 10010.

*CAREER:* Writer of books for children. *Member:* National League of American Pen Women, Authors Guild, Children's Reading Round Table, Friends of Libraries, American Legion Auxiliary. *Awards, honors:* Lewis Carroll Shelf award of University of Wisconsin for *Farmer Hoo and the Baboons;* certificate of appreciation from Mobile Media, 1975; award of recognition from Central Missouri State University for outstanding contribution to children's literature, 1977.

*WRITINGS*—Children's books: *Farmer Hoo and the Baboons,* Delacorte, 1971; *The Hermit Boy,* Delacorte, 1972; *Clabber Biscuits,* Steck, 1973; *A Nutty Business,* Putnam, 1973; *The Empty Grave,* American Educational Publications, 1974; *The Secrets of Madam Renee,* Independence Press, 1975; (contributor) *The Princess Book,* Rand, 1975; *The Ghost Boy,* Independence Press, in press. Contributor of short stories and articles to magazines.

*AVOCATIONAL INTERESTS:* Trees, birds, and all living things; collecting books, especially old ones, people, sunshine.

\*     \*     \*

## CHIU, Hungdah 1936-

*PERSONAL:* Born March 23, 1936, in Shanghai, China; son of Han-ping (a lawyer) and Min-non (Yang) Chiu; married Yuan-yuan Hsieh, May 14, 1966; children: Wei-hsueh (son). *Education:* National Taiwan University, LL.B., 1958; Long Island University, M.A. (with honors), 1962; Harvard University, LL.M., 1962, S.J.D., 1965. *Home:* 6254 Cricket Pass, Columbia, Md. 21044. *Office:* 029 University of Maryland Law School, 500 West Baltimore St., Baltimore, Md. 21201.

*CAREER:* National Taiwan University, Taipei, Taiwan, Republic of China, associate professor of international law, 1965-66; Harvard University, School of Law, Cambridge, Mass., research associate in law, 1966-70, 1972-74; University of Maryland, School of Law, Baltimore, associate professor, 1974-77, professor of law, 1977—. Professor of law, National Chengchi University, Taipei, Taiwan, Republic of China, 1970-72; research fellow, Institute of International Relations, Mucha, Taipei, Taiwan, Republic of China, 1967-73. *Military service:* Chinese Army (Republic of China), 1958-60; became second lieutenant; public defender in Judge-Advocate Office, 1959-60. *Member:* American Society of International Law (member of Panel on China and International Order, 1969-73), Association for Asian Studies, British Institute of International and Comparative Law, International Law Association (Taiwan branch), Chinese Society of Comparative Law (member of executive council).

*WRITINGS: The Capacity of International Organizations to Conclude Treaties,* Nijhoff (The Hague), 1966; (with D. M. Johnston) *Agreements of the People's Republic of China, 1949-67: A Calendar,* Harvard University Press, 1968; *The People's Republic of China and the Law of Treaties,* Harvard University Press, 1972; (with S. C. Leng) *Law in Chinese Foreign Policy,* Oceana, 1972; (editor and contributor) *China and the Question of Taiwan: Document and Analysis,* Praeger, 1973; (co-author) *People's China and International Law: A Documentary Study,* two volumes,

Princeton University Press, 1974; (co-editor) *Legal Aspects of U.S.-Republic of China Trade and Investment,* School of Law, University of Maryland, 1977; (editor and contributor) *Normalizing Relations with the People's Republic of China: Problems, Analysis, and Documents,* School of Law, University of Maryland, 1978.

Books in Chinese: *Hsien-tai Kuo-chi fa wen-t'i* (title means "Selected Problems of Modern International Law"), New Century Publishing Co. (Taipei), 1966; *Chung-Kuo Kuo-chi-fa wen-t'i O lun-chi* (title means "Essays on Chinese International Law Problems"), Taiwan Commercial Press (Taipei), 1968; (editor) *Hsien-tai Kuo-chi fa (ts'an-k'ao wen-chien),* (title means "Modern International Law, Reference Documents"), San-Min Book Co. (Taipei), 1972; (editor) *Hsien-tai Kuo-chi fa* (title means "Modern International Law"), San-Min Book Co., 1973; *Kuan-yu Chung-kuo ling-tu ti kuo-chi wen-t'i lun chi* (title means "Collected Essays on International Law Problems Concerning Chinese Territory"), Taiwan Commercial Press, 1975.

Contributor of articles to professional journals, including *American Journal of International Law, Journal of Asian Studies, China Quarterly, International and Comparative Law Quarterly.*

*WORK IN PROGRESS: China and the Law of the Sea; Justice in China After the Death of Mao;* second edition of *China and the Question of Taiwan;* a supplement to *People's China and International Law.*

\*     \*     \*

## CHOW, Yung-Teh 1916-

*PERSONAL:* Born October 28, 1916, in Wu-Yi County, Chekiang Province, China; son of Fan-Ping (a public school principal) and Hsiu-Ning (Li) Chow. *Education:* National Tsing Hua University, B.A., 1937; University of Chicago, M.A., 1951, Ph.D., 1958. *Politics:* None. *Religion:* None. *Home address:* P.O. Box 5694, University, Ala. 35486.

*CAREER:* National Association for the Advancement of Mass Education, Changsha, China, editor, 1937-39; National Yunnan University, Kunming, Yunnan, China, research assistant of Socio-economic Institute, 1939-41; National Tsing Hua University, Peking, China, research instructor in Institute for Census Research, 1941-46, instructor in sociology, 1946-48; Eastern Michigan University, Ypsilanti, assistant professor of sociology, 1958-61; researcher on Chinese population in Chicago, Ill., 1961-62; Moorhead State College, Moorhead, Minn., associate professor, 1962-65, professor of sociology, 1965-67; Northern Michigan University, Marquette, professor of sociology, 1967-73; University of Alabama, Tuscaloosa, professor of sociology, 1973-74; currently independently researching areas of Chinese sociology. *Member:* American Sociological Association, Population Association of America, Association for Asian Studies, American Association of University Professors, Midwest Sociological Society, Ohio Valley Sociological Society. *Awards, honors:* Wenner-Gren Foundation research grant, 1959; Social Science Research Council grant to travel and research in People's Republic of China, 1972.

*WRITINGS: How to Mobilize the Peasants* (in Chinese), National Association for the Advancement of Mass Education (Changsha), 1938; (with Hsiao-tung Fei) *China's Gentry,* University of Chicago Press, 1953, new edition, Phoenix Publishing, 1968; *Social Mobility in China: Status Careers among the Gentry in a Chinese Community,* Atherton, 1966. Contributor to newspapers and magazines in China and the United States.

*WORK IN PROGRESS: Social Mobility in Shang Hai.*

*SIDELIGHTS:* Yung-Teh Chow told *CA* that he is devoted to making a scientific contribution in sociology, specifically to help bring about more of an understanding of Chinese society. His writing career began when he published an article as a freshman in college. Later he became editor of a student weekly at Hsing Hua University. He published his first book after graduating and found himself becoming more and more serious about his field of study.

Chow adamantly believes in working in seclusion. Over many years he has amassed a personal library of some two thousand books on Chinese sociology. He feels he has been influenced by the writings of Goethe, Anton Chekov, Karl Marx, and Freud.

*BIOGRAPHICAL/CRITICAL SOURCES: Pacific Affairs,* Volume XI, number 1-2, spring-summer, 1967; *Sociology and Social Research,* Volume LI, number 4, July, 1967; *Journal of Asian Studies,* Volume XXVI, number 4, August, 1967; *Journal of American Anthropologists,* Volume XLIX, number 6, December, 1967.

\* \* \*

## CHRISTENSON, Reo M. 1918-

*PERSONAL:* Born June 5, 1918, in Dodge Center, Minn.; son of Arthur S. (a farmer) and Ella (Hoffman) Christenson; married Helen M. Dooling, November 30, 1944; children: Virginia (Mrs. Thomas Helm), Brian. *Education:* University of Redlands, B.A., 1948; University of Michigan, M.A., 1950, Ph.D., 1953. *Religion:* Christian. *Home:* Route 1, Oxford, Ohio 45056. *Office:* Department of Political Science, Miami University, Oxford, Ohio 45056.

*CAREER: Toledo Blade,* Toledo, Ohio, editorial writer, 1953-56; Miami University, Oxford, Ohio, assistant professor, 1956-59, associate professor, 1959-63, professor of political science, 1963—. *Military service:* U.S. Army, 1941-46; became warrant officer junior grade. *Member:* American Political Science Association, Midwest Political Science Association.

*WRITINGS: The Brannan Plan,* University of Michigan Press, 1959; (editor with R. O. McWilliams) *Voice of the People,* McGraw, 1962; *Challenge and Decision,* Harper, 1964, 5th edition, in press; (with Paul Rejai, Alan Engel, Daniel Jacobs, and Herbert Waltzer) *Ideologies and Modern Politics,* Dodd, 1971; *Heresies Right and Left,* Harper, 1972.

\* \* \*

## CHRISTIE, George C(ustis) 1934-

*PERSONAL:* Born March 3, 1934, in New York, N.Y.; son of Custis and Sophie (Velemahitis) Christie; married Susan Monserud, April 20, 1965 (divorced July 18, 1974); married Deborah Carnes, December 20, 1974; children: (first marriage) Constantine George. *Education:* Columbia University, A.B. (with honors), 1955, J.D. (with honors), 1957; Cambridge University, Diploma in International Law, 1962; Harvard University, S.J.D., 1966. *Home:* 17 Stoneridge Cir., Durham, N.C. 27705. *Office:* School of Law, Duke University, Durham, N.C. 27706.

*CAREER:* Admitted to Bar in New York State, 1957, and in District of Columbia, 1958; Covington & Burling, Washington, D.C., associate, 1958-60; University of Minnesota, Minneapolis, associate professor, 1962-65, professor of law, 1965-66; U.S. Department of State, Agency for International Development, Washington, D.C., assistant general

counsel for Near East and South Asia, 1966-67; Duke University, Durham, N.C., professor of law, 1967—. Consultant to President's Commission on Federal Statistics. *Military service:* U.S. Army, 1957. *Member:* American Law Institute, American Bar Association. *Awards, honors:* Fulbright scholarship at Cambridge University, 1961-62.

*WRITINGS: Jurisprudence: Text and Readings on the Philosophy of Law,* West Publishing, 1973; *Sum and Substance of the Law of Torts,* Center for Creative Educational Services, 1978. Contributor of articles and reviews to law journals.

*WORK IN PROGRESS: Cases and Materials on the Law of Torts,* for West Publishing.

\* \* \*

## CHURCH, Ralph (Bruce) 1927-

*PERSONAL:* Born July 9, 1927, in North Wilkesboro, N.C.; son of Rufus Bradshaw (a businessman) and Clara (McNeil) Church; married Evelyn Hester (an assistant professor of Spanish), August 23, 1946; children: Bruce, Emily (Mrs. Vincent Mortimer, Jr.), Rebecca, Lynne, Katrina, Melissa. *Education:* Attended Florence State College (now University), 1946-47; Wake Forest University, A.B., 1949; Columbia University, M.A., 1951; George Washington University, graduate study, 1959-61. *Home:* 2306 Murray Ave., Huntingdon, Pa. 16652. *Office:* Department of English, Juniata College, Huntingdon, Pa. 16652.

*CAREER:* High school English teacher in North Wilkesboro, N.C., 1951-52; high school English and speech teacher in Florence, Ala., 1952-54; Mitchell College, Statesville, N.C., professor of English, acting dean, and assistant to president, 1954-56; Shepherd College, Shepherdstown, W.Va., associate professor of English, 1956-62; Muskingum College, New Concord, Ohio, assistant professor of English, 1962-66; Juniata College, Huntingdon, Pa., associate professor of English and chairman of department, 1966—, and director of writing program. Lecturer, George Washington University, 1960. Chairman, Artists-in-residence Committee, Juniata. *Military service:* U.S. Naval Reserve, 1945-46. *Member:* Modern Language Association of America, American Literature Association, South Atlantic Modern Language Association, American Association of University Professors, Alpha Psi Omega, Pi Delta Epsilon. *Awards, honors:* Southern Universities fellow, 1959-61.

*WRITINGS:* (Author of introduction) Stephen Crane, *The Red Badge of Courage,* Cambridge Book Co., 1968; *Two Loves: Abelard and Heloise* (poetry), Juniata College Press, 1969; (author of introduction) Samuel Clemens, *A Connecticut Yankee in King Arthur's Court,* Cambridge Book Co., 1969; (author of introduction) Herman Melville, *Billy Budd,* Cambridge Book Co., 1970. Editor, *Juniata Studies,* 1976—.

*WORK IN PROGRESS:* A novel and a collection of poetry.

\* \* \*

## CHURCHILL, Edward Delos 1895-1972

December 25, 1895—September 2, 1972; American surgeon. Obituaries: *New York Times,* September 4, 1972.

\* \* \*

## CHURCHMAN, Michael 1929-

*PERSONAL:* Born March 9, 1929, in Indianapolis, Ind.; son of M. Steele (an engineer) and Luita (Curtis)

Churchman; married Jean V. Wood, April 28, 1951; children: Jean Wood, Julia Brooke, Diana Armit. *Education:* Wesleyan University, B.A., 1950; University of Missouri, M.A., 1958; Harvard University, Ed.M., 1964. *Home:* 15 Roslyn Rd., Richmond, Va. 23226. *Office:* St. Catherine's School, Richmond, Va. 23226.

*CAREER:* Kent School, Englewood, Colo., headmaster, 1964-74; St. Catherine's School, Richmond, Va., headmaster, 1974—.

*WRITINGS: Collected Works of Walter Bagehot, Volume IV, Bagehot and the American Civil War,* Harvard University Press, 1968; *The Kent School: 1922-1972,* Star Press (Denver), 1972. Contributor of reviews to professional journals.

*       *       *

## CIANCIOLO, Patricia Jean  1929-

*PERSONAL:* Born October 24, 1929, in Chicago, Ill.; daughter of Michael C. and Lottie Cianciolo. *Education:* Cardinal Stritch College, Ph.B., 1949; University of Wisconsin, M.E., 1954; Ohio State University, Ph.D., 1963. *Home:* 4206 Wabaningo Rd., Okemos, Mich. 48864. *Office:* Michigan State University, 360 Erickson, East Lansing, Mich. 48823.

*CAREER:* Marquette University, Milwaukee, Wis., assistant professor of curriculum and elementary education, 1958-60, 1962-64; Michigan State University, East Lansing, assistant professor, 1964-66, associate professor, 1966-68, professor of children's literature, 1968—. Visiting professor at University of Hawaii, 1968, and University of Nevada, 1971, 1974, and 1977. Specialist for English language arts, Systems Development Corp., 1972—. Chairperson, Newbery Caldecott Committee, 1978. Consultant to Laidlaw Reading Program. *Member:* National Council of Teachers of English, American Library Association, International Reading Association, National Society for the Study of Education, Association for Childhood Education International, Delta Kappa Gamma, Phi Delta Kappa. *Awards, honors:* Ohio State University centennial award, 1970.

*WRITINGS:* (With Jean LePere) *Literary Time Line in American History,* Doubleday, 1969; *Illustrations in Children's Books,* W. C. Brown, 1970, revised edition, 1976; (editor) *Picture Books for Children,* National Council of Teachers of English, 1972; (with Martha King and Robert Emans) *Focus for Language Arts in the Elementary School,* National Council of Teachers of English, 1973; (editor) *Adventuring with Books,* National Council of Teachers of English, 1977. Collaborated in creation of films: "Sharing Time," 1970, "Let's Tell a Story," 1972, "Understanding Instructions," 1972, and "Rhythm, Rhythm, Everywhere," 1973, for Coronet Instructional Films; also author of "Children's Literature" filmstrip series, McGraw, 1973. Contributor to literature journals and national magazines. Children's literature editor, *Michigan Reading Journal,* 1976—.

*       *       *

## CIPLIJAUSKAITE, Birute  1929-

*PERSONAL:* Born April 11, 1929, in Kaunas, Lithuania; daughter of Juozas (a professor of medicine) and Elena (Stelmokaite) Ciplijauskas. *Education:* Lycee Lithuanien, diploma of maturity, 1948; University of Montreal, M.A., 1956; Bryn Mawr College, Ph.D., 1960. *Office:* Department of Spanish, University of Wisconsin, Madison, Wis. 53706.

*CAREER:* University of Wisconsin—Madison, instructor,

1960-61, assistant professor, 1961-64, associate professor, 1964-68, professor of Spanish literature, 1968-73, John Bascom Professor of Spanish Literature, 1973—. Member, Institute for Research in the Humanities, 1974—. *Awards, honors:* Guggenheim fellow, 1967-68; Institute for Research in the Humanities, Madison, Wis., fellow, 1971-72.

*WRITINGS: La soledad y la poesia espanola contemporanea,* Insula (Madrid), 1962; *El poeta y la poesia: Del romanticismo a la poesia social,* Insula, 1966; (editor) Luis de Gongora, *Sonetos completos,* Castalia (Madrid), 1968; (contributor) Ivar Ivask and Juan Marichal, editors, *Luminous Reality: The Poetry of Jorge Guillen,* University of Oklahoma Press, 1969; *Deber de plenitud: La poesia de Jorge Guillen,* SepSetentas (Mexico), 1972; *Baroja: Un estilo,* Insula, 1973; (editor) *Jorge Guillen,* Taurus, 1976.

*WORK IN PROGRESS: Las guerras carlistas: Historia y novela.*

*BIOGRAPHICAL/CRITICAL SOURCES: Books Abroad,* winter, 1970.

*       *       *

## CLAPP, Verner W(arren)  1901-1972

June 3, 1901—June 15, 1972; American librarian, researcher, and developer of methods and hardware for libraries. Obituaries: *New York Times,* June 16, 1972; *Washington Post,* June 16, 1972; *Antiquarian Bookman,* June 26, 1972; *Publishers Weekly,* July 3, 1972; *Current Biography,* September, 1972.

*       *       *

## CLAR, C(harles) Raymond  1903-

*PERSONAL:* Born November 8, 1903, in Guerneville, Calif.; son of Ivon Matthew (a carpenter) and Elizabeth (Hogue) Clar; married Evelyn Mickelberry, April 21, 1928; children: Laura C. (Mrs. Michael Rothkopf), Barbara Ann (Mrs. Franklin Turner). *Education:* University of California, Berkeley, B.S., 1927. *Politics:* Democrat. *Home:* 1681 Parkmead Way, Sacramento, Calif. 95822.

*CAREER:* California State Division of Forestry, Sacramento, 1927-69, began as ranger, became chief deputy state forester. *Member:* Society of American Foresters, Forest History Society (fellow), California Writers' Club, Society of California Pioneers, California Historical Society, Los Californianos, Westerners.

*WRITINGS:* (With Leonard R. Chatten) *Principles of Forest Fire Management,* State of California, 1954; *California Government and Forestry,* State of California, Volume I, 1959, Volume II, 1969; *Quarterdecks and Spanish Grants,* Glenwood, 1971; *Out of the River Mist,* Forest History Society, 1974. Contributor to professional bulletins and histories.

*       *       *

## CLARK, Fred George  1890-1972

November 2, 1890—January 7, 1972; American economist, author, and radio broadcaster. Obituaries: *New York Times,* January 8, 1972.

*       *       *

## CLARK, Jerome L.  1928-

*PERSONAL:* Name legally changed, 1948; born August 6, 1928, in New York, N.Y.; son of Reuben and Eva May (Clark) Rapaport; married Ann Rorabaw (a college English teacher), February 5, 1950; children: Jerry, Alice, Daniel. *Education:* Atlantic Union College, Th.B., 1948; University of Maryland, M.Ed., 1951; Seventh-day Adventist Theological Seminary (now Andrews University), M.A., 1953: University of Southern California, Ph.D., 1959. *Politics:* Independent. *Religion:* Seventh-day Adventist. *Home address:* Box 515, Collegedale, Tenn. 37315. *Office:* Department of History, Southern Missionary College, Collegedale, Tenn. 37315.

*CAREER:* High school instructor and principal in Dayton, Ohio, 1951-52, Monnett, Ohio, 1951-54, and Reedley, Calif., 1954-56; La Sierra College, Arlington, Calif., instructor of history, 1957-58; Loma Linda Union Academy, Loma Linda, Calif., teacher of history, 1958-59; Southern Missionary College, Collegedale, Tenn., assistant professor, 1959-60, associate professor, 1960-65, professor of history and political science, 1965—. *Member:* American Historical Association, Association of Seventh-day Adventist Historians, Phi Alpha Theta.

*WRITINGS: 1844,* Southern Publishing, 1968, Volume I: *Religious Movements,* Volume II: *Social Movements,* Volume III: *Intellectual Movements.* Contributor of articles to *Review* and *Journal of True Education.*

*WORK IN PROGRESS: Crusade against Alcohol: A History of the American Temperance Movement.*

*AVOCATIONAL INTERESTS:* Swimming, stamp collecting, coin collecting, boating, reading, hiking, playing baseball, volleyball.

\* \* \*

## CLARK, John Drury 1907-

*PERSONAL:* Born August 15, 1907, in Fairbanks, Alaska; son of John Albert (an attorney) and Jeanette (Drury) Clark; married Mildred Baldwin, 1943 (divorced, 1962); married Inga Pratt (an artist), 1962 (died, 1970). *Education:* Attended University of Alaska, 1925-27; California Institute of Technology, B.S., 1930; University of Wisconsin, M.S., 1932; Stanford University, Ph.D., 1934. *Politics:* "Eclectic Pragmatist." *Religion:* "Backslid Episcopalian." *Home and office:* Green Pond Rd., Q-D-2, Newfoundland, N.J. 07435.

*CAREER:* Worked for John Wyeth & Brothers, General Electric Co., and others, 1934-39; U.S. Naval Air Rocket Test Station, Dover, N.J., developer of liquid rocket propellants, 1949-60; Picatinny Arsenal, Liquid Rocket Propulsion Laboratory, Dover, N.J., developer of liquid rocket propellants, 1960-70. *Member:* U.S. Naval Institute, Baker Street Irregulars, Trap Door Spiders.

*WRITINGS: Ignition!,* Rutgers University Press, 1972. Contributor of popular science articles and science fiction stories to magazines and journals.

\* \* \*

## CLARK, John R(ichard) 1930-

*PERSONAL:* Born October 2, 1930, in Philadelphia, Pa.; son of Russell L. and Dorothy (Myers) Clark; married Anna Lydia Motto (a professor of classics), November 7, 1959; children: Valerie Molly, Bradford Russell. *Education:* Pennsylvania State University, B.A., 1952; Columbia University, M.A. (with honors), 1956; University of Michigan, Ph.D., 1965. *Home:* 11712 Davis Rd., Tampa, Fla. 33617. *Office:* Department of English, University of South Florida, Tampa, Fla. 33620.

*CAREER:* Bloomfield College, Bloomfield, N.J., instructor in English, 1956-57; Alfred University, Alfred, N.Y., instructor, 1958-61, assistant professor of English, 1963-65; Muhlenberg College, Allentown, Pa., assistant professor of English, 1965-66; City College of the City University of New York, New York City, assistant professor of English, 1966-68; Fordham University, Bronx, N.Y., assistant professor, then associate professor of English, 1968-69; New York University, New York City, associate professor of English and assistant chairman of department, 1969-73, acting chairman of English department of University College, 1972-73, assistant to head of department and graduate advisor, Graduate School of Arts and Sciences, 1972-73; University of South Florida, Tampa, professor of English and chairman of department, 1973—. Adjunct professor, Drew University, 1969; visiting summer professor, University of Michigan, 1968, 1969.

*MEMBER:* American Philological Association, College English Association, American Society for Eighteenth-Century Studies, Modern Language Association of America, National Council of Teachers of English, Rhetoric Society, Northeast Modern Language Association, South Atlantic Modern Language Association, New York State English Council, Michigan Academy of Arts and Science, Greater New York Regional College English Association, Phi Kappa Phi.

*WRITINGS: Form and Frenzy in Swift's "Tale of a Tub,"* Cornell University Press, 1970; (editor) *Satire: That Blasted Art,* Putnam, 1973. Contributor of over seventy articles, satiric short stories, reviews, and translations of Catullus' poems to *Saturday Review, Satire Newsletter, Studies in Philology, Classical Philology, Philological Quarterly, College English,* and other periodicals.

*WORK IN PROGRESS: Satire: Negative Form, Affirmative Art.*

*SIDELIGHTS:* John R. Clark writes: "When I commenced writing 'serious,' 'heavy' prose, my readers believed I was being satiric. Here is an important influence. I have been writing satire (and/or articles about satire) ever since—and no one has noticed the difference. So, as Vonnegut would have it, it goes." *Avocational interests:* Travel, jazz.

*BIOGRAPHICAL/CRITICAL SOURCES: Criticism,* fall, 1970.

\* \* \*

## CLARK, Mary T.

*PERSONAL:* Born in Philadelphia, Pa.; daughter of Francis and Regina (Twibill) Clark. *Education:* Manhattanville College, B.A., 1939; Fordham University, M.A., 1952, Ph.D., 1955; Yale University, postdoctoral fellow, 1968-69. *Religion:* Roman Catholic. *Office:* Department of Philosophy, Manhattanville College, Purchase, N.Y. 10577.

*CAREER:* Manhattanville College, Purchase, N.Y., instructor, 1951-52, assistant professor, 1953-57, associate professor, 1957-61, professor of philosophy, 1961—, chairperson of department, 1966-68, 1971—. *Member:* Metaphysical Society of America, American Philosophical Association, American Catholic Philosophical Association (member of executive council; vice-president, then president, 1975-77), Metropolitan Round Table of Philosophy (chairman, 1960-61, 1970-71). *Awards, honors:* Interracial Justice Award for *Discrimination Today,* 1967; Outstanding Educator of America award, 1971.

*WRITINGS: Augustine: Philosopher of Freedom,* Desclee, 1959; (with H. Casey) *Logic: A Practical Approach,* Regnery, 1963; *Discrimination Today*, Hobbs, Dorman, 1965; *Augustinian Personalism*, Villanova University Press, 1970; (editor) *An Aquinas Reader*, Doubleday, 1972; *The Problem of Freedom*, Prentice-Hall, 1973. Contributor of articles to scholarly journals.

*WORK IN PROGRESS:* Translating theological writings of Marius Victorinus, for Catholic University Press "Fathers of the Church" series.

*SIDELIGHTS:* Mary T. Clark told *CA*, "In all that I read and all that I write, I try to get and to give more insight into the human person and 'personal freedom.'" *Augustine: Philosopher of Freedom* has been translated into Spanish.

\*          \*          \*

### CLARK, Walter Houston   1902-

*PERSONAL:* First syllable of middle name is pronounced "house"; born July 15, 1902, in Westfield, N.J.; son of James Oliver (a lawyer) and Eloise (Houston) Clark; married Ruth-Marie O'Brien, June 24, 1930; children: Walter Houston, Jr., Jonathan. *Education:* Williams College, A.B., 1925; Harvard University, A.M., 1926, Ed.M., 1935, Ph.D., 1944. *Politics:* Independent. *Religion:* Episcopalian. *Home:* 750 Commonwealth Ave., Newton Centre, Mass. 02159.

*CAREER:* Lenox School, Lenox, Mass., instructor in English and Bible, then senior master and acting headmaster, 1926-45; Bowdoin College, Brunswick, Me., instructor in psychology, 1945-47; Middlebury College, Middlebury, Vt., associate professor of psychology and education, 1947-51; Hartford Seminary Foundation, School of Religious Education, Hartford, Conn., associate professor, 1951-52, professor of psychology, 1952-62, dean of school, 1952-62; Andover Newton Theological School, Newton Center, Mass., professor of psychology of religion, 1962-67. Visiting professor at University of Denver, 1948-49, Wesleyan University, Middletown, Conn., 1952-53, Tufts University, 1967-68, and at Furzedown College, London, England, 1969; Finch Lecturer at Fuller Theological Seminary, 1971. President of board of directors, Self-Development Group, 1970-72. *Member:* American Psychological Association, American Association for the Advancement of Science (fellow), Society for the Scientific Study of Religion (co-founder; president, 1948-51, 1964-66), Religious Education Association, Academy of Religion and Psychical Research (president, 1973—).

*WRITINGS: The Oxford Group: Its History and Significance*, Bookman Associates, 1951; *The Psychology of Religion: An Introduction to Religious Experience and Behavior*, Macmillan, 1958; *Chemical Ecstasy: Psychedelic Drugs and Religion*, Sheed, 1969; (with N. H. Malony, J. Daane, and A. R. Tippett) *Religious Experience: Its Nature and Functioning in the Human Psyche*, C. C Thomas, 1973. Contributor to *Encyclopaedia Britannica*, and to religion, psychology, and education journals.

*WORK IN PROGRESS:* Further research in the field of psychedelic drugs and religion.

*SIDELIGHTS:* Several of Walter Houston Clark's books have been translated into Swedish and German.

\*          \*          \*

### CLARKE, Hans Thacher   1887-1972

December 27, 1887—October 21, 1972; American biochemist, educator, editor, and author of books on organic chemistry. Obituaries: *New York Times*, October 22, 1972.

### CLARKE, Howard William   1929-

*PERSONAL:* Born June 12, 1929, in Waterbury, Conn.; son of Justin Chapman and Ellen (Meade) Clarke; married Ursula Nickisch, September 21, 1955; children: Christine, Anne. *Education:* Holy Cross College, A.B., 1950; Harvard University, A.M., 1951, Ph.D., 1960. *Politics:* Democrat. *Religion:* Roman Catholic. *Home:* 3717 Fortunato Way, Santa Barbara, Calif. 93105. *Office:* Department of Comparative Literature, University of California, Santa Barbara, Calif. 93106.

*CAREER:* Boston University, Boston, Mass., instructor in classics, 1956-58, 1959-60; Oakland University, Rochester, Mich., professor of classics, 1960-69; University of California, Santa Barbara, professor of comparative literature, 1969—. *Military service:* U.S. Army, 1953-56; became sergeant. *Member:* Modern Language Association of America, American Philological Association, American Comparative Literature Association, American Institute of Archaeology.

*WRITINGS:* (Translator and author of introduction) Stanislaw Wyspianski, *The Return of Odysseus*, Indiana University Press, 1966; *The Art of the Odyssey*, Prentice-Hall, 1967.

*WORK IN PROGRESS: Homer's Readers: An Historical Introduction to the "Iliad" and the "Odyssey."*

\*          \*          \*

### CLAUSER, Suzanne (P.)   1929-

*PERSONAL:* Born August 25, 1929, in New Rochelle, N.Y.; daughter of Leonard S. (a business executive) and Elizabeth (Jones) Phillips; married Charles E. Clauser (a physical anthropologist), August 28, 1951. *Education:* Indiana University, A.B., 1951. *Politics:* Democrat. *Religion:* None. *Residence:* Yellow Springs, Ohio. *Agent:* International Creative Management, 40 West 57th St., New York, N.Y. 10019.

*CAREER:* Indiana University, Bloomington, research assistant in economics department, 1951-57; scriptwriter and novelist. Member of board of trustees, Dayton Museum of Natural History, 1961, and Glen Helen, Antioch College, 1968. Red Cross Water Safety Aid Instructor, 1959—. *Member:* Writers Guild of America, West. *Awards, honors:* Western Heritage Award for Best Television Western Fiction, 1974, for "Pioneer Woman"; award for best television drama from Population Institute, 1975, for "The Family Nobody Wanted."

*WRITINGS: A Girl Named Sooner*, Doubleday, 1972. Scriptwriter for television series, "Bonanza," 1964-74; also scriptwriter for numerous television specials, 1974-77, including "A Girl Named Sooner," based on her novel of the same title. Contributor to *Blackwood's Magazine*.

*WORK IN PROGRESS:* An historical novel, *Captive Woman*, for Doubleday; a five-hour mini-series, "Little Women," for National Broadcasting Co.; a series pilot, "Harper's Ferry," for NBC.

*SIDELIGHTS:* Suzanne Clauser lived in Rangoon, Burma, 1953-54. *A Girl Named Sooner* has been translated into German and Italian.

\*          \*          \*

### CLELAND, W(illiam) Wendell   1888-1972

December 14, 1888—December 2, 1972; American educator, government official, and specialist in Egyptian affairs. Obituaries: *New York Times*, December 4, 1972.

## CLERC, Charles 1926-

*PERSONAL:* Surname is pronounced Clair; born March 16, 1926, in Pocatello, Idaho; son of Clemence Clerc; married Virginia Wilson, 1946 (divorced, 1949); married Maria Labriola, February 18, 1966 (divorced, 1974); married Sjaan VandenBroeder Fries, 1977; children: (first marriage) Kim (son); (second marriage) Claudette, Caroline, Rebecca. *Education:* Idaho State College (now University), B.A., 1949, B.A., 1955; University of Utah, M.A., 1957; University of Iowa, Ph.D., 1963. *Residence:* Stockton, Calif. *Office:* Department of English, University of the Pacific, Stockton, Calif. 95204.

*CAREER:* Has worked as shipyard steamfitter, ranch hand, railroad worker, seaman, construction worker, newspaper reporter, radio news and sports director, announcer, correspondent, advertising writer, and factory worker; University of Iowa, Iowa City, instructor in English, 1962-63; University of the Pacific, Stockton, Calif., assistant professor, 1963-66, associate professor, 1966-70, professor of English, 1970—, acting chairman of department, 1968-69. Director, National Defense Education Act (NDEA) Institute in Modern Literary Critical Methods, 1968. Has also lectured on television in central California, 1967. *Military service:* U.S. Merchant Marine Cadet Corps, 1944-46; served in Okinawa; received citation, U.S. Army, 1951-53; became lieutenant. *Member:* Modern Language Association of America. *Awards, honors:* Faculty study grant, 1967, and research grants, 1971, and 1974; named to roll of honor, *Best American Short Stories,* for "The Sacrifice," 1968.

*WRITINGS:* (Editor with Louis H. Leiter) *Seven Contemporary Short Novels,* Scott, Foresman, 1969, 2nd edition, 1975. Also author of "The Pillar," a play first produced by Delta College Theater, 1972; author of two novels, *Cool Fire,* 1975, and *King Life,* 1977, and of a short story collection, *Sans Everything and Other Stories,* 1976. Contributor of articles and short stories to literature and history journals, including *Modern Fiction Studies, English Journal, Pacific Review, The Explicator, Satire Newsletter, Western Humanities Review, Southern Exposure,* and *Midwest Quarterly.*

*WORK IN PROGRESS:* Editing and contributing to *Approaches to "Gravity's Rainbow,"* for Indiana University Press; a novel, *Tiger Eye;* a screenplay, "Medusa."

\* \* \*

## CLIFFORD, John E(dward) 1935-

*PERSONAL:* Born November 21, 1935, in Cleveland, Ohio; son of Louis L. and Patricia (Sloan) Clifford; married Nancy L. Krupinski, July 4, 1959; children: Bridget, Christine, Kathleen. *Education:* John Carroll University, B.S.S., 1958; St. Louis University, M.A., 1959; Michigan State University, Ph.D., 1966. *Religion:* Roman Catholic. *Home:* 3 Bobwhite Ct., San Marcos, Tex. 78666. *Office:* Department of Drama, Southwest Texas State University, San Marcos, Tex. 78666.

*CAREER:* Loras College, Dubuque, Iowa, instructor in speech, 1959-62; Dubuque Department of Recreation, Dubuque, director of Eagle Point Theatre, 1960-62, director of creative dramatics, 1960-62; Bradley University, Peoria, Ill., associate professor of theatre and manager of theatre, 1964-73; Murray Park College of Advanced Education, Adelaide, South Australia, visiting lecturer in drama, 1973-75; Southwest Texas State University, San Marcos, associate professor of drama and director of theatre, 1975—. *Member:* Speech Communication Association, American National

Theatre and Academy, American Theatre Association, International Platform Association, Illinois Speech Association, Southwest Theatre Conference, Texas Educational Theatre Association.

*WRITINGS: Educational Theatre Management,* National Textbook Corporation, 1972. Contributor of reviews of books on theatre direction to *Quarterly Journal of Speech.* Editor, *Theatre Southwest.*

*WORK IN PROGRESS:* A textbook on modern dramatic styles.

\* \* \*

## CLINARD, Turner N(orman) 1917-

*PERSONAL:* Surname is pronounced *Cligh*-nard; born March 5, 1917, in Robertson County, Tenn.; son of Zack Norman (a minister) and Maudie (Rawls) Clinard; married Dorothy Smith (a teacher), December 22, 1942; children: Norman Smith, John Alan. *Education:* Bethel College, McKenzie, Tenn., B.A., 1939; George Peabody College for Teachers, M.A., 1941; Vanderbilt University, Ph.D., 1956, postdoctoral study, 1963-64, summers, 1965, 1966; University of Tennessee, postdoctoral study, 1974. *Politics:* "A 'swinging' Democrat." *Home:* Princeton Ave., Emory Acres, Emory, Va. 24327. *Office:* Department of English, Emory and Henry College, Emory, Va. 24327.

*CAREER:* Clergyman of Cumberland Presbyterian Church; teacher in public schools of Springfield, Tenn., 1939-41; pastor in Birmingham, Ala., 1942-45; high school English teacher in Birmingham, 1943-45; Berry Schools, Mount Berry, Ga., chaplain and English teacher, 1945-47; pastor in Nashville, Tenn., 1947-52, and Greeneville, Tenn., 1952-65; Tusculum College, Greeneville, associate professor of English, 1956-65; Emory and Henry College, Emory, Va., professor of English, 1965—, chairman of department, 1974-77, chairman of Humanities Division, 1968-71. Chairman of board of trustees, Memphis Theological Seminary, 1955-64; member of board of trustees, Holston Conference Colleges, 1973-77. Director, Roane Mountain Naturalist Rally, 1971—.

*MEMBER:* Modern Language Association of America, South Atlantic Modern Language Association, Southeastern Renaissance Conference, Nature Conservancy, Audubon Society, Virginia Society for Ornithology, Tennessee Ornithological Society. *Awards, honors:* McConnell fellowship, 1970, to work on *Birds in American Poetry.*

*WRITINGS: The Holy Spirit Comes through the Worshiping Community,* Pioneer Press, 1971; *Words in Season,* Tidings, 1974; *Becoming a Christian,* Tidings, 1976. Contributor of articles and poetry to about sixty journals. Contributing editor and writer of column, "In a Word," for *Cumberland Presbyterian,* 1967—.

*WORK IN PROGRESS: Birds in American Poetry; Responding to God.*

*BIOGRAPHICAL/CRITICAL SOURCES: Greeneville Sun,* July 11, 1968.

\* \* \*

## CLORE, Gerald L(ewis, Jr.) 1939-

*PERSONAL:* Born March 12, 1939, in St. Paul, Minn.; son of Gerald L., Sr. (a rehabilitation executive) and Anna (Ridlen) Clore; married Marilee Sargent (a college teacher and historian), June 16, 1962 (divorced December, 1973); married Judy S. DeLoache (a research psychologist), September 18, 1977. *Education:* Southern Methodist University, B.A., 1961; University of Texas, Ph.D., 1966. *Home:* 305 West Washington, Urbana, Ill. 61801. *Office:* Department of Psychology, University of Illinois, Urbana, Ill. 61801.

*CAREER:* University of Illinois at Urbana-Champaign, assistant professor, 1966-70, associate professor, 1970-75, professor of psychology, 1975—. Visiting professor, Harvard University, 1973. *Member:* American Psychological Association, Psychonomic Society, Society of Experimental Social Psychology.

*WRITINGS:* (With J. S. Wiggins, K. E. Renner, and R. J. Rose) *The Psychology of Personality,* Addison-Wesley, 1971; *Interpersonal Attraction: An Overview,* General Learning Corp., 1975; (with Wiggins, Renner, and Rose) *The Principles of Personality,* Addison-Wesley, 1976. Contributor of articles to *Journal of Personality and Social Psychology* and other journals.

*WORK IN PROGRESS:* Research on interpersonal attraction and dislike.

\*      \*      \*

### CLUBB, O(liver) Edmund   1901-

*PERSONAL:* Born February 16, 1901, in South Park, Minn.; son of Oliver E. (a rancher) and Lillian May (Nichols) Clubb; married Mariann E. H. Smith (an artist), June 30, 1928; children: Oliver E., Jr., Zoe Mariana (Mrs. William H. Gleysteen, Jr.). *Education:* Attended University of Washington, 1922-23; University of Minnesota, B.A., 1927; California College in China, M.A., 1940. *Home:* 276 Riverside Dr., New York, N.Y. 10025.

*CAREER:* Various positions in U.S. Foreign Service, 1928-52; consul general in Vladivostok, U.S.S.R., 1944-46, Mukden, China, 1946, Changchun, China, 1946-47, and Peking, China, 1947-50; Department of State, Office of Chinese Affairs, director, 1950-52. Visiting lecturer at Columbia University, 1959-62, 1964-65, 1967-68, Brooklyn College (now Brooklyn College of the City University of New York), 1959-61, New York University, 1960-63, New School for Social Research, 1962-65, Florida State University, summer, 1965, and Cornell University, summers, 1966-69. Staff editor, Columbia University Research Project on Men and Politics in Modern China, 1960-66; senior research associate, East Asian Institute, Columbia University, 1966-67, 1968-70. *Military service:* U.S. Army, 1918-19. *Member:* Association for Asian Studies, American Association for the Advancement of Slavic Studies, American Academy of Political and Social Sciences, American Society of International Law, Authors League, Diplomatic and Consular Officers Retired, Mongolia Society, Royal Society for Asian Affairs.

*WRITINGS: Twentieth Century China,* Columbia University Press, 1964, revised edition, 1972; (contributor) Raymond L. Gartoff, editor, *Sino-Soviet Military Relations,* Praeger, 1966; *Communism in China, As Reported from Hankow in 1932,* Columbia University Press, 1968; *China and Russia: The "Great Game,"* Columbia University Press, 1971; (advisory editor) *China,* Arno, 1972; *The Witness and I,* Columbia University Press, 1974. Contributor to *Biographical Dictionary of Republican China,* four volumes, Columbia University Press, 1967-71. Contributor of articles and book reviews to magazines. Consulting editor, *Atlas* magazine, 1961-65; contributing editor, *Current History,* 1976—.

*WORK IN PROGRESS:* A book on the United States and the West Pacific.

\*      \*      \*

### COATES, Geoffrey Edward   1917-

*PERSONAL:* Born May 14, 1917, in London, England; son of Joseph Edward and Ada (Finney) Coates; married Winifred Jean Hobbs (a physician), March 28, 1951; children: Helen Mary (Mrs. John Charles Gerdes), Anthony Peter. *Education:* Oxford University, B.A., 1938, B.Sc., 1939, M.A., 1942; University of Bristol, D.Sc., 1954. *Home:* 1801 Rainbow Ave., Laramie, Wyo. 82070.

*CAREER:* Magnesium Metal Corp., Swansea, England, research chemist, 1940-45; University of Bristol, Bristol, England, lecturer in chemistry, 1945-53; University of Durham, Durham, England, professor of chemistry, 1953-68, chairman of department, 1953-68; University of Wyoming, Laramie, professor of chemistry and head of department, 1968-77. *Member:* Chemical Society (London), American Chemical Society, American Institute of Chemists, New York Academy of Science.

*WRITINGS: Organometallic Compounds,* Methuen, 1956, 3rd edition (with M.L.H. Green and Kenneth Wade), 1967; (with Green, Wade, and Paul Powell) *Principles of Organometallic Chemistry,* Methuen, 1968.

\*      \*      \*

### COATES, William Ames   1916-1973

*PERSONAL:* Born January 26, 1916, in Milton, Mass.; son of Frederick Ames (a businessman) and Adelaide (Swift) Coates; married Carolyn Cummings, January 26, 1963; children: In-Ja (daughter). *Education:* Harvard University, A.B. (summa cum laude), 1937, A.M., 1939, Ph.D., 1950. *Politics:* Independent Democrat. *Religion:* Quaker. *Office:* Department of Modern Languages, Kansas State University, Manhattan, Kan. 66504.

*CAREER:* U.S. Government, Washington, D.C., research analyst, 1950-60; University of Ceylon, Peradeniya, Fulbright lecturer in English and linguistics, 1960-62; University of Rochester, Rochester, N.Y., assistant professor of linguistics, 1963-66; Kansas State University, Manhattan, associate professor of linguistics, 1966-73. *Military service:* U.S. Army, 1945-46. *Member:* Linguistic Society of America, International Linguistic Association, Phi Beta Kappa.

*WRITINGS:* (Translator from the Rumanian) Mircea Eliade, *Two Tales of the Occult,* Herder & Herder, 1970. Contributor to linguistics journals and journals of Slavic affairs.

*WORK IN PROGRESS: The Modern Indo-European Languages;* translating another Mircea Eliade story.

*SIDELIGHTS:* William Coates spoke German, French, Italian, Russian, Swedish, Dutch, Spanish, Danish, and Icelandic, and could read most of the other languages of Europe. Coates visited the major Maya sites in Mexico and Guatemala, spent a month in Iceland, and traveled to the Maldive Islands on a wooden sailing ship. *Avocational interests:* Religion, psychic research, music, travel.†

(Died July 8, 1973)

\*      \*      \*

### COATES, Willson H(avelock)   1899-1976

*PERSONAL:* Born August 1, 1899, in Takayama (near Sendai), Japan; son of Canadian missionaries, Harper H. and

Agnes (Wintemute) Coates; married Hilda Altschule (an artist), September 17, 1928. *Education:* Had early schooling in Japan and attended high school in Vancouver, British Columbia; University of British Columbia, B.A., 1920; Oxford University, B.A. (honors), 1923, M.A., 1926; Cornell University, Ph.D., 1926. *Home:* 220 Highland Pkwy., Rochester, N.Y. 14620. *Office:* Department of History, University of Rochester, Rochester, N.Y. 14627.

*CAREER:* University of Rochester, Rochester, N.Y., instructor, 1925-28, assistant professor, 1928-35, associate professor, 1935-47, professor of history, 1947-65, professor emeritus, 1965-76. Visiting professor at Sarah Lawrence College, 1947-48, and Trinity College, Hartford, Conn., 1967. Public panel member, War Labor Board, 1944-45; U.S. Department of State consultant at Lucknow University, 1957. Rochester Police Advisory Board, member, 1963-70, chairman, 1965-70. *Military service:* Canadian Army, Field Artillery, 1918; became sergeant.

*MEMBER:* American Historical Association, Conference on British Studies, American Association of University Professors, Association of American Rhodes Scholars. *Awards, honors:* Rhodes scholar, 1921-23; grants-in-aid of research from Social Science Research Council and American Council of Learned Societies, 1938, 1949, 1971; Folger Shakespeare Library fellowship, 1951.

*WRITINGS:* (Editor and author of introduction and notes) *The Journal of Sir Simonds D'Ewes: From the First Recess of the Long Parliament to the Withdrawal of King Charles from London,* Yale University Press, 1942; *An Analysis of Major Conflicts in Seventeenth-Century England,* New York University Press, 1960; (with Hayden V. White) *The Emergence of Liberal Humanism: An Intellectual History of Western Europe,* McGraw, Volume I: *From the Italian Renaissance to the French Revolution,* 1966, Volume II: *The Ordeal of Liberal Humanism: An Intellectual History of Western Europe; since the French Revolution,* 1970. Contributor of eight articles and seventy reviews to historical journals. Editor, *Journal of British Studies,* Volumes I-IX, 1961-70. Founder and editor, *The Comparative Study in Society and History.*

*WORK IN PROGRESS:* Editing diaries of the Long Parliament for the period January to September, 1642; editing diaries and analysis of the Short Parliament, 1640; *Cultural Interchange between East and West: The Case of Agnes Wintemute and Harper H. Coates in Japan.*†

(Died September 23, 1976)

\* \* \*

## COCOZZELLA, Peter 1937-

*PERSONAL:* Born November 20, 1937, in Monaciloni, (Campobasso), Italy; came to United States in 1954, naturalized in 1960; son of Mike and Angelina (Naimo) Cocozzella; married Carol Ann Hoffmann; children: Angela. *Education:* Regis College, A.B., 1959; St. Louis University, Ph.D., 1966. *Office:* Department of Romance Languages, State University of New York, Binghamton, N.Y. 13901.

*CAREER:* Latin teacher in high school in Denver, Colo., 1959-60; University of Missouri at St. Louis, instructor, 1965-66, assistant professor of Spanish, 1966-67; Dartmouth College, Hanover, N.H., assistant professor of Spanish, 1967-70; State University of New York at Binghamton, assistant professor, 1970-73, associate professor of Spanish language and literature, 1973—. *Member:* Modern Language Association of America, American Association of Teachers

of Spanish and Portuguese, Alpha Sigma Nu. *Awards, honors:* National Endowment for the Humanities summer research fellowship, 1968; Fulbright-Hays fellowship, Spain, 1963-64, 1964-65.

*WRITINGS:* (Editor) Francisco Moner, *Obres catalanes,* Editorial Barcino (Barcelona), 1970; (contributor) Josep Gulsoy and Josep M. Sola-Sole, editors, *Cementiri de Sinera,* Hispam (Barcelona), 1977.

*WORK IN PROGRESS:* Editing Castilian works of Francisco Moner, for Espasa-Calpe; translating modern Catalan works into English.

\* \* \*

## CODER, S(amuel) Maxwell 1902-

*PERSONAL:* Born March 25, 1902, in Straight, Pa.; son of Emmanuel Miller (a machinist) and Abbie (Bailey) Coder; married Elizabeth Maria Dieterle, February 20, 1932; children: Margaret Elizabeth (deceased), Maxine Joyce (Mrs. T. C. B. Howard IV), Donald Maxwell. *Education:* Temple University, B.S. in Ed., 1938; Evangelical Theological College (now Dallas Theological Seminary and Graduate School of Theology), Th.B., 1938, Th.M., 1940. *Politics:* Republican. *Home:* 1860 Sherman Ave., Evanston, Ill. 60201. *Office:* Moody Bible Institute, Chicago, Ill.

*CAREER:* Businessman, 1928-32; ordained to Presbyterian ministry, 1938; pastor at Grace Church, Camden, N.J., 1935-38, Chelsea Church, Atlantic City, N.J., 1938-43, and Philadelphia, Pa., 1944-45; Moody Bible Institute, Chicago, Ill., member of faculty, 1945-69, editor-in-chief, Moody Press, 1945-46, vice-president and dean of education, 1947-69, dean emeritus, 1969—. Speaker at Bible and missionary conferences throughout the world. *Awards, honors:* D.D., Bible Theological Seminary of Los Angeles, 1949.

*WRITINGS*—All published by Moody: *Dobbie: Defender of Malta,* 1946; *Youth Triumphant* (correspondence course), three volumes, 1946; *God's Will for Your Life,* 1950; (editor) *Our Lord Prays for His Own,* 1950; (editor) *The World to Come,* 1954; *Jude: The Acts of the Apostates,* 1955; (with William Evans) *Great Doctrines of the Bible,* 1974; (editor) *Nave's Topical Bible,* 1975; *Israel's Destiny,* 1978. Co-editor with Wilbur M. Smith, "Wycliffe Series of Christian Classics," Moody, 1946—.

*WORK IN PROGRESS: The Olivet Discourse of Christ; The City of Jerusalem; Christian Workers New Testament; Bible Books in Brief.*

*SIDELIGHTS:* S. Maxwell Coder told *CA:* "My primary reason for writing is that 'necessity is laid upon me; yea, woe is unto me if I preach not the gospel' through the printed page (I Cor. 9:26). A second reason is that much theological or religious writing is phrased in language which obscures the meaning it is intended to convey, creating a great need for clarity and simplicity."

\* \* \*

## COE, William C(harles) 1930-

*PERSONAL:* Born October 22, 1930, in Hanford, Calif.; son of Bernard (a farmer) and Bertha (Vaughan) Coe; married second wife, Linda G. Buckner, July 29, 1972; children: (first marriage) Karen A., William V. *Education:* Attended Stanford University, 1948-50; University of California, Davis, B.S., 1958; Fresno State College (now California State University, Fresno), additional study, 1960-61; University of California, Berkeley, Ph.D., 1964. *Home:* 574 East Shields, Fresno, Calif. 93704. *Office:* Department of

Psychology, California State University, Fresno, Calif. 93740.

*CAREER:* Self-employed in earthmoving and landsurveying, Woodland and Hanford, Calif., 1956-60; Langley-Porter Neuropsychiatric Institute, San Francisco, Calif., clinical psychologist, 1964-66; California State University, Fresno, professor of psychology, 1966—. *Military service:* U.S. Air Force, 1952-56; became first lieutenant; received Air Medal with one oak-leaf cluster and Distinguished Flying Cross. *Member:* American Psychological Association, Society for Advancement of Behavior Therapy, Society for Clinical and Experimental Hypnosis, Western Psychological Association, California State Psychological Association, Central California Psychological Association (president, 1967).

*WRITINGS:* (With T. R. Sarbin) *The Student Psychologist's Handbook,* Schenkman, 1969; *Challenges of Personal Adjustment,* Holt, 1972; (with Sarbin) *Hypnotism,* Holt, 1972.

\* \* \*

## COFER, Charles N(orval) 1916-

*PERSONAL:* Born June 1, 1916, in Cape Girardeau, Mo.; son of Charles N. (a merchant) and Ernestine (Osterloh) Cofer; married Justine Donnelly, August 3, 1940; married second wife, Lynette K. Friedrich, July 4, 1976; children: Thomas M., Jonathan C. *Education:* Southeast Missouri State College (now University), A.B., 1937; University of Iowa, M.A., 1937; Brown University, Ph.D., 1940. *Home:* 511 Stoneleigh, Houston, Tex. 77079. *Office:* Department of Psychology, University of Houston, Houston, Tex. 77004.

*CAREER:* George Washington University, Washington, D.C., began as instructor, 1941, assistant professor of psychology, 1946-47; University of Maryland, College Park, associate professor, 1947-51, professor of psychology, 1951-59; New York University, New York, N.Y., professor of psychology, 1959-63; Pennsylvania State University, University Park, professor of psychology, 1963-67; University of Maryland, professor of psychology, 1967-68; Pennsylvania State University, professor of psychology, 1968-76; University of Houston, Houston, Tex., professor of psychology, 1976—. Visiting professor of psychology, University of California, Berkeley, 1962-63. *Military service:* U.S. Naval Reserve, active duty, 1943-46; became lieutenant. *Member:* American Psychological Association, Psychonomic Society, American Association for the Advancement of Science, Sigma Xi.

*WRITINGS: Verbal Learning and Verbal Behavior,* McGraw, 1961; (with B. S. Musgrave) *Verbal Behavior and Learning,* McGraw, 1963; (with M. H. Appley) *Motivation: Theory and Research,* Wiley, 1964; *Motivation and Emotion,* Scott, Foresman, 1972. Editor, *Psychological Review,* 1965-70.

*SIDELIGHTS: Motivation: Theory and Research* has been translated into Spanish and Polish, *Motivation and Emotion* into German, Italian, and Spanish.

\* \* \*

## COHEN, William B(enjamin) 1941-

*PERSONAL:* Born May 2, 1941, in Jakobstad, Finland; son of Walter J. (a physician) and Rosi (Hirschberg) Cohen; married Habiba Suleiman (an assistant college dean), October 25, 1964; children: Natalie, Leslie. *Education:* Pomona College, B.A., 1962; Stanford University, M.A., 1963, Ph.D., 1968. *Politics:* Democrat. *Religion:* Jewish.

*Home:* 615 North Lincoln, Bloomington, Ind. 47401. *Office:* Department of History, Ballantine Hall, Indiana University, Bloomington, Ind. 47401.

*CAREER:* Northwestern University, Evanston, Ill., instructor in history, 1966-67; Indiana University at Bloomington, lecturer, 1967-68, assistant professor, 1968-71, associate professor of history, 1971—, chairman, West European Studies Program, 1978—. *Member:* American Historical Association, French Historical Studies. *Awards, honors:* National Endowment for Humanities grant, 1971-72.

*WRITINGS: Rulers of Empire: The French Colonial Service in Africa,* Hoover Institution Press, 1971; (editor) *Robert Delavignette on the French Empire,* University of Chicago Press, 1977. Contributor of articles to *African Historical Studies, Journal of Contemporary History, French Historical Studies, Journal of the Nigerian Historical Society,* and *Race and Class.*

*WORK IN PROGRESS: French Image of Africa, 1700-1900.*

\* \* \*

## COJEEN, Robert H. 1920-

*PERSONAL:* Born June 5, 1920, in Ishpeming, Mich.; son of John and Lily (Knight) Cojeen; married Billie Jane Cranfield, September 6, 1952; children: Paul, Robert, Christopher. *Education:* University of Michigan, B.B.A., 1946, M.B.A., 1947; Indiana University, D.B.A., 1955. *Home:* 6035 Greenwich Lane, Grand Blanc, Mich. 48439. *Office:* Department of Business Administration, University of Michigan—Flint, Flint, Mich. 48503.

*CAREER:* University of Florida, Gainesville, instructor in accounting, 1947-48; University of Kentucky, Lexington, associate professor of business administration, 1948-56; University of Michigan—Flint, professor and chairman of department of business administration, 1956—. Visiting professor of business administration, University of Pittsburgh, 1965-66; professor of business administration and co-founder of School of Business Administration, Ahmadu Bello University (Zaria, Nigeria), 1965-66. Commissioner, Genesee County Economic Development Commission; member of board of directors, Family Service Agency, 1963-64; member of board of directors, Flint Young Men's Christian Association (YMCA), 1964. *Military service:* U.S. Army, 1942-45; served in Pacific theater of operations. *Member:* Academy of Management, American Accounting Association, National Association of Accountants (president of Saginaw Valley chapter), Association for Education in International Business, Industrial Relations Research Association, Michigan Economic Association, Michigan Accounting Educators.

*WRITINGS:* (Editor) *Cases in Branch Plant Personnel Administration,* Indiana University, 1955; (with William A. Paton and Robert L. Dixon) *Problems and Practice Sets Accompanying Essentials of Accounting,* Macmillan, 1958; *Case Studies in Nigerian Business,* Ahmadu Bello University, University of Pittsburgh, 1966; (editor) *Nigerian Business Materials: Cases, Incidents, Articles,* Ahmadu Bello University, University of Pittsburgh, 1966; (editor) *Personnel Management Cases in Developing Countries,* Graduate School of Business, University of Michigan, 1968. Book reviewer, *Choice.*

*WORK IN PROGRESS:* Research on intercultural management problems in European manufacturing subsidiaries of American corporations.

## COLBURN, C(lyde) William 1939-

*PERSONAL:* Born March 31, 1939, in Bloomington, Ill.; son of Clyde William (a farmer) and Wanda (Simmons) Colburn; married Colette Ann Meismer, August 20, 1960; children: Bill, Jon. *Education:* Illinois Wesleyan University, B.S., 1961; Bowling Green State University, M.A., 1962; Indiana University, Ph.D., 1967. *Politics:* Republican. *Religion:* Methodist. *Home:* 3304 Tacoma, Ann Arbor, Mich. 48104. *Office:* Department of Speech, University of Michigan, Ann Arbor, Mich. 48108.

*CAREER:* University of Michigan, Ann Arbor, assistant professor of speech, 1965—. City councilman, Ann Arbor, Mich., 1972—. *Member:* American Forensic Association, Central States Speech Association, Michigan Speech Association, Speech Communication Association. *Awards, honors:* University of Michigan, Outstanding Service Award, 1968.

*WRITINGS: Strategies for Educational Debate,* Holbrook, 1972; *Communication and Consensus,* Harcourt, 1972.

*WORK IN PROGRESS:* A book on information theory.

\* \* \*

## COLEMAN, Bruce P(umphrey) 1931-

*PERSONAL:* Born June 8, 1931, in Pittsburgh, Pa.; son of Raymond W. (a professor emeritus) and Essie Bee (Pumphrey) Coleman; married Phyllis J. Lloyd, June 9, 1956; children: Roberta J., Lisa R. *Education:* West Virginia University, B.S., 1954; Indiana University, M.B.A., 1958, D.B.A., 1967. *Home:* 1596 Pebblestone Dr., Okemos, Mich. 48864. *Office:* Eppley Center, Michigan State University, East Lansing, Mich. 48823.

*CAREER:* Chesapeake & Potomac Telephone Co. of West Virginia, Charleston, administrative assistant, 1954-55; Kansas State College of Pittsburg (now Pittsburg State College), assistant professor of management, 1958-62; Michigan State University, East Lansing, associate professor of management, 1966—. Adjunct assistant professor, overseas graduate program, Boston University, Mannheim, West Germany, 1973-74. *Military service:* U.S. Air Force, 1955-57. U.S. Air Force Reserve, 1957—; current rank, lieutenant colonel. *Member:* American Institute for Decision Sciences, Academy of Management, Industrial Relations Research Association, Midwest Business Administration Association, Beta Gamma Sigma, Sigma Iota Epsilon.

*WRITINGS:* (With J. W. Bonge) *Concepts for Corporate Strategy: Readings in Business Policy,* Macmillan, 1972; (contributor) N. H. Cuthbert and K. H. Hawkins, editors, *Company Industrial Relations Policies,* Longman, 1973. Contributor of articles to *Business Horizons* and *Research Management.*

\* \* \*

## COLIMORE, Vincent J(erome) 1914-

*PERSONAL:* Born June 27, 1914, in Baltimore, Md.; son of Charles (a restaurateur) and Teresa (Fava) Colimore; married Miriam Holthaus, January 19, 1944; children: Michael, Mary Patricia, Joan Elizabeth, Mark. *Education:* Loyola University, Chicago, Ill., B.A., 1939; Fordham University, M.A., 1953; New York University, Ph.D., 1967. *Religion:* Roman Catholic. *Home:* 10918 Gateview Rd., Cockeysville, Md. 21030. *Office:* Department of Education, Towson State University, York Rd., Towson, Md. 21204.

*CAREER:* Loyola College, Baltimore, Md., 1946-67, became associate professor of modern languages, and chairman of department, tennis coach, 1947-73; Towson State University, Towson, Md., associate professor of education, 1973—. *Military service:* U.S. Army, 1942-45, 1950-51; became staff sergeant; received Bronze Star and two oak leaf clusters. *Member:* American Council of Foreign Language Teachers, Middle States Association of Modern Language Teachers, Maryland Foreign Language Association, Knights of Columbus.

*WRITINGS:* (Translator) Claude Cuenot, *Teilhard de Chardin,* Helicon, 1965; (compiler) *Selected Readings in Existentialism and Education,* MSS Information Corp., 1969; (compiler) *Selected Readings in Modern Language Teaching,* MSS Information Corp., 1969; (compiler) *Selected Readings in Scholasticism and Education,* MSS Information Corp., 1971. Contributor of book reviews to *Best Sellers.*

*WORK IN PROGRESS:* A method of teaching values in schools.

\* \* \*

## COLLIER, Gaylan Jane 1924-

*PERSONAL:* Born July 23, 1924, in Fluvanna, Tex.; daughter of Ben Vivian (a stock farmer) and Narcis (Smith) Collier. *Education:* Abilene Christian College (now University), B.A., 1946; University of Iowa, M.A., 1949; Cornell University, additional study, summer, 1953; University of Denver, Ph.D., 1957. *Religion:* Church of Christ. *Office:* Department of Theatre, Texas Christian University, Fort Worth, Tex. 76129.

*CAREER:* University of North Carolina at Greensboro, instructor in drama, 1947-48; Greensboro College, Greensboro, N.C., assistant professor of drama and acting department head, 1949-50; Abilene Christian College (now University), Abilene, Tex., 1950-60, began as assistant professor, became associate professor of drama and director of theatre; Idaho State University, Pocatello, associate professor of drama, 1960-63; Sam Houston State University, Huntsville, Tex., 1963-67, began as associate professor, became professor of drama; Texas Christian University, Fort Worth, professor of theatre, 1967—, head of acting, 1967—. Visiting lecturer at Idaho State University, 1958, 1959, and University of Wisconsin, 1965. Administrative assistant to director of Children's Theatre Association, 1965-67. Director of repertory theatres in Fort Worth, Tex., 1968, 1969, 1972. *Member:* American Theatre Association (chairman of committee for directory of children's theatres in the United States, 1964-65), American Association of University Professors, Southwest Theatre Conference, Texas Theatre Association.

*WRITINGS: Assignments in Acting,* Harper, 1966. Contributor of articles to *Rocky Mountain Theatre News, Southern Speech,* and *Western Speech.* Editor, *Region Four Children's Theatre Association News.*

*WORK IN PROGRESS:* Articles about "American Theatre History" for journals in her field; dialects for the stage.

*AVOCATIONAL INTERESTS:* Foreign travel.

\* \* \*

## COLLINS, June Irene 1935-

*PERSONAL:* Name legally changed, February 2, 1973; born May 16, 1935, in Sydney, New South Wales, Australia;

daughter of Richard Edward and Joyce (Bayfield) Weatherstone; married Peter Michael Skewes, May 15, 1954 (divorced). *Education:* Attended schools in Sydney, Australia. *Religion:* Church of England. *Home address:* P.O. Box 80571, Seattle, Wash. 98108.

*CAREER:* Self-employed as dancer and theatrical booking agent in Southeast Asia, 1961-69; spent three years in Vietnam before coming to United States in 1969 to testify before the Senate permanent subcommittee on investigations and the committee on government operations. *Member:* Overseas Press Club, Special Forces Decade Association (honorary member).

*WRITINGS:* (With Robin Moore) *The Khaki Mafia,* Crown, 1971.

*WORK IN PROGRESS:* A humorous novel about two girls who become involved in a jewel theft while entertaining in the Orient.

\*      \*      \*

**COLODNY, Robert G.   1915-**

*PERSONAL:* Born August 5, 1915, in Phoenix, Ariz.; son of Omar I. (a scholar) and Pauline (Shenberg) Colodny; married Dorothy Newman, June 15, 1946 (died, 1968); children: Robert Richard. *Education:* University of California, Berkeley, B.A., 1947, M.A., 1948, Ph.D., 1950. *Politics:* Independent. *Religion:* ''Scientific Humanism.'' *Office:* Department of History, University of Pittsburgh, Pittsburgh, Pa. 15213.

*CAREER:* Has worked as a research chemist and journalist; University of Kansas, Lawrence, 1957-59, became professor of history; University of Pittsburgh, Pittsburgh, Pa., associate professor, 1958-67, professor of history and philosophy of science, 1967—. *Military service:* Spanish Republican Army, 1937-38. U.S. Army, 1941-46; became staff sergeant; received Hans Beimler Medal. *Member:* American Historical Association, History of Science Society, American Association for the Advancement of Science.

*WRITINGS: The Struggle for Madrid,* Paine-Whitman, 1959; *The Scientific Revolution of the Seventeenth Century,* University of Pittsburgh Press, 1963; *Spain: The Glory and the Tragedy,* Humanities, 1971; *El Asedio de Madrid* (title means ''The Siege of Madrid''), Ruedo Iberico, 1971; *Biographies of Twelve Great Chemists,* McGraw, 1972; (author of introduction) *Spain: The Unfinished Revolution,* Camelot, 1972; *The Decline and Fall of Modern Europe,* University of Pittsburgh Press, 1972.

Editor: ''Philosophy of Science'' series, University of Pittsburgh Press, Volume I: *Frontiers of Science and Philosophy,* 1962, Volume II: *Beyond the Edge of Certainty,* 1965, Volume III: *Mind and Cosmos: Essays in Contemporary Science and Philosophy,* 1966, Volume IV: *The Nature and Function of Scientific Theories,* 1970, Volume V: *Paradigms and Paradoxes: The Philosophical Challenge of the Quantum Domain,* 1972, Volume VI: *Logic, Laws and Life: Some Philosophical Complications,* 1977. Contributor to professional journals.

*WORK IN PROGRESS: History of Modern Scientific Achievements.*

\*      \*      \*

**COLONY, Horatio   1900-1977**

*PERSONAL:* Born September 22, 1900, in Keene, N.H.; son of Charles Taylor (a manufacturer and banker) and Ellen Luthera (Warren) Colony; married Mary Curtis, November 9, 1946. *Education:* Harvard University, A.B., 1922. *Politics:* Democrat. *Religion:* Unitarian Universalist. *Home:* 199 Main St., Keene, N.H. 03431; and 83 Chestnut St., Boston, Mass. 02108.

*CAREER:* Textile manufacturer. Former director and treasurer, Cheshire Mills, Harrisville, N.H.; former director, Ashuelot National Bank, Keene, N.H. *Member:* Poetry Society of America, New Hampshire Poetry Society, Boston Authors Club, St. Botolph Club (Boston).

*WRITINGS: Free Forester* (novel), Little, Brown, 1935; *The Amazon's Hero* (play), Branden Press, 1972; *The Emperor and the Bee Boy* (play), Branden Press, 1976.

Poems: *A Brook of Leaves,* Badger, 1935; *Birth and Burial,* Meador, 1939; *Bacchus and Krishna,* Branden, 1952; *Demon in Love,* Hampshire, 1955; *Young Malatesta,* R. R. Smith, 1957; *Three Loves the Same,* Bruce Humphries, 1961; *The Early Land,* Bruce Humphries, 1962; *The Flying Ones,* Bruce Humphries, 1964; *The Magic Child,* Branden Press, 1966; *Some Phoenix Blood,* Branden Press, 1969; *Flower Myth,* Branden Press, 1971.

*SIDELIGHTS:* Horatio Colony traveled in most of the countries of the world, the exceptions being mainland China, Iran, and Iraq.†

(Died April 28, 1977)

\*      \*      \*

**COLTON, James B(yers) II   1908-**

*PERSONAL:* Born September 9, 1908, in Newton, Mass.; son of Edward S., Jr. (an education administrator) and E. Leslie (Barnes) Colton; married Ruth S. Ruiter (an alumni secretary), June 29, 1935; children: Charles E., Susan B. (Mrs. Hugh M. Gibbons), Elizabeth W. *Education:* Bowdoin College, A.B., 1931; New York College for Teachers (now State University of New York at Albany), M.A., 1952. *Politics:* Mugwump. *Religion:* Congregational. *Home:* 63 Academy Rd., Albany, N.Y. 12208. *Office:* The Albany Academy, Academy Rd., Albany, N.Y. 12208.

*CAREER:* The Loomis School, Windsor, Conn., teacher of Latin and Greek, 1931-34; The Albany Academy, Albany, N.Y., teacher of Latin, Greek, and humanities, chairman of Latin department and foreign languages department, 1934—. Consultant to Summer Pilot Program, Johns Hopkins University, Baltimore, Md., 1967. *Member:* American Philological Association, Classical Association of the Empire State.

*WRITINGS:* (Translator) *The Surgery of Theodoric,* Appleton, Volume I, 1955, Volume II, 1960; (translator) *John Mirfield on Wounds and Trauma,* Hafner, 1969. Contributor of articles to *New York State Journal of Medicine* and *Journal of Surgery and Gynecology.*

*WORK IN PROGRESS:* Textbooks.

\*      \*      \*

**COMFORT, Howard   1904-**

*PERSONAL:* Born June 4, 1904, in Haverford, Pa.; son of William Wistar (a professor and college president) and Mary L. (Fales) Comfort; married Elizabeth P. Webb, June 3, 1931; children: W. Wistar, Laura W. (Mrs. George F. Kesel). *Education:* Haverford College, A.B., 1924; Princeton University, M.A., 1927, Ph.D., 1932. *Politics:* Republican. *Religion:* Quaker. *Home:* Crosslands 224, Kennett Square, Pa. 19348. *Office:* Department of Classics, Haverford College, Haverford, Pa. 19041.

*CAREER:* Haverford School, Haverford, Pa., teacher of Latin, 1924-26; Hamilton College, Clinton, N.Y., assistant professor of classics, 1929-30; Haverford College, Haverford, began as instructor, became assistant professor, 1932-38, associate professor, 1938-57, professor of classics, 1957-69, professor emeritus, 1969—. Consultant, Prison Industries Reorganization Administration, Washington, D.C., 1936; director of Rome, Italy office, American Friends Service Committee, 1940; cultural attache (United States Information Service), Rome Embassy, 1950-51, Bern Legation, 1951-52.

*MEMBER:* Archaeological Institute of America, American Philological Association (secretary-treasurer, 1946-49; vice-president, 1960-62; president, 1962-63), Rei Cretariae Romanae Fautores (president, 1957-71, honorary president, 1971—), Deutsches Archaeologisches Institut, Accademia Petrarca (Arezzo, Italy), Society of Antiquaries of London (fellow), Classical Club of Philadelphia (president, 1955-56), C. C. Morris Cricket Library Association (president, 1969-77), Merion Cricket Club, Forty (Cricket) Club of London (honorary), Cricket Society of London (honorary).

*WRITINGS:* (Editor and translator) August Oxe, *Corpus Vasorum Arretinorum,* Habelt Verlag, 1968; (with Arturo Stenico, Mario Del Chiaro, and Enrico Paribeni) *Terra Sigillata: La ceramica a rilievo ellenistica e romana,* Istituto della Enciclopedia Italiana, 1968. Contributor of articles and reviews to *American Journal of Archaeology, Acta Rei Cretariae Romanae Fautorum,* and other archaeological journals.

*WORK IN PROGRESS:* Supplement to *Corpus Vasorum Arretinorum;* various articles on Roman ceramic archaeology.

*AVOCATIONAL INTERESTS:* Cricket, water colors, creative ceramics.

\* \* \*

## COMPARETTI, Alice 1907-

*PERSONAL:* Born December 1, 1907, in South Bend, Ind., daughter of Cyrus Edward (a lawyer and judge) and Elizabeth M. (Creed) Pattee; married Ermanno F. Comparetti (a professor of music), August 16, 1938; children: Tanya (Mrs. Roger D. Smith), Roger. *Education:* Rockford College, B.A., 1930; Cornell University, M.A., 1934, Ph.D., 1936. *Home:* 4830 East Pima Cir., Phoenix, Ariz. 85044. *Office:* Department of English, Colby College, Waterville, Me. 04901.

*CAREER:* Colby College, Waterville, Me., instructor, 1936-42, assistant professor, 1942-54, associate professor, 1954-61, professor of English, 1961—. *Member:* American Association of University Professors, Modern Language Association of America, College English Association, Phi Beta Kappa.

*WRITINGS:* *Wordsworth's White Doe of Rylstone,* Cornell University Press, 1937; *Gregory's Angels,* Eerdmans, 1972; *The Hammer of Thor,* Lion Publishing, 1974.

\* \* \*

## CONDON, Robert 1921(?)-1972

1921(?)—June 13, 1972; American television and radio writer. Obituaries: *New York Times,* June 14, 1972.

\* \* \*

## CONKLIN, John E(van) 1943-

*PERSONAL:* Born October 2, 1943, in Oswego, N.Y.; son of Evan Nelson (an insurance salesman) and Susan (Brenner) Conklin; children: Christopher Perry, Anne Tiffany. *Education:* Cornell University, A.B. (cum laude), 1965; Harvard University, Ph.D., 1969. *Home:* 315 Reedsdale Rd., Milton, Mass. 02186. *Office:* Department of Sociology, Tufts University, Medford, Mass. 02155.

*CAREER:* Harvard University, Center for Criminal Justice, Cambridge, Mass., research associate, 1969-70; Tufts University, Medford, Mass., assistant professor, 1970-76, associate professor of sociology, 1976—. *Member:* American Sociological Association, Society for the Study of Social Problems, Law and Society Association, National Council on Crime and Delinquency, Phi Beta Kappa.

*WRITINGS:* *Robbery and the Criminal Justice System,* Lippincott, 1972; (editor) *The Crime Establishment,* Prentice-Hall, 1973; *The Impact of Crime,* Macmillan, 1975; *"Illegal But Not Criminal": Business Crime in America,* Prentice-Hall, 1977. Contributor of articles to scholarly journals.

*WORK IN PROGRESS:* An introductory criminology textbook, completion expected in 1980.

\* \* \*

## CONLON, Denis J. 1932-

*PERSONAL:* Born April 8, 1932, in Stockport, England; son of Arthur and Mildred (Ledwich) Conlon; married Maureen Henry, August 14, 1957. *Education:* University of Nottingham, B.A., 1954, post-graduate certificate in education, 1955; University of London, B.A., 1964, Ph.D., 1972; University of Lille, docteur de l'universite, 1966. *Office:* U.F.S.I.A., University of Antwerp, Prinsstraat 13, 2000 Antwerp, Belgium.

*CAREER:* French department head in Singapore, 1959-63; Memorial University of Newfoundland, St. John's, assistant professor, 1963-67, associate professor of French, 1967-73; University of Antwerp, Antwerp, Belgium, reader in literature, 1970-72, professor of English literature, 1974—. *Military service:* Royal Air Force, flying officer, 1955-58. *Member:* Royal Society of the Arts (fellow).

*WRITINGS:* (Editor) Jean Anouilh, *L'Invitation au chateau,* Cambridge University Press, 1962; (editor) Jean Giraudoux, *La Folle de Chaillot,* Cambridge University Press, 1963; *Anthologie de contes et nouvellas modernes,* Methuen, 1968, 6th edition, 1977; (editor) *Le Rommant de Guy de Warwik,* University of North Carolina Press, 1971; (editor) Jean-Paul Sartre, *Le Diable et le bon Dieu,* Methuen, 1971; (editor) *Witasse le Moine,* University of North Carolina Press, 1972; *English Literature from the Beginning to the Dawn of the Modern Age,* De Nederlandsche Boekhandel, 1974; (editor) *G. K. Chesterton: The Critical Judgments,* Part I: *1900-1937,* Antwerp Studies in English Literature, 1976; (editor) *Richart sans peur,* University of North Carolina Press, 1977. General editor, "Antwerp Studies in English Literature".

*WORK IN PROGRESS:* *Simon de Puille; The Song of Dermot.*

\* \* \*

## CONTRERAS, Heles 1933-

*PERSONAL:* Born August 1, 1933, in Victoria, Chile; son of Domingo and Frieda (Weibel) Contreras; married Gladys Gaete, January 15, 1955; children: Patricio, Moyra, Sandra, Carmen, Leticia. *Education:* University of Conception, Chile, professor of English, 1957; Indiana University, M.A.,

1959, Ph.D., 1961. *Home:* 9611 24th N.W., Seattle, Wash. 98117. *Office:* Department of Romance Languages, University of Washington, Seattle, Wash. 98105.

*CAREER:* University of Conception, Conception, Chile, professor of linguistics, 1961-64; University of Washington, Seattle, visiting assistant professor, 1964-65, assistant professor, 1965-67, associate professor, 1967-77, professor of linguistics, 1977—. *Awards, honors:* Fulbright scholar, 1958-59.

*WRITINGS:* (With Sol Saporta) *A Phonological Grammar of Spanish,* University of Washington Press, 1962; (editor) *Los fundamentos de la gramatica transformacional,* Siglo XXI, 1971; *A Theory of Word Order with Special Reference to Spanish,* North-Holland Publishing, 1976.

\*    \*    \*

## CONWAY, (Mary) Margaret 1935-

*PERSONAL:* Born May 14, 1935, in Terre Haute, Ind.; daughter of Frank J. (a pharmacist) and Mary (Downing) Conway. *Education:* Purdue University, B.A., 1957; University of California, Berkeley, M.A., 1960; Indiana University, Ph.D., 1965. *Office:* Department of Government and Politics, University of Maryland, College Park, Md. 20742.

*CAREER:* University of Maryland, College Park, member of faculty of department of government and politics, 1963—. *Member:* American Political Science Association, Southern Political Science Association, Midwest Political Science Association.

*WRITINGS: Political Analysis: An Introduction,* Allyn & Bacon, 1972, 2nd edition, 1976; *Parties and Politics in America,* Allyn & Bacon, 1976.

*WORK IN PROGRESS: Watergate and the 1974 Election.*

\*    \*    \*

## COOK, Beverly Blair 1926-

*PERSONAL:* Born December 10, 1926, in Chicago, Ill.; daughter of Ross Joseph (a lawyer-executive) and Nita (Hanson) Ulman; married Charles C. Cook, Jr., June 21, 1949 (divorced, 1960); married Cornelius Philip Cotter (a professor of political science), July 31, 1966; children: (first marriage) Linda, C. Randall, David, Gary; (step-children) Cornelia (Mrs. David Calvert), Lawrence, Charles, Steven. *Education:* Wellesley College, B.A., 1948; University of Wisconsin—Madison, M.A., 1949; Claremont University College (now Claremont Graduate School), Ph.D., 1962. *Politics:* Democrat. *Home:* 3965 North Harcourt Pl., Milwaukee, Wis. 53211. *Office:* Department of Political Science, University of Wisconsin, Milwaukee, Wis. 53201.

*CAREER:* Iowa State University, Ames, instructor in political science, 1949-50; California State College at Fullerton (now California State University, Fullerton), assistant professor of political science, 1962-66; University of Wisconsin—Milwaukee, lecturer, 1967-70, associate professor, 1970-74, professor of political science, 1974—. *Member:* American Association for the Advancement of Science, American Political Science Association, American Judicature Society, National Women's Political Caucus, Midwest Political Science Association. *Awards, honors:* American Philosophical Society, grant for research on Kansas Courts, 1967, grant for judicial biography, 1971; Social Science Research Council grant for seventh circuit study, 1969; University of Wisconsin—Milwaukee summer grants, 1970, 1972; Ford Foundation fellowship, 1972-73, for federal district judgeship study; Fromkin grant and lectureship, 1973; Flor-

ence Eagleton grant, 1976-77, to study women judges on urban courts.

*WRITINGS: The Judicial Process in California,* Dickenson, 1967. Contributor of articles to *Kansas Law Review, Judicature, Washington University Law Quarterly, Law and Society Review, Black Law Journal, Western Political Quarterly, Cincinnati Law Review, American Journal of Political Science,* and *American Politics Quarterly.*

*WORK IN PROGRESS:* Contributing two chapters on women judges and Supreme Court decisions on women's rights; a book on women judges; research on the president and judicial appointments and on public opinion and diffuse support for federal judges.

*SIDELIGHTS:* Beverly Cook told *CA:* "The central theme of my research is the exploration of possible explanations for public policy decisions by judges, through environmental variables such as political culture and public opinion, personal variables of ascription and socialization, and structural variables of recruitment and bureaucratization."

\*    \*    \*

## COOK, Mark 1942-

*PERSONAL:* Born December 6, 1942, in Sandown, Isle of Wight; son of Samuel Astbury (a civil servant) and Beatrice (Rawlins) Cook; married Janette McLeod, December 29, 1969. *Education:* Oxford University, B.A., 1965, M.A., 1970, D.Phil., 1971. *Home:* 10, Woodlands Ter., Swansea, Wales. *Office:* Department of Psychology, University College of Swansea, Singleton Park, Swansea, Wales.

*CAREER:* University of Aberdeen, Aberdeen, Scotland, assistant lecturer in psychology, 1968-69; Oxford University, Oxford, England, research officer in psychology, 1969-73; University College of Swansea, Swansea, Wales, lecturer in psychology, 1973—.

*WRITINGS: Interpersonal Perception,* Penguin, 1971; (with Michael Argyle) *Gaze and Mutual Gaze,* Cambridge University Press, 1976; *Love and Attraction,* Pergamon, 1977; (with Robert McHenry) *Sexual Attraction,* Pergamon, 1978.

*WORK IN PROGRESS: Bases of Human Sexual Attraction,* for Academic Press; *Judging People,* for Methuen.

*AVOCATIONAL INTERESTS:* History of transport, driving cars and motorcycles, collecting government survey maps.

\*    \*    \*

## COOK, Warren L. 1925-

*PERSONAL:* Born July 29, 1925, in Spokane, Wash.; son of Silas Warren and Amy (Morris) Cook; married Sandra E. Smith (a physical education instructor and horse breeder), March 15, 1963; children: Susan Amy. *Education:* Attended Washington State University, 1944-46; National University of San Marcos (Lima), B.A., 1950, Doct. Letras, 1955; Yale University, M.A., 1957, Ph.D., 1960. *Home address:* P.O. Box 344, Castleton, Vt. 05735. *Office:* Department of History, Castleton State College, Castleton, Vt. 05735.

*CAREER:* Castleton State College, Castleton, Vt., assistant professor, 1960-63, associate professor, 1963-69, professor of history and anthropology, 1970—, chairman of department of history, 1967-68, member of president's cabinet, 1971-72. Member of Castleton Town Planning Commission, 1971-74. *Member:* American Historical Association, Society for the History of Discoveries, Conference on Latin

American History, American Association of University Professors, American Federation of Teachers, American Philatelic Society, Epigraphic Society, New England Conference on Latin American Studies, Western History Association, Vermont Archaeological Society. *Awards, honors:* Herbert Eugene Bolton Memorial Prize, 1974, for best book in Latin American history.

*WRITINGS:* (Author of bio/bibliographical prologue) B. Salinas y Cordova, *Memorial de las historias del Nuevo Mundo Peru,* University of San Marcos, 1957; *Floodtide of Empire: Spain and the Pacific Northwest: 1543-1819,* Yale University Press, 1973.

*WORK IN PROGRESS:* A book tentatively entitled *Maverick of Massachusetts: Dissenter in New Zion;* a book on the Inca religion.

*SIDELIGHTS:* Warren L. Cook participated in an expedition to the Campa Indians of the Amazon River in Peru in 1947; he has also traveled through Latin America and Europe. *Avocational interests:* Collecting stamps, and assisting wife in breeding Arabian horses.

\* \* \*

## COOLIDGE, Archibald C(ary), Jr. 1928-

*PERSONAL:* Born June 9, 1928, in Oxford, England; son of Archibald Cary (an educator) and Susan (Jennings) Coolidge; married Lillian Merrill, June 29, 1951; children: Lillian, Emily, Sarah, Archibald, Anne, John, Alexander. *Education:* Harvard University, B.A. (magna cum laude), 1951; Brown University, M.A., 1954, Ph.D., 1956. *Office:* Department of English, University of Iowa, Iowa City, Iowa 52240.

*CAREER:* Harvey School, Hawthorne, N.Y., teacher of English, 1946-47; University of Iowa, Iowa City, instructor, 1956-59, assistant professor, 1959-65, associate professor, 1965-74, professor of English, 1974—. *Military service:* U.S. Marine Corps Reserve, active duty, 1945-46. *Member:* Modern Language Association of America, Modern Humanities Research Association, Phi Beta Kappa.

*WRITINGS: Charles Dickens as Serial Novelist,* Iowa State University Press, 1967. Contributor of articles to literature journals.

*WORK IN PROGRESS: Drama before Aristotle;* a book on psychological and philosophic implications of common story patterns not explored by Freud and Jung.

\* \* \*

## COOPER, Paulette 1944-

*PERSONAL:* Born July 26, 1944, in Belgium; daughter of Ted (a diamond exporter and importer) and Stella (Toepfer) Cooper. *Education:* Brandeis University, B.A. (with honors), 1964; City University of New York, M.A., 1968. *Politics:* Democrat. *Religion:* Jewish. *Home and office:* 300 East 40th St., New York, N.Y. 10016. *Agent:* Scott Meredith Literary Agency, Inc., 845 Third Ave., New York, N.Y. 10022.

*MEMBER:* American Medical Writers Association, National Academy of Television Arts and Sciences, Society of Magazine Writers, Mystery Writers of America, Authors Guild, Authors League of America, New York Press Club. *Awards, honors:* Received special award, Mystery Writers of America, 1973, for *The Medical Detectives.*

*WRITINGS: The Scandal of Scientology,* Tower, 1971; *Growing Up Puerto Rican,* Arbor House, 1972; *Let's Find*

*Out about Halloween* (juvenile), F. Watts, 1972; *The Medical Detectives,* McKay, 1973. Author of "Travel Tips," a syndicated column. Contributor of articles to *Cosmopolitan, True, Publishers Weekly, Writer's Digest, Washington Post, New York Times, Medical Opinion,* and other periodicals.

*AVOCATIONAL INTERESTS:* Oriental cooking, travel.

\* \* \*

## COOPERMAN, Hasye 1909-

*PERSONAL:* Born February 2, 1909, in New York, N.Y.; daughter of Efrem and Miriam (Scholar) Cooperman; married N. B. Minkoff (an author, poet, critic, and professor of literature; deceased); children: Amram C., Eli C. *Education:* Hunter College (now Hunter College of the City University of New York), B.A., 1929; Columbia University, M.A., 1930, Ph.D., 1933. *Religion:* Jewish. *Home:* 344 West 85th St., New York, N.Y. 10024. *Office:* New School for Social Research, 66 West 12th St., New York, N.Y. 10011.

*CAREER:* World Publishing Co., Cleveland, Ohio, research editor, *American Language Dictionary,* 1937-43; City College (now City College of the City University of New York), New York City, lecturer in Yiddish literature, 1939-41; New School for Social Research, New York City, 1950—, teacher of comparative and American literature, chairperson of department, 1960-66. *Member:* American Association of University Professors (former president of local chapter), Poetry Society of America, Phi Beta Kappa. *Awards, honors:* American Literary Association National Poetry Award, 1957.

*WRITINGS: The Chase,* Bayard Press, 1932; *The Aesthetics of Stephane Mallarme,* Koffern, 1933, revised edition, Russell & Russell, 1971; *Men Walk the Earth* (poems), William Frederick, 1953; (contributor) Oscar Isaiah Janowsky, editor, *The American Jew: A Reappraisal,* Jewish Publication Society, 1964; (contributor) Morris Adler, editor, *Jewish Heritage Reader,* Taplinger, 1965. Work is represented in many anthologies, including *Golden Year* and *Diamond Anthology.* Contributor of poetry and criticism to periodicals.

*WORK IN PROGRESS: Folk Tendencies in World Literature; The Making of a Woman,* a book of poetry.

*SIDELIGHTS:* Hasye Cooperman told *CA,* "My writing, especially my poetry, defines the delight and sorrows of being human, insights into the young and the mature [and] the men and women who have made and do now make our world."

\* \* \*

## CORBETT, Janice M. 1935-

*PERSONAL:* Born June 3, 1935, in Avoca, N.Y.; daughter of Orlo Charles (a minister) and Margaret (Owen) Corbett. *Education:* Eastern College, St. Davids, Pa., B.A., 1957; Eastern Baptist Theological Seminary, M.R.E., 1959; Temple University, M.S., 1974. *Politics:* Democrat. *Religion:* American Baptist. *Address:* Box 493, Malvern, Pa. 19355. *Office:* American Baptist Churches, Valley Forge, Pa. 19481.

*CAREER:* American Baptist Churches, Board of Education and Publication, Valley Forge, Pa., editor, 1959-61; Jack T. Holmes and Associates, Fort Worth, Tex., assistant in public relations, 1962-64; First Baptist Church, Brockton, Mass., director of Christian education, 1964-66; American

Baptist Churches Board of Education and Publication, editor, 1966-75; *Youth* magazine, Philadelphia, Pa., managing editor, 1976-77; American Baptist Churches, director of communication for board of educational ministries, 1977—. Secretary, Conference of Editors of Church Magazines for Children and Youth, 1969. The New School Cooperative, Wayne, Pa., president, 1971-72, treasurer, 1972-73. *Member:* National Committee for the Support of Public Schools.

*WRITINGS:* (With Curtis E. Johnson) *It's Happening with Youth,* Harper, 1972; *Creative Youth Leadership,* Judson, 1977. Editor, *Action,* 1966—.

*SIDELIGHTS:* Janice Corbett is interested in "alternate models of education, both within the church and within the public sector that are relevant to the changing needs of society and that result in the creation of humane institutions."

\* \* \*

### CORD, William O. 1921-

*PERSONAL:* Born May 1, 1921, in St. Louis, Mo.; son of Jessie O. and Martha (Pratt) Cord; married Marjorie Blackford, January 3, 1942; children: Kimberly A., J. Christian. *Education:* Southeast Missouri State College (now University), B.A., 1943; Washington University, M.A., 1948; University of Colorado, Ph.D., 1960. *Home:* 420 Santa Barbara Ct., Rohnert Park, Calif. 94928. *Office:* Department of Foreign Languages, California State College, Sonoma, Rohnert Park, Calif. 94928.

*CAREER:* St. Louis University High School, St. Louis, Mo., instructor in Spanish and English, 1943-45; Washington University, St. Louis, lecturer in Spanish, 1945-48; St. Louis University, St. Louis, instructor in Spanish, 1948-52; high school department chairman, 1952-55; Fresno State College (now California State University, Fresno), assistant professor, 1958-61, associate professor of Spanish, 1961-63; California State College, Sonoma, Rohnert Park, professor of Spanish, 1963—, chairman, Division of Humanities, 1970-76. Chairman, Cultural Arts Committee, Rohnert Park, 1968-69. *Member:* American Association of Teachers of Spanish and Portuguese. *Awards, honors:* Award from State Government of Michoacan, Mexico, "for service to Mexican literature."

*WRITINGS: Poems y Ensayos Ineditos do Jose Ruben Romero,* Andrea (Mexico), 1963, 2nd edition, 1964; (translator) Jose Ruben Romero, *The Futile Life of Pito Perez,* Prentice-Hall, 1967, editor of publication in Spanish as *La Vida Inutil de Pito Perez,* Prentice-Hall, 1972. Contributor of articles, poetry, and short stories to *Hispania* and *Mexico Today.*

*WORK IN PROGRESS:* Studies on *Der Ring des Nibelungen.*

*AVOCATIONAL INTERESTS:* German opera.

\* \* \*

### CORDIER, Ralph Waldo 1902-

*PERSONAL:* Born June 28, 1902, in Canton, Ohio; son of Wellington Jacob (a highway superintendent) and Ida (Anstine) Cordier; married Esta Brenner, June 3, 1925; children: Sherwood Stanley. *Education:* Manchester College, A.B., 1925; Ohio State University, M.A., 1929, Ph.D., 1934. *Home:* 235 South 13th St., Indiana, Pa. 15701. *Office:* Department of History, Indiana University of Pennsylvania, Indiana, Pa. 15701.

*CAREER:* High school teacher of social studies in North Canton, Ohio, 1925-28, in Columbus, Ohio, 1929-34; Eastern Illinois University, Charleston, supervisor of student teaching in social studies, 1934-36; Clarion State College, Clarion, Pa., head of department of social studies, 1936-46; Indiana University of Pennsylvania, Indiana, chairman of department of social studies, 1946-55, professor of history, 1955—, dean of instruction, 1955-60, of academic affairs, 1960-70. Instructor in history, Franklin Evening University, 1932-34; summer instructor at Manchester College, 1933, 1935, at Ohio State University, 1934. Member, U.S. State Department education team in Morocco, 1965; member of board of directors, American University of Tangiers, 1965; visited University of Sierra Leone to plan seminar, 1966; member of foundation committee, International Christian University of Japan; member of board of directors, Penn-Ram Corp.

*MEMBER:* National Council for the Social Studies (president, 1968), National Education Association, American Historical Association, Foreign Policy Association, Regional Council for International Education (member of executive committee, 1968-72), Pennsylvania Council for the Social Studies (president, 1953; executive secretary, 1958-67), Pennsylvania Historical Association (president, 1958-61), Pennsylvania Historical Foundation (member of board of directors, 1965-70), Pi Gamma Mu, Phi Delta Kappa. *Awards, honors:* Ford Foundation fellowship, 1951-52; distinguished service plaque from Middle States Council for the Social Studies, 1962; LL.D. from Manchester College, 1971.

*WRITINGS*—Published by Rand McNally, except as indicated: *A History for Beginners,* 1948; *A History of Young America,* 1948; *A History of World Peoples,* 1949; *Many Homes,* 1950; *Friendly Neighbors,* 1950; *All Around America,* 1950; (with Hane McGuidan) *Resources in Teaching History in the Middle Grades,* 1950; (editor and contributor) *Course of Study in the Social Studies for Secondary Schools,* Pennsylvania Department of Public Instruction, 1951; *A History of Our United States,* 1953; (with S. K. Stevens and Florence Benjamin) *Exploring Pennsylvania: Its History and Government,* Harcourt, 1953, new edition, 1971. Author of instructional films, including "The Vikings" and "George Washington: National Leader." Contributor of about forty articles to journals. History editor of *Britannica Junior Encyclopaedia.*

*WORK IN PROGRESS:* A book on the teaching of elementary social studies.

*SIDELIGHTS:* Ralph Waldo Cordier and his wife have visited all fifty states and fifty-four foreign countries.

\* \* \*

### CORNGOLD, Stanley Alan 1934-

*PERSONAL:* Born June 11, 1934, in Brooklyn, N.Y.; son of Herman (a margin clerk) and Estelle (Bramson) Corngold; married Marie Josephine Brettle, July 26, 1961 (divorced, 1969); children: Isabel Anna. *Education:* Columbia University, A.B. (with honors), 1957; additional study at University of London, 1957-58, and Columbia University, 1958-59; Cornell University, M.A., 1963, Ph.D., 1968; University of Basel, additional study, 1965-66. *Home:* 20 Erdman Ave., Princeton, N.J. 08540. *Office:* Department of German, Princeton University, Princeton, N.J. 08540.

*CAREER:* University of Maryland, European Division, Heidelberg, Germany, instructor in English, 1959-62; Princeton University, Princeton, N.J., assistant professor, 1966-72, associate professor of German, 1972—. *Military service:* U.S. Naval Reserve, 1951-55. U.S. Army, 1955-57. *Member:* Modern Language Association of America, Phi Beta Kappa. *Awards, honors:* American Council of Learned Societies fellowship, 1965; National Endowment for the Humanities fellowship, 1973; Guggenheim fellowship, 1977.

*WRITINGS:* (Contributor) Willis Barnstone, editor, *Modern European Poetry,* Bantam, 1966; (editor, and author of introduction, notes, and vocabulary) *"Ausgewaehlte Prosa" by Max Frisch,* Harcourt, 1968; (translator, editor, and author of introduction, notes, and critical apparatus) Franz Kafka, *The Metamorphosis,* Bantam, 1972; *The Commentators' Despair: The Interpretation of Franz Kafka's "Metamorphosis",* National University Publications, 1973; (editor and contributor) *Thomas Mann,* Princeton University Press, 1975; (editor) *Aspekte der Goethezeit,* Vandenhoeck & Ruprecht, 1977. Also author of numerous articles on Rousseau, Kafka, Heidegger, Tarm.

*WORK IN PROGRESS: The Intelligible Mood: Aesthetic Experience in Rousseau, Kant, and Hoelderlin.*

\*    \*    \*

## CORRE, Alan D. 1931-

*PERSONAL:* Surname is pronounced Cor-*ray;* born May 2, 1931, in London, England; came to United States in 1955, naturalized citizen; son of Jacob and Edith (Taylor) Corre; married Nita Levy (a social worker), December 18, 1957; children: Jacob I., Giselle A., Raquel L., Isaac D. *Education:* University of London, B.A. (honors), 1951; University of Manchester, M.A., 1953; University of Pennsylvania, Ph.D., 1962. *Home:* 3309 North 45th St., Milwaukee, Wis. 53216. *Office:* Department of Hebrew Studies, University of Wisconsin, Milwaukee, Wis. 53201.

*CAREER:* Rabbi; Congregation Mikveh Israel, Philadelphia, Pa., rabbi, 1955-63; University of Wisconsin—Milwaukee, assistant professor, 1963-65, associate professor, 1965-68, professor of Hebrew studies and chairman of department, 1968—. Research associate, Milwaukee Public Museum. *Member:* Linguistic Society of America, American Association of Sephardic Studies (secretary-treasurer, 1972-75), Wisconsin Academy of Arts, Letters, and Science. *Awards, honors:* Prize of Wisconsin Academy of Arts, Letters, and Science, 1966, for research in humanities; National Endowment for the Humanities fellow, 1967-68; Standard Oil of Indiana Award, 1973, for teaching excellence.

*WRITINGS: A Programmed Hebrew Speller for Colleges* (monograph), Department of Hebrew Studies, University of Wisconsin, 1970; *Daughter of My People,* E. J. Brill, 1971; *Understanding the Talmud,* Ktav, 1972. Contributor to *Encyclopaedia Judaica.*

*WORK IN PROGRESS: History and Culture of Spanish Jewry.*

\*    \*    \*

## CORTES, Juan B(autista) 1925-

*PERSONAL:* Born January 6, 1925, in Alicante, Spain; son of Sebastian S. (a businessman) and Maria (Quirant) Cortes. *Education:* University of Valencia, B.A., 1942; Colegio San Francisco de Borja, Barcelona, Spain, M.A. (philosophy), 1951; Boston College, Ph.D. (theology), 1958; Harvard University, Ph.D. (clinical psychology), 1961. *Politics:* Republican. *Home and office:* Department of Psychology, Georgetown University, Washington, D.C. 20007.

*CAREER:* Entered Roman Catholic Society of Jesus (Jesuits), 1943, ordained priest, 1957; Georgetown University,

Washington, D.C., assistant professor, 1962-65, associate professor, 1965-71, professor of psychology, 1971—. Visiting professor, Escuela Superior de Ciencias Empresariales, Alicante, Spain, summers, 1966—. *Member:* American Psychological Association.

*WRITINGS:* (Contributor) A. D'Agostino, editor, *Family, Church and Community,* Kenedy, 1965; (with Florence M. Gatti) *Delinquency and Crime: A Biopsychosocial Approach,* Academic Press, 1972; (editor and contributor with F. M. Gatti) *Recent Advances in Psychology,* Xerox College Publishing, 1973; (with Gatti) *The Case against Possessions and Exorcisms,* Vantage, 1975. Contributor of articles to *Psychology Today, Biblica, Marianum, Catholic Biblical Quarterly, Journal of Consulting Psychology, Theology Digest, Estudios Biblicos,* and *Journal of Religion and Health.*

*WORK IN PROGRESS: A Unifying Psychology of Life; Delinquency and Crime: An Introduction,* completion expected in 1980; *Psychological Insights,* completion expected in 1981; *Measuring and Increasing Academic Motivation,* completion expected in 1982.

*SIDELIGHTS:* Juan Cortes is proficient in Greek, Latin, English, French, Italian, and Portuguese, in addition to his native Spanish.

\*    \*    \*

## CORY, Daniel 1904-1972

1904—June 18, 1972; American editor and author of children's books and essays. Obituaries: *New York Times,* June 20, 1972.

\*    \*    \*

## COSTA, Gustavo 1930-

*PERSONAL:* Born March 21, 1930, in Rome, Italy; son of Paolo and Ida (Antonangelo) Costa; married Natalia Zalessow (an associate professor of Italian and law), June 8, 1963; children: Dora L. *Education:* University of Rome, Ph.D., 1954; Istituto Italiano per gli Studi Storici, Naples, postdoctoral study, 1954-55. *Home:* 605 Colusa Ave., Berkeley, Calif. 94707. *Office:* Department of Italian, University of California, Berkeley, Calif. 94720.

*CAREER:* University of Rome, Rome, Italy, assistant in history of modern and contemporary philosophy, 1957-60; University of Lyons, Lyons, France, lecturer in Italian, 1960-61; University of California, Berkeley, instructor, 1961-63, assistant professor, 1963-68, associate professor, 1968-72, professor of Italian, 1972—, chairman of department, 1973-76. *Member:* Modern Language Association of America, American Association of Teachers of Italian, Renaissance Society of America, Dante Society of America, American Society for Aesthetics, American Historical Association, American Society for Eighteenth Century Studies. *Awards, honors:* American Philosophical Society grant, 1967; University of California humanities research fellowship, 1970-71; Guggenheim fellowship, 1976-77.

*WRITINGS: La critica omerica di Thomas Blackwell, 1701-1757,* Sansoni, 1959; (contributor) *Saggi e ricerche sul Settecento,* Istituto Italiano per gli Studi Storici, 1968; *La leggenda dei secoli d'oro nella letteratura italiana,* Laterza, 1972; *Le antichitagermaniche nella cultura italiana da Machiavelli a Vico,* Istituto Italiano per gli Studi Filosofici, 1977. Contributor of articles to language journals, and reviews and about sixty bibliographical notes to daily newspapers in Rome.

*WORK IN PROGRESS:* A book on the role of the sublime in Italian culture; a monograph on G. B. Vico.

*SIDELIGHTS:* Gustavo Costa writes: "I consider myself a specialist in the field of intellectual history, dealing with literary and philosophical material. The pivot of my research has always been G. B. Vico, a thinker who can only be correctly understood against the background of seventeenth- and eighteenth-centuries European culture."

\*      \*      \*

## COTNER, Robert Crawford 1906-

*PERSONAL:* Born November 1, 1906, in Cleveland, Ohio; son of Thomas Ewing (a salesman) and Nina Dot (Crawford) Cotner; married Elizabeth Marie Breihan (a public school teacher), January 30, 1943; children: Catherine Elizabeth, Robert Crawford, Jr. *Education:* Baylor University, B.A., 1928; Brown University, M.A., 1929; Harvard University, Ph.D., 1959; also attended University of Texas, University of Mexico, and University of Munich. *Politics:* Democrat. *Religion:* Baptist. *Home:* 2208 Greenlee Dr., Austin, Tex. 78703. *Office:* Department of History, University of Texas, Austin, Tex. 78712.

*CAREER:* First National Bank, Dallas, Tex., teller, 1924-25; Holland's Magazine Co., Dallas, salesman, summers, 1926-28; teacher of history and economics in public schools in Midland, Tex., 1929-30; Henderson State College, Arkadelphia, Ark., member of faculty of history and dean of men, 1931-35; Stetson University, Deland, Fla., member of faculty of history and government, 1935-40, dean of men, 1935-40; University of Texas at Austin, member of faculty of history, 1940—. *Military service:* U.S. Navy, 1942-46; became commander. *Member:* American Historical Association, Organization of American Historians, Southern Historical Association (member of executive committee, 1955-57), East Texas Historical Association (president, 1971-72), Texas State Historical Association, West Texas Historical Association. *Awards, honors:* Lit.D., Baylor University, 1970.

*WRITINGS:* (Editor) Theodore Foster, *Theodore Foster's Minutes: Rhode Island Constitutional Convention, 1790,* Rhode Island Historical Society, 1929, 2nd edition, 1967; (editor) *The Addresses and State Papers of James Stephen Hogg,* University of Texas Press, 1951; (editor with Joe B. Frantz, R. L. Biesele, and others) *Readings in American History,* two volumes, Houghton, 1952, 4th edition, 1976; *James Stephen Hogg: A Biography,* University of Texas Press, 1959; (co-editor) *The Texas State Capitol,* Pemberton, 1968; (editor with others) *Texas Cities and the Great Depression,* Texas Memorial Museum, 1973. Book review editor, *West Texas Historical Association Yearbook,* 1955-75, and *Southwestern Historical Quarterly,* 1966-69.

\*      \*      \*

## COTNER, Thomas E(wing) 1916-

*PERSONAL:* Born October 26, 1916, in Dallas, Tex.; son of Thomas Ewing (a salesman) and Nina Dot (Crawford) Cotner; married Jeanne Booth, December 26, 1941; children: Thomas E., Zachary B., George R. *Education:* Baylor University, B.A., 1937; University of Texas, M.A., 1939, Ph.D., 1947. *Home:* 228 Buxton Rd., Falls Church, Va. 22046. *Office:* Division of International Education, U.S. Office of Education, Washington, D.C. 20202.

*CAREER:* High school teacher of history and civics, Brownwood, Tex., 1937-39; Texas Memorial Museum, Aus-

tin, director of Historical Division, 1939-40; Tulane University, New Orleans, La., instructor in Latin American history, 1940-41; U.S. Office of Education, Washington, D.C., various positions in international exchange and training, 1942-43, 1946-62, deputy associate commissioner of Bureau of International Education, 1962-65, chief of International Exchange and Training Branch, 1965-68, director of Division of International Exchange and Training, 1968-75, chief of International Services and Research Branch, 1975—. Lecturer in Latin American history and government, George Washington University, 1948-53. Member of Falls Church, Va. school board, 1966-69, and of U.S. Delegation to International Conference on Education, Geneva, 1966 and 1977. *Military service:* U.S. Naval Reserve, active duty with Atlantic Fleet, 1943-46; became lieutenant. *Awards, honors:* Medal of Merit of Belgium Government, 1958; Superior Service Award, U.S. Department of Health, Education and Welfare, 1962.

*WRITINGS: Military and Political Career of Jose Joaquin de Herrera,* University of Texas Press, 1949; (editor with Carlos Castenada) *Essays in Mexican History,* University of Texas Press, 1958; *International Educational Exchange: A Selected Bibliography,* U.S. Department of Health, Education and Welfare, 1961. Contributor of articles on exchange and training programs to journals.

\*      \*      \*

## COUDENHOVE-KALERGI, Richard (Nicolas) 1894-1972

November 16, 1894—July 27, 1972; European author and promoter of European unification. Obituaries: *New York Times,* July 29, 1972; *Current Biography,* October, 1972.

\*      \*      \*

## COUND, John J(ames) 1928-

*PERSONAL:* Surname rhymes with "pound"; born February 7, 1928; son of Oliver Edward and Maurice (McGuire) Cound; married Jeanne Bailley, September 25, 1954; children: Edward, William, Thomas, Bronwen. *Education:* George Washington University, B.A., 1949; Harvard University, LL.B., 1952. *Politics:* Democratic-Farmer-Labor. *Religion:* Catholic. *Home:* 6 Wood Duck Lane, St. Paul, Minn. 55110. *Office:* Law School, University of Minnesota, Minneapolis, Minn. 55455.

*CAREER:* U.S. Department of Justice, Washington, D.C., attorney, 1953-56; University of Minnesota, Law School, Minneapolis, professor of law, 1956—. *Military service:* U.S. Army, 1946-48.

*WRITINGS:* (With Arthur R. Miller and Jack H. Friedenthal) *Cases on Civil Procedure,* West Publishing, 1968, 2nd edition, 1974; (with Miller and Friedenthal) *Cases on Pleading, Joinder, and Discovery,* West Publishing, 1968; *Minnesota Criminal Jury Instruction Guides,* West Publishing, 1977. Wrote Supreme Court commentary, radio station KUOM, 1969-71.

*WORK IN PROGRESS:* Criminal jury instructions for Minnesota.

\*      \*      \*

## COUNT, Earl W(endel) 1899-

*PERSONAL:* Born October 22, 1899, in Irvington, N.Y.; son of Elmer Ernest and Viette Ella (Thompson) Count; married Maude A. Poole, July 6, 1928. *Education:* Williams College, A.B., 1922; Northwestern University, postgraduate study, 1924-26, 1927-28; Garrett Theological Seminary, B.D., 1926; University of California, Berkeley, Ph.D., 1935. *Politics:* Liberal Democrat. *Home:* 2616 Saklan Indian Dr., Walnut Creek, Calif. 94595.

*CAREER:* Ordained Episcopal priest, 1932; San Jose State College (now University), San Jose, Calif., 1928-37, began as instructor, became assistant professor of biology; New York Medical College, New York City, 1937-45, began as assistant professor, became associate professor of anatomy; Wenner-Gren Foundation for Anthropological Research, New York City, research associate, 1945-46; Hamilton College, Clinton, N.Y., professor of anthropology, 1946-68, professor emeritus, 1968—, chairman of department, 1946-68. Visiting professor, Brandeis University, summer, 1957, Syracuse University, 1958, Tulane University, 1966, Northwestern University, 1968, and Purdue University, 1978. Guest lecturer at various universities around the country. *Military service:* U.S. Army, 1918; Massachusetts National Guard, 1922-23. *Member:* American Association for the Advancement of Science (fellow), American Anthropological Association (fellow), Phi Beta Kappa, Sigma Xi. *Awards, honors:* National Institutes of Health grant, 1961-62.

*WRITINGS: 4000 Years of Christmas,* Henry Schuman, 1948; *This Is Race,* Henry Schuman, 1950; (translator) M. P. Dragomanov, *The Dualistic Creation of the World,* University of Indiana, 1961; (translator) Bunak, Roginsky, Debets, Levin, and Ceboksarov, *Contemporary Raciology and Racism,* University of Indiana, 1961; (editor and author with G. T. Bowles) *Fact and Theory in Social Science,* Syracuse University Press, 1964; *Das Biogramm: Anthropologische Studien,* S. Fischer Verlag, 1970; *Being and Becoming Human: Essays on the Biogram,* Van Nostrand, 1973. Contributor of anthropological studies to professional journals, and translator. Editor of "Human Biology" section, *Biological Abstracts.* Member of national book committee, *The Key Reports* (Phi Beta Kappa).

*WORK IN PROGRESS:* A monograph, tentatively entitled *In Search of the Biogram.*

*SIDELIGHTS:* Earl Count has resided and traveled in Europe and Japan. He is competent in Bulgarian, German, French, Italian, Russian, Dano-Norwegian, Spanish, and Swedish.

\*        \*        \*

## COVERT, James Thayne 1932-

*PERSONAL:* Born April 20, 1932, in Cimarron, Kan.; son of J. T. (a pharmacist) and Edna (Petty) Covert; married Sally Ann Miller; children: Marcus William, Michael Christopher, Jennifer Ann, Juliann Marie, Elizabeth Ann, Christine Marie. *Education:* University of Portland, B.A. (maxima cum laude), 1959; University of Oregon, M.A., 1961, Ph.D., 1967. *Politics:* Democrat. *Religion:* Roman Catholic. *Home:* 6626 North Curtis, Portland, Ore. 97217. *Office:* Department of History, University of Portland, Portland, Ore. 97203.

*CAREER:* Austin Bros. Drug Co., Portland, Ore. and Spokane, Wash., warehouse manager and assistant buyer, 1950-51, 1952-55; University of Portland, Portland, instructor, 1961-64, assistant professor, 1964-68, associate professor, 1968-71, professor of history, 1971—, chairman of department, 1967—. American Red Cross, director of Northwest Leadership Training Center, 1960, and member of advisory board to Office of Educational Relations, Oregon Trail chapter, 1961-64. *Military service:* Air National Guard,

1950-52, with active duty in U.S. Air Force, 1951-52. *Member:* American Historical Association, American Catholic Historical Association, West Coast Conference on British Studies, Oregon and Southwest Washington Historians, Delta Epsilon Sigma, Phi Alpha Theta. *Awards, honors:* Culligan Faculty Award, 1968, and Distinguished Professor Award (first recipient), both from University of Portland; Danforth associate, 1970-72.

*WRITINGS:* (Editor with Louis Vaccaro) *Student Freedom in American Higher Education,* Teachers College Press, 1969; *A Point of Pride: The University of Portland Story,* University of Portland Press, 1976. Contributor to *New Catholic Encyclopedia* and to journals and newspapers. *University of Portland Review,* assistant editor, 1961-64, managing editor, 1964-68, special consultant, 1968-71.

*WORK IN PROGRESS:* A biography of Mandell Creighton, Victorian churchman and scholar; a mystery novel; children's stories.

*AVOCATIONAL INTERESTS:* Folk music (plays banjo and guitar), wood carving, photography, sports, tree farming, Sherlockiana (founder of Portland's Sherlock Holmes Society).

\*        \*        \*

## COVINGTON, Martin Vaden 1936-

*PERSONAL:* Born February 14, 1936, in San Bernardino, Calif.; son of Vaden Irwin (an inventor) and Dorothy (Stone) Covington; married Bette Marie Wilson, June 20, 1962; children: Matthew Stone, Mark Hunter. *Education:* University of Redlands, B.A. (magna cum laude), 1957; University of California, Berkeley, Ph.D., 1962. *Home:* 45 Sullivan Dr., Moraga, Calif. 94556. *Office:* 3210 Tolman Hall, University of California, Berkeley, Calif. 94720.

*CAREER:* Sacramento State College (now California State University), Sacramento, Calif., acting assistant professor of psychology, 1959; University of California, Berkeley, assistant research psychologist, 1961-64, assistant professor, 1964-67, associate professor of psychology, 1967—, associate research psychologist, 1967—, vice-chairman of department, 1969—, co-director of research project in Institute of Personality Assessment and Research, 1964-69. Visiting scholar, Michigan State University, 1970. *Awards, honors:* Distinguished Teaching Award, University of California, Berkeley, 1976.

*WRITINGS:* (Editor with P. H. Mussen and Jonas Langer) *Trends and Issues in Developmental Psychology,* Holt, 1969; (with R. S. Crutchfield, L. B. Davies, and R. M. Olton) *The Productive Thinking Program,* C. E. Merrill, 1972; (with R. Beery) *Self-Worth and School Learning,* Holt, 1976.

Contributor: J. M. Seidman, editor, *The Child: A Book of Readings,* Holt, 1969; Seidman, editor, *The Adolescent: A Book of Readings,* Holt, 1969; Jerome Hellmuth, editor, *Cognitive Studies,* Volume I, *Special Child,* Brunner, 1969; B. F. Anderson, editor, *The Psychology Experiment,* Brooks/Cole, 1971; I. K. Davis and James Hartley, editors, *Contributions to an Educational Technology,* Butterworth, 1972. Also contributor to *Self-Instructional Learning in the Elementary School, Perspectives in Contemporary Special Education,* Allyn & Bacon, *Readings on Creativity in Education,* Prentice-Hall, and *Experience Learning,* Basic Books. Contributor of articles to professional journals.

## COWGILL, Donald O(len)   1911-

*PERSONAL:* Born May 10, 1911, in Wood River, Neb.; son of Olen and Gertrude (Quisenberry) Cowgill; married Mary Catherine Strain, September 1, 1935; children: Martha Jane (Mrs. Paul Burns), Donald Franklin, Catha Jean. *Education:* Park College, A.B., 1933; Washington University, St. Louis, Mo., A.M., 1935; University of Pennsylvania, Ph.D., 1940. *Home:* 819 Greenwood Ct., Columbia, Mo. 65201. *Office:* Department of Sociology, University of Missouri, Columbia, Mo. 65201.

*CAREER:* Drury College, Springfield, Mo., assistant professor of sociology, 1937-42; Missouri Social Security Commission, Jefferson City, Mo., senior research analyst, 1942-43; Studebaker Corp., South Bend, Ind., research assistant to vice-president, 1943-45; Drake University, Des Moines, Iowa, professor of sociology and head of department, 1945-46; Wichita State University, Wichita, Kan., professor and head of department of sociology and anthropology, 1946-67; University of Missouri—Columbia, professor of sociology, 1967—, professor of rural sociology, 1970—, chairman of departments of sociology and rural sociology, 1970-72. Fulbright lecturer, Chiengmai University, 1964-65; consultant and visiting professor, Mahidol University, 1968-69. Visiting summer professor at University of Missouri, 1948, 1966, at University of Rhode Island, 1968; visiting summer lecturer, Mindolo Ecumenical Centre, Kitwe, Zambia, 1962. University of California, fellow of Inter-University Institute of Social Gerontology, summer, 1959; fellow of Midwest Council for Social Research on Aging, University of Minnesota, summer, 1963. Consultant for Wichita Community Planning Council, 1946-66. *Member:* International Association of Gerontology, American Sociological Association, Gerontological Society, Population Association of America, Midwest Sociological Society (president, 1952-53), Midwest Council for Social Research on Aging (president, 1962-64), Kansas Council on Aging (president, 1961-62).

*WRITINGS: Mobile Homes: A Study of Trailer Life,* American Council of Public Affairs, 1941; (co-author) *Children and Youth in Wichita,* University of Wichita Press, 1954; (co-author) *The People of Wichita,* Center for Urban Studies, University of Wichita, 1962; (contributor) Richard L. Stauber, editor, *Approaches to the Study of Urbanization,* Governmental Research Center, University of Kansas, 1964; (contributor) Arnold M. Rose and Warren A. Peterson, editors, *Older People and Their Social World,* F. A. Davis, 1965; (contributor) Thomas E. Lasswell, John H. Burma, and Sidney H. Aronson, editors, *Life in Society,* Scott, Foresman, 1965; (principal author) *Family Planning in Bangkhen, Thailand,* Center for Population and Social Research, Mahidol University, 1969; (contributor) Adeline M. Hoffman, editor, *The Daily Needs and Interests of Older People,* C. C Thomas, 1970; (co-editor and contributor) *Aging and Modernization,* Appleton, 1972. Writer of research monographs; contributor of about thirty articles to professional journals.

*WORK IN PROGRESS:* A volume on comparative gerontology.

*       *       *

## COX, Edwin B(urk)   1930-

*PERSONAL:* Born April 3, 1930, in Philadelphia, Pa.; son of George Harvey (a salesman) and Lourea (Wessels) Cox; married Myrtle Yates (a teacher), February 18, 1956; children: Edwin Burk, Jr., David George. *Education:* University of Pennsylvania, A.B., 1951, M.A., 1953, Ph.D., 1960. *Residence:* Lexington, Mass. *Office:* Arthur D. Little, Inc., Acorn Park, Cambridge, Mass. 02140.

*CAREER:* University of Pennsylvania, Philadelphia, instructor in statistics, 1951-54, 1956-60; Boston University, Boston, Mass., assistant professor, 1960-62, associate professor, 1962-64, professor of business administration, 1964-68, assistant dean, 1965-68; Arthur D. Little, Inc., Cambridge, Mass., senior management consultant, 1968—. *Military service:* U.S. Air Force, 1954-56; became first lieutenant. *Member:* American Statistical Association (national chairman of section on training, 1965; national council member, 1966-67; member of national board of directors, 1968-70; fellow), American Economic Association, Institute of Management Sciences.

*WRITINGS: Trends in the Distribution of Stock Ownership,* University of Pennsylvania Press, 1963; (editor) *Basic Tables in Business and Economics,* McGraw, 1967; (with John Boot) *Statistical Analysis for Managerial Decisions,* McGraw, 1970, 2nd edition, 1974; (with Martin Ernst) *The Consequences of Electronic Funds Transfer,* National Science Foundation, 1975. Contributor of articles to business and statistics journals.

*WORK IN PROGRESS:* Research on the impact of payments system change in business decisions.

*       *       *

## COX, Kevin R.   1939-

*PERSONAL:* Born March 22, 1939, in Warwick, England; son of George Robert (an internal revenue officer) and Eleanor (Jenkins) Cox; married Marjorie Snell (a piano teacher), February 6, 1965; children: Nicole Denise, Gerard Damian. *Education:* Cambridge University, B.A., 1961; University of Illinois, M.A., 1963, Ph.D., 1966. *Home:* 111 Forest Ridge Dr., Worthington, Ohio 43085. *Office:* Department of Geography, Ohio State University, Columbus, Ohio 43210.

*CAREER:* Ohio State University, Columbus, assistant professor, 1965-68, associate professor, 1968-71, professor of geography, 1971—. *Member:* Association of American Geographers, Canadian Association of Geographers. *Awards, honors:* National Science Foundation grant, 1966.

*WRITINGS:* (Editor with R. G. Golledge) *Behavioral Problems in Geography: A Symposium,* Northwestern University Press, 1969; *Man, Location and Behavior: An Introduction to Human Geography,* Wiley, 1972; *Conflict, Power and Politics in the City: A Geographic View,* McGraw, 1972; (editor with D. R. Reynolds) *Locational Approaches to Power and Conflict,* Sage Publications, 1974; (editor) *Urbanization and Conflict in Market-Societies,* Maaroufa, 1977. Contributor to geography, political science, and sociology journals.

*       *       *

## COYNE, John R(ichard), Jr.   1935-

*PERSONAL:* Born June 2, 1935, in Bangor, Me.; son of John R. (a steamfitter) and Margaret (Grant) Coyne; married Patricia Schaefer, September 10, 1960; children: Jennifer, John III, Amanda, Charity. *Education:* University of Alaska, B.A., 1961, M.A., 1963; University of Denver, M.A., 1965; University of California, Berkeley, graduate study, 1967-69. *Politics:* Republican.

*CAREER:* University of Alaska, College, instructor in English, 1961-63; *National Review* (magazine), New York,

N.Y., associate editor, 1969-71; Arizona State University, Tempe, assistant professor of mass communications, 1971-72; Office of the Vice-President, Washington, D.C., speechwriter, beginning 1972. *Military service:* U.S. Marine Corps, 1953-56; became sergeant.

*WRITINGS: The Kumquat Statement*, Cowles, 1970; *The Impudent Snobs: Agnew versus the Intellectual Establishment*, Arlington House, 1972; (with wife, Patricia S. Coyne) *The Big Breakup: Energy in Crisis*, Sheed, Andrews & McMeel, 1977. Contributor of articles to *National Review* and *The Alternative*.

*WORK IN PROGRESS:* A book on the 1972 elections.

*BIOGRAPHICAL/CRITICAL SOURCES: National Review*, November 17, 1970, December 29, 1970; *Commonweal*, January 8, 1971.†

\* \* \*

## CRAIG, Albert M(orton) 1927-

*PERSONAL:* Born December 9, 1927, in Chicago, Ill.; son of Albert Morton and Adda (Clendenin) Craig; married Teruko Ugaya, July 10, 1953; children: John, Paul, Sarah. *Education:* Northwestern University, B.S., 1949; further study at University of Strasbourg, 1949-50, and Kyoto University, 1951-53; Harvard University, Ph.D., 1959. *Home:* 172 Goden, Belmont, Mass. 02178. *Office:* Department of History, Harvard University, 2 Divinity, Cambridge, Mass. 02138.

*CAREER:* University of Massachusetts—Amherst, instructor in history, 1957-59; Harvard University, Cambridge, Mass., instructor, 1959-60, assistant professor, 1960-63, associate professor, 1963-67, professor of Japanese history, 1967—, director of Harvard-Yenching Institute, 1976—. Fulbright research professor, Kyoto University, 1962-63. *Military service:* U.S. Army, 1946-47. *Member:* Association for Asian Studies, American Historical Association, Shigakkai. *Awards, honors:* Fulbright scholar in France, 1949-50; Guggenheim fellowship, 1967-68; American Council of Learned Societies-Social Science Research Council grant, 1967-68; Japan Foundation senior fellowship, 1975.

*WRITINGS: Choshu in the Meiji: Restoration*, Harvard University Press, 1961; (with Edwin O. Reischauer and John K. Fairbank) *East Asia: The Modern Transformation*, Houghton, 1965; (editor with D. H. Shively), *Personality in Japanese History*, University of California Press, 1971; (with Reischauer and Fairbank) *East Asia: Tradition and Transformation*, Houghton, 1973; (with Reischauer) *Japan: Tradition and Transformation*, Houghton, 1977.

Contributor: Marius S. Jansen, editor, *Changing Japanese Attitudes Toward Modernization*, Princeton University Press, 1965; Robert E. Ward, editor, *Political Development in Modern Japan*, Princeton University Press, 1968; John W. Hall and Jansen, editors, *Studies in the Institutional History of Early Modern Japan*, Princeton University Press, 1968; Ezra F. Vogel, editor, *Modern Japanese Organization and Decision-Making*, University of California Press, 1975. Contributor to historical journals.

*WORK IN PROGRESS:* Studies on Fukuzawa as a translator, on childhood in Japanese society, and on Meiji bureaucracy.

\* \* \*

## CRAIG, Barbara M(ary St. George) 1914-

*PERSONAL:* Born February 14, 1914, in Ottawa, Ontario, Canada; daughter of William Woodham (a clergyman) and Edith (Silcock) Craig. *Education:* Queen's University, Kingston, Ontario, B.A., 1937, M.A., 1939; Bryn Mawr College, Ph.D., 1949; also attended University Centre of the Mediterranean, 1937-38. *Office:* Department of French and Italian, University of Kansas, Lawrence, Kan. 66045.

*CAREER:* Mount Royal College, Calgary, Alberta, instructor in French and German, 1943-46; University of Kansas, Lawrence, instructor, 1947-49, assistant professor, 1949-59, associate professor, 1959-64, professor of French, 1964—, chairman of department of French and Italian, 1976—. *Member:* Modern Language Association of America, Mediaeval Academy of America, Renaissance Society, American Association of University Professors, Pi Delta Phi. *Awards, honors:* Standard Oil award for outstanding teaching, 1973.

*WRITINGS:* (Editor) *L'Estoire de Griseldis*, University Press of Kansas, 1954; (editor with M. E. Porter and J. F. Burks) *La Vie Monseigneur Saint Fiacre*, University Press of Kansas, 1960; (editor) *"La Creacion," "la Transgression," and "l'Expulsion" of the "Mistere du Viel Testament,"* University Press of Kansas, 1968; (contributor) Runte, Niedzielski, and Hendrickson, editors, *Jean Misrahi Memorial Volume*, French Literature Publications Co., 1977; (contributor) R. J. Cormier, editor, *Voices of Conscience*, Temple University Press, 1977.

*WORK IN PROGRESS:* A critical edition of *Sacrifice d'Abraham* from *Mistere du Viel Testament*, and two plays.

*AVOCATIONAL INTERESTS:* Medieval art, architecture, and music, bird-watching, travel.

\* \* \*

## CRAWFORD, Charles O(len) 1934-

*PERSONAL:* Born September 19, 1934, in West Chester, Pa.; son of Olen C. and Agnes I. (Poole) Crawford; married Ruth W. Arms, August 20, 1960; children: Charles O., Jr., Brian L., Timothy B. *Education:* Pennsylvania State University, B.S., 1956, M.S., 1958; Cornell University, Ph.D., 1963. *Home:* 215 Val Verda Dr., Pennsylvania Furnace, Pa. 16865. *Office:* 107 Weaver Bldg., Pennsylvania State University, University Park, Pa. 16802.

*CAREER:* University of Connecticut, Storrs, assistant professor of rural sociology, 1963-65; State Health Department, Harrisburg, Pa., director, Division of Behavioral Science, 1965-71; Pennsylvania State University, University Park, associate professor, 1971-77, professor of rural sociology, 1977—. *Member:* American Sociological Association, American Public Health Association, Rural Sociological Society.

*WRITINGS: Health and the Family: A Medical Sociological Analysis*, Macmillan, 1971; (contributor) E. W. Hassinger and Larry R. Whiting, editors, *Rural Health Services: Organization, Delivery and Use*, Iowa State University Press, 1976. Contributor of articles to *Health Education Monographs, Journal of Northeast Agricultural Economics Council, Public Health Reports, Rural Sociology*, and *Pennsylvania's Health*.

\* \* \*

## CRENSHAW, James L. 1934-

*PERSONAL:* Born December 19, 1934, in Sunset, S.C.; son of B. D. (a minister) and Bessie (Aiken) Crenshaw; married Juanita Rhodes, June 10, 1956; children: James Timothy, David Lee. *Education:* North Greenville Junior College,

A.A., 1954; Furman University, B.A., 1956; Southern Baptist Theological Seminary, B.D., 1960; Hebrew Union College, graduate study, 1963; Vanderbilt University, Ph.D., 1964. *Home:* 3807 Brighton Rd., Nashville, Tenn. 37205. *Office:* Vanderbilt University Divinity School, Nashville, Tenn. 37240.

*CAREER:* Clergyman of Baptist Church; Atlantic Christian College, Wilson, N.C., assistant professor of religion, 1964-65; Mercer University, Macon, Ga., associate professor of religion, 1965-69; Vanderbilt University Divinity School, Nashville, Tenn., 1969—, began as associate professor, currently professor of Old Testament. *Member:* Society of Biblical Literature (president of Southern Section, 1968-69), American Academy of Religion, Catholic Biblical Association, American Association of University Professors. *Awards, honors:* Society for Religion in Higher Education cross-disciplinary fellowship, 1972-73.

*WRITINGS: Prophetic Conflict,* Walter de Gruyter, 1971; (editor with John T. Willis) *Essays in Old Testament Ethics,* Ktav, 1974; *Hymnic Affirmation of Divine Justice,* Scholars' Press, 1976; *Studies in Ancient Israelite Wisdom,* Ktav, 1976; (contributor) *The New English Bible: Oxford Study Edition,* Oxford University Press, 1976; (contributor) D. Knight, editor, *Theology in the Old Testament,* Fortress, 1977; *Samson: A Secret Betrayed, a Vow Ignored,* John Knox, in press; *Gerhard von Rad: From Tradition to the Silence of God,* Word, Inc., in press; (contributor) *Samuel Terrien Festschrift,* Scholars' Press, in press. Also co-author of *Semitics I* and *The Old Testament and Form Criticism,* and contributor to *Structuralism,* edited by S. Wittig and Pickwick, 1976. Associate editor, "SBL" monograph series, 1976—. Contributor of about twenty articles and numerous reviews to journals.

*WORK IN PROGRESS: The Contest of Darius' Pages; Impossible Questions and Tasks;* books on the rhetoric of wisdom, on riddles in the Old Testament, and an introduction to wisdom; essays on the revolution within wisdom research.

*SIDELIGHTS:* James L. Crenshaw works in German, French, Hebrew, Greek, and Aramaic. He told *CA* that he is particularly interested in ancient folklore, as well as Hebrew narrative art.

\* \* \*

## CRISP, C(olin) G(odfrey) 1936-

*PERSONAL:* Born October 12, 1936, in Paeroa, New Zealand; son of Godfrey Richard and Lilian (Parker) Crisp; married Jane Dasherwood Durrant (a lecturer), December, 1961; children: Nicholas. *Education:* Auckland University, B.A., 1957, M.A., 1958; University d'Aix-Marseille, doctorat d'universite, 1964. *Politics:* Socialist.

*CAREER:* Teacher at Tamaki College, Auckland, New Zealand, 1959-61, and in Hampshire, England, 1962; Australian National University, Canberra, Australian Capital Territory, Australia, lecturer in twentieth-century literature and cinema, beginning 1965.

*WRITINGS: Francois Truffaut,* Praeger, 1972.

*WORK IN PROGRESS: French Cinema: 1950-70.*

*AVOCATIONAL INTERESTS:* Pottery, travel, native plants and birdlife of Australia.†

\* \* \*

## CRISPO, John 1933-

*PERSONAL:* Born May 5, 1933, in Toronto, Ontario, Can-

ada; married Melba Baker; children: Carol Ann, Sharon. *Education:* Attended Upper Canada College, 1948-53; Trinity College, Toronto, Ontario, B.Com., 1956; Massachusetts Institute of Technology, Ph.D., 1960. *Office:* Faculty of Management Studies, University of Toronto, Toronto, Ontario, Canada.

*CAREER:* University of Toronto, Toronto, Ontario, assistant professor, 1961-64, associate professor, 1964-65, professor of industrial relations and public policy, 1965—. *Member:* Industrial Relations Research Association, Canadian Industrial Relations Research Institute (former president), International Industrial Relations Association.

*WRITINGS: International Unionism,* McGraw, 1967; *Public Right to Know,* McGraw, 1975; *The Canadian Industrial Relations System,* McGraw, 1978; *Industrial Democracy in Western Europe,* McGraw, 1978.

*WORK IN PROGRESS: Industrial Relations after Wage and Price Controls.*

\* \* \*

## CRONIN, John F(rancis) 1908-

*PERSONAL:* Born October 4, 1908, in Glens Falls, N.Y.; son of Bernard J. and Nora (Reardon) Cronin. *Education:* Catholic University of America, A.B., 1927, M.A., 1928, Ph.D., 1935. *Politics:* Independent. *Home and office:* St. Mary's Seminary, 5400 Roland Ave., Baltimore, Md. 21210.

*CAREER:* Ordained Roman Catholic priest; St. Mary's Seminary, Baltimore, Md., instructor, 1933-37, assistant professor, 1937-40, associate professor, 1940-41, professor of philosophy and economics, 1941-45; U.S. Catholic Conference, Department of Social Action, Washington, D.C., assistant director, 1945-67; St. Mary's Seminary, professor of Christian ethics, 1967—. President, Maryland Project Equality (inter-religious civil-rights program for fair employment), 1968-72. *Member:* American Society of Christian Ethics, Catholic Theological Society of America. *Awards, honors:* Pabst Award, for essay on postwar employment plans, 1944.

*WRITINGS: Economic Analysis and Problems,* American Book Co., 1945; *The Catholic as Citizen,* Helicon, 1963; *Government in Freedom,* Holt, 1965; *Christianity and Social Progress,* Helicon, 1965; *Social Principles and Economic Life,* Bruce, 1966.

\* \* \*

## CROSS, Anthony (Glenn) 1936-

*PERSONAL:* Born October 21, 1936, in Nottingham, England; son of Walter Sidney and Ada (Lawson) Cross; married Margaret Elson, August 11, 1960; children: Jane Louise, Serena Claire. *Education:* Cambridge University, B.A., 1960, Ph.D., 1966; Harvard University, A.M., 1961. *Home:* 42 Arlington Lane, Norwich N0R 78E, England. *Office:* School of European Studies, University of East Anglia, Norwich NR2 2DB, England.

*CAREER:* University of East Anglia, School of European Studies, Norwich, England, lecturer, 1964-69, senior lecturer, 1969-72, reader in Russian, 1972—. Fellow of Center for Advanced Study, University of Illinois, 1968-69; visiting fellow, All Souls College, University of Oxford, 1978. *Member:* British Universities Association of Slavists, GB-USSR Association, British Society for Eighteenth-Century Studies. *Awards, honors:* Frank Knox Memorial Fellowship, Harvard University, 1960-61.

*WRITINGS: Russia under Western Eyes, 1517-1825*, St. Martin's, 1971; *N. M. Karamzin: A Study of His Literary Career, 1783-1803*, Southern Illinois University Press, 1971; (editor and contributor) *Russian Literature in the Age of Catherine the Great*, Willem A. Meeuws, 1976; (compiler) *Anglo-Russian Relations in the Eighteenth Century: Catalogue of an Exhibition*, University of East Anglia, 1977; (editor and contributor) *Great Britain and Russia in the Eighteenth Century: Contacts and Comparisons*, Oriental Research Partners, 1978. General editor of Cass-DaCapo reprint series, "Russia through European Eyes, 1553-1917." Contributor to journals of Slavic studies in Europe, North America, and Soviet Union. Editor, *Study Group on Eighteenth-Century Russia Newsletter;* reviews editor, *Journal of European Studies.*

*WORK IN PROGRESS: 'By the Banks of the Thames':* Russians in Eighteenth-Century Britain; *'By the Banks of the Neva': The British in Eighteenth-Century Petersburg.*

\*  \*  \*

## CROSS, Robert Brandt 1914-

*PERSONAL:* Born December 9, 1914, in Stockton, Calif.; son of LaRue Ackley (an accountant) and Theresa (Brandt) Cross. *Education:* University of California, Los Angeles, A.B., 1937; University of California, Berkeley, M.A., 1939; University of Southern California, Ph.D., 1948. *Politics:* Democrat. *Religion:* Greek Orthodox. *Address:* Box 663, Fayetteville, Ark. 72701. *Office:* Department of Foreign Languages, University of Arkansas, Fayetteville, Ark. 72701.

*CAREER:* University of Southern California, Los Angeles, assistant professor of classics, 1948-57; University of Arkansas, Fayetteville, professor of foreign languages, 1957—. *Military service:* U.S. Army Air Forces, 1942-46. *Member:* Classical Association of the Middle West and South (vice-president for Arkansas division, 1959), Desert Tortoise Council, California Turtle and Tortoise Club.

*WRITINGS:* (Translator from the French) Milo Riguad, *Secrets of Voodoo*, Arco, 1969.

*WORK IN PROGRESS:* Editing, compiling, and translating Latin inscriptions from the French colonial period in the Republic of Haiti.

*SIDELIGHTS:* Robert Cross has traveled extensively in the West Indies, chiefly in Haiti, and in Greece, Italy, France, and Mexico.

\*  \*  \*

## CRUMBAUGH, James C(harles) 1912-

*PERSONAL:* Born December 11, 1912, in Terrell, Tex.; son of Charles Miller (an attorney) and Hallie (Dansby) Crumbaugh; married Edna Bailey, December 31, 1938 (died, 1946); children: Charles Miller II. *Education:* Baylor University, A.B., 1935; Southern Methodist University, A.M., 1938; University of Texas, Ph.D., 1954. *Politics:* Independent. *Religion:* Roman Catholic. *Home:* Tally Arms Condiminium No. 32, Church and 16th Sts., Gulfport, Miss. 39501. *Office:* Veterans Administration Hospital, Gulfport, Miss. 39501.

*CAREER:* Memphis State College (now Memphis State University), Memphis, Tenn., instructor in psychology, 1947-56; MacMurray College, Jacksonville, Ill., associate professor of psychology and head of department, 1957-59; Bradley Center (mental health clinic), Columbus, Ga., research director, 1959-64; Veterans Administration Hospital,

Gulfport, Miss., staff clinical psychologist, 1965—. Consultant to Mix Memorial Fund, 1957, International Graphoanalysis Society, 1968—, and Coastal Mental Health Center, 1971. *Military service:* U.S. Army Air Forces, assistant psychologist, 1942-45. *Member:* American Psychological Association, Southern Society for Philosophy and Psychology, Southeastern Psychological Association, Mississippi Psychological Association, Psi Chi.

*WRITINGS: The Purpose-in-Life Test*, with manual, Psychometric Affiliates, 1969; *Everything to Gain: A Guide to Self-Fulfillment through Logoanalysis*, Nelson-Hall, 1973; *The Seeking of Noetic Goals Test (SONG)*, with manual, Psychometric Affiliates, 1977; *Logotherapy: Now Help for Problem Drinkers*, Nelson-Hall, in press. Contributor of over one-hundred articles to journals.

*WORK IN PROGRESS:* Research on logotherapy as applied to aging, retirement, physical handicaps, imprisonment, and other related areas.

*AVOCATIONAL INTERESTS:* Parapsychology and psychical research.

\*  \*  \*

## CULBERTSON, Paul T(homas) 1905-

*PERSONAL:* Born March 13, 1905, in Ashland, Ore.; son of Thomas A. (a farmer) and Mamie (Wiley) Culbertson; married Jessie D. Durrand; children: Gerard W. *Education:* University of California, Berkeley, A.B., 1931, M.A., 1933; University of Oregon, Ph.D., 1941. *Politics:* Democrat. *Religion:* Protestant (Nazarene). *Home:* 3034 Kellogg St., San Diego, Calif. 92106. *Office:* Point Loma College, 3900 Lomaland Dr., San Diego, Calif. 92106.

*CAREER:* Pasadena College, Pasadena, Calif., assistant professor, 1941-45, associate professor, 1945-49, professor, 1949-75, professor emeritus, 1975—, dean, 1949-65; currently affiliated with Point Loma College, San Diego, Calif. *Member:* Phi Delta Kappa.

*WRITINGS*—All published by Nazarene Publishing: *Introduction to Christian Theology*, 1944; *Building a Bridge to a Better World*, 1948; *More Like the Master*, 1966; *Contemporary Portraits of Old Testament Personalities*, 1973; *Our Battle and Our Hope*, 1976; *Living Portraits from the Old Testament*, 1978.

*WORK IN PROGRESS: Psycho-Spiritual Studies of Bible Personalities.*

\*  \*  \*

## CUMMINS, D. Duane 1935-

*PERSONAL:* Born June 4, 1935, in Dawson, Neb.; son of Delmer H. (a businessman) and Ina Z. (Arnold) Cummins; married Darla Sue Beard, October 6, 1957; children: Stephen, Cristi, Caroline. *Education:* Philips University, B.A., 1957; University of Denver, M.A., 1965; University of Oklahoma, Ph.D., 1974. *Politics:* Democrat. *Religion:* Christian. *Home:* 12760 Shady Creek Lane, St. Louis, Mo. 63141. *Office:* Division of Higher Education, 119 North Jefferson, St. Louis, Mo. 63103.

*CAREER:* History teacher at high school in Denver, Colo., 1957-67, chairman of department, 1959-67; Oklahoma City University, Oklahoma City, Okla., assistant professor, 1967-71, associate professor of history, 1972-74, Darbeth-Whitten Professor of American History, 1974-78, chairman of department, 1969-72, director of Robert A. Taft Institute of Politics and Government, 1970-78, director, Division of

Continuing Education, 1971-72, curator, George H. Shirk Oklahoma History Collection, 1977; Division of Higher Education (Christian Church), St. Louis, Mo., president, 1978—. *Military service:* U.S. Army, Infantry, 1955-57. *Member:* American Historical Association, Organization of American Historians, Western History Association, Oklahoma Association of History Professors (vice-president, 1970).

*WRITINGS*—"Inquiries" series, published by Benziger: Author with William G. White of *The American Revolution,* 1968, revised edition, 1973, *The American Frontier,* 1968, revised edition, 1972, *Origins of the Civil War,* 1971, and *Contrasting Decades,* 1972; sole author of *Consensus and Turmoil,* 1972, and *Consensus and Conflict,* 1978; editor of four other books in the series, *The Federal Period,* 1971, *Our Colonial Heritage,* 1972, *Industrialism: The American Experience,* 1972, and *American Foreign Policy,* 1972. Also author of *Southwestern Palette,* a monograph on Western art. Editor of series of history transparencies published by Keuffel & Esser Corp.

*AVOCATIONAL INTERESTS:* Photography, travel, literature, poetry.

\*    \*    \*

## CURL, James Stevens 1937-
## (Adytum, E. B. Keeling, Parsifal)

*PERSONAL:* Born March 26, 1937, in Belfast, Northern Ireland; son of George Stevens (a businessman) and Sarah (McKinney) Curl; married Eileen Elizabeth Blackstock (a psychiatrist), January 1, 1960; children: Astrid, Ingrid. *Education:* Attended Campbell College, Belfast, 1946-54, and Queens University and Belfast College of Art, 1954-58; Oxford School of Architecture, Dipl. Arch., 1964, Dip. T.P., 1967. *Home:* 5 Clifton Ter., Winchester, Hampshire 5022 5BJ, England.

*CAREER:* Architect and planner, Oxford, England, 1963-69; architectural specialist contributor to *Survey of London,* London, England, 1970-73; Oxford School of Architecture, Oxford, tutor in history of architecture, 1967-73; architect to the Scottish contribution to European Architectural Heritage Year, 1973-75; Hertfordshire County Council, Planning Department, Hertfordshire County, England, principal architect-planner, 1975—. *Member:* Royal Town Planning Institute (fellow), Royal Institute of British Architects, Society of Antiquaries of London (fellow), Society of Antiquaries of Scotland (fellow), Royal Incorporation of Architects in Scotland (fellow), United Oxford and Cambridge University Club, Oxford Civic Society (chairman, 1969-72). *Awards, honors:* Sir Charles Lanyon Prize for measured drawings; traveling scholarship to Germany, 1962.

*WRITINGS: European Cities and Society,* Leonard Hill, 1970; *The Victorian Celebration of Death,* David & Charles, 1972, Partridge Press, 1972; (contributor) *Encyclopedia of Town Planning,* McGraw, 1973; *City of London Pubs,* David & Charles, 1973; *Victorian Architecture,* David & Charles, 1973; *The Erosion of Oxford,* Oxford Illustrated Press, 1977; *English Architecture: An Illustrated Glossary,* David & Charles, 1977. Contributor of articles, some under pseudonyms Adytum, E. B. Keeling, and Parsifal, to *Country Life, Spectator, Oxford Mail, Guardian, Official Architecture and Planning, Oxford, Oxford Magazine, R.I.B.A. Journal,* and other periodicals.

*WORK IN PROGRESS: The Architecture of Death.*

*AVOCATIONAL INTERESTS:* Travel, opera, music, photography, food, humor.

## CURLEY, Michael J. 1900-1972

1900—December 3, 1972; American Redemptorist missionary, historian, educator, and author of religious works. Obituaries: *New York Times,* December 5, 1972.

\*    \*    \*

## CURTIS, Howard J(ames) 1906-1972

December 11, 1906—September 13, 1972; American biologist, educator, editor, and author of books on biophysics and radiology. Obituaries: *New York Times,* September 15, 1972.

\*    \*    \*

## CZERNIAWSKI, Adam 1934-

*PERSONAL:* Born December 20, 1934, in Warsaw, Poland; son of Emil Jerzy (a military officer and civil servant) and Maria (Tynicka) Czerniawski; married Ann Christine Daker (a high school director of studies), July 27, 1957; children: Irena Christine, Stefan Mark Emil. *Education:* University of London, B.A., 1955, B.A., 1967; University of Sussex, M.A., 1968; Oxford University, B.Phil., 1970. *Politics:* Socialist. *Religion:* None. *Home:* 13 King Edward Rd., Rochester, Kent ME1 1UB, England. *Office:* Philosophy Division, Thames Polytechnic, Wellington St., London SE18 6PF, England.

*CAREER:* U.S. Information Agency, Munich, Germany, broadcaster, 1955-57; Northern Assurance Co., London, England, assistant superintendent, 1957-65; Medway College of Design, Rochester, England, lecturer in philosophy and literature, 1970-74; Thames Polytechnic, London, lecturer in philosophy, 1974-77, senior lecturer and acting head of philosophy division, 1977—. *Member:* Royal Institute of Philosophy, Polish Society of Arts and Sciences Abroad, Trinity College Oxford Society. *Awards, honors:* Second prize for young writers, Union of Polish Writers Abroad (London), 1954; Abraham Woursell Foundation grant, University of Vienna, 1965, 1970; poetry prize, Union of Writers Abroad, 1967; poetry award, Koscielski Foundation, 1971; Sulkowski prize for literary criticism, Poet's & Painter's Press, 1971; L'ordre du "Merite Culturel," Polish government, 1975; Polish Writers' Union Translators' Prize (Warsaw), 1977; Translators' Award, Arts Council of Great Britain.

*WRITINGS: Polowanie na jednorozca* (poetry; title means "Hunting the Unicorn"), Poets' & Painters' Press (London), 1956; *Topografia wnetrza* (poetry; title means "Topography of the Interior"), Institut Litteraire (Paris), 1962; *Czesci mniejszej calosci* (short stories; title means "Parts of a Smaller Whole"), Poets' & Painters' Press, 1964; (editor) *Ryby na piasku* (poetry; title means "Fish on the Strand"), Swiderski (London), 1965; *Sen cytadela gaj* (poetry; title means "A Dream, a Citadel, a Grove"), Institut Litteraire, 1966; *Liryka i druk* (literary criticism; title means "Poetry and Print"), Poets' & Printers' Press, 1972; *Widok Delft* (poetry; title means "A View of Delft"), Wydawnictwo Literackie (Krakow, Poland), 1973; *Akt* (short stories), Poets' & Painters' Press, 1975; *Wiersz Wspolczsny* (literary essays; title means "The Contemporary Poem"), Poets' & Painters' Press, 1977.

Translator: Tadeusz Rozewicz, *Faces of Anxiety,* Rapp & Whiting (London), 1969; Rozewicz, *The Card-Index and Other Plays,* Calder & Boyars (London), 1969; Rozewicz, *The Witnesses and Other Plays,* Calder & Boyars, 1970; W. Tatarkiewicz, *History of Aesthetics,* Mouton, 1970; Rozewicz, *Selected Poems,* Penguin, 1976.

Contributing translator: E. Ordon, editor, *Ten Contemporary Polish Stories*, Wayne State University Press, 1958; P. Mayewski, editor, *Antologia wspolczesnej poezji brytyjskiej i amerykanskiej* (title means "Anthology of Contemporary British and American Poetry"), Criterion, 1958, 2nd edition, 1965; June Oppen Degan and others, editors, *San Francisco Review Annual*, New Directions, 1963; A. Gillon and L. Krzyzanowski, editors, *Introduction to Modern Polish Literature*, Twayne, 1964; *Polish Writing Today*, Penguin, 1967; Krzeczkowski, Sito, and Zulawski, editors, *Poeci jezkyka angielskiego* (title means "Poets of the English Language"), [Warsaw], Volume I, 1969, Volume III, 1974; A. N. Bold, editor, *The Penguin Book of Socialist Verse*, Penguin, 1970; J. Harrell and A. Wierzbianska, editors, *Aesthetics in Twentieth-Century Poland*, Bucknell University Press, 1973.

Represented in anthologies, including: *Opisanie z pamieci*, edited by Andrzej Lam, PIW (Warsaw), 1965; *Anthologie de la poesie polonaise*, edited by Constantin Jelenski, Editions du Seuil (Paris), 1965; *Neue Polnische Lyrik*, edited by Karl Dedecius, Moderner Buch-Club (Darmstadt), 1965; *Explorations in Freedom*, edited by L. Tyrmand, Free Press, 1970; *Kolumbowie i wspolczesni*, edited by A. Lam, Czytelnik (Warsaw), 1972, 2nd revised edition, 1976; *Modern Poetry in Translation*, edited by B. Czaykowski, [London], Volume XXIII-XXIV, 1975.

*WORK IN PROGRESS:* Translations of plays by Tadeusz Rozewicz; a book on Descartes.

*BIOGRAPHICAL/CRITICAL SOURCES: Kultura* (Paris), July, 1957; *Kontynenty* (London), April-June, 1962; T. Terlecki, editor, *Literatura polska na obczyznie 1940-1960*, [London], 1964; J. Brzekowski, *Wyobraznia wyzwolona*, [London], 1966; C. Milosz, *The History of Polish Literature*, Macmillan, 1969; T. E. Bird, editor, *Queens Slavic Papers*, [New York], Volume I, 1973; Karl Dedecius, *Uberall ist Polen*, Suhrkamp Verlag, 1974; *Tygodnik Kulturalny* (Warsaw), September 21, 1975; L. M. Bartelski, editor, *Polscy pisarze wspolczesni*, [Warsaw], 1977.

\*     \*     \*

# CZOBOR, Agnes 1920-

*PERSONAL:* Surname is pronounced Zo-bor; born May 13, 1920, in Budapest, Hungary; daughter of Ernest (a lawyer) and Agnes (Lowy) Czobor; married Eugene Katona (an editor), May 18, 1946; children: Agnes. *Education:* Pazmany Peter University of Arts and Sciences (now Eotvos Lorand University), Ph.D., 1972. *Religion:* Roman Catholic. *Office:* Szepmuveszeti Muzeum, Dozsa Gyorgy ut 41, Budapest, Hungary.

*CAREER:* Art critic for daily newspapers and periodicals, Budapest, Hungary, 1945-52; Szepmuveszeti Muzeum (Museum of Fine Arts), Budapest, museologist, 1949-66, deputy keeper of old paintings, 1966-70, keeper of drawings and prints, 1970—. *Member:* Magyar Regeszeti, Muveszettorteneti es Eremtani Tarsulat (Hungarian Society of Archaeology, History of Fine Arts and Numismatics).

*WRITINGS: Caravaggio*, Kepzomuveszeti Alap, 1960; *Barokk muveszet Italiaban* (title means "Baroque Art in Italy"), Kepzomuveszeti Alap, 1961; *Holland Tajkepek* (catalogue of Dutch landscape paintings in Budapest Museum of Fine Arts), Corvina (Budapest), 1967, translation published as *Dutch Landscapes*, Corvina, 1967, Taplinger, 1968; *Malarstwo weneckie pietnasty-osiemnasty wiek*, [Warsaw], 1968; *Rembrandt es koere*, Corvina, 1969, translation by Lili Halapy published as *Rembrandt and His Circle*, Corvina, 1969, Taplinger, 1970, published as *Rembrandt and His Circle in Hungarian Museums*, International Publications Service, 1977; (editor) *A Szepmuveszeti Muzeum* (guidebook), Corvina, 1971, translation by Ruth Pataki and Mari Szilveszter published as *The Budapest Museum of Fine Arts*, Corvina, 1971.

Catalogues: *Az Egri Keptar katalogusa* (catalogue of the Gallery of Eger), 1960; *Csendeletkiallitas* (catalogue for exhibition of still lifes), 1962; *Venezianische Malerei* (catalogue for Dresden exhibition of pictures from Budapest), 1968. Author of several other catalogues for the Budapest Museum of Fine Arts. Contributor to *Enciclopedia Universale dell Arte*, and more than forty articles to art bulletins and periodicals, including *Burlington Magazine*.

*SIDELIGHTS:* Agnes Czobor has made several study tours in Italy and the Netherlands, some of which were made possible by scholarships.

*BIOGRAPHICAL/CRITICAL SOURCES: Alte und Moderne Kunst*, Volumes V-VI, 1970.†

# D

## DACEY, Philip 1939-

PERSONAL: Born May 9, 1939, in St. Louis, Mo.; son of Joseph and Teresa (McGinn) Dacey; married Florence Chard, May 25, 1963; children: Emmett Joseph, Fay Pauline Teresa, Austin Warren. *Education:* St. Louis University, B.A., 1961; Stanford University, M.A., 1967; Iowa University, M.F.A., 1970. *Address:* Box 346, Cottonwood, Minn. 56229. *Office:* Southwest State University, Marshall, Minn. 56258.

CAREER: Peace Corps Volunteer in Eastern Nigeria, 1963-65; University of Missouri—St. Louis, instructor, 1967-68; Southwest State University, Marshall, Minn., associate professor of literature, 1970—. *Awards, honors:* Yankee Poetry Prize for "Storm," 1968; Poet and Critic Prize for "For the Poet's Father, On His Taking Up Gardening Late in Life," 1969; Borestone Mountain Poetry Award, 1974; Discovery Award, 1974; National Endowment for the Arts fellowship, 1975; Minnesota State Arts Council fellowship, 1975; first prize, G. M. Hopkins Memorial Sonnet Competition, 1977; first prize in poetry, *Prairie Schooner,* 1977; Bush fellowship, 1977; Pushcart Prize, 1977.

WRITINGS: *The Beast with Two Backs* (a small pamphlet collection of poetry), Gunrunner Press, 1969; (editor with Gerald Knoll) *I Love You All Day: It Is That Simple* (an anthology of modern poetry), Abbey Press, 1970; *Fish, Sweet Giraffe, The Lion, Snake, and Owl* (a small pamphlet collection of poetry), Back Door Press, 1970; *Four Nudes* (a small pamphlet collection of poetry), Morgan Press, 1971; *How I Escaped from the Labyrinth and Other Poems,* Carnegie-Mellon University Press, 1977. Poems in many anthologies, including: *American Poetry Anthology,* edited by D. Halpern, Avon, 1975; *Heartland II: Poets of the Midwest,* edited by L. Stryk, Northern Illinois University Press, 1975; *Ardis Anthology of New American Poetry,* edited by D. Rigsbee, Ardis, 1977. Contributor of poetry to *Esquire, New York Quarterly, Poetry Northwest, Nation, Paris Review, American Review, Partisan Review, Hudson Review, Shenandoah,* and other periodicals; editor, *Crazy Horse,* 1971-76.

WORK IN PROGRESS: A book-length sequence, *Gerard Manley Hopkins Meets Walt Whitman in Heaven and Other Poems.*

BIOGRAPHICAL/CRITICAL SOURCES: *Shenandoah,* winter, 1971; *Minnesota Daily,* August 8, 1977; *Great River Review,* fall, 1977.

## DALGLISH, Edward R(ussell) 1913-

PERSONAL: Born December 25, 1913, in Paterson, N.J.; son of William Cleland (a mining engineer) and Alice (Smith) Dalglish; married Florence Margaret, 1941. *Education:* Columbia University, B.S., 1943, M.A., 1946, Ph.D., 1955; also studied at Harvard University and Heidelberg University. *Politics:* Conservative Progressive. *Religion:* Southern Baptist. *Home:* 316 Guittard Ave., Waco, Tex. 76706. *Office:* Department of Religion, Baylor University, Waco, Tex. 76703.

CAREER: Gordon Divinity School, Boston, Mass., professor, 1946-52; Eastern Baptist Seminary, Philadelphia, Pa., professor, 1952-66; Baylor University, Waco, Tex., professor of religion, 1966—. Director of major library acquisitions.

WRITINGS: *Psalm Fifty-One in the Light of Ancient Patternism,* E. J. Brill, 1962; *The Book of Judges,* Broadman, 1969; *The Book of Nahum,* Broadman, 1972; *Studies in the Book of Exodus,* Broadman, 1977. Contributor of four hundred articles to *Interpreter's Dictionary of Bible.*

\*    \*    \*

## D'ALONZO, C(onstance) Anthony 1912-1972

1912—July 23(?), 1972; American physician, industrial medical director, and author of books on alcoholism, industrial safety, and other topics. Obituaries: *New York Times,* July 24, 1972.

\*    \*    \*

## DAMM, John S. 1926-

PERSONAL: Born June 21, 1926, in Union City, N.J.; son of William John (an engineer) and Lillian (Meisse) Damm. *Education:* Concordia College, Bronxville, N.Y., A.A., 1945; Concordia Seminary, St. Louis, Mo., B.A., 1947, M.Div., 1951; Columbia University, M.A., 1952, Ed.D., 1963; Harvard University, postdoctoral study, 1972. *Home:* 68 Notre Dame Dr., Creve Coeur, Mo. 63141. *Office:* Christ Seminary-Seminex, 607 North Grand, St. Louis, Mo. 63103.

CAREER: Clergyman of Association of Evangelical Lutheran Churches; teacher and principal at Lutheran school in New York, N.Y., 1947-49; director of education at Lutheran church in Teaneck, N.J., 1951-66; Concordia Seminary, St.

Louis, Mo., assistant professor, 1966-68, associate professor of religious education and liturgy, 1968-72, academic dean, 1972-74; Christ Seminary-Seminex, St. Louis, director of Joint Project for Theological Education, 1974-75, acting president, 1974-75, academic dean, 1974—. Lutheran Church-Missouri Synod, member of board of directors, Commission on Parish Education, and member of curriculum committee, Board of Higher Education. *Member:* Religious Education Association, Lutheran Education Association, Luther Education Society, Society for Worship, Music and Arts. *Awards, honors:* Fulbright scholarship to Germany, 1959-60; University of Muenster Auslands-Kommittee Award, 1960; American Association of Theological Schools postdoctoral scholarship at Harvard University, Graduate School of Business Administration, 1972.

*WRITINGS:* (Editor) *The Teaching of Religion,* Lutheran Education Association, 1965; *Lenten Meditations for Students,* National Lutheran Council, 1966; *Theological Education for Today,* Board of Higher Education, Lutheran Church-Missouri Synod, 1970; *Portals of Prayer,* Concordia, 1971. Chairman of editorial board, Lutheran Education Association; member of editorial committee, *Concordia Theological Monthly.*

*WORK IN PROGRESS:* A popular history of Christian worship, for Concordia; a chapter for a book of educational readings, for Concordia.

\* \* \*

## DAMON, Virgil G. 1895-1972

January 19, 1895—July 9, 1972; American obstetrician and gynecologist, author, and educator. Obituaries: *New York Times,* July 11, 1972. (See index for *CA* sketch)

\* \* \*

## DANCE, E(dward) H(erbert) 1894-

*PERSONAL:* Born November 17, 1894, in Nottingham, England; son of E. G. and Elizabeth (Crampton) Dance; married Ida Harrison, August 3, 1922; children: Janet. *Education:* University of Manchester, M.A., 1917. *Home:* 39 Castlecroft Lane, Wolverhampton WV3 8JX, England.

*CAREER:* Wolverhampton Grammar School, Wolverhampton, England, head of English and history department, 1920-54. Expert consultant in education to Council of Europe. *Member:* Historical Association (England; honorary vice-president).

*WRITINGS: Outlines of British Social History,* Longmans, Green, 1927, 3rd edition, 1948; *The Victorian Illusion,* Heinemann, 1928; *Britain in World History,* Longmans, Green, 1932, also published as *Britain in the Old World, Britain in the Old World and the New,* and *Britain in the Modern World,* 1964; *The World before Britain,* Longmans, Green, 1937; *Christendom and Beyond: The Middle Ages,* Longmans, Green, 1940; *History Without Bias?,* Council of Christians and Jews (England), 1954; (with G. P. Dartford) *Malayan and World History,* Longmans, Green, Book I: *Malaya and the Old World,* 1959, Book II: *Malaya and the New World,* 1960; *Living in Towns,* Longmans, Green, 1960; *History the Betrayer: A Study in Bias,* Hutchinson, 1960, 4th edition, 1969, Greenwood Press, 1975; (with Edouard Bruley) *A History of Europe?* (published in English, French, Italian, Greek, Turkish, and Dutch editions), Sythoff, for Council of Europe, 1960; *Alexander the Great,* Hutchinson Educational, 1964; *The Place of History in Secondary Teaching: A Comparative Study,* Harrap, for

Council of Europe, 1970; *History for a United World,* Harrap, 1971.

Author of history texts published by Longmans, Green as "British and Foreign History" series, latest edition, 1965, composed of *The World before Britain* (supra, 1937), *Europe and the Old World: The Middle Ages* (original title, *Christendom and Beyond: The Middle Ages* [supra 1940]), *New Europe and the New World: From the 16th to the 18th Century,* and *The Modern World Since the Eighteenth Century.*

General editor, "Man's Heritage," series, Longmans, Green, and "Men of Mark" series, Hutchinson. Contributor to educational publications throughout the world.

*WORK IN PROGRESS:* Research and writing on historical prejudice.

*BIOGRAPHICAL/CRITICAL SOURCES: Birmingham Post* (England), August 14, 1971.

\* \* \*

## D'ANGELO, Edward 1932-

*PERSONAL:* Born December 30, 1932, in Brooklyn, N.Y.; son of Salvatore and Mary (Parrino) D'Angelo. *Education:* Oswego State Teachers College (now State University of New York College at Oswego), B.S., 1954; Columbia University, graduate study, 1954-55; New York University, M.A., 1958; State University of New York at Buffalo, Ph.D., 1966; Cornell University, additional study, 1968-69. *Home:* 895 Wood Ave., Bridgeport, Conn. 06604. *Office:* Philosophy Department, University of Bridgeport, Bridgeport, Conn. 06602.

*CAREER:* State University of New York College at Buffalo, assistant professor of philosophy, 1958-64; University of Missouri—Kansas City, assistant professor of philosophy, 1965-68; University of Bridgeport, Bridgeport, Conn., assistant professor of philosophy, 1969—. *Member:* Critical Thinking Association (president), American Philosophical Association. *Awards, honors:* Research grant, University of Missouri, 1968.

*WRITINGS: The Problem of Freedom and Determinism,* University of Missouri Press, 1968; (editor with David H. DeGrood and Dale Riepe) *Contemporary East European Philosophy,* Spartacus, 1970; (editor) *Reflections on Revolution,* Spartacus, 1971; (with DeGrood and Riepe) *Philosophy at the Barricade,* Spartacus, 1971; *The Teaching of Critical Thinking,* Gruener, 1971. Contributor of articles to scholarly journals. Editor, *Philosophical Society Review,* 1960, 1961.†

\* \* \*

## DANHOF, Clarence H(enry) 1911-

*PERSONAL:* Born September 12, 1911, in Sully, Iowa; son of Henry (a minister) and Anna (Brouwer) Danhof; married Gertrude Brussee, June 2, 1937 (died, 1950); married Ruth Ingram, October 2, 1951; children: (first marriage) Sharon (Mrs. Lang D'Atri), Constance (Mrs. Tom Baker), Pamela (Mrs. Dan Benitez), Leslie (step-daughter); (second marriage) Debra. *Education:* Kalamazoo College, A.B., 1932; University of Michigan, M.A., 1933, Ph.D., 1939. *Home:* 26 Beach View Lane, Springfield, Ill. 62707. *Office:* Sangamon State University, Springfield, Ill. 62703.

*CAREER:* Lehigh University, Bethlehem, Pa., assistant professor, later associate professor of economics, 1937-42; National War Labor Board, Washington, D.C., branch chief, Wage Stabilization Division, 1943-44; U.S. Department of Commerce, Washington, D.C., editor, *Survey of Current Business*, 1944-45; U.S. Bureau of the Budget, Washington, D.C., staff of Committee on Records of War Administration, 1945-46, consultant, 1946-47; Princeton University, Woodrow Wilson School of Public and International Affairs, Princeton, N.J., assistant professor of public affairs, 1946-51; U.S. Bureau of the Budget and Office of Defense Mobilization, Washington, D.C., director, Office of Defense History, 1951-53; Tulane University, New Orleans, La., professor of economics, 1953-61; Brookings Institution, Washington, D.C., member of senior staff, 1961-66; George Washington University, Washington, D.C., senior scientist, Program of Policy Studies in Science and Technology, 1966-70; Council of State Governments, Washington, D.C., deputy director, Science and Technology Project, 1971; Sangamon State University, Springfield, Ill., professor of political economy, 1972—. Adjunct professor, American University, 1962-63, George Washington University, 1966-67. Lecturer at Columbia University, 1949, and Johns Hopkins University, 1968-69. Consultant to Commission on Marine Sciences, Engineering and Resources, 1967-68, National Academy of Public Administration, 1969-70, Commission on Government Procurement, 1970-72, and National Science Foundation, 1971.

*MEMBER:* American Economic Association, Economic History Association (vice-president, 1955), Agricultural History Society (president, 1972), Southern Economic Association (vice-president, 1960), Beta Gamma Sigma, Cosmos Club (Washington, D.C.). *Awards, honors:* E. F. Gay Prize of Economic History Association for *Change in Agriculture*.

*WRITINGS: Government Contracting and Technological Change*, Brookings Institution, 1968; *Change in Agriculture: The Northern States, 1820-1870*, Harvard University Press, 1969.

Contributor: H. F. Williamson, editor, *The Growth of the American Economy*, Prentice-Hall, 1944, 2nd edition, 1951; *The United States at War*, U.S. Government Printing Office, 1947; *Change and the Entrepreneur*, Harvard University Press, 1949; A. Dudley Ward, editor, *Goals of Economic Life*, Harper, 1953; Vernon Carstensen, *The Public Lands*, University of Wisconsin Press, 1963; Melvin L. Greenhut and W. Tate Whitman, editors, *Essays in Southern Economic Development*, University of North Carolina Press, 1964; *Toward Balanced Growth: Quantity with Quality*, National Goals Research Staff, 1970; Raphael G. Kasper, editor, *Technology Assessment*, Praeger, 1972. Contributor to economic, business, labor, and agriculture journals. Former member of board of editors, Economic History Association and Southern Economic Association.

*WORK IN PROGRESS:* Two books, *Technological Change: Process and Problems*, and *American Economy since 1945*.

*      *      *

## DANIEL, Pete 1938-

*PERSONAL:* Born November 24, 1938, in Rocky Mount, N.C.; son of Peter Edward and Stella (Hunt) Daniel; married Bonnie Sullivan, June 11, 1961 (divorced, 1972); children: Elizabeth Anne, Laura Elaine. *Education:* Wake Forest University, B.A., 1961, M.A., 1962; University of Maryland, Ph.D., 1970. *Home:* 501 View Park Dr., Apt. 12, Knoxville, Tenn. 37920. *Office:* Department of History, University of Tennessee, Knoxville, Tenn. 37916.

*CAREER:* University of North Carolina at Wilmington, instructor in history, 1963-66; University of Maryland, College Park, assistant editor of Booker T. Washington papers, 1969-70; University of Tennessee, Knoxville, assistant professor, 1971-73, associate professor of history, 1973—. Visiting professor, University of Colorado, 1970, University of Maryland, 1971, University of Massachusetts, 1974-75. *Member:* American Historical Association, Organization of American Historians, Southern Historical Association. *Awards, honors:* Louis Pelzer Prize for "Up from Slavery and Down to Peonage: The Alonzo Bailey Case," from Organization of American Historians, 1970; National Endowment for the Humanities, fellowship, 1970-71, 1978-79, stipend, 1974; American Philosophical Society grant, 1975.

*WRITINGS: The Shadow of Slavery: Peonage in the South, 1901-1969*, University of Illinois Press, 1972; (assistant editor with others) Louis R. Harlan, senior editor, *The Booker T. Washington Papers*, Volume II, University of Illinois Press, 1972; (with Raymond Smock) *A Talent for Detail: The Photographs of Miss Frances Benjamin Johnston, 1889-1910*, Harmony, 1974; *Deep'n As It Come: The 1927 Mississippi Flood*, Oxford University Press, 1977. Member of board of editorial advisors, Booker T. Washington papers. Contributor of articles to history journals.

*AVOCATIONAL INTERESTS:* Photography.

*      *      *

## DANIELS, Elizabeth Adams 1920-

*PERSONAL:* Born May 8, 1920, in Westport, Conn.; daughter of Thomas Davies (a mechanical engineer) and Minnie M. (Sherwood) Adams; married John L. Daniels (a stock broker), March 21, 1942; children: John L., Jr., Eleanor B., Sherwood A. (daughter), Ann S. *Education:* Vassar College, A.B., 1941; University of Michigan, A.M., 1942; New York University, Ph.D., 1954. *Politics:* Democrat. *Home:* 129 College Ave., Poughkeepsie, N.Y. 12603. *Office:* Department of English, Vassar College, Poughkeepsie, N.Y. 12603.

*CAREER:* Vassar College, Poughkeepsie, N.Y., instructor, 1948-54, assistant professor, 1954-60, associate professor, 1960-63, professor of English, 1964—, assistant dean, 1955-58, dean of studies, 1966-72, dean of faculty, 1976—.

*WRITINGS: Jessie White Marco: Risorgimento Revolutionary*, Ohio University Press, 1972. Contributor of articles to scholarly journals.

*WORK IN PROGRESS:* Research on female Victorian writers.

*      *      *

## DANIELS, Farrington 1889-1972

March 8, 1889—June 23, 1972; American physical chemist, researcher in solar energy, educator, and author of books and papers on physics. Obituaries: *New York Times*, June 24, 1972; *Washington Post*, June 24, 1972; *Newsweek*, July 3, 1972; *Current Biography*, September, 1972. (See index for CA sketch)

*      *      *

## DANZIG, Allison 1898-

*PERSONAL:* Born February 27, 1898, in Waco, Tex.; son of Morris (a businessman) and Ethel (Harvith) Danzig; married Dorothy Charlotte Chapman, July 9, 1923; children: Dorothy (Mrs. Shelley Hull), Mimi (Mrs. Charles Christie),

Allison C. *Education:* Cornell University, A.B., 1921. *Home and office:* 13 The Birches, Roslyn, N.Y. 11576.

*CAREER: Brooklyn Eagle,* Brooklyn, N.Y., sports writer, 1921-23; *New York Times,* New York, N.Y., sports writer, 1923-68. Member of board of directors, National Tennis Foundation and Hall of Fame; trustee of National Rowing Foundation, National Art Museum of Sport, and Christopher Morley Knothole Association. Chairman of war fund sports committee, Greater New York Red Cross, 1944-45; also former member of Roslyn auxiliary police force and former trustee, Village of Roslyn Estates. *Military service:* U.S. Army, Infantry, 1918-19; became second lieutenant.

*MEMBER:* National Football Foundation and Hall of Fame (member of honors court; member of board of directors), Lawn Tennis Writers Association of America (former president), Rowing Writers Association of America (former president), U.S. Tennis Writers Association (honorary member), U.S. Naval Academy Athletic Association (honorary member), North American Racquets Association (honorary member), U.S. Court Tennis Association, Authors Guild, International Lawn Tennis Club (honorary member), Circumnavigators Club, Royal Tennis Court of Hampton Court Palace (London), Football Writers Association of New York (former president), Cornell Club of New York, West Side Tennis Club of Forest Hills (honorary member).

*AWARDS, HONORS:* Elected to National Lawn Tennis Hall of Fame and Tennis Museum, 1968; elected to Helms Foundation Rowing Hall of Fame, 1968; received distinguished service awards from National Football Foundation and Hall of Fame, U.S. Lawn Tennis Association, U.S. Professional Lawn Tennis Association, City of New York, and Medical Society of New York; Grantland Rice Award for distinguished sports writing. Also has received awards from Football Writers Association of New York, Philadelphia Sports Writers Association, Yale University Football "Y" Association, National Association of Amateur Oarsmen, Princeton University Athletic Association, West Side Tennis Club, Tennis Umpires Association of the United States, and Cornell Club of New York. Columbia University has instituted Allison Danzig Cup for tennis in his honor; Longwood (Massachusetts) Cricket Club established Allison Danzig Award for tennis writing.

*WRITINGS: The Racquet Game,* Macmillan, 1930; (with John Doeg) *Elements of Lawn Tennis,* Coward, 1931; (editor with Peter Brandwein) *Sport's Golden Age: A Close-Up of the Fabulous Twenties,* Books for Libraries, 1948, 2nd edition, 1969; (editor) *The Greatest Sports Stories from the New York Times,* A. S. Barnes, 1951; *The History of American Football: Its Great Teams, Players, and Coaches,* Prentice-Hall, 1956; (with Joe Reichler) *The History of Baseball: Its Great Players, Teams and Managers,* Prentice-Hall, 1959; *Oh, How They Played the Game: The Early Days of Football and the Heroes Who Made It Great,* Macmillan, 1971; (with Peter Schwed) *Fireside Book of Tennis,* Simon & Schuster, 1972. Sports columnist, *New Yorker,* during 1920's. Contributor to *Encyclopaedia Britannica, Collier's Year Book, Companion to Sports and Games, English Encyclopedia of Tennis,* and *English International Encyclopedia of Sports;* contributor to national periodicals, including *Saturday Evening Post, Collier's,* and *New Yorker.*

*SIDELIGHTS:* Allison Danzig covered the Olympic games in Los Angeles in 1932, in London in 1948, in Helsinki in 1952, in Melbourne in 1956, and in Rome in 1960.

## DAUER, Dorothea W. 1917-

*PERSONAL:* Born June 29, 1917, in Cleve, Germany; U.S. citizen; daughter of Willy Franz (a businessman) and Annemarie (Fischer) Dauer; married Michael S. Watanabe-Dauer (a university professor), September 7, 1937; children: Francis. *Education:* Attended University of Leipzig, 1937-38; Sorbonne, University of Paris, M.A., 1938; Japanese Language School, Tokyo, diploma, 1943; University of California, Berkeley, graduate study, 1950; University of Texas at Austin, Ph.D., 1953; University of Munich, postdoctoral study, 1954-55. *Religion:* Lutheran. *Home:* 242 Kaalawai Pl., Honolulu, Hawaii 96816. *Office:* Department of European Languages and Literature, University of Hawaii, Honolulu, Hawaii.

*CAREER:* State Music Academy, Tokyo, Japan, assistant professor of German and French, 1940-43; Meteorological University, Tokyo, lecturer in scientific German, 1940-43; U.S. Armed Forces, General Headquarters, Tokyo, coordinator, interpreter, information and education officer, 1945-46; U.S. Army Education Center, Tokyo, instructor in German and French, 1946-48; Southwestern University, Georgetown, Tex., assistant professor of German, French, and Japanese, 1948-50; University of Maryland Overseas Program, Munich, Germany, professor of German and dean of women, 1954-55; University of Virginia, Fredericksburg, assistant professor of German and French, 1955-56; Texas Lutheran College, Seguin, associate professor of German, French, and philology, 1956-57; Monmouth College, West Long Branch, N.J., associate professor of German, 1957-63; Kentucky Wesleyan College, Owensboro, professor of German and French and chairman of department of modern languages, 1963-64; Marshall University, Huntington, W.Va., professor of German and chairman of department of modern languages, 1964-66; University of Hawaii, Honolulu, professor of German, 1966—, chairman of German division, 1966-69. *Member:* Modern Language Association of America, American Association of Teachers of German (chairman of Hawaii chapter, 1967-71), Japan American Society.

*WRITINGS: Schopenhauer as Transmitter of Buddhist Ideas,* H. Lange & Co., 1969; (contributor) J. Y. Fraser and N. Laurence, editors, *The Study of Time II,* Springer-Verlag, 1975. Contributor of articles to professional journals.

*WORK IN PROGRESS: Richard Wagner's Buddha Drama "Die Sieger"; Wagner's Jesus of Nazareth;* research on Buddhist influence in Schopenhauer, Wagner, and Nietzsche; research on concept of time in Schopenhauer and Nietzsche.

\*          \*          \*

## DAVID, Heather M(acKinnon) 1937-

*PERSONAL:* Born December 11, 1937, in Kobe, Japan; daughter of Joseph Ayer and Sylvia (Clarke) MacKinnon; children: Laurel Allyson. *Education:* Attended University of Colorado, 1955-56; University of Maryland, B.A., 1959. *Home:* 2506 Eye St. N.W., Washington, D.C. 20037.

*CAREER: American Aviation Publication,* Washington, D.C., associate editor, 1959-67; Fairchild Publications and Capital Cities Broadcasting, Washington, D.C., Pentagon correspondent, 1967-70; Wagner & Baroody (public affairs consultants), Washington, D.C., account executive, 1975—. *Member:* Authors Guild.

*WRITINGS: Wernher Von Braun,* Putnam, 1965; *Admiral Rickover and the Nuclear Navy,* Putnam, 1969; *Operation:*

*Rescue,* Pinnacle, 1971. Contributor of articles to *Encyclopedia Americana Yearbook,* 1968-69, and to *Electronic Design Magazine.*

*WORK IN PROGRESS:* An historical novel.

\*     \*     \*

## DAVID, Lester  1914-

*PERSONAL:* Born October 26, 1914, in New York, N.Y.; son of William and Regina (Roth) David; married Irene Neer (a teacher and former journalist), November 30, 1947; children: Margery Ellen (Mrs. Baran S. Rosen), Susan Helen. *Education:* New York University, B.S., 1934; Columbia University, M.A., 1935. *Office:* 946 Carol Ave., Woodmere, N.Y. 11598.

*CAREER: Brooklyn Eagle,* Brooklyn, N.Y., editor and reporter, 1936-49; professional writer, 1949—. *Military service:* U.S. Army, 1942-46. *Member:* Society of Magazine Writers (former vice-president). *Awards, honors:* Journalism awards from American Dental Association, 1963, American Medical Association, 1964, Family Service Association, 1966, and Arthritis Foundation, 1969.

*WRITINGS: Slimming for Teenagers,* Pocket Books, 1966; *Ted Kennedy: Triumphs and Tragedies,* Grosset, 1971; *Ethel: The Story of Mrs. Robert F. Kennedy,* World Publishing, 1971; *Joan: The Reluctant Kennedy,* Funk, 1974; (with Jhan Robbins) *Jackie and Ari: The Inside Story,* Pocket Books, 1976; (with Robbins) *Richard and Elizabeth,* Crowell, 1977; *The Lonely Lady of San Clemente: The Story of Pat Nixon,* Crowell, 1978. Contributor of nearly a thousand articles to national magazines, including *Reader's Digest, Good Housekeeping, Today's Health,* and *This Week.* Managing editor, *Stars and Stripes,* Paris edition, 1944-45.

*BIOGRAPHICAL/CRITICAL SOURCES: Washington Post,* July 2, 1971, August 31, 1978; *Detroit Free Press,* September 19, 1978.

\*     \*     \*

## DAVID, Martin H(eidenhain)  1935-

*PERSONAL:* Born January 21, 1935, in Heemstede, Netherlands; naturalized U.S. citizen; married Elizabeth Likert, September 7, 1957; children: Peter Rensis, Margaret Meigs, Andrew J. H. *Education:* Swarthmore College, A.B. (with honors), 1955; University of Michigan, M.A., 1957, Ph.D., 1960. *Home:* 207 DuRose Ter., Madison, Wis. 53705. *Office:* Department of Economics, 1180 Observatory Dr., Social Science Bldg., University of Wisconsin, Madison, Wis. 53706.

*CAREER:* University of Wisconsin—Madison, assistant professor, 1961-64, associate professor, 1964-67, professor of economics, 1967—, Social Systems Research Institute, director, 1963-67, chairman, 1970-71. Institute for Social Research, University of Michigan, study director, 1959-61, visiting professor and program director, 1971-72; visiting professor, University of Nairobi, 1974-76. Fiscal economist, U.S. Treasury Department, 1961-62. *Awards, honors:* American Statistical Association fellow; National Science Foundation fellow, 1967-68.

*WRITINGS: Family Composition and Consumption,* North-Holland Publishing, 1962; *Income and Welfare in the United States,* McGraw, 1962; *Alternative Approaches to Capital Gains Taxation* (a survey monograph), Brookings Institution, 1968; *Linkage and Retrieval of Microeconomic Data,* Lexington, 1974.

## DAVIDS, Lewis Edmund  1917-

*PERSONAL:* Born April 21, 1917, in New York, N.Y.; son of William Theodore (a lithographer) and Janet (Reid) Davids; married Anna Ruth Dornbush (a writer), May 29, 1941; children: Janet Ruth (Mrs. Rodney Grantham), Judith Ann (Mrs. Steve Henson), Lewis Edmund, Jr. *Education:* New York University, B.S., 1941, M.B.A., 1942, Ph.D., 1949; additional graduate study at Wake Forest College, 1943, University of Paris, 1945, Southern Methodist University, 1958, and University of Wisconsin, 1966. *Home:* 2401 Topaz Dr., Columbia, Mo. 65201. *Office:* 332 School of Business and Public Administration, University of Missouri, Columbia, Mo. 65201.

*CAREER:* Chase National Bank, New York City, clerk, 1935-39; Williamsburgh Savings Bank, New York City, accountant, 1939-47; Institute of International Finance, New York City, research associate, 1947-48; Bankers Trust Co., New York City, economist, 1948; Drake University, Des Moines, Iowa, assistant professor of finance, 1949-51; Agricultural and Mechanical College of Texas (now Texas A&M University), College Station, professor of business administration, 1951-59; University of Georgia, Athens, professor of finance, 1959-61; University of Missouri—Columbia, Robert E. Lee Hill Professor of Bank Management, 1961—, chairman of finance department, 1977—. Visiting professor in Santiago, Chile, 1959, at Harvard University, 1963; faculty fellow at Northwestern University School of Mortgage Banking, 1967. Chief economic analyst, U.S. Economic Stabilization Agency, Iowa District, 1951; economist, National Committee on Monetary Policy, 1956—. Consultant and member of business and industry boards of directors. *Military service:* U.S. Army Air Forces, 1943-45.

*MEMBER:* American Finance Association (chairman of southern district, 1960), American Economic Association, American Association of University Professors, Midwest Case Research Association (president, 1964-66), Southern Economic Association, Southern Finance Association (president, 1961), Midwest Business Administration Association (director), Midwest Economic Association, Missouri Bankers Association, Alpha Kappa Psi, Lakeshore Estates Association (president, 1966-67), Missouri Country Club. *Awards, honors:* Certificate from Instituto Chileno de Administracion Racional de Empresas, 1959, from Council for International Progress in Management, 1960.

*WRITINGS: Dictionary of Insurance,* Littlefield, 1959, 5th edition, 1977; (with Herbert Spero) *Money and Banking,* 2nd edition (Davids was not associated with earlier edition), Barnes & Noble, 1960, 4th edition, Harper, 1978; *Small Business Founders,* University of Georgia, 1963; *Money and Banking Casebook,* Irwin, 1966; *Banking in Mid-America,* Public Affairs Press, 1970; *Dictionary of Business,* Career Institute, 1970; *Board Policy on Risk Management,* Commerce Publishing, 1977; *The Effective Board Audit,* Commerce Publishing, 1977; *Board Reports for the Bank Director,* Commerce Publishing, 1978; *Dictionary of Banking and Finance,* Littlefield, 1978. Also author of *Conflicts of Interest for Directors and Officers of Financial Institutions, Composition and Compensation of Bank Boards, Bank Director's World, Women: The 'Forgotten' Directors, A Trust Guide for the Bank Director,* and *Behind Board Room Doors,* all published by Commerce Publishing. Contributor to banking journals. Editor of *Bank Board Letter.*

*WORK IN PROGRESS:* Research on bank directors, their role, functions, and contribution to the economy.

*SIDELIGHTS: Money and Banking* has been published in Spanish translation.

## DAVIES, Daniel R. 1911-

*PERSONAL:* Born February 21, 1911, in Plymouth, Pa.; son of John R. (an electrician) and Minnie (Kocher) Davies; married Winifred Evans (an art consultant), June 14, 1946 (divorced July, 1975); married Nancy Church, September 9, 1975; children: (first marriage) Catherine (Mrs. Timothy W. Armistead), Wendy Evans. *Education:* Harvard University, A.B., 1933; Bucknell University, M.A., 1943; Columbia University, Ph.D., 1946. *Politics:* "Casual." *Religion:* "Casual." *Home and office:* 6315 Calle del Caballo, Tucson, Ariz. 85718.

*CAREER:* High school English teacher in Forty-Fort, Pa., 1934-44, head of department, 1940-44; assistant superintendent of schools in Briarcliff, N.Y., 1944-45; Columbia University, Teachers College, New York, N.Y., assistant professor, 1946-49, associate professor, 1949-50, professor of education, 1950-61; Croft Educational Services, Consulting Division, New London, Conn., vice-president, 1961-71, director, Tucson, Ariz, 1966-71; Davies-Brickell Associates, Ltd. (educational consultants), Tucson, president, 1972—. Lecturer, University of Arizona, 1962-64; visiting professor at San Diego State University, 1957, University of New Mexico, 1960, Oklahoma State University, 1963, Texas A & M University, 1964, University of Scranton, 1964, and University of Nebraska, 1971. Coordinator of Cooperative Program in Educational Administration, Middle Atlantic Region, W. K. Kellogg Foundation, 1950-59. *Member:* National Association of School Administrators (life member), National Conference of Professors of Educational Administration (past secretary-treasurer), National Education Association (life member), American Association for the Advancement of Science (fellow). *Awards, honors:* Ford Foundation grant, Europe, 1961.

*WRITINGS:* (With Willard S. Elsbree) *Instructional Personnel Record*, Croft Educational Services, 1945; (with W. F. Hosler) *The Challenge of School Board Membership*, Chartwell, 1949; *The School Board Member in Action*, A.A.S.A., 1949; (with Elwood Prestwood) *Practical School Board Procedures*, Chartwell, 1951; (with Kenneth Herrold) *The Dynamics of Group Action*, eight volumes, Croft Educational Services, 1954-56; (with Vivienne Anderson) *Patterns of Educational Leadership*, Prentice-Hall, 1956; (with Henry Mitchell Brickell) *Davies-Brickell System for School Board Policy-Making and Administration*, Croft Educational Services, 1957, 5th edition, 1978; (with Robert T. Livingston) *You and Management*, Harper, 1958.

(With D. E. Griffiths) *Executive Action*, Croft Educational Services, 1962; *The Administrative Internship*, Center for Applied Research in Education, 1962; (with Margaret Handlong) *Teaching of Art*, Croft Educational Services, 1962; (with Elsbree) *Non-Instructional Personnel Record*, Croft Educational Services, 1962; (with J. Floyd Hall and John T. Greer) *Recruiting Teachers*, Croft Educational Services, 1967; (with James B. Deneen) *New Patterns for Catholic Education*, Croft Educational Services, 1968; *Educational Policy: The Inaugural Lecture*, Memorial University of Newfoundland, 1969; (with Catherine Davies Armistead) *Teacher Education*, National Education Association, 1974. Contributor of articles to education journals. Editor, *School Board Policy Letter*, 1958-72, and *Executive Secretary*, 1962-69.

*SIDELIGHTS:* Since 1964, Daniel R. Davies has served as special consultant in installing the Davies-Brickell system in schools throughout the United States and in several countries of Europe. *Avocational interests:* Tennis, piano, swimming, dancing.

## DAVIES, Morton Rees 1939-

*PERSONAL:* Born January 29, 1939, in Glamorganshire, South Wales; son of William George (a mine worker) and Jennet Gwen (Rees) Davies; married Myra Gwenllian Williams (a school teacher), May 1, 1963; children: Tania Suzanne, Nadia Janine, Ailsa Yvonne, Huw Morton Lee. *Education:* University College, Swansea, University of Wales, B.A., 1961, Diploma in Education, 1962. *Home:* 37 Beryl Rd., Noctorum, Birkenhead, England. *Office:* Department of Political Theory, Social Studies Building, University of Liverpool, Liverpool, England.

*CAREER:* University of Liverpool, Liverpool, England, lecturer in politics, 1964-68, Leverhulme Lecturer in Public Administration, 1968-76, director of public administration studies, 1976—.

*WRITINGS:* (With V. A. Lewis) *Models of Political Systems*, Praeger, 1971.

*WORK IN PROGRESS:* A book and articles on development administration, with special emphasis on agricultural development.

\*　　　\*　　　\*

## DAVIS, Adelle 1904-1974
### (Jane Dunlap)

*PERSONAL:* Name was originally Daisie Adelle Davis; born February 25, 1904, in Lizton, Ind.; daughter of Charles Eugene (a farmer) and Harriette (McBroom) Davis; married George Edward Leisey (an engineer), October, 1943 (divorced, 1953); married Frank Vernon Sieglinger (an accountant), April 23, 1960; children: (first marriage) George Davis Leisey, Barbara Adelle Leisey Frodahl. *Education:* Attended Purdue University, 1923-25; University of California, Berkeley, B.A., 1927; University of Southern California, M.S., 1939; postgraduate work at Columbia University and University of California, Los Angeles. *Religion:* Protestant. *Residence:* Palos Verdes Estates, Calif.

*CAREER:* Received dietetics training at Bellevue and Fordham Hospitals, New York, N.Y., 1927-28; Yonkers Public Schools, Yonkers, N.Y., supervisor of nutrition, 1928-30; consulting nutritionist to physicians and in a health clinic in Oakland, Calif., 1931-33, Los Angeles, Calif., 1934-38, Palos Verdes, Calif., 1948-74. Lecturer on nutrition to numerous organizations, including women's clubs, dental and medical seminars, and colleges and universities. *Member:* International College of Applied Nutrition (honorary fellow). *Awards, honors:* Brazilian Award of Merit, 1971; D.Sc., Plano University, Plano, Tex., 1972; Raymond A. Dart Human Potential Award, 1972.

*WRITINGS:* *Optimum Health*, privately printed, 1935; *You Can Stay Well*, privately printed, 1939; *Vitality Through Planned Nutrition*, Macmillan, 1942, revised edition, 1949; *Let's Cook It Right*, Harcourt, 1947, 3rd edition, revised, New American Library, 1970; *Let's Have Healthy Children*, Harcourt, 1951, 3rd edition, revised and enlarged, 1972; *Let's Eat Right to Keep Fit*, Harcourt, 1954, revised edition, 1970; (under pseudonym Jane Dunlap) *Exploring Inner Space: Personal Experiences Under LSD-25*, Harcourt, 1961; *Let's Get Well*, Harcourt, 1965. Contributor of numerous articles on health and nutrition to periodicals.

*SIDELIGHTS:* "Mass advertising of refined foods has exploited health for money to the extent that it amounts to mass murder," Adele Davis said in *Let's Get Well*. Like this one, most of her now-famous statements on nutrition were based on the assumption that the majority of Americans are badly nourished. Jane Howard quotes her as saying: "'It's just propaganda that the American diet is the best in the world. Commercial people have been telling us those lies for years.'" A veteran nutritionist of almost 40 years who planned special diets for over 20,000 persons suffering from practically every known disease, Davis knew her subject. She was raised on an Indiana farm where "we were better fed. The only things we bought were some coffee, some sugar and salt. We raised all our own meat, eggs, chickens, [grains, fruits, and vegetables]." Although it is commonly believed that she became interested in nutrition through the 4-H clubs she belonged to as a child, Davis told C. Robert Jennings in an interview that "she really came to nutrition by an accident of birth. 'My mother had a stroke of paralysis when I was ten days old. She was never out of bed again. She died when I was seventeen months old. There were no bottle-fed babies then. The only way I could get anything to eat was through a medicine dropper [or from] a spoon. It's the [unconscious] reason I'm in nutrition.'"

Adelle Davis was trained in nutrition through dietetics courses at New York City hospitals in the late 1920's, received a master's degree in biochemistry in 1938, and acted as consulting nutritionist in various clinics in New York and California beginning in the early '30's. According to a *Publishers Weekly* article, "a milk company's promotional pamphlet was her first writing experience, in 1932." She privately published *Optimum Health* in 1935, ignored by publishers. "Only lately," Howard wrote in 1971, "has she savored the sweet, organic taste of public esteem. 'I know how it feels to be sneered at,' she says. 'In the early days I'd get so discouraged I'd cry. For years people thought I was a kooky crank.'" By the early 1970's she was called the "high priestess" or the "guru" of popular nutrition by talk show hosts, "earth mother to the foodists" by *Life* magazine, and "the Hesiod of the burgeoning health-food tribe, the Margaret Mead of nutrition . . . [and the] Oracle of the Oatmeal Cult" by Jennings. At the time of her death (according to the *Washington Post*), her four books on nutrition and health (*Let's Cook It Right, Let's Have Healthy Children, Let's Eat Right to Keep Fit,* and *Let's Get Well*) had sold close to 10,000,000 copies.

In the preface to *Let's Eat Right to Keep Fit,* W. D. Currier, a former National Secretary of the American Academy of Nutrition (now the International College of Applied Nutrition) wrote: "Adelle Davis is the only author I know who can present authoritative, accurate information concerning vital, complicated human nutritional processes in such an interesting and fascinating manner. . . . Even as a physician especially informed and interested in human nutrition I learned much from this book, as I have from hearing the author lecture on many occasions. . . . If the principles set forth in this book were followed by most people, I believe a greater advancement in health would result than from any other occurrence in the history of mankind. It surely represents the basis of preventive medicine."

John Poppy notes that Davis "demands hard work while holding out an offer of salvation. Disdaining fads, she pushes natural foods, not vitamin pills—though in despair over the quality of even her own food, she swallows handfuls of supplements every day." She told Jennings: "Most every disease suffered by humans is caused by inadequate diet that preceded the onset of that illness. Look, I'm not pushing supplements. We *need* them, because our food is absolutely *horrible.*" Her books detail the horrors of overprocessed commercial foods, empty calories, chemical additives, and imitation flavorings and dyes (for example, she claimed that

much of the brown bread on the market today is only overrefined white bread dyed brown to fool the consumer). She blamed many of America's ills, including most diseases, crime, drug abuse, mental instability, depression, and lack of enjoyment of sex, at least partially on malnutrition. In the *Look* article she expressed approval of the recent, youthful natural foods movement: "The thing that impresses me most about the youngsters is that they are totally uninterested in the group of people who try to tell you something simply because they want to make money. They are ready for good whole-grain breads, they do their own baking, do organic gardening to grow their own food, and I think there is great hope for [the country because of] them." Yet she told an interviewer she was wary of "health food" stores. "It's tragic the junk a lot of them sell, the misstatements they make," she said.

As Poppy has noted, Adelle Davis' popularity with the nutrition-conscious public did not make her "the darling of all doctors—perhaps because she scorns their training in nutrition [which she asserts is nonexistent], perhaps because she and other popularizers present as fact some things that are, in an infant science, still unsure." A *Time* article states: "Her emphasis on raw milk, eggs and cheese could be an invitation to overweight and heart trouble. She does insist, to be sure, that proper nutrition is no substitute for medical care. But her grand design of diet could induce the medically naive to ignore symptoms of serious diseases while waiting for vitamins and wheat germ to work their wonders. The Chicago Nutrition Association includes three of her books on its list of works that are not recommended." Davis pointed out that also "not recommended" are the "books of Carlton Fredricks, Dr. Roger Williams, and any person not recommending refined foods." *Time* continued, "Dr. Edward H. Rynearson, professor emeritus of the Mayo Graduate School of Medicine of the University of Minnesota, is even more critical. He has conducted a careful study of her books [which are all carefully footnoted], claims to have found hundreds of errors of fact and interpretation." Davis disagreed, adding, "M.D.'s make hundreds of errors in their own journals." Jennings quotes her as saying that most doctors "don't know a damn thing about nutrition, but at last their apathy is turning to interest. . . . One of the greatest tragedies in America is babies under the care of mothers who do not take the responsibility of seeing that their child is given an adequate diet, or pediatricians who have not been given *one course* in nutrition."

Despite the skepticism of some members of the medical profession, she was literally deluged with requests to speak at meetings of all kinds, requests from individuals seeking nutrition advice, and requests from numerous companies asking for endorsements of their products, especially vitamins. She told Jennings she did not "endorse *anything* whatsoever; it is one area in which I've stayed absolutely clean. I've been a consultant for a couple of dozen vitamin firms, but usually I get fired the first day when I tell them this supplement or that is not very good. By the time I got through with the last one he was *groaning.* They didn't want to have anything to do with me. I said iron destroys vitamin E and to pretend otherwise is just plain dishonest."

Davis told an interviewer that in 1973, when she learned she had bone cancer, her first thought was "I have been a failure. . . . I thought this was for people who drink soft drinks, who eat white bread, who eat refined sugar and so on." But she reviewed her life and realized that from 1924, when she left home, until the early 1950's, she ate "junk food." To this she attributed the cancer. She added that she hoped "her illness would not dishearten people who had held her nutritional advice in high regard."

*AVOCATIONAL INTERESTS:* Tennis (she played singles with her husband every morning), swimming, bridge, sewing, reading, painting.

*BIOGRAPHICAL/CRITICAL SOURCES: Look*, December 15, 1970; *Bookseller*, March 6, 1971; *Vogue*, May, 1971; *Publishers Weekly*, June 21, 1971, June 17, 1974; *McCall's*, August, 1971; *Life*, October 22, 1971; *West Magazine* (of the *Los Angeles Times*), January 16, 1972; *Harper's Bazaar*, June, 1972; *Cosmopolitan*, July, 1972; *Time*, December 18, 1972; *New York Times*, June 1, 1974; *Washington Post*, June 2, 1974.†

(Died May 31, 1974)

\*    \*    \*

## DAVIS, Charles T(ill) 1929-

*PERSONAL:* Born April 14, 1929, in Natchez, Miss.; son of Frank Vincent (a farmer) and Sarah (Till) Davis; married Caecilia Weyer (an art historian), September 8, 1961; children: Bernard, Frank. *Education:* Davidson College, B.A., 1950; St. John's College, Oxford, B.A., 1952, M.A., 1957, D.Phil., 1956. *Home:* 1337 Pine St., New Orleans, La. 70118. *Office:* Department of History, Tulane University, New Orleans, La. 70118.

*CAREER:* Tulane University, New Orleans, La., instructor, 1956-57, assistant professor, 1957-61, associate professor, 1961-64, professor of medieval and Renaissance history, 1964—. *Member:* American Historical Association, Dante Society of America (member of council, 1966-68), Mediaeval Academy of America (member of council, 1973-75), Societa Dantesca Italiana. *Awards, honors:* Rhodes scholar, Oxford University, 1950-53; Fulbright student grant, 1953-55, senior research grant, 1972; American Philosophical Society grants, 1957-58, 1962; Guggenheim fellow, 1959-60; American Council of Learned Societies fellow, 1965-66; National Endowment for the Humanities fellow, 1976-77.

*WRITINGS: Dante and the Idea of Rome*, Clarendon Press (of Oxford University), 1957; (author of introduction) Ubertino da Casale, *Arbor Vite Crudifixe Jesu*, Bottega d'-Erasmo, 1961; (editor) *The Eagle, the Crescent and the Cross*, Appleton, 1967; (editor) *Western Awakening*, Appleton, 1967. Contributor of articles to historical and medieval studies journals. Member of editorial board, *Medievalia et Humanistica* and Speculum Anniversary Monographs.

*WORK IN PROGRESS:* A book on early Tuscan political theory; a book on Ubertino da Casale.

\*    \*    \*

## DAVIS, Dorothy Salisbury 1916-

*PERSONAL:* Born April 26, 1916, in Chicago, Ill.; daughter of Alfred Joseph (a farmer) and Margaret Jane (Greer) Salisbury; married Harry Davis (an actor), April 25, 1946. *Education:* Barat College, A.B., 1938. *Politics:* Democrat. *Home:* Snedens Landing, Palisades, N.Y. 10964. *Agent:* McIntosh & Otis, Inc., 475 Fifth Ave., New York, N.Y. 10017.

*CAREER:* Swift & Co., Chicago, Ill., research librarian and editor of *The Merchandiser*, 1940-46. Member of board of directors, Palisades Free Library, 1967-71. *Member:* Author's League, Mystery Writers of America (president, 1955-56; executive vice president, 1977-78; member of board of directors). *Awards, honors:* Five nominations for "best

mystery novel of the year"; two nominations for "best mystery short story."

*WRITINGS*—Mysteries, except as shown; all published by Scribner: *The Judas Cat*, 1949; *The Clay Hand*, 1950; *A Gentle Murderer*, 1951; *A Town of Masks*, 1952; *Men of No Property* (novel), 1956; *Death of an Old Sinner*, 1957; *A Gentleman Called*, 1958; *Old Sinners Never Die*, 1959; *The Evening of the Good Samaritan* (novel), 1961; *Black Sheep, White Lamb*, 1963; *The Pale Betrayer*, 1965; *Enemy and Brother* (novel), 1966; (with Jerome Ross) *God Speed the Night*, 1968; *Where the Dark Streets Go*, 1969; *Shock Wave*, 1972; *The Little Brothers*, 1973; *A Death in the Life*, 1976.

Editor: *A Choice of Murders*, Scribner, 1958; *Crime Without Murder*, Scribner, 1970, both anthologies of stories by Mystery Writers of America.

*SIDELIGHTS:* Dorothy Davis told *CA*: "I believe the mystery [form] in which I have worked largely, to be a medium highly reflective of its time, morals, social attitudes." And Clifford A. Ridley wrote: "*Where the Dark Streets Go*, ... may certainly be called ... one of the best mystery novels of this or any other year. But to let it go as simply a mystery novel is patently unfair, for *Where the Dark Streets Go* is first-rate fiction by any standard—rich, probing, and ultimately moving." The *Times Literary Supplement* termed it "an inoffensive because intelligent sentimental story, original in invention and in feeling."

Film rights to *God Speed the Night* were sold to Herb Alpert in 1968. In 1970, Otto Preminger and Frank Sinatra, as co-producers, announced the filming of *Where the Dark Streets Go*.

*BIOGRAPHICAL/CRITICAL SOURCES: Times Literary Supplement*, February 23, 1967, August 14, 1970; *Spectator*, November 3, 1967; *Back Stage*, September 15, 1968, November 9, 1968; *Variety*, June 11, 1969, July 1, 1970; *Show Business*, July 5, 1969, July 11, 1970; *National Observer*, January 5, 1970, July 15, 1972; *Newsday*, December 12, 1970; *New York Times*, July 22, 1972; *Saturday Review*, September 9, 1972.

\*    \*    \*

## DAVIS, Robert Ralph, Jr. 1941-

*PERSONAL:* Born October 18, 1941; son of Robert R. (a machinist) and Mary F. (Michalson) Davis; married Freida Carter (a mathematician), December 24, 1959; children: Gregg Warren, Jane Whitney. *Education:* Kent State University, B.A., 1962, M.A., 1964; Michigan State University, Ph.D., 1967. *Home:* 415 Grandview Blvd., Ada, Ohio 45810. *Office:* Department of History and Political Science, Ohio Northern University, Ada, Ohio 45810.

*CAREER:* Ohio Northern University, Ada, associate professor, 1969-75, professor of history, 1975—, chairman of department, 1969-77. *Member:* American Historical Association.

*WRITINGS: A Lexicon of Historical and Political Terms*, Simon & Schuster, 1973; *A Lexicon of Afro-American History*, Simon & Schuster, 1975. Contributor of articles to *Journal of Southern History, American Quarterly, Civil War History, Pennsylvania History, Ohio History, Historian*, and other journals.

\*    \*    \*

## DAVIS, Ronald L(eroy) 1936-

*PERSONAL:* Born September 22, 1936, in Cambridge,

Ohio; son of E. Leroy and Ruth (Dudley) Davis; married Marilyn Bowden, July 3, 1958 (divorced, 1965). *Education:* University of Texas, Main University (now University of Texas at Austin), B.A., 1956, M.A., 1958, Ph.D., 1961. *Politics:* Democrat. *Home:* 6013 E. University Blvd., Dallas, Tex. 75206. *Office:* Department of History, Southern Methodist University, Dallas, Tex. 75222.

*CAREER:* Kansas State College (now Emporia State University), Emporia, assistant professor of history, 1961-62; Michigan State University, East Lansing, assistant professor of humanities, 1962-65; Southern Methodist University, Dallas, Tex., associate professor, 1965-72, professor of history, 1972—, director of oral history project, 1973—. Director, DeGolyer Institute of American Studies, 1974—. *Member:* American Historical Association, Organization of American Historians, Western History Association, Southern Historical Association, Texas State Historical Association, Phi Beta Kappa.

*WRITINGS: A History of Opera in the American West,* Prentice-Hall, 1965; *Opera in Chicago: A Social and Cultural History,* Appleton, 1966; *The Social and Cultural History of the 1920's,* Holt, 1972. Contributor to history, art, and opera journals.

*WORK IN PROGRESS: A History of Music in American Life; When Romance Ends: Hollywood and the American Dream.*

*BIOGRAPHICAL/CRITICAL SOURCES: Yale Review,* spring, 1967.

\*　　\*　　\*

## DAVISON, Roderic H(ollett) 1916-

*PERSONAL:* Born April 27, 1916, in Buffalo, N.Y.; son of Walter Seaman (a minister and professor) and Eloise (Hollett) Davison; married Louise Atherton Dickey, 1949; children: R. John, Richard H. *Education:* Princeton University, A.B., 1937; Harvard University, A.M., 1938, Ph.D., 1942. *Office:* Department of History, George Washington University, Washington, D.C. 20052.

*CAREER:* Princeton University, Princeton, N.J., instructor in history, 1940-42, 1946-47; George Washington University, Washington, D.C., assistant professor, 1947-49, associate professor, 1949-54, professor of history, 1954—, chairman of department, 1960-64. Lecturer in diplomatic history, Johns Hopkins University, School of Advanced International Studies, 1951-58; visiting lecturer, Harvard University, 1960. *Wartime service:* American Friends Service Committee, 1942-44; Civilian Public Service Camp, 1944-46. *Member:* American Historical Association, Middle East Institute (member of board of governors, 1964—; vice president, 1975—), Middle East Studies Association (member of board of directors, 1968-70; president, 1974-75), Society of Religion in Higher Education, American Association of University Professors, Phi Beta Kappa. *Awards, honors:* Social Science Research Council fellow, 1939-40, 1964-65, 1977-78; Ford Foundation fellow, 1953-54; Guggenheim fellow, 1970-71.

*WRITINGS:* (Contributor) Gordon A. Craig and Felix Gilbert, editors, *The Diplomats: 1919-1939,* Princeton University Press, 1953; *The Near and Middle East: An Introduction to History and Bibliography* (booklet), American Historical Association, 1959; (contributor) George F. Howe and others, editors, *Guide to Historical Literature,* Macmillan, 1961; *Reform in the Ottoman Empire: 1856-1876,* Princeton University Press, 1963; (contributor) Dankwart

Rustow and Robert Ward, editors, *Political Modernization in Japan and Turkey,* Princeton University Press, 1964; (contributor) Shirley H. Engle, editor, *New Perspectives in World History,* National Council for the Social Studies, 1964; *Turkey,* Prentice-Hall, 1968; (contributor) William R. Polk and Richard L. Chambers, editors, *Beginnings of Modernization in the Middle East: The Nineteenth Century,* University of Chicago Press, 1968; (contributor) William Haddad and William Ochsenwald, editors, *Nationalism in a Non-National State: The Dissolution of the Ottoman Empire,* Ohio State University Press, 1977; (contributor) Moshe Davis, editor, *With Eyes Toward Zion: Scholars Colloquium on American-Holy Land Studies,* Arno, 1977. Contributor to *Encyclopedia of Islam, Collier's Encyclopedia,* and *Encyclopedia Americana;* contributor of articles to history journals. Member of advisory board of editors, *Middle East Journal,* 1954—.

*WORK IN PROGRESS:* Research on Ottoman diplomatic history in the late nineteenth century.

\*　　\*　　\*

## DAWES, Robyn M(ason) 1936-
## (Braz Cubas)

*PERSONAL:* Born July 23, 1936, in Pittsburgh, Pa.; son of Norman (a professor) and Zita (Hill) Dawes; married Carol J. Reverski, March 2, 1963 (divorced, 1971); children: Jennifer Hill, Molly McDermott. *Education:* Harvard University, A.B., 1958; University of Michigan, M.A., 1960, Ph.D., 1963. *Politics:* Left-wing Democrat. *Religion:* Pantheistic subjectivist. *Home:* 2817 Spring Blvd., Eugene, Ore. 97403. *Office:* Department of Psychology, University of Oregon, Eugene, Ore. 97403.

*CAREER:* Ann Arbor Veterans Administration Hospital, Ann Arbor, Mich., research associate, 1962-63, research psychologist, 1963-67; University of Michigan, Ann Arbor, 1963-67, began as lecturer, became associate professor; University of Oregon, Eugene, associate professor, 1967-71, professor of psychology, 1971—, faculty advisor, students for McCarthy, 1967-68; Oregon Research Institute, Eugene, Ore., research associate, 1967-75. Consultant, *Decision Research,* 1976—. *Member:* American Psychological Association (fellow), American Association for the Advancement of Science, American Statistical Association, Psychometric Society, Society of Multivariate Experimental Psychologists, Sigma Xi.

*WRITINGS:* (With Clyde H. Coombs and Amos Tversky) *Mathematical Psychology: An Elementary Introduction,* Prentice-Hall, 1970; *Fundamentals of Attitude Measurement,* Wiley, 1972. Contributor of about twenty-five articles to psychology journals.

*WORK IN PROGRESS: How to Use Your Head and Statistics at the Same Time, or At Least in Rapid Alternation;* under pseudonym Braz Cubas, *The Collected Work of Braz Cubas.*

\*　　\*　　\*

## DAWSON, George G(lenn) 1925-

*PERSONAL:* Born August 16, 1925, on Shelter Island, N.Y.; son of Harry and Frances (Menafee) Dawson; married Shirley Meader, January 18, 1947. *Education:* New York University, B.S. (summa cum laude), 1956, M.A., 1957, Ph.D., 1959. *Home:* 2292 Arby Ct., Bellmore, N.Y. 11710. *Office address:* Department of Economics, Empire State College of the State University of New York, Box 130, Old Westbury, N.Y. 11568.

*CAREER:* RCA Communications, radio operator, 1947-55; New York University, New York City, part-time instructor, 1957-59, assistant professor, 1959-64, associate professor, 1964-65, professor of social studies, head of Division of Social Studies, and director of Center for Economic Education, 1965-70; Joint Council on Economic Education, New York City, director of research and publications and managing editor of *Journal of Economic Education,* 1970-75; Empire State College of the State University of New York, Old Westbury, dean and professor of economics, 1975—. Director of Peace Corps Somalia Project, 1962-64, working in the field in northern Somalia for one year; teacher of economic courses at First National City Bank, New York. *Military service:* U.S. Navy, 1942-46, 1950-51; became radioman first class.

*MEMBER:* American Economic Association, American Council on Consumer Interests, National Council for the Social Studies, Middle States Council for the Social Studies, New York State Council for the Social Studies, Phi Delta Kappa, Kappa Delta Pi. *Awards, honors:* New York University Founders Day Award, 1956, 1959; first place in Kazanjian Foundation Awards Program for the teaching of economics at college level, 1967; Certificate of Merit from New York State Council on Economic Education, 1971.

*WRITINGS: Communism* and *Freedom* (booklets), Reader's Digest Services, 1962; (with R. H. McClain) *The Collier Quick and Easy Guide to Economics,* Collier Books, 1963, revised edition published as *Economics for Businessmen and Investors,* 1966; *Economics* (review text), Books I-II, Putnam, 1965, revised one-book edition published as *College Level Economics,* American R.D.M., 1968; *Our Nation's Wealth: What You Should Know about Economics in American History* (secondary level text), Scholastic Book Services, 1968; (with Sanford Gordon and Jess Witchel) *The American Economy: Analysis and Policy* (college text), Heath, 1969; (with Gordon) *Introductory Economics* (college text), Heath, 1972, 3rd edition, 1976; *Teaching Economics in American History,* Joint Council on Economic Education, 1978.

Contributor: Herbert I. London, editor, *Social Science Theory, Structure and Application,* New York University Press, 1975; Gladys Bahr and F. K. Bangs, editors, *Foundations of Education for Business,* National Business Education Association, 1975; Norman Lee, editor, *Teaching Economics,* 2nd edition, Heinemann Educational Books, 1975; Steven E. Goodman, editor, *Handbook on Contemporary Education,* Bowker, 1976; *Perspective on Economic Education,* Social Science Education Consortium, 1977.

Other: "Foundations of the American Economy" (taped short course with guidebook), Universal Learning Corp., 1969. Also author of monographs and six teaching guides. Editor, *Economic Education Experiences of Enterprising Teachers,* Volumes IV-XV, Joint Council on Economic Education, 1967-78, and "Economic Topics" series of pamphlets published by Joint Council on Economic Education. Contributor of about sixty articles to journals.

*WORK IN PROGRESS:* Research and evaluation on the teaching of economics.

*AVOCATIONAL INTERESTS:* Gardening, drawing, painting, reading, collecting recordings, swimming, weightlifting.

\* \* \*

## DEAN, Anabel 1915-

*PERSONAL:* Born May 24, 1915, in Deming, N.M.; daughter of Orlee Eugene and May (Wheeler) Stephenson; married William O. Hummel, March 10, 1933; married second husband, Edward M. Dean (an accountant), September 3, 1949; children: (first marriage) David; (second marriage) Stephen Mason, Denise. *Education:* Humboldt State Teachers College (now Humboldt State University), B.A., 1959; further study at California State University, Chico and University of California. *Home:* 2993 Sacramento Dr., Redding, Calif. 96001.

*CAREER:* Enterprise Elementary Schools, Redding, Calif., teacher, 1960—. *Member:* National Education Association, California Teachers Association, Enterprise Elementary Teachers Association. *Awards, honors: Submerge! The Story of Divers and Their Crafts* was chosen as an outstanding science book by National Association of Science Teachers, 1976.

*WRITINGS—Juvenile: About Paper,* Melmont, 1968; *Willie Can Not Squirm,* Denison, 1971; *Willie Can Ride,* Denison, 1971; *Willie Can Fly,* Denison, 1971; *Men under the Sea,* Harvey House, 1972; *The Pink Paint,* Denison, 1972; *Bats, the Night Flyers,* Lerner, 1974; *Animals That Fly,* Messner, 1975; *Strange Partners: The Story of Symbiosis,* Lerner, 1976; *Submerge! The Story of Divers and Their Crafts,* Westminster, 1976; *How Animals Communicate,* Messner, 1977; *Plants That Eat Insects: A Look at Carnivorous Plants,* Lerner, 1977; *Fire! How Do They Fight It?* (Junior Literary Guild selection), Westminster, 1978; *How Animals Defend Themselves,* Messner, 1978.

Published by Benefic: *Exploring and Understanding Oceanography,* 1970; *Exploring and Understanding Heat,* 1970; *Hot Rod,* 1972; *Destruction Derby,* 1972; *Drag Race,* 1972; *Road Race,* 1972; *Stock Race,* 1972; *Indy 500,* 1972; *Junior Rodeo,* 1975; *High Jumper,* 1975; *Harness Race,* 1975; *Steeple Chase,* 1975; *Ride the Winner,* 1975; *Saddle Up,* 1975; *Motorcycle Scramble,* 1976; *Motorcycle Racer,* 1976; *Baja 500,* 1976; *Safari Rally,* 1976; *Grand Prix Races,* 1976; *Le Mans Race,* 1976; "Emergency Squad" series, six books, 1978.

\* \* \*

## DEAN, Jeffrey S. 1939-

*PERSONAL:* Born February 10, 1939, in Lewiston, Idaho; son of Kenneth Franklyn and Margaret (Mitchell) Dean; married Patricia M. Sacht, June 7, 1959 (divorced, 1977); children: Alison Elizabeth, Carrie Margaret. *Education:* Attended University of Idaho, 1957-58; University of Arizona, B.A., 1961, Ph.D., 1967. *Home:* 2505 North Dodge, No. A-3, Tucson, Ariz. 85716. *Office:* Laboratory of Tree-Ring Research, University of Arizona, Tucson, Ariz. 85721.

*CAREER:* University of Arizona, Tucson, research associate, 1964-66, instructor, 1966-67, assistant professor, 1967-72, associate professor, 1972-77, professor of dendrochronology, 1977—. Research associate, Museum of Northern Arizona, Flagstaff, 1971—. *Member:* American Anthropological Association (fellow), Society for American Archaeology (treasurer), American Association for the Advancement of Science, Northern Arizona Society of Science and Art, Arizona Academy of Science, Arizona Archaeological and Historical Society (president, 1968-69), Sigma Xi, Phi Beta Kappa, Phi Kappa Phi.

*WRITINGS: Chronological Analysis of Tsegi Phase Sites in Northeastern Arizona,* University of Arizona Press, 1969. Also author of several monographs on tree ring dates. Contributor to professional journals.

*WORK IN PROGRESS:* Research in the prehistory of northeastern Arizona and in the dendroclimatic reconstruction of paleoenvironmental conditions during the past two thousand years on the Colorado Plateau in Utah, Colorado, Arizona, and New Mexico.

\*       \*       \*

### DEAN, Vera Micheles   1903-1972

March 29, 1903—October 10, 1972; Russian-born American editor, lecturer, and authority on international affairs. Obituaries: *New York Times,* October 12, 1972; *Time,* October 23, 1972.

\*       \*       \*

### DEAN, William D(enard)   1937-

*PERSONAL:* Born July 12, 1937, in South Bend, Ind.; son of William Stover (a rate analyst) and Eleanor (Hatcher) Dean; married Patricia Fletcher (a college professor), September 17, 1960; children: Jennifer, Colin. *Education:* Carleton College, B.A., 1959; attended Union Theological Seminary, New York, N.Y., 1959-60; University of Chicago, M.A., 1964, Ph.D., 1967. *Politics:* Democrat. *Religion:* Protestant. *Home:* 918 South Washington Ave., St. Peter, Minn. 56082. *Office:* Department of Religion, Gustavus Adolphus College, St. Peter, Minn. 56082.

*CAREER:* University of Chicago, Chicago, Ill., assistant to Paul Tillich, 1964-65; Northland College, Ashland, Wis., assistant professor of philosophy and religion, 1966-68; Gustavus Adolphus College, St. Peter, Minn., assistant professor, 1968-73, associate professor of religion, 1973—. Served as delegate from Wisconsin to Democratic National Convention, 1968. *Member:* American Academy of Religion.

*WRITINGS: Coming To: A Theology of Beauty,* Westminster, 1972; (contributor) Jack L. Nelson, editor, *Population and Survival,* Prentice-Hall, 1972; *Love before the Fall,* Westminster, 1976. Contributor to theology journals.

*WORK IN PROGRESS:* A theory of the relation between literary form and religious experience.

\*       \*       \*

### de ARMAS, Frederick A(lfred)   1945-

*PERSONAL:* Born February 9, 1945, in Havana, Cuba; son of Alfredo and Ana (Galdos) de Armas. *Education:* Stetson University, B.A. (magna cum laude), 1965; University of North Carolina at Chapel Hill, Ph.D., 1968. *Home:* 8345 Perkins Rd., Baton Rouge, La. 70810. *Office:* Department of Foreign Languages, Louisiana State University, Baton Rouge, La. 70803.

*CAREER:* Louisiana State University, Baton Rouge, assistant professor, 1968-73, associate professor of Spanish and French, 1973—. *Member:* Modern Language Association of America, American Association of Teachers of Spanish and Portuguese, American Association of Teachers of French, American Comparative Literature Association, Renaissance Society of America, Asociacion Internacional de Hispanistas.

*WRITINGS: The Four Interpolated Stories in the "Roman comique,"* University of North Carolina Press, 1971; *Paul Scarron,* Twayne, 1972; (editor) Luis de Belmonte Bermudez, *El sastre del campillo,* Estudios de Hispanofila, 1975; *The Invisible Mistress: Aspects of Feminism and Fantasy in the Golden Age,* Biblioteca Siglo de Oro, 1976. Contributor to literary journals.

*WORK IN PROGRESS: The Count of Villamediana,* for Twayne; "working on the pictoris art of Lope de Vega."

\*       \*       \*

### DEBICKI, Andrew P(eter)   1934-

*PERSONAL:* Born June 28, 1934, in Warsaw, Poland; son of Roman (a diplomat and professor) and Jadwiga (Dunin) Debicki; married Mary Jo Tidmarsh, December 28, 1959 (died, 1975); children: Mary Beth, Margaret. *Education:* Yale University, B.A. (summa cum laude), 1955, Ph.D., 1960. *Religion:* Roman Catholic. *Home:* 2547 Alabama St., Lawrence, Kan. 66044. *Office:* Department of Spanish and Portuguese, University of Kansas, Lawrence, Kan. 66045.

*CAREER:* Trinity College, Hartford, Conn., instructor in Spanish, 1957-60; Grinnell College, Grinnell, Iowa, assistant professor, 1960-62, associate professor, 1962-66, professor of Spanish, 1966-68; University of Kansas, Lawrence, professor of Spanish, 1968—, University Distinguished Professor, 1976—. Director, National Endowment for the Humanities summer seminar, 1976, 1978. *Member:* Phi Beta Kappa. *Awards, honors:* Danforth research award, summer, 1959; American Council of Learned Societies fellow, 1966-67; Fulbright travel grant, 1966; American Philosophical Society grant, 1969; *Hispania* award for best article, Spanish American literature, 1969-71; Guggenheim fellow, 1971-72; University of Kansas teaching award, 1972.

*WRITINGS: La Poesia de Jose Gorostiza,* Ediciones de Andrea, 1962; *Estudios sobre poesia espanola contemporanea: La generacion de 1924-1925,* Editorial Gredos, 1968; (contributor) Ivar Ivask and Juan Marichal, editors, *Luminous Reality: The Poetry of Jorge Guillen,* University of Oklahoma Press, 1969; *Damaso Alonso,* Twayne, 1970; *La poesia de Jorge Guillen,* Editorial Gredos, 1973; (editor) *Pedro Salinas,* Taurus Ediciones, 1976; (editor) *Antologia de la poesia mexicana moderna,* Tamesis Books, 1977; *Poetas hispanoamericanos contemporaneos: Punto de vista, perspectiva, experiencia,* Editorial Gredos, 1977. Contributor of about thirty articles to language journals. Associate editor, *Hispania,* 1974-80; member of editorial advisory board, *PMLA,* 1976-80.

*WORK IN PROGRESS:* Studies on contemporary Spanish poetry.

\*       \*       \*

### DEBREU, Gerard   1921-

*PERSONAL:* Born July 4, 1921, in Calais, France; son of Camille and Fernande (Decharne) Debreu; married Francoise Bled, June 14, 1945; children: Chantal (Mrs. Paul Teller), Florence (Mrs. Daniel Hanen). *Education:* Attended Ecole Normale Superieure, Paris, 1941-44; University of Paris, Agrege de l'Universite, 1946, D.Sc., 1956. *Home:* 267 Gravatt Dr., Berkeley, Calif. 94705. *Office:* Department of Economics, University of California, Berkeley, Calif. 94720.

*CAREER:* Centre National de la Recherche Scientifique, Paris, France, research associate, 1946-48; University of Chicago, Chicago, Ill., research associate of Cowles Commission for Research in Economics, 1950-55; Yale University, New Haven, Conn., Cowles Foundation associate professor of economics, 1955-60; University of California, Berkeley, professor of economics, 1962—. Yale University, visiting professor of economics, fall, 1961, visiting professor at Cowles Foundation for Research in Economics, fall, 1976; visiting professor at Center for Operations Research,

University of Louvain, fall, 1971, winter, 1972, and University of Canterbury, Christchurch, summer, 1973. *Military service:* French Army, 1944-45. *Member:* Econometric Society (president, 1971), National Academy of Sciences, American Academy of Arts and Sciences (fellow). *Awards, honors:* Rockefeller fellow in United States, Sweden, and Norway, 1948-50; Center for Advanced Study in the Behavioral Sciences fellow, 1960-61; Guggenheim fellow, 1968-69; Erskine fellow at University of Canterbury, summer, 1969; Churchill College overseas fellow, 1972; Senior U.S. Scientist Award, Alexander von Humboldt Foundation, University of Bonn, 1977; Dr.rer.pol.h.c., University of Bonn, 1977.

*WRITINGS: Theory of Value,* Wiley, 1959, new edition, Yale University Press, 1971. Contributor to economics journals. Former associate editor of *International Economic Review.* Member of editorial board of *Journal of Economic Theory;* member of advisory board of *Journal of Mathematical Economics.*

\*    \*    \*

## DEBUS, Allen G(eorge) 1926-

*PERSONAL:* Born August 16, 1926, in Chicago, Ill.; son of George Walter William (a manufacturer) and Edna Pauline (Schwenneke) Debus; married Brunilda Lopez-Rodriguez, August 25, 1951; children: Allen Anthony George, Richard William, Karl Edward. *Education:* Northwestern University, B.S., 1947; Indiana University, A.M., 1949, further study, 1950-51; University College, London, graduate study, 1959-60; Harvard University, Ph.D., 1961. *Residence:* Deerfield, Ill. *Office:* Social Sciences 209, University of Chicago, 1126 East 59th St., Chicago, Ill. 60637.

*CAREER:* Abbott Laboratories, North Chicago, Ill., research and development chemist, 1951-56; University of Chicago, Chicago, Ill., assistant professor, 1961-65, associate professor, 1965-68, professor of history of science, 1968—, director of Morris Fishbein Center for the Study of the History of Science and Medicine, 1971-77. Member of Institute for Advanced Study, 1972-73. Holder of chemical patents.

*MEMBER:* History of Science Society (member of council, 1962-65; program chairman, 1972), American Institute of the History of Pharmacy, American Chemical Society (associate; member of executive committee, History of Chemistry Division, 1969—), American Association for the Advancement of Science (fellow; chairman of electorate nominating committee, Section L, 1974), Internationale Paracelsus Gesellschaft, American Association for the History of Medicine, British Society for the History of Science, Society for the Study of Alchemy and Early Chemistry (member of council, 1967—), Academie Internationale d'Histoire de la Medicine, Academie Internationale d'Histoire des Sciences (corresponding member), Society of Medical History of Chicago (member of council, 1969-77; secretary-treasurer, 1971-72; vice-president, 1972-74; president, 1974-76).

*AWARDS, HONORS:* Social Science Research Council and Fulbright fellow in England, 1959-60; Guggenheim fellow, 1966-67; overseas fellow, Churchill College, Cambridge University, 1966-67, 1969; National Endowment for the Humanities fellow at Newberry Library, 1975-76. Research grants from American Philosophical Society, 1961-62, National Science Foundation, 1961-63, 1971-74, National Institutes of Health, 1962-70, and American Council of Learned Societies, 1966, 1974-75, 1977-78.

*WRITINGS: The English Paracelsians,* Oldbourne, 1965, F. Watts, 1966; (with Robert P. Multhauf) *Alchemy and Chemistry in the Seventeenth Century,* William Andrews Clark Memorial Library, University of California, Los Angeles, 1966; (author of introduction) Elias Ashmole, *Theatrum Chemicum Britannicum,* Johnson Reprint, 1967; *The Chemical Dream of the Renaissance* (lecture at Churchill College, Cambridge University), Heffer, 1968, Bobbs-Merrill, 1972; (editor) *World Who's Who in Science from Antiquity to the Present,* Marquis, 1968.

*Science and Education in the 17th Century: The Webster-Ward Debate,* American Elsevier, 1970; (editor and contributor) *Science, Medicine and Society in the Renaissance: Essays in Honor of Walter Pagel,* two volumes, Neale Watson Academic Press, 1972; (with Brian A. L. Rust) *The Complete Entertainment Discography, 1898-1942,* Arlington House, 1973; (editor and contributor) *Medicine in Seventeenth Century England,* University of California Press, 1974; (author of introduction) John Dee, *The Mathematicall Praeface to the Elements of Geometrie of Euclid of Megara,* Science History Publications, 1975; *The Chemical Philosophy: Paracelsian Science and Medicine in the Sixteenth and Seventeenth Centuries,* two volumes, Science History Publications, 1977. Editor, "History of Science and Medicine" series, University of Chicago Press. Contributor of about seventy articles to professional journals.

*WORK IN PROGRESS: Science and Medicine in the Renaissance: 1450-1650,* for Wiley; *Robert Fludd and His Philosophical Key,* for Science History Publications.

\*    \*    \*

## DECKER, Donald M(ilton) 1923-

*PERSONAL:* Born June 16, 1923, in Detroit, Mich.; son of Royal E. (a businessman) and Mildred (Donaldson) Decker; married Mary Locher, August 20, 1961; children: Catherine Irene, Thomas Royal. *Education:* University of Michigan, B.A., 1949, M.A., 1950; University of California, Los Angeles, Ph.D., 1961. *Religion:* United Methodist. *Home:* 852 West Sonoma, Stockton, Calif. 95204. *Office:* Department of Modern Languages, University of the Pacific, Stockton, Calif. 95211.

*CAREER:* Occidental College, Los Angeles, Calif., instructor in Spanish, 1960; University of California, Davis, assistant professor of Spanish, 1961-63; University of the Pacific, Stockton, Calif., professor of modern languages, 1963—. *Military service:* U.S. Army, 1943-46; received Europe-Africa-Middle East Theater ribbon with three Bronze Stars. *Member:* Modern Language Association of America, American Association of Teachers of Spanish and Portuguese, Teachers of English to Speakers of Other Languages, American Council on the Teaching of Foreign Languages, National Association of Foreign Student Affairs, Phi Beta Kappa, Phi Kappa Phi, Sigma Delta Pi.

*WRITINGS: Mastering the International Phonetic Alphabet,* Simon & Schuster, 1970; *Luis Durand,* Twayne, 1971. Contributor of about twenty articles and reviews to journals of Latin American and Spanish language affairs in North and South America.

*WORK IN PROGRESS: The Use and Teaching of English in Mexico.*

*SIDELIGHTS:* Donald Decker has had eight and a half years of travel and residence in Latin America.

# De GREENE, Kenyon B(renton)

*PERSONAL:* Born in Kansas City, Mo.; son of Charles Arthur (a lawyer) and Leona Helen (Pool) De Greene; children: Karola Alexandra, Kenyon Brenton, Jr., Erika Krystal, Kenyon David Michael. *Education:* University of California, Los Angeles, A.B., 1946, M.A., 1949, Ph.D., 1953. *Home:* 4345 Chaumont Rd., Woodland Hills, Calif. 91364. *Office:* Institute of Safety and Systems Management, University of Southern California, Los Angeles, Calif. 90007.

*CAREER:* Montana State University (now University of Montana), Missoula, assistant professor of psychology, 1953-54; University of California, Far East Program, Tokyo, Japan, lecturer in psychology, 1954-55; System Development Corp., Santa Monica, Calif., human factors scientist, 1956-61; Northrop Corp., Hawthorne, Calif., human factors engineer and scientist, 1961-63; Aerospace Corp., El Segundo, Calif., human factors scientist and manager, 1963-65; University of Southern California, Institute of Safety and Systems Management, Los Angeles, associate professor of human factors, 1965—. *Member:* Society for General Systems Research, American Psychological Association, Human Factors Society, American Association for the Advancement of Science, Institute of Electrical and Electronics Engineers, American Association of University Professors, Sierra Club, Sigma Xi.

*WRITINGS:* (Editor and contributor) *Systems Psychology,* McGraw, 1970; *Sociotechnical Systems: Factors in Analysis, Design, and Management,* Prentice-Hall, 1973; (contributor) Harriet H. Werley and others, editors, *Health Research: A Systems Approach,* Springer, 1976. Contributor to *International Encyclopedia of Neurology, Psychiatry, Psychoanalysis, and Psychology,* edited by Benjamin Wolman, Van Nostrand, 1977, and *Encyclopedia of Professional Management,* edited by Lester Bittel, McGraw, 1978. Contributor of over thirty articles to *Ergonomics, Human Factors, Organization and Administrative Sciences, Behavioral Science,* other scholarly journals, and national and international conference proceedings.

*AVOCATIONAL INTERESTS:* International travel, conservation.

\* \* \*

# de JONG, Gerrit, Jr. 1892-

*PERSONAL:* Born March 20, 1892, in Amsterdam, Netherlands; son of Gerrit (a merchant) and Lijda Marianna (Kuiper) de Jong; married Rosabelle Winegar, September 14, 1911 (died January, 1940); married Thelma Bonham (a professor of education), September 28, 1951; children: (first marriage) Belle Felice (Mrs. Dean E. Van Wagenen), Nola Eloise (Mrs. Clyde E. Sullivan), Carma Rose (Mrs. Richard L. Anderson). *Education:* University of Utah, A.B., 1920, M.A., 1925; further study at National University of Mexico, 1921, and University of Munich, 1927; Stanford University, Ph.D., 1933. *Politics:* Republican. *Religion:* Church of Jesus Christ of Latter-day Saints (Mormon). *Home:* 640 North University Ave., Provo, Utah 84601. *Office:* Department of Modern Languages, Brigham Young University, Provo, Utah 84601.

*CAREER:* Murdock Academy, Beaver, Utah, teacher of music and languages, 1916-18; Latter-day Saints University, Salt Lake City, Utah, teacher of modern languages, 1919-25; Brigham Young University, Provo, Utah, professor of modern languages, 1925—, College of Fine Arts, organizer and dean, 1925-59, dean emeritus, 1959—. Executive director, Centro Cultural Brasil-Estados Unidos, 1947-48.

*Member:* Modern Language Association of America, American Association of Teachers of Spanish and Portuguese, American Musicological Society, Internationale Gesellschaft fuer Musikwissenschaft, Utah Academy of Sciences, Arts and Letters (fellow; president, 1949-50). *Awards, honors:* Distinguished Service Award in arts and letters, Utah Academy of Sciences, Arts, and Letters, 1953; Karl G. Maeser Distinguished Teaching Award, 1960; Distinguished Special Service Award of Brigham Young University, 1967; David O. McKay Humanities Award, 1972.

*WRITINGS: Greater Dividends from Religion,* Deseret, 1950; (contributor) T. Lynn Smith, editor, *Brazil: Portrait of Half a Continent,* University of Florida Press, 1950; *Living the Gospel,* Deseret Sunday School Union, 1958; *The Gospel Today,* Deseret, 1966; *Four Hundred Years of Brazilian Literature,* Brigham Young University Press, 1969; (editor of music and German text) *Die Kinder Singen,* Frankfurt, 1969; (contributor) *Modern Brazil,* University of Florida Press, 1970; *Eternal Progress: The Practicality and Relevance of the Gospel Today,* Bookcraft, 1975.

*AVOCATIONAL INTERESTS:* Music (performs and composes string quartets, symphonies, oratorio, and choral works).

\* \* \*

# DEKMEJIAN, Richard Hrair 1933-

*PERSONAL:* Born August 3, 1933, in Aleppo, Syria; son of Hrant and Vahide (Matossian) Dekmejian; married Anoush Hagopian, September 19, 1954; children: Gregory, Armen, Haig. *Education:* University of Connecticut, B.A., 1959; Boston University, M.A., 1960; Columbia University, Certificate of Middle East Institute, 1964, Ph.D., 1966. *Religion:* Armenian Apostolic. *Home:* 917 Country Club Rd., Binghamton, N.Y. 13901. *Office:* Department of Political Science, State University of New York, Binghamton, N.Y. 13901.

*CAREER:* State University of New York at Binghamton, assistant professor, 1964-69, associate professor, 1969-77, professor of political science, 1977—, master of Hinman Residential College, 1971-72. Visiting professor, Columbia University, spring, 1977, and University of Pennsylvania, fall, 1977. Chairman, World Affairs Council of Binghamton, 1970-72; president of board of directors, Southern Tier Civic Ballet Company, 1973-76. *Military service:* U.S. Army, 1955-57. *Member:* International Political Science Association, Middle East Studies Association, American Political Science Association, Middle East Institute, Pi Sigma Alpha, Phi Alpha Theta.

*WRITINGS: Egypt Under Nasir: A Study in Political Dynamics,* State University of New York Press, 1971; (contributor) Abid al-Marayati, editor, *Contemporary Middle Eastern Governments and Politics,* Duxbury Press, 1972; *Patterns of Political Leadership: Egypt, Israel, Lebanon,* State University of New York Press, 1975. Contributor to journals on international politics and Middle Eastern affairs.

*WORK IN PROGRESS:* A book on Sadat's Egypt.

*SIDELIGHTS:* Richard Dekmejian has traveled throughout Europe and the Middle East; he speaks Turkish, Arabic, French, and Armenian. *Avocational interests:* Singing, violin, folk dancing, classical music, ballet, private business, French wines.

\* \* \*

# de LAGUNA, Frederica (Annis) 1906-

*PERSONAL:* Born October 3, 1906, in Ann Arbor, Mich.;

daughter of Theodore (a professor of philosophy) and Grace (a professor of philosophy; maiden name, Andrus) de Laguna. *Education:* Bryn Mawr College, A.B., 1927; Columbia University, Ph.D., 1933. *Home:* 221 Roberts Rd., Bryn Mawr, Pa. 19010. *Office:* Dalton Hall, Department of Anthropology, Bryn Mawr College, Bryn Mawr, Pa. 19010.

*CAREER:* University of Pennsylvania Museum, Philadelphia, assistant in American section and expedition field director, 1931-35; U.S. Department of Agriculture, Soil Conservation Service, Arizona and New Mexico, associate conservationist, 1935-36; Bryn Mawr College, Bryn Mawr, Pa., lecturer, 1938-41, assistant professor, 1941-42, 1946-49, associate professor, 1949-55, professor of anthropology, 1955-75, professor emeritus, 1975—, chairman of department, 1950-72. Visiting professor at University of Pennsylvania, 1947, 1948, 1949, 1973, 1974, 1975, and University of California, 1959. Assistant on Danish Government's archaeological expedition to western Greenland, 1929; leader of Alaskan expeditions for University of Pennsylvania, 1930-32; joint leader of archaeological and ethnological expeditions to Alaska, for Danish National Museum and University of Pennsylvania, 1933; leader of archaeological expedition to the Yukon River, for University of Pennsylvania and American Philosophical Society, 1935, and to Arizona, for Bryn Mawr College and Museum of Northern Arizona, 1941; other archaeological and ethnological expeditions to Alaska were made in 1949-50, 1952, 1954, 1958, 1960, 1968. *Military service:* U.S. Naval Reserve, active duty, 1942-45; became lieutenant commander.

*MEMBER:* American Association for the Advancement of Science, National Academy of Sciences, American Anthropological Association (president, 1966-67), American Ethnological Society, Society for American Archaeology, Arctic Institute of North America, Society for Pennsylvania Archaeology, Philadelphia Anthropological Society, Sigma Xi. *Awards, honors:* Bryn Mawr College European fellow, 1927; National Research Council fellow, 1936-37; Rockefeller post-war fellow, 1945-46; Viking Fund fellowship, from Wenner-Gren Foundation, 1949; Social Science Council postdoctoral fellow, 1962-63; Lindbarker Award for distinguished teaching, 1972; National Endowment for the Humanities research grant, 1977-78.

*WRITINGS: The Thousand March: Adventures of an American Boy with Garibaldi* (juvenile), Little, Brown, 1930; *A Comparison of Eskimo and Palaeolithic Art,* [New York], 1933; *The Archaeology of Cook Inlet, Alaska,* University of Pennsylvania Press, 1934; *The Arrow Points to Murder* (mystery novel), Doubleday, 1937; *Fog on the Mountain* (mystery novel), Doubleday, 1938; (with Kaj Birket-Smith) *The Eyak Indians of the Copper River Delta, Alaska,* [Copenhagen], 1938; *The Prehistory of Northern North America as Seen from the Yukon,* Society for American Archaeology, 1947; *Chugach Prehistory: The Archaeology of Prince William Sound, Alaska,* University of Washington Press, 1956; (editor) *Selected Papers from the "American Anthropologist,"* Row Peterson, 1960; *The Story of a Tlingit Community,* U.S. Government Printing Office, 1960; (with others) *The Archeology of the Yakutat Bay Area, Alaska,* U.S. Government Printing Office, 1964; *Under Mount Saint Elias: The History and Culture of the Yakutat Tlingit,* Smithsonian Institution, 1972; *Voyage to Greenland: A Personal Initiation into Anthropology,* Norton, 1977. Contributor of articles to anthropology and archaeology journals.

## DELANEY, Norman Conrad 1932-

*PERSONAL:* Born April 13, 1932, in Rockport, Mass.; son of William Lyman and Ardell (Stolpe) Delaney; married Linda Barnett, July 29, 1966; children: Norman Christopher, Stephen Conrad. *Education:* Massachusetts State College at Salem (now Salem State College), B.S. Ed., 1955; Boston University, A.M., 1956; Duke University, Ph.D., 1967. *Home:* 3747 Aransas St., Corpus Christi, Tex. 78411. *Office:* Department of History, Del Mar College, Corpus Christi, Tex. 78404.

*CAREER:* Massachusetts State College at Bridgewater (now Bridgewater State College), instructor in history, 1959-62; Osmania University, Hyderabad, India, Peace Corps teacher of history, 1962-64; University of Houston, Houston, Tex., instructor in history, 1966-67; Del Mar College, Corpus Christi, Tex., assistant professor, 1967-71, associate professor, 1971-74, professor of history, 1974—. *Member:* Association for Gravestone Studies. *Awards, honors:* Mrs. Simon Baruch University Award, United Daughters of the Confederacy, for *John McIntosh Kell of the Raider Alabama,* 1970.

*WRITINGS: John McIntosh Kell of the Raider Alabama,* University of Alabama Press, 1973. Contributor to scholarly journals.

*WORK IN PROGRESS:* Editing Civil War letters of Private Charles Chase from Massachusetts; researching Civil War general John W. Phelps.

\*  \*  \*

## DELDERFIELD, Ronald Frederick 1912-1972

February 12, 1912—June 24, 1972; English playwright, novelist, and chronicler of English life. Obituaries: *New York Times,* June 27, 1972; *Washington Post,* June 28, 1972; *National Obseurver,* July 8, 1972; *Newsweek,* July 10, 1972; *Publishers Weekly,* July 17, 1972.

\*  \*  \*

## De LOACH, Charles F. 1927-

*PERSONAL:* Born December 12, 1927, in Echols County, Ga.; son of Charles F. (a naval stores inspector) and Inez (Mobley) De Loach. *Education:* Attended South Georgia College, 1946, 1948, and Emory University at Valdosta, 1949; University of Georgia, A.B., 1953. *Politics:* Independent. *Religion:* Protestant. *Home:* 405 South Hillcrest, Clearwater, Fla. 33515. *Office: Clearwater Sun,* Myrtle Ave., Clearwater, Fla.

*CAREER: Enterprise Ledger,* Enterprise, Ala., news editor, 1953-55; *Evening Herald,* Rock Hill, S.C., bureau chief and sports editor, 1955-60; Liberty Life Insurance Co., Rock Hill, insurance agent, 1960-61; Carolina Newspapers, York, S.C., editor and part owner, 1961-67; free-lance writer and photographer, 1967-70; *Playground Daily News,* Fort Walton Beach, Fla., reporter and photographer, 1970; *Clearwater Sun,* Clearwater, Fla., photographer, 1971—. *Military service:* U.S. Navy.

*WRITINGS: The Armstrong Error* (nonfiction), Logos International, 1971; *Seeds of Conflict,* Logos International, 1974. Also author of *The Quotable Shakespeare,* and *When Crusaders Fall.* Contributor to *Miami Herald, Jacksonville Journal,* and other publications.

*WORK IN PROGRESS:* A nonfiction book; research into Bible prophecies.

## DENENBERG, Herbert S(idney)  1929-
### (Humpty S. Dumpty)

*PERSONAL:* Born November 20, 1929, in Omaha, Neb.; son of David Aaron and Fannie (Rothenberg) Denenberg; married Naomi Glushakow, June 22, 1958. *Education:* Creighton University, J.D. (cum laude), 1954; Johns Hopkins University, B.S., 1958; Harvard University, LL.M., 1959; University of Pennsylvania, Ph.D., 1962. *Politics:* Democrat. *Religion:* Jewish. *Residence:* Harrisburg, Pa. *Office:* WCAU-TV, City Line and Monument, Philadelphia, Pa. 19131.

*CAREER:* Denenberg & Denenberg (law firm), Omaha, Neb., attorney, 1954-55; University of Iowa, Iowa City, assistant professor of insurance, 1961-62; University of Pennsylvania, Philadelphia, assistant professor, 1962-65, associate professor, 1965-68, Loman Associate Professor, 1968-70, Loman Professor of Insurance, Wharton School of Finance and Commerce, 1970-73; Insurance Commissioner of Pennsylvania, 1971-74; Public Utility Commissioner of Pennsylvania, 1975; WCAU-TV, Philadelphia, talk show panelist, 1974-75, consumer editor and reporter, 1975—. Visiting professor of law, Temple University, 1975. Chartered property and casualty underwriter, 1962; chartered life underwriter, 1965; admitted to practice before U.S. Supreme Court, Supreme Court of Nebraska, U.S. Court of Military Appeals, and District of Columbia Bar. Special counsel, U.S. President's National Advisory Panel on Insurance in Riot-Affected Areas, 1967-68; consultant to U.S. Department of Labor, Small Business Administration, U.S. Civil Rights Commission, Federal Trade Commission, Atomic Energy Commission, U.S. Department of Justice, mayor of Washington, D.C., government of Puerto Rico, States of Wisconsin, Alaska, and Nevada, and other public and private agencies. Director, Pennsylvania Workmen's Compensation Fund and Pennsylvania Coal Mine Subsistence Fund, 1971-74. Member of administrative board, S.S. Huebner Foundation, 1966-71. *Military service:* U.S. Army, 1955-58. U.S. Army Reserve, 1959-64; became captain.

*MEMBER:* American Risk and Insurance Association (president, 1969-70), American Bar Association, International Insurance Law Association (vice-president and scientific secretary of American chapter, 1967—), American Judicature Society, Society of Chartered Property and Casualty Underwriters (member of research board, 1963-66), Nebraska State Bar Association, District of Columbia Bar Association, Pennsylvania Bar Association, National Academy of Sciences Institute of Medicine, Phi Gamma Sigma. *Awards, honors:* Eight awards for articles from *Journal of Risk and Insurance;* Lambert Award, 1972, for "Shopper's Guide" series; National Press Club Awards, 1975, 1976, for best consumer column, 1976, for best consumer journalism; American Osteopathic Association Journalism Award, 1975; Philadelphia Press Club Award for television feature, 1976; American Chiropractic Association Gold Medal Award for Distinguished Health Journalism, 1978; Society of Professional Journalists Award for Excellence in Documentary and Special Reports on TV, 1978.

*WRITINGS:* (With Robert D. Eilers, Joseph J. Melone, G. Wright Hoffman, Chester A. Kline, and H. Wayne Snider) *Risk and Insurance,* Prentice-Hall, 1964, 2nd edition, 1974; (with John Robert Ferrari) *Life Insurance and/or Mutual Funds: A Comparative Analysis of Endowment Life Insurance and the Insured Contractual,* Pageant, 1967; (editor with Spencer L. Kimball) *Insurance, Government, and Social Policy: Studies in Insurance Regulation,* Irwin, 1969;

(with Kimball) *Mass Marketing of Group Property and Liability Insurance* U.S. Government Printing Office, 1970; *The Insurance Trap: Unfair at Any Rate,* Western Publishing, 1972; *Getting Your Money's Worth,* Public Affairs Press, 1974; *Shopper's Guidebook,* Acropolis, 1974; *A Consumer's Guide to Bankruptcy,* Pilot Books, 1975. Also author of series of "Shopper's Guides" as insurance commissioner of Pennsylvania, including *A Shopper's Guide to Hospitals in Philadelphia, A Shopper's Guide to Surgery, A Shopper's Guide to Life Insurance,* and *A Shopper's Guide to Auto Insurance in Pennsylvania.* Contributor of more than two hundred articles and reviews to *Spectator, Congressional Record, Parade, Progressive, Prevention, Los Angeles Times,* and insurance journals; writes occasional articles under pseudonym Humpty S. Dumpty. Assistant editor of *Annals of the Society of Chartered Property and Casualty Underwriters,* 1964-71; columnist for *Pennsylvania Bulletin,* 1975—, *Sales and Marketing Management,* 1975—, *Caveat Emptor,* 1975—, *Omaha Sun,* 1975-76, and *Beaver County Times,* 1975—.

*WORK IN PROGRESS:* A Consumer's Guide to Health Care.

*SIDELIGHTS:* Herbert S. Denenberg, an indefatigable consumer advocate, is the author of the first "no fault" automobile accident compensation law. He told *CA:* "Ideas are still the most powerful force in the world, and if you want to move things and change things, the quickest and most efficient way to do so, in most cases, is to write about problems and solutions. For example, as Insurance Commissioner of Pennsylvania I soon discovered government is our number one consumer fraud, and much of my writing is directed at making government perform."

*BIOGRAPHICAL/CRITICAL SOURCES: Time,* July 10, 1971; *New York Times,* August 8, 1971; *National Observer,* September 18, 1971; *Wall Street Journal,* February 1, 1972; *Saturday Review,* July 1, 1972; *Newsweek,* August 14, 1972; *Parade,* August 28, 1972; Howard Shapiro, *How to Keep Them Honest* (biography), Rodale Press, 1974.

\*          \*          \*

## de NEVERS, Noel (Howard)  1932-

*PERSONAL:* Born May 21, 1932, in San Francisco, Calif.; son of Czeslaw Daniel (a realtor) and Florence (Gorman) de Nevers; married Klancy Clark (a teacher of mathematics), August 23, 1955; children: Clark, Nanette, Renee. *Education:* Stanford University, B.S. in C.E., 1954; Karlsruhe Technical Institute, Karlsruhe, Germany, exchange student, 1954-55; University of Michigan, M.S., 1956, Ph.D., 1959. *Politics:* Democrat. *Religion:* "Not religious." *Home:* 1416 Butler Ave., Salt Lake City, Utah 84102. *Office:* University of Utah, Salt Lake City, Utah 84112.

*CAREER:* Chevron Research Co., research engineer in Richmond and La Habra, Calif., 1958-63; University of Utah, Salt Lake City, assistant professor, 1963-67, associate professor, 1967-71, professor of chemical engineering, 1971—. Fulbright lecturer, University Del Valle, Cali, Columbia, summer, 1974. Engineer, Environmental Protection Agency, U.S. Government, 1971-72. *Member:* American Institute of Chemical Engineers, Air Pollution Control Association, Sierra Club. *Awards, honors:* Outstanding Teacher Award, University of Utah, 1969; Reynolds lectureship, University of Utah, 1973.

*WRITINGS: Fluid Mechanics,* Addison-Wesley, 1970; *Technology and Society,* Addison-Wesley, 1972.

## DeNEVI, Donald P. 1937-

*PERSONAL:* Born July 9, 1937, in Stockton, Calif.; son of Aldo and Adele (Firpo) DeNevi; married Heather Strong Gordon, January 1, 1967. *Education:* University of the Pacific, B.A., 1959, M.A., 1961; University of California, Berkeley, Ed.D., 1966. *Politics:* None. *Office:* Department of Education, California College of Arts and Crafts, Broadway at College, Oakland, Calif. 94618.

*CAREER:* Merritt College, Oakland, Calif., instructor and counselor, beginning 1962; California College of Arts and Crafts, Oakland, member of faculty.

*WRITINGS:* (Compiler) *Sketches of Early California,* Chronicle Books, 1971; (with James C. Stone) *Portraits of America's Universities,* Jossey-Bass, 1971; (compiler with Stone) *Teaching Multi-Cultural Populations,* Van Nostrand, 1971; (compiler) *Racism at the Turn of the Century: Documentary Perspectives 1870-1910,* Leswing, 1973; (compiler with John Bookout and Helen M. Friend) *Tricks & Puzzles,* Silver Dog Press, 1973; *Alcatraz '46: The Anatomy of a Classic Prison Tragedy,* told to DeNevi by Philip Bergen and Clarence Carnes, Leswing, 1974; *Western Train Robberies,* Celestial Arts, 1976; *Earthquakes,* Celestial Arts, 1977; *Tragic Train "The City of San Francisco,"* Superior, 1977; *To the Edges of the Universe: Space Exploration in the 20th Century,* Celestial Arts, 1978; *The Weather Report,* Celestial Arts, 1978. Contributor of about fifty articles to education journals.†

\* \* \*

## DENSEN-GERBER, Judianne 1934-

*PERSONAL:* Born November 13, 1934, in New York, N.Y.; daughter of Gustave Gerber (an attorney) and Beatrice Densen (an attorney); married Michael Baden (chief medical examiner of New York City), June 14, 1958; children: Trissa Austin, Judson Michael, Lindsey Robert, Sarah Densen. *Education:* Bryn Mawr College, B.A. (cum laude), 1956; Columbia University, LL.B., 1959, J.D., 1969; New York University, M.D., 1963. *Religion:* Unitarian Universalist. *Office:* Odyssey Institute, Inc., 24 West 12th St., New York, N.Y. 10011.

*CAREER:* Admitted to New York State Bar, 1961; admitted to practice medicine and surgery in New York, 1967, New Jersey, 1969, New Hampshire, 1971, Utah, 1971, Michigan, 1973, Connecticut, 1973, Louisiana, 1974, New Mexico, 1975, New South Wales, Australia, 1977, and Texas, 1978. French Hospital, New York City, rotating internship, 1963-64; Metropolitan Hospital, New York City, psychiatric residency, 1964-65, researcher in forensic psychiatry, developing the program used at Odyssey House, 1966-67; Odyssey Institute (formerly Odyssey House; psychiatric hospital for rehabilitation of narcotics addicts), New York City, founder, 1967, executive director, 1969—, president of board of directors, 1967—. Delegate, White House Conference on Youth, 1971; member, national Advisory Commission on Criminal Justice Standards and Goals, 1971-74; member, President's Commission on White House Fellows, 1972-76; member of drug experience advisory committee, Department of Health, Education, and Welfare, 1973-76; adviser to members of U.S. Congress and local law enforcement officials. Founder and president, Institute of Women's Wrongs, 1973—; member of professional advisory committee for the study of drug use among children and adolescents, Institute for Child Mental Health; member of board of directors, Simpson Street Development Association, 1969, Hospital Audiences, Inc., 1971—, Extraordinary Events,

Inc., 1973—, First Women's Bank of New York, 1974—, National Coalition for Children's Justice, 1975—, Richmond County Society for the Prevention of Cruelty to Children, 1977—, Mary E. Walker Foundation, 1978, and others. Visiting associate professor of law, University of Utah, 1974-75; adjunct associate professor of law, New York Law School, 1973—. Consultant to public and private health, social work, and crime control agencies.

*MEMBER:* American Medical Association, American Psychiatric Association, American Bar Association, American Academy of Psychiatry and the Law, Society of Medical Jurisprudence, American College of Legal Medicine (fellow), American Academy of Forensic Sciences (fellow), Therapeutic Communities of America (founding member; first vice-president, 1975-76), New York Association of Voluntary Agencies on Narcotics Addiction and Substance Abuse (member of board of directors, 1969—; legal consultant, 1969-71), New York State Medical Society, New York County Medical Society (member of sub-committees on drug abuse and on delivery of health care), New York Women's Bar Association, Women's City Club of New York. *Awards, honors:* American Association of University Women and Hadassah awards, 1970; B'nai B'rith awards, 1971, as woman of achievement.

*WRITINGS:* (Contributor) Chris J. D. Zarafonetis, editor, *Drug Abuse: Proceedings of the International Conference,* Lea & Febiger, 1971; (with daughter, Trissa Austin Baden) *Drugs, Sex, Parents, and You,* Lippincott, 1972; (with Odyssey House staff members) *We Mainline Dreams: The Odyssey House Story,* Doubleday, 1973; *Walk in My Shoes: An Odyssey into Womanlife,* Saturday Review Press, 1976; *Child Abuse and Neglect as Related to Parental Drug Abuse and Other Antisocial Behavior,* National Center of Child Abuse and Neglect, 1978. Columnist for *New York Law Journal,* 1971-72, and *Manchester Union Leader,* 1971-73. Member of board of advisers, *Contemporary Drug Problems,* 1971—; editor, *Journal of Corrective and Social Psychiatry,* 1975.

\* \* \*

## DENTON, Charles F(rederick) 1942-

*PERSONAL:* Born February 20, 1942, in Montreal, Quebec, Canada; immigrated to Puerto Rico, 1963; naturalized U.S. citizen, 1970; son of Fred L. (a management consultant) and Ruth (Lister) Denton; married Louise Lalonde, April 18, 1961; children: Frederick, Mark, Stephen. *Education:* University of the Americas, Mexico City, B.A., 1962; University of Texas at Austin, M.A., 1966, Ph.D., 1969. *Office:* Rectoria, Universidad Nacional de Costa Rica, Heredia, Costa Rica.

*CAREER:* Pan American Airways, San Juan, P.R., assistant station manager, 1963-65; University of Texas at Austin, instructor in government, 1968-69; Wayne State University, Detroit, Mich., assistant professor of political science, 1969-71; California State University, Fresno, dean, School of Social Sciences, 1971-75; National University of Costa Rica, Heredia, director of Institute for Social and Population Studies, 1975—. *Member:* American Political Science Association, Latin American Studies Association. *Awards, honors:* Fulbright-Hays award, Costa Rica, 1967.

*WRITINGS: La Politica del desarrollo en Costa Rica,* Novedades de Costa Rica, 1969; *Patterns of Costa Rican Politics,* Allyn & Bacon, 1971; (with P. L. Lawrence) *Latin American Politics: A Functional Approach,* Chandler Publishing, 1972; (with O. Acuna) *The Family in Costa Rica*

(monograph), UNESCO (Paris), 1978. Contributor of articles to professional journals.

*WORK IN PROGRESS:* Two monographs, *The Politics of University Administration,* and *A Social Ethic for Latin America.*

*SIDELIGHTS:* Charles F. Denton told *CA* he is bilingual (Spanish-English) as he was raised in Latin America, "and happier when I live there."

\* \* \*

## DEON, Michel 1919-

*PERSONAL:* Born August 4, 1919, in Paris, France; son of Paul and Alice (de Fossey) Deon; married Chantal Renaudeau d'Arc, March 15, 1963; children: Alice, Alexander. *Education:* University of Paris, Licence de droit, 1940. *Religion:* Roman Catholic. *Home:* Old Rectory, Tynagh, County Galway, Eire; and Island of Spetsai, Greece.

*CAREER: Action Francaise* (daily newspaper), Paris, France, journalist, 1942-44; *Paris-Match* (weekly), Paris, journalist, 1954-56; author, 1944—. Literary adviser, Plon, 1956-58, and La Table Ronde, 1961-63. *Military service:* French Army, 1939-42. *Awards, honors:* Prix Interallie, 1970, for *Les Poneys sauvages;* Grand Prix du Roman de l'Academie francaise, 1973, for *Un Taxi mauve.*

*WRITINGS*—Fiction, except as noted: *Adieux a Sheila,* Laffont, 1944; *Amours perdues,* Bordas, 1946; *La Princesse de Manfred* (short story), Editions Sun (Lyon), 1949; *Je ne veux jamais l'oublier,* Plon, 1950; *La Corrida,* Plon, 1952; *Des Enfants s'aimaient,* Les Oeuvres Libres, 1953; *Le Dieu pale,* Plon, 1954; *La Tache rose,* Les Oeuvres Libres, 1955; *Tout l'amour du monde* (prose sketches), Plon, Part I, 1956, Part II, 1960; *Lettre a un jeune Rastignac* (pamphlet), Fasquelle, 1956; *Les Trompeuses esperances,* Plon, 1956; (with Salvadore Dali) *Histoire d'un grand livre: Don Quichotte* (nonfiction), illustrated by Dali, Foret, 1957; *Les Gens de la nuit,* Plon, 1958; *L'Armee d'Algerie et la pacification* (nonfiction), Plon, 1959; *La Carotte et le baton,* Plon, 1960; *Le Balcon de Spetsai* (nonfiction), Gallimard, 1961; *Le Rendez-vous de Patmos,* Plon, 1965; *Megalonose: Supplement aux "Voyages de Gulliver"* (pamphlet), La Table Ronde, 1967; *Un Parfum de jasmin* (short stories), Gallimard, 1967; *Les Poneys sauvages,* Gallimard, 1970; *Un Taxi mauve,* Gallimard, 1975; *Les Vingt Ans du jeune homme vert,* Gallimard, 1977; *Mes Arches de Noe,* La Table Ronde, 1978.

Author of text: (Photographs by Patrice Molinard) *La Cote d'Azur,* Editions Mondiales, 1950; *Versailles,* Editions Sun, 1951; (photographs by Molinard) *Le Cote basque et les Pyrenees,* Editions Mondiales, 1951; (photographs by Jean Imbert) *Venise que j'aime,* Editions Sun, 1956, translation by Ruth Whipple Fermaud published as *The Venice I Love,* Tudor, 1957; (photographs by Jacques Boulas) *Iles Baleares,* Hachette, 1958; (photographs by Robert Descharnes) *La Grece que j'aime,* Editions Sun, 1961, translation by Fermaud published as *The Greece I Love,* Tudor, 1961; *Le Portugal que j'aime,* Editions Sun, 1963, translation by Fermaud published as *The Portugal I Love,* Tudor, 1964; (with Nino Franck) *L'Italie que j'aime,* Editions Sun, 1968, translation by Fermaud published as *The Italy I Love,* Tudor, 1968; *Rever de la Grece,* Vilo, 1968; *Londres que j'aime,* Editions Sun, 1970, translation by Fermaud published as *The London I Love,* Tudor, 1970; *Haddelsey's Horses,* Editions Sun, 1978.

Editor: Louis XIV, King of France, *Louis XIV par lui-meme,* Librairie Academique Perrin, 1964; Salvador Dali, *Journal d'un genie,* La Table Ronde, 1964.

Translator: Victor Gollomb, *La Vie ardente d'Albert Schweitzer,* Editions Sun, 1951; Alarcon, *Le Tricorne* (from the Spanish), illustrated by Salvador Dali, Editions du Rocher, 1952; Saul Bellow, *L'Homme de Buridan (Dangling Man),* Plon, 1952.

Other writings include an introduction to Honore de Balzac's *Illusions perdues,* Livre de Poche, 1962, an introduction to *Marivaux's theater,* Livre de Poche, 1966, a chapter in *Prenoms,* Plon, 1967, and articles in periodicals.

*AVOCATIONAL INTERESTS:* Collecting modern paintings and lead soldiers, shooting, horses.

*BIOGRAPHICAL/CRITICAL SOURCES: Livres de France,* special issue, August-September, 1962; Pol Vandromme, *La Droite Buissonniers,* Les Sept Couleurs, 1957; Pierre de Boisdeffre, *Une Histoire vivante de la litterature d'aujourd'hui,* Perrin, 1958; Kleber Haedens, *Une Histoire de la litterature francaise,* Grasset, 1970; *L'Express,* September, 1970; *Matula,* July-August, 1973; Regis Cayrol, *La Droite desabusee et nonchalante,* University Center of Perpignan, 1975.

\* \* \*

## DESCARGUES, Pierre 1925-

*PERSONAL:* Born September 22, 1925, in Montrouge, France; son of Etienne and Alice (Schaub) Descargues; married Catherine Valogne (a painter and writer), April 22, 1950; children: Olivier. *Education:* Studied at Lycee Louis le Grand, Paris, and Sorbonne, University of Paris. *Home:* 6 Rue Boris-Vilde, 92 Fontenay-aux-Roses, France.

*CAREER: Arts* (weekly), Paris, France, art critic, 1946-50; *Les Lettres Francaise* (weekly), Paris, art critic, 1950—; *Tribune de Lausanne* (daily newspaper), Lausanne, Switzerland, correspondent, 1954-69; Radiodiffusion-Television Francaise, Paris, art critic, 1970—. *Member:* International Association of Art Critics. *Awards, honors:* Prix Descartes from French-Holland Association, 1967.

*WRITINGS: Durer,* Somogy, 1954; *Fernand Leger,* Editions Cercle d'Art, 1955; *Picasso,* Editions Universitaires, 1956, new edition, Felicie, 1974; *Le Siecle d'or de la peinture hollandaise,* Somogy, 1956, translation by Stuart Hood published as *Dutch Painting,* Thames & Hudson, 1959; *Le Cubisme,* Somogy, 1956; *La Peinture allemande du XIVeme aux XVIeme siecle,* Somogy, 1958, translation by Stuart Hood published as *German Painting from the 14th to the 16th Centuries,* Thames & Hudson, 1958; *Bernard Buffet* (includes *Bernard Buffet, peintre ou temoin?* by Pierre de Boisdeffre), Editons Universitaires, 1959.

*Lucas Cranach, le aine,* translation by Helena Ramsbotham published as *Lucas Cranach, the Elder,* Oldbourne, 1960, and as *Cranach,* Abrams, 1962; *Le Musee de L'Ermitage,* Somogy, 1961, translation by Katharine Delavenay published as *The Hermitage Museum, Leningrad,* Abrams, 1961, revised edition published as *Art Treasures of the Hermitage,* 1972 (translation published in England as *The Hermitage,* Thames & Hudson, 1961, revised edition, 1967); *Rembrandt et Saskia a Amsterdam,* Payot, 1965; *Vermeer,* published in French and in English translation by James Emmons, Skira (Geneva), 1966; (with Kynaston McShine and Pierre Restany) *Yves Klein* (exhibition catologue), Jewish Museum, Jewish Theological Seminary of America, 1967; *Hals,* published in French and in English translation by James Emmons, Skira, 1968.

*Rebeyrolle,* Maeght, 1970; (with Francis Ponge) *Georges Braque,* Draeger, 1971, English translation published under same title, Abrams, 1971; *Julio Gonzalez*, Musee de Poche, 1971; *Robert Muller*, La Connaissance (Brussels), 1971; *Le Douanier Rousseau: Etude biographique et critique*, Skira, 1972; *Picasso de Draeger*, Draeger, 1974; *Perspective*, Abrams, 1977; *Hartung*, Rizzoli, 1977.

Booklets in "Collection Artistes de ce temps" series, published by Presses Litteraires de France: *Bernard Buffet*, 1949; *Y. Alde*, 1950; *Vieira de Silva*, c. 1950; *Volti*, 1950; *Piaubert*, 1950; *Gili*, 1951; *Rebeyrolle*, 1951; *Bertholle*, 1952; *Gabriel Zendel*, 1952, *J. Dewasne*, 1952.

Other short works and texts of exhibition catalogues: *Jean Aujame*, Galerie de Berri, 1949; *Amedeo Modigliani, 1884-1920*, Braun, 1951; *Bourdelle*, Hachette, 1954; *Jacobsen: Sculptures 1961-1962*, Galerie de France, 1963; *Niki Saint-Phalle: Nanas* (text translated by Frances Frank), Iolas Gallery (New York), 1966; *Francois Fiedler*, Maeght, 1967.

*WORK IN PROGRESS: Goya*, for Alfieri & Lacroix (Milan); articles on Hals and Vermeer for *Encyclopaedia Britannica*.

*BIOGRAPHICAL/CRITICAL SOURCES: Best Sellers*, July 1, 1968; *Time*, December 20, 1971.†

\* \* \*

## DeSHAZO, Elmer Anthony 1924-

*PERSONAL:* Born June 22, 1924, in Winters, Tex.; son of William Thomas and Dott (Jolley) DeShazo; married Helene Ruth Schmidt, 1972 (divorced, 1978); children: Frances Michelle. *Education:* Texas Technological College (now Texas Tech University), B.B.A. (magna cum laude), 1953, M.A., 1954; Indiana University, Ph.D., 1957. *Politics:* Registered Democrat. *Religion:* Christian (nondenominational). *Home:* 822 North Guadalupe St., San Marcos, Tex. 78666. *Mailing address:* P.O. Box 1245, San Marcos, Tex. 78666. *Office:* Department of Political Science, Southwest Texas State University, San Marcos, Tex. 78666.

*CAREER:* International Milling Co., New York, N.Y., export assistant, 1946-49; Southwest Texas State University, San Marcos, instructor, 1957-58, assistant professor, 1958-63, associate professor, 1963-67, professor of political science, 1967—, university coordinator, international programs, 1968—, also instructor in U.S. Air Force Reserve Officers Training Corps at the university, 1958-65. Member, San Marcos Equal Opportunities Committee/Community Relations Service, 1963-66; member, Texas Adult Probation Advisory Council for Hays County, 1968. *Military service:* U.S. Coast Guard Reserve, active duty, 1942-46. U.S. Naval Reserve, 1947-70; presently lieutenant commander (retired).

*MEMBER:* American Political Science Association, International Studies Association (secretary-treasurer, 1969-71, president, 1972-74), Association of World Colleges and Universities, Southwestern Social Science Association, Southwestern Political Science Association, Social Science Club (University of Texas), Pi Gamma Mu, Delta Tau Kappa, Pi Sigma Alpha, Gamma Theta Upsilon, Delta Sigma Pi, Alpha Chi, Phi Eta Sigma.

*WRITINGS:* (Senior editor and contributor) *Documents and Readings in American and Texas Government*, Kendall/Hunt, 1969. Contributor of articles and reviews to professional journals; regular reviewer for Sunday supplement, *Austin American-Statesman*, 1968. Member of editorial board, *International Behavioural Scientist* (publication of Delta Tau Kappa), 1969-70.

## DESIDERATO, Otello 1926-

*PERSONAL:* Born September 18, 1926, in Buia, Italy; naturalized U.S. citizen; son of Robert and Ferma (Bortolotti) Desiderato; married Dorothy Streng (a fund raiser), November 13, 1954; children: David, Laurie. *Education:* Columbia University, A.B., 1949; New York University, M.A., 1951, Ph.D., 1953. *Home:* 150 Mohegan Ave., New London, Conn. 06320. *Office:* Department of Psychology, Connecticut College, New London, Conn. 06320.

*CAREER:* George Washington University, Washington, D.C., research associate of Human Resources Research Office, 1953-54; research psychologist for U.S. Army Signal Corps, 1954-55; Adelphi University, Garden City, N.Y., assistant professor of psychology, 1955-60; Connecticut College, New London, professor of psychology, 1960—, chairman of department, 1960-71. Lecturer, Brooklyn College (now Brooklyn College of the City University of New York), 1955-56. *Military service:* U.S. Army Air Forces, 1946-47. *Member:* American Association for the Advancement of Science (fellow), American Psychological Association, Association for the Advancement of Behavior Therapy, Society for Psychophysiological Research, Psychonomic Society, Eastern Psychological Association, Sigma Xi. *Awards, honors:* National Institute of Mental Health grants, 1957-58, 1959-63, 1971-72; National Science Foundation grant, 1963-65; science faculty fellowship at University of Pennsylvania, 1966-67; National Institute of Health grant, University of Connecticut, 1974-75.

*WRITINGS:* (Editor) *Readings in General Psychology*, MSS Educational Publishing, 1969; (with D. B. Howieson and J. H. Jackson) *Investigating Behavior: Principles of Psychology*, with study guide and instructor's manual, Harper, 1976. Contributor of about thirty articles to psychology journals.

*WORK IN PROGRESS:* Research reports.

\* \* \*

## DETWILER, Donald S(caife) 1933-

*PERSONAL:* Born August 19, 1933, in Jacksonville, Fla.; son of Donald Jacob (a retired naval officer and Federal Aviation Administration official) and Hazel (Scaife) Detwiler; married Ilse Elisabeth Kellner, April 8, 1956; children: Henry. *Education:* George Washington University, B.A., 1954; University of Goettingen, Dr.phil. (cum laude), 1961. *Home:* 201 Travelstead Lane, Carbondale, Ill. 62901. *Office:* Department of History, Southern Illinois University, Carbondale, Ill. 62901.

*CAREER:* Institute of European History, Mainz, Germany, research fellow, 1960-61; Montgomery Junior College, Takoma Park, Md., instructor, 1962-64, assistant professor of history, 1964-65; West Virginia University, Morgantown, assistant professor of history, 1965-67; Southern Illinois University at Carbondale, assistant professor, 1967-70, associate professor, 1970-77, professor of history, 1977—. Consultant to publishers, journals, and foundations. *Military service:* U.S. Air Force, 1954-57; became first lieutenant. *Member:* American Historical Association, Conference Group on Central European History, American Committee on the History of the Second World War (secretary, 1975—), Committee on the History of the Classroom (co-chairman, 1975—), Society for Spanish and Portuguese Historical Studies, Phi Beta Kappa. *Awards, honors:* German exchange scholarships, 1957-58, 1958-59; American Philosophical Society grants, 1969, 1974; American Council of

Learned Societies grant, 1978; German Exchange grant, 1978.

*WRITINGS: Hitler, Franco und Gibraltar die Frage des spanischen Eintritts in den Zweiten Weltkrieg* (title means "Hitler, Franco and Gibraltar: The Question of the Spanish Entry into the Second World War"), Steiner Verlag, 1962; (editor, translator, and author of introduction) Percy Ernst Schramm, *Hitler: The Man and the Military Leader* (translation of studies and documents by Schramm, a war diary officer in Hitler's headquarters, synthesizing his interpretation of Hitler), Quadrangle, 1971; *Germany: A Short History,* Southern Illinois University Press, 1976. Contributor of articles, critical reviews, and reviews to professional journals.

*WORK IN PROGRESS:* Editing a multivolume collection of archival material on World War II.

*        *        *

### DeVITO, Joseph Anthony 1938-

*PERSONAL:* Born August 1, 1938, in New York, N.Y.; son of James and Theresa (DeMartino) DeVito. *Education:* Hunter College (now Hunter College of the City University of New York), B.A., 1960; Temple University, M.A., 1962; University of Illinois, Ph.D., 1964. *Religion:* Roman Catholic. *Home:* 133 East 35th St., New York, N.Y. 10016. *Office:* Department of Communication Arts and Sciences, Queens College of the City University of New York, Flushing, N.Y. 11367.

*CAREER:* Hunter College of the City University of New York, New York, N.Y., instructor in communication, 1964-66; Herbert H. Lehman College of the City University of New York, Bronx, N.Y., assistant professor, 1967-69, associate professor of communication arts and sciences, 1969-71; Queens College of the City University of New York, Flushing, N.Y., professor of communication arts and sciences, 1972—. *Member:* International Communication Association, International Society for General Semantics, Speech Communication Association, Institute of General Semantics, Eastern Communication Association.

*WRITINGS: The Psychology of Speech and Language: An Introduction to Psycholinguistics,* Random House, 1970; (editor) *Communication: Concepts and Processes,* Prentice-Hall, 1971, revised edition, 1976; *General Semantics: Guide and Workbook,* Everett/Edwards, 1971, revised edition, 1974; *Psycholinguistics,* Bobbs-Merrill, 1973; (editor) *Language: Concepts and Processes,* Prentice-Hall, 1973; (with Jill Giattino and T. D. Schon) *Articulation and Voice: Effective Communication,* Bobbs-Merrill, 1975; *The Interpersonal Communication Book,* Harper, 1976; *Instructional Strategies for The Interpersonal Communication Book,* Harper, 1976; *Communicology: An Introduction to the Study of Human Communication,* Harper, 1978. Also author of "General Semantics: Nine Cassette Lectures," Everett/Edwards, 1971. Contributor to speech journals.

*WORK IN PROGRESS: Communication and Sexual Behavior; Movie Quiz.*

*SIDELIGHTS:* Joseph DeVito told *CA:* "From a relatively narrow interest in the psychology of language my interests expanded to encompass the entire range of human communication. Right now I am most interested in the relationship between communication and sexual behavior, the assumption being that we can learn a great deal about each from the other. A related interest is the sociological and psychological dimension of sexual 'deviation' particularly as these relate to communication."

### DEVLIN, John J(oseph), Jr. 1920-

*PERSONAL:* Born September 24, 1920, in Brighton, Mass.; son of John Joseph (a civil engineer) and Mary (Manton) Devlin; married Patricia Riley (a volunteer teacher of the retarded), August 29, 1953; children: Sean, Christopher, Gregory, Justin. *Education:* Boston College, A.B. (cum laude), 1945, M.A., 1950; St. John's Seminary, Brighton, Mass., theological studies, 1945-49; Boston University, Ph.D., 1956. *Politics:* Democrat. *Religion:* Roman Catholic. *Home:* 11 Crescent Rd., Larchmont, N.Y. 10538. *Office:* Liberal Arts Faculty, Fordham University, Bronx, N.Y. 10458.

*CAREER:* Boston College High School, Boston, Mass., instructor in German, 1950-51; Newman Preparatory School, Boston, instructor in languages, 1951, 1953; Newton College of the Sacred Heart, Newton, Mass., part-time instructor in German and European literature, 1952-53; St. Michael's College, Winooski, Vt., instructor, 1953-54, assistant professor of modern languages, 1954-57, chairman of department, 1956-57; Fordham University, Bronx, N.Y., assistant professor, 1957-65, associate professor, 1965-70, professor of Spanish literature, 1970—. Adjunct assistant professor, St. Joseph's Seminary, Dunwoodie, Yonkers, 1965-66; adjunct professor of German, Cathedral College, Douglaston, 1969—. Town of Mamaronek, N.Y., candidate for town council, 1961, candidate for town supervisor, 1963, Democratic district leader.

*MEMBER:* American Association of Teachers of Spanish, Modern Language Association of America (chairman of Franco-German comparative literature group, 1958), American Association of University Professors, Catholic Renascence Society (member of board of directors, 1966—; vice-president, 1970—), Catholic Conference on Cultural and Intellectual Affairs.

*WRITINGS: Spanish Anticlericalism: A Study in Modern Alienation,* Las Americas, 1966; (contributor) Herbert Golden, editor, *Studies in Honor of Samuel M. Waxman,* Boston University Press, 1969; (author of introduction) Benito Perez Galdos, *Doña Perfecta,* Las Americas, 1969; *The Celestina: A Parody of Courtly Love,* Las Americas, 1971.

Translator from the German: Sven Stolpe, *Night Music* (novel), Sheed, 1960; (with Maria von Eroes) Otto Semmelroth, *Mary, Archtype of the Church,* Sheed, 1963. Has done other translations from the German, including *The Plays of Calderon* and the preface to *The Unknown God,* Sheed, 1967. Contributor to *New Catholic Encyclopedia, America,* and professional journals.

*WORK IN PROGRESS:* A new contemporary English translation of the *Vida* of Teresa of Avila, with introduction and notes; a new translation of St. Bonaventura's *Itinerarium Mentis in Deum,* with an introduction by Herbert Musurillo.

*SIDELIGHTS:* John Devlin lived and did research in Spain, 1962-63. *Avocational interests:* Classical music, especially the paino (his wife and children also are amateur classical musicians), bicycling, camping, mountain hiking, swimming, and other recreation "in the quiet of the wilderness."

*        *        *

### DE WAAL, Ronald Burt 1932-

*PERSONAL:* Born October 23, 1932, in Salt Lake City, Utah; son of Jack and Marjorie (Burt) De Waal; married Gayle Lloyd, November 7, 1963; children: Serge, Leslie.

*Education:* University of Utah, B.S., 1955; University of Denver, M.A., 1958. *Politics:* Republican. *Religion:* Unitarian Universalist. *Home:* 5020 Hogan Dr., Fort Collins, Colo. 80521. *Office:* Colorado State University Library, Fort Collins, Colo. 80523.

*CAREER:* University of New Mexico, Albuquerque, special collections librarian, 1958-59; New Mexico Military Institute, Roswell, head librarian, 1959-60; Sperry Utah Co., Salt Lake City, Utah, head librarian, 1961-64; Westminster College, Salt Lake City, head librarian, 1964-66; Colorado State University Library, Fort Collins, humanities librarian and exhibits coordinator, 1966—. *Member:* College Art Association of America, Music Educators National Conference, Music Library Association, National Sculpture Society, Baker Street Irregulars, Praed Street Irregulars, Sherlock Holmes Society of London, Dr. Watson's Neglected Patients (president). *Awards, honors:* John H. Jenkins Award for best bibliography, 1974.

*WRITINGS: The World Bibliography of Sherlock Holmes and Dr. Watson: A Classified and Annotated List of Materials Relating to Their Lives and Adventures, 1887-1972,* New York Graphic Society, 1974. Contributor to literary journals.

*WORK IN PROGRESS:* A five-year supplement to the Sherlock Holmes bibliography.

*SIDELIGHTS:* Ronald De Waal has extensive collections on Beethoven and on Sherlock Holmes; he is "trying to collect everything relating to *the* master composer and *the* master detective." The Beethoven collection includes more than one hundred pieces of sculpture as well as books, records, prints, and paintings. *Avocational interests:* Classical music, reading, handball, mountain climbing, running, ballroom dancing.

*BIOGRAPHICAL/CRITICAL SOURCES: Baker Street Journal,* June, 1972; *Los Angeles Herald Examiner,* February 23, 1975; *Punch,* June 18, 1975.

\* \* \*

### DEWEY, Donald O(dell)  1930-

*PERSONAL:* Born July 9, 1930, in Portland, Ore.; son of Leslie Hamilton (an electrician) and Helen (Odell) Dewey; married Charlotte Neuber, September 21, 1952; children: Leslie Helen, Catherine Dawn, Scott Hamilton. *Education:* University of Oregon, B.A., 1952; University of Utah, M.S., 1956; University of Chicago, Ph.D., 1960. *Politics:* Independent. *Home:* 3891 Hampstead Rd., La Canada, Calif. 91011. *Office:* School of Letters and Science, California State University, Los Angeles, Calif. 90032.

*CAREER:* Managing editor, then city editor of newspapers in Oregon, 1952-54; University of Chicago, Chicago, Ill., instructor in history, 1960-62, assistant editor, *The Papers of James Madison,* 1960-61, associate editor, 1961-62; California State University, Los Angeles, assistant professor, 1962-65, associate professor, 1965-69, professor of history, 1969—, dean of School of Letters and Science, 1970—. Member of statewide academic senate, California State University and Colleges. *Member:* Society of American Historians (member of membership committee), American Society for Legal History (Pacific Coast branch; member of advisory board). *Awards, honors:* American Philosophical Society research grant, 1965; Outstanding Professor Award, California State University, Los Angeles, 1976.

*WRITINGS:* (Associate editor; W. T. Hutchinson, senior editor) *The Papers of James Madison,* Volumes I-III, University of Chicago Press, 1962-64; (editor with S. T. McSeveney, R. D. Burns, and E. R. Fingerhut) *The Continuing Dialogue,* two volumes, Pacific Books, 1964; (editor) *Union and Liberty: Documents in American Constitutionalism,* McGraw, 1969; *Jefferson versus Marshall: The Political Background of Marbury V. Madison,* Knopf, 1970. Contributor to twelve historical journals and to newspapers in Oregon and Utah.

*WORK IN PROGRESS:* A book on the impeachment of federal judges.

\* \* \*

### DICK, Robert C.  1938-

*PERSONAL:* Born May 25, 1938, in Hutchinson, Kan.; son of Frederick C. (stepfather; a truck driver) and Mae (Snell) Dick Markham; married Rebecca F. Caudill, August 4, 1957; children: Shelly, Dana, Allison. *Education:* Hutchinson Junior College (now Hutchinson Community Junior College), A.A., 1958; Kansas State Teachers College, B.S., 1960; University of New Mexico, M.A., 1961; Stanford University, Ph.D., 1969. *Politics:* Democrat. *Religion:* Methodist. *Home:* 127 Harmony Rd., Carmel, Ind. 46032. *Office:* Department of Speech-Theatre-Communications, Indiana—Purdue University, Indianapolis, Ind. 46202.

*CAREER:* Texas Technological College (now Texas Tech University), Lubbock, instructor, 1961-62; Stanford University, Stanford, Calif., instructor, 1962-65; University of New Mexico, Albuquerque, assistant professor, 1965-66 and 1967-70, associate professor of speech, 1970-75; Indiana University—Purdue University at Indianapolis, professor of speech communication and chairman of department, 1975—. Lecturer, San Francisco State College (now University), 1966-67. *Military service:* U.S. Army, National Guard, 1956-60. *Member:* Speech Communication Association, American Forensic Association, Western Speech Communication Association, Northern California Forensic Association (secretary-treasurer, 1964-65), New Mexico Forensic Association (president, 1967-68).

*WRITINGS: Argumentation and Rational Debating,* W. C. Brown, 1972; (contributor) Arthur L. Smith, editor, *Language, Communication, and Rhetoric in Black America,* Harper, 1972; *Black Protest: Issues and Tactics,* Greenwood Press, 1974.

*WORK IN PROGRESS:* A text in advanced public speaking.

\* \* \*

### DICKINSON, Ruth F(rankenstein)  1933-

*PERSONAL:* Born April 6, 1933, in St. Louis, Mo.; daughter of Kenneth F. (a minister) and Lillian (Wendt) Frankenstein; married V. L. Rieck, August 10, 1957 (died, 1963); married Joel R. Dickinson (a professor), June 8, 1965; children: (first marriage) Kristin, Erica; (second marriage) Joey, Alison. *Education:* Valparaiso University, B.A., 1954; attended University of Southern California, Los Angeles, 1954-56; California State College (now University), Los Angeles, M.A., 1961; University of Missouri, additional study, 1967. *Religion:* Lutheran. *Home:* 660 Cedarwood Ct., Mobile, Ala. 36609.

*CAREER:* Lutheran High School, Los Angeles, Calif., teacher of English, 1954-61; Millikin University, Decatur, Ill., instructor, 1964-65; Stephens College, Columbia, Mo., assistant professor of English, 1965-70; Northern Michigan University, Marquette, director of English skills workshop,

1973-75, instructor in English, 1973-77. Staff writer, Upper Peninsula Medical Education Program, 1977. Member of United Fund Board; committee chairman, Hadley Hospital Auxiliary. *Member:* Great Lakes Women's Studies Association (coordinator, 1977).

*WRITINGS:* (With Gary L. Harmon) *Write Now,* Holt, 1972; *Stars of Promise,* Concordia, 1976. Writer of monographs on contemporary literature for Lutheran Church, Missouri Synod, 1966-68.

*       *       *

## DICKSON, Naida  1916-
### (Grace Lee Richardson)

*PERSONAL:* Born April 18, 1916, in Thatcher, Ariz.; daughter of Charles Edmund (a pioneer lawyer, teacher, and doctor) and Daisie (Stout) Richardson; married C. Eugene Dickson, December 25, 1942; children: Charles Edmund and Clarence Eugene (twins). *Education:* Utah State University, B.S., 1940, M.S., 1944. *Politics:* Conservative Republican. *Religion:* Church of Jesus Christ of Latter-day Saints (Mormon). *Home:* 23500 Old Rd. No. 23, Newhall, Calif. 91321.

*CAREER:* Elementary and special education teacher in Payson, Utah, 1939-40, Weber County, Utah, 1943-44, 1947-48, Ontario, Calif., 1953-57, San Bernardino and Riverside Counties, Calif., 1963-68, and Los Angeles County, Calif., 1970-74; founder of Dickson Feature Service (distributor of puzzles), 1976. Social case worker in Cache and Weber Counties, Utah, 1941-43; assistant juvenile librarian, Upland Public Library, 1958-59; correctional counselor, California Institute for Women (prison), 1961-63.

*WRITINGS—For children; self-illustrated, except as indicated:* *The Littlest Helper,* Denison, 1971; *The Best Color* (not self-illustrated), Denison, 1971; *In the Meadow,* Denison, 1971; *I'd Like,* Denison, 1971; *The Story of Harmony Lane,* Golden Press, 1972; *The Toad That Couldn't Hop,* Denison, 1972; *Just the Mat for Father Cat,* Denison, 1972; *About Doctors of Long Ago,* Children's Press, 1972; *The Happy Moon,* Denison, 1972; *Big Sister and Tagalong Teddy,* Denison, 1973; *Biography of a Honeybee,* Lerner Press, 1974. Also author of eighteen puzzle magazines for Circle-a-Word. Contributor of poems and stories to magazines and anthologies. Editor, *Washington Terrace Spokesman,* Ogden, Utah, 1943-44.

*WORK IN PROGRESS:* Five children's books for Denison; research on "Bigfoot" or "Sasquatch," for a book.

*SIDELIGHTS:* Naida Dickson told *CA:* "I got printer's ink in my veins at the age of thirteen when the *Salt Lake Tribune* began a juvenile section called the *Tribune Junior,* which encouraged and published contributions from kids, I drew their first paper doll, constructed their first crossword puzzle, and wrote their first serialized story. I've wanted to see my work in print ever since that heady two and one-half-year experience. I like the permanency and prestige of book authorship, but appreciate also the easy and welcome income from my puzzle magazine work. Words are great fun!"

*       *       *

## Di CYAN, Erwin  1918-

*PERSONAL:* Surname is pronounced De Kine; born February 18, 1918, in Vienna, Austria; son of Emmanuel and Bertha (Blauvelt) Di Cyan; married, wife's name Lucille (deceased); children: Erika Di Cyan Hessman, Adrian Burke. *Education:* University of Bonn, Ph.D., 1933. *Office:* 12 East 41st St., New York, N.Y. 10017.

*CAREER:* Di Cyan & Brown (drug consultants), New York City, director, 1943-72; J. Walter Thompson Co. (advertising agency), New York City, consultant, 1972-78. Writer and lecturer.

*WRITINGS:* (With Robert H. Moser) *Adventures in Medical Writing,* C. C Thomas, 1970; (with Lawrence Hessman) *Without Prescription,* Simon & Schuster, 1972; *Vitamin E and Aging,* Pyramid Publications, 1972; *Vitamins in Your Life,* Simon & Schuster, 1974; *Creativity: Road to Self Discovery,* Harcourt Brace Jovanovich, 1978. Writer of health and medical column, "The Doctor Lets You In," in *Family Weekly,* 1971—. Contributor of reviews to *Archives of Internal Medicine* and other medical journals. Editor of *Monthly Bulletin* of Di Cyan & Brown, 1950-1970; east coast editor of *Brain/Mind Bulletin;* associate editor of *Journal of Psychosomatic Medicine and Dentistry.*

*SIDELIGHTS:* Erwin Di Cyan told *CA:* "I have been asked several times, how come I work and write in such diverse areas as science and the arts? The answer is simple: first, I have never been convinced that one must remain parochial in the devotion to one's career (as long as one can do it adequately), and second, the divisions in knowledge are artificial at best and narrowing at worst. . . . Creativity is a democratic trait and is not limited to painting pictures or composing immortal music; but creativity is a state of mind." *Avocational interests:* Theology, poetry.

*       *       *

## DIESKA, L. Joseph  1913-

*PERSONAL:* Born April 5, 1913, in D. Lehota, Czechoslovakia; son of John (a farmer) and Christina (Kraton) Dieska; married Anna Graca, November 4, 1940; children: Anna Hudec, Joseph. *Education:* Attended State Gymnasium, 1926-31; Slovak State University, Ph.D., 1940. *Religion:* Roman Catholic. *Home:* 2222 Rugby Rd., Dayton, Ohio 45406. *Office:* Department of Philosophy, University of Dayton, Dayton, Ohio 45469.

*CAREER:* Slovak State University, Bratislava, Czechoslovakia, assistant professor of philosophy, 1944-48; Georgetown University, Washington, D.C., assistant professor of languages, 1951-54; University of Dayton, Dayton, Ohio, professor of philosophy, 1960—. Secretary general, Slovak Philosophical Association, 1945-48; director of Philosophical Institute, Slovak Matica, 1945-48. *Member:* American Catholic Philosophical Association.

*WRITINGS:* *Practical Psychology,* Slovak Publishing Co., 1942; *Critical and Intuitive Realism,* Slovak Publishing Co., 1944; *Human Knowledge and Its Validity,* privately printed, 1970. Editor-in-chief, *Slovak Philosophical Review,* 1945-48.

*       *       *

## DIGGINS, John P(atrick)  1935-

*PERSONAL:* Born April 1, 1935, in San Francisco, Calif.; son of James J. (a gardener) and Anne (Norton) Diggins; married Jacy Battles, February 17, 1960 (divorced April, 1977); children: Sean, Nicole. *Education:* University of California, Berkeley, A.B., 1957; San Francisco State College (now University), M.A., 1959; University of Southern California, Ph.D., 1964. *Politics:* Democrat. *Religion:* Ex-Catholic. *Home:* 918 Van Dyke Rd., Laguna Beach, Calif. 92651. *Office:* Department of History, University of California, Irvine, Calif. 92664.

*CAREER:* San Francisco State College (now University), San Francisco, Calif., assistant professor of American intellectual history, 1966-69; University of California, Irvine, associate professor, 1969-72, professor of history, 1972—. Fellow, Churchill College, Cambridge University, 1975-76; visiting professor, Princeton University, 1977-78. *Member:* American Historical Association, American Studies Association, American Council of Learned Societies, American Philosophical Society. *Awards, honors:* National Endowment for the Humanities fellowship, 1972-73, for *Up from Communism;* John H. Dunning Award from American Historical Association, 1973; Guggenheim fellowship, 1975-76.

*WRITINGS: Mussolini and Fascism: The View From America,* Princeton University Press, 1972; *The American Left in the Twentieth Century,* Harcourt, 1973; *Up from Communism: Conservative Odysseys in American History,* Harper, 1975; *The Bard of Savagery: Thorstein Veblen and Modern Social Theory,* Seabury, 1978. Contributor of articles to *American Historical Review, Kenyon Review, Antioch Review, Historian, Journal of Contemporary History,* and other journals.

*WORK IN PROGRESS: Alienation, Modernism, and the Crisis of Authority: The Dilemmas of American Liberal Social Thought, 1880-1975.*

\* \* \*

## DIJKSTRA, Bram (Abraham Jan) 1938-

*PERSONAL:* Surname is pronounced *Dike*-stra; born July 5, 1938, in Tandjung Pandan, Indonesia; son of Abraham Jan and Bertha (Donk) Dijkstra; married Sandra Kanter (a professor of French), February 4, 1964. *Education:* Ohio State University, B.A., 1961, M.A., 1962; University of California, Berkeley, Ph.D., 1967. *Home:* 650 Rimini Rd., Del Mar, Calif. 92014. *Office:* Department of Literature, University of California, San Diego, La Jolla, Calif. 92093.

*CAREER:* University of California, San Diego, La Jolla, 1966—, began as assistant professor, currently associate professor of literature. *Member:* Modern Language Association of America.

*WRITINGS: Faces in Skin,* Oyez, 1965; *The Hieroglyphics of a New Speech: Cubism, Stieglitz and the Early Poetry of William Carlos Williams,* Princeton University Press, 1969; (editor) *A Recognizable Image: William Carlos Williams on Art and Artists,* New Directions, 1978. Contributor of articles to professional journals.

*WORK IN PROGRESS: Art, Ideology and the Structures of the Unconscious; Gustave Moreau and Lautreamont: Art and the Limits of Perception; The Pond and the Spring: Economic Meaning of De Foe's "Roxana."*

*BIOGRAPHICAL/CRITICAL SOURCES: Virginia Quarterly Review,* autumn, 1970.

\* \* \*

## DILL, Alonzo T(homas, Jr.) 1914-

*PERSONAL:* Born June 11, 1914, in New Bern, N.C.; son of Alonzo Thomas (a tobacconist) and Clara Maria (Green) Dill; married Julia Nowitzky (a teacher), August 10, 1949; children: Clara Maria, Alonzo Thomas III. *Education:* University of North Carolina at Chapel Hill, A.B., 1935. *Politics:* Independent. *Religion:* Episcopalian. *Home:* Cypress Ave., Box 625, West Point, Va. 23181. *Office:* Chesapeake Corporation of Virginia, West Point, Va. 23181.

*CAREER:* United Press Associations, Chicago, Ill., reporter, 1935-36; *Raleigh News and Observer,* Raleigh, N.C., reporter, 1936-37; Norfolk Newspapers, Inc., Nor-

folk, Va., associate editor, 1938-52; Tryon Palace Restoration, New Bern, N.C., research director, 1952-55; Jamestown Commission, Williamsburg, Va., public relations director, 1955-58; Chesapeake Corporation of Virginia, West Point, public relations director, 1958—. *Awards, honors:* Ogden Reid fellowship for study abroad, 1949; Charles A. Cannon Cup for research on North Carolina history, 1951.

*WRITINGS: Governor Tryon and His Palace,* University of North Carolina Press, 1958; *Jamestown,* U.S. Department of the Interior, 1959; *Chesapeake: Pioneer Papermaker,* University Press of Virginia, 1968. Also author of booklets on Carter Braxton, William Lee, Francis Lightfoot Lee, and George Wythe for Virginia Bicentennial Commission.

\* \* \*

## DILLON, Wilton S(terling) 1923-

*PERSONAL:* Born July 13, 1923, in Yale, Okla.; son of Earl Henry (an oilman) and Edith (Holland) Dillon; married Virginia Leigh Harris, January 20, 1956; children: Wilton Harris. *Education:* University of California, Berkeley, B.A., 1951; attended Sorbonne, University of Paris, 1951-52, and University of Leiden, 1952; Columbia University, Ph.D., 1961. *Politics:* Democrat. *Religion:* Christian (Episcopal). *Home:* 1446 Woodacre Dr., McLean, Va. 22101. *Agent:* Lurton Blassingame, 60 East 42nd St., New York, N.Y. 10017. *Office:* Smithsonian Institution, Washington, D.C. 20560.

*CAREER:* Information specialist for U.S. Government, and journalist in Tokyo, Japan, 1946-49; Hobart and William Smith Colleges, Geneva, N.Y., instructor in sociology and anthropology, 1953-54; Society for Applied Anthropology, director of Clearinghouse for Research in Human Organization, 1954-56, vice-president, 1956-57; Phelps-Stokes Fund of New York, New York, N.Y., director of research and executive secretary, 1957-63, director, Hazen Foundation research program, Ghana, West Africa, 1961-62, secretary, board of trustees, 1970—; Smithsonian Institution, Washington, D.C., director of seminars, 1969—, liaison with institutions of higher education in the United States and abroad; University of Alabama, Tuscaloosa, adjunct professor of anthropology, 1971—. Lecturer, Teachers College, Columbia University, 1955-56, 1957-58, New School for Social Research, 1959-60; lay reader in cancer hospital in New York, N.Y., 1957-59; lecturer, under the auspices of the U.S. Department of State, at museums in Asia, 1971. President, board of directors, Institute of Intercultural Studies, New York, N.Y.; secretary-treasurer, Institute for Psychiatry and Foreign Affairs, Washington, D.C. Consultant on international programs, Bryn Mawr College. *Military service:* U.S. Army, served in Infantry, 1942-43, and U.S. Army Air Forces, 1943-46; received Asiatic-Pacific ribbon and Philippine Liberation Medal.

*MEMBER:* American Anthropological Association (fellow), Council on Anthropology and Education (fellow), African Studies Association (fellow), Anthropological Society of Washington (president). *Awards, honors:* Grant Foundation research awards, France, 1956, and Ghana, 1970; Ford Foundation travel-study award, West Africa, 1958; U.S. Department of State grant for lecture tour in Asia, 1971.

*WRITINGS: Gifts and Nations: The Obligation to Give, Receive, and Repay,* Humanities, 1969; (editor with John F. Eisenberg) *Man and Beast: Comparative Social Behavior,* Smithsonian Press, 1971; (contributor) Gene Usdin, editor,

*Perspectives on Violence*, Brunner, 1972; (editor) *The Cultural Drama: Modern Identities and Social Ferment*, Smithsonian Press, 1974; (contributor) Owen Gingerich, editor, *The Nature of Scientific Discovery*, Smithsonian Press, 1975; (contributor) George N. Atiyeh, editor, *Arab and American Cultures*, American Enterprise Institute, 1977. Contributor to *Encyclopedia Americana*. Contributor of articles to *New Yorker, New Republic, Kenyon Review, Virginia Quarterly Review, Africa Report*, and *Columbia Forum*.

*WORK IN PROGRESS:* Editing a collection of essays, *Anecdotal Anthropology*; rewriting an unpublished manuscript, *The Observer Observed*; a play, *Fox*; a novel, *The Simple Man*.

*SIDELIGHTS:* Wilton Dillon told *CA* that he is, as a museum official, "increasingly interested in the uses of museums as stages for communicating ideas, and support[s] closer cooperation between scientists and creative artists. . . . I studied anthropology with Margaret Mead and Claude Levi-Strauss, and thus have not yet evolved toward computers and quantification. . . . Anthropology provides a framework for experimenting with writing which combines some techniques of journalism and playwrighting, canons of objectivity notwithstanding. I like to think that first-person narratives are more 'objective' than some other forms because they make clear the perceptions of an identifiable observer, biases and all."

"Though I have never attempted fiction, vignettes and narratives I have written contain the raw material of drama in other forms; without any deliberate intention, stories in retrospect seem to specialize on the interplay of different cultures or civilizations through women (e.g., a German woman harpsichordist and her Japanese maid, or an African paramount chief in New York, or the French painter, Yves Klein, and his British friend, a judo woman, inside El Greco's house in Toledo, or an American bride in a French household getting to know her mother-in-law). Having been exposed to fascinating women all my life in the American South, this is a 'natural' choice of materials, and a basis for admiring the work of Eudora Welty, Flannery O'Connor, Tennessee Williams, and Lillian Hellman. My ambition to write a novel, *The Simple Man*, is inspired by finding Southern elements at work in the French aristocracy; it would be a garnished story of a French officer, back from wars, who marries a lady mayor. Both have been influenced by wartime exposure to Americans. . . . My interests in ritual and liturgy grow out of my training as an anthropologist, a childhood of iconoclasm in the Bible belt, and prior service as an Episcopal lay reader in a cancer hospital in New York City."

*AVOCATIONAL INTERESTS:* Collecting African sculpture and Korean ceramics.

*BIOGRAPHICAL/CRITICAL SOURCES: Village Voice,* August 21, 1969.

* * *

## DINITZ, Simon 1926-

*PERSONAL:* Born October 29, 1926, in New York, N.Y.; son of Morris and Dinah (Schulman) Dinitz; married Mildred H. Stern, August 20, 1949; children: Jeffrey, Thea, Risa. *Education:* Vanderbilt University, B.A. (magna cum laude), 1947; University of Wisconsin, M.A., 1949, Ph.D., 1951. *Politics:* Democratic. *Religion:* Jewish. *Home:* 298 North Cassady, Columbus, Ohio 43209. *Office:* Department of Sociology, Ohio State University, Columbus, Ohio 43210.

*CAREER:* Ohio State University, Columbus, instructor, 1951-55, assistant professor, 1956-59, associate professor, 1959-63, professor of sociology, 1963—, research associate in psychiatry, 1957—, chairman of Research Council, 1969-70, senior fellow, Academy for Contemporary Problems, 1975—. Visiting professor, University of Tel Aviv, 1970, 1971; summer lecturer, University of Wisconsin, 1951, 1952; visiting summer professor at University of Southern California, 1968, and University of Wisconsin, 1969. Member of Columbus Urban Community Task Force, 1969, and of Ohio Governor's Task Force on Corrections, 1971; member, United Nations Social Defence Research Institute, 1969—; member of international advisory board, University of Tel Aviv, 1970—; member of International Symposium on Victimology, Hebrew University, 1972. Consultant to public and private groups, including Buckeyes Boys' Ranch and Columbus Community Mental Health Center. *Military service:* U.S. Navy, 1945-46.

*MEMBER:* American Sociological Association (council member of section on criminology, 1968-71), American Society of Criminology (president, 1970-71), American Psychopathological Association, Society for the Study of Social Problems, Ohio Valley Sociological Association (vice-president, 1968-69), Phi Beta Kappa (honorary member). *Awards, honors:* National Institute of Mental Health research grants, 1958-59, 1959-61, 1963-66, 1966-70; State of Ohio research grants, 1969-70, 1970-72; Hofheimer prize for research from American Psychiatric Association, 1967, for *Schizophrenics in the Community: An Experiment in the Prevention of Hospitalization.*

*WRITINGS:* (With Russell Dynes, Alfred C. Clarke, and Iwao Ishino) *Social Problems: Dissensus and Deviation,* Oxford University Press, 1964; (contributor) Walter C. Reckless and Charles L. Newman, editors, *Interdisciplinary Problems of Criminology,* American Society of Criminology, 1965; (contributor) Paul Hoch and Joseph Zubin, editors, *Psychopathology of Schizophrenia,* Grune, 1966; (with Benjamin Pasamanick and Frank Scarpitti) *Schizophrenics in the Community: An Experiment in Prevention of Hospitalization,* Appleton, 1967; (editor with Reckless) *Critical Issues in the Study of Crime: A Book of Readings,* W. C. Brown, 1968; (with Shirley Angrist, Mark Lefton, and Pasamanick) *Women after Treatment: A Comparison of Treated Mental Patients and Their Normal Neighbors,* Appleton, 1968; (with Clarke and Dynes) *Deviance: Studies in the Process of Stigmatization and Societal Reaction,* Oxford University Press, 1969, 2nd edition, 1975; (contributor) *The Threat of Crime in America* (E. Paul duPont lectures), University of Delaware, 1969.

(With Reckless) *Experimenting with Delinquency Prevention,* Ohio State University Press, 1972; (with Reckless) *The Prevention of Delinquency: An Experiment,* Ohio State University Press, 1972; (with Pasamanick and Ann I. Davis) *Schizophrenics in the New Custodial Community,* Ohio State University Press, 1974; (with Ferracuti and Acosta de Brenes) *Delinquents and Nondelinquents in the Puerto Rico Slum Culture,* Ohio State University Press, 1975; (with Bartollas and Miller) *Juvenile Victimization: The Institutional Paradox,* Halsted, 1976; (with John P. Conrad) *In Fear of Each Other,* Lexington Books, 1977. Also author of research reports. Contributor of about one hundred articles and reviews to psychology journals. Editor, *Criminologica,* 1966-68; member of editorial board, *Excerpta Criminologica,* 1966-68; associate editor, *American Sociological Review,* 1968-71.

**DIVINE, Thomas F(rancis) 1900-**

*PERSONAL:* Born August 23, 1900, in Kansas City, Mo.; son of James F. (a plumbing contractor) and Agnes (Hersen) Divine. *Education:* St. Louis University, B.A., 1923, M.A., 1924; attended Geneva Institute of International Relations, summers, 1935-37; University of London, Ph.D., 1938. *Politics:* Republican. *Home and office:* College of Business Administration, Marquette University, Milwaukee, Wis. 53233.

*CAREER:* Roman Catholic priest; entered Society of Jesus (Jesuits), 1917, ordained priest, 1930; Loyola University, Chicago, Ill., instructor, 1924-26; Creighton University, Omaha, Neb., instructor, 1926-27; Rockhurst College, Kansas City, Mo., assistant professor of social science and assistant dean, 1931-32; Marquette University, Milwaukee, Wis., instructor, 1933-34, assistant professor, 1938-42, professor of economics, 1942-73, director of department of economics, 1942-49, dean of College of Business Administration, 1942-59, dean emeritus, 1973—, founder and director of Labor College, 1942-59. Professor of economics, St. Louis University, 1960-63. Region VI public member, National War Labor Board, 1942-44. Milwaukee Council for a Lasting Peace, vice-president, 1943-44, president, 1944-45. *Military service:* U.S. Navy, 1955; became honorary commodore. *Member:* American Economic Association, Catholic Economic Association (founder and president, 1942-43), Catholic Commission on Intellectual and Cultural Affairs, International Platform Association, Wisconsin Academy of Sciences, Arts, and Letters, Beta Gamma Sigma (member of national executive committee, 1955-63), Pi Gamma Mu.

*WRITINGS: Tariffs and World Peace,* Catholic Association for International Peace, 1934; *Interest,* Marquette University Press, 1959; (contributor) Joseph W. Towle, editor, *Ethics and Standards in American Business,* Houghton, 1964. Contributor to *Encyclopedia Americana* and *New Catholic Encyclopedia;* contributor of articles to professional journals. Editor, *Review of Social Economy,* 1948-59, and *Marquette Business Review,* 1963-77.

*WORK IN PROGRESS:* Research on Ferdinando Galiani and the history of economic analysis.

\*      \*      \*

**DJEDDAH, Eli 1911-**

*PERSONAL:* Born September 23, 1911, in Manchester, England; son of Nessim and Bahia (Ades) Djeddah; married Cynthia Marx. *Education:* Attended Corinth College, Cheltenham, England; National University, M.A.; California Pacific University, Ph.D. *Home:* 2520 Clairmont Dr., San Diego, Calif. 92117. *Office:* Office of the President, La Jolla University, 8939 Villa La Jolla Dr., La Jolla, Calif. 92037.

*CAREER:* Before 1962, employed as operations manager, Campbell & Hall, Boston, Mass., president, Breitbart-Finklestein, New York City, managing director, Carrier, Egypt, and manager of engineering for North Africa, Mitchell Cotts & Co., London, England; Bernard Haldane Associates (executive career counselors), Boston, president, 1962-67, Philadelphia, Pa., principal, 1964-72, Hartford, Conn., president, 1965-67, Los Angeles, Calif., vice-president, 1967-68, San Francisco, Calif., president, 1967-70, New York City, vice-president, 1970-71, San Francisco, president, 1971-77; La Jolla University, La Jolla, Calif., president, 1977—. Member of board of directors, Egyptian Salt & Soda Co., Societe Egyptienne des Eballages Economiques (packaging firm), and Societe de Fayoum (operators of hotels and resorts); president, Lac Maison Country Es-

tates, Quebec. Former honorary secretary, Jewish Hospital, Cairo, Egypt. *Member:* Royal Egyptian Cultural Society, Music Box International, Masons, Rolls Royce Club, Commonwealth Club (San Francisco).

*WRITINGS: Elements of Success,* privately printed, 1970; *Moving Up: How to Get High-Salaried Jobs,* Lippincott, 1971, revised edition, Ten Speed Press, 1978; *Now That I Know Which Side Is Up,* Ten Speed Press, 1976; *Papyrus Flowers,* Allen Co., 1977.

\*      \*      \*

**DOBSON, John M(cCullough) 1940-**

*PERSONAL:* Born July 20, 1940, in Las Cruces, N.M.; son of Donald Duane (a U.S. State Department employee) and Carolyn (Van Anda) Dobson; married Cynthia Davis (a sociologist), August 29, 1963; children: David, Daniel. *Education:* Massachusetts Institute of Technology, B.S., 1962; University of Wisconsin, M.S., 1964, Ph.D., 1966. *Home:* 2019 Kildee St., Ames, Iowa 50010. *Office:* Department of History, Iowa State University, Ames, Iowa 50011.

*CAREER:* Chico State College (now California State University, Chico), assistant professor of history, 1966-67; U.S. Department of State, Washington, D.C., foreign service officer, 1967-68; Iowa State University, Ames, associate professor of history, 1968—. *Member:* American Historical Association, Organization of American Historians, American Association of University Professors.

*WRITINGS: Politics in the Gilded Age: A New Perspective on Reform,* Praeger, 1972; *Two Centuries of Tariffs,* U.S. Government Printing Office, 1976; *America's Ascent: The United States Becomes a Great Power 1880-1914,* Northern Illinois University Press, 1978.

\*      \*      \*

**DOBYNS, Henry F(armer) 1925-**

*PERSONAL:* Born July 3, 1925, in Tucson, Ariz.; son of Henry Farmer (a printer) and Susie Kell (Comstock) Dobyns; married Zipporah Pottenger, 1948 (divorced, 1958); married Cara E. Richards, 1958 (divorced, 1968); married Mary Faith Patterson, August 3, 1968; children: (first marriage) Henry Farmer III, William C., Martha S., Mark McC.; (second marriage) York H. *Education:* University of Arizona, B.A., 1949, M.A., 1956; Cornell University, Ph.D., 1960. *Home:* 1124 East Linden St., Tucson, Ariz. 85719.

*CAREER:* Arizona State Museum, Tucson, Ariz., research associate, 1950-51, 1958-59; Cornell University, Ithaca, N.Y., research associate of department of sociology and anthropology, 1959-63, lecturer and senior research associate of department of anthropology, 1963-66, coordinator of Cornell project in Lima, Peru, 1960-62; University of Kentucky, Lexington, professor of anthropology and chairman of department, 1966-70; Prescott College, Prescott, Ariz., professor of anthropology, 1970-73; University of Wisconsin—Parkside, visiting professor of anthropology, 1974-75. Visiting professor of anthropology, University of Florida, 1977-78. Democratic precinct chairman, Fayette County, Ky. Has conducted research among Walapai, Havasupai, Papago, Gila River Pima, Apache, and Navajo Indians. *Military service:* U.S. Army, 1942-43.

*MEMBER:* American Association for the Advancement of Science (fellow), American Anthropological Association (fellow), Society for Applied Anthropology (fellow), American Society for Ethnohistory (secretary-treasurer, 1968-70;

president, 1976-77), Arizona Academy of Science (honorary fellow), Arizona Historical Society. *Awards, honors:* Malinowski Award from Society for Applied Anthropology, 1951, for article, "Blunders with Bolsas"; co-winner of Anisfield-Wolf award of *Saturday Review,* 1968, for "The American Indian Today"; National Science Foundation fellow, 1956-57; Social Science Research Council fellow, 1959.

*WRITINGS: Papagos in the Cotton Fields, 1950,* [Tucson ], 1951; (editor) *Hepah, California! The Journal of Cave Johnson Couts from Monterey, Nuevo Leon, Mexico, to Los Angeles, California, during the Years 1848-1849,* Arizona Pioneers' Historical Society, 1961; (editor with Mario C. Vazquez, and contributor) *Migracion e Integracion en el Peru,* Editorial Estudios Andinos, 1963; *The Social Matrix of Peruvian Indigenous Communities,* Department of Anthropology, Cornell University, 1964; (with Paul L. Doughty and Allan R. Holmberg) *Measurement of Peace Corps Program Impact in the Peruvian Andes: Final Report,* Department of Anthropology, Cornell University, 1965; (with Holmberg, Morris E. Opler, and Lauriston Sharp) *Recommendations for Future Research on the Processes of Cultural Change,* Department of Anthropology, Cornell Univesity, 1966; (with Holmberg, Opler, and Sharp) *Some Principles of Cultural Change,* Department of Anthropology, Cornell University, 1967; (with Holmberg, Opler, and Sharp) *Strategic Intervention in the Cultural Change Process,* Department of Anthropology, Cornell University, 1967; (with Holmberg, Opler, and Sharp) *Methods for Analyzing Cultural Change,* Department of Anthropology, Cornell University, 1967; (with Susan C. Bourque, Leslie A. Brownrigg, and Eileen A. Maynard) *Factions and Faenas: The Developmental Potential of Checras District, Peru,* Department of Anthropology, Cornell University, 1967; (with Robert C. Euler) *The Ghost Dance of 1889 among the Pai Indians of Northwestern Arizona,* Prescott College Press, 1967; (with Earl W. Morris, Bownrigg, and Bourque) *Coming down the Mountain: The Social Worlds of Mayobamba,* Department of Anthropology, Cornell University, 1968; *Comunidades Campesinas del Peru,* Editorial Estudios Andinos, 1970; (with Euler) *Wauba Yuma's People: The Comparative Socio-Political Structure of the Pai Indians of Arizona,* Prescott College Press, 1970: (with Euler) *The Havasupai People,* [Phoenix ], 1971; (with Euler) *The Hopi People,* [Phoenix ], 1971; *The Apache People* (Coyoteros), [Phoenix ], 1971; (editor with Doughty and Harold D. Lasswell) *Peasants, Power, and Applied Social Change: Vicos as a Model,* Sage Publications, 1971; (with Euler) *The Navajo People,* [Phoenix ], 1972. Also author with Euler of *The Walapai People,* 1976, and *Navajo Indians.*

Contributor: Lyle W. Shannon, editor, *Underdeveloped Areas,* Harper, 1957; R. E. Bolton, editor, *Case Studies to Accompany Getting Agriculture Moving,* Agricultural Development Council, 1967; Stuart Levine and Nancy O. Lurie, editors, *The American Indian Today,* Everett Edwards, 1968; K. R. Anschell, R. H. Brannon, and E. D. Smith, editors *Agricultural Cooperatives and Markets in Developing Countries,* Praeger, 1969; Virgil J. Vogal, editor, *This Country Was Ours: A Documentary History of the American Indian,* Harper, 1972; Deward E. Walker, Jr., editor, *The Emergent Native Americans,* Little, Brown, 1972; *Spanish Colonial Tucson,* University of Arizona Press, 1976; *Historical Native American Demography: A Critical Essay,* Indiana University Press, 1976; (with Doughty) *Peru: A Cultural History,* Oxford University Press, 1976. Contributor of more than one hundred articles and reviews

to *Saturday Review, Arizona Quarterly, Andean Air Mail and Peruvian Times,* and to historical and anthropological journals.

*WORK IN PROGRESS: From Fire to Flood.*

*       *       *

### DOCKRELL, William Bryan 1929-

*PERSONAL:* Born January 12, 1929, in Manchester, England; son of James (an electrical engineer) and Elizabeth (Slater) Dockrell; married Ann Cirilla (a psychologist), June 12, 1954; children: Julia, Helen, Richard, Catherine, Martin, Mark. *Education:* University of Manchester, B.A., 1950; University of Edinburgh, M.Ed., 1952; University of Chicago, Ph.D., 1963. *Home:* The Coachhouse, Inveresk, Musselburgh, Midlothian, Scotland. *Office:* Scottish Council for Research in Education, 16 Moray Pl., Edinburgh, Scotland.

*CAREER:* Education Authority, Manchester, England, psychologist, 1955-58; University of Alberta, Edmonton, assistant professor of educational psychology, 1958-67; Ontario Institute for Studies in Education, Toronto, professor of special education, 1967-71; Scottish Council for Research in Education, Edinburgh, Scotland, director, 1971—. *Military service:* British Army, 1956-57. *Member:* American Psychological Association, American Educational Research Association, British Psychological Association. *Awards, honors:* Senior Imperial Relations fellow, London, 1966-67.

*WRITINGS:* (Editor) *On Intelligence,* Methuen, 1971; (with P. M. Broadfoot) *Pupils in Profile,* Hodder & Stoughton, 1977; (editor with W. Dunn and A. Milne) *Special Education in Scotland,* SCRE Publication, 1978; (editor with D. Hamilton) *New Dimensions in Educational Research,* Hodder & Stoughton, 1978.

*       *       *

### DODGE, Peter 1926-

*PERSONAL:* Born November 12, 1926, in New York, N.Y.; son of Martin (a public relations representative) and D'Etta (Brown) Dodge; married Renata Kanicky de Czachrowa, September 6, 1952; children: Timothy, Christopher. *Education:* Swarthmore College, B.A. (with high honors), 1948; Harvard University, A.M., 1950, Ph.D., 1961. *Politics:* Independent Democrat. *Religion:* None. *Home:* Wadleigh's Fall's Rd., Lee, R.F.D. Newmarket, N.H. 03857. *Office:* Department of Sociology and Anthropology, Social Science Building, University of New Hampshire, Durham, N.H. 03824.

*CAREER:* State University of New York, Harpur College (now State University of New York at Binghamton), Binghamton, instructor in sociology, 1958-61, assistant professor of sociology, history, and anthropology, 1961-64, assistant chairman of Division of Social Sciences, 1962-64; University of New Hampshire, Durham, associate professor of sociology, 1964—, director of graduate program in sociology, 1967-71. Visiting professor, University of Wales, 1973. *Military service:* U.S. Army, 1945-46. *Member:* American Sociological Association, Latin American Studies Association, American Association of University Professors. *Awards, honors:* Fulbright grant, University of Brussels, 1954-55, 1955-56; State University of New York grant for Belgian research, 1963; grants from University of New Hampshire and State of New York for research in Brazil and Surinam, 1965; Rockefeller Visiting Scholar Award, Institute of Latin American Studies, Columbia University, 1965-66; postdoctoral fellow, Institute for Comparative Sociology, Indiana University, summer, 1968; grant from Joint Committee on Latin American Studies of Social Science Research Council and American Council of Learned Societies for research in Brazil, 1968-69.

*WRITINGS: Beyond Marxism: The Faith and Works of Hendrik de Man,* Nijhoff, 1966; (editor and translator) *Hendrik de Man, Socialist Critic of Marxism: A Documentary Study,* Princeton University Press, 1978. Contributor to *International Encyclopedia of the Social Sciences;* contributor to professional journals.

*WORK IN PROGRESS:* The family firm in Sao Paulo, Brazil.

\* \* \*

## DOIG, Jameson W. 1933-

*PERSONAL:* Born June 12, 1933, in Oakland, Calif.; son of James Rufus and Mary (Jameson) Doig; married Joan Nishimoto, October 8, 1955; children: Rachel, Stephen, Sarah. *Education:* Dartmouth College, B.A., 1954; Princeton University, M.P.A., 1958, M.A., 1959, Ph.D., 1961. *Home:* 12 College Rd., Princeton, N.J. 08540. *Office:* Department of Politics, Woodrow Wilson School of Public and International Affairs, Princeton University, Princeton, N.J. 08540.

*CAREER:* Brookings Institution, Washington, D.C., research assistant and research associate, 1959-61; Princeton University, Princeton, N.J., assistant professor, 1961-67, associate professor, 1967-70, professor of politics and public affairs in department of politics and at Woodrow Wilson School of Public and International Affairs, 1970—, director of research program in criminal justice, 1973—. Visiting professor, John Jay College of Criminal Justice of the City University of New York, 1967-68, 1970-72. Committee chairman, New Jersey Governor's Council against Crime, 1967-70; member of Correctional Master Plan Policy Council, 1974—, governor's Juvenile and Adult Justice Advisory Committee, 1975—, and Advisory Council on Corrections, 1977— (all New Jersey). Consultant to Fels Fund, 1966-68, to New Jersey Department of Community Affairs, 1969-70, to Guggenheim Foundation, 1970—, to governor of New Jersey on revision of parole statutes, 1975—, to Center for Administrative Justice, 1972-77, and to Police Foundation, 1977-78; member of board of directors, New Jersey Association on Correction, 1971—. *Military service:* U.S. Navy, 1954-56; became lieutenant junior grade. *Member:* American Political Science Association, American Society for Public Administration (member of executive committee of criminal justice section, 1977—), American Correctional Association, Policy Studies Organization, National Association of Schools of Public Affairs and Administration (member of executive committee, 1973-74).

*WRITINGS:* (With Dean E. Mann) *The Assistant Secretaries,* Brookings Institution, 1965; *Metropolitan Transportation Politics and the New York Region,* Columbia University Press, 1966; (with David T. Stanley and Mann) *Men Who Govern,* Brookings Institution, 1967; (contributor) Duane Lockard, editor, *Governing the States and Localities,* Macmillan, 1969.

Contributor: Lyle C. Fitch and Annamarie H. Walsh, editors, *Agenda for a City,* Sage Publications, 1970; M. N. Danielson, editor, *Metropolitan Politics,* Little, Brown, 1971; S. M. Davidson and P. E. Peterson, editors, *Urban Politics and Public Policy,* Praeger, 1973; John A. Gardiner and Michael Mulkey, editors, *Crime and Criminal Justice,* Lexington-Heath, 1975; G. Frederickson and C. Wise, edi-

tors, *Public Administration and Public Policy,* Lexington-Heath, 1977. Contributor of reviews to *American Political Science Review, Political Science Quarterly,* and *Public Policy;* contributor of articles to journals of political affairs.

*WORK IN PROGRESS:* The role of government in urban development; police behavior; patterns of power and justice in prisons.

\* \* \*

## DOMMEYER, Frederick Charles 1909-

*PERSONAL:* Born January 12, 1909, in Pensacola, Fla.; son of F. C. (a musician) and Christine B. (Levi) Dommeyer; married Mariam Pankov, July 1, 1937; children: Barbara Pauline (Mrs. Michael King), Carl Dennis, Curt John. *Education:* Union College, Schenectady, N.Y., A.B., 1932; additional study at Oxford University, 1933-34, and University of Hamburg, 1934; Brown University, M.A., 1935, Ph.D., 1937. *Politics:* Republican. *Religion:* Unitarian-Universalist. *Home:* 1352 Happy Valley Ave., San Jose, Calif. 95129. *Office:* Department of Philosophy, San Jose State University, San Jose, Calif. 95114.

*CAREER:* Brown University, Providence, R.I., instructor in philosophy, 1937-38; Syracuse University, Syracuse, N.Y., instructor in philosophy, 1938-44; St. Lawrence University, Canton, N.Y., assistant professor, 1944-47, associate professor of philosophy, 1947-58; San Jose State University, San Jose, Calif., professor of philosophy, 1958—. Tully Cleon Knoles Lecturer, University of the Pacific, 1964. Member of board of directors, California Parapsychology Research Group. *Military service:* New York State National Guard, 1929-31. *Member:* Parapsychological Association, American Society for Psychical Research, Academy of Parapsychology and Medicine. *Awards, honors:* Rhode Island English-Speaking Union fellow at Oxford University, 1933-34.

*WRITINGS:* (Editor) *In Quest of Value,* Chandler Publishing, 1963; *Body, Mind, and Death,* Spartan Book Store, 1965; (editor) *Current Philosophical Issues,* C. C Thomas, 1966; (with others) *Logics,* Chandler Publishing, 1966. Contributor of articles and reviews to professional journals. Member of board of review, *Psychic.*

*WORK IN PROGRESS: Sixty Years of Psychical Research at Stanford University.*

\* \* \*

## DONART, Arthur C(harles) 1936-
### (Anton Donat)

*PERSONAL:* Born June 21, 1936, in Peoria, Ill.; son of Arthur Joseph (an electrician) and Virginia (Andrews) Donart; married Frances Arlene Gritton (an elementary teacher), June 11, 1960; children: Susan Anne, Christine Michelle, Stephen Arthur, Lorraine Kay. *Education:* St. Ambrose College, B.A., 1962; Western Illinois University, M.S., 1969, C.A.S., 1970. *Politics:* Independent Democrat. *Religion:* Roman Catholic.

*CAREER:* Elementary school teacher in Andover, Ill., 1964-67; high school English teacher in Orion, Ill., 1967-69, and East Moline, Ill., 1969-70; Western Illinois University, Macomb, assistant professor of English, beginning 1970. *Military service:* U.S. Army, parachutist, 1955-57. *Member:* National Council of Teachers of English, College English Association, Conference on English Education, Phi Delta Kappa.

*WRITINGS:* (With Alfred J. Lindsey) *The Student Speaks*

*Out,* W. C. Brown, 1972. Contributor to education journals. Author of "Comment on Education," a monthly newspaper column. Author of articles under pseudonym Anton Donat.

*WORK IN PROGRESS: Research in the Teaching of Composition; Smile for the Teacher.*††

\*     \*     \*

## DONHEISER, Alan D. 1936-

*PERSONAL:* Born October 1, 1936, in Merrick, N.Y.; son of Sidney (a salesman) and Agnes (Hennessy) Donheiser; married Madeline Falzone, July 3, 1964; children: Andrew. *Education:* Villanova University, B.S., 1958; New York University, M.A., 1963, D. Public Administration, 1966. *Home and office:* 67 Churchill Ave., Arlington, Mass. 02174.

*CAREER:* Tax Foundation Inc., New York City, research associate, 1961-64; New York University, New York City, research scientist, 1964-66, lecturer, 1969-70; Regional Plan Association, New York City, chief economist, 1969-70; Arthur D. Little, Inc., Cambridge, Mass., senior economist, 1966-69, 1970—. Chief economist, Regional Planning Association (New York), 1969-70. *Military service:* U.S. Air Force, 1958-59. U.S. Air Force Reserve, 1958-64. *Member:* National Tax Association. *Awards, honors:* New York University Founders Day Award, 1967; Arthur D. Little Presidential Citations, 1967 and 1971.

*WRITINGS:* (With Dick Netzer and others) *Financing Government in New York City,* New York University, 1967; (with Robert Fraser and Thomas Miller) *Civil Aviation Development: A Policy and Operations Analysis,* Praeger, 1972.

*WORK IN PROGRESS: Aviation policy.*†

\*     \*     \*

## DONNELLAN, Michael T(homas) 1931-

*PERSONAL:* Born November 7, 1931, in Galway, Ireland; son of John J. and Nora (McNamara) Donnellan. *Education:* National University of Ireland, Dip. Social Sc., 1954; St. Mary's Theologate, Techny, Ill., further study, 1958-62; Catholic University of America, M.A., 1964, Ph.D., 1972; also studied at Universities of Paris and Salzburg, 1966-68. *Religion:* Roman Catholic. *Office:* Humanities Division, Siena Heights College, Adrian, Mich. 49221.

*CAREER:* St. Patrick's College, Donamon Castle, Ireland, instructor in biblical foundations, 1964-67; Belmont College, Belmont, N.C., instructor in contemporary religious thought, 1970-71; Catholic University of America, Washington, D.C., instructor in religion, 1971-73; University of Dayton, Dayton, Ohio, assistant professor of religious studies, 1973-75; Siena Heights College, Adrian, Mich., associate professor, 1975—, chairman of Social Science/Humanities Division, 1976-78. Instructor in graduate program at St. John College, Cleveland, Ohio, summers, 1969-72; visiting scholar, University of Michigan, 1978-79. Has conducted workshops for religion teachers and lectured in adult education programs. *Member:* American Academy of Religion, College Theology Society, American Association of Higher Education, American Association of Community and Junior Colleges. *Awards, honors:* Fellow in Academic Leadership Development Program, 1977-78; Lilly Foundation award, Colorado College, summer, 1977.

*WRITINGS:* (With Sean O'Riordan) *Young Christians Today,* Volume III, Geoffrey Chapman, 1967; *What to Believe: Changing Patterns in Religious Education,* Gill &

Macmillan (Dublin), 1968; *We Together,* Divine Word Publications, 1971; (editor with James Ebben) *Values Pedagogy in Higher Education,* Office of Professional Development, Siena Heights College, 1978. Also author of scripts for a series of religious television programs. Contributor of articles to theology and education journals.

\*     \*     \*

## DONOVAN, John C(hauncey) 1920-

*PERSONAL:* Born February 9, 1920, in New York, N.Y.; son of Michael J. and Myrtie (Tucker) Donovan; married Beatrice Witter, September 9, 1947; children: Carey, Christine, Martha, John. *Education:* Bates College, A.B., 1942; Harvard University, M.A., 1948, Ph.D., 1949. *Politics:* Democrat. *Home:* 56 Federal St., Brunswick, Me. 04011. *Office:* Bowdoin College, Brunswick, Me. 04011.

*CAREER:* Bates College, Lewiston, Me., instructor, 1949-51, assistant professor, 1951-53, associate professor, 1953-57, professor of government, 1957-59; administrative assistant to U.S. Senator Edmund S. Muskie, 1959-62; executive assistant to Secretary of Labor W. Willard Wirtz, 1962-64; U.S. Department of Labor, Washington, D.C., U.S. Manpower administrator, 1964-65; Bowdoin College, Brunswick, Me., DeAlva Stanwood Alexander Professor of Government, 1965—. Chairman, Maine State Democratic Committee, 1957-58; member of board of directors, Center for Governmental Studies; consultant to Ford Foundation and Center for Research in Social Systems; member of board of trustees, University of Maine, 1972—. *Military service:* U.S. Navy, 1942-46; served in Pacific; became lieutenant junior grade. *Member:* Northeastern Political Science Association, Phi Beta Kappa. *Awards, honors:* Distinguished Service Award, U.S. Department of Labor, 1965; grants from Ford Foundation and U.S. Department of Labor, for study in England, 1969-70.

*WRITINGS: Congressional Campaign: Maine Elects a Democrat,* Holt, 1957; *The Politics of Poverty,* Pegasus, 1967, revised edition, 1973; *The Policy Makers,* Pegasus, 1970; *The Cold Warriors,* Heath, 1974; (general editor) *Democracy at the Crossroads,* Praeger, 1978. Contributor of articles to political science and social science journals.·

*BIOGRAPHICAL/CRITICAL SOURCES: New Republic,* July 6, 1968; *Polity,* summer, 1976.

\*     \*     \*

## DORNER, Peter Paul 1925-

*PERSONAL:* Born January 13, 1925, in Luxemburg, Wis.; son of Peter (a farmer) and Monica (Ditmann) Dorner; married Lois Hartnig (a Red Cross worker), December 26, 1950; children: Cathy, Greg, Paul, Sara, Carrie. *Education:* University of Wisconsin, B.S., 1951; University of Tennessee, M.S., 1953; Harvard University, Ph.D., 1959. *Home:* 541 Woodside Ter., Madison, Wis. 53711. *Office:* Department of Agricultural Economics, University of Wisconsin, Madison, Wis. 53706.

*CAREER:* Harvard University, Cambridge, Mass., instructor in agricultural economics and economics, 1957-58; University of Wisconsin—Madison, professor of agricultural economics, 1959—; University of Chile, Santiago, professor of agricultural economics, 1963-65; Council of Economic Advisors, Washington, D.C., senior staff economist, 1967-68. Consultant to the Commission on Rights, Liberties, and Responsibilities of the American Indians, AID Washington D.C. and field missions in Latin America, President's

Panel on the World Food Supply, United Nations and UNDP, Harvard Development Advisory Service in Ethiopia, and U.S. Department of Labor. *Military service:* U.S. Army, Pacific Theater, 1944-46. *Member:* American Economic Association, American Agricultural Economic Association, Association for Evolutionary Economics.

*WRITINGS:* (Editor and contributor) *Land Reform in Latin America: Issues and Cases,* University of Wisconsin, 1971; *Land Reform and Economic Development,* Penguin, 1972; (editor and contributor) *Cooperative and Commune: Group Farming in the Economic Development of Agriculture,* University of Wisconsin Press, 1977. Contributor of research articles to *Yale Review, Journal of Land Economics, Inter-American Economic Affairs, American Journal of Agricultural Economics,* and other professional journals; also contributor of book reviews to periodicals. Member of editorial council, *Land Economics,* 1961—, *American Journal of Agricultural Economics,* 1968-71.

*WORK IN PROGRESS:* Research on economic development, agricultural development, land reform, rural poverty, and agricultural policies.

\* \* \*

## DOROCH, Efim Yakovlevitch 1908(?)-1972

1908(?)—August (?), 1972; Russian historian. Obituaries: *L'Express,* August 28-September 3, 1972.

\* \* \*

## DORRIES, William (Lyle) 1923-

*PERSONAL:* Born April 4, 1923, in Denison, Tex.; son of William A. and Hattie (Seal) Dorries; married Virginia Julian, December 21, 1947; children: David, Martha. *Education:* East Texas State University, B.S., 1942; Agricultural and Mechanical College of Texas (now Texas A&M University), M.S., 1952, Ph.D., 1955. *Religion:* Baptist. *Home:* 101 Kings Lane, Commerce, Tex. 75428. *Office:* Department of Economics-Finance, East Texas State University, Commerce, Tex. 75428.

*CAREER:* Auburn University, Auburn, Ala., assistant professor, 1954-55; East Texas State University, Commerce, instructor, 1955-56, assistant professor, 1956-57, associate professor, 1957-67, professor of economics and finance, 1967—, chairman of department, 1970—. Director, Blossom Telephone Company, 1963—; member of tax equalization boards of city and public schools, 1968, 1972—. *Military service:* U.S. Army Air Forces, 1943-46. *Member:* American Economic Association, Southwestern Social Science Association, Texas Association of College Teachers, Phi Delta Kappa, Delta Sigma Pi, Omicron Delta Epsilon.

*WRITINGS:* (With Frances Potts and John Lewis) *Texas in Maps,* East Texas State University Press, 1966; (with Arthur A. Smith and James R. Young) *Personal Finance,* C. E. Merrill, 1974. Contributor of articles to *Southwestern Social Science Quarterly.*

\* \* \*

## DORSEN, Norman 1930-

*PERSONAL:* Born September 4, 1930, in New York, N.Y.; son of Arthur and Tanya (Stone) Dorsen; married Harriette Koffler, November 25, 1965; children: Jennifer, Caroline, Anne. *Education:* Columbia University, B.A., 1950; Harvard University, LL.B., 1953; London School of Economics and Political Science, London, additional study, 1955-56. *Home:* 146 Central Park West, New York, N.Y. 10023. *Of-*

*fice:* School of Law, New York University, 40 Washington Sq. S., New York, N.Y. 10012.

*CAREER:* Law clerk to Calvert Magruder, chief judge of U.S. Court of Appeals for First Circuit, 1956-57, to Justice John M. Harlan of U.S. Supreme Court, 1957-58; Dewey, Ballantine, Bushby, Palmer & Wood, New York City, law clerk, 1958-60; New York University, School of Law, New York City, professor of constitutional law, 1961—. American Civil Liberties Union, New York City, general counsel, 1968-76, chairman of board of directors, 1976—. Chairman and secretary, review panel on new drug regulation, U.S. Department of Health, Education, and Welfare. Chairman, Committee for Public Justice; director of special committee on courtroom conduct, New York City Bar Association. *Military service:* U.S. Army, 1953-55; became first lieutenant. *Member:* American Law Institute, American Bar Association.

*WRITINGS:* (Editor with Thomas Irwin Emerson and David Haber) *Political and Civil Rights in the United States,* Little, Brown, Volume I, 3rd edition (Dorsen was not associated with earlier editions), 1967, 4th edition, 1976, Volume II, 3rd edition (Dorsen was not associated with earlier editions), 1967, 4th edition, 1978; *Frontiers of Civil Liberties* (preface by Robert F. Kennedy), Pantheon, 1968; *Discrimination and Civil Rights* (abbreviated version of Volume II, 3rd edition of *Political and Civil Rights in the United States),* Little, Brown, 1969; (editor) *The Rights of Americans; What They Are–What They Should Be: Essays Commemorating the 50th Anniversary of the American Civil Liberties Union,* Pantheon, 1971; (with Leon Friedman) *Disorder in the Court: Report of the Association of the Bar of the City of New York Special Committee on Courtroom Conduct,* Pantheon, 1973; (editor with Stephen Gillers) *None of Your Business: Government Secrecy in America,* Viking, 1974. Contributor to law journals.

*AVOCATIONAL INTERESTS:* Baseball, mystery stories, country living.

*BIOGRAPHICAL/CRITICAL SOURCES: Saturday Review,* November 9, 1968; *New York Times Book Review,* November 24, 1968; *New York Times,* December, 1976.

\* \* \*

## DOTY, James Edward 1922-

*PERSONAL:* Born May 8, 1922, in Lakewood, Ohio; son of Ordello Luce and Margaret (McCurdy) Doty; married Mary Merciel Smith, September 8, 1943; children: Mark Allen, David Wesley, Martha Suzanne. *Education:* Mount Union College, A.B., 1944; Boston University, S.T.B. (cum laude), 1947, Ph.D., 1959; also studied at Harvard University and Oxford University. *Address:* 3333 South Alameda 1-D, Corpus Christi, Tex. 78411.

*CAREER:* Ordained Methodist minister, 1945; pastor of Methodist churches in Alliance, Ohio, 1942-43, Hatteras Island, N.C., 1943-44, Salem, Mass., 1947-51, and Lynn, Mass., 1951-57; Indiana Area of the Methodist Church, Indianapolis, director of pastoral care and counseling, 1957-66; Baker University, Baldwin City, Kan., president, 1966-73; Corpus Christi Pastoral Counseling Center, Corpus Christi, Tex., director, 1973—. Psychological counselor, Boston Dispensary, 1948-49; member of faculty, Boston Center for Adult Education, 1949-53. Special lecturer at Union Theological Seminary, Buenos Aires, Argentina, 1962, Methodist Theological Seminary, Sao Paolo, Brazil, 1962, Epworth Theological Seminary, Salisbury, Rhodesia, 1963, Methodist Theological Seminary, Mulungwishi, Congo, 1964, and

Trinity Theological College, Singapore, 1967. World Methodist Family Life Committee, treasurer, 1971—, and chairman of North American section. Member of first student Christian Movement Conference in postwar Germany, University of Heidelberg, summer, 1947; delegate to World Family Life Consultation, Birmingham, England, 1966. WFBM-Television, "Insight," panelist for weekly broadcast, 1957-66; has appeared in national television programs; has founded twelve pastoral care and counseling centers in New England and the Midwest.

*MEMBER:* American Psychological Association, American Association of Pastoral Counselors (fellow), American Association of Marriage and Family Counselors, Southwest Texas Conference of the United Methodist Church, Associated Independent Colleges of Kansas (president, 1968-69), Kansas Foundation for Private Colleges (president, 1970-71), Sigma Alpha Epsilon, Corpus Christi Country Club, Neuces Club, Rotarian. *Awards, honors:* D.D., Mount Union College, 1965; D.D., De Pauw University, 1966; Boston University School of Theology distinguished alumnus, 1971.

*WRITINGS: The Pastor as Agape Counselor,* John Woolman, 1964; *Postmark Lambarene: A Visit with Albert Schweitzer,* John Woolman, 1965; (editor) *Authentic Man Encounters God's World,* Baker University Press, 1967; (editor) *Students Search for Meaning,* Lowell Press, 1971. Contributor of articles to religious magazines and newspapers.

*WORK IN PROGRESS: The Church and Counseling; Albert Schweitzer: Reverence for Life.*

\* \* \*

## DOWLING, Joseph A(lbert)　1926-

*PERSONAL:* Born November 10, 1926, in Dalmuir, Scotland; naturalized U.S. citizen; son of Joseph Albert (a soldier) and Maud (Mitchell) Dowling; married Sylvia Minkin, June 16, 1956; children: David, Kathryn, Juliet, Marc. *Education:* Lincoln Memorial University, A.B., 1948; New York University, M.A., 1951, Ph.D., 1958. *Politics:* Democrat. *Home:* R.D. 1, Zionsville, Pa. 18092. *Office:* Department of History, Lehigh University, Bethlehem, Pa. 18018.

*CAREER:* Shorter College, Rome, Ga., instructor in English and history, 1952-53; Bates College, Lewiston, Me., instructor in cultural heritage, 1955-58; Lehigh University, Bethlehem, Pa., assistant professor, 1958-61, associate professor, 1961-67, professor of history, 1967—, distinguished professor, 1974. *Military service:* U.S. Army, 1945-46. *Member:* American Historical Association, Organization of American Historians, American Studies Association (president of middle Atlantic states section, 1969-70).

*WRITINGS:* (Editor with Merle Curti, Willard Thorp, and Carlos Baker) *American Issues: The Social Record,* Lippincott, 1971; (contributor) Lawrence Leder, editor, *The Colonial Legacy,* Harper, 1971. Contributor to professional journals.

*WORK IN PROGRESS:* A psycho-historical study of American millenarianism.

\* \* \*

## DOWNS, Jacques M.　1926-

*PERSONAL:* Born February 11, 1926, in Detroit, Mich.; son of Jacques S. (a newspaperman) and Elizabeth (Watson) Downs; married Eva M. von Huene (an educational supervisor of Head Start Program), February 14, 1960; children:

Andreae, Jonathan, Alexander. *Education:* University of California, Berkeley, A.B., 1948, M.A., 1950; Georgetown University, Ph.D., 1961. *Politics:* Democratic. *Religion:* Congregational. *Home address:* Box 356A, Kennebunkport, Me. 04046. *Office:* Department of History, St. Francis College, Biddeford, Me. 04005.

*CAREER:* Department of State, Washington, D.C., analyst, 1955-58, Port of Spain, Trinidad, vice-consul, 1958-59; St. Francis College, Biddeford, Me., instructor, 1961-62, assistant professor, 1962-65, associate professor, 1966-71, professor of American history, 1971—, head of department, 1967—. *Military service:* U.S. Army, 1951-54. *Member:* American Historical Association, Society for Historians of American Foreign Relations, Economic History Association, Society for the History of Technology.

*WRITINGS:* (Editor with Arthur M. Johnson) *Case Studies in Business History and Economic Life,* D. H. Mark, 1970. Contributor of articles to *Business History Review, Pacific History Review, Rhode Island History.*

*WORK IN PROGRESS:* A study of the American community at Canton, 1784-1844; first American diplomatic mission to China, 1843-44; American commercial diaspora, 1783-1860.

\* \* \*

## DOYNO, Victor A(nthony)　1937-

*PERSONAL:* Born July 12, 1937, in Chicago, Ill.; son of Victor A. (a salesman) and Sally (Finnegan) Doyno; married Ellen J. Kuchar, August 22, 1959; children: David, Ken, Anna Jo. *Education:* University of Miami, Oxford, Ohio, B.A., 1959; Harvard University, M.A., 1960; Indiana University, Ph.D., 1966. *Religion:* Unitarian Universalist. *Home:* 80 Meadowbrook Rd., Williamsville, N.Y. 14221. *Office:* Department of English, State University of New York, Buffalo, N.Y. 14214.

*CAREER:* Rutgers University, New Brunswick, N.J., instructor in English, 1964-65; Princeton University, Princeton, N.J., instructor in English, 1965-66; State University of New York at Buffalo, assistant professor, 1966-69, associate professor of English, 1969—, associate dean of undergraduate education, 1977-78.

*WRITINGS: Parthenophil and Parthenophe,* Southern Illinois University Press, 1971. Contributor to literature journals.

*WORK IN PROGRESS:* Research on Mark Twain, film, and genetic criticism.

\* \* \*

## DRAKE, Richard Bryant　1925-

*PERSONAL:* Born August 5, 1925, in Ames, Iowa; son of G. Bryant (a minister) and Alberta (Stimpson) Drake; married Julia Leland Angevine (a musician), September 5, 1945; children: Anne Elizabeth, John Bryant, Margaret Ellen. *Education:* Doane College, A.B., 1948; University of Chicago, M.A., 1950; Emory University, Ph.D., 1957. *Politics:* Democrat. *Religion:* Congregationalist. *Home:* 110 Van Winkle Grove, Berea, Ky. 40403. *Office:* Department of History, Berea College, Berea, Ky. 40404.

*CAREER:* Piedmont College, Demorest, Georgia, professor of history, 1950-53; Agnes Scott College, Decatur, Georgia, instructor in history, 1955-56; Berea College, Berea, Kentucky, instructor, 1956-57, assistant professor, 1957-61, associate professor, 1961-67, professor of history and political science, 1967—, chairman of department, 1958—. Berea Planning and Zoning Committee, chairman, 1958-70. *Military service:* U.S. Naval Reserve, 1943-48. *Member:* American Historical Association, Southern Historical Association, American Studies Association (regional president, 1967), American Association of University Professors (state vice-president, 1970-72).

*WRITINGS:* (Editor) *An Appalachian Reader,* Berea College, 1970; *Mountaineers and Americans,* Berea College, 1976. Contributor of articles to *Mountain Life and Work, Journal of Southern History, Negro History Bulletin,* and *The Churchman.* Editor, *Appalachian Notes,* 1973—.

*WORK IN PROGRESS: A History of Appalachian America; Of Mountains, Technology, and History.*

\* \* \*

## DRANGE, Theodore M. 1934-

*PERSONAL:* Surname rhymes with "range"; born March 14, 1934, in New York, N.Y.; son of Louis Magnus (a carpenter) and Enni Maria (Seppa) Drange; married Annette Lee Soy, August 12, 1959; children: Susan, Michael. *Education:* Brooklyn College (now Brooklyn College of the City University of New York), B.A., 1955; Yale University, additional study, 1955-56; Cornell University, Ph.D., 1963. *Politics:* Democrat. *Religion:* None. *Home:* 521 Meridan St., Morgantown, W.Va. 26505. *Office:* Department of Philosophy, West Virginia University, Morgantown, W.Va. 26505.

*CAREER:* Brooklyn College of the City University of New York, Brooklyn, N.Y., instructor in philosophy, 1960-62; University of Oregon, Eugene, instructor, 1962-63, assistant professor of philosophy, 1963-65; Idaho State University, Pocatello, assistant professor of philosophy, 1965-66; West Virginia University, Morgantown, assistant professor, 1966-67, associate professor, 1967-74, professor of philosophy, 1974—. *Member:* American Philosophical Association, West Virginia Philosophical Society (vice-president, 1969-70; president, 1970-71).

*WRITINGS: Type Crossings: Sentential Meaninglessness in the Border Area of Linguistics and Philosophy,* Mouton, 1966. Contributor of articles to *Philosophical Studies, Mind, Journal of Critical Analysis, Journal of the West Virginia Philosophical Society,* and *Philosophy and Phenomenological Research.* Editorial associate, *Journal of Critical Analysis,* 1975—.

*WORK IN PROGRESS:* Research in theory of knowledge and philosophy of language.

*SIDELIGHTS:* Theodore Drange told *CA* he is "an expert in the Oriental game of Go, with a rank of 1-dan."

\* \* \*

## DRANSFIELD, Michael (John Pender) 1948-1977
### (Edward Tate)

*PERSONAL:* Born September 12, 1948, in Sydney, New South Wales, Australia; son of John Francis (a company director) and Elspeth (Pender) Dransfield. *Education:* "Dropped out" of University of New South Wales, 1966, and University of Sydney, 1967. *Religion:* "I am of the race that sings under torture." *Address:* "Jumping Creek," Candelo, New South Wales 2550, Australia.

*CAREER:* Has worked as journalist, cleaner, postman, taxation assessor with the Federal Treasury in Australia, farmed his own land, and done on-camera work in television;

full-time writer. *Awards, honors:* Commonwealth Literary Award of Australian Broadcasting Commission, 1963-64; Harri Jones Memorial Prize for poetry, University of Newcastle upon Tyne, 1970; Commonwealth Literary Fund Fellowship, 1973.

*WRITINGS*—Under name Michael Dransfield: *Streets of the Long Voyage* (poems), University of Queensland Press, 1970; (assistant editor) *More Verse by Young Australians,* Rigby, 1971; *The Inspector of Tides* (poems; a section originally published in *Poetry Australia* under pseudonym, Edward Tate), University of Queensland Press, 1972; *Drug Poems,* Macmillan, 1972; *Memoirs of a Velvet Urinal* (poems), Maximus Books, 1975.

*WORK IN PROGRESS:* Researching for several prose works, "ranging from fiction to art monograph to early Australian history."

*SIDELIGHTS:* Michael Dransfield once told *CA* that he was born scion of an ancient baronial line, but soon escaped society and defected to the counter-culture. He continued: "The world poisons itself, ours is a sick age but the victims are the poor, the minorities. Cities exemplify the worst of man's nature." His lifestyle involved "living on my farm without the 'benefits' of western civilization."

*AVOCATIONAL INTERESTS:* "Getting into conservation, forest living, wandering, music, gold prospecting."†

(Died November 11, 1977)

\* \* \*

## DREYFUS, Edward A(lbert) 1937-

*PERSONAL:* Born March 27, 1937, in New York, N.Y.; son of Herbert and Estelle (Soussi) Dreyfus. *Education:* City College (now City College of the City University of New York), B.B.A., 1958, M.S., 1960; University of Kansas, Ph.D., 1964. *Office:* 921 Westwood Blvd., Los Angeles, Calif. 90024.

*CAREER:* Licensed psychologist and family, child, and marital counselor in state of California; licensed school psychologist in state of New York; City of New York, Bureau of Child Welfare, New York, N.Y., social investigator 1959-60; clinical psychology trainee in Veterans Administration hospitals in Kansas, 1961-63; Kansas University Medical Center, Kansas City, clinical psychologist, 1961-62; Kansas Reception and Diagnostic Center, Topeka, clinical psychologist, 1962-64; Veterans Administration Hospital, Topeka, Kan., clinical psychology intern, 1963-64; Veterans Administration Hospital, Palo Alto, Calif., clinical psychologist, 1964-65; clinical psychologist in private practice, 1965—. University of California, Los Angeles, associate director, Student Counseling Center, 1965-73, guest lecturer, School of Social Welfare, 1968—, instructor in psychology, 1969, lecturer, School of Dentistry, 1971-72, assistant clinical professor, department of psychiatry, 1977—. Field assessment officer and consultant, Peace Corps, 1968-70; supervisor and member of board of directors, Southern California Counseling Center, 1969-76; instructor, California School of Professional Psychology, 1970—; member of field faculty, Goddard College, 1971-74. Member of faculty, Lendenwood College, 1975-76. Member of attending professional staff, Calabasas Hospital-Neuropsychiatric Center.

*MEMBER:* American Psychological Association, American Association of Marriage and Family Counselors, American Association of Sex Educators, Counselors, and Therapists, Western Psychological Association, California State Psychological Association, California State Marriage and

Family Counselors Association, Los Angeles County Psychological Association, Los Angeles Society of Clinical Psychologists, Psi Chi.

WRITINGS: (Contributor) Carleton Beck, editor, *Guidelines for Guidance,* W. C. Brown, 1966; (contributor) Arthur Nikelly, editor, *Techniques for Behavioral Changes,* C. C Thomas, 1971; *Youth: Search for Meaning,* C. E. Merrill, 1972; *Adolescence: Theory and Experience,* C. E. Merrill, 1976. Contributor of about a dozen articles to professional journals.

WORK IN PROGRESS: *Single Fatherhood.*

\* \* \*

**DREYFUSS, Henry 1904-1972**

March 2, 1904—October 5, 1972; American industrial designer, and author of books on design and symbols. Obituaries: *New York Times,* October 6, 1972. (See index for *CA* sketch)

\* \* \*

**DRIBBEN, Judith Strick 1923-**

PERSONAL: Born November 5, 1923, in Rovno, Ukraine; daughter of Alexander (an industrialist) and Rachel (Pisiuk) Strick; married Edward Charles Dribben, January 12, 1954. *Education:* Attended Hebrew Gymnasium and University Ivana Franki, Lvov. *Politics:* "With the government in Israel." *Religion:* Jewish. *Agent:* Toni Strassman, 130 East 18th St., New York, N.Y. 10003.

CAREER: Became a spy at seventeen when her home town in the Ukraine was overrun by the Germans, taking a job as a maid to facilitate leading Nazi officers into partisan traps; eventually captured by the Gestapo, she survived three prisons, including Auschwitz, before escaping during a forced march; fought in the Russian Army, then fled to join the Irgun in Palestine; became a captain in the Israeli Army, its first woman intelligence officer, and military commander of Sde Boker, Negev, 1952-54; later managed a kibbutz; translator and collator, working in Russian, English, German, and French, for Israel Program for Scientific Translations, Jerusalem, 1969—.

WRITINGS: *And Some Shall Live,* Keter, 1969; *A Girl Called Judith Strick* (autobiographical; foreword by Golda Meir), Cowles, 1970; *Good Morning, Life!,* Maariv, 1971. Author of series of short stories on territories occupied after the Six Days War.

WORK IN PROGRESS: *The Arabs That I Knew.*

SIDELIGHTS: In addition to Hebrew and the languages in which she translates, Judith Dribben understands Ukrainian, Italian, Spanish, and Arabic.

BIOGRAPHICAL/CRITICAL SOURCES: *Publishers' Weekly,* April 27, 1970; *Best Sellers,* July 15, 1970; *Baltimore Sun,* July 19, 1970.††

\* \* \*

**DROUIN, Francis M. 1901-**

PERSONAL: Born July 1, 1901, in Ottawa, Ontario, Canada; son of Arthur (a painter) and Maud (Lafleur) Drouin. *Education:* Laval University, B.A., 1923; Dominican College, Ottawa, Ontario, Ph.L., 1930; University of Fribourg, S.T.D., 1934. *Home:* 27 Bartlett St., Lewiston, Me. 04240.

CAREER: Ordained Roman Catholic priest of the Order of Preachers (Dominicans), 1928; professor of sacred theology,

1934-37; high school principal in Lewiston, Me., 1941-43; Dominican College, Ottawa, Ontario, prior, 1952-55; retreat master throughout United States and Canada, 1952-71; St. Ann's Church, Fall River, Mass., assistant pastor, beginning 1972. *Member:* American Theological Association, American Academy of Religion.

WRITINGS: *Autor des berceaux,* Levrier, 1937; *The Sounding Solitude: Meditations for Religious Women,* Alba, 1971. Contributor to *Etudes Medievales, Homiletic Pastoral Review, Emmanuel,* and other journals.

WORK IN PROGRESS: *The Theology of the Spirit.*†

\* \* \*

**DRUMMOND, Ian (Macdonald) 1933-**

PERSONAL: Born June 4, 1933, in Vancouver, British Columbia, Canada; son of George Finlayson (a professor) and Laura (a teacher; maiden name, Milne) Drummond. *Education:* University of British Columbia, B.A., 1954; University of Toronto, M.A., 1955; University of London, graduate study, 1957-58; Yale University, Ph.D., 1959. *Politics:* Liberal. *Religion:* Anglican. *Home:* 149 South Dr., Toronto, Ontario, Canada. *Office:* Department of Political Economy, University of Toronto, Toronto, Ontario, Canada M5S 1A1.

CAREER: Yale University, New Haven, Conn., instructor in economics, 1958-60; University of Toronto, Toronto, Ontario, lecturer, 1960-62, assistant professor, 1962-65, associate professor, 1965-71, professor of economics, 1971—, chairman of department of political economy, 1977—. Visiting professor at Princeton University and University of Edinburgh. Technical officer in Economic and Research Bureau, Canadian Department of Labour, 1961. Consultant to various Canadian governmental agencies. *Military service:* Royal Canadian Air Force Reserve, 1951-54; became flight lieutenant. *Member:* American Economic Association, Economic History Association, Canadian Economics Association, Royal Commonwealth Society, Economic History Society of Great Britain, Royal Economic Society.

WRITINGS: *The Canadian Economy: Structure and Development,* Irwin, 1965, 2nd edition, 1972; *Canada's Trade with the Communist Countries of Eastern Europe,* Private Planning Association, 1965; *British Economic Policy and the Empire, 1919-1939,* Allen & Unwin, 1972; *Imperial Economic Policy, 1917-1939,* Allen & Unwin, 1974; *Economics: Principles and Policies in an Open Economy,* Irwin, 1976. Contributor to economics journals. Managing editor, *Canadian Journal of Economics and Political Sciences,* 1965-67, *Canadian Journal of Economics,* 1967-69.

WORK IN PROGRESS: *The Floating Pound and the Sterling Area, 1931-1939.*

\* \* \*

**DUBIN, Samuel Sanford 1914-**

PERSONAL: Born March 12, 1914, in Newark, N.J.; son of Benjamin and Anna (Kaiser) Dubin; married Lydia Symons, October 9, 1943; children: Michael, Constance, David, Deborah. *Education:* Oberlin College, A.B., 1938; Columbia University, M.A., 1939; University of Illinois, Ph.D., 1950. *Home:* 102 Hillcrest Ave., State College, Pa. 16801. *Office:* Department of Psychology, 215 Shields Bldg., Pennsylvania State University, University Park, Pa. 16802.

CAREER: Menninger Clinic, Topeka, Kan., intern psychologist, 1939-40; Joseph E. Seagram, Louisville, Ky., psychologist, 1941-43; University of Colorado, Medical Center, Denver, Colo., chief psychologist, 1946-47; University of Illinois at Urbana-Champaign, instructor, 1947-49, research associate, 1949-50, assistant professor of psychology, 1950-52; U.S. Department of the Army, Personnel Research Department, Washington, D.C., supervisory psychologist, 1952-56; Pennsylvania State Department of Health, Harrisburg, research psychologist, 1957-60; Pennsylvania State University, University Park, Pa., professor of psychology, 1961—. Diplomate in industrial and organization psychology, American Board of Professional Psychologists, 1973; certified psychologist, Pennsylvania State Board of Psychologist Examiners, 1974. Lecturer, University of Maryland Overseas Program, 1966-67; visiting NATO lecturer in Europe, 1973; Sigma Xi lecturer in eastern United States, 1974-75, 1976-78; U.S. Information Agency lecturer in Asia, 1975, in Asia and Africa, 1976; keynote speaker at U.S. Civil Service Interstate Training Agency and Electric Energy Association. Director of numerous symposia and workshops. Consultant to Pennsylvania Research Associates, 1970-71, Westinghouse Corp., 1972-73, Industrial Management Institute, Tehran, Iran, 1974, National Science Foundation, 1977, and numerous other companies, organizations, and institutions. *Military service:* U.S. Army, 1943-46; became lieutenant colonel.

*MEMBER:* International Association of Applied Psychology (member of professional affairs executive committee, 1977), American Psychological Association (fellow; president of Division of Business and Industrial Psychology, 1966-68; member of task force on continuing education, 1976), National Science Foundation (member of steering committee on continuing education in science and engineering, 1976-77), American Society for Engineering Education, American Association of University Professors, Pennsylvania Psychological Association (fellow), Sigma Xi. *Awards, honors:* Invitation Lecture Tour Award, American Society of Chemical Engineers, 1971-72, 1972-73; Research Award, National University Extension Association, 1973.

*WRITINGS: Professional Obsolescence,* English Universities Press, 1971, Heath, 1972; (editor and contributor) *Motivation for Professional Updating,* Heath, 1972; (contributor) *Productivad y Dissarolla,* Centre National de Productivad, 1974; (contributor) *Education Yearbook,* Macmillan, 1975; *Keeping Up-to-Date,* American Management Association, in press.

Monographs; published by Pennsylvania State University, except as indicated: *Continuing Professional Education Needs of Engineers,* 1965; *Managerial and Supervisory Educational Needs of Business and Industry,* 1967; *Continuing Education Needs of National Resource Managers and Scientists,* 1971; *Maintaining Professional and Technical Competence of Older Engineers,* American Society for Engineering Education, 1973; *Adults as Learners,* 1974; (with others) *Management Development in Iran,* Industrial Management Institute, 1974; *Educational Needs Assessment,* 1978; *Women in Management,* 1978.

Contributor to *New York Times* and *Chicago Daily News;* contributor to numerous journals, including *Design News, Engineering Education, Continuing Engineering Studies Newsletter, Vocational Guidance Quarterly, Training and Development Journal, American Psychologist,* and *Adult Education.* Editor, *Continuing Education,* 1969-70.

*SIDELIGHTS:* Samuel Dubin writes: "Professional obsolescence and updating is a problem that confronts every professional including managers. As scientific information advances and technology proliferates, every scientist, engineer, technician and manager will have to cope with rapid changes and gaps in knowledge that will interfere with the performance of his job. This issue became critical in the 1950's when the knowledge explosion and rate of technological change accelerated at a rapid pace. As a result knowledge is doubling every seven to ten years; hence, undergraduate and graduate education is changing by approximately fifty percent every seven years. The impact of these events is that every professional must now be concerned with lifelong learning if he or she is to remain competent. We now recognize that keeping up-to-date is a multidimensional problem. It is strongly influenced by personal motivation and the work environment. The latter includes such conditions as organization climate, the job, manager-subordinate relations, peer interaction and management policy.... I became aware of the importance of this problem during my research on continuing education needs of engineers and scientists.''

\*    \*    \*

## DuBRUCK, Alfred J(oseph)  1922-

*PERSONAL:* Born October 5, 1922, in Detroit, Mich.; son of Alfred P. and Mary E. (Haverty) DuBruck; married Edelgard Else Conradt (a professor), June 15, 1957; children: Alfred John. *Education:* University of Michigan, B.A., 1949, M.A., 1950, Ph.D., 1962; also studied at University of Grenoble, 1950-51, and University of Lille, 1951-52. *Home:* 2045 South Hammond Lake Dr., West Bloomfield, Mich. 48033. *Office:* Department of Modern Languages, Oakland University, Rochester, Mich. 48063.

*CAREER:* Kalamazoo College, Kalamazoo, Mich., instructor, 1958-62; Oakland University, Rochester, Mich., assistant professor 1962-65, associate professor, 1965-71, professor of French, 1971—. *Military service:* U.S. Army, 1942-46. *Member:* Modern Language Association of America, American Association of University Professors.

*WRITINGS: Gerard de Nerval and the German Heritage,* Mouton & Co., 1965.

*WORK IN PROGRESS:* A book, *Theater of Nerval.*

\*    \*    \*

## DUCORNET, Erica  1943-
## (Rikki)

*PERSONAL:* Born April 19, 1943, in Canton, N.Y.; married Guy Ducornet (a painter and potter); children: Jean-Yves. *Education:* Bard College, B.A., 1962. *Home:* 49260 Le Puy-Notre Dame, Maine-et-Loire, France.

*CAREER:* Writer and illustrator. Drawings have been exhibited widely, notably in Czechoslovakia, 1966, Museum of West Berlin, 1969, 1972, Museum of Lille (France), 1973, Museum of Fine Arts (Belgium), 1974, and at International Surrealist Exhibition, Chicago, 1977. Began a puppet theatre for children, 1972. With husband, creator of game "Le Nouveau Jeu de Loto,'' 1975.

*WRITINGS—Fiction:* (Adapter and illustrator) *The Blue Bird* (juvenile), Knopf, 1970; (with husband, Guy Ducornet) *Shazira Shazam and the Devil* (juvenile; Junior Literary Guild Selection), Prentice-Hall, 1970; (under name Rikki) *The Butcher's Tales,* Intermedia, 1978.

Poetry; under name Rikki: *From the Star Chamber,* Fiddlehead, 1974; (self-illustrated) *Wild Geraniums,* Actual Size Press, 1975; (self-illustrated) *Weird Sisters,* Intermedia, 1976; *Knife Notebook,* Fiddlehead, 1977; *The Illustrated Universe,* Aya Press, 1978.

Illustrator: Paris Leary and Muriel DeGre, *The Jack Spratt Cookbook,* Doubleday, 1965; Guy Ducornet, *Silex de l'avenir* (poems), Pierre Jean Oswald, 1966; Mme. Leprince de Beaumont, *Beauty and the Beast* (translated from the French by P. H. Muir), Knopf, 1968; Guy Ducornet, *Trophees en selle* (poems), Traces, 1970; (under name Rikki; with Guy Ducornet) *Bouche a bouche* (erotic game book), Soror, 1975; (under name Rikki) Susan Musgrave, *Gullband,* J. J. Douglas, 1975; (under name Rikki) Matt Cohen, *The Leaves of Louise,* McClelland & Stewart, 1978.

Work represented in anthologies, including: *The Stonewall Anthology,* University of Iowa Press, 1974, *Minute Fictions,* 1976, 1977, and *La Domaine internationale du surrealism,* Le Puits de l'Ermite, 1978. Contributor of short stories and poetry to *Canadian Fiction, Radical America, Arsenal, Prism, Phases, Tri-Quarterly, Mundus Artium, Review Two, Malahat Review, Eleobore,* and other periodicals.

*WORK IN PROGRESS:* A novel, *Somnolencil,* to be published in Canada; a collage book for children.

\*     \*     \*

## DUFF, Margaret K.
### (Maggie Duff)

*PERSONAL:* Born in Cleveland, Ohio; daughter of Harvey Edward and Dulcie (Crim) Kapp; married Cloyd E. Duff (a musician), October 26, 1940; children: Jonathan Kapp, Barbara Duff Anderson. *Education:* Butler University, A.B., 1937; Case Western Reserve University, M.L.S., 1966; also studied at Cleveland Institute of Art. *Home:* 15515 Van Aken, Apt. 5, Shaker Heights, Ohio 44120. *Office:* Cuyahoga County Public Library, Cleveland, Ohio 44114.

*CAREER:* Cuyahoga County Public Library, children's librarian in Solon Branch, Ohio, 1966-70, specialist in children's work in Cleveland, Ohio, 1970—. Has exhibited paintings and sculptures in Cleveland and Indiana, and in private exhibits. Member of boards of trustees, Cleveland Orchestra Women's Committee, 1960-65, and Cleveland Institute of Music Women's Committee, 1970—. *Member:* Women's National Book Association, Ohio Library Association, Mu Phi Epsilon, Pi Beta Phi.

*WRITINGS*—Under name Maggie Duff: *Jonny and His Drum* (juvenile), Walck, 1972; *Rum Pum Pum,* Macmillan, 1978. Contributor to *Top of the News* and to library journals.

*SIDELIGHTS:* Margaret Duff received an artist's diploma in violin. *Avocational interests:* Music, art, books.

\*     \*     \*

## DUFFUS, R(obert) L(uther) 1888-1972

July 10, 1888—November 28, 1972; American reporter, editorial writer, biographer, historian, and essayist. Obituaries; *New York Times,* November 30, 1972.

\*     \*     \*

## DUFFY, Bernard C. 1902-1972
### (Ben Duffy)

January 2, 1902—September 1, 1972; American advertising executive and writer on advertising and publicity. Obituaries: *New York Times,* September 2, 1972.

\*     \*     \*

## DUGGINS, James (Harry), Jr. 1933-

*PERSONAL:* Born December 21, 1933, in Kansas City,

Mo.; son of James H. (a civil engineer) and Alberta (Greathouse) Duggins. *Education:* San Francisco State College (now University), B.A., 1961, M.A., 1964; University of California, Berkeley, Ph.D., 1970. *Home:* 69 Beaver St., San Francisco, Calif. 94114. *Office:* Department of Secondary Education, San Francisco State University, 1600 Holloway Ave., San Francisco, Calif. 94132.

*CAREER:* Mission High School, San Francisco, Calif., English teacher, 1962-65; Laney College, Oakland, Calif., instructor in English, 1965-69; San Francisco State University, San Francisco, 1969—, began as associate professor, currently professor of secondary education. *Military service:* U.S. Navy, 1951-54; served as a journalist. *Member:* International Reading Association, National Council of Teachers of English.

*WRITINGS: Teaching Reading for Human Values in High School,* C. E. Merrill, 1972; (with Daniel Fader, Tom Finn, and Elton McNeil) *New Hooked on Books,* Berkley Publishing, 1976. Contributor to education journals. Guest editor, *Phi Delta Kappan,* April, 1971.

\*     \*     \*

## DUMBLETON, William A(lbert) 1927-

*PERSONAL:* Born December 31, 1927, in Troy, N.Y.; son of Albert F. and Anne (Dougherty) Dumbleton; married Susanne Murphy, January 29, 1966; children: Kathleen, Timothy Albert, Molia. *Education:* New York College for Teachers (now State University of New York at Albany), B.A., 1950, M.A., 1952; University of Pennsylvania, Ph.D., 1966; University College, Dublin, M.A., 1971. *Home:* 51 Lenox Ave., Albany, N.Y. 12203. *Office:* Department of English, State University of New York at Albany, Albany, N.Y. 12203.

*CAREER:* State University of New York at Albany, assistant professor, 1956-63, associate professor of English, 1963—, director of undergraduate program in English, 1976—. Visiting professor at American University, Cairo, Egypt, 1964, and Union College, Schenectady, N.Y., 1965-66. *Member:* Modern Language Association of America, International Association for Study of Anglo-Irish Literature, American Committee for Irish Studies.

*WRITINGS: The Literary Relationship of Gerard Manley Hopkins and Robert Bridges,* University of Pennsylvania, 1967. Also editor of *The Sleep of the King and the Sword of Dermot,* by James Cousins, DePaul University Press. Contributor to *Ariel, Thought, Eire-19, Carleton Newsletter,* and other periodicals.

*WORK IN PROGRESS: James Cousins and the Irish Literary Renaissance; Stone in the Midst of All: Perspective in Irish Literature.*

\*     \*     \*

## DUNCAN, Pam 1938-

*PERSONAL:* Born August 16, 1938, in Oshkosh, Wis.; daughter of James F. (a professor) and Gladys (Killam) Duncan. *Education:* Wisconsin State College, Oshkosh (now University of Wisconsin—Oshkosh), B.A., 1958; University of Chicago, M.A., 1961; University of Wisconsin, Ph.D., 1968. *Home:* 424 Goldstream Rd., Victoria, British Columbia, Canada. *Office:* Department of Psychology, University of Victoria, Victoria, British Columbia, Canada.

*CAREER:* Wisconsin State Department of Public Welfare, Division of Corrections, Madison, psychologist, 1962-66; Milton College, Milton, Wis., assistant professor of psychology, 1966-67; University of Victoria, Victoria, British Columbia, assistant professor of psychology, 1967—. Consulting psychologist for Saanich Police Department, 1971—, and Department of Human Resources, 1976—. *Member:* American Association for the Advancement of Science, British Columbia Psychological Association.

*WRITINGS:* (Editor) *Readings in Contemporary Psychology,* Simon & Schuster, 1968. Contributor to *Child Development, Perceptual and Motor Skills,* and *Psychological Record and Focus.*

*WORK IN PROGRESS: Psychopathology and Canadian Literature;* research in client-active systematic desensitization, children's perceptions of parents, and patterns of laterality, aggression, and sexual deviance.

*AVOCATIONAL INTERESTS:* Strong interest in animals, breeding, environmental conditions, and sports.

\* \* \*

## DUNHAM, Lowell 1910-

*PERSONAL:* Born October 14, 1910, in Wellston, Okla.; son of James A. (a realtor) and Lola (Neeley) Dunham; married Frances C. Ranson (a professor), November 5, 1943; children: Kenneth Eugene. *Education:* University of Oklahoma, A.B., 1932, M.A., 1935; University of California, Los Angeles, Ph.D., 1955; further study at Royal Shakespeare Theatre School (Stratford-on-Avon), summer, 1969. *Politics:* Democrat. *Home:* 439 Chautauqua, Norman, Okla. 73069. *Office:* Department of Modern Languages, 202 Kaufman Hall, 780 Van Vleet Oval, University of Oklahoma, Norman, Okla. 73069.

*CAREER:* Latin and Spanish teacher in high school in Idabel, Okla., 1935-36; Central State College (now University), Edmond, Okla., instructor, 1936-37, assistant professor of Spanish, Latin, and French, 1937-40; Federal Bureau of Investigation (FBI), Washington, D.C., special agent, 1940-42, assistant special agent in charge of office in San Juan, Puerto Rico, 1942-46; University of Oklahoma, Norman, assistant professor, 1946-56, associate professor, 1956-60, professor of modern languages, 1960—, chairman of department, 1957—. *Member:* American Council of Teachers of Foreign Languages (vice-president, 1970; president, 1971), American Association of Teachers of Spanish and Portuguese (director of national placement bureau, 1959—), Modern Language Association of America, South Central Modern Language Association (vice-president, 1972; president, 1973), Phi Beta Kappa. *Awards, honors:* Andres Bello Literary Prize, Venezuelan Academy of Languages, 1949, for *Manuel Diaz Rodriguez: Maestro del estilo;* Juan de Castellanos Literary Prize, Miles M. Sherover Foundation, 1958, for *Romulo Gallegos: Vida y obra;* Knight of the Order of Liberator Simon Bolivar, 1976.

*WRITINGS:* (Editor) Romulo Gallegos, *Dona Barbara,* Appleton, 1942; (editor with Ramon Lavandero) Miguel de Unamuno, *Cuenca Iberica: Lenguaje y paisaje,* Lucero Editorial Seneca, 1943; *Manuel Diaz Rodriguez: Maestro del estilo,* Tipografia Americana-Caracas, 1949; (editor) Romulo Gallegos, *Una posicion en la vida: Collected Essays of R. Gallegos,* Humanismo, 1955; *Romulo Gallegos: Vida y obra,* Libreria Studium, 1957; (translator and editor) Alfonso Caso, *The Aztecs: The People of the Sun,* University of Oklahoma Press, 1958; *Manuel Diaz Rodriguez: Vida y obra,* Libreria Studium, 1959; (translator and editor with James H. Abbott) Leopoldo Zea, *The Latin American Mind,* University of Oklahoma Press, 1963; (editor with Ivar Ivask) *The Cardinal Points of Borges,* University of Okla-

homa Press, 1971; *Romulo Gallegos: An Oklahoma Encounter and the Writing of the Last Novel,* University of Oklahoma Press, 1974. Contributor of articles to Spanish journals.

*SIDELIGHTS:* Lowell Dunham has traveled through Europe and South and Central America. He was a personal friend of Venezuela's former president Romulo Gallegos, and was acquainted with other Venezuelan presidents, Betancourt, Leoni, and Caldera. *Avocational interests:* Cooking, collecting antique American cut crystal.

\* \* \*

## DUNLAP, Aurie N(ichols) 1907-1977

*PERSONAL:* Born September 4, 1907, in New York, N.Y.; son of Aurie Joseph (a custom house broker) and Gertrude (Nichols) Dunlap; married R. Alene Tubbs, 1932; children: A. David (deceased). *Education:* Union College, Schenectady, N.Y., A.B., 1929; Columbia University, A.M., 1931, Ph.D., 1955. *Politics:* Republican. *Home:* 1623 Eaton Ave., Bethlehem, Pa. 18018.

*CAREER:* Teacher of social studies in public high schools in Somerville, N.J., 1933-36, and Pelham, N.Y., 1936-47; Sampson College, Sampson, N.Y., assistant professor of history and government, 1947-48; Lehigh University, Bethlehem, Pa., assistant professor, 1948-57, associate professor, 1957-72, professor of international relations, beginning 1972. Member of Pelham Defense Council, Pelham, N.Y., 1942-45, Citizens' Urban Renewal Enterprise, Bethlehem, Pa., 1958-61, and Foreign Policy Association, Pa., 1948-61. *Member:* American Society of International Law, Westchester County Teachers' Association (president, 1945-46).

*WRITINGS: The Teaching of International Relations in the Secondary School,* Lehigh University, 1965; (editor) *Basic Cases in Public International Law,* MSS Educational Publishing, 1971; (editor) *Readings on National and Regional Foreign Policies,* MSS Educational Publishing, 1971; (editor) *Readings on National and Regional Foreign Policies: Supplement,* MSS Educational Publishing, 1973. Contributor of articles and reviews to *Union College Symposium, Lehigh Alumni Bulletin, Annals of American Academy of Political and Social Science,* and *Call-Chronicle* newspapers.

*WORK IN PROGRESS:* A text on national and regional foreign policies.†

(Died May 19, 1977)

\* \* \*

## DUNLAP, Leslie W(hittaker) 1911-

*PERSONAL:* Born August 3, 1911, in Portland, Ore.; son of Frederick Cephus (a contractor) and Alice (Taylor) Dunlap; married Marie Neese, April 15, 1933; children: Lesley Eileen (Mrs. William Lawrence), Bruce Michael. *Education:* University of Oregon, B.A., 1933; University of Freiburg, graduate study, 1933-34; Columbia University, A.M., 1938, B.S. (library service), 1939, Ph.D., 1944. *Home:* 326 Hutchinson Ave., Iowa City, Iowa 52240. *Office:* University of Iowa Libraries, Iowa City, Iowa 52240.

*CAREER:* New York Public Library, New York, N.Y., reference and general assistant, 1936-41; University of Wisconsin Library, Madison, head of acquisitions department, 1942-45; Library of Congress, Washington, D.C., assistant chief of general reference and bibliography division and assistant chief of manuscript division, 1945-49; University of British Columbia, Vancouver, librarian, 1949-51; University of Illinois Library, Urbana, associate director and professor, 1951-58; University of Iowa, Iowa City, director of libraries, 1958-70, dean of library administration, 1970—. Chairman of board of directors for Center for Research Libraries, 1964-65; consultant and examiner for North Central Association Commission on Institutions of Higher Education, 1965—; member, National Commission on Libraries and Information Science, 1971-75; member of executive committee, Midwest Regional Library Network, 1976-77. Member of board, United States Capitol Historical Society and Jay N. Darling Foundation.

*MEMBER:* American Association for State and Local History, American Library Association, Association of College and Research Libraries, Manuscript Society, Iowa Library Association (president, 1969), Phi Beta Kappa.

*WRITINGS:* (Editor) *The Letters of Willis Gaylord Clark and Lewis Gaylord Clark,* New York Public Library, 1940; (compiler) *Our New Army: A Compilation of Recent Publications,* New York Public Library, 1941; *American Historical Societies, 1790-1860,* privately printed, 1944; *Readings in Library History,* Bowker, 1972. Also co-editor of *The Publication of American Historical Manuscripts,* 1975. Contributor to library and historical journals.

\*    \*    \*

## DUNN, Catherine M(ary) 1930-

*PERSONAL:* Born March 5, 1930, in San Diego, Calif.; daughter of Perley Barton and Amelia (Timmerman) Dunn. *Education:* Immaculate Heart College, B.M., 1951, M.A., 1962; University of California, Los Angeles, Ph.D., 1967. *Politics:* Republican. *Religion:* Roman Catholic. *Residence:* Northridge, Calif. *Office:* Department of English, California State University, 1811 Nordhoff St., Northridge, Calif. 91330.

*CAREER:* High school teacher, 1952-59; Immaculate Heart College, Los Angeles, Calif., instructor in English, 1960-66; California State University, Northridge, assistant professor, 1967-70, associate professor, 1970-74, professor of English, 1974—. *Member:* Modern Language Association of America, Philological Association of the Pacific Coast, Southern California Renaissance Society. *Awards, honors:* National Endowment for the Humanities grant, 1973-75.

*WRITINGS:* (Editor) *The Logike of Peter Ramus,* Renaissance Editions, 1969; (editor) Henry Cornelius Agrippa, *Of the Vanitie and Uncertaintie of Artes and Sciences,* Renaissance Editions, 1974; (contributor) Marlene Springer, editor, *What Manner of Woman: Essays on English and American Life and Literature,* New York University Press, 1977. Contributor of articles to *Shakespeare Quarterly.* Editor of *Renaissance Editions.*

*WORK IN PROGRESS:* A translation and critical edition of Julius Caesar Scaliger's *Poetices Libri Septem;* an article on J. C. Scaliger for *Milton Encyclopedia.*

*SIDELIGHTS:* Catherine Dunn originated the Renaissance Editions Series at California State University, Northridge.

\*    \*    \*

## DUNN, William L(awrence, Jr.) 1924-

*PERSONAL:* Born April 19, 1924, in Richmond, Va.; son of William Lawrence, Sr. and Emily (Noble) Dunn; married Elizabeth Olechnovitch (a language teacher), June 12, 1948; children: Olga, William Mark, Alexandra, Lawrence Alexis. *Education:* Lynchburg College, B.S., 1947; Duke University, Ph.D., 1953. *Home:* 4614 King William Rd., Rich-

mond, Va. 23225. *Office address:* Philip-Morris Research Center, P.O. Box 26583, Richmond, Va. 23261.

*CAREER:* Veterans Administration Hospital, Richmond, Va., clinical psychologist, 1954-61; Philip-Morris Research Center, Richmond, associate principal scientist, 1961-75, principal scientist, 1975—. *Military service:* U.S. Naval Reserve, 1942-46; became lieutenant. *Member:* American Psychological Association, Virginia Psychological Association (president, 1966-67), Virginia Board of Psychologists Examiners (chairman, 1968-71).

*WRITINGS:* (Editor) *Smoking Behavior, Incentives and Motives,* V. H. Winston & Sons, 1972. Contributor of articles to *Journal of Personality, World Tobacco Journal.*

*WORK IN PROGRESS:* Investigations of the explanation for cigarette smoking.

\*    \*    \*

## DURATSCHEK, (Mary) Claudia 1894-
### (Sister Mary Claudia Duratschek)

*PERSONAL:* Born March 2, 1894, in Wecehaza, Hungary; daughter of Frank J. (a farmer) and Clara (Filibek) Duratschek. *Education:* Creighton University, Ph.B., 1934; Marquette University, M.A., 1940; Catholic University of America, Ph.D., 1943. *Politics:* Republican. *Home:* Sacred Heart Convent, Yankton, S.D. 57078.

*CAREER:* Roman Catholic nun of the Order of St. Benedict; teacher and principal of junior and senior high schools, 1916-1939; Mount Marty College, Yankton, S.D., professor of history and political science, 1943-70, professor emeritus, 1970—, head of department, 1950-69.

*WRITINGS: The Beginnings of Catholicism in South Dakota,* St. Meinrad Press, 1943; *Crusading along Sioux Trails,* St. Meinrad Press, 1947; *Travelers on the Way of Peace,* privately printed, 1955; *Under the Shadow of His Wings,* North Plains Press, 1971. Contributor of articles to *New Catholic Encyclopedia* and *Dakota Panorama.*

*WORK IN PROGRESS: Builders of God's Kingdom: The History of the Catholic Church in South Dakota.*

\*    \*    \*

## DUROCHE, Leonard L(eRoy) 1933-

*PERSONAL:* Born June 3, 1933, in Kansas City, Mo.; son of Eugene Addison and Mary Elizabeth (Godfrey) Duroche; married Mary Betz (a technical editor), July 10, 1955; children: Leonard, Jr., Matthew, Lucy, Timothy. *Education:* University of Kansas, A.B., 1955, M.A., 1957; Stanford University, Ph.D., 1965. *Politics:* Democrat. *Religion:* Unitarian-Universalist. *Home:* 5015 Harriet Ave. S., Minneapolis, Minn. 55419. *Office:* Department of German, University of Minnesota, Minneapolis, Minn. 54455.

*CAREER:* State University of New York at Binghamton, instructor in German, 1961-65; Dartmouth College, Hanover, N.H., assistant professor of German, 1965-70; University of Minnesota, Minneapolis, associate professor of German, 1970—. Visiting assistant professor, Stanford University, summer, 1969. President, Norwich Development Association (Vermont), 1969-70. Director, National Endowment for the Humanities Summer Institutes, 1975, 1977. Advisor, National Center for the Humanities, 1977—. *Military service:* U.S. Navy, 1955-56. *Member:* International Association for Philosophy and Literature (member of executive committee, 1976-80; chairman of executive committee, 1976-77), Modern Language Association of America, American Association of Teachers of German, American Comparative Literature Association, Hoelderlin-Gesellschaft, Society for Phenomenology and Existential Philosophy, Northeast Conference on Language (adviser, 1966-70). *Awards, honors:* Fulbright fellowships, 1960, 1972-73; Society for the Humanities fellow, 1968-69.

*WRITINGS: Aspects of Criticism: Literary Study in Present-Day Germany,* Mouton, 1967. Contributor of articles and reviews to language and art journals. Member of editorial board, *Philosophy and Literature,* 1977—.

*WORK IN PROGRESS: Literature and Phenomenology: Foundations of an Existential-Phenomenological Aesthetic,* completion expected in 1980; a study of existentialist antecedents in German romanticism; research on mythic structure in nineteenth-century German literature.

*AVOCATIONAL INTERESTS:* Music, natural history, ornithology, conservation, trout fishing, wild foods.

\* \* \*

## DURR, Frederick R(oland) E(ugene) 1921-1978 (Fred Durr)

*PERSONAL:* Born July 16, 1921, in Washington, D.C.; son of Frederick George (an accountant) and Sara (Huddleston) Durr; married LaRaine Partington, September 7, 1947; children: LaRaine, Geoffrey, Linda, Diane. *Education:* Marietta College, A.B., 1949; University of Miami, Coral Gables, Fla., M.A., 1955; Ohio State University, Ph.D., 1961. *Office:* Department of Business and Economics, Salisbury State College, Salisbury, Md. 21801.

*CAREER:* College of William and Mary, Williamsburg, Va., associate professor of economics, 1961-62; University of Delaware, Newark, professor of urban economics, 1962-71; Florida International University, Miami, associate dean, 1971-72; Salisbury State College, Salisbury, Md., chairman of department of economics, 1972-78. Member of education faculty, Sales and Marketing Executives-International, New York, N.Y., beginning 1966. Served as consultant for Bell Telephone Co. of Pennsylvania, Westinghouse Corporation, Delaware Racing Commission, and Delaware State Highway Department. *Military service:* U.S. Coast Guard, 1942-46, 1951-54; became lieutenant. *Member:* American Economic Association, Southern Economic Association.

*WRITINGS:* (Under name Fred Durr) *The Urban Economy,* Intext, 1971.

Monographs: *The Economy of the Wilmington Metropolitan Region: Current Status and Future Prospects,* Division of Urban Affairs, University of Delaware, 1963; (with Robert W. Cook) *An Economic Base Study of the Greater Wilmington Region,* Division of Urban Affairs, University of Delaware, 1963. Also author, with Baline Schmidt and Eugene Johnson, of a monograph, *The Economic Impact of Horse Racing on the State of Delaware,* 1973.†

(Died, 1978)

\* \* \*

## DVORETZKY, Edward 1930-

*PERSONAL:* Born December 29, 1930, in Houston, Tex.; son of Max (a salesman) and Anna Lea (Greenfield) Dvoretzky; married Charlotte Silversteen, August 1, 1953; children: Toban. *Education:* Rice University, B.A., 1953; Harvard University, M.A., 1954, Ph.D., 1959. *Home:* 2035 Ridgeway Dr., Iowa City, Iowa 52240. *Office:* Department of German, University of Iowa, Iowa City, Iowa 52240.

*CAREER:* Rice University, Houston, Tex., instructor, 1956-59, assistant professor, 1959-64, associate professor of German, 1964-67; University of Iowa, Iowa City, professor of German and chairman of department, 1967—. *Member:* Modern Language Association of America, Lessing Society, American Association of Teachers of German, Midwest Modern Language Association (chairman of German section, 1970-71), Phi Beta Kappa, Delta Phi Alpha. *Awards, honors:* Fulbright fellowship in Germany, 1953, 1958; Old Gold research fellowship, 1968.

*WRITINGS:* (Translator and author of introduction) Gotthold Ephriam Lessing, *Emilia Galotti,* Ungar, 1962; *The Enigma of "Emilia Galotti,"* Nijhoff, 1963; *The Eighteenth-Century English Translations of "Emilia Galotti,"* Rice University Press, 1966; *Lessing: Dokumente zur Wirkungsgeschichte 1755-1968,* Kuemmerle, Volume I, 1971, Volume II, 1972. Contributor of articles and reviews to language and other journals.

*WORK IN PROGRESS:* Translating Lessing's *Miss Sara Sampson* into English; a novel.

\* \* \*

## DYER, George E(dward) 1928-1974

*PERSONAL:* Born December 9, 1928, in Allen, W. Va.; son of Lew M. (a construction engineer) and Ruby (Scragg) Dyer; married Grace Wellman, May 28, 1949; children: Carl W. *Education:* Anderson College, B.S., 1958; Texas Tech College (now University), M.A., 1960, Ph.D., 1967. *Politics:* Democrat. *Religion:* Church of God. *Home:* 60 Belmont Dr., Little Rock, Ark. 72204.

*CAREER:* High school teacher in Big Spring, Tex., 1958-63; Howard County Junior College, Big Spring, instructor in political science, 1961-63; Texas Tech College (now University), Lubbock, instructor in political science, 1963-66; University of Arkansas at Little Rock, assistant professor, 1966-69, associate professor of political science, beginning 1969. Research assistant, Little Rock Chamber of Commerce, 1967; chairman, Pulaski County Election Study Committee, 1968-69; president, Academic Press of Arkansas, 1972. *Member:* American Political Science Association, American Association of University Professors (president of University of Arkansas at Little Rock chapter, 1970-72), Southwestern Social Science Association.

*WRITINGS:* (With others) *Politics in Arkansas: The Constitutional Experience,* Academic Press of Arkansas, 1972; (contributor) Johnye Mathews, *Composition for Composition,* Little, Brown, 1972.

*WORK IN PROGRESS:* Editor with Richard Griffin, *The New Southern Politics,* for Chandler Publishing.†

(Died September 5, 1974)

\* \* \*

## DYK, Walter 1899-1972

September 30, 1899—December 23, 1972; German-born American anthropologist, educator, and author of Navajo biographies and other works. Obituaries: *New York Times,* December 25, 1972.

\* \* \*

## DYOTT, George (Miller) 1883-1972

1883—August 2, 1972; American lecturer, photographer, explorer, and author of books on foreign countries. Obituaries: *New York Times,* August 3, 1972.

# E

**EARHART, H(arry) Byron   1935-**

*PERSONAL:* Born January 7, 1935, in Aledo, Ill.; son of Kenneth Harry and Mary (Haack) Earhart; married Virginia Margaret Donaho, September 2, 1956; children: Kenneth Clark, David Charles, Paul William. *Education:* Attended Knox College, 1953-56; University of Chicago, B.D. and M.A., 1960, Ph.D., 1965; also attended Columbia University, 1962, and Tohoku University, 1962-65. *Home:* 3814 Stonegate Rd., Kalamazoo, Mich. 49007. *Office:* Department of Religion, Western Michigan University, Kalamazoo, Mich. 49001.

*CAREER:* Vanderbilt University, Nashville, Tenn., visiting assistant professor of religions, 1965-66; Western Michigan University, Kalamazoo, assistant professor, 1966-69, associate professor, 1969-75, professor of religion, 1975—. Instructor, International Summer School in Asian Studies, Ewha Womans University, Seoul, South Korea, 1973. Advisor on Far Eastern religion to *Encyclopaedia Britannica. Member:* Association for Asian Studies, American Academy of Religion, American Society for the Study of Religion. *Awards, honors:* Fulbright fellowship to Japan, 1962-65, and to Korea, 1973; National Foundation for the Humanities grant, summer, 1969; American Council of Learned Societies and Social Science Research Council joint grant on East Asia, summer, 1970.

*WRITINGS:* (Contributor) *Studies of Esoteric Buddhism and Tantrism,* Koyasan University, 1965; (contributor) J. M. Kitagawa and others, editors, *The History of Religion: Essays on the Problems of Understanding,* University of Chicago Press, 1967; *Japanese Religion: Unity and Diversity,* Dickenson, 1969, 2nd edition, 1974; *The New Religions of Japan: A Bibliography of Western-Language Materials,* Sophia University Press, 1970; *A Religious Study of the Mount Haguro Sect of Shugendo: An Example of Japanese Mountain Religion,* Sophia University Press, 1970; *Religion in the Japanese Experience: Sources, Interpretations, and Illustrations,* Dickenson, 1973; (contributor) *Religious Ferment in Asia,* University Press of Kansas, 1974. Also contributor to *A Mountaineering Aesthetic;* translator from the Japanese, Shigeyoshi Murakami, *Japanese Religion: The Past Century.* Contributor to history of religions and Asian studies journals. Editor, *Religious Studies Review,* 1976—.

*WORK IN PROGRESS:* Research on the Japanese new religions.

*SIDELIGHTS:* H. Byron Earhart told *CA:* "Almost all my published writing has been on aspects of Japanese religion, but my first serious interest in the study of religion began when I was a student at Knox College, and John Collier, Sr. introduced me to the richness of the vision of the American Indians. During graduate school at the University of Chicago I continued this interest while studying under Mircea Eliade, and wrote an M.A. thesis on the world view of the Zuni Indians. But I was attracted to the study of Japanese religion, because it featured both active folk religion and more highly organized world religions. Study of Japanese language under Edwin McClellan, Japanese Buddhism under Shoson Miyamoto, and Japanese religion under Joseph M. Kitagawa prepared me for dissertation research in Japan under the supervision of Ichiro Hori. While in Japan from 1962 to 1965, I did additional language work and read Japanese materials on Shugendo, a highly syncretistic folk religious movement, and observed all the surviving rituals of the Shugendo headquarters around Mount Haguro in northeast Japan.

"Since completion of my doctoral dissertation in 1965, I have been teaching in the general area of East Asian religions, but almost all my research and writing has been concerned with Japanese religion. The fascination for the never-ending variety of Japanese religion that first attracted me to this subject still holds my attention. This subject includes elaborate shrine and temple rituals, as well as simple rice-transplanting celebrations, the national religion of Shinto as well as the Indian import of Buddhism and the Chinese imports of Confucianism and Taoism, a rich and varied tradition of several thousand years, as well as dynamic new movements.

"My first work in this area focused on the earlier historical period and the broad sweep of Japanese religious history, but increasingly my attention has been directed to the 'new religions' that have become conspicuous during the past hundred years. I collected information on the Japanese new religions during a 1969 trip to Japan, and gathered comparative information while observing Korean new religions during a 1973 trip to Korea. Soon I hope to begin writing a book on the Japanese new religions, in which I will attempt to assess the form and status of religion in contemporary Japan. Long-range plans include the possibility of a case study of one or more Japanese new religions, and perhaps a comparative study of new religions in East Asia. A number of other monographs on Japanese religion are planned, when time allows. In all my writings I am attempting to convey to the Western reader aspects of a tradition that never fails to interest me. I count myself lucky to be able to work full time in a field that I enjoy, and to write on topics of my own choice.''

\* \* \*

## EASTMAN, Ann Heidbreder 1933-
### (Margaret Ann Heidbreder)

*PERSONAL:* Born August 31, 1933, in Minneapolis, Minn.; daughter of H. Willis (in life insurance) and Margaret (Hislop) Heidbreder; married Arthur M. Eastman (head of English department, Virginia Polytechnic Institute and State University), 1973. *Education:* University of Michigan, B.A. (with honors), 1955; additional study at Columbia University, 1956-57, and New York University, 1957-59. *Religion:* Episcopalian. *Home:* 716 Burruss Dr. N.W., Blacksburg, Va. 24060.

*CAREER:* Macmillan Co., New York City, in sales promotion and editorial assistant, 1955-56; Alfred A. Knopf, Inc., New York City, promotion director and editorial assistant, 1956-57; Holt, Rinehart & Winston, New York City, assistant social studies editor, 1957-59; McGraw-Hill Book Co., New York City, promotion assistant in children's book department, 1959; Henry Z. Walck, Inc., New York City, school and library consultant, publicity director, and sales promotion manager, 1959-63; Random House, New York City, school and library consultant, 1963-64; Association of American Publishers, New York City, senior associate for education and library services, research director of National Book Committee, coordinator of Educational Media Selection Centers Program, program director of National Library Week Program, 1964-71; Harcourt Brace Jovanovich, New York City, director of education and library services, 1972-73; Chatham College, Pittsburgh, Pa., director of admissions, 1975-77; free-lance marketing, library, and conference consultant, 1977—. Organizer and officer, Publishers Library Promotion Group; organizer of Executive Women's Council of Pittsburgh. Member of advisory committee of the White House Conference on Library and Information Services, 1977—.

*MEMBER:* International Reading Association, Women's National Book Association (past vice-president; president of New York chapter, 1971-73; organizer of Pittsburgh chapter, 1975; national president, 1976—), American Library Association, American Association of School Librarians, Association for Supervision and Curriculum Development, National Council of Teachers of English, American National Standards Institute, Publishers Library Promotion Group (organizer and past officer), League of Women Voters, Zonta, Phi Beta Kappa, Phi Kappa Phi, Delta Gamma.

*WRITINGS*—All published under name Margaret Ann Heidbreder: (Editor) *The Buck Hill Falls Report: The School and Library Market*, Association of American Publishers, 1967; (with John Rowell) *Educational Media Selection Centers: Identification and Analysis of Current Practices*, American Library Association, 1971; (with C. P. Bomar and C. A. Nemeyer) *Guide to the Development of Educational Media Selection Centers*, American Library Association, 1972. Contributor to library and education journals, including *Publishers' Weekly, Library Journal,* and *School Libraries.*

*WORK IN PROGRESS:* With husband, Arthur M. Eastman, editing an autobiography of John Wrenshall.

## EBERSOLE, A(lva) V(ernon), Jr. 1919-

*PERSONAL:* Born June 27, 1919, in Liberal, Kan.; son of Alva V. (a civil servant) and E. Lucia (Cash) Ebersole; married Carmen Iranzo (a writer), September 24, 1949. *Education:* Mexico City College, B.A., 1949, M.A., 1951; University of Kansas, Ph.D., 1957. *Home:* 1510 Smith Level Rd., Chapel Hill, N.C. 27514. *Office:* Department of Romance Languages, University of North Carolina, Chapel Hill, N.C. 27514.

*CAREER:* Pacific School of Languages, San Diego, Calif., instructor in Spanish, 1951-52; University of Illinois, Urbana, instructor in Spanish, 1957-59; University of Massachusetts—Amherst, assistant professor, 1959-61, associate professor of Spanish, 1961-62; Adelphi University, Garden City, N.Y., professor of Spanish and chairman of department, 1962-68; University of North Carolina at Chapel Hill, professor of Spanish, 1968—. *Military service:* U.S. Marine Corps, 1937-41. U.S. Naval Reserve, 1944-45. *Member:* American Association of Teachers of Spanish and Portuguese, Modern Language Association of America, Asociación Internacional de Hispanistas, American Association of University Professors, Sigma Delta Pi, Pi Delta Phi.

*WRITINGS: El ambiente español visto por Juan Ruiz de Alarcón,* Castalia, 1959; (editor) Calderón de la Barca, *La desdicha de la voz,* Castalia, 1963; (editor) Juan Ruiz de Alarcón, *Obras completas,* Castalia, 1966; (editor) Guillén de Castro, *El Narciso en su opinión,* Taurus, 1968; *Cinco cuentistas contemporáneos,* Prentice-Hall, 1969; *Selección de comedias del Siglo de Oro español,* Castalia, 1974; (editor) Juan Ruiz de Alarcón, *La verdad sospechosa,* Catedra, 1976. Contributor to journals. Founder and editor, *Hispanófila,* 1957—; editor, *Estudios de Hispanófila,* and *Colección Siglo de Oro.*

*WORK IN PROGRESS:* A study of the complete works of Lope de Vega.

*AVOCATIONAL INTERESTS:* Music (presents concerts, with wife, specializing in Spain's Golden Age).

\* \* \*

## ECKARDT, A(rthur) Roy 1918-

*PERSONAL:* Born August 8, 1918, in Brooklyn, N.Y.; son of Frederick William (an electrician) and Anna (Fitts) Eckardt; married Alice Lyons (a free-lance writer), September 2, 1944; children: Paula Jean, Stephen Robert. *Education:* Brooklyn College (now Brooklyn College of the City University of New York), B.A., 1942; Yale University, B.D., 1944; Columbia University, Ph.D., 1947. *Politics:* Democrat. *Home:* Beverly Hill Rd., Box 619A, Coopersburg, Pa. 18036. *Office:* Department of Religious Studies, Maginnes Hall, Lehigh University, Bethlehem, Pa. 18015.

*CAREER:* Clergyman of United Methodist Church; Hamline University, St. Paul, Minn., assistant professor of philosophy and religion, 1946-47; Lawrence College, Appleton, Wis., assistant professor of religion, 1947-50; Duke University, Durham, N.C., assistant professor of religion, 1950-51; Lehigh University, Bethlehem, Pa., associate professor, 1951-56, professor of religion, 1956—, head of department, 1951—. Visiting professor of Jewish studies, City University of New York, 1973. Member of Committee of Church and Jewish People, World Council of Churches, 1964—; vice-president, Christians Concerned for Israel, 1970—; member of advisory council, Clinical Forum for Conscience, Medical Research Foundation. Member of board of directors and sponsor, American Professors for Peace in the Middle East;

sponsor, Youth Committee for Democracy and Peace in the Middle East. Member of council of fellows, National Institute on the Holocaust; member of board of directors, National Committee on American Foreign Policy.

*MEMBER:* American Academy of Religion (president, 1956), American Philosophical Association, American Society of Christian Ethics, Society for the Scientific Study of Religion, American Association of University Professors, Pi Gamma Mu. *Awards, honors:* Ford Foundation fellow at Harvard University, 1955-56; Distinguished Alumnus Award of Brooklyn College, 1963; Lilly Foundation fellow at Cambridge University, 1963-64; National Foundation for Jewish Culture fellow, 1968-69; L.H.D., Hebrew Union College—Jewish Institute of Religion, 1969; Rockefeller fellow, University of Tuebingen, 1975-76. Recipient with wife, Alice L. Eckardt, of Human Relations Award of American Jewish Committee of Philadelphia, 1971, Myrtle Wreath Achievement Award of Allentown chapter of Hadassah, 1971, and of Achievement Award of Eastern Pennsylvania Hadassah, 1975.

*WRITINGS: Christianity and the Children of Israel,* Kings Crown Press, 1948; *The Surge of Piety in America,* Association Press, 1958; *Elder and Younger Brothers: The Encounter of Jews and Christians,* Scribner, 1967; (editor) *The Theologian at Work,* Harper, 1968; (with wife, Alice Eckardt) *Encounter with Israel: A Challenge to Conscience,* Association Press, 1970; *Your People, My People,* Quadrangle, 1974. Also author, with Alice Eckardt, of *Long Night's Journey into Day,* 1978.

Contributor: Harold E. Fey and Margaret Frakes, editors, *The Christian Century Reader,* Association Press, 1962; Gregory Baum, editor, *Ecumenical Theology Today,* Paulist Press, 1964; George A. F. Knight, editor, *Jews and Christians,* Westminister, 1965; Gerald H. Anderson, editor, *Christian Mission in Theological Perspective,* Abingdon, 1967; *The Anatomy of Peace in the Middle East,* American Academic Association for Peace in the Middle East, 1969; James E. Wood, Jr., editor, *Jewish-Christian Relations in Today's World,* Baylor University Press, 1971; Harold Hart, editor, *Punishment,* Hart Publishing, 1972.

Editor of booklet, *Christianity in Israel,* American Academic Association for Peace in the Middle East, 1971. Contributor to more than fifteen scholarly journals. Editor, *Journal of American Academy of Religion,* 1961-69.

*WORK IN PROGRESS:* Research in the theology of politics.

*SIDELIGHTS:* "Reinhold Niebuhr has had a tremendous influence on my thought and theological viewpoint," Eckardt writes. "He brought together a profound understanding of human nature in the individual and society with a keen perception of how political and social institutions must be devised to protect and foster both."

*BIOGRAPHICAL/CRITICAL SOURCES:* Alan Davies, *Anti-Semitism and the Christian Mind,* Herder & Herder, 1964; *New York Times Book Review,* April 7, 1968; *Christian Century,* April 24, 1968, March 10, 1971; *Commentary,* June, 1968; *Western Humanities Review,* summer, 1968; Frank E. Talmage, *Disputation and Dialogue,* Ktav, 1975.

*              *              *

**ECKARDT, Alice L(yons)   1923-**

*PERSONAL:* Born April 27, 1923, in Brooklyn, N.Y.; daughter of Henry Egmont (an executive) and Almira (Palmer) Lyons; married A. Roy Eckardt (a professor of re-

ligion), September 2, 1944; children: Paula Jean, Stephen Robert. *Education:* Oberlin College, B.A., 1944; Lehigh University, M.A., 1966. *Politics:* Democrat. *Religion:* Protestant. *Home:* Beverly Hill Rd., Box 619A, Coopersburg, Pa. 18036. *Office:* Department of Religious Studies, Lehigh University, Bethlehem, Pa. 18015.

*CAREER:* Time, Inc., New York, N.Y., personnel interviewer and supervisor of office staff, 1944-46; Wisconsin Telephone Co., Appleton, commercial representative, 1947-48; Lehigh University, Department of Religious Studies, Bethlehem, Pa., lecturer, 1972-75, assistant professor, 1976—. Research associate for Rockefeller Foundation project in West Germany and Great Britain, 1975-76. Sponsor, Christians Concerned for Israel, 1971—; vice-president, American Friends of Nes Ammin, 1972—. *Member:* American Academy of Religion, American Professors for Peace in the Middle East, League of Women Voters, Lehigh University Women's Club (president, 1960-61), Wednesday Club. *Awards, honors:* Recipient with husband of Human Relations Award of American Jewish Committee of Philadelphia, 1971, Myrtle Wreath Achievement Award of Allentown chapter of Hadassah, 1971, and of Achievement Award of Eastern Pennsylvania Hadassah, 1975.

*WRITINGS:* (With husband, A. Roy Eckardt, and illustrator) *Encounter with Israel: A Challenge to Conscience,* Association Press, 1970. Also author, with A. Roy Eckardt, of *Long Night's Journey into Day,* 1978. Contributor to *Christian Century, Congress Bi-Weekly, Lutheran Forum,* and other periodicals.

*WORK IN PROGRESS: How Christianity Paved the Way to Auschwitz.*

*AVOCATIONAL INTERESTS:* British history, English churches, brass rubbing, birds, wildflowers, gardening.

*BIOGRAPHICAL/CRITICAL SOURCES: Christian Century,* March 10, 1971; Frank E. Talmage, *Disputation and Dialogue,* Ktav, 1975.

*              *              *

**ECKERT, Horst   1931-**
**(Janosch)**

*PERSONAL:* Born March 11, 1931, in Zaborze, Poland; son of Johann (a shopkeeper) and Hildegard E. (Glodny) Eckert. *Education:* Attended gymnasium in Zaborze, 1940-43, and textile design school in Krefeld, Germany, 1947-49. *Religion:* None.

*CAREER:* Author and illustrator of children's books.

*WRITINGS—*All under pseudonym Janosch and all self-illustrated except as indicated: *Onkel Poppoff kann auf Baeume fliegen,* Domino, 1964; *Das Auto hier heisst Ferdinand,* Deutscher Buecherbund, 1965; *Das Apfelmaennchen,* Parabel, 1965, translation published as *Just One Apple,* Walck, 1966; *Heute um neune hinter der Scheune,* Parabel, 1965, translation published as *Tonight at Nine,* Walck, 1967; *Ratemal, wer suchen muss,* Parabel, 1966; *Hannes Strohkopp und der unsichtbare Indianer,* Parabel, 1966; *Leo Zauberfloh: Oder, Wer andern eine Grube graebt,* Domino, 1966; *Poppoff und Piezke,* Parabel, 1966; *Der Josa mit der Zauberfiedel,* Parabel, 1967, translation published as *Joshua and the Magic Fiddle,* World Publishing, 1968; *Schlafe, lieber Hampelmann,* Parabel, 1967; *Raubenkoenig Muckelbass,* Domino, 1967; *Herr Wurzel und sein Zauberkuenstler,* Paulus, 1968; *Boellerbam und der Vogel,* Middelhauve, 1968, translation by Refna Wilkin published as *Bollerbam,* Walck, 1969; *Has Anyone Seen Paul? Who Will Be He?,* translated from the German by Margaret Green, Dobson, 1969; *Der Maeuse-Sheriff: Luegengeschicten aus dem Wilden Western, er logen von einer Maus,* Bitter Verlag, 1969; *Das Regenauto,* Ellermann (Munich), 1969, translation published as *The Magic Auto,* Crown, 1971; *Ach lieber Schneeman,* Parabel, 1969, translation published as *Dear Snowman,* World Publishing, 1970; *Drei Raeuber und ein Raben Koenig,* Parabel, 1969, translation by Elizabeth Shub published as *The Thieves and the Raven,* Macmillan, 1970.

*Leo Zauberfloh; oder die Leowenjagd in Oberfimmel,* Bitter Verlag, 1970; *Komm nach Iglau, Krokodil,* Parabel, 1970, translation published as *The Crocodile Who Wouldn't Be King,* Putnam, 1971; *Cholonek oder der liebe Gott aus Lehm,* Bitter Verlag, 1970; *Flieg Vogel flieg,* Parabel, 1971; *Loewe Spring,* Parabel, 1971; *Ene bene Bimmelbahn,* Parabel, 1971; *Lari fari Mogelzahn,* Parabel, 1971; *Gottfried Wilhelm Leibniz Scriptores rerum Brunsvic ensium,* Klostermann Verlag, 1971; *Autos Autos viel Autos,* illustrated by Friedrich Kohlsaat, Beltz Verlag, 1971; *Janosch erzahlt Grimms Marchen,* Beltz Verlag, 1972; *Bilder und Gedichte fuer Kinder,* Westermann Verlag, 1972; *Schulfiebel I,* Westermann Verlag, 1972; *Ich bin ein grosser Zottelbaer,* Parabel, 1972; *Wohin Rast die Feuerwehr,* [Munich], 1972; *Familie Schmidt,* Rowohlt Verlag, 1974; *Hottentotten gruene Motten,* Rowohlt Verlag, 1974; *Das starke Auto Ferdinand,* Parabel, 1975, translation published as *The Yellow Auto Named Ferdinand,* Carolrhoda, 1973; *Sacharin im Salat* (novel), Bertelsmann, 1976; *Die Globeriks,* Globi-Verlag, 1976; *Die Loewenreise,* Beltz, 1976; *Oh wie schoen ist Panama,* Beltz, 1976; *Das grobe Janosch Buch,* Beltz, 1976; *Die Maus hat rote Struempfe an Beltz,* Beltz, 1978; *Kasper Loeffel und seine gute Oma,* Parabel, 1978; *Ein Mann ein Kahn die Maus das Haus,* Parabel, 1978; *Das kleine Hasenbuch,* Parabel, 1978; *Schnuddelbuddel sagt gutnacht,* Parabel, 1978; *Baerenzirkus Zampano,* Parabel, 1978; *Ich sag du bist ein Baer,* Beltz, 1978; *Traumstunde fuer Siebenschlaefer,* Beltz, 1978. Also author and illustrator of numerous other juvenile books.

Illustrator: Mischa Damjan; *Filipo und sein Wunderpinsel,* Nord-Sued Verlag, 1967, translation published as *The Magic Paintbrush,* Walck, 1967; Jozef Wilkon, *Die Loewenkinder,* Middelhauve, 1968; Hans-Joachim Gelberg, *Die Stadt der Kinder,* Bitter Verlag, 1969; Jack Prelutzky, *Lazy Blackbird, and Other Verses,* Macmillan, 1969; Hans Baumann, *Der Wunderbare Ball Kada lupp,* Betz (Munich), 1969, translation published as *Gatalop: The Wonderful Ball,* Walck, 1971; Beverly Cleary, *Die Maus auf dem Motorrad,* Union Verlag, 1972; Cleary, *Mauserich Ralf Haut ab,* Union Verlag, 1972; Walter D. Edmonds, *Das Mausehaus,* Loewes Verlag, 1972; Anne Rose, *How Does the Czar Eat Potatoes?,* Lothrop, 1973; James Kruess, *Der Kleine Flax,* Oetinger Verlag, 1975; *Die Kikerikikiste,* Parabel, 1978; *Bombo,* Parabel, 1978; *Bombo kann alles,* Parabel, 1978; *Wasja kauft den Hund im Sack,* Thienemann, 1978; *Der Weihnachtsstern,* Oetinger Verlag, 1978; *Kaese Kaese,* Mosaik Verlag, 1978. Also illustrator of *Bonko,* by Hans Baumann, 1972, and *Die lustigen Abenteur des Kasperl larifari,* by Franz Graf von Pacci, 1972.

*BIOGRAPHICAL/CRITICAL SOURCES: New York Times,* November 3, 1968; *National Observer,* November 4, 1968.

\*     \*     \*

## ECKHARDT, Tibor 1888-1972

1888—September 3, 1972; Hungarian diplomat, lecturer, and historian. Obituaries: *New York Times,* September 5, 1972.

## EDMAN, David 1930-

*PERSONAL:* Born January 9, 1930, in Worcester, Mass.; son of Victor Raymond (an educator) and Edith (Olson) Edman; married Evelyn Buck, June 10, 1956; children: Sarah, Peter, Brita. *Education:* Wheaton College, Wheaton, Ill., B.A., 1955; Columbia University, M.A., 1959; Union Theological Seminary, B.D., 1959. *Religion:* Episcopal. *Home and office:* 26 Browns Ave., Scottsville, N.Y. 14546.

*CAREER:* Ordained Episcopal priest, January 10, 1959; Christ Church, Bronxville, N.Y., curate, 1959-62; Church of Christ the King, Stone Ridge, N.Y., priest-in-charge, 1962-65; Rochester Institute of Technology, Rochester, N.Y., chaplain, 1965-69; Grace Church, Scottsville, N.Y., rector, 1969—. *Military service:* U.S. Army, Corps of Engineers, 1951-53; became first lieutenant.

*WRITINGS: Of Wise Men and Fools,* Doubleday, 1972; *A Bit of Christmas Whimsy,* Concordia, 1974. Contributor of articles to *Reader's Digest, Christian Century, Christian Herald, The Living Church,* and other magazines.

*WORK IN PROGRESS:* A novel about an old minister who dreams of a trip to the Holy Land.

*SIDELIGHTS:* David Edman writes, "A life-long fascination with words has led me to the conviction that I would prefer being a failure as a writer than a success at anything else."

\*     \*     \*

## EDMONDS, Vernon H. 1927-

*PERSONAL:* Born December 18, 1927, in Clinton, Okla.; son of Clarence Lee (a farmer) and Mary Jane (Hurd) Edmonds; married Gloria Graves King, August 26, 1955; children: Kevin V. *Education:* Oklahoma State University, B.A., 1954; Purdue University, M.S., 1955; University of Missouri, Ph.D., 1962. *Politics:* Democrat. *Religion:* None. *Home:* 2 Travis Lane, Williamsburg, Va. 23185. *Office:* Department of Sociology, College of William and Mary, Williamsburg, Va. 23185.

*CAREER:* High school teacher of sociology and biology in Salem, Ind., 1955-56; Cottey Junior College, Nevada, Mo., instructor in sociology, 1956-58; University of South Florida, Tampa, 1960-63, began as instructor, became assistant professor of sociology; Florida State University, Tallahassee, assistant professor of sociology, 1963-67; College of William and Mary, Williamsburg, Va., 1967—, began as associate professor, currently professor of sociology. *Military service:* U.S. Army Air Forces, 1946-47; U.S. Air Force, 1947-49. *Member:* American Sociological Association, American Civil Liberties Union (chairman for Florida and member of national board of directors, 1965-67), Southern Sociological Society.

*WRITINGS:* (With others) *Human Behavior,* Volume II, W. C. Brown, 1962; (with others) *Social Behavior,* McGraw, 1964, 2nd edition, 1967. Contributor to sociology journals.

*WORK IN PROGRESS:* Writing on rightist ideology, universal themes, definition, and measurement, on a tentative theory of its acceptance and origination, and on personality correlates of conservative and rightest ideology.

\*     \*     \*

## EDWARDS, Jerome E(arl) 1937-

*PERSONAL:* Born March 11, 1937, in Seattle, Wash.; son of Earl C. (an auto mechanic) and Ora (Eckhart) Edwards;

married Elsie Hradsky (a teacher), November 6, 1971. *Education:* Yale University, B.A., 1958; University of Chicago, M.A., 1960, Ph.D., 1966. *Politics:* Democrat. *Religion:* Protestant. *Home:* 385 Bret Harte Ave., Reno, Nev. 89509. *Office:* Department of History, University of Nevada, Reno, Nev. 89507.

*CAREER:* University of Nevada, Reno, instructor, 1965-66, assistant professor, 1966-72, associate professor of history, 1972—. *Member:* American Historical Association, Organization of American Historians, Nevada Historical Society.

*WRITINGS: The Foreign Policy of Col. McCormick's Tribune, 1929-1941,* University of Nevada Press, 1971.

*WORK IN PROGRESS:* A political study of Nevada Senator Patrick A. McCarran.

\*     \*     \*

### EDWARDS, Julia Spalding   1920-

*PERSONAL:* Born October 6, 1920, in Louisville, Ky.; daughter of James P. and Margaret (Walthen) Edwards. *Education:* Barnard College, B.A., 1940; Columbia University, M.S., 1942, additional graduate study, 1966. *Home:* 2801 New Mexico Ave. N.W., Apt. 1110, Washington, D.C. 20007. *Office:* World Affairs Bureau, 2801 New Mexico Ave. N.W., Suite 1110, Washington, D.C. 20007.

*CAREER: Baltimore Sun,* Baltimore, Md., reporter, 1942-44; *Chicago Daily News,* Chicago, Ill., re-writer, 1944-45; *Stars and Stripes,* Germany, correspondent, 1946-47, Frankfurt bureau chief, 1948; Pulliam Newspapers, Washington, D.C., correspondent, 1949-50; U.S. Information Agency, Washington, D.C. and Tokyo, Japan, editor, 1951-52; Worldwide Press Service, New York City, managing editor, 1953-54; Research Institute of America, New York City, director of public information, 1955-56; free-lance writer and editor, New York City, 1957-67; World Affairs Bureau, Washington, D.C., director, 1968—. Final report writer, Conference on International Exchanges in the Arts; press coordinator, Sixth Conference on International Education. Business and economic writer for *Business International* and *Business Week. Member:* Overseas Press Club (Washington chairman, 1969-73), American Newspaper Women's Club, Authors Guild, National Press Club.

*WRITINGS: The Occupiers,* Fleet Press, 1967. Contributor of articles to magazines and newspapers in Korea, Vietnam, Germany, Japan, China, and more than 100 other countries.

\*     \*     \*

### EDWARDS, P(rior) Max(imilian) H(emsley)   1914-

*PERSONAL:* Born August 13, 1914, in Pau, France; son of Alfred Culmer (a dental surgeon) and Amy Louisa (Hemsley) Edwards. *Education:* University of British Columbia, B.A., 1949; Columbia University, M.A., 1952; Harvard University, M.A., 1956; University of Pennsylvania, Ph.D., 1959; studied in London, England, earning L.R.A.M., 1938, F.T.C.L., A.R.C.M., 1939. *Religion:* Episcopalian. *Home:* 3835 Clarndon Rd., Victoria, British Columbia, Canada V8N 4A4. *Office:* Department of French, University of Victoria, Victoria, British Columbia, Canada.

*CAREER:* University of Otago, Dunedin, New Zealand, lecturer in Russian, 1959-64; University of Victoria, Victoria, British Columbia, associate professor of modern languages, 1964—. Affiliated with Instituto Cultural Venezolano-Britanico, Caracas, Venezuela, 1942-46, director,

1945-46. *Member:* Incorporated Guild of Church Musicians (England), Canadian Association of Hispanists, Canadian Linguistic Association, Universala Esperanta Asocio (Rotterdam), Philological Association of the Pacific Coast.

*WRITINGS:* (Compiler with A. G. Juilland and Ica Juilland) *Frequency Dictionary of Rumanian Words,* Mouton (The Hague), 1965; (with A. G. Juilland) *The Rumanian Verb System,* Mouton, 1971.

*WORK IN PROGRESS:* Russian morphological analysis; a study of the compositions of C. W. Orr; a study of the artificial international languages proposed; research on language-learning and language-teaching; an analysis of the French verbal system.

*AVOCATIONAL INTERESTS:* Ufology—the study of unidentified flying objects.

\*     \*     \*

### EDWARDS, Rem B(lanchard, Jr.)   1934-

*PERSONAL:* Born October 2, 1934, in Washington, Ga.; son of Rem Blanchard, Sr. (a postmaster) and Opal (Vickers) Edwards; married Louise Blalock (a piano teacher), August 5, 1962; children: Rem B. III, Cherron Suzanne. *Education:* Emory University, A.B., 1956, Ph.D., 1962; Yale University, B.D., 1959. *Politics:* Democrat. *Religion:* Methodist. *Home:* 8709 Longmeade Dr., Knoxville, Tenn. 37919. *Office:* Department of Philosophy, University of Tennessee, Knoxville, Tenn. 37916.

*CAREER:* Jacksonville University, Jacksonville, Fla., assistant professor of philosophy, 1962-66; University of Tennessee, Knoxville, associate professor of philosophy, 1966—. *Member:* American Association of University Professors, American Philosophical Association, Society for the Philosophy of Religion, Southern Society for Philosophy and Psychology, Tennessee Philosophical Association, Phi Beta Kappa. *Awards, honors:* Danforth graduate fellow, 1956-62.

*WRITINGS: Freedom, Responsibility and Obligation,* Nijhoff, 1969; *Reason and Religion: An Introduction to the Philosophy of Religion,* Harcourt, 1972. Also author of *Qualitative Hedonism,* and *God, Freedom, and Enlightenment in Early American Philosophy.* Contributor of articles to *Mind, Continuum, The Monist, Philosophy of Science, American Philosophical Quarterly, The Personalist, Southern Journal of Philosophy, The New Scholasticism,* and *The Journal of Value Inquiry.*

*SIDELIGHTS:* Rem Edwards' areas of specialization in philosophy are ethics, metaethics, philosophy of religion, epistemology and American philosophy.

\*     \*     \*

### EFFINGER, Geo(rge) Alec   1947-

*PERSONAL:* Born January 10, 1947, in Cleveland, Ohio; son of George Paul and Ruth (Uray) Effinger. *Education:* Attended Yale University, 1965 and 1969, and New York University, 1968. *Politics:* ''Intermittent.'' *Religion:* ''A sort of nervous curiosity.'' *Home address:* Box 15183, New Orleans, La. 70175. *Agent:* Jane Rotrosen, 318 East 51st St., New York, N.Y. 10022.

*CAREER:* Free-lance writer. Writer for Marvel Comic Books, New York, N.Y., 1971—. *Member:* Authors Guild, Science Fiction Writers of America.

*WRITINGS: What Entropy Means to Me,* Doubleday, 1972; *Relatives,* Harper, 1973; *Mixed Feelings,* Harper,

1974; (with Gardner Dozois) *Nightmare Blue,* Berkley Publishing, 1975; *Irrational Numbers,* Doubleday, 1976; *Those Gentle Voices,* Warner Brothers, 1976; *Felicia,* Putnam, 1976; *Death in Florence,* Doubleday, 1978. Also author of *Dirty Tricks,* 1978. Contributor of over one hundred stories to anthologies and magazines.

*WORK IN PROGRESS: Blood Pinball,* for Dell; *Teflon,* for Doubleday; *Steal,* for Playboy Press.

*SIDELIGHTS:* Effinger told *CA:* "When I first began to write, seeing one of my stories in a magazine or one of my books on a shelf in a store was exciting. Unfortunately, that excitement wanes, although the excitement of the creative act itself never diminishes. Now, after eight years and a dozen books, my own gratification must come from somewhere else. I am glad, therefore, that I have many goals yet unachieved; I cannot imagine being able to write merely for the checks, as if writing were nothing more than a job. Writing is a joy, but the source of the joy is internal, now. The visible results mean less to me: the physical books, the money deposited in the bank, the reviews. I write for fun, and for a kind of self-challenge. I dare myself to develop a difficult idea. I do not know about my popularity among critics and readers, but as long as I get a kick out of watching my struggling characters, then I will stay at the typewriter. When that thrill ends, I think I will find something else to do. Maybe I'll be a professional bowler."

\* \* \*

### EFIRD, James M(ichael) 1932-

*PERSONAL:* Born May 30, 1932, in Kannapolis, N.C.; son of James R. (in textiles) and I. Z. (Christy) Efird; married Joan Shelf, June 30, 1951 (divorced November, 1971); married Vivian Poythress, March 7, 1975; children: (first marriage) Whitney Michelle. *Education:* Davidson College, A.B., 1954; Louisville Presbyterian Seminary, B.D., 1958; Duke University, Ph.D., 1962. *Religion:* Presbyterian. *Home:* 2609 Heather Glen Rd., Durham, N.C. 27712. *Office:* Duke University Divinity School, Durham, N.C. 27706.

*CAREER:* Ordained minister of Presbyterian Church, 1958; Duke University Divinity School, Durham, N.C., assistant professor, 1962-68, associate professor of Biblical studies, 1968—, director of academic affairs, 1971-75. *Member:* Society of Biblical Literature and Exegesis, Phi Beta Kappa.

*WRITINGS:* (Editor and contributor) *The Use of the Old Testament in the New and Other Essays,* Duke University Press, 1972; *These Things Are Written: An Introduction to the Religious Ideas of the Bible,* John Knox, 1978; *Daniel and Revelation: A Layman's Guide to Apocalyptic Literature,* Judson, 1978. Also author of *New Testament Introduction,* and *Luke and Acts: A Layman's Guide to Early Christian History,* both 1978. Contributor of articles to *Presbyterian Journal.*

*WORK IN PROGRESS: Proverbs, Job, and Ecclesiastes: A Layman's Guide to Wisdom Literature; Mark and Matthew: A Layman's Guide to the Gospels; Introduction to New Testament Greek.*

\* \* \*

### EGBERT, Donald Drew 1902-1973

May 12, 1902—January 3, 1973; American educator, scholar, and author of books on art, archaeology, and architecture. Obituaries: *New York Times,* January 5, 1973. (See index for *CA* sketch)

### EGGENSCHWILER, David 1936-

*PERSONAL:* Born October 11, 1936, in Canton, Ohio; son of Robert William (a machinist) and Gladys (Bernhardt) Eggenschwiler; married Jean Gilbertson (a teaching assistant), March 26, 1962; children: Jonathan. *Education:* Harvard University, B.A., 1958; Arizona State University, M.A., 1961; Stanford University, Ph.D., 1965. *Home:* 2553½ Third St., Santa Monica, Calif. 90405. *Office:* Department of English, University of Southern California, Los Angeles, Calif. 90007.

*CAREER:* University of Minnesota, Minneapolis, assistant professor of English, 1964-66; University of Southern California, Los Angeles, associate professor of English, 1966—. *Military service:* U.S. Army, 1958-59. U.S. Air Force Reserve, 1959-64.

*WRITINGS: The Christian Humanism of Flannery O'Connor,* Wayne State University Press, 1972. Contributor of articles to professional journals, including *Studies in Romanticism, Victorian Poetry, English Language Notes, 19th Century Fiction, Renaissance Studies in Scottish Literature,* and *Concerning Poetry.*

*WORK IN PROGRESS:* Studies of disunity in modern fiction.

\* \* \*

### EHRET, Christopher 1941-

*PERSONAL:* Born July 27, 1941, in San Francisco, Calif.; married, 1963; children: one. *Education:* University of Redlands, B.A., 1963; Northwestern University, M.A., 1966, Ph.D., 1969. *Office:* Department of History, University of California, Los Angeles, Calif. 90024.

*CAREER:* University of California, Los Angeles, assistant professor, 1968-72, associate professor of African history, 1972—. *Member:* Kenya Historical Society, Historical Society of Tanzania. *Awards, honors:* Ford Foundation grant, 1971-74.

*WRITINGS: Southern Nilotic History: Linguistic Approaches to the Study of the Past,* Northwestern University Press, 1971; *Ethiopians and East Africans: The Problem of Contacts,* East African Publishing House, 1972. Contributor to professional journals.

\* \* \*

### EHRLICH, Amy 1942-

*PERSONAL:* Born July 24, 1942, in New York, N.Y.; daughter of Max (an author) and Doris (Rubenstein) Ehrlich. *Education:* Attended Bennington College, 1960-62, 1963-65. *Address:* Box 75, East Haven, Vt. 05837.

*CAREER:* Early jobs for short periods included teacher in day care center, fabric colorist, and hospital receptionist; Dell Publishing Co., Inc., New York, N.Y., children's book editor.

*WRITINGS—All juvenile: Zeek Silver Moon,* Dial, 1972; (adaptor for young readers) Dee Brown, *Wounded Knee* (originally published as *Bury My Heart at Wounded Knee*), Holt, 1974; *The Everyday Train,* Dial, 1977.

*SIDELIGHTS:* Amy Ehrlich told *CA:* "As a child, I was an avid reader. Books were my escape, a private world that I could retreat to. But I also learned history, geography, psychology, and ethics from the experiences of characters in fiction. When I work on my books, I go back into my own childhood and try to recreate the vividness of life to me at that time. And now that I have my own child, I see it all over again through his eyes. Writing for children is not easy, but it's a wonderful responsibility."

*    *    *

## EIBLING, Harold Henry  1905-197(?)

*PERSONAL:* Born August 5, 1905, in Dola, Ohio; son of Henry Williams (a civil servant) and Sarah (Stanyer) Eibling; married Evelyn Agner, August 14, 1929; children: Judith Anne (Mrs. Robert C. Ackerman), Stephen Harold, David Michael. *Education:* Ohio Northern University, B.Sc., 1926; Ohio State University, M.A., 1932, Ph.D., 1950. *Religion:* Presbyterian.

*CAREER:* Teacher, principal, and superintendent of schools in Findlay, Ohio, 1926-36; superintendent of schools in Maumee, Ohio, 1936-47, Elyria, Ohio, 1947-49, Akron, Ohio, 1949-50, Canton, Ohio, 1950-56, and Columbus, Ohio, 1956-71; educational consultant, beginning 1971. Member of board of control, Ohio Pupils and Teachers Reading Circle, 1942; member of executive committee, National Reading Council. Member of board of trustees, Ohio Northern University, beginning 1960; member of board of directors of City National Bank, Columbus Savings & Loan Association, Columbus Boys Club, Center of Science and Industry, and American Red Cross.

*MEMBER:* American Association of School Administrators (president, 1970-71), Phi Delta Kappa, Alpha Phi Gamma, Kappa Phi Kappa, Masons, Rotary. *Awards, honors:* D.Sc., Mount Union College, 1953; Ph.D., Ohio Northern University, 1959; Freedoms Foundation educator's medal, 1963; LL.D., Miami University, Oxford, Ohio, 1963; Liberty Bell Award, from Columbus Bar Association, 1964; honor award from State of Ohio Department of Education, 1971; also recipient of many awards from institutions in and around Columbus, Ohio.

*WRITINGS*—All published by Laidlaw Brothers: *Great Names in American History,* 1965; *Our Country,* 1965; *Our Beginnings in the Old World,* 1965; *The Story of America,* 1965; *History of Our United States,* 1966; *Foundations of Freedom,* 1973; *Challenge and Change,* 1973. Contributor of articles to education journals.

*WORK IN PROGRESS:* A historical novel on man's achievements through the ages.

*AVOCATIONAL INTERESTS:* Travel (to Europe, Australia, and New Zealand).†

(Deceased)

*    *    *

## EICHNER, Maura  1915-
### (Sister Maura)

*PERSONAL:* Born May 5, 1915, in Brooklyn, N.Y.; daughter of Andrew and Mary (Doyle) Eichner. *Education:* College of Notre Dame of Maryland, A.B., 1941; Catholic University of America, M.A., 1942; additional study at Johns Hopkins University, 1944, University of Notre Dame, 1955, University of London, 1961, and University of Minnesota, 1966. *Home and office:* College of Notre Dame of Maryland, Baltimore, Md. 21210.

*CAREER:* Roman Catholic nun, member of School Sisters of Notre Dame (S.S.N.D.); teacher at Catholic junior high school in Annapolis, Md., 1936-38, and at Notre Dame Preparatory School, Baltimore, Md., 1938-41; College of Notre Dame of Maryland, Baltimore, instructor, 1942-48, assistant professor, 1948-53, associate professor, 1953-67, professor

of English, 1967—, chairperson of department, 1954-74. Participant, Maryland Poetry-in-the-Schools program. Member of advisory committee, Maryland Arts Council. *Member:* National Council of Teachers of English, College English Association, Association of Departments of English, Maryland English Association. *Awards, honors:* Awards for distinguished teaching from Catholic School Press Association, 1956, Freedoms Foundation, 1960, and Lindback Foundation, 1961; three awards from *Lyric* (magazine).

*WRITINGS*—Poems; under name Sister Maura: *Initiate the Heart,* Macmillan, 1946; *The Word Is Love,* Macmillan, 1958; *Bell Sound and Vintage,* Contemporary Poetry, 1966; *Walking on Water,* Paulist/Newman, 1972. Also author of booklets, *Come Christmas,* 1950, *Christmas Convocation,* 1961, and *The Fall of a Sparrow,* 1966. Poems have been recorded for collections at Lamont Library, Harvard University, and at Library of Congress. Contributor of poetry to periodicals, including *America, Accent, Commonweal, New York Times, Poetry,* and *Yale Review;* contributor of articles and reviews to *Critic, Renascence, Spirit,* and *Thought.*

*WORK IN PROGRESS: What We Women Know,* poems.

*    *    *

## EINBOND, Bernard Lionel  1937-

*PERSONAL:* Born May 19, 1937, in New York, N.Y.; son of Hyman and Julia (Parsont) Einbond; married Linda Sue Saxe, February 20, 1977. *Education:* Columbia University, A.B., 1958, M.A., 1960, Ph.D., 1966. *Religion:* Jewish. *Home:* 250 Cabrini Blvd., New York, N.Y. 10033. *Office:* Department of English, Herbert H. Lehman College of the City University of New York, Bronx, N.Y. 10468.

*CAREER:* Radio station WCED, Dubois, Pa., disc jockey, 1958-59; Columbia University, New York City, preceptor in English, 1961-63; Hunter College of the City University of New York, New York City, instructor in English, 1964-68; Herbert H. Lehman College of the City University of New York, Bronx, N.Y., assistant professor, 1968-72, associate professor of English, 1973—, chairman of department, 1976—. *Member:* Haiku Society of America (vice-president, 1972; president, 1975), American Association of University Professors. *Awards, honors:* Keats Poetry Prize, United Kingdom, 1975.

*WRITINGS: Samuel Johnson's Allegory,* Mouton, 1971. Poems anthologized in *Live Poetry,* edited by Kathleen S. Koppell, Holt, 1971, and *The Haiku Anthology,* Anchor Books, 1974. Contributor of poems to various magazines.

*WORK IN PROGRESS: The Coming Indoors and Other Poems.*

*    *    *

## EISENBERG, Maurice  1902-1972

February 24, 1902—December 13, 1972; German-born American cellist, teacher, and editor of music scores. Obituaries: *New York Times,* December 14, 1972.

*    *    *

## EISENMENGER, Robert Waltz  1926-

*PERSONAL:* Born June 30, 1926, in New York, N.Y.; son of Walter S. and Mary Emily (Brenner) Eisenmenger; married Carolyn Lois Shaver, October 11, 1952; children: Anne Waltz, Katherine Carol, Lisa Ellen. *Education:* Amherst College, B.A. (cum laude), 1949; Yale University, M.F., 1951; Harvard University, M.P.A., 1955, Ph.D., 1964.

*Home:* 92 Woodland St., South Natick, Mass. 01760. *Office:* Federal Reserve Bank of Boston, 30 Pearl St., Boston, Mass. 02106.

*CAREER:* U.S. Department of Interior, Bureau of Land Management, Washington, D.C., forestry aid, 1951, forest economist, 1952-53, forester, 1953-54; Federal Reserve Bank of Boston, Boston, Mass., resource economist, 1955-59, industrial economist, 1959-61, acting director, 1961-63, director of resources, 1965—, vice-president, 1965-69, senior vice-president, 1969—. Lecturer, Wellesley College, 1969. New England Board of Higher Education, member, 1970-72, vice-chairman, 1972-74, chairman, 1974. New England Natural Resources Center, trustee, 1971—, clerk, 1973-74, treasurer, 1974—. Trustee, Bacon Free Public Library. *Military service:* U.S. Naval Reserve, 1944-46. *Member:* American Economic Association, National Association of Business Economists, New England Natural Resources Center, New England Board of Higher Education, Boston Economic Club (vice-president, 1972—). *Awards, honors:* Littauer fellow at Harvard University, 1959-60; Wells Prize and New England Council Publications Prize, 1963.

*WRITINGS: The Dynamics of Growth in New England's Economy, 1870-1964,* Wesleyan University Press, 1967. Contributor to professional journals.

*WORK IN PROGRESS:* Writing on the impact of the proposed new financial structure on mortgage markets.†

\* \* \*

## EKBLAW, Sidney E(verette) 1903-

*PERSONAL:* Born March 24, 1903, in Rantoul, Ill.; son of Andrew (a farmer) and Ingrid (Johnson) Ekblaw; married Luella M. Arends, November 8, 1931 (died, 1951); married Jean H. Christensen, August 30, 1952; children: (first marriage) Keith, Linda; (second marriage) Karen, Karla, Kroy. *Education:* University of Illinois, A.B., 1929, M.S., 1930; Clark University, Ph.D., 1934. *Religion:* Lutheran. *Home:* 5741 North Invergordon Rd., Scottsdale, Ariz. 85253.

*CAREER:* U.S. Geological Society, Washington, D.C., assistant calculator, 1927; Illinois State Geological Society, Urbana, assistant geologist, 1928-32; *Economic Geography,* Worcester, Mass., editorial assistant, 1933-34; University of Missouri—Kansas City, 1934-70, became professor of geography; Arizona State University, Tempe, visiting professor, 1970-73. *Member:* American Geographical Society, American Association for the Advancement of Science, American Meteorological Society, American Geophysical Union, Association of American Geographers, National Council for Geographic Education (2nd vice-president, 1961; first vice-president, 1962; president, 1963), Phi Beta Kappa, Sigma Xi.

*WRITINGS:* (With D. C. Ridgley) *Influence of Geography on Our Economic Life,* Gregg, 1938; (with Ridgley) *Problems in Economic Geography,* Gregg, 1938; (contributor) G. Etzel Pearcy, *World Political Geography,* Crowell, 1948; (with Donald J. D. Mulkerne) *Economic and Social Geography,* McGraw, 1958; (with Mulkerne) *Workbook in Economic and Social Geography,* McGraw, 1958; *Exercises in Earth Science,* McCutchan, 1970.

\* \* \*

## EKKER, Charles 1930-

*PERSONAL:* Born August 13, 1930, in New Orleans, La.; son of Marguerite (Bruszko) Ekker; married Gertrude Joyce Arneson, August 23, 1952; children: Charlotte, Elizabeth, David, Stephen. *Education:* Louisiana State University,

B.A., 1948, M.A., 1954; Southern Illinois University, additional study, 1971. *Home address:* Route 3, Box 194, Carbondale, Ill. 62901.

*CAREER:* Louisiana State University, Baton Rouge, instructor in English as a second language, summers, 1946-50, instructor in Spanish and Portuguese, 1953-57; Instituto Cultural Peruano, Lima, Peru, chief executive and academic administrator, 1957-59; Instituto Brasil-Estados Unidos, Vitoria, Brazil, chief executive, 1959-66; Southern Illinois University, Carbondale, member of staff, beginning 1966. *Military service:* U.S. Army, 1950-53; became captain. *Member:* Latin American Studies Association, American Association of Teachers of Spanish and Portuguese.

*WRITINGS:* (Translator) Furtado Celso, *Obstacles to Development in Latin America,* Doubleday-Anchor, 1970. Managing editor, *Specialia,* a multidisciplinary journal. Author of "A Vitoria do Progresso," a movie script, and of television and radio scripts in English, Spanish, and Portuguese for international broadcasting.

*AVOCATIONAL INTERESTS:* Stamp collecting, travel.††

\* \* \*

## EKMAN, Paul 1934-

*PERSONAL:* Born February 15, 1934, in Washington, D.C. *Education:* Attended University of Chicago, 1949-52; New York University, B.A., 1954; Adelphi University, M.A., 1955, Ph.D., 1958. *Home:* 3811 16th St., San Francisco, Calif. 94114. *Office:* Department of Psychology, University of California, 401 Parnassus Ave., San Francisco, Calif. 94143.

*CAREER:* University of California, School of Medicine, San Francisco, research psychologist at Langley Porter Neuropsychiatric Institute, 1960-72, professor of psychology, 1972—. *Military service:* U.S. Army, Medical Corps, 1958-60; became first lieutenant. *Member:* American Psychological Association (fellow), American Association for the Advancement of Science (fellow), Federation of American Sciences. *Awards, honors:* National Institute of Mental Health research scientist awards, 1966, 1970, 1977.

*WRITINGS:* (With Wallace V. Friesen and Phoebe Ellsworth) *Emotion in the Human Face,* Pergamon, 1972; *Darwin and Facial Expression,* Academic Press, 1973; *Unmasking the Face,* Prentice-Hall, 1975.

\* \* \*

## ELBERT, Edmund J(oseph) 1923-

*PERSONAL:* Born May 5, 1923, in Brooklyn, N.Y.; son of John Francis (a draftsman) and Agnes (Carr) Elbert. *Education:* Cathedral College of the Immaculate Conception Seminary, B.A., 1949, D.D., 1949; Catholic University of America, Ph.D., 1956; St. John's University, Jamaica, N.Y., additional study, 1964-65. *Home:* 78 Split Rock Rd., Syosset, N.Y. 11791.

*CAREER:* Roman Catholic priest; Cathedral College, Douglaston, N.Y., professor of human and behavioral sciences, 1955-68; counselor and therapist at numerous mental health clinics in Nassau and Suffolk counties, 1968—; private practice in Hewlett, N.Y., as counselor and therapist of adolescent, marriage, and family problems, 1972—.

*WRITINGS: I Understand: A Handbook for Counseling in the Seventies,* Sheed, 1971; *Youth: The Hope of the Harvest,* Sheed, 1972. Author of weekly newspaper column,

''Man and His Behavior,'' 1969-71; author of occasional articles on man and his problems.

*WORK IN PROGRESS: Problems Faced By Man Today In His Daily Living;* two articles, ''Alcoholism in Our Current Society'' and ''Unmarried Mothers in Our High Schools.''†

\*      \*      \*

## ELLENDER, Raphael 1906-1972

February 22, 1906—September 21, 1972; American artist, instructor, and author of books on drawing and art. Obituaries: *New York Times,* September 26, 1972.

\*      \*      \*

## ELLINGTON, James W(esley) 1927-

*PERSONAL:* Born August 4, 1927, in Grange City, Ky.; son of William Oscar (a landowner) and Nell (Keerans) Ellington. *Education:* University of Chicago, Ph.B., 1947, Ph.D., 1958. *Home address:* Storrs Rd., Mansfield Center, Conn. 06250. *Office:* Department of Philosophy, University of Connecticut, Storrs, Conn. 06268.

*CAREER:* University of Washington, Seattle, assistant professor of philosophy, 1956-57; State University of New York at Stony Brook, assistant professor of philosophy, 1958-61; University of Connecticut, Storrs, assistant professor, 1961-64, associate professor, 1964-72, professor of philosophy, 1972—. *Member:* American Philosophical Association.

*WRITINGS:* (Translator) Immanuel Kant, *Metaphysical Principles of Virtue,* Bobbs-Merrill, 1964; (translator) Kant, *Metaphysical Foundations of Natural Science,* Bobbs-Merrill, 1970; (translator) Kant, *Prolegomena to Any Future Metaphysics,* Hackett, 1977. Contributor of articles to *Dictionary of Scientific Biography.*

*AVOCATIONAL INTERESTS:* French and Chinese cuisine, classical music, science.

\*      \*      \*

## ELLIOTT, Jan Walter 1939-

*PERSONAL:* Born November 8, 1939, in Indianapolis, Ind.; son of James Whitcomb (a technician) and Mary Francis (Montgomery) Elliott; married Marilyn Kay House, November 17, 1963 (divorced March, 1978); children: Brian Walter, Bradley William. *Education:* Purdue University, B.S., 1961; University of Southern California, M.S., 1964, D.B.A., 1967. *Office:* Department of Business Administration and Economics, University of Wisconsin, Milwaukee, Wis. 53217.

*CAREER:* California State College at Los Angeles (now California State University, Los Angeles), assistant professor of economics, 1966-67; University of Wisconsin—Milwaukee, associate professor, 1967-72, professor of economics and business administration, 1972—. *Member:* American Economic Association, American Finance Association, Econometric Society, Western Finance Association, Financial Management Association.

*WRITINGS: Economic Analysis for Management Decisions,* Irwin, 1973; *Macroeconomic Analysis,* Winthrop, 1975.

*WORK IN PROGRESS: The Effect of Wealth on Consumption.*

\*      \*      \*

## ELLIS, James 1935-

*PERSONAL:* Born December 7, 1935, in Painesville, Ohio;

son of Delmont James (a businessman) and Louise (King) Ellis; married Virginia Ridley (an English professor), September 7, 1963. *Education:* Oberlin College, B.A., 1957; New York University, graduate study, 1957-58; University of Iowa, M.A., 1960, Ph.D., 1964. *Home:* 131 Cold Hill, Granby, Mass. 01033. *Office:* Department of English, Mount Holyoke College, South Hadley, Mass. 01075.

*CAREER:* University of Rochester, Rochester, N.Y., instructor in English, 1961-62; Mount Holyoke College, South Hadley, Mass., instructor, 1962-64, assistant professor, 1964-69, associate professor, 1969-72, professor of English, 1972—. Director, Highfield Theatre, Falmouth, Mass., 1955, 1957, 1959-60. *Member:* Modern Language Association of America, American Society for Theatre Research, Society for Theatre Research, Research Society for Victorian Periodicals, Theatre Library Association, Gilbert and Sullivan Society. *Awards, honors:* Woodrow Wilson fellowship, 1957; National Endowment for the Humanities junior fellowship, 1966, senior stipend, 1977.

*WRITINGS:* (Editor) *The Bab Ballads of W. S. Gilbert,* Harvard University Press, 1970; (advisory editor) *Waterloo Directory of Victorian Periodicals, 1824-1900,* Wilfrid Laurier University Press, 1976. Contributor to *Theatre Survey XVIII,* 1976. Member of editorial board, *Massachusetts Review,* 1969-75; co-editor, *Victorian Periodicals Newsletter,* 1970-73.

*WORK IN PROGRESS:* Co-editing *The London Stage, 1800-1900: A Calendar of Performances;* advisory editor, *English and American Drama of the Nineteenth Century.*

*AVOCATIONAL INTERESTS:* Collecting books on the nineteenth-century theatre.

\*      \*      \*

## ELLIS, M(arion) LeRoy 1928-

*PERSONAL:* Born March 27, 1928, in Georgetown, S.C.; son of Bucanan C. (a salesman) and Ola Belle (Dukes) Ellis. *Education:* University of South Carolina, B.A., 1948, M.A., 1950; Universite d'Aix-Marseille, Doctorat d'Universite, 1955. *Home:* 4060 Kenneth St., Beaumont, Tex. 77705. *Office address:* Box 10049, Lamar University Station, Beaumont, Tex. 77710.

*CAREER:* French government assistant, 1950-51; *The State,* Columbia, S.C., reporter, 1956-57; Virginia Polytechnic Institute, Blacksburg, assistant professor of English, 1957-60, associate professor French and Spanish, 1961-63; Erskine College, Due West, S.C., professor of French and head of language department, 1960-61; Lewis and Clark College, Portland, Ore., professor of French, 1964-68; North Texas State University, Denton, professor of French, 1968-69; Lamar University, Beaumont, Tex., professor of French, 1969—, head of department of modern languages, 1969—, organizer of Lamar Overseas Study Program at University of Strasbourg. *Military service:* U.S. Air Force, 1951-53; became second lieutenant. *Member:* American Association of Teachers of French (East Texas Chapter, president, 1971-72), Sabine Area Language Teachers Association (president, 1970-71), South Central Modern Language Association, Texas Foreign Language Association, Phi Beta Kappa. *Awards, honors:* Chevalier in Order of Palmes Academiques, 1967; Officier in Order of Palmes Academiques, 1977.

*WRITINGS: Prose classique,* Ginn-Blaisdell, 1966. Contributor of articles to *Bulletin of the Association of Departments of Foreign Languages* and *Le Journal Francais.*

*WORK IN PROGRESS:* The Contemporary French Theater.

*SIDELIGHTS:* M. LeRoy Ellis has organized the Lamar Overseas Study Program with groups studying at the University of Strasbourg, France, 1971, 1973, 1975, and 1977.

\* \* \*

## ELSMERE, Jane Shaffer 1932-

*PERSONAL:* Born May 22, 1932, in Andrews, Ind.; daughter of Kenneth L. and Margarette (Wiese) Shaffer; married Robert T. Elsmere (a professor at Ball State University), January 3, 1953; children: Eva. *Education:* Manchester College, B.S., 1953; Indiana University, A.M., 1958, Ph.D., 1962. *Religion:* Church of the Brethren. *Home address:* R.R. 7, Box 228-I, Muncie, Ind. 47302.

*CAREER:* High school teacher in Indiana, 1953-60; Manchester College, North Manchester, Ind., assistant professor of history, 1962-63; Ball State University, Muncie, Ind., assistant professor of history, 1964-67. *Member:* American Historical Association, Organization of American Historians, Indiana Historical Society.

*WRITINGS: Henry Ward Beecher: The Indiana Years, 1837-1847,* Indiana Historical Society, 1973. Contributor of articles to *Indiana Social Studies Quarterly* and *Georgia Historical Quarterly.*

*WORK IN PROGRESS: Samuel Chase, Patriot and Judge.*

*AVOCATIONAL INTERESTS:* Reading, travel.

\* \* \*

## EMENHISER, JeDon A(llen) 1933-

*PERSONAL:* Born May 19, 1933, in Clovis, N.M.; son of Glen A. (a banker) and Opal (Sasser) Emenhiser; married Patricia Burke, January 27, 1954; children: Melissa. *Education:* University of Redlands, A.B., 1955; University of Minnesota, Ph.D., 1962. *Politics:* Democrat. *Religion:* Presbyterian. *Home:* 1500 Bayside Rd., Arcata, Calif. 95521. *Office:* School of Behavioral and Social Sciences, Humboldt State University, Arcata, Calif. 95521.

*CAREER:* University of Redlands, Redlands, Calif., instructor in political science, 1959-60; Utah State University, Logan, 1960-77, began as instructor, became professor of political science; Humboldt State University, Arcata, Calif., professor of political science and dean of School of Behavioral and Social Sciences, 1977—. Fulbright professor of political science, University of Saigon, 1964-65; research director, Utah Legislative Council, 1966; academic administrative intern, Colgate University, 1972-73. Member of board of directors, Exchange Bank. Also produced and directed "The Hawks and the Doves," a series, for KUSU-Television, 1967-68. *Member:* American Political Science Association, American Association of University Professors, American Society of Public Administration. *Awards, honors:* American Council on Education fellowship, 1972-73.

*WRITINGS: Utah's Governments,* National Press, 1964; (editor) *The Dragon on the Hill: Utah's 38th Legislature, Analysis and Comment,* University of Utah Press, 1970; (editor) *Rocky Mountain Urban Politics* (monograph), Utah State University, 1971; *Implementing a Tenure Quota: The Bamford College Case,* University Council for Educational Administration, 1977. Contributor to history, science, and political science journals.

*WORK IN PROGRESS: Government and the Individual,* a textbook; research on academic administration, and on computer simulations of political systems.

\* \* \*

## EMERY, Robert F(irestone) 1927-

*PERSONAL:* Born January 18, 1927, in Kenton, Ohio; son of Clayton Sprague (a physician) and Sarah Webster (Firestone) Emery; married Phyllis Swanson (a librarian), 1957; children: Ross David, Ann Elaine, Hope Roberta. *Education:* Oberlin College, B.A., 1951; University of Michigan, M.A., 1952, Ph.D., 1956. *Politics:* Republican. *Religion:* Methodist. *Home:* 3421 Shepherd St., Chevy Chase, Md. 20015. *Office:* 20th St. and Constitution Ave. N.W., Washington, D.C. 20551.

*CAREER:* Board of Governors of Federal Reserve System, Washington, D.C., economist, 1955—. Adjunct professor of economics, Southeastern University, Washington, D.C., 1960—. *Military service:* U.S. Merchant Marine, Cadet Corps, 1945-47. *Member:* American Economic Association. *Awards, honors:* Fulbright fellowship, 1953-54.

*WRITINGS: The Financial Institutions of Southeast Asia: A Country-by-Country Study,* Praeger, 1971. Contributor of articles to *Asian Survey, Oriental Economist, Far Eastern Survey, Inter-American Economic Affairs, Kyklos,* and *National Banking Review.*

*WORK IN PROGRESS: The Japanese Money Market.*

\* \* \*

## ENGBERG, Holger L(aessoe) 1930-

*PERSONAL:* Born July 17, 1930, in Koege, Denmark; son of Viggo L. (a professor) and Ellen (Rasmussen) Engberg; married Lillemor Andersen, September 15, 1955; children: Lisbet, Niels Peter. *Education:* University of Copenhagen, B.A., 1951, M.A., 1955; London School of Economics and Political Science, summer study, 1956; Columbia University, Ph.D., 1963. *Religion:* Protestant. *Home:* 375 Riverside Dr., New York, N.Y. 10025. *Office:* Graduate School of Business Administration, New York University, 100 Trinity Pl., New York, N.Y. 10006.

*CAREER: Berlingske Tidende,* Copenhagen, Denmark, economist, 1955-57; Columbia University, New York City, lecturer, in banking and finance, 1958-62; New York University, Graduate School of Business Administration, New York City, assistant professor, 1962-65, associate professor of finance, 1965—, secretary to the faculty, 1971-73, director of doctoral program, 1970-71. Visiting professor, University of Ghana, 1973-76. Lecturer, U.N. Workshop on Financial Planning, Tanzania, 1969. Columbia University Seminar on Contemporary Africa, associate, 1965—, co-chairman, 1978-79. External thesis examiner, Makerere University, Kampala, Uganda, 1970. Consultant, Contact Associates Ltd. (Accra, Ghana), 1974-76. *Member:* Danish Economic Society, American Finance Association, African Studies Association, American Economic Association, Academy of International Business, American Association of University Professors, Ghana Institute of Management, Economic Society of Ghana, African Association of Management and Public Administration.

*WRITINGS: French Money and Capital Markets and Monetary Management,* Institute of Finance, New York University, 1965; (with John Fayerweather and Jean Boddewyn) *International Business Education: Curriculum Planning,* New York University Press, 1966; (with Boddewyn,

Fayerweather, Peter Franck, Ashok Kapoor, and Walter Ness), *World Business Systems and Environments,* International Textbook Company, 1972. Contributor of articles to *Journal of Finance, Journal of Modern African Studies, Economic Geography,* and other journals. Editor, *Journal of Management Studies* (Ghana), 1973-76.

\* \* \*

## ENGEL, Alan S(tuart) 1932-

*PERSONAL:* Born January 31, 1932, in Chicago, Ill.; son of Julius (a businessman) and Marian (Maltz) Engel; married Sondra Utanoff (a librarian), December 25, 1954; children: Reed, Drew. *Education:* Northern Illinois University, B.S.Ed., 1952; University of Chicago, M.A., 1953; Ohio State University, graduate study, 1953; Northwestern University, Ph.D., 1960. *Home:* 558 Melissa Dr., Oxford, Ohio 45056. *Office:* Department of Political Science, Miami University, Oxford, Ohio 45056.

*CAREER:* Wright Junior College, Chicago, Ill., instructor in social science, 1956-58; Miami University, Oxford, Ohio, assistant professor, 1960-65, associate professor, 1965-71, professor of political science, 1971—, assistant chairperson of department, 1974—. Instructor, Ohio Peace Officer Training Council, 1967—; consultant to police academies on human relations training, Hamilton, Ohio, 1967—. *Member:* American Political Science Association, Law and Society Association, Midwest Political Science Association, Ohio Association of Economists and Political Scientists, Pi Sigma Alpha, Omicron Delta Kappa, Phi Eta Sigma.

*WRITINGS:* (With Reo Christenson, Dan Jacobs, Paul Rejai, and Herbert Waltzer) *Ideologies and Modern Politics,* Dodd, 1971, 2nd edition, 1975; *The Justice Game,* Glencoe Press, 1974. Contributor of articles to periodicals, including *Progressive, Current, Washington Post, Junior College Journal,* and *Midwest Journal of Political Science.*

*WORK IN PROGRESS:* Research in constitutional law, civil rights and liberties, and law enforcement.

\* \* \*

## ENGEL, S(rul) Morris 1931-

*PERSONAL:* Born March 3, 1931, in Promow, Poland; Canadian citizen; son of Isaac (a rabbi) and Feige-Leah (Pasha) Engel; married Phyllis Chisvin, December 25, 1953; children: Michael, Hartley. *Education:* University of Manitoba, B.A., 1953, M.A., 1955; University of Toronto, Ph.D., 1959. *Office:* School of Philosophy, University of Southern California, Los Angeles, Calif. 90007.

*CAREER:* University of New Brunswick, Fredericton, assistant professor of philosophy, 1959-61; University of Southern California, Los Angeles, assistant professor, 1962-64, associate professor, 1964-72, professor of philosophy, 1972—, acting director of School of Philosophy summer sessions, 1966—. *Member:* American Philosophical Association, Royal Institute of Philosophy, Canadian Philosophical Association, Mind Association. *Awards, honors:* Canada Council fellow, 1961-62.

*WRITINGS:* (Translator) S. Ansky, *The Dybbuk,* Comet Press, 1953, 2nd edition, Nash Publishing, 1974; (translator) Rachmil Bryks, *A Cat in the Ghetto,* Bloch Publishing, 1959, revised edition, Behrman, 1977; *The Problem of Tragedy,* Brunswick Press, 1960; (contributor) Keith C. Brown, editor, *Hobbes Studies,* Basil Blackwell, 1965; (contributor) Robert Paul Wolff, editor, *Kant: A Collection of Critical Essays,* Doubleday, 1967; *Language and Illumination:*

*Studies in the History of Philosophy,* Nijhoff, 1969; *Wittgenstein's Doctrine of the Tyranny of Language: An Historical and Critical Examination,* Nijhoff, 1971; *The Strata of Argument,* St. Martin's, 1973; *With Good Reason: An Introduction to Informal Fallacies,* St. Martin's, 1976. Also author of "The Art of Thinking," television series produced by University of Southern California and broadcast on KNXT-TV, 1973-74. Contributor of more than thirty articles and reviews to journals. Editorial consultant to *Magill's Encyclopedia of Literature.*

\* \* \*

## ENGELBERG, Edward 1929-

*PERSONAL:* Born January 21, 1929, in Germany; naturalized U.S. citizen; son of Jakob and Paula (Weber) Engelberg; married Elaine A. Rosen (a high school teacher), July 27, 1950; children: Stephen Paul, Michael Joseph, Elizabeth Joyce. *Education:* Brooklyn College (now Brooklyn College of the City University of New York), A.B. (with honors), 1951; University of Oregon, M.A., 1952; Cambridge University, additional study, 1955-56; University of Wisconsin, Ph.D., 1957. *Politics:* Independent. *Religion:* Jewish. *Home:* 58 Turning Mill Rd., Lexington, Mass. 02173. *Office:* Brandeis University, Waltham, Mass. 02154.

*CAREER:* Has worked as a diamond cutter and a salesman of children's clothing; University of Michigan, Ann Arbor, instructor, 1957-60, assistant professor, 1960-64, associate professor of English, 1964-65; Brandeis University, Waltham, Mass., associate professor, 1965-67, professor of comparative literature, 1967—, chairman of department of Romance languages and comparative literature, 1972-75, chairman of joint program of literary studies, 1971-75. *Member:* Modern Language Association of America, American Comparative Literature Association, American Association of University Professors, Eastern Comparative Literature Conference (member of executive committee), Phi Beta Kappa. *Awards, honors:* Fulbright fellow, Cambridge University, 1955-56; American Council of Learned Societies travel grant, summer, 1970; National Endowment for the Humanities senior fellow, 1975-76.

*WRITINGS: The Vast Design: Patterns in W. B. Yeats's Aesthetic,* Oxford University Press, 1964; (editor) *The Symbolist Poem: The Development of the English Tradition,* Dutton, 1967; *The Unknown Distance: From Consciousness to Conscience, Goethe to Camus,* Harvard University Press, 1972. Contributor of articles, essays, and reviews to journals in his field.

*WORK IN PROGRESS: Naive and Sentimental Poetry; Matthew Arnold, Walter Pater and the Image of Germany.*

\* \* \*

## ENGLER, Richard E(mil), Jr. 1925-

*PERSONAL:* Born December 31, 1925, in Los Angeles, Calif.; son of Richard Emil (a machinist) and Janet (Thompson) Engler. *Education:* University of California, Los Angeles, B.A., 1949; University of Southern California, M.A., 1953, Ph.D., 1957. *Politics:* Democrat. *Religion:* Presbyterian. *Home:* 1225 Martha Custis Dr. No. 1518, Alexandria, Va. 22302. *Office:* Roy Littlejohn Associates, Inc., 1328 New York Ave. N.W., Washington, D.C. 20005.

*CAREER:* Child Welfare League of America, New York City, research sociologist, 1957-59; Ramo Wooldridge Corp., Denver, Colo., human factors scientist, 1959-60; System Development Corp., Falls Church, Va., social scientist, 1961-66; Greenleigh Associates, New York City, senior consultant, 1966-67; senior associate with social policy consulting firms in Washington, D.C., 1968-70; Roy Littlejohn Associates, Inc., Washington, D.C., senior associate, 1971-75, vice-president, 1975—. Consultant to Inner City Development Corp. and Afro-American Bicentennial Corp. *Military service:* U.S. Army, 1944-46, 1950-52; became sergeant. *Member:* American Sociological Association, Society for Applied Anthropology (fellow), American Academy of Political and Social Science, American Association for the Advancement of Science, Authors Guild of Authors League of America.

*WRITINGS:* (With Henry A. Maas) *Children in Need of Parents,* Columbia University Press, 1959; *The Challenge of Diversity,* Harper, 1964; (with William W. Chenault) *Social and Behavioral Factors in the Implementation of Local Survival,* Human Sciences Research, 1967.

*WORK IN PROGRESS: On Continuing a Revolution: The Nurture of Social Organism in America.*

\* \* \*

## ENGLISH, Earl (Franklin) 1905-

*PERSONAL:* Born January 29, 1905, in Lapeer, Mich.; son of Robert W. (an engineer) and Esther (Bell) English; married Ceola Bartlett, June 13, 1930; children: Esther Dawn, Barbara Lu. *Education:* Western Michigan University, A.B., 1928, B.S., 1932; Purdue University, graduate study, 1932-33; State University of Iowa, M.A., 1937, Ph.D., 1944. *Home:* 2205 Bluff Blvd., Columbia, Mo. *Office:* School of Journalism, University of Missouri, Columbia, Mo. 65201.

*CAREER:* University of Iowa, Iowa City, associate professor of psychology of advertising, 1942-44; University of Missouri—Columbia, professor of psychology of advertising, 1944—, dean of School of Journalism, 1951-70. Member of board of directors, Lee Enterprises, Inc., 1970—. Member of accrediting committee, American Council on Education for Journalism, 1946-49; European lecturer, U.S. State Department, 1965. *Member:* American Society of Newspaper Editors, American Association of Schools and Departments of Journalism, Association for Education in Journalism, American Council on Education in Journalism (chairman, appeals committee, 1972-75), Northwest Missouri Presidents Association, Sigma Delta Chi, Kappa Tau Alpha, Kappa Alpha Mu, Alpha Delta Sigma, Sigma Xi. *Awards, honors:* National Editorial Association, award of merit, 1958.

*WRITINGS: Exercises in High School Journalism,* University of Iowa Press, 1937; (with Clarence Hach, R. Nafziger, and others) *Introduction to Journalism Research,* University of Louisiana Press, 1949; *Scholastic Journalism,* Iowa State University Press, 1951, 6th edition, 1977. Editor, *Iowa Publisher,* 1942-45.

\* \* \*

## ENLOE, Cynthia H(olden) 1938-

*PERSONAL:* Born July 16, 1938, in New York, N.Y.; daughter of Cortez F. (a physician) and Harriett (Goodridge) Enloe. *Education:* Connecticut College, B.A. (cum laude), 1960; University of California, Berkeley, M.A., 1963, Ph.D., 1967. *Office:* Department of Government, Clark University, Worcester, Mass. 01610.

*CAREER:* University of California, Berkeley, acting instructor in political science, 1966-67; Miami University, Oxford, Ohio, assistant professor, 1968-71, associate professor of political science, 1971-72; Clark University, Worcester, Mass., associate professor, 1972-77, professor of government, 1977—. *Member:* American Political Science Association, International Studies Association, Association for Asian Studies, Asia Society, Phi Sigma Alpha. *Awards, honors:* National Endowment for the Humanities grant, 1969; Fulbright lecturer in political science, University of Guyana, Georgetown, Guyana, 1971-72; Council on Foreign Relations fellow, 1974-75.

*WRITINGS: Multi-Ethnic Politics: The Case of Malaysia,* Center for South and Southeast Asia Studies, University of California, 1970; *Ethnic Conflict and Political Development,* Little, Brown, 1973; *Politics of Pollution in a Comparative Perspective,* Longman, 1975; (co-author) *Development and Diversity in Southeast Asia,* McGraw, 1977. Contributor of articles to journals, including *Pacific Affairs,* and *International Studies Quarterly.*

*WORK IN PROGRESS: Police, Military, and Ethnicity: Foundations of State Power,* for Transaction Books; research on the politics of manpower in multi-national corporations.

\* \* \*

## ENROTH, Clyde A(dolph) 1926-

*PERSONAL:* Born April 26, 1926, in Minneapolis, Minn.; son of Johan Werner (a foreman) and Walborg (Hedberg) Enroth; married Theresa Louise McElwee (an English instructor), September 27, 1947; children: Daniel Gordon, Kate Jane, Sarah Theresa. *Education:* University of Minnesota, B.A., 1947, M.A., 1949, Ph.D., 1956. *Politics:* Democrat. *Religion:* Unitarian Universalist. *Home:* 3200 Cutter Way, Sacramento, Calif. 95818. *Office:* Department of English, California State University, Sacramento, Calif. 95819.

*CAREER:* University of Minnesota, Minneapolis, instructor in English, 1950-56; California State University, Sacramento, assistant professor, 1956-61, associate professor, 1961-66, professor of English, 1966—, assistant chairman, Division of Humanities and Fine Arts, 1963-64. Fulbright Professor of American Literature, Cairo University, 1964-65, and University of Sao Paulo, 1971-72; visiting professor of American Studies, University of Nottingham, 1973-74. State College Program in Ireland, 1970, 1971. *Military service:* U.S. Navy, 1943-46, 1951-53; became lieutenant commander. *Member:* American Association of University Professors, American Federation of Teachers, Association of California State College Professors (vice-president, 1963-64), English Council of the California State Colleges (president, 1961-62).

*WRITINGS:* (Editor) *Early Modern Poets,* Holt, 1969; (editor) *Joyce and Lawrence,* Holt, 1969. General editor, *Major British Authors,* Holt, 1970, and "Aspects of English," Holt. Contributor to *Twentieth Century Literature.*

*AVOCATIONAL INTERESTS:* Photography, music, scuba diving.

\* \* \*

## EPPS, Preston H(erschel) 1888-

*PERSONAL:* Born April 26, 1888, in Pittsylvania County, Va.; son of Robert Martin and Tabitha (Cumi) Epps; married Stella Wadsworth, August 30, 1916 (died June 4, 1934); married Miriam Rightmire, June 23, 1935; children: (first marriage) Aida F., Barbara (Mrs. Thomas S. Deering, Jr.), Marjory (Mrs. Joe E. Mitchell). *Education:* University of North Carolina at Chapel Hill, B.A., 1915, M.A., 1916;

University of Chicago, Ph.D., 1928. *Home:* 28 Hayes Rd., Chapel Hill, N.C. 27514.

*CAREER:* Teacher and assistant principal in high school in Atlanta, Ga., 1916-28; Furman University, Greenville, S.C., professor of classics, 1928-38; University of North Carolina at Chapel Hill, associate professor, 1938-42, professor, 1942-54, Kenan Professor of Greek, 1955-60, emeritus Kenan Professor, 1960—. *Member:* Phi Beta Kappa.

*WRITINGS:* (Editor and translator) Aristotle, *The Poetics of Aristotle,* University of North Carolina Press, 1942; (editor) George Howe and Gustave A. Harrer, *Greek Literature in Translation,* Harper, revised edition (Epps was not associated with earlier edition), 1948; (translator) Homer, *The Odyssey,* Macmillan, 1965; *Thoughts from the Greeks,* University of Missouri Press, 1969. Contributor to philology journals.

*AVOCATIONAL INTERESTS:* Music.

\*     \*     \*

## ERICKSEN, Kenneth J(errold) 1939-

*PERSONAL:* Born June 7, 1939, in Everett, Wash.; son of Frank L. (a Lutheran minister) and Evelyn (Carlson) Ericksen. *Education:* Pacific Lutheran University, B.A., 1961; Rice University, M.A., 1963, Ph.D., 1967. *Religion:* Lutheran. *Home:* 3321 Lavina Dr., Forest Grove, Ore. 97116. *Office:* Department of English, Linfield College, McMinnville, Ore. 97128.

*CAREER:* Linfield College, McMinnville, Ore., assistant professor, 1965-68, associate professor, 1968-75, professor of English, 1975—, chairman of humanities division, 1968-69, acting head of department, 1968-71, head of department, 1973—. Chapman College, Orange, Calif., World Campus Afloat, communications professor, 1972. *Member:* American Association of University Professors, Modern Language Association.

*WRITINGS:* (With Warren L. Clare) *Multimmediate: Multimedia and the Art of Writing,* Random House, 1972; (editor) James Shirley, *The Young Admiral* (critical, old-spelling edition), Garland Publishing, 1978.

\*     \*     \*

## ERIKSON, Stanley 1906-

*PERSONAL:* Born August 17, 1906, in Chicago, Ill.; son of Charles F. (a newspaper publisher) and Selma C. (Dahlstrom) Erikson; married Lila L. Ellstrom, June 12, 1937; children: Robert S., Allen F. (deceased). *Education:* University of Wisconsin, B.A., 1929; Northwestern University, J.D., 1933, Ph.D., 1939. *Religion:* Episcopalian. *Home:* 3932 Eighth Ave., Rock Island, Ill. 61201.

*CAREER:* Rockford College, Rockford, Ill., assistant professor of political science, 1944-48; Augustana College, Rock Island, Ill., professor of political science, 1948-74, professor emeritus, 1974—. *Member:* American Political Science Association, Midwest Political Science Association.

*WRITINGS:* (With Thomas J. Bellows and Herbert R. Winters) *Political Science: Introductory Essays and Readings,* Duxbury Press, 1971; (with Bellows and Winters) *People and Politics: An Introduction to Political Science,* Wiley, 1977.

*WORK IN PROGRESS:* A textbook for introductory course in political science with Thomas J. Bellows and Herbert R. Winters.

## ERNSTING, Walter 1920-
### (Clark Darlton)

*PERSONAL:* Born June 13, 1920, in Koblenz, Germany; son of Martin and Grete (Risse) Ernsting; married Ursula Kaiser, November 2, 1942; children: Robert, Sonja. *Education:* Realgymnasium Essen-Bredeney, Abitur, 1938. *Residence:* West Germany. *Agent:* (U.S. representative) Forrest J. Ackerman, 2495 Glendower Ave., Hollywood, Calif. 90027.

*CAREER:* Professional writer and translator of science fiction in Germany and Austria, 1954—. Literary agent for American and English science fiction, representing the British agent Ted Carnell, and the Ackerman Agency in Germany, Switzerland, and Austria. *Military service:* German Army, 1939-45; served in Russia where he was held prisoner of war until 1950. *Member:* Deutscher Schriftstellerverband; various science fiction clubs in Europe. *Awards, honors:* Winner of prize for best German science fiction novel five times.

*WRITINGS*—Under pseudonym Clark Darlton, except as indicated: *Ufo am Nachthimmel,* Erich Pabel, 1955; *Der Mann, Der Die Zukunft stahl,* Erich Pabel, 1955; (with Raymond Z. Gallun) *Ring um die Sonne,* Erich Pabel, 1956; *Die Zeit ist gegen uns,* Erich Pabel, 1956; *Und Satan wird kommen,* Erich Pabel, 1956; *Ueberfall aus dem Nichts,* Zwei Schwalben, 1956; *Raum ohne Zeit,* Erich Pabel, 1957; *Das Ewige Gesetz,* Erich Pabel, 1957; *Befehl aus der Unendlichkeit,* Erich Pabel, 1957; *Finale,* Erich Pabel, 1957; *Schwelle zur Ewigkeit,* Erich Pabel, 1957; *Planet Lerks III,* Erich Pabel, 1957; *Attentat auf Sol,* A Moewig, 1958; *Zurueck aus der Ewigkeit,* A. Moewig, 1958; *Die galaktische Foederation,* A. Moewig, 1958; *Das Leben endet nie,* Erich Pabel, 1958; *Die Strahlenden Staedte,* Doerner, 1958; *Planet YB-23,* A. Moewig, 1958; *Vater der Menschheit,* A. Moewig, 1958; *Der Sprung ins Ungewisse,* Doerner, 1958; *Der Tod kam von den Sternen,* Doerner, 1958; *Experiment gelungen,* Doerner, 1959; *Raumschiff der toten Seelen,* Doerner, 1959; *Geheime Order fuer Andromeda,* A. Moewig, 1959; *Wanderer zwischen drei Ewigkeiten,* Doerner, 1959; (with Jesco von Puttkamer) *Das Unsterbliche Universum,* Zimmermann, 1959; *Der fremde Zwang,* Zimmermann, 1959.

*Die Zeitlosen,* Zimmermann, 1960; *Welt ohne Schleier,* Zimmermann, 1960; (with Jack Williamson) *Als die Sonne erlosch,* Erich Pabel, 1960; *Das Erbe von Hiroshima,* A. Moewig, 1960; *Die letzte Zeitmaschine,* Zimmermann, 1960; *Der Eisenfresser,* Erich Pabel, 1961; (under name Walter Ernsting) *Das Marsabenteuer* (juvenile), Sigbert Mohn, 1963; (under name Walter Ernsting) *Das Weltraumabenteuer* (juvenile), Sigbert Mohn, 1964; (under name Walter Ernsting) *Das Planetenabenteuer* (juvenile), Sigbert Mohn, 1965; (compiler with Robert Artner) *Am Ende der Fuercht* (anthology), Wilhelm Heyne, 1966; (with Artner) *Leben aus der Asche,* A. Moewig, 1967; (with Artner) *Der Strahlende Tod,* A. Moewig, 1967; *Der Sprung ins Jenseits,* Wilhelm Heyne, 1968; *Todesschach,* A. Moewig, 1968; *Der tag, an dem die Goetter Starben* (title means "The Day the Gods Died"), Bantam, 1975.

"Perry Rhodan" series: Creator, with Karl-Herbert Scheer, and author or co-author of over 120 books, A. Moewig, 1961-72, translations by Wendayne Ackerman, with subtitle "Peacelord of the Universe," Ace Books, 1969—. Also author of "Hurricane" series, fourteen books, published by A. Moewig and Erich Pabel, 1958-65.

Editor and translator: "Utopia-Grossband" series (translations of English and American science ficiton novels), Erich Pabel, 1954; "Terra-Sonderband" series (translations of science fiction novels from all countries), A. Moewig, 1958; "Terra" series, A. Moewig, 1958. Translator of about one hundred other science fiction novels for various German publishers. Editor, and translator of series, *Utopia* (first German science fiction magazine with translations), Erich Pabel, 1955-57, and German edition of *Magazine of Fantasy and Science Fiction*, Heyne, 1965.

*SIDELIGHTS:* The "Perry Rhodan" series now includes 850 titles published in German and 114 published in English. Since 1961, numerous authors have written books featuring the characters created by Ernsting and Scheer; these include Klaus Mahr, Willi Voltz, W. W. Shols, and Hanna Kneifel.

Many of Walter Ernsting's science fiction novels have been translated into Italian, Hungarian, and Serbo-Croatian. The "Perry Rhodan" series has been published in France, the Netherlands, and Japan.

*AVOCATIONAL INTERESTS:* Swimming, sailing, "a bit of skin-diving," and traditional jazz.

\* \* \*

## ESCANDON, Ralph 1928-

*PERSONAL:* Born May 21, 1928, in Barranquilla, Colombia; son of Antonio J. (a businessman) and Leonor (Hernandez) Escandon; married Lena Hilda Moore (an elementary school teacher), June 6, 1955; children: Willie, Rafael. *Education:* Union College, Lincoln, Neb., B.A., 1957; University of Nebraska, M.A., 1959; University of Omaha, additional study, 1966-67; Interamerican University, Saltillo, Mexico, Ph.D., 1968. *Religion:* Seventh-day Adventist. *Home:* 280 Washburn, Angwin, Calif. 94508. *Office:* Department of Modern Languages, Pacific Union College, Angwin, Calif. 94508.

*CAREER:* University of Nebraska, Lincoln, instructor in Spanish, 1958-60; Creighton University, Omaha, Neb., instructor in Spanish, 1960-62; Cali Junior Academy, Cali, Colombia, principal, 1962-66; University of Omaha (now University of Nebraska at Omaha), assistant professor of Spanish literature, 1966-67; Pacific Union College, Angwin, Calif., associate professor of Latin American literature and history, 1968—, chairman of department of modern languages, 1977—. *Member:* Phi Sigma Iota.

*WRITINGS: Curiosidades matematicas,* Editorial Novaro, 1965; *Excentricidades y rarezas,* Editorial Novaro, 1967; *Anecdotas favoritas,* Editorial Novaro, 1970; *Humo y Ceniza* (novel), Editorial Iztaecittuatl, 1972; *Have Fun Being a Christian,* Review & Herald, 1973; *Adelante entusiasta juventud,* Editorial Novaro, 1973; *El origen de muchas cosas,* Editorial Novaro, 1973; *Smoke and Ashes* (novel), Dorrance, 1973; *Curiosidades Biblicas,* Editorial Novaro, 1975; *Sendros de Victoria,* Pacific Press Publishing Association, 1977; *Para usted que quierre ser escritor,* [Miami], 1977; *Intermediate Spanish,* Home Study Institute, 1978.

*WORK IN PROGRESS: Caprichos del Idioma,* for Editorial Novaro; *Pensamientos inolvidables; Prote ja a sus hijos contra la delincuencia.*

\* \* \*

## ESCHHOLZ, Paul A(nderson) 1942-

*PERSONAL:* Born October 15, 1942, in Hartford, Conn.; son of Paul Arthur (an electrical engineer) and Leone (Anderson) Eschholz; married Eva Lillian Paquin, May 28,

1966; children: William Edward, Sarah Lynn, Ulrich Paul, Karen Louise. *Education:* Wesleyan University, B.A., 1964; University of Vermont, M.A., 1966; University of Minnesota, Ph.D., 1971. *Religion:* Roman Catholic. *Home address:* R.F.D., Westford, Vt. 05494. *Office:* Department of English, University of Vermont, Burlington, Vt. 05401.

*CAREER:* University of Vermont, Burlington, instructor in English, 1969-71; Johnson State College, Johnson, Vt., instructor in English, 1971; University of Vermont, assistant professor, 1971-75, associate professor of English, 1975—. *Member:* Modern Language Association of America, College English Association, National Council of Teachers of English, American Name Society, American Dialect Society, North East Modern Language Association, New England Association of Teachers of English, Vermont Historical Society, Chittenden County Historical Society, Rowland E. Robinson Memorial Association.

*WRITINGS:* (Editor with Virginia Clark and Alfred Rosa) *Language: Introductory Readings,* St. Martin's, 1972, 2nd edition, 1977; (with Arthur W. Biddle) *Literature of Vermont: A Sampler,* University Press of New England, 1973; (editor with Clark and Rosa) *Language Awareness,* St. Martin's, 1974, 2nd edition, 1978; (editor) *Critics on William Dean Howells,* University of Miami Press, 1975; (contributor) Rowland E. Robinson, editor, *Vermont: A Study of Independence,* Tuttle, 1975; (with Rosa) *Bibliography of Contemporary British and American Fiction, 1950-1970,* Gale, 1977; (editor with Rosa) *Subject and Strategy: A Rhetoric Reader,* St. Martin's, 1978. Contributor to academic journals. Co-editor of *Exercise Exchange: For Teachers of English in High Schools and Colleges.*

*WORK IN PROGRESS:* The dialect writings of and an unpublished biography of Ethan Allen by Rowland Evans Robinson, 1833-1900; writing on W. D. Howells and Henry James, and on rhetoric and the writing process.

\* \* \*

## ESKIN, Frada 1936-

*PERSONAL:* Born July 15, 1936, in Birmingham, England; daughter of Joshuah (a clergyman) and Ethel (Cohen) Eskin; married Percy Wilenski (a physicist), September 18, 1960. *Education:* University of Sheffield, M.B.Ch.B., 1960; University of Manchester, D.P.H., 1966. *Religion:* Jewish. *Office:* Department of Community Medicine, Stopford Bldg., University of Manchester, Oxford Rd., Manchester, England.

*CAREER:* Derbyshire County, England, senior medical officer for maternal and child welfare, 1966-68; Sheffield Corporation, Sheffield, England, senior medical officer for handicapped persons, 1968-70; Sheffield Regional Hospital Board, Sheffield, assistant senior medical officer, 1970-74; specialist in community medicine, Barnsley Area Health Authority, 1974-75; University of Manchester, Department of Community Medicine, Manchester, England, director of Unit for Continuing Education, 1975—. *Member:* British Medical Association, Faculty of Community Medicine, Manchester Medical Society.

*WRITINGS: Medical Notes for Social Workers,* John Wright, 1971. Contributor to *Change Agents at Work,* 1978. Contributor of articles to journals in her field.

*WORK IN PROGRESS:* Research on management teams in the National Health Service.

## ESPINASSE, Albert    1905-1972
### (Pierre Brasseur)

December 22, 1905—August 14, 1972; French actor and playwright. Obituaries: *New York Times,* August 16, 1972.

\* \* \*

## ETEROVICH, Francis Hyacinth    1913-

*PERSONAL:* Surname is accented on second syllable, "e" pronounced "a"; born October 4, 1913, in Pucisca, Croatia; son of Lovro (a mailman) and Marija (Petrovic) Eterovich. *Education:* Dominican School of Philosophy and Theology, Dubrovnik, diploma, 1937; Dominican School of Theology, Louvain, Belgium, lectorate, 1939; Croatian State University, Zagreb, classics diploma, 1944; Dominican University, Le Saulchoir, France, Ph.D., 1948; University of Chicago, A.M., 1965. *Office:* Department of Philosophy, DePaul University, Chicago, Ill. 60614.

*CAREER:* College of St. Joseph (now University of Albuquerque), Albuquerque, N.M., instructor in sociology, 1953-56; College of St. Teresa, Winona, Minn., assistant professor of philosophy, 1957-61; DePaul University, Chicago, Ill., professor of philosophy, 1962—. *Member:* American Philosophical Association, American Academy of Political and Social Science, American Association for the Advancement of Slavic Studies, Croatian Academy of America, Center for the Study of Democratic Institutions.

*WRITINGS:* (Editor) *Croatia—Land, People, Culture,* University of Toronto Press, Volume I, 1964, Volume II, 1970, Volume III, 1978; (editor, compiler, and publisher) *Directory of Scholars, Artists, and Professionals of Croatian Descent in the United States and Canada,* [Chicago], 1963, 1965, 1970; *Approaches to Morality,* Harcourt, 1966; *Approaches to Natural Law,* Exposition Press, 1972; (author of analysis and commentary) Aristotle, *Nicomachian Ethics,* University Press of Washington, 1978.

\* \* \*

## EVANS, J(ames) A(llan) S(tewart)    1931-

*PERSONAL:* Born March 24, 1931, in Galt, Ontario, Canada; son of David Arthur (a farmer) and Isabella Jane (Stewart) Evans; married Eleanor Lynn Ward, June 16, 1964; children: James Arthur Laird, Cecily Eleanor, Andrew Lindsay. *Education:* Victoria College, Toronto, B.A., 1952; Yale University, M.A., 1953, Ph.D., 1957; also attended American School of Classical Studies, Athens, Greece, 1954-55. *Politics:* Conservative. *Religion:* Anglican. *Home:* 2967 West 43rd Ave., Vancouver, British Columbia, Canada. *Office:* Buchanan Bldg., University of British Columbia, Vancouver, British Columbia, Canada.

*CAREER:* University of Western Ontario, Waterloo College, London, assistant professor of classics, 1955-60; University of Texas at Austin, assistant professor of classics, 1961-62; McMaster University, Hamilton, Ontario, professor of history, 1962-71; University of British Columbia, Vancouver, professor of classics, 1972—. Visiting special lecturer in classics, University of Toronto, 1960-61. *Member:* Canadian Classical Association, Canadian Historical Association, American Philological Society, American Institute of Archaeology.

*WRITINGS: Economic History of an Egyptian Temple in Greco-Roman Egypt,* Yale University Press, 1961; *Procopius,* Twayne, 1972; *Polis and Imperium: Studies in Honour of Edward Togo Salmon,* Hakkert, 1974. Editor, *Waterloo Review,* 1958-60; editor, *Vergilius,* 1963-71; literature editor,

*Commentator,* 1963-71; reviews editor, *Bulletin of the American Society of Papyrologists,* 1970-76; editor, *Studies in Medieval and Renaissance History,* 1977—.

*WORK IN PROGRESS: Herodotus,* for Twayne.

\* \* \*

## EVANS, John X(avier)    1933-

*PERSONAL:* Born September 22, 1933, in Bennington, Vt.; son of Francis X. and Doris (Ryan) Evans; married Rosemarie Appenzeller, January 2, 1960; children: John X., Elizabeth Marie. *Education:* Holy Cross College, A.B., 1955; Yale University, M.A., 1956, Ph.D., 1966. *Religion:* Catholic. *Office:* Department of English, Arizona State University, Tempe, Ariz. 85281.

*CAREER:* Arizona State University, Tempe, associate professor of English, 1964—. *Military service:* U.S. Army, 1957-58. *Member:* American Association of University Professors, Amici Thomas Mori, Renaissance Society of America, Catholic Record Society. *Awards, honors:* National Endowment for the Humanities fellowship, 1969-70; American Philosophical Society fellowship, summer, 1970.

*WRITINGS: The Works of Sir Roger Williams,* Clarendon Press, 1972. Contributor of articles and reviews to *Shakespeare Quarterly, Texas Studies in Literature and Language, Moreana, Recusant History,* and *Ampleforth Journal.*

*WORK IN PROGRESS:* A study of Tudor Recusant literature; a study of the "interior paradise" in Renaissance literature and the visual arts.

\* \* \*

## EVANS, Laurence    1923-

*PERSONAL:* Born August 10, 1923, in Manchester, England; U.S. citizen; son of William Griffith and Anne Mabel (Iley) Evans; married Elizabeth Taylor, November 30, 1946; children: Cornelia Anne, Elizabeth Iley, Thomas Laurence. *Education:* Attended Columbia University, 1947-48; University of Maine, B.A., 1951; Johns Hopkins University, Ph.D., 1957. *Home:* 712 Murray Hill Rd., Binghamton, N.Y. 13903. *Office:* Department of History, State University of New York, Binghamton, N.Y. 13901.

*CAREER:* University of Maine at Orono, extension lecturer in business law, 1951, instructor in economics, 1952; National Academy of Sciences, Washington, D.C., professional assistant in international relations, 1956-57; U.S. Department of State, Washington, D.C., diplomatic historian, 1957-60; researcher in American Middle East policy in the Middle East and Europe, 1960-61; Loyola College, Baltimore, Md., lecturer in Middle East history, 1962; Johns Hopkins University, Baltimore, research associate in School of Advanced International Studies, 1962-63; U.S. Department of State, senior diplomatic historian, 1963-65; Simon Fraser University, Burnaby, British Columbia, associate professor of history, 1965-67; State University of New York at Binghamton, professor of history, 1967—. Consultant in social sciences to College of Marine Studies, University of Delaware, 1970-71. *Member:* Phi Beta Kappa. *Awards, honors:* American Council of Learned Societies-Social Science Research Council grant, 1960-61; Rockefeller Foundation grant, 1962-63.

*WRITINGS:* (Contributor) *Worldmark Encyclopedia of the Nations,* Worldmark, 1963; (co-author) *Foreign Relations of the United States,* U.S. Department of State, Volume IV: *1943,* 1964, Volume V: *1944,* 1965, Volume VIII: *1945,*

1967; *United States Policy and the Partition of Turkey,* Johns Hopkins Press, 1965; (contributor) H. J. Bass, editor, *The State of American History,* Quadrangle, 1970; (editor and contributor) Martin W. Wilmington, *The Middle East Supply Center,* State University of New York Press, 1971. Also author of classified monographs on U.S. policy in Asia; contributor of articles and reviews to journals.

*WORK IN PROGRESS:* Research for *The United States and the Middle East in World War II, 1939-1947,* completion awaiting declassification of documents.

\* \* \*

## EVANS, Rupert N. 1921-

*PERSONAL:* Born April 6, 1921, in Terre Haute, Ind.; son of Loren N. (a teacher) and Hazel (Rupert) Evans; married Barbara Jean Barbre, June 29, 1941; children: Ellen Anne (Mrs. Roger Collins), Catherine Nell (Mrs. Ron Westman), Nancy Jean. *Education:* Indiana State University, B.S., 1946; Purdue University, M.S., 1949, Ph.D., 1950. *Home:* 1842 Maynard Dr., Champaign, Ill. 61820. *Office:* 188 Education Building, University of Illinois, Urbana, Ill. 61801.

*CAREER:* University of Illinois at Urbana-Champaign, assistant professor, 1950-51, associate professor, 1952-55, professor of vocational and technical education, 1956—, dean of College of Education, 1963-68. Fulbright lecturer in Japan, 1957-58. *Awards, honors:* Dr. Vocat. Ed., Purdue University, 1970.

*WRITINGS:* (With Charles Porter) *Experimental Basic Electronics,* McKnight, 1958; (with Garth Mangum and Pragan) *Education for Employment,* Wayne State University Press, 1969; (editor with David Terry) *Changing the Role of Vocational Teacher Education,* McKnight, 1971; (with Ed Herr) *Foundations of Vocational Education,* C. E. Merrill, 1971, 2nd edition, 1978; (with Kenneth Hoyt, Edward Mackin, and Mangum) *Career Education: What It Is and How to Do It,* Olympus Publishing, 1972, 2nd edition, 1974; (with Hoyt and Mangum) *Career Education in the Middle/Junior High School,* Olympus Publishing, 1973; (with Hoyt, Mangum, and Ella Bowen) *Career Education in the High School,* Olympus Publishing, 1977. Contributor to vocational education journals.

*WORK IN PROGRESS:* Studies of vocational education students and teachers.

\* \* \*

## EVERSON, Ida Gertrude 1898-

*PERSONAL:* Born March 1, 1898, on Staten Island, N.Y.; daughter of George (a banker) and Ida (Miller) Everson. *Education:* Barnard College, A.B., 1920; Columbia University, M.A., 1929, Ph.D., 1945. *Office:* Department of English, Wagner College, 631 Howard Ave., Staten Island, N.Y. 10301.

*CAREER:* American Book Company, New York City, editor's assistant, 1920-22; Columbia University, New York City, library assistant, 1928-38; Hunter College (now Hunter College of the City University of New York), New York City, instructor in English, 1938; Brooklyn College (now Brooklyn College of the City University of New York), Brooklyn, N.Y., instructor in English, 1936-46; Wagner College, Staten Island, N.Y., professor of English, 1949-69, professor emeritus, 1969—. Visiting professor, Illinois College, Jacksonville, Ill., 1968-69. *Member:* Modern Language Association of America, American Association of University Professors, American Association of Retired Persons.

*WRITINGS: George Henry Calvert: American Literary Pioneer,* Columbia University Press, 1944, reprinted, 1975. Contributor of articles to *American Literature, Maryland Historical Magazine, Modern Drama, New England Quarterly.*

*WORK IN PROGRESS:* Irish literary renaissance; American literature of the nineteenth century.†

\* \* \*

## EWEN, Robert B. 1940-

*PERSONAL:* Born March 30, 1940, in Brooklyn, N.Y.; son of David (an author) and Hannah (Weinstein) Ewen. *Education:* Cornell University, B.A., 1961; University of Illinois, M.A., 1963, Ph.D., 1965. *Home:* 8101 Camino Real, Miami, Fla. 33143. *Office:* Department of Psychology, Florida International University, Tamiami Trail, Miami, Fla. 33144.

*CAREER:* New York University, New York, N.Y., assistant professor, 1965-72, associate professor of psychology, 1972-73, assistant chairman of department, 1971-73; Florida International University, Miami, adjunct associate professor of psychology, 1974—. Staff psychologist, Lincoln Institute for Psychotherapy, 1971-72. *Member:* American Psychological Association, Phi Kappa Phi, Psi Chi.

*WRITINGS:* (With James J. Kirkpatrick, Richard S. Barrett, and Raymond A. Katzell) *Testing and Fair Employment,* New York University Press, 1968; *Opening Leads,* Prentice-Hall, 1970; (with Joan Welkowitz and Jacob Cohen) *Introductory Statistics for the Behavioral Sciences* (with workbook), Academic Press, 1971, 2nd edition, 1976; (editor) *Charles Goren Presents the Precision System,* Chancellor Hall, 1971; (editor) C. C. Wei, *The Simplified Precision System,* Barclay Bridge Supplies, 1972; *Doubles for Penalties, Takeout, and Profits,* Prentice-Hall, 1973; *Preemptive Bidding,* Prentice-Hall, 1975; *Contract Bridge: A Concise Guide,* F. Watts, 1975; *The Teenager's Guide to Bridge,* Dodd, 1976; *Getting It Together,* F. Watts, 1976; *Choosing the College for You,* F. Watts, 1976. Contributor to publications for bridge players.

*WORK IN PROGRESS: An Introduction to the Theory of Personality,* for Academic Press.

# F

**FAGUNDO, Ana Maria 1938-**

*PERSONAL:* Born March 13, 1938, in Tenerife, Spain; daughter of Ramon (a teacher) and Candelaria (Guerra) Fagundo. *Education:* Escuela Professional de Comercio, Profesora Mercantil, 1957; University of Redlands, B.A., 1962; University of Washington, Seattle, M.A., 1964, Ph.D.,1967. *Religion:* Roman Catholic. *Home:* 3305 Wickham Dr., Riverside, Calif. 92505. *Office:* Department of Literature and Language, University of California, Riverside, Calif. 92502.

*CAREER:* University of California, Riverside, 1967—, began as assistant professor, currently associate professor of contemporary Spanish literature. *Member:* American Association of Teachers of Spanish and Portuguese.

*WRITINGS*—Poetry, except as indicated: *Brotes,* privately printed, 1965; *Isla adentro,* Graceta de las Artes (Tenerife), 1969; *Diario de una muerte,* Alfaguara Editorial (Madrid), 1970; *Vida y obra de Emily Dickinson* (literary criticism), Alfaguara Editorial, 1972; *Configurado tiempo,* Editorial Oriens, 1974; *Invencion de la luz,* Editorial Vosgos, 1978. Contributor of more than forty poems to literary magazines in the United States and Spain; contributor of short stories, articles, reviews, and literary criticism to journals. Founder and editor-in-chief of *Alaluz,* Spanish-language poetry and short story journal, 1969—.

*WORK IN PROGRESS: El banquete de los sonambulos,* short stories; research in twentieth-century poetry, especially Spanish and American; *Poetas espanoles de posguerra; Literatura norteamericana contemporanea: 1950-75.*

*BIOGRAPHICAL/CRITICAL SOURCES: Poesia Espanola,* February, 1967, April, 1970, January, 1971; *Cuadernos Americanos* (Mexico), March/April, 1970; *Ceres,* December 15, 1970; *Revista de estudios Hispanicos* (United States), January, 1972; *Estafeta Literaria,* July, 1978.

\*　　\*　　\*

**FAIRLEY, M(ichael) C(harles) 1937-**

*PERSONAL:* Born May 13, 1937, in Sittingbourne, Kent, England; son of Charles Frederick and Dorothy (Kay) Fairley; married Patricia Cockell, March 30, 1960; children: Jacqueline. *Education:* Studied at Medway and Maidstone Colleges of Art, 1954-62, receiving full technological certificate in printing; Garnett College of Education, London, teacher's certificate, 1966. *Religion:* Church of England. *Home:* 10 Torrington Dr., Potters Bar, Herts, England. *Office:* Paper and Paper Products Industry Training Board, Star House, Potters Bar, Herts, England.

*CAREER: East Kent Gazette,* Sittingbourne, England, printer, 1954-63; Thanet School of Art, Margate, England, lecturer in printing, 1964-71; Printing Industry Research Association, Leatherhead, Surrey, England, deputy head of training, 1971-75; Paper and Paper Products Industry Training Board, Star House, Potters Bar, Herts, England, deputy planning and information manager, 1975—. *Member:* Institute of Printing, Association of Teachers of Printing, National Graphical Association, Institute of Management in Printing.

*WRITINGS: Safety, Health, and Welfare in the Printing Industry,* Pergamon, 1968; *Materials Handling in the Printing Industry,* Pergamon, 1970; *Print: Technological Change and the Printing Craftsman,* National Graphical Association, 1971; *The Printing Processes-Screen Process,* Printing Industry Research Association, 1972; *The Principles of Moisture Measurement of Paper and Board,* Printing Industry Research Association, 1973. Also author of a wide range of information, careers, and training publications for the Paper and Paper Products Industry Training Board, 1975—. Contributor to *Encyclopaedia of Occupational Health and Safety;* regular contributor to *Print* (journal), 1969-71, and occasional contributor to other periodicals.

*SIDELIGHTS:* M. C. Fairley told *CA:* "The main aim of almost all of the books or publications I have written or contributed to has been to explain the nature of industrial problems or technology in a clear, concise and interesting way. This developed from my years as a lecturer in technical education where much of the existing text book or lecture material was too complex for the average reader."

\*　　\*　　\*

**FALERO, Frank, Jr. 1937-**

*PERSONAL:* Born December 22, 1937, in New York, N.Y.; married Sara Ann Schucker, June 26, 1959; children: Lisa Ann, Sara Francine. *Education:* St. Petersburg Junior College, A.A., 1962; University of South Florida, B.A. (with honors), 1964; Florida State University, M.S., 1965, Ph.D., 1967. *Office:* Department of Economics, California State College, Bakersfield, Calif. 93305.

*CAREER:* Federal Reserve Bank of Richmond, Va., research economist, 1967; Virginia Polytechnic Institute and State University, Blacksburg, assistant professor of economics, 1967-72; California State College, Bakersfield, 1972—, began as associate professor, currently professor of economics. Fulbright visiting professor, Universidad del Pacifico, Lima, Peru, 1968-69. Consultant to mission to Ethiopia, U.S. Agency for International Development, 1970—. *Military service:* U.S. Army, 1955-58. *Member:* American Economic Association, Royal Economic Society (fellow), American Association for the Advancement of Science, American Arbitration Association, Regional Science Association, Southern Economic Association, Alpha Kappa Psi, Beta Gamma Sigma, Phi Kappa Phi, Delta Tau Kappa, Omicron Delta Epsilon. *Awards, honors:* Resources for the Future grant, 1969; honorable mention for the teaching of economics by Kazanjian Foundation, 1971, from Joint Council on Economic Education.

*WRITINGS: Elementos basicos de econometria con applicaciones al Peru,* Universidad del Pacifico, 1969; *Monetary History of Honduras, 1950-1968,* University Press of Kentucky, 1972; (contributor) *Kazanjian Awards 1971,* Joint Council on Economic Education, 1972. Contributor of about twenty articles to economic journals.

*WORK IN PROGRESS: Observaciones sobre el progreso technico; An Alternative Concept of the Demand for Money in a Developing Country; Macro-Development Game; The Negative Effects of Foreign Investment; The Economics of Academia; Money, Exports, Government Spending, and Income in Ethiopia, 1961-1967.*

\* \* \*

## FANT, Louis J(udson), Jr. 1931-

*PERSONAL:* Born December 13, 1931, in Greenville, S.C.; son of Louie Judson and Hazeline (Reid) Fant; married Lauralea Irwin (a teacher), June 12, 1954; children: Lynn, Layne (son), Lesa (daughter), Lorn (son). *Education:* Baylor University, B.A., 1953; Columbia University, M.A., 1955; University of Maryland, additional graduate study, 1958-67. *Politics:* Democrat. *Religion:* Unitarian Universalist. *Home:* 18819 Vintage St., Northridge, Calif. 91324. *Office:* California State University, Northridge, Calif. 91324.

*CAREER:* New York School for the Deaf, White Plains, elementary teacher, 1955-58; Gallaudet College, Washington, D.C., associate professor of education, 1958-67; National Theatre of the Deaf, New York, N.Y., actor and administrator, 1967-70; California State University, Northridge, lecturer in special education and drama, 1970—. Actor on stage and in films; sign language interpreter and member of Registry of Interpreters for the Deaf. *Member:* National Association of the Deaf, Convention of American Instructors of the Deaf, Screen Actors Guild, Actors' Equity Association, American Federation of Television and Radio Artists.

*WRITINGS: Say It with Hands,* National Association of the Deaf, 1964; *Ameslan: An Introduction to American Sign Language,* Joyce Media, 1972; *Sign Language,* Joyce Media, 1977.

*SIDELIGHTS:* Louis Fant's books are based on the concept that sign language (the fourth most-used language in the United States according to government surveys) must be studied just as any other language is. Both of his parents are deaf.

## FARAU, Alfred 1904-1972

December 10, 1904—November 14, 1972; Austrian-born American psychologist, psychotherapist, and author of poems, plays, and books on the human personality. Obituaries: *New York Times,* November 15, 1972.

\* \* \*

## FARCA, Marie C. 1935-

*PERSONAL:* Born June 6, 1935, in Philadelphia, Pa.; daughter of George (a quality control manager) and Catherine (Candea) Farca. *Education:* University of Pennsylvania, B.S. Ed., 1957. *Residence:* Bucks County, Pa. *Agent:* Scott Meredith Literary Agency, Inc., 845 Third Ave., New York, N.Y. 10022.

*CAREER:* Teacher in public schools in Trenton, N.J. area. Demonstration teacher, Trenton State College, 1963-69. Free-lance photographer, using her own slides to create educational filmstrips. *Member:* National Education Association, New Jersey Education Association, Alpha Omicron Pi.

*WRITINGS: Earth* (science-fiction), Doubleday, 1972; *Complex Man* (science fiction), Doubleday, 1973.

*WORK IN PROGRESS:* A new novel.

*SIDELIGHTS: Earth* and *Complex Man* have been published together in a French edition by Editions de Noel (Paris), 1974. *Avocational interests:* Travel abroad, including eastern and western Europe and Africa.

*BIOGRAPHICAL/CRITICAL SOURCES: Trenton Times,* May 28, 1972.

\* \* \*

## FARICY, Robert L(eo) 1926-

*PERSONAL:* Born August 29, 1926, in St. Paul, Minn.; son of Roland Joseph (an attorney) and Clare (Sullivan) Faricy. *Education:* United States Naval Academy, B.S., 1949; St. Louis University, M.A., 1954, Ph.L., 1955; Lyon-Fourviere Institute (France), S.T.L., 1963; Catholic University of America, S.T.D., 1966. *Religion:* Roman Catholic. *Home and office:* Gregorian University, Piazza della Pilotta 4, 00187, Rome, Italy.

*CAREER:* Roman Catholic priest of the Society of Jesus (Jesuits); entered 1950, ordained, 1962; Catholic University of America, Washington, D.C., assistant professor of theology and spirituality, 1966-71; Gregorian University, Rome, Italy, professor of spirituality, 1971—. *Military service:* U.S. Navy, 1944-50; became an ensign. *Member:* Catholic Theological Society of America, College Theology Society, American Teilhard de Chardin Association (member of advisory board).

*WRITINGS: Teilhard de Chardin's Theology of the Christian in the World,* Sheed, 1967; *Building God's World,* Dimension, 1976; *Spirituality for Religious Life,* Paulist/Newman, 1976; (with M. Flick and G. O'Collins) *What Are They Saying about the Cross?,* Paulist/Newman, 1978. Contributor of articles to *Theological Studies, Gregorianum, Civilta Cattolica, Thomist, Spiritual Life, Theology Today,* and other periodicals.

*WORK IN PROGRESS:* A practical book on prayer and meditation; a book on Christian faith and Marxist philosophy partly based on a shorter study; a book on celibate Christian community and charismatic renewal.

*SIDELIGHTS:* Robert L. Faricy told *CA:* "I write from a

Christian faith perspective about Jesus Christ, who he is for us, and who we are for him. My purpose is to bring to expression the interpersonal relationships that we all have with him, and in him with one another. So, hopefully, more aware of life's meaning and of its joy and its solemnity, the reader (and the writer) may live it more fruitfully. In other words, I write about love, God's love for us and how we can love him back.''

\*　　　\*　　　\*

## FARIES, Clyde J. 1928-

*PERSONAL:* Born July 8, 1928, in Macomb, Ill.; son of Darcy O. and Inez (McIntosh) Faries; married Elizabeth Thomas (a teacher); children: Dixie (Mrs. Jorge Dominquez), Dora Jean, David, Doug. *Education:* Southeast Missouri State College (now University), B.S., 1950; University of Michigan, M.A., 1954; University of Missouri, Ph.D., 1965. *Home:* 227 Jana Rd., Macomb, Ill. 61455. *Office:* Department of Speech, Western Illinois University, Macomb, Ill. 61455.

*CAREER:* Teacher of English and speech in a Missouri high school, 1950-52; teacher in Michigan schools, 1952-55; Lincoln College, Lincoln, Ill., instructor in speech, 1955-57; Georgia Southern College, Statesboro, assistant professor of speech, 1957-63; Murray State College (now University), Murray, Ky., member of faculty, 1963-66; Western Illinois University, Macomb, teacher of speech education, rhetoric, public address, and oral interpretation, 1966—. *Military service:* U.S. Army, 1946-47. *Member:* Speech Communication Association, Religious Speech Communication Association, Central States Speech Association, Illinois Speech-Theatre Association.

*WRITINGS: Assignments in Speech,* Kendall/Hunt, 1969; (contributor) De Witte Holland, editor, *Preaching in American History,* Abingdon, 1969; (contributor) Holland, editor, *Sermons in American History,* Abingdon, 1971; (contributor) *American Issues,* W. C. Brown, 1973. Contributor of articles to *Quarterly Journal of Speech, Forensic, Journal of Mississippi History, Preaching,* and *Illinois Speech and Theater Journal.*

*WORK IN PROGRESS: Mississippi Private,* a biography of Private John Allen.

\*　　　\*　　　\*

## FARIGOULE, Louis 1885-1972
### (Jules Romains)

August 26, 1885—August 14, 1972; French novelist, poet, playwright, essayist, and founder of the philosophy of unanimism. Obituaries: *New York Times,* August 18, 1972; *L'Express,* August 21-27, 1972; *Newsweek,* August 28, 1972; *Time,* August 28, 1972.

\*　　　\*　　　\*

## FARMER, Gene 1919-1972

August 20, 1919—June 20, 1972; American editor. Obituaries: *New York Times,* June 22, 1972; *Publishers Weekly,* July 3, 1972; *Time,* July 3, 1972.

\*　　　\*　　　\*

## FARR, David M. L. 1922-

*PERSONAL:* Born December 19, 1922, in Vancouver, British Columbia, Canada; son of Arthur Morice and Mary (Marlatt) Farr; married Joan R. Fisher, September 5, 1946;

children: Christopher, Timothy, Jeremy. *Education:* University of British Columbia, B.A., 1944; University of Toronto, M.A., 1946; Oxford University, Ph.D., 1952. *Home:* 942 Echo Dr., Ottawa, Ontario, Canada KIS 5C9. *Office:* Department of History, Carleton University, Ottawa, Ontario, Canada KIS 5B6.

*CAREER:* Dalhousie University, Halifax, Nova Scotia, lecturer in Canadian history, 1946-47; Carleton University, Ottawa, Ontario, 1947—, began as lecturer, currently professor of history, dean of arts, 1963-69. Visiting professor, University of British Columbia, 1957-58, Duke University, 1960. *Military service:* Royal Canadian Naval Volunteer Reserve, 1944-45. *Member:* Canadian Historical Association (English language secretary, 1948-50, 1952-57; vice-president, 1976-77; president, 1977-78), Canadian Institute of International Affairs.

*WRITINGS: The Colonial Office and Canada 1867-1887,* University of Toronto Press, 1955; (with J. S. Moir and S. R. Mealing) *Two Democracies,* Ryerson, 1963; (with Moir) *The Canadian Experience,* Ryerson, 1969.

*WORK IN PROGRESS:* Studying Canadian external relations and Canada-United States relations.

\*　　　\*　　　\*

## FASANA, Paul James 1933-

*PERSONAL:* Born July 20, 1933, in Bingham Canyon, Utah; son of Oreste G. and Mary (Rolando-Calcio) Fasana. *Education:* University of California, Berkeley, B.A., 1959, M.L.S., 1960. *Politics:* Democrat. *Religion:* Roman Catholic. *Home:* 115 Central Park W., Apt. 27E, New York, N.Y. 10023. *Office:* Research Libraries, New York Public Library, 42nd St. and 5th Ave., New York, N.Y. 10018.

*CAREER:* New York Public Library, New York City, cataloger in Circulation Division, 1960-61; ITEK Laboratories, Lexington, Mass., systems engineer, 1961-63; U.S. Air Force Cambridge Research Laboratory Library, Bedford, Mass., chief of cataloging, 1963-64; Columbia University Libraries, New York City, assistant coordinator of cataloging, 1964-66, assistant to the director for library automation, 1966-71; Collaborative Library Systems Development, New York City, secretary to planning council, 1968-71; New York Public Library, chief of preparation services, Research Libraries, 1971—. Lecturer in library schools of McGill University, 1966-69, University of Montreal, 1968-69, Rutgers University, 1970-71, Graduate School and University Center of the City College of the City University of New York, 1974-76; lecturer or speaker at seminars for American Management Association and information science and library associations. Consultant, Inforonics, Inc., 1963-68, Center for Urban Education, 1965-66, Harvard University, 1965—, Metropolitan Applied Research Center, Inc., 1968-71, New Jersey Department of Higher Education, 1970-72.

*MEMBER:* American Library Association (member of board of directors, Information Science and Automation Division, 1966-67, 1971—; member of board of directors, Resources and Technical Services Division, 1970—; member of council, 1970-73), American Society for Information Science (member of council, 1971—), New York Technical Service Librarians (president, 1971-72).

*WRITINGS:* (Contributor) *Automation and Scientific Communication,* American Documentation Institute, 1963; (editor with L. Denis, and contributor) *Proceedings: Colloque sur les implications administratives de l'automatisa-*

*tion dans les bibliotheques,* Montreal University Press, 1968; (editor) *Electronic Data Processing Concepts,* American Society for Information Science, 1968; (editor) *Elements of Information Systems,* American Society for Information Science, 1968; (with others) *A Computer Based System for Reserve Activities in a University Library,* Columbia University Libraries, 1969; (editor with Allen Veaner, and contributor) *The Collaborative Library Systems Development Project,* M.I.T. Press, 1971; *The Columbia University Libraries Integrated Technical Services System: Acquisition,* U.S. National Science Foundation, 1971. Author or editor of other reports on automated routines and mechanization for libraries and library orientated organizations. Contributor to numerous library journals.

\* \* \*

## FATIO, Louise 1904-

*PERSONAL:* Born August 18, 1904, in Lausanne, Switzerland; daughter of Alfred and Elisa (Chenevard) Fatio; married Roger Antoine Duvoisin (a writer and illustrator of children's books), July 25, 1925; children: Roger, Jacques. *Education:* Attended boarding school in Basel and College des Jeunes Filles in Geneva. *Address:* P.O. Box 116, Gladstone, N.J. 07934.

*CAREER:* Began to gather ideas for her own books while helping her husband with his writing for children. *Member:* Authors Guild. *Awards, honors: The Happy Lion* received first prize for a juvenile book from the West German Government, 1956 (it was published in German, 1955).

*WRITINGS*—All illustrated by her husband, Roger Duvoisin: *The Christmas Forest,* Aladdin Books, 1950; *Anna, the Horse,* Aladdin Books, 1951; *The Happy Lion,* Whittlesey House, 1954; *The Happy Lion in Africa,* Whittlesey House, 1955; *A Doll for Maria,* Whittlesey House, 1957; *The Happy Lion Roars,* Whittlesey House, 1957; *The Three Happy Lions,* Whittlesey House, 1959; *The Happy Lion's Quest,* Whittlesey House, 1961; *Red Bantam,* Whittlesey House, 1963; *The Happy Lion and the Bear,* Whittlesey House, 1964; *The Happy Lion's Vacation,* McGraw, 1967; *The Happy Lion's Treasure,* McGraw, 1971; *The Happy Lion's Rabbits,* McGraw, 1973; *Hector Penguin,* McGraw, 1974; *Hector and Christina,* McGraw, 1977.

*WORK IN PROGRESS:* Two children's books, for McGraw.

*SIDELIGHTS:* Louise Fatio and her husband live and write in rural New Jersey, leaving their hillside home to do some extensive traveling every year. *Avocational interests:* Growing flowers, the animals on their land, music, reading.

*BIOGRAPHICAL/CRITICAL SOURCES: Book World,* October 1, 1967; *Young Reader's Review,* November, 1967; *New York Times Book Review,* January 21, 1968; Lee Bennet Hopkins, *Books Are by People,* Citation, 1969.

\* \* \*

## FEAGIN, Joe R(ichard) 1938-

*PERSONAL:* Surname is pronounced *Fay*-gin; born May 6, 1938, in San Angelo, Tex.; son of Frank J. (a geophysicist) and Hannah (Griffin) Feagin; married Clairece Y. Booher, September 1, 1959; children: Michelle, Trevor. *Education:* Baylor University, B.A., 1960; Harvard University, Ph.D., 1966. *Office:* Department of Sociology, University of Texas, Austin, Tex. 78712.

*CAREER:* University of Massachusetts—Boston, instructor in sociology, 1965-66; University of California, Riv-

erside, assistant professor of sociology, 1966-70; University of Texas at Austin, associate professor, 1970-75, professor of sociology, 1975—. Research assistant, Joint Center for Urban Studies, Harvard University and Massachusetts Institute of Technology, 1964-65. *Member:* American Sociological Association, Southwestern Sociological Association, Southwestern Social Science Association. *Awards, honors:* Pulitzer Prize nomination, 1974, for *Ghetto Revolts.*

*WRITINGS: Subsidizing the Poor,* Heath Lexington, 1972; *Ghetto Revolts,* Macmillan, 1973; *The Urban Scene,* Random House, 1973; *Subordinating the Poor,* Prentice-Hall, 1975; *Racial and Ethnic Relations,* Prentice-Hall, 1978; (with wife, Clairece Feagin) *Discrimination American Style: Institutional Racism and Sexism,* Prentice-Hall, 1978. Contributor of articles to sociology, public opinion, and political science journals. Advisory editor, *Social Science Quarterly;* associate editor, *Journal of Voluntary Action Research.*

*AVOCATIONAL INTERESTS:* Chess.

\* \* \*

## FEAL-DEIBE, Carlos 1935-

*PERSONAL:* Born March 6, 1935, in La Coruna, Spain; son of Andres and Isabel (Deibe) Feal; married Gisele Carrat, November 16, 1962; children: Sophie, Helene. *Education:* University of Madrid, B.A., 1957, Ph.D., 1963. *Home:* 265-B Scamridge, Buffalo, N.Y. 14221. *Office:* Department of Modern Languages and Literatures, State University of New York, Buffalo, N.Y. 14260.

*CAREER:* University of Lyon, Lyon, France, lecturer in Spanish, 1960-61; University of Nantes, Nantes, France, lecturer in Spanish, 1963-66; University of Michigan, Ann Arbor, assistant professor of Spanish, 1966-69; State University of New York at Buffalo, associate professor, 1969-75, professor of Spanish, 1975—. *Member:* American Association of University Professors, Modern Language Association of America, American Association of Teachers of Spanish. *Awards, honors:* Faculty research fellowship, University of Michigan, 1969; faculty research fellowship, State University of New York, 1970, 1974.

*WRITINGS: La Poesia de Pedro Salinas,* Gredos (Madrid), 1965, 2nd edition, 1971; *Eros y Lorca,* Edhasa (Barcelona), 1973; *Unamuno: El Otro y Don Juan,* Planeta (Madrid), 1976.

\* \* \*

## FEARON, John D(aniel) 1920-

*PERSONAL:* Born May 23, 1920, in St. Cloud, Minn.; son of Francis H. and Hazel (Bernick) Fearon. *Education:* St. Albert's College, B.A., 1943, S.T.B., 1945, S.T.Lic. and S.T.Lr., 1947. *Politics:* Democrat. *Office address: Western Dominican,* P.O. Box 3045, Oakland, Calif. 94609.

*CAREER:* Roman Catholic priest of Dominican Order; St. Albert's College, Oakland, Calif., instructor in philosophy, 1947-52; St. Dominic's Parish, Los Angeles, Calif., assistant pastor, 1952-55; Mount St. Mary's College, Los Angeles, Calif., instructor in religious studies, 1955-58; St. Albert's College, assistant professor of theology, 1958-62; Seattle University, Seattle, Wash., assistant professor, 1963-67, associate professor of theology, 1967-71; St. Francis College, Loretto, Pa., assistant professor in department of religious studies, 1972-73; *Western Dominican,* Oakland, Calif., editor, 1973—. Assistant chaplain to District of Columbia penal institutions, 1946-47. *Member:* Catholic

Theological Society of America, American Catholic Philosophical Association, Religious Education Association, American Academy of Religion, College Theology Society, American Association of University Professors, Association of Dominican College Teachers of the Western Province (chairman, 1964-69). *Awards, honors:* Research grants from Seattle University, 1966, 1970.

*WRITINGS: Graceful Living,* Newman, 1956; *Sin,* McGraw, 1969. Assistant editor for moral theology of *New Catholic Encyclopedia.* Contributor of about twenty articles to *America, Commonweal, Ave Maria,* and other religious journals.

\*        \*        \*

## FEDDER, Edwin H(ersh) 1929-

*PERSONAL:* Born January 21, 1929, in Baltimore, Md.; son of William S. and Rose Fedder; married Ruth Weger (a social worker), September 19, 1954; children: Jane, David. *Education:* University of Maryland, B.A., 1950; American University, M.A., 1953, Ph.D., 1957; additional study at Hague Academy of International Law, 1961, and Oak Ridge Institute of Nuclear Studies, 1963. *Home:* 559 Stratford, St. Louis, Mo. 63130. *Office:* Center for International Studies, University of Missouri, St. Louis, Mo. 63121.

*CAREER:* Public school teacher in Maryland, 1954-56; University of Pittsburgh, Pittsburgh, Pa., instructor in political science, 1956-59; Hollins College, Hollins College, Va., assistant professor, 1959-61, associate professor of politics, 1962-65, chairman of department, 1964-65; Ohio State University, Columbus, visiting associate professor of political science and Mershon research fellow, 1965-67; University of Missouri—St. Louis, associate professor, 1967-68, professor of political science, 1968—, director of Center for International Studies, 1967—. Visiting lecturer at West Virginia University, summer, 1957, at University of Illinois, 1964; visiting fellow, London School of Economics and Political Science, University of London, summer, 1970.

*MEMBER:* International Studies Association (founder and president of south section, 1964-65; president of midwest section, 1972-73), Committee on Atlantic Studies, Midwest Political Science Association, Missouri Political Science Association, Pi Sigma Alpha. *Awards, honors:* Danforth Foundation faculty grants, 1960-61.

*WRITINGS: Prolegomena to the Theory of Alliance,* Mershon Center, Ohio State University, 1966; (with James A. Robinson) *The United States and NATO,* Mershon Center, Ohio State University, 1967; (with Robinson) *Beyond Hegemony,* Mershon Center, Ohio State University, 1967; (contributor) Joseph Dunner, editor, *Handbook of World History,* Philosophical Library, 1967; (editor) *Methodological Concerns in International Studies,* Center for International Studies, University of Missouri, 1970; (editor and contributor) *NATO in the Seventies,* Center for International Studies, University of Missouri, 1970; (editor) *The United Nations: Problems and Prospects,* Center for International Studies, University of Missouri, 1971; (contributor) Robinson, editor, *Political Science Annual,* Volume III, Bobbs-Merrill, 1972; John Lovell and Philip Kronenberg, editors, *The New Civil-Military Relations: The Agonies of Adjustment to Post Vietnam Realities,* Transaction, 1973; *NATO: The Dynamics of Alliance in the Postwar World,* Dodd, 1973. Contributor of about twenty articles to journals of political affairs. Member of board of editors, *International Studies Quarterly,* 1970—.

*WORK IN PROGRESS:* With Frederic S. Pearson, *Theory in International Relations,* for Dodd.

## FEDER, Ernest 1913-

*PERSONAL:* Born August 23, 1913, in Berlin, Germany; came to U.S., 1939; naturalized, 1944; married; children: one daughter. *Education:* Attended London School of Economics and Political Science, 1936; University of Geneva, Ph.D., 1938; University of California, Berkeley, M.S., 1948. *Office:* FAO Regional Office, Providencia 871, Casilla 10095, Santiago, Chile.

*CAREER:* Legal assistant at various law firms in Geneva, Switzerland, 1935-38; EPA Insurance Co., Geneva, legal advisor, 1938-39; apprentice farmer on various farms in U.S., 1939-41; owner-operator of dairy farm, Monee, Ill., 1941-46; Arizona State University, Tempe, assistant professor of economics and agricultural economics, 1949; South Dakota State University, Brookings, associate professor of agricultural economics, 1949-54; University of Nebraska, Lincoln, associate professor of agricultural economics, 1954-61; Universidad del Valle, Cali, Colombia, professor of land economics, 1961-62; Organization of American States (OAS), Washington, D.C., chief of agricultural program, 1963-64; United Nations, New York, N.Y., advisor on land reform and agricultural development, Economic Commission for Latin America (ECLA), in Washington, D.C., 1964-68, chief of agricultural section in Mexico office of ECLA, 1968-69, project or mission director with Food and Agriculture Organization (FAO), in Ceylon, 1969-70, in Rome, Italy, 1970, in Lima, Peru, 1970-71, in Santiago, Chile, 1971—. Fulbright professor, Graduate School of Economics, University of Chile, 1958-59. Agricultural economics advisor or consultant to various government organizations; visiting professor, Latin American Institute, Free University of Berlin, Berlin, Germany, 1972—.

*WRITINGS: The Rape of the Peasantry: Latin America's Landholding System,* Doubleday, 1971; (compiler) *Gewalt und Ausbeutung,* Hoffmann & Cape, 1973.

Contributor: Rodolfo Stavenhagen, editor, *Agrarian Problems and Peasant Movements in Latin America,* Doubleday-Anchor, 1970; T. Shanin, editor, *Peasants and Peasant Society,* Penguin (London), 1971. Contributor of articles and papers on land conditions and agrarian reform in Latin America, and reviews, to various journals, including *Economica Colombiana, American Journal of Economics and Sociology, Estudios Agrarios* (Mexico), *Trimestre Economico* (Mexico), *Wirtschaftdienst* (Hamburg), *Journal of Farm Economics, Mundo Nuevo* (Buenos Aires), and *America Latina* (Rio de Janeiro).†

\*        \*        \*

## FEENSTRA, Henry John 1936-

*PERSONAL:* Born February 24, 1936, in Hamilton, Ontario, Canada; son of Tjebbe (a farmer) and Alberdina (Reurink) Feenstra; married Jane Vandervelde, August 27, 1960; children: Renee Michelle, Thomas Harrison Jacob. *Education:* University of Western Ontario, B.A., 1962, M.A., 1965, Ph.D., 1967. *Home address:* R.R. 3, Chatsworth, Ontario, Canada. *Office address:* Box 100, Markdale, Ontario, Canada.

*CAREER:* London Board of Education, London, Ontario, psychologist, 1967-69; Philippine Normal College, Manila, psychologist, 1969-71; Grey County Board of Education, Ontario, psychologist, 1971—. *Member:* International Association of Applied Psychologists, Canadian Psychological Association, Ontario Psychological Association.

*WRITINGS:* (With H. S. Zingle, C. Safran, A. E. Hobol, and J. H. Hassard) *Decision-Making,* Holt, 1969.

## FEIL, Hila 1942-

*PERSONAL:* Born June 29, 1942, in New York, N.Y.; daughter of Robert (a writer) and Dorothy (a writer; maiden name, Crayder) Newman; married Gerald Feil (a film director), February 2, 1967; children: Anna. *Education:* Attended Barnard College, 1960-62. *Office:* c/o Feil Productions, 36 West 62nd St., New York, N.Y. 10023.

*CAREER:* Worked for many years as a writer, researcher, and editor of films and television series. *Awards, honors:* Emmy and Peabody Awards for contributions to "The 20th Century" and "The 21st Century" series.

*WRITINGS: The Windmill Summer* (juvenile), Harper, 1972; (translator into French) Shel Silverstein, *L'Arbre au grand coeur,* Harper, 1973; *The Ghost Garden* (juvenile), Atheneum, 1975. Also author and co-narrator for "New Guinea: Patrol into the Unknown," a special program for National Broadcasting Co. (NBC).

*SIDELIGHTS:* In 1969, Hila Feil accompanied her husband to New Guinea to film traditional ceremonies and cultures of the inhabitants, and on an expedition to establish contact with a group of people who had never seen anyone from the outside.

\* \* \*

## FELLOWS, Hugh P. 1915-

*PERSONAL:* Born April 25, 1915, in Cottondale, Fla.; son of Clyde Michael (a businessman and farmer) and Maud (Shomaker) Fellows; married Sara Hamilton, May 25, 1940 (divorced, July, 1947); children: Judith Anne Stanley. *Education:* Bob Jones University, B.A., 1935; Northwestern University, M.A., 1937; New York University, Ph.D., 1955. *Politics:* Independent. *Religion:* Episcopalian. *Residence:* Tampa, Fla. *Agent:* Bertha Klausner International Literary Agency, Inc., 71 Park Ave., New York, N.Y. 10016. *Office:* Department of Speech, Hillsborough Community College, Tampa, Fla. 33622.

*CAREER:* University of Florida, Gainesville, special lecturer in speech, 1940-41; City College (now City College of the City University of New York), New York City, coordinator of speech, 1947-51; New York University, New York City, associate professor and coordinator of speech in Division of General Education, 1955-64; University of Tampa, Tampa, Fla., professor of speech and chairman of speech and drama department, 1964-76; Hillsborough Community College, Tampa, Fla., adjunct professor of speech, 1976—. Summer professor in Japan and the United States and in England. Consultant to industry and to private clients. Director of professional summer theaters in New Milford, Conn., 1946, Kennebunkport, Me., 1949-51, and Santa Fe, N.M., 1958. *Military service:* U.S. Naval Reserve, combat pilot, 1941-45; became lieutenant senior grade; served in Pacific; received combat medal. *Member:* Speech Communication Association of America, Florida Speech and Hearing Association. *Awards, honors:* Fulbright scholar in England, 1951-52; Library of Congress citation for recording *Talking Books.*

*WRITINGS: Dark Needs No Candles,* Kaleidograph Press, 1941; *The Art and Skill of Talking with People,* Prentice-Hall, 1964. Contributor of articles to periodicals.

*WORK IN PROGRESS:* Three books, *Fresh from the Dryer,* an "expo" of the beauty salon business, *Executive Training in Communication,* with film strips, and *Dear Professor,* a collection of letters; *Speech: Sense and Nonsense.*

## FELS, Rendigs 1917-

*PERSONAL:* Born June 11, 1917, in Cincinnati, Ohio; son of Clifford G. and Estella (Rendigs) Fels; married Beatrice Baker, December 27, 1941; children: Charles W. B., Carmichael. *Education:* Harvard University, A.B., 1939, Ph.D., 1948; Columbia University, A.M., 1940. *Home:* 917 Westview Ave., Nashville, Tenn. 37205. *Office address:* Box 1664, Station B, Vanderbilt University, Nashville, Tenn. 37235.

*CAREER:* Vanderbilt University, Nashville, Tenn., assistant professor, 1948-52, associate professor, 1952-56, professor of economics, 1956—, chairman of department of economics and business administration, 1962-65, 1977—. Visiting professor at Stanford University, 1955, and Salzburg Seminar in American Studies, 1963. Chairman, Universities-National Bureau Committee for Economic Research, 1962-67; consultant to Economic Development Institute, University of Nigeria, 1963. *Military service:* U.S. Army Air Forces, 1942-46; became major. *Member:* American Economic Association (secretary-treasurer, 1970-75; treasurer, 1975—), American Association of University Professors, Southern Economic Association (president, 1967-68).

*WRITINGS: History of American Business Cycles, 1865-97,* University of North Carolina Press, 1959; *Challenge to the American Economy: An Introduction to Economics,* Allyn & Bacon, 1961, 2nd edition, 1966; (editor and author of introduction and summary) Joseph A. Schumpeter, *Business Cycles,* abridged edition, McGraw, 1964; *The Law of Supply and Demand: A Programmed Approach,* Allyn & Bacon, 1966; (with C. Elton Hinshaw) *Forecasting and Recognizing Business Cycle Turning Points,* National Bureau of Economic Research, 1968; (contributor) Keith G. Lumsden, editor, *Recent Research in Economics Education,* Prentice-Hall, 1970; (editor with Robert G. Uhler) *Casebook of Economic Problems and Policies,* West Publishing, 1974, 4th edition (with Stephen Buckles and Walter Johnson), 1979. Co-author of workbooks for *Modern Economics,* 2nd edition, Harcourt, 1953, and *Challenge to the American Economy,* Allyn & Bacon, 1962. Contributor of about thirty articles to economics journals. Member of board of editors, *Southern Economic Journal,* 1952-55, *American Economic Review,* 1959-61, and *Journal of Economic Education,* 1969—.

*WORK IN PROGRESS:* Further research in economic education.

\* \* \*

## FELTSKOG, E(lmer) N. 1935-

*PERSONAL:* Born July 7, 1935, in Chicago, Ill.; son of Elmer N. and Helen (Tengwald) Feltskog; married Cathryn Rupert, September 12, 1959. *Education:* Augustana College, B.A., 1957; Washington State University, M.A., 1959; University of Illinois, Ph.D., 1965. *Politics:* Mugwump. *Religion:* Lutheran.

*CAREER:* University of Wisconsin—Madison, assistant professor, 1965-68, associate professor of English, 1968. *Member:* American Civil Liberties Union, American Association of University Professors, Modern Language Association.

*WRITINGS:* (Editor) Francis Parkman, *The Oregon Trail,* University of Wisconsin Press, 1969; (editor) Washington Irving, *Mahomet and His Successors,* University of Wisconsin Press, 1970.

*WORK IN PROGRESS: Trilogy of Power;* book-length manuscripts on Jack London, Albert H. Lewis, and Richard Harding Davis; editorship of the Randolph Papers.††

\*     \*     \*

## FENNELLY, Catherine 1918-

*PERSONAL:* Born October 24, 1918, in Staten Island, N.Y.; daughter of Patrick (a typographer) and Catherine (Schrowang) Fennelly. *Education:* Notre Dame College of Staten Island, B.A., 1939; Columbia University, M.A., 1940; Yale University, Ph.D., 1946. *Religion:* Roman Catholic. *Home:* 20 Ridgewood Ter., North Haven, Conn. 06473. *Agent:* McIntosh & Otis, Inc., 475 Fifth Ave., New York, N.Y. 10017. *Office:* Old Sturbridge Village, Sturbridge, Mass. 01566.

*CAREER:* Albertus Magnus College, New Haven, Conn., instructor in history, 1945-51; Old Sturbridge Village, Sturbridge, Mass., research associate, 1951-56, director of research and publications, 1956-66, editor, 1966—. Assistant to state historian and co-editor, *Legislative Records,* State of Connecticut, 1946-51. Research associate, American Red Cross, 1948. *Member:* American Historical Association, League of American Pen Women, College Club (Boston), Connecticut Historical Society, New Haven Colony Historical Society. *Awards, honors:* Litt.D., New England College, 1970.

*WRITINGS: Life in an Old New England Country Village,* Crowell, 1969; *Connecticut Women in the Revolutionary Era,* edited by Glenn Weaver, Pequot, 1976.

Editor of booklet series, published by Old Sturbridge Village: (And author) *The New England Village Scene;* (and author) *Something Blue: Some American Views on Staffordshire; Country Stores in Early New England; New England Clocks at Old Sturbridge Village;* (and author) *New England Character and Characters;* (and author) *Old Sturbridge Village: A Guidebook; Architecture in Early New England; Customs on the Table Top; Glass in New England; Early New England Pottery; Country Art in New England: 1790-1840; Child Life in New England: 1790-1840;* (and author) *Textiles in New England: 1790-1840; Early New England Gardens: 1620-1840;* (and author) *Town Schooling in Early New England: 1790-1840; Food, Drink, and Recipes of Early New England; A Primer of New England Crewel Embroidery; The Village Mill in Early New England; Herbs and Herb Cookery through the Years; Medicine in New England: 1790-1840; Rum and Reform in Old New England;* (and author) *Country Garb in Early New England;* (and author) *The Country Lawyer in New England: 1790-1840; Roads and Travel in New England: 1790-1840; Floor Coverings in New England before 1850; The ABC's of Canvas Embroidery; Glass Paperweights at Old Sturbridge Village; Printed Cottons at Old Sturbridge Village; The XYZ's of Canvas Embroidery; New England Militia Uniforms and Accoutrements; A Tour of Old Sturbridge Village.*

*WORK IN PROGRESS:* Editing the journal of Ruth Henshaw Bascom, a nineteenth-century housewife, artist, teacher, and advocate of village rights.

\*     \*     \*

## FENNER, H(arry) Wolcott 1911-1972

March 24, 1911—October 14, 1972; American promoter, circus executive, and editor. Obituaries: *New York Times,* October 17, 1972. (See index for *CA* sketch)

## FENNER, James 1923-

*PERSONAL:* Born December 31, 1923, in New York, N.Y.; son of Abner L. (a lawyer) and Edna (Stern) Fenner. *Education:* University of Michigan, B.A., 1945; Columbia University, A.M., 1948. *Home:* 60 Cole St., Bridgeport, Conn. 06604. *Office:* Department of Economics, University of Bridgeport, Bridgeport, Conn. 06602.

*CAREER:* Monmouth Junior College (now Monmouth College—Junior College Division), Long Branch, N.J., assistant professor of economic history, 1948; University of Bridgeport, Bridgeport, Conn., assistant professor, 1949-71, associate professor of economics, 1972—. *Military service:* U.S. Army, 1943-46. *Member:* American Economic Association.

*WRITINGS:* (With Llewellyn M. Mullings) *Economic Development,* MSS Publishing, 1971.

\*     \*     \*

## FENNER, Theodore (Lincoln) 1919-

*PERSONAL:* Born February 13, 1919, in Hornell, N.Y.; son of James Lewis and Grace (Coleman) Fenner; married Lee Ullmann, April 20, 1946. *Education:* Columbia University, B.S., 1951, M.A., 1953, Ph.D., 1967. *Residence:* Potsdam, N.Y.

*CAREER:* Western Electric Co., New York City, systems analyst, 1955-58; Socony-Mobil Oil Corporation, New York City, systems analyst, 1959-62; Flint College of University of Michigan (now University of Michigan—Flint), assistant professor of English, 1965-68; Clarkson College of Technology, Potsdam, N.Y., assistant professor of humanities, 1968-72; State University of New York College at Potsdam, adjunct professor of English, 1976—. *Military service:* U.S. Army Air Forces, 1944-45; became staff sergeant; received Air Medal. *Member:* Modern Language Association of America, American Association of University Professors, American Civil Liberties Union.

*WRITINGS: Leigh Hunt and Opera Criticism: The "Examiner" Years, 1808-1821,* University Press of Kansas, 1972. Contributor of articles to *Musical Quarterly, Studies in Romanticism,* and *Dance Chronicle.*

\*     \*     \*

## FENTON, John H(arold) 1921-

*PERSONAL:* Born September 9, 1921, in Canton, Ohio; son of John Harold (a steel superintendent) and Margaret (Hanbuechen) Fenton; children: Margaret, John, Jr. *Education:* University of Kentucky, A.B., 1948, M.A., 1951; Harvard University, Ph.D., 1956. *Home:* 75 Memorial Dr., Amherst, Mass. 01002. *Office:* Department of Political Science, University of Massachusetts, Amherst, Mass. 01002.

*CAREER:* Commonwealth of Kentucky, Frankfort, budget analyst, 1949-51; Oak Ridge Institute of Nuclear Studies, Oak Ridge, Tenn., head of department of management services, 1951-53; Tulane University, New Orleans, La., instructor in political science, 1955-57; Michigan State University, East Lansing, assistant professor of political science, 1957-59; University of Massachusetts—Amherst, professor of political science, 1959—, Commonwealth Professor, 1961—. *Military service:* U.S. Army, 1940-45. *Member:* American Political Science Association, American Association for the Advancement of Science, Northeastern Political Science Association. *Awards, honors:* Social Science Research Council grant, 1962.

*WRITINGS: Midwest Politics,* Holt, 1966; *People, Parties and Politics,* Scott, Foresman, 1966; (with L. W. Koenig, G. S. Schuber, L. D. Musolf, and L. I. Radway) *American National Government,* Scott, Foresman, 1971. Contributor to political science journals and to *Harper's.*

*WORK IN PROGRESS:* Studying election turnout.

\*     \*     \*

### FERBER, Robert 1922-

*PERSONAL:* Born February 13, 1922, in New York, N.Y.; son of Samuel and Dinah (Rosenthal) Ferber; married Marianne Abeles (an economist), August 18, 1946; children: Don, Ellen. *Education:* City College (now City College of the City University of New York), B.S., 1942; University of Chicago, M.A., 1945, Ph.D., 1951; Columbia University, graduate study, 1946-47. *Home:* 606 South Western Ave., Champaign, Ill. 61820. *Office:* Survey Research Laboratory, 414 David Kinley Hall, University of Illinois, Urbana, Ill. 61801.

*CAREER:* University of Chicago, Cowles Commission for Research in Economics, Chicago, Ill., research assistant, 1943-44; Industrial Surveys Co., Chicago, chief statistician, 1943-45; de Vegh & Co., New York, N.Y., economist and statistician, 1945-47; University of Illinois at Urbana-Champaign, research assistant professor, 1949-51, research associate professor, 1951-55, professor of economics and professor of marketing, research professor of economics in Bureau of Economic and Business Research, 1955—, and director of Survey Research Laboratory, 1965—. *Member:* International Association for Research on Income and Wealth, American Marketing Association (president, 1969-70), American Economic Association, American Statistical Association (fellow; member of council), Econometric Society, Association for Consumer Research, Latin American Studies Association. *Awards, honors:* Master scholar award from Ford Foundation, 1963; Hall of Fame in Distribution award, 1964.

*WRITINGS: Statistical Techniques in Market Research,* McGraw, 1949; (editor with Hugh G. Wales) *Marketing Research: Selected Literature,* W. C. Brown, 1952; (with Donald F. Blankertz and Wales) *Cases and Problems in Marketing Research,* Ronald, 1954; (with Wales) *A Basic Bibliography on Marketing Research,* American Marketing Association, 1956, 2nd revised edition, 1963; (co-editor) *Motivation and Market Behavior,* Irwin, 1958; (with Wales) *The Effectiveness of Pharmaceutical Promotion,* University of Illinois Press, 1958; (with P. J. Verdoorn) *Research Methods in Economics and Business,* Macmillan, 1962; (with Blankertz and Sidney Hollander, Jr.) *Marketing Research: A Managerial Approach,* Ronald, 1964; (editor) *Determinants of Investment Behavior,* Columbia University Press, 1967; (with Wallace Wilson) *Education in the Health Fields for the State of Illinois,* Illinois State Board of Higher Education, 1968; (editor with Daniel M. Slate) *Systems: Research and Applications for Marketing,* Bureau of Economic and Business Research, University of Illinois, 1968; (editor) *Handbook of Marketing Research,* McGraw, 1974.

Contributor: *Consumer Behavior: Research on Consumer Reactions,* Harper, 1958; *The Quality and Economic Significance of Anticipations Data,* Princeton University Press, 1960; *Demographic and Economic Change in Developed Countries,* Princeton University Press, c. 1961; *Flow-of-Funds Approach to Social Accounting,* National Bureau of Economic Research, 1962; Julius Gould and W. L. Kolb, editors, *A Dictionary of the Social Sciences,* Free Press,

1964; Arthur M. Ross, editor, *Employment Policy and the Labor Market,* University of California Press, 1965; *The Measurement and Interpretation of Job Vacancies,* National Bureau of Economic Research, 1966; Thomas T. Murphy and John R. Malone, editors, *The Complex Mission of the Business Schools in a Dynamic Society,* University of Notre Dame Press, 1966; Arnold Zellner, editor, *Readings in Economic Statistics and Econometrics,* Little, Brown, 1968. Writer of a dozen monographs on marketing topics; contributor of more than one hundred articles and reviews to journals. Forum editor, *Journal of Marketing,* 1955-63; editor of *Journal of Marketing Research,* 1964-69, and *Journal of Consumer Research,* 1977—; *Journal of American Statistical Association,* associate editor, coordinating and applications editor, 1969-76.

\*     \*     \*

### FERNANDEZ, Joseph A. 1921-

*PERSONAL:* Born April 15, 1921, in Richmond, Va.; son of Jose Maria (a cook) and Generosa (Alvarez) Fernandez; married M. J. Esther Moro (a teacher), September 18, 1963. *Education:* University of Pennsylvania, A.B., 1948, M.A., 1951; University of Toulouse, diplome, 1949; University of Madrid, Dr. en F. y L., 1953. *Politics:* Democrat. *Religion:* Roman Catholic. *Home:* 1212 South Wright Rd., Greenville, N.C. 27834. *Office:* Department of Foreign Languages and Literatures, East Carolina University, Greenville, N.C. 27834.

*CAREER:* University of Pennsylvania, Philadelphia, instructor in Spanish, 1953-55; Military Sea Transportation Service, New York, N.Y., seaman, 1955-56, 4th officer, 1956-60; University of Pennsylvania, lecturer in Spanish, 1960-61; Military Sea Transportation Service, 4th officer, 1961-63; Consejo Superior de Investigaciones Cientificas, Madrid, Spain, researcher, 1963-64; Georgetown University, Washington, D.C., assistant professor of Spanish, 1964-66; East Carolina University, Greenville, N.C., assistant professor, 1966-68, professor of Spanish, 1968—, chairman of department of Romance languages, 1968-73. *Military service:* U.S. Navy, 1941-47. U.S. Naval Reserve, 1947-71; became lieutenant.

*MEMBER:* Modern Language Association of America, American Association of Teachers of French, American Association of Teachers of Spanish and Portuguese, Oficina Internacional de Informacion y Observacion del Espanol, Pedagogical Seminar for Romance Philology, American Dialect Society, Sociedad Espanola de Linguistica, South Atlantic Modern Language Association. *Awards, honors:* Fulbright-Hays researcher "A" grant, Madrid, 1964.

*WRITINGS: El habla de Sisterna,* Consejo Superior de Investigaciones Cientificas, 1960; (with Antonio Quilis) *Curso de fonetica y fonologia espanolas,* Consejo Superior de Investigaciones Cientificas, 1964, 8th edition, 1975; (translator into Spanish) Robert Lado, *Linguistica Contrastiva: Lenguas y Culturas,* Alcala, 1973. Contributor to Spanish and French journals. Assistant editor, *Hispanic Review,* 1953-55, 1960-61; member of editorial board, "Collectanea Phonetica," 1964—.

*WORK IN PROGRESS:* A study of dialogue in novels of Galdos; research on Spanish dialects based on field work.

\*     \*     \*

### FERRIS, Theodore P(arker) 1908-1972

December 23, 1908—November 26, 1972; American clergyman, educator, and author of books on religious themes. Obituaries: *New York Times,* November 28, 1972.

\* \* \*

## FERSH, Seymour H. 1926-

*PERSONAL:* Born March 24, 1926, in Poughkeepsie, N.Y.; son of David (a salesman) and Lillian (Hambourg) Fersh; married Harriet Fein, August 31, 1947; children: Donald, Susan, Maryl. *Education:* New York College for Teachers (now State University of New York at Albany), B.A., 1949, M.A., 1950; Yale University, additional study, 1952; Columbia University, additional study, 1953; New York University, Ph.D., 1955. *Home:* 315 Highland Ave., Upper Montclair, N.J. 07043. *Office:* Department of Education, Fairleigh Dickinson University, Rutherford, N.J. 07070.

*CAREER:* Social studies teacher in New Paltz, N.Y., 1950-55; New Jersey State College, Montclair, 1955-61, began as assistant professor, became professor of history; The Asia Society, New York, N.Y., education director, 1961-73; Fairleigh Dickinson University, Rutherford, N.J., professor of education, 1973—. Fulbright professor, India, 1958-59. Assistant director of summer Asian studies program, Rutgers University, New Brunswick, N.J., 1960-66. *Military service:* U.S. Army, 1944-46; became sergeant; received Purple Heart. *Member:* Association for Asian Studies, American Historical Association, National Council for the Social Studies. *Awards, honors:* New York State University at Albany distinguished alumni award, 1971.

*WRITINGS: The View from the White House: Annual Message to Congress,* Public Affairs Press, 1961; *India and South Asia,* Macmillan, 1965, revised edition, 1970; *Learning about Peoples and Cultures,* McDougal, Littell, 1974; *Asia: Teaching About/Learning From,* Teachers College Press, 1978. Contributor of articles to *Social Education.*

\* \* \*

## FESHBACH, Seymour 1925-

*PERSONAL:* Born June 21, 1925, in New York, N.Y.; son of Joseph (a furrier) and Fannie (Katzman) Feshbach; married Norma Deitch (a professor), August 16, 1947; children: Jonathan Stephen, Laura Elizabeth, Andrew David. *Education:* College of the City of New York (now City College of the City University of New York), B.S., 1947; Yale University, M.A., 1948, Ph.D., 1951. *Religion:* Hebrew. *Office:* University of California, 405 Hilgard Ave., Los Angeles, Calif. 90024.

*CAREER:* University of Pennsylvania, Philadelphia, assistant professor, 1952-57, associate professor of psychology, 1957-63; University of Colorado, Boulder, professor of psychology, 1963-64; University of California, Los Angeles, professor of psychology, 1964—, chairman of department, 1977—, director of Fernald School, 1964-73. Chairman of Psychology Training Grant Committee and member of national panel, National Institutes of Mental Health. *Military service:* U.S. Army, 1943-46, 1950-52; became first lieutenant. *Member:* American Psychological Association, American Association for the Advancement of Science, Society for Research in Child Development, International Applied Psychology Association, Western Psychological Association (president, 1976-77), Phi Beta Kappa, Sigma Xi. *Awards, honors:* Townsend Harris Medal, Alumni Association of the City College of New York, 1972.

*WRITINGS:* (Editor with Richard Jessor) *Cognition, Personality and Clinical Psychology,* Jossey-Bass, 1967; (with

Robert D. Singer) *Television and Aggression,* Jossey-Bass, 1970; (contributor) Paul Henry Mussen, editor, *Carmichael's Manual of Child Psychology,* Volume II, Wiley, 1970. Contributor to psychology journals. Consulting editor, *Journal of Abnormal Psychology* and *Developmental Psychology.*

*WORK IN PROGRESS:* Research on children's aggression, and on sex and aggression.

*AVOCATIONAL INTERESTS:* Politics, theater, history, European travel.

\* \* \*

## FICKERT, Kurt J(on) 1920-

*PERSONAL:* Born December 19, 1920, in Pausa, Germany; son of Kurt Alfred (a mechanic) and Martha (Saerchinger) Fickert; married Lynn B. Janda, August 6, 1946; children: Linda (Mrs. Robert Alexander), Jon, Chris. *Education:* Hofstra College (now University), A.B., 1941; New York University, M.A., 1947, Ph.D., 1952. *Politics:* Independent. *Religion:* Lutheran. *Home:* 33 South Kensington Pl., Springfield, Ohio 45504. *Office:* Department of German, Wittenberg University, Springfield, Ohio 45501.

*CAREER:* Hofstra College (now University), Hempstead, N.Y., instructor, 1947-52, assistant professor of German, 1952-53; Florida State University, Tallahassee, instructor in German, 1953-54; Fort Hays Kansas State College, Hays, assistant professor of German and English, 1954-56; Wittenberg University, Springfield, Ohio, assistant professor, 1956-60, associate professor, 1960-67, professor of German, 1967—. *Military service:* U.S. Army Air Forces, 1942-45; served in Pacific theater. *Member:* American Association of Teachers of German, American Association of University Professors, Ohio Poetry Day Association (president, 1971-75), Sigma Kappa Alpha, Phi Eta Sigma. *Awards, honors:* Fullbright grant for teachers of German, Germany, 1957; Stephen Vincent Benet Narrative Poem Award, 1968, for "Struggle with Loneliness," from *Poet Lore;* citation for meritorious achievement, Society for German-American Studies, 1973; New England Prize, *Lyric* (magazine), 1976.

*WRITINGS: To Heaven and Back: The New Morality in the Plays of Friedrich Duerrenmatt,* University Press of Kentucky, 1972. Work is also represented in *Anthology of German Poetry,* Anchor Books, 1960. Contributor of articles to *German Quarterly, Monatshefte, Modern Fiction Studies, Contemporary Literature, Books Abroad, Explicator,* and *Modern Drama,* of poems to *Lyrica Germanica, German-American Studies, Poet Lore, Bitterroot, Poetry Venture, Speak Out, Lunatic Fringe, Change, Southern Humanities Review,* and *Lyric,* and of a translation of a story from German to *Dimension.*

*WORK IN PROGRESS: The Conscience of Us All: The "Dichter" as Ideal in the Work of Hermann Hesse; Kafka's Doubles.*

\* \* \*

## FIELD, G(eorge) W(allis) 1914-

*PERSONAL:* Born March 5, 1914, in Cobourg, Ontario, Canada; son of George Henry (a physician) and Mary (Gearing) Field; married Eleanor Woodger (a teacher), August 28, 1949; children: Christopher, Michael, John, Jane. *Education:* University of Toronto, B.A., 1935, M.A., 1946, Ph.D., 1948; University of California, Los Angeles, graduate study, 1946-47. *Religion:* Anglican. *Home:* 6 Edgar Ave., Toronto, Ontario, Canada M4W 2A9. *Office:* Department of German, Victoria College, University of Toronto, Toronto, Ontario, Canada M5S 1A1.

*CAREER:* High school teacher in Ontario, 1936-38, and at Canadian Academy, Kobe, Japan, 1938-40; taught at Queen's University, Kingston, Ontario, 1947; University of Toronto, Toronto, Ontario, lecturer, 1948-49, assistant professor, 1950-56, associate professor, 1957-61, professor of German, 1962—. *Military service:* Canadian Army, 1940-45. Canadian Army Reserve, 1946—; present rank lieutenant colonel; received Canadian Efficiency Decoration and Canadian Forces Decoration. *Member:* Modern Language Association of America, Canadian Association of University Teachers, Canadian Association of University Teachers of German, Royal Canadian Military Institute.

*WRITINGS:* (Editor) *A Heine Verse Selection,* Macmillan (London), 1966; (editor) *Fontane: Irrungen, Wirrungen,* Macmillan (London), 1968; *Hermann Hesse,* Twayne, 1970; *A Literary History of Germany: The Nineteenth Century, 1830-1890,* Benn, 1975; *Hermann Hesse: Kommentar zu Samtlichen Werken,* Akademischer Verlag, 1977; (contributor) M. Pfeifer, editor, *Hermann Hesse Weltweite Wirkung,* Suhrkamp, 1977. Contributor of articles and reviews to *German Quarterly, German Life and Letters, Monatshefte, University of Toronto Quarterly, Queen's Quarterly,* and *Seminar.*

*WORK IN PROGRESS:* Writing on Theodor Fontane and Guenter Grass.

*BIOGRAPHICAL/CRITICAL SOURCES: Books Abroad,* spring, 1971.

\*    \*    \*

## FIELD, John P(aul) 1936-

*PERSONAL:* Born September 21, 1936, in Newton, Mass.; son of Paul Shenfelder (a lawyer) and Signe (Pihl) Field; married Wenda Watts, September 29, 1962. *Education:* Bowdoin College, A.B., 1958; Harvard University, M.B.A., 1960; University of Michigan, graduate study, 1961; University of Cincinnati, M.A., 1967, Ph.D., 1970. *Home address:* Indiantown Rd., R.D. 2, Glenmoore, Pa. 19343. *Office:* School of Arts and Letters, West Chester State College, West Chester, Pa. 19380.

*CAREER:* Procter & Gamble Co., Cincinnati, Ohio, staff assistant, 1961-63, assistant brand manager, 1963-65, assistant copy supervisor, 1965-66; West Chester State College, West Chester, Pa., associate professor, 1970-74, professor of English, 1974—, coordinator of graduate studies in English, 1975-77, acting dean, School of Arts and Letters, 1976—. *Military service:* U.S. Army, 1958-66; became captain. *Member:* Phi Beta Kappa. *Awards, honors:* Woodrow Wilson fellow, 1961-62.

*WRITINGS: Richard Wilbur: A Bibliographical Checklist,* Kent State University Press, 1971.

*WORK IN PROGRESS: Cases for Composition,* a writing text, with Robert H. Weiss, for Little, Brown.

\*    \*    \*

## FIELD, Mark G(eorge) 1923-

*PERSONAL:* Born June 17, 1923, in Lausanne, Switzerland; U.S. citizen; son of Jacques and Mary (Imbert) Field; married Anne Murray, August 28, 1948; children: Alexander James, Michael Bayard, Andrew Murray, Elizabeth Imbert. *Education:* Attended Hamilton College, 1941-42; Harvard University, A.B. (cum laude), 1948, A.M., 1950, Ph.D.,

1955. *Home:* 40 Peacock Farm Rd., Lexington, Mass. 02173. *Office:* Department of Sociology, Boston University, 96 Cummington Street, Boston, Mass. 02215; and Russian Research Center, Harvard University, 1737 Cambridge St., Cambridge, Mass. 02138.

*CAREER:* Beth Israel Hospital, Boston, Mass., associate director of medical care study, 1955-57; Joint Commission on Mental Illness and Health, Cambridge, Mass., research associate, 1957-59; Harvard University, Cambridge, lecturer, department of social relations, 1957-61, research associate, Russian Research Center, 1959-61, 1963—; University of Illinois, Urbana, associate professor of sociology, 1961-62; Boston University, Boston, professor of sociology, 1962—. Harvard University, visiting professor, summers, 1961-63, 1965-67, research associate, program on Technology and Society, 1966-67, lecturer on sociology, Medical School, 1971-72, visiting lecturer on health services administration, School of Public Health, 1972—. Assistant sociologist, Massachusetts General Hospital, Boston, 1964—; research associate in Family and Child Health Division, Childrens Hospital, Boston, 1972-74. Consultant to Arthur D. Little, Inc., Cambridge, Mass., 1962-63 and 1966-67, World Health Organization, Geneva, Switzerland, 1969, and Medical School and School of Public Health, Harvard University, 1971-72. Member of planning group on comparative communist societies, American Council of Learned Societies; member of joint committee on Soviet studies, American Council of Learned Societies-Social Science Research Council, 1971-75. *Military service:* U.S. Army, 1944-47; served in France, Germany, and Austria.

*MEMBER:* International Sociological Association (chairman of research committee on medical sociology, 1970—), American Sociological Association (fellow), American Public Health Association (fellow), American Association for the Advancement of Slavic Studies, American Association for the Advancement of Science, American Association of University Professors, American Association Against Involuntary Mental Hospitalization, Cahiers de Sociologie et Demographie Medicales, Societe de Demographie, Economie et Sociologie Medicales. *Awards, honors:* U.S. Public Health Service research grants, 1959-76; American Council of Learned Societies fellowship, 1968-69.

*WRITINGS: Organization of Medical Services in the Soviet Union* (monograph), Human Resources Research Institute, 1954; *Doctor and Patient in Soviet Russia,* foreword by Paul Dudley White, Harvard University Press, 1957; *The Social Environment and Its Effect on the Soviet Scientist* (monograph), Associates for International Research, 1959; (with Morris S. Schwartz, Charlotte Green Schwartz, and others) *Social Approaches to Mental Patient Care,* Columbia University Press, 1964; *Soviet Socialized Medicine: An Introduction,* Free Press, 1967; *Technology, Medicine and Society: Effectiveness, Differentiation and Depersonalization* (monograph), Program on Technology and Society, Harvard University, 1968; (author of foreword) Nancy Rollins, *Child Psychiatry in the Soviet Union,* Harvard University Press, 1972; (with Ralph E. Berry, Jr., Dieter Koch-Weser, John Karefa-Smart, and Mark Thompson) *Evaluating Health Program Impact: The U.S.-Yugoslav Cooperative Research Effort,* Lexington Books, 1974; (editor and contributor) *The Social Consequences of Modernization in Communist Countries,* Johns Hopkins University Press, 1976.

Contributor: Ronald Freedman and others, *Principles of Sociology: A Text with Readings,* revised edition, Holt,

1956; Raymond G. McCarthy, editor, *Drinking and Intoxication*, Free Press, 1959.

Thomas Fitsimmons and others, *U.S.S.R.: Its People, Its Society, Its Culture*, Human Relations Area File Press, 1960; Cyril E. Black, editor, *The Transformation of Russian Society*, Harvard University Press, 1960; George Z. F. Bereday and Jaan Pennar, editors, *The Politics of Soviet Education*, Praeger, 1960; Alex Inkeles and Kent Geiger, editors, *Soviet Society: A Book of Readings*, Houghton, 1961; Seymour M. Lipset and Neil J. Smelser, editors, *Sociology: The Progress of a Decade*, Prentice-Hall, 1961; Harry Schwartz, editor, *The Many Faces of Communism*, Berkley Publishing, 1962; S. N. Eisenstadt, editor, *Comparative Social Problems*, Columbia University Press, 1964; W. Richard Scott and Edmund Volkart, editors, *Medical Care: Readings in the Sociology of Medical Institutions*, edition with new preface, Wiley, 1966; Donald W. Treadgold, editor, *Soviet and Chinese Communism: Similarities and Differences*, University of Washington Press, 1967; Hugh Freeman and James Farndale, editors, *New Aspects of the Mental Health Services*, 2nd edition, Pergamon, 1967; S. Kirson Weinberg, editor, *The Sociology of Mental Disorders: Analyses and Readings in Psychiatric Sociology*, Aldine, 1967; Allen Kassof, editor, *Prospects for Soviet Society*, Praeger, 1968; Donald E. Brown, editor, *The Role and Status of Women in Soviet Society*, Teachers College Press, 1968; I. E. Purkis and U. F. Matthews, editors, *Medicine in the University and the Community of the Future*, Dalhousie University, 1969.

Georgene Seward and Robert Williamson, editors, *Sex Roles in Changing Society*, Random House, 1970; Alan Sheldon, Frank Baker, and Curt McLaughlin, editors, *Systems and Medical Care*, M.I.T. Press, 1970; John G. Eriksen, editor, *The Development of Soviet Society: Plan and Performance*, Institute for the Study of the USSR (Munich), 1970; Everett I. Mendelsohn, Judith P. Swazey, and Irene Taviss, editors, *Human Aspects of Biological Innovation*, Harvard University Press, 1971; Alex Inkeles and Bernard Barber, editors, *Stability and Social Change: Essays in Honor of Talcott Parsons*, Little, Brown, 1971; *Medicine and Society: Contemporary Medical Problems in Historical Perspective*, American Philosophical Library Society, 1971; Judith M. Bardwick, editor, *Readings in the Psychology of Women*, Harper, 1972; E. Gartley Jaco, editor, *Patients, Physicians and Illness*, Free Press, 1972; Ellen Mickiewicz, editor, *Handbook of Soviet Social Science Data*, Free Press, 1973; Margaret S. Archer, editor, *Current Research in Sociology*, Mouton, 1974; *Medicine in Chinese Cultures: Comparative Studies of Health Care in Chinese and Other Societies*, U.S. Government Printing Office, 1975; Manfred Pflanz and Elizabeth Schach, editors, *Cross-National Sociomedical Research: Concepts, Methods, Practices*, Georg Thieme Verlag, 1976; Charles Leslie, editor, *Asian Medical Systems: A Comparative Study*, University of California Press, 1976; M. Sokolowska, M. J. Holowka, and A. Ostrowska, editors, *Health, Medicine, Society*, D. Reidel, 1976; Ray Elling and Sokolowska, editors, *Medical Sociologists at Work*, Transaction Books, 1977; John D. Stoeckle, editor, *Doctor-Patient Encounters*, Prodist Press, in press; Frederic J. Fleron, editor, *Technology and Communist Culture: The Socio-Cultural Impact of Technology Transfer under Socialism*, Praeger, in press.

Writer of monographs on Soviet and American pharmaceutical systems. Contributor to *McGraw-Hill Encyclopedia of Russian and the Soviet Union*; contributor of articles and reviews to sociology and medical journals in United States,

France, Switzerland, Germany, and Italy. Editorial consultant, *International Journal of Psychiatry*, 1964; foreign correspondent, *Cahiers de Sociologie et Demographie Medicales* (Paris), 1971—.

*WORK IN PROGRESS: Soviet Medicine and Medical Organization: A Contribution to a Comparative Analysis*; articles for publication in journals.

*SIDELIGHTS:* Mark Field told *CA:* "Ever since I can remember, I have held writers in some kind of awe. Perhaps it was the distance between the printed text and the creator of that text that added a touch of mystery in my mind. Who was that person, unknown and unseen to me, who could fashion texts and express ideas and affect others (including myself)? I think it was that power that impressed me. As a sociologist I have enjoyed writing, crafting so to speak, lovingly going over the draft, correcting, changing, adding, modifying. My manuscripts usually look very messy because of all the changes: bits of papers are stapled or scotch-taped; inserts are added; rarely is a single line left untouched. The manuscript is objective evidence of the time, the effort, the intellect invested in it. And then I like to compare, in my mind at least, the finished polished printed product and to superimpose upon it the messy and sweaty and much-corrected final draft from which the final product emerged. The metaphor that this process evokes is that of a fine bottle of wine that has lain for several years behind the woodpile, covered with dirt, sand, cobwebs. And then you carefully uncork it, and from it flows a red liquid that is the antithesis of the outside of the bottle: clear, clean and good to the taste. Of course, sometimes, the wine has turned into undrinkable vinegar!

"I think writing is a struggle against death: one hopes that what one has written will survive one; that others, unknown to you, will also be influenced, instructed, affected by what you put down on paper. And of course, in the academic world, publishing is an important asset in professional survival. Finally, writing is a difficult task; although enjoyable, it can be exasperating and painful. In academia one exposes oneself all the time to the critiques of one's colleagues for what one writes. One day, I would like to write a novel, i.e. to write as I please, using my imagination, rather than having to worry about documenting, footnoting, and defending every statement."

Field is fluent in Russian and French and speaks some German. He lectures and writes informally about his trips to the Soviet Union, where he visited medical and other institutions in 1946, 1961, 1963, 1964, 1974, and twice in 1975.

\*          \*          \*

## FIFE, Robert Oldham    1918-

*PERSONAL:* Born December 15, 1918, in DuQuoin, Ill.; son of Earl Hanson (a minister) and Mabel (Oldham) Fife; married LaVada Gilfilen (a tutor), March 28, 1941; children: Wayne Earl, Gloria Lynn (Mrs. Michael Stephen Lacy), Robert Dean. *Education:* Johnson Bible College, B.A., 1940; University of Glasgow, additional study, 1945, 1946; Butler University, B.D., 1950; Indiana University, Ph.D., 1960. *Politics:* Independent. *Home:* 915 Lincoln Ave., Johnson City, Tex. 37601.

*CAREER:* Minister of Christian churches in Etowah, Tenn., 1937-41, Alma, Neb., 1941-43, Hoquiam, Wash., 1945-47, and Plainfield, Ind., 1949-54; Milligan College, Milligan College, Tenn., associate professor, 1954-61, professor of history and chairman of department, beginning 1961. Visiting professor, Pepperdine University, 1970-71. Fellow,

University of Southern California, 1970-71. Member of executive committee, World Convention of Churches of Christ. *Military service:* U.S. Army, chaplain, 1943-46; became major; received Bronze Star Medal. *Member:* American Historical Association, American Academy of Political and Social Science, Disciples of Christ Historical Society (life member), Theta Phi, Phi Alpha Theta, Phi Kappa Phi.

*WRITINGS: Christ Our Hope,* Manhattan Christian College, 1964; (with Ronald E. Osborn and David Edwin Harrell) *Disciples and the Church Universal,* Disciples of Christ Historical Society, 1967; *Teeth on Edge,* Baker Book, 1971; *Under the Chapel Spire,* Baker Book, 1972. Contributor of articles to religious magazines.

*WORK IN PROGRESS: Renewal of the Family; The Church in the Age.*

*AVOCATIONAL INTERESTS:* Music, fly fishing, handcrafts, athletics, camping, travel.†

\* \* \*

## FIRCHOW, Peter (Edgerly) 1937-

*PERSONAL:* Surname is pronounced *Fir*-show; born December 16, 1937, in Needham, Mass.; son of Paul (a businessman) and Marta (Loria-Montenegro) Firchow; married Evelyn Scherabon (a professor), 1969. *Education:* Harvard University, B.A., 1959, M.A., 1961; University of Wisconsin, Ph.D., 1965; also studied at University of Vienna, 1959-60. *Home:* 135 Birnamwood Dr., Burnsville, Minn. 55378. *Office:* Department of English, University of Minnesota, Minneapolis, Minn. 55455.

*CAREER:* University of Michigan, Ann Arbor, assistant professor of English, 1965-67; University of Minnesota, Minneapolis, associate professor of English and comparative literature, 1967—, chairman of comparative literature program, 1972—. *Member:* Modern Language Association of America, American Comparative Literature Association, Midwest Modern Language Association (vice-president, 1976-77; president, 1977-78). *Awards, honors:* Fellow, Institute for Advanced Studies in the Humanities, University of Edinburgh, 1977.

*WRITINGS:* (Translator and editor) Friedrich Schlegel, *Lucinde and the Fragments,* University of Minnesota Press, 1971; *Aldous Huxley: Satirist and Novelist,* University of Minnesota Press, 1972; *The Writer's Place: Interviews on the Literary Situation in Contemporary Britain,* University of Minnesota Press, 1974. Contributor of articles to literary journals.

*WORK IN PROGRESS: The Modern Past: Aspects of Modern British Literature;* with wife, E. S. Firchow, *Hammer and Pen: Stories from the Other Germany,* for Twayne.

\* \* \*

## FISCH, Harold 1923-

*PERSONAL:* Name in Israel is Aharon Harel-Fisch; born March 25, 1923, in Birmingham, England; son of Solomon (a rabbi) and Rebecca (Swift) Fisch; married Frances Joyce Roston (a high-school teacher), August 26, 1947; children: Malcolm, David, Brian, Shifra, Eli. *Education:* University of Sheffield, B.A. (first class honors), 1946; Oxford University, B.Litt., 1948. *Religion:* Jewish. *Office:* Department of English, Bar-Ilan University, Ramat-Gan, Israel.

*CAREER:* University of Leeds, Leeds, England, lecturer in English, 1947-57; Bar-Ilan University, Ramat-Gan, Israel,

associate professor, 1957-64, professor of English, 1964—, rector of university, 1968-71. Visiting professor at Brown University, 1965, and University of Maryland, 1971-72. Member of the Council of Broadcasting Authority (Israel). *Military service:* Royal Naval Volunteer Reserve, 1942-45; became sub-lieutenant; served in Atlantic theater. *Member:* Land of Israel Movement, Israel-American Association (member of council).

*WRITINGS: The Dual Image: The Figure of the Jew in English and American Literature,* World Jewish Congress, 1959, revised and enlarged edition, 1971; *Jerusalem and Albion: The Hebraic Factor in Seventeenth-Century Literature,* Schocken, 1964; (translator) *The Haggada,* Koren Publishers, 1965; (translator) *Tora and Haftarot,* Koren Publishers, 1967; (editor) Richard Overton, *Mans Mortalitie,* Liverpool University Press, 1968; (translator) *The Jerusalem Bible,* Koren Publishers, 1969; *Hamlet and the Word: The Covenant Pattern in Shakespeare,* Ungar, 1971; *S. Y. Agnon,* Ungar, 1975; *The Zionist Revolution: A New Perspective,* St. Martin's, 1978. Contributor to *Commentary, Midstream, Haaretz, Shakespeare Survey,* and other journals in the United States and Israel.

*WORK IN PROGRESS:* A book on archetypal motifs in nineteenth- and twentieth-century literature; a book on the theory of criticism exploring the difference between the sacred and the profane.

\* \* \*

## FISCHER, Ernst 1899-1972

July 3, 1899—August 1, 1972; Austrian editor, poet, translator, social activist, and critic. Obituaries: *New York Times,* August 2, 1972; *L'Express,* August 7-13, 1972.

\* \* \*

## FISCHER, Robert H. 1918-

*PERSONAL:* Born April 26, 1918, in Williamsport, Pa.; son of M. Hadwin (a clergyman and seminary professor) and Alice (Gortner) Fischer; married Edna Mae Black (a teacher), September 5, 1942; children: Susan K. (Mrs. James L. Wade III). *Education:* Gettysburg College, A.B., 1939; Lutheran Theological Seminary, Gettysburg, Pa., B.D., 1942; Yale University, Ph.D., 1947. *Politics:* Republican. *Home:* 5324 Central Ave., Western Springs, Ill. 60558. *Office:* Lutheran School of Theology at Chicago, 1100 East 55th St., Chicago, Ill. 60615.

*CAREER:* Lutheran clergyman; held ministerial posts in Hartland, Vt., 1944-45, and Sunbury, Pa., 1947-49; Lutheran School of Theology at Chicago, Chicago, Ill., professor of historical theology, 1949—. Lutheran tutor, Mansfield College, Oxford University, 1957-58; research fellow, University of Tuebingen, 1964-65; guest professor, Kirchliche Hochschule, 1973. Director, Maywood Seminary Choir, 1949-67; accompanist and assistant director, Suburban Veterans Chorus, 1949—. Participant in five International Luther-Research Congresses.

*MEMBER:* American Theological Society (president, Midwest Division, 1961-62; secretary-treasurer, Midwest Division, 1964—), American Society for Reformation Research (president, 1954), American Society of Church History, North American Academy of Ecumenists, Lutheran Historical Conference (vice-president, 1972-76), Phi Beta Kappa, Phi Gamma Delta. *Awards, honors:* American Association of Theological Schools postdoctoral fellowship.

*WRITINGS:* (Translator) Martin Luther, *Large Cate-*

*chism*, Muhlenberg, 1959; (editor and translator) *Luther's Works*, Volume XXXVII, Muhlenberg, 1961; (contributor) F. H. Littell, editor, *Reformation Studies*, John Knox, 1962; (translator) Franz Lau, *Luther*, Westminster Press, 1963; (contributor) Vilmos Vajta and Hans Weissgerber, *The Church and the Confessions*, Fortress, 1963; (translator) Robert Stupperich, *Melanchthon*, Westminster Press, 1965; *Luther* (biography), Lutheran Church Press, 1966; (contributor) Herbert Neve and B. A. Johnson, editors, *The Maturing of American Lutheranism*, Augsburg, 1968; (editor) *Franklin Clark Fry: A Palette for a Portrait*, Lutheran Quarterly, 1972; (contributor) Vajta, editor, *The Lutheran Church Past and Present*, Augsburg, 1977; (editor) *A Tribute to Arthur Voobus: Studies in Early Christian Literature and Its Environment, Primarily in the Syrian East*, Lutheran School of Theology at Chicago, 1977. Publications include arrangements of three sacred choral numbers. Contributor to *Lutheran* and *Luther-Jahrbuch*.

*WORK IN PROGRESS:* Continuing studies studies in Luther's thought and in nineteenth-century American Lutheranism.

\*     \*     \*

## FISHER, Louis 1934-

*PERSONAL:* Born August 17, 1934, in Norfolk, Va.; son of Louis (in public relations) and Marjorie (Leyden) Fisher; children: Ellen Beckwith, Joanna Leyden. *Education:* College of William and Mary, B.S., 1956; New School for Social Research, Ph.D., 1967. *Home:* 4108 Southend Rd., Rockville, Md. 20853. *Office:* Library of Congress, Washington, D.C. 20540.

*CAREER:* Miles-Samuelson (advertising agency), New York City, writer, 1960-62; *Plastics Technology* (magazine), New York City, assistant editor, 1962-63; Queens College of the City University of New York, Flushing, N.Y., assistant professor of political science, 1967-70; Library of Congress, Congressional Research Service, Washington, D.C., specialist, 1970—. Adjunct professor of political science, American University, 1975-77, Georgetown University, 1976-77. *Military service:* U.S. Army, 1957-59; became first lieutenant. *Member:* American Political Science Association. *Awards, honors:* National Science Foundation fellow, 1965-67; Louis Brownlow Book Award from the National Academy of Public Administration, 1976, for *Presidential Spending Power*.

*WRITINGS: President and Congress: Power and Policy*, Free Press, 1972; *Presidential Spending Power*, Princeton University Press, 1975; *"The Constitution between Friends": Congress, President, and the Law*, St. Martin's, 1978. Contributor of articles to political science, law, and American studies journals, and to national magazines, including *New Leader, Nation,* and *Progressive*.

*WORK IN PROGRESS:* A study of the federal pay procedures; an article on public law issues.

*SIDELIGHTS:* Louis Fisher told *CA*, "I . . . flounder about, grabbing . . . [at] the isolated fragments of our governmental system, trying to breathe new life into such discarded disciplines as public law and political economy."

\*     \*     \*

## FISHER, Roger (Dummer) 1922-

*PERSONAL:* Born May 28, 1922, in Winnetka, Ill.; son of Walter Taylor (a lawyer) and Katharine (Dummer) Fisher; married Caroline Speer, September 18, 1948; children: El-

liott Speer, Peter Ryerson. *Education:* Harvard University, A.B., 1943, LL.B. (magna cum laude), 1948. *Home:* 16 Fayerweather St., Cambridge, Mass. 02138. *Office:* Law School, Harvard University, Cambridge, Mass. 02138.

*CAREER:* Attorney; admitted to the Bar of Massachusetts, 1948, Bar of Washington, D.C., 1950, and the Bar of U.S. Supreme Court, 1956; Economic Cooperation Administration, Paris, France, assistant to the general counsel, 1948-49; Covington & Burling (law firm), Washington, D.C., attorney, 1950-56; Department of Justice, Washington, D.C., assistant to solicitor general, 1956-58; Harvard University, Cambridge, Mass., lecturer, 1958-60, professor of law, 1960-76, Williston Professor of Law, 1976—. Consultant on international security affairs to Department of Defense, 1962-68; member of board of trustees, Hudson Institute, 1962—; member of board of directors, Public Interest Communication Services, Inc., 1976—, Overseas Development Council, 1977—, International Peace Academy, 1977—. *Military service:* U.S. Army Air Forces, 1942-46; became first lieutenant. *Member:* American Academy of Arts and Sciences (fellow), American Society of International Law, Commission to Study the Organization of Peace, Council on Foreign Relations, World Affairs Council (Boston, vice-president, 1972—). *Awards, honors:* Guggenheim fellow, 1965-66; Peabody Award, 1970, for television series, "The Advocates"; Tom Phillips Memorial Award, United Press International New England, 1969, for Best Television Public Service Program, "Harvard, Where Do We Go from Here."

*WRITINGS:* (Editor, contributor, and author of introduction) *International Conflict and Behavioral Science*, Basic Books, 1964; (with Richard Falk, Michael Cardozo, and William Burke) *Essays on Intervention*, Ohio State University Press, 1964; *International Conflict for Beginners*, Harper, 1969; *Dear Israelis, Dear Arabs*, Harper, 1972. Originator and executive editor of "The Advocates," national public television series, 1969-70.

*WORK IN PROGRESS: International Law: The Compliance Problem.*

*BIOGRAPHICAL/CRITICAL SOURCES: New Yorker*, September 27, 1969; *Christian Science Monitor*, October 16, 1969; *Washington Post*, October 22, 1969; *New Republic*, October 25, 1969; *New York Times Book Review*, November 9, 1969; *Christan Century*, May 13, 1970; *Financial Times* (London) February 25, 1971; *Time*, October 9, 1972.

\*     \*     \*

## FITZGERALD, Barry Charles 1939-

*PERSONAL:* Born October 13, 1939, in Melbourne, Victoria, Australia; son of John Charles (a textile foreman) and Eileen (Maddern) Fitzgerald; married Anna Kemper, January 8, 1966; children: Michelle, Jacqueline, Paul, Ellen. *Education:* Melbourne Teachers' College, Trained Primary Teachers Certificate, 1958; University of Melbourne, B.A., 1966, B.Ed., 1970; Monash University, M.Ed., 1972; Western Michigan University, Ed.D., 1973. *Home:* Smythes Creek, Victoria, Australia 3351. *Office:* Ballarat College of Advanced Education, Ballarat, Victoria, Australia.

*CAREER:* Elementary teacher in Benalla and Melbourne, Victoria, Australia, 1959-64; Educational Research, Melbourne, Victoria, research assistant, 1965-66; Strathmore High School, Melbourne, Victoria, senior English master, 1967-69; Monash Teachers' College, Melbourne, Victoria, lecturer-in-charge of English teaching method, 1970-72; Western Michigan University, Kalamazoo, Mott intern,

1972-73; director of community education in Buchanan, Mich., 1973-74; Ballarat College of Advanced Education, Ballarat, Victoria, head of department of school and community studies, 1975-76, head of School of Education, 1976—. *Member:* International Communication Association, International Community Education Association, Australian Community Education Association, Sociological Association of Australia and New Zealand, Victorian Institute for Educational Research, Phi Delta Kappa.

*WRITINGS:* (With P. D. Rousch) *Personal English Program,* F. W. Cheshire, 1969; *Background to Politics,* International Publications Service, 1970. Compiler of supplement of Australian and New Zealand words for *Chamber's Modern English Dictionary.* Contributor to education journals and research bulletins. Editor, Ballarat College of Advanced Education Occasional Papers in Education series.

\* \* \*

## FITZGERALD, Gerald (Pierce) 1930-

*PERSONAL:* Born April 29, 1930, in Boston, Mass.; son of Pierce Joseph (a teacher) and Eleanor (Burrell) Fitzgerald; married Vera Blass (a journalist), December 20, 1953; children: Gerald Blass, Anna Lucy. *Education:* Harvard University, A.B., 1952, A.M., 1956, Ph.D., 1963. *Home:* 220 High St., Duxbury, Mass. 02332. *Office:* Department of English, Boston University, Boston, Mass. 02215.

*CAREER:* Harvard University, Cambridge, Mass., instructor in history, literature, and Romance languages, 1962-63; Boston University, Boston, Mass., assistant professor, 1963-66, associate professor, 1967-73, professor of English, 1973—, University Professor, 1973-74, 1977—. *Military service:* U.S. Army, Medical Corps, 1952-55. *Member:* Modern Language Association of America, Renaissance Society of America.

*WRITINGS: The Wordless Flesh* (poems), Identity Press, 1960; (translator) Renato Poggiolo, *The Theory of the Avant-garde,* Harvard University Press, 1968; *Daughters of Earth, Sons of Heaven* (poems), Identity Press, 1969. Contributor of translations to literature journals and reviews to newspapers and magazines.

*WORK IN PROGRESS: Waking in Traffic and Other Poems;* collection of poems translated from Italian; a book on the minor poems of Edmund Spenser.

\* \* \*

## FITZGERALD, John Joseph 1928-

*PERSONAL:* Born October 17, 1928, in North Adams, Mass.; son of John Francis and Frances (Kelley) Fitzgerald; married Margaret McEneny, June 19, 1954; children: Catherine, Joan, Stephen, Thomas, Joseph, Michael. *Education:* University of Notre Dame, A.B., 1949; St. Louis University, A.M., 1953; Tulane University, Ph.D., 1962. *Home:* 124 Pearse Rd., Swansea, Mass. 02777. *Office:* Department of Philosophy, Southeastern Massachusetts University, North Dartmouth, Mass. 02747.

*CAREER:* University of Notre Dame, Notre Dame, Ind., instructor, 1958-61, assistant professor of philosophy, 1961-66; Southeastern Massachusetts University, North Dartmouth, professor of philosophy, 1966—, chairman of faculty senate, 1970-72, president of faculty federation, 1973-76. *Military service:* U.S. Coast Guard, 1953-56. U.S. Coast Guard Reserve, 1956-77; retired as captain. *Member:* American Philosophical Association, American Catholic Philosophical Association, American Association of University

Professors, American Federation of Teachers, Charles S. Peirce Society.

*WRITINGS: Peirce's Theory of Signs as Foundation for Pragmatism,* Mouton, 1966. Contributor of articles to *New Scholasticism, International Philosophical Quarterly,* and *Transactions* of the Charles Peirce Society.

*WORK IN PROGRESS:* Further study of Peirce's theory of signs.

\* \* \*

## FITZGERALD, Laurine Elisabeth 1930-

*PERSONAL:* Born August 24, 1930, in New London, Wis.; daughter of Thomas F. (a manufacturer) and Laurine (Branchflower) Fitzgerald. *Education:* Northwestern University, B.S., 1952, M.A., 1953; Michigan State University, Ph.D., 1959. *Home:* 3715 Pan Ko Tuk Lane, Oshkosh, Wis. 54901. *Office:* 330 Dempsey Hall, Graduate School, University of Wisconsin, Oshkosh, Wis. 54901.

*CAREER:* Kendall College, Evanston, Ill., social program coordinator and residence director, 1951-53; Northwestern University, Evanston, Ill., instructor in Psycho-Educational Clinic, 1952-53; Wisconsin State College (now University of Wisconsin), Whitewater, instructor in English, director of Developmental Reading Laboratory, and head resident-director, 1953-55; Indiana University at Bloomington, residence area director in teaching and counseling, 1955-57; Michigan State University, East Lansing, instructor in counseling, 1958-59; University of Denver, Denver, Colo., assistant professor of psychology and education and associate dean of students, 1959-62; University of Minnesota, Minneapolis, assistant professor of counseling, 1962-63; Michigan State University, associate professor of counseling, personnel services, and educational psychology, 1963-68, professor of administration and higher education, 1968-74, assistant dean of students, 1963-70, associate dean of students, 1970-74; University of Wisconsin—Oshkosh, professor of counselor education, dean of Graduate School, and director of North East Wisconsin Regional Graduate Center, 1974—. Visiting lecturer, University of Oklahoma, 1961; visiting professor, Oregon State University, 1977. Member of North Central Association accrediting teams. Certified consulting psychologist in States of Minnesota and Colorado. Consultant in student personnel administration to fifty colleges and universities.

*MEMBER:* American Psychological Association, American Personnel and Guidance Association, American College Personnel Association (secretary, 1965-67; member of executive board, 1968-70; chairman of Women's Task Force, 1970-71), Association for Counselor Education and Supervision, American Association for Higher Education, National Association of Women Deans and Counselors (vice-president, 1972-74), National Education Association, American Association of University Professors, Women's Equity Action League (archivist, 1970-74; national recording secretary, 1972-73), Michigan Psychological Association, Michigan Association of Women Deans and Counselors (president, 1967-69), Wisconsin College Personnel Association, American Association of University Women, Beta Beta Beta, Alpha Lambda Delta, Psi Chi, Mortar Board, Delta Kappa Gamma, Zonta International. *Awards, honors:* Elin Wagner research fellowship, 1963-64; National Federation of Business and Professional Women's Clubs fellowship, 1966-67; Harriet Meyer Education Award, Michigan Association of Women Deans and Counselors, 1977; Contribution Award, Women's Equity Action League, 1978.

*WRITINGS:* (Editor with Walter F. Johnson and Willa Norris) *College Student Personnel: Readings and Bibliographies,* Houghton, 1970; (editor with L. Harmon, J. M. Birk, and M. F. Tanney) *Counseling Women,* Brooks/Cole, 1978. Contributor of more than seventy articles to journals. Editor, *Journal of College Student Personnel,* 1977-82.

\* \* \*

## FLAIANO, Ennio 1910-1972

1910—November 20, 1972; Italian playwright, novelist, critic, and screenwriter. Obituaries: *New York Times,* November 21, 1972.

\* \* \*

## FLANDERS, Ned A. 1918-

*PERSONAL:* Born February 21, 1918, in Paso Robles, Calif.; son of Fred A. (a teacher) and Ona (Leland) Flanders; married Mary Powell, 1943; children: Margaret (Mrs. Peter Darby), Kathleen (Mrs. William Rich). *Education:* University of California, Berkeley, A.B., 1940; Oregon State College (now University), B.S. (E.E.), 1944; University of Chicago, M.A., 1947, Ph.D., 1949. *Home and office:* 1 Spyglass Hill, Oakland, Calif. 94618.

*CAREER:* High school science teacher in Richmond and Pacific Grove, Calif., 1941; elementary teacher in Oakland, Calif., 1941-42; University of Minnesota, Minneapolis, assistant professor, 1949-52, associate professor of education, 1952-61; University of Michigan, Ann Arbor, professor of educational research, 1961-70; Far West Laboratory for Educational Research and Development, Berkeley, Calif., associate laboratory director for teacher education, 1970-75; currently self-employed researcher on teaching. Member of School Board in Golden Valley, Minn., 1958-61. Visiting summer professor, University of California, Berkeley, 1952. *Military service:* U.S. Army, Signal Corps, 1942-46; became first lieutenant. *Member:* American Educational Research Association (member of executive committee, 1966-69), Association for Supervision and Curriculum Development, California Educational Research Association, Phi Delta Kappa. *Awards, honors:* Fulbright research scholar in New Zealand, 1957; U.S. Office of Education research grants, 1958-60, 1959-61, 1961-62, 1963-69, 1976-78; Center for Advanced Study in the Behavioral Sciences fellow, 1969-70.

*WRITINGS: Teaching with Groups,* Burgess, 1954; (contributor) B. N. Phillips and others, editors, *Psychology at Work in the Elementary Classroom,* Harper, 1960; (contributor) Werret Wallace Charters and N. L. Gage, editors, *Readings in the Social Psychology of Education,* Allyn & Bacon, 1963; (contributor) A. A. Bellack, editor, *Theory and Research in Teaching,* Teachers College Press, 1963; (with Edmund J. Amidon) *The Role of the Teacher in the Classroom,* Paul S. Amidon Associates, 1963; (contributor) B. J. Biddle and W. J. Ellena, editors, *Contemporary Research on Teacher Effectiveness,* Holt, 1964; (contributor) F. R. Cyphert and E. Spaights, editors, *An Analysis and Projection of Research in Teacher Education,* College of Education, Ohio State University, 1964; (author of introduction and contributor) E. J. Amidon and J. B. Hough, editors, *Interaction Analysis: Theory, Research, and Application,* Addison-Wesley, 1967; (contributor) Anita Simon and E. G. Boyer, editors, *Mirrors for Behavior: An Anthology of Classroom Observation Instruments,* Volume II, Research for Better Schools, 1967; (author of introduction) Dwight William Allen and Kevin Ryan, *Microteaching,* Addison-Wesley, 1969; *Analyzing Teaching Behavior,* Addison-

Wesley, 1970; (contributor) *Teachers and the Learning Process,* Prentice-Hall, 1971. Contributor of more than sixty articles to encyclopedias and journals.

*WORK IN PROGRESS:* A case study of dissemination and utilization of "Flanders Interaction Analysis Categories" (1976-78).

\* \* \*

## FLASCH, Joy 1932-

*PERSONAL:* Born March 23, 1932, in Denison, Tex.; daughter of Robert H. (a water well driller) and Ersa Lois (Griffin) Childers; married Harold Andrew Flasch (a farmer), July 15, 1956; children: Christopher John, Julie Lois, Jeanine Laurie. *Education:* Southeastern State College (now Southeastern Oklahoma State University), B.A., 1951; Oklahoma State University, M.A., 1954, Ed.D., 1969; also studied at University of Colorado, University of Tulsa, and Langston University. *Religion:* Lutheran. *Home address:* Route 1, Box 167, Coyle, Okla. 73027. *Office:* Department of English, Langston University, Langston, Okla. 73050.

*CAREER:* English and physical education teacher in high school in Ardmore, Okla., 1951-53; Oklahoma State University, Stillwater, instructor in English, 1954-60, 1961-62; Langston University, Langston, Okla., instructor, 1964-66, assistant professor, 1966-68, associate professor, 1968-69, professor of English and foreign languages, 1969—, coordinator of humanities, 1970-72, acting chairman of department of communication, 1974, chairman, 1976—. *Member:* National Council of Teachers of English, Oklahoma Council of Teachers of English, Kappa Delta Pi.

*WRITINGS: Melvin B. Tolson,* Twayne, 1972. Contributor of articles to *Modern Drama, Satire Newsletter,* and *Oklahoma Librarian.*

*SIDELIGHTS:* The book *Melvin B. Tolson* came into being, Joy Flasch told *CA,* "as a result of my having the opportunity to know Prof. Melvin B. Tolson when I became one of the first white teachers to teach at Langston University.... I was fascinated with the intellect and talent of Dr. Tolson, who, although he had published poetry as early as 1944, had been virtually ignored by the literary world with the exception of some few critics, such as Karl Shapiro, Allen Tate, Robert Frost, etc. Since no book-length work had been written about him, I hoped to bring this long-ignored poet of excellence to public attention."

\* \* \*

## FLEISCHER, Nathaniel S. 1888(?)-1972

1888(?)—June 25, 1972; American journalist and authority on boxing. Obituaries: *New York Times,* June 26, 1972; *L'Express,* July 3-9, 1972; *Time,* July 10, 1972.

\* \* \*

## FLEMING, George J(oseph) 1917-

*PERSONAL:* Born January 21, 1917, in Chicago, Ill.; son of George Joseph (an association secretary) and Elizabeth (Young) Fleming; married Lenore Moe, 1950. *Education:* Loyola University, Chicago, Ill., A.B., 1938; Catholic University of America, M.A., 1939, Ph.D., 1950. *Politics:* Democrat. *Religion:* Roman Catholic. *Home:* 11225 King Dr., Chicago, Ill. 60628. *Office:* Department of History, Calumet College, Hammond, Ind.

*CAREER:* Xavier University, Cincinnati, Ohio, instructor

in history, 1942-44; University of Detroit, Detroit, Mich., instructor in history, 1945-51; Great Books Foundation, Chicago, Ill., assistant academic director, 1951-53; *American People's Encyclopedia,* Chicago, secondary editor in history, 1954-58; Follett Publishing Co., Chicago, social studies editor, 1958-62; Calumet College, Hammond, Ind. (formerly East Chicago, Ind.), assistant professor, 1962-64, associate professor, 1964-70, professor of history, 1970—, chairman of department, 1964—. Editor in history and geography, *World Book Encyclopedia,* 1960-61. Lecturer at Catholic University of America, 1945-46, and Loyola University, Chicago, 1959-62. *Member:* American Historical Association, Organization of American Historians, American Catholic Historical Association, Chicago Historical Association, Historians of Metropolitan Chicago (director, 1970—; vice-president, 1971-73; president, 1973-75), Civil War Round Table (director, 1971-73).

*WRITINGS: Canal at Chicago,* Catholic University Press, 1950; (editor with John Bettenbender) *Famous Battles,* Dell, 1970. Contributor to *Catholic Historical Review.*

*WORK IN PROGRESS:* A biography of General John A. Logan (1826-1886), tentatively entitled *Logan of Illinois,* completion expected in 1978.

\* \* \*

## FLESCHER, Irwin 1926-

*PERSONAL:* Born June 12, 1926, in New York, N.Y.; son of Max (a waiter) and Gussie (Spiegel) Flescher; married Adele Kransdorf, December 20, 1953; children: Jonathan, Mark, Judy. *Education:* Long Island University, B.S., 1949; New York University, M.A., 1950; Columbia University, Ph.D., 1960. *Religion:* Jewish. *Home:* 33 Canterbury Lane, Roslyn Heights, N.Y. 11577. *Office:* 225 Locust Lane, Roslyn Heights, N.Y. 11577.

*CAREER:* New York State Department of Labor, New York City, placement counselor, 1952-55; Bureau of Child Guidance, New York City, staff psychologist, 1955-58; clinical psychologist in private practice, Roslyn Heights, N.Y., 1959—; East Williston Public Schools, East Williston, N.Y., school and research psychologist, 1960—; clinical associate, Psychological Services Institute, 1967—; Long Island University, Long Island, N.Y., adjunct associate professor, 1971—. *Military service:* U.S. Army Air Forces, 1944-46. *Member:* American Psychological Association, New York State Psychological Association, New York Society of Clinical Psychologists, New York Academy of Sciences, Nassau County Psychological Association (president, 1972-73), Sigma Xi.

*WRITINGS: Children in the Learning Factory,* Chilton, 1972. Contributor of articles to *Genetic Psychology Monographs* and *Journal of Psychology.* Member of editorial advisory board, *Nassau County Psychological Association Newsletter,* 1966—.

\* \* \*

## FLETCHER, Robert H. 1885(?)-1972

1885(?)—November 20, 1972; American engineer, public relations manager, novelist, poet, and song writer. Obituaries: *New York Times,* November 23, 1972.

\* \* \*

## FLIER, Michael S(tephen) 1941-

*PERSONAL:* Born April 20, 1941, in Los Angeles, Calif.; son of Albert Alfred (a clockshop owner) and Bonnie (Burnkrant) Flier. *Education:* University of California, Berkeley, A.B., 1962, M.A., 1964, Ph.D., 1968. *Office:* Department of Slavic Languages, 405 Hilgard Ave., University of California, Los Angeles, Calif. 90024.

*CAREER:* University of California, Los Angeles, assistant professor, 1968-73, associate professor of Slavic languages, 1973—. Visiting acting assistant professor, University of California, Berkeley, summer, 1968. *Member:* Linguistic Society of America, International Linguistic Association, American Association of Teachers of Slavic and East European Languages, Linguistics Association of Great Britain. *Awards, honors:* Inter-University grant for study in Russia, 1966-67; International Research and Exchanges Board fellowship, 1971, for study in Russia and Czechoslovakia, 1978, for research in Russia, Belorussia, and the Ukraine.

*WRITINGS:* (Contributor) Dean S. Worth, editor, *The Slavic Word,* Mouton, 1972; (contributor) Demetrius J. Koubourlis, editor, *Topics in Slavic Phonology,* Slavica, 1974; (editor) *Slavic Forum: Essays in Slavic Linguistics and Literature,* Mouton, 1974; *Aspects of Nominal Determination in Old Church Slavic,* Mouton, 1974; (contributor) L'ubomir Durovic and others, editors, *Studia Linguistica Alexandro Vasilii filio Issatschenko Collegis et Amieis oblata,* De Ridder (Paris), 1977; (contributor) Richard D. Brecht and Dan E. Davidson, editors, *Soviet-American Russian Language Contributions,* G & G Press, 1978; (contributor) Henrik Birnbaum and others, editors, *American Contributions to the Eighth International Congress of Slavists,* Slavica, 1978. Also contributor to *Phonology in the 1970's,* edited by D. L. Goyvaerts. Contributor of articles and reviews to language journals, including *Russian Linguistics, International Journal of Slavic Linguistics and Poetics, Slavic and East European Journal, Language, Slavic Review, Journal of Linguistics,* and *Russian Review.*

\* \* \*

## FLINT, John E(dgar) 1930-

*PERSONAL:* Born May 17, 1930, in Montreal, Quebec, Canada; son of Alfred Edgar and Sarah (Pickup) Flint; married Sheila Doreen Curran, June 15, 1951; children: Helen Sarah, Richard John James. *Education:* St. John's College, Cambridge, B.A. (honors), 1952, M.A., 1954; Royal Holloway College, London, Ph.D., 1957. *Home:* 5711 Southwood Dr., Halifax, Nova Scotia, Canada. *Office:* Department of History, Dalhousie University, Halifax, Nova Scotia, Canada.

*CAREER:* University of London, King's College, London, England, assistant lecturer, 1954-56, lecturer, 1956-63, reader in history, 1963-67; Dalhousie University, Halifax, Nova Scotia, professor of history, 1967—, head of department, 1968—. Visiting professor, University of California, Santa Barbara, 1960-61; visiting professor and head of department, University of Nigeria, Nsukka, 1963-64. British adviser to the federal government of Nigeria, 1963-64. *Member:* Canadian Historical Association (council member), Historical Society of Nigeria, Canadian African Studies Association, American Historical Association, Atlantic Association of Historians, Royal Historical Society (fellow). *Award, honors:* Fulbright fellowship, 1960-61.

*WRITINGS: Sir George Goldie and the Making of Nigeria,* Oxford University Press, 1960; (editor) *Mary Kingsley's Travels in West Africa,* F. Cass, 1764; (editor) *Mary Kingsley's West African Studies,* F. Cass, 1965; *Nigeria and Ghana,* Prentice-Hall, 1966; *Books on the British Empire and Commonwealth,* Oxford University Press, 1967;

*Cecil Rhodes*, Little, Brown, 1974; (editor) *Cambridge History of Africa*, Volume V: *1790-1870*, Cambridge University Press, 1976. Contributor of articles to *Journal of African History, Canadian Journal of African Studies, African Historical Studies*, and other journals.

*WORK IN PROGRESS:* A study of British decolonization in Africa.

\* \* \*

## FLOWER, (Harry) John 1936-

*PERSONAL:* Born July 2, 1936, in Toronto, Ontario, Canada; son of Henry George and Doris (Vardy) Flower. *Education:* York University, B.A. (honors). *Religion:* Anglican. *Home:* 395 Elm Rd., Toronto, Ontario, Canada M5M 3W3. *Office:* 350 Bloor St. E., Toronto, Ontario, Canada.

*CAREER:* Worked for Commerce General Insurance Co., Toronto, Ontario, 1964-71; Shaw & Begg Ltd, Toronto, member of staff, 1971—. *Member:* Glenn Miller Society (London), Lawrence Park Tennis Club.

*WRITINGS: Moonlight Serenade: A Bio-Discography of the Glenn Miller Civilian Band*, Arlington House, 1972.

*WORK IN PROGRESS: I Sustain the Wings*, a bio-discography of the Glenn Miller Army Air Forces Orchestra.

\* \* \*

## FLOYD, Troy S(mith) 1920-

*PERSONAL:* Born January 31, 1920, in Rampart, Alaska; son of Ernest Marion (a miner) and Ruth (Smith) Floyd; married Dorothy I. Ballard, July 2, 1951; children: Phyllis, Larry. *Education:* University of Missouri, B.J., 1948, A.M., 1949; University of California, Berkeley, Ph.D., 1959. *Politics:* Democrat. *Religion:* Presbyterian.

*CAREER: La Junta Tribune*, La Junta, Colo., managing editor, 1949-50; International News Service, Denver, Colo., staff correspondent, 1950-51; University of New Mexico, Albuquerque, assistant professor, 1959-65, associate professor, 1965-72, professor of history, 1972-74. *Military service:* U.S. Army, 1942-46, 1951-52; became first lieutenant. *Member:* American Association of University Professors, Conference on Latin American History, United Nations Association—U.S.A.

*WRITINGS:* (Editor and translator) *The Bourbon Reformers and Spanish Civilization*, Heath, 1966; *The Anglo-Spanish Struggle for Mosquitia*, University of New Mexico Press, 1967.

*WORK IN PROGRESS: Origins of Spanish Civilization in the Caribbean, 1492-1526.* †

\* \* \*

## FLYNN, Paul P(atrick) 1942-

*PERSONAL:* Born October 1, 1942, in Worcester, Mass.; son of Paul E. (in electronics) and Eileen (Sullivan) Flynn; married Sandra Marie Clark, December 21, 1968; children: Erin, Elizabeth. *Education:* College of the Holy Cross, B.S., 1964; Boston College, J.D., 1967; Southern Methodist University, LL.M., 1968, S.J.D., 1972. *Home:* 221 South Norton Ave., Los Angeles, Calif. 90004. *Office:* 3440 Wilshire Blvd., Suite 601, Los Angeles, Calif. 90010.

*CAREER:* Admitted to the Massachusetts State Bar, 1968, and to the California State Bar, 1975; Drake University, Des Moines, Iowa, assistant professor of law and assistant dean of Law School, 1968-70; director of Drug Abuse Authority,

Office of the Governnor, State of Iowa, 1970-71; Southwestern University, School of Law, Los Angeles, Calif., 1971-75, began as associate professor, became professor of law. Private practice of law, 1967—. Consultant to Polk County (Iowa) Crime Commission, 1969-70, and Iowa State Crime Commission, 1970. *Member:* American Bar Association, Massachusetts Bar Association, California State Bar Association, Los Angeles County Bar Association.

*WRITINGS: Aviation Law: Cases and Materials*, Drake University, 1969, 2nd edition, Southwestern Press, 1972; *Legal Skills and Professional Responsibility*, Drake University, 1970; *Professional Responsibility in California*, Southwestern Press, 1976. Member of editorial board, *Sui Juris*, 1967; editor of *Iowa Academy of Trial Lawyers, Proceedings*, 1969, 1970.

*WORK IN PROGRESS:* Liability in aviation congestion in the United States.

\* \* \*

## FLYNT, Wayne 1940-

*PERSONAL:* Born October 4, 1940, in Pontotoc, Miss.; son of James H. (a manager) and Mae (Moore) Flynt; married Dorothy Smith, August 20, 1965; children: David, Sean. *Education:* Samford University, A.B. (magna cum laude), 1961; Florida State University, M.S., 1962, Ph.D., 1965. *Politics:* Democrat. *Religion:* Baptist. *Home:* 1224 Pene Lane, Auburn, Ala. 36830. *Office:* Department of History, Auburn University, Auburn, Ala. 36830.

*CAREER:* Samford University, Birmingham, Ala., assistant professor, 1965-68, associate professor of history, 1968-77; Auburn University, Auburn, Ala., chairman of history department, 1977—. *Member:* Labor Historians, American Association of University Professors, Association of Southern Labor Historians, Southern Historical Association, Florida Historical Association, L.Q.C. Lamar Society. *Awards, honors: Duncan U. Fletcher: Dixie's Reluctant Progressive* was awarded Rembert Patrick Memorial Award as best book on Florida history, 1971, and Award of Merit from Association for State and Local History.

*WRITINGS: Duncan U. Fletcher: Dixie's Reluctant Progressive*, Florida State University Press, 1971; (contributor) James W. Gibson, editor, *Reader in Speech Communication*, McGraw, 1971; (contributor) H. Brandt Ayers and Thomas H. Naylor, editors, *You Can't Eat Magnolias*, McGraw, 1972; (contributor) Gary M. Fink and Merl E. Reed, editors, *Essays in Southern Labor History*, Greenwood Press, 1977; *Cracker Messiah: Governor Sidney J. Catts of Florida*, Louisiana State University Press, 1977. Contributor of articles to history, speech, and social science journals.

*WORK IN PROGRESS:* Research on the social thought of Southern evangelical Protestants since the Civil War.

\* \* \*

## FOGLE, French R(owe) 1912-

*PERSONAL:* Born February 28, 1912, in Marietta, Ohio; son of Charles Enoch (a minister) and Emma (Edgar) Fogle; married Caroline Bennett, January 28, 1955. *Education:* Marietta College, A.B., 1933; Drew Theological Seminary, graduate study, 1933-34, 1936; Columbia University, M.A., 1938, Ph.D., 1949. *Home:* 4236 Via Padova, Claremont, Calif. 91711.

*CAREER:* Columbia University, New York City, instructor in English, 1937-40; College of the City of New

York (now City College of the City University of New York), New York City, instructor in English, 1940-41; Barnard College, New York City, instructor, 1946-49, assistant professor of English, 1949-51; Huntington Library, San Marino, Calif., Renaissance research staff member, 1951-57; Claremont Graduate School, Claremont, Calif., professor of English literature, 1957-77, professor emeritus, 1977—. *Military service:* U.S. Marine Corps, 1942-45; became colonel; received Silver Star. *Member:* Modern Language Association of America, Milton Society of America (president, 1956), Philological Association of the Pacific Coast (vice-president, 1969; president, 1970), Renaissance Conference of Southern California (president, 1956-57, 1969-70), Phi Beta Kappa. *Awards, honors:* D.Litt., Marietta College, 1958.

*WRITINGS:* (With F. A. Patterson) *An Index to the Columbia Edition of Works of John Milton,* Columbia University Press, 1940; *A Critical Study of William Drummond of Hawthornden,* Kings Crown, 1952; (editor) *Complete Poetry of Henry Vaughan,* Doubleday, 1964, revised edition, Norton, 1969; (editor) John Milton, *Complete Prose Works,* Volume V: *History of Britain,* Yale University Press, 1971. Member of editorial boards, *Huntington Library Quarterly* and *Duquesne Studies in Language and Literature.*

*WORK IN PROGRESS:* Seventeenth-century English literature and history; biography of Alice, Countess Dowager of Derby (1559-1637).

*AVOCATIONAL INTERESTS:* All sports, gardening, books, printing, and music.

\* \* \*

### FOLEY, (Mary) Louise Munro 1933-

*PERSONAL:* Born October 22, 1933, in Toronto, Ontario, Canada; daughter of William Angus (a pharmacist) and Mary (Nicholls) Munro; married Donald J. Foley (a California National Guard officer), August 9, 1957; children: Donald, William. *Education:* Attended University of Western Ontario, 1951-52, and Ryerson Institute of Technology, 1952-53; California State University, Sacramento, B.A. (honors), 1976. *Politics:* Independent. *Religion:* Presbyterian. *Home and office:* 5010 Jennings Way, Sacramento, Calif. 95819.

*CAREER:* CHOK Radio, Sarnia, Ontario, copy editor, 1953-54; CJSP Radio, Leamington, Ontario, copy editor, 1954-56; KLIX-TV, Twin Falls, Idaho, copy editor, 1956-58; KGMS Radio, Sacramento, Calif., copy editor, 1958-60; copy chief (retail) for Breuner's, Weinstock's, and Rhodes' department stores, 1961-65; currently lecturer in extension program, California State University, and editor, School of Social Work, California State University, Sacramento. *Member:* National League of American Penwomen, California Writer's Club. *Awards, honors:* Advertising Club of Sacramento award, 1971, "for excellence in creative, effective advertising in the field of brochures"; Literary Achievement award, Sacramento Regional Arts Council, 1974; National League of American Pen Women awards, first place, 1974, for television script, first place, 1975, for nonfiction article, second place, 1975, for film script, and first place, 1977, for song lyrics.

*WRITINGS: The Caper Club,* Random House, 1969; *No Talking,* Western Publishing, 1970; *Sammy's Sister,* Western Publishing, 1970; *A Job for Joey,* Western Publishing, 1970; *Somebody Stole Second,* Delacorte, 1972; (editor) *Stand Close to the Door,* School of Social Work, California State University, Sacramento, 1976. Editor, *. . . of human*

*interest* (quarterly newsletter of School of Social Work, California State University, Sacramento).

*WORK IN PROGRESS:* Two nonfiction career books for young readers; research project in the management of human services.

*SIDELIGHTS:* Louise Foley enjoys writing "'fun' fiction for kids—rather than moralistic stories—[I] believe kids need escapist reading just as much as adults." She adds: "I'm happy to see the trend toward more non-sexist books for young readers and hope that girls will be given more role options and fewer stereotyped models in current fiction."

\* \* \*

### FONTENOT, Mary Alice 1910-

*PERSONAL:* Surname is pronounced *Fon*-te-no; born April 16, 1910, in Eunice, La.; daughter of Elias Valrie and Kate (King) Barras; married Sidney J. Fontenot, September 6, 1925 (died, 1963); married Vincent L. Riehl, Sr., November 14, 1966; children: (first marriage) Edith (Mrs. Burton Ziegler), R. D. (deceased), Julie (Mrs. Michael Landry). *Education:* Attended school in Eunice, La. *Religion:* Roman Catholic. *Home:* 431 Holden Ave., Lafayette, La. 70506. *Office: Crowley Post-Signal,* Crowley, La. 70526.

*CAREER: New Era,* Eunice, La., reporter, columnist, and women's news writer, 1946-50; *Eunice News,* Eunice, editor, 1950-53; *Daily World,* Opelousas, La., columnist, 1953-57; *Daily Advertiser,* Lafayette, La., women's news reporter, 1958-60; *Rayne Tribune,* Rayne, La., editor, 1960-62; *Daily World,* area editor, 1962-69, columnist, 1969-71; *Crowley Post-Signal,* Crowley, La., columnist, 1977—. *Member:* League of American Pen Women, Louisiana Press Women. *Awards, honors:* First prize from National Press Women, 1966; Louisiana Literary Award, Louisiana Library Association, 1976, for *Acadia Parish, La.: A History to 1900.*

*WRITINGS*—Published by Claitors: *The Ghost of Bayou Tigre* (juvenile), 1964; (editor) *Quelque Chose Douce* (cookbook), 1964; (editor) *Quelque Chose Piquante* (cookbook), 1966; (with husband, Vincent L. Riehl, Sr.) *The Cat and St. Landry* (biography), 1972; (editor with Mercedes Vidrine) *Beaucoup Bon* (cookbook), 1973; (with Paul B. Freeland) *Acadia Parish, La.: A History to 1900,* 1976.

"Clovis Crawfish" juvenile series; published by Claitors: *Clovis Crawfish and His Friends,* 1962; *. . . and the Big Betail,* 1963; *. . . and the Singing Cigales,* 1964; *. . . and Petit Papillon,* 1966; *. . . and the Spinning Spider,* 1968; *. . . and the Curious Craupaud,* 1970; *. . . and Michelle Mantis,* 1976.

*WORK IN PROGRESS:* With Dorothy B. McNeely, a second volume of Acadia Parish history, completion expected in 1980.

\* \* \*

### FORBES, Joanne R. (Triebel) 1930-

*PERSONAL:* Born January 17, 1930, in Flint, Mich.; daughter of Robert C. and Eva (Rhoden) Triebel; married John D. Forbes (an industrial relations manager), September 15, 1951; children: Scott, Jody Ann, Jill, Jenny. *Education:* Michigan State University, B.A., 1952; Assumption College, M.A., 1973. *Religion:* Protestant. *Home:* 311 Neck Rd., Lancaster, Mass. 01523.

*CAREER:* Caseworker in Child Welfare Division in the states of Maryland, Virginia, and Ohio, 1952-57; affiliated with Child Conservation League and Red Cross Swimming program, Ohio, 1957-64; probation officer in Lake George, N.Y., 1965-67; family therapist at North Central Massachusetts Mental Health Center, 1975—. *Member:* American Association of University Women, Welsh Pony and Cob Society of America (member of national board of directors), Groton Pony Club (member of executive board).

*WRITINGS: So Your Kids Want a Pony,* Stephen Greene, 1973. Contributor of articles to *Western Horseman, Management Review,* and other journals.

*WORK IN PROGRESS:* A book on family relations in a democratic society which deals with parental attitudes in programming children for the social responsibility to live in freedom and maintain good family relationships, tentatively entitled *The Love Go Round.*

*AVOCATIONAL INTERESTS:* Working with children, their horses, and ponies.

\* \* \*

### FORBIS, William H. 1918-

*PERSONAL:* Born February 4, 1918, in Missoula, Mont.; son of Clarence J. (an architect) and Josephine (Hunt) Forbis; married Marie Vincent, December 12, 1943 (died, 1969); married Deborah Hall, September 19, 1970; children: (first marriage) Peter Vincent, Steven Jenks, Barbara Belle; (second marriage) William Hall. *Education:* University of Montana, B.A., 1939. *Politics:* Democrat. *Office: Money* Magazine, Time-Life Building, New York, N.Y. 10020.

*CAREER: Panama American,* Panama, Republic of Panama, city editor, 1940-42; *Nation,* Panama, city editor, 1946-49; *Time,* Panama correspondent, 1949-51, New York City, writer, 1951-58, senior editor, 1958-67; Time-Life News Service, Rio de Janeiro, Brazil, correspondent, 1967-69; *Money,* New York City, senior editor, 1978—.

*WRITINGS:* (Contributor and editor) *John Gunther's Inside Australia,* Harper, 1972; *The Cowboys,* Time-Life Books, 1972; *Japan Today,* Harper, 1975.

*WORK IN PROGRESS:* A journalistic book about Iran.

\* \* \*

### FORD, Richard Brice 1935-

*PERSONAL:* Born August 27, 1935, in Youngstown, Ohio; son of Robert T. (a real estate broker) and Katherine (McMillen) Ford; married Nancy Becker; children: Andrew, Linda, Jonathan, Sarah, Daniel. *Education:* Denison University, B.A., 1957; Yale University, M.A.T., 1959; University of Denver, Ph.D., 1966. *Home:* 14 Algonquin Rd., Worcester, Mass. 01609. *Office:* Department of History, Clark University, Worcester, Mass. 01610.

*CAREER:* Teacher in public schools in Bronxville, N.Y., 1959-60, and Denver, Colo., 1960-61; Kent School, Englewood, Colo., chairman of history department, 1961-64; Carnegie-Mellon University, Pittsburgh, Pa., assistant professor of history, 1964-68; Clark University, Worcester, Mass., associate professor of history, 1968—. Member of board of directors, International Film Foundation and Oxford Committee for Famine Relief-America. *Member:* American Historical Association, African Studies Association.

*WRITINGS: Tradition and Change in Four Societies: An Inquiry Approach,* Holt, 1968, revised edition, 1974; (with L. Berry) *People, Places and Change,* Holt, 1976.

*WORK IN PROGRESS: Environmental Trends in Africa.*

### FORER, Lucille K(remith)

*PERSONAL:* Surname is pronounced For-*ay;* born in Springfield, Ill.; daughter of William Frederick and JoAnne (Teubner) Kremith; married Bertram R. Forer (a clinical psychologist), September 27, 1941; children: Stephen, William Robert. *Education:* University of Southern California, M.A., 1949, Ph.D., 1953. *Religion:* Protestant. *Home and office:* 19854 Pacific Coast Hwy., Malibu, Calif. 90265.

*CAREER:* California State College (now University), Los Angeles, assistant professor of psychology, 1951-55; clinical psychologist in private practice, 1953—, currently in Malibu, Calif. National executive secretary, Psi Chi, 1952-56; consultant, Larri E. Welty Center of Educational Therapy; member of board of directors, Psychological Center of Los Angeles and Psychologists in Clinical and Independent Practice. *Member:* Society for Personality Assessment (fellow), International Psychological Association, American Association of University Women, American Psychological Association, Western Psychological Association, California State Psychological Association, California League of Women Voters, Los Angeles County Psychological Association, Malibu Authors' Society, Malibu Township Council, Los Angeles Graphics Council.

*WRITINGS: Birth Order and Life Roles,* C. C Thomas, 1969; *The Birth Order Factor,* David McKay, 1976. Contributor to professional and popular publications. Editor, Los Angeles County Psychological Association *Newsletter,* 1975—.

*WORK IN PROGRESS:* A book on psychological self-help; articles on birth order.

*SIDELIGHTS:* Lucille Forer told *CA:* "Studies of psychologists indicate that they show an early interest in 'being a writer.' I was no exception, filling notebooks from age 7 or so with fanciful (and simple) tales. For the budding psychologist, this written expression probably indicates concern about human relationships and an attempt to make some sense of them by imagining ways they should go. The fact that my own interest was in real, and not fictional life, is suggested by my turning completely away from imaginative themes to my present more or less scientific writings in psychological areas."

*AVOCATIONAL INTERESTS:* Art, international travel, politics.

\* \* \*

### FORNO, Lawrence J(oseph) 1943-

*PERSONAL:* Born October 2, 1943, in New York, N.Y.; son of Felice M. (a lawyer) and Marie (Elmi) Forno; married Susan Senter (an artist), December 28, 1968. *Education:* Attended Institut Catholique de Paris, 1963-64; Fordham University, A.B., 1965; Columbia University, M.A., 1967, Ph.D., 1970.

*CAREER:* Drew University, Madison, N.J., assistant professor of French, 1970; State University of New York College at Brockport, assistant professor of French, 1970-71; University of Hawaii, Honolulu, assistant professor of French, 1971-74; University of Kentucky, Lexington, associate professor, beginning 1974. *Member:* Modern Language Association of America, American Association of Teachers of French (president, Hawaii chapter, 1972-73), American Society for Eighteenth Century Studies, Phi Beta Kappa. *Awards, honors:* State University of New York research grant, 1971.

*WRITINGS: Robert Challe: Intimations of the Enlighten-*

*ment,* Fairleigh Dickinson University Press, 1972. Contributor of articles to *French Review, Studies on Voltaire, Studies on Burke.*

WORK IN PROGRESS: *Diderot and Russell: A Study in Comparative Philosophy.*†

\* \* \*

### FORSYTH, George H(oward), Jr. 1901-

*PERSONAL:* Born September 2, 1901, Highland Park, Ill.; son of George H. and Sarah (Brockunier) Forsyth; married former wife, Eleanor Marquand, February 5, 1927; married Mary Isom Hayes, August 18, 1942 (died, November 6, 1958); married Ilene Haering (an art historian), June 4, 1960; children: (first marriage) Eleanor, Mary Blaikie (Mrs. Robert R. Worth), Allan; (second marriage) Hope G. *Education:* Princeton University, A.B., 1923, M.F.A., 1927, attended Institute for Advanced Study, 1935-36, 1945. *Home:* 5 Geddes Heights, Ann Arbor, Mich. 48104. *Office:* Kelsey Museum of Archaeology, University of Michigan, Ann Arbor, Mich. 48104.

*CAREER:* Princeton University, Princeton, N.J., instructor, 1927-31, assistant professor of art and archaeology, 1931-42; University of Michigan, Ann Arbor, professor of art history, 1947-72, head of department, 1947-61, director of Kelsey Museum, 1961-68, research professor, 1969-72. Research associate, Freer Gallery, Smithsonian Institution, 1954, 1956, 1960. *Military service:* U.S. Naval Reserve, 1942-45; became lieutenant. *Member:* Mediaeval Academy of America, Societe Francaise d'Archeologie, College Art Association (director, 1949, 1954), International Center of Medieval Art (member of board of advisors, 1961-70), Dumbarton Oaks Center for Byzantine Studies (member of board of scholars, 1958-72), Royal Society of Arts, Phi Beta Kappa, Phi Kappa Phi. *Awards, honors:* Mediaeval Academy fellow, 1924-25; Rockefeller Foundation research grant, 1946; Guggenheim fellow, 1953; Mediaeval Academy of America, Haskins Medal, 1955.

*WRITINGS: The Church of St. Martin at Angers,* Princeton University Press, 1951; (with Kurt Weitzmann) *The Monastery of St. Catherine at Mount Sinai: The Church and Fortress of Justinian,* Volume I (plates), University of Michigan Press, 1972. Contributor of articles to *Art Bulletin, Dumbarton Oaks Papers, Bulletin Monumental,* and other journals.

WORK IN PROGRESS: *The Monastery of St. Catherine at Mount Sinai: The Church and Fortress of Justinian,* Volume I (text), for University of Michigan Press.

\* \* \*

### FORSYTH, Ilene (Haering) 1928-

*PERSONAL:* Born August 21, 1928, in Detroit, Mich.; daughter of Austin Federick and Eleanor (Middleton) Haering; married George H. Forsyth (an archaeologist), June 4, 1960. *Education:* University of Michigan, A.B., 1950; Columbia University, A.M., 1955, Ph.D., 1960. *Home:* 5 Geddes Heights, Ann Arbor, Mich. 48104. *Office:* Department of the History of Art, University of Michigan, Ann Arbor, Mich. 48104.

*CAREER:* Barnard College, New York City, lecturer in art history, 1955-58; Columbia University, New York City, instructor in art history, 1959-61; University of Michigan, Ann Arbor, lecturer, 1961-63, assistant professor, 1963-68, associate professor, 1968-74, professor of art history, 1974—. Member, Institute for Advanced Study, Princeton, 1977.

*Member:* Mediaeval Academy of America, International Center of Medieval Art (member of board of directors, 1970—), College Art Association, Societe Francaise d'Archeologie, Academie des Sciences, Arts et Belles-Lettres de Dijon. *Awards, honors:* Fulbright grant, 1958-59; Rackham grants, 1965, 1972; American Council of Learned Societies grant, 1972; Charles R. Morey Book Award, College Art Association of America, 1974, for *The Throne of Wisdom.*

*WRITINGS: The Throne of Wisdom: Wood Sculptures of the Madonna in Romanesque France,* Princeton University Press, 1972. Contributor of articles to *Art Bulletin, Art Quarterly, Speculum,* and other journals.

WORK IN PROGRESS: Research on Romanesque stone sculpture in Burgundy, France.

\* \* \*

### FORT, Williams Edwards, Jr. 1905-

*PERSONAL:* Born September 29, 1905, in Birmingham, Ala.; son of Williams Edwards (a lawyer and circuit court judge) and Adele (Brooks) Fort; married Margrette Bullard, July 4, 1942; children: Adele Fort (Mrs. Jefferson R. Kirkpatrick), William E. III. *Education:* Georgia School of Technology (now Georgia Institute of Technology), B.S., 1930; Duke University, M.A., 1932, Ph.D., 1934. *Religion:* Church of Jesus Christ of Latter-day Saints (Mormon). *Home:* 1275 Fort Lane, Pleasant Grove, Utah 84062. *Office:* Brigham Young University, Provo, Utah 84601.

*CAREER:* Mercer University, Macon, Ga., professor of economics and chairman of Division of Economics and Business Administration, 1934-38; Winthrop College, Rock Hill, S.C., associate professor of business administration and philosophy, 1938-42; Rollins College, Winter Park, Fla., professor of philosophy and psychology, 1942-59; Deep Springs College, Deep Springs, Calif., president, 1959-61; Americanism Educational League, Buena Park, Calif., director, 1961-68; Brigham Young University, Provo, Utah, associate professor of religion and philosophy, 1968-72, professor emeritus, 1972—. *Member:* American Philosophical Association, Southern Society for Philosophy and Psychology, Phi Kappa Phi, Beta Gamma Sigma, Pi Gamma Mu.

*WRITINGS:* (With Richard Vetterli) *The Socialist Base of Modern Totalitarianism,* McCutchan, 1970; (with Vetterli) *The Socialist Revolution,* Clute, 1971. Contributor of articles to social science journals. Former contributing editor, *Florida Times-Union.*

WORK IN PROGRESS: Bibliographical research.

*AVOCATIONAL INTERESTS:* Travel.

\* \* \*

### FOSDICK, Raymond B(laine) 1883-1972

June 9, 1883—July 18, 1972; American lawyer, statesman, government official and consultant, and author of biographies, histories, and books on other subjects. Obituaries: *New York Times,* July 19, 1972; *Washington Post,* July 20, 1972; *Current Biography,* September, 1972.

\* \* \*

### FOTTLER, Myron David 1941-

*PERSONAL:* Born September 5, 1941, in Boston, Mass.; son of Myron Dustin and Anna (Curley) Fottler; married Carol Ann Szczepaniak (a teacher), August 11, 1972. *Education:* Northeastern University, B.S., 1962; Boston University, M.B.A. (with distinction), 1963; Columbia University, Ph.D., 1970. *Home:* 128 Vestavia Hills, Northport, Ala. 35476. *Office:* Graduate School of Business, University of Alabama, University, Ala. 35486.

*CAREER:* State University of New York at Buffalo, lecturer, 1967-70, assistant professor of industrial relations and of environmental analysis and policy, 1970-75; University of Iowa, Iowa City, associate professor, 1975-76; University of Alabama, University, associate professor of human resources management and health care management, 1976—. *Member:* Industrial Relations Research Association, Academy of Management.

*WRITINGS: Manpower Substitution in the Hospital Industry,* Praeger, 1972. Contributor of thirty articles to industrial relations, economics, management, and health care journals.

*WORK IN PROGRESS:* With Trevor Bain, *Determinants of Occupational Choice;* research on physician utilization of nurse practitioners, employee acceptance of various innovations, and the impact of various work scheduling innovations.

*SIDELIGHTS:* Myron Fottler told *CA:* "My writings are typically a quantitative and scientifically based attempt to measure the impact of people on the functioning of organizations. I don't believe in a dichotomy between the humanistic and the scientific. Both perspectives are necessary for important research."

\*        \*        \*

## FOULKES, A(lbert) Peter   1936-

*PERSONAL:* Born October 17, 1936, in Yorkshire, England; son of Henry and Cavell (O'Mara) Foulkes; married Joy French, 1960; children: Imogen, Juliet. *Education:* Sheffield University, B.A., 1958; Cologne University, graduate study, 1958-59; McMaster University, M.A., 1960; Tulane University, Ph.D., 1963. *Office:* Department of German, University of Wales, Cardiff, Wales.

*CAREER:* University of Mississippi, University, assistant professor of German, 1961-63; University of Illinois, Urbana, assistant professor of German, 1963-65; Stanford University, Stanford, Calif., 1965-72, began as assistant professor, became professor of German literature, associate dean of humanities and sciences, 1970-72; University of Konstanz, Konstanz, Federal Republic of Germany, Alexander von Humboldt senior research fellow in linguistics, 1972-74; University of Stirling, Stirling, Scotland, reader in German, 1974-77; University of Wales, Cardiff, professor of German and head of department, 1977—. Visiting professor of comparative literature, University of Mainz, 1976.

*WRITINGS: The Reluctant Pessimist: A Study of Franz Kafka,* Mouton, 1967; *Deutsche Novellen von Tiech bis Hauptmann,* Houghton, 1969; *Das Deutsche Drama von Kleis bis Hauptmann,* Houghton, 1972; *The Search for Literary Meaning,* Lang, 1975; *The Uses of Criticism,* Lang, 1976.

*WORK IN PROGRESS:* Research on Heine's early aesthetic theories; a book on propaganda and literature.

*AVOCATIONAL INTERESTS:* Travel, hiking, gardening.

\*        \*        \*

## FOWKE, Edith (Margaret)   1913-

*PERSONAL:* Surname is pronounced like "folk"; born April 30, 1913, in Lumsden, Saskatchewan; daughter of William Marshall (a garage proprietor) and Margaret (Fyffe)

Fulton; married Franklin George Fowke (an engineer), October 1, 1938. *Education:* University of Saskatchewan, B.A. (with high honors), 1933, M.A., 1937. *Home:* 5 Notley Pl., Toronto, Ontario, Canada M4B 2M7. *Office:* Room S706, York University, 4700 Keele St., Downsview, Ontario, Canada.

*CAREER:* Has worked as an editor, prepared radio programs for CBC, and worked for various magazines; York University, Downsview, Ontario, associate professor, 1971-76, professor of English, 1976—. *Member:* Canadian Folk Music Society (director, 1960—), American Folklore Society (fellow), English Folk Dance and Song Society, Association of Canadian University Teachers of English, Canadian Authors Association, Mensa Canada, Writers Union of Canada. *Awards, honors:* Medal from Association of Canadian Children's Librarians, 1970, for *Sally Go Round the Sun;* LL.D., Brock University, 1974; D.Lit., Trent University, 1975; Order of Canada (CM), 1978.

*WRITINGS:* (With Richard Johnston) *Folk Songs of Canada,* Waterloo Music Co., 1954; (with Johnston) *Folk Songs of Quebec,* Waterloo Music Co., 1957; (with Alan Mills) *Canada's Story in Song,* Gage, 1960; (with Joe Glazer) *Songs of Work and Freedom,* Roosevelt University, 1960, reprinted as *Songs of Work and Protest,* Dover, 1973; *Traditional Singers and Songs from Ontario,* Folklore Associates, 1965; (with Johnston) *More Folk Songs of Canada,* Waterloo Music Co., 1967, reprinted as *Folk Songs of Canada II,* 1978; *Sally Go Round the Sun* (juvenile), McClelland & Stewart, 1969; *Lumbering Songs from the Northern Woods,* University of Texas Press, 1970; (editor) *Canadian Vibrations Canadiennes,* Macmillan, 1972; *Penguin Book of Canadian Folk Songs,* Penguin, 1973; *Folklore of Canada,* McClelland & Stewart, 1976; *Ring around the Moon,* McClelland & Stewart, 1977.

*WORK IN PROGRESS: A Bibliography of Canadian Folklore in English,* with Carole Carpenter.

*SIDELIGHTS:* Edith Fowke has produced the following recordings: "Folk Songs of Ontario," "Irish and British Songs from the Ottawa Valley," "Lumbering Songs from the Ontario Shanties," "Songs of the Great Lakes," "LaRena Clark: Canadian Garland," "Tom Brandon of Peterborough," "Ontario Ballads and Folksongs," and "Far Canadian Fields."

*BIOGRAPHICAL/CRITICAL SOURCES: Canadian Forum,* December, 1968.

\*        \*        \*

## FOX, George (Richard)   1934-

*PERSONAL:* Born September 8, 1934, in Camden, N.J.; son of George Julius (an engineer) and Lillian (Geist) Fox; married Helen Gray, March 26, 1960; children: Karen. *Education:* University of Missouri, B.A., 1958. *Politics:* Independent. *Religion:* Protestant. *Residence:* Woodland Hills, Calif. *Agent:* Paul R. Reynolds, 12 East 41st St., New York, N.Y. 10017.

*CAREER: Evening News,* Perth Amboy, N.J., reporter, 1959-61; Magazine Management Company, New York, N.Y., 1962-68, began as associate editor, became editorial director. *Military service:* U.S. Air Force, 1951-55. *Member:* Writers Guild of America.

*WRITINGS: Without Music,* Holt, 1971; *Amok,* Simon & Schuster, 1978. Co-author of screenplay, "Earthquake," 1974. Contributor of articles and short stories to *Paris Review, Saturday Evening Post, Esquire, Playboy,* and other periodicals.

*WORK IN PROGRESS:* Currently writing a novel.

*BIOGRAPHICAL/CRITICAL SOURCES: Washington Post,* June 6, 1978.

\* \* \*

### FOX, Grace (Estelle) 1899-

*PERSONAL:* Born December 25, 1899, in Washington, D.C.; daughter of Edmund Kelly (a realtor) and Florence Eyster (Weaver) Fox. *Education:* Vassar College, B.A., 1922; Columbia University, M.A., 1925, Ph.D., 1940. *Religion:* Lutheran. *Home:* 1709 S St. N.W., Washington, D.C. 20009.

*CAREER:* Choate School, Brookline, Mass., teacher of history, 1927-29; Sarah Lawrence College, Bronxville, N.Y., member of the history faculty, 1929-35; U.S. Office for Foreign Relief and Rehabilitation Operations, Washington, D.C., historian, 1943; United Nations Relief and Rehabilitation Administration, Washington, D.C., historian, 1944-49; American University, Washington, D.C., lecturer in history, 1953-57; Goucher College, Towson, Md., lecturer in history, 1953, 1954. Visiting lecturer, Workers' Educational Association Summer School, Oxford, 1932. Member of board of directors, Barney Neighborhood House, 1960-74; member of board of directors and executive committee, International Student House, 1966—. *Member:* Association for Asian Studies, Asiatic Society of Japan, International House of Japan, Sino-American Cultural Society (treasurer, 1958; member of board of directors, 1975—), Sulgrave Club. *Awards, honors:* Social Science Research Council grants, Admiralty and Foreign Office Archives, 1939, 1954; American Council of Learned Societies grant, 1940; American Philosophical Society grant, 1954.

*WRITINGS: British Admirals and Chinese Pirates: 1832-1869,* Kegan Paul, 1940; (with George Woodbridge and others) *UNRRA: The History of the United Nations Relief and Rehabilitation Administration,* three volumes, Columbia University Press, 1950; (author of introduction) John Black, *Young Japan,* two volumes, Oxford University Press, 1968; *Britain and Japan: 1858-1883,* Clarendon Press, 1969. Contributor of articles to political science and history journals in Canada and the United States.

*WORK IN PROGRESS:* Research on Japan's control of the opium trade, 1722-1937; research on Japan's opium policies, 1945-1971.

*AVOCATIONAL INTERESTS:* Music, gardening, dogs, horses.

*BIOGRAPHICAL/CRITICAL SOURCES: Times Literary Supplement,* October 16, 1970.

\* \* \*

### FOX, Uffa 1898-1972

January 15, 1898—October 26, 1972; English yachtsman, designer, and author of books on yacht design and sailing. Obituaries: *New York Times,* October 27, 1972; *Antiquarian Bookman,* December 4, 1972.

\* \* \*

### FOX, Vernon (Brittain) 1916-

*PERSONAL:* Born April 25, 1916, in Boyne Falls, Mich.; son of John Lorenzo (a teacher) and Ethel (Hamilton) Fox; married Laura Grace Ellerby (a teacher), March 22, 1941; children: Karen (Mrs. Richard Root), Vernon, Jr., Loraine (Mrs. James K. Farley). *Education:* Michigan State University, A.B., 1940, certificate in social work, 1941, M.A., 1943, Ph.D., 1949. *Politics:* None. *Religion:* Methodist. *Home:* 644 Voncile Ave., Tallahassee, Fla. 32303. *Office:* School of Criminology, Florida State University, Tallahassee, Fla. 32306.

*CAREER:* Starr Commonwealth for Boys, Albion, Mich., psychological caseworker and athletic director, 1941-42; Michigan Department of Corrections, Jackson and Chelsea, psychologist, 1942-49; State Prison of Southern Michigan, Jackson, deputy warden in charge of individual treatment, 1949-52; Florida State University, Tallahassee, associate professor, 1952-56, professor of criminology, 1956—, chairman of department, 1956-71. Consultant to U.S. Department of Justice, Law Enforcement Assistance Administration. Member of board of visitors, U.S. Army Military Police School, 1971—. *Military service:* U.S. Army, 1945-46; became sergeant.

*MEMBER:* American Correctional Association, American Sociological Association, National Association of Social Workers, American Association of University Professors, National Council on Crime and Delinquency, American Society of Criminology. *Awards, honors:* Delta Tau Kappa award, 1963, for service to the social sciences; Florida State University Alumni Professor of the year, 1970; Florida Correctional Association first annual award, 1970, for contributions to criminology.

*WRITINGS: Violence behind Bars,* Vantage Press, 1956; *Guidelines for Corrections Programs in Community and Junior Colleges,* American Association of Junior Colleges, 1969; (co-author) *Crime and Law Enforcement,* Southern Newspaper Publishers Association, 1971; *Introduction to Corrections,* Prentice-Hall, 1972, 2nd edition, 1977; *Handbook for Volunteers in Juvenile Court,* National Council of Juvenile Court Judges, 1973; (with Neil Chamelin and Paul Whisenand) *Introduction to Criminal Justice,* Prentice-Hall, 1975, 2nd edition, 1979; *Introduction to Criminology,* Prentice-Hall, 1976; *Community-Based Corrections,* Prentice-Hall, 1977; (with Burton Wright) *Criminal Justice and the Social Sciences,* Saunders, 1978. Contributor of about seventy articles to criminology and sociology journals.

*WORK IN PROGRESS: Correctional Institutions,* for Prentice-Hall; *Juvenile Delinquency Control,* for Glencoe Press.

*SIDELIGHTS:* The Vernon B. Fox Collection of papers, memorabilia, and publications, is contained in the Archives of Contemporary History at the University of Wyoming.

\* \* \*

### FRADKIN, Elvira (Thekla) Kush 1890(?)-1972

1890(?)—December 18, 1972; American social activist and author of books on nuclear disarmament, peace, and women's rights. Obituaries: *New York Times,* December 20, 1972.

\* \* \*

### FRANCIS, Nelle (Trew) 1914-

*PERSONAL:* Born June 29, 1914, in Prague, Okla.; daughter of William Benjamin (a cotton ginner) and Mary (Trew) Francis. *Education:* Hardin-Simmons University, B.A., 1934; University of Texas, Main University (now University of Texas at Austin), M.A., 1942, Ph.D., 1961. *Religion:* Baptist. *Home:* 601 East Maryland, Ruston, La. 71270. *Office:* Department of English, Louisiana Tech University, Ruston, La. 71270.

*CAREER:* Texas Western College (now University of Texas at El Paso), instructor in English, 1946-54; University of Texas, Main University (now University of Texas at Austin), instructor in English, 1958-59; Arlington State College (now University of Texas at Arlington), assistant professor of English, 1961-63; University of Texas at El Paso, assistant professor of English, 1965-67; Louisiana Tech University, Ruston, associate professor of English, 1967—.

*WRITINGS:* (With John Warren Smith) *Patterns for Prose Writing: From Notes to Themes,* Scott, Foresman, 1969. Contributor of articles to *Delta Kappa Gamma Bulletin* and *Western Review.*

*       *       *

## FRANCOEUR, Robert T(homas)   1931-

*PERSONAL:* Born October 18, 1931, in Detroit, Mich.; son of George Antoine (a steel consultant) and Julia Ann (Russell) Francoeur; married Anna Kotlarchyk (an accountant), September 24, 1966; children: Nicole Lynn, Danielle Ann. *Education:* Sacred Heart College, B.A., 1953; St. Vincent College, M.A., 1958; University of Detroit, M.S., 1961; University of Delaware, Ph.D., 1966; also studied at Fordham University and Johns Hopkins University. *Politics:* Democrat. *Religion:* Roman Catholic. *Home:* 2 Circle Dr., Rockaway, N.J. 07866. *Office:* Department of Biology, Fairleigh Dickinson University, Madison, N.J. 07940.

*CAREER:* Fairleigh Dickinson University, Madison, N.J., instructor, 1965-66, assistant professor, 1966-70, associate professor of experimental embryology and social biology, beginning 1970, currently professor of human sexuality and embryology and chairman of biological sciences. Frequent lecturer at colleges, universities, and professional conferences; has appeared on national and local television and radio programs. Has completed documentary programs for Public Broadcasting Authority of New Jersey and Canadian Broadcasting Corp. (CBC); consultant for ''Death: The Invention of Life,'' a film. Adviser to Institute for the Scientific Study of Human Sexual Potentials and to Sandstone Foundation for Community Systems Research. *Member:* World Future Society, National Council on Family Relations, Society for the Scientific Study of Sex (Eastern chapter secretary), Groves Conference on Marriage and the Family.

*WRITINGS: Evolving World, Converging Man,* Holt, 1970; *Utopian Motherhood: New Trends in Human Reproduction,* Doubleday, 1970, revised edition, A. S. Barnes, 1972; (author of introduction) Beatrice Bruteau, *Worthy Is the World: The Hindu Philosophy of Sri Aurobindo,* Fairleigh Dickinson University Press, 1971; (contributor) Kenneth Vaux, editor, *To Create a Different Future: Religious Hope and Technological Planning,* Friendship, 1972; (contributor) Seymour Farber and Joseph Alioto, editors, *Teilhard de Chardin: In Quest of the Perfection of Man,* Fairleigh Dickinson University Press, 1972; *Eve's New Rib: Twenty Faces of Sex, Marriage and Family,* Harcourt, 1972; (with wife, Anna K. Francoeur) *Hot and Cool Sex: Cultures in Conflict,* Harcourt, 1974; (editor with A. K. Francoeur) *The Future of Sexual Relations,* Prentice-Hall, 1974. Contributor of articles to scientific and national magazines, including *Forum, Journal of Sex Research,* and *Journal of Marriage and Family.*

*WORK IN PROGRESS: An Operational Decision Workbook on Biomedical Ethics; Learning to Become a Sexual Person; Religious Covenants for Alternate Lifestyles.*

*BIOGRAPHICAL/CRITICAL SOURCES: Newsweek,* November 23, 1970; *Medical World News,* November 27, 1970; *Baltimore Sun,* February 7, 1971.

*       *       *

## FRANK, Benis M.   1925-

*PERSONAL:* Given name rhymes with ''Dennis''; born February 21, 1925, in Amsterdam, N.Y.; son of Victor Bernard (a pharmacist) and Sarah (Gray) Frank; married Marylouise Swatowicz (a registered nurse), October 8, 1960; children: Karen, Victor, Jennifer. *Education:* Attended University of Connecticut, 1942-43, 1946-49, A.B., 1949; Clark University, candidate for M.A. *Home:* 12501 Killian Lane, Bowie, Md. 20715. *Office:* History and Museums Division, Headquarters, U.S. Marine Corps, Washington, D.C. 20380.

*CAREER:* Assistant buyer for department stores in St. Louis, Mo., 1954-56, and Bridgeport, Conn., 1956-57; Franklin Simon, Westport, Conn., assistant manager, 1957-58; Central States Paper & Bag Co., New York, N.Y., salesman, 1958-59; King School, Stamford, Conn., teacher of history, 1959-60; Headquarters, U.S. Marine Corps, History and Museums Division, Washington, D.C., historian, 1961—, head of oral history section, 1966—. *Military service:* U.S. Marine Corps, 1943-46. U.S. Marine Corps Reserve, 1947-60; resigned as captain. *Member:* American Military Institute, Society for Army Historical Research, American Committee on the History of the Second World War, Oral History Association, Company of Military Historians. *Awards, honors:* Meritorious Civilian Service Award.

*WRITINGS: A Brief History of the 3d Marines,* Historical Division, Marine Corps, 1962, revised edition, 1970; *A Brief History of Marine Corps Roles and Missions,* Historical Division, Marine Corps, 1962; *Denig's Demons and How They Grew,* Marine Corps Combat Correspondents Association, 1967; (with H. I. Shaw) *Victory and Occupation: History of U.S. Marine Corps Operations in World War II,* U.S. Government Printing Office, 1969; *Okinawa: Touchstone to Victory,* Ballantine, 1970; *Halsey,* Ballantine, 1973. Contributor to military journals.

*WORK IN PROGRESS:* Conducting highly classified interviews relating to Vietnam; a monograph on Marine Special Landing Force operations in Vietnam; research on the Shanghai Volunteer Corps, the Marine Navajo code talkers of World War II, and other areas in military history.

*AVOCATIONAL INTERESTS:* Military music, with emphasis on bagpipes.

*       *       *

## FRANK, Charles Raphael (Jr.)   1937-

*PERSONAL:* Born May 15, 1937, in Pittsburgh, Pa.; son of Charles R. (a banker) and Lucille (Briscoe) Frank; married Susan Patricia Backman, March 9, 1963 (divorced June, 1977); married Eleanor Sebastian, July 19, 1977; children: (first marriage) Elizabeth Grace, Stephen Raphael; (second marriage) Paul Sebastian, Philip Sebastian. *Education:* Rensselaer Polytechnic Institute, B.S., 1959; Princeton University, M.A., 1961, Ph.D., 1963. *Home:* 3127 Rittenhouse St., Washington, D.C. 20015.

*CAREER:* U.S. Steel Research Center, Monroeville, Pa.; operations research analyst, summer, 1960, 1961; Makerere University, Kampala, Uganda, lecturer in economics and research fellow of East African Institute of Social Research, 1963-65; Yale University, New Haven, Conn., assistant professor of economics, 1965-67; Princeton University,

Princeton, N.J., associate professor, 1967-70, professor of economics and international affairs, 1970—, associate director of research program in economic development at Woodrow Wilson School, 1967-69, director, 1969-72; Brookings Institution, Washington, D.C., senior fellow, 1972-74; U.S. Department of State, Washington, D.C., member of policy planning staff, 1974-77, deputy assistant secretary of state for economic and social affairs, 1977—. Member of working party on transport and communications, Uganda Second Five Year National Plan, 1966-71. Consultant to U.S. Agency for International Development, 1966—, World Bank, 1969—, United Nations Economic Commission for Asia and the Far East, 1969, and to other public groups. *Member:* American Economic Association, Econometric Society, African Studies Association, Council on Foreign Relations.

*WRITINGS: The Sugar Industry in East Africa,* East African Publishing House and East African Institute of Social Research, 1965; (with B. Van Arkadie) *Economic Accounting and Development Planning,* Oxford University Press, 1969; *Production Theory and Indivisible Commodities,* Princeton University Press, 1969; *Debt and Terms of Aid,* Overseas Development Council, 1970; *Statistics and Econometrics,* Holt, 1971; *Foreign Trade and Domestic Aid,* Brookings Institution, 1977; (editor with Richard Webb) *Income Distribution: Policies and Projects in Developing Countries,* Brookings Institution, 1977.

Contributor: J. Preston Layton, editor, *Proceedings of the Princeton University Conference on Aerospace Methods for Revealing and Evaluating Earth's Resources,* Princeton University Press, 1970; Gustav Ranis, editor, *Government and Economic Development,* Yale University Press, 1971; *Seminar on Korea's Foreign Trade and Balance of Payments in Economic Development,* Korea University Press, 1971; Ronald G. Ridker and Howard Lubell, editors, *Employment and Unemployment Problems of the Near East and South Asia,* Vikas Publications, 1971; Peter J. M. McEwan and Ronald B. Sutcliffe, editors, *The Study of Africa,* 2nd edition, Methuen, 1972. Contributor of more than twenty-five articles and reviews to economics journals.

\* \* \*

### FRANK, Murray 1908-1977

*PERSONAL:* Born May 10, 1908, in New York, N.Y.; son of Paul and Pauline (Waxman) Frank; married Freidel Itzkowitz (a teacher), April 7, 1935; children: Paul Allen, David Elliot, Judith Sharon. *Education:* Attended New York University, 1929-31; Jewish Teachers Seminary, teacher's diploma, 1933; George Washington University, B.A., 1936; American University, M.A., 1937, postgraduate study, 1937-40. *Politics:* Democrat. *Religion:* Jewish. *Home and office:* 11724 Auth Lane, Silver Spring, Md. 20902.

*CAREER:* Teacher of history and literature in schools in Washington, D.C., 1937-41; U.S. Government, Washington, D.C., economic analyst, 1941-45; Washington, D.C. correspondent for newspapers in New York City, London, Israel, and Argentina, 1945-49; administrative assistant to U.S. Congressmen from New York and Connecticut and part-time newspaper correspondent, 1949-70; Washington, D.C. correspondent for *Jewish Daily Forward,* New York City, and newspapers in Israel and Argentina, 1970-77. Consultant on Jewish affairs to Congressman Sol Bloom (chairman, Foreign Affairs Committee of U.S. House of Representatives), 1946-49. Instructor, College of Jewish Studies, 1949-52, and Temple Sinai, 1956-58. Member of board of

directors, National Committee for Labor Israel, 1968-77; member of national executive committee, Labor Zionist Alliance, 1970-77. Former national director of information, B'nai B'rith; director, United Jewish Endowment Fund, 1970-74; delegate to National Jewish Leadership Conference on the Middle East, 1970, and to Ad Hoc Committee for the Conference on Human Rights and Genocide, 1970; vice-president, Washington Committee for Shaare Zedek Hospital in Jerusalem; chairman, Israel Histadrut Council of Greater Washington, and delegate to Histadrut Jubilee Conference, Israel, 1970. Director and announcer, "Voice of Israel" (radio program), 1958-61. *Member:* American Historical Association, American Academy of Political and Social Science, Congressional Press Gallery, State Department Correspondents Association, J. L. Peretz Writers Club, Farband Labor Zionist Organization (president, 1968-77), United Jewish Appeal (vice-president of government division), Workmen's Circle, YIVO-Yiddish Scientific Institute.

*WRITINGS: Fisheries of Latin America,* U.S. Department of Commerce, 1944; (with Lloyd J. Hughlett) *Industrialization of Latin America,* McGraw, 1946; *This Is B'nai B'rith: Book of Facts,* B'nai B'rith, 1947, revised edition, 1949; *Medinat Yisrael in Unzere Tayg* (title means "Israel in Our Days"), Naileben, 1972. Contributor to magazines in the United States and abroad. Editor, *B'nai B'rith News,* 1945-47.

*BIOGRAPHICAL/CRITICAL SOURCES: Washington Post,* October 21, 1977.†

(Died October 19, 1977)

\* \* \*

### FRANKO, Lawrence G. 1942-

*PERSONAL:* Born November 3, 1942, in Kingston, N.Y.; son of Michael and Lanra (Zielinski) Franko; married Marjorie Greep, December 21, 1963; children: Frederick, Tania. *Education:* Harvard University, A.B. (cum laude), 1963, D.B.A., 1969; Fletcher School of Law and Diplomacy, M.A. (international relations), 1964, M.A. (law and diplomacy), 1965. *Office:* Centre d'Etudes Industrielles, 4 Chemin de Conches, 1211 Geneva, Switzerland.

*CAREER:* Tunisian Government, Tunis, Tunisia, technical assistant, 1966-67; Harvard University, Cambridge, Mass., research assistant, School of Business, 1968-69; Centre d'Etudes Industrielles, Geneva, Switzerland, faculty member, management of international operations, 1969—. *Awards, honors:* McKinsey Prize for best article in *European Business,* 1971.

*WRITINGS: Joint Venture Survival in Multinational Corporations,* Praeger, 1971; *European Business Strategies in the United States: Meeting the Challenge of the World's Largest Market,* Business International (Geneva), 1971; *The Multinational Company in Europe: Some Key Problems,* Longman, 1973; *The European Multinationals: A Renewed Challenge to American and British by Business,* Harper, 1976.

\* \* \*

### FRASER, Russell A(lfred) 1927-

*PERSONAL:* Born May 31, 1927, in Elizabeth, N.J.; son of Roger John (a businessman) and Mary Louise (Narden) Fraser; married Eleanor Jane Phillips, May 31, 1947; children: Karen Mildred, Alexander Varennes. *Education:* Dartmouth College, A.B., 1947; Harvard University, M.A.,

1949, Ph.D., 1950. *Home:* 2105 Tuomy Rd., Ann Arbor, Mich. 48104. *Office:* 2619 Haven Hall, University of Michigan, Ann Arbor, Mich. 48104.

*CAREER:* University of California, Los Angeles, instructor in English, 1950; Duke University, Durham, N.C., instructor, 1952-55, assistant professor of English, 1955-56; Princeton University, Princeton, N.J., assistant professor, 1956-61, associate professor of English, 1961-65, associate dean of Graduate School, 1962-65; Vanderbilt University, Nashville, Tenn., professor of English and chairman of department, 1965-68; University of Michigan, Ann Arbor, professor of English and chairman of department, 1968—. Researcher at British Museum, Cambridge University Library, and Bodleian Library, Oxford, 1951-52; visiting professor, Columbia University, 1962-63; lecturer at Free University of Berlin, Charles University of Prague, and National University of Hungary, 1965; resident, Institute for Advanced Study, Princeton, 1976. *Military service:* U.S. Naval Reserve, 1944-46. *Member:* Modern Language Association of America, Renaissance Society of America, Shakespeare Society, American Association of University Professors, Authors Guild. *Awards, honors:* American Council of Learned Societies grants, 1951-52, 1960, 1968; American Philosophical Society grants, 1951-52, 1960, 1963; National Science Foundation grant, 1964-67; Guggenheim fellow, 1973-74; Rockefeller resident scholar at Villa Serbelloni, Bellagio, 1975; National Endowment for the Humanities fellow, 1978-79.

*WRITINGS: The Court of Venus,* Duke University Press, 1955; (contributor) Harvey Goldberg, editor, *American Radicals: Some Problems and Personalities,* Monthly Review Press, 1957; *The Court of Virtue,* Rutgers University Press, 1961; *Shakespeare's Poetics,* Routledge & Kegan Paul, 1962, Vanderbilt University Press, 1966; (editor) William Shakespeare, *King Lear,* New American Library, 1963; *Selected Writings of Oscar Wilde,* Houghton, 1969; *The War against Poetry,* Princeton University Press, 1970; *An Essential Shakespeare: Nine Plays and the Sonnets,* Macmillan, 1972; (contributor) Sylvan Barnet and others, editors, *The Complete Signet Shakespeare,* Harcourt, 1972; *The Dark Ages and the Age of Gold,* Princeton University Press, 1973; (with N. Rabkin) *Drama of the English Renaissance,* two volumes, Macmillan, 1976; *The Language of Adam,* Columbia University Press, 1977. Contributor of more than fifty articles to *Yale Review, Sewanee Review, Kenyon Review, Nation,* and other periodicals.

*BIOGRAPHICAL/CRITICAL SOURCES: Hudson Review,* summer, 1967.

\*    \*    \*

**FRAZEE, Charles A(aron)   1929-**

*PERSONAL:* Born July 4, 1929, in Rushville, Ind.; son of Charles Aaron (in politics) and Frances (Geraghty) Frazee; married Kathleen Siegert, September 10, 1971. *Education:* St. Meinrad College, A.B., 1951; Catholic University of America, M.A., 1954; American School of Classical Studies, Athens, Greece, summer graduate study, 1960; Indiana University, Ph.D. and Certificate of Russian and East European Institute, 1965. *Home:* 726 Paris Way, Placentia, Calif. 92670. *Office:* Department of History, California State University, Fullerton, Calif. 92634.

*CAREER:* Marian College, Indianapolis, Ind., instructor, 1956-59, assistant professor, 1959-65, associate professor of history, 1965-69; Indiana University at Bloomington, visiting assistant professor of history, 1969-70; California State

University, Fullerton, professor of history, 1970—. Researcher in western Europe, 1963, Athens, Greece, 1964, the Balkans, summer, 1966, and Tunisia, summer, 1968. *Member:* American Historical Society, American Society of Church History, Modern Greek Studies Association. *Awards, honors:* American Philosophical Society grant, summer, 1972; National Endowment for the Humanities grant, summer, 1976.

*WRITINGS: The Orthodox Church and Independent Greece,* Cambridge University Press, 1969; (contributor) J.T.A. Kovmoulides, editor, *Greece in Transition,* Zeno, 1977. Also contributor to *The Religious Heritage of Southern California,* Francis Weber, editor, 1976. Contributor to historical journals.

*WORK IN PROGRESS: The Catholic Church in the Ottoman Empire,* completion expected in 1978.

*BIOGRAPHICAL/CRITICAL SOURCES: Spectator,* March 28, 1969.

\*    \*    \*

**FREEMAN, Donald McKinley   1931-**

*PERSONAL:* Born April 22, 1931, in Asheville, N.C.; son of Major M. (a machinist) and Bertha (Wright) Freeman; married Ina Benner, September 1, 1955. *Education:* Wake Forest College (now University), B.A., 1954; University of Rhode Island, M.A., 1955; University of North Carolina at Chapel Hill, Ph.D., 1963. *Politics:* Democrat. *Religion:* Presbyterian. *Home:* 1617 27th St., Apt. 603, Lubbock, Tex. 79405. *Office:* Department of Political Science, Texas Tech University, Lubbock, Tex. 79409.

*CAREER:* Hollins College, Roanoke, Va., instructor in politics, 1962-63; University of North Carolina at Charlotte, assistant professor of political science, 1963-65; University of Arizona, Tucson, associate professor of political science, 1965-69; University of West Florida, Pensacola, professor of political science and chairman of department, 1969-77; Texas Tech University, Lubbock, visiting professor of political science, 1977—. North Carolina editor for Congressional elections, Columbia Broadcasting System, Inc. (CBS), 1964; consultant on survey research, Data Surveys, Phoenix, Ariz., 1967-68. Precinct chairman, Charlotte, N.C. and Tucson, Ariz.; chairman, Humphrey for president committee, southern Arizona, 1968, Pensacola, 1972. *Member:* American Political Science Association, Southern Political Science Association, Western Political Science Association, Southwestern Political Science Association. *Awards, honors:* National Convention fellow, National Center for Education in Politics, 1964.

*WRITINGS:* (Editor and author of introduction with William J. Crotty and Douglas S. Gatlin) *Political Parties and Political Behavior,* Allyn & Bacon, 1966, 2nd edition, 1972; (editor and contributor) *Foundation of Political Science: Research, Methods, and Scope,* Free Press, 1977. Contributor to *Social Science Quarterly.* Member of board of editors, *Western Political Quarterly,* 1969-75.

*WORK IN PROGRESS: Political Parties,* a textbook, and a basic text for a first course in American government.

\*    \*    \*

**FREESTROM, Hubert J.   1928-**

*PERSONAL:* Born April 19, 1928, in Chicago, Ill.; son of Edward Charles (an ironworker) and Emma (Parmentier) Freestrom. *Education:* Attended St. Mary's College, Winona, Minn., 1945; DePaul University, B.Sc., 1950, M.A., 1957. *Home:* O.S. 540 Summit Ave., Villa Park, Ill. 60181.

*CAREER:* Board of Education, Chicago, Ill., science teacher, 1952-53, 1955-65, science consultant, 1965—. *Military service:* U.S. Army, Adjutant General's Corps, 1953-55. *Member:* National Science Teachers Association, American Association for the Advancement of Science, National Science Supervisors Association.

*WRITINGS*—With Bernard R. Osterberger and F. Alvin Blackman; all published by Benefic: *The Five Senses,* 1970; *Place and Space,* 1970; *Things Around Us,* 1971; *One and More,* 1971; *How Much-How Many,* 1971; *All and Part,* 1971. Producer of educational slides for Visualcraft, 1969.

*AVOCATIONAL INTERESTS:* Chess; any outdoor activity.††

\* \* \*

## FREILICH, Morris 1928-

*PERSONAL:* Born July 26, 1928, in Warsaw, Poland; naturalized U.S. citizen; son of Harry (a cantor) and Sura (Kashket) Freilich; married Natalie Ashkanozy (a psychologist), February, 1954; children: Harold, Steven. *Education:* Brooklyn College (now Brooklyn College of the City University of New York), B.A., 1952; Columbia University, Ph.D., 1960. *Religion:* Jewish. *Home:* 28 Elwin Rd., Natick, Mass. 01760. *Office:* Department of Sociology-Anthropology, Northeastern University, Boston, Mass. 02115.

*CAREER:* Accountant with chartered accountancy firm, London, England, 1947-49; University of Akron, Akron, Ohio, instructor in anthropology and sociology, 1959-61; Northern Illinois University, DeKalb, assistant professor of anthropology, 1961-63; Washington University, St. Louis, Mo., associate professor of anthropology, 1963-66; Northeastern University, Boston, Mass., associate professor, 1966-70, professor of anthropology, 1971—. Has done field work among the Mohawk Indians and in Trinidad and Israel. *Member:* American Anthropological Association, Society for Social Studies of Science, Northeastern Anthropological Association. *Awards, honors:* National Institute of Mental Health grants, 1960, 1961, 1963.

*WRITINGS:* (Editor and contributor) *Marginal Natives: Anthropologists at Work,* Harper, 1969; (editor and contributor) *The Meaning of Culture,* Xerox College Publishing, 1972.

Contributor: J. D. Jennings and E. A. Hoebel, editors, *Readings in Anthropology,* McGraw, 1967; Stanford Gerber, editor, *The Family in the Caribbean,* Institute of Caribbean Studies, University of Puerto Rico, 1968. Contributor to *International Encyclopedia of the Social Sciences* and to sociology and anthropology journals.

*WORK IN PROGRESS: Fieldwork: Society and Culture from the Inside.*

\* \* \*

## FRIED, Joseph P. 1939-

*PERSONAL:* Born June 16, 1939, in Brooklyn, N.Y.; son of Irving (a truckman) and Ruth (Schulman) Fried; divorced; children: Susan Deborah. *Education:* Columbia University, B.A., 1960. *Home:* 101 Clark St., Brooklyn, N.Y. 11201. *Office:* News Department, *New York Times,* 229 West 43rd St., New York, N.Y. 10036.

*CAREER: New York Times,* New York, N.Y., copy boy, news clerk, news assistant, and picture deskman, 1960-67, reporter, 1967—. *Military service:* U.S. Army, 1963-65. *Member:* Authors Guild, Urban Writers Society.

*WRITINGS:* (Editor with G. Feissel, and contributor) *American Government and Political Science,* Monarch, 1962; *Housing Crisis U.S.A.,* Praeger, 1971; (contributor) *Crisis in Urban Housing,* H. W. Wilson, 1974. Contributor of articles to magazines, including *Saturday Review, New York Times Magazine, Writer, American History Illustrated,* and *Nation.*

*WORK IN PROGRESS:* Articles on current affairs and urban affairs.

*BIOGRAPHICAL/CRITICAL SOURCES: Writer,* December, 1964; *New York Times Book Review,* November 28, 1971.

\* \* \*

## FRIEDELBAUM, Stanley H(erman) 1927-

*PERSONAL:* Born October 6, 1927, in New York, N.Y.; son of Nathan and Rose (Werner) Friedelbaum; married Clara Armel (a teacher and librarian), February 22, 1953; children: Barbara Ann. *Education:* Brooklyn College (now Brooklyn College of the City University of New York), A.B. (magna cum laude), 1947; Rutgers University, A.M., 1948; Columbia University, Ph.D., 1955. *Home:* 35 Foxwood Dr., Somerset, N.J. 08873. *Office:* Department of Political Science, Rutgers University, New Brunswick, N.J. 08903.

*CAREER:* Rutgers University, New Brunswick, N.J., assistant professor, 1958-61, associate professor, 1961-64, professor of political science, 1964—. *Member:* American Political Science Association, American Association of University Professors, American Association for Public Administration (vice-president of local chapter, 1957), Pi Sigma Alpha. *Awards, honors:* Rutgers University research council faculty fellow, 1965-66; citation of honor from the sixth annual Writer's Conference, 1973, for *Contemporary Constitutional Law.*

*WRITINGS: Municipal Government in New Jersey,* Rutgers University Press, 1954; (with Benjamin Baker) *Government in the United States,* Houghton, 1966; *Contemporary Constitutional Law,* Houghton, 1972; (contributor) Kurland, editor, *1974 Supreme Court Review,* University of Chicago Press, 1975; (contributor) Rosenthal and Blydenburgh, editors, *Politics in New Jersey,* Eagleton Institute, 1975; (contributor) Wasby, editor, *Civil Liberties: Policy and Policy Making,* Heath, 1976. Contributor of articles to law and history journals.

*WORK IN PROGRESS: Human Freedom: A View from the States; Civil Liberties in the Burger Court.*

*SIDELIGHTS:* Stanley Friedelbaum believes that analysis in constitutional law need not be "tiresome or mired in technicalities." He feels that there is room for graceful language and pleasing style, and that traditional conflicts over such issues as judicial review should be matters of widespread interest and excitement. Friedelbaum told *CA* that "the application of a pseudo-scientific methodology, no matter how elaborate, is not a substitute for creativity, sound reasoning, and urbane writing."

\* \* \*

## FRIEDL, Ernestine 1920-

*PERSONAL:* Born August 13, 1920, in Szegled, Hungary; U.S. citizen; daughter of Nicholas and Ethel (Neudorfer) Friedl; married Harry L. Levy (vice-chancellor emeritus, City University of New York), September 27, 1942. *Education:* Hunter College (now Hunter College of the City University of New York), A.B., 1941; Columbia University, Ph.D., 1950. *Politics:* Democrat. *Religion:* Jewish. *Home:* 3080 Colony Rd., Durham, N.C. 27705. *Office:* Department of Anthropology, Duke University, Durham, N.C. 27706.

*CAREER:* Wellesley College, Wellesley, Mass., instructor in anthropology, 1944-46; Queens College of the City University of New York, Flushing, N.Y., 1947-74, assistant professor, 1955-61, associate professor, 1962-65, professor of anthropology, 1965-74, chairman of department, 1964-68, executive officer of Ph.D. program in anthropology, 1969-70; Duke University, Durham, N.C., professor of anthropology, 1973—, chairman of department, 1973-78. *Member:* American Anthropological Association (fellow; president, 1975), American Academy of Arts and Sciences (fellow), American Association for the Advancement of Science (fellow), American Ethnological Society (president, 1967), Northeastern Anthropological Association (president, 1971), Phi Beta Kappa. *Awards, honors:* Fulbright and Wenner-Gren Foundation Award, for *Vasilika,* 1955-56; National Science Foundation grant, 1964-67.

*WRITINGS: Vasilika: A Village in Modern Greece,* Holt, 1962; (contributor) Bernard J. Siegel, editor, *Biennial Review of Anthropology, 1963,* Stanford University Press, 1963; (contributor) Julian Alfred Pitt-Rivers, *Mediterranean Countrymen,* Mouton, 1964; (contributor) Peggy Golde, editor, *Women in the Field: Anthropological Experiences,* Aldine, 1970; *Women and Men: An Anthropologist's View,* Holt, 1975; (contributor) J. Peristiany, editor, *Mediterranean Family Structure,* Cambridge University Press, 1976. Contributor of articles and reviews to *American Anthropologist, Human Organization,* and *Anthropological Quarterly.*

\*      \*      \*

### FRIEDLANDER, Walter A(ndreas) 1891-
### (Walter Andreas Kraft)

*PERSONAL:* Born September 20, 1891, in Berlin, Germany; son of Hugo (an industrialist) and Ernestine (Lichtenstein) Friedlaender; married Li Bergmann (an artist and physiotherapist), February 8, 1919; children, Dorothee (Mrs. Albert Mindlin). *Education:* Studied at University of Berlin and University of Munich; University of Berlin, B.A., 1914, A.M., 1918, Ph.D., 1920. *Home:* 6437 Regent St., Oakland, Calif. 94618. *Office:* School of Social Welfare, University of California, Berkeley, Calif. 94720.

*CAREER:* Juvenile court judge in Potsdam, Germany, 1920-21; admitted to bar, Berlin, Germany, 1921; alderman and commissioner for child welfare and public assistance, Berlin, Germany, 1921-33; lecturer and professor of social studies at Institute for Social Pedagogics and other institutions, Berlin, Germany, 1927-33; Social and Legal Service for Refugees, Paris, France, executive director, 1933-36; University of Chicago, Chicago, Ill., lecturer in School of Social Service Administration, 1937-43; University of California, Berkeley, lecturer, 1943-48, associate professor, 1948-55, professor of social welfare, 1955-59, professor emeritus, 1959—. Visiting professor at German Academy of Political Science, 1951-52, Free University of Berlin (as Fulbright senior lecturer), 1956-57, Michigan State University, 1959-60, University of Minnesota, 1963-64, University of Cologne, 1966, and Free University of Berlin, 1967. President, German Child Welfare League, 1931-33; chairman, International Committee on Social Welfare, 1946—; member, National Commission on International Social Welfare, 1965.

*MEMBER:* National Association of Social Workers, Amer-

ican Public Welfare Association, American Association of University Professors, National Conference of Social Work, Council on Crime and Delinquency, Deutsche Vereinigung fuer Jugendgerichte, Deutscher Vereinigung fuer oeffentliche und private Fuersorge. *Awards, honors:* Named social worker of the year by Golden Gate (San Francisco) chapter of National Association of Social Workers, 1971.

*WRITINGS: Grundzuege des Jugendrechts* (title means "Principles of Child Welfare Legislation"), Ernst Oldenburg, 1924; (with Otto Heimerich) *Die Bekaempfung der Arbeitslosigkeit* (title means "The Fight Against Unemployment"), O. Haase, 1927; (with Theodor Tichauer) *Das Recht der Jugend* (title means "The Charter of Youth"), J.H.W. Dietz, 1930; *Jugendrecht und Jugendpflege* (title means "Child Welfare Legislation and Protection"), Arbeiterjugend-Verlag, 1930; (with Earl D. Myers) *Child Welfare in Germany before and after Naziism,* University of Chicago Press, 1940; *Introduction to Social Welfare,* Prentice-Hall, 1955, 5th edition, 1979; (with Henry S. Maas, Gisela Konopka, and Genevieve W. Carter) *Concepts and Methods of Social Work,* Prentice-Hall, 1958, 2nd revised edition, 1976; *Individualism and Social Welfare: An Analysis of the System of Social Security and Social Welfare in France,* Free Press, 1962; *Helene Simon: Ein Leben fuer soziale Gerechtigkeit,* Hauptausschuss fuer Arbeiterwohlfahrt, 1962; *International Social Welfare,* Prentice-Hall, 1975.

Contributor: *Menschenbildung* (title means "Education of Mankind"), Schwetschke, 1921; *Jugendnot* (title means "The Distress of Youth"), Ernst Oldenburg, 1922; *Die Zusammenarbeit der oeffentlichen und der freien Jugendhilfe in den Jugendaemtern* (title means "The Cooperation between Public and Private Child Welfare Agencies in the Child Welfare Bureaus"), F. A. Herbig, 1926; *Die Durchfuehrung des Jugendgerichtsgesetzes als Personenfrage* (title means "The Realization of the Juvenile Court Law as a Problem of Personnel"), O. Braun, 1927; *Der Jugendhelfer* (title means "The Youth Guide"), Hensel & Co., 1927; *Lehrbuch der Wohlfahrtspflege* (title means "Textbook of Social Welfare"), Hauptausschuss fuer Arbeiterwohlfahrt, 1927; *Das Buch des Kindes* (title means "The Book of the Child"), Akademische Deutsche Verlagsanstalt, 1930; *Children, Young People, and Unemployment,* Save the Children International Union, 1933; *Lebendige Oekumene: Festschrift fuer F. Siegmund-Schultze zum 80 Geburtstag,* Luther-Verlag, 1966. Author of articles written under pseudonym Walter Andreas Kraft.

*SIDELIGHTS:* Walter Friedlander told *CA* that he hopes his work will "help to create an interprofessional awareness of the need to overcome the present spirit of wars, slavery, (and) destruction of the rare resources of this earth." *Introduction to Social Welfare* has been translated into Chinese, Spanish, Portuguese, and Turkish, and *Concepts and Methods of Social Work* into Italian, German, Spanish, Hindi, and Turkish.

\*      \*      \*

### FRIEDMAN, Paul 1899-1972

June 23, 1899—October 12, 1972; Polish-born American psychiatrist, educator, and authority on suicide. Obituaries: *New York Times,* October 13, 1972.

\*      \*      \*

### FRILLMANN, Paul W. 1911-1972

June 12, 1911—August 19, 1972; American missionary,

fund-raising executive, and author of books on China. Obituaries: *New York Times,* August 23, 1972. (See index for *CA* sketch)

\*     \*     \*

## FRIML, Rudolph 1879-1972

December 7, 1879—November 12, 1972; Czech-born American composer of operettas for stage and screen. Obituaries: *New York Times,* November 14, 1972; *L'Express,* November 20-26, 1972; *Newsweek,* November 27, 1972; *Time,* November 27, 1972; *Antiquarian Bookman,* December 4, 1972.

\*     \*     \*

## FROST, James A(rthur) 1918-

*PERSONAL:* Born May 15, 1918, in Manchester, England; U.S. citizen; son of Harry Arthur (a minister) and Janet (Wilson) Frost; married Elsie Mae Lorenz, September 14, 1942; children: Roger, Janet, Elise. *Education:* Columbia University, B.A., 1940, M.A., 1941, Ph.D., 1949. *Home:* 17 Neal Dr., Sunsbury, Conn. 06070. *Office address:* Executive Offices, Connecticut State Colleges, P.O. Box 2008, New Britain, Conn. 06050.

*CAREER:* High school history teacher in Nutley, N.J., 1946-47; State University of New York College at Oneonta, instructor in American history, 1947-49, assistant to the president, 1949-52, dean of the college, 1952-64; State University of New York at Albany, associate provost for academic planning, 1964-65, university dean for four-year colleges, 1965-68, vice-chancellor for university colleges, 1968-71, provost for undergraduate education, 1971-72; executive director, Connecticut State Colleges, 1972—. Smith-Mundt professor, University of Ceylon, 1959-60; acting president, State University of New York College at New Paltz, 1967. Member of Commission on Higher Education, Middle States Association of Colleges and Secondary Schools, 1966-72, of Patent Processes Board, State University of New York, 1970-74, and of Committee on Research and Development, College Entrance Examination Board, 1971-76. *Military service:* U.S. Army Air Forces, 1941-46; became major. *Member:* American Historical Association, New York State Historical Association (fellow). *Awards, honors:* Rockefeller Foundation grant, 1959.

*WRITINGS: Life on the Upper Susquehanna,* King's Crown Press, 1951; (with D. Ellis, H. Syrett, and H. J. Carman) *A History of New York State,* Cornell University Press, 1957, 2nd edition, 1967; (with Ellis and W. Fink) *New York: The Empire State,* Prentice-Hall, 1961, 4th edition, 1974; (with R. A. Brown, Ellis, and Fink) *The Evolution of American Democracy,* Follett, 1968, 2nd edition, 1969. Contributor to encyclopedias, yearbooks, and historical journals. Member of editorial board, State University of New York Press, 1964-72; member of editorial advisory board, *Connecticut Review,* 1972-76.

\*     \*     \*

## FROST, Richard T. 1926-1972

December 30, 1926—November 9, 1972; American educator, political scientist, editor, and corporation executive. Obituaries: *New York Times,* November 11, 1972. (See index for *CA* sketch)

\*     \*     \*

## FRUMAN, Norman 1923-

*PERSONAL:* Born December 2, 1923, in New York, N.Y.; son of Nathan and Minnie (Goodman) Fruman; married Doris Frankel (a teacher), June 15, 1958; children: Jessica, Sara, David. *Education:* City College (now City College of the City University of New York), B.A., 1946; Columbia University, M.A., 1948; post graduate study, University of Paris, 1950-51; New York University, Ph.D., 1960. *Home:* 8704 East Duarte Rd., San Gabriel, Calif. 91175. *Office:* Department of English, California State University, Los Angeles, Calif. 90032.

*CAREER:* Best Syndicated Features, New York City, editor, 1951-54; free-lance writer, New York City, 1954-59; California State University, Los Angeles, assistant professor, 1959-62, associate professor, 1962-66, professor of English, 1966—. Fulbright professor at University of Tel-Aviv, 1964-65, University of Clermont-Ferrand, 1971-72, and University of Nice, 1972; associate professor, University of Clermont-Ferrand, 1977-78. Advisor to film, "Coleridge: The Fountain and the Cave," 1974. *Military service:* U.S. Army, Infantry, 1943-45; became first lieutenant; received two Bronze Star Medals. *Member:* Modern Language Association of America, American Association of University Professors, International P.E.N.

*WRITINGS:* (Editor with Marvin Laser) *J. D. Salinger: Reviews, Essays, Critiques,* Odyssey, 1963; *Coleridge: The Damaged Archangel,* Braziller, 1971. Contributor of articles to popular and scholarly journals.

*WORK IN PROGRESS: The Idea of Originality in the Arts.*

*SIDELIGHTS:* Norman Fruman's book *Coleridge: The Damaged Archangel* elicited the following response from critic Thomas Lask: "No book I think will do more to indicate the dimensions of the 'problem of Coleridge' than Mr. Fruman's. In the process he will make every reader rethink his conclusions as to the nature and meaning of the Romantic movement, the nationalism of literature, the trustworthiness of literary evidence, the relation of language to the ideas and sensibility of an age."

*BIOGRAPHICAL/CRITICAL SOURCES: New York Times,* December 24, 1971.

\*     \*     \*

## FRY, C(harles) George 1936-

*PERSONAL:* Born August 15, 1936, in Piqua, Ohio; son of Sylvan Jack and Lena Freda Marie (Ehle) Fry; married Brigitte Gertrud Langer, December 28, 1961 (divorced October 2, 1970); married Christel Heischmann (a businesswoman), November 24, 1971. *Education:* Capital University, B.A. (with honors), 1958; Ohio State University, M.A., 1961, Ph.D., 1965; Evangelical Lutheran Theological Seminary, B.D. (with honors), 1962, M.Div., 1977; Winebrenner Theological Seminary, D.Min., 1978. *Politics:* Republican. *Home:* 158 West Union St., Circleville, Ohio. *Office:* Department of Historical Theology, Concordia Theological Seminary, Fort Wayne, Ind. 46815.

*CAREER:* Clergyman of Lutheran Church, vicar in Columbus, Ohio, 1961-62; Wittenberg University, Springfield, Ohio, instructor in history, 1962-63; pastor in Columbus, 1963-66; Capital University, Columbus, instructor, 1963-65, assistant professor, 1966-71, associate professor of religion and history, 1971-75; Concordia Theological Seminary, Fort Wayne, Ind., associate professor of historical theology and director of missions education, 1975—. Visiting professor, Damavand College, 1973-74, Concordia Lutheran Seminary, St. Catharines, Ontario, 1978; visiting lecturer, Wittenberg University, 1971; visiting theologian at churches in Columbus, Ohio, 1971-72. Member of North American executive committee, Fellowship of Faith for the Muslims; member of North American Conference on Muslim Evangelization, 1977-78.

*MEMBER:* American Historical Association, American Academy of Religion, Conference on Faith and History, Foundation for Reformation Research (Ohio representative), Turkish-American Association, United Nations Association for the United States, International Platform Association, American Association of University Professors, Organization of American Historians, Ohio Historical Society, Ohio Academy of History, Phi Alpha Theta, Kappa Alpha Pi. *Awards, honors:* Regional Council for International Education research grant for study in Turkey, 1969.

*WRITINGS: The Supper Guest,* Ohio State University Printing, 1971; (with James R. King) *The Middle East: Crossroads of Civilization,* C. E. Merrill, 1973.

Editor: (With Donald E. Bensch, and contributor) *The Middle East in Transition,* Capital University Press, 1970; (with James L. Burke, and contributor) *The Past in Perspective,* MSS Educational Publishing, 1971; (with Burke, and contributor) *The Emergence of the Modern World, 1300-1815,* MSS Educational Publishing, 1971; (with Burke, and contributor) *The Search for a New Europe, 1919-1971,* MSS Educational Publishing, 1971; (with James R. King) *An Anthology of Middle Eastern Literature from the Twentieth Century,* Wittenberg University, 1974; *Ten Contemporary Theologians,* Concordia Theological Seminary, 1976; (with King) *An Anthology of Middle Eastern Literature from the Twentieth Century,* Wittenberg University, 1974.

*WORK IN PROGRESS: A History of Lutheranism in America, 1619-1933; A History of Islam.*

*AVOCATIONAL INTERESTS:* Hiking, painting, science fiction.

* * *

### FRY, Howard T(yrrell) 1919-

*PERSONAL:* Born September 15, 1919; son of Lindsay Bowring and Edith Alice (Finch) Fry. *Education:* Pembroke College, Cambridge, organ scholar, 1938-39; Cambridge University, B.A., 1948, Ph.D., 1967. *Office:* James Cook University of North Queensland, Townsville, Queensland, Australia.

*CAREER:* Served in British Army, 1940-42, and as pilot in Royal Air Force, 1943-46, 1951-55; James Cook University of North Queensland, Townsville, Queensland, Australia, senior lecturer in Southeast Asian history, 1968—. *Member:* Royal Geographical Society (fellow), Royal Commonwealth Society (fellow).

*WRITINGS: Europe and the U.S.A.: A Revision Course in History, 1763-1870,* Dent, 1965; *Alexander Dalrymple (1737-1808) and the Expansion of British Trade,* University of Toronto Press for Royal Commonwealth Society, 1970; (with J. M. Thomson and Isobel McBryde) *The Significance of Cook's Endeavour Voyage* (three bicentennial lectures), James Cook University of North Queensland, 1970. Contributor to *Mariner's Mirror* and history journals.

*WORK IN PROGRESS: The Mountain Province, North Luzon: The Integration of a Cultural Minority Group in the Philippines.*

*AVOCATIONAL INTERESTS:* Formerly flying and sailing; classical music.

### FUCHS, Daniel 1934-

*PERSONAL:* Born August 12, 1934, in New York, N.Y.; son of Isaac (a manufacturer) and Sadie (Fox) Fuchs; married Cara Skoler, January 25, 1959; children: Margot Lynn, Sabrina. *Education:* Columbia University, A.B., 1955, Ph.D., 1960; Brandeis University, A.M., 1956. *Politics:* Democrat. *Religion:* Jewish. *Home:* 155 Elm St., Tenafly, N.J. 07670. *Office:* Department of English, College of Staten Island of the City University of New York, Staten Island, N.Y. 10301.

*CAREER:* Rensselaer Polytechnic Institute, Troy, N.Y., instructor in English, 1960-61; University of Michigan, Ann Arbor, instructor in English, 1961-62; University of Chicago, Chicago, Ill., instructor, 1962-64, assistant professor of English, 1962-67; College of Staten Island of the City University of New York, assistant professor, 1968-70, associate professor of English, 1970—. Fulbright lecturer in American literature at University of Nantes, 1967-68, and University of Vienna, 1975-76. *Awards, honors:* Norman Foerster Prize, for "Ernest Hemingway: Literary Critic," an essay in *American Literature,* 1965; City University of New York faculty research grant, 1972-73; fellow, Yaddo writer's colony, 1975, 1977.

*WRITINGS: The Comic Spirit of Wallace Stevens,* Duke University Press, 1963; (contributor) Marston LaFrance, editor, *Patterns of Commitment in American Literature,* University of Toronto Press, 1967; (contributor) Arthur Waldhorn, editor, *Ernest Hemingway,* McGraw, 1972; (contributor) Linda Wagner, editor, *Five Decades of Hemingway Criticism,* Michigan State University Press, 1974; (contributor) Duane Macmillan, editor, *The Stoic Strain in American Literature,* University of Toronto Press, 1977; (contributor) *Americana-Austriaca,* Braumuller Verlag, in press. Contributor to literature journals.

*WORK IN PROGRESS: Saul Bellow,* a critical study, completion expected in 1979.

*AVOCATIONAL INTERESTS:* Sports, camping, classical music, enology, museums, travel.

* * *

### FUEGI, John 1936-

*PERSONAL:* Born May 9, 1936, in London, England; son of Adolf Frank and Winifred (Burgess) Fuegi; married Penny Peoples, August 11, 1962; children: Stefan Carl, Aaron Douglass. *Education:* Pomona College, B.A. (with honors), 1961; University of Southern California, Ph.D., 1967. *Home:* 2701 Curry Dr., Adelphi, Md. 20783. *Office:* Department of Comparative Literature, University of Maryland, College Park, Md. 20783.

*CAREER:* Free University of Berlin, Berlin, Germany, lecturer in American studies, 1965-67; University of Wisconsin—Milwaukee, assistant professor, 1967-69, associate professor, 1969-72, professor of comparative literature, 1972-76; University of Maryland, College Park, professor of comparative literature and director of comparative literature program, 1976—. Visiting professor at Harvard University, summer, 1974, and at Free University of Berlin, summer, 1977. President, Flare Films. *Military service:* U.S. Navy, 1956-58. *Member:* Modern Language Association of America, International Brecht Society, International and American Comparative Literature Society, American Federation of Labor-Congress of Industrial Organizations (AFL-CIO; president of Local 79, 1970-73).

*WRITINGS:* (Editor with Eric Bentley, Reinhold Grimm,

and Jost Hermand) *Brecht Heute/Brecht Today,* Atheneum, Volume I, 1971, Volume II, 1972, Volume III, 1974; *The Essential Brecht,* University of Southern California Press, 1972. Author of "Genesis," a film script, 1961. Editor, *Brecht Jahrbuch,* 1974-77.

*WORK IN PROGRESS: The Violent Art: A Study of Violence in the Drama.*

\* \* \*

## FUJITA, Tamao 1905-

*PERSONAL:* Born November 11, 1905, in Tokyo, Japan; son of Akira (a history professor) and Ayako (Wada) Fujita; married Yuri Goto, March 2, 1934; children: Atsuko (Mrs. Iwase Kaiichiro), Shigeru, Sakiko (Mrs. Atsushi Ideno). *Education:* Waseda University, B.A., 1930. *Home:* 2-49 Sakuradai, Nerima-ku, Tokyo, Japan.

*CAREER: Chuo-Koron-Sha,* Tokyo, Japan, chief editor and director, 1933-70. Visiting professor, University of Hawaii, 1968. Member of board of directors of Children's Welfare Committee, Welfare Ministry. *Member:* Japan Pen Club (member of board of directors, 1969), Juvenile Literature Association of Japan (president). *Awards, honors:* Award of Juvenile Literature Association of Japan, and Japan Nursery Rhymes award.

*WRITINGS: Bokuwa kaizoku* (title means "I Am a Pirate"), Froebel Kan, 1965; *Utano nakano Nihongo* (title means "Japanese Language in Songs"), Asahi Shimbun, 1965; *Kenchan Asobimasho* (title means "Let's Play Together, Kenchan"), Kodan Sha, 1966; *Ojiisan to Violin* (title means "The Old Man and His Violin"), Shiko-Sha, 1969, translation by Kota Taniuchi published as *The North Star Man,* F. Watts, 1970; *Maigo no Ohmu* (title means "The Missing Parrot"), Shiko-Sha, 1970, translation by Tiyoko Tucker published as *The Boy and the Bird,* John Day, 1971; *Nihon doyoshi* (title means "History of Japanese Children's Songs"), Akane Shobo, 1971; *Kaidai sengo Nihon doyo nenpyo* (title means "Annotated Bibliography and Chronology of Post-war Japanese Children's Songs"), Tokyo Shoseki, 1977. Contributor to *World Encyclopedia for Children* and *World's Masterpieces for Children.*

*WORK IN PROGRESS:* A novel for young readers about the death of a father; a study of the Japanese language.

\* \* \*

## FULLER, Helen 1914(?)-1972

1914(?)—September 15, 1972; American journalist, editor, and author of books on political affairs. Obituaries: *New York Times,* September 24, 1972.

\* \* \*

## FULLER, Miriam Morris 1933-

*PERSONAL:* Born February 1, 1933, in Big Stone Gap, Va.; daughter of Charles Edward (an interior decorator) and Verta E. (in business with husband; maiden name Warner) Morris; married Foster D. Fuller (a professor of vocational education), June 7, 1958; children: Foster D., Jr., Gary Morris. *Education:* Swift Memorial Junior College, Diploma, 1951; Virginia State College, B.S., 1954; University of Illinois, M.S., 1968. *Politics:* Independent. *Religion:* Presbyterian. *Home:* 728 Glendale, Jefferson City, Mo. 65101.

*CAREER:* High school librarian and teacher of stenography, Bland High School, Big Stone Gap, Va., 1954-64; high school librarian in Appalachia, Va., 1964-67; elementary school librarian in Urbana, Ill., 1967-71. Summer instructor, University of Illinois, 1969. *Member:* National Association for the Education of Young Children, Missouri Library Association, Illinois Parent-Teacher Association (life member), Delta Kappa Gamma, Alpha Kappa Alpha. *Awards, honors:* Shields–Howard Poetry Award; Central Missouri State University award in recognition of outstanding contributions to children's literature, 1973.

*WRITINGS: Literature Appreciation Kit,* twelve volumes, C. E. Merrill, 1970; *Phillis Wheatley: America's First Black Poetess,* Garrard, 1971. Also author with Marion Leonard, *Correlating Library Skill with Classroom Instruction.* Contributor to education and religious journals.

*WORK IN PROGRESS:* A picture book with Jeanne B. Morris; an annotated booklist of ethnic books for young children.

\* \* \*

## FULLERTON, Gail Jackson 1927-
### (Gail J. Putney, Gail Putney Fullerton)

*PERSONAL:* Born April 29, 1927, in Lincoln, Neb.; daughter of Earl Warren and Gladys (Marshall) Jackson; married Snell Wallace Putney, July 28, 1950 (divorced, 1966); married Stanley J. Fullerton (a painter and sculptor), March 27, 1967; children: (first marriage) Gregory S., Cindy G. *Education:* University of Nebraska, B.A., 1949, M.A., 1950; University of Oregon, Ph.D., 1954. *Home:* 226 Wave Crest Ave., Santa Cruz, Calif. 95060. *Agent:* Gerard McCauley, 159 West 53rd St., Suite 27-A, New York, N.Y. 10019. *Office:* Executive Offices, San Jose State University, San Jose, Calif. 95192.

*CAREER:* Drake University, Des Moines, Iowa, lecturer in sociology, 1955-57; Florida State University, Tallahassee, assistant professor of sociology, 1957-59; San Jose State University, San Jose, Calif., associate professor, 1963-72, professor sociology, 1972—, dean of graduate studies and research, 1972-76, executive vice president, 1977—. Member of executive committee, Council of Graduate Schools in the United States, 1976-77. *Member:* International Sociological Association, National Council on Family Relations, American Sociological Association, American Association for the Advancement of Science, Pacific Sociological Association, Phi Beta Kappa.

*WRITINGS:* (Under name Gail J. Putney, with Snell Putney) *Normal Neurosis,* Harper, 1964, published as *The Adjusted American,* 1966; (under name Gail Putney Fullerton) *Survival in Marriage,* Holt, 1972, 2nd edition, 1977.

\* \* \*

## FULTON, Norman 1927-

*PERSONAL:* Born July 5, 1927, in Sedalia, Mo.; son of Homer L. and Nora Pauline (Stuart) Fulton; married Amparo Olias, July 16, 1966. *Education:* Central Missouri State College (now University), B.S., 1948; University of Rochester, Ed.M., 1955; University of Madrid, licentiate, 1965, Ph.D., 1966. *Home:* 926 Bloomfield Ave., Glen Ridge, N.J. 07028. *Office:* Department of Spanish and Italian, Montclair State College, Upper Montclair, N.J. 07043.

*CAREER:* U.S. Embassy, Madrid, Spain, chief of protocol, 1956-61; St. Olaf College, Northfield, Minn., professor of Spanish, 1966-68; Bradley University, Peoria, Ill., professor of Spanish and chairman of department of foreign languages, 1968-72; Montclair State College, Upper Montclair, N.J., professor of Spanish and chairman of department of Spanish and Italian, 1972—. *Military service:* U.S. Army, 1950-52. *Member:* American Association of Teachers of Spanish and Portuguese, American New Jersey Federation of Teachers of Foreign Languages. *Awards, honors:* National Investigator of Spain, 1966.

*WRITINGS: The Heritage of Spain* (pamphlet), U.S. Embassy Press, 1958; *Relaciones Diplomaticas entre Espana y los Estados Unidos, a Finales del Siglo XVIII* (title means "Diplomatic Relations between Spain and the United States at the End of the Eighteenth Century"), University of Madrid Press, 1970.

*WORK IN PROGRESS: A Cultural History of Spain.*

\*     \*     \*

## FURNESS, Edna L(ue) 1906-

*PERSONAL:* Born January 26, 1906, in Wausa, Neb.; daughter of Frank A. and Nellie (Swanson) Furness. *Education:* University of Colorado, B.A. and B.E., 1928, M.A., 1940, Ph.D., 1952; National University of Mexico, summer study, 1930, 1931, 1937. *Religion:* Protestant. *Home:* 725 South Alton Way, Windsor Gardens, Denver, Colo. 80231. *Agent:* Charles R. Byrne, 1133 Avenue of the Americas, New York, N.Y. 10036.

*CAREER:* High school teacher in Colorado, 1928-33, and Wyoming, 1933-39; Southern Colorado State College, Pueblo, instructor in Spanish, 1942-45; Casper Junior College, Casper, Wyo., instructor in English and modern languages, 1945-47; University of Wyoming, Laramie, assistant professor, 1947-52, associate professor, 1952-55, professor of English and foreign languages, 1955-61; Kearney State College, Kearney, Neb., professor of language and literature, 1961-72, professor emeritus, 1972—. Visiting summer professor at Adams State College, 1945, University of Denver, 1946, Central Michigan University, 1947, and University of Tennessee at Chattanooga, 1948.

*MEMBER:* National Education Association (life member), National Council of Teachers of English, Daughters of the American Revolution, Society of Children's Book Writers, Phi Sigma Iota, Kappa Delta Pi, Pi Lambda Theta, Pi Delta Phi, Delta Kappa Gamma, Gamma Phi Beta, P.E.O. Sisterhood. *Awards, honors:* Fellow, University of Colorado, 1939-40, 1950-51; trustee fellowship, Smith College, 1941-42; Rockefeller fellowship for inter-American studies, 1944; faculty research grant, University of Wyoming, 1957; Coe fellow in American studies, 1959; Delta Kappa Gamma postdoctoral scholarship at University of Denver, 1960-61; U.S. Office of Education humanities grant, 1965, 1967, 1971, 1972; *Poet Lore* Translation Prize, 1969.

*WRITINGS:* (With Gertrude Boyd) *Diagnostic and Instructional Procedures in the Language Arts,* Curriculum and Research Center, University of Wyoming, 1956; *Spelling for the Millions,* Appleton, 1964, 2nd edition, Thomas Nelson, 1977; (with Roy P. Ludtke) *New Dimensions in the Teaching of English,* Pruett, 1967.

Contributor: Oscar S. Causey, editor, *The Reading Teacher's Reader,* Ronald, 1958; James Magary and John Eichorn, editors, *The Exceptional Child,* Holt, 1960; Lester D. Crow, Alice Crow, and Walter Murray, editors, *Teaching in the Elementary School,* Longmans, Green, 1961; James C. MacCampbell, editor, *Readings in the Language Arts in the Elementary School,* Heath, 1964; Paul S. Anderson, editor, *Linguistics in the Elementary School Classroom,* Macmillan, 1971; Hal D. Funk and DeWayne Tri-

plett, editors, *Language Arts in the Elementary School,* Lippincott, 1972. Articles included in other collections of readings.

Publications include *Furness Test of Aural Comprehension of Spanish,* National Textbook Corp., and monographs. Contributor of more than 80 articles, 150 reviews, and 40 translations of plays, poetry, and stories to about twenty journals.

*WORK IN PROGRESS: Image of the Schoolteacher in Literature;* an anthology of children's stories; a bilingual edition of South American stories; a collective biography of distinguished women; translation of Spanish American poetry and prose; research on Arabic influence in English and Spanish vocabularies; haiku; *Mediterranean Magic,* a travelogue.

*BIOGRAPHICAL/CRITICAL SOURCES: Booklist,* September 15, 1976.

\*     \*     \*

## FURNISS, Edgar S(tephenson) 1890-1972

April 15, 1890—July 17, 1972; American educator, dean, and economist. Obituaries: *New York Times,* July 19, 1972.

\*     \*     \*

## FUSON, Benjamin Willis 1911-

*PERSONAL:* Born February 17, 1911, in Canton, China; son of Chester Garfield and Phebe (Meeker) Fuson; married Daisylee McClure, June 18, 1938; children: Linda, David W. *Education:* College of Emporia, A.B., 1932; University of Kansas, M.A., 1933; State University of Iowa, Ph.D., 1942. *Politics:* Independent. *Religion:* Society of Friends (Quaker). *Home address:* Box 354, Route 1, Louisa, Ky. 41230.

*CAREER:* First Sun Yat-Sen University, Canton, China, instructor in English, 1933-34, 1936; Lingnan University, Canton, editorial worker, 1934-36; Allahabad Christian College, Allahabad, India, instructor in English, 1936-37; Berea College, Berea, Ky., instructor in English, 1937-40; Mary Baldwin College, Staunton, Va., associate professor of English, 1942-44; Bridgewater College, Bridgewater, Va., associate professor of English, 1944-46; Lynchburg College, Lynchburg, Va., associate professor of English, 1946-48; Park College, Parkville, Mo., associate professor of English, 1948-58; University of Meshed, Meshed, Iran, Fulbright-Mundt Professor of English, 1958-60; Kansas Wesleyan University, Salina, professor of English, 1960-76, professor emeritus, 1976—. Visiting professor of English, Kobe College, Nishinomiya, Japan, 1966-67, 1973-74; part-time instructor of Asian literature at Prestonburg Community College and Ashland Community College, 1976-77. President, Fellowship House, Kansas City, 1955. *Member:* Modern Language Association of America, National Council of Teachers of English, American Association of University Professors, Kansas Association of Teachers of English (president, 1964-66), Lambda Iota Tau. *Awards, honors:* First award from National University Extension Association, for *Oriental Literature Study Guide,* 1970.

*WRITINGS: Browning and His English Predecessors in the Dramatic Monolog,* State University of Iowa, 1948; *Centennial Bibliography of Kansas Literature,* Kansas Wesleyan Press, 1961, sequel: *1960-1970,* 1971; *Oriental Literature Study Guide,* Independent Study Center, University of Kansas, 1970; *Islamic Literature Study Guide,* Independent Study Center, University of Kansas, 1977. Contributor of book reviews to *Library Journal,* 1961-72, and *Choice,* 1975—; contributor of articles to *Kobe College Studies* (Japan).

*SIDELIGHTS:* Benjamin Fuson told *CA* that "world travel, and residence in China, India, Iran, and Japan as teacher, plus longtime convictions against war and militarism, led to my little monograph *Anti-War Poems by Asian Poets: 'White the Bones of Men'*—a relatively unexplored field." He adds he hopes to do a "book-length anthology of Asian peace poems. I'm also working toward an eventual autobiography, while fighting encroachment of multiflora rose briars on our seventy-acre east Kentucky 'holler.'"

# G

## GAENG, Paul A. 1924-

PERSONAL: Born August 17, 1924, in Budapest, Hungary; naturalized U.S. citizen; son of Hans P. and Theresa (Brule) Gaeng; married Joan E. Gallagher (a college professor), April 6, 1968. Education: Received secondary education in Zurich, Switzerland; University of Geneva, Diploma, 1947; Columbia University, M.A., 1950, Ph.D., 1965. Religion: Protestant. Home: 2 Colony West Dr., Champaign, Ill. 61820. Office: 2090 FLB, University of Illinois at Urbana-Champaign, Urbana, Ill. 61801.

CAREER: McGraw-Hill Book Co., New York, N.Y., editorial assistant, 1950-54; Montclair Academy, Montclair, N.J., head of language department, 1957-63; Montclair State College, Upper Montclair, N.J., assistant professor, 1964-66, associate professor, 1966-68, professor of foreign languages, 1968-69, head of department of languages, 1966-69; University of Virginia, Charlottesville, associate professor of Romance philology, 1969-72; University of Cincinnati, Cincinnati, Ohio, professor of Romance languages and literature, and head of department, 1972-76; University of Illinois at Urbana-Champaign, professor of French and head of department, 1976—. Adjunct professor at Hofstra University, 1963, 1964, Queens College of the City University of New York, 1966, and Columbia University, 1968; visiting instructor at Columbia University, summers, 1967, 1969. Military service: Swiss Army, 1944-45. Member: Modern Language Association of America, American Society of Geolinguistics (treasurer, 1965-68), American Association of University Professors, Societe de Linguistique Romane.

WRITINGS: An Inquiry into the Influences of the Germanic Superstratum on the Vocabulary and Phonetic Structure of Gallo-Romance, Montclair State College, 1968; An Inquiry into Local Variations in Vulgar Latin as Reflected in the Vocalism of Christian Inscriptions, University of North Carolina Press, 1969; Introduction to the Principles of Languages, Harper, 1971; (editor) Studies in Honor of Mario Pei, University of North Carolina Press, 1972; (with Mario Pei) The Story of Latin and the Romance Languages, Harper, 1976; A Study of Noun Inflection in Latin Inscriptions, University of North Carolina Press, 1977. Contributor to philology journals, including Modern Language Studies, Romance Notes, and Revista di Studi Classici.

WORK IN PROGRESS: Research on Latin Christian inscriptions.

SIDELIGHTS: Paul Gaeng is fluent in seven languages. Avocational interests: Classical music.

\* \* \*

## GALANSKOV, Yuri 1939(?)-1972

1939(?)—November 4, 1972; Russian editor, poet, and dissident. Obituaries: New York Times, November 9, 1972; Newsweek, November 20, 1972; Antiquarian Bookman, December 4, 1972.

\* \* \*

## GALBRAITH, Jean 1906-
### (Correa, Judith Green)

PERSONAL: Born March 28, 1906, in Tyers, Victoria, Australia; daughter of Matthew (a farmer) and Amy (Ladson) Galbraith. Education: Attended state school in Tyers for seven years (intermittently because of poor health). Politics: None. Religion: Christadelphian. Residence: Tyers, Victoria 3844, Australia.

CAREER: Botanist and nature writer; lecturer in botany at Council of Adult Education spring schools, 1963-71. Member: Wild Life Preservation Society of Australia (life member), Native Plants Preservation Society, Society for Growing Australian Plants (honorary life member), National Parks Association (life member), Latrobe Valley Naturalists Club (honorary life member), Field Naturalists Club of Victoria (honorary member). Awards, honors: Australian Natural History Medallion for 1970.

WRITINGS: Garden in a Valley, Horticultural Press, 1939; Wildflowers of Victoria, Colorgravure Publications, 1950, 3rd edition, Longmans (Melbourne), 1967; Grandma Honeypot (juvenile), Angus & Robertson, 1962; From Flower to Fruit, Longmans (Melbourne), 1965; Fruits, Longmans (Melbourne), 1966; The Wonderful Butterfly: The Magic of Growth in Nature (juvenile), Angus & Robertson, 1968; (contributor) Patricia Wrightson, editor, Beneath the Sun, William Collins, 1972; (editor) Winifred Waddell, Wildflower Diary, Native Plants Preservation Society, 1976; A Field Guide to Wildflowers of South East Australia, Collins, 1977. Poems included in Music of Faith, Christadelphian, 1954.

Writer of scripts on nature subjects for Australian Broadcasting Commission. Contributor of articles, stories, and poems to many magazines, including monthly article under pseudonym Correa in Australian Garden Lover, 1926-76; writes for another magazine under pseudonym Judith Green.

*SIDELIGHTS:* Jean Galbraith does "fairly fulltime writing" when not traveling about Australia on botanical studies and collecting for her own herbarium and Victorian National Herbarium. Her motivation: "Helping others to see and enjoy those things that are a joy to me, and to protect them."

*AVOCATIONAL INTERESTS:* Music, reading, gardening, "all beautiful things."

*BIOGRAPHICAL/CRITICAL SOURCES: Victorian Naturalist,* October, 1970, July-August, 1977; *Melbourne Age,* July 2, 1977; *Victorian National Parks Association Journal,* November, 1977.

\* \* \*

## GALLAGHER, Louis J(oseph) 1885-1972

July 22, 1885—August 14, 1972; American Jesuit college administrator and educator. Obituaries: *New York Times,* August 16, 1972.

\* \* \*

## GAPANOV, Boris 1934(?)-1972

1934(?)—July 25, 1972; Russian Hebraist. Obituaries: *New York Times,* July 26, 1972.

\* \* \*

## GARBER, Lee O(rville) 1900-

*PERSONAL:* Born March 28, 1900, in Weston, Ill.; son of Chriss S. (a farmer) and Ida J. (Roeseler) Garber; married Gertrude H. Simpkins, August 15, 1921; children: Elizabeth Anne (Mrs. Paul M. Hutton), William Lee. *Education:* Studied law at Bloomington Law School, 1919-20; Illinois Wesleyan University, B.S., 1920; University of Illinois, M.S., 1925; University of Chicago, Ph.D., 1932. *Home:* 208 North Third St., Fairbury, Ill. 16739.

*CAREER:* Teacher and administrator in public schools in Illinois, 1920-25; Butler University, Indianapolis, Ind., 1926-33, began as instructor, became assistant professor; State Teachers College (now Mankato State College), Mankato, Minn., professor, 1933-41; Lake Forest College, Lake Forest, Ill., professor and head of department of education, 1941-43, 1945-46; Tennessee Valley Authority, Knoxville, education specialist, 1946-48; University of Pennsylvania, Philadelphia, 1948-67, began as associate professor, became professor of education, professor emeritus, 1967—; Illinois State University, Normal, professor of educational administration, 1967-72. *Military service:* U.S. Army, American Expeditionary Forces, 1918. U.S. Army Air Forces, 1943-45; became captain. *Member:* National Organization on Legal Problems of Education (secretary, 1954-56; president, 1965).

*WRITINGS: Education as a Function of the State: Its Legal Implications,* Educational Test Bureau, 1934, also printed privately as *The Legal Implications of the Concept of Education as a Function of the State,* 1934; *Handbook of School Law,* Croft, 1954; *The Law and the Teacher in Pennsylvania,* Educational Service Bureau, University of Pennsylvania, 1955, enlarged edition (with Charles M. Micken), Interstate, 1971; (with Robert L. Drury and Roger M. Shaw) *The Law and the Ohio Teacher,* Interstate, 1956, 2nd edition published as *The Law and the Teacher in Ohio,* 1966; (with William A. Yeager) *Legal Powers and Duties of Pennsylvania Boards of School Directors,* Educational Service Bureau, University of Pennsylvania, 1959; (with H. Hayes Smith) *The Law and the Teacher in Illinois,* Interstate, 1965, revised edition (with Ben Hubbard), 1976; (with

Micken) *The Commonwealth, the Law, and the Teacher: A Manual for Pennsylvania Teachers,* Interstate, 1963, revised edition, 1978; (with William J. Hageny) *The Law and the Teacher in New York State,* Interstate, 1967; (with Eugene Benedetti) *The Law and the Teacher in California,* Interstate, 1967; (with Floyd G. Delon) *The Law and the Teacher in Missouri,* Interstate, 1971, 2nd edition, 1977; (with Hubbard) *Illinois School Board Members and the Law,* Interstate, 1971.

With Newton Edwards: "The School Law Casebook" series, Interstate, Volume I: *The Public School in Our Governmental Structure,* 1962, 2nd edition, 1970, Volume II: *The Law Relating to the Creation, Alteration, and Dissolution of School Districts,* 1962, Volume III: *The Law Governing Teaching Personnel,* 1962, 2nd edition, 1970, Volume IV: *The Law Governing Pupils,* 1962, 2nd edition, 1969, Volume V: *The Law Governing School Board Members and School Board Meetings,* 1963, Volume VI: *Tort and Contractual Liability of School Districts and School Boards,* 1963, Volume VII: *The Law Governing School Property and School-Building Construction,* 1964, Volume VIII: *The Law Governing the Financing of Public Education,* 1964.

Editor: (With E. Duncan Grizzell) *Critical Issues and Trends in American Education,* American Academy of Political and Social Science, 1949; (and contributor) *Law and the School Business Manager,* Interstate, 1957; *Current Legal Concepts in Education,* University of Pennsylvania Press, 1966; John A. Stoops, *Religious Values in Education,* Interstate, 1967; Newton Edwards, *The Courts and the Public Schools,* revised 3rd edition (Garber was not associated with earlier editions), University of Chicago Press, 1971.

Writer of annual publication, *The Yearbook of School Law,* published by Interstate, 1950-71, with Edmund Reutter as collaborator on 1967-70 editions, and Reynolds Seitz as collaborator on 1971 edition. Contributor of more than 250 articles and reviews to periodicals, including a monthly article in *Nation's Schools,* 1951-71.

\* \* \*

## GARFUNKEL, Louis X. 1897(?)-1972

1897(?)—November 1, 1972; American restauranteur and writer. Obituaries: *New York Times,* November 3, 1972.

\* \* \*

## GARNER, (Samuel) Paul 1910-

*PERSONAL:* Born August 15, 1910, in Yadkinville, N.C.; son of Samuel W. and Ila Jane (Hoots) Garner; married Ruth Bailey, August 25, 1934; children: Thad Barclay, Walter Samuel, Sarah Jane. *Education:* Duke University, A.B., 1932, A.M., 1934; Columbia University, further graduate study, 1936; University of Texas, Ph.D., 1940. *Office:* College of Commerce and Business Administration, University of Alabama, University, Ala. 35486.

*CAREER:* Duke University, Durham, N.C., instructor in economics, 1934-35; Mississippi State University, State College, instructor, 1935-36, assistant professor of accounting, 1936-37; University of Texas, Main University (now University of Texas at Austin), instructor in accounting, 1937-39; University of Alabama, University, associate professor, 1939-43, professor of accounting, 1943—, head of department, 1949-55, dean of College of Commerce and Business Administration, 1954-71. Certified public accountant in

Texas, 1938, in Alabama, 1942; member of firm, Knight & Garner (certified public accountants), University, Ala., 1942-49; member of board of directors, First Federal Savings and Loan Association, Tuscaloosa, Ala., 1963-75. Comer Foundation lecturer at University of Georgia, 1957; Price-Waterhouse Foundation lecturer at Georgia State College, 1964; distinguished lecturer at University of South Dakota, 1963, Virginia Polytechnic Institute, 1966, and other colleges. Consultant on education to U.S. Comptroller General, 1955-61, U.S. Office of Education, 1965-70, and U.S. Department of Defense, 1965-69; conducted special education assignments for Department of State and other agencies in Europe, on twenty-three trips, 1957-72, in Turkey, 1958, Far East, 1960, 1966, 1968, 1969, 1972, South America, 1962, 1965, and Africa, 1964. U.S. Council for International Progress in Management, member, 1961—, member of board of directors, 1965-68; member, International University Contact for Management Education, 1963—; member of board of directors, International Committee for Accounting Cooperation, Inc., 1966—.

MEMBER: American Accounting Association (president, 1951), National Association of Certified Public Accountants Examiners, Society of Expert Accountants of France, American Association of Collegiate Schools of Business (president, 1964-65), Association for Education in International Business, Financial Executives Institute of America, American Institute of Certified Public Accountants, Alabama Society of Certified Public Accountants, Phi Beta Kappa, Beta Gamma Sigma (member of national executive committee, 1961-66), Sigma Alpha Epsilon, Beta Alpha Psi, Omicron Delta Kappa, Alpha Kappa Psi, Pi Tau Chi, Pi Gamma Mu, Omicron Delta Epsilon. Awards, honors: Alpha Kappa Psi Foundation Award, 1962; D.Ec., Pusan National University, Korea, 1966; L.L.D., University of Alabama, 1971; Dow-Jones award, 1976.

WRITINGS: (With George Hillis Newlove) Elementary Cost Accounting, Heath, 1941, revised edition, 1949; (with Newlove) Advanced Accounting, Heath, Volume I, 1950, Volume II, 1951; Evolution of Cost Accounting to 1925, University of Alabama Press, 1954; (contributor) Morton Backer, editor, Handbook of Modern Accounting Theory, Prentice-Hall, 1955; (contributor) Education for the Professions, U.S. Office of Education, 1954; (contributor) W. E. Thomas, editor, Readings in Cost Accounting, Budgeting and Control, Southwestern Publishing, 1955, revised edition, 1960; (editor with K. B. Berg) Readings in Accounting Theory, Houghton, 1966. Contributor to business and accounting journals in United States, Turkey, Italy, Netherlands, Switzerland, Greece, Japan, Korea, India, Germany, France, Philippines, and Canada. Member of editorial advisory board, Management International, 1964—; member of editorial board, Accounting Review, 1966-69, and Essays in International Business (annual), 1967—.

*　　*　　*

## GARRETT, Romeo Benjamin 1910-

PERSONAL: Born February 2, 1910, in Natchez, Miss.; son of Charles Edward (a dairyman) and Ponkie (Duncan) Garrett; married Naomi Sanders, November 29, 1945. Education: Dillard University, B.A., 1932; Bradley University, M.A., 1947; New York University, Ph.D., 1963. Home: 304 West Seventh Ave., Peoria, Ill. 61605. Office: Department of Sociology, Bradley University, Peoria, Ill. 61606.

CAREER: Baptist minister; New Orleans Welfare Department, New Orleans, La., social worker, 1932-34; Works

Progress Administration (WPA), New Orleans, supervisor, 1934-42; Bradley University, Peoria, Ill., instructor, 1947-49, assistant professor, 1949-56, associate professor, 1956-70, professor of sociology, 1970—. Member of board of directors, Peoria Goodwill Industries, Inc., and Visiting Nurses Association of Peoria. Associate minister, Zion Baptist Church. Member: International Student Friendship Foundation (member of board of directors), American Sociological Association, American Anthropological Association, Association for the Study of Negro Life and History, American Historical Society, American Gerontological Society, American Association of University Professors, National Association for the Advancement of Colored People (member of board of directors), Mid-West Sociological Society, Illinois Sociological Society, Peoria Academy of Science (chairman, anthropological section). Awards, honors: LL.D., Natchez College, 1949.

WRITINGS: Famous First Facts about Negroes, Arno, 1972.

WORK IN PROGRESS: The Presidents and the Negro; Puns for Fun; The Negro in Peoria.

*　　*　　*

## GARRIGUE, Jean 1914-1972

December 8, 1914—December 27, 1972; American poet. Obituaries: New York Times, December 28, 1972; Publishers Weekly, January 22, 1973. (See index for CA sketch)

*　　*　　*

## GARRISON, Karl C(laudius) 1900-

PERSONAL: Born August 14, 1900, in Gaston County, N.C.; son of Rufus J. (a farm owner) and Susie (Mauney) Garrison; married Ruby Heafner, 1924 (divorced, 1942); married Linnea Malmborg, 1943; children: (first marriage) Karl Claudius, Jr. Education: Attended Lenoir Rhyne College, 1917-18, 1919-21; George Peabody College for Teachers, B.S., 1922, Ph.D., 1927; University of North Carolina, M.S., 1926. Politics: Independent Democrat. Religion: Lutheran. Office: Department of Educational Psychology, University of Georgia, Athens, Ga. 30601.

CAREER: George Peabody College for Teachers, Nashville, Tenn., instructor in educational psychology, 1927-28; North Carolina State College, (now North Carolina State University at Raleigh), Raleigh, professor of psychology and chairman of department, 1928-40; Central Connecticut State College, New Britain, professor of education and psychology, 1941-46; Georgia State College for Women (now Georgia College), Atlanta, professor of psychology, 1946-47; Frostburg State College, Frostburg, Md., dean of instruction, 1947-48; University of Georgia, Athens, professor of education and chairman of department of educational psychology, 1948-65, professor emeritus, 1965—. Visiting professor of education, Old Dominion College, 1965—. Member: American Psychological Association (fellow), Council for Exceptional Children, American Educational Research Association, National Education Association, Southeastern Psychological Association, Southern Society for Philosophy and Psychology, Phi Delta Kappa, Phi Kappa Phi, Kappa Delta Pi, Kappa Phi Kappa, Psi Chi, Pi Gamma Mu. Awards, honors: Lenoir Rhyne College distinguished alumni award, 1962.

WRITINGS: (With brother, Sidney C. Garrison) The Psychology of the Elementary School Subjects, Johnson Publishing Co. (Richmond), 1929; Psychology of Adolescence,

Prentice-Hall, 1934, 7th edition (with son, Karl Claudius Garrison, Jr.), 1975; (with S. C. Garrison) *Fundamentals of Psychology in Secondary Education,* Prentice-Hall, 1936; *The Psychology of Exceptional Children,* Ronald, 1940, 4th edition (with Dewey G. Force), 1965; *Growth and Development,* Longmans, Green, 1950, revised edition, 1959; (contributor) J. Stanley Gray, editor, *Psychology in Use,* 2nd edition, American Book Co., 1951; (contributor) Gray, *Psychology in Industry,* McGraw, 1952; (with Gray) *Educational Psychology,* Appleton, 1955, 3rd edition (with Robert A. Magoon), 1972; (editor with Magoon) *Special Education for the Exceptional,* Sargent, 1955; (contributor) A. A. Roback, editor, *Present-Day Psychology,* Philosophical Library, 1956; (with Albert J. Kingston and Harold Bernard) *Child Psychology,* Scribner, 1966; (with Franklin R. Jones) *Psychology of Human Development,* World Publishing, 1969. Contributor of about seventy articles to education and psychology journals.

*WORK IN PROGRESS:* With Gilbert Ragland, 5th edition of *The Psychology of Exceptional Children.*†

\*     \*     \*

## GASSNER, Julius S(tephen)   1915-

*PERSONAL:* Born September 22, 1915, in New York, N.Y.; son of Julius and Barbara (Arlitsch) Gassner; married Renee Staring (a registered nurse), February 13, 1943; children: Jules L., Stephen T., John C., Elizabeth M., Martin C., Thomas A. *Education:* St. Peter's College, A.B., 1937; Fordham University, M.A., 1940; University of Minnesota, further study, 1951-52. *Politics:* Democrat. *Religion:* Roman Catholic. *Address:* P.O. Box 478, Corrales, N.M. 87048. *Office:* University of Albuquerque, Albuquerque, N.M. 87140.

*CAREER:* St. Thomas College, St. Paul, Minn., instructor in politics, 1947-52; University of Southwestern Louisiana, Lafayette, assistant professor of history, 1952-57; University of Albuquerque, Albuquerque, N.M., assistant professor, 1957-60, associate professor, 1961-73, professor of politics and history, 1973—. Instructor, College of St. Catherine, 1950-52. *Military service:* New York National Guard, 1937-40. New York State Guard, 1941-42. U.S. Army, 1942-46. U.S. Army Reserve, 1947-67; became major. *Member:* American Political Science Association, American Association of University Professors, Hakluyt Society, Cambridge Philological Society.

*WRITINGS:* (Translator) Jean-Francois de La Perouse, *Voyages and Adventures of La Perouse,* University of Hawaii Press, 1969.

*WORK IN PROGRESS:* Translating *Voyage autour de Monde,* by Louis Antoine de Bougainville.

*SIDELIGHTS:* Julius Gassner wrote *CA,* "My interest in La Perouse and Bougainville was stimulated by a prolonged visit to the Solomon Islands in 1944 and by the gradual realization of the great imbalance in American culture between the widespread familiarity with Capt. James Cook and the nearly total ignorance of the French explorers who were his contemporaries." *Avocational interests:* Travel, Greek and Roman archaeology, and numismatics.

\*     \*     \*

## GATES, Arthur Irving   1890-1972

1890—August 24, 1972; American educator. Obituaries: *New York Times,* August 25, 1972.

## GELD, Ellen Bromfield   1932-

*PERSONAL:* Born April 25, 1932, in Paris, France; daughter of Louis (the author) and Mary (Wood) Bromfield; married Carson Zachary Geld (a farmer); children: Stephen, Robin, Michael, Kenneth, Christina. *Education:* Attended Cornell University. *Politics:* "As little government as possible." *Religion:* None. *Home:* Fazenda Pau d'Alho, Cx.2 Tiete, Sao Paulo, Brazil. *Agent:* Paul R. Reynolds, Inc., 12 East 41st St., New York, N.Y. 10017.

*CAREER:* O Estadode Sao Paulo (newpaper), Sao Paulo, Brazil, author of column, "Suplemento Agricola." *Member:* Alto Conselho do Secretario de Agricultura for the State of Sao Paulo.

*WRITINGS:* *Strangers in the Valley,* Dodd, 1957; *The Jungley One,* Dodd, 1957; *The Heritage,* Harper, 1962; *The Garlic Tree,* Doubleday, 1970; *A Timeless Place,* Doubleday, 1971; *The Dreamers,* Doubleday, 1973; *A Winter's Reckoning,* Doubleday, 1976. Contributor to *Correio Agropecuaria* and *Latin American Daily Post;* also contributor to *Reader's Digest.*

*WORK IN PROGRESS:* A novel with "Brazil diamond mining region background."

*SIDELIGHTS:* Ellen Bromfield Geld told *CA:* "In my routine on the farm, no day is complete if I haven't written something [with which] I am fairly well satisfied. I imagine that is how one must feel about any profession if he loves it."

*BIOGRAPHICAL/CRITICAL SOURCES: New York Times Book Review,* February 1, 1970; *Best Sellers,* February 15, 1970; *National Review,* April 21, 1970.

\*     \*     \*

## GEORGE, Roy E(dwin)   1923-

*PERSONAL:* Born February 17, 1923, in Liverpool, England; son of Frederick W. (a tugboat captain) and Minnie (Crabtree) George; married Jean Morgan, September 12, 1949; children: Michele, Karen. *Education:* University of London, B.Sc., 1949, Ph.D., 1967; University of Bristol, M.A., 1956. *Home:* 147 Joffre St., Dartmouth, Nova Scotia, Canada. *Office:* Dalhousie University, Halifax, Nova Scotia, Canada.

*CAREER:* South Western Gas Board, Bath, England, assistant personnel manager, 1949-56; National Coal Board, Burnley, England, areas staff manager, 1956-60; St. Mary's University, Halifax, Nova Scotia, assistant professor of commerce, 1960-63; Dalhousie University, Halifax, associate professor, 1963-65, professor of commerce, 1965—. Consultant to Canadian government agencies, private industry, and trade unions. Member of board of directors, Maritime Chamber of Commerce, 1971-72. *Military service:* Royal Air Force, flight sergeant, 1941-46. *Member:* Canadian Economics Association, Canadian Association of University Teachers (vice-president, 1965-66; treasurer, 1966-67). *Awards, honors:* Canada Council leave fellowship and research grant.

*WRITINGS: Technological Redundancy in a Small Isolated Society,* Industrial Relations Centre, McGill University, 1969; *Leader and Laggard: Manufacturing Industry in Nova Scotia, Quebec and Ontario,* University of Toronto Press, 1970; *The Life and Times of Industrial Estates Limited,* Institute of Public Affairs, Dalhousie University, 1974.

*WORK IN PROGRESS:* Research on corporate bankruptcies in Canada.

## GERBER, William 1908-

*PERSONAL:* Born July 12, 1908, in Philadelphia, Pa.; son of Samuel (a store owner) and Fanny (Kramer) Gerber; married Sylvia R. Wigdor, August 6, 1933; children: Louis M. W. *Education:* University of Pennsylvania, B.A. (with honors), 1929; George Washington University, M.A., 1932; Johns Hopkins University, graduate study, 1932-33, 1935-36; Columbia University, Ph.D., 1945. *Politics:* Independent. *Religion:* Jewish. *Home:* 3077 Chestnut St. N.W., Washington, D.C. 20015.

*CAREER:* U.S. Department of State, Washington, D.C., member of staff, Office of Historical Adviser, Division of Research and Publication, 1930-41, assistant to chief of division, 1941-44, alternate representative to interdepartmental committee for acquisition of foreign publications, 1942-44, assistant chief of current research branch, Division of Historical Policy Research, 1946-48, chief of special studies section, Historical Division, 1948-57, foreign service officer, 1957-60; U.S. Department of Labor, Washington, D.C., chief of British Commonwealth section, Division of Foreign Labor Conditions, 1958-60, chief of research branch, 1960-62, acting deputy chief of division, 1962-65, deputy chief, 1965-68; Editorial Research Reports, Washington, D.C., writer, 1968-71; *Congressional Quarterly,* Washington, D.C., writer and indexer, 1971-72. Washington Hall Junior College, instructor in philosophy and world literature, 1955-57, acting director of Division of Humanities, 1956-57; lecturer in philosophy at University of Maryland, 1959-60, 1963-72, and at American University, 1962. Consultant, Harvard University Program on Technology and Society, 1968-69. *Member:* American Philosophical Association, Washington Philosophy Club, Phi Beta Kappa.

*WRITINGS: The Department of State of the United States,* U.S. Government Printing Office, 1942; *The Domain of Reality,* King's Crown Press, 1946; (with Letitia A. Lewis) *Freedom of Information in American Policy and Practice,* U.S. Department of State, 1948; (with Edwin S. Costrell) *The Department of State: 1930-55,* U.S. Government Printing Office, 1955; (contributor) S. D. Kertesz, editor, *American Diplomacy in a New Era,* University of Notre Dame Press, 1961; *The Mind of India,* Macmillan, 1967; *American Liberalism,* Twayne, 1975. Author of public affairs pamphlets for Editorial Research Reports. Contributor to *Encyclopedia of Philosophy;* contributor of articles to American, British, and Belgian journals.

*WORK IN PROGRESS:* A book on ways of achieving equanimity.

*BIOGRAPHICAL/CRITICAL SOURCES: Books Abroad,* spring, 1968.

*       *       *

## GERNERT, Eleanor Towles 1928-

*PERSONAL:* Born September 7, 1928, in New York, N.Y.; daughter of Oliver Phelps (a professor) and Cecile Helene (Long) Towles; married J. Wayne Harris, September 6, 1957 (divorced April, 1967); married Max Riley Gernert (an architect), July 4, 1970. *Education:* Attended Hofstra College (now Hofstra University), 1946-48; Smith College, B.A., 1950; University of Paris, postgraduate study, 1954. *Politics:* Democrat. *Home:* 958 Hartzell St., Pacific Palisades, Calif. 90272. *Office:* Rand Corp., 1700 Main St., Santa Monica, Calif. 90408.

*CAREER:* Henry E. Huntington Library and Art Gallery, San Marino, Calif., searcher in literature, history, and art of

England and the United States, 1950-55, executive secretary to director, 1955-60, editor of library publications, 1956-60; Rand Corp., Santa Monica, Calif., research editor, 1960—. *Military service:* U.S. Marine Corps Reserve, 1949-59; became second lieutenant. *Member:* Rand Cercle Francais (secretary, 1960—).

*WRITINGS: A Guide for the Preparation of Indexes,* Rand Corp., 1965; (editor with Dale L. Morgan) William Marshall Anderson, *The Rocky Mountain Journals of William Marshall Anderson: The West in 1834,* Huntington Library, 1967. Editor, *Notary Newsletter,* 1967-68.

*WORK IN PROGRESS:* Editing *The Gold Rush Diaries of Vincent A. Hoover.*

*SIDELIGHTS:* Eleanor Gernert has followed the 1834 trail of William Marshall Anderson to verify his journals; she has also toured Japan to study bonsai culture.

*       *       *

## GERSTER, Georg (Anton) 1928-

*PERSONAL:* Born April 30, 1928, in Winterthur, Switzerland; son of Charles (a businessman) and Emilie (Mattmann) Gerster; married Isabel Hummel, April 24, 1954; children: Franziska Barbara, Thomas Philipp. *Education:* University of Zurich, Ph.D., 1953. *Home:* Tobelhusstrasse 24, 8126 Zumikon-Zurich, Switzerland.

*CAREER: Weltwoche* (weekly newspaper), Zurich, Switzerland, science editor, 1950-56; free-lance writer and photographer specializing in science reports, 1956—. Photographs shown in traveling exhibitions, "Kirchen im Fels," 1968-69, "Der Mensch auf seiner Erde," 1975—, and at Swissair pavilions at Basel Trade Fair, annually, 1965-71; the Swissair exhibitions were on North America, 1965, Africa, 1966, South America, 1967, North America, 1968, Japan, 1969, worldwide, 1970, and United States, 1971. *Awards, honors:* Goldene Blende (Germany), 1973; Ehrengabe des Kts. Zurich, 1974; Prix Nadar (Paris), 1976, for *Der Mensch auf seiner Erde;* Anerkennungs-gabe der Stadt Winterthur, 1977.

*WRITINGS*—Self-illustrated, except as indicated: *Die leidigen Dichter: Goethes Auseinandersetzung mit dem Dichter* (not illustrated), Artemis-Verlag, 1954; *Eine Stunde mit . . .* (interviews with scientists), Ullstein, 1956, reissued as *Aus der Werkstatt des Wissens,* Series I, 1962, published with further interviews as *Aus der Werkstatt des Wissens,* Series II, 1958; *Sahara: Reiche, fruchtbare Wueste,* Ullstein, 1959, translation by Stewart Thomson published as *Sahara,* Barrie & Rockliff, 1960, published in America as *Sahara: Desert of Destiny,* Coward, 1961; *Sinai: Land der Offenbarung,* Ullstein, 1961, 2nd edition with new preface, Atlantis-Verlag, 1970; *Augenschein in Alaska: Eindruecke von einer Reise durch den 49. Staat der USA* (five reports on Alaska), Scherz, 1961; *Nubien: Goldland am Nil,* Artemis-Verlag, 1964; Kazimierz Michalowski, *Faras, die Kathedrale aus dem Wuestensand,* Benziger-Verlag, 1967; (with assistance of David R. Buxton and others) *Kirchen im Fels: Entdeckungen in Aethiopien* (summary of three years of exploration in Ethiopian Highlands), Kohlhammer, 1968, revised and enlarged edition, Atlantis-Verlag, 1972, translation of first edition by Richard Hosking published as *Churches in Rock: Early Christian Art in Ethiopia,* preface by Emperor Haile Selasie I, Phaidon, 1970; (with Christiane Desroches-Noblecourt) *Die Welt rettet Abu Simbel,* Koska, 1968, also published in English as *The World Saves Abu Simbel,* Koska, 1969; *Frozen Frontier* (brochure on Antarctica), U.S. Information Agency, 1968; *Countdown fuer die*

*Mondlandung* (brochure on U.S. Apollo program), Verlag der Neuen Zuercher Zeitung, 1969; Robert A. Fernea, *Nubians in Egypt: Peaceful People*, University of Texas Press, 1973; *Aethiopien: Das Dach Afrikas*, Atlantis-Verlag, 1974; *Der Mensch auf seiner Erde: Eine Befragung in Flugbildern* (aerial photography), Atlantis-Verlag, 1975, translation by Renee Meddemmen and Stanley Mason published as *Grand Design: The Earth from Above*, Paddington, 1976.

Writer of commentaries for motion pictures, "Wunder der Wueste" and "Elefanten fuer Buddha." Regular contributor, both as photographer and writer, to *Neue Zuercher Zeitung* (Zurich); photographic essays have been published by Time-Life Books, *National Geographic* (Washington, D.C.), *Sunday Times Magazine* (London), *Paris-Match*, and *Geo* (Hamburg).

*BIOGRAPHICAL/CRITICAL SOURCES: New York Times Book Review*, June 14, 1970; *Times Literary Supplement*, September 18, 1970; *Economist*, October 16, 1976; *Christian Science Monitor*, November 24, 1976; *National Observer*, December 4, 1976; *Newsweek*, December 13, 1976.

\* \* \*

## GETTLEMAN, Marvin E. 1933-

*PERSONAL:* Born September 12, 1933, in New York, N.Y.; son of Arthur A. (a pharmacist) and Pauline (Antopol) Gettleman; married Marge Nissenson, January 1, 1953 (divorced, 1968); married Susan Braiman (a psychotherapist and writer), May 4, 1969; children: (first marriage) Daniel, Todd; (second marriage) Eva, Rebecca. *Education:* College of the City of New York (now City College of the City University of New York), B.A. (cum laude), 1957; Johns Hopkins University, M.A., 1959, Ph.D., 1972. *Politics:* Democratic Socialist. *Religion:* None. *Home:* 110 West 94th St., New York, N.Y. 10025. *Agent:* Joan Daves, 515 Madison Ave., New York, N.Y. 10022. *Office:* Polytechnic Institute of New York, 333 Jay St., Brooklyn, N.Y. 11201.

*CAREER:* City College of the City University of New York, New York, N.Y., lecturer in government, 1959-63; Polytechnic Institute of New York, Brooklyn, N.Y., began as lecturer, became assistant professor, 1963-69, associate professor, 1969-77, professor of history, 1978—. Guest lecturer at University of Texas, Vassar College, State University of New York at Stony Brook, and other institutions. Consultant to project on privacy, Association of the Bar of the City of New York. Member of board of sponsors, *Catalyst: A Socialist Journal of the Social Services. Member:* American Historical Association, Organization of American Historians, Committee of Concerned Asian Scholars, Socialist Scholars Conference (member of steering committee, 1966-69), New American Movement, Mid-Atlantic Radical Historians Organization, Phi Beta Kappa. *Awards, honors:* Woodrow Wilson fellowship, 1957-59; Rabinowitz Foundation fellowship, 1968; National Endowment for the Humanities fellowship, 1973-74; National Historical Publications and Records Commission fellowship, 1977-78.

*WRITINGS:* (Editor) *Vietnam: History, Documents, and Opinions*, Fawcett, 1965, 2nd revised edition (preface by David Schoenbrun), New American Library, 1970; (with David Mermelstein) *The Great Society Reader: The Failure of American Liberalism*, Random House, 1967; (with Susan Millman and Eleanor Leacock) *Theory, Data, and Analysis: A Book of Readings*, Polytechnic Institute of Brooklyn, 1969; (editor with wife, Susan Gettleman, Lawrence Kaplan, and Carol Kaplan) *Conflict in Indochina: Historical*

*Perspectives on the Widening War in Laos and Cambodia*, Random House, 1970; (with Mermelstein) *The Failure of American Liberalism: After the Great Society*, Random House, 1971; *The Dorr Rebellion: A Study in American Radicalism, 1833-1849*, Random, 1973; *An Elusive Presence: The Discovery of John H. Finley and His America*, Nelson-Hall, 1978. Contributor of more than twenty-five articles and reviews to *Science and Society, In These Times, Nation, Commonweal*, and other journals. Regular reviewer for *Choice*. Member of editorial board, *Science and Society*.

*WORK IN PROGRESS: Roots of the Second American Enlightenment: The Johns Hopkins University Seminary of History and Politics, 1877-1912*, for Johns Hopkins Press; *Rehearsal for McCarthyism: The Rapp-Coudert Investigation and Communism in New York City Municipal Colleges, 1935-1942*, for Random House.

*BIOGRAPHICAL/CRITICAL SOURCES: New York Times Book Review*, January 7, 1968, February 21, 1971, September 16, 1973; *Journal of American History*, March, 1974; *New England Quarterly*, March, 1974.

\* \* \*

## GEYMAN, John P. 1931-

*PERSONAL:* Born February 9, 1931, in Santa Barbara, Calif.; son of Milton John (a physician) and Betsy (Payne) Geyman; married Emogene Deichler (a teacher), June 9, 1956; children: John Matthew, James Caleb, William Sabin. *Education:* Princeton University, A.B., 1952; University of California, M.D., 1960. *Politics:* Republican. *Religion:* Unitarian. *Home:* 2325 92nd Ave. N.E., Bellevue, Wash. 98004. *Office:* School of Medicine, University of Washington, Seattle, Wash. 98004.

*CAREER:* Private practice of medicine, Mount Shasta, Calif., 1963-69; director of family practice residency program at Community Hospital of Sonoma County, Santa Rosa, Calif., and assistant clinical professor of ambulatory and community medicine at School of Medicine, University of California, San Francisco, 1969-71; University of Utah, College of Medicine, Salt Lake City, associate professor of community and family medicine, and chairman, Division of Family Practice, 1971-72; University of California, Davis, School of Medicine, professor of family practice, vice-chairman of Department of Family Practice, and director of family practice residency program, 1972-76; University of Washington, Seattle, professor of family medicine and chairman of department, 1977—. Trustee, College of Siskiyous, 1969. *Military service:* U.S. Navy, 1952-55; became lieutenant junior grade. *Member:* American Academy of Family Physicians, Society of Teachers of Family Medicine, American Board of Family Practice (fellow).

*WRITINGS: The Modern Family Doctor and Changing Medical Practice*, Appleton, 1971. Contributor to medical journals. Founding editor, *Journal of Family Practice*, 1974—.

\* \* \*

## GHISELLI, Edwin E(rnest) 1907-

*PERSONAL:* Born June 28, 1907, in San Francisco, Calif.; son of Ernest J. (a broker) and Emma (Baron) Ghiselli; married Louisa Hickox, August 13, 1938; children: William, John, David. *Education:* University of California, Berkeley, A.B., 1930, M.A., 1933, Ph.D., 1936. *Home:* 427 Boynton Ave., Berkeley, Calif. 94707. *Office:* Department of Psychology, University of California, Berkeley, Calif. 94720.

*CAREER:* Harvard University, Cambridge, Mass., National Research Council fellow and research associate, 1936-37; Cornell University, Ithaca, N.Y., assistant in psychology, 1937-38; University of Maryland, College Park, instructor in psychology, 1938-39; University of California, Berkeley, assistant professor, 1939-43, associate professor, 1943-48, professor of psychology, 1948—. *Military service:* U.S. Army Air Forces, 1941-46; became lieutenant colonel. *Member:* American Psychological Association.

*WRITINGS:* (With C. W. Brown) *Personnel and Industrial Psychology,* McGraw, 1948, 2nd edition, 1955; (with Brown) *The Scientific Method in Psychology,* McGraw, 1950; *Theory of Psychological Measurement,* McGraw, 1964; *The Validity of Occupational Aptitude Tests,* Wiley, 1966; *Managerial Thinking,* Wiley, 1966; *Explorations in Managerial Talent,* Goodyear Publishing, 1971. Contributor to *Japan Economic Journal.*

\* \* \*

## GIBSON, Frank K. 1924-

*PERSONAL:* Born January 10, 1924, in Morgantown, W.Va.; son of F. K. and Sarah (Donaldson) Gibson; married Rose Helen Forys, March 4, 1946; children: Terence Keith, Bruce Gregory. *Education:* West Virginia University, A.B., 1947, M.A., 1948; University of North Carolina, Ph.D., 1953. *Politics:* Democrat. *Home:* Barnett Shoals Rd., Route 3, Athens, Ga. 30601. *Office:* Baldwin Hall, University of Georgia, Athens, Ga. 30601.

*CAREER:* West Virginia University, Morgantown, instructor in political science, 1948-49, 1951-52; University of Virginia, Charlottesville, assistant professor of political science and research assistant, 1953-55; University of Georgia, Athens, director of Bureau of Public Administration, 1956-57; University of Virginia, associate professor of political science and research associate, 1957-59; University of Georgia, associate professor, 1959-66, professor of political science, 1966—, director of graduate studies, 1967-70, director of graduate program in public administration, 1971—. Consultant to International City Managers Association, federal and state agencies, and other public groups. *Military service:* U.S. Army Air Corps, 1942-44; became technical sergeant; received Air Medal with eight oak-leaf clusters. *Member:* American Political Science Association, American Society for Public Administration, American Association of University Professors, Southern Political Science Association.

*WRITINGS:* (Contributor) Dwight Waldo, editor, *Strengthening Management for Democratic Government,* American Society for Public Administration, 1959; (with E. S. Overman) *County Government in Virginia,* University Press of Virginia, 1961; (contributor) *The Future of Outdoor Recreation in the Atlanta Standard Metropolitan Statistical Area,* U.S. Government Printing Office, 1963; (editor with R. T. Golembiewski and Geoffrey Cornog) *Public Administration: Readings in Institutions, Processes, and Behavior,* Rand McNally, 1966, 3rd edition, 1977; (with Golembiewski) *Managerial Behavior and Organizational Demands,* Rand McNally, 1968, 2nd edition, F. E. Peacock, 1978; (contributor) *Reapportionment in Georgia,* Institute of Government, University of Georgia, 1970; *Atlanta Makes a Decision: A Study in Organizational Politics,* Syracuse University Press, 1970. Writer of about twenty monographs on political science topics; contributor of about twenty articles to professional journals.

*WORK IN PROGRESS:* Evaluation of Social Program, with James E. Prather.

## GICOVATE, Bernard 1922-

*PERSONAL:* Born April 21, 1922, in Santos, Brazil; came to United States in 1944, naturalized in 1952; son of Jose (a realtor) and Clara B. Gicovate; married Alice Echeverz (a teacher), July 4, 1944; children: Henry S. *Education:* University of Buenos Aires, Dr.Litt., 1943; Bowdoin College, B.A., 1945; University of North Carolina, M.A., 1946; Harvard University, Ph.D., 1952. *Residence:* San Francisco, Calif. *Office:* Department of Spanish and Portuguese, Stanford University, Stanford, Calif. 94305.

*CAREER:* University of Oregon, Eugene, assistant professor of Spanish, 1949-55; Tulane University, New Orleans, La., associate professor, 1955-60, professor of Spanish, 1960-65; Stanford University, Stanford, Calif., professor of Spanish and comparative literature, 1965—, chairman of department of Spanish and Portuguese, 1966—.

*WRITINGS:* *Julio Herrera y Reissig and the Symbolists,* University of California Press, 1957; *La poesia de Juan Ramon Jimenez,* Asomante, 1959; *Conceptos fundamentales de literatura comparanda,* Asomante, 1962; *Ensayos sobre poesia hispanica,* De Andrea, 1967; *Saint John of the Cross,* Twayne, 1971; *La poesia de J. R. Jimenez: Obra en marcha,* Ariel, 1973; *Garcilaso de la Vega,* Twayne, 1975. Contributor of articles and reviews to *Hispanic Review* and other journals.

\* \* \*

## GILGEN, Albert R(udolph) 1930-

*PERSONAL:* Born September 19, 1930, in Akron, Ohio; son of Albert (a metalsmith) and Jeannette (Rufer) Gilgen; married Carol E. Keyes (a writer and investor), August 1, 1954; children: DeForest, Jeanne Elizabeth, Albert Pruyn. *Education:* Princeton University, A.B., 1952; Kent State University, M.A., 1962; Michigan State University, Ph.D., 1965. *Religion:* Roman Catholic. *Office:* Department of Psychology, University of Northern Iowa, Cedar Falls, Iowa 50613.

*CAREER:* General Tire and Rubber Co., Akron, Ohio, management trainee, 1955-56, assistant manager of quality control, 1956-57; Sumner Realty Co., Akron, salesman, 1957-60; Beloit College, Beloit, Wis., assistant professor, 1965-70, associate professor of psychology, 1970-73; University of Northern Iowa, Cedar Falls, professor of psychology and head of department, 1973—. Fulbright-Hays exchange lecturer in psychology, University College, Galway, Ireland, 1971-72. *Military service:* U.S. Navy, 1952-55; became lieutenant junior grade. *Member:* American Psychological Association.

*WRITINGS:* (Editor) *Contemporary Scientific Psychology,* Academic Press, 1970. Contributor to American and Irish psychology journals.

*WORK IN PROGRESS:* A book about the recent history of American psychology.

\* \* \*

## GILHOOLEY, Leonard 1921-

*PERSONAL:* Born October 9, 1921, in Brooklyn, N.Y.; son of Francis Girard (a member of the U.S. Army) and Anne (Flynn) Gilhooley. *Education:* Attended Catholic University of America, 1939-42; Loyola College, Baltimore, A.B., 1944; St. John's University, Jamaica, N.Y., M.Ed., 1949; Boston College, M.A., 1955; Fordham University, Ph.D., 1959. *Politics:* Independent. *Religion:* Christian. *Home:* 40 Chesnut Ridge Rd., Montvale, N.J. 07645. *Office:* Department of English, Fordham University, East Fordham Rd., Bronx, N.Y. 10458.

*CAREER:* Catholic University of America, Xaverian College, Washington, D.C., assistant professor, 1961-63, associate professor of English, 1963-66, academic dean, 1963-66; Fordham University, Bronx, N.Y., assistant professor, 1966-70, associate professor of English, 1970—. *Member:* Modern Language Association of America, Emerson Society, Gustave Weigel Society, American Association of University Professors. *Awards, honors:* Faculty fellowship, Fordham University, 1970-71.

*WRITINGS: Contradiction and Dilemma,* Fordham University Press, 1972; *No Divided Allegiance,* Fordham University Press, in press. Staff editor for literature, *New Catholic Encyclopedia,* fifteen volumes, McGraw, 1967. Contributor of articles and reviews to *America, Thought,* and other periodicals.

*WORK IN PROGRESS:* Two books, *Henry Adams and the American Idea* and *The Education of E. L. Godkin;* several articles on literary topics and figures.

\* \* \*

## GITTLER, Joseph B(ertram) 1912-

*PERSONAL:* Born September 21, 1912, in New York, N.Y.; son of Morris and Toby (Rosenblatt) Gittler; married Lami Shapiro, June 28, 1934 (died, 1966); married Susan Wolters (a senior employment counselor), September 15, 1968; children: (first marriage) Josephine. *Education:* University of Georgia, B.S., 1934, M.A., 1936; University of Chicago, Ph.D., 1941. *Religion:* Jewish. *Office:* Ferkhauf Graduate School of Humanities and Social Sciences, Yeshiva University, 55 Fifth Ave., New York, N.Y. 10003.

*CAREER:* University of Georgia, Athens, 1936-43, began as instructor, became associate professor of sociology; Drake University, Des Moines, Iowa, professor of sociology and head of department, 1943-45; Iowa State College of Agriculture and Mechanic Arts (now Iowa State University of Science and Technology), Ames, 1945-54, began as associate professor, became professor of sociology; University of Rochester, Rochester, N.Y., professor of sociology and chairman of department of sociology and anthropology, 1954-61, chairman of university reorganization committee, 1956-58, director of Center for the Study of Group Relations, 1954-60; Queensborough Community College of the City University of New York, Bayside, N.Y., dean of faculty, 1961-66, director of College Discovery Program, 1963-66; Yeshiva University, New York, N.Y., professor of sociology, Graduate School of Education, 1961-63, part-time adjunct professor, 1963-66, university professor of sociology, 1966—, dean of Ferkhauf Graduate School of Humanities and Social Sciences, 1966-77, director of Center for the Study of Minority Groups, 1968-72. Research associate for Virginia State Planning Board, 1942-43; research consultant, U.S. Army Air Forces, 1943; research associate in sociology, University of Chicago, summer, 1944; member of Iowa State Committee on Atomic Energy Education, 1947; member of Rochester council, New York State Commission Against Discrimination, 1955-60; Woodrow Wilson Fellowship Foundation, member of regional selection committee, 1956-58, chairman of committee, 1957-58; member of board of directors, Rochester Council of Social Agencies, 1958-59; member of council of fellows, Crozer Seminary, Upland Institute, 1961-70; member of advisory board, Rose F. Kennedy Center for Mental Retardation, 1966—; member of board of trustees, Center for Urban Education, New York

City, 1968-75. National co-chairman of Commission on Educational Organizations, National Conference of Christians and Jews, 1952; member of committee on university relations, Office of the Mayor, New York City.

*MEMBER:* International Organization for the Study of Group Tensions, American Sociological Association (fellow), National Council for the Social Studies, American Educational Research Association, Association for Higher Education, Society for the Study of Social Problems, Society for Values in Higher Education (fellow), Eastern Sociological Society, New York Academy of Sciences (fellow), Phi Beta Kappa. *Awards, honors:* Walter B. Hill prize in philosophy, University of Georgia, 1934; fellow, Rockefeller Foundation, 1938-39.

*WRITINGS: Social Thought among the Early Greeks,* University of Georgia Press, 1940; *Virginia's People,* Virginia State Planning Board, 1944; *Social Dynamics,* McGraw, 1952; (contributor) Edward C. McDonagh and Eugene S. Richards, editors, *Ethnic Relations in the United States,* Appleton, 1953; (with first wife, Lami Gittler) *Your Neighbor Near and Far: A Handbook in Intercultural Education for Extension Workers,* Iowa State College Press, 1955; (editor and contributor) *Understanding Minority Groups,* Wiley, 1956, revised edition, 1964; (editor and contributor) *Review of Sociology: Analysis of a Decade,* Wiley, 1957; (contributor) W. S. Hunsberger, editor, *New-Era in the Non-Western World,* Cornell University Press, 1957; (contributor) Franklin Patterson, editor, *Citizenship in a Free Society: Education for the Future,* National Council for the Social Studies, 1960. Contributor of about thirty articles to professional journals; contributor to *American Educator Encyclopedia* and *American Encyclopedia.* Editor, *Midwest Sociologist,* 1945-48, and *Ethnic Minorities in the United States,* 1977.

*WORK IN PROGRESS: Sociology of Jews in the United States.*

\* \* \*

## GLAHE, Fred R(ufus) 1934-

*PERSONAL:* Born June 30, 1934, in Chicago, Ill.; son of Frederick William (an executive) and Frances (Welch) Glahe; married Nancy S. Behrent, June 24, 1961. *Education:* Purdue University, B.S., 1957, M.S., 1962, Ph.D., 1964. *Religion:* Anglican Church of North America. *Home:* 1970 Glenwood Dr., Boulder, Colo. 80302. *Office:* Department of Economics, University of Colorado, Boulder, Colo. 80302.

*CAREER:* General Motors Corp., Allison Division, Indianapolis, Ind., engineer, 1957-61; Battelle Memorial Institute, Columbus, Ohio, research economist, 1964-65; University of Colorado, Boulder, assistant professor, 1965-68, associate professor, 1968-73, professor of economics, 1973—. *Military service:* U.S. Army, 1958; became second lieutenant. U.S. Army Reserve, 1958-64; became captain. *Member:* American Economic Association, Mont Pelerin Society, Invisible Hand Society.

*WRITINGS:* (Editor) *Readings in Econometric Theory,* Colorado Associated Universities Press, 1970; (editor) Kenneth Boulding, *Collected Papers of Kenneth Boulding,* Volumes I-II: *Economics,* Colorado Associated Universities Press, 1971-72; *Introduction to Macroeconomic Theory and Policy,* Harcourt, 1972, 2nd edition, 1977; *Adam Smith and the Wealth of Nations,* Colorado Associated Press, 1978.

*WORK IN PROGRESS: Microeconomics: Theory with Applications,* for Harcourt.

\*     \*     \*

### GLASER, Edward 1918-1972

December 26, 1918—August 29, 1972; Viennese-born American educator, authority on Spanish and Portuguese literature, and author of books on historical and religious themes. Obituaries: *New York Times,* September 1, 1972.

\*     \*     \*

### GLAZIER, Lyle (Edward) 1911-

*PERSONAL:* Born May 8, 1911, in Leverett, Mass.; son of Harry Lee and Mertie (Briggs) Glazier; married Amy Niles (a teacher), 1939; children: Laura Mary, Susan Carol, Alis Louise. *Education:* Middlebury College, A.B. (cum laude), 1933, A.M., 1937; Harvard University, Ph.D., 1950. *Politics:* "None." *Religion:* "None." *Home:* R.D. 2, Bennington, Vt. 05201. *Office:* State University of New York, Buffalo, N.Y. 14214.

*CAREER:* Principal of grade school in Northfield, Mass., 1934-35; Mount Hermon School for Boys, Gill, Mass., instructor and house master, 1935-37; Bates College, Lewiston, Me., instructor in English, 1937-41; Tufts University, Medford, Mass., instructor in English, 1941-45; State University of New York at Buffalo, began as assistant professor, 1947, professor of English, 1963-72, professor emeritus, 1972—. Fulbright professor and chairman of American literature at Istanbul University, 1961-63; Hacettepe University, Ankara, Fulbright lecturer, 1968-69, visiting professor, 1970-71; U.S. Information Service lecturer in India, 1971; staff member of Fulbright seminars in India, 1970-71. Vice-president, Orchard Park Board of Education, 1953-59. Consultant, John Jay College of Criminal Justice of the City University of New York, 1966. *Member:* Modern Language Association of America, American Studies Association, American Association of University Professors, Gay Academic Union, Heterosexual Joy. *Awards, honors:* American Council of Learned Societies faculty fellow, 1951-52.

*WRITINGS*—Poems, except as noted: *Orchard Park and Istanbul,* Big Mountain Press, 1965; *You Too,* Istanbul Matbaasi, 1969; *The Dervishes,* Istanbul Matbaasi, 1971; *V D (Voices of the Dead),* Istanbul Matbaasi, 1971; *Decadence and Rebirth: Representative American Novels* (criticism), Hacettepe University Press, 1971; *Two Continents* (chapbook), Vermont Council on the Arts, 1976. Poems have been published in *New Yorker, Partisan Review, Beloit Poetry Journal, Mouth of the Dragon, Fag Rag,* and other literary reviews, a story in *Story Magazine,* and articles in American and Turkish journals. Represented in *Asian Response to American Literature,* 1971.

Unpublished work includes six novels, a collection of topical essays, a book on contemporary American fiction, and a book on Black literature.

*WORK IN PROGRESS:* Poetry and a chapter of his unpublished novel, *Stills of a Moving Picture,* to be included in *Erotica* for Smyrna Press.

*SIDELIGHTS:* Lyle Glazier has this to say about his unpublished materials: "Trade publishers recommend university presses; university press editors recommend trade. I keep busy, play Bach."

\*     \*     \*

### GLOVACH, Linda 1947-

*PERSONAL:* Surname is pronounced *Glo*-vack; born June 24, 1947, in Rockville Centre, N.Y.; daughter of John Maurice (a maintenance engineer) and Elvira (Martone) Glovach. *Education:* Attended Farmingdale University, 1965-66, Art Students League of New York, 1966-68, and California Art Center College of Design, 1969. *Politics:* Liberal. *Home and office:* 60 Little East Neck Rd., Babylon, Long Island, N.Y. 11702.

*CAREER:* Free-lance artist. Has worked as a secretary and a hostess at Disneyland, Calif. Speaker in grade schools in Brentwood, N.Y. *Member:* Defenders of Wildlife, Catholic Society for Welfare of Animals, Library Club of Bayshore. *Awards, honors:* Art Students League of New York award for book illustration, 1970.

*WRITINGS*—Children's books, all self-illustrated: *Hey, Wait for Me! I'm Amelia,* Prentice-Hall, 1971; *The Cat and the Collector,* Prentice-Hall, 1972; *The Little Witch's Black Magic Cookbook,* Prentice-Hall, 1972; *Little Witch's Black Magic Book of Disguises,* Prentice-Hall, 1973; *Little Witch's Black Magic Book of Games,* Prentice-Hall, 1974; *Little Witch's Christmas Book,* Prentice-Hall, 1974; *Little Witch's Halloween Book,* Prentice-Hall, 1975; *The Little Witch's Thanksgiving Book,* Prentice-Hall, 1976; (with Charles Keller) *The Little Witch Presents a Monster: Joke Book,* Prentice-Hall, 1976.

*WORK IN PROGRESS:* A novel for teenagers, entitled *Laura's Story;* several children's books; research on San Juan Capistrano mission in California, for a picture book for children.

*SIDELIGHTS:* Linda Glovach has lived one year in Haiti. *Avocational interests:* Traveling, gardening, and raising cats and Afghan hounds.

\*     \*     \*

### GLUECK, Eleanor T(ouroff) 1898-1972

April 12, 1898—September 25, 1972; American criminologist, researcher, and author of books on criminal law, the nature and prevention of juvenile delinquency, and prison practice. Obituaries: *New York Times,* September 26, 1972; *Current Biography,* November 1972. (See index for *CA* sketch)

\*     \*     \*

### GODBOLD, E(dward) Stanly, Jr. 1942-

*PERSONAL:* Born March 15, 1942, in Rembert, S.C.; son of Edward Stanly (a farmer) and Louise (James) Godbold. *Education:* Duke University, B.A., 1963, M.A., 1968, Ph.D., 1970; Southern Methodist University, B.D., 1966. *Office address:* Drawer H, Mississippi State University, Starkville, Miss. 39762.

*CAREER:* University of Tennessee, Chattanooga, assistant professor of history, 1969-70; Valdosta State College, Valdosta, Ga., assistant professor of history, 1970-77; Mississippi State University, Starkville, associate professor of history, 1977—. *Member:* American Historical Association, Organization of American Historians, American Studies Association, American Association of University Professors, Southern Historical Association.

*WRITINGS: Ellen Glasgow and the Woman Within,* Louisiana State University Press, 1972.

*WORK IN PROGRESS:* A biography of Christopher Gadsden.

## GOETZ, Ignacio L. 1933-

*PERSONAL:* Born August 10, 1933, in Caracas, Venezuela; son of Federico L. (a banker) and Ilse (Roemer) Goetz; married Katherine Griggs, August 21, 1965; children: Christine, Mariella, Sonya. *Education:* Pontifical Athenaeum, Poona, India, B.A. (with honors), 1956; St. Mary's College, Kurseong, India, B.D. (with honors), 1963; Columbia University, M.A., 1965; New York University, Ph.D., 1968. *Home:* 386 California Ave., Uniondale, N.Y. 11553. *Office:* 107 Barnard Hall, Hofstra University, Hempstead, N.Y. 11550.

*CAREER:* Ordained a Roman Catholic priest, 1962; teacher of English at junior high school in Baroda, India, 1957-59; St. Stanislaus' College, Hazaribagh, India, lecturer in exegesis, 1963-64; Hofstra University, Hempstead, N.Y., special assistant professor, 1966-68, assistant professor of philosophy of education, 1968—, director, special studies program, 1972—. *Member:* Philosophy of Education Society, American Association of University Professors, American Teilhard de Chardin Association, Middle Atlantic States Philosophy of Education Society, Kappa Delta Pi, Sigma Delta Pi. *Awards, honors:* Hofstra University, Teacher of the Year Award, 1971, and Faculty Distinguished Service Award, New College, 1977.

*WRITINGS:* (Translator) *Pavitra Gulabmala*, Anand Press (Anand, India), 1961; (editor) *No Schools*, MSS Educational Publishing, 1971; *The Psychedelic Teacher*, Westminster, 1972. Contributor to education, philosophy, and theology journals, including *Educational Theory, Teilhard Review,* and *Journal of Negro Education.*

*WORK IN PROGRESS:* Three books completed and awaiting publication, *The Emergence of the Human, Meditations on Albert Camus,* and *Creativity-Theoretical and Socio-Cosmic Reflections;* another book, *Zen in the Art of Teaching.*

*SIDELIGHTS:* Ignacio L. Goetz speaks French, Gujarati, Latin, and Hindi, and reads Italian, Greek, Portuguese, Sanskrit, and German.

\*     \*     \*

## GOFFART, Walter (Andre) 1934-

*PERSONAL:* Surname is accented on first syllable; born February 22, 1934, in Berlin, Germany; son of Francis-Leo (a Belgian diplomat) and Andree (Steinberg) Goffart; married Ellen Schadek, May 19, 1961 (divorced, January 12, 1977); children: Vivian, Andrea. *Education:* Harvard University, A.B. (magna cum laude), 1955, A.M., 1956, Ph.D., 1961; also attended Ecole Normale Superieure and Ecole des Hautes Etudes (Paris), 1957-58. *Residence:* Toronto, Ontario, Canada. *Office:* Department of History, University of Toronto, Toronto, Ontario, Canada.

*CAREER:* University of Toronto, Toronto, Ontario, lecturer, 1960-63, assistant professor, 1963-66, associate professor, 1966-71, professor of history, 1971—, Centre for Medieval Studies, academic secretary, 1969-71, 1972—, acting director, 1971-72. Visiting assistant professor of history, University of California, Berkeley, 1965-66; visiting fellow, Institute for Advanced Studies, Princeton, N.J., 1967-68; visiting fellow, Dumbarton Oaks Center for Byzantine Studies, 1973-74. *Member:* American Historical Association, Mediaeval Academy of America (councillor, 1977—). *Awards, honors:* American Council of Learned Societies fellow, 1973-74.

*WRITINGS: The Le Mans Forgeries: A Chapter from the*

*History of Church Property in the 9th Century,* Harvard University Press, 1966; *Caput and Colonate: Towards a History of Late Roman Taxation,* University of Toronto Press, 1974; (translator with Marshall Baldwin) Carl Erdmann, *The Origin of the Crusade,* Princeton University Press, 1978. Contributor to professional journals.

*WORK IN PROGRESS: Roman Land Tax and Barbarian Settlement;* research on late Roman and early medieval historiography and economic history.

\*     \*     \*

## GOIST, Park Dixon 1936-

*PERSONAL:* Born September 7, 1936, in Seattle, Wash.; son of Clarence Edwin and Helen (Hunter) Goist; married Doris Francis (an anthropologist), June 28, 1964. *Education:* University of Washington, Seattle, B.A., 1958; University of Rochester, Ph.D., 1967. *Home:* 2697 Euclid Heights Blvd., Cleveland Heights, Ohio 44106. *Office:* Case Western Reserve University, Cleveland, Ohio 44106.

*CAREER:* Case Western Reserve University, Cleveland, Ohio, instructor, 1966-67, assistant professor, 1967-71, associate professor of American studies, 1971—. Executive secretary, Citizens for Effective Heights Government, 1973-74. Democratic precinct committeeman. *Military service:* U.S. Naval Air Reserve, 1954-62. *Member:* American Studies Association, American Historical Association, Organization of American Historians, Ohio-Indiana American Studies Association (member of executive board).

*WRITINGS:* (Editor with Jack Tager) *The Urban Vision: Selected Interpretations of the Modern American City,* Dorsey, 1970; *From Main Street to State Street: Town, City and Community in America,* Kennikat, 1977. Contributor to *American Quarterly, American Studies, Journal of the American Institute of Planners,* and *Urban and Social Change Review.*

*WORK IN PROGRESS: The Long Journey,* a historical novel dealing with the Oregon Trail.

\*     \*     \*

## GOLDBERG, Joseph P(hilip) 1918-

*PERSONAL:* Born May 1, 1918, in Brooklyn, N.Y.; son of Max and Fanny (Steltzer) Goldberg; married Selma Takiff (a teacher), 1943; children: Seth M., Lise A. *Education:* College of the City of New York (now City College of the City University of New York), B.S.S., 1937; Columbia University, M.A., 1938, Ph.D., 1950. *Home:* 707 Stonington Rd., Silver Spring, Md. 20902. *Office:* Bureau of Labor Statistics, U.S. Department of Labor, Washington, D.C. 20212.

*CAREER:* High school teacher in New York, N.Y., 1938-42; National War Labor Board, Washington, D.C., economist, 1942-46; Public Affairs Institute, Washington, D.C., labor specialist, 1948-49; Bureau of Labor Statistics, Washington, D.C., labor economist, 1949-51; Wage Stabilization Board and Office of Economic Stabilization, Washington, D.C., economist, 1951-53; Bureau of Labor Statistics, assistant chief in office of publications, 1953-54, special assistant to commissioner, 1954—. Lecturer, American University, 1948-49; research associate, Harvard University, 1957; research associate, University of Michigan, 1964-69. Economic adviser, Joint Congressional Committee on Labor-Management Relations, 1949; governmental adviser and representative for International Labor Organization at sixteen maritime conferences in Geneva, Naples, Genoa, Mare del Plato, Argentina, Oslo, and London, 1956-76; chairman of U.S. delegation to conferences on professional and salaried employees, 1967, 1974.

*MEMBER:* American Economic Association, Industrial Relations Research Association (president of chapter, 1964-65; member of chapter executive committee, 1962-65; member of national executive board, 1973-76), Phi Beta Kappa. *Awards, honors:* Yale Fund for Merchant Seamen Studies grant, 1947; Meritorious Service Award, U.S. Department of Labor, 1962; Eminent Service Award, Commissioner of Bureau of Labor Statistics, 1973.

*WRITINGS: The Maritime Story,* Harvard University Press, 1957, revised edition, 1958; (with H. M. Levinson, C. M. Rehmus, and M. L. Kahn) *Modernization of the Maritime Industry in Collective Bargaining and Technological Change in American Transportation,* Northwestern University Press, 1971. Contributor of articles on maritime economics and labor, public employees, and international labor organizations to labor, history, and political science journals.

*WORK IN PROGRESS:* Research on public employee organization developments, longshoremen in the United States and abroad, the International Labor Organization, and Merchant Marine policies and impact on seamen.

\*          \*          \*

## GOLDE, Peggy   1930-

*PERSONAL:* Born September 29, 1930, in St. Louis, Mo. *Education:* Antioch College, A.B., 1953; Harvard University, Ph.D., 1963. *Home:* 960 North San Antonio Rd., Los Altos, Calif. 94022.

*CAREER:* Dayton Art Institute, Dayton, Ohio, art teacher and lecturer, 1953; Antioch College, Dayton, worked in public relations, 1953-54; Age Center of New England, Boston, Mass., interviewer and research assistant, 1957-58; Harvard University, Medical School, Cambridge, Mass., research associate, 1964-65; Stanford University, School of Medicine, Stanford, Calif., assistant professor of psychiatry, and lecturer in department of anthropology, 1968-74; counselor in private practice, 1975—. Received Marriage, Family, and Child Counselor's License in 1975. *Member:* American Anthropological Association, Society for Applied Anthropology, Society for American Anthropology, American Association for the Advancement of Science. *Awards, honors:* National Science Foundation grant, 1971.

*WRITINGS:* (Editor) *Women in the Field,* Aldine, 1970. Also author, with others, of *Encounter: Confrontations in Self and Interpersonal Awareness.*

\*          \*          \*

## GOLDFARB, Russell M.   1934-

*PERSONAL:* Born August 13, 1934, in Yonkers, N.Y.; married Clare Rosett, August 11, 1957; children: Eric, Jennifer. *Education:* New York University, B.A., 1954, M.A., 1957; Indiana University, Ph.D., 1961. *Office:* Department of English, Western Michigan University, Kalamazoo, Mich. 49001.

*CAREER:* Western Michigan University, Kalamazoo, instructor, 1960-61, assistant professor, 1961-64, associate professor, 1964-71, professor of English, 1971—. *Military service:* U.S. Army, 1954-56; became first lieutenant.

*WRITINGS:* (Contributor) Anne Szalkowski, editor, *Readings for Communication,* University of Michigan Press,

1961; *Sexual Repression and Victorian Literature,* Bucknell University Press, 1970; *Spiritualism and Nineteenth-Century Letters,* Fairleigh Dickinson University Press, 1977. Contributor of articles to *Research Studies, Journal of Popular Culture, Victorian Poetry, Journal of Aesthetics and Art Criticism, Midwest Quarterly, University Review,* and other journals.

*WORK IN PROGRESS:* A book, *The Survivor in Victorian Literature.*

\*          \*          \*

## GOLDFRIED, Marvin R(obert)   1936-

*PERSONAL:* Born January 24, 1936, in Brooklyn, N.Y.; son of Samuel and Anna (Ozer) Goldfried; married Anita Powers, December 23, 1967; children: Daniel, Michael. *Education:* Brooklyn College (now Brooklyn College of the City University of New York), B.A. (cum laude), 1957; University of Buffalo (now State University of New York at Buffalo), Ph.D., 1961. *Office:* Department of Psychology, State University of New York, Stony Brook, N.Y. 11794.

*CAREER:* Veterans Administration Hospitals, Buffalo, N.Y., and Palo Alto, Calif., psychology trainee, 1958-60; Buffalo State Hospital, Buffalo, senior clinical psychologist, 1960-61; University of Buffalo (now State University of New York at Buffalo), instructor in psychology, 1960-61; University of Rochester, Rochester, N.Y., assistant professor of psychology, 1961-64; State University of New York at Stony Brook, assistant professor, 1964-66, associate professor, 1966-71, professor of psychology, 1971—, director of psychological services, 1964-68. Summer instructor, Brooklyn College of the City University of New York, 1961; visiting professor, Bar-Ilan University, 1970-71; visiting research assistant, University of California, Berkeley. Certified psychologist in State of New York; diplomate in clinical psychology of American Board of Professional Psychology. Research consultant, Alcoholism Treatment Center, Rochester, N.Y., 1963-65; consultant on behavior modification, Teachers College, Columbia University, 1967-68. Consultant to Upward Bound, State University of New York at Stony Brook, and to Child Development Specialist Program, Florida State University.

*MEMBER:* American Psychological Association (fellow), American Association of University Professors, Parents Without Partners (member of advisory board, Suffolk chapter), Eastern Psychological Association, New York State Psychological Association, Suffolk County Psychological Association, Sigma Xi, Psi Chi. *Awards, honors:* Ebsary Foundation study grant, 1963-65; National Institute of Mental Health grants, 1964, 1966-68, 1967-71, 1973-79.

*WRITINGS:* (Contributor) C. D. Spielberger, editor, *Current Topics in Clinical and Community Psychology,* Volume I, Academic Press, 1969; (with I. B. Weiner and G. Stricker) *Rorschach Handbook of Clinical and Research Applications,* Prentice-Hall, 1971; (editor with Michael Merbaum, and contributor) *Behavior Change through Self-Control,* Holt, 1973; (with G. C. Davison) *Clinical Behavior Therapy,* Holt, 1976. Also author of numerous professional papers and colloquia. Contributor of more than fifty articles to professional journals. Editorial consultant to *Psychological Review,* 1960, *Quarterly Journal of Studies on Alcohol,* 1969, 1971, 1972, and *Journal of Abnormal Psychology,* 1972; contributing editor, *Clinical Psychologist,* 1969-71; associate editor, *Cognitive Research and Therapy,* 1977—.

## GOLDSMITH, Ilse Sondra (Weinberg) 1933-

*PERSONAL:* Born September 9, 1933, in Germany; daughter of Joseph and Bettina (Bendit) Weinberg; married Alfred Goldsmith (an optometrist), February, 1956; children: Jeffrey Mitchell, Stephen Blaine. *Education:* Hunter College (now Hunter College of the City University of New York), B.A., 1955; State University College at Albany (now State University of New York at Albany), M.A., 1960. *Home:* Park Court, Middletown, N.Y. 10940.

*CAREER:* Mt. Sinai Hospital, New York, N.Y., research chemist, 1954-56; General Electric Co., Schenectady, N.Y., research chemist, 1956-60; teacher in Middletown, N.Y. President, Horton Hospital Auxiliary, 1971-72. *Member:* American Chemical Society, University Club (president, 1961).

*WRITINGS*—Juveniles: *Anatomy for Children,* Sterling, 1964, revised edition published as *Human Anatomy for Children: Your Body and How It Works,* Dover, 1969; *Complete Science Course,* Sterling, 1968; *Why You Get Sick and How You Get Well,* Sterling, 1971.

*WORK IN PROGRESS: Sandy's Castle,* fiction for children.

*BIOGRAPHICAL/CRITICAL SOURCES: Times-Herald Record* (Middletown, N.Y.), June 18, 1964, November 29, 1970.†

\* \* \*

## GOLON, Serge(anne) 1903-1972

1903—July 12, 1972; French geochemist and novelist. Obituaries: *L'Express,* July 31-August 6, 1972.

\* \* \*

## GOODMAN, Elaine 1930-

*PERSONAL:* Born January 23, 1930, in New York, N.Y.; daughter of Abraham and Dorothy (Dean) Egan; married Walter Goodman (a writer), February 10, 1951; children: Hal, Bennet. *Education:* Syracuse University, B.A., 1951; University of Reading, Reading, England, M.A., 1953. *Religion:* Jewish. *Home:* 4 Crest Dr., White Plains, N.Y. 10607.

*MEMBER:* Phi Beta Kappa. *Awards, honors:* Christopher Award, 1971, for *The Rights of the People.*

*WRITINGS:* (With husband, Walter Goodman) *The Rights of the People,* Farrar, Straus, 1971; (with W. Goodman) *The Family, Yesterday, Today, and Tomorrow,* Farrar, Straus, 1975.

\* \* \*

## GOODMAN, Jay S. 1940-

*PERSONAL:* Born January 16, 1940, in St. Louis, Mo.; son of Harold M. (a merchant) and Minnie (Frumer) Goodman; married Ellen Safier, June 15, 1963; children: Robert F. *Education:* Beloit College, B.A., 1961; Stanford University, M.A., 1963; Brown University, Ph.D., 1966. *Office:* Department of Government, Wheaton College, Norton, Mass. 02766.

*CAREER:* Wheaton College, Norton, Mass., instructor, 1965-66, assistant professor, 1966-70, associate professor, 1970-73, professor of government, 1973—. Alternate delegate, Democratic National Convention, 1968. *Member:* International Political Science Association, American Political Science Association, Midwest Political Science Association. *Awards, honors:* Woodrow Wilson fellow, 1961, 1962; Woodrow Wilson dissertation fellow, 1964-65.

*WRITINGS: The Democrats and Labor in Rhode Island: 1952-1962,* Brown University Press, 1967; (with C. Peter Magrath and Elmer E. Cornwell, Jr.) *The American Democracy,* Macmillan, 1969, second edition, 1973; (with Cornwell) *The Politics of the Rhode Island Constitution Convention,* National Municipal League, 1969; (editor) *Perspectives on Urban Politics,* Allyn & Bacon, 1970; (with Wayne R. Swanson and Cornwell) *Politics and Constitutional Reform: The Maryland Experience, 1966-1968,* Washington Center for Metropolitan Studies, 1970; (with Swanson and Cornwell) *State Constitutional Conventions,* Praeger, 1975; *The Dynamics of Urban Government and Politics,* Macmillan, 1975, 2nd edition, in press.

\* \* \*

## GOODMAN, Paul 1911-1972

September 9, 1911—August 2, 1972; American lecturer, psychotherapist, humanist, polemicist, essayist, poet, novelist, and social critic. Obituaries: *New York Times,* August 4, 1972; *Newsweek,* August 14, 1972; *L'Express,* August 14-20, 1972; *Publishers Weekly,* August 14, 1972; *Time,* August 14, 1972; *Current Biography,* October, 1972. (See index for *CA* sketch)

\* \* \*

## GOODRICH, Foster E(dward) 1908-1972

August 12, 1908—December 12, 1972; American business executive and writer on sales promotion. Obituaries: *New York Times,* December 13, 1972.

\* \* \*

## GOODWIN, Craufurd D(avid) W(ycliffe) 1934-

*PERSONAL:* Born May 23, 1934, in Montreal, Quebec, Canada; son of George and Roma (Stewart) Goodwin; married Nancy Sanders, June 7, 1958. *Education:* McGill University, B.A., 1955; Duke University, Ph.D., 1958. *Home address:* P.O. Box 957, Hillsborough, N.C. 27278. *Office:* Department of Economics, Duke University, Durham, N.C. 27706.

*CAREER:* Courtauld's Canada Ltd., Montreal, Quebec, economic research assistant, summer, 1955; University of Windsor, Windsor, Ontario, lecturer in economics, 1958-59; Duke University, Durham, N.C., visiting assistant professor of economics and executive secretary of Commonwealth Studies Center, 1959-60; Australian National University, Canberra, honorary research fellow, 1960-61; York University, Toronto, Ontario, assistant professor of economics, 1961-62; Duke University, assistant professor, 1962-63, associate professor, 1963-68, professor of economics, 1968—, assistant to provost, 1962-64, assistant provost, 1964-68, vice-provost for International Studies, 1969-71, director of International Programs, 1969-71. Officer in Charge of European and International Affairs, Ford Foundation, 1971-77. *Member:* American Economic Association, Economic History Association, Canadian Economics Association.

*WRITINGS*—All published by Duke University Press, except as indicated: *Canadian Economic Thought,* 1961; *Economic Enquiry in Australia,* 1966; (with W. B. Hamilton and Kenneth Robinson) *A Decade of the Commonwealth: 1955-1964,* 1966; (editor with I. B. Holley) *The Transfer of Ideas,* 1968; (editor with R. D. C. Black and A. W. Coat) *The Marginal Revolution in Economics,* 1973; *The Image of Australia,* 1974; (editor and contributor) *Exhortation and*

Controls: The Search for a Wage-Price Policy, 1945-71, Brookings Institution, 1975. Editor, History of Political Economy.

\* \* \*

## GOOSSEN, Irvy W. 1924-

PERSONAL: Surname is pronounced Go-sen; born June 2, 1924, in Rosenort, Manitoba, Canada; son of Jacob F. (a machine shop owner) and Marie (Wiebe) Goossen; married Imogene Evelyn Unruh (operator of a foster home); children: Alta Lena, Mervin Gene. Education: Northern Arizona University, B.A., 1972. Religion: Mennonite. Home: 12902 Sahuoro, Peoria, Ariz. 85345. Office: Northern Arizona University, Faculty Box 5776, Flagstaff, Ariz. 86001.

CAREER: Worked as a garage mechanic, 1945-46, and as a farmer in Kansas, 1946-49; Church of God in Christ (Mennonite), missionary on reservation of Navajo Indians at Greasewood, Wide Ruins, and Salina Springs, Ariz., 1951-67; Northern Arizona University, Flagstaff, instructor in Navajo, 1967—, member of committee on Indian education. Consultant to northern Arizona and New Mexico schools with Navajo children.

WRITINGS: Navajo Made Easier, Northland Press, 1967; Go and Tell, Gospel Publishers, 1968; Let's Read Navajo, Northern Arizona Supplementary Education Center, 1968; They're People Too, Flagstaff Chamber of Commerce, 1970; (with Barbara Hall) Kee's Home, Northland Press, 1972; (contributor of translations) Karl W. Luckert, The Navajo Hunter Tradition, University of Arizona Press, 1975. Also contributor of translations and transcriptions, Navajo Mountain and Rainbow Bridge Religion, Volume I, by Luckert, Museum of Northern Arizona.

SIDELIGHTS: Irvy W. Goossen believes that the Indian, who is ready and willing, should have a chance to contribute his unique abilities to American society. He thinks much more could be written to help bring the Indian and non-Indian together.

\* \* \*

## GORDON, Donald Ramsay 1929-

PERSONAL: Born September 14, 1929, in Toronto, Ontario, Canada; son of Donald and Maisie Gordon; married an anesthetist, December 21, 1953; wife's name Helen Elizabeth; children: Donald John, Bruce, Keith. Education: Queen's University, B.A. (with honors), 1953; University of Toronto, M.A., 1955; London School of Economics and Political Science, graduate study, 1956-63, now Ph.D. candidate. Home: 134 Iroquois Place, Waterloo, Ontario, Canada N2L 2S5.

CAREER: Canadian Press, Toronto, Ontario, writer and filing editor, 1949-55; Financial Post, Toronto, Ontario, assistant editor, 1955-56; affiliated with Clyde Brothers Circus, Oklahoma City, Okla., 1956; European correspondent in London, England for Canadian Broadcasting Corp., 1957-63; University of Calgary, Calgary, Alberta, assistant professor, 1963-65, associate professor of political science, 1965-66; University of Waterloo, Waterloo, Ontario, assistant professor, 1966-67, associate professor of political science, 1967-69, associate professor in Faculty of Arts, part-time, 1969-70; Earthrise, Inc., Ottawa, Ontario, director and project coordinator, 1970; University of Waterloo, associate professor of political science, part-time, 1970-71, associate professor in Arts 100 Project, 1971-72, associate professor of Arts 100 communications, 1972-75; consultant, 1975—.

Member, Royal Commission on the Status of Women in Canada, 1967; research consultant to Senate Committee on the Mass Media in Canada, 1969-70, and to Royal Commission on Violence in the Communications Industry, 1976-77. Co-host of "20,000,000 Questions" on CBS Television, 1966-67.

MEMBER: Canadian Political Science Association, Canadian Broadcasting League, Canadian Institute of International Affairs, Association of Canadian Radio and Television Artists, University Film Association, Kropotkin Institute (director, 1960—). Awards, honors: Ford Foundation communications fellowship, 1954; International Institute of Education travel and research award, 1962-63; Canada Council research award, 1969.

WRITINGS: Language, Logic, and the Mass Media, Holt, 1966; (contributor) J. King Gordon, editor, Canada as a Middle Power, Canadian Institute of International Affairs, 1966; The New Literacy, University of Toronto Press, 1971. Writer of pamphlets and reports, including "Mass Media and the Rule of Law in Canada," report for Task Force on Government Information, 1969. Contributor to Canadian Commentator, Saturday Night, MacLean's, Toronto Globe and Mail, Times, Guardian, Spectator, New Statesman, Jerusalem Post, Financial Post, Toronto Star, and other publications, and to television in Canada, the United States, and England.

WORK IN PROGRESS: A children's saga, The Rock Candy Bandits; a film/print documentary, Political Journalism; poems, Monogamism and Declining Years.

SIDELIGHTS: Donald Ramsay Gordon told CA, "Since being converted to empirical monogamism, I have abandoned plans to move to St. Helena and am experimenting with alternate philosophies which might replace empiricism."

\* \* \*

## GORDON, Edmund Wyatt 1921-

PERSONAL: Born June 13, 1921, in Goldsboro, N.C.; son of Edmund Taylor and Mabel (Ellison) Gordon; married Susan Elizabeth Gitt, November 6, 1948; children: Edmund T., Christopher W., Jessica G., Johanna S. Education: Howard University, B.S., 1942, B.D., 1945; American University, M.A., 1950; additional study at Jefferson School of Social Sciences, 1951-52, and New York University Medical Center, 1954-56; Columbia University, Ed.D., 1957. Home: Cooper Morris Dr., Pomona, N.Y. 10970. Office: Teachers College, Columbia University, New York, N.Y. 10027.

CAREER: Ordained minister of Presbyterian Church, 1945, field missionary, 1945-46; Howard University, Washington, D.C., assistant dean of men, 1946-50; Morningside Community Center and Mental Health Service, New York City, assistant director and counseling psychologist, 1951-52; clinical posts in psychology and psychiatry at New York Medical College, New York City, Jewish Hospital of Brooklyn, and Morris J. Solomon Clinic for the Rehabilitation of Retarded Children, 1952-60; Harriett Tubman Clinic for Children, New York City, founder and co-director, 1953-59; Yeshiva University, New York City, lecturer in special education, 1959-60, associate professor, 1960-65, professor of education and chairman of department of educational psychology and guidance at Ferkauf Graduate School, 1960-68, research assistant professor of pediatrics at Albert Einstein College of Medicine, 1961—; Columbia University, Teachers College, New York City, professor of education and chairman of department of guidance, 1968-73, director of

National Center for Research and Information on Equal Educational Opportunity, 1968-73, director of Institute for Urban and Minority Education, 1973—. Visiting lecturer, Long Island University, 1958-59; visiting professor, Harvard University, summer, 1966. Consultant, U.S. Office of Education, 1964-66, member of research grants review panel, 1964—; director of Division of Research and Evaluation, Project Head Start, Office of Economic Opportunity, 1965-67. Member of editorial board, American Orthopsychiatric Association.

*MEMBER:* American Psychological Association (fellow), American Association for the Advancement of Science (fellow), American Educational Research Association (member of executive council), American Orthopsychiatric Association (fellow), American Personnel and Guidance Association, Association of Black Psychologists, Society for Research on Child Development, Educational Research Association of New York State, New York State Psychological Association (division president, 1965-66).

*WRITINGS:* (With Doxey A. Wilkerson) *Compensatory Education for the Disadvantaged: Programs and Practices—Preschool through College,* College Entrance Examination Board, 1966.

Contributor: Ross Stagner, editor, *The Dimensions of Human Conflict,* Wayne State University Press, 1967; *Higher Education in Revolutionary Decades,* McCutchan, 1967; Jerome Hellmuth, editor, *Disadvantaged Child,* Brunner, Volume II: *Special Child,* 1968, Volume III, 1970; David R. Cook, editor, *Guidance for Education in Revolution,* Allyn & Bacon, 1971; Robert Cancro, editor, *Intelligence: Genetic and Environmental Influences,* Grune, 1971. Contributor to other collections, to *New York Times Annual Education Review,* and to journals. Editor, *Journal of American Orthopsychiatry,* 1978—; member of editorial committee, *American Educational Research Journal.*

\* \* \*

## GORDON, Guanetta Stewart

*PERSONAL:* Born in Kansas City, Mo.; daughter of Samuel Lewis (a veterinarian) and Minnie Anna (Brown) Stewart; married Lynell F. Gordon (a retired colonel, U.S. Army); children: Stewart (a concert pianist and composer), Krista Sharon (Mrs. Reginald T. Morris; adopted daughter). *Education:* Studied at Baker University and University of Kansas. *Home:* 11847 Hacienda Dr., Sun City, Ariz. 85351.

*CAREER:* Taught school in earlier years, wrote scripts for radio programs, and performed in talent shows and plays; writer. *Member:* National League of American Pen Women (recording secretary, 1952-54; registrar, 1962-64; first vicepresident, 1970-72), Poetry Society of America, World Poetry Society Intercontinental, American Poetry League, Federation of Chaparral Poets, Poetry Society of Virginia, Arizona Poetry Society, Kansas Authors. *Awards, honors:* More than 200 awards on state and national levels for poetry and short stories, including first award for a love sonnet in World Poetry Day contest, 1966, Kansas Poet of the Year awards, Federation of Chaparral Poets, 1966-71, and distinguished service citation from World Poetry Society, 1970, for "The Dream Reaper."

*WRITINGS—Poems:* *Songs of the Wind,* illustrated by Eleanor Guarino, McGregor & Werner, 1952; *Under the Rainbow Arch,* Windfall Press, 1963; *Petals from the Moon,* Golden Quill, 1971; *Shadow within the Flame,* Golden Quill, 1973; *Above Rubies: Women of the Bible,* illustrated by Pat Scher and Jeanne Thompson, Golden Quill, 1976;

*Red Are the Embers,* Golden Quill Press, in press. Poetry has appeared in various anthologies. Contributor to *Saturday Evening Post, Popular Romances, Bardic Echoes, Encore, Sandcutters, Lyric, Poetry Digest, American Bard, Muse,* and many other poetry journals.

*WORK IN PROGRESS:* *The Aurora Tree,* a historical novel.

*SIDELIGHTS:* Guanetta Gordon spent five years in Europe as an Army wife, mainly in Germany where she and her husband adopted a four-year-old girl. Ms. Gordon's manuscripts and publications are on deposit in the Kansas Room of University of Kansas Library.

\* \* \*

## GORDON, Leonard A. 1938-

*PERSONAL:* Born January 17, 1938, in New York, N.Y.; son of Reuben (a textile executive and professional athlete) and Rose (Slutsky) Gordon; married Carol Jean Meadows, 1977. *Education:* Amherst College, B.A., 1959; Harvard University, M.A., 1961, Ph.D., 1969. *Home:* 276 Riverside Dr., New York, N.Y. 10025. *Office:* Department of History, Brooklyn College of the City University of New York, Brooklyn, N.Y. 11210.

*CAREER:* Columbia University, New York City, instructor, 1967-69, assistant professor of history, 1969-73; Brooklyn College of the City University of New York, Brooklyn, N.Y., associate professor, 1973-77, professor of history, 1978—. *Member:* American Historical Association, Association for Asian Studies, Committee of Concerned Asian Scholars, Phi Beta Kappa. *Awards, honors:* American Philosophical Association grant, 1972; Fulbright-Hays senior faculty research grant, 1972-73; Watumull Prize of the American Historical Association, 1974, for *Bengal: The Nationalist Movement, 1876-1940;* American Institute of Indian Studies grants, 1976, 1977.

*WRITINGS:* (With Barbara Stoler Miller) *A Syllabus of Indian Civilization,* Columbia University Press, 1971; *Bengal: The Nationalist Movement, 1876-1940,* Columbia University Press, 1974. Contributor to Asian and African studies journals.

*WORK IN PROGRESS:* A history of twentieth-century Bengal, concentrating on the period 1930-1947, and a political biography of Subhas and Sarat Bose.

*SIDELIGHTS:* "I was raised to take an interest in political movements, especially those in what we now call the Third World," Leonard A. Gordon says. "To some extent I identify with these peoples and their continuing struggles and to some extent I feel the collective guilt we must all feel for the way in which the Government of the United States contributes to the oppression of these people. So I both identify with the Indians and Bengalis about whom I have written and write and feel somewhat detached from them. I have some of my best friends in India, but feel that U.S. action in the Third World is making it ever more difficult for Americans to communicate with and understand Asians and Africans."

\* \* \*

## GORMAN, Ralph 1897-1972

October 4, 1897—October 17, 1972; American Roman Catholic priest, editor, and writer on religious themes. Obituaries: *New York Times,* October 19, 1972.

## GORMAN, T. Walter   1916(?)-1972

1916(?)—August 5, 1972; American network radio and television director and adapter for stage and television. Obituaries: *New York Times,* August 7, 1972.

\*   \*   \*

## GOTTERER, Malcolm H(arold)   1924-

*PERSONAL:* Born March 11, 1924, in New York, N.Y.; son of Abbey S. and Matilda (Saks) Gotterer; married Shirley J. Lasher, October 19, 1957; children: David Abbey. *Education:* Curtiss-Wright Technical Institute, Los Angeles, Certificate in Aeronautical Engineering, 1942; Suffolk University, B.S., 1955, M.S. in B.A., 1956; Harvard University, D.B.A., 1960. *Home:* 6400 Southwest 112th St., Miami, Fla. 33156. *Office:* Department of Mathematical Sciences, Florida International University, Tamiami Trail, Miami, Fla. 33144.

*CAREER:* Employed in industry as industrial engineer, chief industrial engineer, management consultant, and assistant to the president, 1946-54; Harvard University, Graduate School of Business Administration, Boston, Mass., instructor in business administration, 1956-57; University of California, Berkeley, began as lecturer, became assistant professor of business administration, 1959-62; Georgia Institute of Technology, Atlanta, associate professor of industrial management, 1962-64; Pennsylvania State University, University Park, professor of computer science and of business administration, 1965-68, professor of computer science, 1968-73; Florida International University, Miami, professor of computer science, 1972—. Consultant to U.S. Government agencies, nonprofit organizations, and business. *Military service:* U.S. Army, 1943-45.

*MEMBER:* Association for Computing Machinery, Institute of Electrical and Electronic Engineers, Association for Educational Data Systems. *Awards, honors:* Social Science Research Council grant, 1962, 1965; postdoctoral fellow at International Business Machines (IBM) Systems Research Institute, 1964, and Johns Hopkins University, 1968-69.

*WRITINGS:* (With S. S. Aidlin) *Engineering Economy,* New York State Society of Professional Engineers, 1950; *Profitable Small Plant Management,* Conover-Mast Publications, 1955; *La Gestion de l'enterprise,* S.A.D.E.P. Editions (Paris), 1957; (with Robert Malcom) *Computers in Business: A FORTRAN Introduction,* International Textbook Co., 1968; *A Bibliography of Computer Management,* Auerbach, 1970; *Gotterer on Direct Access File Techniques* (workbook), two volumes, Edutronics, 1971; (with Malcom and Frank Luh) *Computers in Administration: A FORTRAN IV Introduction,* Intext, 1973.

Contributor: Frederick E. Balderston and A. C. Hoggatt, editors, *Symposium on Simulation Models,* South-Western, 1963; *Computers and You, the User,* Computer Society of Canada, 1967; Allen Kent, Orrin E. Taulbee, and Gordon D. Goldstein, editors, *Electronic Handling of Information,* Thompson Book Co., 1967; *Information Systems for Jamaica in the 70's,* Government of Jamaica, 1970. Editor, *Proceedings of the Third Annual Computer Personnel Research Conference,* Association for Computing Machinery, 1965. Contributor of articles to professional journals. Member of editorial executive committee and editorial board, *IAG Technical Quarterly;* member of editorial board, *Management Informatics.*

*WORK IN PROGRESS: Data Base and File Organization,* to be published by Auerbach.

## GOTTESMAN, Irving I(sadore)   1930-

*PERSONAL:* Born December 29, 1930, in Cleveland, Ohio; son of Bernard (an insurance broker) and Virginia (Weitzner) Gottesman; married Carol Applen, 1970; children: Adam. *Education:* Illinois Institute of Technology, B.S., 1953; University of Minnesota, Ph.D., 1960. *Home:* 2118 Folwell St., St. Paul, Minn. 55108. *Office:* Department of Psychology, University of Minnesota, Minneapolis, Minn. 55455.

*CAREER:* A. H. Wilder Child Guidance Clinic, St. Paul, Minn., fellow in clinical psychology, 1957-59; Veterans Administration Hospital, Minneapolis, Minn., clinical psychology trainee, 1959-60; Harvard University, Cambridge, Mass., lecturer in psychology, 1960-63; University of North Carolina Medical School, Chapel Hill, clinical assistant professor, 1963-64, associate professor of psychology, 1964-66; University of Minnesota, Minneapolis, associate professor, 1966-68, professor of psychology, 1968—, director of training program in behavioral genetics, 1966—. Diplomate in clinical psychology of American Board of Examiners in Professional Psychology. U.S. Public Health Service special fellow in psychiatric genetics, Maudsley Hospital, University of London Institute of Psychiatry, 1963-64; Guggenheim fellow, Psykologisk Institut, Copenhagen, Denmark, 1972-73. David C. Wilson Lecturer, University of Virginia Medical School, 1967. Consultant to U.S. Department of Defense, 1962-63, and U.S. Veterans Administration. *Military service:* U.S. Navy, 1953-56; became lieutenant.

*MEMBER:* American Psychological Association, Society for Research in Child Development, American Society for Human Genetics, American Eugenics Society (member of research council), Behavior Genetics Society (chairman of public and professional affairs), American Association of University Professors, American Psychopathological Association, Royal College of Psychiatrists (associate member), American Civil Liberties Union, Minnesota Human Genetics League (vice-president), Sigma Xi. *Awards, honors:* R. Thornton Wilson Prize in genetic and preventive psychiatry from Eastern Psychiatric Research Association, 1965; Hofheimer Prize for Research from American Psychiatric Association, 1973, for *Schizophrenia and Genetics.*

*WRITINGS:* (Editor with James Shields) *Men, Mind, and Heredity: The Selected Papers of Eliot Slater on Psychiatry and Genetics,* Johns Hopkins Press, 1971; (with Shields) *Schizophrenia and Genetics: A Twin Study Vantage Point,* Academic Press, 1972.

Contributor: Norman Ellis, editor, *The Handbook of Mental Deficiency: Psychological Theory and Research,* McGraw, 1963; Steven Vandenberg, editor, *Methods and Goals in Human Behavior Genetics,* Academic Press, 1965; Brendan Maher, editor, *Progress in Experimental Personality Research,* Academic Press, 1966; Thomas Lowry, editor, *Hyperventilation and Hysteria,* C. C Thomas, 1967; Martin Manosevitz, Gardner Lindzey, and Delbert Thiessen, editors, *Behavioral Genetics: Method and Research,* Appleton, 1968; D. C. Glass, editor, *Biology and Behavior: Genetics,* Rockefeller University Press and Russell Sage, 1968; Martin Deutsch, Irwin Katz, and Arthur Jensen, editors, *Social Class, Race, and Psychological Development,* Holt, 1968; Theo Dobzhansky, M. K. Hecht, and W. C. Steere, editors, *Evolutionary Biology,* Appleton, 1968; S. Vandenberg, editor, *Progress in Human Behavior Genetics,* Johns Hopkins Press, 1968; David Rosenthal and Seymour Kety, editors, *The Transmission of Schizophrenia,* Pergamon, 1968; Paul Mussen, John Conger, and Jerome Kagan, editors, *Readings in Child Development,* 2nd edition, Harper, 1969.

D. N. Robinson, editor, *Heredity and Achievement,* Oxford University Press, 1970; E. N. Gale and N. L. Corah, editors, *Origins of Abnormal Behavior,* Addison-Wesley, 1971; C. T. Morgan and Richard King, editors, *Readings for an Introduction to Psychology,* McGraw, 1971; *New Considerations in Child Development,* Day Care and Child Development Council of America, 1971; R. M. Allen and others, editors, *The Role of Genetics in Mental Retardation,* 1972; Willard Hartup, editor, *The Young Child,* National Association for the Education of Young Children, 1972; Lee Ehrman and Gilbert Omenn, editors, *Genetic Endowment and Environment in the Determination of Behavior,* Academic Press, 1972; A. Pick, editor, *Minnesota Symposium on Child Psychology,* University of Minnesota Press, 1974; (with J. Shields and L. L. Heston) Fieve, Rosenthal, and Brill, editors, *Genetic Research in Psychiatry,* Johns Hopkins Press, 1975; Schaie, Anderson, McClearn, and Money, editors, *Developmental Human Behavior Genetics,* Heath, 1975; (with Shields) B. A. Maher, editor, *Progress in Experimental Personality Research,* Academic Press, 1977; (with B. Bell, S. Mednick, and J. Sergeant) Mednick and K. O. Christiansen, editors, *Bio-social Bases of Criminal Behavior,* Halsted, 1977; L. C. Wynne, R. L. Cromwell, and S. Matthysse, editors, *The Nature of Schizophrenia,* Wiley, 1978; W. T. Reich, editor, *Encyclopedia of Bioethics,* Free Press, 1978; (with R. R. Golden) R. L. Spitzer and D. F. Klein, editors, *Current Issues in Psychiatric Diagnosis,* Raven Press, 1978; (with D. R. Hanson) G. M. van Praag, M. H. Lader, O. J. Rafaelsen, and E. J. Sachar, editors, *Handbook of Biological Psychiatry,* Volume I, Dekker, 1978.

Contributor of over fifty articles to psychology and psychiatry journals. Associate editor, *Social Biology, American Journal of Human Genetics,* and *Behavior Genetics.*

*WORK IN PROGRESS:* Writing on genetics in psychiatry and other topics.

\*      \*      \*

## GOVE, Philip Babcock 1902-1972

June 27, 1902—November 15, 1972; American educator, editor, and writer on the English language. Obituaries: *New York Times,* November 17, 1972; *Publishers Weekly,* November 27, 1972; *Antiquarian Bookman,* December 4, 1972. (See index for *CA* sketch)

\*      \*      \*

## GRAHAM, Fred P(atterson) 1931-

*PERSONAL:* Born October 6, 1931, in Little Rock, Ark.; son of Otis Livingstone (a clergyman) and Lois (Patterson) Graham; married Lucile McCrea, December 28, 1961; children: Grier, Michael, Alyse. *Education:* Yale University, B.A., 1953; Vanderbilt University, LL.B., 1959; Oxford University, diploma in law, 1960. *Home:* 2909 Cleveland Ave. N.W., Washington, D.C. 20008. *Agent:* Sterling Lord Agency, 660 Madison Ave., New York, N.Y. 10021. *Office:* 2020 M St. N.W., Washington, D.C. 20036.

*CAREER:* Private practice of law in Nashville, Tenn., 1960-62; United States Senate Judiciary Subcommittee on Constitutional Amendments, Washington, D.C., chief counsel, 1962-63; special assistant to Secretary of Labor W. Willard Wirtz, Washington, D.C., 1963-65; *New York Times,* Washington, D.C., Supreme Court correspondent, 1965-72; Co-

lumbia Broadcasting System, Washington, D.C., law correspondent for CBS News, 1972—. *Military service:* U.S. Marine Corps Reserve, 1953-56; became first lieutenant. *Awards, honors:* Gavel Award from American Bar Association, 1971, for *The Self-Inflicted Wound;* recipient of three "Emmy" awards from National Academy of Television Arts and Sciences, 1973; George Foster Peabody Broadcasting Award, 1974.

*WRITINGS: The Self-Inflicted Wound,* Macmillan, 1970; *The Alias Program,* Little, Brown, 1977.

*SIDELIGHTS:* Written while Fred Graham was the *New York Times* Supreme Court correspondent, *The Self-Inflicted Wound* is an account of the Warren Court's decisions on criminal law, particularly the Miranda vs. Arizona case in which the court ruled that a person must be told at the time of his arrest of his rights to counsel and to remain silent, and of the fact that anything said can be used against him. The *Newsday* reviewer calls the book an "eminently fair-minded appraisal of the Warren Court.... Graham makes it perfectly clear that crime in the streets *is* a menacing problem and that the average citizen has every right to be frightened. As a totally frank reporter he also makes it clear that the upsurge in such crime has come largely from the Negro community. As a fair-minded writer he lays the blame at the door of the white community, whose neglect and prejudice has created some of the most abominable ghettos in the presumably civilized Western world."

*The Alias Program* discusses the Justice Department's program to relocate and provide new identities for persons involved in organized crime who are willing to testify against their former cohorts. The *Book List* reviewer notes that "Graham argues vehemently that the alias program has not been successful; conceived under wraps and initiated without adequate forethought, it is incapable of handling the complexity of establishing foolproof aliases. Graham has raised the curtain on a potential hornet's nest." The book focuses on Jerry Zelmanowitz, who James R. Silkenat describes in *Business Week* as "a rather seedy, essentially nonviolent, upwardly mobile New Jersey crook who became Paul Maris, a lionized San Francison-based manufacturing executive, after he testified for the government. Unfortunately for Zelmanowitz-Maris, despite his success after relocation, the cover provided by the Justice Department proved illusory." The government's bungling of Zelmanowitz's new identity included failure to provide birth records in the city in which Maris was supposedly born, failure to establish records with the high school and college Maris was said to have attended, and failure to establish in government files his supposed background in military intelligence. In a fight for control of his company, Maris' false identity was questioned and, eventually, parts of his true identity became known. Maris disappeared and has apparently established a more successful and secure identity for himself without the government's interference. In his book, Graham discusses the problems with this alias program, not only from the witnesses' viewpoint, but the ethical, legal, and practical implications for society as well. Although as Paul Maris, Jerry Zelmanowitz seems to have dealt ethically and nonviolently with the people he met, not all witnesses given new identities behave in a similar manner. Silkenat calls the book "most impressive as a rollicking adventure story; the hero (such as he is) survives in the end, but just barely. Written with the pace and color of a novel, this most informative book is presented in the same scholarly, compassionate tone we are accustomed to hearing from Graham in his reports on radio and television."

*BIOGRAPHICAL/CRITICAL SOURCES: Newsday,* November 7, 1970; *Washington Post,* November 10, 1970; *New York Times Book Review,* November 22, 1970, August 28, 1977; *New Yorker,* December 26, 1970; *Book List,* September 1, 1977; *Business Week,* October 10, 1977.

\*     \*     \*

### GRAVES, Charles Parlin   1911-1972
### (John Parlin)

January 23, 1911—August 2, 1972; American author of children's books. Obituaries: *New York Times,* August 4, 1972; *Publishers Weekly,* August 14, 1972. (See index for *CA* sketch)

\*     \*     \*

### GRAY, J(esse) Glenn   1913-1977

*PERSONAL:* Born May 27, 1913, near Mifflintown, Pa.; married Ursula Werner, 1947; children: Elizabeth, Charlotte. *Education:* Juniata College, A.B. (magna cum laude), 1936; University of Pittsburgh, M.A., 1938; Columbia University, Ph.D., 1941. *Home:* 17 West Buena Ventura, Colorado Springs, Colo. 80907. *Office:* Department of Philosophy, Colorado College, Colorado Springs, Colo. 80903.

*CAREER:* Juniata College, Huntingdon, Pa., instructor in philosophy, 1936-38; Swarthmore College, Swarthmore, Pa., and University of Pennsylvania, Philadelphia, instructor in philosophy, 1945-46; U.S. Military Government in Germany, education officer, 1946-47; Haverford College, Haverford, Pa., assistant professor of philosophy, 1947-48; Colorado College, Colorado Springs, associate professor, 1948-52, professor of philosophy and chairman of department, 1952-77. Visiting professor, Graduate Center, New School for Social Research, 1973. Consultant, National Endowment for the Humanities, 1969-73; member of advisory group, Library of Congress. *Military service:* U.S. Army, 1941-45; became second lieutenant. *Awards, honors:* Ford Foundation faculty fellow, 1954-55; Fulbright research professor in Germany, 1954-55; Guggenheim fellow, 1961-62; National Council on the Arts and Humanities senior fellow, 1967-68; Aspen Center for Humanistic Studies, scholar-in-residence, summer, 1969; LL.D., Juniata College, 1971.

*WRITINGS: Hegel's Hellenic Ideal,* King's Crown Press, 1941, new edition published as *Hegel and Greek Thought,* Harper, 1968; *The Warriors: Reflections on Men in Battle,* Harcourt, 1959, revised edition, with introduction by Hannah Arendt, Harper, 1967; *The Promise of Wisdom: An Introduction to Philosophy of Education,* Lippincott, 1968; (translator with Fred D. Wieck, and author of introduction) Martin Heidegger, *What Is Called Thinking?,* Harper, 1968; (editor and author of introduction) *G. W. F. Hegel, on Art, Religion, Philosophy: Introductory Lectures to the Realm of Absolute Spirit,* Harper, 1970; *Understanding Violence Philosophically and Other Essays,* Harper, 1970.

Contributor: Earl McGrath, editor, *The Humanities in Higher Education,* W. C. Brown, 1949; George L. Kline, editor, *European Philosophy Today,* Quadrangle, 1965; Edward N. Lee and Maurice Mandelbaum, editors, *Phenomenology and Existentialism,* Johns Hopkins Press, 1967; John Anton, editor, *Naturalism and Historical Understanding,* State University of New York Press, 1967; Nathan A. Scott, Jr., editor, *The Modern Vision of Death,* John Knox, 1967; *Ideas and Style,* Odyssey, 1968; Coulos, Somer, and Wilcox, editors, *Literature and Rhetoric,* Scott, Foresman, 1969.

General editor of works of Martin Heidegger in English translation, Harper, 1965-77. Contributor of numerous articles and reviews to *New York Times, Western Humanities Review, Commentary,* and other publications.†

(Died October 30, 1977)

\*     \*     \*

### GREEN, Donald Ross   1924-

*PERSONAL:* Born August 12, 1924, in Holyoke, Mass.; son of Donald R. and Constance (McLaughlin) Green; married Mary Reese, 1950; children: Alice Angell, Mitchell Reese. *Education:* Yale University, B.A., 1948; University of California, Berkeley, M.A., 1954, Ph.D., 1958. *Office:* CTB/McGraw-Hill, Del Monte Research Park, Monterey, Calif. 93940.

*CAREER:* George School, George School, Pa., instructor in mathematics, 1948-50; University of California Medical School, San Francisco, statistician at Cancer Research Institute, 1953-56; University of California, Berkeley, associate in education, 1957; Emory University, Atlanta, Ga., instructor, 1957-58, assistant professor, 1958-63, associate professor of education and psychology, 1963-67; CTB/McGraw-Hill, Monterey, Calif., senior research psychologist and director of research, 1967—. Visiting lecturer, University of Victoria, summer, 1968. *Military service:* U.S. Army, 10th Mountain Division, 1943-45. *Member:* American Psychological Association, American Association for the Advancement of Science, American Educational Research Association.

*WRITINGS:* (With W. E. Gauerke) *If the Schools Are Closed: A Critical Analysis of the Private School Plan* (booklet), Southern Regional Council, 1959; *Educational Psychology,* Prentice-Hall, 1964; (with J. A. Jordan, W. J. Bridgeman, and C. V. Brittain) *Black Belt Schools: Beyond Desegregation* (booklet), Southern Regional Council, 1965; (with R. L. Henderson) *Reading for Meaning in the Elementary School,* Prentice-Hall, 1969; (editor with M. P. Ford and G. B. Flamer) *Measurement and Piaget,* McGraw, 1971; (editor) *The Aptitude-Achievement Distinction,* CTB/McGraw-Hill, 1973; (editor with M. J. Wango) *Achievement Testing of Minority Students for Program Education,* CTB/McGraw-Hill, 1978. Contributor to *Proceedings* of American Psychological Association, American Educational Research Association, and International Reading Association, and to journals.

\*     \*     \*

### GREENBAUM, Fred   1930-

*PERSONAL:* Born November 6, 1930, in Brooklyn, N.Y.; son of David (a baker) and Rose (Jaegar) Greenbaum; married Ann Teresa Corsini (a social work therapist), May 3, 1954; children: Jonathan Michael, Theodore Newell. *Education:* Brooklyn College (now Brooklyn College of the City University of New York), B.A., 1952; University of Wisconsin, M.A., 1953; Columbia University, Ph.D., 1962. *Politics:* Democrat. *Home:* 118 Meadbrook Rd., Garden City, N.Y. 11530. *Office:* Department of History, Queensborough Community College of the City University of New York, Bayside, N.Y. 11364.

*CAREER:* Brooklyn College (now Brooklyn College of the City University of New York), New York, N.Y., lecturer in history, 1957-60; Queens College of the City of New York (now Queens College of the City University of New York), Flushing, N.Y., lecturer in history, 1960-61; Queensborough Community College of the City University of New York, Bayside, N.Y., instructor, 1961-62, assistant professor, 1962-67, associate professor, 1967-70, professor of history, 1970—. Lecturer, Cooper Union, 1961. *Military service:* U.S. Army, 1953-55; served in Signal Corps. *Member:* American Historical Association, Organization of American Historians, Professional Staff Congress.

*WRITINGS:* (Contributor) Daniel Walden, editor, *American Reform: The Ambiguous Legacy,* Ampersand Press, 1967; (editor with Pedro T. Meza) *Readings in Western Civilization: Early Modern Period,* McCutchan, 1970; *Fighting Progressive, Edward P. Costigan,* Public Affairs Press, 1971; *Robert Marion La Follette,* Twayne, 1975; (contributor) Hans Trefousse, editor, *Towards a New View of America,* Burt Franklin, 1977. Contributor to *Encyclopedia Judaica;* contributor of articles on American progressive and labor history to *Social Science, Arizona and the West, Labor History, New Politics, Pacific Historian,* and other journals.

*WORK IN PROGRESS: Progressives and the New Deal.*

*SIDELIGHTS:* Fred Greenbaum told *CA:* "Research and writing are important adjuncts of teaching. These activities bring depth to classroom analysis and enable the teacher more adequately to evaluate the work of other authors. Historical writing should not affect pretended profundity through the use of verbose complexity. Nor should the historian burden the general reader with historiographical pedantry. Sparring with colleagues should be reserved for professional journals. The purpose of the historian should be to communicate with the reading public as simply, concisely and lucidly as possible."

\*  \*  \*

## GREENE, A(lvin) C(arl) 1923-
### (Arthur C. Randolph, Mateman Weaver)

*PERSONAL:* Born November 4, 1923, in Abilene, Tex.; son of Alvin Carl and Marie (Cole) Greene; married Betty Jo Dozier, May 1, 1950; children: Geoffrey, Mark, Eliot, Meredith Elizabeth. *Education:* Attended Phillips University, 1942, and Kansas State College of Pittsburg (now Pittsburg State University), 1943; Abilene Christian College (now University), B.A., 1948; graduate study at Hardin-Simmons University, 1951, and University of Texas at Austin, 1968-70. *Religion:* Presbyterian. *Home and office:* 4934 Crooked Lane, Dallas, Tex. 75229. *Agent:* Peter Matson, Harold Matson Co., Inc., 22 East 40th St., New York, N.Y. 10016.

*CAREER: Abilene Reporter-News,* Abilene, Tex., member of staff, 1948-52, amusements editor, 1952-59; *Dallas Times Herald,* Dallas, Tex., book editor and editorial columnist, 1960-68, editor of editorial page, 1963-65; KERA-Television, Dallas, executive producer, 1970-71, news commentator, 1970-77. Owner of book store in Abilene, 1952-57; special instructor and head of department of journalism, Hardin-Simmons University, 1957, University of Texas at Austin, 1973, and Southern Methodist University, 1976. *Military service:* U.S. Navy and U.S. Marines, 1942-46; served in Pacific theater and China; became pharmacist's mate second class. *Member:* Texas Institute of Letters (president, 1969-71). *Awards, honors:* Texas Institute of Letters award, 1963 and 1973; award from National Conference of Christians and Jews, 1964; Dobie-Paisano fellowship, 1968.

*WRITINGS: A Personal Country,* Knopf, 1969; (editor and contributor) *Living Texas: A Gathering of Experiences,*

Encino Press, 1970; *The Last Captive,* Encino Press, 1972; *The Santa Claus Bank Robbery,* Knopf, 1972; (contributor) John Graves, editor, *Growing Up in Texas,* Encino Press, 1972; *Dallas: The Deciding Years,* Encino Press, 1973; *A Christmas Tree,* Encino Press, 1973; *Views in Texas,* Encino Press, 1974; *A Place Called Dallas,* Dallas County Heritage Society, 1975; (contributor) Evelyn Oppenheimer and Bill Porterfield, editors, *The Book of Dallas,* Doubleday, 1976. Executive editor of *Southwestern Historical Quarterly,* 1968-69.

*BIOGRAPHICAL/CRITICAL SOURCES: New Yorker,* March 14, 1970; *Detroit News,* July 23, 1972; *Dallas Times Herald Sunday Magazine,* October 30, 1977.

\*  \*  \*

## GREENFIELD, Jeff 1943-

*PERSONAL:* Born June 10, 1943, in New York, N.Y.; son of Benjamin (a lawyer) and Helen (a teacher; maiden name, Greenwald) Greenfield; married Harriet Carmichael (an actress), May 11, 1968; children: Casey Carmichael (daughter). *Education:* University of Wisconsin, B.A. (with honors), 1964; Yale University, LL.B. (with honors), 1967. *Home:* 322 West 72nd St., New York, N.Y. 10023. *Agent:* Sterling Lord Agency, 660 Madison Ave., New York, N.Y. 10021.

*CAREER:* Legislative aide to late Senator Robert Kennedy, Washington, D.C., 1967-68; assistant to Mayor John Lindsay, New York City, 1968-70; Garth Associates, New York City, consultant, 1970-76.

*WRITINGS:* (With Jerry Bruno) *The Advance Man,* Morrow, 1971; (with Jack Newfield) *A Populist Manifesto: The Making of a New Majority,* Praeger, 1972; *No Peace, No Place,* Doubleday, 1973; *Tiny Giant* (juvenile), Raintree, 1975; *The World's Greatest Team: A Portrait of the Boston Celtics, 1957-1969,* Random House, 1976; *Television: The First Fifty Years,* Abrams, 1977. Contributor to national magazines.

*BIOGRAPHICAL/CRITICAL SOURCES: Newsday,* July 10, 1971; *New York Times,* November 11, 1977.

\*  \*  \*

## GREENWOOD, Gordon E(dward) 1935-

*PERSONAL:* Born August 21, 1935, in Jasonville, Ind.; son of Arthur Lee (owner of a pest control business) and Annette (Goodman) Greenwood; married Linda Jane Williams (a secondary school teacher), June 23, 1957; children: Joseph Arthur, Richard Roy, Donald Edward. *Education:* Indiana State University, B.S., 1958, M.A., 1962; Indiana University, Ed.D., 1967. *Home:* 3962 Southwest Fourth Place, Gainesville, Fla. 32601. *Office:* 513 Weil Hall, University of Florida, Gainesville, Fla. 32611.

*CAREER:* High school teacher in Dowagiac, Mich., 1958-60, and Terre Haute, Ind., 1960-65; University of Florida, Gainesville, assistant professor, 1967-72, associate professor, 1972-76, professor of psychological foundations of education, 1976—. Visiting professor, Indiana University, 1968. Director of Florida Follow Through research and development grant, and consultant to Project Follow Through in ten states. *Member:* American Educational Research Association.

*WRITINGS:* (Contributor) Ira J. Gordon, editor, *Reaching the Child through Parent Education: The Florida Approach,* Institute for the Development of Human Resources, University of Florida, 1969; *Problem Situations in Teaching,*

Harper, 1971; (contributor with Leonard Kaplan) Gordon, editor, *Building Effective Home-School Relationships,* Allyn & Bacon, 1976; (contributor) *Improving College and University Teaching Yearbook,* Oregon State University Press, 1976. Contributor to study guides for teaching texts; contributor to professional journals, including *Science Education, Journal of Teacher Education,* and *Journal of Educational Psychology.*

\* \* \*

## GREET, William Cabell 1901-1972

January 28, 1901—December 19, 1972; American educator, editor, and authority on American dialects and pronunciation. Obituaries: *New York Times,* December 21, 1972; *Washington Post,* December 22, 1972.

\* \* \*

## GREGORY, Roy 1935-

*PERSONAL:* Born March 7, 1935, in London, England. *Education:* Brasenose College, Oxford, M.A., 1961; Nuffield College, Oxford, D.Phil., 1962. *Politics:* Labour. *Home:* 2A, Grove Park Gardens, Chiswick, London W4, England. *Office:* Department of Politics, University of Reading, Reading, Berkshire RG6 2AH, England.

*CAREER:* Queens College, Dundee, Scotland, lecturer in political science, 1962-64; University of Reading, Reading, England, lecturer, 1964-73, reader, 1973-75, professor of politics, 1975—. Elected member, County Borough of Reading Council, 1966-69. *Member:* Political Studies Association, Royal Institute of Public Administration.

*WRITINGS: The Miners and British Politics, 1906-1914,* Oxford University Press, 1968; *The Price of Amenity: Five Studies in Conservation and Government,* St. Martin's, 1971; *The Parliamentary Ombudsman,* Allen & Unwin, 1973. Contributor of articles to *Political Studies, Public Administration,* and *International Journal of Environmental Studies.*

*WORK IN PROGRESS:* Additional research on the British Parliamentary Commissioner for Administration.

\* \* \*

## GRIFFIN, Donald (Redfield) 1915-

*PERSONAL:* Born August 3, 1915, in Southampton, N.Y.; son of Henry Farrand (an author) and Mary (Redfield) Griffin; married Ruth Marion Castle, September 6, 1941 (divorced August 9, 1965); married Jocelyn Crane (a zoologist), December 16, 1965; children: (first marriage) Nancy Jean (Mrs. Rex Jackson), Janet Redfield (Mrs. Freeman K. Abbott, Jr.), Margaret Louise, John Hadley. *Education:* Harvard University, B.S., 1938, M.A., 1940, Ph.D., 1942. *Home:* 1 West 67th St., New York, N.Y. 10023. *Office:* Rockefeller University, New York, N.Y. 10021.

*CAREER:* Harvard University, Cambridge, Mass., research associate and junior fellow, psycho-acoustic laboratory, fatigue laboratory, and biological laboratory, 1942-46; Cornell University, Ithaca, N.Y., assistant professor, 1946-47, associate professor, 1947-52, professor of zoology, 1952-53; Harvard University, professor of zoology, 1953-65, chairman of department, 1962-65; Rockefeller University, New York, N.Y., professor of animal behavior, 1965—, member of board of trustees, 1973-76. Lecturer, Lowell Institute, 1942; senior research zoologist, New York Zoological Society, 1965—.

*MEMBER:* National Academy of Sciences, American Philosophical Society, American Academy of Arts and Sciences, American Physiological Society, American Society of Zoologists, Ecological Society of America, Phi Beta Kappa, Sigma Xi. *Awards, honors:* Elliot Medal, National Academy of Sciences, for *Listening in the Dark,* 1961; Phi Beta Kappa Science Prize, 1966, for *Bird Migration;* D.Sc., Ripon College, 1967.

*WRITINGS: Listening in the Dark,* Yale University Press, 1958; *Echoes of Bats and Men,* Doubleday, 1959; *Animal Structure and Function,* Holt, 1962, 2nd edition (with Alvin Novick), 1970; *Bird Migration,* Doubleday, 1964; *The Question of Animal Awareness,* Rockefeller University Press, 1976. Contributor of science articles to magazines and professional journals.

*WORK IN PROGRESS:* Research on animal behavior, with special emphasis on animal orientation and communication, bird navigation, and echolocation of bats.

\* \* \*

## GRIFFITH, Albert J(oseph, Jr.) 1932-

*PERSONAL:* Born June 5, 1932, in Fort Worth, Tex.; son of Albert Joseph (a newspaperman) and Dorothy (Byron) Griffith; married Elizabeth Jansing, January 26, 1957; children: Katherine Celine, John Harold, Carol Elizabeth, Mark Byron. *Education:* St. Edward's University, B.A., 1953; University of Texas, M.A., 1954, Ph.D., 1959. *Home:* 6218 Rue Sophie, San Antonio, Tex. 78238. *Office:* Department of English, Our Lady of the Lake University, San Antonio, Tex. 78285.

*CAREER:* Our Lady of the Lake University, San Antonio, Tex., instructor, 1958-61, assistant professor, 1961-64, associate professor, 1964-66, professor of English, 1966—, vice-president for development and public relations, 1969-72, director of humanities division, 1974, vice-president and dean of academic affairs, 1974—. *Military service:* U.S. Army, 1954-56. *Member:* Modern Language Association of America, National Council of Teachers of English, South Central Modern Language Association, Conference of College Teachers of English of Texas, Texas Joint English Committee for School and College (former district chairman), English Teacher's Club of San Antonio (former president).

*WRITINGS: Peter Taylor,* Twayne, 1971. Work represented in anthologies, including *Beginnings,* Sheed, 1956, *The New Guest Room Book,* Sheed, 1957, and *France and North America: The Revolutionary Experience,* 1974. Contributor to literature journals and national periodicals, including *Commonweal, America, Explicator, Shenandoah,* and *Choice.*

*WORK IN PROGRESS:* Research on mixed media literature and on the Southern literary renaissance.

\* \* \*

## GRIFFITHS, Michael C(ompton) 1928-

*PERSONAL:* Born April 7, 1928, in Cardiff, Wales; son of Charles Idris Ewart and Myfanwy (Jones) Griffiths; married Valerie Kipping (a theological teacher), July 21, 1956; children: John Anderson, Elizabeth Bronwen, Nigel Timothy, Stephen Glyndwr. *Education:* Peterhouse College, Cambridge, B.A., 1952; Ridley Hall, Cambridge, M.A., 1954. *Religion:* Christian. *Permanent address:* 8 Ellis Ave., Onslow Village, Guildford, Surrey, England. *Office:* 2 Cluny Rd., Singapore 10.

*CAREER:* Inter-Varsity Fellowship, traveling secretary, 1954-57; Overseas Missionary Fellowship, missionary in Japan, 1958-68, general director in Singapore, 1969—. *Military service:* Royal Army Medical Corps, 1947-49; became corporal.

*WRITINGS: Consistent Christianity,* Inter-Varsity Fellowship, 1960; *Christian Assurance,* Inter-Varsity Fellowship, 1962; *Take My Life,* Inter-Varsity Fellowship, 1967; *Give Up Small Ambitions,* Inter-Varsity Fellowship, 1970; *Three Men Filled with Spirit,* Overseas Missionary Fellowship, 1970; *Take Off Your Shoes,* Overseas Missionary Fellowship, 1971; *Cinderella with Amnesia,* Inter-Varsity Fellowship, 1975; *Changing Asia,* Lion Publishing, 1977; *Cinderella's Betrothal Gifts,* Overseas Missionary Fellowship, 1978. Contributor to journals and newspapers.

*WORK IN PROGRESS:* Several books.

*SIDELIGHTS:* Michael C. Griffiths has travelled widely in the Far East, Europe, Australia, New Zealand, South Africa, and North America. He speaks Japanese fairly well, and knows some German. Editions of his books have been published in German, Chinese, Japanese, Indonesian, Vietnamese, Urdu, French, Portuguese, Dutch, Swedish, Hungarian, and Korean.

\* \* \*

## GRIMES, Joseph E(vans) 1928-

*PERSONAL:* Born December 10, 1928, in Elizabeth, N.J.; son of Homer Winder (a minister) and Ruby (Evans) Grimes; married Barbara Fornasero (a missionary-linguist), March 1, 1952; children: Marilyn Kay, Charles Edward, Keith Douglas. *Education:* Wheaton College, Wheaton, Ill., B.A., 1950; Cornell University, M.A., 1958, Ph.D., 1960. *Religion:* Christian. *Office:* Department of Modern Languages and Linguistics, Cornell University, Ithaca, N.Y. 14853.

*CAREER:* Summer Institute of Linguistics, Mexico City, Mexico, field investigator and consultant, 1950—; Cornell University, Ithaca, N.Y., associate professor, 1967-76, professor of linguistics, 1976—. *Member:* Linguistic Society of America, American Anthropological Association, Association for Computational Linguistics, Asociacion de Linguistica y Filologia de la America Latina, Association for Computing Machinery.

*WRITINGS:* (With John B. McIntosh) *Huichol-Spanish Dictionary,* Summer Institute of Linguistics (Mexico), 1954; *Huichol Syntax,* Mouton, 1964; (translator) *Huichol New Testament,* American Bible Society, 1968; *Phonological Analysis,* Summer Institute of Linguistics, 1969; (editor) *Languages of the Guianas,* Summer Institute of Linguistics, 1972; *The Thread of Discourse,* Mouton, 1975; *Network Grammars,* Summer Institute of Linguistics, 1975. Contributor of articles to *Language, International Journal of Linguistics, American Anthropologist,* and other journals.

*WORK IN PROGRESS: Language Variation and Limits to Communication,* with Gary Simons.

*SIDELIGHTS:* Grimes has travelled in Mexico, Colombia, Surinam, Brazil, Chile, Argentina, Paraguay, India, Nepal, Indonesia, Australia, New Guinea, the Philippines, Ghana, Ivory Coast, Papua, and Nigeria, and is fluent in Huichol and Spanish.

\* \* \*

## GROENE, Janet 1936-

*PERSONAL:* Born May 6, 1936, in Hudson, N.Y.; daughter of Irving E. and Ida E. (Maycock) Hawkins; married Gordon H. Groene (a writer-photographer), April 16, 1955. *Education:* Attended Baldwin-Wallace College, 1953-55; also attended Youngstown University and Danville Junior College. *Religion:* Lutheran-Missouri Synod. *Address:* c/o David McKay Co., 750 Third Ave., New York, N.Y. 10017.

*WRITINGS: Cooking on the Go,* Grosset, 1971; *The Galley Book,* McKay, 1977; (with husband, Gordon H. Groene) *Living aboard Your Recreation Vehicle,* McKay, 1978. Contributor of articles to boating, camping, and aviation magazines, and other publications. Editor, *Heritage of Vermilion County,* 1964-66; contributing editor, *Rudder,* 1970—.

*WORK IN PROGRESS: Preventative Boat Maintenance,* with husband, Gordon H. Groene.

*SIDELIGHTS:* The Groenes lived aboard their twenty-nine-foot sailboat for four years, then they added a motorhome and lived on the go for five more years on both land and sea. They have now chosen a home base in central Florida as a workshop/office and continue travels by boat, recreation vehicle, and air.

\* \* \*

## GROSSMAN, Jean Schick 1894-1972
### (Alice Barr Grayson)

1894—October 29, 1972; American authority on education and family life. *Obituaries: New York Times,* October 30, 1972.

\* \* \*

## GRUMELLI, Antonio 1928-

*PERSONAL:* Born January 17, 1928, in Alanno, Pescara, Italy; son of Leonardo (a government employee) and Rosaria (Aromatario) Grumelli. *Education:* Catholic University of the Sacred Heart, Milan, Dr. (political and social science), 1956; Pontifical Lateran University, Dr. (canon law), 1958; Columbia University, additional study in sociology, 1960-61. *Home:* Liberazione 53, Chieti, Italy 166100. *Office:* Secretariat for Non-Believers, Vatican City, Rome, Italy 00120.

*CAREER:* Ordained a Roman Catholic diocesan priest, 1950; University of Chieti, Chieti, Italy, professor of sociology, 1965—; The Vatican, Rome, Italy, undersecretary of Secretariat for Non-Believers, 1966—; Papal Urban University, Rome, professor of sociology, 1974—. Convener of First International Symposium on "The Culture of Unbelief," Rome, 1969; rapporteur at other international and national congresses in Los Angeles, Yugoslavia, and elsewhere. *Member:* International Sociological Association, Conference Internationale de Sociologie Religieuse, American Sociological Association, Society for the Scientific Study of Religion, Centro Nazionale di Difesa e Prevenzione Sociale. *Awards, honors:* Commendatore of Republic of Italy (special title, bestowed by President of Italy).

*WRITINGS: Aspetti sociologici dell'evoluzione demografica in Abruzzo,* Editoriale Cultura e Documentazione, 1960; *Problemi socio-economici della montagna,* Unione Nazionale Comuni ed Enti Montani, 1961; *Sociologia del Cattolicismo,* Anonima Veritas Editrice, 1965; *Mondo in trasformazione,* Anonima Veritas Editrice, 1965; *Problematica pastorale,* Anonima Veritas Editrice, 1966; *Amicizia e socialita,* Anonima Veritas Editrice, 1967; (with others) *L'Uomo oggi,* Anonima Veritas Editrice, 1968; (with others)

*Ateismo e secolarizzazione,* Cittadella Editrice, 1969; (with others) *Il Divorzio in una societa democratica,* Scuola Editrice, 1969; (with others) *Dialogo ad una svolta,* Edizioni Pastorali, 1969.

*Il Prete nella citta secolare,* Anonima Veritas Editrice, 1971; (editor with Rocco Caporale) *The Culture of Unbelief: Studies and Proceedings from the First International Symposium on Belief, Rome,* University of California Press, 1971; (with others) *L'Educazione familiare oggi,* Scuola Editrice, 1972; *Ateismo, secolarizzazione e dialogo,* Anonima Veritas Editrice, 1974; *Pastorale e promozione umana,* Carabba, 1976; (with others) *Giovani e futuro della fede,* Studium, 1977.

*SIDELIGHTS:* Antonio Grumelli's prime interest as undersecretary of the Secretariat for Non-Believers (Vatican) "is the promotion of the scientific study of the phenomenon of contemporary unbelief and of promoting an open dialogue between Christians and those not affiliated with any particular religion or religious body."

\*        \*        \*

## GRUN, Bernard 1901-1972

1901—December 28, 1972; Czech-born English composer, conductor, editor, translator, and author of books on composers and on other musical topics. Obituaries: *New York Times,* December 29, 1972.

\*        \*        \*

## GRUNDSTEIN, Nathan D(avid) 1913-

*PERSONAL:* Born September 19, 1913, in Ashland, Ohio; son of Samuel Lewis (a scrap dealer) and Rose (Kolinsky) Grundstein; married Dorothy Deborah Davis, November 12, 1938; children: Miriam (Mrs. Bruce Levin), Margaret (Mrs. Rachmat Kartadjoemena), Leon D., Robert H. *Education:* Ohio State University, B.A., 1935, M.Sc., 936; Syracuse University, Ph.D., 1943; George Washington University, LL.B. (converted to J.D.), 1951. *Religion:* Jewish. *Home:* 2872 Washington Blvd., Cleveland Heights, Ohio 44118. *Office:* School of Management, Case Western Reserve University, Cleveland, Ohio 441106.

*CAREER:* U.S. Government, Washington, D.C., posts in Office of Solicitor, Department of Agriculture, 1939-40, and Food and Drug Administration, 1940-41, administrative assistant and analyst in Labor Division, Office of Production Management, 1941-43, assistant to vice-chairman for labor production, 1943-45, principal policy analyst, Office of the Executive Secretary, War Production Board, 1945-47; Wayne State University, Detroit, Mich., assistant professor, 1947-49, associate professor, 1949-54, professor of public law and administration, 1954-58; University of Pittsburgh, Graduate School of Public and International Affairs, Pittsburgh, Pa., visiting professor, 1958-60, professor of administration, 1960-64; Case Western Reserve University, Cleveland, Ohio, professor of public management science, 1964-68, professor of political science, 1968-70, professor of management, 1968—, director of graduate program in public management science, 1964—, chairman of policy committee, School of Management, 1969-70. Consultant to numerous federal departments, and state and local governments on a wide range of issues, projects, and programs.

*MEMBER:* Institute of Management Sciences, Society for General Systems Research, Urban and Regional Information Systems Association, American Society for Political and Legal Philosophy, Phi Beta Kappa, Order of the Coif.

*WRITINGS: General Management of Michigan State Government* (monograph), Detroit Bureau of Governmental Research, c.1950; (editor with J. Forrester Davison) *Administrative Law: Cases and Readings,* Bobbs-Merrill, 1952; *Presidential Delegation of Authority in Wartime* (collection of articles originally published in *George Washington Law Review*), University of Pittsburgh Press, 1961; (editor with Davison) *Administrative Law and the Regulatory System,* Lerner Law Book Co., 1966, revised edition, 1968; *Ethical Decisions of City Managers,* International City Management Association, 1968.

Contributor: *Industrial Mobilization for War,* Volume I, U.S. Government Printing Office, 1947; Harold D. Lasswell and Harlan Cleveland, editors, *Ethics and Bigness,* Harper, 1962; A. G. Feldt, editor, *Selected Papers on Operational Gaming,* Center for Housing and Environmental Studies, Cornell University, 1966; H. J. Schmandt and Warner Bloomberg, editors, *The Quality of Urban Life,* Sage Publications, 1969; J. E. Rickert and S. L. Hale, editors, *Urban and Regional Information Systems: Past, Present, and Future,* Urban and Regional Information Systems Association, 1970; F. G. Brown and T. P. Murphy, editors, *Emerging Patterns in Urban Administration,* Heath, 1970. Co-author of monographs on regulatory procedure for U.S. Department of Agriculture, 1940-41. Contributor to legal and urban affairs journals.

*WORK IN PROGRESS: Law and the Adaptation of Enterprise Management;* research project on the future as an adaptive concept.

*SIDELIGHTS:* Nathan Grundstein told *CA:* "My professional education, my occupation as a university academic, and my experience in consulting and public employment, has always crossed both management and law. The power of these two fields of learning and practice is their focus on the regulation of humans. It is not management technology nor administrative law, but the regulation of humans that is the ground of all my writings. I have finally moved to that level of understanding where I am able to deal directly with some of the fundamentals of humans in relation to the morality and design of systems of human regulation. My object is to establish a foundation whereby humans may be enabled to enlarge their own regulative capabilities as against imposed systems for their regulation."

\*        \*        \*

## GUERNSEY, James Lee 1923-

*PERSONAL:* Born June 22, 1923, in Henryville, Ind.; son of Thomas (a farmer) and Cloe (Turner) Guernsey; married Ruth Schulthise (a teacher), August 18, 1946; children: Ernest, Carol. *Education:* Indiana State Teachers College (now Indiana State University), B.S., 1947; Indiana University, M.A., 1948; Northwestern University, Ph.D., 1953. *Politics:* Independent. *Religion:* Protestant. *Home:* 4221 Hulman St., Terre Haute, Ind. 47803. *Office:* Department of Geography, Indiana State University, Terre Haute, Ind. 47809.

*CAREER:* Indiana State Teachers College (now Indiana State University), Terre Haute, instructor, 1948-51, assistant professor of geography, 1951-53; University of Louisville, Louisville, Ky., assistant professor, 1953-56, associate professor of geography, 1956-57; Indiana State University, associate professor, 1957-60, professor of geography, 1960—, director of River Basin Research Center, 1961—. Consultant to numerous energy and environmental groups. *Military service:* U.S. Army Air Forces, 1942-45. *Member:*

Association of American Geographers, Sigma Xi, Gamma Theta Upsilon, Phi Kappa Phi.

*WRITINGS: Our Physical Environment,* University of Louisville Press, 1957; *Principles of Geography,* Barron's, 1959, revised edition, 1976; *Principles of Physical Geography,* Barron's, 1964; *Conserving American Resources,* Prentice-Hall, 1972. Contributor of over sixty articles to professional journals.

*WORK IN PROGRESS:* Research on state and national land use policies and surface mining reclamation programs.

\*     \*     \*

## GUNN, Neil M(iller)   1891-1973

November 8, 1891—January 15, 1973; Scottish playwright, novelist, and short story writer. Obituaries: *New York Times,* January 17, 1973.

\*     \*     \*

## GUTENBERG, Arthur W(illiam)   1920-

*PERSONAL:* Born November 10, 1920, in Darmstadt, Germany; son of Beno and Hertha (Dernburg) Gutenberg; married Natalie Shapiro, February 9, 1947 (divorced October, 1973); married Barbara H. Frankling, August, 1974; children: (first marriage) Jeff S. and Arlan P. (twins), Lee F., Susan B. and Diane H. (twins). *Education:* University of California, Berkeley, B.A.S. (engineering), 1942, B.S. (business administration), 1946, M.B.A., 1947; Stanford University, Ph.D., 1955. *Address:* P.O. Box 278, San Gabriel, Calif. 91778. *Office:* Department of Management, University of Southern California, University Park, Los Angeles, Calif. 90007.

*CAREER:* Fresno State College (now California State University, Fresno), Fresno, Calif., instructor in business administration, 1948-51; Arizona State University, Tempe, assistant professor of business administration, 1951-60, director, Bureau of Business Services, 1951-57; University of Southern California, Los Angeles, associate professor, 1960-69, professor of management, 1969—, coordinator of graduate studies for minorities, 1971-77. Consulting editor, Intext. Has also been an editor and a business executive. *Military service:* U.S. Army, 1942-45; became first lieutenant. *Member:* American Statistical Association (member of national council, 1970), American Economic Association, American Academy of Management, American Academy for the Advancement of Science, American Association of University Professors, Southern California Statistical Association (president, 1968-69).

*WRITINGS:* (With Val Albrecht) *Profitable Studio Management,* Amphoto Publishing, 1964, 2nd edition, 1972; (with Gene Richman) *Dynamics of Management,* Intext, 1968; *Pharmacy Management,* University of Southern California Press, 1976. Contributor of over sixty articles to scholarly journals in the United States and abroad.

*WORK IN PROGRESS:* An applied management book for practicing managers.

*AVOCATIONAL INTERESTS:* Photography, stamp collecting, travel, books on history, anthropology, and behavior.

\*     \*     \*

## GUTHRIE, Judith Bretherton   1905(?)-1972

1905(?)—July 25, 1972; English opera singer, playwright, and widow of Sir Tyrone Guthrie. Obituaries: *New York Times,* July 26, 1972.

# H

## HAAS, Michael 1938-

*PERSONAL:* Born March 26, 1938, in Detroit, Mich.; son of Mark Leo (a broadcaster) and Isabelle (Helm) Haas. *Education:* Stanford University, B.A., 1959, Ph.D., 1964; Yale University, M.A., 1960. *Home:* 469 Ena Rd., Apt. 2903, Honolulu, Hawaii 96815. *Office:* Department of Political Science, University of Hawaii, Honolulu, Hawaii 96822.

*CAREER:* University of Hawaii, Honolulu, assistant professor, 1964-67, associate professor, 1967-71, professor of political science, 1971—. *Member:* American Political Science Association, International Political Science Association, International Studies Association, Peace Science Society.

*WRITINGS:* (With Henry S. Kariel) *Approaches to the Study of Political Science,* text edition, Chandler Publishing, 1970; (compiler) *International Organization: An Interdisciplinary Bibliography,* Hoover Institution, 1973; (editor) *International Systems: A Behavioral Approach,* text edition, Chandler Publishing, 1974; *International Conflict,* text edition, Bobbs-Merrill, 1974; *Basic Documents of Asian Regional Organizations,* four volumes, Oceana, 1974. Contributor to political science journals.

\*     \*     \*

## HAAS, Raymond Michael 1935-

*PERSONAL:* Born February 13, 1935, in Bordentown, N.J.; son of Joseph Luther (an expediter) and Helen Victoria (Hartmann) Haas; married Mary Elizabeth Ryan (a teacher), August 29, 1959; children: Joseph Raymond, Jeanne Marie, Jennifer Ann, Lauretta Mary. *Education:* Rider College, B.S., 1956; Lehigh University, M.B.A., 1958; Indiana University, D.B.A., 1961. *Residence:* Morgantown, W.Va. *Office:* Stewart Hall, West Virginia University, Morgantown, W.Va. 26506.

*CAREER:* West Virginia University, Morgantown, assistant dean of College of Business and Economics, 1967-68, acting dean, 1968-69, assistant to the president, 1969-71, provost for planning, 1971—. Member, Common Council of Morgantown and citizens advisory committee of Planning Commission of Morgantown; chairman, Monongalia County Planning Commission, and Morgantown Housing Authority; president, West Virginia League of Municipalities. *Military service:* U.S. Air National Guard, 1953-61; became

staff sergeant. *Member:* American Marketing Association, Society for College and University Planning, Beta Gamma Sigma.

*WRITINGS: Long-Range Planning for Small Businesses,* Indiana University Press, 1964; *Long-Range New Product Planning in Business: A Conceptual Model,* West Virginia University, 1965; *Science, Technology, and Marketing,* American Marketing Association, 1966. Contributor to *Planning for Higher Education.* Member of editorial board, *Appalachian Review;* member of advisory board, *Victorian Poetry.*

\*     \*     \*

## HABLUTZEL, Philip 1935-

*PERSONAL:* Surname is accented on first syllable; born August 23, 1935, in Flagstaff, Ariz.; son of Charles Edward (a physicist) and Electa (Cain) Hablutzel; married Diane Gregart Duvel, October 11, 1963 (divorced, 1968). *Education:* Louisiana State University, B.A., 1958; attended University of Heidelberg, 1959-60, 1962-64; University of Chicago, M.A., 1961, J.D., 1967. *Politics:* Republican. *Home:* 5631 South Dorchester Ave., Chicago, Ill. 60637.

*CAREER:* Office of Economic Opportunity, Chicago Regional Office, Chicago, Ill., deputy director of regional legal services, 1966, acting director, 1967; American Bar Foundation, Chicago, Ill., research attorney, 1967-68, senior research attorney, 1968-71; Chicago-Kent College of Law, Illinois Institute of Technology, Chicago, Ill., assistant professor of trusts and corporations, beginning 1971. Lecturer, in psychology and urban sociology, City Colleges of Chicago, 1967-71; member of board of directors, Hyde Park-Kenwood Community Conference, 1971-74.

*MEMBER:* American Bar Association, American Judicature Society, Law and Society Association, American Psychology-Law Society, National Organization on Legal Problems of Education, Association of American Law Schools, American Political Science Association (founding member of conference group on German politics), American Association for the Advancement of Science, American Civil Liberties Union (member of Illinois board of directors, 1970—), Illinois State Bar Association, Chicago Bar Association, Chicago Council of Lawyers, Chicago Audubon Society (member, board of directors, 1972—).

*WRITINGS:* (With Julian H. Levi, Louis Rosenberg, and

James White) *Model Residential Landlord-Tenant Code,* American Bar Foundation, 1969; (with Ray Garrett and Willard P. Scott) *Model Business Corporation Act Annotated,* three volumes, West Publishing, 2nd edition (Hablutzel was not associated with earlier edition), 1971; *Teleclass Study Guide for Business 211: Business Law,* City Colleges of Chicago, 1974. Contributor to *Journal of Property Management.* Editor of Audubon Society journal, 1973—.

*WORK IN PROGRESS: Legal Problems of Public School Teaching;* preparing television scripts for a course in business law for Chicago Television College.

*AVOCATIONAL INTERESTS:* Photography.†

\* \* \*

## HACHEY, Thomas E(ugene) 1938-

*PERSONAL:* Born June 8, 1938, in Lewiston, Me.; son of Leo Joseph and Margaret M. (Johnson) Hachey; married Jane Beverly Whitman (an administrative assistant and editor), June 9, 1962. *Education:* St. Francis College, B.A. (cum laude), 1960; Niagara University, M.A., 1961; St. John's University, Ph.D., 1965. *Politics:* Independent. *Religion:* Anglican. *Home:* 663 North 75th St., Wauwatosa, Wis. 53233. *Office:* Department of History, Marquette University, Milwaukee, Wis. 53213.

*CAREER:* Marquette University, Milwaukee, Wis., instructor, 1964-65, assistant professor, 1965-69, associate professor, 1969-76, professor of Anglo-Irish history, 1976—. Visiting professor at School of Irish Studies, Dublin, summer, 1970-1972. *Member:* American Historical Association, Conference of British History, American Committee for Irish Studies (treasurer, 1971—).

*WRITINGS:* (With Ralph Weber) *Voices of Revolution: Rebels and Rhetoric,* Dryden, 1972; (editor) *The Problem of Partition: Peril to World Peace,* Rand McNally, 1972; (editor) *Anglo-Vatican Relations, 1914-1939: Annual Reports of the British Minister to the Holy See,* G. K. Hall, 1972; *Confidential Dispatches,* New University Press, 1974; *Britain and Irish Separatism: From the Fenians to the Free State,* Rand McNally, 1977. Contributor of articles to *Irish University Review, Eire-Ireland, Church History, Journal of Church and State, Wisconsin Magazine of History, Journal of International Relations, Journal of Negro History,* and other journals.

*WORK IN PROGRESS:* A monograph in progress on Anglo-Irish relations, tentatively entitled *A Dominion Departs the Commonwealth: The Irish Secession, 1937-48.*

\* \* \*

## HACKETT, Marie G. 1923-

*PERSONAL:* Born June 25, 1923, in Boston, Mass.; daughter of Timothy A. (an engineer) and Mary (Reardon) Gannon; married Paul Hackett (an author), September 27, 1944; children: Christine, Regina (Mrs. Paul O'Neil), John, Paula. *Education:* Emmanuel College, Boston, Mass., B.A., 1944; University of California, Santa Barbara, M.A., 1965; University of California, Berkeley, Ph.D., 1968. *Politics:* Democrat. *Religion:* Catholic.

*CAREER:* Mount St. Mary College, Los Angeles, Calif., English teacher, 1956-58; Santa Paula High School, Santa Paula, Calif., English teacher, 1962-66; University of California, Berkeley, research educator, 1968-69; Florida State University, Tallahassee, assistant professor of educational psychology, beginning 1969. *Member:* International Reading Association, National Council of Teachers of English,

American Psychological Association, American Association for the Advancement of Science, American Educational Research Association.

*WRITINGS: The Cliff's Edge* (autobiographical), McGraw, 1954; *Success in the Classroom: An Approach to Instruction,* Holt, 1971. Contributor of articles to *Redbook, Reader's Digest,* and professional journals.

*WORK IN PROGRESS:* A book, *Design of Instruction;* professional and popular articles related to a study of the reading abilities of 20,000 students.

*SIDELIGHTS:* Marie Hackett's interest is to show that minority or economically disadvantaged students are able to learn as well and with as much competence as middle and upper class children. She believes that learning depends upon a proper diagnostic instructional program. She is also interested in the higher educational opportunities for women and the opportunities open to them as a result of their education.†

\* \* \*

## HAGAN, Charles B(anner) 1905-

*PERSONAL:* Born January 27, 1905, in Irwin, Va.; son of Patrick C. (a farmer) and Nannie (Dingus) Hagan; married Dorothy Veinus (a professor), April 18, 1938; children: Patricia Gray Hagan Kuwayama, John Lee. *Education:* Emory and Henry College, A.B., 1926; University of Virginia, A.M., 1928; Harvard University, graduate study, 1931-32; Duke University, Ph.D., 1933. *Home:* 1400 Hermann Dr., Houston, Tex. 77004.

*CAREER:* Emory and Henry College, Emory, Va., instructor in history and economics, 1928-29; Duke University, Durham, N.C., graduate assistant in economics, 1930-31; University of Illinois, Urbana, instructor, 1934-35, assistant professor, 1937-46, associate professor, 1946-52, professor of political science, 1952-67; Smith College, Northampton, Mass., instructor in political science, 1935-37; University of Houston, Houston, Tex., professor of political science, 1967-75. Visiting lecturer in political science, Harvard University, 1942-44; Fulbright lecturer, Sydney, Australia, 1957-58, 1966; visiting professor of political science, Duke University, 1971-72. Intelligence officer, U.S. Department of State, 1951-52. *Member:* American Political Science Association, American Association of University Professors, Australian Political Studies Association, Midwestern Political Science Association, Southern Political Science Association, Phi Beta Kappa. *Awards, honors:* Carnegie fellow in international law, 1931-32.

*WRITINGS:* (With Neil Garvey) *Blueprint for America,* Science Research Associates, 1954, 2nd edition, 1967; (with E. S. Redford) *American Government and the Economy,* Macmillan, 1965. Contributor of articles to political science, history, and law journals.

\* \* \*

## HAGE, Jerald 1932-

*PERSONAL:* Surname rhymes with "vague"; born September 27, 1932, in St. Paul, Minn.; son of Jewell Thore (a manager) and Margaret (Rhuel) Hage; married Madeleine Cottenet, January 27, 1966; children: Martin, Rebecca. *Education:* University of Wisconsin, B.B.A., 1955; Columbia University, Ph.D., 1963. *Religion:* Catholic. *Home:* 1909 Carver St., Madison, Wis. 53713. *Office:* Department of Sociology, University of Wisconsin, Madison, Wis. 53706.

*CAREER:* University of Wisconsin—Madison, 1963—, began as lecturer, professor of sociology, 1971—. *Military service:* U.S. Navy, 1955-58; became lieutenant junior grade. *Member:* American Sociological Association, American Social History Association.

*WRITINGS:* (With Michael Aiken) *Social Change in Complex Organizations,* Random House, 1970; *Techniques and Problems in Theory Construction in Sociology,* Wiley, 1972; (with Koya Azumi) *Organizational Systems: A Text-Reader in the Sociology of Organizations,* D. C. Heath, 1972; *An Organizational Theory of Cybernetic Control,* Wiley, 1974; (with Aiken and others) *Coordinating Human Services,* Jossey-Bass, 1975. Associate editor of *Administrative Science Quarterly,* 1968-71, and *Social Forces,* 1972—.

*WORK IN PROGRESS: Theories of Organizations, Statics and Dynamics; The Rise of the Welfare State in Western Europe 1871-1971,* with Edward Gargan and Robert Hanneman.

*SIDELIGHTS:* Jerald Hage's long-term objective is to help underdeveloped countries become more developed in the way *they* desire.

*       *       *

## HAIDU, Peter 1931-

*PERSONAL:* Born March 7, 1931, in Paris, France; married Marilene Edrei, January 25, 1968; children: Rachel, Noah. *Education:* University of Chicago, B.A., 1951; Columbia University, Ph.D., 1966. *Office:* Department of French, University of Illinois, Urbana, Ill. 61801.

*CAREER:* Columbia University, New York, N.Y., instructor in French, 1960-68; Yale University, New Haven, Conn., assistant professor of French, 1968-72; University of Virginia, Charlottesville, associate professor of French, 1972-74; University of Illinois at Urbana-Champaign, professor of French, 1974—. *Military service:* U.S. Army, 1953-55.

*WRITINGS: Aesthetic Distance in Chretien de Troyes: Irony and Comedy in Cliges and Perceval,* Droz (Geneva), 1968; *Lion-queue-coupee: L'Ecart symbolique chez Chretien de Troyes,* Droz, 1972; (editor) *Approaches to Medieval Romance,* Yale French Studies, Yale University, 1974.

*WORK IN PROGRESS: Semiotics of Medieval Narrative.*

*       *       *

## HAIMAN, Franklyn S(aul) 1921-

*PERSONAL:* Surname is pronounced *Hay*-man; born June 23, 1921, in Cleveland, Ohio; son of Alfred W. (an attorney) and Stella (Weiss) Haiman; married Louise Goble, June 11, 1955; children: Mark, Eric. *Education:* Western Reserve University (now Case Western Reserve University), A.B., 1942; Northwestern University, M.A., 1946, Ph.D., 1948. *Politics:* Democrat. *Home:* 824 Ingleside Pl., Evanston, Ill. 60201. *Office:* Department of Communication Studies, Northwestern University, 1822 Sheridan Rd., Evanston, Ill. 60201.

*CAREER:* Northwestern University, Evanston, Ill., 1948—, began as instructor, currently professor of communication studies and urban affairs. *Member:* American Civil Liberties Union (chairman of Illinois division, 1964-75; member of national board of directors, 1967—; national secretary, 1976—), Speech Communication Association (chairman of Commission on Freedom of Speech, 1961-65, 1971-72), American Psychological Association, American

Association of University Professors, Phi Beta Kappa. *Awards, honors:* Intellectual Freedom Award, Illinois Library Association, 1967; Outstanding Scholarly Article award, Speech Communication Association, 1967-72.

*WRITINGS: Group Leadership and Democratic Action,* Houghton, 1951; (with Dean C. Barnlund) *The Dynamics of Discussion,* Houghton, 1960; *Freedom of Speech: Issues and Cases,* Random House, 1965; *Freedom of Speech,* National Textbook Co., 1976. Contributor of articles to *Quarterly Journal of Speech, Speech Monographs, Journal of Communication, Journal of Social Psychology, Northwestern University Law Review,* and other journals.

*WORK IN PROGRESS: Communication in America: Freedom and Restraint.*

*       *       *

## HAIMOWITZ, Morris L(oeb) 1918-

*PERSONAL:* Born June 5, 1918, in New York, N.Y.; son of Sam and Frieda (Paster) Haimowitz; married Natalie Reader (a psychologist), December 31, 1948; children: Carla, Myrna, Louise. *Education:* University of Florida, B.A., 1941, M.A., 1942; University of Chicago, Ph.D., 1951; also attended University of Hawaii and Harvard University. *Home and office:* 1101 Forest Ave., Evanston, Ill. 60202.

*CAREER:* Chicago City College, Wright Branch (now Wright Junior College), Chicago, Ill., social psychologist, 1950-55, 1957-60; Chicago Public Schools, Chicago, assistant director, 1960-61, director of human relations, 1961-67; Chicago City Colleges, Chicago, coordinator of adult education, 1967-69; professor of social sciences, Wright and Loop branches, 1969—. Co-director, Haimowoods Institute, 1973—. Consultant to many organizations. *Military service:* U.S. Army Air Forces, 1942-46; became first lieutenant; received Bronze Star Medal. *Member:* International Transactional Analysis Association (member of board of trustees, 1966-67), American Sociological Association, Phi Beta Kappa. *Awards, honors:* Recipient of various social science research grants.

*WRITINGS:* (Editor with wife, Natalie Haimowitz) *Human Development: Selected Readings,* Crowell, 1958, 3rd edition, 1968; (with N. Haimowitz) *Suffering Is Optional: The Myth of the Innocent Bystander,* Haimowoods Press, 1977. Author with N. Haimowitz of "Child Psychology," Chicago Public Schools, 1960-68. Contributor of articles to sociology journals.

*WORK IN PROGRESS: Research on the effects of psychotherapy on behavior.*

*       *       *

## HAINES, Gail Kay 1943-

*PERSONAL:* Born March 15, 1943, in Mt. Vernon, Ill.; daughter of Samuel Glen (an atomic plant foreman) and Audrey (Goin) Beekman; married Michael Philip Haines (an oral surgeon), May 8, 1964; children: David Michael, Cindy Lynn. *Education:* Washington University, St. Louis, Mo., A.B., 1965. *Home:* 4145 Lorna Court S.E., Olympia, Wash. 98503.

*CAREER:* Mallinckrodt Chemical Works, St. Louis, Mo., analytical chemist, 1965-66; writer, 1969—.

*WRITINGS—All juvenile: The Elements,* F. Watts, 1972; *Fire,* Morrow, 1975; *Explosives,* Morrow, 1976; *Supercold/Superhot,* F. Watts, 1976; *What Makes a Lemon Sour?,* Morrow, 1977.

*WORK IN PROGRESS: Poison; Human Intelligence.*

*SIDELIGHTS:* Gail Kay Haines writes: "I have always been fascinated by science, especially reading and writing about it. Chemistry is my favorite, because it is the science I know the most about, but writing books keeps me learning all kinds of things from up-to-minute research to ancient history. I think children want more than just the basic science information they get in school—they want to know what is going on today and what the future holds, and that is what other juvenile non-fiction writers and I try to explore."

\* \* \*

## HALL, Elizabeth Cornelia 1898-

*PERSONAL:* Born March 17, 1898, in Meriden, Conn.; daughter of Arthur Elisha (a chemical engineer) and Mabel Edith (David) Hall. *Education:* Radcliffe College, A.B., 1921; School of Horticulture, Ambler, Penn., diploma, 1922-24; Columbia University, M.S., 1928. *Politics:* Republican. *Religion:* Congregationalist. *Home:* 2976 Marion Ave., Bronx, N.Y. 10458. *Office:* Horticultural Society of New York, 128 West 58th St., New York, N.Y. 10019.

*CAREER:* Horticultural Society of New York, New York City, head librarian, 1930-37, senior librarian, 1968—; New York Botanical Garden, New York City, head librarian, 1937-64, associate curator of education, 1965-67, librarian emeritus, 1968—. *Member:* English Speaking Union, Horticultural Society of New York, Garden Club of America, Society of Woman Geographers, Torrey Botanical Club. *Awards, honors:* Horticultural citation from American Horticultural Society, 1969; Men's Garden Club of New York, Woman Gardener of the Year award, 1969.

*WRITINGS: Printed Books: 1481-1900 in the Horticultural Society of New York,* Horticultural Society of New York, 1970. Contributor of book reviews to *Library Journal, New York Botanical Garden, Garden Magazine, Monthly Bulletin* of Horticultural Society of New York, and *Reprint Bulletin.*

*SIDELIGHTS:* For the past ten years Elizabeth Cornelia Hall has been an assistant guide on numerous garden tours in the United States, the Orient, Europe, the West Indies, Mexico, and South America.

\* \* \*

## HALL, Thor 1927-

*PERSONAL:* Given name is pronounced Tor; born March 15, 1927, in Larvik, Norway; son of Jens Martin (a master builder) and Margit Elvira (Petersen) Hall; married Gerd Hellstroem, July 15, 1950; children: Jan Tore. *Education:* University of Oslo, Ex. Art., 1946; Scandinavian Methodist Seminary, Dipl. Th., 1950; Selly Oak College, graduate study, 1950-51; Duke University, M.R.E., 1959, Ph.D., 1962. *Home:* 1102 Montvale Circle, Signal Mountain, Tenn. 37377. *Office:* Department of Philosophy and Religion, University of Tennessee, Chattanooga, Tenn. 37401.

*CAREER:* Clergyman of United Methodist Church; assistant pastor and minister in Norway, 1946-47, 1951-53; Methodist Church in Norway, national director of Christian education, 1953-57; minister in Ansonville, N.C., 1958-59, and Durham, N.C., 1960-62; Duke University, Divinity School, Durham, assistant professor, 1962-68, associate professor of preaching and theology, 1968-72; University of Tennessee at Chattanooga, distinguished professor of religious studies, 1972—. Guest lecturer or preacher at U.S. military installations in the United States, Europe, and Turkey, and at Dav-

idson College, University of Miami, Wake Forest University, Randolph Macon College, and other institutions; James Sprunt Lecturer, Union Theological Seminary in Virginia, 1970; visiting professor, University of Oslo, spring, 1977. Member of General Board of Evangelism, United Methodist Church, 1969-72.

*MEMBER:* Society for the Scientific Study of Religion, American Academy of Religion, Society for Philosophy of Religion, Institute of Homiletical Studies of Western North Carolina Conference (vice-president, 1965-71). *Awards, honors:* American Association of Theological Schools faculty fellowship, 1968-69.

*WRITINGS: Jesu Laere om synd,* Norsk Forlagsselskap, 1958; (editor) *The Unfinished Pyramid: Ten Sermons by Charles P. Bowles,* Parthenon, 1967; (contributor) Richard A. Goodling, editor, *The Church's Ministry to the Homebound,* General Board of Education of Methodist Church, 1967; *A Theology of Christian Devotion,* Upper Room, 1969; *A Framework for Faith,* E. J. Brill, 1970; (contributor) Charles W. Kegley, editor, *The Philosophy and Theology of Anders Nygren,* Southern Illinois University Press, 1970; *The Future Shape of Preaching,* Fortress, 1971; *Whatever Happened to the Gospel,* Tidings, 1973; *Advent-Christmas,* Fortress, 1975; (contributor) Robert P. Clark, editor, *America in Crisis: The Human Implications of Two Hundred Years of Growth,* University of Tennessee at Chattanooga, 1976; (editor) *A Directory of Systematic Theologians in North America,* Council on the Study of Religion, 1977; *Anders Nygren,* Word, Inc., 1978. Contributor, *Kristelig Familiebok,* Forlaget Kristne Bokverk, 1957-58; contributor of about twenty articles to theology journals, including *Theology Today, Religion in Life, Christian Century,* and *Duke Divinity School Review.*

*WORK IN PROGRESS:* Writing on philosophy of religion, on systematic theology, and on Scandinavian religious thought; *Systematic Theology Today; Lift up Your Hearts; A History of the Interpretation of the Atonement,* a long-term project.

*AVOCATIONAL INTERESTS:* Golf, motoring, music, skiing.

*BIOGRAPHICAL/CRITICAL SOURCES: Duke Divinity School Bulletin,* November, 1962; *Religion och metafysik,* Diakonistyrelsens Bokfoerlag, 1966; Charles W. Kegley, editor, *The Philosophy and Theology of Anders Nygren,* Southern Illinois University Press, 1970; *Christian Century,* December 15, 1971; Benkt-Erik Benktson, *Adam-Vem Aer Du?,* Haakan Ohlson, 1976.

\* \* \*

## HALLO, William W. 1928-

*PERSONAL:* Born March 9, 1928, in Kassel, Germany; son of Rudolf (an art historian and curator) and Gertrude (Rubensohn) Hallo; married Edith Sylvia Pinto (in urban studies), June 22, 1952; children: Ralph Ethan, Jacqueline Louise. *Education:* Harvard University, B.A., (magna cum laude), 1950; University of Leiden, graduate study, 1950-51; University of Chicago, M.A., 1952, Ph.D., 1955. *Home:* 245 Blake Rd., Hamden, Conn. 06517. *Agent:* Georges Borchardt, Inc., 145 East 52nd St., New York, N.Y. 10022. *Office:* Babylonian Collection, Yale University, New Haven, Conn. 06520.

*CAREER:* University of Chicago, Oriental Institute, Chicago, Ill., research assistant, 1954-56; Hebrew Union College-Jewish Institute of Religion, Cincinnati, Ohio, instructor, 1956-58, assistant professor of Bible and Semitic languages, 1958-62; Yale University, New Haven, Conn., associate professor, 1962-65, professor of Assyriology, 1965-75, William M. Laffan Professor of Assyriology and Babylonian Literature, 1976—, assistant curator of Babylonian Collection, 1962-63, curator, 1963—. Delegate, Third World Congress of Jewish Studies, Jerusalem, Israel, 1961, Fourth World Congress, 1965, Sixth World Congress, 1973, and Seventh World Congress, 1977. *Member:* American Oriental Society (chairman of program committee, 1964, 1972; chairman of sectional committee for Ancient Near East, 1971-78), Society of Biblical Literature, Association for Jewish Studies (incorporator; member of executive committee, 1970-71; vice-president, 1972-74), Conference on Jewish Philosophy. *Awards, honors:* Fulbright scholar in the Netherlands, 1950-51; American Philosophical Society grants, 1961, 1965; Guggenheim fellow, 1965-66; M.A., Yale University, 1965.

*WRITINGS: Early Mesopotamian Royal Titles: A Philologic and Historical Analysis,* American Oriental Society, 1957; (contributor) Edward F. Campbell, Jr. and David Noel Freedman, editors, *Biblical Archaeologist Reader 2,* Doubleday, 1964; (contributor) Maurice Stanley Friedman, editor, *Worlds of Existentialism: A Critical Reader,* Random House, 1964; (contributor) David W. McKain, editor, *Christianity: Some Non-Christian Appraisals,* McGraw, 1964; (editor and contributor) *Essays in Memory of E. A. Speiser,* American Oriental Society, 1968; (with J.J.A. van Dijk) *The Exaltation of Inanna,* Yale University Press, 1968; (contributor) Leon Jick, editor, *The Teaching of Judaica in American Universities,* Ktav, 1970; (translator) Franz Rosenzweig, *The Star of Redemption* (translated from 2nd edition, published in 1930), Holt, 1971; (with William Kelley Simpson) *The Ancient Near East: A History,* Harcourt, 1971; (editor) *Tabulae Cuneiformes a F. M. Th. de Liagre Boehl Collectae,* Volume III: *Sumerian Archival Texts,* Netherlands Institute for the Near East, 1973.

Contributor to anniversary volumes for A. Leo Oppenheim, Benno Landsberger, W. F. Albright, Albrecht Goetze, F. M. Th. de Liagre Boehl, Theodore Gaster, I. J. Gelb, Thorkild Jacobsen, S. N. Kramer, A. Salonen, Tom Jones, H. L. Ginsberg, and J. J. Finkelstein.

Contributor to *Hebrew Union College Annual* and to encyclopedias and dictionaries of Hebrew and Bible studies; contributor of more than fifty articles and reviews to learned journals. Associate editor for American Oriental Society, 1965-71; Yale Near Eastern Researches, member of editorial committee, 1968—, editor, 1971—; member of editorial board, "Yale Oriental" series and "Babylonian Inscriptions . . . Nies" series, 1971—.

*WORK IN PROGRESS: The Royal Correspondence of Larsa; Sumerian Royal Hymns and Related Genres; The Pentateuch and Ancient Near Eastern Literature.*

*       *       *

## HALPERT, Stephen 1941-

*PERSONAL:* Born July 3, 1941, in Providence, R.I.; son of Robin (a philatelist) and Ruth (Silverstein) Halpert; married Melinda O'Donnell, 1962 (divorced, 1970); married Brenda Lyons (a poet), 1971 (divorced, 1978); children: (first marriage) Sean Michael. *Education:* Attended Emerson College, 1964. *Politics:* "Eclectic." *Home:* 314 Newtonville Ave., Newton, Mass. 02160. *Office: Fusion* Magazine, 909 Beacon St., Boston, Mass. 02215.

*CAREER:* D. C. Heath & Co., Boston, Mass., advertising coordinator in college department, 1964-66; Little, Brown & Co., Boston, sales and promotion manager in Law Book Division, 1966-67; Warren, Gorham & Lamont, Inc., Boston, director of Book Division, 1967-69; Financial Publishing Co., Boston, senior editor, 1969-70, director of Faneuil Press, 1969-70; *Fusion* (magazine), Boston, associate editor, 1969—; free-lance advertising and marketing consultant, 1970—. Publisher and co-editor of *Outpost* (magazine), 1977. Regional consultant, Law Science Institute, 1970-71; member of faculty, Cambridge Center for Adult Education, 1969.

*WRITINGS:* (Editor with Richard Johns) *A Return to Pagany: The History, Correspondence and Selections from a Little Magazine, 1929-1933,* introduction by Kenneth Rexroth, Beacon Press, 1969; (with Thomas Murry) *Witness of the Berrigans,* Doubleday, 1972; (with Brenda Halpert) *Brahmins and Bullyboys,* Houghton, 1973. Contributor to literary magazines and law journals. Editor, *Scribe,* 1963-64; managing editor, *Criminal Law Bulletin,* 1968-69; literary consultant, *Boston Review of the Arts,* 1970-71; co-editor, *New Age Spiritual Directory,* 1978.

*WORK IN PROGRESS: Music for a New Earth,* a book of poems; studies in the occult sciences; a play.

*       *       *

## HALSEY, Martha T. 1932-

*PERSONAL:* Born May 5, 1932, in Richmond, Va.; daughter of James D. and Martha (Taliaferro) Halsey. *Education:* Goucher College, A.B., 1954; State University of Iowa, M.A., 1956; Ohio State University, Ph.D., 1964. *Politics:* Democrat. *Religion:* Episcopalian. *Home:* 110 East Foster Ave., No. 503, State College, Pa. 16801. *Office:* Pennsylvania State University, 350 North Burrowes Building, University Park, Pa. 16802.

*CAREER:* Pennsylvania State University, University Park, assistant professor, 1964-70, associate professor of Spanish, 1970—. *Member:* American Association of Teachers of Spanish and Portuguese, Modern Language Association of America, American Association of University Professors. *Awards, honors:* American Philosophical Society grant, 1970.

*WRITINGS:* (Editor with Donald Bleznick) Buero Vallejo, *Madrugada,* text book edition, Ginn, 1969; *Antonio Buero Vallejo,* Twayne, 1973. Contributor of articles and reviews to literary journals including *Hispania, Romanic Review, Romance Notes, Comparative Literature Studies, Contemporary Literature,* and *Revista de Estudios Hispanicos.* Editorial associate, *Modern International Drama,* and *Kentucky Romance Quarterly.*

*WORK IN PROGRESS:* A study of the recent generation of Spanish playwrights, including Carlos Muniz, Antonio Gala, Ricardo Buded, Lauro Olmo, and Martin Recuerda.

*       *       *

## HALVERSON, William H(agen) 1930-

*PERSONAL:* Born July 28, 1930, in Sebeka, Minn.; son of Arthur William (a farmer) and Clara (Hagen) Halverson; married Marolyn Sortland, August 25, 1951; children: Lynn, Kay, Beth, Susan, Carol. *Education:* Augsburg Seminary (now Augsburg College), B.A., 1951, B.Th., 1955, Th.M., 1957; Princeton University, M.A., 1959, Ph.D., 1961. *Politics:* Independent. *Religion:* Lutheran. *Home:* 2330 Nayland Rd., Columbus, Ohio 43220. *Office:* University College, Ohio State University, 1050 Carmack Rd., Columbus, Ohio 43210.

*CAREER:* Princeton Theological Seminary, Princeton, N.J., instructor in philosophy, 1957-59; Augsburg College, Minneapolis, Minn., assistant professor, 1959-61, associate professor, 1961-65, professor of philosophy and chairman of department, 1959-67; Ohio State University, Columbus, associate dean of University College, 1967—. *Member:* American Philosophical Association, Mind Society.

*WRITINGS: A Concise Introduction to Philosophy,* Random House, 1967, 3rd edition, 1976. Contributor of articles to theology and philosophy journals, including *Mind, Journal of Religion,* and *Pacific Journal of Philosophy.*

\* \* \*

## HAMBLIN, Dora Jane 1920-

*PERSONAL:* Born June 15, 1920, in Bedford, Iowa; daughter of Allen W. (a newspaperman) and Grace (Sailor) Hamblin. *Education:* Coe College, B.A., 1941; Northwestern University, M.S., 1942. *Politics:* Independent. *Religion:* Protestant. *Home and office:* Villa Le Arcate, Trevignano Romano 00069, Italy. *Agent:* Paul R. Reynolds, Inc., 12 East 41st St., New York, N.Y. 10017.

*CAREER: Cedar Rapids Gazette,* Cedar Rapids, Iowa, reporter and photographer, 1942-44; American National Red Cross, began as "doughnut girl" in New Guinea and Germany, became public relations employee, 1944-47; *Life,* New York City, 1948-69, began as reporter, became correspondent in Paris, France, London, England, and Chicago, Ill., bureau chief in Rome, Italy, 1957-60, writer and staff writer in New York City, 1960-68, covered Space Center in Houston, Tex., 1968-69; free-lance writer living in Italy, 1969—. Etruscan expert for U.S. travel agencies. *Member:* Authors Guild, Theta Sigma Phi, Phi Beta Kappa. *Awards, honors:* D.Litt., Coe College, 1968.

*WRITINGS: Pots and Robbers,* Simon & Schuster, 1970; (with Gene Farmer) *First on the Moon: A Voyage with Neil Armstrong, Michael Collins, Edwin E. Aldrin, Jr.,* Little, Brown, 1970; (contributor) *Italy* (revised edition of book first published in 1961), Time-Life, 1972; (contributor) *Life before Man,* Time-Life, 1972; *Buried Cities and Ancient Treasures,* Simon & Schuster, 1973; *First Cities,* Time-Life, 1973; (with Mary Jane Grunsfield) *The Appian Way, a Journey,* Random House, 1974; *The Etruscans,* Time-Life, 1975; *That Was the LIFE,* Norton, 1977. Contributor to *Sports Illustrated, Smithsonian, Signature, Classic,* and other periodicals.

*WORK IN PROGRESS:* Articles for *Smithsonian;* research on Carthage; work on her memoir; *My Heart Belongs,* an autobiography of Mary Martin, for Morrow.

*SIDELIGHTS:* In a review of *That Was the LIFE,* a book about *Life* magazine, Jane Howard writes: "No two sets of *Life* memories will mesh. The phenomenon lasted 36 years, after all, and spanned the globe. Most of us, of course, had hearts of gold and winning wits behind our arrogant facades, but not all, and Hamblin isn't shy about saying who she thinks the exceptions were.... Gusto animates this memoir."

Dora Jane Hamblin began her love affair with Italy and with archaelogy, which "have come to dominate" her life, on a six-day leave from the Red Cross in 1947; she returned in 1969, built a villa on a lake, and became a free-lance writer. She told *CA:* "No doubt there is too much of beauty and fascination in any country for one lifetime to absorb, but I find it most poignantly true in Italy. I love to share my pleasure by writing about it for others."

*AVOCATIONAL INTERESTS:* Tennis, gardening.

*BIOGRAPHICAL/CRITICAL SOURCES: Life,* January 18, 1963, April 1, 1966, December 20, 1968; *New York Times,* April 20, 1970; *New York Times Book Review,* July 5, 1970, May 15, 1977.

\* \* \*

## HAMBURG, Carl H(einz) 1915-

*PERSONAL:* Born March 12, 1915, in Hindenburg, Germany; son of Sal and Jenny (Lewin) Hamburger; children: Darcy, Toni, Kai. *Education:* University of Breslau, certificates, 1934, 1935; University of Bordeaux, Diplome, 1936; Columbia University, M.A., 1940, Ph.D., 1948. *Home:* 1314 Audubon St., New Orleans, La. 70118. *Office:* Department of Philosophy, Tulane University, Tilton Hall, New Orleans, La. 70118.

*CAREER:* Worked as an editorial assistant in New York, N.Y., 1941-43; Tulane University, New Orleans, La., assistant professor, 1948-52, associate professor, 1953-59, professor of philosophy, 1960—. Summer visiting professor, Columbia University, 1964. Consultant to UNESCO and American University and field staff, and to Dartmouth College, 1964. *Military service:* U.S. Army, 1943-46; served in Pacific theater. *Member:* American Philosophical Association, Center for Study of American Institutions. *Awards, honors:* Carnegie research grant, 1949, 1951, 1957; Ford Foundation faculty fellowship, 1952-53; Tulane University research grant, 1960, 1969, 1977.

*WRITINGS:* (Contributor) Paul E. Schilpp, editor, *The Philosophy of E. Cassirer,* Northwestern University Press, 1949; *Symbol and Reality: Studies in the Philosophy of Ernst Cassirer,* Nijhoff, 1956, 2nd edition, 1970; (contributor) Silvano Arieti, editor, *American Handbook of Psychiatry,* Basic Books, 1959; (contributor) *UNESCO Dictionary of Social Science Concepts,* UNESCO, 1964; (contributor) *Cassirer's Philosophie—Begroff,* Kohlhammer, 1966; (contributor) Kahlman Silvert, editor, *The Social Reality of Scientific Myth,* American Universities Field Staff, 1969. Contributor of about two dozen articles to social science and philosophy journals.

*WORK IN PROGRESS:* Volume II of *Symbol and Reality.*

\* \* \*

## HAMBY, Alonzo L. 1940-

*PERSONAL:* Born January 13, 1940, in Humansville, Mo.; son of David A. (a merchant) and Lila (Summers) Hamby; married Joyce Ann Litton, June 6, 1967. *Education:* Southeast Missouri State College (now University), B.A., 1960; Columbia University, M.A., 1961; University of Missouri, Ph.D., 1965. *Politics:* Democrat. *Home:* 16 Euclid Dr., Athens, Ohio 45701. *Office:* Department of History, Ohio University, Athens, Ohio 45701.

*CAREER:* Ohio University, Athens, assistant professor, 1965-69, associate professor, 1969-75, professor of history, 1975—. Manuscript evaluator for Holmes & Meier, and several journals, reviews, and university presses. *Member:* American Historical Association, Organization of American Historians, Southern Historical Association, Ohio Academy of History, Phi Alpha Theta. *Awards, honors:* Woodrow Wilson fellow, 1960-61; National Defense Education Act fellow, 1962-64; Harry S Truman Institute grants, 1964, 1966, 1967, 1969; American Philosophical Society grant, 1967; Ohio University Research Fund grants, 1967, 1976; John C. Baker fellow, fall, 1969; National Endowment for the Humanities fellow, 1972-73; also recipient of David

D. Lloyd Prize, Ohio Academy of History Award, and Phi Alpha Theta First Book Award, all for *Beyond the New Deal: Harry S. Truman and American Liberalism.*

*WRITINGS:* (Editor) *The New Deal: Analysis and Interpretation,* Weybright, 1969; *Beyond the New Deal: Harry S. Truman and American Liberalism,* Columbia University Press, 1973; (editor) *Harry S. Truman and the Fair Deal,* Heath, 1974; *The Imperial Years: The United States since 1939,* Weybright, 1969; (editor) *Access to the Papers of Recent Public Figures: The New Harmony Conference,* Organization of American Historians for the Joint Committee on Historians and Archives, 1978. Contributor to *Encyclopaedia Britannica.* Contributor of articles and reviews to numerous periodicals, including *Review of Politics, Historian, Journal of American History,* and *American Historical Review.*

*WORK IN PROGRESS: Harry S. Truman: An Interpretative Biography; Makers of Contemporary Politics: FDR to Richard Nixon;* a project entitled "The Structure of Politics in Post World War II America."

\* \* \*

## HAMILTON, Marshall Lee 1937-

*PERSONAL:* Born August 2, 1937, in El Centro, Calif.; son of Marshall L. (a shoe store manager) and Marie (Fitzgerald) Hamilton; married Sara McElligott, July 1, 1958; children: William James, Gregory Lee, Monica Lynn. *Education:* Attended Santa Ana College, 1955-57; Long Beach State College (now California State University, Long Beach), B.A., 1959, M.A. (with honors), 1961; University of Texas, Ph.D., 1964. *Home address:* Eden Mills, Ontario, Canada. *Office:* Department of Psychology, University of Guelph, Guelph, Ontario, Canada.

*CAREER:* Clinical psychology trainee at Veterans Administration Hospital, Temple, Tex., 1962, 1964, and Veterans Administration Mental Hygiene Clinic, San Antonio, Tex., 1963; University of Texas at Austin, special instructor in psychology, 1963-64; Langley Porter Neuropsychiatric Institute, San Francisco, Calif., U.S. Public Health Service fellow and clinical psychology intern, 1964-65; San Jose State College (now University), San Jose, Calif., assistant professor of psychology, 1965-66; Washington State University, Pullman, assistant professor, 1966-70, associate professor of psychology in department of child and family studies, 1970-72; University of Guelph, Guelph, Ontario, associate professor of psychology, 1972—. *Member:* American Psychological Association, Canadian Psychological Association, Western Psychological Association, Psi Chi. *Awards, honors:* U.S. Public Health Service research grant, 1968; Canada Council grant, 1973; Health and Welfare Canada grant, 1975.

*WRITINGS:* (Editor with Donn Byrne) *Personality Research: A Book of Readings,* Prentice-Hall, 1966; *Father's Influence on Children,* Nelson-Hall, 1977. Contributor to *Inter-National Encyclopedia of Neurology,* and to *Psychiatry, Psychoanalysis, Developmental Psychology, Psychology, Journal of Experimental Psychology,* and other professional journals.

*WORK IN PROGRESS:* With Donn Byrne, a revised edition of *Personality Research: A Book of Readings.*

\* \* \*

## HAMILTON, W(illiam) B(askerville) 1908-1972

March 7, 1908—July 17, 1972; American historian and editor. Obituaries: *New York Times,* July 20, 1972. (See index for *CA* sketch)

\* \* \*

## HAMLIN, Gladys E(va)

*PERSONAL:* Born in Sioux Falls, S.D.; daughter of Norman O. (a farmer) and Nellie (Dunlap) Hamlin. *Education:* University of Chicago, Ph.B., 1926; Columbia University, M.A., 1937. *Home:* 229 Beach Ave., Ames, Iowa 50010.

*CAREER:* Normal training supervisor in high schools in Sioux Falls, S.D., 1926-29, and Manning, Iowa, 1929-31; Duke University, Durham, N.C., instructor in art history, 1938-39; American Council of Learned Societies, Committee on Preservation of Art Treasures in War Areas, New York, N.Y., research assistant, 1944-45; American Commission for Protection and Salvage of Artistic and Historic Monuments in War Areas, Washington, D.C., research assistant, 1945-46; National Gallery of Art, Washington, D.C., docent, 1946-49; Iowa State University, Ames, associate professor of art history, 1949-73. *Member:* Society of Architectural Historians, American Association of University Women, National Photographic Society, Iowa Society for the Preservation of Historic Landmarks, Ames Camera Club (president, 1963-64). *Awards, honors:* Institute of International Education scholar, University of London, summer, 1936.

*WRITINGS: The Sculpture of Fred and Mabel Torrey,* Borden Publishing, 1969. Contributor to *Iowa Journal of History and Politics* and *College Art Journal.*

*SIDELIGHTS:* Gladys E. Hamlin has conducted tours to the Orient, Europe, and areas of the South Pacific and Mediterranean. She has been a star exhibitor in the Photographic Society of America.

\* \* \*

## HAMLIN, Griffith Askew 1919-

*PERSONAL:* Born February 24, 1919, in Richmond, Va.; son of Charles Hunter (a teacher) and Mary (Griffith) Hamlin; married Margaret Geneva Cook (a teacher), June 1, 1943; children: Griffith Askew, Jr., John Charles. *Education:* Atlantic Christian College, B.A., 1939; Lexington Theological Seminary, M.Rel.Ed., 1942; Duke University, B.D., 1946; Iliff School of Theology, Th.D., 1953; Southern Illinois University, M.S. in Ed., 1968. *Politics:* Democrat. *Home:* 201 Lynn Ave., Fulton, Mo. 65251. *Office:* William Woods College, Fulton, Mo. 65251.

*CAREER:* Minister of Christian Churches (Disciples of Christ) in Hampton, Va., 1951-57, and Goldsboro, N.C., 1957-61; William Woods College, Fulton, Mo., registrar of the college and chairman of humanities, 1961—. *Member:* American Academy of Religion, Smithsonian Associates, Missouri Philosophical Society, National Trust for Historic Preservation.

*WRITINGS: The Old Testament: Its Intent and Content,* Christopher, 1959; *In Faith and History: The Story of William Woods College,* Bethany Press, 1965; *Monticello: The Biography of a College,* Monticello College Foundation, 1976.

*SIDELIGHTS:* Griffith Askew Hamlin told *CA:* "My writing usually is the result of an interest developing out of my college teaching. I do not attempt to write fiction, but some of the persons and places about which I write develop into a true story as exciting as any fiction. Perhaps it gives proof to the old adage that truth is stranger than fiction."

## HANCOCK, Mary A. 1923-

*PERSONAL:* Born March 21, 1923, in Berlin, Wis.; daughter of Gaylord and Alice (Van Fossen) Hancock. *Education:* Mitchell College, Statesville, N.C., A.A., 1943. *Home:* 5 Golf St., Apt. A, Asheville, N.C. 28801.

*WRITINGS*—Juveniles: *Menace on the Mountain,* Macrae, 1968; *The Thundering Prairie,* Macrae, 1969.

*SIDELIGHTS: Menace on the Mountain* was dramatized and produced on NBC-TV by World of Disney, August, 1970.

\* \* \*

## HANDSCOMBE, Richard 1935-

*PERSONAL:* Born February 19, 1935, in England; son of James C. and Dorothy M. (Jenkins) Handscombe. *Education:* Cambridge University, B.A., 1959, Cert. Ed., 1960, M.A., 1962; University of Leeds, P.D.E.S.L., 1964. *Office:* Department of English, Glendon College, 2275 Bayview Ave., Toronto, Ontario, Canada M4N 3M6.

*CAREER:* Nuffield Foreign Languages Project, Leeds, England, research director, 1964-67; Glendon College, Toronto, Ontario, 1967—, began as associate professor, currently professor of English. Business director of R. & J. Handscombe Ltd. *Military service:* Royal Air Force, 1954-56.

*WRITINGS:* (With Jon Ancevich) *Castle Zaremba,* two volumes, O.E.C.A. Queen's Printer, 1970.

*WORK IN PROGRESS:* Research on stylistics and children's language.

\* \* \*

## HANKS, Lucien M(ason) 1910-

*PERSONAL:* Born March 25, 1910, in Madison, Wis.; son of Lucien M. and Mary Esther (Vilas) Hanks; married Jane Richardson (an anthropologist), December 28, 1938; children: Peter Vilas, Tobias Richardson, Nicholas Fox Walton. *Education:* University of Wisconsin, B.A., 1931; Columbia University, Ph.D., 1936. *Residence and office:* North Bennington, Vt. 05257.

*CAREER:* Wisconsin State Prison, Waupun, Wis., psychologist, 1936-37; University of Illinois, Urbana, instructor in psychology, 1937-42; Bennington College, Bennington, Vt., 1942-69, began as assistant professor, became professor of psychology and anthropology. Affiliated with Southeast Asia Program of Cornell University, Ithaca, N.Y., 1952-57. Psychologist, Office of Strategic Services, Washington, D.C., 1943-45. *Member:* Association for Asian Studies, American Anthropological Association, Society for the Psychological Study of Social Issues, New England Psychological Association. *Awards, honors:* Received Bronze Star as a civilian in Office of Strategic Services, 1943-45; Fulbright research scholar in Thailand, 1953-54; National Science Foundation grant, 1963-66.

*WRITINGS:* (With wife, Jane R. Hanks) *Tribe under Trust,* University of Toronto Press, 1948; (editor with J. R. Hanks and R. L. Sharp) *Ethnographic Notes on Northern Thailand,* Cornell University Press, 1965; *Rice and Man,* Aldine-Atherton, 1972; (with Sharp) *Bang Chan: Social History of a Rural Community in Thailand,* Cornell University Press, 1978.

*WORK IN PROGRESS: The Discovery of Muang T'ing: Transformations of the Thai Borderlands.*

## HANLEY, Katharine Rose 1932-

*PERSONAL:* Born September 27, 1932, in Orange, N.J.; daughter of James Leo (a dentist) and Eleanor (Ryan) Hanley. *Education:* Attended Laval University, 1953, and Heidelberg University, 1955; Manhattanville College of the Sacred Heart (now Manhattanville College), A.B., 1954; Catholic University of Louvain, Belgium, Ph.B., 1955, Ph.L., 1958, Ph.D., 1961. *Religion:* Christian, Roman Catholic. *Office:* Philosophy Department, Le Moyne College, Syracuse, N.Y. 13214.

*CAREER:* Seton Hall University, South Orange, N.J., instructor in philosophy, 1955; Le Moyne College, Syracuse, N.Y., instructor, 1961-62, assistant professor, 1962-67, associate professor of philosophy, 1967—, chairman of department, 1968—. *Member:* American Catholic Philosophical Association (member of executive committee, 1970-73), American Philosophical Association, Metaphysical Society of America, American Association of University Professors, Society for Phenomenology and Existential Philosophy, Societe Internationale de Philosophie Medievale. *Awards, honors:* Belgian American Educational Foundation fellow, 1956-58; American Association of University Women fellow, 1958-60; Danforth Foundation grant, 1968; National Endowment for the Humanities fellow, 1973-74.

*WRITINGS:* (With James Donald Monan) *A Prelude to Metaphysics: The Meaning of Being Interrogated through Reflection and History,* Prentice-Hall, 1967; (contributor) Christopher Mooney, editor, *Prayer: Problem of Dialogue with God,* Paulist-Newman, 1969. Consultant editor, *New Scholasticism,* 1971—.

*WORK IN PROGRESS:* Research on subjective consciousness of fault and values in transition.

*AVOCATIONAL INTERESTS:* Skiing, golf, and dance.†

\* \* \*

## HANSEN, Terrence Leslie 1920-1974

*PERSONAL:* Born November 1, 1920, in Logan, Utah; son of Leslie (a farmer) and Salome (Toolson) Hansen; married Glenna Mavis Anderson, August 6, 1947; children: Terrence Leslie, Jr., Michael John, Angela Jeanne, Christine Lee. *Education:* University of Utah, B.A., 1946; Stanford University, M.A., 1949, Ph.D., 1951. *Religion:* Church of Jesus Christ of Latter-day Saints (Mormon). *Home:* 2105 North Oak Lane, Provo, Utah 84601. *Office:* Language Training Mission, Brigham Young University, Provo, Utah 84601.

*CAREER:* Union College, Schenectady, N.Y., assistant professor of Spanish, 1951-52; University of California, Riverside, assistant professor of Spanish, 1952-58; Brigham Young University, Provo, Utah, associate professor, 1958-60, professor of Spanish, 1960-74, president of Language Training Mission, 1970-74. President of Central American Mission, Church of Jesus Christ of Latter-day Saints, 1964-67. Consultant to Division of Manpower Development, U.S. Office of Education, 1972. *Member:* American Association of Teachers of Spanish and Portuguese, American Folklore Society. *Awards, honors:* Guggenheim fellow, 1958.

*WRITINGS: The Types of the Folktale in Cuba, Puerto Rico, the Dominican Republic, and Spanish South America,* University of California Press, 1957; *Espanol para jovenes* (title means "Spanish for Young People"), Brigham Young University Press, 1963; *Espanol para misioneros* (title means "Spanish for Missionaries"), Deseret, 1964; *Por-*

*tugues para missionarios* (title means "Portuguese for Missionaries"), Deseret, 1964; (with Ernest J. Wilkins) *Espanol a lo vivo* (title means "Living Spanish"), text edition with teacher's manual, Level I, Ginn, 1964, 4th edition, 1978, Level II, Ginn, 1966, 2nd edition, Xerox College Publications, 1972; *Deutsche fuer Missionare* (title means "German for Missionaries"), Deseret, 1965; (editor with Wilkins and Ann C. Jervis) *Por los senderos de lo hispanico: Cuentos y teatro minusculo* (title means "Along Hispanic Ways"), Xerox College Publications, 1971; (with Wilkins and J. Barry Nielsen) *Beginning German: A Practical Approach*, text edition with teacher's manual, workbook, and tapes, Level I, Xerox College Publications, 1972; (with Wilkins and Jon G. Enos) *Le Francais vivant* (title means "Living French"), text edition with teacher's manual, workbook, and tapes, Level I, Xerox College Publications, 1972, Level II, Wiley, 1978.†

(Died May 17, 1974)

\*      \*      \*

## HANSON, Richard S(imon)   1931-
### (Simon Hanson)

*PERSONAL:* Born February 8, 1931, in Minneapolis, Minn.; son of Simon E. B. (a farmer) and Ina (Nelson) Hanson; married Rita Anna Sumbs, September 2, 1954; children: Rebecca, Randall, Reuben (deceased), Rodney. *Education:* Luther College, B.A., 1953; Luther Theological Seminary, B.Th., 1957, M.Th., 1959; Harvard University, Ph.D., 1963. *Home:* 905 Pearl St., Decorah, Iowa 52101. *Office:* Luther College, Decorah, Iowa 52101.

*CAREER:* Clergyman of Lutheran Church; Luther Theological Seminary, St. Paul, Minn., instructor in religion, 1957-60; Lutheran assistant pastor in St. Paul, 1958-60; Luther College, Decorah, Iowa, associate professor of religion, 1963—. Has traveled and worked in Israel and in Turkey as archaeologist in special fields of numismatics and paleography. *Member:* American Society for Oriental Research.

*WRITINGS: The Psalms in Modern Speech*, Fortress, 1968; *Kingdoms of Man and the Kingdom of God*, Augsburg, 1971; *The Serpent Was Wiser*, Augsburg, 1972; *The Future of the Great Planet Earth*, Augsburg, 1972; (contributor) F. M. Cross and W. E. Lemke, editors, *Magnalia Dei*, Doubleday, 1976; (contributor) E. M. Meyers and others, *Ancient Synagogue Excavations at Khirbet Shema' Upper Galilee, Israel, 1970-72*, Duke University Press, 1977; *Meiron II: The City Coins of Tyre* (monograph), American Schools of Oriental Research, in press. Contributor to *Bulletin* of American Society for Oriental Research and to *New Catholic Encyclopedia*.

*WORK IN PROGRESS:* Three manuscripts in the field of Biblical theology; various articles on numismatics and archeology.

\*      \*      \*

## HANSON, Robert Carl   1926-

*PERSONAL:* Born November 5, 1926, in Wichita, Kan.; son of Otto Albert (a farmer) and Alma (Larson) Hanson; married Margaret Bremner, January 1, 1950 (divorced, 1969); children: Steven, Holly, Juliana. *Education:* University of California, Berkeley, A.B., 1949, M.A., 1951, Ph.D., 1955; Harvard University, graduate study, 1951-52. *Office:* Department of Sociology, University of Colorado, Boulder, Colo. 80309.

*CAREER:* Michigan State University, East Lansing, 1955-

60, began as instructor, became assistant professor of sociology and anthropology; University of Colorado, Boulder, assistant professor, 1960-62, associate professor, 1963-66, professor of sociology, 1966—, research program director of Institute of Behavioral Science, 1965-74. Member of U.S. Office of Education Study Commission on Undergraduate Education; consultant to Denver Juvenile Court and other agencies. *Military service:* U.S. Army, 1944-46. *Member:* American Sociological Association, American Association for the Advancement of Science, Peace Research Society International, American Association of University Professors, American Civil Liberties Union, American Federation of Teachers, Pacific Sociological Association.

*WRITINGS:* (With Lyle Saunders) *Nurse-Patient Communication*, U.S. Public Health Service, 1967; (with Richard Jessor, Theodore D. Graves, and Shirley L. Jessor) *Society, Personality, and Deviant Behavior: A Study of a Tri-Ethnic Community*, Holt, 1968. Contributor to *American Sociological Review, American Journal of Sociology, Human Organization, Journal of Health and Human Behavior, Social Science Research, International Migration Review, Nursing Research*, and *American Behavioral Scientist*.

*WORK IN PROGRESS:* Research on dialectical methodology.

\*      \*      \*

## HARDEN, Oleta Elizabeth (McWhorter)   1935-

*PERSONAL:* Born November 22, 1935, in Jamestown, Ky.; daughter of Stanley V. and Myrtie (Stearns) McWhorter; married Dennis Clarence Harden (a credit manager), July 23, 1966. *Education:* Western Kentucky University, B.A., 1956; University of Arkansas, M.A., 1958, Ph.D., 1965. *Politics:* Republican. *Religion:* Methodist. *Home:* 2618 Big Woods Trail, Fairborn, Ohio 45324. *Office:* Department of English, Wright State University, Dayton, Ohio 45431.

*CAREER:* Southwest Missouri State College (now University), Springfield, instructor in English, 1957-58; Murray State University, Murray, Ky., instructor in English, 1959-61; Northeastern State College, Tahlequah, Okla., assistant professor of English, 1963-65; Wichita State University, Wichita, Kan., assistant professor of English, 1965-66; Wright State University, Dayton, Ohio, assistant professor, 1966-68, associate professor, 1968-72, professor of English, 1972—, assistant chairman of department, 1967-70, assistant dean of College of Liberal Arts, 1971-73, associate dean, 1973-74, executive director of General University Services, 1974-76. *Member:* College English Association, Modern Language Association of America, American Association of University Professors, College English Association of Ohio. *Awards, honors:* Liberal arts research grant, Wright State University, 1968; Wright State Foundation grant, 1972.

*WRITINGS: Maria Edgeworth's Art of Prose Fiction*, Mouton & Co., 1971.

*WORK IN PROGRESS:* Writing on Maria Edgeworth and on Jane Austen; research on English Romantic poets, nineteenth-century fiction, and seventeeth-century English literature to 1660.

*SIDELIGHTS:* Reviewing *Maria Edgeworth's Art of Prose Fiction*, a *Choice* critic called Oleta Elizabeth Harden's book an "admirably concise and yet thorough survey of Maria Edgeworth's voluminous output from the early children's tales to the late novels. . . . A valuable introduction for the general reader." And Richard J. Finneran has called it "the best book-length study of (Edgeworth's) fictional techniques and literary theories."

Harden told *CA:* "Thomas Wolfe has admirably expressed my greatest dream: 'I will go everywhere and see everything. I will meet all the people I can. I will think all the thoughts, feel all the emotions I am able, and I will write, write, write....'" She has travelled extensively in Europe and the Americas.

*BIOGRAPHICAL/CRITICAL SOURCES: Choice,* May, 1972; Richard J. Finneran, *Anglo-Irish Literature: A Review of Research,* Modern Language Association, 1976.

\* \* \*

## HARDER, Eleanor (Loraine) 1925-

*PERSONAL:* Born January 23, 1925, in Waterloo, Iowa; daughter of Clarence Austin (a businessman) and Helen (Carr) Brown; married Raymond W. Harder, Jr. (an advertising executive), September 4, 1948; children: Daniel W., Julia Ann. *Education:* University of California, Los Angeles, B.A., 1949. *Politics:* Democrat. *Religion:* Methodist. *Home:* 3548 Military Ave., Los Angeles, Calif. 90034.

*CAREER:* Started performing for children as a teen-ager when she toured with her own marionette show; later acted in professional theatre company touring Southern California; producer for children's theatre company presenting plays she and her husband wrote, 1965-67; teacher of writing class, University of California Extension, Los Angeles, 1969—. *Member:* Actors' Equity Association, American Society of Composers, Authors and Publishers, American Federation of Television and Radio Artists, Women in Communications, P.E.O. Sisterhood, Delta Delta Delta. *Awards, honors:* Second prize, Seattle Junior Programs Playwriting Contest, 1962, for *Good Grief, a Griffin;* best play award, Montana State Drama Festival, 1964, for *Annabelle Broom;* best play award, National Thespian Society, 1968, for *Beauty and the Lonely Beast.*

*WRITINGS: Darius and the Dozer Bull* (juvenile), Abingdon, 1971.

Musical plays for children; with husband, Raymond W. Harder, Jr., except as indicated: *Annabelle Broom,* Music Theatre International, 1959; *Good Grief, a Griffin,* Anchorage Press, 1968; (sole author) *Beauty and the Lonely Beast,* Pioneer Drama Service, 1969; *Sacramento Fifty Miles,* Anchorage Press, 1969; *The Near-Sighted Knight and the Far-Sighted Dragon,* Anchorage Press, 1977. Also author of a musical play, "Darius and the Dozer Bull," adapted from her juvenile book. Other writings for children include filmstrips and radio and television programs.

*WORK IN PROGRESS:* With her husband, a musical drama, "How Shall We Sing."

*SIDELIGHTS:* Eleanor Harder told *CA* that in writing *Annabelle Broom* she and her husband "enjoyed working together on it so much that we have continued doing musicals over the years." Sometimes, she added, "the whole family gets into the act—my husband designing the sets, our son, Dan, playing drums, and our daughter, Julie, acting and singing."

*BIOGRAPHICAL/CRITICAL SOURCES: Los Angeles Times,* July 20, 1969.

\* \* \*

## HARDING, Harold F(riend) 1903-

*PERSONAL:* Born July 30, 1903, in Niagara Falls, N.Y.; son of Robert and Florence Alice (Friend) Harding; married Elizabeth A. Reeves, September 5, 1935; children: Daniel

R., Robert R. and Susan F. (twins). *Education:* Hamilton College, A.B., 1925; Cornell University, M.A., 1929, Ph.D., 1937; attended University of London, summer, 1933; U.S. Army Command and General Staff College, graduate, 1944. *Politics:* Independent. *Home:* 4433 North Stanton, No. 407, El Paso, Tex. 79902. *Office:* Department of Speech, University of Texas, El Paso, Tex. 79968.

*CAREER:* Iowa State College (now Iowa State University of Science and Technology), Ames, instructor in public speaking, 1925-27; Cornell University, Ithaca, N.Y., instructor in public speaking, 1928-31; George Washington University, Washington, D.C., assistant professor, 1931-38, associate professor, 1938-44, professor, 1944-46, Chauncey M. Depew Professor of Speech and executive officer of department, 1946; Ohio State University, Columbus, professor of speech, 1946-66; University of Texas at El Paso, Benedict Professor of Speech, 1966—. Commandant, Fort Hayes Army Reserve School, 1950-57; member of educational survey commission, Command and General Staff College, 1956. Consultant to Battelle Memorial Institute, 1960-66. Visiting professor at University of British Columbia, summer, 1964; visiting professor of speech, University of California, Santa Barbara, 1965-66. *Military service:* U.S. Army Reserve, 1929-64, with active duty, mainly in Pacific theater, 1941-45; commander of 83rd Infantry Division, 1961-64; retired as major general; received (in World War II) Bronze Star Medal and Legion of Merit with oak-leaf cluster. *Member:* Institute for Strategic Studies (London), International Phonetics Association, Modern Language Association of America, Reserve Officers Association of the United States, Delta Sigma Rho (national treasurer, 1937-41; trustee, 1948-53), Delta Kappa Epsilon, Pi Delta Epsilon. *Awards, honors:* Rockefeller Foundation fellowship, 1946; L.H.D., Hamilton College, 1962.

*WRITINGS: English Rhetorical Theory: 1750-1800,* Cornell University Press, 1937; (editor) *The Age of Danger: Major Speeches on American Problems,* Random House, 1952; (editor with Sidney J. Parnes) *A Source Book for Creative Thinking,* Scribner, 1962; (editor) Hugh Blair, *Lectures on Rhetoric and Belles Lettres,* Southern Illinois University Press, 1965; (editor) *The Speeches of Thucydides,* Coronado, 1972. Editor, *Quarterly Journal of Speech,* 1948-51.

*WORK IN PROGRESS: Burke's Leading Ideas, Our Two Nations: F. D. R. and King George VI.*

\* \* \*

## HARDY, Richard E(arl) 1938-

*PERSONAL:* Born October 11, 1938, in Victoria, Va.; son of Clifford E. and Louise (Hamilton) Hardy. *Education:* Virginia Polytechnic Institute (now Virginia Polytechnic Institute and State University), B.S., 1960; Virginia Commonwealth University, M.S., 1962; University of Maryland, A.G.S., 1964, Ed. D., 1966. *Religion:* Baptist. *Office:* Department of Rehabilitation Counseling, Virginia Commonwealth University, Richmond, Va. 23284.

*CAREER:* Virginia Commission for the Visually Handicapped, Richmond, rehabilitation counselor, 1961-63; U.S. Department of Health, Education, and Welfare (HEW), Washington, D.C., rehabilitation adviser, 1963-66; South Carolina Department of Rehabilitation, Columbia, chief psychologist, 1966-68; Virginia Commonwealth University, Richmond, associate professor of rehabilitation counseling, chairman of department, and director of graduate studies, 1967—. Member of Richmond's Comprehensive Health Planning Commission, Governor of Virginia's Commission on Problems of Aging, and Commission on Employment of the Handicapped. *Member:* National Rehabilitation Association (national program chairman, 1972), American Psychological Association, American Correctional Association, American Personnel and Guidance Association, American Rehabilitation Counseling Association, Association for Counselor Education and Supervision, National Employment Counselors Association, Vocational Evaluation and Work Adjustment Association, National Vocational Guidance Association.

*WRITINGS:* (With Hubert M. Clements and Jack A. Duncan) *The Unfit Majority: A Research Study of the Rehabilitation of Selective Service Rejectees in South Carolina,* South Carolina Vocational Rehabilitation Department, 1967; *The Anxiety Scale for the Blind* (monograph), American Foundation for the Blind, 1968.

With John G. Cull; published by C. C Thomas, except as indicated: (Editors) *Social and Rehabilitation Services for the Blind,* 1972; (editors) *Vocational Rehabilitation: Profession and Process,* 1972; (editors) *Applied Psychology in Law Enforcement and Corrections,* 1973; *Applied Volunteerism in Community Development,* foreword by Lenore Romney, 1973; *Climbing Ghetto Walls: Disadvantagement, Delinquency, and Rehabilitation,* 1973; *Vocational Evaluation for Rehabilitation Services,* 1973; (editors) *Drug Dependence and Rehabilitation Approaches,* 1973; *Adjustment to Work,* 1973; (editors) *Understanding Disability for Social and Rehabilitation Services,* 1973; (editors) *The Big Welfare Mess: Public Assistance and Rehabilitation Approaches,* 1973; *Introduction to Correctional Rehabilitation,* 1973; (editors) *Law Enforcement and Correctional Rehabilitation,* 1973; *The Neglected Older American: Social and Rehabilitation Services,* 1973; (editors) *Rehabilitation of the Urban Disadvantaged,* 1973; *Fundamentals of Criminal Behavior and Correctional Systems,* 1973.

(Editors) *Educational and Psychological Aspects of Deafness,* 1974; (editors) *Group Counseling and Therapy Techniques in Special Settings,* 1974; (editors) *Mental Retardation and Physical Disability,* 1974; *Rehabilitation of the Drug Abuser with Delinquent Behavior: Case Studies and Rehabilitation Approaches in Drug Abuse and Delinquency,* 1974; (editors) *Severe Disabilities: Social and Rehabilitation Approaches,* 1974; (editors) *Therapeutic Needs of the Family: Problems, Descriptions, and Therapeutic Approaches,* 1974; (editors) *Modification of Behavior of the Mentally Ill: Rehabilitation Approaches,* 1974; *Modification of Behavior of the Mentally Retarded: Applied Principles,* 1974; *Organization and Administration of Drug Abuse Treatment Programs: National and International,* 1974; (editors) *Administrative Techniques of Rehabilitation Facility Operations,* 1974; *Behavior Modification in Rehabilitation Settings: Applied Principles,* 1974; (editors) *Career Guidance for Young Women: Considerations in Planning Professional Careers,* 1974; (editors) *Techniques and Approaches in Marital and Family Counseling,* 1974; (editors) *Alcohol Abuse and Rehabilitation Approaches,* 1974; *Rehabilitation Techniques in Severe Disability: Case Studies,* 1974; (editor) *Creative Divorce through Social and Psychological Approaches,* 1974; (editors) *Counseling and Rehabilitating the Diabetic,* 1974; (editors) *Counseling High School Students: Special Problems and Approaches,* 1974; (editors) *Deciding on Divorce: Personal and Family Considerations,* 1974; *Types of Drug Abusers and Their Abuses,* 1974; *Volunteerism: An Emerging Profession,* 1974; *Problems of Adolescents: Social and Psychological Approaches,* 1974; (edi-

tors) *Psychological and Vocational Rehabilitation of the Youthful Delinquent,* 1974.

*Counseling and Rehabilitating the Cancer Patient,* 1975; *Organization and Administration of Service Programs for the Older American,* 1975; *Drug Language and Lore,* 1975; *Fundamentals of Juvenile Criminal Behavior and Drug Abuse,* 1975; *Services of the Rehabilitation Facility,* 1975; *Problems of Disadvantaged and Deprived Youth,* 1975; (editors) *Rehabilitation Facility Approaches in Severe Disabilities,* 1975; (editors) *Career Guidance for Black Adolescents: A Guide to Selected Professional Occupations,* 1975; *Counseling Strategies with Special Populations,* 1975; (editors) *Problems of Runaway Youth,* 1976; *Considerations in Rehabilitation Facility Development,* 1976; *Hemingway: A Psychological Portrait,* Banner Books International, 1977; *Physical Medicine and Rehabilitation Approaches in Spinal Cord Injury,* 1977; *Vocational Rehabilitation: Profession and Process,* 1977.

Editor, "Social and Rehabilitation Psychology" series, C. C Thomas, 1972—. Contributor to professional journals. Associate editor, *Journal of Voluntary Action Research,* 1972—.

*SIDELIGHTS:* Richard Hardy has traveled throughout Europe, the Near East, Mexico, Canada, and the Caribbean. *Avocational interests:* Boating, water skiing, banjo, flying (he is a licensed airplane pilot).†

\*　　\*　　\*

## HARE, F(rederick) Kenneth 1919-

*PERSONAL:* Born February 5, 1919, in Wylye, Wiltshire, England; became Canadian citizen, 1951; son of Frederick Eli and Irene (Smith) Hare; married Suzanne Alice Bates, 1941 (marriage dissolved, 1952); married Helen Neilson Morrill, December 26, 1953; children: (first marriage) Christopher John; (second marriage) Elissa, Robin. *Education:* University of London, B.Sc. (first class honors), 1939; University of Montreal, Ph.D., 1950. *Home:* 91 Great Oak Dr., Islington, Ontario, Canada. *Office:* Institute for Environmental Studies, University of Toronto, Toronto, Ontario, Canada M5S 1A1.

*CAREER:* University of Manchester, Manchester, England, assistant lecturer in geography, 1940-41; McGill University, Montreal, Quebec, assistant professor, 1945-49, associate professor, 1949-52, professor of geography amd meteorology, 1952-64, chairman of geography department, 1950-62, dean of Faculty of Arts and Sciences, 1962-64; University of London, London, England, professor of geography and head of department at King's College, 1964-66, master of Birkbeck College, 1966-68, fellow of King's College, 1967—; University of British Columbia, Vancouver, president, 1968-69; University of Toronto, Toronto, Ontario, professor of geography and physics, 1969-76, university professor, 1976—, director of Institute for Environmental Studies, 1974—; Department of the Environment, Canadian Government, Ottawa, Ontario, director-general of research coordination (on leave from University of Toronto), 1972-73. Visiting scientist, University of Wisconsin, 1969. Chairman of board, Arctic Institute of North America, 1963; member of board of directors of Resources for the Future (U.S.), 1969—, John Wiley & Sons, 1973—, and Wiley Publishers of Canada, 1973—; member of National Research Council (Canada), 1962-64, Advisory Committee on Natural Resources (United Kingdom), 1965-66, and Natural Environment Research Council (United Kingdom), 1965-68. Vice-chairman, Thea and Leon Koerner Foundation, 1968-69; trustee of Stanstead College, 1956-77,

Canadian-Scandinavian Foundation, 1956-60, and Thomas Coram Fields Trust, 1967. *Wartime service:* British Air Ministry, meteorologist, 1941-45.

*MEMBER:* Royal Society of Canada (fellow), Canadian Association of Geographers (president, 1963-64), Royal Meteorological Society (president, 1967-68), Royal Geographical Society, Royal Canadian Geographical Society (fellow), Canadian Geographical Society, Arctic Institute, American Geographical Society (fellow), American Meteorological Society (fellow), Glaciological Society, Geographical Association, Institute of British Geographers, American Association for the Advancement of Science (fellow), Geologists' Association, Canadian Meteorological and Oceanographic Society, Athenaeum Club (London).

*AWARDS, HONORS:* Meritorious Achievement Citation, Association of American Geographers, 1961; President's Prize, Canadian branch of Royal Meteorological Society, 1961, 1962; Patterson Medal, Atmospheric Environment Service (Canada), 1973; Massey Medal, Royal Canadian Geographical Society, 1974; Patron's Medal, Royal Geographical Society, 1977. LL.D., Queen's University of Kingston, 1964, and University of Western Ontario, 1968; D.Sc., McGill University, 1969, Adelaide University, 1974, and York University, 1978.

*WRITINGS: The Restless Atmosphere,* Hutchinson, 1953, 4th edition, Harper, 1966; (with L. Dudley Stamp) *Physical Geography for Canada,* Longmans, Green, 1953; (with Svenn Orvig) *The Arctic Circulation,* Arctic Meteorology Research Group, McGill University, 1958; *A Photo-Reconnaissance Survey of Labrador-Ungava,* Department of Mines and Technical Surveys (Ottawa), 1959; *On University Freedom in the Canadian Context* (Plaunt lectures at Carleton University), University of Toronto Press, 1967; (with M. K. Thomas) *Climate Canada,* Wiley, 1974; (editor with R. A. Bryson, and contributor) *Climates of North America,* Elsevier Scientific Publishing, 1974; (with A. M. Aikin and J. M. Harrison) *The Management of Canada's Nuclear Wastes,* Department of Energy, Mines and Resources (Ottawa), 1977.

Contributor: *Geography,* Odhams, 1948; L. Dudley Stamp and S. W. Wooldridge, editors, *The London Essays in Geography* (memorial volume to L. R. Jones), Harvard University Press, 1950; Griffith Taylor, editor, *Geography in the Twentieth Century,* Philosophical Library, 1951; *Compendium on Meteorology,* American Meteorological Society, 1951; George W. Hoffman, editor, *A Geography of Europe,* Ronald, 1953, 3rd edition, 1969; R. R. Platt, editor, *Finland and Its Geography,* American Geographical Society, 1955; *Melanges geographiques canadiens offerts a Raoul Blanchard,* University of Laval Press, 1959; G. Johnston and W. Roth, editors, *The Church in the Modern World,* Ryerson, 1967; Arnold Court, editor, *Eclectic Climatology,* Association of Pacific Coast Geographers, 1968; H. Steppler, editor, *The Food Resources of Mankind,* Agri-World Press, 1968; John Warkentin, editor, *Canada: A Geographical Interpretation,* Methuen, 1968; *Memorial Volume to Sir Dudley Stamp,* Institute of British Geographers, 1969; *Desertification and Its Causes,* Pergamon Press for United Nations Environmental Programme, 1977.

Author of regional studies and technical reports for Air Ministry (London), and co-author of education studies in Canada. Contributor of more than sixty articles to *Arctic, Weather,* and other scientific journals. Associate editor (in the past or currently), *Geographical Review, Journal of Applied Meteorology, Environmental Research, Geograf-* *iska Annaler, Environmental Geology,* and *Journal of Biogeography.*

*WORK IN PROGRESS:* Research on nuclear waste disposal problems; preparations for World Climate Conference and United Nations World Climate Programme.

*SIDELIGHTS:* F. Kenneth Hare told *CA:* "The social applications of science need not be gibberish. They touch on great issues, and should be written as far as possible in the literary tradition. To write anything is hard work. To write well is still harder—and possibly requires the right genes, as well as genius. I don't have either—so I sweat my papers out."

*AVOCATIONAL INTERESTS:* Singing in choirs, playing the piano, and music generally; gardening, watching the sky and landscape.

\*   \*   \*

### HARGREAVES, Mary W(ilma) M(assey) 1914-

*PERSONAL:* Born March 1, 1914, in Erie, Pa.; daughter of Albert Edward (a factory foreman) and Bess (Childs) Massey; married Herbert Walter Hargreaves (a college professor), August 24, 1940. *Education:* Bucknell University, A.B., 1935; Radcliffe College, M.A., 1936, Ph.D., 1951. *Politics:* Democrat. *Religion:* Methodist. *Home:* 237 Cassidy Ave., Lexington, Ky. 40502. *Office:* Department of History, University of Kentucky, Lexington, Ky. 40506.

*CAREER:* Business School, Harvard University, Cambridge, Mass., research editor, 1937-39; University of Kentucky, Lexington, research editor, 1952—, assistant professor, 1964-69, associate professor, 1969-73, professor of history, 1973—. *Member:* American Association of University Women (branch president, 1957-59; member of state board, 1957-69), American Historical Association, Organization of American Historians, Agricultural History Society (member of executive committee, 1969-72), American Association of University Professors, Southern Historical Association, Phi Beta Kappa (chapter secretary, 1964-69; chapter president, 1970-71), Phi Alpha Theta, Sigma Tau Delta.

*WRITINGS: Dry Farming in the Northern Great Plains,* Harvard University Press, 1957; (editor with James F. Hopkins) *The Papers of Henry Clay,* University Press of Kentucky, Volume I, 1959, Volume II, 1961, Volume III, 1963, Volume IV, 1971, Volume V, 1973. Contributor of articles to *Agricultural History* and other historical publications.

*WORK IN PROGRESS:* Continuing research on readjustment of agriculture in northern Great Plains.

\*   \*   \*

### HARING, Philip S(myth) 1915-

*PERSONAL:* Born October 7, 1915, in White Plains, N.Y.; son of Clarence Henry (a professor) and Helen (Garnsey) Haring; married Ellen Newton Stone, December, 1942 (divorced, 1951); married Jacqueline Kolle (a curator and archivist), March 8, 1952; children: (second marriage) Tori (Helen Victoria). *Education:* Harvard University, B.A., 1937; University of Chicago, M.A., 1953, Ph.D., 1954. *Home:* 30 Hillcrest Dr., Galesburg, Ill. 61401. *Office:* Knox College, Galesburg, Ill. 61401.

*CAREER:* Boston University, Boston, Mass., assistant professor of public relations, 1948-51; Northwestern University, Evanston, Ill., lecturer in political science, 1953-54; Knox College, Galesburg, Ill., assistant professor, 1954-60, associate professor, 1960-69, professor of political science,

1969-73, Robert Murphy Professor of Political Science, 1973-77, professor of political philosophy, 1977—. *Military service:* U.S. Navy Reserve, active duty, 1940-42.

*WRITINGS: Political Morality,* Schenkman, 1970; (contributor) Michael A. Weinstein, editor, *The Political Experience,* St. Martin's, 1972. Contributor to *American Political Science Review* and other journals.

*AVOCATIONAL INTERESTS:* Painting, prints, architecture, and travel.

\*    \*    \*

## HARLOW, Samuel Ralph    1885-1972

July 20, 1885—August 21, 1972; American religious educator. Obituaries: *New York Times,* August 23, 1972. (See index for *CA* sketch)

\*    \*    \*

## HARMON, Gary L.    1935-

*PERSONAL:* Born August 16, 1935, in Aurora, Neb.; son of Vyrle Martin (an engineer) and Esther (Koberstein) Uehling; married Susanna Marie Pollock (an editor), December 27, 1960; children: Thomas Thorburn, James Matthias, Nathan Martin. *Education:* Hastings College, B.A., 1956; Indiana University, M.A., M.A.T., Ph.D., 1966; also studied at Michigan State University, University of Michigan, and University of Geneva. *Religion:* "Humanist." *Home:* 3419 Beauclerc Rd., Jacksonville, Fla. 32217. *Office:* Department of English, University of North Florida, Jacksonville, Fla. 32216.

*CAREER:* Flint Community College, Flint, Mich., instructor in English, 1960-64; Morehead State University, Morehead, Ky., associate professor of English, chairman of Division, and director of English graduate studies, 1966-67; Stephens College, Columbia, Mo., division and department chairman for English, 1967-71; University of North Florida, Jacksonville, professor of literature and English and chairman of department, 1971—. *Member:* College English Association, Modern Language Association of America, American Studies Association, Popular Culture Association, Popular Culture Association in the South (president, 1977; executive secretary, 1977-78), National Council of Teachers of English, American Association of University Professors.

*WRITINGS:* (With R. F. Dickinson) *Write Now!,* Holt, 1970, revised edition published as *Write Now!: Substance—Strategy—Style,* 1972; *Scholar's Market: An International Directory of Periodicals Publishing Literary Scholarship,* Ohio State University Library, 1974; (editor with Peter F. Parshall) *Fiction and Its Readers,* Harcourt, 1979. Contributor of articles to professional journals.

*WORK IN PROGRESS: Florida's Novelists, Poets, and Playwrights;* editing *"Matters of the Deepest Importance": America's Popular Culture.*

\*    \*    \*

## HARMS, Robert T(homas)    1932-

*PERSONAL:* Born April 12, 1932, in Peoria, Ill.; son of Wilbert E. (a businessman) and Mildred (Thomas) Harms; married Sirpa Aaltonen (a nurse), July 1, 1956; children: Kirsti, Ritva, Eerik, Timo. *Education:* University of Chicago, A.B. (with honors), 1952, A.M., 1956, Ph.D., 1960; additional study at University of Helsinki, 1954-56, and Leningrad State University, 1962-63. *Religion:* Lutheran.

*Home:* 2609 Deerfoot Trail, Austin, Tex. 78704. *Office:* Department of Linguistics, University of Texas, Austin, Tex. 78712.

*CAREER:* Chicago Lutheran Theological Seminary, Chicago, Ill., special instructor, 1958; University of Texas at Austin, instructor, 1958-61, assistant professor, 1961-64, associate professor, 1965-67, professor of linguistics, 1967—, chairman of department, 1973-77. Visiting professor at Columbia University, 1960, 1965, and Ohio State University, 1964. *Member:* Linguistic Society of America, Phi Beta Kappa. *Awards, honors:* Fulbright scholar in Finland, 1954-56, research grant in Finland, 1968; American Council of Learned Societies grant, 1960-61, 1962; Inter-University travel grants in Leningrad, 1962-63, in Hungary, 1967-68.

*WRITINGS: Estonian Grammar,* Indiana University Press, 1962; *Finnish Structural Sketch,* Indiana University Press, 1964; *Introduction to Phonological Theory,* Prentice-Hall, 1968; (editor with Emmon Bach) *Universals in Linguistic Theory,* Holt, 1968. Contributor of article on Uralic languages to *Encyclopaedia Britannica.* Contributor of about thirty articles and reviews to professional journals.

*WORK IN PROGRESS:* Writing on historical linguistics, the relationship between phonetics and phonology, the Estonian and Lapp languages.

\*    \*    \*

## HARNETTY, Peter    1927-

*PERSONAL:* Born June 6, 1927, in Brighton, England; Canadian citizen; son of Edward and Anne (McKeon) Harnetty; married Claire Demers, September, 1956; children: Richard. *Education:* University of British Columbia, B.A. (with honors), 1953; Harvard University, A.M., 1954, Ph.D., 1958. *Home:* 3026 West 34th Ave., Vancouver, British Columbia, Canada. *Office:* Department of Asian Studies, University of British Columbia, Vancouver, British Columbia, Canada V6T 1W5.

*CAREER:* University of British Columbia, Vancouver, instructor, 1958-61, assistant professor, 1961-65, associate professor, 1965-72, professor of history, 1972—, head of department of Asian studies, 1975—. *Member:* Association for Asian Studies, Economic History Association, Historical Association, Canadian Society for Asian Studies. *Awards, honors:* Woodrow Wilson fellow, 1953-54; Social Science Research Council fellow, 1956-57; Nuffield Foundation fellow, 1964-65; Canada Council senior fellow, 1964-65, 1971-72.

*WRITINGS: Imperialism and Free Trade: Lancashire and India in the Mid-Nineteenth Century,* University of British Columbia Press, 1972. Contributor of articles to journals, including *English Historical Review, Economic History Review, Agricultural History, Journal of British Studies,* and *South Asian Review. Pacific Affairs,* associate editor 1966-69, member of editorial board, 1969—.

*WORK IN PROGRESS: Social and Economic Change in Central India, 1854-1920.*

*SIDELIGHTS:* Peter Harnetty visited India in 1945-46, 1964-65, and 1971-72.

\*    \*    \*

## HARPOLE, Patricia Chayne    1933-

*PERSONAL:* Born November 14, 1933, in Two Harbors, Minn.; daughter of Cecil Ceylon (a postal clerk) and Nanna E. (Green) Chayne; children: Tracey, Leslie, Kimberly.

*Education:* University of Minnesota, B.A., 1955; University of Denver, M.A. in L.S., 1962. *Home:* 928 Goodrich Ave., St. Paul, Minn. 55105. *Office:* Minnesota Historical Society, 690 Cedar St., St. Paul, Minn. 55101.

*CAREER:* St. Paul Public Library, St. Paul, Minn., library assistant, 1955-60; University of Denver Library, Denver, Colo., library assistant, 1961-62; Minnesota Historical Society, St. Paul, reference librarian, 1963-71, head of reference division, 1971—, assistant chief librarian, 1972-78, chief of reference library, 1978—. Has taught adult education courses in genealogical research for St. Paul, South St. Paul, and Minneapolis, Minn. school systems, 1964—. *Member:* Minnesota Library Association, Minnesota Genealogical Society (founder; president, 1969-70).

*WRITINGS:* (Editor with Mary D. Nagle) *Minnesota Territorial Census, 1850,* Minnesota Historical Society, 1972. Editor, *Minnesota Genealogist,* 1969—.

*WORK IN PROGRESS:* A revised edition of *Minnesota Biographies* first published by the Minnesota Historical Society in 1912; an index of architectural publications with Minnesota imprints.

\* \* \*

## HARRELL, David Edwin, Jr. 1930-

*PERSONAL:* Born February 22, 1930, in Jacksonville, Fla.; son of David Edwin (a physician) and Mildred (Lee) Harrell; married Adelia Roberts, September 7, 1954; children: Mildred Susan, David Edwin III, Elinor Elizabeth, Marilyn Lee, Harold Robert. *Education:* David Lipscomb College, B.A., 1954; Vanderbilt University, M.A., 1958, Ph.D., 1962. *Office:* Department of History, University of Alabama, Birmingham, Ala. 35294.

*CAREER:* East Tennessee State University, Johnson City, assistant professor, 1961-64, associate professor of history, 1964-66; University of Oklahoma, Norman, associate professor of history, 1966-67; University of Georgia, Athens, associate professor of history, 1967-70; University of Alabama in Birmingham, professor of history, 1970-76, chairman of department, 1970-74, University Scholar in History, 1976—. Senior Fulbright lecturer, University of Allahabad (India), 1976-77. Special lecturer at universities and conferences in India, Bangladesh, and the United States, including East Tennessee State University, 1968, Madras Christian College, 1977, and University of Iowa, 1978. *Member:* American Historical Association, American Studies Association, American Society of Church History, Organization of American Historians, Disciples of Christ Historical Society (member of board of trustees, 1968-73), American Catholic Historical Society, Southern Historical Association (member of various committees, 1968-79). *Awards, honors:* Faculty research grants, University of Alabama in Birmingham, 1972, 1973, 1975, 1977; Institute of Ecumenical and Cultural Research fellow, 1974.

*WRITINGS: Quest for a Christian America: A Social History of the Disciples of Christ,* Volume I, Disciples of Christ Historical Society, 1966; (with Robert O. Fife and Ronald E. Osborn) *The Disciples and the Church Universal,* Disciples of Christ Historical Society, 1967; *White Sects and Black Men in the Recent South,* Vanderbilt University Press, 1971; *The Social Sources of Division in the Disciples of Christ: A Social History of the Disciples of Christ,* Volume II, Publishing Systems, 1973; *All Things Are Possible: The Healing and Charismatic Revivals in Modern America,* Indiana University Press, 1975. Contributor of more than twenty articles and reviews to historical journals.

Co-general editor of series "Minorities in Modern America," for Indiana University Press.

*WORK IN PROGRESS: Religion in the South,* a volume in series "New Perspectives on the South," for University of Kentucky Press; a biography of Oral Roberts.

\* \* \*

## HARRINGTON, Elbert W(ellington) 1901-

*PERSONAL:* Born January 27, 1901, in De Motte, Ind.; son of Charles G. (a carpenter) and Elizabeth Alma (Hilton) Harrington; married Marjorie Mayberry (an elementary school teacher), November 2, 1929; children: Rodney E., Charles D. *Education:* University of Northern Iowa, B.A., 1926; University of Iowa, M.A., 1930, Ph.D., 1938. *Politics:* Democrat. *Religion:* Methodist. *Home:* 1043 Valley View Dr., Vermillion. S.D. 57069. *Office:* University of South Dakota, Vermillion, S.D. 57069.

*CAREER:* High school teacher in Iowa, 1926-28; Wisconsin State University, River Falls (now University of Wisconsin—River Falls), professor of government and speech, 1930-31; Mayville State College, Mayville, N.D., professor of history and speech, 1931-36, dean of men, 1933-36; University of Colorado, Boulder, assistant professor of speech, 1937-45; University of South Dakota, Vermillion, professor of speech, 1945-67, chairman of department of speech and dramatic arts, 1945-55, dean of College of Arts and Sciences, 1948-67, dean emeritus and professor of communication, 1967—. *Member:* Speech Communication Association (life member), Central State Speech Association, South Dakota Education Association (life member), South Dakota State Historical Association (life member), Rotary Club (past president), Delta Sigma Rho, Tau Kappa Alpha.

*WRITINGS: Rhetoric and the Scientific Method of Inquiry: A Study in Invention,* University of Colorado Studies, 1948; *Procrustes on the Campus: Fourth Annual Lecture on Liberal Education,* College of Arts and Sciences, University of South Dakota, 1956; (contributor) Loren Reid, editor, *American Public Address: Studies in Honor of Albert Craig Baird,* University of Missouri Press, 1961; *Janus on the Campus: Status of the Liberal Arts,* Dakota Press, 1972. Contributor of about a dozen articles to speech journals. Associate editor, *Quarterly Journal of Speech.*

*AVOCATIONAL INTERESTS:* Travel, reading, writing, fishing.

\* \* \*

## HARRIS, Alice Kessler 1941-

*PERSONAL:* Born June 2, 1941, in Leicester, England; daughter of Zoltan and Ilona (Elefant) Kessler; married Jay Evans Harris, August 28, 1960 (divorced, 1974); children: Ilona Kay. *Education:* Goucher College, B.A. (cum laude), 1961; Rutgers University, M.A., 1963, Ph.D., 1968. *Home:* 141 East 88th St., New York, N.Y. 10028. *Office:* Department of History, Hofstra University, Hempstead, N.Y. 11550.

*CAREER:* Hofstra University, Hempstead, N.Y., assistant professor of history, 1968-73; Sarah Lawrence College, Bronxville, N.Y., professor of history and women's studies, 1974-76, director of Women's Studies Program, 1974-76; Hofstra University, associate professor of history, 1977—, co-director of Center for the Study of Work and Leisure, 1977—. Member, Metropolitan Conference, 1972—, and Columbia University Seminar in American Civilization. *Member:* American Association of University Professors

(Hofstra; treasurer, 1969-71), American Historical Association, Organization of American Historians, Women in the Historical Profession (member of coordinating committee), American Studies Association, American Civil Liberties Union (member of academic freedom committee, 1971-77), Berkshire Conference of Women Historians. *Awards, honors:* National Endowment for the Humanities fellowship, 1976-77; Radcliffe Institute fellowship, 1977.

*WRITINGS:* (Editor with Blanche Cook and Ronald Radosh) *Past Imperfect: Alternative Essays in American History,* Random House, 1972; (author of introduction) William Ladd, *On the Duty of Females to Promote the Cause of Peace,* Garland, 1972; (author of introduction) George Cone Beckwith, *The Peace Manual; or, War and Its Remedies,* Garland, 1972; (author of introduction) Anzia Yezierska, *Bread Givers,* Braziller, 1975; *Social History of Women Wage-Earners,* Oxford University Press, in press.

Contributor: *Cooperative History of the United States,* Dushkin, 1974; Richard Edwards and others, editors, *Labor Market Segmentation,* Lexington Books, 1975; Ronald Grele, editor, *Envelopes of Sound,* Precedent Publishing, 1975; Bernice Carroll, editor, *Liberating Women's History,* University of Illinois Press, 1976.

*WORK IN PROGRESS:* Research on women in the labor movement.

\*     \*     \*

### HARRIS, Sheldon H(oward)   1928-

*PERSONAL:* Born August 22, 1928, in Brooklyn, N.Y.; son of Peter and Bertha Harris; married Sheila J. Black, 1955; children: Robin, David. *Education:* Brooklyn College (now Brooklyn College of the City University of New York), A.B. (cum laude), 1949; Harvard University, A.M., 1950; Columbia University, Ph.D., 1958. *Home:* 17144 Nanette St., Granada Hills, Calif. 91344. *Office:* Department of History, California State University, Northridge, Calif. 91326.

*CAREER:* Brooklyn College (now Brooklyn College of the City University of New York), Brooklyn, N.Y., instructor in history, 1957-58; Bradford Durfee College of Technology (now Southeastern Massachusetts University), New Bedford, associate professor of social sciences, 1958-63; California State University, Northridge, assistant professor, 1963-66, associate professor, 1966-69, professor of history, 1969—. Visiting professor, University of California, Los Angeles, 1966. *Member:* American Historical Association, Organization of American Historians, California Council for the Social Studies, San Fernando Valley Area Council for the Social Studies. *Awards, honors:* Rogers Benjamin Foundation award, 1962; American Council of Learned Societies research grant, 1963-64; American Philosophical Society grant for research in England, 1971.

*WRITINGS: Paul Cuffe and the African Return,* Simon & Schuster, 1972; *President Johnson's Decision to Intervene in Vietnam,* American Education Publication, 1972; *Prohibition,* Xerox Education Publications, 1973. Contributor of about ten articles to *Commonweal, American Neptune,* and other periodicals.

*WORK IN PROGRESS:* A book tentatively entitled *Those Extraordinary Twins: Mark Twain and H. H. Rogers;* research for a book on English Quakers and their influence on the American anti-slavery movement.

### HARRISON, Lowell H(ayes)   1922-

*PERSONAL:* Born October 23, 1922, in Russell Springs, Ky.; son of Chester A. and Cecil (Hayes) Harrison; married Elaine M. Maher (an archivist), December 23, 1948. *Education:* Western Kentucky University, A.B., 1947; New York University, M.A., 1948, Ph.D., 1951; London School of Economics and Political Science, graduate study, 1951-52. *Politics:* Democrat. *Religion:* Methodist. *Home:* 704 Logan Ave., Bowling Green, Ky. 42101. *Office:* Department of History, Western Kentucky University, Bowling Green, Ky. 42101.

*CAREER:* New York University, New York, N.Y., instructor in history, 1947-50, assistant director of foreign student center, 1950-51; West Texas State University, Canyon, associate professor, 1952-57, professor of history and chairman of department, 1957-67, chairman of Division of Social Sciences, 1961-67; Western Kentucky University, Bowling Green, professor of history, 1967—. Former member, City Commission of Canyon, Tex. *Military service:* U.S. Army, 1943-45. *Member:* National Historical Society, Organization of American Historians, Southern Historical Association, Kentucky Historical Society, Filson Club. *Awards, honors:* Fulbright scholar in London, 1951-52; West Texas State University Faculty Excellence award, 1965; Minnie Stevens Piper Foundation Faculty award, 1966; commendation from American Association for State and Local History, 1970, for *John Breckinridge: Jeffersonian Republican;* Western Kentucky University Faculty Research award, 1971.

*WRITINGS: American History Examinations,* Arco, 1948; (with G. Derek West, Lonnie J. White, and Ernest R. Archambeau) *Battles of Adobe Walls and Lyman's Wagon Train,* Panhandle-Plains Historical Society, 1964; *John Breckinridge: Jeffersonian Republican,* Filson Club, 1969; (with James D. Bennett) *A Guide to Historical Research and Writing,* Western Kentucky University Press, 1970, revised edition, 1974; *The Civil War in Kentucky,* University Press of Kentucky, 1975; *George Rogers Clark and the War in the West,* University Press of Kentucky, 1976; (editor with Nelson Dawson) *A Kentucky Sampler: Essays from the Filson Club History Quarterly, 1926-1976,* University Press of Kentucky, 1977; *The Antislavery Movement in Kentucky,* University Press of Kentucky, 1978. General editor, "Kentucky Bicentennial Bookshelf," fifty volumes, 1975—. Contributor of over 150 articles to *William and Mary Quarterly, Great Plains Journal, Civil War Times Illustrated,* and other journals. Co-editor of *Panhandle-Plains Historical Review,* 1957-67.

*WORK IN PROGRESS:* Writing on historical topics, especially on the early national period, the Civil War, and Kentucky history.

*SIDELIGHTS:* Lowell Harrison told *CA:* "I have been especially interested in the past few years in preparing three volumes for the 'Kentucky Bicentennial Bookshelf.' This series has presented a particular challenge since they are limited to approximately 120 pages and are supposed to satisfy both scholars in the field and members of the general reading public. In an effort to add freshness to the subjects, I have made extensive use of primary sources. Each manuscript could have been completed in half the time if it could have been twice as long."

\*     \*     \*

### HARSTAD, Peter Tjernagel   1935-

*PERSONAL:* Born November 13, 1935, in Madison, Wis.;

son of Adolph M. (a clergyman) and Martha (Tjernagel) Harstad; married Carolyn A. Schneider, August 10, 1957; children: Linda, Karen, Mark, Kristen, David. *Education:* Attended Bethany Lutheran College, 1953-55; University of Wisconsin, B.S., 1957, M.S., 1959, Ph.D., 1963. *Religion:* Lutheran. *Home:* 9 Caroline Court, Iowa City, Iowa 52240. *Office:* Iowa State Historical Society, Centennial Building, 402 Iowa Ave., Iowa City, Iowa 52240.

*CAREER:* University of Wisconsin—Madison, assistant university archivist, 1962-63; Idaho State University, Pocatello, assistant professor, 1963-66, associate professor, 1966-70, professor of history, 1970-72; State Historical Society of Iowa, Iowa City, director, 1972—. Visiting professor, University of Iowa, 1970-71; visiting summer professor, University of Washington, Seattle, 1970. *Member:* American Historical Association, American Association for the History of Medicine, Organization of American Historians, Western History Association, Idaho Historical Society, Wisconsin Historical Society. *Awards, honors:* Ford Foundation fellow, 1967-68.

*WRITINGS:* (Contributor) Harry N. Scheiber, editor, *The Old Northwest: Studies in Regional History, 1787-1910,* Lincoln Publishing, 1969; (editor and author of introduction and appendix) *Reminiscences of Oscar Sonnenkalb: Idaho Surveyor and Pioneer,* Idaho State University Press, 1972. Contributor of numerous articles to historical journals.

\* \* \*

## HART, Edward L. 1916-

*PERSONAL:* Born December 28, 1916, in Bloomington, Idaho; son of Alfred A. (a government employee and farmer) and Sarah C. (Patterson) Hart; married Eleanor May Coleman (a musician), December 15, 1944; children: Edward Richard, Paul L., Barbara, Patricia. *Education:* University of Utah, B.S., 1939; University of Michigan, M.A., 1941; Oxford University, D.Phil., 1950. *Politics:* Democrat. *Religion:* Church of Jesus Christ of Latter-day Saints (Mormon). *Home:* 1401 Cherry Lane, Provo, Utah 84601. *Office:* Department of English, A230 JKBA, Brigham Young University, Provo, Utah 84601.

*CAREER:* University of Utah, Salt Lake City, instructor in English, 1946; University of Washington, Seattle, assistant professor of English, 1949-52; Brigham Young University, Provo, Utah, assistant professor, 1952-55, associate professor, 1955-59, professor of English, 1959—. Visiting professor of English, University of California, Berkeley, 1959-60; visiting professor, Arizona State University, summer, 1968. *Military service:* U.S. Navy, Japanese language translator and interpreter, 1942-46; became lieutenant. *Member:* Modern Language Association of America, American Society for Eighteenth-Century Studies (charter member), Rocky Mountain Modern Language Association (president, 1958), Utah Academy of Sciences, Arts, and Letters, Phi Beta Kappa, Phi Kappa Phi (president of local chapter, 1971-73). *Awards, honors:* Rhodes scholar, Oxford University, 1939; American Council of Learned Societies fellow, 1942; American Philosophical Society grant, 1964; Redd Award in Humanities, Utah Academy, 1976; College of Humanities Distinguished Faculty Award, Brigham Young University, 1977.

*WRITINGS:* (Editor) John Nichols, *Minor Lives: A Collection of Biographies,* Harvard University Press, 1971; (editor) *Instruction and Delight,* Brigham Young University Press, 1976. Contributor of articles to *PMLA, Shakespeare Quarterly, Studies in English Literature, Western Humani-*

ties *Review, Literature and Psychology,* and other journals, and of poems to *Beloit Poetry Journal, Western Humanities Review,* and other periodicals.

*WORK IN PROGRESS:* A biography of James H. Hart; editing Warton manuscripts in British Museum; research on the writings of John Nichols.

\* \* \*

## HART, John Fraser 1924-

*PERSONAL:* Born April 5, 1924, in Staunton, Va.; son of Freeman H. (a professor) and Jean (Fraser) Hart; married Meredith Davis, February 5, 1949; children: Richard Laird, Meredith Anne. *Education:* Attended Hampden-Sydney College, 1939-40; Emory University, A.B., 1943; Northwestern University, M.A., 1949, Ph.D., 1950. *Office:* Department of Geography, University of Minnesota, Minneapolis, Minn. 55455.

*CAREER:* University of Georgia, Athens, assistant professor, 1949-53, associate professor of geography, 1953-55; Indiana University at Bloomington, assistant professor, 1955-58, associate professor, 1958-63, professor of geography, 1963-67, acting head of department, 1956-58; University of Minnesota, Minneapolis, professor of geography, 1967—. *Military service:* U.S. Naval Reserve, 1944-46, 1955; became lieutenant commander. *Member:* Association of American Geographers, Royal Scottish Geographical Society (fellow), Pierce County Geographical Society. *Awards, honors:* Medal of University of Liege, 1960, for contributions to geography; Association of American Geographers citation, 1969, for meritorious contributions to geography; National Council of Georgia Education award, 1971, for teaching of geography.

*WRITINGS: British Moorlands,* University of Georgia Press, 1955; *Geographic Manpower,* Association of American Geographers, 1966; *Southeastern United States,* Van Nostrand, 1966; *United States and Canada,* Ginn, 1967; (editor) *Regions of the United States,* Harper, 1973; *Manpower in Geography,* Association of American Geographers, 1973; *The Look of the Land,* Prentice-Hall, 1975. Editor of *Annals* of the Association of American Geographers, 1970-75.

*WORK IN PROGRESS: This World of Ours.*

\* \* \*

## HARTLEY, L(eslie) P(oles) 1895-1972

December 30, 1895—December 13, 1972; English novelist, short story writer, and critic. Obituaries: *New York Times,* December 14, 1972; *Time,* December 25, 1972. (See index for *CA* sketch)

\* \* \*

## HARTSHORNE, Thomas L(lewellyn) 1935-

*PERSONAL:* Born June 28, 1935, in Madison, Wis.; son of Llewellyn Harold (a clerk) and Emma (Bossart) Hartshorne; married Joan Taliaferro (a choreographer-teacher), February 1, 1958. *Education:* University of Wisconsin, B.A., 1955, Ph.D., 1965; attended Brown University, 1955-56. *Home:* 4589 Emerson Rd., South Euclid, Ohio 44121. *Office:* Department of History, Cleveland State University, Cleveland, Ohio 44115.

*CAREER:* Kent State University, Kent, Ohio, assistant professor of history, 1962-66; Cleveland State University, Cleveland, Ohio, associate professor of history, 1966—.

*Military service:* U.S. Army, 1959-61. *Member:* Organization of American Historians, American Studies Association, Popular Culture Association.

*WRITINGS: The Distorted Image: Changing Conceptions of the American Character since Turner,* Case Western Reserve University Press, 1968. Contributor of reviews to *Cleveland after Dark.*

*WORK IN PROGRESS:* An article on changing aesthetic ideas in U.S. in the 1920's; research for a book on U.S. cultural history since 1945.

*SIDELIGHTS:* Thomas Hartshorne is especially interested in dealing with America's arts in a truly historical manner, that is, to deal with works of art, and with popular culture as well, as "documents" which can be used by a historian to illuminate the past.

*       *       *

**HARVEY, Lashley Grey   1900-**

*PERSONAL:* Born December 18, 1900, in California, Mo.; son of Alexander Nunn (a banker and farmer) and Ella (Inglish) Harvey; married Ernestine Dow, August 7, 1926 (died July, 1974); children: David Dow. *Education:* William Jewell College, A.B., 1925; Stanford University, A.M., 1930; graduate study at Williams College, 1932, Northwestern University, 1932, and University of Michigan, 1935; Harvard University, Ph.D., 1942. *Politics:* Democrat. *Home and office:* 109 West Aurora St., California, Mo. 65018.

*CAREER:* High school teacher in Missouri, Montana, and Wyoming, 1924-26; high school principal in Greybull, Wyo., 1926-29; Adams State Teachers College (now Adams State College of Colorado), Alamosa, Colo., 1930-36, began as assistant professor, became associate professor of economics and political science; University of New Hampshire, Durham, assistant professor of government and executive secretary of Bureau of Government Research, 1938-42, 1945-46; Boston University, Boston, Mass., assistant professor, 1946-47, associate professor, 1947-49, Maxwell Professor of Government and Citizenship, 1949-66, professor emeritus, 1966—, chairman of department of government, 1948-56, director of Bureau of Public Administration, 1947-66. Fulbright professor, London School of Economics and Political Science, University of London, 1951-52; visiting professor, University of Ankara, 1953-54, Norfolk State College, 1968, and College of the Holy Cross, 1968-69. Member, United Nations mission to establish the Public Administration Institute for Turkey and the Middle East, 1953-54. *Military service:* U.S. Naval Reserve, 1942-45; became lieutenant commander; served at Pearl Harbor and Saipan. *Member:* American Political Science Association, American Society for Public Administration, National Municipal League, New England Political Science Association (secretary, 1948-49), Massachusetts City and Town Managers Association (honorary member), Maine Municipal League (honorary member), New Hampshire Municipal League (co-founder).

*WRITINGS:* (With Frank C. Spencer) *Colorado: Its Government and History,* Herrick Book, 1934; *Bibliography of State and Local Government in New England,* Bureau of Public Administration, Boston University, 1952; (contributor) *Presidential Nominating Politics,* Johns Hopkins Press, 1952; (contributor) Belle Zeller, editor, *American State Legislatures,* Crowell, 1954; (contributor) Paul David, editor, *The Northeast Politics,* Johns Hopkins Press, 1954; *A Guide to Governmental Procurement Techniques,* Inter-

continental Book, 1965; *Water: Methods of Use and Conservation,* Intercontinental Book, 1966. Contributor to *Encyclopaedia Britannica.* Contributor of more than one hundred articles to public administration journals.

*WORK IN PROGRESS:* State and local government in New England.

*       *       *

**HARVEY, O. J.   1927-**

*PERSONAL:* Born August 27, 1927, in Corinne, Okla.; son of Joseph Marion (a farmer) and Nina Inez (Little) Harvey; married Mary Christine Minton (a teacher), November 17, 1950. *Education:* Attended Oklahoma State University, 1945; University of Oklahoma, B.A., 1950, M.A., 1951, Ph.D., 1954. *Home:* 435 South 68th St., Boulder, Colo. 80303. *Office:* Department of Psychology, University of Colorado, Boulder, Colo. 80302.

*CAREER:* University of Colorado, Boulder, assistant professor, 1958-60, associate professor, 1960-62, professor of psychology, 1962—. *Military service:* U.S. Navy, 1946-47. *Member:* American Psychological Association, American Educational Research Association. *Awards, honors:* Social Science Research Post-Doctoral fellow, Yale University, 1954-55; Center for Advanced Study, Stanford University, fellow, 1965-66; Career Development award, National Institute of Mental Health, 1966-71.

*WRITINGS:* (With David E. Hunt and Harold M. Schroder) *Conceptual Systems and Personality Organization,* Wiley, 1961; (editor) *Motivation and Social Interaction,* Ronald, 1963; (editor) *Experience, Structure and Adaptability,* Springer Publishing, 1966. Contributor of over fifty articles to psychology journals.

*       *       *

**HASLEY, Louis (Leonard)   1906-**

*PERSONAL:* Surname is pronounced *Haze*-lee; born November 3, 1906, in Amana, Iowa; son of Joseph Peter (a farmer) and Emma (Hirt) Hasley; married Lucile Hardman (a free-lance writer and painter), June 19, 1935; children: Mrs. Albert Ysordia, Mrs. Paul Lombardi (deceased), Daniel L. *Education:* University of Notre Dame, A.B., 1930, A.M., 1931; summer graduate study at Columbia University, 1932, University of Chicago, 1933, and University of Wisconsin, 1936. *Politics:* Democrat. *Religion:* Roman Catholic. *Home:* 3128 Wilder Dr., South Bend, Ind. 46615.

*CAREER:* Secretary and law office clerk, 1924-26; University of Notre Dame, Notre Dame, Ind., instructor, 1931-34, assistant professor, 1934-37, associate professor, 1937-43, professor of English, 1943-72, professor emeritus, 1972—, assistant dean of College of Arts and Letters, 1942-49, assistant chairman of department of English, 1959-64. Forever Learning Institute, professor and member of advisory board, 1974—. *Member:* Indiana College English Association (president, 1970-71).

*WRITINGS:* (Editor) *The Best of Bill Nye's Humor,* College & University Press, 1972. Contributor of short stories, poems, humor, essays, and articles to scholarly and general periodicals.

*SIDELIGHTS:* Louis Hasley wrote *CA:* "Since retirement I confine myself mostly to writing serious poetry and humor. My volunteer work at Forever Learning Institute I find a rewarding way to 'pay somebody back' for the generous help given me by others along the way."

## HASSING, Per 1916-

*PERSONAL:* Born February 7, 1916, in Bureaa, Sweden; son of Hjalmar M. (a merchant) and Sigrid (Johannessen) Hassing; married Ruth Karen Heggoey (a registered nurse), August 16, 1941; children: Arne, Ase Hassing Blake. *Education:* Methodist School of Theology, Gothenburg, Sweden, Dipl.Th., 1937; Hartford Seminary Foundation, M.A., 1948; American University, Ph.D., 1960. *Politics:* "Independent voter." *Home:* 17 Glendale Rd., Lake Junaluska, N.C. 28745.

*CAREER:* Ordained to ministry of United Methodist Church, 1937; minister in Norway, 1937-39, in Rhodesia, 1939-59; Boston University, School of Theology, Boston, Mass., professor of world Christianity, 1960-78, professor emeritus, 1978—. *Member:* African Studies Association (fellow), Association of Professors of Missions, Society for African Church History, International Association for Mission Studies, Norwegian-American Historical Association. *Awards, honors:* American Association of Theological Schools grant, 1967-68.

*WRITINGS:* (Contributor) Helge Alm, editor, *Vaar Misjon,* Norsk Forlagsselskap, 1956; (contributor) Paul S. King, editor, *Missions in Rhodesia,* Inyati Centenary Trust, 1959; (contributor) N. R. Bennett, editor, *Leadership in Eastern Africa: Six Political Biographies,* Boston University Press, 1968; (contributor) Stephen Neill, Gerald H. Anderson, and John Goodwin, editors, *Concise Dictionary of the Christian World Mission,* Lutterworth, 1971. Contributor to journals in the United States and Norway.

*WORK IN PROGRESS:* Research on theological education in east Africa.

\*    \*    \*

## HASTINGS, Arthur Claude 1935-

*PERSONAL:* Born May 23, 1935, in Neosho, Mo.; son of Chauncey Arthur (in insurance) and Mildred (Mace) Hastings; married Sandra Joan Gray, March 21, 1969. *Education:* Tulane University, B.A., 1957; Northwestern University, M.A., 1958, Ph.D., 1962. *Home and office:* 2451 Benjamin Dr., Mountain View, Calif. 94040.

*CAREER:* University of Nevada, Reno, assistant professor of speech, 1960-63; Stanford University, Stanford, Calif., member of faculty of department of speech, 1963-71; California State University, San Jose (now San Jose State University), lecturer in speech communication, 1971-72; Hastings Associates Consulting Services, Mountain View, Calif., president, 1972—. Visiting summer professor, University of California, Santa Barbara, 1963; adjunct professor, John F. Kennedy University, 1977—. *Member:* Speech Communication Association of America, International Society for General Semantics, Parapsychology Association.

*WRITINGS:* (With Russel R. Windes) *Argumentation and Advocacy,* Random House, 1965. General editor of Macmillan's "Speech and Communication" series.

*WORK IN PROGRESS:* Language, consciousness, and reality; reasoning processes; parapsychological phenomena.

\*    \*    \*

## HATCH, William H(enry) P(aine) 1875-1972

1875—November 11, 1972; American New Testament scholar and author of religious works. Obituaries: *New York Times,* November 13, 1972.

## HATTON, Robert Wayland 1934-

*PERSONAL:* Born February 5, 1934, in Columbus, Ohio; son of Wayland Charles and Ida Catherine (Eblin) Hatton; married Marlene Tuller, June 25, 1954; children: Marc, Heidi, Kevin. *Education:* Capital University, B.A. (magna cum laude), 1957; Middlebury College, M.A. (summa cum laude), 1959; also studied at Ohio State University and University of Madrid. *Politics:* Republican. *Religion:* Baptist. *Home:* 6565 Calgary Ct., Columbus, Ohio 43229. *Office:* Department of Modern Languages, Capital University, Columbus, Ohio 43209.

*CAREER:* Teacher of Spanish and biology in public schools in Columbus, Ohio, 1958-60; U.S. Information Service, Bogota, Colombia, Binational Center director, 1960-62; Ohio Wesleyan University, Delaware, instructor in modern languages, 1962-63; Capital University, Columbus, assistant professor, 1963-66, associate professor, 1966-71, professor of modern languages, 1971—, acting chairman of department, 1965-68, chairman of department, 1976—. Resident director, North American college students in Colombia, 1963; escort interpreter in Spanish, U.S. Department of State, 1966-69; consecutive translator, World Weightlifting Congress, 1970. Member of study abroad committee, Regional Council on International Education. *Member:* American Association of Teachers of Spanish and Portuguese, American Council on the Teaching of Foreign Languages, Taurine Bibliophiles of America, Ohio Modern Language Teachers Association, Columbus Modern Language Teachers Association. *Awards, honors:* Faculty growth award, American Lutheran Church, 1965, 1967, 1971, 1973, 1975, 1977; Capital University Praestantia Award for distinguished teaching, 1969.

*WRITINGS:* (Editor with Frank Sedwick) *La Gloria de don Ramiro,* Heath, 1966; (editor with Dan Romani and Gene Allsup) *Hombre hispanico,* with teacher's manual, C. E. Merrill, 1970; (contributor of photographs) Agnes Brady and Harley Oberhelman, *Espanol Moderno I,* C. E. Merrill, 1970; *Los Clarines del miedo,* Ginn, 1971; (with Gordon Jackson) *The Bullfight: A Teaching and Study Guide,* Advancement Press of America, 1974. Contributor to *Hispania, Spanish Today, Ohio History, Foreign Language Annals,* and other journals.

*WORK IN PROGRESS:* Articles on the history of cheerleading, on Ohio author Louis Bromfield, and on asking questions and getting answers.

*SIDELIGHTS:* Robert Hatton has traveled all over the world and has lived in Spain and Colombia. He told *CA* that he and his wife were married on the television program "Bride and Groom."

\*    \*    \*

## HAUBERG, Clifford A(lvin) 1906-

*PERSONAL:* Born January 12, 1906, in Fergus Falls, Minn.; son of Andrew (a bricklayer) and Anna (Langness) Hauberg; married Marguerite Pooley, April 6, 1936; children: Ann Marie Wilson, Jan Leslie Witcraft, Marguerite Sue. *Education:* University of Minnesota, B.S. in Ed., 1931, M.A., 1940, Ph.D., 1950. *Politics:* Independent Democrat. *Religion:* Methodist. *Home:* Route 5, Northfield, Minn. 55057.

*CAREER:* High school teacher of social studies and principal in Braham, Minn., 1931-37; high school teacher in Cristobal, Canal Zone, Panama, 1937-45; University of Minnesota, Minneapolis, assistant professor of history, 1945-47;

St. Olaf College, Northfield, Minn., assistant professor, 1947-50, associate professor, 1950-64, professor of history, 1964-72, chairman of department, 1965-69. Latin-American consultant for world affairs program conducted by Hill Family Foundation and Winton Fund. *Member:* American Historical Association, Hispanic American Historical Association, Mississippi Valley Historical Association, American Association of University Professors, Phi Delta Kappa, Phi Alpha Theta. *Awards, honors:* Social Science Research Council grant, 1952-53.

*WRITINGS: Latin American Revolutions,* Denison, 1968; *Puerto Rico and the Puerto Ricans,* Twayne, 1974. Contributor to *Grolier Encyclopedia* and professional journals, including *Current History.*

*WORK IN PROGRESS:* Revised edition of *Latin American Revolutions;* an autobiography, *Has the Blue Hen Laid an Egg Today?*

*SIDELIGHTS:* Clifford Hauberg told *CA* that his chief motive in writing has been "to help make the world a better place to live by clarifying and thus ameliorating the causes that often lead to man's greatest holocausts—wars." *Avocational interests:* Hunting, fishing, golf, bridge.

*       *       *

### HAUSKNECHT, Murray       1925-

*PERSONAL:* Born October 28, 1925, in New York, N.Y.; son of David (a businessman) and Celia (Schulsinger) Hausknecht; married Ellen Rosenbaum (a teacher), 1950; children: David, Gina. *Education:* College of the City of New York (now City College of the City University of New York), B.S., 1948; Columbia University, M.A., 1950, Ph.D., 1961. *Residence:* Long Island City, N.Y. *Office:* Department of Sociology, Herbert H. Lehman College of the City University of New York, Bronx, N.Y. 10468.

*CAREER:* Herbert H. Lehman College of the City University of New York, Bronx, N.Y., instructor, 1961-64, assistant professor, 1964-67, associate professor, 1967-70, professor of sociology, 1970—. *Military service:* U.S. Army, 1943-46. *Member:* American Sociological Association, Eastern Sociological Society.

*WRITINGS: The Joiners,* Bedminster, 1962; (editor with Jewel Bellush) *Urban Renewal: People, Politics and Planning,* Doubleday, 1967.

*       *       *

### HAWLEY, Amos H(enry)       1910-

*PERSONAL:* Born December 5, 1910, in St. Louis, Mo.; son of Amos H. (an engineer) and Margaret B. (Holtzclaw) Hawley; married Gretchen Haller, September 5, 1937; children: Steven Amos, Margie Lynne, Susan Esther, Patrice Ann. *Education:* Attended Miami University, Oxford, Ohio, 1929-30; University of Cincinnati, A.B., 1936; University of Michigan, A.M., 1938, Ph.D., 1941. *Home:* 407 Brookside Dr., Chapel Hill, N.C. 27514. *Office:* Department of Sociology, University of North Carolina, Chapel Hill, N.C. 27514.

*CAREER:* University of Michigan, Ann Arbor, instructor, 1941-44, assistant professor, 1944-47, associate professor, 1947-51, professor of sociology, 1951-66, chairman of department, 1952-61, director of Social Science Research Project, 1946-65; University of North Carolina at Chapel Hill, professor, 1966-71, Kenan Professor of Sociology, 1971—. Visiting professor, University of the Philippines, 1953-54. Director of census, Aruba, Netherlands Antilles, 1960;

member of U.S. Committee on International Exchange of Persons, 1962-66; adviser to Prime Minister's Office, Thailand, 1964-65; demographic adviser to government of Malaysia, 1973-74. Senior consultant to Office of Operations Research, Department of the Army, 1945-48, Human Behavior Research Office, Department of the Air Force, 1945-48, and Housing and Home Finance Agency, 1950-53; consultant to Ford Foundation on demographic research and training in the Caribbean area, 1966-68; member of National Academy of Sciences advisory committee to Department of Housing and Urban Development, 1969-74, and of executive committee, Behavioral Sciences Division, National Academy of Sciences, 1970-78.

*MEMBER:* International Union for the Scientific Study of Population, Population Association of America (vice president, 1955; president, 1971-72), American Association for the Advancement of Science (fellow), American Sociological Association (president, 1978), Sociological Research Association, American Academy of Arts and Sciences, Southern Sociological Society. *Awards, honors:* Fulbright grant for research in Italy, 1959; Litt.D. from University of Cincinnati, 1977.

*WRITINGS: The Population of Michigan 1840-1960: An Analysis of Growth, Distribution, and Composition,* Bureau of Government, University of Michigan, 1949; (author of foreword) Don J. Bogue, *The Structure of the Metropolitan Community,* University of Michigan Press, 1949; *Human Ecology: A Theory of Community Structure,* Ronald, 1950; (with Ronald Freedman, Werner S. Landecker, and Horace Miner) *Principles of Sociology,* Holt, 1952, revised edition, 1956; *The Changing Shape of Metropolitan America,* Free Press, 1955; *The Population of Aruba: An Analysis Based on the Census of 1960,* Office of Vital Statistics and Census (Aruba), 1960; (editor and author of introduction) *R. D. McKenzie on Human Ecology,* University of Chicago Press, 1968; (with Basil Zimmer) *Metropolitan Area Schools: Resistance to District Reorganization,* Sage Publications, 1968; (with Zimmer) *The Metropolitan Community: Its People and Government,* Sage Publications, 1970; *Urban Society: An Ecological Approach,* Ronald, 1971; (editor) *Freedom of Choice in Housing,* National Academy of Sciences, 1972; (editor) *Segregation in Residential Areas,* National Academy of Sciences, 1973; (editor) *Man and Environment,* New Viewpoints, 1975; *Toward an Understanding of Metropolitan America,* Canfield Press, 1975; (editor with Vincent Rock) *Metropolitan America in Contemporary Perspective,* Sage Publications, 1975.

Contributor: Edwin Stone and others, *Public Administration in the Philippines,* University of the Philippines Press, 1955; Philip Hauser and O. D. Duncan, editors, *The Study of Population,* University of Chicago Press, 1959; Morris Janowitz, editor, *Community Political Systems,* Free Press, 1961; Rene Konig, editor, *Handbuch der empirischen Sozialforschung,* Enke Verlag, 1962, revised edition, 1967; Ronald Freedman, editor, *Population: The Vital Revolution,* Doubleday-Anchor, 1964; Bernard Berelson and others, editors, *Family Planning and Population Programs,* University of Chicago Press, 1965; S. J. Behrman, Leslie Corsa, and Ronald Freedman, editors, *Fertility and Family Planning: A World View,* University of Michigan Press, 1969; Hans-Georg Gadamer, editor, *Nieu Anthropologie,* George Thieme Verlag, 1972; J. V. Ferreira and S. S. Jha, editors, *The Outlook Tower: Essays on Urbanization in Memory of Patrick Geddes,* Popular Prakashan (Bombay), 1975.

Writer of tape, "Urbanization in the Modern World,"

McGraw-Hill Sound Seminars, 1969. Editor, American Sociological Association *Series on Issues and Trends in Sociology,* 1968-71. Contributor to *A Dictionary of the Social Sciences, Encyclopaedia Britannica, Worterbuch der Soziologie,* and *International Encyclopedia of the Social Sciences;* contributor of about fifty articles and forty reviews to journals.

\* \* \*

## HAYASHI, Tetsumaro 1929-

*PERSONAL:* Born March 22, 1929, in Sakaide, Japan; son of Tetsuro (a clergyman) and Shieko (Honjyo) Hayashi; married Skiko Sakuranti, April 14, 1960; children: Richard Hideki. *Education:* Okayama University, B.A., 1953; Wilmington College, Wilmington, Ohio, further study, 1954-55; University of Florida, M.A., 1957; Kent State University, M.A. in L.S., 1959, Ph.D., 1968. *Politics:* Democrat. *Home:* 1405 North Kimberly Lane, Muncie, Ind. 47306. *Office:* Department of English, Ball State University, Muncie, Ind. 47306.

*CAREER:* Culver-Stockton College, Canton, Mo., assistant professor of English and associate director of library, 1959-63; Kent State University, Kent, Ohio, instructor in English, 1965-68; Ball State University, Muncie, Ind., assistant professor, 1968-72, associate professor of English, 1972—. *Member:* Modern Language Association of America, John Steinbeck Society of America (co-founder; director, 1966—), American Library Association, Shakespeare Association of America, Association for Asian Studies, Midwest Modern Language Association. *Awards, honors:* Folger Shakespeare Library senior fellowship, 1972; American Philosophical Society fellowship, 1975; American Council of Learned Societies fellowship, 1976.

*WRITINGS: Amerika bunka sobyo* (title means "Sketches of American Culture"), Tarumi Shobo (Tokyo), 1960; *John Steinbeck: A Concise Bibliography, 1930-65,* Scarecrow, 1967, updated edition published as *A New Steinbeck Bibliography, 1929-71,* 1973; *Arthur Miller Criticism, 1930-1967,* Scarecrow, 1969, 2nd edition published as *An Index to Arthur Miller Criticism,* 1976; *A Textual Study of "A Looking Glass for London and England," by Thomas Lodge and Robert Greene,* Ball State University, 1969; (editor) Thomas Lodge and Robert Green, *A Looking Glass for London and England: An Elizabethan Text* (based on Hayashi's doctoral thesis), Scarecrow, 1970; *Robert Greene Criticism: A Comprehensive Bibliography,* Scarecrow, 1971; (editor with Richard Astro) *Steinbeck: The Man and His Work* (proceedings of Steinbeck Conference), Oregon State University Press, 1971; *Shakespeare's Sonnets: A Record of 20th Century Criticism,* Scarecrow, 1972; (editor) *Steinbeck's Literary Dimension,* Scarecrow, 1973; *A Textual Study of Robert Greene's Orlando Furioso,* Ball State University Press, 1973; *A Study Guide to Steinbeck: A Handbook to His Major Works,* Scarecrow, 1974; *A Study Guide to Steinbeck's "The Long Valley,"* Pierian, 1976; (with Kenneth D. Swan) *Steinbeck's Prophetic Vision of America,* Taylor University, 1976; (editor) *John Steinbeck: A Dictionary of His Fictional Characters,* Scarecrow, 1976; *The Poetry of Robert Greene,* Ball State University Press, 1977. Contributor of more than fifty articles to journals in America, Japan, and India, and twelve short stories to American periodicals. General editor, "Steinbeck Monograph" series. Editor, *Steinbeck Quarterly,* 1968—.

## HAYS, Richard D. 1942-

*PERSONAL:* Born November 12, 1942, in West Frankfort, Ill.; son of Arthur H. (an executive) and Dorothy Ramona (Polson) Hays; married Carolyn Sue Brewer, May 30, 1964; children: Kristin Anne, Karin Leigh. *Education:* Purdue University, B.S.M.E., 1965, M.S.I.A., 1966; Indiana University, D.B.A., 1969. *Home:* 5933 Chestnut St., New Orleans, La. 70115. *Office:* Graduate School of Business Administration, Tulane University, New Orleans, La. 70118.

*CAREER:* Duncan Electric Co., Lafayette, Ind., assistant design engineer, 1965; Indiana University, Bloomington, state analyst, 1966-68; Tulane University, New Orleans, La., associate professor of international business and organizational behavior, 1969—. President, Development Group, Inc., 1972—. *Member:* American Society of Mechanical Engineers, Society for International Development, Association for Education in International Business, American Institute for the Decision Sciences.

*WRITINGS:* (With Christopher Korth and Manucher Roudiani) *International Business: An Introduction to the World of the Multinational Firm,* Prentice-Hall, 1972. Contributor to business journals.

*SIDELIGHTS: International Business* has been translated into Spanish.†

\* \* \*

## HEAD, Constance 1939-

*PERSONAL:* Born March 1, 1939, in San Antonio, Tex.; daughter of C. C. and Ruby Mae (Barron) Head. *Education:* Trinity University, B.A., 1959; Duke University, B.D., 1963, M.A., 1967, Ph.D., 1968. *Home address:* Route 66, Box 92-A, Cullowhee, N.C. 28723. *Office:* Department of History, Western Carolina University, Cullowhee, N.C. 28723.

*CAREER:* Western Carolina University, Cullowhee, N.C., 1967—, currently professor of history and religion. *Awards, honors:* National Endowment for the Humanities Younger Humanist fellowship, 1972-73.

*WRITINGS: Justinian II of Byzantium,* University of Wisconsin Press, 1972; *The Emperor Julian,* Twayne, 1976; *Imperial Twilight,* Nelson–Hall, 1977. Contributor of articles to *Mankind, Byzantion, Archivum Historiae Pontificiae, History Today,* and other journals.

\* \* \*

## HEADINGS, Mildred J. 1908-

*PERSONAL:* Born June 22, 1908, in McAlisterville, Pa.; daughter of Isaac G. (a physician) and Mary L. (Moore) Headings. *Education:* Bucknell University, A.B. (cum laude), 1929; Cornell University, M.A., 1931, Ph.D., 1938; also attended Sorbonne, University of Paris, 1931-32, Zimmern School of International Studies, Geneva, 1935, and Columbia University. *Politics:* Democrat. *Religion:* Presbyterian.

*CAREER:* Teacher of history and French at Miss Wright's School, Bryn Mawr, Pa., 1933-36, and Hannah More Academy, Reisterstown, Md., 1937-38; Linden Hall, Lititz, Pa., teacher of history, 1938-40; Hood College, Frederick, Md., instructor, 1942-44, assistant professor, 1944-46, associate professor, 1947-49, professor of history, 1950-62. *Member:* American Historical Association, French Historical Society, Societe d'Histoire Moderne, American Association of University Professors, American Association of University

Women, League of Women Voters, Women's Democratic League of Frederick County.

*WRITINGS: French Freemasonry under the Third Republic,* Johns Hopkins Press, 1949, 2nd edition, 1971. Contributor to journals.

*WORK IN PROGRESS: The Relationship of the French Radical Party to the French Masonic Lodges, 1858-1906.*

*SIDELIGHTS:* Mildred Headings' independent research has involved two and a half years of residence in Paris; other travel has included Canada, Central and South America, Russia, the Near East, and western Europe.†

\*     \*     \*

## HEATH, G. Louis   1944-

*PERSONAL:* Born September 4, 1944, in Portola, Calif.; son of Sam Reuben (a railroad worker) and Laura (Klemetson) Heath. *Education:* University of California, Berkeley, B.A., 1966, M.A., 1967, Ph.D., 1969. *Religion:* Humanist. *Home:* 806 West Locust, Bloomington, Ill. 81701. *Office:* Department of Education, Illinois State University, Normal, Ill. 61761.

*CAREER:* Illinois State University, Normal, 1969—, currently associate professor of education. Consultant to Illinois Commission on Human Relations, 1969—. Visiting summer professor, McGill University, 1972, University of British Columbia, 1973, Dalhousie University, 1974, University of New Brunswick, 1975, University of Regina, 1976, and Memorial University of Newfoundland, 1977. *Member:* American Educational Studies Association.

*WRITINGS:* (Contributor) William W. Brickman and Stanley Lehrer, editors, *Conflict and Change on the Campus: The Response to Student Hyperactivism,* Society for the Advancement of Education, 1970; *Red, Brown, and Black Demands for Better Education,* Westminster, 1972; *The Hot Campus: The Politics That Impede Change in the Technoversity,* Scarecrow, 1973; *The New Teacher: Changing Patterns of Authority and Responsibility in the American Schools,* Harper, 1973; (contributor) Dwight Allen, editor, *Controversies in Education,* Saunders, 1974; *Vandals in the Bomb Factory: The History and Literature of the Students for a Democratic Society,* Scarecrow, 1976; *Off the Pigs!: The History and Literature of the Black Panther Party,* Scarecrow, 1976; *The Black Panther Leaders Speak,* Scarecrow, 1976; *Mutiny Does Not Happen Lightly: The Literature of the American Resistance to the Vietnam War,* Scarecrow, 1976. Also author of *The Indians of Canada: History, Documents, Bibliography,* and *Death in the Trenches: A Young World War One Soldier's Letters Home to Newfoundland.* Contributor of over fifty articles to periodicals. Contributing editor, *Interracial Review.*

*WORK IN PROGRESS: Maple Leaf Six: An American Professor's Memoirs of Six Summers Teaching in Canadian Universities.*

*SIDELIGHTS:* G. Louis Heath wrote *CA:* "I enjoy the emotional reward that arrives when someone writes me or approaches me after class and says, 'This chapter made me angry about the plight of the American Indian' or 'This book made me think in a new way.' This is what I'm about: writing about social concerns in a popular way. I know I can teach many more people through my writings then I can possibly address personally. That idea, the idea that a teacher can say something valuable and critical about his society and be heard, and not be sent to a concentration camp or mental hospital, or be outright killed, as is the case in some socie-

ties, is at least a small part of what compels me. Also, more importantly, there is that mixture of pleasure and pain that is the sado-masochistic joy of writing and, of course, my ego and writer's pride, and the fact that I am a resolute loner who likes barriers about him such as an unlisted phone number and an underground reserved parking space at the university. These factors, plus whatever blind forces animate me, have moved me through about fifty published articles, seven published books, and two manuscripts unpublished to date."

\*     \*     \*

## HEDGES, William L(eonard)   1923-

*PERSONAL:* Born February 16, 1923, in Arlington, Mass.; son of James B. (a college professor) and Nina (Leonard) Hedges; married Elaine Catherine Ryan (a college professor), June 28, 1956; children: Marietta, James Leonard. *Education:* Haverford College, B.A., 1946; University of Paris, additional study, 1949-50; Harvard University, Ph.D., 1954. *Home:* 317 Hawthorn Rd., Baltimore, Md. 21210. *Office:* Department of English, Goucher College, Baltimore, Md. 21204.

*CAREER:* University of Wisconsin—Madison, instructor in English, 1953-56; Goucher College, Baltimore, Md., assistant professor, 1956-62, associate professor, 1962-67, professor of English, 1967—, head of department, 1968-71, 1977-78, head of program in American studies, 1972—. Visiting assistant professor, University of California, Berkeley, 1957-58. *Military service:* U.S. Army, 1943-45; became sergeant; received Purple Heart. *Member:* Modern Language Association of America, Phi Beta Kappa. *Awards, honors:* Fulbright fellow in Paris, 1949-50; American Council of Learned Societies fellow, 1963-64.

*WRITINGS:* (Contributor) Perry Miller, editor, *Major Writers of America,* Harcourt, 1962; *Washington Irving: An American Study, 1802-1832,* Johns Hopkins Press, 1965; (contributor) Hennig Cohen, editor, *Landmarks of American Writing,* Basic Books, 1969; (contributor) Matthew J. Bruccoli, editor, *The Chief Glory,* Southern Illinois University Press, 1973; (contributor) Leo Lemay, editor, *The Oldest Revolutionary,* University of Pennsylvania Press, 1976. Contributor to professional journals and *Baltimore Sun.* Member of editorial board, *Early American Literature,* 1971-74.

*WORK IN PROGRESS: American Literature in the Age of Adams and Jefferson; Land and Imagination: The Rural American Dream.*

\*     \*     \*

## HEGARTY, Ellen   1918-
### (Sister M[ary] Loyola Hegarty)

*PERSONAL:* Born February 5, 1918, in Cork, Ireland; U.S. citizen; daughter of Michael (a music teacher) and Elizabeth (Kearney) Hegarty. *Education:* Loyola University, New Orleans, La., B.S., 1948; Dominican College, Houston, Tex., B.A., 1951; Catholic University of America, M.A., 1954; California State University, Long Beach, M.P.A., 1977. *Home and office:* Sisters of Charity of the Incarnate Word, 6510 Lawndale Ave., Houston, Tex. 77023.

*CAREER:* Roman Catholic religious of Sisters of Charity of the Incarnate Word; Dominican College, Houston, Tex., instructor, 1954-56, associate professor of English, 1956-70; Sisters of Charity of the Incarnate Word (religious order),

Houston, director of studies, 1956-70; St. Anthony High School, Long Beach, Calif., teacher of English, 1970-77; St. Mary Medical Center, Long Beach, assistant administrator, 1977-78; St. Joseph Villa, Salt Lake City, Utah, administrator, 1977-78; Sisters of Charity of the Incarnate Word, superior general, 1978—. Juniorate director, Villa de Matel, Houston, 1969-70; member of board of directors, St. Mary's Hospital, Long Beach, Calif., 1970-77. Registered pharmacist in State of Louisiana.

*WRITINGS*—Under name, Sister M(ary) Loyola Hegarty: *Serving with Gladness: The Origin and History of the Congregation of the Sisters of Charity of the Incarnate Word,* Bruce, 1967. Contributor to *New Catholic Encyclopedia* and *Catholic Encyclopedia for School and Home.*

\* \* \*

## HEGGOY, Alf Andrew 1938-

*PERSONAL:* Born December 15, 1938, in Algiers, Algeria; naturalized U.S. citizen, 1959; son of W. N. (a missionary and author) and Hariet (Berggreen) Heggoy; married Carol Purkis, June, 1963 (divorced August, 1977); children: Ingrid, Eric and Brian (twins). *Education:* Randolph-Macon College, B.A., 1959; Duke University, M.A., 1961, Ph.D., 1963. *Politics:* Independent. *Religion:* Methodist. *Address:* P.O. Box 274, Danielsville, Ga. 30631. *Office:* Department of History, University of Georgia, Athens, Ga. 30601.

*CAREER:* Researcher in France and North Africa, 1963-65; University of Georgia, Athens, assistant professor, 1965-69, associate professor, 1969-77, professor of history, 1977—. Visiting assistant professor of history, North Carolina Wesleyan College, 1962-63; social science analyst, U.S. Army Research Office, summer, 1963. Volunteer fireman, Danielsville, Ga., 1974—. *Member:* Middle East Studies Association, African Studies Association, American Association of University Professors, French Colonial Historical Society (vice-president, 1974-75; president, 1976-78), Southern Historical Association, Pi Gamma Mu, Phi Alpha Theta. *Awards, honors:* Institute of International Education grant, 1963-64; Army Research Office of Durham grant, 1964-65; selected outstanding honors professor, University of Georgia, 1972, 1974; Joseph H. Parlss Award, 1974, for excellence in the teaching of history.

*WRITINGS: The African Policies of Gabriel Hanotaux,* University of Georgia Press, 1972; *Insurgency and Counterinsurgency in Algeria,* Indiana University Press, 1972. Contributor to *Muslim World, African Historical Studies, African Studies Review, International Journal of Middle East Studies,* and other publications. Editor, *Proceedings* of the French Colonial Historical Society, 1975-78.

*WORK IN PROGRESS: Oral Sources for North African Studies; Social and Intellectual History of Algeria,* completion expected in 1980.

*SIDELIGHTS:* Alf Heggoy is fluent in French and Norwegian, and reads Spanish, Danish, Swedish, German, and Italian.

\* \* \*

## HELLER, Celia S(topnicka)

*PERSONAL:* Born in Stryj, Poland; daughter of Emanuel (a businessman) and Ida (Rosenman) Heller. *Education:* Brooklyn College (now Brooklyn College of the City University of New York), B.A., 1950; Columbia University, M.A., 1952, Ph.D., 1962. *Home:* 15 West 72nd St., New York, N.Y. 10023. *Office:* Department of Sociology,

Hunter College of the City University of New York, 695 Park Ave., New York, N.Y. 10021.

*CAREER:* University of Cartagena, Cartagena, Colombia, lecturer in sociology, 1955-56; Vassar College, Poughkeepsie, N.Y., lecturer in sociology, 1963-64; Hunter College of the City University of New York, New York, N.Y., 1964—, began as assistant professor, professor of sociology, 1971—. Visiting professor at Tel Aviv University and Bar-Ilan University, 1970-71. *Member:* American Sociological Association (fellow), American Association for the Advancement of Science, American Professors for Peace in the Middle East (member of executive board), New York Academy of Science. *Awards, honors:* Grants from National Institute of Mental Health, 1962, 1970, Ford Foundation, 1962, and Memorial Foundation for Jewish Culture, 1968.

*WRITINGS: Mexican American Youth: Forgotten Youth at the Crossroads,* Random House, 1966; *Structured Social Inequality,* Macmillan, 1969; *New Converts to the American Dream,* College & University Press, 1971; *On the Edge of Destruction: Jews in Poland between the Two World Wars,* Columbia University Press, 1977. Contributor to sociology journals and to magazines, including *Commonweal* and *Commentary.*

\* \* \*

## HELLWIG, Monika Konrad 1929-
## (Mary Cuthbert)

*PERSONAL:* Born December 10, 1929, in Breslau, Germany; daughter of Rudolf (an economist) and Marianne (a sculptress; maiden name, Blaauw) Hellwig; children: Erica, Michael. *Education:* University of Liverpool, LL.B., 1949, C.S.Sc., 1951; Catholic University of America, M.A., 1956, Ph.D., 1968. *Politics:* "Fabian socialist persuasion." *Religion:* Roman Catholic. *Home:* 3826 T St. N.W., Washington, D.C. 20007. *Office:* Georgetown University, Washington, D.C. 20057.

*CAREER:* Family Service Society, Liverpool, England, case worker, 1951-52; St. Therese Junior College, Philadelphia, Pa., assistant professor of theology, 1956-62; Pius XII International Center, Rome, Italy, worked at English language desk, 1964-66; Georgetown University, Washington, D.C., lecturer, 1967-68, assistant professor, 1968-71, associate professor, 1971-77, professor of theology, 1977—. Has lectured to church groups around the world.

*WRITINGS*—All published by Pflaum, except as indicated: *What Are the Theologians Saying?,* 1971; *The Meaning of the Sacraments,* 1972; *Christian Creeds: A Faith to Live By,* 1973; *Tradition,* 1974; *The Eucharist and the Hunger of the World,* Paulist/Newman, 1976. Contributor to professional and popular journals, occasionally under pseudonym, Mary Cuthbert.

*WORK IN PROGRESS:* A book on Christian theology and Judaism; *Death and Hope.*

*SIDELIGHTS:* Monika Hellwig told *CA,* "I shall write as long as people keep asking me questions about the Christian faith and heritage."

\* \* \*

## HELM, Bertrand P. 1929-

*PERSONAL:* Born February 20, 1929; married Carolyn Wall, June 11, 1960; children: Kelly Carolyn, Michael Hollett. *Education:* University of Texas at Austin, B.A. (cum laude), 1952, M.A., 1959; Union Theological Seminary,

New York, N.Y., B.D., 1955; Tulane University, Ph.D., 1966. *Home:* 733 McCann, Springfield, Mo. 65804. *Office:* Department of Philosophy, Southwest Missouri State University, Springfield, Mo. 65802.

*CAREER:* Northwestern State College of Louisiana (now Northwestern State University of Louisiana), Natchitoches, teacher of philosophy, 1961-64; Southwest Missouri State University, Springfield, teacher of philosophy, 1966—. *Military service:* U.S. Army, 1948-50. *Member:* American Philosophical Association.

*WRITINGS:* (Editor) *The Systematic Philosophy of James K. Feibleman,* Springer-Verlag, 1971. Contributor of articles and book reviews to *Saturday Review, Journal of History of Ideas, Journal of History of Philosophy,* and *Journal of General Education.*

\* \* \*

## HEMDAHL, Reuel Gustaf    1903-1977

*PERSONAL:* Born June 20, 1903, in Princeton, Ill.; son of Gustaf Emil (a minister) and Selma (Anderson) Hemdahl; married Bernice Lillian Johnson, August 3, 1933; children: Ann Venette (Mrs. Richard Weston), Karen Gail (Mrs. Robert Coit, Jr.), Joyce Jeanine. *Education:* Augustana College, Rock Island, Ill., B.A., 1925; University of Chicago, graduate study, 1927-29; Northwestern University, Ph.D., 1932.

*CAREER:* Caseworker in Chicago, Ill., 1932-34; Chicago Adult Education Program of Work Projects Administration (WPA), Chicago, assistant superintendent, 1935-42; Pennsylvania Economy League, Pittsburgh, research associate, 1942-44; South Dakota State College (now University), Brookings, assistant professor of history, 1944-46; University of Louisville, Louisville, Ky., assistant professor, 1946-50, associate professor, 1950-57, professor of political science, 1957-69, professor emeritus, beginning 1969. Director, City of Louisville, Department of Urban Redevelopment, 1952-53; Louisville and Jefferson County Planning and Zoning Commission, member, 1954-61, chairman, 1958-61. Consultant to city government. *Member:* American Political Science Association, American Society for Public Administration, National League of Cities.

*WRITINGS: Digest of Redevelopment Contracts,* National Association of Housing and Redevelopment Officials, 1955; *Urban Renewal,* Scarecrow, 1959; *Cologne and Stockholm: Urban Planning and Land-Use Controls,* Scarecrow, 1971.

*WORK IN PROGRESS:* Research on human and social potentials of people-oriented urban planning for urban centers in the United States.

*SIDELIGHTS:* Reuel Hemdahl told *CA:* "In 1932, when I received my Ph.D. in political science there were no teaching positions available (depths of the Depression); therefore I accepted a position as caseworker in the Chicago 'Black Belt.' There I received my best education—the human problems of the slums, in which I have been concerned ever since. At a later date, this concern led me to urban renewal and city planning, even though I had no academic background in either. My disappointment in both has been the lack of concern about the human element—people. City planning in our society has become a species of low-level gadgeteering instead of a sincere effort to provide the good life for the total population."†

(Died August, 1977)

## HEMPHILL, Martha Locke    1904-1973

*PERSONAL:* Born July 25, 1904, in Fort Dodge, Iowa; daughter of Charles Alison (an artist) and Maude Lillian (Preston) Locke; married Lester G. Hemphill (a teacher), October 31, 1925 (deceased); children: Shirley (Mrs. James J. Magarian), Lester, Mary (Mrs. J. R. Swihart), JoEllen. *Education:* Attended Morningside College, 1922-23, University of Chicago, 1923-26, and Colorado State University, summers, 1927-29; National Children's Center, Green Lake, Wis., graduate. *Politics:* Democrat. *Religion:* Protestant. *Home:* 1617 Hobson Rd., Fort Wayne, Ind. 46805. *Office:* Crescent Avenue United Methodist Church, 1232 Crescent Ave., Fort Wayne, Ind. 46805.

*CAREER:* Ginn & Co., Boston, Mass., member of editorial department, 1923-26; South Wayne Baptist Church, Fort Wayne, Ind., director of nursery school, 1943-47; Crescent Avenue United Methodist Church, Fort Wayne, Ind., director of ministry for children and families, beginning 1957. Instructor in early childhood education, Fort Wayne Campus, Purdue University, beginning 1967. National Laboratory School teacher in Chicago, Ill., San Diego, Calif., and Green Lake, Wis. Member of board of directors, Child Care of Allen County; member, Martin Luther King Montessori School Board. *Member:* National Association for the Education of Young Children, Association for Childhood Education International, Midwest Association for the Education of Young Children, Indiana Association for the Education of Young Children.

*WRITINGS*—All published by Judson: *The Threes at Vacation Church School* (juvenile), 1953, revised edition, 1963; *Thank You God* (juvenile), 1963; *When Children Worship* (a compilation), 1963; *A Book about Jesus* (juvenile), illustrations by Al Fiorentino, 1969; *Christmas* (juvenile), 1969; *Are You My Friend?* (juvenile), illustrations by Joanne Isaac, 1969; *Partners in Teaching Young Children,* 1972; *Weekday Ministry with Young Children: A Manual for the Church Nursery School,* 1973. Contributor to *Baptist Leader* and other religious magazines.

*BIOGRAPHICAL/CRITICAL SOURCES: Ontario Bible College,* June, 1972.†

(Died October 17, 1973)

\* \* \*

## HENDERSON, G(eorge) P(oland)    1920-

*PERSONAL:* Born April 24, 1920, in London, England; son of George James and Emma (Wilson) Henderson; married Shirley Prudence Ann Cotton (a publisher), April 27, 1953; children: Crispin Alastair Poland, Antony James Willis. *Education:* Attended University of London, 1939-40. *Home:* Rivendell, The Avenue, Beckenham, Kent BR3 2ES, England. *Office:* CBD Research Ltd., 154 High St., Beckenham, Kent BR3 1EA, England.

*CAREER:* Guildhall Library, London, England, commercial reference librarian, 1938-63; Kelly's Directories Ltd., Kingston, Surrey, England, director, 1963-66; CBD Research Ltd., Beckenham, Kent, England, director, 1966—. *Military service:* Royal Artillery, 1940-46; became captain. *Member:* Association of Special Libraries and Information Bureaux (honorary treasurer, 1974-76), Association of British Directory Publishers (chairman, 1975-76), European Association of Directory Publishers (president, 1976-78), Industrial Marketing Research Association, European Association for Industrial Marketing Research, British Direct Mail Marketing Association.

*WRITINGS:* (With Ian Gibson Anderson) *Current British Directories,* CBD Research, 1953; *European Companies: A Guide to Sources of Information,* CBD Research, 1961; *Current European Directories,* CBD Research, 1969; (editor with wife, S.P.A. Henderson) *Directory of British Associations,* CBD Research, 1970.

*SIDELIGHTS:* G. P. Henderson wrote *CA* that he is a "collector and auction-attender, dabbler in languages, traveller by road to out-of-the-way places."

\* \* \*

## HENDERSON, S(hirley) P(rudence) A(nn) 1929-

*PERSONAL:* Born February 8, 1929, in London, England; daughter of Kenneth Willis (a librarian) and Grace Mildred (de Vaney) Cotton; married George Poland Henderson (a publisher), April 27, 1953; children: Crispin Alastair Poland, Antony James Willis. *Education:* Educated in England. *Home:* Rivendell, The Avenue, Beckenham, Kent BR3 2ES, England. *Office:* CBD Research Ltd., 154 High St., Beckenham, Kent, BR3 1EA, England.

*CAREER:* Guildhall Library, London, England, library assistant, 1946-53; Direct Mail Group, London, research assistant, 1953-55; CBD Research Ltd., Beckenham, Kent, England, director, 1961—.

*WRITINGS:* (Editor with husband, G. P. Henderson) *Directory of British Associations,* CBD Research, 1970.

*WORK IN PROGRESS:* Sixth edition of *Directory of British Associations.*

*AVOCATIONAL INTERESTS:* First aid, gardening, local and English history, reading, and travelling.

\* \* \*

## HENDRICKS, Frances Wade Kellam 1900-

*PERSONAL:* Born November 20, 1900, in Blanco, Tex.; daughter of John Watson (a cotton merchant) and Lucy (Dignan) Kellam; married Henry George Hendricks (an economics professor and author), June 14, 1929. *Education:* Attended Southwest Texas State College (now University), 1917-20; University of Texas, B.A., 1922, M.A., 1925; University of Illinois, Ph.D., 1931. *Politics:* Independent. *Religion:* Methodist. *Home:* 130 Stanford Dr., San Antonio, Tex. 78212.

*CAREER:* Stephen F. Austin State College (now University), Nacogdoches, Tex., assistant professor of history, 1927-28; University of San Antonio (absorbed by Trinity University, 1942), San Antonio, Tex., professor of history, 1936-42; Trinity University, San Antonio, associate professor, 1942-46, professor of history, 1946-68, chairman of department, 1942-58, 1961-66. *Member:* American Historical Association, Texas State Historical Association, San Antonio Historical Society (president, 1957). *Awards, honors:* Piper Professorship of Minne Stevens Piper Foundation, 1966; Distinguished Service award, Trinity University, 1968.

*WRITINGS:* (Translator with Beatrice Berler) Mariano Azuela, *Two Novels of the Mexican Revolution, The Underdogs* [and] *Trials of a Respectable Family,* Principia Press of Trinity University, 1963; (editor with Berler) *Las Tribulaciones de una Familia Decente,* Macmillan, 1966; (translator with Berler) Leopoldo Zea, *Latin America and the World,* University of Oklahoma Press, 1969; (translator with Berler) Hugo Laterre Cabal, *The Revolution in the Latin American Church,* University of Oklahoma Press, 1978.

*WORK IN PROGRESS:* With Beatrice Berler, translating *La Luciernaga* by Mariano Azuela; writing *History of the Southwest Texas Methodist Hospital.*

*AVOCATIONAL INTERESTS:* Volunteer work at a San Antonio hospital; travel.

\* \* \*

## HENKEL, Stephen C. 1933-

*PERSONAL:* Born November 6, 1933, in Orange, N.J.; son of Marvin Victor (an insurance executive) and E. Jean (Nufer) Henkel; married Carol E. Pippitt, June 17, 1955; children: Charlie, Laird. *Education:* Princeton University, B.S.M.E., 1955; Rutgers University, M.B.A., 1963. *Home:* 4 Woodland Dr., Darien, Conn. 06820. *Office:* N. L. Industries, 1230 Avenue of the Americas, New York, N.Y. 10020.

*CAREER:* M. W. Kellogg Co., New York City, engineer and administrator, 1955-65; Esso Chemical Co., New York City, executive in planning, marketing, and finance, 1965-72; N. L. Industries (formerly National Lead Industries), New York City, business planning manager, 1972-74, manager of business analysis, 1974—. *Military service:* U.S. Air Force, 1958. U.S. Air Force Reserve, 1958-66. *Member:* Planning Executives Institute, Noroton Yacht Club, Darien Boat Club, Darien Winter Commodores. *Awards, honors:* Darien Art Show awards for oil paintings, 1970, 1971.

*WRITINGS:* (Self-illustrated) *Bikes,* Chatham Press, 1972. Contributor to *Yachting.*

\* \* \*

## HENLE, Faye (?)-1972

(?)—November 24, 1972; American financial columnist, broadcaster, and lecturer. Obituaries: *New York Times,* November 26, 1972; *Publishers Weekly,* December 18, 1972.

\* \* \*

## HENLE, James 1891(?)-1973

1891(?)—January 9, 1973; American publisher and writer. Obituaries: *New York Times,* January 11, 1973; *Washington Post,* January 12, 1973; *Time,* January 22, 1973; *Publishers Weekly,* January 22, 1973.

\* \* \*

## HENRY, Harold Wilkinson 1926-

*PERSONAL:* Born July 22, 1926, in Maryville, Tenn.; son of Oscar Pleas (a banker) and Carrie (Wilkinson) Henry; married Zurma Mounce, August 27, 1949; children: Patricia (Mrs. John Edward Bleazey), Diana, Michael, Phyllis (Mrs. Daniel I. Gammon), Bruce. *Education:* Maryville College, B.S., 1948; University of Tennessee, M.S., 1959; University of Michigan, Ph.D., 1965. *Religion:* Protestant. *Home:* 8020 Bennington Dr., Knoxville, Tenn. 37919. *Office:* Department of Industrial Management, University of Tennessee, Knoxville, Tenn. 36916.

*CAREER:* High school teacher in Maryville, Tenn., 1950-52; Union Carbide Nuclear Co., Oak Ridge, Tenn., junior physicist, 1952-56, associate physicist, 1956-60; University of Michigan, Ann Arbor, radiation physicist, 1960-64; University of Tennessee, Knoxville, assistant professor, 1965-66, associate professor, 1966-74, professor of industrial management, 1974—. Technical and project management specialist for National Aeronautics and Space Administration, 1967, 1968, 1969, 1971. *Military service:* U.S. Navy,

1944-46. *Member:* North American Society for Corporate Planners, Academy of Management, Planning Executives Institute, Health Physics Society.

*WRITINGS: Long-Range Planning Practices in Forty-five Industrial Companies,* Prentice-Hall, 1967; *Pollution Control: Corporation Responses,* American Management Association, 1974. Contributor of articles to *Michigan Business Review, Tennessee Survey of Business, National Contract Management Journal, Management Review, Long Range Planning,* and *Planning Review.*

*WORK IN PROGRESS: Corporation Strategic Planning Systems.*

*AVOCATIONAL INTERESTS:* Cattle breeder.

\* \* \*

## HERBST, Jurgen (F. H.) 1928-

*PERSONAL:* Born February 22, 1928, in Braunschweig, Germany; U.S. citizen; son of Hermann (a research librarian) and Annemaria (Otto) Herbst; married Susan Allen, September 16, 1951; children: Christian, Annemaria, Stephanie. *Education:* Attended University of Goettingen, 1947-48; University of Nebraska, B.A., 1950; University of Minnesota, M.A., 1952; Harvard University, Ph.D., 1958. *Politics:* Democrat. *Office:* University of Wisconsin, Madison, Wis. 53706.

*CAREER:* Wesleyan University, Middletown, Conn., instructor, 1958-59, assistant professor, 1959-65, associate professor of history, 1965-66; University of Wisconsin—Madison, professor of educational policy studies and of history, 1966—. Visiting lecturer, Yale University, 1962-64; Fulbright lecturer in Germany, 1963; International Research and Exchanges Board scholar, 1977. *Member:* American Historical Association, American Studies Association, Organization of American Historians, History of Education Society, New England American Studies Association (president). *Awards, honors:* American Council of Learned Societies grant, 1960; National Endowment for the Humanities grant, 1972-73; National Institute of Education grant, 1973-76.

*WRITINGS:* (Editor) Josiah Strong, *Our Country,* Harvard University Press, 1963; *The German Historical School in American Scholarship,* Cornell University Press, 1965. Contributor to *Harvard Educational Review, Perspectives in American History, Educational Theory, Proceedings* of American Philosophical Society, and *History of Education Quarterly.*

*WORK IN PROGRESS: Legal History of American Universities.*

\* \* \*

## HERFINDAHL, Orris C. 1918-1972

June 15, 1918—December 16, 1972; American economist and authority on natural resources and the environment. Obituaries: *Washington Post,* December 27, 1972. (See index for *CA* sketch)

\* \* \*

## HERMANNS, William 1895-

*PERSONAL:* Born July 23, 1895, in Koblenz, Germany; son of Michael (a merchant) and Bertha (Wolff) Hermanns. *Education:* University of Berlin, M.A., 1924; University of Frankfurt, Ph.D., 1926. *Office:* Department of Foreign Languages, San Jose State University, San Jose, Calif. 95192.

*CAREER:* After release as French prisoner of war, 1920, prepared for diplomatic career with League of Nations, Geneva, Switzerland, and was associated with League of Nations Union as honorary member on peace committees in Berlin, London, and Boston, 1924-45; a "German radical," he fled his native land during World War II; Harvard University, Cambridge, Mass., research and lecturer at summer sessions, at intervals, 1940-45; San Jose State University, San Jose, Calif., assistant professor, 1946-54, associate professor, 1954-62, professor of German, 1962-65, professor emeritus, 1965—. Worked for Office of Strategic Services, Washington, D.C., 1944. *Member:* Tau Delta Phi (honorary). *Military service:* German Army, volunteer in World War I; served in France where he was taken prisoner at Verdun; became sergeant; received Iron Cross and Cross of Honor.

*WRITINGS: Mary and the Mocker,* Our Sunday Visitor, 1953; *The Holocaust: From a Survivor of Verdun,* Harper, 1972. Also author of book of poems, *Passion and Compassion,* privately printed. Author of poems and educational plays in German and poems in English.

*WORK IN PROGRESS: Conversations with Einstein; War and Conscience,* conversations with Niemoeller, Speer, and others; *Seed of the Last Days,* reminiscences on philosophy and people; *Journal of a Professor,* experiences with students and their problems; *Theology of Violence,* personal experiences with Goebbels, Hitler, Piux XII, Mussolini; treatise on Mao Tse-tung; *Liddy Belova,* story of a German Jewess in France during World War II; *Poor Kaiser, Poor Germany, Poor God; Ich liche mein Schnicksal,* a collection of German poems and experiences.

*SIDELIGHTS:* William Hermanns' original manuscript of *The Holocaust* was translated by a French general for France's archives shortly after World War I.

\* \* \*

## HERNANDEZ, Frances 1926-

*PERSONAL:* Born April 6, 1926, in St. Louis, Mo.; daughter of Kenneth Gearhart (an electrical engineer) and Bertha Mildred (a biochemist; maiden name, Walton) Baker; married John Whitlock Hernandez (dean of engineering at New Mexico State University), December 2, 1951. *Education:* Purdue University, B.S., 1948, M.S., 1959; University of New Mexico, M.A., 1950, Ph.D., 1963. *Politics:* Republican. *Religion:* Unitarian. *Address:* P.O. Box 3196, Las Cruces, N.M. 88001. *Office:* Department of English, University of Texas, El Paso, Tex. 79968.

*CAREER:* Elementary teacher in a bilingual program in Santa Fe, N.M., 1954-58; Purdue University, Lafayette, Ind., instructor in Spanish, 1958-59; Northeastern University, Boston, Mass., instructor in English, 1964-65; New Mexico State University, Las Cruces, assistant professor of English, 1965-67; University of Texas at El Paso, associate professor of English, 1967—, assistant dean, College of Liberal Arts, 1974-77. Visiting professor, St. John's College, Annapolis, Md., 1963-64, and University of Bosphorus, Istanbul, Turkey, 1973-74. Fulbright senior professor, Catholica University of Chile, Santiago, Chile, 1970; exchange professor, University of Puerto Rico, Rio Piedras, Puerto Rico, 1973. *Member:* Modern Language Association of America, College English Association (president of Rocky Mountain chapter, 1976-77, and south central chapter, 1976-78), National Association for the Advancement of Colored People, American Association of University Women, League of Women Voters, Planned Parenthood Association, South Central Modern Language Association, Rocky Mountain Modern Language Association (member of executive board, 1974-78), Conference of College Teachers of English of Texas (member of executive council, 1971-73), Mortar Board (honorary member), Phi Kappa Phi, Delta Kappa Gamma, Alpha Xi Delta.

*WRITINGS: Katherine Anne Porter and Julio Cortazar: The Craft of Fiction,* Texas Tech University Press, 1972; *The Turks with the Grand Catalan Company, 1306-1316* (monograph), Press of the University of Bosphorus, 1974; *The Catalan Chronicle of Francisco de Mondcada,* Texas Western Press, 1975; *Only the Wind: Legends of the Onas of Tierra del Fuego,* Pajarito Press, 1978. Contributor to numerous academic journals.

*WORK IN PROGRESS:* English translations of two novels by Ramon Sender, *Bizancio* and *Cronus y la senora con rabo.*

*SIDELIGHTS:* Frances Hernandez told *CA:* "I am primarily an academic, involved in teaching, research, travel, campus politics, administrative responsibilities, and professional organizations. But writing, so essential for prestige and promotion in my vocation, is also my hobby and greatest pleasure. I prefer nonfiction—and know that when I die it will be with my study still stacked with note cards and folders for projects that have absorbed me."

\* \* \*

## HERR, Edwin L. 1933-

*PERSONAL:* Born November 23, 1933, in Carlisle, Pa.; son of S. Leon Herr; married Patricia Greene, July 27, 1963; children: Amber Leigh, Christopher Alan, Alicia Estelle. *Education:* Shippensburg State College, B.S., 1955; Columbia University, M.A., 1959, Professional Diploma in Guidance, 1961, Ed.D., 1963. *Home:* 860 Saxton Dr., State College, Pa. 16801. *Office:* 201 Social Science Bldg., Pennsylvania State University, University Park, Pa. 16802.

*CAREER:* High school business teacher in Carlisle, Pa., 1956-57, in Paterson, N.J., 1957-59; high school director of guidance in Saddle Brook, N.J., 1959-62; State University of New York at Buffalo, assistant professor, 1963-65, associate professor of counselor education, 1965-66; Pennsylvania Department of Public Instruction, Harrisburg, director of Bureau of Guidance Services, 1966-68; Pennsylvania State University, University Park, professor of education, 1968—, head of department of counselor education, 1972—, assistant dean for graduate studies, 1972—, head of division of counseling and educational psychology, 1976—. Visiting professor, University of Reading, 1967; summer extension professor, Temple University, 1967, 1968; auxiliary professor, Lebanon Valley College, 1967-68; visiting lecturer, University of Puerto Rico, 1970. Visiting fellow, National Institute for Careers, Education and Counseling, Cambridge, England, 1976. Consultant to national, state, and local government, to school boards, and to universities. *Military service:* U.S. Air Force and U.S. Air Force Reserve, 1952-68; became captain.

*MEMBER:* International Association of Applied Psychology, International Association for Educational and Vocational Guidance, American Psychological Association, American Personnel and Guidance Association, National Vocational Guidance Association (professional member), American School Counselors Association, Association for Counselor Education and Supervision (senator and member of executive council, 1969-71; president of North Atlantic region, 1970-71; president, 1973), American Educational

Research Association, Association of College Admissions Counselors, American Vocational Association, Pennsylvania Psychological Association (fellow), Phi Delta Kappa, Kappa Delta Pi, Pi Omega Pi, Phi Sigma Pi.

*WRITINGS:* (Contributor) *Preparing School Counselors in Educational Guidance,* College Entrance Examination Board, 1967; (with Stanley H. Cramer) *Guidance of the College-Bound Student: Problems, Practices, Perspectives,* Appleton, 1968; (with Robert F. Cox) *Group Techniques in Guidance,* Pennsylvania Department of Public Instruction, 1968; *Decision-Making and Vocational Development,* Houghton, 1970; (with Cramer, Charles N. Morris, and Thomas Frantz) *Research and the School Counselor,* Houghton, 1970; (editor with James C. Hansen, and contributor) *Group Guidance and Counseling in the Schools,* Appleton, 1971; (with Cramer) *Vocational Guidance and Career Development in the Schools: Toward a Systems Approach,* Houghton, 1972; *Review and Synthesis of Foundations for Career Education,* Center for Vocational and Technical Education, Ohio State University, 1972; *Vocational Guidance and Human Development,* Houghton, 1974; *Conditions for Educational Reform: An Analysis,* U.S. Office of Education, 1975; *The Emerging History of Career Education,* U.S. Office of Education, 1976; *Schools and Career,* McGraw, 1977; *Foundations of Vocational Education,* Merrill Co., 1978. Contributor of more than 130 articles to professional journals. Member of editorial board, *School Counselor,* 1966-69, *Vocational Guidance Quarterly,* 1969—; editor, *Pennsylvania Guidance Keynotes,* 1968-69; *Counselor Education and Supervision,* associate editor, 1969-70, editor-elect, 1970, editor, 1971.

\* \* \*

## HERRESHOFF, Lewis Francis 1890-1972

November 11, 1890—December 3, 1972; American yacht designer and writer on boats and sailing. Obituaries: *New York Times,* December 4, 1972. (See index for *CA* sketch)

\* \* \*

## HERRMANN, Klaus J(acob) 1929-

*PERSONAL:* Born July 21, 1929, in Cammin, Germany; son of Felix F. (a merchant) and Hertha (Steinbach) Herrmann; married Shirley Mackie, July 27, 1965; children: Stephanie, Marcus. *Education:* University of Minnesota, B.A., 1954, M.A., 1958, Ph.D., 1960. *Politics:* Republican. *Religion:* Jewish Reformed. *Home:* 25 Henley Ave., Mount Royal, Quebec, Canada. *Office:* Department of Political Science, Concordia University, Sir George Williams Campus, Blvd. Maisonneuve, Montreal, Quebec, Canada.

*CAREER:* University of Maryland, European Division, Heidelberg, Germany, lecturer in political science, 1960-62; American University, Washington, D.C., assistant professor of political science, 1963-65; Concordia University, Sir George Williams Campus, Montreal, Quebec, associate professor of political science, 1965—. Guest professor, Hochschule fuer Politik (Munich), 1966—. *Military service:* U.S. Army, 1948-52, 1954-57; became first lieutenant. *Member:* Leo Baeck Institute, Gesellschaft fuer Geistesgeschichte, Canadian Political Science Association, American Council for Judaism.

*WRITINGS: The Third Reich and German-Jewish Organizations: 1933-34,* Carl Heymanns, 1969. Contributor to *Middle East Journal, American University Law Review,* and other journals.

*WORK IN PROGRESS:* A book on Dr. Max Naumann's "Association of National-German Jews."

\* \* \*

## HERRON, William George 1933-

*PERSONAL:* Born March 21, 1933, in Englewood, N.J.; married, 1957; children: Judith, Rachel, Lia, Mara. *Education:* College of the Holy Cross, B.A., 1954; Fordham University, M.A., 1957, Ph.D., 1960; Adelphi University, additional study, 1973. *Home and office:* 5 Pascack Rd., Woodcliff Lake, N.J. 07675.

*CAREER:* Manhattanville College of the Sacred Heart, Purchase, N.Y., instructor in psychology, 1957-58; St. Vincent's Hospital, New York City, intern in clinical psychology, 1958-59; St. Bonaventure University, St. Bonaventure, N.Y., associate professor of psychology and chairman of department, 1959-65; private practice of clinical psychology, 1961—. Professor and co-director of clinical training, St. John's University, Jamaica, N.Y., 1965—. Supervisory clinical psychologist, Cattaraugus County Mental Health Clinic, 1961-65; psychologist, Randolph Children's Home, Randolph, N.Y., 1961-63; director, Cattaraugus County Mental Health Board; chief psychologist, West Bergen Mental Health Center, 1966-70.

*WRITINGS:* (With Robert E. Kantor) *Reactive and Process Schizophrenia,* Science & Behavior Books, 1966; (with others) *Contemporary School Psychology,* Intext, 1970, revised edition, Carroll Press, in press; *F. Quantmeyer Hose No. 7* (novel), Exposition, 1972.

*SIDELIGHTS:* William George Herron told *CA,* "I write to be heard, understood, and published, and to stay in touch with myself."

\* \* \*

## HERTZ, Peter Donald 1933-

*PERSONAL:* Born June 2, 1933, in Berlin, Germany; son of Richard Otto (a German foreign officer) and Feliza (Vorwerk) Hertz; married Nancy Augustus, June 6, 1962 (divorced July 8, 1977); married Andrea-Maria Ohmes, December 4, 1977; children: Vicki, Terry, Kathryn. *Education:* Stanford University, A.B., 1957, Ph.D., 1967; Columbia University, M.A., 1964. *Politics:* Democrat. *Home:* 162 West Fourth St., Oswego, N.Y. 13126. *Office:* Department of German, State University of New York College, Oswego, N.Y. 13126.

*CAREER:* University of Redlands, Redlands, Calif., instructor in German, 1960-61; State University of New York College at Oswego, associate professor, 1965-71, professor of German, 1971—, director of International Education, 1972-75, director of Wuerzburg Exchange Program, 1975-76. Assistant to president, State University of New York at Stony Brook, 1971-72. *Member:* Modern Language Association of America, American Association of Teachers of German. *Awards, honors:* American Council on Education fellow, 1971-72.

*WRITINGS:* (Translator) Martin Heidegger, *On the Way to Language,* Harper, 1971. Contributor of articles to *Georgia Review, Topic, Western Humanities Review,* and other literature and humanities journals.

*WORK IN PROGRESS:* An assessment of recent German and French theories of literary communication.

## HERZ, Peggy 1936-
### (Peggy Hudson)

*PERSONAL:* Born December 16, 1936, in Hamburg, Iowa; daughter of Virgil and Eva (Rood) Dilts; married James A. Hudson (a free-lance writer), July 9, 1966 (divorced, 1972); married Edgar L. Herz (an insurance agent), November 9, 1972. *Education:* Syracuse University, B.A., 1959. *Home:* 220 East Saddle River Rd., Saddle River, N.J. 07458. *Office:* Scholastic Magazines and Book Services, 50 West 44th St., New York, N.Y. 10036.

*CAREER:* Scholastic Magazines and Book Services, New York, N.Y., radio and television editor, 1961—. *Member:* National Academy of Television Arts and Sciences, Phi Beta Kappa, Theta Sigma Phi.

*WRITINGS*—Under name Peggy Hudson; all published by Scholastic Book Services: *Words to the Wise,* 1967; *TV Today,* 1968; *TV 70,* 1969; *TV 71,* 1970; *TV 72,* 1971; *The Television Scene,* 1971; *With the Osmonds,* 1973.

Under name Peggy Herz: *TV Time Seventy-Four,* 1974; *TV Close-Ups,* 1975; *All about "Rhoda,"* 1975; *TV People,* 1975; *All about "Mash,"* 1976; *TV's Top Ten Shows and Their Stars,* 1976; *TV Talk,* 1976; *TV Talk 2,* 1977; *The Truth about Fonzie,* 1977; *TV's Fabulous Faces,* 1977; *TV Talk 3,* 1978; *Nancy Drew and the Hardy Boys,* 1978.

*WORK IN PROGRESS:* Research for another book about television.

\* \* \*

## HERZKA, Heinz (Stefan) 1935-

*PERSONAL:* Born February 1, 1935, in Vienna, Austria; son of Hans and Else (Freistadt) Herzka; married Irene Langsam (a social worker), 1960; children: Marc, Michael, Ruth. *Education:* Studied at University of Zurich, University of Basel, and at clinics in England and the Netherlands; University of Zurich, M.D., 1961. *Home:* Allmendstrasse 18, CH8 309 Wallisellen, Switzerland. *Office:* Tagesklinik, Toblerstrasse 101, 8044 Zurich, Switzerland.

*CAREER:* Child psychiatrist and pediatrician in Zurich, Switzerland, 1968—. Lecturer in child psychiatry and professor of child psychopathology, University of Zurich.

*WRITINGS*—All books on child psychology and child psychiatry, except as indicated: *Spielsachen fuer das gesunde und das behinderte Kind,* Schwabe, 1964, revised edition, 1974; *Das Gesicht des Saeuglings,* Schwabe, 1965; *Die Sprache des Saeuglings,* Schwabe, 1967; *Das Kind im geistigen Klima,* Francke, 1968; *Do in den roten Stiefein* (juvenile picture book), illustrations by Heiri Steiner, Artemis-Verlag, 1969, translation by Elizabeth D. Crawford published as *Robin in Red Boots,* Harcourt, 1970; (with Bernardo Ferrari) *Das Kind von der Geburt bis zur Schule,* Schwabe, 1972, revised edition, 1978; *Kinderpsychiatrische Krankheitsbilder,* Schwabe, 1978.

\* \* \*

## HESCHEL, Abraham Joshua 1907-1972

1907—December 23, 1972; Polish-born American Jewish theologian and author. Obituaries: *New York Times,* December 24, 1972; *Washington Post,* December 26, 1972. (See index for *CA* sketch)

\* \* \*

## HESLEP, Robert D(urham) 1930-

*PERSONAL:* Born December 18, 1930, in Houston, Tex.;

son of Norman Gordon and Lady (Davis) Heslep; married Joelyn Miller, February 15, 1964; children: one son. *Education:* Texas Christian University, B.A., 1955; University of Chicago, M.A., 1957, Ph.D., 1963. *Home:* 285 Hancock Lane, Athens, Ga. 30605. *Office:* College of Education, University of Georgia, Athens, Ga. 30602.

*CAREER:* Pestalozzi-Froebel Teachers College, Chicago, Ill., lecturer in educational philosophy, 1959-61; Harvard School, Chicago, instructor in English and history, 1958-63; Edinboro State College, Edinboro, Pa., associate professor of education and philosophy, 1963-65; University of Georgia, Athens, professor of philosophy of education, 1965—. *Military service:* U.S. Army, 1952-54; became sergeant; received Bronze Star. *Member:* American Association of University Professors, Philosophy of Education Society (president, 1976-77), Southeast Philosophy of Education Society (president, 1971-72), Georgia Philosophical Society. *Awards, honors:* Designated an "Outstanding Educator of 1971," Outstanding Educators of America, Chicago, Ill.

*WRITINGS: Thomas Jefferson and Education,* Random House, 1969; (editor) *Philosophy of Education, 1971,* Philosophy of Education Society, 1971; (with W. T. Blackstone) *Social Justice and Preferential Treatment,* University of Georgia Press, 1977. Contributor of articles to *Educational Theory, Studies in Philosophy and Education, Harvard Educational Review, Emory University Quarterly,* and *Journal of Thought.*

*WORK IN PROGRESS:* Research and essays concerning the concept of action as an alternative to the concept of behavior in educational research.

*AVOCATIONAL INTERESTS:* Fresh water fishing and organic vegetable gardening.

*      *      *

## HESLIN, Richard 1936-

*PERSONAL:* Born January 5, 1936, in Providence, R.I.; son of John Edward (an electrician) and Catherine (Locke) Heslin; married Marsha McMichael, September 21, 1957; children: Bruce, Tracy, Paul, Andrea. *Education:* Rhode Island College, Ed.B., 1957; University of California, Berkeley, additional study, 1960-61; Harvard University, A.M., 1963; University of Colorado, Ph.D., 1966. *Politics:* Democrat. *Religion:* Presbyterian. *Home:* 2812 Henderson St., West Lafayette, Ind. 47906. *Office:* Department of Psychological Sciences, Purdue University, West Lafayette, Ind. 47907.

*CAREER:* Institute for Naval Studies, Cambridge, Mass., member of scientific staff, 1962-63; Purdue University, Lafayette, Ind., assistant professor, 1966-71, associate professor of psychology, 1971—. Co-director of workshops, University Associates, Indianapolis. *Military service:* U.S. Navy, 1957-60; became lieutenant. *Member:* American Psychological Association, Psychonomic Society, Midwestern Psychological Association, Sigma Xi.

*WRITINGS:* (Contributor) O. J. Harvey, editor, *Experience, Structure, and Adaptability,* Springer Publishing, 1966; (contributor) C. W. Backman and P. F. Secord, editors, *Problems in Social Psychology,* McGraw, 1966; (with J. William Pfeiffer and John E. Jones) *The Use of Instruments in Human Relations Training,* University Association Press, 1972, revised edition, 1977; (contributor) J. A. Howard and L. E. Ostlund, editors, *Buyer Behavior,* Random House, 1973. Contributor to psychology and business journals. Editorial consultant, *Journal of Applied Social Psychology, Journal of Personality and Social Psychology, Sociometry, Personality and Social Psychology Bulletin,* and *Environmental Psychology and Nonverbal Behavior.*

*      *      *

## HESLOP, J. Malan 1923-

*PERSONAL:* Born June 18, 1923, in Taylor, Utah; son of Jesse and Zella (Malan) Heslop; married Fae Stokes (a secretary), May 1, 1944; children: Paul, Lyn (Mrs. Tom Osmond), Scott, Ann (Mrs. Dean Coleman), Don. *Education:* Utah State University, B.S., 1949. *Religion:* Church of Jesus Christ of Latter-day Saints (Mormon). *Home:* 80 Edgecombe Dr., Salt Lake City, Utah 84103. *Office:* Deseret News, 30 East First S., Salt Lake City, Utah 84110.

*CAREER:* Free-lance photographer in Logan, Utah, 1946-49; news photographer in Salt Lake City, Utah, 1949-69; *Deseret News,* Salt Lake City, editor, 1969—. *Military service:* U.S. Army, photographer, 1943-46.

*WRITINGS*—All with Dell Van Orden; published by Deseret, except as indicated: *Joseph Fielding Smith: A Prophet among the People,* 1971; *From the Shadow of Death,* 1973; *Marie Osmond in Black and White,* 1974; *Happy Birthday Marie,* 1974; *How to Write Your Personal History,* Book Craft, 1976; *How to Make Your Book of Remembrance,* Book Craft, 1977. Also author of "Copy Boy," a play in three acts.

*WORK IN PROGRESS:* A teen novel; a religious book about proverbs.

*      *      *

## HESTER, James J. 1931-

*PERSONAL:* Born September 21, 1931, in Anthony, Kan.; son of Simon Fredric and Ada B. (Smith) Hester; married Adrienne Davis, October 1, 1955; children: Michael, Randy, David. *Education:* University of New Mexico, B.A., 1953; University of Arizona, Ph.D., 1961. *Politics:* Moderate. *Religion:* Unitarian. *Home:* Jamestown, Star Route, Boulder, Colo. 80302. *Office:* Department of Archaeology, University of Colorado, Boulder, Colo. 80302.

*CAREER:* Museum of New Mexico, Santa Fe, assistant curator, 1959-64; Southern Methodist University, Dallas, Tex., adjunct professor of archaeology, 1964-65; National Institutes of Health, Bethesda, Md., scientist administrator, 1965-67; University of Colorado, Boulder, 1967—, currently professor of archaeology. Managing partner, H. P. Charolais Associates, Boulder, 1971—. *Military service:* U.S. Air Force, 1954-56; became first lieutenant. *Member:* Society for American Archaeology, American Quaternary Association, Society for Applied Anthropology, Explorers Club (chairman of Rocky Mountain Group).

*WRITINGS:* (With A. E. Dittert, Jr. and Frank W. Eddy) *An Archaeological Survey of the Navajo Reservoir,* Museum of New Mexico, 1961; *Early Navajo Migrations and Acculturation in the Southwest,* Museum of New Mexico, 1962; *The Reconstruction of Past Environments,* Fort Burgwin Research Center, 1964; *Prehistoric Settlement Patterns in the Libyan Desert,* University of Utah, 1971. Editor of *Southwestern Lore,* 1967-68, 1972—.

*WORK IN PROGRESS: Paleoecology of the Bella Bella Region,* British Columbia.

## HETTINGER, Herman Strecker   1902-1972

1902—October 2, 1972; American financial and stockholder relations counsel, editor, and author of works on finance, music, advertising, and other topics. Obituaries: *New York Times,* October 7, 1972.

\*     \*     \*

## HETZLER, Stanley Arthur   1919-

*PERSONAL:* Born February 20, 1919, in Miamisburg, Ohio; son of Stanley Ray (a farmer) and Clemma (Ballard) Hetzler; married Esther Granger (a college professor), December 31, 1965; children: Stanley Stephen, Lance Royce-Tristan. *Education:* Ohio State University, B.A., 1940, Ph.D., 1952. *Home:* 1560 President St., Yellow Springs, Ohio 45387. *Office:* Department of Sociology, University of Dayton, 300 College Park Ave., Dayton, Ohio 45409.

*CAREER:* U.S. Government, research sociologist, 1952-57; American University of Beirut, Beirut, Lebanon, assistant professor of sociology, 1958-59; North American Rockwell, Columbus, Ohio, project director, 1959-64; University of Costa Rica, San Jose, distinguished lecturer in sociology, 1965-66; Colorado State University, Fort Collins, professor of sociology, 1966-67; Central State University, Wilberforce, Ohio, professor of sociology and director of International Center, 1968-70; University of Dayton, Dayton, Ohio, professor of sociology, 1970—. Social psychologist, Wright-Patterson Air Force Base, 1952-58; research associate, Ritchie & Associates, Inc., 1959-60; research sociologist, County Public Welfare Department, Ohio, 1961-62, and North American Aviation Corp., 1962-65. *Member:* American Sociological Association. *Military service:* U.S. Army, 1942-46; became captain.

*WRITINGS:* (With Roger W. Nett) *An Introduction to Electronic Data Processing Systems,* Free Press, 1959; *Technological Growth and Social Change: Achieving Modernization,* Praeger, 1969; *Applied Measures for Promoting Technological Growth,* Routledge & Kegan Paul, 1973. Contributor to sociology journals.

*WORK IN PROGRESS:* Two books, *The Sociology of Drama,* and *On the Theories of Urban Change and Population Fluctuation.*

\*     \*     \*

## HEWES, Dorothy W.   1922-

*PERSONAL:* Born April 15, 1922, in Milan, Ill.; daughter of Raymond and Maude Walker; married David D. Hewes (a psychotherapist), June 11, 1949; children: Andrew, Christopher, Rosemary, John. *Education:* Iowa State University, B.A., 1943; University of California, Berkeley, additional study, 1946-48; Mills College, additional study, 1948-51; San Fernando Valley State College (now California State University, Northridge), M.A., 1969; Union Experimenting College and University, Ph.D., 1975. *Home:* 9840 Alto Dr., La Mesa, Calif. 92041. *Office:* San Diego State University, San Diego, Calif. 92115.

*CAREER:* Consultant or director of early childhood education programs, 1946—; California State College, Bakersfield, adjunct assistant professor, 1971-75; San Diego State University, San Diego, Calif., associate professor, 1975—. *Military service:* U.S. Marine Corps, 1943-45; became staff sergeant. *Member:* National Association for the Education of Young Children (vice-president), Psychological Association, National Women's Political Caucus.

*WRITINGS:* (With Barbara Hartman) *Early Childhood*

*Education: A Workbook for Administrators,* R and E Research—Early Childhood Division (Palo Alto, Calif.), 1972, 2nd edition, 1974; (contributor) *Rationale for Day Care Services: Programs vs. Policies,* Human Sciences Press, 1975. Has authored television and radio scripts for educational programs. Contributor of articles to *Young Children* and other journals in her field.

*WORK IN PROGRESS: Frederich Froebel: Education for Self Esteem; Discipline in the Victorian Kindergarten.*

\*     \*     \*

## HEWSON, John   1930-

*PERSONAL:* Born December 19, 1930, in Tugby, England; son of George Arthur (an Anglican clergyman) and Margery (Shaw) Hewson; married Irene O'Neill, April 18, 1954; children: Anne, Jean, Paul. *Education:* University of London, B.A. (honors), 1952, certificate in education, 1953; Laval University, M. es Arts, 1958, D. de l'U, 1960. *Home:* 11 Howley Ave. Extension, St. John's, Newfoundland, Canada. *Office:* Department of Linguistics, Memorial University, St. John's, Newfoundland, Canada.

*CAREER:* Memorial University, St. John's, Newfoundland, assistant professor, 1960-64, associate professor, 1964-68, professor of linguistics, 1968—. *Military service:* Royal Canadian Air Force Reserve, 1961—; honorary aide-de-camp to Governor General of Canada, 1972-74. *Member:* Linguistic Society of America, Canadian Linguistics Association (executive member), Linguistic Association of Great Britain, Philological Society.

*WRITINGS: Oral French Pattern Practice,* Gage, 1963; *La Pratique du Francais,* Gage, 1966; *Article and Noun in English,* Mouton, 1972. Also author, *The Beothuk Vocabularies,* 1977. Contributor of about forty articles and reviews to scholarly journals.

*WORK IN PROGRESS:* Research on computer assisted protolanguage reconstruction; American Indian languages (Algonkian Family); the phenomenon of language; a book, tentatively entitled *An Introduction to Linguistic Mechanisms.*

\*     \*     \*

## HIGGINS, A(lbert) C(orbin)   1930-

*PERSONAL:* Born November 1, 1930, in New York, N.Y.; son of Albert Corbin and Joyce (McManus) Higgins; married Anne Nichols (an author), June 8, 1957; children: Brigitte, Sean, Jessica, Alexandra, Martha. *Education:* Fordham University, B.S., 1952, M.A., 1957; University of North Carolina, Ph.D., 1964. *Politics:* Democrat. *Religion:* Roman Catholic. *Address:* R.D. 1, Johnstown, N.Y. 12095. *Office:* Department of Sociology, State University of New York at Albany, 1400 Washington Ave., Albany, N.Y. 12203.

*CAREER:* Watts Hospital School of Nursing, Durham, N.C., instructor in sociology, 1956-59; Louisiana State University in New Orleans, instructor in sociology, 1959-61; University of North Carolina at Chapel Hill, lecturer in sociology, 1961-64; State University of New York Upstate Medical Center, Syracuse, assistant professor of administrative medicine, 1964-69; Syracuse University, Syracuse, assistant professor of sociology, 1964-69; State University of New York at Albany, associate professor of sociology, 1969—, co-director of Evaluation of the Urban Center of the Capital District. Director of various projects at State University of New York Upstate Medical Center and Syracuse University. *Military service:* U.S. Air Force, 1952-54. *Member:* American Academy, American Association for the Advancement of Science, American Association of University Professors, American Public Health Association, American Sociological Association, Eastern Sociological Society, Southern Sociological Society, New York State Public Health Association, Central New York Sociological Society.

*WRITINGS:* (With William P. Richardson and Richard G. Ames) *The Handicapped Children of Alamance County, North Carolina,* Nemours Foundation, 1965; (contributor) Irwin Deutscher and Elizabeth Thompson, editors, *Among the People: Encounters with the Poor,* Basic Books, 1968. Contributor of articles to *Sociometry, American Journal of Public Health,* and *Journal of Medical Education.* Contributor of book reviews to journals in his field.

*WORK IN PROGRESS: Professions in Society; The Social Meanings of Professional Judgment;* several articles.

\*　　\*　　\*

## HIGGINS, W(illiam) Robert 1938-

*PERSONAL:* Born January 28, 1938, in Gaffney, S.C.; son of James Thomas, Sr. (a civil engineer) and Willie (Davis) Higgins; married Eva Poythress (an historian), September 3, 1966; children: Mirabeau Lamar. *Education:* University of South Carolina, B.A., 1959, M.A., 1967; University of Michigan, graduate study, 1964-65; Duke University, Ph.D., 1970. *Politics:* Democrat. *Religion:* Episcopalian.

*CAREER:* College of Charleston, Charleston, S.C., instructor in history, 1964; Murray State University, Murray, Ky., assistant professor, 1968-71, associate professor of history, beginning 1971. Visiting lecturer in early American history, Emory University, 1965; visiting assistant professor, Duke University, summer, 1972. *Military service:* U.S. Navy, 1959-63. U.S. Naval Reserve, 1963-71; became lieutenant commander. *Member:* American Historical Association, Organization of American Historians, American Association of University Professors, United States Naval Institute, Southern Historical Association, South Carolina Historical Association, William L. Clements Associates, Pi Alpha Theta, Omicron Delta Kappa. *Awards, honors:* National Endowment for the Humanities fellowship, 1973-74.

*WRITINGS: The Slave Trade of Colonial South Carolina,* University of South Carolina Press, 1973. Contributor of articles and reviews to *South Atlantic Quarterly, South Carolina Historical Magazine, American Historical Review, Journal of Southern History,* and *Journal of Introductory History.*

*WORK IN PROGRESS: A Financial History of Revolutionary South Carolina; Colonial Charleston.*†

\*　　\*　　\*

## HIGHSMITH, Richard M(organ), Jr. 1920-

*PERSONAL:* Born August 29, 1920, in Portland, Ore.; son of Richard M., Sr. and Laura S. (Jones) Highsmith; married Marijane Harkema, June 14, 1942 (divorced, 1967); children: Jill (Mrs. James N. Kelly), Brooke (Mrs. Larry M. Bewley), Nan (Mrs. Bobby Copeland), Richard M. III, April. *Education:* Central Washington State College, B.A., 1941; University of Washington, M.A., 1946, Ph.D., 1950. *Religion:* Presbyterian. *Home:* 3024 Firwood Dr., Corvallis, Ore. 97330. *Office:* Department of Geography, Oregon State University, Corvallis, Ore. 97331.

*CAREER:* Oregon State University, Corvallis, assistant

professor, 1947-50, associate professor, 1950-55, professor of geography, 1955—, head of department, 1964—. *Military service:* U.S. Marine Corps, 1942-46; became first lieutenant; received Silver Star. *Member:* Association of American Geographers, American Association for the Advancement of Science, Association of Pacific Coast Geographers (president, 1964-65), Sigma Xi.

*WRITINGS:* (With J. Granville Jensen) *Pendleton: World's Round-up City,* Pendleton Public Schools, 1950; (with Jensen) *The Little Fork Santiam River Basin: Its Resources and Their Potentials,* Benton-Lincoln Electric Cooperative, 1951; *The West End of Umatella County: Resource Development and Prospects,* Pacific Power & Light Co., 1953; (with Jensen) *Resources and Potentials of the Grande Ronde and Imnaha Basins,* Walla Walla District Corps of Engineers, 1953; (editor with others and contributor) *Atlas of Pacific Northwest: Resources and Development,* Oregon State University Press, 1953, 5th edition, 1974; (with O. H. Heintzelman) *World Regions Map,* Chandlers, 1953; (editor with Ida Mohn and Bernard Lindenstein) *Directory of Northwest Resource Organizations,* Department of Natural Resources, Oregon State College, 1953; (contributor) Otis W. Freeman and H. H. Martin, editors, *The Pacific Northwest,* 1954; (with Heintzelman) *World Regional Geography,* Prentice-Hall, 1955, 4th edition, 1973; (with Jensen) *Geography of Commodity Production,* Lippincott, 1958, 2nd edition, 1963; *Atlas of Oregon Agriculture,* Oregon Agricultural Experiment Station, 1958; (with Heintzelman) *Aids to Understanding World Regional Geography,* Prentice-Hall, 1958, 2nd edition, 1964; (with Heintzelman, Jensen, and R. D. Rudd) *Case Studies in World Geography, Occupance, and Economy Types,* Prentice-Hall, 1961; (with Jensen and Rudd) *Conservation in the United States,* Rand McNally, 1962, 2nd edition, 1969; (with Ray M. Northam) *World Economic Activities: A Geographic Analysis,* Harcourt, 1968.

Contributor to *Yearbook,* Association of Pacific Coast Geographers, Volume IX, 1947, Volume XII, 1950, Volume XXVII, 1965. Contributor to *World Book Encyclopedia, Grolier's New Book of Knowledge,* and *Encyclopedia Americana.* Also contributor of articles to *Economic Geography, Journal of Geography, Scientific Monthly, Northwest, Proceedings of the Institute of Northwest Resources, Pacific Northwest Quarterly, Geographical Review, Foreign Agriculture, Professional Geographer, Louisiana Studies, Pacific Northwest Geographer,* and *Journal of Developing Areas.*

*WORK IN PROGRESS: Atlas of Pacific Northwest,* 6th edition.

\*　　\*　　\*

## HILL, (Charles) Fowler 1901(?)-1973

1901(?)—January 4, 1973; American journalist, book reviewer, and novelist. Obituaries: *New York Times,* January 6, 1973.

\*　　\*　　\*

## HILL, J(ohn) C(ampbell) 1888-

*PERSONAL:* Born April 25, 1888, in Glasgow, Scotland; son of John (a shipbuilder) and Margaret (McGregor) Hill; married Margaret Elizabeth Park, February 7, 1917; children: Sir John McGregor, Andrew Campbell, Malcolm Campbell. *Education:* University of Glasgow, Teachers' Certificate, 1911; University of Durham, B.Sc., 1914, M.Sc., 1923; University of Manchester, additional study. *Home:* 280 Kew Rd., Kew Gardens, Surrey TW9 3EE, England.

CAREER: Rutherford College, Newcastle upon Tyne, England, science master, 1914-15, 1918-20; Chester Training College, Chester, England, lecturer in geography, 1920-25; University of London, King's College, London, England, lecturer in education, 1925-30; London County Council, London, inspector of schools, 1930-54. Tutor in psychology for Workers' Educational Association, 1923-30, and University of London Extension Board, 1926-30; educational adviser, Hampstead Child Therapy Clinic, 1954-77. Military service: British Army, Infantry, 1915-19; served in France; became major on the staff; mentioned in despatches, 1917. Member: British Psychological Society (fellow), Royal Mid-Surrey Golf Club.

WRITINGS: Dreams and Education, Methuen, 1926; The Teacher in Training, Allen & Unwin, 1935, 2nd edition, 1946; Introduction to Geography, Oxford University Press, 1937; Introduction to History, Oxford University Press, 1937; Introduction to Science, Oxford University Press, 1937; Introduction to Mathematics, Oxford University Press, 1937; Introduction to Citizenship, Oxford University Press, 1941; Teaching and the Unconscious Mind, International Universities Press, 1971. Contributor to British Journal of Medical Psychology and London Head Teacher.

SIDELIGHTS: J. C. Hill has made five visits to the United States. Teaching and the Unconscious Mind has been published in Italian, Spanish, and Portuguese.

*   *   *

HILL, John S(tanley) 1929-
(Stan Wiley)

PERSONAL: Born May 12, 1929, in Winfield, Kan.; son of John R. (a businessman) and Lola (Wiley) Hill; married Lucy Robinson, December 27, 1955; children: Rob, Ros. Education: University of Kansas, B.S., 1951, M.A., 1956; University of Wisconsin, Ph.D., 1960. Politics: Democrat. Religion: Methodist. Home: Colony Apartments, No. 506, San Marcos, Tex. 78666. Office: Graduate School, Southwest Texas State University, San Marcos, Tex. 78666.

CAREER: Ohio University, Athens, instructor in English, 1959-62; Illinois State University, Normal, associate professor, 1962-67, professor of English, 1967-77; Southwest Texas State University, San Marcos, professor of English and dean of graduate school, 1977—. Military service: U.S. Army, 1951-53; became sergeant; received Bronze Star. Member: Modern Language Association of America, National Council of Teachers of English, College English Association, Midwest Modern Language Association.

WRITINGS: Thesis Handbook, Illinois State University Press, 1964; Checklist of Frank Norris, C. E. Merrill, 1970. Contributor of over thirty articles to professional journals. Writer of short stories under pseudonym Stan Wiley.

WORK IN PROGRESS: American Naturalism; The American City.

*   *   *

HILL, Lee H(alsey) 1899-1974

PERSONAL: Born March 8, 1899, in Toms River, N.J.; son of David (a banker) and Anna P. (Applegate) Hill; married Helen Woltram, December 25, 1922; children: Lee H., Jr. Education: Cornell University, E.E., 1922. Politics: Republican. Religion: Methodist. Home: 225 Plymouth Rd., West Palm Beach, Fla. 33405. Office: Hill-Donnelly Corp., 2907 Bay to Bay Blvd., P.O. Box 14417, Tampa, Fla. 33609.

CAREER: Design and development engineer, Westing-house Electric and Manufacturing Co., 1922-28; manager of transformer division, American Brown Boveri Co., 1928-30; Allis-Chalmers Manufacturing Co., Milwaukee, Wis., manager of Transformer Division, 1931-41, vice-president, 1941-47; Rogers, Slade & Hill, Inc. Management Consultants, New York, N.Y., chairman, 1947-66; Hill-Donnelly Corp., Tampa, Fla., president, beginning 1965; Florida Air Lines, Tampa, president, beginning 1969. Military service: U.S. Army, 1917-18; became second lieutenant. Member: Institute of Electrical and Electronics Engineers, Direct Mail Advertising Association, Commerce Club of Tampa.

WRITINGS: Transformers, International Textbook Co., 1940; Management at the Bargaining Table, McGraw, 1942; Pattern for Good Labor Relations, McGraw, 1944; (contributor) Louis G. Silverberg, editor, The Wagner Act after Ten Years, Bureau of National Affairs, 1945; (contributor) J. K. Lassen, editor, Business Management Handbook, McGraw, 1951-52; Upward in the Black, Prentice-Hall, 1969; (contributor) H. B. Maynard, editor, Handbook of Business Administration, McGraw, 1969.††

(Died January 27, 1974)

*   *   *

HILL, Roscoe E(arl) 1936-

PERSONAL: Born July 4, 1936, in Lincoln, Neb.; son of Roscoe S. and Ruth (Davis) Hill; married Nancy Klenk (a teacher), January 29, 1959; children: Stephen, Jennifer. Education: Carleton College, B.A. (cum laude), 1958; Union Theological Seminary, New York, N.Y., additional study, 1958-59, summer, 1962; Albert Ludwigs Universitat, Freiburg, Germany, additional study, 1959-61; University of Chicago, M.A., 1963, Ph.D., 1968. Office: College of Arts and Sciences, University of Denver, Denver, Colo. 80208.

CAREER: Carleton College, Northfield, Minn., instructor in philosophy, 1961-62; University of Illinois, Chicago, teaching assistant, 1965-66; Yale University, New Haven, Conn., lecturer, 1967-68, assistant professor of philosophy, 1968-73; University of Denver, Denver, Colo., associate professor of philosophy, 1973—, associate dean of College of Arts and Sciences, 1977—. Awards, honors: Fulbright Scholar, Freiburg, Germany, 1959-61; Morse fellowship for research, Yale University, 1971-72.

WRITINGS: (Editor with Malcolm Feeley) Affirmative School Integration, Sage Publications, 1969. Contributor of articles to Law and Society Review, Yale Law Journal, and New York Law Review.

BIOGRAPHICAL/CRITICAL SOURCES: Nation, May 26, 1969.

*   *   *

HILL, West T(hompson), Jr. 1915-

PERSONAL: Born January 18, 1915, in Louisville, Ky.; son of West Thompson and Mary (Bewley) Hill; married Dorothy Thompson (curator of McDowell House), June 6, 1939; children: Paula (Mrs. Michael Collins), Judith (Mrs. David W. Wilson). Education: Georgetown College, A.B., 1937; Columbia University, M.A., 1941; University of Iowa, Ph.D., 1954. Politics: Democrat. Religion: Presbyterian. Home: 254 East Lexington, Danville, Ky. 40422. Office: Department of Dramatic Arts, Centre College of Kentucky, Danville, Ky. 40422.

CAREER: Centre College of Kentucky, Danville, assistant professor, 1946-54, associate professor, 1954-61, professor of dramatic art, 1961—, director of college theatre, 1946—.

*Military service:* U.S. Army, Infantry, 1944-46; received Purple Heart. *Member:* American Education Association, Kentucky Historical Association, Filson Club, Omicron Delta Kappa.

*WRITINGS: The Early Theatre in Kentucky: 1790-1820,* University Press of Kentucky, 1971. Contributor of articles and reviews to *Theatre Arts, Filson Club Historical Quarterly,* and *Pennsylvania Magazine of History.*

*WORK IN PROGRESS: Kentucky Theatre; All You Need to Know about the Theatre.*

*SIDELIGHTS:* West Hill has travelled to the British Theatre Seminar in London and has made many trips to Europe. *Avocational interests:* Fishing.

\* \* \*

## HILL, William Joseph 1924-

*PERSONAL:* Born March 30, 1924, in North Attleboro, Mass.; son of William Edward (a truck driver) and Rita (Lanteigne) Hill. *Education:* Providence College, A.B., 1945; Pontifical Faculty of the Dominican House of Studies, Washington, D.C., S.T.B., 1949, S.T.L., S.T.Lr., 1951; University of St. Thomas, Rome, S.T.D., 1953. *Home:* 487 Michigan Ave., Washington, D.C. 20017. *Office:* Catholic University of America, Washington, D.C. 20017.

*CAREER:* Ordained Roman Catholic priest of the Order of Preachers (Dominicans); Pontifical Faculty of Theology at Dominican House of Studies, Washington, D.C., professor of systematic theology, 1954-71; Catholic University of America, Washington, D.C., associate professor of systematic theology, 1971—. Summer lecturer at Immaculata College, Immaculata, Pa., 1951, Dunbarton College of Holy Cross, 1953, Marygrove College, 1953, 1954, Carlow College, 1955, 1956, and Providence College, 1957-64. Vice-president, Dominican Faculty of Theology, Washington, D.C.; vice-regent of studies, Dominican Province of St. Joseph in U.S.A., 1966-70. *Member:* Catholic Theological Society of America. *Awards, honors:* Master of Sacred Theology (highest honorary title of theology in Dominican Order), 1967; Providence College, D.R.E., 1976.

*WRITINGS:* (Editor and translator) St. Thomas, *Hope,* McGraw, 1966; *Knowing the Unknown God,* Philosophical Library, 1971. Contributor of scholarly articles to *Proceedings, Thomist, Journal of Religion, New Scholasticism, Theological Studies,* and *New Catholic Encyclopedia.* Editor-in-chief, *Thomist,* 1975—. Member of editorial board, *New Catholic Encyclopedia,* 1974— and *Communio,* 1977—.

*WORK IN PROGRESS:* Research in various problems related to Trinitarian theology.

\* \* \*

## HILLGARTH, J(ocelyn) N(igel) 1929-

*PERSONAL:* Born September 22, 1929, in London, England; son of Alan Hugh (a naval officer) and Mary (Gardner) Hillgarth; married Nina Pantaleoni (a university administrator), February 25, 1966. *Education:* Attended Eton College, 1943-47; Queens' College, Cambridge, B.A., 1950; Cambridge University, M.A., 1954, Ph.D., 1957. *Office:* Pontifical Institute of Mediaeval Studies and Centre for Medieval Studies, University of Toronto, 59 Queens Park CR E, Toronto, Ontario, Canada M5S 2C4.

*CAREER:* Warburg Institute, London, England, senior research fellow, 1959-62; Institute for Advanced Study,

Princeton, N.J., member, 1963-64; Harvard University, Cambridge, Mass., assistant professor of history, 1965-70; Boston College, Boston, Mass., professor of history, 1970-77; University of Toronto, Pontifical Institute of Mediaeval Studies and Centre for Medieval Studies, Toronto, Ontario, professor of history, 1977—. Visiting lecturer, University of Texas at Austin, 1964-65. *Member:* American Historical Association, Mediaeval Academy of America. *Awards, honors:* Guggenheim fellow, 1968-69.

*WRITINGS: The Conversion of Western Europe, 350-750,* Prentice-Hall, 1969; *Ramon Lull and Lullism in Fourteenth-Century France,* Clarendon Press, 1971; *The Spanish Kingdoms, 1250-1516,* Oxford University Press, Volume I, 1976, Volume II, in press.

*WORK IN PROGRESS:* Research on royal finances and on popular religion in 14th century Spain.

\* \* \*

## HINE, Frederick R. 1925-

*PERSONAL:* Born November 16, 1925, in Cincinnati, Ohio; son of Fred L. (a salesman) and Alma (Waltamath) Hine; married Corinne L. Kopp, September 16, 1948; children: Frederick C. *Education:* Yale University, B.S., 1946, M.D., 1949. *Home:* 2317 Prince St., Durham, N.C. 27707. *Office:* Duke University Medical Center, Durham, N.C. 27710.

*CAREER:* Charity Hospital, New Orleans, La., interne, 1949-50; Tulane University, New Orleans, psychiatric resident, School of Medicine, 1950-53, instructor in psychiatry, 1952-59; Southeast Louisiana Hospital, New Orleans, staff psychiatrist, 1953-54, director of training and research, 1954-58, clinical director, 1958; Duke University, Medical Center, Durham, N.C., began as assistant professor, became associate professor, 1959-71, professor of psychiatry, 1971—.

*WRITINGS: Introduction to Psychodynamics: A Conflict-Adaptational Approach,* Duke University Press, 1971; (with Eric Pfeiffer) *Behavioral Science: A Selective View,* Little, Brown, 1972.

\* \* \*

## HINNEBUSCH, William A(quinas) 1908-

*PERSONAL:* Born July 10, 1908, in Pittsburgh, Pa.; son of John Frederick (a bookkeeper) and Anna M. Hinnebusch. *Education:* St. Thomas College, River Forest, Ill., B.A., 1932; Catholic University of America, M.A., 1936; Oxford University, D.Phil., 1939. *Home and office:* Dominican House of Studies, 487 Michigan Ave. N.E., Washington, D.C. 20017.

*CAREER:* Roman Catholic priest of Order of Preachers (Dominicans); Providence College, Providence, R.I., professor of medieval history, 1939-50; Convento Santa Sabina, Historical Institute, Rome, Italy, researcher in Dominican history, 1950-53; Pontifical Institute of Theology of Immaculate Conception College (Dominican House of Studies), Washington, D.C., professor of church history, 1955-75. *Member:* American Catholic Historical Association, Mediaeval Academy of America. *Awards, honors:* D.H.L., Providence College, 1969.

*WRITINGS: The Early English Friars Preachers,* Historical Institute of Santa Sabina, 1951; *Dominican Spirituality: Principles and Practice,* Thomist Press, 1965; *History of the Dominican Order,* Alba, Volume I, 1966, Volume II, 1973; *Renewal in the Spirit of St. Dominic,* Dominicana Press,

1968. Contributor to *New Catholic Encyclopedia, Encyclopedia Americana, Catholic Encyclopedia of Home and School,* and *Encyclopaedia Britannica.*

*WORK IN PROGRESS:* Third and fourth volumes of *History of the Dominican Order,* for Alba.

\* \* \*

## HIRST, David W(ayne) 1920-

*PERSONAL:* Born January 26, 1920, in Meriden, Conn.; son of James Firth and Mabel (Oeffinger) Hirst; married Barbara Kortum (a research secretary), September 13, 1947. *Education:* Attended Ohio Wesleyan University, 1940-41; University of Connecticut, B.A., 1950; Northwestern University, M.A., 1952, Ph.D., 1962. *Politics:* Democrat. *Religion:* Protestant. *Home:* 229 Hartley Ave., Princeton, N.J. 08540. *Office:* Department of History, Princeton University, Princeton, N.J. 08540.

*CAREER:* National College of Education, Evanston, Ill., instructor in history, 1954-55; Library of Congress, Washington, D.C., 1955-56, began as assistant, became head of recent manuscript section, Manuscript Division; University of Maryland, College Park, instructor in history, 1956-59; Princeton University, Princeton, N.J., senior research historian, department of history, 1960—. *Military service:* U.S. Army Air Forces, 1942-46; flight radio operator in China-Burma-India theater; received Distinguished Flying Cross, Air Medal with two oak-leaf clusters, and five battle stars. *Member:* American Historical Association, Organization of American Historians, Society for the History of American Foreign Relations, Southern Historical Association.

*WRITINGS:* (Editor) *Woodrow Wilson, Reform Governor: A Documentary Narrative,* Van Nostrand, 1965. Associate editor, *The Papers of Woodrow Wilson,* twenty-three volumes, Princeton University Press, 1966-77.

*WORK IN PROGRESS:* Further volumes of the projected forty-plus of *The Papers of Woodrow Wilson;* a study of American society during World War I; a short interpretive biography of Wilson, for schools and colleges; an interpretive analysis of Wilson's presidency.

\* \* \*

## HITCHMAN, James H. 1932-

*PERSONAL:* Born November 17, 1932, in Los Angeles, Calif.; son of Walter Harold (a public relations executive) and Millicent (Milligan) Hitchman; married Marie Corner, January 23, 1955; children: Matthew, Suzanne, Daniel. *Education:* Willamette University, B.A., 1954; University of California, Berkeley, M.A., 1955, Ph.D., 1965. *Office:* History Department, Western Washington University, Bellingham, Wash. 98225.

*CAREER:* Westminster College, Salt Lake City, Utah, admissions counselor, 1958-60; Portland State College (now University), Portland, Ore., 1963-66, became assistant professor of history; Western Washington University, Bellingham, assistant professor, 1966-69, associate professor, 1969-73, professor of history, 1973—, assistant academic dean, 1966, dean of students, 1967-69. Member of board of trustees, Willamette University. *Military service:* U.S. Marine Corps, 1955-58; became first lieutenant. *Member:* American Historical Association, Society for Historians of American Foreign Relations, North American Society for Oceanic History, Washington State Historical Society, Bellingham Yacht Club. *Awards, honors:* Portland State College award, 1966, for outstanding teaching; National Endowment for the Humanities award, 1976.

*WRITINGS: Leonard Wood and Cuban Independence, 1898-1902,* Nijhoff, 1971; *The Port of Bellingham 1920-70,* Western Washington State College, 1972; *The Waterborne Commerce of British Columbia and Washington, 1850-1970,* Western Washington University Press, 1976. Also contributor, J. W. Scott, editor, *Essays in Honor of Keith Murray,* 1978. Contributor to *The Americas, Pacific Northwest Quarterly, American Neptune,* and *Journal of Inter-American Studies and World Affairs.*

*WORK IN PROGRESS:* Articles on higher education in the Pacific Northwest.

\* \* \*

## HIXSON, William B(utler), Jr. 1940-

*PERSONAL:* Born November 8, 1940, in New York, N.Y.; son of William Butler (an actor) and Mary (Thomas) Hixson; married Vivian Scott (an assistant professor of sociology), May 29, 1965. *Education:* Pomona College, B.A., 1961; Columbia University, M.A., 1963, Ph.D., 1969. *Office:* Department of History, Morrill Hall, Michigan State University, East Lansing, Mich. 48824.

*CAREER:* Michigan State University, East Lansing, instructor, 1966-69, assistant professor, 1969-71, associate professor of history, 1971—. *Member:* American Historical Association, Organization of American Historians. *Awards, honors:* Pelzer Award, Organization of American Historians, 1968, for "Moorfield Storey and the Struggle for Equality," published in *Journal of American History.*

*WRITINGS: Moorfield Storey and the Abolitionist Tradition,* Oxford University Press, 1972. Contributor to *American Scholar, Commonweal, Journal of American History,* and *New England Quarterly.*

\* \* \*

## HOBEN, John B. 1908-

*PERSONAL:* Born May 30, 1908, in Chicago, Ill.; son of Allan T. (an educator) and Jessie (Lindsay) Hoben; married Jean Graham, January 28, 1935; children: Celia (Mrs. Miodrag Beljakovic), Anne (Mrs. Richard Broussard), Carol (Mrs. Jon Muth). *Education:* Colgate University, A.B., 1930; University of Michigan, M.A., 1931. *Politics:* Democrat. *Religion:* Baptist. *Home:* Preston Hill Rd., Hamilton, N.Y. 13346. *Office:* English Department, Colgate University, Hamilton, N.Y. 13346.

*CAREER:* Western Michigan University, Kalamazoo, instructor in English and public speaking, 1933-34; Kalamazoo College, Kalamazoo, Mich., instructor in speech and English history, 1934-37; Colgate University, Hamilton, N.Y., instructor in public speaking, 1937-43, assistant professor, 1943-48, associate professor, 1948-63, professor of English, 1964-76, director of English communication, 1948-57. President, Hamilton Democratic Club, 1943-44. *Member:* American Association of University Professors, Phi Beta Kappa, Kappa Delta Rho (national director, 1956-60).

*WRITINGS:* (With E. T. Adams) *The American Idea,* Harper, 1942; (with E. J. McGrath) *Communication in General Education,* W. C. Brown, 1948; *A Pocket Full of Rye,* Mid-York Press, 1965; *A Crooked Stile,* Mid-York Press, 1970; *Cockleshell,* Colgate University Press, 1974. Contributor to *American Literature, New York History, Harper's,* and *Philobiblon.*

*WORK IN PROGRESS: The Clock Struck One.*

## HODGES, Henry (Woolmington MacKenzie) 1920-

*PERSONAL:* Born July 19, 1920, in Oxfordshire, England; son of George M. W. and Barbara K. (Webber) Hodges; married Bernadette J. Davies, February 20, 1965; children: Hugh, Penelope. *Education:* Attended St. John's College, Cambridge, 1938-40, and University of London, 1951-53. *Politics:* None. *Religion:* None. *Home:* 271 College St., Kingston, Ontario, Canada. *Office:* Art Conservation Programme, Queen's University, Kingston, Ontario, Canada.

*CAREER:* Queen's University of Belfast, Belfast, Northern Ireland, lecturer in archaeology, 1953-57; University of London, Institute of Archaeology, London, England, lecturer, 1957-69, senior lecturer in archaeological technology, 1969-74; Queen's University, Kingston, Ontario, professor of artifact conservation, 1974—. *Military service:* Royal Naval Volunteer Reserve, Air Branch, observer, 1940-44. *Member:* International Institute for Conservation of Historic and Artistic Works (fellow).

*WRITINGS: Artifacts: An Introduction to Primitive Technology,* Praeger, 1964 (published in England as *Artifacts: An Introduction to Early Materials and Technology,* John Baker, 1964); (with M. Maitland Howard and Edward Pyddoke) *Ancient Britons: How They Lived,* John Baker, 1969, Praeger, 1970; *Technology in the Ancient World,* Knopf, 1970; *Pottery: A Technical History,* Hamlyn House, 1972. Contributor to archaeology journals.

*WORK IN PROGRESS: Technology in the Medieval World,* for Penguin.

*AVOCATIONAL INTERESTS:* Making pottery; food preparation and cooking.

*BIOGRAPHICAL/CRITICAL SOURCES: Best Sellers,* November 1, 1970.

\* \* \*

## HODGINS, Bruce W(illard) 1931-

*PERSONAL:* Born January 29, 1931, in Kitchener, Ontario, Canada; son of Stanley Earl (a teacher) and Laura Belle (Turel) Hodgins; married Carol Edith Creelman (a physiotherapist), July 24, 1958; children: Shawn Prescott, Geoff Stanley (sons). *Education:* University of Western Ontario, B.A., 1953; Queen's University at Kingston, M.A., 1955; Duke University, Ph.D., 1965. *Politics:* New Democratic Party. *Home:* 7 Engelburn Pl., Peterborough, Ontario, Canada. *Office:* Department of History, Trent University, Peterborough, Ontario, Canada.

*CAREER:* Prince of Wales College (now University of Prince of Wales), Charlottetown, Prince Edward Island, instructor in history, 1955-58, 1961-62; University of Western Ontario, London, assistant professor of history, 1962-65; Trent University, Peterborough, Ontario, assistant professor, 1965-67, associate professor, 1967-72, professor of history, 1972—. Fellow in history, Australian National University, 1970. Director, Camp Wanapitei, Temagami, Ontario. Candidate for Parliament, New Democrat Party, 1968; former member of Ontario provincial council.

*MEMBER:* Canadian Historical Association (member of council, 1961-64), Royal Commonwealth Society, United Nations Association of Canada (member of national policy council, 1965-72; president of national administrative council, 1967-69), Ontario Confederation of University Faculty Associations (member of executive board, 1971-72), Ontario Historical Society. *Awards, honors:* Centenary Medal of Canadian Government, 1967; Cruikshank Award of Ontario Historical Society, 1968.

*WRITINGS: John Sandfield Macdonald: 1812-1872,* University of Toronto Press, 1971; (editor with Robert Page) *Canadian History since Confederation: Essays and Interpretations,* Dorsey, 1972; (editor with Bowles, Hanley, and Rawlyk) *The Indian: Assimilation, Integration, or Separation,* Prentice-Hall, 1972; *Canadiens, Canadians and Quebecois,* Prentice-Hall, 1974; *Paradis of Temagami, 1848-1926,* Highway Bookshop, 1976; (editor with Benidickson and Rawlyk) *The Canadian North: Source of Wealth or Vanishing Heritage,* Prentice-Hall, 1977; (with Wright and Heick) *Federalism in Canada and Australia; The Early Years,* Wilfrid Laurier Press, 1978. Member of editorial board, *Alternatives,* 1971—.

*WORK IN PROGRESS: The Temagami Experience: A Story of Man's Impact upon His Environment,* completion expected in 1980.

*SIDELIGHTS:* With his wife and children, Bruce Hodgins drove from Ireland to Ceylon, via Turkey, Iran, Afghanistan, and India, thence by boat to Perth and overland from Perth to Canberra, 1969-70. He has traveled more than eight thousand miles by canoe in the Canadian north, frequently with his wife.

\* \* \*

## HOEHNER, Harold W. 1935-

*PERSONAL:* Born January 12, 1935, in Sangerfield, N.Y.; son of Walter Jacob (a farmer) and Mary (Siegel) Hoehner; married Virginia Alice Bryan, February 6, 1934; children: Stephen Harold, Susan Heidi, David Mark, Deborah Marie. *Education:* Barrington College, Barrington, R.I., B.A. (with honors), 1958; Dallas Theological Seminary, Th.M., 1962, Th.D. (with honors), 1965; Cambridge University, Ph.D., 1968; Tuebingen University, additional study, 1976-77. *Home:* 6538 Ridgemont Dr., Dallas, Tex. 75214. *Office:* Dallas Theological Seminary, 3903 Swiss Ave., Dallas, Tex. 75204.

*CAREER:* Pastor of Congregational Church in Manitou, Okla., 1958-60; ordained to ministry in Grace Bible Church, Dallas, Tex., 1962; supply preacher in England, 1964-67; Dallas Theological Seminary, Dallas, assistant professor of Bible exposition, 1968-72, assistant professor, 1972-77, professor of New Testament literature and exegesis and chairman of department, 1977—, director of doctoral studies, 1975—. Part-time instructor, Southern Bible Training School, 1960-64. *Member:* Society of Biblical Literature, Evangelical Theological Society, Studiorum Novi Testamenti Societas, Delta Epsilon Kai.

*WRITINGS:* (Contributor) Ernest Bammel, editor, *The Trial of Jesus* (festschrift for C. F. D. Moule), S.C.M. Press, 1970; *Herod Antipas,* Cambridge University Press, 1972; (contributor) Richard N. Lengenecker and Merrill C. Tenney, editors, *New Dimensions in New Testament Study,* Zondervan, 1974; *Chronological Aspects of the Life of Christ,* Zondervan, 1977. Assistant editor, *Bibliotheca Sacra.*

*WORK IN PROGRESS:* Articles for *Zondervan Pictorial Encyclopedia of the Bible, Wycliffe Bible Encyclopedia,* and *The Expositor's Bible Commentary.*

\* \* \*

## HOFFMAN, Robert L. 1937-

*PERSONAL:* Born July 11, 1937, in Washington, D.C.; son of Jay Louis (a psychiatrist) and Clara (a teacher; maiden name, Friedman) Hoffman; married Sheilah Valerie Doty (a psychologist), September 20, 1958; children: Tobias, Susannah, Rebecca. *Education:* Harvard University, A.B., 1959; Brandeis University, M.A., 1961, Ph.D., 1968. *Religion:* Quaker. *Home:* 1013 Washington Ave., Albany, N.Y. 12206. *Office:* Department of History, State University of New York, Albany, N.Y. 12222.

*CAREER:* U.S. Air Force Cambridge Research Laboratories, Bedford, Mass., physicist (part-time), 1959-61; University of Vermont, Burlington, instructor in history, 1964-65; Rensselaer Polytechnic Institute, Troy, N.Y., instructor in history, 1965-68; State University of New York at Albany, assistant professor, 1968-74, associate professor of history, 1974—. *Member:* American Historical Association, American Association of University Professors, War Resisters League, Fellowship of Reconciliation.

*WRITINGS:* (Editor) *Anarchism,* Aldine-Atherton, 1970; *Revolutionary Justice: The Social and Political Theory of P. J. Proudhon,* University of Illinois Press, 1972. Contributor of articles to *Journal of International Affairs, Historian,* and *Dissent.*

*WORK IN PROGRESS: More Than a Trial: The Struggle Over Captain Dreyfus,* completion expected in 1979; *Mystiques and Machines.*

*SIDELIGHTS:* Robert L. Hoffman told *CA:* "My earlier writing clarified complex political ideas, in part by placing them in their original historical contexts. Now I work in the opposite direction, using such ideas to reveal the history of which they are a part. I still concentrate upon politics, but to do so I go much more into literature, the arts, and popular attitudes. In all I emphasize reactions against modern culture, and how seemingly wrong-headed or mad ideas and sentiments reveal historical process. This process involves me because the present is only the latest moment in it, and refined historical consciousness is essential to knowing ourselves."

\* \* \*

## HOFFMANN, Ann (Marie) 1930-

*PERSONAL:* Born May 6, 1930, in Abingdon, Berkshire, England; daughter of Cecil Duncan (a schoolmaster) and Irene (White) Hoffmann. *Education:* Attended school in London, England. *Religion:* Church of England. *Home and office:* Forest Lodge, Broadwater Forest, Tunbridge Wells TN3 9JP, England.

*CAREER:* Architectural Press Ltd., London, England, secretary to book production manager, 1948-50; World Health Organization (WHO), Geneva, Switzerland, secretary, 1952; International Court of Justice, The Hague, Netherlands, secretary, 1953-57, administrative assistant, 1958-59; Organization for European Economic Cooperation (OEEC), Paris, France, private secretary to legal adviser, 1957-58; private secretary and researcher to author Robert Henriques, 1959-62; Conference Services Ltd., London, administrative assistant, 1963-66; Authors' Research Services, Tunbridge Wells, Kent, England, principal, 1966—. *Member:* Society of Indexers, Society of Women Writers and Journalists, Society of Genealogists.

*WRITINGS: The Dutch: How They Live and Work,* Praeger, 1971, revised edition, 1973; *Research: A Handbook for Writers and Journalists,* Midas Books, 1975; *Bocking Deanery: The Story of an Essex Peculiar,* Phillimore, 1976; *Lives of the Tudor Age,* Osprey, 1977; *Majorca,* David & Charles, 1978.

*WORK IN PROGRESS:* An updated and expanded edition of *Research: A Handbook for Writers and Journalists,* completion expected, 1979; a novel; historical and biographical research for other writers.

*SIDELIGHTS:* Ann Hoffmann told *CA:* "My working time is divided between researching for other writers and writing my own books in varying proportions each year. Both are creatively satisfying in their different ways, but I sometimes long to get away from *facts* and to write something entirely out of my own imagination." *Avocational interests:* Travel, theatre, and cooking.

*BIOGRAPHICAL/CRITICAL SOURCES: Sussex Express,* September 5, 1969; *Sussex Life,* May, 1971.

\* \* \*

## HOGENDORN, Jan S(tafford) 1937-

*PERSONAL:* Born October 27, 1937, in Lahaina, Hawaii; son of Paul Earl and Helen (Stafford) Hogendorn; married Dianne Hodet (a professor of classics), September 6, 1960; children: Christiaan Paul. *Education:* Wesleyan University, Middletown, Conn., B.A., 1960; London School of Economics and Political Science, M.Sc., 1962, Ph.D., 1966; additional study at Harvard University, 1962-63. *Politics:* Democrat. *Religion:* Unitarian Universalist. *Home:* R.F.D. 1, North Vassalboro, Me. 04962. *Office:* Department of Economics, Colby College, Mayflower Hill, Waterville, Me. 04901.

*CAREER:* Boston University, Boston, Mass., instructor in economics, 1963; Colby College, Waterville, Me., assistant professor, 1966-69, associate professor of economics, 1969—, Grossman Professor of Economics, 1976, chairman of department, 1972—. Ford Foundation professor of development economics, Robert College, Istanbul, Turkey, 1971-72; Fulbright professor of economic history, Ahmadu Bello University, 1975—. Associate, Columbia University, 1977—. *Member:* American Economic Association, Royal Economic Society, African Studies Association, Society for Religion in Higher Education (fellow), American Association of University Professors, Phi Beta Kappa. *Awards, honors:* Fulbright fellow in England, 1960-61; Danforth fellow, 1965-66.

*WRITINGS:* (Contributor) Carl Eicher and Carl Liedholm, editors, *Growth and Development of the Nigerian Economy,* Michigan State University Press, 1970; *Managing the Modern Economy,* Winthrop, 1972. Also author of "Understanding Modern Economics," a series of programs for Maine educational television, 1969.

*WORK IN PROGRESS: Economic Initiative and African Peasant Production,* for Cambridge University Press series, "Colonialism in Africa"; a sequel to *Managing the Modern Economy;* a book on the colonial experience with agriculture in Northern Nigeria.

*SIDELIGHTS:* Jan Hogendorn lived in Africa in 1965.

\* \* \*

## HOGUE, Arthur R(eed) 1906-

*PERSONAL:* Born November 16, 1906, in Pittsburgh, Pa.; son of Walter Jenkins and Gertrude (Dickerson) Hogue; married Elizabeth Steinbrecher, June 28, 1937; children: David Barclay. *Education:* Oberlin College, A.B., 1928; Harvard University, M.A., 1929, Ph.D., 1937. *Politics:* Republican. *Religion:* Presbyterian. *Home:* 2121 High St., R.R. 3, Bloomington, Ind. 47401. *Office:* Department of History, Indiana University, Bloomington, Ind. 47401.

CAREER: Hanover College, Hanover, Ind., associate professor, 1935-37, professor of history, 1937-48, academic dean, 1945-48; University of Illinois at Urbana–Champaign, assistant professor of history, 1948-50; Indiana University at Bloomington, associate professor, 1950-66, professor of history, 1966-74, professor emeritus, 1974—. Member: Selden Society, American Historical Association, American Society of Legal History, Mediaeval Academy of America, Indiana Historical Society, Phi Beta Kappa.

WRITINGS: (Editor) Carl Schurz, *Charles Sumner: An Essay,* University of Illinois Press, 1951; *Origins of the Common Law,* Indiana University Press, 1966. Contributor of articles or reviews to *American-German Review, Journal of Modern History, Indiana Magazine of History, Speculum,* and other professional journals.

WORK IN PROGRESS: Research on English legal history.

AVOCATIONAL INTERESTS: Farming and livestock breeding.

BIOGRAPHICAL/CRITICAL SOURCES: *South Atlantic Quarterly,* autumn, 1968.

*    *    *

## HOLADAY, Allan Gibson 1916-

PERSONAL: Born January 16, 1916, in Grand Ledge, Mich.; son of Robert Clayton (a merchant) and Effie (Hooks) Holaday; married Ruby Lees, September 30, 1945; children: Scott, Bruce. Education: Miami University, Oxford, Ohio, B.A., 1938; Cornell University, M.A., 1939; George Washington University, Ph.D., 1943. Politics: Democrat. Religion: Methodist. Home: 308 East Colorado Ave., Urbana, Ill. 61801. Office: 100 English Bldg., University of Illinois, Urbana, Ill. 61801.

CAREER: University of Illinois at Urbana–Champaign, instructor, 1942-47, assistant professor, 1947-55, associate professor, 1955-59, professor of English, 1959—. Member: Modern Language Association of America, Modern Humanities Research Association, Cambridge Bibliographical Society, Phi Beta Kappa, Phi Eta Sigma, Delta Phi Alpha.

WRITINGS: *Thomas Heywood's "The Rape of Lucrece,"* University of Illinois Press, 1950; (translator with Gerald Markley) *The Life of Lazarillo De Tormes,* Bobbs-Merrill, 1954; (editor) *The Plays of George Chapman,* University of Illinois Press, 1970. Contributor of articles on Renaissance English literature to professional journals. Editor, *Illinois Studies in Language and Literature.*

WORK IN PROGRESS: *George Chapman's Tragedies.*

*    *    *

## HOLBIK, Karel 1920-

PERSONAL: Born September 9, 1920, in Prague, Czechoslovakia; naturalized U.S. citizen; son of Karel and Katherine (Krouzel) Holbik; married Olga Rehacek, September 10, 1956; children: Thomas. Education: Charles University, Prague, J.D., 1947; University of Detroit, M.B.A., 1950; University of Wisconsin, Ph.D., 1956; attended Harvard University Law School, 1958-60. Home: 313 Country Club Rd., Newton, Mass. 02159. Office: United Nations, CH 2606, New York, N.Y. 10017.

CAREER: University of Detroit, Detroit, Mich., instructor in economics, 1948-49; Bank of America, San Francisco, Calif., researcher, 1951-52; Lafayette College, Easton, Pa., assistant professor of economics, 1955-58; Boston University, Boston, Mass., assistant professor, 1958-61, associate

professor, 1961-66, professor of economics, 1966-76; United Nations, New York, N.Y., chief of Section for Development of Financial Institutions, 1976—. Visiting professor, University of Brussels, 1969-70. Resident economics consultant, U.S. Naval War College, 1964-65. Member: Royal Economic Society, Association for Comparative Economics, American Economic Association, American Finance Association. Awards, honors: West German, Italian, and Romanian research and travel grants.

WRITINGS: *Italy in International Cooperation,* CEDAM, (Padua), 1959; (with Henry Myers) *Postwar Trade in Divided Germany,* Johns Hopkins Press, 1964; (with Myers) *West German Foreign Aid 1956-66,* Boston University Press, 1968; (editor with Phillip Grub) *American-East European Trade,* National Press, 1968; *The U.S., the U.S.S.R. and the Third World,* Weltarchiv (Hamburg), 1968; (with Philip Swan) *Trade and Industrialization in the Central American Common Market: The First Decade,* Bureau of Business Research, University of Texas, 1972; *Monetary Policy in Twelve Industrial Countries,* Federal Reserve Bank of Boston, 1973; *Industrialization and Employment in Puerto Rico,* University of Texas, 1975.

*    *    *

## HOLDEN, Raymond (Peckham) 1894-1972 (Richard Peckham)

April 7, 1894—June 26, 1972; American editor, poet, novelist, and author of children's books. Obituaries: *New York Times,* June 27, 1972; *Washington Post,* June 28, 1972; *Time,* July 10, 1972. (See index for *CA* sketch)

*    *    *

## HOLDEN, Vincent F. 1911-1972

April 21, 1911—August 23, 1972; American Paulist priest, historian, archivist, biographer, and early advocate of ecumenism. Obituaries: *New York Times,* August 24, 1972.

*    *    *

## HOLDREN, Bob R. 1922-

PERSONAL: Born September 13, 1922, in Pendleton, Ind.; son of Henry Ray and Della J. (Reynolds) Holdren; married Betty L. Claytor, August 17, 1947 (died, 1960); married Wilma M. Jelmeland (a research assistant), February 29, 1968; children: Kathleen Joan, Susan Jane, Michaela Wynne. Education: Indiana University, A.B., 1948, M.A., 1949; Yale University, Ph.D., 1959. Home: 111 Lynn Ave., Ames, Iowa 50010. Office: Department of Economics, Iowa State University, Ames, Iowa 50010.

CAREER: Bates College, Lewiston, Me., assistant professor of economics, 1952-55; Williams College, Williamstown, Mass., assistant professor of economics, 1955-58; Iowa State University, Ames, assistant professor, 1958-61, associate professor, 1961-68, professor of economics, 1968—. Economic advisor to Governor Edmund Muskie, Maine, 1954, and to Berkshire Development Committee, 1956-58. Military service: U.S. Army, 1942-46; became first lieutenant. Member: American Economic Association, American Association of University Professors.

WRITINGS: *The Structure of a Retail Market and the Market Behavior of Retail Units,* Prentice-Hall, 1960, 2nd edition, Iowa State University Press, 1968; (with Blaine Roberts) *Theory of Social Process: An Economic Analysis,* Iowa State University Press, 1972. Contributor to numerous professional journals.

*WORK IN PROGRESS:* A book on economic theory, research on theory of multiproduct firm; research on applying learning theory to decision under imperfect knowledge.

\*    \*    \*

## HOLISHER, Desider 1901-1972

February 2, 1901—August 11, 1972; Hungarian-born journalist, educator, photographer, and author of books on religious subjects. Obituaries: *New York Times,* August 13, 1972. (See index for *CA* sketch)

\*    \*    \*

## HOLLAND, Glen A. 1920-

*PERSONAL:* Born February 20, 1920, in Elm Springs, Ark.; son of Clyde Ervin and Georgianna (Myers) Holland; married Marjorie Jean Stanfield (a remedial teacher), June 6, 1943; children: Nancy Jean, Glenn Stanfield. *Education:* Stanford University, B.A. (with great distinction), 1941; Yale University, M.A., 1945, Ph.D., 1947. *Home:* 10469 Lindbrook Dr., Los Angeles, Calif. 90024. *Office:* 1322 Second St., No. 8, Santa Monica, Calif. 90401.

*CAREER:* Connecticut College for Women (now Connecticut College), New London, instructor in psychology, 1944-46; Pomona College, Claremont, Calif., assistant professor of psychology, 1946-49; University of California, Los Angeles, assistant professor of psychology, 1949-55; clinical psychologist in private practice, 1955—, currently in Santa Monica, Calif. *Member:* International Transactional Analysis Association (clinical member), American Psychological Association, Phi Beta Kappa, Sigma Xi.

*WRITINGS: Fundamentals of Psychotherapy,* Holt, 1965; (contributor) Raymond J. Corsini, editor, *Current Psychotherapies,* F. T. Peacock, 1973.

\*    \*    \*

## HOLLAND, James R. 1944-
### (J. H. Rand)

*PERSONAL:* Born February 20, 1944, in St. Louis, Mo.; son of Rand and Thelma (Robinson) Holland; married Helen Devine, February 18, 1972; children: Danielle, James Randolph. *Education:* Attended Principia College, 1962-64; Ohio University, B.F.A., 1966; Missouri University, additional study, 1967. *Residence:* Boston, Mass. *Office:* 208 Commonwealth Ave., Boston, Mass. 02116.

*CAREER: National Geographic,* Washington, D.C., photographic trainee, summer, 1966, contract photographer, 1967-68; Christian Science Center, Boston, Mass., film producer, 1969—. Photographs exhibited at Missouri University, Ohio University, and Truman Library; films have appeared on national and British television. *Awards, honors:* National Press Photographers awards, 1967, 1968, 1969; World Press Competition award, 1967; *Newsweek*/Bolex documentary film award, 1969; Industrial Photography Competition award, 1970; International Film and Television Festival of New York award, 1971.

*WRITINGS: The Amazon,* A. S. Barnes, 1971; *Mr. Pops,* Barre, 1972; *Tanglewood,* foreword by Michael Tilson Thomas, Barre, 1973. Author of more than a dozen documentary film scripts. Contributor to *World Book Encyclopedia;* contributor to photography, sociology, and popular journals, and to newspapers. Also contributor of articles under pseudonym J. H. Rand.

*WORK IN PROGRESS: Serpent Handlers.*

*AVOCATIONAL INTERESTS:* Renovating old city houses.

\*    \*    \*

## HOLLANDER, Paul 1932-

*PERSONAL:* Born October 3, 1932, in Budapest, Hungary; son of Jeno and Elsa (Kaszab) Hollander; married second wife, Mina Harrison; children: (first marriage) Sarah. *Education:* University of London, B.A., 1959; University of Illinois, M.A., 1960; Princeton University, Ph.D., 1963. *Office:* Department of Sociology, University of Massachusetts, Amherst, Mass. 01002.

*CAREER:* Harvard University, Cambridge, Mass., assistant professor of sociology, 1963-68; University of Massachusetts—Amherst, associate professor, 1968-74, professor of sociology, 1974—. *Awards, honors:* Guggenheim fellow, 1974-75.

*WRITINGS:* (Editor) *American and Soviet Society: A Reader in Comparative Sociology and Perception,* Prentice-Hall, 1969; *Soviet and American Society: A Comparison,* Oxford University Press, 1973.

*WORK IN PROGRESS:* A book on the two roles of intellectuals: social critic and utopia seeker.

\*    \*    \*

## HOLLANDER, Stanley C(harles) 1919-

*PERSONAL:* Born August 2, 1919, in Baltimore, Md.; son of Abraham A. (a manufacturer's agent) and Selma (Langfeld) Hollander; married Selma Dorothy Jacobs (an artist-craftsman), December 16, 1956. *Education:* New York University, B.S., 1941; American University, M.A., 1946; University of Pennsylvania, Ph.D., 1954. *Office:* Department of Marketing, Michigan State University, East Lansing, Mich. 48823.

*CAREER:* Office of Price Administration, Washington, D.C., business analyst, 1943-45, consultant, 1946; Charles Stores Co., New York, N.Y., analyst, 1945-47; University of Buffalo (now State University of New York at Buffalo), instructor in marketing, 1947-49; University of Pennsylvania, Philadelphia, instructor, 1949-54, associate professor of marketing, 1956-58; University of Minnesota, Minneapolis, assistant professor of economics and marketing, 1954-56; Michigan State University, East Lansing, associate professor, 1958-59, professor of marketing, 1959—. *Member:* American Marketing Association, American Economic Association, American Collegiate Retailing Association, Economic History Association, Midwest Marketing Association, Southern Marketing Association, Beta Gamma Sigma, Eta Mu Pi, Phi Kappa Phi.

*WRITINGS: Sales Devices Throughout the Ages,* J. Meier Co., 1953; *History of Labels: A Record of the Past Developed in the Search for the Origins of an Industry,* A. Hollander Co., 1956; *A Special Interest Bibliography on Discount Selling, Retail Price-Cutting, and Resale Price Controls,* American Marketing Association, 1956; (with Harry J. Ostland) *Small Business Is Big Business,* University of Minnesota Press, 1956; (editor) *Retail Price Policies,* 2nd edition (Hollander was not associated with earlier edition), Bureau of Business and Economic Research, Michigan State University, 1959; *The Rise and Fall of a Buying Club,* Bureau of Business and Economic Research, Michigan State University, 1959; (editor) *Explorations in Retailing,* Bureau of Business and Economic Research, Michigan State University, 1959; (with Gary A. Marple) *Henry Ford:*

*Inventor of the Supermarket?*, Bureau of Business and Economic Research, Michigan State University, 1960; (compiler) *Business Consultants and Clients: A Literature Search on the Marketing Practices and Problems of the Management Research and Advisory Professions,* Bureau of Business and Economic Research, Michigan State University, 1963, revised edition, 1973; *Restraints on Retail Competition,* Bureau of Business and Economic Research, Michigan State University, 1965; (editor) *Passenger Transportation: Readings Selected from a Marketing Viewpoint,* Bureau of Business and Economic Research, Michigan State University, 1968; (editor with Reed Moyer) *Markets and Marketing in Developing Economies,* Irwin, 1968; *Multinational Retailing,* Bureau of Business and Economic Research, Michigan State University, 1970; (with D. J. Duncan and C. F. Phillips) *Modern Retailing Management,* Irwin, 1972, revised edition (with Duncan), 1977; (editor with J. Boddewyn) *Public Policy Toward Retailing in Selected Countries,* Lexington, 1973. Contributor of numerous articles to professional journals. Member of editorial boards of *Journal of Marketing, Journal of Retailing, Retail and Distribution Management,* and *Michigan State University Business Topics.*

*WORK IN PROGRESS:* Research in marketing history.

\*    \*    \*

## HOLLEY, I(rving) B(rinton), Jr.    1919-

*PERSONAL:* Born February 8, 1919, in Hartford, Conn.; son of Irving B. (a businessman) and Mary (Sharp) Holley; married Janet Carlson, October 9, 1945; children: Janet Turner (Mrs. Hans H. Wegner), Jean Carlson (Mrs. William F. Schmidt III), Susan Sharp. *Education:* Attended Oxford University, 1937; Amherst College, B.A., 1940; Yale University, M.A., 1942, Ph.D., 1947. *Religion:* Episcopalian. *Home:* 2506 Wrightwood Ave., Durham, N.C. 27705. *Office:* Department of History, Duke University, Durham, N.C. 27706.

*CAREER:* Industrial College of Armed Forces, member of faculty, 1945-47; Duke University, Durham, N.C., instructor, 1947-50, assistant professor, 1950-54, associate professor, 1954-61, professor of history, 1961—. Visiting professor, U.S. Military Academy, 1974-75. Associate staff member, Army Research Office, 1963-72. Member of advisory committee on history, National Aeronautics and Space Administration (NASA), 1974—. Consultant to U.S. Department of Army, 1947; Health Planning Council of Central North Carolina, member, 1964-72, chairman, 1971-72; consultant on NASA Project Saturn with University of Alabama, Huntsville, Ala., 1967-71; advisory committee chairman, Air Force Historical Program, 1970—; member, Department of Defense advisory committee on R.O.T.C. affairs, 1971—. Trustee, Air Force Historical Foundation, 1973—, and American Military Institute, 1973—. *Military service:* U.S. Army Air Forces, 1942-47. U.S. Air Force Reserve, 1947—, current rank major general. *Member:* American Historical Association, Organization of American Historians, Society for History of Technology (advisory council, member, 1967), American Institute of Aeronautics and Astronautics (associate fellow, 1966—), Phi Beta Kappa (Duke University chapter president, 1970-71). *Awards, honors:* Social Science Research Council awards, 1955-56, 1961-62; Smithsonian Institution fellow, 1968-69.

*WRITINGS: Ideas and Weapons,* Yale University Press, 1953; *Buying Aircraft,* U.S. Government Printing Office, 1963; (contributor) M. Kranzberg and C. W. Purcell, Jr.,

editors, *Technology in Western Civilization,* Oxford University Press, 1967; (editor with C.D.W. Goodwin) *The Transfer of Ideas,* South Atlantic Press, 1968; *An Enduring Challenge: The Problem of Air Force Doctrine,* U.S. Air Force Academy, 1974. Also author of several volumes to the "U.S. Air Force Historical Study" series. Reviewer for *Technology and Culture, Journal of Southern History, Aerospace Historian, South Atlantic Quarterly,* and *Science.* Member of editorial board, *South Atlantic Quarterly,* 1966—; member of advisory board, *Aerospace Historian,* 1969—.

*WORK IN PROGRESS:* A biography of Brigadier General John M. Palmer (U.S. Military Academy, 1892).

\*    \*    \*

## HOLMAN, Harriet R.    1912-

*PERSONAL:* Born October 28, 1912, in Anderson, S.C.; daughter of Arthur E. and Olive (Brownlee) Holman. *Education:* Winthrop College, A.B., 1934; University of Michigan, A.M., 1939; Duke University, Ph.D., 1948. *Home:* 117 Victoria Cir., Andersen, S.C. 29621. *Office:* Department of English, Clemson University, Clemson, S.C. 29631.

*CAREER:* Teacher in public schools in South Carolina, 1934-41; Winthrop College, Rock Hill, S.C., instructor in English, 1942-43, reference librarian, 1949-52; Duke University, Durham, N.C., reference librarian, 1944-49; Erskine College, Due West, S.C., professor of English and chairman of department, 1952-60; Clemson University, Clemson, S.C., associate professor, 1960-70, professor of English, 1970-78, professor emerita, 1978—. *Member:* Modern Language Association of America, South Atlantic Modern Language Association.

*WRITINGS:* (Editor) *The Verse of Floride Clemson,* University of South Carolina Press, 1965; *John Fox and Tom Page: As They Were,* Field Research Projects (Miami), 1970; (editor) *North African Journal of T. N. Page,* Field Research Projects, 1970; (editor) Rosewell Page, *When I Was a Little Boy,* Field Research Projects, 1970; (editor) T. N. Page, *Mediterranean Winter,* Field Research Projects, 1971. Contributor of articles to *New England Quarterly, Southern Literary Journal, Georgia Review, American Notes and Queries,* and other journals.

*WORK IN PROGRESS:* Studies in Poe; an edition of T. N. Page's journals; a biography of T. N. Page.

\*    \*    \*

## HOLMER, Paul L(eroy)    1916-

*PERSONAL:* Born November 14, 1916, in Minneapolis, Minn.; son of Paul E. (a civil servant) and Elsie (Johnson) Holmer; married Phyllis J. Schulberg (a teacher), October 18, 1944; children: Paul, Linnea (Mrs. David Wren), Jonathan. *Education:* Attended University of Chicago, 1936; University of Minnesota, B.A., 1940, M.A., 1942; Yale University, Ph.D., 1946. *Politics:* Democrat. *Religion:* Lutheran. *Home:* 43 Swarthmore St., Hamden, Conn. 06517. *Office:* Stuart House, Yale University, 409 Prospect St., New Haven, Conn. 06510.

*CAREER:* Yale University, New Haven, Conn., instructor in philosophy, 1945-46; University of Minnesota, Minneapolis, instructor, 1946-48, assistant professor, 1948-50, associate professor, 1950-55, professor of philosophy, 1955-60; Yale University, professor of philosophical theology, 1960—. Visiting professor at Garrett Theological Seminary, 1951, Maywood Theological Seminary, 1952, Northwestern

University, 1952, College of the Pacific, 1957, Dartmouth College, 1957, Sacramento State College (now California State University, Sacramento), 1958, Moorehead State College, 1963, Oxford University, 1964-65, and University of California, 1970. *Awards, honors:* Fulbright research scholar and Swenson-Kierkegaard fellow, University of Copenhagen, 1953-54; Guggenheim fellow, 1964-65; Christian X Lecturer, Copenhagen, 1970; recipient of 4 honorary degrees, including L.H.D., University of North Dakota, 1960.

*WRITINGS: Philosophy and the Common Life* (Knoles lectures), Stanford University Press, 1958; (editor) *Discourses,* Harper, 1958; *Theology and the Scientific Study of Religion,* Denison, 1961; *Doubt and Frustration,* Thomas Nelson, 1965; (editor) Kierkegaard, *Edifying Discourses,* Augsburg, 1967; *C. S. Lewis: The Shape of His Faith and Thought,* Harper, 1976. Editorial consultant, Princeton University Press, 1970—, and Princeton Theological Seminary, 1976.

*WORK IN PROGRESS:* A book on Kierkegaard; *Emotions;* a translation of Kierkegaard's *Letters.*

*SIDELIGHTS:* Paul L. Holmer reads and speaks Danish, Swedish, and Norwegian, and he reads Latin, German, and French.

\* \* \*

## HOLMES, Edward M(orris) 1910-

*PERSONAL:* Born September 27, 1910, in Montclair, N.J.; son of Edward Huntington and Helen (Sinsabaugh) Holmes; married Jane Marshall Colyer (a librarian), June 27, 1936; children: Caroline (Mrs. Lawrence E. Marsh), Virginia, Constance (Mrs. Daniel McCarthy). *Education:* Dartmouth College, A.B., 1933; University of Maine, M.Ed., 1954; Brown University, M.A., 1956, Ph.D., 1962. *Politics:* Democrat. *Religion:* "Unaffiliated." *Office:* Department of English, E-M Building, University of Maine, Orono, Me. 04473.

*CAREER:* Has worked as a clerk, salesman, stage carpenter, seaman, business manager of a health cooperative, news reporter, and organizer of fishermen's cooperatives and credit unions; principal of high school in Princeton, Me., 1944-45; head of English department of high school in Ellsworth, Me., 1947-54; Farmington State Teachers College (now University of Maine at Farmington), instructor in English, 1954-55; University of Maine at Orono, instructor, 1956-62, assistant professor, 1962-64, associate professor, 1964-68, professor of English, 1968-74, Lloyd Elliot Professor of English, 1974-77, professor emeritus, 1977—. Visiting professor, Prince of Wales College, Prince Edward Island, 1968-69. Second selectman, Town of Tremont, 1946-47. *Awards, honors:* Emily Clark Balch Prize, 1971, for "Drums Again."

*WRITINGS: Faulkner's Twice-Told Tales: His Re-Use of His Material,* Mouton, 1966; *Driftwood,* Puckerbrush Press, 1972. Represented in *The Best American Short Stories of 1972,* edited by Martha Foley, Houghton, 1972. Contributor of about fifty stories and articles to New England journals.

\* \* \*

## HOLMES, Kenneth L(loyd) 1915-

*PERSONAL:* Born January 14, 1915, in Montreal, Quebec, Canada; naturalized U.S. citizen; son of James Sails (a clergyman) and Ruby Alice (Renshaw) Holmes; married Inez L'Adelle Rawlings, August 23, 1941; children: Donald Clifford, Stephen Lloyd. *Education:* University of Redlands, B.A., 1938; Berkeley Baptist Divinity School, B.D., 1945, M.A., 1948; University of Oregon, Ph.D., 1962. *Politics:* Democrat. *Religion:* Society of Friends (Quaker). *Home:* 410 Orchard St., Monmouth, Ore. 97361. *Office:* Department of History, Oregon College of Education, Monmouth, Ore. 97361.

*CAREER:* American Baptist Convention, pastor in Moscow, Idaho, 1948-53 (now a Quaker); Linfield College, McMinnville, Ore., assistant professor, 1954-61, associate professor, 1961-64, professor of history, 1964-67, dean of men, 1955-59; Oregon College of Education, Monmouth, professor of history, 1967—. Special writer, *Portland Oregonian,* 1953-60. *Member:* English-Speaking Union, American Historical Association, American Association for the Advancement of Science, Royal Geographical Society (London; fellow), Fellowship of Reconciliation, Northwest Scientific Association (president, 1976-77), Hudson's Bay Record Society.

*WRITINGS:* (Editor and contributor) *Linfield's Hundred Years* (centennial history), Binfords, 1956; (contributor) LeRoy Hafen, editor, *Mountain Men and the Fur Trade,* Arthur Clark, Volumes II, III, VI, VII, VIII, IX, 1964—; *Ewing Young, Master Trapper,* Binfords for Peter Binford Foundation, 1967; (with Judith Farmer) *Historical Atlas of Early Oregon,* text edition, Geographic & Area Study Publications, 1973. Author of column, "Pages from the Past," appearing in twenty Pacific northwest newspapers, 1962-66. Contributor to *Encyclopedia Americana, Dictionary of Canadian Biography,* and to magazines, Quaker journals, and newspapers.

*WORK IN PROGRESS:* Research on science as a motive for the enlightenment explorers and on Japanese drifts across the Pacific; a work on Sir Francis Drake, with particular reference to his activities on the Pacific Coast of North America, 1579; *Black Pioneers of Early Oregon.*

*SIDELIGHTS:* "There is a demand on professors to 'produce' research and writing," Kenneth L. Holmes told *CA.* "I have been writing for years because it is my highest joy to do so. Research is my detective work, comparable to the pursuits of my most famous 'relative,' Sherlock Holmes."

\* \* \*

## HOLT, Robert T. 1928-

*PERSONAL:* Born July 26, 1928, in Caledonia, Minn.; son of Oscar M. and Olga (Matson) Holt; married, December 14, 1957; wife's name, Shirley (a college teacher); children: Susan, Ann, Sharon. *Education:* Hamline University, A.B., 1950; Princeton University, M.P.A., 1952, Ph.D., 1957. *Home:* 1937 Kenwood Parkway, Minneapolis, Minn. 55405. *Office:* Department of Political Science, University of Minnesota, Minneapolis, Minn. 55455.

*CAREER:* University of Minnesota, Minneapolis, member of political science department, 1956—, director, Center for Comparative Studies in Technological Development and Social Change, 1967—. Fellow, Center for Advanced Study in the Behavioral Sciences, Palo Alto, Calif., 1961-62. *Military service:* U.S. Army. *Member:* American Political Science Association, International Studies Association, Midwest Political Science Association.

*WRITINGS: Radio Free Europe,* University of Minnesota Press, 1958; (with Robert W. van de Velde) *Strategic Psychological Operations and American Foreign Policy,* University of Chicago Press, 1960; (editor with John E. Turner)

*Soviet Union: Paradox and Change,* Holt, 1962; (contributor) Don Martindale, editor, *Functionalism in the Social Sciences,* American Academy of Political and Social Science, 1965; (with Turner) *The Political Basis of Economic Development: An Exploration in Comparative Political Analysis,* Van Nostrand, 1966; (with Turner) *Political Parties in Action: The Battle of Barons Court,* Free Press, 1969; (contributor) James N. Rosenau, editor, *Linkage Politics,* Free Press, 1969; (editor with Turner) *The Methodology of Comparative Research,* Free Press, 1970; (contributor) Fred W. Riggs, editor, *Frontiers of Development Administration,* Duke University Press, 1971.

*WORK IN PROGRESS:* The Analysis of Complex Social Systems.

\* \* \*

## HOLTER, Don W. 1905-

*PERSONAL:* Born March 24, 1905, in Lincoln, Kan.; son of Henry O. (a minister) and Lenna (Mater) Holter; married Isabelle Elliott, June 20, 1931; children: Phyllis (Mrs. Robert Dunn), Martha (Mrs. Robert Hudson), Heather (Mrs. Lee Ellis). *Education:* Baker University, A.B., 1927; Garrett Theological Seminary, B.D., 1930; University of Chicago, Ph.D., 1934. *Politics:* Independent. *Home:* 7725 Briar St., Prairie Village, Kan. 66208.

*CAREER:* Ordained clergyman of United Methodist Church; Union Theological Seminary, Manila, Philippines, professor of church history, 1935-40, president, 1940-45; Garrett Theological Seminary, Evanston, Ill., professor of church history and missions, 1949-58; Saint Paul School of Theology, Kansas City, Mo., president, 1959-72; United Methodist Church, Lincoln, Neb., bishop of Nebraska area, 1972-76. *Awards, honors:* D.D., Baker University, 1948; LL.D., Dakota Wesleyan University, 1967; D.D., Saint Paul School of Theology, 1973.

*WRITINGS:* (Contributor) William Ketcham Anderson, editor, *Christian World Missions,* Parthenon Press, 1946; *Fire on the Prairie: Methodism in the History of Kansas,* Methodist Publishing House, 1969.

\* \* \*

## HOLTZMAN, Wayne H(arold) 1923-

*PERSONAL:* Born January 16, 1923, in Chicago, Ill.; son of Harold H. (a businessman) and Ida Lillian (Manney) Holtzman; married Joan King, August 23, 1947; children: Wayne Harold, Jr., James K., Scott E., Karl H. *Education:* Northwestern University, B.S., 1944, M.S., 1947; Stanford University, Ph.D., 1950. *Politics:* Democrat. *Religion:* Methodist. *Home:* 3300 Foothill Dr., Austin, Tex. 78731. *Office:* Hogg Foundation for Mental Health, University of Texas, Austin, Tex. 78712.

*CAREER:* University of Texas at Austin, assistant professor, 1949-53, associate professor, 1953-59, professor of psychology and education, 1959-70, Hogg Professor of Psychology and Education, 1970—, associate director of Hogg Foundation for Mental Health, 1955-64, dean of College of Education, 1964-70, president of Hogg Foundation for Mental Health, 1970—. Social Science Research Council, member of board of directors, 1957-63, chairman of committee on learning and the educational process, 1966-71; co-chairman of science committee, U.S. National Commission to UNESCO, 1963-66; National Science Foundation, member of advisory committee for computing activities, 1970—, chairman, 1972—; member of computer science and

engineering board, National Academy of Sciences, 1971—; Learning Research and Development Center, member of board of visitors, 1969—, chairman, 1976; member of executive committee, International Social Science Council, 1976—; member of advisory committee, Medicine in the Public Interest, 1977—; consultant or member of advisory panels to U.S. Public Health Service, Social Security Administration, Surgeon General, National Institute of Mental Health, U.S. Office of Education, Educational Commission of the States, and other groups. Member of board of directors, El Centro de Investigaciones Sociales (Mexico), 1960—, Southwest Educational Development Laboratory, 1969-76, and Science Research Associates, 1974—. Conference of Southwest Foundations, member of board of directors, 1976—, vice-president, 1977-78; trustee, Educational Testing Service, 1972—; secretary-general, International Union of Psychological Science, 1972—. *Military service:* U.S. Navy, 1943-46; became lieutenant junior grade.

*MEMBER:* American Psychological Association (fellow; representative to International Union of Psychological Science, 1970-72; president), American Statistical Association, American Association for the Advancement of Science (fellow), Interamerican Society of Psychology (vice-president, 1962-64; president, 1966-67), International Council of Psychology (fellow), Psychometric Society, Society for Projective Techniques (fellow), Society of Multivariate Experimental Psychology, American Association of University Professors, American Association for Educational Research, Southwestern Psychological Association (president, 1958-59), Philosophical Society of Texas, Texas Psychological Association (president, 1956-57), Sigma Xi, Phi Delta Kappa. *Awards, honors:* Faculty research fellow, Social Science Research Council, 1953-54; Helen D. Sargent Memorial Award, Menninger Foundation, 1962; Center for Advanced Study in Behavioral Sciences fellow, 1962-63.

*WRITINGS:* (With J. S. Thorpe, J. D. Swartz, and E. W. Herron) *Inkblot Perception and Personality,* University of Texas Press, 1961; (editor with R. L. Sutherland, and others) *Personality Factors on the College Campus,* Hogg Foundation for Mental Health, University of Texas, 1962; (with B. M. Moore) *Tomorrow's Parents,* University of Texas Press, 1965; (with J. F. Santos, and others) *The Peace Corps in Brazil,* International Office, University of Texas, 1966; (with O. G. Brim, Jr. and R. S. Crutchfield) *Intelligence: Perspectives 1965,* Harcourt, 1966; *Computer-Assisted Instruction: Testing and Guidance,* Harper, 1971; (with others) *Interpretacion de Manchas de Tinta,* translated by Jose Huerta Ibarra, Editorial Trillas (Mexico), 1971; (with William F. Brown) *A Guide to College Survival,* Prentice-Hall, 1972; (with R. Diaz-Guerrero and Swartz) *Personality Development in Two Cultures,* University of Texas Press, 1975; *Introductory Psychology,* Harper, 1978.

Contributor: I. A. Berg and B. M. Bass, editors, *Objective Approaches to Personality Assessment,* Van Nostrand, 1959; C. W. Harris, editor, *Problems in Measuring Change,* University of Wisconsin Press, 1963; S. Tomkins and S. Messick, editors, *Computer Simulation of Personality,* Wiley, 1963; Mazafer and C. W. Sherif, editors, *Family Structure of Youth Attitudes,* Aldine, 1965; B. I. Murstein, editor, *Handbook of Projective Techniques,* Basic Books, 1965; R. Glaser, editor, *Organization for Research,* American Educational Research Association, 1966; J. P. Hill, editor, *Minnesota Symposia on Child Psychology,* Volume II, University of Minnesota Press, 1968; A. I. Rabin, editor, *Introduction to Modern Projective Techniques,* Springer-Verlag, 1968; N. S. Endler, and others, editors, *Contempo-*

*rary Issues in Developmental Psychology,* Holt, 1968; Hugo Leipziger-Pierce, editor, *Planning Versus or for the Individual,* School of Architecture, University of Texas, 1968; M. H. Appley, editor, *Adaption-Level Theory,* Academic Press, 1971.

Co-author of research reports for U.S. Air Force on psychiatric screening of flying personnel. Contributor to *Seventh Mental Measurements Yearbook,* and to *International Encyclopedia of the Social Sciences, Encyclopedia of Education, International Encyclopedia of Psychiatry, Psychology, and Neurology,* and *Encyclopedia of Educational Research;* contributor of about ninety articles and twenty reviews to scientific journals.

Editor, Harper & Row Psychology Series, 1963—, and *Journal of Educational Psychology,* 1966-72; consulting editor, *Psychological Bulletin,* 1957-64, *Multivariate Behavioral Research,* 1966-68, *Psychology in the Schools,* 1966-70, *Revista Interamericana de Psicologia,* 1967—, and to *Applied Psychological Measurement;* member of American Psychological Association council of editors, 1966-72, and of publication board, 1968-71.

\*    \*    \*

## HOLZMAN, Philip Seidman 1922-

*PERSONAL:* Born May 2, 1922, in New York, N.Y.; son of Barnet and Natalie (Seidman) Holzman; married Hannah Abarbanell, September 18, 1946; children: Natalie Kay, Carl David, Paul Benjamin. *Education:* City College (now City College of the City University of New York), B.A. (with honors), 1943; University of Kansas, Ph.D., 1952; attended Topeka Institute for Psychoanalysis, 1949-54. *Home:* 7A Soldiers Field Park, Boston, Mass. 02163. *Office:* Department of Psychology, Harvard University, Cambridge, Mass. 02138.

*CAREER:* Menninger Foundation, Topeka, Kan., senior psychologist and training psychoanalyst, 1949-68; University of Chicago, Chicago, Ill., professor of psychiatry and psychology, 1968-77; Chicago Institute for Psychoanalysis, Chicago, training and supervising psychoanalyst, 1968-77; Harvard University, Cambridge, Mass., member of department of psychology, 1977—. Member, Mayor's Commission on Human Relations, Topeka, 1963-68. *Military service:* U.S. Army, 1943-46; became first lieutenant. *Member:* American Psychological Association (fellow), American Psychoanalytic Association, American Psychopathological Association, American Psychosomatic Society, American Association for the Advancement of Science, Boston Psychoanalytic Society.

*WRITINGS:* (With R. Gardner, G. Klein, H. Linton, and D. Spence) *Cognitive Control,* International Universities Press, 1959; *Psychoanalysis and Psychopathology,* McGraw, 1970; (with Karl Menninger) *Theory of Psychoanalytic Technique,* Basic Books, 1973; (with Morton M. Gill) *Psychology versus Metapsychology,* International Universities Press, 1976. Member of board of editors, *Bulletin of the Menninger Clinic, Psychological Issues,* and *Psychosomatic Medicine;* consulting editor, *Contemporary Psychology, Schizophrenia Bulletin,* and *Social Service Review;* assistant editor, *Journal of the American Psychoanalytic Association.*

*WORK IN PROGRESS:* A report of research on disordered perceptual functioning in schizophrenia.

## HOOD, David Crockett 1937-

*PERSONAL:* Born April 21, 1937, in Tulsa, Okla.; son of Reginald Craig (a newspaper distributor) and Cathleen Sue (Crockett) Hood; married Lacey Joan Laylander (a reading specialist), October 21, 1961; children: Carl Victor, Mark Peter. *Education:* University of California, Santa Barbara, B.A., 1961; University of Southern California, Ph.D., 1966. *Home:* 3600 Wisteria St., Seal Beach, Calif. 90740. *Office:* Department of History, California State University, Long Beach, Calif. 90801.

*CAREER:* Wichita State University, Wichita, Kan., assistant professor of history, 1965-66; California State University, Long Beach, assistant professor, 1966-70, associate professor, 1970-75, professor of history, 1975—. Acting director, American Indian Studies Program, 1971, 1974-75. *Member:* Society for Promotion of Hellenic Studies, Society for the Promotion of Roman Studies.

*WRITINGS:* (Editor) *The Rise of Rome,* Heath, 1970. Editor, Southern California Wilderness Management Plan publications.

*WORK IN PROGRESS:* A Roman historiography.

*SIDELIGHTS:* David Crockett Hood reads French, Latin, Italian, Greek, Spanish, and German. Backpacking is a major hobby. He and his wife spent a year riding around Europe on a motorscooter.

\*    \*    \*

## HOOD, Donald W(ilbur) 1918-

*PERSONAL:* Born July 12, 1918, in New Castle, Pa.; son of Charles and Ida (Blews) Hood; married Betty Jackson, November, 1945; children: Rebecca Jean, Barbara Joan, Susan Marie. *Education:* Pennsylvania State University, B.S., 1940; Oklahoma State University, M.S., 1942; Agricultural and Mechanical College of Texas (now Texas A&M University), Ph.D., 1950. *Home address:* P.O. Box 57, Friday Harbor, Wash. 98250. *Office:* Friday Harbor Laboratories, University of Washington, Friday Harbor, Wash. 98250.

*CAREER:* Chemist with E. I. duPont de Nemours & Co., 1942-43, Manhattan Project, 1944, and Hanford Engineering Works, 1944-46; Texas A&M University, College Station, instructor, 1946-47, assistant professor, 1950-54, associate professor, 1954-60, professor of chemistry, 1960-65; University of Alaska, College, professor of marine science, 1965-76, director of Institute of Marine Science, 1965-77, professor emeritus, 1977—; currently affiliated with Friday Harbor Laboratories, University of Washington, Friday Harbor. National Science Foundation, member of panel on oceanography, 1967-70, and member of panel of International Decade of Oceanography, 1972-76. Co-chairman, International Conference on Port and Ocean Engineering under Arctic Conditions, Norway, 1971, and International Symposium for Bering Sea Study, Japan, 1972; chairman, Gordon Research Conference on Chemical Oceanography, 1972.

*MEMBER:* American Chemical Society, American Society of Limnology and Oceanography (vice-president, 1969), American Association for the Advancement of Science, American Geophysical Union, Geochemical Society, Federated Societies of Pollution and Waste Control, Marine Technology Society, Sigma Xi, Phi Lambda Upsilon, Phi Kappa Phi.

*WRITINGS:* (Editor) *Organic Matter in Natural Waters,* Institute of Marine Science, University of Alaska, 1970; (editor) *Impingement of Man on the Oceans,* Interscience, 1971; (editor) *Environmental Studies of Port Valdez,* Institute of Marine Science, University of Alaska, 1973; (editor) *Assessment of the Arctic Environment,* Institute of Marine Science, University of Alaska, 1976; (editor) *Oceans Handbook,* Dekker, in press. Author or co-author of more than eighty scientific papers. Editor, *Marine Science Communications,* 1974—.

*WORK IN PROGRESS:* Editing proceedings of International Symposium for Bering Sea Study.

*AVOCATIONAL INTERESTS:* Outdoor activities.

\* \* \*

## HOPKINS, Jasper Stephen, Jr. 1936-

*PERSONAL:* Born November 8, 1936, in Atlanta, Ga.; son of Jasper Stephen, Sr. (a barber) and Willie Ruth (Sorrow) Hopkins; married Gabriele Voigt, December 13, 1967. *Education:* Wheaton College, Wheaton, Ill., A.B., 1958; Harvard University, A.M., 1959, Ph.D., 1963. *Office:* Department of Philosophy, University of Minnesota, Minneapolis, Minn. 55455.

*CAREER:* Case Western Reserve University, Case Institute of Technology, Cleveland, Ohio, assistant professor, 1963-68; University of Arkansas, Fayetteville, associate professor, 1969; University of Massachusetts—Boston, associate professor, 1969-70; University of Minnesota, Minneapolis, associate professor, 1970-74, professor of philosophy, 1974—. *Awards, honors:* National Endowment for the Humanities fellowship for research in Munich, 1967-68; American Council of Learned Societies fellowship for research in Paris, 1973-74.

*WRITINGS:* (Editor, translator, and author of introduction with Herbert Richardson) Anselm of Canterbury, *Truth, Freedom, and Evil: Three Philosophical Dialogues* (also see below), Harper, 1967; (translator and author of introduction with Richardson) Anselm of Canterbury, *Trinity, Incarnation, and Redemption: Theological Treatises* (also see below), Harper, 1970; *A Companion to the Study of St. Anselm,* University of Minnesota Press, 1972; (editor and translator with Richardson) *Anselm of Canterbury,* Edwin Mellon Press, Volume I, 1974, Volume II (based on *Truth, Freedom, and Evil: Three Philosophical Dialogues,* Harper, 1967), 1976, Volume III (based on *Trinity, Incarnation, and Redemption: Theological Treatises,* Harper, 1970), 1976, Volume IV: (sole editor and translator) *Hermeneutical and Textual Problems in the Complete Treatises of St. Anselm,* 1976.

*WORK IN PROGRESS:* A Concise Introduction to the Philosophy of Nicolaus Cusanus.

\* \* \*

## HOPKINS, Thomas J(ohns) 1930-

*PERSONAL:* Born July 28, 1930, in Champaign, Ill.; son of Sewell Hepburn (a college teacher) and Pauline (Cole) Hopkins; married Frances LeFoy Skinner, December 22, 1956; children: Katherine M., Susan L., Nicholas J., Patrick S. *Education:* College of William and Mary, B.S., 1953; Massachusetts Institute of Technology, B.S., 1953; Yale University, B.D., 1958, M.A., 1959, Ph.D., 1962. *Politics:* Democrat. *Religion:* Protestant. *Home:* 323 North West End Ave., Lancaster, Pa. 17603. *Office:* Department of Religious Studies, Franklin and Marshall College, Lancaster, Pa. 17604.

*CAREER:* Franklin and Marshall College, Lancaster, Pa.,

assistant professor, 1961-67, associate professor, 1967-72, professor of religious studies, 1972—. Director, India Study Program of the Central Pennsylvania Consortium, Mysore, India, 1971—. *Member:* Association for Asian Studies, American Oriental Society, American Academy of Religion, American Society for the Study of Religion.

*WRITINGS:* (Contributor) Milton Singer, editor, *Krishna: Myths, Rites, and Attitudes,* East-West Center, 1966; *The Hindu Religious Tradition,* Dickenson, 1971; (contributor) Robert A. McDermott, editor, *Six Pillars: Introduction to the Major Works of Sri Aurobindo,* Conochocheague Association, 1974.

*WORK IN PROGRESS:* A source book on the Hindu religious tradition; research on Hindu religious history.

\* \* \*

## HORN, John L(eonard) 1928-

*PERSONAL:* Born September 7, 1928, in St. Joseph, Mo.; son of John L. (a sailor) and Nellie Rae (Weldon) Horn; married Darlene Dimmitt, November 15, 1950 (divorced, 1954); married Bonnie Colleen Hoskins, July 30, 1955; children: (second marriage) John Leonard, Jr., James Bryan, Julie Lynn, Jennifer Lee. *Education:* University of Denver, B.A., 1956; University of Melbourne, further study, 1956-57; University of Illinois, A.M., 1961, Ph.D., 1965. *Home:* 196 South Corona, Denver, Colo. 80209. *Office:* Department of Psychology, University of Denver, Denver, Colo. 80210.

*CAREER:* University of Denver, Denver, Colo., assistant professor, 1961-65, associate professor, 1965-69, professor of psychology, 1969—. Research associate, University of Illinois, summer, 1964; postdoctoral fellow, University of Wisconsin, summer, 1965; visiting lecturer, University of California, Berkeley, 1967. Visiting research associate, Institute of Psychiatry, University of London, 1972-73. Trustee, Institute for Research in Moral and Personality Adjustment; member of board of directors, Metropolitan Group Homes. *Military service:* U.S. Army, 1950-52.

*MEMBER:* American Psychological Association (fellow), American Association for the Advancement of Science (fellow), Psychometric Society, Society of Multivariate Experimental Psychology, Phi Beta Kappa, Sigma Xi, Phi Kappa Phi, Phi Delta Theta, Psi Chi. *Awards, honors:* Fulbright fellowship to Australia, 1956-57; U.S. Office of Education postdoctoral fellowship, 1965.

*WRITINGS:* (With R. B. Cattell) *The Handbook for the Motivational Analysis Test,* Institute for Personality and Ability Testing, 1962, revised edition, 1964; *Concepts and Methods of Correlational Analysis,* text edition, Holt, 1976.

Contributor: Cattell, editor, *Handbook of Multivariate Experimental Psychology,* Rand McNally, 1966; L. R. Goulet and P. B. Baltes, editors, *Life-Span Development Psychology,* Academic Press, 1970; A. R. Mahrer, editor, *New Approaches in Personality Classification,* Columbia University Press, 1970; P. D. Knott, editor, *Student Activism,* W. C. Brown, 1971; R. H. Dreger, editor, *Multivariate Personality Research,* Claitor's Book Store, 1971; Cattell and Dregor, editors, *Handbook of Modern Personality Theory,* Appleton, 1973; N. Rosenberg, editor, *Contributions to an Understanding of Alcoholism,* U.S. Government Printing Office, 1973; J. R. Royce, editor, *Contributions to Multivariate Analysis to Psychological Theory,* Academic Press, 1973; S. Gerson and A. Raskin, editors, *Genesis and Treatment of Psychologic Disorders in the Elderly,* Raven Press,

1975; S. Hooks, P. Kurtz, and M. Todorovich, editors, *The Ethics of Teaching and Scientific Research*, Prometheus Books, 1977; R. T. Osborne, C. E. Noble, and N. Weyl, editors, *Human Variation: The Biopsychology of Age, Race, and Sex*, Academic Press, 1978; P. B. Baltes, editor, *Lifespan Development and Behavior*, Academic Press, 1978. Also contributor to *Constancy and Change in Human Development*, edited by O. G. Brim and J. Kagan, in press.

Articles have been reprinted in fifteen books. Contributor to other volumes, to *International Encyclopedia of Neurology, Psychiatry, Psychoanalysis and Psychology*, to *International Lexicon of Psychology*, and of more than fifty articles to professional journals. Member of editorial board, *Journal of Educational Measurement*, 1968-69, *Multivariate Behavioral Research*, 1968-69, and *Applied Psychological Measurement*, 1976—.

*SIDELIGHTS:* John Horn writes: "I am basically a lazy, hedonistic person, orphaned at an early age and subsequently incapable of adapting to many of the conditions to which normal people readily adapt; I was lucky to find the sanctuary known as the university: it provides a protected environment for some kinds of poorly adapted creatures. In this environment I have been able to do some thinking and writing. I am very grateful to the society that provides such sanctuaries.

"My good fortune in this respect may indicate a principle: some work that is important for a civilized society (which is not to say that my work is of this kind) is best promoted through non-profit means, as in a university. Here one can take the long view and try things for which there is little chance of success but which, if successful, genuinely improve conditions in this universe. Much science, art and literature can be produced only under such circumstances. Thus, all of us should be grateful for a society that provides the sanctuaries to which I have referred."

\*     \*     \*

### HORN, Siegfried H(erbert) 1908-

*PERSONAL:* Born March 17, 1908, in Wurzen, Saxony, Germany; son of Albin Ernst (an airplane pilot) and Klara (Kertscher) Horn; married Jeanne Rothfusz, October 4, 1933 (died July 28, 1970); married Jeanne Kirkwood, February 29, 1976. *Education:* Walla Walla College, B.A., 1947; Seventh-day Adventist Theological Seminary, M.A., 1948; University of Chicago, Ph.D., 1951. *Religion:* Seventh-day Adventist. *Home:* 379 Ridge View Dr., Pleasant Hill, Calif. 94523.

*CAREER:* Netherlands East Indies Union Mission of Seventh-day Adventists, Java and Sumatra, missionary teacher, 1932-40; imprisoned as a civil internee in the Far East and India, 1940-46 (continued as teacher during this period); teacher at Walla Walla College, College Place, Wash., 1946-47, and University of Chicago, Chicago, Ill., 1948-50; Andrews University, Berrien Springs, Mich., professor of archaeology and history of antiquity, 1951-76, dean, 1973-76. Director of American Center for Oriental Research in Amman, Jordan, 1970-71; archaeological advisor to the Department of Antiquities of the Government of Jordan, 1970-71. *Member:* Palestine Exploration Fund (London), Egypt Exploration Society (London), American Oriental Society, German Orient-Gesellschaft (Berlin), Deutscher Palaestina Verein (Wiesbaden).

*WRITINGS:* (With Lynn H. Wood) *Chronology of Ezra 7*, Review & Herald, 1953, 2nd edition, 1970; *Light from the Dustheaps*, Review & Herald, 1955; *Entdeckungen zwischen Nil und Euphrat*, Advent-Verlag (Zurich), 1957, 2nd edition, 1966; *The Spade Confirms the Book*, Review & Herald, 1957; *Pietre che parlano*, Advent-Verlag (Florence), 1958; *Seventh-Day Adventist Bible Dictionary*, Review & Herald, 1960; *Records of the Past Illuminate the Bible*, Review & Herald, 1963; (with Roger S. Boraas) *Heshbon 1968, 1971, 1973* (three monographs), Andrews University Press, 1969, 1973, 1975; *Der Spaten bestaetigt die Bibel*, Saatkorn Verlag (Hamburg), 1970; *Mit dem Spaten an biblischen Staetten*, Unions Verlag (Stollberg), 1972; *Lapio ja Raamattu*, Kirjatoimi (Finland), 1976; *Opgravingen befestigen de Bijbel*, Vitgeverij Veritas (The Hague), 1977. Contributor of articles to *Journal of Near Eastern Studies*, *Bulletin of the American Schools of Oriental Research*, *Biblical Archaeologist*, *Bibliotheca Orientalis*, *Ex Oriente Lux*, and *Revue Biblique*. Editor, *Andrews University Seminary Studies*, 1963-74.

*WORK IN PROGRESS:* Publication of the results of the excavations at Heshbon (Jordan), conducted under Horn's direction; revision of *Seventh-Day Adventist Bible Dictionary*.

*SIDELIGHTS:* Siegfried H. Horn has traveled repeatedly around the world and in all continents except South America. He has been in the Near East twenty-one times in the last twenty-six years. From 1968-73 he was director of the archaeological expedition excavating Heshbon (Tell Hesban) in Jordan, of which the fifth campaign took place in 1976 under the direction of Lawrence T. Geraty.

\*     \*     \*

### HORNER, Thomas Marland 1927-

*PERSONAL:* Born February 7, 1927, in Cross Creek, N.C.; son of William McKinley and Dorothy (Baines) Horner. *Education:* Elon College, A.B., 1946; Duke University, M.Div., 1949; Columbia University, Ph.D., 1955. *Politics:* Independent. *Home:* 615 Frenchmen St., New Orleans, La. 70116.

*CAREER:* Episcopalian clergyman; Horace Mann School, Riverdale, N.Y., chaplain, 1954-55; Philadelphia Divinity School, Philadelphia, Pa., associate professor of Old Testament, 1957-69; Philadelphia Community College, Philadelphia, instructor in world history, 1970-71; Bethesda Episcopal Church, Saratoga Springs, N.Y., associate rector, beginning 1971. *Member:* American Hellenic League, General Society of the War of 1812, New York Society of the Sons of the Revolution, Historical Society of Pennsylvania, St. Andrew Society of Philadelphia, Masonic Order. *Awards, honors:* Sealantic Fund grant for study in Greece, 1968.

*WRITINGS:* (Translator from the German) Hermann Gunkel, *Psalms*, Fortress, 1967; *Student Aids to Old Testament Study*, Philadelphia Divinity School Bookstore, 1970; *Sex in the Bible*, Tuttle, 1973; *Jonathan Loved David: Homosexuality in Biblical Times*, Westminster, 1978.

*WORK IN PROGRESS:* A novel on Sappho.

*SIDELIGHTS:* Thomas Horner told *CA:* "One of my greatest interests at the moment is the Women's Liberation Movement, and I want to do everything I can do it promote it—by writing, speaking, or whatnot."

\*     \*     \*

### HORNSBY, Alton, Jr. 1940-

*PERSONAL:* Born September 3, 1940, in Atlanta, Ga.; son of Alton (an auto painter) and Lillie (Newton) Hornsby;

married Anne R. Lockhart, June 5, 1965; children: Alton III, Angela. *Education:* Morehouse College, B.A., 1961; University of Texas, Main University (now University of Texas at Austin), M.A., 1962; University of Texas at Austin, Ph.D., 1969. *Residence:* Atlanta, Ga. *Office:* Department of History, Morehouse College, 223 Chestnut S.W., Atlanta, Ga. 30314.

*CAREER:* Tuskegee Institute, Tuskegee Institute, Ala., instructor in history, 1962-65; Morehouse College, Atlanta, Ga., assistant professor, 1968-71, associate professor, 1971-74, professor of history, 1974—, chairman of department, 1971—. *Member:* American Historical Association, Association for Study of Negro Life and History, American Association of University Professors, Association of Social and Behavioral Scientists, Southern Historical Association, Phi Alpha Theta. *Awards, honors:* Woodrow Wilson fellow, 1961-62.

*WRITINGS: In the Cage: Eyewitness Accounts of the Freed Negro in Southern History, 1877-1929,* Quadrangle, 1971; *The Black Almanac,* Barron's, 1972, 4th edition, 1977. Editor, *Journal of Negro History,* 1976—.

*WORK IN PROGRESS:* Research on effects of slave unrest and rebellion on the status of freed Negroes in the antebellum South.

\*     \*     \*

## HOROWITZ, Leonard M(artin) 1937-

*PERSONAL:* Born March 1, 1937, in Baltimore, Md.; son of Jack (a wholesaler) and Bertha (Belson) Horowitz; married Suzanne R. Larsen (a psychologist), January 16, 1966; children: Jonathan Richard, Jeremy Daniel. *Education:* Johns Hopkins University, B.A. and M.A., 1957, Ph.D., 1960. *Home:* 480 La Mesa Court, Portola Valley, Calif. 94025. *Office:* Department of Psychology, Stanford University, Stanford, Calif. 94305.

*CAREER:* Stanford University, Stanford, Calif., 1960—, began as assistant professor, currently professor of psychology, vice-chairman of department, 1976—. *Member:* American Psychological Association, Phi Beta Kappa, Sigma Xi. *Awards, honors:* Woodrow Wilson fellow, 1957-58; Fulbright fellow, University College, University of London, 1958-59; National Institute of Mental Health fellow, 1972-73.

*WRITINGS: Elements of Psychological Statistics,* McGraw, 1974. Contributor of articles to psychology journals. Consulting editor, *Journal of Experimental Psychology.*

*WORK IN PROGRESS:* Research on cognitive processes and abnormal psychology.

\*     \*     \*

## HOUGH, Louis 1914-

*PERSONAL:* Born February 3, 1914, in Oakland City, Ind.; son of Ray (a superintendent of schools) and Louise (Stone) Hough. *Education:* University of Chicago, A.B., 1936, A.M., 1942, Ph.D., 1952. *Home:* 6847 Alden Dr., Union Lake, Mich. 48085. *Office:* School of Business, Wayne State University, Detroit, Mich.

*CAREER:* Miami University, Athens, Ohio, associate professor of economics, 1942-46; University of Denver, Denver, Colo., associate professor of economics, 1946-48; University of Pittsburgh, Pittsburgh, Pa., associate professor of statistics, 1948-54; University of Toledo, Toledo, Ohio, professor of economics and head of department, 1954-59; senior

research economist, Dunlap & Associates, Connecticut, 1959-60; Wayne State University, School of Business, Detroit, Mich., director of Bureau of Business Research, 1960—, professor of business administration, 1965—. *Member:* American Statistical Association, American Economic Association, Green Lake Association.

*WRITINGS: Principles of Economics,* Pitman, 1954; *Principles of Advertising,* Pitman, 1955; *Corporate Finance,* Pitman, 1956; *Modern Research for Administrative Decisions,* Prentice-Hall, 1971. Contributor to economics journals.

*WORK IN PROGRESS: Statistical Research Methods.†*

\*     \*     \*

## HOUSTON, Robert 1935-

*PERSONAL:* Born November 13, 1935, in Baltimore, Md.; son of Samuel and Florine (Dunlap) Houston; married Greta Sykes, June 9, 1959; children: Anthony, Cassandra, Danielle, Erika. *Education:* University of Maryland, B.S., 1963. *Politics:* Independent. *Religion:* Protestant. *Home:* 1512 East Chase St., Baltimore, Md. 21213. *Office:* c/o Mr. Howard Chapnick, 450 Park Avenue South, New York, N.Y. 10016.

*CAREER:* Professional photographer, 1966—. *Military service:* U.S. Army, 1958-60. *Awards, honors:* Award from Eastman Kodak for photographic excellence, 1967.

*WRITINGS: Legacy to an Unborn Son,* Beacon Press, 1971.

*WORK IN PROGRESS:* Three screenplays.††

\*     \*     \*

## HOWARD, Alan 1934-

*PERSONAL:* Born April 28, 1934, in Brooklyn, N.Y.; son of David and Frances (Ziff) Howard; married Kajorn Lekhakul (a program officer), February 19, 1964. *Education:* Stanford University, B.A., 1955, M.A., 1958, Ph.D., 1962. *Home:* 250 Kawaihae St., No. 11-B, Honolulu, Hawaii 96825. *Office:* Department of Anthropology, University of Hawaii, 2550 Campus Rd., Honolulu, Hawaii 96822.

*CAREER:* Ford Center for Advanced Study in the Behavioral Sciences, Palo Alto, Calif., research assistant, 1956-59; Cabrillo College, Aptos, Calif., instructor in sociology and anthropology, 1961-62; Bernice P. Bishop Museum, Honolulu, Hawaii, anthropologist, 1963-71, acting chairman of department of anthropology, 1970-71; University of Hawaii, Honolulu, part-time assistant professor, 1963-64, lecturer and instructor, 1965-68, professor of anthropology, 1971—, research at East-West Population Institute, 1971—. Visiting lecturer in social anthropology, University of Auckland, 1962-63; visiting lecturer, Institute for Cultural Sociology, Copenhagen, Denmark, 1969. Consultant to Hawaii Department of Education, Peace Corps, and other agencies. *Military service:* U.S. Army Reserve, 1954-62.

*MEMBER:* American Anthropological Association (fellow), Association for Social Anthropology in Oceania (member of executive committee, 1971-73). *Awards, honors:* National Institute of Mental Health researcher on Polynesian island of Rotuma, 1959-60, researcher in Hawaii, 1965-68, 1969-70; Human Ecology Fund grant, 1962; National Science Foundation grant, 1970-72.

*WRITINGS:* (Editor with Genevieve A. Highland and others, and contributor) *Polynesian Culture History: Essays in Honor of Kenneth P. Emory,* Bishop Museum Press, 1967;

(editor with Ronald Gallimore, and contributor) *Studies in a Hawaiian Community: Na Makamaka O Nanakuli*, Bishop Museum Press, 1968; *Learning to Be Rotuman*, Teachers College Press, 1970; (editor and contributor) *Polynesia: Readings on a Culture Area*, Chandler Publishing, 1971; *Households, Families and Friends in a Hawaiian-American Community*, East-West Population Institute, 1971; *Ain't No Big Thing: Coping Strategies in a Hawaiian-American Community*, University of Hawaii Press, 1973.

Contributor: H. C. Lindgren, editor, *Contemporary Research in Social Psychology*, Wiley, 1963; Sol Levine and Norman A. Scotch, editors, *Social Stress*, Aldine, 1970; Vern Carroll, editor, *Adoption in Eastern Oceania*, University of Hawaii Press, 1970; W. P. Lebra, editor, *Culture and Mental Health Research in Asia and the Pacific*, University of Hawaii Press, 1973. Contributor of about thirty-five articles to anthropology journals. Member of manuscript review committee, *Behavioral Science*, 1971-73.

\*      \*      \*

## HOWARD, Thomas   1930-

*PERSONAL:* Born April 11, 1930, in Tampa, Fla.; son of William Herman and Mildred (Clark) Howard; married Anne Smith (a school librarian), June 26, 1954; children: Catherine, Judith, Alice. *Education:* University of Richmond, B.A., 1951. *Religion:* Presbyterian. *Home:* 7914 Stuart Hall Rd., Richmond, Va. 23229. *Office:* Richmond *Times-Dispatch*, 333 East Grace, Richmond, Va. 23219.

*CAREER:* United Press International (UPI), Raleigh, N.C., staff correspondent, 1953; *Newport News Daily Press*, Newport News, Va., reporter, 1955-57; *Richmond Times-Dispatch*, Richmond, Va., reporter and editor, 1957—, state editor, 1972—. Copy editor, *Pacific Stars and Stripes* (Tokyo), 1965; lecturer in journalism, University of Richmond, 1968-69. *Military service:* U.S. Army Reserve, 1948-62; became first lieutenant. *Awards, honors:* National Headliners Award, 1977.

*WRITINGS:* (Editor) *Black Voyage: Eyewitness Accounts of the Atlantic Slave Trade*, Little, Brown, 1971. Contributor to national periodicals, including *Fortune*, *Time*, and *Newsweek*, and to newspapers. Virginia correspondent, *McGraw-Hill World News*, 1965-72.

*WORK IN PROGRESS:* Research on a relationship between a national "guilt complex" and Southern race relations.

\*      \*      \*

## HOWARTH, William Louis   1940-

*PERSONAL:* Born November 26, 1940, in Minneapolis, Minn.; son of Nelson Oliver (an attorney) and Mary (Prindiville) Howarth; married Barbara Ann Brown (a teacher), August 16, 1963; children: Jennifer Lynn, Jeffrey Todd. *Education:* University of Illinois, B.A. (with honors), 1962; University of Virginia, M.A., 1963, Ph.D., 1967. *Home:* 45 Knoll Dr., Princeton, N.J. 08540. *Office:* Department of English, McCosh 22, Princeton University, Princeton, N.J. 08540.

*CAREER:* Princeton University, Princeton, N.J., instructor, 1966-68, assistant professor, 1968-73, associate professor of English, 1973—. *Member:* Modern Language Association of America, American Studies Association, Thoreau Society (president, 1975), Phi Beta Kappa. *Awards, honors:* Huntington Library fellow, 1968; John E. Annan Bicentennial Preceptor, 1970-73; National Endowment for the Humanities fellow, 1976-77.

*WRITINGS:* (Editor) *A Thoreau Gazetteer*, Princeton University Press, 1970; (editor) *Twentieth-Century Interpretations of Poe's Tales*, Prentice-Hall, 1971; *The Literary Manuscripts of Henry David Thoreau*, Ohio State University Press, 1974; (editor) *The John McPhee Reader*, Farrar, Straus, 1976. Contributor to literature journals.

*WORK IN PROGRESS:* Editing volumes of Thoreau's journal; a critical study of Thoreau's journal; editor-in-chief and director of textual center for *The Writings of Henry D. Thoreau*.

\*      \*      \*

## HOYT, Elizabeth E(llis)   1893-

*PERSONAL:* Born January 27, 1893, in Augusta, Me.; daughter of William A. (a teacher) and Fannie (Ellis) Hoyt. *Education:* Boston University, A.B., 1913; Harvard University, A.M., 1924, Ph.D., 1925. *Residence:* Round Pond, Me. 04564.

*CAREER:* National Industrial Conference Board, New York, N.Y., research worker, 1917-21; Iowa State University, Ames, associate professor, 1925-28, professor of economics, 1928-72. Instructor, Wellesley College, 1917-21. Has done extensive research abroad in such countries as Japan, China, Guatemala, Jamaica, former British East Africa (Uganda, Kenya, Tanzania). *Member:* American Economic Association, American Association of University Professors. *Awards, honors:* Fulbright fellow at Makerere University, Uganda, 1950-51; Ford Foundation fellow in Jamaica, 1957-58.

*WRITINGS:* *Primitive Trade*, Kegan Paul, 1926, published as *Economic Classic*, Augustus M. Kelly, 1968; *Consumption of Wealth*, Macmillan, 1928; *Consumption in Our Society*, McGraw, 1938; *Income of Society*, Ronald, 1950; *American Income and Its Use*, Harper, 1954; *Choice and the Destiny of Nations*, Philosophical Library, 1969.

*WORK IN PROGRESS:* Communication with African libraries and the Africanization of education.

*SIDELIGHTS:* Elizabeth Hoyt told *CA* that she is currently involved in "plans and efforts toward greater communication between international philanthropies and academic institutions, especially universities, working in international fields. At present international philanthropies function largely apart from contacts with the research of academic institutions, although this research casts a good deal of light on international need and opportunities for international development and means toward it. At present the response from twelve international philanthropies has been poor. Ten have either not replied or said they knew enough without the help of academic research. These ten are all connected with religious groups. Two philanthropies not connected with religious groups have supported our efforts at communication."

\*      \*      \*

## HSIN-HAI, Chang   1898(?)-1972

1898(?)—December 5, 1972; Chinese diplomat, educator, and author of novels and books on Asian-American relations. Obituaries: *New York Times*, December 7, 1972.

\*      \*      \*

## HSIUNG, James Chieh   1935-

*PERSONAL:* Surname is pronounced as "shone"; born July 23, 1935, in Kaifeng, Honan, China; son of Kung-Che (an educator) and Ying-chih (Hsieh) Hsiung; children: Susette Lynn, Paul Eric, Cynthia Cheryl. *Education:* National Taiwan University, B.A., 1955; Southern Illinois University, M.A., 1961; Columbia University, Ph.D., 1967. *Office:* Department of Politics, New York University, 25 Waverly Place, New York, N.Y. 10003.

*CAREER:* Broadcasting Corp. of China, Taipei, Taiwan, editor and producer, 1956-58; *China News,* Taipei, associate editor for foreign affairs, 1957-58; Columbia University, New York City, lecturer in Chinese, 1961-67; New York University, New York City, assistant professor, 1967-69, associate professor, 1969-75, professor of politics, 1975—, director of East Asian studies, 1969-73, director of undergraduate studies in politics, 1971-73, director of graduate studies in politics, 1973-75. Lecturer in political science, Rutgers University, 1966-67. Member of board of directors, National Chinese-American Civic Association, 1971-72. *Member:* American Political Science Association, Association for Asian Studies, International Studies Association, American Society of International Law, Asian-American Assembly for Policy Research (director of foreign policy committee). *Awards, honors:* First prize for essay, "Asian Student," 1963.

*WRITINGS:* (Contributor) William Richardson, editor, *China Today,* Maryknoll Publications, 1969; *Ideology and Practice: The Evolution of Chinese Communism,* Praeger, 1970; *Law and Policy in China's Foreign Relations,* Columbia University Press, 1972; (contributor) Shao-chuan Leng, Hungdah Chiu, and others, editors, *Law in Chinese Foreign Policy,* Oceana, 1972; (contributor) Jerome A. Cohen and others, editors, *China's Practice of International Law,* Harvard University Press, 1973; (editor) *The Logic of Maoism,* Praeger, 1974.

*WORK IN PROGRESS: Politics of Normalization in U.S.-China Relations.*

\* \* \*

## HUDDLE, Frank, Jr. 1943-

*PERSONAL:* Born May 9, 1943; son of Franklin Pierce (a writer) and Clare (Scott) Huddle. *Education:* Brown University, A.B., 1965; attended Columbia University, 1965-66; Harvard University, M.A., 1972, Ph.D., 1978. *Home:* 2405 Nemeth Ct., Alexandria, Va. 22306.

*CAREER:* Peace Corps, Libya, assistant Arabic coordinator, 1968-69; Foreign Service officer, 1975; former English teacher in Jeddah, Saudi Arabia. *Member:* Phi Beta Kappa.

*WRITINGS: Let's Go: Europe,* Dutton, 1972. Contributor of articles to *Harvard Journal of Asiatic Studies* and *Seventeen* magazine.

*WORK IN PROGRESS: Trekking in Nepal.*

*SIDELIGHTS:* Frank Huddle knows Russian, German, Arabic, Persian, Nepali, and other languages; he has travelled to Central Asia, Nepal, and Middle East. *Avocational interests:* Piano, photography.

\* \* \*

## HUDGENS, A(lice) Gayle 1941-
### (Gayle Hudgens Watson)

*PERSONAL:* Born April 20, 1941, in Artesia, N.M.; daughter of J. Don (an independent oilman) and Evelyn (Magrill) Hudgens; divorced; children: Hal Watson III, Amy Cecile Watson. *Education:* University of New Mexico, B.A., 1963; University of Texas, M.L.S., 1967, M.A.,

1977, Ph.D., 1979. *Home:* 1619 Forest Trail, Austin, Tex. 78703.

*CAREER:* Governor's Office, Austin, Tex., assistant to press secretary, 1963-64; University of Texas at Austin, reference librarian, Latin American Collection, 1966; De-Golyer Foundation Library, Dallas, Tex., archivist, 1968-69; Southern Methodist University, Dallas, Tex., library consultant to history department, 1969, Ibero-American bibliographer, 1969-71; part-time writer, 1971-75; University of Texas at Austin, social science research assistant, Institute of Latin American Studies, 1976-77, educational consultant to dean of College of Education, and to Community College Leadership Program, 1977; El Paso Community College, El Paso, Tex., coordinator of Management Improvement Program, 1978. Researcher in Brazil, 1972. Part-time Spanish language coordinator and reference librarian, Austin Public Library, 1976-77. *Member:* American Association of University Women, American Library Association, American Field Service Returnee Association, Phi Sigma Iota, Phi Kappa Phi, Kappa Kappa Gamma. *Awards, honors:* Ford Foundation scholarship, 1964-66; Sid Richardson Foundation fellowship, 1977-79.

*WRITINGS:* (Under name Gayle Hudgens Watson) *Colombia, Ecuador and Venezuela: An Annotated Guide to Reference Materials in the Humanities and Social Sciences,* Scarecrow, 1971. Contributor to periodicals, including *Nation* and *Southwestern Heritage.*

*WORK IN PROGRESS:* A biographical study of Maria Leopoldina, wife of Pedro I, Emperor of Brazil; research on the similarities in the political development of Texas and Rio Grande do Sul, Brazil; *Rio Grande Realms; Literacy Acquisition in the Culturally Different Adult Student: A Neuropsychological View; Discovery and Hope in College: Toward Holistic Literacy.*

*SIDELIGHTS:* A former model, A. Gayle Hudgens was selected Miss Wool of America by the American Wool Industry in 1961. She told *CA* that she has been "vitally interested in Latin America" since she was an American Field Service exchange student in Cordoba, Argentina in 1958. She added, "I see society facing several serious problems: overpopulation, pollution, war, human rights (status of women, loss of identity), illiteracy.... I want to contribute in my small way to better understanding among the peoples of the world."

\* \* \*

## HUDSON, Michael C(raig) 1938-

*PERSONAL:* Born June 2, 1938, in New Haven, Conn.; son of Robert Bowman (a public television executive) and Joan (Loram) Hudson; married Vera Wahbe, (a biologist and ecologist), June 16, 1963; children: Leila, Aida. *Education:* Swarthmore College, B.A., 1959; Yale University, M.A., 1960, Ph.D., 1964; Princeton University, certificate in Arabic, 1961. *Office:* Department of Middle East Studies, Georgetown University, Washington, D.C. 20057.

*CAREER:* Swarthmore College, Swarthmore, Pa., instructor in political science, 1963-64; Brooklyn College of the City University of New York, Brooklyn, N.Y., assistant professor of political science, 1964-70; Johns Hopkins University, School of Advanced International Studies, Washington, D.C., associate professor of political science, 1970-75; Georgetown University, Washington, D.C., 1975—, currently director of Center for Contemporary Arab Studies and member of faculty of School of Foreign Service. Lecturer at colleges and universities in Egypt, Lebanon, Qatar, the United Arab Emirates, Turkey, the West Bank, and Israel. *Member:* American Political Science Association, Middle East Institute, Middle East Studies Association, International Studies Association. *Awards, honors:* Overbrook Prize, Yale University, 1961; recipient of Ford and Guggenheim fellowships, and American Philosophical Society grants.

*WRITINGS: The Precarious Republic: Political Modernization in Lebanon,* Random House, 1968; (with Charles L. Taylor) *World Handbook of Political and Social Indicators* Yale University Press, 2nd edition (Hudson was not associated with first edition), 1972; *Arab Politics: The Search for Legitimacy,* Yale University Press, 1977. Contributor of articles to political science journals.

*WORK IN PROGRESS:* Research on the civil war in Lebanon, on the politics of development planning in Egypt, Saudi Arabia, Iraq, and Yemen, and on Palestinian politics.

*BIOGRAPHICAL/CRITICAL SOURCES: American Political Science Review,* December, 1969; *Middle East Journal,* summer, 1969, spring, 1978; *Comparative Politics,* April, 1970.

\*     \*     \*

## HUGHES, Robert    1929(?)-1972

1929(?)—July 24, 1972; American documentary filmmaker and editor of books on film. Obituaries: *New York Times,* July 26, 1972.

\*     \*     \*

## HUHTA, James K(enneth)    1937-

*PERSONAL:* Surname is pronounced *Who*-tah; born August 27, 1937, in Ashtabula, Ohio; son of Otto (a laborer) and Helmi (Kauppinen) Huhta; married Mary Foye Perry, December 28, 1958; children: Rebecca Foye, Mary Suzanne. *Education:* Baldwin-Wallace College, A.B., 1959; University of North Carolina at Chapel Hill, M.A., 1963, Ph.D., 1965. *Home:* 507 East Northfield Blvd., Murfreesboro, Tenn. 37130. *Office:* Department of History, Middle Tennessee State University, Murfreesboro, Tenn. 37132.

*CAREER:* North Carolina State University, Raleigh, instructor in history, 1963-65; Middle Tennessee State University, Murfreesboro, assistant professor, 1965-69, associate professor, 1969-73, professor of history, 1973—, director of historic preservation studies, 1974—, assistant vice-president for academic affairs, 1975—. Reviewer, National Heritage Trust Task Force. *Military service:* U.S. Army Reserve, 1956-62. *Member:* American Association for State and Local History, Organization of American Historians (life member), Institute of Early American History and Culture, National Geographic Society, Nordic Association for American Studies, American Association of University Professors (Tennessee chapter; president, 1971-72; secretary-treasurer, 1972-74), National Trust for Historic Preservation, Association for Preservation Technology (member of board of directors of preservation action and research committee), Society of Architectural Historians, Tennessee Historical Society, Phi Alpha Theta, Omicron Delta Kappa.

*WRITINGS: A College Instructor's Manual in American History,* two volumes, Ronald, 1968; (editor with William S. Powell and Thomas J. Farnham) *The Regulators in North Carolina, 1759-1776: A Documentary History,* North Carolina State Department of Archives and History, 1971. Contributor to history journals.

*WORK IN PROGRESS:* Research on preservation education, historic zoning, architectural and cultural resource survey techniques.

*AVOCATIONAL INTERESTS:* Travel, camping.

\*     \*     \*

## HULICKA, Irene M(ackintosh)    1927-

*PERSONAL:* Born January 27, 1927, in Gull Lake, Saskatchewan, Canada; daughter of George A. (a farmer) and Violet (Rose) Mackintosh; married Karel Hulicka (a professor), May 27, 1957; children: Charles Hulicka Mackintosh. *Education:* University of Saskatchewan, B.A., 1947, H.Ec., 1948, M.A., 1949; University of Alberta, B.Ed., 1952; University of Nebraska, Ph.D., 1954. *Home:* 98 University Ave., Buffalo, N.Y. 14214. *Office:* Department of Psychology, State University of New York College at Buffalo, 1300 Elmwood Ave., Buffalo, N.Y. 14222.

*CAREER:* University of Oklahoma, Norman, assistant professor of psychology, 1955-59; Veterans Administration Hospital, Buffalo, N.Y., research and clinical psychologist, 1959-65; D'Youville College, Buffalo, professor of psychology and chairman of department, 1965-68; State University of New York College at Buffalo, professor of psychology, 1967—, chairperson of department, 1967-72, Faculty of Natural and Social Sciences, acting dean, 1975-76, dean, 1976—. Principal psychologist, Cornell Aeronautical Laboratories (Bangkok), summer, 1969; associate director, Center for the Study of Psychotherapy (Madrid), 1970—. *Member:* American Psychological Association, American Gerontological Association (fellow), Eastern Psychological Association. *Awards, honors:* Research grants from National Science Foundation and National Institutes of Health.

*WRITINGS:* (With husband, Karel Hulicka) *Soviet Institutions, the Individual and Society,* Christopher, 1967; *Hemiplejias: Prevencion, Tratamiento, Rehabilitacion,* Editorial Cientifico-Medica, 1968; (contributor) *The Slow Learner,* Philosophical Library, 1969; *Rehabilitacion: Del Deficiente mental,* Editorial Cientifico-Medica, 1970; *Rehabilitacion infantil,* Editorial Cientifico-Medica, 1972; *Empirical Studies in the Psychology and Sociology of Aging,* Crowell, 1977. Contributor of about one hundred articles to scientific journals in the United States and abroad.

*WORK IN PROGRESS:* Experimental research on age differences in latitude of choice.

\*     \*     \*

## HULL, Denison Bingham    1897-

*PERSONAL:* Born March 25, 1897, in Chicago, Ill.; son of Morton Dennison (a lawyer) and Katharine Louise (Bingham) Hull; married Marion Walker, May 29, 1926; children: Morton Denison, Lyman Walker, Katharine Bingham (Mrs. Attallah Kappas), Eunice Larned (Mrs. Edmond T. Drewsen, Jr.). *Education:* Harvard University, A.B., 1919, M. Arch., 1923. *Politics:* Republican. *Religion:* Unitarian Universalist.

*CAREER:* Architect in private practice, 1927—. President, Otarion, Inc. (hearing aids manufacturer), Chicago, Ill., 1939-56; 208 South LaSalle St. Corp, Chicago, member of board of directors, 1945-67, president, 1967—. Served as trustee, vice-chairman, chairman, and treasurer, Meadville/Lombard Theological School, 1938-67; former member of visiting committee of School of Design and Visual Arts, Harvard University, and Division of Humanities, University of Chicago. Legislative Voters League of Illinois, director, 1938-39, secretary, 1939-42; North Shore Country Day

School, Winnettka, Ill., director, 1938-52, president, 1945-46; Winnetka Park Board, commissioner, 1939-45, president, 1940, vice-president, 1941-45; chairman of Chicago committee, Fight for Freedom, Inc., 1941-42; member of Board of directors of Evanston Hospital, 1949-54, and Harvard Alumni Association, 1954-58. Trustee of Provident Hospital, Chicago, 1930, First Unitarian Society, 1936-44, Hunt Servants Benefit Foundation, 1953-63, and American Farm School, Thessaloniki, Greece, 1969—; president of board of trustees, Music Center of North Shore, 1953-61; governing life member, Art Institute of Chicago. *Military service:* U.S. Army, Infantry, 1918-1919; became second lieutenant.

*MEMBER:* American Institute of Architects (vice-president of local chapter, 1936-38), Archaeological Institute of America (member of local chapter executive committee, 1968), Harvard Foundation for Advanced Study and Research (member of council, 1952-63), Masters Foxhounds Association, Indian Hill Club (Winnetka), Cliff Dwellers (Chicago), Fox River Valley Hunt (Barrington, Ill.). *Awards, honors:* L.H.D., Meadville/Lombard Theological School, 1965; Gold Cross of Order of Phoenix (Greece), 1966.

*WRITINGS: Thoughts on American Fox Hunting,* McKay, 1958; (translator from the Greek) *Aesop's Fables: Told by Valerius Babrius,* University of Chicago Press, 1960; *Hounds and Hunting in Ancient Greece,* University of Chicago Press, 1964; (translator from the Greek) *Digenis Akritas: The Two Blood Border Lord,* Ohio University Press, 1972. Contributor of articles and poems to architecture, medical, and Greek journals, and to *Chicago Tribune.*

*WORK IN PROGRESS:* Translating Homer's *Odyssey;* an anthology of Greek translations for the young at heart.

*SIDELIGHTS:* Denison Bingham Hull told *CA:* "After reading translations of the Greek to school classes from 6th grade up for the last four years, I'm more than ever convinced of the 'relevance' (a tiresome word) of the classics to modern life; and of the irrelevance of organized religion to the modern world. My own church has fallen down on the greatest need of the day, a new religion (science is no substitute), and I'm getting too old to do anything about it. But reading the classics to the young is very rewarding—and eye-opening. They *love* it. But can I do it well enough?"†

\*    \*    \*

## HULL, Eugene L(eslie)   1928-

*PERSONAL:* Born October 8, 1928, in Budapest, Hungary; U.S. citizen; married Robina Martin (an educator), April 13, 1953; children: Marla Jeanne, Bradford. *Education:* New York University, B.S., 1957; Seton Hall University, M.A., 1959; New School for Social Research, additional study, 1960-61. *Home:* 10760 Northeast Second Court, Miami, Fla. 33161. *Office:* Barry College, Miami, Fla. 33161.

*CAREER:* St. Louis University, St. Louis, Mo., instructor in accounting, 1959-60; Iona College, New Rochelle, N.Y., lecturer in finance, 1960-64; Trenton State College, Trenton, N.J., assistant professor of economics, 1961-66; Plymouth State College, Plymouth, N.H., assistant professor of business administration and chairman of department, 1966-67; Lake Superior State College, Sault Ste. Marie, Mich., associate professor of business administration, 1967-68; Parsons College, Fairfield, Iowa, associate professor of business administration, 1968-70; Barry College, Miami, Fla., vice-president for business affairs, 1970—. *Member:* National Association of College and University Business Officers,

College and University Personnel Association, American Accounting Association.

*WRITINGS: Money and Banking: College Level,* Monarch, 1965; *The Putnam Collegiate Guide to Accounting,* Putnam, 1966. Author of weekly financial column in *Sault Ste. Marie Evening News.*

*WORK IN PROGRESS:* Research on economic management of Catholic women's colleges in the United States.†

\*    \*    \*

## HUNGERFORD, Edward Buell   1900-

*PERSONAL:* Born January 19, 1900, in New Britain, Conn.; son of Frederick Buell (a lawyer) and Mary Lee (Post) Hungerford; married Alice Nora Thomas, 1931; children: Susan (Mrs. Donald Bennett McEvoy), Thomas. *Education:* Trinity College, Hartford, Conn., A.B., 1921; Harvard University, M.A., 1922, Ph.D., 1928. *Home:* Meinert Rd., Montague, Mich.

*CAREER:* Beloit College, Beloit, Wis., instructor in English, 1922-23; Harvard University, Cambridge, Mass., tutorial instructor in English, 1925-26, 1927-28; Northwestern University, Evanston, Ill., assistant professor, 1928-51, associate professor, 1951-58, professor of English, 1958-68. *Military service:* U.S. Naval Reserve, 1942-45; became lieutenant commander. *Member:* Friends of Literature (member of advisory board, 1960—). *Awards, honors:* Friends of Literature award, 1966, for services to literature for children.

*WRITINGS: Shores of Darkness* (on classical mythology), Columbia University Press, 1941, new edition, World Publishing, 1963; *Fighting Frigate* (juvenile fiction), Wilcox & Follett, 1947; *Emergency Run* (juvenile fiction), Wilcox & Follett, 1948; *Escape to Danger* (juvenile fiction), Wilcox & Follett, 1949; *Forbidden Island* (juvenile fiction), Wilcox & Follett, 1950; *Forge for Heroes* (juvenile fiction), Wilcox & Follett, 1952; (editor and author of introduction) *Poets in Progress,* Northwestern University Press, 1962; *Recovering the Rhythms of Poetry,* Scott, Foresman, 1966. Contributor of about sixty articles and reviews to *Chicago Tribune* and other publications. Founder and editor of *Tri-Quarterly,* 1958-64.

*WORK IN PROGRESS:* A volume of Shakespearean studies, tentatively entitled *The Magician in the Forest.*

\*    \*    \*

## HUNT, H(arry) Draper   1935-

*PERSONAL:* Born January 25, 1935, in Boston, Mass.; son of Jarvis (an attorney) and Philomena (Blaine) Hunt; married Elaine Gaza, June 22, 1958; children: Victoria, Harry Draper IV. *Education:* Harvard University, A.B. (cum laude), 1957; Columbia University, M.A., 1960, Ph.D., 1968. *Home:* 94 Coach Rd., South Portland, Me. 04106. *Office:* Department of History, University of Maine at Portland-Gorham, Portland, Me. 04103.

*CAREER:* Hunter College of the City University of New York, New York, N.Y., lecturer in history, 1962-65; University of Maine at Portland-Gorham, Portland, instructor, 1965-66, assistant professor, 1966-69, associate professor, 1969-72, professor of history, 1972—. Chairman of advisory board, South Portland Public Library, 1977. *Member:* American Historical Association, Organization of American Historians, Maine Historical Society (vice-president, 1977-78), Illinois State Historical Society, Friends of South Portland Public Library (president, 1976-78), Phi Kappa Phi (charter member). *Awards, honors:* Distinguished Scholar Award, University of Maine at Portland-Gorham, 1976.

*WRITINGS: Hannibal Hamlin of Maine: Lincoln's First Vice-President,* Syracuse University Press, 1969; *The Blaine House: Home of Maine's Governors,* Maine Historical Society, 1974; *Brother against Brother: Understanding the Civil War Era,* J. Weston Walch, 1977.

*SIDELIGHTS:* H. Draper Hunt has been a collector of Lincolniana since the age of nine.

\*     \*     \*

## HUNT, J(oseph) McVicker   1906-

*PERSONAL:* Born March 19, 1906; son of Robert Sanford (a farmer and stock raiser) and Carrie Pearl McVicker (Loughborough) Hunt; married Esther Dahms (a former director of Planned Parenthood), December 25, 1929; children: Judith Ann, Carol Jean (Mrs. George M. Epple). *Education:* University of Nebraska, B.A., 1929, M.A., 1930; Cornell University, Ph.D., 1933; postdoctoral study at Columbia University, 1933-34, and Clark University, 1934-35. *Religion:* Unitarian-Universalist. *Home:* 1807 Pleasant Cir., Urbana, Ill. 61801. *Office:* Department of Psychology, University of Illinois, Champaign, Ill. 61820.

*CAREER:* University of Nebraska at Lincoln, visiting instructor, fall, 1935; St. Elizabeth Hospital, Washington, D.C., research associate, spring, 1936; Brown University, Providence, R.I., 1936-46, began as instructor, became associate professor of psychology; Community Service Society of New York, Institute of Welfare Research, New York, N.Y., director, 1946-51; University of Illinois at Urbana-Champaign, professor of psychology, 1951-74, professor of education, 1967-74, professor emeritus, 1974—. Chairman, White House Task Force on Early Childhood, 1966-67; psychological consultant, School of Aviation Medicine (Randolph Air Force Base), 1951-54. American Psychological Foundation, member of board of trustees, 1953-59, president of board, 1953-54, 1958-59; member of board of trustees, Elizabeth McCormick Memorial Fund, 1954-62.

*MEMBER:* American Academy of Psychotherapy, American Academy for the Advancement of Science (fellow; council member, 1967-70), American Psychological Association (member of board of directors, 1949-53, 1970-73; president, 1951-52), American Sociological Association, American Statistical Association, Eastern Psychological Association (president, 1947-48). *Awards, honors:* Sc.D., Brown University, 1958; award for excellence in research from National Personnel and Guidance Association, 1960; D.Sc., University of Nebraska, 1967; Distinguished Scholar Award, Hofstra University, 1973; American Psychological Association, Distinguished Contribution Award from division twelve, 1973, G. Stanley Hall Award from division seven, 1976; Helen Elaine Meyer O'Neal Lectureship Award in Developmental Pediatrics, University of Nebraska Medical School, 1977.

*WRITINGS:* (Editor) *Personality and the Behavior Disorders,* two volumes, Ronald, 1944; (with L. S. Kogan) *Measuring Results in Social Casework: A Manual on Judging Movement,* Family Service Association of America, 1950; (with Kogan and Phillis Bartelme) *A Follow-up Study of the Results of Social Casework,* Family Service Association of America, 1953; *Intelligence and Experience,* Ronald, 1961; *The Challenge of Incompetence and Poverty,* University of Illinois Press, 1969; (editor) *Human Intelligence,* Transaction Books, 1972; (with I. C. Uzgiris) *Assessment in Infancy: Ordinal Scales of Psychological Development,* University of Illinois Press, 1975; *Experience and Early Development* (Heinz Memorial Lectures), Clark University Press, 1977. Contributor of about 175 articles to psychology, psychiatry, sociology, and education journals. Editor, *Journal of Abnormal and Social Psychology,* 1950-56.

*WORK IN PROGRESS:* Writing on research on social class and language skills, on the relation of accuracy of mothers' knowledge of their children's abilities and the development advancement of the children, and on a pedagogy for infancy and early childhood.

*SIDELIGHTS:* J. McVicker Hunt told *CA,* "I am trying to learn what fosters and what hampers early psychological development, and I would like to help the parents from the poverty sector utilize the knowledge we have about what fosters development to enable them to bring their children to the age when they enter school with the knowledge and skills required to cope effectively with traditional schools."

\*     \*     \*

## HUNTER, Doris A.   1929-

*PERSONAL:* Born June 29, 1929, in Grand Rapids, Mich.; daughter of William James and Dorothy (Champion) Leenhouts; married Howard E. Hunter (a professor), July 5, 1957; children: Amy, Bruce. *Education:* Albion College, B.A., 1951; Boston University, S.T.B., 1955, Ph.D., 1958. *Home and office:* 3 Madison Ave. W., Winchester, Mass. 01890.

*CAREER:* Boston University, Boston, Mass., assistant professor of humanities, 1967-73, counselor to women students; Bentley College, Waltham, Mass., adjunct assistant professor of philosophy, 1973; Northeastern University, Lincoln College, Boston, lecturer in philosophy, 1974. *Member:* American Philosophical Association, Society for Religion, Arts and Contemporary Culture, American Association of University Professors.

*WRITINGS:* (Editor with George Estey) *Nonviolence: A Reader in the Ethics of Action,* Ginn, 1970; (editor with Estey) *Violence: A Reader in the Ethics of Action,* Ginn, 1971; (contributor with husband, Howard Hunter) Peyton Richter, editor, *Utopia, Dystopia,* General Learning Press, 1975; *Introducing Religion,* Holt, in press.

\*     \*     \*

## HUNTER, J(ohn) F(letcher) M(acGregor)   1924-

*PERSONAL:* Born September 8, 1924, in Toronto, Ontario, Canada; son of Robert G. (a lawyer) and Blair (MacGregor) Hunter; married Monica Stewart, May 20, 1955; children: Stephen, James, Alison, Baye. *Education:* University of Toronto, B.A., 1947, M.A., 1950; University of Edinburgh, Ph.D., 1956. *Politics:* "Leftish." *Religion:* None. *Home:* 3 Lumley Ave., Toronto, Ontario, Canada M4G 2X3. *Office:* Department of Philosophy, University of Toronto, Toronto, Ontario, Canada M57 1A1.

*CAREER:* Merchant seaman, 1943-45; University of Edinburgh, Edinburgh, Scotland, assistant lecturer in moral philosophy, 1952-54; University of Toronto, Toronto, Ontario, lecturer, 1954-60, assistant professor, 1960-66, associate professor, 1966-74, professor of philosophy, 1974—.

*WRITINGS: Essays after Wittgenstein,* University of Toronto Press, 1973; *Intending,* Canadian Monograph Series, 1978. Contributor of articles to philosophy journals.

*WORK IN PROGRESS:* Research in philosophical psychology; another book on Wittgenstein.

*AVOCATIONAL INTERESTS:* Cabinet making, boat building, baroque music, and sailing.

## HURLEY, W(illiam) Maurice 1916-

*PERSONAL:* Born November 12, 1916; son of James Daniel and Jane (Ashley) Hurley; married Kathryn Ann Chambers (a social case worker), September 22, 1938; children: James David, Olivia Kay (Mrs. Gerald Smith), William Michael. *Education:* University of Tulsa, B.A., 1940, M.A., 1947; Southwestern Baptist Theological Seminary, B.D., 1949; University of Oklahoma, Ed.D., 1961. *Home:* Ouachita Hills, Arkadelphia, Ark. *Office:* Department of Psychology, Ouachita Baptist University, Arkadelphia, Ark. 71923.

*CAREER:* Clergyman of Baptist Church; Oklahoma Baptist University, Shawnee, assistant professor of psychology, 1948-52; minister of Baptist churches in Bartlesville, Okla., 1952-55, McGregor, Tex., 1955-57, and Tomball, Tex., 1957-60; Ouachita Baptist University, Arkadelphia, Ark., professor of psychology and chairman of department, 1960—, dean of students, 1961-63. Part-time psychologist, Arkansas State Hospital, 1966-69; director of Hospital Improvement Program Project, Arkansas Children's Colony, 1971-72. *Member:* American Psychological Association, Christian Association for Psychological Studies, Arkansas State Mental Health Association (vice-president), Arkansas Psychological Association, Southwestern Psychological Association.

*WRITINGS: Ouch! My Conscience,* Eerdmans, 1953; *The Peril of Hostility,* McCutchan, 1966. Contributor to *Administration.*

*WORK IN PROGRESS:* Research on personality, self-concept, and Christian psychology.

\* \* \*

## HURST, Charles G., Jr. 1928-

*PERSONAL:* Born June 14, 1928, in Atlanta, Ga.; son of Charles G. and Pearl (Ashley) Hurst; married Beverly Scott, February 22, 1963; children: Carolyn, James R., Frederick A., Robert A., Ronald C. (deceased), Christopher, Chaverly. *Education:* Wayne State University, B.S., 1953, M.A., 1959, Ph.D., 1961. *Office:* Daniel Hale Williams University, 5247 West Madison St., Chicago, Ill. 60644.

*CAREER:* Howard University, Washington, D.C., assistant professor, 1961-67, associate professor, 1967-69, professor of audiology, 1969, associate dean of college of liberal arts, 1961-68; Malcolm X College, Chicago, Ill., president, 1969-72; founder and president, Malcolm X Educational Foundation, 1972-75; Daniel Hale Williams University, Chicago, founder and president, 1975—. *Member:* Acoustical Society of America, Speech Communication Association of America, American Association for the Advancement of Science, National Education Association, American Association of University Professors, Society for Research in Child Development. *Awards, honors:* Grant from Office of Education to study psycho-social correlates of culturally induced behavioral differences, 1963.

*WRITINGS: Passport to Freedom: Education and the Humanism of Malcolm X,* Shoe String, 1972. Contributor of articles to *Journal of Speech and Hearing Disorders* and *Journal of Negro Education.*

*WORK IN PROGRESS: Black Powerlessness; Black and Brown Together.*

*BIOGRAPHICAL/CRITICAL SOURCES: Tuesday Magazine,* March, 1972; *College and University Business,* June, 1972; *Playboy,* July, 1972.

## HURWITZ, Howard L(awrence) 1916-

*PERSONAL:* Born June 10, 1916, in Brooklyn, N.Y.; son of William (a businessman) and Dora (Berger) Hurwitz; married Nettie Schifrin, August 31, 1941; children: Donald. *Education:* Brooklyn College (now Brooklyn College of the City University of New York), B.A., 1936; Columbia University, M.A., 1937, Ph.D., 1943. *Religion:* Jewish. *Home:* 166-15 Grand Central Pkwy., Jamaica, N.Y. 11432.

*CAREER:* High school teacher in New York City, 1938-53; assistant high school principal in New York City, 1953-66; Long Island City High School, Long Island City, N.Y., principal, 1966-77. Adjunct associate professor of education, St. Johns University, 1959-68. Member of advisory board, Jamaica Jewish Center, 1960-65. *Military service:* U.S. Army Air Forces, 1942-45; became technical sergeant. *Member:* Council of Supervisors and Administrators (vice-president, 1975-77), Administrative Assistants Association (president, 1962-64), Association of Teachers of Social Studies in the City of New York (president, 1952-53).

*WRITINGS: Theodore Roosevelt and Labor in New York State,* Columbia University Press, 1943; *Quiz Refresher in World History,* Keystone Education Press, 1952, 7th edition, 1966; *Review Survey of American History,* Keystone Education Press, 1955, 7th edition, 1968; (with Frederick Shaw) *Economics in a Free Society,* Oxford Book Co., 1962, 3rd edition, 1965; (with Shaw) *Mastering Basic Economics,* Oxford Book Co., 1962, 3rd edition, 1970; *An Encyclopedic Dictionary of American History,* Washington Square Press, 1968, 3rd edition, 1974; *Donald: The Man Who Remains a Boy,* Pocket Books, 1973; (with Shaw and Jacob Irgang) *Using Economics,* Sadlier, 1975. Author of semi-weekly column which appears in *Trib* (New York). Contributor of several hundred articles and reviews to educational journals.

*WORK IN PROGRESS: The Fighting Principal,* completed and awaiting publication.

*SIDELIGHTS:* Howard Hurwitz's book, *Donald: The Man Who Remains a Boy,* is the biography of his mentally retarded son. A reviewer for *Publishers Weekly* calls the book ''a detailed and harrowing account of his parents' valiant efforts to educate Donald and provide him with some skill by which he could achieve a measure of independence. Hurwitz seems to have been unstintingly honest about the tensions and hardships Donald's condition has caused these two basically ordinary people.'' The book is now being considered for motion picture production. Hurwitz's latest book, *The Fighting Principal,* is under consideration as a television series.

*BIOGRAPHICAL/CRITICAL SOURCES: Publishers Weekly,* October 8, 1973; *Teacher,* October, 1974; *Best Sellers,* October 1, 1974.

\* \* \*

## HUTCHISON, Jane Campbell 1932-

*PERSONAL:* Born July 20, 1932, in Washington, D.C.; daughter of James Paul (a cartographer) and Leone (Warrick) Hutchison. *Education:* Western Maryland College, B.A., 1954; Oberlin College, M.A., 1958; University of Utrecht, further study, 1960-61; University of Wisconsin, Ph.D., 1964. *Office:* Elvehjem Art Center, University of Wisconsin, Madison, Wis. 53706.

*CAREER:* U.S. Navy Department, Taylor Model Basin, Washington, D.C., draftsman, 1954-55; Toledo Museum of Art, Toledo, Ohio, research librarian, 1957-58; University of

Wisconsin—Madison, assistant professor, 1964-69, associate professor, 1964-74, professor of art history, 1975—, chairman of department, 1977—. Visiting assistant professor of art history, Temple University, summer, 1967. Consultant to National Endowment for the Humanities. *Member:* Mediaeval Academy of America, College Art Association, American Association of University Professors, Midwest Art History Society, Madison Art Association, University Club. *Awards, honors:* Fulbright scholar, 1960-61.

*WRITINGS: The Housebook Master,* Collectors Editions, 1972; *Dutch and Flemish Paintings of the Seventeenth Century from Private Collections* (exhibition catalogue), Elvehjem Art Center, University of Wisconsin—Madison, 1974; (contributor) Reinhold Grimm and Jost Hermand, editors, *Deutsche Feier,* Athenaion (Wiesbaden, Germany), 1977. Contributor to art journals.

*SIDELIGHTS:* Jane Hutchison's particular interests are in northern European painting and graphics of the fifteenth century.

# I

## IMERTI, Arthur D. 1915-

PERSONAL: Born July 2, 1915, in New York, N.Y.; son of Vincent and Agata (Catalani) Imerti; married Frances Prochep, March 25, 1951. Education: City University of New York, B.A., 1939; Fordham University, M.A., 1945; University of Mexico, further study, summer, 1946; Columbia University, Ph.D., 1969. Home: 69 Fifth Ave., New York, N.Y. 10003.

CAREER: Imerti Modern Language Institute, New York City, director and teacher of Romance languages, 1943-50; John Marshall College, Jersey City, N.J., assistant professor of Spanish, 1947; Yeshiva University, New York City, assistant professor of speech, 1950-59; New School for Social Research, New York City, professor of Italian and Spanish, 1951-71, chairman of department of foreign languages, 1960-64; City University of New York, New York City, adjunct associate professor of Spanish, 1973-74. Member: American Association of Teachers of Italian, Renaissance Society of America, America-Italy Society. Awards, honors: American Foundation for the Blind travel grants, 1946, 1949.

WRITINGS: (Editor and translator) Giordano Bruno, The Expulsion of the Triumphant Beast, Rutgers University Press, 1964; Vincenzo Catalani: Neopolitan Jacobin, Jurist, Reformer, Coronado Press, 1976. Contributor to Pan-American and Occupations.

WORK IN PROGRESS: Before the Curtain Falls: Confessions of a Blind Humanist, an autobiography.

SIDELIGHTS: Arthur D. Imerti wrote CA: "I have devoted my life to the propagation of Italian culture in the United States. Undoubtably my most significant contribution is my widely acclaimed edition and translation of Giordano Bruno's The Expulsion of the Triumphant Beast, the only complete edition in English of what is probably Bruno's most controversial work. It is used by scholars in the fields of Renaissance philosophy, literature and history."

Imerti explained that his book on Vincenzo Catalani (1769-1843) "is the first biography of that eminent but almost forgotten jurist, humanist, parliamentarian, moral philosopher, feminist and fighter for Italian freedom and unification. He was a man of utmost integrity, dedication and commitment to the noblest principles. This uncompromising idealist was twice arrested by the Bourbon authorities and exiled from the Kingdom of Naples in 1800. Upon his return in 1806, he

was imprisoned for two years, because of his criticism of the policies of King Joseph Bonaparte.

"My autobiography, Before the Curtain Falls: Confessions of a Blind Humanist, is a frank account of one who has triumphed over almost insurmountable odds to become a recognized teacher, scholar and author."

\*  \*  \*

## INBER, Vera Mikhailovna 1893-1972

1893—November 11, 1972; Russian poet and journalist. Obituaries: New York Times, November 15, 1972; Antiquarian Bookman, December 4, 1972.

\*  \*  \*

## INEZ, Colette 1931-

PERSONAL: Born June 23, 1931, in Brussels, Belgium; married second husband, Saul A. Stadtmauer (a free-lance writer), July 26, 1964. Education: Hunter College of the City University of New York, B.A., 1961. Home: 5 West 86th St., New York, N.Y. 10024.

CAREER: Held various jobs, including posts with Recreation Magazine, International Theater Magazine, the New York office of Le Figaro, and the Sephardi Foundation, 1948-61; New York University, New York City, adult education teacher, 1962; high school and private school teacher in New York City, 1961-71; teacher in anti-poverty and English-for-the-foreign-born programs in New York City, 1965-70; poet-in-the-schools in Binghamton, N.Y. and Pittsburgh, Pa., 1973-74; New School, New York City, instructor in poetry workshop, 1974—; Denison University, Granville, Ohio, lecturer in poetry, 1974—; State University of New York at Stonybrook, lecturer in poetry, 1975-76; Kalamazoo College, Kalamazoo, Mich., poet-in-residence, 1976—. Poetry reader at Library of Congress, Lamont Library, Harvard University, and at other libraries, colleges, and cafes, 1967—. Director of Poetry Society of America. Awards, honors: National League of American Pen Women poetry award, 1962; Osgood Warren national first prize award, Poetry Society of New England, 1967; Marion Reedy National Award, Poetry Society of America, 1972; Great Lakes Colleges Association national first prize book award, 1972, for The Woman Who Loved Worms; National Endowment for the Arts fellowship, 1974-75; Kreymborg National Poetry Award, Poetry Society of America, 1975;

New York State Creative Artists Public Service (CAPS) fellowship, 1975.

*WRITINGS: The Woman Who Loved Worms and Other Poems,* Doubleday, 1972; *Alive and Taking Names and Other Poems,* Ohio University Press, 1977. Poetry represented in several anthologies, including *Quickly Aging Here: Some Poets of the 1970's,* edited by Geof Hewitt, Doubleday, 1969, *Live Poetry: Thoughts for the Seventies,* edited by K. S. Koppell and others, Holt, 1971, *In the Belly of the Shark,* Random House, 1972, *Love, Etc.,* Doubleday, 1973, *Rising Tides,* edited by Laura Chester, Simon & Schuster, 1973, *We Became New,* edited by Lucille Iverson, Bantam, 1975, and *I Hear My Sisters Saying,* edited by Carol Koneck and others, Crowell, 1976. Contributor of numerous poems to periodicals in the United States and abroad, including *Antioch Review, Nation, New York Times, Beloit Poetry Journal, Minnesota Review, Poetry Australia, Hudson Review, Poetry, New Republic, American Poetry Review, Chicago Review,* and *Humanist.*

*WORK IN PROGRESS:* A book of poetry, tentatively entitled *The Dance of Adolph and Eva.*

*AVOCATIONAL INTERESTS:* Painting, drawing, the piano, and naturalist interests.

*BIOGRAPHICAL/CRITICAL SOURCES: Their Place in the Heat,* Road Runner Press, 1971.

\*      \*      \*

### INGRAM, (Mildred Rebecca) Bowen (Prewett)

*PERSONAL:* Born in Gordonsville, Tenn.; daughter of Austin Lemuel (a lawyer and businessman) and Frances (Gold) Prewett; married Daniel Taylor Ingram, May 28, 1925 (deceased); children: Alice Gordon (Mrs. George Whitfield Holcomb), Daniel Taylor, Jr., John Gold Lawrence. *Education:* Attended Cumberland University (now Cumberland College of Tennessee), 1924. *Politics:* Democrat. *Religion:* Episcopalian. *Home:* Moran Rd., Route 11, Franklin, Tenn. 37064.

*CAREER:* U.S. Army, Lebanon Maneuver Headquarters, Lebanon, Tenn., civilian employee, 1943-45. *Member:* Tennessee Historical Society. *Awards, honors:* Award of Phoenix, Cumberland College of Tennessee, 1967.

*WRITINGS—Novels: If Passion Flies,* Dodd, 1945; *Light as the Morning,* Houghton, 1954; *Milbry,* Crown, 1972. Contributor to library journals and national magazines, including *New Yorker, Seventeen,* and *Town and Country.*

*WORK IN PROGRESS:* A novel, *The Lake.*

*BIOGRAPHICAL/CRITICAL SOURCES:* John N. Bradbury, *Renaissance in the South,* University of North Carolina Press, 1963.

\*      \*      \*

### IRVING, T(homas) B(allantine)    1914-

*PERSONAL:* Born July 20, 1914, in Preston (now Cambridge), Ontario, Canada; naturalized U.S. citizen; son of William John (a machinist) and J. Christina (MacIntyre) Irving; married Amanda Antillon, August 31, 1950 (divorced, 1955); married Evelyn Uhrhan (a professor), June 30, 1961; children: (first marriage) Diana (Mrs. Arthur McClellan), Lillian (Mrs. Lic. L. I. de Vides), Nichol. *Education:* University of Toronto, B.A., 1937; University of Montreal, M. es L., 1938; Princeton University, Ph.D., 1940. *Religion:* Muslim. *Home:* 1840 Azrock Dr., Knoxville, Tenn. 37914. *Office:* 611A McClung Tower, University of Tennessee, Knoxville, Tenn. 37916.

*CAREER:* University of California, Berkeley, instructor in Spanish, 1940-42; Carleton University, Ottawa, Ontario, instructor in Spanish (concurrent with naval service), 1942-44; Colegio Nueva Granada, Bogota, Columbia, director, 1944-45; Wells College, Aurora, N.Y., assistant professor of Romance languages, 1945-46; University of Minnesota, Minneapolis, assistant professor, 1948-52, associate professor, 1952-63, professor of Spanish and Arabic, 1963-65; North Central College, Naperville, Ill., professor of modern languages and chairman of department, 1965-67; University of Guelph, Guelph, Ontario, professor of Spanish, 1967-69; University of Tennessee, Knoxville, professor of Spanish, 1969—. University of San Carlos of Guatemala, visiting professor, 1946-48, and summers, 1950, 1952, 1955, 1956, 1959, director of summer school, 1946-48; visiting professor, University of Texas, 1960-61, University of Libya, 1973. Consultant on Spanish publications, Minneapolis Moline Co., 1952-56. *Military service:* Royal Canadian Naval Volunteer Reserve, 1942-44; became lieutenant.

*MEMBER:* International Institute of Ibero-American Literature, American Association of Teachers of Spanish and Portuguese, American Oriental Society, Mediaeval Academy of America, Middle East Institute, Middle East Studies Association, Society of Geography and History (Guatemala; honorary member), Honduran Academy of Geography and History (honorary member), Latin American Studies Association, American Association of University Professors, South Atlantic Modern Language Association. *Awards, honors:* Fulbright research fellow at College of Arts, Baghdad, Iraq, 1958-59.

*WRITINGS:* (Editor) Jose Mills, *Aventuras en Centro-America* (text edition of two novelettes), Houghton, 1951; *Falcon of Spain* (biography), M. Ashraf (Lahore), 1954, 2nd edition, 1962; (editor with Robert Kirsner) *Paisajes del sur* (Latin American cultural anthology), Ronald, 1954; *Dario y la patria,* Ministerio de Gubernacion (Managua), 1959; (editor and translator) *Selections from the Noble Reading* (Quranic anthology), Unity Publishing (Cedar Rapids), 1968. Contributor to professional journals. Editor, *Muslim Life,* 1963-65.

*WORK IN PROGRESS:* Translating *Qur'an* into contemporary English; compiling an anthology, *The Maya's Own Words.*

*SIDELIGHTS:* T. B. Irving has pursued his interest in the peripheral cultures to Spanish—the Arabs in Spain, the Aztecs in Mexico, and the Mayas in Central America—on travels to those areas and in Africa and the Middle East.

\*      \*      \*

### ISEMINGER, Gary    1937-

*PERSONAL:* Born March 3, 1937, in Middleboro, Mass.; son of Boyd Austin (a lawyer) and Harriet (Hudson) Iseminger; married Andrea Grove (a teacher), December 18, 1965; children: Andrew, Ellen. *Education:* Wesleyan University, B.A., 1958; Yale University, M.A., 1960, Ph.D., 1961. *Home:* 401 Prairie St., Northfield, Minn. 55057. *Office:* Department of Philosophy, Carleton College, Northfield, Minn. 55057.

*CAREER:* Yale University, New Haven, Conn., instructor in philosophy, 1961-62; Carleton College, Northfield, Minn., instructor, 1962-63, assistant professor, 1963-68, associate professor, 1968-73, professor of philosophy, 1973—, chairman of department, 1972-75. *Member:* American Philosophical Association, Phi Beta Kappa. *Awards, honors:* Woodrow Wilson fellow, 1958; National Endowment for the Humanities grant, summer, 1971.

*WRITINGS: An Introduction to Deductive Logic*, Appleton, 1968; (editor) *Logic and Philosophy: Selected Readings*, Appleton, 1968; (contributor) L. Aagaard-Mogensen, editor, *Culture and Art*, Humanities, 1976; (contributor) Ruediger Bittner and Peter Pfaff, editors, *Das Aesthetische Urteil*, Kiepenheuer & Witsch, 1977. Contributor to philosophy journals.

*WORK IN PROGRESS:* Research on aestethics and on argument analysis.

*AVOCATIONAL INTERESTS:* Singing, composing, conducting, and playing percussion instruments.

\*          \*          \*

## IVASK, Ivar Vidrik 1927-

*PERSONAL:* Born December 17, 1927, in Latvia (annexed by Soviet Union, 1940); naturalized U.S. citizen; son of Vidrik and Ilze (Guters) Ivask; married Astrid Harmanis (a writer), February 26, 1949. *Education:* Attended University of Marburg, 1946-49; University of Minnesota, M.A., 1950, Ph.D., 1953. *Politics:* Democrat. *Religion:* Protestant. *Residence:* Norman, Okla. *Office:* World Literature Today, 630 Parrington Oval, Norman, Okla. 73019.

*CAREER:* St. Olaf College, Northfield, Minn., assistant professor, 1952-57, associate professor, 1958-63, professor of German, 1964-67, acting head, 1956-57, head of department, 1964-67; University of Oklahoma, Norman, professor of modern languages and editor of *World Literature Today* (formerly *Books Abroad;* international literary quarterly), 1967—. *Military service:* U.S. Army, Medical Corps, 1954-56. *Member:* Modern Language Association of America, American Association of Teachers of German, South Central Modern Language Association, American Society for Friendship with Switzerland, Estonian Learned Society, Institute of Estonian Language (University of Stockholm), Estonian P.E.N. in Exile, P.E.N. American Center, Association for the Advancement of Baltic Studies, Phi Beta Kappa.

*WRITINGS: Taehtede taehendus* (title means "The Meaning of Stars"), Eesti Kirjanike Kooperatiiv (Lund, Sweden), 1964; *Paev astub kukesammul* (title means "The Day Arrives with a Rooster's Step"), Eesti Kirjanike Kooperatiiv, 1966; *Gespiegelte Erde*, Ungar, 1967; (editor with Juan Marichal) *Luminous Reality: The Poetry of Jorge Guillen*, University of Oklahoma Press, 1969; *Ajaloo aiad* (title means "The Garden of History"), Eesti Kirjanike Kooperatiiv, 1970; (editor with Lowell Dunham) *The Cardinal Points of Borges*, University of Oklahoma Press, 1971; (editor with Gero von Wilpert) *Moderne Weltliteratur*, Alfred Kroener (Stuttgart), 1972; (editor with von Wilpert) *World Literature since 1945*, Ungar, 1973; (editor) *The Perpetual Present: The Poetry and Prose of Octavio Paz*, University of Oklahoma Press, 1973; *Oktoober Oklahomas* (title means "October in Oklahoma"), Eesti Kirjanike Kooperatiiv, 1973; *Verikivi* (title means "Bloodstone"), Eesti Kirjanike Kooperativ, 1976; (editor with Jaime Alazraki) *The Final Island: The Fiction of Julio Cortazar*, University of Oklahoma Press, 1978.

*WORK IN PROGRESS: Heimito von Doderer*, for Twayne.

*SIDELIGHTS:* Ivar Vidrik Ivask organized the Oklahoma Conferences on Writers of the Hispanic World, and the Books Abroad/Neustadt International Prize for Literature. He told *CA* that he has recently taken up drawing and has illustrated *Verikivi*, his fifth book of verse.

Ivask is competent in German, Finnish, French, and Spanish, as well as Latvian and Estonian.

*BIOGRAPHICAL/CRITICAL SOURCES: Books Abroad*, winter, 1970.

# J

## JACKSON, Douglas N. 1929-

PERSONAL: Born August 14, 1929, in Merrick, N.Y.; son of Douglas N. (a retail merchant) and Caya (Cramer) Jackson; married Lorraine J. Morlock (a teacher and consultant), July 28, 1962; children: Douglas, Diana, Charles Theodore VI. Education: Cornell University, B.Sc., 1951; Purdue University, M.Sc., 1952, Ph.D., 1958. Residence: London, Ontario, Canada. Office: Department of Psychology, University of Western Ontario, London, Ontario, Canada N6A 5C2.

CAREER: Menninger Foundation, Topeka, Kan., postdoctoral fellow, 1955-56; Pennsylvania State University, University Park, 1956-64, began as assistant professor, became associate professor of psychology; University of Western Ontario, London, senior professor of psychology, 1964—. Visiting associate professor of psychology, Stanford University, 1962-64; visiting scholar, Educational Testing Service, 1971—. Member: American Psychological Association, Canadian Psychological Association, Psychometric Society, Society of Multivariate Experimental Psychology (president, 1976), Sigma Xi.

WRITINGS: Personality Organization in Cognition, Psychological Issues, 1960; (editor with Samuel Messick) Problems in Human Assessment, McGraw, 1967; Manual to the Personality Research Form, Research Psychologists Press, 1967; Jackson Personality Inventory, Research Psychologists Press, 1976; Jackson Vocational Interest Survey, Research Psychologists Press, 1977. Contributor of more than one hundred articles to scientific journals.

WORK IN PROGRESS: A monograph on the perception of personality; a book on personality assessment.

*     *     *

## JACKSON, Herbert G., Jr. 1928-

PERSONAL: Born March 19, 1928, in Newark, N.Y.; son of Herbert G. and Cecilia (Bolles) Jackson; married Caryl Mae Warren, August 27, 1949. Education: Tufts University, B.A., 1949. Residence: Lincoln Park, N.J. 07035. Office: William Paterson College of New Jersey, Wayne, N.J. 07470.

CAREER: Times-Union, Rochester, N.Y., reporter, 1949-57, assistant city editor, 1957-62, city editor, 1962-67; self-employed full-time writer, 1967-73; William Paterson College of New Jersey, Wayne, assistant professor of communi-

cations, 1973—. Military service: U.S. Navy, 1945-47. Member: Society of Professional Journalists, Association for Education in Journalism, Sigma Delta Chi.

WRITINGS: The Spirit Rappers, Doubleday, 1972; A Century of the Telephone in Rochester, New York, Rochester Telephone Corp., 1978. Contributor of articles to several magazines.

*     *     *

## JACKSON, Jacquelyne Johnson 1932-

PERSONAL: Born February 24, 1932, in Winston-Salem, N.C.; daughter of James Albert (an educator) and Beulah (an educator; maiden name, Crosby) Johnson; married Frederick A. S. Clarke, August 26, 1955 (divorced, 1959); married Murphy Jackson (a car salesman), May 15, 1962; children: (second marriage) Viola Elizabeth. Education: University of Wisconsin—Madison, B.S., 1953, M.S., 1955; Ohio State University, Ph.D., 1960; postdoctoral study at University of Colorado, summer, 1961, and Duke University Medical Center, 1966-68. Politics: Democrat. Religion: Episcopalian. Address: P.O. Box 8522, Durham, N.C. 27707. Office: Duke University Medical Center, P.O. Box 3003, Durham, N.C. 27710.

CAREER: Duke University, Medical Center, Durham, N.C., instructor, 1967-68, assistant professor, 1968-71, associate professor of medical sociology, 1971—. Visiting professor of sociology, St. Augustine's College, 1969—. Consultant to National Center for Health Statistics and to U.S. Senate Special Committee on Aging. Member: Association of Social and Behavioral Scientists (former president and current executive secretary), Caucus of Black Sociologists (chairman), National Council on Family Relations (member of executive committee), American Sociological Association, National Caucus on the Black Aged (secretary), Gerontological Society (fellow; member of executive committee of Psychological and Social Science Section), American Association of University Professors, Southern Sociological Society, North Carolina Sociological Association, North Carolina Women's Political Caucus, Groves Conference on Marriage and Family, Tuskegee Civic Association, Carver Research Foundation of Tuskegee Institute (member of board of trustees). Awards, honors: National Science Foundation fellow, 1961.

WRITINGS: These Rights They Seek, Public Affairs

Press, 1962. Contributor of articles to professional journals, and to *Afro-American* and *Ebony*. Associate editor, *Social Forces;* editor, *Journal of Health and Social Behavior, Afro-American,* and *Journal of Social and Behavioral Sciences.*

*WORK IN PROGRESS: Race Relations and Social Policy,* for Prentice-Hall; a book on the black aged, with Robert Kastenbaum, for Springer Publishing; research on black women, with a book expected to result.

*AVOCATIONAL INTERESTS:* International travel.

\*     \*     \*

## JACKSON, John N(icholas) 1925-

*PERSONAL:* Born December 15, 1925, in Nottingham, England; son of Alexander (a teacher and clergyman) and Phyllis E. (Oldfield) Jackson; married Kathleen M. Nussey, May, 1951; children: Andrew, Susan, Paul. *Education:* University of Birmingham, Birmingham, England, B.A., 1949; University of Manchester, Ph.D., 1960. *Religion:* Anglican. *Home:* 80 Marsdale Dr., St. Catharines, Ontario, Canada. *Office:* Department of Geography, Brock University, St. Catharines, Ontario, Canada.

*CAREER:* Herefordshire County Council, Herefordshire, England, research officer, 1950-53; Hull County Borough, Hull, England, senior planning assistant, 1954-56; University of Manchester, Manchester, England, lecturer in geography, 1956-65; Brock University, St. Catharines, Ontario, professor of applied geography, 1965—, head of department, 1965-70. *Military service:* Royal Navy. *Member:* Royal Town Planning Institute.

*WRITINGS: Surveys for Town and Country Planning,* Hutchinson University Library, 1963; *Recreational Development and the Lake Erie Shore,* Niagara Region Development Council, 1968; *The Industrial Structure of the Niagara Region,* Brock University, 1971; *The Canadian City: Space, Form, Quality,* McGraw-Ryerson, 1972; (editor with J. Forrester) *Practical Geography,* McGraw-Ryerson, 1972; *Welland and the Welland Canal,* Mika, 1975; *St. Catharines, Ontario: Its Early Years,* Mika, 1976; *A Planning Appraisal of the Welland Urban Community,* Department of Public Works (Ottawa), 1976; *Land Use Planning in the Niagara Region,* Niagara Region Study Review Commission, 1976.

*WORK IN PROGRESS: Railway Development in the Niagara Region; Urban Characteristics and the Changing Regional Format in the Niagara Peninsula, 1900 to Present; The Niagara Frontier: Social Change across the International Border; Urban Form, Regional Growth: Quality, Expectations and Reality in Western Europe and North America.*

\*     \*     \*

## JACOBS, Clyde E(dward) 1925-

*PERSONAL:* Born January 19, 1925, in Herington, Kan.; son of Harry Charles (an engineer) and Jessie (Tarbill) Jacobs. *Education:* University of Kansas, A.B., 1946; University of Paris, further study, 1946-47; University of Michigan, M.A., 1948, Ph.D., 1952. *Politics:* Republican. *Religion:* Roman Catholic. *Home:* 1005 Cornell Dr., Davis, Calif. 95616. *Office:* Department of Political Science, University of California, Davis, Calif. 95616.

*CAREER:* University of California, Davis, instructor, 1952-54, assistant professor, 1954-60, associate professor, 1960-63, professor of political science, 1963—, chairman of de-

partment, 1960-66. City of Davis, councilman, 1960-64, member of planning commission, 1960-62, chairman of personnel board, 1966-72. *Member:* American Political Science Association, Western Political Science Association, Phi Beta Kappa, Phi Kappa Phi, Delta Sigma Rho, Pi Sigma Alpha, Beta Theta Pi.

*WRITINGS: Law Writers and the Courts,* University of California Press, 1954; *Justice Frankfurter and Civil Liberties,* University of California Press, 1961; (with A. D. Sokolow) *California Government,* Macmillan, 1966, 2nd edition, 1970; (with J. F. Gallagher) *The Selective Service Act,* Dodd, 1967; *The Eleventh Amendment and Sovereign Immunity,* Greenwood Press, 1972. Contributor to political science and legal journals.

*WORK IN PROGRESS: Comparative Freedom of Expression: The United States and Western Europe.*

\*     \*     \*

## JACOBS, Milton 1920-

*PERSONAL:* Born August 9, 1920, in Braddock, Pa.; son of Charles (a salesman) and Sarah (Weiss) Jacobs; married Colette Benhaim (an art dealer), December 10, 1944; children: Renee Jacobs Payne, David Carroll. *Education:* George Washington University, B.A., 1948, M.A., 1950; Catholic University of America, Ph.D., 1956. *Politics:* Democrat. *Religion:* Judaism. *Home:* 123 Plains Rd., New Paltz, N.Y. 12561. *Office:* Department of Anthropology, State University of New York College, New Paltz, N.Y. 12561.

*CAREER:* U.S. Department of the Air Force, Washington, D.C., research psychologist, 1950-52; George Washington University, Washington, D.C., research anthropologist, 1952-54; U.S. Department of Agriculture, Washington, D.C., research anthropologist, 1954-57; City College of New York (now City College of the City University of New York), New York, N.Y., lecturer in sociology and anthropology, 1957-61; American University, Washington, D.C., research anthropologist, 1961-66; University of Maryland, College Park, lecturer in anthropology, 1966; State University of New York College at New Paltz, professor of anthropology, 1966—. Lecturer in anthropology, Catholic University of America, Washington, D.C., 1954-57; visiting professor of anthropology, Georgetown University, Washington, D.C., summer, 1968. *Military service:* U.S. Army Air Forces, 1942-45. *Member:* American Anthropological Association, Senate Professional Association (New Paltz Chapter, president, 1971-72, 1972-73), Sigma Xi.

*WRITINGS: A Study of Culture Stability and Change: The Moroccan Jewess,* Catholic University of America Press, 1956; (with Alexander R. Askenasy and Norita P. Scott) *Resettlement in Latin America: An Analysis of Thirty-five Cases,* American University, 1966. Contributor of articles to *Anthropological Quarterly, Social Forces, Anthropos, American Anthropologist, Journal of the Siam Society,* and *Jewish Journal of Sociology.*

*WORK IN PROGRESS:* Analysis of flora and fauna in *The Old Testament;* a cross-cultural study of emotions and nonverbal behavior.

\*     \*     \*

## JACOBSON, Ethel

*PERSONAL:* Born in Paterson, N.J.; daughter of Alfred H. (a manufacturer) and Helen (Gould) Sonntag; married Louis John Jacobson, November 25, 1923; children: Dorcas Gould

(Mrs. C. William Salzmann), Noel Hoyt (Mrs. William G. Lamkin). *Education:* Attended Parsons School of Design, New York, Syracuse University, Ohio Wesleyan University, National Academy of Design, and studied art and music privately. *Politics:* "No party (but my politics somewhat pre-date William McKinley)." *Religion:* Lutheran. *Home:* 108 Buena Vista, Fullerton, Calif. 92633; and Route 1, Box 172, Mammoth Lakes, Calif. 93546 (summers).

*CAREER:* Writer and book reviewer; speaker at writer's conferences and for other groups; judge of writing contests. Writer for Braille Institute, 1952—. *Member:* P.E.N. International (member of board of directors, Los Angeles chapter, 1966-68; vice-president, 1968), California Writers Guild (member of board of directors, 1966-70), Southern California Women's Press Club, Chaparral Poets, Freedoms Foundation at Valley Forge. *Awards, honors:* Awards from Friends of the Library, University of California, Irvine, for *I'll Go Quietly,* 1967, and *Who, Me?,* 1971.

*WRITINGS: Larks in My Hair* (poems), Courier Press (Placentia, Calif.), 1952; *Mice in the Ink* (poems), self-illustrated, Progress Press, 1955; *Diamonds for Your Jubilee* (commemorative verse), Orange County Historical Society, 1964; *I'll Go Quietly* (poems), Triangle Press (Dallas), 1966; *The California Dream* (historical ode), Orange County Historical Society, 1968; *Curious Cats* (prose and verse), Funk, 1969; *Who, Me?* (poems), Triangle Press, 1970; *The Cats of Sea-Cliff Castle* (non-fiction), Ward Ritchie, 1972.

Poetry included in over forty anthologies, including *Best Poems of the Times,* Viking, 1971. Former reviewer for *Chicago Tribune;* reviewer for *St. Louis Post Dispatch,* 1967—, and for *Santa Ana Register,* 1968—. Contributor of over 5000 poems, as well as fiction, satire, and reviews to numerous publications, including *Saturday Evening Post, McCall's, Good Housekeeping, Arizona Highways, New York Times, Christian Science Monitor, Author and Journalist, Saturday Review, New Yorker, Instructor, Atlantic, Gourmet, Look, Reader's Digest,* and *Family Weekly.* Editor, *Guilder* (publication of California Writers Guild), 1966-68.

*WORK IN PROGRESS:* Several books; reviews and criticism.

*SIDELIGHTS:* Ethel Jacobson writes: "I feel I was lucky to be reared in a houseful of books with people who read. So I read. But with writing, as with a buzz saw, you soon can't let someone else have all the excitement; you want to try it yourself. By the second grade I was writing reams that, mercifully, are long forgotten (can't think how I frittered away the whole first grade). But I'm stubborn. I keep trying, hoping I'll begin to get the hang of it one fine day.

"I've always lived with a private menagerie of all the animals I could find, always including cats that always turned out to be female. I didn't finish college, thinking it would be more educational to marry an engineer (it was). . . . I like all critters, including varmints like bats, coyotes, and snakes, preferring them to the human variety that is ruining this pleasant land.

"The English language, I'm convinced, is man's greatest invention. It can soar to sublimest heights or (which fascinates me more) kick up its heels in the zaniest fun and games. The sixteenth century was a literary carnival. Today bureaucrats, educationists, and social scientists have contorted the language into pompous imbecilities, a sort of institutional pig Latin so grotesque that you're sure it must be a sick 'in' joke. But these jokers are as serious as they are smug. Our schools are the world's most extravagant manufacturers of illiterates, producing each year greater marvels of incompetence.

"I began writing for no nobler reason than that I found it more entertaining to scribble than to bite my nails or chew bubble gum. The current scene? Literary excellence and good taste have been deep-sixed. You can still find them, but look what you must scavenge through, as I must in my business, to find them. To aspiring writers: Try aspirin and a cold compress. It may go away. If not, master your craft, discover that wallowing in a quagmire isn't the only game in town—and enough of you may make our trade respectable again. Good luck!"

The Jacobsons divide their time between Southern California and the High Sierras, where they live on a trout stream seven thousand feet up on a mountain that juts almost twice that high.

\* \* \*

## JACOBSON, Sheldon A(lbert) 1903-

*PERSONAL:* Born June 25, 1903, in New York, N.Y.; son of Albert Edward (a photographic chemist) and Rosalie H. Hartogensis) Jacobson; married Annette Chesin, May 4, 1939; children: Eric Sheldon, Ira Sheldon, Ruth Anne. *Education:* College of the City of New York (now City College of the City University of New York), A.B., 1922; Yale University, M.D., 1928. *Politics:* Independent. *Religion:* Jewish. *Home:* 6413 Buena Vista Dr., Vancouver, Wash. 98661.

*CAREER:* Montefiore Hospital, New York City, resident pathologist, 1928-30; Hospital for Joint Diseases, New York City, assistant pathologist, 1931-36; Crown Heights Hospital, Brooklyn, N.Y., pathologist, 1936-40; U.S. Veterans Administration Hospital, Wichita, Kan., pathologist, 1946-49; U.S. Veterans Administration Hospital, Vancouver, Wash., pathologist, 1949-72. Clinical professor of pathology and director of bone tumor registry, University of Oregon Medical School, 1956—. *Military service:* U.S. Naval Reserve, 1930-61; active duty, 1940-46; became captain.

*MEMBER:* International Academy of Pathology, College of American Pathologists, American Society of Clinical Pathologists, American Association of Pathologists and Bacteriologists, Pan American Medical Association (life member), Pacific Northwest Society of Pathologists (president, 1963-64), Western Orthopedic Association (honorary member), Vancouver Optimist Club (president, 1966-67), Jewish Educational Association (Portland; president, 1960-62), Sea Explorer Ship Dragon (Vancouver; chairman, 1956-69), Alpha Omega Alpha, Sigma Xi. *Awards, honors:* Gold Medal exhibit, American Academy of Orthopedic Surgeons, 1934; Bronze Medal exhibit, American Society of Clinical Pathologists, 1968.

*WRITINGS: Fleet Surgeon to Pharaoh,* Oregon State University Press, 1971; *Comparative Pathology of the Tumors of Bone,* C. C Thomas, 1971. Contributor of medical papers to journals.

*WORK IN PROGRESS: The Man Who Moved the World,* a historical novel; medical papers.

*AVOCATIONAL INTERESTS:* Cruising under sail, skiing, and camping.

*BIOGRAPHICAL/CRITICAL SOURCES: Best Sellers,* June 15, 1971.

## JAFFE, Eugene D. 1937-

*PERSONAL:* Born January 9, 1937, in New York, N.Y.; son of Isidor Ira and Sadye (Holstein) Jaffe; married Liora Mayerfeld-Maor, August 15, 1965; children: Iris Michal, Nurit Adi. *Education:* University of Pennsylvania, B.S., 1958, Ph.D., 1966; New York Univesity, M.B.A., 1961. *Office:* College of Business, St. John's University, Jamaica, N.Y. 11439.

*CAREER:* Silk City Electrical Supply Co., Newburgh, N.Y., vice-president, 1958-61, 1965-66; University of Pennsylvania, Management Science Center, Philadelphia, instructor in marketing, 1962-64; St. John's University, Jamaica, N.Y., assistant professor, 1966-70, associate professor of marketing, 1971—. Lecturer, Iona College, 1965-66; visiting assistant professor of business administration, Rutgers University, summer, 1968. Director of special projects, Erdos & Morgan Research, Inc., 1969-71. Consultant to Litton Industries, 1967, Famous Schools, 1968, Grolier, Inc., 1968, Edward E. Emanuel Co., 1972—, and Economic Development Administration, New York, N.Y., 1972—. *Member:* American Marketing Association. *Awards, honors:* Automatic Retailers of America award, 1963-64; St. John's University President's Advisory Council research grant, 1965; Foundation for Economic Education fellowship in business, 1968.

*WRITINGS: American Investment and Operations in Israel,* Bureau of Business Research, St. John's University, 1969; (contributor) *Comparative Management and Marketing,* Scott, Foresman, 1969; *Marketing Principles Text and Study Guide,* School of Continuing Education, New York Institute of Technology, 1971; *Sales Management Study Guide,* School of Continuing Education, New York Institute of Technology, 1972; (editor) *Social, Cultural and Economic Changes in the 70's,* Emanuel Publishing Co., 1972; *Grouping: A Strategy for International Marketing,* American Management Association, 1974; (with Stephen Hilbert) *Barron's How to Prepare for the Admission Test for Graduate Study in Business,* Barron's, 1975, revised edition published as *Barron's How to Prepare for the Graduate Management Admission Test,* 1977. Contributor of articles to *California Management Review, Business Horizons, University of Washington Business Review,* and *University of Houston Business Review.*†

\*    \*    \*

## JAMES, Estelle 1935-

*PERSONAL:* Born December 1, 1935, in Bronx, N.Y.; daughter of Abraham and Lee Dinerstein; married Ralph C. James, 1957; married second husband, Harry Lazer (a professor), June 27, 1971; children: (first marriage) Deborah, David. *Education:* Cornell University, B.S., 1956; Massachusetts Institute of Technology, Ph.D., 1961. *Office:* Office of the Provost of Social and Behavioral Sciences, State University of New York, Stony Brook, N.Y. 11790.

*CAREER:* University of California, Berkeley, lecturer in economics, 1964-65; Stanford University, Stanford, Calif., acting assistant professor of economics, 1965-67; State University of New York at Stony Brook, associate professor, 1967-72, professor of economics, 1972—, research associate, Economic Research Bureau, 1967-72, provost of social and behavioral sciences, 1975—. *Member:* American Economics Association, Phi Kappa Phi, Omicron Delta Epsilon. *Awards, honors:* National Science Foundation faculty research grant, 1970-72.

*WRITINGS:* (With Ralph C. James) *Hoffa and the Teams-*

*ters: A Study of Union Power,* Van Nostrand, 1965. Contributor of articles and reviews to economics and industrial relations journals.

*WORK IN PROGRESS:* Research on resource allocation and economic efficiency in nonprofit institutions, with particular reference to universities.

\*    \*    \*

## JANKOWSKY, Kurt Robert 1928-

*PERSONAL:* Born April 23, 1928, in Loewen, Germany; son of Hans and Maria (Scholz) Jankowsky; married Ellen H. Heimes, December 30, 1960; children: Andreas R., Fabian H. *Education:* Muenster University, Staatsexamen, 1956, Ph.D., 1956; Staatliches Studienseminar Bochum, M.E., 1958. *Religion:* Roman Catholic. *Home:* 6506 76th St., Bethesda, Md. 20034. *Office:* Department of German, Georgetown University, 36th and O Sts., Washington, D.C. 20057.

*CAREER:* Poona University, Poona, India, postgraduate lecturer in German, 1958-62; Georgetown University, Washington, D.C., assistant professor, 1962-67, associate professor, 1967-72, professor of German linguistics, 1972—, chairman of department, 1964—. *Member:* Societas Linguistica Europea, Linguistic Society of India, Linguistic Society of America, Modern Language Association of America, American Association of Teachers of German.

*WRITINGS: Die Versauffassung bei Gerard Manley Hopkins, den Imagisten und T. S. Eliot,* Max Hueber, 1967; *The Neogrammarians: A Re-evaluation of Their Place in the Development of Linguistic Science,* School of Language and Linguistics, Georgetown University, 1968, revised edition, Mouton, 1972; (editor) *Georgetown University Round Table on Languages and Linguistics,* Georgetown University Press, 1973. Contributor to *Orbis* and *Babel.*

*WORK IN PROGRESS: The Emergence of Lexicology as a Linguistic Science; Time Concepts in Indo-European Languages;* research on problems of synchronic and historical linguistics.

\*    \*    \*

## JARVIS, F(rank) Washington 1939-

*PERSONAL:* Born June 24, 1939, in Pittsburgh, Pa.; son of Frank W. (a businessman) and Prudence (Crandall) Jarvis. *Education:* Harvard University, B.A., 1961; Cambridge University, M.A., 1963; Episcopal Theological School, M.Div., 1964. *Office:* University School, 2785 S.O.M. Center Rd., Chagrin Falls, Ohio 44022.

*CAREER:* Clergyman of Episcopal Church; senior curate in Cleveland, Ohio, 1964-71; University School, Chagrin Falls, Ohio, teacher, 1971—. Overseer, Case Western Reserve University, Cleveland; trustee, Harvard Club, Cleveland.

*WRITINGS: Come and Follow: An Introduction to Christian Discipleship,* Seabury, 1972; *Prophets, Poets, Priests, and Kings: The Old Testament Story,* Seabury, 1974.

*WORK IN PROGRESS: A Short History of Israel; Plutarch's Lives: A New Translation.*†

\*    \*    \*

## JEAN, Gabrielle (Lucille) 1924-
## (Sister Jean de Milan)

*PERSONAL:* Born April 8, 1924, in Lowell, Mass.; daughter of Alfred (an electrician) and Claudia (Guillemette) Jean. *Education:* Rivier College, A.B., 1954; Boston College, M.Ed., 1957, Ph.D., 1961. *Home:* 975 Varnum Ave., Lowell, Mass. 01854. *Office:* D'Youville Manor, 981 Varnum Ave., Lowell, Mass. 01854.

*CAREER:* Roman Catholic nun of Order of Sisters of Charity, Ottawa, name in religion, Sister Jean de Milan; science and mathematics teacher in Roman Catholic high school for girls, Lowell, Mass., 1954-59; Marillac College, Normandy, Mo., instructor in psychology and education, 1961-62; Rivier College, Nashua, N.H., assistant professor of psychology and education, 1962-64; Rhode Island College, Providence, associate professor of psychology, 1964-71, chairman of department, 1967-69; Roger Williams College, Bristol, R.I., professor of psychology, 1972-74; House of Affirmation, Whitinsville, Mass., staff psychologist, 1974-76; D'Youville Manor Nursing Home, Lowell, Mass., administrator, 1976—. Instructor in sociology and psychology, School of Nursing, St. Joseph's Hospital, 1957-61; part-time teacher, University of Rhode Island, 1971-72. *Member:* American Psychological Association, American Educational Research Association, American Personnel and Guidance Association, National Vocational Guidance Association, Psychologists Interested in Religious Issues.

*WRITINGS*—Editor: Bernhard Haering, *Shalom: Peace,* Farrar, Straus, 1967; Haering, *Acting on the Word,* Farrar, Straus, 1968; Haering, *A Theology of Protest,* Farrar, Straus, 1970; Haering, *Hope Is the Remedy,* St. Paul, 1971, Doubleday, 1972; Haering, *Medical Ethics,* Fides, 1973, revised edition, Fides/Claretion, 1975; Haering, *Faith and Morality in a Secular Age,* Doubleday, 1973; *Sin in a Secular Age,* Doubleday, 1974; *Beatitudes—The Social Dimension,* [St. Paul, England], 1976. Contributor of articles to religious and psychological journals.

\*          \*          \*

## JEDAMUS, Paul 1923-

*PERSONAL:* Born February 1, 1923, in Wausau, Wis.; son of Paul (an electrical engineer) and Erma (Manecke) Jedamus; married Mary Lu Miller, September 9, 1952; children: Julith, Laurel, Carolyn, Allison. *Education:* University of Wisconsin, B.S., 1944, M.B.A., 1949, Ph.D., 1955. *Home:* Red Hill Rd., Boulder, Colo. 80302. *Office:* University of Colorado, Boulder, Colo. 80302.

*CAREER:* Marathon Corp., Rothschild, Wis., chemical engineer, 1944-45; University of Colorado, Boulder, 1953—, currently professor of business statistics, director of institutional research, 1964-68. *Military service:* U.S. Army, 1945-47. *Member:* Institute for Management Science, American Statistical Association, Association for Institutional Research, Beta Gamma Sigma, Sigma Iota Epsilon, Delta Sigma Pi.

*WRITINGS:* (With Robert Frame) *Business Decision Theory,* McGraw, 1969; (with Robert Taylor and Frame) *Statistical Analysis for Business Decisions,* McGraw, 1976. Editor-in-chief, *New Directions for Institutional Research.*

*WORK IN PROGRESS:* Research on management of higher education.

\*          \*          \*

## JEFFREY, Adi-Kent Thomas 1916-

*PERSONAL:* Given name is pronounced Odd-ie-kent; born October 1, 1916, in Atlantic City, N.J.; daughter of Adolph Alexander (a lawyer) and Helen (Rowe) Thomas; married Gilbert Jeffrey (a mechanical engineer), January 17, 1942; children: Lynda Elizabeth. *Education:* Barnard College,

B.A., 1938. *Home:* 927 Cybus Way, Southampton, Pa. 18966. *Agent:* Toni Mendez, 140 East 56th St., New York, N.Y. 10022. *Office:* New Hope Art Shop, 37 North Main, New Hope, Pa. 18938.

*CAREER:* Vera Maxwell (fashion designer), New York City, model, 1938-39; National Broadcasting Co., New York City, host of overseas radio talk show, "Around New York," 1939; John Wanamaker (department store), Philadelphia, Pa., fashion copywriter, 1959-60; now lecturer on ghosts and investigator of psychic phenomena. Taught for several years in adult education creative writing programs. *Member:* American Society of Journalists and Authors, American Association of University Women, Overseas Press Club of America, Daughters of the American Revolution, Bucks County Historical Society, Bucks County Writers' Guild (past president), Philadelphia Children's Reading Round Table.

*WRITINGS:* *They Dared Niagara,* Follett, 1968; *Witches and Wizards,* Cowles, 1971; *Ghosts in the Valley,* New Hope, 1971; *Dictionary of the Supernatural,* New Hope, 1972; *More Ghosts in the Valley,* New Hope, 1973; *The Bermuda Triangle,* Warner Books, 1973; *Triangle of Terror,* Warner Books, 1974; *They Dared the Devil's Triangle,* Warner Books, 1975; *Across the Land from Ghost to Ghost,* New Hope, 1975; *Ghosts of the Revolution,* New Hope, 1976; *Parallel Universe,* Warner Books, 1977. Contributor to *Saga, Man's Magazine, Bride's Magazine,* and other periodicals. Columnist for *Bucks County Courier-Times,* 1963-68; historical editor for *Bucks County Life Magazine,* 1965-68; regular contributor to *Philadelphia Evening Bulletin,* 1968-70.

*WORK IN PROGRESS:* Researching a book on true close encounters of the third kind.

*BIOGRAPHICAL/CRITICAL SOURCES: Philadelphia Evening Bulletin,* October 29, 1971; *Philadelphia Sunday Bulletin,* October 31, 1971.

\*          \*          \*

## JEFFREY, Lloyd Nicholas 1918-

*PERSONAL:* Born November 26, 1918, in Temple, Okla.; son of Nicholas Ephraim (a cattleman) and Eunice (Greenland) Jeffrey; married Virginia Coleman, August 11, 1945; children: Michael Alan, Nikki Ann. *Education:* University of Texas, B.A., 1939, M.A., 1947, Ph.D., 1951. *Politics:* Democrat. *Religion:* Methodist. *Home:* 625 Linwood Dr., Denton, Tex. 76201. *Office:* Department of English, North Texas State University, Denton, Tex. 76203.

*CAREER:* University of Texas at Austin, instructor in English, 1948-50; East Central State College (now East Central Oklahoma State University), Ada, Okla., associate professor of English, 1951-55; North Texas State University, Denton, professor of English, 1955—. *Military service:* U.S. Army, 1941-46; became captain; received Bronze Star and Purple Heart. *Member:* Modern Language Association of America, College English Association, Keats-Shelley Association, Classical Association of Middle West and South, South Central Modern Language Association (section chairman, 1963, 1966), Texas Association of College Teachers (local chapter president, 1965-66).

*WRITINGS:* *Thomas Hood,* Twayne, 1972; (with others) *Fears Related to Death and Suicide,* Mss Information, 1974; *Shelley's Knowledge and Use of Natural History,* Humanities, 1976. Contributor of articles to *College English, Western Folklore, Psychoanalytical Review, Journal*

*of Humanistic Psychology, New Mexico Quarterly, Bulletin of Bibliography, Explicator, Keats-Shelley Journal, Classical Journal, Notes and Queries,* and *CEA Critic.* Associate editor, *Studies in the Novel,* 1969—.

*WORK IN PROGRESS:* A critical work on Shelley; various articles on Shakespeare, romantic poetry, and classical studies.

*AVOCATIONAL INTERESTS:* Animals, wild nature, and surf-fishing.

\* \* \*

### JEFFS, Julian 1931-

*PERSONAL:* Born April 5, 1931, in Sedgley, England; son of Alfred Wright (a stockbroker) and Irene (Davies) Jeffs; married Deborah Bevan, May 21, 1966; children: Daniel, Alexander, Benjamin. *Education:* Attended Downing College, Cambridge, B.A., 1953, M.A., 1957. *Politics:* "Vague." *Religion:* Unitarian. *Home:* Church Farm House, East Ilsley, Newbury, Berkshire, England. *Agent:* John Johnson, 3 Albemarle St., London W.1, England. *Office:* Francis Taylor Building, Temple, London E.C.4, England.

*CAREER:* Barrister of Gray's Inn, the Inner Temple, and Midland and Oxford, England; recorder of the Crown Court. *Military service:* Royal Navy, 1949-50. *Member:* Circle of Wine Writers (honorary treasurer, 1965-70; chairman, 1970-72; vice-president, 1975), Garrick Club, Reform Club, Saintsbury Club, Beefsteak Club. *Awards, honors:* Prize of Office International de la Vigne et du Vin, 1962, for *Sherry;* Glenfiddich Book Award, 1974, for *Little Dictionary of Drink.*

*WRITINGS: Sherry,* Faber, 1961, 2nd edition, 1970; (editor with Robert Harling) *Wine,* Conde Nast Publications, 1966; (contributor) A. L. Armitage, editor, *Torts,* Sweet & Maxwell, 1969; *The Wines of Europe,* Taplinger, 1971; *Little Dictionary of Drink,* Pelham, 1971; *The Dictionary of World Wines, Liqueurs, and Other Drinks,* Pagurian, 1975; (with T. A. Blanco White, Robin Jacob and W. R. Cornish) *Encyclopedia of United Kingdom and European Patent Laws,* Sweet & Maxwell, 1977. Contributor to *House & Garden* (British edition), *Vogue* (British edition), *Decanter,* and other publications. Editor, *Wine & Food,* 1965-67.

*WORK IN PROGRESS: A Beginner's Guide to Wine;* editing a volume of the letters of Maurice Baring.

*SIDELIGHTS:* "Come of a hard drinking family," Julian Jeffs writes. *Avocational interests:* "Like walking, old cars (own and drive a 1935 Rolls Royce), have a collection of musical boxes, and am devoted to Spain."

\* \* \*

### JENKINS, Dorothy Helen 1907-1972

1907—December 10, 1972; American editor and authority on gardening. Obituaries: *New York Times,* December 12, 1972.

\* \* \*

### JENNINGS, James M(urray) 1924-

*PERSONAL:* Born October 28, 1924, in Tulsa, Okla.; son of Edward Paul (an auditor) and Eleanor (Easton) Jennings; married Aija Vilcins (a secretary), December 24, 1946; children: James M., Jr., Linda Doris. *Education:* Attended Virginia Polytechnic Institute, 1943-44; George Washington University, A.A., 1949, B.A., 1950; Syracuse University,

additional study, 1953-56; Cornell University, additional study, 1954-55; University of North Carolina, M.A., 1955. *Religion:* American Baptist. *Home:* 1858 Chatfield Rd., Columbus, Ohio 43221. *Office address:* James M. Jennings Associates Co., P.O. Box 5762, Columbus, Ohio 43221.

*CAREER:* University of Pittsburgh, Pittsburgh, Pa., associate professor and acting head of department, 1956-59; Battelle Memorial Institute, Columbus, Ohio, researcher, 1959-65; James M. Jennings Associates Co., Columbus, president, 1965—. Chairman of Upper Arlington Planning Commission, 1975—. *Military service:* U.S. Army, served in infantry and Air Forces, 1943-45; became staff sergeant; received Bronze Star. *Member:* American Society of Consulting Planners, American Industrial Development Council (national chairman for consultants), National Association of Business Economists, American Society of Planning Officials, Urban Land Institute, American Economic Association, Association of American Geographers, American Geographical Society, Regional Science Association, Great Lakes States Industrial Development Council, North East Industrial Development Council, Ohio Society of Consulting Planners (board member, 1967—; secretary-treasurer, 1967-69; treasurer, 1977—), Ohio Planning Conference (vice-president, 1970—; president, 1973-75).

*WRITINGS:* (With John H. Thompson) *Manufacturing in the St. Lawrence Area,* Syracuse University Press, 1968. Also author of *Comprehensive Plan: Monroe County, Ohio,* and *Comprehensive Plan: Noble County, Ohio.* Editor, *Ohio Planning Conference Newsletter,* 1969-72.

*WORK IN PROGRESS: Land Use and Socio-Economics of Power Plant Siting.*

*AVOCATIONAL INTERESTS:* Reading, coin and stamp collecting, outdoor activities, travel, family.

\* \* \*

### JERSILD, Paul T(homas) 1931-

*PERSONAL:* Born May 28, 1931, in Blair, Neb.; son of Hans Christian (a clergyman) and Carrie (Sinamark) Jersild; married Marilyn Steffensen, August 28, 1954; children: Ann, Austin, Amy, Aaron. *Education:* Dana College, B.A., 1953; University of Nebraska, M.A., 1955; Wartburg Seminary, B.D., 1959; University of Heidelberg, additional study, 1960-61; University of Muenster, Dr. Theol., 1962. *Politics:* Democrat. *Religion:* Lutheran. *Home:* 10401 South Leavitt, Chicago, Ill. 60643. *Office:* Department of Theology, St. Xavier College, 3700 West 103rd St., Chicago, Ill. 60655.

*CAREER:* Ordained minister of Lutheran Church, 1962; St. Matthew Lutheran Church, Palmyra, Wis., pastor, 1962-64; Luther College, Decorah, Iowa, assistant professor of religion, 1964-69; St. Xavier College, Chicago, Ill., associate professor, 1969-76, professor of theology, 1976—. *Member:* American Association of University Professors, American Academy of Religion, American Society of Christian Ethics.

*WRITINGS:* (Editor with Dale A. Johnson) *Moral Issues and Christian Response,* Holt, 1971, revised edition, 1976; *Invitation to Faith,* Augsburg, 1978. Contributor of articles to *Lutheran Quarterly, Dialog,* and *Concordia Theological Monthly.*

*WORK IN PROGRESS:* Research on current developments in Roman Catholic theology.

\* \* \*

### JOFEN, Jean 1922-

*PERSONAL:* Born November 13, 1922, in Vienna, Austria;

daughter of Moses and Stella (Meisels) Blech; married Jacob Jofen (dean of Beth Joseph Rabbinic Seminary), March 26, 1944; children: Aaron, Fay (Mrs. Maurice Roth), Mordechai, Michelle (Mrs. Mordechai Tendler). *Education:* Brooklyn College (now Brooklyn College of the City University of New York), B.A., 1943; Brown University, M.A., 1945; Columbia University, Ph.D., 1953. *Religion:* Jewish. *Home:* 1684 52nd St., Brooklyn, N.Y. 11204. *Office:* Department of Germanic and Slavic Languages, Bernard M. Baruch College of the City University of New York, 17 Lexington Ave., New York, N.Y. 10010.

*CAREER:* Yeshiva University, Stern College for Women, New York City, assistant professor, 1957-61, associate professor of Germanic and Slavic languages, 1961-63; Bernard M. Baruch College of the City University of New York, New York City, professor of Germanic and Slavic languages and head of department, 1963—. *Member:* Modern Language Association of America, American Psychological Association, American Association of University Women, Lexicological Institute (The City University of New York).

*WRITINGS*—All published by Edwards Brothers, except as indicated: *A Linguistic Atlas of Eastern European Yiddish,* 1964; *Yiddish for Beginners,* 1965; *Das letzte Geheimnis,* Franke Verlag (Bern, Switzerland), 1972; *Hebrew for Beginners,* 1974; *Chinese for Beginners,* 1975. Editor, *Elizabethan Concordance,* Olms Verlag, 1978.

\* \* \*

### JOHNSON, Dale A(rthur) 1936-

*PERSONAL:* Born March 13, 1936, in Duluth, Minn.; son of Arthur B. (a civil engineer) and Luella (Dahlman) Johnson; married Norma J. Freeman, September 23, 1958; children: Eric, Kristin, Stephanie. *Education:* Colgate University, B.A., 1957; Oxford University, B.A., 1959, M.A., 1963; Lutheran School of Theology, Chicago, B.D., 1962; Union Theological Seminary, New York, N.Y., Th.D., 1967. *Religion:* Lutheran. *Home:* 2860 Sugartree Rd., Nashville, Tenn. 37215. *Office:* Divinity School, Vanderbilt University, Nashville, Tenn. 37240.

*CAREER:* Luther College, Decorah, Iowa, assistant professor of religion, 1965-69; Vanderbilt University, Divinity School, Nashville, Tenn., assistant professor, 1969-74, associate professor of church history, 1974—, director of continuing education, 1973-77. *Member:* American Society of Church History, American Academy of Religion, American Association of University Professors.

*WRITINGS:* (Editor with Paul T. Jersild) *Moral Issues and Christian Response,* Holt, 1971, revised edition, 1976.

*WORK IN PROGRESS:* Research on Victorian religion, and research on church and state.

\* \* \*

### JOHNSON, E(dgar) A(gustus) J(erome) 1900-1972

January 31, 1900—August 17, 1972; American educator, economist, historian, and consultant to U.S. and foreign governments. Obituaries: *New York Times,* August 19, 1972; *Time,* August 28, 1972. (See index for *CA* sketch)

\* \* \*

### JOHNSON, Edward A(ndrew) 1915-

*PERSONAL:* Born February 11, 1915, in Brooklyn, N.Y.; son of Edward Andrew (a real estate broker) and Clara I. (Roesler) Johnson; married Mary C. Cook (a secretary),

June 18, 1949. *Education:* St. Francis College, Brooklyn, N.Y., B.A. (magna cum laude), 1936; St. John's University, Jamaica, N.Y., M.A., 1940, Ph.D., 1950. *Religion:* Roman Catholic. *Home:* 1361 East 16th St., Brooklyn, N.Y. 11230. *Office:* Department of English, St. John's University, Grand Central and Utopia Pkwys., Jamaica, N.Y. 11432.

*CAREER:* Brooklyn Botanic Garden, Brooklyn, N.Y., instructor in horticulture and botany, 1932-38; high school teacher of biology, English, and history in Brooklyn, 1936-42; St. John's University, Jamaica, N.Y., assistant professor, 1950-54, associate professor, 1954-57, professor of English, 1957—, chairman of department, 1958-61. Frequent television lecturer, "Shakespeare's Tragedies," 1978—. Member of board of directors, Greenfield Civil Association, 1968—; member of board of trustees, St. Francis Preparatory School, 1971-77. *Military service:* U.S. Army, Infantry, 1942-46; served in Europe; became captain; received Bronze Star Medal. *Member:* Modern Language Association of America, National Council of Teachers of English, National Catholic Education Association, American Association of University Professors, Shakespeare Association of America, Catholic Renascence Society, International Platform Association, Browning Institute. *Awards, honors:* St. John's University President's medal, 1971.

*WRITINGS:* (Contributor) Frank N. Magill, editor, *Masterpieces of Catholic Literature,* two volumes, Salem Press, 1964; *The Vision of Shakespeare,* St. John's University Press, 1968. Contributor of scholarly articles to literature journals.

\* \* \*

### JOHNSON, Ellen H. 1910-

*PERSONAL:* Born November 25, 1910, in Warren, Pa.; daughter of Jacob August (a businessman) and Hulda (Hedlund) Johnson. *Education:* Oberlin College, B.A., 1933, M.A., 1935; further study at Sorbonne, University of Paris, Harvard University, and University of Uppsala. *Religion:* Lutheran. *Residence:* Oberlin, Ohio. *Office:* Allen Art Building, Oberlin College, Oberlin, Ohio 44074.

*CAREER:* Toledo Museum of Art, Toledo, Ohio, librarian and member of staff, department of education, 1936-39; Oberlin College, Oberlin, Ohio, art librarian and part-time instructor, 1939-45, instructor, 1945-50, assistant professor, 1950-58, associate professor, 1958-64, professor of art history, 1964-77, professor emeritus, 1977—, honorary curator of modern art, Allen Art Museum, 1973—. Visiting professor, University of Wisconsin, 1950-51; visiting lecturer, Uppsala University, 1960-61; U.S. commissioner, New Delhi Triennale of Contemporary World Art, 1968. *Member:* American-Scandinavian Foundation (honorary fellow), College Art Association of America, American Association of University Professors.

*WRITINGS: Cezanne,* Purnell & Sons, 1967; *Claes Oldenburg,* Penguin, 1971; *Modern Art and the Object,* Harper, 1976. Contributor of articles to art journals. Museum editor, *Art Journal.*

\* \* \*

### JOHNSON, Harold Scholl 1929-

*PERSONAL:* Born November 15, 1929, in Hamburg, N.Y.; son of William Rae and Julia (Scholl) Johnson. *Education:* St. Lawrence University, B.A., 1951; Syracuse University, M.A., 1957; University of Michigan, Ph.D., 1963. *Politics:* Democrat. *Home address:* P.O. Box 828, East Lansing,

Mich. 48823. *Office:* 135 Snyder Hall, Michigan State University, East Lansing, Mich. 48823.

*CAREER:* Michigan State University, East Lansing, assistant professor, 1965-69, associate professor, 1969-72, professor of political science, 1972—. *Military service:* U.S. Army Reserve, 1948-58. *Member:* American Political Science Association, American Society of International Law, United Nations Association of the United States of America (Michigan division president, 1969-70), American Society for Public Administration, International Studies Association, American Judicature Society, Phi Delta Kappa, Tau Kappa Alpha, Pi Sigma Alpha, Omicron Delta Kappa. *Awards, honors:* Ford Foundation grant, 1964-65.

*WRITINGS: Self-Determination within the Community of Nations,* Sijthoff, 1967; (with Baljit Singh) *International Organizations: A Classified Bibliography,* Asian Studies Center, Michigan State University, 1969. Contributor to political science journals.

*WORK IN PROGRESS:* Analysis of the concept of self-determination as it relates to principles of world order.

*       *       *

## JOHNSON, Harvey L(eroy)   1904-

*PERSONAL:* Born September 12, 1904, in Cleburne, Tex.; son of John Andrew (a railroad engineer) and Ida May Johnson; married Margaret Burkhardt (a teacher), August 31, 1950; children: Harvey L., Jr., Harold F. *Education:* Howard Payne College, B.A., 1925; University of Texas, M.A., 1928; University of Pennsylvania, Ph.D., 1940. *Politics:* Democrat. *Religion:* Baptist. *Home:* 5307 Dumfries, Houston, Tex. 77096. *Office:* Department of Spanish, University of Houston, Houston, Tex. 77004.

*CAREER:* High school teacher in New Mexico, 1925-26; Victoria Junior College, Victoria, Tex., instructor in Spanish, 1928-30; Rice Institute (now University), Houston, Tex., instructor in Spanish, 1930-36; Cedar Crest College, Allentown, Pa., professor of Spanish, 1937-40; Northwestern University, Evanston, Ill., instructor, 1940-43, assistant professor, 1943-45, associate professor, 1945-50, professor of Spanish and Portuguese, 1950-51; Indiana University at Bloomington, professor of Spanish and Portuguese and chairman of department, 1951-65; University of Houston, Houston, professor of Spanish and Portuguese, 1965-75, professor emeritus, 1975—. U.S. Department of State visiting lectureship in Uruguay, Paraguay, Argentina, Peru, and Bolivia, 1948. Consultant to U.S. Library of Congress and U.S. Department of Health, Education and Welfare. Chairman of executive committee, Institute of Hispanic Culture of Houston, 1969-70.

*MEMBER:* Modern Language Association of America, Association for Latin American Studies, American Association of University Professors, Academy of Geography (Sucre, Bolivia; corresponding member), Instituto Internacional de Literatura Iberoamericana, Asociacion Internacional de Hispanistas, Association of College Honor Societies (national president, 1953-55), South Central Modern Language Association, Midwest Council for Latin American Studies (president, 1961-62), Southwestern Council for Latin American Studies (president, 1969-70), Texas Association of College Teachers (chapter president, 1968-69), Houston Area Teachers of Foreign Languages (president, 1972-73), Phi Kappa Phi, Phi Sigma Iota (president, 1952-55), Kappa Delta Pi (chapter president, 1969-70), Alpha Chi, Sigma Delta Pi. *Awards, honors:* American Council of Learned Societies grant for research on Colombian theater,

1942; senior research fellow of Newberry Library, Chicago, 1973; grant from American Philosophical Society, 1973.

*WRITINGS: Triunfo de los Santos,* University of Pennsylvania Press, 1941; *La America Espanola: Panorama Cultural,* Oxford University Press, 1949; (author of prologue and annotations) Antonio Garcia Gutierrez, *El diablo nocturno,* Andrea, 1956; (translator and author of introduction) Ignatio M. Altamirano, *La Navidad en las montanas,* University of Florida Press, 1961; *Aprende a hablar espanol,* Ginn, 1963, laboratory manual, Blaisdell, 1965. Contributing editor, *Handbook of Latin American Studies.*

*WORK IN PROGRESS:* A critical edition of the diary of Andres de Avendano (1696); a critical edition of the novel, *Cadete mexicano,* written in 1833; a book, *The Virgin of Guadalupe in Mexican Culture.*

*       *       *

## JOHNSON, Joseph E(arl)   1946-
## (Hal Fitzgerald)

*PERSONAL:* Born August 14, 1946, in Ann Arbor, Mich.; son of Earl C. (an attorney) and Leila (Micheel) Johnson. *Education:* Attended Kearney State College, 1964-65, and Nebraska Wesleyan University, 1965-70. *Politics:* Democrat. *Religion:* Episcopalian. *Home address:* Route 1, Box 16, Anselmo, Neb. 68813. *Office:* Quest Associates, 6844 Leighton Ave., Lincoln, Neb. 68507.

*CAREER:* Quest Associates, Lincoln, Neb., president, 1969—. Tutor to Indian children, 1970; probation officer in Lancaster County, 1970. Director of local unit, Nebraskans for McGovern, Broken Bow, 1972; county chairman and area coordinator, Democratic Party, 1972. *Member:* American Political Science Association. *Awards, honors:* American High School Poetry Association award for *Of the Universe, God and Men.*

*WRITINGS: Shall Earth and Man Survive?* (monograph), Nebraska Wesleyan University, 1969; *A Political Biography of William Jennings Bryan,* Nebraska Wesleyan Reference Division, 1971. Author of *Of the Universe, God and Men,* 1964, *The Power of Politics, the Power of People,* 1967, and of a play, "The Temptation of the Father." Science writer, *Custer County Chief.*

*WORK IN PROGRESS:* Research on constitutional amendment procedures and conventions; research on exobiology and on theology.

*AVOCATIONAL INTERESTS:* Sciences, history, reading, music, travel, tennis, and golf.†

*       *       *

## JOHNSON, Margaret   1926-

*PERSONAL:* Born August 15, 1926, in Grand Rapids, Mich.; daughter of Joseph J. and Bedelia (Kamel) Haggai; married Vern Johnson (a quality control supervisor), January 16, 1947; children: Cynthia (Mrs. Donald Bergstrom), Richard, David, Daniel. *Education:* Attended Moody Bible Institute, 1945. *Politics:* Republican. *Religion:* Protestant. *Residence:* Canoga Park, Calif.

*CAREER:* Formerly employed as a secretary.

*WRITINGS—*All published by Zondervan: *Eighteen: No Time to Waste,* 1971; *Chocolate Malts and Nickel Sodas,* 1976; *At Home before Dark,* 1978.

*WORK IN PROGRESS: Giving Birth Naturally,* for Zondervan.

SIDELIGHTS: Margaret Johnson's first book is the story of her 18-year-old daughter who was killed in a head-on automobile collision, along with two other teen-agers. She had committed her life to Christian service, perhaps as a missionary. Avocational interests: Music, singing in a 150-voice church choir.

*     *     *

## JOHNSON, Merle Allison 1934-
### (Pastor X)

PERSONAL: Born February 14, 1934, in Damascus, Ark.; son of Merle Allison, Sr. (a shoe store owner) and Ambra (Parish) Johnson; married Mary Catherine Hall, October 23, 1954; children: Marsha Susan, Karla Kay. Education: Ouachita Baptist University, B.A., 1956; Southwestern Baptist Theological Seminary, B.D.; additional study at Southern Baptist Theological Seminary. Politics: Independent. Home: 309 Prospect, Siloam Springs, Ark. 72761.

CAREER: Minister in Baptist churches in Lake Village, Ark., 1960-65, and Malvern, Ark., 1965-69; minister of Methodist church in Eudora, Ark., 1969-71; United Methodist Church, Siloam Springs, Ark., minister, 1971-75; First United Methodist Church, Forrest City, Ark., minister, 1975—. Member: Society of Biblical Literature and Exegesis, American Schools of Oriental Research, Yokefellow Institute, Rotary Club.

WRITINGS: (Under pseudonym Pastor X) How to Murder a Minister, Revell, 1970; Beyond Disenchantment, Revell, 1972; Ancient Fires for Modern Man, Tidings, 1973; The Kingdom Seekers, Abingdon, 1973; Religious Roulette and Other Dangerous Games Christians Play, Abingdon, 1975; Sermons for Christian Seasons, Abingdon, 1976. Contributor of articles to religious periodicals. Author of column in Malvern Daily Record, 1967-69.

WORK IN PROGRESS: Research on the youth movement, for a book for Abingdon Press.

BIOGRAPHICAL/CRITICAL SOURCES: Hot Springs Sentinel-Record, May 21, 1970; Arkansas Gazette, February 27, 1971.

*     *     *

## JOHNSON, Richard A(ugust) 1937-

PERSONAL: Born April 18, 1937; son of Cecil August (an attorney) and Esther (Nelson) Johnson; married Michaela Memelsdorff (an artist and writer), August 20, 1960; children: Nicholas August, Patrick Michael. Education: Swarthmore College, B.A., 1959; Yale University, additional study, 1959-60; Cornell University, Ph.D., 1965. Politics: Independent Liberal. Religion: Episcopalian. Home: 27 Ashfield Lane, South Hadley, Mass. 01075. Office: Department of English, Mount Holyoke College, South Hadley, Mass. 01075.

CAREER: University of Virginia, Charlottesville, member of English department, 1963-65; Mount Holyoke College, South Hadley, Mass., associate professor, 1965-74, professor of English and chairman of department, 1974—. Member: American Association of University Professors, Modern Language Association of America, Phi Beta Kappa.

WRITINGS: Man's Place: An Essay on Auden, Cornell University Press, 1972. Contributor of articles and reviews to Virginia Quarterly Review, Yale Review, Sewanee Review, Parnassus: Poetry In Review, and other journals.

WORK IN PROGRESS: A comparative study of Anthony Powell and C. P. Snow.

## JOHNSON, Robert Erwin 1923-

PERSONAL: Born February 3, 1923, in Coos Bay, Ore.; son of Franz Oscar (a farmer) and Agnes (Sandquist) Johnson; married Vivian Ellis, December 19, 1959. Education: Attended Oregon State College (now University), 1946-48; University of Oregon, B.A., 1951, M.A., 1953; Claremont Graduate School, Ph.D., 1956. Politics: Democrat. Home: 61 The Downs, Tuscaloosa, Ala. 35401. Office address: University of Alabama, Box 1936, University, Ala. 35486.

CAREER: University of Alabama, University, assistant professor, 1956-63, associate professor, 1963-67, professor of history, 1967—. Military service: U.S. Coast Guard, 1941-46. U.S. Naval Reserve, active duty, 1951-52; became quartermaster first class. Member: American Historical Association, Society for Nautical Research, World Ship Society, Naval Historical Foundation, United States Naval Institute, Phi Beta Kappa.

WRITINGS: Thence Round Cape Horn: The Story of United States Naval Forces on Pacific Station, 1818-1923, U.S. Naval Institute, 1963; Rear Admiral John Rodgers: 1812-1882, U.S. Naval Institute, 1967. Contributor of articles and reviews to scholarly journals.

WORK IN PROGRESS: Studying U.S. naval policy in the Far East up to 1897; research on the U.S. Navy between 1865-1895.

*     *     *

## JOHNSON, Van L(oran) 1908-

PERSONAL: Born January 18, 1908, in Medford, Wis.; son of William and Rossie (Olson) Johnson; married Marjorie Jean Carr, June 30, 1934; children: Karen Christine (Mrs. James V. Detore), Eric V. Education: University of Wisconsin, B.A., 1930, M.A., 1931, Ph.D., 1935; Oxford University, B.A., 1934, M.A., 1938. Home: 1056 Hedley Dr., San Luis Obispo, Calif. 93401. Office: Department of Classics, Tufts University, Medford, Mass. 02155.

CAREER: University of Wisconsin—Madison, instructor in classics, 1936-37; Tufts University, Medford, Mass., instructor, 1937-41, assistant professor, 1941-46, associate professor, 1946-52, professor of Latin, 1952-73, professor emeritus, 1973—, head of department, 1952-69. Member: American Association of Rhodes Scholars, Phi Beta Kappa. Awards, honors: Rhodes scholarship, 1931-34.

WRITINGS: Roman Origins of Our Calendar, American Classical League, 1958, 3rd edition, 1974; (editor) Tenuis Musa (Latin poems), Tufts University Press, 1960. Translator of Andromache included in Six Greek Plays, Dryden, 1955. Contributor of articles to journals in his field.

WORK IN PROGRESS: Latin epigrams.

AVOCATIONAL INTERESTS: Sculpture.

*     *     *

## JOHNSTON, William M(urray) 1936-

PERSONAL: Born December 11, 1936, in Brookline, Mass.; son of Ivan Murray (a professor) and Mildred (Williamson) Johnston; married Cheryl McCartney, July 6, 1968; children: Ian Andrew, Alexander Murray. Education: Harvard University, A.B., 1958, Ph.D., 1966. Home: 35 McClure St., Amherst, Mass. 01002. Office: Department of History, University of Massachusetts, Amherst, Mass. 01002.

CAREER: University of Massachusetts—Amherst, assistant professor, 1966-70, associate professor, 1970-75, professor of history, 1975—. *Member:* American Historical Association. *Awards, honors:* Austrian History award, Austrian History Institute, 1969, for *The Austrian Mind.*

*WRITINGS: The Formative Years of R. G. Collingwood,* Nijhoff, 1967; *The Austrian Mind: An Intellectual and Social History, 1848-1938,* University of California Press, 1972.

\*     \*     \*

## JONES, Margaret E. W.  1938-

*PERSONAL:* Born February 4, 1938, in New York, N.Y.; daughter of Theodore T. and Malvina (Wald) Weitzner; married Joseph R. Jones (a professor of Spanish), March 30, 1964; children: Alison Margaret. *Education:* State University College of Education (now State University of New York at Albany), B.A., 1959; University of Wisconsin, M.A., 1961, Ph.D., 1963. *Office:* Department of Spanish, University of Kentucky, Lexington, Ky. 40506.

*CAREER:* Salem College, Winston-Salem, N.C., assistant professor of Spanish, 1963-64; North Carolina College at Durham (now North Carolina Central University), assistant professor, 1964-66, associate professor of Spanish, 1966-67; University of Kentucky, Lexington, associate professor, 1967-75, professor of Spanish, 1975—, associate dean of graduate school, 1977—. *Member:* Modern Language Association of America, American Association of Teachers of Spanish and Portuguese, American Association of University Professors, American Association of University Women, South Atlantic Modern Language Association.

*WRITINGS: The Literary World of Ana Maria Matute,* University Press of Kentucky, 1970; *Delores Medio,* Twayne, 1974; (co-author) *A Brief History of Spanish Literature,* Littlefield, 1974. Contributor to foreign language journals.

*WORK IN PROGRESS:* A book on the contemporary Spanish novel, for Twayne.

*BIOGRAPHICAL/CRITICAL SOURCES: Books Abroad,* spring, 1971.

\*     \*     \*

## JONES, W(illiam) T(homas)  1910-

*PERSONAL:* Born April 29, 1910, in Natchez, Miss.; son of W. T. (a physician) and Mary (Chamberlain) Jones; married Molly Mason (a professor of psychology), March 29, 1941; children: Jeffrey, Gregory. *Education:* Swarthmore College, B.A. (with highest honors), 1931; Oxford University, B.Litt., 1933; Princeton University, M.A., 1936, Ph.D., 1937. *Office:* Department of Philosophy, California Institute of Technology, 1201 East California Blvd., Pasadena, Calif.

*CAREER:* Pomona College, Claremont, Calif., assistant professor, 1941-45, associate professor, 1945-49, professor of philosophy, 1950-72; California Institute of Technology, Pasadena, professor of philosophy, 1972—. Nimitz Professor of Social and Political Philosophy, Naval War College, 1953-54; resident scholar, Rockefeller Foundation (Villa Serbelloni), 1966, 1970; visiting professor, California Institute of Technology, 1970-72. *Military service:* U.S. Naval Reserve, active duty, 1942-45; became lieutenant commander. *Member:* American Philosophical Association (president of Pacific Division, 1969-70), Phi Beta Kappa. *Awards, honors:* Rhodes scholar, Oxford University, 1931-33; Proctor postdoctoral fellow, 1937-38; Ford faculty fellow, 1955-56; Guggenheim fellow, 1958-59.

*WRITINGS: Morality and Freedom in the Philosophy of Kant,* Oxford University Press, 1940; *Masters of Political Thought,* Volume II: *Machiavelli to Bentham,* Houghton, 1947; *A History of Western Philosophy,* Houghton, 1952, 2nd revised edition published in five separate volumes, Volume I: *The Classical Mind,* 1969, Volume II: *The Medieval Mind,* 1969, Volume III: *Hobbes to Hume,* 1969, Volume IV: *Kant and the Nineteenth Century,* 1975, Volume V: *The Twentieth Century to Wittgenstein and Sartre,* 1975; *The Romantic Syndrome: Toward a New Method in Cultural Anthropology and History of Ideas,* Nijhoff, 1961; *Facts and Values,* Philosophical Institute, University of the Pacific, 1961; (editor with M. O. Beckner, R. J. Fogelin, and F. Sontag) *Approaches to Ethics: Representing Selections from Classical Times to the Present,* McGraw, 1962, 3rd edition, 1977; *The Sciences and the Humanities: Conflict and Reconciliation,* University of California Press, 1965.

\*     \*     \*

## JOSIPOVICI, Gabriel  1940-

*PERSONAL:* Born October 8, 1940, in Nice, France; son of Jean (a writer) and Sacha (Rabinovitch) Josipovici. *Education:* Studied at Victoria College, Cairo, Egypt, 1950-56, and Cheltenham College, 1956-57; St. Edmund Hall, Oxford, B.A., 1961. *Home:* 60 Prince Edwards Rd., Lewes, Sussex, England. *Agent:* John Johnson, Clerkenwell House, 45-7 Clerkenwell Green, London EC1R OHT, England. *Office:* Arts Building, University of Sussex, Falmer, Brighton, England.

*CAREER:* University of Sussex, Falmer, Brighton, England, lecturer in English and comparative literature, 1963-74, reader in English, 1974—. *Awards, honors:* Sunday Times award, 1970, for the play "Evidence of Intimacy."

*WRITINGS: The Inventory* (novel), M. Joseph, 1968; *Words* (novel), Gollancz, 1971; *The World and the Book* (criticism), Macmillan, 1971, 2nd edition, 1978; *Mobius the Stripper* (stories and short plays), Gollancz, 1974; (author of introduction) *Portable Saul Bellow,* Viking, 1974; *The Present* (novel), Gollancz, 1975; (editor) *The Modern English Novel: The Reader, the Writer and the Work,* Harper, 1976; *Migrations* (novel), Harvester Press, 1977; *Four Stories,* Menard Press, 1977; *The Lessons of Modernism* (criticism), Macmillan, 1977. Also author of plays: "Dreams of Mrs. Fraser," "Evidence of Intimacy," "Marathon," "Playback," "A Life," "AG," and "Vergil Dying." Contributor to *Adam International Review, Critical Quarterly, Encounter, European Judaism, Transatlantic Review, Tempo, Listener,* and *New York Review of Books.*

*WORK IN PROGRESS:* A novel; a radio play, with composer Jonathan Harvey.

*SIDELIGHTS:* "Gabriel Josipovici is a born writer not afraid of the dark," believes John Mellors, a critic for *Listener.* "He asks questions, mainly in dialogue, both in his stories and short plays, about identity, truth, memory, death, and the relationships between mind and body and writer and words."

Although known mostly for his plays and novels, Josipovici has edited two books of criticism. One of these, *The Modern English Novel: The Reader, the Writer and the Work,* began rather informally when Josipovici, associates, and a group of friends were discussing novels and their authors. They decided to write, then combine their essays on a number of their favorite authors and their writings. A reviewer for the *Times Literary Supplement* wrote of Josipovici's contribution: ''Great literary criticism is the most evasive of achievements. Gabriel Josipovici seems blessed with all the gifts: a lucid style, vast imaginative energy, a huge storehouse of reading, a living concern for art, as well as a certain self-conscious humility at this whole buzz and fuzz in the face of aesthetic experience.''

*BIOGRAPHICAL/CRITICAL SOURCES: New Statesman,* December 17, 1971; *Times Literary Supplement,* February 25, 1972; *Listener,* January 9, 1975; *Contemporary Literary Criticism,* Volume VI, Gale, 1976.

\*    \*    \*

## JOYNER, Charles W. 1935-

*PERSONAL:* Born January 5, 1935, in Spartanburg, S.C.; son of Winston G. (an engineer) and Kelly (Paul) Joyner; married Jean Dusenbury, January 8, 1963; children: Hannah Ruth, Wesley Winston. *Education:* Presbyterian College, B.A., 1956; University of South Carolina, M.A., 1959, Ph.D. (history), 1968; University of Pennsylvania, Ph.D. (folklore and folklife), 1977. *Office:* Department of History, St. Andrews Presbyterian College, Laurinburg, N.C. 28352.

*CAREER:* Pfeiffer College, Martin, Tenn., assistant professor of history, 1963-65; University of Tennessee at Martin, assistant professor of history, 1965-66; St. Andrews Presbyterian College, Laurinburg, N.C., associate professor of history, 1966-70, associate professor of history and anthropology, 1970—, chairman of American studies program, 1966—. *Military service:* U.S. Army, 1955-60. *Member:* American Folklore Society, American Studies Association, Organization of American Historians, American Association of University Professors, Southern Historical Association. *Awards, honors:* National Endowment for Humanities research grant, 1969, for field work in folklore; Piedmont University Center Grants, 1970, 1972; Social Science Research Council grant, 1974-75; Newberry Library fellowship in family and community history, 1977.

*WRITINGS: Folk Song in South Carolina,* University of South Carolina Press, 1971. Contributor of articles and reviews to *Journal of American Folklore, North Carolina Folklore, American Quarterly, Southern Humanities Review, Humane Learning in a Changing Age, Keystone Folklore Quarterly, Southern Folklore Quarterly, Journal of Southern History, American Anthropologist.*

*WORK IN PROGRESS:* Study of slave folklife on rice plantations of South Carolina low country; study of acculturation of African and British musical folk culture in the American South.

*SIDELIGHTS:* Charles Joyner told *CA:* ''My special interest is the relationship between folklore and history, both as fields of study and as academic disciplines. I am also interested in every aspect of the American South—its history, folklore, politics, literature, and sociology.''

\*    \*    \*

## JULIN, Joseph R. 1926-

*PERSONAL:* Born July 5, 1926, in Chicago, Ill.; son of George A. and Jennie E. Julin; married wife, Dorothy, 1952; children: Pamela, Thomas, Diane, Linda. *Education:* Attended George Washington University, 1946-49; Northwestern University, B.S.L., 1950, LL.B., 1952, J.D., 1971. *Home:* 2240 Northwest 7th Lane, Gainesville, Fla. 32601. *Office:* College of Law, University of Florida, Gainesville, Fla. 32601.

*CAREER:* Attorney; Schuyler, Stough & Morris, Chicago,

Ill., law partner, 1952-59; University of Michigan, Ann Arbor, associate professor, 1959-62, professor of law, 1962-70, associate dean, 1958-70; University of Florida, Gainesville, professor of law and dean, College of Law, 1970—. Chairman and member of executive committee, Institute of Continuing Legal Education. *Military service:* U.S. Army, 1944-46; became staff sergeant. *Member:* American Bar Association.

*WRITINGS:* (With Olin Browder and Roger Cunningham) *Basic Property Law,* West Publishing, 1966. Editor of American Bar Association newsletter, *Real Property, Probate and Trust Law.*

\*    \*    \*

## JULITTE, Pierre (Gaston Louis) 1910-

*PERSONAL:* Born May 24, 1910, in Chevannes, France; son of Henri (a professor) and Marguerite (Pierre) Julitte; married Anne-Marie Baudot, April 14, 1936; children: Jean-Pierre, Alain. *Education:* Institut National Agronomique, Ingenieur agronome, 1930; Ecole Superieure d'Electricite, Diplome, 1932; Ecole Nationale du Genie Rural et des Eaux et Forets, additional study, 1932. *Religion:* Roman Catholic. *Home:* 25 Rue d'Orleans, 92 Neuilly-sur-Seine, France.

*CAREER:* Rural engineer at Nantes and then Angers, France, 1933-39; joined General de Gaulle in London, England, 1940, and served on his staff; parachuted into France in May, 1941, to organize the French Resistance; imprisoned by Gestapo in March, 1943, and held in German concentration camps until freed by British Forces in April, 1945; served with French Foreign Office, 1945-51, in administration of the French Occupation Zone in Germany, 1946-51, and as governor of Province of Treves, 1948-51; privately employed as consultant, 1951-71. *Member:* Club de la Maison de la Chasse et de la Nature (Paris). *Awards, honors:* Commander de la Legion d'honneur, Compagnon de la Liberation, Croix de Guerre, and other decorations for wartime work; Commander du Merite agricole, 1963; Prix litteraire de la Resistance, 1965, for *L'Arbre de Goethe.*

*WRITINGS:* (With Marcel Sailly) *Les Destinees de la France se jouent,* privately printed, 1945; (with Paul Pezard) *L'Eau a la ferme et aux champs,* Hachette, 1958; *Les Eaux de consommation et leur traitment,* Editions Eyrolles, 1964; *L'Arbre de Goethe* (autobiographical), Presses de la Cite, 1965, translation by Francis Price published as *Block 26: Sabotage at Buchenwald,* Doubleday, 1971.

\*    \*    \*

## JUNG, Hwa Yol 1932-

*PERSONAL:* Born May 17, 1932, in Chinju, Korea; son of Maeng Kwon and Ho Jum (Hwang) Jung; married Petee Beth Schwartz (a mathematician), June 18, 1960; children: Michael, Eric. *Education:* Emory University, B.A., 1957, M.A., 1958; University of Florida, Ph.D., 1962. *Politics:* Democrat. *Office:* Department of Political Science, Moravian College, Bethlehem, Pa. 18018.

*CAREER:* Moravian College, Bethlehem, Pa., assistant professor, 1962-64, associate professor, 1964-72, professor of political science, 1972—, chairman of department, 1962-64. *Member:* American Political Science Association, Society for Phenomenology and Existential Philosophy, International Political Science Association, Phi Beta Kappa.

*WRITINGS: The Foundation of Jacques Maritain's Political Philosophy,* University of Florida Press, 1961; *Existential Phenomenology and Political Theory,* Regnery, 1972;

*Beyond Technological Rationality: The Harmony of Man and Nature,* International Documentation Center, 1972.

*WORK IN PROGRESS: Ecology: A Philosophic Perspective, East and West; Phenomenology and Political Theory; Contemporary Political Theory.*

*AVOCATIONAL INTERESTS:* Ecology.

*BIOGRAPHICAL/CRITICAL SOURCES: American Political Science Review,* September, 1972.†

\*     \*     \*

## JURJEVICH, Ratibor-Ray (Momchila) 1915-

*PERSONAL:* Born August 24, 1915, in Ristovac, Yugoslavia; naturalized U.S. citizen, 1956, spelling of surname changed at this time; son of Momchila and Ljubica (Milovanovic) Djurdjevich; married Vera Petnicki, October 31, 1947. *Education:* University of Edinburgh, B.Sc., 1938; George Williams College, M.S., 1953; University of Denver, Ph.D., 1958. *Religion:* Eastern Orthodox. *Home and office:* 916 Red Mountain Dr., Glenwood Springs, Colo. 81601.

*CAREER:* Young Men's Christian Association (YMCA), Italy and Germany, secretary, 1945-50; Medical Center, Chicago, Ill., member of staff, 1951-52; Northside Community Center, Denver, Colo., program director, 1952-54, executive director, 1954-58; State Training School for Girls, Morrison, Colo., clinical psychologist, 1958-60; Psychiatric Clinic, Lowry Air Force Base, Denver, chief psychologist, 1961-70; Denver Court Consultation Service, General Hospital, Denver, psychologist, 1970-72; Denver County Jail, Denver, chief psychologist, 1972-73; entered private practice in clinical psychology, 1973—. Diplomate in clinical psychology, American Board of Professional Psychology, 1975. *Member:* American Psychological Association, Christian Association for Psychological Studies, Colorado Psychological Association.

*WRITINGS: No Water in My Cup: Experiences and a Controlled Study of Psychotherapy of Delinquent Girls,* Libra, 1968; (editor) *Direct Psychotherapy: Twenty-eight American Originals,* two volumes, University of Miami Press, 1973; *The Hoax of Freudism: A Study of Brainwashing the American Professionals and Laymen,* Dorrance, 1974.

*WORK IN PROGRESS: Freud, Witches and Satanists: Sex Cults and Secular Foibles; Freud's Atheistic Religion.*

*SIDELIGHTS:* Ratibor-Ray Jurjevich told *CA:* "My main impetus for writing is my strong belief that Freud and Freudians as well as behaviorists and other scientistic psychologists have done a serious disservice to contemporary humans. They have distorted the self-image, animalized the soul and contributed to sub-human behaviors in families, societies, and in personal morality.... I hope that at least some readers will return to rationality and responsible reactions and will become liberated from irrationality and emotionality with which modern psychology is permeated."

# K

**KAFKER, Frank A.   1931-**

*PERSONAL:* Born December 18, 1931, in Brooklyn, N.Y.; son of Robert (a businessman) and Ida (Schear) Kafker; married Serena Lipton, December 20, 1953; children: Scott Lewis, Roger Bruce. *Education:* Columbia University, B.A., 1953, M.A., 1954, Ph.D., 1961. *Home:* 10586 Adventure Lane, Cincinnati, Ohio 45242. *Office:* Department of History, University of Cincinnati, Cincinnati, Ohio 45221.

*CAREER:* Corning Community College, Corning, N.Y., instructor, 1958-59, assistant professor, 1959-61, associate professor of history, 1961-62; University of Cincinnati, Cincinnati, Ohio, assistant professor, 1962-66, associate professor, 1966-72, professor of history, 1972—. *Member:* American Historical Association, American Society for Eighteenth-Century Studies, Society for French Historical Studies, Societe francaise d'Etude du XVIII siecle, American Association of University Professors, Ohio Academy of History. *Awards, honors:* Taft faculty fellow, University of Cincinnati, 1965, 1972, 1978.

*WRITINGS:* (Editor with J. M. Laux) *The French Revolution: Conflicting Interpretations,* Random House, 1968, 2nd edition, 1976. Contributor to *Encyclopedia Americana* and to *Revue d'Histoire Moderne, Diderot Studies,* and other journals.

*WORK IN PROGRESS:* A collective biography of the contributors to Diderot's *Encyclopedia.*

\*     \*     \*

**KAHN, Ely Jacques   1884-1972**

June 1, 1884—September 5, 1972; American architect, educator, consultant, and writer on design. Obituaries: *New York Times,* September 6, 1972.

\*     \*     \*

**KAIN, Richard Y(erkes)   1936-**

*PERSONAL:* Born January 20, 1936, in Chicago, Ill.; son of Richard Morgan (a professor) and Louise (Yerkes) Kain; married Helen Buchanan, December 16, 1961; children: Helen, Karen, Susan. *Education:* Massachusetts Institute of Technology, B.S., 1957, S.M., 1959, Sc.D., 1962. *Home:* 4802 Maple Rd., Edina, Minn. 55424. *Office:* Electrical Engineering Department, University of Minnesota, Minneapolis, Minn. 55455.

*CAREER:* Massachusetts Institute of Technology, Cambridge, assistant professor, 1962-66; University of Minnesota, Minneapolis, associate professor, 1966-77, professor of electrical engineering, 1977—. Consultant to UNIVAC, 1969-76, and Honeywell, 1975—. *Member:* Institute of Electrical and Electronics Engineers, American Association for the Advancement of Science, Association for Computing Machinery, Sigma Xi, Eta Kappa Nu.

*WRITINGS: Automata Theory: Machines and Languages,* McGraw, 1972.

\*     \*     \*

**KAISER, Walter (Jacob)   1931-**

*PERSONAL:* Born May 31, 1931, in Bellevue, Ohio; son of Walter Kaiser; married Neva Goodwin Rockefeller, December 17, 1966; children: David Walter, Miranda Margaret. *Education:* Harvard University, A.B. (magna cum laude), 1954, Ph.D., 1960. *Office:* Department of Comparative Literature, 404 Boylston Hall, Harvard University, Cambridge, Mass. 02138.

*CAREER:* Harvard University, Cambridge, Mass., instructor, 1960-62, assistant professor, 1962-65, associate professor, 1965-69, professor of English and comparative literature, 1969—, chairman of department, 1969—. Vice-director, Villa I Tatti, Florence, Italy. Trustee, Rosenbach Foundation. *Member:* American Comparative Literature Association, Renaissance Society of America, Modern Greek Studies Association, Boston Library Society (trustee). *Awards, honors:* Harvard Faculty Prize, 1963, for *Praisers of Folly.*

*WRITINGS: Praisers of Folly: Erasmus, Rabelais, Shakespeare,* Harvard University Press, 1963; (editor and author of notes, glossary, and introduction) *Essays of Montaigne Translated by John Florio,* Houghton Mifflin, 1964; (translator and author of introduction) *Three Secret Poems by George Seferis,* Harvard University Press, 1969.

*BIOGRAPHICAL/CRITICAL SOURCES: Comparative Literature,* fall, 1968.

\*     \*     \*

**KAMM, (Jan) Dorinda   1952-**

*PERSONAL:* Born October 17, 1952, in Hempstead, N.Y.; daughter of John Frederick (an accountant) and Janice (Snediker) Kamm. *Education:* Graduated from high school in Franklin Square, New York. *Home:* 82 New Hyde Park Rd., Franklin Sq., New York, N.Y. 11010.

*CAREER:* Writer.

*WRITINGS: Cliff's Head* (gothic novel), Lenox Hill, 1972; *Devil's Doorstep* (gothic novel), Lenox Hill, 1973; *The Marly Stones* (murder mystery), Zebra Publications, 1977.

*WORK IN PROGRESS:* A revision of a previous work entitled *Shadow Game;* a novel of political intrigue set in and around Miami, Fla.

*SIDELIGHTS:* Dorinda Kamm told *CA* that, as a young writer, she feels that what she produces in her early years is especially important. She sees it as an encouragement to others her age who want to write yet lack the direction to achieve something. Kamm feels that many beginning writers think they lack the maturity and education to attempt a writing career. She thinks they should work *now,* "when the desire is greatest and the reward is so much sweeter."

*AVOCATIONAL INTERESTS:* Reading, collecting poetry, animals, long walks.

\* \* \*

## KAMRANY, Nake M. 1934-

*PERSONAL:* Born August 29, 1934, in Kabul, Afghanistan; son of Shair M. and Fia (Farukh) Kamrany; married Barbara Gehlke, December 6, 1957 (divorced September, 1967); children: Shair John, Lilia Joy. *Education:* University of California, Los Angeles, B.S., 1959; University of Southern California, M.A. and Ph.D., 1962. *Home:* 1106 Kagawa St., Pacific Palisades, Calif. 90272. *Office:* Department of Economics, University of Southern California, Los Angeles, Calif. 90007.

*CAREER:* University of Southern California, Los Angeles, lecturer, 1960-62, assistant professor of economics, 1962-63; Battelle Memorial Institute, Columbus, Ohio, senior economist, 1963-65; University of Southern California, associate professor of economics, 1965-66; System Development Corp., Santa Monica, Calif., senior social scientist, 1965-69; International Bank for Reconstruction and Development (World Bank), Washington, D.C., senior economist, 1969-71; University of Southern California, associate professor, 1971-72, director of economic research and professor of economics, Information Sciences Institute, 1972—, currently director of Program in Productivity and Technology. Visiting professor, University of California, Los Angeles, 1966-68. Consultant to the United Nations and the U.S. Government. *Member:* Society for International Development, Association for Asian Studies, American Economic Association, Association for Comparative Economics, Association for Afghanistan Studies. *Awards, honors:* Clune Award of University of Southern California, 1960, 1961, 1962.

*WRITINGS:* (Contributor) H. R. Hamilton, editor, *Systems Simulation for Regional Analysis,* M.I.T. Press, 1968; *Peaceful Competition in Afghanistan: American and Soviet Models for Economic Aid,* Communication Service Corp., 1969; (with John Elliott) *Technology, Productivity, and Public Policy: A National Needs Analysis,* Center for Policy Alternatives, Massachusetts Institute of Technology, 1975; (editor) *The New Economics of the Less Developed Countries: Changing Perceptions in the North-South Dialogue,* Westview, 1978. Contributor of articles and reviews to journals in his field.

*WORK IN PROGRESS: Economics of Technology* and *Contemporary Economic Issues.*

*SIDELIGHTS:* Nake Kamrany told *CA:* "[I] write to express and record my ideas concerning the major issues confronting the individual, the family, the city, the nation, and the international community. This pursuit draws me into a continuous questioning of the role of men and women to achieve a dynamic definition of the quality of life."

\* \* \*

## KANG, Younghill 1903-1972

1903—December 11, 1972; Korean-born American novelist, poet, translator, and educator. Obituaries: *New York Times,* December 14, 1972.

\* \* \*

## KANWAR, Mahfooz A. 1939-

*PERSONAL:* Born September 16, 1939, in Pakistan; son of Muhammad Ismail and Nasiban Kanwar; married, December 25, 1968; wife's name, Shahnaz B.; children: Samina P., Tariq A., Tahir A. *Education:* University of the Punjab, B.A., 1962, M.A. (criminology-sociology), 1964; University of Texas, El Paso, graduate study, 1965-66; University of Waterloo, M.A. (sociology), 1968, additional graduate study, 1968. *Office:* Department of Sociology, Mount Royal College, Calgary, Alberta, Canada.

*CAREER:* High school teacher in Khanewal, West Pakistan, 1958; University of Waterloo, Waterloo, Ontario, lecturer in sociology at St. Jerome's College, 1967-68, assistant lecturer at Renison College, 1968-69; South Waterloo Memorial Hospital, Galt, Ontario, instructor in School of Nursing, 1968-69; Mount Royal College, Calgary, Alberta, instructor in sociology, 1969—. Summer instructor, Waterloo Lutheran University, 1969; part-time instructor, University of Calgary, 1969-70. Has done field research in Canada and Pakistan, including research among beggars in Lahore, West Pakistan, 1962-63, and among murderers at New Central Jail, Multan, West Pakistan, 1963-64, summer, 1971, 1975. *Member:* Canadian Sociology and Anthropology Association, American Sociological Association, International Sociological Association, Pakistan Sociological Association, Pakistan-Canada Association, Western Association of Sociology and Anthropology, John Howard Society.

*WRITINGS: Changing Social Trends in the Muslim World,* Mount Royal College Press, 1970; (contributor) George Kurian, editor, *Comparative Studies in Religion and Society,* Simon & Schuster, 1971; (editor) *Sociological Perspectives of Family,* Mount Royal College Press, 1971; (editor) *The Sociology of Family: An Interdisciplinary Approach,* Shoe String, 1971; (editor and contributor) *Sociology of Criminal Behavior,* Simon & Schuster, 1972; *Sociology of Religion: Changing Conceptions in the Structure of Islam,* Mount Royal College Press, 1974. Also author of *Beggary as a Social Problem in Pakistan,* Mount Royal College Press. Contributor to sociology journals.

*WORK IN PROGRESS: Murder: A Sociological Study of Homicide in Pakistan.*

\* \* \*

## KANZER, Mark 1908-

*PERSONAL:* Born December 6, 1908, in New York, N.Y.; son of Edward M. (a teacher) and Susan (Shaw) Kanzer; married Viva Schatia (a physician), June 3, 1938 (died, 1971); children: Paul, Alan. *Education:* Yale University, B.S., 1928; Harvard University, M.A., 1929; University of Berlin, M.D., 1934. *Home:* 16 Sunny Ridge Rd., Harrison,

N.Y. 10528. *Office:* 120 East 36th St., New York, N.Y. 10016.

*CAREER:* Psychoanalyst; State University of New York, Downstate Medical Center, Brooklyn, N.Y., assistant professor, 1949-50, associate professor, 1950-56, clinical professor of psychiatry, 1956—. *Military service:* U.S. Army, 1943-46; became major. *Member:* American Psychoanalytic Association (councillor-at-large, 1969-73).

*WRITINGS: The Unconscious Today,* International Universities Press, 1969; (editor with Jules Glenn) *Freud and His Self-Analysis,* Jason Aronson, 1978; (editor with Glenn) *Freud and His Patients,* Jason Aronson, 1978. Member of editorial board, *Journal of the American Psychoanalytic Association, International Journal of Psychoanalytic Psychotherapy,* and *American Imago.*

\*     \*     \*

**KARPF, Holly W.   1946-**

*PERSONAL:* Born December 20, 1946, in Washington, D.C.; daughter of James A. (a journalist) and Nancy (a lawyer; maiden name Fraenkel) Wechsler; married David A. Karpf (a clinical psychologist), August 20, 1967. *Education:* Finch College, B.A., 1968; Hunter College of the City University of New York, graduate study, 1968-69; Long Island University, M.A., 1971.

*CAREER:* Yorktown High School, Yorktown Heights, N.Y., psychology teacher, beginning 1971.

*WRITINGS:* (With father, James A. Wechsler and mother, Nancy F. Wechsler) *In a Darkness,* Norton, 1972.

*WORK IN PROGRESS:* Research in social psychology, specifically helping behavior in children.

*SIDELIGHTS:* Holly Karpf told *CA: "In a Darkness* is my first effort at writing for publication and was prompted by my love for my brother and my vocational pursuit of psychology."†

\*     \*     \*

**KARSTEN, Peter   1938-**

*PERSONAL:* Born July 27, 1938, in New Haven, Conn.; son of Paul Daggett and Ceil (O'Brien) Karsten; married Bonnie Klein, June 26, 1965; children: Heather, Adam, Amanda. *Education:* Yale University, B.A., 1960; University of Wisconsin, Ph.D., 1968. *Politics:* Democrat. *Home:* 309 Overdale Rd., Pittsburgh, Pa. 15221. *Office:* Department of History, University of Pittsburgh, Pittsburgh, Pa. 15260.

*CAREER:* University of Pittsburgh, Pittsburgh, Pa., 1967—, professor of history, 1977—. *Military service:* U.S. Navy, 1960-63; became lieutenant junior grade. Consultant to Center for Defense Information and Hudson Institute. *Member:* Organization of American Historians, American Historical Association, American Military Institute, Conference on Peace Research in History, Inter-University Seminar on Armed Forces and Society.

*WRITINGS: The Naval Aristocracy: The Golden Age of Annapolis and the Emergence of Modern American Navalism,* Free Press, 1972; (contributor) J. Israel, editor, *Building the Organizational Society,* Free Press, 1972; (contributor) John Lovell and Philip Kronenberg, editors, *The New Civil-Military Relations,* Transaction, 1973; (contributor) K. Knorr, editor, *Historical Dimensions of National Security Problems,* University of Kansas Press, 1977; *Law, Soldiers, and Combat: The Causes of War Crimes and*

*Their Prevention,* Greenwood Press, 1978; *Soldiers and Society,* Greenwood Press, 1978; *Patriot Heroes and Political Change: Three Centuries of Patriot-Worship in England and America,* University of Wisconsin Press, 1978; (with A. F. Allen and P. Howell) *Threats,* Arms Control Center, University of Pittsburgh, 1978. Contributor of articles to *Military Affairs, Foreign Policy, American Quarterly,* and other journals. Member of editorial board, *Armed Forces and Society.*

*WORK IN PROGRESS:* Research on the consequences of tourism.

\*     \*     \*

**KATICIC, Radoslav   1930-**

*PERSONAL:* Born July 3, 1930, in Zagreb, Croatia, Yugoslavia; son of Natko (a university professor) and Ivana (Benesic) Katicic; married Ionna Michailidu, July 2, 1958; children: Natko, Doroteja, Antigona. *Education:* University of Zagreb, Ph.D., 1959. *Politics:* None. *Religion:* Roman Catholic. *Home:* Gornje Prekrizje 51, Croatia, Yugoslavia. *Office:* Faculty of Philosophy, University of Zagreb, Dure Salaja 3, Zagreb, Croatia, Yugoslavia.

*CAREER:* University of Zagreb, Zagreb, Croatia, Yugoslavia, assistant professor, 1961-66, associate professor, 1966-72, professor of general linguistics, 1972—. *Member:* Societe linguistique de Paris, Societas linguistica Europaea, Linguistic Society of America.

*WRITINGS: A Contribution to the General Theory of Comparative Linguistics,* Mouton, 1970, Humanities, 1971; (co-editor) Stjepan Ivsic, *Slavenska poredbena gramatika,* Skolska Knjiga (Zagreb), 1970; *Jerikoslovni ogledi,* Skolska Knjiga, 1971; *Stara indijska knjizevnost: Matica hrvatska,* Nakladni zavod Matice hrvatske, 1973; *Ancient Languages of the Balkans,* Volume I, Mouton, 1976, Humanities, 1977, Volume II, Humanities, 1977.

*SIDELIGHTS:* In addition to Croat and Serbian, Katicic is competent in German, modern Greek, French, and English.†

\*     \*     \*

**KATO, Shuichi   1919-**

*PERSONAL:* Born September 19, 1919, in Tokyo, Japan; son of Shin'ichi (a doctor) and Oriko (Masuda) Kato. *Education:* Tokyo University, M.D., 1950. *Home:* Kaminoge 1-8-16, Tokyo, Japan. *Office:* International College, Sophia University, Tokyo, Japan.

*CAREER:* University of British Columbia, Vancouver, professor of Asian studies and fine art, 1960-69; Free University of Berlin, West Berlin, Germany, professor of Asian studies and sociology, 1969-72; Sophia University, International College, Tokyo, Japan, professor of comparative culture, 1976—. Visiting lecturer in Japanese history, Yale University, 1974-76.

*WRITINGS: Tominaga Nakamoto, a Tokugawa Iconoclast,* University of British Columbia, 1967; *Hitsuji no Uta* (autobiography), Iwanami, 1969; (contributor) Francois Bondy, editor, *So Sehen Sie Deutschland,* Seewald Verlag, 1970; *Form, Style, Tradition,* University of California Press, 1971; *The Japan-China Phenomenon,* Paul Norbury Publications, 1974; *History of Japanese Literature, The First Thousand Years,* Macmillan, 1978. Contributor to professional journals.

*WORK IN PROGRESS:* A book on modern Japanese attitudes toward death, with Robert Lifton and Michael Reich, for Yale University Press; *History of Japanese Literature, The Last Five Hundred Years.*

\* \* \*

## KATZ, Bobbi 1933-

*PERSONAL:* Born May 2, 1933, in Newburgh, N.Y.; daughter of George and Margaret (Kahn) Shapiro; married Harold D. Katz (an optometrist), July 15, 1956 (separated March, 1977); children: Joshua, Lori. *Education:* Goucher College, B.A. (with honors), 1954; also studied at Hebrew University of Jerusalem, 1955-56. *Politics:* Peace Activist, registered Democrat. *Religion:* Unitarian. *Home and office:* 10 Maple Rd., Cornwall-on-Hudson, N.Y. 12520.

*CAREER:* Began career as a free-lance writer and fashion editor in New York, N.Y., 1954-55; Department of Welfare, Newburgh, N.Y., social worker, 1956-59; Headstart, Newburgh, social worker, 1966-67. Creative writing consultant, Greater Cornwall School District; chairman, Orange County Sane and Citizens for Peace, 1960-61, Arts in Action, 1969-71; education chairman, Newburgh NAACP, 1964-67. Conducts poetry and creative writing workshops for children, teachers, and librarians. *Member:* Authors League of America.

*WRITINGS: I'll Build My Friend a Mountain,* Scholastic Book Services, 1972; *Nothing But a Dog,* Feminist Press, 1972; *Upside-Down and Inside-Out,* F. Watts, 1973; *The Manifesto and Me–Meg,* F. Watts, 1974; *Rod and Reel Trouble,* Albert Whitman, 1974; *1,001 Words,* F. Watts, 1975; *Snow Bunny,* Albert Whitman, 1976; *Volleyball Jinx,* Albert Whitman, 1977. Contributor of poetry and articles to anthologies and magazines.

*WORK IN PROGRESS:* Several anthologies of poetry and a first-person novel.

*SIDELIGHTS:* Bobbi Katz writes: "I write for children because I desperately want to return childhood to them. I hope to join those writers and artists who delight, sensitize, and give hope to children." She has reading and speaking competence in French, Spanish, and Hebrew.

\* \* \*

## KATZ, John Stuart 1938-

*PERSONAL:* Born June 21, 1938, in Cincinnati, Ohio; son of Maurice G. (a sales representative) and Helen (Klein) Katz; married second wife, Judith T. Milstein (a professor and psychologist), October 1, 1967; children: (second marriage) Jesse. *Education:* Miami University, Oxford, Ohio, B.A., 1960; Columbia University, M.A., 1961; Harvard University, Ed.D., 1967. *Home:* 37 Colin Ave., Toronto, Ontario, Canada. *Office:* Department of Film, Faculty of Fine Arts, York University, Toronto, Ontario, Canada.

*CAREER:* High school English teacher in Watertown, Mass., 1962-63; Harvard resident supervisor, public schools of Newton, Mass., 1965-67; University of Toronto, Toronto, Ontario, assistant professor of education at Ontario Institute for Studies in Education, 1967-71, director of film-literature study project, 1967-71; York University, Toronto, Ontario, visiting lecturer in film, 1971—, associate professor of film, 1971—, chairman of department, 1974-76, 1977—. Visiting scholar, University of California, Berkeley, 1976-77. Member of Canadian selection committee, UNESCO International Centre of Films for Children and Young People. Member of board of directors, John Grierson Film Seminars, 1964-66, Toronto Film Society, 1968-70, Cana-

dian Film Institute, 1975-77, and Young Filmmakers' Exchange. Member, International Seminar on Teaching of English (York, England), 1971. *Member:* Modern Language Association of America, University Film Association, Society for Cinema Studies. *Awards, honors:* British Council fellowship, 1967.

*WRITINGS:* (With Joseph Hansen and others) *A Folklore-Mythology Based Curriculum,* Newton School Foundation, 1966; (contributor) *Screen Education in Canadian Schools,* Canadian Education Association, 1969; (editor and contributor) *Perspectives on the Study of Film,* Little, Brown, 1971; (contributor) *Challenge and Change in the Teaching of English,* Allyn & Bacon, 1971; (with Curt Oliver and Forbes Aird) *A Curriculum in Film,* Ontario Institute for Studies in Education Press, 1972; (contributor) *Popular Media and the Teaching of English,* Goodyear Publishing, 1972. Producer and co-director of documentary films; producer of student-made films. Contributor of about twenty-five articles and reviews to journals. Member of editorial board, *Harvard Educational Review,* 1966-67; editorial consultant, *Journal of Aesthetic Education,* 1972-75.

*WORK IN PROGRESS:* An autobiographical film.

\* \* \*

## KAVENAGH, W(illiam) Keith 1926-

*PERSONAL:* Born November 11, 1926, in Springfield, Mass.; son of Carl John and Jeannette (Kelly) Kavenagh; married Joan Carol Davis (a psychologist), August 14, 1955; children: Renee, Pamela, Claudia. *Education:* Oberlin College, A.B., 1950; Columbia University, A.M., 1959; New York University, Ph.D., 1966; Hofstra University, J.D., 1977. *Politics:* Independent. *Home:* 215 South Gillette Ave., Bayport, N.Y. 11705. *Office:* Legal Aid Society, Appeals Bureau, Stony Brook, N.Y.

*CAREER:* Has worked as radio operator, assistant buyer for retail stores, and salesman; teacher of high school social studies, Sayville, N.Y., 1958-60; Dowling College, Oakdale, N.Y., assistant professor of history, 1960-66; State University of New York at Stony Brook, assistant professor of history, 1966-74; admitted to Bar of New York State, 1978; Legal Aid Society, Appeals Bureau, Stony Brook, attorney, 1978—. Lecturer on colonial charters and on charter rights of states and towns; has served as consultant to U.S. Department of Justice and American Civil Liberties Union. *Military service:* U.S. Maritime Service, radio officer, 1944-47, 1948, 1949; became lieutenant junior grade. *Member:* American Bar Association, New York Bar Association.

*WRITINGS: Foundations of America: Basic Colonial Documents, 1492-1763,* three volumes, Bowker, 1973; *Vanishing Tidelands: Land and the Law in Suffolk County, N.Y., 1640-Present,* New York Sea Grant Institute, in press. Contributor to *Historical Methods Newsletter.*

\* \* \*

## KAVET, Robert 1924-

*PERSONAL:* Born January 25, 1924, in Seattle, Wash.; son of Alexander A. (a salesman) and Ann (O'Donnell) Kavet; married Geraldine M. Beck, February 14, 1952; children: William Anthony, Lorreta Marie. *Education:* San Jose State College (now University), B.A., 1950. *Politics:* Democrat. *Religion:* Roman Catholic. *Office:* Sunland Marketing Inc., 3000 Sand Hill Rd., Menlo Park, Calif. 94025.

*CAREER:* Lawrys Foods Inc., Los Angeles, Calif., western sales manager, 1957-63; Foote, Cone & Belding (advertising agency), Los Angeles, merchandising supervisor, 1963-64; The Squirt Company (beverage manufacturer), Sherman Oaks, Calif., sales promotion manager, 1964-69; Sun-Maid Raisin Growers, Kingsburg, Calif., advertising merchandise manager, 1969-72; Sunland Marketing Incorporated, Menlo Park, Calif., advertising public relations manager, 1972—. *Military service:* U.S. Navy, 1942-46. *Member:* Sales Promotion Executives Association, Theta Chi, Alpha Delta Sigma.

*WRITINGS: The Dirty Boy,* Lerner, 1971. Also author of speeches and slide and trade show presentations.

*WORK IN PROGRESS:* Children's stories and cook books.††

*        *        *

## KAWAHITO, Kiyoshi 1939-

*PERSONAL:* Born March 9, 1939, in Manchuria; holds Japanese citizenship; son of Sadao (a physician) and Sumako (Ueda) Kawahito; married Erna van der Schaaf (a Dutch citizen), August 30, 1971. *Education:* Attended Osaka University of Foreign Studies, 1957-60; Oklahoma City University, B.S., 1963; University of Maryland, M.B.A., 1965, Ph.D., 1971. *Home:* 406 Second Ave., Murfreesboro, Tenn. 37130. *Office:* Department of Economics and Finance, Middle Tennessee State University, Murfreesboro, Tenn. 37132.

*CAREER:* University of Maryland, College Park, instructor in economics, 1968-71; Middle Tennessee State University, Murfreesboro, assistant professor, 1971-74, associate professor of economics, 1975—. Escort-interpreter at intervals, U.S. Department of State, 1965—. *Member:* American Economic Association, Society for International Development, Association for Asian Studies.

*WRITINGS: The Japanese Steel Industry,* Praeger, 1972; *America's Face Abroad,* Dorrance, 1972; (with Hans Mueller) *Steel Industry Economics,* Japan Iron & Steel Exporters' Association, 1978.

*WORK IN PROGRESS:* Research in steel industry economics; a comparative study of Japanese-United States business and economics.

*AVOCATIONAL INTERESTS:* Sports (played baseball and basketball on high school and university teams in Japan).

*BIOGRAPHICAL/CRITICAL SOURCES: Cleveland Plain Dealer,* June 20, 1972.

*        *        *

## KAWIN, Bruce F. 1945-

*PERSONAL:* Born November 6, 1945, in Los Angeles, Calif.; son of Morris Kawin (a certified public accountant) and Marjorie (a certified psychologist; maiden name, Rosenkranz) Kawin Toomim. *Education:* Columbia University, A.B. (cum laude), 1967; Cornell University, M.F.A., 1969, Ph.D., 1970. *Politics:* "Pacifist." *Religion:* Jewish. *Home:* 915 15th St., Boulder, Colo. 80309. *Office:* Department of English, University of Colorado, Boulder, Colo. 80309.

*CAREER:* Wells College, Aurora, N.Y., assistant professor of English, film history, and filmmaking, 1969-73; University of California, Riverside, lecturer in English and film, 1973-75; University of Colorado, Boulder, associate professor of English and film, 1975—. Specialist in film analysis, American Film Institute, Center for Advanced Film Studies.

*WRITINGS: Slides* (poems), Angelfish Press, 1970; *Telling*

*It Again and Again: Repetition in Literature and Film,* Cornell University Press, 1972; *Faulkner and Film,* Ungar, 1977; *Mindscreen: Bergman, Godard, and the Language of First-Person Film,* Princeton University Press, 1978. Also author of an unpublished book, "Notes on a Haunted Form: Self-Conscious Fiction from *Moby-Dick* to *The Golden Notebook.*" Contributor of poems and reviews to periodicals including *Film Quarterly* and *Take One.*

*WORK IN PROGRESS: The Space Between,* poems; *Madman's Belfry,* a novel; *The Selected Screenplays of William Faulkner;* an annotated edition of the final shooting script of "The Big Sleep."

*SIDELIGHTS:* Bruce Kawin told *CA:* "I have always considered myself a poet first and a critic second, but have had incredible difficulty getting anybody to give my poems a serious reading. In the meantime I turn out speculative criticism, most of it having to do with the metaphysics of narration in literature and film. *Mindscreen* is, I think, the best of these; it's the most serious contribution to film theory I'm liable to make."

*        *        *

## KAYE, Philip A. 1920-

*PERSONAL:* Born July 3, 1920, in Highmore, S.D.; son of Albert Arnot (an insurance agent) and Bennie Bee (Foote) Kaye; married Hilda Zoe Bruning, October 22, 1945; children: Marjorie (Mrs. Patric Omeara), Nancy. *Education:* Dakota Wesleyan University, A.B., 1942; Iliff Theological Seminary, Th.M., 1945, M.R.E., 1953; Denver University, M.A., 1947, Ph.D., 1955. *Politics:* Democrat. *Religion:* Methodist. *Home:* 5635 Madison Ave., Lincoln, Neb. 68507. *Office:* Department of Speech, Nebraska Wesleyan University, Lincoln, Neb. 68504.

*CAREER:* Dakota Wesleyan University, Mitchell, S.D., 1947-56, became professor of speech and department chairman; Nebraska Wesleyan University, Lincoln, Neb., 1956—, began as associate professor, currently professor of speech and chairman of department. Host on KUON-TV "Bookshelf" program. *Military service:* U.S. Navy, 1945-46. *Member:* International Communication Association, Speech Communication Association, Nebraska Speech Association. *Awards, honors:* Trustee Distinguished Teaching Award, Nebraska Wesleyan University, 1970.

*WRITINGS: Preparing Speeches of Substance: The Analysis Method,* Wesleyan University Press, 1970. Co-author of "He's Gone Away," a musical produced in 1951.

*WORK IN PROGRESS: Practical Persuasion,* a text.

*        *        *

## KAYSER, Elmer Louis 1896-

*PERSONAL:* Born August 27, 1896, in Washington, D.C.; son of Samuel Louis (a civil servant) and Susan (Huddleston) Kayser; married Margery Ludlow, February 13, 1922; children: Katherine Ludlow (Mrs. Arthur Hallett Page III). *Education:* George Washington University, B.A., 1917, M.A., 1918; Columbia University, Ph.D., 1932. *Religion:* Episcopalian. *Home:* 2921 34th St. N.W., Washington, D.C. 20008. *Office:* Room 500, Library, George Washington University, Washington, D.C. 20006.

*CAREER:* George Washington University, Washington, D.C., instructor, 1917-20, assistant professor, 1920-24, associate professor, 1924-32, professor of history, 1932-67, professor emeritus, 1967—, secretary of university, 1918-29, dean of Division of University Students, 1932-62, dean emeritus, 1967—, university historian, 1962—. *Member:* American Historical Association (treasurer, 1957—), American Association of University Professors, Institute of Judicial Administration, Columbia Historical Society (vice-president, 1970-72).

*WRITINGS: Grand Social Enterprise,* Columbia University Press, 1932; *Manual of Ancient History,* Public Affairs Press, 1937; *Washington's Bequest to a National University,* George Washington University, 1965; *The George Washington University,* George Washington University, 1966; *Luther Rice, Founder of Columbian College,* George Washington University, 1966; *Bricks without Straw,* Appleton, 1970; *A Medical Center: The Institutional Development of Medical Education in George Washington University,* George Washington University, 1973.

\*      \*      \*

## KEALEY, Edward J(oseph) 1936-

*PERSONAL:* Born August 1, 1936, in New York, N.Y.; son of John E. and Margaret (Lyon) Kealey. *Education:* Manhattan College, A.B., 1958; Johns Hopkins University, M.A., and Ph.D., 1962. *Religion:* Roman Catholic. *Home:* 5639 186th St., Flushing, N.Y. 11365. *Office:* Department of History, Holy Cross College, Worcester, Mass. 01610.

*CAREER:* Holy Cross College, Worcester, Mass., 1962—, began as associate professor, currently professor of history; University of Massachusetts Labor Relations Institute, Amherst, lecturer, 1969—. *Member:* American Historical Association, Mediaeval Academy of America, Catholic Historical Association, American Association of University Professors, Conference of British Studies, Society of Religion in Higher Education, Massachusetts Archaeological Association.

*WRITINGS: Roger of Salisbury, Viceroy of England,* University of California Press, 1972.

*WORK IN PROGRESS: Anglo-Norman Studies; British and New World Archaeology.*

*SIDELIGHTS:* Edward Kealey did archaeological field-work in Britain.

\*      \*      \*

## KEEFE, Donald Joseph 1924-

*PERSONAL:* Born July 14, 1924, in Hamilton, N.Y.; son of Donald John and Frances Katherine (Balmes) Keefe. *Education:* Colgate University, B.A., 1949; Georgetown University, J.D., 1951; Fordham University, Ph.L., 1958; Woodstock College, S.T.L., 1963; Gregorian University, S.T.D., 1967. *Home:* 3601 Lindell Blvd., St. Louis, Mo. 63108. *Office:* 3634 Lindell Blvd., St. Louis, Mo. 63108.

*CAREER:* Roman Catholic priest of the Society of Jesus (Jesuits); Canisius College, Buffalo, N.Y., 1966-70, became assistant professor of religious studies; St. Louis University, St. Louis, Mo., assistant professor, 1970-73, associate professor of dogmatic and systematic theology, 1973-76, professor of theological studies, 1976—. *Military service:* U.S. Navy, 1943-46, 1951-53. *Member:* Catholic Biblical Association, Institute for Theological Encounter of Science and Technology.

*WRITINGS: Thomism and the Ontological Theology of Paul Tillich: A Comparison of Systems,* E. J. Brill, 1971.

*WORK IN PROGRESS:* Working on a book which will propose an ontology of sacrament.

*SIDELIGHTS:* Donald Keefe told *CA:* "My major profes-

sional interest is now focused upon the ontology of the Eucharist, seen from within the Catholic tradition; I consider this to be the central theological concern of contemporary Christianity. I have also been interested in the application of the notion of sacrament to law."

\*      \*      \*

## KEITH, Herbert F. 1895-

*PERSONAL:* Born April 10, 1895, in Cattaraugus, N.Y.; son of Fred L. and Clare (Cox) Keith; married Maria Surudjiewa. *Home:* Wanakena, N.Y. 13695.

*CAREER:* Worked as a guide in the Adirondack Mountain area. *Military service:* U.S. Army, 1919, 1942-48. *Member:* Veterans of Foreign Wars.

*WRITINGS: Man of the Woods,* Adirondack Museum, Syracuse University Press, 1972.

\*      \*      \*

## KEITHLEY, George 1935-

*PERSONAL:* Born July 18, 1935, in Chicago, Ill.; son of James Balliet and Helen (Stuart) Keithley; married Mary Zoe Marhoefer, November 5, 1960; children: Elizabeth, Clare, Christopher. *Education:* Duke University, A.B., 1957; Stanford University, graduate study, 1957-58; University of Iowa, M.F.A., 1960. *Politics:* Democrat. *Home:* 1302 Sunset Ave., Chico, Calif. 95926. *Agent:* (Theatrical) Samuel Liff, William Morris Agency, Inc., 1350 Avenue of the Americas, New York, N.Y. 10019; (literary) Patricia Berens, Sterling Lord Agency, Inc., 660 Madison Ave., New York, N.Y. 10021. *Office:* Department of English, California State University, Chico, Calif. 95926.

*CAREER:* Has worked as hotel desk clerk, groundskeeper at a race track, interviewer, copy writer, and copy-boy for a television station; University of Iowa, Iowa City, instructor in literature and business writing, 1961-62; California State University, Chico, instructor, 1962-65, assistant professor, 1966-69, associate professor, 1970-71, professor of American literature and poetry, 1973—. Free-lance writer, 1965-66, 1969-70, 1972, and 1977. Editorial consultant, W. W. Norton & Co., Inc., California State University Press, University Press of Kentucky, and Harcourt, Brace, Jovanovich, Inc. *Member:* Poetry Society of America, Dramatists Guild, New England Poetry Club. *Awards, honors:* DiCastagnola Award, Poetry Society of America, 1973, for *Song in a Strange Land;* Leighton Rollins Award, New England Poetry Club, and Duke Players Playwriting award, both 1977, for "The Best Blood of the Country."

*WRITINGS: The Donner Party* (epic poem), Braziller, 1972; (editor with Charles V. Genthe) *Themes in American Literature,* Heath, 1972; *Song in a Strange Land* (poems), Braziller, 1974. Also author of a play, "The Best Blood of the Country." Contributor of over one hundred poems to literature journals and national magazines, including *Harper's,* and of short stories to *North American Review,* and other journals.

*WORK IN PROGRESS:* Two books of poems; a novel.

*AVOCATIONAL INTERESTS:* Sports, travel, theatre, music.

*BIOGRAPHICAL/CRITICAL SOURCES: San Francisco Sunday Examiner & Chronicle,* January 30, 1972; *Sacramento Bee,* February 12, 1972; *Nashville Tennessean,* March, 1972; *New York Times,* March 11, 1972.

## KELEHER, Will(iam Aloysius)  1886-1972

1886—December 18, 1972; American lawyer, politician, and New Mexico historian. Obituaries: *Washington Post,* December 21, 1972.

* * *

## KELLEY, William T(homas)  1917-

*PERSONAL:* Born February 4, 1917, in Jersey City, N.J.; son of William Scholes (a manufacturer) and Elsie (Thomas) Kelley; married Barbara Bacher (a textile designer), May 16, 1945; children: Thomas B. *Education:* University of Toronto, B.A., 1939; University of Pennsylvania, M.B.A., 1941, Ph.D., 1951. *Religion:* Society of Friends (Quaker). *Home:* 608 Spruce Lane, Villanova, Pa. 19085. *Office:* Wharton School, University of Pennsylvania, Philadelphia, Pa. 19104.

*CAREER:* War Shipping Administration, Washington, D.C., associate economist, 1942-43; University of Pennsylvania, Wharton School, Philadelphia, instructor, 1946-51, assistant professor, 1951-55, associate professor, 1955-65, professor of marketing and communications, 1963—. Consultant to businesses, including DuPont, General Motors, U.S. Travel Service, and Agency for International Development (AID). *Military service:* U.S. Army, Transportation Corps, 1943-46; became first lieutenant. *Member:* American Marketing Association, American Economic Association, American Academy of Advertising.

*WRITINGS:* (With Ralph Bodek) *House Purchasing Motivations,* Municipal Publications, 1960; (with E. L. Brink) *Management of Promotion,* Prentice-Hall, 1963; *Marketing Intelligence,* Staples, 1968; *The New Consumerism,* Grid Publishing, 1973. Contributor of about twenty-five articles to business and marketing journals. Member, editorial board, *Journal of Marketing,* 1966—.

*WORK IN PROGRESS: Social Aspects of Marketing; Geriatric Marketing.*

*AVOCATIONAL INTERESTS:* Travel, art, music (plays organ).

* * *

## KELLING, Hans-Wilhelm  1932-

*PERSONAL:* Born August 15, 1932, in Schwerin, Germany; son of Wilhelm (a state official) and Aenne (Hinkfoth) Kelling; married Joyce Kay Coy, June 10, 1958; children: Sven Warren, Kareen Joyce, Kirsten Inge, Kerryl Aenne. *Education:* Brigham Young University, B.A., 1958; Stanford University, M.A., 1967, Ph.D., 1967. *Religion:* Church of Jesus Christ of Latter-day Saints. *Home:* 2840 Apache Lane, Provo, Utah 84601. *Office:* Department of German, 323 McKay, Brigham Young University, Provo, Utah 84601.

*CAREER:* Brigham Young University, Provo, Utah, assistant professor, 1962-67, associate professor, 1967-72, professor of German, 1972—. *Member:* American Association of Teachers of German, Modern Language Association of America, Rocky Mountain Modern Language Association (section chairman, 1968-69). *Awards, honors:* Woodrow Wilson fellow, 1958, 1962.

*WRITINGS:* (With Marvin Folson) *Deutsche Aufsatzhilfe,* Brigham Young University Press, 1967, revised edition, 1969; *The Idolatry of Poetic Genius in German Goethe Criticism,* Herbert Lang (Berne), 1970; (with Folson) *Deutsch-Wie Man's Sagt und Schreibt,* Holt, 1972; *Deutsche Kulturgeschichte,* Holt, 1974.

*WORK IN PROGRESS:* Articles on Goethe, Goethe criticism and contemporary German culture.

* * *

## KELLY, Edward H(anford)  1930-

*PERSONAL:* Born August 9, 1930, in Yonkers, N.Y.; son of Charles Edward (a journeyman) and Grace (Williams) Kelly; married Barbara Trizinsky, September 3, 1954; children: Kathleen, Carol Ann, Gregory, John. *Education:* State University of New York at Albany, A.B., 1962, M.A., 1963; University of Rochester, Ph.D., 1970. *Office:* Department of English, State University of New York College, Oneonta, N.Y. 13820.

*CAREER:* New York Central Railroad, New York, N.Y., freight sales department employee, 1948-59; State University of New York at Albany, instructor in English, 1963-65; Monroe Community College, Rochester, N.Y., assistant professor of English, 1967-68; State University of New York College at Oneonta, associate professor of English, 1968—. *Military service:* Enlisted Reserve Corps, 1950-56. *Member:* Modern Language Association of America, American Association of University Professors. *Awards, honors:* Lovenheim Award for a short story, 1962; State University of New York research award, summer, 1971; Clark Memorial Library postdoctoral fellowship, University of California, Los Angeles, summer, 1972.

*WRITINGS:* (Editor) *Moll Flanders* (critical edition), Norton, 1972. Contributor to scholarly journals.

*WORK IN PROGRESS: Petronius in England and America; Book of Recent Hoaxes.*

* * *

## KELLY, Philip John  1896-1972

May 25, 1896—November 4, 1972; American advertising man and author of books on sales promotion and aging. Obituaries: *New York Times,* November 8, 1972. (See index for *CA* sketch)

* * *

## KENNEDY, Kieran A.  1935-

*PERSONAL:* Born July 14, 1935, in Newbridge, County Kildare, Ireland; son of Patrick (a police officer) and Margaret (Callaghan) Kennedy; married Finola Flanagan (a university lecturer), June 21, 1966; children: Kieran Francis, Ruth Margaret, Michael Brendan, Susan Edel, Lucy. *Education:* University College, Dublin, Diploma in Public Administration, 1956, B.Comm. (first class honors), 1958, M.Econ.Sc. (first class honors), 1960; Nuffield College, Oxford, B.Phil., 1963; Harvard University, Ph.D., 1968. *Religion:* Roman Catholic. *Home:* 12 Richelieu Park, Sydney Parade Ave., Dublin 4, Ireland. *Office:* Economic and Social Research Institute, 4 Burlington Rd., Dublin 4, Ireland.

*CAREER:* Irish Civil Service, Dublin, Ireland, executive officer in Department of Industry and Commerce, 1954-58, administrative officer in Department of Finance, 1958-65, assistant principal officer, 1965-70; Economic and Social Research Institute, Dublin, senior research officer, 1968-71, director, 1971—. Economic consultant, Central Bank of Ireland, Dublin, 1970-71. Lecturer in economics, University College, Dublin, 1965—. Member, Irish Council of the European League for Economic Cooperation, 1971—, Committee for the Administration of the Ford Foundation Grant for Social Science Research in Ireland, 1973-75, and National Economic and Social Council, 1973—. *Member:* American Economic Association, Statistical and Social Inquiry Society of Ireland (member of council, 1973—), Royal Irish Academy (elected member).

*WRITINGS: Productivity and Industrial Growth: The Irish Experience,* Clarendon Press, 1971; (with B. R. Dowling) *Economic Growth in Ireland: The Experience since 1947,* Barnes & Noble, 1975; (with R. Bruton) *The Irish Economy,* Commission of the European Communities, 1975; *The ESRI Research Plan 1976-80 and Background Analysis,* Economic and Social Research Institute, 1976. Contributor to economic journals. Member of editorial board, *Economic and Social Review,* 1971—, and *Quarterly Economic Commentary* of the Economic and Social Research Institute, 1971—.

*WORK IN PROGRESS: Analysis of Employment Creation Measures in Ireland.*

\* \* \*

## KENNEDY, Leonard Anthony 1922-

*PERSONAL:* Born September 6, 1922, in Oldham, England; son of John (a textile operator) and Margaret (Robinson) Kennedy. *Education:* University of Toronto, B.A., 1944, M.A., 1947, Ph.D., 1958. *Religion:* Catholic. *Office:* Department of Philosophy, St. Thomas More College, University of Saskatchewan, Saskatoon, Saskatchewan, Canada S7N 0W6.

*CAREER:* University of Saskatchewan, Saskatoon, assistant professor of philosophy, 1948-52, 1955-60; University of Toronto, Toronto, Ontario, assistant professor of philosophy, 1960-63; University of Windsor, Windsor, Ontario, assistant professor, 1963-67, associate professor, 1967-72, professor of philosophy, 1972-77; University of Saskatchewan, St. Thomas More College, professor of philosophy and principal, 1977—. *Member:* Canadian Philosophical Association, American Catholic Philosophical Association.

*WRITINGS: The Universal Treatise of Nicholas of Autrecourt,* Marquette University Press, 1971; (editor) *Renaissance Philosophy: New Translations,* Mouton, 1972. Contributor of articles to *Modern Schoolman, New Scholasticism, Franciscan Studies, Medieval Studies, Culture, Vivarium, Archives d'Histoire Doctrinale et Litteraire du Moyen Age,* and *Archivo Teologico Granadino.*

\* \* \*

## KENNEDY, Robert E(mmet), Jr. 1937-

*PERSONAL:* Born October 7, 1937, in Chicago, Ill.; son of Robert Emmet (a newspaper editor) and Rosetta (Vinson) Kennedy; married Joyce Steele, June 25, 1960; children: Robert Emmet III. *Education:* University of Missouri—Columbia, B.A. (with distinction), 1959; Columbia University, M.A., 1961; University of California, Berkeley, Ph.D., 1967. *Home address:* P.O. Box 675, Rush City, Minn. 55069. *Office:* Department of Sociology, University of Minnesota, Minneapolis, Minn. 55455.

*CAREER:* University of Minnesota, Minneapolis, assistant professor, 1967-72, associate professor of sociology, 1972—, associate chairman, 1973-75, director of graduate studies, 1976—. *Military service:* U.S. Army, 1961-63; became first lieutenant. *Member:* American Sociological Association, Population Association of America, International Union for the Scientific Study of Population.

*WRITINGS: The Irish: Emigration, Marriage and Fertility,* University of California Press, 1973; (contributor) H. Y. Tien and F. D. Bean, editors, *Comparative Family and Fer-*

*tility Research,* E. J. Brill, 1974; (contributor) K.C.W. Kammeyer, editor, *Population Studies,* 2nd edition, Rand McNally, 1975; (contributor) A. G. Dworkin and R. J. Dworkin, editors, *The Minority Report,* Praeger, 1976. Contributor to *American Journal of Sociology* and *American Sociological Review.*

*WORK IN PROGRESS: Ethnicity,* with William Petersen, for University of California Press.

\* \* \*

## KENNY, W. Henry 1918-

*PERSONAL:* Born September 28, 1918, in New Albany, Ind.; son of Herbert Philip and Alice Marie (Terstegge) Kenny. *Education:* St. Joseph's College, Rensselaer, Ind., A.B., 1939; Loyola University, Chicago, Ill., Ph.L., 1946, S.T.L., 1952; St. Louis University, Ph.D., 1959. *Office:* Chicago Province of the Society of Jesus, 509 North Oak Park Ave., Oak Park, Ill. 60302.

*CAREER:* Loyola Academy, Chicago, Ill., instructor in physics, 1946-49; St. Louis University, St. Louis, Mo., instructor in philosophy, 1954-56; Xavier University, Cincinnati, Ohio, 1957-67, began as instructor, became professor of philosophy, chairman of department, 1962-67; Loyola University of Chicago, Chicago, associate professor of philosophy, 1967-69; University of Detroit, Detroit, Mich., associate professor of philosophy, 1969-70; Chicago Province of the Society of Jesus, provincial assistant for communities and apostolates, 1973—, Director of African Retreats, 1973-75; St. Paul's Major Seminary, Bussere (Wau), Sudan, professor of philosophy, 1975—. *Member:* Jesuit Philosophical Association (president, 1972-73), Catholic Philosophical Association, American Teilhard de Chardin Association.

*WRITINGS: A Path through Teilhard's Phenomenon,* Pflaum, 1970.

\* \* \*

## KENT, George O(tto) 1919-

*PERSONAL:* Born October 2, 1919, in Vienna, Austria; U.S. citizen; married Gertrude Eben (a librarian), July 16, 1946 (divorced, 1977); married Marthe Beckett, May, 1977. *Education:* Columbia University, B.S., 1948, M.A., 1949; Oxford University, D.Phil., 1958. *Home:* 9919 La Duke Dr., Kensington, Md. 20795. *Office:* Department of History, University of Maryland, College Park, Md. 20742.

*CAREER:* U.S. Air Force, Eglin Air Force Base, Fla., historian, 1951-53; U.S. Department of State, Washington, D.C., historian, 1953-66; Library of Congress, Washington, D.C., historian, 1966-70; University of Maryland, College Park, professor of history, 1970—. Instructor, Florida State University, 1951-52; occasional lecturer, George Washington University, 1960-68. Consultant, American Commission for the Study of War Documents, 1953-58. *Military service:* U.S. Army, 1942-46. *Member:* American Historical Association, International Club (Washington).

*WRITINGS:* (Editor) *A Catalog of Files and Microfilms of the German Foreign Ministry Archives: 1920-45,* four volumes, Stanford University Press, 1962-72; *Arnim and Bismarck,* Oxford University Press, 1968; *Bismarck and His Times,* Southern Illinois University Press, 1978. Editor, *News from the Center* (publication of Library of Congress), 1967-70.

\* \* \*

## KERPELMAN, Larry C(yril) 1939-

*PERSONAL:* Born January 27, 1939, in Baltimore, Md.;

son of Morris Eugene (a case worker) and Fannie (Kurland) Kerpelman; married Joan Paksarian (a social psychologist), August 12, 1967; children: one. *Education:* Johns Hopkins University, B.A., 1958; University of Rochester, Ph.D., 1963.

*CAREER:* Institute for Juvenile Research, Chicago, Ill., senior research associate in psychology, 1963-66; University of Illinois College of Medicine, Chicago, assistant professor of psychology, 1964-66; University of Massachusetts—Amherst, assistant professor of psychology, 1966-72; Editorial Consultant Service, Amherst, co-director, 1971—. Lecturer, Northwestern University, 1964-65. Consultant to United States Veterans Administration, 1966-72, Protestant Youth Center, 1967, Northampton Public Schools, 1970-72, and National Endowment for the Humanities, 1972-73. *Member:* American Association for Advancement of Science, American Association of University Professors, American Psychological Association, Eastern Psychological Association, New England Psychological Association, Psychonomic Society, Western Massachusetts Psychology Interest Group (member of steering committee, 1972), Amherst Environmental Concerns Committee. *Awards, honors:* American Psychological Association travel grant to U.S.S.R., 1966; U.S. Office of Education research grant, 1968-69; university faculty growth grant, University of Massachusetts, 1970.

*WRITINGS: Activists and Nonactivists: A Psychological Study of American College Students,* Behavioral Publications, 1972. Also author of *Student Activism and Ideology in Higher Education Institutions,* report for U.S. Department of Health, Education, and Welfare, 1970. Contributor of articles to *Journal of Counseling Psychology, Child Development, Journal of Experimental Psychology, Educational and Psychological Measurement, American Journal of Ophthalmology.* Editor of *Research Bulletin.*

*WORK IN PROGRESS: Manual for the Activity Scale;* research in political behavior and attitudes, consultation, and problems in scientific and technical communication.

*AVOCATIONAL INTERESTS:* Cabinetmaking, pottery, camping.†

\*      \*      \*

## KERR, Elizabeth M.   1905-

*PERSONAL:* Born January 25, 1905, in Sault Ste. Marie, Mich.; daughter of John Arthur (a bookkeeper) and Katherine (Hirth) Kerr. *Education:* University of Minnesota, B.A., 1926, M.A., 1927, Ph.D., 1941. *Politics:* Democrat. *Religion:* Congregational. *Home:* 4259 North Sercombe Rd., Milwaukee, Wis. 53216.

*CAREER:* Tabor College, Hillsboro, Kan., instructor in English, 1929-30; University of Minnesota, Minneapolis, instructor in English, 1930-37, 1938-43; College of St. Catherine, St. Paul, Minn., instructor in English, 1937-38; Rockford College, Rockford, Ill., assistant professor of English, 1943-45; University of Wisconsin—Milwaukee, instructor, 1945-55, associate professor, 1955-59, professor of English, 1959-70. *Member:* Modern Language Association of America, American Association of University Women, Dickens Society, Society for Study of Southern Literature, Phi Kappa Phi.

*WRITINGS: Bibliography of the Sequence Novel,* University of Minnesota Press, 1950, Octagon, 1972; (with Ralph Aderman) *Aspects of American English,* Harcourt, 1962, revised edition, 1971; *Yoknapatawpha,* Fordham University

Press, 1969, 2nd edition, 1976; *Faulkner's Gothic Domain,* Kennikat, 1978.

*WORK IN PROGRESS: The Evolution of Yoknapatawpha; William Faulkner's Yoknapatawpha: The Keystone in the Universe.*

*SIDELIGHTS:* Elizabeth Kerr told *CA:* "My doctoral dissertation on the sequence novel was the basis of my work on Faulkner. From the study of Faulkner I have become interested in modern American Gothic fiction and in Gothic elements in Dickens. I have spent considerable time in Faulkner's home town, Oxford, Miss. In travels in the British Isles, I have explored Joyce's Dublin and Dickens's London and other places associated with Dickens.

"The continued proliferation of sequence novels and the adaptation of both old and new sequence novels for television series confirm my conviction that the sequence novel is a significant development in the literature of the twentieth century.... My study of works in a series has accustomed me to take a broad view and to deal with interrelationships between separate works, and to make much use of comparing and contrasting authors and their works. I think in terms of configurations and spectrums rather than of single forms and colors."

\*      \*      \*

## KESSELMAN, Mark J.

*PERSONAL:* Son of Paul Kesselman; married Wendy Spiegel (a writer and singer). *Education:* Cornell University, B.A., 1959; University of Chicago, M.A., 1961, Ph.D., 1965. *Office:* Columbia University, 420 West 118th St., New York, N.Y. 10027.

*CAREER:* Columbia University, New York, N.Y., assistant professor, 1964-69, associate professor, 1969-73, professor of political science, 1973—. *Member:* Phi Beta Kappa. *Awards, honors:* Guggenheim fellowship, 1968-69.

*WRITINGS: The Ambiguous Consensus,* Knopf, 1967; *The Politics of Power,* Harcourt, 1975. Contributor to political science and sociology journals in America and abroad.

\*      \*      \*

## KIBLER, William W.   1942-

*PERSONAL:* Born January 22, 1942, in Rochester, N.Y.; son of Charles J. (a research chemist) and Ruth (Westcott) Kibler; married Nancy Schwan, June 29, 1968. *Education:* University of Notre Dame, A.B., 1963; University of North Carolina, M.A., 1966, Ph.D., 1968. *Home:* 2315 Village Circle, Austin, Tex. 78745. *Office:* 113 Sutton Hall, University of Texas, Austin, Tex. 78712.

*CAREER:* University of Texas at Austin, assistant professor, 1969-73, associate professor of French, 1973—. *Member:* International Arthurian Society, Societe Rencesvals, American Association of Teachers of French, Modern Language Association of America, South Central Modern Language Association. *Awards, honors:* Fulbright fellowship to France, 1963-64.

*WRITINGS:* (Translator of Surselvan texts) R. R. Bezzola, editor, *The Curly-Horned Cow: An Anthology of Swiss-Romance Poems and Stories,* P. Owen, 1971; (editor) *Eleanor of Aquitaine, Patron and Politician,* University of Texas Press, 1976. Contributor of articles to *Speculum* and other scholarly journals in North America and Europe.

*WORK IN PROGRESS:* Edition and facing translation of Chretien de Troyes' *Chevalier de la Charrete;* an edition of

*Lion de Bourges,* an Old French epic, completion expected in 1979.

*SIDELIGHTS:* William Kibler told *CA:* "My principal interest is in Old French literature and in making it more widely available and appreciated by the modern public, whence my interest in editions and translation. I am also interested in furthering the minor Romance tongues, Romansh and Catalan."

\* \* \*

## KIEPPER, Shirley Morgan 1933- (Shirley Morgan)

*PERSONAL:* Born December 11, 1933, in Dorset, England; came to United States in 1948; daughter of Leslie M. and Margaret (Andrews) Morgan; divorced; children: Stephanie, Christopher. *Education:* University of New Hampshire, B.A. (cum laude), 1955; State University of New York at Oneonta, M.S., 1965. *Politics:* Independent. *Religion:* Episcopalian. *Home and office:* Emma Willard Children's School, Troy, N.Y. 12181.

*CAREER:* Robert Freeman Advertising, London, England, fashion copywriter, 1955-56; George Dawson Advertising, Concord, N.H., copywriter, 1957-58; kindergarten teacher in Valatie, N.Y., 1962-66, and Guilderland, N.Y., 1966-71; Montessori teacher in Loudonville, N.Y., 1971-72; Emma Willard Children's School, Troy, N.Y., nursery teacher, co-director, 1972—. *Member:* National Association for the Education of Young Children, American Montessori Association, Society of Children's Book Writers.

*WRITINGS*—Under name Shirley Morgan: *Rain, Rain, Don't Go Away* (juvenile), Dutton, 1972. Contributor of articles to education journals and newspapers.

*WORK IN PROGRESS*—For children: *Miscellaneous Bear; Charlie's Big, Huge, Enormous Bicycle.*

*SIDELIGHTS:* Shirley Morgan Kiepper told *CA:* "As a teacher of young children, I read a great many children's books to my classes. Thus I have a first-hand sense of what children enjoy. Many of my ideas come from conversations with children, others from experiences with my own two children. I love to write. I find that I often don't know where my writing is going until I sit down at the typewriter and begin working!"

*BIOGRAPHICAL/CRITICAL SOURCES: Albany Times Union,* May 11, 1972; *Manchester Union Leader,* August 9, 1972.

\* \* \*

## KILEY, Frederick 1932-

*PERSONAL:* Born January 4, 1932, in Waltham, Mass.; son of Thomas Francis (a driver) and Jane M. (Greene) Kiley; married Audrey Jeane Cate, April 24, 1954; children: Michael, Catherine, Stephanie. *Education:* University of Massachusetts, B.A., 1953; Trinity University, San Antonio, Tex., M.A., 1959; Denver University, Ph.D., 1965; attended Vietnamese Language School, 1968. *Politics:* Independent. *Permanent home:* 40 West Woodmen Rd., Colorado Springs, Colo. 80919. *Office:* Office of the Secretary of Defense—History, 5C328, The Pentagon, Washington, D.C. 20301.

*CAREER:* U.S. Air Force, 1954—; present rank, colonel. Instructor at Air Force and Navy schools, 1954-62; U.S. Air Force Academy, instructor, 1962-63, assistant professor, 1963-65, associate professor, 1965-68, tenure associate pro-

fessor of English, 1969-74; Office of the Secretary of Defense, Washington, D.C., historian, 1974—. Adjunct instructor in English, University of Colorado, University of Denver, University of Maryland, 1962-69. Served as an advisor with Vietnamese Air Force, 1969. *Member:* Modern Language Association of America, National Council of Teachers of English, College English Association, Rocky Mountain Modern Language Association, Colorado Language Arts Society, South Atlantic Modern Language Association, Conference on College Composition and Communication, American Historical Association. *Awards, honors*—Military: Bronze Star Medal, Purple Heart, among others.

*WRITINGS:* (Editor with J. M. Shuttleworth) *Satire from Aesop to Buchwald,* Bobbs-Merrill, 1971; (author of critical introduction) William Shakespeare, *Macbeth,* Apollo, 1971; (editor with Walter McDonald) *A "Catch-22" Casebook,* Crowell, 1972; (author of critical introduction) William Shakespeare, *Titus Andronicus,* Apollo, 1973; (editor with Tony Dater) *Listen, the War: A Collection of Poetry about the Viet-Nam War,* U.S. Air Force Academy Association of Graduates, 1973. Also author of ·Department of Defense Style Sheet, and filmstrip "Joseph Heller's *Catch-22,*" 1975. Contributor to *Journal of English-Teaching Techniques, East-West Review, Critique,* and other journals. Contributing editor, *New Directions in English,* Harper, 1973-74.

*WORK IN PROGRESS:* A full-length history, *The American Prisoner of War Experience in Southeast Asia;* a critical study of Chaucer's *Canterbury Tales;* a study of Donne's Holy Sonnets.

*SIDELIGHTS:* Frederick Kiley wrote *CA:* "Since 1974, when fate and circumstance thrust me into writing history, I have found that the historian has much in common with the journalist. Gathering facts is no problem; sorting them to make judgments is. The moment one selects, one judges, and that selecting implies a responsibility to the truth which historian and journalist similarly face. Not so with one who writes fiction, for he creates his truth or, more often, creates his own perception of an old truth, and his responsibility is to that perception. When the maker of fiction, journalist, or historian deserts his responsibility, he becomes politician, preacher, pander, or polemicist. As he avoids responsibility, he slays truth and manacles art—he settles for the cheap shot. Art *is* long and life short."

\* \* \*

## KILSON, Marion 1936-

*PERSONAL:* Born May 8, 1936, in New Haven, Conn.; daughter of Joannes Gregorius (a physician) and Emily (Greene) Dusser de Barenne; married Martin Kilson (a professor), August 8, 1959; children: Jennifer, Peter, Hannah. *Education:* Attended Barnard College, 1954-56; Radcliffe College, B.A., 1958; Stanford University, M.A., 1959; Harvard University, Ph.D., 1967. *Home:* 4 Eliot Rd., Lexington, Mass. 02173. *Office:* 3 James St., Cambridge, Mass. 02138.

*CAREER:* University of Massachusetts—Boston, instructor, 1966-67, assistant professor of anthropology, 1967-68; Radcliffe Institute, Cambridge, Mass., scholar, 1968-70; Simmons College, Boston, Mass., associate professor of sociology, 1969-73; Newton College, Newton, Mass., professor of sociology and chairman of department, 1973-75; Radcliffe Institute, director of research, 1975-77, director of institute, 1977—. *Member:* American Anthropological Association (fellow), American Sociological Association (fellow), Phi Beta Kappa.

*WRITINGS: Kpele Lala: Ga Religious Songs and Symbols,* Harvard University Press, 1971; *African Urban Kinsmen,* St. Martin's, 1974; *Royal Antelope and Spider,* Press of the Langdon Associates, 1976. Contributor of articles to sociology and anthropology journals.

\*     \*     \*

### KIM, C(hong-) I(k) Eugene   1930-

*PERSONAL:* Born November 2, 1930, in Seoul, Korea; son of Hong-gi and Mibo (Chang) Kim; married, August 30, 1964; wife's name, Hiroko Helen; children: Margaret C., Adlai C. *Education:* Attended Seoul National University, 1948-49; King College, Bristol, Tenn., B.A., 1952; Vanderbilt University, M.A., 1954; Stanford University, Ph.D., 1959. *Home:* 1030 Berkshire Dr., Kalamazoo, Mich. 49007. *Office:* Department of Political Science, Western Michigan University, Kalamazoo, Mich. 49008.

*CAREER:* Communications Affiliates, Inc., Marplan Division, New York City, study director, 1959-60; Black Hills Teachers' College (now Black Hills State College), Spearfish, S.D., assistant professor of political science, 1960-61; Western Michigan University, Kalamazoo, assistant professor, 1961-66, associate professor, 1966-69, professor of political science, 1970—. Executive director, Korea Research & Publications, Inc., Kalamazoo, Mich., 1964—. Member of governing council, Inter-University Seminar on Armed Forces and Society, 1975—. *Member:* American Political Science Association, Association for Asian Studies (chairman of executive committee, Korean committee, 1969-70, 1974-75), Korean Political Science Association, Midwest Political Science Association. *Awards, honors:* American Philosophical Society research grants, 1965-67; Western Michigan University faculty research fellowship, 1966, 1973; Inter-University Seminar on Armed Forces and Society fellow, 1969; Social Science Research Council grant, 1973.

*WRITINGS:* (Editor) *A Pattern of Political Development: Korea,* Korea Research & Publications, 1964; (with Han-kyo Kim) *Korea and the Politics of Imperialism,* University of California Press, 1968; (editor with Ch'angboh Chee) *Aspects of Social Change in Korea,* Korea Research & Publications, 1969; (editor) *Korean Unification: Problems and Prospects,* Korea Research & Publications, 1973; (editor with Y. W. Kihl) *Party Politics and Elections in Korea,* Research Institute on Korean Affairs, 1976; (with L. Ziring) *An Introduction to Asian Politics,* Prentice-Hall, 1977. Contributor to political science journals, particularly in the Asian field.

*WORK IN PROGRESS: The Military in the Politics of South Korea,* completion expected in 1979.

\*     \*     \*

### KIM, Chin W.   1936-

*PERSONAL:* Born March 22, 1936, in Choongju, Korea; son of Hyonggi (a professor) and Kyongok (Lee) Kim; married Beverly Jean Kircher, June 14, 1964; children: Joseph Hosu, Daniel Hyonsu. *Education:* Yonsei University, Korea, B.A., 1958; Washington State University, B.A., 1962; University of California, Los Angeles, M.A., 1964, Ph.D., 1966. *Home:* 1603 Sheridan Rd., Champaign, Ill. 61820. *Office:* Department of Linguistics, University of Illinois, Urbana, Ill. 61801.

*CAREER:* University of Illinois at Urbana-Champaign,

1967—, began as assistant professor, currently professor of linguistics. *Military service:* Korean Air Force, 1958-61; became first lieutenant. *Member:* Korean Linguistic Society, Linguistic Society of America. *Awards, honors:* American Council of Learned Societies fellow, 1965-66; Massachusetts Institute of Technology postdoctoral fellow, 1966-67.

*WRITINGS:* (Editor with H. Stahlke) *Papers in African Linguistics,* Linguistic Research, 1971; *The Making of the Korean Language,* Center for Korean Studies, University of Hawaii, 1974.

*WORK IN PROGRESS:* Books on *Korean Phonology* and *Foundation of Phonetics.*

*SIDELIGHTS:* Chin Kim is familiar with French, German, Korean, Mongolian, Swahili, and Yoruba.

\*     \*     \*

### KIM, Kwan-Bong   1936-

*PERSONAL:* Born June 21, 1936, in Yosu, Korea; son of In-Che (a businessman) and Soon-Ye (Cho) Kim; married Yun-Sook Hong (an assistant professor of linguistics), February 7, 1959; children: Jung-Woo, Peter Jung-Suk. *Education:* University of Pennsylvania, B.S., 1959, M.A., 1960; University of London, Ph.D., 1969. *Home:* 409-62 Jung-nung-dong, Sungbuk-Ku, Seoul, Korea. *Office:* Hanyang University, 8-2 Haengdang-dong, Sungdong-Ku, Seoul, Korea.

*CAREER:* Hanyang University, Seoul, Korea, assistant professor, 1969-70, associate professor, 1970-72, professor of political science, 1972—. Member of Central Committee, Democratic Republican party of Korea, 1970-72. Consultant to Korean Ministry of Culture and Information, 1970-71. *Military service:* Army of Rupublic of Korea, 1961-63; became sergeant. *Member:* Korean Political Science Association, Korean Association of International Relations, Korean Institute of International Studies (research associate).

*WRITINGS: The Korea-Japan Treaty Crisis and the Instability of the Korean Political System,* Praeger, 1971.†

\*     \*     \*

### KINDRED, Wendy (Good)   1937-

*PERSONAL:* Born December 19, 1937, in Detroit, Mich.; daughter of Charles Roger and Ida (Berndt) Good; married Michael Kindred (a professor of law), December 27, 1960 (divorced, 1968); children: Audrey Lauren and Jessica Berit (twins). *Education:* Attended Western College for Women (now Western College), 1955-56 and University of Vienna, 1956-57; University of Chicago, B.F.A., 1959, M.F.A., 1963. *Home:* 9 Afred St., Fort Kent, Me. 04743. *Office:* University of Maine, Fort Kent, Me. 04743.

*CAREER:* High school teacher of art in Harvey, Ill., 1960-62; School of Fine Arts, Addis Ababa, Ethiopia, teacher of art history and graphics, 1965-69; University of Maine at Fort Kent, assistant professor of art, 1973—. Coordinator, Children's Community Workshop School, New York, N.Y., 1971. Painter and graphic artist; writer and illustrator of books for children. *Awards, honors:* Bread Loaf Writer's Conference, fellowship in children's literature, 1971; Fehsenfeld Award for Painting, Indiana Artists Exhibition at Indianapolis Museum of Art, 1973.

*WRITINGS—*Self-illustrated children's books: *Negatu in the Garden,* McGraw, 1971; *Ida's Idea,* McGraw, 1972; *Lucky Wilma,* Dial, 1973; *Hank and Fred, Fred and Hank,*

Lippincott, 1976. Art writer for *Voice of Ethiopia* (newspaper) and illustrator for *Addis Reporter* (magazine), 1969.

*WORK IN PROGRESS:* Adult short stories.

*SIDELIGHTS:* Wendy Kindred has lived out of the United States half her adult life, including five years in Ethiopia where her children were born, and in Greece, Austria, and France. She told *CA*, "I still have the feeling that I am just visiting the U.S. The foreignness I feel in my own country makes our national preoccupations and characteristics appear as startling to me as they would to a visiting Danakil. My own personal evolution seems comparatively obvious and simple, but is often in conflict with the culture and even the sub-cultures of this country. These contradictions have become the pivot of my present writing."†

\*　　\*　　\*

### KING, James T(errell) 1933-

*PERSONAL:* Born April 22, 1933, in Hastings, Neb.; son of James Mervin (a professor) and Evelyn (Cobb) King. *Education:* Hastings College, A.B., 1955; University of Nebraska, A.M., 1957, Ph.D., 1962. *Politics:* Democrat. *Religion:* Presbyterian. *Home:* 308 South Second St., River Falls, Wis. 54022. *Office:* Department of History, University of Wisconsin, River Falls, Wis. 54022.

*CAREER:* Theodore Roosevelt National Memorial Park, Medora, N.D., historian, 1959; University of Nebraska, Lincoln, instructor in history, 1960-61; University of Wisconsin—River Falls, assistant professor, 1962-64, associate professor, 1964-66, professor of history, 1966—, director of Area Research Center, 1964—. Visiting associate professor, University of Nebraska, 1965. *Member:* American Historical Association, Organization of American Historians, Western History Association (member of council, 1970-73), Colorado State Historical Society, Nebraska State Historical Society. *Awards, honors:* Henry E. Huntington grant, 1966; James L. Sellers Memorial Prize from Nebraska State Historical Society, 1970, for "A Better Way: General George Crook and the Ponca Indians."

*WRITINGS: War Eagle: A Life of General Eugene A. Carr,* University of Nebraska Press, 1964; (editor and author of introduction) C. T. Brady, *Indian Fights and Fighters,* University of Nebraska Press, 1971; (contributor) Lonnie J. White, editor, *Hostiles and Horse Soldiers,* Pruett, 1972; (editor and author of introduction) G. B. Grinnell, *Two Great Scouts and Their Pawnee Battallion,* University of Nebraska Press, 1973; (with Walker D. Wyman) *A Centennial History: The University of Wisconsin—River Falls 1874-1974,* University of Wisconsin—River Falls Press, 1975. Contributor to *Encyclopedia of the American West;* contributor to history journals.

*WORK IN PROGRESS: George Crook: A Biography;* research into the career of Cheyenne Chief Tall Bull, completion expected in 1979.

*AVOCATIONAL INTERESTS:* Photography, travel.

\*　　\*　　\*

### KING, Richard G. 1922-

*PERSONAL:* Born December 31, 1922, in Cambridge, Mass.; son of John Fitch and Hilda (Clark) King; married Mary Louise Mears, June 21, 1944; children: John, Richard. *Education:* Williams College, A.B., 1943; Harvard University, M.A., 1950, Ed.D., 1958. *Office:* School of Education, University of Alabama, Birmingham, Ala. 35294.

*CAREER:* High school teacher of English, Spanish, and mathematics in South Byfield, Mass., 1946-48; Harvard University, Cambridge, Mass., director, Office of Tests, 1952-54; College Entrance Examination Board, New York, N.Y., assistant director, 1954-56; Harvard University, associate director of admissions and financial aid, Harvard College, 1956-60, director of Office for Graduate Career Plans, 1960-66, lecturer in education and research associate of Center for the Study of Education and Development, 1963-70, coordinator of high school project in Nigeria, 1963-64, field director of Central American project in higher education, 1964-65; University of Alabama in Birmingham, professor of educational research, 1970—. Part-time instructor in German, Northeastern University, 1949-50. Executive secretary, Commission on Higher Education, New England Association of Colleges and Secondary Schools, 1957-64. Consultant to Ford Foundation, 1963—. *Military service:* U.S. Navy, Submarine Service, 1943-46. U.S. Naval Reserve, 1942-65; became captain.

*MEMBER:* American Statistical Association, Psychometric Society, National Council on Measurement in Education, American Personnel and Guidance Association, American Association for the Advancement of Science, Comparative Education Society, American Educational Studies Association, Alabama Education Association (president, 1973-74).

*WRITINGS:* (With Noel McGinn and Russell Davis) *The Technology of Instruction in Mexican Universities,* Education and World Affairs, 1968; (with McGinn, David Kline, and Alfonso Rangel Guerra) *The Provincial Universities of Mexico: An Analysis of Growth and Development,* Praeger, 1971. Contributor to education journals.†

\*　　\*　　\*

### KING, T(homas) J(ames) 1925-

*PERSONAL:* Born July 25, 1925, in Philadelphia, Pa.; son of Thomas James (a business executive) and Ellen (Clark) King; married Joan Harding, June 17, 1950; children: Hilary, Charles, Rufus, Emily, Mary. *Education:* Princeton University, A.B., 1948; Columbia University, M.A., 1958, Ph.D., 1963. *Home:* 80 Saw Mill Rd., New City, N.Y. 10956. *Office:* Department of English, City College of the City University of New York, New York, N.Y. 10031.

*CAREER:* Stage manager for several Broadway plays, business manager and director at summer theatres, 1948-56; Columbia University, New York City, instructor in English, 1961-65; Dartmouth College, Hanover, N.H., assistant professor, 1965-67; City College of the City University of New York, New York City, assistant professor, 1968-74, associate professor of English, 1975—. Visiting assistant professor of English, Columbia University, 1968. *Military service:* U.S. Army Air Forces, 1943-45; served as a navigator in Pacific theatre. *Member:* Modern Language Association of America, Society for Theatre Research, Renaissance Society of America, Princeton Club of New York.

*WRITINGS: Shakespeare Staging, 1599-1642,* Harvard University Press, 1971.

*WORK IN PROGRESS: The King's Men on Stage: Four Manuscript Playbooks from Shakespeare's Company, 1611-1631.*

\*　　\*　　\*

### KINGSBURY, Jack Dean 1934-

*PERSONAL:* Born November 19, 1934, in Los Angeles, Calif.; son of Carl Clinton (a contractor) and Amelia (Ewert)

Kingsbury; married Barbara Louise Schmidt (an executive secretary), October 15, 1961. *Education:* California Concordia College, A.A., 1954; Concordia Seminary, St. Louis, B.A., 1956, B.D., 1959; University of Tuebingen, additional study, 1959-60; University of Basel, Dr. Theol., 1967. *Politics:* Independent. *Office:* Department of New Testament, Union Theological Seminary in Virginia, 3401 Brook Rd., Richmond, Va. 23227.

*CAREER:* Lutheran clergyman, ordained, 1968; assisting pastor at Mount Olive Lutheran Church, Minneapolis, Minn.; Luther Theological Seminary, St. Paul, Minn., assistant professor, 1968-72, associate professor of New Testament theology, beginning 1972; currently associate professor of New Testament at Union Theological Seminary in Virginia, Richmond. *Member:* Society of Biblical Literature, American Academy of Religion, Studiorum Novi Testamenti Societas, Catholic Biblical Association.

*WRITINGS: The Parables of Jesus in Matthew 13: A Study in Redaction-Criticism,* John Knox, 1969; *Matthew: Structure, Christology, Kingdom,* Fortress, 1975; (with David Randolph) *Pentecost One,* Fortress, 1975; *Matthew,* edited by Gerhard Krodel, Fortress, 1977. Book review editor, *Dialog,* 1972—.

*WORK IN PROGRESS: The Theology of Matthew;* and a book dealing with the theology of Mark.

*SIDELIGHTS:* Jack Dean Kingsbury lived in Germany and Switzerland a total of seven years. In addition to speaking German fluently, he reads French, Latin, Greek, and Hebrew.

\*        \*        \*

## KINGSLEY, Michael J.    1918(?)-1972

1918(?)—July 17, 1972; American mystery writer and business executive. Obituaries: *New York Times,* July 19, 1972.

\*        \*        \*

## KINKADE, Richard P(aisley)    1939-

*PERSONAL:* Born January 7, 1939, in Los Angeles, Calif.; son of Joseph Marion (a physician) and Elizabeth (Paisley) Kinkade; married Raquel Liebes, June 2, 1962; children: Kathleen, Richard, Jr., Scott Philip. *Education:* Yale University, B.A., 1960, Ph.D., 1965. *Home:* 12 Brookside Lane, Mansfield, Conn. 06250. *Office:* Department of Romance and Classical Languages, University of Connecticut, Storrs, Conn. 06268.

*CAREER:* University of Arizona, Tucson, assistant professor, 1965-69, associate professor of Romance languages, 1969-71; Emory University, Atlanta, Ga., professor of Romance languages, 1971-77, chairperson of department, 1971-74, director of graduate studies in Spanish, 1971-75, chairperson of Committee of Foreign Languages and Classics, 1976-77; University of Connecticut, Storrs, professor of Romance languages and head of department of Romance and classical languages, 1977—. Visiting professor, department of Spanish and Portuguese, Yale University, 1977. Emory University, associate member of Graduate Institute of Liberal Arts, 1971-77, chairperson of John Gordon Stipe Lectureship Committee, 1972-74, member of University Committee on Educational Policy, 1972-75, member of University Library Policy Committee, 1973-76, member of governing committees of Hispanic and Latin American Studies Program and Medieval and Renaissance Program, 1975-77. Chairperson of various symposia at Kentucky Foreign Language Conference, 1973 and 1977, Tenth Conference of

Medieval Studies, Medieval Institute, 1975, and at International Courtly Literature Society, University of Georgia, 1977. Consultant, National Endowment for the Humanities, 1976-77.

*MEMBER:* International Association of Hispanists, Modern Language Association of America (member of Bibliography and Research Committee, 1972-75; chairperson of Spanish Section, 1974, 1977; member of executive committee, 1974-78; divisional delegate to national delegate assembly, 1976-78), American Association of Teachers of Spanish and Portuguese, Medieval Academy of America, Academy of American Research Historians on Medieval Spain, American Council on the Teaching of Foreign Languages, South Atlantic Modern Language Association (chairperson of Medieval Section, 1973; member of executive committee, 1973-76), Southeastern Medieval Association, Connecticut Council of Language Teachers. *Awards, honors:* Graduate College Research Support Committee grants, University of Arizona, 1966, 1967, and 1970; summer travel grants, Emory University, 1972, 1974; American Council of Learned Societies travel grant, 1974; National Endowment for the Humanities research grant, 1978-79.

*WRITINGS: Los "Lucidarios" espanoles* (critical edition), Editorial Gredos (Madrid), 1968; (contributor) Staubach, Guerrero, and Bonilla, *Espanol: Lengua Activa 2,* Ginn, 1970; (contributor) *Estudios Literarios de Hispanistas Norteamericanos Dedicados a Helmut Hatzfeld,* HISPAM (Barcelona), 1974; (contributor with J. A. Zahner) *Homenaj a Agapito Rey,* Indiana University Press, in press. Also contributor to *Actas del Primer Congreso Internacional sobre el Arcipreste de Hita,* 1973, and *Actas del Congreso Internacional de Hispanistas,* 1978. Contributor to professional journals. Member of editorial boards, *Kentucky Romance Quarterly, Vortice, Revista de Estudios Hispanicos,* and *Studia Humanitas.*

*WORK IN PROGRESS:* A critical edition of Gonzalo de Berceo's *Los milagros de nuestra Senora,* for Editorial Catedra; an edition of *La Vida de San Amaro: La leyenda de San Brandan en la Espana medieval,* with Dana A. Nelson; an edition of *La semeianca de mundo,* with James F. Burke, for University Press of Kentucky; a text and anthology of medieval Spanish literature with John E. Keller.

*SIDELIGHTS:* Richard Kinkade has traveled extensively in Mexico and Central America, and has lived in Spain.

\*        \*        \*

## KINNAMON, Keneth    1932-

*PERSONAL:* Born December 4, 1932, in Dallas, Tex.; son of David Ernest (an attorney) and Gladys Lucille (Page) Kinnamon; married Francisca Guillen; children: John, Louis, Theodore. *Education:* University of Texas, Main University (now University of Texas at Austin), B.A., 1953; Harvard University, A.M., 1954, Ph.D., 1966. *Residence:* Champaign, Ill. *Office:* University of Illinois, 100 English Building, Urbana, Ill. 61801.

*CAREER:* University of Illinois at Urbana-Champaign, instructor, 1965-66, assistant professor, 1966-70, associate professor, 1970-73, professor of English, 1973—, associate head of department, 1975-77, head of department, 1977—, associate of Center for Advanced Study. *Member:* Modern Language Association of America (committee member), American Studies Association, College English Association (committee member), College Language Association, Phi Beta Kappa. *Awards, honors:* National Endowment for the Humanities summer stipend, 1969.

*WRITINGS:* (Editor with Richard K. Barksdale) *Black Writers of America: A Comprehensive Anthology,* Macmillan, 1972; *The Emergence of Richard Wright: A Study in Literature and Society,* University of Illinois Press, 1972; (editor) *James Baldwin: A Collection of Critical Essays,* Prentice-Hall, 1974. Contributor to literature journals and national periodicals, including *Nation* and *American Literature.*

*WORK IN PROGRESS:* A comprehensive annotated guide to Richard Wright; research on John Brown and the American imagination and on W. E. B. Du Bois.

*SIDELIGHTS:* Keneth Kinnamon is competent in Spanish, French, German, Latin, and Old and Middle English. *Avocational interests:* Mexico and Mexican culture.

\* \* \*

## KINNEAR, Michael 1937-

*PERSONAL:* Born August 13, 1937, in Saskatoon, Saskatchewan, Canada; son of William S. and Agnes (Read) Kinnear; married Elizabeth Mary Preston, July 4, 1964; children: David, Andrew, Sara, Lucy. *Education:* University of Saskatchewan, B.A. (with distinction), 1960; University of Oregon, M.A., 1961; St. Antony's College, Oxford, D.Phil., 1965. *Religion:* Anglican. *Home:* 754 Cloutier Dr., Winnipeg, Manitoba, Canada R3V 1L2. *Office:* Department of History, University of Manitoba, Winnipeg, Manitoba, Canada.

*CAREER:* University of Manitoba, Winnipeg, associate professor of history, 1965—. Senior research associate, St. Antony's College, Oxford University, 1972-73. Chairman, Manitoba Ethnic Mosaic Congress. *Member:* American Historical Association, Canadian Historical Association, Canadian Association of University Teachers. *Awards, honors:* Woodrow Wilson fellow, 1960-61; Canada Council scholarship research grants, 1965-72; Canada Council leave fellowship, 1972-73.

*WRITINGS: The British Voter,* Cornell University Press, 1968; *The Fall of Lloyd George,* Macmillan, 1973. Also author of *The Campaign Guide (British Conservative Party)* and editor of *Gleanings and Memoranda.* Contributor of book reviews to *Winnipeg Free Press.*

*WORK IN PROGRESS:* A book on the British Liberal Party (1918-1945) and a book on American voting patterns.

*AVOCATIONAL INTERESTS:* Collecting postage stamps of political interest.

\* \* \*

## KINNEY, Arthur F(rederick) 1933-

*PERSONAL:* Born September 5, 1933, in Cortland, N.Y.; son of Arthur Frederick, Sr. and Gladys Elorsie (Mudge) Kinney. *Education:* Syracuse University, B.A. (magna cum laude), 1955; Columbia University, M.S., 1956; University of Michigan, Ph.D., 1963. *Residence:* 25 Hunter Hill Dr., Amherst, Mass. 01002. *Agent:* McIntosh & Otis, Inc., 475 Fifth Ave., New York, N.Y. 10017. *Office:* Department of English, University of Massachusetts, Amherst, Mass. 01002.

*CAREER:* Yale University, New Haven, Conn., instructor in English, 1963-66; University of Massachusetts—Amherst, assistant professor, 1966-68, associate professor, 1968-74, professor of English, 1974—, director, bachelor's degree program in individual studies. Affiliate associate professor of English, Clark University, Worcester, Mass.,

1971—. *Military service:* U.S. Army, chaplain, 1966-68. *Member:* Modern Language Association of America (chairman of Conference of Editors of Learned Journals, 1971-73), National Council of Teachers of English, College English Association, American Studies Association, Renaissance Society of America, Northeast Modern Language Association (executive secretary, 1971-73), New England College English Association (member of board of directors, 1971-73), Michigan Academy of Arts and Letters, Phi Beta Kappa, Phi Kappa Phi, Rho Delta Phi. *Awards, honors:* Jules M. and Avery Hopwood Major Award for Writing, 1961; Breadloaf scholar, 1962; Morse fellow, Yale, 1964, 1965, 1966; senior fellow, Huntington Library, 1972; senior fellow, Folger Shakespeare Library, 1973; Fulbright-Hays fellow, New College, Oxford, 1976; senior fellow, National Endowment for the Humanities, 1977.

*WRITINGS: Bear, Man, and God: Seven Approaches to Faulkner's "The Bear,"* Random House, 1964, revised edition, 1971; *Symposium,* Houghton, 1968; *On Seven Shakespearean Tragedies,* Scarab, 1968; *Symposium on Love,* Houghton, 1969; *On Seven Shakespearean Comedies,* Scarab, 1969; (author of critical and textual notes) H. R., *Mythomystes (1623),* Scolar Press, 1972; *Rogues, Vagabonds, and Sturdy Beggars,* Imprint Society, 1973; *Titled Elizabethans: A Directory of Elizabethan State and Church Officers and Knights with Peers of England, Scotland, and Ireland, 1558-1603,* Shoe String, 1973; *Elizabethan Backgrounds,* Shoe String, 1974; *Dorothy Parker,* Twayne, 1978. Also author of *Markets of Bawdrie: The Dramatic Criticism of Stephen Gosson,* 1975, and of *Faulkner's Narrative Poetics: Style as Vision,* 1978. Editor, *English Literary Renaissance;* supervisor of "English Literary Renaissance Monographs."

*WORK IN PROGRESS: Tudor and Stuart England,* for Houghton; *Nicholas Hilliard's "Arte of Limning"; Humanist Poetics.*

*SIDELIGHTS:* Arthur Kinney told *CA:* "My writing career began when I adapted the Book of Ruth for a Sunday school Easter play; I was eleven at the time, and the production of that play, to local acclaim anyway, insured my career as a writer. Later teen-age journalism gave way to fiction and that to criticism. Now I try to interpret the people, events, and literature of the Elizabethan period—Shakespeare and his age—to those who want some fresh critical interpretations which begin in the background of the age. Writing helps me to think, for writing, I find, not only clarifies one's thought, but fixes it, as if in photographer's acid, in semi-permanent form. Not only the ideas, then, but the expression become vital—since the way you say things defines what it is you are saying—and I find that writing, even more than research and judgement, leads me to new ideas I had not been fully conscious of before sitting down at the typewriter."

\* \* \*

## KIRK, Donald 1938-

*PERSONAL:* Born May 7, 1938, in New Brunswick, N.J.; son of Rudolf (an English professor) and Clara (Marburg) Kirk; married Susanne C. Smith (a book editor), May 31, 1965. *Education:* Princeton University, A.B., 1959; University of Chicago, M.A., 1965; Columbia University, certificate in international reporting program, 1965. *Politics:* Independent. *Religion:* Protestant. *Home:* 33 East End Ave., New York, N.Y. 10028.

*CAREER:* Reporter for newspapers in New York, N.Y.

and Chicago, Ill., 1960-64; correspondent from Asia, 1965-74; *Chicago Tribune,* Chicago, far eastern correspondent in Tokyo, Japan, 1971-74, New York and United Nations correspondent, 1975-76. *Military service:* U.S. Army, 1959. *Member:* Overseas Press Club of America, American Society of Journalists and Authors, Authors Guild, Foreign Correspondents Club of Japan, Foreign Correspondents' Club (Hong Kong). *Awards, honors:* Chicago Newspaper Guild award for feature writing, 1961; citations from Overseas Press Club for reports on Asia, 1967, 1971, and 1972; Edward Scott Beck award, 1972; Overseas Press Club award for best article on Asia, 1973; George Polk Memorial Award for foreign reporting, 1974; Murrow fellow, Council on Foreign Relations, 1974-75.

*WRITINGS:* (Contributor) Eugene Fodor, editor, *Fodor's Japan and East Asia* (annual travel guide), McKay, 1968-72; *Wider War: The Struggle for Cambodia, Thailand and Laos,* Praeger, 1971; (contributor) Fodor, editor, *Fodor's Southeast Asia* (annual travel guide), 1973-78; (contributor) Donnell and Joiner, editors, *Electoral Politics in Vietnam,* Heath, 1974; *Tell It to the Dead: Memories of a War,* Nelson-Hall, 1975; (contributor) Zasloff and Brown, editors, *Communism in Indo China: New Perspectives,* Heath, 1975. Contributor of articles on Asia to national periodicals, including *New York Times Magazine, New Leader,* and *True.*

*WORK IN PROGRESS:* Research on the Vietnam war and on U.S. foreign affairs.

\*    \*    \*

## KIRK, James A(lbert) 1929-

*PERSONAL:* Born January 20, 1929, in L'Anse, Mich.; son of Orman A. (a school administrator) and Gladys (Tremaine) Kirk; married Lois E. Grubaugh (a children's librarian), August 19, 1956; children: Robert A., Aletha K., Ann Louise. *Education:* Hillsdale College, A.B., 1951; Iliff School of Theology, Th.M., 1954, Th.D., 1959. *Home:* 1919 East Cornell, Denver, Colo. 80210. *Office:* Department of Religion, University of Denver, Denver, Colo. 80208.

*CAREER:* Ordained minister of Congregational Church, 1954; minister of First Congregational Church, Arriba, Colo., 1951-59; University of Denver, Denver, Colo., 1959—, currently professor of religious studies. Research fellow, Center for the Advanced Study of Philosophy, University of Madras, 1967-68; adjunct faculty member, Iliff School of Theology. Member of Committee on Church and Ministry, Rocky Mountain Conference, United Church of Christ. *Member:* American Academy of Religion (regional president, 1963-64, 1970-71; member of board of directors, 1970-72), Association for Asian Studies, American Association of University Professors. *Awards, honors:* Society for Religion in Higher Education fellowship in Asian religions, 1968-69; Doshisha University, Center for Study of Japanese Religions research fellowship, 1968.

*WRITINGS:* (Editor) *Stories of the Hindus: An Introduction through Texts and Interpretations,* Macmillan, 1972; (with Carl A. Raschke and Mark C. Taylor) *Religion and the Human Image,* Prentice-Hall, 1977. Contributor of articles and reviews to *Choice* and *Iliff Review.*

*WORK IN PROGRESS:* Research on philosophy in Asian religions.

*SIDELIGHTS:* James Kirk told *CA* that his first book "reflects an interest in approaching Asian religion as Asians do, through popular materials, simple lessons, and non-technical style."

## KIRKHAM, E. Bruce 1938-

*PERSONAL:* Born January 11, 1938, in White Plains, N.Y. *Education:* Lehigh University, B.A., 1961, M.A., 1963; University of North Carolina at Chapel Hill, Ph.D., 1968. *Office:* Department of English, Ball State University, Muncie, Ind. 47306.

*CAREER:* Ball State University, Muncie, Ind., assistant professor, 1968-74, associate professor of English, 1974—. Executive secretary, Friends of the Alexander M. Bracken Library, 1976—. *Member:* Modern Language Association of America, American Studies Association, Edgar Allan Poe Society, Society for the Study of Southern Literature, Society for the Study of Midwestern Literature, Manuscripts Society, Midwest Modern Language Association.

*WRITINGS:* (Editor) *Indices to American Literary Annuals and Gift Books: 1825-1865,* Research Publications, 1975; *The Building of Uncle Tom's Cabin,* University of Tennessee, 1977. Editor, *Forum* of Ball State University.

*WORK IN PROGRESS:* Editing *The Complete Letters of Harriet Beecher Stowe.*

\*    \*    \*

## KIRKWOOD, Kenneth P. 1899-1968

*PERSONAL:* Born April 14, 1899, in Brampton, Ontario, Canada; son of John Campbell (a journalist) and Lottie Valentine (Porter) Kirkwood; married Christine de Czerwinski (a librarian), December 3, 1960; stephchildren: Jacek S. Christians, Roman Christians. *Education:* University of Toronto, B.A., 1922; London School of Economics and Political Science, graduate study, 1922-23; Columbia University, M.A., 1927, fellow in public law, 1927-28 (completed requirements for Ph.D. except for dissertation).

*CAREER:* Instructor in history at International College, Smyrna, Turkey, 1923-25, Appleby College, Oakville, Ontario, 1925-26, and at Columbia University, New York City, Brooklyn Law School, Brooklyn, N.Y., and Teaching Division of the Long Island College Hospital (now State University of New York Downstate Medical Center), Brooklyn, 1926-27; joined Canadian Diplomatic Service, 1928, and held appointments in Washington, D.C., Tokyo, Japan, 1929-39, and The Hague, Netherlands, 1939-40; consul in Greenland, 1940-41; first secretary, counsellor, and charge d'affaires in Buenos Aires, Argentina, 1941-46; charge d'affaires with rank of minister, Warsaw, Poland, 1947-50; high commissioner to Pakistan, 1951-54; first Canadian ambassador to Egypt and first Canadian minister to Lebanon, 1954-56; high commissioner to New Zealand, 1956-57; special assignment with Historical Division, Department of External Affairs, Ottawa, Ontario, writing the history of the department, 1957-59. Adviser to Canadian Delegation at United Nations General Assembly, Paris, France, 1948; Canadian delegate to United Nations General Assembly, New York City, 1954. *Military service:* Royal Naval Air Service and Royal Air Force, flight lieutenant, 1917-19. Later served on reserve duty in Canada as officer in Royal Canadian Air Force and Queen's Own Rifles (Militia).

*MEMBER:* Royal Geographical Society (fellow), American Geographical Society (fellow), Canadian Geographical Society (fellow), United Nations Association (Canada); other Asian and Canadian societies. *Awards, honors:* George V Jubilee Medal; George VI Coronation Medal; Elizabeth II Coronation Medal.

*WRITINGS:* (With Arnold J. Toynbee) *Turkey,* Benn, 1926, Scribner, 1927, reprinted, Greenwood, 1976; *In Gar-*

*dens of Proserpine* (poems), privately printed (Tokyo), 1930; *Song in My Heart* (poems), privately printed (Tokyo), 1932; *Travel Dust* (poems), privately printed (Tokyo), 1932; *Lyrics and Sonnets,* privately printed (Tokyo), 1934; *Time's Tavern* (poems), privately printed (Tokyo), 1935; *Unfamiliar Lafacadio Hearn,* Hokuseido Press (Tokyo), 1936; *Abstractions* (thoughts and comments), privately printed (Tokyo), 1937; *Renaissance in Japan: A Cultural Survey of the Seventeenth Century,* privately printed (Tokyo), 1938, new edition, foreword by Toynbee, Tuttle, 1970; *Under Argentine Skies* (travel), Artes Graficas (Buenos Aires), 1945; *Excursions among Books,* Mitchell's Bookstore (Buenos Aires), 1945; *Maud: An Essay on Tennyson's Poem,* privately printed (Ottawa), 1951; *A Garden in Poland* (booklet of notes on Chopin), privately printed (Karachi), 1953; *Did Shakespeare Visit Denmark?,* privately printed (Karachi), 1953; *Ophelia of Elsinore,* privately printed (Ottawa), 1958; *The Immortal Memory of Robert Burns,* privately printed (Ottawa), 1958; *Preface to Cairo: A Survey of Pre-Cairo in History and Legend,* privately printed (Ottawa), 1958; *The Diplomat at Table: A Social and Anecdotal History through the Looking Glass,* Scarecrow, 1974. Writer of pamphlets on mountaineering in Japan and other topics. Unpublished and unprinted works include several volumes of literary manuscripts and his memoirs and poems.†

(Died September 26, 1968)

\* \* \*

## KIRSCH, Leonard Joel 1934-1977

*PERSONAL:* Born July 6, 1934; son of David and Anne (Joel) Kirsch; married wife, Elena A. (an editor), March 13, 1961; children: Lara Dela. *Education:* University of Pittsburgh, B.A., 1956; Harvard University, A.M., 1958, Ph.D., 1967; attended University of Moscow, 1960-61. *Home:* 28 Mason St., Lexington, Mass. *Office:* Department of Economics, University of Massachusetts, 100 Arlington St., Boston, Mass. 02116.

*CAREER:* Simmons College, Boston, Mass., instructor in economics, 1965-67; University of Massachusetts—Boston, associate professor of economics and chairperson of department, 1967-77. Associate of Russian Research Center, Harvard University, 1967-77. Consultant to United Auto Workers, 1967-77. *Member:* American Economic Association, Association for the Study of Soviet-type Economics.

*WRITINGS:* (Editor with Marshall I. Goldman) *Applied Principles of Economics,* McGraw, 1967; (editor) V. I. Raitsin, *Planning the Standard of Living According to Consumption Norms,* International Arts & Sciences Press, 1969; *Soviet Wages: Changes in Structure and Administration since 1956,* M.I.T. Press, 1972. Contributor to economics journals.†

(Died July 5, 1977)

\* \* \*

## KITZINGER, Sheila 1929-

*PERSONAL:* Born March 29, 1929, in Taunton, England; daughter of Alexander and Clare (Bond) Webster; married Uwe W. Kitzinger (dean of European School of Management Studies, Fontainebleau, France); children: Celia, Nell, Tess, Polly, Jenny. *Education:* Ruskin College, Oxford, Diploma in Social Anthropology (with distinction), 1951; St. Hugh's College, Oxford, B.Litt. (research degree in anthropology), 1956. *Politics:* Labour. *Religion:* Quaker. *Home:*

The Manor, Standlake, near Witney, Oxfordshire, England. *Agent:* Hilary Rubinstein, A. P. Watt & Son, 26/28 Bedford Row, London WC1R 4HL, England. *Office:* National Childbirth Trust, 9 Queensborough Ter., London W.2, England.

*CAREER:* University of Edinburgh, Edinburgh, Scotland, researcher on race relations in Britain, 1951-53; National Childbirth Trust, London, England, prenatal teacher and counselor, 1958—. Lecturer in England for Department of Education and Science, at universities and teacher training colleges, and to nurses and social workers; lecturer in United States for International Childbirth Education Association and American Society for Psychoprophylaxis in Obstetrics, 1972; has also lectured and conducted workshops in Canada, Sweden, and South Africa. *Member:* Institute of Health Educators. *Awards, honors:* Joost de Blank Award for research, 1972.

*WRITINGS: The Experience of Childbirth,* Gollancz, 1962, 4th edition, Taplinger, 1972; *An Approach to Antenatal Teaching* (booklet), National Childbirth Trust, 1968; *Giving Birth: The Parents' Emotions in Childbirth,* Gollancz, 1971, Taplinger, 1972; (editor) *Episiotomy: Physical and Emotional Aspects,* National Childbirth Trust, 1972; *Counselling for Childbirth,* Bailliere Tindall, 1977; *Journey through Birth* (cassette tapes), International Childbirth Education Association, 1977; *Women as Mothers,* Fontana Books, 1978; (editor with John Davis) *The Place of Birth,* Oxford University Press, 1978.

Contributor: Alioune Diop, editor, *Les Etudiants Noirs parlent,* Presence Africaine, 1952; M. L. Kellmer Pringle, editor, *Caring for Children,* Longmans, Green, 1969, Humanities, 1970; Michael Horowitz, editor, *Peoples and Cultures of the Caribbean,* Natural History Press, 1971; Margaret Laing, editor, *Women on Women,* Sidgwick & Jackson, 1972. Contributor of articles and reviews to *New Society, Vogue, Nursing Mirror, Journal for the Scientific Study of Religion,* and other periodicals.

*WORK IN PROGRESS: The Good Birth Guide;* a book on breastfeeding for Penguin; a book on birth at home for Oxford University Press.

*SIDELIGHTS:* Sheila Kitzinger writes: ''Birth, like death, is an experience in which we all share. It can either be a disruption in the flow of human existence, a fragment which has little or nothing to do with loving and being loved or with the passionate longing which created the baby, or it can be lived with beauty and dignity, and labour itself be a celebration of joy. Birth is a part of a woman's very wide psychosexual experiences and is intimately concerned with her feelings about and sense of her own body, her relations with others, her role as a woman, and the meaning of her personal identity. I feel that in choosing to write about childbirth I am at the hub of life.''

*AVOCATIONAL INTERESTS:* Painting.

\* \* \*

## KLASS, Sheila Solomon 1927-

*PERSONAL:* Born November 6, 1927, in New York, N.Y.; daughter of Abraham Louis (a presser) and Virginia (Glatter) Solomon; married Morton Klass (a professor of anthropology), May 2, 1953; children: Perri Elizabeth, David Arnold, Judith Alexandra. *Education:* Brooklyn College (now Brooklyn College of the City University of New York), B.A., 1949; University of Iowa, M.A., 1951, M.F.A., 1953. *Religion:* Jewish. *Home:* 330 Sylvan Ave.,

Leonia, N.J. 07605. *Agent:* Aaron M. Priest, 150 East 35th St., New York, N.Y. 10016. *Office:* Department of English, Manhattan Community College of the City University of New York, 1633 Broadway, New York, N.Y. 10019.

*CAREER:* Worked as an aide in a psychopathic hospital in Iowa City, Iowa, 1949-51; English teacher in junior high school in New York City, 1951-57; Manhattan Community College of the City University of New York, New York City, 1965—, began as assistant professor, currently associate professor of English. Guest at Yaddo colony, 1974. *Member:* International P.E.N. *Awards, honors:* Bicentennial Prize from Leonia Drama Guild, 1976, for one-act play, "Otherwise It Only Makes One Hundred Ninety-Nine."

*WRITINGS: Come Back on Monday,* Abelard, 1960; *Everyone in This House Makes Babies,* Doubleday, 1964; *Bahadur Means Hero,* Gambit, 1969. Contributor of short stories and humorous articles to *Hadassah, Manhattan Mind, New York Times,* and other publications.

*WORK IN PROGRESS:* A collection of humorous essays on suburban living, *The Bedroom of Columbia;* a long play set in India, "The Accounting."

*SIDELIGHTS:* Sheila Solomon Klass told *CA:* "I've been a writer since adolescence and I know it's a unique and chronic madness. I have my first rejection slip from the *New Yorker,* dated October 11, 1948. It reads 'I'm afraid the vote went against the Solomon pieces. We found them a bit too fragmentary, sorry to say.' As a young writer, I was greatly encouraged by this: to be too fragmentary for the *New Yorker* surely meant talent. This is the twenty-ninth year of uninterrupted rejection slips from them to me. Perhaps there is some commemorative token they award after thirty years of such a stable, harmonious relationship. I hope so.

"I write because writing is supreme pleasure. Creating a story on paper is a peculiar joy unlike any other. Just the writing itself is the first reward. Later, if a relative or a friend reads the work and admires it, the delight is heightened. Then, if an editor likes it well enough to print it, the delight bursts all boundaries. And if the book is printed and makes money, that is sheer ecstacy. But it is irrelevant to the writing itself. This pleasure in the act of writing makes teaching writing a delightful job. What I'm doing is introducing students to the highest high in the whole world—the high that is achieved by creating new and wonderful works out of their own heads.

"My life and what happens around me, what I hear about and read about—these are the sources that initiate the act of writing. But, almost immediately, imagination takes over and the story acquires its own energy and direction. What *really* happened is not pertinent. It's forgotten. Fiction is not autobiography. It is experience transmuted by the imagination in inexplicable ways. It has its own truth and its own life. I rarely remember after finishing a story or a book what actually happened and what I made up. An idea simply nags and nags—like a child requiring attention—and it doesn't go away until the writing. Then, and only then, there is peace.

"I hope my writing entertains, for while it may instruct the mind, or purge the emotions, or ennoble the spirit, if it doesn't offer diversion I feel it is unsuccessful. I have an attic room in which I write. Silence and seclusion are all that I require, rare treasures not easily come by in a busy household. Early morning is the best time of day for me, very early before the others are up. I've concluded that the longest distance on earth for the writer who is also a mother and a wife is the distance from the kitchen to the typewriter. I'm becoming quite adept as a long-distance runner."

## KLEIN, A(braham) M(oses)   1909-1972

February 14, 1909—August 21, 1972; Canadian lawyer, poet, and Talmudic and Joycean scholar. Obituaries: *Detroit News,* August 22, 1972; *New York Times,* August 23, 1972.

\* \* \*

## KLEIN, Arnold William   1945-

*PERSONAL:* Born February 27, 1945, in Mt. Clemens, Mich. *Education:* University of Pennsylvania, B.A. (cum laude), 1967, M.D., 1971. *Politics:* Democrat. *Religion:* Jewish. *Home:* 435 North Roxbury Dr., Beverly Hills, Calif. 90210. *Office:* Medical Center, University of California, Los Angeles, Calif. 90024.

*CAREER:* Clinical clerk at Veterans Hospital and Cedars of Lebanon Hospital, Miami, Fla., summer, 1968; Cedars-Sinai Medical Center, Los Angeles, Calif., intern in medicine, 1971-72; University of Pennsylvania, School of Medicine, Philadelphia, resident in dermatology, 1972-73; University of California, Los Angeles, Medical Center, resident in dermatology, 1973-75, chief dermatologic resident, 1975—, assistant professor of dermatology. Physician in private practice; certified by American Board of Dermatology in 1977. Attending physician, Cedars-Sinai Medical Center, Century Hospital, Midway Hospital, and Los Angeles New Hospital; president of psoriasis treatment centers in Los Angeles, Encino, and Orange County; founder, Switchboard Center (a program for young adults with problems); lecturer on drug abuse in Florida, Maine, and Pennsylvania. *Member:* American Academy of Dermatology, American Venereal Disease Association, Society for Investigative Dermatology, Pepper Medical Society, Los Angeles Medical Society, Phi Beta Kappa, Sigma Tau Sigma, Alpha Epsilon Delta. *Awards, honors:* Honey scholarship, 1967; Measey scholarship, 1967; Philadelphia Foundation fellowship, 1970; Public Health Service postdoctoral grant, 1970.

*WRITINGS: Drug-Trip Abroad: American Drug Refugees in Amsterdam and London,* University of Pennsylvania Press, 1972. Contributor of articles on drug abuse to medical journals and to *U.S. News and World Report.*

*WORK IN PROGRESS:* Assisting in the writing of a book on tactile communication.

*SIDELIGHTS:* Arnold William Klein has worked with members of the World Health Organization Expert Committee on Drug Dependence, while studying drug addiction, especially of Americans abroad, in hospitals in London and Amsterdam.

\* \* \*

## KLEIN, Mina C(ooper)

*PERSONAL:* Born in England; married H. Arthur Klein (an author). *Education:* Attended schools in Canada, California, New York, and University of Berlin. *Home address:* Box 3, Malibu, Calif. 90265.

*CAREER:* Author and editor. *Member:* Authors League of America.

*WRITINGS*—All with husband, H. Arthur Klein: (Translator with others) *Hypocritical Helena, Plus a Plenty of Other Pleasures* (verses based on picture-stories of German artist-satirist, Wilhelm Busch), Dover, 1962; (translator with others) *Max and Moritz, with Many More Mischief-Makers* (verses from Wilhelm Busch), Dover, 1962; (editor) *Surf's Up!: An Anthology of Surfing,* Bobbs-Merrill, 1966; *Peter Bruegel the Elder, Artist of Abundance,* Macmillan, 1968; *Great Structures of the World,* World Publishing, 1968.

*Temple beyond Time: The Story of the Site of Solomon's Temple,* Van Nostrand, 1970; *Israel, Land of the Jews: A Survey of 43 Centuries,* Bobbs-Merrill, 1972; *Kaethe Kollwitz: Life in Art,* Holt, 1972; *The Kremlin, Citadel of History,* Macmillan, 1973; (editor and translator) B. Traven, *The Kidnapped Saint and Other Stories,* Lawrence Hill, 1975; *Hitler's Hang-ups: An Adventure in Insight,* Dutton, 1976.

*AVOCATIONAL INTERESTS:* Travel, music, reading.

\* \* \*

## KLEINBAUER, W(alter) Eugene 1937-

*PERSONAL:* Born June 15, 1937, in Los Angeles, Calif.; married Julianne Van Horn; children: Christopher, Mark. *Education:* University of California, Berkeley, B.A., 1959; Princeton University, Ph.D., 1967. *Office:* Department of Fine Arts, Indiana University, Bloomington, Ind. 47401.

*CAREER:* University of California, Los Angeles, assistant professor, 1965-72, associate professor of art history, 1972; Indiana University at Bloomington, associate professor of art history and chairman of department of fine arts, 1973-76, professor of fine arts, 1977—. Member of board of directors, International Center of Medieval Art, 1970-73, 1974-76.

*WRITINGS: Modern Perspectives in Western Art History: An Anthology of Twentieth-Century Writings on the Visual Arts,* Holt, 1971; (editor) Ernst Kitzinger, *The Art of Byzantium and the Medieval West: Selected Studies,* Indiana University Press, 1976. Contributor of over twenty articles to scholarly journals.

*WORK IN PROGRESS: The Aisled Tetraconch,* for Princeton University Press.

\* \* \*

## KLEMER, Richard Hudson 1918-1972

February 6, 1918—September 11, 1972; American educator, psychologist, and author of books on marriage and sexuality. Obituaries: *New York Times,* September 14, 1972. (See index for *CA* sketch)

\* \* \*

## KLEMPNER, John 1898(?)-1972

1898(?)—July 30, 1972; American novelist and film writer. Obituaries: *New York Times,* August 2, 1972.

\* \* \*

## KNAPP, Joseph G(rant) 1900-

*PERSONAL:* Born November 22, 1900, in Loveland, Colo.; son of Mason E. (a teacher and agriculturalist) and Florence Amy (White) Knapp; married Carol Maud West, February 13, 1929; children: Sheila (Mrs. Daniel P. Woodard), John Laurence. *Education:* Attended Colorado A&M College (now Colorado State University), 1918-19, and University of Illinois, 1920-21; University of Nebraska, B.Sc., 1922, M.A., 1923; Stanford University, Ph.D., 1929. *Home:* 7119 Fairfax Rd., Bethesda, Md. 20014.

*CAREER:* Stanford University, Stanford, Calif., fellow of Food Research Institute, 1924-25; Brookings Institution, Washington, D.C., member of staff, Institute of Economics, 1926-29, 1944-46; North Carolina College of Agriculture and Mechanic Arts (now North Carolina State University at Raleigh), associate professor in charge of agricultural marketing and associate agricultural economist, 1929-34; Farm Credit Administration, Washington, D.C., senior agricul-

tural economist, 1934-36, principal agricultural economist, 1936-48, associate and then acting chief, Cooperative Research and Service Division, 1948-53; U.S. Department of Agriculture, Farmer Cooperative Service, administrator, 1954-66. Consultant on American cooperative enterprise problems; as independent consultant has made studies of cooperative enterprise in Ireland, England, and Brazil.

*MEMBER:* American Economic Association, American Farm Economics Association, American Marketing Association (president of Washington chapter, 1956-57), Phi Kappa Psi, Alpha Kappa Psi, Sigma Nu, Cosmos Club (Washington, D.C.). *Awards, honors:* Pioneer Award of American Institute of Cooperation, 1964, for outstanding service to American agriculture and farmer cooperatives; D.Sc. from University of Nebraska and North Carolina State University at Raleigh, both 1967; Ellerbe Award from Cooperative Foundation, 1975, for "devoted dedication to cooperatives as an author, historian, teacher, philosopher, and public servant."

*WRITINGS:* (With Edwin Griswold Nourse) *The Cooperative Marketing of Livestock,* Brookings Institution, 1931; *The Hard Winter Wheat Pools: An Experiment in Agricultural Marketing Integration,* University of Chicago Press, 1933; *E. A. Stokdyk: Architect of Cooperation,* American Institute of Cooperation, 1953; *Seeds That Grew: A History of the Cooperative Grange League Federation Exchange,* Anderson House, 1960; *Farmers in Business,* American Institute of Cooperation, 1963; *An Appraisement of Agricultural Cooperation in Ireland,* Irish Department of Agriculture, 1964; *An Analysis of Agricultural Cooperation in England,* Agricultural Central Cooperative Association (London), 1965; (with others) *Great American Cooperators,* American Institute of Cooperation, 1967; *The Glen Haven Story* (family memoirs), privately printed, 1967; *The Rise of American Cooperative Enterprise: 1620-1920,* Interstate, 1969; *The Advance of American Cooperative Enterprise,* Interstate, 1973. Writer of reports and articles relating to agricultural marketing and agricultural cooperation.

*WORK IN PROGRESS:* A final volume of his history of cooperative enterprise covering the era from 1946 to the present and a biography of Edwin G. Nourse, a cooperative theorist and first chairman of the Council of Economic Advisers.

*SIDELIGHTS:* Joseph Knapp told *CA,* "Looking back on my long career, I feel that my writings have contributed to the sound development of cooperative enterprise as an important part of our American competitive free enterprise system."

*AVOCATIONAL INTERESTS:* Hiking, reading, traveling.

\* \* \*

## KNIGHT, Ione Kemp 1922-

*PERSONAL:* Born December 9, 1922, in Greensboro, N.C.; daughter of Thomas Benton (a merchant) and Ione (Kemp) Knight. *Education:* Meredith College, A.B., 1943; University of Pennsylvania, A.M., 1944; University of North Carolina at Chapel Hill, Ph.D., 1954. *Religion:* Baptist. *Address:* P.O. Box 7, Madison, N.C. 27025. *Office:* Department of English, Meredith College, Raleigh, N.C. 27611.

*CAREER:* Shorter College, Rome, Ga., professor of English and head of department, 1953-56; Meredith College, Raleigh, N.C., associate professor, 1956-73, professor of

English, 1973—. *Member:* Modern Language Association of America, College English Association, American Association of University Women, South Atlantic Modern Language Association.

*WRITINGS: Wimbledon's Sermon,* Duquesne University Press, 1966.

*WORK IN PROGRESS:* A biography of Elizabeth Elstob.

\*     \*     \*

### KNIGHT, W(illiam) Nicholas 1939-

*PERSONAL:* Born April 18, 1939, in Mount Vernon, N.Y.; son of Nicholas William (a banker) and Elinor (Cochrane) Knight; married Susan Harrison, September 2, 1961; children: Pauline Atlee, Nathaniel Harrison, Jessica Mudge, Portia Drake. *Education:* Amherst College, B.A. (cum laude), 1961; University of California, Berkeley, M.A., 1963; Indiana University, Ph.D., 1968. *Religion:* Christian Scientist. *Home:* 1313 Whitney Lane, Rolla, Mo. 65401. *Agent:* Arthur Pine Associates, Inc., 1780 Broadway, New York, N.Y. 10019. *Office:* Department of Humanities, University of Missouri, Rolla, Mo. 65401.

*CAREER:* Wesleyan University, Middletown, Conn., assistant professor of English and Shakespeare, 1966-75; University of Missouri—Rolla, professor of English and chairman of humanities department, 1975—. Renaissance consultant for *Choice. Member:* Modern Language Association of America, American Association of University Professors, National Council of Teachers of English, Renaissance Society. *Awards, honors:* Ford Foundation fellow, 1970-71; award for excellence in teaching from American Departments of English, 1972-73.

*WRITINGS:* "The Death of J.K." (produced Off-Off Broadway at Cubiculo Theatre, December, 1971), published in *London Review,* winter, 1969-70; *Shakespeare's Hidden Life: Shakespeare at the Law, 1585-1595,* Mason & Lipscomb, 1973. Contributor of articles to periodicals, including *Review of English Studies, Erasmus Review, Comparative Drama,* and *Shakespeare Newsletter.*

*WORK IN PROGRESS: Julius Caesar and Shakespearean Revenge Tragedy,* for University of Missouri Press; *Equity in Law and Drama,* for Princeton University Press; *Kennedy and the Assassination Archetype.*

*BIOGRAPHICAL/CRITICAL SOURCES: Paris Review,* winter, 1968-1969; *New York Times,* August 19, 1971; *Folger Library Newsletter,* December, 1971.

\*     \*     \*

### KNIGHT, Walker L(eigh) 1924-

*PERSONAL:* Born February 6, 1924, in Henderson, Ky.; son of Cooksey Bennett (a journalist) and Rowena (Henderson) Knight; married Iva Nell Moseley, November 10, 1943; children: Walker, Jr., Kenneth Wayne, Nelda Denise, Emily Jill. *Education:* Baylor University, B.A., 1949. *Politics:* Independent. *Religion:* Baptist. *Home:* 1008 Forrest Blvd., Decatur, Ga. 30030. *Office:* 1350 Spring St. N.W., Atlanta, Ga. 30309.

*CAREER:* Baptist Standard Publishing, Dallas, Tex., associate editor, 1950-59; bureau chief, Baptist Press, 1959; Home Mission Board, Southern Baptist Convention, Atlanta, Ga., editorial secretary, 1959—. *Military service:* U.S. Army Air Forces, 1943-46. *Member:* Baptist Public Relations, Baptist Press Association, Associated Church Press, Common Cause.

*WRITINGS: Panama, Land Between,* Home Mission Board, Southern Baptist Convention, 1965; *Struggle for Integrity,* Word Books, 1970; *See How Love Works,* Broadman, 1971; (compiler) *Jesus People Come Alive,* Tyndale, 1971; (compiler) *Weird World of the Occult,* Tyndale, 1972; *Seven Beginnings,* Home Mission Board, Southern Baptist Convention, 1976. Editor of *Home Missions Magazine.*

*WORK IN PROGRESS:* A book on civilian and military chaplaincy, for Home Mission Board, Southern Baptist Convention.

\*     \*     \*

### KNIGHTS, Peter R(oger) 1938-

*PERSONAL:* Born May 8, 1938, in Melrose, Mass.; son of George Brownbill and Ruth (Rother) Knights. *Education:* Attended Massachusetts Institute of Technology, 1955-57; Johns Hopkins University, B.A., 1959; graduate study at Universitaet zu Koeln, 1959-60, Westfaelische Wilhelms Universitaet, 1960, and Cornell University, 1960-62; University of Wisconsin, M.A., 1965, Ph.D., 1969. *Politics:* "Usually Democratic." *Religion:* "Deist." *Home:* 205 Hilda Ave., Apt. 1710, Willowdale, Ontario, Canada M2M 4B1. *Office:* Department of History, York University, Downsview, Ontario, Canada M3J 1P3.

*CAREER: Burlington Standard-Press,* Burlington, Wis., centennial supplements editor and general assignments reporter, summer, 1964; University of Pittsburgh, Pittsburgh, Pa., Andrew Mellon Postdoctoral Fellow in History, 1968-69; University of Illinois at Urbana-Champaign, assistant professor of journalism, 1969-71; York University, Downsview, Ontario, associate professor of history, 1971—. *Member:* Organization of American Historians, Economic History Association, Social Science History Association, Society for the History of Technology. *Awards, honors:* Fulbright scholar, 1959-60; National Endowment for the Humanities research grant, 1972-73; Canada Council leave fellowship, 1976-77.

*WRITINGS: The Press Association War of 1866-1867,* Association for Education in Journalism, 1967; (contributor) Stephan Thernstrom and Richard Sennett, editors, *Nineteenth-Century Cities,* Yale University Press, 1969; *The Plain People of Boston: A Study in City Growth,* Oxford University Press, 1971; (contributor) Tamara K. Hareven, editor, *Anonymous Americans,* Prentice-Hall, 1971. Contributor of articles to journalism and history journals. Member of editorial board, *Historical Methods Newsletter.*

*WORK IN PROGRESS:* Research on internal migration to and through Boston, 1850-1880, completion expected in 1980; research on social and economic backgrounds of the political leaders of Boston, 1830-1930.

\*     \*     \*

### KNIPE, Humphry 1941-

*PERSONAL:* Born September, 1941, in Kimberley, South Africa; son of Victor and Gertrude Knipe. *Education:* Attended Selborne College, East London, South Africa; Rhodes University, South Africa, B.A., 1962, U.E.D., 1964. *Address:* c/o Souvenir Press Ltd., 43 Great Russell St., London WC1B 3A, England.

*CAREER: Pretoria News,* Pretoria, South Africa, reporter, 1962-63; teacher in South African schools, 1965-66; worked as a reporter on a London newspaper, 1967-68; full-time writer, 1969—.

*WRITINGS:* (With George Maclay) *The Dominant Man: The Pecking Order in Human Society,* Delacorte, 1972.

*WORK IN PROGRESS:* Researching and writing another book in the field of dominance and "peak experiences."†

\* \* \*

## KOBLER, (Mary) Turner S. 1930-

*PERSONAL:* Born September 1, 1930, in Shreveport, La.; daughter of H. Frank (a fieldman for U.S. Department of Agriculture) and Jennie (Turner) Spenser; married J. F. Kobler (an associate professor at North Texas State University), February 8, 1952; children: Laura, Linda. *Education:* Louisiana State University, B.A., 1951; University of Houston, M.A., 1961; University of Texas, Ph.D., 1968. *Home:* 2206 Picadilly Lane, Denton, Tex. 76201. *Office:* Department of English, Texas Woman's University, Denton, Tex. 76204.

*CAREER: Baton Rouge Morning Advocate,* Baton Rouge, La., reporter, 1951-52; Department of Defense, Washington, D.C., research analyst, 1952-53; University of Texas at Arlington, instructor in English, 1964-68; Texas Woman's University, Denton, assistant professor, 1968-70, associate professor of English, 1970—.

*MEMBER:* College English Association, National Council of Teachers of English, American Association of University Professors, American Association of University Women, South Central Modern Language Association, Conference of College Teachers of English, Theta Sigma Phi (honorary).

*WRITINGS: Alice Marriott,* Steck-Vaughn, 1969. Contributor to journals.

*WORK IN PROGRESS:* A critical study of Rebecca West.†

\* \* \*

## KOCHMAN, Thomas 1936-

*PERSONAL:* Born May 19, 1936, in Berlin, Germany; son of Max (a certified public accountant) and Ellen (Samson) Kochman; married Alexandra Diachenko, January 28, 1961; children: Adrienne, Switlana. *Education:* College of the City of New York (now City College of the City University of New York), B.A., 1958; New York University, M.A., 1962, Ph.D., 1966. *Religion:* Jewish. *Home:* 5453 North Virginia Ave., Chicago, Ill. 60625. *Office:* Department of Speech and Theater, University of Illinois at Chicago Circle, Chicago, Ill. 60680.

*CAREER:* English teacher in high school in New York, N.Y., 1961-66; Northeastern Illinois State College (now Northeastern Illinois University), Chicago, assistant professor, 1966-69, associate professor of linguistics, 1969-70; University of Illinois at Chicago Circle, Chicago, associate professor, 1970-74, professor of communication, 1974—. *Military service:* U.S. Army Reserve, active duty, 1959-60. *Member:* Modern Language Association of America, American Anthropological Association, Linguistic Society of America, Speech Communication Association, Society for Applied Anthropology, American Association of University Professors, Gompers Park Chess Club.

*WRITINGS:* (Editor) *"Rappin' and "Stylin Out": Communication in Urban Black America,* University of Illinois Press, 1972. Contributor of articles to professional journals.

*WORK IN PROGRESS: Cognitive and Communicative Patterns: Mainstream and Afro-American.*

*SIDELIGHTS:* Thomas Kochman told *CA,* "One of my main goals in writing is to promote a greater public awareness of those cultural and social factors that affect inter-

group communication, to merge in effect, anthropology with the public interest while satisfying my own inclinations towards social activism." *Avocational interests:* Travel, chess, tennis.

\* \* \*

## KOEHLER, G(eorge) Stanley 1915-

*PERSONAL:* Born March 27, 1915, in West Orange, N.J.; son of M. Raymond (business personnel) and Katherine (Goff) Koehler; married Gene McIlvaine (a teacher), June 16, 1951; children: Margaret, Raymond, Jenny, Jamison, Mary Anne. *Education:* Princeton University, B.A., 1936, M.A., 1938, Ph.D., 1942; Harvard University, M.A., 1937. *Home:* 54 Hills Rd., Amherst, Mass. 01002. *Office:* Bartlett Hall, University of Massachusetts, Amherst, Mass. 01002.

*CAREER:* Oklahoma State University, Stillwater, instructor in English, 1938-40; University of Kansas, Lawrence, instructor in English, 1946; Yale University, New Haven, Conn., instructor in English, 1946-50; University of Massachusetts—Amherst, professor of English, 1950—. Visiting professor, Amherst College, Amherst, Mass., 1963-64, and University of Freiburg, 1976-77. Director of Chautauqua Writer's Workshop, Chautauqua, N.Y., 1962-70. *Military service:* U.S. Navy Reserve, 1942-46; became lieutenant. *Member:* Modern Language Association of America, Milton Society, Phi Beta Kappa.

*WRITINGS:* (With L. Barron, D. Clark, and R. Tucker) *A Curious Quire,* University of Massachusetts, 1962; *The Fact of Fall: Poems,* University of Massachusetts, 1969. Contributor of poetry to *New Poems by American Poets #2,* edited by Rolfe Humphries, Ballantine, 1957. Contributor of poems to *Sewanee Review, Yale Review, Massachusetts Review,* and *Voices;* contributor of articles to *Studies in Philology, Journal of American Folklore, Fabula, Massachusetts Review, Paris Review,* and *Milton Studies.* Poetry editor, *Massachusetts Review.*

*WORK IN PROGRESS:* A book of poems; a book on William Carlos Williams.

\* \* \*

## KOENIG, Duane (Walter) 1918-

*PERSONAL:* Born June 6, 1918, in Kinde, Mich.; son of Adolph Joseph (a professional city manager) and Blossom (Gane) Koenig; married Duronda Reynolds (a writer), May 24, 1952. *Education:* University of Wisconsin, B.A., 1939, M.A., 1941, Ph.D., 1943. *Religion:* Protestant. *Home:* 427 Giralda Ave., Coral Gables, Fla. 33134. *Office:* Department of History, Box 8051, University of Miami, Coral Gables, Fla. 33124.

*CAREER:* University of Missouri—Columbia, assistant professor of European history, 1943-45; University of Miami, Coral Gables, Fla., assistant professor, 1945-48, associate professor, 1948-56, professor of European history, 1956—. Visiting associate professor of history, University of Alaska, Fairbanks, 1950-51, 1952-53. *Member:* American Historical Association, American Catholic Historical Association (member of executive council, 1963-66), The Historical Association (London), Society for Italian Historical Studies, Dante Society of America (Harvard), Dante Alighieri Society (honorary member), Florida College Teachers of History (president, 1968-69). *Awards, honors:* University of Miami humanities grant for overseas study, 1971.

*WRITINGS:* (Editor) *Historians and History: Essays in Honor of C. W. Tebeau,* University of Miami Press, 1966.

Also author of monthly syndicated column, "A Historian's Notebook," in two dozen foreign newspapers. Contributor of travel articles to *Chicago Tribune, New York Times, Travel,* and *Ships and the Sea;* contributor of about 40 articles and 100 book reviews to historical journals.

*WORK IN PROGRESS:* A book in two volumes: *Italian Armies in Russia, 1812, 1855, 1918-19, 1941-43.*

\* \* \*

## KOENIG, Samuel 1899-1972

March 29, 1899—December 29, 1972; Austrian-born American sociologist and anthropologist, educator, and author of books on immigration and contemporary society. Obituaries: *New York Times,* December 31, 1972. (See index for *CA* sketch)

\* \* \*

## KOHAK, Erazim V. 1933-

*PERSONAL:* Born May 21, 1933, in Prague, Czechoslovakia; son of Miloslav (a journalist) and Zdislava (Prochazkova) Kohak; children: Mary Zdislava, Susan Bozena, Katherine Macpherson. *Education:* Colgate University, B.A., 1954; Yale University, M.A., 1957, Ph.D., 1958. *Religion:* Episcopalian. *Address:* P.O. Box 6, Jaffrey, N.H. 03452. *Office:* Department of Philosophy, Boston University, 232 Bay State Rd., Boston, Mass. 02215.

*CAREER:* Gustavus Adolphus College, St. Peter, Minn., assistant professor of philosophy, 1958-60; Boston University, Boston, Mass., assistant professor, 1960-66, associate professor, 1966-71, professor of philosophy, 1971—. Visiting professor of philosophy, Bowling Green State University, 1971. *Member:* American Philosophical Association, Society for Phenomenology and Existential Philosophy, Czechoslovak Society for Arts and Sciences, Phi Beta Kappa.

*WRITINGS:* (Translator and author of introduction) Paul Ricoeur, *Freedom and Nature,* Northwestern University Press, 1966; (editor and translator) Thomas G. Masaryk, *Masaryk on Marx,* Bucknell University Press, 1972; (with Heda Kovaly) *The Victors and the Vanquished,* Horizon Press, 1972; (with Kovaly) *Na vlastni kuzi,* Sixty-eight Publishers (Toronto), 1972; *Narod v nas,* Sixty-eight Publishers, 1978; *Idea and Experience,* University of Chicago Press, 1978. Regular contributor to *Dissent, Commonweal,* and *Harper's.* Member of editorial board, *Dissent* and *Philosophical Forum.*

*WORK IN PROGRESS: The Rights of the Human; Love and Labor.*

*SIDELIGHTS:* Erazim V. Kohak has been exiled twice from his Czechoslovakian homeland. He told *CA* that he writes "a book or article in Czech for every book or article I write in English. Even though English is not my native language, one of my essays, 'The Roads Less Travelled,' is used . . . as a sample of English prose in high school instruction." *Na vlastni kuzi* has been translated into Norwegian, Spanish and Japanese; parts of the work have been translated into English and serialized by the British Broadcasting Corp.

\* \* \*

## KOHEN-RAZ, Reuven 1921-

*PERSONAL:* Born April 28, 1921, in Bukov, Czechoslovakia; emigrated to Palestine, 1939; son of Kamil (an engineer) and Zdenka (Ascher) Kohen; married Zipporeth Raz (a psychologist); children: Noa, Achi, Odeya. *Education:* Teacher Seminary and Jerusalem Music Seminary, teaching diploma, 1947; University of Zurich, Ph.D., 1954. *Religion:* Jewish. *Home:* Shmaryahu Levin 11, Jerusalem, Israel. *Office:* Department of Special Education, Hebrew University, Jerusalem, Israel.

*CAREER:* Ben-Shemen Youth Village, Jerusalem, Israel, teacher, 1947-48, 1949-50; Department for Special Education of Youth Aliya, Jewish Agency, Jerusalem, chief clinical psychologist, 1955-58; Hebrew University, Jerusalem, research fellow, 1957, lecturer in developmental psychology and special education, 1958, lecturer in juvenile delinquency, Institute of Criminology, 1962-64, senior lecturer, 1964-74, associate professor and head of department of special education, 1974—. Chief clinical psychologist at Observation Center for Juvenile Delinquents, Ministry of Social Welfare, and at Child Guidance Clinic, Ministry of Health, Jerusalem, 1960—. Senior research psychologist for behavioral development, Jerusalem Center for Child and Family Care, 1971—. Visiting associate professor, Stanford University, 1968-70; visiting professor, Sorbonne, University of Paris, 1975, and University of Genoa, 1976. *Military service:* British Army, served in Palestinian Units during World War II, 1942-46; Israeli Defense Army, 1948-59. *Member:* Israel Psychological Association.

*WRITINGS: Hapsycholog bema 'arecht hachinuch* (title means "The Psychologist in the Education Services"), Jewish Agency, 1959; *Hitpatchut kalit begil hitbagrut* (title means "Emotional Development in Adolescence"), Ministry of Education and Szold Foundation, 1961; *Shikum noar oleh kshe histaglut bekibbutz* (title means "Rehabilitation of Disturbed Immigrant Youth in a Kibbutz"), Youth Aliya and Szold Foundation, 1963, published as *From Chaos to Reality,* Gordon & Breach, 1972; *Ekronot ha-higyenah hanafshit* (title means "Principles of Mental Hygiene"), Youth and Pioneer Department, Jewish Agency, 1964; *Al saf hahitbagrut* (title means "The Threshold of Adolescence"), Achiassaf (Tel Aviv), 1967, published as *The Child from 9 to 13: The Psychology and Psychopathology of Preadolescence and Early Puberty,* Aldine-Atherton, 1971; *Psychobiological Aspects of Cognitive Growth,* Academic Press, 1977.

Contributor of articles on child psychology, juvenile delinquency, and related subjects to various periodicals, including *Megamoth, Hed Hagan, Zeitschrift fuer Experimentelle und Angewandte Psychologie, Scripta Hierosolymitana, Urim, Perceptual and Motor Skills Monographs, Genetic Psychology Monographs, Journal of Consulting Psychology, Journal of Child Psychology and Psychiatry, Diseases of the Nervous System, Child Development, Pediatrics,* and to *Educational Encyclopedia* and *Proceedings* of several congresses.

*WORK IN PROGRESS: Problems and Prospects of Contemporary Special Education.*

*SIDELIGHTS:* Reuven Kohen-Raz told *CA,* "My chief aim of research is to widen the area of interdisciplinary activity between education, psychology, biology, and medicine in child development and special education."

\* \* \*

## KOLARS, Frank 1899-1973

October 28, 1899—January 6, 1973; American educator, novelist, and syndicated feature writer. Obituaries: *New York Times,* January 7, 1973. (See index for *CA* sketch)

## KOLB, Erwin J(ohn) 1924-

*PERSONAL:* Born August 6, 1924, in Bay City, Mich.; son of John Frederick (a foundry worker) and Lydia (Lutz) Kolb; married A. Bernice Homm, August 29, 1949; children: Kathryn Kay, Peter Lewis, David Lowell. *Education:* Attended Concordia College, Milwaukee, 1942-44; Concordia Seminary, St. Louis, A.B., 1945, B.D., 1949, S.T.M., 1953, Th.D., 1967; Washington University, St. Louis, graduate study, 1951-52; Southern Illinois University, M.S. in Ed., 1963. *Politics:* Republican. *Home:* 20 Lake Dr., Troy, Ill. 62294. *Office:* Department of Evangelism, Lutheran Church-Missouri Synod, 500 North Broadway, St. Louis, Mo. 63102.

*CAREER:* Clergyman of Lutheran Church-Missouri Synod; pastor of churches in Cottage Hills, Highland, Bethalto, and Centralia, Ill., 1949-63; Concordia Teachers College, Seward, Neb., dean of the chapel, 1963-71, assistant professor and dean of men, 1966-67, associate professor of theology, 1963-72; Lutheran Church-Missouri Synod, St. Louis, executive secretary for evangelism, 1972—. Adviser, National Lutheran Parent-Teacher League. *Military service:* U.S. Marine Corps, 1945-47. U.S. Army Reserve, 1950—; present rank, colonel. *Member:* Lutheran Academy for Scholarship, Lutheran Education Association, Lutheran Human Relations Association, Concordia Historical Institute, Reserve Officers Association of the United States, Military Chaplains Association of the U.S.A., Lions International.

*WRITINGS: Christian Discipline,* Family Life Committee, Lutheran Church-Missouri Synod, 1960; *Christian Conversation about Sex,* Concordia, 1967; *Conversion,* Department of Evangelism, Lutheran Church-Missouri Synod, 1969; *A Lutheran Understanding of Evangelism,* Department of Evangelism, Lutheran Church-Missouri Synod, 1976.

\*     \*     \*

## KOLB, Lawrence 1911-1972

June 16, 1911—November 18, 1972; American psychiatrist, educator, research director, and author of books on mental health and current psychiatric practice. Obituaries: *New York Times,* November 19, 1972.

\*     \*     \*

## KONICK, Marcus 1914-

*PERSONAL:* Born October 22, 1914, in Philadelphia, Pa.; son of Joseph (a dress manufacturer) and Josephine (Barkus) Konick; married Evelyn Goldstein (a musician), November 24, 1940; children: John Carl, Cynthia Louisa. *Education:* Temple University, B.S., 1936; University of Pennsylvania, M.A., 1937, Ph.D., 1953. *Religion:* Reform Jewish. *Home:* 1214 North Hillview St., Lock Haven, Pa. 17745. *Office:* Lock Haven State College, Lock Haven, Pa. 17745.

*CAREER:* Harrison Art Advertising, Philadelphia, Pa., advertising copywriter and artist, 1938-42; teacher of English in high schools in Philadelphia, 1942-60; Department of Public Instruction, Harrisburg, Pa., director of Bureau of Instructional Materials and Services, 1960-66; Lock Haven State College, Lock Haven, Pa., director of Division of Humanities, 1966-73, director of academic services, 1973-75, director of international education and associate dean of arts and sciences, 1975—. Associate professor of English and education, Lebanon Valley College and Elizabethtown College, 1961-66.

*MEMBER:* National Council of Teachers of English (committee member), Modern Language Association of America, Pennsylvania Learning Resources Association, Pennsylvania Council of Teachers of English (president, 1957-58), Association of Chief State School Audiovisual Officers (president, 1966), Association of Chief State Television Authorities (vice-president, 1966), Allegheny Educational Broadcasting Council (member of board of directors, 1966—), Philadelphia English Club (president, 1956), Rotary Club, B'nai B'rith, Phi Delta Kappa. *Awards, honors:* Pennsylvania Department of Public Instruction award for distinguished contribution to education, 1964; Pennsylvania Learning Resources Association award, 1966; medal for "Science in Service of the People" from Marie Curie Sklodowska University, Lublin, Poland, 1977.

*WRITINGS:* (Editor with National Council of Teachers of English Committee on Playlist, and contributor) *Guide to Play Selection,* Appleton, 1958; (editor and contributor) *Plays for Modern Youth,* Globe Book, 1961; (editor) *Six Complete World Plays,* Globe Book, 1963; (editor with Lewis G. Sterner) *Tales in Verse,* Globe Book, 1963; (editor) *The Rubaiyat of Omar Khayyam by Edward Fitzgerald,* Avon, 1967.

Full-length plays and musicals produced: "The Iron Cross," "What Ain't We Got," "Skullduggery on the Bayou," "Anything but the Truth," "Pucker up, Kate," and "The Schmahta Game."

One-act plays produced: "Philadelphia Interlude," "The Atom and Oak Ridge, Tennessee," "Horn of Plenty" (series of four radio plays), "The Forbidden Christmas," "Equal Rights," "The Battle of the Clouds," "The Choice," "A Life of My Own," "The Christmas Spirit," "A Woman in the House," "The Gravy Train," "Christmas for the Boss," "Talking Turkey," "The Angels Sing," "Junior Prom," "Everybody Does It," "Pilgrims of Today," "Legend of Twin Rock," "Aladdin," and "Beowulf."

Also author of "The Wife of Bath," 1976. Contributor of articles to literature and audiovisual journals.

*AVOCATIONAL INTERESTS:* Painting, carving, collecting, theatrical masks, theater, music, travel.

\*     \*     \*

## KOOB, Derry D(elos) 1933-

*PERSONAL:* Born February 26, 1933, in Willoughby, Ohio; son of Raymond O. and Doris (Hern) Koob. *Education:* Kent State University, B.Sc., 1954; Ohio State University, M.Sc., 1956; Cornell University, Ph.D., 1959. *Politics:* Independent. *Home address:* Route 1, Box 303, Pisgah Forest, N.C. 28768. *Office:* Department of Biology, Brevard College, Brevard, N.C. 28712.

*CAREER:* Wellesley College, Wellesley, Mass., assistant professor of biology, 1959-63; Ohio State University, Institute of Polar Studies, 1963-68, assistant professor of phycology, 1964-68; Battelle Memorial Institute, Columbus, Ohio, research limnologist, 1968-69; Utah State University, Logan, associate professor of limnology, 1970-74; Brevard College, Brevard, N.C., associate professor of biology, 1974—. *Member:* National Science Teachers Association, Wilderness Society, National Wildlife Federation, American Institute of Biological Sciences, Sierra Club, Friends of the Earth, Sigma Xi.

*WRITINGS:* (With W. E. Boggs) *The Nature of Life,* Addison-Wesley, 1972. Contributor to American Geographical Society's "Antarctic Folio" series. Contributor of articles to *Journal of Phycology* and *Antarctic Journal of the United States.*

*WORK IN PROGRESS:* Research on freshwater biology of nonpolluted ecosystems—effects of incipient eutrophication.

*SIDELIGHTS:* Derry Koob has conducted expeditions for the Institute of Polar Studies, Columbus, Ohio, to Greenland, Aleutian Islands and Antarctica to study algal production in lakes. *Avocational interests:* Back-packing, gourmet cooking, cinematography.

\*      \*      \*

## KOPLITZ, Eugene D(e Vere)  1928-

*PERSONAL:* Born April 30, 1928, in Withee, Wis.; son of Henry Lee and Lilliam (Chase) Koplitz; married Betty Joyce Theiler, 1953; children: Stephanie Jane, Pamela Jean, David Kent. *Education:* Wisconsin State University, B.S., 1950; University of Wisconsin, M.S., 1955, Ph.D., 1958. *Politics:* Independent. *Religion:* Congregational. *Office:* Department of Psychology, University of Northern Colorado, Greeley, Colo. 80631.

*CAREER:* High school teacher in Barron, Wis., 1950-52; University of Northern Colorado, Greeley, assistant professor, 1958-61, associate professor, 1961-65, professor of psychology, 1966—, associate dean for honors program, 1967-74. *Military service:* U.S. Army, instructor in ballistic meteorology at Fort Sill, Okla., 1952-54. *Member:* American Psychological Association, American Personnel and Guidance Association (member of executive council, 1966-69), Student Personnel Association for Teacher Education (member of executive committee, 1961-70; president, 1967-68), Association for Counselor Education and Supervision, American Association of University Professors, Phi Delta Kappa, Pi Epsilon Delta, Masons.

*WRITINGS: Guidance in the Elementary School: Theory, Research and Practice,* W. C. Brown, 1968; (contributor) C. D. Beck, editor, *Philosophical Guidelines for Counseling,* W. C. Brown, 1971. Contributor to education journals.

*WORK IN PROGRESS:* A textbook, *Educational Psychology for Teachers.*

\*      \*      \*

## KOPP, Sheldon B(ernard)  1929-

*PERSONAL:* Born March 29, 1929, in New York, N.Y.; married Marjorie Ice (an editor), February 3, 1953; children: Jonathan, David, Nicholas. *Education:* New York University, B.A., 1949; Brooklyn College (now Brooklyn College of the City University of New York), graduate study, 1949-51; New School for Social Research, M.A., 1953, Ph.D., 1960. *Religion:* Jewish. *Home:* 2911 Covington Rd., Silver Spring, Md. 20910. *Office:* 5225 Connecticut Ave. N.W., Washington, D.C. 20015.

*CAREER:* Intern and clinical psychologist in New Jersey state institutions and agencies, 1951-53; University of Colorado, Boulder, extension instructor in psychology, 1954; Trenton State Hospital, Trenton, N.J., clinical psychologist and acting department head, 1955-60; District of Columbia Comprehensive Mental Health Center, Washington, D.C., chief clinical psychologist in adult program, 1961-66; private practice as psychotherapist, Washington, D.C., 1962—; George Washington University, Washington, D.C., associate clinical professor of psychology, 1964-70. Psychotherapy supervisor, Pastoral Counseling and Consultation

Centers, 1969—. Member of field faculty, Humanistic Psychology Institute, 1976—. *Military service:* U.S. Army, 1953-55. *Member:* American Academy of Psychotherapists, American Psychological Association, District of Columbia Psychological Association, Psi Chi.

*WRITINGS*—Published by Science & Behavior Books, except as indicated: *Guru,* 1971; *If You Meet a Buddha on the Road, Kill Him,* 1972; *The Hanged Man,* 1974; (with Claire Flanders) *The Hidden Meanings,* 1975; *The Naked Therapist,* Robert R. Knapp, 1976; *This Side of Tragedy,* 1977; *Back to One,* 1977. Contributor of over fifty articles to journals. Member of editorial boards, *Voices,* 1970-77, and *Pilgrimage,* 1972-77.

*WORK IN PROGRESS: An End to Innocence,* for Macmillan.

\*      \*      \*

## KORBEL, Josef  1909-1977

*PERSONAL:* Born September 20, 1909, in Kysperk, Czechoslovakia; came to United States in 1948, naturalized citizen in 1957; son of Arnost (a businessman) and Olga (Ptackova) Korbel; married Anna M. Spieglova, April 20, 1935; children: Madeleine Jana (Mrs. Joseph M. P. Albright), Anna Katherine (Mrs. G. Silva), John Joseph. *Education:* Attended Sorbonne, University of Paris, 1928-29; Charles University, Prague, J.D., 1933. *Religion:* Roman Catholic. *Home:* 2335 South Madison St., Denver, Colo. 80210. *Office:* Graduate School of International Relations, University of Denver, Denver, Colo. 80210.

*CAREER:* Czechoslovak Diplomatic Service, 1934-48, with assignments in Ministry of Foreign Affairs, Prague, 1934-36, as press attache at Czechoslovak Legation, Belgrade, Yugoslavia, 1937-38, personal secretary to Jan Masaryk, London, England, 1939-40, head of broadcasting department, Czechoslovak Government-in-Exile, London, 1940-45, chief of cabinet to Masaryk, Prague, 1945, and ambassador to Yugoslavia, Belgrade, 1945-48; University of Denver, Denver, Colo., professor of international relations, 1949-69, Andrew W. Mellon Professor of International Studies, 1969-77, dean of Graduate School of International Studies, 1959-69, director of Social Science Foundation, 1959-69. Research fellow at Russian Research Center, Harvard University, 1957; visiting fellow, St. Antony's College, Oxford University, 1963; senior research fellow at European Institute, Columbia University, 1968. Member of United Nations Commission for Kashmir, 1948-49. *Military service:* Czechoslovak Army, first lieutenant, 1933-34.

*MEMBER:* International Studies Association, American Political Science Association, American Association for the Advancement of Slavic Studies, Council on Foreign Relations, Czechoslovak Society of Arts and Sciences in America, Rocky Mountain Association for Slavic Studies (president, 1973-74), Phi Beta Kappa. *Awards, honors:* University of Denver lectureship award for research, 1958; Outstanding Educators of America, 1971.

*WRITINGS: Tito's Communism,* University of Denver Press, 1951; *Danger in Kashmir,* Princeton University Press, 1954, revised edition, 1966; *The Communist Subversion of Czechoslovakia, 1938-1948: The Failure of Coexistence,* Princeton University Press, 1959; *Poland between East and West: Soviet and German Diplomacy Toward Poland, 1919-1933,* Princeton University Press, 1963; *Detente in Europe: Real or Imaginary?,* Princeton University Press, 1972; *Twentieth-century Czechoslovakia: The Meaning of Its History,* Columbia University Press, 1977. Also author of pamphlets published by Canadian Institute of International Affairs, *The Captive Nations*, 1955, and *Trouble in the Satellites*, 1957. Contributor to *World Politics, Foreign Affairs, New Leader, East Europe*, and other journals.†

(Died July 18, 1977)

\* \* \*

**KORMENDI, Ferenc   1900-1972**

February 12, 1900—July 20, 1972; Hungarian-born American novelist, critic, and editor for Voice of America. Obituaries: *New York Times*, July 21, 1972; *Washington Post*, July 21, 1972.

\* \* \*

**KORT, Wesley A(lbert)   1935-**

*PERSONAL:* Born June 8, 1935, in Hoboken, N.J.; son of Arthur H. (a pastor) and Jeanette (Schrik) Kort; married Phyllis May Hoekstra, December 17, 1960; children: Anne Catherine, Eva Deane, Alexander Wesley. *Education:* Calvin College, A.B., 1956, Calvin Theological Seminary, B.D., 1959; University of Chicago, M.A., 1961, Ph.D., 1965. *Religion:* Presbyterian. *Home:* 3514 Winding Way, Durham, N.C. 27706. *Office:* Department of Religion, Duke University, Durham, N.C. 27702.

*CAREER:* Princeton University, Princeton, N.J., instructor in religion, 1963-65; Duke University, Durham, N.C., assistant professor, 1965-70, associate professor, 1970-77, professor of religion, 1977—, assistant dean of graduate school, 1970-71, associate dean of the college, 1973-74. Co-chairman, Cooperative Program in Humanities of Duke University and University of North Carolina at Chapel Hill, 1970-72. *Member:* Conference on Christianity and Literature (member of board of directors, 1971—), American Association of University Professors. *Awards, honors:* Rockefeller Foundation doctoral fellowship, 1962-63; Outstanding Professor Award from Duke University student government, 1968.

*WRITINGS: Shriven Selves: Religious Problems in Recent American Fiction*, Fortress, 1972; *Narrative Elements and Religious Meaning*, Fortress, 1975. Contributor of articles to *Comparative Literature Studies, Thought, Anglican Theological Review*, and other theological and literary journals.

*WORK IN PROGRESS: American Fiction and Religious Anthropology.*

\* \* \*

**KOSSMANN, Rudolf R(ichard)   1934-**

*PERSONAL:* Born December 1, 1934, in Jakarta, Indonesia; son of Rudolf E. A. and Mabel C. (van der Hoop) Kossmann; married Anna M. d'Aniello (a teacher of Latin and Italian), June 9, 1962; children: Robert J., Marc R., Eduard R. *Education:* University of Leyden, Cand. Litt., 1956, Drs. Litt., 1962, Dr. Litt., 1969; postdoctoral study at Princeton University, 1959-60. *Home:* 45 Peach Rd., R.D. 1, Poughkeepsie, N.Y. 12601. *Office:* Department of English, State University of New York College, New Paltz, N.Y. 12561.

*CAREER:* State University of New York College at New Paltz, instructor, 1962-63, assistant professor, 1963-64, associate professor, 1964-72, professor of English, 1972—. Lecturer in English language and literature, University of Groningen, 1968-69. *Military service:* Royal Dutch Army,

Medical Corps, 1954-56; became first lieutenant. *Member:* Modern Language Association of America, American Studies Association, American Association of University Professors.

*WRITINGS: Henry James: Dramatist*, Wolters-Noordhoff, 1969. Contributor of articles to Dutch journals.

*WORK IN PROGRESS: A Concise History of American Literature*, for foreign students.

\* \* \*

**KOSTER, R(ichard) M(orton)   1934-**

*PERSONAL:* Born March 1, 1934, in Brooklyn, N.Y.; son of Harry (a surgeon) and Lily (Silverstein) Koster; married Otilia Tejeira (a dancer), July 18, 1959; children: Ricardo, Lily. *Education:* Yale University, B.A., 1955; New York University, M.A., 1962. *Politics:* Democrat. *Home:* Calle 47, No. 9, Panama, Republic of Panama. *Agent:* Paul R. Reynolds, 12 East 41st St., New York, N.Y. 10017. *Office address:* Florida State University, Canal Zone Branch, P.O. Box 930, Albrook, Canal Zone 09825.

*CAREER:* National University of Panama, Panama City, Panama, teacher of English, 1960-61; Florida State University, Canal Zone Branch, Albrook, 1964—, began as lecturer, currently associate professor of English. Free-lance correspondent, Copley New Service, 1964-67. Democratic national committeeman for Canal Zone, 1966—; delegate to Democratic National Convention, 1964, 1968, 1972, and 1976. *Military service:* U.S. Army, Counter Intelligence Corps, 1956-59. *Member:* Authors Guild, American Association of University Professors. *Awards, honors:* National Book Award nomination, 1973, for *The Prince*.

*WRITINGS: The Prince* (novel), Morrow, 1972; *The Dissertation* (novel), Harper Magazine Press, 1973; *Mandragon* (novel), Morrow, 1979. Contributor to periodicals.

*SIDELIGHTS: The Prince* has been translated into French and Spanish.

*BIOGRAPHICAL/CRITICAL SOURCES: Detroit News*, February 6, 1972; *New York Times*, February 22, 1972; *Washington Post*, April 22, 1972.

\* \* \*

**KOTZIN, Michael C(harles)   1941-**

*PERSONAL:* Born May 6, 1941, in Chicago, Ill.; son of Solomon (a manufacturer) and Ann (Brickman) Kotzin; married Judith Walchirk, August 9, 1964; children: Daniel, Joshua, Abigail. *Education:* University of Chicago, B.A., 1962; University of Minnesota, M.A., 1965, Ph.D., 1968. *Religion:* Jewish. *Office:* Department of English, Tel-Aviv University, Ramat-Aviv, Tel-Aviv, Israel.

*CAREER:* Tel-Aviv University, Tel-Aviv, Israel, lecturer, 1968-72, senior teacher of English literature, 1972—. *Member:* Modern Language Association of America, Dickens Society. *Awards, honors:* Honorable mention, University of Chicago folklore contest, for *Dickens and the Fairy Tale.*

*WRITINGS: Dickens and the Fairy Tale*, Bowling Green University Popular Press, 1972. Contributor of articles to periodicals, including *Art Journal, Folklore*, and *Studies in Short Fiction.*

*WORK IN PROGRESS:* Research on Dickens; research on the literary fairy tale in the nineteenth century.

## KOWALSKI, Frank 1907-

*PERSONAL:* Born October 18, 1907, in Meriden, Conn.; son of Frank and Mary (Miller) Kowalski; married Helene Bober (a writer and artist), October 20, 1931; children: Carol Helene (Mrs. Richard F. Rudy), Barry Frank. *Education:* U.S. Military Academy, B.S., 1930; Massachusetts Institute of Technology, M.S., 1936; Columbia University, graduate study, 1945. *Politics:* Democrat. *Home:* 7204 Regent Dr., Alexandria, Va. 22307.

*CAREER:* U.S. Army, career officer, 1930-58, retiring as colonel; U.S. Congress, Washington, D.C., Democratic representative from Connecticut, 1959-63, served as member of House Armed Services Committee. Served in Army as chief of staff, U.S. advisory group, Japan, 1950-52. *Awards, honors*—Military: Legion of Merit (with oak leaf cluster), Bronze Star Medal.

*WRITINGS: Rearmament of Japan,* Simul Press, 1971. Contributor of articles on military management and politics to journals.

*WORK IN PROGRESS: Politics in Connecticut;* a political-military analysis; research on the implications of the Viet Nam war for American life; research on the life of Polish immigrants, 1910-1920.

*SIDELIGHTS:* Frank Kowalski told *CA:* ". . . Organizing Japan's new military forces, under subterfuge of forming police forces [, I] saw my nation at its worst, trampling on the Japanese constitution which we forced upon Japan. In the Democratic Convention at Hartford, Conn., [I] witnessed democracy crushed by political bosses, saw delegates without souls dance like puppets to the orders of their mentors—while the public cared more for their cosmetics, pleasures and TV programs than their rights. Unless a leadership dedicated to human rights rather than special interests arises in the country America is finished as a useful entity of humanity."

*AVOCATIONAL INTERESTS:* Inventing (holds six patents).

\*       \*       \*

## KRACMAR, John Z. 1916-

*PERSONAL:* Born May 13, 1916, in Bohumin, Czechoslovakia; married September, 1948; wife's name, Herma. *Education:* Charles University, Prague, doctorate in law and economics, 1938. *Home:* 25 The Cedars, London W. 13, England. *Office:* 94 Uxbridge Rd., London W. 6, England.

*CAREER:* Attorney in Prague, for some years; operated own export business in Prague and Brussels; Singer Sewing Machine Co., New York, N.Y., economist, 1954-68, European Division, London, England, manager of marketing research, 1965—. Lecturer at New York University, for American Management Association, and other institutions and firms.

*WRITINGS: Marketing Research in the Developing Countries: A Handbook* (foreword by Jan Tinbergen, winner of Nobel Prize for economics, 1969), Praeger, 1971. Contributor of about one thousand articles on economics, politics, and architecture to newspapers published in English, German, and Czech.

*SIDELIGHTS:* Proceeds from John Z. Kracmar's book are being donated to the College of Europe of Bruges, Belgium, to provide a scholarship for students from developing countries. The book is being translated into Spanish and Japanese.

*BIOGRAPHICAL/CRITICAL SOURCES: New Commonwealth,* Number 5, 1971; *Business Abroad,* July, 1971; *Business Asia,* July 30, 1971; *International Executive,* summer, 1971; *Economic Trends,* October 16, 1971; *Journal of Marketing,* April, 1972.

\*       \*       \*

## KRAFT, Robert Alan 1934-

*PERSONAL:* Born March 18, 1934, in Waterbury, Conn.; son of Howard Russell and Marian (Northrup) Kraft; married Carol Wallace (an elementary school teacher), June 11, 1955; children: Cindy Lee, Scott Wallace, Todd Alan, Randall Jay. *Education:* Wheaton College, Wheaton, Ill., A.B., 1955, A.M., 1957; Harvard University, Ph.D., 1961. *Home:* 11 Conwell Dr., Maple Glen, Pa. 19002. *Office:* Department of Religious Thought, University of Pennsylvania, Box 36, College Hall, Philadelphia, Pa. 19104.

*CAREER:* University of Manchester, Manchester, England, assistant lecturer in New Testament studies, 1961-63; University of Pennsylvania, Philadelphia, assistant professor, 1963-68, associate professor, 1968-76, professor of religious studies, 1976—, chairperson of department, 1977—. Coordinator, Philadelphia Seminar on Christian Origins. *Member:* Society of Biblical Literature, Studiorum Novi Testamenti Societas, International Organization for Septuagint and Cognate Studies. *Awards, honors:* Guggenheim fellow, 1969-70; American Council of Learned Societies fellow, 1975-76.

*WRITINGS: The Apostolic Fathers: A New Translation and Commentary,* Thomas Nelson, Volume III: *Barnabas and the Didache,* 1965; (with Pierre Prigent) *Epitre de Barnabe* (Sources Chretiennes 172), Les Editions du Cerf, 1971; (translator and editor with Gerhard Krodel) Walter Bauer and Georg Strecker, *Orthodoxy and Heresy in Earliest Christianity,* Fortress, 1971; *Septuagintal Lexicography,* Society of Biblical Literature, 1972; (with Ann-Elizabeth Purintun) *Paraleipomena Jeremiou* (Texts and Translations I), Society of Biblical Literature, 1972; *Testament of Job* (Texts and Translations V), Society of Biblical Literature, 1974. Contributor of articles and reviews to religious studies journals and anthologies. Editor, "Society of Biblical Literature Monograph Series," 1967-72; editor, "Society of Biblical Literature Texts and Translations: Pseudepigrapha Series," 1973—.

*WORK IN PROGRESS:* Inventory of papyri and related materials in the University of Pennsylvania Museum; research on Christian transmission and adaptation of Jewish traditions and literature.

*SIDELIGHTS:* Robert Kraft works in Aramaic and Syriac, Hebrew, Greek, Latin, Coptic, German, and French. He has toured Israel and participated in European congresses.

\*       \*       \*

## KRAMER, Eugene F(rancis) 1921-

*PERSONAL:* Born September 9, 1921, in New York, N.Y.; son of Hubert Eugene and Ann (Grimes) Kramer; married Alice Elizabeth Hinson (an antiquarian book-dealer). *Education:* University of Rochester, B.S., 1947, M.A., 1948; Ohio State University, Ph.D., 1955. *Office:* New York State Department of Education, 99 Washington Ave., Albany, N.Y. 12224.

*CAREER:* Monroe County, New York, social caseworker, 1951-53, historian, 1953-56; New York State Education Department, Albany, associate curator of history, 1956-66, editor of Schuyler Papers, 1966— . *Military service:* U.S. Army Air Forces, 1942-45; became technical sergeant; received Distinguished Flying Cross, Air Medal, six battle stars on Asiatic Campaign Ribbon. *Member:* American Historical Association, New York State Historical Association, Albany Institute.

*WRITINGS:* (Editor) *Major General Philip Schuyler's Public Papers on Saratoga Campaign,* New York University Press, 1972. Also author of a pamphlet, *Collecting Historical Artifacts,* for American Association for State and Local History.

*WORK IN PROGRESS:* Continuing editing of Schuyler papers.†

\*      \*      \*

## KRAMER, Milton D. 1915-1973

1915—January 11, 1973; American public relations director, educator, government consultant, and author of books on transport and highway safety. Obituaries: *New York Times,* January 12, 1973.

\*      \*      \*

## KRASNER, William 1917-

*PERSONAL:* Born June 8, 1917, in St. Louis, Mo.; son of Sam and Bryna (Persov) Krasner; married Juanita Frances Frazier, October 12, 1956; children: David E., Daniel A., Larry S., James N. *Education:* Attended Washington University, St. Louis, Mo., 1935-36 and U.S. Army Air Forces Weather Schools, 1942-45; Columbia University, B.S., 1948. *Home and office:* 538 Berwyn Ave., Berwyn, Pa. 19312.

*CAREER:* Free-lance writer, 1948-62; writer and producer for television series "Eye on St. Louis," 1958; Washington University, St. Louis, Mo., staff writer for *WU Magazine,* 1962; *Trans-action* (magazine of the social sciences), co-founder, articles editor, and chief writer, 1963-69; senior associate editor, *SK & F Psychiatric Reporter,* 1969; University of Pennsylvania, School of Medicine, Philadelphia, writer and editor, 1969-72, currently consultant on free-lance basis. Ghost writer. *Military service:* U.S. Army Air Forces, weather observer, teacher, forecaster, researcher, 1942-46; served in Central Pacific. *Awards, honors:* Award for excellence from National Institute of Arts and Letters, 1955.

*WRITINGS: Walk the Dark Streets* (mystery), Harper, 1949; *The Gambler,* Harper, 1950; *North of Welfare* (mystery; first chapter published as short story in *Ellery Queen's Mystery Magazine*), Harper, 1954; *The Stag Party,* Harper, 1957; *Drug-Trip Abroad: American Drug-Refugees in Amsterdam and London,* University of Pennsylvania Press, 1972. Also writer and/or producer of about a hundred movie, television, and radio documentary programs, and radio plays, a feature-length movie, a play, and dramatizations of novels for television. Contributor to national periodicals, including *Holiday, Harper's,* and *Saturday Evening Post,* and to newspapers and journals in the United States and England.

*WORK IN PROGRESS:* Two suspense novels.

*SIDELIGHTS:* William Krasner told *CA:* "For the past twenty years I have concentrated on what might be considered the holy cause of translating academic and social science jargon into English. Alas, judging by what I see and hear daily, I have writ on water."

A dramatization of *Walk the Dark Streets* was produced by CBS, and shown five times on network television. *North of Welfare* has been adapted for the stage.

\*      \*      \*

## KRAUCH, Velma 1916-

*PERSONAL:* Born September 21, 1916, in West Los Angeles, Calif.; married William Krauch (an advertising executive), June 12, 1937 (died December 4, 1972); children: William Karl, Nikki Ann (Mrs. John Lee). *Education:* Santa Monica City College, A.A., 1955; Immaculate Heart College, B.A., 1975; University of California, Los Angeles, adult teaching credential, 1976; also attended San Fernando Valley State College (now California State University, Northridge). *Home and office:* 675 Seville Lane, Vacaville, Calif. 95688.

*CAREER:* Adult educator in senior centers; free-lance writer. Conductor of workshops for National Council on the Aging. *Member:* American Association of University Women, California Council for Adult Education, Solano County Historical Society.

*WRITINGS: Three Stacks and You're Out,* VanLee Enterprise, 1971.

*AVOCATIONAL INTERESTS:* Travel, photography (as a journalistic tool and art form), decorative crafts, flower arranging, painting.

\*      \*      \*

## KRAUSHAAR, Otto F(rederick) 1901-

*PERSONAL:* Born November 19, 1901, in Clinton, Iowa; son of Otto Christian (a college president) and Marie (Staehling) Kraushaar; married Maxine MacDonald, November 26, 1926; children: Jo Anne (Mrs. Henry Poss). *Education:* University of Iowa, A.B., 1924, A.M., 1927; Harvard University, Ph.D., 1933. *Politics:* Independent Democrat. *Home:* 1606 Park Ave., Baltimore, Md. 21217.

*CAREER:* University of Iowa, Iowa City, instructor in philosophy, 1926-27; Harvard University and Radcliffe College, Cambridge, Mass., instructor in philosophy, 1927-29, 1930-33; Smith College, Northampton, Mass., assistant professor, 1933-36, associate professor, 1936-38, professor of philosophy, 1938-48; Goucher College, Towson, Md., president, 1948-67; Harvard University, visiting research associate, 1967-71. Visiting professor at University of Kansas, 1929-30, Amherst College, 1938-47, and Mount Holyoke College, 1947. Trustee of Calvert School, Samuel Ready School, 1950-60, Park School, 1952-61, and Bryn Mawr School, 1954-58. Member of Maryland Commission on Human Relations, 1950-56; chairman of Maryland Commission to Study State Aid to Nonpublic Schools, 1969-71; chairman of Mayor's Panel on Baltimore Symphony Orchestra. *Military service:* U.S. Army Air Forces, Education Officer, 1942-45; became lieutenant colonel; served in Egypt, Iran, Newfoundland, Greenland, Iceland, Labrador, Algiers, Morocco, Philippines, Guam, Saipan, Okinawa, Japan, and Korea; received Legion of Merit.

*MEMBER:* American Philosophical Association, ACTION (member of board of directors, 1962-64), Century Association (New York, N.Y.), Johns Hopkins University Club. *Awards, honors:* Nine honorary degrees, including LL.D. from Smith College, 1948, Dickinson College, 1948, Brandeis University, 1958, and Johns Hopkins University, 1963; CAPE Award for distinguished service to American education, 1977.

*WRITINGS: Lotze and James,* privately printed, 1940; *Kierkegaard in English,* privately printed, 1942; (editor with Max H. Fisch) *Classic American Philosophers,* Appleton, 1951; *American Nonpublic Schools: Patterns of Diversity,* Johns Hopkins Press, 1972; *Private Schools: From The Puritans to the Present,* Phi Delta Kappa Educational Foundation, 1976; *Schools in a Changing City: An Overview of Baltimore's Private Schools,* Sheridan Foundation, 1976. Associate editor, *Journal of Philosophy,* 1936-42.

*WORK IN PROGRESS: Baltimore's Adopt-a-School Program; A History of Nonpublic Schools.*

\*       \*       \*

**KREFETZ, Ruth    1931-1972**
   **(Ruth Marossi)**

October 6, 1931—June 10, 1972; Viennese-born American artist and author of books on financial subjects. Obituaries: *New York Times,* June 16, 1972. (See index for *CA* sketch)

\*       \*       \*

**KREIDER, Carl    1914-**

*PERSONAL:* Born September 26, 1914, in Wadsworth, Ohio; son of Lloyd Stanley (a banker) and Adelia (Stover) Kreider; married Evelyn Burkholder, June 8, 1939; children: Alan Fetter, Rebecca Elizabeth (Mrs. Weldon Pries), Stephen Carl, Thomas Edmund. *Education:* Goshen College, B.A., 1936; Princeton University, M.A., 1938, Ph.D., 1941; postgraduate study at London School of Economics and Political Science, 1938-39, and Brookings Institution, 1939-40. *Politics:* Independent Democrat. *Religion:* Mennonite. *Home:* 1121 South Eighth St., Goshen, Ind. 46526. *Office:* Department of Economics, Goshen College, Goshen, Ind. 46526.

*CAREER:* Goshen College, Goshen, Ind., assistant professor, 1940-44, professor of economics, 1944—, dean, 1944-70, president, 1950-51, 1970-71, provost, 1971-72. International Christian University, Tokyo, Japan, dean, 1952-56, visiting professor, 1972-73; professor of economics, Haile Selassie I University, Addis Ababa, Ethiopia, 1963-64. Chairman of overseas committee, Mennonite Board of Missions. *Member:* American Economic Association, Association of Higher Education, Mennonite Historical Society, North Central Association of Colleges.

*WRITINGS: The Anglo-American Trade Agreement,* Princeton University Press, 1943; *Helping Developing Countries,* Herald Press, 1968; (with Delton Franz and Andrew Shelley) *Let My People Choose,* Herald Press, 1969; *Care for One Another,* Herald Press, 1972. Contributor of articles to *Christian Living* (monthly), 1949-64, *American Economic Review, Quarterly Journal of Economics,* and *American Political Science Review.* Managing editor, *Mennonite Quarterly Review,* 1974—.

\*       \*       \*

**KREINGOLD, Shana    1889(?)-1972**

1889(?)—September 8, 1972; Russian-born Israeli educator, and author of a popular biography of her sister, Golda Meir. Obituaries: *New York Times,* September 9, 1972; *L'Express,* September 18-24, 1972.

\*       \*       \*

**KRENTS, Harold Eliot    1944-**

*PERSONAL:* Born November 5, 1944, in New York, N.Y.; son of Milton Ellis (a radio and television producer) and Irma (Kopp) Krents; married Katherine Williams (a teacher), June 12, 1971. *Education:* Harvard University, B.A. (cum laude), 1967, J.D., 1970; Oxford University, D.P.L., 1974. *Office:* Surrey, Karasik & Morse, 1156 15th St. N.W., Washington, D.C. 20003.

*CAREER:* Admitted to the Bar of New York State, 1971; Surrey, Karasik & Morse (law firm), Washington, D.C., partner, 1971—. *Member:* American Bar Association, New York Bar Association.

*WRITINGS: To Race the Wind,* Putnam, 1972.

*SIDELIGHTS:* Harold Krents told *CA:* "I am prototype for the main character of Leonard Gershe's play *Butterflies Are Free.* I gave the story its inspiration—the play's plot is *not* my story; its spirit is."

*BIOGRAPHICAL/CRITICAL SOURCES: Life,* February 6, 1970; *Detroit News,* June 25, 1972.

\*       \*       \*

**KREYCHE, Gerald F.    1927-**

*PERSONAL:* Born June 19, 1927, in Kenosha, Wis.; son of Harold Joseph (a clerk) and Henrietta (Otemann) Kreyche; married Eleanor Ann Okon, June 19, 1948; children: Geraldine (Mrs. Jon Malmberg), Laurence, James, Carolyn, Richard, Paul. *Education:* DePaul University, B.A., 1950, M.A., 1951; University of Ottawa, Ph.D., 1958. *Politics:* Democrat. *Religion:* Roman Catholic. *Home:* 2551 Fontana Dr., Glenview, Ill. 60025. *Office:* Department of Philosophy, DePaul University, 2323 North Seminary, Chicago, Ill. 60614.

*CAREER:* DePaul University, Chicago, Ill., assistant professor, 1952-60, associate professor, 1960-65, professor of philosophy, 1965—, chairman of department, 1961—. Visiting professor, Chair of Human Development, St. Mary's College, Winona, Minn. Planner and conductor of workshops on a variety of subjects, including philosophy, birth control, education, and the urban crisis. Lecturer to numerous groups. Member of various academic committees at DePaul University. Member of board of directors, Civitas Dei Foundation, 1969—. Has appeared on radio and television; conducted a series of radio broadcasts entitled "What Do You Think?," WFMF-FM, Chicago. Member of board of advisors, University Press of America; curriculum consultant to Fontbonne College and Maryville College, St. Louis, 1969, to University of Dayton, 1971, and to Frostburg State Collge, Maryland. *Military service:* U.S. Army, 1945-46; became staff sergeant. *Member:* American Philosophical Association, American Catholic Philosophical Association (president, 1972-73; acting secretary of Midwest Regional Conference, 1961—), National Catholic Education Association. *Awards, honors:* Danforth Associate grants, 1971, 1972; DePaul Distinguished Service award, 1969.

*WRITINGS:* (Editor with Jesse Mann) *Reflections on Man,* Harcourt, 1966; (editor with Mann) *Perspectives on Reality,* Harcourt, 1966; (editor with Mann) *Approaches to Morality,* Harcourt, 1966; (contributor) Frank N. Magill, editor, *Masterpieces of Catholic Literature in Summary Form,* Salem Press, 1966; (contributor) Robert Apostol, editor, *Human Values in a Secular World,* Humanities, 1970; (contributor) Helmut Loiskandl, editor, *Man and Society,* Kendall/Hunt, 1971; *Thirteen Thinkers,* University Press of America, 1976. Contributor to *New Catholic Encyclopedia;* contributor of articles and reviews to *Critic, Ave Maria, New World,* and other religious and scholarly journals. Senior philosophy editor, *Intellect;* associate editor, *Listening;* member of editorial board, *Journal of Existential Psychiatry.*

*WORK IN PROGRESS:* A book on interdisciplinary man.

*AVOCATIONAL INTERESTS:* Literature of the early west, camping, golf, chess, playing guitar.

\* \* \*

## KRINSKY, Carol Herselle 1937-

*PERSONAL:* Born June 2, 1937, in New York, N.Y.; daughter of David (a school principal) and Jane (Gartman) Herselle; married Robert D. Krinsky (an actuary), January 25, 1959; children: Alice, John. *Education:* Smith College, B.A., 1957; New York University, M.A., 1960, Ph.D., 1965. *Office:* Department of Fine Arts, New York University, Washington Sq., New York, N.Y. 10003.

*CAREER:* New York University, New York, N.Y., 1965—, began as assistant professor, currently associate professor of art history and co-director of urban design studies program. Lecturer on art. *Member:* College Art Association, Society of Architectural Historians (member of board of directors), Victorian Society, Classical America, National Trust (United States and Great Britain), Municipal Art Society.

*WRITINGS:* (Editor and author of introduction) Vitruvius, *De Architectura,* Wilhelm Fink Verlag, 1969; *Rockefeller Center,* Oxford University Press, 1978. Contributor to *New Catholic Encyclopedia* and *Columbia Encyclopedia;* contributor to art journals.

*WORK IN PROGRESS:* A book on European synagogues.

\* \* \*

## KROHN, Ernst C(hristopher) 1888-1975

*PERSONAL:* Born December 23, 1888, in New York, N.Y.; son of Ernst L. (a musician) and Emma (Haueisen) Krohn. *Education:* Attended high school one year; studied piano under his father until 1910 and under Ottmar Moll, 1910-25. *Home:* 428 East Jackson Rd., St. Louis, Mo. 63119.

*CAREER:* Teacher of piano privately in St. Louis, Mo., 1909-1959, and as first assistant to Ottmar Moll, 1913-34; Washington University, St. Louis, lecturer in history of music, 1938-53; St. Louis University, St. Louis, lecturer in history of music and director of music department, 1953-63. Honorary curator, Gaylord Music Library, Washington University, 1963-75. Organist for five years. *Member:* International Musicological Society, International Association of Music Libraries, American Musicological Society (honorary member), Music Library Association, Mediaeval Academy of America, Renaissance Society of America, Missouri State Music Teachers Association, Missouri Historical Society, Piano Teachers Round Table, Musicians Guild of St. Louis (honorary member).

*WRITINGS: A Century of Missouri Music,* privately printed, 1924, expanded and updated edition published as *Missouri Music,* Da Capo, 1971; *The History of Music; An Index to the Literature Available in a Selected Group of Musicological Publications,* [St. Louis], 1958, reprinted, Da Capo, 1973; *Music Publishing in the Middle Western States before the Civil War,* Information Coordinators, 1972. Also author of about one hundred essays on music history.

*WORK IN PROGRESS: Music Publishing in St. Louis;* his memoirs.

*SIDELIGHTS:* Ernst C. Krohn collected a musical library

of ten thousand volumes, which he sold to Washington University, where he was honorary curator of Gaylord Music Library. "Deeply interested in art, but have no talent," he told *CA.* "My grandfather and three uncles were artists."

*BIOGRAPHICAL/CRITICAL SOURCES: St. Louis Post-Dispatch,* November 28, 1971; *American Musicological Society Newsletter,* August 15, 1975; *Music Library Association Journal,* September, 1975.†

(Died March 21, 1975)

\* \* \*

## KRUEGER, Anne O. 1934-

*PERSONAL:* Born in 1934 in Endicott, N.Y.; daughter of Leslie A. (a physician) and Dora (Wright) Osborn; married William R. Krueger, 1953 (divorced, 1957); children: Kathleen Suzanne. *Education:* Oberlin College, B.A., 1953; University of Wisconsin, M.S., 1956, Ph.D., 1958. *Home:* 1865 Roselawn Ave., St. Paul, Minn. 55113. *Office:* Department of Economics, University of Minnesota, Minneapolis, Minn. 55455.

*CAREER:* University of Wisconsin—Madison, instructor in economics, 1958-59; University of Minnesota, Minneapolis, assistant professor, 1959-63, associate professor, 1963-66, professor of economics, 1966—, research associate of Upper Midwest Economic Study, 1962-64. International economist, Bankers' Trust Co., 1961-62; National Bureau of Economic Research, research associate, 1969-76, member of senior research staff, 1977—. Consultant to U.S. Agency for International Development, 1965-72, Upper Midwest Research and Development Council, 1966, and National Science Foundation, 1971—. *Member:* American Economic Association (vice-president, 1977), Midwest Economic Association (president, 1973). *Awards, honors:* National Science Foundation grant, 1966-69.

*WRITINGS:* (Contributor) Theodore Morgan, George Betz, and N. K. Choudhry, editors, *Readings in Economic Development,* Wadsworth, 1963; (with James M. Henderson) *National Growth and Economic Change in the Upper Midwest,* University of Minnesota Press, 1965; (with Henderson) *Economic Growth and Adjustment in the Upper Midwest, 1960-75: A Supplement to the Upper Midwest Economic Study,* Upper Midwest Research and Development Council, 1967; (contributor) Bruce M. Russett, editor, *Economic Theories of International Politics,* Markham, 1968; (contributor) *Foreign Trade and Economic Development,* Economic and Social Studies Conference Board (Istanbul), 1968; (contributor) *Rural Poverty in the United States,* President's National Advisory Commission on Rural Poverty, 1968.

(Editor with Wontack Hong) *Trade and Development in Korea,* University Press of Hawaii, 1975; *Benefits and Costs of Import-Substitution: A Micro-Economic Study,* University of Minnesota Press, 1975; *Foreign Trade Regimes and Economic Development: Turkey,* Columbia University Press, 1975; (contributor) Willy Sellekaerts, editor, *Essays in Honor of Jan Tinbergen,* Macmillan, 1977; *Foreign Trade Regimes and Economic Development: Liberalization Attempts and Consequences,* Ballinger, 1978; *Trade and Aid in Korea's Development,* Harvard University Press, 1979.

\* \* \*

## KRZYZANOWSKI, Jerzy R(oman) 1922-

*PERSONAL:* Born December 10, 1922, in Lublin, Poland;

son of Julian (a professor) and Emilia Krzyzanowski; married Elzbieta Kuraszkiewicz, September 12, 1948; children: Krzysztof, Justyn, Daniel. *Education:* University of Warsaw, M.A., 1959; University of Michigan, Ph.D., 1965. *Religion:* Roman Catholic. *Home:* 4546 Crompton Dr., Columbus, Ohio 43220. *Office:* Department of Slavic Languages, Ohio State University, 1841 Millikin Rd., Columbus, Ohio 43210.

*CAREER:* University of California, Berkeley, lecturer in Slavic languages, 1959-60; University of Michigan, Ann Arbor, lecturer in Slavic languages, 1960-63; University of Colorado, Boulder, assistant professor of Slavic languages, 1963-64; University of Kansas, Lawrence, associate professor of Slavic languages, 1964-67, director of Slavic Institute, 1964; Ohio State University, Columbus, professor of Slavic languages and literature, 1967—. *Member:* American Association for the Advancement of Slavic Studies, American Association of Teachers of Slavic and East European Languages, Association for the Advancement of Polish Studies (president), Polish Institute of Arts and Sciences, Polish-American Historical Association, Phi Beta Kappa, Delta Tau Kappa.

*WRITINGS:* (Editor) Ernest Hemingway, *Rzeka dwuch serc,* [Warsaw], 1962, 6th edition, 1976; *Ernest Hemingway,* Wiedza Powszechna, 1963; (editor with Sigmund S. Birkenmayer) *A Modern Polish Reader,* Pennsylvania State University, 1970; *Wladyslaw Stanislaw Reymont,* Twayne, 1972. Contributor of articles to Polish and Slavic literature journals.

*WORK IN PROGRESS: The General: The Story of Leopold Okuliki;* a research project, *Boleslaw Prus.*

\* \* \*

## KUBOTA, Akira 1932-

*PERSONAL:* Born August 30, 1932, in Sacramento, Calif.; son of Otohei (a businessman) and Honami Kubota. *Education:* University of Tokyo, B.A., 1957; University of Michigan, M.A., 1962, Ph.D., 1966. *Politics:* Democrat. *Religion:* "No affiliation." *Office:* Department of Political Science, University of Windsor, Windsor, Ontario, Canada.

*CAREER:* University of Michigan, Ann Arbor, research associate, Survey Research Center and Center for Japanese Studies, 1966-70; University of Windsor, Windsor, Ontario, assistant professor, 1970-71, associate professor of political science, 1971—. *Military service:* U.S. Army, 1957-59; served in Europe. *Member:* American Political Science Association, Canadian Political Science Association, Association for Asian Studies, International House of Japan.

*WRITINGS: Higher Civil Servants in Postwar Japan: Their Social Origins, Educational Backgrounds, and Career Patterns,* Princeton University Press, 1969.

*WORK IN PROGRESS:* Research on Japanese voting behavior; a comparative study of Canadian and American political attitudes and behavior.

\* \* \*

## KUFELDT, George 1923-

*PERSONAL:* Born November 4, 1923, in Chicago, Ill.; son of Henry (a fruit grower) and Lydia (Dorn) Kufeldt; married Kathryn Rider, July 24, 1943 (died, 1956); married Claudena Eller (an elementary school teacher), June 21, 1957; children: (first marriage) Anita Kay (Mrs. Jeffery W. Shelton), Kristina Sue (Mrs. James Ely Schmidt). *Education:* Anderson College, A.B., 1945, Th.B., 1946, B.D., 1953;

Dropsie University, Ph.D., 1974. *Home:* 907 North Nursery Rd., Anderson, Ind. 46012. *Office:* School of Theology, Anderson College, Anderson, Ind. 46011.

*CAREER:* Ordained minister of Church of God, 1949; minister in Homestead, Fla., 1948-50, Cassopolis, Mich., 1954-57, and Lansdale, Pa., 1957-61; Anderson College, Anderson, Ind., professor of religion (Old Testament), 1961—. *Member:* National Association of Professors of Hebrew, Society of Biblical Literature, Wesleyan Theological Society, American Hellenic Educational Progressive Association.

*WRITINGS:* (Author of commentary) *The Wesleyan Bible Commentary,* Volume II: *The Book of Proverbs,* Eerdmans, 1968.

*AVOCATIONAL INTERESTS:* Gardening.

\* \* \*

## KUHN, William Ernst 1922-

*PERSONAL:* Born February 15, 1922, in St. Gall, Switzerland; naturalized U.S. citizen in 1955; son of Ernst Ulrich and Fanny (Eisenhut) Kuhn; married Barbara Ann Carlson (a teacher), July 4, 1952; children: Jacqueline Ann, John Boyd, Jerrald Walter. *Education:* St. Gall Graduate School of Economics, Business and Public Administration, M.A., 1946, Ph.D., 1949; University of Kansas, graduate study, 1947-48. *Politics:* None. *Religion:* Unitarian Universalist. *Home address:* Route 1, Box 101B, Bennet, Neb. 68317. *Office:* Department of Economics, University of Nebraska, Lincoln, Neb. 68588.

*CAREER:* Augustana College, Sioux Falls, S.D., assistant professor of economics, 1949-52; University of Wyoming, Laramie, assistant professor, 1952-57, associate professor of economics, 1957-62; Federal Reserve Bank, Chicago, Ill., international economist, 1962-64; Roosevelt University, Chicago, professor of economics, 1965-66; University of Nebraska, Lincoln, professor of economics, 1966—. Fulbright lecturer at University of Dacca, 1964-65, and in Liberia, 1969-70; visiting professor, St. Gall Graduate School of Economics, Business and Public Administration, 1970-71. Researcher and translator, Union Bank of Switzerland, Zurich, 1958-59; research consultant, Continental Illinois National Bank & Trust Co., Chicago, 1965. *Military service:* Swiss Army, World War II. *Member:* American Economic Association, Missouri Valley Economic Association. *Awards, honors:* Ford Foundation faculty research fellow at University of Washington, Seattle, 1960.

*WRITINGS: Der Rueckschlag der amerikanischen Konjunktur in Jahre 1937,* Fehr'sche Buchhandlung, 1949; *The Evolution of Economic Thought,* South-Western, 1963, 2nd edition, 1970; *History of Nebraska Banking: A Centennial Retrospect,* Bureau of Business Research, University of Nebraska, 1968; (translator) Erich Schneider, *Joseph A. Schumpeter: Leben und Werk eines grossen Sozialoekonomen,* Bureau of Business Research, University of Nebraska, 1975.

\* \* \*

## KUHNS, Richard (Francis, Jr.) 1924-

*PERSONAL:* Born May 3, 1924, in Chicago, Ill.; son of Richard Francis (a lawyer) and Helen (Kuh) Kuhns; married Margaret Portis, June 5, 1944; children: Frederick. *Education:* Dartmouth College, B.A., 1947; University of California, Berkeley, additional study, 1947-49; Columbia University, Ph.D., 1955. *Office:* Department of Philosophy, Columbia University, New York, N.Y. 10027.

*CAREER:* Dartmouth College, Hanover, N.H., instructor in philosophy, 1949-50; Columbia University, New York, N.Y., instructor, 1950-54, assistant professor, 1954-60, associate professor, 1960-62, professor of philosophy, 1962—. *Military service:* U.S. Army, Infantry, 1943-46. *Member:* American Philosophical Association, American Society for Aesthetics. *Awards, honors:* Distinguished book award from Van Am Society, Columbia University, 1971.

*WRITINGS: The House, the City, and the Judge: The Growth of Moral Awareness in the Oresteia,* Bobbs-Merrill, 1962; (with Albert Hofstadter) *Philosophies of Art and Beauty: Selected Readings in Aesthetics from Plato to Heidegger,* Random House, 1964; *Structures of Experience,* Basic Books, 1971. Contributor of articles to journals, including *Journal of Philosophy, Journal of Aesthetics,* and *Philosophical Forum.*

\* \* \*

## KUIC, Vukan 1923-

*PERSONAL:* Born February 17, 1923, in Sarajevo, Yugoslavia; son of Simeon and Aglaja (Homiuka) Kuic; married Louise Cobb, August 31, 1957; children: Angela, Sonja, Mira, Tanja, Simeon, Elena. *Education:* Attended College of Commerce (Vienna), 1942-44, and University of Trieste, 1945-46; University of Colorado, Boulder, M.A., 1953; University of Chicago, Ph.D., 1958. *Religion:* Serbian Orthodox. *Home:* 745 Westover Rd., Columbia, S.C. 29210. *Office:* Department of Government and International Studies, University of South Carolina, Columbia, S.C. 29028.

*CAREER:* University of Alabama, Tuscaloosa, instructor, 1956-58, assistant professor, 1958-63, associate professor of political science, 1963-66; University of South Carolina, Columbia, professor of political science, 1966—. Visiting fellow, Center for the Study of Democratic Institutions, Santa Barbara, Calif., 1965-66. *Member:* American Political Science Association, International Political Science Association, World Future Society, Southern Political Science Association.

*WRITINGS:* (Editor) Yves Simon, *The Tradition of Natural Law: A Philosopher's Reflections,* Fordham University Press, 1965; (editor) Simon, *Work, Society, and Culture,* Fordham University Press, 1971; (contributor) Tinsley E. Yarbrough, Don H. DeMyer, and John P. East, editors, *Politics '72: Trends in Federalism,* East Carolina University, 1972. Contributor to political science journals.

*WORK IN PROGRESS: Federalism and Contemporary Political Science; The Silences of the Constitution;* research on work, leisure, culture, and the future; research on the contribution of Yves Simon to political thought.

## KUNZ, Phillip Ray 1936-

*PERSONAL:* Born July 19, 1936, in Bern, Idaho; son of Parley Peter (a farmer) and Hilda (Stoor) Kunz; married Joyce Sheffield, March 18, 1960; children: Jay Phillip, Jenifer, Jody, Johnathan, Jana. *Education:* Brigham Young University, B.S. (cum laude), 1961, M.S., 1962; University of Michigan, Ph.D., 1967. *Politics:* Democrat. *Religion:* Church of Jesus Christ of Latter-day Saints (Mormon). *Home:* 3040 Navajo, Provo, Utah 84601. *Office:* Department of Sociology, Brigham Young University, Provo, Utah 84601.

*CAREER:* Lyman Latter-day Saints Seminary, Lyman, Wyo., principal, 1962-63; Eastern Michigan University, Ypsilanti, instructor in sociology, 1964; University of Wyoming, Laramie, assistant professor of sociology, 1967-68; Brigham Young University, Provo, Utah, associate professor, 1968-73, professor of sociology, 1973—. Director, Institute of Genealogical Studies. Consultant to Bonneville Research Corp., Provo Police Department, and other public and industrial organizations. *Military service:* U.S. Army, 1954-56. *Member:* International Platform Association, American Sociological Association, American Council on Family Relations, Society for the Scientific Study of Religion, Religious Research Association, Groves Conference on Marriage and the Family, Rocky Mountain Social Science Association, Phi Kappa Phi, Sigma Xi, Alpha Kappa Delta. *Awards, honors:* National Science Foundation fellowship, 1962; National Institute of Mental Health fellow, 1963; Maeser Research Award, 1977.

*WRITINGS:* (With Merlin Brinkerhoff) *Utah in Numbers, Comparisons, Discussion, and Trends,* Brigham Young University Press, 1969; (with Spencer Condie) *Man in His Social Environment,* Simon & Schuster, 1970; (with Brinkerhoff) *Complex Organizations and Their Environments,* W. C. Brown, 1972. Contributor of over sixty articles and reviews to sociology journals.

*WORK IN PROGRESS:* Writing on family topics, including polygamy, divorce, the family through four generations, and others.

\* \* \*

## KURIHARA, Kenneth Kenkichi 1910-1972

January 8, 1910—June 13, 1972; Japanese-born American economist, educator, researcher, and author of books on economic development. Obituaries: *New York Times,* June 14, 1972. (See index for *CA* sketch)

# L

## La CASCE, Steward 1935-

*PERSONAL:* Surname is pronounced La-*Case;* born January 19, 1935, in Fryeburg, Me.; son of Elroy O. (a headmaster) and Marion (Steward) La Casce. *Education:* Bowdoin College, B.A., 1956; Columbia University, Ph.D., 1966. *Home:* 12 Edgewood Dr., Essex Junction, Vt. 05452.

*CAREER:* Boston University, Boston, Mass., assistant professor of English, 1965-71; National Student Volunteer Program, Boston, editor, 1971-72; Vermont Institute of Community Involvement, Burlington, Vt., president and founder, 1972—. *Member:* Phi Beta Kappa.

*WRITINGS:* (With Terry Belanger) *The Art of Persuasion,* Scribner, 1972. Author of four articles on Jonathan Swift; editor of several pamphlets on student volunteer activities.

\* \* \*

## LACCETTI, (Silvio) Richard 1941-

*PERSONAL:* Born January 14, 1941, in Teaneck, N.J.; son of Silvio Anthony (a businessman) and Stella (Nappi) Laccetti. *Education:* Columbia University, A.B., 1962, M.A., 1963, Ph.D., 1967. *Home:* 117 Shaler Ave., Fairview, N.J. 07022. *Office:* Department of Humanities, Stevens Institute of Technology, Castle Point, Hoboken, N.J. 07030.

*CAREER:* Stevens Institute of Technology, Hoboken, N.J., instructor, 1965-67, assistant professor, 1967-73, associate professor of humanities, 1973—. Grants administrator, New Jersey Department of Community Affairs, 1969-74; executive director and board chairman, North Bergen Drug Program, 1970-72; chairman of Hudson County Bicentennial Congress, 1974-76, and Citizenship Institute, 1974-75. Advisor, Hudson County prosecutor's office, 1968-70; consultant to New Jersey Regional Drug Abuse Agency, 1970, and North Hudson Mayor's Council, 1971-72; planning consultant, UNICO National Humanities program, 1976. *Member:* American Historical Association, Forum of Contemporary History. *Awards, honors:* Fulbright fellow, 1965.

*WRITINGS:* (Editor with H. Druks) *Cities and Civilization,* Speller, 1971; *Dialogue on Drugs,* Exposition, 1974; (editor) *New Jersey Colleges and Vocational Schools,* William H. Wise, 1976. Consulting editor, "Books about New Jersey" series, William H. Wise. Contributor of articles to *Manchester Union Leader, Southwestern Law Review,* and *Forum.*

*WORK IN PROGRESS:* Editing, *Focus on New Jersey: A Casebook for New Jersey Studies.*

*SIDELIGHTS:* Richard Laccetti writes: "I consider myself first and foremost a Humanist and I consciously infuse my writings with a general humanistic quality. Whether I am dealing with drug abuse, political issues, urban problems, or career education, my work is never done unless I have engaged the reader's mind to consider related questions of meaning, of values, and of truth."

\* \* \*

## LACOMBE, Gabriel 1905(?)-1973

1905(?)—January 3, 1973; French journalist and news bureau director. Obituaries: *L'Express,* January 8-14, 1973.

\* \* \*

## LACY, Dan (Mabry) 1914-

*PERSONAL:* Born February 28, 1914, in Newport News, Va.; son of Tolbert Hardy (a lawyer) and Ann Electa (Boatwright) Lacy; married Hope Lenore Leiken, December 14, 1946; children: Philip Tolbert, Dudley Boatwright, Elizabeth Hardy. *Education:* University of North Carolina, A.B., 1933, A.M., 1935. *Politics:* Democrat. *Religion:* Unitarian Universalist. *Home:* 52 West Clinton Ave., Irvington, N.Y. 10533. *Office:* McGraw-Hill, Inc., 1221 Ave. of the Americas, New York, N.Y. 10020.

*CAREER:* Works Progress Administration, Raleigh, N.C. and Washington, D.C., state supervisor for North Carolina and assistant national director of historical records survey, 1936-41; U.S. National Archives, Washington, D.C., assistant archivist, 1941-47; U.S. Library of Congress, Washington, D.C., deputy chief assistant librarian, 1947-51; U.S. State Department, Washington, D.C., director of Information Center Services, 1951-53; American Book Publishers Council, New York City, managing director, 1953-66; McGraw-Hill, Inc., New York City, senior vice-president of McGraw-Hill Book Co., 1966-74, senior vice-president and executive assistant to the president, 1974—. Member of National Advisory Commission on Libraries, 1967-69, and National Commission on New Technological Uses of Copyrighted Works, 1976—. Trustee, Irvington, N.Y. Public Library, 1960-70. *Member:* P.E.N., Authors Guild. *Awards, honors:* Superior Service Medal, U.S. State Department, 1952; Litt.D., University of North Carolina, 1968.

*WRITINGS:* (Co-editor) *Historical Records of North Carolina,* three volumes, North Carolina Historical Commission, 1938-40; *The Library of Congress: A Sesquicentenary Review,* Library of Congress, 1950; *Books and the Future: A Speculation,* New York Public Library, 1956; *Freedom and Communications,* University of Illinois Press, 1961, revised edition, 1965; *The Meaning of the American Revolution,* New American Library, 1964; *The White Use of Blacks in America,* Atheneum, 1972; *The Lost Colony,* F. Watts, 1972; *The Colony of Virginia,* F. Watts, 1973; *The Lewis and Clark Expedition: 1804-1806,* F. Watts, 1974; *The Colony of North Carolina,* F. Watts, 1975; (with John L. Stage) *The Birth of America,* Grosset, 1975; *The Abolitionists,* McGraw, 1977.

*SIDELIGHTS: The Meaning of the American Revolution* has editions in Spanish in Argentina, in Arabic in Egypt and Lebanon, and in Chinese in Hong Kong.

\* \* \*

## LAFFAN, Kevin (Barry)  1922-
### (Kevin Barry)

*PERSONAL:* Born May 24, 1922, in Reading, Berkshire, England; son of Patrick (a photographer) and Amelia (Old) Laffan; married Jeanne Thompson, 1952; children: Michael, Paul, David. *Religion:* Atheist. *Home:* The Grange, Colworth, Chichester, Sussex, England. *Agent:* E. Wax, ACTAC, 16 Cardogan Lane, London SW1, England.

*CAREER:* Actor, director, and playwright; artistic director of Everyman Theatre, Reading, England, 1950-56. *Awards, honors:* Associated Television Ltd. Award, 1959, for "Cut in Ebony"; Irish Life Drama Award at Dublin Festival, 1967, for "The Superannuated Man"; National Union of Students Award, 1969, and *Sunday Times* Award, 1970, both for *Zoo Zoo Widdershins Zoo.*

*WRITINGS*—Plays: *Zoo Zoo Widdershins Zoo* (comedy; first produced at Leicester University, 1968), Faber, 1969; *It's a Two-Foot-Six-Inches-above-the-Ground World* (comedy; first produced in Bristol at Theatre Royal, 1969; produced on the West End at Wyndham's Theatre, February 9, 1970; also see below), Faber, 1970.

Unpublished plays: "Cut in Ebony," 1956; (under name Kevin Barry) "First Innocent," first produced in Reading, England at Everyman Theatre, 1957; (with Peter Jones) "Angie and Bernie," produced in Guilford, England at Yvonne Arnaud Theatre, 1965; "The Superannuated Man" (comedy-tragedy), first produced in Watford, England at Palace Theatre, May 18, 1970; "There Are Humans at the Bottom of My Garden," first produced in London, 1972; "Strictly for the Birds" (comedy), first produced, 1973; "Never So Good," produced in London at Africa Centre, May, 1976; "The Wandering Jew," produced in London, 1978.

Films: "It's a Two-Foot-Six-Inches-above-the-Ground World" (based on play with same title), produced by Betty Box and Ralph Thomas, 1972; "Best Pair of Legs in the Business" (based on television play with same title; see below), produced by Leslie Grade Ltd., 1972.

Television plays and series: "Lucky for Some," produced for ATV, January, 1968; "The Best Pair of Legs in the Business," produced on Yorkshire TV, May, 1968; "You Can Only Buy Once," produced on Yorkshire TV, September, 1968; "Castlehaven" (serial), produced on Yorkshire TV, March, 1969—February, 1970; "Decision to Burn," pro-

duced on Yorkshire TV, June—October, 1970; "A Little Learning," 1970; "Fly on the Wall" (trilogy), produced on Yorkshire TV, September, 1971; "The Designer," 1971; "The General," 1971; "Emmerdale Farm" (serial), produced on Yorkshire TV, beginning in October, 1972; "Justicer" (series), 1973; "The Reformer," 1973; "Getting Up," 1973; (with Bill McIlwraith) "Beryl's Lot" (series), 1973; "After the Wedding Was Over," 1975; "It's a Wise Child," 1975; "All Saints" (series), 1978. Also author of radio play, "Portrait of an Old Man," 1961.

*SIDELIGHTS:* A reviewer for *Variety* writes of Kevin Laffan's "It's a Two-Foot-Six-Inches-above-the-Ground World": "The play's title is not only elusive but could be damaging. This is not a wacky opus. It's billed as a comedy and is often very funny in both spoken line and situation. But it's also serious, for the author, whom a program note informs us is the third of 12 children born in England of Irish parents, has written a bitterly anti-Catholic tract." The play revolves around a Catholic couple with three children; the wife, who doesn't want another child, has refused to sleep with her husband for ten months. The *Variety* reviewer continues: "The husband-wife skirmishing works beautifully to illumine the larger clash between intellect and faith, which is what the playwright is really up to. Laffan has invested all this with entertaining vitality—characters of dimension in believable circumstance."

Harold Hobson, writing in *Christian Science Monitor,* finds "that the play is uproariously funny, and that Mr. Laffan displays in it a touching sympathy with all his principal characters. He has no villains." However, Hobson does take issue with what he views as the playwright's one-sided approach. "Mr. Laffan will not admit that there is any rational argument against oral contraception," Hobson writes, "and this gives his play a feeling of bias. There is no reason why he should not let his priest have the worst of the dispute, but his play would be all the better if he were not so obviously determined that this should be so. There are doubtless many foolish priests in the world, but for his play Mr. Laffan should have chosen an intelligent one, as, for example, Shaw would certainly have done."

*BIOGRAPHICAL/CRITICAL SOURCES: Variety,* September 24, 1969, February 18, 1970; *Observer Review,* January 25, 1970; *Punch,* January 28, 1970; *Christian Science Monitor,* January 30, 1970; *Stage,* May 27, 1971, September 23, 1971; *Plays and Players,* June, 1971.

\* \* \*

## LAITE, William Edward, Jr.  1932-

*PERSONAL:* Born August 19, 1932, in Tampa, Fla.; son of Edward William (a merchant) and Frances (Regener) Laite; married Marilyn M. Meeks (a teacher), August 7, 1953; children: W. E. III (deceased), Jennifer Lynn, Kathrina Francis, Kelly Marilyn. *Education:* University of Georgia, B.S., 1954, M.Ed. *Politics:* Democrat. *Religion:* Methodist. *Home:* 2948 Crestline Dr., Macon, Ga. 31204. *Office:* Bill Laite District Co., 1820 Seventh St., Macon, Ga. 31206.

*CAREER:* Triangle Chemical Co., Macon, Ga., product development, 1955-59; Town and Country Pest Control, Inc., Macon, president and owner, 1959—; Laite Contracting Co., Macon, president and owner, 1959—; Tifton Brick and Block, Tifton, Ga., president and owner, 1970—; Atlas Weight Co., Fairburn, Ga., president and owner, 1970—; Georgia Department of Offender Rehabilitation, Atlanta, Ga., chief, construction section, Correction Industries Division, beginning 1972; owner, Bill Laite District Co.

(wholesale beer company), Macon. Member of Georgia House of Representatives, 1963-65, 1967-68; Georgia state legislative chairman, United Cerebral Palsy Foundation. Lecturer with American Program Bureau, Boston, Mass.

*WRITINGS: U.S. vs. William Laite,* Acropolis Books, 1972.

*WORK IN PROGRESS: Survival Kit for Jail and Prison.*

\*    \*    \*

### LAM, Charlotte (Dawson) 1924-

*PERSONAL:* Born June 17, 1924, in Mexia, Tex.; daughter of Arden Earl and Maude (Merrifield) Dawson; married Marvin B. Lam, March 28, 1951 (divorced, 1959); children: Vicki Nell (Mrs. Paul Parks, Sr.), Mary Lynn (Mrs. Richard Lenz), Bradford Earl. *Education:* University of Oklahoma, B.S., 1956, Ph.D., 1967; Southeastern State College (now Southeastern Oklahoma State University), M.T., 1961. *Home:* 826 North Bryan St., Weatherford, Okla. 73096. *Office:* Southwestern Oklahoma State University, Weatherford, Okla. 73096.

*CAREER:* Elementary school teacher in Springer, Okla., 1950-51, Ione, Wash., 1956-59, Mead, Okla., 1960-61, and Lawton, Okla., 1961-62; Cameron State Agricultural College, Lawton, teacher of English and speech, 1962-64; remedial reading editor in Oklahoma City, Okla., 1966-67; Southwestern Oklahoma State University, Weatherford, member of faculty teaching education and psychology, 1967—. Editor of educational materials, Economy Co. *Member:* National Education Association, International Reading Association, American Association of University Professors, Southwest Reading Council, Oklahoma Education Association, Oklahoma Reading Council, Kappa Delta Pi, Kappa Kappa Iota.

*WRITINGS: Context Clues for Second Grade,* Continental Publishing, 1972. Contributor to reading journals.

*WORK IN PROGRESS: The Organization and Supervision of Reading Programs.*

*AVOCATIONAL INTERESTS:* Playing bridge (holds an accredited bridge teacher certificate).

\*    \*    \*

### LAMBERT, Roy Eugene 1918-

*PERSONAL:* Born November 16, 1918, in Tacoma, Wash.; son of Ulric Eugene and Florence (Reisen) Lambert; married Ruth Margaret Price (a professor), August 25, 1945; children: Leslie Anne, Lorraine Ruth, Lynne Marie, Larry Roy. *Education:* University of Washington, Seattle, B.A., 1949, M.A., 1950; University of Illinois, Ph.D., 1957. *Home:* 1403 Northwest Ninth Ave., Gainesville, Fla. 32601. *Office:* Department of Humanities, University of Florida, Gainesville, Fla. 32601.

*CAREER:* Texas Technological College (now Texas Tech University), Lubbock, assistant professor of linguistics, 1957-58; University of Florida, Gainesville, associate professor of humanities and cybernetics, 1959—. Member of Gainesville Little Theater and Gainesville Civic Ballet. *Military service:* U.S. Army, 1941-45, 1951-53; became lieutenant colonel. *Member:* American Dialect Society, Modern Language Association of America, Academy of Social and Political Scientists, Lichnos, University Professors for Academic Order, Audubon Society, Phi Beta Kappa, Pi Sigma Lambda. *Awards, honors:* Faculty development grants, 1965, 1972.

*WRITINGS:* (With Merlin C. Cox, Gould Sadler, and wife, Ruth Lambert) *Twentieth-Century Values,* MSS Educational Publishing, 1970. Contributor of articles to linguistics and cybernetics journals.

\*    \*    \*

### LAMBERTS, J(acob) J. 1910-

*PERSONAL:* Born July 3, 1910, in Rochester, N.Y.; son of Lambertus J. (a clergyman) and Anna (Dick) Lamberts; married Louise Kieft (a teacher), October 17, 1942; children: Mary. *Education:* Calvin College, B.A., 1931; University of Michigan, M.A., 1949, Ph.D., 1954; University of Groningen, graduate study, 1949-50. *Politics:* Democrat. *Religion:* Presbyterian. *Home:* 237 Broadmor Dr., Tempe, Ariz. 85282. *Office:* Department of English, Arizona State University, Tempe, Ariz. 85281.

*CAREER:* Before turning to teaching was weekly newspaper editor; Northwestern University, Evanston, Ill., instructor, 1953-55, assistant professor of English, 1955-60; Arizona State University, Tempe, associate professor, 1960-63, professor of English, 1963—. Visiting lecturer, University of Minnesota, 1958-59. *Military service:* U.S. Army Air Forces, 1942-45; editor of *Caribbean Breeze,* official publication of 6th Air Force; became sergeant. *Member:* Modern Language Association of America, Linguistic Society of America, National Council of Teachers of English. *Awards, honors:* Fulbright scholar in the Netherlands, 1949-50.

*WRITINGS: A Short Introduction to English Usage,* McGraw, 1972.

Translator from the Dutch: J. H. Bavinck, *The Riddle of Life,* Eerdmans, 1958; Gerrit C. Berkouwer, *Recent Developments in Roman Catholic Thought,* Eerdmans, 1958. Contributor to linguistic and other professional journals and to religious periodicals.

*WORK IN PROGRESS:* A study of English usage with special attention to popular attitudes toward language differences.

\*    \*    \*

### LANDWEHR, Arthur J. II 1934-

*PERSONAL:* Born March 8, 1934, in Northbrook, Ill.; son of Arthur J. and Alice E. (Borchardt) Landwehr; married Avonna Lee Mitchell (an artist), September 19, 1953; children: Arthur J. III, Andrea Lee. *Education:* Drake University, B.A., 1956; Garrett Theological Seminary, B.D., 1959; additional study at University of Chicago, Ecumenical Institute, and Contemporary Theology Institute. *Home:* 310 Church St., Evanston, Ill. 60201. *Office:* First United Methodist Church, 1630 Hinman, Evanston, Ill. 60201.

*CAREER:* Clergyman of United Methodist Church; pastor in Lyndon, Ill., 1956-59, Marseilles, Ill., 1959-65, Lisle, Ill., 1965-69, and Elmhurst, Ill., beginning 1969; currently pastor of First United Methodist Church, Evanston, Ill. Lecturer at Northern Illinois University, Lawrence University, Elmhurst College, St. Bede Abbey, St. Procopius College, and Garrett Theological Seminary. Founder, Ecumenical Insights (lay-centered ecumenical movement); field supervisor, Evangelical Theological Seminary. Member of Chicago Conference of Religion and Race and Church Federation of Greater Chicago. Trustee, Garrett Evangelical Theological Seminary. *Member:* American Association for the Advancement of Science, American Academy of Religion, International Society for General Semantics, American Theological Association (vice-chairman of board of trustees), Psi Chi, Phi Sigma Tau, Rotary Club.

*WRITINGS: In the Third Place,* Abingdon, 1972.

*WORK IN PROGRESS: Authority—Who Needs It?,* a book on the nature of authority within human experience, and its place within the discipline of theological reflection.

\*          \*          \*

## LANE, E(ugene Numa)   1936-

*PERSONAL:* Born August 13, 1936, in Washington, D.C.; son of George Sherman (a professor) and Colette (Resweber) Lane; married Carol Gault, August 22, 1964; children: Michael, Helen. *Education:* Princeton University, A.B., 1958; Yale University, M.A., 1960, Ph.D., 1962. *Politics:* Independent. *Religion:* Episcopalian. *Home:* 813 Maupin Rd., Columbia, Mo. 65201. *Office:* 420 General Classroom Bldg., University of Missouri, Columbia, Mo. 65201.

*CAREER:* University of Virginia, Charlottesville, assistant professor of classics, 1962-66; University of Missouri—Columbia, associate professor of classics, 1966—. *Member:* Archaeological Institute of America, American Philological Association, Classical Association of Middle West and South.

*WRITINGS: Corpus Inscriptionum Religionis Dei Menis,* Volume I, Brill, 1971. Contributor of articles to *Hesperia, Berytus, Anatolian Studies, Muse.*

*WORK IN PROGRESS:* Second volume of *Corpus Inscriptionum Religionis Dei Menis.*

\*          \*          \*

## LANE, Gary   1943-

*PERSONAL:* Born March 25, 1943, in New York, N.Y.; son of Edward and Frances (Berman) Lane; married Bonnie Greenberg, December 31, 1975. *Education:* Oberlin College, B.A., 1964; University of Michigan, M.A., 1965, Ph.D., 1973. *Home:* 13639 Coleridge, San Antonio, Tex. 78217. *Office:* Department of English, University of Texas, San Antonio, Tex. 78285.

*CAREER:* Muhlenburg College, Allentown, Pa., instructor in modern poetry and creative writing, 1969-72; University of Michigan, Ann Arbor, visiting lecturer in creative writing, 1972-74; University of Miami, Coral Gables, Florida, assistant professor of English, 1974-76; University of Texas at San Antonio, associate professor of English, 1976—. *Member:* Modern Language Association of America, Poetry Society of America.

*WRITINGS:* (Editor) *A Word Index to Joyce's Dubliners,* Haskell House, 1972; (editor) *A Concordance to the Poems of Theodore Roethke,* Scarecrow, 1972; (editor) *A Concordance to the Poems of Hart Crane,* Haskell House, 1972; (editor) *A Concordance to the Poems of Marianne Moore,* Haskell House, 1972; (editor) *A Concordance to Personae: The Shorter Poems of Ezra Pound,* Haskell House, 1972; *I Am: A Study of E. E. Cummings' Poems,* University Press of Kansas, 1976; (editor) *A Concordance to the Poems of Dylan Thomas,* Scarecrow, 1976; *Inscape* (poems), Blue Lion Press, 1977; (editor) *Sylvia Plath: A Bibliography,* Scarecrow, 1978; (editor and contributor) *Sylvia Plath: New Essays on the Poetry,* Johns Hopkins Press, in press. Contributor of poems to *Arcade, The Blackbird Circle, Monmouth Review* and other periodicals. Contributor of articles to *Explicator, Studies in Short Fiction* and other periodicals.

*WORK IN PROGRESS: The Poetry of Sylvia Plath,* probably from Johns Hopkins Press; *Henry's Rest: New Essays on the Poetry of John Berryman,* probably from University of Texas Press; a new volume of poetry.

*AVOCATIONAL INTERESTS:* Chess, tennis.

\*          \*          \*

## LANGNER, Nola   1930-

*PERSONAL:* Born September 24, 1930, in New York, N.Y.; daughter of Gerald B. (owner of an advertising agency) and Elsie (Feigenbaum) Spiero; married Thomas S. Langner (a research professor of sociology at Columbia University), February 21, 1953; children: Lisa, Josh, Eli, Gretchen and Belinda (twins). *Education:* Attended Vassar College, 1948-50; Bennington College, B.A., 1952. *Home and studio:* 271 Central Park W., New York, N.Y. 10024. *Agent:* Marilyn Marlow, Curtis Brown, Ltd., 575 Madison Ave., New York, N.Y. 10022.

*CAREER:* After college worked briefly doing paste-ups for movie magazines published by Ideal Publishing Co., New York City; illustrator at TV Art Studio, New York City, 1953-54; writer and illustrator of children's books. *Awards, honors: Miss Lucy* was named by *New York Times* as one of the outstanding picture books of 1969; Horn Book award for illustrations, *Boston Globe,* 1975, for *Scram, Kid!.*

*WRITINGS*—Self-illustrated juveniles: *Miss Lucy,* Macmillan, 1969; *Go and Shut the Door,* Dial, 1971; *Joseph and the Wonderful Tree,* Addison-Wesley, 1972; (adapter) *Cinderella,* Scholastic Book Services, 1972; *Dusty,* Coward, 1976; *Rafiki,* Viking, 1977.

Illustrator: Flora Fifield, *Pictures for the Palace,* Vanguard, 1958; Robert Pack, *The Forgotten Secret,* Macmillan, 1959; Ann McGovern, *Who Has a Secret?,* Houghton, 1963; Pack, *How to Catch a Crocodile,* Knopf, 1964; Sidney Simon, *Henry the Uncatchable Mouse,* Norton, 1964; McGovern, *Little Wolf,* Abelard, 1965; Aileen Olsen, *Bernadine and the Water Bucket,* Abelard, 1966; Charles House, *The Lonesome Egg,* Norton, 1968; Harold Longman, *The Kitchen-Window Squirrel,* Parents' Magazine Press, 1969; *Hi Diddle Diddle,* Scholastic Book Services, 1970; McGovern, *Scram, Kid!,* Viking, 1974; Marcia Newfield, *Six Rags Apiece,* Warne, 1976; McGovern, *Half a Kingdom,* Warne, 1977.

*SIDELIGHTS:* Nola Langner says that she has "always loved children's books—particularly my early German ones (I learned German as a small child). I love movies and dance," she continues, "and think of picture books as moving along like animation and dance choreography.... We travel a lot with our children and places I've seen seem to crop up as background material or story ideas. My children are by now very good travelers and also very good book critics. I test out my writing with them (as well as art) and they keep me from anything which is dishonest, or which doesn't really fit with the story. Children have a good sense of what's true and real. Even in a fantasy story, illogic is quickly spotted."

Langner and her husband built their own summer and weekend house in Connecticut. They have seven Siamese cats, which explains why cats frequent her books.

\*          \*          \*

## LANTZ, Herman R.   1919-

*PERSONAL:* Born June 17, 1919, in New York, N.Y.; son of Abraham and Sarah (Alpert) Lantz; married June 5, 1948; children: Sarah and Rachel. *Education:* Kent State University, B.S., 1942; Ohio State University, M.A., 1947, Ph.D.,

1950. *Office:* Department of Sociology, Southern Illinois University, Carbondale, Ill. 62901.

*CAREER:* Ohio State University, Columbus, instructor, 1948-50; Norwich State Hospital, Norwich, Conn., researcher and counselor, 1950-51; Southern Illinois University at Carbondale, assistant professor, 1951-54, associate professor, 1954-59, professor of sociology, 1959—. Research fellow, Harvard University, Center for the Study of History of Liberty in America, 1962-63; scholar, Princeton University, summer, 1965. *Military service:* U.S. Army Air Forces, 1942-46. *Member:* American Sociological Association, Pi Gamma Mu, Alpha Kappa Delta.

*WRITINGS:* (With assistance of J. S. McCrary) *People of Coal Town,* Columbia University Press, 1958; (with Eloise C. Snyder) *Marriage: An Examination of the Man-Woman Relationship,* Wiley, 1962, 2nd edition, with *Workbook,* 1969; (with Gunnar Boalt) *Universities and Research: Observations on the United States and Sweden,* Wiley, 1970; (with Boalt and Erling Ribbing) *Resource Allocation Among Academic Departments,* Almqvist & Wiksell, 1971; (with Boalt) *The Sociology of the Chivalrous Orders,* Norstedt & Soners, 1971; (with Boalt and Helena Herlin) *Research and Career,* Almqvist & Wiksell, 1971; *A Community in Search of Itself: A Case History of Cairo, Illinois,* Southern Illinois University Press, 1971.

Contributor: William Foster and Morris Caldwell, editors, *Analysis of Social Problems,* Stackpole, 1954; Arthur Shostock and William Gomberg, editors, *Blue-Collar World,* Prentice-Hall, 1964; Mildred B. Kantor, editor, *Mobility and Mental Health,* C. C Thomas, 1965. Contributor of twenty-six articles to professional journals. General editor and author of foreword to most volumes, "Perspectives in Sociology," seven books, Southern Illinois University Press, 1964-71.

*       *       *

## LAPPE, Frances Moore  1944-

*PERSONAL:* Surname is pronounced La-*pay;* born February 10, 1944, in Pendleton, Ore.; daughter of John Gilmer (a meteorologist) and Ina (Skrifvars) Moore; married Marc Alan Lappe (a biology research associate), November 12, 1967 (divorced November, 1977); children: Anthony, Anna. *Education:* Attended American University, 1962-63; Earlham College, A.B., 1966; University of California, Berkeley, additional study, 1968. *Home:* 239 Precita Ave., San Francisco, Calif. 94110. *Agent:* Joan Raines, Raines & Raines, 475 Fifth Ave., New York, N.Y. 10017. *Office:* Institute for Food and Development Policy, 2588 Mission St., San Francisco, Calif. 94110.

*CAREER:* Philadelphia Neighborhood Renewal Program, Philadelphia, Pa., community organizer, 1967-69; Institute for Food and Development Policy, San Francisco, Calif., founder and staff member, 1975—.

*WRITINGS: Diet for a Small Planet,* Ballantine, 1971, 2nd edition, 1975; (with Joseph Collins) *Food First: Beyond the Myth of Scarcity,* Houghton, 1977. Contributor to numerous publications, including *New Internationalist, Renaissance Universal, CNI Weekly Report, American Freedom from Hunger Foundation Bulletin, Nutrition Action, Home Echos, East-West Journal, World Future Studies, Boston Globe, Journal of Nutrition Education, Ceres, Mother Jones, Social Scientist,* and *Vegetarian Times.*

*WORK IN PROGRESS:* Articles and pamphlets on the work of people throughout the world for food self-reliance.

*SIDELIGHTS:* In *Food First: Beyond the Myth of Scarcity,* Frances Moore Lappe and Joseph Collins present the argument that starvation and hunger are not caused by insufficient food supplies to feed the world's population, by unfavorable climate or weather conditions, or by archaic farming methods employed by underdeveloped countries. The problem, according to Lappe and Collins, is instead rooted in the centralized control of farmland and in the colonialization of underdeveloped countries by Western nations. Quite simply, it is more profitable to sow "cash" crops than basic food products adequate to feed the local populations. According to John L. Hess, the book states "that there is enough land in the world, but much of it is idle or badly used, and there is enough food, but much of it is wasted or badly distributed."

The authors of *Food First* write that during the great famine of 1974 the African nation of Mali actually increased its export of peanuts; much of the donated rice sent to Bangladesh during the famine rotted because the natives could not afford to buy it. Mexico, a country whose high infant death rate is closely associated with hunger and malnutrition, exports large amounts of winter vegetables to the United States; one-half to two-thirds of certain winter vegetables consumed in this country are imported from Mexico. Mark Hertsgaard cites other examples: "The croplands of India and Vietnam, and of other European colonies in Asia, were used throughout the late nineteenth and early twentieth centuries to produce wheat and rice for export, while many of the rural poor in those regions went hungry.... Regions which had been largely self-reliant before colonial intervention became highly vulnerable to any disruption in the supply of imported food. Control over the resources used to grow food had been lost."

Emma Rothschild writes that "the vision of *Food First* is more political and cultural than technological. The authors believe that villages and countries must become 'self-reliant' in food. Communities should set out, as their first priority, to produce food for local consumption and to manufacture the tools and fertilizers that they need." Acquiring this self-reliance would require massive land reform and some return of control and ownership of local farming land to the people who live on it and away from multinational corporations. Rothschild continues, "[Lappe and Collins] see elements of this equitable agrarian life in China, and to a larger extent in those capitalistic countries such as Taiwan and Japan where land and rural incomes are fairly equally distributed."

In an interview with Janet Somerville for Canada's "Ten Days for World Development" program, Lappe states: "Very clearly, people can feed themselves. There is no physical limit-problem at the present time on the world's capacity to feed everyone well. There is enough grain alone produced—without counting all the potatoes, beans, nuts, fruits, vegetables and other foods that people eat—to provide 3000 calories each day for every man, woman and child on earth. And that's the amount the average American eats. So the problem is not scarcity. Scarcity is a scare word that makes people not look at underlying causes and helps the people who are benefitting from the present way things are operating—helps them avoid coming to terms with what changes are necessary for all of us to be able to eat. ... What we've concluded—and this is something the facts have led us to, not some preconceived bias—is this: the only way people will be fed is if the majority of people are themselves in control of, and actively participating in, the production process. As a peasant said recently in India—no matter how much the land is producing, if you don't have land, you don't eat."

*BIOGRAPHICAL/CRITICAL SOURCES: Publishers Weekly,* August 2, 1971, May 9, 1977; *American Forests,* May, 1972; *Book World,* July 10, 1977; *New York Times Book Review,* July 17, 1977; *New York Times,* August 3, 1977; *Guardian Weekly,* September 4, 1977; *Progressive,* December, 1977; *Christian Science Monitor,* January 12, 1978.

\* \* \*

## LASHER, Faith B. 1921-

*PERSONAL:* Born January 26, 1921, in Lincoln County, Mont.; daughter of Benjamen and Clara (Weaver) Nelson; married Richard L. Hoppie, 1944 (died, 1958); married Don R. Lasher, 1962; children: Michael Jay. *Education:* St. Patrick's School of Nursing, Missoula, Mont., R.N., 1944. *Religion:* Protestant. *Home:* 119 Water St., Gaithersburg, Md. 20760.

*CAREER:* Registered nurse and licensed real estate saleswoman. *Member:* Women in Communications.

*WRITINGS: Hubert Hippo's World* (juvenile), Childrens Press, 1971. Contributor of fiction, poems, and articles to *Primary Treasure, Happy Times, Wee Wisdom, Rotarian, Bottle News, Women's Circle, American Collector, Spinning Wheel, Antique Trader, Southeast Trader* and *Collectors News,* and other magazines.

*WORK IN PROGRESS:* A series of articles on antiques and collectibles.

*SIDELIGHTS:* Faith Lasher told *CA:* "I began writing when my son was a baby as a mental stimulus. My first efforts were stories for young children. Later I did some articles for them and also some poetry. Several years ago I interviewed a collector of American Indian pottery. That was so much fun, and sold so quickly, that I immediately did another 'collector' article. Now I keep busy with a steady program of covering antique shows, interviewing collectors and doing research articles about antiques or collectibles. Occasionally for a change of pace I do an article which consists mainly of a collection of recipes or I interview a craftsperson and write up their approach to their craft. Illustrations are vital for this type of writing so along the way I learned the rudiments of photography and do my own developing and printing for the black and white photos. Although the books are great I enjoy doing articles because each requires only a short time of concentrated work, then I'm free until ready to start another."

*AVOCATIONAL INTERESTS:* Photography, vegetable gardening.

*BIOGRAPHICAL/CRITICAL SOURCES: National Antiques Review,* September, 1975.

\* \* \*

## LATANE, Bibb 1937-

*PERSONAL:* Surname is pronounced Latin-*a;* born July 19, 1937, in New York, N.Y.; son of Henry A. (an economist) and Felicite (Bibb) Latane; married Jane Arbiter; children: Julia, Claire, Henry. *Education:* Yale University, B.A., 1958; University of Minnesota, Ph.D., 1963. *Office:* Behavioral Sciences Laboratory, Ohio State University, Columbus, Ohio 43210.

*CAREER:* Columbia University, New York, N.Y., 1961-68, began as instructor, became associate professor; Ohio State University, Columbus, associate professor, 1968-70, professor of psychology, 1970—, director of Behavioral Sci-

ences Laboratory, 1976—. *Member:* Society for Personality and Social Psychology (president, 1977-79). *Awards, honors:* Socio-psychological prize of the American Association for the Advancement of Science, and Century Psychology award, both 1970, for *The Unresponsive Bystander;* Guggenheim fellowship, 1974-75.

*WRITINGS:* (With J. M. Darley) *The Unresponsive Bystander: Why Doesn't He Help?,* Appleton, 1970. Contributor of about sixty articles to journals.

\* \* \*

## LAUB, (Martin) Julian 1929-

*PERSONAL:* Born January 17, 1929, in New York, N.Y.; son of Max A. (a manager) and Pauline (Green) Laub; married Naomi Klauber, October 3, 1953; children: Beth. *Education:* New York University, B.S.M.E., 1951; Alfred University, M.S., 1962; Cornell University, Ph.D., 1970. *Home:* 532 Sibley Pl., Delmar, N.Y. 12054. *Office:* New York State Department of Environment Conservation, 50 Wolf Rd., Albany, N.Y. 12201.

*CAREER:* State University of New York Agricultural and Technical College at Alfred (now Alfred State College), 1959-66, became professor of environmental technology and chairman of department; Cornell University, Ithaca, N.Y., professor and research associate, 1967-70; New York State Department of Environment Conservation, Albany, principal planner, 1969—. Consultant engineer and planner for Eastern Engineer and Planner Association. *Military service:* U.S. Army, Corps of Engineers, 1944-46; became staff sergeant. *Member:* American Society of Mechanical Engineers, American Institute of Planners, American Society of Planning Officials. *Awards, honors:* U.S. Office of Education grant, 1969; New York State Department of Education grant, 1969.

*WRITINGS: Heating and Air Conditioning Practice,* Holt, 1963; *College and Community Development: A Socio-economic Analysis for Urban Regional Growth,* Praeger, 1970.

*WORK IN PROGRESS:* A book on public affairs, *State Government Efficiency and Effectiveness;* papers on planning and environment.

*SIDELIGHTS:* Julian Laub is concerned with various aspects of urban development. He enjoys the theatre, art, literature, and travel.

\* \* \*

## LAUER, Theodore E. 1931-

*PERSONAL:* Born February 4, 1931, in Beloit, Wis.; son of Theodore E. and Lolita Posey (Rambo) Lauer; married Kathryn Jones; children: David, Barbara, Betsy, Robert. *Education:* Millikin University, B.A., 1953; Washington University, LL.B., 1956; University of Michigan, S.J.D., 1958. *Home:* 13 Calle de Valle, Santa Fe, N.M. 87501. *Office:* Lauer & Lauer, 319 Johnson St., Santa Fe, N.M. 87501.

*CAREER:* Admitted to the Bar of the State of Missouri, 1956, and New Mexico Bar, 1974; private practice of law, and partner in law firm of Cave and Lauer, Fulton, Mo., 1958-62; Callaway County, Mo., prosecuting attorney, 1961-62; University of Missouri—Columbia, lecturer, 1960-62, assistant professor, 1962-65, associate professor, 1965-69, professor of law, 1969-71; St. Louis University, National Juvenile Law Center, St. Louis, Mo., deputy director, 1970-71, director, 1971-74; Lauer and Lauer, Santa Fe, N.M., partner, 1974—. Visiting professor of law, St. Louis University, 1970-74. State chairman, New Mexico Council on Crime and Delinquency, 1978—. Legal services consultant, Office of Economic Opportunity, 1967-70; reporter, Missouri Supreme Court Committee on Rules of Practice and Procedure in Juvenile Court, 1969-72. *Member:* American Bar Association, New Mexico Criminal Defense Lawyers Association (president, 1976—). *Awards, honors:* Order of the Coif, 1956.

*WRITINGS:* (With Dominic B. King and W. L. Ziegler) *Water Resources and the Law,* University of Michigan Press, 1958; *Missouri Water Law,* University of Missouri, 1966; (with Donald B. King, C. A. Kuenzel, N. O. Littlefield, and B. Stone) *Commercial Transactions Under the Uniform Code,* Matthew Bender, 1968, revised edition, 1974; (with J. A. Cannon, R. M. Faust, C. E. Miller, and P. D. Piersma) *Law and Tactics in Juvenile Cases,* St. Louis University Press, 1972, 2nd edition, 1974. Regular contributor to various law journals.

*WORK IN PROGRESS:* Newsletter and commentaries on New Mexico criminal law.

\*     \*     \*

## LAUGHLIN, Ledlie Irwin   1890-1977

*PERSONAL:* Born April 26, 1890, in Pittsburgh, Pa.; son of James Ben and Clara (Young) Laughlin; married Roberta M. Howe, September 25, 1925; children: Leighton H., James B., Ledlie I., Jr., Robert M. *Education:* Princeton University, B.S., 1912. *Politics:* Independent. *Religion:* Presbyterian. *Home:* Drakes Corner Rd., Princeton, N.J. 08540.

*CAREER:* Jones & Laughlin Steel Corp., Pittsburgh, Pa., various positions in rolling mills and on open hearth furnaces, 1912-18, sales work, 1920-28, district manager of Buffalo office, 1922-28, director of board, 1922-64; Princeton University, Princeton, N.J., 1928-53, began as assistant director of admissions, became director of admissions and adviser to freshmen. Member of board of directors, Princeton Hospital; reader and contributor, Recordings for the Blind, Princeton; head of building fund drive, Princeton Y.M.C.A. and Y.W.C.A. *Military service:* U.S. Army, Infantry, 1917-19; became captain.

*WRITINGS: Pewter in America: Its Makers and Their Marks,* Volumes I and II, Houghton, 1940, 2nd edition, Barre, 1969, Volume III, Barre, 1971; *Joseph Ledlie and William Moody, Early Pittsburgh Residents: Their Background and Some of Their Descendants,* University of Pittsburgh Press, 1961. Contributor of articles to *Antiques* and other periodicals and bulletins.

*SIDELIGHTS:* Ledlie Laughlin, who had a fine collection of American pewter, did research in that subject for over forty-five years.†

(Died February 7, 1977)

\*     \*     \*

## LAWS, G(eorge) Malcolm, Jr.   1919-

*PERSONAL:* Born January 4, 1919, in Philadelphia, Pa.; son of George M. (a physician) and Elizabeth H. (Williams) Laws; married Beatrice Elfreth, June 10, 1950; children: Susan E., Katherine A., George M. III, Elizabeth A. *Education:* Attended Princeton University, 1937-40; University of Pennsylvania, A.B., 1942, A.M., 1946, Ph.D., 1949. *Politics:* Republican. *Religion:* Episcopalian. *Home:* 422 Penn Rd., Wynnewood, Pa. 19096. *Office:* Department of English, University of Pennsylvania, Philadelphia, Pa. 19104.

*CAREER:* University of Pennsylvania, Philadelphia, assistant instructor, 1942-44, instructor, 1944-55, assistant professor, 1955-59, associate professor, 1959-66, professor of English, 1966—. *Member:* American Folklore Society, Merion Cricket Club, Union Benevolent Association (vice-president), Philobiblon Club.

*WRITINGS: Native American Balladry,* American Folklore Society, 1950, revised edition, 1964; *American Balladry from British Broadsides,* American Folklore Society, 1957; (contributor) Horace P. Beck, editor, *Folklore in Action,* American Folklore Society, 1962; (contributor) Tristram P. Coffin, editor, *Our Living Traditions,* Basic Books, 1968; (contributor) W. Paul Elledge and Richard L. Hoffmann, editors, *Romantic and Victorian: Studies in Memory of William H. Marshall,* Fairleigh Dickinson University Press, 1971; *The British Literary Ballad,* Southern Illinois University Press, 1972.

*WORK IN PROGRESS:* A study of nineteenth-century British and American humor.

*AVOCATIONAL INTERESTS:* Collecting books.

\*     \*     \*

## LEACOCK, Eleanor Burke   1922-

*PERSONAL:* Born July 2, 1922, in Weehawken, N.J.; daughter of Kenneth (a critic and philosopher) and Lily Mary (Batterham) Burke; married Richard Leacock (a film maker), December 27, 1941; married second husband, James Haughton (a community organizer), August 3, 1966; children: (first marriage) Elspeth, Robert, David, Claudia. *Education:* Barnard College, B.A. (cum laude), 1944; Columbia University, M.A., 1946, Ph.D., 1952. *Home:* 135 Duane St., New York, N.Y. 10013. *Office:* Department of Anthropology, City College of the City University of New York, Convent Ave. and 138th St., New York, N.Y. 10031.

*CAREER:* Field worker among Harrison Indians of British Columbia, 1945, among Montagnais-Naskapi Indians of Quebec, Newfoundland, and Labrador, 1950-51; Cornell University, Medical College, Ithaca, N.Y., research assistant in department of psychiatry, 1952-55; Queens College of the City of New York (now Queens College of the City University of New York), Flushing, N.Y., lecturer in department of anthropology and sociology, 1955-56; U.S. Department of Health, Education and Welfare, Washington, D.C., special consultant to Behavioral Studies Section, 1957-58; co-director of research on problems in suburban interracial housing in Teaneck, N.J., 1958-60; Bank Street College of Education, New York City, senior research associate of schools and mental health project, 1958-65; Polytechnic Institute of Brooklyn, Brooklyn, N.Y., lecturer in department of history and economics, 1962-63, associate professor, 1963-67, professor of anthropology, 1967-72; City College of the City University of New York, New York City, professor of anthropology and chairman of the department, 1972—. City College of the City University of New York, part-time lecturer, 1956-60, summer lecturer, 1966, 1967; part-time lecturer at Washington Square College, New York University, 1960-61.

*MEMBER:* American Association for the Advancement of Science (secretary of section on anthropology, 1962-66), American Anthropological Association (fellow; member of executive board, 1971-73), Society for Applied Anthropology (fellow; member of executive committee, 1972-75), American Indian Ethnohistoric Society (secretary-treasurer, 1961-65), Society for the Psychological Study of Social Issues, American Ethnological Society, Phi Beta Kappa.

*Awards, honors:* Wenner Gren Foundation grant to do research on child training in Switzerland and Italy, 1948-49; Rabinowitz Foundation and National Research Council grants to do research in Zambia, East Africa, 1970-71.

*WRITINGS:* (Editor and author of introduction) Lewis Henry Morgan, *Ancient Society,* Meridian Books, 1963; (with Martin Deutsch and Joshua A. Fishman) *Toward Integration in Suburban Housing: The Bridgeview Study,* Anti-Defamation League of B'nai B'rith, 1965; *Teaching and Learning in City Schools: A Comparative Study,* Basic Books, 1969; (editor with Nancy Lurie) *North American Indians in Historical Perspective,* Random House, 1971; (editor) *Culture of Poverty: A Critique,* Simon & Schuster, 1971; (editor and author of introduction), Frederick Engels, *Origin of the Family, Private Property, and the State,* International Publishers, 1972.

Contributor: Marian W. Smith, editor, *Indians of the Urban Northwest,* Columbia University Press, 1949; Alexander Leighton and others, editors, *Explorations in Social Psychiatry,* Basic Books, 1957; Yehudi A. Cohen, editor, *Social Structure and Personality: A Casebook,* Holt, 1961; Joseph Zubin, editor, *Field Studies in the Mental Disorders,* Grune, 1961; Arno A. Bellack, editor, *Theory and Research in Teaching,* Teachers College Press, 1963; Glen D. Mills, editor, *Elementary School Guidance and Counseling: An Introduction through Essays and Commentaries,* Random House, 1969; Annette T. Rubinstein, editor, *Schools against Children: The Case for Community Control,* Monthly Review Press, 1970; Melvin L. Silberman, editor, *The Experience of Schooling,* Holt, 1971; Murray Wax, editor, *Anthropological Perspectives on Education,* Basic Books, 1971; Courtney Cazden and others, editors, *Functions of Language in the Classroom,* Teachers College Press, 1971. Contributor of about thirty articles and reviews to anthropology, history, and education journals.

*WORK IN PROGRESS: Labrador Winter,* with William Duncan Strong, for Columbia University Press.

*BIOGRAPHICAL/CRITICAL SOURCES: New York Times Book Review,* September 14, 1969.

\* \* \*

## LEACOCK, Ruth 1926-

*PERSONAL:* Born January 30, 1926, in Chicago, Ill.; daughter of Adam and Alma (Stein) David; married Seth Leacock (a professor), May 10, 1949. *Education:* University of Chicago, Ph.B., 1945; University of Wisconsin, B.A., 1948; University of California, M.A., 1952, Ph.D., 1959. *Home:* Rt. 1, Box 179, Mansfield Center, Conn. 06250.

*CAREER:* Southeast Junior College, Chicago, Ill., instructor in social science, 1960-62; Indiana University, Gary, lecturer in history, 1963-64; Central Connecticut State College, New Britain, associate professor of history, 1965-77. *Member:* American Historical Association.

*WRITINGS:* (With husband, Seth Leacock) *Spirits of the Deep,* Doubleday, 1972.†

\* \* \*

## LEAKEY, Louis (Seymour Bazett) 1903-1972

August 7, 1903—October 1, 1972; British anthropologist, educator, and author of books on man's African ancestry, whose fossil discoveries at Africa's Olduvai Gorge revolutionized the field of anthropology. Obituaries: *New York Times,* October 2, 1972; *Newsweek,* October 16, 1972.

## LEAR, John 1909-

*PERSONAL:* Born August 10, 1909, near Allen, Pa.; son of Charles (a carpenter) and Esther May (Sourbeer) Lear; married Dorothy Leeds, September 26, 1931 (died May 9, 1965); married Marie Nesta, August 28, 1966. *Education:* Attended New York University, 1949. *Home:* 505 North Lake Shore Dr., Chicago, Ill. 60611.

*CAREER: Daily Local News,* Mechanicsburg, Pa., editor, 1927-28; *Patriot,* Harrisburg, Pa., reporter, 1928-34; Associated Press, early day editor in Philadelphia, Pa., 1934, assistant night editor in Chicago, Ill., 1935, special news service editor in New York City, 1936-39, roving correspondent on the South American continent, Buenos Aires, Argentina, 1940-41, Latin American specialist in Washington, D.C., 1941; Office of the Governor, San Juan, Puerto Rico, coordinator of information, 1942-43; Press Association, New York City, radio news writer, 1943; free-lance writer, 1944-48; *Steelways* (magazine), New York City, managing editor, 1948-49; *Colliers,* New York City, chief articles editor, 1949-50, associate editor, 1950-53; International Business Machines (IBM), New York City, communications consultant to T. J. Watson, Jr., 1953-54; Research Institute of America, New York City, special consultant on atomics and automation, 1954-55; *Saturday Review,* New York City, science editor, 1956-71, senior editor, 1971-72; Bauer Engineering, Inc., Chicago, vice-president for communications, 1972; Bauer, Sheaffer & Lear, Inc., Chicago, vice-president and chief editor, 1972-75; Keifer & Associates, chief editor, 1975-76; *Atlas World Press Review,* New York City, contributing editor, 1976—. American correspondent, *New Scientist* (London), 1956-62; member of board of advisers, *Harper Dictionary of Contemporary Usage,* 1970—. Consultant to Russell Sage Foundation, 1967-68, Institute for Social Research, University of Michigan, 1972-73, Office of Technology Assessment, U.S. Congress, 1975-76, National Academy of Sciences forum, 1976, and Rockefeller Foundation, 1977.

*MEMBER:* Sigma Delta Chi. *Awards, honors:* Distinguished Public Service Award, Sigma Delta Chi, 1950, 1961; Headliners Award, 1950; George Westinghouse Science Writing Award, American Association for the Advancement of Science, 1951; Albert Lasker Award for Medical Journalism, 1952; D.Sc., Dickinson College, 1968; citation from Deadline Club (New York, N.Y.), 1971; Ford Foundation study and travel grant.

*WRITINGS: Forgotten Front,* Dutton, 1942; *Kepler's Dream,* University of California Press, 1965.

Contributor: John Haverstick, editor, *The Saturday Review Treasury,* Simon & Schuster, 1957; *World Today,* Shinozaki Shorin (Tokyo), 1958; M. Shutte and Erwin R. Steinberg, editors, *Personal Integrity,* Norton, 1961; Dean Albertson, editor, *Eisenhower as President,* Hill & Wang, 1963; Newman P. Birk and Genevieve Birk, editors, *Ideas and Style,* Odyssey, 1968; Frank L. Bergmann, editor, *Essays,* W. C. Brown, 1970; Hermann K. Bleitrau and James F. Downs, editors, *Human Variation: Readings in Physical Anthropology,* Glencoe Press, 1971; Alfred Balk and James Boylan, editors, *Our Troubled Press,* Little, Brown, 1971; Doris Asmundsson, editor, *Doom of A Dream,* Chandler Publishing, 1971; Robert H. Mayer and Joseph L. Subbiando, *Borrowed Time: Literature on Man and His Environment,* Wadsworth, 1972; James Armstrong, *Voyages of Discovery,* Wiley, 1972; Maxwell Honorton, editor, *Dimensions of the Future,* Holt, 1974; Richard Howell, editor, *ASFE Institute of Professional Practice Seminar One, 1975,* Risk Analysis & Research Corp., 1975.

*WORK IN PROGRESS:* A book on the recombinant DNA controversy, *The Genetic Time Bomb;* a biography of Marie Tharp.

\* \* \*

## LEBOW, Victor 1902-

*PERSONAL:* Born December 26, 1902, in Brooklyn, N.Y.; son of Robert and Sarah (Seidel) Lebow; married Leah Markel, December 17, 1924; children: Nina Beth Lebow Reed. *Education:* Studied in evening classes at College of the City of New York (now City College of the City University of New York), 1919-25. *Home:* 11 Riverside Dr., Apt. 13-E West, New York, N.Y. 10023.

*CAREER:* Sales manager of chain store group while still in his twenties, and employed in various capacities in other businesses, 1919-34; Chester H. Roth Co., Inc. (now Kayser-Roth Corp.), New York, N.Y., sales promotion manager, 1934-36, sales and advertising manager, 1936-46, vice-president-marketing, 1946-50; marketing consultant to various U.S. and foreign corporations, 1950-71. Co-chairman, Columbia University Seminar on Economic Planning—Public and Private. Consultant and member of board of directors, Faberge, Inc. Trustee, Research Institute for the Study of Man.

*WRITINGS: Free Enterprise: The Opium of the American People,* Oriole Editions, 1972. Contributor to *Progressive, Harper's, Nation, Challenge,* and to university and business publications.

*WORK IN PROGRESS:* A book on the role of American capitalism in the world.

\* \* \*

## LEBOWITZ, Naomi 1932-

*PERSONAL:* First syllable of surname sounds like "deb"; born February 6, 1932, in St. Louis, Mo.; daughter of Julius (a rabbi) and Mildred (Dubin) Gordon; married Albert Lebowitz (an attorney and writer), November 26, 1953; children: Joel, Judith. *Education:* Attended Sorbonne, University of Paris, 1951-52; Wellesley College, B.A., 1953; Washington University, St. Louis, Mo., M.A., 1955, Ph.D., 1962. *Religion:* Jewish. *Home:* 743 Yale Ave., University City, Mo. 63130. *Office:* English Department, Washington University, St. Louis, Mo. 63130.

*CAREER:* Washington University, St. Louis, Mo., professor of English and comparative literature. *Awards, honors:* American Association of University Women fellowship, 1966-67; Guggenheim fellowship, 1972-73.

*WRITINGS:* (Editor) *Discussions of Henry James,* Heath, 1962; *The Imagination of Loving: Henry James,* Wayne State University Press, 1963; *Humanism and the Absurd in the Modern Novel,* Northwestern University Press, 1971; *Italo Svevo,* Rutgers University Press, 1978. Contributor of articles to *Kenyon Review, Perspective, Sewanee Review, Toronto Quarterly, Criticism.*

*BIOGRAPHICAL/CRITICAL SOURCES: South Atlantic Quarterly,* winter, 1967.

\* \* \*

## Le CLERCQ, Jacques Georges Clemenceau 1898-1972

### (Paul Tanaquil)

June 27, 1898—August 29, 1972; Austrian-born American educator, poet, and authority on French literature and Ro-

mance languages. Obituaries: *New York Times,* September 3, 1972.

\* \* \*

## LEE, Elizabeth Briant 1908-

*PERSONAL:* Born September 9, 1908, in Pittsburgh, Pa., daughter of William Wolfer (a personnel manager) and Adah May (Riley) Briant; married Alfred McClung Lee (a social scientist), September 15, 1927; children: Alfred McClung III, Briant Hamor. *Education:* University of Pittsburgh, B.A., 1930, M.A., 1931; Yale University, Ph.D., 1937. *Religion:* Humanist-Friend. *Home:* 100 Hemlock Rd., Short Hills, N.J. 07078. *Office:* Irish Culture-and-Personality Project, Graduate School and University Center of the City University of New York, New York, N.Y.

*CAREER:* Wayne University (now Wayne State University), Detroit, Mich., lecturer in sociology, 1944-46; Brooklyn College (now Brooklyn College of the City University of New York), Brooklyn, N.Y., lecturer in sociology, 1949-50; Hartford Theological Seminary, Hartford, Conn., lecturer in sociology, 1951-53; Connecticut College for Women (now Connecticut College), New London, visiting associate professor of sociology and acting chairman of department, 1953-54; Universita Cattolica del Sacro Cuore, Milan, Italy, research associate of Center for Sociological Research, 1957-58; Fairleigh Dickinson University, Rutherford, N.J., lecturer in sociology and anthropology, 1962-63, 1965-66; Graduate School and University Center of the City University of New York, New York, N.Y., associate director of Irish Culture-and-Personality Project, 1965—. Field researcher in Ireland, 1955, 1958, 1961, 1967, 1970, 1975, in Italy and Sicily, 1957-58, 1960-61, 1967, 1970. U.S. Department of State lecturer in Pakistan, India, Syria, Lebanon, Italy, Austria, Belgium, Germany, and Iceland, 1967. Participant, New Jersey State Conference of International Women's Year, 1977.

*MEMBER:* American Sociological Association (fellow), Society for the Study of Social Problems (co-organizer; vice president, 1977-78; life member), Irish Sociological Association (honorary member), Association for Humanist Sociology (co-organizer; president, 1978), Sociologists for Women in Society, Eastern Sociological Society (secretary-treasurer, 1956-57, 1958-59), Summit (N.J.) Art Center, Summit (N.J.) College Club, Kappa Kappa Gamma. *Awards, honors:* Annual merit award, Eastern Sociological Society, 1974.

*WRITINGS:* (Editor with husband, Alfred McClung Lee) *The Fine Art of Propaganda,* Harcourt, 1939, revised edition, Octagon, 1972; (editor with A. M. Lee) *Social Problems in America,* Holt, 1949, revised edition, 1955; (editor with Arnold N. Rose and others) *Mental Health and Mental Disorder,* Norton, 1955; (with A. M. Lee) *Marriage and the Family,* Barnes & Noble, 1961, revised edition, 1967. Contributor of articles and reviews to journals and magazines.

*WORK IN PROGRESS:* Statistical study of the life histories of more than 800 eminent American women; special studies of Irish and Sicilian families.

*AVOCATIONAL INTERESTS:* Painting—has exhibited many paintings; gardening, especially roses and irises.

\* \* \*

## LEE, Harold N(ewton) 1899-

*PERSONAL:* Born August 6, 1899, in Seattle, Wash.; son of George Hewit (a minister) and Nettie Anna (Cooke) Lee;

married Norma Soule, June 6, 1924; children: Walter Cooke, Donald Soule. *Education:* Attended George Fox College, 1917-19; University of Oregon, B.A., 1922, M.A., 1924; Harvard University, Ph.D., 1930. *Home and office:* 801 Broadway, New Orleans, La. 70118.

*CAREER:* Tulane University, Newcomb College, New Orleans, La., assistant professor, 1925-36, associate professor, 1936-43, professor of philosophy, 1943-70, professor emeritus, 1970—. Instructor and tutor in philosophy, Harvard University, 1930-31. *Member:* American Philosophical Association, American Society for Aesthetics, Association for Symbolic Logic, American Studies Association, Mind Association, American Association of University Professors (member of council, 1945-48; second vice-president, 1954-56), Southwestern Philosophical Society (president, 1945-46), Southern Society for Philosophy and Psychology (president, 1948-49), Charles S. Peirce Society, American Forestry Association, National Parks and Conservation Association, American Civil Liberties Union, Phi Beta Kappa, Sierra Club, Audubon Society, Wilderness Society. *Awards, honors:* L.H.D., Tulane University, 1976.

*WRITINGS: Perception and Aesthetic Value,* Prentice-Hall, 1938, Johnson Reprint, 1967; (editor and contributor) *Essays on the Theory of Value and Valuation by Members of the Southwestern Philosophical Conference,* Burgess, 1945; (contributor) Ray Lepley, editor, *Value: A Cooperative Inquiry,* Columbia University Press, 1949; (contributor) Lepley, editor, *The Language of Value,* Columbia University Press, 1957; *Symbolic Logic: A Textbook for Non-Mathematicians,* Random House, 1961; *Percepts, Concepts, and Theoretic Knowledge,* Memphis State University Press, 1973. Contributor of more than forty articles to academic journals.

*AVOCATIONAL INTERESTS:* Travel in western U.S. mountains, landscape and flower photography.

\*　　\*　　\*

## LEE, Ronald 1934-

*PERSONAL:* Born August 12, 1934, in Montreal, Quebec, Canada; son of Helen Lee; married Marie Duchesne, September, 1958; children: Delilah, Linda, Dianna, Steven Eli, Helen. *Education:* Sir George Williams University, graduate of general course, 1953. *Politics:* "I vote for what I feel is the right man regardless of the party." *Religion:* "Nominal Muslim." *Home:* 5037 Park Ave., Montreal, Quebec, Canada. *Agent:* Mrs. May Ebbet Cutler, Montreal, Quebec, Canada.

*CAREER:* Has worked as carnival hand, door-to-door salesman, department store salesman, office clerk, house painter, stove mechanic, and plater-mechanic; Canadian Import Co. Ltd., Montreal, Quebec, clerk, 1949-55; traveled with Canadian Gypsies for research purposes, 1955-60; business machinery mechanic, 1960-65; Montreal Military & Maritime Museum, Montreal, assistant curator, 1965-69; John Piper Studio, Richmond, England, master model builder, 1969-70; Globe Publications, Montreal, staff writer, beginning 1970; currently investigative reporter, *National Examiner,* Montreal. *Awards, honors:* Awards from Canadian Government for three ship models built for Expo 67; Canada Council grant to compile data on Gypsies of Canada.

*WRITINGS: Goddam Gypsy* (an autobiographical novel), Tundra Books, 1971, Bobbs-Merrill, 1972; *The Gypsies of Canada,* Tundra Books, in press. Contributor to *Journal of the Gypsy Lore Society.* Collaborator on Canadian Broad-

casting Corp. (CBC) documentary program, "Gypsies of Canada," 1965.

*WORK IN PROGRESS: The London Gypsies,* an ethnographic novel, for Tundra Books.

*SIDELIGHTS:* Ronald Lee is a Gypsy, and speaks Romany, French, Spanish, Italian, Serbo-Croat, Greek, Hindustani, and Mohawk Indian. He has lived in London and traveled through Europe, Mexico, and Central America. He told *CA:* "I am motivated, primarily, as a writer, to present the true facts surrounding my people, the Romany or Gypsies as they are commonly called, to present them as they really are, both the sociological aspect and the culture, language, history, etc., so that an accurate picture will be available to the general public which I feel will help eradicate the present prejudice and preconceived ideas which hinder the integration of the Gypsies into the mainstream of society." *Goddam Gypsy* has been translated into German.

*AVOCATIONAL INTERESTS:* Playing bouzouki (plays semi-professionally, with or without a band); ship-model building, history, and linguistics.

*BIOGRAPHICAL/CRITICAL SOURCES: Canada Month,* October, 1962; *Montreal Star,* December 11, 1965, March 8, 1969; *Canadian Magazine,* May 6, 1972.

\*　　\*　　\*

## LEE, Tanith 1947-

*PERSONAL:* Born September 19, 1947, in London, England; daughter of Bernard and Hylda (Moore) Lee. *Education:* Attended secondary school in Catford, London, England, and studied art. *Residence:* London, England.

*CAREER:* Librarian, writer.

*WRITINGS*—Juvenile: *The Dragon Hoard,* Farrar, Straus, 1971; *Animal Castle,* Farrar, Straus, 1972; *Princess Hynchatti,* Macmillan (London), 1972, Farrar, Straus, 1973.

Young adult; all published by Macmillan: *Companions on the Road,* 1975; *The Winter Players,* 1976; *East of Midnight,* 1977.

Adult fantasy and science fiction; all published by Daw Books: *The Birthgrave,* 1975; *The Storm Lord,* 1976; *Don't Bite the Sun,* 1976; *Drinking Sapphire Wine,* 1977; *Volkhavaar,* 1977; *Vazkor, Son of Vazkor,* 1978; *Quest for the White Witch,* 1978; *The Prince of Demons,* 1978.

Radio plays: "Bitter Gate," broadcast by British Broadcasting Corp., June, 1977; "Red Wine," broadcast by British Broadcasting Corp., December, 1977. Contributor of a long short story to an anthology, 1978.

*WORK IN PROGRESS:* A fantasy novel and a science fiction novel, for Daw Books; a fantasy novel for older children, *The Castle of Dark;* a play for BBC; numerous short stories.

*SIDELIGHTS:* Tanith Lee told CA: "I began to write, and continue to write, out of the sheer compulsion to fantasize. I can claim no noble motives, no aspirations that what comes galloping from my biro will overthrow tyranny, unite nations or cause roses to bloom in the winter snow. I just want to write, can't stop, don't want to stop, and hope I never shall.

"As a writer who has been lucky enough to make writing her profession, I am most undisciplined and erratic. One day I will commence work at four in the afternoon and persevere until four the next morning. Sometimes I start at four in the morning, and go on until physical stamina gives out. Sometimes I get stuck on some knotty problem, (how do you describe the emotions of a man who finds he is a god? What will he do now he knows? Is there any point in his doing anything? Yes. What?) and worry about said problem for days, pen poised, eyes glazed. Frequently I race through 150 pages in a month, and then stick for three months over one page. It's a wonder to me I get anything done. But I do, so presumably it's all right.

"I admire far too many writers to make a list. I'm always discovering new ones to admire. Some operate in the Fantasy/Science Fiction field; a lot don't. I think I can say that I've been influenced by everything I've read and liked. But I'm influenced by symphonies and concertos, too, by paintings and by films. And sometimes by people. A character. A sentence."

*Don't Bite the Sun* has been translated into Swedish. Several other books are "in the pipeline" for Italy, France, and Germany.

*AVOCATIONAL INTERESTS:* Past civilizations (Egyptian, Roman, Inca), psychic powers (their development, use, and misuse), music.

*BIOGRAPHICAL/CRITICAL SOURCES: Spectator,* April 22, 1972, November 11, 1972; *Books and Bookmen,* May, 1972; *Times Literary Supplement,* July 14, 1972, November 3, 1972, April 2, 1976, October 1, 1976; *Observer,* November 26, 1972, February 15, 1976, November 28, 1976; *History Today,* December, 1975.

\*       \*       \*

## LEHISTE, Ilse   1922-

*PERSONAL:* Surname is pronounced *Lay*-histey; born January 31, 1922, in Tallinn, Estonia; daughter of Aleksander and Julie Marie (Sikka) Lehiste. *Education:* Studied at University of Tartu, 1942-43, and University of Leipzig, 1943-44; University of Hamburg, Dr.Phil., 1948; University of Michigan, Ph.D., 1959. *Religion:* Lutheran. *Residence:* Columbus, Ohio. *Office:* Department of Linguistics, Ohio State University, Columbus, Ohio 43210.

*CAREER:* University of Hamburg, Hamburg, Germany, member of faculty, 1948-49; Kansas Wesleyan University, Salina, associate professor of Germanic philology, 1950-51; Detroit Institute of Technology, Detroit, Mich., associate professor of modern languages, 1951-56; University of Michigan, Ann Arbor, research associate in acoustic phonetics, Communication Science Laboratory, 1957-63; Ohio State University, Columbus, associate professor, 1963-65, professor of linguistics, 1965—, chairman of department, 1965-71. Visiting professor at University of Cologne, 1965, University of California, Los Angeles, 1966, and University of Vienna, 1974.

*MEMBER:* Linguistic Society of America (member of executive committee, 1971-73), Modern Language Association of America, Acoustical Society of America (fellow), International Society of Phonological Sciences, Societas Linguistica Europaea, American Association for the Advancement of Science, American Association of University Women. *Awards, honors:* National Science Foundation research grants, 1961-63, 1963-65, 1972; Guggenheim fellowships, 1969, 1975-76; Center for Advanced Study in the Behavioral Sciences, fellow, 1975-76; Doctor of the University, University of Essex, 1977.

*WRITINGS:* (With Gordon E. Peterson) *Studies of Syllable Nuclei,* two volumes, Speech Research Laboratory, University of Michigan, 1959-60; *An Acoustic-Phonetic Study of Internal Open Juncture,* S. Karger, 1960; (with Pavle Ivic) *Accent in Serbocroation: An Experimental Study,* Michigan Slavic Materials, 1963; *Acoustical Characteristics of Selected English Consonants,* Research Center in Anthropology, Folklore, and Linguistics, Indiana University, 1964; *Some Acoustic Characteristics of Dysarthric Speech,* S. Karger, 1965; *Consonant Quantity and Phonological Units in Estonian,* Indiana University, 1966; (editor) *Readings in Acoustic Phonetics,* M.I.T. Press, 1967; *Suprasegmentals,* M.I.T. Press, 1970. Contributor of more than 120 articles and reviews to scholarly journals; some of the articles have been issued as separate reprints by Acoustical Society of America.

*WORK IN PROGRESS:* Acoustic phonetic studies of several languages; Serbo-Croatian accentology.

\*       \*       \*

## LEHMANN, Johannes   1929-

*PERSONAL:* Born September 7, 1929, in Madras, India; son of Arno (a professor) and Gertrud (Harstall) Lehmann; married Ruth Lindenberg, 1956; children: Christine, Maria. *Education:* Studied at University of Halle-Saale, University of Edinburgh, and Free University of Berlin; University of Berlin, Ph.D. *Home:* 8 Degerlocherstrasse, Stuttgart, Germany. *Office:* Sueddeutscher Rundfunk, Stuttgart, Germany.

*CAREER:* Lutheran World Federation, Geneva, Switzerland, news editor, 1955-60; German Press Agency, Hamburg, Germany, news editor, 1960-63; Sueddeutscher Rundfunk (Radio Stuttgart), Stuttgart, Germany, head of literature department, 1963—. *Member:* Deutscher Schriftstellerverband (writer's association).

*WRITINGS:* (Editor) *Christliche Erziehung heute* (title means "Christian Education Today"), Ehrenwirth, 1964; (editor) *Ist der Glaube krank? Glaubwuerdigkeit und Unglaubwuerdigkeit der Glaeubigen* (title means "Is the Faith Ill?"), Quell, 1966; (editor) *In allen Zungen: Geistliche Reden durch 15 Jahrhunderte* (title means "In All Tongues: Spiritual Speeches in Fifteen Centuries"), Ehrenwirth, 1966; (translator with Norbert Brieger and Barbara Beuys) *Gute Nachricht fuer Sie* (title means "Good News for You"), Bibelanstalt, 1967; (editor) *Motive des Glaubens: Eine Ideengeschichte des Christentums in 18 Gestalten* (title means "Motives of Faith"), Furche, 1968; *Mao, Marx und Jesus: Ein Vergleich in Zitaten* (title means "Mao, Marx and Jesus: A Comparison in Quotes"), Jugenddienstverlag, 1969; *Jesus-Report: Protokoll einer Verfaelschung,* Econ Verlag, 1970, translation by Michael Heron published as *Rabbi J.,* Stein & Day, 1971; *Die Jesus GMBH* (title means "The Jesus Ltd."), Econ Verlag, 1972; *Die Hethiter: Volk der tausend Gotter,* Bertelsmann Verlag, 1975, translation by Maxwell Brownjohn published as *The Hittites: People of a Thousand Gods,* Viking, 1977; *Die Kreuzfahrer* (title means "The Cruisadors"), Bertelsmann Verlag, 1976; *Die Staufer: Glanz und Elend eines deutschen Kaisergeschlechts* (title means "Staufer: Glory and Downfall of a German Kaiser-house"), Bertelsmann Verlag, 1978. Writer of radio plays and features. Contributor to journals.

*WORK IN PROGRESS:* Short stories; research on early Christianity and mythology in the Near East.

*SIDELIGHTS:* In addition to German, Johannes Lehmann is competent in Greek, Latin, Hebrew, English, and French. He has traveled in the United States, Near East, and throughout Europe. His *Jesus Report* has been published in Sweden, Denmark, Netherlands, France, and England, and in a paperback edition in Germany.

## LEIBOLD, (William) John 1926-

*PERSONAL:* First syllable of surname rhymes with "sigh"; born February 8, 1926, in Cincinnati, Ohio; son of Albert William (a realtor) and Helen (Metz) Leibold; married Anne Lecot (a librarian), July 7, 1951; children: Mathew, Helen, Frank. *Education:* Xavier University, Ph.B., 1949; attended Sorbonne, University of Paris, 1949-51. *Home:* 927 East Concordia Dr., Tempe, Ariz. 85282. *Office:* Williams Air Force Base, Chandler, Ariz. 85224.

*CAREER:* U.S. Air Force, management analysis officer in Seville, Spain, 1959-70, in Tempe, Ariz., 1970—. *Military service:* U.S. Marine Corps, 1943-46.

*WRITINGS: This Is the Bullfight* (photographic illustrations by Luis Arenas), A. S. Barnes, 1971; *Portrait of the Bullfight* (short stories), Sunrise Press, 1976. Co-publisher and managing editor, *Guidepost* (Madrid, Spain), 1957-59.

*WORK IN PROGRESS:* A book describing the basic principles of organic management; a long narrative which deals with the theme of friendship.

*SIDELIGHTS:* John Leibold lived and travelled in Europe from 1949 to 1970. He spent more than fifteen years in Madrid and Seville working on the Spanish base program and studying the bullfight.

\* \* \*

## LEIBOWITZ, Rene 1913-1972

February 17, 1913—August 28, 1972; Polish-born French composer, conductor, and music critic. Obituaries: *New York Times,* August 30, 1972; *L'Express,* September 4-10, 1972.

\* \* \*

## LEIGHTON, Albert C(hester) 1919-

*PERSONAL:* Born September 6, 1919, in Chester, N.H.; son of Arthur Edmund (a farmer) and Sarah (Edwards) Leighton; married Estella R. Dietel, January 17, 1958; children: Cedric Edmund George. *Education:* University of California, Berkeley, A.B., 1960, M.A., 1961, Ph.D., 1964. *Home address:* R.D. 5 Dumas Rd., Oswego, N.Y. 13126. *Office:* History Department, State University of New York College, Oswego, N.Y. 13126.

*CAREER:* U.S. Army, 1937-57; retired as captain; received Commendation Medal with oak leaf cluster; State University of New York College at Oswego, professor of medieval history, 1964—, coordinator of medieval studies, 1975—. Fulbright professor, University of Munich, 1978-79. Speaker at International Congresses on economic history and history of science. *Member:* American Historical Association, Mediaeval Academy of America, American Cryptogram Association, Mensa, Society for the History of Technology, Delta Phi Alpha. *Awards, honors:* State University of New York summer research fellowships, 1967, 1968; fellow, Medieval Seminar, 1971—; fellow, Duke University Medieval Institute, 1976.

*WRITINGS: Transport and Communication in Early Medieval Europe,* Barnes & Noble, 1972. Contributor to *Encyclopedia Americana, Technology and Culture, Jahrbuecher fuer Geschichte Osteuropas, Historia Mathematica, Cryptologia,* and *Zeitschrift fuer bayerische Landesgeschichte.*

*WORK IN PROGRESS:* Coordinating research in historical cryptanalysis-codebreaking as an auxiliary science for the historian.

*SIDELIGHTS:* Albert Leighton's *Transport and Commu-nication in Early Medieval Europe* is "a skilful and scholarly synthesis," said a *Times Literary Supplement* reviewer. Although John Beeler of the *American Historical Review* wrote "this is not a very well organized study," the *Choice* reviewer praised it for "precisely the kind of scholarship social history demands. . . . This book will be consulted and argued with for years to come."

Leighton has travelled in Europe, Russia, Korea, Japan, and Taiwan, and works in German, French, and Latin.

*BIOGRAPHICAL/CRITICAL SOURCES: Times Literary Supplement,* October 6, 1972; *Choice,* December, 1972; *Business History Review,* fall, 1973; *Geographical Review,* October, 1973; *American Historical Review,* October, 1973.

\* \* \*

## LEISERSON, Michael 1939-

*PERSONAL:* First syllable of surname is pronounced "lye"; born February 12, 1939, in Chicago, Ill.; son of Avery and Winifred (Smith) Leiserson; married Martha McCaughtry, June, 1962 (divorced, 1964); married Michiko Ishikawa, January 1, 1966; children: Naomi, Ken. *Education:* Princeton University, B.A., 1961; Yale University, M.A., 1963, Ph.D., 1966. *Home:* 2420 Prince St., Berkeley, Calif. 94705. *Office:* Department of Political Science, University of California, Berkeley, Calif. 94720.

*CAREER:* University of California, Berkeley, 1967—, began as instructor, currently assistant professor of political science. *Member:* American Political Science Association, Association of Asian Studies. *Awards, honors:* Fulbright fellowship to Japan, 1965-67.

*WRITINGS: The Study of Coalition Behavior,* Holt, 1970; *The End of Politics in America: Experience and Possibilities,* Little, Brown, 1972.†

\* \* \*

## LEITER, Louis (Henry) 1921-

*PERSONAL:* Surname is pronounced Lighter; born February 22, 1921, in Cleveland, Ohio; son of Christopher Joseph and Susan (Holy) Leiter. *Education:* Attended University of Southern California, 1946-48, and University of Chicago, 1948-49; University of Iowa, A.B., 1950, M.A., 1953; Brown University, Ph.D., 1960. *Home:* 1168 South Country Club Blvd., Stockton, Calif. 95204. *Office:* English Department, University of the Pacific, Stockton, Calif. 95204.

*CAREER:* University of Idaho, Moscow, instructor in English, 1953-55; Ripon College, Ripon, Wis., instructor in English, 1955-56; Brown University, Providence, R.I., instructor in English, 1957-59; University of Nebraska, Lincoln, assistant professor of English,1959-63; University of the Pacific, Stockton, Calif., associate professor of English, 1963—. Lecturer in Finland at University of Oulu and University of Javaskalya, 1967-68. *Military service:* U.S. Aviation Service, 1939-41; U.S. Army Air Forces, 1941-45; became staff sergeant. *Member:* Mediaeval Academy of America, Philological Association of Central California. *Awards, honors:* University of Nebraska research grant, 1960.

*WRITINGS: Approaches to the Novel,* Chandler Publishing, 1963; *Seven Contemporary Short Novels* (American), Scott, Foresman, 1970, 2nd edition, 1975. Contributing editor, *College English,* 1963-70. Contributor of essays to critical journals.

*WORK IN PROGRESS: Dictionary of Film Symbolism.*

\*     \*     \*

**LEMAITRE, Georges E(douard)   1898-1972**

November 26, 1898—August 11, 1972; Algerian-born American educator, diplomat, and authority on French literature and art. Obituaries: *New York Times,* August 13, 1972. (See index for *CA* sketch)

\*     \*     \*

**LEMON, James Thomas   1929-**

*PERSONAL:* Born July 2, 1929, in West Lorne, Ontario, Canada; son of Victor Earl (a retailer) and Grace (Sharratt) Lemon; married Carolyn Jean Miller (a teacher), September 13, 1958; children: Margaret, Janet, Catherine. *Education:* University of Western Ontario, B.A., 1955; Yale University, B.D., 1958; University of Wisconsin, M.S., 1961, Ph.D., 1964. *Politics:* New Democratic Party. *Religion:* United Church of Canada. *Home:* 78 Walmer Rd., Toronto, Ontario, Canada M5R 2X7. *Office:* Department of Geography, University of Toronto, Toronto, Ontario, Canada M5S 1A1.

*CAREER:* Clergyman of United Church of Canada, serving Iron Bridge, Ontario, 1958-60; University of California, Los Angeles, assistant professor of geography, 1964-67; University of Toronto, Toronto, Ontario, assistant professor, 1967-68, associate professor, 1968-72, professor of geography, 1973—. Chairman, Confederation of Resident and Ratepayer Associations, 1973; director, Community Living Program, 1975-78; trustee, Toronto Board of Education, 1977—. Active participant in national and city politics. *Member:* Canadian Association of Geographers, Canadian Association of American Studies, Social Science History Association. *Awards, honors:* Beveridge Prize, American Historical Association, 1972, for *The Best Poor Man's Country;* Guggenheim fellow, 1974-75.

*WRITINGS: The Best Poor Man's Country: A Geographical Study of Early Southeastern Pennsylvania,* Johns Hopkins, 1972. Contributor of articles to professional journals.

*WORK IN PROGRESS:* A book on *Urban Historical Geography* that will compare Toronto's development to U.S. cities of comparable size; studies on the theory of place and community.

\*     \*     \*

**LEMONS, J. Stanley   1938-**

*PERSONAL:* Born June 14, 1938, in Louisville, Ky.; son of Leland Carol (a minister) and Lena May (Lusk) Lemons; married Nancy Jane Simmons, September 3, 1960. *Education:* William Jewell College, A.B., 1960; University of Rochester, M.A., 1962; University of Missouri, Ph.D., 1967. *Politics:* Independent. *Religion:* Baptist. *Home:* 103 High Service Ave., North Providence, R.I. 02911. *Office:* Department of History, Rhode Island College, Providence, R.I. 02908.

*CAREER:* Ohio State University, Columbus, instructor in history, 1965-67; Rhode Island College, Providence, assistant professor, 1967-71, associate professor, 1971-76, professor of history, 1976—. *Member:* Organization of American Historians, American Historical Association, New England Historical Association, Providence Preservation Society.

*WRITINGS: The Woman Citizen: Social Feminism in the*

1920's, University of Illinois Press, 1973; (editor) *Aspects of the Black Experience,* Rhode Island Committee for the Humanities, 1975. Contributor of articles to *Journal of American History, Labor History, American Quarterly, Rhode Island History,* and *Missouri Historical Review.*

*WORK IN PROGRESS:* A study of ultra-conservatism in the 1920's; teaching social and cultural history through multi-media.

\*     \*     \*

**LEMOS, Ramon M(arcelino)   1927-**

*PERSONAL:* Born July 7, 1927, in Mobile, Ala.; son of Marcelino and Marie Louise (Moore) Lemos; married Mamie Lou McCrory, December 26, 1951; children: Noah Marcelino, William Ramon, Christopher Tait, John Paul. *Education:* University of Alabama, B.A., 1951; Duke University, M.A.,1953, Ph.D., 1955; University of London, postdoctoral study, 1955-56. *Politics:* Democrat. *Religion:* Episcopalian. *Home:* 6960 Southwest 82nd Court, Miami, Fla. 33143. *Office:* Department of Philosophy, University of Miami, Coral Gables, Fla. 33124.

*CAREER:* University of Miami, Coral Gables, Fla., instructor, 1956-58, assistant professor, 1958-62, associate professor, 1962-67, professor of philosophy, 1967—, chairman of department, 1971—. *Military service:* U.S. Marine Corps, 1945-49; became sergeant. *Member:* American Philosophical Association, Metaphysical Society of America, Aristotelian Society, American Catholic Philosophical Association (Florida Chapter, president, 1971), Southern Society for Philosophy & Psychology, Florida Philosophical Association (president, 1963).

*WRITINGS: Experience, Mind, and Value: Philosophical Essays,* E. J. Brill, 1969; (contributor) Harold Zellner, editor, *Assassination,* Schenkman, 1974; *Rousseau's Political Philosophy: An Exposition and Interpretation,* University of Georgia Press, 1977; *Hobbes and Locke: Power and Consent,* University of Georgia Press, 1978. Contributor of articles to *Theoria, Philosophy & Phenomenological Research, International Philosophical Quarterly, Ratio, Studium Generale,* and other journals.

*WORK IN PROGRESS: Morality and Politics.*

\*     \*     \*

**LEONARD, V. A.   1898-**

*PERSONAL:* Born January 13, 1898, in Cleburne, Tex.; son of Anderson and Mary (Martin) Leonard; married Imogene McFall, June 21, 1935; children: Sherry Sue (Mrs. George J. Simchuk), Marylin Kay. *Education:* Texas Wesleyan College, B.S., 1939; Texas Christian University, M.A., 1940; Ohio State University, Ph.D., 1949. *Address:* P.O. Box 2184, Denton, Tex. 76201.

*CAREER:* Police Department of City of Berkeley, Berkeley, Calif., patrolman, investigative officer, and identification expert, 1925-32; Police Department of City of Fort Worth, Fort Worth, Tex., superintendent commanding Records and Identification Division, 1934-39; Washington State University, Pullman, professor of police science and administration, 1941-63, professor emeritus, 1963—, chairman of department, 1941-56. Visiting professor, Chinese Central Police College, Taipei, Taiwan, 1971-72. *Military service:* U.S. Army, 1918. *Member:* International Association of Chiefs of Police, International Association for Identification (past president and honorary life member of Texas Division), Academy of Criminal Justice Sciences (honorary life member), Academy for Scientific Interrogation (past president and past chairman of board of directors; now part of American Polygraph Association), American Polygraph Association (honorary life member), Sociedad Cubana de Policiologia y Criminalistica (honorary life member, 1949). *Awards, honors:* Founder's Award, Academy of Criminal Justice Sciences, 1976.

*WRITINGS: Police Communication Systems,* University of California Press, 1938; *Survey and Reorganization of the Seattle Police Department,* City of Seattle, 1945; *Police Organization and Management,* and Study Guide, Foundation Press, 1950, 5th edition (with Harry W. More), 1978; *The Police of the Twentieth Century* (senior high school students), Foundation Press, 1964; (with More) *The General Administration of Criminal Justice* (university text), Foundation Press, 1967; *Police Science for the Young American* (sixth through tenth grade), C. C Thomas, 1968; *The Police Enterprise: Its Organization and Management,* C. C Thomas, 1968; *Police Personnel Administration,* C. C Thomas, 1968; *The Police, the Judiciary, and the Criminal,* C. C Thomas, 1969, 2nd edition, 1975; *The Police Records System,* C. C Thomas, 1969; *The Police Communications System,* C. C Thomas, 1969; *Police Patrol Organization,* C. C Thomas, 1970; *The Police Detective Function,* C. C Thomas, 1970; *Criminal Investigation and Identification,* C. C Thomas, 1971; *Police Traffic Control and Regulation,* C. C Thomas, 1972; *Police Crime Prevention,* C. C Thomas, 1972; *Police Pre-Disaster Preparation,* C. C Thomas, 1973; *The Police Imperative: Challenge of a Democratic Society,* West Publishing, 1979. Editor, "Police Science" series, C. C Thomas, 1952—. Contributor to professional journals. Associate editor, *Journal of Criminal Law and Criminology,* 1944-56; editor of *Police,* 1952-61.

*WORK IN PROGRESS: Introduction to Police Service and the Criminal Justice System.*

*SIDELIGHTS:* V. A. Leonard told *CA:* "I write for several reasons—the creative pleasure of turning a sentence or a paragraph that come up to my standards. Words can be a powerful thing and when the writing is equal to the occasion, they can seize the reader to ignite the imagination and through cross-fertilization, lead to the indefinite birth of new ideas. After the completion of the manuscript for the first edition of *Police Organization and Management,* it took me three months to put together the first sentence that launched the book at the beginning of the first chapter. Sometimes, it doesn't come quick and easy.

"Secondly, I am interested in attracting the best human material available into the police services, and it is safe to say that the best is none too good in meeting the demands placed upon the police in a modern social order. In the third place, a profession demands an adequate literature and I have in a small way made some contribution to the cause. Furthermore, though I retired in 1963, the rocking chair—and I have a nice one about 200 years old—has never seemed very attractive to me."

*The Police, the Judiciary, and the Criminal,* according to A. F. Wilcox, "traces how the courts in the United States have sought to uphold the liberty of the individual by safeguarding the rights of the accused while at the same time protecting the law-abiding public against lawlessness. The efforts made by eminent judges to balance the scales of justice make fascinating reading. . . . One of the merits of this book is that Professor Leonard treats the leading cases in depth, giving clear summaries of the facts and quoting at length relevant passages, not only from the decisions but alsofrom the

dissenting opinions which are so often much more trenchant and convincing than those of the majority. . . . Professor Leonard's book can be thoroughly recommended to all who are disposed to believe that the existing procedure governing the investigation of crime and the rules of evidence in our own criminal courts are capable of improvement."

Reviewing *Police Crime Prevention,* Lee E. Lawder writes: "The police have an important role as they are usually the first contact with the child who gets into trouble. They have the best opportunity to inaugurate preventive programs and the balance of this book contains material aimed at reducing the opportunity for crime. This wanders into the realm of public relations. There are reprints of pamphlets on how to protect a home against burglars, burglary and hold-up alarm systems, a message to women which gives advice on many subjects on how to protect themselves. The object is: if we can reduce the opportunity for crime, it is a giant step in reducing the incidence."

When asked his opinion of the current literature in his field, Leonard remarked to *CA,* "Seemingly, the criminal justice system as a whole is being over-worked, and suggests the need for individual attention to the basics—the police, the prosecutor, the courts, corrections, parole and probation, punishment, rehabilitation, role of the people and the community, role of the media, the challenge of delinquency and crime prevention, with appropriate recognition of an emerging new discipline, behavioral medicine."

Leonard organized and developed the four-year curriculum leading to the Bachelor's and Master's degrees in Police Science and Administration at Washington State University in 1941. One of his books, *Police Organization and Management,* was translated into Vietnamese under the auspices of the U.S. Department of State.

*BIOGRAPHICAL/CRITICAL SOURCES: Journal of Criminal Law, Criminology and Police Science,* December, 1972; *Law and Order,* February, 1973; *Abstracts on Police Science,* March/April, 1973, May/June, 1973; *Medical Book News,* July, 1973; *Police Journal,* July/September, 1973, April, 1974; *Washington Policeman,* March, 1976; *Journal of Contemporary Law,* spring, 1976; *Police Chief,* April, 1977; *Criminal Law Review,* August, 1977.

\* \* \*

## LEONARD, William N. 1912-

*PERSONAL:* Born December 12, 1912, in Pittsburgh, Pa.; son of Burt Hayes (a writer) and Mabel (Norris) Leonard; married Elizabeth Waugh (a professor), August 24, 1939; children: Virginia W., John W. *Education:* University of Virginia, B.A., 1936; University of Texas, M.A., 1938; Columbia University, Ph.D., 1945. *Politics:* Democrat. *Religion:* Unitarian. *Home:* 20 Glenville Rd., Greenwich, Conn. 06830. *Office:* Department of Economics, Herbert H. Lehman College of the City University of New York, Bronx, N.Y. 10468.

*CAREER:* University of Connecticut, Storrs, 1939-42, began as instructor, became assistant professor of economics; War Production Board, Washington, D.C., office of civilian requirements, industrial analyst, 1942-45; Trans-World Airlines, Kansas City, Mo., assistant coordinator of planning, 1945-46; Rutgers University, New Brunswick, N.J., chairman of economics department, 1946-49; Pennsylvania State University, University Park, professor of economics and commerce and department chairman, 1949-53; Hofstra University, Hempstead, N.Y., professor of economics and department chairman, 1953-74; Herbert H.

Lehman College of the City University of New York, Bronx, N.Y., professor of economics and department chairman, 1974—. Consultant to secretary of interior, 1950-51, Federal Trade Commission, 1968-69, Senate Antitrust and Monopoly Subcommittee, 1969—. Chairman, Nassau County Planning Commission, 1962-65. *Member:* American Economic Association, American Association for the Advancemnt of Science, New York State Economics Association (vice-president, 1971-72; president, 1972-73), Phi Beta Kappa, Raven Society (University of Virginia), Hempstead Rotary Club (president, 1972-73). *Awards, honors:* National Science Foundation grant, 1971-73, for research and development in economic growth; Fulbright lecturer in Haiti, 1974.

*WRITINGS: Railroad Consolidation under the Transportation Act of 1920,* Columbia University Press, 1946, reprinted, AMS Press, 1971; *Business Size, Market Power and Public Policy,* Crowell, 1969. Contributor of articles to *Journal of Political Economy, Current History, Challenge, Transportation Journal,* and *American Economic Review.*

*WORK IN PROGRESS:* Articles on research and development in economic growth; a book on industrial organization.

*SIDELIGHTS:* William Leonard has traveled extensively in Europe, Asia, and the Caribbean. His interests include tennis, swimming, and golf.

\*    \*    \*

## LeROY, Gaylord C. 1910-

*PERSONAL:* Born September 28, 1910, in Aspinwall, Pa.; son of Albert E. and Rhoda (Clarke) LeRoy; married Eva Spiro, 1942; children: Stephen, John. *Education:* Oberlin College, A.B., 1930; Harvard University, A.M., 1931, Ph.D., 1935. *Home:* 1552 Edge Hill Rd., Abington, Pa. 19001. *Office:* Department of English, Temple University, Philadelphia, Pa. 19122.

*CAREER:* University of Maine, Orono, instructor in English, 1934-38; University of Hawaii, Honolulu, instructor, 1938-40, assistant professor of English, 1941-46; Temple University, Philadelphia, Pa., assistant professor, 1946-53, associate professor, 1953-60, professor of English, 1960-76, professor emeritus, 1977—. *Member:* Modern Language Association of America.

*WRITINGS: Perplexed Prophets,* University of Pennsylvania Press, 1953; *Marxism and Modern Literature,* American Institute for Marxist Studies, 1967; (editor with Ursula Beitz) *Preserve and Create: Essays in Marxist Literary Criticism,* Humanities, 1973; (contributor) Norman Rudich, editor, *Weapons of Criticism: Marxism and the Literary Tradition,* Ramparts, 1976.

*WORK IN PROGRESS:* Work in Marxist literary criticism and aesthetics.

*SIDELIGHTS:* Gaylord LeRoy cites two motives for his study of Marxism. The first is his "search for the meaning of a cycle of experience that began with a religious childhood . . . and culminated in an adult interest in Marxism and socialism. What are the continuities (immense, I believe) and the discontinuities (also considerable) between the first and final stages of this cycle?" He continues, "A further motive [is] to help restore sanity on great and inescapable issues of our time after the distortions stemming from McCarthyism and the Cold War." Portions of *Marxism and Modern Literature* have appeared in Russian translation in a book honoring the American bicentennial.

## LESTER, Anthony 1936-

*PERSONAL:* Born July 3, 1936, in London, England; son of Harry (a barrister) and Kate (Cooper) Lester; married Catherine Wassey (a barrister), July 29, 1971; children: Gideon, Maya. *Education:* Trinity College, Cambridge, B.A., 1960; Harvard University, LL.M., 1962. *Politics:* Labour. *Religion:* None. *Home:* 38 Half Moon Lane, London SE24 9HO, England. *Office:* 2 Hare Court, Temple, London E.C.4, England.

*CAREER:* Barrister, author, and broadcaster. Appointed Queen's Counsel, 1975; special adviser to Home Secretary Roy Jenkins, 1974-76. Governor, London School of Economics, 1971-72; member of board of overseers, University of Pennsylvania Law School, 1977—. *Military service:* British Army, Royal Artillery, 1955-57; became second lieutenant. *Member:* Justice, National Council of Civil Liberties, Amnesty International, Society of Labour Lawyers, Runnymede Trust (trustee), Fabian Society (honorary treasurer, 1968-72; chairman, 1972), Garrick Club.

*WRITINGS:* (Joint editor) C. N. Shawcross and K. M. Beaumont, *Air Law,* 3rd edition (Lester was not associated with earlier editions), Butterworths, 1964; (editor) Roy Jenkins, *Essays and Speeches,* Collins, 1967, Chilmark, 1968; (with Geoffrey Bindman) *Race and Law in Great Britain,* Harvard University, 1972. Contributor to legal journals, political magazines, and newspapers.

*BIOGRAPHICAL/CRITICAL SOURCES: Times Literary Supplement,* November 30, 1967.

\*    \*    \*

## LEUBA, Clarence J(ames) 1899-

*PERSONAL:* Born July 3, 1899, in Bryn Mawr, Pa.; son of James Henry (a professor) and Berthe (Schopfer) Leuba; married Frances Briggs, May 28, 1926; children: Richard, Edward, Roger, Elizabeth (Mrs. G. Chapman Petersen), Katharine (Mrs. Alan Glos). *Education:* Haverford College, B.A., 1920; Harvard University, M.A., 1921; Syracuse University, Ph.D., 1929. *Home:* 1320 President St., Yellow Springs, Ohio 45387. *Office:* Department of Psychology, Antioch College, Yellow Springs, Ohio 45387.

*CAREER:* Syracuse University, Syracuse, N.Y., instructor, 1928-29; Bryn Mawr College, Bryn Mawr, Pa., lecturer, 1929-30; Antioch College, Yellow Springs, Ohio, associate professor, 1930-37, professor of psychology, 1937—, chairman of department, 1930—. Visiting professor or lecturer at Indiana University, 1941, University of California, Los Angeles, 1949, and Wright State University, 1965-68. Served with American Friends Service Committee in Germany, 1921-22; research analyst, U.S. Strategic Bombing Survey, Germany, 1945. *Military service:* U.S. Army, 1918; honorable discharge. *Member:* American Psychological Association (president of division II, 1970-71), Midwestern Psychological Association, Ohio Psychological Association (president, 1962-63). *Awards, honors:* Distinguished Service Award from Ohio Psychological Association, 1971.

*WRITINGS: Ethics in Sex Conduct,* Association Press, 1948; *The Natural Man,* Doubleday, 1954; *Sexual Nature of Man,* Doubleday, 1954; *Man: A General Psychology,* Holt, 1961; *Personality: Interpersonal Relations and Self Understanding,* Merrill Books, 1962; (with Arthur Morgan) *A Road to Creativity: Arthur Morgan, Engineer, Educator, Administrator,* Christopher, 1971. Contributor of numerous articles to educational and scientific journals.

*WORK IN PROGRESS:* Articles for newspapers and magazines on current issues.

## LEVANT, Oscar 1906-1972

December 27, 1906—August 14, 1972; American pianist, film actor, composer, radio and television personality, and wit. Obituaries: *New York Times,* August 15, 1972; *Newsweek,* August 28, 1972; *Time,* August 28, 1972; *Current Biography,* October, 1972.

\* \* \*

## LEVITCH, Joel A. 1942-

*PERSONAL:* Born October 5, 1942, in Kansas City, Mo.; son of David and Frances (Brand) Levitch; married Judith Rabicoff, June 16, 1963; children: Mark Jason, Timothy Justin. *Education:* Yale University, B.A., 1964, M.A., 1966. *Home:* 2621 Palisade Ave., Riverdale, N.Y. 10463. *Agent:* Marilyn Marlowe, Curtis Brown Ltd., 575 Madison Ave., New York, N.Y. 10022.

*CAREER:* Jason Films, New York, N.Y., owner and president, 1968—. Writer of syndicated feature articles, 1973—. *Awards, honors:* CINE Gold Eagle, 1969; blue ribbon from American Film Festival, 1970; gold medal from Atlanta Film Festival, 1970; and thirty-two others.

*WRITINGS:* (With Laurel F. Vlock) *Contraband of War,* Funk, 1969.

\* \* \*

## LEVY, Fred D(avid), Jr. 1937-

*PERSONAL:* Born October 10, 1937, in Chicago, Ill.; son of Fred David and Anne (Adler) Levy; married Judy Reinach, June 12, 1960; children: Sally Ann, Patricia Louise, Sharon Lea. *Education:* Purdue University, B.S., 1959; Yale University, M.A., 1960, Ph.D., 1966. *Home:* 10318 Folk St., Silver Spring, Md. 20902.

*CAREER:* Syracuse University, Syracuse, N.Y., instructor, 1964-65, assistant professor, 1965-72, associate professor of economics, beginning 1972; U.S. Agency for International Development (USAID), Rio de Janeiro, Brazil, economic adviser, 1967-69; consultant to U.S. Agency for International Development, 1969-72, and U.S. Treasury Department, 1972—. *Member:* American Economic Association, American Society for Public Administration, Latin American Studies Association, Society for International Development, National Platform Association, National Planning Association.

*WRITINGS: Economic Planning in Venezuela,* Praeger, 1968; *Documentos para o Planejamento da Economia Brasileira,* Interamerican University Foundation, 1971; (with Sidney C. Sufrin) *Basic Economics: Analysis of Contemporary Problems and Politics,* with workbook and instructor's manual, Harper, 1973. Contributor to *Collier's Encyclopedia;* contributor of articles on economic planning and foreign technical assistance to journals in his field.

*WORK IN PROGRESS: Unions in Developing Countries,* with S. C. Sufrin, for publication by General Learning Corp.†

\* \* \*

## LEVY, Robert J(oseph) 1931-

*PERSONAL:* Born June 27, 1931, in Philadelphia, Pa.; son of Bert (a salesman) and Jane (Kotkin) Levy; married Roberta Kaplan (a judge), August 16, 1959; children: Valerie, Jonathan, Joshua. *Education:* Kenyon College, A.B., 1952; University of Pennsylvania, J.D., 1957. *Home:* 2250 Lee Ave. N., Minneapolis, Minn. 55422. *Office:* University of Minnesota Law School, Minneapolis, Minn. 55455.

*CAREER:* U.S. Department of Justice, trial attorney, antitrust division, 1957-59; University of Minnesota, Minneapolis, associate professor, 1959-62, professor of family law, 1962—. Fellow, Center for Advanced Study in the Behavioral Sciences, Palo Alto, Calif., 1967-68. Member of Minnesota Governor's Committee for Children & Youth, 1959; consultant to Administrative Conference of U.S., 1961; lecturer, Salzburg (Austria) Seminar in American Institutions, 1977. *Military service:* U.S. Army, 1952-54; became sergeant; received Bronze Star. *Member:* American Law Institute.

*WRITINGS:* (Editor and contributor with Caleb Foote and Frank E. A. Sander) *Cases and Materials on Family Law,* Little, Brown, 1966, 2nd edition, 1972; *Uniform Marriage and Divorce Legislation,* National Conference Commissioners on Uniform State Laws, 1968; (editor and contributor with Thomas P. Lewis and Peter Martin) *Cases on Social Welfare and the Individual,* Foundation, 1971.

*WORK IN PROGRESS:* Empirical study of custody adjudication following divorce.

\* \* \*

## LEWIS, Jack P(earl) 1919-

*PERSONAL:* Born March 13, 1919, in Midlothian, Tex.; son of Pearl Gaunce (a farmer) and Anna Elizabeth (Holland) Lewis; married Lynell Carpenter, August 3, 1943 (died, 1975); children: John Robert, Jerry Wayne. *Education:* Abilene Christian College (now University), B.A., 1941; Sam Houston State Teacher's College (now Sam Houston State University), M.A., 1944; Harvard University, S.T.B., 1947, Ph.D., 1953; Hebrew Union College, Ph.D., 1962. *Religion:* Church of Christ. *Home:* 1132 South Perkins Rd., Memphis, Tenn. 38117. *Office:* Harding Graduate School of Religion, 1000 Cherry Rd., Memphis, Tenn. 38117.

*CAREER:* Minister, serving in churches in Texas, Rhode Island, and Kentucky, 1941-54; Harding Graduate School of Religion, Memphis, Tenn., associate professor, 1954-57, professor of Bible, 1957—. Member of board of directors, University Christian Center, Oxford, Miss., 1966—. *Member:* Society of Biblical Literature, American Academy of Religion, National Association of Professors of Hebrew, Evangelical Theological Society. *Awards, honors:* American Schools of Oriental Research (Jerusalem), Thayer fellow, 1967-68; *Twentieth Century Christian,* Christian Education Award, 1968.

*WRITINGS: The Minor Prophets,* Baker Book, 1966; *The Interpretation of Noah and the Flood in Jewish and Christian Literature,* E. J. Brill (Leiden), 1968; *Historical Backgrounds of Bible History,* Baker Book, 1971; (editor) *The Last Things,* R. B. Sweet, 1972; *The Gospel of Matthew* (commentary), two volumes, R. B. Sweet, 1976. Contributor of articles to *Journal of Bible and Religion.* Member of editorial board, *Restoration Quarterly,* 1957—, and *Journal of Hebraic Studies,* 1969—.

*WORK IN PROGRESS: The Day after Domes Day—A History of the Bishop's Bible;* an evaluation of English translations of the Bible, *Scripture for the Boy Who Drives the Plow.*

*SIDELIGHTS:* Jack Lewis has a reading knowledge of German, French, Hebrew, Aramaic, Greek, and Latin. He is a tour leader for Wholesale Tours International, Inc. *Avocational interests:* Woodwork, flying, photography.

## LI, Tien-yi 1915-

*PERSONAL:* Born March 14, 1915, in Juyang, Honan, China; son of Kuei-hsin and Hsin Li; married Julia Liu (a computer programmer and analyst), September 14, 1963; children: Norman. *Education:* Nankai University, B.A., 1937; Yale University, M.A., 1946, Ph.D., 1950. *Home:* 4532 Kipling Rd., Upper Arlington, Ohio 43220. *Office:* Department of East Asian Languages and Literatures, Ohio State University, Columbus, Ohio 48210.

*CAREER:* Yale University, New Haven, Conn., instructor, 1948-51, assistant professor, 1951-59, associate professor, 1959-62, professor of Chinese literature and culture, 1962-69; Ohio State University, Columbus, Mershon Professor of Chinese Literature and History, 1969—, chairman of East Asian Languages and Literatures, 1971-75; University of Hong Kong, chairman of department of history and director of Institute of Chinese Studies, 1976-77. Lecturer in Far Eastern history, Smith College, 1951-52; research fellow, Institute of Humanistic Sciences, Kyoto University, 1955-56; visiting professor of Chinese literature and history, Indiana University, 1960-61; lecturer in Chinese history, University of Hawaii, summer, 1963. Columbia University, member of University Seminar on Modern China and University Seminar on Traditional China; correspondence research fellow, Academia Sinica, 1964—; honorary research fellow, China Academy, 1967—. *Member:* American Historical Association, Association for Asian Studies, American Oriental Society, Chinese Language Teachers Association. *Awards, honors:* Morse fellow, 1955-56; American Council of Learned Societies East Asian fellow, 1963-64.

*WRITINGS: A Study of Thomas Hardy,* Commercial Press (Shanghai), 1938; *The Dictatorship of the People's Democracy* (an annotated text), Institute of Far Eastern Languages, Yale University, 1951 (revised edition issued as *On the People's Democratic Dictatorship,* Far Eastern Publications, 1965); *Chinese Newspaper Manual,* Institute of Far Eastern Languages, Yale University, 1952, revised edition, 1962; *Woodrow Wilson's China Policy: 1913-1917,* Twayne, 1952; (editor with Wuchi Liu) *Readings in Contemporary Chinese Literature,* six volumes, Institute of Far Eastern Languages, Yale University, 1953-58, revised edition, Far Eastern Publications, 1964-68; (editor) *Selected Readings in Chinese Communist Literature,* Institute of Far Eastern Languages, Yale University, 1954, revised edition, Far Eastern Publications, 1967; (editor) *Ku-chin hsiao-shuo,* two volumes, World Book Co. (Taipei), 1958; (editor) *Ching-shih t'ung-yen,* two volumes, World Book Co., 1958; (editor) *Hsing-shih heng-yen,* three volumes, World Book Co., 1959; (editor) *Erh-k'o P'o-an Ching-ch'i,* Cheng Chung Book Co., 1960; (editor) George A. Kennedy, *The Selected Works of George A. Kennedy,* Far Eastern Publications, 1964; (editor) *P'o-an ching-ch'i,* two volumes, Union Press (Hong Kong), 1967; (editor) *Chinese Fiction: A Bibliography of Books and Articles in Chinese and English,* Far Eastern Publications, 1968; (editor) *The History of Chinese Literature: A Selected Bibliography,* Far Eastern Publications, 1968, revised edition, 1970; *Chinese Historical Literature,* Union Press, 1977. Contributor of many articles to journals in his field. Secretary and editor, *Tsing Hua Journal of Chinese Studies;* editor, Far Eastern Publications and *Chinese Culture.*

*WORK IN PROGRESS:* Research on Chinese fiction and on Chinese-American relations.

*AVOCATIONAL INTERESTS:* Photography, travel.

## LICHTENBERG, Philip 1926-

*PERSONAL:* Born October 1, 1926, in Schenectady, N.Y.; son of Chester (an engineer-physicist) and Bertha (Stein) Lichtenberg; married Elsa Russell (a librarian), June 15, 1949; children: Erik Russell, Andrew Adam, Thomas Philip, Peter Alexander. *Education:* Attended Rose Polytechnic Institute, 1944, and Indiana University, 1945; Western Reserve University (now Case Western Reserve University), B.S., 1948, M.A., 1950, Ph.D., 1952. *Home:* 25 Lowry's Lane, Rosemont, Pa. 19010. *Office:* Bryn Mawr College, 300 Airdale Rd., Bryn Mawr, Pa. 19010.

*CAREER:* Harvard University, Cambridge, Mass., research fellow in clinical psychology, 1951-52; New York University, New York, N.Y., research assistant professor of psychology, 1952-54; Michael Reese Hospital, Chicago, Ill., research psychologist, 1954-57; New York State Department of Mental Hygiene, Syracuse, N.Y., research psychologist (social), 1957-61; Bryn Mawr College, Bryn Mawr, Pa., 1961—, began as associate professor, professor of social research, 1968—. *Military service:* U.S. Army Air Forces, 1944-46; became sergeant. *Member:* American Psychological Association, American Association for the Advancement of Science, Council on Social Work Education, American Association of University Professors, Eastern Psychological Association, Pennsylvania Psychological Association.

*WRITINGS:* (With Robert Kohrman and Helen MacGregor) *Motivation for Child Psychiatry Treatment,* Russell, 1960; *Psychoanalysis: Radical and Conservative,* Springer Publishing, 1969; (with Dolores G. Norton) *Cognitive and Mental Development in the First Five Years of Life,* U.S. Government Printing Office for U.S. Department of Health, Education and Welfare, 1970. Contributor to psychology, social work, and sociology journals.

*WORK IN PROGRESS:* Research on social workers in unions.

\*      \*      \*

## LIEB, Robert C. 1944-

*PERSONAL:* Born March 29, 1944, in Pittsburgh, Pa.; son of Robert C. and Katherine (Boyle) Lieb; married Lorraine Kopchik, July 8, 1967; children: Kristin Jennifer. *Education:* Duquesne University of the Holy Ghost, B.S., 1966; University of Maryland, M.B.A., 1968, D.B.A., 1970. *Residence:* Lexington, Mass. *Office:* College of Business Administration, Northeastern University, Boston, Mass. 02115.

*CAREER:* University of Maryland, College Park, instructor in business administration, 1969-70; Northeastern University, Boston, Mass., College of Business Administration, assistant professor, 1970-73, associate professor of transportation and coordinator of transportation programs, 1973—. Consultant for U.S. Department of Transportation, Interstate Commerce Commission, American Track (Amtrak) of the National Railroad Passenger Corp., and private firms. Member of synthesis and advisory panel, committee of transportation, National Academy of Sciences. Member of board of directors, Northeastern University Press. *Member:* American Society of Traffic and Transportation, American Economic Association, Beta Gamma Sigma.

*WRITINGS: Freight Transportation: A Study of Federal Intermodal Ownership Policy,* Praeger, 1972; *Labor in the Transportation Industries,* Praeger, 1974; *Transportation: The Domestic System,* Reston, 1978. Contributor to transportation and economics journals.

## LIHANI, John 1927-

*PERSONAL:* Surname is pronounced Le-*hon*-ey; born March 24, 1927, in Hnusta, Czechoslovakia; son of John (a molder) and Susanna (Jablonska) Lihani; married Emily G. Kolesar (a librarian), September 9, 1950; children: J. Brian, Robert P., David L. *Education:* Western Reserve University (now Case Western Reserve University), B.S. (magna cum laude), 1948; Ohio State University, M.A., 1950; Tulane University, further study, 1950-51; University of Texas, Ph.D., 1954; postdoctoral study at Yale University and University of Madrid. *Religion:* Lutheran. *Office:* Department of Spanish, University of Kentucky, Lexington, Ky. 40506.

*CAREER:* University of Texas at Austin, instructor in Spanish, 1953-54; Yale University, New Haven, Conn., instructor, 1954-58, assistant professor of Spanish, 1958-62; University of Pittsburgh, Pittsburgh, Pa., associate professor of Spanish, 1962-69; University of Kentucky, Lexington, professor of Spanish, 1969—. Member of board of directors, National Confederation of American Ethnic Groups, 1969-71. *Member:* Modern Language Association of America, American Association of Teachers of Spanish and Portuguese, Comparative Romance Linguistics Group, American Association of University Professors, Phi Beta Kappa. *Awards, honors:* Morse fellow, 1960-61; Fulbright professor in Colombia, 1965-66; International Research and Exchanges award, 1974; American Philosophical Society award, 1977.

*WRITINGS:* (Editor) Lucas Fernandez, *Farsas y eglogas,* Las Americas, 1969; *El lenguaje de Lucas Fernandez,* Instituto Caro y Cuervo, 1973; *Lucas Fernandez,* Twayne, 1973. Contributor of articles to language and Romance studies journals. Member of editorial board, *Kentucky Romance Quarterly;* associate editor, *Bulletin of the Comediantes;* founding editor, *La coronica.*

*WORK IN PROGRESS: Bartolome de Torres Naharro,* for publication by Twayne; research on Spanish linguistics, Spanish medieval and renaissance literature, comparative Romance linguistics, and Indo-European languages.

*SIDELIGHTS:* John Lihani speaks Spanish, Slovak, French, Italian, Portuguese, Russian, Polish, Czech, Serbo-Croatian, German, and has studied Latin, Sanskrit, Greek, and Roumanian. He has traveled extensively in Europe and North and South America.

\*   \*   \*

## LILIENTHAL, Alfred M. 1913-

*PERSONAL:* Born December 25, 1913, in New York, N.Y.; son of Herbert and Lottye (Kohn) Lilienthal. *Education:* Cornell University, B.A., 1934; Columbia University, LL.D., 1938. *Politics:* Independent Republican. *Religion:* Hebrew. *Residence:* New York, N.Y. *Office: Middle East Perspective,* 850 Seventh Ave., New York, N.Y. 10019.

*CAREER:* U.S. Department of State, Washington, D.C., political expert, 1942-43, 1945-47; attorney, Washington, D.C., 1947-49; member of the Bar of the State of New York; has worked as lecturer on foreign affairs and historian; *Middle East Perspective,* New York, N.Y., editor and publisher, 1968—; accredited journalist to the United Nations. Served as counsel to American-Arab Association for Commerce and Industry; consultant to first U.S. delegation to United Nations. *Military service:* U.S. Army, 1943-45; served in Middle East. *Member:* National Republican Club, Cornell Club of New York, Sons and Daughters of Nantucket.

*WRITINGS: What Price Israel?,* Regnery, 1953; *There Goes the Middle East,* Devin, 1957; (contributor) E. D. Anderson, editor, *Issues and Conflicts: Studies in Twentieth-Century American Diplomacy,* University of Kansas, 1958; *The Other Side of the Coin,* Devin, 1965; (contributor) Gary V. Smith, editor, *Zionism: The Dream and the Reality,* Barnes & Noble, 1974; *The Zionist Connection: Still, What True Israel?,* Dodd, in press. Contributor of articles to magazines. Author of monthly column "The Turbulent Middle East."

*WORK IN PROGRESS:* Research on Semitism and anti-Semitism in the Middle East, and on suppression of free speech and debate on the Middle East.

*SIDELIGHTS:* Alfred M. Lilienthal is regarded as the leading anti-Zionist in the United States; his studies have allowed him to interview such world leaders as Nasser, Sadat, Faisal, and Hussein, and to be the only Jewish journalist visiting both sides of the Middle East conflict on a regular basis.

\*   \*   \*

## LIND, Sidney Edmund 1914-

*PERSONAL:* Born June 6, 1914, in New York, N.Y.; son of Philip and Esther (Bernstein) Lind; married Ilse Dusoir, 1942 (divorced, 1962); married Antoinette Vigliotti, January 24, 1963 (divorced, 1975); children: (first marriage) Peter E. *Education:* College of the City of New York (now City College of the City University of New York), B.S., 1937; New York University, M.A., 1939, Ph.D., 1948. *Address:* c/o Department of English, Brooklyn College of the City University of New York, Brooklyn, N.Y. 11210.

*CAREER:* New York University, New York, N.Y., instructor in English, 1946; Rutgers University, New Brunswick, N.J., instructor, 1947-50; Brooklyn College of the City University of New York, Brooklyn, N.Y., instructor, 1950-56, assistant professor, 1956-62, associate professor, 1962-70, professor of English, 1970-77. *Military service:* U.S. Army, 1941-46; became captain.

*WRITINGS:* (With Robert Hollander) *Literature in English,* American Book Co., 1966; (with Hollander) *The Art of the Story,* American Book Co., 1968. Author of numerous articles on American literature and book reviews.

\*   \*   \*

## LINDBECK, (K.) Assar (E.) 1930-

*PERSONAL:* Born January 26, 1930, in Umeaa, Sweden; son of Carl (a county social welfare supervisor) and Eugenia (Sundelin) Lindbaeck; married Dorothy Nordlund, 1953; children: Dan, Maria. *Education:* University of Uppsala, Pol. mag., 1952; University of Stockholm, Fil.lic., 1957, Fil.dr., 1963. *Home:* Oestermalmsgaton 50, 11426 Stockholm, Sweden. *Office:* Institute for International Economic Studies, University of Stockholm, 106 91 Stockholm, Sweden.

*CAREER:* Swedish Government, Treasury Department, Stockholm, part-time employee, 1953-54, member of economic secretariat, 1955-56; Rockefeller Foundation fellow at Yale University, New Haven, Conn., Federal Reserve Board, Washington, D.C., and University of Michigan, Ann Arbor, 1957-58; University of Stockholm, Stockholm, Sweden, lecturer, 1959-60, docent (reader), 1962-63, acting professor of economics, 1963; Stockholm School of Economics, Stockholm, professor of economics, 1964-71; University of Stockholm, professor of international economics and director of Institute for International Economic Studies, 1971—. Visiting assistant professor, University of Michigan, 1958; Wesley Clair Mitchell Research Professor, Columbia University, 1968-69; Ford Rotating Research Professor, University of California, Berkeley, 1969; visiting fellow, National University of Australia, summer, 1970; Irving Fisher Visiting Professor, Yale University, 1976-77. Organization for Economic Co-operation and Development, member of expert group on agriculture and economic growth, 1964-65, of expert group on fiscal policy, 1966-68, and of McCracken group on noninflationary growth, 1975-77. Expert, Swedish Department of Domestic Affairs, 1964-66; economic advisor, Swedish Central Bank, 1964-68, 1971-74; member, Swedish Social Science Research Council, 1965-68; member, Swedish Government Research Council, 1969—. Member of selection committee for prize in economic sciences, in honor of Alfred Nobel, Swedish Government Council for Economic Planning, 1969—. *Member:* Royal Swedish Academy of Engineering Sciences, Royal Academy of Sciences, Finnish Academy of Sciences, Danish Academy of Sciences, American Economic Association (honorary member). *Awards, honors:* Ahrenberg Prize of Swedish Academy of Science, 1964.

*WRITINGS: Statsbudgetens verkningar paa konjunkturutvecklingen* (title means "The Short-Run Effects of the Government Budget"), Treasury Department (Stockholm), 1956; *The "New" Theory of Credit Control in the United States: An Interpretation and Elaboration,* Almqvist & Wiksell, 1959, 2nd edition, 1962; (with Ragnar Bentzel and Ingemar Staahl) *Bostadsbristen: en studie av prisbildningen paa bostads marknaden* (title means "The Housing Shortage: A Study of the Price System in the Housing Market"), Industriens Ufredningsinstitut, 1963; *A Study of Monetary Analysis,* Almqvist & Wiksell, 1963; (with Odd Gulbrandsen) *Jordbrukspolitikens maal och medel* (title means "Aims and Means of Agricultural Policy"), Almqvist & Wiksell, 1966; *Monetary-Fiscal Analysis and General Equilibrium,* Yrjoe Jahnssonin Saeaetioe, 1967; (contributor) L. E. Ericsson and Matts Hellstroem, editors, *Vaelstaandsklyftor och standardhoejning,* Prisma, 1967; *Theories and Problems in Swedish Economic Policy in the Post-War Period,* published as supplement to *American Economic Review,* June, 1968; *Svensk ekonomisk politik: Problem och teorier under efterkrigstiden,* Aldus/Bonnier, 1968; (with Gulbrandsen) *Jordbruksnaeringens ekonomi,* Almqvist & Wiksell, 1969, translation by Patrick Hort published as *The Economics of the Agriculture Sector,* North-Holland Publishing, 1971; *Den nya vaensterns politiska ekonomi,* Aldus/Bonnier, 1970, his own translation published as *The Political Economy of the New Left: An Outsider's View,* Harper, 1971; *Swedish Economic Policy,* Macmillan, 1972.

Contributor to published conference volumes of International Economic Association Conference of the Economic Problems of Housing and Problems of Economic Planning, and of expert groups for Organization for Economic Co-operation and Development. Contributor to *Encyclopaedia Britannica* and contributor of about fifty articles to economic journals.

*          *          *

## LINDBERG, Lucile 1913-

*PERSONAL:* Born June 10, 1913, in Essex, Iowa; daughter of Elmer and Sadie (Barnes) Lindberg. *Education:* Northwest Missouri State College (now University), B.S., 1936; Northwestern University, M.A., 1941; Columbia Univer-

sity, Ed.D., 1952. *Home:* 152-72 Melbourne Ave., Flushing, N.Y. 11367. *Office:* Department of Education, Queens College of the City University of New York, Flushing, N.Y. 11367.

*CAREER:* Has worked as an elementary school teacher, 1932-47; Queens College of the City University of New York, Flushing, N.Y., assistant professor, 1947-57, associate professor, 1957-60, professor of education, 1960—. Has lectured in New Zealand, 1966, 1970, Australia, 1969, 1970, 1972, 1974, 1975, and the Philippines, 1970. Consultant to Campus Films, New York, N.Y. *Member:* Association for Childhood Education Inter-National (vice-president, 1959-61; president, 1961-63), Committee for Early Childhood Education, New York State Council for Children (president, 1956), Queens County Mental Health Society (president, 1959-61), Kappa Delta Pi, Delta Kappa Gamma, Pi Gamma Mu, Alpha Phi Sigma. *Awards, honors:* Fulbright lecturer in Australia, 1964.

*WRITINGS: The Democratic Classroom,* Teachers College Press, 1954; *Teaching Primary Children,* Beacon Press, 1957; *Exploring Beginnings,* Beacon Press, 1958; *Those First School Years,* Department of Elementary School Principals, 1960; *Kindergarten for Today's Children,* Follett, 1967; *Early Childhood Education,* Allyn & Bacon, 1976. Associate editor, *New Era,* 1957-68.

*          *          *

## LINDEN, Kathryn (Wolaver) 1925-

*PERSONAL:* Born August 13, 1925, in Albion, Ind.; daughter of Harry Robert and Maida (Hough) Evans; married John H. Wolaver (a physician), May 4, 1945 (divorced, 1952); married James D. Linden (a psychologist), December 13, 1963; children: (first marriage) John H., Robert G., James W., Kathryn L. *Education:* Purdue University, B.S. (with distinction), 1957, M.S., 1959, Ph.D., 1964. *Home:* 2401 South Ninth St., Lafayette, Ind. 47905. *Office:* Department of Education, Purdue University, Lafayette, Ind. 47907.

*CAREER:* Worked as a high school teacher, 1957-61; Purdue University, Lafayette, Ind., instructor, 1963, assistant professor, 1963-70, associate professor, 1970-76, professor of educational psychology, 1976—. Visiting lecturer in education, University of Hawaii, Honolulu, 1969; lecturer in educational psychology, University of Reading, Reading, England, 1972. *Member:* American Psychological Association, American Educational Research Association, National Council on Measurement in Education.

*WRITINGS:* (With James D. Linden) *Modern Mental Measurement: A Historical Perspective,* Houghton, 1968; (with Linden) *Tests on Trial,* Houghton, 1968; (contributor) B. Shertzer and J. Linden, editors, *Fundamentals of Individual Analysis,* Houghton, in press. Contributor of articles to *Journal of Teacher Education, Educational Technology, Teaching of Psychology,* and other educational and psychological journals.

*WORK IN PROGRESS:* Research in classroom measurement and evaluation; research in instructional modules for educational psychology courses; *Measuring Classroom Behaviors.*

*AVOCATIONAL INTERESTS:* Reading of history and historical literature.

*          *          *

## LINGIS, Alphonso Frank 1933-

*PERSONAL:* Born November 24, 1933, in Crete, Ill.; son of

Alphonso William (a farmer) and Anna (Korshus) Lingis. *Education:* Loyola University, Chicago, Ill., B.A., 1954; University of Louvain, Ph.D., 1960. *Home:* 132½ East Prospect Ave., State College, Pa. 16801. *Office:* Pennsylvania State University, 242 Sparks, University Park, Pa. 16802.

*CAREER:* Duquesne University, Pittsburgh, Pa., instructor, 1959-60, assistant professor, 1960-66; Pennsylvania State University, University Park, associate professor of philosophy, 1966—. *Member:* American Philosophical Association, Society for Phenomenology and Existential Philosophy.

*WRITINGS*—Translator: Emmanuel Levinas, *Totality and Infinity,* Duquesne University Press, 1960; Maurice Merleau-Ponty, *The Visible and the Invisible,* Northwestern University Press, 1960; Levinas, *Existence and Existents,* Nijhoff, 1978.

*WORK IN PROGRESS: The Phantasm; The French Erotogenic Zone: French Existential Theories of the Libido.*

\* \* \*

# LINK, Eugene P(erry) 1907-

*PERSONAL:* Born September 4, 1907, in Paris, Ill.; son of Nethaniah (a pharmacist) and Lidabelle Link; married Beulah Meyer (a teacher), 1938; children: Martha (Mrs. Charles Casey), Eugene Perry, Jr., Bruce George. *Education:* College of Emporia, B.A., 1929; University of Chicago, graduate study, 1929-31; Union Theological Seminary, New York, B.D., 1933; Columbia University, Ph.D., 1941. *Home:* 12 Gravelly Point, Mounted Rd. 8, Plattsburgh, N.Y. 12901. *Office:* Department of History, State University of New York College at Plattsburgh, Plattsburgh, N.Y. 12901.

*CAREER:* Ordained in Congregational Church, 1933; Mt. Hermon School, Mt. Hermon, Mass., master in history, 1933-37; Limestone College, Gaffney, S.C., assistant professor of sociology, 1938-40; State Woman's College, Rock Hill, S.C., professor of sociology and chairman of department, 1941-44; Montclair State Teachers College (now Montclair State College), Upper Montclair, N.J., associate professor of social science, 1944-46; University of Denver, Denver, Colo., professor of sociology and chairman of department, 1946-50; State University of New York College at New Paltz, professor of social science and dean of division of social science, 1950-63; State University of New York College at Plattsburgh, research professor of American social history, 1963-70, professor emeritus of labor history, 1970—. Fulbright lecturer in India, 1954-55, 1959-60; consultant to Agency for International Development team in India, Columbia University, 1963.

*MEMBER:* American Historical Association, Association of American Historians, American Association for the History of Medicine, National Council on Family Relations (secretary, 1948-50), John Dewey Society, United States-China Friendship Association (president, 1975-77), United University Professions, (officer of New York State chapter, 1972-77), International History of Medicine Society (elected member), State University Federation of Teachers (vice-president, 1970-72), New York State Federation of College Teachers (vice-president, 1970—), Tri-State Council on Family Relations (president, 1958-60).

*WRITINGS: Democratic-Republican Societies,* Columbia University, 1942, reprinted, Octagon, 1965; *Victories in the Villages,* National Council on Educational Research and

Training (India), 1965. Contributor of articles on social history, particularly American medical history, to journals.

*WORK IN PROGRESS: Humanitarian Tradition in American Medicine;* a biography of Harry F. Ward, social gospel leader in the U.S.

\* \* \*

# LIPPITT, Ronald O. 1914-

*PERSONAL:* Born March 21, 1914, in Jackson, Minn.; son of Walter Otis (a teacher) and Lois (Garvey) Lippitt; married Rosemary N. Smith, August 13, 1937 (died, 1957); married Peggy Brunelle, August 8, 1959; children: (first marriage) Lawrence, Carolyn McCarthy, Martha. *Education:* Springfield College, B.S., 1936; University of Iowa, M.A., 1938, Ph.D., 1940. *Home and office:* 1916 Cambridge, Ann Arbor, Mich. 48104.

*CAREER:* Massachusetts Institute of Technology, Cambridge, associate professor of social psychology and program director of Research Center for Group Dynamics, 1945-48; University of Michigan, Ann Arbor, associate professor, 1948-52, professor of sociology and psychology, 1956—, program director of Research Center for Group Dynamics of Institute for Social Research, 1948-74. President of Human Resource Development Associates of Ann Arbor. *Member:* American Psychological Association, American Sociological Association, Society for Applied Anthropology, Society for Research in Child Development, American Educational Research Association, National Training Laboratories Institute for Applied Behavioral Science, Social Science Education Consortium.

*WRITINGS: Training for Community Relations,* Harper, 1950; (with J. Watson and B. Westby) *The Dynamics of Planned Change,* Harcourt, 1958; (with Richard Schmuck and Mark Chesler) *Problem Solving to Improve Classroom Learning,* Science Research Associates, 1966; (with Charles Jung and Robert Fox) *Retrieving Social Science Knowledge for Secondary Curriculum Development,* Social Science Education Consortium, 1966; *The World of Troubled Youth,* Addison-Wesley, 1967; (with Fox and Lucille Schaible) *Behavioral Science Series* (Grades 4-6), Science Research Associates, 1968; (with wife, Peggy Lippitt, and Jeffrey Eiseman) *A Cross-Age Helping Package,* Institute for Social Research (Ann Arbor), 1969, revised edition, 1971; *The Generation Mix,* Jewish Family Service of Los Angeles, 1969; *The Forgotten Consumer: The Child,* Social Science Education Consortium, 1969; (with Fox) *A Framework for Social Science Education,* Social Science Education Consortium, 1969; (with Schaible) *SRA Social Science Laboratory Units,* Science Research Associates, 1969.

*Psychopathology of Adolescence,* Grune, 1970; *The Neglected Learner,* Social Science Education Consortium, 1970; (with Eva Schindler-Rainman) *The Volunteer Community: Creative Use of Human Resources,* Learning Resources, Inc., 1971; (with Fox and Schindler-Rainman) *Images of Potentiality: Toward a Humane Society,* Center for a Voluntary Society, 1972; (with Schindler-Rainman) *Team Training for Community Change,* University of California, Riverside, 1972; (with Schindler-Rainman) *Taking Your Meetings out of the Doldrums,* University Associates, 1975; (with Gordon Lippitt) *Consulting Process in Action,* University Associates, 1978.

Contributor: *Curriculum Change: Direction and Process,* Association for Supervision and Curriculum Development, 1966; Richard Miller, editor, *Perspectives on Educational Change,* Meredith, 1966; Eli Bower and William Hollister, editors, *Behavioral Science Frontiers in Education,* Wiley, 1967; Irving Morrissett, editor, *Social Sciences in the Schools: A Search for Rationale,* Holt, 1968; John Clausen, editor, *Socialization and Society,* Little, Brown, 1968; Louis J. Rubin, editor, *Improving In-Service Education: Proposals and Procedures for Change,* Allyn & Bacon, 1971. Contributor of more than thirty articles to encyclopedias and professional journals.

*WORK IN PROGRESS:* Writing on educational research topics, on community change, on laboratory training.

\* \* \*

## LISCA, Peter 1925-

*PERSONAL:* Born February 1, 1925, in Sardinia, Italy; son of Gavin (a laborer) and Mary (Maiore) Lisca; married Dorothy Patterson, September 3, 1947 (divorced, 1972); married Amy Bushnell, December 6, 1975; children: (first marriage) Andreana, Piera; (second marriage) Catherine, Colleen. *Education:* Attended University of California, 1948-49; Santa Barbara State College (now University of California, Santa Barbara), B.A., 1950; University of Wisconsin, M.S., 1951, Ph.D., 1955. *Home:* 3510 Northwest 33rd Pl., Gainesville, Fla. 32605. *Office:* Department of English, University of Florida, Gainesville, Fla. 32611.

*CAREER:* Has worked as a chemical operator and an assistant chemist; Women's College of the University of North Carolina (now University of North Carolina at Greensboro), instructor in English, 1954-56; University of Washington, Seattle, instructor, 1956-57, assistant professor of English, 1957-58; University of Florida, Gainesville, assistant professor, 1958-64, associate professor, 1964-69, professor of English, 1969—. Smith-Mundt Lecturer in American Literature, University of Zaragosa, 1959-60; Fulbright professor of American literature, University of Warsaw, 1972-73. Reader of advanced placement exams for Educational Testing Service. Consultant and writer, Lee Mendelson Studio production entitled "Forty Years of American Life as Seen in the Work of John Steinbeck." Consultant and participant, Steinbeck Conference at San Jose State College (now University). *Member:* Modern Language Association of America, Steinbeck Society (associate editor), International Oceanographic Institute, South Atlantic Modern Language Association. *Awards, honors:* Alumni honors scholarship, University of California; University of Florida humanities research grant and graduate faculty research grant.

*WRITINGS: The Wide World of John Steinbeck,* Rutgers University Press, 1958; (editor) *"The Grapes of Wrath": Text and Criticism,* Viking, 1972; (editor) *Essays in American Literature: Irving to Steinbeck,* University of Florida Press, 1972; *John Steinbeck: Nature and Myth,* Crowell, 1978.

Contributor: Tedlock and Wicker, editors, *Steinbeck and His Critics,* University of New Mexico Press, 1957; Bluestone and Rabkin, editors, *Shakespeare's Contemporaries,* Prentice-Hall, 1961; Max Westbrook, editor, *The Modern American Novel,* Random House, 1966; K. Ledbetter, editor, *A Critical Guide to John Steinbeck,* American R. D. M. Corp., 1967; Agnes Donohue, editor, *A Casebook on "The Grapes of Wrath,"* Crowell, 1968; Richard Astro and T. Hayashi, editors, *Steinbeck: The Man and His Work,* University of Oregon Press, 1971; John Pick, editor, *A Critical Guide to "The Windhover,"* Merrill, 1969; *The Grapes of Wrath* (critical edition), Viking, 1972; Deakin and Lisca, editors, *From Irving to Steinbeck, Studies of American Literature,* University of Florida Press, 1972; Robert M.

Davis, editor, *Twentieth Century Views,* Prentice-Hall, 1972; Hayashi, *A Study Guide to Steinbeck's Long Valley,* Piernian Press, 1976. Also author of poetry and of professional papers presented to learned societies. Contributor to *Colliers Encyclopedia* and *Encyclopaedia Britannica;* contributor of articles to literature journals.

*AVOCATIONAL INTERESTS:* Skindiving, boating, music (has studied voice professionally), and ecology and conservation.

\* \* \*

## LIST, Ilka Katherine 1935-
(Ilka Maidoff)

*PERSONAL:* Surname List legally re-adopted in 1974; born November 22, 1935, in Orange, N.J.; daughter of Albert and Phyllis (Carrington) List; married Jules Maidoff, August 28, 1959 (divorced, August, 1967); children: Lee David, Jonah Asher, Natasha Katherine. *Education:* Attended Cornell University, Reed College, and St. Andrew's University; University of Maine at Orono, B.S., 1975; State University of New York College at New Paltz, M.F.A., 1978. *Home and office:* 201 West 89th St., New York, N.Y. 10024.

*CAREER:* Brooklyn Friends School, Brooklyn, N.Y., teacher of sculpture, print-making, and women's lib, 1969—. Sculptor-member, Environment Gallery, New York, N.Y., 1967—. *Member:* New York Society of Women Artists. *Awards, honors: Seashore Life* was chosen by Children's Book Council as one of thirty-three best books of 1971; residence fellowship at Yaddo Foundation, 1972.

*WRITINGS:* (Under name Ilka Maidoff) *Let's Explore the Shore,* Obolensky, 1962; (self-illustrated with Arabelle Wheating) *Questions and Answers about Seashore Life,* Four Winds, 1971; *Grandma's Beach Surprise,* new edition, 1975; (author with Albert List, Jr., and self-illustrated) *A Walk in the Forest: The Woodlands of North America,* Crowell, 1977.

*WORK IN PROGRESS:* Sculptures commissioned for public housing in Maine.

*SIDELIGHTS:* Ilka List told *CA:* "Writing for me serves as intense distillation of experience. It involves responsibility and choice in trying to get words to correspond accurately to experience. It involves an attempt to catch fleeting associations and poetic imaginings and relate these to one's more objective experience. It can be a painful or exhilerating process, depending on how it goes. Words have a music for me that has to sound right—so often a single paragraph can involve hours of work. I feel most of the pleasure comes from the knowledge that you have managed to communicate something to someone and perhaps conveyed something of your own slant on things in a way that can be deeply felt.

"If I have something difficult to work on, I can discipline myself to start working on it by promising myself a walk, a treat, a shower—something pleasant to occur after an hour ... of work. Then I sit down and do some more.... I go over and over and over things until they sound right, until there is a flow, and until the words hold the right combination of seriousness, humor, imagination, speculation."

*AVOCATIONAL INTERESTS:* Horses and goats.

\* \* \*

## LIVERGOOD, Norman D(avid) 1933-

*PERSONAL:* Born September 21, 1933, in Syracuse, Kan.; son of Donald (a merchant) and Bessie (Tucker) Livergood;

married Beverly J. Walker (an artist), 1961 (divorced); married Nanette Vawter, 1976; children: (first marriage) two; (second marriage) one. *Education:* Phillips University, B.A., 1955; Yale University, B.D., 1958, M.A., 1959, Ph.D., 1962. *Home:* 25 West Grant St., Healdsburg, Calif. 95448. *Office:* California Institute of Asian Studies, 3494 21st St., San Francisco, Calif. 94140.

*CAREER:* St. Lawrence University, Canton, N.Y., assistant professor of philosophy, 1961-62; Ohio Wesleyan University, Delaware, Ohio, assistant professor of philosophy, 1962-63; Frostburg State College, Frostburg, Md., professor of philosophy, 1963-65; Southern Illinois University, Edwardsville, associate professor of philosophy, 1965-69; self-employed as teacher, consultant, 1969-72; California Institute of Asian Studies, San Francisco, professor of philosophical psychology, 1973—. Group counselor, St. Louis Institute for Rational Living, St. Louis, Mo., 1967-69. Part-time instructor, Santa Rosa Junior College, 1973; University of California, Berkeley, director of studies for the Association for Democratic Preparation, 1972—, summer university professor, 1973. *Member:* American Philosophical Association.

*WRITINGS:* (Contributor) Bradford E. Gale, editor, *Contemporary Accents in Liberal Religion*, Beacon Press, 1960; *Activity in Marx's Philosophy*, Nijhoff, 1967; *How to Become a Modern Guru (in Forty Nights)*, Association for Meaningful Active Learning (Healdsburg, Calif.), 1974; *Walter Lippmann and the Continuing American Revolution*, Santa Rosa Junior College, 1976.

*WORK IN PROGRESS:* Studying Sufism; *The President of the World*, a novel.

*       *       *

## LLEWELLYN-JONES, Derek   1923-

*PERSONAL:* Born April 29, 1923, in Cheshire, England; son of John Glyn (a physician) and Olivia (Baile) Llewellyn-Jones; married Elizabeth Kirkby (an actress), February 22, 1947; children: Anthony, Deborah, Robert. *Education:* University of Dublin. *Politics:* Radical. *Religion:* Humanist. *Home:* Awabakal, Owen's Rd., Martinsville, New South Wales 2265, Australia. *Agent:* Lis Kirkby, 589 South Dowling St., Surry Hills, New South Wales, Australia. *Office:* University of Sydney Medical School, Sydney, Australia.

*CAREER:* University of Sydney, Sydney, New South Wales, Australia, associate professor of obstetrics and gynaecology, 1965—. President, Zero Population Growth (Australia), 1971—. *Awards, honors:* Order of the British Empire, 1963.

*WRITINGS: Fundamentals of Obstetrics and Gynaecology,* Faber, Volume I, 1969, Volume II, 1970, 2nd edition, 1978; *Everywoman,* Taplinger, 1971, revised edition, Faber, 1978; *Human Reproduction and Society,* Faber, 1974; *People Populating,* Faber, 1975; *Sex and VD,* Faber, 1975.

*WORK IN PROGRESS: Everyman Today; Fat People Are Fat Because . . .* , a study in food habits in the western world.

*       *       *

## LLOYD, Norman   1909-

*PERSONAL:* Born November 8, 1909, in Pottsville, Pa.; son of David (a businessman) and Annie (Holstein) Lloyd; married Ruth Rohrbacher (a musician and educator), April 10, 1933; children: David Walter, Alex. *Education:* New York University, B.S., 1932, M.A., 1936. *Residence:* Greenwich, Conn.

*CAREER:* New York University, New York City, lecturer in music, 1936-45; Sarah Lawrence College, Bronxville, N.Y., professor of music, 1936-46, conductor of chorus, 1945-48; Juilliard School, New York City, professor of music, 1946-63; Oberlin College, Oberlin, Ohio, dean of Conservatory, 1963-65; Rockefeller Foundation, New York City, director for arts and humanities, 1965-72; free-lance consultant in the arts, 1973—. Also a professional performer and composer. *Member:* American Society of Composers, Authors, and Publishers (ASCAP), American Federation of Musicians. *Awards, honors:* Annual awards from American Society of Composers, Authors, and Publishers, 1962-72.

*WRITINGS:* (With Margaret Boni) *Fireside Book of Folksongs,* Simon & Schuster, 1947; (with Boni) *Fireside Book of American Songs,* Simon & Schuster, 1952; (with Arnold Fish) *Fundamentals of Sight Singing,* Dodd, 1963; *Golden Encyclopedia of Music,* Western Publishing, 1968; (with wife, Ruth Lloyd) *American Heritage Songbook,* American Heritage, 1971; (contributor) Margaret Mahoney, editor, *Arts on the Campus,* Graphic Arts Press, 1971; (with R. Lloyd) *Keyboard Improvisation,* Dodd, 1973.

*       *       *

## LLOYD GEORGE (OF DWYOR), Frances (Louise Stevenson)   1888(?)-1972

1888(?)—December 5, 1972; English secretary and later wife to David Lloyd George, former Prime Minister of England. Obituaries: *New York Times,* December 7, 1972.

*       *       *

## LOCKERBIE, D(onald) Bruce   1935-

*PERSONAL:* Born August 25, 1935, in Capreol, Ontario, Canada; son of Ernest Arthur (a minister) and Jeanette (Honeyman) Lockerbie; married Lory Quayle (a teacher), December 15, 1956; children: Donald Bruce, Jr., Kevin John, Ellyn Beth. *Education:* New York University, A.B., 1956, M.A., 1963; also attended Wheaton College, Wheaton, Ill., 1956-57. *Politics:* Independent. *Religion:* Episcopalian. *Home:* 12 Chub Hill Rd., Stony Brook, N.Y. 11790. *Office:* Stony Brook School, Stony Brook, N.Y. 11790.

*CAREER:* Stony Brook School, Stony Brook, N.Y., chairman of Fine Arts department, 1957—. Visiting professor of English, Wheaton College; Staley Foundation lecturer at several colleges. *Member:* National Council of Teachers of English (member of Commission on English Curriculum), Cum Laude Society, New York Athletic Club.

*WRITINGS: Billy Sunday,* Word Books, 1965; (with Thomas C. Pollock) *The Macmillan English Series,* twelve volumes, Macmillan, 1969; (with Lincoln Westdal) *Success in Writing,* Addison-Wesley, 1970; *Purposeful Writing,* Addison-Wesley, 1972; *The Way They Should Go,* Oxford University Press, 1972; *The Liberating Word: Art and the Mystery of the Gospel,* Eerdmans, 1974; *Education of Missionaries' Children: The Neglected Dimension of World Mission,* William Carey Library, 1975; *The Apostles' Creed: Do You Really Believe It?,* Victor, 1977; *A Man under Orders: Lt. General William K. Harrison, Jr.,* Harper, 1978. Contributor of articles to religion and literature journals. General editor, "Major American Authors," Holt, 1970.

*WORK IN PROGRESS: While the Music Lasts,* with Werner Janssen.

## LOCKLIN, Gerald (Ivan) 1941-

*PERSONAL:* Born February 17, 1941, in Rochester, N.Y.; son of Ivan Ward and Esther (Kindelen) Locklin; married Mary Alice Keefe; married second wife, Maureen McNicholas; children: (first marriage) James, Heidi, Rebecca; (second marriage) Blake, John. *Education:* St. John Fisher College, B.A., 1961; University of Arizona, M.A., 1963, Ph.D., 1964. *Office:* Department of English, California State University, Long Beach, Calif. 90801.

*CAREER:* California State College at Los Angeles (now California State University, Los Angeles), instructor in English, 1964-65; California State University, Long Beach, 1965—, began as associate professor, currently professor of English. *Member:* Phi Beta Kappa.

*WRITINGS: Sunset Beach,* Hors Commerce Press, 1967; *The Toad Poems,* Runcible Spoon Press, 1970, new edition, Venice Poetry Company, 1975; *Poop, and Other Poems,* Mag Press, 1973; *Toad's Europe,* Venice Poetry Co., 1973; *Locked In,* True Gripp Press, 1973; (with Koertge and Stetler) *Tarzan and Shane Meet the Toad,* Russ Haas Press, 1975; *The Chase: A Novel,* Duck Down Press, 1976; *The Criminal Mentality,* Red Hill Press, 1976; *The Four-Day Work Week and Other Stories,* Russ Haas Press, 1977; *Frisco Epic,* Russ Haas Press, in press; *Toad's Sabbatical,* Venice Poetry Co., in press. Also author of play "The Dentist." Contributor of numerous reviews to *Los Angeles Times* and *Long Beach Independent Press-Telegram,* and of articles to *Coast;* contributor of poems and stories to literary magazines, including *Wormwood Review* and *Transpacific.*

*WORK IN PROGRESS:* Poems, stories, novels, plays, and literary criticism.

\*        \*        \*

## LOCKWOOD, Lee 1932-

*PERSONAL:* Born May 4, 1932, in New York, N.Y.; son of Arthur H. and Ruth (Edinberg) Lockwood; married Joyce Greenfield, June 14, 1964; children: Andrew, Gillian. *Education:* Boston University, B.A., 1954; Columbia University, graduate study, 1956-59. *Residence:* Newton, Mass. *Office:* Black Star Publishing Co., Inc., 450 Park Ave. S., New York, N.Y. 10016.

*CAREER:* Editor of *Contemporary Photographer Quarterly,* 1963-67; Black Star Publishing Co., Inc., New York, N.Y., currently photographer. Producer-director of documentary film, *The Holy Outlaw,* N.E.T. Journal, 1970. *Military service:* U.S. Army, 1954-56. *Member:* Authors Guild of America, Authors League of America. *Awards, honors:* Overseas Press Club Award for best distinguished foreign reporting, 1967; Rockefeller fellow in educational television, WGBH-TV, Boston, Mass., 1967-68.

*WRITINGS: Castro's Cuba, Cuba's Fidel,* Macmillan, 1967, revised edition, Vantage, 1970; *Conversation with Eldridge Cleaver/Algiers,* McGraw, 1970; (with Daniel Berrigan) *Absurd Convictions, Modest Hopes,* Random House, 1972.

*SIDELIGHTS:* Lee Lockwood made his first visit to Cuba in 1958 as a free-lance photo-journalist covering the fall of Batista when Fidel Castro took over Cuba. He returned in 1959 for a year on other assignments, and in 1964 to cover the July 26 independence celebrations for *Newsweek.* He spent three months in Cuba doing research and taking photographs, and devoted one week to an interview with Castro which was included in *Castro's Cuba, Cuba's Fidel.*

Most of the critics agree that *Castro's Cuba, Cuba's Fidel* is well worth reading. "The author's questions are tough and penetrating and they elicited the same kind of answers," writes a *Harper's* reviewer, adding, "The lively record deserves and encourages serious study." Claude Julien feels that the book "permits the educated man concerned with forming his own opinion without prejudice to inform himself on a problem that interests not only America but the world. . . . A first rate psychological document, this book is also a historical one in that it contains information necessary to the understanding of several controversial questions, such as the priority given agriculture in the development of the Cuban economy. . . . The only flaws . . . are factual errors that seem unaccountable [although they] do not lessen [the book's] value."

Jose Yglesias considers the book to be "frequently lively and informative and its long interview with Fidel—the heart of the book—is of major importance, one which the Cubans themselves read with considerable interest. . . . He is a photographer, and when he tells us about Cuba with his camera, he is at his best. It is in [these pictures], not in the chapters of reportage, that his feeling for the landscape, the Cubans, and the Cuban revolution comes through."

Lockwood told *Publishers' Weekly* that the only part of the book edited by Fidel Castro was the interview itself, and he made only minor changes at that. The author had "'expected some kind of strong reaction from him,'" but found Castro "'liked the interview very much and thought he hadn't been misinterpreted.'"

*BIOGRAPHICAL/CRITICAL SOURCES: Life,* April 7, 1967; *Publishers' Weekly,* May 1, 1967; *New York Times Book Review,* May 21, 1967; *Harper's,* June, 1967; *New Republic,* July 8, 1967; *Book World,* August 18, 1968; *Washington Post,* May 20, 1970.

\*        \*        \*

## LOEWEN, James W. 1942-

*PERSONAL:* Born February 6, 1942, in Decatur, Ill.; son of David Frank (a physician) and Winifred (Gore) Loewen; married Patricia Hanrahan, October 26, 1968 (divorced, January, 1976); children: Bruce Nicholas, Lucy Catherine. *Education:* Attended Mississippi State University, 1963; Carleton College, B.A., 1964; Harvard University, M.A., 1967, Ph.D., 1968. *Politics:* Independent. *Religion:* Unitarian-Universalist. *Office:* Department of Sociology, University of Vermont, Burlington, Vt. 05401.

*CAREER:* Tougaloo College, Tougaloo, Miss., assistant professor, 1968-70, associate professor of sociology, 1970-75, chairman of department of sociology and anthropology, 1969-73; University of Vermont, Burlington, associate professor of sociology, 1975—. Co-director of Mississippi History Project. *Member:* American Sociological Association, Southern Sociological Society, Mississippi Historical Society.

*WRITINGS: The Mississippi Chinese: Between Black and White,* Harvard University Press, 1971; (with Charles Sallis and others) *Mississippi: Conflict and Change,* Pantheon, 1974. Contributor to national journals and professional publications.

*WORK IN PROGRESS: Essential Sociology,* a core introductory text; research on school desegregation in Mississippi.

\*        \*        \*

## LOEWENSTEIN, Louis Klee 1927-

*PERSONAL:* Born June 22, 1927, in San Francisco, Calif.;

son of Louis (a retailer) and Helen (Klee) Loewenstein; married Marcella DeCray (a musician), May 27, 1961 (divorced, 1972); married Joan A. Nelson (a student), June 26, 1977; children: (first marriage) Louis DeCray, Lael Kimberly. *Education:* University of Virginia, B.S., 1949; Columbia University, M.S., 1958; University of Pennsylvania, M.C.P., 1960, Ph.D., 1962. *Home and office:* 3858 Jackson St., San Francisco, Calif. 94118.

*CAREER:* Arthur D. Little, Inc., San Francisco, Calif., consultant, 1963-67; University of California, Berkeley, real estate economist, 1967-68; San Francisco State College (now University), San Francisco, Calif., 1968-71, became professor of urban studies; University of California, Berkeley, lecturer in real estate, 1972—. Acting professor of urban planning, Stanford University, 1974-76. *Member:* Lambda Alpha (international president, 1978-79). *Awards, honors:* Ford Foundation grant, 1977.

*WRITINGS: The Location of Residences and Work Places,* Scarecrow, 1965; (contributor) H. Wentworth Eldredge, editor, *Introduction to Urban Planning and Urbanism,* Doubleday, 1967; (contributor) T. Milton Nelson, editor, *Urban Problems and Techniques,* Chandler-Davis, 1970; (contributor) Goodman, editor, *A Reader on Urban Politics,* Allyn & Bacon, 1970; (editor) *Urban Studies,* Free Press, 1971, 2nd edition, 1977; Robert Dentler, editor, *Urban Problems: Perspectives and Solutions,* Rand McNally, 1977.

*WORK IN PROGRESS: The New York State Urban Development Corporation: A Noble Experiment.*

*SIDELIGHTS:* Louis Klee Loewenstein told CA: "I consider myself to be a broker of information between laymen—the general public—and persons who are 'on the leaning edge of knowledge' in the field of city planning."

*       *       *

## LOGAN, James Phillips 1921-

*PERSONAL:* Born April 27, 1921, in Frenchtown, N.J.; son of Robert Lee and Elizabeth (Schenck) Logan; married Joanne Marie Solie (a school director), September 7, 1945; children: Donald, Jan Louise, Derek. *Education:* Princeton University, A.B., 1943; Harvard University, M.B.A., 1949; Columbia University, Ph.D., 1960. *Politics:* Independent. *Religion:* Unitarian Universalist. *Home:* 2046 East Fourth St., Tucson, Ariz. 85719. *Office:* College of Business and Public Administration, University of Arizona, Tucson, Ariz. 85721.

*CAREER:* Thomas & Skinner Steel Products Co., Indianapolis, Ind., clerk, 1946-47; St. Lawrence University, Canton, N.Y., instructor in management, 1950-51; Columbia University, New York, N.Y., lecturer in management, 1951-54; Dartmouth College, Hanover, N.H., assistant professor of business administration, 1954-58; Columbia University, 1958-68, began as assistant professor, became associate professor of management; University of Arizona, Tucson, professor of management, 1968—. *Military service:* U.S. Army Air Forces, 1943-46; became captain. *Member:* American Economic Association, Academy of Management, American Association for the Advancement of Science, American Association of University Professors.

*WRITINGS:* (With William H. Newman) *Management of Expanding Enterprises,* Columbia University Press, 1954; (with Newman) *Business Policies and Management,* South-Western Publishing, 1959, subsequent editions published under varying titles, 6th edition as *Strategy, Policy and Central Management,* 1971.

*WORK IN PROGRESS:* Research on boards of directors of corporations, evaluation of business management, and processes of strategy formation.

*AVOCATIONAL INTERESTS:* Travel ("almost anywhere").††

*       *       *

## LOGANBILL, G. Bruce 1938-

*PERSONAL:* Born September 6, 1938, in Newton, Kan.; son of Oscar J. and Warrene Rose Loganbill. *Education:* Bethel College, North Newton, Kan., B.A., 1956; University of Kansas, M.A., 1958; Michigan State University, Ph.D., 1961; Martin Palmer Institute of Logopedics, logopedic pathology postdoctoral certificate, 1965. *Religion:* Episcopalian. *Home:* 101 Claremont Ave., Belmont Shore, Long Beach, Calif. 90803. *Office:* Department of Speech Communication, California State University, Long Beach, Calif. 90840.

*CAREER:* California State University, Long Beach, associate professor of logopedic pathology, 1968-73, professor of speech communication, 1973—. International Interpretive Theatre Alliance, president and artist critic, 1970-77; member of Governor's Conference on Aging, 1971. Professional baritone soloist. *Member:* International Association of Logopedics and Phoniatrics, International Association for Melody Programmed Therapy of Speech, International Phonetics Society, American Speech and Hearing Association, Exceptional Children's Conference, Speech Communication Association, Norsk Logopedlag of Norway, Speech Communication Association of the Pacific, Western Speech Association, California Speech and Hearing Association, California Speech Association, Pi Eta Delta.

*WRITINGS: Prose, Poetry, Drama: A Study in Oral Interpretation,* Sansyusya, (Tokyo), 1972; *The Bases of Voice, Articulation and Pronunciation,* Sansyusya, 1972. Contributor to *Folia Phoniatrica.* Associate editor, *Speech Abstracts;* referee, *Western Speech.*

*       *       *

## LONG, Louise

*PERSONAL:* Daughter of George Ware (a stockbroker) and Annie Lee (Loveless) Long. *Education:* Huntingdon College, A.B.; Northwestern University, M.A., 1945; Garrett Theological Seminary, B.D., 1946. *Politics:* Democrat. *Religion:* Methodist. *Home:* 45251 Fern Dr., Mendocino, Calif. 95460.

*CAREER:* Served as a Protestant chaplain for twenty-six years, of which twenty-one were in the state of California. The Methodist California-Nevada Conference, board of ordained ministry, 1972-77, member of committee on ecumenical affairs, and business committee, 1973-76. *Member:* American Association of University Women, California State Employees Association, Mendocino Study Club.

*WRITINGS: Door of Hope,* Abingdon, 1972.

*WORK IN PROGRESS:* A book, tentatively entitled *Gruesome Twosome,* about two prisoners "released as cured, who raped, killed, dismembered, and ate a girl."

*       *       *

## LONG, Richard A(lexander) 1927-
### (Ric Alexander)

*PERSONAL:* Born February 9, 1927, in Philadelphia, Pa.; son of Thaddeus B. and Lela (Washington) Long. *Educa-*

*tion:* Temple University, A.B., 1947, M.A., 1948; further study at University of Pennsylvania and University of Paris; University of Poitiers, D.es L., 1965. *Office:* Department of English, Atlanta University, Atlanta, Ga. 30314.

*CAREER:* West Virginia State College, Institute, instructor in English, 1949-50; Morgan State College, Baltimore, Md., assistant professor, 1951-64, associate professor of English, 1964-66; Hampton Institute, Hampton, Va., professor of English and French, 1966-68; Atlanta University, Atlanta, Ga., professor of English, 1968—. Visiting lecturer in Afro-American Studies, Harvard University, 1970-72. *Military service:* U.S. Army, 1944-45. *Member:* Modern Language Association of America, College Language Association (president, 1971-72), Modern Humanities Research Association, American Association of Museums, Linguistics Society of America, Southeastern Conference on Linguistics. *Awards, honors:* Fulbright scholar, University of Paris, 1957-58.

*WRITINGS:* (Editor with Albert Berrian) *Negritude: Essays and Studies,* Hampton Institute Press, 1967; (editor with Eugenia Collier) *Afro-American Writing: An Anthology of Prose and Poetry,* New York University Press, 1972; *Ascending and Other Poems,* Du Sable Museum, 1975.

Author of dramatic works under name Ric Alexander: "The Pilgrim's Pride" (sketches), 1963; "Stairway to Heaven" (gospel opera), 1964; "Joan of Arc" (folk opera), 1964; "Reasons of State" (play), 1966; "Black Is Many Hues" (play), 1969. Member of editorial boards, *Phylon* and *Black Books Bulletin.*

*WORK IN PROGRESS:* Editing works of Alain Locke; editing and writing works on African art.

\* \* \*

**LONGMAN, Mark Frederic Kerr 1916-1972**

November 12, 1916—September 6, 1972; English publisher and bookman. Obituaries: *New York Times,* September 8, 1972; *Publishers Weekly,* September 18, 1972; *Antiquarian Bookman,* October 16, 1972.

\* \* \*

**LOOMIS, Stanley 1922-1972**

December 21, 1922—December 18, 1972; American historian. Obituaries: *New York Times,* December 22, 1972. (See index for *CA* sketch)

\* \* \*

**LOPEZ-REY, Jose 1905-**

*PERSONAL:* Born May 14, 1905, in Madrid, Spain; son of Leocadio (a physician) and Filomena (Rey) Lopez; married Maria Victoria Gonzalez Mateos, 1933 (divorced, 1939); married Justa Arroyo (a college professor), November 25, 1946; children: (first marriage) Margarita Lopez-Rey Gonzalez (Mrs. Luis Fernandez Plaza). *Education:* Instituto del Cardenal Cisneros, B.A., 1925; University of Madrid, Licenciado en Filosofia y Letras, 1929, Doctor en Filosofia y Letras, 1935; also studied at University of Florence and University of Vienna. *Home:* Callejon de la Sierra 3, Ciudad Santo Domingo, Algete (Madrid), Spain.

*CAREER:* University of Madrid, Madrid, Spain, professor of art history, 1932-39; Smith College, Northampton, Mass., lecturer in Spanish and twentieth-century art, 1940-45; New York University, Institute of Fine Arts, New York City, lecturer, 1951-53, associate professor, 1953-64, professor of fine arts, 1964-73, professor emeritus, 1973—. Research fellow in art history, Center of Historical Studies, 1932-39; adviser on fine arts, Ministry of Education (Madrid), 1933-39; general commissioner for Spain, International Art Exhibition (Venice), 1936; sponsor, International University of Art (Florence), 1969—; vice-president, International Foundation for Art Research (New York City), 1970—.

*WRITINGS: Antonio del Pollaiuolo y el fin del Quattrocento,* Hauser y Menet (Madrid), 1935; *Goya y el mundo a su alrededor,* Sudamericana (Buenos Aires), 1947; *Goya's Caprichos: Beauty, Reason and Caricature,* two volumes, Princeton University Press, 1953; *A Cycle of Goya's Drawings: The Expression of Truth and Liberty,* Faber, 1956; *Velazquez: A Catalogue Raisonne of His Oeuvre,* Faber, 1963; *Velazquez' Work and World,* Faber, 1968; *Velazquez: The Artist as a Maker,* Bibliotheque des Arts (Lausanne), in press. Contributor of articles to *Art Quarterly, Art Bulletin, Saturday Review, Gazette des Beaux-Arts, Archivo Espanol de Arte, Arte Espanol, Apollo, Critica d'Arts.*

*WORK IN PROGRESS: Velazquez,* for Arnoldo Mondadori (Milan); *Goya in His Time and After.*

\* \* \*

**LORD, Donald Charles 1930-**

*PERSONAL:* Born August 21, 1930, in Derby, Conn.; married Kathleen Anderson (an opera singer), February 8, 1954; children: Maurita Beth, Sean Christopher. *Education:* Oberlin College, B.A., 1957; Western Reserve University (now Case Western Reserve University), M.A., 1960, Ph.D., 1964. *Politics:* Independent. *Religion:* Presbyterian. *Office:* Department of History, Unity College, Unity, Me. 04988.

*CAREER:* Junior high school teacher in Oberlin, Ohio, 1957-58, and in Maple Heights, Ohio, 1959-60; Western Ontario University, London, lecturer in history, 1962-63; State University of New York College at Plattsburgh, assistant professor of history, 1963-64; Hampton Institute, Hampton, Va., assistant professor of history, 1964-67; Eastern Kentucky University, Richmond, assistant professor of history, 1964-67; Texas Woman's University, Denton, associate professor of history, 1967-73; Unity College, Unity, Me., professor of history, 1973-78. Editor, Jones Kenilworth Publishing Co. Consultant to U.S. Air Force program on black history. President, Denton Christian Pre-School.

*WRITINGS: Mo Bradley and Thailand,* Eerdmans, 1969; *The Lovesong of Emelie Bradley,* Eerdmans, 1971; *John F. Kennedy,* Barron's, 1977; (with Robert M. Calhoon and others) *Issues Past and Present,* two volumes, Heath, 1978. Contributor of twenty articles to history and education journals.

*WORK IN PROGRESS: King John the First: Image Making in the White House.*

\* \* \*

**LORD, Frederic Mather 1912-**

*PERSONAL:* Born November 12, 1912, in Hanover, N.H.; son of Frederic Pomeroy and L. Jeannette (Mather) Lord; married Shirley Arlene Hanfman, June 15, 1946 (divorced July, 1975); children: John, Eric. *Education:* Dartmouth College, B.A., 1936; University of Minnesota, M.A., 1943; Princeton University, Ph.D., 1951. *Office:* Educational Testing Service, Princeton, N.J. 08540.

*CAREER:* U.S. Civil Service Commission, Washington,

D.C., principal assistant, 1941-44; Carnegie Foundation, Graduate Record Office, New York City, research assistant, 1944-45, head of tabulating department, 1945-46; American Council on Education, Cooperative Test Service, New York City, assistant director of research department, 1946-49, statistical analysis head in Statistical Service Division, 1949; Educational Testing Service, Princeton, N.J., research associate, 1949-60, senior research psychologist and chairman of psychometric research group, 1960—. Visiting professor of psychology, Princeton University, 1959-71; Brittingham Visiting Professor of Educational Psychology, University of Wisconsin, 1963-64; visiting lecturer in psychology, University of Pennsylvania, 1969.

*MEMBER:* Psychometric Society (president, 1958-59), American Psychological Association (fellow), American Statistical Association (fellow), Institute of Mathematical Statistics (fellow), Phi Beta Kappa, Sigma Xi.

*WRITINGS: A Theory of Test Scores* (monograph), Psychometric Society, 1952; (with Melvin R. Novick) *Statistical Theories of Mental Test Scores,* Addison-Wesley, 1968. Contributor of articles to psychology, mathematics, statistics, and education journals.

*WORK IN PROGRESS:* Research on statistics and mental test theory.

\* \* \*

## LOSONCY, Lawrence J. 1941-

*PERSONAL:* Surname is accented on second syllable; born September 12, 1941, in Detroit, Mich.; son of Joseph Michael (a businessman) and Rose (Laus) Losoncy; married Mary Jan Sibley (a teacher and researcher), August 16, 1965; children: David Lawrence, John Michael, Kristen Mary. *Education:* Sacred Heart Seminary College, B.A., 1963; St. John's Seminary, additional study, 1963-65; University of Detroit, M.A., 1968; Wayne State University, Ph.D., 1971. *Politics:* Democrat. *Religion:* Roman Catholic. *Home:* 1701 West Virgin Ave., Tulsa, Okla. 74127. *Office:* Oral Roberts University, Tulsa, Okla. 74145.

*CAREER:* School music teacher and church organist in Lincoln Park, Mich., 1965-68; University of Detroit, Detroit, Mich., instructor in philosophy, 1968; high school religion teacher in Southgate, Mich., 1968-69; Wayne State University, Detroit, instructor in philosophy of education, 1969; Hi-Time Publisher, Elm Grove, Wis., editor, 1969; U.S. Catholic Conference, Washington, D.C., director of Adult Education Division, project director for national study, "The Church's Expanding Role in Adult Education," 1970-72; currently a practising professional marriage and family counselor. Adjunct associate professor, Oral Roberts University. National consultant, U.S. Catholic Conference.

*WRITINGS: Common Sense Vision: A Philosophy of Religious Education,* privately printed, 1968; *For Parents: Teaching Religion at Home,* privately printed, 1969; (with wife, Mary Jan Losoncy) *Love,* Ave Maria Press, 1970; (with Mary Jan Losoncy) *Sex and the Adolescent,* Ave Maria Press, 1971; *The ABC's of Adult Education,* Volume I, U.S. Catholic Conference, 1971; *Land of Promise,* Dimension Books, 1972; *Religious Education and the Life Cycle,* Catechetical Communications, 1977. Editor of bimonthly "Focus '72," monthly "Financial Aid," and monthly "Footprints."

*WORK IN PROGRESS: When Your Child Needs a Hug.*

*SIDELIGHTS:* Lawrence Losoncy told *CA:* "I have found working and writing in the service of other people to be a

source of unending satisfaction. Our challenge today in literature and in life is to uphold the dignity and individual rights of each person in the face of technology and bureaucracy. Literature has always been such a force for humanizing ourselves." •

\* \* \*

## LOSONCY, Mary Jan 1942-

*PERSONAL:* Born June 8, 1942, in Muskegon, Mich.; daughter of Harold D. (an industrial executive) and Lois (Gibbs) Sibley; married Lawrence J. Losoncy (national adult education director for U.S. Catholic Conference), August 16, 1965; children: David Lawrence, John Michael, Kristen Mary. *Education:* Attended Nazareth College, Kalamazoo, Mich., 1960-62; Mercy College, Detroit, Mich., B.S., 1965; Marygrove College, additional study, 1965-67; Tulsa University, additional study, 1977—. *Religion:* Roman Catholic. *Home:* 1701 West Virgin Ave., Tulsa, Okla. 74127.

*CAREER:* Mercy Hospital, Muskegon, Mich., nurses aid, 1964; high school home economics and English teacher in Highland Park, Mich., 1965; elementary teacher in Lincoln Park, Mich., 1966; teacher of developmental psychology in community program in Southgate, Mich., 1967; U.S. Catholic Conference, Washington, D.C., research assistant in Adult Education Division, 1971-72.

*WRITINGS:* (With husband, Lawrence J. Losoncy) *Love,* Ave Maria Press, 1970; (with L. J. Losoncy) *Sex and the Adolescent,* Ave Maria Press, 1971. Contributor to magazines.

*WORK IN PROGRESS:* The current role of liberated but non-radical woman; growth in family life from shared income responsibility and shared child-raising; value and goal decision to order priorities and free men and women from traditional inhibitions.

\* \* \*

## LOTZ, James Robert 1929-

*PERSONAL:* Born January 12, 1929, in Liverpool, England; son of John Bowyer (a railway worker) and Mary (Hutcheon) Lotz; married Pat Wicks (a free-lance editor and librarian), December 12, 1959; children: Annette Mary, Fiona Suzanne. *Education:* University of Manchester, B.A. (honors), 1952; McGill University, M.Sc., 1957; University of British Columbia, additional study, 1964-65 ("ejected from institution"). *Religion:* Christian. *Home address:* Box 3393, Halifax South P.O., Halifax, Nova Scotia, Canada B3J 3J1.

*CAREER:* Spent some time in Africa as trader after leaving England, and served with the special constabulary in the Kano riots in Nigeria, 1953; later wrote advertising copy in Ottawa, Ontario; Canadian Government, Department of Indian Affairs and Northern Development, Ottawa, Ontario, community planning officer, then research officer, 1960-66; Canadian Research Centre for Anthropology, Ottawa, associate director, 1966-71; St. Francis Xavier University, Coady International Institute, Antigonish, Nova Scotia, assistant professor of community development, 1971-73; free-lance writer, teacher, research worker, and consultant, 1973—. *Military service:* Royal Air Force, radio technician, 1947-49. *Member:* Writer's Union of Canada. *Awards, honors:* Queen's Commendation for brave conduct in Kano riots.

*WRITINGS: Northern Realities: Exploitation of the Cana-*

*dian North,* Follett, 1971; (editor with wife, Pat Lotz, and contributor) *Pilot, Not Commander: Essays in Memory of Diamond Jenness,* Canadian Research Centre for Anthropology, St. Paul University, 1971; (co-author) *Cape Breton Island,* David & Charles, 1974; *Understanding Canada: Regional and Community Development in a New Nation,* NC Press, 1977; *Death in Dawson,* General Publishing, 1978. Contributor of about three hundred articles, technical papers, and reviews to Canadian, American, British, Italian, and German journals; also has written for *New York Times Book Review.*

*WORK IN PROGRESS:* A book on an arctic expedition based on personal involvement; a series of murder mysteries with an authentic northern background.

\*     \*     \*

## LOUNSBURY, Myron O. 1940-

*PERSONAL:* Born February 9, 1940, in New York, N.Y.; son of Myron Horton (a construction worker) and Margaret (Osborn) Lounsbury; married Lynann Rudert (a part-time teacher), August 24, 1963; married second wife, Jill Hardwicke (a part-time teacher); children: (first marriage) Jennifer Ann, Heather Margaret; (second marriage) Nathaniel Hardwicke. *Education:* Duke University, B.A. (summa cum laude), 1961; University of Pennsylvania, M.A., 1962, Ph.D., 1966. *Office:* University of Maryland, College Park, Md. 20740.

*CAREER:* University of Maryland, College Park, 1965—, began as assistant professor, currently professor of American studies, director of American studies program, 1974-77. *Member:* American Studies Association (Chesapeake chapter president, 1970-72), Popular Culture Association, Phi Beta Kappa, Phi Kappa Phi. *Awards, honors:* Woodrow Wilson fellowship, 1961-62; Excellence in Teaching Award, University of Maryland, 1968.

*WRITINGS: The Origins of American Film Criticism, 1909-1939,* Arno, 1972. Contributor to *Popular Culture Journal.*

*WORK IN PROGRESS:* Researching various projects, film criticism 1940 to the present; intellectual traditions of American studies; study of the comparative arts; intellectual and artistic communities in America since 1890.

\*     \*     \*

## LOVE, Barbara J. 1937-

*PERSONAL:* Born February 27, 1937, in Glen Ridge, N.J.; daughter of Egon (a hosiery manufacturer) and Lois (Crane) Love. *Education:* Attended Purdue University, 1955-57; Syracuse University, B.A., 1959. *Home:* 43 Fifth Ave., New York, N.Y. 10003. *Agent:* Anita Diamant, Writers' Workshop, Inc., 51 East 42nd St., New York, N.Y. 10017. *Office: Folio* Magazine, 125 Elm St., New Canaan, Conn. 06840.

*CAREER:* American School, Florence, Italy, teacher of English and mathematics, 1959-61; New York Lumber Trade Journal, New York City, 1961-62; *Sponsor* (magazine), New York City, production editor, 1962-63, associate editor, 1963-65, senior editor, 1965-67; Columbia Broadcasting System (CBS) Television Network, New York City, editor and writer, 1967-69; Foremost Americans Publishing Corp., New York City, president, editor of *Foremost Women in Communications,* 1969-72; *Supermarketing* (magazine), New York City, associate editor, beginning 1972; currently affiliated with *Folio* (magazine), New Canaan,

Conn. Public relations consultant, ABC Sports, 1963-64. *Member:* National Organization for Women, Advertising Women of New York, Gay Liberation, Theta Sigma Phi.

*WRITINGS:* (Contributor with Sidney Abbott) Vivian Gornick and Barbara K. Moran, editors, *Woman in Sexist Society: Studies in Power and Powerlessness,* Basic Books, 1971; (with Abbot) *Sappho Was a Right-On Woman: A Liberated View of Lesbianism,* Stein & Day, 1972.†

\*     \*     \*

## LOVELACE, Marc Hoyle 1920-

*PERSONAL:* Born June 5, 1920, in Henrietta, N.C.; son of Arsola Crawford (a professor) and Maude (a teacher; maiden name White) Lovelace; married Mary Gibson (a teacher), May 10, 1941; children: Lynn (Mrs. Francis Fenderson, Jr.), Noel. *Education:* High Point College, A.B., 1940; Southern Baptist Theological Seminary, Th.M., 1943, Th.D., 1946; additional study at University of Chicago, 1949, Duke University, 1950, University of Pennsylvania, summer, 1950, American School of Oriental Research, Jerusalem, 1955-56, Oxford University, 1964-65, Harvard University, 1975. *Politics:* Democrat. *Home:* 925 North Sans Souci Ave., DeLand, Fla. 32720. *Office:* Department of History, Stetson University, Box 1260, DeLand, Fla. 32720.

*CAREER:* Wake Forest College (now University), Winston-Salem, N.C., associate professor of religion, 1946-52; Southeastern Seminary, Wake Forest, N.C., professor of archaeology, 1952-68; Stetson University, DeLand, Fla., professor of history, 1968—. *Member:* American Academy of Religion, Archaeological Institute of America, American Historical Society, Society of Biblical Literature and Exegesis, North Carolina Art Society, International Relations Club of Volusia County, Omicron Delta Kappa, Phi Alpha Theta, Kappa Delta Pi. *Awards, honors:* Carnegie Foundation grants, 1948-49, 1949-50, 1950-51, 1951-52; American Schools of Oriental Research fellow, 1955-56; Outstanding Educator in America award, 1970, 1971, 1973; William Hugh McEniry Award for Teaching Excellence, Stetson University, 1974-75.

*WRITINGS: Compass Points for Old Testament Study,* Abingdon, 1972. Contributor of articles to *The Interpreter's Dictionary of the Bible,* and to literature and religion journals.

*WORK IN PROGRESS: In Quest of a Reason: Essays for Lay Theologians, Profiles of Archaeology,* completion expected in 1979; *Greek Keys to the Past,* 1982.

*SIDELIGHTS:* Marc Lovelace told *CA:* "I find truth in the statement that one does not become a person until he has expressed himself in an art form; and one has not really lived until he has said what he has to say. Writing is one art form which I enjoy; the other is teaching, whereby I can write into the lives of students a challenge to express themselves also." Lovelace has participated in archaeological excavations in the Near East, 1951-65, and has conducted student tours of Europe and the Near East. He has competence in Hebrew, Greek, French, German, Arabic, and Latin, and has studied voice, piano, and clarinet for several years.

\*     \*     \*

## LOVIN, Clifford R(amsey) 1937-

*PERSONAL:* Born August 14, 1937, in Enka, N.C.; son of Carl Wesley (a minister) and Lois (Failing) Lovin; married June Lowder (a nurse), September 20, 1959 (divorced, 1975); married Frances Wickham (a medical record administrator),

August 9, 1977; children: (first marriage) April Marie, Clifford Ramsey, Jr., Mary Elizabeth. *Education:* Davidson College, B.A., 1957; University of North Carolina, M.A., 1962, Ph.D., 1965. *Politics:* Democrat. *Religion:* Methodist. *Home address:* Box CL, Cullowhee, N.C. 28723. *Office:* Department of History, Western Carolina University, Cullowhee, N.C. 28723.

*CAREER:* Central Wesleyan College, Central, S.C., assistant professor of history, 1965-67; Western Carolina University, Cullowhee, N.C., professor of history, 1967—, director of Mountain Heritage Center, 1977—. President and member of board of directors, Twin-State Development Association. *Military service:* U.S. Army, 1957-60. *Member:* American Historical Association. Agricultural History Society.

*WRITINGS: European Diplomacy in the Contemporary World,* Western Carolina University Press, 1969. Contributor of articles to *Journal of the History of Ideas, Agricultural History, Zeitschrift fuer Agrargeschichte und Agrarsoziologie,* and *East European Quarterly.*

*WORK IN PROGRESS:* Book on the Nazi agricultural policy and the Supreme Economic Council.

\* \* \*

## LOW, Anthony 1935-

*PERSONAL:* Born May 31, 1935, in San Francisco, Calif.; son of Emerson and Clio (Caroli) Low; married Pauline Mills, December 28, 1961; children: Louise, Christopher, Georgianna, Elizabeth, Peter, Catherine. *Education:* Harvard University, A.B., 1957, M.A., 1959, Ph.D., 1965. *Home:* 18 Greenacres Ave., Scarsdale, N.Y. 10583. *Office:* Department of English, 19 University Pl., New York University, New York, N.Y. 10003.

*CAREER:* University of Washington, Seattle, assistant professor of English, 1965-68; New York University, New York, N.Y., associate professor of English, 1968—. *Military service:* U.S. Army, 1959-62. *Member:* Modern Language Association of America, Milton Society of America, Renaissance Society of America, Modern Humanities Research Association, Phi Beta Kappa.

*WRITINGS:* (Contributor) James D. Simmonds, editor, *Milton Studies,* University of Pittsburgh Press, 1969; *Augustine Baker,* Twayne, 1970; *The Blaze of Noon: A Reading of "Samson Agonistes,"* Columbia University Press, 1974. Contributor of articles and reviews to literature journals.

*WORK IN PROGRESS: Devotional Modes in Seventeenth-Century English Poetry,* for New York University Press.

\* \* \*

## LOW, Lois Dorothea 1916-
### (Dorothy Mackie Low, Lois Paxton)

*PERSONAL:* Born July 15, 1916, in Edinburgh, Scotland; daughter of Basil Alexander and Alice (Thorpe) Pilkington; married William Mackie Low (an actuary); children: Roderick, Murray. *Education:* Attended Edinburgh Ladies' College (now Mary Erskine School). *Politics:* None. *Religion:* Church of England ("plus and minus"). *Home:* High View, Shawcross Rd., West Runton, Norfolk, England. *Agent:* A. M. Heath & Co., Ltd., 40-42 William IV St., London WC2N 4DD, England.

*CAREER:* Has worked at various times in stockbroking, in insurance, as professional reader, and literary agent; novelist. *Member:* Romantic Novelists' Association (chairman, 1969-71), Crime Writers Association, National Book League.

*WRITINGS—*Under name Dorothy Mackie Low: *Isle for a Stranger,* Hurst & Blackett, 1962, Ace Books, 1968; *Dear Liar,* Hurst & Blackett, 1963; *A Ripple on the Water,* Hurst & Blackett, 1964; *The Intruder,* Hurst & Blackett, 1965; *A House the Country,* Hurst & Blackett, 1968; *To Burgundy and Back,* Hurst & Blackett, 1970, Ace Books, 1972.

Under pseudonym Lois Paxton: *The Man Who Died Twice,* Hurst & Blackett, 1969, Ace Books, 1970; *The Quiet Sound of Fear,* Hawthorn, 1971; *Who Goes There?,* Hurst & Blackett, 1972.

Stories have been serialized in *Woman's Realm.* Contributor to *Woman's Own, Good Housekeeping, Woman's Weekly,* and other British and continental magazines for women.

*WORK IN PROGRESS:* A novel, *The Cypress Grove; Concert Pitch.*

*SIDELIGHTS:* Lois Low writes: "Love cities for stimulation, country for peace and relaxation. Favorite occupation [is] listening to good conversation." Low's books have been published in all Scandinavian languages, French, Dutch, Italian, German, Spanish, Portuguese, Serbo-Croatian, and Icelandic. *Avocational interests:* People, books, the theatre, cinema, pictures (gallery variety).

\* \* \*

## LOWERY, Thomas V(incent) 1919-

*PERSONAL:* Born December 22, 1919, in Providence, R.I.; son of Thomas Francis (an ironworker) and Beatrice (Connor) Lowery; *Education:* Rhode Island College, Ed.B., 1941; Providence College, Ph.B., 1946; University of Notre Dame, M.A., 1948. *Politics:* Independent. *Religion:* Catholic. *Home:* 11 Elmcrest Ave., Providence, R.I. 02908.

*CAREER:* LaSalle Academy, Prividence, R.I., English teacher, 1942-47, instructor in English, 1951-69, chairman of department, 1961-69, 1977—, assistant principal, 1969-77. Extension lecturer in English, Rhode Island College, Providence, 1951-61, and University of Rhode Island, Kingston, 1963-71. *Member:* Modern Language Association of America, National Council of Teachers of English, National Catholic Educational Association, Council for Basic Education.

*WRITINGS: A Book of Modern American Poetry,* Harcourt, 1970.

*WORK IN PROGRESS: An Introduction to Linguistics.*

\* \* \*

## LOWI, Theodore J(ay) 1931-

*PERSONAL:* Born July 9, 1931, in Gadsden, Ala.; son of Alvin R. (a businessman) and Janice (Haas) Lowi; married Angele Daniel, May 11, 1963; children: Anna, Jason. *Education:* Michigan State University, B.A., 1954; Yale University, M.A., 1955, Ph.D., 1961. *Home:* 101 Delaware, Ithaca, N.Y. 14850. *Office:* Department of Government, Cornell University, Ithaca, N.Y. 14850.

*CAREER:* Columbia University, New York, N.Y., research associate in New York government and politics, 1956-57, Ford Foundation fellow, 1958-59; Cornell University, Ithaca, N.Y., instructor, 1959-61, assistant professor of government, 1961-65; University of Chicago, Chicago, Ill., associate professor, 1965-68, professor of government, 1968-72; Cornell University, John L. Senior Professor of American Institutions, 1972—. Lecturer at universities throughout United States, England, and Europe. *Member:* American Academy of Arts and Sciences, American Political Science Association (member of council), Policy Studies Organization (president, 1976-77), Midwest Political Science Association (member of executive council). *Awards, honors:* J. Kimbrough Owen Award of American Political Science Association, 1962; Social Science Research Council fellow, 1963-64; Guggenheim fellow, 1967-68; D.H., Oakland University, 1972; Center for Advanced Study in the Behavioral Sciences fellow, 1977-78; National Endowment for the Humanities fellow, 1977-78; Ford Foundation fellow, 1977-78.

*WRITINGS:* (Editor) *Legislative Politics U.S.A.: Congress and the Forces That Shape It,* Little, Brown, 1962, 3rd edition, 1973; *Bases in Spain* (booklet), Bobbs-Merrill, for Inter-University Case Program, 1963; *At the Pleasure of the Mayor: Patronage and Power in New York City, 1898-1958,* Free Press, 1964; (co-author) *The Pursuit of Justice,* Harper, 1964; (editor and author of introduction) *Private Life and Public Order: The Context of Modern Public Policy,* Norton, 1968; *The End of Liberalism: Ideology, Policy, and the Crisis of Public Authority,* Norton, 1969; *The Politics of Disorder,* Basic Books, 1971; (co-author) *Poliscide,* Macmillan, 1976; *American Government: Incomplete Conquest,* Holt, 1976. Contributor to anthologies, political science journals, and popular periodicals, including *Nation, Washington Monthly, New York Times, Public Interest,* and *American Political Science Review.*

*                    *                    *

**LOWRY, Charles W(esley)    1905-**

*PERSONAL:* Born March 31, 1905, in Checotah, Okla. (then Indian Territory); son of Charles Wesley (a businessman) and Sue (Price) Lowry; married Edith Clark, June 14, 1930 (divorced, 1957); married Kate Rowe Holland, January 11, 1960; children: (first marriage) Harriet Richards (Mrs. J. Kimball King), Charles Wesley III, Atherton Clark, James Meredith Price. *Education:* Washington and Lee University, B.A., 1926; Harvard University, M.A., 1927; Episcopal Theological School, Cambridge, Mass., B.D., 1930; Oxford University, D.Phil., 1933. *Politics:* Republican. *Address:* Box 1829, Pinehurst, N.C. 28374.

*CAREER:* Ordained deacon, Protestant Episcopal Church, 1930, and priest, 1931; traveling fellow of Episcopal Theological School, 1930-32; University of California, Berkeley, chaplain to Episcopalians, 1933-34; Protestant Episcopal Theological Seminary in Virginia, Alexandria, professor of systematic theology, 1934-43; All Saint's Episcopal Church, Chevy Chase, Md., rector, 1943-53; Foundation for Religious Action, Inc., Washington, D.C., president, 1953—. Minister, Village Chapel, Pinehurst, N.C., 1966-73. Lecturer at Seabury-Western Theological Seminary, 1947, Divinity School of the Protestant Episcopal Church, 1949-50, and General Staff College, Naval War College, Air War College, National War College, and other service colleges; more recently lecturer in philosophy and political science at Sandhills Community College, Southern Pines. President, American Peace Society, 1958-61; national chairman, Jefferson Davis Hall of Fame Committee, 1960—.

*MEMBER:* American Political Science Association, American Theological Society (vice-president, 1949-50; treasurer, 1955-72), National Press Club, Phi Beta Kappa, Omicron Delta Kappa, Rotary International (district governor, 1970-71), Chevy Chase Club. *Awards, honors:* George Wash-

ington Medal of Freedoms Foundation at Valley Forge, 1955, 1959, 1961, 1968; D.D., Washington and Lee University, 1959.

*WRITINGS:* (Contributor) A. C. Zabriskie, editor, *Anglican Evangelicalism,* Church Historical Society, 1943; *The Trinity and Christian Devotion,* Harper, 1946; (contributor) *Lenten Counsellors,* Mowbray (London), 1951; *Communism and Christ,* Morehouse, 1952, revised edition, Collier Books, 1962; *Conflicting Faiths: Christianity versus Communism,* Public Affairs Press, 1953; (contributor) Frank Dean Gifford, editor, *The Anglican Pulpit Today,* Morehouse, 1953; *To Pray or Not to Pray! Handbook on Church and State,* University Press of Washington, D.C., 1962, 3rd edition, 1969; *The Kingdom of Influence,* Village Press (Pinehurst), 1969. Columnist, *Pinehurst Outlook,* 1977—. Contributor to *Encyclopedia of Religion.* Editor, *Blessing of Liberty,* 1956—.

*WORK IN PROGRESS:* A study of William Temple, scholar-archbishop.

*                    *                    *

**LUBAR, Joel F.    1938-**

*PERSONAL:* Born November 16, 1938, in Washington, D.C.; son of Raymond and Barbara (Pollack) Lubar; married Judith Ostrovsky (a teacher and social worker), June 18, 1961; children: Sandra Gita, Edward Justin. *Education:* University of Chicago, B.S., 1960, Ph.D., 1963. *Home:* 1809 Tanager Lane, Knoxville, Tenn. 37919. *Office:* 305 Austin, Peay Bldg., University of Tennessee, Knoxville, Tenn. 37916.

*CAREER:* University of Rochester, Rochester, N.Y., assistant professor of psychology, 1963-67; University of Tennessee, Knoxville, associate professor, 1967-71, professor of psychology, 1971—. Co-director, Southeastern Biofeedback Institute. *Member:* American Psychological Association, Psychonomic Society, American Association for the Advancement of Science, Society for Neuroscience, Biofeedback Society of America (president of Tennessee branch), American Association of University Professors, Eastern Psychological Association, Southeastern Psychological Association, New York Academy of Sciences, Sigma Xi. *Awards, honors:* National Institute of Mental Health grants; National Science Foundation grant.

*WRITINGS: Biological Foundations of Behavior,* Kendall/Hunt, 1969; *A Primer of Physiological Psychology,* and study guide, Harper, 1971; *A First Reader in Physiological Psychology,* Harper, 1972. Contributor of about forty articles to psychology and biomedical journals.

*WORK IN PROGRESS:* Comparison of septal and frontal ablation in rats and cats in complex operant tasks; studies of the operant control of brain rhythm in humans and animals; the effect of septal ablation and stimulation on evoked response in cortical and subcortical areas in the visual system; research on the control of epileptic seizures and hyperactivity in children using biofeedback; researching for a popular book on modern frontiers in brain research.

*AVOCATIONAL INTERESTS:* Travel, experimental horticulture, music.

*                    *                    *

**LUCAS, John    1937-**

*PERSONAL:* Born June 26, 1937, in Devonshire, England; married Pauline van Meeteren; children: Ben, Emma. *Education:* University of Reading, B.A., 1959, Ph.D., 1965.

*Politics:* Socialist. *Religion:* None. *Home:* 19 Devonshire Ave., Beeston, Nottinghamshire, England. *Office:* Department of English, University of Loughborough, Leicestershire LE11 3TU, England.

*CAREER:* University of Reading, Reading, England, lecturer in English, 1961-64; University of Nottingham, Nottingham, England, lecturer, 1964, senior lecturer, 1971-75, reader in English, 1975-77; University of Loughborough, Leicestershire, England, professor of English and drama, 1977—. Visiting professor at Universities of Maryland and Indiana, 1967-68.

*WRITINGS:* (With John Goode and David Howard) *Tradition and Tolerance in Nineteenth Century Fiction,* Barnes & Noble, 1966; (editor and author of introduction and notes) *A Selection from George Crabbe,* Longmans, Green, 1967; *The Melancholy Man: A Study of Dickens's Novels,* Barnes & Noble, 1970; (editor and author of introduction) *Literature and Politics in the Nineteenth Century* (essays), Barnes & Noble, 1971; *About Nottingham,* Byron Press, 1971; *A Brief Bestiary* (poems), Pecten Press, 1972; *Chinese Sequence* (poems), Sceptre Press, 1972; *Arnold Bennett: A Study of His Fiction,* Methuen, 1975; *Egillssaga: The Poems,* Dent, 1975; (editor) W. H. Mallock, *The New Republic,* Leicester University Press, 1975; *The Literature of Change,* Barnes & Noble, 1977; *The 1930's: A Challenge to Orthodoxy,* Harvester Press, 1978.

*WORK IN PROGRESS:* A critical study of Elizabeth Gashel; *Social History of the English Novel, 1918-1938.*

*AVOCATIONAL INTERESTS:* Jazz, sports, beer.

\* \* \*

## LUCAS, Robert Harold 1933-

*PERSONAL:* Born August 22, 1933, in Portland, Ore.; son of Harold Irvin and Adryne (Kidney) Lucas. *Education:* University of Oregon, B.A., 1954; Columbia University, M.A., 1958, Ph.D., 1966. *Home:* 2306 Crestview Dr. S., Salem, Ore. 97302. *Office:* Department of History, Willamette University, Salem, Ore. 97301.

*CAREER:* University of California, Irvine, assistant professor of European history, 1966-73; Willamette University, Salem, Ore., associate professor of European history, 1973—. *Military service:* U.S. Army, 1954-56. *Member:* Mediaeval Academy of America. *Awards, honors:* Fulbright scholar, University of Paris, 1959-60; American Philosophical Society research grant, 1970.

*WRITINGS:* (Editor) Christine de Pisan, *Livre du corps de Policie* (a critical edition), Droz, 1967. Contributor of articles to scholarly journals.

*WORK IN PROGRESS:* Research on propaganda and public opinion during the Hundred Years War.

*AVOCATIONAL INTERESTS:* Gem cutting, bookbinding.

\* \* \*

## LUOMALA, Katharine 1907-

*PERSONAL:* Born September 10, 1907, in Cloquet, Minn.; daughter of John Erland and Eliina (Forsness) Luomala. *Education:* University of California, Berkeley, A.B., 1931, M.A., 1933, Ph.D., 1936. *Office:* Department of Anthropology, University of Hawaii, 2424 Maile Way, Honolulu, Hawaii 96822.

*CAREER:* University of California, Berkeley, art research assistant, 1941; U.S. Department of Agriculture, Bureau of Agricultural Economics, Division of Program Surveys, Washington, D.C., social science analyst and study director, 1942-44; U.S. Department of the Interior, War Relocation Authority, Washington, D.C., social science analyst and assistant head of community analysis section, 1944-46; University of Hawaii, Honolulu, assistant professor, 1946-48, associate professor, 1948-52, professor of anthropology, 1952-73, professor emeritus, 1973—, chairman of department, 1954-57. Senior visiting research associate in anthropology, Smithsonian Institution, 1966-67. Honorary associate in anthropology, Bishop Museum, 1941—. *Member:* American Folklore Society (fellow), American Anthropological Association (fellow), Polynesian Society, International Society for Folk-Narrative Research (vice-president for Oceania, 1962—), Phi Beta Kappa, Sigma Xi. *Awards, honors:* American Association of University Women fellowship, 1937-38; Bishop Museum—Yale Fellowship, 1938-40; Wenner-Gren Foundation fellowship for anthropological research, 1948-49; Guggenheim fellowships, 1956, 1960.

*WRITINGS: Navaho Life of Yesterday and Today,* National Park Service, Western Museums Laboratories, U.S. Department of the Interior, 1938; *Oceanic, American Indian and African Myths of Snaring the Sun,* Bishop Museum, 1940; (with E. H. Spicer, A. T. Hansen, and M. K. Opler) *Impounded People: Japanese Americans in the Relocation Centers,* War Relocation Authority, U.S. Department of the Interior, 1946; *Maui-of-a-thousand-tricks: His Oceanic and European Biographers,* Bishop Museum, 1949; *The Menehune of Polynesia and Other Mythical Little People of Oceania,* Bishop Museum, 1951; *Ethnobotany of the Gilbert Islands,* Bishop Museum, 1953; *Voices on the Wind: Polynesian Myths and Chants,* Bishop Museum, 1955.

Contributor to *Encyclopedia of Literature, Funk & Wagnalls Standard Dictionary of Folklore, Mythology, and Legend,* and *Encyclopedia of Poetry and Poetics;* contributor of articles to folklore and anthropology journals. *Journal of American Folklore,* associate editor, 1947-52, editor, 1952-53; editor, *News from the Pacific,* 1951.

*WORK IN PROGRESS: Polynesian Puppets and Marionettes; Birds in Gilbertese Myths and Customs; Autobiography and Culture of a Diegueno Medicine Man;* research on ethnology of the Gilbert Islands, on the Diegueno Indians of California, on the mythology of Polynesia and Micronesia, and on the Gilbert Islands material culture in museums.

\* \* \*

## LURIA, Maxwell Sidney 1932-

*PERSONAL:* Born February 5, 1932, in Trenton, N.J.; son of Samuel Jerome (a haberdasher) and Etta (Gurney) Luria. *Education:* Rutgers University, B.A., 1953; University of Bordeaux, additional study, 1955; Princeton University, Ph.D., 1965. *Religion:* Jewish. *Address:* Box 2221, Trenton, N.J. 08607. *Office:* Department of English, Temple University, Philadelphia, Pa. 19122.

*CAREER:* Rutgers University, New Brunswick, N.J., instructor in English, 1963-65; Temple University, Philadelphia, Pa., assistant professor, 1965-69, associate professor of English, 1969—. *Military service:* U.S. Army, 1956-58. *Member:* Modern Language Association of America, Mediaeval Academy of America, Phi Beta Kappa. *Awards, honors:* Fulbright study grant, 1954-55.

*WRITINGS:* (With Bernard Forer) *The ABCD of Successful College Writing,* Kendall/Hunt, 1971; (with Richard Hoffman) *Middle English Lyrics,* Norton, 1973. Contributor of articles to *Studies in Philology, English Studies,* and *Texas Studies in Literature and Language.*

*WORK IN PROGRESS:* Variorum edition of Chaucer's "Second Nun's Tale"; an edition of medieval English romances; a critical study of Chaucer; studies in patterns of order in Chaucer, Shakespeare, Mozart, and R. Strauss.

*SIDELIGHTS:* Maxwell Luria told *CA:* "The largest influence on my scholarship is the late Ernst Curtius; on my writing, Mozart; on my ideas, D. W. Robertson, Jr.; on my morals, J. K. Steen; on my manners, R. L. Hoffman; on my style of life, R. L. Patten; on my expectations, Richard Brewer."

\* \* \*

## LUSCHEI, Eugene C(harles)  1928-

*PERSONAL:* Surname is pronounced *Loo*-shy; born June 17, 1928, in Kimball, Neb.; son of Erich Gustav (a teacher) and Helen (Mills) Luschei; married (divorced, 1976). *Education:* University of Nebraska, B.A., 1949, M.A., 1951; Oxford University, D.Phil., 1959. *Politics:* Independent. "Further left than right on most issues." *Home* (summer): Kinnikinnik, Sylvan Lane, Box 428, Truro, Mass. 02666. *Office:* Department of Philosophy, Brown University, Providence, R.I. 02912.

*CAREER:* University of North Carolina at Chapel Hill, assistant professor of philosophy, 1959-64; Brown University, Providence, R.I., associate professor of philosophy, 1964—. Visiting professor at Pennsylvania State University, 1964, and University of California, Santa Cruz, 1967. *Member:* American Philosophical Association, American Association of University Professors, American Association of Rhodes Scholars. *Awards, honors:* Rhodes scholar, Oxford University, 1951-54.

*WRITINGS: The Logical Systems of Lesniewski,* North-Holland Publishing, 1962; (contributor) Storrs McCall, editor, *Polish Logic: 1920-1939,* Oxford University Press, 1967. Contributor to *Encyclopaedia Britannica;* contributor of articles to journals in his field.

*WORK IN PROGRESS:* A book on logic; a book on semantics; research on meaning and symbolism.

\* \* \*

## LUTZKER, Edythe  1904-

*PERSONAL:* Born June 25, 1904, in Berlin, Germany; naturalized U.S. citizen; daughter of Russian-born parents, Solomon (a cabinetmaker) and Sophia (Katz) Levine; married Philip Lutzker (employed in sales promotion), June 14, 1924; children: Michael, Arthur, Paul. *Education:* Took a commerical course, 1918-22, resumed her education after children were grown, and received high school diploma when she was forty-six; City College (now City College of the City University of New York), New York, N.Y., B.A., 1954; Columbia University, M.A., 1959. *Politics:* Liberal Democrat. *Religion:* Humanist. *Address:* 201 West 89th St., New York, N.Y. 10024.

*CAREER:* Author and researcher, 1959—. Has read research papers and lectured at numerous conventions and seminars. *Member:* Societe Internationale d'Histoire de la Medecine, International Alliance of Women, Pan Pacific and Southeast Asia Women's Association of the U.S.A., Fawcett Society, History of Science Society, International Society of the History of Medicine, American Society for Microbiology, American Historical Association, American Association for the History of Medicine, American Associa-

tion of University Women, Jewish Academy of Arts and Sciences, Zionist Organization of America, Waldemar M. Haffkine International Memorial Committee, Common Cause, Fawcett Society (London), League of Women Voters of New York City. *Awards, honors:* American Philosophical Society grants for research on Edith Pechey-Phipson, 1964, and for research on W. Mordecai Haffkine, 1965; National Library of Medicine grants for further work on Pechey Phipson's biography, 1966, and on Haffkine's biography, 1968-71, 1972-74.

*WRITINGS: Women Gain a Place in Medicine* (juvenile), edited by Daniel Greenberg, McGraw, 1969; *Edith Pechey-Phipson, M.D.: The Story of England's Foremost Pioneering Woman Doctor,* Exposition Press, 1973. Has published numerous research papers, lectures, and addresses. Contributor of many research articles to various journals including *Orient/West, Journal of Indian Medical Profession, Medica Judaica, Journal of Medical Women's Federation,* and others.

*WORK IN PROGRESS:* A biography of W. Mordecai Haffkine, Jewish scientist who developed first effective vaccine against cholera in 1892, and against bubonic plague in 1896.

*SIDELIGHTS:* Edythe Lutzker received her high school diploma when she was forty-six. "The B.A. I got when I was fifty. I was the oldest woman in the college, and I was in the first graduating class in which women got a degree," Lutzker explained to *CA.*

\* \* \*

## LYDENBERG, John  1913-

*PERSONAL:* Born March 22, 1913, in White Plains, N.Y.; son of Harry Miller and Madeleine (Day) Lydenberg; married Marion Evans, June 15, 1940 (died, 1967); married Helene Rioux, November 13, 1969 (divorced, 1972); married Mary Jane Dee, July, 1973; children: (first marriage) Steven David, Ann Elisabeth. *Education:* Oberlin College, A.B., 1934; Harvard University, M.A., 1938, Ph.D., 1946. *Politics:* Democratic. *Home:* 715 South Main St., Geneva, N.Y. 14456. *Office:* Department of English, Hobart and William Smith Colleges, Geneva, N.Y. 14456.

*CAREER:* Hobart and William Smith Colleges, Geneva, N.Y., assistant professor, 1946-49, associate professor, 1949-55, professor of English and American studies, 1955—. Fulbright lecturer, University of Aix-en-Provence, 1960-61, 1968-69; visiting professor at Scripps College, 1950-51, University of Minnesota, 1953-54, and Stanford University, 1964. Member, Geneva City Council, 1964; delegate to Democratic National Convention, 1968. *Member:* American Historical Association, Modern Language Association of America, American Studies Association, American Studies Association of New York (president, 1959-60), Colonial Society of Massachusetts, Phi Beta Kappa.

*WRITINGS: Dreiser: A Collection of Critical Essays,* Prentice-Hall, 1971.

Contributor: Harvey Goldberg, editor, *American Radicals,* Monthly Review Press, 1957; Gerald Willen, editor, *A Casebook on Henry James's The Turn of the Screw,* Crowell, 1960; Edward Lueders, editor, *The College and Adult Reading List of Books in Literature and the Fine Arts,* Washington Square Press, 1962; *Essays on Determinism in American Literature,* Kent State University Press, 1964; Francis Utley and others, editors, *Bear, Man, and God,* Random House, 1964; John B. Vickery, editor, *Myth and*

*Literature,* University of Nebraska Press, 1966; Allen Belkind, editor, *Dos Passos, the Critics, and the Writer's Intention,* Southern Illinois University Press, 1971; David Sanders, editor, *Views of "U.S.A.,"* C. E. Merrill, 1971. Contributor of articles and reviews to *South Atlantic Quarterly, New Leader, Nation, Saturday Review, American Quarterly,* and other periodicals.

*WORK IN PROGRESS:* Writing on Dos Passos; *Harvard in the 1930's.*

\* \* \*

## LYFORD, Joseph Philip 1918-

*PERSONAL:* Born August 4, 1918, in Chicago, Ill.; son of Philip (an artist) and Ruth (Pray) Lyford; married Jean Thomas (a teacher), February 16, 1963; children: Amy Jean, Joseph Philip, Jr. *Education:* Harvard University, A.B. (cum laude), 1947. *Home:* 216 Crestview Dr., Orinda, Calif. 94563. *Office:* School of Journalism, University of California, Berkeley, Calif.

*CAREER:* Public Education Association, New York City, staff director, 1953-55; University of California, Berkeley, professor of journalism, 1965—. Information officer, Fund for the Republic, Santa Barbara, Calif., 1955-66; Fund for Peace, Inc., New York City, president, 1969-71, trustee, 1969—. Formerly consultant to U.S. Senate subcommittee on executive reorganization; consultant to Public Broadcasting Laboratory, 1968; consultant to Center for the Study of Democratic Institutions, 1966—. Press secretary to Connecticut governor Chester Bowles, 1949-50; executive secretary, U.S. Senator William Benton, 1950; candidate for U.S. House of Representatives from Connecticut, 1952, 1954. *Military service:* U.S. Navy, 1942-1946; became lieutenant. *Member:* Council on Foreign Relations. *Awards, honors:* Sidney Hillman Award, 1967, for nonfiction book, *The Airtight Cage.*

*WRITINGS: Candidate* (monograph), Eagleton Institute, Rutgers University, 1955; *The Agreeable Autocracies,* Oceana, 1959; *The Talk in Vandalia,* Harper, 1961; *The Airtight Cage,* Harper, 1966. Contributor of articles to *Saturday Review, New Republic, Bulletin of American Association of University Professors, America, Center.* Assistant editor, *New Republic,* 1946-48.

*WORK IN PROGRESS:* Research on impact of mass media on modern society; a sociological study of the city of Berkeley, Calif.

*AVOCATIONAL INTERESTS:* Joseph Lyford enjoys painting and gardening. He has traveled in Western Europe, U.S.S.R., China, and Japan.

\* \* \*

## LYNGSTAD, Alexandra Halina 1925-

*PERSONAL:* Born January 21, 1925, near Warsaw, Poland; daughter of Leonid (a landowner) and Sophia (Schapierydze-Winogradov) Danielewicz; married, 1941; married second husband, Sverre Lyngstad (a professor of English), May 15, 1953 (divorced, 1975); children: (first marriage) Janusz; (second marriage) Karin. *Education:* Hunter College (now Hunter College of the City University of New York), B.A., 1958; Columbia University, M.A., 1962, additional study, 1962-65; Herbert H. Lehman College of City University of New York, certification for secondary school teaching of German and Russian, 1972. *Residence:* Riverdale, N.Y.

*CAREER:* International Refugee Organization, Salzburg, Austria, secretary and interpreter, 1947-51; Voice of America, New York City, radio reader, 1951-53; Maureen Cloak Co., Inc., New York City, fashion model, 1954-60; instructor in Russian at Rutgers University, New Brunswick, N.J. and Hunter College of the City University of New York, New York City, 1960-63; Fordham University, New York City, instructor in Russian, 1963-71; lecturer in Russian at J. F. Kennedy Adult Education Center, 1973—. Free-lance interpreter for Soviet delegations to the U.S. *Member:* American Association for Teachers of Slavic and East European Languages, Delta Phi Alpha.

*WRITINGS:* (Translator and author of introduction with Sverre Lyngstad) Lev Tolstoy, *Childhood, Boyhood, and Youth,* Washington Square Press, 1968; (with Sverre Lyngstad) *Ivan Goncharov,* Twayne, 1972; *Dostoevskij and Schiller,* Mouton, 1975. Contributor to *Slavic and East European Journal.*

*SIDELIGHTS:* Alexandra Lyngstad speaks Russian, German, Czech, and French, in addition to Polish, and has traveled through northern and western Europe.

\* \* \*

## LYNGSTAD, Sverre 1922-

*PERSONAL:* Born April 30, 1922, in Norway; son of Bernhard Theodor (a farmer) and Anna Lyngstad; married Alexandra Halina Danielewicz, May 15, 1953 (divorced, 1975); children: Karin. *Education:* Oslo University, B.A. (English), 1943, B.A. (history), 1946; University of Washington, Seattle, M.A., 1949; New York University, Ph.D., 1960. *Home:* 180 Park Row, New York, N.Y. *Office:* Department of English, New Jersey Institute of Technology, 323 High St., Newark, N.J. 07102.

*CAREER:* City College, (now City College of the City University of New York), New York, N.Y., lecturer in English, 1954-55; Hofstra College (now University), Long Island, N.Y., instructor in English, 1955-60; Queens College of the City of New York (now Queens College of the City University of New York), Flushing, N.Y., instructor in English, 1960-62; New Jersey Institute of Technology, Newark, N.J., assistant professor, 1962-65, associate professor, 1965-68, professor of English, 1968—. *Member:* Modern Language Association of America, American Comparative Literature Association, Society for the Advancement of Scandinavian Study, American-Scandinavian Foundation, International Society for the Study of Time.

*WRITINGS:* (Translator) Sven Hassel, *Comrades of War,* Fawcett, 1963; (translator with Alexandra Halina Lyngstad) Lev Tolstoy, *Childhood, Boyhood, and Youth,* Washington Square Press, 1968; (with Alexandra Halina Lyngstad) *Ivan Goncharov,* Twayne, 1972; (translator) Erik Krag, *Dostoevsky: The Literary Artist,* Humanities, 1976; *Jonas Lie,* Twayne, 1977. Contributor to *Encyclopedia of Poetry and Poetics.*

*WORK IN PROGRESS:* Two books on time in the novel, one of which is an edition of critical articles; a critical study of Sigurd Hoel, a twentieth-century Norwegian novelist and critic.

\* \* \*

## LYNN, Richard 1930-

*PERSONAL:* Born February 20, 1930, in London, England; son of Richard and Ann (Freeman) Lynn; married Susan Maher (a lecturer in history), December 31, 1955; children: Emma, Sophia, Matthew. *Education:* Kings College, Cambridge, B.A., 1953, Ph.D., 1956. *Politics:* Conservative.

*Home:* Dunderg House, Coleraine, Londonderry, Northern Ireland. *Office:* Department of Psychology, New University of Ulster, Coleraine, Londonderry, Northern Ireland.

*CAREER:* Exeter University, Devon, England, lecturer, 1956-67; Economic and Social Research Institute, Dublin, Ireland, professor of psychology, 1967-72; New University of Ulster, Coleraine, Londonderry, member of faculty, department of psychology, 1972—. *Military service:* British Army, 1949.

*WRITINGS: Arousal, Attention, and the Orientation Reaction,* Pergamon Press, 1966; *Personality and National Character,* Pergamon Press, 1971; *An Introduction to the Study of Personality,* Macmillan, 1971; *The Entrepreneur,* Allen & Unwin, 1974.

*WORK IN PROGRESS: National Differences in Personality and Intelligence.*

\*       \*       \*

## LYON, Thomas Edgar, Jr.   1939-

*PERSONAL:* Born May 13, 1939, in Salt Lake City, Utah; son of Thomas Edgar (a professor) and Hermana (Forsberg) Lyon; married Cheryl Larsen, June 12, 1962; children: Thomas Rex, Ann Marie, Jennifer, Gregory, Peter. *Education:* University of Utah, B.A., 1963; University of California, Los Angeles, Ph.D., 1967. *Religion:* Church of Jesus Christ of Latter-day Saints. *Home:* 3008 North 175 East, Provo, Utah 84601. *Office:* Department of Spanish and Portuguese, Brigham Young University, Provo, Utah.

*CAREER:* University of Oklahoma, Norman, assistant professor of Spanish and Portuguese, 1967-69; assistant professor of Spanish and Portuguese, University of Wisconsin, 1969-72; Brigham Young University, Provo, Utah, professor of Spanish and Portuguese, 1972—. Visiting professor, University of California, Los Angeles, 1967. *Military service:* U.S. Army, 1957; U.S. Army Reserve, 1956-1964. *Member:* Modern Language Association of America, American Association of Teachers of Spanish & Portuguese, Phi Beta Kappa. *Awards, Honors:* National Endowment for the Humanities award, 1968; American Council of Learned Societies fellowship, 1972.

*WRITINGS: Juan Godoy,* Twayne, 1972. Contributor of articles to journals.

*WORK IN PROGRESS: The Role of Religion in Latin American Literature.*

*SIDELIGHTS:* Thomas Edgar Lyon told *CA:* "Writing is a way of staying 'alive.' All of my articles have come from ideas first used in the classroom and later refined into writing. The process of getting new ideas and then painstakingly working them into print is the most vital academic exercise I perform. I am, however, bothered by the volume of senseless writing that takes itself too seriously; I would prefer to see most of it remain in the author's head (or wastebasket—perhaps the same receptacle) and let me enjoy the trees in the forest instead of being burdened by unread books in the library."

# M

**MAASS, Joachim 1901-1972**

1901—October 15, 1972; German-born educator, poet, essayist, and novelist. Obituaries: *New York Times,* October 16, 1972.

\* \* \*

**MacARTHUR, Robert H(elmer) 1930-1972**

April 7, 1930—November 1, 1972; Canadian-born American authority on population biology. Obituaries: *New York Times,* November 2, 1972.

\* \* \*

**MacCAULEY, Sister Rose Agnes 1911-**

*PERSONAL:* Born April 8, 1911, in New York, N.Y.; daughter of John Henry and Helen (Mernin) MacCauley. *Education:* College of Mount St. Vincent, B.A., 1947; Fordham University, M.A. (English), 1956; Manhattan College, M.A. (theology), 1969. *Politics:* Democrat (liberal). *Home:* 110 Melton Rd., Rye, N.Y. 10580. *Office:* Elizabeth Seton College, Yonkers, N.Y. 10701.

*CAREER:* Roman Catholic nun; member of the order of Sisters of Charity of New York; teacher of English at Catholic high schools in New York, N.Y., 1947-69; Elizabeth Seton College, Yonkers, N.Y., assistant professor, 1969-74, associate professor of English and theology, 1974—. *Member:* College Theology Society, American Academy of Religion, Society of Biblical Literature.

*WRITINGS: Vision 20/20: Twenty Psalms for the 20th Century,* Fides, 1971.

*WORK IN PROGRESS:* A sequel to *Vision 20/20.*

*SIDELIGHTS:* "My career is teaching, not writing," Sister Rose Agnes MacCauley told *CA,* "and my teaching is an expression of my ministry as a Sister of Charity. I think I would say that my motivating factor is a desire to communicate to others the joy that my deep faith in a loving God has brought me. The book, *Vision 20/20,* is an expression of my prayer life, and my teaching is, so to speak, an extension of my prayer life. Writing and teaching are for me opportunities to share with others the richness I have drawn from life."

\* \* \*

**MacCOMBIE, John 1932-**

*PERSONAL:* Born March 7, 1932, in Providence, R.I.; son

of Herbert Elden (a clergyman) and Amy Amanda (Campbell) MacCombie. *Education:* Yale University, B.A., 1953, Ph.D., 1965. *Home:* "Sandridge," Sagamore, Mass. 02561. *Office:* Department of French, University of Massachusetts, Boston, Mass. 02125.

*CAREER:* Phillips Exeter Academy, Exeter, N.H., instructor in French, 1953-54; University of Massachusetts—Amherst, instructor, 1955-57, 1961-65, assistant professor, 1965-69, Boston Campus, associate professor, 1969-75, professor of French, 1975—, chairman of department, 1965-70, 1973-76. *Member:* American Association of Teachers of French (president of eastern Massachusetts chapter, 1969). *Awards, honors:* Scholarship from Government of France, 1960-61.

*WRITINGS: The Prince and the Genie: A Study of Rimbaud's Influence on Claudel,* University of Massachusetts Press, 1972. Contributor of translation to *Massachusetts Review.*

*WORK IN PROGRESS:* Translating *Les Illuminations* and *Une Saison en enfer* by Rimbaud, with preface and notes; translating *Connaissance de l'Est* by Claudel; research on the life and works of Marcel Bealu; art in Claudel's work.

*AVOCATIONAL INTERESTS:* Playing piano (has presented recitals for twenty-five years; presently preparing a concert series for Boston area), composition for piano, voice, and orchestra, collecting contemporary art.

\* \* \*

**MACHOL, Robert E(ngel) 1917-**

*PERSONAL:* Born October 16, 1917, in New York, N.Y.; son of Morris R. (an engineer) and Claudia (Engel) Machol; married Florence Guttman, September 8, 1946; children: Margot E., Kennard D. *Education:* Harvard University, A.B., 1938; University of Michigan, M.S., 1953, Ph.D., 1957. *Home:* 2020 Orringtor Ave., Evanston Ill. 60202. *Office:* Graduate School of Management, Northwestern University, Evanston, Ill. 60201.

*CAREER:* Purdue University, Lafayette, Ind., professor of electrical engineering, 1958-61; Conductron Corp., Ann Arbor, Mich., vice-president, 1961-64; University of Illinois at Chicago Circle, professor of systems engineering and head of department, 1964-67; Northwestern University, Graduate School of Management, Evanston, Ill., professor of systems, 1967—. Lecturer at Waseda University (Japan),

347

1957, and University of Michigan, 1957-58. *Military service:* U.S. Naval Reserve, active duty, 1940-46; became lieutenant commander. *Member:* Operations Research Society of America (president, 1971-72), Institute of Management Sciences.

*WRITINGS:* (With H. H. Goode) *System Engineering,* McGraw, 1957; (editor) *Information and Decision Processes,* McGraw, 1960; (editor) *Recent Developments in Information and Decision Processes,* Macmillan, 1962; (editor) *System Engineering Handbook,* McGraw, 1965; *Elementary Systems Mathematics,* McGraw, 1976; (editor) *Management Science in Sports,* North-Holland Publishing, 1976; (editor) *Optimal Strategies in Sports,* North-Holland Publishing, 1977. Editor-in-chief, ''TIMS Studies in the Management Sciences'' series, 1977—. Contributor to professional journals.

*WORK IN PROGRESS:* Research on mathematical models of large-scale systems; research on mathematical taxonomy, with special application to mushrooms.

*SIDELIGHTS:* Robert E. Machol's books have been translated into French, Japanese, and Russian. *Avocational interests:* Collecting books on mushrooms (has ''probably the finest private library'' of these books).

\*　　　\*　　　\*

### MacINTOSH, J(ohn) J(ames)　1934-

*PERSONAL:* Born July 30, 1934, in North Bay, Ontario, Canada. *Education:* University of New Zealand, B.A., 1957, M.A., 1958; Oxford University, B. Phil., 1961. *Office:* Department of Philosophy, University of Calgary, Calgary, Alberta, Canada.

*CAREER:* University of Auckland, Auckland, New Zealand, junior lecturer, 1959; Oxford University, Oxford, England, research lecturer at Merton College, 1961-63, fellow of St. John's College, 1963-66; University of Calgary, Calgary, Alberta, associate professor, 1966-70, professor of philosophy, 1970—. *Member:* Mind Association, Aristotelian Society. *Awards, honors:* Canada Council research fellowship, 1970-71.

*WRITINGS:* (Editor with S. C. Coval) *The Business of Reason,* Humanities, 1969; (editor with Terence Penelhum) *The First Critique: Reflections on Kant's Critique of Pure Reason,* Wadsworth, 1969. Contributor to philosophy journals.

*WORK IN PROGRESS:* Research on personal identity.

\*　　　\*　　　\*

### MACKENZIE, Compton (Edward Montague)　1883-1972

January 17, 1883—November 30, 1972; English poet, novelist, biographer, and playwright. Obituaries: *New York Times,* December 1, 1972; *Sunday Times* (London), December 3, 1972; *Newsweek,* December 11, 1972; *Publishers Weekly,* December 11, 1972; *Time,* December 11, 1972; *L'Express,* December 11-17, 1972. (See index for *CA* sketch)

\*　　　\*　　　\*

### MACKENZIE, Kenneth Donald　1937-

*PERSONAL:* Born December 20, 1937, in Salem, Ore.; son of Kenneth Victor (a physicist) and Dorothy (Miniker) Mackenzie; married Sally McHenry; children: Dorothy Jane, Carolyn Beta, Susan Gamma, Nancy Delta. *Educa-*

*tion:* University of California, Berkeley, A.B., 1960, Ph.D., 1964. *Politics:* Republican. *Religion:* Agnostic. *Home:* 502 Millstone Dr., Lawrence, Kan. 66044. *Office:* University of Kansas, 311 Summerfield Hall, Lawrence, Kan. 66044.

*CAREER:* Carnegie-Mellon University, Pittsburgh, Pa., assistant professor of industrial administration, 1964-67; University of Pennsylvania, Philadelphia, associate professor of industry, 1967-71; University of Waterloo, Waterloo, Ontario, professor of management sciences and psychology, 1969-72; University of Kansas, Lawrence, Edmund P. Learned Distinguished Professor of Business Administration, 1972—. President of Organizational Systems, Inc. *Military service:* U.S. Marine Corps Reserve, Infantry, 1956-60; California Army National Guard, 1960-64; became lieutenant. *Member:* American Psychological Association, American Management Associations, International Communications Association, American Association for the Advancement of Science, Institute of Management Sciences, Econometric Society, Operations Research Society of America, Psychometric Society, Beta Gamma Sigma. *Awards, honors:* Ford Foundation fellowship; research grants from National Science Foundation, Canada Council, and National Research Council of Canada.

*WRITINGS:* (With M. Hinich) *An Introduction to Continuous Probability Theory,* C. E. Merrill, 1968; *A Theory of Group Structures,* Gordon & Breach Science Publishers, Volume I: *Basic Theory,* Volume II: *Empirical Tests,* 1976; *Organizational Structures,* AHM Publishing, 1978. Editor of five volumes of ''Organizational Behavior'' series, AHM Publishing. Contributor of over thirty articles to professional journals.

\*　　　\*　　　\*

### MACKEY, William Francis　1918-

*PERSONAL:* Born January 26, 1918, in Winnipeg, Manitoba, Canada; son of Thomas Clutterbuck (a publisher) and Margaret (Kennedy) Mackey; married Ilonka Schmidt (a university professor), 1949; children: Ilona, Ariane. *Education:* University of Manitoba, B.A., 1940; Laval University, M.A., 1942; Harvard University, A.M., 1948; University of Geneva, D.Litt., 1965. *Home:* 2010 Helene Boule St., Ste-Foy 10, Quebec, Canada.

*CAREER: Lake Winnipeg News,* Winnipeg, Manitoba, editor and publisher, 1938-40; *Winnipeg Tribune,* Winnipeg, reporter, 1940-41; University of London, London, England, senior lecturer in linguistic method, 1948-50; Laval University, Quebec, Quebec, associate professor, 1950-55, professor of English philology and linguistics, 1954-61, professor of language didactics, 1961-67, founder-director of International Center for Research on Bilingualism, 1967-70. Federal Commissioner of Bilingual Districts (Canada), 1972-75. Visiting professor at University of Alberta, University of Moncton, University of Texas, University of California, Los Angeles, and University of Nice; Adair Memorial Lecturer at McGill University, 1966. Member of Humanities Research Council (Canada), Science Council of Canada, Intergovernmental Committee on European Migration (Geneva), and Committee for Education of Poles in the United Kingdom (London). Consultant to Royal Commission on Bilingualism, British Broadcasting Corp., Canada Council, Ford Foundation, U.S. Department of Health, Education, and Welfare, United Nations Educational, Scientific, and Cultural Organization (UNESCO), Irish Government Language Attitudes Research Committee, and Commonwealth Office of Education (Australia). *Military service:* Canadian Army, reserve officer, 1933-47; became captain.

*MEMBER:* Linguistic Society of America, International Phonetics Association, Permanent International Committee of Linguistics, Societe de linguistique de Paris, Canadian Linguistic Association, Royal Society of Canada (fellow).

*WRITINGS:* (With A. V. P. Elliott and J. A. Noonan) *Listen and Speak* (bilingual edition), Volumes I-II, Chaix, 1950, unilingual edition published by Macmillan, 1953; *English Pronunciation Drills,* Laval University Press, 1951; (with wife, Ilonka S. Mackey, and I. A. Richards) *German through Pictures,* Washington Square Press, 1953; *English for Migrants,* Intergovernmental Committee for European Migration (Geneva), 1957, two-volume *Teaching Manual,* 1958; *Language Teaching Analysis,* Longmans, Green (London), 1965, University of Indiana Press, 1967; (with M. S. Mepham) *Mechanolinguistic Method Analysis,* Royal Commission on Bilingualism (Ottawa), 1966; *Bilingualism as a World Problem,* English and French editions, Harvest House, 1967; (with Michael P. West) *The Canadian Reader's Dictionary,* Longmans Canada, 1968.

(With Jean-Guy Savard) *Le Vocabulaire disponible du francais,* two volumes, Didier, 1971; (editor and translator in part) *L'Enseignement des langues et l'ecolier* (translation of *Languages and the Young School Child,* edited by H. H. Stern), UNESCO Education Institute (Hamburg), 1971; (translator with Lorne Laforge) *Principes de didactique analytique,* Didier, 1972; *Bilingual Education in a Binational School,* Newbury House, 1972; *International Bibliography on Bilingualism,* Laval University Press, 1972; *La Distance Interlinguistique,* Centre International de Recherche sur la Bilinguisme, 1972.

*Education bilingue et education biculturelle: tour d'horizon sur les politiques contemporaines,* [Paris], 1974; (editor with Albert Verdoodt) *The Multinational Society,* Newbury House, 1975; *Bilinguisme et contact des langues,* Klincksieck (Paris), 1976; (with G. Bibeau and others) *Independent Study of Language Training in the Public Service,* 12 volumes, Public Service Commission (Canada), 1976; (with Von N. Beebe) *Bilingual Schools for a Bicultural Community: Miami's Adaptation to the Cuban Refugees,* Newbury House, 1977; (with Jacob Ornstein and others) *The Bilingual Education Movement: Essays on its Progress,* Texas Western Press, 1977; (editor with Theodore Andersson) *Bilingualism in Early Childhood,* Newbury House, 1977; *Irish Language Promotion: Potentials and Constraints,* Institiuid Teangeolaiochta Eireann (Dublin), 1977; *Le Bilinguisme canadien: bibliographie analytique et guide du chercheur,* International Center for Research on Bilingualism, in press; (editor with Jacob Ornstein) *Sociolinguistic Studies in Language Contact: Methods and Cases,* Laval University Press, in press.

Author of preface: Jean-Guy Savard, *Analytical Bibliography of Language Tests,* Laval University Press, 1961; Savard and J. C. Richards, *L'Utilite du vocabulaire fondamental francais,* Laval University Press, 1970; L. A. Jakobovits, *Foreign Language Learning,* Newbury House, 1970; R. K. Chiu, *Language Contact and Language Planning in China,* Laval University Press, 1970; Lorne Laforge, *La Selection en didactique analytique,* Laval University Press, 1972; Heinz Kloss, *The American Tradition,* Newbury House, 1977; John Mallea, *Quebec's Language Policy,* Laval University Press, 1977; J.-G. Belle-Isle, *Dictionnaire technique general anglais-francais,* Beauchemin-Dunod, 1977.

Contributor: P. R. Leon, editor, *Applied Linguistics and the Teaching of French,* Centre Educatif et Culturel (Montreal),

1967; W. R. Lee, editor, *English Language Teaching Selections,* Oxford University Press, 1967; H. H. Stern, editor, *Languages and the Young School Child,* Oxford University Press, 1968; Joshua Fishman, editor, *Readings in the Sociology of Language,* Mouton, 1968; E. Firchow and others, editors, *Studies for Einar Haugen,* Mouton, 1972; Joshua Fishman, editor, *Advances in the Sociology of Language,* Mouton, Volume 2, 1972; J. W. Oller and J. C. Richards, editors, *Focus on the Learner,* Newbury House, 1973; R. P. Fox, editor, *Essays on Teaching English as a Second Language and as a Second Dialect,* National Council of Teachers of English, 1973; J.-G. Savard and Richard Vigneault, editors, *Multilingual Political Systems: Problems and Solutions,* Laval University Press, 1975; Harald Haarmann, editor, *Sprachen und Staaten,* Stiftung Europa-Kolleg (Hamburg), Volume 2, 1976; Hans R. Runte and Albert Valdman, editors, *Identite culturelle et francophonie dans les Ameriques,* Indiana University Research Center for Language and Semiotic Studies, 1976; Henri Giordan and Alain Ricard, editors, *Diglossie et litterature,* Maison des sciences de l'homme (Bordeaux, France), 1976; Marina Burt, Dulay Finocchiario, and Mary Finocchiario, editors, *Viewpoints on English as a Second Language,* Regents (New York City), 1977; Bernard Spolsky and Robert Cooper, *Frontiers of Bilingual Education,* Newbury House, 1977; B. P. Sibayan and A. B. Gonzalez, editors, *Language Planning and the Building of a National Language,* Linguistic Society of the Philippines (Manila), 1977.

Publications include three booklets for Canadian Citizenship Branch, Department of Citizenship and Immigration: *Reading Materials in Controlled Vocabularies,* 1957; *Expressioni Communi Inglesi,* 1961; *Allegemeine Englische Redewendungen,* 1961. Contributor to linguistic monographs published by Georgetown University Press and to symposia and conference proceedings. General editor of ''Studies in Bilingual Education'' series, published by Newbury House, 1972— . Contributor to *Encyclopaedia Britannica* and *Foreign Language Annals;* contributor of over one hundred articles to magazines and learned journals in Europe and America. Member of editorial board, *Revue de phonetique appliquee* (Belgium), *Language Problems and Language Planning,* and *Studi italiani di linguistica teoria e applicata* (Italian).

*WORK IN PROGRESS:* *The Study of Bilingualism,* a basic theoretical book, for Oxford University Press; *La Disponibilite: Fondements scientifique et problemes de sondage; Le Bilinguisme: Lectures,* for Klincksieck (Paris); *Language Irredentism; Interintelligibility of Dialects and Languages; The Covering Power of English Words; Vexatious Labels; Language Survival.*

*SIDELIGHTS:* William Francis Mackey's interest in language contact dates from the age of five during residence in a bilingual school. This interest increased after a shipboard meeting with Ilonka Schmidt (his wife), who is fluent in ten languages. He writes: ''The basic theme [of his motivation] is the relativity and indeterminacy of everything human. The basic method is to replace the stilted categorizations of the past by the more realistic approximations; for example, to use scales instead of categories, indices instead of value judgments. Categorization is the basis for ethnic, linguistic and racial prejudice.''

\*    \*    \*

## MACKEY, William J., Jr. 1902(?)-1972

1902(?)—July 2, 1972; American sportsman and authority on bird decoys. Obituaries: *New York Times,* July 5, 1972.

## MACKWORTH, Jane F. 1917-

*PERSONAL:* Born September 15, 1917, in Melbourne, Victoria, Australia; daughter of Walter Hugh C. S. (a captain, Royal Navy) and Dorothy (Wooldridge) Thring; married Norman H. Mackworth (a research psychologist), June 12, 1941; children: Jean Clare (Mrs. David Surry), Alan K., Hugh F. *Education:* Cambridge University, B.A. (first class honors), 1940, M.A., 1942, Ph.D., 1945, M.B. and B.Chir., 1954. *Home:* 16232 Camellia Ter., Los Gatos, Calif. 95030.

*CAREER:* Cambridge University, Cambridge, England, research on war gases at Biochemical Institute, 1940-42, psychological research on high-speed decision making and eye movements with Applied Psychology Research Unit, Medical Research Council, 1954-58; Defence Research Medical Laboratories, Toronto, Ontario, research on memory, eye movements, perception, and vigilance, 1960-65; Radcliffe College, Cambridge, Mass., fellow of Radcliffe Institute, 1967—. Consultant to Rutgers University, 1970-71, and Aphasia Institute, Stanford University, 1971-72; reading consultant, 1972-76; Santa Clara Valley Medical Center, San Jose, medical consultant, 1976—, co-principal investigator of Head Injury Trauma Center, 1977—.

*WRITINGS: Vigilance and Habituation,* Penguin, 1969; *Vigilance and Attention,* Penguin, 1970. Contributor of more than thirty articles to medical and psychology journals.

\* \* \*

## MACNEILL, Earl S(chwom) 1893-1972

October 2, 1893—December 14, 1972; American lawyer, lecturer, and writer on legal subjects. Obituaries: *New York Times,* December 16, 1972.

\* \* \*

## MacNEISH, Richard S(tockton) 1918-

*PERSONAL:* Born April 29, 1918, in New York, N.Y.; son of Harris Franklyn (a teacher) and Elizabeth (Stockton) MacNeish; married June Helm, 1945 (divorced, 1960); married Phyllis Walters, September 26, 1963; children: (second marriage) Richard Roderick, Alexander Stockton. *Education:* University of Chicago, B.A., 1940, M.A., 1944, Ph.D., 1949. *Politics:* "Roosevelt Democrat." *Religion:* None. *Home:* 33 Kirkland Dr., Andover, Mass. 01810. *Office:* Robert S. Peabody Foundation for Archaeology, Box 71, Andover, Mass. 01810.

*CAREER:* University of Michigan, Ann Arbor, North American aboriginal fellow, 1946-47; National Museum of Canada, Ottawa, Ontario, anthropologist, 1949-55, chief of archaeology section, 1955-64; University of Calgary, Calgary, Alberta, head of archaeology department, 1964-68; Robert S. Peabody Foundation for Archaeology, Andover, Mass., director, 1968—. *Military service:* U.S. Army, 1943-44.

*MEMBER:* American Anthropological Association (fellow), Society for American Archaeology (president, 1971-72), American Academy of Arts and Sciences (fellow), Union Internationale des Sciences Prehistoriques et Protohistoriques (member of permanent council), Arctic Institute of North America (fellow), International Congress of Americanists, American Association for the Advancement of Science, International Circumpolar Anthropological Committee, Institute of Andean Research (member of executive committee), British Academy of Science, National Academy of Sciences, Societe des Americanistes Musee de l'Homme, Sigma Psi.

*AWARDS, HONORS:* Guggenheim fellowship, 1954; National Science Foundation and Rockefeller Foundation fellowships, 1960; Spinden Medal for Archaeology, 1964; Lucy Wharton Drexel Medal of University of Pennsylvania Museum, 1965; Addison Emery Verrill Medal of Peabody Museum, Yale University, 1966; honorary distinguished professor, University Nacional de San Cristobal de Huamanga, 1970; Albert Vincent Kidder Award of American Anthropological Association, 1971; recipient of Cornplanter Medal.

*WRITINGS:* (With F. C. Cole) *Kincaid: A Prehistoric Illinois Metropolis,* University of Chicago Press, 1951; *Iroquois Pottery Types: A Technique for the Study of Iroquois Prehistory,* National Museum of Canada, 1952; *An Introduction to the Archaeology of Southeastern Manitoba,* National Museum of Canada, 1958; (with Donald Wray) *The Weaver Site: Twenty Centuries of Illinois Prehistory,* Illinois State Museum, 1961; (with Hugh Raup and Frederick Johnson) *Investigations in the Southwest Yukon,* Peabody Foundation for Archaeology, 1964; (with others) D. S. Byers, editor, *Prehistory of the Tehuacan Valley,* University of Texas Press, for Peabody Foundation for Archaeology, Volume I: *Environment and Substance,* 1967, Volume II: *The Non-Ceramic Artifacts,* 1967, Volume III: *Ceramics of the Tehuacan Valley,* 1970, (with Volume IV became general editor) Volume IV: *The Chronology of Tehuacan,* 1972, Volume V: *Excavations and Reconnaissance,* 1975, Volume VII: *The Central Peruvian Prehistoric Interaction Sphere,* 1975; (author of introduction) *Early Man in America,* text edition, W. H. Freeman, 1973. Also author of *The Science of Archaeology,* 1978, and *The Prehistory of the Ayacucho Valley,* Volume III, in press.

Contributor: J. B. Griffin, editor, *Archaeology of Eastern United States,* University of Chicago Press, 1952; Joseph R. Caldwell, editor, *New Roads to Yesterday,* Basic Books, 1966; John A. Graham, editor, *Ancient Mesoamerica,* Peek Publications, 1966; W. S. Laughlin and R. S. Osborne, editors, *Human Variations and Origins,* Freeman, Cooper, 1967; Paul Deprez, editor, *Population and Economics,* University of Manitoba Press, 1970. Contributor to *Middle American Handbook* and *Encyclopedia of History and Geography.*

Publications (bibliography runs to more than 170 items) include site analysis and interpretation, technical studies, archaeological summaries and theoretical works, popular articles, and reviews. Writer of newspaper series, "Archaeological Discoveries in Northern Mexico," International News Service, 1949.

*WORK IN PROGRESS:* Volume VI of *Prehistory of the Tehuacan Valley,* entitled *Energy and Culture in Ancient Tehuacan;* research on the origins of agriculture in Ayachucho, Peru.

*SIDELIGHTS:* "As a research scientist," Richard S. MacNeish writes, "whatever literary endeavors I become involved in are the reporting of my scientific endeavors."

\* \* \*

## MADISON, Winifred

*PERSONAL:* Born in Pawtucket, R.I.; daughter of Louis S. (a businessman) and Sara (Colitz) Law; married John H. Madison (a professor), August 18, 1942; children: Deborah, Michael, Jamie, Roger. *Education:* Attended Mt. Holyoke College; University of California, Davis, B.A., 1964. *Home:* 1300 Pine Lane, Davis, Calif. 95616. *Agent:* Raines & Raines, 475 Fifth Ave., New York, N.Y. 10017.

*CAREER:* Writer; has taught creative writing at University of California, Davis, and at extension; her paintings and batiks have been shown at many exhibitions in California. Coordinator, Davis Conference on Realism and Fantasy in Children's Literature, 1977. *Member:* California Writers Club, Phi Beta Kappa.

*WRITINGS*—All juvenile: *Maria Luisa*, Lippincott, 1971; *Max's Wonderful Delicatessen*, Little, Brown, 1971; *Growing Up in a Hurry*, Little, Brown, 1973; *Bird on the Wing*, Little, Brown, 1973; *Becky's Horse*, Four Winds, 1975; *Marinka, Katinka and Me (Susie)*, illustrations by Pope Miller, Bradbury Press, 1975; *The Mysterious Caitlin McIver*, Follett, 1975; *Getting Out*, Follett, 1976; *The Party That Lasted All Summer*, Little, Brown, 1976; *Call Me Danica*, Four Winds, 1976; *The Genessee Queen*, Delacorte, 1977. Contributor of articles to *Writer*.

*SIDELIGHTS:* Winifred Madison told *CA:* "Sometimes when I am asked why I write for children and young people, I am not sure what to say. Possibly there is a child that lingers within this adult, a child that speaks when I begin to write.

"'Where do your stories come from?' is another of those unanswerable questions. Anything may set off a story, a chance remark, an encounter, a memory of something long forgotten that unaccountably rises to the surface ... it almost never works the same way twice. For the most part I believe that stories generate spontaneously, crying 'Write me! Write me!' and giving me no peace until I set them down.

"Some of my stories are amusing and others, unfortunately, show a sadder side of life and growing up, but I could not end a story without a whisper of hope."

\* \* \*

## MAHLER, Jane Gaston 1906-

*PERSONAL:* Surname is pronounced *May*-ler; born April 21, 1906, in Dallas, Tex.; daughter of William Henry and Elizabeth (Wathen) Gaston; married Charles Henry Mahler (a physician), August 14, 1943 (died, 1968). *Education:* University of Wisconsin, A.B., 1927; Columbia University, A.M., 1930, Ph.D., 1950; Sorbonne, University of Paris, Certificate of Ecole d'Art et Archeologie, 1938. *Religion:* Protestant. *Residence:* Charleston, S.C.

*CAREER:* Columbia University, Barnard College, New York, N.Y., instructor, 1935-50, assistant professor, 1950-56, associate professor of art history, 1956-64, member of university Graduate Faculty of art history and archeology, 1942-68, professor emeritus, 1969—. Has researched art in Japan, Korea, Manchuria, Russia, China, Turkey, Iran, Afghanistan, India, Ceylon, Nepal, Vietnam, Burma, Thailand, Cambodia, Taiwan, and throughout Europe. Organized bicentennial exhibition in Charleston, S.C., entitled "Women to Remember, 1670-1800: A View of Their Times," 1976-77. *Member:* American Oriental Society, Society of Architectural Historians, Repertoire Internationale des Medievistes (France), Society of Woman Geographers, Asia Society (member of board of trustees, 1959-69), National Society of Colonial Dames of America, Vineyard Conservation Society, Chinese Art Society (member of board of governors, 1943-65), Historical Society of South Carolina, Huguenot Society of South Carolina, Dukes County Historical Society, Garden Club of Martha's Vineyard, Garden Club of Charleston, Preservation Society of Charleston, Century Club of Charleston (president, 1972-73). *Awards, honors:* Carnegie grant to study in Paris, 1938;

Barnard faculty research fellowship, 1955; Asia Foundation grant, 1955; American Association of University Women Marion Talbott fellowship, 1955.

*WRITINGS:* (With Everard Upjohn and Paul Wingert) *History of World Art*, Oxford University Press, 1949; (contributor of Oriental sections) Bernard Myers, editor, *Encyclopedia of World Painting*, Crown, 1955; (editor-in-chief) *Art Treasures of Asia*, four volumes, Tuttle, 1958-60; *Westerners among the Figurines of the T'ang Dynasty of China*, Istituto Italiano per il Medio ed Estremo Oriente, 1959; (contributor) Theodore Bowie, editor, *East-West in Art*, Indiana University Press, 1966. Contributor to *Encyclopedia of World Art*, *Saturday Review*, and art journals. Member of board of editors, *Archives of Asian Art*.

*WORK IN PROGRESS: The Golden Age of Burma in Pagan.*

*SIDELIGHTS:* Jane Gaston Mahler told *CA* that her published books have resulted from her research and academic career, and she has "intended to extend knowledge in my area of Art History and Archaeology of Asia—but, from childhood on, my spontaneous urge is to write poetry inspired by the world of Nature, or verses for special occasions (for fun), or narratives based on the many adventures in my years of rather hazardous travel." She went on to say that "this is a time of frustration for most Art Historians who need publishers willing to bring out books with color plates; the cost is so great that they cannot take a chance on a book that may not be a big seller."

\* \* \*

## MAIER, Pauline (Rubbelke) 1938-

*PERSONAL:* Born April 27, 1938, in St. Paul, Minn.; daughter of Irvin Louis (a fireman) and Charlotte (Winterer) Rubbelke; married Charles Steven Maier (a college professor), June 17, 1961; children: Andrea Nicole, Nicholas Winterer, Jessica Elizabeth Heine. *Education:* Radcliffe College, A.B., 1960; Harvard University, Ph.D., 1968. *Religion:* Roman Catholic. *Home:* 60 Larchwood Dr., Cambridge, Mass. 02138. *Office:* Department of Humanities, Massachusetts Institute of Technology, Cambridge, Mass. 02139.

*CAREER:* University of Massachusetts—Boston, assistant professor, 1968-72, associate professor of history, 1972-77; University of Wisconson—Madison, Robinson Edwards Professor of History, 1977-78; Massachusetts Institute of Technology, Cambridge, professor of history, 1978—. *Awards, honors:* Fulbright scholar, London School of Economics and Political Science, University of London, 1960-61.

*WRITINGS: From Resistance of Revolution: Colonial Radicals and the Development of American Opposition to Britain, 1765-1776*, Knopf, 1972.

*WORK IN PROGRESS:* Research on the "Old Revolutionaries" of 1776, resulting in a book to be published by Knopf.

\* \* \*

## MAKTARI, Abdulla M. A. 1936-

*PERSONAL:* Born November 17, 1936, in Aden, Arabia; son of Muhammad A. G. and 'Aisha (Hasan) Maktari; married 'Aisha Nasir (a teacher), August 5, 1966; children: Maysun, Muna. *Education:* University of London, Diploma in Islamic and Comparative Laws, 1961; University of California, Los Angeles, M.A., 1964; Cambridge University,

Ph.D., 1968. *Home:* D4 Shaikh Uthman, Aden, South Yemen.

*CAREER:* Pan American Hadramawt Oil Co., Aden, Arabia, member of administrative staff and consultant, 1964-65; consultant to local governments of Hadramawt and Lahj, Arabia, 1964-67; Ministry of Agriculture, South Yemen, consultant on agricultural laws, 1968-69; Bank of South Arabia (nationalized), member of board of directors, 1969-70; University of Malaya, Kuala Lumpur, lecturer in Islamic law and insititutions. Consultant on Wadi Jizan Irrigation Project, Saudi Arabia. *Awards, honors:* Commonwealth scholar for research in Islamic and customary law at Cambridge University, 1965-68.

*WRITINGS: Water Rights and Irrigation Practices in Lahj: A Study of the Application of Customary and Shri'ah Law in South-West Arabia,* Cambridge University Press, 1971. Co-editor, *Dirasat* (Arabic-English bimonthly), Aden, 1964-66.

*WORK IN PROGRESS:* An approach to Islamic law as interpreted by the Shafi'i school.††

\* \* \*

## MALCOLM, Norman 1911-

*PERSONAL:* Born June 11, 1911, in Selden, Kan.; son of Charles Claude and Ada (Wingrove) Malcolm; married Leonida Morosova, February 12, 1944 (divorced); married Ruth Riesenberg, October 28, 1976; children: (first marriage) Christopher, Elizabeth. *Education:* University of Nebraska, B.A., 1933; Harvard University, M.A., 1938, Ph.D., 1940; also attended Cambridge University, 1938-40. *Politics:* Democrat. *Religion:* Episcopalian. *Residence:* Ithaca, N.Y. *Office:* Department of Philosophy, Cornell University, Ithaca, N.Y. 14850.

*CAREER:* Princeton University, Princeton, N.J., instructor in philosophy, 1940-42 and 1946; Cornell University, Ithaca, N.Y., assistant professor, 1947-50, associate professor, 1950-55, professor of philosophy, 1955—, Susan Linn Sage Professor of Philosophy, 1965. Visiting professor at University of California, Los Angeles, 1964. *Military service:* U.S. Navy, 1942-45; became lieutenant. *Member:* American Philosophical Association (president of Eastern Division, 1972), American Association of University Professors, American Academy of Arts and Science. *Awards, honors:* Guggenheim fellow, 1946-47; Hibben research fellow, Princeton University, 1952; Fulbright research fellow, University of Helsinki, Finland, 1960-61; Center for Advanced Study in the Behavioral Sciences fellow, 1968-69.

*WRITINGS: Ludwig Wittgenstein: A Memoir,* Oxford University Press, 1958; *Dreaming,* Routledge & Kegan Paul, 1959; *Knowledge and Certainy,* Prentice-Hall, 1963; *Problems of Mind,* Harper, 1971; *Memory and Mind,* Cornell University Press, 1977; *Thought and Knowledge,* Cornell University Press, 1977.

*AVOCATIONAL INTERESTS:* Walking, sailing, skiing, running.

\* \* \*

## MALONEY, Joan M(arie) 1931-

*PERSONAL:* Born May 7, 1931, in Washington, D.C.; daughter of Frank (an attorney) and Arline (Smith) Maloney. *Education:* Trinity College, Washington, D.C., A.B., 1953; Georgetown University, M.A., 1958, Ph.D., 1961. *Politics:* Independent. *Address:* Box 364, North Chatham, Mass. 02650. *Office:* Department of History, Salem State College, Salem, Mass. 01960.

*CAREER:* Seton Hall University, South Orange, N.J., research associate, 1961-62; Rosemont College, Rosemont, Pa., assistant professor of contemporary history, 1962-64; Salem State College, Salem, Mass., professor of Asian history, 1964—. Associate director of Research Institute on Sino-Soviet Bloc, Washington, D.C., 1959—. *Member:* American Association of University Professors, Association of Asian Studies, American Historical Association, American Catholic Historical Association (member of executive council, 1970-73).

*WRITINGS:* (With Peter S. H. Tang) *Communist China: The Domestic Scene 1949-67,* Seton Hall University Press, 1968. Editor of seven books in the area of contemporary Chinese studies.

*WORK IN PROGRESS: Thousand Year Dream: Maoism and Feminism.*

\* \* \*

## MANCEWICZ, Bernice Winslow 1917-

*PERSONAL:* Born April 12, 1917, in Grand Rapids, Mich.; daughter of John (a seaman) and Edna (Gelmuss) Winslow; married John Joseph Mancewicz, October 14, 1939 (divorced, February, 1976); children: Carol Jeanne (Mrs. James Sudzik), Marcia Lynne, Mark. *Education:* Attended Meinzinger Art School, 1940-42, and School of the Art Institute of Chicago, 1942. *Home:* 229 Covell Ave. N.W., Grand Rapids, Mich. 49504. *Office: Grand Rapids Press,* Grand Rapids, Mich. 49502.

*CAREER:* Began career as a fashion artist, 1942-44; WLAV, radio copy writer, 1944-46; *Grand Rapids Herald,* Grand Rapids, Mich., fashion editor, 1946-50; *Grand Rapids Press,* Grand Rapids, fashion editor, 1950-53, feature writer and art editor, 1962—. Employed with United Fund Public Relations, Grand Rapids, 1953-59; freelance artist, 1959-62. Grand Valley Artists Civic Theater, worked on publicity for five years, member of board for two years. *Member:* National Book Women's Association, Ad Club (president, 1957-58).

*WRITINGS: Alexander Calder: A Pictorial Essay,* Eerdmans, 1969, revised edition, Imperial Masterpieces Gallery (Grand Rapids, Mich.), 1978.

*WORK IN PROGRESS:* A novel on the newspaper world.

*SIDELIGHTS:* In 1968, Bernice Mancewicz wrote twenty-three feature articles in twenty-two days while in Europe. She has photographed Princess Grace, Yousuf Karsh, Barnaby Conrad, Alexander Calder, Dinah Shore, Liberace, Klaus Perls, and other famous persons.

\* \* \*

## MANCHEL, Frank 1935-

*PERSONAL:* Born July 22, 1935, in Detroit, Mich.; son of Lee and Olga (Fluhr) Manchel; married Sheila Wachtel, 1958; children: Steven Lloyd, Gary Howard. *Education:* Ohio State University, A.B., 1957; Hunter College (now Hunter College of the City University of New York), M.A., 1960; Columbia University, Ed.D., 1966. *Home:* 5 Cranwell Ave., South Burlington, Vt. 05401. *Agent:* Julian Bach, Jr., 3 East 48th St., New York, N.Y. 10017. *Office:* Office of the Dean, College of Arts and Sciences, University of Vermont, Burlington, Vt. 05401.

*CAREER:* High school instructor in English, New Rochelle, N.Y., 1958-64; Southern Connecticut State College, New Haven, assistant professor of English, 1964-67; University of Vermont, Burlington, associate professor of English and speech, 1967-71, professor of communication and theater, 1971-77, associate dean of College of Arts and Sciences, 1977—, director of La Mancha Project in Composition (cooperative program with Vermont high schools, exploring techniques in improving writing skills). Visiting professor, University of Bridgeport, summer, 1967. *Military service:* U.S. Army, Medical Corps, 1957. U.S. Army Reserve, 1957-63. *Member:* National Council of Teachers of English, American Federation of Film Societies (chairman of executive board), Society for Cinema Studies (member of executive committee), American Film Institute, British Film Institute. *Awards, honors:* Simmonds Foundation grant for research in England, 1970.

*WRITINGS: Movies and How They Are Made* (juvenile), Prentice-Hall, 1968; *When Pictures Began to Move* (juvenile), illustrations by James Caraway, Prentice-Hall, 1968; *When Movies Began to Speak* (juvenile), Prentice-Hall, 1969; *Terrors of the Screen* (Junior Literary Guild selection), Prentice-Hall, 1970; (contributor) Sheila Schwartz, editor, *Readings in the Humanities*, Macmillan, 1970; *Cameras West* (Junior Literary Guild selection), Prentice-Hall, 1972; *Black Projections*, Prentice-Hall, 1973; *Film Study: A Resource Guide*, Fairleigh Dickinson University Press, 1973; *Yesterday's Clowns: The Rise of Film Comedy*, F. Watts, 1973; *The Talking Clowns*, F. Watts, 1976; *An Album of Great Science Fiction Films*, F. Watts, 1976; *Women on the Hollywood Screen*, F. Watts, 1977. Contributor of articles and reviews to film and other professional journals.

*SIDELIGHTS:* Frank Manchel believes that "the demand for comedy of all kinds seems to be a permanent fixture of society. When life goes sour, people want to laugh. It is not unusual, therefore, that the most popular figures in film history have been great jesters. . . . The comedian's art is based on the difference between what is and what is possible. . . . Their aim, which has been the aim of all great comedy since the beginning of time, is to criticize the world in the belief that things can be better."

*BIOGRAPHICAL/CRITICAL SOURCES: Variety*, January 15, 1969, October 22, 1969; *Saturday Review*, August 16, 1969.

\* \* \*

## MANDEL, Adrienne Schizzano 1934-

*PERSONAL:* Born October 10, 1934, in Italy; U.S. citizen; daughter of Andrew (a builder) and Concetta (Livoti) Schizzano; married Oscar Mandel (a professor), 1960. *Education:* Hunter College (now Hunter College of the City University of New York), A.B., 1954; Columbia University, M.A., 1955; University of California, Ph.D., 1970. *Home:* 979 Casiano Rd., Los Angeles, Calif. 90049. *Office:* Department of Foreign Languages, California State University, 18111 Nordhoff St., Northridge, Calif. 91324.

*CAREER:* California Institute of Technology, Pasadena, lecturer in French, 1964-65; California State University, Northridge, assistant professor, 1965-68, associate professor of French, 1968—. Escort and interpreter, U.S. Department of State, 1966—. *Member:* Modern Language Association of America, Philological Association of the Pacific Coast.

*WRITINGS:* (Contributor) Oscar Mandel, editor, *The Theatre of Don Juan*, University of Nebraska Press, 1963; (translator and editor with husband, Oscar Mandel) *Seven Comedies of Marivaux*, Cornell University Press, 1968; *La Celestina Studies: A Thematic Survey and Bibliography*,

*1824-1970*, Scarecrow, 1971. Contributor of translations of theater journals, including *First Stage* and *Drama and Theatre*.

*WORK IN PROGRESS:* Translating *Las mocedades del Cid*, by Guillen de Castro; research on the nature of the comic in Nolant de Fatouville.†

\* \* \*

## MANDEL, Ernest 1923-

*PERSONAL:* Born April 5, 1923; married Gisela Scholtz. *Education:* Attended Free University of Brussels; Sorbonne, University of Paris, Diplome; Free University of Berlin, Doktor. *Home:* 127 Rue Jos. Impens, Brussels 1030, Belgium. *Office:* Free University of Brussels, Brussels, Belgium.

*CAREER:* Free University of Brussels, Brussels, Belgium, professor. Visiting professor, Free University of Berlin, 1970-71; Alfred Marshall Visiting Professor of Economics, Cambridge University, 1978. Member of economic studies commission, Belgian Trade Union Federation, 1955-63.

*WRITINGS: Introduction to Marxist Economic Theory*, Pathfinder Press, 1968; *Marxist Economic Theory*, Monthly Review Press, 1968; *Contradictions of Imperialism: Europe vs. America?*, Monthly Review Press, 1970; *The Formation of the Economic Thought of Karl Marx*, Monthly Review Press, 1971; *The Decline of the Dollar: A Marxist View of the International Monetary Crisis*, Monad Press, 1972; *Workers Control, Workers Councils, Workers Self-Management*, Penguin, 1973; *An Introduction to Marxism*, Ink Link Books, 1977; *Late Capitalism*, New Left Books, 1978; *A Critique of Eurocommunism*, New Left Books, in press. Editor, *La Gauche*; co-editor, *Intercontinental Press*.

*BIOGRAPHICAL/CRITICAL SOURCES: Times Literary Supplement*, July 16, 1970.

\* \* \*

## MANDEL, Jerome 1937-

*PERSONAL:* Surname is pronounced with accent on second syllable; born November 17, 1937, in Cleveland, Ohio; son of William and Rose (Abraham) Mandel; married Miriam Bauer (a teacher and editor), December 23, 1964; children: Jessica Rifke, Naomi Iliana. *Education:* Oberlin College, A.B., 1959; Ohio State University, M.A., 1961, Ph.D., 1966. *Office:* Department of English, Clemson University, Clemson, S.C. 29631.

*CAREER:* Rutgers University, New Brunswick, N.J., assistant professor, 1966-72; Clemson University, Clemson, S.C., associate professor, 1972-76, professor of Medieval English, 1976—. Visiting professor, University of Haifa, 1976-77; associate professor, Tel Aviv University, 1977—. Reader for *Chaucer Review. Member:* International Arthurian Society, College English Association, Modern Language Association of America, Mediaeval Academy of America, Modern Humanities Research Association. *Awards, honors:* Rutgers faculty fellowship, 1968-69; Andrew Mellon postdoctoral fellowship, 1969-70; Anthologist of the Year award, New Jersey Association of Teachers of English, 1972, for *Medieval Literature and Folklore Studies.*

*WRITINGS:* (Editor with Martin Stevens) *Old English Literature: Twenty-Two Analytical Essays*, University of Nebraska Press, 1968; (editor with Bruce A. Rosenberg) *Medieval Literature and Folklore Studies: Essays in Honor of Francis Lee Utley*, Rutgers University Press, 1970. Contributor of articles to *Yearbook of English Studies*, and to

*Modern Philology, Papers on Language and Literature, Chaucer Review, Shakespeare Quarterly, Studies in Medieval Culture, Neuphilologische Mitteilungen, James Joyce Quarterly, D. H. Lawrence Review, French Review, French Review Mosaic,* and *Criticism.*

*WORK IN PROGRESS:* Translations of *Evec and Enide, The Knight of the Cart, Cliges,* and *Yvain; Order in the Fragments of the Canterbury Tales.*

*        *        *

## MANE, Robert   1926-

*PERSONAL:* Born August 19, 1926, in Annot, France; son of Rene and Marguerite (Blanc) Mane; married Josette Schnuer (a teacher), June 20, 1957; children: Pierre-Antoine, Michele. *Education:* Sorbonne, University of Paris, agregation d'anglais, 1955, doctorat d'etat, 1968. *Home:* 6 rue de Coarraze, Pau 64, France. *Office:* Faculte des Lettres, University of Pau, Pau 64, France.

*CAREER:* University of Pau, Pau, France, professor of African and Afro-American literature, 1964—, chairman of department of American studies, 1964—. Visiting professor of Afro-American literature, Federal University of Cameroon; director of graduate studies program in African literature, University of Abidjan. *Member:* French Association for Commonwealth Studies (secretary).

*WRITINGS: Hamlin Garland: L'Homme et L'Ouevre,* Didier, 1968; *Henry Adams on the Road to Chartres,* Harvard University Press, 1971. Also author of *Commonwealth: Essays and Studies,* 1975, 1976, 1978. Editor of ''Echos du Commonwealth'' series, 1974—.

*WORK IN PROGRESS:* A double volume of *Commonwealth, Essays and Studies* entitled *The African Novel: A Comparative Study* and *La Litterature Canadienne Anglaise.*

*        *        *

## MANGALAM, J(oseph) J(oseph)   1924-

*PERSONAL:* Born February 16, 1924, in Trichur, India; married Sylvia Verin, 1956; children: Harry-Joseph, Kunjalichi Theadora. *Education:* University of Punjab, B.Sc., 1944, M.Sc., 1950; Cornell University, Ph.D., 1957. *Politics:* Democrat. *Religion:* Quaker. *Home:* 1388 Bedford Highway, Bedford, Nova Scotia, Canada. *Office:* 313B Forrest Building, Dalhousie University, Halifax, Nova Scotia, Canada.

*CAREER:* Forman College, Lahore, Pakistan, lecturer in chemistry, 1950-52, head of department of sociology, 1957-60; University of Punjab, Lahore, West Pakistan, head of sociology department, 1957-60; University of Kentucky, Lexington, assistant professor of rural sociology, Experimental Station, 1960-67; Dalhousie University, Halifax, Nova Scotia, professor of sociology and anthropology, 1971—. Consultant to Peace Corps, 1961. *Awards, honors:* Fulbright travel grant, 1952; Asia Foundation research grant, 1958-60; Rockefeller Foundation research grant, 1961-62; Canada Council research grants, 1967 and 1977.

*WRITINGS: Human Migration,* University Press of Kentucky, 1968; (with Lee Taylor and W. Reeder) *Internationalizing Rural Sociology,* New York State College of Agriculture, 1970; (with H. K. Schwarzweller and J. S. Brown) *Mountain Families in Transition,* University of Pennsylvania Press, 1972.

*WORK IN PROGRESS:* Research on problems of college

students in Pakistan and on higher education and development.

*        *        *

## MANKIN, Paul A.   1924-

*PERSONAL:* Born July 11, 1924, in Berlin, Germany; came to United States in 1939; son of Curt E. (an engineer) and Nelly (Hachenburger) Mankin; married Carol Chaitin, July 11, 1957 (divorced, 1973); children: Eric David, Nina Claudia. *Education:* University of California, Los Angeles, A.A., B.A., 1948, M.A., 1952; attended Universite de Grenoble, 1948-49; Yale University, Ph.D., 1959. *Office:* Department of French and Italian, University of Massachusetts, Amherst, Mass. 01003.

*CAREER:* University of Massachusetts—Amherst, teacher of French and comparative literature, 1963—. Guest professor, University of Freiburg, Germany, 1969-70; exchange professor in Avignon, France, 1972-73; visiting professor, Monterey Institute of Foreign Studies, 1974. Director of Grenoble study program, 1976, and of Western European studies, University of Massachusetts, 1977—. Recording artist for Folkways Records. Consultant to *Encyclopaedia Britannica* and dictionaries of literature. *Military service:* U.S. Army, Counter Intelligence Corps, 1943-45; became sergeant. *Member:* American Association of University Professors, American Comparative Literature Association, Modern Language Association of America, American Association of Teachers of French, Pi Delta Phi. *Awards, honors:* Fulbright travel grant; Italian government grant.

*WRITINGS: Anthologie d'humour francais,* Scott, Foresman, 1970; *Precious Irony: The Theatre of Jean Giraudoux,* Mouton, 1971. Contributor of articles to literary and scholarly journals.

*WORK IN PROGRESS: Marcel Ayme,* for Twayne Books.

*        *        *

## MANNERS, Gerald   1932-

*PERSONAL:* Born August 7, 1932, in Durham; England; son of George William (a civil servant) and Louise (Plumpton) Manners; married Anne Sawyer, July 11, 1959; children: Carolyn, Christopher, Katharine. *Education:* St. Catharine's College, Cambridge, B.A., 1954, M.A., 1958. *Home:* Rodinghead, Ashridge Park, Berkhamsted, Hertfordshire, England. *Office:* University College, University of London, Gower St., London W.C.1, England.

*CAREER:* University of Wales, University College of Swansea, Swansea, lecturer in economic geography, 1957-67; University of London, University College, London, England, reader in geography, 1967—. Visiting scholar, Resources for the Future, Inc., Washington, D.C., 1964-65. Member of board of directors, Economic Associates Ltd., and Location of Offices Bureau. Member of South East Economic Planning Council. Governor, Cavendish School. *Military service:* Royal Air Force, flying officer, 1955-57. *Member:* Institute of British Geographers (member of council, 1967-70), Royal Geographical Society (fellow), Royal Society of Arts (fellow), Regional Studies Association, Maconochie Foundation.

*WRITINGS: The Geography of Energy,* Hutchinson, 1964, revised edition, 1971; (editor) *South Wales in the Sixties,* Pergamon, 1964; *The Changing World Market for Iron Ore, 1950-1980: An Economic Geography,* Johns Hopkins Press, 1971; (editor with Michael Chisholm) *Spatial Policy Prob-*

*lems of the British Economy,* Cambridge University Press, 1971; (editor) *Regional Developments in Britain,* Wiley, 1972.

*WORK IN PROGRESS:* Research on economics of office location and regional development and on western European energy markets.

\* \* \*

## MANNING, Clarence A(ugustus) 1893-1972

April 1, 1893—October 4, 1972; American educator and authority on Slavic languages and literature. Obituaries: *New York Times,* October 6, 1972.

\* \* \*

## MANNING, Peter K(irby) 1940-

*PERSONAL:* Born September 27, 1940, in Salem, Ore.; son of Kenneth G. and Esther A. (Gibbard) Manning; married Victoria Shaughnessy, September 3, 1961; children: three. *Education:* Willamette University, B.A., 1961; Duke University, M.A., 1963, Ph.D., 1966. *Home:* 626 Kedzie Dr., East Lansing, Mich. 48823. *Office:* Department of Sociology, 201 Berkey Hall, Michigan State University, East Lansing, Mich. 48823.

*CAREER:* Duke University, Durham, N.C., instructor, 1964-65; University of Missouri—Columbia, assistant professor, 1965-66; Michigan State University, East Lansing, assistant professor, 1966-70, associate professor of sociology, 1970-74, professor of sociology and psychiatry, 1974—. Visiting research fellow, Goldsmith's College, University of London, 1972-73; visiting fellow, Law Enforcement Assistance Administration, National Institute of Law Enforcement and Criminal Justice, 1974-75; visiting professor, Portland State University, 1976, and Purdue University, 1977. *Member:* International Sociological Association, Society for the Study of Social Problems (chairman of social problems theory section, 1971—; member of program committee, 1978), National Deviancy Conference, American Sociological Association, Society for the Study of Symbolic Interaction, Association of Humanist Sociology, Royal Anthropological Institute (fellow), Western Society of Criminology, Midwest Sociological Society, Ohio Valley Sociological Society (section head of Medical Sociology, 1967; program chairman, 1970), Pi Gamma Mu.

*WRITINGS:* (Editor with Marcello Truzzi) *Youth and Sociology,* Prentice-Hall, 1972; (editor with Robert B. Smith, and contributor) *Social Science Methods: An Introduction,* Free Press, 1972; (editor) *Youth: Divergent Perspectives,* Wiley, 1973; (with Martine Zucker) *The Sociology of Mental Health and Illness,* Bobbs-Merrill, 1976; *Police Work: The Social Organization of Policing,* M.I.T. Press, 1977; (editor with John Van Maanen) *Policing: Controlling the Streets,* Goodyear Publishing, 1978.

Contributor: Jack D. Douglas, editor, *Understanding Everyday Life,* Aldine, 1970; Russell Kleis, editor, *Social Relevance in Continuing Education,* Continuing Education Service, Michigan State University, 1970; Douglas, editor, *Crime and Justice in American Society,* Bobbs-Merrill, 1971; James Henslin, editor, *The Sociology of Sex,* Appleton, 1971; Henslin, editor, *Down to Earth Sociology,* Free Press, 1972; (with Horacio Fabrega, Jr.) Douglas and Robert A. Scott, editors, *Theoretical Perspectives on Deviance,* Basic Books, 1972; Douglas, editor, *Research on Deviance,* Random House, 1972; Douglas, editor, *Introductory Sociology,* Free Press, 1972; (with C. Richard Fletcher,

Larry T. Reynolds, and James O. Smith) Paul Roman and Harrison Trice, editors, *Current Perspectives in Psychiatric Sociology,* Science House, 1972; (with Fabrega) George Psathas, editor, *Phenomenological Sociology,* Wiley, 1973; R. J. Havighurst, editor, *Youth,* National Society for the Study of Education, 1975; Niederhoffer and Blumberg, editors, *The Ambivalent Force,* Dryden, 1976; R. Blankenship, editor, *Colleagues in Organizations,* Wiley, 1977; (with L. J. Redlinger) P. E. Rock, editor, *Politics and Drugs,* Transaction Books, 1977; Douglas and Johnson, editors, *Official Deviance,* Lippincott, 1977; Sagarin, editor, *Fundamentals of Sociology,* Holt, 1977.

Consulting editor, "Principal Themes of Sociology" series, W. C. Brown, 1971—. Contributor of articles and reviews to journals, including *Sociological Quarterly, Social Forces, Contemporary Sociology,* and *British Journal of Criminology. Sociological Quarterly,* member of editorial review board, 1969—, reviews-features editor, 1972-73; *Urban Life,* new ethnographies editor, 1972-75, editor, 1978—; member of editorial review boards, *American Sociological Review,* 1975—, and *Humanist Sociology,* 1977—.

*WORK IN PROGRESS: Social Control and Social Regulation* for W. C. Brown; *The Problematics of Social Problems* for Wiley; editing *Formal Sociology* for Routledge & Kegan Paul; *The Narcs' Game;* numerous articles for professional journals.

\* \* \*

## MANTELL, Leroy H. 1919-

*PERSONAL:* Born September 14, 1919, in New York, N.Y.; son of Felix S. (an electrician) and Lillian E. (Wasserman) Mantell; married Loretta C. Collins, May, 1943 (divorced, 1953); married Ursula Berta Oomen (a professor at the University of Bonn, Germany), July 6, 1968; children: (first marriage) Robert E. *Education:* George Washington University, B.A., 1942, M.A., 1945, D.B.A., 1959. *Religion:* Jewish. *Home:* Ippendorfer Allee 39, 5300 Bonn, West Germany.

*CAREER:* U.S. Government employee, 1939-62; Nasson College, Springvale, Me., professor of economics and business, 1962-66; Georgetown University, Washington, D.C., associate professor of management, 1966-69; George Washington University, Washington, D.C., associate professor of management, 1969-72; U.S. Department of Commerce, Washington, D.C., senior policy analyst, Office of Telecommunications, 1972-73; Executive Office of the President, Washington, D.C., chief economist in Office of Telecommunications Policy, 1973-75. *Military service:* U.S. Air Force Reserve, 1949-72; became major. *Member:* Omicron Delta Epsilon.

*WRITINGS:* (With Francis P. Sing) *Economics for Business Decisions,* McGraw, 1972. Contributor to papers on applications of general systems theory to linguistic models in *Folia Linguistica* and other publications. Contributor to business and trade journals.

*WORK IN PROGRESS:* A book on organizational systems, an application of general systems theory to management.

*AVOCATIONAL INTERESTS:* Photography, painting, hiking.

\* \* \*

## MANWELL, Reginald D. 1897-

*PERSONAL:* Born December 24, 1897; son of John P. (a

clergyman) and Stella (Dickinson) Manwell; married Elizabeth Skelding Moore, August 6, 1930 (died, 1964); children: John Parker, Henry Dickinson. *Education:* Amherst College, A.B., 1919, A.M., 1926; Johns Hopkins University, Sc.D., 1928. *Politics:* Democrat. *Religion:* Unitarian Universalist. *Home:* Hoag Lane, Fayetteville, N.Y. 13066. *Office:* 26A Lyman Hall, Syracuse University, Syracuse, N.Y. 13210.

*CAREER:* West Virginia Wesleyan College, Buckhannon, professor of biology and chairman of department, 1928-29; Johns Hopkins University, Baltimore, Md., instructor in protozoology, 1929-30; Syracuse University, Syracuse, N.Y., assistant professor, 1930-33, associate professor, 1933-36, professor of zoology, 1936-63, professor emeritus and research associate, 1963—. Teacher of parasitology, Rocky Mountain Biological Laboratory, summers, 1929, 1948-54; visiting professor of zoology, Mountain Lake Biological Station, University of Virginia, summer, 1961. *Military service:* U.S. Army, 1943-45; became captain.

*MEMBER:* American Society of Parasitologists, Society of Protozoologists (former vice-president and president), Rocky Mountain Biological Laboratory (trustee; former vice-president and president), Sigma Xi, and numerous other scientific societies. *Awards, honors:* Sigma Xi annual research award, 1959; Sc.D., Syracuse University, 1963; American Association for the Advancement of Science fellow; New York Academy of Science fellow.

*WRITINGS:* (With Paul F. Russell, Luther S. West, and George MacDonald) *Practical Malariology,* Saunders, 1946, revised edition, Oxford University Press, 1963; *The Church across the Street,* Beacon Press, 1947, revised edition, 1962; *Introduction to Protozoology,* St. Martin's, 1961, revised edition, Dover, 1967. Contributor of about one hundred seventy-five articles to scientific journals. Member of editorial board, *Journal of Parasitology,* and *Journal of Protozoology,* 1954-58.

*AVOCATIONAL INTERESTS:* Travel, music.

*       *       *

## MAO, James C. T. 1925-

*PERSONAL:* Born November 3, 1925, in Shanghai, China; son of Ho-yuan (a businessman) and Hwa-mei (Tai) Mao; married Petrina Tai, June 14, 1955; children: Stephen, Jeffrey. *Education:* Northwestern University, M.B.A., 1950, Ph.D., 1954. *Office:* Department of Finance, University of British Columbia, Vancouver, British Columbia, Canada V6T 1W5.

*CAREER:* University of Michigan, Ann Arbor, instructor, 1954-56, assistant professor, 1956-58, associate professor, 1959-64, professor of finance, 1964-67; University of British Columbia, Vancouver, professor of finance, 1967—.

*WRITINGS: Quantitative Analysis of Financial Decisions,* Macmillan, 1969; *Corporate Financing Decisions,* Pavan, 1976.

*       *       *

## MARANDA, Pierre 1930-

*PERSONAL:* Born March 27, 1930, in Quebec, Canada; son of Lucien and Marie-Alma (Rochette) Maranda; married Elli Kongas (a university professor), March 12, 1962; children: Erik, Nicolas. *Education:* Laval University, B.A., 1949; Universite de Montreal, M.A., 1953, L.Ph., 1955; Harvard University, Ph.D., 1966. *Home:* 1080 Avenue Des Braves, Quebec, Quebec, Canada G1K 7P4. *Office:* Universite Laval, Quebec, Quebec, Canada G1K 7P4.

*CAREER:* Harvard University, Cambridge, Mass., research fellow, 1964-68; Ecole Pratique des Hautes Etudes, Paris, France, research director, 1968-69; University of British Columbia, Vancouver, associate professor of anthropology, 1969-74; visiting professor, College de France, 1974; Laval University, Quebec, Quebec, research professor, 1975—. Member of board of directors, International Centre for Semantics and Linguistics, University of Urbino, Urbino, Italy. *Member:* Canadian Sociology and Anthropology Association (president, 1972-73), Social Science Research Council of Canada (member of board of directors), American Anthropological Association (fellow), American Folklore Society, Association of Social Anthropologists for Oceania, Royal Society of Canada (fellow), Societe des Oceanistes (Paris). *Awards, honors:* Harvard University Milton Fund, 1966-68; National Institutes of Health grants, 1966-69; Canada Council grants, 1970-78; Medaille du College de France, 1975.

*WRITINGS:* (With wife, Elli Kongas) *Structural Models in Folklore and Transformational Essays,* Mouton, 1962, 2nd revised and enlarged edition, 1971; (editor with Jean Pouillon) *Echanges et Communications,* Mouton, 1970; (with Elli Kongas) *Structural Analysis of Oral Tradition,* University of Pennsylvania Press, 1971; *Introduction to Anthropology: A Self-Guide,* Prentice-Hall, 1972; (editor) *Mythology,* Penguin, 1972; *French Kinship: Structure and History,* Mouton, 1974; (editor) *Soviet Structural Folkloristics,* Mouton, 1974.

Contributor: June Helm, editor, *Essays on the Verbal and Visual Arts,* University of Washington Press, 1967; Bernard Jaulin and Jean-Claude Gardin, editors, *Calcul et formalisation dans les sciences de l'homme,* CNRS (Paris), 1968; Philippe Richard and Robert Jaulin, editors, *Anthropologie et calcul,* Nouvelle Societe d'Editions (Paris), 1971; Antonino Butitta and Antonino Pasqualino, editors, *Structures et genres de la litterature ethnique,* Association for the Preservation of Oral Traditions (Palermo), 1972. Contributor of about twenty papers to scientific journals.

*WORK IN PROGRESS:* A book on the Lau people of Malaita, Solomon Islands; a book on computers in semantic anthropological analysis; a book on mythic dynamisms and popular subdiscourse.

*SIDELIGHTS:* Pierre Maranda did two years of field work in Lau Lagoon, Malaita, Solomon Islands.

*       *       *

## MARANELL, Gary M. 1932-

*PERSONAL:* Born September 15, 1932, in Hartley, Iowa; son of Michael M. (a farmer) and Carolyn (Williamson) Maranell; married Roberta Castle (divorced, 1976); married Martha Oldham (a librarian), July 31, 1977; children: (first marriage) Michael, Kimberly, Mark, Carrie. *Education:* University of Iowa, B.A., 1955, M.A., 1957, Ph.D., 1959. *Politics:* Liberal Democrat. *Religion:* Congregationalist. *Home:* 821 Alabama, Lawrence, Kan. 66044. *Office:* Department of Sociology, University of Kansas, Lawrence, Kan. 66044.

*CAREER:* University of Iowa, Iowa City, instructor in sociology, 1957-59; University of Arkansas, Fayetteville, assistant professor of sociology and anthropology, 1959-63; University of Kansas, Lawrence, assistant professor, 1963-67, associate professor, 1967-70, professor of sociology, 1970—. *Member:* American Sociological Association (fellow), Midwest Sociological Society, Alpha Kappa Delta.

WRITINGS: Scaling: A Source Book for Behavioral Scientists, Aldine, 1974; Responses to Religion, University Press of Kansas, 1974. Contributor to professional journals.

WORK IN PROGRESS: Research on marriage and divorce patterns, divorce from 1940 to the present; a study of marital compatibility; update of work on presidential greatness.

*      *      *

## MARCHIONE, Margherita Frances 1922-

PERSONAL: Born February 19, 1922, in Little Ferry, N.J. Education: Georgian Court College, A.B., 1943; Columbia University, A.M., 1949, Ph.D., 1960. Home: Villa Walsh, 455 Western Ave., Morristown, N.J. 07960. Office: College of Education, Fairleigh Dickinson University, Madison, N.J. 07940.

CAREER: Roman Catholic nun of order of Religious Teachers Filippini; teacher in parochial and private high schools, 1943-54; Villa Walsh College, Morristown, N.J., instructor in languages, 1954-65; Fairleigh Dickinson University, Madison, N.J., assistant professor, 1965-72, associate professor of Italian, 1972—, chairman of foreign languages department, 1967-68. Director of language institute, U.S. Office of Education, summer, 1968; director of Italian Institute, University of Salerno, and N.D.E.A. Italian Institute, summer, 1972, and lecturer at other institutions in Europe, 1972. Religious Teachers Filippini, Morristown, vocation promotion directress, 1954-66, secretary, 1960-66, treasurer, 1966-78. Consultant and representative, Gallery of Modern Art, summers, 1968-69.

MEMBER: Associazione Internazionale Professori di Italiano, Modern Language Association of America, American Association of Teachers of Italian, American Association of University Professors. American Italian Historical Association (member of executive council, 1977-79), American Institute of Italian Studies (president), American Italian Association, American Council on the Teaching of Foreign Languages, United Nations Association, Amici di Don Clemente Rebora, New Jersey Catholic Historical Records Commission, New Jersey Foreign Language Teachers Association. Awards, honors: National Defense Education Act grant in French, University of Kentucky, 1962; Fulbright scholar at University of Rome, 1964; National Defense Education Act grant, Italian Institute, 1968; American-Italian Women of Achievement Award in education, 1971; New Jersey Bicentennial Commission grant, 1974-75; Woman of the Year award, 1976; New Jersey Foreign Language Teachers Association award for outstanding contribution to foreign language education, 1977; Literary Luminary of New Jersey citation, 1977; Kosciuszko Foundation grant, 1977; Premio della Cultura award, 1977; Cavaliere dell'Ordine della Stella della Solidarieta Italiana (highest award of Italian Republic), conferred by president of Italy, 1977; Fairleigh Dickinson University research grant, 1977-78.

WRITINGS: L'Imagine Tesa, Edizioni di Storia e Letteratura, 1960, revised and enlarged edition, 1974; (editor with S. Eugene Scalia) "Carteggio di Giovanni Boine," Edizioni di Storia e Letteratura, Volume I: Carteggio Boine-Prezzolini, 1971, Volume II: Carteggio Boine-Cecchi, 1972, Volume III: Giovanni Boine: Amici del "Rinnovamento," 1977; (editor with Guillermo del Olmo) Foreign Language: Teaching and Learning, Fairleigh Dickinson University Press, 1971; (editor and translator) Twentieth Century Italian Poetry, Fairleigh Dickinson University Press, 1972; (editor and translator) Philip Mazzei: Jefferson's "Zealous Whig,"

American Institute of Italian Studies, 1975; Lettere di Clemente Rebora, Edizioni di Storia e Letteratura, 1976. Also author of "FLES Italian Series: Materials for Teaching Italian, Kindergarten Through Grade 4," Villa Walsh College, 1960. Contributor to A Bicentennial Anthology, edited by Francis J. Manno. Contributor of articles and translations to journals in United States and Italy.

WORK IN PROGRESS: Editing The Papers of Philip Mazzei.

SIDELIGHTS: Margherita Marchione told CA: "We should be proud of our heritage as Italian-Americans. We are part of the mosaic of ethnic cultures that make America the land we love. Now is the time to encourage the study of Italian culture; to unite our efforts and improve the image of the Italian immigrants who brought with them, together with their skills, an appreciation of nature and the arts, reverence for family, love of community, loyalty to their customs and traditions, faith in their adopted nation. There is no more fascinating story than theirs—their failures, tragedies, accomplishments, successes and, above all, their hopes."

*      *      *

## MARCUS, Harold G. 1936-

PERSONAL: Born April 8, 1936, in Worcester, Mass.; son of Abraham and Eva (Golden) Marcus; married Susanne Salomon, August, 1957 (divorced, 1967); married Elizabeth Johnston (an editor), August, 1968. Education: Clark University, B.A. (with honors), 1958; Boston University, M.A., 1959, Ph.D., 1964. Home: 415 Orchard, East Lansing, Mich. 48823. Office: Department of History, Michigan State University, East Lansing, Mich. 48824.

CAREER: Haile Selassie I University, Addis Ababa, Ethiopia, visiting assistant professor of history, 1961-63; Howard University, Washington, D.C., assistant professor of history, 1963-68; Michigan State University, East Lansing, associate professor, 1968-74, professor of history, 1974—. Member: American Historical Association, African Studies Association, Royal Geographical Society (fellow). Awards, honors: Grants from Hoover Institution, 1965, 1968, from Smithsonian Institution, 1966, from Institute of International Education, 1969-70, and from Social Science Research Council, 1970, 1976-77.

WRITINGS: (Contributor) Challenge and Response in Internal Conflict, Volume III, American University Press, 1967; (contributor) Norman Bennett, editor, Leadership in Eastern Africa, Boston University Press, 1968; (contributor) L. H. Gann and Peter Duignan, editors, Colonialism in Africa, 1870-1960, Cambridge University Press, 1969; The Modern History of Ethiopia and Somalia: A Critical Bibliography, two volumes, Hoover Institution, in cooperation with Smithsonian Institution, 1972; The Life and Times of Menilek II: Ethiopia, 1844-1913, Clarendon Press, 1975. Contributor of over sixty articles and reviews to historical and African affairs journals.

WORK IN PROGRESS: A biography of Haile Selassie I of Ethiopia.

*      *      *

## MARDEN, Charles F(rederick) 1902-

PERSONAL: Born April 17, 1902, in Newport, N.H.; son of Albion S. (a physician) and Laura (McEachern) Marden; married Freda Wobber, July 28, 1930; children: Philip W. Education: Dartmouth College, B.A., 1923; Columbia University, M.A., 1926, Ph.D., 1935. Politics: Liberal Democrat. *Religion:* Protestant. *Home and office:* Highwood-Easton Ave., Somerset, N.J. 08873.

*CAREER:* Rutgers University, New Brunswick, N.J., instructor, 1928-35, assistant professor, 1935-57, associate professor, 1957-62, professor of sociology, 1962-67; Holy Cross College, Worcester, Mass., professor of sociology, 1967-70, professor emeritus, 1970—. Reconciliation master, Superior Court of New Jersey, 1957-60; president, Urban League of New Brunswick; member of New Brunswick Tuberculosis and Health Leagues; former member, Franklin Township Planning Board; former chairman, Franklin Township Human Rights Commission. *Member:* American Sociological Association, Eastern Sociological Association.

*WRITINGS: Rotary and Its Brothers,* Princeton University Press, 1935; *Minorities in American Society,* American Book Co., 1952, 4th edition (with Gladys Meyer), Van Nostrand, 1973.

*WORK IN PROGRESS:* A fifth edition of *Minorities in American Society,* with Gladys Meyer, for Van Nostrand.

*        *        *

## MARGENAU, Henry     1901-

*PERSONAL:* Born April 30, 1901, in Bielefeld, Germany; naturalized U.S. citizen; son of Frederick and Karoline (Wagemann) Margenau; married Louise Margarethe Noe, May 28, 1932; children: Rolf Carl, Annemarie Louise, Henry F., Jr. *Education:* Midland Lutheran College, A.B., 1924; University of Nebraska, M.Sc., 1926; Yale University, Ph.D., 1929. *Home:* 173 Westwood Rd., New Haven, Conn. 06525. *Office:* 44 S.P.L., Yale University, New Haven, Conn. 06520.

*CAREER:* University of Nebraska, Lincoln, instructor in physics, 1926-27; Yale University, New Haven, Conn., assistant professor, 1931-40, associate professor, 1940-45, professor of physics, 1945-47, professor of physics and natural philosophy, 1947-49, Eugene Higgins Professor of Physics and Natural Philosophy, 1949—. Member of Institute for Advanced Study, 1939-40; member of radiation weapons committee, Institute for Defense Analysis. Distinguished visiting professor, University of Pennsylvania, 1959; visiting professor at University of Heidelberg, University of Fribourg, University of Tokyo, University of California, University of Washington, Seattle, Whitman College, Haverford College, and Carleton College. Member of World Council of Churches Committee on Atomic War, 1954-56. Consultant to Lockheed Aviation Co., RAND Corp., U.S. Air Force, and U.S. Navy.

*MEMBER:* International Academy of Philosophy of Science, American Academy of Arts and Sciences, Philosophy of Science Association (president, 1950-60). *Awards, honors:* L.H.D., Carleton College, 1954; D.Sc., University of Nebraska, 1957, Hartwick College, 1964; LL.D., Dalhousie University, 1960, Rhode Island College, 1962; D.Pub.Serv., Midland College, 1965. Michigan State University Centennial award, 1955; DeVane Medal, 1971.

*WRITINGS:* (With R. D. Lindsay) *Foundations of Physics,* Wiley, 1936, Dover, 1942; (with G. M. Murphy) *Mathematics of Physics and Chemistry,* Van Nostrand, Volume I, 1943, 2nd edition, 1956, Volume II, 1964; *Nature of Physical Reality,* McGraw, 1950; *Open Vistas,* Yale University Press, 1963; *Ethics and Science,* Van Nostrand, 1966; *Theory of Intermolecular Forces,* Pergamon, 1969; (editor) *Integrative Principles of Modern Thought,* Gordon & Breach, 1972. Consulting editor, Time-Life Science Series.

Contributor of about two hundred research articles to journals.

*WORK IN PROGRESS: Philosophy of Quantum Mechanics.*

*        *        *

## MARGOLIS, Joseph     1924-

*PERSONAL:* Born May 16, 1924, in Newark, N.J.; son of Harry J. (a dentist) and Bluma (Goldfarb) Margolis; married Cynthia Baimas, April 14, 1948 (divorced, 1968); married Clorinda G. Hunter (a clinical psychologist), August 24, 1968; children: (first marriage) Paul, Michael, Ellen; (second marriage) Ann, Jennifer. *Education:* Drew University, B.A., 1947; Columbia University, M.A., 1950, Ph.D., 1953. *Home:* 422 Catharine St., Philadelphia, Pa. 19147. *Office:* Department of Philosophy, Temple University, Philadelphia, Pa. 19122.

*CAREER:* Cooper Union, New York City, lecturer in philosophy, 1953; Columbia University, New York City, lecturer in philosophy, 1954; Long Island University, New York City, instructor, 1947-54, assistant professor of philosophy, 1954-56; University of South Carolina, Columbia, assistant professor of philosophy, 1956-58; University of Cincinnati, Cincinnati, Ohio, associate professor, 1960-64, professor of philosophy, 1964-65, senior research associate in psychiatry, 1960-65; University of Western Ontario, London, professor of philosophy and head of department, 1965-67; Temple University, Philadelphia, Pa., professor of philosophy, 1968—. Visiting assistant professor at Trinity College, Hartford, Conn., 1955, 1956; visiting associate professor, Northwestern University, 1958; visiting assistant professor, University of California, Berkeley, 1958-59; visiting professor, Columbia University, 1960, 1965, University of Minnesota, 1964, University of Toronto, 1967-68, University of Utah, 1968, University of Calgary, 1968, and New York University, 1970-71. *Military service:* U.S. Army, 1943-45; received Purple Heart.

*MEMBER:* American Philosophical Association, American Association of University Professors. *Awards, honors:* National Institutes of Mental Health special fellow, 1962-63; Canada Council grant, 1967, 1968.

*WRITINGS:* (Editor) *Philosophy Looks at the Arts,* Scribner, 1962, 2nd edition, Temple University Press, 1978; *The Language of Art and Art Criticism,* Wayne State University Press, 1965; *Psychotherapy and Morality,* Random House, 1966; (editor) *Contemporary Ethical Theory,* Random House, 1966; (editor) *An Introduction to Philosophical Inquiry,* Knopf, 1968, 2nd edition, 1978; (editor) *Fact and Existence,* University of Toronto Press, 1969.

*Values and Conduct,* Oxford University Press, 1971; *Knowledge and Existence,* Oxford University Press, 1973; *Negativities: The Limits of Life,* C. E. Merrill, 1975; *Persons and Minds,* D. Reidel, 1977; *Art and Philosophy,* Humanities, 1978. Contributor to *Encyclopaedia Britannica.* Contributor of about two hundred articles and reviews to learned journals and popular magazines, including *American Scholar, Humanist, Nation,* and *Society.* Contributing editor, *Book Forum,* 1972—; member of advisory board, *Social Theory and Practice,* 1972—; editor, *Philosophical Monographs,* 1975—.

*WORK IN PROGRESS: Perception and Language; Humane Issues.*

## MARKEL, Lester 1894-1977

*PERSONAL:* Born January 9, 1894, in New York, N.Y.; son of Jacob Leo (a banker) and Lillian (Hecht) Markel; married Meta Edman, April 3, 1917; children: Helen. *Education:* Attended College of the City of New York (now City College of the City University of New York), 1912-13; Columbia School of Journalism, Litt.B., 1914. *Politics:* Independent. *Home:* 135 Central Park W., New York, N.Y. 10023. *Office:* 10 Columbus Cir., New York, N.Y. 10019.

*CAREER: New York Tribune,* New York City, late night editor, 1915-19, assistant managing editor, 1919-23; *New York Times,* New York City, Sunday editor, 1923-65, associate editor, 1965-69; free-lance writer and editorial consultant, 1969-77. Moderator and editor of television program, "News in Perspective," 1963-69. Distinguished visiting professor, Fairleigh Dickinson University, 1969-77. *Member:* International Press Institute (founder), American Society of Newspaper Editors, Council on Foreign Relations. *Awards, honors:* Litt.D., New School for Social Research, 1953; Dr. Humane Letters, Bates College, 1953.

*WRITINGS:* (Editor with others) *Public Opinion and Foreign Policy,* Harper, 1958; *What You Don't Know Can Hurt You: A Study of Public Opinion and Public Emotion,* Public Affairs Press, 1972, revised edition, Quadrangle, 1973; (editor) *World in Review,* Rand McNally, 1972; (with Audrey March) *Global Challenge to the United States: A Study of the Problems, the Perils, and the Proposed Solutions Involved in Washington's Search for a New Role in the World,* Fairleigh Dickinson University Press, 1976. Contributor of articles to *Harper's, Saturday Review,* and *Atlantic.*†

(Died October 23, 1977)

\* \* \*

## MARLOR, Clark Strang 1922-

*PERSONAL:* Born November 18, 1922, in Camden, N.J.; son of Alan F. (a freight agent) and Laura (Strang) Marlor. *Education:* Carnegie-Mellon University, B.F.A., 1945; University of Michigan, M.A., 1946; New York University, D.Ed., 1961. *Residence:* Brooklyn, N.Y. *Office:* Department of Speech and Dramatic Art, Adelphi University, Garden City, N.Y. 11530.

*CAREER:* Kalamazoo College, Kalamazoo, Mich., instructor, 1946-47; Miami University, Oxford, Ohio, instructor, 1947-50; Queens College (now Queens College of the City University of New York), Flushing, N.Y., instructor, 1950-55; Adelphi University, Garden City, N.Y., 1956—, began as associate professor, currently professor of speech art and coordinator of M.A. program in speech arts and educational theatre. *Member:* American Association of University Professors, American Theatre Association, Speech Communication Association (chairman of Readers Theatre Bibliography Committee), Victorian Society in America, Salmagundi Club (honorary member).

*WRITINGS:* (With Dorothy Mulgrave and Elmer Baker) *Bibliography of Speech and Allied Areas,* Chilton, 1962; *A History of the Brooklyn Art Association,* James F. Carr, 1970. Contributor to *Antiques Magazine.*

*WORK IN PROGRESS: The Society of Independent Artists, 1917-1944.*

*SIDELIGHTS:* Clark Marlor has traveled extensively in England and Japan and has visited the Scandinavian countries, France, Switzerland, Italy, Greece, Turkey, Lebanon, Egypt, India. Thailand, Republic of China, and Philippines. *Avocational interests:* Gardening, swimming, and antiques.

## MARRINER, Ernest (Cummings) 1891-

*PERSONAL:* Born October 16, 1891, in Bridgton, Me.; son of Willis E. (a grocer) and Margie (Whitney) Marriner; married Eleanor Creech, June 17, 1917 (deceased); children: Ernest C., Jr., Ruth Eleanor (Mrs. Eugene Szopa). *Education:* Colby College, A.B., 1913; Suffolk University, A.M., 1937. *Politics:* Republican. *Religion:* Baptist. *Home:* 17 Winter St., Waterville, Me. 04901. *Office:* Colby College, Waterville, Me. 04901.

*CAREER:* Teacher at Hebron Academy, Hebron, Me., 1913-20; Maine representative, Ginn & Co., 1921-23; Colby College, Waterville, Me., professor of English, 1923-60, librarian, 1923-29, dean of men, 1929-46, dean of faculty, 1946-57, historian, 1960—. Trustee, Thomas College, 1963—; member of State Archives Board of Maine; member of State Board of Education of Maine, 1949-72. Presents weekly radio program devoted to history of Maine communities. *Member:* American Association for State and Local History, New England Association of College Deans, Maine League of Historical Societies, Maine Folklore Society, Waterville Historical Society (president, 1962-76). *Awards, honors:* L.H.D., Colby College, 1954, University of Maine, 1957; award of merit from American Association for State and Local History, 1966; Litt. D., Thomas College, 1975; Marriner Hall of Colby College, the Marriner Library of Thomas College, and the Marriner Assembly Room of Waterville Historical Society were named in his honor.

*WRITINGS*—All published by Colby College Press: *Kennebec Yesterdays,* 1954; *Remembered Maine,* 1957; *History of Colby College,* 1962; *Man of Mayflower Hill,* 1966. Contributor to *Down East.*

\* \* \*

## MARSH, Leonard (Charles) 1906-

*PERSONAL:* Born September 24, 1906, in England; son of William James Andersen (a contractor) and Anne (Underwood) Marsh; married Beatrice Wright (a radio producer), July 1, 1946. *Education:* University of London, B.Sc. (first class honors), 1928; McGill University, M.A., 1930, Ph.D., 1940. *Politics:* "Radical humanist." *Religion:* Unitarian Universalist. *Home:* 3405 West 18th Ave., Vancouver, British Columbia, Canada.

*CAREER:* McGill University, Montreal, Quebec, director of social sciences research, 1931-41; Dominion Government, Ottawa, Ontario, research adviser, Committee on Reconstruction, 1941-44; United Nations Relief and Rehabilitation Administration, senior information officer, Washington, D.C., London, and Geneva, 1944-46; University of British Columbia, Vancouver, research professor, School of Social Work, and special lecturer, School of Architecture, 1947-64, professor of educational sociology, faculty of education, 1964-72, professor emeritus, 1972—.

*MEMBER:* Community Planning Association of Canada, Canadian Association for Adult Education, Canadian Sociology and Anthropology Association, United Nations Association, World Association of World Federalists, Amateur Chamber Music Players. *Awards, honors:* LL.D., York University, 1977, and McMaster University, 1978.

*WRITINGS: Canadians In and Out of Work,* Oxford University Press, 1940; *Report on Social Security for Canada,* Queen's Printer, 1943; *Rebuilding a Neighbourhood,* University of British Columbia, 1950; *Communities in Canada,* McClelland & Stewart, 1970; *At Home with Music,* Versatile Publishing (Vancouver), 1972; *Cats We Have Known,* Versatile Publishing, 1973; *Education in Action,* Versatile Publishing, 1973. Editor, "McGill Social Research" series, 1930-40. Contributor to journals and magazines.

*WORK IN PROGRESS: Educational Imperatives for the 1970's,* a book on the need for international and community education.

*AVOCATIONAL INTERESTS:* Playing violin, viola, and violoncello, with chamber music groups.

\* \* \*

## MARSHALL, Charles Burton 1908-

*PERSONAL:* Born March 25, 1908, in Catskill, N.Y.; son of Caleb C. (a brick manufacturer) and Alice (Beeman) Marshall; married Doris L. Smith (divorced, 1958); married Betty L. O'Brien (a secretary), August 1, 1958; children: (first marriage) Charles R., Jean (Mrs. Charles E. Vickery). *Education:* Attended Texas College of Mines and Metallurgy (now University of Texas at El Paso), 1927-30; University of Texas, A.B., 1931, A.M., 1932; Harvard University, Ph.D., 1939. *Home:* 4106 North Randolph St., Arlington, Va. 22207. *Office:* Suite 1700, 1500 Wilson Blvd., Arlington, Va. 22209.

*CAREER:* Consultant to Intergovernmental Committee on Refugees, 1946-47; staff consultant, Committee on Foreign Affairs, U.S. House of Representatives, 1947-50; member of policy planning staff, U.S. Department of State, 1950-53; political advisor to prime minister of Pakistan, 1955-57; research associate, Washington Center of Foreign Policy Research, 1957—; visiting scholar, Carnegie Endowment for International Peace, 1958-59; alumni visiting professor of international studies, University of North Carolina, 1960-61; School of Advanced International Studies, Washington, D.C., professor of international politics, 1965-75. Centennial visiting professor, Texas A & M University, 1976. *Military service:* U.S. Army, 1942-46; became lieutenant colonel. *Member:* Council on Foreign Relations, Washington Institute of Foreign Affairs, Cosmos Club, Harvard Club of Washington.

*WRITINGS: The Limits of Foreign Policy,* Holt, 1954, enlarged edition, Johns Hopkins Press, 1968; *The Exercise of Sovereignty,* Johns Hopkins Press, 1965; *The Cold War: A Concise History,* F. Watts, 1965; *Crisis over Rhodesia: A Skeptical View,* Johns Hopkins Press, 1967.

*WORK IN PROGRESS:* A memoir concerning Dean Acheson's ideas; a study of political issues pertinent to southern Africa in international affairs, especially the South West Africa (Namibia) issue.

*SIDELIGHTS:* Charles Marshall visited southern Africa in 1965, 1966, 1968, 1971, 1972, and 1974.

*BIOGRAPHICAL/CRITICAL SOURCES:* Henry Paolucci, *Peace, War, and the Presidency,* McGraw, 1968.

\* \* \*

## MARSHALL, Helen E(dith) 1898-

*PERSONAL:* Born October 25, 1898, in Braman, Okla.; daughter of David Conwell (a blacksmith) and Laura (Souter) Marshall. *Education:* College of Emporia, A.B., 1923; University of Chicago, M.A., 1929; Duke University, Ph.D., 1934. *Religion:* Christian Science. *Home:* 960 Tanglewood Dr., Mountain Home, Ark. 72653.

*CAREER:* Teacher in public schools of Kansas, Colorado, and New Mexico, 1916-31; University of New Mexico,

Albuquerque, instructor in history, 1930-31; Eastern New Mexico College (now University), Portales, professor of history, and head of department of social science, 1934-35; Illinois State University, Normal, 1935-67, began as instructor, became professor of American history. Consultant to American Nurses Association Historical Committee, 1965-66. *Member:* American Historical Association, Organization of American Historians, National Press Woman's Association, United Nations Association of U.S.A., Illinois Woman's Press Association, Phi Beta Kappa, Delta Kappa Gamma, Phi Alpha Theta. *Awards, honors:* U.S. Public Health Grant for research on Mary Adelaide Nutting, 1964 and 1965.

*WRITINGS: Dorothea Dix: Forgotten Samaritan* (Book-of-the-Month Club alternate, 1937), University of North Carolina Press, 1937, reprinted, 1967; *Grandest of Enterprises,* Illinois State University Press, 1956; *The Eleventh Decade,* Illinois State University Press, 1967; *Mary Adelaide Nutting: Pioneer in Modern Nursing,* Johns Hopkins Press, 1972. Contributor of articles to *World Book, Education Today, Journal of Illinois Historical Society,* and *New Mexico Quarterly.*

*WORK IN PROGRESS:* Biography of Jesse Fell of Bloomington, Illinois; Souters and Marshalls, a family saga.

\* \* \*

## MARSHALL, Howard D(rake) 1924-1972

April 9, 1924—August 15, 1972; American economist and educator. Obituaries: *New York Times,* August 22, 1972. (See index for *CA* sketch)

\* \* \*

## MARSHALL, Robert G. 1919-

*PERSONAL:* Born February 19, 1919, in Houston, Tex.; son of Luther P. (a businessman) and Nancy (May) Marshall; married Kathryn Keller, August 27, 1949; children: Christoph, Ann, Philip. *Education:* Rice University, B.A., 1941, M.A., 1946; Yale University, Ph.D., 1950. *Politics:* Independent. *Religion:* Episcopalian. *Office:* Department of Modern Languages, Sweet Briar College, Sweet Briar, Va. 24595.

*CAREER:* Yale University, New Haven, Conn., instructor in French, 1947-49; Texas Woman's University, Denton, assistant professor of French, 1949-51; Wells College, Aurora, N.Y., assistant professor, 1951-55, associate professor, 1955-57, professor of Romance languages, 1957-72, chairman of department, 1955-72; Sweet Briar College, Sweet Briar, Va., professor of French and director of Junior Year in France, 1972—. *Military service:* U.S. Army, 1942-45; became captain. *Member:* American Association of Teachers of French, Modern Language Association of America. *Awards, honors:* American Council of Learned Societies grant, 1954; Danforth Foundation grant, 1957; Fulbright grant for research in Rome, 1959-60.

*WRITINGS:* (Editor with Frederic C. St. Aubyn) Jean Paul Sartre, *Les Mouches,* Harper, 1963; (editor with Marion Sonnenfeld) *Wert und Wort,* Wells College Press, 1965; (editor and author of notes with St. Aubyn) *Trois Pieces surrealistes,* Appleton, 1969; (editor) *Short-Title Catalog of Books Printed in Italy and of Books in Italian Printed Abroad, 1501-1600,* three volumes, G. K. Hall, 1970. Contributor to language journals.

*WORK IN PROGRESS:* Translating *Histoire d'une Grecque moderne* for publication in English as *A Greek Girl's Story* (provisional title).

*AVOCATIONAL INTERESTS:* Working in theater (has directed several French plays).

\* \* \*

## MARSZALEK, John F(rancis, Jr.) 1939-

*PERSONAL:* Surname is pronounced *Mars*-ah-lack; born July 5, 1939, in Buffalo, N.Y.; son of John F. (a grocer) and Regina (Sierakowski) Marszalek; married Jeanne A. Kozmer, October 16, 1965; children: John F. III, Christopher H., James S. *Education:* Canisius College, A.B., 1961; University of Notre Dame, A.M., 1963, Ph.D., 1968. *Religion:* Roman Catholic. *Home:* 108 Grand Ridge, Starkville, Miss. 39759. *Office:* Department of History, Mississippi State University, Starkville, Miss. 39762.

*CAREER:* Canisius College, Buffalo, N.Y., instructor, 1967-68; Gannon College, Erie, Pa., assistant professor, 1968-72, associate professor of history, 1972-73; Mississippi State University, Starkville, associate professor of history, 1973—. *Military service:* U.S. Army, 1965-67; became captain. *Member:* American Historical Association, Organization of American Historians, Mississippi Historical Society. *Awards, honors:* National Endowment for the Humanities Summer Award for Younger Humanists, 1971; American Council of Learned Societies grant, 1973-74.

*WRITINGS: Court Martial: A Black Man in America,* Scribner, 1972; (with Sadye Wier) *A Black Businessman in White Mississippi, 1886-1974,* University Press of Mississippi, 1977. Contributor to *Dictionary of American Biography.* Contributor of articles and reviews to *American Heritage, Civil War Times Illustrated, Northwest Ohio Quarterly, Duquesne Review, Ohio History,* and other journals.

*WORK IN PROGRESS: Civil War/Reconstruction Diary of Miss Emma Holmes of Charleston, S.C.,* for Louisiana State University Press; *Sherman's Other War: The General and the Civil War Press;* a book-length study of black congressman George Washington Murray; articles on black perceptions in late nineteenth-century America and on Civil War generals.

\* \* \*

## MARTIN, Boyd A(rcher) 1911-

*PERSONAL:* Born March 3, 1911, in Cottonwood, Idaho; son of Archer Olmstead (a farmer) and Norah Claudine (Imbler) Martin; married Grace Charlotte Swingler, December 29, 1933; children: (adopted) William Archer, Michael Archer. *Education:* University of Idaho, student, 1929-30, 1935-36, B.S., 1936; Pasadena Junior College, student, 1931-32; Stanford University, A.M., 1936, Ph.D., 1943. *Home:* 1314 Walenta Dr., Moscow, Idaho 83843. *Office:* Institute of Human Behavior, University of Idaho, Moscow, Idaho 83843.

*CAREER:* University of Idaho, Moscow, instructor in political science, 1938-39; Stanford University, Stanford, Calif., acting instructor in political science, 1939-40; University of Idaho, instructor, 1940-43, assistant professor, 1943-44, associate professor, 1944-47, professor, 1947-70, William E. Borah Distinguished Professor of Political Science, 1970—, head of department of social sciences, 1947-55, assistant dean of College of Letters and Sciences, 1947-55, dean of College of Letters and Sciences, 1955-70, director of Bureau of Public Affairs Research, 1959—, and Institute of Human Behavior, 1970—. Stanford University, visiting associate professor, summer, 1946, visiting professor of political sci-

ence, 1952. Chairperson, William E. Borah Foundation on the Outlawry of War, 1947-55; member of Commission to Study the Organization of Peace. Chairperson of humanities section, regional meetings of UNESCO in Denver and San Francisco; research affiliate, American Association for the United Nations. Member of DuPont Educational Conference, 1957; Northwest Conference on Higher Education, member of steering committee, 1960-67, president, 1966-67. Chairperson, Idaho Advisory Council on Higher Education, 1964-67; member of Constitutional Revision Commission of the State of Idaho, 1965-70; chairperson, Idaho Partners of the Americas, 1971. Consultant to Idaho Municipal League.

*MEMBER:* American Political Science Association (member of executive council, 1952-53), Foreign Policy Association, American Society for Public Administration, American Association of University Professors, Western Political Science Association (president, 1950), Pacific Northwest Political Science Association, Phi Beta Kappa, Phi Gamma Mu, Kappa Delta Pi, Alpha Phi Omega, Delta Phi, Pi Sigma Alpha.

*WRITINGS: The Direct Primary in Idaho,* Stanford University Press, 1947; (with Joseph S. Roucek and others) *Introduction to Political Science,* Crowell, 1950; (with others) *Strengthening the United Nations,* Harper, 1957; (contributor) Frank H. Jonas, editor, *Western Politics,* University of Utah Press, 1961, revised edition published as *Politics in the American West,* 1969, *Supplement,* 1971; (editor with Ray C. Jolly and Glenn W. Nichols) *State and Local Government in Idaho: A Reader,* Bureau of Public Affairs Research, University of Idaho, 1970. Also author of *Idaho Voting Trends: Party Realignment and Percentage of Votes for Candidates, Parties, and Elections, 1890-1974,* 1975. Contributor to political science and other journals. State editor, *National Municipal Review;* member of editorial board, *Western Political Quarterly.*

*SIDELIGHTS:* Boyd Martin traveled more than five thousand miles by car through Iron Curtain and communist countries of Europe in 1960. In 1964 he represented the Department of State in the Alliance for Progress program in Ecuador, and in 1970 traveled widely in Africa. He also has toured in the Middle East, China, and southern Asia.

\* \* \*

## MARTIN, Geoffrey John 1934-

*PERSONAL:* Born March 9, 1934, in London, England; son of Charles Walter (an education officer) and Elizabeth K. (Doughty) Martin; married Norma Jean Bechtel, January, 1965; children: Thaddius Stuart, Amanda Gale. *Education:* London School of Economics and Political Science, B.Sc., 1956; Kings College, London, P.G.C.E., 1957; University of Florida, M.A., 1958. *Home:* 82 Banks Rd., Fairfield, Conn. 06430. *Office:* Department of Geography, Southern Connecticut State College, New Haven, Conn. 06515.

*CAREER:* Eastern Michigan University, Ypsilanti, assistant professor of geography, 1959-65; Wisconsin State University, Platteville (now University of Wisconsin—Platteville), assistant professor of geography, 1965-66; Southern Connecticut State College, New Haven, professor of geography, 1966—, chairperson of department, 1976—. *Member:* Association of American Geographers (chairperson, committee on association history and archives). *Awards, honors:* National Council for Geographic Education grant, 1968, for *Mark Jefferson: Geographer;* American Council of Learned Societies Grant-in-Aid for *Ellsworth Huntington: His Life and Thought;* American Philosophical Society grant for *The Life and Thought of Isaiah Bowman.*

WRITINGS: Mark Jefferson: Geographer, Eastern Michigan University, 1968; Ellsworth Huntington: His Life and Thought, Archon Books, 1973.

WORK IN PROGRESS: The Life and Thought of Isaiah Bowman; The History of the Association of American Geographers, with P. E. James.

AVOCATIONAL INTERESTS: International chess playing.

*    *    *

## MARTIN, Wendy 1940-

PERSONAL: Born March 15, 1940, in Coral Gables, Fla.; daughter of Earl E. (an engineer) and Teresa (deLuca) Martin. Education: University of California, Berkeley, B.A., 1962; University of California, Davis, Ph.D., 1968. Office: Department of English, Queens College of the City University of New York, Flushing, N.Y. 11367.

CAREER: Queens College of the City University of New York, Flushing, N.Y., assistant professor of American literature, 1968—. Member: Modern Language Association of America, American Studies Association.

WRITINGS: (Author of critical preface) Susanna Rowson, Charlotte Temple: A Tale of Truth, Charlotte's Daughter, [and] Reuben and Rachel (three novels), Garrett Press, 1971; (contributor) Vivian Gornick and Barbara K. Moran, editors, Women in Sexist Society, Basic Books, 1971; (editor) The American Sisterhood: Feminist Writings from Colonial Times to the Present, Harper, 1972; (editor) A Chronological Reading of Adrienne Rich's Poetry, Norton, 1974. Also author of a monograph on Adrienne Rich for Scribner, 1977, and contributor to Essays in Contemporary American Humor, 1977. Contributor to literary criticism journals. Editor-in-chief, Women's Studies: An Interdisciplinary Journal, 1972—.

*    *    *

## MARTINI, Virgilio 1903-
### (Letrusco)

PERSONAL: Born May 3, 1903, in Fiesole, Firenze, Italy; son of Luigi (a mason) and Annunziata (Manzani) Martini; married Tina Volpi (a schoolteacher), July 16, 1955; children: Sandra. Education: Attended technical secondary school in Florence, receiving his diploma at seventeen. Politics: "I detest politics and all political parties." Religion: "Until fourteenth year of age Catholic; then agnostic." Home: Stentatoio di San Francesco, 50065 Pontassieve, Firenze, Italy.

CAREER: Left Florence at the age of eighteen to see the world, working in Rome, Milan, Paris, and then in fifteen countries of South and Central America at an assortment of jobs, including hod carrier, cowboy, teacher of Italian and French and translator from those languages and Spanish, bank clerk, advertising writer, caricaturist, assistant to playwrights, salesman for a vermouth company, reporter, and book publisher; founder, owner, and manager of Coccodrillo, Firenze, Italy, 1954-55, Giornale di Jesolo, Jesolo, Italy, 1963-64, Tritone, Jesolo, 1965, and La Voce di Jesolo, Jesolo, 1965-72.

WRITINGS: Il mondo senza donne (novel; originally published under pseudonym Letrusco), Aliprandi & Martini (Guayaquil, Ecuador), 1936, translation by Emile Capouya published as The World without Women, Dial, 1971; L'Eta imbecille (autobiography to age eighteen), Guanda (Parma, Italy), 1948; La Terra sensa il sole (novel based on his play,

"Tornare un passo indietro," written in 1922, but never performed; first published in Venice magazine, Ridotto, February, 1956), Guanda, 1948; (translator from the Spanish) Ramon Diaz Sanchez, Mene (novel), Casa Editrice La Croce del Sud, 1966; La Liberta Sotto i carri armati (novel), Edizioni Tritone (Jesolo), 1972; L'allegra terza guerra mondiale (novel), Edizioni Equatore (Firenze), 1977.

Author of "Il Giro del mondo in 66 giorni," a booklength log of a sea journey from Genoa to Genoa, by way of Africa, Australia, Oceania, and America, published in installments in Voce di Jesolo, May-December, 1971; also author of two unpublished novels, "Il naso alla finestra," and "La selva ascura," and a play, "La Cociata dei miliardari." Contributor to magazines and newspapers in Italy and various countries of South America.

SIDELIGHTS: In a review of Il mondo senza donne, Paul Theroux writes: "Notes of distinct fatuousness are struck throughout the story, but the satire is a success. What begins as a peculiarly Italian nightmare, a phalanx of mincing pederasts scourging motherhood—the triumph of the epicene—becomes universalized into a parable of mankind's folly. Most of it is the best kind of satire made of a vision essentially humane. If Signor Martini's three other novels have not been translated into English, it's about time they were." C. L. Markmann feels that Martini "leaves no aspect of mankind or its works unbloodied—as far as one can determine, at any rate—in this hilariously depressing projection of its future.... Certainly if the book achieves the audience it deserves, [it] will inspire the most stupendous united 'defense' front that any agitprop fantasist could conceive." Catharine Stimpson agrees that Martini is ruthless in his depiction of the human race: "It is easy for a man with Martini's theory of history to be a prophet.... The pattern of his narrative is comic. Yet the tale of malevolence in perpetuity creates a chill skepticism about the efficacy of human will ... Martini's theory sacrifices individuals to the great cycles of history. All of his characters are blatant stereotypes—the Jew a crafty banker, the black a jungle boy, the homosexual a hostile queen, the woman a whore who loves her work.... [He] really likes no one. The absence of warmth is characteristic of satire, but Martini's refusal to permit any good feeling between his characters makes him seem nasty."

Il mondo senza donne has been Martini's most troublesome—and most successful book. When copies of the original publication were sent to Italy, they were "sequestrated" by the Fascist government and Martini was placed on the official blacklist. Not until 1954 was the novel published in Italy, and then in installments in Coccodrillo, a weekly literary magazine. Edizioni Coccodrillo followed up with a bound edition, which brought official action before the Court of Justice in Florence. That prosecution failed, but action against the book was carried to the Court of Appeals in 1956, again with vindication. The novel now is in its seventh Italian printing and has been published in French, Portuguese, Danish, and Swedish translations, as well as in English. Although Il mondo senza donne is Martini's favorite work, he has great fondness for the unperformed play on which he based his other published novel, La Terra senza il sole. He was nineteen when he wrote "Tornare un passo indietro," set in Rome in the year 5000. According to Martini, Pirandello read the manuscript, liked it, and recommended the play to his producer and editor—without success. The author's view of his play fifty years later: "It is excellent and very present and could be a great success."

The play was written in Rome, the novel adaptation in Paris, the novel, Il mondo senze donne, in Ecuador, and L'Eta *imbecille* in Colombia, Paraguay, Argentina, Chile, Peru, Ecuador, and Venezuela. In all, Martini has visited more than forty countries, traveling by every means from tramp steamer to cruise ship, cattle wagon to sleeping car, World War I surplus plane to jet, a bus full of swine to a Mercedes, and by motorcycle, bicycle, pirogue, and on foot. He speaks "very bad" English and Portuguese, but has a translator's ability in French and Spanish.

*BIOGRAPHICAL/CRITICAL SOURCES: Roma,* September 3, 1970; *Kirkus Review,* May 15, 1971; *Journal of Library History,* May 17, 1971; *New Republic,* July 24, 1971; *Atlantic,* August, 1971; *Saturday Review,* August 7, 1971; *Book World,* August 8, 1971; *Nation,* August 30, 1971.

\* \* \*

## MARTON, Endre 1910-

*PERSONAL:* Born October 29, 1910, in Budapest, Hungary; son of Ernoe and Sharon Marton; married Ilona Nyilas (a teacher), December 24, 1943; children: Juli Marton Weber, Kati Marton Wetzel, Andrew Thomas. *Education:* Budapest University, B.A., 1932, Ph.D., 1936. *Religion:* Calvinist Protestant. *Home:* 4213 Leland St., Chevy Chase, Md. 20015.

*CAREER:* Associated Press (AP), Washington, D.C., staff writer, specializing in European, Middle Eastern, and African affairs, diplomatic correspondent. Adjunct professor, School of Foreign Service, Georgetown University. *Member:* White House Correspondents Association, State Department Correspondents Association (past president), Overseas Writers Club (former president). *Awards, honors:* George Polk Award, 1957; Overseas Writers Presidential Award, 1957; Headliners Club Award, 1957.

*WRITINGS: The Forbidden Sky,* Little, Brown, 1971.

*SIDELIGHTS:* In a review of *The Forbidden Sky,* John B. Vought writes: "Endre Marton's remarkable little book is the story of Budapest, 1956. He is uniquely qualified to write of those times, having experienced them as few observers could. He was at once observer and participant—as a political prisoner of the system, and was a Western correspondent whose activity was continually suspect by the authorities.... His particular contribution is to document the little anecdotes and incidents which give a human dimension to the Hungarian uprising. He tells, for example, of the young teenagers, who, having destroyed a Soviet tank, are then in great haste to be home in time for supper lest they incur their mother's wrath.... This is a patriot's tribute to his homeland, and simultaneously an American journalist's appreciation of a tumultous uprising which he observed from beginning to end."

*BIOGRAPHICAL/CRITICAL SOURCES: Detroit News,* January 30, 1972.

\* \* \*

## MARVIN, Philip (Roger) 1916-

*PERSONAL:* Born May 1, 1916, in Troy, N.Y.; son of George G. and Marjorie (Moston) Marvin; married Grace E. Meerbach (an educator), August 22, 1942. *Education:* Rensselaer Polytechnic Institute, B.S., 1937; Indiana University, M.B.A. and D.B.A., 1951; LaSalle University, LL.B., 1954; Institute of Chartered Financial Analysts, C.F.A., 1963. *Home:* 2750 Weston Ridge Dr., Cincinnati, Ohio 45239. *Office:* School of Business, University of Cincinnati, Cincinnati, Ohio 45221.

*CAREER:* General Electric Co., New York City, engineer, 1937-42; Bendix Aviation Corp., New York City, director of chemical and metallurgical engineering, 1943-44; Milwaukee Gas Specialty Co., Milwaukee, Wis., director of research and development, 1945-52; Commonwealth Engineering Co., New York City, vice-president and director, 1952-54; American Viscose Corp., New York City, corporate staff consultant, 1955-56; American Management Association, New York City, manager of Division of Research and Development, 1956-64; Clark, Cooper, Field & Wohl, Inc., New York City, president and director, 1964-65; University of Cincinnati, Cincinnati, Ohio, professor of business administration and dean, 1965—. Lecturer, Bridgeport Engineering Institute, 1937-43, and Junior College of Connecticut, 1940-41; lecturer in war training program, Yale University, 1941-44; lecturer, U.S. Air Force Institute of Technology, 1953-55. Consultant to U.S. Army Air Forces and U.S. Navy, 1944; consultant to National Aeronautics and Space Administration Manned Spacecraft Center.

*MEMBER:* National Academy of Television Arts and Sciences, Newcomen Society, Society of Authors (London, England), Authors Guild, Institute of Directors (London), Institute of Chartered Financial Analysts, New York Society of Security Analysts, Sigma Xi, Tau Beta Pi, Beta Gamma Sigma.

*WRITINGS: Top-Management and Research,* Research Press, 1953, 2nd edition, 1956; *Administrative Management,* Research Press, 1954, 2nd edition, 1954; *Planning New Products,* Penton, Volume I, 1958, Volume II, 1964; *Management Goals: Guidelines and Accountability,* Dow-Jones-Irwin, 1968; *Multiplying Management Effectiveness,* American Management Association, 1971; *Developing Decisions for Action,* Dow-Jones-Irwin, 1971; *Man in Motion,* Dow-Jones-Irwin, 1972; *Product Planning Simplified,* American Management Association, 1972. Also author of filmstrips, "Product Pioneering," 1957, "Detecting and Developing Business for the Future," 1958, "Corporate Development Function," 1959, "Signposts," 1960, "Basic Building Blocks," 1961, "Keys to Ideas," 1962, "F.E.A.D.," 1962, "Steps to Productive Programs," 1963, and "Planning Effective Programs," 1964.

\* \* \*

## MARWICK, M(axwell) G(ay) 1916-

*PERSONAL:* Born June 4, 1916, in Richmond, Natal, South Africa; son of Robert Arthur (a lawyer) and Alice (Angus) Marwick; married Nora Margaret Joan Paton, June 30, 1941; children: Paul David, Robin Leslie. *Education:* Natal University College (now University of Natal), B.A. (with distinction), 1938, University Education Diploma, 1939, M.A. (with distinction), 1945; University of South Africa, B.A., 1950; University of Cape Town, Ph.D., 1961. *Home:* 27 Fewings St., Toowong, Queensland 4066, Australia. *Office:* School of Humanities, Griffith University, Nathan, Queensland 4111, Australia.

*CAREER:* Natal Education Department, Natal, South Africa, teacher of geography, principally at Sastri College, Durban, 1940-45; Colonial Social Science Research Council, research fellow in central Africa, 1946-47; South African Native College (now University College of Fort Hare), Fort Hare, senior lecturer in psychology, 1948-49; University of Natal, Durban, South Africa, lecturer, 1950-53, senior lecturer in sociology, 1953-56, acting director, Institute for Social Research, 1955-56; University of the Witwatersrand, Johannesburg, South Africa, professor of social anthropology and head of department of social anthropology and

African administration, 1957-63; Monash University, Clayton, Victoria, Australia, professor of anthropology and sociology and chairman of department, 1963-68; University of Stirling, Stirling, Scotland, professor of sociology and head of department, 1968-75; Griffith University, Nathan, Queensland, Australia, senior lecturer, 1975-76, reader in humanities, 1976—, acting chairperson of School of Humanities, 1977-78. Simon senior research fellow, University of Manchester, 1962; distinguished visiting professor, Western Michigan University, summers, 1965, 1968, 1970; Florence Purington Visiting Lecturer, Mount Holyoke College, spring, 1968.

*MEMBER:* Royal Anthropological Institute of Great Britain and Northern Ireland (fellow), Association of Social Anthropologists of the British Commonwealth, Australian Anthropological Society, Sociological Association of Australia and New Zealand (president, 1965-67), Australian Institute of Aboriginal Studies.

*WRITINGS: The Modern Family in Social-Anthropological Perspective* (pamphlet; inaugural lecture at University of the Witwatersrand), Witwatersrand University Press, 1958; *Sorcery in Its Social Setting: A Study of the Northern Rhodesian Cewa,* Humanities, 1965; (editor) *Witchcraft and Sorcery,* Penguin, 1970; (author of foreword) Mia Brandel-Syrier, *Reeftown Elite,* Africana Publishing, 1971.

Contributor: Prudence Smith, editor, *Africa in Transition,* Faber, 1958; Raymond Apthorpe, editor, *Social Research and Community Development,* Rhodes-Livingstone Institute, 1961; John Middleton, editor, *Magic, Witchcraft, and Curing,* Natural History Press, 1963; Meyer Fortes and Germaine Dieterlen, editors, *African Systems of Thought,* Oxford University Press, for International African Institute, 1965; Colin Cave, editor, *Man and Morals,* Adult Education Centre (Wangaratta, Victoria), 1966; A. L. Epstein, editor, *The Craft of Social Anthropology,* Tavistock Publications, 1967; H. A. Finlay, editor, *Divorce, Society and the Law,* Butterworth & Co. (Melbourne), 1969; Richard Cavendish, editor, *Man, Myth and Magic,* Purnell & Sons, 1972; *In Memoriam Antonio Jorge Dias,* Instituto de Alta Cultura (Lisbon), 1974. Also contributor to *Encyclopaedia Britannica,* 1974. Contributor to *Listener, Meanjin Quarterly, Africa,* and other journals. Joint editor, *African Studies* (Johannesburg), 1957-63; notes and news editor, *Australian Journal of Sociology,* 1965-67.

*WORK IN PROGRESS:* An article on aspects of African urban life for a *festschrift* for emeritus professor Eileen Krige; field work on alternative life-styles in eastern Australia.

*SIDELIGHTS:* ''A year's sabbatical in England in 1962 and first experience of living in a free country helped me make up my mind to become a voluntary exile from South Africa,'' M. G. Marwick writes. He became an Australian citizen by registration while living there, and is now a citizen of the United Kingdom. He is fluent in Cewa, less so in Zulu, and has a reasonable knowledge of Afrikaans.

\*     \*     \*

## MARX, Gary T. 1938-

*PERSONAL:* Born October 1, 1938, in Hanford, Calif.; son of Donald and Ruth Marx; married Phyllis A. Rakita. *Education:* University of California, Los Angeles, B.A., 1960; University of California, Berkeley, M.A., 1962, Ph.D., 1966. *Office:* Department of Urban Studies and Planning, Massachusetts Institute of Technology, 77 Massachusetts Ave., Cambridge, Mass. 02139.

*CAREER:* Traveled around the world, preparing for the study of comparative race and ethnic relations, 1963-64; University of California, Berkeley, research associate, Survey Research Center, 1965-67, lecturer in sociology, 1966-67; Harvard University, Cambridge, Mass., assistant professor of social relations, 1967-69, lecturer, 1969-73, research associate, Harvard-Massachusetts Institute of Technology Joint Center for Urban Studies, 1967-73; Massachusetts Institute of Technology, Cambridge, associate professor, 1973—. Visiting associate professor or lecturer, Boston College, spring, 1973, University of California, summer, 1974, Wellesley College, fall, 1975, Boston University, spring, 1976. Consultant to National Advisory Commission on Civil Disorder, 1967, Urban Institute, 1970—, and Police Foundation, 1971—. *Member:* American Sociological Association, American Political Science Association, Society for the Study of Social Problems, Society for the Psychological Study of Social Issues. *Awards, honors:* Guggenheim fellow in England and France, 1970-71.

*WRITINGS: The Social Basis of the Support of a Depression Era Extremist: Father Coughlin,* Survey Research Center, University of California, Berkeley, 1962; *Protest and Prejudice,* Harper, 1967, edition with postscript, Torchbooks, 1969; (editor with others) *Confrontation: Psychology and the Problems of Today,* Scott, Foresman, 1970; (editor) *Radical Conflict: Tension and Change in American Society,* Little, Brown, 1971; (with others) *Inquiries in Sociology,* Allyn & Bacon, 1972; (editor) *Muckraking Sociology: Research as Social Criticism,* Transaction Books, 1972; (reviser with N. Goodman) *Society Today,* 3rd edition, Random House, 1978; (editor with Goodman) *Sociology: Classic and Popular,* Random House, in press.

Contributor: C. E. Lincoln, editor, *Is Anybody Listening to Black America?,* Seabury, 1968; M. Minnis and W. Cartwright, editors, *Readings in Deviant Behavior and Social Problems,* W. C. Brown, 1968; C. Bonjean and N. Glenn, editors, *Blacks in America: An Anthology,* Chandler Publishing, 1969; P. Washburn and C. Larson, editors, *Power, Participation and Ideology,* McKay, 1969; M. Goldschmid, editor, *The Negro American and White Racism,* Holt, 1970; C. Anderson, editor, *Sociological Essays and Research: Introductory Readings,* Dorsey, 1970; J. F. Szwed, editor, *Black Americans: A Second Look,* Basic Books, 1970; P. Rose, editor, *Study of Society,* Random House, 1970; H. Nelsen, and others, editors, *The Black Church in America,* Basic Books, 1971; G. Gaviglio and D. Rays, editors, *Society as It Is,* Macmillan, 1971; D. Boesel and P. Rossi, editors, *Cities under Siege,* Basic Books, 1971; D. A. Wilkinson, editor, *Black Revolt: Strategies of Protest,* McCuchan Publishing, 1972; G. Thielbar and S. Feldman, editors, *Issues in Social Inequality,* Little, Brown, 1972; E. Greer, editor, *Black Political Power: A Reader,* Allyn & Bacon, 1972; M. Wolfgang and J. Short, editor, *Collective Violence,* Aldine, 1972; S. Guterman, editor, *The Personality Patterns of Black Americans,* Glendessary, 1972; C. Glock, editor, *Religion in Sociological Perspective,* Wadsworth, 1973; S. McNall, editor, *The Sociological Perspective,* Little, Brown, 1973; B. Franklin and F. Kohout, editors, *Social Psychology and Everyday Life,* McKay, 1973; S. Wasby, editor, *American Government and Politics,* Scribner, 1973; B. Beit-Hallahmi, eidtor, *Research in Religious Behaviour,* Brooks/Cole, 1974; W. Newman, editor, *The Social Meanings of Religion,* Rand McNally, 1974; C. Reasons, editor, *Criminology: A Radical Perspective,* Goodyear, 1974; R. Evans, editor, *Social Movements,* Rand McNally, 1974; J. Rosenbaum and C. Sederberg, editors, *Vigilantism,* University of Pennsylvania, 1975. Contributor to *Encyclopaedia Britannica;* also contributor to *Nations, Phylon, New Republic, Annals* of American Academy of Political and Social Science, *Harvard Review,* and other journals. Associate editor, *Social Problems,* 1969—.

*WORK IN PROGRESS:* With Nathan Glazer, *Race and Ethnic Relations: Social Movements and Social Policy,* for Houghton; with T. Cottle and G. Platt, *Image and Concept; Social Control and Irony.*

\* \* \*

## MARX, Paul 1920-

*PERSONAL:* Born May 8, 1920, in St. Michael, Minn.; son of George (a farmer) and Elizabeth (Rauw) Marx. *Education:* St. John's University, Collegeville, Minn., B.A., 1943; Catholic University of America, Ph.D., 1957. *Home and office:* St. John's University, Collegeville, Minn. 56321.

*CAREER:* Roman Catholic priest of Order of St. Benedict (Benedictines); St. John's University, Collegeville, Minn., associate professor, 1956-71, professor of sociology, 1971—. Member of National Catholic Family Life Committee, 1959-61; founder and director of Marriage and Family Life Workshop; founder and executive director, Human Life Centers, 1974—. Lecturer to U.S. Air Force chaplains, 1968; tutor, International College, Los Angeles, 1977—; also has lectured widely on topics pertaining to marriage and family life. Member of board of directors, Minnesota Citizens Concerned for Life, 1969-77, and Minnesota Council on Family Relations, 1970-76. Consultant on marriage and family life in Australia, 1971.

*MEMBER:* American Sociological Society, American Anthropological Association, American Catholic Liturgical Conference (member of board of directors, 1956-59). *Awards, honors:* American Catholic Sociological Society Award for best book of research, 1957, for *Virgil Michel and the Liturgical Movement.*

*WRITINGS: Virgil Michel and the Liturgical Movement,* Liturgical Press, 1957; *The Death Peddlers: War on the Unborn,* St. John's University Press, 1971; *Death without Dignity,* Liturgical Press, 1976. Also author of *The Mercy Killers,* 1974. Contributor to *America, Social Order,* and other journals.

*WORK IN PROGRESS:* Research on abortion and its effects, both personal and social.

\* \* \*

## MARXHAUSEN, Joanne G. 1935-

*PERSONAL:* Born August 7, 1935, in Seward, Neb.; daughter of Albert Frederick and Lillian (Firnhaber) Prochnow; married Benjamin W. Marxhausen (a professor of art), April 6, 1958; children: Kim, Matthew, Vaughn. *Education:* Attended Concordia Teachers College, Seward, Neb., 1953-54. *Religion:* Lutheran Church—Missouri Synod. *Home:* 815 Cope Ave. W., St. Paul, Minn. 55113.

*WRITINGS*—All juveniles; published by Concordia, except as indicated: *Thank God for Circles,* illustrated by Dan Johnson, Augsburg, 1971; *3 in 1: A Picture of God,* illustrated by husband, Benjamin W. Marxhausen, 1973; *The Mysterious Star,* illustrated by Susan Stoehr Morris, 1974; *Advent Calendar Banner Kit,* 1974; *See His Banners Go,* 1975; *I Am,* illustrated by B. W. Marxhausen, 1975; *If I Should Die/If I Should Live,* illustrated by B. W. Marxhausen, 1975. Also author of two booklets, *Posters,* and *Banners,* for Concordia's "A Nice Place to Live" series.

*WORK IN PROGRESS: If All the World Were Green;* "I Am" series, for Concordia, based on her book of the same title.

*SIDELIGHTS:* Joanne Marxhausen writes: "A career as author happened to me as what seems to me to be the result of 'seeking first the Kingdom of God.' Feeding His lambs and His sheep are my first concern, and so, as wife and mother, preparation of family devotions has been a very important part of my daily activity. I think that my books, all of them being of a religious nature, have come as a result of keeping my mind constantly open to ideas from God for feeding the Gospel of Christ to my family. I believe it is the Holy Spirit who motivates me to write for publication, He who provides the enthusiasm and encouragement I need to carry them out to the point of submitting them for publication even though many other activities 'busy-up' my days."

\* \* \*

## MASON, Betty (Oxford) 1930-

*PERSONAL:* Born October 10, 1930, in Sikes, La.; daughter of Reuben E. and Della (Killebrew) Oxford; married David E. Mason, August 11, 1950 (divorced, 1964); children: David, Paul. *Education:* Louisiana State University, B.S., 1950, M.E.D., 1967; University of Florida, M.Ed., 1967. *Office:* Florida Southern College, Lakeland, Fla. 33802.

*CAREER:* Teacher in Louisville, Ky., 1950-52, Atlanta, Ga., 1952-53, and Baton Rouge, La., 1962-66; Florida Southern College, Lakeland, instructor in elementary education and educational psychology, 1966—. *Member:* Kappa Delta Pi.

*WRITINGS*—Juvenile: *The Story of Joseph,* Convention Press, 1966; *I Go to School,* Broadman, 1971. Curriculum writer for Southern Baptist Convention, 1957—.††

\* \* \*

## MASON, Julian D(ewey), Jr. 1931-

*PERSONAL:* Born March 25, 1931, in Washington, N.C.; son of Julian Dewey (a salesman) and Lillie (Spencer) Mason; married Elsie May, June 9, 1954; children: Christopher, Rebecca, Emily. *Education:* University of North Carolina, A.B., 1953, Ph.D., 1962; George Peabody College for Teachers, M.A., 1954. *Politics:* Democrat. *Religion:* Quaker. *Home:* 5909 Ruth Dr., Charlotte, N.C. 28215. *Office:* Department of English, University of North Carolina at Charlotte, Charlotte, N.C. 28223.

*CAREER:* High school English teacher in Bristol, Tenn., 1954-55; University of Maryland Overseas Program, Gelnhausen, Germany, part-time instructor in English, 1956-57; University of North Carolina, Chapel Hill, instructor, 1960-62, assistant professor of English and director of student aid, 1962-66; University of North Carolina at Charlotte, assistant professor, 1966-68, associate professor, 1968-72, professor of English, 1972—, chairperson of department, 1977—, assistant to chancellor, 1967, American studies coordinator, 1974-77. Specialist in American cultural history, Library of Congress, 1968-70. *Military service:* U.S. Army, 1955-57. *Member:* Modern Language Association of America, American Studies Association, College Language Association, Society for Study of Southern Literature, South Atlantic Modern Language Association (chairperson of American literature section, 1976-77), Southeastern American Studies Association (member of executive committee, 1972-74; president, 1976-77), Order of the Golden Fleece, Phi Beta Kappa.

*WRITINGS: Search Party* (poems), Pageant, 1953; (editor) *The Poems of Phillis Wheatley,* University of North Carolina Press, 1966; (contributor) Louis D. Rubin, Jr., editor, *A Bibliographical Guide to the Study of Southern Literature,* Louisiana State University Press, 1969. Contributor of articles to *Mississippi Quarterly, Early American Literature, Southern Literary Journal, Quarterly Journal of the Library of Congress, American Speech, Southern Humanities Review,* and other journals; contributor of poems to *Carolina Quarterly, Crucible,* and *Barnstormer.*

*WORK IN PROGRESS:* Three books, one on Owen Wister, one on the South in 1776, and one a revision of his Ph.D. dissertation, *The Critical Reception of American Negro Authors in American Magazines, 1800-1885;* poems, short stories, articles, and research.

*AVOCATIONAL INTERESTS:* Collecting rare books, primarily American.

\*        \*        \*

## MASSMAN, Virgil Frank   1929-

*PERSONAL:* Born July 19, 1929, in New Munich, Minn.; son of Anton Herman (a farmer) and Christine (Eichoff) Massman; married Mary Nancy Bachhuber (a nurse), August 23, 1958; children: Samuel, Donna, Ruth Ann, Sara Ann. *Education:* St. John's University, Collegeville, Minn., B.A., 1957; University of Minnesota, M.A. (English) and M.A. (library science), 1960; University of Michigan, Ph.D., 1970. *Home:* 3411 Vivian Ave., St. Paul, Minn. 55112. *Office:* J. J. Hill Reference Library, Fourth & Market Sts., St. Paul, Minn. 55102.

*CAREER:* Bemidji State College, Bemidji, Minn., reference librarian, 1960-65; University of South Dakota, Vermillion, associate professor of English, 1965-66, director of libraries, 1966-71; J. J. Hill Reference Library, St. Paul, Minn., executive director, 1971—. Visiting professor, School of Library Science, University of Denver, summer, 1965. Chairperson, Minnesota Educational Computing Consortium Library Committee, 1976-77. *Military service:* U.S. Army, 1953-55. *Member:* American Association of University Professors, American Library Association, Minnesota Library Association, South Dakota Library Association (president, 1970-71), Minnesota State Library Planning Council.

*WRITINGS: Faculty Status for Librarians,* Scarecrow, 1972; (contributor) Bill Katz and Joel J. Schwartz, editors, *Library Lit: The Best of 1971,* Scarecrow, 1972; (contributor) *Academic Libraries by the Year 2000: Essays Honoring Gerald Orne,* Bowker, 1977. Also producer of film, "Travels in the Interior of North America," 1972. Contributor to professional journals. Member of editorial board, *Journal of Academic Librarianship.*

*WORK IN PROGRESS:* Research on book selection as it affects library use and on on-line data base searching.

\*        \*        \*

## MATARAZZO, James M.   1941-

*PERSONAL:* Born January 4, 1941, in Stoneham, Mass.; son of Angelo Michael (a candy-maker) and Anna (Finamore) Matarazzo; married Alice M. Keohane, September 3, 1966; children: James M., Jr., Susan Eileen. *Education:* Boston College, B.S., 1963, M.A., 1972; Simmons College, M.S., 1965; University of Pittsburgh, Ph.D. candidate. *Home:* 146 Cottage Park Rd., Winthrop, Mass. 02152. *Office:* School of Library Science, Simmons College, 300 The Fenway, Boston, Mass. 02115.

*CAREER:* Massachusetts Institute of Technology, Cambridge, assistant science librarian, 1965-67, documents librarian, 1967-68, serials librarian, documents librarian, and head of technical reports, 1968-69; Simmons College, School of Library Science, Boston, Mass., lecturer, 1968, instructor, 1969-70, assistant professor, 1971-73, associate professor of library science, 1973—, acting assistant director, 1974-75, assistant dean, 1975-77, assistant dean for student affairs, 1977—. *Member:* Special Libraries Association (chairman of education committee, Boston chapter, 1969-72).

*WRITINGS: Library Problems in Science and Technology,* Bowker, 1971; (co-editor) *Scientific, Technical, and Engineering Societies Publications in Print, 1974-75,* Bowker, 1974; (editor) *The Serials Librarian,* Faxon, 1975; (co-editor) *Scientific, Medical, and Engineering Societies Publications in Print, 1976-77,* Bowker, 1977. Contributor to library journals.

*WORK IN PROGRESS:* New edition of *Scientific, Medical, and Engineering Societies Publications in Print;* research on corporate libraries and the reasons for their closure.

\*        \*        \*

## MATHEWS, H(arry) Lee   1939-

*PERSONAL:* Born June 17, 1939, in Cincinnati, Ohio; son of William T. (a businessman) and Martha (Wise) Mathews; married Patricia Dana, October 4, 1964; children: Sarah, Martha, Colin, Alix. *Education:* University of Illinois, B.S., 1961; Ohio State University, M.B.A., 1963, Ph.D., 1966. *Home:* 6347 Plesenton Dr., Worthington, Ohio 43085. *Office:* Department of Marketing, Hagerty Hall, Ohio State University, Columbus, Ohio 43210.

*CAREER:* Mellon National Bank & Trust Co., Pittsburgh, Pa., research consultant, marketing research department, 1967-68; Pennsylvania State University, University Park, assistant professor, 1965-69, associate professor, 1969-72, professor of marketing, 1972-77, chairperson of department, 1975-77; Ohio State University, Columbus, professor of marketing and chairperson of faculty of marketing, 1977—. Partner, Marketing Management Development Group (consultants), University Park, 1970-77. *Member:* American Marketing Association, Order of Artus, Beta Gamma Simga.

*WRITINGS:* (With John W. Slocum, Jr.) *Marketing Strategies in the Commercial Bank Credit Card Field* (monograph), American Bankers Association, 1968; *Causes of Personal Bankruptcies* (monograph), Bureau of Business Research, Ohio State University, 1969; (contributor) David L. Sparks, editor, *Broadening the Concept of Marketing,* American Marketing Association, 1970; (with Ira J. Dolich and David T. Wilson) *Analysis and Decision Making: Cases in Marketing Management,* Prentice-Hall, 1971. Contributor of articles to professional and popular journals.

*WORK IN PROGRESS:* Research on the effect of sociological and psychological variables on credit decision by consumers, funded in part by Gulf Oil Foundation; research on the impact of sophisticated applications of electronic data processing on purchasing decisions, funded by National Association of Purchasing Managers; other studies on industrial buyer decision making and on the effect of perceived risk on bank loyalty.

## MATHIS, F(erdinand) John 1941-

*PERSONAL:* Born December 9, 1941, in Rockford, Ill.; son of F. John (an office machines repairman) and Jean K. (Vorwald) Mathis; married Linda R. McGinnis, February, 1962; children: John Kenneth, Laura Katheleen. *Education:* University of California, Riverside, B.A., 1963, M.A., 1964; University of Iowa, Ph.D., 1966. *Home:* 1214 Alima Ter., LaGrange Park, Ill. 60525. *Office:* Continental Illinois National Bank, 231 South LaSalle St., Chicago, Ill. 60693.

*CAREER:* University of Illinois at Chicago Circle, assistant professor of economics, 1966-68; State University of New York College at Brockport, associate professor of economics, 1968-70; Chase Manhattan Bank, New York, N.Y., economist and second vice-president, 1970-71; Continental Illinois National Bank, Chicago, vice-president and international economist, 1971—. *Member:* American Economic Association, Society for International Development, Midwest Economic Association. *Awards, honors:* Organization of American States postdoctoral fellow, 1967.

*WRITINGS:* (Editor with Walter Krause) *International Economics and Business: Selected Readings,* Houghton, 1968; *Problems and Progress of the Latin American Common Market* (monograph), Pan American Union, 1968; *The Latin American Common Market: Economic Disparity and Benefit Diffusion* (monograph), Georgia State College, 1968; *Economic Integration in Latin America: The Problems and Prospects of LAFTA,* Bureau of Business Research, University of Texas at Austin, 1969; (contributor) Ronald Hilton, editor, *The Movement toward Latin American Unity,* Praeger, 1969; (with Krause) *Latin America and Economic Integration: Regional Planning for Development,* University of Iowa Press, 1970; (contributor) *La Integracion Latinoamericana: Un Reto para la mujer Latinoamericana,* Organization of American States, 1970; (editor) *Offshore Lending by U.S. Commercial Banks,* Bankers Association for Foreign Trade/Robert Morris Associates, 1975. Contributor of articles to economics and business journals.

*WORK IN PROGRESS:* Research on international economic and financial developments, United States balance of payments, country risk analysis, and foreign exchange rate forecasting.

\*    \*    \*

## MATHIS, (Gerald) Ray 1937-

*PERSONAL:* Born April 2, 1937, in Sanford, Miss.; son of Paul M. (a machinist) and LaVerne (a teacher; maiden name Morris) Mathis; married Mary Kathryn Pugh (a sociology instructor), December 28, 1958; children: John Paul, Charles Ray. *Education:* Snead Junior College, A.A., 1957; Birmingham-Southern College, B.A., 1958; Duke University, M.Div., 1962; University of Georgia, M.A., 1963, Ph.D., 1967. *Home address:* Route 1, Mathews, Ala. 36052. *Office:* Department of History, Troy State University, Troy, Ala. 36081.

*CAREER:* Snead Junior College, Boaz, Ala., instructor in history, 1964-65; Georgia Southern College, Statesboro, assistant professor, 1966-69; Troy State University, Troy, Ala., professor of history, 1969—. *Member:* American Historical Association, Organization of American Historians, Southern Historical Association, Society for the Study of Southern Literature, Georgia Historical Society, Alabama Historical Society, Phi Beta Kappa, Phi Theta Kappa, Omicron Delta Kappa, Phi Kappa Phi, Phi Alpha Theta.

*Awards, honors:* American Philosophical Society grant, 1968.

*WRITINGS:* (Co-author) *Introduction and Index to Dent Journals,* University of Alabama, 1977; *J. H. Dent: South Carolina Planter on the Alabama Frontier,* University of Alabama, 1978.

Editor: *Pilgrimage to Madison: Correspondence Concerning the Georgia Party's Inspection of the University of Wisconsin, November 1904,* University of Georgia, 1970; *T. W. Reed's History of the University of Georgia: 1885-89,* University of Georgia Libraries, 1974; *College Life in the Reconstruction South,* University of Georgia Libraries, 1974; (co-editor) *John Harry Dent Farm Journals, 1840-1892,* University of Alabama, 1977. Contributor to professional journals.

*WORK IN PROGRESS:* *Walter B. Hill and the Savage Ideal; Southern History and Myth As They Relate to the Search for National Character.*

\*    \*    \*

## MATSUBA, Moshe 1917-
### (Avraham C[haim] Ben-Yosef)

*PERSONAL:* Name changed to Matsuba in 1973; born January 15, 1917, in Golders Green, Hendon, Middlesex, England; son of Joseph and Frances Lilian May (Lynes) Welsman; married Mitsko Matsumura, 1973. *Education:* Attended Clark's College, London, 1929-33, Pitman's College, 1937; University of London, B.Com., 1947, B.Sc., 1954. *Politics:* Socialist. *Religion:* (Very) liberal Jewish. *Home:* Kibbutz Akan, Shin Shizen Noen, Nakasetsuri, Tsurui Mura, Akan Gun, Hokkaido 085-12, Japan.

*CAREER:* Tailor's shop assistant, shorthand-typist, and shipping clerk in various firms in London, England, 1933-50. Kibbutz member in Israel, 1950-71, in Japan, 1972—. *Military service:* Israeli army, 1953-66.

*WRITINGS:* (Under name Avraham C. Ben-Yosef) *The Purest Democracy in the World,* Herzl Press, 1963; (under name Avraham C. Ben-Yosef) *Ancient History: The Twentieth Century,* Sargent, 1970; (with Zenzo Kusakari and Michael Steinbach) *Communes of Japan,* Japanese Commune Movement, 1977. Editor, *Commumanity.*

*SIDELIGHTS:* Moshe Matsuba has briefly toured Europe from Spain to Sweden and Austria, Yugoslavia, and Greece; his basic interests are sociology, politics, and classical music. He has "long since thrown over the establishment for the counter-society, specifically in anarchist kibbutzism, transferring from Israel to Japan on account of disagreement with Israeli foreign policy." Japan, he notes, "has had its own communes even longer than Israel.... I can only hope that a few others may be attracted by my statements and example to reverse our slavery to money-making and our dire alienation from nature and healthy culture, by means of the modern constructive anarchism ... of communal living."

*AVOCATIONAL INTERESTS:* Geography, geology, travel, transport, architecture, silverware, ceramics, painting, literature, animals, philosophy, evolution, and futurology.

*BIOGRAPHICAL/CRITICAL SOURCES:* Leonard Woolf, *The Journey Not the Arrival Matters,* Hogarth Press (London), 1969.

## MATTHIS, Raimund Eugen 1928-

PERSONAL: Born June 3, 1928, in La Grande, Ore.; son of Frederick and Una (Tameris) Matthis; married Bette Kenton, March 5, 1954 (divorced June, 1971); children: Leslie Jeanine, Mark Frederick. Education: University of Puget Sound, B.A., 1958; University of Washington, M.L.S., 1960. Home: 1502 North Mason, Tacoma, Wash. 98406. Office: University of Puget Sound, North 15th and Warner, Tacoma, Wash. 98416.

CAREER: Pierce County Public Library, Tacoma, Wash., reference librarian, 1960-63; University of Puget Sound, Tacoma, Wash., 1963—, currently technical services librarian. Consultant on conversion to the Library of Congress classification system, Pacific Lutheran University and Tacoma Community College, 1965—. Military service: U.S. Army, 1949-53; became sergeant.

WRITINGS: (With W. Desmond Taylor) Adopting the Library of Congress Classification System: A Manual of Methods and Techniques for Application or Conversion, Bowker, 1971.

WORK IN PROGRESS: A book of poetry.†

\*     \*     \*

## MATTILL, A(ndrew) J(acob), Jr. 1924-

PERSONAL: Born August 2, 1924, in St. Joseph, Mo.; son of Andrew Jacob (an accountant) and Ruth Florence (Hanne) Mattill; married Mary Elizabeth Bedford, March 31, 1960. Education: University of Chicago, B.A., (with honors), 1949; Evangelical Theological Seminary, Naperville, Ill., B.D., 1952; Vanderbilt University, Ph.D., 1959. Home address: Route 2, Box 49, Gordo, Ala. 35466.

CAREER: Armour & Co., South St. Joseph, Mo., assistant to paymaster, 1943-46; ordained to ministry of Evangelical United Brethren Church, 1952, transferred ordination and membership to Churches of God in North America, 1966, dropped ordination and membership, 1977; pastor of church in Vassar, Kan., 1952-54; Berry College, Mount Berry, Ga., 1958-62, began as assistant professor, became associate professor of Bible; Livingstone College, Salisbury, N.C., professor of Bible, 1962-65; Winebrenner Theological Seminary, Findlay, Ohio, Bucher Professor of New Testament and registrar, 1965-75; private scholar, engaged in New Testament research on a farm near Gordo, Ala., 1975—. Part-time minister, Liberty Universalist Church, Louisville, Miss., 1977—. Military service: U.S. Army, 1945-47; served in France, became sergeant. Member: Society of Biblical Literature. Awards, honors: Scholarship through New York University for postdoctoral work in Israel, 1959; American Association of Theological Schools grant for sabbatical year in Germany, 1972-73.

WRITINGS: The Wets Are All Wet (booklet), Christian Action League, 1965; (with wife, Mary Elizabeth Mattill) A Classified Bibliography of Literature on the Acts of the Apostles, E. J. Brill, 1966; (translator; Paul Feine and Johannes Behm, revisers) W. G. Kuemmel, Introduction to the New Testament, 14th revised edition, Abingdon, 1966; The Church in a Revolutionary World (booklet), Central Publishing House of the Churches of God in North America, 1968; (contributor) W. W. Gasque and R. P. Martin, editors, Apostolic History and the Gospel, Paternoster, 1970; A Religious Odyssey (booklet), Scott Recording Laboratory, 1977; (contributor) C. H. Talbert, editor, North American Perspectives on Luke-Acts, Scholars Press, in press. Contributor of articles and reviews to religious journals.

WORK IN PROGRESS: Studies on the purpose and eschatology of Luke Acts and on Unitarian Christology.

\*     \*     \*

## MAULE, Christopher J(ohn) 1934-

PERSONAL: Born July 18, 1934, in Kent, England; son of William H. F. and Hilda M. M. (Wild) Maule; married Jeannette G. Filleul, July 10, 1962; children: Nicola, Andrew. Education: University of British Columbia, B.A., 1961; Queen's University, M.A., 1964; London School of Economics and Political Science, Ph.D., 1966. Home: 14 Bedford Crescent, Ottawa, Ontario, Canada K1K 0E4. Office: Department of Economics, Carleton University, Ottawa, Ontario, Canada K1S 5B6.

CAREER: Carleton University, Ottawa, Ontario, lecturer, 1962-64; University of London, London School of Economics and Political Science, London, England, tutor, 1964-66; McMaster University, Hamiton, Ontario, assistant professor of economics, 1966-70; Carleton University, 1970—, began as associate professor, currently professor of economics and international affairs. Military service: British Army, 1952-54; became lieutenant. Member: Canadian Institute of International Affairs, Canadian Economic Association, American Economic Association, Royal Economic Society. Awards, honors: Grants from British Council, 1964, 1965, and 1969; research grant from Canadian Donner Foundation, 1968; research grant from McMaster University, 1968; research grants from Canada Council, 1969, 1971, and 1977; research grant from McLean Foundation, 1970; publication grant from Social Science Research Council, 1971.

WRITINGS: (Editor and contributor with Isaiah A. Litvak) Foreign Investment: The Experience of Host Countries, Praeger, 1970; (with Litvak and Richard D. Robinson) Dual Loyalty, McGraw, 1971.

WORK IN PROGRESS: Economics and Politics of Foreign Investment; Studies of the Modern Corporation, Domestic and Foreign.

\*     \*     \*

## MAUNG, Mya 1933-

PERSONAL: Born January 5, 1933, in Kyaiklatt, Burma; son of U Kauk and Daw Aye (Myaing) Maung. Education: University of Rangoon, B.A., 1954; Massachusetts Institute of Technology, additional study, fall, 1954; University of Michigan, M.A., 1957; Catholic University of America, Ph.D., 1961. Religion: Buddhist. Office: Department of Finance, Boston College, Chestnut Hill, Mass. 02167.

CAREER: Rangoon University, Rangoon, Burma, tutor in logic, 1953-54; Asia Foundation, Rangoon, director of research, 1961-62; Defense Services Academy, Maymyo, Burma, head of department of economics, 1962-63; Kansas State Teachers College, Emporia (now Emporia State University), assistant professor of economics, 1963-64; South Dakota State University, Brookings, assistant professor of economics, 1964-66; Boston College, Chestnut Hill, Mass., associate professor, 1966-75, professor of economics, 1975—. Research associate in international development studies, Fletcher School of Law and Diplomacy, 1969-71. Member: American Economic Association, Association for Asian Studies, American Academy of Political and Social Sciences, Pi Gamma Mu.

WRITINGS: Burma and Pakistan: A Comparative Study of Development, Praeger, 1971; Two Models of Foreign Devel-

*opment Banks: Mexico and Finland,* Center for Community Economic Development (Cambridge), 1973.

*WORK IN PROGRESS:* A textbook, *Basic Finance,* for Harper.

\* \* \*

## MAURER, John G. 1937-

*PERSONAL:* Born May 22, 1937, in Evansville, Ind.; son of John George, Jr. (a personnel director) and Mildred (Lintzenich) Maurer; married Marianne Fischer, 1973; children: two daughters. *Education:* University of Detroit, B.S., 1960; Michigan State University, M.B.A., 1962, Ph.D., 1967. *Home:* 1095 Hackberry Cir., Rochester, Mich. 48063. *Office:* School of Business Administration, Wayne State University, 5201 Cass, Detroit, Mich. 48202.

*CAREER:* Wayne State University, Detroit, Mich., assistant professor, 1965-69, associate professor of management and organization sciences, 1969—, chairman of department, 1972-74, dean for academic programs, 1974—. *Member:* American Sociological Association, Academy of Management, Beta Gamma Sigma, Sigma Iota Epsilon.

*WRITINGS: Work Role Involvement of Industrial Supervisors,* Graduate School of Business Administration, Michigan State University, 1969; (editor) *Readings in Organization Theory: Open-System Approaches,* Random House, 1971. Also author of numerous papers presented to learned societies. Contributor to sociology and management journals.

*WORK IN PROGRESS:* Research on job involvement.

\* \* \*

## MAXWELL, Sister Mary 1913-

*PERSONAL:* Born June 4, 1913, in Buffalo, N.Y.; daughter of John L. (a dentist) and Elizabeth (Dwyer) Maxwell. *Education:* Mt. St. Joseph College (now Medaille College), B.S., 1940, M.A. (English), 1954; Rosary College, M.A. (library science), 1944. *Politics:* Republican. *Religion:* Roman Catholic. *Home:* 634 Central Ave., Dunkirk, N.Y. 14048. *Office:* Cardinal Mindszenty High School, Central Ave., Dunkirk, N.Y. 14048; and Medaille College, Agassiz Circle, Buffalo, N.Y. 14214 (summer).

*CAREER:* Roman Catholic nun of order of the Sisters of St. Joseph (S.S.J.); Cardinal Mindszenty High School, Dunkirk, N.Y., teacher of English and chairman of department; Medaille College, Buffalo, N.Y., professor during summer sessions. *Member:* National Council of Teachers of English, National Educational Association, National Catholic Education Association, National Catholic Library Association (coordinator for conventions), American Association of University Women, New York State Council of English (coordinator for conventions).

*WRITINGS: Like a Swarm of Bees,* Society of Saint Paul, 1962; *Witness to Christ,* Paulist Press, 1967. Contributor of articles and poetry to professional journals and current magazines.

*WORK IN PROGRESS:* Articles for professional journals.

\* \* \*

## MAYER, Milton 1908-

*PERSONAL:* Born August 24, 1908, in Chicago, Ill.; son of Morris Samuel (a salesman) and Louise (Gerson) Mayer; married Bertha Hagedorn Tepper, September 13, 1929 (divorced, 1945); married Jane Stoddard, August 6, 1947; chil-

dren: Julie (Mrs. Robert Vognar), Amanda (Mrs. Theodore B. Stinchecum), Rock, Richard. *Education:* Attended University of Chicago, 1925-28. *Politics:* Independent. *Religion:* Jewish; member of Religious Society of Friends (Quakers). *Home:* 3066 Rio Rd., Carmel, Calif. 93923. *Agent:* Harold Ober Associates, 40 East 49th St., New York, N.Y. 10017.

*CAREER:* Worked for newspapers, colleges, and universities at home and abroad, 1929-64; University of Massachusetts—Amherst, professor of English, 1964-73. Professor of humanities, Windham College, 1968—; visiting tutor, University of Frankfurt, 1952, School of Humanities (Switzerland), 1955—, University of Prague, 1964, University of Paris, 1973, and University of Louisville, 1977; visiting professor of humanities, Max Planck Institute, Germany, 1978. Lecturer for American Friends Service Committee and Jewish Peace Fellowship. Consultant to Center for the Study of Democratic Institutions. *Awards, honors:* George Polk Memorial Award for journalism; Benjamin Franklin Citation for journalism; Communicator of the Year award, University of Chicago.

*WRITINGS: They Thought They Were Free: The Germans, 1933-45,* University of Chicago Press, 1955; (editor) *The Tradition of Freedom,* Oceana, 1958; (with Mortimer J. Adler) *The Revolution in Education,* University of Chicago Press, 1958; *What Can a Man Do?,* University of Chicago Press, 1964; (with others) *Humanistic Education and Western Civilization,* Holt, 1965; (with others) *Anatomy of Anti-Communism,* Schocken, 1967; *The Art of the Impossible: A Study of the Czech Resistance,* Center for the Study of Democratic Institutions, 1969; *If Men Were Angels,* Atheneum, 1972; *The Nature of the Beast,* University of Massachusetts Press, 1975. Contributor to magazines and journals in the United States and abroad. Roving editor, *Progressive Magazine.*

*WORK IN PROGRESS:* A biography of Robert Maynard Hutchins; an anthology of the works of Robert Maynard Hutchins.

\* \* \*

## MAYFIELD, Robert C(harles) 1928-

*PERSONAL:* Born October 15, 1928, in Abilene, Tex.; son of Percy Anderson and Fay (Hicks) Mayfield; married Loraine Poindexter, September 3, 1952; children: Julie, Jennifer, Mark, Randy. *Education:* Texas Christian University, B.A. (summa cum laude), 1952; Indiana University, M.A., 1953; University of Washington, Seattle, Ph.D., 1961. *Politics:* Independent. *Religion:* Christian. *Home:* 325 Goddard Ave., Brookline, Mass. 02146. *Office:* External Programs, Boston University, 705 Commonwealth Ave., Boston, Mass. 02215.

*CAREER:* Indiana University at Bloomington, lecturer in geography, 1954-56; Southeastern State College (now Southeastern Oklahoma State University), Durant, assistant professor of geography, 1958-60; Texas Christian University, Fort Worth, associate professor of geography, 1961-64; University of Texas at Austin, associate profsssor, 1964-68, professor of geography, 1968-71, acting chairman of department, 1967-69, chairman of department, 1969-71; Boston University, Boston, Mass., professor of geography, 1971—, chairman of department, 1972-77, vice-president for external programs, 1977—. Official delegate of the National Academy of Sciences to the Regional Conference of Southeastern Asian Geographers, Kuala Lumpur, Malaysia, 1962. *Military service:* U.S. Air Force, Air Training Command, 1946-49.

*MEMBER:* Association of American Geographers, American Geographical Society, National Council for Geographic Education, Regional Science Association, Association for Asian Studies, Sigma Xi. *Awards, honors:* National Academy of Science—National Research Council, Field Research Program, 1957-58; Fulbright-Hays fellowship, 1966-67, for innovation diffusion field study; Agricultural Development Council grant for travel and field expenses to India, summer, 1968; received travel award to the Twenty-First International Geographical Congress.

*WRITINGS: The Spatial Structure of a Selected Interpersonal Contact: A Regional Comparison of Marriage Distances in India,* Northwestern University, 1967; (editor with Paul Ward English) *Man, Space, and Environment: Concepts in Contemporary Human Geography,* Oxford University Press, 1972. Contributor of articles to *Quantitative Geography, Annals of the Association of American Geographers, Journal of Geography, Geographical Review,* and other journals.

*WORK IN PROGRESS:* Research on interpersonal communication structures in 395 villages in South India (Mysore State) as a part of an effort to simulate by Monte Carlo methods the diffusion of agricultural innovation there.

\* \* \*

## MAYHEW, Edgar deNoailles 1913-

*PERSONAL:* Born October 1, 1913, in Newark, N.J.; son of Alfred F. (a broker) and Alice (Richardson) Mayhew. *Education:* Amherst College, B.A., 1935; Yale University, M.A., 1939; Johns Hopkins University, Ph.D., 1941. *Home:* 613 Williams St., New London, Conn. 06320. *Office:* Lyman Allyn Museum, New London, Conn. 06320.

*CAREER:* Johns Hopkins University, Baltimore, Md., instructor in fine arts, 1941-42; St. Mark's School, Southborough, Mass., instructor in history, 1942-44; Wellesley College, Wellesley, Mass., instructor in fine arts, 1944-45; Connecticut College, New London, assistant professor, 1945-62, associate professor, 1962-66, professor of art history, 1966—; Lyman Allyn Museum, New London, curator, 1950-62, associate director, 1962-68, director, 1968—. Connecticut Commission on the Arts, member, 1966—, chairman, 1971-73. Member of board of directors, Lawrence Hospital and Goodspeed Opera Foundation. *Member:* American Association of Museums, Antiquarian and Landmarks Society of Connecticut (member of board of directors), New London Historical Society (member of board of directors), and other historical and preservation societies. *Awards, honors:* American Philosophical Society grant for research, 1967.

*WRITINGS:* (With Charles Singleton) *The Book of the Courtier,* Doubleday, 1959; *Sketches by Thornhill in the Victoria and Albert Museum,* H.M.S.O., 1968; *New London County Furniture,* Eastern Press, 1974. Contributor to *Antiques.*

*WORK IN PROGRESS:* A documentary history of the American interior.

\* \* \*

## MAZIARZ, Edward A(nthony) 1915-

*PERSONAL:* Surname is accented on first syllable; born March 6, 1915, in Milwaukee, Wis.; son of John (a laborer) and Mary (Matusiak) Maziarz. *Education:* St. Charles Seminary, Carthagena, Ohio, graduate, 1940; Catholic University of America, A.M., 1941; St. Joseph's College, Rensse-

laer, Ind., B.S. (magna cum laude), 1944; University of Michigan, M.S., 1945; University of Ottawa, Ph.D., 1949; summer graduate study at University of Virginia, 1944, Laval University, 1946, and American University, 1962. *Residence:* Chicago, Ill. *Office:* Department of Philosophy, Loyola University, Chicago, Ill. 60626.

*CAREER:* Roman Catholic priest of Congregation of the Most Precious Blood (C.PP.S.); Marian College, Fond du Lac, Wis., instructor in philosophy, 1941-42; St. Joseph's College, Rensselaer, Ind., instructor, 1942-47, assistant professor, 1947-54, associate professor, 1954-58, professor of philosophy and mathematics, 1958-64, academic dean, 1955-63, professor of philosophy at Calumet Campus, 1964-66; Loyola University, Chicago, Ill., professor of philosophy, 1966—. *Member:* American Association for the Advancement of Science, American Philosophical Association, American Catholic Philosophical Association, American Mathematical Association, Association for Symbolic Logic, Catholic Theological Society of America, History of Science Society, Philosophy of Science Association, Society for the Scientific Study of Religion, Phi Eta Sigma, Delta Epsilon Sigma (national president, 1961-63). *Awards, honors:* National Science Foundation summer fellowship, 1959.

*WRITINGS: The Philosophy of Mathematics,* Philosophical Library, 1950; (contributor) *Philosophical Studies in Honor of the Very Rev. Ignatius Smith, O.P.,* Paulist Press, 1952; (translator) F. J. Thonnard, *A Short History of Philosophy,* Desclee, 1955, 2nd revised edition, 1960; (translator) Gaspar Lefebvre, *Redemption through the Blood of Jesus,* Paulist Press, 1960; (with Thomas Greenwood) *Greek Mathematical Philosophy,* Ungar, 1968; (with Edmund F. Byrne) *Human Being and Being Human: Man's Philosophies of Man,* Appleton, 1969. Contributor to *New Catholic Encyclopedia, Catholic Encyclopedia for School and Home,* and *Encyclopedia of World Biography;* contributor of about thirty articles and reviews to philosophy journals. Founder and editorial advisor, *Philosophy Today,* 1957-59; associate editor, *Philosophia Mathematica.*

*WORK IN PROGRESS:* Editing *Values in the Human Future;* a contribution to *Corpus Theology Dictionary;* writing on history and philosophy of science.

\* \* \*

## MAZO, Earl 1919-

*PERSONAL:* Born July 7, 1919, in Warsaw, Poland; son of Samuel George and Sonia (Portugal) Mazo; married Rita Vane, June 15, 1941; children: Judith, Mark. *Education:* Clemson College (now University), graduate, 1940. *Politics:* Independent. *Religion:* Jewish. *Home:* 5915 Nebraska Ave. N.W., Washington, D.C. 20015. *Office:* Woodrow Wilson International Center for Scholars, Smithsonian Institution, 1000 Jefferson Ave. N.W., Washington, D.C. 20560.

*CAREER:* Member of staff, *Charleston News and Courier* and *Greenville News,* 1939-41; *Camden Courier,* Camden, N.J., political correspondent, 1946-49; *New York Herald Tribune,* Washington D.C., political correspondent, 1949-63; *New York Times,* New York, N.Y., political correspondent, 1963-65; *Reader's Digest,* Washington D.C., writer, 1965-71; Smithsonian Institution, Woodrow Wilson International Center for Scholars, Washington, D.C., fellow, 1972—. *Military service:* U.S. Army Air Forces, World War II; became first lieutenant; received five Air Medals, two presidential citations, and Bronze Star Medal. *Member:* National Press Club, Overseas Press Club.

WRITINGS: Richard Nixon: A Political and Personal Portrait, Harper, 1959; The Great Debates, Center for Democratic Institutions, 1961; Nixon: A Political Portrait, Harper, 1968.

WORK IN PROGRESS: A book on political polling.

BIOGRAPHICAL/CRITICAL SOURCES: New York Times Book Review, August 4, 1968, January 19, 1969.

\*    \*    \*

## McCAFFERY, Margo (Smith)   1938-

PERSONAL: Born September 29, 1938, in Corsicana, Tex.; daughter of Marley William and Mary Katherine (Adams) Smith; married Robert Charles McCaffery (an art dealer), July 4, 1965; children: Melissa Ruth. Education: Attended Navarro Junior College, summer, 1955; Baylor University, B.S., 1959; Vanderbilt University, M.S., 1961. Politics: Democrat. Religion: None. Home: 1458 Berkeley, Apartment 1, Santa Monica, Calif. 90404.

CAREER: Registered nurse. Texas Women's University, Dallas, instructor in surgical nursing, 1958-59; Vanderbilt University, Nashville, Tenn., assistant professor of nursing of children and chairman of department, 1961-62; University of California, Los Angeles, instructor, 1962-65, assistant professor of pediatric nursing, 1965-70, junior research nurse, 1962-63, post-graduate research nurse, 1963; consultant in nursing care of patients with pain, 1970—.

WRITINGS: Nursing Practice Theories Related to Cognition, Bodily Pain and Man-Environment Interactions, University of California at Los Angeles Student's Store, 1968; Nursing Management of the Patient with Pain, Lippincott, 1972, 2nd edition, in press. Contributor of articles to nursing journals.

WORK IN PROGRESS: Further work on ways the nurse can assist the patient with pain.

SIDELIGHTS: Margo McCaffery told CA: "Part of my motivation to learn and write about pain comes from my observation that pain relief is a low priority in patient care; consequently many patients suffer pain needlessly. Nurses spend more time with patients with pain than do any other members of the health team, and that means they can make a special contribution to the care of patients with pain."

\*    \*    \*

## McCAFFREY, Joseph A.   1940-

PERSONAL: Born April 14, 1940, in New York, N.Y.; son of Daniel James (owner of a tavern) and Alice M. (Dineen) McCaffrey; children: David Conan. Education: Aquinas Institute of Philosophy, Ph.B., 1963, M.A. and Ph.L., 1964; Pontifical University of St. Thomas Aquinas, Rome, Italy, Ph.D., 1969; University of Iowa, M.A., 1974. Home: 1103 Blanchard, Davenport, Iowa 52804. Office: President, Palmer Junior College, Davenport, Iowa 52803.

CAREER: St. Ambrose College, Davenport, Iowa, instructor, 1964-67, assistant professor, 1967-72, associate professor of philosophy, 1972—, assistant dean, 1973-74, associate dean, 1974-75, academic dean, 1975-77; Palmer Junior College, Davenport, president, 1977—. Member, Davenport Human Relations Commission, 1967-70, Davenport Board of Education, 1970-73, Iowa Board of Medical Examiners, 1976—, and Davenport Civil Service Commission, 1977—. Member: American Philosophical Association, American Catholic Philosophical Association, American Association of University Professors, National School Board Association, Iowa Association of School Boards.

WRITINGS: Homosexuality: Toward a Moral Synthesis (book-length monograph), Catholic Book Agency, 1969; (editor) The Homosexual Dialectic, Prentice-Hall, 1972. Contributor to Catholic World and other denominational publications.

WORK IN PROGRESS: Fathers of the Church on Sexual Ethics; Business Ethics; a novel.

SIDELIGHTS: Joseph A. McCaffrey speaks French, Italian, and Latin, and reads Spanish and Greek.

\*    \*    \*

## McCALLUM, George E(dward)   1931-

PERSONAL: Born February 17, 1931, in Pittsburgh, Pa.; son of Herschel James (a commercial artist) and Irma (Posch) McCallum. Education: University of California, Berkeley, B.A., 1952, Ph.D., 1965. Religion: Roman Catholic. Home: 310A Grant St., De Pere, Wis. 54115. Office: Department of Economics, St. Norbert College, De Pere, Wis. 54115.

CAREER: Gannon College, Erie, Pa., instructor in economics, 1959-61; Interstate Commerce Commission, Washington, D.C., economist, 1962; Gannon College, Erie, Pa., assistant professor of economics, 1963-67; St. Norbert College, De Pere, Wis., associate professor of economics, 1967—, faculty chairman, 1969-70. Consultant to Upper Great Lakes Regional Commission and to Wisconsin Department of Transportation; member of Board of Directors, RAIL Foundation and of Railroad Passengers, 1977—. Secretary, Erie Metropolitan Transit Commission, 1965-66, and Erie Metropolitan Transit Authority, 1966-67. Member of transportation advisory committee, University of Wisconsin extension; member of Common Cause and Public Citizen. Military service: U.S. Army, 1954-56. Member: American Association of University Professors (president of Gannon chapter, 1966-67; secretary of St. Norbert chapter, 1967-68, president, 1968-69), American Economic Association, American Society of Traffic & Transportation, Railway and Locomotive Historical Society, National Railway Historical Society, National Association of Railroad Passengers (northwest Pennsylvania regional chairman, 1970—), Phi Beta Kappa, Phi Eta Simga, Siera Club.

WRITINGS: New Techniques in Railroad Ratemaking, Washington State University, 1968. Contributor to Economic Journal.

WORK IN PROGRESS: A study of the effects of differential government regulatory and promotional policies on intermodal competition in transportation; LRV ("light rail") solution to urban transportation problems.

SIDELIGHTS: George E. McCallum feels strongly about the "incredibly ill-conceived government policies on intercity transportation!" He has traveled extensively in Canada, Central America, Europe, North Africa, U.S.S.R., and Japan.

AVOCATIONAL INTERESTS: Chamber music, public speaking, railway history.

\*    \*    \*

## McCARDLE, Carl W(esley)   1904(?)-1972

1904(?)—July 10, 1972; American reporter and foreign correspondent. Obituaries: New York Times, July 12, 1972; Washington Post, July 12, 1972.

## McCARTHY, Thomas N.   1927-

*PERSONAL:* Born July 24, 1927, in Medford, Mass.; son of Thomas Martin and H. Ruth (McCarthy) McCarthy; married Ruth G. Patterson, July 4, 1958; children: Thomas M., David P., Paul N., Margaret R. *Education:* Catholic University of America, A.B., 1950, M.A., 1952; Ottawa University, Ph.D., 1956. *Religion:* Roman Catholic. *Home:* 205 Roberts Ave., Glenside, Pa. 19038. *Office:* Department of Psychology, La Salle College, Philadelphia, Pa. 19141.

*CAREER:* Consulting psychologist, Glenside, Pa., 1956-70; La Salle College, Philadelphia, Pa., assistant professor, 1956-60, associate professor, 1960-64, professor of psychology, 1964—, vice-president of student affairs, 1970—, La Salle College Counseling Center, assistant director, 1952-59, director, 1959-69. *Military service:* U.S. Navy, 1945-46. *Member:* American Association of Higher Education, National Association of Student Personnel Administrators, American Association of University Administrators, American Psychological Association, American Personnel and Guidance Association, American College Personnel Association, National Vocational Guidance Association, Association of Evaluation and Measurement in Guidance, Eastern Psychological Association, Pennsylvania Psychological Association (fellow), Pennsylvania Personnel and Guidance Association.

*WRITINGS: Assessment of Candidates for the Religious Life,* Cara, 1968; (contributor) W. C. Bier, editor, *Psychological Testing for Ministerial Selection,* Fordham University Press, 1970. Also author of *The Called and the Chosen: A Psychological Study of Candidates to Church Vocations.* Contributor of about fifteen articles to theology and education journals.

*       *       *

## McCASH, June Hall   1938-
### (June Hall Martin)

*PERSONAL:* Born June 8, 1938, in Newberry, S.C.; daughter of James DeLeon (a U.S. Army officer) and Williemaye (Stone) Hall; married Marvin Hampton Martin, April 8, 1961 (divorced, 1971); married William Barton McCash, June 26, 1974; children: (first marriage) Michael Hall, Christopher Brenden. *Education:* Agnes Scott College, B.A., 1960; Emory University, M.A., 1963, Ph.D., 1967; also studied in Paris, 1958-59. *Politics:* Democrat (usually). *Religion:* Episcopal. *Home:* 135 Cherry La., Murfreesboro, Tenn. 37130. *Office:* Department of Foreign Languages, Middle Tennessee State University, Box 262, Murfreesboro, Tenn. 37130.

*CAREER:* Methodist Publishing House, Nashville, Tenn., editorial assistant, 1961; Brandon Hall, Dunwoody, Ga., teacher, 1961-62; Emory University, Atlanta, Ga., instructor, 1964-67; Middle Tennessee State University, Murfreesboro, assistant professor, 1967-70, associate professor, 1970-75, professor of foreign languages, 1975—, director of honors program, 1973—. Actor and director of Little Theatre, Murfreesboro, Tenn. *Member:* American Association of University Professors (secretary of M.T.S.U. chapter, 1970-71, vice-president, 1971-72), Modern Language Association of America, National Collegiate Honors Council, American Association of Teachers of French, South Atlantic Modern Language Association, Tennessee Philological Association, Phi Sigma Iota, Alpha Mu Gamma. *Awards, honors:* Faculty research grant, Middle Tennessee State University, 1970; National Endowment for the Humanities research grant, 1975.

*WRITINGS:* (Under name June Hall Martin) *Love's Fools: Aucassin, Troilus, Calisto, and the Parody of the Courtly Lover,* Tamesis Books, 1972. Contributor of articles and reviews to *Romance Notes, Southern Humanities Review,* and *Comparative Literature.*

*WORK IN PROGRESS:* A biography of Marie de Champagne.

*AVOCATIONAL INTERESTS:* Photography, theatre.

*       *       *

## McCLAIN, Carl S.   1899-

*PERSONAL:* Born February 28, 1899, in Altona, Ind.; son of A. H. (a minister) and Livicy (Harper) McClain; married Eunice Spruce (a teacher), December 24, 1928; children: Barbara, Ruth (Mrs. Roger Boothe), Carol (Mrs. Bill Sloan). *Education:* Olivet Nazarene College, B.A., 1923; University of Illinois, M.A., 1932; attended Northwestern University, 1945-46. *Politics:* Republican. *Religion:* Nazarene. *Home:* 111 North Convent Ave., Bourbonnais, Ill. 60914. *Office:* Department of English, Olivet Nazarene College, Kankakee, Ill. 60901.

*CAREER:* Olivet Nazarene College, Kankakee, Ill., 1923-72, began as teacher, became professor of English language and literature, professor emeritus, 1972—, dean, 1930-54, registrar, 1954-62. Treasurer for Kankakee Valley Airport Authority. *Member:* Modern Language Association of America, National Council of Teachers of English, College English Association, Conference on Christianity and Literature, Kappa Phi Delta, Sigma Tau Delta, Phi Delta Lambda. *Awards, honors:* Litt.D., Olivet Nazarene College, 1954; recognition by International Church of the Nazarene for dedicated service to Christian Higher Education, 1960.

*WRITINGS: Morals and the Movies,* Beacon Press, 1970. Contributor of articles to religion journals.

*       *       *

## McCLOSKEY, Paul N., Jr.   1927-

*PERSONAL:* Born September 29, 1927, in San Bernardino, Calif.; son of Paul N. (an attorney) and Vera (McNabb) McCloskey; married Caroline Wadsworth (a real estate agent), August 6, 1949 (divorced, 1973); children: Nancy, Peter, John, Kathleen. *Education:* Stanford University, B.A., 1950, LL.B., 1953. *Home:* 1344 29th St. N.W., Washington, D.C. 20007. *Office:* Room 205, Cannon House Office Building, Washington, D.C. 20515.

*CAREER:* Admitted to California Bar, 1953; deputy district attorney, Alameda County, Calif., 1953-54; Costello & Johnson, Palo Alto, Calif., attorney, 1955-56; McCloskey, Wilson, Mosher & Martin, Palo Alto, Calif., founding partner, 1956-67; elected to U.S. House of Representatives from 11th District of California in special election, 1967, re-elected, 1968—. Co-chairman, Young Lawyers for Nixon-Lodge, 1960; conference chairman, California Republican League, 1967; member of Republican Congressional "truth squad," 1968. President, Stanford Area Youth Plan, 1960-66, and Palo Alto Fair Play Council, 1965-67. Candidate for presidential nomination at Republican National Convention, 1972. *Military service:* U.S. Navy, 1945-47. U.S. Marine Corps, 1950-52; became second lieutenant; received Navy Cross, Silver Star for gallantry, and Purple Heart. *Member:* Conference of Barristers of State Bar of California (president, 1961-62), Santa Clara County Bar Association (trustee, 1965-67), Palo Alto Area Bar Association (president, 1960-61), Sierra Club.

*WRITINGS: Truth and Untruth,* Simon & Schuster, 1972.

\* \* \*

## McCLURE, Ron 1941-

*PERSONAL:* Born March 5, 1941, in Pittsburgh, Pa.; son of Charles (a mechanic) and Alda (Dimpel) McClure; married Gail Louise Campbell, March 4, 1969. *Education:* University of Wyoming, B.A., 1972. *Politics:* None. *Religion:* None. *Residence:* Laramie, Wyo.

*CAREER:* Professional free-lance musician, 1965—.

*WRITINGS: Rawlins,* Dial, 1972.

*WORK IN PROGRESS: Parades Make Me Cry,* a novel.††

\* \* \*

## McCOY, D(onald) E(dward) 1923-

*PERSONAL:* Born November 7, 1923, in Stanberry, Mo.; son of William Arthur and Gretchen (Frederick) McCoy; married Mary Sue Kearny, August 31, 1946 (died, 1967); married Anne Marie Barnes, December 13, 1968; children: (first marriage) Janet Sue, William K., Barbara Anne; (second marriage) Tina Marie. *Education:* University of Kansas City (now University of Missouri—Kansas City), B.A., 1946, M.A., 1948; University of Illinois, Ph.D., 1952; University of Kansas, graduate study, 1947-49. *Home:* 1138 Westmoor Pl., St. Louis, Mo. 63131. *Office:* D. E. McCoy Associates, 634 West Port Plaza, St. Louis, Mo. 63141.

*CAREER:* University of Kansas, Lawrence, instructor in English, 1947-49; University of Minnesota, Minneapolis, instructor, 1952-54, assistant professor of literature and writing, 1954-56, chairman of department, 1955-56; University of Illinois at Urbana—Champaign, assistant professor of humanities, 1956-61, chairman of department of verbal communication, 1957-61; Principia College, Elsah, Ill., associate professor, 1961-67, professor of English, 1967-68; University of Missouri—St. Louis, visiting professor of English, 1968-70; D. E. McCoy Associates, St. Louis, Mo., principal, 1970—. Dynamic Productions, Inc., director of research and development, 1971-73, vice-president, 1973-75; president of McCoy & Ross, Inc., 1975—. President of Communication Centers of America, 1977—. *Military service:* U.S. Army, 1942-46. U.S. Air Force Reserve, 1951—; present rank, captain. *Member:* Modern Language Association of America, American Society for Training and Development, International Platform Association, International Institute of Arts and Letters (Geneva; fellow), Sigma Tau Delta.

*WRITINGS: Keys to Good Instruction,* Shell Oil Co., 1958, 3rd edition, 1967; (with T. J. Kallsen) *Rhetoric and Reading: Order and Idea,* Dodd, 1962. Contributor of articles to *School and Society,* and of book reviews to *Christian Science Monitor.* Editor, *Word Study,* Merriam, 1958-70; editorial consultant, Oxford University Press, Dodd, Mead & Co., and Scott, Foresman & Co.

*WORK IN PROGRESS: The Shell Oil Company Yesterday and Today; Petroleum and the Prerogatives of Power,* with M. B. Huldgraf; research on the literary correspondence of George Henry Boker and Bayard Taylor and its illumination of the "Philadelphia Circle."

\* \* \*

## McCOY, Ralph E(dward) 1915-

*PERSONAL:* Born October 1, 1915, in St. Louis, Mo.; son of Melvin Walter (a printer) and Luella Pearl (Geitz) McCoy; married Melba Elizabeth McKibben, September 8, 1940; children: Robert Allan, David Lawrence. *Education:* Illinois Wesleyan University, A.B., 1937; University of Illinois, B.S.L.S., 1939, M.S., 1950, Ph.D., 1956. *Politics:* Democrat. *Religion:* Methodist. *Home:* 1902 Chautauqua, Carbondale, Ill. 62901.

*CAREER:* High school teacher in Marissa, Ill. 1937-38; University of Illinois, Urbana, assistant librarian, College of Agriculture, 1938-39; Illinois State Library, Springfield, editor of publications and administrative assistant, 1939-43; U.S. Army, Quartermaster Technical Library, Fort Lee, Va., librarian, 1946-48; University of Illinois, librarian (assistant professor), Institute of Labor and Industrial Relations, 1948-55; Southern Illinois University at Carbondale, director of libraries, 1955-70, special assistant to vice-president for planning, 1963-64, dean, 1970-76, dean emeritus, 1976—. Member of committee on libraries, Illinois State Board of Higher Education, 1969-76. Carbondale Public Library Board, member, 1961-74, president, 1966-74; Shawnee Systems Library Board, founder, member, 1964-71; chairman of Depository Library Council to Public Printer, 1972-75; member of Illinois State Archives Advisory Board, 1973-77. Library consultant to Library Division of U.S. Office of Education and various universities. *Military service:* U.S. Army, 1943-46, became captain.

*MEMBER:* American Library Association (member of council, 1966; representative to American Council on Education, 1970-72), Association of College and Research Libraries (president, 1966), Center for Research Libraries (member of council, 1965-76; member of board of directors, 1972-74), Bibliographical Society of America, American Association of University Professors, American Civil Liberties Union, Ulysses S. Grant Association (member of board, 1970—), Illinois Library Association (president, 1960), Illinois State Historical Society, Beta Phi Mu, Phi Kappa Phi, Caxton Club.

*AWARDS, HONORS:* First annual award for outstanding contribution to the profession, Illinois Library Association, 1961; Intellectual Freedom Award, Scarecrow Press Award of American Library Association, and Joseph L. Andrews Bibliographic Award of American Association of Law Libraries, all in 1969 for *Freedom of the Press.*

*WRITINGS: Permanent Interment of World War II Dead,* U.S. Army, 1949; *University of Illinois Library Resources in Labor and Industrial Relations,* Institute of Labor and Industrial Relations, University of Illinois, 1949; *Personnel Administration for Libraries,* American Library Association, 1953; *History of Labor and Unionism: A Bibliography,* Institute of Labor and Industrial Relations, University of Illinois, 1953; (with John Clifford) *"The President of the United States": An Exhibition of Manuscripts, Letters, and Documents* (exhibition catalogue), Southern Illinois University Library, 1960; (contributor) R. B. Downs, editor, *Resources of Missouri Libraries,* Missouri State Library, 1966; *Freedom of the Press: An Annotated Bibliography,* Southern Illinois University Press, 1968; *Freedom of the Press: A Bibliocyclopedia (1967-1977),* Southern Illinois University Press, 1978. Also author of *Theodore A. Schroeder, the Cold Enthusiast: A Bibliography,* Southern Illinois University Library.

Contributor to library and other academic journals. Editor, *Illinois Libraries,* 1939-43, *ILA Record,* 1948-50, *Bibliographic Contributions,* Institute of Labor and Industrial Relations, University of Illinois, 1952-55, *Bibliographic Contributions,* Southern Illinois University Library, 1958—;

member of advisory board, "Collected Works of John Dewey," five volumes of which have been published, 1961—.

SIDELIGHTS: Ralph E. McCoy told CA: "My interest in freedom of the press grew out of experience as a student editor in 1937 and continued with work on a doctoral dissertation, Literary Censorship in Massachusetts, . . . teaching a seminar on the subject . . . , writing two books on press freedom, and assembling (over a period of 25 years) a book collection on freedom of the press which now numbers some 7,000 items."

\*     \*     \*

## McDANIEL, Roderick D.    1927-

PERSONAL: Born August 25, 1927, in El Centro, Calif.; son of Henry Terry (a blacksmith) and Myrtle (Willey) McDaniel; married Dona Colleen Gamby (a businesswoman), April 14, 1946; children: Sean Monroe, Stephen Douglas. Education: University of Southern California, B.A., 1951, Ed.D., 1967; Long Beach State College (now California State University, Long Beach), M.A., 1959. Home: 2051 Via Madonna, Lomita, Calif. 90717. Office: Palos Verdes Peninsula Unified School District, 38 Crest Rd., Rolling Hills, Calif. 90274.

CAREER: Teacher in La Puente, Calif., 1952-53; Torrance Unified School District, Torrance, Calif., teacher, principal, and director of media, 1953-68; Xerox Corp., Santa Ana, Calif., vice-president in professional library service, 1968-69; Palos Verdes Peninsula Unified School District, Rolling Hills, Calif., curriculum director, 1970-75, teacher and librarian at Rolling Hills High School, 1975—. Visiting lecturer, University of Southern California. Military service: U.S. Army, paratrooper, 1946-47. Member: Association for Supervision and Curriculum Development, California Library and Media Educators Association.

WRITINGS: Resources for Learning, Bowker, 1971. Contributor to audiovisual journals.

WORK IN PROGRESS: A novel of the life and times of an apprentice law clerk in 18th century London, tentatively entitled Gwilliamson; a novel of the Phillipine Revolution, 1898-1902, tentatively entitled Henry and the Revolutionary.

AVOCATIONAL INTERESTS: Gardening, painting, handcrafts, reading, travel.

\*     \*     \*

## McDAVID, John E., Jr.    1934-

PERSONAL: Born November 2, 1934, in Charleston, W.Va.; son of John E. (a banker) and Elizabeth (Rodgers) McDavid; married second wife, Sandra Warden, April 9, 1977; children: (first marriage) Stephen A., Catherine A., John E. III; (second marriage) Michael, Lynda, Gregory. Education: Ohio State University, B.S., 1956, M.B.A., 1962, Ph.D., 1966. Politics: Republican. Religion: Presbyterian. Home: 668 Clearview Hghts., Charleston, W.Va. 25312. Office: National Bank of Commerce, Charleston, W.Va. 25302.

CAREER: Ohio Valley Capital Corporation, Cincinnati, Ohio, vice-president and treasurer, 1963-65; Xavier University, Cincinnati, professor of business administration, 1965-72; East Tennessee State University, Johnson City, Tenn., professor and chairman of department of business administration, 1972—. Director, National Bank of Commerce of Charleston, W.Va., 1966—; director and advisor to president, Muncy Corporation, Springfield, Ohio. Member of board of directors, Charleston Symphony Orchestra. Mili-

tary service: U.S. Air Force; served as fighter pilot. U.S. Air Force Reserve; current rank lieutenant colonel. Member: American Marketing Association (president, Cincinnati chapter, 1968-69), Sales and Marketing Executives, Boy Scouts of America (member of executive board, Buckskin Council).

WRITINGS: Small Business Management, McGraw, 1972.

WORK IN PROGRESS: Collecting material for a book, Contemporary Marketing Problems and Bank Management.

AVOCATIONAL INTERESTS: Hunting and fishing; pilot (holds instructor rating).

\*     \*     \*

## McDAVID, Virginia (Glenn)    1926-

PERSONAL: Born August 9, 1926, in Minneapolis, Minn.; daughter of Lester Truxtun (an engineer) and Anna (Wurtz) Glenn; married Raven I. McDavid, Jr. (a professor at University of Chicago), June 7, 1950; children: Glenn, Raven III, Thomas, Ann. Education: University of Minnesota, B.A., 1946, M.A., 1948, Ph.D., 1956. Religion: Episcopalian. Home: 5736 South Blackstone, Chicago, Ill. 60637. Office: English Department, Chicago State University, Chicago, Ill. 60628.

CAREER: Kent State University, Kent, Ohio, instructor in English, 1956-57; Chicago State University, Chicago, Ill., professor of English, 1957—; co-director and partner (with husband) of language research services, 1962—. Member: Modern Language Association of America, Linguistic Society of America, National Council of Teachers of English, American Association of University Professors, Midwest Modern Language Association, Phi Beta Kappa.

WRITINGS: (With William Card) 99 Exercises for College Composition, Scott, Foresman, 1962; (with Macklin Thomas) Basic Writing, privately printed, 1971; English Usage, Random House, 1972; (with Thomas) Writing Today's English, Harper, 1977. Associate editor, Linguistic Atlas of the North Central States; editor, Illinois Schools Journal, and Publication of the American Dialect Society.

\*     \*     \*

## McDONALD, William Francis    1898-1976

PERSONAL: Born November 15, 1898, in Philadelphia, Pa.; son of Matthew Patrick (a telegrapher) and Mary Ann (Given) McDonald; married Mildred Norma Lee, April 27, 1931; children: Jo Ann (Mrs. Harry C. Avery), Nancy Lee (Mrs. Guy Allen Gladson, Jr.), Molly (Mrs. Sydney S. Shoemaker). Education: Georgetown University, B.A., 1923; Oxford University, B.A. (first class honors), 1927, M.A., 1930; Cornell University, Ph.D., 1929. Politics: Democrat. Religion: Roman Catholic. Home: 423 Arden Rd., Columbus, Ohio 43214. Office: Department of History, Ohio State University, Columbus, Ohio 43210.

CAREER: Cornell University, Ithaca, N.Y., instructor in classics, 1928-29; University of Minnesota, Minneapolis, assistant professor of ancient history, 1929-30; Cornell University, assistant professor of classics, 1930-31; Ohio State University, Columbus, associate professor, 1931-36, professor of ancient history, 1936-69, professor emeritus, 1972-76. Member: American Historical Association, American Oriental Society, American Philology Association, American Catholic History Association, Phi Beta Kappa. Awards, honors: Research grant, American Council of Learned Societies, 1943-45.

*WRITINGS: Federal Relief Administration and the Arts: The Origins and Administrative History of the Arts Projects of the Works Progress Administration,* Ohio State University Press, 1969; (editor) *Criminal Justice and the Victim,* Sage Publications, Inc., 1976.†

(Died August 7, 1976)

* * *

## McDOUGALL, John Lorne 1900-

*PERSONAL:* Born January 1, 1900, in Tayside, Ontario, Canada; son of Duncan M. (a commercial traveler) and Isabel M. (McGregor) McDougall; married Blossom Mackenzie, June 4, 1927 (died, 1968); married Elinor D. Matthews, December 29, 1969; children: (first marriage) Duncan M., H. John, Helen McDougall Treble, Janet McDougall Johnston. *Education:* University of Toronto, B.A., 1921, M.A., 1923; graduate study at London School of Economics and Political Science, 1923-24, and Harvard University, 1924-25. *Politics:* Conservative. *Religion:* Anglican. *Home:* 253 Albert St., Kingston, Ontario, Canada K7L 3V4.

*CAREER:* University of Texas at Austin, instructor, 1925-26; University of Toronto, Toronto, Ontario, lecturer, 1926-27; Canadian General Securities Ltd., chief statistician, 1927-31; Queens's University, Kingston, Ontario, 1932-70, began as assistant professor, became professor of economics. Visiting fellow, Princeton University, 1949-50. Alderman, City of Kingston, 1971-74. *Member:* Royal Economic Society, Canadian Economics Association.

*WRITINGS: Canadian Pacific: A Brief History,* McGill University Press, 1968. Also author of *The Foundations of National Wellbeing,* published by Ryerson, and *Railway Wage Rates, Employment and Pay,* published by Longmans, Green. Contributor of articles to professional journals.

*SIDELIGHTS:* John Lorne McDougall told *CA:* "Currently my interests are in the editing of manuscripts for publication and in free-lance journalism on economic events. Clarity and accuracy are always a challenge; I enjoy it."

* * *

## McELROY, Davis Dunbar 1917-

*PERSONAL:* Born August 1, 1917, in San Francisco, Calif.; son of Chester Earl (an electrician) and Violet (Humann) McElroy; married Lucille Beauvaise, August, 1942 (divorced, 1962); married Suzanne Saunders, May 25, 1962; children: (second marriage) Joy Lynn. *Education:* University of California, Berkeley, A.B., 1949; University of Edinburgh, Ph.D., 1952. *Politics:* Democrat. *Religion:* None. *Home:* 811 North Washington, Centralia, Wash. 98531. *Office:* Department of English, Centralia College, Centralia, Wash. 98531.

*CAREER:* Matson Navigation Co., San Francisco, Calif., marine engineer, 1940-42; Washington State University, Pullman, assistant professor, 1962-68, associate professor of English, 1962-70; Centralia College, Centralia, Wash., chairman of English department, 1970—. *Military service:* U.S. Navy, 1942-46; became lieutenant.

*WRITINGS: Existentialism and Modern Literature,* Philosophical Library, 1963; *The Study of Literature,* Philosophical Library, 1965; *Scotland's Age of Improvement,* Washington State University Press, 1970. Contributor to literature journals.

*WORK IN PROGRESS: Three Existential Heroes: Don Juan, Faust, and Don Quixote.*

## McGAUGHEY, (Florence) Helen 1904-

*PERSONAL:* Born March 1, 1904, in Roachdale, Ind.; daughter of Charles E. (a lawyer and banker) and Sallie E. (Brumfield) McGaughey. *Education:* Attended Western College for Women (now Western College), 1922-23; DePauw University, A.B., 1926; Middlebury College, A.M., 1932; also attended Indiana University and Indiana State University. *Politics:* Independent. *Religion:* Christian Church (Disciples of Christ). *Home:* 136 South 25th St., Terre Haute, Ind. 47803. *Office:* Department of English, Indiana State University, Terre Haute, Ind. 47809.

*CAREER:* High school English teacher in Kentland, Ind., 1926-27, and Cloverdale, Ind., 1927-28; head of English department in high school in Plymouth, Ind., 1928-34, supervising teacher in Greencastle, Ind., 1935-46; Indiana State University, Terre Haute, assistant professor, 1946-56, associate professor, 1956-60, professor of English, 1960-70, professor emeritus, 1970—. Member of Terre Haute Symphony board, 1963-65, 1967-69. *Member:* International Poetry Society (fellow), International Academy of Poets (founding fellow), National Arts Club, National League of American Pen Women, World Poetry Society International, Academy of American Poets, Centro Studie Scambi Internazionali (Rome), Indiana Federation of Poetry Clubs, Pen and Brush Club, Daughters of the American Revolution, Wedgewood Collectors' Society, Metropolitan Opera Guild, Delta Delta Delta, Alpha Phi Gamma, Delta Kappa Gamma. *Awards, honors:* DePauw University Alumni Citation, 1959; Diploma Signalazione and Poet Laureate Award in English, from Centro Studie Scambi Internazionali, 1962; American Poets Fellowship Society publication grant, 1967.

*WRITINGS: Wind Across the Night,* Emory University Press, 1938; *Music in the Wind,* Emory University Press, 1941; *Spring Is a Blue Kite,* Emory University Press, 1946; *Reaching for the Spring,* Exposition, 1958; *Selected Poems,* Centro Studi, 1961; *Shadows,* Centro Studi, 1965; *Petals from a Plum Tree,* Prairie Press, 1967. Editor of and contributor to *The History of Greencastle Christian Church, Greencastle, Indiana, 1830-1972.* Author of *Songs of Sorrow* (songs; contains "Unseasonal," "Had I but Known," "Thought Wave," "At the River Curve," "If a Leaf but Fall," and "Holy Night"), with music by Jon J. Polifrone, and of librettos for Polifrone, "The Dispossessed" and "Written in the Stars." Has adapted "Holy Night" for orchestra and chorus, with music by Jeffrey King. Contributor of essays and poems to magazines and newspapers, including *Christian Science Monitor* and *New York Sun.*

*WORK IN PROGRESS: Speak to the Stones,* a book of poems.

*SIDELIGHTS:* Helen McGaughey told *CA:* "My writing began almost assuredly from my experiences at the Bread Loaf School of English, Middlebury, Vermont: the inspiration of the setting, the contact with contemporary writers, and the necessity for putting into words the experiences of living. My poems, and essays, are a revelation of self."

* * *

## McGIMSEY, Charles Robert III 1925-

*PERSONAL:* Born June 18, 1925, in Dallas, Tex.; son of Charles Robert, Jr. (a businessman) and Ellen (Parks) McGimsey; married Elizabeth Conger (a photographer), December 20, 1949; children: Charles Robert, Brian Keith, Mark Douglass. *Education:* Attended Vanderbilt University, 1942-43, and University of the South, 1943-44; University of New Mexico, B.A., 1949; Harvard University, M.A., 1954, Ph.D., 1958. *Home:* 435 Hawthorn, Fayetteville, Ark. 72701. *Office:* University of Arkansas Museum, Fayetteville, Ark. 72701.

*CAREER:* University of Arkansas, Fayetteville, 1957—, began as instructor, professor of anthropology and chairman of department, 1969—, director of University of Arkansas Museum, 1959—. Director, Arkansas Archeological Survey, 1967—. Consultant to National Park Service. Member of National Committee on the Recovery of Archeological Remains. *Military service:* U.S. Naval Reserve, 1943—, active duty, 1943-47. *Member:* American Anthropological Association (fellow), Society for American Archaeology (member of executive committee, 1971-73; vice-president, 1973-74; president, 1974-75), American Association of Museums, Arkansas Archeological Society (editor, 1960-72). *Awards, honors:* Distinguished Service Award, Society for American Archaeology, 1975.

*WRITINGS:* (With G. R. Willey) *The Monagrillo Culture of Panama,* Peabody Museum of Archaeology and Ethnology, 1955; *Indians of Arkansas,* Arkansas Archeological Survey, 1970; *Public Archeology,* Seminar Press, 1972; (with H. A. Davis) *The Management of Archeological Resources,* Society for American Archaeology, 1977. Contributor of eighty articles to journals.

*WORK IN PROGRESS:* Research on Arkansas archeology.

\* \* \*

## McGUIRE, Martin C. 1933-

*PERSONAL:* Born December 12, 1933, in Shanghai, China; son of Martin C. and Margaret (Walsh) McGuire; married Mary Alice Delaney, October 9, 1965; children: Walsh, John, Constance. *Education:* U.S. Military Academy, B.S., 1955; Oxford University, B.A., 1958, M.A., 1962; Harvard University, Ph.D., 1964. *Home:* 4531 28th St. N.W., Washington, D.C. 20008. *Office:* Department of Economics, University of Maryland, College Park, Md. 20742.

*CAREER:* Harvard University, Cambridge, Mass., instructor in economics, 1964; Office of Secretary of Defense, Washington, D.C., economist, 1964-65; U.S. Economic Development Administration, Washington, D.C., director of program analysis, 1965-67; University of Maryland, College Park, associate professor, 1967-71, professor of economics, 1971—. Ford Foundation visiting professor, University of California, Berkeley. *Military service:* U.S. Army, 1955-61; became captain. *Awards, honors:* Rhodes scholar, 1955; National Science Foundation grant.

*WRITINGS: Secrecy and the Arms Race,* Harvard University Press, 1965.

Contributor: Roland McKean, editor, *Issues in Defense Economics,* Columbia University Press, 1967; Bruce M. Russett, *Economic Theories of International Politics,* Markham, 1968; Kenneth E. Boulding and Martin Pfaff, editors, *Redistribution to the Rich and the Poor,* Wadsworth, 1972; Wallace E. Oates, editor, *Financing the New Federalism,* Resources for the Future (Washington, D.C.), 1975.

*WORK IN PROGRESS: Economic Theory of Government Decisions.*

\* \* \*

## McINTYRE, William (Alexander) 1916-

*PERSONAL:* Born December 17, 1916, in Bozeman, Mont.; son of Cornelius Alexander and Annie (McDonnell) McIntyre; married Nancy Fair (a writer), September 15, 1948; children: Megan Catherine. *Education:* University of California, Los Angeles, B.Ed., 1938; Instituto Meschini, Rome, Italy, courses in Italian language and literature, 1951-52. *Home:* 31257 East Nine Dr., Laguna Niguel, Calif. 92677. *Office address:* Gala Books, P.O. Box 659, Laguna Beach, Calif. 92652.

*CAREER:* Walt Disney Studio, Burbank, Calif., 1938-41, became assistant director and assistant animator; *Esquire,* New York City, humor-cartoon editor, 1948; *Reporter,* New York City, art editor, 1949-50; art director of various publications in Milan and Rome, Italy, 1950-54; *True,* New York City, associate editor and humor editor, 1954-60; collaborator with Virgil Partch on syndicated cartoons, 1960-66; Gala Books (specialized gift books and cookbooks), Laguna Beach, Calif., publisher, 1969—. *Military service:* U.S. Marine Corps, 1942-46; became major. *Member:* Southern California Book Publishers Association, Delta Epsilon.

*WRITINGS*—Editor, except as indicated: *Crazy Cartoons by VIP,* Fawcett, 1956; *Best Cartoons from True,* Fawcett, 1958; (author of text; cartoons by Virgil Partch) *VIP Tosses a Party,* Simon & Schuster, 1959; *The Sexperts,* Dell, 1970; *Off-Collar Cartoons,* Dell, 1971. Contributor of ideas and cartoons to *New Yorker,* 1946-47, and articles to *New York Times Magazine,* 1958-59.

\* \* \*

## McKAY, Alexander G(ordon) 1924-

*PERSONAL:* Born December 24, 1924, in Toronto, Ontario, Canada; son of Alexander Lynn (a public health specialist) and Marjory (Nicoll) McKay; married Helen Jean Zulauf (a high school teacher), December 24, 1964; stepchildren: Julie Anne Stephanie Fraser, Danae Helen Fraser. *Education:* University of Toronto, B.A., 1946; Yale University, M.A., 1947; Princeton University, A.M., 1948, Ph.D., 1950. *Politics:* Liberal. *Religion:* Anglican. *Home:* 1 Turner Ave., Hamilton, Ontario, Canada L8P 3K4. *Office:* Faculty of Humanities, McMaster University, Hamilton, Ontario, Canada L8S 4L8.

*CAREER:* Instructor at Wells College, Aurora, N.Y., 1949-50, and University of Pennsylvania, Philadelphia, 1950-51; lecturer in classical philology at University of Manitoba, Winnipeg, 1951-52, and Mount Allison University, Sackville, New Brunswick, 1952-53; Waterloo College, Waterloo, Ontario, assistant professor, 1953-54, associate professor of classical philology, 1954-55; University of Manitoba, assistant professor of classical philology, 1955-57; McMaster University, Hamilton, Ontario, assistant professor, 1957-59, associate professor, 1959-61, professor of classics, 1961—, chairman of department, 1962-68, 1976-79, dean of Faculty of Humanities, 1968-73. Director, Classical Summer School of Vergilian Society, Cumae, Italy, 1957-72; visiting professor, University of Colorado, summers, 1961, 1964, 1965, and at University's Hellenic Institute, Athens, Greece, 1966. President of Architectural Conservancy of Ontario, 1966-67, Hamilton Philharmonic Orchestra, 1968-70, Hamilton Chamber Music Society, 1968-71, and Hamilton and Region Arts Council, 1971-73.

*MEMBER:* Royal Society of Canada (fellow; honorary editor, 1968—), Classical Association of Canada (vice-president, 1970-72; president, 1978-80), Vergilian Society of America (vice-president, 1960-72; president, 1972-74), Archaeological Institute of America, American Philological

Association, American Classical League, Classical Association of the Atlantic States, Classical Association of the Middle West and South (president, 1972-73), Men's Canadian Club of Hamilton (president, 1972-73).

*WRITINGS:* (Compiler) *Naples and Compania: Texts and Illustrations,* Vergilian Society of America, 1962; (with D. M. Shepherd) *Roman Lyric Poetry: Catullus and Horace,* St. Martin's, 1969; *Vergil's Italy,* New York Graphic Society, 1970; *Cumae and the Phlegraean Fields,* Cromlech Press, 1972; *Naples and Coastal Campania,* Cromlech Press, 1972; (with Shepherd) *Roman Satire,* St. Martin's, 1975; *Houses, Villas and Palaces in the Roman World,* Cornell University Press, 1975; *Vitruvius, Architect and Engineer,* Macmillan, 1978. Member of editorial board, *Arethusa,* 1967; contributing editor, *Classical World* and *Vergilius;* executive editor, *Cultural History of Canada,* 1975—.

*WORK IN PROGRESS: Vergil: A Study,* for Twayne; *Vergil's "Eclogues," "Georgics" and "Aeneid,"* for Teubner Gesellschaft; *The Roman City,* for Macmillan (Toronto); *Aeschylean Stagecraft,* for Hakkert.

\*    \*    \*

## McKEAN, Keith F.   1915-

*PERSONAL:* Born August 18, 1915, in Beaver Falls, Pa.; son of Arthur (a lawyer) and Eleanor (Ferguson) McKean; married Catherine Stevenson, October 31, 1942 (divorced, 1965); married Joan Sanford Canter, September 26, 1969; children: Kevin, Bruce. *Education:* Williams College, A.B., 1938; University of Chicago, A.M., 1940; University of Michigan, Ph.D., 1949. *Politics:* Independent. *Home:* 824 Hudson Rd., Cedar Falls, Iowa 50613. *Office:* Baker 210, University of Northern Iowa, Cedar Falls, Iowa 50613.

*CAREER:* University of Toledo, Toledo, Ohio, instructor in English, 1940-42; North Carolina State University, Raleigh, associate professor, 1949-55, professor of general studies, 1955-61; Elmira College, Elmira, N.Y., professor of English, 1961-68, chairman of department, 1966-68; University of Northern Iowa, Cedar Falls, professor of English, 1968—, department chairman, 1968-71. *Military service:* U.S. Army Air Forces, 1942-46; became first lieutenant. *Member:* Modern Language Association of America, American Association of University Professors. *Awards, honors:* Ford Foundation faculty fellowship for post-doctoral work at Yale University, 1954-55; University of North Carolina research and development grant, 1959-60; Inter-University Committee on Economic Development in the South grant, 1961-62.

*WRITINGS:* (Author of introduction) *On Modern Poets,* Meridian, 1959; *Cross Currents in the South,* Swallow Press, 1960; *The Moral Measure of Literature,* Swallow Press, 1961; (editor with S. Kumar) *Critical Approaches to Fiction,* McGraw, 1968; (editor and contributor with Charles Wheeler) *World of Informative and Persuasive Prose,* Holt, 1971.

\*    \*    \*

## McKEATING, Henry   1932-

*PERSONAL:* Born January 15, 1932, in Cumberland, England; son of Thomas Gallantry (a miner) and Edith (Hodgson) McKeating; married Margaret D. Mercer (a teacher), August 17, 1957; children: Helen Margaret, Katherine Mary, Jane Elizabeth, Richard Thomas. *Education:* Attended Handsworth Theological College, Birmingham, England, 1951-55, and University of Strasbourg, 1955-56;

University of London, B.D., 1955, M.Th., 1958, Ph.D., 1966 (all external degrees). *Home:* 9 Templeoak Dr., Wollaton, Nottingham NG8 2SF, England. *Office:* Department of Theology, University of Nottingham, Nottingham NG7 2RD, England.

*CAREER:* Methodist minister in pastoral work, 1956-59; University of Nottingham, Nottingham, England, lecturer in theology, 1959—. *Member:* Society for Old Testament Study.

*WRITINGS:* (Contributor) R.P.C. Hanson, editor, *Difficulties for Christian Belief,* Macmillan, 1967; (contributor) *A Sourcebook of the Bible for Teachers,* S.C.M. Press, 1969; *Living with Guilt,* S.C.M., 1970; *Amos, Hosea and Micah,* Cambridge University Press, 1971; *God and the Future,* S.C.M., 1974, Judson, 1975.

\*    \*    \*

## McKENNA, J(ohn) W(illiam)   1938-

*PERSONAL:* Born July 23, 1938, in West Warwick, R.I.; son of James A. and Jeanne (Chagnon) McKenna; married Elizabeth Davis, December 16, 1961; children: Christopher Davis, Edward Telford. *Education:* Amherst College, B.A., 1960; Columbia University, M.A., 1961; Cambridge University, Ph.D., 1965. *Home:* 1444 Old Gulph Road, Villanova, Pa.; and Bayview House, Southport, Me. *Office:* Department of History, Haverford College, Haverford, Pa. 19041.

*CAREER:* Brooklyn College of the City University of New York, Brooklyn, N.Y., lecturer in history, 1962-63; Homerton College, Cambridge, England, acting lecturer, 1964-65; Brooklyn College, instructor in history, 1965-66; University of California, Riverside, assistant professor of history, 1966-69; Haverford College, Haverford, Pa., Walter D. and Edith M. L. Scull Associate Professor of English Constitutional History, 1969—. Instructor in history, Columbia University, New York, N.Y., summer, 1963. *Member:* Royal Historical Society (fellow), Conference on British Studies, American Historical Association, Mediaeval Academy of America, Boothbay Harbor (Me.) Yacht Club. *Awards, honors:* Fulbright Fellow, Clare College, Cambridge, 1963-65.

*WRITINGS: The Lancastrian Kings,* Cambridge University Press, 1973; (editor) *The Borzoi History of England,* Volume IV (sources and readings), Knopf, 1973; *Richard III,* Holt, 1973. Contributor to *Encyclopedia Americana* and *Colliers Encyclopedia.* Contributor of scholarly articles and reviews to *English Historical Review, Speculum,* and *Journal of Warburg Institutes.*

*WORK IN PROGRESS: Joan of Arc: Sources and Readings; Kingship and Propaganda in Fifteenth Century England; The Origins of Modern Propaganda.*

*AVOCATIONAL INTERESTS:* Sailing, skiing, gardening.†

\*    \*    \*

## McKENNEY, Ruth   1911-1972

November 18, 1911—July 25, 1972; American humorist and Marxist. Obituaries: *New York Times,* July 25, 1972; *Washington Post,* July 28, 1972; *Newsweek,* August 7, 1972; *Publishers Weekly,* August 14, 1972; *Antiquarian Bookman,* September 25, 1972; *Current Biography,* October, 1972.

\*    \*    \*

## McKERN, Sharon S(mith)   1941-

*PERSONAL:* Born February 14, 1941, in Austin, Tex.;

daughter of Douglas Hudson and Jeanette (McPhail) Smith; married Thomas W. McKern (a physical anthropologist), July 19, 1966. *Education:* Attended University of Texas, 1966. *Politics:* Independent. *Home:* 2181 Hillside, Coquitlam, British Columbia, Canada.

*MEMBER:* American Anthropological Association, Human Ecological Association, Theta Sigma Phi.

*WRITINGS:* (With husband, Thomas W. McKern) *Human Origins: An Introduction to Physical Anthropology,* Prentice-Hall, 1969; (with T. W. McKern) *Tracking Fossil Man: An Adventure in Evolution,* Praeger, 1970; *Exploring the Unknown: Mysteries in American Archaeology,* Praeger, 1972; *The Many Faces of Man,* Lothrop, 1972; (with T. W. McKern) *Living Prehistory: An Introduction to Physical Anthropology and Archaeology,* Cummings, 1974. Contributor of articles to *Science Digest, Mankind, Sexology, Nature and Science, Children's Friend, Jack and Jill,* and *Highlights for Children.*

*WORK IN PROGRESS:* Articles on captive breeding programs.

*SIDELIGHTS:* Sharon McKern tells *CA* her main interest is "anthropology—the science of man. Directly or indirectly, we all bear the costs of scientific research. We've a right to expect to share in scientific discoveries. And no field promises so much excitement as anthropology. This is the discipline which seeks to explain human actions and attitudes, the patterns for which are buried in the distant past. I can't imagine writing full-time about anything else."†

\*    \*    \*

## McKINNEY, David Walter, Jr.  1920-

*PERSONAL:* Born February 3, 1920, in Gurdon, Ark.; son of David Walter (a railroad mechanic) and Grace (Cunningham) McKinney; married Tyra Elizabeth Bass (divorced, 1951); married Edna Helen Rochlin; children: (first marriage) David W. III, Elana Duvonne (Mrs. James Prude), Hurron Bernard; (second marriage) Nicole Camille, Carla Serena, Barry Martin. *Education:* Arkansas Agricultural, Mechanical and Normal College (now University of Arkansas at Pine Bluff), A.B., 1941; Wayne University (now Wayne State University), M.A., 1946; University of Wisconsin, Ph.D., 1960. *Home:* 62 Ermosa Crescent, Guelph, Ontario, Canada N1E 5Z4. *Office:* Department of Sociology, University of Guelph, Guelph, Ontario, Canada N16 2W1.

*CAREER:* University of Chicago, Chicago, Ill., instructor, 1949-51; Brooklyn College of the City University of New York, Brooklyn, N.Y., 1953-68, began as instructor, became assistant professor of sociology; University of Guelph, Guelph, Ontario, 1966—, began as associate professor, currently professor of sociology. Visiting professor of sociology, State University of New York College at Plattsburg, fall, 1970. Consultant to City of New York Commission on Human Rights, 1965-66, 1967, Thomas Y. Crowell Co., 1966, and New York State Temporary Commission to Revise the Social Services Law, 1971. *Member:* American Academy of Political and Social Science, Society for the Study of Social Problems, American Association of University Professors, Eastern Sociological Society, New York Academy of Science, Sigma Xi, Alpha Kappa Delta.

*WRITINGS: The Authoritarian Personality Studies: An Inquiry into the Failure of Social Science Research to Produce Demonstrable Knowledge,* Mouton, 1971. Guest editor, "Papers on the Social Sciences," 1971, 1973. Contributor of about ten articles to social science journals.

## McKINNON, Robert Scott  1937-

*PERSONAL:* Born October 27, 1937, in Portland, Ore.; son of Angus (a YMCA secretary) and Vivian (Moggy) McKinnon; married Suzanne Reavley Cook, July 5, 1960; children: Christopher Kevin, Wendy Clare. *Education:* Attended Oakland Junior College; University of Montana, B.Ed.; graduate study at University of Massachusetts, University of Utah, University of Montana, Hollins College, and Eastern Montana College. *Home:* 1608 7th St. S., Great Falls, Mont. 59405. *Office:* Charles M. Russell High School, Great Falls, Mont. 59401.

*CAREER:* Charles M. Russell High School, Great Falls, Mont., English teacher, for thirteen years. *Member:* National Education Association, Montana Education Association, Great Falls Teacher Association. *Awards, honors:* Masquer Writing Award, University of Montana, for one-act play, "Sport of Kings."

*WRITINGS: Moose, Bruce and the Goose* (juvenile), Bobbs-Merrill, 1969; *To Yellowstone: A Journey Home* (juvenile), Holt, 1975. Author of plays, "Sport of Kings," "Gabriel Blow Your Horn," and "The Kissin' River." Contributor of articles on boat trips and swimming to newspaper supplements and miner magazines.

*SIDELIGHTS:* Robert McKinnon is a veteran YMCA swimming champion, coached the Great Falls (Mont.) Swim Club for seven years, and teaches learn-to-swim programs in his own indoor backyard pool which he built himself. He also raises and races greyhounds, and has taken several river raft and boat trips in several states, totaling thousands of miles. Johnson Motors, Alcoa Aluminum, and Crestliner Boats chronicled McKinnon's trip on the wild Salmon River in a film entitled "The River Busters."

*BIOGRAPHICAL/CRITICAL SOURCES: Kirkus Reviews,* October 1, 1969; *New York Times Book Review,* November 30, 1969, January 11, 1976.

\*    \*    \*

## McLEAN, Sammy Kay  1929-

*PERSONAL:* Born September 29, 1929, in Eldorado, Kan.; son of Kermit Kooper and Lillian Ruth (McCool) McLean; married Margaret Smith, 1954 (divorced, 1965); married Deborah Teague, 1976. *Education:* University of Oklahoma, B.A., 1952; University of Michigan, M.A., 1957, Ph.D., 1963. *Office:* Department of Germanic Languages and Literature, University of Washington, Seattle, Wash. 98195.

*CAREER:* Dartmouth College, Hanover, N.H., instructor, 1961-63, assistant professor of German language and literature, 1963-65; University of Maryland Overseas Program, London, England, lecturer in German, 1965-67; University of Washington, Seattle, assistant professor, 1967-73, associate professor of German and comparative literature, 1973—. *Military service:* U.S. Air Force, 1952-56; became staff sergeant; served as musician. *Member:* International Brecht Society, American Association of University Professors, Seattle Film Society, Seattle Jazz Society. *Awards, honors:* Fulbright study grant, 1958-59; Dartmouth College comparative studies grant, 1963.

*WRITINGS: The Baenkelsang and the Work of Bertolt Brecht,* Mouton, 1972. Author of poems and of essays on Brecht and Kafka; translator of poems from German.

*WORK IN PROGRESS:* Poems and essays.

*SIDELIGHTS:* Sammy Kay McLean told *CA,* "I try to

bring the processes of imaginative and scholarly writing together in the classes I teach, in the process of teaching.''

\*　　\*　　\*

## McLEOD, Wallace (Edmond) 1931-

*PERSONAL:* Born May 30, 1931, in Toronto, Ontario, Canada; son of Angus Edmond (a printing pressman) and Mary A. E. (Shier) McLeod; married Elizabeth M. Staples (a teacher), July 24, 1957; children: Betsy, John, James, Angus. *Education:* University of Toronto, B.A., 1953; Harvard University, A.M., 1954, Ph.D., 1966; also studied at American School of Classical Studies, Athens, Greece, 1957-59. *Politics:* Conservative. *Religion:* Presbyterian. *Home:* 399 St. Clements Ave., Toronto, Ontario, Canada M5N 1M2. *Office:* Victoria College, University of Toronto, Toronto, Ontario, Canada M5S 1K7.

*CAREER:* Trinity College, Hartford, Conn., instructor in classical languages, 1955-56; University of British Columbia, Vancouver, instructor in classics, 1959-61; University of Western Ontario, London, lecturer in classics, 1961-62; University of Toronto, Victoria College, Toronto, Ontario, assistant professor, 1962-66, associate professor, 1966-74, professor of classics, 1974—, associate chairman of undergraduate classics department, 1975—. *Member:* Classical Association of Canada, American Philological Association, Society of Archer-Antiquaries, Ancient Free and Accepted Masons. *Awards, honors:* Canada Council leave fellowship, 1970-71.

*WRITINGS: Composite Bows from the Tomb of Tutankhamun,* Oxford University Press, 1970; (editor and contributor) *Beyond the Pillars: More Light on Freemasonry,* Grand Lodge of Canada, 1973; (editor and contributor) *Meeting the Challenge: The Lodge Officer at Work,* Grand Lodge of Canada, 1976. Contributor of articles and reviews to professional journals. *Phoenix,* associate editor, 1965-70, acting editor, 1973.

*WORK IN PROGRESS: Inscribed Pottery from the Middle Bronze Age at Lerna; Archery Equipment from the Tomb of Tutankhamun; Crusaders' Castles of the Argolid; History of Freemasonry in Ontario.*

*SIDELIGHTS:* Wallace McLeod participated in archaeological excavations at Lerna, Greece, and Gordion, Turkey, in 1958.

\*　　\*　　\*

## McMAHON, Thomas 1923(?)-1972

1923(?)—June 19, 1972; American educator and literary critic. Obituaries: *New York Times,* June 20, 1972.

\*　　\*　　\*

## McMANNERS, John 1916-

*PERSONAL:* Born December 25, 1916, in Durham, England; son of Joseph (a clergyman of Church of England) and Ann (Marshal) McManners; married Sarah Carruthers Errington, December 27, 1952; children: Hugh, Helen, Peter, Ann. *Education:* Oxford University, B.A. (first class honors), 1938, M.A., 1946; University of Durham, Diploma in Theology, 1947. *Home and office:* Christ Church, Oxford University, Oxford OX1 1DP, England.

*CAREER:* Clergyman, Church of England, 1947—; Oxford University, St. Edmund Hall, Oxford, England, fellow and chaplain, 1948-56; University of Sydney, Sydney, New South Wales, Australia, professor of history, 1960-68; University of Leicester, Leicester, England, professor of history, 1968-72; Oxford University, Regius Professor of Ecclesiastical History, 1973—. Senior visiting fellow, All Souls College, Oxford University, 1967-68; visiting professor of British Academy, Institut Catholique, Paris, 1972; trustee, National Portrait Gallery, London, 1971—. *Military service:* British Army, 1939-45; became major; decorated Officer, Order of King George I of the Hellenes. *Member:* Australian Academy of the Humanities (fellow), British Academy (fellow).

*WRITINGS:* (Editor with John M. Wallace-Hadrill *France: Government and Society,* Methuen, 1957, 2nd edition, 1970; *French Ecclesiastical Society under the Ancient Regime: A Study of Angers in the Eighteenth Century,* Manchester University Press, 1960; (with R. M. Crawford) *The Future of the Humanities in the Australian Universities* (booklet), Melbourne University Press, for Australian Humanities Research Council, 1965; *Lectures on European History, 1789-1914: Men, Machines and Freedom* (sequel to J. M. Thompson's *Lectures on Foreign History, 1494-1789*), Basil Blackwell, 1966, Barnes & Noble, 1967, reprinted as *European History, 1789-1914: Men, Machines, and Freedom,* Harper, 1969; *The Social Contract and Rousseau's Revolt against Society* (his inaugural lecture at University of Leicester), Leicester University Press, 1968; *The French Revolution and the Church,* S.P.C.K., for Church Historical Society, 1969, Harper, 1970; *Church and State in France,* S.P.C.K. for Church Historical Society, 1972; (contributor) D. Baker, editor, *Church, Society, and Politics,* Basil Blackwell, 1975; (contributor) Baker, editor, *Religious Motivations: Biographical and Sociological Problems for the Church Historian,* Basil Blackwell, 1978. Contributor to *New Cambridge Modern History,* Volumes VI and VIII.

*WORK IN PROGRESS:* Further studies on French ecclesiastical life in the eighteenth century; *Death and the Enlightenment.*

*AVOCATIONAL INTERESTS:* Tennis, squash.

\*　　\*　　\*

## McMASTER, Juliet 1937-

*PERSONAL:* Born August 2, 1937, in Kisumu, Kenya; daughter of Sydney Herbert (a British colonial administrator) and Sylvia (Hook) Fazan; married Leonard Sutton, January 7, 1961 (divorced, 1967); married Rowland Douglas McMaster (a university professor), May 10, 1968; children: (second marriage) Rawdon, Lindsey. *Education:* St. Anne's College, Oxford, B.A. (honors), 1959; Mt. Holyoke College, additional study, 1959-60; University of Alberta, M.A., 1962, Ph.D., 1965. *Residence:* Edmonton, Alberta, Canada. *Office:* Department of English, University of Alberta, Edmonton, Alberta, Canada T69 2E5.

*CAREER:* University of Alberta, Edmonton, assistant professor, 1965-70, associate professor, 1970-76, professor of English, 1976—. *Member:* Modern Language Association of America, Association of Canadian University Teachers of English (president), Canadian Fencing Association, Victorian Studies Association of Western Canada (president).

*WRITINGS: Thackeray: The Major Novels,* University of Toronto Press, 1971; (editor) *Jane Austen's Achievement,* Barnes & Noble, 1976. Also author of *Trollope's Palliser Novels, Jane Austen on Love,* and a television script about Hogarth. Contributor to literature journals.

*AVOCATIONAL INTERESTS:* Fencing, ceramic sculpture.

## McNALLY, Raymond T. 1931-

*PERSONAL:* Born May 15, 1931, in Cleveland, Ohio; son of Michael Joseph and Marie (Kinkoff) McNally. *Education:* Attended University of Paris, 1951-52; Fordham University, A.B. (highest honors), 1953; Free University of Berlin, Ph.D., 1956; University of Leningrad, postdoctoral studies, 1961. *Politics:* Democrat. *Office:* Carney Hall 201, Boston College, Chestnut Hill, Mass. 02167.

*CAREER:* John Carroll University, Cleveland, Ohio, instructor in history, 1956-58; Boston College, Chestnut Hill, Mass., assistant professor, 1958-61, associate professor, 1962-69, professor of history, 1970—, director of Slavic and East European Center, 1964-74. Fulbright faculty research appointment to Romania, 1969-70. *Member:* American Association of Slavic Studies, American Historical Society. *Awards, honors:* American Exchange Scholar to the U.S.S.R., 1961; American Philosophical Society research grant, 1961; American Council of Learned Societies and Social Science Research Council grant, 1965.

*WRITINGS: The Major Works of Peter Chaadayev,* University of Notre Dame Press, 1969; *Chaadayev and His Friends: An Intellectual History of Peter Chaadayev and His Russian Contemporaries,* Diplomatic Press, 1971; (with Radu Florescu) *In Search of Dracula,* New York Graphic Society, 1972; (with Floresen) *Dracula: A Biography of Vlad the Impaler, 1431-1476,* Hawthorne, 1973; *A Clutch of Vampires,* New York Graphic Society, 1974. Contributor of articles to *Forschungen zur Osteuropaischen Geschichte, Slavic and East European Review, Russian Review, Slavic Review, Journal of the History of Ideas, Jahrbucher fuer Geschichte Osteuropas.*

*SIDELIGHTS:* Raymond McNally's "*In Search of Dracula* is a bit overpackaged," writes John Skow. "But the authors have done fine work in assembling documents and tales from Dracula's own time." The *Time* reviewer also notes that *In Search of Dracula* clears its subject "of one notable charge: by examining Rumanian, Russian, German and French folklore of the 15th century, in which Dracula figures vividly, it establishes that he was not a vampire."

*BIOGRAPHICAL/CRITICAL SOURCES: Atlantic,* November, 1972; *New York Times Book Review,* January 14, 1973; *Time,* January 15, 1973; *Saturday Review,* February, 1973; *Commonweal,* March 2, 1973; *Choice,* April, 1973; *Harper's,* April, 1973.

\* \* \*

## McNICOLL, Robert E. 1907-

*PERSONAL:* Born February 4, 1907, in St. Louis, Mo.; son of Thomas Stewart (a writer) and Frances (Edwards) McNicoll; married Hortensia Ares, June 5, 1942; children: Robert, Edward, Elizabeth. *Education:* University of Miami, Coral Gables, Fla., A.B., 1931; Duke University, M.A., 1936, Ph.D., 1938. *Politics:* Democrat. *Home:* 5401 Alhambra Circle, Coral Gables, Fla. 33146.

*CAREER:* University of Miami, Coral Gables, Fla., teacher of Latin-American history, 1933-46; employed by U.S. Government, 1946-64; University of Miami, teacher of Latin American history and affairs, 1965-74, professor of history emeritus, 1974—.

*WRITINGS: Furthering Inter-American Education,* University of Miami, 1942; (with Paul Kramer) *Latin-American Panorama,* Putnam, 1968. General editor, *Journal of Inter-American Studies,* 1959-64.

## McNIECE, Harold Francis 1923-1972

March 20, 1923—December 27, 1972; American legal educator. Obituaries: *New York Times,* December 29, 1972.

\* \* \*

## MEAD, Walter B(ruce) 1934-

*PERSONAL:* Born May 25, 1934, in Cedar Rapids, Iowa; son of Otis Bruce (a railroader) and Emma (Schluntz) Mead. *Education:* Carleton College, B.A., 1956; Yale University, B.D., 1960; Duke University, M.A., 1962, Ph.D., 1968. *Home:* 700 North Fell Ave., Normal, Ill. 61761. *Office:* Department of Political Science, Illinois State University, Normal, Ill. 61761.

*CAREER:* Ordained Methodist minister; Lake Forest College, Lake Forest, Ill., instructor in political science, 1963-67; Illinois State University, Normal, assistant professor, 1967-71, associate professor of political science, 1971—. *Member:* American Political Science Association, American Association of University Professors, Southern Political Science Association.

*WRITINGS: Extremism,* Presbyterian Church, 1966; *Extremism and Cognition: Styles of Irresponsibility in American Society,* Kendall-Hunt, 1971. Contributor of about twenty articles to political science journals.

*WORK IN PROGRESS:* Research on value theory, with a book expected to result.

*AVOCATIONAL INTERESTS:* Architecture.

\* \* \*

## MECKLEY, Richard F(redrick) 1928-

*PERSONAL:* Born September 20, 1928, in Newark, Ohio; son of Harold Arthur (an auto repairman) and Francis (Davis) Meckley; married Jessie Mae Cooperrider, September 11, 1953; children: William Allen, Sue Ann. *Education:* Ohio University, B.S.Ed., 1953; Ohio State University, M.A., 1959, Ph.D., 1967. *Politics:* Independent. *Religion:* Protestant. *Home:* 1266 Braewick Dr., Morgantown, W.Va. 26505. *Office:* Department of Education Administration, West Virginia University, Morgantown, W.Va. 26506.

*CAREER:* Jacksontown High School, Jacksontown, Ohio, teacher, 1954-57, principal, 1957-59; Lakewood High School, Hebron, Ohio, principal, 1959-61; Toronto High School, Toronto, Ohio, principal, 1961-64; Ohio State University, Center for Vocational and Technical Education, Columbus, research associate, 1964-66, project director, 1967-69; West Virginia University, Kanawha Valley Graduate Center, Morgantown, assistant professor, 1969-72, associate professor, 1972-75, professor of education administration, 1975—, chairman of department, 1972-75. Member of the Citizen's Advisory Committee to the Westerville, Ohio Board of Education, 1967-69. *Member:* American Association of School Administrators, Ohio Valley Principal's Association (secretary, 1963-64), Phi Delta Kappa.

*WRITINGS:* (With Arthur E. Wohlers, Marion J. Conrad, and others) *A Cooperative Study of Educational Needs for the World of Work,* Ohio State University, 1965; (with Wohlers and Conrad) *A Study of School Building Needs in the Springfield Local School District, Clark County, Ohio,* Ohio State University, 1965; (with Conrad, William J. Griffith, and H. Paul Snyder) *Education Facilities Needs of the Liberty-Perry School Corporation, Selma, Indiana,* Ohio State University, 1966; (with Griffith, Conrad, and others)

*Educational Facilities for Springfield Public Schools,* Ohio State University, 1966; (with Griffith, Conrad, and James W. Clark) *School Building Needs of the Southwestern City Schools,* Ohio State University, 1966; (with Wohlers, Conrad, and Daniel Heisler) *Educator's Specifications for the Eastland Vocational School,* Ohio State University, 1967; (with Ivan E. Valentine and Zane McCoy) *A Guide to Systematic Planning for Vocational and Technical Education Facilities,* The Center for Vocational and Technical Education, 1968; (with Valentine and Conrad) *A General Guide for Planning Facilities for Occupational Preparation Programs,* The Center for Vocational and Technical Education, 1969.

(With Valentine and McCoy) *Simulation Training in Planning Vocational Education Programs and Facilities,* The Center for Vocational and Technical Education, 1970; (with Dick C. Rice) *Supervision and Decision-Making Skills in Vocational Education: A Training Program Utilizing Simulation Techniques,* The Center for Vocational and Technical Education, 1970; (with David A. Puzzuoli) *Toward the 21st Century,* College of Human Resources and Education, West Virginia University, 1971; *Planning Facilities for Occupational Education Programs,* C. E. Merrill, 1972; *Handbook of West Virginia School Law,* West Virginia University Press, 1976, 2nd edition, in press. Also author of *A Study of Facilities and Finances of Kanawha County Catholic Schools.* Contributor of articles to *Ohio Schools, NEA Journal, American Vocational Journal* and numerous other periodicals.

\* \* \*

## MEDLICOTT, Alexander G(uild), Jr. 1927-

*PERSONAL:* Born May 15, 1927, in Springfield, Mass.; son of Alexander Guild and Allethaire (Estey) Medlicott; married Suzanne Rykken, June 15, 1949; children: Alexander III, Peter, Susan. *Education:* Dartmouth College, B.A., 1950; Trinity College, Hartford, Conn., M.A., 1958; University of Washington, Seattle, Ph.D., 1962. *Politics:* Independent. *Office:* Department of English, University of Connecticut, Storrs, Conn. 06268.

*CAREER:* Has worked as a salesman and newspaper editor and writer; University of Connecticut, Storrs, assistant professor, 1964-67, associate professor, 1967-72, professor of English, 1972—. *Military service:* U.S. Army, paratrooper, 1944-46. *Member:* Modern Language Association of America.

*WRITINGS:* (Editor and author of introduction) *The Female Marine,* DaCapo Press, 1966. Contributor of articles to journals in his field.

*WORK IN PROGRESS:* Editing the journals of George Ticknor and Anna Eliot.

*AVOCATIONAL INTERESTS:* Conservation, mountain climbing, ecology, backpacking.

\* \* \*

## MEEHAN, Eugene J(ohn) 1923-

*PERSONAL:* Born September 16, 1923, in Peckville, Pa.; son of James (an accountant) and Anna (Harvilchuck) Meehan; married Ruth J. Patterson, 1946 (divorced, 1949); married Alice Elizabeth McCuskey, September 26, 1949; children: (first marriage) Kathleen Ann, Eileen. *Education:* Attended University of Kentucky, 1946; Ohio State University, B.A., 1950, M.A., 1951; London School of Economics, Ph.D., 1954, postdoctoral study, 1954-57. *Home:* 125 Fron-

tenac Forest, Frontenac, Mo. 63131. *Office:* Department of Political Science, University of Missouri, St. Louis, Mo. 63131.

*CAREER:* U.S. Department of the Air Force, assistant chief of education and libraries in London, England, 1953-57; U.S. Armed Forces Institute, Madison, Wis., educational adviser, 1957-58; Rutgers University, New Brunswick, N.J., lecturer, 1958-60, assistant professor of political science, 1960-65; Brandeis University, Waltham, Mass., associate professor of political science, 1965-68; University of Illinois at Urbana-Champaign, professor of political science, 1969-70; University of Missouri—St. Louis, professor of political science, 1970—. Consultant to Inter-American Foundation, 1973—, and U.S. Agency for International Development (USAID). *Military service:* U.S. Army Air Forces, 1942-45; became captain; received Distinguished Flying Cross. *Member:* American Political Science Association, American Society for Legal and Political Philosophy, Public Choice Society, Southern Political Science Association, Midwest Political Science Association.

*WRITINGS: Introductory Social Studies,* U.S. Government Printing Office, 1957; *Introductory Physical Science,* U.S. Government Printing Office, 1959.

*The British Left Wing and Foreign Policy: A Study of the Influence of Ideology,* Rutgers University Press, 1960; (with Paul A. Samuelson and Robert Bierstedt) *Modern Social Science,* McGraw, 1964; *The Theory and Method of Political Analysis,* Dorsey, 1965; (with John P. Roche and Murray S. Stedman, Jr.) *The Dynamics of Modern Government,* McGraw, 1966; *Contemporary Political Thought: A Critical Study,* Dorsey, 1967; *Explanation in Social Science: A System Paradigm,* Dorsey, 1968; *Value Judgment and Social Science: Structures and Processes,* Dorsey, 1969.

*Foundations of Political Analysis: Empirical and Normative,* Dorsey, 1971; (contributor) Wolfram F. Hanreider, editor, *Comparative Foreign Policy,* McKay, 1972; (contributor) George Graham, editor, *The Post-Behavioral Era,* McKay, 1972; *Public Housing Policy: Convention Versus Reality,* Center for Urban Policy Research, Rutgers University, 1975; (contributor) Stuart S. Nagel, editor, *Policy Studies and the Social Sciences,* Lexington Books, 1975; (contributor) Frank P. Scioli, Jr. and Thomas J. Cook, editors, *Methodologies for Analyzing Public Policies,* Lexington Books, 1975; *The Distribution of Public Assistance and Benefits in the St. Louis Metropolitan Area, 1970-1977,* Metropolitan Data Center (St. Louis), 1975; (contributor) Donald Phares, editor, *A Decent Home and Environment,* Ballinger, 1977. Contributor to political science journals. Member of editorial board, *Journal of Politics.*

*WORK IN PROGRESS: Argument in the Social Sciences: Structures and Processes; The Quality of Governmental Performance: The Case of Public Housing.*

\* \* \*

## MEHRENS, William A(rthur) 1937-

*PERSONAL:* Born September 20, 1937, in Lordsburg, N.M.; son of Arthur W. and Gertrude (Spatz) Mehrens; married Bethel Wulf (a teacher), March 22, 1959; children: Lori Beth, Machell Ann. *Education:* University of Nebraska, B.S. in Educ., 1958, M.Ed., 1959; University of Minnesota, Ph.D., 1965. *Religion:* Lutheran. *Home:* 2193 Butternut Dr., Okemos, Mich. 48864. *Office:* 462 Erickson Hall, Michigan State University, East Lansing, Mich. 48824.

*CAREER:* Mathematics teacher and counselor in public high schools of Minneapolis, Minn., 1959-63; University of Minnesota, Minneapolis, instructor in measurement evaluation, 1964-65; Michigan State University, East Lansing, assistant professor, 1965-67, associate professor, 1967-70, professor of educational psychology, 1970—. Assistant director, National Assessment Program, Ann Arbor, Mich., 1968-69. *Member:* American Education Research Association, American Psychological Association, National Council on Measurement in Education, National Society for Study of Education, Psychometric Society, Phi Delta Kappa.

*WRITINGS:* (With Robert Ebel) *Principles of Educational and Psychological Measurement,* Rand McNally, 1967; (with I. Lehmann) *Standardized Tests in Education,* Holt, 1969, 2nd edition, 1975; (with H. Clarizo and Robert Craig) *Contemporary Issues in Educational Psychology,* Allyn & Bacon, 1970, 3rd edition, 1977; (with Lehmann) *Educational Research: Readings in Focus,* Holt, 1971; (with Lehmann) *Measurement and Evaluation in Education and Psychology,* Holt, 1973; (with Clarizo and Craig) *Contemporary Educational Psychology: Concepts, Issues, Applications,* Wiley, 1975; *Readings in Measurement and Evaluation in Education and Psychology,* Holt, 1976. Contributor to periodicals.

*WORK IN PROGRESS:* Second edition of *Measurement and Evaluation in Education and Psychology,* for Holt.

\* \* \*

## MEIGS, Peveril   1903-

*PERSONAL:* Surname rhymes with "legs"; born May 5, 1903, in Flushing, N.Y.; son of Peveril, Jr. (a foreign exchange broker) and Lorena (Stewart) Meigs; married Yvonne Lieben, May 7, 1928; children: Willard, Nancy (Mrs. Michael Brandriss). *Education:* University of California, Berkeley, A.B., 1925, Ph.D., 1932. *Politics:* Democrat. *Religion:* Unitarian Universalist. *Home:* 147 Pelham Island Rd., Wayland, Mass. 01778.

*CAREER:* San Francisco State Teachers College (now San Francisco State University), San Francisco, Calif., instructor in geography, 1929; Chico State College (now California State University), Chico, Calif., assistant professor, 1929-32, associate professor, 1932-41, professor of geography, 1941-42; U.S. Office of Strategic Services, Washington, D.C., 1942-44, began as geographer, became research analyst; Joint Intelligence Study Publishing Board, Washington, D.C., 1944-47, began as editor, became editor-in-chief; Arctic Institute of North America, Washington, D.C., analyst for Arctic bibliography project, 1948-49; U.S. Department of the Army, Quartermaster Corps, Earth Sciences Division, geographer, then chief of research section in Washington, D.C., 1949-53, and at Quartermaster Research and Engineering Center, Natick, Mass., 1953-65, becoming chief of Earth Sciences Division. Visiting professor at Louisiana State University, 1938-39, American University and George Washington University, 1948. Chairman of Arid Zone Commission, International Geographical Union, 1950-68. State chairman of Progressive Party, California, 1936-38; elected member of Democratic Town Committee, Wayland, 1968-80.

*MEMBER:* American Geographical Society (honorary member), Royal Geographical Society (London; fellow), Association of American Geographers, American Association for the Advancement of Science, American Civil Liberties Union, New England Historic Genealogical Society, Bostonian Society, Phi Beta Kappa. *Awards, honors:* Research grants from Social Science Research Council and American Philosophical Society.

*WRITINGS: The Dominican Mission Frontier of Lower California (Mexico),* University of California Press, 1935, reprinted, Johnson Reprint, 1968; *Climates of California* (booklet), California State Department of Education, 1938; *The Kiliwa Indians of Lower California (Mexico),* University of California Press, 1939; (with Nels Bengtson and William Van Royen) *Fundamentals of Economic Geography,* 3rd edition, Prentice-Hall, 1950; *Geography of Coastal Deserts,* UNESCO, 1966.

Contributor: P. E. James and C. F. Jones, editors, *American Geography: Inventory and Prospect,* Syracuse University Press, for Association of American Geographers, 1954; Edmund C. Jaeger, *The North American Deserts,* Stanford University Press, 1957; G.H.T. Kimble, *Tropical Africa,* Twentieth Century Fund, 1960; W. G. McGinnies and B. J. Goldman, editors, *Arid Lands in Perspective,* American Association for the Advancement of Science and University of Arizona Press, 1969.

Author of thirty-five government publications (restricted) on geography and climate of the countries of Africa, Far East, and southern Europe, 1942-43, and editor or editor-in-chief of series of Joint Army-Navy Intelligence Studies (JANIS) dealing chiefly with Far Eastern countries from New Guinea to Manchuria. Contributor to *Encyclopedia of Science and Technology;* contributor to geography journals, including *Pacific Coast Archaeological Society Quarterly, UNESCO Arid Zone Series,* and *New England Historic Genealogical Society Quarterly,* and to periodicals, including *Nation* and *Westways.*

*WORK IN PROGRESS:* Field and library research on the tide mills of the Atlantic Coast for articles and a book.

*SIDELIGHTS:* Peveril Meigs told *CA:* "At the time of my retirement, I was considered a desert expert, having written books and articles on deserts and travelled in Europe, Asia, and South America. When I retired, I decided to go into an entirely new field, the study of tide mills, because they fascinated me and no one had done much work on them. Tide mills were of great historic importance to the American colonies on the Atlantic Coast, and their sites and even their dams are available to generate tidal power now, with minimum harm to the environment."

*AVOCATIONAL INTERESTS:* Photography ("which I use to illustrate my books and articles and to give exhibits"), nature, people, gardening, chess, and civil liberties.

\* \* \*

## MEISENHOLDER, Robert   1915-

*PERSONAL:* Born March 15, 1915, in Mitchell, S.D.; son of Bernard Augst and Louise (Koenig) Meisenholder; married Myra Roseland, December 26, 1939; children: Joan, Leslie, Richard. *Education:* University of South Dakota, B.A., 1936; University of Michigan, J.D., 1939, S.J.D., 1942. *Residence:* Bellevue, Wash. *Office:* School of Law, University of Washington, Seattle, Wash. 98105.

*CAREER:* Chadbourne, Wallace, Parke & Whiteside, New York, N.Y. (attorneys), associate, 1940-43, 1946-47; University of Miami, Coral Gables, Fla., professor of law, 1947-51; U.S. Navy Department, General Counsel, Dayton, Ohio, associate attorney, 1951-52; University of Cincinnati, Cincinnati, Ohio, professor of law, 1952-54; University of Washington, Seattle, professor of law, 1954—. Visiting professor of law at Emory University, summer, 1948, University of Arizona, summer, 1950, and University of Michigan, 1958-59. Reporter, Washington Judicial Council Civil Rules Projects, 1955-60, 1965-68. Member, Washington Judicial Council Task Force on Rules of Evidence, 1976-77. *Military service:* U.S. Naval Reserve, Japanese language officer, active duty, 1943-46; became lieutenant.

*MEMBER:* American Association of University Professors, American Wireless Association, New York State Bar Association, Ohio Bar Association, Washington State Bar Association (chairman of committee on federal rules, 1970-73), Seattle-Kings County Bar Association (chairman of judicial administration section, 1970-73), Phi Beta Kappa, Tau Kappa Alpha, Delta Tau Delta, Order of Coif.

*WRITINGS: Washington Evidence Law and Practice,* with supplements, West Publishing, 1965; *West's Federal Forms,* with supplements, West Publishing, Volume II (Meisenholder was not associated with Volume I), 1967, Volume III, 1968, revised edition published as Volume IIIA, 1977, Volume IV, 1970; (with Claude Brown, Delmar Karlen, George Neff Stevens, and Allan Vestal) *Procedure before Trial,* West Publishing, 1968; (with others) *McCormick on Evidence,* 2nd edition (Meisenholder was not associated with first edition), West Publishing, 1972; (with Kenneth Broun) *Problems in Evidence,* West Publishing, 1973; (with Karlen, Stevens, and Vestal) *Civil Procedure,* West Publishing, 1975. Contributor of articles to law journals.

*WORK IN PROGRESS:* Revision of *Problems in Evidence;* volumes IIA and IIB of *West's Federal Forms.*

\* \* \*

## MELLINKOFF, Ruth 1924-

*PERSONAL:* Born December 18, 1924, in Marshall, Minn.; daughter of N. Ben and Dorothy (Aaron) Weiner; married David Mellinkoff (a professor of law), July 10, 1949; children: Daniel. *Education:* University of Minnesota, B.A., 1947; University of California, Berkeley, M.A., 1963; University of California, Los Angeles, Ph.D., 1967, postdoctoral study, 1970—. *Home:* 744 Holmby Ave., Los Angeles, Calif. 90024.

*WRITINGS: Something Special Cookbook,* Ritchie, 1959, revised edition, 1971; *The Uncommon Cookbook,* Ritchie, 1968; *The Horned Moses in Medieval Art and Thought,* University of California Press, 1970; *The Just Delicious Cook Book,* Ritchie, 1974.

*WORK IN PROGRESS: Cain as an Image of Evil in the Middle Ages;* another cookbook.

\* \* \*

## MELLON, William Knox, Jr. 1925-
### (Knox Mellon)

*PERSONAL:* Born October 20, 1925, in Houston, Tex.; son of William Knox (an oil executive) and Zelma Mellon; married second wife, Carlotta Herman (a history professor), June 8, 1972. *Education:* Pomona College, B.A., 1950; Claremont College (now Claremont Graduate School), M.A., 1953; Claremont Graduate School, Ph.D., 1972. *Politics:* Democrat. *Home:* 1235 42nd St., Sacramento, Calif. 95819. *Office:* Department of History, Immaculate Heart College, 2021 North Western Ave., Los Angeles, Calif. 90027.

*CAREER:* University of California, Los Angeles, teaching assistant, 1953-55; Mount San Antonio College, Walnut, Calif., instructor in history, 1955-60; Immaculate Heart College, Los Angeles, Calif., 1960—, currently professor of his-

tory. Executive secretary, State Historic Resources Commission, 1975—; State Historic Preservation officer, 1977—. Democratic nominee, U.S. Congress, 1962. *Military service:* U.S. Army, 1942-46; became second lieutenant. U.S. Army Reserve; retired. *Member:* Oral History Association (treasurer).

*WRITINGS*—Under name Knox Mellon: (With Harry Carroll) *Development of Civilization,* Scott, Foresman, Volume I, 1961, Volume II, 1962; (with Miriam Chrisman) *As It Was, as It Is: People and Issues in the Western World,* Scott, Foresman, Volume I, 1972, Volume II, 1972.

\* \* \*

## MELTON, William 1920-

*PERSONAL:* Born November 24, 1920, in Detroit, Mich.; son of William Ray (an advertising copy writer) and Marguerite (Hale) Melton; married Cleola May Smith, July 19, 1942; children: Judith Ann Melton Phipps, Carole Jean Melton Bommarito, Nancy Sue Melton DuFau, Patricia Louise Melton Bereznay. *Education:* Attended College of Puget Sound (now University of Puget Sound), 1938-40; University of Southern California, B.A., 1950, M.S., 1952. *Politics:* Republican. *Home:* 1310 South Ironwood St., La Habra, Calif. 90631. *Office:* Occidental Life of California, Los Angeles, Calif. 90051.

*CAREER:* California Test Bureau (educational publishing firm), Monterey, Calif., production manager, 1948-63; Smith-Kitten Advertising, Los Angeles, Calif., production manager, 1966-67; Occidental Life of California (insurance company), Los Angeles, second vice-president of sales promotion, 1967—. *Military service:* U.S. Army Air Forces, 1942-46; became first lieutenant. *Member:* Mystery Writers of America, P.E.N. International (executive vice-president of Los Angeles center), Hollywood Authors Club, Orange County Press Club, Phi Delta Kappa.

*WRITINGS: I Get My Best Ideas in Bed,* Nash Publishing, 1971; *Nine Lives to Pompeii,* McKay, 1974. Book columnist for *Los Angeles Times* and Santa Ana *Register.* Contributor to *Journal of Educational Psychology.*

*WORK IN PROGRESS: The Drosophila Affair.*

*SIDELIGHTS:* William Melton told *CA:* "I write to entertain and strictly as a hobby on weekends. Any time I can work in my first love—archaeology—I do. [I was] inspired by John O'Hara, Alistair MacLean, and Ellery Queen." *Avocational interests:* Travel, collecting books, collecting Benny Goodman jazz recordings, archaeology.

\* \* \*

## MELZI, Robert C. 1915-

*PERSONAL:* Born March 12, 1915, in Milan, Italy; became U.S. citizen; son of Enrico (a businessman) and Bice (Miglia) Melzi; married Marie C. D'Amico, January 11, 1948; children: Robert H., Marie L., James E. *Education:* University of Padua, Padua, Italy, D. in L., 1938; University of Pennsylvania, M.A., 1951, Ph.D., 1963. *Home:* 132 Bentley Ave., Bala Cynwyd, Pa. 19004. *Office:* Department of Languages, Widener College, Chester, Pa. 19013.

*CAREER:* University of Pennsylvania, Philadelphia, assistant instructor in Romance languages, 1949-53; interpreter of French and Italian, U.S. Department of Justice, 1953-56; Prudential Insurance Co., Philadelphia, Pa., staff manager, 1953-58; Plymouth Whitemarsh High School, Plymouth Meeting, Pa., teacher, 1958-62; Millersville State College, Millersville, Pa., associate professor of languages, 1962-63;

Widener College, Chester, Pa., professor of Romance languages, 1963—. *Member:* American Association of Teachers of Italian (regional coordinator for Pennsylvania), Modern Language Association of America, American Dante Society, Renaissance Society of America. *Awards, honors:* Cavaliere of Star of Solidarity from Republic of Italy, 1971.

*WRITINGS: Castelvetro's Annotations to the Inferno,* Mouton, 1966; (co-author) *Renaissance Drama,* Northwestern University Press, 1966; *The New College Italian and English Dictionary,* AMSCO School Publications, 1976. Regular contributor to *Italica* and *Forum Italicum.*

\*      \*      \*

## MENARD, H(enry) William   1920-

*PERSONAL:* Born December 10, 1920, in Fresno, Calif.; son of Henry William (a businessman) and Blanche (Hodges) Menard; married Gifford Merrill, September 21, 1946; children: Andrew O., Elizabeth M., Dorothy M. *Education:* California Institute of Technology, B.S., 1942, M.S., 1947; Harvard University, Ph.D., 1949. *Home:* 7948 Roseland Dr., La Jolla, Calif. 92037. *Office address:* Scripps Institution of Oceanography, P.O. Box 109, La Jolla, Calif. 92037.

*CAREER:* Navy Electronics Laboratory, San Diego, Calif., began as oceanographer, became supervisor of oceanography, 1949-51; University of California, San Diego, La Jolla, associate professor of geology at Institute of Marine Resources and Scripps Institution of Oceanography, 1955-61, professor, 1961—, acting director, Institute of Marine Resources, 1967-68. On leave to serve in Office of Science and Technology, Executive Office of the President, Washington, D.C., 1965-66. Visiting professor at California Institute of Technology, 1959; visiting geoscientist, American Geological Institute; lecturer for American Academy of Arts and Sciences, at Royal Ontario Museum, Cambridge University, Oxford University, Yale University, Harvard University, Stanford University, and a number of other universities in England and United States. Member of oceanographic advisory committee, U.S. Navy, member of advisory panel IDOE, National Science Foundation, 1972-73; National Academy of Sciences, member of ocean science committee, 1971-72, of committee on science and public policy, 1972-75, and of Commission on Natural Resources, 1976—. National Academy of Sciences, member of summer study panels on Everglades Jetport, 1969, and Kennedy Airport, 1970. Member or chief scientist on twenty oceanographic expeditions in the Pacific, South American, and Aleutian waters, 1949-77.

*MEMBER:* National Academy of Sciences, American Academy of Arts and Sciences, American Association of Petroleum Geologists, American Geophysical Union (fellow), Geological Society of America (fellow), California Academy of Sciences (fellow), Sigma Xi. *Awards, honors:* Co-recipient of Society of Economic Paleontologists and Mineralogists Award for outstanding paper, 1954; Guggenheim fellowship, 1962; overseas fellowship at Churchill College, Cambridge University, 1970-71; Shepard Medal, 1977.

*WRITINGS: Marine Geology of the Pacific,* McGraw, 1964; *Anatomy of an Expedition,* McGraw, 1969; *Science: Growth and Change,* Harvard University Press, 1971; *Geology, Resources and Society,* W. H. Freeman, 1974; *Oceans: Our Continuing Frontier,* Publishers, Inc., 1976.

Contributor: *Deep-Sea Research,* Volume I, Pergamon, 1954; M. N. Hill, editor, *The Sea,* Interscience, Volume

III, 1963, Volume IV, Part II, 1971; *Pacific Basin Biogeography,* Bernice Pauahi Bishop Museum Press, for National Academy of Sciences, 1963; *Marine Geology,* Volume III, Elsevier, 1965; *Physics and Chemistry of the Earth,* Volume VI, Pergamon, 1966; R. A. Phinney, editor, *History of the Earth's Crust,* Princeton University Press, 1968; K. K. Turekian, editor, *The Late Cenoziac Glacial Ages,* Yale University Press, 1971; E. C. Robertson, editor, *The Nature of the Solid Earth,* McGraw, 1972. Contributor of about eighty articles to other symposia, professional journals, and scientific magazines; reviewer for *Science* and *Journal of Geophysical Research, Journal of Geology,* and *Earth and Planetary Science Letters.*

*WORK IN PROGRESS:* Technical research papers; two contemporary novels.

\*      \*      \*

## MENGES, Karl (Heinrich)   1908-

*PERSONAL:* Surname is pronounced *Men*-ges, with a hard "g"; born April 22, 1908, in Frankfurt am Main, Germany; son of Heinrich (a civil court inspector) and Johanna (Keim) Menges; married Valesca M. Treppner, January 22, 1938 (divorced April, 1947); married Natalie Cornaja, December 3, 1951; children: (first marriage) Konstantin, Natalie. *Education:* Attended University of Frankfurt, 1926-27, and University of Munich, 1927-28; University of Berlin, Ph.D., 1932. *Religion:* Roman Catholic. *Residence:* Germany.

*CAREER:* Academy of Sciences, Berlin, Germany, research fellow, 1933-36; University of Ankara, Ankara, Turkey, professor of Russian language and literature, 1937-40; Columbia University, New York, N.Y., visiting lecturer, 1940-41, lecturer, 1941-47, associate professor, 1947-56, professor of Altaic philology, 1956-76. Visiting summer professor at University of California, Berkeley, 1945, 1946, and University of Washington, Seattle, 1947, 1960. Consultant, Chinese history project, University of Washington, Seattle, and Columbia University, 1942-76.

*MEMBER:* Societe Finno-Ougrienne (Helsinki), Societe d'Iranologie (Tehran), Societe Asiatique (Paris), Societas Uralo-Altaica (Hamburg), International Association of Tamil Research (Madras), Royal Central Asian Society (London), Ukranian Academy of Arts & Sciences in the U.S., Kunglig Humanistiska Vetenskaps-Samfundet i Uppsala. *Awards, honors:* Bronze Medal of University of Helsinki, 1960, 1968; Gold Medal of University of Uppsala, 1968; Guggenheim fellowship, 1972.

*WRITINGS:* (Editor) Nikolai F. Katanov, *Volkskundliche Texte aus Ost-Tuerkistan,* Akademie der Wissenschaften und der Literatur, 1933; *Qaraqalpaq Grammar* (German manuscript translated by Leora P. Cunningham), King's Crown Press, 1947; *The Oriental Elements in the Vocabulary of the Oldest Russian Epos, "The Igor Tale,"* Linguistic Circle of New York, 1951; *Introduction to Old Church Slavic,* Department of Slavic Languages, Columbia University, 1953; *Glossar zu den volkskundlichen Texten aus Ost-Tuerkistan II,* Akademie der Wissenschaften und der Literatur, 1954; *Das CaYatajische in der persischen Darstellung von Mirza Mahdi Xan,* Akademie der Wissenschaften und der Literatur, 1957; (with Bernhard Geiger) *People and Languages of the Caucasus,* Mouton Co., 1959; *Morphologische Probleme,* Harrassowitz, 1960; *Tungusen und Ljao,* Deutsche Morgenlaendische Gesellschaft, 1968; *The Turkic Languages and Peoples: An Introduction to Turkic Studies,* Harrassowitz, 1968.

Also editor of *Altajische Studien,* a collection of works in

Altaic languages. Contributor to *Handbuch der Orientalistik,* Volume V, E. J. Brill, 1968. Contributor of more than one hundred articles to scholarly journals. Co-editor, *Central Asiatic Journal,* Leiden and Wiesbaden, since its founding in 1954.

*WORK IN PROGRESS:* Two books, *Japanese and Altaic* and *The Turkic Elements in South-Slavic,* Volume I: *Serbo-Croatian;* research in comparative and historical grammar of the Tungus languages and in the Dravido-Altaic genetic relationship; other etymological studies.

*SIDELIGHTS:* Books on travel and exploration in eastern Europe and Asia attracted Menges in his early boyhood, and as a young Slavist and Orientalist he became a traveler. But he was prevented by the political situation of the 1930's on "from following in the footsteps of the great explorers of archaeology and linguistics of Central Asia ... down to these days when Central Asia is still forbidden land. I was lucky to have travelled extensively in the USSR in 1928-29 and participated in an ethnological-linguistic expedition in Tadzikistan and Oezbekistan, 1929. On later expeditions I was in Persia, Afghanistan, and Soviet Turkistan."

*BIOGRAPHICAL/CRITICAL SOURCES:* N. N. Poppe, *Introduction to Altaic Linguistics,* Harrassowitz, 1965.†

\*     \*     \*

## MENIKOFF, Barry 1939-

*PERSONAL:* Born January 2, 1939, in Brooklyn, N.Y.; son of Frank (a grocer) and Blanche Menikoff; children: Carrie, Alec, Aaron. *Education:* Brooklyn College (now Brooklyn College of the City University of New York), B.A., 1960; University of Wisconsin, M.S., 1962, Ph.D., 1966. *Politics:* Independent. *Religion:* Jewish. *Home:* 2729 Peter St., Honolulu, Hawaii 96816. *Office:* Department of English, University of Hawaii, 1733 Donaghho Rd., Honolulu, Hawaii 96822.

*CAREER:* University of Hawaii, Honolulu, assistant professor, 1965-70, associate professor of English, 1970—. Visiting associate professor of English, Southern California, 1976-78. Fulbright lecturer in English, University of Santiago, Santiago, Spain, 1968-69. *Member:* Modern Language Association of America, Philological Association of the Pacific Coast, American Association of University Professors, National Council of Teachers of English (former state chairman of achievement awards, 1966-68). *Awards, honors:* University of Hawaii Merit Award, 1968, 1970.

*WRITINGS:* (Editor with R. A. Rees) *The Short Story: An Introductory Anthology,* Little, Brown, 1969, 2nd edition, 1975; (contributor) *Fifteen American Authors Before 1900,* University of Wisconsin Press, 1971. Contributor to *Dictionary of Literary Biography,* Gale, 1978. Also contributor of essays and reviews on Henry James and American and Victorian fiction to *Style, English Studies, Journal of Modern Literature, Nineteenth-Century Fiction,* and *CLA Journal.*

*WORK IN PROGRESS:* A reevaluation of Robert Louis Stevenson.

*SIDELIGHTS:* Barry Menikoff told *CA:* "Although coming of age in Brooklyn must be one of the more tired subjects of contemporary life, I must admit to being one of that group of youngsters who lived in ghetto libraries and on cement playgrounds. I can't remember a time when I haven't read and lived imaginatively through literature. New York gave me as well, my semi-fluent Spanish and has thus indirectly influenced my interest and travel 'habits': I spent a year in Spain and in New Mexico." Menikoff worked

during an eight-year period as a waiter in upstate New York, and says: "The time I spent in New York working with Cubans and Colombians and Dominicans in hotels helped me use my Spanish and certainly added to my interest if not affection for Spanish culture."

\*     \*     \*

## MENYUK, Paula 1929-

*PERSONAL:* Born October 2, 1929, in New York, N.Y.; daughter of Leon (a businessman) and Helen (Weissman) Nichols; married Norman Menyuk (a physicist), March 5, 1950; children: Curtis, Diane, Eric. *Education:* New York University, B.S., 1951; Boston University, D.Ed., 1961. *Home:* 162 Mason Ter., Brookline, Mass. 02146. *Office:* Department of Education, Boston University, 232 Bay State Rd., Boston, Mass. 02215.

*CAREER:* High school speech and English teacher in New York, N.Y., 1951-52; Massachusetts General Hospital, Boston, speech therapist, 1952-54; Massachusetts Institute of Technology, Cambridge, researcher and lecturer in speech, 1964-72; Boston University, Boston, professor of psycho-linguistics, 1972—. Consultant to hearing and speech division, Childrens Hospital Medical Center. Vice-president, Brookline Council for Public Schools. *Member:* Linguistic Society of America, Society for Research in Child Development, American Speech and Hearing Association (fellow). *Awards, honors:* National Institute of Mental Health postdoctoral fellow, 1961; Fulbright fellow, 1971; Distinguished Service Award from Massachusetts Speech and Hearing Association, 1976.

*WRITINGS: Sentences Children Use,* M.I.T. Press, 1969; *Acquisition and Development of Language,* Prentice-Hall, 1971; *Language and Maturation,* M.I.T. Press, 1977. Contributor to speech journals.

*WORK IN PROGRESS:* A research project, "Patterns of Language Development in Children at Risk"; acquisition of the speech sound system, language acquisition of children with neurophysiological problems, and written language of the deaf.

\*     \*     \*

## MERITT, Lucy Shoe 1906-
### (Lucy T. Shoe)

*PERSONAL:* Born August 7, 1906, in Camden, N.J.; daughter of William Bonaparte (a safety engineer) and Mary (Dunning) Shoe; married Benjamin Dean Meritt (a professor), November 7, 1964. *Education:* Bryn Mawr College, B.A., 1927, M.A., 1928, Ph.D., 1935; fellow at American School of Classical Studies at Athens, 1929-34; fellow at American Academy in Rome, 1936-37, research fellow, 1949-50. *Religion:* Protestant. *Home:* 712 West 16th St., Austin, Tex. 78701. *Office:* University of Texas, Austin, Tex. 78712.

*CAREER:* Mount Holyoke College, South Hadley, Mass., assistant professor, 1937-42, associate professor of art, archaeology, and Greek, 1942-50, chief counselor of students, 1943-47; American School of Classical Studies, Athens, Greece, editor of publications, 1950-72. University of Texas at Austin, visiting professor, 1973-74, 1975-76, visiting scholar, 1973—. Member of Institute for Advanced Study, Princeton, N.J., 1948-49, 1950-73. Visiting professor of archaeology, Washington University, St. Louis, Mo., 1958, 1960; visiting lecturer in archaeology, Princeton University, 1959. Member of excavation staff at Cosa, 1950 and at Morgantina, 1957. *Member:* International Association of Classical Archaeology (correspondent), German Archaeological Institute (corresponding member), Archaeological Institute of America (recorder, 1960-68, 1971, acting general secretary, 1962, president Princeton Society, 1963-67), Society of Architectural Historians, Alumni Association of American School of Classical Studies (secretary-treasurer, 1940-75), Classical Society of American Academy in Rome (president, 1952). *Awards, honors:* L.H.D., Brown University, 1974; received gold medal for distinguished archaeological achievement, Archaeological Institute of America.

*WRITINGS: Profiles of Greek Mouldings,* American School of Classical Studies (Athens), 1936; *Profiles of Western Greek Mouldings,* American Academy in Rome, 1952; *Etruscan and Republican Roman Mouldings,* American Academy in Rome, 1965. Contributor of archaeological articles to *Hesperia, Berytus, Studi Etruschi.* Contributor to several encyclopedias.

*WORK IN PROGRESS: Architectural Fragments From Excavations in Athenian Agora;* a history of the second fifty years of American School of Classical Studies at Athens.

\*        \*        \*

## MERRY, Henry J(ohn)   1908-

*PERSONAL:* Born September 28, 1908, in Pontiac, Mich.; son of Earl D. (an engineer) and Lillian (Eck) Merry. *Education:* University of Michigan, A.B., 1931, J.D., 1936; American University, M.A., 1952; Harvard University, LL.M., 1954; University of London, Ph.D., 1957. *Religion:* Protestant. *Home and office:* 555 East Williams St., Ann Arbor, Mich. 48108.

*CAREER:* Private practice of law, 1937-46; U.S. Bureau of Internal Revenue, Washington, D.C., member of Excess Profits Tax Council, 1946-52, chairman of council, 1947-52; Mutual Security Agency, Paris Regional Office, Paris, France, assistant controller, 1952-53; Michigan State University, East Lansing, lecturer in political science, 1957-58; U.S. Library of Congress, Washington, D.C., attorney for legislative reference service, 1958-60; Northern Illinois University, DeKalb, associate professor of political science, 1960-62; Purdue University, Lafayette, Ind., assistant professor of political science, 1962-65, associate professor of political science at Calumet Campus, 1965-74, professor emeritus, 1974—. *Awards, honors:* Ross Essay Award from American Bar Association, 1954.

*WRITINGS: Montesquieu's System of Natural Government,* Purdue University Studies, 1970; *Constitutional Function of Presidential–Administrative Separation,* University Press of America, 1978. Contributor to *Western Political Quarterly, American Bar Association Journal, Minnesota Law Review,* and *Midwest Political Science Journal.*

\*        \*        \*

## MERSKY, Roy M.   1925-

*PERSONAL:* Born September 1, 1925, in New York, N.Y.; son of Irving and Rose (Mendelson) Mirsky; married Deena Hersh, February 3, 1951; children: Alisa Judith, Deborah Ann, Ruth Elizabeth. *Education:* University of Wisconsin, B.S., 1948, LL.B., 1952, M.A.L.S., 1953; other courses at London School of Economics and Political Science and Oxford University, 1949, Sorbonne, University of Paris, 1950, and Yale University, 1954. *Home:* 1419 Gaston Ave., Austin, Tex. 78703. *Office:* Law Library, University of Texas, 2500 Red River, Austin, Tex. 78705.

*CAREER:* Practicing attorney in Wisconsin, 1952-54; staff of Milwaukee Public Library and municipal reference librarian at City Hall, Milwaukee, Wis., 1953-54; Yale University, Law Library, New Haven, Conn., assistant librarian and chief of readers and reference services, 1954-59; Washington Supreme Court Law Library, Olympia, director, 1959-63, and concurrently commissioner of Washington Supreme Court Reports; University of Colorado, Boulder, professor of law and law librarian, 1963-65; University of Texas at Austin, professor of law and law librarian, 1965—, director of research, 1965—. Interim director, Jewish National and University Library, Hebrew University of Jerusalem, 1972-73. Consultant to Office of Economic Opportunity Legal Services, National College of State Trial Judges, Microform Reference Publishers, Auerbach Corp., State University of New York at Albany, Brigham Young University, Oral Roberts University, and other institutions and firms. *Military service:* U.S. Army, Combat Infantry, 1944-46; received four battle stars for service in Europe, Combat Infantry Badge, and Bronze Star.

*MEMBER:* Association of American Law Schools (chairman, committee on index to legal periodicals), American Trial Lawyers Association, American Association of Law Libraries, State Bar of Texas (member of committee on computerized legal research), Texas Library Association, Texas Association of College Teachers, American Civil Liberties Union (member of board of directors, central Texas chapter), Southwest Intergroup Relations Council (counsel), Scribes.

*WRITINGS:* (Editor with J. Myron Jacobstein) *Water Law Bibliography 1847-1965,* Jefferson Law Book Co., 1966, Supplement I, 1969; (editor) *Law Books for Non-Law Libraries and Laymen: A Bibliography,* Oceana, 1969; (with Jacobstein) "Classics in Legal History" series, W. S. Hein, 1970; (editor with Jacobstein) *Ten-Year Index to Periodical Articles Related to Law (1958-1968),* Glanville, 1970; (editor with Jacobstein) *Legislative History of Title 28,* William Gaunt, 1971; (with Jacobstein) *Fundamentals of Legal Research,* Foundation Press, 1977; (with Albert Blaustein) *The First Hundred Justices,* Shoe String, 1978; (with Robert Berring and James McCue) *Author's Guide to Journals in Law, Criminal Justice and Criminology,* Haworth Press, 1978. Also editor with Jacobstein, *The Supreme Court of the United States Hearings and Reports on Successful and Unsuccessful Nominations of Supreme Court Justices by the Senate Judiciary Committee, 1916-1972,* 1975, and supplement, 1977. Book review editor, *Law Library Journal,* 1960-72; contributing editor, *Criminal Law Bulletin,* 1972; associate editor, *Real Estate Law Journal,* 1972—.

*WORK IN PROGRESS: Law Books for the Non-Law Librarian.*

\*        \*        \*

## METAXAS, B(asil) N(icolas)   1925-

*PERSONAL:* Born July 6, 1925, in London, England; son of Nicolas B. and Razi (Metaxa) Metaxas; children: Aikaterini. *Education:* Columbia University, B.Sc., 1950, additional study, 1950-51; London School of Economics and Political Science, Ph.D., 1967. *Politics:* "No politics." *Religion:* Greek Orthodox. *Home:* 29A South Ealing Rd., London W.5, England. *Office:* Department of Economics, Ealing Technical College, Ealing, London, England.

*CAREER:* Merchant seaman, 1945-46; clerk in an import-export firm, New York, N.Y., 1951-53; engaged in shipping management, London, England, 1953-67; Ealing Technical

College, Ealing, London, lecturer in economics, 1967-68, senior lecturer, 1968-73, principal lecturer of economics of transport, 1973—. Visiting lecturer of maritime economics, Polytechnic of Central London, 1973—. Consultant to United Nations Conference on Trade and Development, 1967, International Bank for Reconstruction and Development, 1969, World Bank, 1969-70, and to private businesses and small shipping firms of Greek origin. *Member:* Institute of Chartered Shipbrokers (fellow), Institute of Transport (corporate member), Maritime Economists' Group.

*WRITINGS: The Economics of Tramp Shipping,* Athlone Press, 1971. Also co-author of *The Impact of Flags of Convenience.* Contributor of articles on shipping to *Journal of Transport Economics and Policy,* and other journals. Also contributor of articles in Greek on economics, maritime economics, and the socio-economics of Hellenes living abroad to journals.

*SIDELIGHTS:* B. N. Metaxas told *CA:* "Writing is a creative art. There is no better craft than writing if one wishes to contribute to the development of a subject which is at the stage of its genesis. I am writing mainly because it is my aim to contribute as much as I can to the development of maritime economics." *Avocational interests:* Art, travel.

\*   \*   \*

## MEYER, Ben F. 1927-

*PERSONAL:* Born November 5, 1927, in Chicago, Ill.; son of Ben F. (a banker) and Mary (Connor) Meyer; married Denise Oppliger, March 27, 1969. *Education:* University of Santa Clara, S.T.M., 1958; Biblical Institute, Rome, Italy, S.S.L., 1961; Gregorian University, Rome, Italy, S.T.D. (summa cum laude), 1965. *Politics:* Democrat. *Religion:* Roman Catholic. *Home:* 2160 Lakeshore Rd., Apt. 1008, Burlington, Ontario, Canada. *Office:* Department of Religious Studies, McMaster University, Hamilton, Ontario, Canada.

*CAREER:* Graduate Theological Union, Berkeley, Calif., assistant professor of religion, 1965-68; McMaster University, Hamilton, Ontario, associate professor, 1969-74, professor of religious studies, 1974—. *Member:* Society of Biblical Literature, Catholic Biblical Association, Studiorum Novi Testamenti Societas. *Awards, honors:* Fulbright fellow, Germany, 1964-65; Canada Council fellowship in Greece and Switzerland, 1976-77.

*WRITINGS: The Man for Others,* Bruce, 1970; *The Church in Three Tenses,* Doubleday, 1971. Contributor to religious journals.

*WORK IN PROGRESS: The Aims of Jesus; A New Mankind.*

*SIDELIGHTS:* Ben Meyer has traveled throughout the Near East, Europe, and South America; he reads ten languages and speaks five.

\*   \*   \*

## MEYER, Louis A(lbert) 1942-

*PERSONAL:* Born August 22, 1942, in Johnstown, Pa.; son of Louis Albert (a retired career soldier) and Martha (Keytack) Meyer; married Annetje Lawrence (a teacher), May 28, 1966; children: Matthew, Nathaniel. *Education:* University of Florida, A.B., 1964; Boston University, M.F.A., 1973. *Home:* 191 Captain Pierce Rd., Scituate, Mass. 02066.

*CAREER:* Painter. Teacher at Rockland High School, Rockland, Mass. *Military service:* U.S. Navy, 1964-68; became lieutenant. *Member:* Boston Visual Arts Union.

*WRITINGS*—Self-illustrated, for children: *The Gypsy Bears,* Little, Brown, 1970; *The Clean Air and Peaceful Contentment Dirigible Airline,* Little, Brown, 1971.

*WORK IN PROGRESS:* A juvenile novel dealing with the Impressionist period in France.†

\*   \*   \*

## MEYER, Robert H. 1934-

*PERSONAL:* Born September 22, 1934, in Santa Ana, Calif.; son of Fred and Minola (Holt) Meyer; married Isabel Marie Goncalves, June 17, 1961; children: Suzanne Marie, Christopher Robert. *Education:* Attended University of San Francisco, 1952-54; Sacramento State College (now California State University, Sacramento), B.A., M.A., 1962; University of California, Davis, Ph.D., 1966. *Politics:* Democrat. *Address:* P.O. Box 311, Lincoln, Calif. 95648. *Office:* Department of English, Sierra College, Rocklin, Calif. 95677.

*CAREER:* University of California, Davis, teaching associate, 1962-63; American River College, Sacramento, Calif., instructor in English, 1963-66; University of Santa Clara, Santa Clara, Calif., assistant professor of English, 1966-73; San Jose State University, San Jose, Calif., lecturer, 1973-75; Sierra College, Rocklin, Calif., instructor in English, 1975—. *Military service:* U.S. Army, 1957-1958; California Army National Guard, 1958-62; became sergeant. *Member:* Modern Language Association of America, National Council of Teachers of English, American Association for the Advancement of Science, American Association of University Professors, California College and University Faculty Association.

*WRITINGS: Anatomy of a Theme,* Glencoe Press, 1969; (with Joseph Subbiondo) *Borrowed Time: Literature on Man and His Environment,* Wadsworth, 1972. Contributor to *English Journal.*

*WORK IN PROGRESS: Anatomy for Writers: Rhetoric; The Last Quest,* a science fiction short story; a book on the Oriental martial arts; a volume of poems.

*SIDELIGHTS:* Robert Meyer told *CA:* "I'm a teacher who likes to write and a writer who likes to teach. Writing allows me to relive my experiences and then to share them with others. As my craft improves, I hope someday that my more meaningful experiences will become art." *Avocational interests:* "I am a 'Shodan'—a black belt in Kenpo-Karate and a student of Escrima (Phillipine fencing) and the Wing Chun style of Kung Fu."

\*   \*   \*

## MEZA, Pedro Thomas 1941-

*PERSONAL:* Born September 2, 1941, in New York, N.Y.; son of Louis (a technician) and Elizabeth (Gibson) Meza; married Rose Althaus; children: Winifred Elizabeth Clarke. *Education:* New York University, B.A. (with highest honors), 1962, M.A., 1963, Ph.D.,1967. *Politics:* Democrat. *Religion:* Protestant. *Home:* 50-10 215 St., Bayside Hills, N.Y. 11364. *Office:* History Department, Queensborough Community College of the City University of New York, Bayside, N.Y. 11364.

*CAREER:* Bronx Community College of the City University of New York, Bronx, N.Y., lecturer in history, 1966-67; Queensborough Community College of the City University of New York, Bayside, N.Y., assistant professor, 1967-74, associate professor of history, 1974—. *Member:* American Historical Association, American Association of University Professors, Conference on British Studies.

WRITINGS: (Editor with Fred Greenbaum) *Readings in Western Civilization: The Early Modern Period,* Mc-Cutchan, 1970. Contributor to *Historical Magazine of the Protestant Episcopal Church.*

WORK IN PROGRESS: A study of the reaction of the Church of England to the Act of Toleration of 1689.

SIDELIGHTS: Pedro Meza told *CA,* "My historical research centers mainly about problems of church and state relations in England." Meza has traveled in Canada, Mexico, England, France, Belgium, the Netherlands, and Spain.

\*　　　\*　　　\*

## MEZZROW, Milton 1890(?)-1972
### (Mezz Mezzrow)

1890(?)—August 5, 1972; Expatriate American jazz clarinetist. Obituaries: *Washington Post,* August 10, 1972.

\*　　　\*　　　\*

## MICHALOS, Alex C. 1935-

PERSONAL: Born August 1, 1935, in Cleveland, Ohio; son of Charles and Josephine (Pucci) Michalos; married Barbara Lee Fitch (a Ph.D. business candidate), September 7, 1957; children: Cynthia, Theodore, Stephanie. *Education:* Western Reserve University (now Case Western Reserve University), B.A., 1957; University of Chicago, M.A., 1961, B.D., 1961, Ph.D., 1965. *Politics:* "Independent dove." *Religion:* None. *Home:* R.R. 2, Acton, Ontario, Canada. *Office:* Department of Philosophy, University of Guelph, Guelph, Ontario, Canada.

CAREER: St. Cloud State College, St. Cloud, Minn., assistant professor of philosophy, 1962-64; State University of New York College at Plattsburgh, assistant professor of philosophy, 1964-66; University of Guelph, Guelph, Ontario, associate professor of philosophy, 1966-69; University of Pittsburgh, Pittsburgh, Pa., visiting associate professor of philosophy, 1969-70; University of Guelph, professor of philosophy, 1970—, director of social indicators research programme, 1976—. *Military service:* Ohio National Guard, 1953-56. U.S. Army Reserve, 1956-61; became sergeant. *Member:* Canadian Philosophical Association (secretary, 1968), American Philosophical Association, Philosophy of Science Association, American Association for the Advancement of Science, Society for Health and Human Values, American Academy of Political and Social Science, Society for Social Studies of Science, Canadian Sociology and Anthropology Association, Canadian Civil Liberties Association, Public Choice Society, Society for Value Inquiry.

WRITINGS: *Principles of Logic,* Prentice-Hall, 1969; *Improving Your Reasoning,* Prentice-Hall, 1970; *The Popper-Carnap Controversy,* Nijhoff, 1971; *Foundations of Decision-Making,* Canadian Association for Publishing Philosophy. Contributor to more than a dozen professional journals. Founder and editor, *Social Indicators Research.*

WORK IN PROGRESS: *North American Social Report,* a comparative social report for Canada and the United States, a six-year projected five-volume study.

\*　　　\*　　　\*

## MICKEL, Emanuel John, Jr. 1937-

PERSONAL: Born October 11, 1937, in Joliet, Ill., son of Emanuel J. (a laborer) and Mildred (Newton) Mickel; married Kathleen Russell, May 31, 1959; children: Jennifer,

Chiara, Heather. *Education:* Louisiana State University, B.A., 1959; University of North Carolina, M.A., 1961, Ph.D., 1965. *Home:* 117 North Park Ridge Rd., Bloomington, Ind. 47401. *Office:* Department of French, Indiana University, Bloomington, Ind. 47401.

CAREER: University of Nebraska, Lincoln, assistant professor, 1965-67, associate professor, 1967-68; Indiana University at Bloomington, associate professor, 1968-73, professor of French literature, 1973—. *Military service:* U.S. Army, 1961-63; became captain. *Member:* Mediaeval Academy of America, Modern Language Association of America, Societe Rencesvals.

WRITINGS: *The Artificial Paradises in French Literature,* Volume I, University of North Carolina Press, 1969; (co-editor) *Studies in Honor of Alfred G. Engstrom,* University of North Carolina Press, 1972; *Marie de France,* Twayne, 1974; *The Old French Crusade Cycle,* Volume I, University of Alabama, 1977. Contributor of scholarly articles to *Speculum, Romania, Romance Notes, Modern Philology, Modern Language Quarterly, Studi Francesi, Studies in Philology, Romanische Forschungen Zeitschrift fuer Romanische Philologie,* and other journals.

WORK IN PROGRESS: The second volume of *The Artificial Paradises.*

SIDELIGHTS: Emanuel John Mickel, Jr. reads Latin, French, Provencal, German, Spanish, Portuguese, Italian, and Arabic.

\*　　　\*　　　\*

## MIDDLEBROOK, (Norman) Martin 1932-

PERSONAL: Born January 24, 1932, in Boston, England; married Mary Sylvester, September 7, 1954; children: Jane, Anne, Catherine. *Education:* Attended schools in England. *Politics:* None. *Religion:* Roman Catholic. *Home and office:* 48 Linden Way, Boston, Lincolnshire, England. *Agent:* A. P. Watt & Son, 26-28 Bedford Row, London, England.

CAREER: Poultry farmer in Boston, England, 1956—. *Military service:* British Army, 1950-52.

WRITINGS: *The First Day on the Somme,* Penguin, 1971, Norton, 1972; *The Nuremberg Raid,* Morrow, 1974; *Convoy,* Penguin, 1976, Morrow, 1977; (contributor) Edward Marshal and Michael Carver, editors, *The War Lords,* Weidenfeld & Nicolson, 1976; (with Patrick Mahoney) *Battleship,* Penguin, 1977.

WORK IN PROGRESS: *The Kaiser's Battle; The Battle of Hamburg;* editing, *The Diaries of Private Bruckshaw,* for Scholarly Press.

AVOCATIONAL INTERESTS: Golf, skiing, local government.

\*　　　\*　　　\*

## MIDDLETON, David L. 1940-

PERSONAL: Born March 5, 1940, in Grand Forks, N.D.; son of Arthur L. (a farmer) and Claudia (Solberg) Middleton; married Mary Hogue, June 6, 1964; children: Benjamin, Hilary. *Education:* Jamestown College, B.A., 1961; Purdue University, M.A., 1965; University of Wisconsin, Ph.D., 1969; also studied at International Christian University, Tokyo, Japan. *Residence:* Gilby, N.D. 58235. *Office:* Department of English, Trinity University, San Antonio, Tex. 78284.

CAREER: Trinity University, San Antonio, Tex., associate professor of Renaissance literature, 1969—.

*WRITINGS:* (Compiler and editor with Harry B. Caldwell) *English Tragedy, 1370-1600: Fifty Years of Criticism,* Trinity University Press, 1971. Contributor to Shakespeare journals.

*WORK IN PROGRESS:* A collection of English history plays; a book on plays about the legendary period of English history.

\* \* \*

## MIERS, Earl Schenck 1910-1972
### (David William Meredith)

May 27, 1910—November 17, 1972; Editor and author whose work includes American history, biography, fiction, and sports. Obituaries: *New York Times,* November 19, 1972; *Publishers Weekly,* December 11, 1972. (See index for *CA* sketch)

\* \* \*

## MIGNANI, Rigo 1921-

*PERSONAL:* Born June 11, 1921, in Florence, Italy; son of Ettore and Gemma (Carcassi) Mignani; married Gerda Rueckle, August 27, 1951. *Education:* University of Florence, Dott. in Lettere, 1945; University of Washington, Ph.D., 1957. *Home:* 5 Riverside Dr., A. 1006, Binghamton, N.Y. 13905. *Office:* Department of Romance Languages, Harpur College, State University of New York, Binghamton, N.Y. 13901.

*CAREER:* Harvard University, Cambridge, Mass., instructor in Italian, 1948-51; State University of New York at Binghamton, Harpur College, Binghamton, assistant professor, 1955-62, associate professor, 1962-72, professor of Romance philology, 1972—. *Member:* American Association of Teachers of Spanish, American Association of Teachers of Italian, Modern Language Association of America, Mediaeval Academy of America, Dante Society, Modern Humanities Research Association.

*WRITINGS:* (With A. S. Bernardo) *Ritratto dell' Italia,* Heath, 1968, 2nd edition, 1978; (translator with M. Di Cesare) J. Ruiz, *The Book of Good Love,* State University of New York Press, 1970; *Un canzoniere italiano del secolo XIV,* Sansoni-Licosa, 1974; (with Di Cesare) *Ruiziana: Research Materials for the Study of Juan Ruiz Libro de buen Amor,* State University of New York Press, 1977; (with Di Cesare) *Concordance to the Libro de buen amor,* State University of New York Press, 1977; (with Di Cesare) *Concordance to the Complete Writings of George Herbert,* Cornell University Press, 1977.

*WORK IN PROGRESS: Introduction to Provencal Poetry.*

\* \* \*

## MIKHAIL, E(dward) H(alim) 1928-

*PERSONAL:* Born June 29, 1928, in Cairo, Egypt; emigrated to Canada in 1966; son of Halim and Mathilda (Phares) Mikhail; married Isabelle Bichai, July 22, 1954; children: May, Carmen. *Education:* Cairo University, B.A. (with honors), 1947, B.Ed., 1949; Trinity College, Dublin, D.E.S., 1959; University of Sheffield, Ph.D., 1966. *Politics:* Conservative. *Religion:* Christian. *Home:* 2109 Scenic Dr., Lethbridge, Alberta, Canada. *Office:* Department of English, University of Lethbridge, Lethbridge, Alberta, Canada.

*CAREER:* Cairo University, Cairo, Egypt, 1949-66, began as lecturer, became assistant professor; University of Leth-

bridge, Lethbridge, Alberta, associate professor, 1966-72, professor of English, 1972—. *Member:* International Association for the Study of Anglo-Irish Literature, Canadian Association for Irish Studies, Modern Language Association of America, Association of Canadian University Teachers of English, British Drama League, James Joyce Foundation. *Awards, honors:* Six Canada Council research grants, 1967-74.

*WRITINGS: Social and Cultural Setting of the 1890's,* Garnstone Press (London), 1969; *John Galsworthy the Dramatist: A Bibliography of Criticism,* Whitston, 1971; (editor) *Sean O'Casey: A Bibliography of Criticism,* Macmillan, 1972; *Comedy and Tragedy,* Whitson, 1972; *A Bibliography of Modern Irish Drama 1899-1970,* Macmillan, 1972; *Dissertations on Anglo-Irish Drama,* Macmillan, 1973; (editor with John O'Riordan) *The Sting and the Twinkle: Conversations with Sean O'Casey,* Macmillan, 1974; (editor) *J. M. Synge: A Bibliography of Criticism,* Macmillan, 1975; *Contemporary British Drama 1950-1976: An Annotated Critical Bibliography,* Macmillan, 1976; *J. M. Synge: Interviews and Recollections,* Macmillan, 1977; *W. B. Yeats: Interviews and Recollections,* two volumes, Macmillan, 1977; *English Drama 1900-1950: A Guide to Information Sources,* Gale, 1977; *Lady Gregory: Interviews and Recollections,* Macmillan, 1977; *Oscar Wilde: An Annotated Bibliography of Criticism,* Macmillan, 1978.

*WORK IN PROGRESS: Brendan Behan: An Annotated Bibliography of Criticism; Brendan Behan: Interviews and Recollections; James Joyce: Interviews and Recollections; An Annotated Bibliography of Modern Anglo-Irish Drama.*

\* \* \*

## MILENKOVITCH, Michael M. 1932-

*PERSONAL:* Born June 15, 1932, in Belgrade, Yugoslavia; son of Milutin (an army officer) and Darinka (a dentist; maiden name Mladenovic) Milenkovitch; married Deborah Duff, June 25, 1960; children: Andrew Duff, Catharine Margaret. *Education:* Ohio Wesleyan University, B.A., 1956; Columbia University, M.I.A., Ph.D., 1964. *Home:* 425 Riverside Dr., New York, N.Y. 10025. *Office:* Department of Political Science, Herbert H. Lehman College of the City University of New York, Bedford Park Blvd., Bronx, N.Y.

*CAREER:* Herbert H. Lehman College of the City University of New York, Bronx, N.Y., 1964—, currently associate professor of political science. *Member:* American Political Science Association, American Association for the Advancement of Slavic Studies, American Association of University Professors.

*WRITINGS: The View from Red Square: A Critique of Cartoons from Pravda and Izvestia, 1947-1964,* Hobbs Dorman, 1966; (editor with wife, Deborah Milenkovitch) *Milovan Djilas: Parts of a Lifetime,* Harcourt, 1975; (editor) *Milovan Djilas: An Annotated Bibliography, 1928-1975,* University Microfilm, 1976.

*WORK IN PROGRESS: Milovan Djilas: His Life and Works; Yugoslav Marxism and Marxist Humanism: Retrospect and Prospect.*

\* \* \*

## MILES, Elton (Roger) 1917-

*PERSONAL:* Born May 25, 1917, in Coryell, Tex.; son of A. L. (a cottonseed oil miller) and Ozelle (Rogers) Miles; married Lillian Neale, July 19, 1941; children: Harry Mc-

Cauley, Adrienne. *Education:* Baylor University, A.B., 1939; North Texas State Teachers College (now North Texas State University), M.A., 1946; University of Texas, Ph.D., 1949. *Politics:* Democrat. *Religion:* Presbyterian. *Home:* 505 East Hendryx Ave., Alpine, Tex. 79830. *Office:* English Department, Sul Ross State University, Alpine, Tex. 79830.

*CAREER:* Sul Ross State University, Alpine, Tex., associate professor, 1949-52, professor of English, 1952—, department chairman, 1952-77. *Military service:* U.S. Army, 1941-46. *Member:* Southwestern American Literature Association (president, 1971), Western American Literature Association, Texas Folklore Society (president, 1954).

*WRITINGS:* (Editor and author of introduction) Will Tom Carpenter, *Lucky Seven: Autobiography of a Cowman,* University of Texas Press, 1957; (editor and author of introduction) Walter Fulcher, *The Way I Heard It: Tales of the Big Bend,* University of Texas Press, 1958; *Southwest Humorists,* Steck, 1967; (author of introduction) H. Allen Smith, *The Best of H. Allen Smith,* Trident, 1972; *Tales of the Big Bend,* Texas A & M University Press, 1976. Contributor of articles to publications of the Texas Folklore Society. Also author of "Who's Hubie" and "The Law West of the Pecos," regionally produced plays.

\*　　　\*　　　\*

## MILLER, Arthur B(urton)   1922-

*PERSONAL:* Born January 22, 1922, in Des Moines, Iowa; son of Howard W. and Amy (Edson) Miller; married Lucy Smith, September 11, 1942; children: Frederick Alan, David Paul. *Education:* Whitworth College, B.A., 1949, B.Ed., 1950; University of Oregon, M.A., 1962, Ph.D., 1964. *Religion:* United Church of Christ. *Home:* 1312 East Glen Ave., Peoria Heights, Ill. 61614. *Office:* 4906 Prospect Rd., Peoria Heights, Ill. 61614.

*CAREER:* State University of New York College at Oneonta, assistant professor of rhetoric and public address, 1963-65; Washington State University, Pullman, assistant professor of rhetoric and public address, 1965-67; Northern Michigan University, Marquette, associate professor of rhetoric and public address, 1967-68; Park College, Kansas City, Mo., professor of rhetoric and public address and acting chairman, 1968-70; University of Akron, Akron, Ohio, associate professor and director of rhetoric and public address, 1970-72; Central Baptist Theological Seminary, Kansas City, associate professor, 1972-74; Northwestern University, Evanston, Ill., visiting scholar, 1974-75; Peoria Heights Congregational Church, Peoria Heights, Ill., pastor, 1975—. *Military service:* U.S. Coast Guard, 1941-45. *Member:* Speech Communication Association.

*WRITINGS:* (With Remo P. Fausti) *Elements of Deliberative Debating,* Wadsworth, 1969; *Modes of Public Speaking,* Wadsworth, 1971. Contributor of essays to *Journal of the American Forensic Association, Speech Monograph,* and *Philosophy and Rhetoric.*

*WORK IN PROGRESS:* An essay on the history of eighteenth-century English rhetorical theory, and three essays concerning rhetoric and interpreting the New Testament.

*SIDELIGHTS:* Arthur Miller told *CA:* "How does one beget a manuscript? As a writer of non-fiction I write as I feel constrained to do so in the context of sharing significant insights. For me, those insights seem to appear spontaneously during periods of conversation, reading and reflec-

tion. In particular, I find that seminal writers of western thought provoke my thinking and read them, *not* because they *put* ideas into my mind, but because they stimulate me to reflect creatively. I refer, for example, to the great minds of the past, for instance Thales, Plato, and Aristotle in particular, to de Chardin, Heidegger, Husserl, and Kierkegaard of the modern era." Miller continues: "I jot down an idea that I think significant, and the context in which it arose, in sufficient detail to allow me to recall images for perusal. After living with an idea for a sufficient time and allowing it to mature I make a judgment as to its worth to myself and to others. If I think that there is a sound reason for my wanting readers to believe what I wish to say then I proceed to build a design for adapting that idea to readers."

\*　　　\*　　　\*

## MILLER, Daniel Adlai II   1918-

*PERSONAL:* Born May 21, 1918, in Princeton, Ind.; son of Clarence Isaac (a merchant) and Christine (Walker) Miller; married Jean Hart, October 29, 1945; children: Claudia Miller Congleton, Dan III, Debra Miller Forrest, Lisa, Kent, Kathleen. *Education:* Hanover College, A.B., 1940; University of Michigan, M.A., 1946, Ph.D., 1964. *Politics:* Democrat. *Religion:* Methodist. *Home:* 328 East Brumfield, Princeton, Ind. 47670. *Office:* Department of History, Indiana State University, Evansville, Ind. 47708.

*CAREER:* Oakland City College, Oakland City, Ind., 1962-66, became assistant professor of social sciences; Indiana State University, Evansville, associate professor, 1966-72, professor of history, 1972—, chairperson of Division of Social Sciences, 1966—. *Military service:* U.S. Army, Horse Cavalry and Signal Corps, 1941-45; served in Southwest Pacific. *Member:* American Historical Association, Indiana Academy of Social Sciences.

*WRITINGS: Sir Joseph Yorke and Anglo-Dutch Relations, 1774-1780,* Mouton, 1970.

*WORK IN PROGRESS:* A biography of Smith Miller, Indiana legislator; a biography of Sir Joseph Yorke, British ambassador to the Netherlands.

\*　　　\*　　　\*

## MILLER, Ed(die) L(eRoy)   1937-

*PERSONAL:* Born April 6, 1937, in Los Angeles, Calif.; son of William Don and Georgia (Davidson) Miller; married Yvonne Marie Farrar, July 6, 1956 (divorced June 13, 1975); children: Terryl, Timothy, Tad. *Education:* Attended Pepperdine College (now University), 1955-56; Compton College, A.A., 1957; University of Southern California, B.A., 1959, M.A., 1960, Ph.D., 1965; University of Basel, Switzerland, additional study, 1973-74. *Politics:* Democratic Party. *Religion:* Lutheran. *Home:* 4160 Evans Dr., Boulder, Colo. 80303. *Office:* Department of Philosophy, University of Colorado, Boulder, Colo. 80302.

*CAREER:* University of Southern California, Los Angeles, research assistant, 1960-61, 1962; Bendix Computer, Los Angeles, Calif., junior mathematician, 1961-62; California Lutheran College, Thousand Oaks, instructor in philosophy, 1962-64; St. Olaf College, Northfield, Minn., assistant professor of philosophy, 1964-66; University of Colorado, Boulder, assistant professor, 1966-70, associate professor, 1970-76, professor of philosophy and religious studies, 1976—. Director of University of Colorado Theology Forum. *Member:* American Philosophical Association, Studiorum Novi Testamentum Societas.

*WRITINGS:* (Editor) *Classical Statements on Faith and Reason,* Random House, 1970; (editor) *Philosophical and Religious Issues,* Dickinson, 1971; *God and Reason,* Macmillan, 1972. Contributor of articles and reviews to *Personalist, Lutheran Quarterly, Journal of the History of Philosophy, Classical Journal, Thedogische Zeitschrift,* and other journals.

*WORK IN PROGRESS: The Meaning of Faith,* and *Jesus and the Future;* research in progress in New Testament studies and Greek philosophy.

\* \* \*

## MILLER, Hubert John 1927-

*PERSONAL:* Born December 9, 1927, in Hays, Kan.; son of John Jacob (a farmer) and Barbara (Bollig) Miller; married Doris Mutz, August 24, 1957; children: John, Michael, Paul, David, Christopher, Vincent, Marie. *Education:* University of Dayton, B.A., 1951; St. Louis University, M.A., 1954; Loyola University of Chicago, Ph.D., 1965. *Politics:* "Tend to be Democrat." *Religion:* Roman Catholic. *Home:* 1516 Ivy Lane, Edinburg, Tex. 78539. *Office:* Department of History, Pan American University, Edinburg, Tex.

*CAREER:* Escuela Americana, El Salvador, Central America, teacher, 1955-56; Instituto de Ingeles, El Salvador, Central America, director, 1956; St. Mary's University, San Antonio, Tex., assistant professor, 1960-65, associate professor, 1965-71; Pan American University, Edinburg, Tex., associate professor of Latin American history, 1971—. Member of board of directors, Texas Colleges and University Bicentennial Committee. *Member:* Latin American Studies Association, American Historical Association, American Association of University Professors, Texans for Educational Advancement of Mexican Americans (former vice-president, acting president). *Awards, honors:* Smith-Mundt Exchange grant, 1959-60; Tinker Foundation grant, 1968; International Education of the Border States University Consortium on Latin America grant, 1977.

*WRITINGS*—All published by New Santander Press, except as indicated: (Contributor) Ralph Lee Woodward, editor, *Positivism in Latin America 1850-1900,* Heath, 1971; *Hernan Cortes: Conquistador and Colonizer,* with teaching manual, 1972; *Bartolome de Las Casas: Protector of the Indians,* 1972; *Church and State Question in Guatemala 1871-1885,* University of San Carlos of Guatemala, 1973; *Antonio de Mendoza: First Viceroy of Mexico,* 1973; *Juan de Zumarraga: First Bishop of Mexico,* 1973; *Jose Vasconcelos: A Man for All the Americas,* 1978.

*WORK IN PROGRESS: Jose de Escandon: Colonizer of Northeastern Mexico and the Valley; Miguel Hidalgo: Father of Mexican Independence.*

*SIDELIGHTS:* Hubert Miller told *CA,* "I believe that the traditional teaching of U.S. history survey courses has neglected the Mexican American heritage that flows from Mexico to the U.S."

\* \* \*

## MILLER, Lynn H(ellwarth) 1937-

*PERSONAL:* Born October 2, 1937, in Dodge City, Kan.; son of Louis F. and Janet (Hellwarth) Miller. *Education:* University of Kansas, A.B., 1959, M.A., 1962; Graduate Institute of International Studies, Geneva, Switzerland, additional study, 1959-60; Princeton University, Ph.D., 1966. *Residence:* Philadelphia, Pa. *Office:* Department of Political Science, Temple University, Philadelphia, Pa. 19122.

*CAREER:* University of California, Los Angeles, assistant professor of political science, 1965-69; Temple University, Philadelphia, Pa., associate professor of political science, 1969—, associate dean of Graduate School, 1973—. *Member:* American Political Science Association, American Society of International Law, International Studies Association.

*WRITINGS: Organizing Mankind: An Analysis of Contemporary International Organization,* Holbrook, 1972; (with Ronald N. Pruessen) *Reflections on the Cold War,* Temple University Press, 1974. Special editor, *International Conciliation,* 1968, 1969.

\* \* \*

## MILLER, Norman 1933-

*PERSONAL:* Born November 29, 1933, in New York, N.Y.; son of Arthur (an insurance agent) and Pearl (Doudera) Miller; married Natalie Brigham, October, 1956; married Lori Brown, December 25, 1970 (divorced, 1975); children: (first marriage) Carrie Ellen. *Education:* Antioch College, A.B., 1956; Northwestern University, M.S., 1957, Ph.D., 1959. *Home:* 17031 Bollinger Dr., Pacific Palisades, Calif. 90272. *Office:* Department of Psychology, University of Southern California, Los Angeles, Calif. 90007.

*CAREER:* Yale University, New Haven, Conn., assistant professor of psychology, 1959-65; University of California, Riverside, associate professor of psychology, 1965-66; University of Minnesota, Minneapolis, professor of psychology, 1966-70; University of Southern California, Los Angeles, professor of psychology, 1970—, Mendel B. Silberberg Professor of Psychology, 1973, chairperson of department, 1972—. *Member:* American Psychological Association (fellow), American Sociological Association, American Association for the Advancement of Science, Society of Experimental Social Psychology. *Awards, honors:* National Institute of Mental Health special research fellow, 1967-68; Jame McKeen Cattell fellowship, 1977.

*WRITINGS:* (With Charles A. Kiesler) *Attitude Change: A Critical Analysis of Theory and Data,* Wiley, 1970; (with Harold B. Gerard) *School Desegregation: A Long Range Study,* Plenum, 1975. Contributor to professional journals. Editorial consultant, *Journal of Personality and Social Psychology* and *Journal of Experimental Social Psychology.*

\* \* \*

## MILLER, Norman C(harles) 1934-

*PERSONAL:* Born October 2, 1934, in Pittsburgh, Pa.; son of Norman C. (a physician) and Elizabeth (Burns) Miller; married Mary Ann Rudy, June 15, 1957; children: Norman, Jr., Mary Ellen, Teresa, Scott. *Education:* Pennsylvania State University, B.A., 1956. *Religion:* Roman Catholic. *Home:* 5604 Ontario Cir., Sumner, Md. 20016. *Office:* 245 National Press Building, Washington, D.C. 20045.

*CAREER: Wall Street Journal,* Washington, D.C., reporter, 1960-73, bureau chief, 1973—. *Military service:* U.S. Navy, 1956-60; became lieutenant junior grade. *Member:* Sigma Delta Chi, Pi Kappa Alpha. *Awards, honors:* Pulitzer Prize, 1964, for reporting; George Polk Award, 1964.

*WRITINGS: The Great Salad Oil Swindle,* Coward, 1965.

\* \* \*

## MILLER, Oscar J. 1913-

*PERSONAL:* Born December 18, 1913, in Pittsburgh, Pa.;

son of Oscar Stephen (a salesman) and Charlotte (Hug) Miller. *Education:* St. Mary's Seminary, Perryville, Mo., B.A., 1935, additional study, 1935-39; Northwestern University, M.A., 1944. *Home and office:* St. Mary's Seminary, Houston, Tex.

*CAREER:* Ordained Roman Catholic priest of Congregation of the Mission (Vincentian Fathers), 1939; St. Vincent's College, Cape Girardeau, Mo., instructor in science and prefect, 1939-41; St. John's Seminary, Camarillo, Calif., instructor in biology, English, speech, and preaching, and dean of men, 1941-56; St. Mary's Seminary, Perryville, Mo., instructor in speech and preaching, academic dean, and registrar, 1956-62; Kenrick Seminary, St. Louis, Mo., instructor in preaching, liturgy, and catechetics, and dean of men, 1962-67; De Andreis Seminary, Lemont, Ill., instructor in preaching and treasurer, 1967-77; St. Mary's Seminary, Houston, Tex., professor of communications and homiletics, 1977—. *Member:* Speech Association of America, Catholic Homiletic Society (now Christian Preaching Conference; president, 1966-68).

*WRITINGS:* (With brother, Charles Miller) *To Sow the Seed,* Joseph F. Wagner, 1967; (with C. Miller) *Communicating Christ,* Joseph F. Wagner, 1970; (with C. Miller and James Robert) *Announcing the Good News,* Alba, 1971; (contributor) Maury Smith, editor, *Retreat for Religious Women,* Paulist/Newman, in press. Also author, *Breaking the Bread,* Alba.

\*      \*      \*

## MILLER, (Mitchell) Peter 1934-

*PERSONAL:* Born January 6, 1934, in New York, N.Y.; son of Lloyd Samuel (a bond salesman) and Mary (Mitchell) Miller; married Margaret Mahaffy, 1960 (divorced, 1968); children: Dorothy, Hilary. *Education:* University of Toronto, B.A., 1955. *Politics:* Liberal. *Religion:* None. *Address:* P.O. Box 398, Waterbury, Vt. 05676.

*CAREER:* Free-lance photographer and writer. Assistant to photographer Yousuf Karsh, Ottawa, Ontario, 1956; *Life,* New York, N.Y., reporter and writer, 1957-63; *Eastern Skiing* and *Vermont Skiing,* Stowe, Vt., editor, 1963-68; Actionpix, Inc., Waterbury, Vt., president, 1967—. *Military service:* U.S. Army, photographer based in Paris, 1955-58. *Member:* American Society of Magazine Photographers.

*WRITINGS: 30,000 Mile Ski Race,* Dial, 1972; (with Larry Benoit) *How to Bag the Biggest Buck of Your Life,* Whitetail Press, 1973. Contributor of articles and photographs to popular magazines, including *Sports Afield,* and other outdoor life and travel magazines. Contributing photographer, *Signature;* contributing editor, *Ski.*

*WORK IN PROGRESS:* A picture book on skiing; a book on the changing face of New England, illustrated with photographs; further research and writing on skiing and other outdoor sports.

*AVOCATIONAL INTERESTS:* Skiing, hunting, fishing, mountain climbing, wine, food, travel.

*BIOGRAPHICAL/CRITICAL SOURCES: Ski,* September, 1977, December, 1977; *Outdoor Life,* October, 1977.

\*      \*      \*

## MILLER, Rob(ert) Hollis 1944-

*PERSONAL:* Born February 10, 1944, in Colfax, Wash.; son of Wayne Clyde Miller (a vice-president of an engineering firm) and Vivien (Godsey) Miller Waite; married

Kathleen Edvalson (a secretary and free-lance writer), November 19, 1966; children: Myshkin Blake, Ammon Aloysha, Hollis Bayes. *Education:* Eastern Oregon College, B.A., 1970; Washington State University, M.A., 1972. *Religion:* Church of Jesus Christ of Latter-day Saints (Mormon). *Address:* P.O. Box 516, Union, Ore. 97883.

*CAREER:* Missionary in Belgium and Holland, 1963-65; U.S. census taker in Union, Ore., 1970; lookout fireman and trail crewman, summers, U.S. Forest Service, 1966-73; beekeeper in Oregon, 1975—. *Awards, honors: Story* Citation of Honor, for short story, "One Night the Green Knight," 1970-71.

*WRITINGS: Ghrist Mill II* (poems), Ramah Press, 1971. Contributor of short stories to men's magazines, of reviews to literary journals, including *Measure* and *West Coast Review,* and of poems to many little literary magazines, including *St. Andrews Review, Rolling Stone, Human Voice,* and *Dialogue.* Editor, *Middle R,* 1967-68, and *Beancan* (newspaper), 1969-70; co-editor, *Azimuth.*

*WORK IN PROGRESS: Last One Down,* a novel; *Campground Is One Word;* poetry.

\*      \*      \*

## MILLHAM, C(harles) B(lanchard) 1936-

*PERSONAL:* Born November 1, 1936, in Liberal, Kan.; son of Charles Blanchard (a printer) and Abbie (Lowrance) Millham; married Betty Jo Brickler (a research associate), June 29, 1960; children: Michael. *Education:* Attended Carleton College, 1954-56; Iowa State University, B.S., 1958, M.S., 1961, Ph.D., 1962. *Politics:* Independent. *Home:* 1135 Clifford, Pullman, Wash. 99163. *Office:* Department of Computer Science, Washington State University, Pullman, Wash. 99163.

*CAREER:* Iowa State University, Ames, instructor, 1962-64, assistant professor of mathematics, 1964-66; Washington State University, Pullman, assistant professor of mathematics, 1966-69, associate professor, 1969-74, professor of computer science and mathematics, 1974—. Fulbright professor, University of Jordan, 1976-77. *Member:* Society for Industrial Applied Mathematics, Mathematical Programming Society, Mathematical Association of America, Operations Research Society.

*WRITINGS:* (With Gerhard Tintner) *Mathematics and Statistics for Economists,* Holt, 1970. Contributor of about twenty articles to professional journals.

*WORK IN PROGRESS:* Research on economic costs of diversion of water to California, on bimatrix games, and on energy supply, demand, and use optimization models.

*AVOCATIONAL INTERESTS:* Boating, camping.

\*      \*      \*

## MILLIS, Walter 1899-1968

March 16, 1899—March 17, 1968; American author and journalist specializing in military, political, and foreign affairs. Obituaries: *New York Times,* March 18, 1968; *Washington Post,* March 19, 1968; *Time,* March 29, 1968; *Books Abroad,* spring, 1969. (See index for *CA* sketch)

\*      \*      \*

## MILLS, Belen Collantes 1930-

*PERSONAL:* Born October 15, 1930, in Abuyog, Leyte, Philippines; daughter of Ricardo Enrile (a lawyer) and Epifania (Tomines) Collantes; married Ralph A. Mills (an economist), July 3, 1957; children: Belinda Lee, Roger Ainslee. *Education:* Leyte Normal College, Philippines, elementary teacher certificate, 1950; Leyte Colleges, B.S., 1954; Indiana University, M.S., 1956, Ed.D., 1967. *Home:* 2205 Amelia Circle, Tallahassee, Fla. 32304. *Office:* Department of Early Childhood Education, Florida State University, Tallahassee, Fla.

*CAREER:* Leyte Normal College, Philippines, critic teacher, 1950-55; National Economic Council, Manila, Philippines, executive assistant, 1957-59; Lake Erie College, Painesville, Ohio, instructor in education, 1963-64; Indiana University at Bloomington, research assistant, 1964-66; West Georgia College, Carrollton, assistant professor of education, 1966-68; Florida State University, Tallahassee, associate professor of early childhood education, 1968—. Consultant in early childhood education to various counties in Georgia, Louisiana, and Florida. *Member:* Association of Childhood Education International, National Association for the Education of Young Children, American Association of University Professors, National Organization for Women. *Awards, honors:* Smith-Mundt/Fulbright scholar, 1955.

*WRITINGS: Understanding the Young Child and His Curriculum,* Macmillan, 1972; (with husband Ralph A. Mills) *Designing Instructional Strategies for Young Children,* W. C. Brown, 1972.

*WORK IN PROGRESS:* Two books to be co-authored with husband, Ralph A. Mills, *A Systematic Guide for Competent Teaching: A Diagnostic-Prescriptive Approach,* and *A Liberated Woman-A Liberated Man.*

\* \* \*

## MILORADOVICH, Milo 1901(?)-1972

1901(?)—October 28, 1972; American operatic soprano, investment adviser, and author of cookbooks. Obituaries: *New York Times,* October 29, 1972.

\* \* \*

## MINSHULL, Evelyn 1929-

*PERSONAL:* Born February 4, 1929, in Templeton, Pa.; daughter of Harry Grant (a carpenter) and Clara Lillian (Kammerdiener) White; married Fred Minshull (an applicator), June 22, 1951; children: Valerie, Melanie, Michael (deceased), Robin. *Education:* Edinboro State College, B.S., 1951; Slippery Rock State College, M.Ed., 1972. *Religion:* United Methodist. *Residence:* Mercer, Pa. *Office:* Commodore Perry High School, R. D. 1, Hadley, Pa. 16130.

*CAREER:* Art teacher in public schools in Pleasantville, Pa., 1951-52, Glendale, Ariz., 1952-53, and Mercer, Pa., 1953-56; Commodore Perry High School, Hadley, Pa., teacher of English, 1967—, and teacher in gifted children's program. Member of board and member of tutorial faculty, St. David's Christian Writers' Conference, 1975—. *Member:* National Education Association, Pennsylvania State Education Association.

*WRITINGS*—Juvenile; all published by Westminster, except as indicated: *Nine Fine Gifts,* Parents' Magazine Press, 1962; *The Ghost of Crabtree Hall,* 1970; *The Dune Witch,* 1972; *Firebug!,* 1974; *Madame Pastry and Meow,* 1975; *But I Thought You Really Loved Me,* 1976. Contributor of articles, stories, and poems to various magazines.

*WORK IN PROGRESS:* A picture book, *The Cornhusk Doll,* to be published by Herald Press; a book of teacher meditations; projects aimed at juvenile and young adult audiences; further meditational poems.

*SIDELIGHTS:* Evelyn Minshull told *CA:* "At school, I am deeply involved in fostering creative writing. Since 1967, have been developing a creative writing program which begins in the elementary, and have organized an annual Writers' Day for interested high school students, in which a panel of published writers work with the students."

\* \* \*

## MITCHELL, Memory F(armer) 1924-

*PERSONAL:* Born January 21, 1924, in Raleigh, N.C.; daughter of James S. (an editor and Baptist minister) and Foy (Johnson) Farmer; married B. W. Blackwelder, July 14, 1955 (divorced February, 1960); married Thornton W. Mitchell (a North Carolina state archivist), September 7, 1963; children: (second marriage) James Thornton and David Wingate (twins). *Education:* Meredith College, A.B., 1944; Cornell University, additional study, 1944-45; University of North Carolina at Chapel Hill, J.D., 1946, M.A., 1949. *Politics:* Democrat. *Religion:* Baptist. *Home:* 2431 Medway Dr., Raleigh, N.C. 27608. *Office:* North Carolina Division of Archives and History, 109 East Jones St., Raleigh, N.C. 27611.

*CAREER:* Meredith College, Raleigh, N.C., instructor in history, 1949-50; North Carolina State Board of Public Welfare, Raleigh, administrative assistant, 1950-54; Cabarrus County Domestic Relations Court, Concord, N.C., judge, 1954-55; North Carolina Division of Archives and History, Raleigh, records management supervisor, 1956-61, historical publications administrator, 1961—. Trustee, Olivia Raney Library, 1961-69; former director, Raleigh Community Ambassador Project.

*MEMBER:* Organization of American Historians, American Association of University Women (president of Raleigh branch, 1961-63), Southern Historical Association (member of council, 1976—), North Carolina State Bar, North Carolina Literary and Historical Association (secretary-treasurer, 1975-77), Historical Society of North Carolina (president, 1973-74), Wake County Historical Society. *Awards, honors:* Named "woman of the year," Raleigh, N.C. 1961; Robert D. W. Connor Award, 1973.

*WRITINGS: Legal Aspects of Conscription and Exemption in North Carolina, 1861-1865,* University of North Carolina Press, 1965; (editor) *Messages, Addresses, and Public Papers of Terry Sanford: Governor of North Carolina, 1961-1965,* State of North Carolina, 1966; (editor) *Messages, Addresses, and Public Papers of Daniel Killian Moore: Governor of North Carolina, 1965-1969,* State of North Carolina, 1971; (editor) *Addresses and Public Papers of Robert Walter Scott: Governor of North Carolina, 1969-1973,* Division of Archives and History, State of North Carolina, 1974. Contributor of articles to history journals. Editor, *North Carolina Historical Review,* 1962—; member of editorial board, *American Archivist,* 1972-74.

*AVOCATIONAL INTERESTS:* Travel, painting in oils (has had two one-woman art shows at Meredith College), cooking.

\* \* \*

## MITCHELL, Otis C. 1935-

*PERSONAL:* Born January 10, 1935, in Spearville, Kan.; son of Otis C. and Joeanna E. (Woodring) Mitchell; married Darlene Foley, August 20, 1966. *Education:* Wichita State University, A.B., 1957; Kansas State College at Pittsburg (now Pittsburg State University), M.A., 1960; University of

Kansas, Ph.D., 1963. *Politics:* Democrat. *Religion:* None. *Home address:* R.F.D. 2, Hidden Valley Lake, Lawrenceburg, Ind. 47025. *Office:* Department of History, University of Cincinnati, Cincinnati, Ohio 45221.

*CAREER:* Wichita State University, Wichita, Kan., instructor in history, 1963-64; University of Cincinnati, Cincinnati, Ohio, assistant professor, 1964-69, associate professor, 1969-75, professor of history, 1975—. Has appeared as host on educational television programs. *Military service:* U.S. Army, Counter Intelligence Corps, 1957-59. *Member:* American Historical Association, Conference Group of Central European Historians, American Association of University Professors, Phi Alpha Theta.

*WRITINGS: The Western Cultural Way,* W. C. Brown, 1965; *Two Totalitarians,* W. C. Brown, 1965; *A Concise History of Western Civilization,* Van Nostrand, 1968, 2nd edition, Burgess, 1976; (with Walter C. Langsam) *The World Since 1919,* Macmillan, 1971; (editor) *Nazism and the Common Man: Essays in German History,* Burgess, 1972; *Fascism: An Introductory Perspective,* Moore Publishing, 1978. Contributor of articles to professional journals.

*WORK IN PROGRESS:* "Turning Points in Western History," first volume on French Revolution.

*AVOCATIONAL INTERESTS:* Painting in oils; golf.

\* \* \*

## MOAK, Samuel K(uhn) 1929-

*PERSONAL:* Born December 15, 1929, in Yonan, Korea; came to United States in 1957; son of Yong Moon (a landowner) and Ham Am (Park) Moak; married Soon Wha (a nutritionist), April 10, 1945; children: Joanne K. *Education:* Colorado State University, B.S., 1959; University of Kentucky, M.S., 1962; North Carolina State University, Ph.D., 1966. *Politics:* Republican. *Religion:* Presbyterian. *Office:* Department of Business Administration, Covenant College, Lookout Mountain, Tenn. 37350.

*CAREER:* North Carolina State University, Raleigh, instructor in economics, 1965-66; Campbell College, Buies Creek, N.C., assistant professor of economics, 1966-67; University of Richmond, Richmond, Va., assistant professor, 1967-71, associate professor of economics, beginning 1971; currently affiliated with department of business administration, Covenant College, Lookout Mountain, Tenn. *Military service:* Korean Army, 1950-56; became a captain. *Member:* American Economic Association, American Agricultural Economic Association, National Economist Club, Korean Economic Society, Gamma Sigma Delta, Beta Epsilon.

*WRITINGS:* (With K. J. Lee) *The Church Finance,* Jung Yeon Publishing Co. (Korea), 1968; (contributor) G. S. Tolley, editor, *Study of U.S. Agricultural Adjustment,* API Series 48, North Carolina State University, 1970; (with Thomas C. Sanders) *Macroeconomics in the Modern Environment,* University of Richmond, 1973. Contributor of articles to *Asian Forum* and *The Korean Economist.*

*WORK IN PROGRESS: Church Financial Management.*

*SIDELIGHTS:* Moak has travelled in Asia, Latin America, and Europe. In addition to English and Korean, he speaks Japanese, and some German.†

\* \* \*

## MOBLEY, Harris W(itsel) 1929-

*PERSONAL:* Born June 19, 1929, in Hinesville, Ga.; son of Clarence B. and Olga L. Mobley; married Vivian Anderson (a teacher), June 25, 1950; children: Stephen Michael, Laura Jane, John Mark. *Education:* Armstrong College, A.A., 1953; Mercer University, A.B., 1955; Columbia Theological Seminary, additional study, 1955-56; Southeastern Baptist Theological Seminary, B.D., 1959; Hartford Seminary Foundation, M.A., 1965, Ph.D., 1966. *Home:* 2 Niver Rd., Statesboro, Ga. 30453. *Office:* Georgia Southern College, P.O. Box 3995, Statesboro, Ga. 30453.

*CAREER:* Student minister in Goldsboro, N.C.,1956-59; Baptist missionary in Ghana, doing research and developing training programs for missionaries, 1959-62; Board of Education, Hartford, Conn., director of African studies curriculum for honors program, 1965-66; Georgia Southern College, Statesboro, associate professor of anthropology and sociology, 1966—. Consultant, U.S. Research and Development Corp., New York, N.Y., 1967—; consultant-trainer, Human Resources Institute, Savannah, Ga., 1969-70. *Military service:* U.S. Marine Corps, 1946-48, 1950-51. *Member:* American Anthropological Association (fellow), African Studies Association (fellow), Southern Anthropological Society.

*WRITINGS: The Ghanaian's Image of the Missionary,* E. J. Brill, 1970.

*WORK IN PROGRESS:* An introductory text in anthropology, for Prentice-Hall.

\* \* \*

## MOFFETT, Martha (Leatherwood) 1934-

*PERSONAL:* Born January 3, 1934, in Pell City, Ala.; daughter of William E. (a teacher) and Martha (Funderburk) Leatherwood; married Robert Knight Moffett (an editor and writer), January 31, 1955; children: Cameron, Tyler, Kirsten. *Education:* University of Alabama, B.S., 1954; Columbia University, M.S.,1972. *Home:* 740 Rider Rd., Boynton Beach, Fla. 33435. *Agent:* Charles Neighbors, 240 Waverly Pl., New York, N.Y.

*CAREER: New Book of Knowledge,* New York City, head of proof department, 1964-66; *American Heritage Dictionary,* New York City, senior copy editor, 1966-68. Active in the peace movement and local co-operative and school organizations. *Member:* Forum of Writers for Young People.

*WRITINGS:* (With husband, Robert Knight Moffett) *The Whale in Fact & Fiction,* Quist, 1967; (with R. Moffett) *First Book of Dolphins,* Watts, 1971; (editor) *Great Love Poems,* five volumes, World Publishing, 1971; *A Flower Pot Is Not a Hat,* Dutton, 1972; *The Common Garden,* Berkley, 1977.

*WORK IN PROGRESS:* A political novel; a book of short stories; poetry.

*SIDELIGHTS:* Martha Moffett told *CA:* "Everything in the small, isolated, raw mining town in the mountains of northeast Alabama is removed by more than time from the life I lead now—it is all a world away. I grew up dreaming of escape, of life in a great city; reading books that I hoped would lead me there."

*BIOGRAPHICAL/CRITICAL SOURCES: New York Times Book Review,* September 24, 1967.

\* \* \*

## MOLENAAR, Dee 1918-

*PERSONAL:* Born June 21, 1918, in Los Angeles, Calif.; son of Peter and Marina Molenaar, both natives of the Netherlands; married Colleen Haag, October 9, 1954; children: Patrice Ann, Karen Marina, Peter Cornelius, David Christian. *Education:* Attended Los Angeles City College, one year; University of Washington, Seattle, B.Sc., 1950. *Home address:* P.O. Box 62, Burley, Wash. 98322. *Office:* Water Resources Division, U.S. Geological Survey, Tacoma, Wash.

*CAREER:* Milked cows, drove trucks, and worked for a taxidermy studio and other shops in Los Angeles, Calif., and vicinity, 1936-39; summit and glacier guide on Mount Rainier, summers, 1940-41; photographer with Allied Advertising Artists, Los Angeles, Calif., 1945-46; co-operator of Mount Rainier Guide Service, summer, 1947, and summer seasonal ranger, Mount Rainier National Park, 1948-49; permanent park ranger, Mount Rainier National Park, 1950-52; civilian adviser in U.S. Army's Mountain and Cold Weather Training Command, Camp Carson and Camp Hale, Colo., 1952-53; geologist for Phillips Petroleum Co. in southeastern Alaska, Colorado, and Utah, 1954-55; geologist with Division of Water Resources, Washington State Department of Conservation, Olympia, 1956-66; geologist-hydrologist and technical reports editor with Water Resources Division, U.S. Geological Survey, Tacoma, Wash., 1966—. Mountaineering since 1936—; member of Mount St. Elias Alaskan expedition, 1946, third American Karakoram expedition to world's second highest peak, K2, 1953, Mount McKinley rescue expedition, 1960, and National Geographic Society-Boston Museum of Science expedition to Mount Kennedy, Yukon Territory, 1965; has made more than fifty ascents of Mount Rainier over twelve different routes. Photographer, lecturer, painter, and cartographer. *Military service:* U.S. Coast Guard, photographer, 1941-45; served in Aleutians and central Pacific.

*MEMBER:* American Alpine Club, Mountaineers, Wilderness Society, Association of Earth Science Editors, North Cascades Conservation Council, Mountain Rescue Association (charter member, Seattle unit), Appalachian Mountain Club (honorary corresponding member). *Awards, honors:* Special award, Washington State Governor's Writers Day Awards, 1972, for *The Challenge of Rainier.*

*WRITINGS:* (Contributor) *Mountaineering: Freedom of the Hills* (textbook), Mountaineers, 1960; (contributor) *Climber's Guide to the Cascade and Olympic Mountains of Washington,* American Alpine Club, 1960; *The Challenge of Rainier: A Record of the Explorations and Ascents, Triumphs and Tragedies on the Northwest's Greatest Mountain,* Mountaineers, 1971, 2nd edition, 1973.

Author or co-author of geologic studies and bulletins on water resources. Art and cartographic work has been published in climbing and exploring guides for the Cascade and Olympic Mountains, Olympic seashore and Olympic Peninsula, Death Valley, and Mount Rainier National Park. Photographic work includes the documentary film, ''Ascent of Liberty Ridge'' for KOMO-TV. Illustrations have appeared in *National Geographic.* Contributor of numerous articles to periodicals including *Summit, Off Belay,* and *Backpacker.* Northwest editor, *Summit.*

*SIDELIGHTS:* Dee Molenaar told *CA:* ''I suppose my enjoyment of writing began way back in grade school, but my first literary effort was done while serving in the military in the Central Pacific during World War II—an article published in a mountaineering journal, describing pre-war guiding experiences on Mount Rainier.... I'd like to do another book someday, a sort of light-veined dissertation on my own experiences and observations of climbing and

climbers over the past 40 years. Of course, as I grow older my writing becomes increasingly more retrospective, as I look back on the early days of American mountaineering, in the 1920's and 1930's when it was still fashionable to ask the eternal, 'Why do you climb?' It is easy to wax nostalgic over those times, before the advent of modern mountaineering, when climbers began to take their mountains—and themselves—so seriously. Although mountaineering has always been considered a physically and psychologically challenging activity, it should also be fun.'' Molenaar continues, ''My early favorites among writers, and those probably most affecting my interest in writing, have been John Muir, Thoreau, Ernest Thompson Seton, James Willard Shultz, Zane Grey, all writing of the outdoors and rugged individualism.''

\*     \*     \*

### MONAGHAN, Patrick C. 1903(?)-1972

1903(?)—November 8, 1972; American public relations and marketing consultant. Obituaries: *New York Times,* November 10, 1972.

\*     \*     \*

### MONTESI, Albert Joseph 1921-

*PERSONAL:* Born January 10, 1921, in Memphis, Tenn.; son of Alex (a groceryman) and Amelia (Boldreghini) Montesi. *Education:* University of Tennessee, student, 1946-47; Northwestern University, B.S., 1949; University of Michigan, M.A., 1950; University of Denver, additional study, 1950-51; Pennsylvania State University, Ph.D., 1955. *Politics:* Democrat. *Religion:* Roman Catholic. *Home:* 22 Benton Pl., St. Louis, Mo. 63104. *Office:* Department of English, St. Louis University, 221 North Grand, St. Louis, Mo. 63103.

*CAREER:* St. Louis University, St. Louis, Mo., assistant professor, 1957-62, associate professor, 1962-71, professor of English, 1971—. President, Benton Place Association. *Military service:* U.S. Army Air Forces, 1942-46; became staff sergeant. *Member:* Modern Language Association of America, National Council of Teachers of English, James Joyce Society, American Association of University Professors. *Awards, honors:* American Council of Learned Societies grant, 1961-62.

*WRITINGS: Micrograms* (poems), Mayhurst Press, 1971; *Windows and Mirrors* (poems), Cornerstone, 1977. Contributor to *New Catholic Encyclopedia* and *Catholic Encyclopedia for Home and School;* contributor of articles to literature journals. Editor, *Twentieth Century Literature.* Poetry editor, *St. Louis Literary Supplement,* 1977.

*WORK IN PROGRESS: Poetry of the American Twenties.*

\*     \*     \*

### MONTHERLANT, Henry (Milon) de 1896-1972

April 21, 1896—September 21, 1972; French novelist and playwright. Obituaries: *New York Times,* September 23, 1972; *L'Express,* September 25-October 1, 1972; *Newsweek,* October 2, 1972; *Antiquarian Bookman,* October 16, 1972.

\*     \*     \*

### MOONEY, Christopher F(rancis) 1925-

*PERSONAL:* Born February 23, 1925, in Bayonne, N.J.; son of Christopher and Frances (Behan) Mooney. *Education:* Loyola University, Chicago, Ill., A.B., 1950, M.A., 1954; Woodstock College, S.T.L., 1958; Institut Catholique,

Paris, S.T.D., 1964; University of Pennsylvania, law studies, 1976—. *Home:* 5841 Overbrook Ave., Philadelphia, Pa. 19131. *Agent:* Marilyn Marlow, Curtis Brown, Ltd., 575 Madison Ave., New York, N.Y. 10022.

*CAREER:* Roman Catholic priest of the Society of Jesus (Jesuits); Canisius College, Buffalo, N.Y., professor of theology, 1959-61; St. Peter's College, Jersey City, N.J., professor of theology, 1959-61; Fordham University, New York City, professor of theology, 1964-69, chairman of department, 1965-69; Woodstock College, New York City, president of the college, 1969-74; Yale University, Law School, New Haven, Conn., graduate fellow, 1974-75; St. Joseph's College, Philadelphia, Pa., visiting professor, 1975-76. *Member:* Catholic Biblical Association, Catholic Theological Society of America, Society for the Scientific Study of Religion, Religious Education Association, American Academy of Religion. *Awards, honors:* Best scholarly article of the year award, Catholic Press Association, 1964, for "Anxiety in Teilhard de Chardin"; National Catholic Book Award, 1966, for *Teilhard de Chardin and the Mystery of Christ.*

*WRITINGS: Teilhard de Chardin and the Mystery of Christ,* Harper, 1966; (editor and author of introduction) *The Presence and Absence of God,* Fordham University Press, 1969; (editor and author of introduction) *Prayer: The Problem of Dialogue with God,* Paulist Press, 1969; *The Making of Man,* Paulist Press, 1971; *Man Without Tears,* Harper, 1975; *Religion and the American Dream,* Westminster, 1977. Member of editorial board, *Concilium,* 1970—; contributor of articles to *Theological Studies, Harvard Theological Review, Downside Review, Scripture, Religious Education, Social Research, Continuum,* and other journals.

*WORK IN PROGRESS:* Study of the relationships between freedom and equality in the context of American pluralism.

\*      \*      \*

## MOORE, Carey Armstrong 1930-

*PERSONAL:* Born March 5, 1930, in Baltimore, Md.; son of Carey Armstrong (a realtor) and Grace (Bell) Moore; married Patricia Emlet (an educator), December 31, 1952; children: Kathleen Anne, Stephen Loudon, David Saddler, Bruce Edward. *Education:* Gettysburg College, A.B., 1952; Lutheran Theological Seminary at Gettysburg, B.D., 1956; Johns Hopkins University, Ph.D., 1965; Hebrew Union College, Jerusalem, Israel, additional study, 1967-68. *Politics:* Democrat. *Home:* 452 Baltimore St., Gettysburg, Pa. 17325. *Office:* Department of Religion, Gettysburg College, Gettysburg, Pa. 17325.

*CAREER:* Gettysburg College, Gettysburg, Pa., instructor, 1955-56, assistant professor, 1959-65, associate professor, 1966-68, professor of religion, 1969—. Visiting professor of Hebrew, Lutheran Theological Seminary at Gettysburg, 1965-66; archaeological field supervisor, Hebrew Union College, Jerusalem, Israel, 1965-68. Trustee, Adams County Public Library. *Member:* National Association of Professors of Hebrew, Archaeological Institute of America, American Schools of Oriental Research, American Association of University Professors, Adams County Historical Society (vice-president), Gettysburg Photographic Society (president), Phi Beta Kappa.

*WRITINGS: Esther: Introduction, Translation, and Notes,* Doubleday, 1971; (editor with H. Bream and R. Heim) *A Light unto My Path: Old Testament Studies in*

*Honor of J. M. Myers,* Temple University Press, 1974; *Daniel, Ester and Jeremiah: The Additions,* Doubleday, 1977; *The Book of Esther: An Anthology of Scholarly Articles,* Ktav, in press. Contributor to theological journals.

*SIDELIGHTS:* Carey Armstrong Moore has traveled extensively in the Near East, and has participated in archaeological excavations at Gezer, Dan and Hebron, Israel. He is competent in Semitic and Indo-European languages.

\*      \*      \*

## MOORE, Jane Ann 1931-

*PERSONAL:* Born March 11, 1931; daughter of Charles William (a minister) and Margaret Lois (Timmons) Stoneburner; married William Frederick Moore (a clergyman), November 25, 1961; children: Deborah Ann. *Education:* Ohio Wesleyan University, B.A., 1952; Yale University, B.D., 1956; Boston University, M.A., 1961, Ph.D., 1966. *Politics:* Democrat. *Office:* Department of Sociology, Howard University, Washington, D.C. 20001.

*CAREER:* Ordained minister of United Church of Christ; minister in churches in Barton, Vt., 1956-57, and Columbus, Ohio, 1957-59; Boston University, Boston, Mass., instructor, 1961-63; Howard University, Washington, D.C., assistant professor of sociology and African studies, 1967—. *Member:* American Sociological Association, African Studies Association, Eastern Sociological Association, Washington, D.C. Sociological Association.

*WRITINGS:* (Editor) *Cry Sorrow, Cry Joy: Selections from Contemporary African Writers,* Friendship, 1971. Also author of *The Middle Society: Five Orientations toward Husband-Wife Roles in West African Novels.*

*WORK IN PROGRESS: Sociology of Occupations in Africa; Methods and Techniques of Research in Africa.*†

\*      \*      \*

## MOORE, John A(ndrew) 1918-1972

May 10, 1918—June 22, 1972; American educator and authority on classical Greek poetry. Obituaries: *Washington Post,* June 24, 1972.

\*      \*      \*

## MOORE, John Norton 1937-

*PERSONAL:* Born June 12, 1937, in New York, N.Y.; son of William Thomas (a nuclear engineer) and Lorena (Norton) Moore; married Patricia Diane Morris (an artist), January 26, 1963. *Education:* Drew University, A.B., 1959; Duke University, LL.B. (with distinction), 1962; University of Illinois, LL.M., 1965; Yale Law School, Fellow of the National Institute of Health, 1965-66. *Home address:* Route 3, Box 43, Charlottesville, Va. 22901. *Office:* University of Virginia School of Law, Charlottesville, Va. 22901.

*CAREER:* Attorney; admitted to Bars of Florida, 1962, Illinois, 1963, Virginia, 1969, District of Columbia, 1974, and U.S. Supreme Court, 1973; University of Florida, Gainesville, assistant professor of law, 1963-65; University of Virginia, Charlottesville, associate professor, 1965-68, professor of international law, 1968-76, Walter L. Brown Professor of Law, 1976—, director, Center for Oceans Law and Policy; U.S. Department of State, counselor on international law, 1972-73. Chairman, U.S. National Security Council Task Force on the Law of the Sea; U.S. ambassador to Third United Nations Conference on the Law of the Sea, 1973-76. Consultant in international law to Naval War

College and National War College; member of Council on Foreign Relations; member of U.S. delegation to United Nations, 1972-75; member of State Department Advisory Panel on International Law. Fellow of Berkeley International Legal Studies Program, 1963. *Member:* International Law Association, American Society of International Law (member of executive council and board of review and development), American Bar Association (chairman, Committee on International Law and Use of Force), Phi Beta Kappa, Cosmos Club, Order of the Coif. *Awards, honors:* Sesquicentennial Fellow of Center for Advanced Studies at the University of Virginia, 1971-72; fellow, Woodrow Wilson International Center for Scholars, 1976; alumni achievement award in the arts, Drew University, 1976; Phi Beta Kappa Award for *Law and the Indo-China War.*

*WRITINGS: Law and the Indo-China War,* Princeton University Press, 1972; (editor) *The Arab-Israeli Conflict,* three volumes, Princeton University Press, 1972, abridged edition, 1977; (editor) *Law and Civil War in the Modern World,* Johns Hopkins University Press, 1975. Author of numerous articles on oceans policy, national security, and congressional-executive relations in foreign policy. Member of editorial board, *American Journal of International Law,* 1972, and *Marine Technology Society Journal,* 1976—.

*WORK IN PROGRESS:* Writing *The Red, White and Blue Whale: A National Oceans Program for the United States;* editing two volumes of readings in international law for the *Naval War College Review.*

\* \* \*

## MOOS, Malcolm C(harles) 1916-

*PERSONAL:* Born April 19, 1916, in St. Paul, Minn.; son of Charles John (an insurance executive and politician) and Katherine Isabelle (Grant) Moos; married Margaret Tracy Gager (an art librarian), June 29, 1945; children: Malcolm, Katherine, Grant, Ann, Margaret. *Education:* University of Minnesota, B.A., 1937, M.A., 1938; University of California, Berkeley, Ph.D., 1942. *Office address:* Fund for the Republic, Inc., P.O. Box 4068, Santa Barbara, Calif. 93103.

*CAREER:* League of Minnesota Municipalities, Minneapolis, research assistant, 1938-39; University of Alabama, University, research assistant in Bureau of Public Administration, 1941-42; University of Wyoming, Laramie, assistant professor of political science, 1942; Johns Hopkins University, Baltimore, Md., assistant professor, 1942-46, associate professor, 1946-52, professor of political science, 1952-61, 1963; adviser on public affairs to the five Rockefeller brothers, New York City, 1961-63; Columbia University, New York City, professor of public law and government, 1963-65; Ford Foundation, New York City, director of policy and planning, 1964-66, director of office of government and law, 1966-67; University of Minnesota, Minneapolis, president, 1967-74; Fund for the Republic, Inc., Santa Barbara, Calif., president, 1974—. Visiting professor, University of Michigan, 1955. Republican National Convention, alternate delegate, 1952, delegate, 1956; chairperson, Republican State Central Committee of Maryland, 1954-58; consultant, administrative assistant, and special assistant to President Dwight D. Eisenhower, 1957-61. Member, Baltimore City Jail Commission, 1953-55, President's Commission on Campaign Costs, 1961-62, Commission on Political Activity of Government Employees, 1966—, President's Task Force on Priorities in Higher Education, 1969—, and British-North American Committee, 1969—. Member of boards of directors, Harry S Truman Library Institute, 1968—, American

Council on Education, 1971-74, and National Public Affairs Center for Television, 1972—; Carnegie Foundation, member of board of trustees, 1969—, member of executive committee, 1971-73. Consultant to Maryland Commission on Organization of State Government, 1952-54.

*MEMBER:* American Political Science Association, National Association of State Universities and Land-Grant Colleges (vice-chairman of federal relations committee, 1970—), Political Economy Club, Minnesota Historical Society (member of executive council, 1968-71), Phi Beta Kappa, Century Association. *Awards, honors:* LL.D., Ohio Northern University, 1960, University of North Dakota and Georgetown University, 1968, Johns Hopkins University, 1969, University of Notre Dame, 1973, and University of Maryland, 1974; Litt.D., College of St. Thomas, 1970.

*WRITINGS: State Penal Administration in Alabama,* Bureau of Public Administration, University of Alabama, 1942; (with Wilfred E. Binkley) *A Grammar of American Politics: The National Government,* Knopf, 1949, revised edition published as *Grammar of American Politics: The National, State, and Local Governments,* 1952; *Politics, Presidents, and Coattails,* Johns Hopkins Press, 1952; (with Paul T. David) *Presidential Nominating Politics in 1952,* Johns Hopkins Press, 1954; (with Thomas L. Cook) *Power through Purpose: The Bases of American Foreign Policy,* Johns Hopkins Press, 1954; (editor) H.L. Mencken, *A Carnival of Buncombe,* Johns Hopkins Press, 1956; *The Republicans: A History of Their Party,* Random House, 1956; (with Francis Rourke) *The Campus and the State,* Johns Hopkins Press, 1959; (with Stephen Hess) *Hats in the Ring,* Random House, 1960; *Dwight D. Eisenhower* (children's book), Random House, 1964. Also author of recording, "The Crisis of the Contemporary Presidency: A Democratic View," Center for the Study of Democratic Institutions, 1975. Associate editor of *Baltimore Evening Sun,* 1945-48.†

\* \* \*

## MORAN, Ronald (Wesson, Jr.) 1936-

*PERSONAL:* Born September 9, 1936, in Philadelphia, Pa.; son of Ronald Wesson (an engineer) and Julia (Hagymasi) Moran; married Jane Edith Hetzler, January 31, 1959; children: Sally and R. Wesson III (twins). *Education:* Colby College, B.A., 1958; Louisiana State University, M.A., 1962, Ph.D., 1966. *Home:* 114 Princess Lane, Clemson, S.C. 29631. *Office:* Department of English, Clemson University, Clemson, S.C. 29631.

*CAREER:* Louisiana State University, Baton Rouge, instructor in English, 1963-66; University of North Carolina at Chapel Hill, assistant professor, 1966-69, associate professor, 1969-75, assistant dean of College of Arts and Sciences, 1972-75; Clemson University, Clemson, S.C., professor of English and head of department, 1975—. Fulbright lecturer in West Germany, 1969-70. *Member:* Modern Language Association of America, South Atlantic Modern Language Association.

*WRITINGS: So Simply Means the Rain,* Claitor's, 1965; *Louis Simpson,* Twayne, 1972; (with George S. Lensing) *Four Poets and the Emotive Imagination,* Louisiana State University Press, 1976. Contributor to literary journals and to *Commonweal.*

*WORK IN PROGRESS:* A book of poems.

## MOREAU, John Adam   1938-

*PERSONAL:* Born February 27, 1938, in New York, N.Y.; son of Charles Ellis and Christina (Kreag) Moreau; married Linda Ann Swanson, February 21, 1970. *Education:* Northwestern University, B.S.J., 1960; Fordham University, M.A., 1961; University of Virginia, Ph.D., 1964. *Politics:* Liberal. *Religion:* Catholic. *Office: Chicago Tribune,* 435 North Michigan Ave., Chicago, Ill. 60611.

*CAREER:* Reporter for California newspapers and the *Washington Post,* Washington, D.C., 1962-1967; *Chicago Sun-Times,* Chicago, Illinois, reporter, rewriteman, deskman, editorial writer, 1967-71, Latin American correspondent, 1971-72; *Chicago Tribune,* Chicago, Latin American correspondent, 1972—. *Member:* Chicago Press Club, Sigma Delta Chi. *Awards, honors:* Fellowships from American Political Science Association and Inter American Press Association, for study of Latin American affairs.

*WRITINGS: Randolph Bourne: Legend and Reality,* Public Affairs Press, 1966. Contributor of scholarly articles to various journals.

*WORK IN PROGRESS:* A biography of Paxton Hibben, diplomat and historian.†

\*     \*     \*

## MORGAN, Charles H(ill)   1902-

*PERSONAL:* Born September 19, 1902, in Worcester, Mass.; son of Paul Beagary and Lessie (Maynard) Morgan; married Janet Barton, September 14, 1928; children: Audrey E. (Mrs. Carlton D. Leaf), George S. B., Prudence Gilbert (Mrs. Edward C. Eppich). *Education:* Harvard University, A.B., 1924, A.M., 1926, Ph.D., 1928; American School of Classical Studies at Athens, postdoctoral study, 1928-29. *Home:* 22 Snell St., Amherst, Mass. 01002. *Agent:* McIntosh & Otis, Inc., 475 Fifth Ave., New York, N.Y. 10016.

*CAREER:* Bryn Mawr College, Bryn Mawr, Pa., lecturer in archaeology, 1929-30; Amherst College, Amherst, Mass., assistant professor, 1930-34, associate professor, 1934-38, professor of fine arts and director of Mead Art Building, 1938-68, professor emeritus, 1968—. American School of Classical Studies at Athens, visiting professor, 1933-34, assistant director, 1935-36, director, 1936-38, chairman of managing committee, 1950-60. Chairman of department of art, Trinity College, Hartford, Conn., 1964-66. Trustee of American International College and American Farm School, Salonika, Greece. *Military service:* U.S. Army Air Forces, 1942-46; served overseas three years; became colonel; received Legion of Merit and Belgian Croix de Guerre with palms.

*MEMBER:* Authors Guild, Century Association, Delta Kappa Epsilon. *Awards, honors:* Grand Cross, Royal Order of the Phoenix (Greece), 1953; L.H.D., University of Vermont, 1960, Amherst College, 1972; Litt.D., Trinity College, Hartford, Conn., 1965.

*WRITINGS: Corinth XI: The Byzantine Pottery,* Harvard University Press, 1942; *Life of Michelangelo,* Reynal, 1960; *George Bellows: Painter of America,* Reynal, 1965; *The Amherst College Art Collection,* Amherst College Press, 1972. Contributor to art and archaeology journals. Editor, *Hesperia,* 1936-38.

*WORK IN PROGRESS:* A "true" history of Greek sculpture; a cookbook "for the man who wants to make a big show with very little effort."

*SIDELIGHTS:* Charles Morgan says that he wrote *Corinth*

*XI* "because there was no general study of Byzantine pottery, and one was needed," on Michelangelo because "no brief biography had appeared for half a century," on Bellows because "it seemed important to get this out while some of his friends were still alive," and on the Amherst art collection because "most of it was formed under my direction."

\*     \*     \*

## MORGAN, Dan   1925-

*PERSONAL:* Born December 24, 1925, in Holbeach, Lincolnshire, England; son of Cecil (a tailor) and Lilian Kate (Morley) Morgan. *Education:* Educated in Spalding, Lincolnshire, England. *Home and office:* 1 Chapel Lane, Spalding, Lincolnshire PE11 1BP, England. *Agent:* Laurence Pollinger Ltd., 18 Maddox St., London W1R OEU, England; and Robert P. Mills, Ltd., 156 East 52nd St., New York, N.Y. 10022.

*CAREER:* Has worked as a musician; Dan Morgan (a menswear retail business), Spalding, Lincolnshire, England, managing director, 1958—. *Military service:* British Army, Medical Corps, 1947-48.

*WRITINGS: Playing the Guitar,* Bantam, 1967.

Science fiction: *The New Minds,* Avon, 1969; *The Several Minds,* Avon, 1969; *Mind Trap,* Avon, 1970; (with John Kippax) *A Thunder of Stars,* Ballantine, 1970; (with Kippax) *Seed of Stars,* Ballantine, 1972; *The High Destiny,* Berkley, 1973; (with Kippax) *The Neutral Stars,* Ballantine, 1973; *Inside,* Berkley, 1974; *The Country of the Mind,* Corgi Books, 1975; *The Concrete Horizon,* Millington Books, 1976. Contributor to anthologies, including *New Writings in SF;* contributor to science fiction magazines in Great Britain and the United States.

*SIDELIGHTS:* Dan Morgan told *CA:* "My writing career is in the deep freeze at the moment (1977) and looks like remaining so for some years to come, as I am committed to full-time business activity. This is regrettable, but the plain fact is that I can earn a much more comfortable standard of living as a businessman than I can as a writer and I'm too darned old to relish the idea of starving for my art. Maybe one day I'll be able to get back to writing seriously (i.e., novels), but don't hold your breath—business is expanding and I'm more and more involved."

\*     \*     \*

## MORGAN, Patrick M.   1940-

*PERSONAL:* Born December 6, 1940, in Syracuse, N.Y.; son of George A. and Mary (Cartin) Morgan; married Marilyn A. Kelly (a college administrator and high school teacher), August 24, 1964; children: Kelly Sue, Christopher, Kimberly. *Education:* Harpur College of State University of New York (now State University of New York at Binghamton), B.A., 1962; Yale University, M.A., 1963, Ph.D., 1967. *Politics:* Democrat. *Home:* Southeast 535 Dexter St., Pullman, Wash. 99163. *Office:* Department of Political Science, Washington State University, Pullman, Wash. 99164.

*CAREER:* Washington State University, Pullman, assistant professor, 1967-72, associate professor, 1972-77, professor of political science, 1977—. Member, Inter-University Seminar on Armed Forces and Society. *Member:* American Political Science Association, International Studies Association, American Committee on East-West Accord. *Awards, honors:* Woodrow Wilson International Center for Scholars fellow, 1973-74; American Council on Education fellow, 1976-77.

*WRITINGS:* (Editor with Terrence Cook) *Participatory Democracy*, Canfield Press, 1971; *Theories and Approaches to International Politics*, Consensus Publishers, 1972, 2nd edition, Page-Ficklin/Transaction, 1975; *Deterrence: A Conceptual Analysis*, Sage Publications, 1977.

*WORK IN PROGRESS:* A third edition of *Theories and Approaches to International Politics;* a study of deterrence in practice.

* * *

## MORGAN, Ruth P. 1934-

*PERSONAL:* Born March 30, 1934, in Berkeley, Calif.; daughter of Ervin J. (a professor) and Thelma (Precesang) Prouse; married Vernon E. Morgan (a chemical engineer), June 3, 1956; children: Glenn E. *Education:* University of Texas, B.A. (summa cum laude), 1956; Louisiana State University, M.A., 1962, Ph.D., 1966. *Office:* Office of the Director, Master of Liberal Arts Program, Southern Methodist University, Dallas, Tex. 75222.

*CAREER:* Southern Methodist University, Dallas, Tex., assistant professor, 1966-70, associate professor, 1970-74, professor of political science, 1974—, director, liberal arts graduate program, 1976—. *Member:* International Political Science Association, American Political Science Association, American Association of University Professors, Academy of Political Science, Southern Political Science Association, Western Political Science Association, Southwestern Social Science Association. *Awards, honors:* Southern Methodist University, "Outstanding Professor," 1969, 1974, "M" Award for outstanding service, 1972.

*WRITINGS: The President and Civil Rights*, St. Martin's, 1970.

*WORK IN PROGRESS: The Cartoon Presidency.*

*AVOCATIONAL INTERESTS:* Travel, photography, flute.

* * *

## MORGAN, Thomas (Bruce) 1885(?)-1972

1885(?)—July 8, 1972; Welsh-born American journalist and author of books on contemporary events. Obituaries: *New York Times*, July 11, 1972.

* * *

## MORLEY, Samuel A. 1934-

*PERSONAL:* Born April 7, 1934, in Aberdeen, Wash.; son of William R. (a businessman) and Louise (Scoville) Morley; married Monica DaRosa, December 19, 1959; children: Samuel, William, Edward. *Education:* Yale University, B.A., 1956; University of California, Berkeley, Ph.D., 1965. *Home:* 6011 Dunham Springs Rd., Nashville, Tenn. 37205. *Office:* Department of Economics, Vanderbilt University, Nashville, Tenn. 37235.

*CAREER:* U.S. Department of State, Washington, D.C., foreign service officer, 1958-59; rancher operating Lone Creek Ranch, Lonerock, Ore., 1959-61; University of California, Berkeley, research economist, 1965-67, coordinator of Brazil Development Assistance Program, 1967-68; University of Wisconsin—Madison, assistant professor, 1968-73, associate professor of economics, 1973-75; Vanderbilt University, Nashville, Tenn., professor of economics, 1975—. Visiting assistant professor, Rice University, 1971—. Employment research expert, United Nations mission to Brazil, 1975-76. *Military service:* U.S. Army.

*Awards, honors:* Grants from Ford Foundation, 1969, Social Science Research Council, 1971, and National Science Foundation (for study of foreign investment in Brazil), 1972-73.

*WRITINGS: Stabilizing an Economy: A Comparison of Stabilization Programs in Chile, Brazil and Korea* (monograph), Agency for International Development, 1969; *The Economics of Inflation*, Dryden, 1971; (contributor) M. Buescu, editor, *Essays in Honor of Octavio Gouvea de Bulhoes*, [Rio de Janeiro], 1972; (contributor) Alfred Stepan, editor, *Brazil in the 1960s*, Yale University Press, 1973; (contributor) Manning Nash, editor, *Essays on Economic Development and Cultural Change in Honor of Bert F. Hoselitz*, University of Chicago Press, 1977; *Inflation and Unemployment*, Dryden Press, in press. Contributor of articles and reviews to professional journals.

*WORK IN PROGRESS:* Employment, income distribution and growth in Brazil.

* * *

## MORRIS, Henry M(adison, Jr.) 1918-

*PERSONAL:* Born October 6, 1918, in Dallas, Tex.; son of Henry M. (a realtor) and Emily Ida (Hunter) Morris; married Mary Louise Beach (a librarian), January 24, 1940; children: Henry M. III, Kathleen (Mrs. Leslie Bruce), John, Andrew, Mary, Rebecca. *Education:* Rice University, B.S.C.E. (with distinction), 1939; University of Minnesota, M.S., 1948, Ph.D., 1950. *Politics:* Republican. *Religion:* Independent Baptist. *Home:* 6733 El Banquero Pl., San Diego, Calif. 92119. *Office:* Institute for Creation Research, Christian Heritage College, 2716 Madison Ave., San Diego, Calif. 92116.

*CAREER:* Member of Texas State Highway Department, Houston, Tex., 1938-39; International Boundary and Water Commission, El Paso, Tex., junior engineer, 1939-41, assistant hydraulic engineer, 1941-42; Rice University, Houston, instructor in civil engineering, 1942-46; University of Minnesota, St. Anthony Falls Hydraulic Laboratory, Minneapolis, instructor, 1946-50, assistant professor of civil engineering, 1950-51, research project leader, 1947-51; University of Southwestern Louisiana, Lafayette, professor of civil engineering, 1951-56, head of department, 1951-56, acting dean of engineering, fall, 1956; Southern Illinois University, Carbondale, professor of applied science, 1957; Virginia Polytechnic Institute and State University, Blacksburg, professor of hydraulic engineering and chairman of department of civil engineering, 1957-70; Christian Heritage College, San Diego, Calif., director of Institute for Creation Research, 1970—, vice-president for academic affairs, 1970—.

*MEMBER:* American Association for the Advancement of Science (fellow), American Society of Civil Engineers (fellow), American Scientific Affiliation (fellow), American Geophysical Union, American Geological Institute, American Society for Engineering Education, Engineers Council for Professional Development, Creation Research Society (president, 1967—), Evolution Protest Movement (member of council, 1968—), Phi Beta Kappa, Sigma Xi, Tau Beta Pi, Chi Epsilon. *Awards, honors:* LL.D., Bob Jones University, 1966.

*WRITINGS:* (With R. S. Stephens) *Report on the Rio Grande Water Conservation Investigation*, El Paso International Boundary and Water Commission, 1942; *That You Might Believe*, Good Books, 1946; (with C. L. Larson) *Hydraulics of Flow in Culverts*, University of Minnesota Press, 1948; *A New Concept of Flow in Rough Conduits*, University of Minnesota Press, 1950; *The Bible and Modern Science,* Moody, 1951, revised edition, 1968; (with John C. Whitcomb) *The Genesis Flood,* Presbyterian & Reformed, 1961; *The Twilight of Evolution,* Baker Book, 1963; *Applied Hydraulics in Engineering,* Ronald, 1963, revised edition (with J. M. Wiggert), 1972; *Science, Scripture, and Salvation,* Baptist Publications, 1965, revised edition, 1971; *Studies in the Bible and Science,* Presbyterian & Reformed, 1966; *Evolution and the Modern Christian,* Baker Book, 1968; *Hydraulics of Energy Dissipation,* Virginia Polytechnic Institute and State University, 1968.

*Biblical Cosmology and Modern Science,* Craig, 1970; *The Bible Has the Answer,* Craig, 1971, 2nd edition, 1976; (editor with others) "Science and Creation" series (eight student books and nine teacher books), Creation Science, 1971; *A Biblical Manual on Science and Creation,* Institute for Creation Research, 1972; *The Remarkable Birth of Planet Earth,* Institute for Creation Research, 1972; (editor) *Scientific Creationism,* Creation-Life, 1974; *Many Infallible Proofs,* Creation-Life, 1974; *The Troubled Waters of Evolution,* Creation-Life, 1975; (editor) *The Battle for Creation,* Creation-Life, 1976; *The Genesis Record,* Creation-Life, 1976; *Education for the Real World,* Creation-Life, 1977; *The Scientific Case for Creation,* Creation-Life, 1977. Contributor of about a hundred seventy-five articles on hydraulics and on the Bible to technical journals, magazines, and newspapers.

*WORK IN PROGRESS:* A popular level book on Christian apologetics; a scientific commentary on the Book of Psalms.

\* \* \*

## MORRIS, Norval 1923-

*PERSONAL:* Born October 1, 1923, in Auckland, New Zealand; son of Louis and Vera (Burke) Morris; married Elaine Richardson; children: Gareth, Malcolm, Christopher. *Education:* University of Melbourne, LL.B., 1941, LL.M., 1947; University of London, Ph.D., 1950. *Home:* 1207 East 50th St., Chicago, Ill. 60615. *Office:* Law School, University of Chicago, 1111 East 60th St., Chicago, Ill. 60637.

*CAREER:* University of Chicago, Chicago, Ill., Julius Kreeger Professor of Law and Criminology, and dean of the Law School. *Military service:* Australian Army, 1941-45; served in Pacific. *Member:* American Bar Association (member of Commission on Corrections). *Awards, honors:* Award from Government of Japan.

*WRITINGS: The Habitual Criminal,* Longmans, Green, 1950; *Studies in Criminal Law,* Oxford University Press, 1964; (with Gordon Hawkins) *The Honest Politician's Guide to Crime Control,* University of Chicago Press, 1970; (with Hawkins) *Crime and Modern Society: America's Dilemma,* University of Tokyo Press, 1971; (editor with Mark Perlman) *Law and Crime: Essays in Honor of Sir John Barry,* Gordon & Breach, 1972; *The Future of Imprisonment,* University of Chicago Press, 1974; (with Hawkins) *Letter to the President on Crime Control,* University of Chicago Press, 1977. Contributor of articles to law journals.

*BIOGRAPHICAL/CRITICAL SOURCES: Observer Review,* June 21, 1970; *Times Literary Supplement,* September 18, 1970.

\* \* \*

## MORRIS, William O. 1922-

*PERSONAL:* Born December 2, 1922, in Fairmont, W.

Va.; son of William Otis (a printer) and Flora (Preston) Morris; married Hazel I. Kolbus, May 28, 1948; children: Barbara Ann, Melinda Lou. *Education:* College of William and Mary, A.B., 1944; University of Illinois, LL.B., 1946, J.D., 1968. *Religion:* Lutheran. *Home:* 644 Bellaire Dr., Morgantown, W. Va. 26505. *Office:* Law School, West Virginia University, University Ave., Morgantown, W. Va. 26506.

*CAREER:* Attorney at law. West Virginia University, Law School, Morgantown, associate professor, 1958-61, professor of law, 1961—, lecturer in dental jurisprudence. Visiting professor at numerous universities in the United States and Europe, including University of Texas at Hastings, University of California, Stetson University, Loma Linda University, University of Muenster, City College of London, University of Mainz, and George Washington University. Fulbright professor, Westfalish-Wilhelm University, 1963. Legal advisor and consultant to comptroller of currency, U.S. Treasury Dept., 1961-66; consultant to legislative committees of West Virginia legislature. *Military service:* U.S. Army, 1945. *Member:* State Bar of Illinois, State Bar of Virginia, Bar of the Supreme Court of the United States.

*WRITINGS: Dental Litigation,* Michie Co., 1972, 2nd edition, 1977; *The Law of Domestic Relations,* Michie Co., 1973; *Veterinarian in Litigation,* VM Publishing, 1976; *Statutes and Cases on Domestic Relations,* West Virginia University, 1977. Also author of taped lectures. Contributor of more than twenty-five articles to law and banking journals.

\* \* \*

## MORRISON, Frank M. 1914-

*PERSONAL:* Born January 29, 1914; son of Dougal Lawrence (a farmer) and Jennie (Manning) Morrison; married Vivian Desermeau, October 30, 1936; children: Patricia (Mrs. Romaine DeFrain), Diana (Mrs. Jimmy Thomas). *Education:* Attended General Motors Technology school, 1944-45; attended University of Michigan, 1959-60; studied at University of Tampa and University of Florida, 1962-63. *Politics:* Republican. *Home:* 4419 Trilby Ave., Tampa, Fla. 33616.

*CAREER:* Self-employed as a custom cabinet maker, 1952—. Taught creative writing for Tampa Recreation Department and for the Hillsborough County School System. *Member:* West Coast Writer's Guild (president), St. Petersburg Writer's Club (president).

*WRITINGS: Adventure Stories for Boys,* Denison, 1969; *Golden Ditches,* Denison, 1970. Contributor of approximately 100 articles and short stories to periodicals in the United States and Canada.

*WORK IN PROGRESS: The Secrets of the Smokies,* a 33,000 word juvenile adventure story; a book on bread.

*SIDELIGHTS:* Frank Morrison is interested in traveling, especially in the Central and South American countries. Both his books have been transcribed to Braille.

*BIOGRAPHICAL/CRITICAL SOURCES: Tampa Tribune,* January 28, 1970, April 6, 1971.

\* \* \*

## MORRISON, Kristin (Diane) 1934-

*PERSONAL:* Born April 22, 1934, in Los Angeles, Calif.; daughter of Robert Wood and Mary-Louise (Allec) Morrison. *Education:* Immaculate Heart College, B.A., 1957;

St. Louis University, M.A., 1960; Harvard University, Ph.D., 1966. *Home:* 358 Arborway, Boston, Mass. 02130. *Office:* Department of English, Boston College, Chestnut Hill, Mass.

*CAREER:* Immaculate Heart College, Los Angeles, Calif., instructor in English, 1960-61; South Carolina State College, Orangeburg, professor of English, 1966-67; New York University, Washington Square College of Arts and Sciences, New York, N.Y., assistant professor of English, 1967-69; Boston College, Chestnut Hill, Mass., associate professor of English, 1969—. Member of selection committee for Kent fellowships, Danforth Foundation, 1969—. *Member:* American Association of University Professors, Women's Equity Action League. *Awards, honors:* Woodrow Wilson fellow, 1958; Kent fellow, 1964.

*WRITINGS:* (With Michael Anderson, Jacques Guicharnaud, and Jack D. Zipes) *Crowell's Handbook of Contemporary Drama,* Crowell, 1971; *In Black and White,* Free Press, 1972. Contributor to scholarly journals.

*WORK IN PROGRESS:* A study of the drama of Samuel Beckett.

\* \* \*

## MORSE, David 1940-

*PERSONAL:* Born December 15, 1940, in Vinita, Okla.; son of Wilbur L. (a lawyer) and Edna (Ruanna) Morse; married Virginia Ardell Vest, February 3, 1962 (divorced, 1972); married Ann Shapiro, 1977; children: Scott, Robert, Eli Sunrise. *Education:* University of Iowa, B.A., 1962, M.A., 1965. *Home:* 433 East Main St., Norwich, Conn. 06030. *Office:* Department of English, Mohegan Community College, Norwich, Conn.

*CAREER:* Has worked as a photographer, graphic artist, and file clerk; English teacher in high schools in Connecticut, 1965-69; American School in London, London, England, English teacher, 1969-70; Mohegan Community College, Norwich, Conn., part-time instructor in English, 1971—. English teacher, Neighborhood Youth Corps, 1971-72. *Member:* Mobilization for Survival.

*WRITINGS: Grandfather Rock,* Delacorte, 1972. Contributor to *Media and Methods,* and *Yankee.*

*WORK IN PROGRESS:* "Nonfiction concerned with survival of the species."

\* \* \*

## MORSE, Donald E. 1936-

*PERSONAL:* Born March 3, 1936, in Boston, Mass.; son of Everett I. and Mary (Harrower) Morse; married Elaine Perkins, June 30, 1962; children: Sean David, Christopher Andrew. *Education:* Williams College, B.A., 1958; attended Union Theological Seminary, 1958-60, and University of London, summer, 1961; University of Connecticut, M.A., 1963, Ph.D., 1965. *Politics:* Democrat. *Religion:* Bokononist. *Home:* 860 Knox, Birmingham, Mich. 48008. *Office:* English Department, Oakland University, Rochester, Mich. 48063.

*CAREER:* University of Connecticut, Storrs, Conn., instructor in English, 1960-62; Williamantic State College, Williamantic, Conn., instructor in English, 1962-63; Babson College, Wellesley, Mass., assistant professor of literature, 1963-67; Oakland University, Rochester, Mich., assistant professor, 1967-69, associate professor, 1969-74, professor of English, 1974—. Host of "The Folk Show," WQRS-FM,

Detroit, Mich., nightly folkmusic program, 1969-73. Eighteenth Congressional district secretary, Michigan Democratic Party, 1968-73; member, Birmingham Board of Canvassers, 1972-78. *Member:* International Association for the Study of Anglo-Irish Literature, American Association of University Professors (Oakland University chapter; member of bargaining council, 1970-71, 1971-72, president, 1975-77), Modern Language Association of America, American Council for Irish Studies, Michigan Academy (religious studies chairman, 1971-72), College English Association (executive secretary, 1971-77). *Awards, honors:* University Faculty Research Fellow, summer, 1969; Roothbert Fund fellow; Society for Values in Higher Education fellow, 1976.

*WRITINGS: The Choices of Fiction,* Winthrop, 1973. Contributor of numerous articles and reviews on W. H. Auden and on Irish literature to *Renascence, American Notes & Queries, English Language Notes, The Michigan Academician, Journal of Modern Literature,* and other periodicals; contributor of original satire to *C E A Critic;* contributor of book reviews to *Choice* and other periodicals. Editor, *C E A Forum* and *C E A Critic,* 1976-77.

*WORK IN PROGRESS:* Satire and Religion in 18th Century England; Modern Irish Literature; Novels of J. P. Donleavy.

*SIDELIGHTS:* Donald E. Morse has a "lively interest in things Irish, especially the literature," and has lived and travelled extensively in Ireland.

\* \* \*

## MORTENSEN, C. David 1939-

*PERSONAL:* Born September 26, 1939, in Chicago, Ill.; son of David (an administrator) and Muriel (Powell) Mortensen; married Judith Sharp (a teacher), September 10, 1960; children: Deborah, Lance. *Education:* Bethel College, St. Paul, Minn., B.A., 1962; University of Minnesota, M.A., 1964, Ph.D., 1967. *Home:* 5126 Tomahawk Trail, Madison, Wis. 53705. *Office:* Department of Communication Arts, University of Wisconsin, Madison, Wis. 53706.

*CAREER:* Bethel College, St. Paul, Minn., chairperson of department of speech communication, 1964-67; University of Washington, Seattle, assistant professor of speech communication science, 1967-70; University of Wisconsin—Madison, associate professor, 1970-77, professor of communications, 1977—, director of Center for Communication Research, 1972-74. Member of board of directors, Friends of WHA-TV. *Member:* International Communication Association, Speech Communication Association.

*WRITINGS:* (With Kenneth K. Sereno) *Foundations of Communication Theory,* Harper, 1970; *Communication: The Study of Human Interaction,* McGraw, 1972; *Basic Readings in Communication Theory,* Harper, 1973, 2nd edition, 1978; (with Sereno) *Advances in Communication Theory,* Harper, 1973. Associate editor, *Quarterly Journal of Speech,* 1972-77.

*WORK IN PROGRESS: Symbolic Killing.*

\* \* \*

## MORTON, Richard (Everett) 1930-

*PERSONAL:* Born November 8, 1930, in Liverpool, England; son of Harold (an accountant) and Florence (Hughes) Morton; married Beryl Cooper, August 3, 1959; children: James Cooper, Timothy Dwight. *Education:* University of Wales, B.A., 1952; Oxford University, B.Litt., 1955. *Politics:* None. *Religion:* None. *Home:* 6 Valleyview Ct., Dundas, Ontario, Canada. *Office:* Department of English, McMaster University, Hamilton, Ontario, Canada.

*CAREER:* University of the Witwatersrand, Johannesburg, South Africa, lecturer in English, 1955-59; Lake Erie College, Painesville, Ohio, assistant professor of English, 1960-62; McMaster University, Hamilton, Ontario, assistant professor, 1962-66, associate professor, 1966-70, professor of English, 1970—, chairman of department, 1976—. Lecturer at Universities of Canada Shakespeare Seminar, Stratford, Ontario, 1963, and University of Birmingham Shakespeare Seminar, Stratford, England, 1971. *Member:* Canadian Association of University Teachers, Northeastern Modern Language Association, Oxford Society, Oxford Union. *Awards, honors:* American Council of Learned Societies grant, 1962; Canada Council fellowship, 1968-69, 1971.

*WRITINGS:* (Editor with W. M. Peterson) John Gay, *Three Hours after Marriage,* Lake Erie College Press, 1962; (editor) Anne Killigrew, *Poems,* Scholar's Reprint Series, 1967; *The Works of Dylan Thomas,* Forum, 1970; *The Poetry of W. B. Yeats,* Forum, 1971; (editor with P. S. Fritz) *The Eighteenth Century Woman,* Hakkert, 1976; (editor with J. Browning) *1776,* Hakkert, 1976; *The Poems of Sir Aston Cokayne,* Cromlech, 1977. Contributor of articles on seventeenth- and eighteenth-century literature to professional journals.

*WORK IN PROGRESS:* Editing plays of James Shirley, for Oxford University Press.

\*        \*        \*

## MOSELEY, J(oseph) Edward 1910-1973

*PERSONAL:* Born May 15, 1910, in Jackson, Tenn.; son of Joseph Edward (a banker and real estate broker) and Addie Frances (Smith) Moseley; married Florence Louise Alexander, March 24, 1934 (divorced, 1942); married Dorothy Louise Lomax, December 13, 1947. *Education:* Spokane University, A.B., 1932; University of Chicago, M.A., 1937. *Politics:* Democrat. *Home:* 5155 Atherton South Dr., Indianapolis, Ind. 46219.

*CAREER:* Clergyman of Christian Church (Disciples of Christ); *Christian-Evangelist,* St. Louis, Mo., associate editor, 1934-43; *Seattle Times,* Seattle, Wash., copy editor, 1944; Agencies of Christian Church, Indianapolis, Ind., publicity director, 1945-48, co-editor of *Christian Crusader,* 1946-48; National Benevolent Association, St. Louis, feature writer, 1956-73. *Member:* Society of American Archivists, Disciples of Christ Historical Society (charter member and trustee, 1941-71; president, 1941-47; chairman of board, 1958; trustee emeritus, 1971-73), Manuscript Society, Sigma Delta Chi. *Awards, honors:* Litt.D., Culver-Stockton College, 1966.

*WRITINGS:* (Editor with George A. Campbell) *My Dad: Preacher, Pastor, Person,* Bethany Press, 1938; *Using Drama in the Church,* Bethany Press, 1939, revised edition, 1955; *Disciples of Christ in Georgia,* Bethany Press, 1954; (editor) *Evangelism: Commitment and Involvement,* Bethany Press, 1965; (compiler) *The Spanish-Speaking People of the Southwest,* Council on Spanish-American Work, 1966; *The Many Faces of Aging,* Bethany Press, 1968. Editorial consultant, columnist, and contributing editor of *World Call,* 1945-67; contributing editor of *Discipliana,* 1960-73; editor of *Evangelism Bulletin,* 1964-68.

*WORK IN PROGRESS:* A history of the United Christian Missionary Society of the Christian Church (Disciples of Christ).†

(Died October 30, 1973)

## MOSHER, Frederick C(amp) 1913-

*PERSONAL:* Born July 5, 1913, in Oberlin, Ohio; son of William E. (a professor) and Laura (Camp) Mosher; married Edith Kern (a professor), 1940; children: Alice, James, David. *Education:* Dartmouth College, B.A. (magna cum laude), 1934; Syracuse University, M.S., 1939; Harvard University, D.P.A., 1953. *Politics:* Democrat. *Home:* 1823 Yorktown Dr., Charlottesville, Va. 22901. *Office:* Department of Government and Foreign Affairs, University of Virginia, 232 Cabell Hall, Charlottesville, Va. 22901.

*CAREER:* Syracuse University, Syracuse, N.Y., professor of political science, 1947-58; University of California, Berkeley, professor of political science, 1958-68; University of Virginia, Charlottesville, Doherty Professor, 1968—. Professor of Administrative Sciences, University of Bologna, 1957-59. *Military service:* U.S. Army Air Forces, 1942-45; became major; received Legion of Merit. *Member:* National Academy of Public Administration, Public Personnel Administration, American Political Science Association, American Society for Public Administration, Phi Beta Kappa. *Awards, honors:* Syracuse University, Maxwell Public Service Award, 1968; Louis Brownlow Memorial Book Prize, 1969, for *Democracy and the Public Service.*

*WRITINGS:* (With Salvatore Cimmino) *Elementi di scienza dell' "aministrazione,"* [Milan], 1959; *Program Budgeting: Theory and Practice,* Chicago Public Administration Service, 1954; *Personnel for the New Diplomacy,* Carnegie Endowment, 1962; (with Orville F. Poland) *Costs of American Governments,* Dodd, 1964; *Governmental Reorganizations: Cases and Commentary,* Bobbs-Merrill, 1967; *Democracy and the Public Service,* Oxford University Press, 1968; (with John Harr) *Programming Systems and Foreign Affairs Leadership,* Oxford University Press, 1970; (editor) *Watergate: Implications for Responsible Government,* Basic Books, 1974; (editor) *American Public Administration: Past, Present, Future,* University of Alabama Press, 1975; (editor) *Basic Documents of American Public Administration, 1776-1950,* Holmes & Meier, 1976. Editor-in-chief, *Public Administration Review,* 1951-54.

\*        \*        \*

## MOSKOW, Michael H. 1938-

*PERSONAL:* Born January 7, 1938, in Paterson, N.J.; son of Jacob and Sylvia (Edelstein) Moskow; married Constance Bain, December 18, 1966; children: Robert, Eliot. *Education:* Lafayette College, A.B., 1959; University of Pennsylvania, M.A., 1962, Ph.D., 1965. *Home:* 4442 Hawthorne St. N.W., Washington, D.C. 20016.

*CAREER:* High school teacher of English and history in Paterson, N.J., 1960-61; Drexel Institute of Technology (now Drexel University), Philadelphia, Pa., instructor in economics, 1963-64; Lafayette College, Easton, Pa., instructor in economics, 1964-65; Drexel Institute of Technology, assistant professor of management, 1965-67; Temple University, Philadelphia, Pa., associate professor of economics, and director of Bureau of Economics and Business Research, 1967-69; U.S. President's Council of Economic Advisers, Washington, D.C., senior staff economist, 1969-71; U.S. Department of Labor, Washington, D.C., executive director of construction industry collective bargaining commission, 1970-72, deputy under-secretary, 1971-72, assistant secretary for policy, evaluation, and research, 1972-73; U.S. Department of Housing and Urban Development, Washington, D.C., assistant secretary for policy development and research, beginning 1973. Consultant to Associated Council for the Arts, Rockefeller Brothers Fund, and other public and private agencies. *Military service:* U.S. Army, 1959-60; became first lieutenant. *Member:* American Arbitration Association (member of national panel of arbitrators), American Economics Association, Industrial Relations Research Association.

*WRITINGS: Teachers and Unions,* University of Pennsylvania Press, 1966; (with Myron Lieberman) *Collective Negotiations for Teachers,* Rand McNally, 1966; (editor with Stanley Elam) *Employment Relations in Higher Education,* Phi Delta Kappa, 1966; (editor with Elam and Lieberman) *Readings on Collective Negotiations in Public Education,* Rand McNally, 1967; *Labor Relations in the Performing Arts: An Introductory Survey,* Associated Council for the Arts, 1969; (with J. Joseph Lowenberg and Edward C. Koziara) *Collective Bargaining in Public Employment,* Random House, 1970; (editor with Lowenberg) *Collective Bargaining in Government,* Prentice-Hall, 1972. Contributor of more than twenty articles to professional journals.†

\*        \*        \*

## MOULTON, Harland B.   1925-

*PERSONAL:* Born April 5, 1925, in Mankato, Minn.; son of Claud W. (a dentist) and Laura (Buell) Moulton; married Patty Nelson (a business manager), August 28, 1948; children: Stephanie Jo Hoestetter, Pamela Garcia Almazon, Bretton N., Bradley H. *Education:* University of Minnesota, B.A., 1947, M.A., 1949, Ph.D., 1969. *Politics:* Independent. *Religion:* Unitarian Universalist. *Home:* 6927 Churchill Rd., McLean, Va. 22101. *Office:* National War College, Fort McNair, Washington, D.C. 20315.

*CAREER:* U.S. Air Force, Strategic Air Command (SAC), Omaha, Neb., civilian employee in war plans and policy, 1950-62; U.S. Arms Control and Disarmament Agency, Washington, D.C., arms controller, 1962-71; American University, Washington, D.C., teacher of graduate seminar in U.S. national security policy, 1969—. Teacher of courses in arms control and national security policy, National War College, 1969—.

*WRITINGS: Superiority and Parity: The U.S. and the Strategic Arms Race, 1961-1971,* Greenwood Press, 1973; (co-editor) *International Issues and Perspectives,* Industrial College of the Armed Forces, 1976. Contributor to *Orbis.*

\*        \*        \*

## MOULTON, Phillips P(rentice)   1909-

*PERSONAL:* Born December 24, 1909, in Cleveland, Ohio; married Mary Cochran (a social worker), June 14, 1947; children: Kathy, Larry. *Education:* Ohio Wesleyan University, B.A., 1931; further study at University of Marburg, 1931-32, Princeton Theological Seminary, 1940-41, and Boston University, summers, 1941, 1942; Yale University, B.D., 1942, Ph.D., 1949. *Politics:* Independent. *Religion:* Methodist and Quaker. *Home and office:* 225 Brookside Dr., Ann Arbor, Mich. 48105.

*CAREER:* Cleveland Guidance Service, Cleveland, Ohio, research director and counselor, 1936-38; Cleveland State University, Cleveland, instructor in philosophy and religion, 1938-40; Federal Council of Churches, New York City, national director of university Christian mission, 1946-49; University of Chicago, Chicago, Ill., director of chapel house and coordinator of religious activities, 1949-51; Union Theological Seminary, New York City, lecturer in religion and higher education, 1951-54; Simpson College, Indianola,

Iowa, chairman of department of philosophy and religion, 1954-58; University of North Dakota, Grand Forks, professor of religion, 1958-65, chairman of department, 1962-64, president of Wesley College, 1958-63; Adrian College, Adrian, Mich., professor of philosophy, 1965-76; University of Michigan, Ann Arbor, Center for Study of Higher Education, visiting scholar, 1976-78. Danforth professor at Boston University, summer, 1953, and Garrett Theological Seminary, summer, 1954; chairman, National Danforth Campus-Community Workshop, Sarah Lawrence College, summer, 1957; speaker at International Philosophy Congress, Vienna, 1968.

*MEMBER:* American Academy of Religion (president of Midwest section, 1961-62), American Society of Christian Ethics, American Philosophical Association, Philosophic Society for the Study of Sport, Midwest Faculty Christian Fellowship (president, 1957-58), Phi Beta Kappa, Omicron Delta Kappa, Delta Sigma Rho. *Awards, honors:* Postdoctoral fellowship, Haverford College, 1965, 1967-68; American Philosophical Society grant, 1967-68; award of merit, American Association of State and Local History, 1972, for *Journal and Major Essays of John Woolman.*

*WRITINGS: Community Resources in Cleveland, Ohio,* National Youth Administration in Ohio, 1937; (with William E. Kerstetter) *Experiment in General Education,* Methodist Publishing House, 1957; *Violence: Or Aggressive Nonviolent Resistance,* Pendle Hill, 1971; *Journal and Major Essays of John Woolman,* Oxford University Press, 1971; *The Living Witness of John Woolman,* Pendle Hill, 1973. Also author of *Guidelines for Intercollegiate Athletics in Small Colleges,* 1978. Contributor to about twenty professional journals.

*WORK IN PROGRESS:* Research on Society of Friends and pacifism.

\*        \*        \*

## MOUNTSIER, Robert   1888(?)-1972

1888(?)—November 23, 1972; American editor, aviation and automotive expert, and author of books on the armed forces and on economics. Obituaries: *New York Times,* November 25, 1972.

\*        \*        \*

## MOYES, Norman Barr   1931-

*PERSONAL:* Born August 26, 1931, in Fairmont, W.Va.; son of Roland Dare (a journalist) and Lillian (Barr) Moyes; married Rose Marie Kohlmeyer, June 10, 1964; children: Christine Marie, Mark David, Elizabeth Anne. *Education:* West Liberty State College, B.A., 1953; West Virginia University, M.A., 1956; Syracuse University, Ph.D., 1965. *Politics:* Independent. *Religion:* Methodist. *Home:* 239 Clark Rd., Brookline, Mass. 02146. *Office:* Boston University, 640 Commonwealth Ave., Boston, Mass. 02215.

*CAREER:* Syracuse University, Syracuse, N.Y., instructor, 1960-65; *Syracuse Post Standard,* Syracuse, copy editor, 1962-65; Boston University, Boston, Mass., associate professor, 1965—; *Boston Herald Traveler,* Boston, Sunday feature editor, 1967-74; *Boston Herald American,* Boston, Sunday editor, 1974—. Consultant to the President's Commission on Causes of Violence, and to the U.S. Civil Service Commission, 1966; member of communications committee, Urban Coalition, 1968. *Military service:* U.S. Army, Signal Corps, 1953-55. *Member:* American Association of University Professors, Sigma Delta Chi.

*WRITINGS:* (With David Manning White) *Journalism in the Mass Media,* Ginn, 1970. Writer of numerous magazine articles.

*WORK IN PROGRESS: Battle Eye: The History of American Combat Photography.*

*   *   *

## MUELLER, John E(rnest)   1937-

*PERSONAL:* Born June 21, 1937, in St. Paul, Minn.; son of Ernst A. (a manufacturer) and Elsie (Schleh) Mueller; married Judith A. Reader, September 6, 1960; children: Karl, Karen, Susan. *Education:* University of Chicago, A.B., 1960; University of California, Los Angeles, M.A., 1963, Ph.D., 1965. *Politics:* Democrat. *Home:* 246 Roslyn St., Rochester, N.Y. 14619. *Office:* Department of Political Science, University of Rochester, Rochester, N.Y. 14627.

*CAREER:* University of Rochester, Rochester, N.Y., assistant professor, 1965-69, associate professor, 1969-72, professor of political science, 1972—.

*WRITINGS:* (Editor) *Approaches to Measurement in International Relations,* Appleton, 1969; *War, Presidents and Public Opinion,* Wiley, 1973; *Films on Ballet and Modern Dance,* American Dance Guild, 1974; *Dance Film Directory,* Princeton Books, in press. Author of "Film," a column in *Dance,* 1974—. Contributor of articles to political science journals.

*WORK IN PROGRESS:* Research on Vietnam policy; research on the value of dance films.

*   *   *

## MULLIGAN, Raymond A(lexander)   1914-

*PERSONAL:* Born January 11, 1914, in New York, N.Y.; son of John J. (a fire captain) and Margaret (Carmody) Mulligan; married Virginia A. Worland, January 12, 1945; children: Barry, Kevin, Brian, Marianne. *Education:* New York University, B.S., 1937; Fordham University, M.A., 1939; Indiana University, Ph.D., 1950. *Home:* 6901 Big Bear Dr., Tucson, Ariz. 85715. *Office:* Department of Public Administration, University of Arizona, BPA, Tucson, Ariz. 85721.

*CAREER:* DePauw University, Greencastle, Ind., assistant professor, 1946-52, associate professor of sociology, 1952-53; University of Arizona, Tucson, associate professor, 1953-59, professor of sociology and public administration, 1959—. *Member:* American Sociological Association, American Society for Public Administration, American Society for Corrections, Western Correctional Society, Arizona Correctional Society, Pima County Correctional Society.

*WRITINGS: Welfare Policies and Administration in Arizona,* Arizona Academy, 1963; (with Hazel Fredericksen) *The Child and His Welfare,* 3rd edition (Mulligan was not associated with earlier editions), W. H. Freeman, 1972. Contributor of articles to numerous journals.

*SIDELIGHTS:* A Spanish translation of *The Child and His Welfare* has been published in Mexico.

*   *   *

## MULLINGS, Llewellyn M.   1932-

*PERSONAL:* Born December 14, 1932, in Jamaica, West Indies; son of Beresford C. and Hannah A. Mullings; married Pearl E. Bell, June 20, 1956. *Education:* Attended West Indies College, 1950-51; Atlantic Union College, A.B., 1960; Clark University, A.M., 1961, Ph.D., 1964. *Office:*

Office of the Dean, College of Business, University of Bridgeport, Bridgeport, Conn. 06602.

*CAREER:* Manager of book store in Mandeville, Jamaica, 1953-55; Bahamas Mission of Seventh-day Adventists, Nassau, Bahamas, secretary-treasurer, 1956-58; University of Bridgeport, Bridgeport, Conn., instructor, 1963-64, assistant professor, 1964-68, associate professor of economics, 1968-73, assistant dean, 1973-74, dean of College of Business, 1974—. Member of board of directors, Pioneer Valley Academy; member of board of trustees, Atlantic Union College. *Member:* American Economic Association, National Association of Business Economists, Royal Economic Society (fellow), Southern New England Conference of Seventh-Day Adventists (member of executive committee).

*WRITINGS:* (With James Fenner) *Economic Development,* MSS Educational Publishing, 1971.

*WORK IN PROGRESS: Towards Exchange Stability: Lessons for Third World Countries.*

*   *   *

## MURPHY, Edward J.   1927-

*PERSONAL:* Born July 16, 1927, in Springfield, Ill.; son of Martin J. and Linda (Pihlaja) Murphy; married Mary Ann Hansen, June 19, 1954; children: Ann, Martin, James, John, Mary, Thomas, Patrick, Michael, Stephen. *Education:* University of Illinois, B.S., 1949, LL.B., 1951. *Religion:* Catholic. *Home:* 11891 Vistula Rd., Osceola, Ind. 46561. *Office:* Notre Dame Law School, Notre Dame, Ind. 46556.

*CAREER:* University of Notre Dame, Notre Dame, Ind., assistant professor, 1957-63, associate professor, 1963-65, professor of law, 1965-75, Thomas J. White Professor, 1975—. *Military service:* U.S. Army, 1946-47. *Member:* American Bar Association, Illinois State Bar Association.

*WRITINGS:* (With Richard Speidel) *Studies in Contract Law,* Foundation Press, 1970, 2nd edition, 1978; *Life to the Full,* Our Sunday Visitor, 1978.

*   *   *

## MURRAY, Lois Smith   1906-

*PERSONAL:* Born October 9, 1906, in West, Texas; daughter of Walter Clarence (a farmer) and Cora (Casey) Smith; married Lowell N. Douglas, 1931 (died, 1946); married John D. Murray, 1954 (died, 1962); children: (first marriage) Lowell C., Dell Douglas Everton. *Education:* Baylor University, A.B. (magna cum laude), 1927, A.M., 1929; attended University of Chicago, 1930, and University of Texas, 1952-53. *Religion:* Baptist. *Home address:* Rt. 2, Box 18, McGregor, Tex. 76657. *Office:* Department of English, Baylor University, Waco, Tex. 76703.

*CAREER:* Baylor University, Waco, Tex., instructor, 1931-40, assistant professor, 1940-44, associate professor, 1944-46, professor of English, 1946—; Murray Grain Co., McGregor, Tex., president, 1962—. Lecturer, University of Texas, University of Delaware, University of Wisconsin, and University of Chicago. Consultant in human relations and lecturer, 1951—. Member of Goodwill Industries Board, Waco, Tex. *Member:* Modern Language Association of America, American Association of College Teachers of English, American Association of University Professors, Texas Association of College Teachers of English, McLennan County Mental Health Society, Sigma Tau Delta. *Awards, honors:* Waco Citizenship Award, 1946; Litt.D., Howard Payne College, 1954; American Ideals of Freedom Foundation award, 1961.

WRITINGS: *Through Heaven's Backdoor*, Baylor University, 1951; *Effective Living*, Harper, 1961; *Baylor at Independence*, Baylor University, 1972. Contributor of numerous articles and poems to journals.

WORK IN PROGRESS: Editing a biography of David Guion, Texas composer and musician; editing Bronte's "Juvenalia."†

\* \* \*

## MUSSELMAN, Vernon A(rmor) 1912-

PERSONAL: Born April 20, 1912, in Kansas City, Mo.; son of David Schyler and Myrtle May (South) Musselman; married Jean MacLeod, September 6, 1943; children: Donald Lee, Catherine Anne (Mrs. Edwin Melton). *Education:* Southwestern State College, Weatherford, Okla., B.S., 1930; University of Oklahoma, Ed.M., 1938, Ed.D., 1946. *Politics:* Democrat. *Religion:* Baptist. *Home:* 1956 Hart Rd., Lexington, Ky. 40502. *Office:* College of Education, University of Kentucky, Lexington, Ky. 40506.

CAREER: High school and junior college teacher in Oklahoma, 1930-41; University of Oklahoma, Norman, assistant professor of business education, 1941-43; University of Denver, Denver, Colo., associate professor of business education, 1946-48; University of Kentucky, Lexington, professor of business education, 1948—. *Military service:* U.S. Naval Reserve, 1943-46; became lieutenant. *Member:* National Business Education Association (past president), National Association for Business Teacher Education, National Education Association (life member), Southern Business Education Association (past president), Delta Pi Epsilon.

WRITINGS: (With Hilton D. Shepherd) *Introduction to Modern Business*, Prentice-Hall, 1950 (3rd and subsequent editions by Musselman and Eugene H. Hughes), 7th edition, 1977; (with others) *Improving the High School Program Through Unit Teaching*, College of Education, University of Kentucky, 1952; (with Ray G. Price) *General Business for Everyday Living*, McGraw, 1954, 4th edition (with Curtis Hall as additional co-author), 1972; (with J. Marshall Hanna) *Teaching Bookkeeping and Accounting*, McGraw, 1960, 2nd edition, 1978; *Methods in Teaching Basic Business Subjects*, Interstate, 1971, 3rd edition, 1975; *Lesson Plans in Accounting*, Interstate, 1978.

\* \* \*

## MUSSULMAN, Joseph A(gee) 1928-

PERSONAL: Born November 20, 1928, in East St. Louis, Ill.; son of Boyd (a merchant) and Susan (Ellis) Mussulman; married E. Jo-Anne Stafford (administrative assistant, Montana Arts Council), June 15, 1950; children: Eleanor, Claudia. *Education:* Northwestern University, B.Mus., 1950, M.Mus., 1951; Syracuse University, Ph.D., 1966. *Home:* 2318 43rd St., Missoula, Mont. 59801. *Office:* Department of Music, University of Montana, Missoula, Mont. 59801.

CAREER: St. Cloud Teachers College (now St. Cloud State College), St. Cloud, Minn., instructor in music, 1951-52; Northwestern University, Evanston, Ill., assistant to dean of music, 1952-54; Ripon College, Ripon, Wis., assistant professor of music, 1954-57; University of Montana, Missoula, assistant professor, 1957-66, associate professor, 1966-71, professor of music, 1971—. Conductor, Missoula Symphony Chorale. *Member:* Pi Kappa Lambda, Phi Kappa Phi. *Awards, honors:* Danforth grant, 1961, 1963, 1965; National Endowment for the Humanities grant, 1967.

WRITINGS: *Music in the Cultured Generation: A Social History of Music in America, 1870-1900*, Northwestern University Press, 1971; *The Uses of Music: An Introduction to Music in Contemporary American Life*, Prentice-Hall, 1974. Contributor of articles to music journals.

WORK IN PROGRESS: *Dear People . . . Robert Shaw*, a biography of the conductor, completion expected in 1978.

\* \* \*

## MYERS, Patricia 1929-

PERSONAL: Born May 15, 1929, in Goodland, Kan.; daughter of William Bryan and Roxanna (Harris) Myers. *Education:* Texas College of Arts and Industries (now Texas A & I University), B.A., 1951; University of Texas, Main University (now University of Texas at Austin), M.Ed., 1954, Ed.D., 1963. *Home:* 8058 Broadway, Apt. 143-S, San Antonio, Tex. 78209. *Office:* Education Service Center, Region 20, 1550 Northeast Loop 410, San Antonio, Tex. 78209.

CAREER: Certified psychologist by Texas State Board of Examiners of Psychologists; Texas public schools, speech therapist, 1952-55; teacher, 1955-56; Texas Rehabilitation Center, Gonzales, teacher of exceptional children, 1956-60; Louisiana State University, New Orleans, assistant professor of education, 1963-64; Our Lady of the Lake College, San Antonio, Tex., associate professor of speech, 1964-70, professor of communication disorders, 1970-73, coordinator of diagnostic services, Harry Jersig Speech and Hearing Center, 1964-70, chairman of department of communication disorders, 1970-73; Education Service Center, Region 20 (state agency), San Antonio, director of special education services, 1973—. Lecturer at Cerebral Palsy workshop, University of Texas at Austin, 1965-66; member of advisory committee for preparing teachers of children with learning disabilities, Southern Regional Education Board, 1966-67; lecturer in special study institute on evaluation of minimally brain injured children, Texas Education Agency, 1967. Consultant to Project Headstart, 1967-71.

MEMBER: American Speech and Hearing Association, American Psychological Association, Association for Children with Learning Disabilities, Council for Exceptional Children (vice-president, 1972-73; president, Division for Children with Learning Disabilities, 1974-75).

WRITINGS: (Contributor) Sister M. Arthur Carrow, editor, *Theoretical Approaches to Language Disorders*, Harry Jersig Speech and Hearing Center, 1967; (with Donald Hammill) *Methods for Learning Disorders*, Wiley, 1969, 2nd edition, 1976. Contributor of articles to professional journals.

\* \* \*

## MYERS, Robert Manson 1921-

PERSONAL: Born May 29, 1921, in Charlottesville, Va.; son of Horwood Prettyman (a clergyman) and Matilda Manson (Wynn) Myers. *Education:* Vanderbilt University, B.A. (summa cum laude), 1941; Columbia University, M.A., 1942, Ph.D., 1948; Harvard University, M.A., 1943. *Home:* 2101 Connecticut Ave. N.W., Washington, D.C. 20008. *Office:* Department of English, Taliaferro Hall, University of Maryland, College Park, Md. 20742.

CAREER: Yale University, New Haven, Conn., instructor in English, 1945-47; College of William and Mary, Williamsburg, Va., assistant professor of English, 1947-48; Tulane University, Newcomb College, New Orleans, La., assistant professor of English, 1948-54; Brearley School, New York, N.Y., member of English faculty, 1954-56; chairman of department of English at high school in Manassas, Va., 1956-58; University of Maryland, College Park, assistant professor, 1959-63, associate professor, 1963-68, professor of English, 1968—. Fulbright professor, University of Rotterdam, 1958-59. *Member:* Modern Language Association of America, American Society for Eighteenth-Century Studies, Jane Austen Society, Society for Eighteenth-Century Theatre Research, Phi Beta Kappa. *Awards, honors:* Fulbright research scholar at University of London, 1953-54; National Book Award, 1973, for *The Children of Pride.*

*WRITINGS: Handel's Messiah: A Touchstone of Taste,* Macmillan, 1948; *From Beowulf to Virginia Woolf,* Bobbs-Merrill, 1952; *Handel, Dryden, and Milton,* Bowes, 1956; *Restoration Comedy,* Dietz, 1961; (editor) *The Children of Pride* (Jones family letters; also see below), one volume, Yale University Press, 1972, augmented and revised edition, Popular Library, Volume I: *Many Mansions (1854-1857),* 1977, Volume II: *The Finger of Providence (1857-1860),* 1977, Volume III: *The Edge of the Sword (1860-1861),* 1977, Volume IV: *The God of Battles (1862-1863),* 1977, Volume V: *The Wings of the Wind (1863-1865),* 1977, Volume VI: *The Night Season (1865-1868),* 1978; (editor) *A Georgian at Princeton* (Jones family letters; also see below), Harcourt, 1976.

Plays, all based on Jones family letters: "The Night Season" (based on *The Children of Pride*), presented by the author numerous times, 1972-77, at various American universities and libraries, produced in London by BBC-Radio, October, 1978; "The Courtship of Mary Jones" (based on unpublished letters), produced in Washington, D.C., summer, 1976; "Voices of Pride" (based on *The Children of Pride*), produced in Washington, D.C., summer, 1977. Also author of "A Georgian at Princeton," based on book of same title, not yet produced.

*WORK IN PROGRESS:* Another volume of Jones family letters, *The Courtship of Mary Jones.*

*SIDELIGHTS:* Robert Manson Myers' *The Children of Pride,* a collection of letters of a prominent Georgian family between 1854 and 1868, is "extraordinary social history," writes Jonathan Yardley. The *New Republic* critic continues, the book "enlarges our understanding of [a] traumatic period in American history as few others have done.... It is, I think, a great and indispensable book." Reynolds Price, reviewing the book for the *Washington Post,* calls it "the best book known to me which is concerned with the daily lives and minds of upper- and middle-class white Southerners during the war." Reynolds praises the "selection and abridgement by which this scattered mass of miscellaneous papers is finally made to reveal both the minutiae of a vanished life and the controlling, extraordinarily complex moral vision which created that life." A *Newsweek* reviewer writes, "Myers has edited superbly, refraining from narrative links or footnotes." The author told an interviewer that *The Children of Pride* is a "documentary novel," arranged so that the reader can experience history "intimately! Unfiltered! Without any twentieth century hand stepping in."

*A Georgian at Princeton* is another series of Jones family letters, in the same style as *The Children of Pride.* It is "an interesting further record of a fascinating family ... but its interest is pale in comparison with its predecessor," notes the *Choice* reviewer.

*AVOCATIONAL INTERESTS:* The American Civil War, cinema, antiques, playing the piano and harpsichord, restoring old houses.

*BIOGRAPHICAL/CRITICAL SOURCES: Newsweek,* April 24, 1972; *New York Times Book Review,* May 7, 1972; *New Republic,* May 13, 1972; *America,* June 3, 1972; *Times Literary Supplement,* June 9, 1972; *National Review,* September 1, 1972; *Virginia Quarterly Review,* autumn, 1972, autumn, 1976; *American Literature,* November, 1972; *Journal of American History,* December, 1972; *Saturday Review,* December 2, 1972; *American Scholar,* winter, 1972-73; *New Yorker,* February 12, 1976; *Best Sellers,* June, 1976; *Choice,* July/August, 1976.

# N

## NACHTMANN, Francis Weldon 1913-

*PERSONAL:* Born January 16, 1913, in Springfield, Mo.; son of Francis X. and Effie (Myers) Nachtmann; married Mary Margaret Hickey, August 17, 1949; children: Christine (Mrs. Herbert J. Sliger, Jr.), Rita, Julianne (Mrs. Robert Aberle), Gregory. *Education:* St. Louis University, A.B., 1934; Middlebury College, M.A., 1941; University of Illinois, Ph.D., 1958. *Religion:* Roman Catholic. *Home:* 610 West John St., Champaign, Ill. 61820. *Office:* Department of French, University of Illinois, Urbana, Ill. 61801.

*CAREER:* Western Military Academy, Alton, Ill., instructor in Spanish, Latin, English, and history, 1937-42, 1946-48; University of Illinois at Urbana-Champaign, instructor, 1948-59, assistant professor, 1959-62, associate professor, 1962-67, professor of French, 1967—, coordinator of language laboratory, 1959-65. *Military service:* U.S. Army, 1942-45, 1951-53; became major; received Bronze Star Medal. U.S. Army Reserve, 1945-68; retired as lieutenant colonel. *Member:* Modern Language Association of America, American Association of Teachers of French (national executive secretary, 1969—), American Council on the Teaching of Foreign Languages, Rotary International.

*WRITINGS: French Review for Reading Improvement,* Macmillan, 1966; (contributor) G. Mathieu, editor, *Advances in Teaching of Foreign Languages,* Volume II, Pergamon, 1966; *Exercises in French Phonics,* Scott, Foresman, 1970.

\* \* \*

## NAGOURNEY, Peter (Jon) 1940-

*PERSONAL:* Born October 10, 1940; son of Rove and Ann (Hecht) Nagourney. *Education:* City College of the City University of New York, B.A., 1961; University of Chicago, M.A., 1962, Ph.D., 1971; University College, London, graduate study, 1966-67. *Home:* 68-29 Dartmouth St., Forest Hills, N.Y. 11375. *Office:* Department of English, Wayne State University, Detroit, Mich. 48202.

*CAREER:* University of California, Santa Barbara, acting assistant professor of English, 1967-70; Wayne State University, Detroit, Mich., assistant professor of English, 1973—. *Member:* Modern Language Association of America, Popular Culture Association, American Association of University Professors, Augustan Reprint Society, Midwest Modern Language Association. *Awards, honors:* Fulbright-Hays grant to London, England, 1966-67.

*WRITINGS:* (Editor with Susan Steiner) *Growing Up American,* Wadsworth, 1972. Contributor of articles to *College English* and *Scholia Satyrica;* contributor of fiction to *Tracks: A Journal of Artists' Writings.* Poetry editor, *Chicago Review,* 1964-66.

*WORK IN PROGRESS:* A study of biography, *The Theoretical Foundations of Literary Biography;* an investigation of popular reading, *The Literature of Everyday Life;* a satirical novel, *The Silver Pharaoh;* work on a documentary series for public television, "The Critic in America."

*AVOCATIONAL INTERESTS:* Aikido (holds a 2nd degree black belt), photography.

\* \* \*

## NAHAL, Chaman 1927-

*PERSONAL:* Born August 2, 1927, in India; son of Gopal Das and Jamuna (Devi) Nahal; married Sudarshna Rani (a teacher), 1955; children: Ajanta (daughter), Anita. *Education:* Delhi University, M.A., 1948; University of Nottingham, Ph.D., 1961. *Home:* 2/1 Kalkaji Extension, New Delhi 110019, India. *Agent:* John Farquharson Ltd., Bell House, Bell Yard, London WC2, England; and Collier Associates, 280 Madison Ave., New York, N.Y. 10016. *Office:* Department of English, Delhi University, Delhi 110007, India.

*CAREER:* Delhi University, Institute of Postgraduate Studies, Delhi, India, chairman of department of English, 1963—. Associate professor of English, Long Island University, 1968-70. *Awards, honors:* British Council Scholar, University of Nottingham, 1959-61; Fulbright fellow, Princeton University, 1967-68; Sahitya Akademi (national academy of letters) award, and Federation of Indian Publishers' award for excellence in creative writing, 1977, both for *Azadi.*

*WRITINGS: A Conversation with J. Krishnamurti,* Arya, 1965; *The Weird Dance* (short stories), Arya, 1965; (editor) *Drugs and the Other Self,* Harper, 1970; *D. H. Lawrence: An Eastern View,* A. S. Barnes, 1970; *The Narrative Pattern in Ernest Hemingway's Fiction,* Fairleigh Dickinson University Press, 1971; *My True Faces* (novel), Hind Books, 1973; *Azadi* (novel; title means "Freedom"), Houghton, 1975; *Into Another Dawn* (novel), Sterling, 1977.

*WORK IN PROGRESS:* A satire on the anglicized Indians; a novel about the sense of identity in contemporary India.

SIDELIGHTS: Chaman Nahal told CA: "What prompts me to write fiction is the small and the under-privileged: the world is teeming with them. I try to make some sense of this vast drama in which most of us are obliged to live with handicaps—and not of our own making!"

BIOGRAPHICAL/CRITICAL SOURCES: D. H. Lawrence, fall, 1971; Barbara J. Harrison, Learning about India, State University of New York Press, 1977.

*    *    *

## NAPOLITAN, Joseph  1929-

PERSONAL: Born March 6, 1929; son of Pasquale and Lucy (Anzalotti) Napolitan; married Mary T. Nelen, October 13, 1952; children: Christine, Joseph, Jr., Luke, Martha. Education: American International College, B.A., 1952. Politics: Democrat. Home: 276 Longhill St., Springfield, Mass. 01108. Office: 121 Chestnut St., Springfield, Mass. 01103.

CAREER: Joseph Napolitan Associates, Inc., Springfield, Mass., president, 1956—; Public Affairs Analysts, Inc., Washington, D.C., president, 1969—. Military service: U.S. Army, 1946-48. Member: American Association of Political Consultants (founder and past president), International Association of Political Consultants (co-founder and past president).

WRITINGS: The Election Game and How to Win It, Doubleday, 1972.

BIOGRAPHICAL/CRITICAL SOURCES: New York, April 10, 1972.

*    *    *

## NASH, Gary B.  1933-

PERSONAL: Born July 27, 1933, in Philadelphia, Pa.; son of Ralph C. and Edith (Baring) Nash; married Mary Workum, December 20, 1955 (divorced); children: Brooke, Robin, Jennifer, David. Education: Princeton University, A.B., 1955, Ph.D., 1964. Home: 16174 Alcima Ave., Pacific Palisades, Calif. 90272. Office: Department of History, University of California, Los Angeles, Calif. 90024.

CAREER: Princeton University, Princeton, N.J., assistant professor of history, 1964-66; University of California, Los Angeles, assistant professor, 1964-68, associate professor, 1968-72, professor of history, 1972—. Military service: U.S. Navy, 1955-58; became lieutenant junior grade. Member: American Historical Association. Awards, honors: Guggenheim fellow, 1969-70.

WRITINGS: Quakers and Politics: Pennsylvania, 1681-1726, Princeton University Press, 1968; The Great Fear: Race in the Mind of America, Holt, 1970; Class and Society in Early America, Prentice-Hall, 1970; Red White, and Black: The Peoples of Early America, Prentice-Hall, 1974.

WORK IN PROGRESS: The Urban Crucible: Politics and Society in Pre-Revolutionary Boston, New York and Philadelphia.

BIOGRAPHICAL/CRITICAL SOURCES: Virginia Quarterly Review, spring, 1969.

*    *    *

## NAYLOR, Penelope  1941-

PERSONAL: Born January 13, 1941, in New York, N.Y.; daughter of Lester Owen and Elaine (Connolly) Naylor; divorced. Education: Attended Smith College; also studied sculpture in Spain with Otto Georg Hitzberger, 1960. Residence: New York, N.Y.

CAREER: Professional painter, 1963-70, exhibiting in group shows in United States, Spain, Portugal, and Africa, and in one-woman shows in New York, 1966, and Portugal, 1969; Travel Marketing Co., New York, N.Y., creative director, 1973-74, 1977—. Incorporator, Jesse Tree Press, Inc., 1977. Marketing consultant on task force study groups for major travel firms. Awards, honors: Spring Book Award, Chicago Tribune, 1973, for Black Images; American Institute of Graphic Arts certificate of excellence, 1974, for Black Images.

WRITINGS—Juvenile: Sculpture: The Shapes of Belief, F. Watts, 1971; (self-illustrated) Spider World, F. Watts, 1972; Black Images: The Art of West Africa, photographs by Lisa Little, Doubleday, 1973. Also author of travel writing for major travel firms, and scripts on the family, and child psychology for Butterick Educational Films, 1976.

Illustrator: Laura Baker, A Tree Called Moses, Atheneum, 1966; Bernice Kohn, Ferns: Plants without Flowers, Hawthorn, 1968; Francine Klagsbrun, The First Book of Spices, F. Watts, 1968; D. X. Fenten, Plants for Pots, Lippincott, 1969; Alvin Silverstein and Virginia Silverstein, Bionics: Man Copies Nature's Machines, McCall Publishing, 1970; Fred Warren and Lee Warren, The Music of Africa, Prentice-Hall, 1970.

WORK IN PROGRESS: An art book on symbols, tentatively entitled Markings; a fictional work, tentatively entitled Sunshine Cake; design and illustrations for a book on African animals to be researched in Kenya in collaboration with an animal behaviorist; editing and design for a book on the Kalahari bushman in collaboration with two anthropologists.

SIDELIGHTS: Penelope Naylor's award-winning book, Black Images: The Art of West Africa, combines translations of African poetry with photographs of sculpture contained in New York's Museum of Primitive Art. The writer for Kirkus Reviews calls the work "an exceptional book for its striking design, its sensitive and dramatic photography, and especially the awesome beauty of the masks, figures and ritual objects reproduced. Naylor's sequence unobtrusively follows the sacred, cyclical 'rhythm of creation,' so that mother-and-child and ancestor figures come first, then items associated in turn with boy and girl societies, initation rites, and community rituals." The Chicago Tribune reviewer finds that "both the poetry and the art are beautiful; the photographs are of excellent quality, and the book is handsome in design and typography. The text is imbued with a sense of appreciation of the dignity and complexity of the West African peoples whose artistic tradition Penelope Naylor expresses. The presentation is so impressive that the book may well encourage further investigation of African art."

BIOGRAPHICAL/CRITICAL SOURCES: Kirkus Reviews, May 1, 1973; Chicago Tribune, May 1, 1973; St. Louis Post Dispatch, June 10, 1973; Arts d'Afrique Noire, autumn, 1973; Africana Journal, Volume II, 1974.

*    *    *

## NEBYLITSYN, Vladimir Dmitrievich  1930(?)-1972

1930(?)—October 9(?), 1972; Russian experimental psychologist. Obituaries: New York Times, October 11, 1972.

*    *    *

## NELSON, Carnot E(dward)  1941-

PERSONAL: Given name is pronounced Car-no; born February 20, 1941, in Milwaukee, Wis.; son of Max T. and

Marion (Roth) Nelson; married Alice Katz (a lawyer), September 1, 1963; children: Jeremy, Seth. *Education:* Attended U.S. Naval Academy, 1959-60; University of Wisconsin, B.S., 1963; Columbia University, Ph.D., 1966. *Home:* 727 South Edison, Tampa, Fla. 33606. *Office:* Department of Psychology, University of South Florida, Tampa, Fla. 33620.

*CAREER:* Emory University, Atlanta, Ga., assistant professor of sociology, 1966-67; Johns Hopkins University, Baltimore, Md., assistant professor of psychology and research associate, Center for Research in Scientific Communication, 1967-71; University of South Florida, Tampa, associate professor, 1971-77, professor of psychology, 1977—. *Member:* American Psychological Association (fellow), Society for the Social Study of Science, American Educational Research Association, American Association for the Advancement of Science. *Awards, honors:* U.S. Office of Education research grant, 1971; National Institute of Education fellow, 1977-78.

*WRITINGS:* (Editor with D. K. Pollock, and contributor) *Communication among Scientists and Technologists,* Heath, 1970; (with W. D. Garvey, Nan Lin, and Kazuo Tomita) *Information Exchange Associated with National Scientific Meetings in Relation to the General Process of Communication in Science,* Center for Research in Scientific Communication, Johns Hopkins University, 1970; (contributor) Richard Christie and Florence Geis, editors, *Machiavellianism,* Academic Press, 1970; (contributor) R. A. Dershimer, editor, *The Educational Research Community: Its Communication and Social Structure,* American Educational Research Association, 1970; *Evaluation of Professional Psychology,* American Psychological Association, 1973. Collaborator on a number of technical reports published by Center for Research in Scientific Communication, Johns Hopkins University. Contributor to *Science, Professional Geographer,* and to sociology, psychology, and educational research journals.

*WORK IN PROGRESS:* Research on scientific communication in educational research and the utilization of scientific and technical information.

\* \* \*

## NELSON, Charles R(owe)   1942-

*PERSONAL:* Born August 21, 1942, in Milwaukee, Wis.; son of Elmer R. (a geologist) and Julia (Hydar) Nelson; married Kathleen Yoerg (an urban planner), 1969. *Education:* Yale University, B.A., 1963; University of Wisconsin, M.A., 1967, Ph.D., 1969. *Home:* 10648 Durland N.E., Seattle, Wash. 98125. *Office:* Department of Economics, DK 30, University of Washington, Seattle, Wash. 98195.

*CAREER:* University of Chicago, Chicago, Ill., assistant professor, 1969-73, associate professor of business economics, 1973-75; University of Washington, Seattle, Wash., professor of economics, 1975—. *Member:* American Education Association, American Finance Association, Econometric Society. *Awards, honors:* Irving Fisher graduate monograph award, 1970; National Science Foundation grant, 1972-73.

*WRITINGS: The Term Structure of Interest Rates,* Basic Books, 1972; *Applied Time Series Analysis,* Holden-Day, 1973. Contributor to *American Economic Review, Journal of the American Statistical Association, Journal of Political Economy, Econometrica,* and *Journal of Econometrics.*

*WORK IN PROGRESS:* Research in econometrics and macroeconomics.

## NELSON, Donald F.   1929-

*PERSONAL:* Born July 17, 1929, in Minneapolis, Minn.; son of Alfred S. (a die-maker) and Esther (Helwig) Nelson; married Barbara Messner (an interior decorator), February 18, 1956; children: Philip, Michelle. *Education:* University of Minnesota, B.A. (magna cum laude), 1953; studied at University of Munich, Germany, 1957; University of Minnesota, M.A., 1963, Ph.D., 1966. *Politics:* "Temperamentally incapable of embracing." *Home:* 665 Sheridan Ave., Columbus, Ohio 43210.

*CAREER:* Ohio State University, Columbus, instructor, 1962-66, professor of German and comparative literature, beginning 1966. *Military service:* U.S. Army, Intelligence, 1954-56; served as interpreter. *Member:* Phi Beta Kappa.

*WRITINGS: Portrait of the Artist as Hermes,* University of North Carolina Press, 1971. Author of articles on Thomas Mann and Nietzsche.

*WORK IN PROGRESS: Literature versus Life,* concerned with existentialist literary criticism; *The Ethics of Masochism* (Rousseau, Dostoyevsky, Hesse, Kafka).

*SIDELIGHTS:* Donald F. Nelson told *CA:* "The two greatest influences in my career as a writer and teacher have been psychoanalysis and myth. In myth man discovers the necessity of a redefinition of the term 'individuality.' In psychoanalysis or depth psychology I see a tremendous ethical potential, a moral commitment: 'know thyself.' Hitherto associated with the clinic and available only to a moneyed elite, psychoanalysis must be incorporated into the present trend toward democratization. There can be no social liberation without psychological liberation."†

\* \* \*

## NELSON, John Oliver   1909-

*PERSONAL:* Born May 14, 1909, in Pittsburgh, Pa.; son of John Evon (an oil executive) and Margaret (Dodds) Nelson; married Jane Bone (a clergywoman), February 11, 1961; children: Richard C. D. *Education:* Princeton University, B.A., 1930; McCormick Theological Seminary, B.D., 1933; Yale University, Ph.D., 1935. *Politics:* Democrat. *Home and office:* Kirkridge, Bangor, Pa. 18013.

*CAREER:* Ordained minister of Presbyterian church, 1935; pastor in Pittsburgh, Pa., 1935-40; Presbyterian Board of Christian Education, Philadelphia, Pa., director of department of life work, 1940-45; Federal Council of Churches of Christ (now National Council of Churches of Christ), New York, N.Y., director of commission on ministry, 1945-50; Yale University, Divinity School, New Haven, Conn., professor of Christian vocation, director of field work, 1950-64; Kirkridge Retreat and Study Center, Bangor, Pa., director, 1964-74, adviser, 1974—. Adjunct professor, Drew University, 1975; headmaster, School at Kirkridge, 1969-70. Secretary, Presbyterian Council on Theological Education, 1943-46; chairman of study commission on vocations, World Council of Churches, 1950-54, of National Fellowship of Reconciliation, 1950-55, of War Nation Church Study Group, 1963-74, and of Ecumenical Institute of Spirituality, 1972—; National Council of Churches, chairman of United Christian Mission, 1954-61, member of commission on architecture, 1963-66, chairman of department of evangelism, 1963-66; chairman of the board, Turning Point Alcoholism Rehabilitation Center, 1968-70; member of national board, YMCA, 1957-70; member of board of advisers, Earlham School of Religion, 1965-72, 1977—; member of advisory council, Princeton Chapel, 1965-69. *Member:* Princeton

Club (New York). *Awards, honors:* Litt. D., Westminster College, 1952; Sertoma Club man of the year (N.J., eastern Pa., Del.), 1975.

*WRITINGS: America Inherits Religion,* Delphian Society, 1938; *Look at the Ministry,* Association Press, 1946; *Young Laymen, Young Church,* Association Press, 1948; (editor) *The Student Prayerbook,* Association Press, 1953; (editor) *Work and Vocation,* Harper, 1954; *Vocation and Protestant Religious Occupations,* Vocational Guidance Manuals, 1963; *Dare to Reconcile,* Friendship, 1969. Editor, *Intercollegian,* 1943-50. Association Press, chairman, 1950-70.

*WORK IN PROGRESS: Careers in Religion,* for Vocational Guidance Manuals.

\*    \*    \*

## NESPOJOHN, Katherine V(eronica)   1912-

*PERSONAL:* Born June 25, 1912, in Bridgeport, Conn.; daughter of Oliver Francis (a production engineer) and Nora (Herlihy) Merillat; married Joseph B. Nespojohn (a postal employee), August 13, 1948; children: Nora Mary. *Education:* Columbia University, B.S., 1938, M.A., 1942; additional study at University of California, Berkeley, 1942, and Fairfield University, 1965-68. *Religion:* Roman Catholic. *Home:* 1643 Noble Ave., Bridgeport, Conn. 06610. *Agent:* Florence Alexander, 50 East 42nd St., New York, N.Y.

*CAREER:* Elementary and high school teacher in Stratford, Conn., 1936-46; University of Bridgeport, Bridgeport, Conn., instructor in biology, 1942-49; teacher in elementary and high school in Fairfield, Conn., 1943-53, science consultant, 1953-68. *Member:* National Education Association, Connecticut Education Association, Fairfield Education Association.

*WRITINGS*—Juvenile: *Animal Eyes,* Prentice-Hall, 1965; *Worms,* illustrated by Haris Petie, F. Watts, 1972.

*WORK IN PROGRESS: Animal Ears.* †

\*    \*    \*

## NETTLEFORD, Rex M.

*PERSONAL:* Born in Falmouth, Trelawney, Jamaica; son of Charles Nettleford and Lebertha Palmer. *Education:* University of the West Indies, B.A. (honors), 1956; Oxford University, B.Phil., 1959. *Office:* Department of Extra-Mural Studies, University of the West Indies, P.O. Box 42, Mona, Kingston 7, Jamaica.

*CAREER:* University of the West Indies, Mona, Kingston, Jamaica, member of department of extra-mural studies, 1959—, professor, 1975—, acting director of extra-mural studies, 1967-71, director of extra-mural studies, 1971—, resident tutor of Jamaica, 1959-61, staff tutor in government and political education, 1961-63, director of studies, Trade Union Education Institute, 1963—. International Labor Organization (United Nations), fellow, 1965-66, lecturing on West Indian labor and industrial relations in the Philippines and Israel; associate fellow, Center for African and African-American Studies at Atlanta University, 1970; visiting lecturer at Texas Southern University, Temple University, Harvard University, and University of Delaware, 1970-71; visiting professor, Centre des Etudes Industrielles, Geneva, Switzerland, 1973—. Member of Jamaica Technical Mission to West Africa and Ethiopia, 1962; leader of cultural missions to United States, Canada, United Kingdom, Mexico, Cuba, Australia, West Germany, and the eastern Caribbean; governor, International Development Research Centre, Ottawa, Ontario. Member of Jamaica Arts Devel-

opment Council, 1962-63, Jamaica Public Services Commission, 1976—, and Inter-American Committee on Culture, Organization of American States; member of board of directors, Jamaica Broadcasting Corp. and National Continental Corp.; chairman of Institute of Jamaica, 1973—, and Jamaica Tourism Product Development Co., 1974—. Founder and artistic director, Jamaica National Dance Theatre Co.; cultural advisor to prime minister of Jamaica, 1972—. *Member:* Academy of Arts and Sciences of Puerto Rico (corresponding member). *Awards, honors:* Rhodes scholar at Oxford University, 1958-59; Issa scholar, 1958; Order of Merit (Jamaica), 1976.

*WRITINGS:* (With M. G. Smith and F. R. Augier) *The Rastafari in Jamaica,* Institute of Social and Economic Studies, University of the West Indies, 1960; (with John Hearne) *Our Heritage,* Department of Extra-Mural Studies, University of the West Indies, 1963; (editor and author of introduction and notes) Louise Bennett, *Jamaica Labrish,* Collins-Sangster, 1965; (editor) *Trade Union and Industrial Relations Terms* (booklet), Trade Union Education Institute, University of the West Indies, 1967; *Roots and Rhythms: Jamaica's National Dance Theatre,* photographs by Maria La Yacona, Deutsch, 1969, Hill & Wang, 1970; *Mirror Mirror: Identity, Race and Protest in Jamaica,* Collins-Sangster, 1970, edition with new preface published as *Identity, Race and Protest in Jamaica,* Morrow, 1971; (editor and author of introduction) *Manley and the New Jamaica,* Longmans, Green, 1971; *Report on Worker Participation in Jamaica,* [Kingston, Jamaica], 1975; *Caribbean Cultural Identity: The Case of Jamaica,* Institute of Jamaica, 1978.

Contributor: (Author of introductory essay) Walter Jekyll, editor, *Jamaican Song and Story,* Dover, 1966; John Lowe, editor, *Adult Education and Nation Building,* Edinburgh University Press, 1970; T. G. Munroe and Rupert Lewis, editors, *Readings in Government,* Department of Government, University of the West Indies, 1971; Phillip Weiner and John Fisher, editors, *Violence and Aggression,* Rutgers University Press, 1974; *Tourism and Its Effects in the Caribbean,* Guyana, 1975; *The Struggle for Equal Opportunity: Struggles for Social Welfare Action,* Columbia University Press, 1977; (author of introductory essay) *Dread and the Rastafari of Jamaica,* Joseph Owens, 1977. Editor, "Labour Education" series and "Occasional Papers in Industrial Relations" series. Contributor to *Caribbean Quarterly, Times* (London), and other publications. Editor, *Caribbean Quarterly,* 1967—; chairman of editorial board, *Jamaica Journal* (publication of Institute of Jamaica).

*WORK IN PROGRESS:* Compiling with Louise Bennett, and editing and annotating, *Jamaican Proverbs; Myth and Reality in Folklife;* writing *Documents in Caribbean Labour.*

\*    \*    \*

## NEVITT, H(enry) J(ohn) Barrington   1908-

*PERSONAL:* Born June 1, 1908, in St. Catharines, Ontario, Canada; son of Robert Barrington (a clergyman) and Selma L. (Melville) Nevitt; married Constance Elsie Johnson, June 28, 1941; children: Richard Barrington, Amy Becker. *Education:* University of Toronto, B.A.Sc., 1934; McGill University, M.Eng., 1945; also studied at University of Santander in Spain, 1933, and University of Western Ontario, 1960. *Religion:* Christian. *Home:* 2 Clarendon Ave., Apt. 207, Toronto, Ontario, Canada M4V 1H9.

*CAREER:* Worked as a Marconi radio operator and trained

as a bush pilot; Zavod Elektropribor, Leningrad, Soviet Union, research and development engineer for microwave radio test equipment, 1932-33; Northern Electric Co., Montreal, Quebec, trainee and then industrial engineer, 1934-39; Canadian Pacific Telegraph and Defence Communications Ltd., Montreal, systems engineer, 1939-44; systems engineer with RCA Victor, Montreal, and later with RCA International Division, New York, N.Y., 1944-47; Telefonaktiebolaget L. M. Ericsson, Stockholm, Sweden, consultant to senior management on projects in Europe and the Americas, 1947-60, residing in South America, 1950-60; independent consultant in Canada, first on Royal Commission for Government Organization, then on Canadian Government Communication Satellite program, and on various assignments for private companies, 1961-64; Ontario Development Corp., Toronto, director of innovations and training, 1964-76. Lecturer at Sir George Williams College. Honorary correspondent, Centre for Industrial Development, United Nations. Honorary director, Institut fuer Informationsentwicklung, Vienna, Austria. Consultant on international communication, effects of technological innovation, and management by pre-vision (MBP).

*MEMBER:* Institute of Electrical and Electronic Engineers (fellow), Institution of Electrical Engineers (United Kingdom; fellow), American Association for the Advancement of Science (fellow), Engineering Institute of Canada (fellow), Society for General Systems Research, American Management Association (consulting member), Discoveries International (Tokyo and Rome), Association of Professional Engineers of the Province of Ontario.

*WRITINGS:* (Contributor) Don Toppin, editor, *This Cybernetic Age,* Human Development Corp., 1969; (contributor) T. H. Bonaparte and J. E. Flaherty, editors, *Peter Drucker: Contributions to Business Enterprise,* New York University Press, 1970; (with Marshall McLuhan) *Take Today: The Executive as Dropout,* Harcourt, 1972; (contributor) Stanley Winkler, editor, *Computer Communications: Impacts and Implications,* Institute of Electrical and Electronic Engineers, 1972; (contributor) Jean-Pierre Gravier, editor, *Management Horizon 1980,* [Paris], 1972; (contributor) Jacques Roger, editor, *Seminari Interdisciplinari di Venezia: La Teoria dell' Informazione,* Il Mulino (Bologna), 1974; (contributor) Anthony Debons and William J. Cameron, editors, *Perspectives in Information Science,* Noordhoff (Leyden), 1975. Contributor to *Explorations* and to business and technical journals.

*WORK IN PROGRESS:* Continuing research, in collaboration with the Centre for Culture and Technology at University of Toronto, on the physical, psychic, and social effects of man's technological extensions, past and present, by process pattern recognition.

*SIDELIGHTS:* H. J. Barrington Nevitt writes that he is "particularly interested in sharpening perception of intercultural barriers to communication, stimulating the processes of invention, and anticipating the effects of innovation by using all our wits and senses. [I am] now involved in exploring the conflicts and complementarities of art and science, East and West, in order to organize current ignorance for continuing dialogue to transform breakdowns into breakthroughs." He has a working knowledge of French, German, Spanish, Portuguese, Italian, Swedish, and Russian, obtained along with a smattering of other languages, through work and residence abroad.

## NEWALL, Venetia 1935-

*PERSONAL:* Born June 29, 1935, in London, England; daughter of Charles George and Joan (Barrett) Tubbs; married John N. F. Newall (a businessman), March 14, 1959. *Education:* Sorbonne, University of Paris, Diploma in French, 1954; St. Andrews University, M.A., 1958. *Religion:* Church of England. *Office:* Department of English, University College, University of London, Gower St., London WC1E 6BT, England.

*CAREER: Times,* London, England, travel correspondent, 1962-67; University of London, London, university extension lecturer in department of extra-mural studies and honorary research fellow of University College, 1971—. Visiting tutor, University of Keele, 1970; visiting lecturer at University of Pennsylvania, University of Texas, Indiana University, University of Kansas, State University of New York College at Buffalo, and University of Edinburgh. *Member:* Royal Society of Arts (fellow), Royal Geographical Society (fellow), International Society for Folk Narrative Research, International Folk Music Council, Society for Folk Life Studies (committee member), American Folklore Society (life member), Folklore Society (honorary secretary, 1967—), University Womens Club. *Awards, honors:* International Folklore Prize from University of Chicago, 1971, for *An Egg at Easter.*

*WRITINGS: An Egg at Easter: A Folklore Study,* Indiana University Press, 1971; *The Folklore of Birds and Beasts,* Shire Publications, 1971; (editor) *The Witch Figure: Essays in Honour of Katharine M. Biggs,* Routledge & Kegan Paul, 1973; *The Encyclopedia of Witchcraft and Magic,* Hamlyn, 1974. General editor, "The Folklore of the British Isles" series. Contributor to *Reader's Digest* and to folklore journals in the United States and England.

*SIDELIGHTS:* Venetia Newall's collections include twelve-hundred-fifty traditionally-decorated Easter eggs, as well as Albanian costume and folk art, and Eskimo masks and carvings.

*BIOGRAPHICAL/CRITICAL SOURCES: Books and Bookmen,* June, 1971.

\*    \*    \*

## NEWELL, William T(hrift) 1929-

*PERSONAL:* Born April 9, 1929, in Oklahoma City, Okla.; son of William Thrift and J. Fay (Kendrick) Newell; married Rosemary Louise Hinkley, November 20, 1954; children: Laura Louise, Scott Jeffrey, Cheryl Lynne. *Education:* University of Colorado, B.S., 1952; University of Denver, M.B.A., 1955; University of Texas, Main University (now University of Texas at Austin), Ph.D., 1962. *Home:* 4830 Northeast 42nd St., Seattle, Wash. 98105. *Office:* Department of Management and Organization, Graduate School of Business Administration, DJ-10, University of Washington, Seattle, Wash. 98195.

*CAREER:* Mine & Smelter Supply Co., Denver, Colo., assistant department manager, 1947-54; KFML-FM Radio, Denver, announcer and engineer, 1954-55; University of Texas, Main University (now University of Texas at Austin), instructor in management, 1956-60; University of Washington, Seattle, assistant professor, 1960-63, associate professor of management, 1963-69; Institute for the Study of Management Methods (IMEDE), Lausanne, Switzerland, professor of management, 1969-70; University of Washington, professor of management, 1969—, chairman of department of management and organization, 1976—. *Member:*

Institute of Management Sciences, American Institute of Decision Sciences, Academy of Management, Alpha Kappa Psi, Beta Gamma Sigma. *Awards, honors:* Alfred P. Sloan Faculty Fellow, Massachusetts Institute of Technology, 1963-64; H. B. Maynard Book of the Year Award, American Institute of Industrial Engineers, 1970, for *Simulation in Business and Economics.*

*WRITINGS: Long-Range Planning Policies and Practices,* Bureau of Business Research, University of Texas, 1963; (with A. N. Schreiber, R. A. Johnson, R. C. Meier, H. C. Fischer) *Cases in Manufacturing Management,* McGraw, 1965; (with Meier) *Simulation in Business and Economics,* Prentice-Hall, 1969; (with Johnson and R. C. Vergin) *Operations Management: A Systems Concept,* Houghton, 1972; (contributor) Harold Guetzkow, Philip Kotler, and Randall L. Schultz, editors, *Simulation in Social and Administrative Science,* Prentice-Hall, 1972; (with Johnson and Vergin) *Production and Operations Management: A Systems Concept,* Houghton, 1974.

*WORK IN PROGRESS:* Computer simulation models of business, economic, social, and ecological systems; managerial long-range planning; interdisciplinary research management.

\* \* \*

### NEWKIRK, Glen A. 1931-

*PERSONAL:* Born August 23, 1931, in Strawn, Kan.; son of Brice L. and Lena (Schellenger) Newkirk; married Peggy Myrick (a diagnostic reading instructor), March 24, 1957; children: David Glen, Heather Colleen, Rebecca Erin. *Education:* Kansas State Teachers College (now Emporia State University), B.S., 1953, M.A., 1956; University of Denver, Ph.D., 1966. *Home:* 6041 Walnut, Omaha, Neb. 68106. *Office:* Department of English, University of Nebraska, 60th and Dodge, Omaha, Neb. 68101.

*CAREER:* Colorado State University, Fort Collins, instructor in English, 1957-58; Southwest Missouri State College (now University), Springfield, instructor in English, 1958-61; Southwestern College, Winfield, Kan., assistant professor of English, 1961-63; University of Nebraska at Omaha, assistant professor, 1963-67, associate professor, 1967-71, professor of English, 1971—. *Member:* Modern Language Association of America, Renaissance Society of America.

*WRITINGS:* (Editor) *Contemporary Issues,* Scott, Foresman, 1971; (contributor) *England in the Age of Shakespeare,* University of Nebraska at Omaha, 1976.

*WORK IN PROGRESS:* A modern adaptation of Count Romei's *Courtier's Academie.*

\* \* \*

### NEWMAN, Daisy 1904-

*PERSONAL:* Born May 9, 1904, in Southport, Lancashire, England; daughter of James (a merchant) and Ella (Calman) Neumann; married Richard Newman, 1928; children: Ellen Newman Rothchild, John Nicholas. *Education:* Ethical Culture School, New York, 1922; attended schools in Switzerland and France; attended Radcliffe College, 1922-23. *Home and office:* 42 Todd Pond Rd., Lincoln, Mass. 01773. *Agent:* Curtis Brown Ltd., 575 Madison Ave., New York, N.Y. 10022.

*CAREER:* Radcliffe College, Cambridge, Mass., director of Music Center and head resident of Holmes Hall, 1957-62; affiliate, North House, Harvard University.

*WRITINGS: Timothy Travels,* Coward, 1928; *Sperli the Clockmaker,* Macmillan, 1932; *Now that April's There,* Lippincott, 1945; *Diligence in Love,* Doubleday, 1951; *Dilly,* Hodder & Stoughton, 1951, published as *The Autumn's Brightness,* Macmillan, 1955; *Mount Joy,* Atheneum, 1968; *A Procession of Friends, Quakers in America,* Doubleday, 1972; *I Take Thee, Serenity,* Houghton, 1975. Contributor of articles to *Saturday Review, Ladies Home Journal, New Yorker,* and *New York Times.*

*WORK IN PROGRESS:* A novel.

*BIOGRAPHICAL/CRITICAL SOURCES: Young Readers' Review,* May, 1968; *National Observer,* October 21, 1968.

\* \* \*

### NEWMAN, Joseph W(illiam) 1918-

*PERSONAL:* Born March 31, 1918, in Manhattan, Kan.; son of Porter Joseph (an insurance agent) and Nettie B. (Humfeld) Newman; married Susan Elizabeth Masters (a social worker), August 16, 1958; children: Amy Louise, Jane Elizabeth. *Education:* Kansas State University, B.S., 1939, M.S., 1941; Harvard University, M.B.A., 1947, D.C.S., 1957. *Office:* Department of Marketing, College of Business and Public Administration, University of Arizona, Tucson, Ariz. 85721.

*CAREER:* Bureau of Advertising, Inc., New York, N.Y., Chicago market and media analyst, 1947-49; University of Michigan, Ann Arbor, instructor in marketing, 1949-51; Harvard University, Boston, Mass., instructor, 1951-53, assistant professor of marketing, 1953-60; Stanford University, Stanford, Calif., associate professor of marketing, 1960-65; University of Michigan, professor of marketing, 1965-73; University of Arizona, Tucson, professor of marketing and chairman of department, 1973—. *Military service:* U.S. Naval Reserve, 1942-47; became lieutenant. *Member:* American Marketing Association (director, 1961-63; vice-president, 1963-64), Association for Consumer Research, Academy of Marketing Science, Beta Gamma Sigma, Sigma Delta Chi.

*WRITINGS: Motivation Research and Marketing Management,* Division of Research, Graduate School of Business Administration, Harvard University, 1957; (editor with Harper Boyd) *Advertising Management,* Irwin, 1965; *On Knowing the Consumer,* Wiley, 1966; *Marketing Management and Information,* Irwin, 1967; *Management Applications of Decision Theory,* Harper, 1971; (contributor) A. Woodside, J. Sheth, and P. Bennett, editors, *Consumer and Industrial Buying Behavior,* North-Holland, 1977. Contributor of articles to *Harvard Business Review, Journal of Marketing Research, Journal of Consumer Research, Journal of Marketing,* and other journals. Member of editorial board, *Journal of Marketing Research,* 1974—.

*WORK IN PROGRESS:* Research on nature of consumer purchase decision process, and on consumer satisfaction.

\* \* \*

### NEWMAN, Katharine D. 1911-

*PERSONAL:* Born August 17, 1911, in Philadelphia, Pa.; daughter of C. Victor and Harriet (Hetherington) Dealy; married Morton Newman, May 11, 1946 (divorced, 1968); children: Deborah (Mrs. Stanley J. Silverstein), Ruth. *Education:* Temple University, B.S. in Ed. (summa cum laude), 1933; University of Pennsylvania, M.A., 1937, Ph.D., 1961. *Religion:* Episcopalian. *Home:* 14732A Carfax Ave., Tustin, Calif. 92680. *Office:* Department of English, University of Southern California, Los Angeles, Calif. 90007.

*CAREER:* Teacher of English in Philadelphia, Pa. senior high schools, 1934-46, and in Abington, Pa., 1963-67; University of Minnesota, Minneapolis, instructor in English, 1946-47; Temple University Community College, Philadelphia, Pa., instructor in English, 1959; Moore College of Art, Philadelphia, Pa., associate professor of English, 1961-63; West Chester State College, West Chester, Pa., associate professor, 1967-69, professor of English, 1969-77, co-director of Ethnic Cultures Workshops, 1971-75, director of Institute for Ethnic Studies, 1975-77; University of Southern California, Los Angeles, adjunct staff member in department of English, 1977—. Exchange professor, Cheyney State College, spring, 1971. Associate editor of Planning Committee for a History of Ethnic Literatures, 1977—. *Member:* Modern Language Association of America (member of executive committee of Division of Ethnic Studies in Language and Literature, 1977—; member of delegate assembly, 1977—), Conference of Editors of Learned Journals, Society for the Study of Multi-Ethnic Literature of the United States (MELUS; founder and first chairperson, 1973-74), National Council of Teachers of English, College Language Association, National Association of Interdisciplinary Ethnic Studies, Philological Association of the Pacific Coast.

*WRITINGS: The American Equation: Literature in a Multi-Ethnic Culture,* Allyn & Bacon, 1971; (editor) *Ethnic American Short Stories,* Pocket Books, 1975. Editor, *Bulletin* of Philadelphia Art Alliance, 1937-45, *Melus Newsletter,* 1974-77, and *Journal* of the Society for the Study of Multi-Ethnic Literature of the United States, 1978—.

*WORK IN PROGRESS: Towards an American Aesthetic,* essays on the impact of multiethnicity of American literature.

*SIDELIGHTS:* Katharine Newman told *CA:* "For a decade, all that I have done, as administrator, editor, teacher, book-reviewer, and author has been directed toward expanding the definition of American literature to include all forms of literary expression by all Americans, regardless of the language used by the speaker/writer/creator. Now there are many people with the same goal, and, through our efforts, there will come a revolution in academic thinking, a great change in the contents of American literature courses, and a wide variety of exciting literary works for all readers. To perform their critical task appropriately, scholars will use the componential approach, that is, they will look to see the importance of the ethnic component in each book. They will be able to evaluate the importance of our diversity in our literature. And writers will feel free to write out of their own backgrounds and cultural value-systems, sure that there are readers able to comprehend and accept them. There is much to be done yet!"

\*　　\*　　\*

### NICHOLS, Roy F(ranklin)   1896-1973

March 3, 1896—January 11, 1973; American historian, educator, and authority on nineteenth-century American history. Obituaries: *New York Times,* January 13, 1973; *Washington Post,* January 13, 1973. (See index for *CA* sketch)

\*　　\*　　\*

### NICHOLSON, Ranald (George)   1931-

*PERSONAL:* Born July 5, 1931, in Edinburgh, Scotland; son of Ramsay Thomas A. and Susan (Wilson) Nicholson. *Education:* University of Edinburgh, M.A., 1953; Oxford University, D.Phil., 1961. *Politics:* Radical Conservative. *Religion:* Presbyterian. *Home:* Rockhill Castle, High Craigmore, Isle of Bute, Scotland.

*CAREER:* University of Edinburgh, Edinburgh, Scotland, lecturer in Scottish history, 1960-67; University of Guelph, Guelph, Ontario, 1967-78, began as associate professor, became professor of history. *Military service:* Royal Air Force, 1953-56; became flight lieutenant.

*WRITINGS: Edward III and the Scots,* Oxford University Press, 1965; *Scotland: The Later Middle Ages,* Oliver & Boyd, 1974, revised edition, 1978; (editor with Peter McNeill) *An Historical Atlas of Scotland, c.400-c.1600,* St. Andrews University, 1975. Contributor to Scottish and English history journals.

*WORK IN PROGRESS: Scotland's Wars with England,* for Batsford.

*SIDELIGHTS:* Ranald Nicholson told *CA,* "I look forward to attempting to write historical fiction."

\*　　\*　　\*

### NICKLAUS, (Charles) Frederick   1936-

*PERSONAL:* Born January 19, 1936, in Columbus, Ohio; son of Charles Frederick and Effie (Fiedler) Nicklaus. *Education:* Ohio State University, B.F.A., 1957. *Home:* 241 East 73rd St., New York, N.Y. 10021.

*CAREER:* Editor; has worked both free-lance and for various publishers, including Columbia University Press, 1966-72, and Simon & Schuster, Inc. Poetry consultant for the Asia Society, New York, N.Y. *Member:* Poetry Society of America.

*WRITINGS—Poems: The Man Who Bit the Sun,* New Directions, 1964; *Cut of Noon,* David Lewis, 1971. Poetry included in *Borestone Mountain Poetry Awards, 1959,* edited by Lionel Stevens and others, Pacific Books, 1960. Contributor of poetry to *Antaeus, New York Times, Prairie Schooner, Voices, Poetry* (Chicago), *New Directions,* and numerous other periodicals.

*WORK IN PROGRESS:* Two volumes of poetry, *Snow Blindness* and *The Hunting Flight.*

*SIDELIGHTS:* Frederick Nicklaus writes: "I have been influenced little by contemporary events or the current 'literary scene.' Although my poetry has been strongly colored by travel, a sense of place, it has for some time been a poetry of introspection and personal human conflict. It is a poetry of understated tension."

\*　　\*　　\*

### NIGRO, Felix A(nthony)   1914-

*PERSONAL:* Born August 8, 1914, in Brooklyn, N.Y.; married Edna Helen Nelson, July 28, 1938; children: Lloyd G., Kirsten F. *Education:* University of Wisconsin, B.A., 1935, M.A., 1936, Ph.D., 1948. *Home:* 199 West View Dr., Athens, Ga. 30602. *Office:* 203A Baldwin Hall, University of Georgia, Athens, Ga. 30601.

*CAREER:* Public Administration Service, Chicago, Ill., member of staff, 1937-38; Social Science Research Council, Committee on Public Administration, Washington, D.C., researcher, 1938-39; National Resources Planning Board, Washington, D.C., administrative analyst, 1939-40; National Youth Administration, Washington, D.C., chief of classification, 1940-42; Office of Emergency Management,

Washington, D.C., senior classification officer, 1942-43; War Shipping Administration, Washington, D.C., administrative analyst, 1943-44; National Housing Agency, Washington, D.C., assistant personnel officer, 1944-45; United Nations Relief and Rehabilitation Administration, Washington, D.C., management analyst, 1945-46; Griffenhagen & Associates, Chicago, staff member, 1946-47; University of Texas, Main University (now University of Texas at Austin), assistant professor of political science, 1948-49; University of Puerto Rico, Rio Piedras, visiting professor of public administration, 1949-51; Florida State University, Tallahassee, associate professor of public administration, 1951-52; Institute of Inter-American Affairs, Montevideo, Uruguay, and El Salvador, public administration field consultant, 1952-54; J. L. Jacobs & Co. (management consultants), Chicago, senior associate, 1954; University of Puerto Rico, associate professor of public administration, 1954-56; United Nations Advanced School of Public Administration, San Jose, Costa Rica, lecturer in personnel administration, 1956-57; Southern Illinois University, Carbondale, professor of government, 1957-61; San Diego State College (now University), San Diego, Calif., professor of political science, 1961-65; University of Delaware, Newark, Charles P. Messick Professor of Public Administration, 1965-69; University of Georgia, Athens, professor of political science, 1969—. Lecturer at United Nations International Training Center (El Salvador), 1951, Pan-American Sanitary Bureau on Water Finance and Administration regional conference (Mexico), 1960, and Public Administration Center (Guatemala), 1961; lecturer in personnel administration, School of Public Administration (Spain), 1975. Visiting professor at University of Southern California, spring, 1960, summers, 1966-68, San Jose State College (now University), summer, 1961, University of Delaware, summer, 1963, University of Wisconsin, summer, 1964, and North Carolina State University, 1969; Simon fellow, University of Manchester, fall, 1972. Member of New Castle County (Delaware) Personnel Board, 1967-69; member of City of Newark (Delaware) Board of Ethics, 1967-69. Arbitrator, Federal Mediation and Conciliation Service; arbitrator and factfinder, Florida Public Employment Relations Commission. Consultant to Venezuela's Ministry of Health, 1952, Uruguay's Ministry of Health, 1952-53, and Venezuela's Ministry of Finance, 1958.

*MEMBER:* International Personnel Management Association, National Academy of Administration, American Society for Public Administration, American Political Science Association, Society for Personnel Administration, American Association of University Professors, National Labor Panel, American Arbitration Association, Phi Beta Kappa, Phi Kappa Phi, Phi Eta Sigma.

*WRITINGS: University Training for the Public Service* (pamphlet), Civil Service Assembly, 1938; *Recruitment of Firemen* (pamphlet), Public Administration Service, 1940; (editor) *Public Administration: Readings and Documents,* Rinehart, 1951; *Conferencias sobre Gerencia Administrativa,* Government of El Salvador, 1951; *Conferencias sobre Administracion de Personal,* Government of El Salvador, 1953; *El Concepto Moderno de Administracion de Personal* (pamphlet), Government of Guatemala, 1956; *Administracion de Personal: United Nations,* United Nations Advanced School of Public Administration (Central America), 1957; *Public Personnel Administration,* Holt, 1959; *Modern Public Administration,* Harper, 1965, 4th edition (with son, Lloyd G. Nigro), 1977; *Management-Employee Relations in the Public Service,* Public Personnel Administration, 1969; (with L. G. Nigro) *The New Public Personnel Administra-*

tion, F. E. Peacock, 1976. Contributor of about sixty articles in Spanish and English to professional journals.

*WORK IN PROGRESS:* A fifth edition of *Modern Public Administration,* with Lloyd G. Nigro; research on British civil service and labor relations in government.

\*    \*    \*

### NISBETT, Richard E.    1941-

*PERSONAL:* Born June 1, 1941, in Littlefield, Tex.; son of R. Wayne (in insurance) and Helen (King) Nisbett; married Susan Isaacs (a Ph.D. student), June 29, 1969. *Education:* Tufts University, A.B., 1962; Columbia University, Ph.D., 1966. *Residence:* Ann Arbor, Mich. *Office:* Department of Psychology, 3068 Institute of Social Research, University of Michigan, Ann Arbor, Mich. 48109.

*CAREER:* Yale University, New Haven, Conn., assistant professor of psychology, 1966-71; University of Michigan, Ann Arbor, associate professor, 1971-76, professor of psychology, 1976—. *Member:* American Psychological Association, Society of Experimental Social Psychology.

*WRITINGS:* (With Edward E. Jones, David K. Kanouse, Harold H. Kelley, Stuart Valins, and Bernard Weiner) *Attribution: Perceiving the Causes of Behavior,* General Learning Press, 1972; (editor with H. S. London) *Thought and Feeling: Cognitive Alteration of Feeling States,* Aldine, 1974. Contributor to psychology journals. Editorial consultant to *Journal of Personality and Social Psychology, Journal of Experimental Social Psychology,* and *Cognitive Psychology.*

*WORK IN PROGRESS:* With Lee Ross, *Human Inference,* for Prentice-Hall.

\*    \*    \*

### NISSMAN, Albert    1930-

*PERSONAL:* Born February 23, 1930, in Philadelphia, Pa.; son of Meyer J. and Pauline (Slifkin) Nissman; married Blossom Snoyer (a teacher and counselor), December 27, 1953 (divorced, November 21, 1975); married Minnie Reba Berman, May 29, 1977; children: (first marriage) Debra Beth, David Arthur. *Education:* Temple University, B.S. in Ed., 1952, Ed.M., 1956; Pennsylvania State University, Ed.D., 1965. *Politics:* Independent. *Religion:* Jewish. *Home:* 24 Needlepoint Lane, Garfield Park North, Willingboro, N.J. 08046. *Office:* School of Education, Rider College, 2083 Lawrenceville Rd., P.O. Box 6400, Lawrenceville, N.J. 08648.

*CAREER:* Substitute teacher in Philadelphia, Pa., 1952-53; Bristol Township School District, Bristol, Pa., teacher, and later chairman of department of English and social studies, 1953-63; Rider College, Lawrenceville, N.J., assistant professor of English and education, 1966-70, associate professor of education, 1970-74, professor of education, 1974—. *Member:* National Education Association, Society of Professors of Education, American Educational Studies Association, American Association of University Professors, American Educational Research Association, Brith Shalom, B'nai B'rith, Phi Delta Kappa, Phi Kappa Phi. *Awards, honors:* Author Award of New Jersey Association of Teachers of English, 1969, for *Fragments/Figments;* Patriotic Civilian Award, Department of Army, 1975; Author Award of New Jersey Institute of Technology, 1976, for *Operation Classroom;* Christian R. and Mary F. Lindback Foundation Award for Distinguished Teaching, 1977.

*WRITINGS: Fragments/Figments* (poems), privately printed, 1967; (with Jack Lutz) *Organizing and Developing a Summer Professional Workshop,* Shoe String, 1971; *Operation Classroom: A Direct Experience Approach,* New Voices Publishing, 1975. Contributor of poems to literary journals and articles to education journals.

*WORK IN PROGRESS: Teaching English and Social Studies; The Teacher-Image in the American Short Story;* book manuscripts on the teaching of values and the teaching of poetry.

*SIDELIGHTS:* Albert Nissman writes: "Teaching is my *raison d'etre,* my reason for being. One can not be a successful teacher unless he is a willing learner. Writing is another facet of teaching. One can not be a successful writer unless he, too, is a willing learner.

"For me, then, teaching, writing, and learning are mutually dependent for their very survival. Teaching is more direct; I can see, at least superficially, some impact. In writing, I have a one-to-one relationship with students unknown. Teaching a lesson leaves no tangible residue; a finished book, article, or poem is the concrete expression of teaching and learning. Teaching is a gregarious art; writing is a lonely art; both are nourished by learning."

\* \* \*

## NISSMAN, Blossom S. 1928-

*PERSONAL:* Born February 23, 1928, in Yonkers, N.Y.; daughter of Arthur R. and Rose (Strauss) Snoyer; children: Debra Beth, David Arthur. *Education:* Temple University, B.S., 1951; Trenton State College, M.A., 1969; Rutgers University, Ed.D., 1976. *Home:* 1 Glen Stewart Dr., Ewing, N.J. 08618. *Office:* Central Burlington County Region for Special Education, c/o Westhampton School, Mount Holly, N.J. 08060.

*CAREER:* Elementary teacher in Elkins Park, Pa., 1951-53, Fallsington, Pa., 1953-57, and Bristol, Pa., 1964-66; Willingboro School District, Willingboro, N.J., elementary teacher, 1966-69, learning disabilities teacher and consultant, 1970-72; Central Burlington County Region for Special Education, Mt. Holly, N.J., specialist in curriculum and instruction, 1972-76, coordinator, 1976—. Adjunct assistant professor at Rider College and Trenton State College, 1969—. *Member:* National Education Association, American Personnel and Guidance Association, American School Counselor Association, Association for Counselor Education and Supervision, New Jersey Education Association, New Jersey Personnel and Guidance Association, Delta Kappa Gamma, Delta Kappa Pi. *Awards, honors:* Elected Willingboro (N.J.) Woman of the Year, 1976.

*WRITINGS*—With Martin Stamm, except as indicated: *Ask the Counselor,* Chandler-Davis, 1970; *Alphabet Land,* Chandler-Davis, 1970; *New Dimensions in Elementary Guidance* (adult text), Rosen Press, 1971; *Your Child and Drugs,* Guidance Awareness Publications, 1973; *What You Always Wanted to Know about Tests,* Guidance Awareness Publications, 1974; *Implications and Applications of Assessment Procedures for Counselors and Teachers,* Guidance Awareness Publications, 1976; *Practical Guidelines for Space-Age Children,* Guidance Awareness Publications, 1977; (sole author) *Model of Middle School Guidance,* Allyn & Bacon, 1978. With Stamm, writer of weekly column, "Ask the Counselor," in *Burlington County Times.* Contributor of more than forty articles to professional journals. Member of editorial board and coordinator of publications, New Jersey Personnel and Guidance Association.

*WORK IN PROGRESS: Developing Assessment Tools for Measuring Potential;* further books in a series to develop awareness on the elementary level (*Alphabet Land* was the first in this series).

\* \* \*

## NOBLE, G(eorge) Bernard 1892-1972

July 11, 1892—November 28, 1972; American historian, educator, senator, and U.S. Government official. Obituaries: *New York Times,* November 30, 1972. (See index for *CA* sketch)

\* \* \*

## NOLDE, O(tto) Frederick 1899-1972

June 30, 1899—June 17, 1972; American clergyman, educator, crusader for peace and religious freedom, and author of books on religious themes. Obituaries: *New York Times,* June 19, 1972; *Washington Post,* June 22, 1972; *Newsweek,* July 3, 1972; *Current Biography,* September, 1972. (See index for *CA* sketch)

\* \* \*

## NORD, Walter R(obert) 1939-

*PERSONAL:* Born July 2, 1939, in Mt. Kisco, N.Y.; son of Arthur William (a pipe-fitter) and Elizabeth (Reimstedt) Nord; married Ann Feagan (a psychologist), June 10, 1967. *Education:* Williams College, B.A., 1961; Cornell University, M.S., 1963; Washington University, Ph.D., 1967. *Home:* 7430 Gannon, St. Louis, Mo. 63130. *Office:* School of Business, Washington University, St. Louis, Mo. 63130.

*CAREER:* Washington University, St. Louis, Mo., 1967—, assistant professor, 1967-71, currently professor of organizational psychology. *Member:* American Psychological Association, Academy of Management, Phi Kappa Phi, Beta Gamma Sigma.

*WRITINGS: Concepts and Controversy in Organizational Behavior,* Goodyear Publishing, 1972, 2nd edition, 1976; (with P. Frost and V. Mitchell) *Organizational Reality: Observations from the Firing Line,* Goodyear Publishing, 1978. Contributor of articles to *Psychological Bulletin, Personnel Administration, Organizational Behavior, Human Performance, Journal of Applied Psychology, American Psychologist, Journal of Applied Behavioral Science,* and *Organization Dynamics.*

*WORK IN PROGRESS:* Writing on the social exchange theory and critical analysis of organizational psychology.

*SIDELIGHTS:* Walter R. Nord told *CA,* "Much of my work is directed to analysis of modern organizations and how to make them contribute to human welfare."

\* \* \*

## NORTON, Boyd 1936-

*PERSONAL:* Born April 8, 1936, in Pawtucket, R.I.; son of Boyd Earl (a guard) and Edith (Eastman) Norton; married Barbara M. Cooksey (a librarian), July 25, 1959; children: Jean Anne, Scott. *Education:* Michigan Technological University, B.S., 1960. *Politics:* Democrat. *Religion:* None. *Home:* 33481 Stransky Rd., Evergreen, Colo. 80439.

*CAREER:* Free-lance photographer; Phillips Petroleum Atomic Energy, Idaho Falls, Idaho, physicist, 1960-67; Idaho Nuclear Corporation, Idaho Falls, section chief, 1967-69; The Wilderness Society, Denver, Colo., western field representative, 1969-71. *Member:* Sierra Club, Friends of the Earth (Rocky Mountain representative, 1971—).

WRITINGS: Snake Wilderness, Sierra Club, 1972; The Grand Tetons, Viking, 1974; Rivers of the Rockies, Rand McNally, 1975; Alaska: Wilderness Frontier, foreword by Cecil D. Andrus, Reader's Digest Press, 1977; The Backroads of Colorado, Rand McNally, 1977.

SIDELIGHTS: Boyd Norton is also a photographer whose pictures have appeared in numerous books, including America the Beautiful, Wildflowers of the Mountains, Wildflowers of the Desert, and in such magazines as Life, Popular Photography, Audubon, Smithsonian, Reader's Digest, American Heritage, and many others. Norton writes: "My photography and writing are directed along rather limited lines. Basically I specialize in the beauty of wilderness, in the discovery of the intrinsic values of unspoiled life and land, and in the preservation of our remaining wild lands. Too little of our planet remains free of man's disruptive influence. I don't wish to contribute to the deterioration of this remainder." He travels frequently on river raft trips, backpacking, and mountain climbing expeditions.†

*     *     *

NORTON, David L. 1930-

PERSONAL: Born March 27, 1930, in St. Louis, Mo.; son of Cecil Vallat (a civil engineer) and Ruth (Essick) Norton; married second wife, Mary F. Kille, August 22, 1970; children: (first marriage) Anita Lee, Ronald Vallet, Peter Daniel; (second marriage) Timothy Tucker, Cory Dana. Education: Washington University, St. Louis, Mo., B.S., 1952, M.A., 1962; Boston University, Ph.D., 1968. Religion: Humanism. Home: 6 Windflower Dr., Meadowood, Newark, Del. 19711. Office: Department of Philosophy, University of Delaware, Newark, Del. 19711.

CAREER: Smokejumper (parachute firefighter), 1950; U.S. Geological Survey, uranium prospector in Alaska for Trace Elements Unit, 1951; California Highway Department, San Francisco, Calif., civil engineer, 1953-54; Norton Co. (architectural designers), St. Louis, Mo., architectural engineer, 1954-58; Ethical Society of St. Louis (civic and religious institution), St. Louis, associate leader, 1958-62; Ethical Society of Boston, Boston, Mass., leader, 1962-66; University of Delaware, Newark, associate professor of philosophy, 1966—. Held summer jobs as forest firefighter, 1946, 1947, 1949, and as coal miner, 1948. Military service: U.S. Air Force, 1952-53; became second lieutenant. Member: American Ethical Union, American Philosophical Association, Society for the Advancement of American Philosophy, National Trust for Scotland, Audubon Society.

WRITINGS: (Editor with wife, Mary F. Kille) Philosophies of Love, Chandler Publishing, 1971; Personal Destinies: A Philosophy of Ethical Individualism, Princeton University Press, 1976. Contributor of about two dozen articles to Ethics, Review of Metaphysics, Journal of Value Inquiry, and other journals. Critic for St. Louis Post-Dispatch, 1958-63.

WORK IN PROGRESS: Political Individualism: A Eudaimonistic Prospective.

AVOCATIONAL INTERESTS: Painting, bird-watching, motorcycling.

*     *     *

NOWACKI, Walenty 1906-

PERSONAL: Born January 26, 1906, in Sieradz, Poland; son of Marcin (a farmer) and Jozefa (Lyczka) Nowacki; married Alina Patocka, August 31, 1941 (died May 10, 1942); married Halina Krystyna Pindar (a clerk), August 4, 1959; children: (first marriage) Przemyslaw. Education: Polytechnic Institute, Lwow, Poland, Dip.Ing., 1928. Politics: "Active all life as an anticommunist in Poland." Religion: Roman Catholic. Home: 67-34 Austin St., Forest Hills, N.Y. 11375. Office: Engineering Index, Inc., 345 East 47th St., New York, N.Y. 10017.

CAREER: Assistant professor of chemical engineering at Polytechnic Institute, Lwow, Poland; researcher and engineer with chemical firms in Warsaw, Poland, 1928-36; Polish Government, Warsaw, assistant to Minister of Industry and Commerce, 1937-39; owner and manager of chemical and plastics processing factory, Warsaw, Poland, 1940-64; plastics processing engineer, Augsburg, Germany, 1964-66; Engineering Index, Inc. (scientific and technical information service), New York, N.Y., editor, abstracting and indexing material from books and magazines in five languages, 1966—. Holder of eight Polish patents in chemistry field. Military service: Fought with Polish forces in the war against Soviet Union, 1920. Pilot in World War II, shot down by Luftwaffe at the beginning of the war in Poland, 1939.

WRITINGS: Revolution without Revolution: A New Approach to Old Ideas, Gaus, 1970. Co-editor of an ideological-political magazine, Zadruga, published in Poland between the world wars.

WORK IN PROGRESS: The Law of Inversely Proportional Stupidity.

SIDELIGHTS: Walenty Nowacki describes himself as "an individual with two natures: the one of an engineer and scientist, and the other of a politician and philosopher." He spent thirty-eight years under three dictatorships, and that is why his "interest in writing about politics could be realized only after settling down in the United States in 1966." As all his life he had been an "enthusiastic admirer of the American economy and political system, [I] experienced a great personal tragedy when at first hand [I] learned the truth about the U.S. political reality, namely that the policy-shapers in Washington are leading this nation to catastrophe." Because his first book, "which attempted to reverse the existing trend by submitting a Great Program of National Reconstruction, did not stir up any discussion, [I have] formulated 'The Universal Law of Civilizational Progress,' which explains the suicidal behavior of American society. This law, which constitutes the theoretical basis of [my] Work in Progress, reads: 'There is an inverse correlation between civilizational progress of a society and logical thinking capability of its members; the higher the level of science and technology, the lower the understanding of interhuman relations.'"

In his youth, Nowacki was an alpinist, then a participant in international car and balloon races. He also flew his own sport plane and gliders, and competed in ski racing and jumping. Since his arrival in the United States he has visited most of the states and national parks and other points of interest.

*     *     *

NOYCE, Gaylord B. 1926-

PERSONAL: Born July 8, 1926, in Burlington, Iowa; son of Ralph Brewster (a clergyman) and Harriet (Norton) Noyce; married Dorothy Caldwell (a school psychologist), May 25, 1949; children: Elizabeth Ann, Karen Virginia, Timothy Brewster. Education: Miami University, Oxford, Ohio, B.A., 1947; Yale University, M.Div., 1952. Home: 56 Morse St., Hamden, Conn. 06517. Office: Divinity School,

Yale University, 409 Prospect St., New Haven, Conn. 06520.

*CAREER:* Clergyman of United Church of Christ; Robert College, Istanbul, Turkey, instructor in mathematics, 1947-49; assistant minister of Congregational church in Lexington, Mass., 1952-54; pastor of community church in Raleigh, N.C., 1954-60; Yale University, Divinity School, New Haven, Conn., assistant professor, 1960-65, associate professor of pastoral theology, 1965—. *Military service:* U.S. Navy, 1944-46.

*WRITINGS: The Church Is Not Expendable,* Westminster, 1969; *The Responsible Suburban Church,* Westminster, 1970; *Survival and Mission for the City Church,* Westminster, 1975.

\*    \*    \*

## NOYES, Charles Edmund   1904-1972

1904—August 2, 1972; American editor, government official, and writer on economics. Obituaries: *New York Times,* August 4, 1972.

\*    \*    \*

## NOYES, Morgan Phelps   1891-1972

March 29, 1891—June 20, 1972; American clergyman, educator, and writer on religious subjects. Obituaries: *New York Times,* June 22, 1972. (See index for *CA* sketch)

\*    \*    \*

## NOYES, Nell Braly   1921-

*PERSONAL:* Born June 27, 1921, in Olden, Tex.; daughter of Samuel Rodgers (a telegrapher) and Ruby (Holton) Braly; married William Edwin Noyes (an Air Force officer and civil servant), June 24, 1950; children: Patrice Elaine, Michael Steven, Sue Ellen, Faye Marie. *Education:* University of Texas, Main University (now University of Texas at Austin), B.A., 1941. *Home:* 2011 Brown, Wichita Falls, Tex. 76309. *Office:* School of Health Care Sciences, United States Air Force, Sheppard Air Force Base, Tex.

*CAREER:* Legal secretary; has worked as editor of weekly newspaper in western Texas, secretary to general manager of American aircraft corporation in Japan, Spanish-English secretary in Latin American department of a New York hotel, and teacher of conversational Spanish in adult education classes; foreign service clerk in Office of Military Attache, American Embassy, Tegucigalpa, Honduras, 1943-45, and Santiago, Chile, 1945-46; Noyes Bookland (Christian book store), Wichita Falls, Tex., owner and manager, 1965-74; United States Air Force, civil service employee in School of Health Care Sciences, Sheppard Air Force Base, Tex., 1974—.

*WRITINGS: Your Future as a Secretary,* Rosen Press, 1963, 2nd edition, 1970; (contributor) James A. Adair, editor, *God's Power to Triumph,* Prentice-Hall, 1965.

*WORK IN PROGRESS: In a Persian Palace,* an historical novel on the life of Queen Esther.

\*    \*    \*

## NOZICK, Martin   1917-

*PERSONAL:* Born June 28, 1917, in New York, N.Y.; son of Solomon (a milliner) and Mary (Seidman) Nozick. *Education:* Brooklyn College (now Brooklyn College of the City University of New York), B.A., 1936; Columbia University, M.A., 1941, Ph.D., 1953. *Home:* 420 East 55th St., New York, N.Y. 10022. *Office:* Ph.D. Program in Spanish, Graduate School and University Center of the City University of New York, Rm. 106, 33 West 42nd St., New York, N.Y. 10036.

*CAREER:* Brooklyn College (now Brooklyn College of the City University of New York), Brooklyn, N.Y., instructor in Romance languages and literature, 1943-46; Colgate University, Hamilton, N.Y., instructor in Romance languages and literature, 1946-47; Oberlin College, Oberlin, Ohio, instructor in Romance languages and literature, 1947-49; Queens College of the City University of New York, Queens, N.Y., professor of Romance languages, 1949-73; Graduate School and University Center of the City University of New York, New York, N.Y., chairman of Ph.D. Program in Spanish, 1973—. *Member:* American Association of Teachers of Spanish and Portuguese, Modern Language Association of America.

*WRITINGS:* (With Beatrice P. Patt) *The Generation of 1898 and After,* Dodd, 1960; (with Patt) *Spanish Literature 1700-1900,* Dodd, 1965; *Miguel de Unamuno,* Twayne, 1971; (compiler with Patt) *Spanish Literature since the Civil War,* Dodd, 1973. Editor of series, "Selected Works of Miguel de Unamuno," for Bollingen and Princeton University Press, 1967—.

\*    \*    \*

## NUNN, Henry L(ightfoot)   1878-1972

1878—September 15, 1972; American business executive and economist. Obituaries: *New York Times,* September 20, 1972.

# O

## OATES, Wallace Eugene 1937-

*PERSONAL:* Born March 21, 1937, in Los Angeles, Calif.; son of Eugene A. (a business executive) and Irene (Young) Oates; married Mary Irby (a college teacher), September 6, 1959; children: Catherine, Christopher, Mary Nora. *Education:* Stanford University, M.A., 1959, Ph.D., 1965. *Home:* 43 Murray Pl., Princeton, N.J. 08540. *Office:* Department of Economics, Princeton University, Princeton, N.J. 08540.

*CAREER:* San Diego State College (now University), San Diego, Calif., instructor in economics, part-time, 1961-62; San Jose State College (now University), San Jose, Calif., instructor in economics, part-time, 1962-65; Princeton University, Princeton, N.J., assistant professor, 1965-71, associate professor, 1971-74, professor of economics, 1974—. *Military service:* U.S. Navy, 1959-62; became lieutenant junior grade. *Member:* American Economic Association, National Tax Association.

*WRITINGS: Fiscal Federalism,* Harcourt, 1972; *Introduction to Econometrics,* Harper, 1974; *The Theory of Environmental Policy,* Prentice-Hall, 1975. Contributor of articles to *American Economic Review, Quarterly Journal of Economics,* and *Journal of Political Economy.*

*WORK IN PROGRESS: Economics, Environmental Policy, and the Quality of Life,* with William Baumol, for Prentice-Hall; a study of state and local government finance.

\*    \*    \*

## O'CONNOR, Patricia Walker 1931-

*PERSONAL:* Born April 26, 1931, in Memphis, Tenn.; daughter of Shade Wilson (a college president) and Lillie (Mullins) Walker; married David Evans O'Connor, April 4, 1953 (divorced, 1965); children: Michael Peter, Erin Anne. *Education:* Attended Florida State University, 1949-51, and University of Havanna, summer, 1949; University of Florida, B.A.E., 1953, M.A., 1954, Ph.D., 1962. *Home:* 727 Dixmyth Ave., Cincinnati, Ohio 45220. *Office:* Department of Romance Languages, University of Cincinnati, Cincinnati, Ohio 45221.

*CAREER:* University of Cincinnati, Cincinnati, Ohio, instructor, 1962-63, assistant professor, 1963-67, associate professor, 1967-72, professor of Romance languages, 1972—. *Member:* Modern Language Association of America, American Association of Teachers of Spanish and Portuguese, American Association of University Professors, Midwest Modern Language Association, Phi Beta Kappa. *Awards, honors:* Taft grants, 1965, 1972; American Philosophical Society grant, 1971.

*WRITINGS: Women in the Theater of Gregorio Martinez Sierra,* American Book Co., 1967; *Gregorio and Maria Martinez Sierra,* Twayne, 1977; (editor with Anthony M. Pasquariello), *El tragaluz,* Scribner, 1977. Contributor to Spanish literature journals. Member of editorial staff, *Modern International Drama, Hispanofila,* and *Anales de la novela de posguerra;* editor, *Estreno* (Spanish theater journal).

*WORK IN PROGRESS:* Research on contemporary Spanish theater, censorship in the theater, women in literature, and the contemporary Spanish novel.

*SIDELIGHTS:* Patricia Walker O'Connor told *CA* that her father was a positive influence in her life. "He was delighted to have a girl [and] did not see sex as a barrier to accomplishment. These are exciting times to be a woman!" *Avocational interests:* Travel through Europe, the Caribbean, Mexico, and Canada.

\*    \*    \*

## O'CONNOR, William E(dmund) 1922-

*PERSONAL:* Born March 26, 1922, in Boston, Mass.; son of William Edward (a teacher) and Marguerite (O'Neill) O'Connor. *Education:* Brown University, A.B., 1942; George Washington University, M.A., 1947; American University, Ph.D., 1970. *Home:* Sandy Park Apartments, No. 619, 1049 Brentwood Dr., Daytona Beach, Fla. 32017. *Office:* Embry-Riddle Aeronautical University, Regional Airport, Daytona Beach, Fla. 32014.

*CAREER:* U.S. Department of State, Washington, D.C., foreign affairs officer, 1944-50; Civil Aeronautics Board, Washington, D.C., foreign affairs analyst, 1951-54, assistant chief of division, 1955-71; Embry-Riddle Aeronautical University, Daytona Beach, Fla., assistant professor, 1972-75, associate professor, 1975—. *Member:* American Society of International Law, Society for International Development, Mensa, Delta Phi Epsilon, Phi Kappa Phi, Pi Sigma Alpha.

*WRITINGS: Economic Regulation of the World's Airlines: A Political Analysis,* Praeger, 1971; *An Introduction to Airline Economics,* Praeger, in press.

## ODAHL, Charles Matson  1944-

*PERSONAL:* Born July 1, 1944, in Fresno, Calif.; son of Albert Charles (a college professor) and Audrey (Weinberg) Odahl; married Linda Kay Vosseler, December 20, 1968; children: Charlynn Anne. *Education:* Fresno State College (now California State University, Fresno), B.A. (summa cum laude), 1966, M.A. (with distinction), 1968; Pacific College, further study, 1966-67; University of California, San Diego, Ph.D., 1976. *Politics:* Independent. *Religion:* Friends. *Home:* 1412 North Fifth St., Boise, Idaho 83702. *Office:* Department of History, Boise State University, Boise, Idaho 83707.

*CAREER:* Palm Springs High School, Palm Springs, Calif., teacher of world history and humanities, 1968-71; Boise State University, Boise, Idaho, assistant professor of ancient and medieval history, 1975—. Has lectured on art and history in high schools and higher institutions, and for cultural clubs. European tour leader for Students Travel Abroad, New York, N.Y., summer, 1969, and Study Tours, Sherman Oaks, Calif., summer, 1971. *Member:* American Historical Association, Society for Ancient Numistics, American Numistic Society, Fellowship of Reconciliation, Society for Church History, Rocky Mountain Medieval and Renaissance Association, Phi Kappa Phi.

*WRITINGS: The Catilinarian Conspiracy,* College & University Press, 1971; *The Western Heritage Explorer,* Study Tours, 1971; (contributor) H. T. Parker, editor, *Problems of Modern European History,* Moore Publishing, 1978. Contributor to *Journal of the Society for Ancient Numismatics.*

*WORK IN PROGRESS: The Gospel or the Sword: A Study in Early Christian Attitudes toward War and Military Service;* two articles.

*AVOCATIONAL INTERESTS:* Collecting Roman coins, European travel, weight training, running, swimming, and camping.

\* \* \*

## ODEN, William E(ugene)  1923-

*PERSONAL:* Born February 26, 1923, in Chickasha, Okla.; son of Carroll Elmer (an independent businessman) and Lonas Elizabeth (Humphrey) Oden; married Francis Xen Harris, June 17, 1950; children: David, Barbara, Sarah. *Education:* Attended Bethany College, Bethany, Okla., 1941-42; University of Oklahoma, B.A., 1946, M.A., 1949; further study at University of Wisconsin, 1950-51; Indiana University, Ph.D., 1957. *Politics:* Democrat. *Religion:* Episcopalian. *Home:* 4614 West 14th St., Lubbock, Tex. 70416. *Office:* Graduate School, Texas Tech University, Lubbock, Tex. 79406.

*CAREER:* Texas Tech University, Lubbock, instructor, 1948-56, assistant professor, 1956-57, associate professor, 1957-65, professor of government, 1965—, director of Texas Tech University Center at Junction, 1971—, associate dean of Graduate School, 1977—. Chairman of Institute of Rural Analysis and Development; president of Guadalupe Neighborhood Center; member of Mayor's Council on United Nations. Consultant to State Legislative Bureau for Constitutional Revision (Texas), 1961. *Member:* American Political Science Association, Southern Political Science Association, Southwestern Social Science Association, Western Political Science Association, Western Social Science Association (president, 1975-76), Rocky Mountain Social Science Association (member of council, 1969-72).

*WRITINGS: Constitutional Revision: A Study of the Texas*

*Constitution,* Texas Legislative Council, 1960; *The Constitution of Texas: Municipal and County Government* (monograph), Arnold Foundation, Southern Methodist University, 1961; (with Dan Nimmo) *The Texas Political System,* Prentice-Hall, 1972.

\* \* \*

## O'DOHERTY, E(amonn) F(elchin)  1918-

*PERSONAL:* Born February 10, 1918, in Dublin, Ireland; son of Seamus and Catherine (Gibbons) O'Doherty. *Education:* University College, Dublin, B.A., 1938, M.A., 1939; Cambridge University, Ph.D., 1945. *Politics:* None. *Home:* 33 Louvain St., Dublin 14, Ireland. *Office:* Faculty of Philosophy, University College, National University of Ireland, Dublin 4, Ireland.

*CAREER:* Roman Catholic priest and honorary prelate; National University of Ireland, University College, Dublin, lecturer, 1945-49, professor of logic and psychology, 1949—, head of department, 1949, dean of Faculty of Philosophy, 1971—. Visiting professor at Catholic University of America, 1962, and Seton Psychiatric Institute, Baltimore, 1962-68; Forwood Lecturer at University of Liverpool, 1965-66. Has lectured extensively on psychological and religious topics in North America, Australia, Africa, and western Europe.

*MEMBER:* British Psychological Society (fellow), Royal Irish Academy (former member of council), International Round Table for the Advancement of Counselling (vice-chairman), Ergonomics Research Society (former member of council).

*WRITINGS:* (Editor with S. Desmond McGrath) *The Priest and Mental Health,* Clonmore & Reynolds, 1962, Alba, 1963; *Religion and Personality Problems,* Alba, 1964; *Vocation, Formation, Consecration and Vows,* Alba, 1971 (published in Ireland in two volumes as *Vocation and Formation* and *Consecration and Vows,* Gill & Macmillan, 1971); *Psychology of Vocation,* Faversham Press, 1972; *The Religious Psychology of the Elementary School Child,* Alba, 1973; *The Religious Psychology of the Adolescent,* Alba, 1973; *Human Psychology,* University College (Dublin), Volumes I and II, 1976, Volume III, 1977; *Religion and Psychology,* Alba, 1978.

\* \* \*

## OGAWA, Dennis Masaaki  1943-

*PERSONAL:* Born September 7, 1943, in Manzanar, Calif.; son of Frank T. and Alice Ogawa. *Education:* University of California, Los Angeles, Ph.D., 1969. *Office:* American Studies Department, University of Hawaii, Honolulu, Hawaii 96822.

*CAREER:* University of Hawaii, Honolulu, member of faculty of American studies, 1971—. Consultant for Japanese American Research Center; State Foundation History and Humanities trustee. *Member:* International Communication Association.

*WRITINGS: From Japs to Japanese,* McCutchan, 1970; *Jan Ken Po,* University Press of Hawaii, 1973; *Kodomo No Tume Ni: For the Sake of Our Children,* University Press of Hawaii, 1977. Contributor of articles to *International Communication Journal, Journal of Black Studies,* and *Race.*

*WORK IN PROGRESS: Interethnic Communication.*

*SIDELIGHTS:* Dennis Masaaki Ogawa wants "to encourage and promote the study of Japanese Americans in the

U.S.,'' and ''to suggest that the human experience of this ethnic group contributes to man's knowledge of himself and society.''

\* \* \*

## O'GORMAN, Richard F. 1928-

PERSONAL: Born July 22, 1928, in St. Louis, Mo.; son of Paul J. and Dorothy (Hogan) O'Gorman; married Rita Bruusgaard, June 30, 1959; children: Nina, Alexandra. Education: Washington University, B.A., 1955, M.A., 1957; University of Pennsylvania, Ph.D., 1962. Home address: R.R. 2, West Branch, Iowa 52358. Office: Department of French and Italian, University of Iowa, Iowa City, Iowa 52240.

CAREER: Indiana University at Bloomington, 1962-67, began as assistant professor, became associate professor of French; University of Iowa, Iowa City, 1967—, currently professor of French and chairman of department of French and Italian. Military service: U.S. Navy, submarine service, 1946-48. Member: Modern Language Association of America, Modern Humanities Research Association, Mediaeval Academy of America. Awards, honors: Senior fellow, National Endowment for the Humanities, 1972-73.

WRITINGS: (With Robert Hellman) Fabliaux, Crowell, 1965. Contributor of articles to Manuscripta, Romance Philology, Romania, Zeitschrift fuer Romanische Philologie, and Revue de l'histoire des textes.

WORK IN PROGRESS: A critical edition of Robert De Boron's Joseph D'Arimathie.

\* \* \*

## OHLINGER, Gustavus 1877-1972

July 15, 1877—June 12, 1972; American lawyer, educator, and author of legal studies. Obituaries: New York Times, June 14, 1972.

\* \* \*

## OHLSEN, Merle M(arvel) 1914-

PERSONAL: Born March 3, 1914, in Willow Lake, S.D.; son of Nick P. (a farmer) and Dora (Riter) Ohlsen; married Helen Oistad, August 5, 1939; children: Marilyn (Mrs. Jacob Saathoff), Linda (Mrs. Allen Ferreira), Barbara (Mrs. Charles Lawe), Ronald M. Education: Winona State Teachers College (now Winona State College), B.E., 1938; University of Illinois, A.M., 1941; University of Iowa, Ph.D., 1946. Politics: Democrat. Religion: Lutheran. Home address: R.R. 22, Box 699, Terre Haute, Ind. 47802. Office: Department of Psychology, Indiana State University, Terre Haute, Ind. 47809.

CAREER: Elementary school teacher in Carpenter, S.D., 1934-35; junior high school science teacher in Winona, Minn., 1938-39; junior high school mathematics teacher in Champaign, Ill., 1939-41; senior high school principal in Sioux Center, Iowa, 1941-43; University of Iowa, Iowa City, instructor in mathematics, 1943-44; senior high school chemistry teacher in Iowa City, Iowa, 1944-45; Washington State University, Pullman, assistant professor, 1945-47, associate professor of education, 1947-50; University of Illinois at Urbana–Champaign, associate professor, 1950-53, professor of educational psychology, 1953-69; Indiana State University, Terre Haute, Holmstedt Distinguished Professor of Guidance and Psychological Services, 1969—. Roy Roberts Distinguished Visiting Professor, University of Missouri—Kansas City, 1967-68. Member of Synod execu-

tive board of the Lutheran Church in America for Illinois, 1965-69, for Indiana, 1972-75. Member: American Psychological Association, American Personnel and Guidance Association (president, 1969-70). Awards, honors: Distinguished alumni award, 1960, from Winona State Teachers College (now Winona State College).

WRITINGS: Guidance: An Introduction, Harcourt, 1955; Modern Methods in Elementary Education, Holt, 1959; Evaluation of Group Techniques in the Secondary Schools, Cornell University Press, 1963; Guidance Services in the Modern School, Harcourt, 1964, 2nd edition, 1974; Group Counseling, Holt, 1970, 2nd edition, 1977; Counseling Children in Groups, Holt, 1973. Contributor of more than ninety articles to education journals.

\* \* \*

## OLIVER, W. Andrew 1941-

PERSONAL: Born October 16, 1941, in Loughborough, England; son of Richard George and Joyce (Faulks) Oliver; married Jane Gosham, August 24, 1963 (divorced, 1971); married Hendrikje Kolkman, April 8, 1972; children: (first marriage) Simon, Matthew. Education: Emmanuel College, Cambridge, B.A., 1963, M.A., 1966; Universite Laval, Ph.D., 1967. Office: Department of French, Trinity College, University of Toronto, Toronto, Ontario, Canada M5S 1H8.

CAREER: University of Toronto, Trinity College, Toronto, Ontario, 1966—, currently professor of French literature. Member: Association des amis d'Andre Gide, Society for French Studies, Canadian Association of University Teachers. Awards, honors: Commonwealth scholarship, 1963-66; Canada Council leave fellowship, 1972-73.

WRITINGS: (Editor) Benjamin Constant, Adolphe, Macmillan (London), 1968; Benjamin Constant: Ecriture et conquete du moi, Minard (Paris), 1970; (editor) Raymond Radiguet, Le Bal du comte d'Orgel, Minard, 1978; (editor) Radiguet, Le Fantome du devoir, Minard, 1978; (editor and contributor) Andre Gide: Perspectives contemporaines, Minard, 1978; Michel, Pierre, Paul, Job: Intertextualite de la lecture dans "L'Immoraliste" d'Andre Gide, Minard, 1978.

WORK IN PROGRESS: Critical editions of Andre Gide's Genevieve and L'Ecole des Femmes.

\* \* \*

## OLSHEWSKY, Thomas M(ack) 1934-

PERSONAL: Born November 20, 1934, in Springfield, Mo.; son of Valentine and Louise Marie (McClellan) Olshewsky; married Vera Eloise Brown, December 27, 1956 (divorced, 1965); married Katherine Hutcheson Bihl (a teacher), October 29, 1966 (divorced, 1974); married Judith Stuart Withers Burris, November, 1977; children: (first marriage) Steven James, Irene Louise, John Courtney; (second marriage) Katherine Elizabeth; (third marriage) Kimberly, James Clinton, Todd. Education: Wabash College, A.B. (cum laude), 1956; New College, Edinburgh, additional study, 1957-58; McCormick Theological Seminary, B.D., 1960; Emory University, Ph.D., 1965; postdoctoral study at State University of New York at Buffalo, 1971 and 1974, and in Athens and Rome, 1976. Politics: Democrat. Office: Department of Philosophy, University of Kentucky, Lexington, Ky. 40506.

CAREER: Presbyterian minister. Parsons College, Fairfield, Iowa, assistant professor of philosophy, 1962-63; Coe

College, Cedar Rapids, Iowa, assistant professor of philosophy, 1963-66; University of Kentucky, Lexington, assistant professor, 1966-69, associate professor of philosophy, 1969—, acting chairperson of department, 1977—, director of graduate studies in philosophy, 1969-71, and 1976-77, chairperson of Arts and Sciences Faculty Council, 1970-72, director of undergraduate studies, 1972-73, chairperson of program in linguistics, 1973—. Church Community Service, member of board of directors, 1967-70, vice-chairman of board, 1969-70.

*MEMBER:* American Philosophical Association, Society for Ancient Greek Philosophy, Mind Association, American Society for Value Inquiry, Society for the Advancement of American Philosophy, Linguistics Society of America, Southern Society for Philosophy and Psychology, Iowa Philosophical Society (secretary, 1965-66), Kentucky Philosophical Society (vice-president, 1970-71; president, 1971-72), Phi Beta Kappa, Tau Kappa Alpha, Eta Sigma Phi. *Awards, honors:* University of Kentucky summer research fellowships, 1967 and 1970; University of Kentucky teacher improvement fellowships, 1974 and 1977.

*WRITINGS:* (Editor) *Problems in the Philosophy of Language,* Holt, 1969. Editor of *The Philosophy of Logical Atomism* and author of *Good Reasons and Persuasive Force: A Manual for Argumentation;* also author of numerous papers presented to learned societies and conferences. Contributor of articles and reviews to philosophy journals.

*WORK IN PROGRESS: Toward Understanding Persons; Language, Thought, and Reality.†*

\* \* \*

## OLSON, Harry F(erdinand) 1901-

*PERSONAL:* Born December 28, 1901, in Mt. Pleasant, Iowa; son of Frans O. (a farmer) and Nelly (Benson) Olson; married Lorene Johnson, June 11, 1935. *Education:* University of Iowa, B.E., 1924, M.S., 1925, Ph.D., 1928, E.E., 1932. *Politics:* Republican. *Religion:* Lutheran. *Home:* 71 Palmer Sq. W., Princeton, N.J. 08540.

*CAREER:* RCA Corp., Princeton, N.J., research scientist, 1928-32; RCA Corp., Camden, N.J., director of acoustical research, 1932-42; RCA Laboratories, Princeton, director of acoustical and electromechanical laboratory, 1942-59, vice-president in acoustical research, 1959-66, consultant, 1966-70. *Member:* Institute of Electrical and Electronic Engineers, Society of Motion Picture Engineers, Acoustical Society of America (president, 1952), Audio Engineering Society (president, 1959), National Academy of Sciences, Sigma Xi, Tau Beta Pi. *Awards, honors:* D.Sc., Iowa Wesleyan College, 1939; John Potts Medal, Audio Engineering Society, 1952; Warner Medal, Society of Motion Picture and Television Engineers, 1955; John Scott Medal, City of Philadelphia, 1956; John Ericson Medal, American Society of Swedish Engineers, 1963; Emile Berliner Award, 1965; Kelly Award, 1967; Consumer Electronics Award, 1969; Lamme Medal, Institute of Electrical and Electronic Engineers, 1970; Silver Medal, Acoustical Society of America, 1974.

*WRITINGS: Dynamical Analogies,* Van Nostrand, 1942; *Acoustical Engineering,* Van Nostrand, 1957; *Musical Engineering,* McGraw, 1960; *Music, Physics and Engineering,* Dover, 1968; *Modern South Reproduction,* Van Nostrand, 1972. Consulting editor, *Encyclopaedia Britannica* and *McGraw-Hill Encyclopedia of Science and Technology.* Editor, *Journal of Audio Engineering Society,* 1960-70; associate editor, *Journal of Acoustical Society of America,* 1942-72.

\* \* \*

## OLSON, James C(lifton) 1917-

*PERSONAL:* Born January 23, 1917, in Bradgate, Iowa; son of Arthur Edwin (a businessman) and Albertina (Anderson) Olson; married Vera B. Farrington, June 6, 1941; children: Elizabeth (Mrs. Steven R. Goldring), Sarah Margaret. *Education:* Morningside College, A.B., 1938; University of Nebraska, M.A., 1939, Ph.D., 1942. *Religion:* Protestant. *Home:* 1900 South Providence Rd., Columbia, Mo. 64110. *Office:* University of Missouri—Kansas City, 5100 Rockhill Rd., Kansas City, Mo. 64110.

*CAREER:* Northwest Missouri State Teachers College (now Northwest Missouri State University), Maryville, instructor in history, summers, 1940-42; University of Nebraska, Lincoln, lecturer, 1946-54, associate professor, 1954-56, professor, 1956-58, Martin Professor of History, 1962-65, chairman of department, 1956-65, associate dean of Graduate College, 1965-66, dean, 1966-68, vice-chancellor for graduate studies and research, 1968; University of Missouri—Kansas City, chancellor, 1968-76, interim president, 1976-77, president, 1977—. Lecturer, Municipal University of Omaha (now University of Nebraska at Omaha), 1947-50; visiting professor at College of Mexico, 1962, and University of Colorado, summer, 1965. Consultant to U.S. Air Force and U.S. Department of Defense. Director, Nebraska State Historical Society, 1946-56; member of board of directors, State Federal & Loan Association, Standard Milling Co., and United Telecommunications, Inc.; chairman of board of directors, Mid-America Arts Alliance; president of Missouri Council on Public Higher Education; vice-president of Kansas City Public Television 19, Inc.; member of board of trustees, Midwest Research Institute. Member of College of Electors, Hall of Fame for Great Americans, Nebraska Hall of Agricultural Achievement, Nelson Gallery Foundation, and William R. Nelson Trust. Group secretary, Great Plains Conference on Higher Education, 1956; participant in National Security Forum, Air War College, Air University, 1957. Participated in "The Great Plains Trilogy," a series for Educational Radio and Television Center. *Military service:* U.S. Army Air Forces, 1942-46; became first lieutenant.

*MEMBER:* American Association for State and Local History (member of council, 1948-56; regional vice-president, 1956-62; president, 1962-64), American Association of University Professors (vice-president of University of Nebraska chapter, 1958-59), Association of Urban Universities (vice-president, 1972-73; president, 1973-75), American Historical Association, Council for Basic Education (charter member), Organization of American Historians (secretary-treasurer, 1953-57; member of executive committee, 1963-66), Harry S Truman Library Institute (member of board of directors), Western History Association, Nebraska History and Social Studies Teachers Association (president, 1957-58), Nebraska Writers Guild (president, 1951-53), Nebraska State Historical Society (member of executive board, 1957-68; president, 1962-68; honorary life member), Mississippi Valley Historical Association (secretary-treasurer, 1953-56), Kansas City Museum Association (member of board of trustees), Kansas City Museum of Science and Industry (member of board of governors), Phi Beta Kappa, Phi Kappa Phi, Pi Gammu Mu, Omicron Delta Kappa, Rotary Club of Columbia, Missouri. *Awards, honors:* Annual award, Alpha Epsilon Rho (national honorary radio-television fraternity),

1955; Montana Heritage Award, State Historical Society of Montana, 1958; Woods faculty fellowship, University of Nebraska, 1959-60; LL.D., Morningside College, 1968.

*WRITINGS: J. Sterling Morton,* University of Nebraska Press, 1942, reprinted, 1972; (with George E. Condra and Royce Knapp) *The Nebraska Story,* University Publishing Co., 1951; (contributor) W. F. Craven and J. L. Cate, editors, *The Army Air Forces in World War II,* University of Chicago Press, Volume II, 1951, Volume V, 1953; (editor and author of introduction) James H. Kyner, *End of Track,* University of Nebraska Press, 1961; *History of Nebraska,* University of Nebraska Press, 1955, 2nd edition, 1966; (with wife, Vera Farrington Olson) *Nebraska Is My Home,* University Publishing Co., 1956, 2nd edition, 1965; (with V. F. Olson) *This Is Nebraska,* University Publishing Co., 1960, 2nd edition, 1968; *Red Cloud and the Sioux Problem,* University of Nebraska Press, 1965. Author of several columns appearing in Nebraska newspapers, 1946-56. Contributor to *Encyclopedia Americana, Encyclopaedia Britannica, Collier's Encyclopedia,* and *World Book Encyclopedia;* contributor of articles and reviews to history journals. Editor, *Nebraska History,* 1946-56; member of editorial board, *Mississippi Valley Historical Review.*

*       *       *

## O'MALLEY, Joseph James   1930-

*PERSONAL:* Born October 20, 1930, in Chicago, Ill.; son of Joseph Nugent (a meatcutter) and Alice (King) O'Malley; married Ruth Serrao, April 16, 1961; children: Ruth, Joseph, James, Deborah. *Education:* Loyola University (Chicago), B.A., 1960; Marquette University, Ph.D., 1965. *Home:* 3617 North Maryland Ave., Shorewood, Wis. 53211. *Office:* Department of Philosophy, Marquette University, Milwaukee, Wis. 53233.

*CAREER:* Alverno College, Milwaukee, Wis., part-time instructor, 1964-65; Marquette University, Milwaukee, instructor, 1965-68, assistant professor, 1968-72, associate professor of philosophy, 1972—, assistant chairman, 1968-74, chairman of department, 1974-77. *Military service:* U.S. Naval Reserve, 1953-57. *Member:* American Catholic Philosophical Association, Metaphysical Society of America, Hegel Society of America (member of executive council, 1971-72; secretary, 1972-74), Society for the Study of Neoplatonic Philosophy, International Society for Metaphysics.

*WRITINGS:* (Editor and translator) Karl Marx, *Critique of Hegel's "Philosophy of Right,"* Cambridge University Press, 1970; (contributor) S. Avineri, editor, *Varieties of Marxism,* Nijhoff, 1977. Contributor to *Revue des questions scientifiques, Review of Politics, Political Studies,* and *International Review of Social History.*

*WORK IN PROGRESS:* Research in socio-political thought of Marx and Hegel.

*       *       *

## O'NEILL, William   1927-

*PERSONAL:* Born October 16, 1927, in London, England; son of William (an engineer) and Maud (Crowley) O'Neill; married Roberta Hisu (an administrative secretary), October 27, 1962; children: Brendan Lopaka, Shivaun Alika. *Education:* King's College, London, B.A. (first class honours in Classics), 1947; University College, London, M.A. (with distinction), 1956; University of Liverpool, Ph.D., 1961; Graduate Theological Union, M.A.T., 1974. *Politics:* Democrat. *Religion:* Catholic. *Home:* 286 30th St., San Francisco, Calif. 94131.

*CAREER:* University of Wellington, Wellington, New Zealand, assistant professor of classics, 1957-59; University of Southern California, Los Angeles, assistant professor of ancient and medieval philosophy, 1961-64; Graduate Theological Union, Institute of Lay Theology, Berkeley, Calif., lecturer in existentialism, 1968-72. Lecturer in classics, philosophy, history, and music, Berkeley Extension, University of California, San Francisco, 1967-70; professor of world philosophy, International Pioneer Academy, San Francisco, 1971-72. Member of education committee, Academy of World Studies, 1972-76.

*WRITINGS:* (Translator and author of commentary) *Proclus: Alcibiades I,* Nijhoff, 1965, 2nd edition, 1971; (contributor) Rosamond Kent Sprague, editor, *Translations of the Sophists,* University of South Carolina Press, 1973. Contributor of articles to *Phronesis, New Catholic Encyclopedia, Vivarium, The Personalist,* and *Revue des etudes Augustiniennes.* Editor, *The Wonersh Magazine,* 1949-50.

*WORK IN PROGRESS: Augustine: Philosophical Texts Translated; The Social and Political Thought of Washington, Adams, Jefferson, and John Quincy Adams;* abridgements and modern versions of mystical works; theological papers on clericalism and Christianity, lay persons and clerics, and community and charity.

*SIDELIGHTS:* William O'Neill is interested in contemporary existentialism, classical New Orleans jazz, and western mysticism, especially the early English mystics. He told *CA* that he "has been involved in liturgy groups and adult religious education," and sees "a great need for contemporary theology."

*       *       *

## OPPENHEIMER, Joan L(etson)   1925-

*PERSONAL:* Born January 25, 1925, in Ellendale, N.D.; daughter of Maurice Devillo (a teacher) and Lola (Jones) Letson; married Robert Gridley, April 10, 1943 (divorced, 1953); married Elwyn S. Oppenheimer, June 19, 1953; children: (first marriage) Donald B., Jeffrey L.; (second marriage) Debra L. *Education:* Attended Northwestern University, 1944, and Southwestern College, 1966-70. *Politics:* Democrat. *Religion:* Protestant. *Home:* 1663 Mills St., Chula Vista, Calif. 92010. *Agent:* Jay Garon-Brooke Associates, 415 Central Park West, 17D, New York, N.Y. 10025. *Office:* Department of English, Southwestern College, Chula Vista, Calif. 92010.

*CAREER:* First National Bank, Chicago, Ill., clerk, 1942-43; Federal Bureau of Investigation (FBI), Chicago, stenographer, 1943-45; U.S. Gauge Co., Chicago, secretary, 1945; Lever Brothers, Chicago, secretary, 1946; Rohr Corp., secretary, 1952-53; Southwestern College, Chula Vista, Calif., instructor in creative writing, 1977—.

*WRITINGS—For young people: The Coming Down Time,* Transition Press, 1969; *Run for Your Luck,* Hawthorn, 1971; *The Nobody Road,* TAB Books, 1974; *On the Outside, Looking In,* TAB Books, 1975; *Francesca, Baby,* TAB Books, 1976; *The Lost Summer,* TAB Books, 1977; *The Millionairess,* Scholastic Books, 1978; *Walk beside Me, Be My Friend,* Scholastic Books, 1978; *One Step Apart,* Tempo Books, 1978; *No Laughing Matter,* Tempo Books, 1978. Stories included in anthologies: *Today's Stories from Seventeen,* Macmillan, 1971; *Short Story Scene,* Globe, 1974; *Dreamstalkers,* Economy Co., 1975; *Oceans and Orbits,* Laidlaw Brothers, 1977. Contributor to popular magazines, including *Redbook, Woman's Day, Extension, Seventeen, Ingenue, Co-Ed, Boys' Life, Chatelaine,* and *Alfred Hitchcock Mystery Magazine.*

*SIDELIGHTS:* Joan L. Oppenheimer told *CA:* "I began writing for young people [ages 10 to 18] because it is a group facing so many serious problems in today's world. I felt strongly that a young reader might be interested in a fictional character facing a problem, learning to cope and perhaps gaining some insight into possible solutions.

"Whenever I can, I go to the young people involved with the problems I cover in fiction (drugs, alcohol, broken homes, foster homes, etc.) and get their own views. This can cover anything from family to friends to school to the way they see the world today. When I have enough material to live comfortably in a teenaged mind for several months, I am ready to write the book already in rough outline.

"The feedback from these books has been tremendous. My young readers seem to appreciate honesty in the handling of problems they are already familiar with. They develop a greater understanding of these problems and of others who struggle with them—and they write to tell me so. In my opinion, these letters are one of the greatest rewards in writing for young people."

Both *Francesca, Baby* and *The Millionairess* have been made into ABC-TV afternoon specials. *Francesca, Baby,* the story of two young girls and their alcoholic mother, is being distributed as an educational tool by Walt Disney Productions. "It is marvelous to know that it can help children cope with this tremendous problem," Joan Oppenheimer commented. "And it obviously helps children understand others who are less fortunate than they in such home situations. I am, therefore, a writer who frequently weeps over her fan mail!"

*BIOGRAPHICAL/CRITICAL SOURCES: Star-News* (National City, Calif.), August 21, 1969; Philadelphia *Inquirer,* January 9, 1972.

\* \* \*

## O'QUINN, Hazel Hedick

*PERSONAL:* Born in Austin, Tex.; daughter of John David (a state employee) and Era (Allen) Hedick; married Trueman E. O'Quinn (an associate justice in Texas court of civil appeals), November 26, 1929; children: Kerry Hedick, Trueman E., Jr. *Education:* University of Texas, Main University (now University of Texas at Austin), B.A., 1926. *Politics:* "Generally Democrat." *Religion:* Methodist. *Home:* 2300 Windsor Rd. E., Austin, Tex. 78703.

*CAREER:* Has worked as an advertising copy-writer and as assistant secretary of the state senate of Texas. *Member:* Austin State Official Ladies's Club, Austin Lawyers' Wives' Club, Theta Sigma Phi.

*WRITINGS: Rhyming at the Kitchen Sink,* Jenkins Publishing, 1971. Also compiler of *Texas Legislative Manual,* 1964. Contributor of stories to newspapers.

*WORK IN PROGRESS: The Stories Pop Told.*

*SIDELIGHTS:* Hazel Hedick O'Quinn told *CA* that she found herself "writing more and more rhymes, usually with a humorous twist, for gift cards, thank you notes...." She put them together to form *Rhyming at the Kitchen Sink.*

\* \* \*

## ORGAN, Troy Wilson 1912-

*PERSONAL:* Born October 25, 1912, in Edgar, Neb.; son of William Roscoe and Millie (Sugden) Organ; married Lorena May Dunlap, June 28, 1937; children: Kent, Nancy (Mrs. William O. Paton). *Education:* Hastings College, B.A.,

1934; McCormick Theological Seminary, B.D., 1937; State College of Iowa (now University of Northern Iowa), M.A., 1939, Ph.D., 1941; University of Hawaii, postdoctoral study, 1949. *Home:* 65 Second St., Athens, Ohio 45701.

*CAREER:* Parsons College, Fairfield, Iowa, assistant professor and assistant dean, 1941-44, associate professor of philosophy and acting dean, 1944-45; University of Akron, Akron, Ohio, professor of philosophy, 1945-46; Pennsylvania College for Women (now Chatham College), Pittsburgh, Pa., professor of philosophy, 1946-54; Ohio University, Athens, professor of philosophy, 1954-77. *Member:* American Philosophical Association, Indian Philosophical Congress, Ohio Philosophical Association (president, 1961-64). *Awards, honors:* Ford Foundation fellowship, 1952; Fulbright senior research grants to India, 1958-59, 1965-66; Baker Fund Award, 1965.

*WRITINGS: An Index to Aristotle,* Princeton University Press, 1949; *The Examined Life,* Houghton, 1956; *The Self in Indian Philosophy,* Mouton, 1964; *The Art of Critical Thinking,* Houghton, 1965; *The Hindu Quest for the Perfection of Man,* Ohio University Press, 1970; *Hinduism: Its Historical Development,* Barron's, 1974; *Western Approaches to Eastern Philosophy,* Ohio University, 1975.

\* \* \*

## ORNATI, Oscar A(braham) 1922-

*PERSONAL:* Born July 11, 1922, in Trieste, Italy; came to United States in 1939, naturalized citizen, 1943; son of Julius (a businessman) and Anna (Klar) Ornati; married Winifred Benes, 1946; children: Lee, Susan, Molly. *Education:* Hobart College, B.A., 1949; Harvard University, M.A., 1950, Ph.D., 1955. *Politics:* Democrat. *Religion:* Jewish. *Home:* 147 Edgars Lane, Hastings-on-Hudson, N.Y. 10706. *Office:* Department of Management, Graduate School of Business, New York University, 100 Trinity, New York, N.Y. 10003.

*CAREER:* Cornell University, New York State School of Industrial and Labor Relations, Ithaca, N.Y., assistant professor of economics, 1952-57; New School for Social Research, New York City, associate professor, 1957-61, professor of economics, 1961-66; New York University, New York City, professor of economics and management, 1966—. Visiting professor in Trieste, Italy, 1955-56. Principal, Arthur Young & Co., 1973-78. Chief of economic development, Office of Economic Opportunities (OEO), 1965-66. Vice-president, Humanic Designs Corp., Manhasset, N.Y., 1969-73. Appointed to New York State Task Force on Poverty; director, National Committee on American Foreign Policy; director, Council on Municipal Performance. Consultant to Human Relations Area Files, India, 1955, and to First Minister of Republic of Indonesia, 1960; arbitrator in public and private labor disputes. *Military service:* U.S. Army, interpreter for Allied Military Government in Italy, 1943-46; received Order of the British Empire. *Member:* American Economic Association, Industrial Research Association.

*WRITINGS: Jobs and Workers in India,* Cornell University Press, 1955; *Poverty Amid Affluence,* Twentieth Century Fund, 1965; *Transportation Needs of the Poor,* Praeger, 1971; (with Katzell, Yamkelovich, Fein, and Nash) *Work, Productivity and Job Satisfaction,* Harcourt, 1975. Also author of *E.E.O.: Avoiding Compliance Headaches,* and *How to Eliminate Discriminatory Practices: A Guide to EEO Compliance.* Contributor of numerous articles to professional journals.

## ORRELL, John (Overton) 1934-

*PERSONAL:* Surname rhymes with "quarrel"; born December 31, 1934, in Maidstone, England; son of William Ramsden (a chemist) and Mabel (Hallam) Orrell; married Wendy Phillips, June 23, 1956; children: Katherine, David. *Education:* University College, Oxford, B.A., 1958, M.A., 1964; University of Toronto, M.A., 1959, Ph.D., 1964. *Home:* 11423 58th Ave., Edmonton, Alberta, Canada. *Office:* Department of English, University of Alberta, Edmonton, Alberta, Canada.

*CAREER:* University of Alberta, Edmonton, 1961—, currently professor of English. *Military service:* Royal Air Force, National Service, 1953-55.

*WRITINGS:* (Editor) *Studies of Major Works in English,* Oxford University Press, 1968; (editor) John Sandilands, *Western Canadian Dictionary and Phrase Book,* University of Alberta Press, 1977. Writer of documentary television and film scripts for Canadian Broadcasting Corp. and educational television. Contributor of articles to journals in his field.

*WORK IN PROGRESS: The Theatre Plans of Inigo Jones;* work on Shakespeare's Globe Theatre in the context of Elizabethan building and architecture.

\* \* \*

## ORSINI, Joseph E(mmanuel) 1937-

*PERSONAL:* Born June 1, 1937, in Bayonne, N.J.; son of Giuseppe (a laborer) and Carmela (Amore) Orsini. *Education:* Seton Hall University, B.A., 1960, M.A., 1965; Rutgers University, Ed.D., 1973. *Religion:* Roman Catholic. *Home:* 42 West 50 St., Bayonne, N.J. 07002. *Office:* Campus Ministry, Rutgers University, New Brunswick, N.J.

*CAREER:* Entered priesthood in Diocese of Camden, N.J., ordained Roman Catholic priest, 1964; Camden Catholic High School, Cherry Hill, N.J., philosophy teacher, 1964-68; Paul VI High School, Haddon Heights, N.J., religion teacher, 1968-70; Don Bosco College, Newton, N.J., professor of education, 1970-72; Church of St. Edward, Pine Hill, N.J., Diocese of Camden, associate pastor, 1972-77; Rutgers University, New Brunswick, N.J., member of campus ministry and associate director of Charismatic Renewal, 1977—. National chaplain of Unico National (Italian-American professional organization), 1965—.

*WRITINGS: Hear My Confession: A Catholic Priest Finds Power in Christianity,* Logos International, 1971, revised edition (includes *The Anvil;* see below), 1976; *An Educational History of the Pentecostal Movement,* Rutgers University, 1973; *The Anvil,* Logos International, 1974; *Papa Bear's Favorite Italian Dishes,* Logos International, 1976; *The Cost in Pentecost,* Logos International, 1977.

*SIDELIGHTS:* Joseph E. Orsini's *Hear My Confession* has sold over 250,000 copies and has been translated into Spanish, Italian, and Chinese. He has appeared on the "Mike Douglas Show."

\* \* \*

## ORWEN, (Phillips) Gifford

*PERSONAL:* Born in Rochester, N.Y.; son of William Rodman (an insurance agent) and Florence E. (Miller) Orwen; married Mary Ryan (a painter), May 3, 1947; children: Michael. *Education:* University of Rochester, A.B., A.M.; Cornell University, Ph.D., 1937. *Religion:* Episcopa-

lian. *Home:* 66 Center St., Geneseo, N.Y. 14454. *Office:* Foreign Language Department, State University of New York College, Geneseo, N.Y. 14454.

*CAREER:* U.S. Department of State, Washington, D.C., worked at Italian desk, 1946-48; U.S. Department of Defense, Washington, D.C., administrator, 1948-60; Bethany College, Bethany, W.Va., professor, 1960-62; State University of New York College at Geneseo, 1962—, currently professor and chairman of foreign language department. President, Geneseo Community Chest, 1965-68; chairman, Livingston County Heart Fund drive. *Military service:* U.S. Army, 1941-45. *Member:* Dante Society, Modern Language Association of America, American Association of University Professors, American Association of Teachers of French, American Association of Teachers of Italian, National Committee for Promotion of Italian in Higher Education, State University of New York Faculty Association (chairman of foreign language section, 1962-66). *Awards, honors:* Cornell-Strasbourg fellowship, 1936; New York State Research Foundation grant, 1966-68.

*WRITINGS: Italian Reference Grammar,* King's Crown Press, 1943; *Introduction to Italian,* S. F. Vanni, 1966, 2nd edition, 1971; *Upgrade Your Italian,* S. F. Vanni, 1970; *Handbook of French Phonetics,* State University of New York College at Geneseo, 1976; *A Study of Cecco Angiolieri,* University of North Carolina, in press. Contributor of articles to *French Review, Italica, Modern Language Journal.*

*WORK IN PROGRESS: Introduction to Italian Poetry; J. F. Regnard, A Study.*

*AVOCATIONAL INTERESTS:* Music, travel, and collecting pre-Columbian art.

\* \* \*

## OST, John William Philip 1931-

*PERSONAL:* Born February 14, 1931, in Brooklyn, N.Y.; son of John Hans (a machinist) and Johanna (Stoehr) Ost; married Nina Abrahams, December, 1954 (divorced, 1967); married Janice Valdora Humphrey, November 27, 1967; children: (first marriage) Daniel, Martha, J. Michael, Jessica; (second marriage) Joseph, Jane, Jennet. *Education:* Duke University, B.A., 1953, Ph.D., 1960; North Carolina State College, additional study, 1956-57. *Politics:* Democrat. *Religion:* Lutheran.

*CAREER:* Indiana University at Bloomington, member of psychology faculty, 1962-69; Northern Michigan University, Marquette, associate professor and head of department, 1969-72, professor of psychology, beginning 1972. Founder and advisor of Christian Helpers Interested in Retarded People (CHIRP), Marquette, Mich. *Military service:* U.S. Navy, 1953-56; became lieutenant commander. *Member:* American Psychological Association, Psychonomic Society, Sigma Xi.

*WRITINGS: Psychology: A Laboratory Manual,* Academic Press, 1969. Contributor to psychology journals.

*WORK IN PROGRESS: Psychology of Learning and Cognition.*††

\* \* \*

## OSTROM, Thomas M. 1936-

*PERSONAL:* Born March 1, 1936, in Mishawaka, Ind.; son of Alfred S. and Marion (Eggleston) Ostrom; married Diana Forrest, August 30, 1958; children: Lisa, Steven. *Education:*

Wabash College, A.B., 1958; University of North Carolina at Chapel Hill, Ph.D., 1964. *Office:* Department of Psychology, Ohio State University, 404-C West 17th, Columbus, Ohio 43210.

*CAREER:* Ohio State University, Columbus, 1964—, currently professor of psychology. *Member:* American Psychological Association, American Association for the Advancement of Science.

*WRITINGS:* (Co-editor with A. Greenwald and T. Brock) *Psychological Foundations of Attitudes,* Academic Press, 1968. Contributor to *Journal of Personality and Social Psychology, Journal of Experimental Social Psychology, Journal of Applied Social Psychology.*

*WORK IN PROGRESS:* Two books, *Attitude Theory* and *Research Methods.*

\* \* \*

**OTTEN, Terry (Ralph) 1938-**

*PERSONAL:* Born April 15, 1938, in Dayton, Ky.; son of Henry Howard and Alyce (Lucille) Otten; married (Linda) Jane Sharp, August 20, 1960; children: Keith Andrew, Julie Anne. *Education:* Georgetown University, A.B. (cum laude), 1959; University of Kentucky, M.A., 1961; Ohio University, Ph.D., 1966. *Home:* 104 East Third St., Springfield, Ohio 45504. *Office:* English Department, Wittenberg University, Springfield, Ohio 45501.

*CAREER:* Western Kentucky State College (now Western Kentucky University), Bowling Green, instructor in English, 1961-63; Ohio University, Athens, instructor in English, 1963-66; Wittenberg University, Springfield, Ohio, 1966—, began as associate professor, currently professor of English. *Member:* National Council of Teachers of English, Common Cause, Modern Language Association of America, Byron Society, Ohio English Association. *Awards, honors:* National Endowment for the Humanities research grant, 1972; Wittenberg University Distinguished Teacher award, 1975.

*WRITINGS: The Deserted Stage: The Search for Dramatic Form in Nineteenth-Century England,* Ohio University Press, 1972. Contributor of critical essays to *Journal of Aesthetics, Comparative Drama, Discourse, Renascence, Research Studies, South Atlantic Quarterly, Bucknell Review, College Literature,* and other scholarly journals.

*WORK IN PROGRESS:* A study of the relationship between tragedy and serious melodramas in Western literature; a study of nineteenth-century narrative poetry; a study of the myth of "The Fall" in modern literature.

\* \* \*

**OWEN, Reginald 1887-1972**

August 5, 1887—November 5, 1972; English stage and film actor, novelist, and playwright. Obituaries: *New York Times,* November 7, 1972.

\* \* \*

**OWEN, Wilfred 1912-**

*PERSONAL:* Born December 19, 1912, in Birmingham, England. *Education:* Harvard University, A.B., 1934. *Home:* 4539 32nd Rd. N., Arlington, Va. 22207. *Office:* Brookings Institution, 1775 Massachusetts Ave. N.W., Washington, D.C. 20036.

*CAREER:* Brookings Institution, Washington, D.C., senior fellow, 1946—. Adviser on transport, Conference on Natural Resources of Organization of American States, Cuba, 1958; member of transport survey mission, Government of Japan, 1956; adviser to planning commission, Government of Pakistan, 1958, 1960; adviser to Waseda University and Tokyo University, director of task force on transport policy of the U.S. Secretary of Commerce, and coordinator of meeting on transportation of the United Nations Economic Commission for Asia and the Far East, Bangkok, 1960; adviser on transportation, World Bank Transport Survey, Columbia, 1961; U.S. delegate to United Nations Conference on Science and Technology, Geneva, 1963; member, World Bank Economic Mission to India, 1964-65, 1966, 1969; member of urban transport committee, Office of Science and Technology, Organization for Economic Co-operation and Development, 1967—; chairman of steering committee for Southeast Asia Transport Survey, Asian Development Bank, Manila, 1968-71; member of committee on transportation, National Academy of Engineering, 1971—; general rapporteur and U.S. delegate, Conference on Transportation, Urban Development and Environment of the Economic Commission of Europe, June, 1976; chairman, National Academy of Sciences panel on urbanization, transportation, and communications of the United Nations Conference on Science and Technology for Development, 1979. Consultant to U.S. Bureau of the Budget, 1962, United Nations Economic Commission for Asia and the Far East, Bangkok, 1963, and Economic Development Institute and Urban Projects Department of World Bank, 1972.

*WRITINGS: Automotive Transportation,* Brookings Institution, 1948; *National Transportation Policy,* Brookings Institution, 1969; (with Charles L. Dearing) *Toll Roads and the Problem of Highway Modernization,* Brookings Institution, 1951; *The Metropolitan Transportation Problem,* Brookings Institution, 1956, revised edition, 1966; *Cities in the Motor Age,* Viking, 1959; *Strategy for Mobility: Transportation for the Developing Countries,* Brookings Institution, 1964; (with Ezra Bowen) *Wheels,* Life Science Books, 1967; *Distance and Development: Transport and Communications in India,* Brookings Institution, 1968; *The Accessible City,* Brookings Institution, 1972; *Transportation for Cities,* Brookings Institution, 1976. Also author of *Urban Planet,* in press.

\* \* \*

**OWINGS, Loren C(lyde) 1928-**

*PERSONAL:* Born September 29, 1928, in San Fernando, Calif.; son of Claude H. and Hedwig (Zellmann) Owings; married Elizabeth Ann Leonard, August 9, 1961; children: Rebecca Ann, Suzannah Beth, Johanna Mary. *Education:* University of California, Berkeley, A.B., 1953, M.A., 1957, M.L.S., 1963. *Politics:* Democratic. *Home address:* Route 1, Box 2340, Davis, Calif. 95616. *Office:* University Library, University of California, Davis, Calif. 95616.

*CAREER:* Junior high school teacher of social studies in Lompoc, Calif., 1961-62; University of California, Davis, Library, loan librarian, 1963-69, collection development librarian, 1969—. Editorial consultant, AMS Press, 1971-72, and *Agricultural History. Military service:* U.S. Army, 1954-56. *Member:* Organization of American Historians, Agricultural History Society, Wilderness Society, Sierra Club.

*WRITINGS: The American Communitarian Tradition: A Guide to the Sources in the University of California, Davis, Library,* University Library, University of California, Davis, 1971; *Environmental Values, 1860-1972,* Gale, 1976.

*WORK IN PROGRESS: Quest for Walden: The "Country Book" in American Popular Literature.*

# P

## PACKER, Arnold H. 1935-

*PERSONAL:* Born February 26, 1935, in Brooklyn, N.Y.; son of Bernard I. and Lillian (Goldman) Packer; married Marcia Jacobs, June 16, 1956; children: Martin, Debrin, Lawrence. *Education:* Brooklyn Polytechnic Institute, B.M.E., 1956; Sacramento State College (now California State University, Sacramento), M.S.B.A., 1965; University of North Carolina, Ph.D., 1969. *Home:* 2921 Tilden St. N.W., Washington, D.C. 20008. *Office:* U.S. Department of Labor, 200 Constitution Ave. N.W., Washington, D.C. 20210.

*CAREER:* Aerojet-General Corp., Sacramento, Calif., information systems analyst, 1961-65; Research Triangle Institute, Research Triangle Park, N.C., project leader, 1965-69; Office of Management and Budget, Washington, D.C., member of director's staff, 1969-71; Committee for Economic Development, Washington, D.C., staff economist, 1971-74; U.S. Senate, Committee on the Budget, Washington, D.C., chief economist, 1974-77; U.S. Department of Labor, Washington, D.C., assistant secretary for policy, evaluation, and research, 1977—. *Member:* American Economic Association, Operations Research Society (chairman of educational sciences section, 1972-73), Econometric Society, Institute of Management Science.

*WRITINGS: Models of Economic Systems: A Theory for Their Development and Use,* M.I.T. Press, 1972. Contributor of articles to *American Economic Review, Journal of the Operations Research Society,* and *Review of Economics and Statistics.*

*WORK IN PROGRESS:* Research on national priorities.

\*        \*        \*

## PACKER, Herbert L(eslie) 1925-1972

*PERSONAL:* Born July 24, 1925, in Jersey City, N.J.; married Nancy Huddleston (a university professor), March 15, 1958; children: Ann Elizabeth, George Huddleston. *Education:* Yale University, B.A., 1944, J.D., 1949. *Politics:* Democrat. *Religion:* None. *Home:* 807 San Francisco Ter., Stanford, Calif. 94305. *Office:* School of Law, Stanford University, Stanford, Calif. 94305.

*CAREER:* Attorney associated with Washington, D.C. firm; Stanford University, Stanford, Calif., assistant professor, 1956-57, associate professor, 1957-59, professor, 1959-71, Jackson Eli Reynolds Professor of Law, 1971-72, vice-provost, 1967-69. Member of Attorney General's Committee on Poverty and Administration of Federal Criminal Justice, 1961-63; chairman of committee for credential revocation procedures, California State Board of Education, 1962-63; contributor to revision of California penal code, 1964-69. *Military service:* U.S. Navy, 1944-46. *Member:* American Law Institute, Elizabethan Club (Yale University), Mory's Association (Yale University), Phi Beta Kappa. *Awards, honors:* Ford Foundation fellow, 1960-61; Rockefeller Foundation fellow, 1963-64; American Council of Learned Societies fellow, 1963-64; Order of the Coif triennial award, 1970, for *The Limits of the Criminal Sanction;* Guggenheim fellowship, 1971.

*WRITINGS: Ex-Communist Witnesses: Four Studies in Fact Finding,* Stanford University Press, 1962; *The State of Research in Anti-Trust Law,* Walter Meyer Institute of Law, 1963; *The Limits of the Criminal Sanction,* Stanford University Press, 1968; (with Thomas Ehrlich) *New Directions in Legal Education,* McGraw, 1972, abridged edition, 1973. Contributor to *American Scholar, Commentary, New Republic,* and *New York Review of Books,* among other periodicals.

*WORK IN PROGRESS:* A history of the U.S. Court of Appeals for the Second Circuit; a biography of Jerome Frank, tentatively entitled, *The Intellectual as Activist.*

*BIOGRAPHICAL/CRITICAL SOURCES: New Republic,* January 4, 1969; *Nation,* April 21, 1969; *New York Times,* December 8, 1972; *Washington Post,* December 15, 1972.†

(Died December 6, 1972)

\*        \*        \*

## PAL, Pratapaditya 1935-

*PERSONAL:* Born September 1, 1935, in Sylhet, India (now Bangladesh); son of Gopesh Chandra (a businessman) and Bidyut Kana (Dam) Pal; married Chitralekha Bose, April 20, 1968; children: Shalmali. *Education:* Delhi University, B.A. (honors), 1956; Calcutta University, M.A., 1958, D.Phil., 1962; Corpus Christi College, Cambridge, Ph.D., 1965. *Residence:* Los Angeles, Calif. *Office:* Los Angeles County Museum of Art, 5905 Wilshire Blvd., Los Angeles, Calif. 90036.

*CAREER:* Museum of Fine Arts, Boston, Mass., keeper of Indian collections, 1967-69; Los Angeles County Museum of

Art, Los Angeles, Calif., curator of Indian and Islamic art, 1970—. Lecturer at Harvard University, 1968-69, and University of Southern California, 1970—. *Member:* Asiatic Society (Calcutta), Royal Asiatic Society (London), Asia Society (New York), American Committee for the History of South Asian Art, Tibetan Foundation (member of board of directors).

*WRITINGS: Ragamala Paintings in the Museum of Fine Arts,* [Boston], 1967; *The Art of Tibet,* Asia Society and New York Graphic Society, 1969; (with H. C. Tseng) *Lamaist Art,* Boston Museum of Fine Art and New York Graphic Society, 1969; (with Jan Fontein) *Oriental Art,* Boston Museum of Fine Art and New York Graphic Society, 1969; *Vaisnava Iconology in Nepal,* Asiatic Society (Calcutta), 1970; *Indo-Asian Art,* Walters Art Gallery Library, 1971; *Krishna: The Cowherd King,* Los Angeles County Museum of Art, 1972; (editor) *Aspects of Indian Art,* Los Angeles County Museum of Art, 1972; (editor) Katherine Otto-Dorn and others, *Islamic Art: The Nasli M. Heeramaneck Collection,* Los Angeles County Museum of Art, 1973; *The Arts of Nepal,* E. J. Brill, Volume I: *Sculpture,* 1974; *Bronzes of Kashmir,* Hacker, 1974; *Buddhist Art in Licchavi, Nepal,* Los Angeles County Museum of Art, 1974; *Nepal: Where the Gods Are Young,* Asia Publishing House, 1975; (with Catherine Glynn) *The Sensuous Line: Indian Drawings from the Paul F. Walter Collection,* Los Angeles County Art Museum, 1976; *The Sensuous Immortals,* M.I.T. Press, 1977.

*WORK IN PROGRESS: The Arts of Nepal,* Volume II: *Painting.*

*     *     *

## PALANDRI, Angela (Chih-ying) Jung 1926-

*PERSONAL:* Born August 6, 1926, in Peking, China; daughter of Ting (a teacher) and Mary H. (Wang) Jung; married Guido Palandri (a librarian), July 7, 1956; children: Michael, James. *Education:* Fu-Jen University of Peking, B.A., 1946; University of Washington, Seattle, M.A., 1949, M.L.S., 1954, Ph.D., 1955. *Home:* 1770 Skyline Blvd., Eugene, Ore. 97403. *Office:* Department of Chinese and Japanese, University of Oregon, Eugene, Ore. 97403.

*CAREER:* University of Oregon, Eugene, librarian, 1954-56, instructor of Chinese, 1955-56; Harper Hospital Medical Library, Detroit, Mich., reference librarian, 1957-59; University of Oregon, instructor in English, 1960-62, assistant professor, 1962-69, associate professor, 1969-74, professor of Chinese, 1974—. Director, University of Oregon graduate summer residence, Taiwan, 1965, 1968. *Member:* Association for Asian Studies, Committee of Concerned Asian Scholars, Chinese Teachers Association, Modern Language Association of America, Philological Association of the Pacific Coast. *Awards, honors:* Fu-Jen University fellow, 1965.

*WRITINGS:* (Translator) *Sun Moon Collection,* Mei-Ya Publishers, 1968; (editor and translator) *Modern Verse from Taiwan,* University of California Press, 1972; *Yuan Chen,* Twayne, 1977; *Italian Images of Ezra Pound,* Mei-ya Publishers, in press.

*WORK IN PROGRESS: Twentieth Century Chinese Women Writers.*

*     *     *

## PALANGE, Anthony (Jr.) 1942-

*PERSONAL:* Born September 17, 1942, in New Haven,

Conn.; son of Anthony (a truck driver) and Thomasina (Fusco) Palange. *Education:* Attended University of New Haven and Herbert Berghoff Studio, New York, N.Y. *Home:* 9 Harwich St., East Haven, Conn. 06512.

*CAREER:* Has worked as an office clerk, teletypist, cashier, and payroll clerk; playwright. *Military service:* U.S. Army, 1964.

*WRITINGS: The Ultimate Weapon* (novel), Apollo, 1971. Also author of "Just Happy," a play about Sarah Bernhardt, "The Triumph of Osiris," an opera based on the ancient Egyptian passion play, and "The Ultimate Weapon," a screenplay.

*WORK IN PROGRESS: On Both Sides of the Family,* a novel tracing Italian immigrants through four generations.

*     *     *

## PALMATIER, Robert Allen 1926-

*PERSONAL:* Born July 22, 1926, in Kalamazoo, Mich.; son of Karl Ernest (a farmer) and Cecile (Chase) Palmatier; married Marion Babilla (a dispatcher), December 21, 1946; children: David, Denise. *Education:* Western Michigan University, B.A., 1950, M.A., 1955; University of Michigan, Ph.D., 1965. *Home:* 1326 Hardwick, Kalamazoo, Mich. 49002. *Office:* Department of Linguistics, Western Michigan University, Kalamazoo, Mich. 49008.

*CAREER:* Western Michigan University, Kalamazoo, instructor, 1955-57, assistant professor, 1957-64, associate professor, 1964-67, professor of English, 1967-68, professor of linguistics and chairman of the department, 1968—. Visiting professor, W. K. Kellogg Foundation Latin American Orientation Program, Kalamazoo College, summers, 1964-68. *Military service:* U.S. Army, 1944-46; served in Italy. *Member:* Modern Language Association of America, Linguistic Society of America, National Council of Teachers of English, Michigan Linguistic Society.

*WRITINGS: A Descriptive Syntax of the Ormulum,* Mouton, 1969; *A Glossary for English Transformational Grammar,* Appleton, 1972. Contributor to *Journal of English Linguistics.* Editor, *The Informant.*

*WORK IN PROGRESS: A Bibliography of Language Recordings,* with Rex Wilson and Ann Shannon.

*SIDELIGHTS:* Palmatier told *CA* that he is "extremely interested in the teaching and learning of—and preparation of materials for—critical (uncommonly taught, neglected, exotic, esoteric) languages." He has personally supervised the teaching of Serbo-Croatian, Swahili, Korean, Brazilian Portuguese, Mandarin Chinese, and Modern Hebrew.

*     *     *

## PALMER, Michael D. 1933-

*PERSONAL:* Born September 23, 1933, in Bowen, Queensland, Australia; son of Frederick Walter (an Anglican priest) and Elsie (Dixon) Palmer; married Margaret Drabble (a teacher), August 6, 1960; children: Matthew, Martha, Emma. *Education:* Attended Ardingly College, Sussex, England, 1942-52; St. Edmund Hall, Oxford, B.A., 1957, M.A., 1961. *Religion:* Church of England. *Home:* 13 Denham Rd., Epsom, Surrey, England. *Office:* DeBurgh School, Merefield Gardens, Tadworth, Surrey, England.

*CAREER:* Aldenham School, Elstree, England, history master, 1958-63; City of Leicester School, Leicester, England, senior history master, 1963-68; Rickmansworth School, Rickmansworth, England, senior history master,

1968-72; Littlehampton School, Littlehampton, Sussex, deputy headmaster, 1972-77; DeBurgh School, Tadworth, Surrey, England, headmaster, 1977—. Lay reader, St. Mary's Church, Rickmansworth. *Military service:* British Army, Royal Engineers, 1952-54; became lieutenant. *Member:* Leicester Historical Association (secretary, 1966-68). *Awards, honors:* Schoolmaster fellow at Christ Church, Oxford University, 1970.

*WRITINGS*—Published by Batsford, except as indicated: *Government*, 1970; *Cities*, 1971; *Ships and Shipping*, 1971; *Henry VIII*, Longman, 1971; *Warfare*, 1972; *World Population*, 1974; *World Resources and Energy*, 1975.

\* \* \*

## PALMORE, Erdman B. 1930-

*PERSONAL:* Born June 3, 1930, in Tokuyama, Japan; son of Peyton Lee, Sr. (a missionary) and Jean (McAlpine) Palmore; married Barbara Murray, August 23, 1952 (divorced, 1962); married Priscilla Shook, June 1, 1963; children: (first marriage) Karen, Julia. *Education:* Duke University, B.A., 1952; University of Chicago, M.A., 1954; Columbia University, Ph.D., 1959. *Politics:* Democrat. *Religion:* Unitarian-Universalist. *Home:* 19 Scott Pl., Durham, N.C. 27705. *Office:* Box 3003, Medical Center, Duke University, Durham, N.C. 27710.

*CAREER:* Columbia University, New York City, research assistant sociologist with Bureau of Applied Social Research, 1956-58; Finch College, New York City, chairman of department of sociology, 1958-60; Yale University, New Haven, Conn., assistant professor of sociology, 1960-63; Social Security Administration, Baltimore, Md., research sociologist, 1963-67; Duke University, Durham, N.C., associate professor, 1967-72, professor of medical sociology, 1972—. Chairman, Ecumenical Housing Opportunities, Inc., 1971-74. Sociology editor, College & University Press, 1961-64. Consultant, National Institute of Child Health and Human Development, U.S. Public Health Service, 1968-75, and Project FIND, National Center on Aging, 1969-71. *Military service:* U.S. Army, 1954-56. *Member:* American Sociological Association, Gerontological Society, American Association of University Professors, Southern Sociological Society (secretary, 1974-77), Phi Beta Kappa. *Awards, honors:* Danforth fellow, 1952-59.

*WRITINGS:* (Editor) *Normal Aging*, Duke University Press, Volume I, 1970, Volume II, 1974; (editor) *Prediction of Life Span*, Heath, 1971; *The Honorable Elders*, Duke University Press, 1975; *International Handbook on Aging*, Greenwood Press, 1978. Contributor of more than fifty articles to professional journals.

*WORK IN PROGRESS: Stress and Adaptation; Successful Aging; Normal Aging*, Volume III.

\* \* \*

## PALOCZI-HORVATH, George 1908-1973

1908—January 3, 1973; Hungarian journalist and author of political biographies. Obituaries: *New York Times*, January 6, 1973; *L'Express*, January 15-21, 1973. (See index for *CA* sketch)

\* \* \*

## PANO, Nicholas C(hristopher) 1934-

*PERSONAL:* Born October 12, 1934, in Stoneham, Mass.; son of Vasil Vangjel (a grocer) and Margaret (Phillips) Pano; married Joan Alves, August 16, 1958. *Education:* Tufts

University, A.B., 1956; Johns Hopkins University, M.A., 1958. *Home:* 1137 Bobby Ave., Macomb, Ill. 61455. *Office:* Department of History, Western Illinois University, Macomb, Ill. 61455.

*CAREER:* Parsons College, Fairfield, Iowa, instructor in history, 1961-62; Western Illinois University, Macomb, assistant professor, 1963-74, associate professor of history, 1975—. *Member:* American Historical Association, American Association for the Advancement of Slavic Studies, American Association of University Professors, McDonough County Young Republicans (vice-president, 1964-65; president, 1965-66).

*WRITINGS: The People's Republic of Albania*, Johns Hopkins Press, 1968. Contributor to several reference works. Contributor of about two dozen articles to professional journals. General editor, *Journal of Developing Areas;* member of board of managing editors, *Southeast Europe.*

*WORK IN PROGRESS:* A book on the Albanian Communist Party; research for a biography of Bishop Fan Noli.

*AVOCATIONAL INTERESTS:* Hiking, gardening, and photography.

\* \* \*

## PANZER, Pauline (Richman) 1911(?)-1972

1911(?)—October 29, 1972; American novelist. Obituaries: *New York Times*, October 31, 1972.

\* \* \*

## PAPANDREOU, Andreas G(eorge) 1919-

*PERSONAL:* Surname is pronounced Pap-an-*dray*-ou; born February 5, 1919, in Chios, Greece; came to United States, 1940, naturalized citizen, 1944; son of George (Premier of Greece, 1964-65) and Sophia (Mineyko) Papandreou; married Christine Rassias, January, 1941; married Margaret Chant, August 30, 1951; children: George, Sophia, Nicholas, Andreas. *Education:* University of Athens, law student, 1937-40; Harvard University, M.A., 1942, Ph.D., 1943. *Politics:* Panhellenic Socialist Movement (Greece). *Religion:* Greek Orthodox. *Home:* Kastri Kifissias, Athens, Greece.

*CAREER:* Harvard University, Cambridge, Mass., instructor in economics, 1943-44, 1946-47; University of Minnesota, Minneapolis, associate professor of economics, 1947-50; Northwestern University, Evanston, Ill., associate professor of economics, 1950-51; University of Minnesota, professor of economics, 1951-55; University of California, Berkeley, professor of economics, 1955-63, chairman of department, 1956-59; Center of Economic Research, Athens, Greece, director, 1961-64; Greek Government, Athens, minister to the Prime Minister, 1964, Minister of Co-ordination, 1965, deputy in Parliament, 1964-67; University of Stockholm, Stockholm, Sweden, professor of economics, 1968-69; York University, Toronto, Ontario, professor of economics, 1969—; Greek Government, deputy in Parliament, 1974—. Chairman, Panhellenic Liberation Movement (PAK), 1968-74; chairman, Panhellenic Socialist Movement (PASOK), 1974—. Wicksell lecturer in Stockholm, 1966; Benjamin Fairless lecturer at Carnegie-Mellon University, 1969; Edmund Burke Bicentenary lecturer at Trinity College, University of Dublin, 1970. Economic adviser, Bank of Greece, 1961-62. *Military service:* U.S. Naval Reserve, 1944-46.

*MEMBER:* American Economic Association, Royal Economic Society. *Awards, honors:* Social Science Research Council faculty research fellow, 1952-55; Fulbright and Guggenheim fellow, 1959-60.

*WRITINGS:* (With Arthur Naftalin and others) *An Introduction to Social Science: Personality, Work, Community,* three volumes in one, Lippincott, 1953, 3rd edition, 1961; (with J. T. Wheeler) *Competition and Its Regulation,* Prentice-Hall, 1954; *Economics as a Science,* Lippincott, 1958; *A Strategy for Greek Economic Development,* Center of Economic Research (Athens), 1962; *Fundamentals of Model Construction in Macroeconomics,* Center of Economic Research, 1962; *Introduction to Macroeconomic Models,* Center of Economic Research, 1965; *Democracy and National Renascence,* Fexis (Athens), 1966; *Mot en Totalitaer Vaerld?* (title means "Toward a Totalitarian World?"), Norstedts (Stockholm), 1969; *Man's Freedom,* Columbia University Press, 1970; *Democracy at Gunpoint: The Greek Front,* Doubleday, 1970; *Paternalistic Capitalism,* University of Minnesota Press, 1972.

Contributor: B. F. Haley, editor, *Survey of Contemporary Economics,* Volume II, Irwin, 1952; L. H. Clark, editor, *Consumer Behaviour,* New York University Press, 1954; *Linear Economics,* Graduate School of Industrial Studies (Athens), 1960; Jan Olov Hedlund, *Stenar i Munnen,* Bonnier, 1969. Contributor to *Les Temps Modernes,* by Jean-Paul Sartre, 1969; contributor to *Encyclopaedia of Economics and Accountancy, Encyclopaedia Britannica,* and periodicals.

*SIDELIGHTS:* Three of Papandreou's books have been translated into a total of seven languages.

*BIOGRAPHICAL/CRITICAL SOURCES: Washington Post,* May 29, 1970; *New York Review of Books,* September 24, 1970.

\*    \*    \*

## PAREDES, Americo 1915-

*PERSONAL:* Accent in both names falls on second syllable; born September 3, 1915, in Brownsville, Tex.; son of Justo (a rancher) and Clotilde (Manzano) Paredes; married Consuelo Silva, August 13, 1939; married Amelia Nagamine, May 28, 1948; children: Americo, Jr., Alan, Vicente, Julia. *Education:* University of Texas, B.A., 1951, M.A., 1953, Ph.D., 1956. *Politics:* Independent. *Religion:* No denomination. *Home:* 3106 Pinecrest Dr., Austin, Tex. 78757. *Office:* SRH 1/326, University of Texas, Austin, Tex. 78712.

*CAREER:* University of Texas at Austin, 1954—, currently professor of English and anthropology, director, Folklore Center, 1957-70, director, Mexican-American Studies Program, 1970—. *Military service:* U.S. Army, 1944-46; served in Infantry. *Awards, honors:* Guggenheim fellow; cash prizes for short stories.

*WRITINGS: With His Pistol in His Hand: A Border Ballad and Its Hero,* University of Texas Press, 1958; (author of notes and translator) Edward Larocque Tinker, editor, *Corridos & Calaveras,* University of Texas Press, 1961; (translator) Daniel Cosio Villegas, *American Extremes,* University of Texas Press, 1964; (editor with Richard M. Dorson) *Folktales of Mexico,* University of Chicago Press, 1970; (editor with Ellen Stekert) *The Urban Experience and Folk Tradition,* University of Texas Press, 1971; (editor with Raymund Paredes) *Mexican-American Authors,* Houghton, 1972; (editor with Richard Bauman) *Toward New Perspectives in Folklore,* University of Texas Press, 1972; *A Texas-Mexican Cancionero,* University of Illinois Press, 1976; (ed-

itor) *Humanidad: Essays in Honor of George I. Sanchez,* University of California Press, 1977. Editor, *Journal of American Folklore,* 1968-73.

*WORK IN PROGRESS:* Editing a collection of jests, and legendary narratives told by Mexicans and Mexican-Americans with Anglo-Americans as subject; editing a glossary and study of derogatory names for Anglos and Mexican-Americans.

\*    \*    \*

## PARKER, Donald Dean 1899-

*PERSONAL:* Born October 3, 1899, in Street, Md.; son of Albert George (a Presbyterian minister) and Jessie (Bewley) Parker; married Florence Myrtle Patterson, 1928; children: Mary Frances (Mrs. Russell D. Rasmussen), Bonnie Jean (Mrs. Leo H. Janos), Florence Patricia (Mrs. Kenneth D. Moore), Jessie Bewley (Mrs. John F. Strauss), Donald Dean, Jr. *Education:* Park College, B.A., 1922; additional study at University of Illinois, 1922, McCormick Theological Seminary, 1926, University of Chicago, 1926-27, 1935-36, and University of Washington, Seattle, 1927-28; University of Washington, Seattle, M.A., 1932; University of Chicago, B.D., and Ph.D., 1936. *Politics:* Independent. *Home:* Westminster Gardens, 1420 Santo Domingo Ave., Duarte, Calif. 91010.

*CAREER:* Ordained to Presbyterian ministry; Shantung Christian University, Tsinan, China, librarian and teacher of English, 1922-25; Union High School, Manila, Philippines, principal, 1930-35; Lake Forest College, Lake Forest, Ill., librarian, 1936-37; Park College, Parkville, Mo., assistant professor of history, 1937-40; Historical Record Survey for Missouri, assistant state supervisor, 1940-42; American Red Cross, Fort Leonard Wood, Mo., and Kansas City, Mo., field director, 1942-43; South Dakota State University, Brookings, professor of history and head of department of history and political science, 1943-65, professor emeritus, 1965—. *Member:* South Dakota State Historical Society.

*WRITINGS: Local History: How to Gather It, Write It, and Publish It,* Social Science Research Council, 1944; *Founding Presbyterianism in South Dakota,* privately printed, 1963; (editor) *The Recollections of Philander Prescott: Frontiersman of the Old Northwest, 1819-1862,* University of Nebraska Press, 1966; *Gabriel Renville, Young Sioux Warrior,* Exposition Press, 1973. Also author of *Presbyterian Missionary Work in North India, 1923-1960,* 1975. Compiler of twenty-four South Dakota county histories, of denominational histories of South Dakota, 1964, and of a number of mimeographed regional and family history titles, some of them book-length. Author of weekly column, "Know Your State," in *Sioux Falls Argus,* 1951-66, and contributor to other South Dakota newspapers.

*WORK IN PROGRESS:* Research on the early history of Santa Fe, N.M., and on the history of the Presbyterian church there; early South Dakota history.

*SIDELIGHTS:* Donald Parker has visited about forty countries in Asia and Europe, and has made four trips to Mexico.

\*    \*    \*

## PARRISH, John A(lbert) 1939-

*PERSONAL:* Born October 19, 1939, in Louisville, Ky.; son of James W. (a minister) and Lucille (Blair) Parrish; married Joan Claudia Marian, March 24, 1962; children: Susan, Lynn, Mark. *Education:* Duke University, B.A., 1961; Yale University, M.D., 1965. *Home:* 11 Newton St.,

Weston, Mass. 02193. *Agent:* Gerard McCauley Agency, Inc., 209 East 56th St., New York, N.Y. 10022. *Office:* Massachusetts General Hospital, 32 Fruit St., Boston, Mass. 02114.

*CAREER:* University of Michigan, Ann Arbor, intern, 1965-66, resident in internal medicine, 1966-67; Harvard Medical School and Massachusetts General Hospital, Boston, Mass., resident in dermatology, 1969-71, chief resident in dermatology, 1971-72, associate professor of dermatology and clinical assistant in dermatology, 1972—, Nolan Scholar in Photobiology, 1972. Junior associate in medicine, Peter Bent Brigham Hospital, 1972—; consultant in dermatology to Robert B. Brigham Hospital and Children's Hospital Medical Center, 1972—. *Military service:* U.S. Marine Corps, 1967-68; received Vietnamese Cross of Gallantry with Gold. U.S. Navy, 1968-69; became lieutenant commander.

*WRITINGS: 12, 20 & 5: A Doctor's Year in Vietnam,* Dutton, 1972; *Dermatology and Skin Care,* McGraw, 1975; (with others) *Between You and Me: A Sensible and Authorative Guide to the Care and Treatment of Your Skin,* Little, Brown, 1978. Contributor of poetry to *Harper's* and other periodicals, of editorials and reviews to *Boston Globe,* and of articles to medical journals.

*WORK IN PROGRESS:* A novel.

\* \* \*

## PARSONS, Louella (Oettinger) 1881-1972

August 6, 1881—December 9, 1972; American gossip columnist and Hollywood celebrity. Obituaries: *New York Times,* December 10, 1972; *Time,* December 18, 1972.

\* \* \*

## PASCAL, Gerald Ross 1907-

*PERSONAL:* Born August 3, 1907, in Raritan, N.J.; son of Anthony (a businessman) and Mary (Ross) Pascal; married second wife, Lalla Sullivan (a psychologist), September 14, 1964; children: (first marriage) Walter, Lawrence, Christopher, Roy Darby. *Education:* University of California, Berkeley, A.B., 1940; Harvard University, A.M., 1942; Brown University, Ph.D., 1948. *Home:* 3718 Kings Hwy., Jackson, Miss. 39216. *Office:* Medical Tower Bldg., Jackson, Miss. 39216.

*CAREER:* Massachusetts General Hospital, Boston, extern, 1941-42; Harvard University, Cambridge, Mass., researcher in personality, 1942-45; Butler Hospital, Providence, R.I., chief psychologist, 1946-49; University of Pittsburgh, Pittsburgh, Pa., associate professor of psychology, 1949-52; University of Tennessee, Knoxville, professor of psychology and director of clinical training, 1951-64; University of Mississippi, Medical School, Jackson, professor of research psychology, 1964-66, clinical professor, 1966—; Pascal Clinic, Jackson, Miss., director, 1964—. Research psychologist, Western Psychiatric Institute and Clinic, 1949-51; professional adviser to Hinds City Mental Health Association, Goodwill Industries, Miracle House, and to Cerebral Palsy Center. *Military service:* U.S. Army Air Forces, 1943-46; became first lieutenant.

*MEMBER:* American Psychological Association (fellow), American Academy of Psychotherapists, Society of Projective Techniques (fellow), Society for Experimental and Clinical Hypnosis, Mississippi Psychological Association.

*WRITINGS:* (With Barbara J. Suttell) *Bender Gestalt Test: Quantification and Validity for Adults,* Grune, 1951; *Behav-*

*ioral Change in the Clinic: A Systematic Approach,* Grune, 1959; (with W. O. Jenkins) *Systematic Observation of Gross Human Behavior,* Grune, 1961; *Behind the Screen: A Biographical Study,* Christopher, 1969. Contributor of more than fifty articles to medical and psychological journals.

*WORK IN PROGRESS: Diagnostic Interview in Psychology and Psychiatry.*

\* \* \*

## PATRICK, Walton Richard 1909-

*PERSONAL:* Born September 9, 1909, in Collins, Miss.; son of John Richard (a farmer) and Annie (Welch) Patrick; married Miriam Morris, August 28, 1937. *Education:* Mississippi State University, B.S., 1933; Louisiana State University, M.A., 1934, Ph.D., 1937. *Home:* 365 Cary Dr., Auburn, Ala. 36830.

*CAREER:* Louisiana State University, Baton Rouge, instructor, 1937-40, assistant professor of English, 1940-45; Auburn University, Auburn, Ala., associate professor, 1946-47, professor of English and head of department, 1947-77. *Military service:* U.S. Army, 1942-46; became major; served in European Theater. *Member:* South Atlantic Modern Language Association, Alabama College English Teachers Association, Phi Kappa Phi. *Awards, honors:* Ford Foundation faculty fellow, 1953-54.

*WRITINGS:* (Compiler with C. H. Cantrell) *Southern Literary Culture: A Bibliography of Masters' and Doctors' Theses Through 1948,* University of Alabama Press, 1953; (editor with Eugene Current-Garcia) *American Short Stories: 1820 to the Present,* Scott, Foresman, 1953, revised edition, 1964; (editor with Current-Garcia) *What Is the Short Story?,* Scott, Foresman, 1961; (editor with Current-Garcia) *Realism and Romanticism: An Approach to the Novel,* Scott, Foresman, 1962; *Ring Lardner,* Twayne, 1963; (editor with Current-Garcia) *Short Stories of the Western World,* Scott, Foresman, 1969. Contributor of articles and reviews to scholarly journals. Member of editorial board, *Studies in Short Fiction.*

*WORK IN PROGRESS:* A literary history of the American short story from 1870 to 1915, part of a three-volume history of the American short story, for Twayne.

\* \* \*

## PATTERSON, Charles H(enry) 1896-

*PERSONAL:* Born November 29, 1896, in Wellsboro, Pa.; son of John D. (a farmer) and Amy (Bacon) Patterson; married Ruth Swingle, June 14, 1922; children: Donald C., Marilyn Ruth (Mrs. Charles E. Baer). *Education:* Columbia Union College, A.B., 1917; University of Nebraska, A.M., 1921, Ph.D., 1924. *Politics:* Republican. *Religion:* Presbyterian. *Home and office:* 3252 South 39th St., Lincoln, Neb. 68506.

*CAREER:* University of Nebraska, Lincoln, instructor, 1924-27, assistant professor, 1927-37, associate professor, 1937-47, professor of philosophy, 1947-67, chairman of department, 1950-62. Visiting professor of philosophy at Boston University, summer, 1935, Iliff School of Theology, summer, 1952, University of Southern California, summer, 1957, Doane College, 1968, and Nebraska Wesleyan University, 1969. Member of local, regional, and national boards of directors, Young Men's Christian Association (YMCA); member of board of directors, Lincoln City Library. *Member:* American Philosophical Association, American Academy of Religion, American Association of University

Professors (local president), Mountain Plains Philosophical Association, Phi Beta Kappa.

*WRITINGS: Problems in Logic,* Macmillan, 1926; *Principles of Correct Thinking,* Longmans, Green, 1937; *Moral Standards,* Ronald, 1949, revised edition, 1957; *Philosophy of the Old Testament,* Ronald, 1953; *Western Philosophy,* Cliff's Notes, Volume I, 1970, Volume II, 1971; *Introduction to Philosophy,* Cliff's Notes, 1972; *Berkeley's Philosophical Works,* Cliff's Notes, 1972.

\*    \*    \*

## PATTERSON, Mary H(agelin)    1928-1973

1928—January 5, 1973; American novelist. Obituaries: *New York Times,* January 6, 1973.

\*    \*    \*

## PATTON, Rob(ert Warren)    1943-

*PERSONAL:* Born June 15, 1943, in Chicago, Ill.; son of Robert Lee (a professor) and Mary Louise (Trask) Patton. *Education:* Cornell University, B.A., 1966, M.F.A., 1970. *Home:* 532 Leonard Ave., DeKalb, Ill. 60115.

*CAREER:* Cornell University, Ithaca, N.Y., instructor, 1970-71, lecturer in English, 1971-72; Northern Illinois University, DeKalb, instructor in English, 1976-77.

*WRITINGS: Thirty-Seven Poems: One Night Stanzas,* Ithaca House, 1970; *Dare* (poems), Ithaca House, 1977.

*WORK IN PROGRESS:* Poetry.

\*    \*    \*

## PAYNE, LaVeta Maxine    1916-

*PERSONAL:* Born February 20, 1916, in Lebanon, Kan.; daughter of Verne Hobert and Flossie (Whitaker) Payne. *Education:* Union College, Lincoln, Neb., B.A., 1940; University of Nebraska, M.A., 1943, Ph.D., 1952; Assumption College, additional study, 1965; Atlantic Union College, B.A., 1966. *Politics:* Non-partisan. *Religion:* Seventh-day Adventist. *Address:* Route 4, Box 160-20, Cleburne, Tex. 76031.

*CAREER:* Elementary school teacher in Smith County, Kan., 1934-35, and Lincoln, Neb., 1940-41; teacher at Shenandoah Valley Academy, New Market, Va., 1941-46, Platte Valley Academy, Shelton, Neb., 1946-50, and University of Nebraska Extension Division, Lincoln, 1950-51; Columbia Union College, Takoma Park, Md., associate professor of education, 1951-59; Atlantic Union College, South Lancaster, Mass., professor of education and chairman of Division of Education, 1959-66; Southern Missionary College, Collegedale, Tenn., professor of education and psychology, beginning 1966. Associate professor of education, Newbold College, Bracknell, Berkshire, England, 1955-57.

*MEMBER:* National Education Association, American Psychological Association, American Association of University Professors, National Society for the Study of Education (Chattanooga branch), Authors and Artists Club, Daughters of the American Revolution. *Awards, honors:* Authors and Artists Club awards for poetry, short stories, and a television skit.

*WRITINGS: Called to Teach a Sabbath School Class,* with teacher's manual and student's workbook, Review & Herald, 1969; *Careers in Secondary Teaching,* Southern Publishing, 1971. Contributor to religious journals.

*AVOCATIONAL INTERESTS:* Travel and china painting.†

## PAYNTON, Clifford T.    1929-

*PERSONAL:* Born July 30, 1929, in Barrhead, Alberta, Canada; married Gladys Eileen Sitter, July 2, 1955; children: Cheralyn Tamara, Scott Thomas. *Education:* Seattle Pacific College, B.A. (magna cum laude), 1958; University of Washington, Seattle, M.A., 1961, Ph.D., 1964. *Office:* Department of Sociology, California State College, San Bernardino, Calif. 92403.

*CAREER:* University of Washington, Seattle, acting instructor in sociology, 1962-63; University of California, Los Angeles, acting assistant professor of sociology, 1964-65; York University, Toronto, Ontario, assistant professor of sociology, 1965-68; California State College, San Bernardino, associate professor, 1968-72, professor of sociology, 1972—, chairman of department, 1970—. Visiting summer instructor at Seattle Pacific College, 1962, and at McMaster University, 1964. *Member:* American Sociological Association, Eastern Sociological Association, Pacific Sociological Association, Alpha Kappa Delta, Alpha Kappa Sigma.

*WRITINGS:* (Editor with Robert Blackey, and contributor) *Why Revolution? Analyses of the Causes of Revolution,* Schenkman, 1971; (with Blackey) *Revolution and the Revolutionary Ideal,* Schenkman, 1976. Contributor to sociology journals.

\*    \*    \*

## PEARSON, Lester B(owles)    1897-1972

April 23, 1897—December 27, 1972; Canadian politician, statesman, and winner of the Nobel Peace Prize in 1957. Obituaries: *New York Times,* December 28, 1972; *Washington Post,* December 29, 1972; *L'Express,* January 1-7, 1973; *Newsweek,* January 8, 1973; *Time,* January 8, 1973.

\*    \*    \*

## PEDEN, Margaret Sayers    1927-

*PERSONAL:* Surname is pronounced *Pea*-den; born May 10, 1927, in West Plains, Mo.; daughter of Harvey Monroe (a horseman) and Eleanor Green (James) Sayers; married Robert Norwine, August, 1949 (divorced, 1961); married William Harwood Peden (a professor and writer), September 18, 1965; children: (first marriage) Kerry (Mrs. James Dunning), Kyle Robert; (second marriage) Eliza (Mrs. Carl Mitchell), Sally Monroe (stepdaughters). *Education:* University of Missouri—Columbia, A.B., 1948, M.A., 1963, Ph.D., 1966. *Politics:* Independent. *Religion:* Protestant. *Home:* 408 Thilly Ave., Columbia, Mo. 65201. *Office:* 11 Arts and Science, University of Missouri, Columbia, Mo. 65201.

*CAREER:* University of Missouri—Columbia, assistant professor, 1966-70, associate professor, 1970-75, professor of Spanish, 1975—, former chairperson of department of Romance languages. *Member:* Modern Language Association of America, American Association of Teachers of Spanish and Portuguese, American Translators' Association, Missouri Modern Language Association, Phi Sigma Iota, Sigma Delta Pi. *Awards, honors:* Byler Distinguished Professor Award, University of Missouri—Columbia, 1977.

*WRITINGS—Translator:* Emilio Carballido, *The Norther,* University of Texas Press, 1968; Carballido, *The Golden Thread and Other Plays,* University of Texas Press, 1970; Egon Wolff, *Paper Flowers* (play), University of Missouri Press, 1971; (with Lysander Kemp) Octavio Paz, *The Siren and the Seashell* (critical essays), University of Texas Press, 1976; Horacio Quiroga, *The Decapitated Chicken and*

*Other Stories,* University of Texas Press, 1976; *Terra Nostra,* Farrar, Straus, 1976; *Nina Huanca,* Viking, 1977; Carlos Fuentes, *The Hydra Head,* Farrar, Straus, 1978. Contributor of articles to linguistics and literature journals. Member of numerous editorial advisory boards.

*WORK IN PROGRESS: Elemental Odes,* for Farrar, Straus.

\* \* \*

## PELISSIER, Roger    1924-1972

December 30, 1924—August 29, 1972; French authority on oriental languages and literature. Obituaries: *L'Express,* September 4-10, 1972. (See index for *CA* sketch)

\* \* \*

## PENDAR, Kenneth    1906-1972

December 22, 1906—December 7, 1972; American diplomat. Obituaries: *New York Times,* December 8, 1972.

\* \* \*

## PERERA, Thomas Biddle    1938-

*PERSONAL:* Born November 20, 1938, in New York, N.Y.; son of Lionel Cantoni (a banker) and Dorothy (Biddle) Perera; married Gretchen Gifford (a nurse), August 28, 1960; children: Daniel Gifford, Thomas Biddle, Jr. *Education:* Columbia University, A.B., 1961, M.A., 1963, Ph.D., 1968. *Home:* 11 Squire Hill Rd., Caldwell, N.J. 07006. *Office:* Department of Psychology, Montclair State College, Upper Montclair, N.J. 07043.

*CAREER:* Columbia University, Barnard College, New York, N.Y., instructor, 1966-68, assistant professor of psychology, 1968-74, visiting associate professor, 1974—, founder and director of psychophysiology laboratory, 1969-74; Montclair State College, Upper Montclair, N.J., associate professor of psychology and director of psychophysiology laboratory, 1974—. Senior research scientist, New York State Psychiatric Institute, 1964-71. Licensed psychologist in State of New York. Camp counselor, Camp Killooleet, Hancock, Vt., 1956—. Consultant to American Association of State Psychology Boards, 1974—, to National Science Foundation, and to various colleges and organizations. *Member:* American Psychological Association, American Association for the Advancement of Science (life member), Biofeedback Research Association, Amateur Radio Relay League, Aircraft Owners and Pilots Association, MENSA, National Speleological Society, Eastern Psychological Association, New York Academy of Sciences, Sigma Xi.

*WRITINGS:* (With Wallace Orlowsky) *Who Will Wash the River?,* Coward, 1970; (with Orlowsky) *Who Will Clean the Air?,* Coward, 1971; (with wife, Gretchen G. Perera) *Louder and Louder,* F. Watts, 1973; (with G. G. Perera) *Your Brain Power,* Coward, 1975. Also author of numerous scientific papers presented to learned societies. Contributor to professional journals.

*WORK IN PROGRESS:* Research on the electrical activity of the human nervous system, environmental pollution, and computers.

*AVOCATIONAL INTERESTS:* Ham radio, flying, spelunking, and computers.

\* \* \*

## PERLBERG, Mark    1929-

*PERSONAL:* Born February 19, 1929, in Palisade, N.J.; son of Emanuel and Rene (Levinson) Perlberg; married Anna Nessy Backer (a social work administrator), February 4, 1953; children: Katherine, Julie. *Education:* Hobart College, B.A., 1950; Columbia University, graduate study, 1950-52. *Politics:* Independent. *Religion:* Jewish. *Home:* 612 Stratford Pl., Chicago, Ill. 60657.

*CAREER: Time,* Chicago, Ill., contributing editor, 1955-56, correspondent, 1956-60; *The World Book Encyclopedia Yearbook,* Chicago, senior editor, 1961-67; *Encyclopaedia Britannica,* Chicago, principal editor, 1967-72; *Prism* (publication of the American Medical Association), Chicago, managing editor, 1972-75; free-lance writer, 1976—. *Military service:* U.S. Army, 1952-54; served in Korea and Japan; became sergeant. *Member:* Poetry Center (Chicago; founding member). *Awards, honors:* Robert Ferguson Memorial Award, Friends of Literature (Chicago), 1970, for *The Burning Field.*

*WRITINGS: The Burning Field* (poems), Morrow, 1970. Poetry represented in anthologies, including *Best Poems of 1964: Borestone Mountain Poetry Awards,* edited by Waddell Austin, Pacific Books, 1965, *The New Yorker Book of Poems,* edited by Howard Moss, Viking, 1969, *Poetry Brief,* edited by William Cole, Macmillan, 1971, and *Pick Me Up,* edited by Cole, Macmillan, 1972; translator, with Lee Feigon, of classical Chinese poetry published in *Sunflower Splendor: Three Thousand Years of Chinese Poetry,* Doubleday, 1975.

*WORK IN PROGRESS: The Feel of the Sun,* a second book of poems.

*SIDELIGHTS:* Mark Perlberg told *CA:* "As I have grown older I have come to feel that the poet's job and privilege is to keep alive and to extend, for his comparatively small audience, the realm of the spirit. I use 'spirit' here in the nonmystical, secular sense. Further, the poet is interested in learning how to truly stay alive before his time runs out. Perhaps his poetry, among other things, is a record, a presentation of his sense of aliveness. This—and the pleasure others take in reading his poems—is his contribution, plus whatever he manages to do along the way to keep the language (which he loves) a living, vital thing."

\* \* \*

## PERLS, Eugenia Soderberg    1904(?)-1973

1904(?)—January 9, 1973; Swedish novelist, journalist, and author of children's stories. Obituaries: *New York Times,* January 11, 1973.

\* \* \*

## PERRY, David Thomas    1946-

*PERSONAL:* Born November 6, 1946, in Saginaw, Mich.; son of Frank L. (a minister) and Dorma (Smith) Perry; married Autumn Gayl Creeks (a high school English teacher and church secretary), September 18, 1970. *Education:* Asbury College, B.A., 1969, graduate study at Asbury Theological Seminary and Southwestern Baptist Theological Seminary. *Home:* 1225 Rice Mill Rd., Macon, Ga. 31206. *Office:* Glenwood Hills Baptist Church, 3225 Rice Mill Rd., Macon, Ga. 31206.

*CAREER:* Pastor of Presbyterian church in Harrodsburg, Ky., 1966-67; minister of youth for Methodist church in Cynthiana, Ky., 1968-70; Asbury Theological Seminary, Wilmore, Ky., minister of revival, 1970-71; University Baptist Church, Fort Worth, Tex., minister of young adults, 1971-72; Paul Anderson Youth Home, Vidulia, Ga., counselor, 1972-73; Wrens United Methodist Church, Wrens, Ga., pastor, 1973-75; Glenwood Hills Baptist Church, Macon, Ga., pastor, 1975—.

*WRITINGS: Rolling for Jesus,* Broadman, 1972.

*WORK IN PROGRESS: In Christ, Delighted!; Thirty Days of Prayer.*

*BIOGRAPHICAL/CRITICAL SOURCES:* William S. Cannon, *The Jesus Revolution,* Broadman, 1971; *Home Missions,* June-July, 1971.

\*    \*    \*

## PERRY, Joseph M(cGarity)  1936-

*PERSONAL:* Born September 22, 1936, in Marietta, Ga.; son of William H. (a manager) and Rubye (McGarity) Perry; married Ethelia Crews, June 22, 1962; children: Laura, Linda. *Education:* Emory University, A.B., 1958; Georgia State College of Business Administration (now Georgia State University), M.B.A., 1961; Northwestern University, M.A., 1964, Ph.D., 1966. *Home:* 3336 Hollycrest Blvd., Orange Park, Fla. 32073. *Office address:* Department of Economics, University of North Florida, P.O. Box 17074, Jacksonville, Fla. 32216.

*CAREER:* Sears, Roebuck & Company, Atlanta, Ga., mail order inspector, 1957-61; Northwestern University, Evanston, Ill., lecturer in economics, 1963-64; University of Florida, Gainesville, assistant professor of economics, 1964-71; University of North Florida, Jacksonville, associate professor, 1971-74, professor of economics, 1974—, chairperson of department, 1971—. Manuscript consultant to Harcourt, Brace, Jovanovich, Inc., 1969—, Houghton Mifflin, Inc., 1970—, and W. W. Norton, Inc., 1971; consultant to regional and national business and law firms, 1972—. *Military service:* U.S. Army Reserve, 1954-62; became operations sergeant. *Member:* American Economic Association, American Association for Advancement of Science, Economic History Society, Economic History Association, Association for Evolutionary Economics, Southern Economic Association, Phi Beta Kappa, Omicron Delta Epsilon, Beta Gamma Sigma, Delta Sigma Pi.

*WRITINGS:* (With Frank W. Tuttle) *An Economic History of the United States,* Southwestern Co., 1970; *Instructor's Manual For An Economic History of the United States,* Southwestern Co., 1970; *The Impact of Immigration on Three American Industries, 1865-1914,* Arno, 1978. Contributor of articles and reviews to scholarly journals.

*WORK IN PROGRESS: History of Association for University Business and Economic Research;* a textbook in managerial economics.

\*    \*    \*

## PESSEN, Edward  1920-

*PERSONAL:* Born December 31, 1920, in New York, N.Y.; son of Abraham and Anna (Flashberg) Pessen; married Adele Barlin, November 25, 1940; children: Beth (Mrs. Michael Shub), Abigail (Mrs. Richard Wolf), Dinah, Jonathan, Andrew. *Education:* Columbia University, B.A., 1947, M.A., 1948, Ph.D., 1954. *Home:* 853 East 18th St., Brooklyn, N.Y. 11230. *Office:* Department of History, Bernard M. Baruch College of the City University of New York, 17 Lexington Ave., New York, N.Y. 10010; and Graduate Center of the City University of New York, 33 West 42nd St., New York, N.Y. 10036.

*CAREER:* College of the City of New York (now City College of City University of New York), New York City, lecturer in history, 1948-54; Fisk University, Nashville, Tenn., associate professor of history, 1954-56; Staten Island Community College (now Staten Island Community College of the City University of New York), Staten Island, N.Y., professor of history and head of department of social and humanistic studies, 1956-70; Graduate Center of the City University of New York, New York City, professor, 1968-72, distinguished university professor of history, 1972—; Bernard M. Baruch College of the City University of New York, New York City, professor, 1970-72, distinguished university professor of history, 1972—. *Military service:* U.S. Army, Infantry, 1944-45; received Purple Heart and Bronze Star. *Member:* American Historical Association, Organization of American Historians, Southern Historical Association. *Awards, honors:* First prize, State University of New York competition for essays on the improvement of teaching, 1959; first prize, Daughters of the Founders and Patriots of America essay competition, 1966; Pulitzer Prize nomination, 1968, for *Most Uncommon Jacksonians;* National Book Award nomination, 1974, for *Riches, Class, and Power before the Civil War;* Guggenheim fellow, 1977-78.

*WRITINGS: Most Uncommon Jacksonians: The Radical Leaders of the Early Labor Movement,* State University of New York Press, 1967; *Jacksonian American: Society, Personality, and Politics,* Dorsey, 1969, revised edition, 1978; (editor and contributor) *New Perspectives on Jacksonian Parties and Politics,* Allyn & Bacon, 1969; *Riches, Class, and Power before the Civil War,* Heath, 1973; (editor and contributor) *Three Centuries of Social Mobility in America,* Heath, 1974; (editor) *Jacksonian Panorama,* Bobbs-Merrill, 1976; (editor and contributor) *The Many-Faceted Jacksonian Era,* Greenwood Press, 1977.

Contributor: James Bugg, Jr., editor, *Jacksonian Democracy: Myth or Reality?,* Holt, 1964; J. Godechot, editor, *La Presse Ouvrier, 1819-1850,* Centre National de la Recherche Scientifique (Paris), 1966; Charles Rehmus and Doris McLaughlin, editors, *Labor and American Politics,* University of Michigan Press, 1966; Howard Quint, Dean Albertson, and Milton Cantor, editors, *Main Problems in American History,* Dorsey, 1968, revised edition, 1978.

Frank Otto Gatell, editor, *Essays in Jacksonian America,* Holt, 1970; J. R. Johnson, J. A. Hall, and C. D. Farquhar, editors, *Selected Readings in American History,* San Jacinto College Press, 1970; Herbert J. Bass, editor, *The State of American History,* Quadrangle, 1970; Michael McGiffert, editor, *American Social Thought before the Civil War,* Addison-Wesley, 1972; Armin Rappaport and Richard Traina, editors, *Source Problems in American History,* Macmillan, 1972; Ari Hoogenboom and Olive Hoogenboom, editors, *An Interdisciplinary Approach to American History,* Prentice-Hall, 1973; Harry Sievers, editor, *Six Presidents from the Empire State,* Sleepy Hollow Restorations, 1974; John Garraty and J. Sternstein, editors, *Encyclopaedia of American Biography,* Harper, 1974; Herbert G. Gutman, editor, *Readings in American Social History,* Prentice-Hall, 1974; J. H. Cary and J. Weinberg, editors, *The Social Fabric: American Life from 1607 to the Civil War,* Little, Brown, 1975; R. L. Garner and P. E. Stebbins, editors, *Individualism and Community: A Thematic Approach to the History of the United States,* Pennsylvania State University Press, 1975; A. F. Davis and H. D. Woodman, editors, *Conflict and Consensus in Early American History,* Heath, 1976; J. S. Ezell and others, editors, *Readings in American History,* Houghton, 1976; P. Stewart and J. L. Bugg, editors, *Jacksonian Democracy,* Dryden, 1976;

Philip C. Dolce and George H. Shaw, editors, *Power and the Presidency,* Scribner, 1976; Richard B. Morris, editor, *Bicentennial History of the American Worker,* U.S. Department of Labor, 1976.

Contributor to *Political Science Quarterly, New York History, Pennsylvania History, American Historical Review, Dissent, Encyclopaedia Britannica,* and other publications.

*WORK IN PROGRESS: American Society in the Early Nineteenth Century,* for Heath; *Social Mobility: A Short Text,* for Praeger; *Social Mobility in American History,* for Yale University Press.

*SIDELIGHTS:* Edward Pessen writes: "In recent years I have come to regard history as more art than science. Perhaps on reflection the two categories are not as irreconcilable as we sometimes assume they are. Good art requires vast knowledge. Good science best reveals itself in luminous prose and is perhaps no less subjective than is art. In any case, my ideal is to write a history that combines the qualities of the two. My tactics are to try to write good sentences—clear, varied, carriers of important and perhaps interesting intellectual freight. My strategy is to put these sentences at the disposal of what I trust are searching questions about the past. My professional ideology is to follow the evidence along the perverse paths it often takes and to question the past not only about what happened but also about what did not happen and why."

*BIOGRAPHICAL/CRITICAL SOURCES: New York Times,* June 20, 1968.

\* \* \*

## PETERSON, Edwin (Lewis) 1904-1972

October 11, 1904—November 24, 1972; American educator. Obituaries: *New York Times,* November 25, 1972.

\* \* \*

## PETERSON, Elmer 1930-

*PERSONAL:* Born September 2, 1930, in Albert Lea, Minn.; son of Elmer R. and Bertha H. (Glemmestad) Peterson; married Judith Leuthold, March, 1954; children: Eric, Kristin. *Education:* Carleton College, B.A., 1952; Middlebury College, M.A., 1957; University of Colorado, Ph.D., 1962. *Religion:* Episcopalian. *Office:* Colorado College, Colorado Springs, Colo. 80903.

*CAREER:* Colorado College, Colorado Springs, assistant professor, 1961-65, associate professor, 1965-70, professor of French, 1970-77, director of development and special projects, 1977—. *Military service:* U.S. Naval Reserve, active duty as air intelligence officer, 1952-55; became lieutenant. *Member:* American Association of University Professors, American Association of Teachers of French, Modern Language Association of America, Association of Dada-Surrealism, Societe d'Etude du XXe.

*WRITINGS: Tristan Tzara,* Rutgers University Press, 1971; (with Michel Sanouillet) *Salt Seller,* Oxford University Press, 1973; (with Sanouillet) *The Essential Writings of Marcel Duchamp,* Thames & Hudson, 1974; (with Sanouillet) *Duchamp de Signe,* Flammarion, 1974. Contributor to *Colorado College Studies, Boston University Journal,* and *Dada Surrealism.*

*WORK IN PROGRESS:* A study of Paul Dermee and Celine Arnauld; a critical bibliography of French literature.

## PETERSON, Helen Stone 1910-

*PERSONAL:* Born May 12, 1910, in Binghamton, N.Y.; daughter of George Fordyce and May (Cox) Stone; married Arthur Howard Peterson (treasurer of Cornell University), July 7, 1934; children: George E., Arthur H., Jr. *Education:* Oberlin College, A.B., 1932; Smith College, G.S.S., 1933. *Politics:* Independent. *Home:* 519 Caswell Rd., Chapel Hill, N.C. 27514.

*CAREER:* Community Service Society, New York, N.Y., social worker, 1934-36; Connecticut State Department of Health, Hartford, mental hygienist, 1936-39. *Member:* National Association of Social Workers.

*WRITINGS*—All juveniles; published by Garrard: *Henry Clay,* 1964; *Jane Addams,* 1965; *Abigail Adams,* 1967; *Roger Williams,* 1968; *Electing Our Presidents,* 1970; *Susan B. Anthony,* 1971; *Sojourner Truth,* 1972; *Give Us Liberty: The Story of the Declaration of Independence,* 1973; *The Making of the U.S. Constitution,* 1974; *The Supreme Court in America's Story,* 1976. Contributor to *Jack and Jill, Children's Activities,* and to education journals.

\* \* \*

## PETKAS, Peter (James) 1945-

*PERSONAL:* Born May 15, 1945, in Houston, Tex.; son of James Peter (an oil drilling contractor) and Grace (Nicholson) Petkas; married Martha Alexander, June 22, 1968. *Education:* Yale University, B.A. (cum laude), 1967; University of Texas, J.D., 1970. *Home:* 1519 Varnum St. N.W., Washington, D.C. 20011. *Office:* Office of Management and Budget, 244 Old Executive Office Bldg., Washington, D.C. 20503.

*CAREER:* Attorney with Ralph Nader's Public Interest Research Group, 1970-72, and Ralph Nader's Corporation Accountability Research Group, 1971-73; Clearinghouse for Professional Responsibility, Washington, D.C., executive director, 1971-73; Southern Governmental Monitoring Project, Atlanta, Ga., associate director, 1973-74, director, 1974-75; Southern Regional Council, Atlanta, executive director, 1976-77; President's Reorganization Project, Washington, D.C., director of project management staff, 1977—. *Military service:* U.S. Army Reserve, 1968-74. *Member:* American Bar Association, District of Columbia Bar Association.

*WRITINGS:* (Editor and contributor with Kate Blackwell and Ralph Nader) *Whistle Blowing,* Grossman, 1972.

\* \* \*

## PHILLIPS, Clifton J(ackson) 1919-

*PERSONAL:* Born April 11, 1919, in Olean, N.Y.; son of Charles Clifton (a machinist) and Edith (Grey) Phillips; married Rachel Martin, July, 1952; children: Peter, Elaine, Alexis, Patience. *Education:* Hiram College, B.A., 1941; Starr King School of Religious Leadership, Th.B., 1944; Harvard University, M.A., 1950, Ph.D., 1954. *Religion:* Unitarian Universalist. *Home:* 422 Anderson St., Greencastle, Ind. 46135. *Office:* Department of History, DePauw University, Greencastle, Ind. 46135.

*CAREER:* U.S. Department of Defense, civilian official in military government, Kobe, Japan, 1946-49; DePauw University, Greencastle, Ind., instructor, 1954-55, assistant professor, 1955-58, associate professor, 1958-64, professor of history, 1964—. Fulbright lecturer in American studies, Seoul, Korea, 1968-69. *Military service:* U.S. Army, 1944-46; became master sergeant. *Member:* American Historical Association, Association for Asian Studies, Indiana Historical Society. *Awards, honors:* Fulbright scholar in Taiwan, 1962; award of merit from American Association for State and Local History, 1969, for *Indiana in Transition: The Emergence of an Industrial Commonwealth, 1880-1920.*

*WRITINGS: Indiana in Transition: The Emergence of an Industrial Commonwealth, 1880-1920,* Indiana Historical Society, 1968; *Protestant America and the Pagan World: The First Half Century of the American Board of Commissioners for Foreign Missions, 1810-1860,* Harvard University Press, 1969; (contributor) John K. Fairbank, editor, *Missionary Enterprise in China and America,* Harvard University Press, 1974. Contributor to historical journals.

*WORK IN PROGRESS:* The Protestant missionary movement in China and Korea.

\*      \*      \*

**PHILLIPS, Dorothy S(anborn)   1893-1972**

January 6, 1893—June 23, 1972; American short story writer. Obituaries: *New York Times,* June 25, 1972.

\*      \*      \*

**PHILLIPS, E(wing) Lakin   1915-**

*PERSONAL:* Born April 29, 1915, in Higginsville, Mo.; son of Charles Brown (a merchant) and Martha T. (Lakin) Phillips; married Gloria T. Liebner (a sociological researcher), April 30, 1949; children: Charles William, Piper Jeanne, Nonie Elizabeth, Kirk Lakin. *Education:* Central Missouri State College (now University), B.S., 1937; University of Missouri, M.A., 1940; University of Minnesota, graduate study, 1940-42, 1946-48, Ph.D., 1949. *Politics:* "Liberal Democrat/independent." *Religion:* Unitarian Universalist. *Home:* 11416 Vale Rd., Oakton, Va. 22124. *Office:* Department of Psychology, George Washington University, Washington, D.C. 20006.

*CAREER:* Psychologist with schools in St. Paul, Minn., 1946-47, and Minneapolis, Minn., 1947-48; George Washington University, Washington, D.C., 1948—, began as assistant professor, became associate professor, 1952, currently professor of psychology. Clinical psychologist, Arlington County Guidance Center, 1949-56; executive director, School for Contemporary Education (school for handicapped children and adolescents), 1967—. Member of professional advisory board, National Society for Autistic Children. Consultant, National Orthopaedic & Rehabilitation Hospital, 1952—. *Military service:* U.S. Army and U.S. Army Air Forces, 1942-45; became technical sergeant.

*MEMBER:* American Psychological Association (fellow), Association for Advancement of Behavior Therapy, American Association for the Advancement of Science, National Society for Autistic Children, Eastern Psychological Association, Southeastern Psychological Association, Virginia Psychological Association, Virginia Academy of Science, District of Columbia Psychological Association.

*WRITINGS:* (With Isabel R. Berman and Harold B. Hanson) *Intelligence and Personality Factors Associated with Poliomyelitis Among School Age Children,* Society for Research in Child Development, 1948; *Psychotherapy: A Modern Theory and Practice,* Prentice-Hall, 1956; (with James F. Gibson) *Psychology and Personality,* Prentice-Hall, 1957; (with Daniel N. Wiener and Norris G. Haring) *Discipline, Achievement, and Mental Health,* Prentice-Hall, 1960, 2nd edition, 1972; (with Haring) *Educating Emotionally Disturbed Children,* McGraw, 1962; (with Wiener) *Short-Term Psychotherapy and Structured Behavior*

*Change,* McGraw, 1966; (with Wiener) *Training Children in Self-Discipline and Self-Control,* Prentice-Hall, 1972; (with Haring) *Analysis and Modification of Classroom Behavior,* Prentice-Hall, 1972; *Counseling and Psychotherapy: A Behavioral Approach,* Wiley, 1977; *Day to Day Anxiety Management,* Robert E. Krieger, 1977.

\*      \*      \*

**PICKETT, Carla   1944-**

*PERSONAL:* Born June 10, 1944, in Jacksonville, Fla.; daughter of Calvin R. and Catharine (Lapteff) Underdown; married Jack A. Pickett (a social worker), September 3, 1966; children: Helen. *Education:* Attended University of Maryland and Neighborhood Playhouse School of the Theatre. *Residence:* San Diego, Calif.

*CAREER:* Has worked as an actress and singer on stage, in films, and in television; presently employed by city of San Diego, Calif.

*WRITINGS: Calvin Crocodile and the Terrible Noise* (juvenile), illustrated by Carroll Dolezal, Steck, 1972.

*WORK IN PROGRESS:* Several children's stories.†

\*      \*      \*

**PIERCE, Roy   1923-**

*PERSONAL:* Born June 24, 1923, in New York, N.Y.; son of Roy Alexander and Elizabeth (Scott) Pierce; married Winnifred Poland, July 19, 1947. *Education:* Cornell University, B.A., 1947, M.A., 1948, Ph.D., 1950. *Home:* 211 McCotter Dr., Ann Arbor, Mich. 48103. *Office:* Department of Political Science, University of Michigan, Ann Arbor, Mich. 48104.

*CAREER:* Smith College, Northampton, Mass., instructor, 1950-51, assistant professor of political science, 1951-56; University of Michigan, Ann Arbor, associate professor, 1959-64, professor of political science, 1964—, director of Center for Western European Studies, 1972-75. Summer lecturer, Columbia University, 1959 and Stanford University, 1966; Fulbright summer lecturer in Nice, France, 1960; visiting professor, University of Oslo, winter, 1976. *Military service:* U.S. Army Air Forces, 1943-46; became staff sergeant. *Member:* American Political Science Association, Society for French Historical Studies.

*WRITINGS: Contemporary French Political Thought,* Oxford University Press, 1966; *French Politics and Political Institutions,* Harper, 1973. Contributor to political affairs journals.

*WORK IN PROGRESS:* With Philip E. Converse, a book on representative government in France.

*BIOGRAPHICAL/CRITICAL SOURCES: New York Review of Books,* April 6, 1967; *Virginia Quarterly Review,* spring, 1967.

\*      \*      \*

**PIERIK, Robert   1921-**

*PERSONAL:* Born December 29, 1921; son of Theodore Henry (a building contractor) and Christine Cecilia (Smith) Pierik; married Marilyn Anne Bowers (a librarian), July 25, 1964; children: David Vincent, Donald Lesley. *Education:* Los Angeles City College, A.A., 1947; University of Oregon, B.S., 1952; University of Southern California, M.A., 1960. *Residence:* Gresham, Ore.

*CAREER:* Has worked as a salesman and decorator for large department store chains in Los Angeles, Calif., a script and transcription writer for KHJ-Radio, Hollywood, Calif., and an elementary and high school teacher; instructor of language arts and drama at Warner Pacific College, Portland, Ore., and Mt. Hood Community College, Gresham, Ore. Concert chairman, Foothill Community Concert Association, San Gabriel Valley, Calif., 1966-69. *Military service:* U.S. Coast Guard Reserve, active duty, 1942-45. *Member:* National Education Association.

*WRITINGS*—Juvenile: *Niccobarbus and the Bear* (play), Harlequin, 1956; *Hansel and Gretel* (play adaption), Harlequin, 1958; (with Mildred Allen Butler) *Beauty and the Beast* (play adaption), Harlequin, 1958; (with Butler) *In the Forest of Fancy* (play), Harlequin, 1960; *Archy's Dream World* (novel), Morrow, 1972; (contributor) Sylvia Engdahl, editor, *Anywhere, Anywhere,* Atheneum, 1976.

*WORK IN PROGRESS: Nichol's Worth,* a novel for children.

*AVOCATIONAL INTERESTS:* Gardening, camping, hiking, fishing.†

\*    \*    \*

## PIKE, Diane Kennedy 1938-

*PERSONAL:* Born January 24, 1938, in Norfolk, Neb.; daughter of George Edward (a businessman) and Arlene Alice (Wyant) Kennedy; married James Albert Pike (theologian and Episcopal bishop), December 20, 1968 (died, 1969). *Education:* Stanford University, B.A., 1959; Columbia University, M.A., 1964. *Politics:* Democrat. *Religion:* Christian (Methodist). *Home and office address:* P.O. Box 7601, San Diego, Calif. 92107.

*CAREER:* United Methodist Church, Board of Missions, Montevideo, Uruguay, teacher of English, 1960-62; Willow Glen High School, San Jose, Calif., teacher, 1964-65; Palo Alto First United Methodist Church, Palo Alto, Calif., director of youth and children's work, 1965-67; New Focus Foundation, Santa Barbara, Calif., executive director, 1967-69; author and lecturer, 1969—. *Member:* Women's International League for Peace and Freedom, Well-Being: A National Association for Human Community, World Future Society, Common Cause, Fellowship of Reconciliation, P.E.O., Lambda Iota Tau.

*WRITINGS:* (With husband, James A. Pike) *The Other Side,* Doubleday, 1968; *Search,* Doubleday, 1970; (with R. Scott Kennedy) *The Wilderness Revolt,* Doubleday, 1972; (with Arleen Lorrance) *Channeling Love Energy,* L. P. Publications, 1974; *Life Is Victorious: How to Grow through Grief,* Simon & Schuster, 1976; *Cosmic Unfoldment: The Individualizing Process as Mirrored in the Life of Jesus,* L. P. Publications, 1976; *My Journey into Self,* L. P. Publications, 1977.

*WORK IN PROGRESS:* A book on Paul, disciple of Jesus and founder of Christianity; a book on the love project principles as pathways to inner, interpersonal, and international peace; a book on human sexuality as a mirror of the cosmic process of uniting polarities.

*SIDELIGHTS:* Diane Kennedy Pike writes: "I consider my writings to be an outgrowth of my life and work, rather than an end in themselves. My style is very personal, inviting the reader to share my own inner processes as I reflect upon them. Thus I write from the inside of my experiences out, rather than reflecting objectively on the experiences of others from the outside in. My writing style reflects my conviction that each of us learns from our own life experiences, not from those of others. When we share with others, or read

their thoughts and ideas and experiences, we take into ourselves those elements that are meaningful because they match our own experience and knowing and we feel confirmed (sometimes we call it guided) in our chosen direction and growth. We are nurtured by one another as we grow, but no one is an expert about anything but his own experience.

"Since 1972, I have been working with Arleen Lorrance as a group facilitator through The Love Project. The Love Project is an alternative to frustration, negativity, hostility, anger, and competition. It is a way of life based on six principles which focus one's awareness on the life process of choice and help one to remain an open channel for universal love energy. Arleen and I travel all around the country and the world, practicing the application of these principles to our own lives and sharing in that practice with others who seek to be more loving. It is a joyful work, and most of what I write is an expression of that work and of my own process of growth."

*BIOGRAPHICAL/CRITICAL SOURCES: Newsweek,* November 11, 1968; *Washington Post,* December 19, 1968; *New York Times,* December 19, 1968; *Book World,* December 29, 1968; *The Christian Century,* May 21, 1969.

\*    \*    \*

## PILAPIL, Vicente R. 1941-

*PERSONAL:* Born April 5, 1941, in Cebu City, Philippines; son of Francisco Sanchez (a landowner) and Nieves (Ramas) Pilapil; married Mercedes Diaz-Alonso, July 13, 1964 (divorced, 1967). *Education:* University of San Carlos, Philippines, B.A. (magna cum laude), 1959; Catholic University of America, M.A., 1961, Ph.D., 1964. *Home:* 1644 Kaweah Dr., Pasadena, Calif. 91105. *Office:* Department of History, California State University, Los Angeles, Calif. 90032.

*CAREER:* Georgetown University, Washington, D.C., lecturer in sociology, 1962; Loyola College, Baltimore, Md., instructor, 1963-64; assistant professor of history, 1964-65; State University of New York College at Cortland, Cortland, N.Y., assistant professor of history, 1967-68; California State University, Los Angeles, assistant professor, 1970-72, associate professor of history, 1972—. Visiting assistant professor of history, University of California, Los Angeles, 1968-69. *Member:* American Historical Association, Society of Spanish and Portuguese Historians, Iberian Social Studies Association. *Awards, honors:* American Philosophical Society grant, 1969; Social Science Research Council grant, 1970.

*WRITINGS: Alfonso XIII,* Twayne, 1969. Contributor of articles to history and current affairs journals.

*WORK IN PROGRESS:* Further research on the reign of Alfonso XIII.

*AVOCATIONAL INTERESTS:* Travel.†

\*    \*    \*

## PITKIN, Dorothy (Horton) 1899(?)-1972

1899(?)—June 26, 1972; American author of books for girls. Obituaries: *New York Times,* June 28, 1972; *Washington Post,* June 28, 1972.

\*    \*    \*

## PLANTE, David 1940-

*PERSONAL:* Born March 4, 1940, in Providence, R.I.; son of Anaclet Joseph Adolph and Albina (Bison) Plante. *Edu-*

*cation:* Boston College, B.A., 1961; also attended University of Louvain. *Home:* 30A Overstrand Mansions, Prince of Wales Dr., London S.W. 11, England. *Agent:* Deborah Rogers, 5-11 Mortimer St., London W.1, England.

*CAREER:* Writer.

*WRITINGS*—Novels, except as indicated: *The Ghost of Henry James,* Gambit, 1970; *Slides,* Gambit, 1971; *Relatives,* J. Cape, 1972; *The Darkness of the Body,* J. Cape, 1974; (contributor) Giles Gordon, editor, *Beyond Words: Eleven Writers in Search of a New Fiction* (collection), Hutchinson, 1975; *Figures in Bright Air,* Gollancz, 1976; *The Family,* Farrar, Straus, 1978.

*WORK IN PROGRESS:* A novel.

*SIDELIGHTS:* In a review of *The Ghost of Henry James,* Jonathan Raban writes: "Plante, in a splendidly intelligent and ambitious first novel, takes on James with the mixture of love, parody, and emulation. . . . The novel has a prismatic shape; broken into 67 very short chapters; each of which embodies an oblique and fragmentary dialogue. . . ." Richard Freedman believes that "the ghost of Henry James would gibber and quake if it could know of the carryings-on in this talented but perverse first novel. . . ." He calls the book ". . . overrich and too highly technicolored, festering in elegant decadence, and ideal for inhaling with a Campari-and-soda."

According to Anthony Bailey, *Slides* uses Nathaniel Hawthorne's *The Marble Faun* "as a touchstone, detected as if with radar through the gloom, echoing sometimes firm and sometimes weak responses. One measure of *Slides'* success is that the words a reader feels bound to use in describing it are those of either Mr. Plante or Hawthorne. . . . In a time when many books seem full of vicarious lechery, [Plante's] descriptions of sexual activity possess an honest and moving precision. . . . I would conclude that, having made such mysterious and skillful use of Henry James in his first book, and of Hawthorne in this, Mr. Plante seems fully equipped to achieve great magic with Mr. Plante." In writing about the characters in *Slides,* all of whom are in their early twenties, Jonathan Strong states: "Despite their four-letter word vocabularies, puritanical guilt still operates in the minds of these young people. This is no novel of communal love. In that sense it is an honest novel, because no love comes free. But Plante never lets us understand why his five characters are so obsessed with and disturbed by their emotional relations, and therefore it is also a disappointing book."

Thomas LeClair feels that *Relatives* "proceeds through a chronological series of brief tableaux in which little happens but much is suggested by the hushed, almost soap-opera tone Plante falls into. The characters talk and talk and talk 'to extend themselves until they reached the edges of a sustaining context,' but the context achieved at the end of the novel has no more significance to the reader than a fence around a dreary house of mirrors. . . . Some may call *Relatives* a sensitive book because of its fragility, but I think the fineness of perception Plante attempts occurs only occasionally. His people aren't capable of a revealing experience or language because they're empty, not the echoing emptiness of Beckett's speakers or the vacancy of relativity that Plante implies, but that squeezed-out quality that results when a writer presses too hard and too often for Meaning."

Reviewing *The Darkness of the Body,* Valentine Cunningham writes: "The author's constantly deadpan tone and his persistent vagueness about people and places—the refusal to specify which cities or countries are being lived and loved in, on the grounds that it's inner topography that mat-

ters most—suggest the choreographer never letting his dancers try for spontaneity. But the cool unspecificity is in fact played so successfully against the bouts of explicitness as to justify and enhance both these extremes of pitch and tone." A *Times Literary Supplement* reviewer says that "there is some evidence of talent and style in certain phrases, occasional descriptions and in one sustained scene where the two main characters are briefly sympathetic in the context of some alien fiesta. For the most part, however, the behaviour of the characters is childishly perverse and many of the metaphysical passages of reflective description seem hopelessly inflated."

In discussing *Figures in Bright Air,* Susannah Clapp calls Plante "a thoughtful writer, capable of producing fine flashes of prose. His latest novel . . . abandons even the intermittent verisimilitude of his previous books: it describes in long and excited swirls of prose the kind of fictions people use to describe themselves and their relations with others—and the implications of writing fiction." Neil Hepburn writes: "In spite of boiling-oil reviews that have repulsed his previous assaults upon the stronghold of Castle Naturalism, David Plante continues resolutely with his siege, a literary Gawain bent on rescuing the English novel from durance vile. And an appallingly lonely and dangerous business it must be: there are few enough in England willing to allow justice to his cause, let alone to encourage him in it. Its sponsors, living and dead, are all abroad, where they harbour the strangest notions about what the novel, given its liberty, will do for us all." Duncan Fallowell feels that "if compared to the wisecracking polychromatics of very modern writing Plante's *avant-gardisme* seems *passe,* pre-Beckett even, a feeling of affectation because the unfamiliarity of the content is not confirmed by an equivalently original attitude to language, it is because David Plante is not a major writer. But he is much more interesting than many of those claimed as 'major,' since he brings the good news that the novel is still alive and edging forward here and there along a broad front to prove that 'entertainment,' 'good yarn,' and 'diversion,' are ultimately get-out clauses from the energetic responsibilities of creating."

*BIOGRAPHICAL/CRITICAL SOURCES: Times Literary Supplement,* March, 1970, April 16, 1971, July 7, 1972, February 1, 1974, July 2, 1976; *New Statesman,* March 13, 1970, March 12, 1971, June 16, 1972, February 1, 1974, April 2, 1976; *Spectator,* March 14, 1970, March 27, 1971, February 2, 1974, April 10, 1976; *Observer,* March 15, 1970, March 14, 1971, June 18, 1972, January 27, 1974, April 4, 1976; *Listener,* March 19, 1970, March 18, 1971, June 15, 1972, February 7, 1974, April 1, 1976; *Publishers Weekly,* June 29, 1970, June 7, 1971, August 26, 1974; *Kirkus Reviews,* July 1, 1970, June 15, 1971; *Book World,* November 1, 1970; *New York Review of Books,* November 5, 1970; *New York Times Book Review,* November 29, 1970, December 6, 1970, August 22, 1971, October 20, 1974; *Bookseller,* March, 1971; *Choice,* March, 1971; *Books and Bookmen,* May, 1971, July, 1972; *Guardian Weekly,* June 24, 1972, February 2, 1974; *Contemporary Review,* April, 1974; *Contemporary Literary Criticism,* Volume VII, Gale, 1977.

\*     \*     \*

## PLATIG, E(mil) Raymond 1924-

*PERSONAL:* Born March 29, 1924, in Clayton, N.J.; son of Raymond Emil and Frieda (Schumann) Platig; married Rachel Large Weidmen, November 10, 1973; children: (previous marriage) Betsy Miriam, Harvey John. *Education:* Albion College, A.B., 1948; Emory University, M.A., 1949;

University of Chicago, Ph.D., 1957. *Residence:* Washington, D.C. *Office:* Office of External Research, Bureau of Intelligence and Research, U.S. Department of State, 21st and C Sts., Washington, D.C. 20520.

*CAREER:* Millsaps College, Jackson, Miss., instructor, 1949-50, assistant professor of history, 1950-51; University of Denver, Denver, Colo., assistant professor, 1953-59, associate professor of international relations, 1959-61, member of staff of Social Science Foundation, 1953-61; Carnegie Endowment for International Peace, New York, N.Y., director of studies, 1961-66; U.S. Department of State, Bureau of Intelligence and Research, Washington, D.C., director of Office of External Research, 1966—. *Military service:* U.S. Army Air Forces, 1943-46; served in Canada and the South Pacific; became sergeant.

*MEMBER:* International Studies Association, Council on Foreign Relations, Phi Beta Kappa, Omicron Delta Kappa. *Awards, honors:* Rockefeller Foundation grants, 1960-61; Superior Honor Award, U.S. Department of State, 1969, 1973.

*WRITINGS: Our American Foreign Policy,* Science Research Associates, 1956, revised edition, 1956; *The United States and World Affairs,* Laidlaw Brothers, 1959, revised edition, 1967; *The United States and the Soviet Challenge,* Laidlaw Brothers, 1960, revised edition, 1967; (contributor) Howard J. Taubenfeld, editor, *Space and Society,* Oceana, 1964; *International Relations Research: Problems of Evaluation and Advancement,* Carnegie Endowment, 1966; (contributor) Dagmar Horna Perman, editor, *Bibliography and the Historian,* American Bibliographic Center/Clio Press, 1967; (contributor) Norman D. Palmer, editor, *A Design for International Relations Research: Scope, Theory, Methods and Relevance,* American Academy of Political and Social Science, 1970; (contributor) Douglas E. Knight, Huntington W. Curtis, and Lawrence J. Fogel, editors, *Cybernetics, Simulation, and Conflict Resolution,* Spartan, 1971; (contributor) Fred W. Riggs, editor, *International Studies: Present Status and Future Prospects,* American Academy of Political and Social Science, 1971; (contributor) Kenneth W. Thompson, editor, *Ethics and Foreign Policy,* Council on Religion and International Affairs, 1977. Contributor of articles to political science journals and Denver newspapers.

\* \* \*

## PLOWMAN, Edward E(arl)  1931-

*PERSONAL:* Born September 27, 1931, in Hanover, Pa.; son of Edward E., Sr. (retired from U.S. Army) and Roberta (Geiman) Plowman; married Rose Orazi, June, 1952; children: Gary E., Gail E., Beth A., J. Philip. *Education:* Philadelphia Bible Institute, diploma, 1952; Wheaton College, B.A., 1954; Dallas Theological Seminary, Th.M., 1958. *Residence:* Annandale, Va. *Office: Christianity Today* Magazine, 1014 Washington Bldg., Washington, D.C. 20005.

*CAREER:* Ordained to Baptist ministry, 1958; First Baptist Church, National City, Calif., youth minister, 1958-60; Park Presidio Baptist Church, San Francisco, Calif., pastor, 1960-70; *Christianity Today,* Washington, D.C., assistant editor, 1970-72, news editor, 1972—. Press relations consultant to American Baptist Churches of the West, 1965-70. *Awards, honors:* Evangelical Press Association award, 1971, and Religious Heritage of America special award in religious journalism, 1972, for coverage of The Jesus Movement.

*WRITINGS: The Jesus Movement in America,* Pyramid,

1971; *Washington: Christians in the Corridors of Power,* Tyndale, 1975. Contributor of articles to *Power, Private Pilot, Moody Monthly, Washington Post, Christianity Today,* and *Campus Life.*

*AVOCATIONAL INTERESTS:* Color photography, hiking, fishing, travel, and camping.

\* \* \*

## PLUM, Lester Virgil  1906-1972

February 19, 1906—December 25, 1972; American economist, lecturer, and investment counselor. Obituaries: *New York Times,* December 27, 1972. (See index for *CA* sketch)

\* \* \*

## PLUMMER, Mark A(llen)  1929-

*PERSONAL:* Born June 1, 1929, in Seneca, Mo.; son of Maynard Osa and Venta Plummer; married Betty Jean Smith (an instructor), 1953; children: Robert Allen, Lisa Ann. *Education:* Attended University of Missouri, 1947-49; Kansas State College (now Pittsburg State University), B.S., 1951, M.S., 1952; University of Kansas, Ph.D., 1960. *Home:* 504 Hovey, Normal, Ill. 61761. *Office:* Department of History, Illinois State University, Normal, Ill. 61761.

*CAREER:* Illinois State University, Normal, assistant professor, 1960-64, associate professor, 1964-68, professor of history, 1968—, chairperson of department, 1973-76. Fulbright lecturer, National Taiwan University, 1965-66. *Military service:* U.S. Army, 1952-54. *Member:* American Historical Association, Organization of American Historians.

*WRITINGS: Frontier Governor: Samuel J. Crawford of Kansas,* University Press of Kansas, 1971; (contributor) Frank N. Magill, editor, *Great Events from History,* Volume II, Salem Press, 1975.

\* \* \*

## POCHMANN, Henry A(ugust)  1901-1973

*PERSONAL:* Born January 5, 1901, in Round Top, Tex.; son of Henry G. and Clara (Ebner) Pochmann; married Ruth Fouts (an author), September 11, 1928; children: Virginia P. (Mrs. Theodore Patrick Weis). *Education:* Southwest Texas State Teachers College (now Southwest Texas State University), B.A., 1923; University of Texas, M.A., 1924; University of North Carolina, Ph.D., 1928. *Home:* 524 Inwood Lane, Nacogdoches, Tex. 75961.

*CAREER:* Stephen F. Austin Teachers College (now Stephen F. Austin State University), Nacogdoches, Tex., assistant professor of English, 1924-26; University of North Carolina at Chapel Hill, instructor in English, 1926-28; Louisiana State University, Baton Rouge, associate professor of English, 1928-30; University of Mississippi, University, professor of English and head of department, 1930-32; Mississippi State University, State College, professor of English, 1932-38, dean of graduate school, 1935-38; University of Wisconsin—Madison, professor of English, 1938-71, emeritus professor, 1971-73. *Member:* Modern Language Association of America, Madison Literary Club (president, 1960-61), Phi Beta Kappa, Sigma Alpha Epsilon, Alpha Chi. *Awards, honors:* Rockefeller Foundation fellow, 1936-37, 1939; Huntington Library fellow, 1947; Loubat Prize, 1958, for *German Culture in America;* Distinguished Alumnus plaque designating him the "Best Scholar Ever Graduated from Southwest Texas State University," awarded posthumously, 1975; Henry A. Pochmann Professorship has been established at the University of Wisconsin.

*WRITINGS: Washington Irving,* American Book Co., 1934; (with Gay W. Allen) *Masters of American Literature,* two volumes, Macmillan, 1949, published as *Introduction to Masters of American Literature,* Southern Illinois University Press, 1969; *New England Transcendentalism and St. Louis Hegelianism,* Carl Schurz Memorial Foundation, 1949; *Bibliography of German Culture in America,* University of Wisconsin Press, 1953; *German Culture in America, 1600-1900: Philosophical and Literary Influences,* University of Wisconsin Press, 1957; (editor with E. N. Feltskog) Washington Irving, *Mahomet and His Successors,* University of Wisconsin Press, 1970. General editor, *The Complete Works of Washington Irving,* twenty-eight volumes, University of Wisconsin Press, 1969-73. Contributor to journals.

*AVOCATIONAL INTERESTS:* Hunting, fishing, billiards, golf.†

(Died, 1973)

\*    \*    \*

## POLIN, Raymond 1918-

*PERSONAL:* Born August 9, 1918, in Westport, Mass.; son of Israel (an artist) and Ida (Posnick) Polin; married Constance Fay Caplan, November 9, 1957; children: Jane Louise, Lawrence Wayne, Kenneth Lee, Ellen Lynn, Theodore Lewis. *Education:* Attended Yonkers Collegiate Center, 1935-37; New York University, B.A., 1940, M.A., 1941, Ph.D., 1959. *Politics:* Democrat. *Religion:* Jewish. *Home:* 25 Tunstall Rd., Scarsdale, N.Y. 10583. *Office:* Department of Political Science, St. John's University, Jamaica, N.Y. 11439.

*CAREER:* U.S. War Department, New York City, civilian chief clerk at New York Port of Embarkation, 1941-44; Preparatory Academy, New York City, instructor in history, English, and economics, 1944-46; Long Island University, Brooklyn, N.Y., instructor, 1946-49, assistant professor of history and government, 1949-59; Yeshiva University, New York City, assistant professor of government and chairman of department of secondary education, 1959-62; St. John's University, Jamaica, N.Y., associate professor, 1962-67, professor of political science, 1967—. Visiting associate professor of government, New York University, 1961-67. Member of advisory curriculum committee to New York Superintendent of Schools, 1960-62; director, Multi-Ethnic Curriculum and Teacher Training Task Force (Mt. Vernon, N.Y.), 1969-70.

*MEMBER:* American Political Science Association, American Historical Association, American Academy of Political and Social Science, National Council for the Social Studies, Middle States Council for the Social Studies (president, 1968-70), New York Historical Society. *Awards, honors:* Dean Harry J. Carman Memorial Medal, Middle States Council for the Social Studies, 1965, for *Marxian Foundations of Communism;* Eisenhower Award, ROTC Instructor Group, Department of the Army, 1971.

*WRITINGS: Marxian Foundations of Communism,* Regnery, 1966. Contributor of articles and reviews to academic journals and newspapers.

*WORK IN PROGRESS: Modern Government and Constitutionalism,* for Nelson-Hall; *Democracy and the Isms;* research on New York's contribution to the Declaration of Independence; Platonic and Aristotelian approaches to constitutionalism.

## POLK, Edwin Weiss 1916-

*PERSONAL:* Born January 9, 1916, in Lincoln, Neb.; son of Ralph W. (a teacher and author) and Freda (Zimmerman) Polk; married Margaret Rose Connor (a teacher), June 24, 1939; children: Brent W. (deceased), Carole M. (Mrs. Steven H. Gillesby), Gayle Marie (Mrs. Mark Hoffman). *Education:* Western Michigan University, B.S., 1937; Wayne State University, M.Ed., 1948. *Politics:* Republican. *Religion:* Presbyterian. *Home:* 4915 Elm Gate Dr., Orchard Lake, Mich. 48033.

*CAREER:* Teacher of graphic arts in public school in Detroit, Mich., 1937-43, and vocational teacher, Detroit, 1950-63; Lessinger Junior High School, Detroit, vocational department head, 1963—. *Military service:* U.S. Navy; became lieutenant commander; received Bronze Star Medal and Purple Heart. *Member:* Michigan Industrial Education Society, Retired Officers Association.

*WRITINGS:* (With father, Ralph W. Polk) *The Practice of Printing,* Charles A. Bennett, 7th edition (Edwin Polk was not associated with earlier editions), 1971; (with R. W. Polk) *Elementary Platen Presswork,* Charles A. Bennett, 4th edition (Edwin Polk was not associated with earlier editions), 1971.

*WORK IN PROGRESS:* Research on German PT boats of World War II and on the history of the German Navy.

\*    \*    \*

## POLK, Ralph Weiss 1890-1978

*PERSONAL:* Born January 26, 1890; son of Marcellus D. and Ella (Weiss) Polk; married Freda Marie Zimmerman (died January 20, 1978); children: Edwin Weiss. *Education:* Attended Winona State College, Hiram College, University of Nebraska, Wisconsin State University, and Wayne State University. *Religion:* Protestant.

*CAREER:* Teacher. *Member:* Graphic Arts Education Guild (honorary life member).

*WRITINGS: The Practice of Printing,* Charles A. Bennett, 1916, 7th edition (with son, Edwin Weiss Polk), 1971; *Elementary Platen Presswork,* Charles A. Bennett, 1928, 4th edition (with E. W. Polk), 1971; *Composition Manual,* Printing Industry of America, 1950.†

(Died January 26, 1978)

\*    \*    \*

## POLLACK, Reginald 1924-

*PERSONAL:* Born July 29, 1924, in Middle Village, Long Island, N.Y.; son of Sam (a tailor and artist) and Gussie Pollack; married third wife, Kerstin Birjitta Soederlund; children: (second marriage) Jane Olivia, Maia Jaquine. *Education:* Studied as apprentice to Moses Soyer, 1941, under Wallace Harrison, 1946-47, and at Academie de la Grande Chaumiere, Paris, 1948-52. *Politics:* Liberal. *Religion:* Jewish. *Home and studio:* 205 River Bend Rd., Great Falls, Va. 22066.

*CAREER:* Artist; lived and painted in France, 1948-59, then in New York and Hollywood before settling in Virginia; visiting critic in art at Yale University, New Haven, Conn., 1962-63; instructor at Cooper Union, New York, N.Y., 1963-64; visiting artist, Materials Research Lab, Pennsylvania State University, 1977—. Trustee, Washington Project of the Arts, 1976—. Has had over thirty-five one-man shows at Peridot Gallery, New York, 1949-72, at other galleries in Paris, New York, Los Angeles, San Francisco,

La Jolla, Scranton, Washington, D.C., and Chicago; work has been in group exhibitions every year since 1948, including shows at Museum of Modern Art, Whitney Museum, Everhart Museum, Pennsylvania State University, Carnegie International, Corcoran Biennial, Pennsylvania Academy Annual, a number of Paris exhibits, in Rome, Ankara, Tokyo, and in Smithsonian Institution traveling exhibit, "The American Landscape," 1968; represented in collections of Museum of Modern Art, Whitney Museum, Brooklyn Museum, Hirshhorn Museum, Collection de l'Etat (Paris), Tel Aviv Museum, Worcester Museum, University of Glasgow, Rockefeller Institute, Yale University Library, and other public, private, and corporate collections. Developer of technique used by Collectors Graphics, Inc., to produce original lithographs by artists of the New York School on high speed rotary offset presses, 1959-63; presently forming an art and science research studio, The Electronic Art Studio in Washington, D.C., for the creation of works in artistic and educational areas utilizing tools of electronic capabilities, including lasers and computers. *Military service:* U.S. Army and U.S. Army Air Forces, 1941-45; served in Pacific theater.

*AWARDS, HONORS:* Prix Neuman, Jewish Museum (Paris), 1952; Prix Othon Friesz (Paris), 1956, 1957; Prix des Peintres Etranger (Paris), 1958; Ingram-Merrill Foundation grants in painting, 1964, 1970-71.

*WRITINGS: The Magician and the Child* (juvenile), Atheneum, 1971.

Illustrator: John Hollander, *The Quest of the Gole,* Atheneum, 1966; Merrill Pollack, *O Is for Overkill: A Survival Alphabet,* Viking, 1968. Also illustrator, Bill Martin, Jr., compiler, *Collected Folk Tales from All Countries,* Holt, and Seneca, *Oedipus,* Doubleday.

Films: "The Creative Process," Kahana Productions, 1967; "Contextures-Riots-Decade 60," Kahana Productions, 1968.

*WORK IN PROGRESS:* Painting; work with the Materials Research Lab, Pennsylvania State University.

*AVOCATIONAL INTERESTS:* Food, wine, travel, music, architecture, and other arts.

\*   \*   \*

## POLLIO, Howard R.   1937-

*PERSONAL:* Surname is pronounced Polly-o; born July 5, 1937, in New York, N.Y.; son of Donald and Ellen (Mittleman) Pollio; married Marilyn Dyller, January 25, 1959; children: David Erik, Michele Suzanne, Jonathan Meyer. *Education:* Brooklyn College (now Brooklyn College of the City University of New York), B.A., 1957, M.A., 1959; University of Michigan, Ph.D., 1962. *Home:* 7501 Sheffield Dr., Knoxville, Tenn. *Office:* Department of Psychology, 301 Austin Peay Bldg., University of Tennessee, Knoxville, Tenn. 37916.

*CAREER:* University of Tennessee, Knoxville, assistant professor, 1962-64, associate professor, 1964-68, professor of psychology, 1969—. Visiting professor, University of Guelph, 1972. Senior research fellow, University of London, 1968-69, and Cambridge University, 1975-76. Consultant to Fellowship Division of U.S. Public Health Service, 1969-73, and to National Institute of Alcohol and Alcohol Abuse, 1972—. *Member:* American Psychological Association, Psychonomic Society, American Association of University Professors (president of University of Tennessee chapter, 1977-78), Southeastern Psychological Association,

Eastern Tennessee Psychological Association (vice-president, 1963-64), Sigma Xi, Psi Chi, Phi Kappa Phi. *Awards, honors:* U.S. Public Health Service research fellowships, 1968, 1969, 1972; outstanding teacher award, 1971.

*WRITINGS: The Structural Basis of Word Association,* Mouton, 1966; (contributor) Theodore R. Dixon and D. L. Horton, editors, *Verbal Behavior and General Behavior Theory,* Prentice-Hall, 1968; *Learning,* 2nd edition (Pollio was not associated with earlier edition), Prentice-Hall, 1972; *The Psychology of Symbolic Activity,* Addison-Wesley, 1972; (contributor with R. Mers and W. Lucchesi) J. H. Goldstein and P. E. McGhee, editors, *The Psychology of Humor,* Academic Press, 1972; (contributor with J. Edgerly) A. Chapman and H. Foot, editors, *Research in Humor and Laughter,* Wiley, 1976; (with J. Barlow, H. Fine, and M. R. Pollio) *Psychology and the Poetics of Growth: Figurative Language in Psychotherapy and Education,* Halsted, 1977; *Behavior and Existence: An Empirical Introduction to Humanistic Psychology,* Brooks/Cole, 1978. Contributor to psychology journals.

\*   \*   \*

## POLLOCK, John L(eslie)   1940-

*PERSONAL:* Born January 28, 1940, in Atchison, Kan.; son of Leslie R. and Margaret Belle (Endebrock) Pollock; married Carol L. Halvorson, June 23, 1962; children: Erika Christine, Katherine Heather. *Education:* University of Minnesota, B.A. (magna cum laude), 1961; University of California, Berkeley, Ph.D., 1965. *Home:* 66 Boxwood Lane, Fairport, N.Y. 14450. *Office:* Department of Philosophy, University of Rochester, Rochester, N.Y. 14627.

*CAREER:* State University of New York College at Buffalo, assistant professor, 1965-68, associate professor, 1968-71; University of Rochester, Rochester, N.Y., associate professor, 1971-76, professor of philosophy, 1976—. *Member:* American Philosophical Association, Association for Symbolic Logic, Phi Beta Kappa. *Awards, honors:* Woodrow Wilson fellow, 1961-62; American Council of Learned Societies fellow, 1972.

*WRITINGS: An Introduction to Symbolic Logic,* Holt, 1969; *Knowledge and Justification,* Princeton University Press, 1974; *Subjunctive Reasoning,* D. Reidel, 1976. Contributor of articles to philosophy and logic journals.

*WORK IN PROGRESS: Language and Thought,* a treatise on the philosophy of language and the philosophy of logic.

\*   \*   \*

## POOR, Henry Varnum   1914(?)-1972

1914(?)—October 10, 1972; American lawyer, diplomat, educator, editor, and author of political and legal works. Obituaries: *New York Times,* October 11, 1972.

\*   \*   \*

## POSTEUCA, Vasile   1912-1972

1912—December 6, 1972; Rumanian-born American poet and educator. Obituaries: *New York Times,* December 7, 1972.

\*   \*   \*

## POTTER, E. B.   1908-

*PERSONAL:* Born December 27, 1908, in Norfolk, Va.; son of Judson Rice (a grocer) and Fannie (Beacham) Potter; married Grace Brauer, May 21, 1954; children: Katherine

Anne, Lorraine Frances. *Education:* University of Richmond, B.A., 1929; University of Chicago, M.A., 1940. *Home:* 2 Brice Rd., Annapolis, Md. 21401. *Agent:* Curtis Brown Ltd., 575 Madison Ave., New York, N.Y. 10022.

*CAREER:* Teacher in high schools, 1931-41; U.S. Naval Academy, Annapolis, Md., member of history faculty, 1941-77. Has lectured widely on naval history. *Military service:* U.S. Naval Reserve, active duty, 1941-46; served in Pacific theater, 1943-45; became commander. *Member:* U.S. Naval Institute, American Historical Association, American Association of University Professors. *Awards, honors:* Author Award of Merit, U.S. Naval Institute, 1977, for *Nimitz;* Alfred Thayer Mahan Award, Navy League of the United States, 1977.

*WRITINGS:* (With others) *American Sea Power since 1775,* Lippincott, 1947; (with others) *The United States and World Sea Power,* Prentice-Hall, 1955; (with C. W. Nimitz) *Sea Power: A Naval History,* Prentice-Hall, 1960; (with Nimitz) *The Great Sea War,* Prentice-Hall, 1961; *The Naval Academy Illustrated History of the United States Navy,* Crowell, 1971; *Nimitz,* Naval Institute Press, 1976.

*WORK IN PROGRESS:* Revised edition of *Sea Power: A Naval History.*

\*     \*     \*

## POTTER, Van Rensselaer   1911-

*PERSONAL:* Born August 27, 1911, in Day County, S.D.; son of Arthur Howard (a farmer) and Evangeline (Herpel) Potter; married Vivian Christensen, August 3, 1935; children: Karin Evangeline (Mrs. Peter N. Simon), John Howard, Carl Tobin. *Education:* South Dakota State University, B.S., 1933; University of Wisconsin, M.S., 1936, Ph.D., 1938. *Home:* 163 North Prospect Ave., Madison, Wis. 53705. *Office:* McArdle Laboratory, Department of Oncology, University of Wisconsin, Madison, Wis. 53706.

*CAREER:* Biochemist; University of Wisconsin, McArdle Laboratory, Madison, 1940—, currently professor of oncology, assistant director, 1958-72. Hubert Lecturer, British Association for Cancer Research, 1978. American Cancer Society, member of research advisory council, 1965-68, member of council on analysis and projection. *Member:* American Association for Cancer Research (member of board of directors, 1955-58, 1972-75; president, 1975), American Society for Cell Biology (president, 1964-65), American Society of Biological Chemists, American Academy of Arts and Sciences (fellow), National Academy of Science. *Awards, honors:* Paul Lewis Medal and award in enzyme chemistry, American Chemical Society, 1947; D.S., South Dakota State College (now University), 1959; Bertner Foundation award for outstanding achievement in fundamental cancer research, 1961; G. H. A. Clowes award, American Association for Cancer Research, 1964.

*WRITINGS: Enzymes, Growth and Cancer,* C. C Thomas, 1950; *DNA Model Kit,* Burgess, 1959; *Nucleic Acid Outlines,* Burgess, 1960; *Bioethics: Bridge to the Future,* Prentice-Hall, 1971. Contributor of more than 250 articles to professional journals. Editor, *Methods in Medical Research,* 1947.

*WORK IN PROGRESS:* Research on biochemistry of cancer, bioethics, and humanistic biology, with publications expected to result.

*AVOCATIONAL INTERESTS:* Conserving the Wisconsin woodland, travel.

## POUND, Ezra (Loomis)   1885-1972
### (William Atheling, Alfred Venison)

October 30, 1885—November 1, 1972; American expatriate, poet, translator, editor, essayist, and man of letters. Obituaries: *New York Times,* November 2, 1972; *Detroit Free Press,* November 2, 1972; *L'Express,* November 6-12, 1972; *Antiquarian Bookman,* November 13, 1972; *Newsweek,* November 13, 1972; *Publishers Weekly,* November 13, 1972; *Time,* November 13, 1972. (See index for *CA* sketch)

\*     \*     \*

## POWELL, Meredith (Ann)   1936-

*PERSONAL:* Born June 28, 1936, in Baltimore, Md.; daughter of Winters Meredith and Mary Catherine (Lindenberger) Cook; married Charles Kendall Powell (a Western Electric employee), May 28, 1955; children: Gloria Ann, R. Craig, Jan Catherine. *Education:* Dundalk Community College, A.A., 1973; Towson State University, B.S., 1975. *Residence:* Baltimore, Md.

*CAREER:* Has worked as a sales clerk, bank teller and file clerk, telephone company service representative, and substitute teacher; high school teacher in Baltimore, Md., 1975-78; author. Recording secretary for Parent Staff Association, Catonsville Cerebral Palsy Center, 1963.

*WRITINGS:* (With sister, Gail Yokubinas) *What to Be?* (rhyming verse), illustrated by Richard Mlodock, Childrens Press, 1972. Contributor to literary journals. Author of "Meet the People," in *Magpie* (college newsletter).

*WORK IN PROGRESS:* Three children's books.

\*     \*     \*

## POWERS, Thomas   1940-

*PERSONAL:* Born December 12, 1940, in New York, N.Y.; son of Joshua Bryant (a publisher) and Susan (Moore) Powers; married Candace Molloy, August 21, 1965; children: Amanda, Susan, Cassandra. *Education:* Yale University, B.A., 1964. *Home:* 43 West 10th St., New York, N.Y. 10011. *Agent:* Karen Hitzig, 34 Gramercy Park, New York, N.Y. 10003.

*CAREER: Rome Daily American,* Rome, Italy, reporter, 1965-67; United Press International, New York, N.Y., reporter, 1967-70. *Awards, honors:* Pulitzer Prize for national reporting, 1971.

*WRITINGS: Diana: The Making of a Terrorist,* Houghton, 1971; *The War at Home: Vietnam and the American People, 1964-68,* Grossman, 1973.

*WORK IN PROGRESS: The Man Who Kept Secrets: Richard Helms and the CIA,* for Houghton.

\*     \*     \*

## PRESCOTT, Peter S(herwin)   1935-

*PERSONAL:* Born July 15, 1935, in New York, N.Y.; son of Orville (a writer and critic) and Lilias (Ward-Smith) Prescott; married Anne Lake (a professor of English), June 22, 1957; children: David Sherwin, Antonia Courthope. *Education:* Harvard University, A.B. (magna cum laude), 1957; Sorbonne, University of Paris, additional study, 1957-58. *Politics:* Democrat. *Agent:* Sterling Lord Agency, 660 Madison Ave., New York, N.Y. 10021.

*CAREER:* E. P. Dutton & Co., New York City, senior editor, 1958-67; *Women's Wear Daily,* New York City, literary editor, 1964-68; *Look,* New York City, book review editor,

1968-71; *Newsweek,* New York City, general editor and book critic, 1971—. Instructor, Publishers' School for Writers, 1964-65; Constable of town of New Canaan, 1969—. *Military service:* U.S. Army Reserve, 1958-64. *Member:* Authors Guild (member of council, 1971—; foundation vice-president, 1972—), Authors League of America (member of council, 1973-76), International P.E.N. (member of executive board, American Center, 1974-76), National Book Critics Circle (founding member; member of advisory board), Century Association, Coffee House, Country Club of New Canaan, Phi Beta Kappa. *Awards, honors:* Guggenheim fellow, 1977.

*WRITINGS: A World of Our Own: Notes on Life and Learning in a Boys' Preparatory School,* Coward, 1970; *Soundings: Encounters with Contemporary Books,* Coward, 1972; *A Darkening Green: Notes from the Silent Generation,* Coward, 1974.

*WORK IN PROGRESS:* A study of juvenile justice in New York City.

*AVOCATIONAL INTERESTS:* Listening to Bach and Mozart, French wines, collecting Chinese and Japanese paintings and Japanese prints, tennis.

*BIOGRAPHICAL/CRITICAL SOURCES: New York Times,* October 14, 1970; *Washington Post,* October 16, 1970; *Newsweek,* October 26, 1970; *Best Sellers,* December 1, 1970.

\*    \*    \*

## PRICE, William 1938-

*PERSONAL:* Born September 27, 1938, in Wenatchee, Wash.; son of T. M. (an orchardist) and Margaret (Batterton) Price; married Aida Keshishian (a research consultant), June 25, 1966; children: Susan, Jennie. *Education:* Wenatchee Valley College, A.A., 1958; attended Texas Western College (now University of Texas at El Paso), 1962-63. *Home:* 292 Clermont Ave., Brooklyn, N.Y. 11205. *Agent:* Brandt & Brandt, 101 Park Ave., New York, N.Y. 10017.

*CAREER:* Greime & Fasken Theatres, Wenatchee, Wash., manager, 1957-59; Del Monte Foods, Wenatchee, fruit inspector, 1958-61; apartment house manager in Seattle, Wash., 1960-61; orchardist in Malaga, Wash., 1963; General Dynamics, Groton, Conn., security clearance investigator, 1964; United Nations, New York, N.Y., clerk, 1965-68; Ryder Truck Lines, Brooklyn, N.Y., tracer of lost freight, 1968; part-time stagehand, Brooklyn, N.Y. *Military service:* U.S. Army, 1961-63. *Awards, honors:* National Foundation for the Arts and Humanities fellowship, 1974-75.

*WRITINGS: The Potlatch Run* (novel), Dutton, 1971. Contributor of short fiction to *Climax, Saturday Evening Post,* and *Evergreen Review* and of articles to *Frontier Times, American Heritage,* and *True West.*

*BIOGRAPHICAL/CRITICAL SOURCES: Best Sellers,* July 1, 1971.

\*    \*    \*

## PRICE, Wilson T(itus) 1931-

*PERSONAL:* Born March 28, 1931, in Seattle, Wash.; son of Wilson T. (an engineer) and Dorothy (Gagne) Price; married Jeanette Jones, May 4, 1971; children: Diana. *Education:* Washington State University, B.S. in M.E., 1957; University of Pittsburgh, M.S. in M.E., 1958; San Jose State College (now University), M.S. (math), 1962. *Home:* 5450

Bacon Rd., Oakland, Calif. 94619. *Office:* Department of Business, Merritt College, 12500 Campus Dr., Oakland, Calif. 94619.

*CAREER:* Westinghouse Electric Corp., Pittsburgh, Pa., engineer, 1957-58, engineer in Sunnyvale, Calif., 1958-61; Lockheed Missiles & Space Co., Sunnyvale, Calif., consultant, 1961-62; Merritt College, Oakland, Calif., professor of data processing, 1961—. *Military service:* U.S. Army, 1953-55. *Member:* Association for Educational Data Systems.

*WRITINGS*—All published by Holt, except as indicated: (With Kenneth P. Swallow) *Elements of Computer Programming,* 1965, 2nd edition, 1970; (with Merlin C. Miller) *Elements of Data Processing Mathematics,* 1967, 2nd edition, 1970; *Elements of IBM 1130 Programming,* 1968; *Elements of Basic Fortran IV Programming,* 1969, 2nd edition, 1975; *Business Programming the IBM 1130,* 1970; *Introduction to Data Processing,* 1972, 2nd edition, Harcourt, 1977; (with Jack Olson) *Elements of Cobol Programming,* Dryden, 1977.†

\*    \*    \*

## PRITCHARD, R(onald) E(dward) 1936-

*PERSONAL:* Born July 27, 1936, in Rawalpindi, Pakistan; son of Charles E. (a soldier & civil servant) and Alice (Hitchens) Pritchard; married Susan Gaffney, September, 1963; children: John Edward, Anna Louise. *Education:* Balliol College, Oxford, B.A. (first class honors), 1960. *Home:* "Treetops," Welsh Row, Nantwich, Cheshire, England. *Office:* Department of English, University of Keele, Staffordshire ST5 5BG, England.

*CAREER:* William Penn School, Dulwich, London, England, teacher, 1963; Madeley College of Education, Staffordshire, England, lecturer, 1963-65; University of Keele, Staffordshire, lecturer in English literature, 1965—. Assistant examiner, Oxford and Cambridge Examination Board, 1963-72; B. Ed. examiner, University of Keele, 1968—; external assessor for colleges, University of Birmingham, 1972-75. *Military service:* Royal Air Force, junior technician, 1955-57.

*WRITINGS: D. H. Lawrence: Body of Darkness,* Hutchinson University Press, 1971, University of Pittsburgh Press, 1972.

*WORK IN PROGRESS:* A study of the poetry of Edmund Spenser.

\*    \*    \*

## PROCTOR, William (Gilbert, Jr.) 1941-

*PERSONAL:* Born October 11, 1941, in Atlanta, Ga.; son of William Gilbert, Sr. (a controller) and Maud (Moore) Proctor; married Priscilla Moore (a writer), June 17, 1967. *Education:* Harvard University, B.A., 1963, J.D., 1966. *Religion:* Methodist. *Home and office:* 7 Peter Cooper Rd., Apt. 1F, New York, N.Y. 10010. *Agent:* Bill Adler, 1230 Sixth Ave., New York, N.Y. 10020.

*CAREER: New York Daily News,* New York City, writer-reporter, 1969-73; free-lance writer, 1973—. Trustee, Park Avenue United Methodist Church. Literary consultant, Creative Christians. *Military service:* U.S. Marine Corps, 1966-69; served as judge advocate and military judge; became captain. *Member:* Texas Bar Association, Harvard Club of New York City.

*WRITINGS: Survival on the Campus: A Handbook for Christian Students,* Revell, 1972; *Jews for Jesus,* Revell,

1974; *Help Wanted: Faith Required*, Revell, 1974; *The Commune Kidnapping*, Pyramid Publications, 1975; *The Art of Christian Promotion*, Revell, 1975; (senior contributing author) *Jesus the Living Bread*, Logos International, 1976; *Women in the Pulpit*, Doubleday, 1976; *RX: The Christian Love Treatment*, Doubleday, 1976; *PDA: Personal Death Awareness*, Prentice-Hall, 1976; *On the Trail of God*, Doubleday, 1977. Contributor to magazines and newspapers.

*WORK IN PROGRESS:* Ghost-writing several books; an exercise book.

\* \* \*

## PRUNTY, Merle C(harles) 1917-

*PERSONAL:* Born March 2, 1917, in St. Joseph, Mo.; son of Merle Charles (a college administrator) and Mae (Holliday) Prunty; married Eugenia Wyatt, June 3, 1939; children: Mary Merle (Mrs. Paul Howard), Eugene Wyatt, Florence Holliday (Mrs. James M. Lauritsen). *Education:* University of Missouri, B.S., 1939, A.B., 1940, M.A., 1940; Clark University, Ph.D., 1944. *Home:* 255 Terrell Dr., Athens, Ga. 30606. *Office:* Department of Geography, University of Georgia, Athens, Ga. 30602.

*CAREER:* Mississippi State College, Columbus, assistant professor, 1942-43, associate professor of geography, 1943-46; University of Georgia, Athens, professor of geography, 1946—, Alumni Foundation Distinguished Professor of Geography, 1969—, head of department of geography and geology, 1946-61, and of department of geography, 1961-70, acting vice-president for academic affairs, 1977, senior faculty adviser to president, 1977-78. Assistant chancellor, University System of Georgia, 1951; visiting professor, Northwestern University, 1954; lecturer at colleges and universities, including Antioch College, 1959, University of Utah, 1965, Duke University, 1967, University of Wisconsin, 1968, University of Kentucky, 1972, University of Minnesota, 1975, University of North Carolina, 1976, and University of South Carolina, 1978. Consultant to U.S. President's Committee on Equal Employment Opportunity, 1961-64, to U.S. Office of Education, 1964-67, to Educational Testing Service, 1964-69, and to industrial and private institutions. *Military service:* U.S. Naval Reserve, 1943-46; became lieutenant.

*MEMBER:* International Geophysical Union, American Geographical Society, Association of American Geographers (member of executive committee, 1953-55, 1967-69; president of Southeastern Division, 1953-55; honorary life member of Southeastern Division), National Council on Geographic Education (member of board of directors, 1966-69), Georgia Academy of Science, Tennessee Academy of Science, Phi Kappa Phi, Alpha Kappa Delta, Sigma Nu. *Awards, honors:* Field research award, Association of American Geographers, 1955; Guggenheim fellow, 1957-58; research awards from Michael Foundation, 1961, Social Science Research Council, 1964, and U.S. Department of Interior, 1967-71.

*WRITINGS:* (Contributor) Fred E. Dohrs, Lawrence M. Sommers, and Donald R. Petterson, editors, *Readings in Geography*, Crowell, 1955; *The Central Gulf South*, Nelson Doubleday, 1960; (editor and contributor) *Festschrift: Clarence F. Jones*, Northwestern University Press, 1962; (contributor) Karl Raitz and J. Fraser Hart, editors, *Topographic Maps Illustrating Aspects of the Cultural Geography of the United States*, Department of Geography, University of Minnesota, 1970; *This Favored Land*, Mac-

millan, 1971; (with E. B. Fincher) *Lands of Promise*, Macmillan, 1971. Contributor to *World Book, Encyclopedia Americana, Chamber's Encyclopedia, Encyclopedia of Southern History,* and *Encyclopaedia Britannica;* contributor to *Geographical Review, Economic Geography, Annals of the Association of American Geographers, Southeastern Geographer, Professional Geographer, Die Erde,* and other periodicals.

*WORK IN PROGRESS: Birdsong: Biography of a Nineteenth and Twentieth Century Georgia Plantation;* studies in industrial/agricultural resource management; *Economic Geography of the Southern Piedmont*, a long-range project.

\* \* \*

## PURDY, Ken W(illiam) 1913-1972

April 28, 1913—June 7, 1972; American editor, journalist, short story writer, and authority on automobiles. Obituaries: *New York Times*, June 8, 1972; *Washington Post*, June 9, 1972; *Newsweek*, June 19, 1972; *Time*, June 19, 1972; *Antiquarian Bookman*, June 26, 1972; *Publishers Weekly*, July 3, 1972.

\* \* \*

## PURTILL, Richard L. 1931-

*PERSONAL:* Born March 12, 1931, in Chicago, Ill.; son of Joseph T. (a businessman) and Bertha (Walker) Purtill; married Elizabeth Banks (a statistician), June 20, 1959; children: Mark, Timothy, Steven. *Education:* University of Chicago, B.A., 1958, M.A., 1960, Ph.D., 1965; University of California, Los Angeles, postgraduate study, 1960-62. *Politics:* Independent. *Religion:* Roman Catholic. *Home:* 1708 Douglas Ave., Bellingham, Wash. 98225. *Office:* Department of Philosophy, Western Washington University, Bellingham, Wash. 98225.

*CAREER:* Western Washington University, Bellingham, instructor, 1962-65, assistant professor, 1965-68, associate professor, 1968-72, professor of philosophy, 1972—, acting chairman of department, 1970-71. Visiting lecturer, San Francisco State College (now University), 1968-69. Textbook consultant to Prentice-Hall, and other publishers. *Military service:* U.S. Army, 1949-52; became sergeant. *Member:* American Philosophical Association, American Association of University Professors, Sierra Club. *Awards, honors:* National Endowment for the Humanities summer grant, 1970.

*WRITINGS: Logic for Philosophers*, Harper, 1971; *Logical Thinking*, Harper, 1972; *Lord of the Elves and Eldils: Philosophy and Fantasy in C. S. Lewis and J. R. R. Tolkien*, Zondervan, 1974; *Reason to Believe*, Eerdmans, 1974; (contributor) Thomas Beauchamp, editor, *Ethics and Public Policy*, Prentice-Hall, 1975; *Philosophically Speaking*, Prentice-Hall, 1975; *Thinking about Ethics*, Prentice-Hall, 1976; (contributor) Peter J. Schakel, editor, *The Longing for a Form: Essays on the Fiction of C. S. Lewis*, Kent State University Press, 1977; *Thinking about Religion*, Prentice-Hall, 1978. Contributor of over thirty articles to philosophy journals. Associate editor, *International Journal for the Philosophy of Religion*, 1975—.

*WORK IN PROGRESS: Argument, Refutation, and Proof: An Introduction to Logic*, for Canfield Press; a fantasy novel based on Greek mythology, tentatively entitled *The Golden Griffin's Feather*.

*SIDELIGHTS:* Richard Purtill told *CA:* "Most of my books are basically textbooks, though many of them have had some tradebook sales. The textbooks are extensions of my teaching, just as my philosophical articles are extensions of my philosophical thinking and arguing. But I have had a continuing interest in fiction, especially fantasy fiction as evidenced by my studies of C. S. Lewis and J. R. R. Tolkien, and my last three textbooks have employed fictional elements in one way or another: a dialogue between imaginary philosophers in *Philosophically Speaking,* short stories or parables introducing chapters in the two 'Thinking about' books. When I complete revisions on my current project, another logic book, I will begin intensive writing on my next project, a fantasy novel based on Greek mythology. The idea was suggested by a visit to Greece with my wife in the summer of 1976 and by extensive reading in classical archeology and mythology since then.

"Further in the future are more 'Thinking about' books, probably *Thinking about the Arts* and *Thinking about Science.* My interests, both inside of philosophy and outside of it, are very broad: I think that the world is full of interesting subjects. I feel that good teaching and good writing depend on several elements. First, a real enthusiasm by the teacher or writer for his or her subject. Second, a fair amount of imagination and intuition to enable us to create something genuinely new or give really fresh insights. And finally, a certain amount of logic, method, and discipline to keep us close to reality and truth and to prevent enthusiasms and imagination from running away with us. Two of my favorite authors are C. S. Lewis and G. K. Chesterton, both of whom exhibited these qualities. The contemporary novelist whose next books I most look forward to is the Scottish novelist, Jane Duncan, from whom I have learned a great deal."

# Q

**QUALTER, Terence H(all) 1925-**

*PERSONAL:* Born April 15, 1925, in Eltham, New Zealand; son of Michael Frederick (a railroad employee) and Mary (Hall) Qualter; married Shirley Anne Card, May 21, 1951; children: Karen, Matthew, Paul, Adam. *Education:* University of New Zealand, B.A., 1951; University of London, Ph.D., 1956. *Politics:* New Democrat. *Religion:* Roman Catholic. *Home:* 249 Stonybrook Dr., Kitchener, Ontario, Canada. *Office:* Department of Political Science, University of Waterloo, Waterloo, Ontario, Canada.

*CAREER:* University of Waterloo, Waterloo, Ontario, lecturer, 1960-61, assistant professor, 1961-64, associate professor, 1964-68, professor of political science, 1968—, chairman of department, 1970-73. *Military service:* Royal New Zealand Air Force, 1944-46.

*WRITINGS: Propaganda and Psychological Warfare,* Random House, 1962; *The Election Process in Canada,* McGraw (Canada), 1970; *The New Polis: Graham Wallas and the Great Society,* University of Toronto Press, in press.

\* \* \*

**QUIGLEY, Carroll 1910-1977**

*PERSONAL:* Born November 9, 1910, in Boston, Mass.; son of William Francis and Mary F. (Carroll) Quigley; married Lillian Fox (a writer), May 22, 1937; children: Denis Carroll, Thomas Fox. *Education:* Harvard University, A.B. (with high honors), 1933, A.M., 1934, Ph.D., 1938. *Politics:* Independent. *Religion:* Roman Catholic. *Home:* 4448 Greenwich Pkwy. N.W., Washington, D.C. 20007. *Office:* Department of History, Georgetown University, Washington, D.C. 20007.

*CAREER:* Princeton University, Princeton, N.J., instructor in history, 1935-37; Harvard University, Cambridge, Mass., instructor and tutor in history, government, and economics, 1938-41; Georgetown University, School of Foreign Service, Washington, D.C., lecturer, 1941-47, professor of history, 1947-76. Scholar-in-residence, Fairfax County Schools, Va.; lecturer at Brookings Institution, beginning 1960, U.S. Department of State Foreign Service Institute, beginning 1961, and U.S. Department of Agriculture Graduate School, beginning 1967. Collaborator, Smithsonian Institution, 1957-62. Industrial College of the Armed Forces, consultant and lecturer, beginning 1951, honorary member of faculty, beginning 1968; consultant to U.S. House of Representatives Committee on Astronautics and Space Exploration, 1958, U.S. Navy, 1964, and U.S. Air Force, 1966.

*MEMBER:* International Society for the Comparative Study of Civilizations (council member, beginning 1971), American Historical Association, American Anthropological Association, American Association for the Advancement of Science, Academy of Political Science, English-Speaking Union of the Commonwealth (London; life), Royal Commonwealth Society (London), Anthropological Society of Washington, Harvard Club of Washington. *Awards, honors:* Harvard traveling fellowship to archives of Paris and Milan, 1937-38; Georgetown University Vicennial gold medal, 1962, and 175th Anniversary medal of merit, 1964.

*WRITINGS: Evolution of Civilizations,* Macmillan, 1961; *Tragedy and Hope: A History of the World in Our Time,* Macmillan, 1966; *The World since 1939: A History,* Collier, 1968. Contributor of numerous articles to scholarly publications. Member of board of editors, *Current History,* beginning 1959; book reviewer, *Washington Sunday Star,* 1965-72.

*BIOGRAPHICAL/CRITICAL SOURCES: New York Times,* December 9, 1965; Matthew Melko, *The Nature of Civilizations,* Porter Sargent, 1970.†

(Died January 3, 1977 in Washington, D.C.)

\* \* \*

**QUINTO, Leon 1926-**

*PERSONAL:* Born May 18, 1926, in New York, N.Y.; son of Henry and Frieda (Jacobs) Quinto. *Education:* Columbia University, B.A., 1946, M.A., 1948, Ph.D., 1952. *Politics:* Republican. *Home:* 200 East 66th St., New York, N.Y. 10021. *Office:* 219 East 42nd St., New York, N.Y. 10017.

*CAREER:* Mayor's Committee on Management Survey, New York City, research associate, 1950-51; Pennsylvania State University, University Park, assistant professor of economics, 1952-55; Lehman Brothers, New York City, financial analyst in industrial department, 1955-56; IBM Corp., New York City, economist, 1957—. *Member:* Royal Economic Society, American Economic Association.

*WRITINGS: Municipal Income Taxation in the U.S.,* Mayor's Committee on Management Survey of City of New

York, 1952; (with Claude W. Burrill) *Computer Model of a Growth Company*, Gordon & Breach, 1972. Contributor to *Econometrica*.

\* \* \*

## QUONG, Rose Lanu  1879(?)-1972

1879(?)—December 14, 1972; Chinese actress, lecturer, author, and translator. Obituaries: *New York Times*, December 16, 1972.

# R

**RACE, Jeffrey 1943-**

*PERSONAL:* Born July 29, 1943, in Norwalk, Connecticut; son of Victor A. (an executive) and Charlotte (Van Croix) Bissell; married Chumsri Rukwanichpong, July 22, 1972. *Education:* Harvard University, B.A., 1965, M.A., 1971, Ph.D., 1973. *Agent:* Marie Rodell-Frances Collin Literary Agency, 141 East 55th St., New York, N.Y. 10022. *Office:* 20 Chester St., Somerville, Mass. 02144; and P.O. Box 2, Rangsit, Thailand.

*CAREER:* Investment consultant; writer.

*WRITINGS: War Comes to Long An: Revolutionary Conflict in a Vietnamese Province,* University of California Press, 1972; (contributor) John W. Lewis, editor, *Peasant Rebellion and Communist Revolution in Asia,* Stanford University Press, 1974. Contributor of articles to scholarly journals.

*BIOGRAPHICAL/CRITICAL SOURCES: New York Review of Books,* March 9, 1972; *Economist,* March 11, 1972; *Times Literary Supplement,* March 17, 1972; *New York Times Book Review,* May 14, 1972; *Washington Post,* May 20, 1973; *Perspective,* December, 1974.

\*   \*   \*

**RADER, (John) Trout (III) 1938-**

*PERSONAL:* Born August 23, 1938, in Corpus Christi, Tex.; son of John Trout II (a water well contractor) and Elizabeth (Snyder) Rader; married Deanna Ibera, July 30, 1966; children: Katherine Ann, Martha Wendale, David Vincent, Sarah Josephine. *Education:* University of Texas, B.A., 1956; Yale University, M.A., 1960, Ph.D., 1963. *Religion:* Presbyterian. *Home:* 7737 West Biltmore, Clayton, Mo. 63105. *Office:* Department of Economics, Washington University, St. Louis, Mo. 63130.

*CAREER:* University of Missouri—Columbia, assistant professor of economics, 1962-64; University of Illinois at Urbana-Champaign, assistant professor of economics, 1964-65; Washington University, St. Louis, Mo., associate professor, 1965-70, professor of economics, 1970—. Visiting professor at University of Rochester, spring, 1971, and at universities in Louvain, Belgium, fall, 1971. *Member:* Econometric Society. *Awards, honors:* National Science Foundation research grant, 1965-70.

*WRITINGS: Economics of Feudalism,* Gordon & Breach,

1971; *Theory of Microeconomics,* Academic Press, 1972. Also author of *Theory of General Economic Equilibrium,* 1972.

\*   \*   \*

**RAHN, Joan Elma 1929-**

*PERSONAL:* Born February 5, 1929, in Cleveland, Ohio; daughter of George William (a salesman) and Elsie (Thiele) Rahn. *Education:* Western Reserve University (now Case Western Reserve University), B.S., 1950; Columbia University, M.A., 1952, Ph.D., 1956. *Religion:* Lutheran. *Home:* 1656 Hickory St., Highland Park, Ill. 60035.

*CAREER:* Thiel College, Greenville, Pa., assistant professor, 1956-58, associate professor of biology, 1958-59; Ohio State University, Columbus, instructor in botany, 1959-60; International School of America (traveling school visiting world capitals), Columbus, Ohio, instructor in general biology, 1960-61; Lake Forest College, Lake Forest, Ill., assistant professor of biology, 1961-67; free-lance writer and photographer, 1967—. Instructor of biology, Elgin Community College, summer, 1972. *Member:* American Institute of Biological Sciences, Botanical Society of America, American Association for the Advancement of Science, Botanical Club of Wisconsin, Sigma Xi. *Awards, honors:* Joint Committee of National Science Teachers Association and Children's Book Council named the following outstanding science books for children: *Seeing What Plants Do, Grocery Store Botany, How Plants Travel,* and *How Plants Are Pollinated;* Society of Midland Authors Distinguished Service Award, 1974, for *How Plants Travel.*

*WRITINGS*—All published by Atheneum, except as indicated: *Botany Simplified,* Barnes & Noble, 1969, reprinted as *Botany,* Cliffs Notes; *Seeing What Plants Do,* 1972; *How Plants Travel,* 1973; *Biology: The Science of Life,* with study guide, Macmillan, 1974; *Grocery Store Botany,* 1974; *Microbiology,* Cliffs Notes, 1974; *More about What Plants Do,* 1975; *How Plants Are Pollinated,* 1975; *The Metric System,* 1976; *Alfalfa, Beans & Clover,* 1976; (contributor) Marianne Carus and others, editors, *Reading Is Fun,* Open Court, 1976; (contributor) Carus and others, editors, *A Trip through Wonderland,* Open Court, 1976; *Grocery Store Zoology,* 1977; *Nature in the City: Plants,* Raintree, 1977; *Seven Ways to Collect Plants,* 1978; *Watch It Grow, Watch It Change,* in press. Photographic essays have been published in *This Day, National Wildlife, Chicago Tribune*

*Sunday Magazine,* and *Milwaukee Journal;* other photographs published in *National Geographic, Industry Week, Encyclopaedia Britannica,* and various periodicals. Contributor of articles to *Encyclopedia Americana, Wonderland of Knowledge, Woman's World,* and other magazines. Former member of editorial advisory board and contributing editor, *World of Science;* former member of science advisory staff for publications of LaPine Scientific Co., Chicago.

*WORK IN PROGRESS:* A second edition of *Biology: The Science of Life.*

\* \* \*

## RANDALL, Laura 1935-

*PERSONAL:* Born November 18, 1935, in New York, N.Y.; daughter of Bernard (an accountant) and Frances (Friedman) Rosenbaum; married Francis Ballard Randall (a professor of history), June 11, 1957; children: David. *Education:* Barnard College, B.A., 1957; University of Massachusetts, M.A., 1959; Columbia University, Ph.D., 1962. *Home:* 425 Riverside Dr., New York, N.Y. 10025. *Office:* Hunter College of the City University of New York, 695 Park Ave., New York, N.Y. 10021.

*CAREER:* Federal Reserve Bank, New York City, economist, 1961-63; Queens College of the City University of New York, Flushing, N.Y., assistant professor of economics, 1963-67; Columbia University, New York City, visiting scholar, 1967-68; Hunter College of the City University of New York, New York City, assistant professor of economics, 1968—. Part-time teacher at Bernard M. Baruch College of the City University of New York, 1963, at Columbia University, 1964-66. *Member:* Latin American Studies Association, American Economic Association. *Awards, honors:* Social Science Research Council grants, 1967, 1971.

*WRITINGS: Economic Development, Evolution, and Revolution,* Heath, 1964; *A Comparative Economic History of Latin America: Argentina, Brazil, Mexico, and Peru, 1500-1914,* four volumes, University Microfilms, 1977; *An Economic History of Argentina,* Columbia University Press, 1977. Contributor to *Commonweal, Ararat,* and other journals.

*AVOCATIONAL INTERESTS:* Music, reading science fiction.

\* \* \*

## RANGER, Paul 1933-

*PERSONAL:* Born June 10, 1933, in Surrey, England; son of Percy Charles (an accountant) and Dorothy (Cook) Ranger. *Education:* Attended College of St. Mark and St. John, Trinity College of Music, London, 1953-55, Open University, 1971-73, and Bristol University, 1975-76. *Home:* 38 Coombe Hill Crescent, Thame, Oxfordshire, England. *Office:* John Stripe Theatre, King Alfred's College of Education, Winchester, England.

*CAREER:* Teacher of speech, Royal School for the Deaf, Birmingham, England; deputy head and acting head, Boutcher School, Bermondsey, London; King Alfred's College of Education, Winchester, England, senior lecturer in drama, 1968—, theatre coordinator, John Stripe Theatre. Adjunct professor, California State University, Fresno; director, British theatre seminar, University of London. Examiner in speech to the London College of Music; assessor in drama to the School of Education, University of Southampton; examiner in theatre arts, Associated Examining Board. Free-lance producer, actor, and drama adjudi-

cator. *Member:* Society of Teachers of Speech and Drama (member of council), Association of Drama Tutors (convenor of colleges of higher education), British Federation of Music Festivals (adjudicating member), Association of Teachers in Colleges and Departments of Education.

*WRITINGS: Experiments in Drama,* University of London Press, 1971; *The Lost Theatres of Winchester,* Hampshire Field Club, 1976. Reviewer and member of editorial board, *Speech and Drama.*

*WORK IN PROGRESS:* A biography of Henry Thornton (1750-1818), manager of the Theatre Royal, Windsor, and eighteen provincial theatres.

\* \* \*

## RANLY, Ernest W. 1930-

*PERSONAL:* Born February 19, 1930, in Cassella, Ohio; son of Peter Nicholas (a farmer) and Sophia (Speck) Ranly. *Education:* University of Dayton, B.A., 1952; St. Louis University, M.A., 1958, Ph.D., 1963. *Address:* Apartado 36, La Oroya, Peru.

*CAREER:* Ordained Roman Catholic priest of the Society of the Precious Blood, June, 1956; St. Joseph's College, Rensselaer, Ind., assistant professor, 1963-66, associate professor of philosophy, 1967-73; currently doing pastoral work in the Central Andes of Peru. Catholic University of America, visiting associate professor of philosophy, 1969-70. *Member:* American Catholic Philosophical Association. *Awards, honors:* Indiana Consortium for International Programs grant, India, summer, 1971; Fr. Edwin G. Kaiser Faculty Scholarship, St. Joseph's College, 1973.

*WRITINGS: Scheler's Phenomenology of Community,* Nijhoff, 1964. Contributor to philosophy journals, household periodicals, and national magazines, including *Cross Currents, America, Commonweal,* and *Thought.*

*WORK IN PROGRESS:* Studies in liberation theology and the construction of local theologies.

*SIDELIGHTS:* Ernest Ranly writes that he "moved into pastoral work . . . to identify with poor and the working class in a struggling less-developed country of the Third World. I still continue to read and to publish, but I feel that what I say now smacks more of the reality of life than before."

\* \* \*

## RANSOM, William R. 1876-1973

January 18, 1876—January 9, 1973; American mathematician, educator, and author. Obituaries: *New York Times,* January 11, 1973.

\* \* \*

## RAPAPORT, Ionel F. 1909(?)-1972

1909(?)—September 9, 1972; Rumanian-born American psychiatrist, educator, and author of books on Mongolism and mental deficiency. Obituaries: *New York Times,* September 12, 1972.

\* \* \*

## RAPP, Doris Jean 1929-

*PERSONAL:* Born August 31, 1929, in Erie, Pa.; daughter of Charles William and Zoanne (Wyland) Rapp; married Stanley Mysko, Jr., August 31, 1957. *Education:* University of Buffalo, B.A. (magna cum laude), 1950, M.A., 1954; New York University, M.D., 1955. *Politics:* Conservative. *Religion:* "Christian, no affiliation." *Home and office:* 1405 Colvin Blvd., Buffalo, N.Y. 14223.

*CAREER:* Pediatric allergist, Buffalo, N.Y. *Member:* Phi Beta Kappa.

*WRITINGS: Allergies and Your Child,* Holt, 1972, published as *Questions and Answers about Allergies and Your Child,* Drake, 1974; (with A.W. Frankland) *Allergies: Questions and Answers,* Heinemann (London), 1976; *Hyperactive Child and Allergies: A Parents' Guide,* Monarch, in press. Contributor of articles to medical journals.

*AVOCATIONAL INTERESTS:* Tennis, nature study, ornithology.

\* \* \*

## RASKIN, Marcus G.   1934-

*PERSONAL:* Born April 30, 1934, in Milwaukee, Wis.; son of Benjamin Sam (self-employed in plumbing and heating) and Anna (Goodman) Raskin; married Barbara Judith Bellman, June 9, 1957; children: Erika Bay, Jamin Ben, Noah Annin. *Education:* University of Chicago, A.B., 1954, J.D., 1957. *Home:* 1820 Wyoming Ave. N.W., Washington, D.C. 20009. *Office:* Institute for Policy Studies, 1901 Q St. N.W., Washington, D.C. 20009.

*CAREER:* Legislative counsel to twelve Democratic Congressmen, Washington, D.C., 1958-61; National Security Council, Washington, D.C., member of special staff, 1961-63, member of eighteen-nation disarmament delegation at Geneva, Switzerland, 1962; Executive Office of the President, Washington, D.C., education adviser to Bureau of Budget, 1963; White House Office of Science and Technology, consultant on education, 1963-65; Presidential Panel on Educational Research and Development, member, 1963-65; Institute for Policy Studies, Washington, D.C., co-founder and co-director, 1963-77. Member of "Boston Five," acquitted by jury. Trustee, Antioch College, 1965-71. Lecturer at Harvard University, Stanford University, Yale University, and other institutions; has appeared on network television programs. *Member:* P.E.N. *Awards, honors:* Distinguished fellow, Institute for Policy Studies.

*WRITINGS:* (With Richard J. Barnet) *After Twenty Years: Alternatives to the Cold War in Europe,* Random House, 1965; (editor with Bernard Fall) *The Viet-Nam Reader,* Random House, 1965; *Being and Doing: From Deliberation to Liberation,* Random House, 1971; (with Ralph Stavins and Richard J. Barnet) *Washington Plans an Aggressive War,* Random House, 1971; *Notes on the Old System,* McKay, 1974; *The Federal Budget and Social Reconstruction,* Transaction, 1978; *National Security,* Transaction, 1978. Staff editor of Congressional *Liberal Papers,* 1958-61; contributing editor, *Ramparts,* 1965-68. Contributor to *Scientific American, New York Review,* and other publications.

*WORK IN PROGRESS: The Common Good.*

*SIDELIGHTS:* Lawrence Stern, reviewing *Washington Plans an Aggressive War* for the *Washington Post,* wrote: "One of the virtues of this three-part book is that it addresses itself to the pre-eminent issue of the Pentagon Papers revelation: that vast power that has been invested in a small circle of governmental mandarins to crank up a war for which little public consensus had been obtained and for which there is no immediate issue of national survival."

*BIOGRAPHICAL/CRITICAL SOURCES: Motive,* November, 1968; *Washington Post,* October 18, 1971.

\* \* \*

## RATH, R. John   1910-

*PERSONAL:* Born December 12, 1910, in St. Francis, Kan.; son of John and Barbara (Schauer) Rath; married Isabel Jones, June 26, 1937; children: Laurens John (deceased), Isabel Ferguson. *Education:* University of Kansas, A.B., 1932; University of California, Berkeley, A.M., 1934; Columbia University, Ph.D., 1941. *Politics:* Democrat. *Religion:* Presbyterian. *Home:* 7811 Fairdale, Houston, Tex. 77042. *Office:* Department of History, Rice University, Houston, Tex. 77001.

*CAREER:* University of Arkansas, Fayetteville, instructor in history, 1936-37; College of Puget Sound (now University of Puget Sound), Tacoma, Wash., instructor in history and government, 1938-39; Lindenwood College, St. Charles, Mo., head of department of history and political science, 1939-41; Mississippi State College for Women, Columbus, associate professor of history, 1941-43; University of Georgia, Athens, assistant professor of history, 1946-47; University of Colorado, Boulder, associate professor of history, 1947-51; University of Texas at Austin, professor of history, 1951-63; Rice University, Houston, Tex., Mary Gibbs Jones Professor of History, 1963—. Visiting professor at University of Wisconsin, 1955-56, University of Colorado, summer, 1958, Duke University, 1962-63. *Military service:* U.S. Army, United Nations Relief and Rehabilitation Administration (UNRRA), U.S. Zone, Germany, Bureau of Documentation and Tracing, chief of Division of Documentary Evidence, 1945-46.

*MEMBER:* American Historical Association, Conference Group for Central European History (chairman, 1969-70), Southwestern Social Science Association (president, 1976-77; chairman of history section, 1972-73), Southern Historical Association (chairman of European section, 1961-62), Austrian Academy of Sciences (corresponding member), Deputazione di Storia Patria Res le Venezia (corresponding member). *Awards, honors:* Social Science Research Council fellow, Austria and Italy, 1937-38; Guggenheim fellow, Italy, 1956-57; awarded First Class Honor Cross in Art and Literature by Government of Austria, 1963.

*WRITINGS: The Fall of the Napoleonic Kingdom of Italy,* Columbia University Press, 1941; *The Viennese Revolution of 1848,* University of Texas Press, 1957; *L'amministrazione austriaca nel Lombardo Veneto: 1814-1821,* Archivio Economico dell' Unificazione Italiana, 1959; *The Austrian Provisional Government in Lombardy-Venetia: 1814-15,* University of Texas Press, 1969. Contributor of more than a hundred articles and reviews to journals in his field. Founder and editor, *Austrian History News Letter,* 1959-63, and *Austrian History Yearbook,* 1965—; associate editor, *Journal of Central European Affairs,* 1947-51.

*WORK IN PROGRESS:* Research on the Austrian government in Lombardy-Venetia, 1815-1821.

\* \* \*

## RAUP, H(allock) F(loyd)   1901-

*PERSONAL:* Born January 15, 1901, in Athens, Pa.; son of Henry F. (a clerk) and Esther (Myer) Raup; married Lillian James, July 7, 1927; children: Elizabeth Marie Raup McClelland, Henry Armstrong. *Education:* Attended University of California, Los Angeles, 1920-22; University of California, Berkeley, B.S., 1924, M.S., 1927, Ph.D., 1935. *Religion:* Protestant. *Residence:* Kent, Ohio. *Office:* Kent State University, Kent, Ohio 44240.

*CAREER:* University of California, Los Angeles, instructor in geography, 1935-40; Eastern Washington State College (now University), Cheney, assistant professor of geography, 1940-43; U.S. Department of the Interior, Washington,

D.C., researcher, U.S. Board on Geographical Names, 1943-45; Kent State University, Kent, Ohio, professor of geography, 1945-70, head of department, 1945-63, professor emeritus, 1970—. *Member:* Association of American Geographers, American Name Society, California Historical Society.

*WRITINGS:* (With Otis W. Freeman) *Essentials of Geography,* McGraw, 1948, 2nd edition with *Study Guide* and *Instructor's Manual,* 1959; *Fundamentals of Global Geography,* U.S. Air Force (Montgomery, Ala.), 1955; (editor) *Letters of a Pennsylvania Chaplain from the Siege of Petersburg,* privately printed (London), 1961; (editor) *Travels of the Naturalist Charles A. Lesueur,* Kent State University Press, 1966; (editor with Clyde Smith) *Ohio Geography: Selected Readings,* Kendall/Hunt, 1973.

Contributor: Otis W. Freeman and W. H. Martin, editors, *The Pacific Northwest,* Wiley, 1942; John Garland, editor, *The North American Midwest,* Wiley, 1955; Freeman and John Morris, editors, *World Geography,* McGraw, 1958, 3rd edition, 1972.

Author of monographs on Anaheim and San Bernardino, Calif., University of California Publications in Geography. Contributor of about forty articles to professional journals. Editor, *Professional Geographer,* 1963-72, and Kent State University Research Publications.

*WORK IN PROGRESS:* Research on communal societies on the American frontier and on Ohio geographical names.

\* \* \*

## RAVITCH, Norman 1936-

*PERSONAL:* Born November 22, 1936, in New York, N.Y.; son of Louis and Sylvia (Schwey) Ravitch; married Sara Ann Silva, March 24, 1972; children: Nicholas Louis. *Education:* Queens College of the City of New York (now Queens College of the City University of New York), B.A., 1957; Princeton University, M.A., 1959, Ph.D., 1962. *Home:* 5225 Stonewood Dr., Riverside, Calif. 92506. *Office:* Department of History, University of California, Riverside, Calif. 92502.

*CAREER:* Philadelphia Museum College of Art (now Philadelphia College of Art), Philadelphia, Pa., instructor in humanities, 1961-62; University of California, Riverside, assistant professor, 1962-67, associate professor, 1967-75, professor of humanities, 1975—, associate dean of humanities, 1970-75. *Member:* American Historical Association, Phi Beta Kappa. *Awards, honors:* Fulbright scholar, University of Paris, 1960-61; American Philosophical Society and American Council of Learned Societies grant, 1966.

*WRITINGS: Sword and Mitre,* Mouton & Co., 1966; *Images of Western Man,* three volumes, Wadsworth, 1973. Contributor to *Church History, Historical Journal, Journal of the American Academy of Religion, Catholic Historical Review,* and other periodicals.

*WORK IN PROGRESS:* Work on the historical interpretations of human catastrophe.

\* \* \*

## RAY, John R(obert) 1921-

*PERSONAL:* Born August 27, 1921, in Alderson, W. Va.; son of Irene (Thomas) Ray; married Mirka M. Putro (a librarian), March 27, 1948. *Education:* Indiana University, A.B., 1954, M.A., 1955; Florida State University, further study, 1956; Ohio State University, Ph.D., 1972. *Address:*

P.O. Box 488, Fairborn, Ohio 45324. *Office:* Department of Geography, Wright State University, Dayton, Ohio 45435.

*CAREER:* University of Miami, Coral Gables, Fla., instructor, 1955-58, assistant professor of geography, 1958-64; Wright State University, Dayton, Ohio, assistant professor, 1964-74, associate professor, 1974-77, professor of geography, 1978—, chairman of department, 1972—. Lecturer in geography, Florida State University, summer, 1961; instructor in geography at Indiana University, summer, 1963, and Miami University, Oxford, Ohio, summer, 1964. Member of Florida Governor's Committee on Resource-Use in Education, 1958-64; delegate, Southern States Work Conference on Educational Problems, 1961-63. *Military service:* U.S. Army, 1942-46; became technical sergeant; received two Bronze Star Medals. *Member:* Association of American Geographers, American Geographical Society, American Society of Photogrammetry (president, Ohio chapter), Royal Geographical Society (fellow). *Awards, honors:* Research grants, Wright State University, 1974, 1975.

*WRITINGS:* (With Robert H. Fuson) *Laboratory Exercises in Physical Geography,* with answer book, W. C. Brown, 1960, 3rd edition, 1973; (with Fuson) *Problems in World Cultural Geography,* W. C. Brown, 1960, 2nd edition, 1967; (with Fuson) *Resource Conservation in the United States,* W. C. Brown, 1961; (contributor) Raul A. Deju, editor, *Extraction of Minerals and Energy: Today's Dilemmas,* Ann Arbor Science Publications, 1974. Contributor of articles to *East Lakes Geographer, Ohio Journal of Science,* and other periodicals.

*WORK IN PROGRESS:* Research on attitudes toward strip mining for coal and reclamation in Ohio: a spatial analysis.

\* \* \*

## RAYMOND, Ellsworth (Lester) 1912-

*PERSONAL:* Born May 8, 1912, in Fort Ann, N.Y.; son of Herman Lester (a doctor) and Euretta (Brown) Raymond; married Anna Palasova, October 3, 1942; children: Alan Gregory, Catherine Anne. *Education:* University of Michigan, A.B., 1933, M.A., 1935, Ph.D., 1952. *Politics:* Republican. *Religion:* Anglican. *Home:* 33 Greenwich Ave., Apt. 6D, New York, N.Y. 10014. *Office:* Department of Politics, New York University, Washington Sq., New York, N.Y. 10003.

*CAREER:* U.S. Embassy, Moscow, U.S.S.R., researcher on Soviet politics and economics, 1938-43; U.S. War Department, Washington, D.C., section chief and researcher on Soviet economics, 1944-46; director of U.S. Government research project on Soviet propaganda, Washington, D.C., 1947; New York University, New York, N.Y., lecturer, 1949-52, assistant professor, 1952-55, associate professor, 1955-75, professor of Russian area studies, 1975—. Consultant to Armco International. *Military service:* U.S. Army, 1944-46; military intelligence service; reached civilian equivalent of lieutenant colonel. *Member:* American Political Science Association. *Awards, honors:* American Council of Learned Societies fellow, 1937; Hoover Institution fellow, 1948; Ford Foundation fellow at University of Geneva, 1961-62; New York State fellow, 1963.

*WRITINGS:* (Translator) *Industrial Management in the U.S.S.R.,* Public Affairs Press, 1950; *Soviet Economic Progress,* Holt, 1957; *The Soviet State,* Macmillan, 1968, 2nd edition, New York University Press, 1977; (with John Stuart Martin) *A Picture History of Eastern Europe,* Crown,

1971. Contributor to *National Review, American Legion, Reader's Digest, Saturday Evening Post, Catholic Digest,* and other periodicals.

*WORK IN PROGRESS: Soviet Crisis Diplomacy.*

*AVOCATIONAL INTERESTS:* Music and music arranging.

\* \* \*

### READER, W(illiam) J(oseph) 1920-

*PERSONAL:* Born November 20, 1920, in Westonsuper-Mare, Somerset, England; son of Kenneth Joseph and Ethel Mary (Till) Reader; married Ann Maffett (a doctor), July 6, 1950; children: Humphrey Stephen, Roger James. *Education:* Jesus College, Cambridge, B.A., 1947, Ph.D., 1971. *Politics:* Conservative. *Religion:* "Vague." *Home:* 67 Wood Vale, London N10 3DL, England. *Agent:* Campbell Thomson & McLaughlin Ltd., 31 Newington Green, London N16 9PU, England.

*CAREER:* Unilever Ltd., London, England, employed in various capacities, 1947-64; historian for Imperial Chemical Industries, London, 1965-75, Metal Box Ltd., London, 1969-76, and Bowater Corp., 1977—. Visiting professor, University of Delaware, 1973, 1976. *Military service:* British Army, Royal Corps of Signals, 1940-45; became captain. *Member:* Royal Historical Society (fellow), Economic History Society.

*WRITINGS:* (With C. H. Wilson) *Men and Machines: A History of D. Napier & Son,* Weidenfeld & Nicolson, 1958; *Unilever: A Short History,* Unilever House, 1960; *Life in Victorian England,* Putnam, 1964; *Professional Men: The Rise of the Professional Classes in Nineteenth-Century England,* Basic Books, 1966; *Architect of Air Power: The Life of the First Viscount Weir of Eastwood 1877-1959,* Collins, 1968; *Hard Roads and Highways, S.P.D. Limited, 1918-1968,* Batsford, 1969; *Imperial Chemical Industries: A History,* Oxford University Press, Volume I: *The Forerunners,* 1970, Volume II: *The First Quarter-Century 1926-52,* 1975; *The Weir Group: A Centenary History,* Weidenfeld & Nicolson, 1971; *The Middle Classes,* Batsford, 1972; *Victorian England,* Batsford, 1973; *Metal Box: A History,* Heinemann, 1976; (contributor) Leslie Hannah, editor, *Management Strategy and Business Development,* Macmillan (London), 1976.

*WORK IN PROGRESS:* A study of the influences leading to voluntary enlistment for the Great War in the United Kingdom, tentatively entitled *King and Country;* a study of the work of road surveyor J. L. McAdam and his sons, tentatively entitled *McAdam;* a history of Bowater Corp.

*SIDELIGHTS:* W. J. Reader sees history "as it used to be regarded, that is as a branch of imaginative literature rather than as in any way a science, though it differs from novels and drama in relying almost exclusively on written evidence to feed the imagination and requiring strict and explicit distinction between matters of fact and flights of fancy." He has traveled widely in Europe, Asia, tropical Africa, and North America.

*BIOGRAPHICAL/CRITICAL SOURCES: New Statesman,* August 4, 1967; *Times Literary Supplement,* April 8, 1977.

\* \* \*

### REAGAN, Thomas (James) B(utler) 1916-
(Jim Thomas)

*PERSONAL:* Surname rhymes with "pagan"; born December 14, 1916, in Oklahoma City, Okla.; son of Thomas Harper (a member of fire department) and Margaret (Butler) Reagan. *Education:* Attended Oklahoma City University, 1935, and University of Oklahoma, 1936-37. *Religion:* Roman Catholic. *Home:* 5020 Salzburg, Berchtesgadnerstrasse 36A, Austria. *Agent:* Toni Strassman, 130 East 18th St., New York, N.Y. 10003.

*CAREER:* Oklahoma City (Okla.) Fire Department, fireman, 1936-40; self-employed commercial pilot and flight instructor, 1941; U.S. Army, 1942-46, 1949-52, became captain; various minor jobs while writing in spare time, 1953-61; full-time writer of mystery novels, 1961—. *Member:* Mystery Writers of America, Crime Writers Association (London), Authors Guild of America.

*WRITINGS: Bank Job,* Dodd, 1964; *The Big Fall,* Hammond, Hammond, 1967; *An Unkindness of Ravens,* Hammond, Hammond, 1967; *The Caper,* Putnam, 1969; *Blood Money,* Putnam, 1970; *The Inside-Out Heist,* Putnam, 1970; (under pseudonym Jim Thomas) *Cross Purposes,* McCall Books, 1971.

*WORK IN PROGRESS: Cross Questions,* under pseudonym Jim Thomas; a second mystery novel, tentatively entitled *Murder in the Alps.*

*SIDELIGHTS:* Thomas Reagan's favorite reading is mystery novels and he believes that some of the best fiction being produced today comes from mystery writers. The encouragement of several of them, notably Davis Dresser (who writes as Brett Halliday), and Helen McCloy [is] responsible, he says, for "any success I may have achieved in the field." He has lived and traveled in other countries of Europe and the West Indies, but thinks Salzburg, his present home, is "the most beautiful city I've ever seen." Most of his books have been translated into French and German, and several into additional languages.

*AVOCATIONAL INTERESTS:* Music, photography, spectator sports.

*BIOGRAPHICAL/CRITICAL SOURCES: Books and Bookmen,* January, 1968; *New York Times Book Review,* March 9, 1969; *Bookseller,* May 1, 1971.†

\* \* \*

### REBATET, Lucien 1903-1972

1903—August 24, 1972; French journalist and author. Obituaries: *L'Express,* September 4-10, 1972.

\* \* \*

### RECKLESS, Walter Cade 1899-

*PERSONAL:* Born January 19, 1899, in Philadelphia, Pa.; son of Walter Boggs (a salesman) and Ann Eliza (Cade) Reckless; married Martha Goodall Washington; children: Walter Washington. *Education:* University of Chicago, Ph.B., 1921, Ph.D., 1925. *Politics:* Independent. *Religion:* Episcopalian. *Home:* 6044 Dublin Rd., Dublin, Ohio 43017. *Office:* Ohio State University, 1775 South College Rd., Columbus, Ohio 43210.

*CAREER:* Vanderbilt University, Nashville, Tenn., professor of sociology, 1924-40; Ohio State University, Columbus, professor of criminology, 1940-69. Visiting professor at University of Michigan, 1940, and University of Muenster, 1960; distinguished visiting professor, Florida State University, 1969-72. Technical assistance expert on corrections administration (India), United Nations, 1951-52. Member of board of directors, Joint Commission on Correctional Manpower and Training. *Military service:* U.S. Army Reserve, 1917-18. *Member:* International Criminological Association (member of advisory council), American Criminological Society (president, 1963-66), National Council on Crime and Delinquency, American Correctional Association, American Society of Criminology, Phi Beta Kappa, Beta Theta Pi. *Awards, honors:* Edwin Sutherland Award of American Society of Criminology, 1965.

*WRITINGS:* (With E. T. Krueger) *Social Psychology,* Longmans, Green, 1931; (with Mapheus Smith) *Juvenile Delinquency,* McGraw, 1932; *Vice in Chicago,* University of Chicago Press, 1933; *Criminal Behavior,* McGraw, 1940; *The Crime Problem,* Appleton, 1950, 5th edition, 1973; *Die Kriminalitaet in U.S.A.,* de Gruyter, 1962; *American Criminology: New Directions,* Appleton, 1973. Contributor of articles to criminology journals.

*WORK IN PROGRESS:* Research on measurement of impact of prisons and reformatories on inmates; research on youth development and a program for prevention of delinquency.

*AVOCATIONAL INTERESTS:* Music (plays classical violin), foreign travel, theater and ballet (especially Russian).

\*          \*          \*

## REDMOND, Gerald 1934-

*PERSONAL:* Born April 13, 1934, in Dundee, Scotland; son of Edward James Redmond; married Margaret Pender, July 13, 1957; children: Paul, Philip, Gary. *Education:* Loughborough College, teacher's certificate and diploma, 1959; University of Massachusetts, M.S., 1969; University of Alberta, Ph.D., 1972. *Religion:* Church of England. *Office:* Department of Physical Education, University of Alberta, Edmonton, Alberta, Canada T6G 2H9.

*CAREER:* School teacher in England, 1957-65; University of Otago, Dunedin, New Zealand, lecturer in physical education, 1965-68; University of Massachusetts—Amherst, assistant professor of physical education, 1972-73, head soccer coach, 1972-73; University of Alberta, Edmonton, associate professor of physical education, 1973—. *Military service:* Royal Air Force, 1952-55.

*WRITINGS: The Caledonian Games in Nineteenth-Century America,* Fairleigh Dickinson University Press, 1971; *North America's Sporting Heritage: A Guide to Halls of Fame, Sports Museums and Special Collections,* A. S. Barnes, 1974; *Soccer Practice,* Lebel Enterprises, 1978. Contributor of about thirty articles to professional journals. Editor, *New Zealand Journal of Health, Physical Education and Recreation,* 1965-68; book review editor, *Journal of Sport History,* 1973-78.

*WORK IN PROGRESS:* Further research on sports history; a special project for the Royal Society of Canada.

\*          \*          \*

## REED, Joseph W(ayne), Jr. 1932-

*PERSONAL:* Born May 31, 1932, in St. Petersburg, Fla.; son of Joseph Wayne (a printer) and Gertrude (Cain) Reed; married Lillian Craig (a writer, under name Kit Reed), December 10, 1955; children: Joseph McKean, John Craig, Katherine Hyde. *Education:* Yale University, B.A., 1954, M.A., 1958, Ph.D., 1961. *Politics:* Democrat. *Religion:* Episcopalian. *Home:* 45 Lawn Ave., Middletown, Conn. 06457. *Agent:* Hilary Rubinstein, A. P. Watt & Son, 26-28 Bedford Row, Strand, London W.C.2, England. *Office address:* Department of English, Box S, Wesleyan Station, Middletown, Conn. 06457.

*CAREER:* Yale University Library, New Haven, Conn., research assistant, 1956-60; Wesleyan University, Middletown, Conn., instructor, 1960-61, assistant professor, 1961-67, associate professor, 1967-71, professor of English, 1971—, chairman of department, 1971-73. Lecturer for U.S. State Department and U.S. Information Service in Canada, India, and Nepal, 1974. Research consultant, Time-Life Books. Has exhibited paintings in galleries and museums in the United States and abroad, including Portal Gallery (London), Mini-Musee (New York), Ponce Museum (Puerto Rico) and National Miniature Show. *Military service:* U.S. Naval Reserve, active duty, 1954-56; became lieutenant junior grade. *Member:* Modern Language Association of America, Johnsonians, Yale Elizabethan Club. *Awards, honors:* Three awards for paintings exhibited in National Miniature Show, 1972.

*WRITINGS:* (Editor with George R. Creeger) *Selected Prose and Poetry of the Romantic Period,* Holt, 1964; *English Biography in the Early Nineteenth Century: 1801-38,* Yale University Press, 1966; (editor with W. S. Lewis) Horace Walpole, *Castle of Otranto,* Oxford University Press, 1969; (editor with Jeanine Basinger and John Frager) *Working with Kazan,* Wesleyan Film Program, 1971; (editor with Lewis) Horace Walpole, *Family Correspondence,* Yale University Press, 1972; (editor) Barbara Bodichon, *American Diary: 1857-8,* Routledge & Kegan Paul, 1972; *Faulkner's Narrative,* Yale University Press, 1973; (editor with F. A. Pottle) *Boswell, Laird of Auchinleck, 1778-1782,* McGraw, 1977. Contributor to literature journals.

*WORK IN PROGRESS:* Working on problems of film narrative.

\*          \*          \*

## REEVE, Richard M(ark) 1935-

*PERSONAL:* Born June 20, 1935, in Provo, Utah; son of Mark J. (a teacher) and Myre (Wiscombe) Reeve; married V. Karen Brickey, December 13, 1963; children: Susan, Christine, Celia. *Education:* University of Utah, B.A., 1960; Universidad Nacional Autonoma de Mexico, summer study, 1959, 1960; University of Illinois at Urbana-Champaign, M.A., 1962, Ph.D., 1967. *Religion:* Church of Jesus Christ of Latter-day Saints. *Home:* 13135 Morningside Way, Los Angeles, Calif. 90066. *Office:* Department of Spanish and Portuguese, University of California, Los Angeles, Calif. 90024.

*CAREER:* University of Illinois at Urbana-Champaign, instructor in Spanish, 1965-66; Ohio State University, Columbus, Ohio, assistant professor of Spanish, 1966-68; University of California, Los Angeles, assistant professor, 1968-76, associate professor of Spanish, 1976—. *Member:* Modern Language Association of America, American Teachers of Spanish and Portuguese, Instituto Internacional de Literatura Iberoamericana.

*WRITINGS: An Annotated Bibliography on Carlos Fuentes,* Hispania, 1970; (with Gerardo Luzuriaga) *Antologia de Teatro Hispanoamericana,* Fondo de Cultura (Mexico), 1972. Book review editor, *Nueva Narrativa Hispanoamericana,* 1970-75; member of editorial board, *Collier's Encyclopedia,* 1968—; editorial consultant, *Hispamerica,* 1972-75.

\*          \*          \*

## REEVES, Donald 1952-

*PERSONAL:* Born September 23, 1952, in Detroit, Mich.;

son of George Leo and Phinette (Hunter) Reeves. *Education:* Attended Knox College, Jamaica, West Indies, and Cornell University. *Agent:* Kenneth Hagood, 10 Columbus Cir., New York, N.Y. 10019.

*CAREER:* Has worked as a veterinarian's aide, 1968-69, and a steel packer, 1970; Metro Media, New York City, television interviewer, 1970; Harlem Sports Foundation, New York City, track coach, 1970; *New York Times,* New York City, consultant and writer, beginning 1972. Consultant to Board of Mediation of Community Disputes.

*WRITINGS: Notes of a Processed Brother,* Pantheon, 1972.

*WORK IN PROGRESS: The Marginal Man,* a novel.

*BIOGRAPHICAL/CRITICAL SOURCES: New York Times,* February 24, 1970.†

\*        \*        \*

## REGIN, Deric (Wagenvort)

*PERSONAL:* Born in Amsterdam, Netherlands; U.S. citizen; son of J. Paul D. (a naval officer) and Jeannette (Wagenvoort) Riegen; married Nancy Farrand (a librarian), 1953. *Education:* Received B.A. from Amsterdam College; Yale University, M.A., 1954; Columbia University, Ph.D., 1964. *Home:* 601 West 115th St., Apt. 93A, New York, N.Y. 10025. *Agent:* Keuls Autearsrechten Bureau, Amsterdam, Netherlands.

*CAREER:* Rutgers University, New Brunswick, N.J., assistant professor of European history, 1966-67; Brooklyn College of the City University of New York, Brooklyn, N.Y., adjunct associate professor of European history, 1970-72. Instructor (part-time), Columbia University, summer, 1966. Dramaturge, Municipal Theatre (Amsterdam). *Member:* American Historical Association. *Awards, honors:* Annual award from Dutch Government, 1951, for drama; Fulbright fellow, 1952; Dutch Benevolent Society fellow, 1953.

*WRITINGS: Het Spelkarakter van de Griekse Dichtkunst* (literary criticism), Kroonder, 1946; *Inleiding tot de Dramatologie* (literary criticism), [Amsterdam], 1948; *Kleine Prins* (drama), Het Toneel, 1951; *Het Oponthoud* (drama), Bottenburg, 1952; *Freedom and Dignity: The Historical and Philosophical Thought of Schiller,* Nijhoff, 1965; *Culture and the Crowd: A Cultural History of the Proletarian Era,* Chilton, 1968; *Sources of Cultural Estrangement,* Mouton & Co., 1969; *Reflections from a Prison* (poems), Outposts (London), 1971; *Traders, Artists, Burghers: A Cultural History of Amsterdam in the Seventeenth Century,* Humanities, 1976. Contributor of articles and poems to literary journals in England, Europe, and the United States. Editor, *Het Toneel;* literary editor, *Palaestra.*

*WORK IN PROGRESS:* A study of the relationships between the American, English, and Dutch revolutions, tentatively entitled *The Atlantic Revolution.*

\*        \*        \*

## REID, Charles L(loyd)  1927-

*PERSONAL:* Born August 13, 1927, in Bowling Green, Ky.; son of Fred Baird and Bonnie (Lee) Reid; married Frances McCain, October 17, 1948; children: Jeffrey Alan, Sylvia Marie. *Education:* Bethel College, McKenzie, Tenn., B.A. (summa cum laude), 1951; Duke University, M.A., 1954, Ph.D., 1960. *Politics:* Democrat. *Religion:* None. *Home:* 465 Catalina Ave., Youngstown, Ohio 44504. *Office:*

Department of Philosophy, Youngstown State University, Youngstown, Ohio 44503.

*CAREER:* Bethel College, McKenzie, Tenn., assistant professor, 1954-57, associate professor, 1957-61, professor of philosophy, 1962-65; Edinboro State College, Edinboro, Pa., associate professor, 1965-68, professor of philosophy, 1968; Youngstown State University, Youngstown, Ohio, associate professor, 1968-76, professor of philosophy, 1976—. Lecturer in logic, University of Tennessee at Martin, 1963-65. *Military service:* U.S. Army, 1945-48; became staff sergeant. *Member:* National Council for Critical Analysis, Tri-State Philosophical Association (founder and chief executive officer, 1966-71), Ohio Educational Association, Ohio Philosophical Association.

*WRITINGS: Basic Philosophical Analysis,* Dickenson, 1971. Contributor to philosophy journals.

*WORK IN PROGRESS: Choice and Action;* with Thomas A. Shipka, *Readings in Philosophy of Justice.*

*AVOCATIONAL INTERESTS:* History.

\*        \*        \*

## REID, Seerley  1909(?)-1972

1909(?)—July 21, 1972; American audio-visual education specialist, educator, bibliographer, and author on educational subjects. Obituaries: *Washington Post,* July 24, 1972.

\*        \*        \*

## REID, Sue Titus  1939-

*PERSONAL:* Born November 13, 1939, in Bryan, Tex.; daughter of Andrew Jackson, Jr. and Lorraine (Wylie) Titus. *Education:* Texas Woman's University, B.S. (with honors), 1960; University of Missouri, M.A., 1962; University of Iowa, J.D., 1972. *Home:* 7021 58th Ave. N.E., Seattle, Wash. *Office:* School of Law, University of Washington, Seattle, Wash.

*CAREER:* Cornell College, Mount Vernon, Iowa, instructor, 1963-65, assistant professor, 1965-69, associate professor of sociology, 1969-72, acting chairman of department, 1969-72; admitted to Iowa State Bar, 1972; Coe College, Cedar Rapids, Iowa, associate professor of sociology and chairman of department, 1972-74; University of Washington, School of Law, Seattle, associate professor, 1974—. Visiting summer professor, University of Nebraska, 1970; visiting distinguished professor of law and sociology, University of Tulsa, 1977-78. Executive associate, American Sociological Association, 1976-77. *Member:* American Sociological Association, American Society of Criminology, American Bar Association, Midwest Sociological Society (member, board of directors, 1970-72), Iowa Bar Association.

*WRITINGS:* (Editor with David L. Lyon) *Population Crisis: An Interdisciplinary Perspective,* Scott, Foresman, 1972; *Crime and Criminology,* Dryden, 1976. Contributor to professional journals.

*WORK IN PROGRESS:* A revision of *Crime and Criminology;* a book on corrections.

\*        \*        \*

## REINMUTH, Oscar William  1900-

*PERSONAL:* Born October 11, 1900, in St. Louis, Mo.; son of Henry (an engineer) and Mina (Wullschlager) Reinmuth; married Catherine Anne McNaughton, June 3, 1925; children: Oscar McNaughton. *Education:* Clinton College, A.B., 1921; University of Chicago, graduate study, 1921-22;

University of Nebraska, A.M., 1928; Princeton University, Ph.D., 1931. *Home:* 2808 San Pedro, Austin, Tex. 78705. *Office:* Department of Classics, University of Texas, Austin, Tex. 78712.

*CAREER:* University of Nebraska, Lincoln, instructor, 1928-29, assistant professor, 1931-35, associate professor of classics and acting head of department, 1935-37; University of Oklahoma, Norman, professor of classical languages and literatures, 1937-41, head of department, 1937-41; University of Texas at Austin, professor of classics, 1941-72, professor emeritus, 1972—. Visiting professor at University of Illinois, 1937, University of Colorado, 1948, and American School of Classical Studies, Athens, Greece, 1971-72. *Military service:* U.S. Army, 1943-46; became lieutenant colonel. *Member:* American Philological Association (director, 1954-58), American Classical League, American Society of Papyrologists (director, 1966-68), Classical Association of Middle West and South, Archaeological Institute. *Awards, honors:* Litt.D., University of Louisville, 1948; Fulbright Research scholar in Greece, 1951.

*WRITINGS: The Foreigners in the Athenian Ephebia,* University of Nebraska Press, 1929; *The Prefect of Egypt from Augustus to Diocletian,* Dietrichische Verlagsbuchhandlung, 1935, revised edition, Scientia, 1963; (contributor) P. Coleman-Norton, editor, *The Greek Political Experience,* Princeton, 1942; *The Ephebic Inscriptions of the Fourth Century B.C.,* E. J. Brill, 1972. Contributor of articles to journals in his field.

*WORK IN PROGRESS: The Ephebic Inscriptions of the Hellenistic Period,* for E. J. Brill.

*BIOGRAPHICAL/CRITICAL SOURCES:* Marshall Knappen, *And Call It Peace,* University of Chicago Press, 1947.

\* \* \*

### REJAI, Mostafa 1931-

*PERSONAL:* Born March 11, 1931, in Tehran, Iran. *Education:* University of California, Los Angeles, Ph.D., 1964. *Office:* Department of Political Science, Miami University, Oxford, Ohio 45056.

*CAREER:* Miami University, Oxford, Ohio, assistant professor, 1964-67, associate professor, 1967-70, professor of political science, 1970—.

*WRITINGS:* (Editor and contributor) *Democracy: The Contemporary Theories,* Atherton, 1967; (editor) *Mao Tsetung on Revolution and War,* Doubleday, 1969; (co-author) *Ideologies and Modern Politics,* Dodd, 1971, 2nd edition, 1975; (editor and contributor) *Decline of Ideology?,* Aldine–Atherton, 1971; *The Strategy of Political Revolution,* Doubleday, 1973; *The Comparative Study of Revolutionary Strategy,* McKay, 1977. Contributor to political science journals in the United States and abroad.

*WORK IN PROGRESS: Leaders of the Revolution.*

\* \* \*

### RENDON, Armando B. 1939-

*PERSONAL:* Born May 20, 1939, in San Antonio, Tex.; son of Gilbert and Florence (Reyna) Rendon; married Helen Zoma (a program manager), June 17, 1961; children: Mark, Gabrielene, Paul, John. *Education:* St. Mary's College of California, B.A., 1961. *Politics:* Democrat. *Home:* 3643 Veazey St. N.W., Washington, D.C. 20008. *Office:* Latino Institute, American University, McKinley Building 254, Washington, D.C. 20016.

*CAREER:* ATM Systems (a Chicano consultant firm), Washington, D.C., vice-president, 1971—; American University, Washington, D.C., assistant professor of social sciences and director of Latino Institute, 1975—. Member of board of advisors, Children's Television Workshop, 1971; member of board of trustees, University of the District of Columbia, 1976—; chairman of board of directors, Spanish Educational Development Center, 1977—. Secretary, National Mexican American Anti-Defamation Committee. Washington, D.C. delegate to Democratic Central Committee. *Awards, honors:* Council on Interracial Books for Children, runner-up in third annual competition, winner of 1970 competition; travel and study award from Ford Foundation, 1973-74.

*WRITINGS: Chicano Manifesto,* Macmillan, 1971; (photographer) *We, the Mexican Americans,* Bureau of Census, 1970. Work represented in anthologies, *Mexican Americans in the U.S.,* Schenkman, 1970, *Introduction to Chicano Studies,* Macmillan, 1973, and *We Are Chicanos,* Washington Square Press, 1973. Also author of "We Mutually Pledge," a report of the National Hispanic Leadership Conference, "The Chicano Press," and "Chicanos and the Mass Media." Author of "Chicano America," a television script; "New Accent on Science," a film script; and "El Chicano in Washington." Contributor of articles to *Civil Rights Digest, La Luz, City, D.C. Gazette, Washington Post,* and Council on Interracial Books for Children *Bulletin.*

*WORK IN PROGRESS:* Research for a sequel to *Chicano Manifesto,* dealing with similar problems on the international, rather than the national, level.

\* \* \*

### RESTON, James B(arrett), Jr. 1941-

*PERSONAL:* Born March 8, 1941, in New York, N.Y.; son of James Barrett (a writer) and Sarah Jane (a writer; maiden name, Fulton) Reston; married Denise Brender Leary, June 12, 1971. *Education:* University of North Carolina at Chapel Hill, B.A., 1963; attended Oxford University, 1961-62. *Home address:* Route 3, Box 90, Hillsborough, N.C. 27278. *Agent:* Carol Brandt, Brandt & Brandt, 101 Park Ave., New York, N.Y. 10017. *Office:* Department of English, University of North Carolina, Chapel Hill, N.C.

*CAREER:* U.S. Department of the Interior, Washington, D.C., speech writer for Secretary of the Interior Udall, 1963-64; *Chicago Daily News,* Chicago, Ill., reporter, 1964-65; University of North Carolina at Chapel Hill, lecturer in creative writing, 1971—. Community organizer, Neighborhood Youth Corps (New York, N.Y.), summers, 1969, 1970. *Military service:* U.S. Army, 1965-68; became sergeant. *Member:* Authors Guild.

*WRITINGS: To Defend, to Destroy,* Norton, 1971; (contributor) Murray Polner, editor, *When Can I Come Home Again,* Doubleday, 1972; *The Amnesty of John David Herndon,* McGraw, 1973; (with Frank Mankiewicz) *Perfectly Clear: Nixon from Whittier to Watergate,* Quadrangle, 1973; *The Knock at Midnight,* Norton, 1975; *The Innocence of Joan Little: A Southern Mystery,* Quadrangle, 1977. Scriptwriter for David Frost, "The Nixon Interviews," 1976-77.

*WORK IN PROGRESS:* "Sherman's Laurels," a play.

*SIDELIGHTS:* Roger Wilkins states in his review of *The Innocence of Joan Little:* "To millions, . . . Joan Little was a martyr-heroine of the purest sort and the administrators of

North Carolina justice were evil incarnate—anti-woman and anti-black. James Reston, a diligent and sensitive journalist . . . undertook to cut through the collective imagination of those years and through the myths that it spawned . . . to examine what actually happened and how those myths were made.''

*AVOCATIONAL INTERESTS:* Woodcrafting on a lathe, vegetable gardening, the Orient.

*BIOGRAPHICAL/CRITICAL SOURCES: New York Times,* December 17, 1977.

\* \* \*

## REUMAN, Robert E(verett) 1923-

*PERSONAL:* Born February 16, 1923, in Foochow, China; son of Otto G. (a minister) and Martha Lydia (Bourne) Reuman; married Dorothy Ann Swan (a music professor), September 2, 1949; children: Martha Claire, David Alan, Jonathan Robert, Ann Evalyn, Elizabeth Linda. *Education:* Middlebury College, A.B., 1945; University of Pennsylvania, M.A., 1946, Ph.D., 1949. *Politics:* Democrat. *Religion:* Quaker and Unitarian Universalist. *Home:* Marston Ave., Waterville, Me. 04901. *Office:* Department of Philosophy, Colby College, Waterville, Me. 04901.

*CAREER:* Temple University, Philadelphia, Pa., instructor in philosophy, 1947-49; Lafayette College, Easton, Pa., instructor, 1953-54, assistant professor of philosophy, 1954-56; Colby College, Waterville, Me., assistant professor, 1956-59, associate professor, 1959-69, professor of philosophy, 1969—, chairman of department of philosophy and religion, 1977—. American Friends Service Committee, worked in China, 1949-51, and Germany, 1951-53; Quaker International Affairs Representative, Germany, 1964-66; member of board of directors, American Friends of Le College Cevenol. *Wartime service:* Civilian public service as conscientious objector to military duty, 1943-46. *Member:* American Philosophical Association, Society for Values in Higher Education, American Association of University Professors, Danforth Associates (New England regional chairman, 1963-64).

*WRITINGS: Mauern,* Verlag Leonhard Friedrich, 1965; *Walls,* Pendle Hill, 1966; (with James E. Bristol, Holland Hunter, James H. Laird, Sidney Lens, Milton Mayer, Athan Theoharis, and Bryant Wedge) *Anatomy of Anti-Communism,* Hill & Wang, 1969. Contributor to professional journals.

*WORK IN PROGRESS: Social Values and Social Structures.*

\* \* \*

## REWOLDT, Stewart H(enry) 1922-

*PERSONAL:* Born January 26, 1922, in Dundee, Ill.; son of Frank Frederick (a carpenter) and Elsa (Schultz) Rewoldt; married Allison Hilliard, December 28, 1946; children: Gregory, Jeffrey, Thomas. *Education:* University of Michigan, B.B.A., 1946, M.B.A., 1947, Ph.D., 1952. *Home:* 1213 Manhattan Dr., Ann Arbor, Mich. 48103. *Office:* Graduate School of Business Administration, University of Michigan, Ann Arbor, Mich. 48104.

*CAREER:* University of Michigan, Ann Arbor, instructor in marketing, 1947-52; Indiana University at Bloomington, assistant professor, 1953-55, associate professor of marketing, 1955-56; University of Michigan, associate professor, 1956-60, professor of marketing, 1960—. Visiting professor and adviser to Institute for Research in Productivity, Wa-

seda University, Tokyo, 1959-60; visiting professor, Netherlands School of Economics, Rotterdam, 1971. *Military service:* U.S. Army, 1943-46. *Member:* American Economic Association, American Marketing Association, International Sales/Marketing Executives.

*WRITINGS: Economic Effects of Marketing Research,* Bureau of Business Research, University of Michigan, 1953; (contributor) Charles N. Davisson, *The Marketing of Automotive Parts,* Bureau of Business Research, University of Michigan, 1954; (editor) *Frontiers in Marketing Thought,* Bureau of Business Research, Indiana University, 1955; (with J. D. Scott and M. R. Warshaw) *Introduction to Marketing Management: Text and Cases,* Irwin, 1969, 3rd edition, 1977. Contributor of articles and reviews to business journals.

*WORK IN PROGRESS:* With J. D. Scott and M. R. Warshaw, a fourth edition of *Introduction to Marketing Management.*

\* \* \*

## REXINE, John E(fstratios) 1929-

*PERSONAL:* Born June 6, 1929, in Boston, Mass.; son of Efstratios John (a businessman) and Athena (Glekas) Rexine; married Elaine Lavrakas, June 16, 1957; children: John E., Jr., Athena Elisabeth, Michael Constantine. *Education:* Harvard University, A.B. (magna cum laude), 1951, A.M., 1953, Ph.D., 1964. *Politics:* Independent. *Religion:* Greek Orthodox. *Home:* R.D. 2, Spring St., Hamilton, N.Y. 13346. *Office:* 216-217 Lawrence Hall, Colgate University, Hamilton, N.Y. 13346.

*CAREER:* Brandeis University, Waltham, Mass., instructor in humanities, 1955-57; Colgate University, Hamilton, N.Y., instructor, 1957-60, assistant professor, 1960-64, associate professor, 1964-68, professor of classics, 1968—, acting chairman of department of classics, 1962, chairman, 1964-72, director of Division of University Studies, 1969-72, director of Division of Humanities, 1972—, associate dean of faculty, 1973-74, acting dean of faculty, 1977-78. Associate, Center for Neo-Hellenic Studies, 1965—. *Military service:* U.S. Army, 1953-55. *Member:* American Philological Association, Mediaeval Academy of America, American Classical League, Modern Greek Studies Association, American Council on the Teaching of Foreign Languages, Society for the Advancement of Education, British Institute of Archaeology at Ankara, American Society for Neo-Hellenic Studies (member of advisory board, 1967—), Greek Humanistic Society (honorary member), Classical Association of the Atlantic States, Phi Beta Kappa, Eta Sigma Phi. *Awards, honors:* Fulbright scholar in Greece, 1951-52; Danforth grant, 1959-60; Helicon Society Phoutrides Gold Medal, 1962, for contributions to Greek studies; Asian studies fellowship from Colgate University, 1965-66.

*WRITINGS: Solon and His Political Theory,* William-Frederick, 1958; *Religion in Plato and Cicero,* Philosophical Library, 1959; (with Andreas Kazamias, Paul Nash, Henry Perkinson, and others) *The Educated Man,* Wiley, 1965; (with Thomas Spelios and Harry J. Psomiades) *A Pictorial History of Greece,* Crown, 1967. Contributor to *McGraw-Hill Encyclopedia of World Biography,* 1973. Contributor of several hundred articles and reviews to publications in the United States and abroad. Contributing editor of *Hellenic Chronicle,* 1952—; book review editor of *Athene,* 1957-67, of *Orthodox Observer,* 1957—, of *Modern Language Journal,* 1977—; managing editor, 1959-60, associate editor, 1960-67, member of editorial advisory board, 1967—, of *Greek Or-*

thodox *Theological Review;* associate editor of *Diakonia,* 1971—; assistant editor of *Helios,* 1976—; editor of *Classical Outlook,* 1977—.

*WORK IN PROGRESS: Thucydides and Tacitus on the Nature of Power.*

\* \* \*

## REYNOLDS, John J(oseph) 1924-

*PERSONAL:* Born June 25, 1924, in Redwood City, Calif.; son of John J. and Margaret (O'Malley) Reynolds. *Education:* University of California, Berkeley, B.A., 1946, M.A., 1948, Ph.D., 1956. *Home:* 83-15 169th St., Jamaica, N.Y. 11432. *Office:* Department of Spanish, St. John's University, Jamaica, N.Y. 11439.

*CAREER:* University of Arizona, Tucson, instructor, 1950-56, assistant professor of Spanish, 1956-60; St. John's University, Jamaica, N.Y., assistant professor, 1960-62, associate professor, 1962-66, professor of Spanish, 1966—. *Member:* Modern Language Association of America, Renaissance Society of America, Modern Humanities Research Association, American Association of Teachers of Spanish and Portuguese, American Council on the Teaching of Foreign Languages, American Association of University Professors, Comediantes, OFINES (Madrid), Asociacion Internacional de Hispanistas, Phi Beta Kappa, Alpha Mu Gamma, Sigma Delta Pi.

*WRITINGS:* (With T. D. Houchin) *A Directory for Spanish-Speaking New York,* Quadrangle, 1971; *Juan Timoneda,* Twayne, 1975. Contributor to *New Catholic Encyclopedia;* contributor of articles to language journals.

*SIDELIGHTS:* John Reynolds has traveled through Europe, Mexico, and Canada, and has resided in Spain.

\* \* \*

## RIBNER, Irving 1921-1972

August 29, 1921—July 2, 1972; American Shakespearean scholar, educator, and author and editor of books on Elizabethan drama. Obituaries: *New York Times,* July 4, 1972. (See index for *CA* sketch)

\* \* \*

## RICE, Allan Lake 1905-

*PERSONAL:* Born March 1, 1905, in Philadelphia, Pa.; son of Earle C. and Georgene (Smith) Rice; married Rigmor Hallqvist, November 6, 1943; children: Deborah, Suzanne (Mrs. Lawrence Henry), Christopher. *Education:* University of Pennsylvania, A.B., 1927, M.A., 1928, Ph.D., 1932. *Home address:* Box 492, Kimberton, Pa. 19442.

*CAREER:* Princeton University, Princeton, N.J., instructor in German, 1930-36; University of Pennsylvania, Philadelphia, assistant professor of German and Swedish, 1936-47; Ursinus College, Collegeville, Pa., professor of German and Swedish, 1947-75; free-lance translator in ten languages, 1975—. Professor of Swedish, Augustana College, summers, 1948, 1950. *Military service:* U.S. Naval Reserve, assistant naval attache, active duty, 1942-45; served in Sweden and Finland; became commander. *Member:* Phi Beta Kappa. *Awards, honors:* Decorated by King of Sweden, 1970.

*WRITINGS: Swedish: A Practical Grammar,* Fortress Press, 1958, 3rd edition, 1968; *German: A Practical Grammar,* Ursinus College Supply Store, 5th edition, 1972. Contributor of articles on model railroading to periodicals.

*WORK IN PROGRESS: The New Approach to Swedish Grammar.*

*AVOCATIONAL INTERESTS:* Model railroading (trolley-car era).

\* \* \*

## RICE, Donald L. 1938-

*PERSONAL:* Born August 5, 1938, in East Greenwich, R.I.; son of Walter Lewis and Edna (Tunnicliff) Rice; married Dorothy Bundy, May 20, 1961; children: Aaron Lewis. *Education:* Attended Urbana College, 1960-62, Skidmore College, 1976-77. *Politics:* "Armchair anarchist." *Religion:* Unitarian. *Home:* 1109 West Vine St., Mt. Vernon, Ohio 43050.

*CAREER:* Worked for various newspapers in Ohio, Wisconsin, Rhode Island, Massachusetts, 1957-66; Cooper-Bessemer (engine manufacturer), Mt. Vernon, Ohio, technical editor, 1966-72; Photo Documents Corp., Mt. Vernon, production manager, 1972-73; free-lance advertising, 1973—. *Awards, honors:* Ohio Arts Council playwriting prize, 1974, for "The Situation on Earth."

*WRITINGS: The Agitator: A Schism Anthology,* American Library Association, 1972; *Publish Your Own Magazine,* McKay, 1978. Also author of play, "The Situation on Earth," 1974. Contributor of satires, short stories, poetry, and plays to periodicals. Founder and editor of *Schism: A Journal of Divergent American Opinions,* 1969-75.

*WORK IN PROGRESS:* "Uncounted books, plays, short stories, etc."

*SIDELIGHTS:* Donald L. Rice told *CA* that one of his major interests is "the phenomenon of social change. Though I never believe them myself, I enjoy reading and publishing the many panacean schemes offered to cure all our social ills—and I have a special fondness for out-and-out crackpots. (After all, today's crackpot ideas are tomorrow's political realities.)" He continues: "In my own writings . . . I shy away from giving answers, believing that it is the satirist's job to provoke and to pose questions. Perhaps, though, I've simply grown timid—having seen how foolish 'The Truth' appears in print—and rather than risk being ridiculed myself, I prefer the relatively safe occupation of shooting at easy targets set up by others."

\* \* \*

## RICHARDS, James O(lin) 1936-

*PERSONAL:* Born October 25, 1936, in Poplar Bluff, Mo.; son of Olin D. and Wanda (Shearon) Richards; married Barbara Elise Streetman (a church secretary), June 15, 1958; children: Jaimee Elise, Allison Paige. *Education:* Georgetown College, Georgetown, Ky., B.A. (summa cum laude), 1958; University of Illinois, M.A., 1960, Ph.D., 1962. *Residence:* Pine Lakes, Thomaston, Ga. 30286. *Office:* Department of Social Science, Gordon Junior College, Barnesville, Ga. 30204.

*CAREER:* Kentucky Southern College, Louisville, Ky., instructor, 1962-63, assistant professor, 1963-66, associate professor of history, 1966-68, chairman of department, 1964-68; Macon Junior College, Macon, Ga., associate professor of history, 1968-73; Gordon Junior College, Barnesville, Ga., professor of history and chairman of social sciences, 1973—. *Member:* American Historical Association, Conference on British Studies, Urban History Group (United States), Urban History Group (England). *Awards, honors:* Woodrow Wilson fellow, 1958-59.

*WRITINGS: Party Propaganda Under Queen Anne: The General Elections of 1702-1713*, University of Georgia Press, 1972.

*WORK IN PROGRESS:* Research on attitudes towards the city in Victorian England, with a book expected to result.

*AVOCATIONAL INTERESTS:* Gardening, bee-keeping, wood-working.

\*     \*     \*

## RICHARDSON, Cyril Charles   1909-1976

*PERSONAL:* Born June 13, 1909, in London, England; came to United States, 1931, naturalized, 1939; son of Charles Willerton (a merchant) and Kate (Bunker) Richardson; married Louise Burbank Shattuck, February 13, 1945. *Education:* University of Saskatchewan, A.B. (with distinction), 1930; Emmanuel College, Saskatoon, L.Th. (with high honors), 1931; Union Theological Seminary, New York, S.T.M. (summa cum laude), 1932, Th.D., 1934; also studied at University of Goettingen, 1933, University of Dijon, 1935, and University of Basel, 1936. *Politics:* Democrat. *Home:* 99 Claremont Ave., New York, N.Y. 10027. *Office:* Union Theological Seminary, 3041 Broadway, New York, N.Y. 10027.

*CAREER:* Ordained deacon, Protestant Episcopal Church, 1934, and priest, later that year; Union Theological Seminary, New York, N.Y., instructor, 1934-35, assistant professor, 1935-39, associate professor, 1939-49, Washburn Professor of Church History, 1949-76, dean of graduate studies, 1954-74, Union Scholar, 1974-76. Adjunct professor of religion, Columbia University, 1962-76. Mere Preacher, Cambridge University, 1961; member, National Council Commission on Worship. *Member:* American Society of Church History, American Theological Society, Duodecim (founder and secretary, 1937-43). *Awards, honors:* D.D., Emmanuel College, Saskatoon, 1949, General Theological Seminary, N.Y., 1972.

*WRITINGS: The Christianity of Ignatius of Antioch*, Columbia University Press, 1935, reprinted, AMS Press, 1967; *The Church through the Centuries*, Scribner, 1938, reprinted, AMS Press, 1977; *The Sacrament of Reunion: A Study in Ecumenical Christianity*, Scribner, 1940; *Zwingli and Cranmer on the Eucharist* (M. Dwight Johnson memorial lecture), Seabury-Western Theological Seminary, 1949; (abridger) *The Pocket Bible: The Old and New Testaments in the King James Version* (abridgement of *The Bible Designed to Be Read as Living Literature*), Pocket Books, 1951; (editor and translator in collaboration with Eugene R. Fairweather, Edward R. Hardy, and Massey H. Shepherd, Jr.) *Early Christian Fathers*, Westminster, 1953, reprinted, Macmillan, 1970; (editor with Hardy) *Christology of the Later Fathers*, Westminster, 1954; *The Doctrine of the Trinity*, Abingdon, 1958; (reviser with others) Williston Walker, *A History of the Christian Church*, 3rd edition (Richardson was not associated with earlier editions), Scribner, 1959.

Contributor: Paul B. Maves, editor, *The Church and Mental Health*, Scribner, 1953; E. F. Johnson, editor, *Religious Symbolism*, Harper, 1954; Roy W. Battenhouse, editor, *A Companion to St. Augustine*, Oxford University Press, 1955; Simon Doniger, editor, *Healing, Human and Divine*, Association Press, 1957; Harold R. Landon, editor, *Living Thankfully*, Seabury, 1961; Henry P. Van Dusen, editor, *Christianity on the March*, Harper, 1963; S. H. Miller and G. E. Wright, editors, *Ecumenical Dialogue at Harvard*, Harvard University Press, 1964.

Writer of hymn, ''God of the Prairies'' in *Canadian Hymnal* (Anglican). Contributor to religious and theological periodicals in the United States and Europe. Member of editorial board, *Anglican Theological Review* and *Review of Religion*.

*BIOGRAPHICAL/CRITICAL SOURCES: New York Times*, November 17, 1976.†

(Died November 16, 1976)

\*     \*     \*

## RIEPE, Dale (Maurice)   1918-

*PERSONAL:* Born June 22, 1918, in Tacoma, Wash.; son of Roland (in railroad management) and Martha (Johnson) Riepe; married Olave Patricia Hoyle, 1938 (divorced, 1947); married Charleine Williams, 1948; children: (second marriage) Kathrine Leigh, Dorothy Lorraine. *Education:* University of Washington, Seattle, B.A., 1944; University of Michigan, M.A., 1946, Ph.D., 1954; additional graduate study at University of Hawaii, 1949, Banaras Hindu University, 1951, Madras University, 1952, and Waseda University, 1956. *Home:* 48 Capen Blvd., Buffalo, N.Y. 14214. *Office:* State University of New York at Buffalo, 605 Baldy Hall, Amherst Campus, Buffalo, N.Y. 14261.

*CAREER:* Northern Pacific Railway, Seattle, Wash., clerk, 1936-43; Puget Sound Bridge and Dredging Co., Seattle, Wash., electrician, 1942-45; Carleton College, Northfield, Minn., instructor in philosophy, 1948-51; University of South Dakota, Vermillion, assistant professor of philosophy, 1952-54; University of North Dakota, Grand Forks, associate professor, 1954-59, professor of philosophy, 1959-62, head of department, 1954-62; C. W. Post College, Long Island University, Greenvale, N.Y., professor of philosophy and associate director of humanities, 1962-63; State University of New York at Buffalo, professor of philosophy, 1963—, associate dean of Graduate School, 1964-65. Exchange lecturer, University of Manitoba, 1955; Fulbright lecturer, University of Tokyo, 1957-58; visiting lecturer, Western Washington State College, 1961.

*MEMBER:* American Philosophical Association, Conference on Asian Affairs (secretary, 1955), American Oriental Society, Society for Asian Studies, American Archaeological Society, American Association of University Professors, Society for American Philosophy (chairman, 1960), Society for Creative Ethics, Society for the Philosophical Study of Marxism (founding secretary, 1962; publications secretary, 1974—), Alpha Pi Zeta. *Awards, honors:* Fulbright scholar in India, 1951-52; Royal Asiatic Society fellow, 1960; Carnegie fellow, 1960-61; American Philosophical Society grant, 1963; State University of New York Research Foundation grants, 1964, 1968, 1969, 1972, 1973; American Institute of Indian Studies research fellow, 1966-67, London School of Oriental and African Studies grant, 1971.

*WRITINGS: The Naturalistic Tradition in Indian Thought*, University of Washington Press, 1961; (editor with Jack Pustilnik) *The Structure of Philosophy*, Littlefield, 1966; *The Philosophy of India and Its Impact on American Thought*, C. C Thomas, 1970; (editor with David H. DeGrood and John Somerville) *Radical Currents in Contemporary Philosophy*, Warren Green, 1971; (editor with DeGrood and Edward D'Angelo) *Reflections on Revolution*, Spartacus, 1971; (co-editor) *Contemporary East European Philosophy*, Spartacus, 1971; (editor with DeGrood and D'Angelo) *Philosophy at the Barricade*, Spartacus, 1971; (editor) *Phenomenology and Natural Existence: Essays in*

*Honor of Marvin Farber,* State University of New York Press, 1973; (with Paul K. Crosser and DeGrood) *East-West Dialogues: Foundations and Problems of Revolutionary Praxis,* Gruner, 1973; *Contemporary Trends in Asiatic Philosophy,* Gordon & Breach, in press. Also author of *Explorations,* 1977. Contributor to philosophic and literary journals in the United States, India, Japan, and England. Editorial associate, *Humanist;* associate editor of *Chinese Studies in Philosophy* and of *Chinese Studies in History.*

*WORK IN PROGRESS:* Book on contemporary Indian philosophy; a novel, *The Owl Flies by Day.*

\* \* \*

## RIGG, A(rthur) G(eorge) 1937-

*PERSONAL:* Born February 17, 1937, in Wigan, England; son of George William (a businessman) and Alice (Rose) Rigg; married Jennifer Dickie (a novelist), July 4, 1964. *Education:* Oxford University, B.A., 1959, M.A., 1962, D.Phil., 1966. *Home:* 423 Roehampton Ave., Toronto, Ontario, Canada. *Office:* Centre for Medieval Studies, University of Toronto, 39 Queen's Park, Toronto, Ontario, Canada M5S 1A1.

*CAREER:* Oxford University, Oxford, England, lecturer in English, 1961-66; Stanford University, Stanford, Calif., assistant professor of English, 1966-68; University of Toronto, Centre for Medieval Studies, Toronto, Ontario, associate professor, 1968-76, professor of medieval studies, 1976—, acting director, 1976-78. *Member:* Mediaeval Academy of America.

*WRITINGS: Glastonbury Miscellany of the Fifteenth Century,* Clarendon Press, 1968; (editor) *The English Language: A Historical Reader,* Appleton, 1968; (editor) *Editing Medieval Texts Written in England,* Garland, 1977; (editor) *The Poems of Walter of Wimborne,* Pontifical Institute, 1978. Contributor to medieval studies journals. General editor, "Toronto Mediaeval Latin Texts."

*WORK IN PROGRESS:* Studying Goliardic manuscripts of England in the thirteenth, fourteenth, fifteenth, and sixteenth centuries.

\* \* \*

## RIMLINGER, Gaston V. 1926-

*PERSONAL:* Born August 16, 1926, in Strasbourg, France; son of Victor J. and Anne (Glaser) Rimlinger; married Lorraine Stewart, September 1, 1951; children: Yvonne, Claire, Frank, Catherine, Christopher. *Education:* University of Washington, Seattle, B.A. (summa cum laude), 1951; University of California, Berkeley, Ph.D., 1956. *Politics:* Democrat. *Religion:* Roman Catholic. *Home:* 1927 Wroxton Rd., Houston, Tex. 77005. *Office:* Department of Economics, Rice University, Houston, Tex. 77001.

*CAREER:* Interpreter for the U.S. Military Government in Germany, 1945-47; Princeton University, Princeton, N.J., instructor, 1955-57, assistant professor of economics, 1957-60; Rice University, Houston, Tex., professor of economics, 1960-69, 1972—, head of department, 1960-69. Advisor, Ford Foundation, West Africa, 1969-72; member of board of directors of Houston Vocational Guidance Service, 1966-69 and American International School, Lagos, Nigeria, 1971-72. *Member:* American Economic Association, Economic History Association, Association for Social Economics, Southwestern Social Science Association, Southern Economic Association, Phi Beta Kappa. *Awards, honors:* Ford Foundation Faculty fellow, 1964.

*WRITINGS: Welfare Policy and Industrialization in Europe, America, and Russia,* Wiley, 1971; *Indigenization and Management Development in Nigeria,* Lagos, 1974. Contributor of articles to *Journal of Economic History, Quarterly Journal of Economics, Southern Economic Journal, Comparative Studies in Society and History, Industrial and Labor Relations Review, Western Journal of Economics, International Review of Social History, Social Science Quarterly, Harvard Business Review* and other journals.

*WORK IN PROGRESS:* Volume VIII of "Cambridge Economic History of Europe," *Labor and Social Policy in Continental Europe.*

\* \* \*

## RIOPELLE, Arthur J. 1920-

*PERSONAL:* Born April 22, 1920, in Thorp, Wis.; son of Wilfred G. (a physician) and Ann Marie (Schroeder) Riopelle; married Mary Jane Astell, May 2, 1942; children: Mary Ann, James Michael, Jean Elizabeth. *Education:* University of Wisconsin, B.S., 1941, M.S., 1948, Ph.D., 1950. *Home:* 9710 Highland Rd., Baton Rouge, La. 70810. *Office:* Department of Psychology, Louisiana State University, Baton Rouge Campus, Baton Rouge, La. 70803.

*CAREER:* Emory University, Atlanta, Ga., 1950-57, assistant professor, then associate professor of psychology; U.S. Army, Medical Research Laboratory, Fort Knox, Ky., director of Psychology Division, 1957-59; Yerkes Laboratories of Primate Biology, Orange Park, Fla., director, 1959-62; Tulane University, Delta Regional Primate Research Center, Covington, La., director, 1962-71; Louisiana State University, Baton Rouge, professor of psychology, 1971—. *Member:* American Psychological Association, American Physiological Society, American Association for the Advancement of Science, Animal Behaviour Society, Sigma Xi, Phi Kappa Phi.

*WRITINGS:* (Contributor) A. Schrier, H. F. Harlow and F. Stollnitz, editors, *Behavior of Nonhuman Primates,* Academic Press, 1965; (editor) *Problem Solving in Animals,* Penguin, 1967; (contributor) *The Marvels of Animal Behavior,* National Geographic Society, 1972. Contributor to *Encyclopedia Americana;* contributor of articles and reviews to professional journals.

\* \* \*

## RITTER, Jess(e P., Jr.) 1930-

*PERSONAL:* Born October 16, 1930; son of Jesse P. (a fire chief) and Merle E. Ritter; married, August 29, 1949; wife's name, Lorna J.; children: Carolyn, Jeri, Lorna, Paul, Eric. *Education:* Kansas State Teachers College (now Emporia State University), B.A., 1956; University of Arkansas, M.A., 1960, Ph.D., 1963. *Home:* 4035 Tokay Dr., Napa, Calif. 94558. *Office:* Department of English, San Francisco State University, 1600 Holloway, San Francisco, Calif. 94132.

*CAREER:* Eastern Washington State College (now Eastern Washington University), Cheney, instructor in English, 1957-59; North Texas State University, Denton, instructor in English, 1960-62; Northern Illinois University, DeKalb, 1963-68, member of faculty of English; San Francisco State University, San Francisco, Calif., professor of English, 1968—. *Military service:* U.S. Navy, 1951-54. *Member:* English Council of California State Colleges.

*WRITINGS:* (With William Robinson) *Beyond Survival,* Heath, 1971; (with Grover Lewis) *Focus/Media,* Chandler

Publishing, 1972; *B. B. King and the Blues,* Straight Arrow Press, 1972. Author of "Santa Rita," a screenplay. Work is also included in *The Vonnegut Statement* and *A Catch-22 Reader.* Contributor to magazines and newspapers, including *Rolling Stone* and *Village Voice.* Columnist and entertainment editor, *Kansas City Times & Star,* 1974-76.

*WORK IN PROGRESS: Territory Blues,* a book about jazz, country-western, and blues music of the American southwest.

*AVOCATIONAL INTERESTS:* Making furniture, beer, and wine, processing and growing food, collecting country lore.

\*     \*     \*

**ROADEN, Arliss L. 1930-**

*PERSONAL:* Born September 27, 1930, in Bark Camp, Ky.; son of J. S. (a railroadman) and Ethel (Killian) Roaden; married Mary Etta Mitchell, September 1, 1951; children: Janice, Sharon. *Education:* Attended Cumberland Junior College, 1947-48; Carson-Newman College, A.B. (cum laude), 1951; University of Tennessee, M.S., 1958, Ed.D., 1961. *Politics:* Democrat. *Religion:* American Baptist. *Home:* 1155 North Dixie Ave., Cookeville, Tenn. 38501. *Office:* Office of the President, Tennessee Technological University, Cookeville, Tenn. 38501.

*CAREER:* Public school teacher in Williamsburg, Ky., 1949-50; Municipal Housing Commission, Paducah, Ky., management aide, 1953-55; Oak Ridge Institute of Nuclear Studies, Inc., Oak Ridge, Tenn., staff associate, 1957-59; Auburn University, Auburn, Ala., assistant professor of educational foundations, 1961-62; Ohio State University, Columbus, assistant professor, 1962-64, associate professor, 1964-67, professor of education, 1967-74, associate dean of College of Education, 1968-69, acting dean of College of Education, 1969-70, vice-provost for graduate affairs, 1970-72, dean of graduate school, 1970-74, vice-provost for research, 1972-74; Tennessee Technological University, Cookeville, president, 1974—. Visiting professor at Marshall University, 1961, University of Southern California, 1964, and Indiana University, 1967. Consultant to higher educational institutions. Member of executive committee, Urban Education Coalition, Columbus Metropolitan Area, 1969—; vice-chairman, Phi Delta Kappa Foundation, 1969—. Member of board of governors, Ecumenical Education Committee, Columbus Metropolitan Area Church Board, 1968—; member of general assembly, Ohio Council of Churches, 1972—. Director, First National Bank of Cookeville. *Military service:* U.S. Army, Signal Corps, 1951-53.

*MEMBER:* American Association for the Advancement of Science, American Academy of Political and Social Science, American Educational Research Association, American Association for Higher Education, National Association of Land Grant Universities and State Colleges, National Society for the Study of Education, Phi Kappa Phi, Kappa Delta Pi, Kappa Phi Kappa, Phi Delta Kappa. *Awards, honors:* Outstanding alumnus, Cumberland College, 1968; Phi Delta Kappa International research grant, 1968; centennial award for distinguished alumni and faculty, College of Education, Ohio State University, 1970.

*WRITINGS: The Assessment of School Performance in Big City School Systems,* Educational Resources Information Center, 1969; *Formal Programs for Training Educational Research Development, and Dissemination Personnel,* Education Resources Information Center, 1969; *Citizen*

*Participation in School Affairs in Two Southern Cities,* Educational Resources Information Center, 1969; (editor) *Problems of School Men in Depressed Urban Centers,* Ohio State University, 1969; (co-author) *Research Involvement and Productivity of American Educational Research Association Members,* Laboratory of Educational Research, University of Colorado, 1970; (co-author) *A Case for Installing the Research Assistantship as a Formal Component in Educational Research,* American Educational Research Task Force on Training Research and Research-Related Personnel, 1970; (with Blaine R. Worthen) *The Research Assistantship and Subsequent Research Productivity,* Phi Delta Kappa, 1972; (with Worthen) *The Research Assistantship: Recommendations for Colleges and Universities,* Phi Delta Kappa, 1975.

Contributor: Marilyn Gittell, editor, *Educating an Urban Population,* Sage Publications, 1968; D. L. Clark and J. E. Hopkins, editors, *A Study of Roles for Researchers in Education,* Indiana University Research Foundation, 1968. Contributor to *Educational Researcher, Journal of Educational Research, Research in Education, Theory into Practice,* and other publications. Member of editorial board, *Journal of Higher Education,* 1970—.†

\*     \*     \*

**ROARK, Dallas M(organ) 1931-**

*PERSONAL:* Born December 15, 1931, in Birchwood, Tex.; son of Franklin A. (a farmer) and Mattie (White) Roark; married Elaine Joyce Musial (a teacher), March 19, 1955; children: Lyman, Dalaine. *Education:* Northern Baptist College, Th.B., 1954; University of Iowa, M.A., 1958, Ph.D., 1963. *Politics:* Independent. *Home:* 945 Elm, Emporia, Kan. 66801. *Office:* Emporia State University, 1200 Commercial, Emporia, Kan. 66801.

*CAREER:* Pastor of Baptist churches in Bonaparte, Iowa and West Branch, Iowa, 1956-60; Wayland Baptist College, Plainview, Tex., instructor, 1960-63, assistant professor, 1963-65, associate professor of religion, 1965-66; Emporia State University, Emporia, Kan., professor of philosophy, 1966—. *Member:* American Academy of Religion, Southwestern Philosophical Society.

*WRITINGS:* (Editor) *Wayland Lectures,* Wayland Press, 1962; *The Christian Faith,* Broadman, 1969; *Dietrich Bonhoeffer,* Word Books, 1972. Contributor to religious journals.

*WORK IN PROGRESS: Introduction to Philosophy,* completion expected in 1979.

\*     \*     \*

**ROBERTS, Carol A. 1933-**

*PERSONAL:* Born March 5, 1933, in Pottsville, Pa.; daughter of Charles Benjamin (an advertising manager for Sears, Roebuck) and Lotus (Knowlton) Roberts. *Education:* Shippensburg State College, B.S. in Ed., 1955; Middlebury College, M.A., 1960; Temple University, M.S. *Home:* 308 Arby's Rd., Harrisburg, Pa. 17109.

*CAREER:* Elementary teacher in Harrisburg, Pa., 1955-63; Shippensburg State College, Shippensburg, Pa., assistant professor of English, 1963-67; elementary teacher in Harrisburg, 1967—. *Member:* National Education Association, American Association of University Professors, Academy of American Poets, National Federation of State Poetry Societies (3rd vice-president, 1976), American Poetry League, Pennsylvania State Education Association, Pennsylvania Poetry Society (vice-president, 1975-76), South & West, Inc., Keysner Poets (vice-president, 1969-70, 1971-72, 1974-76; president, 1973-74), Harrisburg Manuscript Club (vice-president, 1974-76), Kappa Delta Pi. *Awards, honors:* National Federation of State Poetry Societies, first prize, 1971, 1972, and 1976, and third prize, 1976, for poems; publication award, South & West, Inc., 1971; first prize, Harrisburg Manuscript Club, 1973, for short story; grand prize, Pennsylvania Poetry Society, 1974.

*WRITINGS: A nemish named Lovable,* South & West, 1972. Poems have appeared in prize poem collections of Pennsylvania Poetry Society and National Federation of State Poetry Societies and in *Time of Singing, A Goodly Heritage,* and other collections and poetry journals.

*WORK IN PROGRESS:* Four collections of poems, *Book Read Backwards* (historical poems), *This Morning as Usual, aspects of it,* and *letters to you* (love poems); a collection of short stories, not yet titled.

*AVOCATIONAL INTERESTS:* Rocks and minerals, Welsh literature, metaphysics, painting, photography, music, jazz dance, drama, ecology and wildlife.

\* \* \*

## ROBERTS, Henry L(ithgow) 1916-1972

September 27, 1916—October 17, 1972; American educator, magazine editor, book reviewer, and author of books on Eastern Europe and international relations. Obituaries: *New York Times,* October 18, 1972.

\* \* \*

## ROBERTS, John M(ilton) 1916-

*PERSONAL:* Born December 8, 1916, in Omaha, Neb.; son of John Milton (a contractor) and Ruth Elizabeth (Kohler) Roberts; married Marie Louise Kotouc, May 22, 1941 (died, 1958); married Joan Marilyn Skutt, October 22, 1961; children: (first marriage) Tania Marie, Andrea Louise; (second marriage) James Barton, John Milton, Jr. *Education:* University of Nebraska, A.B. (with distinction), 1937; University of Chicago, graduate student, 1937-39; Yale University, Ph.D., 1947. *Home:* 122 Kent Dr., Pittsburgh, Pa. 15241. *Office:* Department of Anthropology, University of Pittsburgh, Pittsburgh, Pa. 15260.

*CAREER:* University of Minnesota, Minneapolis, assistant professor of anthropology, 1947-48; Harvard University, Cambridge, Mass., assistant professor of social anthropology, 1948-53; University of Nebraska, Lincoln, associate professor, 1953-55, professor of anthropology, 1955-58; Cornell University, Ithaca, N.Y., professor of anthropology, 1958-71; University of Pittsburgh, Pittsburgh, Pa., Andrew W. Mellon Professor of Anthropology, 1971—. Fellow, Center for Advanced Study in the Behavioral Sciences, 1956-57; professor of comparative cultures, Naval War College, 1969-70. Intermittent field researcher among the Ramah Navaho and Zuni, 1946—. *Military service:* U.S. Army, Infantry, 1942-45; became captain; received Silver Star and Bronze Star.

*MEMBER:* American Anthropological Association (fellow), American Ethnological Society (president, 1960), American Folklore Society, American Society for Political and Legal Philosophy, American Association for the Advancement of Science (fellow), American Sociological Association (fellow), American Psychological Association, Royal Anthropological Institute (fellow), Linguistic Society of America, Society for American Archaeology, Society for

Applied Anthropology, Northeastern Anthropological Conference (president, 1966-67), Phi Beta Kappa, Sigma Xi.

*WRITINGS: Three Navaho Households: A Comparative Study in Small Group Culture,* Peabody Museum of American Archaeology and Ethnology, Harvard University, 1951; (with Watson Smith) *Zuni Law,* Peabody Museum of American Archaeology and Ethnology, Harvard University, 1954. Author or co-author of other monographs on the Zuni.

Contributor: Edgar A. Schuler and others, editors, *Readings in Sociology,* Crowell, 1960; Sol Saporta, editor, *Psycholinguistics: A Book of Readings,* Holt, 1961; Florence Kluckhohn and Fred L. Strodtbeck, *Variations in Value Orientations,* Row, Peterson, 1961; Ward Goodenough, editor, *Explorations in Cultural Anthropology: Essays in Honor of George Peter Murdock,* McGraw, 1964; Clellan S. Ford, editor, *Cross-Cultural Approaches: Readings in Comparative Research,* Human Relations Area File Press, 1967; John W. Loy, Jr. and Gerald S. Kenyon, editors, *Sport, Culture and Society: A Reader for the Sociology of Sport,* Macmillan, 1969; William P. Morgan, editor, *Contemporary Readings in Sport Psychology,* C. C Thomas, 1970; Paul Kay, editor, *Explorations in Mathematical Anthropology,* M.I.T. Press, 1971; J. Roland Pennock and John W. Chapman, editors, *Privacy, Nomos XIII,* Atherton, 1971; John M. Gumperz and Dell H. Hymes, editors, *Directions in Sociolinguistics: Ethnography of Communication,* Holt, 1972. Contributor of articles and reviews to anthropology, psychology, and sociology journals.

\* \* \*

## ROBEY, Ralph W(est) 1899-1972

August 29, 1899—July 5, 1972; American economist, educator, editor, columnist, and author of books on banking, real estate, and related subjects. Obituaries: *New York Times,* July 7, 1972; *Current Biography,* September, 1972.

\* \* \*

## ROBINSON, Fred Colson 1930-

*PERSONAL:* Born September 23, 1930, in Birmingham, Ala.; son of Emmett Colson (a salesman) and Hope (Bennett) Robinson; married Helen Caroline Wild, June, 1959; children: Lisa Karen, Eric Wild. *Education:* Birmingham-Southern College, B.A., 1952; University of North Carolina, M.A., 1953; Ph.D., 1960. *Office:* Department of English, Yale University, New Haven, Conn.

*CAREER:* Stanford University, Stanford, Calif., instructor, 1960-62, assistant professor of English, 1962-65; Cornell University, Ithaca, N.Y., assistant professor, 1965-66, associate professor of English, 1966-67; Stanford University, associate professor of English, 1967-71, professor of English philology, 1971-72; Yale University, New Haven, Conn., professor of English, 1972—. *Military service:* U.S. Army, instructor in guided missiles, 1954-56. *Member:* Modern Language Association of America (chairman of Old English group, 1972; chairman of English I section, 1972—), Early English Text Society, Mediaeval Academy of America (councillor, 1977-80), Linguistic Society of America. *Awards, honors:* American Council of Learned Societies fellow, 1968-69; Guggenheim fellow, 1975-76; American Academy of Arts and Sciences fellow, 1976—.

*WRITINGS: Old English: A Select Bibliography,* University of Toronto Press, 1970. Contributor to linguistics and literary journals, encyclopedias and essay collections. Member of editorial board: *Anglo-Saxon England, Journal*

*of English Linguistics, Names,* and Early English Manuscripts in Facsimile.

*WORK IN PROGRESS:* Research in Old English poetry and the English language.

\* \* \*

## ROBINSON, Gustavus H. 1881-1972

January 11, 1881—September 11, 1972; American lawyer, educator, government consultant, and author of works on admiralty and international law. Obituaries: *New York Times,* September 13, 1972.

\* \* \*

## ROBINSON, William H(enry) 1922-

*PERSONAL:* Born October 29, 1922, in Newport, R.I.; son of Julia W. S. Robinson; married Doris Carol Johnson (an administrative assistant), June 8, 1948. *Education:* New York University, B.A., 1951; Boston University, M.A., 1957; Harvard University, Ph.D., 1964. *Home:* 42 Stephen Hopkins Court, Providence, R.I. 02904. *Office:* Department of English, Rhode Island College, Providence, R.I. 02908.

*CAREER:* Prairie View Agricultural and Mechanical College, Prairie View, Tex., instructor in English, 1951-53; Agricultural and Technical College of North Carolina (now North Carolina Agricultural and Technical State University), Greensboro, member of English faculty, 1956-61, 1964-66; Boston University, Boston, Mass., associate professor of English and humanities, 1966-68; Howard University, Washington, D.C., professor of English, 1968-70; Rhode Island College, Providence, professor of English and director of black studies, 1970—. Community lecturer on black studies. *Military service:* U.S. Army, 1942-45; received Bronze Star. *Member:* College Language Arts Association, Association for Study of Negro Life and Culture, American Association of University Professors.

*WRITINGS:* (Editor) *Early Black American Poets: Selections, with Biographical and Critical Introductions,* W. C. Brown, 1969; (editor) *Early Black American Prose,* W. C. Brown, 1970; (editor) *Nommo: An Anthology of Modern Black African and Black American Literature,* Macmillan, 1972; *Phillis Wheatley in the Black American Beginnings,* Broadside, 1975; (editor) *The Proceedings of the Free African Union Society and the African Benevolent Society, Newport, Rhode Island, 1780-1824,* Rhode Island Urban League, 1976; *New England Black Letters,* Boston Public Library, 1978. Also author of several dozen scripts for educational radio, stage, and television productions. Contributor to literature journals.

*WORK IN PROGRESS: The Literature of Black America: A Critical Study; Black and Yankee Me,* an autobiography; research on the early black American novel; *Phillis Wheatley: A Bibliography; Critical Essays on Phillis Wheatley.*

\* \* \*

## ROCHESTER, J. Martin 1945-

*PERSONAL:* Born November 24, 1945, in Baltimore, Md.; son of Harry Louis (a pharmacist) and Sophie (Persky) Rochester; married Ruth M. Kirsh (a vocational counselor), August 3, 1969. *Education:* Loyola College, Baltimore, Md., A.B., 1966; Syracuse University, Ph.D., 1973. *Office:* Center for International Studies, University of Missouri, St. Louis, Mo. 63121.

*CAREER:* Syracuse University, International Relations Program, Syracuse, N.Y., research associate, 1970-72; University of Missouri—St. Louis, Center for International Studies, research associate, 1972-74, assistant professor of political science, 1974—. *Member:* American Political Science Association, International Studies Association.

*WRITINGS:* (With William D. Coplin) *Learning Package #2: Foreign Policy Decision-Making,* Markham, 1971; *Learning Package #3: Dyadic Disputes before the Permanent Court of International Justice, the International Court of Justice, League of Nations, and United Nations,* Markham, 1971. Contributor to *American Political Science Review, Review of Politics, Western Political Quarterly, International Studies Quarterly,* and other journals.

*WORK IN PROGRESS:* Research on comparative analysis of international organizations and international systems.

\* \* \*

## ROCKLAND, Michael Aaron 1935-

*PERSONAL:* Born July 14, 1935, in New York, N.Y.; son of Milton (a high school teacher) and Bess (Sherry) Rockland; married Mae Shafter (an artist), September 4, 1955; children: David, Jeffrey, Keren. *Education:* Hunter College (now Hunter College of the City University of New York), B.A., 1955; University of Minnesota, M.A., 1960, Ph.D., 1968. *Politics:* Democrat. *Religion:* Jewish. *Home:* 8 Madison St., Princeton, N.J. 08540. *Office:* American Studies Department, Douglass College, Rutgers University, New Brunswick, N.J. 08903.

*CAREER:* U.S. Foreign Service, assistant cultural attache in Spain and Argentina, 1961-68; State of New Jersey, Trenton, executive assistant to Chancellor of Higher Education, 1968-69; Rutgers University, Douglass College, New Brunswick, N.J., associate professor of American studies and director of department, 1969—, assistant dean, 1969-71. Director of Casa Americana Cultural Center, Madrid, 1965-67. *Military service:* U.S. Navy, medic, 1955-57; served in Japan. *Member:* American Studies Association (vice-president of Middle Atlantic chapter, 1970-71; president, 1971-72), Popular Culture Association.

*WRITINGS:* (Translator and author of introductory essay) Domingo Faustino Sarmiento, *Travels in the United States in 1847* (History Book Club selection), Princeton University Press, 1970; (editor) Julian Marias Aguilera, *America in the Fifties and Sixties: Julian Marias on the United States,* Pennsylvania State University Press, 1972; *The American Jewish Experience in Literature,* University of Haiti, 1975; (with wife, Mae S. Rockland) *The Jewish Yellow Pages,* Schocken, 1976. Also author of a filmscript for National Educational Television, "Three Days on Big City Waters," 1974. Contributing editor, *New Jersey Monthly,* 1977—.

*WORK IN PROGRESS: Homes on Wheels,* for Rutgers University Press.

\* \* \*

## ROCKWELL, Kiffin Ayres 1917-

*PERSONAL:* Name legally changed, 1955; born October 8, 1917, in Wilkesboro, N.C.; son of Leonidas Braxton (a minister) and Agnes (Rockwell) Hayes; married Elsa Refling Andresen, April 8, 1960; children: Kiffin Yates III, Erling Andresen Jordan. *Education:* Duke University, A.B.,1939; University of North Carolina, M.A., 1941, Ph.D., 1952. *Politics:* Southern Democrat. *Religion:* Episcopalian. *Home address:* Route 5, Box 393, Prairie Rd., Beloit, Wis. 53511.

CAREER: University of Tennessee, Knoxville, instructor in classics, 1955-56; University of Illinois at Urbana-Champaign, instructor in classics, 1956-57; Beloit College, Beloit, Wis., assistant professor of classics, 1957-61; College of Charleston, Charleston, S.C., associate professor of classics, 1961-62; Northern Illinois University, DeKalb, associate professor of history, 1963-77. *Military service:* U.S. Army, 1942-45; became first lieutenant; received Bronze Star Medal with "V" device.

WRITINGS: (With W. A. MacQueen) *Latin Poetry of Andrew Marvell,* University of North Carolina, 1965. Contributor to classics journals. Advisory and contributing editor, *Appalachian Heritage,* 1973—.

\* \* \*

## ROHNER, Ronald P(reston) 1935-

PERSONAL: Born April 17, 1935, in Crescent City, Calif.; son of Preston Eugene (a U.S. Army colonel) and Leta Chandler (Dorsey) Rohner; married Evelyn Constance Parker, March 27, 1957; children: Preston Clark, Ashley Chandler (daughter). *Education:* University of Oregon, B.S., 1958; Stanford University, M.A., 1960, Ph.D., 1964. *Home:* 10 Sumner Dr., Storrs, Conn. 06268. *Office:* Department of Biocultural Anthropology, University of Connecticut, Storrs, Conn. 06268.

CAREER: American School of Tangier, Morocco, teacher and resident dormitory director, 1958-59; University of Connecticut, Storrs, assistant professor, 1964-67, associate professor of anthropology, 1967-75, professor of anthropology and human development, 1975—. Director, Rejection-Acceptance Project, 1964—. Visiting scholar, University of Washington, Seattle, 1971; senior research scientist, Boys Town Center for the Study of Youth Development, Catholic University, 1975-77. Field researcher in an Oregon mental hospital, summers, 1956, 1957, among Kwakiutl Indians of British Columbia, 1962-63, 1964, 1971, in a Turkish village, summer, 1970. Member of board of directors, Natchaug Hospital, Inc., 1977—. *Military service:* U.S. Army, 1953-55.

MEMBER: American Anthropological Association (fellow), American Psychological Association, International Society for the Study of Behavioral Development, Society for Psychological Anthropology, Society for Cross-Cultural Research (co-founder; member of executive council, 1972-76), International Association for Cross-Cultural Psychology (member of executive council, 1976-78), Current Anthropology (associate member), Northeastern Anthropological Association. *Awards, honors:* Ford Foundation behavioral science fellowship, 1961-62; National Science Foundation fellowship, 1966; American Philosophical Society grants, 1965-67.

WRITINGS: (Contributor) June Helm, editor, *Pioneers of American Anthropology,* University of Washington Press, 1966; *The People of Gilford: A Contemporary Kwakiutl Village,* National Museum of Canada, 1967; (editor) *The Ethnography of Franz Boas: Letters and Diaries of Franz Boas Written on the Northwest Coast from 1886 to 1931,* University of Chicago Press, 1969; (with wife, Evelyn C. Rohner) *The Kwakiutl: Indians of British Columbia,* Holt, 1970; (contributor) J. L. Elliott, editor, *Minority Canadians,* Prentice-Hall of Canada, 1971; (with Evelyn C. Rohner) *They Love Me, They Love Me Not: A Worldwide Study of the Effects of Parental Acceptance and Rejection,* Human Relations Area File Press, 1975; (contributor) R. W. Brislin, W. J. Lonner, and S. Bochner, editors, *Cross-Cultural*

*Perspectives on Learning,* Sage Publications, 1975; *International Directory of Scholars Interested in Human Development in Cross-Cultural Perspective,* Boys Town Center, 1976; (contributor) L. L. Adler, editor, *Issues in Cross-Cultural Research,* New York Academy of Sciences, 1977; (contributor) G. D. Spidler, editor, *Native North Americans,* Holt, 1977; *Parental Acceptance and Rejection: A Critical Review of Research and Theory* (monograph), Human Relations Area File Press, 1978. Also contributor to *Problems in Cross-Cultural Psychology,* edited by Y. H. Poortiga. Contributor of more than twenty articles to anthropology and psychology journals. Member of editorial board, *Reviews in Anthropology,* 1973—, and *Child Abuse and Neglect: The International Journal,* 1977—; advisory editor, *Behavior Science Research,* 1974-77; editor, Society for Cross-Cultural Research *Newsletter,* 1976-79.

WORK IN PROGRESS: *Field Manual for the Study of Parental Acceptance and Rejection,* completion expected in 1979.

\* \* \*

## ROHRLICH, George F(riedrich) 1914-

PERSONAL: Born January 6, 1914, in Vienna, Austria; came to United States in 1938; naturalized citizen; son of Egon (an attorney) and Rosa (Tenzer) Rohrlich; married Laura Ticho (a research economist), February 3, 1946; children: Susannah T., David E., Daniel M. *Education:* University of Vienna, Dr. Jur., 1937; Consular Academy of Vienna, diplomate, 1938; Harvard University, Ph.D., 1943. *Politics:* Democrat. *Religion:* Jewish. *Home:* 7913 Jenkintown Rd., Cheltenham, Pa. 19012. *Office:* School of Business Administration, Temple University, Philadelphia, Pa. 19122.

CAREER: Sweet Briar College, Sweet Briar, Va., instructor in economics and government, 1942-45; U.S. Office of Strategic Services, Washington, D.C., consultant and senior analyst, 1944-45; U.S. Department of State, Washington, D.C., senior economic analyst, 1945-47; Supreme Commander for Allied Powers, Social Security Division, Public Health and Welfare Section, Tokyo, Japan, chief of economic analysis branch, 1947-50; U.S. Social Security Administration, Bureau of Old Age and Survivors Insurance, Baltimore, Md., chief of disability research branch, 1950-53; U.S. Department of Labor, Bureau of Employment Security, Unemployment Insurance Service, Washington, D.C., chief of Division of Actuarial and Financial services, 1953-59, chief of Division of Program and Legislation, 1957-58; International Labour Office, Social Security Division, Geneva, Switzerland, senior staff member, 1959-64; University of Chicago, Chicago, Ill., visiting professor of social policy and economics, 1964-67; Temple University, Philadelphia, Pa., professor of economics and social policy, 1967—, director of Institute for Social Economics and Policy Research, 1968—. Research associate, National Planning Association, 1950-52. Senior staff member, President's Commission on Veterans' Pensions, 1955-56. Guest professor, University of Trieste, Institute for Comparative Labor Law and Social Security, 1966; senior lecturer in social policy, Columbia University, 1968-69. U.S. observer, First International Conference of Social Security Actuaries and Statisticians (Brussels), 1956; general reporter, Sixth International Congress on Labor Law and Social Legislation (Stockholm), 1966; member, World Health Organization-International Labour Office Joint Committee of Experts on Personal Health Care and Social Security, 1970; external collaborator, Puerto Rican Commission on Universal

Health Insurance, 1973-74; expert consultant on socio-economic policies and programs, National Planning Department of the Government of Colombia; director of research, Commission on an Integral Social Security System (Puerto Rico), 1975-76. Technical adviser, National Commission on Railroad Retirement, 1971-72; consultant, National Commission on State Workmen's Compensation Laws, 1972; member of board of directors, Regional Health and Welfare Council of Greater Philadelphia, 1968-70.

*MEMBER:* International Society for Labor Law and Social Legislation, American Association for the Advancement of Science, Association for Social Economics (member of executive council, 1975-76; first vice-president, 1978), Association for Evolutionary Economics, American Economic Association, Industrial Relations Research Association (charter member), American Risk and Insurance Association, Eastern Economic Association. *Awards, honors:* Harvard refugee scholar, 1939-41; Brookings Institute fellow, 1942.

*WRITINGS:* (With Louis Hartz, Charles M. Hardin, and William S. McCauley) *Civil-Military Relations: Bibliographical Notes on Administrative Problems of Civilian Mobilization,* Public Administration Service, 1940; *Funds and Accounts in the Federal Government,* Graduate School of Public Administration, Harvard University, 1944; (with Margaret T. Mettert) *Japanese Social Insurance Systems,* Supreme Commander for the Allied Powers, 1951; (with Robert M. Ball and Robert J. Myers) *Pensions in the United States,* U.S. Government Printing Office, 1952; *Veterans' Non-Service-Connected Pensions,* U.S. Government Printing Office, 1956; (editor) *Report on the Asian Regional Training Course in Social Security Administration,* International Labour Office, 1961; *Benefits in the Case of Industrial Accidents and Occupational Diseases,* four volumes, International Labour Office, 1962-64; (contributor) *Essays in Honor of Makoto Suetka,* Seibundo, 1965; (contributor) Sar A. Levitan and others, editors, *Towards Freedom from Want,* Harper, 1968; (contributor) George R. Iden, editor, *Federal Programs for the Development of Human Resources,* U.S. Government Printing Office, 1968.

(Editor and contributor) *Social Economics for the 1970's: Programs for Social Security, Health and Manpower,* Dunellen, 1970; (contributor) Joseph W. Eaton, editor, *Migration and Social Welfare,* National Association of Social Workers, 1971; (contributor) Michael S. March, editor, *Staff Papers Supporting the Report to the President and the Congress by the Commission on Railroad Retirement,* Volume III: *The Relationship of the Railroad Retirement System to Old-Age, Disability, and Survivors' Insurance within the National Social Security Framework,* U.S. Government Printing Office, 1972; (contributor) C. Arthur Williams, Jr., editor, *Compendium on Workmen's Compensation,* U.S. Government Printing Office, 1973; (contributor) *Collected Papers* (monograph), Volume II, Polish Academy of Sciences, 1973; *Social Economics—Concepts and Perspectives* (monograph), Academic Publishers, 1974; (contributor) *Apendices del Informe de la Comision Sobre Seguro de Salud Universal,* Commission on Universal Health Insurance (Puerto Rico), 1974; (editor) *Environmental Management: Economic and Social Dimensions,* Ballinger, 1976. Contributor to *Encyclopedia of Social Work,* National Association of Social Workers, Volume II, 16th edition, 1971, 17th edition, 1977. Contributor of about thirty-five articles to professional journals.

*WORK IN PROGRESS: Foundations of Social Policy:*

*Theoretical and Applied Aspects of Social Economics,* completion expected in 1980.

*SIDELIGHTS:* George Rohrlich told *CA:* "I am interested in reconnecting the field of economics to the broader social setting in which it operates—and which, in its turn, is part and parcel of our environment or habitat. Obviously, this suggests a holistic perspective. John Maurice Clark (1884-1963)—in my view the most perceptive among American economists—has had the greatest and most lingering impact upon my thinking. His challenge to the economics profession, posed more than half a century ago, was to formulate the 'one consistent set of laws' which governs *both* 'free exchange' *and* 'social reform.' It is this challenge which informs and motivates my own quest for what he called 'an economics of responsibility' in lieu of the 'economics of irresponsible conflict.'"

\*          \*          \*

## ROMER, Alfred 1906-

*PERSONAL:* Born August 9, 1906, in Pleasantville, N.Y.; son of Henry Hunt (a businessman) and Jessie (McEwan) Romer; married Emily Korstad, September 6, 1933 (died, 1960); children: Henry F., Anne G. (Mrs. Edward A. Teppo), William Stuart. *Education:* Williams College, B.A., 1928; California Institute of Technology, Ph.D., 1935. *Politics:* Democrat. *Religion:* Unitarian Universalist. *Home:* 7 Pine St., Canton, N.Y. 13617. *Office:* Department of Physics, St. Lawrence University, Canton, N.Y. 13617.

*CAREER:* Whittier College, Whittier, Calif., assistant professor of physics and mathematics, 1933-39, professor of physics, 1939-43; Vassar College, Poughkeepsie, N.Y., associate professor of physics, 1943-46; St. Lawrence University, Canton, N.Y., associate professor, 1946-57, professor, 1957-63, Henry Priest Professor of Physics, 1963-73, professor emeritus, 1973—. Research fellow, Harvard University, 1940-41; fellow, Princeton University, 1955-56; visiting staff member, Educational Services, Inc., 1962-63; visiting professor of history, University of California, Santa Barbara, 1975. Consultant to U.S. Agency for International Development (USAID) and University Grants Commission of India. *Member:* American Association of Physics Teachers, American Physical Society, History of Science Society, Society for the History of Technology, American Association for the Advancement of Science, American Association of University Professors, Phi Beta Kappa, Sigma Xi, Omicron Delta Kappa, Sigma Pi Sigma.

*WRITINGS: The Restless Atom,* Doubleday, 1960; (editor) *The Discovery of Radioactivity and Transmutation,* Dover, 1964; (editor) *Radiochemistry and the Discovery of Isotopes,* Dover, 1970. Acting editor, *American Journal of Physics,* 1962.

\*          \*          \*

## ROMERO, Patricia W. 1935-

*PERSONAL:* Born July 28, 1935, in Columbus, Ohio; daughter of Warren Arthur Watkins (a farmer); children: Stephen, Arthur, Jeffrey. *Education:* Central State College (now University), B.A., 1964; Miami University, Oxford, Ohio, M.A., 1965; Ohio State University, Ph.D., 1971. *Politics:* Democrat. *Religion:* Episcopalian.

*CAREER:* Central State University, Wilberforce, Ohio, instructor in history, 1964-65; Association for the Study of Negro Life and History, Washington, D.C., research associate, 1965-68; United Publishing Corp., Washington, D.C., editor-in-chief, 1968-70; Association for the Study of Negro Life and History, research associate, 1970-72; University of South Florida, Tampa, visiting lecturer, 1972-74. Visiting lecturer, Findlay College, 1969. *Member:* American Historical Association, Organization of American Historians, African Studies Association, Association for the Study of Negro Life and History, Southern Historical Association, Phi Alpha Theta. *Awards, honors:* Negro history research grant, Southern Historical Association, 1965-66; Ford Foundation grant, 1969.

*WRITINGS:* (With Charles H. Wesley) *Negro Americans in the Civil War,* Publishers, 1967; (editor) *I, Too, Am America,* Publishers, 1968, revised edition, 1970; (editor) *In Black America,* United Publishing, 1969; *In Pursuit of African Culture,* United Publishing, 1972. Associate editor, *Negro History Bulletin,* 1966-68; research editor, *Negro Life and History,* ten volumes, International Library.

*WORK IN PROGRESS: Carter G. Woodson: A Prophet Looking Backward.*†

\* \* \*

## ROOSENBURG, Henriette 1920-1972

1920—June 21, 1972; Dutch-born reporter and writer who chronicled her World War II experiences in the anti-Nazi underground. Obituaries: *New York Times,* June 22, 1972; *Publishers Weekly,* July 3, 1972.

\* \* \*

## ROSE, Nancy (Ann) 1934-

*PERSONAL:* Born May 6, 1934, in Chamberlain, S.D.; daughter of Milton Leroy and Helen (Matson) Mortensen; married Robert J. Rose (a realtor), September 13, 1952 (divorced May 31, 1977); children: Randy, Julie, Kenton, Bruce, Stewart, Melissa, Philip. *Education:* Graduated from high school in Brainerd, Minn., in 1951. *Home:* 215 Oak Hill Dr., Green Bay, Wis. 54301.

*CAREER:* Free-lance writer for local and state newspapers and copywriter for advertising agencies, 1962—. Director, Institutional Writing Program in Wisconsin prisons, 1969—; librarian, Brown County Mental Hospital, 1967—. *Member:* National Federation of State Poetry Societies, Wisconsin Regional Writers Association, Wisconsin Fellowship of Poets, Green Bay Writer's Club, Scripters Manuscript Group (leader, 1970—), Allouez Writers (director, 1971), Harlequin Players, Inc. *Awards, honors:* Wisconsin Regional Writers Jade Ring awards, 1967 and 1973, for juvenile fiction, 1970, for adult fiction, and 1976, for poetry; Indiana University Award, short story division, 1971; National Writers Digest Short Story Awards, 6th place, 1974; Council for Wisconsin Writers Awards, 3rd Place, 1978, for published short fiction. Prize winner in other regional and national contests, 1971, 1973, 1974.

*WRITINGS: Funny-Talk Freddy,* Denison, 1970; *Yelly Kelly,* Denison, 1970; *Dragon of Cobblestone Castle,* Denison, 1970; *Motherless Bug,* Denison, 1971. Editor, "The Artist's Notebook," a weekly newspaper column, 1970-71. Contributor of over 150 stories, articles and essays to magazines and newspapers, including *True Experience, True Story, Women's Day,* and the Green Bay *Press-Gazette.*

*WORK IN PROGRESS:* A novel, *The House on the Dunes.*

*AVOCATIONAL INTERESTS:* Piano, tennis, golf, and theatre (acting and directing).

*BIOGRAPHICAL/CRITICAL SOURCES:* Green Bay, Wisconsin *Press-Gazette,* October 1, 1967, July 20, 1972.

\* \* \*

## ROSEN, Barbara 1929-

*PERSONAL:* Born April 10, 1929, in Nelson, Lancashire, England; daughter of Frank M. and Elsie (Draycott) Cooper; married William Rosen (an English professor), August 13, 1960; children: Judith, Susan. *Education:* Royal Holloway College, London, B.A., 1949; University of Birmingham, Ph.D., 1970. *Religion:* Society of Friends (Quaker). *Home:* Stonemill Rd., Storrs, Conn. 06268. *Office:* Department of English, University of Connecticut, Storrs, Conn. 06268.

*CAREER:* Teacher of English in Yorkshire, England, 1952-55; University of Wisconsin—Madison, instructor in English, 1958-60; University of Connecticut, Storrs, assistant professor of English, 1971—.

*WRITINGS:* (Editor with husband, William Rosen) *Shakespeare: Julius Caesar,* New American Library, 1963; *Witchcraft,* Edward Arnold, 1969, Taplinger, 1972. Contributor of articles and poems to literature journals.

*WORK IN PROGRESS:* Research on Shakespeare and dramatic genres.

*SIDELIGHTS:* Barbara Rosen told *CA:* "[I] became interested in witchcraft at the time of the McCarthy hearings in America, and continue interest in the whole question of popular panics, delusions and misuse of reason and information. Misuse of language in politics, advertising and propaganda is of overwhelming importance here; that is why I think English teaching so important." *Avocational interests:* Drama, puppets.††

\* \* \*

## ROSEN, James Alan 1908(?)-1972

1908(?)—October 10, 1972; American gynecologist, obsterician, lecturer, and author of books on medical subjects. Obituaries: *New York Times,* October 12, 1972.

\* \* \*

## ROSENBAUM, Samuel R(awlins) 1888-1972

September 28, 1888—November 10, 1972; American lawyer and author of works on musical and legal subjects. Obituaries: *New York Times,* November 11, 1972.

\* \* \*

## ROSENBERG, J(ehiol) Mitchell 1906-

*PERSONAL:* Born August 26, 1906, in Bayonne, N.J.; son of Israel (a rabbi) and Sarah (Greenburg) Rosenberg; married Helen Emanuel (a school teacher), March 22, 1956. *Education:* New York University, B.A., 1927; Columbia University, LL.B., 1930, M.A., 1939; New School for Social Research, Ph.D., 1969. *Politics:* Democrat. *Religion:* Jewish. *Home:* 901 Ave. H, Brooklyn, N.Y. 11230. *Office:* New York State Department Justice Services, 80 Centre St., New York, N.Y.

*CAREER:* Assistant district attorney for Kings County, Brooklyn, N.Y., 1940-76; New York State Department Justice Services, New York, N.Y., senior attorney, 1976—. Assistant professor of political science, University of Rhode Island, 1967-68; lecturer in political science, Brooklyn College of the City University of New York, 1968-70, and New School for Social Research, 1970-76; lecturer in social science, Kingsborough Community College of the City University of New York, 1970; adjunct assistant professor of criminal justice, Long Island University, 1974. American Jewish Congress, president of Brooklyn division, 1971-74, member of National Governing Council and Committee on Law and Social Action; speaker, United Jewish Appeal. *Member:* American Political Science Association, Brooklyn Bar Association.

*WRITINGS: The Story of Zionism,* Bloch Publishing, 1946; *Jerome Frank: Jurist and Philosopher,* Philosophical Library, 1970; *Our Crime Riddled Society,* University Press of America, 1978.

\*     \*     \*

## ROSENBLOOM, Noah H. 1915-

*PERSONAL:* Born September 29, 1915, in Radom, Poland; son of Michael and Sarah Leah (Weingelb) Rosenbloom; married Pearl Cohen, May 16, 1946; children: Leah Marion, Michaelle Nathanyah. *Education:* Yeshiva University, B.R.E. and Rabbi, 1942, D.H.L., 1948; Columbia University, M.A., 1945; New York University, Ph.D., 1958. *Home:* 357 Remsen Ave., Brooklyn, N.Y. 11212. *Office:* Stern College, Yeshiva University, 253 Lexington Ave., New York, N.Y. 10016.

*CAREER:* Rabbi in Steubenville, Ohio, 1942-43, Philadelphia, Pa., 1944-48, and Brooklyn, N.Y., 1949—; Hunter College (now Hunter College of the City University of New York), New York City, instructor in Hebrew literature, 1949-54; Yeshiva University, New York City, professor of Hebraic philosophy and literature, 1954—. *Member:* Rabbinical Council of America.

*WRITINGS: Luzzatto's Ethico: Psychological Interpretation of Judaism,* Yeshiva University Press, 1965; *Tradition in an Age of Reform,* Jewish Publication Society, 1976. Contributor to Jewish philosophical and theological journals. Member of editorial board, *Tradition.*

*WORK IN PROGRESS: The Threnodist and Threnody of the Holocaust; Epic and Tradition.*

\*     \*     \*

## ROSENKRANZ, Richard S. 1942-

*PERSONAL:* Born February 17, 1942, in Jersey City, N.J.; son of Milton (a lawyer) and Zelda (Ginsberg) Rosenkranz. *Education:* Yale University, B.A., 1964; Columbia University, M.S., 1968. *Politics:* Independent. *Religion:* "Hebrew-Christian Pantheist." *Agent:* Anita Gross, International Famous Agency, 1301 Sixth Ave., New York, N.Y. 10019.

*CAREER:* Worked as a folksinger, New York City, 1965; WGLI (a radio station), Babylon, N.Y., assistant news director, 1966; WINS (a radio station), New York City, copy boy, 1966; Westinghouse Broadcasting Co., Washington, D.C., radio correspondent from the U.S. Congress, 1966-67. *Awards, honors:* Fulbright fellow, l'Institut des Etudes Politiques, Paris, 1964-65; *Across the Barricades* was nominated for a Pulitzer Prize in history, 1972.

*WRITINGS: Across the Barricades,* Lippincott, 1971. Author of radio documentaries.

*WORK IN PROGRESS:* A revised edition of *Across the Barricades,* tentatively entitled *The White Niggers of Avery;* a book of poetry; a book on contemporary politics, religion, and science fiction.†

## ROSENTHAL, Donald B. 1937-

*PERSONAL:* Born July 14, 1937, in Brooklyn, N.Y. *Education:* Brooklyn College (now Brooklyn College of the City University of New York), B.A. (summa cum laude), 1958; University of Chicago, M.A., 1960, Ph.D., 1964. *Office:* State University of New York at Buffalo, Amherst Campus, Buffalo, N.Y. 14261.

*CAREER:* State University of New York at Buffalo, assistant professor, 1964-68, associate professor, 1968-72, professor of political science, 1972—. *Member:* American Political Science Association, Association for Asian Studies, American Society for Public Administration. *Awards, honors:* American Institute of Indian Studies fellow, 1963-64; postdoctoral fellowship from University of Chicago Committee on Southern Asia, 1966-67; joint grant from American Institute of Indian Studies and Social Science Research Council-American Council of Learned Societies for research in India, 1970; National Association of Schools of Public Affairs and Administration fellow, 1977-78.

*WRITINGS:* (With Robert L. Crain and Elihu Katz) *The Politics of Community Conflict,* Bobbs-Merrill, 1969; *The Limited Elite,* University of Chicago Press, 1971; (editor) *The City in Indian Politics,* Thomson Press (India), 1976; *The Expansive Elite,* University of California Press, 1977.

Contributor: James Q. Wilson, editor, *City Politics and Public Policy,* Wiley, 1968; Terry N. Clark, editor, *Community Structure and Decision-Making,* Chandler Publishing, 1968; Rajni Kothari, editor, *Caste in Indian Politics,* Orient Longmans, 1970. Contributor of about twenty articles and reviews to political science journals.

*WORK IN PROGRESS:* A study of intergovernmental relations in the Buffalo metropolitan area.

\*     \*     \*

## ROSS, Janet 1914-

*PERSONAL:* Born April 19, 1914, in Duluth, Minn.; daughter of Guy W. C. (a professor of political science) and Helen (Mason) Ross. *Education:* University of Minnesota, B.A., 1935, M.A., 1941; University of Iowa, Ph.D., 1960. *Home:* 118 Alden Rd., Muncie, Ind. 47304. *Office:* Department of English, Ball State University, Muncie, Ind. 47306.

*CAREER:* University of Minnesota, Minneapolis, instructor in English and counselor, 1946-47; University of Wyoming, Laramie, instructor in guidance, 1947-49; Florida State University, Tallahassee, instructor in English, 1949-52; University of Iowa, Iowa City, instructor in English, 1952-57; Macalester College, St. Paul, Minn., assistant professor of English, 1957-60; University of British Columbia, Vancouver, instructor in English, 1960-61; Ball State University, Muncie, Ind., assistant professor, 1961-64, associate professor, 1964-69, professor of English, 1969—. Fulbright secondary school teacher in Heerenveen, Netherlands, 1954-55. *Member:* Linguistic Society of America, Modern Language Association of America, National Council of Teachers of English, National Association for Foreign Student Affairs, Teaching English as a Second Language. *Awards, honors:* Danforth summer grant, 1963.

*WRITINGS:* (Co-author) *Workbook for Factual Prose,* Scott, Foresman, 1956; (with E. Paul Torrance) *Social Studies in Minnesota Schools,* Bureau of Educational Research, University of Minnesota, 1960; (with Gladys Doty) *Language and Life in the U.S.A.: A Textbook in English as a Foreign Language,* two volumes, Harper, 1960, 3rd edition, 1972; (with Doty) *Writing English,* Harper, 1965; (co-author) *Tests of English as a Foreign Language,* Cooperative Test Service, 1965. Contributor of articles and reviews to journals.

\* \* \*

## ROSSI, Ernest Lawrence 1933-

*PERSONAL:* Born March 26, 1933, in Bridgeport, Conn.; son of Angelo (a carpenter) and Mary (De Libro) Rossi; married Sheila Peabbles (a clinical psychologist), August 10, 1962; children: Lisa, April. *Education:* University of Connecticut, B.S., 1954; Washington State University, M.S., 1957; Temple University, Ph.D., 1961. *Office:* 11980 San Vincente Blvd., Los Angeles, Calif. 90049.

*CAREER:* Clinical psychologist in private practice, Los Angeles, Calif., 1962—; Analytical Psychology Clinic, Los Angeles, member of staff and clinic committee, 1969—; University of California, Los Angeles, member of extension faculty, 1972—. C. G. Jung Institute of Los Angeles, member of executive board, 1975, training analyst, 1976. Volunteer consultant, Westminister Neighborhood Association, Watts, Calif. *Member:* International Association of Analytical Psychology (Jungian Psychology), American Psychological Association, American Society of Clinical and Experimental Hypnosis. *Awards, honors:* U.S. Public Health fellow, 1961-62, 1962-64.

*WRITINGS: Dreams and the Growth of Personality: Expanding Awareness in Psychotherapy,* Pergamon, 1972; (with Milton H. Erickson) *Hypnotic Realities: The Induction of Clinical Hypnosis and Forms of Indirect Suggestion,* Irvington, 1976. Contributor of articles and reviews to more than ten psychology journals and magazines. Member of editorial board, *American Journal of Clinical Hypnosis,* 1977—.

*WORK IN PROGRESS: Hypnotherapy: An Exploratory Casebook,* with Erickson, completion expected in 1978.

*SIDELIGHTS:* Ernest Rossi told *CA:* ''All my writing is an effort to explain something to myself. My first book, *Dreams and the Growth of Personality,* was written while in post-doctoral training.... The director of my program did not want me to present some unusually interesting material [about] a patient who I [considered] a psychological genius. The director felt [that] I was too inexperienced and would make a fool of myself before the august body of psychoanalysts.... I wrote it all up in the form of a book that some people now feel is [a] valid extension of classical psychoanalytic theory. My second book, *Hypnotic Realities,* was my effort to understand the teachings of another genius, Milton H. Erickson. My third book, *Hypnotherapy: An Exploratory Casebook,* is yet another effort to understand and extend our current understanding of the process of psychotherapy. I write because I can clearly see how my mind is inferior to others'; the writing is the scaffolding I throw up in order to reach what I feel I should know.''

\* \* \*

## ROTH, Hal 1927-

*PERSONAL:* Born January 15, 1927, in Cleveland, Ohio; son of Lee (a musician) and Gertrude (Knapp) Roth; married Margaret Hale-White, October 17, 1960. *Education:* University of California, Berkeley, A.B., 1953. *Address:* Box 835, Camden, Me. 04843.

*CAREER:* Author and journalist since 1953. *Military service:* U.S. Army Air Forces, 1944-46; U.S. Air Force, 1950-51. *Member:* American Society of Magazine Photographers,

Authors Guild, Cruising Club of America, Seven Seas Cruising Association. *Awards, honors:* Blue Water Medal of the Cruising Club of America, 1972.

*WRITINGS: Pathway in the Sky,* Howell-North Books, 1965; *Two on a Big Ocean,* Macmillan, 1972; *After 50,000 Miles,* Norton, 1977. Contributor of over two hundred articles to national and regional publications.

*WORK IN PROGRESS:* New books.

\* \* \*

## ROTHENBERG, Joshua 1911-

*PERSONAL:* Born July 1, 1911, in Sandomir, Poland; son of Abraham Moses and Ida (Fishman) Rothenberg; married Frieda Ost (a clerk), September, 1940; children: Joseph. *Education:* University of Warsaw, M.A., 1934; Rutgers University, M.A., 1951; Simmons College, M.S., 1969. *Residence:* Waltham, Mass. *Office:* Department of Near Eastern and Judaic Studies, Brandeis University, Waltham, Mass. 02154.

*CAREER:* Brandeis University, Waltham, Mass., senior research associate, 1965-68, lecturer in contemporary Jewish studies, beginning 1967, currently assistant professor of near-eastern and Judaic studies, head of Library Judaica Department, 1968—. *Member:* American Association for the Advancement of Slavic Studies, Association for Jewish Studies, American Association of University Professors.

*WRITINGS: Shimon Dubnov,* Farband L.Z.O., 1961; (with Robert Szulkin) *Gleanings from Yiddish Literature,* Brandeis University, 1968; *An Annotated Bibliography of Writings on Judaism in the Soviet Union: 1960-1965,* Brandeis University, 1969; *Judaica Reference Materials: An Annotated Bibliography,* Brandeis University, 1971; *The Jewish Religion in the Soviet Union,* Ktav, 1971.

*WORK IN PROGRESS:* Research on Jewish life in eastern Europe and on Yiddish literature.

\* \* \*

## ROTHENBERG, Robert E(dward) 1908-

*PERSONAL:* Born September 27, 1908, in New York, N.Y.; son of Simon (a psychoanalyst) and Caroline (Baer) Rothenberg; married Lillian Lustig (a hospital administrator), June 8, 1933 (deceased); married Eileen F. Kessler, November 3, 1977; children: (first marriage) Robert Philip, Lynn Barbara (Mrs. Richard L. Kay). *Education:* Cornell University, A.B., 1929, M.D., 1932. *Home:* 35 Sutton Pl., New York, N.Y. 10022. *Office:* 870 Fifth Ave., New York, N.Y. 10021.

*CAREER:* Certified by American Board of Surgery, 1942; Jewish Hospital of Brooklyn, Brooklyn, N.Y., intern, 1932-35; Royal Infirmary of Edinburgh, Edinburgh, Scotland, postgraduate surgeon, 1934-35; State University of New York Downstate Medical Center, Brooklyn, clinical assistant professor of environmental medicine and community health, 1950-60; First Army, Fort Jay, N.Y., civilian consultant surgeon, 1960-66; attending surgeon at French Hospital, New York, N.Y. and Jewish Hospital of Brooklyn, 1966-75, and Cabrini Hospital Center, 1975—. Chairman, Central Medical Group of Brooklyn, 1946-60; member of Medical Group Council of Health Insurance Plans, 1946-64; member of board of directors, Health Insurance Plan of Greater New York, 1954-64; member of medical advisory board, Hotel Workers and Association Health Plan, 1952-65. *Military service:* U.S. Army, surgeon, 1942-45; served in European theater; became lieutenant colonel.

*MEMBER:* American College of Surgeons, American Medical Association, American Geriatric Society, American Public Health Association, New York County Medical Society, Kings County Medical Society, Brooklyn Surgical Society, Alpha Omega Alpha.

*WRITINGS:* (With Karl Pickard) *Group Medicine and Health Insurance in Action,* Crown, 1949; (editor and compiler) *Understanding Surgery,* McGraw, 1955, revised edition, Trident, 1965; (compiler and editor) *The New Illustrated Medical Encyclopedia,* four volumes, Abradale Press, 1959, 9th edition, 1978; (editor) *The New American Medical Dictionary and Health Manual,* World Publishing, 1962, 3rd revised edition, 1977; *Health in the Later Years,* New American Library, 1964, revised edition, 1972; (editor) *Reoperative Surgery,* McGraw, 1964; (editor) *The New Illustrated Child Care Encyclopedia,* twelve volumes, Dell, 1966; (editor) *The Doctors' Premarital Medical Adviser,* Grosset, 1969; (editor) *The Fast Diet Book,* Grosset, 1971; (editor) *The New Complete Encyclopedia of Medicine,* twenty volumes, Abradale Press, 1971; *Our Family Medical and Health Record Book,* Abradale Press, 1972; *The Complete Surgical Guide,* Simon & Schuster, 1973, published as *The New Understanding Surgery; the Complete Surgical Guide,* New American Library, 1976; *What Every Patient Wants to Know,* New American Library, 1975; *The Complete Book of Breast Care,* Crown, 1975; *First Aid,* Crown, 1976; *Disney's Growing up Healthy,* Danbury Press, Volume I: *What Goes On inside Us,* 1976, Volume II: *How We Behave,* 1976, Volume III: *Avoiding Sickness and Accidents,* 1976, Volume IV: *Our Illnesses,* 1976. Contributor of about twenty-five articles to medical journals.

*AVOCATIONAL INTERESTS:* Collecting art (French impressionists, American twentieth-century art, and primitive art), travel.

\*      \*      \*

## ROTHMAN, Esther P.    1919-

*PERSONAL:* Born November 25, 1919, in New York, N.Y.; daughter of Max and Annie (Reiner) Pomeranz; married Arthur M. Rothman (a dentist), April 13, 1946; children: Amy. *Education:* Hunter College (now Hunter College of the City University of New York), B.A., 1942; Columbia University, M.A., 1946; College of the City of New York (now City College of the City University of New York), M.A., 1955; New York University, Ph.D., 1957. *Home:* 200 East 16th St., New York, N.Y. *Agent:* Mary Yost, 141 East 55th St., New York, N.Y. 10022.

*CAREER:* Livingston School, New York, N.Y., 1958—, currently principal. Psychologist in private practice, 1958. *Member:* American Psychological Association, American Association of Orthopsychiatry.

*WRITINGS:* (With Pearl Berkowitz) *Disturbed Child,* New York University Press, 1958; (with Berkowitz) *Public Education for Disturbed Children in New York City,* C. C Thomas, 1963; *The Angel inside Went Sour,* McKay, 1970; *Troubled Teachers,* McKay, 1977.

\*      \*      \*

## ROTHMAN, Joel    1938-

*PERSONAL:* Born April 6, 1938, in New York, N.Y.; son of David and Gladys Rothman; married Katy Hidalgo (a teacher), April, 1960; married second wife, Marilyn Amsel (a teacher), January 31, 1971; children: (first marriage) Ivan, Andrea. *Education:* Brooklyn College of the City University of New York, B.A., 1962; Hunter College of the City University of New York, M.S., 1965; Columbia University, further study. *Politics:* "Depends." *Religion:* Atheist. *Home:* 3 Sheridan Sq., New York, N.Y. 10014.

*CAREER:* Professional musician (percussionist), 1953—, and publisher of his own percussion method books; teacher of music, science, and reading in elementary schools of New York, N.Y., 1962—.

*WRITINGS—Juvenile:* (With Ruthven Tremain) *Secrets with Ciphers and Codes,* Macmillan, 1969; (with Bruce Roberts) *At Last to the Ocean: The Story of the Endless Cycle of Water,* Crowell-Collier, 1971; *Night Lights,* Albert Whitman, 1972; *A Moment in Time,* Scroll Press, 1972; *I Can Be Anything You Can Be,* Scroll Press, 1973; *Once There Was a Stream,* Scroll Press, 1973; *The Antcyclopedia,* Phinmarc Books, 1974; *Which Is Different?,* Doubleday, 1975; *How to Play Drums,* Albert Whitman, 1976. Writer of more than seventy manuals on percussion methods, 1961-77.

\*      \*      \*

## ROTHSCHILD, Alfred    1894(?)-1972

1894(?)—September 11, 1972; German-born American business executive and Shakespearean scholar. Obituaries: *New York Times,* September 13, 1972.

\*      \*      \*

## ROTHWELL, V(ictor) H(oward)    1945-

*PERSONAL:* Born April 11, 1945, in Hyde, Cheshire, England; son of Harry (a manager) and Hilda (Holland) Rothwell; married Margaret Cowin (a midwife), March 27, 1971; children: two daughters. *Education:* University of Nottingham, B.A., 1966; University of Leeds, Ph.D., 1969. *Office:* History Department, William Robertson Building, University of Edinburgh, George Square, Edinburgh, Scotland.

*CAREER:* University of Exeter, Exeter, England, tutor in history, 1969-70; University of Edinburgh, Edinburgh, Scotland, lecturer in history, 1970—.

*WRITINGS: British War Aims and Peace Diplomacy, 1914-1918,* Clarendon Press, 1971. Contributor to various professional journals.

*WORK IN PROGRESS:* A book on British foreign policy, 1941-47, that deals with East-West relations, completion expected in 1982, for J. Cape.

\*      \*      \*

## ROUDIEZ, Leon S(amuel)    1917-

*PERSONAL:* Surname is pronounced *Roo*-dee-ay; born November 18, 1917, in Bronxville, N.Y.; son of Leon Samuel (an officer, U.S. Army) and Louise (Horan) Roudiez; married Jacqueline Strich, May 7, 1945; children: Genevieve, Francis. *Education:* College Stanislas, B.S., 1936; University of Paris, LL.B., 1939; Columbia University, M.A., 1940, Ph.D., 1950. *Politics:* Independent (socialist). *Religion:* None. *Home:* 38 Taylor Dr., Closter, N.J. 07624. *Office:* 513 Philosophy Hall, Columbia University, New York, N.Y. 10027.

*CAREER:* Columbia University, New York, N.Y., instructor in French, 1946-50; Pennsylvania State University, University Park, instructor, 1950-51, assistant professor, 1951-55, associate professor of French, 1955-59; Columbia University, associate professor, 1959-62, professor of

French, 1962—, chairman of department, 1971-74. *Military service:* U.S. Army, Signal Corps, 1941-46; became captain. *Member:* American Association of Teachers of French, Modern Language Association of America.

*WRITINGS: Maurras jusqu'a l'Action Francaise,* Andre Bonne, 1957; *Michel Butor,* Columbia University Press, 1965; (editor) Justin O'Brien, *Contemporary French Literature,* Rutgers University Press, 1971; *French Fiction Today,* Rutgers University Press, 1972. *French Review,* managing editor, 1953-62, editor, 1962-65.

*WORK IN PROGRESS:* Studies in contemporary French prose fiction, especially that of Michel Butor.

\* \* \*

## ROUHANI, Fuad   1907-

*PERSONAL:* Born October 23, 1907, in Teheran, Iran; son of Ali-Akbar (a government official) and Parvine (Tayereh) Rouhani; married Rouhanieh Fath-Aazam, September 17, 1927; children: Guity (Mrs. Abdul-Reza Hosseinpour), Negar (daughter). *Education:* University of London, LL.B. (with honors), 1937, LL.M., 1940; University of Paris, Doctorat de specialite, 1968. *Home and office:* 16 Khiaban Rasht, Teheran, Iran.

*CAREER:* Anglo-Iranian Oil Co., Teheran and Abadan, Iran, legal adviser, 1940-51; National Iranian Oil Co., Teheran, chief legal adviser, 1951-54, member of board of directors, 1954-64, deputy chairman, 1956-64; Secretary general, Organization of Petroleum Exporting Countries (O.P.E.C.), 1961-64; special adviser to the prime minister, 1964-65; Regional Cooperation for Development (of Iran, Pakistan, Turkey), Teheran, secretary general, 1965-68; independent consultant on international and industrial law, 1968—. Visiting professor of Iranian studies, Columbia University, 1964-65, Teheran University, 1965-67. Legal adviser to Central Bank of Iran, 1972—. *Military service:* Iranian Army, Mountain Artillery, 1932-33. *Member:* International Law Association, Philharmonic Society of Teheran (founder). *Awards, honors:* Decorated Order of Taj; Commandatore dell' Ordine Al Merito della Repubblica Italiana.

*WRITINGS: A History of the O.P.E.C.,* Praeger, 1971. Also author of *Tarikhe Melli Shodane Sanati Naft dar Iran* (title means "A History of the Nationalization of Oil in Iran").

Translator: (Into Persian) Plato, *Republic,* Royal Publishing Society, 1956; (into French) Attar, *Mystical Poems,* Albin Michel, for UNESCO, 1958; (into Persian) Benedetto Croce, *Breviario di Esthetica,* Royal Publishing Society, 1968; (into Persian) Carl Jung, *Answer to Job,* Royal Publishing Society, 1971. Also translator (into Persian) of Carl Jung's *Psychology and Religion.*

*WORK IN PROGRESS:* Research on two heretical movements in Iran in the nineteenth century and on psychological motifs in Persian mystical poems, myths, and legends.

*SIDELIGHTS:* Fuad Rouhani writes: "The principal motivation in my research work is to stress the fact, supported by historical and other material, that religious bias and fanaticism are one of the most pernicious conditions of the human mind, since they are purely accidental in their origin, false in their content, and detrimental to the cause of human fellowship and international peace."

*AVOCATIONAL INTERESTS:* Music, philosophy, religions, languages.

## ROUSH, John H., Jr.   1923-

*PERSONAL:* Born February 3, 1923, in Portland, Ore.; son of John H. and Josephine Roush; married Virginia Beans, February 24, 1951; children: Paul, Ellard, Michael. *Education:* John F. Kennedy University, B.A. and M.P.A.; Western Colorado University, Ph.D. in Business Administration; graduated from U.S. Army War College, Industrial College of the Armed Forces, Command and General Staff College, and Foreign Service Institute. *Politics:* Republican. *Religion:* Roman Catholic. *Home:* 27 Terrace Ave., Kentfield, Calif. 94904.

*CAREER:* Business consultant. *Military service:* U.S. Army Reserve, 1942-75, with active duty during World War II; served as assistant military attache to Norway; became colonel. *Awards, honors:* George Washington Honor Medal, Freedoms Foundation of Valley Forge, 1969, 1970, for essays; Medal of Merit, Boy Scouts of America, for distinguished adult volunteer work.

*WRITINGS: Hornets in Our Home: Civil Disturbances and Their Effects upon U.S. National Security,* Adams Press, 1971; *The Problems of Civil Disturbances as They Relate to Public Administration,* Adams Press, 1973; *Management Audits of Subordinate Claims Offices of National Insurance Companies,* Adams Press, 1974; *Successfully Fishing Lake Tahoe,* Adams Press, 1976. Contributor of articles on insurance, the military, hunting, and fishing to periodicals.

*WORK IN PROGRESS: Dubious Defector,* a novel about international espionage, completion expected in 1978.

\* \* \*

## ROWAN, Helen   1927(?)-1972

1927(?)—June 23, 1972; American editor and writer on education. Obituaries: *New York Times,* June 25, 1972; *Washington Post,* June 26, 1972.

\* \* \*

## ROWE, James N(icholas)   1938-

*PERSONAL:* Born February 8, 1938, in McAllen, Tex.; son of Lee Delavan and Florence (Survillo) Rowe; married Jane Carolline Benson (a television actress), December 27, 1969; children: one daughter. *Education:* U.S. Military Academy, B.S., 1960. *Politics:* Republican. *Home:* 13601 Esworthy Rd., Potomac, Md. 20854. *Agent:* Mitchell Hamilburg Agency, 292 South La Cienega Blvd., Suite 212, Beverley Hills, Calif. 90211.

*CAREER:* U.S. Army officer, 1960-74; prisoner of war, 1963-68, after being captured while serving in Vietnam as Special Forces first lieutenant; subsequent assignments included Army General Staff, POW-MIA (prisoner of war-missing in action) Planning and Training Program, and Defense Intelligence Agency; retired as major; candidate for state office in Texas, 1975; full-time writer, 1975—. *Member:* Explorers Club (New York). *Awards, honors—Military:* Silver Star, Bronze Star Medal with oak-leaf cluster, Purple Heart with oak-leaf cluster, Meritorious Service Medal. *Other:* American Patriot Award of Freedoms Foundation of Valley Forge, 1969; named one of outstanding young men of America by U.S. Junior Chamber of Commerce, 1970; George Washington Honor Medal of Freedoms Foundation of Valley Forge, 1974; Legion of Honor, International Supreme Council of Order of De-Molay.

*WRITINGS: Five Years to Freedom* (autobiographical),

Little, Brown, 1971; *Southeast Asia Survival Journal,* U.S. Department of the Air Force, 1971; (with Robin Moore) *The Washington Connection,* Condor, 1977; *The Judas Squad* (novel), Little, Brown, 1977.

*WORK IN PROGRESS: Elsa; Memoirs of an Undercover Agent.*

*SIDELIGHTS:* On October 29, 1963, Lieutenant James N. Rowe and two other Green Berets were captured when the South Vietnamese unit with which they were serving as advisers was ambushed by Viet Cong guerillas in the Mekong Delta. The prisoners were taken to a camp in the U Minh Forest, known as the "Forest of Darkness," a communist sanctuary for over thirty years in the extreme south of Vietnam. Here Rowe spent most of the five years of his captivity locked in a bamboo cage three feet wide, six feet long, and four feet high. He had already made three unsuccessful escape attempts when, on December 31, 1968, while transporting him to another camp, his captors were attacked by American helicopters. Rowe seized the opportunity to hit a guard on the head and run into the open waving his arms. The helicopter crews, thinking he was a Viet Cong, circled to fire at him, but the last moment he was recognized as an American and rescued.

The story of Rowe's sixty-two months as a prisoner of war is told in his autobiographical work, *Five Years to Freedom.* In a review of the book, Robin Moore writes: "Anyone who thinks he is qualified to express opinions on conditions in Indo-China must read *Five Years to Freedom* or hold his peace. For true insight into the ideology and methodology of the communist machine in Southeast Asia it is difficult to recall a book as explicit, revealing, and exciting as this one. . . . From a literary standpoint the book is written with the clarity and immediacy only top professionals achieve. Major Rowe's book was not ghosted or 'told to' anyone. The horror, unrelenting misery, pain, and extreme mental pressure that Nick Rowe lived through for five years stab out from the pages of the book." Betty Donovan calls it "a searing story, a true story, told without florid adjectives. Because of the low-key, factual words with which Nick Rowe tells his story, the impact is shattering."

In another review, however, Brother Berchmans Downey says that he found the book "dull. Rowe must have a photographic memory, for every smallest detail, geographical, conversational, or medical, of his prison experience seems to be included. His recording of minutiae can be boring indeed. On the whole, the treatment [the prisoners] received seldom approaches the bestiality of the atrocities inflicted by Americans on Vietnamese prisoners of war as described in Mark Lane's . . . *Conversations with Americans.* Throughout Rowe's book runs the sad assumption that an American life is more valuable than a Vietnamese life, and a deplorable lack of understanding of the meaning of the brotherhood of man. Rowe's courage, endurance, and knowledge of things military is remarkable; his book, in my opinion, is overblown and pedantic." And E. J. Cutler writes: "Rowe's reconstruction of his capture and life as a prisoner is extraordinarily vivid and detailed. But for all its dramatic qualities (which are considerable), the book remains parochial to the point of being an anachronism. Rowe's convictions are simple, strong, and unexplained. He finds his captors cruel although they kept him alive for five years; he never stops to think what the fate of a Vietcong lieutenant captured by 'our side' might be. For him the role of American adviser in Vietnam approaches the messianic. He often comments with hurt, confusion, and above all resentment on the fact that Americans could protest a war against people who were holding him prisoner. In the last five years the nation has slowly developed the ability to see the Vietnam War for what it is; Rowe has a lot of catching up to do."

James N. Rowe told *CA:* "The completion of my first book, *Five Years to Freedom,* awakened an urge within me which I did my utmost to suppress. Logic argued against it; economic realities prohibited it; common sense agonized in opposition to it. Four years lapsed before I acknowledged the fact that the urge not only had survived, but had grown in proportion to arguments urging continued suppression. I wanted to write, not as a part-time hobby, but to devote all of my efforts to writing as a profession.

"I wrote my first novel, *The Judas Squad,* after returning to Washington in 1975. This was followed by collaboration with my good friend, Robin Moore, on an investigative work about the inner workings of Washington politics. I consider myself fortunate to have had my first efforts published. There is tremendous reinforcement for a novice author in finding that his works are acceptable to those in the business who see thousands of manuscripts a year from equally struggling beginners.

"After completing an autobiographical work, a novel, and an investigative non-fiction book, I find myself most at ease with a well-researched novel. Factual settings and frameworks for the plot add the authenticity I seek when selecting novels for my own reading pleasure. James Michener, of course, is at the top of my list of contemporary authors. After reading a novel, I like to feel that I've learned something rather than just having spent a number of pleasant hours in a non-existent environment. Also, in this vein, subtle truths are conveyed to the reader in a more palatable form than the same in a more didactic format.

"The highly competitive nature of the current literary field and overwhelming number of titles printed each year makes writing a precarious profession in an economic sense. It is no longer merely a matter of excellence of style or writer's ability, but a combination of ability, choice of a marketable topic, and subsequent publicity hype so necessary to lift a particular title away from the hundreds of others surrounding it on the bookshelf. Patience, proficiency, and persistence are the writer's armor against 'the slings and arrows of outrageous fortune.' I find the satisfaction and enjoyment of creating a book a reward in itself, but one has also to consider eating and paying bills. In the days of famine, I put ideas of the great American novel in my 'hold' basket and look for ideas my publisher has a reasonable chance of selling.

"Our household and future plans have been adapted to my writing and differ radically from what we envisioned a short time ago. We're buying a small farm in Virginia which will be ideal both for my writing and for our animals (four horses, our daughter's Welsh pony, two German shepherds and two poodles). This, contrasted with the busy, suburban environment necessary for convenience in the nine-to-five world of the commuting businessman. Graduate work has been shifted from International Relations to English Literature and I hope, in the future, to be able to combine my writing with teaching."

Rowe is a qualified parachutist who has made more than 250 jumps, both military and free-fall. Sport parachuting is one of the hobbies he shares with his wife, who has made over 140 jumps; the others are sports cars and scuba diving. He speaks, reads, and writes German, Vietnamese, and Chinese Mandarin, and speaks Spanish.

*BIOGRAPHICAL/CRITICAL SOURCES: New York*

*Times,* January 3, 1969, January 4, 1969; *Time,* January 10, 1969; *Washington Post,* February 16, 1969, November 23, 1969, June 8, 1971; James N. Rowe, *Five Years to Freedom,* Little, Brown, 1971; *Cincinnati Post and Times Star,* May 29, 1971; *Best Sellers,* June 15, 1971; *Boston Herald-Traveler,* June 27, 1971; *Reader's Digest,* January, 1972.

\* \* \*

## ROWLAND, Benjamin, Jr. 1904-1972

December 2, 1904—October 3, 1972; American art critic, historian, and painter. Obituaries: *New York Times,* October 5, 1972.

\* \* \*

## ROXAS, Savina A.

*PERSONAL:* Born in New York, N.Y.; daughter of Peter Mario (a clothier) and Rose (Muscillo) Dagnessa; married Richard A. Roxas (an electrical engineer), September 2, 1939; children: Dianne (Mrs. Ross K. Lindsey), Rita A. *Education:* Duquesne University, B.A., 1957; Carnegie-Mellon University, M.L.S., 1960; University of Pittsburgh, Ph.D., 1970. *Home and office:* 265 Sleepy Hollow Rd., Pittsburgh, Pa. 15216.

*CAREER:* Carnegie-Mellon University, Pittsburgh, Pa., reference librarian, 1960-61; Duquesne University, Pittsburgh, cataloger and instructor in library science, 1961-64; University of Pittsburgh, Pittsburgh, instructor in library science, 1964-70; Clarion State College, Clarion, Pa., professor of library science, 1970-73; currently a library consultant. *Member:* American Library Association, Special Library Association, American Association of University Professors, Pennsylvania Library Association, Pittsburgh Bibliophiles Society, Beta Phi Mu, Psi Chi, Sigma Tau Delta, American Wind Symphony Women's Association, Women's Association of Pittsburgh Symphony Society, Pittsburgh Playhouse, South Hills College Club. `

*WRITINGS: Library Education in Italy: An Historical Survey, 1870-1969,* Scarecrow, 1971. Contributor of articles and of translations from Spanish and Portuguese to *Encyclopedia of Library and Information Science* and *Library Review.*

*WORK IN PROGRESS: Notable Italian Librarians,* completion expected in 1978.

\* \* \*

## RUBIN, Israel 1923-

*PERSONAL:* Born June 8, 1923, in Sighet, Romania; came to United States in 1947; naturalized citizen; son of Menachem Eliezer (a ritual slaughterer) and Rochel (Tischler) Rubin; married Anna Halberstam, March 14, 1951; children: Edward, Haya Rahel, Miriam Esther. *Education:* University of Pittsburgh, B.A. (magna cum laude), 1958, Ph.D., 1965. *Home:* 3520 Bendemeer Rd., Cleveland Heights, Ohio 44118. *Office:* Department of Sociology, Cleveland State University, Cleveland, Ohio 44115.

*CAREER:* Participant in observation study of a Jewish Orthodox community in New York, N.Y., 1960-61; Northwestern University, Evanston, Ill., instructor in sociology, 1961-62; University of Minnesota, Minneapolis, instructor in sociology and social science, 1962-66; Cleveland State University, Cleveland, Ohio, associate professor, 1966-74, professor of sociology, 1974—. Member of board, Telshe Yeshiva (Wickliffe, Ohio), Cleveland Hebrew Academy, and Cleveland Bureau of Jewish Education. *Member:* Amer-

ican Sociological Association, American Association of University Professors, Ohio Valley Sociological Society.

*WRITINGS: Satmar: An Island in the City,* Quadrangle, 1972. Contributor of articles to sociology and anthropology journals.

*SIDELIGHTS:* Israel Rubin told *CA:* "As an orthodox Jew of Hasidic background I have a lifelong interest in orthodoxy in general and Hasidism in particular. As a sociologist my interest lies in comprehension of the process of control in maintaining minority cultures in a modern industrial setting."

Jacob Neusner says in his review of *Satmar: An Island in the City:* "Israel Rubin gives us an intelligent, thoughtful, profound, and sympathetic account of a small community of Jewish Orthodox immigrants.... He provides a full sociological picture of the Satmar community, its historical background, religion, family and education, economics, politics, and welfare. Throughout, he asks the primary questions: What keeps the community together? What preserves its character against change? Why do people participate in the community? How does the community perpetuate itself?"

*BIOGRAPHICAL/CRITICAL SOURCES: Annals* of the American Academy of Political and Social Sciences, May, 1973; *Social Forces,* September, 1974.

\* \* \*

## RUBIN, Jacob A. 1910-1972
### (J. Odem)

July 1, 1910—December 28, 1972; Austrian-born American editor, journalist, and writer on contemporary affairs, the Middle East, and other topics. Obituaries: *New York Times,* December 29, 1972. (See index for *CA* sketch)

\* \* \*

## RUBULIS, Aleksis 1922-

*PERSONAL:* Born October 11, 1922, in Latvia. *Education:* Baltic University, M.A., 1949, Ph.D., 1951. *Religion:* Roman Catholic. *Office:* Department of Modern Languages, University of Notre Dame, Notre Dame, Ind. 46556.

*CAREER:* Barry College, Miami, Fla., instructor in German and Russian, 1961-62; Niagara University, Niagara University, N.Y., assistant professor of German and Russian, 1962-65; University of Notre Dame, Notre Dame, Ind., associate professor of modern languages, 1965—. *Military service:* Latvian Legion, 1944-45; received Silver Medal. *Member:* Modern Language Association of America. *Awards, honors:* Research grant for study at British Museum and at Universities of Helsinki, Hamburg, and Uppsala, summer, 1968.

*WRITINGS: Ar navi uz tu* (title means "Friendship with Death"), Skirmants, 1954; *Via Tua* (title means "Your Road"), Kalnajs, 1956; *Katram savs* (title means "Each to His Own"), Kalnajs, 1956; *Latvian Literature,* Daugavas Vanags, 1964; *Baltic Literature,* University of Notre Dame, 1970; *Uz Latgali* (title means "To Latgale"), Stars, 1975. Contributor of more than three hundred fifty articles on literature, linguistics, art, and ancient history to scholarly journals.

*SIDELIGHTS:* Aleksis Rubulis speaks about a dozen languages.

*BIOGRAPHICAL/CRITICAL SOURCES: Books Abroad,* spring, 1971.

## RUDY, Willis  1920-

*PERSONAL:* Born January 25, 1920, in New York, N.Y.; son of Philip (a pharmacist) and Rose (Handman) Rudy; married Dorothy L. Richardson (an English professor), January 31, 1948; children: Dorothy Elizabeth, Willa Catherine. *Education:* City College (now City College of the City University of New York), B.S.S., 1939; Columbia University, M.A., 1940, Ph.D., 1949. *Politics:* "Independent liberal." *Religion:* Christian Unitarian-Universalist. *Home:* 161 West Clinton Ave., Tenafly, N.J. 07670. *Office:* Department of History, Fairleigh Dickinson University, Teaneck, N.J. 07666.

*CAREER:* City College (now City College of the City University of New York), New York, N.Y., instructor in history, 1939-49; Harvard University, Cambridge, Mass., professor of history of American education, 1949-53; Massachusetts State College, Worcester, professor of history, 1953-63; Fairleigh Dickinson University, Teaneck, N.J., professor of history, 1963—. Visiting professor at New York University, 1953, Harvard University, 1953, 1957-58, and University of Illinois, 1960. Research historian, U.S. Army Procurement Agency, Quartermaster Corps, 1952. Columbia University, Institute of Higher Education, associate, 1958-59, University Seminars associate, 1968-72. *Member:* American Historical Association, Organization of American Historians, Phi Beta Kappa.

*WRITINGS: The College of the City of New York: A History, 1847-1947,* City College Press, 1949, reprinted, Arno, 1976; (with John S. Brubacher) *Higher Education in Transition,* Harper, 1958, 2nd revised edition, 1976; *The Evolving Liberal Arts Curriculum: A Historical Review of Basic Themes,* Teachers College Press, 1960; *Schools in an Age of Mass Culture,* Prentice-Hall, 1965; (with Peter Sammartino) *The Private Urban University,* Fairleigh Dickinson University Press, 1966.

*WORK IN PROGRESS: The University in History,* for Jossey-Bass, completion expected in 1980.

*BIOGRAPHICAL/CRITICAL SOURCES: American Historical Review,* July, 1950; *New York Times Book Review,* September 21, 1958; *Harvard Educational Review,* fall, 1965; *Change,* October, 1976.

\*     \*     \*

## RUEF, John S.  1927-

*PERSONAL:* Born January 24, 1927, in Chicago, Ill.; son of John E. (an engineer) and Leota (Rice) Ruef; married Jane Holt (a typographer), October 11, 1951; children: Marcus, Adam, Seth, Sarah. *Education:* University of Chicago, B.A., 1945; Seabury-Western Theological Seminary, B.D., 1950, S.T.M., 1955; Harvard University, Th.D., 1960. *Home and office:* Nashotah House, Nashotah, Wis. 53058.

*CAREER:* Vicar of Episcopal parish in Park Forest, Ill., 1950-54; Berkeley Divinity School, New Haven, Conn., professor of New Testament, 1960-71; associate rector of Episcopal church in Charlottesville, Va., 1971-72; Diocese of Western New York, Buffalo, director of lay studies, 1972-74; Nashotah House, Nashotah, Wis., dean, 1974—. Member of board of directors, Yale University Ecumenical Continuing Education Center. *Member:* Society of Biblical Literature, Columbia University Seminar in New Testament Studies, Church Society for College Work (fellow), St. John's Parish (Washington, D.C.; fellow).

*WRITINGS: Understanding the Gospels,* Seabury, 1963; *The Gospels and the Teachings of Jesus,* Seabury, 1967; *Paul's First Letter to Corinth,* Penguin, 1971.

*WORK IN PROGRESS: Ethics in the New Testament; The Sacraments in the New Testament; Worship in the New Testament.*

\*     \*     \*

## RULON, Philip Reed  1934-

*PERSONAL:* Born February 20, 1934, in Delaware, Iowa; son of Wayne M. and R. Hannah Rulon; married Janice Kay Brown, December 16, 1961 (divorced, October 6, 1975); married Annette K. Rulon, January 2, 1976; children: Philip Scott, Douglas Matthew; adopted children: Yvonne Winkler Thompson, William Payne Thompson, Ann Marie Thompson. *Education:* Washburn University, B.A., 1963; Kansas State Teachers' College (now Emporia State University), M.A., 1965; Oklahoma State University, Ed.D., 1967; University of Texas, postdoctoral study, 1974. *Politics:* Democrat. *Religion:* Episcopalian. *Home:* 1407 North Aztec, Flagstaff, Ariz. 86001. *Office:* Department of History, Northern Arizona University, Flagstaff, Ariz. 86002.

*CAREER:* Oklahoma State University, Stillwater, instructor in history, 1964-67; Northern Arizona University, Flagstaff, 1967—, began as assistant professor, currently associate professor of history. Summer lecturer at Oklahoma State University, 1965, at Kansas State Teachers' College (now Emporia State University), 1967, 1969. Consultant to Arizona Council on the Humanities and Public Policy. Member of committee on history in the classroom, National Advisory Board. *Military service:* U.S. Army, 1957-59. *Member:* American Historical Association, History of Education Society, Society for History Education, National Council for the Social Sciences, Oklahoma Academy of Science, Phi Kappa Phi, Phi Alpha Theta. *Awards, honors:* Recipient of eleven research grants from Northern Arizona University, and of grants from Lyndon Baines Johnson Foundation, American Historical Association, and U.S. Office of Education.

*WRITINGS: Oklahoma State University: A History,* Oklahoma State University Press, 1972; (contributor) Clifford Trafzer, editor, *The Blue Coats,* University of Oklahoma Press, in press. Author of professional papers. Contributor of numerous articles to education and history journals.

*WORK IN PROGRESS: The Educational Thought of Lyndon Baines Johnson,* for Nelson-Hall.

*SIDELIGHTS:* "The current book on Lyndon Baines Johnson uses a biographical format to relate the story of American national education policy since the turn of the twentieth century," Philip Reed Rulon told *CA.* He continued by saying that his "writing on this project is interspersed with short essays on the teaching of history and on educational leadership in America. In many ways the essay format is more comfortable than the longer book form because it is possible to convey a point of view more quickly in print. Education is the only institution to touch the lives of all Americans and the system must be understood by the general public if we are to have accurate information on the character of the people of this country."

\*     \*     \*

## RUNKLE, Gerald  1924-

*PERSONAL:* Born January 5, 1924, in Akron, Ohio; son of Frank I. (a businessman) and Alberta (Abbett) Runkle; married Audrey Colchin, June 24, 1947; children: Randall, Elizabeth, Sarah. *Education:* Oberlin College, A.B., 1948; Yale University, M.A., 1950, Ph.D., 1951. *Politics:* Democrat.

*Home:* 445 Buena Vista, Edwardsville, Ill. 62025. *Office:* Department of Philosophy, Southern Illinois University, Edwardsville, Ill. 62025.

*CAREER:* University of Georgia, Atlanta Division (now Georgia State University), assistant professor, 1951-55, associate professor of philosophy, 1955; Doane College, Crete, Neb., associate professor of philosophy, 1955-59; Southern Illinois University, Edwardsville, associate professor, 1959-64, professor of philosophy, 1964—, chairman of department, 1959-64, dean, School of Humanities, 1964-73. *Military service:* U.S. Army Air Forces, 1942-46; became lieutenant. *Member:* American Association of University Professors, American Society for Political and Legal Philosophy, American Philosophical Association.

*WRITINGS: A History of Western Political Theory,* Ronald, 1968; *Anarchism: Old and New,* Dell, 1972; *Good Thinking,* Holt, 1978. Contributor of articles to *Atlanta Economic Review, Theology Today, Ethics, Journal of Politics, Comparative Studies in Society and History, Darshana International,* and *Journal of the History of Philosophy.*

*WORK IN PROGRESS:* A study of condemned revolutionists and their final statements before execution, tentatively entitled *The Rest Is Silence.*

\* \* \*

## RUTHERFORD, Phillip Roland 1939-

*PERSONAL:* Born October 13, 1939, in Paris, Tex.; son of Phillip Zachery (an auto mechanic) and Dorine (White) Rutherford; married Lou Carolyn May (a college administrator), May 29, 1961; children: Phillip Terrell, Kristopher Paul. *Education:* East Texas State University, B.A., 1962, M.A., 1964, Ph.D., 1966. *Politics:* Democrat. *Religion:* Methodist. *Home:* 15 Lawn Ave., Gorham, Me. 04038. *Office:* Department of English, University of Maine, Gorham, Me. 04038.

*CAREER:* University of Maine at Portland-Gorham, assistant professor, 1966-68, associate professor, 1968-70, professor of English, 1970—, chairman of department, 1971—. Delegate to Maine Democratic Convention. Member of Democratic Town Committee and Cumberland County Democratic Committee; member of board of directors, South Central Names Institute; Maine chairman of Survey of United States Place Names. *Member:* American Association of University Professors (Maine treasurer, 1972—), American Names Society (state chairman), Southern Conference of Modern Language Association.

*WRITINGS: Dissertations in Linguistics, 1900-1964,* Center for Applied Linguistics, 1968; *The Dictionary of Maine Place Names,* Wheelwright, 1971. Contributor to journals, including *Down East Magazine, Kansas Historical Quarterly, Civil War Times Illustrated.*

*WORK IN PROGRESS:* Research in pronunciation of Maine place names, in linguistic bibliography, and in other place names.

\* \* \*

## RUTKOWSKI, Edwin H(enry) 1923-

*PERSONAL:* Born July 15, 1923, in Chicago, Ill.; son of Walter and Marie (Stander) Rutkowski; married Rose Marie Citro (a nurse and teacher), October 12, 1952; children: Sara Ann, Michael David. *Education:* University of Chicago, M.A., 1950; Columbia University, Ph.D., 1960. *Home:* 3112 Cortland Dr., Vestal, N.Y. 13850. *Office:* Department of Political Science, State University of New York, Binghamton, N.Y. 13901.

*CAREER:* University of Detroit, Detroit, Mich., 1956-67, began as instructor, became associate professor of political science, chairman of department, 1963-67; State University of New York at Binghamton, associate professor of political science, 1967—. Danforth Foundation associate, 1970—. *Member:* American Political Science Association, New York State Political Science Association (member of executive council, 1972-73; president, 1973-74). *Awards, honors:* State University of New York faculty research fellowships, 1968-69 and 1969-70, faculty exchange scholar to Moscow State University, 1977.

*WRITINGS: The Politics of Military Aviation Procurement, 1926-1934: A Study in the Political Assertion of Consensual Values,* Ohio State University Press, 1966; (contributor) Arthur S. Banks, editor, *Political Handbook of the World,* McGraw, 1978. Contributor of articles to *Commonweal, Papers of the Michigan Academy of Science, Arts, and Letters.*

\* \* \*

## RYBACK, Eric 1952-

*PERSONAL:* Born March 19, 1952, in Detroit, Mich.; son of Ernest (an attorney) and Patricia (Wernig) Ryback. *Education:* Attended University of Denver, 1971-73; Idaho State University, B.A., 1976. *Politics:* "Non-Partisan." *Religion:* Roman Catholic. *Home:* 45236 Sunrise Lane, Belleville, Mich. 48111. *Office:* Horizons Unlimited, P.O. Box 147, Pocatello, Idaho 83201.

*CAREER:* Horizons Unlimited (mountaineering, backpacking, and rock climbing school and guide service), Pocatello, Idaho, director, 1976—; junior high school teacher in Pocatello, 1978—. Lecturer to conservation and camping enthusiasts. *Awards, honors:* Certificate of achievement from Appalachian Trail Conference, 1969, for hiking the Appalachian Trail in one trek; certificate of accomplishment from U.S. Forest Service, 1970, for completing Pacific Crest hike in one trek.

*WRITINGS: The High Adventure of Eric Ryback,* Chronicle Publishing, 1971; (with brother, Tim Ryback) *The Ultimate Journey: Canada to Mexico down the Continental Divide,* Chronicle Books, 1973; (contributor) James R. Hare, editor, *Hiking the Appalachian Trail,* Rodale Press, 1975. Contributor to magazines including *Southern Living, Backpacker, National Geographic School Bulletin,* and *Colorado.*

*SIDELIGHTS:* Alone, Eric Ryback hiked the 2,023 mile Appalachian trail from Maine to Georgia, in 1969, as well as the Pacific Crest 2,500 mile trail from Canada to Mexico. On his latest trek (1972), he hiked the length of the Continental Divide. He was accompanied by his brother Tim to the halfway point and then continued his trip alone. Ryback has also served as photographer for Tim's "Viking Journey," in which they rowed and sailed a handmade Viking ship, built to one-fourth scale, from Arcadia National Park in Maine to New York Harbor in 1976. *Avocational interests:* Cross-country skiing, kayaking, rafting, tennis, biking, and fly fishing.

*BIOGRAPHICAL/CRITICAL SOURCES: Ann Arbor News,* June 16, 1972.

\* \* \*

## RYCHLAK, Joseph F(rank) 1928-

*PERSONAL:* Surname is pronounced *Rish*-lock; born December 17, 1928, in Cudahy, Wis.; son of Joseph Walter and

Helen (Bieniek) Rychlak; married Lenora Smith, June 16, 1956; children: Ronald, Stephanie. *Education:* University of Wisconsin, B.S., 1953; Ohio State University, M.A., 1954, Ph.D., 1957. *Home:* 690 Cardinal Dr., Lafayette, Ind. 47905. *Office:* Department of Psychological Sciences, Purdue University, Lafayette, Ind. 47907.

*CAREER:* Florida State University, Tallahassee, assistant professor of psychology, 1957-58; Washington State University, Pullman, assistant professor of psychology and director of Human Relations Center, 1958-61; St. Louis University, St. Louis, Mo., associate professor, 1961-65, professor of psychology, 1965-69; Purdue University, Lafayette, Ind., professor of psychology, 1969—. Research consultant for management progress study, American Telephone & Telegraph Corp., 1957—. *Military service:* U.S. Army Air Forces, 1946-47; U.S. Air Force, 1947-49; became sergeant. *Member:* American Psychological Association (fellow), Society for Projective Techniques (fellow), Phi Beta Kappa. *Awards, honors:* Honored for "outstanding contribution to human understanding and welfare" by the International Association for Social Psychiatry, 1971.

*WRITINGS: A Philosophy of Science for Personality Theory,* Houghton, 1968; *Introduction to Personality and Psychotherapy,* Houghton, 1973; (editor) *Dialectic: Humanistic Rationale for Behavior and Development,* Karger, 1976; *The Psychology of Rigorous Humanism,* Wiley-Interscience, 1977.

\*          \*          \*

### RYDER, Norman B(urston)    1923-

*PERSONAL:* Born August 24, 1923, in Hamilton, Ontario, Canada; son of William George (a tire dealer) and Jean (Crouchley) Ryder; married Helen Barbour, May 3, 1947; children: Anne (Mrs. Eric Anderson), Paul. *Education:* McMaster University, B.A., 1944; University of Toronto, M.A., 1946; Princeton University, A.M., 1949, Ph.D., 1951. *Politics:* "Radical Liberal." *Religion:* None. *Home:* 14 Toth Lane, Rocky Hill, N.J. 08553. *Office:* Office of Population Research, Princeton University, 21 Prospect St., Princeton, N.J. 08540.

*CAREER:* Dominion Bureau of Statistics, Ottawa, Ontario, demographer, 1950-51; University of Toronto, Toronto, Ontario, lecturer in sociology and statistics, 1951-54; Scripps Foundation Research on Population Problems, Miami, Ohio, demographer, 1954-56; University of Wisconsin—Madison, assistant professor, 1956-58, associate professor, 1958-61, professor of sociology, 1961-71; Princeton University, Princeton, N.J., professor of sociology, 1971—. *Military service:* Royal Canadian Navy, 1943-45, became sublieutenant. *Member:* American Sociological Association, Population Association of America (president, 1972—), International Union for the Scientific Study of Population,

American Academy of Arts and Sciences (fellow), American Statistical Association (fellow).

*WRITINGS:* (With C. F. Westoff) *Reproduction in the United States: 1965,* Princeton University Press, 1971; *The Contraceptive Revolution,* Princeton University Press, 1977. Contributor of about sixty articles to scientific journals. Editor, *American Sociological Review,* 1966-69.

\*          \*          \*

### RYMES, Thomas Kenneth    1932-

*PERSONAL:* Born October 24, 1932, in Toronto, Ontario, Canada; son of Henry John and Margery (Downing) Rymes; married Elizabeth Anne Bull, September 22, 1956; children: Carolyn, Paul, John. *Education:* University of Manitoba, B.A., 1955; McGill University, M.A., 1958, Ph.D., 1968. *Office:* Department of Economics, Carleton University, Ottawa, Ontario, Canada K1S 5B6.

*CAREER:* Dominion Bureau of Statistics, Ottawa, Ontario, economist, 1958-63; Carleton University, Ottawa, assistant professor, 1963-66, associate professor, 1966-70, professor of economics, 1970—. *Member:* Canadian Economics Association, International Association for Research in Income and Wealth.

*WRITINGS: On Concepts of Capital and Technical Change,* Cambridge University Press, 1971.

*WORK IN PROGRESS: The Theory of Capital and Money.*

\*          \*          \*

### RYNEW, Arden N.    1943-

*PERSONAL:* Born September 8, 1943, in Chicago, Ill.; son of Nicholas (a traffic controller) and Dorothy (Mitchell) Rynew; married Sari F. Posen (a music instructor), April 24, 1966. *Education:* Attended Detroit Society of Arts and Crafts, 1961-63; University of Michigan, B.S., 1965, M.F.A. (painting and printmaking), 1967; New York University, M.F.A. (film and television production), 1972.

*CAREER:* Adrian College, Adrian, Mich., instructor in art, 1967-68; art teacher in public schools in Valhalla, N.Y., 1968-70. Director of personal creative film-art-literary unit, C.H.A.N.C.E., Inc., 1967—. *Member:* American Film Institute, College Art Association of America, Michigan Academy of Art, Science, and Letters.

*WRITINGS: Filmmaking for Children,* Pflaum, 1971, revised edition, 1975. Also creator of films: "Flood Light," 1968; "Monuments," 1969; "Four Ladies on Stage" (documentary); "Checkmate/Stalemate," 1971.

*WORK IN PROGRESS: Chrome Plated Reality;* "I Seem to be a Verb," a film based on book of the same name by Buckminster Fuller; "There's No Substitute," a comedy about city schools.†

# S

**SAARINEN, Aline B(ernstein Louchheim)  1914-1972**

March 25, 1914—July 13, 1972; American art critic and television correspondent. Obituaries: *New York Times,* July 15, 1972; *Time,* July 24, 1972; *Newsweek,* July 24, 1972; *Current Biography,* September, 1972.

\*  \*  \*

**SACHER-MASOCH, Alexander  1902(?)-1972**

1902(?)—August 18, 1972; Austrian novelist. Obituaries: *L'Express,* August 28-September 3, 1972.

\*  \*  \*

**SACHS, Murray  1924-**

*PERSONAL:* Born April 10, 1924, in Toronto, Ontario, Canada; son of Thomas (a tailor) and Sarah (Roth) Sachs; married Miriam Blank, September 14, 1961; children: Deborah Ruth, Aaron Jacob. *Education:* University of Toronto, B.A., 1946; Columbia University, M.A., 1947, Ph.D., 1952. *Politics:* Independent. *Religion:* Jewish. *Home:* 280 Highland Ave., West Newton, Mass. 02165. *Office:* Department of French, Brandeis University, Waltham, Mass. 02154.

*CAREER:* University of California, Berkeley, instructor in French, 1948-50; University of Detroit, Detroit, Mich., lecturer in French, 1951-52; Williams College, Williamstown, Mass., assistant professor of French, 1954-60; Brandeis University, Waltham, Mass., professor of French, 1960—. *Member:* Modern Language Association of America, Association of Teachers of French, Modern Humanities Research Association (England), Association Internationale Des Etudes Francaises. *Awards, honors:* Palmes Academiques by government of France, 1971.

*WRITINGS:* (Editor with E. M. Grant and R. B. Grant) *French Stories, Plays and Poetry,* Oxford University Press, 1959; *The Career of Alphonse Daudet,* Harvard University Press, 1965; *The French Short Story in the Nineteenth Century,* Oxford University Press, 1969; *Anatole France: The Short Stories,* Edward Arnold, 1974; (contributor) Michael Issacharoff, editor, *Languages de Flaubert,* Lettres Modernes, 1976. Contributor of articles to various professional journals.

*WORK IN PROGRESS:* A study of the career of Gustave Flaubert, completion expected in 1979; a study of the emergence of the short story as a new literary genre, in Europe and in America, completion expected in 1982.

*SIDELIGHTS:* Murray Sachs is fluent in French, can read German, Spanish, Yiddish, and has an "acquaintance" with five other languages.

\*  \*  \*

**SACKTON, Alexander H(art)  1911-**

*PERSONAL:* Born January 30, 1911, in Galveston, Tex.; name legally changed in 1944; son of Tobias (a business executive) and Mathilda (Littman) Sakowitz; married Ivria Adlerblum, May 11, 1944; children: Tobias, David, Margaret, Elisabeth. *Education:* University of Pennsylvania, B.S., 1931; Cambridge University, B.A. (honors), 1934, M.A., 1936; Harvard University, Ph.D., 1941. *Home:* 2525 Spring Lane, Austin, Tex. 78703. *Office:* Department of English, University of Texas, Austin, Tex. 78712.

*CAREER:* Agricultural and Mechanical College of Texas (now Texas A&M University), College Station, instructor in English, 1936-38; University of Delaware, Newark, assistant professor of English, 1945-46; University of Texas at Austin, assistant professor, 1946-50, associate professor, 1950-65, professor of English, 1965—. Visiting associate professor of English, Brandeis University, 1954-55. *Military service:* U.S. Army Air Forces, 1941-45; became first lieutenant. *Member:* Modern Language Association of America, Humanities Research Association, American Association of University Professors.

*WRITINGS: Rhetoric as a Dramatic Language in Ben Jonson,* Columbia University Press, 1948, Octagon Books, 1967; *The T. S. Eliot Collection of the University of Texas at Austin,* Humanities Research Center, University of Texas at Austin, 1975.

*WORK IN PROGRESS: Poems on Literary Subjects in Seventeenth Century England.*

\*  \*  \*

**SAMAY, Sebastian  1926-**

*PERSONAL:* Surname is pronounced Sam-*ay;* born June 10, 1926, in Pecol, Hungary; son of Edwin (a psychologist) and Maria (Wurdak) Samay. *Education:* Benedictine Gymnasium, Koeszeg, Hungary, Diploma, 1945; Ecole Secondaire des Humanitees International, Innsbruck, Austria, Diploma, 1948; St. Vincent College, Latrobe, Pa., B.A. (summa cum laude), 1956; Catholic University of Louvain, Ph.D. (summa cum laude), 1963. *Politics:* Democrat. *Home and office:* St. Vincent College, Latrobe, Pa. 15650.

*CAREER:* Roman Catholic priest of Benedictine Order; St. Vincent College, Latrobe, Pa., chairman of department of philosophy, 1966-69, associate professor of philosophy, 1967—, socius of clerical students, 1967-70, director of institutional research, 1974. Visiting lecturer, National University of Ireland, Dublin, 1970. *Member:* American Catholic Philosophical Association, Metaphysical Society of America, American Benedictine Academy, Western Pennsylvania Philosophical Society.

*WRITINGS: Reason Revisited: The Philosophy of Karl Jaspers,* University of Notre Dame Press, 1971.

\* \* \*

## SAMORA, Julian 1920-

*PERSONAL:* Born March 1, 1920, in Pagosa Springs, Colo. *Education:* Adams State College, B.A., 1942; Colorado State University, M.S., 1947; University of Wisconsin, additional study, 1948-49; Washington University, St. Louis, Mo., Ph.D., 1952. *Office:* Department of Sociology, University of Notre Dame, Notre Dame, Ind. 46556.

*CAREER:* High school teacher in Walsenburg, Colo., 1942-43; Adams State College, Alamosa, Colo., instructor, 1944-45; University of Colorado, School of Medicine, Denver, assistant professor of preventive medicine and public health, 1955-57; Michigan State University, East Lansing, assistant professor of sociology and anthropology, 1957-59; University of Notre Dame, Notre Dame, Ind., professor of sociology, 1959—, head of department, 1963-66. Visiting professor at University of New Mexico, 1954, Michigan State University, 1955, Universidad Nacional de Colombia, 1963, University of California, Los Angeles, 1964, and University of Texas, 1971. Past or present commissioner of President's Commission on Rural Poverty, National Upward Bound, President's Commission on Income Maintenance Programs, Colorado Anti-Discrimination Commission, and Indiana Civil Rights Commission. Has done field work in the United States, Colombia, and the U.S.-Mexico border area. Consultant to U.S. Commission on Civil Rights, U.S. Public Health Service, National Endowment for the Humanities, Ford Foundation, and other public and private groups.

*WRITINGS:* (Contributor) Benjamin Paul, editor, *Health, Culture, and Community,* Russell Sage, 1955; (contributor) James K. Skipper, Jr. and Robert C. Leonard, editors, *Social Interaction and Patient Care,* Lippincott, 1965; *La Raza: Forgotten Americans,* University of Notre Dame Press, 1966; (contributor) W. Richard Scott and Edmund H. Volkart, editors, *Medical Care: Readings in the Sociology of Medical Institutions,* Wiley, 1966; (with Richard A. Lamanna) *Mexican Americans in a Midwest Metropolis: A Study of East Chicago,* Graduate School of Business Administration, University of California, Los Angeles, 1967; (with E. Galarza and H. Gallegos) *Mexican-Americans in the Southwest,* McNally & Loftin, 1969; *Los Mojados: The Wetback Story,* University of Notre Dame Press, 1971; (with P. V. Sirnon) *A History of the Mexican American People,* University of Notre Dame Press, 1977. Contributor of about twenty articles to sociology journals.

\* \* \*

## SAMPSON, Edward E. 1934-

*PERSONAL:* Born December 4, 1934, in Chicago, Ill.; son of Theodore R. and Beatrice Sampson; married Marya Marthas, March 17, 1972. *Education:* University of California, Los Angeles, B.A., 1956; University of Michigan, Ph.D., 1960. *Politics:* "Variable." *Religion:* "Personal." *Office:* Department of Sociology, Clark University, Worcester, Mass. 01610.

*CAREER:* University of California, Berkeley, assistant professor, 1960-66, associate professor of psychology, 1966-70; Brunel University, Uxbridge, England, lecturer, 1970-71; Clark University, Worcester, Mass., visiting professor, 1971-72, professor of sociology and adjunct professor of psychology, 1972—, former chairman of sociology department.

*WRITINGS: Approaches, Contexts, and Problems of Social Psychology,* Prentice-Hall, 1964; *Student Action and Protest,* Jossey-Bass, 1970; *Social Psychology and Contemporary Society,* Wiley, 1971, 2nd edition, 1976; *Ego at the Threshold,* Delta, 1975; (with wife, Marya Marthas) *Group Process for the Health Professions,* Wiley, 1977.

*WORK IN PROGRESS: The Charisma Factor.*

\* \* \*

## SAMRA, Cal 1931-

*PERSONAL:* Born February 1, 1931, in Flint, Mich.; son of N.H. and Adele (Korban) Samra; married Kathleen Kimmel, October 22, 1966; children: Paul Najeeb, Matthew Kahlil. *Education:* University of Michigan, B.A., 1953.

*CAREER:* Worked as a reporter and editorial director for newspapers and Associated Press in Ann Arbor, Mich., 1950-55; *New York Herald Tribune,* New York City, copy reader, 1956; *Newark Evening News,* Newark, N.J., reporter, 1957-59; free-lance journalist in New York City, 1960-63; American Schizophrenia Foundation (now division of Huxley Institute for Bio-Social Research), New York City, national executive director, 1964-69; *Ann Arbor News,* Ann Arbor, Mich., reporter, columnist, and feature writer, beginning 1969. *Military service:* U.S. Army, Public Information Officer, 1953-55. *Member:* Society for the Emancipation of the American Male (president, 1969—).

*WRITINGS: Schizophrenia,* University Books, 1966; *The Feminine Mistake,* Nash Publishing, 1971. Editor, *The Men's Section.*

*WORK IN PROGRESS:* A book on psychiatry.

*AVOCATIONAL INTERESTS:* Photography, tennis, basketball, touch football, swimming.††

\* \* \*

## SANDERS, Jack T(homas) 1935-

*PERSONAL:* Born February 28, 1935, in Grand Prairie, Tex.; son of Eula Thomas (a drycleaner) and Mildred Madge (Parish) Sanders; married Patricia Chism, August 9, 1959 (deceased); children: Collin Thomas. *Education:* Texas Wesleyan College, B.A., 1956; Emory University, M.Div., 1960; Claremont Graduate School and University Center (now Claremont Graduate School), Ph.D., 1963; University of Tuebingen, additional study, 1963-64. *Politics:* Democrat. *Home:* 390 50th Ave. E., Eugene, Ore. 97405. *Office:* Department of Religious Studies, University of Oregon, Eugene, Ore. 97403.

*CAREER:* Emory University, Atlanta, Ga., assistant professor of New Testament, 1964-67; Garrett Theological Seminary, Evanston, Ill., visiting assistant professor of New Testament, 1967-68; McCormick Theological Seminary, Chicago, Ill., visiting assistant professor of New Testament, 1968-69; University of Oregon, Eugene, associate professor, 1969-75, professor of religious studies, 1975—, head of department, 1973-76, 1977—. Fellow of the Center for Biblical

Research and Archives of the Society of Biblical Literature, 1976-77. *Member:* Society of Biblical Literature, American Academy of Religion, American Association of University Professors, Studiorum Novi Testamenti Societas, American Civil Liberties Union. *Awards, honors:* Fulbright fellow at University of Tuebingen, 1963-64.

*WRITINGS: The New Testament Christological Hymns: Their Historical Religious Background* (monograph), Cambridge University Press, 1971; *Ethics in the New Testament: Change and Development,* Fortress, 1975. Contributor to journals.

*WORK IN PROGRESS:* A research project on the ethics in Hellenistic Judaism.

\* \* \*

## SANDERSON, Ivan T(erence)   1911-1973
### (Terence Roberts)

*PERSONAL:* Born January 30, 1911, in Edinburgh, Scotland; son of Arthur Buchanan (a whiskey manufacturer who founded the first game reserve in Kenya, East Africa, and who was killed there by a rhinoceros while making a film with Martin Johnson in 1924) and Stella W. W. (Robertson) Sanderson; married Alma Viola Guillaume de Veil, February 18, 1934 (died, 1972); married Sabina Warren (an editor and writer under pseudonym, Marion L. Fawcett), May 4, 1972. *Education:* Attended Trinity College, Cambridge, 1930-32, and Cambridge University and University of London, 1933-34. *Home and office:* R.D. 1, Ivan Rd., Columbia, N.J. 07832. *Agent:* Paul R. Reynolds, Inc., 12 East 41st St., New York, N.Y. 10017.

*CAREER:* Began animal collecting on his own, 1924, and made a solo trip around the world, 1927-29, collecting for British Museum; leader of Percy Sladen Expedition to Cameroon, West Africa, on behalf of British Museum, Royal Society of London, and other institutions, 1932-33; did research at University of London, 1933-35; collected animals in the West Indies (where he also investigated human rabies carried by bats), 1936-37; led scientific expedition to Dutch Guiana, 1938; made an expedition to Jamaica, British Honduras, and Mexico, 1939-40, doing specialized collecting in Mexico for British Museum and Chicago Museum of Natural History; information and overseas press analyst for British Government in New York, 1945-47; took up residence in United States, 1947, and engaged in television and radio work, lecturing, and writing, 1947-58; retired from regular television programs but continued research and writing, 1958-60; senior trade editor and special science editor, Chilton Book Co., Philadelphia, Pa., 1961-65; free-lance writer and editor, 1965-67; science editor of *Argosy,* 1968-70. Former trustee and administrative director of Society for the Investigation of the Unexplained (non-profit scientific corporation), Columbia, N.J., which he organized in 1965. Did his first radio show for British Broadcasting Corp., 1930; began radio and television series in natural science field for National Broadcasting Co. and local stations, 1948; inaugurated first commercial color television program in history for Columbia Broadcasting System, 1950; featured (with live animals) in weekly spot on "Garry Moore Show," 1951-58. Importer of rare animals, 1950-58, exhibiting them at his private roadside zoo in New Jersey, at sports shows, and on television programs. *Military service:* British Naval Intelligence, 1940-45; became commander. *Member:* Royal Geographical Society (fellow), Zoological Society (London; fellow), Linnean Society (London; fellow). *Awards, honors:* M.A., Cambridge University, 1969.

*WRITINGS*—Many self-illustrated: *Animal Treasure* (Book-of-the-Month Club selection), Viking, 1937; *Caribbean Treasure,* Viking, 1939.

*Animals Nobody Knows* (juvenile), Viking, 1940; *Living Treasure,* Viking, 1941, reprinted, 1965; (under pseudonym Terence Roberts) *Mystery Schooner* (Junior Literary Guild selection), Viking, 1941; (editor) *Animal Tales* (anthology), Knopf, 1946.

*How to Know the North American Mammals,* Little, Brown, 1951; *The Silver Mink* (fiction), Little, Brown, 1952; *John and Juan in the Jungle* (juvenile fiction), Dodd, 1953; *Living Mammals of the World,* Hanover House, 1955; (under pseudonym Terence Roberts) *The Status Quo* (fiction), Merlin Press, 1956; *Follow the Whale,* Little, Brown, 1956; *The Monkey Kingdom: An Introduction to the Primates,* Hanover House, 1957.

*Abominable Snowmen: Legend Come to Life,* Chilton, 1961, abridged edition, Pyramid Publications, 1968; *The Continent We Live On,* Random House, 1961 (published in England as *The Natural Wonders of North America,* Hamish Hamilton, 1962), *The Dynasty of Abu,* Knopf, 1962; *Ivan Sanderson's Book of Great Jungles,* Messner, 1965; (with editors of *Country Beautiful*) *This Treasured Land,* Putnam, 1966, published as *The U.S.A.,* Rand McNally, 1971; *Uninvited Visitors: A Biologist Looks at UFO's,* Cowles, 1967; *Things,* Pyramid Publications, 1967; *More "Things,"* Pyramid Publications, 1969.

*Invisible Residents: A Disquisition upon Certain Matters Maritime, and the Possibility of Intelligent Life under the Waters of This Earth,* World Publishing, 1970; *Investigating the Unexplained: A Compendium of Disquieting Mysteries of the Natural World,* Prentice-Hall, 1972; Sabrina Sanderson, editor, *Green Silence: Travels through the Jungles of the Orient,* McKay, 1974.

Contributor to magazines, beginning in 1938, with articles to *Saturday Evening Post, Reader's Digest, American Heritage, Horizon, True, Sports Afield, Saga,* and other periodicals. Feature writer and special reporter for North American Newspaper Alliance.

*SIDELIGHTS:* Ivan Sanderson's bent for travel began as a small child when he accompanied his parents on trips to Europe, the Mediterranean, and the North Atlantic. On his last major trek, in 1959, he made a 60,000-mile trip around the North American Continent, examining its phytogeography and basic biotic ecology. Although he continued to import animals for a few years afterwards, his unique collection of wild animals was destroyed by fire in 1953, and a new collection, plus the zoo itself, by floods in 1955.†

(Died February 19, 1973)

\* \* \*

## SANDOZ, (George) Ellis (Jr.)   1931-

*PERSONAL:* Born February 10, 1931, in New Orleans, La.; son of George Ellis (a dentist) and Ruby (Odom) Sandoz; married Therese Alverne Hubley, May 31, 1957; children: George Ellis III, Lisa Claire Alverne, Erica Christine, Jonathan David. *Education:* Louisiana State University, B.A., 1951, M.A., 1953; graduate study at Georgetown University, 1952-53, and University of Heidelberg, 1956-58; University of Munich, Dr.oec.publ. (magna cum laude), 1965. *Politics:* Democrat. *Religion:* Baptist. *Office:* Department of Political Science, Louisiana State University, Baton Rouge, La. 70803.

*CAREER:* Louisiana Polytechnic Institute, Ruston, instructor, 1959-60, assistant professor, 1960-66, associate professor, 1966-67, professor of political science, 1967-68, director of Center for International Studies, 1966-68; East Texas State University, Commerce, professor of political science and head of department, 1968-78; Louisiana State University, Baton Rouge, professor of political science, 1978—. Member of council, Southwest Alliance for Latin America, 1966-68. Visiting summer scholar, Hoover Institution on War, Revolution, and Peace, 1970. Consultant, National Endowment for the Humanities fellowship program, 1977—. *Military service:* U.S. Marine Corps, 1953-56; became first lieutenant.

*MEMBER:* American Political Science Association (member of council, 1978-79), American Society for Political and Legal Philosophy, Conference for the Study of Political Thought, Southwestern Political Science Association (vice-president, 1972-73; president, 1974-75), Tau Kappa Alpha, Pi Sigma Alpha. *Awards, honors:* Fulbright scholar in Germany, 1964-65; National Endowment for the Humanities research grant, 1976-78.

*WRITINGS: Political Apocalypse: A Study of Dostoevsky's Grand Inquisitor,* Louisiana State University Press, 1971; (contributor) George J. Graham, Jr. and George W. Carey, editors, *The Post Behavioral Era: Perspectives on Political Science,* McKay, 1972; *Conceived in Liberty: American Individual Rights Today,* Duxbury, 1978; *The Philosophy of Eric Voegelin: An Interpretive Introduction,* Basic Books, in press. Contributor of about twenty articles to political affairs journals. Writer of weekly column, "Southerner Abroad," for *Shreveport Journal,* 1956-58; member of board of editors, *Political Science Reviewer,* 1970—, *Journal of Politics,* 1975—; member of editorial board, *Modern Age,* 1971—.

*WORK IN PROGRESS: Americanism: Political Theory and the American Civil Theology,* for Basic Books; editor, *Eric Voegelin's Thought: A Symposium.*

\* \* \*

### SANGER, Marjory Bartlett 1920-

*PERSONAL:* Born February 11, 1920, in Baltimore, Md.; daughter of J. Kemp, Jr. (a lawyer) and Katharine Kendall (Simons) Bartlett. *Education:* Wellesley College, B.A., 1942. *Address:* Box 957, Winter Park, Fla. 32790.

*CAREER:* Massachusetts Audubon Society, Boston, chairman of public relations and assistant editor of *Bulletin,* 1954-57, administrative assistant at nature camp in Barre, Vt., 1955-57. U.S. representative at International Council for Bird Preservation and International Ornithological Congress in England, 1966. Member of advisory board, Rollins College Annual Writers' Conference, 1968-77, and University of South Florida Writer's Conference, 1977-78. *Member:* International Council for Bird Preservation, American Ornithologists' Union, Wilson Ornithological Society, John Bartram Association, Florida Historical Society.

*WRITINGS: The Bird Watchers* (juvenile), Dutton, 1957; *Greenwood Summer* (juvenile), Dutton, 1958; *Mangrove Island,* World Publishing, 1963; *Cypress Country,* World Publishing, 1965; *World of the Great White Heron,* Devin-Adair, 1967; *Checkerback's Journey: The Migration of the Ruddy Turnstone* (juvenile), World Publishing, 1969; *Billy Bartram and His Green World* (juvenile), Farrar, Straus, 1972; *Escoffier,* Farrar, Straus, 1976. Contributor to *Audubon, Florida Magazine,* and *Florida Naturalist.*

*WORK IN PROGRESS:* A juvenile book about a forest; several cookbooks.

*BIOGRAPHICAL/CRITICAL SOURCES: New York Times Book Review,* December 24, 1967.

\* \* \*

### SARACEVIC, Tefko 1930-

*PERSONAL:* Surname is pronounced Sar-a-*che*-vich; born November 24, 1930, in Zagreb, Croatia; came to U.S., 1959; naturalized, 1964; son of Serif (an economist) and Demila (Hasanpasic) Saracevic; married Blanka Kobovac, December 13, 1958; children: Aida, Alan. *Education:* Croatian University, equivalent to B.S., 1957; Western Reserve University (now Case Western Reserve University), M.S., 1962; Case Western Reserve University, Ph.D., 1970. *Home:* 24105 Chardon Rd., Euclid, Ohio 44143. *Office:* School of Library Science, Case Western Reserve University, Cleveland, Ohio 44106.

*CAREER:* Case Western Reserve University, School of Library Science, Cleveland, Ohio, instructor, 1962-64, assistant professor, 1964-66, U.S. Office of Education fellow, 1966-70, associate professor, 1970-74, professor, 1974—. Visiting professor, Brazilian Institute for Bibliography and Documentation, Rio de Janeiro, 1971-77. *Member:* American Society for Information Science (councilor, 1971-74), American Croatian Academic Club (president, 1969-73). *Awards, honors:* Award for outstanding technical paper published in *Proceedings,* American Documentation Institute, 1966, for "The Measurability of Relevance."

*WRITINGS:* (Editor and compiler) *Introduction to Information Science,* Bowker, 1970.

Contributor of articles to *Information Storage and Retrieval, Journal of the American Society for Information Science, Library Journal, American Documentation, Journal of Documentation, Journal of Education for Librarianship,* and other professional journals. Regular contributor to *Proceedings* of American Society for Information Science and American Documentation Institute; author of various technical reports on information retrieval and library science. Member of advisory board, *Annual Review of Information Science and Technology.*

*WORK IN PROGRESS:* Research on the notion of relevance; research on question analysis in information retrieval systems.

\* \* \*

### SARGENT, Ralph M(illard) 1904-

*PERSONAL:* Born May 10, 1904, in Austin, Minn.; son of Charles James and Katherine (Fox) Sargent; married Louise A. Anderson, June 29, 1929; children: Lydia M. (Mrs. Hal G. Meyer), Hugh Alexander. *Education:* Carleton College, B.A., 1925; Yale University, Ph.D., 1931. *Politics:* Democrat. *Religion:* Society of Friends (Quaker). *Home:* 520 Panmure Rd., Haverford, Pa. 19041.

*CAREER:* High school teacher in Minnesota, 1925-26; Carleton College, Northfield, Minn., instructor, 1931-32, assistant professor of English, 1933-34; Knox College, Galesburg, Ill., professor of English, 1937-41; Haverford College, Haverford, Pa., associate professor, 1941-42, professor of English, 1942-47, Gummere Professor of English, 1947-71. Trustee, Highlands Biological Station. *Member:* Renaissance Society of America (member of national council, 1960-62), American Association of University Professors (member of national council, 1956-59), American Society of Plant Taxonomists, Literary Fellowship of Philadelphia (president, 1969-74), Philadelphia Botanical Club (president, 1967-73).

*WRITINGS: At the Court of Queen Elizabeth*, Oxford University Press, 1935; *Books of the Renaissance*, Haverford College, 1952; *Shakespeare's "As You Like It,"* Penguin, 1959; (editor) *Peter Kalm's Travels into North America*, Imprint Society, 1972; *Biology in the Blue Ridge*, Highlands Biological Foundation, 1977. Contributor to literature journals.

*WORK IN PROGRESS: Shakespeare the Artist.*

*SIDELIGHTS:* Ralph Sargent told *CA:* "Writing is a major way of communicating, creating, and preserving human experience. All writers hope to add significantly to this process." *Avocational interests:* Botany, photography, music.

\* \* \*

## SARKAR, (Anil) Kumar 1912-

*PERSONAL:* Born August 1, 1912, in Ranchi, India; son of Surendranath (an officer) and Sarojini (De) Sarkar; married Aruna Mitra (a lecturer in Bengali and English), November 21, 1941; children: Shreela (Mrs. Yogesh Goel), Sujoy. *Education:* St. Columba's College, Hazaribagh, B.A., 1933; Patna College, M.A., 1935; Patna University, Ph.D., 1946, D.Litt., 1960. *Religion:* Hindu. *Home:* 818 Webster St., Hayward, Calif. 94544. *Office:* Department of Philosophy, California State University, Hillary St., Hayward, Calif. 94542.

*CAREER:* Rajendra College, Chapra, India, professor of philosophy, 1940-44; University of Ceylon, Colombo and Peradeniya, senior lecturer, 1944-64; University of New Mexico, Albuquerque, visiting professor, 1964-65; California State University, Hayward, professor of philosophy, 1965—. Visiting professor of west-east philosophy and religion, California Institute of Asian Studies, 1968—. *Member:* Indian Philosophical Congress, American Philosophical Association. *Awards, honors:* Research fellowships from Indian Institute of Philosophy, Patna University.

*WRITINGS: An Outline of Whitehead's Philosophy*, Arthur H. Stockwell (London), 1940; *Moral Philosophy: A Study of Personality*, Kamala Book Stores (Patna), 1943; *Changing Phases of Buddhist Thought*, Bharati Bhawan (Patna), 1968, 2nd edition, 1973; *Whitehead's Four-Principles: From West-East Perspectives*, Bharati Bhawan, 1974. Contributor to several books on Indian and world philosophy, religion, and culture.

*WORK IN PROGRESS:* A text book on Indian philosophy, two volumes.

\* \* \*

## SARTI, Roland 1937-

*PERSONAL:* Born April 16, 1937, in Massa Carrara, Italy; son of Fulvio and Pia (Carli) Sarti; married Rose A. Alia, June 27, 1964; children: Claudia, Daniel. *Education:* College of the City of New York (now City College of the City University of New York), B.A., 1960; Rutgers University, M.A., 1962, Ph.D., 1967. *Politics:* Independent. *Religion:* Roman Catholic. *Home:* 20 Sheerman Lane, Amherst, Mass. 01002. *Office:* Department of History, University of Massachusetts, Amherst, Mass. 01002.

*CAREER:* Ohio State University, Columbus, instructor, 1965-67; University of Massachusetts—Amherst, assistant professor, 1967-72, associate professor of history, 1972—, director of summer school in Bologna, Italy, 1971. *Member:* American Historical Association, Society for Italian Historical Studies, Columbia University Seminar on Modern Italy. *Awards, honors:* Fulbright fellow, 1964-65.

*WRITINGS: Fascism and the Industrial Leadership in Italy: 1919-1940*, University of California Press, 1971; *The Ax Within: Italian Fascism in Action*, New Viewpoints, 1974.

*WORK IN PROGRESS:* Research on Italian peasantry in the twentieth century and on European emigration.

\* \* \*

## SAVAGE, William W(oodrow) 1914-

*PERSONAL:* Born January 9, 1914, in Onley, Va.; son of Frank Howard (a railroad telegrapher) and Florence (Twyford) Savage; married Margaret Jane Clarke; children: Earl R., William W., Jr. *Education:* College of William and Mary, A.B., 1937; University of Chicago, M.A., 1946, Ph.D., 1955. *Politics:* Independent. *Religion:* Methodist. *Home:* 6316 Eastshore Rd., Columbia, S.C. 29206. *Office:* College of Education, University of South Carolina, Columbia, S.C. 29208.

*CAREER:* Has worked as a newspaper reporter, columnist, and correspondent; Virginia Consultation Service, Richmond, counselor, 1939-42, acting director, 1942-45; Virginia State Department of Education, Richmond, assistant state supervisor of guidance and consultation services, 1946-47; Longwood College, Farmville, Va., dean, 1947-52; University of Chicago, Midwest Administration Center, Chicago, Ill., project coordinator, 1952-54, associate director, 1954-56; University of South Carolina, Columbia, professor of education, 1956—, dean of College of Education, 1956-65. Member of visitation and appraisal committee, National Council for Accreditation of Teacher Education, 1964-67. *Member:* American Association of School Administrators, American Association of University Professors.

*WRITINGS: Consultative Services to Local School Systems*, Midwest Administration Center, University of Chicago, 1959; (contributor) William H. Lucio, editor, *Readings in American Education*, Scott, Foresman, 1963; *Interpersonal and Group Relations in Educational Administration*, Scott, Foresman, 1968. Contributor of more than a hundred articles to education journals. Editor, *Work and Training*, Virginia State Board of Education, 1941-47; editor, *Administrator's Notebook*, 1954-56; member of advisory educational board, *School Review*, 1954-56; editor, *University of South Carolina Education Report*, 1957—; member of advisory editorial board, *High School Journal*, 1957-70.

*WORK IN PROGRESS: Major Public Documents in American Education* (tentative title); *America's State Boards of Education*, completion expected in 1979.

\* \* \*

## SAVARESE, Julia

*PERSONAL:* Last syllable of surname rhymes with "lease"; daughter of Frank (an engineer) and Rose (Volpe) Savarese. *Education:* Hunter College (now Hunter College of the City University of New York), B.A. (summa cum laude), 1950; New York Times School of Journalism, graduate study, 1950-52. *Politics:* Conservative. *Religion:* Roman Catholic. *Home and office:* 200 East End Ave., New York, N.Y. 10028. *Agent:* Robert P. Mills Ltd., 156 East 52nd St., New York, N.Y. 10022.

*CAREER: American Home*, New York City, executive editor, 1954-56; *Holiday*, New York City, assistant to publisher, 1956-59; *American Home*, assistant to editor, 1959-63; executive editor, *California Home*, 1963-66; *Holiday*, manager of special projects, 1966-68; *McCall's,* New York City, professional consultant, 1968-71, promotions writer, 1969—; *American Home,* director of promotion, 1972. Freelance writer of novels, plays, and poetry. *Member:* Authors League of America, Dramatists Guild, New Dramatists, Writers Wing of Actors Studio, Advertising Women of New York. *Awards, honors:* Albert Ralph Korn Poetry Award, 1959; Catholic Fiction Award, 1960; Ford Foundation grant for playwriting, 1963; Hallmark Television Award, 1968.

*WRITINGS: Dreaming Spires* (poetry), Dorrance, 1947; *The Weak and the Strong* (novel), Putnam, 1952; *How to Book the Boss* (nonfiction), Rennessance Press, 1967; *Final Proof* (novel), Norton, 1971.

Television scripts produced: "Houses," Omnibus, 1950; "The Outing," Columbia Broadcasting System, 1955; "Ring Around Rosey," National Broadcasting Co., 1964.

Plays: "Nest of Echoes," first produced in New York, N.Y., by New Dramatists, Inc., 1965. Also author of plays, "Rosie," "Child's Play," and "Season of Return," as yet unpublished and unproduced.

Author of regular column, "Side Lights," for *Ladies' Home Journal.* Contributor of short stories and poetry to *Discovery One, This Week, Paris Review,* and other publications.

*WORK IN PROGRESS:* Two novels, *It's a Long Way to L.A.* and *Joy to My Youth;* a play, "A Quiet House"; *Leafy Chirp,* a children's book; *For Those Who Tuned in Late,* a collection of poetry.

*BIOGRAPHICAL/CRITICAL SOURCES: Best Sellers,* May 15, 1971.†

\*      \*      \*

### SAWYERR, Harry (Alphonso Ebun)   1909-

*PERSONAL:* Born October 16, 1909, in Freetown, Sierra Leone; son of Obrien Alphonso Dandeson (a clergyman) and Cleopatra Florence (Omodele) Sawyerr; married Edith Kehinde Edwin, January 23, 1935; children: Ebun Florence Sawyerr Coleman. *Education:* Attended Fourah Bay College; University of Durham, B.A., 1933, M.A., 1936, M.Ed., 1940, M.B.E., 1954, C.B.E., 1963. *Home and office:* Codrington College, St. Johns, Barbados, West Indies.

*CAREER:* Anglican clergyman; University of Sierra Leone, Fourah Bay College, Freetown, Sierra Leone, tutor, 1933-41, 1943-45, lecturer, 1948-52, senior lecturer, 1952-62, professor of theology, 1962-74, chaplain, 1948-56, principal, 1968-74, acting vice-chancellor, 1968, pro vice-chancellor of university, 1968-70, vice-chancellor, 1970-72; Codrington College, St. Johns, Barbados, West Indies, tutor, 1974—, vice-principal, 1975—. Examining chaplain to Bishop of Sierra Leone, 1948—; Canon of St. George's Cathedral, Freetown, 1961—. Secretary of theological advisers board, Province of West Africa, 1952-58; member of Commission on Faith and Order, World Council of Churches, 1962-74; member of committee of directors, Theologia Africana (all-Africa conference of churches), 1972—. President of Milton Margai Teacher Training College, 1960-69; member of Public Service Commission of Sierra Leone, 1968-69; chairman of Sierra Leone Board of Education, 1969-74. John R. Mott lecturer at East Asia Christian Conference, Hong Kong, 1966. Member of faculty committee of arts and general studies, University of the West Indies, 1978. Consultant, Anglican Consultative Council, 1973, Caribbean Conference of Churches, Guyana, 1978.

*MEMBER:* Studiorum Novi Testamenti Societas. *Awards,*

*honors:* Member, Order of the British Empire, 1954, and Commander, 1963; first prize in Thomas Cochrane Essay Prize competition for West Africa, 1960, for "How Can the Church in Africa be Both African and Yet World-Wide"; Sierra Leone Independence Medal, 1961; D.D., University of Durham, 1970; Grand Commander, Order of the Star of Africa (Liberia), 1971.

*WRITINGS: Creative Evangelism,* Lutterworth, 1968; (with W. T. Harris) *The Springs of Mende Belief and Conduct,* Oxford University Press, 1968; (contributor) Kwesi A. Dickson and Paul Ellingworth, editors, *Biblical Revelation and African Beliefs,* Lutterworth, 1969; *God, Ancestor or Creator? Aspects of Traditional Belief in Ghana, Nigeria and Sierra Leone,* Longmans, Green, 1970; *A New Look at Christianity in Africa,* S.C.M. Press, 1972; *One Hundred Years of University Education in Sierra Leone 1876-1976,* [Freeport], 1976. Contributor to *Relevant Theology for Africa,* and *Religion in a Pluralist Society,* 1976. Also contributor of many articles to journals, including *International Review of Missions, Scottish Journal of Theology, Church Quarterly Review, Numen, Caribbean Journal of Religious Studies, Caribbean Journal of African Studies,* and others. General editor and author of "Aureol Pamphlets," 1960-74; editor, *Sierra Leone Bulletin of Religion,* 1962-68; member of editorial board, *Journal of African Religion,* 1966.

*WORK IN PROGRESS: Spirit and Witchcraft.*

*SIDELIGHTS:* Harry Sawyerr visited universities in the United States, 1963, and has attended educational and theological conferences in Canada, England, Belgium, Sweden, India, and a number of African countries. *Avocational interests:* Walking, gardening.

\*      \*      \*

### SCHACHTEL, Ernest G(eorge)   1903-1975

*PERSONAL:* Born June 26, 1903, in Berlin, Germany; naturalized U.S. citizen, 1944; son of Franz Jacob (a lawyer) and Flora (Isaacsohn) Schachtel; married Zeborah Suesholz (a psychologist), January 11, 1952. *Education:* University of Heidelberg, J.D., 1925. *Religion:* Jewish. *Home and office:* 315 West 106th St., New York, N.Y. 10025.

*CAREER:* Psychologist in private practice, beginning 1937. Research associate, International Institute of Social Research, Columbia University, 1935-38; lecturer, New School of Social Research, 1942-58; fellow and supervisory training analyst, William Alanson White Institute of Psychiatry, Psychoanalysis and Psychology, beginning 1946; adjunct professor, New York University, beginning 1961. Consultant to Harvard Law School, 1939-48. *Member:* American Psychological Association (fellow), American Association for the Advancement of Science (fellow), Society for Personality Assessment (fellow). *Awards, honors:* Washington School of Psychiatry fellow, 1945-55; Helen D. Sargent Memorial Prize for contributions to scientific understanding of psychotherapy, 1968.

*WRITINGS: Metamorphosis: On the Development of Affect, Perception, Attention and Memory,* text edition, Basic Books, 1959; *Experiential Foundations of Rorschach's Test,* Basic Books, 1966. Contributor of articles to scientific journals.†

(Died November 28, 1975)

\*      \*      \*

### SCHACHTER, Stanley   1922-

*PERSONAL:* Born April 15, 1922, in New York, N.Y.; son

of Nathan (an investor) and Anna (Fruchter) Schachter; married Marjorie Holbert, 1960; married Sophia Duckworth, June 2, 1967; children: Elijah. *Education:* Yale University, B.S., 1942, M.A., 1944; Massachusetts Institute of Technology, additional study, 1946-48; University of Michigan, Ph.D., 1950. *Home:* 175 Riverside Dr., New York, N.Y. 10024. *Office:* Department of Psychology, Columbia University, New York, N.Y. 10027.

*CAREER:* University of Minnesota, Minneapolis, assistant professor, 1949-52, associate professor, 1954-59, professor of psychology, 1959-61; Columbia University, New York, N.Y., professor of psychology, 1960—. Visiting professor, University of Amsterdam, 1952-53, and Stanford University, 1959-60. Research coordinator, Organization for Comparative Social Research, 1952-54. Consultant to General Electric Corp., National Institute of Mental Health, and to Social Science Research Council. *Military service:* U.S. Army Air Forces, 1944-46; became sergeant. *Member:* American Academy of Arts and Sciences, American Psychological Association, American Association for the Advancement of Science. *Awards, honors:* Fulbright fellow, 1952-53; Guggenheim fellow, 1967-68; prize from American Association for the Advancement of Science, for *The Psychology of Affiliation,* 1959; Distinguished Scientific Contribution Award, American Psychological Association, 1969; Cattell fellow, 1974-75.

*WRITINGS:* (With Festinger and Bock) *Social Pressures in Informal Groups,* Harper, 1950; (with Festinger and Rieckin) *When Prophecy Fails,* University of Minnesota Press, 1956; *The Psychology of Affiliation: Experimental Studies of the Sources of Gregariousness,* Stanford University Press, 1959; *Emotion, Obesity and Crime,* Academic Press, 1971; (with Judith Rodin) *Obese Humans and Rats,* Halsted, 1974. Editor, "Scripta Series in Psychology."

*WORK IN PROGRESS:* Research on eating behavior, obesity, and smoking.

*BIOGRAPHICAL/CRITICAL SOURCES: American Psychologist,* 1970.

\*     \*     \*

### SCHACHTMAN, Max 1903-1972

1903—November 4, 1972; American Trotskyite, lecturer, and radical leader and organizer. Obituaries: *New York Times,* November 5, 1972.

\*     \*     \*

### SCHAEFER, Charles E. 1933-

*PERSONAL:* Born November 15, 1933, in Bridgeport, Conn.; son of William J. (an engineer) and Loretta (Lawrence) Schaefer; married Anne Weldon (a teacher), December 16, 1967. *Education:* Fairfield University, B.B.A., 1955; Fordham University, Ph.D., 1967. *Politics:* Democrat. *Religion:* Roman Catholic. *Home:* 540 Scarsdale Rd., Crestwood, N.Y. 10707. *Office:* Children's Village, Dobbs Ferry, N.Y. 10522.

*CAREER:* Fordham University, Bronx, N.Y., Creativity Center (affiliated with psychology department), executive director, 1966-69; Children's Village, Dobbs Ferry, N.Y., clinical child psychologist, 1970—. *Military service:* U.S. Navy, 1956-60; became executive officer of a minesweeper. *Member:* American Psychological Association, American Educational Research Association. *Awards, honors:* Fairfield University Man-of-the-Year, 1971.

*WRITINGS:* (Editor with Kathleen Mellor) *Young Voices:*

*The Poetry of Children,* Macmillan, 1972; *Becoming Somebody: Creative Activities for Preschool Children,* DOK Publications, 1973; *Developing Creativity in Children,* DOK Publications, 1973; *Therapeutic Use of Child's Play,* Jason Aronson, 1976; *Therapies for Children,* Jossey-Bass, 1977; *How to Influence Children,* Van Nostrand, 1978.

*WORK IN PROGRESS:* A book for parents on how to deal with the everyday problems of children.

*SIDELIGHTS:* Charles Schaefer told *CA:* "I have always had a strong interest in poetry by children. *Young Voices* is an anthology of poems by elementary school children. Every year I conduct a poetry search for elementary school children in the New York metropolitan area."

\*     \*     \*

### SCHAEFER, Josephine O'Brien 1929-

*PERSONAL:* Born November 28, 1929, in New York, N.Y.; daughter of Michael (a truck driver) and Josephine (Rogers) O'Brien; married Louis Charles Schaefer, June 17, 1957 (divorced, August 4, 1971); children: Elizabeth, Laura Ruth. *Education:* Hunter College (now Hunter College of the City University of New York), B.A., 1952; Smith College, M.A., 1953; Stanford University, Ph.D., 1962. *Home:* 5260 Forbes Ave., Pittsburgh, Pa. 15217. *Office:* Department of English, University of Pittsburgh, Pittsburgh, Pa. 15260.

*CAREER:* University of Nebraska, Lincoln, instructor in English, 1953-55; Indiana University at Fort Wayne, lecturer in English literature, 1960-61; Western College, Oxford, Ohio, associate professor of modern English literature, 1961-65; Trinity College, Washington, D.C., associate professor of modern English literature, 1967-70; Western College, professor of modern English literature, 1970-74; University of Pittsburgh, Pittsburgh, Pa., professor of English, 1974—. *Member:* American Association of University Professors, Modern Language Association of America, Phi Beta Kappa. *Awards, honors:* Fulbright fellowships to England, 1959-60, and India, summers, 1965—; National Endowment for the Humanities grant, summer, 1966.

*WRITINGS: The Three-Fold Nature of Reality in the Novels of Virginia Woolf,* Mouton, 1965; (author of afterword with Louise Bogan) *A Writer's Diary,* New American Library, 1968; (contributor) Jacqueline E. M. Latham, editor, *Critics on Virginia Woolf,* Allen & Unwin, 1970; (contributor) Thomas A. Vogler, editor, *Twentieth-Century Interpretations of "To the Lighthouse,"* Prentice-Hall, 1970. Contributor of articles to *New Republic, Modern Fiction Studies, Virginia Woolf Quarterly,* and other periodicals.

*WORK IN PROGRESS:* A study of James Joyce's *Ulysses.*

\*     \*     \*

### SCHAFER, Stephen 1911-1976

*PERSONAL:* Born February 15, 1911, in Budapest, Hungary; came to United States in 1961, naturalized in 1967; son of Sigismund (an attorney) and Irene (Hahn) Schafer; married Lili Reisner (a library assistant), April 22, 1944; children: Andrew. *Education:* Eoetvoes Lorand University, D. Jurisprudence, 1933, Prof. Agregee, 1947. *Home:* 662 Washington St., Brighton, Mass. 02135. *Office:* Department of Criminal Justice, Northeastern University, Boston, Mass. 02115.

*CAREER:* Attorney in Budapest, Hungary, 1932-43; University of Budapest, Budapest, professor of criminal law,

1947-51; lecturer at Polytechnic, London, England, 1957-61; Florida State University, Tallahassee, assistant professor of criminology, 1961-65; Ohio University, Athens, associate professor of sociology, 1965-66; Northeastern University, Boston, Mass., professor of sociology and criminology, 1966-76. Visiting professor of sociology, Boston University, beginning 1967. President of Supervisory Board for Juvenile Delinquency, Budapest, 1946-51. Consultant, English Home Office Research Unit, 1957-61, President's National Crime Commission, 1967-68, and President's Violence Commission, beginning 1969; special consultant, First International Victimology Congress, 1972-73.

*MEMBER:* International Society of Criminology (Paris), International Association of Penal Law, American Society of Criminology (fellow), American Sociological Association, Society for the Study of Social Problems, Institute for the Scientific Treatment of Delinquency (London), Howard League for Penal Reform, Massachusetts Correctional Association (member of board of directors). *Awards, honors:* English Home Office grant, 1957-61; National Institute of Mental Health grants, 1962-64, 1969-70, and 1972-73.

*WRITINGS: Restitution to Victims of Crime,* Stevens, 1960, revised 2nd edition published as *Compensation and Restitution to Victims of Crime,* Patterson Smith, 1970; *The Victim and His Criminal: A Study in Functional Responsibility,* Random House, 1968, published as *Victimology: The Victim and His Criminal,* Reston, 1977; *Theories in Criminology: Past and Present Philosophies of the Crime Problem,* Random House, 1969; (with Richard D. Knudten) *Juvenile Delinquency: An Introduction,* Random House, 1970; *The Political Criminal: The Problem of Morality and Crime,* Free Press, 1974; *Introduction to Criminology,* Reston, 1976; (editor) *Readings in Contemporary Criminology,* Reston, 1976; (editor with Knudten) *Criminological Theory: Foundations and Perceptions,* Lexington Books, 1977. Contributor to professional journals in the United States, Hungary, Switzerland, and England.†

(Died July 29, 1976)

*       *       *

## SCHAFLANDER, Gerald M(aurice)   1920-

*PERSONAL:* Born January 4, 1920, in Detroit, Mich.; son of Samuel and Nell E. Schaflander; married Marjorie Polumbaum, August 14, 1942 (divorced April, 1967); married Victoria Alla (a registered nurse), December 23, 1967; children: (first marriage) Susy, Marley; (second marriage) Justin. *Education:* University of Michigan, B.A., 1942; Harvard University, M.A., 1966. *Politics:* Reform Democrat. *Religion:* Atheist.

*CAREER:* Advertising and marketing executive; professor of sociology. *Military service:* U.S. Army Air Forces, 1942-45; became second lieutenant.

*WRITINGS:* (With Henry Etzkowitz) *Ghetto Crisis,* Little, Brown, 1969; (with Seymour M. Lipset) *Passion and Politics,* Little, Brown, 1971; *Passion, Pot, and Politics,* Little, Brown, 1972; (with Senator Frank Moss) *Advertising on Trial,* Prentice-Hall, in press.

*WORK IN PROGRESS: What Happened to Yossarian?,* an autobiography; research on self-generating change.

*BIOGRAPHICAL/CRITICAL SOURCES: Social Problems,* spring, 1968.†

*       *       *

## SCHARFSTEIN, Zevi   1884-1972

1884—October 11, 1972; Hebrew educator and author of

textbooks for children. Obituaries: *New York Times,* October 12, 1972.

*       *       *

## SCHELLENBERG, James A.   1932-

*PERSONAL:* Born June 7, 1932, in Vinland, Kan.; son of Isaac F. (a farmer) and Tena (Franz) Schellenberg; married Christine Alberti, December 28, 1974; children: (previous marriage) Robert, Franklin. *Education:* Baker University, A.B., 1954; University of Kansas, M.A., 1955, Ph.D., 1959. *Home:* 87 Heritage Dr., Terre Haute, Ind. 47803. *Office:* Department of Sociology and Social Work, Indiana State University, Terre Haute, Ind. 47809.

*CAREER:* Western Michigan University, Kalamazoo, assistant professor, 1959-63, associate professor, 1963-67, professor of sociology, 1967-76; Indiana State University, Terre Haute, professor of sociology and chairman of department of sociology and social work, 1976—.

*WRITINGS: An Introduction to Social Psychology,* Random House, 1970; (editor with Richard R. MacDonald) *Selected Readings and Projects in Social Psychology,* Random House, 1971; *Masters of Social Psychology,* Oxford University Press, 1978.

*       *       *

## SCHENKER, Eric   1931-

*PERSONAL:* Born February 24, 1931, in Vienna, Austria; naturalized U.S. citizen; son of Adolf (an importer) and Olga (Strauss) Schenker; married Virginia Martha Wick, April 14, 1963; children: David, Richard, Robert. *Education:* City College (now City College of the City University of New York), B.B.A. (with honors), 1952; University of Tennessee, M.S., 1955; University of Florida, Ph.D., 1957. *Home:* 2254 West Dunwood Rd., Milwaukee, Wis. 53209. *Office:* School of Business Administration, University of Wisconsin, Milwaukee, Wis. 53201.

*CAREER:* Michigan State University, East Lansing, assistant professor of economics, 1957-59; University of Wisconsin—Milwaukee, assistant professor, 1959-62, associate professor, 1962-65, professor of economics, 1965—, associate dean, College of Letters and Science, 1963-69, associate director, Center for Great Lakes Studies, 1967-74, director, Urban Research Center, 1974-76, dean, School of Business Administration, 1976—. Transportation economist with U.S. Corps of Engineers, summers, 1956, 1957, Agency for International Development in Nigeria, summer, 1966, and U.S. Secretary of Transportation, 1971. Senior member, Milwaukee Board of Harbor Commissioners, 1960-72, chairman, 1963-66. *Military service:* U.S. Army, 1952-54.

*MEMBER:* American Economic Association, National Academy of Sciences (chairman of panel on future port requirements, 1973-76), Transportation Research Forum, Southern Economic Association. *Awards, honors:* Grants from Ford Foundation, 1962, 1963, Transportation Research Foundation, 1964, U.S. Department of Health, Education, and Welfare, 1967-68, National Science Foundation, 1968-70, 1970-72, U.S. Department of Commerce, 1968-77, and U.S. Department of Transportation, 1970-72.

*WRITINGS: The Port of Milwaukee: An Economic Review,* University of Wisconsin Press, 1967; (co-author) *Post Planning and Development as Related to Problems of United States Ports and the United States Coastal Environment,* Cornell Maritime, 1974; (co-author) *Port Develop-*

ment in the United States, National Academy of Science, 1976; (co-author) *The Great Lakes Transportation System*, University of Wisconsin Sea Grant College Program, 1976. Also author and co-author of over 13 monographs. Contributor of many articles to journals in his field.

*WORK IN PROGRESS: Maritime Labor Organizations on the Great Lakes—St. Lawrence Seaway System.*

\* \* \*

## SCHERMERHORN, Richard A(lonzo) 1903-

*PERSONAL:* Surname is pronounced *Sker*-mer-horn; born October 18, 1903, in Evanston, Ill.; son of William D. (a clergyman) and May (Hoffman) Schermerhorn; married Helen K. Karban (a librarian), 1926. *Education:* Dakota Wesleyan University, B.A., 1924; Garrett Biblical Institute (now Garrett Theological Seminary), B.D., 1926; Northwestern University, M.A., 1927; Harvard University, additional study, 1930-31; Yale University, Ph.D., 1931; German University of Prague, additional study, 1931-32. *Home:* 155 North Cambridge Ave., Claremont, Calif. 91711. *Office:* Department of Sociology, Case Western Reserve University, Cleveland, Ohio 44106.

*CAREER:* Professor of philosophy at Kansas Wesleyan College (now University), Salina, 1932-33, and Clark College, Atlanta, Ga., 1933-38; Yale University, New Haven, Conn., General Education Board fellow, 1938-39, honorary fellow, 1939-40; Baldwin-Wallace College, Berea, Ohio, assistant professor of sociology, 1940-47; Rhode Island State College (now University of Rhode Island), Kingston, associate professor of sociology, 1947-48; Case Western Reserve University, Cleveland, Ohio, associate professor, 1948-62, professor of sociology, 1962-72, professor emeritus, 1972—. Visiting professor at University of Lucknow, 1959-60, and Indian Institute of Technology, Kanpur, 1968-70; member of summer faculty at American University, 1957, Salzburg Seminar in American Studies, 1958, and Cornell University, 1965; Fulbright-Hays lecturer at La Trobe University, 1972.

*MEMBER:* American Sociological Association (fellow), Indian Sociological Society, Society for the Study of Social Problems (president, 1958-59), Association for Asian Studies, American Association of University Professors (chairman of Ohio Conference, 1952-53), Phi Kappa Phi. *Awards, honors:* Fulbright grants, 1959-60, 1972.

*WRITINGS: These Our People: Minorities in American Culture*, Heath, 1949; *Society and Power*, Random House, 1961; (compiler) *Psychiatric Index for Interdisciplinary Research: A Guide to the Literature, 1950-1961*, U.S. Government Printing Office, 1964; *Comparative Ethnic Relations: A Framework for Theory and Research*, Random House, 1969; *Communal Violence in India*, Consultative Committee of Indian Muslims, 1976.

Contributor: J. S. Roucek, editor, *Twentieth Century Political Thought*, Philosophical Library, 1946; Howard Becker and Reuben Hill, editors, *Family, Marriage and Parenthood*, 2nd edition, Heath, 1955; Arnold Rose, editor, *Mental Health and Mental Disorder: A Sociological Approach*, Norton, 1955; Howard Becker and Alvin Boskoff, editors, *Modern Sociological Theory in Continuity and Change*, Dryden, 1957. Contributor of more than twenty articles to journals in America and India.

*WORK IN PROGRESS:* A book tentatively entitled, *Ethnic Plurality in India.*

## SCHERTENLEIB, Charles 1905-1972

September 28, 1905—July 29, 1972; American specialist in managerial economics, public and business administration, and author of economic texts. Obituaries: *Washington Post*, August 2, 1972.

\* \* \*

## SCHIFF, Jacqui Lee 1934-

*PERSONAL:* Born January 4, 1934, in Everett, Wash.; daughter of Franklin Albert and Ethel (Forslund) Patterson; divorced, June, 1972; children: Charles, Thomas, Richard. *Education:* San Francisco State College (now University), A.B., 1961; Virginia Commonwealth University, M.S.S.W., 1964. *Religion:* Jewish. *Address:* P.O. Box 237, Alamo, Calif. 94507.

*CAREER:* Schiff Family (cooperative for disturbed patients who are recovering), Alamo, Calif., psychiatric social worker, 1966—; Cathexis Institute, Oakland, Calif., clinical director, 1971—. *Member:* International Transactional Analysis Association. *Awards, honors:* Award from American Psychological Association, 1970, for *All My Children*; Eric Berne Memorial Award, International Transactional Analysis Association, 1974, for research on passivity and discounting.

*WRITINGS:* (With Beth Day) *All My Children*, M. Evans, 1971; (editor) *Cathexis Reader*, Harper, 1975. Contributor of articles to professional journals.

*WORK IN PROGRESS:* A book on child development as it is related to mental disturbances; a book on schizophrenia.

\* \* \*

## SCHILLER, A. Arthur 1902-1977

*PERSONAL:* Born September 7, 1902, in San Francisco, Calif.; son of George Marcus (a public servant) and Bertha Schiller; married Irma Coblentz, August 22, 1926 (died, 1946); married Erna Kaske, January 23, 1947; children: (first marriage) Donald Coblentz, Jerome Paul. *Education:* University of California, Berkeley, A.B., 1924, M.A. and J.D., 1926; University of Munich, additional study, 1929; Columbia University, J.D., 1932. *Politics:* Democrat. *Home:* 145 East St., Oneonta, N.Y. 13820. *Office:* School of Law, Columbia University, New York, N.Y. 10027.

*CAREER:* Columbia University, New York, N.Y., lecturer, 1928-30, assistant professor, 1930-37, associate professor, 1937-49, professor of law, 1939-71, professor emeritus, 1971-77, director of African Law Center, 1965-71. Fulbright lecturer, University of Aberdeen, 1957. Visiting professor at University of Indonesia, 1949, University of Graz, 1949, University of Erlangen, 1949, and Free University of Berlin, 1953. Consultant to New York State Law Revision Commission, 1935, U.S. Treasury Department Tax Division, 1938-40, and Institute for Pacific Relations, 1945, 1950; legal expert, United Nations Commission on Eritrea, 1951, 1952; adviser, Institute for International Legal Studies, University of Istanbul, 1955.

*MEMBER:* Council on Foreign Relations, Societe International des Droits de l'Antiquite, African Law Association in America (founder and president, 1965-67), Ancient Civilization Group (New York; co-founder, 1930), American Association of Papyrologists, Accademia Nazionale dei Lincei (Italy; foreign member). *Awards, honors:* Social Science Research Council grant, University of Munich, 1929-30, University of Indonesia, 1949; Guggenheim fellow, Indonesia, 1949, Greece, Libya, and Italy, 1956, Italy, Switzerland,

and England, 1963; Dr. iuris honoris causa, University of Erlangen, 1950; Ford Foundation travel grants, Africa, 1959, 1963; Rockefeller Foundation fellow, Italy, Switzerland, and England, 1963.

*WRITINGS:* (Author of introduction) *Ten Coptic Legal Texts,* Metropolitan Museum of Art, 1932, reprinted, 1973; *Texts and Commentary for the Study of Roman Law,* Law School, Columbia University, 1936; *Military Law and Defense Legislation,* West Publishing, 1941, succeeding editions published as *Military Law,* 4th edition, 1968; (with Garrard Glenn) *The Army and the Law,* Columbia University Press, 1947; (with Edwin R. Keedy) *Cases in the Law of Agency,* Bobbs-Merrill, 1948; (translator with E. A. Hoebel) Barends ter Haar, *Adat Law in Indonesia,* Institute for Pacific Relations, 1948; (with W. L. Westermann) *Apokrimata: Decisions of Septimius Severus on Legal Matters,* Columbia University Press, 1954; *The Formation of Federal Indonesia: 1945-1949,* van Hoeve, 1955; *Syllabus on African Law,* Law School, Columbia University, 1967; *An American Experience in Roman Law: Writings from Publications in the United States,* Vandenhoeck & Ruprecht, 1971. Contributor of articles to American and foreign legal journals. Editor, *African Law Digest,* 1965-67; editor, *African Law Studies,* 1969.

*WORK IN PROGRESS: Sententiae at Epistolae Hadriani; The Compilations of Customary Law in Northern Ethiopia.*

*SIDELIGHTS:* A. Arthur Schiller traveled extensively, and had a reading knowledge of Latin, Greek, Egyptian (Coptic), French, German, Italian, Spanish, Dutch, and Tigrinya (for his Ethiopic legal studies). *Avocational interests:* Woodworking.†

(Died July 10, 1977)

\*      \*      \*

### SCHLEGEL, Dorothy B(adders)   1910-

*PERSONAL:* Born July 18, 1910, in Harford County, Md.; daughter of John Joseph (a farmer and salesman) and Lucy Alice (Davis) Badders; married Marvin W. Schlegel (a professor), April 9, 1941. *Education:* Dickinson College, B.A., 1932; College of William and Mary, M.A., 1948; University of North Carolina, Ph.D., 1954; University of Frankfurt, additional study, 1954-55; additional summer study at Columbia University, 1933, 1934, Middlebury College, 1936, Western Reserve University (now Case Western Reserve University), 1937, University of Virginia, 1947, 1948, University of Vienna, 1954, and Sorbonne, University of Paris, 1955. *Home:* 476 Linkhorn Dr., Virginia Beach, Va. 23451.

*CAREER:* Junior high school English teacher in York, Pa., 1932-34; high school Latin, French, and English teacher in York, Pa., 1934-47; College of William and Mary, Norfolk, Va., instructor in English, 1948; Longwood College, Farmville, Va., professor of English and comparative literature, 1953-66; Norfolk State College, Norfolk, Va., professor of English, 1966-76. Member of board of directors, Tidewater Fair Housing, 1967-69. *Member:* Modern Language Association of America, National Council of Teachers of English, College English Association, American Society for Eighteenth Century Studies, American Association of University Professors, American Civil Liberties Union, Virginia Association of Teachers of English, Cabell Society (president, 1969-72), Daughters of the American Revolution, Mayflower Society, Virginia Council on Human Relations, Phi Beta Kappa.

*WRITINGS: Shaftesbury and the French Deists,* Univer-

sity of North Carolina Press, 1956; *Writing for Research,* McCutchan, 1964; *James Branch Cabell: The Richmond Iconoclast,* Revisionist Press, 1975. Contributor to academic journals.

*WORK IN PROGRESS: The Engravings of Shaftesbury's "Characteristics";* alchemical, Rosicrucian, and Masonic symbolism in literature.

\*      \*      \*

### SCHLUMBERGER, Daniel   1904-1972

December 19, 1904—October 20, 1972; French archaeologist. Obituaries: *New York Times,* October 22, 1972; *L'Express,* October 30-November 5, 1972.

\*      \*      \*

### SCHMEIDLER, Gertrude Raffel   1912-

*PERSONAL:* Born July 15, 1912, in Long Branch, N.J.; daughter of Harry B. (an attorney) and Clare (Holzman) Raffel; married Robert Schmeidler, August 27, 1937; children: R. James, Richard, Emilie, Kathy. *Education:* Smith College, B.A., 1932; Clark University, M.A., 1933; Radcliffe College, Ph.D., 1935. *Home:* 17 Kent Ave., Hastings-on-Hudson, N.Y. 10706. *Office:* Department of Psychology, City College of the City University of New York, New York, N.Y. 10031.

*CAREER:* Monmouth College, Long Branch, N.J., instructor in psychology, 1937-39; Harvard University, Cambridge, Mass., research associate in psychology, 1941-45; City College of the City University of New York, New York, N.Y., 1945—, began as instructor, currently professor of psychology. Research officer, American Society for Psychical Research. *Member:* American Psychological Association (fellow), American Association for the Advancement of Science, Parapsychological Association (former president), American Society for Psychical Research (vice-president), Phi Beta Kappa, Sigma Xi. *Awards, honors:* McDougall Award from Parapsychology Laboratory, Duke University, 1964; honorary doctorate, El Instituto de Ciencias Parapsicologicas Hispano Americano, 1977.

*WRITINGS: ESP and Personality Patterns,* Yale University Press, 1958; *Extrasensory Perception,* Aldine-Atherton, 1969; *Parapsychology: Its Relation to Physics, Biology, Psychology, and Psychiatry,* Scarecrow, 1976. Contributor of over 150 technical articles to professional journals.

*WORK IN PROGRESS:* Research on how ESP success can be judged; research on whether there is survival of personality after bodily death.

*SIDELIGHTS:* Gertrude Raffel Schmeidler told *CA,* "There are so many fascinating problems in finding out about human potentiality, that there's never any end to doing research on them—and then writing up the results."

\*      \*      \*

### SCHMID, A. Allan   1935-

*PERSONAL:* Born March 12, 1935, in Dawson, Neb.; son of Alfred E. (a farmer) and Florence (Beutler) Schmid; married Alice Todd (a journalist), July, 1956; children: Elizabeth, John. *Education:* University of Nebraska, B.Sc., 1956; University of Wisconsin, M.Sc., 1957, Ph.D., 1959. *Home:* 217 Oakland Dr., East Lansing, Mich. 48823. *Office:* Department of Agricultural Economics, Michigan State University, East Lansing, Mich. 48824.

*CAREER:* Michigan State University, East Lansing, assistant professor, 1959-64, associate professor, 1964-68, professor of agricultural economics, 1968—. Budget analyst, Office of Secretary of the Army, Washington, D.C., 1968-69. Visiting scholar, Resources for the Future, Inc. Consultant to U.S. Department of Agriculture, U.S. Department of Interior, and National Water Commission. *Member:* American Economic Association, Association for Evolutionary Economics, Public Choice Society.

*WRITINGS: Converting Land from Rural to Urban Uses,* Johns Hopkins Press, 1968; *Property, Power, and Public Choice,* Praeger, 1978. Contributor of articles to agriculture, economics, and urban planning journals.

*WORK IN PROGRESS:* A book on community economics; research on government budget analysis.

*AVOCATIONAL INTERESTS:* Local politics, the dulcimer.

\* \* \*

## SCHMIDT, Albert J(ohn) 1925-

*PERSONAL:* Born August 27, 1925, in Louisville, Ky.; son of Christian Carl (a machinist) and Mary (Jann) Schmidt; married Kathryn Jung (a librarian), 1951; children: Christine Elise, Elizabeth Suzanne. *Education:* DePauw University, A.B., 1949; University of Pennsylvania, A.M., 1950, Ph.D., 1953; additional study, Indiana University, 1960-61, and Moscow University, 1962. *Politics:* Democratic party. *Religion:* Congregationalist. *Home:* 1446 Redding Rd., Fairfield, Conn. 06431. *Office:* Office of Vice-President of Academic Affairs, Wahlstrom Library, University of Bridgeport, Bridgeport, Conn. 06604.

*CAREER:* Coe College, Cedar Rapids, Iowa, assistant professor, 1953-56, associate professor, 1956-65, professor of history, 1965; University of Bridgeport, Bridgeport, Conn., Bernhard Professor of History, 1965—, chairman of department, 1965-72, dean, College of Arts and Sciences, 1972-76, vice-president of academic affairs, 1977—. Fellow of Folger Shakespeare Library, 1960; inter-cultural exchange participant to U.S.S.R., 1962. Member of board of directors, Church Housing for Fairfield, Inc.; member of board of directors of Greater Bridgeport Symphony.

*MEMBER:* American Historical Association (life member), Association of American Colleges, American Association for Higher Education, American Association of University Professors, American Association for Advancement of Slavic Studies, Society for Architectural Historians, National Slavic Honor Society, Conference on British Studies, New England Historical Association. *Awards, honors:* Fulbright scholarship, University of London, 1952-53; grants from American Council of Learned Societies, 1963, American Philosophical Society, 1963, 1965; Scholar of Year, University of Bridgeport, 1969.

*WRITINGS:* (Contributor) J. J. Murray, editor, *The Heritage of the Middle West,* University of Oklahoma Press, 1958; *The Yeoman in Tudor and Stuart England,* Cornell University Press, for Folger Shakespeare Library, 1961; (editor) Giles Fletcher, *Of the Rus Commonwealth,* Cornell University Press, for the Folger Shakespeare Library, 1966. Contributor of articles and reviews to numerous journals, including *Huntington Library Quarterly, Journal of Modern History, Slavic Review, Jahrbucher Geschichte Osteuropas, American Historical Review,* and *University of Bridgeport Quarterly,* and to *Yearbook* and *Proceedings,* of the American Philosophical Society.

*WORK IN PROGRESS: The Making of Classical Moscow; Planning and Architecture of Moscow, 1750-1850.*

\* \* \*

## SCHMITT, Gladys 1909-1972

May 30, 1909—October 3, 1971; American novelist. Obituaries: *New York Times,* October 4, 1972. (See index for *CA* sketch)

\* \* \*

## SCHNEIDER, Ben Ross, Jr. 1920-

*PERSONAL:* Born July 7, 1920, in Cincinnati, Ohio; son of Ben Ross (an engineer) and Jean (Taylor) Schneider; married Mackay McCord, May 21, 1949; children: Devon, Ben III, Nicholas, Mackay. *Education:* Williams College, B.A., 1942; Columbia University, M.A., 1947, Ph.D., 1955. *Religion:* Presbyterian. *Home:* 826 East Alton St., Appleton, Wis. 54911. *Office:* Department of English, Lawrence University, Appleton, Wis. 54911.

*CAREER:* University of Cincinnati, Cincinnati, Ohio, instructor in English, 1947-48; University of Colorado, Boulder, instructor in English, 1950-54; Oregon State College (now University), Corvallis, instructor in English, 1954-55; Lawrence University, Appleton, Wis., instructor, 1955-58, assistant professor, 1958-63, associate professor, 1963-69, professor of English, 1969—. *Military service:* U.S. Army, Signal Corps, 1943-46. *Member:* Modern Language Association of America, Society for Theatre Research, Association for Computing Machinery, Royal Society of Arts (fellow).

*WRITINGS: Wordsworth Portraits: A Biographical Catalogue,* Eagle Publications, 1950; *Wordsworth's Cambridge Education,* Cambridge University Press, 1957; (with H. K. Tjossem) *Themes and Research Papers,* Macmillan, 1961; *The Ethos of Restoration Comedy,* Illinois University Press, 1971; *Travels in Computerland,* Addison-Wesley, 1974; (contributor) *The London Stage, 1660-1800,* Southern Illinois University Press, 1978. Contributor to theater and computer journals.

*AVOCATIONAL INTERESTS:* Sailing, skiing.

\* \* \*

## SCHNEIDER, Delwin Byron 1926-

*PERSONAL:* Born May 14, 1926, in Oshkosh, Wis.; son of Julius Frederick (a lumber inspector) and Marie (Berg) Schneider; married Katherine Louise Gesch (a realtor), July 29, 1951; children: Kathi Del (Mrs. Martin Richardson), Mark William, Michael Byron, Lisa Nain. *Education:* Attended Concordia College, Milwaukee, Wis., 1941-46; Concordia Seminary, St. Louis, Mo., B.A., 1948, B.D., 1951; George Pepperdine College (now Pepperdine University), M.A., 1950; Rikkyo University, Ph.D., 1971. *Home:* 8263 Camino del Oro, La Jolla, Calif. 92037. *Office:* University of San Diego, San Diego, Calif. 92110.

*CAREER:* Gustavus Adolphus College, St. Peter, Minn., assistant professor, 1966-69, associate professor of Asian religions, 1969-70; University of San Diego, San Diego, Calif., professor of Asian religions, 1970—. Visiting scholar, Harvard University, 1961-62; director, East Asia Studies Institute; coordinator, Ecumenical Center for World Religions. *Member:* Association for Asian Studies, Japan Society, International House of Japan, American Academy of Religion, Harvard Club, San Diego Yacht Club.

*WRITINGS: Konkokyo: A Japanese Religion,* Tokyo International Institute for the Study of Religion, 1962; *No God but God,* Augsburg, 1969; *Religious Systems and Psychotherapy,* C. C Thomas, 1973.

*WORK IN PROGRESS:* Translating Konkokyo scriptures.

*SIDELIGHTS:* Delwin Schneider travels to Asia each year to teach American students; he spent a summer in a Zen temple in Yokohama.

\*          \*          \*

## SCHONFELD, William R(ost) 1942-

*PERSONAL:* Born August 28, 1942, in New York, N.Y.; son of William A. (a psychiatrist) and Louise (Rost) Schonfeld; married Elena Beortegui, January 23, 1964; children: Natalie Beortegui, Elizabeth-Lynn Beortegui. *Education:* Attended Cornell University, 1960-61; New York University, B.A. (cum laude), 1964; Universite de Bordeaux, additional study, 1964-65; Princeton University, M.A., 1968, Ph.D., 1970. *Home:* 17981 Mann St., Irvine, Calif. 92715. *Office:* School of Social Sciences, University of California, Irvine, Calif. 92715.

*CAREER:* Princeton University, Center of International Studies, Princeton, N.J., assistant in research, 1966-69, research associate, 1969-70; University of California, Irvine, assistant professor, 1970-75, associate professor of political science, 1975—, director of graduate studies, School of Social Sciences, 1970-73. Visiting assistant professor at University of California, Berkeley, summer, 1972. Senior lecturer, Fondation Nationale des Sciences Politiques, Paris, France, 1973-74. Fulbright senior lecturer in France, 1973-74. *Member:* American Political Science Association, American Association of University Professors, Phi Beta Kappa, Pi Sigma Alpha. *Awards, honors:* Fulbright fellow in France, 1964-65; Danforth fellow, 1964-69.

*WRITINGS: Youth and Authority in France: A Study of Secondary Schools,* Sage Publications, Inc., 1971; *Obedience and Revolt: French Behavior toward Authority,* Sage Publications, Inc., 1976. Contributor of articles to *World Politics, Review of Politics, Political Studies, Revue Francaise de Science Politique.*

*WORK IN PROGRESS: Behind Closed Doors: The Organizational Life of Gaullist and Socialist Elites.*

\*          \*          \*

## SCHRADER, Paul Joseph 1946-

*PERSONAL:* Born July 22, 1946, in Grand Rapids, Mich.; son of Charles A. (an executive) and Joan (Fisher) Schrader. *Education:* Calvin College, B.A., 1968; University of California, Los Angeles, M.A., 1970. *Agent:* Jeff Berg, International Creative Management, 9255 Sunset Blvd., Los Angeles, Calif. 90069. *Office: Cinema,* 9667 Wilshire Blvd., Beverly Hills, Calif. 90212.

*CAREER: Free Press,* Los Angeles, Calif., film critic, 1968-69; *Coast,* Beverly Hills, Calif., film critic, 1970; *Cinema,* Beverly Hills, Calif., editor, 1970—; author of screenplays; director. *Member:* Writers Guild of America, West. *Awards, honors: Atlantic* writing contest, first place essay, 1968; *Story: The Magazine of Discovery* writing contest, first place essay, 1968.

*WRITINGS: Transcendental Style in Film,* University of California Press, 1972.

Screenplays: (With brother, Leonard Schrader) "The Yakuza," Warner Bros., 1972; (with Brian DePalma) "Obsession," Columbia, 1975; "Taxi Driver," Columbia, 1976;

(with L. Schrader) "Blue Collar," directed by P. Schrader, Universal, 1977; "Rolling Thunder," American International Pictures, 1977; "Hard Core," Columbia, in production; (with L. Schrader) "Old Boyfriends," Edward Pressman Productions, in production; "American Gigolo," directed by P. Schrader, Paramount, in production. Contributor to *Film Quarterly, Film Comment,* and *Academy Leader.*

*SIDELIGHTS:* Paul Schrader was born and raised within the strict Calvinist Christian Reform Church in Grand Rapids, Michigan. While in his teens, he seriously considered becoming a minister in the church. As a result of his religion's severe rules which forbids attending movies, Schrader did not see his first movie until he was seventeen. It was at this time that he realized the ministry was not for him and resolved that film making was his life's ambition. Several years later, shortly after his graduation from the University of California film school, Schrader, at the age of twenty-seven, sold his first screenplay for $300,000.

It seems odd to many people that a person with such a strict upbringing and strong religious foundation would write the types of screenplays that Schrader has and achieve the early success that he's gained. Within the film industry, Schrader has a reputation of being unpredictable, arrogant, and outrageous at times. According to Terry Curtis Fox of the *Village Voice,* "'Blue Collar' is the single most overtly political movie made for a major Hollywood studio since Abe Polonsky's 'Tell Them Willie Boy Was Here' a decade ago.... The entire film is constructed to propound the notion that race is used in place of class to keep workers on the line. That Schrader, intellectual and theologian manque, should make a schematic movie is not surprising. That the man who wrote 'Taxi Driver,' a textbook example of existential plotting, where not a single action has an exterior motivation, should make a movie ['Blue Collar'] in which every moment is motivated, in which every action of every character can be explained by a specific emotional moment that is also an economic and social fact is, well, astonishing. It is also astonishing that the man whose grand ambition has always been to film the life of Saint Paul—the man who saw the light and codified the church, the conservative figure who made possible the kind of strict, moralistic Christianity against which Schrader rebelled—should make a Marxist tract." In answer to Fox's astonishment Schrader explained: "I don't think it's profitable to pigeonhole people that tightly. It's like saying to an actor, 'You can't play both a fascist and a revolutionary.' Because he'll say, 'Why not? Both the fascist and the revolutionary are inside me.' I could as easily write the story of Rommell and Che Guevara."

Schrader knows just how violent his films have been and he is slowly moving away from some of the violence that weaves through his films. Schrader feels he's "been going through so many changes in the past few years that I'm strobing. I've written four screenplays in which four people get killed—one of the deaths is off-screen. In the past, I'd have killed off four people in the first minute. And even though I prefer writing to directing—it's a more pleasant activity, working on 'Blue Collar' was really rough—I didn't write anything last year and I probably won't have time to write anything this year either." Terry Curtis Fox feels "as his life changes, so does his image. Schrader the violent is turning into Schrader the deal-maker, the businessman. He is appearing more levelheaded. Which, at the moment, is a very good way for him to appear."

"Blue Collar" was the first movie Schrader directed. He had waited for several years to direct his first film, and after the film was completed Schrader remarked: "It's scary. You suddenly realize you are what you want to be. You have to start living in the present, not the future. You have to stop postponing pleasure."

Probably Schrader's most controversial film up until now has been "Taxi Driver." While many critics feel that there was too much violence and sordidness, another group of critics feel that this film shows the reality of New York City and the people who travel its streets at night. In his review of "Taxi Driver," Howard Kissle writes that the movie "is conceived in rich, complex images. Paul Schrader's sensitive screenplay has been directed with great sympathy and power.... An episodic story like this could seem attenuated, but from the moment the film begins, with a Checker cab emerging from one of those clouds of steam that rise ominously from Manhattan streets—a behemoth prowling some godforsaken primitive terrain—the film moves with admirable assurance through its tricky, highly charged psychological milieux." David Sterritt, reviewing for the *Christian Science Monitor*, feels that "certain key shots—last 10 seconds or so, in some cases—tell more about Travis' [the cab driver] perceptions than most movies can convey in whole scenes. 'Taxi Driver' is one of those rare films that use visual discoveries of the adventurous 'experimental' cinema in narrating a full-fledged story. For its blend of rapid-fire story-telling and artful visual insight, 'Taxi Driver' deserves its own niche in recent film history."

On the other hand, Andrew Sarris of *Village Voice* did not feel the movie was quite as powerful. "... There is much to like in 'Taxi Driver' if one doesn't mind the disorder in the narrative. I didn't mind the sordidness, the violence, or the mock-ironic ending. What I did mind about the film was its life-denying spirit, its complete lack of curiosity about the possibilities of people...." Dave Pomeroy writes that Schrader's script lacks direction. "The realism of 'Taxi Driver' is infectious. New York at night is perfectly realized, and the life of the lonely cabbie (who is seen as a nonperson by his fares). The problem is that so much is left unsaid that confusion is the only ultimate result. We know nothing about Travis' background and motivation except too-subtle hints.... What could have been a truly significant film falters under the sight of its vagueness and unrealized ambitions. Moreover, those few moments of blood-letting at the film's end are as violent as anything put on the screen...." Agreeing, Michael Dempsey writes: "If 'Taxi Driver' had unleashed its firestorm, say halfway through its running time and then had gone on to show Travis dealing with the changes in his life brought on by this catharsis and the resulting fame, it might have become an analysis of contemporary confusion rather than an example of it. In any sense of the term, it fails to transcend because its makers are caught in too many contradictions."

*BIOGRAPHICAL/CRITICAL SOURCES: Film Comment*, July, 1973, March, 1976; *Women's Wear Daily*, February 9, 1976; *Village Voice*, February 16, 1976, February 27, 1978; *Christian Science Monitor*, February 19, 1976; *Film Information*, March, 1976; *Film Quarterly*, summer, 1976; *Newsweek*, February 13, 1978; *Variety*, May 17, 1978.

\* \* \*

## SCHULDER, Diane Blossom 1937-

*PERSONAL:* Born December 11, 1937, in New York, N.Y.; daughter of Jacob J. (an attorney) and Hilda (Beim) Schulder; married Robert Abrams (Bronx Borough president), 1974; children: Rachel. *Education:* Columbia Univer-

sity, B.S., 1961, J.D., 1964. *Office:* 350 Fifth Ave., New York, N.Y. 10001.

*CAREER:* Attorney at law; admitted to Bar of the State of New York, 1965. Ms. Schulder originated a course on women and the law, and has taught that course at University of Pennsylvania and New York University. Conducted workshop on divorce at Ackerman Institute for Family Therapy. *Member:* American Academy of Matrimonial Lawyers.

*WRITINGS:* (Contributor) Robin Morgan, editor, *Sisterhood is Powerful*, Random House, 1970; (with Florynce Kennedy) *Abortion Rap*, McGraw, 1971; (contributor) Robert Lefcourt, editor, *Law against the People*, Random House, 1972. Contributor of book reviews to *New Republic, Fortune Society Newsletter;* contributor of articles to *Village Voice, Women's American ORT Reporter*, and *Atlantic Monthly*.

*BIOGRAPHICAL/CRITICAL SOURCES: New York Times*, February 4, 1970; *Newsweek*, July 13, 1970; *New Republic*, May 8, 1971; *Ms.*, April, 1974.

\* \* \*

## SCHULTZE, William Andrew 1937-

*PERSONAL:* Born February 13, 1937, in Washington, Mo.; son of Andrew Byron (a professor) and Eugenia (Homsley) Schultze; married Sharon Petersen, April 10, 1959; children: Blair, David, Carol. *Education:* Nebraska Wesleyan University, B.A. (with honors), 1959; Rutgers University, M.A., 1964, Ph.D., 1967. *Home:* 3816 Aragon Dr., San Diego, Calif. 92115. *Office:* Department of Political Science, San Diego State University, San Diego, Calif. 92115.

*CAREER:* Insurance inspector for retail credit company in Lincoln, Neb., 1959-60; New Brunswick-Raritan Valley Chamber of Commerce, New Brunswick, N.J., director of research in local government, 1961-63; Rutgers University, New Brunswick, instructor in political science, 1963-64; Valparaiso University, Valparaiso, Ind., instructor in political science and director of Community Research Center, 1964-66; Kansas State University, Manhattan, assistant professor of political science, 1966-68; San Diego State University, San Diego, Calif., assistant professor, 1968-69, associate professor, 1970-74, professor of political science, 1974—. *Military service:* Nebraska National Guard, 1954-61; became sergeant first class. *Member:* American Political Science Association, American Academy of Political and Social Sciences, Phi Kappa Phi. *Awards, honors:* U.S. Office of Education research grant, 1967-68; Outstanding Young Men of America, 1972; Fulbright grant, University of Nice, 1976.

*WRITINGS:* (Editor with Ronald C. Moe, and contributor) *American Government and Politics: A Reader*, C. E. Merrill, 1971; (contributor) *Undertaking Community Development*, Institute of Public Affairs, University of Iowa, 1971; (contributor) James A. Riedel, editor, *New Perspectives in State and Local Politics*, Xerox Education Division, Xerox Corp., 1971; *Urban and Community Politics*, Duxbury Press, 1974. Contributor to *Law in American Society* and other political science journals. Associate editor, *Western Political Quarterly*, 1977—.

*WORK IN PROGRESS: The New Politics of Food and Agriculture*.

\* \* \*

## SCHURMAN, D(onald) M. 1924-

*PERSONAL:* Born September 2, 1924, in Sydney, Nova

Scotia, Canada; son of Bertrand Lloyd (a civil servant) and Mabel P. (MacKenzie) Schurman; married Janice M. Reynolds, June 18, 1947 (died, 1973); married Olive T. Higdon, July 6, 1974; children: (first marriage) Michael, Bruce, Angus, David, Julian, Marianne. *Education:* Acadia University, B.A., 1949, M.A., 1950; Cambridge University, M.A., 1952, Ph.D., 1955. *Religion:* Anglican. *Home:* 58 William St., Kingston, Ontario, Canada K7L 2C4. *Office:* Department of History, Queen's University, Kingston, Ontario, Canada.

*CAREER:* Queen's University, Kingston, Ontario, professor of history, 1967—. *Military service:* Royal Canadian Air Force, flying officer, 1945. *Member:* Navy Records Society, Society for Nautical Research, Cambridge Historical Society.

*WRITINGS: The Education of a Navy,* University of Chicago Press, 1965; (contributor) A.M.J. Hyatt, editor, *From the Dreadnought to Polaris,* Copp, 1973; (contributor) *Perspectives of Empire,* Longman, 1973; (contributor) Gerald Tulchinsky, editor, *To Preserve and Defend,* McGill-Queen's University Press, 1976; (contributor with Barry Hunt) Gerald Jordan, editor, *Warfare in the Twentieth Century,* Croom Helm, 1977. Contributor of articles to periodicals.

*WORK IN PROGRESS: Letters of Benjamin Disraeli,* with J. P. Matthews and J. A. W. Gunn.

\*    \*    \*

## SCHUSTER, George    1873-1972

February 4, 1873—July 4, 1972; American winner of the historic round-the-world auto race in 1908 and author of a book recounting its highlights. Obituaries: *New York Times,* July 5, 1972; *Newsweek,* July 17, 1972; *Time,* July 17, 1972; *L'Express,* July 17-23, 1972.

\*    \*    \*

## SCHWARTZ, David C.    1939-

*PERSONAL:* Born February 27, 1939, in New York, N.Y.; son of Milton (a sales manager) and Ethel (Flack) Schwartz; married Sandra Kenyon (a political scientist), October 25, 1970; children: Todd Jeffrey, Meredith Anne. *Education:* Brooklyn College of the City University of New York, B.A., 1960, M.A., 1962; Massachusetts Institute of Technology, Ph.D., 1965. *Religion:* Jewish. *Home:* 112 North Seventh Ave., Highland Park, N.J. 08903. *Office:* Department of Political Science, Rutgers University, New Brunswick, N.J. 08904.

*CAREER:* University of Pennsylvania, Philadelphia, assistant professor of political science, 1965-71; Rutgers University, New Brunswick, N.J., associate professor, 1971-75, professor of political science, 1975—. *Member:* American Political Science Association.

*WRITINGS:* (Contributor) Walter Izard, editor, *Vietnam: Issues and Alternatives,* Schenkman, 1969; (contributor) James C. Davies, editor, *When Men Revolt and Why,* Free Press, 1971; (contributor) Charles F. Herman, editor, *International Crises,* Free Press, 1972; (contributor) Ted R. Gurr and others, editors, *Readings in Political Violence,* Prentice-Hall, 1972; (contributor) Gurr, I. Feierabend, and R. Feierabend, editors, *Anger, Violence and Politics,* Prentice-Hall, 1972; *Political Alienation and Political Behavior,* Aldine, 1973; (author, and editor with Sandra Kenyon Schwartz) *New Directions in the Study of Political Socialization,* Free Press, 1975; (contributor) A. Somit, edi-

tor, *Biology and Politics,* Mouton, 1976. Also author of professional papers. Contributor to *Orbis, Western Political Quarterly, American Behavioral Scientist,* and other periodicals.

*WORK IN PROGRESS: Political Man Is Man Himself.*

*SIDELIGHTS:* David C. Schwartz is "principally concerned with broadening and deepening our understanding of human political phenomena. I think that music, drama, dance, humor, rumor, biology, life events (like marriage, parenthood, divorce)—all are basic to people's political behavior."

\*    \*    \*

## SCHWARTZ, Emanual K.    1912-1973

*PERSONAL:* Born June 11, 1912, in New York, N.Y.; son of Harry (a tailor) and Sarah (Fried) Schwartz; married Reta Shacknove (an artist), February 3, 1943. *Education:* City University of New York, B.S.S., 1932, M.S., 1933; New York University, Ph.D., 1937; New School for Social Research, D.S.Sc., 1948. *Politics:* Democrat. *Religion:* Jewish. *Home:* 12 East 87th St., New York, N.Y. 10028. *Office:* 124 East 28th St., New York, N.Y. 10016.

*CAREER:* Private practice of psychoanalysis in New York City, 1939-73; Post Graduate Center for Mental Health, New York City, assistant dean, 1948-60, associate dean, 1960-63, dean and director of training, 1963-73. Diplomate in clinical psychology from American Board of Professional Psychology; diplomate in clinical hypnosis from American Board of Examiners in Psychological Hypnosis. Adjunct professor of psychology, New York University, 1960-73; clinical professor of psychology, Adelphi University, Garden City, New York, 1960-73. Member of advisory council for psychology, New York State Department of Education, 1957-73; consultant to Veterans Administration, 1960-73. *Military service:* U.S. Army, 1943-46; served in European theatre and North Africa; became first lieutenant.

*MEMBER:* American Psychological Association (fellow), American Association of Group Psychotherapy, American Orthopsychiatric Association, Society for the Psychological Study of Social Issues, Society for Projective Techniques, Psychotherapy Society (president of Eastern group, 1963-64), American Academy of Psychotherapists, Mexican Psychoanalytic Association, New York Psychological Association (chairman of clinical division), New York Society of Clinical Psychologists (president, 1953), Phi Beta Kappa.

*WRITINGS:* (With Alexander Wolf) *Psychoanalysis in Groups,* Grune & Stratton, 1962; (with Wolf) *Beyond the Couch,* Science House, 1970; (with Lewis R. Wolberg) *Group Therapy: An Overview,* Intercontinental Medical Book Co., 1973. Also author of a column, "Facts, Fancies, and Reflections," which appeared in *Human Context* (London).

*WORK IN PROGRESS: Group Psychotherapy; Psychoanalysis and War; The Leader in the Group; Filicide or the Slaughter of Children.*†

(Died January 22, 1973)

\*    \*    \*

## SCHWARZ, Boris    1906-

*PERSONAL:* Born March 13, 1906, in St. Petersburg, Russia; son of Joseph (a pianist) and Rose (Kaplan) Schwarz; married Patricia Yodido, June 15, 1941; children: Joseph J., K. Robert. *Education:* Attended Sorbonne, University of Paris, 1925-26; University of Berlin, cand.phil., 1935; Columbia University, Ph.D., 1950. *Home:* 50-16 Robinson St., Flushing, N.Y. 11355. *Agent:* Georges Borchardt, Inc., 145 East 52nd St., New York, N.Y. 10022.

*CAREER:* Violinist, conductor, and musicologist. Arthur Jordan Conservatory, Indianapolis, Ind., artist-teacher, 1937-38; Settlement Music School, Philadelphia, Pa., member of faculty, 1938-41; Queens College of the City University of New York, Flushing, N.Y., instructor, 1941-47, assistant professor, 1947-57, associate professor, 1957-58, professor of music, 1958-76, chairman of department, 1949-52, 1953-56, founder-conductor, Queens College Orchestral Society, 1946-76; consultant to Columbia Masterworks, 1974—. Concertmaster, Indianapolis Symphony, 1937-38; first violinist, NBC-Toscanini Symphony, 1938-39; member of New Friends Music Quartet, 1950-51. *Member:* American Musicological Society, International Musicological Society, Gesellschaft fuer Musikforschung. *Awards, honors:* Ford Foundation award, 1952; Guggenheim fellow, 1959-60; American Council of Learned Societies cultural exchange fellow, Academy of Science, Moscow, 1962.

*WRITINGS:* (Contributor) Paul H. Lang, editor, *Igor Stravinsky: A New Appraisal,* Norton, 1963; (contributor) Lang, editor, *Contemporary Music in Europe,* Norton, 1965; (contributor) Paul L. Horecki, editor, *Russia and the Soviet Union* (a bibliographical guide), University of Chicago Press, 1965; (editor and translator) Carl Flesch, *Violin Fingering,* Barrie & Rockliff, 1966; *Music and Musical Life in Soviet Union: 1917-1970,* Norton, 1972; *French Instrumental Music between the Revolutions (1789-1830),* Da-Capo, 1978. Contributor to *The New Grove Dictionary of Music and Musicians,* to *Die Musik in Geschichte und Gegenwart,* and to music journals and *Saturday Review.*

*WORK IN PROGRESS:* *The Great Violinists,* for Simon & Schuster; *Two Hundred Years of Russian Music,* for Prentice-Hall.

\* \* \*

## SCHWARZ, Henry G(uenter) 1928-

*PERSONAL:* Born December 14, 1928, in Berlin, Germany; son of Eugene Alfred (a teacher) and Gertrud (Vogel) Schwarz; married Tracy Elizabeth Hogan, June 6, 1970; children: Kenji Eugene. *Education:* University of Wisconsin, B.A., 1954, M.A., 1958, Ph.D., 1963. *Home:* 416 15th St., Bellingham, Wash. 98225. *Office:* Program in East Asian Studies, Western Washington University, Bellingham, Wash. 98225.

*CAREER:* University of the Philippines, Fulbright professorship, 1964-65; University of Washington, Seattle, assistant professor, 1965-69; Western Washington University, Bellingham, professor of history and political science, 1969—, director of Program in East Asian Studies, 1971—. Member of Seattle Committee on Foreign Relations, 1967—. *Military service:* U.S. Army, 1954-56. *Member:* Association for Asian Studies, American Historical Association, Asia Society, China Society, Center of Japanese Political and Social Studies, Mongolia Society, American Association of University Professors, Asian Studies on the Pacific Coast. *Awards, honors:* Inter-University fellowship for field training in Chinese, 1961-62.

*WRITINGS: Leadership Patterns in China's Frontier Regions,* U.S. Department of State, 1964; *China: Three Facets of a Giant,* Manaktalas (Bombay), 1966; *Liu Shao-ch'i and "People's War,"* University of Kansas, 1969; (contributor) Joseph Kitagawa, editor, *Understanding Modern China,*

Quadrangle, 1969; *Chinese Policies towards Minorities,* Western Washington State College, 1971; *Mongolian Short Stories,* Western Washington University, 1975. Contributor of articles to *China Quarterly, Orbis, Journal of Politics, Military Review, World Politics,* and other scholarly journals.

*WORK IN PROGRESS: Bibliotheca Mongolica;* research on the minorities of China.

\* \* \*

## SCHWARZWELLER, Harry K(arl) 1929-

*PERSONAL:* Born October 27, 1929, in Brooklyn, N.Y.; son of Karl (a machinist) and Bertha (Frey) Schwarzweller; married Elizabeth Purdy, August 2, 1958; children: Paul, Thomas, Erica. *Education:* Cornell University, B.S., 1951, M.S., 1955, Ph.D., 1958. *Residence:* Okemos, Mich. *Office:* Department of Sociology, Michigan State University, East Lansing, Mich. 48824.

*CAREER:* University of Kentucky, Lexington, assistant professor of sociology, 1958-68; West Virginia University, Morgantown, Benedum Professor of Sociology, 1968-72; Michigan State University, East Lansing, professor of sociology, 1972—. *Military service:* U.S. Marine Corps, 1952-54. *Member:* American Sociological Association, European Rural Sociological Society, Rural Sociological Society (president, 1977-78). *Awards, honors:* Fulbright fellow, Canterbury Agricultural College, New Zealand, 1955-56; Fulbright fellow, Germany, 1966-67.

*WRITINGS:* (Editor with John Photiodis) *Change in Rural Appalachia,* University of Pennsylvania Press, 1970; (senior author, with James S. Brown and Joseph J. Mangalam) *Mountain Families in Transition,* Pennsylvania State University Press, 1971. Contributor of articles to professional journals. Editor, "Rural Sociological Monographs."

*WORK IN PROGRESS: Career Planning of Rural Youth in Modern Society; Change in a Rural German Village; Social Dimensions of Part-Time Farming in Michigan.*

\* \* \*

## SCOLES, Eugene F(rancis) 1921-

*PERSONAL:* Born June 12, 1921, in Iowa; son of Samuel S. Scoles; married Helen Glawson, September 6, 1942; children: Kathleen Scoles Sohlman, Janene Scoles Bradfeldt. *Education:* University of Iowa, A.B., 1943, J.D., 1945; Harvard University, LL.M., 1949; Columbia University, J.S.D., 1955. *Politics:* Democrat. *Religion:* Methodist. *Home:* 1931 Kimberly Dr., Eugene, Ore. 97405. *Office:* School of Law, University of Oregon, Eugene, Ore. 97403.

*CAREER:* Seyfarth, Shaw & Fairweather, Chicago, Ill., associate attorney, 1945-46; Northeastern University, Boston, Mass., assistant professor, 1946-47, associate professor of law, 1947-48; University of Florida, Gainesville, associate professor, 1949-50, professor of law, 1951-56; University of Illinois at Urbana-Champaign, professor of law, 1956-58; University of Oregon, Eugene, professor of law and dean, 1968-74, Distinguished Professor of Law, 1974—. Visiting professor of law, University of Khartoum, 1964-65. Commissioner, National Conference of Commissioners of Uniform State Laws. *Member:* American Bar Association, Society of Public Teachers of Law, African Law Association, American Law Institute, American College of Probate Counsel, Association of American Law Schools (president, 1978), Illinois State Bar Association, Lane County Bar Association.

*WRITINGS:* (With Edward C. Halbach) *Problems and Materials on Decedents' Estates and Trusts,* Little, Brown, 1963; (editor) Herbert Funk Goodrich, *Handbook of the Conflict of Laws,* West Publishing, 4th edition (Scoles was not associated with earlier editions), 1964; (with Russell J. Weintraub) *Cases on Conflict of Laws,* West Publishing, 1967, 2nd edition 1972; (with Edward C. Halbach) *Problems and Materials on Future Interests,* Little, Brown, 1977.

\*     \*     \*

## SCOTT, Robert Adrian    1901(?)-1972

1901(?)—December 25, 1972; American film writer and producer. Obituaries: *New York Times,* December 27, 1972.

\*     \*     \*

## SEDERBERG, Arelo Charles    1930-

*PERSONAL:* Born May 17, 1930, in Minneapolis, Minn.; son of Charles Otto and Agnes (Enquist) Sederberg; married Donnajean McCarthy, June 10, 1955 (divorced, 1969); children: James William. *Education:* Los Angeles City College, A.A., 1958; California State College at Los Angeles (now California State University, Los Angeles), B.A., 1966. *Politics:* Democrat. *Religion:* Methodist.

*CAREER:* Los Angeles *Mirror,* Los Angeles, Calif., reporter, 1953-62; Los Angeles *Times,* Los Angeles, reporter, 1962-69; Carl Byoir & Associates (Hughes Tool Co. account), Las Vegas, Nev., public relations consultant, 1969—. *Military service:* U.S. Army, 1951-53; served in Korea and Japan.

*WRITINGS: Stock Market Investment Club Handbook: How to Organize, Maintain, and Profit from an Investment Club,* Sherbourne, 1972; *A Collection for J.L.: A Novel of Crisis,* Sherbourne, 1973; *60 Hours of Darkness: A Novel of Terror in Las Vegas,* Sherbourne, 1974, published as *Casine,* Dell, 1977; *How to Kidnap a Millionaire,* Pinnacle Books, 1974. Contributor to *Time, Saturday Review,* and other magazines and newspapers.†

\*     \*     \*

## SEELY, Gordon M.    1930-

*PERSONAL:* Born April 14, 1930, in San Mateo, Calif.; son of Gordon M. (a merchant) and Helen (Fromm) Seely; married Evelyn Keenan, December 27, 1958; children: Clare Evelyn, Helen Louise. *Education:* Stanford University, B.A., 1951, M.A., 1954, 1958, Ph.D., 1963. *Politics:* Republican. *Religion:* Catholic. *Home address:* P.O. Box 279, Belmont, Calif. 94002. *Office:* Department of History, San Francisco State University, San Francisco, Calif. 94132.

*CAREER:* Teacher in California high schools and junior college, 1954-55, 1956-57, 1959-60; San Francisco State University, San Francisco, Calif., professor of history and education, 1960—. *Military service:* U.S. Army, 1951-53; became first lieutenant. *Member:* Organization of American Historians, History of Education Society, Commonwealth Club.

*WRITINGS: Education: For What and for Whom?,* Prentice-Hall, 1970, 2nd edition, 1975.

\*     \*     \*

## SEGAL, Melvin J(ames)    1910-

*PERSONAL:* Born September 18, 1910, in Winthrop, Mass.; son of Joseph (a merchant) and Ida (Swartz) Segal; married Marian Virginia Harris, June 9, 1944; children: Jane Deborah. *Education:* Amherst College, A.B. (magna cum laude), 1932; Harvard University, additional study, 1932-33; University of Illinois, M.A., 1935, Ph.D., 1938. *Politics:* Democrat. *Home:* 531 Kedzie Dr., East Lansing, Mich. 48823. *Office:* Department of Social Science, University College, Michigan State University, East Lansing, Mich. 48823.

*CAREER:* Southern Illinois University at Carbondale, assistant professor of economics, 1937-42; Minimum Wage Board, San Juan, Puerto Rico, chief economist, 1942-43; U.S. National War Labor Board, Washington, D.C., senior economist, 1943-44; Massachusetts Institute of Technology, Cambridge, lecturer in economics, 1944; Michigan State University, East Lansing, assistant professor, 1945-47, associate professor, 1947-54, professor of social science, 1954—. Member of consumers union, National Education Advisory Committee, 1969—. *Military service:* U.S. Army, 1943. *Member:* American Economic Association, Industrial Relations Research Association, Association of General and Liberal Education, Association for Evolutionary Economics, American Association of University Professors, Phi Beta Kappa.

*WRITINGS: Norris-La Guardia Act and the Courts,* American Council on Public Affairs, 1938; (contributor and editor with others) *Problems of Change and Development,* Volume II, Michigan State University Press, 1967. Contributor of articles to labor and social science journals.

*WORK IN PROGRESS: Consumer Sovereignty,* a college text.†

\*     \*     \*

## SEIFMAN, Eli    1936-

*PERSONAL:* Born August 4, 1936, in Brooklyn, N.Y.; son of Alexander (a businessman) and Lillian (Minoff) Seifman; married Gloria Schalit (a program coordinator), December 29, 1957; children: Alysia Robin, David Randall. *Education:* Queens College (now Queens College of the City University of New York), B.A. (magna cum laude), 1957, M.S., 1959; New York University, Ph.D. (with honors), 1965. *Home:* 21 Seward Lane, Stony Brook, N.Y. 11790. *Office:* Department of Education, State University of New York, Stony Brook, N.Y. 11790.

*CAREER:* Junior high school teacher of English and social studies in Flushing, N.Y., 1957-63; Queens College (now Queens College of the City University of New York), Flushing, lecturer in education, 1961-64; State University of New York at Stony Brook, instructor, 1964-65, assistant professor, 1965-67, associate professor, 1967-70, professor of education, 1970—, chairman of department, 1968-70, professor of social science and director of secondary education, 1976—. Visiting lecturer in education, University of Durham, 1977. Consultant to various organizations, including Project Upward Bound, 1966—, and U.S. Department of Labor, U.S. Office of Education, Melton Research Foundation, U.S. Office of Economic Opportunity, and American Historical Association History Education Project. Chairman of tenure review committee, Three Village School District, 1968-69. Member of board of trustees, Associate for Relevant Curriculum. *Member:* American Historical Association, Historical Association (Great Britain), History of Education Society, National Council for the Social Studies, American Association of Colleges of Teacher Education, Long Island Council for the Social Studies, Phi Beta Kappa, Phi Alpha Theta, Sigma Alpha. *Awards, honors:* Minnesota Mining and Manufacturing Age III education grant, 1965.

*WRITINGS: A History of the New York State Colonization*

*Society,* Phelps-Stokes Fund, 1966; (with Martin Feldman) *The Social Studies: Structures, Models, Strategies,* Prentice-Hall, 1969; (with Dwight Allen) *The Teacher's Handbook,* Scott, Foresman, 1971; (with Shi Ming Hu) *Toward a New World Outlook: A Documentary History of Education in the People's Republic of China, 1949-76,* AMS Press, 1976; (with Shu Ming Hu) *Education for Whom?: Contemporary Chinese Education,* University Press of Singapore, 1977.

Author of video tape series, American Historical Association History Education Project, and of numerous reports and papers. Contributor of articles and book reviews to education journals. American Historical Association History Education Project, general editor of occasional paper series, 1970—, editor of *HEP/News Exchange,* 1972—; educational consultant to Thomas Y. Crowell, Co., 1962-63, John Wiley & Sons, Inc., 1967-70, Scott, Foresman and Co., Inc., 1968—, and Prentice-Hall, Inc., 1970—.

*WORK IN PROGRESS:* Research on contemporary Chinese education in the People's Republic of China.

\* \* \*

## SELBY, Henry A. 1934-

*PERSONAL:* Born September 2, 1934, in Toronto, Ontario, Canada; son of David Longland (a physician) and Katherine Elizabeth (Anderson) Selby; married Lucy Garretson (a professor), August 1, 1960; children: Washington Gardner, Mary Theadosia, Thomas Henry Longland. *Education:* University of Toronto, B.A., 1955; University of London, M.A., 1961; Stanford University, Ph.D., 1966. *Office:* Department of Anthropology, University of Texas, Austin, Tex. 78712.

*CAREER:* University of Texas at Austin, instructor, 1966-69, assistant professor, 1969, associate professor of anthropology, 1969-72; Temple University, Philadelphia, Pa., associate professor of anthropology, 1972-77; University of Texas at Austin, professor of anthropology, 1977—. *Military service:* Royal Canadian Navy; became midshipman. *Member:* American Anthropological Association, Sigma Xi.

*WRITINGS: Kinship and Social Organization,* Macmillan, 1968; *A Formal Study of the Myth,* University of Texas Press, 1968; *Zapotec Deviance,* University of Texas Press, 1974; *Social Organization,* W. C. Brown, 1975; (editor with F. Johnston) *Elements of Anthropology,* twelve volumes, W. C. Brown, 1975; *Meaning in Anthropology,* University of New Mexico Press, 1976; *Anthropology: The Biocultural View,* W. C. Brown, 1978. Contributor to academic journals.

\* \* \*

## SELDON, Mary Elisabeth 1921-

*PERSONAL:* Born August 28, 1921, in Changchun, China; married Nicholas N. Seldon (a teacher), 1950; children: Henry Lee, Nicholas Alan, Mary Alexandra. *Education:* Indiana University, A.B., 1942, M.A., 1945, Ph.D., 1959. *Home:* 6563 North Ferguson St., Indianapolis, Ind. 46220. *Office:* Indiana University—Purdue University at Indianapolis, 925 West Michigan St., Indianapolis, Ind. 46202.

*CAREER:* Judson College, Marion, Ala., instructor in history, 1943-44; Indiana University—Purdue University at Indianapolis, instructor, 1949-63, assistant professor, 1963-66, associate professor of modern European history, 1966—. *Member:* American Historical Association.

*WRITINGS:* (With F. Lee Benns) *Europe: 1914-1939,* Appleton, 1965; (with Benns) *Europe: 1939 to the Present,* Appleton, 1965, revised edition, 1971.

*WORK IN PROGRESS:* A third edition of *Europe: 1939 to the Present.*

\* \* \*

## SEMAAN, Khalil I. H. 1920-

*PERSONAL:* Born March 6, 1920, in Safita, Syria; came to United States in 1950, naturalized citizen in 1960; son of Ibrahim and Marta (Khoury) Semaan; married Aline Elofson, May 6, 1960; children: Jan Jeffery, Johan Nicholas, Ingrid Emily Teresa. *Education:* Georgetown University, Certificate of Interpreter (with honors), 1952, B.S., 1954; Columbia University, M.A., 1955, Ph.D., 1958. *Politics:* Independent. *Religion:* Christian. *Home:* 713 Country Club Rd., Binghamton, N.Y. 13903; and 18 Saraya, Safita, Syria. *Office:* Arabic Studies Program, State University of New York, Binghamton, N.Y. 13901.

*CAREER:* New York University, New York City, lecturer in Semitic languages, 1955-56; Columbia University, New York City, lecturer in Arabic, 1957; University of California, Los Angeles, research historian and acting assistant professor of Oriental languages, 1957-59; Library of Congress, Washington, D.C., reference librarian, 1960-62; Afro-Asian Research Institute, Stockholm, Sweden, director, 1962-64; Columbia University, Teachers College, visiting scholar, 1964-65; State University of New York at Binghamton, assistant professor, 1965, associate professor, 1966-70, professor of Arabic, 1970—. Visiting summer professor, Harvard University, 1966.

*WRITINGS: Ash-Shafi'i's Risalah: Basic Ideas,* Ashraf Press, 1962; *Ibn Sina's Risalah on the Points of Articulation of the Speech-Sounds,* Ashraf Press, 1963; *Linguistics in the Middle Ages: Phonetic Studies in Early Islam,* E. J. Brill, 1968; *Murder in Baghdad* (translation of Salah Abd al-Sabur's verse play, *Ma'sat al-Hallaj*), E. J. Brill, 1972. Contributor of more than twenty articles and reviews to *Middle East Journal, New Left Forum, Muslim World,* and other journals in his field.

*WORK IN PROGRESS: College Arabic I; Islam: A Cultural Tradition,* translation of Kahlil Gibran's earlier works.

\* \* \*

## SERVIN, Manuel P(atrick) 1920-

*PERSONAL:* Born August 8, 1920, in El Paso, Tex.; son of Isidro (a mechanic) and Juana (Maldonado) Servin; married Mary Hart, June 14, 1951 (divorced, 1968); children: Mark, Francis, Paul, Margaret Ann. *Education:* Loyola University of Los Angeles, A.B., 1949; Boston College, M.S.W., 1951; University of Southern California, A.M., 1954, Ph.D., 1959. *Politics:* Democrat. *Religion:* Roman Catholic. *Home:* 506 Tulane Dr. N.E., Albuquerque, N.M. 87106. *Office:* Department of History, University of New Mexico, Albuquerque, N.M. 87131.

*CAREER:* Teacher in junior high school in Hollenbeck, Calif., 1955-58; El Camino College, Torrance, Calif., instructor in history, 1958-60; University of Southern California, Los Angeles, assistant professor, 1962-66, associate professor of history, 1966-70; Arizona State University, Tempe, professor of history, beginning 1970; currently affiliated with department of history, University of New Mexico, Albuquerque. *Military service:* U.S. Army Air Forces, 1945-47. *Member:* Southern California Historical Society (trustee, 1969-70), Arizona Historical Society. *Awards, honors:* Award of merit from California Historical Society for editing quarterly journal, 1971.

*WRITINGS:* (Translator, annotator, and author of introduction) *The Apostolic Life of Fernando Consag, Explorer of Lower California,* Dawson's Book Shop, 1968; (with Iris Wilson) *Southern California and Its University: A History of USC, 1880-1964,* Ritchie, 1969; *The Mexican American: An Awakening Minority,* Glencoe Press, 1970, 2nd edition published as *An Awakened Minority: The Mexican Americans,* 1974. Contributor to history journals. Editor, *California Historical Society Quarterly,* 1961-70.

*WORK IN PROGRESS: The Mexican American and the Gospel of Success; La toma de posesion en la epoca de descubrimento* ("Taking Possession in the Age of Discovery").

\*    \*    \*

## SETHI, Narendra Kumar    1935-

*PERSONAL:* Born July 12, 1935, in India; son of Seth Nemichandji (a businessman) and Laxmi Devi (Luhadiya) Sethi; married Kiran Jain (an executive), April 24, 1956; children: Madhu Milind, Manoj Milind, Michelle. *Education:* Agra University, B.A., 1953, M.A., 1955; Calcutta University, M.A., 1956; New York University, M.B.A., 1961, Ph.D., 1962. *Politics:* None. *Religion:* Jain. *Home:* 89-14 Aubrey Ave., Glendale, N.Y. 11227. *Office:* Department of Management, St. John's University, Jamaica, N.Y. 11432.

*CAREER:* St. John's University, Jamaica, N.Y., associate professor, 1966-69, professor of management, 1969—, chairman of department, 1969-72. Partner, Binodiram Balchand & Co. *Member:* Indian Forum for the Professions (president), Academy of Management, Institute for Decision Sciences, Association for International Business Education, Indore Management Association, Malwa Chamber of Commerce. *Awards, honors:* Shell Company assistance grant, 1969-70; Shiram award, 1974.

*WRITINGS: The Word Is Split,* Writers' Workshop (Calcutta), 1961; *Shabda Ki Chalna,* Malvika Prakashan, 1961; *Hindu Proverbs,* Peter Pauper, 1962; *Song Lines of a Day,* Writers' Workshop (Calcutta), 1965; *A Bibliography of Indian Management,* Popular Prakashan, 1966; (contributor) S. B. Prasad, editor, *Management in International Perspective,* Appleton, 1966; *The Setting of Administrative Management in India,* St. John's University Press, 1969; *Management Perspectives,* [Bombay], 1973; *Environmental Management,* [The Hague], 1973. Contributor of about one hundred and fifty articles to management and economic journals in the United States and India.

*WORK IN PROGRESS:* Six books, *A Managerial Critique of Public Relations, Mary Parker Follett: A Historical and Comparative Study of Her Contribution to Management, A Bibliography of Public Relations in Management, A Bibliography of Human Relations in Management, The Managerial Mirage,* and *Managerial Dynamics.*

\*    \*    \*

## SETHNA, Jehangir Minocher    1941-

*PERSONAL:* Born August 31, 1941, in Bombay, India; son of Minocher Jehangirji (a professor and author) and Khorshed (Anklesaria) Sethna; married Katie Minocher Mody (a psychiatrist), 1967. *Education:* St. Xavier's College, Bombay, India, B.A. (with honors), 1961; Bombay University, LL.B., 1963; Harvard University, LL.M., 1964. *Home:* Sethna House, 251 Tardeo Road, Bombay 7, Mahrashtra, India. *Office:* Counsel's Chambers, High Court (Bombay) Annexe, High Court, Bombay, Mahrashtra, India.

*CAREER:* Admitted to Bombay High Court Bar, 1964; Bombay High Court, Bombay, India, counsel and advocate, 1964—. Part-time professor of mercantile and company law, Sydenham College of Commerce and Economics, Bombay.

*WRITINGS: International Legal Controls and Sanctions Concerning the Production and Use of Atomic Energy,* Kothari-Mc Duneil (Bombay), 1966.

Editor of law books by father, Minocher Jehangirji Sethna: *Indian Company Law, with a Full Text of the Indian Companies Act, 1956, as Amended Up to Date,* 7th edition, Lakhani Book Depot (Bombay), 1967, 8th edition, 1978; *Mercantile Law, Including Industrial Law,* 6th edition, Lakhani Book Depot, 1970, 8th edition, 1978; *Society and the Criminal, with Special Reference to the Problems of Crime and Its Prevention, the Personality of the Criminal, Prison Reform and Juvenile Delinquency in India,* 3rd edition, revised and enlarged, Tripathi (Bombay), 1971; *Jurisprudence,* 3rd edition, revised, Abacus Press, 1972. Contributor of legal articles to *Bombay Law Reporter* and to *Radical Humanist* (New Delhi).

\*    \*    \*

## SEYDEL, Mildred (Wooley)
## (Mildred Seydell)

*PERSONAL:* Born in Atlanta, Ga.; daughter of Vasser (a lawyer) and Elizabeth (Rutherford) Woolley; married Paul Bernard Seydel, February 5, 1910 (died, 1942); married Max Seydel (an industrialist), 1947; children: (first marriage) Paul Vasser, John Rutherford. *Education:* Attended Washington Seminary, Atlanta, Ga., Lucy Cobb Institute, and Sorbonne, University of Paris. *Home and office:* 9530 Scott Rd., Route 2, Roswell, Ga. 30075.

*CAREER:* Columnist for *Gazette,* Charleston, W.Va., 1921, *Georgian,* Atlanta, Ga., 1924-39, *Atlanta Journal,* Atlanta, 1948, *Atlanta Constitution,* Atlanta, 1950; owner and editor, *The Think Tank,* 1940-48; owner and editor, *Seydell Quarterly,* 1948-67; owner, Mildred Seydell Publishing Co. Belgian director, World Poetry Day. Member of board of directors, A. G. Rhoades Home. Member of advisory committee, Fellowship in Prayer. *Member:* International Periodic Press, National League of American Pen Women, Association des Journalistes Periodiques Belges et Etrangers, Georgia Press Association, Beta Sigma Phi. *Awards, honors:* Chevalier, Order of Leopold (Belgium).

*WRITINGS*—Under name Mildred Seydell: *Secret Fathers,* Macauley, 1930; *Chins Up,* Grosset, 1939; (editor) *Poetry Profile of Belgium,* Mildred Seydell Publishing Co., 1961; *Come along to Belgium,* Denison, 1969. Also author of *Then I Saw North Carolina,* 1937. Contributor of articles to *Good Housekeeping, Town and Country, Cosmopolitan,* and Hearst newspapers. Member of advisory staff, *Sunshine.*

*WORK IN PROGRESS:* Research on book for preachers.

*SIDELIGHTS:* During the course of her career as a journalist, Mildred Seydel has travelled to Belgium and Ireland in 1927, the Balkan States, Hungary, Turkey, and Greece in 1929, Sweden, Germany, and France in 1931, Africa (from Capetown to Cairo) in 1934, New Zealand and Australia in 1937, Germany and Czechoslovakia in 1938, Finland in 1939, and England and Wales in 1956. Her work has included special reports on such diverse subjects as liquor regulations in Sweden, the history of diamonds and gold in South Africa, and native customs in the Belgian Congo.†

## SHAFER, Robert Jones 1920-

*PERSONAL:* Born January 29, 1920, in South Salem, Ohio; son of Samuel Sullivan (an attorney) and Anna (Jones) Shafer; married Estela Gamiz, November, 1971; children: Susan Shafer Rumphorst, Sally Lura Finch, John Samuel. *Education:* Ohio State University, B.A., 1938; University of California, Los Angeles, M.A., 1944, Ph.D., 1947. *Office:* Department of History, Syracuse University, Syracuse, N.Y. 13210.

*CAREER:* Syracuse University, Syracuse, N.Y., instructor, 1945-47, assistant professor, 1947-53, associate professor, 1953-58, professor of history, 1958—. *Military service:* U.S. Army Reserve, beginning 1949; on active duty, 1951-53; retired as lieutenant colonel. *Member:* American Historical Association, Conference on Latin American History, American Association of University Professors, Reserve Officers Association. *Awards, honors:* Bolton Prize from American Historical Association, 1959, and Silver Pen Award from Journal Fund, 1960, both for *The Economic Societies in the Spanish World, 1763-1821.*

*WRITINGS: The Conquered Place,* Putnam, 1954; *The Economic Societies in the Spanish World, 1763-1821,* Syracuse University Press, 1958; *Mexico: Mutual Adjustment Planning,* Syracuse University Press, 1966; *A Guide to Historical Method,* Dorsey, 1969; *Mexican Business Organizations: History and Analysis,* Syracuse University Press, 1973; *A History of Latin America,* Heath, 1978. Contributor to yearbooks and journals of Spanish-American affairs.

*WORK IN PROGRESS: A History of Road and Trail Transport in Mexico, 1519—; A Special Relation: Mexican-United States Relations.*

\*    \*    \*

## SHAFFER, Dale Eugene 1929-

*PERSONAL:* Born April 17, 1929, in Salem, Ohio; son of William (a foundry worker) and Erma (Gibbons) Shaffer. *Education:* Kent State University, B.S. (cum laude), 1955, M.A.L.S., 1960; Ohio State University, M.A., 1956. *Religion:* Christian. *Home:* 437 Jennings Ave., Salem, Ohio 44450. *Office:* Jennings Library, Salem, Ohio 44460.

*CAREER:* General Electric Co., Schenectady, N.Y., management trainee, 1957-58; Bethany College, Bethany, W.Va., instructor in economics, 1958-59; South Bend Public Library, South Bend, Ind., business and technical librarian, 1960-61; Ohio State Employment Service, Columbus, training specialist, 1962-63; Glenville State College, Glenville, W.Va., head librarian and head of department of library science, 1963-65; Ocean County College, Toms River, N.J., library director, 1965-67; Capital University, Columbus, Ohio, library director, 1968-71; University of Pittsburgh at Johnstown, Johnstown, Pa., library director, 1972-73; Jennings Library, Salem, Ohio, founder and consultant, 1972—. *Military service:* U.S. Air Force, 1948-52; became technical sergeant. *Member:* American Library Association, Society for the Advancement of Management, Ohio Library Association, Ohio Business Teachers Association, Delta Sigma Pi.

*WRITINGS: The Maturity of Librarianship as a Profession,* Scarecrow, 1968. Also author of *The Sha-Frame System of Organizing Pamphlet Literature in Libraries.* Contributor of articles to library journals.

*WORK IN PROGRESS:* Twelve pamphlets on library topics, including "The Filmstrip Collection: Complete Instructions on How to Process and Organize," "The Library Picture File: A Complete System of How to Process and Organize," "The Pamphlet Library," and "The Audio Tape Collection"; a library manual on sources, processing, and organization.

\*    \*    \*

## SHAFFER, Jerome A(rthur) 1929-

*PERSONAL:* Born April 2, 1929, in Brooklyn, N.Y.; son of Joseph and Beatrice (Leibowitz) Shaffer; married Olivia Anne Connery (a psychology teacher), September 3, 1960; children: Diana, David. *Education:* Cornell University, B.A., 1950; Princeton University, Ph.D., 1952; Magdalen College, Oxford, additional study, 1952-53. *Office:* Department of Philosophy, University of Connecticut, Storrs, Conn. 06268.

*CAREER:* Swarthmore College, Swarthmore, Pa., instructor, 1955-58, assistant professor, 1958-64, associate professor of philosophy, 1964-67; University of Connecticut, Storrs, professor of philosophy, 1967—, head of department, 1976. Visiting professor, Princeton University, 1961. *Military service:* U.S. Army, 1953-55. U.S. Army Reserve, 1955-64; became captain. *Member:* American Philosophical Association, Council for Philosophical Studies (executive secretary, 1965—), American Association of University Professors, American Civil Liberties Union, Phi Beta Kappa, Phi Kappa Phi, Fullerton Club (president, 1962-63). *Awards, honors:* Woodrow Wilson fellow, 1950-51; Fulbright scholar in England, 1952-53; American Council of Learned Societies fellow, 1963-64; Center for Advanced Study in the Behavioral Sciences fellow, 1963-64.

*WRITINGS: The Philosophy of Mind,* Prentice-Hall, 1968; *Reality, Knowledge, and Value,* Random House, 1971; (editor) *Violence,* McKay, 1971.

Contributor: G. W. A. Vesey, editor, *Body and Mind,* Allen & Unwin, 1964; John Hick and Arthur McGill, editors, *The Many-Faced Argument,* Macmillan, 1967; John Hosper, editor, *Readings in Philosophical Analysis,* Bobbs-Merrill, 1968; Terence Penelhum and J. J. MacIntosh, editors, *The First Critique,* Wadsworth, 1969; C. V. Borst, editor, *The Mind-Brain Identity Theory,* Macmillan, 1970; W. T. Blackstone, editor, *Meaning and Existence,* Holt, 1971; D. M. Rosenthal, editor, *Materialism and the Mind-Body Problem,* Prentice-Hall, 1971. Contributor to *Encyclopaedia Britannica, Encyclopedia of Philosophy,* and philosophy journals.

\*    \*    \*

## SHAFFER, Thomas Lindsay 1934-

*PERSONAL:* Born April 4, 1934, in Billings, Mont.; son of Cecil Burdette (a rancher) and Margaret (Parker) Shaffer; married Nancy Jane Lehr, March 19, 1954; children: Thomas, Francis, Joseph, Daniel, Brian, Mary, Andrew, Edward. *Education:* University of Albuquerque, B.A., 1958; University of Notre Dame, J.D., 1961. *Politics:* Independent. *Religion:* Christian. *Home:* 18801 Burke St., South Bend, Ind. 46637. *Office:* Law School, University of Notre Dame, Notre Dame, Ind. 46556.

*CAREER:* Barnes, Hickam, Pantzer & Boyd (attorneys), Indianapolis, Ind., associate, 1961-63; University of Notre Dame, Notre Dame, Ind., assistant professor, 1963-66, professor of law, 1966—, associate dean of Law School, 1969-71, dean, 1971—. Visiting professor of law at University of California, Los Angeles, 1970-71, and University of Virginia, 1975-76. *Military service:* U.S. Air Force, 1953-57.

*Member:* American Bar Association, American Law Institute, American College of Probate Counsel, Indiana State Bar Association, Estate Planning Institute (member of advisory board). *Awards, honors:* Emil Brown Preventive Law Prize, 1966; University of Notre Dame presidential citation, 1975.

*WRITINGS: Death, Property and Lawyers,* Dunellen, 1971; *The Planning and Drafting of Wills and Trusts,* Foundation Press, 1972; *Legal Interviewing and Counseling,* West Publishing, 1976; *The Mentally Retarded Citizen and the Law,* Free Press, 1976; *Lawyers, Law, Students, and People,* McGraw, 1977. Contributor of more than 100 articles to legal and popular journals. Editor, *Notre Dame Lawyer,* 1960-61; advisory editor, *Life-Threatening Behavior, American Journal of Jurisprudence,* and *Journal of Legal Education.*

*WORK IN PROGRESS:* An interdisciplinary text in law and psychology, with Robert S. Redmount; a study on lawyers and Christian ethical principles.

\*        \*        \*

### SHAPIRO, Herbert  1929-

*PERSONAL:* Born June 14, 1929, in Jamaica, N.Y.; son of Max and Sophie (Mirkin) Shapiro; married Judith Stock (a social worker), February 3, 1957; children: Mark, Nina. *Education:* Queens College of the City of New York (now Queens College of the City University of New York), B.A., 1952; Columbia University, M.A., 1958; University of Rochester, Ph.D., 1964. *Home:* 3990 Beechwood, Cincinnati, Ohio 45229. *Office:* Department of History, University of Cincinnati, Cincinnati, Ohio 45221.

*CAREER:* Atlanta University Center, Morehouse College, Atlanta, Ga., assistant professor of history, 1962-66; University of Cincinnati, Cincinnati, Ohio, assistant professor, 1966-71, associate professor of history, 1971—.

*WRITINGS:* (Editor with Ella Winter) *World of Lincoln Steffens,* Hill & Wang, 1962; (editor) *The Muckrakers and American Society,* Heath, 1968. Contributor to history, economics, sociology, and literary journals.

*WORK IN PROGRESS:* A biography of Lincoln Steffens.

\*        \*        \*

### SHAPLEY, Harlow  1885-1972

November 2, 1885—October 20, 1972; American astronomer, educator, and editor and author of books on science. Obituaries: *New York Times,* October 21, 1972; *Newsweek,* October 30, 1972.

\*        \*        \*

### SHARLET, Robert (Stewart)  1935-

*PERSONAL:* Born August 11, 1935, in Boston, Mass.; son of Irving A. (a businessman) and Evelyn (Sedersky) Sharlet; children: Jocelyn C., Jeffrey C. *Education:* Brandeis University, B.A. (with honors), 1960; Indiana University, M.A., 1962, Ph.D., 1968. *Home:* 1023 Park Ave., Schenectady, N.Y. 12308. *Office:* Department of Political Science, Union College and University, Schenectady, N.Y. 12308.

*CAREER:* University of Missouri—Columbia, assistant professor of political science, 1965-67; Union College and University, Schenectady, N.Y., assistant professor, 1967-71, associate professor, 1971-76, professor of political science, 1976—, chairman of department, 1972-76. Visiting assistant professor of law, University of Wisconsin, summer,

1965, 1966-67; visiting professor, Columbia University and Yale University, both 1976-77. Research associate, U.S. Arms Control and Disarmament Agency, 1965-67; senior research associate, Research Institute on International Change, Columbia University, 1974—. *Military service:* U.S. Army, 1955-58. *Member:* American Political Science Association, American Association for the Advancement of Slavic Studies. *Awards, honors:* Ford Foundation, foreign area fellow, 1963-65, grant, 1975-78; Inter-University exchange fellow, Moscow University, 1963-64.

*WRITINGS:* (Contributor) F. J. Fleron, editor, *Communist Studies and the Social Sciences,* Rand McNally, 1969; (contributor) R. E. Kanet, editor, *The Behavioral Revolution and Communist Studies,* Free Press, 1971; (with Zigurds L. Zile and Jean C. Love) *The Soviet Legal System and Arms Inspection,* Praeger, 1972; (contributor) R. E. Kanet and Ivan Volgyes, editors, *On the Road to Communism: Essays on Soviet Domestic and Foreign Politics,* University Press of Kansas, 1972; (contributor) R. C. Tucker, editor, *Stalinism,* Norton, 1977; (contributor) Sheila Fitzpatrick, editor, *Cultural Revolution in Russia, 1928-1932,* Indiana University Press, 1978; *The New Soviet Constitution of 1977,* King's Court, 1978. Contributor of articles to political science and law journals.

*BIOGRAPHICAL/CRITICAL SOURCES: Esquire,* September, 1966; Susan Berman, *The Underground Guide to the College of Your Choice,* Signet, 1971.

\*        \*        \*

### SHAW, B(iswanath) N.  1923-

*PERSONAL:* Born October 26, 1923; son of Lingaraj and Lakhmi (Devi) Chaudhury; married May 13, 1956, wife's name Shashikala; married second wife, Dolores Arnold, December 20, 1969; children: (first marriage) Prabhati, Pranati, Minati. *Education:* University of Iowa, M.A., 1965; University of Mississippi, Ed.D., 1971. *Home:* 3909 California Ave., Jackson, Miss. 39213. *Office:* Division of Humanities, Rust College, Rust Ave., Holly Springs, Miss. 38635.

*CAREER:* Tougaloo College, Jackson, Miss., instructor in education, 1965-67; Rust College, Holly Springs, Miss., instructor, 1967-68, assistant professor, 1968-69, associate professor, 1969-71, professor of education, 1971—, chairman of Division of Humanities and director of cooperative education, 1970—. *Member:* Phi Delta Kappa.

*WRITINGS: Academic Tenure in American Higher Education,* Adams Press, 1971.

*WORK IN PROGRESS:* Two books, tentatively entitled *Abolish Academic Tenure?* and *Inter-Disciplinary Approach to Teaching.*†

\*        \*        \*

### SHAW, Ralph R(obert)  1907-1972

May 18, 1907—October 14, 1972; American librarian, publisher, educator, bibliographer, and editor. Obituaries: *New York Times,* October 16, 1972; *Antiquarian Bookman,* October 23-30, 1972.

\*        \*        \*

### SHAW, Richard  1923-

*PERSONAL:* Born May 21, 1923, in Greensboro, N.C.; son of Charles B. and Dorothy (Joslyn) Shaw; married Benita Haines, June 8, 1950 (divorced, 1967); married Janet Noyes (a school nurse teacher), August 12, 1968; children: (first marriage) Karen, Jennifer; (stepchildren) Keith, Steven, Mark, Geoffrey. *Education:* Attended Swarthmore College, 1941-44, and George Washington University, 1944-45; Columbia University, A.B., 1946, M.L.S., 1951; graduate study at Harvard University, 1956, and University of California, Berkeley, 1960. *Home:* 40 Phyllis Dr., Pearl River, N.Y. 10965. *Office:* Department of English, Westchester Community College, Valhalla, N.Y. 10505.

*CAREER:* Columbia University, New York City, instructor in humanities, 1946-48; Brooklyn Public Library, Brooklyn, N.Y., librarian in language and literature, 1948-51; Friends Academy, Dartmouth, Mass., English teacher, 1951-52; English teacher and chairman of department in high school in Orleans, Mass., 1953-57; Bennett College, Millbrook, N.Y., professor of English, 1958-60; *New York Herald Tribune,* New York City, assistant editor of book section, 1961-62; *New York Times,* New York City, rewriter, 1962-63; Richard Shaw (editorial consultant), Pearl River, N.Y., owner, 1964—. Associate professor of English, Westchester Community College, 1969—. *Member:* United Federation of College Teachers.

*WRITINGS—*For children: *Budd's Noisy Wagon,* Warne, 1968; *Who Are You Today?,* Warne, 1970; (editor) *The Owl Book,* Warne, 1970; *Tree for Rent,* Albert Whitman, 1971; (editor) *The Fox Book,* Warne, 1971; (editor) *The Frog Book,* Warne, 1972; *The Kitten in the Pumpkin Patch,* illustrations by Jacqueline Kahane, Warne, 1973; (editor) *The Cat Book,* Warne, 1973; (editor) *The Bird Book,* Warne, 1974; (editor) *Witch, Witch!,* Warne, 1975; (editor) *The Mouse Book,* Warne, 1975; *Call Me Al Raft,* Thomas Nelson, 1975; *Shape up, Burke,* Thomas Nelson, 1977; *An Introduction to Expository Writing* (filmstrip), Prentice-Hall, 1977.

*WORK IN PROGRESS:* A novel; short stories; a play.

*AVOCATIONAL INTERESTS:* Travel in Europe and Latin America, playing tennis, swimming, music, building with wood, living on a boat.

\* \* \*

## SHAW, Robert Byers 1916-

*PERSONAL:* Born October 11, 1916, in Cambridge, Mass.; son of Adrian Vere (an investment adviser) and Helen (Halter) Shaw; married Miriam P. Dorr, July 4, 1940 (divorced, 1963); married Ilse J. Geissler, February 15, 1966. *Education:* Denison University, B.A., 1939; Harvard University, M.B.A. (cum laude), 1939; New York University, Ph.D., 1965. *Religion:* Presbyterian. *Home:* 18 Cedar St., Potsdam, N.Y. 13676. *Office:* School of Management, Clarkson College of Technology, Potsdam, N.Y. 13676.

*CAREER:* United Business Service Co., Boston, Mass., securities analyst, 1939-42; Harvard University, Cambridge, Mass., instructor in finance, 1946-47; U.S. Foreign Service, vice-consul in Glasgow, Scotland, 1948-50, economic officer in Rangoon, Burma, 1950-52; A. Vere Shaw & Co. (investment counsel), New York City, partner, 1952-64; *Magazine of Wall Street,* New York City, editor, 1964-65; Clarkson College of Technology, Potsdam, N.Y., 1965—, began as associate professor of accounting and finance, currently professor of finance. Lecturer in commerce, Rangoon University, 1950-52; visiting lecturer, University of Cape Town, 1973. *Military service:* U.S. Army, 1943-46; served in Pacific; became technical sergeant. *Member:* Institute of Chartered Financial Analysts, Railway and Locomotive Historical Society, American Society in Scotland (first president, 1948-49), St. Lawrence County Historical Society.

*WRITINGS: Down Brakes: A History of Railway Accidents, Safety Precautions, and Operating Practices,* P. R. Macmillan (London), 1961, revised and enlarged edition published as *A History of Railroad Accidents, Safety Precautions and Operating Practices,* Vail-Baillou Press, 1978; *A History of the Comstock Medicine Business and of Dr. Morse's Indian Root Pills,* Smithsonian Institution Press, 1972. Contributor of more than one hundred sixty articles to *Wall Street Journal, Railway Progress, Trains,* and other publications.

*SIDELIGHTS:* Robert Byers Shaw has traveled in every state of the United States and in more than forty foreign countries.

\* \* \*

## SHELDON, Esther K. 1906-

*PERSONAL:* Born April 22, 1906, in Utica, N.Y.; daughter of Fred R. (a teacher) and Myra (Waugh) Keck; married David C. Sheldon, 1935 (divorced, 1940); married James F. Bechtold, July 30, 1948. *Education:* Adelphi College, B.A., 1926; University of Wisconsin, M.A., 1930, Ph.D., 1937. *Politics:* Democrat. *Home:* 3212 South Ocean Blvd., No. 708, Delray Beach, Fla. 33444.

*CAREER:* Queens College of the City University of New York, Flushing, N.Y., instructor, 1940-47, assistant professor, 1947-57, associate professor, 1957-62, professor of English, 1962-68, professor emeritus, 1968—. *Member:* Modern Language Association of America, American Dialect Society, American Name Society, Linguistic Society of America.

*WRITINGS: Thomas Sheridan of Smock-Alley,* Princeton University Press, 1967. Contributor to literature and language journals.

*WORK IN PROGRESS: The Hibernian Academy: An Eighteenth-Century Experiment in Modern Education.*

*BIOGRAPHICAL/CRITICAL SOURCES: Times Literary Supplement,* September 19, 1968; *Yale Review,* winter, 1968.

\* \* \*

## SHEPS, Mindel (Cherniack) 1913-1973

May 20, 1913—January 15, 1973; Canadian-born American physician, biostatistician, and expert on biological factors affecting fertility and reproduction. Obituaries: *New York Times,* January 17, 1973; *Washington Post,* January 17, 1973.

\* \* \*

## SHERIDAN, Thomas L. 1926-

*PERSONAL:* Born December 17, 1926, in New York, N.Y.; son of Thomas L. (an accountant) and Angela (Sheridan) Sheridan. *Education:* Woodstock College, A.B., 1951, M.A., 1953; Catholic Institute of Paris, S.T.D., 1965. *Home:* 2652 Kennedy Blvd., Jersey City, N.J. 07306. *Office:* Department of Theology, St. Peter's College, Jersey City, N.J. 07306.

*CAREER:* Roman Catholic priest of Society of Jesus (Jesuits); Fordham University, New York, N.Y., assistant professor, 1959-62, associate professor of theology, 1965-66; St. Peter's College, Jersey City, N.J., associate professor, 1966-75, professor of theology, 1975—, chairman of department, 1968-76. *Member:* American Association of University Professors, American Academy of Religion, Catholic Theological Society of America, College Theology Society.

*WRITINGS: The Church in the New Testament,* Paulist Press, 1962; *Newman and Justification,* Alba, 1967.

\*    \*    \*

## SHERMAN, Julia A(nn) 1934-

*PERSONAL:* Born March 25, 1934, in Akron, Ohio; daughter of Roy V. (a professor) and Edna (Schultz) Sherman; married Stanley G. Payne (a professor), June 13, 1961; children: Michael. *Education:* Case Western Reserve University, B.A., 1954; University of Iowa, M.A. and Ph.D., 1957. *Office:* Women's Research Institute of Wisconsin, Inc., 202 North Midvale Blvd., Madison, Wis. 53705.

*CAREER:* Veterans Administration Hospital, Iowa City, Iowa, psychology trainee, 1956-57; Iowa State Psychopathological Hospital, Iowa City, U.S. Public Health Service fellow, 1957-58; Minneapolis Veterans Administration Hospital, Minneapolis, Minn., clinical psychologist, 1958-60; Minneapolis Clinic of Psychiatry and Neurology, Minneapolis, clinical psychologist, 1960-62; Professional Service Corps, Los Angeles, Calif., consultant, 1965-66; Lutheran Social Services, Madison, Wis., clinical psychologist, 1971-73; Women's Research Institute of Wisconsin, Inc., Madison, director, 1974—. Teacher in night school, University of Minnesota, 1959-60; University of Wisconsin—Madison, lecturer in psychology of women, 1971-74, lecturer in women's studies, 1975-76, project associate in department of curriculum and instruction, 1974-76. Consultant, Department of Mental Hygiene, State of Wisconsin, 1973-75. *Member:* American Psychological Association, American Association for the Advancement of Science, Association for the Psychological Study of Social Issues, Wisconsin Psychological Association, Phi Beta Kappa, Sigma Xi.

*WRITINGS: On the Psychology of Women: A Survey of Empirical Studies,* C. C Thomas, 1971; *Sex-Related Cognitive Differences: An Essay on Theory and Evidence,* C. C Thomas, 1978; (editor with F. Denmark) *Psychology of Women: Future Directions of Research,* Psychological Dimensions, 1978. Also editor, with E. Beck, of *Prism of Sex: The Equitable Pursuit of Knowledge.* Contributor to *Psychological Reports, Psychological Review,* and other journals.

*WORK IN PROGRESS:* Research on women and mathematics in relation to career development and on education for women.

\*    \*    \*

## SHERMAN, Roger 1930-

*PERSONAL:* Born September 10, 1930, in Jamestown, N.Y.; son of Claire Blanchard and Margaret (Burke) Sherman; married Charlotte Murphy, April 4, 1953; children: Randall, Thomas. *Education:* Grove City College, B.S., 1952; University of Colorado, graduate study, 1956; Harvard University, M.B.A., 1959; Carnegie-Mellon University, M.S., 1965, Ph.D., 1966. *Home:* 1858 Field Rd., Charlottesville, Va. 22903. *Office:* Department of Economics, University of Virginia, Charlottesville, Va. 22901.

*CAREER:* International Business Machines Corporation, New York, N.Y., manager of manufacturing control, 1960-62; University of Virginia, Charlottesville, assistant professor, 1965-68, associate professor, 1969-71, professor of economics, 1971—. Visiting fellow in economics, University of Bristol, 1968-69; Fulbright lecturer, Autonomous University of Madrid, 1972; research fellow, Science Center, Berlin,

1975. *Military service:* U.S. Navy, 1952-55; became lieutenant. *Member:* American Economic Association, Econometric Society, Public Choice Society, Royal Economic Society, Southern Economic Association.

*WRITINGS: Oligopoly: An Empirical Approach,* Heath, 1972; *The Economics of Industry,* Little, Brown, 1973; *Antitrust Perspectives,* Addison-Wesley, 1978. Associate editor of *Applied Economics,* 1971-73; member of editorial board, *Journal of Economics and Business,* 1974—, and *Southern Economics Journal,* 1978—.

\*    \*    \*

## SHERMAN, Steve (Barry) 1938-

*PERSONAL:* Born July 26, 1938, in Los Angeles, Calif.; son of Gene (a newspaperman) and Genevieve (McLaughlin) Sherman; married Mary Claire Lesiask. *Education:* Loyola University of Los Angeles, B.A., 1960, M.A., 1965; University of California, Los Angeles, M.S.L.S., 1967.

*CAREER:* High school English teacher in Glendale, Calif., 1961-63; elementary school teacher in Ruby, Alaska, 1963-64; University of Alaska, Fairbanks, research librarian, 1967-69; *Anchorage Daily News,* Anchorage, Alaska, reporter, 1971; free-lance writer, 1971—.

*WRITINGS: ABC's of Library Promotion,* Scarecrow, 1971; *Bike Hiking,* Dolphin Books, 1974; *The Wood Stove and Fireplace Book,* illustrated by Julia Older, Stackpole, 1976; (with Older) *Appalachian Odyssey: Walking the Trail from Georgia to Maine,* foreword by Edward Abbey, Greene, 1977. Contributor to library journals and to national periodicals, including *Parents' Magazine, Westways, Ellery Queen's Mystery Magazine,* and *Desert.*

*WORK IN PROGRESS: Wild,* a novel; *A Race of Men,* a novel; *Cut Is the Branch,* a memoir; *Dead Father; To Bridge the Gap,* a history, with William Hunt.†

\*    \*    \*

## SHIEH, Francis S(hih-hao) 1926-

*PERSONAL:* Surname is pronounced Shea; born February 7, 1926, in Shanghai, China; naturalized U.S. citizen, 1954; son of Wei-yu (a professor) and Pei-ying (a professor; maiden name Chen) Shieh; married Agnes Lee, November 26, 1955; children: Grace A., Joseph B., Michael C., Francis Christopher. *Education:* St. John's University, Shanghai, China, B.A., 1946; University of San Francisco, graduate study, 1947-48; Georgetown University, M.A., 1950; California State College at Los Angeles (now California State University, Los Angeles), California College Teaching Credential, 1961; University of Maryland, postgraduate study, 1964-70; California National Open University, Ph.D., 1978. *Religion:* Roman Catholic. *Home:* 11201 Woodlawn Blvd., Upper Marlboro, Md. 20870. *Office:* Department of Economics, Prince George's Community College, Largo, Md. 20870.

*CAREER:* Ziwei College, Shanghai, China, professor of social science, 1946-47; Farmers Insurance Group, Los Angeles, Calif., statistician, 1951-52; U.S. Army Language School, Monterey, Calif., instructor in Chinese, 1953-54, 1956-57; International Business Machines Corp., San Jose, Calif., accountant, 1957-58; Immaculate Heart College, Hollywood, Calif., instructor in economics, 1958-61; Aquinas College, Grand Rapids, Mich., assistant professor of economics, 1961-64; RAND Corp., Santa Monica, Calif., member of research staff, department of economics, 1964-

65; Survey & Research Corp., Washington, D.C., chief compiler and special consultant, 1965-66; Prince George's Community College, Largo, Md., professor of economics, 1966—: Visiting professor, Seton Hall University, and other institutions. *Member:* Society of Government Economists, Community College Social Science Association, Atlantic Economic Society.

*WRITINGS: A Glimpse of the Chinese Language: Peking's Language Reforms and the Teaching of Chinese in the United States,* distributed by U.S. Department of Commerce Clearinghouse, 1965; *Keys for Economic Understanding,* Kendall/Hunt, 1971; (chief compiler and special consultant) *Directory of Selected Scientific and Research Institutes in Mainland China,* Hoover Institution, 1971; *Keys to Economic Understanding,* Kendall/Hunt, 1976. Contributor to *Los Angeles Times, Community College Social Science Journal,* and Chinese publications.

*WORK IN PROGRESS:* Research on consumer economics, manpower economics, and American economic development.

\*　　\*　　\*

## SHIPLEY, David O. 1925-

*PERSONAL:* Born June 9, 1925, in Tipton, Mo.; son of Galveston LeeRoy (a teacher) and Frances Arvenia (Redmon) Shipley; married Alberta D. Scott (a public school counselor), January 27, 1952; children: David O., Jr., Donald A. and Darrell A. (twins), Douglas S. *Education:* Baker University, B.A., 1950; Austin Presbyterian Theological Seminary, diploma in English, 1959; Central Baptist Theological Seminary, B.D. and M.Div., 1971. *Home:* 220 East Ashley, Jefferson City, Mo. 65101.

*CAREER:* Presbyterian minister in Kansas, Arkansas, Texas, and Missouri; director of experimental ministries, Northwest Missouri Presbytery, Presbyterian Church in the United States; minister, St. Mark's Church, Kansas City, Mo.; chaplain and major, Kansas City Police Department. Former president, Hester House. *Military service:* U.S. Navy, 1943-46. *Member:* Kansas City Theological Society. *Awards, honors:* Citation from Missouri House of Representatives, for work with police department; outstanding achievement award, from George Washington Carver Neighborhood Center, 1972.

*WRITINGS: Neither Black nor White: The Whole Church for a Broken World,* Word Books, 1971.

*WORK IN PROGRESS: A New Way,* the story of St. Mark's, a church for four denominations; *One Family of Man; The City.*†

\*　　\*　　\*

## SHIRLEY, Hardy L(omax) 1900-

*PERSONAL:* Born November 20, 1900, in Orleans, Ind.; son of Charles Hicks (a plumber) and Maud (Hardy) Shirley; married Mary Hayward Connard, April 22, 1930; children: Frank Connard, Jon Hardy, Emily Knapp (Mrs. Theodore G. Castner, Jr.). *Education:* Indiana University, B.A., 1922; Yale University, Ph.D., 1928. *Home:* 14 Centennial Dr., Syracuse, N.Y. 13207. *Office:* College of Forestry, Syracuse University, Syracuse, N.Y. 13210.

*CAREER:* Teacher in high school in Indiana, 1922; University of Nevada, Reno, instructor, 1922-24, assistant professor of mathematics, 1924-25; Boyce Thompson Institute for Plant Research, Yonkers, N.Y., assistant biochemist, 1927-29; U.S. Forest Service, St. Paul, Minn., associate sil-

viculturist at Lake States Forest Experimental Station, 1929-35, silviculturist, 1935-36, senior silviculturist, 1936-39; U.S. Forest Service, Philadelphia, Pa., director of Allegheny Forest Experimental Station, 1939-42, and Northeastern Forest Experimental Station, 1942-45; Syracuse University, Syracuse, N.Y., assistant dean, College of Forestry, 1945-52, dean, 1952-67, emeritus dean, 1967—. Member of World Forestry Congress in Finland, 1949, India, 1954, Seattle, 1960, Madrid, 1966; delegate to International Union Forest Research Organizations (England), 1956; U.N. Food and Agricultural Organization, chairman of advisory committee on education in forestry, 1956-66; member, Fulbright Selection Committee in Biology and Agriculture, 1957-58; International Union of Forest Research Organizations, member of permanent committee, 1961-66. Has represented U.S. Agency for International Development (USAID) in Turkey and United Nations Food and Agriculture Organization in Pakistan, the Philippines, and Latin America. Study director, President's Advisory Panel on Timber and the Environment. Owner and manager of Shirley Forests. *Military service:* U.S. Army, Officer Reserve Corps, 1929-37; became captain.

*MEMBER:* Society of American Foresters (member of council, 1945-47), American Association for the Advancement of Science (member of council, 1943), Ecological Society of America, Botanical Society of America, Finnish Forestry Society (honorary member), Torch Club, Syracuse Council on Arts and Sciences (president, 1962-65). *Awards, honors:* Oberlaender Trust fellow, Europe, 1935; D.H.C., University of Helsinki, 1955; D.Sc., Syracuse University, 1966.

*WRITINGS: Forestry and Its Career Opportunities,* McGraw, 1952, 4th edition (with Charles Larson), 1978; (with Paul F. Graves) *Forest Ownership for Pleasure and Profit,* Syracuse University Press, 1967. Contributor of about seventy articles to scientific and professional journals. Editor, *Journal of Forestry,* 1946-49.

\*　　\*　　\*

## SHNEIDMAN, J(erome) Lee 1929-

*PERSONAL:* Born June 20, 1929, in New York, N.Y.; son of Bernard Wolf (a jeweler) and Fannia (Raskin) Shneidman; married Conalee Levine (a psychoanalyst), September 3, 1961; children: Philip Adam-Lev, Jack Ben-Zev. *Education:* New York University, B.A., 1951, M.A., 1952; University of Wisconsin—Madison, Ph.D., 1957. *Politics:* Democrat. *Religion:* Hebrew. *Home:* 161 West 86th St., New York, N.Y. 10024. *Office:* Department of History, Adelphi University, Garden City, N.Y. 11530.

*CAREER:* College of the City of New York (now City College of the City University of New York), New York, N.Y., visiting instructor in history, 1956-57; University of Maryland Overseas Program, lecturer in history and government, 1957-58; Fairleigh Dickinson University, Rutherford, N.J., instructor, 1957, 1958-59, assistant professor of history, 1959-62; Brooklyn College of the City University of New York, Brooklyn, N.Y., assistant professor of history, 1962-63; Adelphi University, Garden City, N.Y., assistant professor, 1963-65, associate professor, 1965-71, professor of history, 1971—. Participant in Columbia University Seminar on the History of Legal and Political Thought. *Member:* American Historical Association, Mediaeval Academy of America, American Association of University Professors, Mediaeval Club, Rossica Society of Russian Philately (librarian, 1969—).

WRITINGS: The Rise of the Aragonese-Catalan Empire, 1200-1350, two volumes, New York University Press, 1970; Spain and Franco, 1949-1959, Facts on File, 1973; (with Peter Schwab) John F. Kennedy, Twayne, 1974. Contributor of about thirty-five articles and reviews to journals. Member of editorial board, Indice Historico Espanol, 1963—, and Societas, 1971—.

WORK IN PROGRESS: Research in psychohistory; a psychobiography of Aaron Burr.

\*　　　\*　　　\*

## SHNEOUR, Elie A(lexis)　1925-

PERSONAL: Born December 11, 1925, in Neuilly-sur-Seine, France; son of Zalman (a writer) and Salome (Landau) Shneour; married Joan Haight Brewster, January 22, 1955; children: Mark Z., Alan B. Education: Columbia University, B.A., 1947; University of California, Berkeley, M.A., 1955; University of California, Los Angeles, Ph.D., 1958. Politics: Independent. Residence: La Jolla, Calif. Agent: Sanford Greenburger Associates, Inc., 825 Third Ave., New York, N.Y. 10022. Office: Biosystems Associates Ltd., P.O. Box 1414, La Jolla, Calif. 92038.

CAREER: University of Utah, Salt Lake City, professor of biology, 1965-69; City of Hope Medical Center, Duarte, Calif., researcher in neurosciences, 1969-71; Calbiochem, Inc., La Jolla, Calif., director of research, 1971-74; Biosystems Associates Ltd., La Jolla, president, 1975—. Consultant in biomedical research and management to General Electric Co., North American Aviation, and Melpar Corp., among others. Member of Science Advisory Council, 1976—. Military service: U.S. Army, 1944.

MEMBER: American Society of Biological Chemists, Federation of American Societies for Experimental Biology, American Society for Neurochemistry (member of executive committee), National Academy of Sciences Study Group on Biology and Space Exploration (member of executive committee), International Society for Neurochemistry, Society for Neurosciences, American Chemical Society, American Institute of Biological Sciences, Cousteau Society, New York Academy of Sciences. Awards, honors: John Bard scholar, Columbia University, 1946; William Lockwood Prize, Columbia University, 1957; D.Sc., Bard College, 1968.

WRITINGS: (With Sam Moffat) Life beyond the Earth, Scholastic NSTA, 1965; (editor with Eric Ottessen) Anthology on Space Biology, National Academy of Sciences, 1965; The Malnourished Mind, Doubleday, 1974. Contributor of articles and reviews to professional scientific journals and to newspapers.

SIDELIGHTS: Elie A. Shneour told CA: "My two greatest intellectual loves are scientific research and writing about it. Science has an intrinsic beauty which transcends its possible 'usefulness'; at its best it is a form of art."

\*　　　\*　　　\*

## SHOEMAKER, Donald J(ay)　1927-

PERSONAL: Born July 26, 1927, in Columbus, Ohio; son of Jay B. and Ruth (Howe) Shoemaker; married Phyllis Wynn (a realtor), September 10, 1948; children: Kenton Jay, Craig Charles. Education: Ohio Wesleyan University, B.A., 1951; Ohio State University, M.A., 1952, Ph.D., 1955. Home: 2717 Kent Dr., Carbondale, Ill. 62901. Office: Department of Psychology, Southern Illinois University, Carbondale, Ill. 62901.

CAREER: Served internship in clinical psychology at Veterans Administration hospitals in Chillicothe and Columbus, Ohio, 1951-54; Ohio Juvenile Diagnostic Center, Columbus, assistant psychologist, 1955; University of Illinois at Urbana-Champaign, instructor, 1955-56, assistant professor of psychology, 1956-60, assistant director of Psychological Clinic, 1957-60; Southern Illinois University at Carbondale, associate professor, 1960-66, professor of psychology and speech pathology, 1967—, coordinator of psychological services, 1961—. Consultant to Veterans Administration Clinical Psychology Training Program, 1958—, Illinois Institute for Juvenile Research, 1963-65, Jeanine Schultz Memorial School, 1967-70, and U.S. Department of Justice, Bureau of Prisons, 1967—. Southern Illinois Mental Health Clinic, member of board of directors, president, 1965. Military service: U.S. Army Air Forces, 1945-46. Member: American Psychological Association, Midwestern Psychological Association, Illinois Psychological Association (member of council, 1961-63, 1964-66), Phi Beta Kappa.

WRITINGS: (Contributor) H. C. Quay, editor, Research in Psychopathology, Van Nostrand, 1963; (contributor) Gene R. Medinnus, editor, Readings in the Psychology of Parent-Child Relations, Wiley, 1966; (with Gene J. Brutten) The Modification of Stuttering, Prentice-Hall, 1967; (contributor) Burl B. Gray and Gene England, editors, Stuttering and the Conditioning Therapies, Monterey Institute for Speech and Hearing, 1969; (contributor) Lee E. Travis, editor, Handbook of Speech Pathology and Audiology, Appleton, 1971. Contributor of about fifteen articles to psychology journals.

WORK IN PROGRESS: Research on causes, diagnosis, and treatment of stuttering.

\*　　　\*　　　\*

## SHOWALTER, Ronda Kerr　1942-

PERSONAL: Born October 2, 1942, in Lima, Ohio; daughter of John R. (an engineer) and Arnita (Baier) Kerr; married Graham C. Showalter (an attorney), August 23, 1969. Education: Capital University, B.S., 1964; Indiana University, M.S., 1968. Politics: Republican. Religion: Presbyterian. Home: 36 South Third St., Lewisburg, Pa. 17837. Office: Department of Health Education, Pennsylvania State University, 270 Recreation Bldg., University Park, Pa. 16801.

CAREER: Public school teacher in Spencerville, Ohio, 1964-65; Ohio Northern University, Ada, instructor in physical education, 1965-68; Pennsylvania State University, University Park, assistant professor of health, 1968—. Consultant for Pennsylvania State Continuing Education Programs in sex education and for health text manuscripts for publishing companies. Member: American Association of University Women (education chairman, 1971—), American School Health Association, Young Republicans of Union County.

WRITINGS: (With Brice W. Corder) It's Your Life, Kendall Hunt, 1971; (with Corder) Health Science and College Life, W. C. Brown, 1972, 2nd edition, 1975. Contributor to Journal of School Health.

WORK IN PROGRESS: Creativity in the Teaching of Health.

AVOCATIONAL INTERESTS: Sewing, gourmet cooking, interior decorating, antiques, and travel.†

## SIDER, Robert Dick 1932-

*PERSONAL:* Born March 10, 1932, in Cheapside, Ontario, Canada; son of Earl Morris (a minister) and Elsie (Sheffer) Sider; married Lura Mae Meeds, June 20, 1959; children: Catherine, Michael, Robert. *Education:* University of Saskatchewan, B.A. (honors), 1955, M.A., 1956; Oxford University, B.A. (honors), 1958, M.A., 1964, Ph.D., 1965. *Religion:* Episcopalian. *Home:* 902 Redwood Dr., Carlisle, Pa. 17013. *Office:* Department of Classical Languages, Dickinson College, Carlisle, Pa. 17013.

*CAREER:* High school teacher, 1958-60; Messiah College, Grantham, Pa., associate professor of religion, 1962-68; Dickinson College, Carlisle, Pa., assistant professor, 1968-71, associate professor, 1971-77, professor of classical studies, 1977—. Visiting professor of Greek and Latin, Catholic University of America, 1978-79. *Member:* American Institute of Archaeology, American Philological Association, American Association of Rhodes Scholars, North American Patristic Society (vice-president, 1962; president, 1973), Classical Association of Atlantic States. *Awards, honors:* Rhodes scholar, Oxford University; National Endowment for the Humanities summer fellowship, 1967; American Council of Learned Societies fellow, 1974-75.

*WRITINGS: Ancient Rhetoric and the Art of Tertullian,* Oxford University Press, 1971. Contributor to professional journals. Co-editor of book reviews, *Classical World.*

*WORK IN PROGRESS: History of Christian Letters in North Africa before Islam.*

\* \* \*

## SIEGEL, Paul N. 1916-

*PERSONAL:* Born June 24, 1916, in Paterson, N.J.; son of Nathan (a salesman) and Jennie (Rabinowitz) Siegel; married Edith Zwerling (an antique dealer), January 28, 1948; children: Rosalind (Mrs. Edward Neil Robertson). *Education:* College of the City of New York (now City College of the City University of New York), B.S., 1936; Harvard University, M.A., 1939, Ph.D., 1941. *Politics:* Socialist. *Home:* 101 West 85th St., New York, N.Y. 10024. *Office:* Department of English, Long Island University, Brooklyn, N.Y. 11201.

*CAREER:* University of Connecticut, Storrs, instructor in English, 1946; College of the City of New York (now City College of the City University of New York), New York, N.Y., instructor in English, 1946-49; Ripon College, Ripon, Wis., associate professor, 1949-52, professor of English, 1952-56; Long Island University, Brooklyn, N.Y., professor of English, 1956—, chairman of department, 1956-71. Member of Columbia University seminar on the Renaissance. *Military service:* U.S. Army, Medical Administration Corps, 1941-46; became captain. *Member:* Modern Language Association of America, World Centre for Shakespeare Studies, United Federation of College Teachers. *Awards, honors:* Ford Foundation fellowship, 1952-53.

*WRITINGS:* (Contributor) Arthur D. Matthews and Clark Emory, editors, *Studies in Shakespeare,* University of Miami Press, 1952; *Shakespearean Tragedy and the Elizabethan Compromise,* New York University Press, 1957; (editor) *His Infinite Variety: Major Shakespearean Criticism since Johnson,* Lippincott, 1964; (contributor) Oscar James Campbell and Edward G. Quinn, editors, *The Reader's Encyclopedia of Shakespeare,* Crowell, 1966; *Shakespeare in His Time and Ours,* University of Notre Dame Press, 1968; (contributor) Martin Tucker, editor, *The Criti-*

*ical Temper,* Ungar, 1969; (contributor) Marcia Allentuck, editor, *The Achievement of Isaac Bashevis Singer,* Southern Illinois University Press, 1969; (editor) *Macbeth,* Informatics, 1970; (editor) *Leon Trotsky on Literature and Art,* Pathfinder, 1970. Contributor of more than fifty articles and reviews to literature journals. Editorial consultant, *P.M.L.A.* (journal of Modern Language Association of America).

*WORK IN PROGRESS: The Novel and Social Revolution,* a study of twentieth-century novels, for Pathfinder Press.

*SIDELIGHTS:* Paul Siegel is one of the chief participants in the scholarly controversy over Christian interpretations of Shakespeare. He told *CA:* "From the time I went to college in the 1930's, I have been interested in the study of literature in relation to the intellectual and emotional environment created by changes in the economic basis of society. Most of my scholarship and criticism has been on Shakespeare and English Renaissance literature. In it I have sought to see the literary works I was studying both as products of their society and as works of art. I have also been concerned with the revolutionary events of our epoch and their reflections in literature."

A *Sewanee Review* critic, reviewing *Shakespearean Tragedy and the Elizabethan Compromise,* praises the book for suggesting "a mode of seeing that was valuable to Elizabethan poets but has since been overlooked by most students of Elizabethan poetry." *Renaissance News* calls the book a "courageous and significant contribution to Shakespearean scholarship." But Siegel's *Shakespeare in His Time and Ours* is called "rarely illuminating" by a *Choice* reviewer. The *Times Literary Supplement* critic, reviewing the same book, writes: "Throughout the book [Siegel] claims, with almost mystical authority, to know how 'the Elizabethan audience' responded (unanimously) to certain moments in the plays. . . . And with an elementary critical confusion, the beliefs of individual characters are transposed into the revelations made by the plays themselves."

*BIOGRAPHICAL/CRITICAL SOURCES: Seventeenth Century News,* autumn-winter, 1957; *Sewanee Review,* spring, 1958; *Renaissance News,* winter, 1958; *Books Abroad,* winter, 1958; *Choice,* December, 1968, July/August, 1971; *Times Literary Supplement,* June 19, 1969; *English Language Notes,* December, 1969; *Cineaste,* winter, 1970-71.

\* \* \*

## SILBERSTEIN, Gerard Edward 1926-

*PERSONAL:* Born August 19, 1926, in Cleveland, Ohio; son of Louis (a civil servant) and Blanche (Seizler) Silberstein; married Ruth E. Grun (a historian), December 22, 1961; children: Marian. *Education:* University of California, Berkeley, A.A., 1949, B.A. (summa cum laude), 1951; Harvard University, M.A., 1952, Ph.D., 1962. *Politics:* Democrat. *Religion:* No preference. *Home:* 126 Johnston Blvd., Lexington, Ky. 40503. *Office:* Department of History, University of Kentucky, Lexington, Ky. 40506.

*CAREER:* State University of New York College at Cortland, assistant professor of history, 1962-64; University of Kentucky, Lexington, assistant professor, 1964-68, associate professor, 1968-71, professor of European history, 1971—. *Military service:* U.S. Army, Medical Corps, 1944-46. *Member:* American Historical Association, Southern Historical Association, Omicron Delta Kappa, Phi Beta Kappa, Phi Alpha Theta. *Awards, honors:* Fulbright fellow,

1958-59; Hallam Award for best article, 1967-68; Phi Alpha Theta national award for best book of the year, 1970-71.

*WRITINGS: The Troubled Alliance: German-Austrian Relations, 1914-1917,* University Press of Kentucky, 1970. Contributor to history journals.

*WORK IN PROGRESS: The Moroccan Affair: A Study in European Diplomacy, 1906-1912,* completion expected in 1980; research on the Casablanca incident of 1908.

*AVOCATIONAL INTERESTS:* Travel.

\* \* \*

### SILVERSTEIN, Josef 1922-

*PERSONAL:* Born May 15, 1922, in Los Angeles, Calif.; son of Frank and Betty (Heymanson) Silverstein; married Marilyn Cooper, June 20, 1954; children: Frank Stephen, Gordon Alan. *Education:* University of California, Los Angeles, B.A. (honors), 1952; Cornell University, Ph.D., 1960. *Politics:* Democrat. *Religion:* Jewish. *Home:* 93 Overbrook Dr., Princeton, N.J. 08540. *Office:* Department of Political Science, Rutgers University, New Brunswick, N.J. 08903.

*CAREER:* U.S. Merchant Marine, 1942-53; became second officer listed; Wesleyan University, Middletown, Conn., assistant professor of political science, 1958-64; Rutgers University, New Brunswick, N.J., professor of political science, 1967—, chairman of department, 1977-80. Fulbright lectureships, Burma, 1961-62 and Malaysia, 1967-68. Director of Institute of Southeast Asian Studies, Singapore, 1970-72. *Member:* Association for Asian Studies, American Political Science Association, American Association of University Professors.

*WRITINGS:* (Contributor) G. M. Kahin, editor, *Government and Politics of Southeast Asia,* Cornell University Press, 1959, revised edition, 1964; (editor and contributor) *Southeast Asia in World War II: Four Essays,* Yale University Southeast Asian Studies, 1966; (contributor) S. Lipset and P. Altbach, editors, *Students in Revolt,* Houghton, 1969; (contributor) R. M. Smith, editor, *Southeast Asia: Documents of Political Development and Change,* Cornell University Press, 1974; *Burma: Military Rule and the Politics of Stagnation,* Cornell University Press, 1977. Author of *Asia, the One and the Many,* 20 programs produced on the National Broadcasting Company television, 1967.

*WORK IN PROGRESS: The Problem of National Unity in Burma; Political Ideas and Leadership in Southeast Asia.*

\* \* \*

### SILVERSTEIN, Norman 1922-1974

*PERSONAL:* Born March 15, 1922, in Bronx, N.Y.; son of Morris Silverstein. *Education:* College of the City of New York (now City College of the City University of New York), A.B., 1943; Columbia University, M.A., 1947, Ph.D., 1960. *Home:* 10 West 66th St., New York, N.Y. 10023. *Office:* Department of English, Queens College of the City University of New York, Flushing, N.Y. 11367.

*CAREER:* Syracuse University, Syracuse, N.Y., instructor in English, 1948-51; Queens College of the City University of New York, Flushing, N.Y., instructor, 1953-64, assistant professor, 1964-68, associate professor, 1969-73, professor of English, 1973-74. Fulbright lecturer in American literature, Poland, 1965-66. *Military service:* U.S. Army, 1943-46; became sergeant. *Member:* Modern Language Association of America, English Institute, National Council of Teachers of English, North East Modern Language Association.

*WRITINGS:* (With Roy Huss) *The Film Experience: Elements of Motion Picture Art,* Harper, 1968; (contributor) Maurice Harmon, editor, *The Celtic Master,* Dolmen Press, 1969. Contributor to literature journals and to *Japan Quarterly.* Editor, *Salmagundi;* consulting editor, *James Joyce Quarterly;* advisory editor, *Literature/Film Quarterly.*

*WORK IN PROGRESS: Literature and Film Language,* for Croom Helm.†

(Died July 29, 1974)

\* \* \*

### SIMMONS, Gloria Mitchell 1932-

*PERSONAL:* Born March 7, 1932, in Atlanta, Ga.; daughter of Willie B. and Georgia (Jones) Mitchell; married Henry Eugene Simmons (a college professor), January 2, 1956 (divorced September, 1974); children: Goddess Y., Giselle Y., Gabrielle Y. *Education:* Bennett College, A.B., 1955; Atlanta University, M.S. in L.S., 1957. *Religion:* Episcopalian. *Home:* 4800 Chicago Beach Dr., Apt. 1301 N., Chicago, Ill. 60615. *Office:* Department of Library Science, Chicago City College, Loop Branch, 64 East Lake St., Chicago, Ill. 60601.

*CAREER:* Chicago City College, Loop Branch, Chicago, Ill., librarian, 1967—.

*WRITINGS:* (With Helene Hutchinson) *Black Culture,* Holt, 1972.

\* \* \*

### SIMON, John G. 1928-

*PERSONAL:* Born September 19, 1928, in New York, N.Y.; son of Robert A. and Madeleine (Marshall) Simon; married Claire Bising, June 14, 1958; children: John Kirby. *Education:* Harvard University, A.B., 1950; Yale University, LL.B., 1953. *Office:* Law School, Yale University, New Haven, Conn. 06520.

*CAREER:* Office of Secretary of Army, Washington, D.C., assistant to general counsel, 1956-58; private practice of law, New York, N.Y., 1958-62; Yale University, Law School, New Haven, Conn., faculty member, 1962—, Lines Professor of Law, 1976—. President, Taconic Foundation, 1967—; member of steering committee, National Urban Coalition, 1970—. *Military service:* U.S. Army, 1953-56; became first lieutenant. *Member:* Association of Bar of City of New York, Century Association.

*WRITINGS:* (With C. Powers and J. Gunnemann) *The Ethical Investor-Universities and Corporate Responsibility,* Yale University Press, 1972.

*WORK IN PROGRESS:* Research for book on tax policy with respect to philanthropy.

\* \* \*

### SIMON, Pierre-Henri 1903-1972

January 16, 1903—September 20, 1972; French critic, political philosopher, educator, and novelist. Obituaries: *New York Times,* September 21, 1972; *L'Express,* October 2-8, 1972.

\* \* \*

### SIMPSON, Kirke L(arue) 1882(?)-1972

1882(?)—June 16, 1972; American journalist. Obituaries: *New York Times,* June 17, 1972; *Newsweek,* June 26, 1972; *Time,* June 26, 1972.

## SINGER, Benjamin D. 1931-

*PERSONAL:* Born May 3, 1931, in Detroit, Mich.; son of Albert (a salesman) and Eva (Meth) Singer; married Eleanore Gartner, August 16, 1954; children: Lisa, Heidi. *Education:* Wayne State University, B.A., 1961; University of Pennsylvania, M.A., 1965, Ph.D., 1965. *Politics:* New Democrat. *Home:* 5 Lindbrook Ct., London, Ontario, Canada. *Office:* Department of Sociology, University of Western Ontario, London, Ontario, Canada.

*CAREER: Grosse Pointe Press,* Grosse Pointe, Mich., editor, 1952; Palmer-Pann Corp., Detroit, Mich., advertising manager, 1953-55; Singer-Kingswood Advertising Co., Detroit, president, 1957-61; University of Western Ontario, London, associate professor, 1966-72, professor of sociology, 1972—. Lincoln Filene Visiting Scholar, Dartmouth College, 1972-73. Consultant to Children's Psychiatric Research Institute, and Federal Ministry of Communications (Canada). *Military service:* U.S. Air Force, 1948-50. *Member:* International Association for Mass Communication Research, Canadian Sociological and Anthropological Society, American Sociological Association, American Association for Public Opinion Research. *Awards, honors:* Canada Council Leave Award, 1972-73.

*WRITINGS:* (With R. Osborn and J. Geschwender) *Black Rioters,* Heath, 1970; (editor) *Communications in Canadian Society,* Copp-Clark, 1972, 2nd edition, 1975; *Feedback and Society,* Heath, 1973; (contributor) Alvin Toffler, editor, *Learning for Tomorrow,* Random House, 1974. Contributor to *Social Problems, British Journal of Sociology, Public Opinion Quarterly, Social Science and Medicine, American Journal of Mental Deficiency,* and *Social Policy.*

*WORK IN PROGRESS:* A book entitled *The Sociology of Coping.*

*SIDELIGHTS:* Benjamin D. Singer is concerned with "the individual's struggle with increasingly complex or uncontrollable organization." He told *CA* that one of the causes of this baffling complexity is "the tremendous increase in communications technology which has had precisely the antithetical effect upon humans that it has engendered in bureaucracies."

\*     \*     \*

## SINGH, R. K. Janmeja 1932-

*PERSONAL:* Born November 26, 1932, in Montgomery, Punjab, India (now Pakistan); son of S. Puran and Kishan (Kaur) Singh; children: Ritu K. (daughter). *Education:* Punjab University College, M.A., 1956; Harvard University, graduate study, 1962-63; Center for Training in Community Psychiatry and Mental Health Administration, graduate study, 1964-65; Boston University, Ph.D., 1965. *Home:* 1365 Summit Rd., Berkeley, Calif. 94708. *Office:* Center for Training in Community Psychiatry and Mental Health Administration, 1625 Shattuck Ave., Berkeley, Calif. 94704.

*CAREER:* Malwa Teachers' Training College, Ludhiana, Punjab, India, lecturer in psychology, 1957-58; intern in clinical psychology at Boston State Hospital, Boston, Mass., 1959-60, and Lafayette Clinic, Detroit, Mich., 1960-61; clinical psychologist at Porterville State Hospital, Porterville, Calif., 1961-62, and Santa Clara County Mental Health Services, San Jose, Calif., 1963-64; Napa County Mental Health Services, Napa, Calif., chief psychologist, 1965-66; Center for Training in Community Psychiatry and Mental Health Administration, Berkeley, Calif., assistant director,

1966-68; Genesee County Community Mental Health Services, Flint, Mich., deputy commissioner for preventive services, 1968-70; Michigan State University, East Lansing, assistant clinical professor in department of psychiatry, 1969-70; Center for Training in Community Psychiatry and Mental Health Administration, assistant director, 1969—. Lecturer in medical psychology, University of California, School of Medicine, San Francisco, 1966-68, 1970—. Part-time private practice of clinical psychology and consultant in community mental health. Founding member and trustee, Sikh Foundation of the U.S.A.

*MEMBER:* Inter-American Society of Psychology, American Psychological Association, American Orthopsychiatric Association (fellow), American Public Health Association, California State Psychological Association, Sikh Center.

*WRITINGS:* (With William Tarnower and Ronald Chen) *Community Mental Health Consultation and Crisis Intervention,* Book People, 1971; (contributor) Elias Katz, editor, *Mental Health of the Mentally Retarded,* C. C Thomas, 1972.

*WORK IN PROGRESS: Developing Community Mental Health Services and Skills,* for Aldine.

\*     \*     \*

## SKAGEN, Kiki 1943-
### (Shehnaaz Munshi)

*PERSONAL:* Given name is pronounced *Kick*-ee; surname rhymes with *hay*-gun; born December 9, 1943, in San Diego, Calif.; daughter of Edward Madison (a labor organizer) and Virginia (Barnes) Skagen; married Gulammustafa S. Munshi (a college teacher), March 18, 1971; children: Zia (daughter). *Education:* Swarthmore College, B.A., 1965; University of California, Berkeley, M.A., 1968, M.L.S., 1970. *Address:* Box 208, Julian, Calif. 92036. *Office:* National Media Office, University of California, San Diego, La Jolla, Calif.

*CAREER:* Educational Resources Center, New Delhi, India, bibliographer and library consultant, 1969-70; Callison College, Bangalore, India, resident assistant and librarian, 1970-71; U.S. Educational Foundation in India, Ahmedabad, India, student adviser, 1971-72; University of Wisconsin Medieval India Bibliographical Project, Aligarh, India, field director, 1973-74; Callison College, co-director of India program, 1974-75; University of California, San Diego, La Jolla, national media office program development coordinator, 1976—. *Member:* Association for Asian Studies. *Awards, honors:* Fulbright grant for study in India, 1966-67; National Defense/Foreign Language grants (Hindi-Urdu), 1966-67, 1967-68; fellow, University of Hawaii, East-West Center, 1972.

*WRITINGS:* (Editor with Margaret Cormack) *Voices from India,* Praeger, 1972; (editor) *Indian Reference and Bibliography: Reference Works Published in India 1965-70,* U.S. Office of Education, 1972; (editor) *Guidelines to Academic Opportunities in South Asia,* revised edition (Skagen was not associated with first edition), Center for South/Southeast Asia Studies, 1972; (with Philip Kaushall) *The Growing Years: A Study Guide for the Televised Course,* McGraw, 1977; (with Melvin Kieschnick) *Perspectives on Effective Parenting* (monograph), Del Mar, 1977; *Careers in Education and the New Woman* (monograph), Watts, 1977; (editor) *The Age of Uncertainty: Points of Departure* (readings), Houghton, 1977. Writer of articles under name Shehnaaz Munshi.

*WORK IN PROGRESS: Nonny, Nani,* a children's book set in India, 1920.

*SIDELIGHTS:* Kiki Skagen told *CA* that the book of readings she edited is designed to be used with John Kenneth Galbraith's *The Age of Uncertainty,* to accompany a television course. Skagen has some knowledge of the Hindi and Urdu languages; she is also competent in Spanish.

\*    \*    \*

## SKELTON, John E.    1934-

*PERSONAL:* Born May 10, 1934, in Amarillo, Tex.; son of Floyd Wayne (an accountant) and Lucille (Paddock) Skelton; married Katherine Dow, March 22, 1959; children: Laura Ann, Jeanette Kay, Jeffrey Edward. *Education:* University of Denver, B.A., 1956, M.A., 1962, Ph.D., 1971. *Home:* 402 Howtz St., Duluth, Minn. 55812. *Office:* Computer Center, University of Minnesota, Duluth, Minn. 55812.

*CAREER:* U.S. Naval Ordnance Laboratory, Corona, Calif., mathematician, 1956-59; Burroughs Corp., technical representative in Denver, Colo., 1959-63, applied programmer in Pasadena, Calif., 1963-64, supervisor of scientific systems in Detroit, Mich., 1964-65, account manager in Denver, 1965-67; University of Denver, Denver, Colo., research associate, 1967-71, assistant professor of mathematics, 1971-74; University of Minnesota, Duluth, director of computer center, 1974—. *Member:* Mathematical Association of America, Association for Computing Machinery (chairman of Rocky Mountain chapter), Sigma Xi, Phi Delta Kappa.

*WRITINGS: An Introduction to the BASIC Language,* Holt, 1971; (with W. Dorn and M. Robbins) *Who Runs the Computer?,* Westview Press, 1975.

*WORK IN PROGRESS:* Research on administration of university computing centers; research on computer art.

\*    \*    \*

## SKILTON, John H.    1906-

*PERSONAL:* Born August 17, 1906, in Philadelphia, Pa.; son of Robert Henry (a bookkeeper) and Margaret (Beaton) Skilton. *Education:* University of Pennsylvania, B.A., 1927, M.A., 1928, Ph.D., 1961; Westminster Theological Seminary, M.Div., 1939; additional graduate study at University of Basel, 1939, and Cambridge University, summer, 1939. *Politics:* Independent. *Home:* 930 West Olney Ave., Philadelphia, Pa. 19141. *Office:* Westminster Theological Seminary, Chestnut Hill, Philadelphia, Pa. 19118.

*CAREER:* Clergyman of Orthodox Presbyterian Church; minister in Portland, Me., 1933-39; Westminster Theological Seminary, Philadelphia, Pa., instructor, 1939-42, assistant professor, 1942-49, associate professor, 1949-62, professor, 1962-73, lecturer in New Testament, 1974—, associate dean, 1959-62, dean of students, 1962-63, chairman of department of New Testament, 1962-73. Dean, Reformed Bible Institute of the Delaware Valley, 1976—; minister-in-residence, Robert H. Skilton and Margaret B. Skilton House, 1977—. *Member:* Evangelical Theological Society, Near East Archaeological Society, Phi Beta Kappa, Pi Mu Epsilon, Philomathean Society, Philadelphia Athletic Club.

*WRITINGS:* (Contributor) N. B. Stonehouse and Paul Woolley, editors, *The Infallible Word,* Presbyterian Guardian, 1946, 3rd revised edition, Presbyterian & Reformed, 1968; (editor) *Machen's Notes on Galatians,* Presbyterian & Reformed, 1971; *Think on These Things: Bible Truths for Faith and Life,* Presbyterian & Reformed, 1972.

Editor and contributor; all published by Presbyterian & Re-

formed: *Scripture and Confession,* 1973; *The Law and the Prophets,* 1974; *Studying the New Testament Today,* 1974; *The New Testament Student at Work,* 1975; *The New Testament Student and Theology,* 1976; *The New Testament Student and Bible Translation,* 1978. Contributor to theological and Biblical encyclopedias, dictionaries, and journals.

\*    \*    \*

## SKULICZ, Matthew V.    1944-

*PERSONAL:* Surname is pronounced "sk-you-liks"; born March 26, 1944, in Long Beach, Calif.; son of Matthew Victor (an insurance investigator) and Grace (Parco) Skulicz; married Marleen O'Brien, October 23, 1971. *Education:* Fordham University, A.B., 1965; University of North Carolina, M.A., 1967, Ph.D., 1969. *Politics:* None. *Religion:* "LSD." *Office:* Department of English, University of California, Los Angeles, Calif. 90024.

*CAREER:* University of California, Los Angeles, assistant professor of English, 1969—.

*WRITINGS: Right on Shane* (juvenile), Putnam, 1972.

*SIDELIGHTS:* Skulicz's major interests are "survival, freedom, beauty."†

\*    \*    \*

## SLAUGHTER, Eugene Edward    1909-

*PERSONAL:* Born June 9, 1909, in Pontotoc, Okla.; son of William Curtis (a banker) and Maybelle (Penick) Slaughter; married Dorothy Orrine Truby, December 26, 1933; children: Eugene Edward, Jr. (died, September 23, 1964), Dorothy Joelle Slaughter Bedwell, James William. *Education:* Southeastern State Teachers College (now Southeastern Oklahoma State University), A.B., 1929; Vanderbilt University, A.M., 1930, Ph.D., 1946. *Politics:* Democrat. *Religion:* Disciples of Christ. *Home:* 2020 Acorn Trail, Durant, Okla. 74701. *Office:* Southeastern Oklahoma State University, Durant, Okla. 74701.

*CAREER:* Employed during his undergraduate years as department store salesman and bank stenographer; high school principal and teacher of English, Latin, and mathematics, Albany, Okla., 1927-28; Southeastern Oklahoma State University, Durant, Okla., associate professor, 1932-45, professor of English, 1946-74, professor emeritus, 1974—, head of Division of English, General Humanities, Journalism, and Speech, 1960-74. Chief of modern language branch, U.S. Office of Education, 1965-67. *Military service:* U.S. Navy, 1942-45, 1950-52. U.S. Naval Reserve, 1945-50, 1952-69; retired with rank of captain.

*MEMBER:* Association of Departments of English (member of executive committee, 1969-71), Modern Language Association of America (life member), National Council of Teachers of English (life member; director-at-large, 1967-68), National Education Association (life member), Modern Humanities Research Association (life member), Reserve Officers Association of the United States (life member), U.S. Naval Institute, Naval Reserve Association (life member), Retired Officers Association (life member), South Central College English Association (president, 1961-62), South Central Association of Departments of English (chairman, 1968-69), South Central Modern Language Association, Oklahoma Council of Teachers of English (honorary life member; president of council, 1946), Oklahoma Education Association (life member; member of board of directors, 1958-60), Kappa Delta Pi, Sigma Tau Delta, Rotary Club.

*WRITINGS:* (Contributor) *Essays in Honor of Walter*

*Clyde Curry,* Vanderbilt University Press, 1955; *Virtue According to Love: In Chaucer,* Bookman Associates, 1957; (with others) *The National Interest and the Teaching of English,* National Council of Teachers of English, 1961; (with others) *The National Interest and the Continuing Education of Teachers of English,* 1964. Also co-author of a report on a federally funded teacher-training project, *The Experiment That Worked,* 1976. Contributor of about twenty-five articles and reviews to education journals.

*WORK IN PROGRESS:* Studies in Chaucer's treatment of universals.

\* \* \*

## SLEIGH, Robert Collins, Jr. 1932-

*PERSONAL:* Born November 30, 1932, in Marblehead, Mass.; son of Robert Collins and Clara (Smith) Sleigh; married Phyllis Doliber (a real estate broker), September 5, 1953; children: David, Stephen, Joanne. *Education:* Dartmouth College, B.A., 1954; Brown University, M.A., 1957, Ph.D., 1963. *Politics:* Democrat. *Religion:* None. *Home:* 16 Forestedge Rd., Amherst, Mass. 01002. *Office:* Department of Philosophy, University of Massachusetts, Amherst, Mass. 01002.

*CAREER:* Wayne State University, Detroit, Mich., instructor, 1958-61, assistant professor, 1961-65, associate professor, 1965-69, professor of philosophy, 1969; University of Massachusetts—Amherst, professor of philosophy, 1969—. Visiting assistant professor of philosophy, Dartmouth College, summer, 1965; visiting associate professor, Harvard University, 1965-66; visiting professor of philosophy, University of Michigan, 1973. *Member:* American Philosophical Association, Association for Symbolic Logic. *Awards, honors:* Wayne State University faculty research fellow, 1966; Center for Advanced Study in the Behavioral Sciences fellow, 1967; American Council of Learned Societies fellow, 1967.

*WRITINGS:* (Editor) *Necessary Truth,* Prentice-Hall, 1971. Contributor to *Journal of Philosophy, Nous, Philosophical Studies,* and *Philosophy and Phenomenological Research.†*

\* \* \*

## SLOAN, Edward William III 1931-

*PERSONAL:* Born October 19, 1931, in Cleveland, Ohio; son of Edward William, Jr. (a business executive) and Josephine (Rudolph) Sloan; married Kathleen O'Shea Hunter (a college professor), March 30, 1970; children: Elisabeth, Palmer, Sarah, Michael, Mary. *Education:* Yale University, A.B., 1953, M.A., 1954; Harvard University, M.A., 1960, Ph.D., 1963. *Home:* 13 High St., Farmington, Conn. 06032. *Office:* Department of History, Trinity College, Hartford, Conn. 06106.

*CAREER:* First Boston Corp., New York, N.Y., financial analyst, 1957-59; Trinity College, Hartford, Conn., assistant professor, 1964-68, associate professor, 1968-75, professor of history, 1975—, director, American studies program, 1972-76. Seminar leader and visiting professor, Munson Institute of American Maritime History; reader for advanced placement examinations in American history, Educational Testing Service. Consultant in New Campuses Program, University of California. *Military service:* U.S. Army, military intelligence analyst and instructor in Army Transportation School, 1954-56. *Member:* American Historical Association, Organization of American Historians, American

Association of University Professors, American Studies Association, International Naval Research Organization, United States Naval Institute, Marine Historical Association, Inc., Phi Beta Kappa, Pi Gamma Mu, Delta Psi.

*WRITINGS: Benjamin Franklin Isherwood, Naval Engineer: The Years as Engineer-in-Chief, 1861-1869,* U.S. Naval Institute, 1965; *Maritime History: A Basic Bibliography,* American Library Association, 1972; (contributor) B. W. Labaree, editor, *The Atlantic World of R. G. Albion,* Wesleyan University Press, 1975. Contributor to *Choice.* Consultant in maritime literature, Wesleyan University Press.

*WORK IN PROGRESS: The Maritime Revolution in Steam.*

\* \* \*

## SLOANE, Thomas O. 1929-

*PERSONAL:* Born July 12, 1929, in West Frankfort, Ill.; son of Thomas O. (an auditor) and Blanche (Morris) Sloan; married Barbara Lewis (a teacher), November 1, 1952; children: Elizabeth, David, Emily. *Education:* Southern Illinois University, B.A., 1951, M.A., 1952; Northwestern University, Ph.D., 1960. *Home:* 366 San Carlos Ave., Piedmont, Calif. 94611. *Office:* Department of Rhetoric, University of California, Berkeley, Calif. 94720.

*CAREER:* Southern Illinois University, Carbondale, lecturer in speech, 1956; Washington and Lee University, Lexington, Va., instructor in English, 1958-60; University of Illinois at Urbana-Champaign, assistant professor, 1960-65, associate professor of speech, 1965-70, assistant dean of liberal arts, 1966-67, associate head of department of speech, 1967-68; University of California, Berkeley, professor of rhetoric, 1970—, chairman of department, 1972—. *Military service:* U.S. Naval Reserve, 1952-56; became lieutenant. *Member:* Modern Language Association of America, Speech Communication Association, Renaissance Society of America. *Awards, honors:* Research awards from Huntington Library, 1967, and University of California, Berkeley, 1974.

*WRITINGS:* (Editor) *The Oral Study of Literature,* Random House, 1966; (editor) Thomas Wright, *The Passions of the Minde in Generall* (1604), University of Illinois Press, 1971; (with Joanna H. Maclay) *Interpretation,* Random House, 1972; (with R. B. Waddington) *The Rhetoric of Renaissance Poetry,* University of California Press, 1974. Contributor to literary and speech journals. Associate editor of *Speech Monographs* and of *Quarterly Journal of Speech,* 1972-75.

*WORK IN PROGRESS: The Text: Reading Rhetorically;* developments in English rhetorical theory in the seventeenth century; the rhetoric of modern poetry.

\* \* \*

## SMARIDGE, Norah (Antoinette) 1903-

*PERSONAL:* Born March 30, 1903, in England; daughter of Henry and Heloise Smaridge. *Education:* University of London, B.A. (honors), 1924; further courses at Columbia University and Hunter College (now Hunter College of the City University of New York). *Politics:* Democrat. *Religion:* Catholic. *Home:* 11 Godfrey Rd., Upper Montclair, N.J. 07043.

*CAREER:* Former teacher at Marymount High School and Junior College, New York, N.Y., 1925-35; advertising writer for St. Anthony Guild Press, Paterson, N.J., 1937-48;

professional writer. *Member:* Writers Guild, British Women's Club (Montclair, N.J.).

*WRITINGS*—Mostly for young people: *Atlantic Deception* (adult novel), C. Arthur Pearson, 1938; *Home in the Sky* (adult novel), C. Arthur Pearson, 1938; *Neatos and Litterbugs: Mystery of the Missing Ticket,* Golden Press, 1952, reprinted, 1977; *Ludi, the Little St. Bernard,* Bruce, 1956; *Nando of the Beach,* Bruce, 1958; *Sunday Best* (poems), Bruce, 1959; *Hands of Mercy: The Story of Sister-Nurses in the Civil War,* Benziger, 1960; *Bernard: A Patron Saint,* Sheed, 1960; *Five Gifts from God* (poem), Bruce, 1961, published as *Your Five Gifts,* C. R. Gibson, 1969; *Looking at You,* Abingdon, 1962; *Saint Helena,* St. Anthony Guild Press, 1962; *Pen and Bayonet: The Story of Joyce Kilmer,* Hawthorn, 1962; *The Big Tidy-Up* (poems), Bruce, 1963, reprinted, Golden Press, 1970; *Impatient Jonathan,* Abingdon, 1964; *The Light Within: The Story of Maria Montessori,* Hawthorn, 1965; *Peter's Tent,* Viking, 1965; *A Family Guide to Pets and Hobbies,* Abbey Press, 1965; *Graymoor's Treasury of Meatless Recipes,* Graymoor, 1965; *Watch Out!,* Abingdon, 1965; *Master Mariner: The Adventurous Life of Joseph Conrad,* Hawthorn, 1966; *Feast Days and Fun Days,* Guild Press, 1966; *Famous British Women Novelists,* Dodd, 1967; *The Tallest Lady in the World: The Statue of Liberty,* Hawthorn, 1967; *What a Silly Thing to Do,* Abingdon, 1967; *Long before Forty,* Hawthorn, 1968; *Teacher's Pest* (poems), Hawthorn, 1968; *I Do My Best,* Golden Press, 1968; *Scary Things* (poems), Abingdon, 1969; *Lee's Dad,* L. W. Singer, 1969; *The March King,* L. W. Singer, 1969; *Famous Modern Storytellers for Young People,* Dodd, 1969; *Raggedy Ann: A Thank You, Please, and I Love You Book,* Golden Press, 1969; *The World of Chocolate,* Messner, 1969.

*The Odds and Ends Playground,* Golden Press, 1970; *Audubon: The Man Who Painted Birds,* World Publishing, 1970; *Trailblazers in American Arts,* Messner, 1971; *Where Did Everybody Go? Funny Rhymes About Place Words,* Golden Press, 1971; *Litterbugs Come in Every Size,* Golden Press, 1972; *Time for Everything,* Rand McNally, 1972; (with Hilda Hunter) *The Teen-ager's Guide to Collecting Practically Anything,* Dodd, 1972; *Famous Author-Illustrators for Young People,* Dodd, 1973; *Raggedy Andy: The I Can Do It, You Can Do It Book,* Golden Press, 1973; *You Know Better Than That,* Abingdon, 1973; (with Hunter) *Teen-ager's Guide to Hobbies for Here and Now,* Dodd, 1974; *Choosing Your Retirement Hobby,* Dodd, 1976; *Famous Literary Teams for Young People,* Dodd, 1977; *School Is Not a Missile Range,* Abingdon, 1977; *The Secret of the Brownstone House,* Dodd, 1977.

Book notes published by Barnes & Noble: *Jane Austen: Emma,* 1966; *George Eliot: Middlemarch,* 1967; *George Eliot: Adam Bede,* 1968; *Jane Austen: Sense and Sensibility,* 1969.

Translator: Suzanne Martel, *The City under the Ground,* Viking, 1964; Claude Jean-Nesmy, *Living the Liturgy,* Alba, 1966; Jacques Laclercq, *The Apostolic Spirituality of the Nursing Sister,* Alba, 1967; Francois Amiot, *From Scripture to Prayer: Daily Readings on the Gospels and St. Paul,* four volumes, Alba, 1967. Translator of series of Bible stories from the Italian for C. R. Gibson.

Writer of monthly column, "Book Nook," in *Catholic Weekly.*

*WORK IN PROGRESS: The Story of Cake,* for Abingdon; an easy-reading book, tentatively entitled *The Ghost of Enderby Hall,* for Dodd.

*AVOCATIONAL INTERESTS:* The theater, reading, young people, cats ("I have ten").

*        *        *

## SMART, (Peter) Alastair (Marshall)   1922-

*PERSONAL:* Born April 30, 1922, in Cambridge, England; son of William Marshall (a university professor emeritus) and Isabel (Carswell) Smart; married Marita Christl Lawler-Wilson; children: Lydia Clare Marita, Julian Alastair Carswell. *Education:* University of Glasgow, M.A., 1942; Edinburgh Theological College, G.O.E. examination, 1946; Edinburgh College of Art, D.A., 1949; attended Institute of Fine Arts, New York University, 1954-55. *Office:* Department of Fine Art, University of Nottingham, Nottingham, England.

*CAREER:* University of Hull, Yorkshire, England, staff tutor, 1949-56; University of Nottingham, Nottingham, England, professor of fine art, 1956—. Member of Institute for Advanced Study, Princeton, N.J., 1964-65. Visiting professor, University of Wisconsin—Milwaukee, 1976. *Military service:* British Army, 1942-43. *Member:* Royal Society of Arts (fellow), International Association of Art Critics, Walpole Society, Society of Authors, Association of Art Historians. *Awards, honors:* Commendation from Scottish P.E.N. for first book, *The Life and Art of Allan Ramsay,* 1952; Commonwealth Fund fellowship, 1954-55.

*WRITINGS: The Life and Art of Allan Ramsay,* Routledge & Kegan Paul, 1952; *The Assisi Problem and the Art of Giotto,* Clarendon Press, Oxford, 1971; *The Renaissance and Mannerism in Italy,* Harcourt, 1972; *The Renaissance and Mannerism in Northern Europe and Spain,* Harcourt, 1972; (with A. Brooks) *Constable and His Country,* Elek, 1976; *The Dawn of Italian Painting, 1250-1400,* Phaidon, 1978. Also author of short monographs on Allan Ramsay and Fra Angelico, and of numerous exhibition catalogues, including *Allan Ramsay,* Royal Academy of Arts, 1964, *Introducing Francis Cotes, R.A.,* Nottingham, 1971, and *Thomas Shotter Boys: Centenary Exhibition,* Nottingham and Agnew, 1974. General editor, *Harbrace History of Art,* 1972—.

*WORK IN PROGRESS: Allan Ramsay: Catalogue Raisonne of Portraits,* Paul Mellon Centre for Studies in British Art (London).

*        *        *

## SMELYAKOV, Yaroslav   1913(?)-1972

1913(?)—November 27, 1972; Russian poet. Obituaries: *New York Times,* November 29, 1972.

*        *        *

## SMITH, Arthur L(ee), Jr.   1927-

*PERSONAL:* Born April 19, 1927, in Los Angeles, Calif.; son of Arthur Lee and Nettie (Sullivan) Smith; married Jutta G. Eymert, December 5, 1948; children: Karl William, Scott Alister. *Education:* Attended Bern School of Languages, 1947; Chapman College, B.A., 1951; University of Southern California, M.A., 1952, Ph.D., 1956. *Politics:* Democrat. *Religion:* None. *Home:* 3616 Thorndale Rd., Pasadena, Calif. 91107. *Office:* California State University, 5151 State College Dr., Los Angeles, Calif. 90032.

*CAREER:* Occidental College, Los Angeles, Calif., instructor in European history, 1955-56; California State University, Los Angeles, assistant professor, 1956-62, associate professor, 1962-65, professor of history, 1965—, resident director of international programs in Germany, 1972-73. *Military service:* U.S. Army Air Forces, 1945-47. *Member:* American Historical Association, American Committee on History of World War II, Conference Group for Central European History.

*WRITINGS: The Deutschtum of Nazi Germany,* Nijhoff, 1965; *Churchill's German Army, Wartime Strategy and Cold War Politics, 1943-1947,* Sage Publications, 1977. Contributor of articles to history journals in the United States and abroad.

*WORK IN PROGRESS:* Study of German foreign policy in the Hitler period.

\* \* \*

## SMITH, Clagett G. 1930-

*PERSONAL:* Born December 4, 1930, in Washington, D.C.; married Mary Ellen Wells (a social worker), April, 1960; children: Julie Suzanne, David Paul. *Education:* University of Maryland, B.A. (with first honors), 1953, M.A., 1955; University of Michigan, Ph.D., 1961. *Politics:* Democrat. *Religion:* Unitarian-Universalist. *Office:* Department of Sociology and Anthropology, University of Notre Dame, Notre Dame, Ind. 46556.

*CAREER:* U.S. Naval Medical Research Institute, Bethesda, Md., psychology trainee, 1954-55; Veterans Administration Neuropsychiatric Hospital, Battle Creek, Mich., social psychology fellow, 1956-57; University of Michigan, Ann Arbor, study director at survey research center of Institute for Social Research, 1960-64; University of Wisconsin—Madison, associate professor of social psychology at Center for Advanced Study in Organization Science, and associate professor of sociology at Milwaukee campus, 1964-68; University of Notre Dame, Notre Dame, Ind., professor of sociology and anthropology, 1968—. *Member:* American Psychological Association, American Sociological Association, Society for the Psychological Study of Social Issues, American Academy of Political and Social Science, New York Academy of Sciences, Phi Kappa Phi, Psi Chi. *Awards, honors:* Carnegie Foundation grant, 1960-64.

*WRITINGS:* (Editor with Arnold S. Tannenbaum, Jerald Bachman, and Philip Marcus, and contributor) *Control in Organizations,* McGraw, 1968; (editor) *Conflict Resolution: Contribution of the Behavioral Sciences,* University of Notre Dame Press, 1971; *Mental Hospitals: A Study in Organizational Effectiveness,* Heath Lexington, 1975. Contributor of about twenty-five articles to sociology and psychology journals.

*WORK IN PROGRESS:* Writing on conflict resolution, on mental health systems, and on complex organizations.

\* \* \*

## SMITH, George E. 1938-

*PERSONAL:* Born March 21, 1938, in Chester, Ohio; son of Dale (an insurance man) and Alma Smith; married Maureen Capehart, September 3, 1966; children: Robin, Leslie, Trent. *Education:* Attended Kent State University. *Home address:* R.D. 2, Box 102, New Cumberland, W.Va. 26047.

*CAREER:* Rural mail carrier in New Cumberland, W.Va., 1966—. *Military service:* U.S. Army, Medic, 1955-66; became staff sergeant; received Purple Heart. *Member:* National Association of Letter Carriers (president of local chapter), West Virginia State Association of Letter Carriers (secretary).

*WRITINGS: P.O.W.: Two Years with the Viet Cong,* Ramparts, 1971.

*BIOGRAPHICAL/CRITICAL SOURCES: Ramparts,* July, 1966, September, 1969.††

\* \* \*

## SMITH, Gerald A(lfred) 1921-

*PERSONAL:* Born March 16, 1921, in Canandaigua, N.Y.; son of Hugh E. (a mason) and Teresa (Farrell) Smith; married Margaret Murphy, March 14, 1945; children: Katherine, Anne (Mrs. John Williams), David, Barbara (Mrs. Rene Sylvester), Susan (Mrs. Christopher Sweeney), Stephen, Edward. *Education:* University of Notre Dame, B.A., 1943; University of Rochester, M.A., 1947; Johns Hopkins University, Ph.D., 1957. *Politics:* Democrat. *Religion:* Roman Catholic. *Home:* 7 Elm St., Geneseo, N.Y. 14454. *Office:* Department of English, State University of New York College, Geneseo, N.Y. 14454.

*CAREER:* University of Rochester, Rochester, N.Y., instructor in English, 1947-48; University of Maryland, College Park, instructor in English, 1951-55; Canisius College, Buffalo, N.Y., assistant professor of English, 1955-57; University of Rochester, assistant professor of English, 1957-58; State University of New York College at Geneseo, associate professor, 1958-60, professor of English, 1960—. *Military service:* U.S. Naval Reserve, active duty, 1942-46; became lieutenant. *Member:* Modern Language Association of America, American Association of University Professors, Malone Society.

*WRITINGS:* (Editor) John Marston, *The Fawn,* University of Nebraska, 1965. Contributor of articles to literature journals. Associate editor, *Hopkins Review,* 1950-51.

*WORK IN PROGRESS:* Editing *The Complete Plays of John Marston.*

\* \* \*

## SMITH, Henry Lee, Jr. 1913-1972

July 11, 1913—December 13, 1972; American educator and authority in the fields of anthropology and linguistics. Obituaries: *New York Times,* December 15, 1972; *Washington Post,* December 16, 1972.

\* \* \*

## SMITH, Jean Edward 1932-

*PERSONAL:* Born October 13, 1932, in Washington, D.C.; son of Jean M. and Eddyth (Carter) Smith; married Christine Zinsel, October 24, 1959; children: Sonja, Christopher. *Education:* Princeton University, A.B., 1954; Columbia University, Ph.D., 1964. *Home:* 138 Roxborough Dr., Toronto, Ontario, Canada. *Agent:* Sterling Lord Agency, 660 Madison Ave., New York, N.Y. 10021. *Office:* Department of Political Economy, University of Toronto, Toronto, Ontario, Canada.

*CAREER:* Dartmouth College, Hanover, N.H., assistant professor of government, 1963-65; University of Toronto, Toronto, Ontario, professor of political economy, 1965—. Research assistant, Center for International Studies, Princeton University, 1967-68; visiting scholar, Columbia University, 1970-71. *Military service:* U.S. Army, 1954-61; became captain. *Member:* Canadian Political Science Association, Academy of Political Science. *Awards, honors:* Woodrow Wilson fellow, 1971.

*WRITINGS: The Defense of Berlin,* Johns Hopkins Press,

1963; *Der Weg ins Delimma*, Ullstein, 1965; *Germany beyond the Wall*, Little, Brown, 1969; *The Papers of General Lucius D. Clay: Germany, 1945-1949*, Indiana University Press, 1974. Contributor to literature and political science journals.

*BIOGRAPHICAL/CRITICAL SOURCES: New York Times Book Review*, March 23, 1969; *Christian Science Monitor*, June 10, 1969; *Virginia Quarterly Review*, autumn, 1969; *Canadian Forum*, March, 1970.

\*     \*     \*

## SMITH, Joseph Fielding   1876-1972

July 19, 1876—July 3, 1972; American spiritual leader of the Mormon Church and author of religious works. Obituaries: *New York Times*, July 3, 1972; *National Observer*, July 15, 1972; *Time*, July 19, 1972.

\*     \*     \*

## SMITH, Maxwell A(ustin)   1894-

*PERSONAL:* Born November 3, 1894, in Madison, Wis.; son of Leonard Sewall (a professor) and Lucy (Austin) Smith; married Mary Clyde Farrior, June 1, 1924 (died, 1972); children: Marylen (Mrs. Tom Jackson), Sylvia (Mrs. George Field). *Education:* University of Wisconsin, A.B., 1917, M.A., 1918; Sorbonne, University of Paris, docteur de l'universite, 1920. *Politics:* Independent. *Religion:* Congregationalist. *Home:* 1300 Nylic St., Apt. B, Tallahassee, Fla. 32304.

*CAREER:* Iowa State College of Agriculture and Mechanic Arts (now Iowa State University of Science and Technology), Ames, instructor in French, 1918; University of Wisconsin—Madison, instructor in French, 1920-22; University of Chattanooga, Chattanooga, Tenn., professor of French, 1922-28; University of California, Los Angeles, assistant professor of French, 1928-29; University of Chattanooga, professor, 1929-61, Guerry Professor of French, 1961-65, also served as dean; Florida State University, Tallahassee, visiting professor of French, 1965-70. *Member:* American Association of Teachers of French, Phi Beta Kappa. *Awards, honors:* Chevalier de la Legion d'Honneur, 1961.

*WRITINGS: L'influence des Lakistes sur les romantiques francais*, Jouve, 1920; *Short History of French Literature*, Holt, 1924; (editor) *Short Stories by French Romanticists*, Heath, 1929; (editor with Helen Posgate) *French Short Stories of the Twentieth Century*, Oxford University Press, 1930; (with Posgate) *French Short Stories of the Second Half of the Nineteenth Century*, Macmillan, 1932; (editor with Mary Ruth Smith) Victor Hugo, *Marion De Lorme*, Appleton-Century, 1934; *Knight of the Air: The Life and Works of Antoine de Saint-Exupery*, Pageant, 1956; (editor) *A Saint-Exupery Reader*, Dodd, 1961; (editor) *Giono Selections*, Heath, 1965; *Jean Giono*, Twayne, 1966; *Francois Mauriac*, Twayne, 1970; *Prosper Merimee*, Twayne, 1972. French editor, "Twayne World Authors" series; former editor, *French Review*.

*SIDELIGHTS:* Maxwell Smith told *CA:* "While consulting the multitude of newspapers and magazines about Giono in the Bibliotheque Nationale I received from the former Nazi occupation authorities the same involuntary cooperation that I had experienced with my earlier book on St. Exupery, and later was to find for my volume on Mauriac. To keep as many able-bodied French youths as possible from deportation as workers to Germany, every effort was made by French authorities during the Occupation to find work which

would appear to the Nazis as indispensable. Accordingly a number of young men were employed by the National Library to make dossiers of all the articles which had been published on French authors. As a result I found a fat packet containing every article which had appeared on Giono from 1929 to 1944.

"When I interviewed Francois Mauriac in 1962 while writing my book on him, I questioned him about the French policeman I had seen walking to and fro in front of his apartment. He confirmed to me that the government, feeling him to be in danger, had stationed a security officer permanently there. This was the period when OAS was taking vengeance on all who supported De Gaulle's anti-colonial policy in Algeria and an effort had been made to blow up Mauriac's country home at Malagar. When my wife and I later visited there we were almost knocked over by the same huge watch dog which had appeared on the scene just in time to rout the invaders."

Clifford J. Gallant, reviewing *Francois Mauriac* in *Modern Language Journal*, writes: "Any one who does not read French, or who does for that matter, and who seeks a review of or an introduction to Francois Mauriac, will glean much from this thorough, clear contribution to Mauriac scholarship. Professor Smith brings a great deal that is new on Mauriac the man and his works. This is the book that any Mauriac scholar could wish he had written."

*BIOGRAPHICAL/CRITICAL SOURCES: Modern Language Journal*, December, 1970, November, 1974.

\*     \*     \*

## SMITH, Murphy D(ewitt)   1920-

*PERSONAL:* Born October 16, 1920, in Birmingham, Ala.; son of Murphy Dewitt (a mechanic) and Damie Emmaline (Hogan) Smith. *Education:* University of Tennessee, B.A., 1949, M.A., 1950; further study at University of Pennsylvania. *Office:* American Philosophical Society Library, 105 South Fifth St., Philadelphia, Pa. 19106.

*CAREER:* American Philosophical Society Library, Philadelphia, Pa., manuscripts librarian, 1952-70, associate librarian, 1971—. *Member:* American Library Association, American Historical Association, Society of American Archivists, Manuscripts Society.

*WRITINGS: A Guide to Manuscripts Relating to the American Indian in the Library of the American Philosophical Society*, American Philosophical Society, 1966; *Guide to the Archives and Manuscript Collections of the American Philosophical Society*, American Philosophical Society, 1966; *Oak from an Acorn: A History of the American Philosophical Society Library, 1770-1803*, Scholarly Resources Inc., 1976. Contributor to professional journals.

*WORK IN PROGRESS:* Travel through North America to view Indian remains, with a book expected to result; "wide-ranging travel which I hope to utilize for a personal history of travel in my lifetime."

\*     \*     \*

## SMITH, Neil Homer   1909(?)-1972

1909(?)—August 17, 1972; American foreign correspondent and editor. Obituaries: *New York Times*, August 18, 1972.

\*     \*     \*

## SMITH, Robert D.   1937-

*PERSONAL:* Born December 7, 1937, in Erie, Pa.; son of

Ira Edward and Rozella (Zimmerman) Smith; married Vilma Josefina Monserrate, August 28, 1966; children: Roger Edward, Victor Hermand, Elena Marie. *Education:* Gannon College, B.S., 1959; Pennsylvania State University, M.S., 1964, Ph.D., 1966. *Religion:* Catholic. *Home:* 1587 Morris Rd., Kent, Ohio 44240. *Office:* College of Business, Kent State University, Kent, Ohio 44242.

*CAREER:* Pennsylvania State University, University Park, assistant professor of management, 1964-68; Kent State University, Kent, Ohio, associate professor, 1969-71, professor of administrative sciences, 1972—. Visiting professor at University of Puerto Rico, Rio Piedras, summers, 1971, 1972, and University of South Africa, 1975. Director of executive development programs in Mexico, Puerto Rico, South Africa, Florida, Pennsylvania, and Ohio. *Military service:* U.S. Army, 1960-62; became first lieutenant. *Member:* Academy of Management, American Institute of Decision Sciences, Beta Gamma Sigma, Omicron Delta Kappa, Scabbard and Blade (chapter president).

*WRITINGS:* (With Earl Poe Strong) *Management Control Models,* Holt, 1968; (with Paul S. Greenlaw) *Personnel Management: A Management Science Approach,* International Textbook, 1970; (with Paul Gross) *Systems Analysis and Design for Management,* Dun, Donnelley, 1976; (with Elmer Burack) *Personnel Management: A Human Resource Systems Approach,* West Publishing, 1977.

\* \* \*

## SMITH, Robert Eliot 1899-

*PERSONAL:* Born May 24, 1899, in Arcachon, France; son of Franklin Taylor (a lawyer) and Mary (Eliot) Smith; married Rebecca Perkins, September 15, 1934. *Education:* Harvard University, B.A., 1922, further study, 1931-32. *Politics:* Republican. *Religion:* Episcopalian. *Address:* P.O. Box 1395, Rancho Santa Fe, Calif. 92067.

*CAREER:* Carnegie Institution, Washington, D.C., member of staff, 1930-59; Instituto Nacional de Antropologiae Historia, Cordoba, Mexico, director of excavation, 1960-62; Harvard University, Peabody Museum, Cambridge, Mass., research associate in Middle American ceramics, 1965-68, honorary research associate, 1968—. Special assistant, U.S. Military Attache (Guatemala), 1942-44. *Military service:* U.S. Army, 1918. *Member:* American Anthropological Association (fellow), Society for American Archaeology (fellow), La Sociedad de Geografia e Historiade Guatemala.

*WRITINGS: A Study of Structure A-I Complex at Uaxactun, Peten, Guatemala,* Carnegie Institution, 1937; *Pottery from Chipoc Alta Verapaz, Guatemala,* Carnegie Institution, 1952; *Ceramic Sequence at Uaxactun, Guatemala,* two volumes, Middle American Research Institute, Tulane University, 1955; *The Place of Fine Grange Pottery in Mesoamerican Archaeology,* American Antiquity, 1958; *The Pottery of Mayapan,* two volumes, Peabody Museum, Harvard University, 1971.

*WORK IN PROGRESS: A Ceramic Sequence from the Pyramid of the Sun at Teotihuacan, Mexico,* for Peabody Museum, Harvard University.

*SIDELIGHTS:* Robert Eliot Smith has conducted archaeological studies in Mexico, Guatemala, Honduras, British Honduras, and Salvador.

\* \* \*

## SMYLIE, James H(utchinson) 1925-

*PERSONAL:* Born October 20, 1925, in Huntington,

W.Va.; son of Theodore Shaw (a minister) and Mildred (Hutchinson) Smylie; married Elizabeth Roblee, November 23, 1951; children: Mark Andrew, Margaret Elizabeth, Mary Catherine. *Education:* Washington University, St. Louis, Mo., B.A., 1946; Princeton Theological Seminary, B.D., 1949, Th.M., 1950, Th.D., 1958. *Office:* Union Theological Seminary in Virginia, 3401 Brook Rd., Richmond, Va. 23227.

*CAREER:* Clergyman of United Presbyterian Church in the U.S.A.; First Presbyterian Church, St. Louis, Mo., assistant minister, 1950-52; Princeton Theological Seminary, Princeton, N.J., instructor, 1956-59, assistant professor of church history, 1959-62, director of studies, 1960-62; Union Theological Seminary in Virginia, Richmond, alumni visiting professor, 1962-64, associate professor, 1964-67, professor of American church history, 1967—. Visiting professor at Pittsburgh Theological Seminary, 1964, Perkins School of Theology, summer, 1966, Sweetbriar College, 1974, and Vancouver School of Theology, 1976. *Member:* American Historical Association, American Studies Association, American Catholic Historical Association, Presbyterian Historical Society, American Society of Church History (secretary, 1963-74), Organization of American Historians, American Academy of Religion, Society for the Scientific Study of Religion, Association for the Study of Afro-American Life and History, American Association of University Professors, Southern Historical Association.

*WRITINGS: Into All the World,* John Knox, 1965; *A Cloud of Witnesses,* John Knox, 1965; (contributor) Daniel Callahan, editor, *The Secular City Debate,* Macmillan, 1966; (contributor) Elwyn Smith, editor, *The Religion of the Republic,* Fortress, 1971. Also editor of *Presbyterians and the American Revolution: A Documentary Account,* 1974, and *Presbyterians and the American Revolution: An Interpretive Account,* 1976. Contributor to encyclopedias, dictionaries, and religious and theological journals. Editor, *Journal of Presbyterian History,* 1968—.

\* \* \*

## SMYTHE, Mabel M(urphy) 1918-

*PERSONAL:* Born April 3, 1918, in Montgomery, Ala.; daughter of Harry Saunders (owner of a printing company) and Josephine (Dibble) Murphy; married Hugh H. Smythe (a sociologist), July 26, 1939 (died June 26, 1977); children: Karen Pamela. *Education:* Attended Spelman College, 1933-36; Mount Holyoke College, A.B., 1937; Northwestern University, M.A., 1940; University of Wisconsin, Ph.D., 1942; also studied at New York University, 1949. *Office:* American Embassy, B.P. 817, Yaounde, Cameroon.

*CAREER:* Lincoln University, Jefferson City, Mo., 1942-45, began as assistant professor, became associate professor of economics and business administration, and acting head of department; Tennessee Agricultural and Industrial State College (now Tennessee Agricultural and Industrial State University), Nashville, professor of economics, 1945-46; Brooklyn College (now Brooklyn College of the City University of New York), Brooklyn, N.Y., lecturer in economics, 1946-47; free-lance writer, 1948-51; Shiga University, Shiga, Japan, visiting professor of economics, 1951-53; high school teacher and principal in New York City, 1954-69; City College of the City University of New York, lecturer, 1959-60; Phelps-Stokes Fund, New York City, vice-president and director of research and publications, 1969—; U.S. Ambassador to United Republic of Cameroon (on leave from Phelps-Stokes Fund), 1977—. Member of advisory council, National Assessment of Educational Progress; member of advisory council on African Affairs, U.S. Department of State, 1962-70; member of U.S. Advisory Commission on Educational Exchange, 1961-62, U.S. Advisory Commission on Educational and Cultural Affairs, 1962-65, U.S. National Commission for UNESCO, 1965-70; U.S. delegate, UNESCO, Thirteenth General Conference, 1964. Member of board of trustees, Mount Holyoke College (vice-chairman, 1975-76), Hampshire College (vice-chairman, 1974-77), Connecticut College, International Schools Services (vice-chairman, 1964-71), National Corporation for Housing Partnerships, Cottonwood Foundation, Urban League of Greater New York, 1964-71, Atlantic Foundation (member of executive committee for L.A.W.S. Division, 1968-76), African-American Institute, 1964-65, Lincoln Square Neighborhood Center, Young Women's Christian Association (member of internal affairs committee), 1961-65, Women's African Committee, 1958-64.

*WRITINGS:* (With Alan B. Howes) *Intensive English Conversation,* Kairyudo, 1953; (with husband, Hugh H. Smythe) *The New Nigerian Elite,* Stanford University Press, 1960; (editor with Edgar S. Bley) *Curriculum for Understanding,* Union Free School District 13, 1965; *Black American Reference Book,* Prentice-Hall, 1976; (author of introduction) Theophilus Conneau, *A Slaver's Log Book, or 20 Years Residence in Africa,* Prentice-Hall, 1976.

*SIDELIGHTS:* Mabel Smythe has traveled or lived in Cameroon, Japan, Syria, Malta, France, Spain, Thailand, Nigeria and numerous other countries. *Avocational interests:* Piloting light planes, sewing.

\*    \*    \*

## SMYTHIES, J(ohn) R(aymond) 1922-

*PERSONAL:* Born November 30, 1922, in Naini Tal, Uttar Pradesh, India; son of Evelyn Arthur and Olive (Cripps) Smythies; married Vanna Maria Gattorno (a designer of jewelry), December 2, 1950; children: Adrian, Christopher. *Education:* Cambridge University, B.A., 1942, M.D., 1955, M.Sc., 1958; University of London, M.B., B.Chir., 1945, D.P.M., 1952. *Office:* Department of Psychiatric Research, School of Medicine, University of Alabama, Birmingham, Ala. 35294.

*CAREER:* University of British Columbia, Vancouver, research fellow, 1953-55; Cambridge University, Cambridge, England, research fellow, 1955-57; Maudsley Hospital, London, England, senior registrar, 1959-61; University of Edinburgh, Edinburgh, Scotland, reader in psychiatry, 1961-73; University of Alabama, Birmingham, visiting professor, 1970-73, C. B. Ireland Professor of Psychiatry, 1973—. Consultant to World Health Organization, 1963-68, and Allergan Pharmaceuticals, 1970—. *Military service:* Royal Naval Volunteer Reserve, 1946-48; became surgeon-lieutenant.

*MEMBER:* International Society for Psychoneuroendocrinology (president, 1971—), Royal College of Physicians (fellow), American Society for Pharmacology and Experimental Therapeutics, Society for Biological Psychiatry, Society for Psychical Research, Athenaeum. *Awards, honors:* Nuffield fellowship in medicine, 1955-57.

*WRITINGS: Analysis of Perception,* Humanities, 1956; *Schizophrenia: Chemistry, Metabolism and Treatment,* C. C Thomas, 1963; (editor) *Brain and Mind,* Humanities, 1965; (editor with Harold E. Himwich) *Amines and Schizophrenia,* Pergamon, 1967; (editor) *Science and the E.S.P.,* Humanities, 1967; (with others) *Biological Psychiatry,*

Springer-Verlag, 1968; (editor with Arthur Koestler) *Beyond Reductionism: New Perspectives in the Science of Life,* Macmillan, 1970; *Brain Mechanism and Behavior,* Academic Press, 1970; (with L. Corbett) *Psychiatry for Students of Medicine,* Year Book Medical Publishers, 1977. Editor with Carl J. Pfeiffer, *International Review of Neurobiology,* Volumes I-XIX, 1958-77. Contributor of more than one hundred scientific, medical, and philosophical articles to journals.

*WORK IN PROGRESS:* Research in molecular neurobiology, the biochemistry of schizophrenia, and drug design.

*AVOCATIONAL INTERESTS:* Lapidary, philately, travel.

*BIOGRAPHICAL/CRITICAL SOURCES: Observer Review,* October 8, 1967; *Times Literary Supplement,* November 9, 1967; *National Review,* June 30, 1970.

\*    \*    \*

## SNAILHAM, (George) Richard 1930-

*PERSONAL:* Surname is accented on first syllable; born May 18, 1930, in Clitheroe, Lancashire, England; son of William Rushton (a cotton agent) and Mabel (Wilson) Snailham. *Education:* Keble College, Oxford, B.A. (second class honors), 1953. *Politics:* Conservative. *Religion:* Church of England. *Home:* c/o Officers Mess, R.M.A. Sandhurst, Camberley, Surrey, England. *Office:* Department of Political and Social Studies, Royal Military Academy, Sandhurst, Camberley, Surrey, England.

*CAREER:* Alleyn Court Preparatory School, Westcliff-on-Sea, Essex, England, schoolmaster, 1954-55; Clayesmore School, Iwerne Minster, Dorset, England, schoolmaster, 1955-57; Exeter School, Exeter, Devon, England, head of history department, 1957-65; Royal Military Academy, Sandhurst, Camberley, Surrey, England, senior lecturer in department of political and social studies, 1965—. *Military service:* British Army, 1948-50. *Member:* Royal Geographical Society (fellow), Scientific Exploration Society (member of council), Historical Association, Anglo-Ethiopian Society. *Awards, honors:* Fellowship from Winston Churchill Memorial Trust, 1971.

*WRITINGS: The Blue Nile Revealed,* Chatto & Windus, 1970; (with J. N. Blashford-Snell) *The Expedition Organiser's Guide,* Daily Telegraph, 1970, revised edition, 1978; *A Giant among Rivers,* Hutchinson, 1976; *Sangay Survived,* Hutchinson, 1978. Contributor to *Times Educational Supplement, Geographical Magazine, Expedition,* and *Yachting Monthly.*

*AVOCATIONAL INTERESTS:* Exploration (has been on expeditions to Ethiopia, 1966, 1968, 1969-70, 1972, Zaire, 1971-72, 1974-75, Jamaica, 1973-74, and Ecuador, 1976).

\*    \*    \*

## SNOW, John Hall 1924-

*PERSONAL:* Born January 23, 1924, in Washington, D.C.; son of Chauncey Depew (an economic analyst) and Marion (MacKendrick) Snow; married Mary Bartow Hall (a teacher), July 2, 1949; children: Stephen Hall, Thomas Freeman, Helena Van Cortlandt, Lydia Field. *Education:* Harvard University, A.B., 1947; Columbia University, M.A., 1949; Episcopal Theological School, B.D., 1958. *Politics:* Democrat. *Home:* 15 St. John's Rd., Cambridge, Mass. 02138. *Office:* Episcopal Divinity School, 99 Brattle St., Cambridge, Mass. 02138.

*CAREER:* Episcopal priest; St. Michael's School, Newport, R.I., headmaster, 1951-55; Gould Farm, Monterey, Mass., executive director, 1960-62; Christ Church, Cambridge, Mass., assistant minister, 1962-68; Princeton University, Princeton, N.J., Episcopal chaplain, 1968-72; Episcopal Divinity School, Cambridge, professor of practical theology, 1972—. *Military service:* U.S. Navy, 1945-47. *Member:* Minister's Club, Cambridge Boat Club.

*WRITINGS: On Pilgrimage: Marriage in the Seventies,* Seabury, 1972; *Christian Identity on Campus,* edited by Myron B. Bloy, Jr., Seabury, 1972; (contributor) Richard E. Sherrell, editor, *Ecology, Crisis and New Vision,* John Knox, 1972; *The Gospel in a Broken World,* Pilgrim Press, 1972; (with Victor P. Furnish) *Proclamation: Easter,* Fortress Press, 1975; *I Win, We Lose: The New Social Darwinism and the Death of Love,* Seabury, 1977. Also contributor to *Beyond Survival: Bread and Justice in Christian Perspective* and *Male and Female.* Contributor to theology journals. Editor, *Harvard Advocate.*

*SIDELIGHTS:* John Hall Snow told *CA:* "What I'm primarily interested in, a Christian critique of society and its institutions, doesn't seem to be a category of religious publishing houses, and they don't know how to get my work received nor do they want to spend much on advertising. Consequently I write largely out of inner compulsion and for a small but loyal constituency of readers who know me as a preacher and speaker."

\* \* \*

## SNOW, Vernon F. 1924-

*PERSONAL:* Born November 25, 1924, in Milwaukee, Wis.; son of Melvin Howard (a businessman) and Violet C. (Stalker) Snow; married Emily Jean Wry, June 17, 1949; children: Jonathan. *Education:* Wheaton College, Wheaton, Ill., B.A., 1948; University of Chicago, M.A., 1949; University of Wisconsin, Ph.D., 1953. *Home:* 5161 Winterton Dr., Fayetteville, N.Y. 13066. *Office:* John Ben Snow Foundation, Department of History, Syracuse University, Syracuse, N.Y. 13210.

*CAREER:* University of Oregon, Eugene, instructor in western civilization, 1953-56; University of Wisconsin—Madison, visiting lecturer in English history, 1956-57; University of Oregon, assistant professor of western civilization, 1957-60; University of Montana, Missoula, assistant professor, 1960-61, associate professor of English history, 1962-66; University of Nebraska at Lincoln, professor of English history, 1966-74; Syracuse University, Syracuse, N.Y., president of John Ben Snow Foundation, 1974—. *Military service:* U.S. Army, 1943-46. *Member:* Royal Historical Society (fellow), American Historical Association, British Historical Association, Conference on British Studies, List and Index Society, American Association of University Professors. *Awards, honors:* American Philosophical Society travel and research grants, 1958, 1965, 1969.

*WRITINGS: Essex the Rebel: The Life of Robert Devereux, Third Earl of Essex, 1591-1646,* University of Nebraska Press, 1970; *Parliament in Elizabethan England,* Yale University Press, 1977. Also author of *JBS: The Biography of John Ben Snow,* 1974. Contributor to *World Book Encyclopedia;* contributor of about twenty articles to historical journals in the United States and England.

*WORK IN PROGRESS:* A study of the aristocracy in England, 1640-1660; a monograph on proctorial representation in the House of Lords, 1509-1649; an edition of the Long Parliament diary of Sir Simonds of Ewes (1642-1648).

## SNYDER, Anne 1922-

*PERSONAL:* Born October 3, 1922, in Boston, Mass.; daughter of Nathan (a manufacturer of key blanks) and Marsha (Borochowitz) Reisner; married Louis Snyder (a plant manager), June 15, 1941; children: Sherri Snyder Stevens, Mari-Beth Snyder Bergman, Nathalie. *Education:* Has taken courses at El Camino College, Valley College, University of California, Los Angeles, University of Portland, and Maren Elwood College of Writing, Los Angeles. *Home:* 13937 Wyandotte St., Van Nuys, Calif. 91405. *Agent:* Molson-Stanton Agency, 10889 Wilshire Blvd., Los Angeles, Calif. 90024.

*CAREER:* Television writer, and author; teacher of creative writing for Gifted Children's Association of San Fernando Valley, 1970-76. *Member:* P.E.N. International, Society of Children's Book Writers, Authors Guild, Authors League of America, Women's National Book Association, Writers Guild of America, West, Southern California Council on Literature for Children and Young People. *Awards, honors:* Child Study Association of America selected *50,000 Names for Jeff* as one of the ten best children's books of 1969; *First Step* was given the top juvenile award by Friends of American Writers and was given special honors by National Council of Christians and Jews, both 1976.

*WRITINGS*—Published by Holt, except as indicated: *50,000 Names for Jeff,* 1969; *Nobody's Family,* 1975; *First Step,* 1975; *My Name Is Davy—I'm an Alcoholic* (also see below), 1977; *Kids and Drinking,* CompCare Publications, 1977; *The Old Man and the Mule,* 1978.

Screenplays: "Women—Alive and Well," produced by PMA Association, 1977; "My Name Is Davy—I'm an Alcoholic" (based on book of same title), NBC-TV, in production. Also writer of documentary screenplay, "New Beginnings," 1977.

*WORK IN PROGRESS:* Documentary film dealing with elementary and junior high school children addicted to alcohol; two books, *Timothy Tyler* and *The Little Line.*

*SIDELIGHTS:* Anne Snyder writes: "I was motivated to write *50,000 Names for Jeff* because each of us has a responsibility to help create better understanding between the races. My purpose was to reach the kids—white and black—*before* they became infected with prejudice. Regarded as a bibliotherapeutic specialist, I enjoy writing about the everyday problems young people face today. However, comedy is also one of my loves, and my *first* concern as a writer is to tell a good story in an interesting and dramatic way. For me, entertaining the reader (or audience on TV) is obligatory; if the story instructs, it is a fringe benefit." *My Name Is Davy—I'm an Alcoholic* is being translated into Danish.

\* \* \*

## SNYDER, Fred A. 1931-

*PERSONAL:* Born December 8, 1931, in Conway Springs, Kan.; son of Howard A. (a contractor) and Martha (Smith) Snyder; married Joyce Piotrowski (a teacher), January 13, 1951; children: Allen W., Gwendolyn Kay. *Education:* Wichita State University, B.A., 1957, M.A., 1961; College of Emporia, graduate study, 1961-63; Oklahoma State University, Ed.D., 1964. *Religion:* Lutheran. *Home address:* R.R. 21, Box 239, Terre Haute, Ind. 47802. *Office:* School of Education, Indiana State University, Terre Haute, Ind. 47809.

*CAREER:* School District 120, Sedgwick County, Kan.,

teacher of science, 1953-54, teacher of physical education, 1954-59, chief school administrator, 1959-63, consultant to board of education, 1963-64, elementary school principal, 1964-65; Indiana State University, Terre Haute, student teaching college supervisor, 1965-67, professor of education, 1967—. *Member:* National Education Association, American Association of School Administrators, American Educational Research Association.

*WRITINGS:* (With Duane Peterson) *Dynamics of Elementary School Administration,* Houghton, 1970; (with Ralph Jones) *Developing Skills in Educational Research,* Interstate, 1976; (contributor with Frank Sibrel) *Library Research: A Module,* Research and Development Center for Teacher's Education, 1976; *Perceptions of Future Elementary School Principals,* Curriculum and Development Center, Indiana State University, 1976; (with Joe Ridgley and Bill Clary) *Trends and Curriculum Development,* Curriculum and Development Center, Indiana State University, 1977. Contributor to education journals.

*WORK IN PROGRESS:* Research on the impact that the Madison (Ind.) Consolidated School Organization has upon its environment.

*SIDELIGHTS:* Fred A. Snyder told *CA:* "As a professor of educational administration, I am concerned about sound practices in teaching, research, and the distribution of new found knowledge. My writing endeavors provide an outlet toward all three of these concerns. Writing helps me in my teaching and research endeavors. It also provides a mode of satisfaction that can not be attained in any other way."

\*    \*    \*

### SNYDER, Solomon H(albert) 1938-

*PERSONAL:* Born December 26, 1938, in Washington, D.C.; son of Samuel Simon (a systems analyst) and Patricia (Yakerson) Snyder; married Elaine Borko, June 10, 1962; children: Judith Rhea, Deborah Lynn. *Education:* Attended Georgetown University, 1955-58, M.D. (cum laude), 1962. *Politics:* Democrat. *Religion:* Jewish. *Home:* 2300 West Rogers Ave., Baltimore, Md. 21209. *Office:* Department of Pharmacology, School of Medicine, Johns Hopkins University, 725 North Wolfe St., Baltimore, Md. 21205.

*CAREER:* Johns Hopkins University, School of Medicine, Baltimore, Md., assistant professor, 1966-68, associate professor, 1968-70, professor of psychiatry and pharmacology, 1970—. *Military service:* U.S. Public Health Service, 1963-65; served as senior surgeon. *Member:* American College of Neuropsychopharmacology, American Society for Pharmacology and Experimental Therapeutics, American Psychiatric Association. *Awards, honors:* Outstanding Scientist Award, Maryland Academy of Sciences, 1969; John Jacob Abel Award, American Pharmacology Society, 1970; A. E. Bennett Award, Society for Biological Psychiatry, 1970; Hofheimer Prize of American Psychiatric Association, 1972; Gaddum Award, British Pharmacology Society, 1974; Daniel Efron Award, American College of Neuropsychopharmacology, 1974; F. O. Schmitt Award in Neurosis, Massachusetts Institute of Technology, 1975.

*WRITINGS: Uses of Marijuana,* Oxford University Press, 1971; (editor) *Perspectives in Neuropharmacology,* Oxford University Press, 1972; *Madness and the Brain,* McGraw, 1974; *The Troubled Mind,* McGraw, 1976. Member of editorial board, *Journal of Neurochemistry.*

*WORK IN PROGRESS:* Laboratory research in psychopharmacology and neurotransmitters.

*SIDELIGHTS:* Solomon H. Snyder told *CA* he is "interested in linking psychiatry and basic information on the chemistry of the brain. [I am] also eager to explicate for the general public new scientific studies of brain function and drug action." *Avocational interests:* Playing classical guitar.

*BIOGRAPHICAL/CRITICAL SOURCES: Washington Post,* February 1, 1974.

\*    \*    \*

### SOCOLOW, Robert H(arry) 1937-

*PERSONAL:* Born December 27, 1937, in New York, N.Y.; son of A. Walter (a lawyer) and Edith (Gutman) Socolow; married Elizabeth Anne Sussman (a fiction writer), June 10, 1962; children: David, Seth. *Education:* Harvard University, B.A. (summa cum laude), 1959, M.A., 1961, Ph.D., 1964. *Home:* 37 Laurel Rd., Princeton, N.J. 08540. *Office:* Department of Aerospace-Mechanical Sciences, Princeton University, Princeton, N.J. 08540.

*CAREER:* Yale University, New Haven, Conn., assistant professor of physics, 1966-71; Princeton University, Princeton, N.J., associate professor, 1971-77, professor of environmental sciences, 1977—. *Member:* American Physical Society, Federation of American Scientists, Phi Beta Kappa, Sigma Xi. *Awards, honors:* National Science Foundation postdoctoral fellow, 1964-66; Yale Junior Faculty fellowship, 1970-71; German Marshall Fund and Guggenheim fellowships, 1976-77.

*WRITINGS:* (With John Harte) *Patient Earth,* Holt, 1971; (with Harold Feiveson and Frank Sinden) *Boundaries of Analysis: An Inquiry into the Tocks Island Dam Controversy,* Ballinger, 1976; *Saving Energy in Your Home: Princeton's Experiments at Twin Rivers,* Ballinger, 1978.

\*    \*    \*

### SOKOL, Anthony E. 1897-

*PERSONAL:* Born March 28, 1897, in Vienna, Austria; came to United States in 1924, naturalized in 1934; son of Anton (a merchant) and Klara (Kuban) Sokol; married Martha Hille, October 8, 1927 (died, February, 1938); married Else Mueller, June 23, 1939; children: (first marriage) Otto M. *Education:* Attended Technical University of Vienna, 1918-19, and University of Vienna, 1926-28; State Teachers College (now University of Southern Mississippi), B.A., 1928; Stanford University, M.A., 1930, Ph.D., 1932. *Home:* 1641 Portola Ave., Palo Alto, Calif. 94306. *Office:* Department of Political Science, Stanford University, Stanford, Calif. 94305.

*CAREER:* Stanford University, Stanford, Calif., assistant professor, 1934-39, associate professor, 1939-57, professor of international security affairs, 1957-62, professor emeritus, 1962—, research associate, Hoover Institution, 1930—. Administered U.S. Army Program on the Far East, 1942-45, and a research project for the U.S. government on problems of disarmament in the Far East. Fulbright professor, University of Vienna, 1956-57. *Military service:* Austro-Hungarian Navy, 1915-19; became lieutenant. Royal Dutch Merchant Marine, 1920-23; served in Dutch East Indies. *Member:* U.S. Naval Institute, American Association of University Professors. *Awards, honors:* Received Austrian Honor Cross First Class for Science and Art for his work on the history and civilization of Austria; numerous grants for historical and cultural research.

*WRITINGS: Beruehmte Forscher und Ihre Beitraege,* American Book Co., 1938; *Sea Power in the Nuclear Age,*

Public Affairs Press, 1961; *The Imperial and Royal Austro-Hungarian Navy*, U.S. Naval Institute, 1968. Contributor of numerous articles to military and geography journals.

*WORK IN PROGRESS: Beautiful Women in World Art; Austria: Past and Present; Sea Power in the Ancient Orient;* research on female admirals and pirates.

*SIDELIGHTS:* Several of Anthony Sokol's books have been translated into Japanese and German. *Avocational interests:* Travel, photography, music, art.

*BIOGRAPHICAL/CRITICAL SOURCES: San Jose News,* February 18, 1971.

\*      \*      \*

## SOLTIS, Jonas F(rancis)   1931-

*PERSONAL:* Born June 11, 1931, in Norwalk, Conn.; son of Jonas J., Jr. (a realtor) and Margaret (Soltes) Soltis; married Nancy Schaal (a teacher), September 10, 1955; children: Susan Lynn Shaw, Robin Lee. *Education:* University of Connecticut, B.A. (with honors), 1956; Wesleyan University, M.A.T., 1958; Harvard University, Ed.D., 1964. *Home:* 436 Falmer Ave., Teaneck, N.J. 07666. *Office:* Division of Philosophy and Social Sciences, Teachers College, Columbia University, New York, N.Y. 10027.

*CAREER:* University of Connecticut, Waterbury, instructor in history and philosophy, 1958-60; Wesleyan University, Middletown, Conn., instructor in education, 1962-64; Columbia University, Teachers College, New York, N.Y., professor of philosophy and education, 1964—, director of Division of Instruction, 1971-75, director of Division of Philosophy and the Social Sciences, 1977-79. Consultant to the Addison-Wesley Publishing Company, Reading, Mass., 1965-68. *Military service:* U.S. Air Force, 1950-54. *Member:* Philosophy of Education Society (president, 1975), American Philosophical Association, National Society for the Study of Education, American Educational Research Association, Phi Beta Kappa, Phi Delta Kappa. *Awards, honors:* U.S. Office of Education post-doctoral fellowship in education research, 1968-69.

*WRITINGS: Seeing, Knowing, and Believing,* Allen & Unwin, 1966; *Introduction to the Analysis of Educational Concepts,* Addison-Wesley, 1968, 2nd edition, 1978; (editor with B. Chazan) *Moral Education,* Teachers College Press, 1974. Editor, "Problems in Education" series, Teachers College Press, 1970. Member of editorial board, *Educational Theory,* 1968-70, *Educational Philosophy and Theory,* 1969—, and *Studies in Philosophy and Education,* 1971-75.

\*      \*      \*

## SOMER, John (Laddie)   1936-

*PERSONAL:* Born October 16, 1936, in Wellington, Kan.; son of John Laddie (a farmer) and Hanorra (Garrity) Somer; married Constance Louise Sawyer, November 11, 1961; children: Anne Elizabeth, Joan Leslie, John Joseph. *Education:* St. Benedict's College (now Benedictine College), B.A., 1959; Kansas State Teachers College (now Emporia State University), M.A., 1960; Northern Illinois University, Ph.D., 1971. *Home:* 1224 West St., Emporia, Kan. 66801. *Office:* Department of English, Emporia State University, Emporia, Kan. 66801.

*CAREER:* Emporia State University, Emporia, Kan., 1971—, began as assistant professor, currently associate professor of English. *Member:* Modern Language Association of America, Midwest Modern Language Association.

*WRITINGS:* (With James Coulos and James Wilcox) *Literature and Rhetoric,* Scott, Foresman, 1969; *Dramatic Experience,* Scott, Foresman, 1970; *Narrative Experience,* Scott, Foresman, 1970; (with Joseph Cozzo) *Poetic Experience,* Scott, Foresman, 1970; (with Cozzo) *Literary Experience,* Scott, Foresman, 1971; (with Jerry Klinkowitz) *Innovative Fiction,* Dell, 1972; (with Klinkowitz) *The Vonnegut Statement,* Delacorte, 1973; (with James Hoy) *The Language Experience,* Delta, 1974. Contributor to numerous journals.

*WORK IN PROGRESS:* Co-authoring three books, *Writing under Fire,* for Delacorte, *A Guide to the Scholarship of Contemporary Literature,* and *The Teacher as Artist.*

\*      \*      \*

## SOMMERFELT, Aimee   1892-

*PERSONAL:* Born April 2, 1892, in Oslo, Norway; daughter of Henrik Arnold Thaulow (a psychiatrist) and Toinon (Myblin) Dedichen; married Alf Sommerfelt (a university professor), August 15, 1919 (deceased); children: Wenche Sommerfelt Werring, Annelise Sommerfelt Ziesler, Axel. *Education:* Attended college in Norway and studied and traveled in several other countries. *Religion:* Lutheran. *Home:* Villa Sandbakken, Johan Castbergs v.9, Oslo, Norway. *Agent:* Falk Lewis, American Literary Exchange, 217 W. 18th St., New York, N.Y. 10011.

*CAREER:* Writer for young people, and translator. Member of board of International Kuratorium for children's books and of Board of Film Censors, Norway.

*MEMBER:* Den norske Forfatterforening (Society of Norwegian Authors), Ungdomslitteraturens orfatterlag (Authors of Books for Children and Young People; president), Zonta International (Norwegian section). *Awards, honors:* Six of her books have received the State Prize for children's literature in Norway; Damms Honor Prize, 1959 and 1971 for *The Road to Agra* and *The Dangerous Night;* Jane Addams Children's Book Award of U.S. section of Women's International League for Peace and Freedom, Boys' Clubs of America Junior Book award, and Child Study Association of America Children's Book Award, all 1962, for *The Road to Agra;* Thomas Alva Edison Foundation National Mass Media Award, 1965, for *The White Bungalow;* Hans Christian Andersen International Children's Book Award for *The Road to Agra,* 1962, *The White Bungalow,* 1964, and *My Name Is Pablo,* 1966.

*WRITINGS: Stopp tyven!,* Gyldendal, 1933; *Fire detektiver arbeider med saken,* Gyldendal, 1935; *Trulte,* Gyldendal, 1935; *Trulte i toppform,* Gyldendal, 1937; *16 aar,* Gyldendal, 1938; *Lisbeth,* Gyldendal, 1939; *Ung front* (historical novel), Gyldendal, 1942; *Annabet* (historical novel), Gyldendal, 1947; *Miriam,* Gyldendal, 1949, translation by Pat Shaw Iversen published under same title, Criterion, 1963; *Bare en jentung,* Tiden, 1952, translation by Patricia Crampton published as *No Easy Way,* Criterion, 1968; *Morton og Monica,* Gyldendal, 1953; *Veien til Agra,* N. W. Damms, 1960, translation by Evelyn Ramsden published as *The Road to Agra,* Criterion, 1961; *Den hvite bungalow,* N. W. Damms, 1962, translation by Evelyn Ramsden published as *The White Bungalow,* Criterion, 1964; *Pablo og de andre,* 1964, translation by Patricia Crampton published as *My Name Is Pablo,* Criterion, 1966; *Den farlige nakten,* N. W. Damms, 1971, translation published as *Dangerous Night,* Criterion, in press; *Manuel, Peter og Ram, Tavi og Marik* (short stories), N. W. Damms, 1972; *Etterlyst,* N. W. Damms, 1972.

Translator of about 30 books in English, Danish, French, and Swedish. Columnist. Contributor to Norwegian newspapers.

*SIDELIGHTS:* "My personal interests are reading, writing, travelling, meeting people," Aimee Sommerfelt says. "I try to write books for children and young people—books which I hope will somehow arouse their imagination and interest in the world they live in. (Adults seem to have so many set ideas which they seldom want to change.) Developing countries and race prejudices are problems our children will have to solve, so they might just as well know something about them. In some of my books I have tried to introduce these topics in a more stimulating than gloomy way. At least that has been my intention."

Sommerfelt spent 1959 and 1960 in Palo Alto, Calif., when her husband was visiting professor at the Ford Foundation Center for Advanced Study in the Behavioral Sciences. He was one of the founders of UNESCO, and his early work as a delegate took him and his family to India. Both *The Road to Agra* and *The White Bungalow* were set in India. Many of Aimee Sommerfelt's books have been translated into several languages.

*BIOGRAPHICAL/CRITICAL SOURCES: Young Readers' Review,* April, 1966, October, 1968.†

*       *       *

### SONG, Ben (Chunho)   1937-

*PERSONAL:* Born February 22, 1937, in Seoul, Korea; son of Jae Sung (a mayor) and Moo Han (Kim) Song; married Kathy Lee, October 11, 1960; children: John, Paul, Karen. *Education:* Korean Presbyterian Theological Seminary, Th.B., 1964; also attended Concordia Theological Seminary, Fort Wayne, Ind. *Home:* 716 Fife Hts. Dr. E., Tacoma, Wash. 98424. *Office address:* Teen Life International, P.O. Box 360, Tacoma, Wash. 98401.

*CAREER:* Teen Life International, Tacoma, Wash., minister involved in missionary youth work, 1961—, pastor of St. Luke's Lutheran Korean Mission, 1977—. Teacher in high school in Seoul, Korea, 1963-65. *Military service:* Korean Army, 1957-60. *Awards, honors:* D.H.L., Linda Vista Bible College and Seminary.

*WRITINGS: No Longer an Orphan* (booklet), Teen Life International, 1968; (as told to Cliff Christians) *Born Out of Conflict: The Autobiography of Ben Song,* Zondervan, 1970. Contributor to religious periodicals.

*WORK IN PROGRESS: Searching Generation,* questions and answers from teen-agers.

*       *       *

### SONNENFELD, Marion (Wilma)   1928-

*PERSONAL:* Born February 13, 1928, in Berlin, Germany; came to United States in 1939, naturalized in 1945; daughter of Kurt (an attorney) and Sibylla (Lemke) Sonnenfeld. *Education:* Swarthmore College, B.A. (with high honors), 1950; Yale University, M.A., 1951, Ph.D., 1956. *Home:* 27 Carol Ave., Fredonia, N.Y. 14063. *Office:* Department of Foreign Languages, State University of New York College, Fredonia, N.Y. 14063.

*CAREER:* Smith College, Northampton, Mass., instructor, 1954-59, assistant professor of German, 1959-62; Middlebury German School, Middlebury, Vt., faculty member, 1961-63; Wells College, Aurora, N.Y., associate professor of German, 1962-67, acting chairman of department, 1962-

63, chairman, 1965-67, assistant director of German School, 1964, director, 1965-67; State University of New York College at Fredonia, associate professor, 1967-74, professor of German, 1974—, Distinguished Teaching Professor, 1977—. *Member:* International Germanistenvereinigung, Modern Language Association of America, North East Modern Language Association (chairman, 19th century German, 1972-73). *Awards, honors: The Complete Narrative Prose of C. F. Meyers* was named "outstanding academic book of 1976" by *Choice.*

*WRITINGS:* (Translator and author of introduction) Heinrich Von Kleist, *Amphitryon: A Comedy,* Ungar, 1962; (editor) *Wert und Wort,* Wells College, 1965; (translator and author of introduction) *Three Plays by Hebbel,* Bucknell University Press, 1974; (editor) *Gepraegte Form,* Europaeische Verlag, 1975; (translator with George Folkers and David Dickens) *The Complete Narrative Prose of C. F. Meyers,* Bucknell University Press, 1976. Contributor of articles to *Neophilologus, Symposium,* and *German Quarterly.*

*WORK IN PROGRESS:* Translating Goethe's *Wilhelm Meister* and works of Theodor Fontane.

*       *       *

### SONTAG, Raymond J(ames)   1897-1972

October 2, 1897—October 27, 1972; American educator and historian. Obituaries: *New York Times,* October 29, 1972.

*       *       *

### SOREL, Nancy Caldwell   1934-

*PERSONAL:* Born May 26, 1934, in Kansas City, Mo.; daughter of John K. (a physician) and Ruth (Conkling) Caldwell; married Edward Sorel (an illustrator), May 29, 1965; children: Jenny, Katherine. *Education:* Ohio Wesleyan University, B.A., 1956; University of Edinburgh, Diploma in English Studies, 1957; New York University, M.A., 1965. *Religion:* Society of Friends. *Home address:* R.F.D. 2, Route 301, Carmel, N.Y. 10512.

*CAREER:* Massachusetts Institute of Technology, Cambridge, news writer, 1958-60; *Columbia Encyclopedia,* New York City, staff editor, 1962-63; English language teacher at New School for Social Research and United Nations, New York City, 1963-65; Brooklyn Friends School, Brooklyn, N.Y., English teacher, 1965-66.

*WRITINGS: Word People,* American Heritage Press, 1970; (contributor) David Wallechinsky and Irving Wallace, *The People's Almanac,* Doubleday, 1975; (contributor) Wallechinsky and Wallace, *The People's Almanac II,* Doubleday, 1978.

*       *       *

### SORRELLS, Helen   1908-

*PERSONAL:* Born January 1, 1908, in Stafford, Kan.; daughter of Leonard Wilson (a farmer) and Edna (Kennedy) Sloan; married Adrian R. Sorrells (a technical writer), June 21, 1933; children: Sarah Kennedy (Mrs. Patrick J. McDermott), Susan Eskridge (Mrs. William Patrick Shelly). *Education:* Kansas State College of Agriculture and Applied Science (now Kansas State University), B.S., 1931. *Politics:* Democrat. *Religion:* Episcopalian. *Home:* 221 Tranquillo Rd., Pacific Palisades, Calif. 90272.

*MEMBER:* Poetry Society of America. *Awards, honors:* Borestone Award, 1967, for "Cry Summer"; *Arizona Quar-*

*terly* award for poetry, 1968; National Endowment for the Arts creative writing grant, 1973; Poetry Science of America award, 1973.

*WRITINGS: Seeds as They Fall* (poems), Vanderbilt University Press, 1971. Contributor to literary and popular journals, including *Esquire* and *Reporter.*

*WORK IN PROGRESS:* A second book of poems.

*AVOCATIONAL INTERESTS:* Travel.

\*     \*     \*

### SOULE, Isabel Walker   1898(?)-1972

1898(?)—July 31, 1972; American editor, labor leader, feminist, and writer on politics, labor, China, and other subjects. Obituaries: *New York Times,* August 2, 1972; *Antiquarian Bookman,* September 25, 1972.

\*     \*     \*

### SOUTHERN, Eileen   1920-

*PERSONAL:* Born February 19, 1920, in Minneapolis, Minn.; daughter of Walter Wade (a teacher) and Lilla (Gibson) Jackson; married Joseph Southern (a college professor), August 22, 1942; children: April, Edward. *Education:* University of Chicago, B.A., 1940, M.A., 1941; New York University, Ph.D., 1961; study of piano at Chicago Musical College, Boston University, and Juilliard Institute. *Home:* 115-05 179th St., St. Albans, N.Y. 11434. *Office:* Department of Music, Harvard University, Cambridge, Mass. 02138.

*CAREER:* Concert pianist, 1940—; Prairie View Agricultural and Mechanical College, Prairie View, Tex., instructor in music, 1941-42; Southern University, Baton Rouge, La., assistant professor of music, 1943-45; Claflin College, Orangeburg, S.C., instructor in music, 1947-49; Southern University, assistant professor of music, 1949-51; secondary school music teacher in public schools of New York, N.Y., 1954-60; Brooklyn College of the City University of New York, Brooklyn, N.Y., instructor, 1960-64, assistant professor of music, 1964-68; York College of the City University of New York, Jamaica, N.Y., associate professor, 1968-71, professor of music, 1972-75; Harvard University, Cambridge, Mass., professor of music and Afro-American studies, 1976—. Active in Girl Scouts of America, 1954-63.

*MEMBER:* International Musicological Society, American Musicological Society (member of board of directors, 1973-75), Association for the Study of Negro Life and History, Music Library Association, Renaissance Society, Author's Guild, National Association for the Advancement of Colored People, National Association of Negro Business and Professional Women's Clubs, Alpha Kappa Alpha, Mu Sigma, Young Women's Christian Association (chairperson of management committee for Queens chapter, 1970-73). *Awards, honors:* Citation from Voice of America for activities in promoting black music and culture; achievement award from National Association of Negro Musicians, 1971; award from American Society of Composers, Authors, and Publishers, 1973, for *The Music of Black Americans.*

*WRITINGS: The Buxheim Organ Book,* Institute of Medieval Music, 1963; (contributor) Jan LaRue, editor, *Aspects of Medieval and Renaissance Music,* Norton, 1966; (contributor) Dominique-Rene de Lerma, editor, *Black Music in Our Culture,* Kent State University Press, 1970; *The Music of Black Americans: A History,* Norton, 1971; (editor) *Readings in Black American Music,* Norton, 1971; (editor) *Black Perspectives in Music,* Volume VI, Foundation for

Research in the Afro-American Creative Arts, 1978. Contributor to encyclopedias and music and other scholarly journals. Founder and editor, *The Black Perspective in Music,* 1973—.

*WORK IN PROGRESS: Anonymous Chansons in Two Manuscripts at El Escorial,* for American Institute of Musicology at Rome; *Computer-Assisted Index of Anonymous Chansons of the Mid-Fifteenth Century.*

*BIOGRAPHICAL/CRITICAL SOURCES: New York Post,* July 22, 1971.†

\*     \*     \*

### SOUTHWORTH, Warren H(ilbourne)   1912-

*PERSONAL:* Born February 10, 1912, in Lynn, Mass.; son of Joseph W. (an accountant) and Jennie M. (Orcutt) Southworth; married Ruth S. Redman (a teacher), 1937; children: Joseph W., Evelyn J. Fleming. *Education:* University of Massachusetts, B.S., 1934; Boston University, M.A., 1935; Massachusetts Institute of Technology, Dr. P.H., 1944. *Home:* 3510 Cross St., Madison, Wis. 53711. *Office:* School of Education, University of Wisconsin, Madison, Wis. 53706.

*CAREER:* High school science teacher, 1936-39; Massachusetts Department of Public Health, Boston, research director for school health study, 1941-42; Panzer College, East Orange, N.J., professor of health education and sciences, 1942-44; University of Wisconsin—Madison, associate professor, 1944-52, professor of health education, 1952—, professor of preventive medicine, 1977—, chairman of graduate program in department of curriculum and instruction, 1963-68. Lecturer at Forsythe Dental Infirmary and Boston City Hospital, 1940-41, and New York University, 1943-44; field worker with Federal Venereal Disease Control Program and American Social Health Association, 1944; coordinator of School Health Program, Wisconsin Department of Public Instruction and State Board of Health, 1944-48; medical team coordinator, Wisconsin Office of Civil Defense, 1952-53; acting chairman of Governor's Commission on Nursing Education, 1969; consultant to World Health Organization, 1971, and UNESCO.

*MEMBER:* International Union for Health Education, American Association for Advancement of Science, American Alliance for Health, Physical Education, and Recreation, American Association of University Professors, American College Health Association (fellow, Health Education section), American Public Health Association (fellow, School Health section), American School Health Association (fellow), National Safety Council, Royal Health Society (fellow), Society of Public Health Educators (charter fellow), Society of State Directors of Health, Physical Education, and Recreation, Wisconsin Association for Health, Physical Education, and Recreation, Wisconsin Association for Teacher Education, Wisconsin Family Life Association, Wisconsin Public Health Association, Wisconsin Public Health Council, Wisconsin School Health Council, Wisconsin Lung Association, Dane County Mental Health Association, Madison Anti-Tuberculosis and Respiratory Disease Association, Sigma Xi, Delta Omega, Phi Delta Kappa. *Awards, honors:* William A. Howe Award from the American School Health Association, 1968.

*WRITINGS: Manual for Mobile Medical Team Personnel,* Wisconsin Office of Civil Defense, 1953; (with Arthur F. Davis) *Hygiene,* McGraw, 1954; (with Davis) *Science of Health,* McGraw, 1957; (editor with Fred V. Hein) *Fit to Teach,* American Association for Health, Physical Education, and Recreation, 1957; (editor with Bernice R. Moss and John L. Reichert) *Health Education,* National Education Association and American Medical Association, 1961; *Some Filtered Facts about Smoking and Health,* University of Wisconsin, 1971; *Curriculum Planning and Some Current Health Problems,* UNESCO (Paris), 1974. Contributor of articles to *Archives of Dermatology and Syphilology, Journal of Bacteriology, Journal of School Health, Research Quarterly, Crusader, Journal of the American Public Health Association,* and other professional journals.

*WORK IN PROGRESS: A History of the Wisconsin State School Health Council, 1945-1975.*

*SIDELIGHTS:* Warren Southworth told *CA:* "Realizing that one can not win 'em all, I do get much pleasure out of changing adversity into advantage. It is surprising how often opportunities for this turnabout occur."

*BIOGRAPHICAL/CRITICAL SOURCES: Wisconsin State Journal,* March 5, 1972.

\*      \*      \*

## SPAAK, Paul-Henri    1899-1972

January 25, 1899—July 31, 1972; Belgian statesman and one of the prime movers for a unified Europe. Obituaries: *New York Times,* August 1, 1972; *Washington Post,* August 1, 1972; *L'Express,* August 7-13, 1972; *Newsweek,* August 14, 1972; *Time,* August 14, 1972; *Current Biography,* October, 1972.

\*      \*      \*

## SPARKS, Will    1924-

*PERSONAL:* Born July 15, 1924, in Detroit, Mich.; son of Ray C. and Josephine (DeVerse) Sparks; married Zona B. Kingery, December 29, 1945; children: Johanna, Guy, Robert. *Education:* Attended Knox College, 1943, and Georgetown University, 1944; University of Chicago, Ph.B., 1946. *Politics:* Democrat. *Religion:* Protestant. *Home address:* P.O. Box 27, Herrick Center, Pa. 18430. *Office:* Citibank, 399 Park Ave., New York, N.Y. 10022.

*CAREER:* U.S. Department of Defense, Washington, D.C., assistant to the Secretary of Defense, 1964-65; White House, Washington, D.C., assistant to President Lyndon B. Johnson, 1965-68; International Telephone & Telegraph, New York City, assistant to the chairman, 1970-76; Citibank, New York City, vice-president, 1976—. *Member:* Writers Guild, Authors League of America.

*WRITINGS: Who Talked to the President Last?,* illustrated by J. Vinton Lawrence, Norton, 1971; (with Clairborne Pell) *Power and Policy,* Norton, 1972; *Financial Competition and the Public Interest,* Citicorp, 1978.

\*      \*      \*

## SPATZ, (Kenneth) Chris(topher, Jr.)    1940-

*PERSONAL:* Born March 25, 1940, in Tyler, Tex.; son of Kenneth Christopher (a salesman) and Mary (Harton) Spatz; married Thea Siria (a teacher), May 31, 1961; children: Mark Christopher, Kenneth Siria, Elizabeth Ann. *Education:* Hendrix College, B.A., 1962; Tulane University, M.S., 1964, Ph.D., 1966; University of California, Berkeley, postdoctoral study, 1969-71. *Home:* 615 Davis, Conway, Ark. 72032. *Office:* Department of Psychology, Hendrix College, Conway, Ark. 72032.

*CAREER:* University of the South, Sewanee, Tenn., instructor in psychology, 1966-69; University of Arkansas at

Monticello, associate professor of psychology, 1971-73; Hendrix College, Conway, Ark., associate professor of psychology and chairman of department, 1973—. *Member:* American Psychological Association.

*WRITINGS: A Laboratory Manual for Experimental Psychology,* Appleton, 1970; (with James O. Johnston) *Basic Statistics: Tales of Distributions,* Brooks/Cole, 1976.

*WORK IN PROGRESS:* Animal behavior research.

\*      \*      \*

## SPEIRS, Logan    1938-

*PERSONAL:* Born March 9, 1938, in Riga, Latvia; son of John (a university professor) and Ruth (Tiefentals) Speirs; married Heather Mackenzie, November 26, 1970. *Education:* Downing College, Cambridge, B.A., 1960, M.A., 1965. *Office:* Department of English, University of California, Santa Barbara, Calif. 93106.

*CAREER:* University of Amsterdam, Amsterdam, Netherlands, lecturer in English literature, 1961-68; University of California, Santa Barbara, assistant professor, 1968-72, associate professor of English, 1972—. Part-time lecturer in English literature, University of Nijmegen, 1963-67. *Awards, honors:* University of California humanities grant, 1973.

*WRITINGS: Tolstoy and Chekhov,* Cambridge University Press, 1971. Contributor to professional journals.

*WORK IN PROGRESS:* A book on the nineteenth-century English novel, emphasizing the work of Charles Dickens and Henry James.

*AVOCATIONAL INTERESTS:* Painting, travel.†

\*      \*      \*

## SPEKKE, Arnolds    1887-1972

June 14, 1887—July 27, 1972; Latvian diplomat, educator, scholar in philosophy, philology, and Romance languages, essayist, and author of books on Latvian history and culture. Obituaries: *Washington Post,* July 29, 1972.

\*      \*      \*

## SPENCE, Vernon Gladden    1924-

*PERSONAL:* Born September 27, 1924, in Tangier Island, Va.; son of Vernon L. (a postmaster) and Ruth (Gladden) Spence; married Wanda Smith (a teacher), December 28, 1948; children: John Randolph, Deborah Anne, Kevin Douglas. *Education:* McMurry College, B.A., 1946; Southern Methodist University, M.A., 1947; University of Colorado, Ph.D., 1968. *Religion:* United Methodist. *Home:* 10216 Bushman Dr., Oakton, Va. 22124. *Office:* Department of History, George Mason University, Fairfax, Va. 22030.

*CAREER:* Teacher in public schools in Virginia, Texas, and Colorado, 1947-60; McMurry College, Abilene, Tex., assistant professor, 1960-68, associate professor of history and chairman of department, 1968-70, chairman of Division of Social Sciences, 1969-70; George Mason University, Fairfax, Va., associate professor of history, 1970—. *Member:* American Historical Association, Organization of American Historians, American Association of University Professors, Western History Association, Texas State Historical Association, West Texas State Historical Association, Potomac Corral. *Awards, honors:* Coe Foundation scholarship, 1960.

*WRITINGS: Colonel Morgan Jones: Grand Old Man of Texas Railroading,* University of Oklahoma Press, 1971;

*Judge Legett of Abilene: A Texas Frontier Profile,* Texas A & M University Press, 1977. Contributor to history journals and newspapers.

*WORK IN PROGRESS: Pioneer Women of Abilene,* completion expected in 1980.

\* \* \*

## SPERBER, Perry Arthur 1907-

*PERSONAL:* Born October 11, 1907, in Providence, R.I.; son of Hugo and Hattie S. (Mann) Sperber; married Muriel Hope Reed, September 28, 1939; children: Gayle Patricia (Mrs. Thomas Eugene Freeman), Perry Reed. *Education:* Brown University, B.A., 1928; New York University, M.D., 1932. *Religion:* Baptist. *Home:* 816 Wells Dr., South Daytona, Fla. 32019.

*CAREER:* Private practice of medicine in dermatology and allergy, Providence, R.I., 1937-50, Daytona Beach, Fla., 1951-74. *Military service:* U.S. Army Reserve, 1934-39; became first lieutenant. *Member:* American Medical Association, American Academy of Dermatology, American College of Allergists, American Association for Clinical Immunology and Allergy (past president of Southeastern Region), Florida Medical Association.

*WRITINGS: Treatment of the Aging Skin and Dermatologic Defects,* C. C Thomas, 1965; *Sex and the Dinosaur,* Warren H. Green, 1970; *Drugs, Demons, Doctors, and Disease,* Warren H. Green, 1972. Contributor of articles to medical journals.

*WORK IN PROGRESS:* Research on the immunity mechanism; a novel.

*SIDELIGHTS:* Perry Arthur Sperber told *CA:* "I write because I like to. I can disseminate knowledge." *Avocational interests:* Travel, archaeology, anthropology, marine biology, music.

\* \* \*

## SPERLICH, Peter W. 1934-

*PERSONAL:* Born June 27, 1934, in Breslau, Germany; son of Max and Annelies (Greulich) Sperlich. *Education:* Mankato State College, B.A., 1959; University of Michigan, M.A., 1961, Ph.D., 1966. *Home:* 39 Adeline Dr., Walnut Creek, Calif. 94596. *Office:* 210 Barrows Hall, University of California, Berkeley, Calif. 94570.

*CAREER:* University of California, Berkeley, instructor, 1963-66, assistant professor, 1966-70, associate professor of political science, 1970—. Expert witness in court regarding jury selection processes, industry standards, and consumer affairs. *Member:* American Political Science Association, Law and Society Association, Society for the Psychological Study of Social Issues, International Political Science Association, Phi Kappa Phi. *Awards, honors:* Woodrow Wilson fellow, 1959; Ford Foundation fellow, 1968.

*WRITINGS: Conflict and Harmony in Human Affairs,* Rand McNally, 1971. Contributor of articles to professional journals.

*WORK IN PROGRESS:* Studying blue laws and crimes without victims; research on jury selection processes and the "equal protection" clause; studying public opinion and the American presidency.

*AVOCATIONAL INTERESTS:* Asian and western European travel.

## SPERRY, Margaret 1905-

*PERSONAL:* Born November 1, 1905, in Chicago, Ill.; daughter of Henry Muhlenberg (a civil engineer) and Sara J. (Hoeglund) Sperry; married Ben Russak (president of a publishing company), August 4, 1935. *Education:* University of Wisconsin, B.A., 1925; Columbia University, graduate study in journalism and languages, 1925-26; New York University, graduate study in public relations. *Religion:* Roman Catholic. *Office:* c/o Ben Russak, Crane, Russak & Co., 347 Madison Ave., New York, N.Y. 10017.

*CAREER:* Author and translator; *Daily Eagle,* Brooklyn, N.Y., journalist, 1927-29; Richard Bennett's Summer Theater, New Hope, Pa., stage manager, 1939; *Louisville Courier-Journal,* Louisville, Ky., feature writer for *Sunday Magazine,* 1941-42; Seagram's International Student Program, Louisville, public relations director, 1942-43; U.S. Office of War Information, feature writer in New York, N.Y., 1943-44. Program director, Guild of St. Birgitta, Darien, Conn., 1965-72. *Member:* Authors League of America, Kappa Alpha Theta, Phi Beta Kappa.

*WRITINGS: Golden Wind* (novel), Bonibooks, 1929; *Sun-Way* (novel), Bonibooks, 1930; *Portrait of Eden* (novel), Liveright, 1934; (translator from the Swedish, and adaptor) *The Magician's Cloak* (juvenile), Holt, 1938; (translator from the Norwegian, and adaptor) *The Hen That Saved the World,* John Day, 1952; (translator from the Polish, and adaptor) *Who Can Tell?* (juvenile), Golden Mill Press, 1959; (translator from the Polish, and adaptor) *The Golden Seeds,* Golden Mill Press, 1959; (translated from Scandinavian folklore, and adaptor) *Brides of Darkness and Other Stories,* Meulenhoff, 1960; (translator from the Polish, and adaptor) *Painted Houses,* Golden Mill Press, 1961; (translator from Scandinavian sources, and adaptor) *Scandinavian Stories* (juvenile), F. Watts, 1970; *Dream Harvest and Other Poems,* limited edition, privately printed, 1971; (translator from the Danish, and adaptor) *The Battle of the Bees and Other Stories by Carl Ewald* (juvenile), Crane, Russak, 1977; (translator from the Swedish, and adaptor) *Where Stories Grow,* Crane, Russak, 1977.

Also author of three-act plays, "Barbarica," 1939, "Soft Landing," 1969, "The Holy Terror," 1969, "The Love Trap," 1970, and "Song of the Seine," 1971, of radio plays, and of several unpublished volumes of verse. Contributor of poems and articles to *American-Scandinavian Review.*

*WORK IN PROGRESS:* A trilogy of novels concerning one family, beginning in seventeenth-century Sweden and ending in present-day America; research and translations from Scandinavian folklore.

*SIDELIGHTS:* Erik J. Friis writes that *Scandinavian Stories* contains "some of the best tales and stories created in the Northern lands, tales that will entertain young and old readers alike and almost uniformly will make one stop and reflect on the folk wisdom and the deeper meaning hiding beneath surface events." Feenie Ziner finds "subtlety, sophistication and wry humor in these stories, simple as they may appear. . . . [They] have the feel of a well-worn stone; there is no age limit to their enjoyment. Margaret Sperry's telling is clear and straightforward and infused with a fine sense of drama."

Sperry told *CA* that her "principal motivation in writing my trilogy is to show the relationship between man, nature, and religion. My major interests lie in Scandinavian history, folklore, and languages." She lived and travelled extensively in the Scandinavian countries from 1947 to 1962.

*BIOGRAPHICAL/CRITICAL SOURCES: New York Times,* December 12, 1971; *American-Scandinavian Review,* spring, 1973; *Best Sellers,* spring, 1977; *Publishers Weekly,* spring, 1977.

\*     \*     \*

**SPIES, Werner  1937-**

*PERSONAL:* Born April 1, 1937; son of Anton and Margarete (Kloepfer) Spies; married Monique Chapalain; children: Patrick, Alexandra. *Home:* 31 Ave. de Lattre de Tassigny, F-92340 Bourg-la-Reine, France. *Office:* Staatliche Kunstakademie Duesseldorf, 4000 Duesseldorf, Eiskellerstrasse 1, Germany.

*CAREER:* Currently professor of history of modern art, Staatliche Kunstakademie Duesseldorf, Duesseldorf, Germany. German commissaire of "Paris-Berlin" exhibition, Centre Georges Pompidou. *Member:* Deutsche Akademie fuer Sprache und Dichtung.

*WRITINGS:* (Editor) *Pour Daniel-Henry Kahnweiler,* Gerd Hatje Stuttgart, 1964; (author of introductory text) Max Ernst, *Frottagen,* Gerd Hatje Stuttgart, 1968, translation by Joseph M. Bernstein published as *Max Ernst,* Abrams, 1968 (published in England as *Max Ernst: Frottages,* Thames & Hudson, 1969); *Vasarely,* Gerd Hatje Stuttgart, 1969, translation by Leonard Nims published under same title, Abrams, 1969 (published in England as *Victor Vasarely,* Thames & Hudson, 1971), expanded German edition published as *Victor Vasarely,* M. DuMont Schauberg, 1971, translation by Robert Erich Wolf published under same title, Abrams, 1971.

*Albers,* Gerd Hatje Stuttgart, 1970, translation by Herma published under same title, Abrams, 1970 (published in England as *Joseph Albers,* Thames and Hudson, 1971); *Pablo Picasso: Das Plastiche Werke,* Gerd Hatje Stuttgart, 1971, translation by J. Maxwell Brownjohn published as *Sculpture by Picasso,* Abrams, 1971 (published in England as *Picasso Sculpture,* Thames & Hudson, 1972); *Die Rueckkehr der Schoenen Gaertnerin: Max Ernst, 1950-1970,* M. DuMont Schauberg, 1971, translation by Walter Allen published as *The Return of la Belle Jardiniere: Max Ernst, 1950-1970,* Abrams, 1972; (author of text) Rudolf Hoflehner, *Krieauer Kreaturen,* A. Schroll, 1971; *Max Ernst: Inventar u Widerspruch,* DuMont Schauberg, 1974; *Max Ernst: Die Arche des Max Ernst,* Verlag Beyeler Basel, 1975; *Catalogue Raisonne Max Ernst,* three volumes, Menil Foundation (Houston), 1975-76; *The Running Fence Project: Christo,* Abrams, 1977.

*WORK IN PROGRESS:* Volumes IV-VII of *Catalogue Raisonne Max Ernst; Vox Angelica: Max Ernst and the Situation of the Art in the United States; The Sculpture of Max Ernst.*

*SIDELIGHTS:* Werner Spies' books have also been published in the Netherlands, France, and Japan.

*BIOGRAPHICAL/CRITICAL SOURCES: Times Literary Supplement,* June 26, 1969; *Der Spiegel,* December, 1974; *Die Welt,* February 13, 1975; *Frankfurter Allgemeine Zeitung,* May 17, 1975; *Sueddeutsche Zeitung,* September, 1975; *Neue Zuercher Zeitung,* December 6, 1975, August, 1978; *Burlington Magazine,* March, 1976; *Die Zeit,* July, 1978; *L'Express,* July, 1978; *Le Point,* July, 1978; *Le Figaro,* July, 1978.

\*     \*     \*

**SPINKA, Matthew  1890-1972**

January 30, 1890—October 23, 1972; Czech-born American

clergyman, educator, translator, and author of works on Christianity. Obituaries: *New York Times,* October 25, 1972. (See index for *CA* sketch)

\*     \*     \*

**SPINRAD, Norman  1940-**

*PERSONAL:* Born September 15, 1940, in New York, N.Y.; son of Morris and Ray (Greenhut) Spinrad. *Education:* City College of the City University of New York, B.S., 1961. *Politics:* "Independent Conservative Radical." *Home:* 8463 Utica Dr., Los Angeles, Calif. 90046. *Agent:* Jane Rotrosen, 212 East 48th St., New York, N.Y. 10017.

*CAREER:* Writer. *Member:* Writers Guild of America, Science Fiction Writers of America (vice-president). *Awards, honors:* Prix Apollo, 1974, for *The Iron Dream.*

*WRITINGS: The Solarians,* Paperback Library, 1966; *Agent of Chaos,* Belmont Books, 1967; *The Men in the Jungle,* Doubleday, 1967; *Bug Jack Barron,* Walker & Co., 1969; *Fragments of America,* Now Library Press, 1970; *The Last Hurrah of the Golden Horde,* Avon, 1970; (editor) *The New Tomorrows,* Belmont Books, 1971; *The Iron Dream,* Avon, 1972; *Modern Science Fiction,* Anchor Books, 1974; *No Direction Home,* Pocket Books, 1975; *Passing through the Flame,* Berkeley Publishing, 1975; *Riding the Torch,* Dell, 1978. Author of teleplay, "The Doomsday Machine," for "Star Trek" series. Contributor of fiction to *Playboy, New Worlds, Analog,* and other peridocials; contributor of film criticism to *Free Press* (Los Angeles), *Cinema,* and *Staff.*

*WORK IN PROGRESS: The Children of Hamlin; A World Between.*

*BIOGRAPHICAL/CRITICAL SOURCES: Books and Bookmen,* May, 1970.

\*     \*     \*

**SPRUNT, Alexander, Jr.  1898-1973**

January 16, 1898—January 3, 1973; American ornithologist and museum curator. Obituaries: *New York Times,* January 6, 1973.

\*     \*     \*

**STACK, George J.  1931-**

*PERSONAL:* Born November 8, 1931, in New York, N.Y.; son of George Francis (an accountant) and Elizabeth (Sullivan) Stack; married Claire J. Avena, September 8, 1962; children: Diane Joan, Christopher George. *Education:* Pace College (now University), B.A., 1960; Pennsylvania State University, M.A., 1962, Ph.D., 1964. *Politics:* Independent. *Home:* 40 Sweden Hill Rd., Brockport, N.Y. 14420. *Office:* Department of Philosophy, State University of New York College, Brockport, N.Y. 14420.

*CAREER:* Long Island University, C. W. Post College, Brookville, N.Y., assistant professor of philosophy, 1963-67; State University of New York College at Brockport, professor of philosophy, 1967—. *Military service:* U.S. Army, Infantry, 1951-54; received Distinguished Service Medal. *Member:* American Philosophical Association, Delta Tau Kappa. *Awards, honors:* National Endowment for the Humanities fellowship, 1969.

*WRITINGS: Berkeley's Analysis of Perception,* Humanities, 1970; *On Kierkegaard: Philosophical Fragments,* F. Lokkes Forlag, 1976; *Kierkegaard's Existential Ethics,* University of Alabama Press, 1977; *Sartre's Philosophy of*

*Social Existence,* Warren Green, 1978. Contributor of articles and reviews to philosophy journals. Editorial adviser to *Folia Humanistica* (Barcelona).

*WORK IN PROGRESS: Authenticity and the Hysteric Personality.*

\* \* \*

## STAMM, Martin L. 1917-

*PERSONAL:* Born October 6, 1917, in Elkhart, Ind.; son of Ottomar A. (a minister) and Ottila (Manerow) Stamm; married Hannah M. Kricher, January 30, 1943; children: Martin J., Hannah, Jayne, Marion B. *Education:* Purdue University, B.S., 1940, M.S., 1949, Ph.D., 1959. *Politics:* Independent. *Religion:* Protestant. *Home:* 25 Crown Rd., Trenton, N.J. 08625. *Office:* New Classroom Bldg., No. 380, Trenton State College, Trenton, N.J. 08625.

*CAREER:* English teacher and coach, 1940-42; guidance counselor, 1947-52; Washington High School, South Bend, Ind., head counselor, 1952-56; administrative assistant to superintendent of curriculum in public schools in South Bend, 1956-57, director of guidance and pupil personnel, 1957-63; district director of guidance in public schools in Scotch Plains, N.J., 1964-67; Trenton State College, Trenton, N.J., professor of education, chairperson of student personnel services, and supervisor of graduate program in guidance and counseling, 1967—. Adjunct professor at Purdue University, 1957, Indiana University, 1957, 1960, University of Notre Dame, 1959-60, 1962-63, and New York University, 1966-67; special lecturer, Ohio State University. Consultant to New Jersey Department of State, 1967—. *Military service:* U.S. Navy, 1942-46.

*MEMBER:* American Personnel and Guidance Association, Association for Counselor Education and Supervision, American School Counselor Association, National Education Association, American Board on Counseling Services, American Association of University Professors, Northeastern State Branch Presidents' Association, New Jersey Personnel Guidance Association (president, 1968-69; member of executive council), Purdue University Alumni Association. *Awards, honors:* Author's Award, National Council of Teachers of English, 1972.

*WRITINGS*—All with Blossom S. Nissman: *Alphabet Land,* Chandler-Davis, 1970; *Ask the Counselor,* Chandler-Davis, 1970; *New Dimensions in Elementary Guidance: Practical Procedures for Teachers, Counselors, and Administrators,* Richards Rosen, 1971; *Your Child and Drugs: A Preventative Approach,* illustrated by James Hiteman, Guidance Awareness Publications, 1973; *What You Always Wanted to Know about Tests but Were Afraid to Ask,* Guidance Awareness Publications, 1974; *Implications and Applications of Assessment Procedures for Counselors and Teachers,* Guidance Awareness Publications, 1976; *Practical Guidelines for Space-Age Children,* Guidance Awareness Publications, 1977. Author of weekly column, "Ask the Counselor," in *Burlington County Times.* Contributor to guidance and counseling journals.

*WORK IN PROGRESS:* A book on guidance in the middle school; research on elementary school guidance.†

\* \* \*

## STANFORD, Barbara Dodds 1943-

*PERSONAL:* Born September 4, 1943, in Santa Maria, Calif.; daughter of Alvin Gordon (a school superintendent) and Evelyn (Daily) Dodds; married Gene Stanford (a

teacher and writer), July 26, 1969. *Education:* University of Illinois, B.A. (with honors), 1964; Columbia University, M.A., 1966; University of Colorado, Ph.D., 1973. *Politics:* Democrat. *Religion:* Quaker. *Home:* 25 Talcott Rd., Utica, N.Y. 13502. *Office:* Department of Education, Utica College, Syracuse University, Utica, N.Y. 13502.

*CAREER:* High school English teacher in St. Louis, Mo., 1964-70, in Boulder, Colo., 1970-72; Syracuse University, Utica College, Utica, N.Y., 1973—, currently associate professor of education. Teacher in Upward Bound program, Webster College, 1968. *Member:* National Council of Teachers of English, Women's International League for Peace and Freedom, Fellowship of Reconciliation, Consortium on Peace Research Education and Development, Phi Beta Kappa, Phi Kappa Phi.

*WRITINGS: Negro Literature for High School Students,* National Council of Teachers of English, 1968; *I, Too, Sing America: Black Voices in American Literature,* Hayden, 1971; *On Being Female,* Pocket Books, 1974; *Flight Plan, Small Planet,* Harcourt, 1975; (with Martha Pomainville and Cynthia Blankenship) *Designs for English,* Learning Ventures, 1977; *Teacher's Guide to Peace Education,* Learning Ventures, 1978.

With husband, Gene Stanford: *Learning Discussion Skills through Games,* Citation, 1969; *Journal 3,* Harcourt, 1971; *Journal 4,* Harcourt, 1971; (editors) *Changes,* and *Teacher's Book,* Harcourt, 1971; (editors) *Mix,* and *Teacher's Book,* Harcourt, 1971; *Myths and Modern Man,* Pocket Books, 1972; (editors) *Strangers to Themselves,* Bantam, 1973; (editors) *Love Has Many Faces,* Pocket Books, 1973; *Roles and Relationships,* Bantam, 1976; *Peacemaking,* Bantam, 1976.

Editor with Bethel Bodine and others: *Like It Is,* Addison-Wesley, 1970; *A Place to Be,* Addison-Wesley, 1970; *The Blue Guitar,* Addison-Wesley, 1970; *A Man of His Own,* Addison-Wesley, 1970. Contributor to education journals.

*WORK IN PROGRESS:* Revising, with Karima Amin, *Negro Literature for High School Students.*

\* \* \*

## STANFORD, Gene 1944-

*PERSONAL:* Born July 11, 1944, in Martin, Tenn.; son of Gene Howey (a university business manager) and Verletta (Hearn) Stanford; married Barbara Dodds (a teacher and writer), July 26, 1969. *Education:* Washington University, St. Louis, Mo., A.B., 1966; University of Colorado, M.A., 1971, Ph.D., 1973. *Politics:* Democrat. *Home:* 25 Talcott Rd., Utica, N.Y. 13502. *Office:* Utica College, Syracuse University, Utica, N.Y. 13502.

*CAREER:* High school English teacher in Ladue, Mo., 1966-70; Syracuse University, Utica College, Utica, N.Y., director of teacher education programs, 1973—. *Member:* National Council of Teachers of English, American Personnel and Guidance Association, National Education Association, Phi Delta Kappa. *Awards, honors:* First place in *Scholastic Magazine's* Promising New Practices in Education Contest, 1969.

*WRITINGS: McGraw-Hill Vocabulary,* Books 1-6, McGraw, 1971; (editor) *Generation Rap,* Dell, 1971; *Steps to Better Writing,* Holt, 1972; (with Albert E. Roark) *Human Interaction in Education,* Allyn & Bacon, 1974; (with Chet Cromwell and others) *Becoming,* Lippincott, 1975; (editor with Charles S. Adler and Sheila Morrissey Adler) *We Are But a Moment's Sunlight,* Pocket Books, 1976; (with Deborah Perry) *Death Out of the Closet,* Bantam, 1976; (with

Marie N. Smith) *A Guidebook for Teaching Composition,* Allyn & Bacon, 1977; (with Smith) *A Guidebook for Teaching Creative Writing,* Allyn & Bacon, 1977; *Developing Effective Classroom Groups,* Hart, 1977; (with John Cormican) *A Guidebook for Teaching about the English Language,* Allyn & Bacon, 1978; *Death: A Filmstrip Program,* Winston Press, 1979.

With wife, Barbara Dodds Stanford: *Learning Discussion Skills through Games,* Citation, 1969; *Journal 3,* Harcourt, 1971; *Journal 4,* Harcourt, 1971; (editors) *Changes,* and *Teacher's Book,* Harcourt, 1971; (editors) *Mix,* and *Teacher's Book,* Harcourt, 1971; *Myths and Modern Man,* Pocket Books, 1972; (editors) *Strangers to Themselves,* Bantam, 1973; (editors) *Love Has Many Faces,* Pocket Books, 1973; *Roles and Relationships,* Bantam, 1976; *Peacemaking,* Bantam, 1976. Contributor to education journals.

\*     \*     \*

## STANSBURY, Donald L.   1929-

*PERSONAL:* Born June 21, 1929, in Fullerton, Calif.; son of Burton James (an oil operator) and Bertha (Baxter) Stansbury; married Beverly Ann Wheeler, November 21, 1958; children: Julia Lee. *Education:* Bakersfield College, A.A., 1956; University of California, Los Angeles, B.S., 1958; San Jose State College (now University), M.A., 1966. *Politics:* Republican. *Religion:* No affiliation. *Home:* 2315 A St., Bakersfield, Calif. 93301. *Office:* Department of English, Bakersfield College, Bakersfield, Calif. 93305.

*CAREER:* B. J. Stansbury, Inc. (oil firm), Bakersfield, Calif., vice-president, 1958-62; high school English teacher in San Jose, Calif., 1963-64, and Pacific Grove, Calif., 1964-66; Bakersfield College, Bakersfield, Calif., instructor in English, 1966—. *Military service:* U.S. Air Force, 1950-54. *Member:* National Council of Teachers of English, American Folklore Society, American Association of University Professors, California Teachers Association, Faculty Association of California Community Colleges, California Folklore Society, Sierra Club.

*WRITINGS:* (Editor) *Impact: Short Stories for Pleasure,* Prentice-Hall, 1971; (co-author) *Improving College English Skills,* Scott, Foresman, 1972.

*WORK IN PROGRESS:* An English composition textbook, *Rhetorical Magic;* a novel, *Tribunal;* *Folklore of Flying;* short stories and poetry.

*AVOCATIONAL INTERESTS:* Flying (has been a private pilot since 1955, and has had instrument and commercial ratings and been a flight instructor since 1973).

\*     \*     \*

## STANTON, Phoebe B(aroody)   1914-

*PERSONAL:* Born December 15, 1914, in Freeport, Ill.; married Daniel J. Stanton, February 21, 1948 (died April 19, 1966); children: Michael. *Education:* Mount Holyoke College, B.A. (magna cum laude), 1937; Radcliffe College, M.A., 1939; Stanford University, graduate study, 1939-41; University of London, Ph.D., 1950. *Home:* 2213 Foxbane Sq., Baltimore, Md. 21209. *Office:* Department of History of Art, Johns Hopkins University, 34th and Charles St., Baltimore, Md. 21218.

*CAREER:* U.S. Department of Navy, and U.S. Board of Economic Warfare, Washington, D.C., researcher, 1941-45; Reed College, Portland, Ore., instructor in history, 1945-47; American Foreign Service, London, England, assistant cultural relations officer, 1950-53; Bryn Mawr College, Bryn

Mawr, Pa., lecturer in history of art, 1953-54; Walters Art Gallery, Baltimore, Md., educator, 1954-55; Johns Hopkins University, Baltimore, Md., lecturer, 1955-57, member of faculty of fine arts, 1957—, assistant professor, 1962-68, associate professor, 1968-70, professor of history of art, 1970—, William R. Kenan, Jr. Professor, 1971—. Goucher College, lecturer, 1955-60, adjunct professor of art history, 1960-63. Consultant, U.S. Office of Education. Member, Maryland Governor's Consulting Commission for the National Register of Historic Places; member of Design Advisory Panel, Baltimore Inner Harbor Project, and Architectural Review Board, Charles Center Inner Harbor.

*MEMBER:* Society of Architectural Historians (member of board of directors), Victorian Society (member of board of directors), Victorian Society in America, Phi Beta Kappa. *Awards, honors:* American Philosophical Society grant, 1958; Chapelbrook Foundation grant, 1969; D.Litt., Mount Holyoke College, 1971; National Endowment for the Humanities senior fellowship, 1972-73.

*WRITINGS:* (Contributor) John Summerson, editor, *Concerning Architecture,* Penguin, 1968; (author of introduction and main text) *The Sculptural Landscape of Jane Frank,* A. S. Barnes, 1968; *The Gothic Revival and American Church Architecture: An Episode in Taste, 1840-1856,* Johns Hopkins Press, 1968; *Pugin,* Thames & Hudson, 1971; (contributor) M. Port, editor, *The Houses of Parliament,* Yale University Press, 1976; (contributor) J. L. Altholz, editor, *The Mind and Art of Victorian England,* University of Minnesota, 1976. General editor, "Johns Hopkins Studies in Nineteenth-Century Architecture," Johns Hopkins Press. Architectural critic and commentator, *Baltimore Sun.* Contributor to *Journal of the Royal Institute of British Architects, Architectural Review, Journal of the Society of Architectural Historians, Voice, Process, Architecture,* and other publications.

\*     \*     \*

## STANTON, Royal (Waltz)   1916-

*PERSONAL:* Born October 23, 1916, in Los Angeles, Calif.; son of Everett C. (a teacher) and Alice Joy (Waltz) Stanton; married Norine Parker, June 18, 1939; children: Lynne Anne, Marcia Joy (Mrs. Stephen C. Hall). *Education:* University of California, Los Angeles, B.E., 1939, M.A., 1946; graduate study at University of Southern California, San Diego State College (now University), Long Beach State College (now California State University, Long Beach), San Jose State College (now University), and Occidental College. *Home:* 22301 Havenhurst Dr., Los Altos, Calif. 94022. *Office:* Fine Arts Division, De Anza College, 21250 Stevens Creek Blvd., Cupertino, Calif. 95014.

*CAREER:* Long Beach Polytechnic High School, Long Beach, Calif., instructor, 1946-50; Long Beach City College, Long Beach, chairman, music department, 1950-61; Foothill College, Los Altos Hills, Calif., chairman, Fine Arts Division, 1961-67; De Anza College, Cupertino, Calif., chairman, Fine Arts Division, 1967—. Founder-conductor of The Schola Cantorum (symphonic choir), Cupertino, 1964; music director of The Schola Cantorum in Long Beach, 1953-61, and in the Foothill College District, 1964—. Director, Los Angeles Bach Festival, 1959-60; minister of music, First Congregational Church, Los Angeles, Calif., 1959-60. Guest professor or choral clinician at University of Southern California, University of California, Los Angeles, Occidental College, University of Wisconsin, University of Puget Sound, Kent State University. *Military service:* U.S. Army, 1943-46; became sergeant.

*MEMBER:* American Society of Composers, Authors and Publishers (ASCAP), Music Educators National Conference, American Musicological Society, American Choral Directors Association, National Education Association, Choral Conductors Guild of California, California Junior College Music Educators Association (state president, 1957-59). *Awards, honors:* ASCAP awards, 1968, 1969, 1970, 1971.

*WRITINGS: The Dynamic Choral Conductor,* Shawnee Press, 1971; *Steps to Singing for Voice Classes,* Wadsworth, 1971, 2nd edition, 1976.

Contributor of 76 miscellaneous choral compositions and arrangements to catalogs of Lawson-Gould Music, Theodore Presser, Neil Kjos, Shawnee Press, J. Fischer & Brother, Foster & Hall, Choristers Guild, Harold Flammer, Warner Brothers, and Remick Music; contributor of articles to *Music Educators Journal.*

*SIDELIGHTS:* Royal Stanton studied composition under Arnold Schoenberg at the University of California at Los Angeles from 1938-42, and choral techniques with John Smallman, Robert Shaw, John Finley Williamson, and Roger Wagner.

\*    \*    \*

## STARCH, Daniel 1883-

*PERSONAL:* Born March 8, 1883, in LaCrosse, Wis.; son of Frank and Theresa Starch; married Amy Jane Hopson, August 26, 1913 (deceased). *Education:* Morningside College, B.A., 1903; University of Iowa, M.A., 1904, Ph.D., 1906; Harvard University, postdoctoral study, 1907-08. *Home:* 14 Burgess Rd., Scarsdale, N.Y. 10583. *Office:* Daniel Starch & Staff, Inc., Mamaroneck, N.Y. 10543.

*CAREER:* University of Iowa, Iowa City, instructor in psychology, 1906-07; Wellesley College, Wellesley, Mass., instructor in psychology, 1907-08; University of Wisconsin—Madison, instructor, 1908-12, assistant professor, 1912-17, associate professor of psychology, 1917-20; Harvard University, Cambridge, Mass., lecturer, 1919-20, assistant professor, 1920-23, associate professor of business psychology, 1923-26; Daniel Starch & Staff, Inc. (business research consultants), owner in New York, N.Y., 1926-52, and Mamaroneck, N.Y., 1952-68. Director of research department, American Association of Advertising Agencies, 1924-32. Professor of psychology, University of Washington, Seattle, summer, 1915, and New York University, summer, 1922. *Military service:* U.S. Aviation Service, 1917; became captain. *Member:* American Psychological Association, American Association for the Advancement of Science (fellow), American Marketing Association, Sigma Xi. *Awards, honors:* Sc.D., Morningside College, 1949; Paul D. Converse Award, American Marketing Association, 1951.

*WRITINGS: Educational Psychology* (textbook), Macmillan, 1919; *Principles of Advertising,* McGraw, 1923; *How to Develop Your Executive Ability,* Harper, 1943; *Measuring Advertising Readership and Results,* McGraw, 1966. Contributor to *Encyclopaedia Britannica;* contributor of articles to psychology, education, and business journals.

*WORK IN PROGRESS:* A book about great books.

\*    \*    \*

## STARKE, Aubrey (Harrison) 1905(?)-1972

1905(?)—October 2, 1972; American historian, editor, biographer, and collector of Americana. Obituaries: *New York Times,* October 4, 1972.

## STARKE, Catherine Juanita 1913-

*PERSONAL:* Born April 5, 1913, in Charlotte, N.C.; daughter of Joseph Thomas (a clerk and teacher) and Sadie Lee (Spencer) Gladden; married William Campbell Starke (a publishing executive), October 28, 1939. *Education:* Hunter College (now Hunter College of the City University of New York), B.A., 1936; Columbia University, M.A., 1937, Ed.D., 1963. *Politics:* Independent. *Religion:* Episcopalian. *Residence:* Flushing, N.Y. *Office:* Department of English, Jersey City State College, Jersey City, N.J. 07305.

*CAREER:* St. Paul's High School, Lawrenceville, Va., English teacher, 1938-46; Morgan State College, Baltimore, Md., instructor, 1947-51, assistant professor of English, 1951-56; Jersey City State College, Jersey City, N.J., assistant professor, 1957-60, associate professor, 1960-63, professor of English, 1963—. *Member:* Modern Language Association of America, Center for the Study of Democratic Institutions, Kappa Delta Pi, Pi Lambda Theta.

*WRITINGS: Black Portraiture in American Fiction: Stock Characters, Archetypes, and Individuals,* Basic Books, 1972. Contributor to *Phylon.*

*WORK IN PROGRESS:* The works of Armand Larusse and others who contributed to *Les Cenelles;* prose writings of contemporary young Blacks.

\*    \*    \*

## STARR, Stephen Z. 1909-

*PERSONAL:* Born November 1, 1909, in Budapest, Hungary; son of Alexander and Regina Starr; married Ivy-Jane Edmondson, November 11, 1933; children: George Alexander, Ivy-Elizabeth Starr Minely, Stephen Frederick, Diana Jane Starr Cooper. *Education:* Western Reserve University (now Case Western Reserve University), B.A., 1930; New York University, J.D., 1941. *Politics:* "Mugwump—mostly conservative." *Religion:* Roman Catholic. *Home address:* R.D. 1, Box 64, Cambridge, Vt. 05444.

*CAREER:* Schenley Industries, New York, N.Y., executive, before 1953; Clopay Corp., Cincinnati, Ohio, secretary-treasurer, 1953-73; Cincinnati Historical Society, Cincinnati, director, 1973-78. *Member:* Cincinnati Historical Society, Literary Club (Cincinnati).

*WRITINGS: Colonel Grenfell's Wars,* Louisiana State University Press, 1971; *Jennison's Jayhawkers,* Louisiana State University Press, 1973. Contributor to history journals.

*WORK IN PROGRESS:* A history of cavalry operations in the Civil War, three volumes, for Louisiana State University Press.

\*    \*    \*

## STAUDER, Jack 1939-

*PERSONAL:* Born March 2, 1939, in Pueblo, Colo.; son of J. Richard (a rancher) and Hilma (Johnson) Stauder; married Wunderley Rich (a researcher), August, 1963 (divorced, 1973); children: Samuel, Jeffrey. *Education:* Harvard University, B.A., 1962; Cambridge University, Ph.D., 1968. *Politics:* "Anti-imperialist, pro-socialist." *Home:* 180 East Clinton, New Bedford, Mass. 02740. *Office:* Department of Sociology and Anthropology, Southeastern Massachusetts University, North Dartmouth, Mass. 02747.

*CAREER:* Harvard University, Cambridge, Mass., lecturer in social anthropology, 1968-71; Northeastern University, Boston, Mass., assistant professor of social anthropology,

1971-73; Southeastern Massachusetts University, North Dartmouth, associate professor of sociology and anthropology, 1973—. *Military service:* U.S. Marine Corps Reserve, active duty, 1958-59. *Member:* American Anthropological Association (fellow). *Awards, honors:* Marshall scholarship, 1962-64; Foreign Area fellowship, 1964-67; Wenner-Gren Foundation grant, 1967-68.

*WRITINGS: The Majangir: Ecology and Society of a Southwest Ethiopian People,* Cambridge University Press, 1971. Contributor of articles to publications in his field.

*WORK IN PROGRESS:* Research on history and development of capitalism and imperialism, and on revolution and socialism, special areas include Africa, China, and the Middle East.

\*      \*      \*

## STAVELEY, Gaylord L(ee)   1931-

*PERSONAL:* Born July 12, 1931, in Traer, Iowa; son of Donald D. and Eva (Crawford) Staveley; married Joan Nevills, December 4, 1954; children: Cameron L., Scott N. *Education:* State University of Iowa, B.A., 1953. *Home:* 7395 Loos Dr., Prescott Valley, Ariz. 86312.

*CAREER:* Canyoneers, Inc. (river and trail outfitters), Flagstaff, Ariz., president and chairman of board, 1957—. *Military service:* U.S. Air Force, 1953-55; became first lieutenant. *Member:* Outdoor Writers Association of America.

*WRITINGS: Broken Waters Sing: Rediscovering Two Great Rivers of the West,* Little, Brown, 1971.

*SIDELIGHTS:* Gaylord Staveley told *CA* that he "wrote *Broken Waters Sing* out of concern for the Colorado River, which has been 'discovered, dammed and dirtied' in little more than a century."

\*      \*      \*

## STEADMAN, Mark   1930-

*PERSONAL:* Born July 2, 1930, in Statesboro, Ga.; son of Mark Sidney (an engineer) and Marie (Hopkins) Steadman; married Joan Anderson (an elementary school librarian), March 29, 1952; children: Clay, Todd, Wade. *Education:* Attended Armstrong Junior College, 1947-49; Emory University, A.B., 1951; Florida State University, M.A., 1956, Ph.D., 1963. *Politics:* "Wishy-washy." *Religion:* "Earnest but vague." *Address:* P.O. Box 1224, Clemson, S.C. 29631. *Agent:* Lois Wallace, Wallace & Sheil Agency, Inc., 118 East 61st St., New York, N.Y. 10021. *Office:* Department of English, Clemson University, Clemson, S.C. 29631.

*CAREER:* Has worked as movie usher, florist's delivery boy, rodman on a survey party, advertising copy writer, and newspaper canvasser; Clemson University, Clemson, S.C., instructor, 1957-60, assistant professor, 1960-64, associate professor, 1964-76, professor of American literature, 1976—. Visiting associate professor of American literature, American University (Cairo), 1968-69. *Military service:* U.S. Navy, 1951-53. *Member:* American Association of University Professors, Authors Guild, South Atlantic Modern Languages Association, South Carolina Council on Human Relations.

*WRITINGS: McAfee County* (novel), Holt, 1971; *A Lion's Share* (novel), Holt, 1976.

*WORK IN PROGRESS: Reunion,* a novel; a film adaptation of *McAfee County.*

*SIDELIGHTS:* Mark Steadman told *CA:* "I owe a debt to just about every writer that you could name—after all, I do

teach literature. But I think that the ones that I was most consciously following were—Erskine Caldwell, Sherwood Anderson, Ring Lardner, S. J. Perelman, Faulkner (of course) and Hemingway.... Flannery O'Connor should have been an influence, but wasn't at the time."

\*      \*      \*

## STEDMAN, Jane W(inifred)   1920-

*PERSONAL:* Born June 8, 1920, in Detroit, Mich.; daughter of Gerald E. and Lillian (Houston) Stedman; married George C. McElroy (a teacher), June 9, 1950. *Education:* Wayne University (now Wayne State University), B.A., 1942, M.A., 1943; additional study at University of Edinburgh, 1950-51; University of Chicago, Ph.D., 1955. *Home:* 1411 East 54th Pl., Chicago, Ill. 60615. *Office:* Roosevelt University, 430 South Michigan Ave., Chicago, Ill. 60605.

*CAREER:* Wayne University (now Wayne State University), Detroit, Mich., instructor in English, 1943-50; Roosevelt University, Chicago, Ill., lecturer, 1952-55, assistant professor, 1955-61, associate professor, 1961-66, professor of English, 1966—. Lecturer in English and humanities, University of Chicago, 1954-61, and Indiana University at Gary, 1959-65; visiting professor, University of Chicago, 1975-76. Correspondent for *Opera News,* 1960—. *Member:* Research Society for Victorian Periodicals, American Association of University Professors, Bronte Society, Midwest Victorian Studies Association. *Awards, honors:* Bronte Society prize for article, "The Genesis of the Genii," 1965; American Council of Learned Societies grant in London, 1970-71; Guggenheim fellowship, 1973-74; Fulbright research fellowship, 1973-74.

*WRITINGS:* (Editor and author of introduction) *Gilbert before Sullivan: Six Comic Plays,* University of Chicago Press, 1967.

Contributor: D.T.W. McCord, editor, *What Cheer: An Anthology of British Humorous and Witty Verse Gathered, Sifted and Salted,* Modern Library, 1955; Frank Merkling, editor, *The Opera News Book of "Figaro,"* Dodd, 1967; F. Merkling, editor, *The Opera News Book of "Traviata,"* Dodd, 1967; John Bush Jones, editor, *W. S. Gilbert: A Century of Scholarship and Commentary,* New York University Press, 1970; James Helyar, editor, *Gilbert and Sullivan Papers Presented at the International Conference Held at the University of Kansas in May, 1970,* University of Kansas, Libraries, 1971; Martha Vicinus, editor, *Suffer and Be Still,* Indiana University Press, 1972; Sylvan Barnet and others, editors, *Classic Theatre,* Little, Brown, 1975. Contributor of articles to *American Speech, Modern Philology, Dickensian, Victorian Studies, Nineteenth-Century Theatre Research, Educational Theatre Journal, Opera News,* and other journals; contributor of poems to *New Yorker, Folio, Oyez,* and *Chicago Review.*

*WORK IN PROGRESS:* A critical book on Gilbert and the Victorian stage; research for a biography of W. S. Gilbert.

*SIDELIGHTS:* Jane Stedman told *CA:* "When I was 17, I heard broadcasts of short versions of the Gilbert and Sullivan operas, and from that time I have been devoted to the works of Gilbert and eventually to nineteenth century satire in general. When I began work, the Victorian theatre was not generally treated as a serious literary field; now I hope that I have helped to make it so."

*BIOGRAPHICAL/CRITICAL SOURCES: New York Times Book Review,* October 1, 1967; *Prairie Schooner,* summer, 1968; *Virginia Quarterly Review,* winter, 1968.

## STEELE, Frank 1935-

*PERSONAL:* Born January 13, 1935, in Tuscaloosa, Ala.; son of Frank Pettus (a salesman) and Zeila (Stovall) Steele; married Peggy Myrick (an English teacher), April 27, 1958; children: Carolyn, Nancy. *Education:* University of Alabama, B.A., 1960; University of Chattanooga (now University of Tennessee at Chattanooga), M.Ed., 1964; University of Tennessee, Ed.D., 1968. *Home address:* P.O. Box 245, College Heights, Bowling Green, Ky. 42101. *Office:* Department of English, Western Kentucky University, Bowling Green, Ky. 42101.

*CAREER:* Baylor School for Boys, Chattanooga, Tenn., instructor in English, 1960-64; Webb School, Knoxville, Tenn., instructor in English, 1964-67; University of Tennessee at Martin, acting assistant professor of English, 1967-68; Western Kentucky University, Bowling Green, director of freshman English, 1968—. *Military service:* U.S. Army, 1958-60. *Member:* Modern Language Association of America, South Atlantic Modern Language Association.

*WRITINGS:* (Editor) *Poetry Southeast: 1950-70*, Tennessee Poetry Press, 1968; *Walking to the Waterfall* (poems), Tennessee Poetry Press, 1969. Contributor of poems to journals, including *Prairie Schooner, Southern Poetry Review,* and *Green River Review.* Editor, *Tennessee Poetry Journal,* 1967-68.

*WORK IN PROGRESS:* A book of poems; a study of the poetry of William Stafford.

\* \* \*

## STEELY, John E(dward) 1922-

*PERSONAL:* Born November 7, 1922, in Almyra, Ark.; son of Dempsey Edward (a minister) and Alva (Bledsoe) Steely; married Donna Brown (a teacher), May 21, 1947; children: Deborah Jane (Mrs. S. Bryant Kendrick, Jr.), John Alan. *Education:* Ouachita Baptist College (now University), B.A., 1944; Southern Baptist Theological Seminary, B.D., Th.M., Th.D. *Address:* P.O. Box 1154, Wake Forest, N.C. 27587. *Office:* Department of Historical Theology, Southeastern Baptist Theological Seminary, Wake Forest, N.C. 27587.

*CAREER:* Baptist minister; Southern Baptist College, Walnut Ridge, Ark., professor of religion, 1948-56, dean of administration, 1953-56; Southeastern Baptist Theological Seminary, Wake Forest, N.C., assistant professor, 1956-57, associate professor, 1957-62, professor of historical theology, 1962—. *Member:* American Society of Church History, Baptist Professors of Religion (vice-president, 1960-61; president, 1961-62), Baptist Historical Society. *Awards, honors:* Christian Research Foundation awards for translation of *Das Kirchliche Apostelamt,* by Walter Schmithals, 1966, and *Kyrios Christos,* by Wilhelm Bousset, 1967.

*WRITINGS:* (With Brooks Hays) *The Baptist Way of Life,* Prentice-Hall, 1963.

Translator; published by Abingdon, except as indicated: Walter Schmithals, *The Office of Apostle in the Early Church,* 1969; Wilhelm Bousset, *Kyrios Christos,* 1970; Schmithals, *Gnosticism in Corinth,* 1971; Schmithals, *Paul and the Gnostics,* 1972; Hans Conzelmann, *History of Primitive Christianity,* 1973; W. G. Kuemmel, *The Theology of the New Testament According to Its Major Witnesses: Jesus, Paul, John,* 1973; M. de Jonge, *Jesus: Inspiring and Disturbing Presence,* 1974; Schmithals, *The Apocalyptic Movement,* 1975; Eduard Lohse, *The New Testament Environment,* 1976; Luc Grollenberg, *Bible Reading for the 21st*

*Century,* Consortium, 1976; G. von Rad, *Biblical Interpretations in Preaching,* 1977. Contributor of articles to religious periodicals.

*WORK IN PROGRESS:* Translations from the German, entitled *Jesus: Stranger from Heaven and Son of God,* by M. de Jonge and *The Hellenistic Mystery Religions,* by R. Reitzenstein; a translation of *Geloven Vandaag* by E. Flesseman-van Leer.

\* \* \*

## STEENBERG, Sven 1905-

*PERSONAL:* Born September 23, 1905, in Riga, Latvia; son of Alfred (a priest) and Elisabeth (Baronesse Ungern-Sternberg) Steenberg; married Margot Schmidt, May, 1934; married second wife, Carla Wiechert (a writer), May 8, 1956; children: (first marriage) Marlis, Sven. *Education:* Studied law and film. *Home:* Sebastian Bach Strasse 2, 7012 Fellbach, Stuttgart, West Germany.

*CAREER:* Began career as juridical consultant, 1931-33; businessman in Berlin, Germany, 1933-37; wrote filmscripts and worked as stage manager's assistant, 1937-40; interpreter, 1940-45; businessman and lecturer on Asian and Russian affairs, 1946—.

*WRITINGS: Wlassow: Verraeter oder Patriot?,* Verlag Wissenschaft & Politik, 1968, translation by Abe Farbstein published as *Vlasov,* Knopf, 1970; *Ein neues China–das Modell Taiwan,* Seewald-Verlag, 1976.

Film scripts: "Boris and Irina," produced by Ufa (Berlin), 1936. Writer of radio and television scripts. Contributor to section on Russian history in *Encyclopaedie 2000,* published in Germany.

*BIOGRAPHICAL/CRITICAL SOURCES: Best Sellers,* August 15, 1970.

\* \* \*

## STEIN, Bob 1920-

*PERSONAL:* Born December 12, 1920, in Chicago, Ill.; son of Joseph (a salesman) and Miriam (Goldblatt) Stein; married Marjorie Sachs, May 1, 1949; children: Linda (Mrs. Mark Loewenstein), Lawrence, Michael. *Education:* Attended Wilson Junior College and University of Chicago. *Home:* 1439 Fargo Ave., Chicago, Ill. 60626. *Office:* 20 North Wacker Dr., Chicago, Ill. 60606.

*CAREER:* Vice-president in sales in hotel and club management firm, Chicago, Ill., 1949-56; co-owner of advertising agency, Chicago, 1957—. Lecturer in hotel and restaurant marketing, Michigan State University, 1965-69; vice-president and member of board of directors, Better Boys Foundation (Chicago), 1971—. *Military service:* U.S. Army Air Forces, 1941-45. *Member:* Hotel Sales Management Association (president of Illinois chapter, 1954; vice-president of national chapter, 1955), Business Executives Move for Vietnam Peace (president of Chicago chapter, 1973), International Society of Antique Scale Collectors (founder), Nippersink Community Club (president, 1963-64; member of board of directors, 1965—). *Awards, honors:* Awards from several advertising clubs and graphics arts societies for advertising and sales literature; award from Hotel Sales Management Association for best-coordinated sales campaign in hotel industry, 1953.

*WRITINGS: Marketing in Action for Hotels, Motels, Restaurants,* Hayden, 1971. Contributor to hotel, restaurant, and travel trade journals.

*WORK IN PROGRESS:* Revising *Marketing in Action for Hotels, Motels, Restaurants.*

\* \* \*

**STEIN, Bruno  1930-**

*PERSONAL:* Born July 19, 1930, in Vienna, Austria; son of Leo and Pauline (Lindenbaum) Stein; married Judith Paris (a writer), December 26, 1969. *Education:* New York University, A.B., 1950, A.M., 1952, Ph.D., 1959. *Office:* Department of Economics, New York University, Washington Square, New York, N.Y. 10003.

*CAREER:* New York University, New York, N.Y., assistant professor, 1959-63, associate professor, 1963-68, professor of economics, 1968—, director, Institute of Labor Relations, 1973—. Member of labor arbitration, mediation, and fact-finding panels of state and national arbitration groups. *Military service:* U.S. Army, 1952-54. *Member:* American Economic Association, Industrial Relations Research Association, History of Economics Society, Society of Professionals in Dispute Resolution, American Arbitration Association. *Awards, honors:* Ford Foundation faculty research fellowship, 1968-69.

*WRITINGS: On Relief: The Economics of Poverty and Public Welfare,* Basic Books, 1971; (co-editor) *Incentives and Planning in Social Policy,* Aldine, 1973; *Work and Welfare in Britain and the U.S.A.,* Wiley, 1976. Contributor to economics and industrial relations journals.

*WORK IN PROGRESS:* A book on Social Security.

\* \* \*

**STEIN, Susan M.  1942-**

*PERSONAL:* Born April 5, 1942, in Springfield, Mass.; daughter of Edward Joseph (an accountant) and Fannie (Emerick) Gleeson; married Charles H. Stein (a teacher), August 17, 1963; children: Edward J., Margaret D., Paul C. *Education:* St. Louis University, B.S., 1962, M.A., 1964; also attended Creighton University, 1967, 1975-76, and University of Nebraska at Omaha, 1970. *Religion:* Roman Catholic. *Home:* 9834 Ruggles St., Omaha, Neb. 68134. *Office:* Department of English, Brownell-Talbot School, 400 North Happy Hollow Blvd., Omaha, Neb. 68132.

*CAREER:* University of Missouri—St. Louis, instructor in English, 1964-66; University of Nebraska, Lincoln, instructor in English, 1967-68; University of Nebraska at Omaha, instructor in English, 1974-75; Creighton University, Omaha, instructor of English and education, 1975-76; Brownell-Talbot School, Omaha, teacher of English, 1976—, chairman of department, 1978—. *Member:* Nebraska Writers Guild.

*WRITINGS:* (With Sarah T. Lottick) *Three, Four, Open the Door: Creative Fun for Young Children,* Follett, 1971. Writer of a weekly humor column, Omaha *World Herald,* 1973—. Contributor to regional periodicals and newspapers.

*WORK IN PROGRESS:* A collection of humorous writings.

*SIDELIGHTS:* Susan Stein told *CA:* "If you peruse the racks of paperback books for humor, Erma Bombeck is usually the sole prose writer; the rest of the offerings are cartoons. Why did the twenties support so many more humorists than we do?"

\* \* \*

**STEINBERG, Danny D(avid Charles)  1931-**

*PERSONAL:* Born August 10, 1931, in Toronto, Ontario, Canada; son of William and Rose (Davis) Steinberg; married Miho Tanaka (a university professor), November 2, 1962; children: Kimio (son). *Education:* University of British Columbia, B.A., 1960; University of Hawaii, M.A., 1964, Ph.D., 1966. *Politics:* Left. *Home:* 403 Kuliouou Rd., Honolulu, Hawaii 96821. *Office:* English as a Second Language Department, University of Hawaii, Honolulu, Hawaii 96822.

*CAREER:* University of Illinois at Urbana-Champaign, Institute of Communications Research, postdoctoral fellow, 1967-69; University of Hawaii, Honolulu, assistant professor of English as a second language, 1969—. *Member:* American Association of University Professors (secretary of University of Hawaii chapter, 1971-72). *Awards, honors:* Grants from University of Hawaii Research Council, 1969, 1970, 1971, and U.S. Office of Education, 1971.

*WRITINGS:* (Editor with L. Jakobovits, and contributor) *Semantics: An Interdisciplinary Reader in Philosophy, Linguistics, and Psychology,* Cambridge University Press, 1971; (contributor) F. J. McGuigan, editor, *Contemporary Studies in Psychology,* Appleton, 1971. Also author with wife, Miho Steinberg, of "Reading in the Crib: A Program and Case Study," as yet unpublished. Contributor to *Journal of Experimental Psychology, Working Papers in Linguistics, Language Sciences, Pacific Speech, American Journal of Psychology,* and other publications.

\* \* \*

**STEINBERG, Fred J.  1933-**

*PERSONAL:* Born August 9, 1933, in New York, N.Y.; son of Philip (a dentist) and Freda (Korins) Steinberg; married Elizabeth Cohen (a teacher), June 11, 1961; children: Stacy, Suzan. *Education:* Cornell University, B.S., 1955; Columbia University, M.S., 1956. *Home:* 198 Glen Ave., Glen Rock, N.J. 07452. *Office:* IBM, Old Orchard Rd., Armonk, N.Y. 10504.

*CAREER:* Editorial work for Prentice-Hall, Inc., Englewood Cliffs, N.J., 1957-58, and McGraw-Hill Publishing Co., New York City, 1958-59; International Business Machines Corp., writer in New York City, 1959-68, information manager in Franklin Lakes, N.J., 1968-77, information activities manager in Armonk, N.Y., 1977—. Instructor in economics and business management at New York Institute of Technology, 1964-66, Adelphi University, 1966-68, Kean College of New Jersey, 1974-75, and Ramapo College of New Jersey, 1977—.

*WRITINGS: Computers* (juvenile), F. Watts, 1969. Contributor to magazines.

\* \* \*

**STEINER, Peter O(tto)  1922-**

*PERSONAL:* Born July 9, 1922, in New York, N.Y.; son of Otto Davidson and Ruth (Wurzburger) Steiner; married Ruth Riggs, December 20, 1947 (divorced, 1967); children: Alison Ruth, David Denison. *Education:* Oberlin College, A.B. (magna cum laude), 1943; Harvard University, M.A., 1949, Ph.D., 1950. *Office:* Legal Research Building, Law School, University of Michigan, Ann Arbor, Mich. 48104.

*CAREER:* University of California, Berkeley, instructor, 1949-50, assistant professor of economics, 1950-57; University of Wisconsin—Madison, associate professor, 1957-59, professor of economics, 1959-68; University of Michigan, Ann Arbor, professor of economics and law, 1968—, chairman of department of economics, 1971-74. Visiting professor, University of Nairobi, 1974-75. *Military service:* U.S. Naval Reserve, 1944-46; became lieutenant. *Member:* American Economic Association, American Statistical Association, American Association of University Professors (president, 1976-78). *Awards, honors:* Social Science Research Council faculty research fellow, 1956-59; Guggenheim fellow, 1960-61; Ford Foundation faculty research fellow, 1965-66.

*WRITINGS:* (With William Goldner) *Productivity,* University of California Press, 1952; *An Introduction to the Analysis of Time Series,* Rinehart, 1956; (with Robert Dorfman) *The Economic Status of the Aged,* University of California Press, 1957; (with Richard G. Lipsey) *Economics,* Harper, 1966, 5th edition, 1978; *On the Process of Planning,* Center of Economic Planning and Research, 1968; *Public Expenditure Budgeting,* Studies of Government Finance, Brookings Institution, 1969; *Mergers: Motives, Effects, Policies,* University of Michigan Press, 1975.

Contributor: Wilma Donahue and Clark Tibbits, editors, *The New Frontiers of Aging,* University of Michigan Press, 1957; *The Price Statistics of the Federal Government,* National Bureau of Economic Research, 1961; S. C. Smith and E. N. Castle, editors, *Water Resource Development,* Iowa State University Press, 1964; John Meyer, editor, *Transportation Economics,* Columbia University Press, 1965; Allen V. Kneese and Smith, editors, *Water Research,* Johns Hopkins Press, 1966; Paul MacAvoy, editor, *The Crisis of the Regulatory Commissions,* Norton, 1970; Harry M. Trebing, editor, *Essays on Public Utility Pricing and Regulation,* Institute of Public Utilities, Michigan State University, 1971; *The Economics of Public Finance,* Studies of Government Finance, Brookings Institution, 1974. Contributor of more than thirty articles and reviews to economics and law journals.

*BIOGRAPHICAL/CRITICAL SOURCES: University Bookman,* winter, 1968.

\*    \*    \*

## STEINWEDEL, Louis William   1943-

*PERSONAL:* Born May 18, 1943, in Baltimore, Md.; son of Louis Alfred and Katharine (Hudson) Steinwedel. *Education:* University of Baltimore, B.A., 1961, J.D., 1964; Towson State University, B.S., 1977. *Home:* 2906 Manhattan Ave., Baltimore, Md. 21215.

*CAREER:* Attorney-at-law, Baltimore, Md., 1966—. *Member:* Maryland State Bar Association.

*WRITINGS: Guide to Guns and Hunting,* Topical Review, 1963; *The Mercedes-Benz Story,* Chilton, 1969; (with J. Herbert Newport) *The Duesenberg,* Chilton, 1970; *The Golden Age of Sports Cars,* Chilton, 1972; *The Gun Collector's Fact Book,* Arco, 1975. Contributor of about 125 articles to magazines, including series on classic cars for *Motor Trend* and *Saturday Evening Post.*

*WORK IN PROGRESS:* An employer's guide to unemployment insurance law; a book on classic motor racing.

\*    \*    \*

## STENERSON, Douglas C.   1920-

*PERSONAL:* Born August 29, 1920, in Barron, Wis.; son of Christopher P. and Maxine (Dalton) Stenerson; married Marjorie Barrows, January 11, 1957. *Education:* Harvard University, A.B. (magna cum laude), 1942, I.A., 1943; University of Minnesota, M.A., 1947, Ph.D., 1961. *Religion:* Protestant. *Residence:* Evanston, Ill. *Office:* Department of

English, Roosevelt University, 430 South Michigan Ave., Chicago, Ill. 60605.

*CAREER:* University of Minnesota, Minneapolis, instructor in English, 1947-55; University of Miami, Coral Gables, Fla., assistant professor of English, 1955-57; Macalester College, St. Paul, Minn., assistant professor of English, 1958-59; Winona State College, Winona, Minn., assistant professor, 1959-63, associate professor of English, 1963-67, head of the department, 1966-67; Roosevelt University, Chicago, Ill., associate professor, 1967-68, professor of English and American studies, 1968—. Fulbright visiting professor of American literature, University of Helsinki, 1965-66; visiting professor of American studies, University of Minnesota, 1967. North Central Association of Colleges and Secondary Schools, consultant-examiner associate, 1969-70, consultant-examiner, 1970—. Guest lecturer, H. L. Mencken annual birthday celebration, Enoch Pratt Free Library, 1971. *Military service:* U.S. Army, 1943-46.

*MEMBER:* American Studies Association (Wisconsin-Northern Illinois chapter; vice-president, 1972-73; president, 1973-74), Modern Language Association of America, American Association of University Professors (chapter representative, Minnesota conference, 1963-65; president, Winona State College chapter, 1964-65). *Awards, honors:* McKnight Foundation Humanities award, 1961, for essay "The Literary Apprenticeship of H. L. Mencken"; Roosevelt University faculty research grant, 1970, 1977.

*WRITINGS:* (Author of introduction) Percival Pollard, *Their Day in Court* [1909], Johnson Reprint, 1969; (author of introduction) William Allen White, *A Certain Rich Man* [1909], Johnson Reprint, 1970; *H. L. Mencken: Iconoclast from Baltimore,* University of Chicago Press, 1971. Contributor to *Menckeniana, American Quarterly, American Literature, Journal of the History of Ideas,* and other publications.

*WORK IN PROGRESS:* A book on the Dreiser-Mencken relationship and its significance within the context of American culture.

*AVOCATIONAL INTERESTS:* Travel, music (orchestral and vocal), art history, walks in woods and fields.

\*    \*    \*

## STEPHENS, Edna Buell   1903-

*PERSONAL:* Born June 15, 1903, in Spiro, Okla.; daughter of Charles Ross and Beulah (Hickman) Stephens. *Education:* University of Arkansas, B.A., 1927, M.A., 1933, Ph.D., 1961; University of Colorado, summer graduate study, 1939, 1954; University of North Carolina, summer graduate study, 1946-48; attended International Summer School, Meyerhofen, Austria, 1951. *Politics:* Democrat. *Religion:* Methodist. *Home:* 2616 Tanglewood St., Commerce, Tex. 75428.

*CAREER:* John Brown University, Siloam Springs, Ark., instructor in Spanish, 1933-37; teacher in public schools in Arkansas, 1938-39; teacher in public schools in Texas, 1939-42; U.S. Office of Censorship, El Paso, Tex., deputy assistant censor of Spanish, 1942-45; teacher in public schools in Texas, 1945-49; Frank Phillips College, Borger, Texas, instructor in English, 1949-61; East Texas State University, Commerce, 1961—, professor of English, 1968-73, professor emeritus, 1973—. *Member:* American Association of University Women, Modern Language Association of America, National Council of Teachers of English, College English Association, Conference of College Teachers of English,

South Central Modern Language Association, Texas Association of College Teachers, Texas Poetry Society, Delta Kappa Gamma (treasurer, 1962-64). *Awards, honors:* East Texas State University research grant, 1970, for research on the Haiku and Zen in Hawaiian and Japanese libraries.

*WRITINGS: John Gould Fletcher,* Twayne, 1967; *Plum Petals, and Other Poems,* Cantrell, 1971. Contributor of poems to *Southwest Review, Kaleidoscope, Florida Magazine of Verse,* and *Forthcoming;* contributor of book reviews to *El Paso Herald-Post.* Former book review editor, *Ozark American;* editor *Texas Bulletin,* of American Association of University Women, 1948.

*WORK IN PROGRESS:* An article on John Gould Fletcher; *Influence on Zen Buddhism on American Poetry.*

*SIDELIGHTS:* Edna Stephens' "major interests include modern poetry, Japanese poetry, language study, Zen Buddhism, Oriental art and philosophy (especially Chinese and Japanese), water colors, gardening, ecology. I have done research in Hawaii and Japan, including at the East-West Center, Hamilton Library, Sinclair Library, University of Tokyo Library, National Diet Library (Tokyo), University of Kyoto Library. I am a travel buff, having made several trips to Europe, one to Canada, and many to Mexico.... I consider it important to my career that I was brought up in the country, and that I was read great poetry almost from infancy."†

\*　　\*　　\*

## STEPHENS, Mary Jo 1935-

*PERSONAL:* Born March 10, 1935, in Harlan, Ky.; daughter of H. M. and Edith (Baker) Campbell; married Roger S. Stephens, August 1, 1955; children: Amy. *Education:* Eastern Kentucky State College (now Eastern Kentucky University), B.A. (with highest honors), 1952. *Politics:* Democrat. *Religion:* Protestant. *Home:* 994 Avondale Ave., Cincinnati, Ohio 45229.

*CAREER:* Teacher of English, 1960-65; Cincinnati (Ohio) public schools, librarian, 1965-74. *Member:* American Civil Liberties Union, American Library Association, Council of the Southern Mountains, Independent Voters of Ohio, Ohio Association of School Librarians. *Awards, honors:* Ohioana Library Association award for best work of literature for young people, 1976.

*WRITINGS: Zoe's Zodiac* (juvenile), Houghton, 1971; *Witch of the Cumberlands* (juvenile), Houghton, 1974.

*WORK IN PROGRESS:* A juvenile novel set in Kentucky in the fifties.

\*　　\*　　\*

## STEPHENS, Will Beth 1918-

*PERSONAL:* Born July 14, 1918, in Van Horn, Tex.; daughter of John L. (an attorney) and Meda (Garner) Dodson; married Jack Howard Stephens, February 17, 1944; children: Jack Howard, Jr., Jill Johnstone. *Education:* University of Texas, B.F.A., 1942, M.Ed., 1958, Ph.D., 1964; graduate study at Columbia University, 1942, Tulane University, 1944, and Peabody College, 1959; postdoctoral study at University of Geneva, 1964-65. *Office:* Special Education Program, University of Texas, Dallas, Tex.

*CAREER:* U.S. Corps of Engineers, Laughlin Field, Del Rio, Tex., secretary to commanding officer, 1942; U.S.O.-Y.W.C.A., Del Rio, assistant director, 1942-45; Y.W.C.A., Austin, Tex., young adult director, 1946-47; Smith County

Public Schools, Tyler, Tex., teacher, 1947-48; Tyler Public Schools, Tyler, special education teacher, 1959-60; University of Texas at Austin, research associate, 1962-64; University of Illinois at Urbana-Champaign, research assistant professor, 1965-66; Temple University, Philadelphia, Pa., associate professor, 1966-70, professor of educational psychology (special education), 1970-75; University of Texas at Dallas, head of special education program, 1975—. Member, President's Committee on Mental Retardation, 1971-78; principal investigator, Project on Cognitive Aspects of the Visually Impaired, Bureau of the Handicapped, U.S. Department of Health, Education and Welfare, 1975; member of educational advisory committee, American Foundation for the Blind, and National Association for Retarded Citizens, 1977—; president, Foundation for Exceptional Children, 1978—. Consultant for school systems, universities, and state and local organizations.

*MEMBER:* International Association on Mental Deficiency, Jean Piaget Society (member of international advisory board, 1970—), American Association on Mental Deficiency (vice-president, Educational Division, 1977—), Council on Exceptional Children (president, Division of Mental Retardation, 1975), American Education Research Association, Society for Research in Child Development, American Psychological Association, Eastern Psychological Association, Pennsylvania Psychological Association. *Awards, honors:* Curtain Club award of merit, University of Texas, 1942; post-doctoral fellowship, Vocational Rehabilitation Administration, 1964-65.

*WRITINGS:* (With J. R. Peck) *Success of Young Adult Male Retardates,* University of Texas, 1964; (with Peck and D. Veldman) *Personality and Success Profiles Characteristic of Young Adult Male Retardates,* University of Texas, 1964; (with Peck and D. K. Fooshee) *Texas Screening Battery for Subnormals, Manual,* University of Texas, 1964; (translator and author of introduction) Barbel Inhelder, *The Diagnosis of Reasoning in the Retarded,* John Day, 1968; (with C. K. Miller and J. A. McLaughlin) *The Development of Reasoning, Moral Judgment and Moral Conduct in Retardates and Normals,* Temple University, 1969; (editor and contributor) *Training the Developmentally Young,* John Day, 1971; (author of introduction) Patrick Ashlock and Sister Marie Grant, *Educational Therapy Materials,* C. C Thomas, 1972.

Contributor: *Symposium on Recent Piagetian Research,* Texas Education Agency, 1970; *Teaching Strategies, Methods, and Materials, Selected Convention Papers,* Council for Exceptional Children, 1970; *Selected Convention Papers, 1971,* Council for Exceptional Children, 1971.

\*　　\*　　\*

## STEPHENSON, Gilbert T(homas) 1884-1972

December 17, 1884—June 9, 1972; American banker, lawyer, educator, and author of books on law and finance. Obituaries: *New York Times,* June 10, 1972. (See index for *CA* sketch)

\*　　\*　　\*

## STEPHENSON, Howard 1893-1978

*PERSONAL:* Born September 2, 1893, in Indianapolis, Ind.; son of Samuel Lincoln and Etta Mae (Van Tilburgh) Stephenson; married Ella Jeannette Dalzell, September 20, 1919 (deceased); children: Margaret (Mrs. Leo Foote), Howard Rene, Nina (Mrs. Thomas E. Holland). *Education:* Attended University of Kansas, 1911-12, and New York

University, 1938. *Politics:* Independent. *Religion:* Protestant. *Home:* 2545 Southwest Terwilliger Blvd., Portland, Ore. 97201.

*CAREER:* Newspaperman in United States and Canada, 1912-17; Scripps-Howard Newspapers, Toledo, Ohio, editorial writer, 1919-32; Hearst Magazines, New York City, editor, 1932-37; Westinghouse Electric Co., New York City, eastern publicity manager, 1939-42; Hill & Knowlton, Inc., New York City, public relations counseling executive, 1942-51, vice-president and director, 1947-51; Community Relations, Inc., New York City, founding president, 1947-67. Lecturer in public relations, New York University, 1949-52; professor of public relations and chairman of department, Boston University, 1953-59; director of public relations and professor, Pacific University, 1960-63. *Military service:* U.S. Army, Signal Corps, 1917-18.

*MEMBER:* Public Relations Society of America, National Association of Science Writers, Oregon Association of Editors and Communicators, Oregon Freelance Writers Association (president, 1963). *Awards, honors:* LL.D., Hartwick College, 1953.

*WRITINGS: Glass* (novel), Claude Kendall, 1934; (with Joseph C. Keeley) *They Sold Themselves,* Hillman-Curl, 1937; (with Wesley F. Pratzner) *Publicity for Prestige and Profit,* McGraw, 1953; (editor) *Handbook of Public Relations,* McGraw, 1960, 2nd edition, 1971. Ghostwriter of four other books. Contributor of about 150 articles to magazines.

*WORK IN PROGRESS: How to Survive in the Establishment.*

*BIOGRAPHICAL/CRITICAL SOURCES: New York Times,* January 9, 1978.†

(Died January 6, 1978)

\*    \*    \*

## STERN, Catherine B(rieger)   1894-1973

1894—January 8, 1973; German-born American educator, editor, and author of elementary school textbooks. Obituaries: *New York Times,* January 9, 1973.

\*    \*    \*

## STERN, E. Mark   1929-

*PERSONAL:* Born December 5, 1929, in New York, N.Y.; son of David Samuel and Esther (Swimmer) Stern; married Virginia Underwood, October 11, 1967; children: Sarah Rebecca, Cailean Fraser. *Education:* Boston University, B.A., 1952; Pennsylvania State University, M.S., 1953; Columbia University, Ed.D., 1955; Training Institute of National Psychological Association for Psychoanalysis, certificate in psychoanalysis, 1958. *Politics:* Democrat. *Home and office:* 215 East 11th St., New York, N.Y. 10003.

*CAREER:* Clinical psychologist in private practice in Amagansett and New York City, 1955; New York Clinic for Mental Health, New York City, director of research and chief psychologist, 1957-61; Iona College, Graduate Division of Pastoral Counseling, New Rochelle, N.Y., 1964—, currently professor of psychology; Seton Hall University, South Orange, N.J., 1967-77, became adjunct associate professor of psychology. Faculty member, American Institute for Psychotherapy and Psychoanalysis. Diplomate in clinical psychology, American Board of Professional Psychology, 1976. *Member:* American Psychological Association, American Academy of Psychotherapists, Society for the Scientific Study of Religion, New York State Psychological Association, New York Society of Clinical Psychologists.

*WRITINGS:* (With Bert Marino) *Psychotheology,* Paulist/Newman, 1971; (editor with Alfred Joyce) *Holiness and Mental Health,* Paulist/Newman, 1972. Contributor to *Voices, Journal of Existentialism, Journal of Contemporary Psychotherapy, Psychoanalytic Review, Journal of Clinical Issues in Psychology.* Former editor, *Journal of Pastoral Counseling;* editor, *Voices.*

*SIDELIGHTS:* Stern has "the desire to locate an indigenous American psychotherapy and to highlight and explore areas of convergence in religion and psychotherapy. I'm a radical being in both areas."

\*    \*    \*

## STERN, Ellen Norman   1927-

*PERSONAL:* Born July 10, 1927, in Hannover, Germany; came to United States in 1939, naturalized in 1945; daughter of Leo and Gertrude (Salomon) Norman; married Harold H. Stern (a self-employed sales representative), October 7, 1956; children: Lawrence Norman, Michael Bruce. *Education:* University of Louisville, B.A., 1950. *Politics:* Democrat. *Religion:* Jewish. *Home:* 135 Anbury Lane, Willow Grove, Pa. 19090.

*CAREER:* Production assistant for station WAVE-TV, Louisville, Ky., 1950-55; National Broadcasting Corp., New York City, production assistant, 1955-57; Children's Aid Society, New York City, secretary to director of Foster Home Department, 1957-59; professional writer, 1959—.

*WRITINGS: Embattled Justice: The Story of Louis Dembitz Brandeis* (juvenile), Jewish Publication Society, 1971. Contributor of stories and articles to *Louisville Courier-Journal, Philadelphia Bulletin, Reconstructionist Views, Jewish Digest,* and *World Over.*

*AVOCATIONAL INTERESTS:* Historical subjects.

\*    \*    \*

## STEVENS, Bernice A.

*PERSONAL:* Born in Evansville, Ind.; daughter of Ralph and Stella (Duggins) Stevens. *Education:* Evansville College (now University of Evansville), B.S., 1949; University of Tennessee, M.S., 1951. *Politics:* Conservative Republican. *Address:* P.O. Box 564, Gatlinburg, Tenn. 37738.

*CAREER:* Teacher of jewelry making and other crafts in public schools in Evansville, Ind. and at Evansville College (now University of Evansville), 1946-59; Southern Highland Handicraft Guild, Asheville, N.C., director of education, 1959-62; 12 Designer Craftsmen, Gatlinburg, Tenn., part owner and member of board of directors, 1964-77. Has exhibited jewelry in regional, national, and international shows; has represented U.S. Department of State in encouraging development of crafts in Malaya. Teacher of jewelry making at Unto These Hills Summer School of Crafts, Cherokee, N.C., and Arrowmont, Gatlinburg, summers, 1954-71. Member of board of directors, Southern Highland Handicraft Guild, 1971-77. *Member:* American Association of University Women, Phi Kappa Phi, Delta Kappa Gamma. *Awards, honors:* Ford Foundation fellowship, 1955-56; Delta Kappa Gamma fellowship, 1956.

*WRITINGS:* (Contributor) T. R. Ford, editor, *The Southern Appalachian Region,* University of Kentucky, 1962; *Our Mountain Craftsmen,* Buckhorn Press, 1969; *A Weavin' Woman,* Buckhorn Press, 1971; *To an Earth Beloved* (poems), Buckhorn Press, 1973. Contributor of articles and poems to magazines.

*WORK IN PROGRESS:* Research on early days of craft development in Appalachia.

*AVOCATIONAL INTERESTS:* Travel.

\* \* \*

## STEVENS, William W(ilson) 1914-

*PERSONAL:* Born October 30, 1914, in Huntington, W.Va.; son of William Wilson (a railroad engineer) and Ellen (Rece) Stevens; married Dorothy Powell (a teacher), October 31, 1944; children: William W. III, David W., John L. *Education:* Marshall University, B.A., 1937; Southern Baptist Theological Seminary, Th.M., 1944, Ph.D., 1951. *Address:* P.O. Box 12, Clinton, Miss. 39056. *Office:* Division of Religion, Mississippi College, Clinton, Miss. 39058.

*CAREER:* Worked as dairy and milk sanitarian in Huntington, W.Va., 1938-41; pastor of Baptist churches in Owenton, Ky., 1947-52, and Hodgenville, Ky., 1952-55; Mississippi College, Clinton, professor of Bible and New Testament Greek, 1955—, chairman of Division of Religion, 1967—. *Military service:* U.S. Naval Reserve, chaplain, active duty, 1944-46; became lieutenant. *Member:* Association of Baptist Professors of Religion (president, 1962-63), Society of Biblical Literature, American Academy of Religion.

*WRITINGS: Doctrines of the Christian Religion,* Broadman, 1967; *A Guide for Old Testament Study,* Broadman, 1974; *A Guide for New Testament Study,* Broadman, 1977.

*WORK IN PROGRESS: The March of Protestantism: The Gospel in Triumph.*

\* \* \*

## STEVENSON, Grace Thomas 1900-

*PERSONAL:* Born January 27, 1900, in Morganfield, Ky.; daughter of Lloyd Pius and Martha (Holbrook) Thomas; married Harvey C. Breaks, February 20, 1923 (deceased); married Christopher G. Stevenson, November 7, 1937 (divorced); children: (first marriage) Ellen (Mrs. William G. Nichols), Thomas. *Education:* Attended St. Joseph's College, Kentucky, and Evansville College (now University of Evansville). *Politics:* Democrat. *Religion:* None. *Home and office:* 2833 East Malvern St., Tucson, Ariz. 85716.

*CAREER:* Long Beach Public Library, Long Beach, Calif., children's librarian, 1924-25; Seattle Public Library, Seattle, Wash., assistant supervisor of school libraries, 1927-43; Hunters' Point Naval Shipyard, San Francisco, Calif., head of personnel department, 1943-45; Seattle Public Library, head of adult education department, 1945-51; American Library Association, Chicago, Ill., deputy executive director, 1951-65. Chairman of Seattle Friends of Dance, 1949-51, and Seattle Film Society, 1948-51. *Member:* American Library Association, Adult Education Association of the United States of America (president, 1957-58), Southwestern Library Association, Arizona Library Association, Tucson Symphony Society, Tucson Festival Society, League of Women Voters. *Awards, honors:* Educational Film Library Association award, 1967; named one of ten outstanding librarians by American Library Association, 1976.

*WRITINGS: Arizona Library Survey,* Arizona State University, 1968; *Serra Regional Library System,* San Diego Public Library, 1969; *Library Service across the Border,* Washington State Library, 1969; *ALA Chapter Relationships: National, Regional and State,* American Library Association, 1971. Contributor to library journals.

*AVOCATIONAL INTERESTS:* Travel, antiquities, anthropology, graphic arts, dance.

## STEWART, Desmond (Stirling) 1924-

*PERSONAL:* Born April 20, 1924, in Leavesden, England; son of Roy Mackenzie (a physician) and Agnes Maud (Stirling) Stewart. *Education:* Trinity College, Oxford, M.A. (honors), 1946, B.Litt., 1948. *Religion:* Church of England. *Home:* 8 Sharia Yusif el-Gindi, Bab el-Louk, Cairo, Egypt; and Ilex House, Wells-next-the-Sea, Norfolk, England. *Agent:* Carl D. Brandt, Brandt & Brandt, 101 Park Ave., New York, N.Y. 10017.

*CAREER:* University of Baghdad, Baghdad, Iraq, assistant professor of English, 1948-56; inspector of English in Islamic schools of Beirut, Lebanon, 1956-58; writer with residence mainly in Egypt and other parts of the Middle East, 1958—. Former Middle East correspondent for *Spectator,* London.

*WRITINGS*—Fiction, except as indicated: *The Besieged City* (poems), Fortune Press, 1945; *Leopard in the Grass,* Euphorion Books, 1951, Farrar, Straus, 1952; *The Memoirs of Alcibiades,* Euphorion Books, 1952; *The Unsuitable Englishman,* Farrar, Straus, 1954; *A Woman Besieged,* Heinemann, 1959; *The Men of Friday,* Heinemann, 1961; *The Sequence of Roles* (trilogy), Chapman & Hall, Book I: *The Round Mosaic,* 1965, Book II: *The Pyramid Inch,* 1966, Book III: *The Mamelukes,* 1968; *The Vampire of Mons,* Harper, 1976.

Nonfiction: (With John Haylock) *New Babylon: A Portrait of Iraq,* Collins, 1956; (with Gerald Hamilton) *Emma in Blue: A Romance of Friendship,* Wingate, 1957, Roy, 1958; *Young Egypt,* Wingate, 1958; *Turmoil in Beirut: A Personal Account,* Wingate, 1958; (with the editors of *Life*) *The Arab World* (juvenile), Time-Life, 1962, revised edition, 1968; (with the editors of *Life*) *Turkey* (juvenile), Time-Life, 1965, revised edition, 1969; *Cairo,* Phoenix House, 1965, A. S. Barnes, 1966, subsequent edition published as *Cairo: 5500 Years,* Crowell, 1968 (published in England as *Great Cairo: Mother of the World,* Hart-Davis, 1969); (with the editors of Time-Life Books) *Early Islam,* Time-Life, 1967; *Orphan with a Hoop: The Life of Emile Bustani,* Chapman & Hall, 1967; (with the editors of Newsweek Book Division) *Pyramids and Sphinx,* Newsweek, 1971; *The Middle East: Temple of Janus,* Doubleday, 1971; *Theodor Herzl,* Doubleday, 1974; (with the editors of Newsweek Book Division) *The Alhambra,* Newsweek, 1974; *T. E. Lawrence,* Harper, 1977.

Translator: Plato, *Socrates and the Soul of Man,* Beacon Press, 1951; A. R. Sharkawi, *Egyptian Earth,* Heinemann, 1962; Fathi Ghanem, *The Man Who Lost His Shadow,* Houghton, 1966. Also translator of many Arabic poems into English.

Contributor to *Nation, Spectator, Holiday, Poetry, Encounter, New Statesman* and other Arab and English publications.

*SIDELIGHTS:* In addition to his fluency in Arabic, Desmond Stewart can read German, Spanish, and Turkish, and has a working knowledge of Greek, Latin, Italian, and French.

*BIOGRAPHICAL/CRITICAL SOURCES: Times Literary Supplement,* June 15, 1967; *Observer Review,* June 25, 1967; *New York Times Book Review,* December 3, 1967.†

\* \* \*

## STEWART, Donald Charles 1930-

*PERSONAL:* Born June 24, 1930, in Kansas City, Mo.; son of Charles Allen and Harriet (McTaggart) Stewart; married Patricia Louise Pettepier, June 3, 1955; children: Ellen

Marie, Mary Catherine. *Education:* University of Kansas, B.A., 1952, M.A., 1955; University of Wisconsin, Ph.D., 1962. *Home:* 2328 Timberlane Dr., Manhattan, Kan. 66502. *Office:* Department of English, Kansas State University, Manhattan, Kan. 66506.

*CAREER:* University of Illinois at Urbana-Champaign, instructor, 1962-63, assistant professor of English, 1963-68; Kansas State University, Manhattan, assistant professor, 1968-75, associate professor of English, 1975—. *Member:* Modern Language Association of America, National Council of Teachers of English, Conference on College Composition and Communication, Kansas Association of Teachers of English, Kansas Association of College Teachers of English, Phi Beta Kappa.

*WRITINGS: The Authentic Voice,* W. C. Brown, 1972. Contributor to *Parks and Recreation, Montana: The Magazine of Western History,* and *Fly Fisherman.* Editor, *Kansas English.*

*WORK IN PROGRESS: Five Golden Summers; A Yellowstone Summer; If We Should Fail; Playing with the Big Boys.*

\* \* \*

## STEWART, Elbert Wilton 1916-

*PERSONAL:* Born May 12, 1916, in Huntington Beach, Calif.; son of Justin Henry (a farmer) and Grace A. (Young) Stewart; married Lillian F. Wolfe (a teacher); children: Michael W., Jean L., Mary Alma (Mrs. Randall C. Witt), Karen A. (Mrs. Frederick T. Kearney). *Education:* Santa Ana Junior College, A.A., 1937; University of California, Berkeley, A.B. (with honors), 1939; University of Redlands, M.A., 1958; also did some course work at American University and Fresno State College (now California State University, Fresno).

*CAREER:* Began career as a high school teacher of history; affiliated with Bakersfield College, Bakersfield, Calif., 1958-76; currently a full-time writer. *Military service:* U.S. Army Air Forces, 1941-45. *Member:* American Sociological Association, Southwestern Anthropological Association, California Community College Faculty Association. *Awards, honors:* Grant to attend National Science Foundation Institute in Anthropology, 1963.

*WRITINGS:* (With James A. Glynn) *Introduction to Sociology,* McGraw, 1971, 2nd edition, 1975; *The Troubled Land: Social Problems in Modern America,* McGraw, 1972, 2nd edition, 1976; *Evolving Life Styles: An Introduction to Cultural Anthropology,* McGraw, 1973; *The Human Bond: Introductory Social Psychology,* Wiley, 1978; *Sociology: The Human Science,* McGraw, 1978.

*WORK IN PROGRESS:* A third edition of *Introduction to Sociology,* with Glynn, completion expected in 1979.

*SIDELIGHTS:* Elbert Stewart writes: "My aim in text writing is to present material geared to the needs and interests of the introductory college student. This calls for clarity, an absence of jargon, and the illustration of concepts with examples that are timely, interesting, and relevant to today's youth."

\* \* \*

## STEWART, Fred Mustard 1936-

*PERSONAL:* Born September 17, 1936; son of Simeon (a banker) and Janet (Mustard) Stewart; married Joan Richardson (a theatrical agent), March 18, 1968. *Education:*

Princeton University, A.B., 1954. *Agent:* Don Gold, William Morris Agency, 1350 Ave. of the Americas, New York, N.Y. 10019.

*CAREER:* Novelist. *Military service:* U.S. Coast Guard, 1955-58; became lieutenant junior grade. *Member:* P.E.N.

*WRITINGS—*All novels: *The Mephisto Waltz,* Coward, 1969; *The Methuselah Enzyme,* Arbor House, 1970; *Lady Darlington,* Arbor House, 1971; *The Mannings,* Arbor House, 1973; *Star Child,* Arbor House, 1974; *Six Weeks,* Arbor House, 1976; *A Rage against Heaven,* Viking, 1978.

*WORK IN PROGRESS:* A three-generation American "dynasty" novel, *Parade;* a television series.

*SIDELIGHTS: The Mephisto Waltz,* was filmed by 20th Century-Fox, under the direction of Paul Wendkos, in 1971. Several of Fred Stewart's novels have been translated into German and Italian.

*BIOGRAPHICAL/CRITICAL SOURCES: Saturday Review,* April 19, 1969; *Books,* February, 1970; *Best Sellers,* August 15, 1970.†

\* \* \*

## STEWART, Rosemary (Gordon)

*PERSONAL:* Born in London, England; daughter of William George (a businessman) and Sylvia (Sulley) Stewart; married Ioan Mackenzie James (a professor), July 1, 1961. *Education:* University of British Columbia, B.A.; London School of Economics, M.Sc. and Ph.D. *Religion:* Church of England. *Residence:* Oxford, England. *Office:* Oxford Centre for Management Studies, Kennington, Oxford OX1 5N4, England.

*CAREER:* Acton Society Trust (an independent research institute), London, England, director, 1956-61; University of London, London School of Economics and Political Science, London, fellow in management studies, 1964-66; Centre for Management Studies, Oxford, England, fellow, 1966—. *Member:* Royal Economic Society (fellow), Association of Teachers of Management, British Sociological Association. *Awards, honors:* John Player Award for best management book published in the United Kingdom, 1976, for *Contrasts in Management.*

*WRITINGS:* (Principal author with Nancy Joy and Paul Duncan-Jones) *Management Succession,* Acton Society Trust, 1956; (with Roy Lewis) *The Managers,* New American Library, 1958 (published in England as *The Boss: The Life and Times of the British Businessman,* Phoenix House, 1958, revised edition, 1960); *The Reality of Management,* Heinemann, 1963; *Managers and Their Jobs,* Macmillan (London), 1967; *The Reality of Organizations,* Macmillan (London), 1970, Doubleday, 1972; *How Computers Affect Management,* Macmillan (London), 1971, M.I.T. Press, 1972; *Contrasts in Management,* McGraw (Maidenhead, England), 1976. Contributor of articles to management journals.

*WORK IN PROGRESS:* Research on classifying choices in managerial jobs.

*SIDELIGHTS:* Rosemary Stewart told *CA:* "My books . . . are a by-product of a career spent in research into management. . . . One, a social satire on life in business . . . , gave an opportunity to describe what life in business is like and how people really get on. It was a by-product of a two-year study into management development and management succession in fifty large companies. . . . Two of the books have been popular text books. The other four are research books.

These all try to combine enough material about the research to be useful to academics, but written in a form that will be relevant for managers. My [first priority] in writing is to be helpful to managers but also to contribute to the academic knowledge of the subject.''

BIOGRAPHICAL/CRITICAL SOURCES: Spectator, December 5, 1958; New Society, June 20, 1963; Personnel Management, September, 1967, September, 1976; Financial Times, December 18, 1970; International Management, November, 1971; Economist, October 23, 1971; Management Review and Digest (of British Institute of Management), October, 1977.

*     *     *

## STEYAERT, Thomas A(dolph) 1930-

PERSONAL: Born December 1, 1930, in Lafayette, Ore.; son of Charles Edward (a farmer) and Ida (Erickson) Steyaert; married Kathryn F. Coughlin (an elementary school teacher), August 13, 1955; children: Del F. Education: College of Great Falls, B.A. (social science) and B.S. (biology), 1956; Oregon State University, M.S., 1958; University of California, Berkeley, additional graduate study, 1960-69. Office: Department of Biological Sciences, Diablo Valley College, Pleasant Hill, Calif. 94523.

CAREER: Biology teacher in high schools in Vernonia, Ore., 1955-56, and Concord, Calif., 1958-60; Merritt College, Oakland, Calif., instructor in biology, 1960-61; Diablo Valley College, Pleasant Hill, Calif., instructor in biology, 1961—. Military service: U.S. Navy, hospital corpsman, 1950-54. Member: American Association for the Advancement of Science, American Institute of Biological Sciences, National Association of Biology Teachers, Audubon Society, Bay Area Biologists Society (founder and president).

WRITINGS: Life and Patterns of Order, McGraw, 1971; Biology: A Contemporary View, McGraw, 1975.

WORK IN PROGRESS: Strategies for Survival, for Saunders.

*     *     *

## STILES, Martha Bennett

PERSONAL: Born in Manila, Philippine Islands; daughter of Forrest Hampton and Jane (Bennett) Wells; married Martin Stiles (a professor of chemistry at University of Michigan), 1954. Education: Attended College of William of Mary; University of Michigan, B.S., 1954. Address: Route 1, Paris, Ky. 40361.

AWARDS, HONORS: Avery and Jule Hopwood Award for essays, University of Michigan, 1958; named notable book of the year, Horn Book Magazine, for Darkness over the Land; Central State University of Missouri certificate, 1978, for outstanding contributions to children's literature.

WRITINGS—Youth books: One among the Indians, Dial, 1962; The Strange House at Newburyport, Dial, 1963; Darkness over the Land, Dial, 1966; Dougal Looks for Birds, Four Winds, 1972; James the Vine-Puller, Carolrhoda, 1975; The Star in the Forest: A Mystery of the Dark Ages, Four Winds Press, 1979; Tana and the Useless Monkey, Thomas Nelson, 1979. Contributor of articles to Thoroughbred Record, Maryland Horse, Michigan Quarterly Review, Esquire, New York Times, and other periodicals, and fiction to Ingenue, Seventeen, and literary reviews.

WORK IN PROGRESS: A novel based in sixth-century France.

SIDELIGHTS: Martha B. Stiles told CA: "I have written historical fiction because I am fascinated by why we are as we are."

BIOGRAPHICAL/CRITICAL SOURCES: Book World, March 19, 1967.

*     *     *

## STILLMAN, Richard J. 1917-

PERSONAL: Born February 20, 1917, in Lansing, Mich.; married Ellen Darlene Slater; children: Richard II, Thomas, Ellen. Education: University of Southern California, B.S., 1938; Harvard University, graduate study, 1938-39; attended Command & General Staff School, 1943; Syracuse University, M.S., 1950, Ph.D., 1955; attended Army War College, 1960; attended North Atlantic Treaty Organization Defense College, 1961. Office: Management Department, University of New Orleans, New Orleans, La. 70122.

CAREER: U.S. Army, 1942-65; commissioned 2nd lieutenant in infantry, 1942; retired as colonel; Ohio University, Athens, 1965-67, became professor of business administration, director of Center for Economic Opportunity, and director of management programs; University of New Orleans, New Orleans, La., professor of management, 1967—. Held command and staff positions in Europe, the Far East, and the U.S.A., 1942-65; during World War II served in operations section of Third Army, and as secretary of General Staff to General Patton, 1944-45; U.S. Military Academy, West Point, N.Y., member of staff and faculty, 1952-55; commanded 20th Infantry and Reserve Forces Act regiment, 1956-57; faculty member, NATO Defense College, 1961-63; office of the Secretary of Defense, assistant division chief, Policy Division and Chief Strategic Studies Branch, International Security Affairs, 1963-65. Member: American Association of University Professors, American Economic Association, American Finance Association, Academy of Management, Army-Navy Country Club. Awards, honors—Military: Legion of Merit, Bronze Star, Luxembourg Order of the Crown, Paratrooper Badge, Department of Defense Badge. Civilian: Scouters Award, Boy Scouts of America, 1955; Naval Institute Award, 1966, for essay "The Pentagon's Whiz Kids."

WRITINGS: U.S. Infantry: Queen of Battle, F. Watts, 1965; (with Florette Henri) Bitter Victory, Doubleday, 1970; Guide to Personal Finance: A Lifetime Program of Money Management, Prentice-Hall, 1972, 2nd edition, 1975; Do It Yourself Contracting to Build Your Own Home: A Managerial Approach, Chilton, 1974; Personal Finance Guide and Workbook: A Managerial Approach to Successful Household Recordkeeping, Pelican, 1977; Moneywise, Prentice-Hall, 1978. Contributor of thirty-five articles to professional journals.

WORK IN PROGRESS: A third edition of Guide to Personal Finance: A Lifetime Program of Money Management.

BIOGRAPHICAL/CRITICAL SOURCES: Detroit News, February 22, 1957; New York Times, May 29, 1966; New Orleans Magazine, November, 1972.

*     *     *

## STOCKTON, J. Roy 1893(?)-1972

1893(?)—August 24, 1972; American sports writer and editor. Obituaries: New York Times, August 25, 1972.

*     *     *

## STODDARD, Tom 1933-

PERSONAL: Born February 1, 1933, in Santa Ana, Calif.;

son of William John and Shirley (Alderson) Stoddard; married Roberta Mary Folkman, August 17, 1958 (separated); children: Antigone, Hillary, Marcus, Jana. *Education:* Long Beach City College, A.A., 1953; attended Long Beach State College (now California State University, Long Beach), 1957; San Francisco State College (now University), B.A., 1958. *Politics:* Democrat. *Religion:* None. *Home:* 1520 San Anselmo Ave., Apt. 13, San Anselmo, Calif. 94960.

*CAREER:* U.S. Government, Small Business Administration, San Francisco, Calif., supervisory loan officer, 1959-69; Wells Fargo Bank, San Francisco, vice-president, 1969-74; real estate investor, 1974—. *Military service:* U.S. Air Force, 1953-56.

*WRITINGS: Pops Foster: The Autobiography of a New Orleans Jazzman,* University of California Press, 1971; *Black Jazz on the Barbary Coast,* Storyville Press, 1978. Contributor of articles on history of jazz to magazines.

*WORK IN PROGRESS:* A novel, completion expected in 1978.

\* \* \*

## STOKES, Olivia Pearl 1916-

*PERSONAL:* Born January 11, 1916, in Middlesex, N.C.; daughter of William Harmon and Bessie (Thomas) Stokes. *Education:* New York University, B.S., 1947, M.S., 1948; Columbia University, Ed.D., 1952. *Office:* Educational Consultant, 2050 Seward Ave., Suite 6-F, Bronx, N.Y. 10473.

*CAREER:* Young Women's Christian Association, Uptown Branch, New York City, contact interviewer, 1935-41; Baptist Educational Center, New York City, associate director, 1941-52; Girl Scouts of America, New York City, program consultant, 1952; Massachusetts Council of Churches, Boston, director of department of religious education, 1953-66; National Council of Churches of Christ in the U.S.A., New York City, staff associate in urban education, Division of Christian Education, 1966-73, developed Black Curriculum Resource Center; Herbert H. Lehman College of the City University of New York, New York City, associate professor of education, 1973-76, chairperson for development of a multi-ethnic, multi-cultural teacher education program, developed a graduate teacher education study abroad-ethnic heritage-African program in conjunction with five Nigerian universities; educational consultant, 1976—. Ordained minister, American Baptist Church. Adjunct professor, City College of the City University of New York, 1970-71, Colgate Rochester and Andover Newton Theological Seminaries, 1973-76. Leader of delegates to White House Conferences on Education, 1955, and Youth, 1960, 1970; director, Greater Harlem Comprehensive Guidance Center, 1975—. Consultant, Princeton and Drew Theological Seminaries, Roxbury-North Dorchester Comprehensive Health Center (Boston), and Columbia University Sickle Cell Comprehensive Health Center, 1974-77; also consultant to Education and Ministry Division of National Council of Churches. Lecturer for African Studies Association, Educational Studies Association, National Association for Study of Afro-American Life and History, 1965-74. Trustee, Berea College (Berea, Ky.). Member of the board, Bronx Council of the Arts. Volunteer posts as secretary with National Council of Churches: Department of Racial and Cultural Relations, 1950-60, program board, Division of Christian Education, 1962-64, and Department of Educational Development, 1964-66.

*MEMBER:* National Education Association, American Educational Studies Association, American Association for Higher Education, Adult Education Association, National Association for Public and Continuing Adult Education (life member), Council of National Organizations for Adult Education (first vice-president, 1969-71), Religious Education U.S.A., American Association of University Professors, American Association of University Women, Afro-American Association for the Study of Life and History, African-American Institute's Educators to Africa Association, National Association for the Advancement of Colored People (life member), National Council of Negro Women, Delta Kappa Delta, Pi Lambda Theta, Alpha Kappa Delta, Delta Sigma Theta, League of Women Voters, Friends of City University and Bronx Community College. *Awards, honors:* Guidance citation, Vocational Guidance Center (New York City), 1964; Christian Education Salute from Massachusetts Council of Churches, 1966; Reconciliation Award of Ministerial Interfaith Association, 1969; Mary McLeod Bethune Bicentennial Achievement Award from the National Council of Negro Women, 1975, 1976; certificate of appreciation, Committee on Social Justice, National Association for Public and Adult Education, 1975; Fulbright-Hays fellowship, 1976.

*WRITINGS: Why the Spider Lives in Corners: African Facts and Fun* (juvenile), edited by Louise Crane, Friendship, 1971; *The Beauty of Being Black: Folktales, Poems, and Art from Africa* (juvenile), edited by Crane, Friendship, 1971; (contributor) *If Teaching Is Your Job,* National Baptist Publishing Board of America, 1974. Also contributor to a book on values published by United Presbyterian Program Agency. Contributor to religious education journals. Special issue editor, *Church Woman,* November, 1969; member of editorial board, *Colloquy,* 1969-71; special issue editor, *Spectrum,* July-August, 1971.

*WORK IN PROGRESS: Emerging Role of African Women;* a study on the life of Roland Hayes, an Afro-American tenor.

*SIDELIGHTS:* Olivia Stokes has visited Africa fifteen times since 1958 for educational seminars and as leader of the World Christian Education Institute in Nairobi in 1967. In 1976, she led sixteen graduate students in a six-week study of the Yourba civilization at the University of Ife and University of Ibadan, Nigeria. She has also traveled in a number of countries of Asia, Europe, and Central America.

In the course of her travels, Stokes has acquired an extensive collection of African art which has had two major exhibits in New York City galleries. "Nearly all African art is religious," she writes, "growing out of African traditional religions; thus African art is of a religio-mythological nature. The tribal and social structure is marked by a complex of authority; kings, secret societies, medicine men, etc. Thus every act in the life of the people is expressed in a ritual. And every rite has its sculptured image appropriate for the ceremonial occasions. . . . Two of the striking characteristics of African art are its feeling for the material and the fact that its carvings are done out of the mass of ivory, wood, bronze, and clay. Through these media, African artists express the clan's outlook on the world, combined with the intensity of the people's religious feelings."

*AVOCATIONAL INTERESTS:* Plants, music appreciation, collecting fine art and international dolls.

\* \* \*

## STOKSTAD, Marilyn 1929-

*PERSONAL:* Born February 16, 1929, in Lansing, Mich.;

daughter of Olaf and Edythe (Gardiner) Stokstad. *Education:* Carleton College, B.A., 1950; Michigan State University, M.A., 1953; University of Michigan, Ph.D., 1957; University of Oslo, graduate study, 1951-52. *Home:* 2020 West Ninth St., Lawrence, Kan. 66044. *Office:* Spencer Museum of Art, University of Kansas, Lawrence, Kan. 66044.

*CAREER:* University of Kansas, Lawrence, assistant professor, 1958-62, associate professor, 1962-66, professor of art history, 1966—, chairman of department, 1962-72, associate dean, College of Liberal Arts and Sciences, 1972-76. Curator of medieval art, Nelson Art Gallery, Kansas City, Mo., 1969—. *Member:* College Art Association, American Association of University Professors (member of national council, 1972-75). *Awards, honors:* Fulbright fellow, 1951-52; American Association of University Women fellow, 1954-55; National Endowment for the Humanities grant, 1967-68; National Humanities Institute fellow, 1976-77.

*WRITINGS: Handbook of the Museum of Art,* University of Kansas Press, 1962; *Renaissance Art outside Italy,* W. C. Brown, 1968; (editor with Robert Engass) *Hortus Imaginum,* University of Kansas Press, 1974. Author of twenty-five museum catalogues. Also author of *Santiago de Compostela in the Age of the Pilgrimages* and contributor to *Irish Culture,* edited by H. Orel. Contributor of about a dozen articles to art journals.

*WORK IN PROGRESS:* A book on medieval art.

\*　　　\*　　　\*

### STONE, Edward 1913-

*PERSONAL:* Born August 29, 1913, in Newark, N.J.; son of Alexander (a manufacturer) and Frances (Kurtz) Stone; married Marjorie Selvage, July 21, 1951; children: Edward Selvage, Glenn Davis, Frederick Alexander. *Education:* University of Texas, B.A., 1934, M.A., 1937; Duke University, Ph.D., 1950. *Home:* 49 Graham Dr., Athens, Ohio 45701. *Office:* Ellis Hall, Department of English, Ohio University, Athens, Ohio 45701.

*CAREER:* University of Texas, Main University (now University of Texas at Austin), tutor in English, 1938-39; Newcomb College, New Orleans, La., instructor in English, 1939-42; Duke University, Durham, N.C., instructor in English, 1949-52; Georgia Institute of Technology, Atlanta, assistant professor of English, 1952-53; University of Virginia, Charlottesville, assistant professor of English, 1953-56; Ohio University, Athens, associate professor, 1956-61, professor, 1961—, distinguished professor of English, 1966—, chairman of department, 1958-63. Fulbright lecturer in Mexico, 1966, and Argentina, 1968. *Military service:* U.S. Coast Guard Reserve, 1942-46; became chief petty officer. *Member:* Modern Language Association of America.

*WRITINGS:* (Editor) *Selected Student Prose,* University of Virginia Press, 1955; *Incident at Harper's Ferry,* Prentice-Hall, 1956; *What Was Naturalism? Materials for an Answer,* Appleton, 1959; (editor with William Van O'-Connor) *The Casebook on Ezra Pound,* Crowell, 1959; (editor and contributor) *Henry James: Seven Stories and Studies,* Appleton, 1961; *The Battle and the Books: Some Aspects of Henry James,* Ohio University Press, 1964; (contributor) *Essays on Determinism in American Literature,* Kent State University Press, 1964; *Voices of Despair: Four Motifs in American Literature,* Ohio University Press, 1966; *A Certain Morbidness: A View of American Literature,* Southern Illinois University Press, 1969.

*SIDELIGHTS:* In his review of *A Certain Morbidness: A View of American Literature,* Russel B. Nye says, ''Those who have read Mr. Stone's previous critical essays on American authors will once more find here his ability to invest the familiar with new perceptions, and will recognize the wide range of interests which allows him to see, in sometimes unexpected places, provocative parallels and sensitive analogies that illuminate a passage, a character, a story, or a novel.''

*BIOGRAPHICAL/CRITICAL SOURCES: American Literature,* November, 1971.

\*　　　\*　　　\*

### STONE, Ralph A. 1934-

*PERSONAL:* Born April 7, 1934, in Telluride, Colo.; son of Kenneth and Ruth (Nichols) Stone; married Jeanne L. Sanders, July 4, 1954; children: Michelle, Theresa. *Education:* University of Kansas, B.A., 1956; University of Illinois, M.A., 1958, Ph.D., 1961. *Home:* 1616 South Lincoln, Springfield, Ill. 62704. *Office:* Department of History, Sangamon State University, Springfield, Ill.

*CAREER:* Southern Illinois University at Carbondale, lecturer, 1960-61; Miami University, Oxford, Ohio, assistant professor, 1961-66, associate professor, 1966-70; Sangamon State University, Springfield, Ill., professor of history, 1970—. *Member:* American Historical Association, Organization of American Historians, American Civil Liberties Union. *Awards, honors: The Irreconcilables and the Fight against the League of Nations* was nominated for Pulitzer Prize, 1971.

*WRITINGS:* (Editor) *Wilson and the League of Nations: Why America's Rejection?,* Holt, 1967; *The Irreconcilables and the Fight against the League of Nations,* University Press of Kentucky, 1970; (editor) *John F. Kennedy, 1917-1963: Chronology, Documents, Bibliographical Aids,* Oceana, 1971. Contributor of articles to history journals.

*WORK IN PROGRESS:* A study of co-operative, labor, and socialist movements, 1915-1930.

*AVOCATIONAL INTERESTS:* Wilderness activities.

\*　　　\*　　　\*

### STONES, E(dgar) 1922-

*PERSONAL:* Born October 19, 1922, in Rotherham, Yorkshire, England; son of Edgar (a miner) and Amelia (Osborne) Stones; married Margaret Louise Strathdee, July 17, 1948; children: Stephen Dunlop, Sheila Catherine. *Education:* University of Sheffield, B. A. (honors), 1951, M.A., 1957, Diploma in Education, 1952; University of Manchester, Diploma in Educational Psychology, 1958; University of Birmingham, Ph.D., 1970. *Office address:* School and Institute of Education, University of Liverpool, 19-23 Abercromby Sq., P.O. Box 147, Liverpool L69 3BX, England.

*CAREER:* Royal Air Force, 1938-48, leaving service as sergeant; University of Birmingham, Birmingham, England, lecturer, 1964-72; University of Liverpool, Liverpool, England, professor of education, 1972—. *Member:* British Psychological Society, International Association of Applied Psychology, Association of University Teachers, Association of Teachers in Colleges and Departments of Education (research secretary, 1968—), American Educational Research Association.

*WRITINGS: Introduction to Educational Psychology,* Methuen, 1966; *Learning and Teaching: A Programmed*

*Introduction,* Wiley, 1968; (editor) *Readings in Educational Psychology: Learning and Teaching,* Barnes & Noble, 1970; *Towards Evaluation: Some Thoughts on Tests and Teacher Education,* Educational Review, 1970; (with Dennis Anderson) *Educational Objectives and the Teaching of Educational Psychology,* Barnes & Noble, 1972; (with Sidney Morris) *Teaching Practice: Problems and Perspectives,* Barnes & Noble, 1972; *How Long Is a Piece of String?* (monograph), Society for Research into Higher Education (London), 1975. Contributor to academic journals.

*AVOCATIONAL INTERESTS:* Gardening, walking, playing squash, the theater, listening to music.

\* \* \*

## STOUDEMIRE, Sterling A(ubrey) 1902-

*PERSONAL:* Born September 4, 1902, in Concord, N.C.; son of Palmer (a merchant) and Frances (Cranford) Stoudemire; married Irene Slate, August 15, 1925 (died November 31, 1940); married Mary Arthur Billups, January 30, 1946; children: (first marriage) Marian Slate (Mrs. James Alexander Hawkins); (second marriage) Cranford Stoudemire. *Education:* University of North Carolina, A.B., 1923, A.M., 1924, Ph.D., 1930. *Politics:* Democrat. *Religion:* Episcopalian. *Home:* 712 Gimghoul Rd., Chapel Hill, N.C. 27514. *Office:* 225 Dey Hall, University of North Carolina, Chapel Hill, N.C. 27514.

*CAREER:* University of North Carolina at Chapel Hill, instructor, 1924-30, assistant professor, 1930-33, associate professor, 1933-41, professor of Spanish, 1941-73, professor emeritus, 1973—, chairman of department of Romance languages, 1949-64. *Military service:* U.S. Navy, 1942-46; became lieutenant commander. *Member:* Modern Language Association of America, American Association of Teachers of Spanish, American Name Society (member of board of governors, 1970-72), South Atlantic Modern Language Association (president, 1962).

*WRITINGS:* (With S. E. Leavitt and others) *A Two Year Course in Spanish,* University of North Carolina Extension Bulletin, 1932; (editor with N. B. Adams) *Selections from Perez de Ayala,* Norton, 1934, new edition, Holt, 1948; (with Leavitt) *Elements of Spanish,* Henry Holt, 1935, revised edition, 1938; (with Leavitt) *Vamos a ver: A Spanish Workbook,* Holt, 1936; (with Leavitt) *Vamos a leer,* Holt, 1938, 3rd edition published as *Vamos a leer: Unified Spanish,* Holt, 1967; (editor) *Cuentos de Espana y de America: A Collection of Spanish Short Stories,* Houghton, 1942; (with Leavitt) *Concise Spanish Grammar,* Henry Holt, 1942; (with Leavitt) *Por los siglos: An Anthology of Spanish Readings,* Henry Holt, 1942; (with Leavitt) *Sound Spanish,* Henry Holt, 1950; (with T. B. Stroup) *South Atlantic Studies for Sturgis E. Leavitt,* Scarecrow, 1953; (with Leavitt) *Tesoro de lecturas,* Henry Holt, 1957; (translator and author of critical comment) Gonzalo Fernandez de Oviedo, *Natural History of the West Indies,* University of North Carolina Press, 1959; (translator and author of introduction) Pedro de Cordoba, *Christian Doctrine,* University of Miami Press, 1970. Also author of a study of Hernan Perez de Oliva.

*WORK IN PROGRESS:* Writing on Spanish literature of the exploration of America, and on the nineteenth-century Spanish stage.

*AVOCATIONAL INTERESTS:* Conservation, travel in Spain.

## STOVER, Jo Ann 1931-

*PERSONAL:* Born April 23, 1931, in Peterborough, N.H.; daughter of Arthur Irving (a machinist) and Gladys (Fairfield) Stover; married Paul Pollaro (an artist and teacher), July 16, 1961; children: Lauren, Paul. *Education:* Attended New England School of Art, 1949-51, Massachusetts School of Art, 1953, and Art Students' League, New York, N.Y. 1955. *Religion:* Theist. *Residence:* Hancock, N.H. 03449.

*CAREER:* Has worked as a painter of portraits, landscapes, and non-objective subjects, and as a teacher of nursery school art. Teacher of courses in writing and illustrating children's books, Sharon Arts Center (N.H.). *Awards, honors:* First prize of City Center Gallery, New York, N.Y., 1958, for painting "West Side Story"; Junior Literary Guild awards, 1960, for *If Everybody Did,* and 1961, for *Why . . . ? Because.*

*WRITINGS*—For children; all self-illustrated: *If Everybody Did,* McKay, 1960; *Why . . . ? Because,* McKay, 1961; *Mr. Widdle and the Sea Breeze,* McKay, 1962; *They Didn't Use Their Heads,* McKay, 1963; *I'm in a Family,* McKay, 1965; *The Binnies and the Dogs and Cats from Everywhere,* Knopf, 1971. Contributor to *Kentucky Library Association Bulletin.*

\* \* \*

## STRAHLEM, Richard E(arl) 1909-

*PERSONAL:* Born July 7, 1909, in Logansport, Ind.; son of Earl Ray and Blanche (Snyder) Strahlem; married Betty Jayne Conover (a purchasing agent), February 19, 1944; children: Betty Lou, Richard M., Constance A. *Education:* Indiana University, B.S. (with high distinction), 1932, M.S., 1940. *Politics:* Republican. *Religion:* Protestant. *Home:* 4624 Carriage Lane, Las Vegas, Nev. 89109. *Office:* Department of Accounting, University of Nevada, Las Vegas, Nev. 89154.

*CAREER:* Statistician, State of Indiana, 1934-39; Indiana University at Bloomington, instructor, 1938-40; Purdue University, West Lafayette, Ind., associate professor, 1940-45; University of New Mexico, Albuquerque, associate professor, 1945-46; University of Miami, Miami, Fla., professor, 1946-47; University of New Mexico, professor and controller, 1948-52; State of New Mexico, Santa Fe, state comptroller, 1951, highway commission controller, 1953, state welfare director, 1954; Sacramento State College (now California State University), Sacramento, Calif., associate professor, 1955-59; University of New Mexico, professor and controller, 1959-62; Lockheed Aircraft Corp., Sunnyvale, Calif., internal auditor, 1962-63; University of Nevada, Las Vegas, associate professor, 1963-68, professor of accounting and chairperson of department, 1968—. Certified Public Accountant in Indiana, New Mexico, and Nevada. Lecturer, University of Santa Clara, 1962-63. President, International Teaching Systems, Inc., Albuquerque, N.M., 1961-62. Consultant to Airfleets, Inc., 1950-55, Sands, Inc., 1965-68, and to Flamingo Resort, Inc., 1968—. *Member:* National Association of Accountants, American Accounting Association, American Institute of CPAs, Nevada Society of CPAs, Alpha Kappa Psi, Beta Gamma Sigma, Phi Kappa Phi.

*WRITINGS: Accounting Fundamentals,* Ronald, 1942; (with Charles W. Beese) *Cost Finding,* Alexander Hamilton Institute, 1947; *Cost Control,* Alexander Hamilton Institute, 1957; *Introduction to Accounting,* Dickenson, 1972. Contributor of articles to *Accounting Review* and *Journal of Accountancy.*

*WORK IN PROGRESS: Managing Records.*†

\*     \*     \*

## STRANG, Barbara M(ary) H(ope)   1925-

*PERSONAL:* Born April 20, 1925, in Croydon, Surrey, England; daughter of Frederick A. (an engineer) and Amy (Wood) Carr; married Colin Strang, April 21, 1955; children: Caroline Jane. *Education:* King's College, London, B.A. (honors), 1945, M.A., 1947. *Politics:* None. *Religion:* None. *Office:* School of English, University of Newcastle upon Tyne, Newcastle upon Tyne NE1 7RY, England.

*CAREER:* University of London, Westfield College, London, England, assistant lecturer in English, 1947-50; University of Newcastle upon Tyne, Newcastle upon Tyne, England, lecturer, 1950-63, professor of English language and general linguistics, 1964—, head of School of English, 1970—, member of University Grants committee. *Member:* Philological Society (former member of council), Linguistics Association (founding member; former secretary).

*WRITINGS: Modern English Structure,* Edward Arnold, 1962, St. Martin's, 1963, 2nd edition, revised and expanded, 1968; *A History of English,* Barnes & Noble, 1970. Contributor to several festschrifts, to *Proceedings of IX and X International Congress of Linguists,* and to professional journals.

*WORK IN PROGRESS:* Studies in the history of English vocabulary and syntax.

*SIDELIGHTS:* "Once a keen traveller," Barbara Strang writes, "[I am] now unwilling to proceed further than my mare will take me." She has "some small knowledge of French, German, Latin, Italian, Old English, Icelandic, and Gothic, and even less of some other European languages."

\*     \*     \*

## STRATTON, Porter Andrew   1918-

*PERSONAL:* Born December 31, 1918, in Richland, N.M.; son of Earl Jefferson and Laura (Watson) Stratton, Sr.; married Mary Carter (a teacher), February 7, 1947; children: Steve, John, Jo Beth. *Education:* University of New Mexico, B.A., 1942; Eastern New Mexico University, M.A., 1962; Texas Technological College (now Texas Tech University), Ph.D., 1967. *Politics:* Democrat. *Home:* 1025 Ebony Dr., Edinburg, Tex. 78539. *Office:* Department of History, Pan American University, Edinburg, Tex. 78539.

*CAREER: Portales Tribune,* Portales, N.M., advertising manager, 1946-55, business manager, 1955-57, and advertising manager of *Portales News-Tribune,* 1957-61; Pan American University, Edinburg, Tex., assistant professor, 1964-67, associate professor of history, 1967-71, head of department of social studies, 1971-73, head of department of history, 1973—. *Military service:* U.S. Army Air Forces, 1941-46; became first lieutenant; received Distinguished Flying Cross, Air Medal with three oak leaf clusters, European Theater Medal with four battle stars. *Member:* American Historical Association, Organization of American Historians, Texas Historical Association, Phi Alpha Theta.

*WRITINGS: The Territorial Press of New Mexico: 1834-1912,* University of New Mexico Press, 1969.

*WORK IN PROGRESS:* Research on clashing of cultures in the American Southwest.

\*     \*     \*

## STRAUS, Dorothea   1916-

*PERSONAL:* Born November 25, 1916, in New York, N.Y.; daughter of Alfred (a brewer and engineer) and Alma (Wallach) Liebmann; married Roger W. Straus, Jr. (a publisher), June 27, 1938; children: Roger W. III. *Education:* Sarah Lawrence College, B.A., 1938. *Politics:* Democrat. *Home:* 171 East 70th St., New York, N.Y. 10021. *Agent:* Robert Lescher, 155 East 71st St., New York, N.Y. 10021.

*WRITINGS: Thresholds,* Houghton, 1971; *Showcases,* Bodley Head, 1975; *Palaces and Prisons,* Houghton, 1976. Contributor to national periodicals, including *Harper's* and *Cosmopolitan.*

*WORK IN PROGRESS: Mrs.,* a novel.

*SIDELIGHTS:* A reviewer for *Vogue* writes: "*Thresholds* . . . is nostalgic, but its fragrances are fresh. [Dorothea Straus] does not condemn the present time nor docs she in any belligerent way campaign for the restitution of time past. . . . She pauses on the thresholds of many rooms, regarding the appointments and the occupants from angles of refraction that differ with her age and with her recollected mood and with judgments emended by hindsight. Some of the interiors do not exist for her in fact, but have come into the possession of her memory through family stories handed down, diminished and bedimmed by time, or enlarged and illuminated by romantic yearning. . . . Mrs. Straus likens herself to an archeologist in reconstructing the scenes of her forbears' enterprise and tribulations, the forests of much ramified trees that intertwined." This nostalgia for the past is reflected in Straus's subsequent books, *Showcases* and *Palaces and Prisons.* Christopher Lehmann-Haupt writes in his review of *Palaces and Prisons:* "There is more to this memoir of places and people than coincidental pleasure or pain. The book has something to do with success or failure at putting down roots in America, something to do with the very idea of rootedness in place."

*BIOGRAPHICAL/CRITICAL SOURCES: Vogue,* September 1, 1971; *New York Times,* November 19, 1976.

\*     \*     \*

## STRAUSS, Albrecht B(enno)   1921-

*PERSONAL:* Born May 17, 1921, in Berlin, Germany; son of Bruno (a professor) and Bertha (a writer; maiden name, Badt) Strauss. *Education:* Oberlin College, B.A., 1942; Tulane University, M.A., 1948; Harvard University, Ph.D., 1956. *Religion:* Jewish. *Home:* 2 Dogwood Acres Dr., Chapel Hill, N.C. 27514. *Office:* Department of English, University of North Carolina, Chapel Hill, N.C. 27514.

*CAREER:* Tulane University, New Orleans, La., instructor in English, 1948-49; Brandeis University, Waltham, Mass., instructor in English, 1951-52; Yale University, New Haven, Conn., instructor in English, 1955-59; University of Oklahoma, Norman, assistant professor of English, 1959-60; University of North Carolina at Chapel Hill, assistant professor, 1960-64, associate professor, 1964-70, professor of English, 1970—. *Military service:* U.S. Army, 1942-46, 1949-53; became second lieutenant. *Member:* Modern Language Association of America, American Society for Eighteenth-Century Studies, American Association of University Professors, The Johnsonians, South Central Modern Language Association, Friends of the Harvard College Library.

*WRITINGS:* (Contributor) Harold C. Martin, editor, *Style in Prose Fiction,* Columbia University Press, 1959; (editor with Daniel W. Patterson) *Essays in English Literature of the Classical Period Presented to Dougald MacMillan,* University of North Carolina Press, 1967; (editor with W. J.

Bate) Samuel Johnson, *The Rambler,* Volumes III, IV, and V, Yale University Press, 1969. Contributor to professional journals. Editor, *Studies in Philology,* 1974—.

*WORK IN PROGRESS:* Editing *Roderick Random,* by Tobias Smollett, for Penguin.

\* \* \*

## STREMPEK, Carol Campbell

*PERSONAL:* Born in Bronxville, N.Y.; daughter of Albert J. and Ida (Miressi) Campbell; married Bernard Strempek (a teacher and poet; died, 1964); children: Christopher, Stephen, Lisa. *Education:* University of Michigan, B.A., 1962; Simmons College, M.S., 1967. *Residence:* Brookline, Mass. 02146. *Office:* Curry College Library, Milton, Mass. 02186.

*CAREER:* WLW-D TV, Dayton, Ohio, writer, 1964-65; Federal Reserve Bank of Boston, Boston, Mass., acquisitions librarian, 1967-68; Curry College, Milton, Mass., reference librarian, 1968—.

*WRITINGS:* (With David A. Bower) *Index to "Evergreen Review",* Scarecrow, 1972.

\* \* \*

## STRICKER, George 1936-

*PERSONAL:* Born November 6, 1936, in Bronx, N.Y.; son of Irving (an office manager) and Diana (Coopersmith) Stricker; married Joan Levy, January 16, 1960; children: Jocelyn, Geoffrey. *Education:* University of Chicago, A.B., 1956; University of Rochester, Ph.D., 1960. *Home:* 134 Wooleys Lane, Great Neck, N.Y. 11023. *Office:* Institute of Advanced Psychological Studies, Adelphi University, Garden City, N.Y. 11530.

*CAREER:* University of Rochester, Rochester, N.Y., assistant lecturer, 1959-60, assistant professor of psychology, 1960-61; Goucher College, Baltimore, Md., assistant professor of psychology, 1961-63; Adelphi University, Garden City, N.Y., assistant professor, 1963-65, associate professor, 1965-70, professor of psychology, 1970—, assistant dean of Institute of Advanced Psychological Studies, 1966—. Private practice as clinical psychologist, 1963—. Clinical psychologist at Rochester State Hospital, 1959-60, Atascadero State Hospital, 1960, Sheppard and Enoch Pratt Hospital, 1962-63, and Nassau County Drug Abuse and Addiction Commission, 1969-71. Clinical assistant professor, Cornell University Medical College, 1966-68. Senior research scientist, New York State Narcotics Addiction Control Commission, 1968-70. Consultant, State of California, 1960-61, Eastman Dental Center, 1962-70, Beth Ha Gan School, 1966-68, Episcopal Church, 1967-68, and Queens-Nassau Mental Health Center, 1968—. Chairman, national advisory panel of the American Psychological Association to the CHAMPUS project. Member of New York State Board of Psychology; diplomate in clinical psychology, American Board of Professional Psychology.

*MEMBER:* American Psychological Association (fellow), Society for Projective Techniques and Personality Assessment (fellow), American Association of University Professors, Eastern Psychological Association, New York State Psychological Association (past president), Nassau County Psychological Association, Sigma Xi. *Awards, honors:* U.S. Public Health Service postdoctoral research fellow, 1960-61; U.S. Office of Education research grant, 1963-64; co-recipient of Frank Ritter Award, Rochester Academy of Medicine, 1965, for paper, "Audio Analgesic Effects"; National Institute of Mental Health grant, 1966-68; National Institute of Law Enforcement and Criminal Justice grant, 1969-71.

*WRITINGS:* *The Experimental Induction of Mood,* Office of Naval Research, 1961; (with Melvin Zax) *Patterns of Psychopathology,* Macmillan, 1964; (with Zax) *The Study of Abnormal Behavior,* Macmillan, 1964, 3rd edition, 1974; *Students' Views of the College Environment,* U.S. Office of Education, 1965; (contributor) L. Kingsley, editor, *Selected Papers on Psychotherapy,* Adelphi University, 1968; (contributor) G. D. Goldman and D. S. Milman, editors, *Modern Woman,* C. C Thomas, 1969; (with M. R. Goldfried and I. B. Weiner) *Rorschach Handbook of Clinical and Research Applications,* Prentice-Hall, 1971; (editor with M. Merbaum) *Search for Human Understanding,* Holt, 1971, 2nd edition, 1975; (with F. Weiss) *Kicking It,* Pyramid Publications, 1971; (editor with Goldman) *Practical Problems of a Private Psychotherapeutic Practice,* C. C Thomas, 1972; (editor with Merbaum) *Growth of Personal Awareness,* Holt, 1973. Contributor to *Journal of Social Psychology, Dental Progress, New York State Dental Association, Psychological Reports, Journal of Clinical Psychology, Psychological Review, Journal of Personality, Medical Care, American Psychoanalyst,* and other professional journals.

*WORK IN PROGRESS:* Contributions to books on psychoanalytic psychotherapy and on professional psychology.

\* \* \*

## STRIGHT, Hayden Leroy 1898-1975

*PERSONAL:* Born April 18, 1898, in Sheakleyville, Pa.; son of Leonard Marcus and Cora Ione (Palm) Stright; married Ruth Harris Brown, June 28, 1928; children: Paul Leonard, Richard Hayden, Jean Louise (Mrs. H. Hale Davenport). *Education:* Thiel College, B.A., 1919; Boston University, M.R.E., 1922, M.A., 1929. *Politics:* Republican. *Religion:* American Baptist.

*CAREER:* Minnesota Council of Churches, Minneapolis, Minn., 1929-64, became executive secretary, executive secretary emeritus, 1964-75. President, Association of Council Secretaries, 1952-53; chairman, Governor's Committee on Refugees, 1954. *Member:* Ramsey County Historical Society (president, 1968-70), General Society of Mayflower Descendants (elder general, 1957-66), Assembly of World Council of Christian Education. *Awards, honors:* Thiel College Distinguished Alumni Award, 1966; D.D., Carleton College, 1954.

*WRITINGS: Together: The Story of Church Cooperation in Minnesota,* Denison, 1971. Also author of *A Stright Genealogy: In Particular John Warnock and Elvira Hall Stright and Their Descendents and Ancestors.* Editor of *Minnesota Messenger,* 1930-64.

*SIDELIGHTS:* Hayden Stright was a leader in the building of the Minnesota Protestant Center (now Minnesota Church Center) in Minneapolis, and a plaque was installed, October 24, 1971, recognizing his contribution. He travelled throughout Europe.†

(Died June 29, 1975)

\* \* \*

## STRINGER, Lorene A(dair) 1908-

*PERSONAL:* Born July 18, 1908, in St. Louis, Mo.; daughter of Wiley M. (a businessman) and Mary (Adair) Stringer. *Education:* Washington University, St. Louis, Mo., B.S.W., 1947, M.S.W., 1949. *Home:* 470 Dickson St., Kirkwood, Mo. 63122.

*CAREER:* Washington University clinics and allied hospitals, St. Louis, Mo., psychiatric social worker, 1949-52; St.

Louis County Health Department, Clayton, Mo., school mental health consultant, 1952-59, project director, National Institute of Mental Health grant, 1959-70, community mental health coordinator, 1970-76. Consultant, Office of Child Health, U.S. Department of Health, Education and Welfare, 1978—. *Member:* American Public Health Association (fellow), American Orthopsychiatric Association (fellow), National Association of Social Workers (charter member), Academy of Certified Social Workers (charter member).

*WRITINGS: The Sense of Self,* Temple University Press, 1971.

Contributor: John C. Glidewell, editor, *Parental Attitudes and Child Behavior,* C. C Thomas, 1961; Eli M. Bower and William G. Hollister, editors, *Behavioral Science Frontiers in Education,* Wiley, 1967; Milton F. Shore and Fortune V. Mannino, editors, *Community Mental Health: Problems, Programs, and Strategies,* Behavioral Publications, 1969; Patrick Cook, editor, *Community Psychology and Community Mental Health,* Holden-Day, 1970. Contributor to professional journals. Member of editorial board, *American Journal of Orthopsychiatry,* 1971—, *American Journal of Community Psychology,* 1978—.

*WORK IN PROGRESS:* Guidelines on adolescent health services.

\*　　\*　　\*

## STRONG, John W.　1930-

*PERSONAL:* Born January 22, 1930, in Waterville, Me.; son of Eugene W. (a postal clerk) and Helen (Springfield) Strong; married Carol Ann Boudreau (a librarian), August 27, 1961. *Education:* Colby College, B.A., 1952; Boston University, M.A., 1954; Harvard University, Ph.D., 1964. *Home:* 91 Riverdale Ave., Ottawa, Ontario, Canada K1S 1R1. *Office:* Department of History, Carleton University, Ottawa, Ontario, Canada K1S 5B6.

*CAREER:* Carleton University, Ottawa, Ontario, assistant professor, 1962-65, associate professor, 1965-72, professor of Russian history, 1972—, chairman of history department, 1977—. *Member:* Canadian Association of Slavists (executive member, 1965-78), American Association for the Advancement of Slavic Studies.

*WRITINGS:* (Contributor) Adam Bromke, editor, *The Communist States at the Crossroads,* Praeger, 1965; (editor) *The Soviet Union under Brezhnev and Kosygin,* Van Nostrand, 1971; (contributor) Bromke and T. R. Harmstone, editors, *The Communist States in Disarray,* University of Minnesota Press, 1972; (editor with Bromke) *Gierek's Poland,* Praeger, 1973; (editor with B. R. Bociurkiw) *Religion and Atheism in the U.S.S.R. and Eastern Europe,* Macmillan (London), 1975. Contributor of articles to history journals. Managing editor, *Canadian Slavonic Papers,* 1970-75.

*WORK IN PROGRESS:* Research on Sino-Soviet relations in the 1970's, and on Russian-Central Asian relations in the early nineteenth century.

\*　　\*　　\*

## STRONG, John William　1935-

*PERSONAL:* Born August 18, 1935, in Iowa City, Iowa; son of Frank Ransom and Gertrude (Way) Strong; married Margaret W. Cleary, June 16, 1962; children: Frank Ransom II, Benjamin Waite. *Education:* Yale University, B.A., 1957; University of Illinois, J.D., 1962. *Home:* 2925 Woods-

dale Blvd., Lincoln, Neb. 68502. *Office:* College of Law, University of Nebraska, Lincoln, Neb. 68508.

*CAREER:* University of Kansas, Lawrence, assistant professor, 1964-66; Duke University, Durham, N.C., associate professor, 1967-69; University of Oregon, Eugene, professor of law, 1969-76; University of Nebraska, Lincoln, professor of law and dean, 1977—. *Military service:* U.S. Army, 1957-59.

*WRITINGS:* (With Edward Cleary) *Cases, Materials and Problems on Evidence,* West Publishing, 1969, 2nd edition, 1975; (with Charles McCormick and others) *Handbook on Evidence,* West Publishing, 1972.

\*　　\*　　\*

## STRONG, Jonathan　1944-

*PERSONAL:* Born August 13, 1944, in Evanston, Ill.; son of Jonathan Webster (an architect and manufacturer) and Anne Malinda (Burnham) Strong. *Education:* Harvard University, B.A., 1969. *Home:* 77 Sacramento St., Somerville, Mass. 02143.

*CAREER:* Tufts University, Medford, Mass., lecturer in English, 1969-78. *Awards, honors:* Rosenthal Foundation award from National Institute of Arts and Letters, 1970, for *Tike and Five Stories.*

*WRITINGS: Tike and Five Stories,* Atlantic-Little, Brown, 1969; *Ourselves* (novel), Atlantic-Little, Brown, 1971. Represented in *American Literary Anthology,* edited by George Plimpton and Peter Ardery, and in *Prize Stories 1969: The O. Henry Awards,* edited by William Abrahams, Doubleday, 1970. Also author of *Doing and Undoing,* a novel. Contributor to *Partisan Review, Atlantic, Esquire, Shenandoah, Transatlantic Review,* and *TriQuarterly.*

*WORK IN PROGRESS:* A novel.

*SIDELIGHTS:* Writing about *Tike and Five Stories,* Sara Blackburn states: "The publication of this novella and five stories marks the arrival of a writer who can speak for the sixties as Salinger did for the fifties. Mr. Strong combines a deceptive surface fragility with a tough, direct, and absolutely authoritative sense of who his characters are and what the world is like for them. His remarkable, unaffected spareness is possible and successful because he trusts his reader; his material barely runs to book length, yet it is far more substantial than works twice its size by novelists of great reputation." Phoebe Pettingell's review describes Strong's style: "Above all, [he] has a delicate and sure touch; his sadness never turns sentimental, and he never simplifies his characters' problems. If his subject matter is somewhat limited, he knows how to exploit its nuances."

Strong himself gives this advice to beginning writers: "No one can point out to you books or writers that would make good models for reading or study. You have to follow your own taste, when reading fiction, and read a lot of it. And you should stay away from critical writing as much as possible. You don't learn by having someone tell you how to do a thing like writing. You learn by watching him do it. . . . Once you have the first sentence, the second will come. Writing is organic; it comes in words, not in preconceptions. It can only be broken down into character, plot, and all that, after it has been written." Speaking of his book *Ourselves,* Strong told *CA,* "My personal experience has made my character, and my character has made my novel, but nothing in my novel ever happened and nobody in my novel ever existed, except insofar as we are all bits and pieces of each other."

*BIOGRAPHICAL/CRITICAL SOURCES: New York*

*Times,* April 14, 1969; *Saturday Review,* May 3, 1969; *Nation,* May 19, 1969; *New Leader,* May 26, 1969; *Book World,* July 20, 1969; *Life,* August 24, 1969; *Commonweal,* September 9, 1969; *Best Sellers,* August 1, 1971; *Writer,* October, 1971.

\* \* \*

## STURGIS, James L(averne) 1936-

*PERSONAL:* Born March 13, 1936, in Alvinston, Ontario, Canada; son of Harold Laverne (a teacher) and Alice (West) Sturgis; married Janet Davidson, June 9, 1958; children: Jennifer Claire, John Alexander Laverne, Patrick James Owen. *Education:* University of Western Ontario, B.A., 1958; University of London, M.A., 1963; University of Toronto, Ph.D., 1972. *Home:* 5 Tudor Ct., Tunbridge Wells, Kent, England. *Office:* Birkbeck College, University of London, London, England.

*CAREER:* High school teacher in Red Lake, Ontario, 1958-61; head of high school history department in St. Catharines, Ontario, 1963-66; University of London, Birkbeck College, London, England, lecturer in history, 1969—. *Member:* Association of University Teachers.

*WRITINGS: John Bright and the Empire,* Athlone, 1969; *Adam Beck,* Fitzhenry & Whiteside, 1978.

*WORK IN PROGRESS:* A study on British attitudes toward non-European peoples in the nineteenth century.

*BIOGRAPHICAL/CRITICAL SOURCES: Times Literary Supplement,* April 23, 1970.

\* \* \*

## STURM, John E. 1927-

*PERSONAL:* Born October 6, 1927, in Pittsburgh, Pa.; son of John Edward (a certified public accountant) and Elizabeth (Sexauer) Sturm; married Jean Moses, December 29, 1951. *Education:* Bowdoin College, A.B., 1951; `University of New Hampshire, M.Ed., 1962; University of Massachusetts, C.A.G.S., 1966, Ed.D.

*CAREER:* Hooksett Public Schools, Hooksett, N.H., elementary principal, 1962-63; teacher in elementary schools in Concord, N.H., 1963-65; State University of New York College at Buffalo, assistant professor of education, beginning 1966. Editorial reviewer for Allyn & Bacon, Inc., Holbrook Press, and Van Nostrand-Reinhold Books. *Military service:* U.S. Army, Infantry, 1945-47. *Member:* American Association of School Administrators, American Association of University Professors, Phi Delta Kappa. *Awards, honors:* American Federation of Teachers writing grants, 1966, 1968.

*WRITINGS:* (Editor with John A. Palmer) *Substantive Readings in Education,* Selected Academic Readings, 1968; (editor with Palmer) *Democratic Legacy in Transition: Perspectives on American Education,* Van Nostrand, 1971.

*WORK IN PROGRESS:* Research on the American family, and on administrative theory in education.†

\* \* \*

## SULLIVAN, Marion F. 1899-

*PERSONAL:* Born August 8, 1899, in Bozeman, Mont.; daughter of James Marion and Nettie (Gray) Fly; married C. Edward Sullivan (a rancher), October 10, 1921; children: Reverend Mother Dolores, Jean (Mrs. J. J. Felldin), Eveleen (Mrs. W. D. Corbett), Ellen (Mrs. W. A. Berg). *Education:* University of California, Berkeley, B.A., 1920. *Poli-*

*tics:* Republican. *Religion:* Roman Catholic. *Home and office:* 7327 Garden Highway, Yuba City, Calif. 95991.

*CAREER:* Lincoln Elementary School, Yuba City, Calif., principal, 1920-21; Sierra Gold Nurseries, Inc., Yuba City, secretary-treasurer, 1951-69; Sullivan Orchards, Inc., Yuba City, secretary-treasurer, 1956—. Chairman of American Red Cross at Camp Beale, Calif., 1944-45.

*WRITINGS: Westward the Bells,* Alba, 1971. Contributor to *Flower and Garden* and *Western Fruit Grower.*

*WORK IN PROGRESS:* Research on history of art and various other subjects.

\* \* \*

## SUMMERFIELD, Harry L. 1940-

*PERSONAL:* Born May 8, 1940, in St. Paul, Minn.; son of Harold O. and Phyllis A. Summerfield. *Education:* University of Minnesota, B.A. and B.S., 1962, Ph.D., 1969; Washington University, St. Louis, Mo., M.A., 1966. *Home:* 2611 Woolsey, Berkeley, Calif. 94705.

*CAREER:* Teacher of social studies in West Allis, Wis., 1964-65; U.S. House of Representatives, Washington, D.C., legislative assistant, 1969-70; Georgia State University, Atlanta, assistant professor of urban life and educational administration, 1970-74; Wright Institute, Berkeley, Calif., resident scholar, beginning 1974. Visiting professor of sociology, University of California, 1974—. Research associate, San Francisco Psychoanalytic Institute. Director, Regulatory Review Task Force of California Department of Consumer Affairs. *Awards, honors:* Education Policy Fellowship Program, 1969; U.S. Office of Education grant, 1972; National Institute of Education grant, 1973-76.

*WRITINGS: The Neighborhood Based Politics of Education,* C. E. Merrill, 1971; *Power and Process: The Formulation and Limits of Federal Education Policy,* McCutchan, 1974; *Regulation of Occupations: The Report of the Regulatory Review Task Force,* California State Department of Consumer Affairs, 1978. Also author of a report to the National Institute of Education, *The Tune of the Hickory Stick: A Social Structural/Psychoanalytic Analysis of the Teacher-Child Relationship,* 1976. Contributor of articles to professional journals.

\* \* \*

## SUTHERLAND, Donald 1915-

*PERSONAL:* Born September 27, 1915, in Seattle, Wash.; son of Donald A. (a delegate from Alaska) and Hilda (Evanson) Sutherland; married Gilberte de Save, September 16, 1937. *Education:* Princeton University, B.A., 1936, Ph.D., 1939. *Politics:* "Variable but left of center." *Home:* 1607 Bluebell, Boulder, Colo. 80302.

*CAREER:* University of Colorado, Boulder, 1940-65, became professor of classics. *Military service:* U.S. Army, Infantry, 1943-45. *Awards, honors:* American Council of Learned Societies fellow, 1950.

*WRITINGS: Gertrude Stein: A Biography of Her Work,* Yale University Press, 1951, reissued, 1972; (translator) Euripedes, *Hippolytus in Drama and Myth* (with essay by Hazel E. Barnes), University of Nebraska Press, 1960; (translator, and author of introduction) Aristophanes, *Lysistrata,* Chandler, 1961; (translator, and author of essay) *The Bacchae of Euripides,* Nebraska Wesleyan Press, 1968; (with A. Centeno y Rilova) *On, Romanticism,* New York University Press, 1971; (with Centeno y Rilova) *The Blue*

*Clown,* University of Nebraska Press, 1971. Composer of various libretti. Author of biblical comedy, "My Sister, My Spouse," published in *Prairie Schooner,* 1960. Contributor to *Prairie Schooner, Parnassus, Denver Quarterly.*

*WORK IN PROGRESS:* A literary critique of Homer's *Odyssey.*

\* \* \*

## SUTHERLAND, Robert D(onald) 1937-

*PERSONAL:* Born November 4, 1937, in Blytheville, Ark.; son of Donald C. and Opal (Gillispie) Sutherland; married Marilyn Neufeldt (a registered nurse), July 25, 1959; children: David Scott, Allan Philip. *Education:* University of Wichita (now Wichita State University), B.A., 1959; University of Iowa, M.A., 1961, Ph.D., 1964. *Home:* 501 East Willow, Normal, Ill. 61761. *Office:* Department of English, Illinois State University, Normal, Ill. 61761.

*CAREER:* Illinois State University, Normal, assistant professor, 1964-66, associate professor, 1966-73, professor of English, 1973—. Co-founder of Pikestaff Publications, Inc., 1977. *Member:* Linguistic Society of America, Lewis Carroll Society.

*WRITINGS:* (Contributor) Frederick P. Kroeger and others, editors, *Readings for Rhetoric,* Wadsworth, 1969; *Language and Lewis Carroll,* Mouton & Co., 1970. Also author of a self-illustrated novel, *Sticklewort and Feverfew.* Contributor to English language journals.

*WORK IN PROGRESS:* A novel; several short stories; poetry; research on the theory of meaning and on linguistic obstacles to communication.

\* \* \*

## SUTTON, Larry M(atthew) 1931-

*PERSONAL:* Born February 24, 1931, in Winter Haven, Fla.; son of Clarence F. (a businessman) and Irma L. (Ashley) Sutton; married Margalo Ann Roller (a teacher), October 18, 1951; children: Debra, Jeffrey, Hollee, Jodi. *Education:* Florida Southern College, B.S., 1954; University of Florida, M.Ed., 1965. *Home:* 1000 West Lake Martha Dr., Winter Haven, Fla. 33880. *Office:* Department of English, Polk Junior College, Winter Haven, Fla. 33880.

*CAREER:* Ward's Nursery, Avon Park, Fla., production manager, 1959-64; Polk Junior College, Winter Haven, Fla., professor of English, 1965—. Director, American Red Cross, Winter Haven chapter, 1972. *Military service:* U.S. Army, 1949-51; became sergeant; received three battle stars. *Member:* Modern Language Association of America, Florida Association of Junior Colleges, Florida Council of Teachers of English.

*WRITINGS:* (With Maurice Sutton and R. W. Puckett) *College English: A Beginning,* Holbrook, 1969; (with M. Sutton and Puckett) *A Simple Rhetoric,* Holbrook, 1969; (with Puckett and Dion Brown) *Journeys: An Introduction to Literature,* Holbrook, 1970. Contributor to *Walt Whitman Journal, Real West,* and other publications.

*WORK IN PROGRESS:* A novel entitled *Hearts Aren't Worn on the Sleeve;* an untitled novel illustrating the harsh effects of tradition on new consciousness thinking; *Scarecrow Summer,* a juvenile novel.

*SIDELIGHTS:* Larry Sutton told *CA:* "From the standpoint of fiction, I'm very much interested in the absurd. Writers such as Kurt Vonnegut, Joseph Heller, and Norman Mailer influence me. The matter of choice—or lack of it—as

influenced by tradition, seems to be central to my thinking. I plan to continue trying to write novels, short stories, and articles."

\* \* \*

## SWADOS, Harvey 1920-1972

October 28, 1920—December 11, 1972; American educator, novelist, short story writer, essayist, and social critic. Obituaries: *New York Times,* December 12, 1972; *Newsweek,* December 25, 1972; *Publishers Weekly,* January 15, 1973. (See index for *CA* sketch)

\* \* \*

## SWANN, Brian 1940-

*PERSONAL:* Born August 13, 1940, in Wallsend, Northumberland, England; son of Stanley and Lilyan (Booth) Swann. *Education:* Queens' College, Cambridge, M.A., 1963; Princeton University, Ph.D., 1970. *Home:* 739 Washington St., New York, N.Y. 10014. *Office:* Department of English, Cooper Union, Cooper Sq., New York, N.Y. 10003.

*CAREER:* Teacher at Manchester Grammar School, Manchester, England, 1964; instructor at Princeton University, Princeton, N.J., and Rutgers University, New Brunswick, N.J., 1964-66; worked for British Council and Esso Standard Italiana in Rome, Italy, 1966-67; teacher at Magistero, Cassino, Italy, 1967; Princeton University, assistant professor of English, 1970-72; Cooper Union, New York, N.Y., 1972—, began as assistant professor, currently associate professor of English. *Member:* Modern Language Association of America. *Awards, honors:* John Florio Prize, 1977, for *Shema: Collected Poems of Primo Levi;* National Education Association fellowship for fiction, 1977.

*WRITINGS:* (Editor; translator with Ruth Feldman) *The Collected Poems of Lucio Piccolo,* Princeton University Press, 1972; (editor and translator with Feldman) *Selected Poems of Andrea Zanzotto,* Princeton University Press, 1975; *The Whale's Scars,* New Rivers Press, 1976; *Roots* (poems) New Rivers Press, 1976; (translator with Michael Impey) *Primele Poeme/First Poems of Tristan Tzara,* New Rivers Press, 1976; (translator with Impey) *Selected Poems of Tudor Arghezi,* Princeton University Press, 1976; (translator) *Shema: Collected Poems of Primo Levi,* Menard (London), 1976.

Contributor of essays to American and Italian journals, and poems to *Poetry, Quarterly Review of Literature, Yale Review, New Yorker, Paris Review, Iowa Review, Shenandoah, Chelsea,* and more than thirty other periodicals; also has translated Italian, Anglo-Saxon, and Norse poetry for literary reviews. Reviewer, *Library Journal.* Guest editor, *Mediterranean Review,* for special issue on the Italian cultural scene, 1972.

*WORK IN PROGRESS: Liking the Sky* and *Scenario for a Farce,* both fiction.

\* \* \*

## SWANSON, Harold B(urdette) 1917-

*PERSONAL:* Born March 2, 1917, in Maple Lake, Minn.; son of Albert J. (a farmer) and Hazel (Johnson) Swanson; married Linnea M. Swanson, April 25, 1942; children: Bruce Douglas, Barbara (Mrs. Gregory Brambrink), Beth Marie. *Education:* University of Minnesota, B.A. (magna cum laude), 1939, M.S., 1949; University of Wisconsin—Madison, Ph.D., 1965. *Religion:* Lutheran. *Home:* 2190 South Rosewood Lane, St. Paul, Minn. 55113. *Office:*

Department of Information and Agricultural Journalism, University of Minnesota, St. Paul, Minn. 55101.

*CAREER: Plainview News,* Plainview, Minn., advertising manager, 1939; University of Minnesota, St. Paul, bulletin editor, 1939-42, instructor, 1942-47, assistant professor, 1948-50, associate professor, 1950-57, professor of agricultural journalism, 1957—, head of department of information and agricultural journalism, 1948-74. *Military service:* U.S. Army, 1942-45; became sergeant. *Member:* American Association of Agricultural College Editors (president, 1953-54), National Project in Agricultural Communications, National Agricultural Advertising and Marketing Association, Minnesota Adult Education Association (president, 1972-73), Epsilon Sigma Phi, Gamma Sigma Delta. *Awards, honors:* Honorary state farmer, Minnesota Association of Future Farmers of America, 1949; Superior Service Award, U.S. Department of Agriculture, 1963; Adult Educator of the Year, Minnesota Adult Education Association, 1974; Professional of the Year, American Association of Agricultural College Editors, 1977.

*WRITINGS: Looking Forward to a Career–Agriculture,* Dillon, 1971. Contributor of hundreds of articles to popular magazines and professional journals.

\* \* \*

## SWEARER, Donald K(eeney) 1934-

*PERSONAL:* Born August 2, 1934, in Wichita, Kan.; son of Edward Mays (an oil broker) and Elloise (Keeney) Swearer; married Nancy Chester, June 17, 1964; children: Susan Marie, Stephen Edward. *Education:* Princeton University, A.B., 1956, M.A., 1965, Ph.D., 1967; Yale University, B.D., 1962, S.T.M., 1963. *Politics:* Democrat. *Religion:* Presbyterian. *Residence:* Swarthmore, Pa. *Office:* Department of Religion, Swarthmore College, Swarthmore, Pa. 19081.

*CAREER:* Oberlin College, Oberlin, Ohio, instructor, 1965-67, assistant professor of religion, 1967-70; Swarthmore College, Swarthmore, Pa., associate professor, 1970-73, professor of religion, 1973—. Acting associate professor of religion, University of Pennsylvania, Philadelphia, 1970-72. Administrative assistant, Edward W. Hazen Foundation, 1961-63. Member of advisory council, department of religion, Princeton University, 1970-75. Consultant to the American Broadcasting Co. film on Buddhism, "Be Ye a Lamp unto Yourselves," 1972, Goucher College department of religion evaluation committee, 1976, and the British Broadcasting Co. film on Thai art and culture, 1977. *Member:* American Academy of Religion (vice-president, Middle Atlantic region, 1971-72), Association for Asian Studies (member of board of directors), Siam Society, Asia Society, Society for Values in Higher Education, Phi Beta Kappa. *Awards, honors:* Society for Religion in Higher Education fellowship, 1967-68; National Endowment for the Humanities senior fellow, 1972-73; Ford Foundation Southeast Asia regional fellowship, 1974-75; Social Science Research Council Southeast Asia fellowship, 1977-78.

*WRITINGS: Buddhism in Transition,* Westminster, 1970; (editor) Bikkhu Buddhadasa, *Toward the Truth,* Westminster, 1971; (with Sobhana Dhammasudhi and Eshin Nishimura) *Secrets of the Lotus,* Macmillan, 1971; *Southeast Asia,* Pendulum Press, 1972; (contributor) B. L. Smith, editor, *Tradition and Change in Theravada Buddhism,* E. J. Brill, 1973; (contributor) Heinrich Dumoulin and John Maraldo, editors, *Buddhism in the Modern World,* Macmillan, 1976; *Wat Haripanjaya, the Royal Temple of the Buddha's*

*Relic* (monograph), American Academy of Religion, 1976; *Buddhism,* Argus Communications, 1977; *Dialogue: The Key to Understanding Other Religions,* Westminster, 1977; (contributor) B. L. Smith, editor, *Buddhism and the Legitimation of Power in Thailand,* Anima Books, 1977. Editor, "Third World Countries" series, Pendulum Press, and "Major World Religions" series, Argus Communications. Also contributor to *Religious Festivals of South Asia,* edited by Guy R. Welbon. Contributor to *Journal of the American Academy of Religion, Philosophy East West, Journal of the American Oriental Society, Journal of the Siam Society,* and *Journal of Ecumenical Studies.* Assistant editor for southeast Asia, *Journal of Asian Studies,* 1977—.

*WORK IN PROGRESS: I Take Refuge in the Buddha,* a study of Buddhism in northern Thailand; *Buddhist Ethics: A Comparative Perspective; Monasticism, Christian and Buddhist,* with Patrick Henry; a contribution to *Saivism in South Asia,* edited by Fred Clothey; a translation of *Tamnan Mulsasana, Wat Pa Daeng* with Sommai Premchit, tentatively entitled *The Red Forest Monastery Chronicle of the Founding of Buddhism.*

\* \* \*

## SWEENEY, (Charles) Leo 1918-

*PERSONAL:* Born September 22, 1918, in O'Connor, Neb.; son of John Michael (a farmer) and Ellen Theresa (McDowell) Sweeney. *Education:* St. Louis University, A.B., 1941, Ph.L., 1943, M.A., 1945, S.T.L., 1951; University of Toronto, Ph.D., 1954. *Home and office:* Loyola University, 6525 North Sheridan Rd., Chicago, Ill. 60626.

*CAREER:* Entered Order of Society of Jesus (Jesuits), 1936, ordained Roman Catholic priest, 1949; taught in high school, 1943-46; St. Louis University, St. Louis, Mo., instructor, 1954-58, assistant professor, 1958-62, associate professor, 1962-66, professor of philosophy, 1966-68; visiting professor of philosophy at Creighton University, Omaha, Neb., 1968-70, and Catholic University of America, Washington, D.C., 1970-72; Loyola University of Chicago, Chicago, Ill., visiting professor of philosophy, 1972-74, adjunct research professor, 1974—.

*MEMBER:* Societe Internationale pour l'Etude de la Philosophie Medievale, Metaphysical Society of America, Mediaeval Academy of America, Jesuit Philosophical Association (secretary-treasurer, 1960-63; president, 1965-66), American Catholic Philosophical Association (member of executive council, 1969-71), American Philosophical Association, International Society for Neoplatonism, Society for Ancient Greek Philosophy. *Awards, honors:* American Council of Learned Societies fellowship, 1963-64; two research grants-in-aid, U.S. Office of Education, 1969-70.

*WRITINGS: A Metaphysics of Authentic Existentialism,* Prentice-Hall, 1965; (editor with Vincent Daues and Maurice Hollway, and contributor) *Wisdom in Depth: Philosophical and Theological Essays in Honor of Henry J. Renard,* Bruce, 1966; *Infinity in the Presocratics: A Bibliographical and Philosophical Study,* Nijhoff, 1972.

Contributor: Charles J. O'Neil, editor, *Etienne Gilson Tribute,* Marquette University Press, 1959; Kurt Aland and F. L. Cross, editors, *Studia Patristica,* Akademie-Verlag, 1962; Paul Wilpert, editor, *Die Metaphysick im Mittelalter ihr Ursprung und ihr Bedeutung,* Walter de Gruyter, 1963; Paul Edwards, editor, *Encyclopedia of Philosophy,* Macmillan, 1967; B. M. Lacroix, editor, *Arts liberaux et philosophie au moyen age,* Institut de'Etudes Medievales (Montreal), 1969; John Bradley, editor, *Encyclopedia Dictionary of*

*Christian Doctrine,* Good Will Publishers, 1972; E. G. Weltin, editor, *Great Events of History,* Harper, 1972; R. W. Shahan and F. J. Kovach, editors, *Bonaventure and Aquinas, Enduring Philosophers,* University of Oklahoma Press, 1976. Editor, *Proceedings* of Conventions of the Jesuit Philosophical Association, Woodstock College Press, 1960-63. Contributor to *Mediaeval Studies, Modern Schoolman, New Scholasticism, Collier's Encyclopedia,* and other publications. Associate editor, *Modern Schoolman,* 1956—.

*WORK IN PROGRESS: Infinity in Plato's Philebus: A Bibliographical and Philosophical Study; Infinity in Aristotle; Infinity in Plotinus; Infinity in Proclus and Pseudo-Dionysius;* contributions to *Studies in Honor of Albert the Great, Structure of Being in Neoplatonism,* and *Order and Disorder: The Coincidence of Opposites in the History of Thought.*

*SIDELIGHTS:* Leo Sweeney told *CA:* "John Henry Newman was the first to influence me as a writer and his influence was disastrous. But it was not his fault.... A professor thought that this was the way to teach college students how to write: Read one chapter of a book by Cardinal Newman and then reproduce what he said in our own words but without quoting or paraphrasing [him].... It was torture to do, and I wrote awkwardly and heavily and I hated it all the while. The most helpful influence was Thomas Aquinas.... Every word he wrote was relevant and necessary; each sentence led directly to the next. The whole paragraph was a simple, organic unit. I then began to write in that fashion and the result is that although my writing has to do with very technical topics in philosophy and theology, it is (I think) simple, clear, and organically developed."

\*     \*     \*

**SWEETSER, Wesley D(uaine) 1919-**

*PERSONAL:* Born May 25, 1919, in National City, Calif.; son of Joseph Sherwood and Ella (Haug) Sweetser; married Marceine Dickfos, December 22, 1942; children: Paul, Imogene (Mrs. Thomas Calogero, Jr.), Genelle (Mrs. Richard Lippincott), Wesley, Jr. *Education:* University of Colorado, B.A., 1938, M.A., 1946, Ph.d., 1958. *Home address:* R.D. 5, Box 74, Oswego, N.Y. 13126. *Office:* Department of English, State University of New York College, Oswego, N.Y. 13126.

*CAREER:* U.S. Army Air Forces, 1940-45; University of Colorado, Boulder, instructor in English, 1945-47; Nebraska State Teachers College at Peru (now Peru State College), assistant professor of English, 1948-50; U.S. Air Force, 1951-66, became major; Nebraska Wesleyan College, Lincoln, visiting professor of English, 1966-67; State University of New York College at Oswego, professor of English, 1967—. Served in Australia and Japan during military career. *Member:* Modern Language Association of America.

*WRITINGS:* (Contributor) Brocard Sewell, editor, *Arthur Machen,* St. Albert's Press, 1960; *Arthur Machen,* Twayne, 1964; (with Adrian Goldstone) *A Bibliography of Arthur Machen,* University of Texas Press, 1965; (contributor) Helmut E. Gerber and W. Eugene Davis, editors, *Thomas Hardy: An Annotated Bibliography of Writings about Him,* Northern Illinois University Press, 1973; *A Bibliography of Ralph Hodgson,* privately printed, 1974. Contributor to English journals.

*WORK IN PROGRESS: Colonial Backgrounds in Nineteenth-Century British Literature: Australia, New Zealand, and the South Sea Islands.*

*SIDELIGHTS:* Wesley Sweetser told *CA:* "My purpose in writing is to contribute to one or another of the areas of basic literary scholarship—authentic text, biography, bibliography, or historical background. Literary guides and interpretive criticism merely destroy the student's incentive to think for himself." *Avocational interests:* Fly fishing, tennis, squash, travel abroad.

\*     \*     \*

**SWIFT, Edward 1943-**
   **(Edd Swift)**

*PERSONAL:* Born October 5, 1943, in Woodville, Tex.; son of Edward F. and Pearl Elizabeth (Brown) Swift. *Education:* Hardin-Simmons University, B.S., 1966. *Home:* 150 2nd Ave., New York, N.Y. 10003.

*AWARDS, HONORS:* Second place for paintings in Kappa Pi (international art fraternity) competition, 1965; grants from Wurlitzer Foundation and Ossabaw Island Project.

*WRITINGS:* (Under name Edd Swift) *Ted and Priscilla* (self-illustrated juvenile), Hawthorn, 1971; *Splendora* (novel), Viking, 1978.

*WORK IN PROGRESS:* A novel.†

\*     \*     \*

**SWIGER, Elinor Porter 1927-**

*PERSONAL:* Born August 1, 1927, in Cleveland, Ohio; daughter of Louie Charles (a farmer) and Mary (Shank) Porter; married Quentin G. Swiger (an attorney), February 5, 1955; children: Andrew, Calvin, Charles. *Education:* Ohio State University, B.A., 1949, LL.B. (now J.D.), 1951. *Religion:* Protestant. *Home:* 1933 Burr Oak Dr., Glenview, Ill. 60025.

*CAREER:* Internal Revenue Service, Office of Chief Counsel, Washington, D.C., attorney, 1951-56. *Member:* National League of American Pen Women, Ohio State Bar Association, Chicago Council on Foreign Relations, Chicago Art Institute, Children's Reading Round Table (Chicago), Lyric Opera Association of Chicago, Off-Campus Writer's Workshop (Winnetka), Glenview Volunteer Bureau.

*WRITINGS: Mexico for Kids,* Bobbs-Merrill, 1971; *Europe for Young Travelers,* Bobbs-Merrill, 1972; *The Law and You: A Handbook for Young People,* Bobbs-Merrill, 1973, revised edition, 1975; *Careers in the Legal Profession,* F. Watts, 1977; *Law in Everyday Life,* McDougal, Littell, 1977; *Women Lawyers at Work,* Messner, in press.

*AVOCATIONAL INTERESTS:* Community activities, art, opera, golf.

\*     \*     \*

**SWINFEN, D(avid) B(erridge) 1936-**

*PERSONAL:* Born November 8, 1936, in Kirkcaldy, Fife, Scotland; son of Thomas Berridge (a businessman) and Freda (Harries) Swinfen; married Ann Pettit (a university lecturer), June 2, 1960; children: Tanya, Michael, Katrina, Nicola, Richard. *Education:* Hertford College, Oxford, B.A. (honors), 1960, D.Phil., 1965. *Religion:* Church of England. *Home:* 14 Cedar Rd., Broughty Ferry, Angus, Scotland. *Office:* Department of Modern History, University of Dundee, Dundee, Angus, Scotland.

*CAREER:* University of Dundee, Dundee, Angus, Scotland, lecturer, 1963-75, senior lecturer in history, 1975—. *Military service:* British Army, 1955-57; became lieutenant. *Member:* British Association of American Studies.

WRITINGS: *Imperial Control of Colonial Legislation: 1813-65,* Clarendon Press, 1970; (contributor) Edwards and Shepperson, editors, *Scotland, Europe, and the American Revolution,* Edinburgh University Student Publications, 1976. Contributor to *Juridicial Review.*

WORK IN PROGRESS: Study of Judicial Committee of the Privy Council, 1833-1970.

\* \* \*

## SWINT, Henry L(ee) 1909-

PERSONAL: Born February 6, 1909, in Chambers County, Ala.; son of Charles Henry and Thyra Lee (Floyd) Swint; married Elizabeth Welter, May 30, 1934; children: Barbara Elizabeth (Mrs. Louis E. Underwood), Margaret Ann, Mary Ruth (Mrs. Thomas W. Martin, Jr.). *Education:* Birmingham-Southern College, A.B., 1929; Vanderbilt University, A.M., 1930, Ph.D., 1939. *Religion:* Methodist. *Home:* 3615 Saratoga Dr., Nashville, Tenn. 37205.

CAREER: Louisburg College, Louisburg, N.C., professor of history, 1930-31; King College, Bristol, Tenn., professor of history and political science, 1931-34; Middle Georgia State College, Cochran, associate professor of history, 1934-36; Vanderbilt University, Nashville, Tenn., assistant professor, 1936-46, associate professor, 1946-52, professor of history, 1952-71, Holland N. McTyeire Professor of History, 1971-77, director, Institute on American Democracy, 1963, coordinator of graduate instruction, department of history, 1963-67, secretary of graduate school faculty, 1963—. Woodrow Wilson fellowship program, member of regional committee, 1949-51, chairman, 1950-51. *Military service:* U.S. Army, Military Intelligence, 1944-46, 1951. *Member:* Southern Historical Association, Tennessee Historical Society. *Awards, honors:* Rosenwald research fellow, 1941; Fund for the Advancement of Education fellow, 1952-53.

WRITINGS: *The Northern Teacher in the South, 1862-1870,* Vanderbilt University Press, 1941; (editor) *Dear Ones at Home: Letters from Contraband Camps,* Vanderbilt University Press, 1966. Contributor to *Tennessee Historical Quarterly, Journal of Southern History, Mississippi Valley Historical Review, Wilson Library Bulletin, Social Studies,* and other publications.

\* \* \*

## SYMMONS-SYMONOLEWICZ, Konstantin 1909-

PERSONAL: Born August 5, 1909, in St. Petersburg (now Leningrad), Russia; came to United States in 1939, naturalized in 1948; son of Konstanty (a diplomat) and Lidia (Cherenkov) Symonolewicz; married Krystyna Wiczynska (a psychiatric social worker), February 1, 1951; children: Kristina Maria (Mrs. L. Allen Hunt). *Education:* University of Warsaw, Ph.M., 1931; Columbia University, Ph.D., 1955. *Home address:* 540 Deissler Ct., Meadville, Pa. 16335.

CAREER: Republic of Poland, Warsaw, civil service employee, 1935-40; Alliance College, Cambridge Springs, Pa., assistant professor of Polish language and culture, 1940-42; Polish Government in Exile, London, England, civil service employee, 1943-45; Wilkes College, Wilkes-Barre, Pa., assistant professor, 1945-55, professor of sociology and anthropology, 1956-62; MacMurray College, Jacksonville, Ill., professor of sociology and anthropology, 1962-69; Allegheny College, Meadville, Pa., professor of sociology and anthropology, 1969-76; currently part-time instructor, Gannon College, Erie, Pa. *Member:* American Sociological Association, American Anthropological Association, Amer-

ican Historical Association, Polish Institute of Arts and Sciences in America.

WRITINGS: *Modern Nationalism: Towards a Consensus in Theory,* Polish Institute of Arts & Sciences in America, 1968; *Nationalist Movements: A Comparative View,* Maplewood Press, 1970; (translator and author of introduction) *The Non-Slavic Peoples of the Soviet Union: A Brief Ethnographic Survey,* Maplewood Press, 1972. Contributor to *Polish Review, Comparative Studies in Society and History, Transactions of the Illinois State Academy of Science, Current Anthropology,* and other publications.

\* \* \*

## SYNAN, (Harold) Vinson 1934-

PERSONAL: Born December 1, 1934, in Hopewell, Va.; son of Joseph Alexander (a minister) and Minnis (Perdue) Synan; married Carol Lee Fuqua, August 13, 1960; children: Mary Carol, Virginia Lee, Vinson, Jr., Joseph Alexander III. *Education:* Emmanuel Junior College, diploma, 1955; University of Richmond, B.A., 1958; University of Georgia, M.A., 1964, Ph.D., 1967. *Politics:* Republican. *Office:* Division of Social and Behavioral Sciences, Emmanuel College, Franklin Springs, Ga. 30639.

CAREER: Pentecostal Holiness minister and historian; teacher in senior high schools in Prince George County, Va., 1960-61, and Chesterfield County, Va., 1961-62; Emmanuel College, Franklin Springs, Ga., instructor, 1962-67, chairperson of Division of Social and Behavioral Sciences, 1967—. *Member:* American Historical Society, Southern Historical Society, Society for Pentecostal Studies (founding member; general secretary; president, 1973-74).

WRITINGS: *El Movimiento Pentecostal,* Enrique Chavez (Chile), 1967; *Emmanuel College: The First Fifty Years,* North Washington Press, 1968; *The Holiness-Pentecostal Movement in the United States,* Eerdmans, 1971; *The Old Time Power,* Advocate Press, 1973; *Charismatic Bridges,* Servant, 1974; (editor) *Aspects of Pentecostal-Charismatic Origins,* Logos International, 1975. Also author of *Age of the Holy Spirit,* 1975; author of document of affiliation between Pentecostal Holiness Church (U.S.) and Pentecostal Methodist Church (Chile). Editor of *Newsletter* of Society for Pentecostal Studies.

BIOGRAPHICAL/CRITICAL SOURCES: *Pentecostal Holiness Advocate* (Franklin Springs, Ga.), January 1, 1972.†

\* \* \*

## SYNNESTVEDT, Sig(fried T.) 1924-1977

PERSONAL: Born November 13, 1924; son of Arthur and Gertrude (Tafel) Synnestvedt; married Nadine Smith, September 13, 1947; children: Barbara, Nancy (Mrs. Stephen Mills), Suzanne, Jeannette, Steven. *Education:* Michigan State University, A.B., 1949, A.M., 1950; University of Pennsylvania, Ph.D., 1959. *Office:* Department of History, State University of New York College, Brockport, N.Y. 14420.

CAREER: College of the Academy of the New Church, Bryn Athyn, Pa., instructor, 1950-60, associate professor of history, 1960-68; State University of New York College at Brockport, associate professor, 1968-69, professor of history and chairman of the department, 1969-74. Research associate, University of Pennsylvania, 1960-64. Visiting professor, Pennsylvania State University, 1964-68, University of Vermont, 1966. *Military service:* U.S. Navy, 1943-46. U.S.

Naval Reserve, 1947-57. *Member:* American Historical Association, Organization of American Historians, Association for the Study of African-American History, Phi Alpha Theta, Phi Kappa Phi. *Awards, honors:* University of Pennsylvania postdoctoral fellow, 1964.

*WRITINGS:* (With Henry Teune) *Measuring International Alignments* (monograph), Foreign Policy Institute, University of Pennsylvania, 1965; (contributor) J. W. Reidy, editor, *Strategy for the Americas,* McGraw, 1966; *The Essential Swedenborg,* Twayne, 1970; *The White Response to Black Emancipation: Second Class Citizenship in the U.S. since Reconstruction,* Macmillan, 1972; *Edwin Markham,* Twayne, 1974; (contributor) Robert A. Bauer, editor, *The United States in World Affairs,* University Press of Virginia, 1975. Contributor to *Mankind, Commonweal, Orbis,* and *Current History.*

*WORK IN PROGRESS: The Black Man and the White House: A Study of the Racial Record of the First Families in the Twentieth Century.*†

(Died June, 1977)

# T

## TACEY, William S(anford) 1904-

*PERSONAL:* Born April 29, 1904, in Bethel, N.Y.; son of James R. F. (a farmer) and Anna C. (Sanford) Tacey; married Eleanor Smith, July 29, 1933 (died October 20, 1969); married Evelyn F. Reithmiller, January 1, 1976; children: (first marriage) Mary M. (Mrs. James K. Boatner). *Education:* Geneva College, B.A., 1928; Columbia University, M.A., 1932; Pennsylvania State University, Ed.D., 1960. *Politics:* Republican. *Religion:* Presbyterian. *Home:* 750 Jefferson Dr., Pittsburgh, Pa. 15229. *Office:* Department of Speech, University of Pittsburgh, Pittsburgh, Pa. 15213.

*CAREER:* Teacher in rural schools in Bethel, N.Y., 1922-24; high school social studies and speech teacher in Mc-Keesport, Pa., 1928-46; Pennsylvania State University, University Park, instructor in speech, 1946-47; University of Pittsburgh, Pittsburgh, Pa., 1947—, began as instructor, became professor of speech, professor emeritus, 1974—. Visiting professor of speech at Queens College of the City University of New York, California State University, Long Beach, Pittsburgh Theological Seminary, and Carlow College, Pittsburgh, Pa. Parliamentarian for professional organizations; member of Carlow College president's council, 1969—; secretary-treasurer, Pittsburgh Federal Credit Union, 1960, 1977. Communications consultant to various corporations, 1949—. *Member:* American Institute of Parliamentarians (director, 1972—; editor, 1972-77), American Association of University Professors (former president and secretary of Pittsburgh chapter), Speech Communication Association, Speech Association of Eastern States (editor, 1960-64), Pennsylvania Speech Communication Association (past president and executive secretary).

*WRITINGS: Humor Booklet,* Toastmasters International, 1967; *Business and Professional Speaking,* W. C. Brown, 1970; (contributor) *History of Speech in Pennsylvania,* Pennsylvania Speech Association, 1971. Contributor of articles to journals, including *Speech Teacher, Parliamentary Journal, Pennsylvania Speech Annual,* and *American Management.* Editor, *Today's Speech,* 1960-64, and *CAPP News* (journal of Commission on American Parliamentary Practice), 1970-77.

*WORK IN PROGRESS:* Two books on parliamentary procedure, *A Manual of Parliamentary Practice,* for Macmillan, and *Studying Parliamentary Law;* a children's book, *The Mallard Family at the Retirement Home.*

## TAHA, Hamdy A(bdelaziz) 1937-

*PERSONAL:* Born April 19, 1937, in Egypt; came to the United States in 1959; U.S. citizen; son of Abdelaziz and Kasma Taha; married Karen Terry, May 12, 1965; children: Tarek, Sharif, Maisa. *Education:* Alexandria University, B.S., 1958; Stanford University, M.S., 1962; Arizona State University, Ph.D., 1964. *Home:* 406 Lake Rd., Springdale, Ark. 72764. *Office:* Department of Industrial Engineering, University of Arkansas, Fayetteville, Ark. 72701.

*CAREER:* University of Cairo, Cairo, Egypt, lecturer in operations research, 1964-67; University of Oklahoma, Norman, assistant professor of industrial engineering, 1967-69; University of Arkansas, Fayetteville, associate professor, 1969-75, professor of industrial engineering, 1975—. Registered professional engineer. *Member:* Institute of Management Science, American Institute of Industrial Engineers, Operations Research Society of America. *Awards, honors:* Selected an "Outstanding Educator," 1971, and "Outstanding Researcher," 1976.

*WRITINGS: Operation Research: An Introduction,* Macmillan, 1971, 2nd edition, 1976; *Integer Programming: Theory, Application, and Computation,* Academic Press, 1975.

*WORK IN PROGRESS: Nonlinear Programming: Minimization of Concave Functions.*

\*       \*       \*

## TAKAKI, Ronald T(oshiyuki) 1939-

*PERSONAL:* Born April 12, 1939, in Honolulu, Hawaii; married, 1961; three children. *Education:* College of Wooster, B.A., 1961; University of California, Berkeley, M.A., 1962, Ph.D., 1967. *Office:* Department of Ethnic Studies, University of California, Berkeley, Calif. 94720.

*CAREER:* College of San Mateo, San Mateo, Calif., instructor in American history, 1965-67; University of California, Los Angeles, assistant professor of history, 1967-72; University of California, Berkeley, associate professor of ethnic studies, 1972—. *Member:* American Historical Association. *Awards, honors:* National Endowment for the Humanities fellowship, 1970-71.

*WRITINGS: A Pro-Slavery Crusade: The Agitation to Reopen the African Slave Trade,* Free Press, 1971; *Violence in the Black Imagination,* Putnam, 1972; *A Discontented*

*Civilization: Race and Culture in 19th-Century America,* Knopf, in press. Contributor to history journals.

\*          \*          \*

## TAMNY, Martin 1941-

*PERSONAL:* Born June 17, 1941, in New York, N.Y.; son of Sidney (a salesman) and Rica (Wexler) Tamny; married Myrna N. Kanarek, June 12, 1960; children: Mark, Tara. *Education:* City College of the City University of New York, B.S., 1963, M.A., 1973, Ph.D., 1976. *Home:* 10-24 166th St., Whitestone, N.Y. 11357. *Office:* Department of Philosophy, City College of the City University of New York, New York, N.Y. 10031.

*CAREER:* City College of the City University of New York, New York, N.Y., lecturer, 1964-76, assistant professor of philosophy, 1976—, director of program in history and philosophy of science, 1976—. Adjunct associate professor, Hofstra University. *Member:* Philosophy of Science Association, History of Science Society, American Association of University Professors.

*WRITINGS:* (With Samuel D. Guttenplan) *Logic: A Comprehensive Introduction,* Basic Books, 1971, 2nd revised edition, 1978; (contributor) Matthew Lipman and Ann Margaret Sharp, editors, *Growing Up with Philosophy,* Temple University Press, 1978. Contributor to professional journals.

*WORK IN PROGRESS:* Research on the history of the philosophy of science, and on the philosophical thought of Isaac Newton.

\*          \*          \*

## TANKSLEY, Perry 1928-

*PERSONAL:* Born September 15, 1928, near Lorman, Miss.; son of Lawrence Warren (a millwright) and Myrtle (Emanuel) Tanksley; married Suzanne Mitchell (a teacher), June 1, 1950; children: John, Robert, Perry, Mark. *Education:* Asbury College, B.A., 1951; Emory University, B.D., 1956, M.Div., 1972. *Home:* 1501 Arlington, Clinton, Miss. 39056.

*CAREER:* United Methodist clergyman. President, Allgood Books, 1967—. *Military service:* U.S. Naval Air Corps, 1946.

*WRITINGS*—All published by Revell: *Love Gift,* 1971; *Friend Gift,* 1972; *Light from the Living Bible,* 1973; *We're in This Thing Together,* 1974; *Reach Out and Touch,* 1974.

Devotional books of poetry, all privately printed: *Gift of Love,* 1967; *Gift of Gratitude,* 1968; *Gift of Hope,* 1968; *Gift of Gladness,* 1969; *Gift of Gold,* 1969; *Love Is Eternal,* 1970; *Thanks for Memories,* 1970; *Friendship Gift,* 1970; *Of Silver and Gold,* 1970; *I Call You Friend,* 1970; *To Love Is to Give,* 1970; *Your Life Touched Mine,* 1971; *These Things I've Loved,* 1971; *For the Good Times,* 1975; *Happiness Gift,* 1975; *Love from the Living Bible,* 1976; *Lucky We Found Each Other,* 1976.

Contributor to books of sermons. Contributor of poetry to national periodicals and church publications.

*SIDELIGHTS:* Perry Tanksley told *CA:* "I am a minister of the gospel of Christ and think of myself as a preacher more than a poet. I am always writing with the thought of getting a point across. I've always been involved with people in pain so I write a lot about suffering. Most of my poems find their inspiration in the lives of people I have ministered to. I have never joined a poetry society or submitted my works for academic evaluation. I write for the man on the

street and the man on the tractor and the scrub woman and even small children. One million of my books are published so I think I'm getting fair coverage."

\*          \*          \*

## TARANOW, Gerda

*PERSONAL:* Surname is pronounced *Ta*-ra-no; born in New York, N.Y.; daughter of Samuel and Sabina (Ostro) Taranow. *Education:* New York University, B.A., 1952, M.A., 1955; Yale University, Ph.D., 1961, post-doctoral fellow, 1962-63. *Residence:* New London, Conn. *Office:* Department of English, Connecticut College, New London, Conn. 06320.

*CAREER:* University of Kentucky, Lexington, instructor, 1963-65, assistant professor of English, 1965-66; Syracuse University, Syracuse, N.Y., assistant professor of English, 1966-67; Connecticut College, New London, assistant professor, 1967-70, associate professor, 1970-76, professor of English, 1976—. *Member:* International Federation for Theatre Research, American Society for Theatre Research, Association of Recorded Sound Collections, Modern Language Association of America, La Societe d'Histoire du Theatre, Delta Phi Alpha.

*WRITINGS: Sarah Bernhardt: The Art within the Legend,* Princeton University Press, 1972.

*WORK IN PROGRESS: Sarah Bernhardt's Interpretation of "Hamlet."*

*SIDELIGHTS:* In a review of *Sarah Bernhardt: The Art within the Legend,* Harold Hobson writes: "This book is probably the most elaborate examination of the various components of the skill of an actor or actress of genius that has ever been written for the general public.... Its range of knowledge is immense, its balance of judgement remarkable.... It is in fact an outstanding work, which should be read by all those interested in theatrical art." A reviewer for the *Times Literary Supplement* finds the book "fascinating reading for anyone interested in the mystery of acting.... This careful, sophisticated study has many virtues. The author has interpreted her research with a fine sense of the nature of the theatre. Her scholarship is exact and thorough. Her criticism is objective, even dispassionate. The result is a remarkable account of the artistic history of an actress of genius...."

Gerda Taranow is competent in German, French, Latin, Greek, Hebrew, and Norwegian.

*AVOCATIONAL INTERESTS:* Opera, theatre, dance.

*BIOGRAPHICAL/CRITICAL SOURCES: Detroit News,* February 6, 1972; *Times Literary Supplement,* June 30, 1972; *Books and Bookmen,* September, 1972.

\*          \*          \*

## TARR, Joel A(rthur) 1934-

*PERSONAL:* Born May 8, 1934, in Jersey City, N.J.; married Arlene Green, 1956 (deceased); children: Michael, Joanna. *Education:* Rutgers University, B.S. (with high honors), 1956, M.A., 1957; Northwestern University, Ph.D., 1963. *Office:* Program in Technology and Humanities, Carnegie-Mellon University, Pittsburgh, Pa. 15213.

*CAREER:* Northwestern University, Evanston, Ill., instructor in history, 1959-61; Long Beach State College (now California State University, Long Beach), Long Beach, Calif., instructor, 1961-63, assistant professor of American history, 1963-66; University of California, Santa Barbara, visiting assistant professor of American history, 1966-67; Carnegie-Mellon University, Pittsburgh, Pa., assistant professor, 1967-70, associate professor, 1970-76, professor of history, technology, and urban affairs, 1976—, director of Program in Technology and Humanities, 1975—, co-director of Ph.D. program in applied history and social science, 1977—. *Member:* American Historical Association, Organization of American Historians. *Awards, honors:* American Philosophical Society grants, 1964, 1966; Scaife Fellow, Carnegie-Mellon University, 1967-69; National Foundation for the Humanities junior fellow, 1969-70.

*WRITINGS: A Study in Boss Politics: William Lorimer of Chicago,* University of Illinois Press, 1971; (contributor) Bruce Stave, editor, *Urban Bosses, Machines, and Progressive Reformers,* Heath, 1971; (contributor) Alexander Callow, editor, *American Urban History,* 2nd edition (Tarr was not associated with earlier edition), Oxford University Press, 1973; (consulting editor) *Living in Urban America,* Holt, 1974; (editor) *Patterns in City Growth,* Scott, Foresman, 1975; (contributor) James P. Walsh, editor, *The Irish: America's Political Class,* Arno, 1976; (contributor) Robert P. Sutton, editor, *The Prairie State,* Eerdmans, 1976; (editor) *Retrospective Technology Assessment,* San Francisco Press, 1977.

Contributor of more than thirty articles to professional journals, including *American Heritage, Business History Review, Civil Engineering,* and *Technology & Culture;* contributor of over forty reviews to professional journals and national publications.

*WORK IN PROGRESS: Transportation Innovation and Changing Spatial Patterns in Pittsburgh, 1850-1934; The Social Impacts of Enforced Energy Change;* revising for publication a 1977 report to the National Science Foundation, "Retrospective Assessment of Wastewater Technology in the United States, 1800-1972."

*SIDELIGHTS:* Joel Tarr writes: "My interest for the past few years has been in the interface between technology and society, particularly the city and technology. In addition to this area, I have been attempting to develop the field of Retrospective Technology Assessment. The latter represents an attempt to use history as a means to shed light upon present day technology-society problems and to aid in anticipating technology impacts."

\* \* \*

### TARRANCE, V(ernon) Lance, Jr. 1940-

*PERSONAL:* Born December 4, 1940, in Harlingen, Tex.; son of Vernon Lance and Mary (Rea) Tarrance; married Eugenia Aileen McCuistion, July 2, 1966; children: Vernon Lance III, Halloway McCuistion. *Education:* Washington and Lee University, B.A., 1962, M.A. *Politics:* Republican. *Religion:* Protestant.

*CAREER:* Director of research, Texas Republican Party, 1964-67; Republican National Committee, Washington, D.C., associate director of research, 1967-68, director of research, 1969; U.S. Bureau of the Census, Washington, D.C., special assistant to the director, 1970-72. *Member:* American Political Science Association, American Association for Public Opinion Research, American Academy of Political and Social Science, Pi Sigma Alpha.

*WRITINGS: The Ticket-Splitter: A New Force in American Politics,* Eerdmans, 1972. Editor and compiler of *Texas Precinct Votes '66,* Seagert Publishing, 1967, *Texas Precinct Votes '68,* Southern Methodist University Press, 1970, and *Texas Precinct Votes '70,* University of Texas Press, 1972.

*AVOCATIONAL INTERESTS:* Tennis, golf, and other sports, American history, historic homes and furniture.†

\* \* \*

### TARSAIDZE, Alexandre 1901-1978

*PERSONAL:* Born June 22, 1901, in Tiflis, Georgia, Russia; came to United States, 1923, naturalized citizen, 1928; son of George A. (an oculist) and Princess Elizabeth (Eristov) Tarsaidze; married Madeleine Black, May 25, 1940 (divorced, 1945); married Elizabeth Sverbeyef, November 27, 1947 (divorced, 1952); married Christine Leusch, March 2, 1958 (divorced, 1963). *Education:* Russian Imperial Naval Academy, graduate, 1918. *Religion:* Russian Christian Orthodox. *Home:* 520 East 76th St., New York, N.Y. *Agent:* Mrs. Carlton Cole, Waldorf-Astoria Hotel, New York, N.Y.

*CAREER:* Buyer of diamond jewelry, New York City, 1926-34; Prince Matchabelli Perfumes, New York City, staff member, 1934-35; Parfums Chevalier Garde, New York City, president, 1935-40; Serge Obolensky Associates, Inc. (public relations), New York City, vice-president, 1945-78; Tarsaidze Public Relations, New York City, president, 1955-78. Vice-president, Embassy Films, Inc. *Wartime service:* Civilian employee with U.S. Army Intelligence during World War II. *Member:* Association of Russian Imperial Naval Officers in America, U.S. Naval Institute (associate member), Russian Nobility Association, Russian Genealogical Society.

*WRITINGS: Czars and Presidents: A Story of a Forgotten Friendship,* Obolensky, 1958; *Katia: Wife before God,* Macmillan, 1970. Contributor to magazines.

*WORK IN PROGRESS: Against Russia.*

*SIDELIGHTS:* Tarsaidze was producer of the documentary, "Emperor Nicholas II" (last czar of Russia) from film made in 1896; this is said to be the oldest documentary newsreel film in the world.†

(Died February 25, 1978)

\* \* \*

### TAUBER, Peter 1947-

*PERSONAL:* Accented first syllable of surname is pronounced to rhyme with "now"; born May 19, 1947, in New York, N.Y.; son of Abraham Tajber (a former college dean and president, and professor of English) and Rhea (an elementary school teacher and administrator; maiden name, Sapodin) Tauber. *Education:* Hobart College, B.A., 1968. *Politics:* Democrat. *Agent:* John Cushman Associates, Inc., 25 West 43rd St., New York, N.Y. 10036.

*CAREER: Geneva Times,* Geneva, N.Y., reporter, 1967-68; *New York Times,* New York, N.Y., reporter, 1968-70; free-lance writer, 1970—; comedian appearing on television and radio shows and in nightclubs, 1972—. Administrative assistant, McCarthy for President campaign, 1968. Chairman and member of board of directors, fellow development committee, MacDowell Colony. Member of board of directors, Millay Colony. *Military service:* U.S. Army Reserve, 1969-75. *Awards, honors:* MacDowell Colony fellowships, 1971, 1972, 1973, 1974; Outstanding Young Men of America, 1972; Millay Colony for the Arts fellowship, 1974.

*WRITINGS: The Sunshine Soldiers,* Simon & Schuster, 1971; *The Last Best Hope* (fiction; Book-of-the Month Club selection), Harcourt, 1978. Contributor to magazines and newspapers.

*WORK IN PROGRESS:* A nonfiction work, *A Part of the World;* screenwritings.

*AVOCATIONAL INTERESTS:* Tennis, skiing, science, law.

\* \* \*

## TAYLOR, Desmond 1930-

*PERSONAL:* Born May 27, 1930, in Detroit, Mich.; son of William B. and Elinor (Brown) Taylor; married Ingeborg Krug, October 26, 1957; children: Onica, Erica. *Education:* Emory and Henry College, B.A., 1953; University of Illinois, M.S., 1960. *Politics:* Independent. *Home:* 2225 North Tacoma Ave., Tacoma, Wash. 98403. *Office:* Library, University of Puget Sound, Tacoma, Wash. 98416.

*CAREER:* Warder Public Library, Springfield, Ohio, reference assistant, 1957-59; University of Puget Sound, Tacoma, Wash., reference librarian, 1960-63, library director, 1963—, assistant director of overseas program, 1971-73. Member of Comprehensive Mental Health Board, 1969-72; trustee, Old Tacoma Improvement Club, 1966—. *Military service:* U.S. Army, Security Agency, 1953-56; served in Europe. *Member:* American Association of University Professors, American Library Association, Washington Library Association.

*WRITINGS:* (Contributor) Theodore Samore, editor, *Problems in Library Classification,* Bowker and University of Wisconsin School of Library and Information Sciences, 1968; (contributor) J. Perrault, editor, *Reclassification, Rationale and Problems,* University of Maryland School of Library and Information Services, 1968; (with Raimund Matthis) *Adopting the Library of Congress Classification,* Bowker, 1971. Also author of program notes for Tacoma Symphony Orchestra, 1964—. Contributor of articles to *Library Journal, College and Research Libraries, PMLA Quarterly.*

*WORK IN PROGRESS: Cooperative Resource and Storage Centers.*

*AVOCATIONAL INTERESTS:* Wine collecting and tasting, drawing, wood carving, hiking, and harpsichord making.

\* \* \*

## TAYLOR, Donna June 1949-

*PERSONAL:* Born June 30, 1949, in St. Helena, Calif.; daughter of Charles Richard (an educational supervisor) and June Laura (Hulbert) Taylor; married Dwight Charles Evans (a medical student), June 18, 1972. *Education:* Southern Missionary College, B.A., 1970; Loma Linda University, M.A., 1972. *Religion:* Seventh-day Adventist. *Agent:* Pacific Press Publishing Association, 1350 Villa, Mt. View, Calif.

*CAREER:* General Conference of Seventh-day Adventists, English teacher in Washington, D.C., 1970-71, and in Riverside, Calif., beginning 1972.

*WRITINGS: Green Ink,* Pacific Press Publishing Association, 1971. Contributor of articles to *Insight* magazine, *Guide,* and other denominational papers.

*WORK IN PROGRESS: Hiroshima Diary.*

*SIDELIGHTS:* Donna June Taylor lived most of her life in Latin America (Mexico and Cuba), spent a year in Europe doing schoolwork and spent a year teaching English in Japan. She speaks Spanish and German fluently and a little Japanese. Taylor writes: "I am very much interested in human relations, especially on the international level, and I hope to work to promote understanding among the different countries."†

\* \* \*

## TAYLOR, Florance Walton

*PERSONAL:* Born in Danville, Ill.; daughter of Thomas E. (a physician) and Elizabeth (Burke) Walton; married Mack Taylor (a dental surgeon); children: Thomas E., Betsy, Alan. *Education:* Northwestern University, B.A., 1920; University of Illinois, M.A., 1933. *Politics:* Republican. *Religion:* Presbyterian. *Home:* 2 North Shore Ter., Danville, Ill. 61832.

*CAREER:* Former high school teacher; writer, mainly of historical fiction for young people. Member of board, Vermilion County Children's Home, 1954-60. *Member:* Children's Reading Round Table, Kappa Kappa Gamma, Delta Kappa Gamma, P.E.O. Sisterhood. *Awards, honors:* Merit award, Northwestern University, 1940.

*WRITINGS: With Fife and Drum,* Albert Whitman, 1938; *Vermilion Clay,* Albert Whitman, 1939; *Salt Streak,* Revell, 1939; *Towpath Andy,* Albert Whitman, 1940; *Owen of the Bluebird,* Albert Whitman, 1942; *Navy Wings of Gold,* Albert Whitman, 1955; *Carrier Boy,* Abelard, 1956; *Jim Longknife,* Albert Whitman, 1959; *Gold Dust and Bullets,* Albert Whitman, 1962; "Felipe Adventure" series, Lerner, 1971, seven books: *Ball Two, Corn Festival, From Texas to Illinois, Plane Ride, School Picnic, What Is a Migrant?,* and *Where's Luis?*

*WORK IN PROGRESS:* A juvenile book based on William Henry Harrison's victory at the Battle of Tippecanoe.

*AVOCATIONAL INTERESTS:* Gardening.

\* \* \*

## TAYLOR, Frank J. 1894-1972

October 8, 1894—October 23, 1972; American editor, journalist, free-lance magazine writer, and author of books on U.S. industry and travel. Obituaries: *New York Times,* October 24, 1972. (See index for *CA* sketch)

\* \* \*

## TAYLOR, James B(entley) 1930-

*PERSONAL:* Born October 23, 1930, in Seattle, Wash.; son of Fred William and Gladys (Bentley) Taylor; married Thelma Mary Carmichael (a physical therapist), April, 1963; children: Jonathan Mark. *Education:* Reed College, B.A., 1952; University of Washington, Seattle, M.A., 1956, Ph.D., 1958. *Home:* 3018 Riverview Rd., Lawrence, Kan. 66044. *Office:* School of Social Welfare, Twente Hall, University of Kansas, Lawrence, Kan. 66045.

*CAREER:* University of Washington, Seattle, research assistant professor of sociology, 1958-63; Menninger Foundation, Topeka, Kan., research psychologist, 1963-69, director of department of research, 1969-75; University of Kansas, Lawrence, professor of social welfare, 1976—. *Member:* American Association for the Advancement of Science, American Psychological Association (fellow), American Sociological Association (fellow), American Orthopsychiatric Association (fellow), Society for the Psychological Study of Social Issues (fellow), Council on Social Work Education.

*WRITINGS:* (With L. A. Zurcher and W. H. Key) *Tornado: A Community Responds to Disaster,* University of Washington Press, 1970; (with Jerry Randolph) *Community*

*Worker,* Jason Aronson, 1975. Contributor of about thirty articles to research journals in the applied behavioral sciences field.

*WORK IN PROGRESS:* Research on methods and theory in community psychology.

\* \* \*

## TAYLOR, Morris F. 1915-

*PERSONAL:* Born October 21, 1915, in Mount Morris, N.Y.; son of Joseph Fenton and Mary Emma (Morris) Taylor; married Mariamne Elizabeth Bell, October 13, 1945; children: Mary (Mrs. Frank Pierz), Rebecca (Mrs. James Bingham). *Education:* University of Colorado, B.A., 1939; Cornell University, M.A., 1940. *Politics:* Democrat. *Home:* 120 East Second St., Trinidad, Colo. 81082. *Office:* Department of History, Trinidad State Junior College, Trinidad, Colo. 81082.

*CAREER:* Trinidad State Junior College, Trinidad, Colo., history teacher, 1941—. Fulbright exchange teacher, Bromley, Kent, England, 1960-61. Visiting lecturer, University of Denver, summer, 1966. Member of board of directors, Community Concert Association, Trinidad, Colo. Member of research team, Colorado Heritage Center Exhibits; member of Colorado Historical Records Advisory Committee. *Military service:* U.S. Marine Corps, 1941-42. *Member:* Organization of American Historians, Western History Association, Colorado Archaeological Society (state president, 1955-56), State Historical Society of Colorado (regional vice-president), Colorado History Group (president), Colorado Committee for the Promotion of Historical Studies, New Mexico Historical Society, Trinidad Historical Society (honorary president). *Awards, honors:* American Association for State and Local History certificate of commendation for *Trinidad, Colorado Territory,* 1967; D.H.L., University of Colorado, 1969.

*WRITINGS: A Sketch of Early Days on the Purgatory,* Trinidad State Junior College, 1959; *Pioneers of the Picketwire,* Trinidad State Junior College, 1964; *Trinidad, Colorado Territory,* Trinidad State Junior College, 1966; *First Mail West: Stage Lines on the Santa Fe Trail,* University of New Mexico Press, 1971. Contributor of articles to regional journals.

*WORK IN PROGRESS:* Research on the history of the Southwest, especially land grants, military affairs, Indians, postal history, pastoral industry and history of various ethnic groups; *O. P. McMains: Agent for the Settlers and the Maxwell Land-Grant Conflict,* for University of Arizona Press.

\* \* \*

## TAYLOR, Welford Dunaway 1938-

*PERSONAL:* Born January 3, 1938, in Caroline County, Va.; son of George Welford (a farmer) and Minnie (Durrette) Taylor; married Carole Wickham (a kindergarten director), January 29, 1960; children: Virginia Welford. *Education:* Attended Shenandoah Conservatory of Music, 1955-56; University of Richmond, B.A., 1959, M.A., 1961; University of Maryland, Ph.D., 1966. *Politics:* "Independent Royalist." *Religion:* Episcopalian. *Home:* 5 Calycanthus Rd., Richmond, Va. 23221. *Office:* Department of English, University of Richmond, Richmond, Va. 23173.

*CAREER:* Virginia Commonwealth University, Richmond, instructor in English, 1961-63; University of Richmond, Richmond, assistant professor, 1964-69, associate professor,

1969-73, professor of English, 1973—, chairperson of department, 1969—. Active in real estate sales and investment, 1974—. Chairperson, State Advisory Council on Libraries. *Member:* South Atlantic Modern Language Association, Sherwood Anderson Society (founding member), Virginia Writers Club.

*WRITINGS:* (Editor) Sherwood Anderson, *The Buck Fever Papers,* University Press of Virginia, 1971; (editor) *Virginia Authors Past and Present,* Virginia Association of Teachers of English, 1972; *Amelie Rives (Princess Troubetzkoy),* Twayne, 1973; (contributor) David D. Anderson, editor, *Sherwood Anderson: Dimensions of His Literary Art,* Michigan State University Press, 1976; (contributor) Hilbert H. Campbell and Charles M. Madlin, editors, *Sherwood Anderson: Centennial Studies,* Whitston Publishing, 1976; *Sherwood Anderson,* Ungar, 1977. Author of "The Virginia Corner," a column appearing in *Richmond Times-Dispatch.* Contributor of articles and reviews to literature journals. Editor, *Winesburg Eagle.*

*WORK IN PROGRESS:* A history of the journalistic mask, or persona, in America.

\* \* \*

## TAZEWELL, Charles 1900-1972

June 2, 1900—June 26, 1972; American actor, scriptwriter, and author of children's stories. Obituaries: *New York Times,* June 28, 1972; *Washington Post,* June 29, 1972; *Newsweek,* July 10, 1972; *Time,* July 10, 1972.

\* \* \*

## TEETS, Bruce E. 1914-

*PERSONAL:* Born May 13, 1914, in Terra Alta, W.Va.; son of Ora D. (a farmer) and Mintie (Whitehair) Teets; married Virginia Zinn, June 5, 1939; children: Catherine (Mrs. Leonard Tashman). *Education:* Fairmont State College, A.B., 1938; West Virginia University, M.A., 1941; Duke University, Ph.D., 1955. *Home:* 402 North Chestnut St., Ellensburg, Wash. 98926. *Office:* Department of English, Central Washington University, Ellensburg, Wash. 98926.

*CAREER:* Teacher in public schools in West Virginia and Maryland, 1933-52; Duke University, Durham, N.C., instructor in English, 1952-55; University of Miami, Coral Gables, Fla., assistant professor, 1955-60, associate professor of English, 1960-65; Purdue University, Indianapolis, Ind., professor of English, 1965-68; Central Washington University, Ellensburg, professor of English, 1968—. *Member:* Modern Language Association of America, American Society for Aesthetics, Philological Association of the Pacific Coast.

*WRITINGS:* (Editor and author of introduction and notes) Maria Edgworth, *Castle Rackrent,* University of Miami Press, 1964; (contributor) Natalie Grimes Lawrence and Jack Adolphe Reynolds, editors, *Sweet Smoke of Rhetoric: A Collection of Renaissance Essays,* University of Miami Press, 1964; (editor with Helmut E. Gerber) *Joseph Conrad: An Annotated Bibliography of Writings about Him* (Scholar's Library selection, Modern Language Association Book Club, spring, 1972), Northern Illinois University Press, 1971; (contributor) Adam Gillon and Ludwik Krzyzanowski, editors, *Joseph Conrad: Commemorative Essays,* [New York], 1975; (contributor) Todd K. Bender, editor, *Literary Impressionism in Ford Madox Ford, Joseph Conrad, and Related Writers,* [Madison], 1975. Contributor of articles to *English Literature in Transition* and *Conradiana.*

*WORK IN PROGRESS:* Editing a supplementary volume to *Joseph Conrad: An Annotated Bibliography of Writings about Him.*

*SIDELIGHTS:* Teets told *CA:* "From a real hillbilly of West (By God) Virginia to a square-dancing Westerner who wears cowboy boots, via a major educational experience at Duke University—such, I might somewhat ironically say, has been my career.

"I write scholarly reviews, articles, and books because I need something to do with all my reading in addition to teaching college students. My research gradually settled on Joseph Conrad and his works, which soon became a major interest."

*AVOCATIONAL INTERESTS:* Swimming, bicycling (rides several miles per day).

\*    \*    \*

## ter HAAR, Jaap 1922-

*PERSONAL:* Born March 25, 1922, in Hilversum, Netherlands; son of Jacob E. (a businessman) and Mieke (van Hengel) ter Haar; married Rudi Schurink, November, 1945; children: Jaap, Bart, Saskia and Jeroen (twins). *Education:* Attended schools in Netherlands. *Politics:* "Not much." *Religion:* "Not much either." *Home:* Eikenlaan 57, Hilversum, Netherlands.

*CAREER:* War correspondent with Royal Netherlands Marines in United States and Indonesia, 1945-47; head of transcription service, Radio Netherlands, 1947-55; professional writer, 1955—. *Member:* Dutch Writers Union. *Awards, honors:* City of Rotterdam Award (juvenile jury), 1958, for *Noodweer op de weisshorn;* Bijenkorf Award, 1961, for total work; City of Rotterdam Award (critics jury), 1966, for best book of the year, *Boris;* Sonderpreis for German edition of *De Geschiedenis van Noord-Amerika;* Jan Campert Foundation Award, 1972, for *Geschiedenis van de lage landen.*

*WRITINGS*—Young adult: *Nordweer op de weisshorn,* van Holkema & Warendorf, 1957, translation by Barrows Mussey published as *Danger on the Mountain,* Duell, Sloan & Pearce, 1960; *De Geschiedenis van Noord-Amerika,* van Dishoeck, 1959, translation by Marieke Clarke published as *The Story of America,* Thomas Nelson, 1967; *De Franse Revolutie,* Fibula-van Dishoeck, 1961; (with K. Sprey) *Het romeinse Keizerrijk,* Fibula-van Dishoeck, 1961; *De Geschiedenis van Napoleon,* Fibula-van Dishoeck, 1963; *De Grote sagen van de donkere middeleeuwen,* Fibula-van Dishoeck, 1963; *De Geschiedenis van Rusland,* Fibula-van Dishoeck, 1965; *Koning Arthur,* van Holkema & Warendorf, 1967, translation published as *King Arthur,* Lutterworth, 1971; *Boris,* van Holkema & Warendorf, circa 1967, translation by Martha Mearns published under same title, Blackie & Son, 1969, Delacorte, 1970; *Altijd, overal, iedereen: Het Nederlandsche Roode Kruis 100 jaar* (history of Netherlands Red Cross), Callenbach, 1967; *Bart: Lumberjack in Canada,* van Holkema & Warendorf, 1968; *Bart met geologen naar de Yukon,* van Holkema & Warendorf, 1968; *De zes Falken,* Callenbach, 1968.

Juvenile: "Saskia en Jeroen" series, ten books, van Holkema & Warendorf; "Ernstjan en Snabbeltje" series, nine books, van Holkema & Warendorf, one title in series, translated by Barrows Mussey, published as *Duck Dutch,* Duell, Sloan & Pearce, 1962; "Eelke" series, nine books, van Holkema & Warendorf; "Lotje" series, twelve books, van Holkema & Warendorf, two titles in series, translated by Martha

Mearns, published in England as *Judy at the Zoo,* Blackie & Son, 1969, and *Judy and the Baby Elephant,* Blackie & Son, 1970; (with Rien Poortvliet) *Het Sinterklaasboek,* van Holkema & Warendorf, 1969; (with Poortvliet) *Het Kerstboek,* van Holkema & Warendorf, 1970; *The Little World of Beer Ligthart,* van Holkema & Warendorf, 1973.

Adult: *Geschiedenis van de lage landen,* four volumes, Fibula-van Dishoeck, 1970; *Jacob Simonsz: De rijk, watergeus,* van Holkema & Warendorf, 1972.

Also author of film scripts and radio and television plays.

*SIDELIGHTS:* Jaap ter Haar's books for young people have been translated into ten languages. He has visited America at the invitation of the Department of State and Russia as a guest of the Soviet Writers Union.

*AVOCATIONAL INTERESTS:* Gardening, the theater, films.†

\*    \*    \*

## TERRY, Mark 1947-

*PERSONAL:* Born February 24, 1947, in Seattle, Wash.; son of Roy H. (an artist) and Dorothy (Pride) Terry; married Catherine Burnell, June 19, 1971. *Education:* Attended Pomona College, 1965-67; University of Washington, Seattle, B.A. (cum laude, with distinction), 1969, graduate study, 1975-76; Cornell University, M.A.T., 1971. *Politics:* Independent. *Religion:* Independent. *Residence:* Mercer Island, Wash. *Agent:* Curtis Brown Ltd., 575 Madison Ave., New York, N.Y. 10022. *Office:* Overlake School, 20301 Northeast 108th St., Redmond, Wash. 98052.

*CAREER:* Teacher of human ecology and evolutionary anthropology for Project: Open Future, in high schools in California, 1968-71, and teacher of biology in Portland, Oregon, high school, 1970-71; John Muir Institute for Environmental Studies, Seattle, Wash., conference coordinator, 1971; Oakwood School, North Hollywood, Calif., teacher of social science, 1972-75; Overlake School, Redmond, Wash., science teacher, 1976—. Instructor in environmental education, University of Washington, Seattle, summers, 1976, 1977. *Member:* International Primate Protection League, American Association for the Advancement of Science, Friends of the Earth, Phi Beta Kappa, Phi Delta Kappa.

*WRITINGS:* *Teaching for Survival,* Ballantine, 1971; (with Paul Witt) *Energy and Order,* Friends of the Earth, 1976. Contributor of articles to national magazines, including *Natural History* and *Today's Girl.*

*WORK IN PROGRESS:* Revised edition of *Teaching for Survival;* planning teacher workshops in environmental education.

*AVOCATIONAL INTERESTS:* Has explored wilderness areas in Olympic Mountains, San Rafael wilderness in California, and the Grand Canyon, and has a "great interest in expanding this experience."

\*    \*    \*

## TERRY, Robert W(illiam) 1937-

*PERSONAL:* Born October 5, 1937, in Port Jefferson, N.Y.; son of Isaac (a railroad engineer) and Lillian (Pendleton) Terry; children: Steven James. *Education:* Cornell University, B.S., 1959; Colgate Rochester Divinity School, B.D., 1963; University of Chicago Divinity School, M.A., 1966, Ph.D. candidate, 1972. *Home:* 512 South Main St., Adrian, Mich. 49221. *Office:* 928 Cresenwood Blvd., East Lansing, Mich. 48823.

CAREER: Clergyman of the American Baptist Church; Detroit Industrial Mission, Detroit, Mich., associate director, 1967-73; partner, Neely, Campbell, Gibb, Terry & Dosor, 1973-76; Organizational Leadership, Inc., East Lansing, Mich., partner, 1976—. Visiting lecturer in social ethics, University of Windsor, Windsor, Ontario, 1967-68, and University of Detroit, 1968-70. Member: American Society of Christian Ethics, Michigan Organizational Development Network.

WRITINGS: For Whites Only, Eerdmans, 1970.

WORK IN PROGRESS: Action from the Boundary: An Historical Study of Detroit Industrial Mission: 1956-70.

\* \* \*

## TeSELLE, Eugene (Arthur, Jr.) 1931-

PERSONAL: Born August 8, 1931, in Ames, Iowa; son of Eugene Arthur and Hildegaard (Flynn) TeSelle; married Sallie McFague (a professor), September 12, 1959 (divorced, October, 1976); children: Elizabeth, John. Education: University of Colorado, B.A., 1952; Princeton Theological Seminary, B.D., 1955; Yale University, M.A., 1960, Ph.D., 1963. Politics: Democrat. Home: 2007 Linden Ave., Nashville, Tenn. 37212. Office: Divinity School, Vanderbilt University, Nashville, Tenn. 37240.

CAREER: Ordained Presbyterian minister, 1955; Yale University, New Haven, Conn., instructor, 1962-66, assistant professor of religious studies, 1966-69; Vanderbilt University, Divinity School, Nashville, Tenn., associate professor, 1969-74, professor of church history and theology, 1974—. Member: American Academy of Religion, American Society for Church History, Society for Values in Higher Education.

WRITINGS: Augustine the Theologian, Herder & Herder, 1970; Augustine's Strategy as an Apologist, Villanova University Press, 1974; Christ in Context, Fortress, 1975.

WORK IN PROGRESS: The Emerging Religious Situation.

BIOGRAPHICAL/CRITICAL SOURCES: Christian Century, April 28, 1971.

\* \* \*

## TEZLA, Albert 1915-

PERSONAL: Born December 13, 1915, in South Bend, Ind.; son of Michael and Lucia (Szenasi) Tezla; married Olive Anna Fox (a psychiatric nurse), July 26, 1941; children: Michael William, Kathy Elaine. Education: University of Chicago, B.A., 1941, M.A., 1947, Ph.D., 1952. Home: 5412 London Rd., Duluth, Minn. 55804. Office: Department of English, University of Minnesota, Duluth, Minn. 55812.

CAREER: Employed during his early career as shipping clerk, lathe operator, and secondary teacher; Indiana University, South Bend, instructor in English literature in Extension Division, 1946-48; University of Minnesota, Duluth, insructor, 1949-53, assistant professor, 1953-56, associate professor, 1956-61, professor of English, 1961—. Columbia University, visiting professor of Hungarian literature, 1966, visiting scholar, 1975. Military service: U.S. Navy, 1942-46; became lieutenant; received Purple Heart and Commendation Medal. Member: American Association of University Professors. Awards, honors: Fulbright research fellow in Vienna, 1959-60; American Council of Learned Societies grants, 1961, 1968; Inter-University Committee research

fellow in Budapest, 1963-64; Outstanding Teacher Award, University of Minnesota Student Association, Duluth, 1965; commemorative medal from Institute of Cultural Relations (Budapest), 1970, for contributions to the knowledge of Hungarian culture in the United States; International Research and Exchanges Board research fellowship, 1978; National Endowment for the Humanities research grant, 1978-81.

WRITINGS: An Introductory Bibliography to the Study of Hungarian Literature, Harvard University Press, 1964; (contributor) East Central Europe: A Guide to Basic Publications, University of Chicago Press, 1969; Hungarian Authors: A Bibliographical Handbook, Belknap Press, 1970. Contributor to New Hungarian Quarterly.

WORK IN PROGRESS: Translations of short stories, a novel, The Fifth Seal, and a play, "Night"; Ocean at the Window: An Anthology of Recent Hungarian Literature; The Hazardous Quest: The Hungarian Immigrant Experience in the United States in Letters and Documents; A History of Hungarian Literature during the Nineteenth Century.

\* \* \*

## THACKREY, Russell I. 1904-

PERSONAL: Born December 6, 1904, in Kansas City, Kan.; son of Samuel Isaac (a government employee) and Carrie May (Richards) Thackrey; married Emily E. Sheppeard, June 29, 1928; children: Elizabeth Ann (Mrs. Hardy D. Berry). Education: Kansas State Agricultural College, (now Kansas State University), B.S., 1927, M.S., 1932; University of Minnesota, part-time graduate study, 1938-40. Religion: Episcopalian. Home and office: 510 N St. N.W., Apt. N523, Washington, D.C. 20024.

CAREER: Newspaper reporter in Memphis, Tenn., Wichita, Kan., and Omaha, Neb., 1927-28; Kansas State University of Agriculture and Applied Science (now Kansas State University), Manhattan, instructor, 1928-32, assistant professor of journalism and newspaper correspondent, 1932-35; Associated Press, reporter in Kansas City, Mo., 1935-36, legislative correspondent in Jefferson City, Mo., 1937; University of Minnesota, Minneapolis, assistant professor of journalism, 1937-40; Kansas State University of Agriculture and Applied Science, professor of journalism and head of department, 1940-44, dean of administration and director of Summer School, 1944-47; National Association of State Universities and Land-Grant Colleges, Washington, D.C., executive director, 1947-70, director emeritus, 1970—; freelance writer and consultant, 1970—. National 4-H Club Foundation, secretary and treasurer, 1949-50, chairman of policy committee, Washington International Center, Washington, D.C., 1951-56; member of advisory committee on university relations, Agency for International Development; member of President John F. Kennedy's Task Force on Education, 1960. Military service: U.S. Naval Reserve, active duty, 1943-44; became lieutenant; retired as lieutenant commander.

MEMBER: Nation Press Club, Sigma Delta Chi, Sigma Alpha Epsilon, Scabbard and Blade. Awards, honors: LL.D. from University of New Hampshire and University of Maine, 1955, University of Arkansas, 1959; Kansas State University, 1961, Michigan State University, 1965, University of Wisconsin and University of Vermont, 1970; D.H.L. from University of Delaware, 1961. Presidential award of American College Public Relations Association for service to higher education, 1969.

WRITINGS: The Future of the State University, University of Illinois Press, 1971. Contributor to education and government journals. Revived and edited Kansas Magazine, 1933-35, 1940-43.

WORK IN PROGRESS: Writing on the financing of higher education and on other problems in education.

AVOCATIONAL INTERESTS: Gardening.

*    *    *

**THAYLER, Carl 1933-**

PERSONAL: Born April 29, 1933, in Los Angeles, Calif.; son of Ben and Jean (Rosensweig) Thayler; married Marcia Ann Katz, March 28, 1964; children: Emily Margaret. Education: Kenyon College, B.A., 1968; University of Wisconsin, graduate study, 1968-72.

CAREER: Writer. Has participated in Wisconsin Poetry-in-the-Schools program.

WRITINGS—All poetry: The Drivers, Perishable Press, 1969; Some Ground, Modine Gunch Press, 1970; The Mariposa Suite, Tetrad (London), 1971; The Providings: Poems, 1963-1971, Sumac Press, 1971; Goodrich and the Haggard Ode and the Disfiguration, Capricorn Press, 1972. Also author of a play, "Grail."

WORK IN PROGRESS: More poetry; Trophies, a novel.†

*    *    *

**THEOBALD, Robert 1929-**

PERSONAL: Born June 11, 1929, in Madras, India; son of Raymond and Irene (Pulleine) Theobald; married J. M. Scott. Education: Cambridge University, M.A., 1952; Harvard University, additional study, 1957-58. Home and office: Box 2240, 153½ Jefferson St., Wickenburg, Ariz. 85358.

CAREER: Self-employed socioeconomist. Military service: British Army, 1946-48; became second lieutenant.

WRITINGS: The Rich and the Poor, C. N. Potter, 1960; The Challenge of Abundance, C. N. Potter, 1961; Free Men and Free Markets, C. N. Potter, 1963; (editor) The Guaranteed Income: Next Step in Economic Evolution?, Doubleday, 1966; (editor) Social Policies for America in the Seventies: Nine Divergent Views, Doubleday, 1968; (editor) Committed Spending: A Route to Economic Security, Doubleday, 1968, published as Middle Class Support, Swallow Press, 1972; An Alternative Future for America (essays and speeches), Swallow Press, 1968.

The Economics of Abundance: A Noninflationary Future, Pitman, 1970; An Alternative Future for America II (further essays and speeches), Swallow Press, 1970; (with wife, J. M. Scott) Teg's 1944, Swallow Press, 1972; Futures Conditional, Bobbs-Merrill, 1972; Habit and Habitat, Prentice-Hall, 1972; (with Stephanie Mills) The Failure of Success, Bobbs-Merrill, 1974; Beyond Despair, New Republic, 1976; An Alternative Future for America's Third Century, Swallow Press, 1976. General editor, "Dialogue" series, seven books, Bobbs-Merrill, 1968.

WORK IN PROGRESS: Building the Communications Era.

SIDELIGHTS: Robert Theobald told CA: "I can write because this is one of the ways that I can find to try to help people understand the speed and intensity of the transition between the industrial era and the communications era. This process of change which surrounds all of us will eventually change all our styles of communication. But for the moment we must do the best we can with the tools that we have available to us.

"I am distressed because it seems to me that the whole publishing field has been commercialized to the point that the new young, serious writer has even less chance than used to exist to be recognized. I am distressed because our schools and colleges do little to help people to understand how to read with understanding.

"I hope to find ways to communicate better with my readers and to receive their feedback. My wife and I have tried in many ways, particularly in our participation book Teg's 1944, to get readers to let us know their thinking. It's hard to break through the accumulated traditions which keep the author at a distance."

AVOCATIONAL INTERESTS: Riding, gardening, cats.

BIOGRAPHICAL/CRITICAL SOURCES: New York Times, September 10, 1968.

*    *    *

**THOMAS, Conrad Ward 1914-**

PERSONAL: Born March 24, 1914, in Spokane, Wash.; son of John Nickolas (a shipbuilder) and Stella M. (Sargent) Thomas; married Jeanne Brandenberg, 1944 (divorced, 1955); married Catherine Walsh, 1963 (divorced, 1967); children: (first marriage) Judith, Carol; (second marriage) Jay. Education: University of California, Berkeley, B.S. (with honors), 1936; Columbia University, M.B.A., 1968. Home and office: 11901 Sunset Blvd., Los Angeles, Calif. 90049.

CAREER: Worked internationally in mining engineering and management, 1936-57, and as a consulting mining engineer in Houston, Rome, Madrid, and New York, 1957-68; Thomas Management & Research, Los Angeles, Calif., president, 1968—; Conrad Ward Thomas & Associates (financial consultants), Los Angeles, president, 1971—. Military service: U.S. Naval Reserve; became lieutenant junior grade. Member: American Institute of Mining, Metallurgical and Petroleum Engineers, Sigma Xi, Theta Tau, Tau Beta Pi. Awards, honors: Ford Foundation New Careers fellow, 1967.

WRITINGS: Hedgemanship: How to Make Money in Bear Markets, Bull Markets and Chicken Markets While Confounding Professional Money Managers and Attracting a Better Class of Women, Dow Jones-Irwin, 1970; Risk and Opportunity: A New Approach to Stock Market Profits, Dow Jones-Irwin, 1974; How to Sell Short and Perform Other Wondrous Feats, Dow Jones-Irwin, 1976. Contributor to Barron's.

WORK IN PROGRESS: Utopia; Disaster at Wall Street and Random Walk; research on investment and risk and opportunity measurement.

AVOCATIONAL INTERESTS: Oceanography, the environment, conservation, utopia, international travel.

*    *    *

**THOMAS, Gordon L. 1914-**

PERSONAL: Born December 4, 1914, in Orpington, Kent, England; U.S. citizen; son of Reginald H. and Amelia (Lawrie) Thomas; married Phyllis Marie Lenzner (a journalist), June 21, 1941; children: David A., Kathleen M. (Mrs. Richard Field). Education: Albion College, B.A., 1936; Michigan State University, M.A., 1941; Northwestern University, Ph.D., 1952. Home: 334 North Hagadorn Rd., East Lansing, Mich. 48823. Office: 424 South Kedzie, Michigan State University, East Lansing, Mich. 48824.

CAREER: High school teacher of speech and English in Fenton, Mich., 1936-39; University of Miami, Coral Gables, Fla., instructor in speech and English, 1941-42; Michigan State University, East Lansing, instructor, 1945-52, assistant professor, 1952-56, associate professor, 1956-60, professor of speech, 1960-69, associate chairman of department of communication, 1968-69, assistant dean of communication arts for continuing education, 1969-71, professor, Office of the Dean of Communication Arts, and assistant dean of continuing education, 1971-73, secretary for academic governance, 1973—. City of East Lansing, member of city council, 1959-61, mayor, 1961-71. President, Michigan Municipal League, 1966-67; member of executive board, National League of Cities, 1968-71; president, Michigan Conference of Mayors, 1971; member of Michigan Governor's Commission on Local Government. Staff member of seminars in communication, Agency for International Development, 1958—. Military service: U.S. Army Air Forces, 1941-43. Member: Speech Association of America, Central States Speech Association, Michigan Speech Association, Delta Sigma Rho, Pi Kappa Delta, Phi Kappa Phi.

WRITINGS: (Contributor) David Potter, editor, Argumentation and Debate, Dryden, 1954; (contributor) Haig A. Boxmajian, editor, The Rhetoric of the Speaker, Heath, 1967; (with Potter) The Colonial Idiom, Southern Illinois University Press, 1970. Contributor to speech journals.

SIDELIGHTS: Gordon Thomas traveled and studied in Mexico, 1959, and in Europe, 1965-66.

*   *   *

THOMAS, Keith (Vivian) 1933-

PERSONAL: Born January 2, 1933, in Wick, Glamorganshire, South Wales; son of Vivian Jones (a farmer) and Hilda (Davies) Thomas; married Valerie Little (a teacher), 1961; children: Emily, Edmund. Education: Balliol College, Oxford, M.A., 1959. Office: St. John's College, Oxford University, Oxford OX1 3JP, England.

CAREER: Oxford University, Oxford, England, fellow of All Souls College, 1955-57, tutor in modern history at St. John's College, 1957-78, university reader in modern history, 1978—. Military service: Royal Welsh Fusiliers, 1950-52. Member: Royal Historical Society (fellow; literary director, 1970-75). Awards, honors: Wolfson Literary Award for History, 1972, for Religion and the Decline of Magic.

WRITINGS: Religion and the Decline of Magic, Scribner, 1971; Rule and Misrule in the Schools of Early Modern England, University of Reading, 1976; Age and Authority in Early Modern England, British Academy, 1976.

Contributor: A. Noland and P. P. Wiener, editors, Ideas in Cultural Perspective, Rutgers University Press, 1962; K. C. Brown, editor, Hobbes Studies, Basil Blackwell, 1965; T. Aston, editor, Crisis in Europe, Routledge & Kegan Paul, 1965; K. Miller, editor, Writing in England Today, Penguin, 1968; M. Douglas, editor, Witchcraft Confessions and Accusations, Tavistock Publications, 1970; G. E. Aylmer, editor, The Interregnum, Macmillan, 1972. Contributor of articles and reviews to learned periodicals and weekly newspapers. Member of editorial board, Past and Present.

WORK IN PROGRESS: Social and intellectual history of sixteenth and seventeenth-century England.

*   *   *

THOMAS, Patricia J. 1934-

PERSONAL: Born January 26, 1934, in Sandy Lake, Pa.; daughter of Raeman Carl (a teacher) and Irene (Lee-Griffin) Jack; married Edward W. Thomas (a comptroller), June 28, 1955; children: Terri Lee, Suzanne Gail, William Raeman, Robert Stuart. Education: Attended Westminster College, New Wilmington, Pa., 1952; Pennsylvania State University, B.S., 1956. Politics: Republican. Religion: Church of Jesus Christ of Latter-day Saints (Mormon). Home address: Box 213, East Butler, Pa. 16029.

CAREER: Spencer Gifts, Inc., Atlantic City, N.J., advertising copywriter, beginning 1969. Publicity director, Power Squadron Auxiliary.

WRITINGS: "Stand Back," Said the Elephant, "I'm Going to Sneeze" (juvenile), illustrated by Wallace Tripp, Lothrop, 1971.

WORK IN PROGRESS: Children's books.

AVOCATIONAL INTERESTS: Camping, water sports, volunteer work with Girl Scouts.†

*   *   *

THOMAS, Peter 1928-

PERSONAL: Born May 11, 1928, in Gloucester, England; son of Archibald Donald (a painter-decorator) and Lucy Eleanor Ann (Packer) Thomas; married Brigid Eyres, June 26, 1966 (divorced September, 1973); children: Patrick Dylan, Isobel Arwen. Education: Magdalen College, Oxford, B.A. (honors), 1950, M.A., 1954; Hampshire School of Drama, additional study, 1955-56. Home: 620 Sheridan Dr., Sault Ste. Marie, Mich. 49783. Office: Department of English, Lake Superior State College, Sault Ste. Marie, Mich. 49783.

CAREER: Ringwood Grammar School for Boys, Bournemouth, England, senior master in English and history and deputy headmaster, 1954-56; Court House School for Maladjusted Children, Painswick, Gloucestershire, England, headmaster, 1957; Opoku Ware Secondary School for Boys, Kumasi, Ghana, senior English master, 1958-60; University of Nigeria, Nsukka, lecturer, 1960-63, senior lecturer in English, 1963-65, director of student drama, 1960-64, director of creative writing (verse), 1961-65; University of Utah, Salt Lake City, visiting lecturer in literature and imaginative writing, 1965-68; Mackinac College, Mackinac Island, Mich., junior fellow in English, 1968-69; Lake Superior State College, Sault Ste. Marie, Mich., associate professor, 1969-71, professor of English and humanities, 1971—. British Council lecturer in Ghana and Nigeria, 1959-65; broadcaster for Nigerian Broadcasting Corp., 1961-65. Michigan State Council for the Arts, travelling reader and lecturer for Poetry Michigan, beginning 1969, member of literature committee, 1970-75. Has read his poetry at various poetry readings, seminars, and workshops; has read poetry on many radio programs.

MEMBER: Unicorn Questers Association (founding member). Awards, honors: Poetry prizes from Pennsylvania State Poetry Society, 1966, Utah State Institute of Fine Arts, 1967, Arizona State Poetry Society, 1970, and Southern Writers' Conference, 1970; National Endowment for the Humanities fellowship, 1978; the Peter Thomas collection at Mugar Memorial Library of Boston University was started in 1969.

WRITINGS: Poems from Nigeria, Vantage, 1967; Sun Bells, Unicorn Hunters Press, 1974; (compiler and editor with Philip Bordinat) Revealer of Secrets: Southern Nigerian Folk Tales, African Universities Press, 1975. Writer of radio scripts for Nigerian network and for radio stations in Detroit, Mich. and Sault Ste. Marie, Ontario. Contributor of more than nine hundred poems, articles, and reviews to

*Western Humanities Review, Roanoke Review, Detroit News, Poetry Venture, Galley Sail Review, Africa Report, African Arts,* and other publications in the United States, Europe, India, and West Africa. Editor of "Poet's Corner" column for *Sault Evening News,* 1969-73; editor, *Woods-Runner,* 1970—.

*WORK IN PROGRESS:* Articles on Christopher Okigbo and Wole Soyinka and their place in Nigerian literature; a study of the western novel and western movie as forms of American frontier mythology; *Earth Mother and the Myth Manipulators,* an inquiry into the uses made by modern poets and scholars of ancient goddess myths and cults.

*SIDELIGHTS:* Peter Thomas took his honors degree in England at Oxford University under the author and scholar, C. S. Lewis. He told *CA* that his recent studies have "renewed my interest in 'Muse poets,' the White Goddess, and Arthurian romances by modern novelists."

\* \* \*

### THOMPSON, Donald Neil 1939-

*PERSONAL:* Born April 11, 1939, in Winnipeg, Manitoba, Canada. *Education:* University of Manitoba, B.A., 1959; University of California, Berkeley, Ph.D., 1968. *Home:* 348 Walmer Rd., Toronto, Ontario, Canada. *Office:* Faculty of Administrative Studies, York University, Toronto, Ontario, Canada.

*CAREER:* University of Alberta, Edmonton, associate professor of economics, 1967-69; Harvard University, Cambridge, Mass., senior fellow, 1970-71; York University, Toronto, Ontario, professor of economics, 1971—. Visiting professor, Long Island University, 1969-70. Chief economist and director of research, Royal Commission on Corporate Concentration, 1975-77. Advisor to governments of United States, Canada, Israel, Thailand, and Laos. *Member:* American Economic Association, American Marketing Association.

*WRITINGS: Contractual Marketing Systems,* Heath, 1971; *Franchise Operations and Antitrust Economics,* Heath, 1971; *The Economics of Environmental Protection,* Winthrop, 1972; *Canadian Marketing: Problems and Prospects,* Wiley, 1972; *Problems in Canadian Marketing,* American Marketing Association, 1977.

\* \* \*

### THOMPSON, Ian B(entley) 1936-

*PERSONAL:* Born January 2, 1936, in Yorkshire, England; son of Frank and Winifred (Booth) Thompson; married Helene Marie Lamerant, July 11, 1961; children: Veronique, Marianne, Brigitte, Catherine. *Education:* University of Durham, Durham, England, B.A., 1957, Ph.D., 1960; Indiana University, A.M., 1958. *Home:* 132 Dowanhill St., Glasgow G12, Scotland. *Office:* Department of Geography, University of Glasgow, Glasgow G12 8QQ, Scotland.

*CAREER:* University of Leeds, Leeds, England, assistant lecturer in geography, 1959-62; University of Southampton, Southampton, England, lecturer, 1962-72, senior lecturer, 1972-74, reader in geography, 1974-75; University of Glasgow, Glasgow, Scotland, professor of geography, 1976—. *Member:* Institute of British Geographers.

*WRITINGS: The St. Malo Region, Brittany,* Geographical Field Group, 1968; *Modern France: A Social and Economic Geography,* Butterworth & Co., 1970, Rowman & Littlefield, 1971, revised translation by author published as *La France: Population, Economie, et Regions,* Douin Editeurs

(Paris), 1973; *Corsica,* Praeger, 1971; *The Paris Basin,* Oxford University Press, 1973; *France: A Geographical Study,* Martin Robertson, 1973; *The Lower Rhone and Marseille,* Oxford University Press, 1975. Editor, "Studies in Industrial Geography" series.

*WORK IN PROGRESS:* Research on Mediterranean France and Algeria.

\* \* \*

### THOMPSON, Joe Allen 1936-

*PERSONAL:* Born February 4, 1936, in Carnduff, Saskatchewan, Canada; U.S. citizen; son of T. F. (a pulp mill manager) and Mary (Chrest) Thompson; married Danielle M. Baetens (a university instructor), September 2, 1964; children: Emily Eve, Andrew Allen. *Education:* Walla Walla College, B.A., 1958; Stanford University, M.A., 1960, Ph.D., 1966. *Home:* 773 Lansdowne Cir., Lexington, Ky. 40502. *Office:* Department of History, University of Kentucky, Lexington, Ky. 40506.

*CAREER:* University of Nevada, Reno, instructor in history, 1963-64; University of Arizona, Tucson, instructor in history, 1964-66; University of Kentucky, Lexington, assistant professor, 1966-72, associate professor of history, 1972—, chairman of department, 1976—. *Member:* American Historical Association, Conference of British Studies.

*WRITINGS:* (Editor) *The Collapse of the British Liberal Party,* Heath, 1969; (with Arthur Mejia, Jr.) *The Modern British Monarchy,* St. Martin's, 1971. Contributor to history journals in America, Australia, and England.

*WORK IN PROGRESS:* A monograph on Lord Robert Cecil and the British League of Nations Union and a study of *Traditional Conservatism: Six Perspectives.*

\* \* \*

### THOMPSON, Karl F. 1917-

*PERSONAL:* Born December 31, 1917, in York, Pa.; son of Charles W. (a newspaper editor) and Virginia (Pfeiffer) Thompson; married Jean Adie (a social worker), May 2, 1942; children: Virginia (Mrs. Robert Bemis), David C., Elizabeth A. *Education:* Yale University, B.A., 1941, M.A., 1942, Ph.D., 1950. *Religion:* Episcopalian. *Home:* 550 Collingwood Dr., East Lansing, Mich. 48823. *Office:* Department of Humanities, Michigan State University, East Lansing, Mich. 48823.

*CAREER:* Oberlin College, Oberlin, Ohio, instructor in English, 1948-53; Michigan State University, East Lansing, assistant professor, 1953-59, associate professor, 1959-64, professor of humanities, 1964—, chairman of department, 1968—. *Military service:* U.S. Army Air Forces, 1942-46; became captain. *Member:* Renaissance Society of America, Modern Language Association of America, Phi Beta Kappa, Phi Kappa Phi. *Awards, honors:* Guggenheim fellowship; Folger Library research fellowship.

*WRITINGS:* (Editor) *Classics of Western Thought: Middle Ages, Renaissance, and Reformation,* Harcourt, 1964, revised edition, 1973; *Modesty and Cunning: Shakespeare's Use of Literary Tradition,* University of Michigan Press, 1971. Contributor to literature journals.

*WORK IN PROGRESS:* Further research on Shakespeare.

\* \* \*

### THOMPSON, Laurence G(raham) 1920-

*PERSONAL:* Born July 9, 1920, in Ichowfu, Shantung,

China; U.S. citizen; son of Kenneth K. (an educational missionary) and Bernice (Archer) Thompson; married Grace Russell (a registered nurse), May 29, 1943; children: Ralph L., Kenneth A., Andrew M., Laurie L., Leslie N. *Education:* University of California, Los Angeles, B.A., 1942; Claremont College (now Claremont Graduate School), M.A., 1947, Ph.D., 1954; University of Colorado, graduate study, summer, 1947, summer and fall, 1948. *Home:* 5515 Medea Valley Dr., Agoura, Calif. 91301. *Office:* Department of East Asian Languages and Cultures, Founders Hall 405, University of Southern California, University Park, Los Angeles, Calif. 90007.

*CAREER:* Teacher of social studies and music in public and private schools in California and Colorado, 1946-51; U.S. Foreign Service, cultural attache at American Embassy, Taipei, Taiwan, 1951-53, staff officer in Tokyo, Japan, Singapore, Manila, Philippines, and Hong Kong, 1954-56; Asia Foundation, representative in Korea, 1956-58, in Taiwan, 1958-59; Taiwan Normal University, Taipei, professor of music, 1959-62; Pomona College, Pomona, Calif., visiting assistant professor of Oriental affairs, 1962-63, of Chinese language and literature, 1963-64, assistant professor of Chinese language and literature, 1964-65; University of Southern California, Los Angeles, assistant professor, 1965-67, associate professor, 1967-70, professor of East Asian languages and cultures, 1970—, chairman of department, 1968-70, 1972-76, director, East Asian Studies Center, 1972-76. Visiting professor, California State College (now University), Los Angeles, 1967, summer, 1969; visiting summer professor, California State College, (now University), Fullerton, 1968; visiting professor, University of California, Santa Barbara, 1974. *Military service:* U.S. Marine Corps, 1942-45. U.S. Marine Corps Reserve, 1945-55; became captain. *Member:* Association for Asian Studies, American Oriental Society, Royal Asiatic Society.

*WRITINGS:* (Translator from the French) O. Briere, *Fifty Years of Chinese Philosophy, 1898-1950,* Allen & Unwin, 1956, revised edition, with Dennis Doolan, Praeger, 1965; (translator from the Chinese, and author of introduction and notes) *Ta T'ung Shu: The One-World Philosophy of K'ang Yu-Wei,* Allen & Unwin, 1958; (contributor) J. P. Lo, editor, *K'ang Yu-Wei: A Biography and a Symposium,* University of Arizona Press, 1967; *Chinese Religion: An Introduction,* Dickenson, 1969, 2nd edition, 1975; (editor and contributor) *The Chinese Way in Religion,* Dickenson, 1973; (editor and contributor) *Studia Asiatica: Essays in Felicitation of the Seventy-fifth Anniversary of Professor Ch'en Shou-yi,* Chinese Materials Center, 1975; (compiler) *Studies of Chinese Religion: A Comprehensive and Classified Bibliography of Publications in English, French, and German through 1970,* Dickenson, 1976. Contributor to journals of Asian studies.

*WORK IN PROGRESS:* Translating and editing a contemporary Chinese history of Chinese thought; research and studies aimed at constructing a general theory of Chinese religion; collecting materials for a supplement to *Studies of Chinese Religion.*

\* \* \*

## THOMPSON, Lewis 1915(?)-1972

1915(?)—July 20, 1972; American public relations aide and mystery writer. Obituaries: *New York Times,* July 21, 1972; *Washington Post,* July 24, 1972.

## THOMPSON, Neville 1938-

*PERSONAL:* Born September 5, 1938, in England; married Gail Ann Pidgeon, May 30, 1970. *Education:* McMaster University, B.A., 1962; Princeton University, A.M., 1964, Ph.D., 1967. *Home:* 364 Windermere Rd., London, Ontario, Canada N6G 2K2. *Office:* Department of History, University of Western Ontario, London, Ontario, Canada N6A 3K7.

*CAREER:* Huron College, London, Ontario, lecturer, 1965-67, assistant professor of history, 1967-70; McMaster University, Hamilton, Ontario, assistant professor, 1970-72, associate professor of history, 1972-73; University of Western Ontario, London, associate professor of history, 1973—, chairperson of department, 1973-78.

*WRITINGS: The Anti-Appeasers: Conservative Opposition to Appeasement in the 1930's,* Oxford University Press, 1971.

*WORK IN PROGRESS: Wellington after Waterloo: A Fourth Estate in the Empire.*

\* \* \*

## THOMPSON, Travis I. 1937-

*PERSONAL:* Born July 20, 1937, in Minneapolis, Minn.; son of William Raymond and Loretta (Travis) Thompson; married Sharon Barbara Powers, June 26, 1955; married second wife, Anna Bianca Leyens (a special education coordinator), June 12, 1970; children: Rebecca Lynn, Jennifer Eva, Andrea Laura, Peter Erich. *Education:* University of Minnesota, B.A., 1958, M.A., and Ph.D., 1961. *Home:* 1595 Vincent St., St. Paul, Minn. 55108. *Office:* Department of Psychology, Elliott Hall, University of Minnesota, Minneapolis, Minn. 55455.

*CAREER:* University of Minnesota, Minneapolis, assistant professor, 1963-66, associate professor, 1966-69, professor of psychology, 1969—. Visiting lecturer at Psychologiska Institutionen, University of Uppsala, 1972; visiting lecturer at University of Otago, University of Auckland, and University of Christchurch, New Zealand, 1974. Consultant to U.S. Food and Drug Administration, 1966—, to Partners of the Alliance for Progress, Sao Paulo, Brazil, 1971, and to Illinois Committee on Problems of Drug Dependence. *Member:* American Psychological Association (president of Division 28, 1972; fellow), Behavioral Pharmacology Society (president, 1972), American Association for the Advancement of Science (fellow), Association for the Advancement of Behavior Therapy, American Association for Mental Deficiency. *Awards, honors:* National Science Foundation postdoctoral fellow at Psychopharmacological Laboratory, University of Maryland, 1961-63; U.S. Public Health Service special postdoctoral fellow at Cambridge University, 1967-68.

*WRITINGS:* (With C. R. Schuster) *Behavioral Pharmacology,* Prentice-Hall, 1968; (editor with Roy Pickens and Richard Meisch) *Readings in Behavioral Pharmacology,* Appleton, 1970; (with Pickens) *Stimulus Properties of Drugs,* Appleton, 1971; (with John Grabowski) *Reinforcement Schedules and Multioperant Analysis,* Appleton, 1972; (with Grabowski) *Behavior Modification for the Mentally Retarded,* Oxford University Press, 1972, 2nd edition, 1977; (with W. S. Dockens) *Applications of Behavior Modification,* Academic Press, 1975; (with P. Dews) *Advances in Behavioral Pharmacology,* Academic Press, 1977; (with K. Unna) *Predicting Dependence Liability of Stimulant and Depressant Drugs,* University Park Press, 1977. Contributor to professional journals. Editorial consultant for *Psychopharmacology, Journal of Pharmacology and Experimental Therapeutics, Journal of Experimental Analysis of Behavior, Journal of Applied Behavior Analysis, Behavior Therapy,* and *Mental Retardation.*

*WORK IN PROGRESS:* Research on behavior modification, on mental retardation, and on drug dependence; *Autism: A Guide for Parents,* with wife, A. Thompson; *Teaching Your Retarded Child,* with J. Grabowski; *Behavioral and Biological Psychiatry,* with Eric Errickson; a revision of *Behavioral Pharmacology,* with C. R. Schuster; a book of short, common language poems.

*SIDELIGHTS: Behavior Modification for the Mentally Retarded* has been translated into German, and *Behavioral Pharmacology* has been translated into Japanese.

\*          \*          \*

**THOMSEN, Russel J(ohn)   1941-**

*PERSONAL:* Born December 15, 1941, in Chehalis, Wash.; son of Herman I. and Mabel (Anderson) Thomsen; married Tina Johnsen, August 8, 1965; children: Randy, Gregg. *Education:* Walla Walla College, B.A., 1964; Loma Linda University, M.A. and M.D., 1968. *Religion:* Seventh-day Adventist.

*CAREER:* Latter-day Saints Hospital, Salt Lake City, Utah, intern, 1968-69; University of Utah, Salt Lake City, resident in obstetrics and gynecology, beginning 1969. *Military service:* U.S. Army, Medical Reserve, 1968-72; became captain; active duty in Medical Corps, beginning 1972.

*WRITINGS: Latter-day Saints and the Sabbath,* Pacific Press Publishing Association, 1971; *Seventh-day Baptists: Their Legacy to Adventists,* Pacific Press Publishing Association, 1971; *The Bible Book of Medical Wisdom,* Revell, 1974. Contributor to magazines.†

\*          \*          \*

**THORNBURG, Hershel D(ean)   1936-**

*PERSONAL:* Born October 27, 1936, in Wichita, Kan.; son of Ellis E. and Beulah (Morrison) Thornburg; married Glenda Zimmerman, August 10, 1957; married second wife, Ellen Branson (a dental hygienist), January 26, 1968; children: (first marriage) Marcia, Marchel, (second marriage) Konried, Kristen. *Education:* Friends University, B.A., 1959; Wichita State University, M.Ed., 1966; University of Oklahoma, Ed.D., 1967. *Home:* 1201 East Calle Elena, Tucson, Ariz. 85718. *Office:* College of Education, University of Arizona, Tucson, Ariz. 85721.

*CAREER:* Wichita Public Schools, Wichita, Kan., teacher, 1960-65; University of Oklahoma, Norman, instructor in education, 1966-67; University of Arizona, Tucson, associate professor of education, 1967—. *Member:* American Psychological Association, American Educational Research Association, American Association for the Advancement of Science, American Society for Preventive Dentistry, Society for Adolescent Medicine, National Society for the Study of Education, American Association of Teachers of French, National Council of Family Relations, National Entertainment and Campus Activities Association, Western Psychological Association, Rocky Mountain Psychological Association, Southwestern Psychological Association, Arizona State Psychological Association, Phi Delta Kappa.

*WRITINGS: Sex Education in the Public Schools,* Arizona Education Association, 1969; *An Investigation of Attitudes among Potential Dropouts from Minority Groups during*

*Their Freshman Year in High School,* U.S. Office of Education, 1971; (editor and contributor) *Contemporary Adolescence: Readings,* Brooks-Cole, 1971, 2nd edition, 1975; *Child Development,* W. C. Brown, 1973; *School Learning and Instruction,* Brooks-Cole, 1973; (editor) *School Learning and Instruction: Readings,* Brooks-Cole, 1973; *Psychological Behavior of the Preadolescent Child,* W. C. Brown, 1973; *Adolescent Development,* W. C. Brown, 1973; *Contemporary Adolescence,* Brooks-Cole, 1975; *You and Your Adolescent,* H.E.L.P. Books, 1977; *Punt, Pop: A Male Sex Role Manual,* H.E.L.P. Books, 1977; *The Preteen Years,* H.E.L.P. Books, 1978; *Youth: Transition Years,* H.E.L.P. Books, 1978.

Contributor to *Arizona Teacher, Journal of School Health, College Student Survey, Sexual Behavior, Psychology in the Schools, Adolescence,* and other professional journals.

*WORK IN PROGRESS:* Revised edition of *Contemporary Adolescence.*

*SIDELIGHTS:* Thornburg told *CA:* "My primary research and writing interest now is the continued development of an adequate instructional theory which will better describe the functions of the classroom teacher. Several research studies designed to confirm many of my theoretical concepts are now under way."

\*          \*          \*

**THORNDIKE, (Arthur) Russell   1885-1972**

February 6, 1885—November 7, 1972; English actor and novelist. Obituaries: *New York Times,* November 9, 1972.

\*          \*          \*

**THUESEN, Gerald J(organ)   1938-**

*PERSONAL:* Born July 20, 1938, in Oklahoma City, Okla.; son of Holger G. (a professor) and Helen Thuesen; married Annette Franey, June 10, 1960; children: Karen Elizabeth, Dyan Louise. *Education:* Stanford University, B.S., 1960, M.S., 1961, Ph.D., 1968. *Home:* 4195 Glen Devon Dr. N.W., Atlanta, Ga. 30327. *Office:* Georgia Institute of Technology, Atlanta, Ga. 30332.

*CAREER:* Pacific Telephone Co., San Francisco, Calif., engineer, 1961-62; Atlantic Refining Co., Dallas, Tex., management engineer, 1962-63; University of Texas at Arlington, assistant professor, 1963-64, 1967-68; Georgia Institute of Technology, Atlanta, professor, 1968—. *Member:* American Institute of Industrial Engineers, Operations Research Society of America, Institute of Management Sciences, American Society for Engineering Education (director, 1977-79), Sigma Xi, Stanford Club of Georgia (president, 1970-71). *Awards, honors:* American Society for Engineering Education-National Aeronautics and Space Administration summer faculty fellowship, 1970; Eugene L. Grant award, 1977.

*WRITINGS:* (With W. J. Fabrycky) *Engineering Economy,* 4th edition (Thuesen was not associated with earlier editions; his father was the original author), Prentice-Hall, 1971, 5th edition, 1977; (with Fabrycky) *Economic Decision Analysis,* Prentice-Hall, 1974. Associate editor, *The Engineering Economist.*

*WORK IN PROGRESS:* Research on uncertainty resolution in sequential capital investment decisions.

*AVOCATIONAL INTERESTS:* Basketball (played at Stanford, 1956-60), volleyball, tennis, jogging.

## TIFFANY, Phyllis G. 1932-

*PERSONAL:* Born July 17, 1932, in Little River, Kan.; daughter of Oliver Preston and Clara Pauline (Crandall) Guthrie; married Donald Wayne Tiffany (a clinical psychologist), June 3, 1961; children: Allen Lloyd, Karen Jo. *Education:* University of Kansas, B.A., 1961, M.A., 1967; Kansas State University, Ph.D., 1978. *Home:* 1401 Ash St., Hays, Kan. 67601. *Office:* Department of Psychology, Fort Hays Kansas State College, Hays, Kan. 67602.

*CAREER:* Training Corp. of America, Falls Church, Va., trainer psychologist, 1967-68, project coordinator, 1968, consultant, 1968-69; self-employed consultant to industry, 1969-71; Fort Hays Kansas State College, Hays, 1970—, began as instructor, currently associate professor of developmental psychology. Member of executive board, The House (refuge for alienated youth). *Member:* American Association of University Professors, Midwest Psychological Association, Rocky Mountain Psychological Association, Kansas Psychological Association, Missouri Psychological Association, Psi Chi.

*WRITINGS:* (With husband, Donald W. Tiffany, and J. Cowase) *The Unemployed: A Social-Psychological Portrait,* Prentice-Hall, 1970. Contributor to professional journals. Associate editor, *Newsletter* of Missouri Psychological Association, 1967-69.

*WORK IN PROGRESS:* With Donald W. Tiffany, a book in the area of experience control; research on the Tiffany Experience Control Scale, tentatively entitled *Don't Drown, We'll Throw You a Life Saver.*

\* \* \*

## TING, Jan C(hing-an) 1948-

*PERSONAL:* Born December 17, 1948, in Ann Arbor, Mich.; son of Sik Woo (a physician) and Ging Mei (Kang) Ting; married Helen Page, July 17, 1971. *Education:* Oberlin College, B.A., 1970; University of Hawaii, M.A., 1972; Harvard University, J.D., 1975. *Agent:* Candida Donadio & Associates, Inc., 111 West 57th St., New York, N.Y. 10019. *Office:* Law School, Temple University, Philadelphia, Pa. 19122.

*CAREER:* Temple University, Law School, Philadelphia, Pa., assistant professor of law, 1977—.

*WRITINGS:* An American in China, Paperback Library, 1972.

*WORK IN PROGRESS:* Current research interests are in subjects relating to American jurisprudence.

*SIDELIGHTS:* Jan Ting has travelled extensively in Asia, and he speaks Mandarin Chinese.

\* \* \*

## TINIC, Seha M(ehmet) 1941-

*PERSONAL:* Born November 23, 1941, in Istanbul, Turkey; son of Cevad Ali (a civil servant) and Nezihe (Bahtoglu) Tinic; married Hale Yorukoglu, August 27, 1964; children: Serra (daughter), Atilla (son). *Education:* Robert College, Istanbul, Turkey, B.A., 1964; University of Tulsa, M.B.A., 1966; Cornell University, Ph.D., 1970. *Religion:* Moslem. *Home:* 4012 125th St., Edmonton, Alberta, Canada. *Office:* Faculty of Business Administration, University of Alberta, Edmonton, Alberta, Canada.

*CAREER:* Middle East Technical University, Ankara, Turkey, instructor in marketing, 1966-70; University of Alberta, Edmonton, 1970—, currently professor of finance and

quantitative methods. *Member:* American Economic Association, Institute of Management Sciences, American Finance Association, Canadian Economic Association, Financial Management Association, Western Finance Association, Phi Kappa Phi.

*WRITINGS:* (With R. R. West) *The Economics of the Stock Market,* Praeger, 1971; (with West) *Investing in Securities: An Efficient Market Approach,* Addison-Wesley, in press. Contributor to economics journals.

*WORK IN PROGRESS:* Research on stochastic decision models and their application in stock market operations.

*AVOCATIONAL INTERESTS:* Travel, sports, reading, music.

\* \* \*

## TOBIAS, Andrew P. 1947-

*PERSONAL:* Born April 20, 1947, in New York, N.Y.; son of Seth D. (chairman of an advertising agency) and Audrey J. (president of a national social service organization) Tobias. *Education:* Harvard University, B.A. (cum laude), 1968, M.B.A., 1972. *Agent:* Sterling Lord Agency, 660 Madison Ave., New York, N.Y. 10021.

*CAREER:* Harvard Student Agencies, Inc., Cambridge, Mass., president, 1967-68; National Student Marketing Corp., New York, N.Y., vice-president, 1968-70.

*WRITINGS:* (Editor) *How to Earn (a Lot of) Money in College,* Harvard Student Agencies, Inc., 1968; (with Arnold Bortz and Caspar Weinberger) *The Ivy League Guidebook,* Macmillan, 1968; *Honor Grades on Fifteen Hours a Week,* Collier, 1969; *The Funny Money Game,* Playboy Press, 1971; *Fire and Ice: The Story of Charles Revson,* Morrow, 1974; *The Only Investment Guide You'll Ever Need,* Harcourt, 1977. Contributor to national magazines, including *This Week, Cosmopolitan, Playboy, Esquire,* and *New York Magazine.* Contributing editor, *New York Magazine,* 1972-76, and *Esquire,* 1977—.

*SIDELIGHTS:* In *The Funny Money Game* Tobias, a former executive, tells of the rise and fall of the small conglomerate firm with which he was associated. In a review of the book, A. John Giunta writes: "The company described here is the National Student Marketing Corporation, NSMC for short, but the story which the author narrates is a very common one. It has happened many times over the last several years as mergers and acquisitions of other companies have become a normal way of business expansion. . . . The book gives the reader an inside view of the conglomerate acquisitions that have dominated the economic scene in recent years, and it points out how a number of them have run into financial difficulties while playing the funny money game." S. W. Clements feels that this "very personal tale of the rise and decline of one of America's growth ventures is perhaps a bit too nostalgic and the two concluding chapters show the benefit of hindsight, which—as every seasoned investor learns sooner or later—carries little material reward. . . . It is saddening to read once more how many people fall for the easy money schemes offered up in various guises."

A reviewer for *Library Journal* feels that *Fire and Ice* "is a readable work, but not exactly the 'classic' one reviewer, quoted on the dust jacket, tells us it is. . . . Tobias seems bent on emphasizing the more negative aspects of Revson's character, suggesting as the basis for most of his behavior an inferiority complex that is the result of small physical stature." D. A. Pietrusza disagrees: "Despite the vehemence with which many of Revson's former employees spoke of him, Tobias declined to issue a blanket condemnation of the man and chose instead to write a book which provides a nicely balanced portrait of this throwback to the Gilded Age.''

*The Only Investment Guide You'll Ever Need* was on the *New York Times* Best Seller List for twenty weeks. In a review for the *Times,* Christopher Lehmann-Haupt says: ''There comes a point in the reading of any financial guide when the mind collapses. This usually happens about the point when the book starts asking you if you've thought of option straddles. Suddenly your head won't take in any more. You realize you've already invested 10 times your hypothetical savings, when in fact, because you still owe Bloomingdale's, there isn't ever going to be even one times your hypothetical savings.... Andrew Tobias, in his witty and succinct *The Only Investment Guide You'll Ever Need,* has a pretty sound explanation for these sinking spells. The guides 'that deal with strategies in commodities or options or gold are too narrow. They tell you how you might play a particular game, but not whether to be playing the game at all. The ones that are encyclopedic, with a chapter on everything, leave you pretty much where you were to begin with—trying to choose from a myriad of competing alternatives.' It's all a matter of organizing your priorities, he believes. And the most basic priority is that before you can start making money through financial investment, you have to figure out how to stop losing money through simple squandering.... What Mr. Tobias has to say here is mostly as rational as a pocket-calculator. It's so full of tips and angles that only a booby or a billionaire could not benefit from it.''

*BIOGRAPHICAL/CRITICAL SOURCES: New York Times,* April 21, 1968, August 25, 1976, February 22, 1978, May 21, 1978; *Kirkus Reviews,* August 15, 1971, June 15, 1976; *New York Times Book Review,* August 24, 1971, July 31, 1977; *Saturday Review,* October 16, 1971; *Best Sellers,* December 1, 1971; *Wall Street Journal,* December 20, 1971, December 8, 1976; *Publishers Weekly,* June 7, 1976, June 20, 1977; *Library Journal,* December 1, 1976; *National Review,* May 27, 1977.

*        *        *

## TOBIAS, Phillip V.   1925-

*PERSONAL:* Born October 14, 1925, in Durban, South Africa; son of Joseph Newman and Fanny (Rosendorff) Tobias. *Education:* University of the Witwatersrand, B.Sc., 1946, B.Sc. (Honours in anatomy), 1947, M.B.B.Ch., 1951, Ph.D., 1953, D.Sc., 1967; also attended Emmanuel College, Cambridge, 1955. *Home:* 602 Marble Arch, Goldreich St., Hillbrow, Johannesburg, South Africa. *Office:* Medical School, University of the Witwatersrand, Johannesburg, South Africa.

*CAREER:* University of the Witwatersrand, Medical School, Johannesburg, South Africa, lecturer, 1951-52, senior lecturer, 1953-58, professor of anatomy and head of department, 1959—, member of university council, 1971-74. Visiting professor of physical anthropology, Cambridge University, 1964; Raymond Dart Lecturer, Institute for the Study of Man in Africa, 1968; Raymond Hoffenberg Lecturer, University of Cape Town, 1969; James Arthur Memorial Lecturer, American Museum of Natural History, 1969; A. J. Orenstein Lecturer, Royal Society of Africa, 1971; honorary professor of palaeoanthropology, Bernard Price Institute for Palaeontological Research. President of human palaeontology section, Pan-African Congress on Prehistory,

1959-63; Institute for the Study of Man in Africa, founder, 1956, first president, 1961-68; member of executive board and board of governors, Museums of Man and Science; member of controlling executive, Associated Scientific and Technical Societies of South Africa; member of Joint Council of Scientific Societies of South Africa; member of board of trustees, L. S. B. Leakey Foundation; member of permanent council, Pan-African Congress of Prehistory and Quaternary Studies. Member of advisory board, International Louis Leakey Memorial Institute of African Prehistory.

*MEMBER:* International Association of Human Biologists (founder; member of council), International Union of Prehistoric and Protohistoric Sciences, International Primatological Society, World Federation of Occupational Therapists, Royal Anthropological Institute of Great Britain and Ireland (fellow), Anatomical Society of Great Britain and Ireland, South African Archaeological Society (president, 1964-65), Anatomical Society of Southern Africa (founder; president, 1968-70), Society for the Study of Human Biology (London), American Association of Physical Anthropologists, American Society of Naturalists, Institute of Society, Ethics, and Life Sciences (New York), Royal Society of South Africa (fellow; president, 1970-72), South African Society for Quaternary Research (president, 1969-73), South African Association for the Advancement of Science (vice-president, 1965-66, 1969-70, 1973-76), South African Society of Physiotherapy (honorary vice-president), American Society of Human Genetics, Science Writers' Association of South Africa (president, 1963-64); honorary member of anthropological and geographical societies in Paris, Lisbon, and Vienna, and of Anatomical Society of Israel.

*AWARDS, HONORS:* Abe Bailey traveling bursar to England, 1952-53; British Association Medal, 1953; Nuffield traveling fellow to Cambridge University, 1955; Rockefeller Foundation traveling fellow in United States, 1956; Simon Biesheuvel Medal, 1966; named one of ''Four Outstanding Young Men,'' in South Africa, 1966; South Africa Medal, 1967; senior Captain Scott Medal, 1973.

*WRITINGS: The African in the Universities* (booklet), National Union of South African Students, 1951; *Chromosomes, Sex-Cells and Evolution in a Mammal,* Lund, Humphries, 1956; *Embryos, Fossils, Genes and Anatomy* (inaugural lecture), Witwatersrand University Press, 1960; *The Meaning of Race* (lecture), South African Institute of Race Relations, 1961, 2nd edition, 1972; (with Maurice Arnold) *Man's Anatomy,* Witwatersrand University Press, Volumes I-II, 1963, Volume III, 1964, 3rd edition of all three volumes, 1978; (with Arnold) *Man's Brain,* Witwatersrand University Press, 1963, 2nd edition, 1974; *Olduvai Gorge,* Volume II: *The Cranium of Australopithecus (Zinjanthropus) boisei,* Cambridge University Press, 1967; (with Arnold) *Man's Limbs,* Witwatersrand University Press, 1968; *Man's Past and Future* (Raymond Dart lecture), Witwatersrand University Press, 1969, Humanities, 1970; *The Brain in Hominid Evolution,* Columbia University Press, 1971; *I.Q. and the Nature/Nurture Controversy,* University of Natal, 1974; *The Bushmen,* Human and Rousseau (Cape Town), 1978. Also author of *Olduvai Gorge,* Volume IV, Cambridge University Press, 1978.

Contributor: Roger Summers, *Inyanga: Prehistoric Settlements in Southern Rhodesia,* Cambridge University Press, 1958; Gottfried Kurth, editor, *Evolution und Hominisation,* Gustav Fischer Verlag (Stuttgart), 1962, new edition, 1968; D. H. S. Davis, editor, *Ecological Studies in Southern Africa,* [The Hague], 1964; *Homenaje a Juan Comas, en su 65 aniversario,* Volume II, Editorial Libros de Mexico, 1965; Paul T. Baker and J. S. Weiner, editors, *The Biology of Human Adaptability,* Clarendon Press, 1966; K. P. Oakley and B. G. Campbell, editors, *Catalogue of Fossil Hominids,* Part I: *Africa,* British Museum of Natural History, 1967, 2nd edition, 1977; *Anthropologie und Humangenetik,* Gustav Fischer Verlag, 1968; B. Chiarelli, editor, *Taxonomy and Phylogeny of Old World Primates,* Rosenberg & Sellier (Turin), 1968; P. R. Erlich, R. W. Holm, and P. H. Raven, editors, *Papers on Evolution,* Little, Brown, 1969.

A. K. Ghosh, editor, *Perspectives in Palaeoanthropology: D. Sen Festschrift Volume,* Firma K. L. Mukhopadhyay (Calcutta), 1971; R. Tuttle, editor, *The Functional and Evolutionary Biology of Primates,* Aldine-Atherton, 1972; B. Pachai, editor, *The Early History of Malawi,* Longmans Green (London), 1972; Ashley Montagu, editor, *The Origin and Evolution of Man,* Crowell, 1973; *Problemi Attuali di Scienza e di Cultura,* Accademia Nationale dei Lincei (Rome), 1973; C. Loring Brace and J. Metress, editors, *Man in Evolutionary Perspective,* Wiley, 1973; W. D. Hammond-Tooke, editor, *The Bantu-speaking Peoples of Southern Africa,* Routledge and Kegan Paul, 1974; Y. A. Cohen, editor, *Man in Adaptation: The Biosocial Background,* Aldine, 1974; P. S. Fry, H. J. van Aswegen, and others, editors, *Die Verhaal van die Mensdom,* Human and Rousseau, 1975; F. Salzano, editor, *The Role of Natural Selection in Human Evolution,* Elsevier (Amsterdam), 1975; R. H. Tuttle, editor, *Primate Functional Morphology and Evolution,* Mouton, 1975; G. L. Isaac and E. R. McCown, editors, *Human Origins: Louis Leakey and the East African Evidence,* W. A. Benjamin, 1975; E. S. Watts, F. E. Johnston and G. W. Lasker, editors, *Biosocial Interrelations in Population Adaptation,* Mouton, 1975; A. C. Brown, editor, *A History of Scientific Endeavour in South Africa,* Royal Society of South Africa, 1977.

Author of preface: Antonio de Almeida, *Bushmen and Other Non-Bantu People of Angola,* Institute for the Study of Man in Africa, 1965; A. J. Clement, *The Kalahari and Its Lost City,* Longmans, Green (Cape Town), 1967; E. M. Veenstra, *Micro-Anatomy Practical Notes,* Anatomy Department, Witwatersrand University, 1971; M. Schoonraad, editor, *Rock Paintings of Southern Africa,* South African Association for the Advancement of Science, 1971; G. H. Sperber, *Cranio-facial Embryology: Dental Practitioner's Handbook No. 15,* John Wright, 1973, 2nd edition, 1976; S. Schmidt, *Karate: An Insight into the Basic Concepts,* Perskor Publishers (Johannesburg), 1976.

Contributor to *Atlas of African Prehistory,* University of Chicago Press, 1967, *Britannica Book of the Year, Yearbook of Physical Anthropology, Encyclopaedia Britannica, Science and Humanity Yearbook* (Moscow), *Wissenschaft und Menschheit* (Berlin), and *Standard Encyclopedia of Southern Africa.* Contributor of more than 300 articles to medical, anthropological, and scientific journals.

*WORK IN PROGRESS:* Numerous articles on human evolution.

*SIDELIGHTS:* Phillip Tobias writes: "Human beings are the most wonderful and the most important things in life. They are one of its greatest justifications. It is not surprising that not only their fossilized origins but every aspect of contemporary man fascinates me, inspires me and moves me. Getting to know the men behind the discoveries is always enlightening; what they write and how they think becomes much more intelligible and more meaningful. Their human qualities are seen, felt and understood, and their researches seem to fall into place much more clearly.

"I love writing. The taste of the lovely English language is sweet upon one's intellectual palate, and inspiration often leads me to work throughout the night."

In addition to his studies at Olduvai Gorge, Tobias has made field expeditions to fossil sites at Makapansgat, Sterkfontein, Taung, Chipongwe Cave in Zambia, and other sites. He has carried out research in over a dozen countries in south, east, and central Africa, as well as in Europe, Asia, and America. His human study expeditions have been centered on Bushmen, Griqua, and Tonga peoples. Besides English and Afrikaans, Tobias speaks French and German, and reads Italian and Dutch.

*AVOCATIONAL INTERESTS:* Classical music, collecting old books and stamps, Africana, people.

\* \* \*

## TOBIN, Kay 1930-

*PERSONAL:* Name Kay Tobin is a pseudonym; born January 5, 1930. *Politics:* Gay liberationist. *Office address:* American Library Association/SRRT Task Force on Gay Liberation, P.O. Box 2383, Philadelphia, Pa. 19103.

*CAREER:* American Library Association/Social Responsibilities Round Table, Task Force on Gay Liberation, Philadelphia, Pa., volunteer worker, 1970—. *Member:* Gay Activists Alliance of New York City (founding member, 1969—), Daughters of Bilitis (lesbian organization).

*WRITINGS:* (With Randy Wicker) *The Gay Crusaders,* Paperback Library, 1972. Contributor to *Ladder: A Lesbian Review,* 1963-66; reporter for *Gay* (newspaper), 1969-71.

*SIDELIGHTS:* A Gay activist since 1961, Kay Tobin told *CA* she is "hell-bent on proclaiming that 'Gay is good.'" She specializes in news coverage of the Gay movement, and maintains an extensive, high quality photo file of Gay activism, and of workers in the Gay liberation movement.

\* \* \*

## TOBY, Mark 1913(?)-1972

1913(?)—October 26, 1972; American novelist, radio and television writer, teacher, and sales director. Obituaries: *New York Times,* October 28, 1972; *Publishers Weekly,* November 20, 1972.

\* \* \*

## TOMESKI, Edward Alexander 1930-

*PERSONAL:* Born February 19, 1930, in New Jersey; son of Stanley K. (a manager) and Catherine J. (Lipinski) Tomeski. *Education:* Fairleigh Dickinson University, B.S., 1956; Columbia University, M.S., 1957; New York University, Ph.D., 1971. *Home:* 501 Chicago Blvd., Sea Girt, N.J. 08750. *Office:* Fordham University, Bronx, N.Y. 10458.

*CAREER:* W. R. Grace & Co., New York City, assistant director, 1963-66; Fordham University, Bronx, N.Y., assistant professor, 1966-71, associate professor of management and computers, 1971-76, professor of management, 1976—. Member of X3 Committee on Information Processing, American National Standards Institute. Systems consultant, Mobil Oil Corp., New York City, 1960-63; consultant in New York City, 1966—. *Military service:* U.S. Air Force, 1950-54; became sergeant. *Member:* International Systems Management Association (director and research chairman), Institute of Management Sciences (chairman of College of Managerial Economics). *Awards, honors:* Awards for distinguished service from International Systems Management

Association, 1967, and American Management Association, 1965; national Outstanding Educator award, 1974.

*WRITINGS: The Executive Uses of Computers,* Collier, 1969; *The Computer Revolution: The Executive and the New Information Technology,* Macmillan, 1970; (with Harold Lazarus) *People-Oriented Computer Systems,* Van Nostrand, 1975. Contributor to journals in his field. Former associate editor, Institute of Management Sciences, and *System & Procedures Journal;* contributing editor, *Computers & People.*

*WORK IN PROGRESS:* An introductory text on information systems; a survey on management function.

\*　　\*　　\*

### TOMPKINS, Stuart R(amsay)　1886-1977

*PERSONAL:* Born June 26, 1886, in Lyn, Ontario, Canada; son of Charles Abraham and Martha (McNish) Tompkins; married Edna(jane) Christie, January 27, 1915. *Education:* University of Toronto, B.A., 1909; University of Alberta, M.A., 1924; University of Chicago, Ph.D., 1931. *Politics:* Conservative. *Religion:* United Church of Canada. *Home:* 211 Lagoon Rd., Victoria, British Columbia, Canada V9C 1T1.

*CAREER:* Department of Education, Edmonton, Alberta, chief clerk, 1911-15; high school teacher in Lethbridge, Alberta, 1920-24; Yukon Territory (Canada) schools, superintendent, 1924-28; University of Oklahoma, Norman, associate professor, 1932-42, professor of history, 1942-49, research professor of Russian and Alaskan history, 1949-56, professor emeritus, 1956-77. Visiting professor of history at University of California, Los Angeles, 1945-46, University of Toronto, 1956-57, and Montana State University, 1962. *Military service:* Canadian Expeditionary Force, 1915-19; served in Europe and Siberia; became first lieutenant; received King's Medal. *Member:* American Historical Association, American Association for the Advancement of Slavic Studies. *Awards, honors:* Rockefeller Foundation grants, 1944, 1952; Newberry Library fellow, 1961.

*WRITINGS:* (Contributor) Eugene Anderson and James L. Cate, editors, *Medieval and Historiographical Essays in Honor of James Westfall Thompson* [Chicago], 1937; *Russia through the Ages,* Prentice-Hall, 1940; *Alaska: Promyshlennik and Sourdough,* University of Oklahoma Press, 1945; (contributor) Leonid Strakhovsky, editor, *Handbook of Slavic Studies,* Harvard University Press, 1949; *The Russian Mind: From Peter the Great through the Enlightenment,* University of Oklahoma Press, 1953; *The Russian Intelligentsia: Makers of the Revolutionary State,* University of Oklahoma Press, 1957; *The Triumph of Bolshevism: Revolution or Reaction?,* University of Oklahoma Press, 1967; (contributor) Morgan B. Sherwood, editor, *Alaska and Its History,* University of Washington Press, 1967; (with William Rodney) *Joe Boyle: King of the Klondike,* McGraw, 1974. Contributor of about fifteen articles to history and Slavic studies journals, and to *Alaska Review.*

*BIOGRAPHICAL/CRITICAL SOURCES: New York Review of Books,* January 15, 1967.†

(Died October 11, 1977)

\*　　\*　　\*

### TORGERSEN, Eric　1943-

*PERSONAL:* Born October 6, 1943, in Huntington, N.Y.; son of John (a carpenter) and Louise (Elsbeck) Torgersen; married Paula Novotnak (a poet), May 31, 1969 (divorced,

1974). *Education:* Cornell University, A.B., 1964; University of Iowa, M.F.A., 1969. *Home:* Route 2, Shepherd, Mich. 48883. *Office:* Department of English, Central Michigan University, Mount Pleasant, Mich. 48858.

*CAREER:* Worked with Peace Corps in Ethiopia, 1964-66; Quincy College, Quincy, Ill., instructor in English, 1968-70; Central Michigan University, Mount Pleasant, 1970—, began as instructor, currently associate professor of English.

*WRITINGS: The Carpenter* (poems), Salt Mound Press, 1969; *At War With Friends* (poems), Ithaca House, 1972; *Ethiopia* (novella), Hanging Loose Press, 1977. Contributor of poetry and reviews to periodicals. Founder and former editor of "Poems of the People," a poetry service for the underground press.

*WORK IN PROGRESS:* A new collection of poems, tentatively entitled *My Blindness.*

\*　　\*　　\*

### TOTTEN, W. Fred　1905-

*PERSONAL:* Born June 28, 1905, in Shelby County, Ind.; son of Albert S. (a farmer) and Myrtle Alice (Larrison) Totten; married Ruth McClure Marcum, May 21, 1932; children: Charles Frederick, Mary Carolyn (Mrs. Ramsey N. Behnan). *Education:* DePauw University, B.A. (with distinction), 1927; Indiana University, M.A., 1931, Ph.D., 1943. *Politics:* Independent. *Religion:* Protestant. *Home and office:* 1810 Ramsay Blvd., Flint, Mich. 48503.

*CAREER:* High school teacher of mathematics and physics and athletic coach in New Augusta, Ind., 1927-29; principal in New Bethel, Ind., 1929-34; Indiana University at Bloomington, instructor and critic teacher in mathematics, 1934-38; high school principal in Bedford, Ind., 1938-43, and Marion, Ind., 1943-45; Wabash College, Crawfordsville, Ind., director of admissions, 1945-50; Flint Junior College, Flint, Mich., president, 1950-55; Eastern Michigan University, Ypsilanti, professor in Graduate School, 1955-70; University of South Florida, St. Petersburg, lecturer, 1970-75. Adjunct professor for workshops on more than thirty university and college campuses. Former member of executive board of Flint Council of Social Agencies and Flint Urban League. Consultant in community education.

*MEMBER:* American Association of School Administrators, National Community Education Association, Flint Community Music Association, Flint Council of Churches, Phi Delta Kappa, Rotary International, Rotary Club of Flint. *Awards, honors:* Distinguished Service Award, National Community School Education Association, 1969; Distinguished Service Award, North Central Association of Colleges and Schools; Educational Press Award.

*WRITINGS:* (With C. A. Smith and Harl R. Douglass) *Algebra One,* Row, Peterson, 1954; (with Smith and Douglass) *Algebra Two,* Row, Peterson, 1955; (with Frank J. Manley) *The Community School,* Allied Education Council, 1969; (with Manley) *Community Education and Functions of the Community,* privately printed, 1970; *The Power of Community Education,* Pendell, 1970. Also author of *Annotated Bibliography of Community Education Resources,* privately printed. Contributor to education journals.

*WORK IN PROGRESS: Planning the School Plant for Total Community Use; Community Education: Resource Manual and Guide; Modern Algebra: First Course,* with Gwendolyn Pearson; *You've Gotta Have Bounce; Community Education as Perceived by Frank J. Manley and His Contemporaries,* with Ferris Crawford; *Learning in the*

*Classroom of God and Man,* with Henry Verges; *Love and Learning Can Solve Human Problems.*

SIDELIGHTS: W. Fred Totten told CA: "All of my writing is intended to help people reclaim the soul of the learning process. We need to do those things which will motivate people to strive for things worth being as well as for things worth having. The overworship of money and power must be counteracted by the forces of love and learning.

"At long last we are beginning to see the entire community as the learning laboratory. In fact, for some youth the schoolbuilding may be the worst place in the community for them to learn what they need to know. Therefore we must learn how to relate learning in nature's classroom and learning in the various business, industrial, and professional areas in the community with learning in the classroom."

\* \* \*

## TOULOUSE-LAUTREC, Marie-Pierre (Mapie) de 1901-1972

May 7, 1901—December 30, 1972; French journalist and novelist. Obituaries: *L'Express,* January 8-14, 1973.

\* \* \*

## TOWER, Margene 1939-

PERSONAL: Born September 21, 1939, in Portland, Ore.; daughter of Gordon Eugene and Marjorie (Tryon) Tower; married V. Alton Dohner (a physician), December 5, 1970. *Education:* Oregon State University and University of Oregon, B.S., 1961; University of Colorado, M.S., 1967. *Politics:* "Democrat most of the time." *Religion:* Protestant. *Home:* 604 31st St. W., Billings, Mont. 59102.

CAREER: University of Colorado, Denver, instructor in psychiatric nursing, 1967-68; Denver General Hospital, Community Mental Health Center, Denver, Colo., director of psychiatric nursing, 1968-70; Public Health Service, Indian Health, Billings, Mont., deputy director of area mental health services, 1971—.

WRITINGS: (With Carol D. DeYoung) *Out of Uniform and into Trouble: The Nurse's Role in Community Mental Health Centers,* Mosby, 1971. Contributor to *Journal of Psychiatric Nursing.*

\* \* \*

## TOWLE, Tony 1939-

PERSONAL: Surname rhymes with "bowl"; born June 13, 1939, in New York, N.Y.; son of Erwin W. (an architect) and Mary E. (Rigg) Towle; married Monica Collins, March, 1958; married second wife, Irma Lee Hurley (an actress), December 31, 1966; children: (first marriage) Scott; (second marriage) Rachel Lee. *Education:* Attended Georgetown University, 1957, New York University, 1961-62, Columbia University, 1963, and New School for Social Research, 1963-64. *Politics:* None. *Religion:* None. *Home:* 100 Sullivan St., New York, N.Y. 10012. *Office:* Universal Limited Art Editions, 5 Skidmore Pl., West Islip, N.Y. 11795.

CAREER: Secretary at Universal Limited Art Editions, West Islip, N.Y., 1964—, and Telamon Editions Limited, West Islip, 1970—. *Member:* Poetry Society of America. *Awards, honors:* Gotham Book Mart Avant-Garde Poetry prize, 1963; Wagner College Writer's Conference poetry prize, 1963; Poet's Foundation awards, 1964, 1966; Frank O'Hara Award, 1970, for *North.*

WRITINGS: *Poems,* privately printed, 1966; *After Dinner*

*We Take a Drive into the Night,* Tibor De Nagy, 1968; *North,* Columbia University Press, 1970; *Autobiography, and Other Poems,* Sun/Coach House South, 1977. Contributor to *Art and Literature, New Yorker, Poetry,* and other magazines.

\* \* \*

## TOWNSEND, John Rowe 1922-

PERSONAL: Born May 10, 1922, in Leeds, England; son of George Edmund Rowe and Gladys (Page) Townsend; married Vera Lancaster, July 3, 1948 (died May 9, 1973); children: Alethea Mary, Nicholas John, Penelope Anne. *Education:* Emmanuel College, Cambridge, B.A., 1949, M.A., 1954. *Home:* 19 Eltisley Ave., Cambridge, England.

CAREER: Journalist for *Yorkshire Post,* 1946, and *Evening Standard,* 1949; *Guardian,* Manchester, England, sub-editor, 1949-54, art editor, 1954-55, editor of weekly international edition, 1955-69, children's books editor (part time), 1968—; writer and lecturer, 1969—. Member of Harvard International Seminar, 1956. Visiting lecturer, University of Pennsylvania, 1965, and University of Washington, 1969, and 1971; May Hill Arbuthnot Honor Lecturer, Atlanta, Ga., 1971; Anne Carroll Moore Lecturer, New York Public Library, 1971; Whittall Lecturer, Library of Congress, 1976. *Military service:* Royal Air Force, 1942-46; became flight sergeant.

MEMBER: Society of Authors (Great Britain). *Awards, honors:* Carnegie Medal honors list, 1963, for *Hell's Edge;* Silver Pen award from English Centre of International P.E.N., 1970, "Edgar" award from Mystery Writers of America, and Carnegie Medal honors list, 1969, all for *The Intruder; Trouble in the Jungle, Good-bye to the Jungle, Pirate's Island, The Intruder, Good-night, Prof, Dear, The Summer People,* and *Noah's Castle* appeared on the American Library Association notable books list; *Trouble in the Jungle, The Intruder,* and *A Sense of Story* appeared on the *Horn Book* Honor List.

WRITINGS—Juveniles, except as indicated: *Gumble's Yard,* Hutchinson, 1961, published as *Trouble in the Jungle,* Lippincott, 1969; *Hell's Edge,* Hutchinson, 1963, Lothrop, 1969; *Widdershins Crescent,* Hutchinson, 1965, published as *Good-bye to the Jungle,* Lippincott, 1967; *Written for Children: An Outline of English Children's Literature* (adult), J. Garnet Miller, 1965, Lothrop, 1967, revised edition, Kestrel Books, 1974, Lippincott, 1975; *The Hallersage Sound,* Hutchinson, 1966; *Pirate's Island,* Lippincott, 1968; *The Intruder,* Oxford University Press, 1969, Lippincott, 1970.

*Good-night, Prof, Love,* Oxford University Press, 1970, published as *Good-night, Prof, Dear,* Lippincott, 1971; *A Sense of Story: Essays on Contemporary Writers for Children* (adult), Lippincott, 1971; (editor) *Modern Poetry: A Selection for Young People,* Oxford University Press, 1971, Lippincott, 1974; *The Summer People,* Lippincott, 1972; *Forest of the Night,* Oxford University Press, 1974, Lippincott, 1975; *Noah's Castle,* Oxford University Press, 1975, Lippincott, 1976; *Top of the World,* Oxford University Press, 1976, Lippincott, 1977; *The Xanadu Manuscript,* Oxford University Press, 1977, published as *The Visitors,* Lippincott, 1977. Contributor of articles and reviews to *Guardian, Times Literary Supplement,* and many other publications.

SIDELIGHTS: John Rowe Townsend told CA: "I'd rather write for children than anyone else. They're a responsive audience: eager, unsated, ready to live the story. They won't put up with longwindedness or pomposity, they won't go on reading if they're not enjoying the book, but that's a healthy discipline. I like writing for adults about children's books and trying to get them interested in the books for their own sake; that way we can all share with children and maybe recapture a little of childhood's excitement.''

*BIOGRAPHICAL/CRITICAL SOURCES: Best Sellers,* May 1, 1967, June 1, 1969; *Christian Science Monitor,* May 4, 1967; *Times Literary Supplement,* May 25, 1967, October 16, 1969; *New York Times Book Review,* November 5, 1967, May 26, 1968, August 31, 1969, April 26, 1970, May 2, 1971, November 19, 1972; *Book World,* December 3, 1967, May 5, 1968; *New Society,* December 7, 1967; *New Yorker,* December 16, 1967, December 14, 1968; *Young Readers' Review,* May, 1967, April, 1968; *Books and Bookmen,* July, 1968; *Horn Book,* August, 1970, June, 1971, August, 1971, October, 1971; *Children's Literature Review,* Volume II, Gale, 1976.

\*        \*        \*

## TOY, Henry, Jr. 1915-

*PERSONAL:* Born February 1, 1915, in Easton, Pa.; son of Henry (a salesman) and Pauline (Pfenning) Toy; married Elizabeth Voelker (a production editor), August 31, 1935; children: Tod Jeffrey, Charles Henry. *Education:* University of Pennsylvania, Certificate (with honors), 1939; George Peabody College for Teachers, B.S., 1961, M.A., 1962. *Religion:* Protestant. *Home:* 13100 West 31st Ave., Golden, Colo. 80401. *Office:* 7314 West Colfax Ave., Lakewood, Colo. 80215.

*CAREER:* Atlantic Refining Co., Philadelphia, Pa., accountant, 1933-41; E. I. duPont de Nemours & Co., Wilmington, Del., purchasing agent, 1941-49; National Citizens Council for Better Schools, New York City, president, 1949-59; Robert A. Taft Institute of Government, New York City, executive director, 1962-63; Henry Toy, Jr. & Associates (consultants in education and community relations), Washington, D.C., president, 1963-70; NuToy, Inc. (publishing and consulting), Lakewood, Colo., president, 1970—. Special adviser to chairman, White House Conference on Education, 1954-55; president, Council for Delaware Education, 1946-49; member of planning committee, National Conference on Citizenship, 1951-53; member of board of directors, Center for Information on America, 1962—, and Citizens Scholarship Foundation of America, 1962-73; member of board and secretary, Council on Civic Education, 1964-66.

*MEMBER:* American Association of School Administrators, Sigma Kappa Phi, Phi Delta Kappa, Kappa Delta Pi. *Awards, honors:* Annual Award of National Association of Purchasing Agents, 1949; Centennial Award of Shattuck School, 1958; Lay Citizens Award of Phi Delta Kappa, 1960; Young Man of the Year award of Delaware Junior Chamber of Commerce, 1949; Distinguished Award of Merit of Evening School Alumni Society of the University of Pennsylvania, 1957; Annual Citation of the Classroom Teacher's Association of New York, 1957.

*WRITINGS: Federal Dollars for Scholars,* Nu-Toy, 1970.

Contributor: *Improving Public Education through School Board Action,* University of Pittsburgh Press, 1950; Harold E. Bottrell, editor, *Applied Principles of Educational Sociology,* Stackpole, 1954; Nelson B. Henry, editor, *Citizens Cooperation for Better Schools,* University of Chicago Press, 1954; Jane E. Russell, editor, *National Policies for Education, Health and Social Services,* Doubleday, 1955; Francis S. Chase and Harold Andersen, editors, *The High School in*

*a New Era,* University of Chicago Press, 1958; Marvin D. Alcorn and James M. Linley, editors, *Issues in Curriculum Development,* World Book Co., 1959; *Implications for Education of Prospective Changes in Society,* Citation, 1967. Contributor of articles, principally on citizenship activity, to journals. Co-author with Robert E. Horn of monthly *Guide to Federal Assistance for Education,* Appleton, 1966—.

*WORK IN PROGRESS:* A revised edition of *Federal Dollars for Scholars.*

*BIOGRAPHICAL/CRITICAL SOURCES: Time,* December 6, 1948; *Newsweek,* January 30, 1950, February 1, 1960; *American Magazine,* December, 1951; *Redbook,* February, 1952; Roy E. Larsen, *How to Get Better Schools,* Harper, 1956; James B. Conant, *The American High School Today,* McGraw, 1959.

\*        \*        \*

## TOYNBEE, Jocelyn M(ary) C(atherine) 1897-

*PERSONAL:* Born March 3, 1897, in London, England; daughter of Harry Valpy and Sarah Edith (Marshall) Toynbee. *Education:* Newnham College, Cambridge, M.A., 1919; Oxford University, Ph.D., 1931. *Religion:* Roman Catholic. *Home:* 22, Park Town, Oxford, England.

*CAREER:* Ladies' College, Cheltenham, England, classical mistress, 1920-21; St. Hugh's College, Oxford University, Oxford, England, classical tutor, 1921-24; University of Reading, Reading, England, lecturer in classics, 1924-27; Cambridge University, Cambridge, England, director of studies and lecturer in classics, and fellow of Newnham College, 1927-51, Laurence Professor of Classical Archaeology, 1951-62, emerita, 1962—, honorary fellow of Newnham College, 1962—. *Member:* British Academy (fellow), London Society of Antiquaries (fellow), American Numismatic Society (honorary member). *Awards, honors:* Medal from Royal Numismatic Society, 1948; medal from American Numismatic Society, 1956; D.Litt. from University of Newcastle-upon-Tyne, 1967, and University of Liverpool, 1968.

*WRITINGS: The Hadriani School: A Chapter in the History of Greek Art,* Cambridge University Press, 1934; *Roman Medallions,* American Numismatic Society, 1944; *Some Notes on Artists in the Roman World,* Latomus (Brussels), 1951; *Ars Pacis Reconsidered and Historical Art in Roman Italy,* British Academy, 1953; (with John B. Ward Perkins) *The Shrine of St. Peter and the Vatican Excavations,* Longmans, Green, 1956, Pantheon, 1957; *The Flavian Reliefs from the Palazzo della Cancelleria in Rome,* Oxford University Press, 1957; (contributor) Olive M. Griffiths, *Daglingworth: The Story of a Cotswold Village,* Museum Press, 1959.

*Art in Roman Britain* (catalog of an exhibition), published for Society for the Promotion of Roman Studies by Phaidon, 1962, 2nd edition, 1963; *A Silver Casket and Strainer from the Walbrook Mithraeum in the City of London,* E. J. Brill, 1963; *Art in Britain under the Romans,* Clarendon Press, 1964; *The Christian Roman Mosaic, Hinton St. Mary, Dorset* (monograph), Dorset Natural History and Archaeological Society, 1964; *The Art of the Romans,* Praeger, 1965; *Death and Burial in the Roman World,* edited by H. H. Scullard, Cornell University Press, 1971; (reviser of English translation) Lino Rossi, *Trajan's Column and the Dacian Wars,* Cornell University Press, 1971; *Animals in Roman Life and Art,* Thames & Hudson, 1973; (editor) Donald E. Strong, *Roman Art,* Penguin, 1976.

Contributor to *Journal of Roman Studies, Papers* of British School at Rome, *Numismatic Chronicle, Classical Review, Classical Quarterly, Antiquaries Journal, Archaeologia, Antiquity, Gnomon, Letomus, Proceedings* of British Academy, and other scholarly journals.

*WORK IN PROGRESS:* A book, *Roman Historical Portraits,* for Thames & Hudson; continuing research on various aspects of Roman archaeology.

*AVOCATIONAL INTERESTS:* Foreign travel, especially in "one-time" Roman lands.

\* \* \*

## TRAGER, James 1925-

*PERSONAL:* Born May 27, 1925, in White Plains, N.Y.; son of J. Garfield and Helen (Mosbacher) Trager; married Olivia A. Hirsch, October 1, 1955 (divorced, August, 1967); married Chie Nishio, August 28, 1972; children: (first marriage) Oliver R., Amanda M., James B. *Education:* Harvard University, A.B., 1946; Columbia University, graduate study. *Residence:* New York, N.Y. *Agent:* Curtis Brown Ltd., 575 Madison Ave., New York, N.Y. 10022. *Office:* 1860 Broadway, New York, N.Y. 10023.

*CAREER:* American Institute of Public Opinion, Princeton, N.J., interviewer, 1944; Gimbel's (department store), New York City, advertising copywriter, 1947-48; C. J. LaRoche & Co. (advertising agency), New York City, copywriter, 1948-59; Warwick & Legler, Inc. (advertising agency), New York City, copywriter, 1959-64; Benton & Bowles, Inc. (advertising agency), New York City, copywriter, 1964-66; free-lance writer, 1966—. Teacher, New School for Social Research, New York City, 1966—. Member of Popular Nutrition Education Panel of U.S. Senate Select Committee on Nutrition and Human Needs, 1974. Lecturer to nutrition groups and other organizations in New York, New Jersey, Connecticut, West Virginia, Ohio, Illinois, Iowa and California. *Member:* Society for Nutrition Information, New York Mycological Society, Harvard Club of New York.

*WRITINGS: The Enriched, Fortified, Concentrated, Country-fresh, Lip-smacking, Finger-licking, International, Unexpurgated Foodbook* (history of food through the ages), Grossman, 1970; *The Big, Fertile, Rumbling, Cast-Iron, Growling, Aching, Unbuttoned Bellybook,* Grossman, 1972; *Amber Waves of Grain: The Secret Russian Wheat Sales That Sent American Food Prices Soaring,* Dutton, 1973, revised edition published as *The Great Grain Robbery,* Ballantine, 1975. Contributor to magazines and newspapers, including *Vogue, Sales Management, Family Circle, Epicure,* and *New York Times.* Editor, *Harvard Crimson.*

*WORK IN PROGRESS: World Chronology: The Year by Year Account of Human Events from Prehistory to the Present,* for Holt.

*AVOCATIONAL INTERESTS:* Photography, history, the environment, population problems.

*BIOGRAPHICAL/CRITICAL SOURCES: New York Times,* October 10, 1970; *Best Sellers,* October 15, 1970.

\* \* \*

## TRAGLE, Henry Irving 1914-

*PERSONAL:* Born October 13, 1914, in Richmond, Va.; son of Thomas Elwood (a banker) and Ilse Anna (Zuck) Tragle; married Dorothy Lois Clark, April 23, 1949 (died October 31, 1957); children: Dorothy Cyril Thomason (stepdaughter). *Education:* Attended University of Richmond,

1932-33; University of Massachusetts, B.A., 1966, M.A., 1967, Ph.D., 1971. *Politics:* Independent. *Religion:* Unitarian Universalist. *Home:* 985 North Pleasant St., Amherst, Mass. 01002. *Office:* Graduate School, University of Massachusetts, Amherst, Mass. 01002.

*CAREER:* U.S. Army, 1941-64, entered as a private and retired as lieutenant colonel; served in three campaigns in the European Theater as company commander, 36th Tank Battalion; staff officer, European Army Headquarters, 1949-53; instructor in Reserve Officers Training Corps (ROTC), 1953-56; staff officer, Eighth Army Headquarters, Seoul, Korea, 1959-60; staff officer, European Army Headquarters, Heidelberg, Germany, 1960-64. University of Massachusetts—Amherst, lecturer in history and assistant graduate dean, 1971—. *Member:* American Historical Association, Organization of American Historians, Phi Beta Kappa, Phi Kappa Phi. *Awards, honors*—Military: Bronze Star Medal with "V" device, and three European Theater campaign stars.

*WRITINGS: The Southampton Slave Revolt of 1831,* University of Massachusetts Press, 1971. Contributor to history journals.

*WORK IN PROGRESS:* A study of General Douglas MacArthur's relationship with his father, Lieutenant General Arthur MacArthur, and his mother.

*BIOGRAPHICAL/CRITICAL SOURCES: Virginian-Pilot,* March 17, 1968; *Daily Hampshire Gazette,* February 11, 1970, March 21, 1972; *Richmond News-Leader,* April 16, 1970.

\* \* \*

## TRATTNER, Walter I(rwin) 1936-

*PERSONAL:* Born July 26, 1936, in New York, N.Y.; married Joan Driscoll, 1958; children: Stephen, Anne, David. *Education:* Williams College, B.A., 1958; Harvard University, M.A.T., 1959; University of Wisconsin—Madison, M.S., 1961, Ph.D., 1963. *Home:* 4719 North Elkhart Ave., Milwaukee, Wis. 53211. *Office:* Department of History, University of Wisconsin, Milwaukee, Wis. 53201.

*CAREER:* Northern Illinois University, DeKalb, assistant professor of history, 1963-65; University of Wisconsin—Milwaukee, assistant professor, 1965-67, associate professor, 1967-71, professor of history and social welfare, 1972—. *Member:* American Historical Association, Organization of American Historians, National Conference on Social Welfare, Social Welfare History Group (vice-chairman, 1968-70; chairman, 1970-72).

*WRITINGS: Homer Folks: Pioneer in Social Welfare,* Columbia University Press, 1968; *Crusade for the Children: A History of the National Child Labor Committee and Child Labor Reform in America,* Quadrangle, 1970; *From Poor Law to Welfare State: A History of Social Welfare in America,* Free Press, 1974. Contributor of about twenty articles to professional journals.

*WORK IN PROGRESS: The Federal Government and Social Welfare in Nineteenth Century America.*

\* \* \*

## TRAUTMAN, Donald T. 1924-

*PERSONAL:* Born June 6, 1924, in Cleveland, Ohio; son of William Daniel and Florence (Zimmermann) Trautman; married Susanah Bailie (a landscape architect), August 28, 1954; children: William, Ann, Benjamin. *Education:* Harvard University, A.B. and LL.B. (J.D.), 1951. *Politics:* Independent. *Home:* 20 Craigie St., Cambridge, Mass. 02138. *Office:* Harvard Law School, Cambridge, Mass. 02138.

*CAREER:* U.S. Supreme Court, Washington, D.C., law clerk, 1952-53; Harvard University, Law School, Cambridge, Mass., 1953—, currently professor of law. *Military service:* U.S. Army, 1943-46. *Member:* American Society of International Law. *Awards, honors:* Guggenheim fellow, 1969.

*WRITINGS:* (With David R. Herwitz) *Materials on Accounting,* Foundation Press, 1959; (with Arthur T. von Mehren) *Law of Multistate Problems,* Little, Brown, 1965. Contributor of articles to law reviews.

*WORK IN PROGRESS: Essays on Law of Multistate Problems.*

\* \* \*

## TRAVIS, Charles S. 1943-

*PERSONAL:* Born January 21, 1943, in Washington, D.C.; son of Philip (a lawyer) and Agnes (Sackheim) Travis; married April, 1963, wife's name Margaret; children: Lisa. *Education:* University of California, Berkeley, B.A., 1963; University of California, Los Angeles, M.A., 1965, Ph.D., 1967. *Religion:* None. *Home:* 3825 Sixth St. S.W., Calgary, Alberta, Canada. *Office:* Department of Philosophy, University of Calgary, 2920 24th Ave. N.W., Calgary, Alberta, Canada T2N 1N4.

*CAREER:* University of North Carolina at Chapel Hill, visiting assistant professor, 1966-68, assistant professor of philosophy, 1968-69; University of Calgary, Calgary, Alberta, assistant professor, 1969-73, associate professor of philosophy, 1973—.

*WRITINGS:* (Editor with Jay F. Rosenberg) *Readings in the Philosophy of Language,* Prentice-Hall, 1971; *Saying and Understanding: A Generative Theory of Illocutions,* New York University Press, 1975. Contributor to *Canadian Journal of Philosophy.*

*WORK IN PROGRESS:* Research on reference, identity, and speech acts.†

\* \* \*

## TRAYLOR, W. L. 1929-

*PERSONAL:* Born May 2, 1929, in Visalia, Calif.; son of Wilfred Lowell and Elsie (Lute) Traylor; married Phyllis Ann Jorgensen (a secretary), January 17, 1951; children: Dana, Debra, Lori, Kevin. *Education:* Attended schools in California.

*CAREER:* Airline pilot and flight instructor. *Military service:* U.S. Navy, 1946-48. *Member:* Society of Air Safety Investigators, Aircraft Owners and Pilots Association, Pilot's International Association.

*WRITINGS: Pilot's Guide to an Airline Career,* Aviation Book Co., 1968, 3rd edition, 1971. Author of a column, "Pilot Error," in *Flying.* Contributor to flying magazines.

*WORK IN PROGRESS:* Aviation safety programs; cause and circumstance of aircraft accidents; *The Four Winds,* a novel.†

\* \* \*

## TREAT, Payson J(ackson) 1879-1972

November 12, 1879—June 15, 1972; American historian, educator, and authority on the Far East. Obituaries: *New York Times,* June 16, 1972; *Washington Post,* June 17, 1972.

## TREFOUSSE, Hans Louis 1921-

*PERSONAL:* Surname is pronounced Trayfus; born December 18, 1921, in Frankfurt, Germany; came to United States in 1936, naturalized in 1943; son of George L. (a physician) and Elizabeth (Albersheim) Trefousse; married Rashelle Friedlander (a teacher), January 26, 1947; children: Roger Philip. *Education:* College of the City of New York (now City College of the City University of New York), B.A., 1942; Columbia University, M.A., 1947, Ph.D., 1950. *Politics:* Democrat. *Religion:* Jewish. *Home:* 22 Shore Acres Rd., Staten Island, N.Y. 10305. *Office:* Department of History, Brooklyn College of the City University of New York, Brooklyn, N.Y. 11210.

*CAREER:* Adelphi College, Garden City, N.Y., instructor in history, 1949-50; Brooklyn College of the City University of New York, Brooklyn, N.Y., instructor, 1950-57, assistant professor, 1958-60, associate professor, 1961-65, professor of history, 1966—. Visiting professor at University of Wisconsin—Milwaukee, 1959, 1968, University of Minnesota, 1963, and Johns Hopkins University, 1964. Editorial advisor, Twayne Publishers. *Military service:* U.S. Army, 1942-45; became captain; received Bronze Star with oak-leaf cluster and Purple Heart. U.S. Army Reserve, 1945—; present rank, lieutenant colonel. *Member:* American Historical Association, Organization of American Historians, Reserve Officers Association of the United States, New York Historical Society. *Awards, honors:* Distinguished teaching award, Brooklyn College, 1960; Guggenheim fellow, 1977-78.

*WRITINGS: Germany and American Neutrality, 1939-1941,* A. B. Bookman, 1951; *Ben Butler: The South Called Him Beast,* Twayne, 1957; (editor) *What Happened at Pearl Harbor?,* Twayne, 1958; (author of preface and introductory notes) Gideon Welles, *Civil War and Reconstruction,* Twayne, 1959; (author of preface and introductory notes) Gideon Welles, *Lincoln's Administration,* Twayne, 1960; *Benjamin Franklin Wade: Radical Republican from Ohio,* Twayne, 1963; (editor) *The Cold War,* Putnam, 1965; *The Radical Republicans: Lincoln's Vanguard for Racial Justice,* Knopf, 1969; (editor) *Background for Radical Reconstruction,* Little, Brown, 1970; (editor) *The Causes of the Civil War,* Holt, 1971; *Reconstruction: America's First Effort at Racial Democracy,* Van Nostrand, 1971; *Impeachment of a President: Andrew Johnson, the Blacks, and Reconstruction,* Tennessee University Press, 1975; *Lincoln's Decision for Emancipation,* Lippincott, 1975; (editor) *Toward a New View of America: Essays in Honor of Arthur C. Cole,* Burt Franklin, 1977. Editor of Twayne's "Statesmen and Rulers of the World" series, 1966-76. Contributor to *Far Eastern Quarterly, Antioch Review, Mississippi Valley Historical Review, Civil War History, Encyclopaedia Britannica,* and other publications.

*WORK IN PROGRESS:* A biography of Carl Schurz.

*BIOGRAPHICAL/CRITICAL SOURCES: Book World,* January 12, 1969.

\* \* \*

## TREICHLER, Jessie C(ambron) 1906(?)-1972

1906(?)—July 11, 1972; American educator, librarian, and short story writer. Obituaries: *New York Times,* July 12, 1972.

\* \* \*

## TREUENFELS, Peter 1926-

*PERSONAL:* Surname is pronounced *Troy*-en-fels; born

May 30, 1926; son of Rudolph L. (an economist) and Therese (Paetsch) Treuenfels; married Helen A. Ward, September 1, 1956; children: Anton P., K. Mark, Elizabeth S., Genevieve L., Thomas W., Andrea L., Katherine A. *Education:* New York University, Ph.D., 1957. *Politics:* Democrat. *Religion:* Roman Catholic. *Home:* 5460 Northeast Seventh St., Fridley, Minn. 55421. *Office:* Comten, Inc., 1950 County Road B-2, Roseville, Minn. 55113.

*CAREER:* Aberdeen Proving Ground, Aberdeen, Md., mathematician, 1950-57; Brookhaven National Laboratory, Brookhaven, N.Y., mathematician, 1957-61; Honeywell, Inc., St. Paul, Minn., mathematician, 1961-76; Comten, Inc., Roseville, Minn., systems analyst, 1976—. *Member:* American Mathematical Society, Association for Computing Machinery. *Awards, honors:* National Aeronautics and Space Administration (NASA) award for technical paper, 1967.

*WRITINGS: Looking Forward to a Career: Computers,* Dillon, 1970. Contributor to mathematics and aeronautics journals.

*WORK IN PROGRESS: Careers for Women: Heads of State.*

* * *

**TREVELYAN, Humphrey 1905-**

*PERSONAL:* Surname is pronounced Tre-*vill*-ian; born November 27, 1905, in Hindhead, England; son of George Philip (a clergyman) and Monica (Phillips) Trevelyan; married Violet Margaret Bartholomew, November 10, 1937; children: Susan Anne (Mrs. Harald Busse), Catherine Mary. *Education:* Attended Lancing College, 1919-24; Jesus College, Cambridge, B.A., 1927, M.A., 1965. *Home:* 13 Wilton St., London SW1 X 7AF, England. *Agent:* Curtis Brown Ltd., 1 Craven Hill, London W2 3EW, England. *Office:* General Electric Co. Ltd., 1 Stanhope Gate, London W.1, England.

*CAREER:* Employed in Indian Civil Service and Indian Political Service, 1929-47, and British Diplomatic Service, 1947-65; served as charge d'affairs in Peking, Ambassador in Egypt, Iraq, and Russia, under-secretary at the United Nations; high commissioner in Aden, 1967. Member of boards of directors of General Electric Co. Ltd. and British Petroleum Ltd., 1965-75, and of British Bank of the Middle East, 1965-77; president, Council of Foreign Bondholders; chairman of board of trustees, British Museum; chairman of council, Royal Institute of International Affairs, 1970-77; vice-president, Great Britain-China Committee. *Member:* Beefsteak. *Awards, honors:* Order of the British Empire, 1941; Companion of the Order of the Indian Empire, 1947; Knight Grand Cross of St. Michael and St. George, 1965; created baron, 1968; LL.D., Cambridge University, 1969; D.C.L., University of Durham, 1973; D. Litt., University of Leeds, 1975.

*WRITINGS: The Middle East in Revolution,* Macmillan, 1970, Gambit, 1971; *Worlds Apart,* Macmillan, 1971, published as *Living with the Communists: China,* Gambit, 1972; *The India We Left,* Macmillan, 1972; *Diplomatic Channels,* Gambit, 1973.

*BIOGRAPHICAL/CRITICAL SOURCES: Observer Review,* August 20, 1970.

* * *

**TROXELL, Mary D(earborn) 1907-**

*PERSONAL:* Born February 24, 1907, in St. Louis, Mo.; daughter of John Tilton (a coal merchant) and Elizabeth (Hinchman) Dearborn; divorced; children: James Hinchman Troxell (deceased). *Education:* University of Iowa, B.S., 1931; New York University, M.S., 1962. *Home and office:* 6947 Woodwind Dr., Sarasota, Fla. 33581.

*CAREER:* Buyer of accessories and ready-to-wear in major department stores in Washington, D.C., Brooklyn, N.Y., Detroit, Mich., and Chicago, Ill., 1947-59; Marjorie Webster Junior College, Washington, D.C., head of merchandising program, 1960-62; Fashion Institute of Technology, New York, N.Y., instructor in fashion buying and merchandising, 1962-63; University of Massachusetts—Amherst, assistant professor and co-ordinator of retail merchandising program, 1963-65; Pennsylvania State University, University Park and Altoona, assistant professor and coordinator of associate degree retailing program, 1965-68; University of Hawaii, Honolulu, Hawaii, associate professor and coordinator of fashion merchandising, 1968-73; Iowa State University, Ames, associate professor and coordinator of fashion merchandising program, 1973-76; consultant in fashion merchandising in Sarasota, Fla., 1976—. *Member:* American Marketing Association, American Association of University Professors, American Home Economics Association, The Fashion Group (Honolulu; scholarship chairman, 1969-73), Honorary Retailing Fraternity, Eta Mu Pi.

*WRITINGS: A Study Guide to the Buyer's Manual,* National Retail Merchants Association, 1967; (with Beatrice Judelle) *Fashion Merchandising,* McGraw, 1971, 2nd edition (sole author), 1976. Contributor of articles to *Hosiery and Underwear Review.*

*WORK IN PROGRESS:* College text and reference publications relating to fashion and specific areas of retail merchandising; *Basic Merchandising Mathematics,* for Prentice-Hall.

* * *

**TROYKA, Lynn Quitman 1938-**

*PERSONAL:* Born February 21, 1938, in Philadelphia, Pa.; daughter of Sidney L. (a financier) and Belle (Furman) Quitman; married David Troyka (a corporate executive), August 13, 1965. *Education:* Brandeis University, B.A., 1959; New York University, M.A., 1960, Ph.D., 1973; Columbia University, summer graduate study, 1962, 1966. *Home:* 166-25 Powells Cove Blvd., Beechhurst, N.Y. 11357. *Office:* Department of Basic Skills, Queensborough Community College of the City University of New York, Bayside, N.Y. 11364.

*CAREER:* Teacher in public schools in Hastings-on-Hudson, N.Y., 1960-63; Baldwin School, New York City, English teacher, 1963-64, head of Junior High Division, 1964-67; Queensborough Community College of the City University of New York, Bayside, N.Y., instructor, 1967-69, assistant professor, 1969-72, associate professor, 1972-75, professor of basic skills, 1975—; Graduate School and University Center of the City University of New York, Center of Advanced Study in Education, New York City, professor, 1975—. Reviewer of college English texts for Prentice-Hall and other publishers. Consultant to Educational Testing Service, 1971—. *Member:* National Council of Teachers of English, Conference on College Composition and Communication, American Association of University Professors, Modern Language Association of America, New York State English Council.

*WRITINGS:* (With Jerrold Nudelman) *Steps in Composi-*

*tion,* Prentice-Hall, 1970, alternate edition, 1972, 2nd edition, 1976; (editor) *Guide to Writing,* Harper, 1974; (with Nudelman) *Taking Action: Writing, Reading, Speaking, and Listening through Simulation Games,* Prentice-Hall, 1975; *Structured Reading,* Prentice-Hall, 1978. Contributor to professional journals.

*WORK IN PROGRESS:* Research on community college English instruction, testing, and cognitive style; revised alternate edition of *Steps in Composition.*

\* \* \*

## TRUMAN, Harry S  1884-1972

May 8, 1884—December 6, 1972; American politician, statesman, and President of the United States. Obituaries: *New York Times,* December 27, 1972; *Washington Post,* December 27, 1972; *L'Express,* January 1-7, 1973; *Newsweek,* January 8, 1973; *Time,* January 8, 1973.

\* \* \*

## TRUPIN, James E.  1940-

*PERSONAL:* Born September 19, 1940, in New York, N.Y.; son of Julian Charles and Natalie (Schusterow) Trupin; married Elizabeth Hobbs, November 16, 1974; children: Joshua Eric, Jessica Ceri. *Education:* Attended Antioch College, 1958-60; City College of the City University of New York, B.A., 1963; Clark University, M.A., 1965; London School of Economics and Political Science, additional study, 1966-67. *Politics:* "Inactive left of center." *Religion:* Jewish. *Home and office:* 124 East 84th St., New York, N.Y. 10028.

*CAREER:* Fawcett Publications, Inc., New York City, educational director, beginning 1970; Jet Literary Associates, New York City, currently literary agent. *Member:* Phi Alpha Theta.

*WRITINGS: West Africa: A Background Book from Ancient Kingdoms to Modern Times,* Parents' Magazine Press, 1971; (editor) *In Prison: Writings and Poems about the Prison Experience,* New American Library, 1975.

*AVOCATIONAL INTERESTS:* Skiing, sailing, basketball, woodworking, travel.

\* \* \*

## TUCK, James A(lexander)  1940-

*PERSONAL:* Born June 28, 1940, Tonawanda, N.Y.; son of Stuart F. (a teacher) and Laura (Donovan) Tuck; married Lynn Robins, October 20, 1962; children: James A., Jr., Michael John, Robin, Laura. *Education:* Syracuse University, A.B., 1962, Ph.D., 1968. *Address:* Site 56, Box 32, Mt. Scio Rd., St. John's, Newfoundland, Canada. *Office:* Department of Anthropology, Memorial University of Newfoundland, St. John's, Newfoundland, Canada A1C 5S7.

*CAREER:* Memorial University of Newfoundland, St. John's, assistant professor of archaeology, 1968-71, associate professor of archaeology and chairman of department of sociology and anthropology, 1971—. Provincial archaeologist in Newfoundland and Labrador. Has presented papers at meetings and symposia in the United States and Canada. Consultant, Department of Historical Resources, governments of Newfoundland and Labrador, 1967—. *Member:* Canadian Archaeological Association (president, 1972-74), Society for American Archaeology, American Anthropological Association (fellow), American Association for the Advancement of Science (fellow), New York State Archaeological Association (fellow).

*WRITINGS:* (Contributor) Elisabeth Tooker, editor, *Iroquois Culture, History, and Prehistory,* New York State Museum, 1967; *Onondaga Iroquois Prehistory: A Study in Settlement Archaeology,* Syracuse University Press, 1971; *Prehistory of Saglek Bay, Labrador: Archaic and Palaeo-Eskimo Occupations,* National Museums of Canada, 1975; (with Robert McGhee) *An Archaic Sequence from the Strait of Belle Isle, Labrador,* National Museums of Canada, 1975; *Ancient People of Port au Choix: The Excavation of an Archaic Indian Cemetery in Newfoundland,* Institute of Social and Economic Research, Memorial University of Newfoundland, 1976. Contributor to *Pennsylvania Archaeologist, Scientific American, American Antiquity, Newfoundland Quarterly, Man in the Northeast,* and *Bulletin of the Massachusetts Archaeological Society.*

*WORK IN PROGRESS:* Archaeology of Newfoundland and Labrador.†

\* \* \*

## TUCKER, Gene M(ilton)  1935-

*PERSONAL:* Born January 8, 1935, in Albany, Tex.; son of Raymond H. and Lorene (Crowder) Tucker; married Charlyne Marye Williams, July 27, 1957; children: Teresa Lynne, Rebecca Michelle. *Education:* McMurry College, B.A., (cum laude), 1957; Yale University, B.D., 1960, M.A., 1961, Ph.D., 1963. *Politics:* Democrat. *Religion:* Methodist. *Home:* 2852 Ponderosa Cir., Decatur, Ga. 30033. *Office:* Candler School of Theology, Emory University, Atlanta, Ga. 30322.

*CAREER:* New Haven College (now University of New Haven), New Haven, Conn., instructor in English, 1958-60; University of Southern California, Los Angeles, assistant professor of religion, 1963-66; Duke University Divinity School, Durham, N.C., assistant professor, 1966-69, associate professor of Old Testament, 1966-70; Candler School of Theology, Emory University, Atlanta, Ga., associate professor, 1970-77, professor of Old Testament, 1977—. Ordained elder in United Methodist Church. Member of North Georgia Conference, United Methodist Church. Durham Council on Human Relations, member of board, 1968-70, president, 1969. *Member:* International Organization for the Study of the Old Testament, Society of Biblical Literature (associate in council, 1971-73), American Schools of Oriental Research, American Oriental Society, Institute for Antiquity and Christianity, Old Testament Colloquium, American Academy of Religion, American Association of University Professors.

*WRITINGS: Form Criticism of the Old Testament: Guides to Biblical Scholarship,* edited by J. Coert Rylaarsdam, Fortress, 1971; (contributor) J. M. Efird, editor, *The Use of the Old Testament in the New and Other Essays: Studies in Honor of William Franklin Stinespring,* Duke University Press, 1972; (with J. Maxwell Miller), *Joshua,* Cambridge University Press, 1974; (contributor) *The Oxford Annotated Bible,* Oxford University Press, 1976. Member of editorial board, "Society of Biblical Literature" monograph series, 1970-76. Contributor to *Journal of Biblical Literature, Encyclopedia Americana, Duke Divinity School Review, Explore, New Creation, Catholic Biblical Quarterly,* and other publications. Member of editorial committee, *Duke Divinity School Review,* 1966-70; member of board of consultants, *Journal of the American Academy of Religion,* 1970-77; associate editor, *Old Testament Abstracts,* 1977—.

*WORK IN PROGRESS:* Editing, with Rolf Knierim, and contributing to *Form Critical Handbook to the Old Testament.*

## TUFTY, Barbara 1923-

*PERSONAL:* Born December 28, 1923, in Iowa City, Iowa; daughter of Carl F. (a professor) and Mary (Haman) Taeusch; married Harold G. Tufty (an architectural representative), December 29, 1948; children: Christopher, Karen, Steven. *Education:* Attended Vassar College, 1941-42, and Catholic University, 1943, 1944; Duke University, A.B., 1945. *Home:* 3812 Livingston St. N.W., Washington, D.C. 20015. *Agent:* Lurton Blassingame, 60 East 42nd St., New York, N.Y. 10017. *Office:* National Science Foundation, 1800 G St. N.W., Washington, D.C. 20550.

*CAREER:* National Academy of Sciences, Washington, D.C., science writer, 1970-72; National Science Foundation, Washington, D.C., staff writer, *Mosaic* magazine, 1972—. *Member:* International Wildlife Federation, National Association of Science Writers, American Association for the Advancement of Science, Smithsonian Association, Author's Guild, Bombay Natural History Society (honorary member; writer/librarian), Press Club of Washington, Chi Delta Phi.

*WRITINGS:* (Translator) B. Holas, *Crafts and Culture in the Ivory Coast,* Musee d' Abidjan (Ivory Coast), 1968; *1001 Questions Answered about Natural Land Disasters,* Dodd, 1969; *1001 Questions Answered about Storms and Other Air Disasters,* Dodd, 1970; *Cells: Units of Life,* Putnam, 1972; (contributor) *Women's Book of World Records and Achievements,* Doubleday, 1978. Contributor to *Science News, Houston Chronicle, Iron Age, Canadian Engineering Journal, Power,* and other publications.

*SIDELIGHTS:* Barbara Tufty told *CA:* "Science writing is like walking on the razor's edge; one has to be accurate enough to keep the faith of the scientists and yet be able to write simply and clearly enough to keep the interest of the lay reader. The greatest satisfaction to me comes when I am able to stimulate or awaken the reader's interest in the true beauty and insight of the natural sciences."

\*    \*    \*

## TULCHIN, Joseph S(amuel) 1939-

*PERSONAL:* Born January 13, 1939, in New York, N.Y.; son of Leon (a businessman) and Fanny (Hyman) Tulchin; married Judith Sandra Brown, June 28, 1964; children: Lisa Pauline, Andrew Reuben, Benjamin Charles, Matthew Thomas. *Education:* Amherst College, B.A. (magna cum laude), 1959; Cambridge University, graduate study, 1959-60; Harvard University, Ph.D., 1965. *Office:* Department of History, Hamilton Hall, University of North Carolina, Chapel Hill, N.C., 27514.

*CAREER:* Yale University, New Haven, Conn., instructor, 1964-65, assistant professor of history, 1965-71; University of North Carolina at Chapel Hill, associate professor, 1971-76, professor of history, 1976—. Visiting assistant professor, George Washington University, 1965; visiting lecturer at Universidad del Salvador, Universidad Nacional de Tucuman, Universidad Catolica de Salta, and Universidad Argentina de la Empresa, 1969-70. Consulting editor, Redgrave Information Services.

*MEMBER:* American Historical Association, American Studies Association, Conference on Latin American History, Latin American Studies Association, Society for Historians of American Foreign Relations, American Committee on the History of the Second World War, New England Historical Association, New England Conference on Latin American Studies, Phi Beta Kappa. *Awards,*

*honors:* Stimson Fund research grant, Yale University, 1964-65; Foreign Area fellowship, 1965-66; Morse research fellowship, Yale University, 1969-70; Fulbright-Hays research grant, Yale University, 1969-70; honorable mention, Conference on Latin American History prize, 1970; Fulbright lectureship, Argentina, 1972; National Endowment for the Humanities fellowship and National fellowship, Hoover Institution, 1975-76; Fulbright research grant, Argentina, 1978.

*WRITINGS: The Aftermath of War: The Latin American Policy of the United States 1918-1925,* New York University Press, 1971; (editor with David J. Danelski) *The Autobiographical Notes of Charles Evans Hughes,* Harvard University Press, 1972; (editor and contributor) *Problems in Latin American History,* Harper, 1972; (editor) *Latin America in the Year 2000,* Addison-Wesley, 1975; (editor) *Hemispheric Perspectives on the United States,* Greenwood Press, 1978. General editor, "Cross Currents in Latin American History" series, Harper, 1972—. Contributor to *Current History, Ventures, Criterio, Yale Review,* and other publications. Member of editorial advisory board, *International Interactions;* associate editor, *Latin American Research Review,* 1973—.

*WORK IN PROGRESS: A Traumatic Decade: The Rise of the Radical Party to Power in Argentina 1910-1920; The United States and Latin America: A Conflicted Relationship; The Human Ecology of Argentine Development: The Evolution of Argentine Agriculture, 1880-1930.*

*SIDELIGHTS:* Joseph Tulchin told *CA:* "Much of my writing during the past five years has been in the service of pedagogy. I have tried to improve the quality of materials available for teaching the history of Latin America to undergraduates in the U.S.A. This cycle is drawing to a close with the publication of *Hemispheric Perspectives,* the papers from a conference I organized on the comparative study of U.S. society and history. In the years ahead, I expect to go back to my research on Argentine history."

\*    \*    \*

## TUOHY, William 1941-

*PERSONAL:* Born August 1, 1941, in Chicago, Ill.; son of William Joseph (an entertainer under name Paul Gray) and Eleanore (Dowling) Tuohy; married Lisa Newland, August 13, 1977. *Education:* University of Missouri, B.A., 1965; additional study at Lincoln College, Lincoln, Ill., and University of Miami, Coral Gables, Fla. *Home:* 8611 Southwest 148th Pl., Miami, Fla. 33193.

*CAREER:* Public school teacher in Tinley Park, Ill., 1965-68, in Miami, Fla., 1968-70; currently working with writing groups in schools. *Member:* American Society of Composers, Authors and Publishers.

*WRITINGS—Poetry;* all published by World Publishing: *Seasons of Love,* 1970; *Love Journey,* 1971; *Spring Comes Running,* 1973. Composer of about forty songs; several songs including "Windows," "The Visitor," "Queen of 59," "Power of Love Within," have been recorded by Dion and featured on several of Dion's albums. Also composer of theme song for television show, "Stop the Presses." Author and originator of greeting card line, "Sentiments."

*WORK IN PROGRESS: Empty Pillows: A Dialogue of Love and Love Lost.*

*SIDELIGHTS:* William Tuohy told *CA:* "I grew up listening to Frank Sinatra albums and probably learned more about style, mood and technique from Sinatra than from all my years in college."

## TURNBULL, Bob 1936-

*PERSONAL:* Born November 21, 1936, in San Diego, Calif.; son of Bob III (a teacher) and Amorita (an optometrist; maiden name Treganza) Turnbull; married Julie Elizabeth James (a 1970 Orange Bowl princess and singer), October 8, 1970; children: Bob Kekoakalani. *Politics:* Independent. *Office address:* World Resort Chaplaincies, 227 Lewers St., P.O. Box 15488, Waikiki Beach, Hawaii 96815.

*CAREER:* Former television and motion picture actor in Hollywood for ten years, now known as "the chaplain of Waikiki Beach"; founder and president of non-denominational evangelical corporations, Waikiki Beach Chaplaincy, and Bob Turnbull Christian Association, headquartered in Waikiki Beach, Hawaii. In his Hollywood days, played running roles in the network television programs, "General Hospital," "Man from UNCLE," "For Better or Worse," "Petticoat Junction," and "My Three Sons," and appeared on other programs, including "Ironside," "Dr. Kildare," and "Arrest and Trial"; also acted in "Tora, Tora, Tora," "Camelot," "Spartacus," and a number of other films; presently chaplain with Honolulu Police Department, founder and main speaker at "Sun and Soul Talk," a Sunday worship service for the beach crowd, founder of Hawaii's emergency hotline telephone service, and founder and publisher of *Hawaii Free Paper;* narrator of "Soul Talk," broadcast Sundays over KKUA, 1968—. Speaker at national seminars.

*MEMBER:* National Association of Evangelicals, Fellowship of Christian Athletes, Academy of Motion Picture Arts and Sciences, Screen Actors Guild, American Federation of Television and Radio Artists, Young Americans for Freedom, Oahu Association of Evangelicals, Thalians, Honolulu Press Club.

*WRITINGS:* (Contributor) Ralph Benner and M. J. Clements, *The Young Actor's Guide to Hollywood,* McCann-Erickson, 1962; *Will the Old Bob Turnbull Please Drop Dead,* David C. Cook, 1970, published as *Hawaiian Soul,* Bible Voice, 1978. Also author of religious tracts, *Christ Told the Truth,* American Tract Society, 1964, and *New Christian? Big Deal!,* Good News Publishers, 1966.

*BIOGRAPHICAL/CRITICAL SOURCES:* Robert Stone, *Jesus Has a Man in Waikiki,* Revell, 1972, published as *God's Man for Waikiki,* Bible Voice, 1978.

\*    \*    \*

## TURNER, Charles W(ilson) 1916-

*PERSONAL:* Born November 15, 1916, in Fredericks Hall, Va.; son of Charles Constantine (a merchant) and Edna (Stecher) Turner. *Education:* University of Richmond, B.A., 1937; University of North Carolina, M.A., 1940; University of Minnesota, Ph.D., 1946. *Politics:* Democrat. *Religion:* Baptist. *Home:* 13 University Pl., Lexington, Va. 24450. *Office:* Washington and Lee University, 1 duPont Hall, Lexington, Va. 24450.

*CAREER:* History teacher in high schools in Louisa County, Va., 1937-43; Iowa State College (now Iowa State University), Ames, instructor in history, 1945-46; University of Minnesota, Minneapolis, instructor in history, 1946-47; Washington and Lee University, Lexington, Va., assistant professor, 1946-53, associate professor, 1953-58, professor of history, 1958—. Member of state selection board for Fulbright scholars. *Member:* National Historical Society, Agricultural History Society, Minnesota Historical Society, Rockridge Historical Society (president and member of board of trustees).

*WRITINGS*—Published by McClure Press, except as indicated: *Chessie's Road,* Garrett & Massie, 1956; *Mississippi West,* Garrett & Massie, 1965; *Mrs. McCulloch's Stories of Old Lexington,* 1974; *Medic Fortyniner,* 1975; (editor) Jeremiah Harris, *An Old Field School Teacher's Diary,* 1975; (editor) *Captain Greenlee Davidson's Civil War Letters,* 1975; (editor) *Professor George Irwin's War Letters, 1917-1918,* 1976; *Mrs. McCulloch's Stories,* 1977. Editor of volumes IV and V, *Proceedings* of Rockridge County Historical Society, 1958, 1963. Contributor of articles on economic and local history to professional journals.

\*    \*    \*

## TURNER, Frederick W(illiam) III 1937-

*PERSONAL:* Born June 8, 1937, in Chicago, Ill.; son of Frederick William, Jr. (an attorney) and Frances (Franklin) Turner; married Faythe Duffy (a teacher), November 21, 1959 (divorced, 1972); married Elise R. Preston, 1975; children: (first marriage) Alexandra, Jessica, Charles; (second marriage) Aaron. *Education:* Denison University, B.A., 1959; Ohio State University, M.A., 1961; University of Pennsylvania, Ph.D., 1965. *Home:* 79 Wendell Rd., Shutesbury, Mass. 01072. *Office:* Department of English, University of Massachusetts, Amherst, Mass. 01002.

*CAREER:* High school teacher of English and social studies in Newark, Ohio, 1959-60; Haverford College, Haverford, Pa., instructor in English, 1962-63; University of Rhode Island, Kingston, instructor, 1963-65, assistant professor of English, 1965-67; University of Massachusetts—Amherst, assistant professor, 1967-70, associate professor of English, 1970—. Visiting lecturer in English and native American studies, Dartmouth College, spring, 1975.

*WRITINGS:* (Contributor) Dominic Consolo, editor, *The Rocking Horse Winner,* C. E. Merrill, 1969; (editor and author of introduction and notes) Geronimo and S. M. Barrett, *Geronimo: His Own Story,* Dutton, 1970, revised edition, Cooper (London), 1975; (contributor) N. Field, editor, *Malamud and the Critics,* New York University Press, 1971; (author of introduction) Virginia Irving Armstrong, *I Have Spoken: American History Through the Voices of the Indians,* Swallow Press, 1971; (editor and author of introduction) *The Portable North American Indian Reader,* Viking, 1974, 3rd edition, 1977; *Beyond Geography: An Odyssey of the Western Spirit,* Viking/Penguin, in press. Also author of *Enemies in Peace: Our Treaty Negotiations with the American Indian,* Godine Press; editor and author of introduction and notes, *Adventures and Adventurers in the American Heartland,* Swallow Press. Contributor of articles, essays, and reviews to *American Heritage, Nation, Saturday Review, Massachusetts Review, New York Times, Novel, Evergreen Review,* and *Centennial Review.*

*WORK IN PROGRESS:* "Working backward into the American past," with current interests in travel literature, literature of exploration, cartography, cultural anthropology, folk tradition, and popular culture.

*BIOGRAPHICAL/CRITICAL SOURCES: New York Times,* July 14, 1970.

\*    \*    \*

## TURNER, Jonathan H. 1942-

*PERSONAL:* Born September 7, 1942, in Oakland, Calif.; son of John Hugh (a developer) and Maries R. (Rubell) Turner; married Susan Hainge, September 7, 1967 (divorced, 1971); married Sandra Leer, November 24, 1971;

children: Patricia, Donna, Kenneth. *Education:* University of California, Santa Barbara, B.A., 1965; Cornell University, M.A., 1966, Ph.D., 1968. *Politics:* Democrat. *Home:* 6470 Hawarden Dr., Riverside, Calif. 92506. *Office:* Department of Sociology, University of California, Riverside, Calif. 92502.

*CAREER:* University of Hawaii, Honolulu, assistant professor of sociology, 1968-69; University of California, Riverside, assistant professor, 1969-72, associate professor of sociology, 1972—. *Member:* American Sociological Association.

*WRITINGS: Patterns of Social Organization,* McGraw, 1972; *American Society: Problems of Structure,* Harper, 1972; *The Structure of Sociological Theory,* Dorsey, 1974, 2nd edition, 1978; *Privilege and Poverty in America,* Goodyear Publishing, 1976; *Social Problems in America,* Harper, 1977; *Sociology: Studying the Human System,* Goodyear Publishing, 1978; *Functionalism,* Cummings, 1978.

\* \* \*

## TURNER, Louis (Mark) 1942-

*PERSONAL:* Born August 8, 1942, in Sheerness, England. *Education:* Trinity College, Oxford, B.A., 1964; University of Salford, management diploma, 1965. *Politics:* Social Democrat. *Religion:* None. *Home:* 30 Fortnam Rd., London N19 3NR, England. *Agent:* Michael Sissons, A. D. Peters & Co., 10 Buckingham St., London WC2N 6BU, England. *Office:* Royal Institute of International Affairs, 10 St. James Square, London SW1Y 4LE, England.

*CAREER:* University of Salford, Salford, England, researcher on multinational corporations, 1964-73; Royal Institute of International Affairs, London, England, specialist/fellow, 1973—. Director, Amanda Films Ltd. *Member:* British Institute of Management, Royal Institute of International Affairs, Salzburg Assembly: Impact of New Technology (SAINT).

*WRITINGS: Politics and the Multinational Company* (pamphlet), Fabian Research, 1969; *Invisible Empires,* Harcourt, 1971; *Multinational Companies and the Third World,* Hill & Wang, 1973; *The Golden Hordes: International Tourism and the Pleasure Periphery,* St. Martin's, 1977; *Oil Companies and the International System: A Study in Transnational Relations,* Allen & Unwin, 1978.

*WORK IN PROGRESS:* Research on the international implications of Middle Eastern industrialization.

*BIOGRAPHICAL/CRITICAL SOURCES: Best Sellers,* March 1, 1971; *Washington Post,* March 1, 1971.

\* \* \*

## TURNER, Ralph H(erbert) 1919-

*PERSONAL:* Born December 15, 1919, in Effingham, Ill.; son of Herbert (a photographer) and Hilda Pearl (Bohn) Turner; married Christine Elizabeth Hanks, November 2, 1943; children: Lowell Ralph, Cheryl Christine. *Education:* Pasadena Junior College, A.A., 1939; University of Southern California, B.A., 1941, M.A., 1942; University of Wisconsin, further graduate study, 1942-43; University of Chicago, Ph.D., 1948. *Home:* 1126 Chautauqua Blvd., Pacific Palisades, Calif. 90272. *Office:* Department of Sociology, University of California, 405 Hilgard Ave., Los Angeles, Calif. 90024.

*CAREER:* American Council on Race Relations, research associate, 1947-48; University of California, Los Angeles,

instructor, 1948-50, assistant professor, 1950-55, associate professor, 1955-59, professor of sociology and anthropology, 1959—, chairman of department of sociology, 1963-68. Visiting professor at University of Washington, Seattle, 1960, University of Hawaii, 1962, and University of Georgia, 1975; visiting scholar, Australian National University, 1972. Chairman, Behavior Science Study Section, National Institutes of Health, 1963-64; director-at-large, Social Science Research Council, 1965-66; director, Foundations Fund for Research in Psychiatry, 1970-73. Chairman of panel of public policy implications of earthquake prediction, National Academy of Sciences, 1974—. *Military service:* U.S. Navy, 1943-46; became lieutenant junior grade.

*MEMBER:* American Sociological Association (president, 1968-69), Society for the Study of Social Problems (member of executive committee, 1959), Sociological Research Association, American Council on Family Relations, Pacific Sociological Association (president, 1956-57), Society for the Study of Symbolic Interaction, American Association of University Professors. *Awards, honors:* Social Science Research Council faculty research fellow, 1953-56; senior Fulbright scholar in London, England, 1956-57; Guggenheim fellow, 1964-65.

*WRITINGS:* (With Lewis Killian) *Collective Behavior,* Prentice-Hall, 1957, revised edition, 1972; *The Social Context of Ambition,* Chandler Publishing, 1964; (editor and author of introduction) Robert E. Park, *On Social Control and Collective Behavior,* University of Chicago Press, 1967; *Family Interaction,* Wiley, 1970. Contributor to sociology journals in the United States and Great Britain. Advisory editor, *American Journal of Sociology,* 1954-56; member of editorial staff, *American Sociological Review,* 1955-56; associate editor, *Social Problems,* 1959-62, 1967; advisory editor, *Sociology and Social Research,* 1961-74; editor, *Sociometry,* 1962-64; consulting editor, *Sociological Inquiry,* 1968-73, *Western Sociological Review,* 1975—; member of editorial board, *Mass Emergencies,* 1975—, *International Journal of Critical Sociology,* 1974—; *Annual Review of Sociology,* member of editorial committee, 1973-79, acting editor, 1977-78.

*WORK IN PROGRESS:* Studies on role theory and on the self-conception; research on social effects of earthquake prediction and disaster warning; studies in theories of collective behavior and social movements.

\* \* \*

## TURNILL, Reginald 1915-

*PERSONAL:* Born May 12, 1915; married Margaret Hennings, September 10, 1938; children: two sons. *Education:* Privately educated. *Home and office:* Somerville Lodge, Hillside, Sandgate, Kent, England.

*CAREER:* Industrial correspondent; British Broadcasting Corp. (BBC), London, England, air and defense correspondent (has covered nearly every American space flight and traveled to Moscow for Yuri Gagarin's flight), 1958-76; full-time writer, 1976—. *Military service:* British Army, 1940-46. *Member:* British Interplanetary Society (fellow).

*WRITINGS: Moonslaught: The Story of Man's Race to the Moon,* British Broadcasting Corp., 1969; *The Language of Space,* John Day, 1971; *The Observer's Book of Manned Space Flight,* Warne, 1972, 3rd edition, 1978; *The Observer's Book of Unmanned Space Flight,* Warne, 1974; *Observer's Space Flight Directory,* Warne, 1978.

*WORK IN PROGRESS: Never Enough Good Men: The*

*Story of the Royal Aircraft Establishment, Farnborough,* for R. Hale.

*SIDELIGHTS:* Reginald Turnill has flown over three million miles for the British Broadcasting Corp., and has made over eight thousand radio and television broadcasts. He is now a full-time writer, and says his best work "is always produced ten seconds before the deadline." He prefers to work on factual books "because facts are always so much more unbelievable than fiction."

\*     \*     \*

### TUTEN, Frederic 1936-

*PERSONAL:* Born December 2, 1936, in New York, N.Y.; son of Rex and Madelyn (Scelfo) Tuten; married Simona Morini (a writer), September 9, 1962. *Education:* College of the City of New York (now City College of the City University of New York), B.A., 1959; New York University, M.A., 1964, Ph.D., 1971. *Office:* Department of English, City College of the City University of New York, 137th St. and Convent Ave., New York, N.Y. 10037.

*CAREER:* City College of the City University of New York, New York, N.Y., associate professor of American literature, 1971—.

*WRITINGS:* (Translator with wife, Simona Morini) G. R. Solari, *The House of Farnese,* Doubleday, 1968; (translator with S. Morini) *Charles Baudelaire: Letters from His Youth,* Doubleday, 1970; *The Adventures of Mao on the Long March* (fiction), Citadel, 1971.

\*     \*     \*

### TWEDT, Dik Warren 1920-

*PERSONAL:* Born December 30, 1920, in Minneapolis, Minn.; married; two children. *Education:* University of Minnesota, B.A. (magna cum laude), 1941; Northwestern University, M.S.J., 1948, Ph.D., 1951. *Home:* 57 Bellerive Acres, St. Louis, Mo. 63121. *Office:* Department of Business Administration, University of Missouri, 8001 Natural Bridge Rd., St. Louis, Mo. 63121.

*CAREER:* Precision Hone Co. (automotive tool company), Detroit, Mich., vice-president and general manager, 1941-42; Time Inc., New York, N.Y., public relations and agency supervisor, 1942-46; Clissold Publishing Co., Chicago, assistant promotion manager, 1946-51; Young & Rubicam, Inc. (advertising agency), Chicago, manager of experimental research, 1951-52; manager of experimental research, supervisor on several accounts, Needham, Louis, & Brorby, Inc. (marketing consultants), 1952-56; Kenyon & Eckhardt, Inc. (advertising agency), Chicago, research director and plan board chairman, 1956-57; Leo Burnett Co. (advertising agency), Chicago, senior account executive, 1957-60; Faison & Twedt, Inc. (marketing consultants), Chicago, president, 1960-62; Batten, Barton, Durstine & Osborn, Inc. (advertising agency), Chicago, vice-president, marketing services, and plan board chairman, 1962-63; Oscar Mayer & Co. (food company), Madison, Wis., director of marketing planning and research, 1963-71; U.S. Postal Service, Washington, D.C., executive director, 1972; University of Missouri—St. Louis, professor of marketing, 1972—. Diplomate of American Board of Professional Psychology, 1956; licensed psychologist in Illinois, 1959, Wisconsin, 1965, and Missouri, 1978.

*MEMBER:* Advertising Research Foundation (general conference chairman, 1966), American Association of Public Opinion Research, American Marketing Association (business manager, 1958-63; president, Chicago chapter, 1960; national vice-president, 1962; member of census advisory committee, 1968-72), American Psychological Association (fellow, 1958—; president of consumer division, 1962), American Standards Association (chairman, Task Force on Standard Geographic Units, 1956-67), American Statistical Association, Sigma Delta Chi.

*WRITINGS:* (With Harry Deane Wolfe) *Essentials of the Promotional Mix,* Appleton, 1970; (contributor) *Handbook of Modern Marketing,* McGraw, 1970. Member of editorial review board, American Marketing Association, 1963—.

Contributor to *Encyclopedia of the Social Sciences.* Contributor to numerous marketing and psychology journals, including *Journal of Applied Psychology, Printers' Ink, Journal of Marketing, Annual Review of Psychology, Business Management, Marketing Management, Food Product Development,* and *Marketing Insights.*

\*     \*     \*

### TYLER, William R(oyall) 1910-

*PERSONAL:* Born October 17, 1910, in Paris, France; son of Royall and Elisina (De Castelvecchio) Tyler; married Bettine Mary Fisher-Rowe, July 31, 1934; children: Royall, Matilda Eve (Mrs. William Kenneth Thompson). *Education:* Oxford University, B.A., 1933; Harvard University, A.M., 1941. *Home:* Antigny-Le-Chateau, 21230 Arnay-Le-Duc, France.

*CAREER:* Employed by Guaranty Trust Co., New York City, 1934-38; WRUL (short wave radio station), Boston, Mass., program manager, 1940-42; worked for U.S. Office of War Information in New York City, 1942, North Africa, 1943-44, and France, 1944-45; U.S. Department of State, American Embassy, Paris, France, counselor, 1948-52, consul, 1952-54, Office of Western European Affairs, Washington, D.C., deputy director, 1954-57, director, 1957-58, American Embassy, Bonn, Germany, political counselor, 1958-61, Washington, D.C., deputy assistant Secretary of State for European Affairs, 1961-62, assistant Secretary, 1962-65, U.S. ambassador to Netherlands, 1965-69; Dumbarton Oaks Research Center, Washington, D.C., director, beginning 1969. *Member:* American Academy of Arts and Sciences (fellow), Massachusetts Historical Society (corresponding member), Colonial Society of Massachusetts (honorary member), Phi Beta Kappa (honorary), Cosmos Club (Washington), Tavern Club (Boston), Club of Odd Volumes (Boston). *Awards, honors:* Medal of Freedom, 1945; knight of French Legion of Honor, 1946.

*WRITINGS:* (Translator) Pierre Janssen, *A Moment of Silence,* Atheneum, 1970; *The Sixth Nouvelle Nouvelle,* Club of Odd Volumes, 1971; *Dijon and the Valois Dukes of Burgundy,* University of Oklahoma Press, 1971.

*WORK IN PROGRESS:* Reserarch project involving letters from Franz Liszt to Olga von Meyendorff.

\*     \*     \*

### TYSON, Joseph B(lake) 1928-

*PERSONAL:* Born August 30, 1928, in Charlotte, N.C.; son of Joseph B. (a construction worker) and Lucy (Lewis) Tyson; married Margaret Helms, June 12, 1954; children: Linda S. *Education:* Duke University, A.B., 1950, B.D., 1953; Union Theological Seminary, New York, N.Y., S.T.M., 1955, Ph.D., 1959. *Religion:* Methodist. *Home:* 8636 Capri Dr., Dallas, Tex. 75238. *Office:* Department of Religious Studies, Southern Methodist University, Dallas, Tex. 75275.

*CAREER:* Southern Methodist University, Dallas, Tex., instructor, 1958-60, assistant professor, 1960-65, associate professor, 1965-74, professor of religious studies, 1974—, head of department, 1965-75. *Member:* American Academy of Religion (president of southwestern region, 1968-69), Society of Biblical Literature, Studiorum Novi Testamenti Societas.

*WRITINGS: A Study of Early Christianity,* Macmillan, 1973. Contributor of articles to *Journal of Biblical Literature, Novum Testamentum,* and *New Testament Studies.*

*WORK IN PROGRESS:* Research in early Christianity and its relationship to Judaism; aspects of Pauline Christianity; *Synoptic Abstract,* for Biblical Research Associates.

# U

## UBELL, Earl 1926-

*PERSONAL:* Born June 21, 1926, in Brooklyn, N.Y.; son of Charles Abraham and Hilda (Kramer) Ubell; married Shirley Leitman (executive director of Center for Modern Dance Education), February 12, 1949; children: Lori Ellen, Michael Charles. *Education:* College of the City of New York (now City College of the City University of New York), B.S., 1948. *Religion:* Ethical Culture. *Home:* 682 Broadway, New York, N.Y. 10012. *Agent:* Curtis Brown Ltd., 575 Madison Ave., New York, N.Y. 10022. *Office:* WNBC-TV News, 30 Rockefeller Plaza, New York, N.Y. 10020.

*CAREER: New York Herald Tribune,* New York City, messenger, 1943, secretary, 1943-48, reporter, 1948-53, science editor, 1953-66; WCBS-TV, New York City, science editor, 1966-72, news Poll director, 1972; WNBC-TV News, New York City, director, 1972-76, producer of planned specials, 1976—. Adjunct associate professor of journalism, College of Liberal Arts, New York University, 1971—. Science editor, Mutual Broadcasting System, 1961-62; special science editor, WNEW, 1964-65. President, Council for Advancement of Science Writing, 1960-66; chairman, Center for Modern Dance Education, 1962; president, North Jersey Cultural Council, 1966-72; member of board of directors, Young Men's Hebrew Association of Bergen County, 1968—; member of board of directors, Plenum Publishing Co., 1971—; chairman, Dance Notation Bureau, 1975—. *Military service:* U.S. Navy, 1944-46.

*MEMBER:* National Association of Science Writers (president, 1960-61), American Crystalographic Association, Phi Beta Kappa (president of Gamma chapter, 1975-76). *Awards, honors:* Albert and Mary Lasker Medical Journalism Award, 1957; American Association for the Advancement of Science-Westinghouse Science Writing Award, 1960; Empire State Award for excellence in medical reporting, 1963; Science Writers Award of American Psychological Foundation, 1965; New York State Associated Press Broadcasting Award for excellence in reporting, 1969, 1970; Emmy Award (for New York area) of National Academy of Television Arts and Sciences, 1970; Donald Salmon Award for significant contribution to development of the arts, 1970.

*WRITINGS: The World of Push and Pull* (juvenile), illustrations by Arline Strong, Atheneum, 1964; *The World of* the Living (juvenile), illustrations by Strong, Atheneum, 1965; *The World of Candle and Color* (juvenile), illustrations by Strong, Atheneum, 1969; *How to Save Your Life,* Harcourt, 1973. Also co-author of children's play, "The Dirty Air Is Everywhere," produced by Merry-Go-Rounders. Contributor of more than fifty popular and several scientific articles to magazines, and of more than two thousand articles to newspapers.

*WORK IN PROGRESS:* A book on science for children; a novel; magazine articles.

*SIDELIGHTS:* As a newsman, Earl Ubell has traveled throughout the world and covered such notable events as the first Sputnik flight, 1961, and the first U.S. manned space flight, 1962. He has done scientific research on summer projects at various laboratories—Weizmann Institute, California Institute of Technology, and Jackson Laboratory. All of his spare time is devoted to the development of arts organizations in his home community.

\* \* \*

## UNDERWOOD, (Mary) Betty 1921-

*PERSONAL:* Born July 4, 1921, in Rockford, Ill.; daughter of Clarence Scott (a professor) and Ethel (a professional writer; maiden name, Todd) Anderson; married Raymond P. Underwood (an attorney), November 6, 1943; children: Douglas Mark, Jeffrey Kirk, Barbara Lael. *Education:* Attended University of Hawaii, 1939-40; Pennsylvania State University, A.B., 1942. *Politics:* Democrat. *Religion:* Society of Friends (Quaker). *Home:* 6236 Southwest Tower Way, Portland, Ore. 97221.

*CAREER:* Houghton Mifflin Co., Boston, Mass., reader and assistant editor, 1943-47; George Washington University, Washington, D.C., staff writer in medical public relations, 1969-70; Lane County Council on Alcoholism, Eugene, Ore., office assistant, 1970-71; American Civil Liberties Union, Portland, Ore., assistant to executive director, 1971-72. Member of Governor's Commission on Status of Women; member of board of governors, University of Oregon Art Museum; former chairman of advisory committee, Multnomah County Welfare Commission; member of regional committee, American Friends Service Committee, 1971; member, Oregon Council for Women's Equality, 1971—; coordinator, Oregon International Women's Year, 1975; life member of Reed College Women's

Committee. *Member:* American Association of University Women, National Organization for Women, Womens International League for Peace and Freedom, League of Women Voters, Planned Parenthood Society, Phi Beta Kappa, Phi Kappa Phi, Alpha Lambda Delta, Pi Gamma Mu, Kappa Alpha Theta. *Awards, honors:* Jane Addams Children's Book Award, Womens International League for Peace and Freedom, 1972, for *The Tamarack Tree*.

*WRITINGS: The Tamarack Tree* (juvenile novel), Houghton, 1971; *The Forge and the Forest* (juvenile novel), Houghton, 1975. Contributor to *Childcraft Encyclopedia*.†

\* \* \*

## UNGAR, Sanford J. 1945-

*PERSONAL:* Born June 10, 1945, in Wilkes-Barre, Pa.; son of Max H. (a businessman) and Tillie (Landau) Ungar; married Beth L. Pollock (a physician), November 1, 1969. *Education:* Harvard University, A.B. (magna cum laude), 1966; London School of Economics and Political Science, University of London, M.Sc., 1967. *Home:* 5312 38th St. N.W., Washington, D.C. 20015. *Agent:* Peter Shepherd, 40 East 49th St., New York, N.Y. 10017. *Office: Foreign Policy,* 11 Dupont Circle N.W., Washington, D.C. 20036.

*CAREER: Boston Globe,* Cambridge, Mass., stringer, 1964-66; *Time,* London, England, stringer, 1966-67; United Press International, Paris, France, correspondent, 1967-69; *Newsweek,* Nairobi, Kenya, correspondent, 1969; *Washington Post,* Washington, D.C., staff writer, 1969-73; Adlai Stevenson Institute, Chicago, Ill., resident fellow, 1973-74; *Atlantic,* Washington, D.C., editor, 1975-77; *Foreign Policy,* Washington, D.C., managing editor, 1977—. *Life,* summer internship in New York office, 1965, and in Paris office, 1966; visiting reporter, *Argus* newspapers of South Africa, 1967; feature and editorial writer, *Daily Nation,* Kenya, 1969. Member of board of trustees National Humanities Faculty, Concord, Mass. *Member:* Authors Guild, American Federation of Television and Radio Artists, Washington Press Club, Harvard Club of Washington. *Awards, honors:* American Bar Association Certificate of Merit, 1971, for coverage of Mayday demonstrations.

*WRITINGS:* (With Allan Priaulx) *The Almost Revolution: France-1968,* Dell, 1969; *The Papers & the Papers,* Dutton, 1972; (with R. Heilbroner and others) *In the Name of Profit,* Doubleday, 1972; *FBI: An Uncensored Look behind the Walls,* Little, Brown, 1976. Contributor of articles to journals.

*WORK IN PROGRESS:* A collection of brief biographies of public figures.

\* \* \*

## UNRAU, William E. 1929-

*PERSONAL:* Born August 19, 1929, in Goessel, Kan.; son of William H. and Margaret C. (Epp) Unrau; married Mildred C. Jantz (a piano instructor), August 17, 1953; children: Debbie D., William S. *Education:* Bethany College, Kansas, B.A., 1951; University of Wyoming, M.A., 1956; University of Colorado, Ph.D., 1963. *Politics:* Independent. *Religion:* Independent. *Home:* 1107 West River Blvd., Wichita, Kan. 67203. *Office:* History Department, Wichita State University, Wichita, Kan. 67208.

*CAREER:* Bethany College, Lindsborg, Kan., 1957-1965, became associate professor of history & chairman of department; Wichita State University, Wichita, Kan., professor of history, 1965—. Consultant to Regents Press of Kansas, and

the Los Angeles County Museum; reader for several professional journals. *Member:* Organization of American Historians, Western History Association, Kansas State Historical Society.

*WRITINGS: The Kansa Indians: A History of the Wind People, 1673-1873,* University of Oklahoma Press, 1971; (with H. Craig Miner) *The End of Indian Kansas: A History of Cultural Revolution, 1854-1871,* Regents Press of Kansas, 1977; *Tending the Talking Wire: A Buck Soldier's View of Indian Country,* University of Utah Press, 1978. Contributor of articles to *Western Historical Quarterly, Montana Magazine of Western History, Michigan History, Missouri Historical Society Bulletin, Kansas Historical Quarterly, Colorado Magazine, New Mexico Historical Quarterly.*

*WORK IN PROGRESS:* Research on the American Indian and federal bureaucracy and on the American Indian and Charles Curtis; *The Emigrant Indians of Kansas: A Critical Bibliography,* for Indiana University Press.

\* \* \*

## UROFSKY, Melvin I. 1939-

*PERSONAL:* Born February 7, 1939, in New York, N.Y.; son of Philip and Sylvia (Passow) Urofsky; married Susan Linda Miller (a legislative analyst), August 27, 1961; children: Philip Eric, Robert Ian. *Education:* Columbia University, A.B., 1961, M.A., 1962, Ph.D., 1968. *Politics:* "Democratic-Independent." *Religion:* Jewish. *Home:* 1500 Careybrook Dr., Richmond, Va. 23233. *Office:* Department of History, Virginia Commonwealth University, Richmond, Va. 23284.

*CAREER:* New York State Employment Service, New York City, interviewer, 1962; Robert Saudek Associates, New York City, researcher, 1963; Ohio State University, Columbus, instructor in history, 1964-67; State University of New York at Albany, assistant professor of history and education, 1967-70, assistant dean for innovative education, 1970-72, professor of history in Allen Center, 1972-74; Virginia Commonwealth University, Richmond, 1974—, began as associate professor, currently professor of history and chairman of department. Chairman, Zionist Academic Council, 1976—. Consultant to Robert Saudek Productions, Institute for the Advancement of Urban Education. *Member:* Organization of American Historians, American Zionist Federation (member of national board and executive committee; co-chairman of Commission on Zionist Idealogy); American Jewish Historical Society (member of academic council, 1977—), Richmond Oral History Association (founder; president). *Awards, honors:* National Endowment for the Humanities grants for editing Louis D. Brandeis letters, 1967-74, senior fellowship, 1976-77; American Council of Learned Societies grants-in-aid, 1972, 1978; Jewish Book Council Kaplun Award, 1976.

*WRITINGS: Big Steel and the Wilson Administration: A Study in Business-Government Relations,* Ohio State University Press, 1969; (editor) *Why Teachers Strike: Teachers' Rights and Community Control,* Doubleday-Anchor, 1970; (editor with David W. Levy) *Letters of Louis D. Brandeis,* State University of New York Press, Volume I: *Urban Reformer, 1870-1907,* 1971, Volume II: *People's Attorney, 1907-1912,* 1972, Volume III: *Progressive and Zionist, 1913-15,* 1973, Volume IV: *Mr. Justice Brandeis, 1916-1921,* 1975, Volume V: *Elder Statesman, 1922-41,* 1978; *A Mind of One piece: Brandeis and American Reform,* Scribner, 1971; (editor) *Perspectives on Urban America,* Doubleday, 1973; *American Zionism from Herzl to the Holocaust,* Doubleday, 1975; *We Are One! American Jewry and Israel,* Doubleday, 1978; *Essays on American Zionism,* Herzl Press, 1978. Contributor of numerous articles to scholarly journals and popular periodicals. Member of editorial board, *Midstream,* 1978—.

*WORK IN PROGRESS:* A biography of Rabbi Stephen S. Wise.

\*     \*     \*

## USDIN, Gene (Leonard) 1922-

*PERSONAL:* Born January 31, 1922, in New York, N.Y.; son of I. L. and Eva (Miller) Usdin; married Cecile Weil, 1947; children: Cecile Catherine, Linda Ann, Steven William, Thomas Michael. *Education:* Attended University of North Carolina, 1939-40, and University of Florida, 1940-41; Tulane University, B.S., 1943, M.D., 1946. *Politics:* Democrat. *Home:* 3 Newcomb Blvd., New Orleans, La. 70118. *Office:* 1522 Aline St., New Orleans, La. 70115.

*CAREER:* Private practice of psychiatry, New Orleans, La., 1951—. Tulane University, School of Medicine, assistant professor, 1958-62, associate professor of clinical psychiatry 1962-69; clinical professor of psychiatry, School of Medicine, Louisiana State University, 1970—; professor of psychiatry, Notre Dame Seminary, 1969—. Charity Hospital, visiting physician, 1956-61, senior visiting physician, 1961—; senior psychiatrist, DePaul Hospital, 1957—; Touro Infirmary, senior psychiatrist, 1959-62, chief psychiatrist, 1962-66, director of psychiatric service, 1966-72. American Board of Psychiatry and Neurology, diplomate, 1952, assistant examiner, 1958—. Member of psychiatric consultants committee, American Bar Foundation. *Military service:* U.S. Navy, 1947-49; became lieutenant junior grade.

*MEMBER:* American College of Psychiatrists (fellow; president, 1978), American Psychiatric Association (fellow), Group for the Advancement of Psychiatry, National Association for Mental Health (member of professional and advisory council), American Medical Writers Association, Southern Psychiatric Association (past president), Louisiana Academy of Religion and Mental Health (past chairman), Louisiana Psychiatric Association (past president), Louisiana State Medical Society, New Orleans Society of Psychiatry and Neurology (past president), Insitute of Mental Hygiene (president, 1978).

*WRITINGS:* (Contributor) Jules H. Masserman, editor, *Current Psychiatric Treatment,* Vol. 3, Grune, 1963; (contributor) Ralph Slovenko, editor, *Sexual Behavior and the Law,* C. C Thomas, 1964; (contributor and co-author with Ralph Solvenko) *Psychotherapy, Confidentiality, and Privileged Communications,* C. C Thomas, 1966; (contributor) Jonas R. Rappeport, editor, *The Clinical Evaluation of the Dangerousness of the Mentally Ill Patient,* C. C Thomas, 1967; (contributor) A. W. Sipe, editor, *Hope, Psychiatry's Commitment: Papers Presented to Leo H. Bartemeier,* Brunner, 1970; (author of introduction) John G. Howells, editor, *Modern Perspectives of World Psychiatry,* Brunner, 1971.

Editor: *Psychoneurosis and Schizophrenia,* Lippincott, 1966; *Practical Lectures in Psychiatry for the Medical Practitioner,* C. C Thomas, 1966; *Adolescence: Care and Counseling,* Lippincott, 1967; (with P. A. Martin and others) *A Physician in the General Practice of Psychiatry,* Brunner, 1970; *Perspectives on Violence,* Brunner, 1972; *Psychiatric Forum,* Brunner, 1972; *Sleep Research and Clinical Practice,* Brunner, 1973; *Overview of the Psychotherapies,* Brunner, 1975; *Schizophrenia: Biological and Psychological Perspectives,* Brunner, 1975; *Depression: Clinical, Biological and Psychological Perspectives,* Brunner, 1977; *Psychiatric Medicine,* Brunner, 1977; *Aging: The Process, the People,* Brunner, in press; *Textbook on Psychiatry in Medical Practice,* McGraw, in press. Contributor to "Current Psychiatric Therapies," series, Grune, 1963, to *Proceedings of Inter-American Congress on Forensic Medicine,* C. C Thomas, 1964, and to psychiatry and legal journals. Member of board of editors, *Mental Hygiene;* editor-in-chief, *Journal of Continuing Education in Psychiatry.*

# V

## van CROONENBURG, Engelbert J(ohannes) 1909-

*PERSONAL:* Born February 27, 1909, in The Hague, Holland; came to U.S., 1952; naturalized, 1958; son of Cornelis F. (a business supervisor) and Johanna (Kloosterman) van Croonenburg. *Education:* University of Fribourg, B.A., 1937, M.A., 1940, D.Th., 1941.

*CAREER:* Ordained priest of Roman Catholic Church, 1938; Holy Ghost Seminary, Gemert, Netherlands, professor of theology and philosophy, 1941-52; Duquesne University, Pittsburgh, Pa., assistant professor, 1952-59, associate professor, 1959-62, professor of philosophy, beginning 1962, executive director, Institute of Man, beginning 1964. Retired. *Member:* American Catholic Philosophical Association, Catholic Theological Society of America.

*WRITINGS: Gateway to Reality: An Introduction to Philosophy,* Duquesne University Press, 1963; (with Adrian van Kaam and Susan Muto) *The Emergent Self,* Dimension Books, 1968; (with van Kaam and Muto) *The Participant Self,* Dimension Books, 1970; *Don't Be Discouraged,* Dimension Books, 1973.

*WORK IN PROGRESS:* A study of man's personal development and his relation to the Transcendent.

\*    \*    \*

## Van Der VOORT, Richard Lee 1936-

*PERSONAL:* Born March 7, 1936, in Wayne, Mich.; son of Ralph Lee (a laborer) and Esther (Daroci) Van Der Voort; married third wife, Donna Jean Hardacre (a dental hygienist), May 1, 1971; children: (first marriage) Bethany Lynn, Susan Carol, Walter Alexander; (second marriage) Jennifer Rebecca. *Education:* Michigan State University, B.A., 1959; University of New Mexico, M.A., 1968.

*CAREER:* Trainee insurance adjuster and substitute high school teacher in East Detroit, Mich., 1959-60; high school teacher in Reese, Mich., 1960-61; Iowa State University of Science and Technology, Ames, instructor in English, 1961-64; Alfred State College (now Alfred University), Alfred, N.Y., lecturer in general studies and instructor in English, creative writing and philosophy, 1964-66; Southwestern College, Chula Vista, Calif., instructor in English, 1968; San Diego State College (now University), San Diego, Calif., lecturer, 1969, assistant professor of English at Imperial Valley Campus, Calexico, 1969-70; Alfred University, assistant professor of English, 1970-71; Western Maryland College, Westminster, assistant professor of English and writer in residence, beginning 1971. Has given readings of his own poetry in six states; participant in Poets in the Schools program of Maryland Arts Council. *Military service:* U.S. Army, 1954-56.

*WRITINGS: Very Young Like Me* (novel), Windfall Press, 1969. About one hundred poems and several short stories have been published in fifty periodicals, including *Caravel, Folio, Grande Ronde Review, Poetry Bag, Wisconsin Review,* and other little literary magazines. Editor, *Word* (formerly poetry broadsheet; issued as mimeographed magazine, January, 1970), spring, 1972.

*WORK IN PROGRESS:* Two novels, *Charles: A Novel in Mind-Letters* and *Oedipal Wrecks and Other Misfortunes;* several collections of poetry.†

\*    \*    \*

## VAN DOREN, Mark 1894-1972

June 13, 1894—December 10, 1972; American poet, critic, educator, novelist, playwright, editor, short story writer, essayist, and man of letters. Obituaries: *New York Times,* December 12, 1972; *L'Express,* December 18-24, 1972; *Publishers Weekly,* December 18, 1972; *Newsweek,* December 18, 1972; *Time,* December 25, 1972. (See index for *CA* sketch)

\*    \*    \*

## van FRAASSEN, Bastiaan Cornelis

*EDUCATION:* University of Alberta, B.A. (honors), 1963; University of Pittsburgh, M.A., 1964, Ph.D., 1966. *Office:* Department of Philosophy, University of Toronto, Toronto, Ontario, Canada.

*CAREER:* Yale University, New Haven, Conn., assistant professor, 1966-68, associate professor of philosophy, 1968-69; University of Toronto, Toronto, Ontario, associate professor, 1969, professor of philosophy, 1971—; University of Southern California, Los Angeles, professor of philosophy, 1976—. Visiting professor, Indiana University, 1968-69. *Awards, honors:* Guggenheim fellowship, 1970-71.

*WRITINGS: Introduction to the Philosophy of Time and Space,* Random House, 1970; *Formal Semantics and Logic,* Macmillan, 1971; (with Karel Lambert) *Derivation and Counterexample,* Dickinson, 1972. Contributor of articles to technical journals.

*WORK IN PROGRESS:* Research on philosophy of science and logic.

\* \* \*

## Van ORDEN, M(erton) D(ick) 1921-

*PERSONAL:* Born February 24, 1921, in Austin, Tex.; son of Merton Leroy and Thelma (Murphy) Van Orden; married Nancy Platt, June 9, 1944; children: Anne (Mrs. Stanton Paine Coerr), Richard Platt. *Education:* U.S. Naval Academy, B.S., 1944; Massachusetts Institute of Technology, B.S.E.E., 1949; Harvard University, graduate study, 1953; George Washington University, M.B.A., 1964. *Religion:* Protestant. *Home:* 5953 Woodacre Ct., McLean, Va. 22101.

*CAREER:* U.S. Navy, midshipman, 1941-44, officer, 1944-75, retired with rank of rear admiral; Decisions & Designs, Inc., McLean, Va., currently research analyst.

*WRITINGS: The Book of United States Navy Ships* (juvenile), Dodd, 1969, 3rd edition, in press. Contributor to *U.S. Naval Institute Proceedings* and other military and technical journals.

*SIDELIGHTS:* M. D. Van Orden told *CA:* "I have long been interested in ships, from sail to steam to nuclear power, particularly U.S. Navy ships. I felt the need for communicating to young people the interesting traditions associated with Navy ships and some of the characteristics of modern ships of the Navy. Discussions of ship terminology, ships' names and how they are arrived at, and some brief descriptions of the different types and their missions are believed to be of interest to young men contemplating a Navy career—these motivated my writing of *The Book of United States Navy Ships.*"

\* \* \*

## Van RIPER, Robert 1921-

*PERSONAL:* Born June 18, 1921, in Mount Vernon, N.Y.; son of Austin Millard (an architect) and Gladys (Brownell) Van Riper; married Barbara Jean Jacobs (a portrait painter), December 2, 1944; children: Alexandra Jay, Tracy Anne. *Education:* Oberlin College, B.A., 1943. *Religion:* Protestant. *Home:* 63 Summit Ave., Bronxville, N.Y. 10708. *Agent:* Bill Berger Associates, Inc., 535 East 72nd St., New York, N.Y. 10021.

*CAREER:* Edward L. Bernays (public relations firm), New York City, expediter, 1947-50; N. W. Ayer & Son, Inc. (advertising agency), account representative, New York City, 1950-54, supervisor in charge of public relations, Philadelphia, Pa., 1954-60, director of information services, Philadelphia, 1960-62, vice-president and management director of public relations department, New York City, 1962-67, senior vice-president and managing supervisor, New York City, 1967-73; Financial Accounting Standards Board, Stamford, Conn., public relations counsel, 1973—. Vice president and trustee, Lawrence Hospital. *Military service:* U.S. Naval Reserve, 1943-46; became lieutenant junior grade. *Member:* Franklin Inn (Philadelphia), Holland Society of New York, Bronxville Field Club.

*WRITINGS: A Really Sincere Guy,* McKay, 1958; *The Governor,* Lippincott, 1970. Contributor of articles to business and professional journals.

*WORK IN PROGRESS:* A novel on life within large organizations.

## VANSANT, Carl 1938-

*PERSONAL:* Born February 14, 1938, in Clinton, Mo.; son of Emmett Allen (a farmer and businessman) and Mary Elinor (Howell) Vansant; married Margaret Joan Chiabotta, June 15, 1958; children: Lori Elizabeth, John Ayres. *Education:* University of Missouri—Rolla, B.S.Met.E., 1960; Purdue University, M.S.Met.E., 1963. *Politics:* Independent. *Religion:* Lutheran. *Home:* 10901 Harrison, Kansas City, Mo. 64131. *Office:* Black & Veatch, P.O. Box 8405, Kansas City, Mo. 64114.

*CAREER:* Has worked as a metallurgist, engineer, and systems and operations analyst for Union Carbide, Speedway, Ind., Texas Instruments, Dallas, Operations Research, Inc., Silver Spring, Md., Vertex Corp., Kensington, Md., and Value Engineering Co., Alexandria, Va.; Black & Veatch, Kansas City, Mo., consulting engineer, 1972—. Registered professional engineer in Missouri, Maryland, and District of Columbia. *Military service:* U.S. Army, U.S. Atomic Energy Commission, 1963-65; became captain. *Member:* Phi Kappa Phi, Tau Beta Pi, Alpha Sigma Mu, Sigma Gamma Epsilon.

*WRITINGS: Strategic Energy Supply and National Security,* Praeger, 1971. Contributor of technical articles to professional journals and to *New Scientist* (England).

\* \* \*

## Van SLYKE, Helen (Lenore) 1919-

*PERSONAL:* Born July 9, 1919, in Washington, D.C.; daughter of Frederick H. and Lenore (Siegel) Vogt; married William Woodward Van Slyke, August 9, 1946 (divorced January, 1952). *Home and office:* 350 East 57th St., New York, N.Y. 10022.

*CAREER: Washington Evening Star,* Washington, D.C., fashion editor, 1938-43; *Glamour* (magazine), New York City, beauty editor, 1945-55, promotion director, 1955-60; Henri Bendel, women's apparel, New York City, promotion and advertising director, 1960-61; Norman, Craig & Kummel (advertising agency), New York City, vice-president and creative director, 1961-63; House of Fragrance (Genesco), New York City, president, 1963-68; Helena Rubinstein, New York City, vice-president creative activities, 1968-72; full-time writer and lecturer. Member of Friends of New York Public Library and volunteer worker for Lighthouse for the Blind. *Member:* Fashion Group, Inc. (past president), Advertising Women of New York. *Awards, honors:* Today's Woman award, Cerebral Palsy Foundation, 1977.

*WRITINGS*—All novels: *The Rich and the Righteous,* Doubleday, 1971; *All Visitors Must Be Announced,* Doubleday, 1972; *The Heart Listens,* Doubleday, 1973; *The Mixed Blessing,* Doubleday, 1975; *The Best Place to Be,* Doubleday, 1976; *Always Is Not Forever,* Doubleday, 1977; *Sisters and Strangers,* Doubleday, 1978. Contributor to *Vogue, Harpers Bazaar, Saturday Evening Post,* and *Writer.*

*WORK IN PROGRESS:* A novel.

*SIDELIGHTS:* Helen Van Slyke told *CA:* "I left my executive post in business at age 50-plus to pursue a new career as a novelist. Looking back now, I wonder how I dared such a gamble, and how fortunate I am that it paid off so well in satisfaction and earning! I write long, absorbing novels directed primarily at a woman's audience, though I do have a few male readers. My forte is taking a contemporary theme (widowhood, mother-daughter relationships, inter-racial marriage, etc.) and building around it. By trade and inclination, I'm a story teller and the key to the success of more than five million copies sold is, I think, that I have fulfilled a need for the sentimental but realistic novel with characters readers remember and with whom they can identify.

"*Always Is Not Forever* is now being translated into ten languages. *The Best Place to Be* has been purchased by Ross Hunter for a prime-time television series. I work six days a week, five hours a day. Writing a book takes seven to eight months. 'Promotion' at publication time—travel, appearances, speeches, etc.—consume another two months. Which leaves me relaxation and 'thinking time' of about two months a year. I write to entertain, to please and as a rewarding career, not only financially but in terms of the satisfaction which comes with reader and reviewer response."

*AVOCATIONAL INTERESTS:* Reading, decorating, travel.

*       *       *

## VARDAMAN, Patricia B(lack) 1931-

*PERSONAL:* Born August 4, 1931, in Detroit, Mich.; daughter of John W. and Elsie (Dowd) Black; married George T. Vardaman (a professor of administration), December 18, 1965; children: Pamela (Mrs. Randolph Fincher), George T., Jr. *Education:* University of Denver, part-time study, 1951-67. *Religion:* Methodist. *Address:* P.O. Box 691, Indian Hills, Colo. 80454.

*CAREER:* University of Denver, Colo., typist and billing clerk, 1949-51, administrative assistant and executive secretary in College of Law, 1951-62, assistant to dean of College of Law, 1951-62, assistant to dean of College of Law, 1962-67, systems analyst, 1967-70; Management Associates (consulting firm), Indian Hills, Colo., vice-president and systems analyst, 1967—.

*WRITINGS:* (With husband George T. Vardaman and Carroll C. Halterman) *Cutting Communications Costs and Increasing Impacts,* Wiley, 1970; *Forms for Better Communication,* Van Nostrand, 1971; (with G. T. Vardaman) *Communication in Modern Organizations,* Wiley, 1973; (with G. T. Vardaman) *Successful Writing,* Wiley, 1977.

*       *       *

## VARGISH, Thomas 1939-

*PERSONAL:* Born February 13, 1939, in Granville, N.Y.; son of Andrew (a college teacher) and Frieda (Baer) Vargish; married Linden K. C. Foo (a research technician), June 8, 1963 (divorced, 1975); children: Nicholas. *Education:* Columbia University, B.A., 1960; Merton College, Oxford, M.A., 1963; Princeton University, Ph.D., 1965. *Politics:* Democrat. *Home:* 97 South Main St., Hanover, N.H. 03755. *Office:* Department of English, Dartmouth College, Hanover, N.H. 03755.

*CAREER:* Dartmouth College, Hanover, N.H., assistant professor, 1965-70, associate professor, 1970-75, professor of English, 1975—. *Awards, honors:* Rhodes scholarship, 1960; Woodrow Wilson fellowship (honorary), 1960; Guggenheim fellowship, 1972.

*WRITINGS: Newman: The Contemplation of Mind,* Oxford University Press, 1970. Contributor to *P.M.L.A.* and *Studies in the Novel.*

*WORK IN PROGRESS:* A book on the Victorian novel.

*       *       *

## VARNER, Velma V. 1916-1972

July 2, 1916—November 24, 1972; American editor and librarian. Obituaries: *New York Times,* November 25, 1972; *Publishers Weekly,* December 4, 1972.

*       *       *

## VASIL, R(aj) K(umar) 1931-

*PERSONAL:* Born July 1, 1931, in Amritsar, India; son of Lal Chand and Pushpa Vasil; married Deepa Chopra, January 25, 1957; children: Anamika, Latika. *Education:* Lucknow University, India, M.A., 1953, Ph.D., 1957; University of Malaya, Malaysia, Ph.D., 1967. *Office:* Political Science Department, Victoria University, Wellington, New Zealand.

*CAREER:* Asia Publishing House, Bombay, India, editor, 1959-60; Jadavpur University, Calcutta, India, lecturer in international relations, 1960-67; Victoria University, Wellington, New Zealand, senior lecturer in political science, 1967—. Visiting professor, University of California, Santa Cruz.

*WRITINGS: Politics in a Plural Society, A Study of Non-Communal Political Parties in Malaysia,* Oxford University Press, 1971; *The Malaysian General Election of 1969,* Oxford University Press, 1972.

*WORK IN PROGRESS:* A comparative study of politics in the plural societies of Malaysia, Fiji, Guyana, and Trinidad.†

*       *       *

## VASS, George 1927-

*PERSONAL:* Born March 27, 1927, in Leipzig, Germany; son of Aloysius (a pathologist) and Minna (Blankfeld) Vass; married Theresa Shirley Miller, June 3, 1951; children: Sharon Elaine, Cynthia Diane. *Education:* Washington University, St. Louis, Mo., B.A., 1950; Northwestern University, M.S., 1952. *Religion:* Jewish. *Home:* 9039 Major Ave., Morton Grove, Ill. 60053.

*CAREER: National Jewish Post,* Indianapolis, Ind., managing editor, 1952-55; *Rockford Register-Republic,* Rockford, Ill., copy editor, 1955-58; *Chicago Daily News,* Chicago, Ill., sportswriter, 1958—. *Military service:* U.S. Army, 1945-47. *Member:* Authors Guild, Baseball Writers Association of America, National Hockey League Writers Association. *Awards, honors:* Illinois Associated Press prizes for stories on sports, 1968, 1970, 1971.

*WRITINGS: The Chicago Black Hawks Story,* Follett, 1970; *Champions of Sports* (juvenile), Reilly & Lee, 1970; (with Stan Mikita) *Inside Hockey,* Regnery, 1971; *George Halas and the Chicago Bears,* Regnery, 1971; (with Ferguson Jenkins) *Like Nobody Else,* Regnery, 1973. Contributor to *Baseball Digest* and *Hockey Digest.*

*WORK IN PROGRESS:* A historical novel.

*       *       *

## VAUGHAN, Beatrice 1909(?)-1972

1909(?)—May 30, 1972: American columnist, television personality, and author of cookbooks. Obituaries: *Publishers Weekly,* July 24, 1972; *Antiquarian Bookman,* August 21-28, 1972.

*       *       *

## VAUGHN, Michael J(effery) 1943-

*PERSONAL:* Born May 26, 1943, in Palestine, Tex.; son of Joe E. (a district superintendent for a gas corporation) and Catherine (a hospital administrator; maiden name Wright)

Vaughn; married Martha Ballenger, July 5, 1967; children: Russ Wright, Mary Elizabeth, Sarah Eleanor, Clay Ballenger. *Education:* Baylor University, B.A., 1964, J.D., 1966; Yale University, LL.M., 1967. *Politics:* Republican. *Religion:* Baptist. *Home:* 200 Castle Dr., Waco, Tex. 76710. *Office:* 604 Washington Ave., Waco, Tex. 76701.

*CAREER:* Admitted to the Bar of the State of Texas, 1966. Baylor University, Waco, Tex., assistant professor, 1967-68, associate professor of law, 1968-71; Vaughn & Sullivan, Waco, partner in private practice of law, 1970-74; private practice of law, 1974—. Visiting professor of law, South Texas College of Law, 1971. Justice of the Peace, Cayuga, Tex., 1964-66; chairman of board of directors, Security State Bank of Hedley, Tex. and City State Bank, Wellington, Tex., 1971-75. *Member:* American Bar Association, American Judicature Society, International Academy of Forensic Psychology (fellow; member of board of governors), State Bar of Texas, Sons of Confederate Veterans, Honorary Order of Kentucky Colonels, Masons, Shriners.

*WRITINGS: The History of Cayuga and Crossroads Texas,* Texian Press, 1967; *Appellate Advocacy in Texas,* Baylor University Press, 1968; (with William Quinby DeFuniak) *Principles of Community Property,* University of Arizona Press, revised 2nd edition, 1971. Editor-in-chief, *Baylor Law Review,* 1966; senior editor, *Journal of Psychology* of International Academy of Forensic Psychology, 1968-70.

\* \* \*

## VEIGA, Jose J(acinto da) 1915-

*PERSONAL:* Born February 2, 1915, in Corumba, Goias, Brazil; son of Luiz Pereira and Maria (Jacinto) da Veiga. *Education:* Universidade Federal do Rio de Janeiro, Bachelor, Faculty of Law, 1944. *Home:* Rua Da Gloria 122/1004, Rio de Janeiro, Guanabara ZC 06, Brazil.

*CAREER:* Shop assistant, 1927-35, and civil servant, in Rio de Janeiro, Brazil, 1939-45; radio commentator and foreign correspondent in London, England, 1945-49; city editor for a newspaper in Rio de Janeiro, 1949-51; *Reader's Digest,* Brazilian edition, Rio de Janeiro, employed as magazine editor and editor in charge of condensed books department, 1951-71. *Awards, honors:* Premio Fabio Prado, Brazilian Writers Association, Sao Paulo, 1959, for collection of short stories, *Os Cavalinhos de Platiplanto;* Premio Luiza Claudio de Souza, Pen Club, 1976, for novelette *Os Pecados da Tribo.*

*WRITINGS: Os Cavalinhos de Platiplanto* (short stories), Editora Nitida (Rio de Janeiro), 1959, 9th edition, 1977; *A Hora dos ruminantes* (novelette), Civilizacao Brasileira (Rio de Janeiro), 1966, 8th edition, 1977, translation by Pamela G. Bird published as *The Three Trials of Manirema,* Knopf, 1970; *A Maquina extraviada* (short stories; includes "Acidente em Sumauma," "Domingo de festa," "A Viagem de dez leguas," "Uma Pedrinha na ponte," "Dialogo da relativa grandeza," "Onde andam os didangos?" "Os Novios," "O Largo do Mestrevinte" "Os Cascamorros," "Galo impertinente," "O Cachorro canibal," "A Maquina extraviada," "Tarde de sabado, manha de domingo," and "Na estrada do Amanhece"), Editora Prelo (Rio de Janeiro), 1969, 2nd edition, 1974, translation by Pamela G. Bird published as *The Misplaced Machine,* Knopf, 1970; *Sombras de Reis Barbudos* (novelette), Civilizacao Brasileira, 1972, 4th edition, 1976; *Os Pecados da Tribo* (novelette), Civilizacao Brasileira, 1976.

Stories anthologized in *Caderno de Portugues,* Volume 3,

edited by Tito Avilez, Editora Loqui (Rio de Janeiro), *Antologia do Novo Conto Brasileiro,* edited by Esdras do Nascimento, Editora Jupiter (Rio de Janeiro), 1964, *Literatura Brasileira em Curso,* edited by Dirce Riedel and others, Editora Bloch (Rio de Janeiro), 1968, *Moderne Brasilianische Erzaehlen,* edited by Karl Heupel, Valter Verlag (Olten and Freiburg), 1968, *Antologia Escolar de Contos Brasileiros,* edited by Herberto Sales, Edicoes do Ouro (Rio de Janeiro), 1969, and *Neuvos Cuentistas Brasilenos,* edited by Flavio Macedo Soares, Monte Avila Editores (Caracas), 1969. Contributor of short stories to *Senhor Magazine, Journal do Brasil* (Rio de Janeiro), and *Minas Gerais* Sunday Supplement (Belo Horizonte).

*SIDELIGHTS: The Three Trials of Manirema* is a didactic allegory, according to Virginia Freehafer, a reviewer for *New Republic,* who feels Jose Veiga chose to write in an "aesopian language" to evade Brazilian censors. Freehafer states that the novel is aimed at "the current, overwhelming presence of the United States in Brazil."

Jose J. Veiga told *CA* that he is very interested in contemporary American literature, especially the works of Hemingway, J. D. Salinger, Donald Barthelme, Richard Brautigan, and Kurt Vonnegut, Jr.

*BIOGRAPHICAL/CRITICAL SOURCES: Best Sellers,* August 15, 1970; *New York Times Book Review,* August 30, 1970; *Saturday Review,* September 12, 1970; *New Republic,* December 16, 1970.

\* \* \*

## VEKEMANS, Roger 1921-

*PERSONAL:* Born December 12, 1921, in Brussels, Belgium; son of Emile (a salesman) and Lucie (van Cauwelaert) Vekemans. *Education:* Catholic University of Louvain, Ph.L., 1945, Th.L., 1951; Catholic University of Nijmegen, Doctoraal, 1955. *Politics:* None. *Home:* Calle 142, No. 93-42 (Apartado Aereo 90790), Bogota D.E.8, Colombia. *Office:* Study Center for Development and Integration in Latin America, Calle 17, No. 4-68 of. 401 (Apartado Aereo 20134), Bogota D.E.1, Colombia.

*CAREER:* Roman Catholic priest of Society of Jesus (Jesuits); Social Research and Action Center, Santiago, Chile, founder and director, 1957-64; Catholic University of Chile, Santiago, founder and director of department of sociology, 1959-64; Center for Economic and Social Development in Latin America, Santiago, founder and director, 1960-70; Study Center for Development and Integration in Latin America (CEDIAL), Bogota, Colombia, founder and director, 1970—.

*WRITINGS:* (Compiler and editor) *La tierra y el hombre* (proceedings of Fourth Catholic International Congress on Rural Life), Talleres Graficos del Atlantico (Buenos Aires), 1958; (with others) *America latina y desarrollo social,* two volumes, Herder (Barcelona), for Center for Economic and Social Development in Latin America, 1964; (with Betty Cabezas de Gonzalez and Ismael Silva-Fuenzalida), Hanns-Albert Steger, editor, *Sozio-oekonomische Typologie Lateinamerikas,* Volume III, Verlag Gehlen (Bad Homburg), 1968; (with others) *Marginalidad en America latina: Un ensayo de diagnostico,* Herder, for Center for Economic and Social Development in Latin America, 1968; *Doctrina, ideologia y politica,* Troquel, for Center for Economic and Social Development in Latin America, 1969; *Lo antidialectico en la dialectica de Marx,* Troquel, for Center for Economic and Social Development in Latin America, 1969; *La prerrevolucion latinoamericana,* Troquel, for Center for

Economic and Social Development in Latin America, 1969; (with others) *Poblacion y familia en una sociedad en transicion,* Troquel, for Center for Economic and Social Development in Latin America, 1969; (with Silva-Fuenzalida) *16 estudios de interpretacion social latino-americana,* Center of Intercultural Documentation, 1969.

(With Hernan Pozo) *Iglesia y mundo politico: Sacerdocio y politica,* Herder (Barcelona), 1971, translation by Aloysius Owen and Charles Underhill Quinn published as *Caesar and God: The Priesthood and Politics,* Orbis Books, 1972; (with Pozo and Alberto Maldonado) *Agonia o resurgimiento? Reflexiones teologicas acerca de la "contestacion" en la Iglesia,* Herder (Barcelona), 1972; (with Silva-Fuenzalida) *Hacia la superacion de la marginalidad,* Herder, for Instituto Ecuatoriano de Desarollo Social, 1972; (with Roberto Jiminez) *Desarrollo y revolucion: Iglesia y liberacion,* Study Center for Development and Integration in Latin America, 1972; (with Silva-Fuenzalida) *Marginalidad, promocion popular y neo-marxismo,* Study Center for Development and Integration in Latin America, 1976; (with Joaquin Lepeley) *Temi roventi alla luce del Cuore di Christo,* Centro Volontari della Sofferenza (Rome), 1976; (with Lepeley) *Teologia de la liberacion y Christianos por el Socialismo,* Study Center for Development and Integration in Latin America, 1976.

Contributor: Centre Catholique des Intellectuels Francais, *L'Amerique Latine en devenir: Economie, politique, religion,* Fayard, 1963; William V. D'Antonio and Frederick B. Pike, editors, *Religion, Revolution and Reform: New Forces for Change in Latin America,* Praeger, 1964; John J. Considine, editor, *Social Revolution in the New Latin America: A Catholic Appraisal,* Fides, 1965; Peter Molt, editor, *Lateinamerika,* Eichholz-Verlag, 1965; Charles J. Fleenes and Harry J. Carger, *Religious and Cultural Factors in Latin America,* St. Louis University, 1969; Elaine H. Burnell, editor, *One Spark from Holocaust: The Crisis in Latin America,* Interbook Inc. for the Center for the Study of Democratic Institutions, 1970; *Kirche und Befreiung,* Paul Pattloch, 1975; *Christlicher Glaube und gesellschaftliche Praxis,* Paul Pattloch, 1978. Also author of many published papers on Latin America. Contributor to *Life, Revista Interamericana de Ciencias Sociales* (Washington, D.C.), *Revue Generale Belge, Stimmen der Zeit* (Munich), *Mensaje* (Santiago), and other journals in Latin America, Europe, and the United States.

*WORK IN PROGRESS:* Further studies on the church and "liberation," and on the social typology of Latin American countries.

*SIDELIGHTS:* Roger Vekemans is competent in five languages—French, Flemish, English, German, and Spanish—, and has some ability in Italian and Portuguese.

\* \* \*

## VICKERY, Florence E. 1906-

*PERSONAL:* Born July 6, 1906, in Evansville, Ind.; daughter of Robert K. (a realtor) and Anna (Greiss) Vickery. *Education:* DePauw University, A.B., 1926; University of Chicago, M.A., 1942. *Home and office:* 239 Perry St., Mill Valley, Calif. 94941.

*CAREER:* San Francisco Senior Center, San Francisco, Calif., executive director, 1947-67; University of California, San Francisco, instructor, 1970-72; private consultant practice, 1972—. Instructor of geriatric psychology, Emeritus College of the College of Marin, 1972-78. *Member:* National Association of Social Workers, American Gerontological Society (fellow).

*WRITINGS: Creative Programming for Older Adults,* Association Press, 1972; *The Older Years—Coping with the Changes They Bring,* C. C Thomas, 1978.

\* \* \*

## VIGNONE, Joseph A. 1939-

*PERSONAL:* Surname is pronounced Vin-yone; born August 9, 1939, in Brownsville, Pa.; son of Angelo D. (a laborer) and Angeline (Pappeteria) Vignone; married Maria Roppolo (a librarian), May 5, 1970. *Education:* Duquesne University, B.S. in Ed., 1963; University of Pittsburgh, M.L.S., 1967, Ph.D., 1971. *Politics:* Democrat. *Religion:* Roman Catholic.

*CAREER:* Board of Education, Pittsburgh, Pa., high school teacher and audiovisual coordinator, 1963-67; University of Pittsburgh, Pittsburgh, assistant director, Bureau of Urban Library Research, 1967-71; National Institutes of Health, National Library of Medicine, Bethesda, Md., library associate in biomedical communications, beginning 1971. *Military service:* U.S. Army Reserve, 1957-61. *Member:* Beta Phi Mu.

*WRITINGS: Collective Bargaining Procedures for Public Library Employees: An Inquiry into the Opinions and Attitudes of Public Librarians, Directors, and Board Members,* Scarecrow, 1971. Compiler with Frank B. Sessa, *Pennsylvania Public Library Statistics,* annually, 1966-69.

*WORK IN PROGRESS:* A study of the interface between audiovisual services and traditional services in a library environment.†

\* \* \*

## VINCENT, John Carter 1900-1972

August 19, 1900—December 3, 1972; American diplomat, lecturer, and specialist in Far Eastern affairs. Obituaries: *New York Times,* December 5, 1972.

\* \* \*

## VINCENT, Peter 1944-

*PERSONAL:* Born July 14, 1944, in Philadelphia, Pa.; son of John B. and Margaret Vincent. *Education:* Attended Fordham University, 1962-64; Villanova University, B.A., 1967; San Francisco State College (now University), M.A., 1968. *Residence:* San Francisco, Calif. *Agent:* Georges Borchardt, Inc., 136 East 57th St., New York, N.Y. 10022.

*CAREER:* San Francisco State University, San Francisco, Calif., instructor in creative writing, beginning 1970.

*WRITINGS: Sanglorians Run* (novel), Delacorte, 1971.

*WORK IN PROGRESS: Amelia,* a novel.

\* \* \*

## VLIET, R(ussell) G. 1929-

*PERSONAL:* Born in 1929, in Chicago, Ill.; married Ann Rutherford (a professor of English), 1951; children: Brooke. *Education:* Southwest Texas State College (now University), B.A. and M.A., 1952; Yale University, further study, 1955-56. *Residence:* Stamford, Vt. *Agent:* Lucy Kroll Agency, 390 West End Ave., New York, N.Y. 10024.

*CAREER:* Poet and novelist. *Awards, honors:* Texas Institute of Letters Poetry Award, 1967, 1971; Rockefeller fellowship in fiction and poetry, 1967-68.

*WRITINGS: Events and Celebrations* (poems), Viking, 1966; *The Man with the Black Mouth* (poems), Kayak, 1970;

*Rockspring* (novel), Viking, 1974; *Solitudes* (novel), Harcourt, 1977. Contributor of stories and poems to literary magazines, including *Saturday Review, New American Review, Hudson Review, Massachusetts Review,* and *Field.*

*WORK IN PROGRESS:* A collection of poems; a novel.

*SIDELIGHTS:* As a child, R. G. Vliet spent two years in Samoa; he lived in the Mexican village of Yautepec, 1968-70. *Avocational interests:* Beekeeping; farmsteading.

*BIOGRAPHICAL/CRITICAL SOURCES: Trace,* spring, 1967; *Books and Bookmen,* May, 1967.

* * *

## VLOCK, Laurel F(ox)

*PERSONAL:* Born in New Haven, Conn.; daughter of John J. and Rose Fox. *Education:* Cornell University, B.A.; Queens College of the City University of New York, M.A. *Home:* Ansonia Rd., Woodbridge, Conn. 06525. *Agent:* Curtis Brown Ltd., 575 Madison Ave., New York, N.Y. 10022.

*CAREER:* Producer and moderator of radio programs, 1963-66; producer and moderator of television programs, in Connecticut, 1966—; director of films, 1969—.

*WRITINGS:* (With Joel A. Levitch) *Contraband of War; William Henry Singleton,* Funk, 1970. Contributor of articles to newspapers and magazines.

* * *

## VOLKENING, Henry T. 1902-1972

May 16, 1902—October 18, 1972; American literary agent. Obituaries: *New York Times,* October 20, 1972; *Publishers Weekly,* October 30, 1972.

* * *

## VOLPE, E(rminio) Peter 1927-

*PERSONAL:* Born April 7, 1927, in New York, N.Y.; son of Rocco and Rose (Ciano) Volpe; married Carolyn Thorne (an artist), September 1, 1955; children: Laura E., Lisa L., John P. *Education:* College of the City of New York (now City College of City University of New York), B.S., 1948; Columbia University, M.A., 1949, Ph.D., 1952. *Home:* 1591 Exposition Blvd., New Orleans, La. 70118. *Office:* Department of Biology, Tulane University, New Orleans, La. 70118.

*CAREER:* Tulane University, New Orleans, La., assistant professor, 1952-56, associate professor, 1957-59, professor of biology, 1960—, chairman of department, 1964—. U.S. National Commissioner, UNESCO, 1968-72. *Military service:* U.S. Navy, 1945-46. *Member:* American Association for the Advancement of Science, American Society of Zoologists, American Institute of Biological Sciences, Phi Beta Kappa, Sigma Xi. *Awards, honors:* Newberry Award, Columbia University, 1952; Sigma Xi faculty research award, Tulane University, 1972.

*WRITINGS: Understanding Evolution,* W. C. Brown, 1977, 3rd edition, 1970; *Human Heredity and Birth Defects,* Pegasus, 1971; *Man, Nature and Society,* W. C. Brown, 1975, 2nd edition, 1978. Consulting editor in biology, William C. Brown Co.; associate editor, *Journal of Experimental Psychology;* editor, *American Zoologist.*

* * *

## VOLZ, Marlin M(ilton) 1917-

*PERSONAL:* Born September 3, 1917, in Cecil, Wis.; son

of Edward A. (a farmer and cheesemaker) and Mae C. (Winter) Volz; married Esther R. Krug, August 23, 1941; children: Marlin M., Jr., Mrs. George R. Campbell, Thomas A. *Education:* University of Wisconsin, B.A., 1938, LL.B., 1940, S.J.D., 1945. *Politics:* Democrat. *Religion:* Methodist. *Home:* 1819 Woodfill Way, Louisville, Ky. 40205. *Office:* School of Law, University of Louisville, Louisville, Ky. 40208.

*CAREER:* University of Wisconsin—Madison, assistant professor of law, 1941-50; University of Kansas City (now University of Missouri—Kansas City), professor of law, 1950-58, dean, 1950-58; University of Louisville, Louisville, Ky., professor of law, 1958—, dean, 1958-65. Attorney, War Production Board, 1942-43. County judge pro tem and probate judge, Jefferson County, Ky., 1969—. *Military service:* U.S. Army, 1943-46; became staff sergeant. *Member:* American Bar Association, Federal Bar Association, National Organization on Legal Problems of Education (president, 1963), Kentucky State Bar Association, Wisconsin State Bar Association, Filson Club. *Awards, honors:* LL.D., San Juan School of Law, 1956.

*WRITINGS:* (With Edwin Pick, Katherine Baldwin, and Jack R. DeWitt) *Wisconsin Practice Methods,* West Publishing, 1948; *Drafting Partnership Agreements,* American Law Institute, 1949; (with Frank F. Messer) *Iowa Practice Methods,* West Publishing, 1953; (with James C. Logan, Charles B. Blackmar, and Elmer Hilpert) *Missouri Practice Methods,* West Publishing, 1953, 2nd edition, 1966; (with Frederick J. Moreau and Leonard Thomas) *Kansas Practice Methods,* West Publishing, 1957; (with John Scurlock, Charles N. Carnes, Leo C. Whinery, Dorothy Clarke, and others) *West's Federal Practice Manual,* West Publishing, 1960, 2nd edition, 1970; (with Ralph Petrilli and Lawrence Grauman) *Caldwell's Kentucky Form Book,* 3rd edition (Volz was not associated with earlier editions), W. H. Anderson, 1963; (with William Dolson) *Kentucky Legal Forms,* Volumes III and IV (Volz was not associated with Volumes I and II), Banks-Baldwin, 1965; (with LeRoy Peterson and Richard Rossmiller) *The Law and Public School Operation,* Harper, 1969, 2nd edition, 1978.

*WORK IN PROGRESS: Kentucky Probate Practice,* completion expected in 1978.

* * *

## von DAENIKEN, Erich 1935-

*PERSONAL:* Born April 14, 1935, in Zofingen, Switzerland; son of Otto (a clothing manufacturer) and Lena (Weiss) von Daeniken; married Elisabeth Skaja, July 20, 1960; children: Cornelia. *Education:* Attended College St. Michel, Fribourg, Switzerland, 1949-54. *Home:* im Schachen, 8906 Bonstetten, Switzerland.

*CAREER:* Hotel-keeper and writer.

*WRITINGS*—All translations by Michael Heron: *Erinnerungen an die Zukunft,* Econ-Verlag, 1968, translation published as *Chariots of the Gods? Unsolved Mysteries of the Past,* Putnam, 1969; *Zurueck zu den Sternen: Argumente fuer das Unmoegliche,* Econ-Verlag, 1969, translation published as *Gods Return to the Stars: Evidence for the Impossible,* Putnam, 1971; *Aussaat und Kosmos: Spuren und Plaene ausserirdischer Intelligenzen,* Econ-Verlag, 1972, translation published as *The Gold of the Gods,* Putnam, 1973; *Erscheinungen: Phaenomene, die d. Welt erregen,* Econ-Verlag, 1974, translation published as *Miracles of the Gods: A Hard Look at the Supernatural,* Delacorte Press, 1975; *In Search of Ancient Gods: My Pictorial Evidence for the Impossible,* Delacorte, 1976; *According to the Evidence,* Souvenir, 1977; *Erich von Daeniken's Proof,* Bantam, 1978.

*SIDELIGHTS:* Erich von Daeniken theorizes that *homosapiens* was created by advanced, extra-terrestrial beings who visited earth millenia ago and mated with our ancestors. It is on this premise that von Daeniken's books are based, and he spends much of his time traveling around the world seeking information in support of his theory.

"It is my very Catholic background which started it all," von Daeniken told *Washington Post* reviewer Adam Shaw. In answer to his questions concerning religion, von Daeniken's high school teachers suggested he read the Old Testament. He followed their advice and became especially interested in certain verses of Genesis which to him suggested many gods, rather than one. From then on he felt compelled to study works of other religions and to travel to "South America, Russia, Egypt to see with my own eyes the inscriptions, the monuments, the traces left behind by the 'gods' to let us know they were here," he said to Shaw. He discovered in many of the religions and legends the following recurring theme: "The gods have come down from the sky, often with a loud noise and in fiery vehicles. They 'created' man, went back into the sky, and promised to return."

Throughout his travels, von Daeniken has accumulated such supporting evidence as "the illustrations of [ancient people from outer space] in the thousands-of-years-old rock formations, whether in South America, Alaska, Easter Island, Africa, or Asia which all show headgear that . . . can be likened to the headgear of astronauts, and what was at first supposed to be horns are really antennae," writes reviewer Sister M. Marguerite in *Best Sellers.* "Also, there is in the Palpa Valley a strip of level ground some thirty-seven miles long. From the air, one can make out gigantic lines, laid out geometrically, which look marvelously like a modern landing space for airships. The archaeologists say they are Inca roads; but von Daeniken questions: of what use to the Incas were roads that ran parallel and came to a sudden end?" And in the instance of Elephant Island, the island resembles an elephant only when viewed from great height; how could primitive inhabitants who supposedly named the island have known this?

S. K. Oberbeck, reviewing *The Gold of the Gods* in *Newsweek,* calls the author's style a mixture of "Carlos Castaneda, Ripley's 'Believe It or Not,' and 'Star Trek.'" A *Choice* reviewer writes of *Chariots of the Gods,* "The book undoubtedly deserves a place of honor beside J. Churchward's *The Lost Continent of Mu* and related texts on the lost continent of Atlantis, but it cannot be recommended, in all conscience, for an academic library."

Prominent scientists and proponents of orthodox religion are skeptical of von Daeniken's theories. NASA (National Aeronautics and Space Administration) space engineer Josef F. Blumrich originally agreed with them, then he read The Book of Ezekiel and applied to it modern space technology. He concluded that Ezekiel did indeed see a space ship more advanced than can be built with our present knowledge of nuclear technology. Von Daeniken predicts that his own interpretations of ancient enigmas, now considered unusual, will, in another generation, be taught in college classrooms.

A color documentary, "Erinnerungen an die Zukunft," based on von Daeniken's first two books and produced by Terra Filmkunst, was released in Berlin in April, 1970. Harald Reinl wrote and directed the film, which had its first showing in England as "Memories of the Future" in December, 1970.

National Broadcasting Company (NBC-TV) showed a special based on von Daeniken's theories on January 5, 1973. Produced by Alan Landsburg Productions for Tomorrow Entertainment, a General Electric subsidiary, the special resulted in a sales boom of *Chariots of the Gods.* Von Daeniken reports that 40,000,000 copies of all editions of his books have been sold thus far.

Oscar Dystel, president of Bantam Books, Inc., responded with a "yes" when asked in an interview for *New York* if he felt the von Daeniken following was an offshoot of the interest in UFO's (Unidentified Flying Objects) fifteen years ago. In reference to this following, and to *Chariots of the Gods* in particular, he is quoted as saying: "'We can't find any pattern of sales. Hippies are buying it, college students, Middle America, your uncle and aunt, the sophisticated and the unsophisticated. People seem to be looking for something, and these books provide that something.'"

*BIOGRAPHICAL/CRITICAL SOURCES: Best Sellers,* February 1, 1970; *Book World,* February 22, 1970; *National Review,* February 24, 1970; *Christian Century,* February 25, 1970; *Atlantic,* March, 1970; *Choice,* May, 1970, December, 1971; *New York,* May 7, 1973; *Guardian,* May 30, 1973; *Newsweek,* October 8, 1973; *Washington Post,* December 2, 1973; *New York Post,* December 19, 1973; *Playboy,* August, 1974; *New York Times Book Review,* March 31, 1974.

\* \* \*

## von HERTZEN, Heikki 1913-

*PERSONAL:* Born November 21, 1913, in Viipuri, Finland; son of Ernst Frithiof (a lawyer) and Lyyli Clara (Enquist) von Hertzen; married Siskolahja Laitinen, 1941; married second wife, Berith Peltonen, 1962 (divorced, 1975); children: (first marriage) Heikki, Hannu, Markku; (second marriage) Hannele. *Education:* University of Helsinki, LL.B., 1940; Technological University of Helsinki, D.Sc., 1974. *Religion:* Lutheran. *Home:* Itaeranta 4, Tapiola 02100, Espoo, Finland. *Office:* Asuntosaeaetioe, Tapiontori, Tapiola 02100, Espoo, Finland.

*CAREER:* Suomen Kaesityoelaeisosakepankki (Bank of Finnish Handicraftsmen), branch manager in Helsinki and Tampere, Finland, 1941-43; Family Welfare League, Helsinki, Finland, managing director, 1943-65; Housing Foundation Asuntosaeaetioe, Tapiola, Espoo, Finland, president, 1951-77, executive and planning director, 1951—. Member of expert advisory panel on environmental sanitation, World Health Organization, 1961-77; bureau member, International Federation for Housing and Planning, 1964—. Leader of United Nations European Seminar on Social Aspects of Housing, 1958, and of University of Pennsylvania New Towns' Seminar in Finland, 1965. Member of board, Nordiska Kooperativa och Allmaennyttiga Bostadsfoeretags Organization (organization for non-governmental constructors in Nordic countries), 1960—. *Member:* Deutsche Akademie fuer Staedtebau und Landesplanung (Munich; corresponding member), Royal Town Planning Institute (London; honorary corresponding member). *Awards, honors:* Commander, Order of the Finnish Lion; Commander, Order of the Homayon (Iran); Fritz Schumacher Prize of Stiftung F.V.S., Hamburg, and University of Hannover, 1970, and L'Institut de la Vie award, 1975, both for merits in the field of urban planning, community planning, and housing production.

*WRITINGS: Koti vai Kasarmi* (title means "Homes or Barracks"; pamphlet), Werner Soederstroem Osakeyhtio, 1946; *Social Aspects of Housing: General Objectives,*

United Nations (Geneva), 1960; (with Paul D. Spreiregen) *Building a New Town: Finland's New Garden City, Tapiola,* M.I.T. Press, 1971. Contributor to *Encyclopedia of Urban Planning,* McGraw, 1974, and to journals in his field. Editor-in-chief, *Asuntopolitiikka* (means "Housing Policy"), 1951—, *Lakimies ja yhteiskunta* (means "Lawyer and Society"), 1953-66, and *Valtakunnansuunnittelu* (means "Town and Country Planning"), 1955-66.

*WORK IN PROGRESS: Experiences in Urban Planning and Administration.*

*SIDELIGHTS:* As a bank manager and lawyer, Heikki von Hertzen "became highly concerned with the everyday economic and social difficulties of the ordinary man and his family.... From social and family welfare I progressed to housing, for that is a key to solving most social problems." He also feels that "our towns must be planned for man and his family, for inhabitants, pedestrians and consumers. Economic life and industry, as well as traffic, must be organized according to this principle."

*BIOGRAPHICAL/CRITICAL SOURCES: New York Times,* October 24, 1963; *Washington Post,* December 1, 1963; *Reader's Digest,* British edition, February, 1966; Wolf von Echardt, *A Place to Live,* Seymour Lawrence, 1968; Ann Louise Strong, *Planned Urban Environments,* Johns Hopkins Press, 1971.

\*    \*    \*

## von MIKLOS, Josephine Bogdan    1900-1972

1900—November 2, 1972; Austrian-born American photographer, designer, and writer on gardening and other subjects. Obituaries: *New York Times,* November 3, 1972.

\*    \*    \*

## von MOSCHZISKER, Michael    1918-

*PERSONAL:* Surname is pronounced Mo-*shis*-ker; born December 1, 1918, in Philadelphia, Pa.; son of Robert (a chief justice of Pennsylvania) and Anne (Macbeth) von Moschzisker; married Marjorie Drayton, October 2, 1942; children: Felix, Colette, Lila, Susan. *Education:* Yale University, B.A., 1940; University of Pennsylvania, J.D., 1947. *Politics:* Democrat. *Religion:* Roman Catholic. *Office:* Department of Justice, Room 206, State Office Building, Broad and Spring Garden Sts., Philadelphia, Pa. 19130.

*CAREER:* Attorney-at-law, in private practice, 1947-51, 1954-65; first assistant district attorney, Philadelphia, Pa., 1952-54; Villanova University, Villanova, Pa., instructor in law, 1956-58; *Philadelphia Evening and Sunday Bulletin,* Philadelphia, columnist, 1965-70; *Dublin Evening Press,* Dublin, Ireland, part-time columnist, 1966-67; Committee of Seventy, executive secretary, 1971-73; deputy attorney general of state of Pennsylvania, 1973—. Chairman, Philadelphia Redevelopment Authority, 1956-62. Instructor, Temple University Law School, 1972—. *Military service:* U.S. Army, 1941-45; became captain; served in European theater. *Member:* Montessori Society of Ireland (vice-president, 1964-67).

*WRITINGS:* (With John Bremer) *The School without Walls: Philadelphia's Parkway Program,* Holt, 1971. Contributor to legal journals.

*SIDELIGHTS:* Michael von Moschzisker was primarily a lawyer specializing in criminal defense work until a coronary attack in 1964 led to a two-year residence in Ireland and changed the direction of his interests for a time. The Committee of Seventy which von Moschzisker headed is a nonpartisan voter education and election-watching group.

## von SALOMON, Ernst    1902-1972

1902—August 9, 1972; German novelist, essayist, and screenwriter. Obituaries: *New York Times,* August 10, 1972; *L'Express,* August 14-20, 1972.

\*    \*    \*

## von STADEN, Heinrich    1939-

*PERSONAL:* Born March 2, 1939, in Pretoria, South Africa; son of Eduard P. H. and Heletha (Prinsloo) von Staden; married, 1962; children: two. *Education:* Yale University, B.A., 1961; University of Vienna, graduate study, 1962-63; University of Tuebingen, Dr. Phil., 1968. *Home address:* 1961 Yale Station, New Haven, Conn. 06520. *Office:* Department of Classics, Yale University, New Haven, Conn. 06520.

*CAREER:* University of Tuebingen, Tuebingen, Germany, assistant in classics, 1966-68; Yale University, New Haven, Conn., assistant professor, 1968-73, associate professor of classics, 1973—.

*WRITINGS: The Land and Government of Muscovy: A Sixteenth-Century Account,* translated by Thomas Esper, Stanford University Press, 1967; (editor) A. Bartlett Giamatti, *Western Literature,* Volume I: *The Ancient World,* with instructor's manual for the three-volume edition co-authored by von Staden, Peter Brooks, and John Hollander, Harcourt, 1971.

*WORK IN PROGRESS: Aisthesis,* a book on Hellenistic epistemology.†

\*    \*    \*

## VOSS, E(rnst) Theodore    1928-

*PERSONAL:* Born December 25, 1928, in Hilden, Germany. *Education:* University of Bonn, Ph.D., 1958. *Home:* Lorettostrasse 28, D-7800 Freiburg, Germany. *Office:* Fachber 09, Philipps-Universitat, D-355 Marburg, Germany.

*CAREER:* Schiller-Nationalmuseum, Marbach, Germany, member of staff, 1958-59; J. B. Metzler Publishing Co., Stuttgart, Germany, editor of scholarly books, 1959-65; University of Wisconsin—Madison, assistant professor of German, 1965-67; University of Minnesota, Minneapolis, associate professor of German, 1967-69; Columbia University, New York, N.Y., associate professor of German, 1969-76; University of Marburg, Marburg, Germany, professor of modern German literature, 1976—. *Member:* Internationale Vereinigung fuer germanische Sprach- und Literaturwissenschaft, Modern Language Association of America, Vereinigung der deutscheer Hochschulgermanisten.

*WRITINGS: Erzaehlprobleme des Briefromans,* University of Bonn, 1960; (editor) Johann Jakob Engel, *Ueber Handlung, Gespraech und Erzaehlung,* J. B. Metzler (Stuttgart), 1965; (editor) Johann Heinrich Voss, *Idyllen,* Lambert Schneider (Heidelberg), 1968; (editor) Salomon Gessner, *Idyllen,* Reclam (Stuttgart), 1973. Also author of essays on S. Gessner, H. V. Kleist, F. G. Klopstock, and J. H. Voss. Co-editor, *Sammlung Metzler,* 1959-65; member of editorial board, *Monatshefte,* 1966-67; member of editorial board, *Germanic Review,* 1970-76.

# W

## WADSWORTH, Barry James 1935-

*PERSONAL:* Born July 9, 1935, in Detroit, Mich.; son of William Franklin (a horticulturist) and Winifred (Sutton) Wadsworth; married Eva Partyka, October 11, 1968; children: Barry James, Jr. *Education:* State University College of Education (now State University of New York College at Oswego), B.A., 1957, M.A., 1960; State University of New York at Albany, Ed.D., 1968. *Home:* 147 Mosier St., South Hadley, Mass. 01075. *Office:* Mount Holyoke College, South Hadley, Mass. 01075.

*CAREER:* Worked as a high school teacher in Glen Head, N.Y., 1957-65; University of Colorado, Denver, assistant professor of education, 1968-69; Mount Holyoke College, South Hadley, Mass., assistant professor of psychology and education, 1969—. Member of South Hadley School Committee. *Military service:* U.S. Army, 1958-60. *Member:* American Educational Research Association, Society for Research in Child Development, American Association for the Advancement of Science, Board of Mental Health and Retardation (Holyoke-Chicopee Area).

*WRITINGS: Piaget's Theory of Cognitive Development,* McKay, 1971; *Piaget for the Classroom Teacher,* Longman, 1978.

*WORK IN PROGRESS:* Research in learning disabilities and on children learning to read; a revision of *Piaget's Theory of Cognitive Development;* a book on cognitive development and teaching at the high school level.

\*　　\*　　\*

## WAGER, Willis Joseph 1911-

*PERSONAL:* Surname is pronounced with a hard "g"; born July 24, 1911, in Pittsburg, Kan.; son of Holmes (a businessman) and Joda (Smith) Wager; married Adah Allen, June 29, 1936 (died, 1970); married Inez Morton, May 30, 1971; children: (first marriage) Holmes, Joseph, Geoffrey. *Education:* Washington University, St. Louis, Mo., A.B., 1931, A.M., 1932; University of Frankfurt, student, 1933-34; New York University, Ph.D., 1943. *Politics:* Democrat. *Religion:* Presbyterian. *Home:* 133 Tadlock Rd., Bristol, Tenn. 37620. *Office:* Department of English, King College, Bristol, Tenn. 37620.

*CAREER:* New York University, New York City, instructor in English, 1935-43; G. Schirmer, Inc., New York City, literary editor, 1936-43; Berea College, Berea, Ky.,

associate professor of English, 1943-45; Boston University, Boston, Mass., professor of humanities, 1945-77, professor emeritus, 1977—; King College, Bristol, Tenn., special lecturer in American literature, 1977—. Senior lecturer, Fulbright Commission, Berlin, 1963-64, Istanbul, 1966-68, Tehran, 1968-70. Consultant to Massachusetts Department of Education, Teachers College, Columbia Institute of Higher Education, Studies in Education, Philadelphia, Pa., and Lowell Institute Cooperative Broadcasting Council, Boston, Mass. *Member:* Modern Language Association of America, College English Association, Modern Humanities Research Association, American Musicological Society, Phi Beta Kappa, Sinfonia.

*WRITINGS:* (Editor with Edward Wagenknecht) Mark Twain, *Life on the Mississippi,* Heritage and Limited Editions Clubs, 1944; (with Earl J. McGrath) *Liberal Education and Music,* Columbia University Press, 1962; *From the Hand of Man: A History of the Arts,* two volumes, Boston University Press, 1962-63; *American Literature: A World View,* New York University Press, 1968; (editor, compiler, and author of preface) *Essays on American Literature,* USIS (Tehran), 1969; (translator and supplementer) Karl H. Woerner, *History of Music,* Free Press, 1973; *A Musician's Guide to Copyright and Publishing,* Carousel Publishing Corp., 1975, 2nd edition, 1977. Contributor of articles to *Modern Language Notes, Modern Language Review, Philological Quarterly, Educational Record,* and other journals.

*WORK IN PROGRESS:* Revision of *From the Hand of Man;* English version of Tchaikovsky's textbook on harmony.

*SIDELIGHTS:* "Everything looks impossible until one gets involved in it," Willis Joseph Wager writes. "My mentor, Oscar Cargill, said to start anywhere and then in revision decide what to do with what had been the starting point."

\*　　\*　　\*

## WAGNER, Ken(neth) 1911-

*PERSONAL:* Born June 13, 1911, in Council Bluffs, Iowa; son of Arthur F. and Neva (Kellogg) Wagner; married LaVina Stevens, November 28, 1934; children: Kenneth, Jr., Diane (Mrs. Pat Noravsky), Linda (Mrs. Cleve Rossetti), Cynthia (Mrs. Jerome Ohnstad). *Education:* Attended high school in Iowa. *Religion:* Episcopalian. *Office:* KMSP-TV, 120 South Ninth St., Minneapolis, Minn. 55402.

*CAREER:* Central Printing Co., Mason City, Iowa, art director, 1931-43; Wilton Theater and Photo Studio, Wilton Junction, Iowa, owner and manager, 1944-51; WOC-TV, Davenport, Iowa, 1949-60, began as art and film director, became producer and host on children's program; KMSP-TV, Minneapolis, Minn., producer-host of "Grandpa Ken Show," 1960—. Created lithographs and posters for leading circuses during years 1931-43, and worked one season as a circus clown to get background for circus comic strip.

*WRITINGS*—All self-illustrated: *One Word Story-book,* Golden Press, 1968; *Tony and His Friends,* Golden Press, 1969; *Jack in the Sack,* Golden Press, 1970; *One to Ten and Back Again,* Golden Press, 1972.

*WORK IN PROGRESS:* A book, tentatively entitled *Who Lives Here; Whittler of Whittletown;* a teen-age book based on his life with deaf-mute parents.†

\*    \*    \*

## WAGNER, Rudolph F(red)   1921-

*PERSONAL:* Born August 22, 1921, in Germany; came to United States in 1949, naturalized in 1955; son of Franz (a businessman) and Hedwig (Riedel) Wagner; married Margaret Hatcher, June 10, 1960; children: Karl, Graeme, Clisby. *Education:* College of William and Mary, B.S., 1956; University of Richmond, M.A., 1957; George Washington University, Ph.D., 1967. *Religion:* Lutheran. *Home:* 2007 Pinecliff Dr., Valdosta, Ga. 31601. *Office:* Department of Psychology, Valdosta State College, Valdosta, Ga. 31601.

*CAREER:* Richmond Public Schools, Richmond, Va., chief psychologist, 1959-75, supervisor, pupil personnel, 1975-77; Valdosta State College, Valdosta, Ga., associate professor of psychology, 1977—. Diplomate in school psychology; member of American Board of Professional Psychology. Consultant. *Member:* American Psychological Association.

*WRITINGS:* (Contributor) H. J. Peters and M. J. Bathory, editors, *School Counseling: Prospectives and Procedures,* F. E. Peacock, 1968; (contributor) Werner Correll, editor, *Forschung und Erziehung,* Ludwig Auer, 1968; *Teaching Phonics with Success,* Mafex Associates, 1969; *Dyslexia and Your Child,* Harper, 1971; *Modern Discipline: Behavior Modification in School and Home,* Mafex Associates, 1972; *Helping the Wordblind,* Center for Applied Research in Education, 1976. Contributor to *Journal of School Psychology, Virginia Journal of Education, International Journal of Symbology, Academic Therapy,* and other publications.

*WORK IN PROGRESS:* Research on dyslexia and psycholinguistics.

\*    \*    \*

## WAGNER, Wenceslas Joseph   1917-

*PERSONAL:* Born December 12, 1917, in Poland; naturalized U.S. citizen; son of Joseph W. (a director of railways) and Margaret (Ferrein) Wagner; married Dianne Moc, July 29, 1950 (divorced); children: Joseph V., Alexandra D., Margaret E. *Education:* University of Warsaw, LL.M., 1939; further study at Academy of International Law, the Hague, 1939, 1947, and Institute of Commercial Science S. Brun, Warsaw, 1939-40; University of Paris, Dr.en Droit, 1947; Northwestern University, J.D., 1950, LL.M., 1953, S.J.D., 1957. *Religion:* Roman Catholic. *Home:* 728 Neff Rd., Grosse Pointe, Mich. 48230. *Office:* School of Law, University of Detroit, 651 East Jefferson Ave., Detroit, Mich. 48226.

*CAREER:* Practice of law in Warsaw, Poland, 1939-44, as counsel for Zieleniewski Factories, 1940-44, and junior judge in Warsaw courts, 1941-44; French Institute of Air Transport, Paris, research associate, 1947-48; Fordham University, Bronx, N.Y., visiting professor of literature, 1948-49; Northwestern University, School of Law, Chicago, Ill., teaching fellow in comparative law, 1950-53; University of Notre Dame, Notre Dame, Ind., instructor, 1953-54, assistant professor, 1954-57; associate professor, 1957-61, professor of law, 1961-62; Indiana University at Bloomington, professor of law, 1962-71; University of Detroit, Detroit, Mich., professor of law, 1971—. Visiting professor at University of Paris and University of Rennes, 1959-60, and Cornell University, 1961-62. U.S. Department of State lecturer in Senegal, Morocco, and Algeria, 1960, and on world tour, 1962; lecturer on American law in South and Central America, 1968, in France, 1968-69, summers, 1974, 1975, and at universities in Poland, 1971, summers, 1976, 1977. Legal counsel, German Consulate General for Indiana, 1966-68. Member, Cornell Project on General Principles of Law, 1959—; president, American Council of Polish Cultural Clubs, 1967-69; associate member, International Academy of Comparative law, 1970—; vice-president, International movement of Catholic Jurists "Pax Romana," 1971—; president, Polish-American Congress Bicentennial Committee of Michigan, 1975—. *Military service:* Polish Home Army, 1941-45. Polish Army Abroad, 1945-48; became second lieutenant; received Golden Cross of Merit.

*MEMBER:* American Foreign Law Association (former vice-president); American Association for the Comparative Study of Law (member of board of directors), American Society for Legal History (treasurer, 1962-64), African Law Association (co-founder; former member of board of directors), Society of Legal History (Paris; member of board of directors), Polish Institute of Arts and Sciences in America (president of council, 1971—), World Association of World Federalists (former member of executive council, 1959-61), World Federalists (former member of executive council, 1958-61), Detroit Yacht Club (director of Pelicans Club, 1977—).

*AWARDS, HONORS:* Fulbright grants in France, 1959-60, Netherlands, 1966, Latin America, 1968; grants from Social Science Research Council, 1961, University of Leyden, 1966, American Council of Learned Societies, 1970, 1971, and Kosciuscko Foundation, 1971.

*WRITINGS: Les Libertes de l'Air,* Editions Internationales, 1948; *The Federal States and Their Judiciary: A Comparative Study in Constitutional Law and Organization of Courts in Federal States,* Mouton, 1959; (contributor) Ralph A. Newman, editor, *Essays in Honor of Roscoe Pound,* Bobbs-Merrill, 1962; *International Air Transportation as Affected by State Sovereignty,* Editions Emile Bruylant (Brussels), 1970; (editor with John N. Hazard) *Legal Thought in the United States of America under Contemporary Pressures,* Editions Emile Bruylant, 1970; (editor and contributor) *Polish Law Throughout the Ages: One Thousand Years of Polish Law,* Hoover Institution, 1970; (editor with Hazard, and contributor) *Law in the United States of America in Social and Technological Revolution,* Editions Emile Bruylant, 1974; *Obligations in Polish Law,* Sijthoff International, 1974. Contributor of about 130 articles and book reviews to journals. Member of board of editors, *American Journal of Comparative Law,* 1962—.

*WORK IN PROGRESS:* A book entitled *The Law in the United States of America in the Bicentennial Era,* edited with John N. Hazard; an article, "Brigitte, Jackie, and Photography—A Welcome Publicity or Offensive Invasion of Privacy?''

\* \* \*

## WAINWRIGHT, Charles Anthony 1933-

*PERSONAL:* Born September 14, 1933, in Los Angeles, Calif.; divorced; married Mary Beth Halbmeir, January 10, 1975; children: Colleen, Elizabeth. *Education:* University of Colorado, B.A., 1955. *Home:* 11616 North Miller Rd., Scottsdale, Ariz. 85260. *Agent:* Michael Hamilburg, 1104 South Robertson Blvd., Los Angeles, Calif. 90035. *Office:* Grey Advertising, 3003 North Central Ave., Phoenix, Ariz. 85004.

*CAREER:* North Advertising, Chicago, Ill., vice-president, 1960-64; Tatham-Laird & Kudner (advertising), Chicago, vice-president, 1964-1969; Wainwright, Inc. (advertising), Chicago, president, 1969-77; Grey Advertising, Phoenix, Ariz., senior vice-president and general manager, 1977—. Director of Gamut of Games, Inc., Tree Ltd., and Lifestyle, Inc. *Military service:* U.S. Navy, 1955-57. *Member:* Arizona Club. *Awards, honors:* Awards at Venice Film Festival and Cannes Film Festival; Clio Award; International Broadcast Award.

*WRITINGS: Television Commericals,* Hastings House, 1965; *Successful Management of New Products,* Hastings House, 1969; *The Treasure,* Hastings House, 1977. Writer of motion pictures, ''Together for Days,'' and ''The Gunfighter,'' 1977, and of television series, ''Little Cook.'' Contributor to magazines.

\* \* \*

## WAINWRIGHT, Geoffrey 1939-

*PERSONAL:* Born July 16, 1939, in Barnsley, England; son of Willie and Martha Ann (Burgess) Wainwright; married Margaret Helen Wiles, April 20, 1965; children: Joanna Mary, Catherine, Dominic Mark. *Education:* Gonville and Caius College, Cambridge, B.A., M.A., 1964, B.D., 1972; Wesley College, Headingley, Leeds, England, graduate study, 1962-64; University of Geneva, D.Th., 1969. *Address:* Queen's College, Birmingham 15, England.

*CAREER:* Clergyman of Methodist Church; minister in Liverpool, England, 1964-66; Protestant Faculty of Theology, Yaounde, Cameroon, professor of systematic theology, 1967-73; Queen's College, Birmingham, England, professor of systematic theology, 1973—. Member of World Methodist Council, 1971-81, of English Churches' Unity Commission, 1974-78, and of World Council of Churches' Commission on Faith and Order, 1976—. Governing body member, Society for Promoting Christian Knowledge, 1976—. *Member:* Societas Liturgica (member of council, 1975—). *Awards, honors:* Leverhulme scholarship in Rome, Italy, 1966-67.

*WRITINGS: Christian Initiation,* John Knox, 1969; *Eucharist and Eschatology,* Epworth, 1971, 2nd edition, 1973; *Le Bapteme, acces a l'Eglise,* Editions Cle, (Yaounde), 1972; (editor with C. Jones and E. Yarnold) *The Study of Liturgy,* Oxford University Press, 1978. Contributor of articles and reviews in English, French, and German to theology journals.

*WORK IN PROGRESS: Doxology, a systematic theology from the perspective of worship,* for Epworth.

*AVOCATIONAL INTERESTS:* Playing tennis, watching cricket; art and architecture; reading novels, detective, and spy stories; theatre, jazz; international ecclesiastical diplomacy.

## WAKEFIELD, Donam Hahn 1927-

*PERSONAL:* Born December 20, 1927, in Korea; daughter of Joong Chun and Tu Sun (Pak) Hahn; married John Wakefield (a teacher). *Education:* Attended Japan Women's University, 1943-45, and Sacred Heart School, Peking, China, 1945-46; Seoul National University, B.A., 1949; Marquette University, M.A., 1964; St. Mary's College, Notre Dame, Ind., Ph.D., 1966. *Office:* Department of Religious Studies, University of Santa Clara, Santa Clara, Calif. 95053.

*CAREER:* St. Mary College, Leavenworth, Kan., instructor in theology, 1966-68; Loras College, Dubuque, Iowa, assistant professor of theology, 1968-72; Dominican College, Houston, Tex., lecturer, 1972-75; University of Santa Clara, Santa Clara, Calif., member of staff, 1977—. *Member:* American Academy of Religions.

*WRITINGS: Journey into the Void,* Our Sunday Visitor, 1971.

*WORK IN PROGRESS:* A book on spiritual awareness entitled *Commentary on Prajnaparamita.*

\* \* \*

## WAKEMAN, Geoffrey 1926-

*PERSONAL:* Born August 18, 1926, in Tunbridge Wells, Kent, England. *Education:* Keble College, Oxford, M.A., 1950. *Home:* 28 Pantain Rd., Loughborough, Leicestershire, England. *Office:* Loughborough School of Librarianship, Loughborough, Leicestershire, England.

*CAREER:* Alsager College of Education, Alsager, England, library tutor, 1957-62; Glasgow College of Building, Glasgow, Scotland, library tutor, 1962-64; Loughborough School of Librarianship, Loughborough, England, 1965—, began as lecturer, became senior lecturer in bibliography.

*WRITINGS:* (With Roderick Cave) *Typographia Naturalis,* privately printed, 1967; *Aspects of Victorian Lithography,* privately printed, 1970; *Nineteenth-Century Illustration,* Plough Press, 1970; *English Hand Made Papers Suitable for Bookwork,* Plough Press, 1972; *Victorian Book Illustration,* David & Charles, 1973; (with Gavin Bridson) *Nineteenth-Century Colour Printers,* Plough Press, 1975; *The Production of Nineteenth-Century Colour Illustralia,* Plough Press, 1976. Contributor of articles to bibliographical journals.

\* \* \*

## WALCOTT, Fred G. 1894-

*PERSONAL:* Born September 8, 1894, in Sparta, Mich.; son of Henry Elijah (a farmer) and Charlotte (Thompson) Walcott; married Edith Carlson, August 21, 1919; children: Virginia Mary (Mrs. George E. Beauchamp, Jr.), John W. *Education:* Attended Grand Rapids Junior College, 1923-25; University of Michigan, A.B. (with high distinction), 1928, A.M., 1930, D.Ed., 1945. *Home:* 2401 Vinewood Blvd., Ann Arbor, Mich. 48104.

*CAREER:* Farmer until the age of twenty-nine, when he entered junior college; high school principal in Sparta, Mich., 1925-27; head of high school English department in Negaunee, Mich., 1928-30; University of Michigan, Ann Arbor, instructor at University High School, 1930-45, assistant professor, 1946-50, associate professor, 1950-54, professor of education and of English, 1954-65, head of department of English at University High School, 1937-51. Visiting professor, University of Wisconsin, summer, 1946, and University of Sheffield, 1964-65. *Member:* National Council of Teachers of English, Philosophy of Education Association, John Dewey Society, Michigan Council of Teachers of English, Phi Beta Kappa, Phi Kappa Phi, Phi Delta Kappa.

*WRITINGS:* (With A. J. Marckwardt) *Facts about Current English Usage,* Appleton, for National Council of Teachers of English, 1938; (with R. C. Pooley and W. S. Gray) *Growth in Reading,* Scott, Foresman, Volume I, 1938, Volume II, 1939, Volume III (with Pooley only), 1942; (with C. D. Thorpe and S. P. Savage) *Growth in Thought and Expression,* Sanborn, Volumes I-II, 1940, Volume III (with L. B. Jacobs as additional co-author), 1941; (with Pooley, Gray, and E. S. Thomas) *Read and Think,* Scott, Foresman, 1941; (with Pooley and Gray) *Guiding the Pupil's Growth in Reading,* Scott, Foresman, 1941; (with Pooley and Gray) *Paths and Pathfinders,* Scott, Foresman, 1946; (with Pooley and Gray) *Wonders and Workers,* Scott, Foresman, 1946; (with Pooley and Gray) *Think-and-Do Book,* Scott, Foresman, Book I, 1946, Book II, 1947; (contributor) Virgil E. Herrick and Leland B. Jacobs, editors, *Children and Language Arts,* Prentice-Hall, 1955; *The Origins of Culture and Anarchy: Matthew Arnold and Popular Education in England,* University of Toronto Press, 1970. Also author of unpublished memoirs, *Maybe I Dreamed It.*

Columnist in *Education,* 1958-61. Contributor of about fifty articles and reviews to education journals and bulletins. Former editor, *English Bulletin* (publication of Michigan Council of Teachers of English).

*SIDELIGHTS:* Fred G. Walcott told *CA:* ''Underneath the routines of my teaching, there loomed the evidence of mankind's becoming. Children and youth were marching up an open road. They moved with the impulse of tropism. They were bent on progress and fulfillment, the means of which they might not always fully understand. Deep, mysterious, irrepressible—the impulse arose from within their nature, as instinctive as the flight of birds. Behind them were their parents, grandparents, friends, relatives—society itself—supporting, urging, identifying with their upward tending. Here was the grand pageant of our humanity. This was what it was all about!''

*AVOCATIONAL INTERESTS:* Gardening, music (plays in string quartet), photography, travel.

\* \* \*

## WALDMAN, Anne    1945-

*PERSONAL:* Born April 2, 1945, in Millville, N.J.; daughter of John M. (an English professor and writer) and Frances (a translator; maiden surname LeFevre) Waldman. *Education:* Bennington College, B.A., 1966. *Office:* Naropa Institute, 1111 Pearl St., Boulder, Colo.

*CAREER:* St. Marks Church In-the-Bowery, New York, N.Y., director of Poetry Project, 1968-77. Poet and performer. Co-director and teacher, Jack Kerouac School of Disembodied Poetics, Naropa Institute, 1974—. *Awards and honors:* Dylan Thomas Memorial Award, 1967; National Literary Anthology Award, 1970.

*WRITINGS:* (Editor) *The World Anthology: Poems from the St. Mark's Poetry Project,* Bobbs-Merrill, 1969; *Baby Breakdown,* Bobbs-Merrill, 1970; *Giant Night,* Corinth Books, 1970; *No Hassles,* Kulchur Press, 1971; (editor) *Another World,* Bobbs-Merrill, 1971; *Life Notes,* Bobbs-Merrill, 1973; *Fast Speaking Woman,* City Lights, 1975; *Journals and Dreams,* Stonehill, 1976; *Shaman,* Munich, 1977. Co-editor, Angel Hair Books. Editor, *World* magazine.

*SIDELIGHTS:* The poetry of Anne Waldman, ''usually considered one of the 'New York School' poets,'' has been praised and disparaged; there seem to be no lukewarm responses from the critics. Denis Donoghue writes: ''I found [*Baby Breakdown*] a horrid little monster, a spoiled brat of a thing.... Miss Waldman's verses are babytalk, precocious but not intelligent.'' On the other hand, Gerard Malanga, in a review for *Poetry,* says, ''she moves through language with a simplicity and grace and respect for language that gives her poems power, not only in the way they are written, but in what they have to say....'' Another reviewer, Robert Peters, complains ''I find Waldman's mind predictable, sentimental, self gratifying, and, in short, boring.'' Critics of both persuasions have commented on her poems' ''curiously little emotional content,'' and several have noted that her work is better read aloud. Aram Saroyan notes, ''Waldman's poems are a kind of high-energy shorthand ...'' and praises her ''repetitive, chant-like 'songs,' which bring to mind tribal shaman ceremonies. These latter, which can work hypnotically on an audience but tend to lose some of their magic on the page, point to a whole new emphasis in today's poetry ... which puts the poet once again in the oral tradition.''

*BIOGRAPHICAL/CRITICAL SOURCES: New York Review of Books,* May 6, 1971; *Poetry,* January, 1974; *Parnassus,* fall/winter, 1974; *Margins,* January/February/March, 1976; *New York Times Book Review,* April 25, 1976; *Ms.,* September, 1976; *Contemporary Literary Criticism,* Volume VII, Gale, 1977.

\* \* \*

## WALDRIP, Louise B.    1912-

*PERSONAL:* Born July 13, 1912, in Ft. Worth, Tex.; daughter of Fred G. (an accountant) and Edna E. (Hooks) Baker; married Olen E. Waldrip (a minister), November 1, 1935; children: Anne (Mrs. Andy Davis), John Baker. *Education:* Mary Hardin-Baylor College, B.S., 1937; Baylor University, M.A., 1961; University of Texas, Ph.D., 1967. *Religion:* Baptist. *Home address:* Route 1, Box 125A, Fincastle, Va. 24090.

*CAREER:* San Antonio College, San Antonio, Tex., instructor in English, 1964-65; Baylor University, Waco, Tex., instructor, 1965-66, assistant professor of English, 1966-73; Liberty Baptist College, Lynchburg, Va., professor of English, 1973-77. *Member:* American Association of University Women, Conference of College Teachers of English.

*WRITINGS:* (With Shirley Ann Bauer) *A Bibliography of Katherine Anne Porter,* Scarecrow, 1969.

\* \* \*

## WALKER, Alice    1944-

*PERSONAL:* Born February 9, 1944, in Eatonton, Ga.; daughter of Willie Lee and Minnie Tallulah (Grant) Walker; married Melvyn Rosenman Leventhal (a civil rights lawyer), March 17, 1967 (divorced, 1976); children: Rebecca Grant. *Education:* Attended Spelman College, 1961-63; Sarah Lawrence College, B.A., 1965. *Home:* 50 B Linnaen St., Cambridge, Mass. 02138. *Agent:* Wendy Weil, Julian Bach Literary Agency, 3 East 48th St., New York, N.Y. *Office:* Ms. Magazine Corp., 370 Lexington Ave., New York, N.Y. 10017.

*CAREER:* Teacher of writing and Black literature at Jackson State College and Tougaloo College, Miss., 1968-70; Wellesley College, Wellesley, Mass., lecturer in writing and literature, 1972—; University of Massachusetts, Boston, lecturer in literature, 1972—; *Ms.* Magazine Corp., New York, N.Y., editor, 1974—; Yale University, New Haven, Conn., associate professor of English, 1977—. Fellow, Radcliffe Institute, 1971-73. *Awards, honors:* Breadloaf Writer's Conference, scholar, 1966; Merrill Writing fellowship, 1967; McDowell Colony Fellowship, 1967; National Endowment for the Arts grant, 1969; Rosenthal Award, National Institute of Arts and Letters, 1974, for *In Love and Trouble: Stories of Black Women;* Guggenheim grant in fiction, 1978—.

*WRITINGS: Once* (poems), Harcourt, 1968; *The Third Life of Grange Copeland* (novel), Harcourt, 1970; *Revolutionary Petunias* (poems), Harcourt, 1973; *Langston Hughes* (biography), Crowell, 1973; *In Love and Trouble: Stories of Black Women* (short stories), Harcourt, 1973; *Meridian* (novel), Harcourt, 1976; *"Good Night Willie Lee, I'll See You in the Morning"* (poems), Dial, in press; (editor) *"I Love Myself When I'm Laughing . . ."*, Feminist Press, in press.

*SIDELIGHTS:* "I was curious to know why people in families (specifically black families) are often cruel to each other and how much of this cruelty is caused by outside forces, such as various social injustices, segregation, unemployment, etc.," Alice Walker told *Library Journal.* In *The Third Life of Grange Copeland* she explores this cruelty. "Family relationships are sacred," she continues. "No amount of outside pressure and injustice must make us lose sight of that fact. . . . In the black family, love, cohesion, support, and concern are crucial since a racist society constantly acts to destroy the black individual, the black family unit, the black child. In America black people have only themselves and each other." Paula Meinetz Shapiro writes that "Miss Walker's haunting tale of three generations of a sharecropper's family attempting to overcome white oppression is candid, sensitive and tragic." Jay L. Halio feels the "honest treatment of both past and present, the worst aspects of which Miss Walker does not flinch at, help make *The Third Life* a convincing and stirring novel. So do its firm, tight control and its eloquence: it is no surprise to learn that the author is also a poet."

Nikki Giovanni, reviewing *In Love and Trouble: Stories of Black Women,* writes: "They are not pretty—these short stories—nor happy—as one traditionally thinks of stories about black women and their men, black mothers and their children, old ladies and their gods. I applaud *In Love and Trouble.* . . . I certainly welcome the love Alice so painfully shares." These stories are "terse, ironic and humorous," says Mel Watkins in *New York Times Book Review.* "Alice Walker writes efficiently and economically, and the shorter pieces here, even when thin as fiction, are often prose poems." *Ms.* reviewer Barbara Smith comments: "Even as a black woman, I found the cumulative impact of these stories devastating. . . . I soon realized, however, that the reason these stories saddened me so much was because of their truthfulness. For every one of Walker's fictional women I knew or had heard of a real woman whose fate was all too similar."

"Alice Walker has written a fine, taut novel that accomplishes a remarkable amount," Marge Piercy says, reviewing *Meridian.* "She writes with a sharp, critical sense as she deals with the issues of tactics and strategy in the civil rights movement." A *New Yorker* reviewer disagrees by stating, "The book tries to make itself a parable—more than a mere novel—or trades the prosaic for an inert symbolism that would seem to be intended to elevate the story but instead collapses it."

Like most of her fiction, Alice Walker's books of poetry, *Once* and *Revolutionary Petunias,* have also earned praise. A *Poetry* reviewer has called her "a sensitive, spirited, and intelligent poet. Feeling is channeled into a style that is direct and sharp, honest speech pared down to essentials. Her poems are like pencil sketches which are all graven outline: no shaded areas, no embellishments. Wit and tenderness combine into humanity."

*BIOGRAPHICAL/CRITICAL SOURCES: Book World,* November 3, 1968, November 18, 1973; *Library Journal,* June 15, 1970; *New Leader,* January 25, 1971; *Poetry,* February, 1971; *Southern Review,* Volume IX, number 1, spring, 1973; *American Scholar,* summer, 1973; *Choice,* September, 1973; *Ms.,* February, 1974; *New York Times Book Review,* March 17, 1974, May 23, 1976; *Books Abroad,* Volume XLVII, number 4, autumn, 1974; *New Republic,* September 14, 1974; *Black World,* October, 1974; *Parnassus: Poetry in Review,* spring-summer, 1976; *New Yorker,* June 7, 1976; *Yale Review,* autumn, 1976; *Contemporary Literary Criticism,* Gale, Volume V, 1976, Volume VI, 1976, Volume IX, 1978.

\* \* \*

## WALKER, Ardis Manly 1901-

*PERSONAL:* Born April 9, 1901, in Kernville, Calif.; son of William Brannon (a miner) and Etta (Bole) Walker; married Eva Gayle Mendelssohn, May 27, 1937. *Education:* Attended Fresno State College (now California State University, Fresno), 1921-22, and University of California, Los Angeles, 1924; University of Southern California, B.S., 1927. *Politics:* Democrat. *Home:* 7 Walker Dr., Kernville, Calif. 93238. *Office address:* P.O. Box 37, Kernville, Calif. 93238.

*CAREER:* Bell Telephone Laboratories, New York, N.Y., member of technical staff, 1927-32; free-lance writer and researcher, 1932—; Judicial Court, Kernville, Calif., judge, 1938-48; Kern County, Bakersfield, Calif., supervisor, 1948-52; motel owner and public relations consultant, Kernville, Calif., 1952-64. Former newspaper correspondent. *Member:* National Wildlife Federation, California Historical Society, Kern County Historical Society (former president), Rotary International.

*WRITINGS: Quatrains,* Stockwell, 1930, Sierra Trails Press, 1971; *Sierra Prologue,* Kern County Historical Society, 1938; *Francisco Garces: Pioneer Padre,* Kern County Historical Society, 1946; *Kern River Valley Vignettes,* La Siesta Press, 1966; *Sierra Nevada Sequence,* Sierra Trails Press, 1968; *The Rough and the Righteous,* Paisano, 1971. Also author of a collection of poetry, Sagebrush Press, in press. Contributor of poems and articles to anthologies and to poetry and historical journals.

*WORK IN PROGRESS:* Compiling a book of haiku and a volume of prose poems; research in the westward migration in America; biographies of Joseph Reddeford Walker and Borax Smith.

*SIDELIGHTS:* Ardis Manly Walker has traveled throughout the U.S., West Indies, and Central America, but prefers the Sierra Nevada wilderness. He told *CA:* "[I am] interested particularly in writing poetry and poetic prose expressing a close affinity with nature, the miracles of which I consider the basic source of inspiration."

\* \* \*

## WALKER, James Lynwood 1940-

*PERSONAL:* Born December 19, 1940, in Fayetteville,

N.C.; son of David Franklin and Mary Ann (McNiell) Walker; married Joyce Moore, December 19, 1958; married second wife, Harmon Lamb, July 27, 1963; children: (first marriage) Michael Anthony; (second marriage) David Edward, Angela Lynnette. *Education:* North Carolina College at Durham (now North Carolina Central University), B.A., 1963; Duke University, graduate study, 1963-65; Pacific School of Religion, B.D., 1966; Graduate Theological Union, Ph.D., in conjunction with University of California, Berkeley, 1970. *Home:* 3500 25th Ave. W., No. 424, Seattle, Wash. 98199.

*CAREER:* Graduate Theological Union, Berkeley, Calif., assistant professor of religion and the personality sciences and assistant dean, 1970-73; Pastoral Institute of Washington, Seattle, president, 1973-78; self-employed counselor, consultant, and writer, 1978—.

*WRITINGS: Body and Soul: Gestalt Therapy and Religious Experience,* Abingdon, 1971; (contributor) Robert Williams, editor, *To Live and to Die: When, Why, How,* Springer-Verlag, 1973.

*AVOCATIONAL INTERESTS:* Photography, wood work, music, travel.

\* \* \*

## WALKER, Joseph E(rdman) 1911-

*PERSONAL:* Born July 14, 1911, in Fannettsburg, Pa.; son of Samuel Elmer (a banker) and Adaline (Seibert) Walker; married Rachael Smith, November 29, 1940; children: Robert Smith, John Samuel, Walter Frederick. *Education:* Park College, Parkville, Mo., A.B., 1932; University of Tennessee, M.A., 1933; Temple University, Philadelphia, Pa., Ed.D., 1964. *Politics:* Republican. *Religion:* Presbyterian. *Home:* 422 Hostetter Dr., Millersville, Pa. 17551.

*CAREER:* High school principal in Fannettsburg, Pa., 1934-39; teacher of history and English in high school in Bradford, Pa., 1940-56; Ryder Scott Co. (petroleum engineers), Bradford, researcher, 1941-49; Culligan Water Conditioning, Bradford, researcher, 1949-53; Millersville State College, Millersville, Pa., associate professor, 1956-64, professor of history and sociology, 1964-76, acting chairman of department, 1964. Member of Millersville Borough Council and Millersville Zoning Board of Review, Millersville, Pa. *Member:* American Historical Association, National Historical Association, National Education Association, National Council for the Social Studies, Pennsylvania Historical Association, Pennsylvania Council for the Social Studies (executive committee), Pennsylvania State Education Association, Historical Society of Pennsylvania, Kittochtinny Historical Society, Millersville Recreation Association, Phi Delta Kappa. *Awards, honors:* Research grants from Eleutherian-Hagley Foundation, 1967, and Economic History Association, 1969.

*WRITINGS: Hopewell Village: A Social and Economic History of an Iron-Making Community,* University of Pennsylvania Press, 1966; (editor) *Business and Pleasure in Western Pennsylvania: The 1809 Journal of Joshua Gilpin,* Pennsylvania Historical and Museum Commission, 1972; (editor) *Lancaster County during the American Revolution,* seven volumes, Sutter House, 1974-1976. Also author with Dorothy Dinroe of a play, "Ododo." Contributor of articles to *Labor History, American City, Social Studies, Education, National Education Association Journal, Pennsylvania Magazine of History and Biography, Pennsylvania History, Clearing House, American School Board Journal,* and *School Activities.*

*WORK IN PROGRESS: A Rage for Going Down the Ohio,* a book on travel in Ohio, 1800-1820; *The Lukens Steel Company,* an industrial history book.

*SIDELIGHTS:* Joseph E. Walker told *CA:* "Perhaps the most lasting influence was the experience of growing up as one of a family of nine children in a small town in the mountains of Pennsylvania. It provided freedom to roam and think for oneself yet gave the warmth and care of a closely knit family life." Walker specializes in the early history of the iron industry in the United States and in the American Revolution and Early National Period.

*AVOCATIONAL INTERESTS:* Reading, travel, sports, and collecting coins, bells, and antiques.

*BIOGRAPHICAL/CRITICAL SOURCES: New York Times,* November 11, 1970.

\* \* \*

## WALKER, Kenneth R(oland) 1928-

*PERSONAL:* Born April 12, 1928, in Syracuse, Ind.; son of Carl and Laura (Ford) Walker; married Marylou E. Neff (a librarian), September 10, 1950; children: Elizabeth Ann, Mary Susan. *Education:* Goshen College, B.A., 1949; Indiana University, M.A., 1950, Ph.D., 1952; University of Florida, graduate study, 1951-52; University of Arkansas, M.Ed., 1964. *Religion:* United Methodist. *Home:* R.R. 2, Box 38, Russellville, Ark. 72801. *Office:* Arkansas Tech University, Russellville, Ark. 72801.

*CAREER:* U.S. Air Force, 1952-58, became captain; U.S. Air Force Reserve, 1958—, current rank, colonel; Arkansas Tech University, Russellville, associate professor and assistant dean of College, 1958-65, professor of history, 1965—, dean of School of Arts and Sciences, 1970-72, head of social science and philosophy department, 1972—. Military assignments included posts as historical officer, Historical Division, Research Studies Institute, Air University, Maxwell Air Force Base, as training and education officer at Thule Air Base, Greenland, and as instructor and assistant professor of history at U.S. Air Force Academy. Peace Corps coordinator, 1961-66; chairman of board of directors, Wesley Foundation, 1967; president, Page County Teachers Credit Union, 1977; former president and vice-president, Department of Higher Education.

*MEMBER:* Organization of American Historians, Association of Arkansas College History Teachers, Arkansas Political Science Association, Arkansas Registrars and Deans (former president and vice-president).

*WRITINGS: Days the Presidents Died,* Pioneer Press (Little Rock, Ark.), 1966; *The History of the Midwest,* Pioneer Press, 1972. Contributor to history and education journals.

*SIDELIGHTS:* Kenneth R. Walker writes: "Most of my writing grows out of my teaching. I hold to the educational theory of cognitive restructuring, and thus my writing is for the purpose of organizing and clarifying material to make it more understandable for my students and the general public."

\* \* \*

## WALL, C. Edward 1942-

*PERSONAL:* Born March 3, 1942, in Cherokee, Iowa; son of Clifford Reginald (an implement dealer) and Mabel (Tjossem) Wall; married Mary Ellen Stratton, September 11, 1962; children: Annette Louise, Jannette Marie, Heather

Rae, Christopher Edward. *Education:* University of Iowa, A.B. (with honors), 1964; University of Michigan, M.A.L.S., 1966. *Home:* 3196 Maple Dr., Ypsilanti, Mich. 48197. *Office:* University of Michigan—Dearborn, Dearborn, Mich. 48128; and Pierian Press, 5000 Washtenaw, Ann Arbor, Mich. 48106.

*CAREER:* University of Michigan—Dearborn, head librarian, 1966—. President, Pierian Press, Ann Arbor, Mich., 1968—. *Member:* American Library Association, Association of College and Research Libraries, Association of Educational Communications and Technology, Michigan Library Association, Phi Beta Kappa, Beta Phi Mu. *Awards, honors:* Loleta D. Fyan Award, Michigan Library Association, 1971; Isadore Gilbert Mudge Citation, American Library Association, 1978.

*WRITINGS: Subject Index to New Serial Titles, 1950-1965,* Pierian, 1968; *Periodical Title Abbreviations,* Gale, 1969; (with Ed Przebienda) *Words and Phrases Index,* four volumes, Pierian, 1969-70; *Cumulative Author Index for Poole's Index to Periodical Literature, 1802-1906,* Pierian, 1971. Also author of *Author Index to the A.L.A. Index to General Literature,* 1972, and *Author Index to P.A.I.S. Bulletin, 1965-1969,* 1973. Has written or edited approximately 150 books in his field and written complete periodical issues. Columnist for and contributor of articles to professional journals. Editor-in-chief, *Media Review Digest,* 1970—, *Reference Sciences Review,* 1972—, *Consumers Index to Product Evaluations and Information Sources,* 1973—, *Serials Review,* 1975—, *Index to Free Periodicals,* 1976, and *Best Buys in Print,* 1978—.

*WORK IN PROGRESS:* Numerous reference books; research on Germany military advisers in China, 1927-38; other library related studies.

*SIDELIGHTS:* C. Edward Wall studied the Mandarin Chinese language for five years. *Avocational interests:* Contemporary art, squash.

\* \* \*

## WALLACE, Andrew 1930-

*PERSONAL:* Born November 18, 1930, in Springfield, Ill.; son of Jerry (an Episcopal priest) and Leonora (Swilling) Wallace; married Bernice Deaton, July 26, 1958; children: Andrea, Mary Margaret, Robert Neil Andrew. *Education:* University of Arizona, B.A., 1953, Ph.D., 1968. *Religion:* Episcopalian. *Home:* 493 West Philomena, Flagstaff, Ariz. 86001. *Office:* Department of History, Northern Arizona University, Flagstaff, Ariz. 86001.

*CAREER:* Arizona Historical Society, Tucson, archivist and chief of research, 1963-68; Northern Arizona University, Flagstaff, assistant professor of history, 1968—. *Military service:* U.S. Army, 1953-58; became first lieutenant; Arizona National Guard, 1959-64; became captain. *Member:* American Historical Association (life member), American Military Institute, American Philatelic Society, Western History Association (charter member; council member, 1967-70), Arizona Historical Society, New Mexico Historical Society.

*WRITINGS:* (Editor) *Sources and Readings in Arizona History,* Arizona Historical Society, 1965; *Pumpelly's Arizona,* Palo Verde Press, 1965; *The Image of Arizona,* University of New Mexico Press, 1971. Contributor to *Brand Book,* Tucson Corral of the Westerners, 1967, 1973. Editor, *Journal of Arizona History,* 1964-68.

*WORK IN PROGRESS:* A biography of General August V. Kautz, tentatively entitled *Soldier of Contention.*

## WALLS, David Stuart 1941-

*PERSONAL:* Born October 21, 1941, in Chicago, Ill.; son of John Archer and Elizabeth (Smith) Walls; married Lucia V. Gattone, November 25, 1971; children: Jesse Michael. *Education:* University of California, Berkeley, B.A., 1964; University of Kentucky, M.A., 1972, Ph.D., 1978. *Home:* 114 Woodford Dr., Lexington, Ky. 40504. *Office:* Appalachian Center, University of Kentucky, Lexington, Ky.

*CAREER:* U.S. Department of Health, Education, & Welfare, Washington, D.C., management intern, 1964-65; Office of Economic Opportunity, Washington, D.C., administrative assistant, 1965-66; Appalachian Volunteers, Inc., Prestonsburg, Ky., field coordinator, 1966-69, director, 1969-70; Berea College, Berea, Ky., part-time instructor, 1970; University of Kentucky, College of Social Professions, Lexington, assistant professor, 1974—, director of Appalachian Center, 1977—. Participant in Appalachian Studies Conference. *Member:* American Sociological Association, Society for the Study of Social Problems.

*WRITINGS:* (Editor with John B. Stephenson) *Appalachia in the Sixties: Decade of Reawakening,* University Press of Kentucky, 1972; (contributor) J. W. Williamson, editor, *An Appalachian Symposium,* Appalachian State University Press, 1977; (contributor) Helen M. Lewis and others, editors, *Colonialism in Modern America: The Appalachian Case,* Appalachian Consortium Press, 1978.

*WORK IN PROGRESS:* Research on economic and political power in central Appalachia, and on the coal industry in the United States.

\* \* \*

## WALSH, Edward J(oseph) 1937-

*PERSONAL:* Born July 11, 1937, in Philadelphia, Pa.; son of Edward Joseph (an electrical engineer) and Loretta (Zahn) Walsh; married Rosemary McNichol (a teacher), December 29, 1970; children: Joan, Martin. *Education:* Glen Ellyn College, B.A., 1960; Maryknoll Seminary, New York, N.Y., B.D., 1964, M.Th., 1965; Gregorian University, Rome, S.T.L., 1967; University of Michigan, Ph.D., 1974. *Home:* 720 South Allen, State College, Pa. 16801. *Office:* Department of Sociology, Pennsylvania State University, State College, Pa.

*CAREER:* Ordained a Roman Catholic priest, 1965; College of Saint Thomas, St. Paul, Minn., instructor in theology, 1967-69; left priesthood, 1969; Pennsylvania State University, State College, assistant professor of sociology, 1975—. *Awards, honors:* Richard Fletcher Prize, Dartmouth College, 1965, for essay "The Christian as a Witness"; National Institute of Mental Health fellowship, University of Michigan, 1969-74; dissertation grants from U.S. Department of Labor and National Science Foundation, 1972-74; research grant from Ford Foundation, 1974-75, to study farm worker struggle in California; research initiation grant from Pennsylvania State University, 1976, to study correlates of occupational status.

*WRITINGS: The Christian as a Witness,* Dartmouth Publications, 1965; *Sacraments: Seven or Seventy Times Seven?,* St. Mary's College Press, 1969; *What Do You Think of Christ?,* Pflaum Press, 1971; *Dirty Work, Race, and Self-Esteem,* Institute of Labor and Industrial Relations, University of Michigan-Wayne State University, 1975. Contributor of articles and reviews to *American Sociological Review, Teaching Sociology, Sociology and Social Research, Journal of Social Psychology,* and other periodicals.

*SIDELIGHTS:* After his ordination, Edward Walsh was assigned to study journalism at the University of Missouri—Columbia, and then ordered to withdraw upon publication of a critical article against the stipend system in the August 25, 1965 issue of *National Catholic Reporter.* In his two years in Rome he had a number of serious conflicts with conservative church authorities. Then, upon learning that his teaching contract at the College of St. Thomas would not be renewed because of his leadership of a march of mourning for the assassination of Martin Luther King, Walsh left the priesthood and took up the study of sociology. He is now starting research on the nuclear/solar energy debate and grass roots insurgency against the nuclear industry.

\*     \*     \*

## WALSH, Gillian Paton  1937-
## (Jill Paton Walsh)

*PERSONAL:* Born April 29, 1937, in London, England; daughter of John Llewellyn (an engineer) and Patricia (Dubern) Bliss; married Antony Paton Walsh (a chartered secretary), August 12, 1961; children: Edmund Alexander, Margaret Ann, Helen Clare. *Education:* St. Anne's College, Oxford, degree (honors), 1959. *Politics:* Liberal. *Religion:* None. *Home:* 60 Mount Ararat Rd., Richmond, Surrey, England.

*CAREER:* Teacher of English in London, England, 1959-62. *Member:* Society of Authors. *Awards, honors:* Children's Spring Book Festival Award from *Book World,* 1970, for *Fireweed;* Whitbread Prize, for *The Emperor's Winding Sheet.*

*WRITINGS*—Juvenile books under name Jill Paton Walsh: *Hengest's Tale,* Macmillan (London), 1966, St. Martin's, 1967; *The Dolphin Crossing,* St. Martin's, 1967; (with Kevin Crossley-Holland) *Wordhoard: Anglo-Saxon Stories,* Farrar, Straus, 1969; *Fireweed,* Macmillan, 1969, Farrar, Straus, 1970; *Goldengrove,* Farrar, Straus, 1972; *The Dawnstone,* Hamish Hamilton, 1973; *Toolmaker,* Heinemann, 1973; *The Emperor's Winding Sheet,* Farrar, Straus, 1974; *The Huffler,* Farrar, Straus, 1975; *The Island Sunrise: Prehistoric Britain,* Deutsch, 1975, Seabury, 1976; *Unleaving,* Farrar, Straus, 1976; *Crossing to Salamis,* Heinemann, 1977; *The Walls of Athens,* Heinemann, 1977.

Adult novels under name Jill Paton Walsh: *Farewell, Great King,* Macmillan, 1972; *The Butty Boy,* Macmillan, 1975.

Other: (Editor) *Beowulf,* structural reader edition, Longman, 1975; *Children of the Fox,* Farrar, Straus, 1978.

*SIDELIGHTS:* Jill Paton Walsh told *CA:* "I am interested in nearly everything—the 'butterfly mind' syndrome. I don't understand my motivation, nor do I want to—it might switch off if I understood it." Walsh explained that she writes for children "largely from a belief that a book [should] always . . . be as simple and as readable as the writer can make it, which is to say that it ought to be for children [if at all possible]. A testimony to the effectiveness of this simplicity comes from Pamela Marsh, who says of *Fireweed,* "[It] justifies, at least for once, all those adult readers who turn for their reading to the children's shelf and insist that they find good, well-plotted novels there."

Walsh's books frequently depict scenes from war or from an early Britain. C. S. Hannabus writes that in *The Emperor's Winding Sheet,* as in *The Dolphin Crossing,* "war is used dramatically; it is a place full of real terrors, and [is] not tied down with wishy-washy abstractions about courage and endurance." However, Marie Peel comments that, in *Fire-*

*weed,* "there is some cheating, . . . for the opting-out situation which brings and holds the boy and girl together, alone against hostile authority, is essentially expressive of modern, not wartime, attitudes. This makes for strong emotional validity for young readers, which is important, but [it does it] at a cost. For the emotional truth is isolated from the outside world; there is much skating over of class divisions, in the authors mind, as much as in the details of the story, which amounts to a kind of pretence."

The results of Walsh's "loving absorption" with Anglo-Saxon history and literature are reflected in *Hengest's Tale,* as well as in her other tales of the Old English period. A *Kirkus Service* reviewer states, "Seldom has the gloom and fear of the Dark Ages been induced with such immediacy, nor the shifting demands of primative loyalty and honor been so effectively juxtaposed; and seldom, indeed, does historical fiction sustain such knife-edge suspense throughout."

Walsh is fluent in French, "adequate" in Latin, can read Old English, Icelandic, Italian, and is learning Greek.

*AVOCATIONAL INTERESTS:* Cooking, carpentry.

*BIOGRAPHICAL/CRITICAL SOURCES: Kirkus Service,* January 15, 1967; *New York Times Book Review,* April 9, 1967, July 5, 1970; *Book World,* November 19, 1967; *Books and Bookmen,* December, 1967, February, 1970; *Times Literary Supplement,* October 16, 1969; *Punch,* December 17, 1969; *Christian Science Monitor,* May 7, 1970; *Children's Book Review,* summer, 1974; *Children's Literature Review,* Volume II, Gale, 1976.†

\*     \*     \*

## WALSH, (Michael) Stephen  1942-

*PERSONAL:* Born June 6, 1942, in Chipping Norton, England; son of Michael (an accountant) and Ethel May (Everest) Walsh; married Mary Sophia (Dru); children: one son, one daughter. *Education:* Attended St. Paul's School, 1956-60; Gonville & Caius College, Cambridge, M.A., 1963. *Home:* Cadoc House, Caerleon Gwent, Wales. *Agent:* David Higham Associates Ltd., 5-8 Lower John St., Golden Square, London W1R 4HA, England.

*CAREER:* Free-lance music critic. British Broadcasting Corp. (BBC), London, England, producer, gramophone department, 1964-65; *Listener,* London, England, music critic, 1965-67; *Observer,* London, England, assistant music critic, 1966—. Senior lecturer in twentieth-century music, University College, University of Wales, 1976—. *Member:* Critic's Circle.

*WRITINGS: The Lieder of Schumann,* Cassell, 1971. Contributor to *London Times.*

*AVOCATIONAL INTERESTS:* Singing, playing piano, chess, reading.

\*     \*     \*

## WALTERS, Sister Annette  1910-

*PERSONAL:* Born May 18, 1910, in Elmwood, Wis.; daughter of Emil Albert (a jeweler) and Anna (Berglund) Walters. *Education:* College of St. Catherine, B.A., 1933; University of Minnesota, M.A., 1935, Ph.D., 1941; University of Chicago, graduate study, summers, 1936, 1939, 1941, 1968. *Politics:* Democrat. *Home:* 2317 Western Ave., Davenport, Iowa 52803. *Office:* Department of Psychology, St. Ambrose College, Davenport, Iowa 52803.

*CAREER:* Roman Catholic religious of St. Joseph of Carondelet; College of St. Catherine, St. Paul, Minn., professor of psychology, 1943-60, part-time clinical psychologist, 1941-55, dean of studies, 1957-59; National Catholic Education Association, Washington, D.C., staff member, 1960-64; College of St. Catherine, professor of psychology, 1965-66; St. Ambrose College, Davenport, Iowa, professor of psychology and chairman of department, 1966—. Consultant to religious congregations and orders in United States and Latin America, 1958—. Lecturer and conductor of workshops on mental health; lecturer on renewal at Christ Church, Oxford University, 1967; visiting scholar, University of Chicago, summer, 1968. Iowa delegate to International Women's Year Conference, 1977. Member of board of directors, Minnesota Association of Mental Health, 1957-59, and currently of St. John's Mental Health Institute for Clergyman and Scott County Association for Retarded Children.

*MEMBER:* American Psychological Association (fellow), Religious Education Association (member of board of directors), Illinois-Iowa Association for Children with Learning Disabilities (member of board of directors), Upper Mississippi Valley Psychological Association (member of board of directors), Phi Beta Kappa, Psi Chi, Pi Gamma Mu, Sigma Xi. *Awards, honors:* Fulbright research scholar at Catholic University of Louvain, 1952-53; grants from National Institute of Mental Health, 1958, Quinlan Foundation, 1958, 1977, and Ford Foundation, 1959-60; honorary fellow, University of Minnesota, 1964-65; research fellow, Yale Divinity School, spring, 1975.

*WRITINGS:* (With Gladys Sellew and Sister Ann Harvey) *Nursing of Children,* 6th edition (Sellew was sole author of earlier editions), Saunders, 1948; (with Sister Kevin O'Hara) *Persons and Personality: An Introduction to Psychology,* Appleton, 1953; (editor and author of introduction and commentary) *Readings in Psychology,* Newman, 1963; *Religious in the Constitution of the Church,* Paulist Press, 1966; *Prayer—Who Needs It?* (youth forum book), Thomas Nelson, 1971; (contributor with Sister Ritamary Bradley) M. P. Strommen, editor, *Research on Religious Development,* Hawthorn, 1971. Contributor to psychology, education, and denominational journals.

*WORK IN PROGRESS:* With Sister Ritamary Bradley, *Women in the Church;* a critical evaluation of changes in the church, *Beyond Renewal.*

\*    \*    \*

## WALTZ, Kenneth N(eal)   1924-

*PERSONAL:* Born June 8, 1924, in Ann Arbor, Mich.; son of Christian Benjamin (a house painter) and Luella (Braun) Waltz; married Helen Lindsley, June 4, 1949; children: Kenneth L., Thomas E., Daniel E. *Education:* Oberlin College, A.B., 1948; Columbia University, M.A., 1950, Ph.D., 1954. *Politics:* Democratic. *Religion:* None. *Residence:* Berkeley, Calif. *Office:* Department of Political Science, University of California, Berkeley, Calif. 94720.

*CAREER:* Columbia University, New York, N.Y., lecturer and instructor, 1953-56, assistant professor of political science, 1956-57; Swarthmore College, Swarthmore, Pa., associate professor, 1957-64, professor of political science, 1964-66; Brandeis University, Waltham, Mass., Adlai Stevenson Professor of International Politics, 1966-71; University of California, Berkeley, Ford Professor of Political Science, 1971—. Columbia University, research associate, 1954-64, Columbia fellow in London, 1959-60; research associate of Center for International Affairs Harvard University, 1963-64, 1968-69, and 1972. Lecturer, National, Army, and Naval

War Colleges. Consultant at various times to Hudson Institute, U.S. Department of Health, Education, and Welfare, U.S. Department of State, Los Alamos Scientific Laboratories, and National Science Foundation. *Military service:* U.S. Army, 1944-46, 1951-52; became first lieutenant. *Member:* American Political Science Association (secretary, 1966-67), International Studies Association (president of New England branch, 1966-67), Phi Beta Kappa. *Awards, honors:* Guggenheim fellow, 1976; Institute for the Study of World Politics fellow, 1977.

*WRITINGS: Man, the State, and War,* Columbia University Press, 1959; (contributor) William T. R. Fox, editor, *Theoretical Aspects of International Relations,* University of Notre Dame Press, 1959; *Foreign Policy and Democratic Politics,* Little Brown, 1967; (editor with R. J. Art) *The Use of Force: International Politics and Foreign Policy,* Little, Brown, 1971; (editor with Steven L. Spiegel and contributor) *Conflict in World Politics,* Winthrop, 1971; (contributor) Wolfram Hanrieder, editor, *The United States and Western Europe in the 1970's,* Winthrop, 1974; *Theory of International Politics,* Addison-Wesley, 1978. Contributor to professional journals.

\*    \*    \*

## WALZER, Michael   1935-

*PERSONAL:* Born March 3, 1935, in New York, N.Y.; son of Joseph and Sally (Hochman) Walzer; married Judith Borodovko, June 17, 1956; children: Sarah, Rebecca. *Education:* Brandeis University, B.A., 1956; Harvard University, Ph.D., 1961. *Religion:* Jewish. *Home:* 23 Bellevue Ave., Cambridge, Mass. *Office:* Department of Government, Harvard University, Cambridge, Mass. 02138.

*CAREER:* Princeton University, Princeton, N.J., assistant professor of politics, 1962-66; Harvard University, Cambridge, Mass., associate professor, 1966-68, professor of government, 1968—. *Awards, honors:* Harbison Award, Danforth Foundation, 1971.

*WRITINGS: The Revolution of the Saints,* Harvard University Press, 1965; (editor with Philip Green) *The Political Imagination in Literature,* Free Press, 1968; *Obligations: Essays on Disobedience, War, and Citizenship,* Harvard University Press, 1970; *Political Action: A Practical Guide to Movement Politics,* Quadrangle, 1971; *Regicide and Revolution,* Cambridge University Press, 1974; *Just and Unjust Wars,* Basic Books, 1977. Contributor to philosophy and public policy journals. Member of editorial board, *Dissent;* contributing editor, *New Republic.*

*BIOGRAPHICAL/CRITICAL SOURCES: Nation,* September 28, 1970; *New York Times,* February 4, 1978.

\*    \*    \*

## WANG, (Fred) Fang Yu   1913-

*PERSONAL:* Born February 2, 1913, in Peking, China; son of Huai-ying and Shu-chin (Chu) Wang; married Sum Wai; children: Shao Fang. *Education:* Catholic University, B.A., 1936; Columbia University, M.A., 1946; South China University, LL.D., 1969. *Home:* 12 Farmstead Rd., Short Hills, N.J. 07078. *Office:* Department of Asian Studies, Seton Hall University, South Orange, N.J. 07079.

*CAREER:* Instructor, Yale University, New Haven, Conn.; Seton Hall University, South Orange, N.J., professor of Chinese, 1965—. *Member:* Chinese Language Teachers Association.

*WRITINGS—Published by Yale University, Far Eastern

Publications, except as indicated: *Chinese Dialogues* (intermediate text for spoken Chinese), 1951; *Read Chinese,* Book I (elementary text for written Chinese), 1953; (with Richard Chang) *Read Chinese,* Book III (intermediate text for written Chinese), 1961; *Introduction to Chinese Cursive Script*, with an introduction to the history of Chinese characters, 1962; *Lady in the Painting* (elementary extensive reader, with illustrations), 1962; *Readings on Chinese Culture* (intermediate extensive reader), 1962; *Talks on Chinese Culture,* Chabanel Language Institute (Hsinchu, Taiwan), 1964; *Introduction to Simplified Characters,* temporary edition, 1964; *Chinese Language Study,* RCA Educational Programs, 1964; *Japanese and Korean Language Study,* RCA Educational Programs, 1965; *Mandarin Chinese Dictionary* (Chinese-English), Seton Hall University Press, 1967; *Mandarin Chinese Dictionary* (English-Chinese), Seton Hall University Press, 1971; *An Introduction to Literary Chinese: From Spoken to Literary,* Seton Hall University Press, 1972.

\* \* \*

### WANG, Sabine E(isenberg) 1925-

*PERSONAL:* Born June 4, 1925, in Vienna, Austria; daughter of Selig (a businessman) and Charlotte (Gottfried) Eisenberg; married Leonard J. Wang (a professor of Romance languages), September 11, 1949; children: Sharon, Anne, Ruth. *Education:* Brooklyn College (now Brooklyn College of the City University of New York), B.A., 1946; Columbia University, M.A., 1947. *Politics:* Democrat. *Home:* 1064 East 27th St., Brooklyn, N.Y. 11210. *Office:* Department of French, Rutgers University, Newark, N.J. 07102.

*CAREER:* Columbia University, New York, N.Y., instructor in French, 1948-52; Brooklyn College (now Brooklyn College of the City University of New York), Brooklyn, N.Y., instructor in French, 1952-54; Rutgers University, Newark, N.J., instructor in French, 1968—. *Awards, honors:* French Government prize.

*WRITINGS:* (With husband, Leonard J. Wang) *Le Voyage Imaginaire,* Macmillan, 1970.

*WORK IN PROGRESS:* A study contrasting the work of Kafka and Ionesco.

*SIDELIGHTS:* Sabine Wang has traveled throughout Western Europe and the Middle East.††

\* \* \*

### WARD, Donald 1930-

*PERSONAL:* Born March 16, 1930, in Petaluma, Calif.; son of James E. (an estimator) and Henriette (Gink) Ward; married Mary Louise Moore, June 9, 1958; children: James K., Natalie. *Education:* San Francisco State College (now University), A.B., 1959; University of California, Los Angeles, M.A., 1961, Ph.D., 1965; University of Mainz, Germany, graduate study. *Home:* 4543 Greenbush Ave., Sherman Oaks, Calif. 91423. *Office:* Department of German, University of California, Los Angeles, Calif. 90024.

*CAREER:* University of California, Los Angeles, associate professor, 1965-74, professor of German and folklore, 1974—, director of Center for the Study of Comparative Folklore and Mythology. Associate director of University of California Study Center at the University of Goettingen, Germany, 1969-71. *Military service:* U.S. Air Force, 1950-54; became staff sergeant. *Member:* American Folklore Society, International Society for Ethnology and Folklore, International Society of Folk-Narrative Research, California Folklore Society, Pacific Coast Philology. *Awards, honors:* Alexander von Humboldt fellow, Freiburg, Germany, 1971-72.

*WRITINGS: The Divine Twins: An Indo-European Myth in Germanic Tradition,* University of California Press, 1968. Associate editor of *Abstracts of Folklore Studies,* 1966—; member of board of governors, *Maledicta.* Contributor of articles to *Handbuch des deutschen Volksliedes, Zeitschrift fuer deutsche Philologie, Fabula, Jahrbuch fuer Volkliedforschung, Western Folklore, Deutsche Vierteljahresschrift, Classica et Mediaevalia, German Quarterly, Journal of American Folklore, Myth and Law Among Indo-Europeans.*

*WORK IN PROGRESS:* Satirical folk songs and their function; *Comparative Indo-European Mythology; Heroic Legend and Epic;* parody; *Popular Beliefs and Superstitions from California;* translating and editing *The German Legends of the Brothers Grimm.*

*AVOCATIONAL INTERESTS:* Painting, theatre, opera.

\* \* \*

### WARD, Michael 1939-

*PERSONAL:* Born July 17, 1939, in London, England; son of Percy John and May (Blumfield) Ward; married Rosemary Baker, July 25, 1965; children: Andrew, Rachel, Kylie. *Education:* Exeter University, B.A. (honors), 1961; Cambridge University, M.A., 1966. *Politics:* Conservative. *Religion:* Anglican. *Home:* 2A Waddelow Rd., Waterbeach, Cambridge, England. *Office:* Institute of Development Studies, University of Sussex, Brighton BN1 9RE, England.

*CAREER:* Cambridge University, Cambridge, England, senior research officer in economics, 1963-75, Selwyn College, fellow, 1965, dean, 1971-72, director of studies in economics, 1965-75; University of Sussex, Institute of Development Studies, Brighton, England, fellow, 1975—. Government technical assistance expert on economic development problems and official statistics. *Member:* International Association for Research in Income and Wealth, Royal Economic Society, Association of University Teachers (secretary, Cambridge University, 1963-65).

*WRITINGS: The Role of Investment in the Development of Fiji,* Cambridge University Press, 1972; *The Measurement of Capital,* [Paris], 1976. Also author of *National Income and the Valuation of Stocks.* Contributor of articles to *Economic Journal, Economic Record, Banker, Bankers' Magazine, Business Economist,* and *Review of Income and Wealth.*

*WORK IN PROGRESS: The Measurement of Economic Change.*

\* \* \*

### WARDHAUGH, Ronald 1932-

*PERSONAL:* Born May 17, 1932, in Widdrington, England; Canadian citizen; children: Bruce, Carolyn. *Education:* University of Durham, B.A., 1955; University of Alberta, B.Ed., 1959, Ph.D., 1964; University of Michigan, M.A., 1961. *Home:* 237 Major St., Toronto, Ontario, Canada M5S 2L5. *Office:* Department of Linguistics, University of Toronto, Toronto, Ontario, Canada M5S 1A1.

*CAREER:* University of Michigan, Ann Arbor, assistant professor, 1966-68, associate professor, 1968-72, professor of linguistics, 1972-75, chairman of psycholinguistics program, 1972-75, director of English Language Institute, 1967-

75, director of Center for Research on Language and Language Behavior, 1969-71; University of Toronto, Toronto, Ontario, professor of linguistics and chairman of department, 1975—. *Member:* Linguistic Society of America, Canadian Linguistic Association.

*WRITINGS: Reading: A Linguistic Perspective,* Harcourt, 1969; *Introduction to Linguistics,* with workbook, McGraw, 1972, 2nd edition, 1977; *Topics in Applied Linguistics,* Newbury House Publishers, 1974; *Series r,* Macmillan, 1975; *The Contexts of Language,* Newbury House Publishers, 1976; (editor with H. D. Brown) *A Survey of Applied Linguistics,* University of Michigan Press, 1976. Executive editor, *Language and Language Behavior Abstracts,* 1969-71. Contributor to language journals. Editor, *Language Learning: A Journal of Applied Linguistics,* 1967-69.

\*    \*    \*

## WARFORD, Jeremy J(ames)   1938-

*PERSONAL:* Born July 27, 1938, in Bristol, England; son of G. F. and Alice M. (Griffin) Warford; married Beryl J. Ford, April, 1960; children: Susan Mary, Ian James. *Education:* University of Bristol, B.A., 1963; University of Manchester, Ph.D., 1967. *Office:* International Bank for Reconstruction & Development, 1818 H St. N.W., Washington, D.C. 20433.

*CAREER:* University of Manchester, Manchester, England, lecturer in economics, 1964-68; Brookings Institution, Washington, D.C., research associate in economics, 1968-70; International Bank for Reconstruction & Development, Washington, D.C., economist, 1970—. Consultant, Ministry of Housing and Local Government (England), 1968. *Military service:* Royal Marines, 1956-60.

*WRITINGS: The South Atcham Scheme: An Economic Appraisal,* H.M.S.O., 1968; *Public Policy Toward General Aviation,* Brookings Institution, 1971; (with Roy W. Bahl and Stephen Coelen) *Estimation and Economic Benefits of Water Supply and Sewerage Projects,* Syracuse University Research Corp., 1973. Contributor of articles to economics and tax journals.†

\*    \*    \*

## WARLUM, Michael Frank   1940-

*PERSONAL:* Born November 28, 1940, in Neillsville, Wis.; son of Elliot Clarence (an electrician) and Mida (a high school teacher; maiden name Quinlan) Warlum. *Education:* University of Wisconsin, B.A., 1962, M.A., 1964, Ph.D., 1967. *Home:* 4412 50th Ave. S.W., Seattle, Wash. 98116. *Office:* Shoreline Community College, 16101 Greenwood Ave. N., Seattle, Wash. 98133.

*CAREER:* National Finnish American Festival, Hurley, Wis., assistant, 1964-65; University of Wisconsin—Madison, assistant professor in Office of Community Arts Development, 1966-69; Indiana State Arts Commission, Indianapolis, executive director, 1969-72; Michigan Council for the Arts, Detroit, director of development services, 1972-74; Seattle Repertory Theatre, Seattle, Wash., development director, 1974-76; Shoreline Community College, Seattle, instructor, 1976—.

*WRITINGS:* (With Kenneth Friou, Robert Gard, Ralph Kohlhoff, and Pauline Temkin) *The Arts in the Small Community: A National Plan,* University of Wisconsin, 1969; *Meridian Maiden* (poems), Wisconsin House, 1971. Also author of monographs and study guides. Contributor of poems to anthologies and to little magazines and newspapers.

*WORK IN PROGRESS:* A science fiction novel, *The Moons of Siris;* a textbook in management and administration of the arts, tentatively entitled *Communities and the Arts.*

*SIDELIGHTS:* Michael Warlum told *CA:* "I have always written. Even during long periods when I defined myself as not writing, I have discovered in retrospect that I was, in fact, turning out reams of prose. This compulsive behavior is the result of parents who read to me, even when I was in the sixth and seventh grades, instilling a deep lust for words and for the printed page.

"Only in the last two to three years have I begun serious work in fiction. It is a wonderful feeling to accomplish something lasting, perhaps even exciting, and at the same time to have the sensation of a kid skipping school. My philosophy, I find now, is: To live is to write."

\*    \*    \*

## WARNATH, Charles F.   1925-

*PERSONAL:* Born April 17, 1925, in Philadelphia, Pa.; son of Oscar J. and Ruth (Juers) Warnath; married Maxine Ammer (a professor of psychology), August 20, 1952; children: Steve, Cindy. *Education:* Princeton University, B.A., 1949; Columbia University, M.A., 1951, Ph.D., 1954. *Politics:* Democrat. *Religion:* Unitarian-Universalist. *Home:* 124 Northwest 30th St., Corvallis, Ore. 97330. *Office:* Psychology Department, Oregon State University, Corvallis, Ore. 97331.

*CAREER:* Columbia University, Horace-Mann-Lincoln Institute, New York, N.Y., research associate, 1954-55; University of Nebraska, Lincoln, assistant professor of family life and counselor, Counseling Center, 1955-57; University of Oregon, Eugene, assistant professor of psychology and counselor, Counseling Center, 1957-61; Oregon State University, Corvallis, associate professor, 1961-68, professor of psychology, 1968—, director, Counseling Center, 1961-72. Marriage counselor in private practice. Chairman, State Board of Psychologist Examiners, 1964-67, and Oregon State Commission for the Blind, 1977—. *Military service:* U.S. Marine Corps, 1943-46. *Member:* American Psychological Association (fellow, Division of Counseling), American Personnel and Guidance Association, American Association of Marriage Counselors, Oregon Psychological Association, Oregon Marriage Counselors Association.

*WRITINGS:* (With Donald Super and others) *Vocational Development: A Framework for Research,* Bureau of Publications, Teachers College, 1957; (with Lawrence Stewart) *The Counselor and Society: A Cultural Approach,* Houghton, 1965; *New Myths and Old Realities: College Counseling in Transition,* Jossey-Bass, 1971; (editor) *New Directions for College Counselors,* Jossey-Bass, 1973. *Counseling News and Notes,* associate editor, 1957-60, editor, 1960-61.

*WORK IN PROGRESS:* A book on counseling in schools for parents and school board members.

\*    \*    \*

## WARREN, W(illiam) Preston   1901-

*PERSONAL:* Born January 26, 1901, in New Glasgow, Prince Edward Island, Canada; son of William John (a miller) and Mary Jane (Glover) Warren; married Agnes Archer, August 27, 1929 (died, 1971); married Alice Macleod Holmes, April 28, 1973; children: (first marriage) William Rollin, Heather Lynne Warren West. *Education:*

Acadia University, B.A. (with honors), 1925; Yale University, B.D., 1927, Ph.D., 1929; also attended University of Prague, 1934, and Cambridge University, 1935. *Home and office:* 41 Plymouth St., Bridgewater, Mass. 02324.

*CAREER:* Furman University, Greenville, S.C., associate professor, 1929-31, professor of philosophy, 1931-45; Bucknell University, Lewisburg, Pa., visiting professor, 1945-46, Harris Professor of Philosophy, 1946-71, Roy Wood Sellars Lecturer, 1971, professor emeritus, 1971—, chairman of department and director of University Course Program, 1945-69. Visiting lecturer, University of North Carolina, 1942-43. Educational director, United Service Organizations, 1943-45. *Military service:* Canadian Army, 1917. *Member:* American Philosophical Association, Metaphysical Society of America, Southern Society for the Philosophy of Religion (founding member), Masaryk's Institute.

*WRITINGS: Pantheism in Neo-Hegelian Thought,* Mennonite Press, 1931; (translator) T. G. Masaryk, *Ideals of Humanity,* Allen & Unwin, 1938, revised edition, Bucknell University Press, 1970; *Masaryk's Democracy: A Philosophy of Scientific Thought,* University of North Carolina Press, 1941; (editor) *Principles of Emergent Realism: Essays by R. W. Sellars,* Warren H. Green, 1970; (editor) *Neglected Alternatives: Critical Essays by R. W. Sellars,* Bucknell University Press, 1972; *Roy Wood Sellars,* Twayne, 1975. Contributor to philosophy journals.

*WORK IN PROGRESS:* A manuscript on Douglas Clyde Macintosh, Thomas Garrigue Masaryk, Alfred North Whitehead, and Roy Wood Sellars.

*SIDELIGHTS:* W. Preston Warren writes: "A member of a family of five teachers, three of whom taught on the university level, I became interested in the early thirties in the importance of the sciences for philosophy. This followed the perusal of some books on this subject and five months study in Czechoslovakia where I worked on the philosophy of values and compiled information on T. G. Masaryk's philosophy. This, in turn, led to my volume on *Masaryk's Democracy,* and to a twenty-year University Course Program at Bucknell University."

In reference to his latest work, a manuscript on four philosophers who he lists as his mentors, Warren told *CA:* "Douglas Macintosh ushered me penetratingly into the importance of philosophy for reflection in all areas of concern and accordingly for life. My other mentors, including a considerable number not treated extensively in this study, enlarged and deepened the vistas of philosophy. I hope to show that philosophers as diverse as Masaryk, Macintosh, Whitehead, and Sellars contributed to a unified perspective."

*AVOCATIONAL INTERESTS:* Reading, games, outdoor activities.

\*    \*    \*

## WARSHAW, Jerry 1929-
### (Warsh)

*PERSONAL:* Born June 12, 1929, in Chicago, Ill.; son of Julius (a display designer) and Jeanette (Seamans) Warshaw; married Joyce Milash (a free-lance writer), May 1, 1960; children: Elizabeth. *Education:* Attended Chicago Academy of Fine Arts, 1947-49, Illinois Institute of Design, 1954-55, and Art Institute of Chicago, 1955-56. *Politics:* "Moderate Liberal Independent Democrat, etc." *Religion:* "Non-Active Jewish." *Home and office:* 1319 Crain St., Evanston, Ill. 60202.

*CAREER:* American Adventure Comic Strip, Bennington,

Vt., art assistant, 1950-51; Cartoonist's Studio, Chicago, Ill., illustrator, 1951, 1953-55; O'Grady-Payne Studio, Chicago, illustrator, 1958-59; Visual Arts Studio, Chicago, illustrator, 1965-70; free-lance illustrator, 1970—. Art consultant and designer, Illinois Sesquicentennial Commission, 1965-69. *Military service:* U.S. Army, 1951-53. *Member:* Society of Typographic Arts, Illinois State Historical Society, Chicago Historical Society (life member), Chicago Press Club, Civil War Round Table of Chicago (former president), Evanston Historical Society, Children's Reading Round Table of Chicago (vice-president, 1972-73; former president). *Awards, honors:* Award of merit for art direction for designing and illustrating the *Illinois Intelligencer* (Sesquicentennial Commission newspaper); award of honor for design of official seal and flag, Illinois Sesquicentennial Commission, 1969; award for design of official seal, Illinois Constitutional Convention, 1971.

*WRITINGS*—Self-illustrated: *The I Can't Draw Book,* Albert Whitman, 1971; *The Funny Drawing Book,* Albert Whitman, 1977.

Illustrator: Jule Krisvoy, *New Games to Play,* Follett, 1968; Florence Heide and Sylvia Van Clief, *The New Neighbor,* Follett, 1971; David L. Harrison, *The Case of Og the Missing Frog,* Rand McNally, 1972; W. Burmeister, *The Long View of Lincoln,* Longview Books, 1975; Joel Rothman, *How to Play the Drums,* Albert Whitman, 1977.

All written by Ann Bishop; published by Albert Whitman: *Hey Riddle Riddle,* 1968; *Riddle Red Riddle,* 1969; *Noah Riddle,* 1970; *The Riddle-iculous Rid-Alphabet Book,* 1971; *Chicken Riddle,* 1972; *Merry-Go-Riddle,* 1973; *The Ella Fanny Elephant Riddle Book,* 1974; *Wild Bill Hiccup's Riddle Book,* 1975; *Oh, Riddlesticks,* 1976; *The Riddle Ages,* 1977.

Also illustrator of textbooks for Rand McNally, Scott, Foresman, Sadlier, Economy Co., Benefic, Combined Motivations, and Science Research Associates Reading Program.

*WORK IN PROGRESS: The I Can't Color Book; Don't Draw on Me, I'm a Book; Gilbert and Sullivan for Fun; The Big and Little Animal Book; Draw Yourself a Zoo;* a collection of cartoons from *Marriage* magazine, *The Family Room.*

*AVOCATIONAL INTERESTS:* Civil War, sports cars, model railroads, photography, film, and theatre.

\*    \*    \*

## WARZESKI, Walter C. 1929-

*PERSONAL:* Born December 21, 1929, in Erie, Pa.; son of Francis and Gladys (Pezanowski) Waruszewski; married Mary Joan Dzmura (a teacher); children: Marylee, Julie-Anne, Jeanne Marie, Melanie. *Education:* Gannon College, A.B.; University of Pittsburgh, M.Ed., Ph.D. *Religion:* Catholic. *Home:* 839 Edward St., Allentown, Pa. 18103. *Office:* Department of History, Kutztown State College, Kutztown, Pa. 19530.

*CAREER:* Kutztown State College, Kutztown, Pa., 1964—, currently professor of history, acting vice-president of academic affairs, and dean of School of Arts and Sciences. Visiting professor, Allentown College of St. Francis de Sales, Allentown, Pa., 1965-68. *Member:* American Association of University Professors, American Association for the Advancement of Slavic Studies, American History Association, Phi Delta Kappa, Phi Alpha Theta.

*WRITINGS: Byzantine Rite Rusins of Carpatho-Ruthenia*

*and America,* Byzantine Press, 1971. Contributor to *Ethnic Groups in Pennsylvania.*

*WORK IN PROGRESS:* History of Ruthenia; the Munich Settlement as experienced by minority groups; cultural ramifications of Rusin culture.

\* \* \*

## WASSERSTEIN, Bruce 1947-

*PERSONAL:* Born December 25, 1947; son of Morris (a businessman) and Lola (Schleifer) Wasserstein; married Christine Parrott. *Education:* University of Michigan, B.A. (honors), 1967; Harvard University, M.B.A. (with high distinction), 1971, J.D. (cum laude), 1971; Cambridge University, diploma in comparative legal studies, 1972. *Politics:* Democrat. *Home:* 605 East 82nd St., New York, N.Y. 10028.

*CAREER:* Cravath, Swaine & Moore, New York, N.Y., lawyer, 1972—; First Boston Corporation, Boston, Mass., investment banker, 1977—. Baker scholar, Harvard University. *Awards, honors:* Knox fellow, Cambridge University, 1972.

*WRITINGS:* (Editor with Mark Green) *With Justice for Some: An Indictment of the Law by Young Advocates,* Beacon, 1971; (with Green and Beverly C. Moore, Jr.) *The Closed Enterprise System: The Nader Study of Antitrust Enforcement,* Grossman, 1972; *Corporate Finance Law: A Guide for the Executive,* McGraw, 1978.

*BIOGRAPHICAL/CRITICAL SOURCES: Saturday Review,* August 7, 1971.

\* \* \*

## WATANABE, Ruth T(aiko) 1916-

*PERSONAL:* Born May 12, 1916, in Los Angeles, Calif.; daughter of Kohei and Iwa Watanabe. *Education:* University of Southern California, B. Mus., 1937, A.B., 1939, M.A., and M.Mus., 1941; Columbia University, additional study, 1947; University of Rochester, Ph.D., 1952. *Politics:* Republican. *Home:* 111 East Ave., Rochester, N.Y. 14604. *Office:* Eastman School of Music, University of Rochester, Rochester, N.Y. 14604.

*CAREER:* Instructor in piano and music theory in Los Angeles, Calif., 1934-41; University of Rochester, Rochester, N.Y., counselor of women, 1943-46, instructor in English, 1946-47, instructor in music history, Eastman School of Music, 1946-61, associate professor of musicology, 1961—, Sibley Music Library, staff member in charge of circulation, 1943-47, acting librarian, 1947-48, librarian, 1948—, director of Music Library Institute, 1956—. Program annotator, Rochester Philharmonic Orchestra, 1959—; lecturer and coordinator of music appreciation courses, Rochester Civic Music Association, 1962-76. Music library consultant, 1968—.

*MEMBER:* International Musicological Association, International Association of Music Libraries (vice-president of Commission on Conservatory Libraries, 1971—), Music Library Association (vice-president, 1968-69; former member of board of directors), American Association of University Women (president of Rochester branch, 1969-71), Music Teachers National Association, Modern Language Association of America, American Library Association, Phi Beta Kappa (president, Iota of New York, 1977—), Mu Phi Epsilon, Pi Kappa Lambda (secretary-treasurer, 1976—), Phi Kappa Phi, Delta Kappa Gamma (vice-president, Eta Chapter, 1972—), Delta Phi Alpha, Soroptimist Club of Rochester (president, 1960-61).

*WRITINGS: Five Books of Italian Madrigals,* University of Rochester, 1957; *Introduction to Music Research,* Prentice-Hall, 1967; *Madrigals of Il Verso,* Olschki (Florence), 1977; (contributor) *Grove's Dictionary of Music and Musicians,* Macmillan, 1978. Also editor of *Scribner's Home Library of Music,* Volumes II, VI, VIII. Contributor to library and music journals; member of editorial board, *Notes.*

*WORK IN PROGRESS:* Contributing music section to *Sources of Information in the Humanities,* edited by Thomas P. Slavens; *Handbook on Music Librarianship;* bibliographical studies of music theory; research on Italian madrigals of the 1550's.

\* \* \*

## WATERHOUSE, Larry G(ene) 1944-

*PERSONAL:* Born September 12, 1944, in Sioux City, Iowa; son of Charles L. and Gretchen (Rose) Waterhouse; married Mariann G. Wizard (a writer), October 9, 1970. *Education:* Attended Texas Christian University, 1963-64; University of Texas at Austin, B.A., 1968, graduate study, 1969, 1972; Antioch College, M.Ed., 1978. *Politics:* Socialist. *Address:* Waterwizards Productions, P.O. Box 13313, Austin, Tex. 78711.

*CAREER:* Employed as draftsman, administrator, political organizer, finance clerk, and news editor; writer. Member, Austin Committee Against the War in Viet Nam, 1967-68; staff member, Texas Youth for McCarthy, 1968; member of Texas regional committee, Students for a Democratic Society, 1968-69; minister of community affairs, Fort Ord Movement for a Democratic Military, 1970; Texas regional coordinator, Viet Nam Veterans Against the War, 1971; youth director, Farenthold for Governor Campaign, 1972; director, Human Service Agency, 1975-78. *Military service:* U.S. Army, 1969-70.

*WRITINGS:* (With wife, Mariann G. Wizard) *Turning the Guns Around: Notes on the G.I. Movement,* Praeger, 1971. Contributor to *Texas Ranger, The Rag, Space City News, Monterey County Nose,* and *Right On Post.* Member of editorial board, *Texas Ranger,* 1969.

*WORK IN PROGRESS:* A book on the late sixties set on a campus in the Southwest; a science-fiction novel set in the 1980s.

*SIDELIGHTS:* Waterhouse told *CA:* "I came to writing by necessity rather than by any planning. My research into international politics and history led to my political activism, and my particular roles in activist politics, plus the lack of relevant information on topics of interest and importance, led me into writing. With *Turning the Guns Around,* I felt that an informative book on the changing nature of the military was not only important for people to have access to, but also that the subject had been neglected and ignored by other writers. I found writing the book rewarding and hope to continue to write as my vocation, intermingled with the political activism which will continue to be the basis of my work.

"The conditions of the late '60s and early '70s, which led me to pick up the pen, have evolved in the 70s into a more specific, introspective set of conditions which have directed my energies into projects which require more technical skills and therefore more technical writing. I sense the shifting of conditions again toward a period of time which is beginning where broader communications will occupy a large amount of my time and energy. I look forward to it."

*AVOCATIONAL INTERESTS:* Music (plays guitar), science fiction, psychic phenomena, chess, animals, gardens, film, "digging into historical currents."

\* \* \*

## WATERMAN, Margaret 1909-

*PERSONAL:* Born October 6, 1909, in Athol, Mass.; daughter of Richard Burton (a welfare worker) and Helen R. (Barber) Waterman. *Education:* Mount Holyoke College, A.B., 1931; University of Wisconsin, M.A., 1933, Ph.D., 1942. *Home:* 2941 Monroe St., Madison, Wis. 53711. *Office:* University of Wisconsin, Madison, Wis. 53706.

*CAREER:* University of Colorado, Boulder, instructor in English, 1939-40; Hiram College, Hiram, Ohio, instructor in English, 1941-42; Lake Forest College, Lake Forest, Ill., assistant professor of English, 1942-44; Case Western Reserve University, Cleveland, Ohio, assistant professor, 1945-65, associate professor of English, 1965-73; University of Wisconsin—Madison, associate editor of *Dictionary of American Regional English,* 1973—. Member of editorial staff, University of Wisconsin Press and Howard Allen, Inc., 1944. *Member:* American Association of University Professors, Modern Language Association of America, Phi Beta Kappa.

*WRITINGS: Themecraft,* Howard Allen, 1959; (with Catherine B. Osborn) *Papa Gorski,* Harcourt, 1969. Member of editorial staff, *Dictionary of Americanisms,* University of Chicago Press, 1944-46. Contributor of stories and articles to several magazines, including *Yankee.*

*WORK IN PROGRESS:* Miscellaneous articles and stories.

*AVOCATIONAL INTERESTS:* Travel.

\* \* \*

## WATERS, John F(rederick) 1930-

*PERSONAL:* Born October 27, 1930, in Somerville, Mass.; children: Herbert, Sandra, Lane, Duane. *Education:* University of Massachusetts, B.S., 1959. *Residence:* Mount Desert Island, Me.

*CAREER: Cape Cod Standard Times,* Cape Cod, Mass., reporter, 1959-60; elementary teacher in Falmouth, Mass., 1960-66; full-time writer, 1966—. *Military service:* U.S. Army; became sergeant.

*WRITINGS*—All juvenile: *Marine Animal Collectors,* Hastings House, 1969; *The Sea Farmers,* Hastings House, 1970; *What Does an Oceanographer Do,* Dodd, 1970; *Saltmarshes and Shifting Dunes,* Harvey House, 1970; *The Crab from Yesterday* (Junior Literary Guild selection), Warne, 1970; *Turtles,* Follett, 1971; *Neighborhood Puddle* (Junior Literary Guild selection), Warne, 1971; *Some Mammals Live in the Sea,* Dodd, 1972; *Green Turtle Mysteries,* Crowell, 1972; *The Royal Potwasher,* Methuen, 1972; *Seal Harbor,* Warne, 1973; *The Mysterious Eel,* Hastings House, 1973; *Giant Sea Creatures,* Follett, 1973; *Hungry Sharks,* Crowell, 1973; *Camels: Ships of the Desert,* Crowell, 1974; *Carnivorous Plants,* F. Watts, 1974; *Exploring New England Shores,* Stone Wall Press, 1974; *Victory Chimes,* Warne, 1975; *The Continental Shelves,* Abelard, 1975; *Creatures of Darkness,* Walker & Co., 1975; *Maritime Careers,* F. Watts, 1977.

*WORK IN PROGRESS: Fishing: A First Book;* a junior novel about the shooting of harbor seals on the Maine coast; *A Jellyfish Is not a Fish;* a young people's science book; a book on forensic medicine.

*SIDELIGHTS:* John F. Waters told *CA:* "Recently I have been writing more fiction than non-fiction. It is more enjoyable because I can use my imagination and create people. Writing in any form is fun, but I write because I have to—otherwise I'd suffocate under the pile of unused words!"

\* \* \*

## WATHEN, Richard B. 1917-

*PERSONAL:* Born June 26, 1917, in Jeffersonville, Ind.; son of Otho H. (an executive) and Fay (Duffy) Wathen; married Viola James, August 17, 1940. *Education:* Princeton University, B.A., 1939; Indiana University, J.D., 1942. *Home:* Utica Pike, Jeffersonville, Ind. 47130.

*CAREER:* Attorney-at-law, 1942—. Republican candidate for U.S. Congress from 9th Indiana District, 1970; member, Indiana House of Representatives, 1972—. *Military service:* U.S. Naval Reserve, 1942-69; retired as commander. *Member:* American Bar Association, Indiana Bar Association.

*WRITINGS: Cliffs of Fall* (novel), T. J. Moran's, 1953; *The Only Yankee* (novel), Regnery, 1970. Contributor to *Indiana Magazine of History.* Editor, *Story* (magazine), 1958-60.

\* \* \*

## WATKINS, Gordon R(onald) 1930-

*PERSONAL:* Born December 24, 1930, in Baltimore, Md.; son of Arthur and Harriet (Parker) Watkins; married Martha Flowers, June, 1957; married second wife, Helen Kollas, April 28, 1966 (divorced March, 1977); children: (second marriage) Stefanie Melissa. *Education:* Juilliard School of Music, B.S., 1958, M.S., 1960; Hunter College of the City University of New York, M.A., 1976. *Politics:* Independent Democrat. *Religion:* Episcopalian. *Home:* 675 Lincoln Ave., Brooklyn, N.Y. 11208. *Agent:* Mary Dolan, 667 Madison Ave., New York, N.Y. 10023. *Office:* Toussaint Group, Inc., 420 East 51st St., New York, N.Y. 10022.

*CAREER:* Television and stage actor, classical concert artist, and nightclub entertainer; Rutgers University, Newark Campus, Newark, N.J., instructor in theatre, and director, 1968-70; WCBS-TV, New York City, producer and writer, 1969-70; Toussaint Group, Inc. (Black-oriented television and film productions), New York City, president, 1970—. Producer, director, writer, composer, and musical director for theatres located in Washington, D.C., Montana, New Jersey, and New York, 1960, 1967-70. Assistant professor, Cinema 7 Theater, Hunter College of the City University of New York, 1974-78; instructor in television directing, Institute of New Cinema Artists, 1977-78. Has appeared on Broadway and Off-Broadway in "Kwamina," "Porgy and Bess," "The Prodigal Singer," "South Pacific," and other productions; television credits include "The Defenders," "The Nurses," and "East Side/West Side." *Military service:* U.S. Air Force, Air Weather Service and Special Services, 1947-51; became sergeant.

*MEMBER:* Actors' Equity Association, Screen Actors Guild, American Federation of Television and Radio Artists, American Guild of Variety Artists. *Awards, honors:* National Association of Television Program Executives Award for Excellence in the Performing Arts, 1971, and Ohio State Award for Excellence in Television Production, 1972, both for "Caught in the Middle."

*WRITINGS*—Plays: "College Time," first produced at

Glacier Park Lodge, Montana, summer, 1960; "This Is My County," first produced at Glacier Park Lodge, Montana, summer, 1960; "Tinkerman to the Promised Land," first produced in New York City, April, 1967; "Caught in the Middle," first produced in New York City at Hunter College, 1969 (also see below); *A Lion Roams the Street* (first produced in Burlington, Vt. at Champlain Shakespeare Festival, September, 1968), Breakthrough Press, 1971. Author of television play, "Caught in the Middle" (based on his play of the same title), broadcast on WCBS-TV, December 16, 1970. Also author of "Expostulations of a Watkins," "Sojourner Truth," "Too Late," and "Cages."

Author of film scripts, "Tom Gideon and Friends," "Jockey," "The Silent World of Mildred N," "I Love Harlem," "Mikey, Bubba, and Leroy," "Busted Dreams," "What Happened to Brownsville?," and "Reaching for a Hard Hat." Composer of musical score, Ed Bullins, "A Son Comes Home" and "How Do You Do?"; composer, with Pat Patrick and Harold Wheeler, of musical score, Melvin Van Peebles, "Jesse." Contributor of poetry to *Harlem, U.S.A.*, edited by John H. Clarke. Contributor of articles, short stories, and drama to periodicals, including *New York Times, Freedomways,* and *Millimeter.*

*WORK IN PROGRESS:* "Dora," a full-length drama with music.

\* \* \*

## WATKINS, T(homas) H(enry) 1936-

*PERSONAL:* Born March 29, 1936, in Loma Linda, Calif.; son of Thomas F. (a mailer) and Orel (Roller) Watkins; married Elaine Otakie, January 26, 1957 (divorced); married Ellen J. Parker, June 12, 1976; children: (first marriage) Lisa Lynn, Kevin Blair. *Education:* Attended San Bernardino Valley College, 1954-56; University of Redlands, B.A., 1958; San Francisco State College (now University), graduate study, 1963-64. *Politics:* Neo-populist. *Religion:* None. *Home:* 311 West 82nd St., Apt. 1B, New York, N.Y. 10024. *Office: American Heritage,* 10 Rockefeller Plaza, New York, N.Y. 10020.

*CAREER:* American West Publishing Co., Palo Alto, Calif., managing editor, 1966-69, editor, 1969-70, associate editor, 1970-76; *American Heritage* (magazine), New York, N.Y., member of board of editors, 1976—.

*WRITINGS: San Francisco in Color,* Hastings House, 1968; (with Roger R. Olmsted) *Here Today: San Francisco's Architectural Heritage,* San Francisco Chronicle, 1968; (with others) *The Grand Colorado: The Story of a River and Its Canyons,* American West, 1969.

*California in Color: An Essay on the Paradox of Plenty,* Hastings House, 1970; (with others) *The Water Hustlers,* Sierra Club, 1971; *Gold and Silver in the West: The Illustrated History of an American Dream,* American West, 1971; *California: An Illustrated History,* American West, 1973; *On the Shore of the Sundown Sea,* Sierra Club, 1973; *Mark Twain's Mississippi: The Pictorial History of America's Greatest River,* American West, 1974.

(With Charles S. Watson, Jr.) *The Lands No One Knows: America and the Public Domain,* Sierra Club, 1975; *John Muir's America,* illustrated with photographs by DeWitt Jones, American West, 1976; (with Olmsted) *Mirror of the Dream: An Illustrated History of San Francisco,* Scrimshaw Press, 1976; *Taken by the Wind: Vanishing Architecture of the West,* illustrated with photographs by Ronald Woodall, New York Graphic Society, 1977. Contributor of more than 150 articles to numerous periodicals.

*WORK IN PROGRESS:* A novel, based on the life of his grandfather in the West.

*SIDELIGHTS:* T. H. Watkins says that "some people call me an historian, some a memorialist, some a conservationist, some an environmentalist—they're all wrong. I'd prefer to think of myself *first* as a writer—a writer who happens to work in all these areas, as well as anything else which presents itself. I'm in love with words, with the sound and muscularity of phrases.... At the same time, I cannot deny a profound dependence upon the historical view, for it seems to me that it provides the essential key to understanding—and understanding is the only shield we have against fate and all its consequences."

*BIOGRAPHICAL/CRITICAL SOURCES: New York Times Book Review,* December 14, 1969, December 18, 1977.

\* \* \*

## WATLINGTON, Patricia (Sue) 1933-

*PERSONAL:* Born February 19, 1933, in Hardinsburg, Ky.; daughter of John Russell (a county agricultural agent) and Claudine (Peggs) Watlington. *Education:* University of Kentucky, B.A., 1955; Yale University, M.A., 1958, Ph.D., 1964. *Politics:* Democrat. *Religion:* Episcopalian. *Home:* 363 North Lime, Lexington, Ky. 40508.

*CAREER:* Quinnipiac College, Hamden, Conn., member of history department, 1964-74. *Member:* Southern Historical Association, Kentucky Historical Society, Phi Beta Kappa, Filson Club.

*WRITINGS: The Partisan Spirit: Kentucky Politics, 1779-1792,* Atheneum, 1972.

*WORK IN PROGRESS:* A book on Kentucky agriculture from 1750 to 1803; a novel under a pen name.

\* \* \*

## WATSON, Harold M. 1924-

*PERSONAL:* Born October 29, 1924, in Mt. Hope, Kan.; son of George J. (a postman) and Clara (Shelley) Watson. *Education:* St. Benedict's College, Atchison, Kan., B.A., 1946; Laval University, M.A., 1956; University of Lyon, D.L.L., 1957; University of Colorado, Ph.D., 1965. *Home:* 706 South Highland, Memphis, Tenn. 38111. *Office:* Department of Foreign Languages, Memphis State University, Memphis, Tenn. 38152.

*CAREER:* St. Benedict's College, Atchison, Kan., instructor, 1957-61, assistant professor, 1964-68, associate professor of modern languages, 1968-70, chairman of department, 1967-70; Memphis State University, Memphis, Tenn., associate professor of foreign languages, 1970-73, professor of French, 1973—, head of French section, 1976—. *Member:* Modern Language Association of America, American Association of Teachers of French, American Association of University Professors, Claudel Society (president, 1974-76), American Benedictine Academy, Societe Claudel (Paris). *Awards, honors:* Fulbright scholar, Lyons, France, 1956-57.

*WRITINGS: Claudel's Immortal Heroes: A Choice of Deaths,* Rutgers University Press, 1971. Contributor to literature journals and *American Benedictine Review.* Associate editor, *Claudel Studies,* 1976—.

*WORK IN PROGRESS:* Further research on Claudel.

## WATSON, Sara Ruth 1907-

*PERSONAL:* Born January 7, 1907, in East Cleveland, Ohio; daughter of Wilbur J. (a civil engineer) and Harriett M. (Barnes) Watson. *Education:* Western Reserve University (now Case Western Reserve University), B.A. (magna cum laude), 1928, M.A., 1929, Ph.D., 1932. *Religion:* Unitarian-Universalist. *Home:* 3570 Glen Allen Dr., Cleveland Heights, Ohio 44121. *Office:* Department of English, Cleveland State University, Cleveland, Ohio 44115.

*CAREER:* Western Reserve University (now Case Western Reserve University), Cleveland, Ohio, research associate, 1935-39; Cleveland State University, Cleveland, instructor, 1942-44, assistant professor, 1945-47, associate professor, 1948-56, professor of English, 1950-70, professor emeritus, 1970—. Cleveland Chamber Music Society, program annotator, 1962-78, trustee, 1968-72. Special lecturer, Cleveland Museum of Art, 1935-38. *Member:* Modern Language Association of America, Renaissance Society of America, American Association for the Advancement of Science, Modern Humanities Research Association (life member), Milton Society of America (life member; secretary, 1954-56; member of executive board, 1957-58), Shakespeare Society of America, Viola da Gamba Society, Phi Beta Kappa. *Awards, honors:* History and Heritage Award from Ohio Council of the American Society of Civil Engineers.

*WRITINGS:* (With father, Wilbur J. Watson) *Bridges in History and Legend,* Jansen, 1936; (with David B. Steinman) *Bridges and Their Builders,* Putnam, 1941, revised edition, Dover, 1957; (with sister, Emily Watson) *Famous Engineers,* Dodd, 1950; *V. Sackville-West,* Twayne, 1972. Contributor to science encyclopedias; contributor of more than thirty poems, articles, and reviews to *Westminister Magazine, Musical America,* and to literature and engineering journals.

*WORK IN PROGRESS:* With sister, Emily Watson, *Brothers-in-Arms;* the life of Sir Thomas Sackville; with John Wolfs, *History of Bridges in Cuyahoga County.*

*AVOCATIONAL INTERESTS:* Music.

\*      \*      \*

## WATT, John Robertson 1934-

*PERSONAL:* Born September 7, 1934, in Rugby, England; son of Robert Cameron (an educator) and Barbara (Bidwell) Watt; married Anne Sturgis (a college teacher), December 17, 1960; children: Alison, Fiona, Jennifer. *Education:* Oxford University, B.A., 1957; Harvard University, M.A., 1959; Columbia University, Ph.D., 1967. *Office address:* Bury, Nelson, Watt, P.O. Box 1240, Brattleboro, Vt. 05301.

*CAREER:* Massachusetts Institute of Technology, Cambridge, assistant professor of history, 1967-68; University of Redlands, Johnston College, Redlands, Calif., fellow in history, 1968-74; Windham College, Putney, Vt., academic dean, 1974-76; Bury, Nelson, Watt, Brattleboro, Vt., partner, 1976—. Administrator, Brattleboro Music Center, 1977-78. Organist, Wilmington Congregational Church. *Military service:* British Army, 1952-54; became lieutenant. *Member:* American Historical Association, International House (Japan), Vermont Academy of Arts and Sciences, Windham World Affairs Council.

*WRITINGS: The District Magistrate in Late Imperial China,* Columbia University Press, 1972. Contributor of articles to *China Quarterly, History of the Twentieth Century, Problems in Ch'ing History.*

*WORK IN PROGRESS:* Translation of an eighteenth-cen-

tury Chinese political text; a book of poems; an autobiography.

*AVOCATIONAL INTERESTS:* Music, the arts, Scottish culture.

\*      \*      \*

## WATT, Thomas 1935-

*PERSONAL:* Born June 17, 1935, in Toronto, Ontario, Canada; son of William L. (a printer) and Isabel (Wright) Watt; married Mabs MacPherson, December 19, 1959; children: Kelly, Ruth Anne, Robert. *Education:* University of Toronto, B.P.H.E., 1959, M.Ed., 1969. *Religion:* Christian. *Home:* 73 Elwood Blvd., Toronto, Ontario, Canada M5S 1A1. *Office:* R. 208 Hart House, University of Toronto, Toronto, Ontario, Canada M5S 1A1.

*CAREER:* Board of Education, Toronto, Ontario, teacher in secondary schools, 1959-65; University of Toronto, Toronto, Ontario, lecturer, 1965-70, assistant professor of physical education and hockey coach, 1970—. *Member:* Canadian Hockey Coaches Association, American Hockey Coaches Association, Canadian Association for Health, Physical Education and Recreation, North American Society for Sports Psychology. *Awards, honors:* Named Canadian college coach of the year by Canadian Hockey Coaches Association, 1970-71.

*WRITINGS: How to Play Hockey: A Guide for Young Players and Their Coaches,* Doubleday, 1971.

*WORK IN PROGRESS:* A second hockey book, for Doubleday; *How to Watch Hockey,* with Darryl Sittler; a history of the University of Toronto hockey team.

\*      \*      \*

## WAUGH, Albert E. 1902-

*PERSONAL:* Born September 28, 1902, in Amherst, Mass.; son of Frank A. (a teacher and author) and Alice (Vail) Waugh; married Edith H. Stewart, June 26, 1926; children: John S., Robert E., Dan H. *Education:* Massachusetts Agricultural College (now University of Massachusetts), B.A., 1924; Connecticut Agricultural College (now University of Connecticut), M.S., 1926; University of Chicago, graduate study, 1931-32, 1941-42. *Politics:* Independent. *Religion:* Independent. *Home and office:* 57 Willowbrook Rd., Storrs, Conn. 06268.

*CAREER:* University of Connecticut, Storrs, instructor, 1924-28, assistant professor, 1928-32, associate professor, 1932-37, professor of economics, 1937-65, dean of college of arts and sciences, 1945-50, provost and academic vice-president, 1950-65. Director, Willimantic Trust Company. Member of Connecticut Constitutional Convention, 1965. *Awards, honors:* Award of merit from Connecticut League of Historical Societies, 1970, for *Samuel Huntington: A Biography.*

*WRITINGS: Elements of Statistical Method,* McGraw, 1938, revised edition, 1952; *Statistical Tables and Problems,* McGraw, 1938, revised edition, 1952; *Priciples of Economics,* McGraw, 1947; *Samuel Huntington: A Biography,* Pequot Press, 1968; *Sundials: Theory and Construction,* Dover, 1972.

*WORK IN PROGRESS:* A series of short bucolic essays.

\*      \*      \*

## WAX, Murray L(ionel) 1922-

*PERSONAL:* Born November 23, 1922, in St. Louis, Mo.;

son of Abraham and Helen (Appelman) Wax; married Rosalie A. Hankey (a professor of anthropology), March 5, 1949. *Education:* University of Chicago, B.S., 1942, Ph.D., 1959; University of Pennsylvania, M.A., 1947. *Home:* 7106 Westmoreland Dr., University City, Mo. 63130. *Office:* Department of Sociology, Washington University, St. Louis, Mo. 63130.

*CAREER:* Temple University, Philadelphia, Pa., instructor in philosophy, 1946-47; University of Chicago, Chicago, Ill., instructor in social science, 1948-49; University of Illinois at Chicago Circle, Chicago, instructor in social sciences, 1953-54; Science Research Associates, Chicago, project director, 1954-56; Gillette Corp., Chicago, senior analyst in market research for Toni Co., 1956-58, research supervisor, 1958-59; University of Miami, Coral Gables, Fla., assistant professor of sociology and anthropology, 1959-62; Emory University, Atlanta, Ga., associate professor of sociology, 1962-64, director of Oglala Sioux education research project, 1962-63; University of Kansas, Lawrence, associate professor, 1964-67, professor of sociology, 1967-73, director of Indian education research project, 1965-68, vice-chairman of department and director of graduate studies, 1969-72, chairman of department, 1972-73; Washington University, St. Louis, Mo., professor of sociology and chairman of department, 1973—.

*MEMBER:* American Anthropological Association (fellow), American Association for the Advancement of Science (fellow), American Sociological Association (fellow), Society for Applied Anthropology (fellow; member of executive committee, 1969-72; president, 1975-76), Council on Anthropology and Education (president, 1970), Current Anthropology (associate), Society for the Scientific Study of Religion, Society for the Scientific Study of Sex, American Educational Research Association, Society for the Study of Social Problems (member of executive committee, 1970-73; vice-president, 1972-73), Midwest Sociological Society, Phi Beta Kappa. *Awards, honors:* Social Science Research Council faculty research fellow, 1961; grants from U.S. Office of Education, 1962-63, 1964-65, 1965-68, 1972-73, National Institute of Education, 1973-74, U.S. Office of Economic Opportunity, and Wenner-Gren Foundation for Anthropological Research.

*WRITINGS:* (With wife, Rosalie H. Wax, and Robert V. Dumont, Jr.) *Formal Education in an American Indian Community,* Society for the Study of Social Problems, 1964; *Indian Americans: Unity and Diversity,* Prentice-Hall, 1971; (editor with Stanley Diamond and Fred O. Gearing) *Anthropological Perspectives on Education,* Basic Books, 1971; (editor with Robert W. Buchanan) *Solving "The Indian Problem": The White Man's Burdensome Business,* F. Watts, 1975.

Contributor: Howard S. Becker, Blanche Geer, David Riesman, and Robert S. Weiss, editors, *Institutions and the Person: Essays Presented to Everett C. Hughes,* Aldine, 1968; Stuart Levine and Nancy O. Lurie, editors, *The American Indian Today,* Everett/Edwards, 1968; James A. Clifton, editor, *Introduction to Cultural Anthropology: Essays in the Scope and Method of the Science of Man,* Houghton, 1968; Muzafer Sherif and Carolyn W. Sherif, editors, *Interdisciplinary Relationships in the Social Sciences,* Aldine, 1969.

Otto von Mering and Leonard Kasdan, editors, *Anthropology and the Behavioral and Health Sciences,* University of Pittsburgh Press, 1970; Harry M. Lindquist, editor, *Education: Readings in the Processes of Cultural Transmission,* Houghton, 1970; Eleanor B. Leacock, editor, *The Culture of Poverty: A Critique,* Simon & Schuster, 1971; Howard M. Bahr, Bruce A. Chadwick, and Robert C. Day, editors, *Native Americans Today: Sociological Perspectives,* Harper, 1971; Deward E. Walker, editor, *Nutrition, Growth, and Development of Native American Children,* U.S. Government Printing Office, 1971; Norman R. Yetman and C. Hoy Steele, editors, *Majority and Minority,* Allyn & Bacon, 1971; *The Emergent Native Americans,* Little, Brown, 1971; Paul Olson, Larry Freeman, and James Bowman, editors, *Education for 1984 and After,* U.S. Office of Education, 1971; Wilton S. Dillon, editor, *The Cultural Drama,* Smithsonian Institution Press, 1974; Vine Deloria, Jr., editor, *Indian Education Confronts the Seventies,* Volume III: *Special Program Considerations,* American Indian Resources Associates, 1974.

Also author of numerous research monographs. Contributor of articles and reviews to *Kenyon Review, Phylon, Nebraska History,* and other journals. Member of editorial board, *Human Organization,* 1966—; *Sociological Quarterly,* 1968—, and *Phylon,* 1972—.

\*    \*    \*

## WEAVER, Katherine Grey Dunlap 1910-
### (Kitty Weaver)

*PERSONAL:* Born September 24, 1910, in Frankfort, Ky.; daughter of Arch Robertson (a newspaper editor and columnist) and Rebecca (Johnson) Dunlap; married Henry Byrne Weaver (an attorney and vice-president of Atlantic-Richfield Co.), June, 1933. *Education:* College of William and Mary, A.B., 1932; George Washington University, M.A., 1933; University of Maryland, B.S., 1947; also studied at Sorbonne, University of Paris, 1929, under Alfred Adler in Vienna, 1932, at Georgetown University, 1964-67, and University of Pennsylvania, 1967-68. *Home:* Glengyle, Aldie, Va. 22001. *Agent:* William Morris Agency, 1350 Avenue of the Americas, New York, N.Y. 10019.

*CAREER:* Junior high school teacher of English and reading in St. Petersburg, Fla., 1932-33; poultry farmer in Aldie, Va., 1947-55. Accredited flower show judge, Garden Club of Virginia. Member of ladies board of Manhattan Eye, Ear, Nose and Throat Hospital, New York, N.Y., and of Loudoun Hospital, Loudoun, Va.; co-founder and board member of Fauquier-Loudoun Day Care Center. *Member:* American Committee for Early Childhood Education, International Platform Association, Fauquier-Loudoun Garden Club, Aldie Horticulture Society (past president), Sulgrave Club (Washington, D.C.), Acorn Club (Philadelphia), River Club (New York), Middleburg Tennis Club (Middleburg, Va.).

*WRITINGS:* (Under name Kitty Weaver) *Lenin's Grandchildren,* Simon & Schuster, 1971.

*WORK IN PROGRESS:* A book on older Russian children.

*SIDELIGHTS:* Katherine Weaver has made eight extensive trips to the Soviet Union since 1963, visiting eleven of the fifteen Soviet Republics. In 1970 she and her husband went on safari (photographic) to Africa, in 1971 to India, and in 1972 to Southeast Asia. She has traveled widely in Europe, South America, Middle East, Central Asia, Mexico, Canada, the Republic of China, and the People's Republic of China.

*AVOCATIONAL INTERESTS:* Fox hunting and riding (former field secretary of Piedmont Fox Hounds), tennis, gardening, flower arrangement.

## WEBB, Bernice Larson

*PERSONAL:* Born in Ludell, Kan.; daughter of Carl Godfred (a farmer) and Ida (Tongish) Larson; married Ralph Schear, August 9, 1942 (divorced, July 27, 1956); married Robert M. Webb (a university professor), July 14, 1961; children: (first marriage) William Carl, Rebecca Rae (Mrs. Cowan E. Gentry, Jr.). *Education:* University of Kansas, A.B., 1956, M.A., 1957, Ph.D., 1961; University of Aberdeen, Scotland, graduate study, 1959-60. *Home:* 159 Whittington Dr., Lafayette, La. 70501. *Office:* Department of English, University of Southwestern Louisiana, Lafayette, La. 70503.

*CAREER:* University of Southwestern Louisiana, Lafayette, assistant professor, 1961-67, associate professor of English, 1967—. Visiting associate professor of English, World Campus Afloat, fall, 1972. Coordinator, Poetry-in-the-Schools program, 1974; resource person for poetry readings and fiction and poetry workshops in high schools and colleges, 1977—. Poetry consultant, Lafayette Parish School System, 1976—; poetry consultant and director of workshops, Acadiana Arts Council, 1977—. *Member:* International Platform Association, American Association of University Women (state division editor, 1967-71), Modern Language Association of America, American Folklore Society, American Association of University Professors, National Federation of State Poetry Societies, College English Association, Deep South Writers and Artists Conference, South Central Modern Language Association, South Central College English Association, Louisiana Council of Teachers of English, Louisiana Folklore Society, Louisiana State Poetry Society (corresponding secretary, 1970-74; second vice-president, 1976—; state editor, 1970-75; co-editor, 1976—), Phi Beta Kappa (Southwestern Louisiana Association; secretary-treasurer, 1965-71; vice-president, 1975-76; president, 1976-77). *Awards, honors:* Recipient of over 108 awards in writing competition, 1954—, for poetry, fiction, nonfiction, and drama.

*WRITINGS: The Basketball Man: James Naismith,* University Press of Kansas, 1973; *The 90th Moon,* (one-act play), Edgemoor Publishing Co., 1973; *Beware of Ostriches* (poems), Legacy Publishing (Baton Rouge), 1978. Also author of "Red and Green," a one-act play for children, published in *Grade Teacher,* December, 1963. Contributor of articles, poems, short stories, or reviews to numerous periodicals, including *New Laurel Review, Ball State University Forum, Alaska Review, AAUP Bulletin, Horn Book Magazine, Poem, Epos, Fiddlehead, Kansas City Times, Denver Post, South Atlantic Quarterly, English Journal, Beaver, Louisiana History, Wichita Eagle and Beacon Magazine, Advocate Sunday Magazine, Kansas Magazine, DePaul Literary Magazine,* and *Louisiana Poets.* Editor of *Cajun Chatter,* 1964-66, *The Magnolia,* 1967-71, and *Louisiana Poets,* 1970—.

*WORK IN PROGRESS:* A second volume of poetry; *Women Out of the Way,* a study of nineteenth-century pioneer women in Kansas; *Immigrants On,* a biography of a Swedish immigrant; reviews, essays, articles, and short stories.

\* \* \*

## WEBB, Richard

*PERSONAL:* Born in Bloomington, Ill.; son of John R. and Laura Gail (Gunnett) Webb; married Elizabeth Regina Sterns, 1942; married second wife, Florence Pauline Morse, January, 1949; children: (first marriage) Richelle Regina, Patricia Gail. *Education:* Attended John Brown University, 1930-33. *Residence:* Van Nuys, Calif. *Agent:* Reece Halsey, 8733 Sunset Blvd., Hollywood, Calif. 90069.

*CAREER:* Actor, producer, and author; starred in "Captain Midnight" television series, 1954-58, and in "U.S. Border Patrol" television series, 1959-61; has appeared in fifty-eight motion pictures, including "I Wanted Wings," "I Was a Communist for the FBI," "Carson City," "This Woman Is Dangerous," "Beware of the Blob," "Washington Behind Closed Doors," and in more than two hundred television shows, including "Studio One," "Lights Out," "Mod Squad," "The Time Travelers," "Name of the Game," and "Lassie." Writer and producer of television films, including "The Legend of Eli and Lottie Johl," aired on American Broadcasting Co. in 1966. Lecturer on psychic phenomenon. *Military service:* U.S. Army, First Coast Artillery, 1936-38; served in Panama Canal Zone, U.S. Army, 1941-45; became lieutenant colonel in U.S. Army Reserve. *Member:* Screen Actors Guild, American Federation of Television and Radio Artists, Actors Equity, Reserve Officers Association, Authors League, Writers Guild, Southern California Society for Psychical Research.

*WRITINGS: Great Ghosts of the West,* Nash Publishing, 1971; *Stigmata,* Psychic Magazine, 1973; *These Came Back* (a reincarnation anthology), Hawthorn, 1974.

*WORK IN PROGRESS: Captain Midnight; Shorty Harris; The Little Giant of Panamint Valley,* a novel.

*SIDELIGHTS:* Richard Webb told *CA:* "My writing career began in 1970 when film work had slowed down and I was looking for something to do. It worked! Never having 'taken writing,' it has been interesting to watch the change, the progress in my work. It is still my conviction that unless a person can write, all the writing courses in the country won't accomplish that for the individual. My interest has been writing on a subject which has distinct appeal for me (I can see the beginning, middle, and end in my mind before striking keys on paper) and which I can see as a possible film project. My talent doesn't as yet include being assigned a writing project from someone else and then doing it in a satisfactory manner. Because of my lifelong training I understand screenplays and can do a credible job; with books I can only feel 'Thank God for editors!'"

Discussing the character, Captain Midnight, that he made famous, Webb remarks: "There has been such a renaissance of interest in 'the old heroes,' that I have developed a whole new television series project, with Captain Midnight now in a flying saucer. No, I won't play the character, I'll play his father, Colonel Midnight. He'll probably need some guidance from the Old Man. Hopefully, the new, younger Captain Midnight will be so popular that he too will draw 15,000 fans to a stadium on a personal appearance (when the Captain Midnight program was at the height of its popularity, six million children joined Captain Midnight's 'Secret Squadron' and his personal appearances at a stadium often drew 15,000 children and parents). Fan mail from members of the 'Secret Squadron' has continued to come in over the years."

In 1977, the U.S. Army and the U.S. Army Reserve made a recruiting film entitled "Captain Midnight Makes General", based on the character Webb made famous.

\* \* \*

## WEBB, Ross A. 1923-

*PERSONAL:* Born July 22, 1923, in Westchester, Nova Scotia, Canada; son of William Oswald and Permilla (Purdy)

Webb; married Ruth Keil, June 19, 1954; children: Eric Seth, Alan George. *Education:* Acadia University, A.B. (with honors), 1949; University of Pittsburgh, M.A., 1951, Ph.D., 1956. *Religion:* Episcopal Church. *Home:* 2534 Shiland Dr., Rock Hill, S.C. 29730. *Office:* Winthrop College, Rock Hill, S.C. 29730.

*CAREER:* University of Pittsburgh, Pittsburgh, Pa., instructor, 1950-56; University of Kentucky, Lexington, 1956-57, began as assistant professor, became associate professor of history and director of undergraduate studies in history; Winthrop College, Rock Hill, S.C., professor, 1967-77, Distinguished Professor of History, 1977—, chairman of department of history, government, and geography, 1967-68, dean of faculty and vice-president for academic affairs, 1968-75. Ex-officio member, York County Technical Education Committee, 1968-75. *Military service:* Royal Canadian Air Force, 1941-45; served as liaison officer between industry and air force. *Member:* Organization of American Historians, American Historical Association, Southern Historical Society, Phi Beta Kappa, Phi Kappa Phi, Phi Alpha Theta, Kiwanis (Rock Hill, S.C.).

*WRITINGS: Benjamin Helm Bristow: Border State Politician,* University Press of Kentucky, 1969; (contributor) Richard O. Curry, editor, *Radicalism, Racism, and Party Realignment: The Border States During Reconstruction,* Johns Hopkins Press, 1969.

\* \* \*

## WEBER, Clarence A. 1903-

*PERSONAL:* Born May 2, 1903, in Winfield, Kan.; son of William J. (a minister) and Pearl L. (a university professor) Weber; married Mary E. Beaty, August 7, 1925; children: Betty Lois (Mrs. C. A. Dewey), Jane Ellen (Mrs. Don V. Ruck). *Education:* Illinois College, A.B., 1924; University of Illinois, M.A., 1929; Northwestern University, Ph.D., 1943. *Religion:* Methodist. *Home:* North Eagleville Rd., Storrs, Conn. 06268.

*CAREER:* Superintendent of public schools in Illinois, 1928-45; University of Connecticut, Storrs, 1945—, dean of Fort Trumbull branch, 1946-50, associate professor, then professor of education and acting dean of School of Education, currently professor emeritus. *Member:* National Education Association, American Association of School Administrators, National Retired Teachers Association, Smithsonian Institution, Rotary International (former district governor), Sigma Pi, Phi Delta Kappa.

*WRITINGS: Personnel Problems of School Administrators,* McGraw, 1954; *Fundamentals of Educational Leadership,* McGraw, 1955; *Industrial Leadership,* Chilton, 1959; *Leadership in Personnel Management,* Warren Green, 1970; *Roots of Rebellion,* Warren Green, 1971; *What the People Ought to Know about School Administration,* Interstate, 1971. Contributor to numerous education journals.

*WORK IN PROGRESS: Diamonds in the Driveway,* a series of vignettes developed from experience.

*AVOCATIONAL INTERESTS:* Fishing, boating, photography.

\* \* \*

## WEBER, David J. 1940-

*PERSONAL:* Born December 20, 1940, in Buffalo, N.Y.; son of Theodore C. (an appliance dealer) and Frances J. Weber; married Carol S. Bryant (a teacher), June 16, 1962; children: Scott David, Amy Carol. *Education:* State University of New York College at Fredonia, B.S., 1962; University of New Mexico, M.A., 1964, Ph.D., 1967. *Home:* 6292 Mercedes, Dallas, Tex. 75214. *Office:* Department of History, Southern Methodist University, Dallas, Tex. 75275.

*CAREER:* San Diego State University, San Diego, Calif., assistant professor, 1967-70, associate professor, 1970-73, professor of history, 1973-76; Southern Methodist University, Dallas, Tex., professor of history, 1976—. Fulbright lecturer, University of Costa Rica, 1970. Danforth associate, 1973—. *Member:* American Historical Association, Conference on Latin American History, Organization of American Historians, Western History Association. *Awards, honors:* Border States Regional Library Association best book on Southwest history, 1970-71, *The Taos Trappers: The Fur Trade in the Far Southwest, 1540-1846;* Outstanding Educator of America award, 1973; National Endowment for the Humanities fellowship, 1974-75; *Foreigners in Their Native Land* was selected as one of the outstanding academic books on the history of North America by *Choice,* 1974-75.

*WRITINGS:* (Editor and translator) *The Extranjeros: Selected Documents from the Mexican Side of the Santa Fe Trail, 1825-1828,* Stagecoach Press, 1967; (editor) Albert Pike, *Prose Sketches and Poems Written in the Western Country (with Additional Stories),* Calvin Horn, 1967; (editor) David H. Coyner, *The Lost Trappers,* University of New Mexico Press, 1970; *The Taos Trappers: The Fur Trade in the Far Southwest, 1540-1846,* University of Oklahoma Press, 1971; *Foreigners in Their Native Land: Historical Roots of the Mexican Americans,* University of New Mexico Press, 1973; (editor) *El Mexico Perdido: Ensayos sobre el antiguo norte de Mexico, 1540-1821,* Secretaria de Education Publica, 1976; (editor) *Northern Mexico on the Eve of the United States Invasion: Rare Imprints Concerning California, Arizona, New Mexico and Texas, 1921-1846,* Arno, 1976; (editor with Duane L. Smith) *Fortunes Are for the Few: Letters of a Forty-niner by Charles William Churchill,* San Diego Historical Society, 1977. Contributor to several volumes of *The Mountain Men and the Fur Trade of the Far West,* edited by LeRoy R. Hafen, 1966-72; contributor of over forty articles and reviews to historical journals. Member of board editorial consultants and book review editor of *Journal of San Diego History,* 1971-76.

*WORK IN PROGRESS:* A study of the Mexican northern frontier, 1821-1846; a book.

\* \* \*

## WEBER, J(ohn) Sherwood 1918-

*PERSONAL:* Born September 21, 1918, in Reading, Pa.; son of Milton Kaufman (a mechanic) and Florence (Madeira) Weber; married Olga Svatik (in publishing), November 28, 1960; children: Mark Kenneth, J. Stephen. *Education:* Temple University, A.B., 1939, M.A., 1940; University of Wisconsin, Ph.D., 1947. *Politics:* Independent. *Home address:* Box 116, Cragsmoor, N.Y. 12420. *Office:* Department of English and Humanities, Pratt Institute, Brooklyn, N.Y. 11205.

*CAREER:* University of Wisconsin—Madison, instructor in English, 1940-44; New York University, New York City, instructor in English, 1945-47; Queens College of the City of New York (now Queens College of City University of New York), Flushing, N.Y., instructor in English, 1947-50; Pratt Institute, Brooklyn, N.Y., assistant professor, 1951-55, associate professor, 1955-59, professor of humanities, 1959—, chairman, department of English and humanities, 1963-74, director of dramatics, 1952-58, chairman of English, evening school, 1954-59, provost, 1974-76. Education commentator, Station WINS, New York City. Education consultant, New American Library, 1960-66. *Member:* American Association of University Professors (president, Pratt Institute chapter, 1960-65), National Council of Teachers of English (convention chairman, 1966), College English Association, Modern Language Association of America.

*WRITINGS:* (Editor) *Good Reading,* 16th through 20th editions, New American Library, 1954, 1958, 1962, 1966, 1969; *From Homer to Joyce: A Study Guide to Thirty-Six Great Books,* Holt, 1959. Also author of "Afterwords" to Signet Classic editions. Contributor of articles to *New York Times Book Review, American German, College English, College English Association Critic, Saturday Review,* and other journals.

*WORK IN PROGRESS: The Relevance of the Past.*

*SIDELIGHTS:* Weber told *CA* that most of his writing "grows out of the college classroom," and that the chief effort of his work "has been to show that the great books of the past are of value not only esthetically and for illuminating cultural history, but also because their themes and conflicts are as relevant as today's newspaper or TV newscast."

\*          \*          \*

## WEBSTER, Donald Blake, Jr.   1933-

*PERSONAL:* Born October 14, 1933, in Rochester, N.Y.; son of Donald Blake and Eleanor (Zach) Webster; married Miriam Bonde, September, 1953 (divorced, 1968); married second wife, Elizabeth Lonsdale Minor, January, 1970; children: Nathaniel, Sarah. *Education:* University of Maine, B.A., 1959; University of Rhode Island, M.A., 1961. *Politics:* "Extremely variable." *Religion:* Anglican. *Home:* 113 Kendal Ave., Toronto, Ontario, Canada. *Office:* Royal Ontario Museum, 14 Park, Toronto, Ontario, Canada.

*CAREER:* Royal Ontario Museum, Canadian Department, Toronto, curator, 1966—; University of Toronto, Toronto, Ontario, faculty of graduate studies, associate professor of art history, 1966—. *Military service:* U.S. Air Force, served as meteorologist, 1953-57.

*WRITINGS: Suicide Specials,* Stackpole, 1958; *Early Slip-Decorated Pottery in Canada,* Musson, 1969; *Early Canadian Pottery,* McClelland & Stewart, 1971; *Decorated Stoneware Pottery of North America,* Tuttle, 1971; (editor) *The Book of Canadian Antiques,* McGraw, 1974. Contributor of articles to *American Heritage* and numerous historical journals.

*WORK IN PROGRESS: English-Canadian Furniture of the Eighteenth and Nineteenth Centuries,* Volume I, *The Georgian Period,* for McGraw.

\*          \*          \*

## WEBSTER, Frederick E., Jr.   1937-

*PERSONAL:* Born October 22, 1937, in Auburn, N.Y.; son of Frederick E. (a merchant) and Evelyn (Dudden) Webster; married Mary Alice Powers, December 27, 1957; children: Lynn Marie, Mark Andrew, Lisa Ann. *Education:* Dartmouth College, A.B., 1959, M.B.A. (with distinction), 1960; Stanford University, Ph.D., 1964. *Religion:* Episcopalian. *Home:* Deer Run Farm, Etna, N.H. *Office:* Amos Tuck School of Business Administration, Dartmouth College, Hanover, N.H. 03755.

*CAREER:* Stanford University, Stanford, Calif., acting instructor in marketing, 1963-64; Columbia University, New York, N.Y., assistant professor of marketing, 1964-65; Dartmouth College, Amos Tuck School of Business Administration, Hanover, N.H., assistant professor, 1965-68, associate professor, 1968-72, professor of business administration, 1972—, dean, 1976—. Has taught in management development programs in the United States and abroad, including University of the Witwatersrand, 1968-69, Cambridge University, 1971, and Centre d'Etudes Industrielles, Geneva, Switzerland, 1972—. Director of Vermont Public Radio, and of Vermont Log Buildings, Inc.; trustee, Alice Peck Day Memorial Hospital. *Member:* American Marketing Association.

*WRITINGS:* (Editor) *New Directions in Marketing,* American Marketing Association, 1965; (editor with Kenneth R. Davis, and contributor) *Readings in Sales Force Management,* Ronald, 1968; (with Davis) *Sales Force Management: Text and Cases,* Ronald, 1968; *Marketing Communication: Modern Promotional Strategy,* Ronald, 1971; (with Yoram Wind) *Organizational Buying Behavior,* Prentice-Hall, 1972; *Social Aspects of Marketing,* Prentice-Hall, 1973; *Marketing for Managers,* Harper, 1974.

Contributor: James Bearden, editor, *Personal Selling: Behavorial Science Readings and Cases,* Wiley, 1967; Ralph L. Day, editor, *Concepts for Modern Marketing,* International Textbook, 1968; Robert F. Gwinner and Edward M. Smith, editors, *Sales Strategy: Cases and Readings,* Appleton, 1969; Bernard Morin, editor, *Marketing in a Changing World,* American Marketing Association, 1969; S. H. Britt, editor, *Consumer Behavior in Theory and in Action,* Wiley, 1970; J. A. Barnhill, editor, *Sales Management: Contemporary Perspectives,* Scott, Foresman, 1970; S. Neelamegham, editor, *Marketing Management and the Indian Economy,* Vikas Publications, 1970; R. L. Day and T. E. Ness, editors, *Marketing Models: Behavioral Science Applications,* International Textbook, 1971.

Editor of Wiley's "Marketing Management" series. Contributor of articles and reviews to marketing journals. Member of editorial board, *Journal of Marketing,* and *Industrial Marketing Management.*

*WORK IN PROGRESS:* Research in international marketing strategies, consumerism, industrial buyer behavior, and social criteria in marketing decision making.

*AVOCATIONAL INTERESTS:* Downhill and cross-country skiing, squash, fishing, bird hunting, farming—sheep, chickens, rabbits, gardening.

\*          \*          \*

## WEBSTER, Margaret   1905-1972

March 15, 1905—November 13, 1972; American actress and stage director. Obituaries: *New York Times,* November 14, 1972; *L'Express,* November 20-27, 1972; *Newsweek,* November 27, 1972; *Time,* November 27, 1972.

\*          \*          \*

## WEIDENBAUM, Murray L(ew)   1927-

*PERSONAL:* Born February 10, 1927, in Bronx, N.Y.; son of David and Rose (Warshaw) Weidenbaum; married Phyllis Green, June 13, 1954; children: Susan, James, Laurie. *Education:* City College (now City College of the City University of New York), B.B.A., 1948; Columbia University, M.A., 1949; Princeton University, M.P.A., 1954, Ph.D., 1958. *Politics:* Republican. *Religion:* Jewish. *Home:* 1531

Heirloom Ct., Creve Coeur, Mo. 63141. *Office:* Center for the Study of American Business, Washington University, St. Louis, Mo. 63130.

*CAREER:* State of New York, Department of Labor, New York, research economist, 1948-49; U.S. Bureau of the Budget, Executive Office of the President, Washington, D.C., fiscal economist, 1949-57; General Dynamics Corp., Convair Division, Fort Worth, Tex., economist, 1957-58; Boeing Co., Seattle, Wash., corporate economist, 1958-63; Stanford Research Institute, Stanford, Calif., senior economist, 1963-64; Washington University, St. Louis, Mo., associate professor, 1964-66, professor of economics, 1966—, chairman of department, 1966-69, 1971-74, director of Center for the Study of American Business, 1975—. Assistant Secretary of the Treasury, U.S. Department of the Treasury, Washington, D.C., 1969-71. Member of business research advisory council, U.S. Department of Labor, 1959-63; executive secretary, Presidential Committee on the Economic Impact of Defense and Disarmament, 1964; director of economic research program, National Aeronautics and Space Administration, 1964-69. Member of committee on government operations and expenditures, U.S. Chamber of Commerce, 1959-63, chairman of subcommittee on military and international budgets, 1960-63; member of committee on science, technology and regional growth, National Academy of Sciences, 1967-68. Consultant to U.S. Department of State, Congressional Joint Economic Committee, and other government bodies. *Military service:* U.S. Army, 1945. *Member:* National Economists Club (member of board of governors), American Economic Association, American Statistical Association, Cosmos Club (Washington, D.C.). *Awards, honors:* Distinguished Writers Award, Georgetown University, 1971.

*WRITINGS: Prospects for Reallocating Public Resources: A Study in Federal-State Fiscal Relations,* American Enterprise Institute for Public Policy Research, 1967; *Prospects for the American Economy during the Post-Vietnam Period,* Department of Economics, Washington University (St. Louis), 1967; *The Modern Public Sector: New Ways of Doing the Government's Business,* Basic Books, 1969; *Economics of Peace Time Defense,* Praeger, 1974; *Business, Government, and the Public,* Prentice-Hall, 1977. Also author of studies published by Washington University. Regular columnist, *Dun's Review.* Contributor to economic journals and to popular periodicals, including *Saturday Review.* Member of board of editors, *Journal of Economic Issues.*

*WORK IN PROGRESS: Government Power and Business Performance.*

\* \* \*

## WEIHOFEN, Henry 1904-

*PERSONAL:* Pronounced Why-Hofen; born June 17, 1904, in Chicago, Ill.; son of Henry (an upholsterer) and Alma (Wolowsky) Weihofen; married Caroline Walsh, September 10, 1934; children: William Henry. *Education:* Attended Northwestern University, 1918-19; University of Chicago, Ph.B., 1926, J.D., 1928, J.S.B., 1930. *Politics:* Democrat. *Religion:* Unitarian Universalist. *Home:* 908 Avenida Cielito N.E., Albuquerque, N.M. 87110. *Office:* University of New Mexico Law School, Albuquerque, N.M. 87106.

*CAREER:* University of Colorado, Boulder, professor of law, 1932-41; U.S. Department of Justice, Washington, D.C., attorney, 1944-48; University of New Mexico, Albuquerque, professor of law, 1948—. *Member:* American Psychiatric Association (honorary fellow), New Mexico State

Bar Association, New Mexico Conference of Social Welfare (president, 1956-57), Albuquerque Area Council on Alcoholism (president, 1964-65). *Awards, honors:* Isaac Ray Award of the American Psychiatric Association.

*WRITINGS:* (With Manfred S. Guttmacher) *Psychiatry and the Law,* Norton, 1952; *Mental Disorder as a Criminal Defense,* Dennis, 1954; *Legal Writing Style,* West Publishing, 1961; (with Sol Rubin) *The Law of Criminal Correction,* West Publishing, 1963; (with Richard C. Allen and Elyce Z. Ferster) *Mental Impairment and Legal Incompetency,* Prentice-Hall, 1968; (with Harrop A. Freeman) *Clinical Law Training: Interviewing and Counseling,* West Publishing, 1972. Contributor of articles to law reviews and other professional journals.

\* \* \*

## WEIL, Roman L(ee) 1940-
## (Eli Worman)

*PERSONAL:* Surname is pronounced Weel; born May 22, 1940, in Montgomery, Ala.; son of Roman Lee (an attorney) and Charlotte (Alexander) Weil; married Cherie Buresh (a librarian), December 28, 1963; children: Alexis Cherie, Charles Alexander Roman, Lacey Lorraine. *Education:* Yale University, B.A., 1962; Carnegie-Mellon University, M.S.I.A., 1965, Ph.D., 1966. *Home:* 726 Sheridan Rd., Evanston, Ill. 60202. *Office:* Graduate School of Business, University of Chicago, 5836 South Greenwood Ave., Chicago, Ill. 60637.

*CAREER:* Carnegie-Mellon University, Pittsburgh, Pa., instructor in mathematics and economics, 1963-65; University of Chicago, Chicago, Ill., instructor, 1965-66, assistant professor, 1966-70, associate professor of management and information sciences, 1970-74, instructor and assistant professor of mathematical economics in Graduate School of Business, 1965-70; Georgia Institute of Technology, Atlanta, Mills B. Lane Professor of Industrial Management, 1974-76; University of Chicago, professor of accounting, 1976—. Visiting associate professor of industrial administration, Carnegie-Mellon University, 1971-72. Certified Public Accountant, 1973. Consultant, Jewel Tea Co., 1965-66, Beverly Bank, 1969-70, Department of Health, Education, and Welfare, United States Public Health Service, 1972; also consultant to International Business Machines, Levi-Strauss, Pillsbury, Sidley & Austin, Marmon Group, and several others. Member of advisory committee on replacement cost implementation, Securities and Exchange Commission, 1976—. *Member:* American Accounting Association, American Institute of Certified Public Accountants, National Association of Accountants, American Economic Association, Econometric Society, Institute of Management Sciences, Illinois Society of Certified Public Accountants. *Awards, honors:* National Science Foundation grant, 1967-79; Graham and Dodd Scroll from Financial Analysts Federation, 1975, for "Inflation Accounting: What Will General Price Level Adjusted Income Statements Show?"

*WRITINGS:* (With Sidney Davidson, James S. Schindler, and Clyde P. Stickney, under own name and under the pseudonym Eli Worman) *Accounting: The Language of Business,* Thomas Horton, 1974, 3rd edition (with Davidson and Stickney) 1979; (with Davidson and Schindler) *Fundamentals of Accounting,* 5th edition (Weil was not associated with previous editions), Dryden, 1975; (with Davidson and Stickney) *Inflation Accounting: A Guide for the Accountant and the Financial Analyst,* McGraw, 1976; (editor with Robert F. Vancil, and contributor) *Replacement Cost Ac-*

*counting: Readings on Concepts, Uses, and Methods,* Thomas Horton, 1976; (with Davidson, Schindler, and Stickney) *Financial Accounting: An Introduction to Concepts, Methods, and Uses,* Dryden, 1976, 2nd edition (with Davidson and Stickney), 1979; (with Davidson and others) *Financial Reporting by State and Local Government Units,* Center for Management of Public and Non-Profit Enterprise of the University of Chicago, 1977; (editor with Davidson, and contributor) *Handbook of Modern Accounting,* 2nd edition (Weil was not associated with first edition), McGraw, 1977; (editor with Davidson, and contributor) *Handbook of Cost Accounting,* McGraw, 1978; (with Davidson, Stickney, and Schindler) *Managerial Accounting: An Introduction to Concepts, Methods, and Uses,* Dryden, 1978.

Contributor: Ralph Willoughby, editor, *Sparse Matrices and Their Applications,* IBM Data Processing, 1969; J. M. Lishan and D. T. Crary, editors *Investment Process,* International Textbook Co., 1970; H. Raupach, E. Fels, and E. Boettcher, editors, *Jahrbuch der Wirtschaft Osteuropas,* Gunter Olzog Verlag, 1970; E. J. Elton and M. J. Gruber, editors, *Security Evaluation and Portfolio Analysis,* Prentice-Hall, 1972; Largay and Livingston, editors, *Accounting for Changing Prices,* Wiley, 1976; H. Aaron, editor, *Inflation and Income Tax,* Brookings Institution, 1976; William S. Eastman, Jr., editor, *Inflation Accounting/Indexing and Stock Behavior,* Faulkner, Dawkins, & Sullivan, 1976; R. Henry and O. Moeschlin, editors, *Mathematical Economics and Game Theory,* Springer-Verlag, 1977.

Contributor to *Econometrica, Journal of Business, Management Science, Journal of Finance,* and other publications. Associate editor, *Managment Science,* 1970-76, *Accounting Review,* 1975—; departmental editor, *Communications of the Association for Computing Machinery,* 1971-73; editor, 25th anniversary issue of *Communications of the Association for Computing Machinery,* July, 1972.

*WORK IN PROGRESS:* Various articles for journals.

\* \* \*

## WEINBERG, Florence M(ay) 1933-

*PERSONAL:* Born December 3, 1933, in Alamogordo, N.M.; daughter of Steven Horace (an educator) and O. Gladys (Edgington) Byham; married Kurt Weinberg (a university professor), May 8, 1955. *Education:* Park College, A.B., 1954; University of Iowa, graduate study, 1954-55; University of British Columbia, M.A., 1963; University of Rochester, Ph.D., 1968. *Home:* 290 Forest Hills Rd., Rochester, N.Y. 14625. *Office:* Department of Modern Languages and Classical Studies, St. John Fisher College, Rochester, N.Y. 14618.

*CAREER:* University of British Columbia, Vancouver, library assistant, 1955-62; St. John Fisher College, Rochester, N.Y., assistant professor, 1967-70, associate professor, 1970-75, professor of French and Spanish literature, 1975—, head of department, 1972—. Consultant-panelist, National Foundation on the Arts and Humanities, and National Endowment for the Humanities, 1977-78. *Member:* Modern Language Association of America, American Association of University Professors, American Association of Teachers of French, American Comparative Literature Association, Northeast Modern Language Association, Delta Epsilon Sigma.

*WRITINGS: The Wine and the Will,* Wayne State University Press, 1972. Also contributor, Barbara C. Bowen, editor, *The French Renaissance Mind: Studies Presented to W. G. Moore,* 1976. Contributor of articles to journals, in-

cluding *Modern Language Review,* and *Modern Language Notes.*

*WORK IN PROGRESS: History of a Literary Topos; The Hero and the Cave.*

\* \* \*

## WEINBERG, Julius 1922-

*PERSONAL:* Born May 9, 1922, in Cleveland, Ohio; son of Meyer Hirsch (a carpenter) and Sarah (Yellen) Weinberg; married Alezah Dworkin (a social worker), January 7, 1952; children: Naimah, Roni, Shirah. *Education:* Western Reserve University (now Case Western Reserve University), B.A., 1945; University of Michigan, M.A., 1955, Ph.D., 1963. *Politics:* Democrat. *Religion:* Jewish. *Home:* 3361 Norwood Rd., Shaker Heights, Ohio 44122. *Office:* Department of History, Cleveland State University, Cleveland, Ohio 44115.

*CAREER:* Wayne State University, Detroit, Mich., instructor in history, 1962-64; State University of New York College at New Paltz, assistant professor of history, 1964-65; Cleveland State University, Cleveland, Ohio, assistant professor, 1965-67, associate professor, 1967-74, professor of history, 1974—. Lecturer, College of Jewish Studies, Cleveland. *Member:* American Historical Association, Organization of American Historians.

*WRITINGS:* (Editor with Roscoe G. Hinkle and Gisela J. Hinkle) Edward Alsworth Ross, *Social Control,* Press of Case Western Reserve University, 1969; *An Introduction to the History of Soviet Jewry,* Bureau of Jewish Education of Cleveland, 1970; (editor with Richard N. Current and John A. Garraty) *Words That Made American History,* 3rd edition (Weinberg was not associated with earlier editions), Little, Brown, 1972, 4th edition, 1978; *Edward Alsworth Ross and the Sociology of Progressivism,* State Historical Society of Wisconsin, 1972; (author of introduction) Ross, *Sin and Society,* Harper, 1972; (editor with John H. Cary) *The Social Fabric,* Little, Brown, 1975, 2nd edition, 1978. Contributor to encyclopedias and historical journals.

\* \* \*

## WEINFIELD, Henry 1949-

*PERSONAL:* Born January 3, 1949, in Montreal, Quebec, Canada; son of Mortimer and Susanne (Eismann) Weinfield; married Ann Frydman (a teacher). *Education:* City College of the City University of New York, B.A., 1970; State University of New York at Binghamton, M.A. 1973.

*CAREER:* State University of New York at Binghamton, instructor, 1971-73, part-time lecturer, 1973-74. *Awards, honors:* Elias Lieberman Poetry Award, 1968; City College of the City University of New York Theodore Goodman Poetry Award, 1970.

*WRITINGS: The Carnival Cantata* (poems), Unicorn Press, 1971; *Rossignol en Amour* (poems), Half-Ass Press, 1971. Editor, *Promethean,* 1970, and *The Mysterious Barricades,* 1972.

*WORK IN PROGRESS: The Nightingale in Love,* poems; *The Poet King and Other Essays;* editing an anthology of *Promethean* material; translations of French and Latin verse.†

\* \* \*

## WEINRICH, A(nna) K(atharina) H(ildegard) 1933-
### (Sister Mary Aquina)

*PERSONAL:* Born November 4, 1933, in Wuppertal, Germany; daughter of Leo (a teacher) and Anny (Cohnen) Weinrich. *Education:* University College of Rhodesia and Nyasaland, B.A., 1959; University of Manchester, M.A., 1962, Ph.D., 1965. *Office address:* Department of Sociology, University of Dar es Salaam, P.O. Box 35043, Dar es Salaam, Tanzania.

*CAREER:* Roman Catholic nun of Order of Preachers (Dominican). School of Social Work, Salisbury, Rhodesia, lecturer in social anthropology, 1965-66; University of Rhodesia, Salisbury, lecturer, 1966-71, senior lecturer in social anthropology, 1972-75; University of Dar es Salaam, Dar es Salaam, Tanzania, senior lecturer in social anthropology, 1975—. Also Dominican missionary. *Member:* Association of Social Anthropologists.

*WRITINGS: Chiefs and Councils in Rhodesia,* University of South Carolina Press, 1971; *Black and White Elites in the Rural Areas of Rhodesia,* University of Manchester Press, 1973; *African Farmers in Rhodesia: Old and New Peasant Communities in Karangaland,* Oxford University Press, 1975; *Mucheke: Race, Status, and Politics in a Rhodesian Community,* UNESCO (Paris), 1976; *The Tongu People of Lake Kariba,* Mambo Press, 1977. Contributor of chapters to numerous books. Contributor of over forty articles to social studies journals.

*WORK IN PROGRESS: Women in Zimbabwe; Marriage and Family Life in Zimbabwe;* a comparative study of contemplative communities on four continents; *Ujanraa Villages in Tanzania.*

\* \* \*

## WEINSTEIN, Norman Charles 1948-

*PERSONAL:* Born January 26, 1948, in Philadelphia, Pa.; son of Emanuel (a florists' supplier) and Gertrude (Zamarin) Weinstein. *Education:* Bard College, B.A., 1969; State University of New York College at New Paltz, graduate study, 1969-70. *Politics:* Anarchist. *Religion:* Zen Buddhist.

*MEMBER:* Modern Language Association of America.

*WRITINGS: Gertrude Stein and the Literature of the Modern Consciousness,* Ungar, 1970. Editor, *Upriver,* 1964-66, and *Lampeter Muse,* 1967-69.

*WORK IN PROGRESS: The Revised Secret Anatomy of the Body of God,* a long poem.

*SIDELIGHTS:* Weinstein says that he expects eventually to move to Japan. His current interests: "deep image, structural anthropology, poetry of para-noia (re R. Laing and David Cooper) . . . exercise of compassion toward and from human and non human."

\* \* \*

## WEISS, Robert M. 1929-

*PERSONAL:* Born March 30, 1929, in Milwaukee, Wis.; son of Alex (a businessman) and Nellis Weiss; married Joyce Sheffield, July 1, 1951; children: Elaine, Nancy. *Education:* University of Wisconsin, B.B.A., 1950; Marquette University, J.D., 1953. *Office:* Lorinczi & Weiss, 700 North Water St., Milwaukee, Wis. 53202.

*CAREER:* Admitted to the Bar of the State of Wisconsin, 1953; Lorinczi & Weiss, Milwaukee, Wis., attorney at law, 1956—. Instructor in law at Marquette University. Certified Public Accountant, 1956. *Military service:* U.S. Air Force, Judge Advocate Division, 1954-56. *Member:* American Bar Association, Wisconsin Bar Association, Milwaukee Bar Association.

*WRITINGS: How to Maximize Tax Savings in Buying, Operating and Selling Real Property,* Prentice-Hall, 1971.††

\* \* \*

## WEISSKOPF, Walter A(lbert) 1904-

*PERSONAL:* Born November 14, 1904, in Vienna, Austria; came to United States in 1938, naturalized in 1942; son of Emil and Martha (Gut) Weisskopf; married Gertrude F. Rosenfield (a professor of modern languages), April 29, 1937; children: Martin C. *Education:* Attended University of Geneva, 1923, and Cambridge University, 1925; University of Vienna, Dr. Juris, 1927. *Home:* 675 Sharon Park Dr., Unit 319, Menlo Park, Calif. 94025.

*CAREER:* Lawyer in Vienna, Austria, 1927-38; University of Omaha (now University of Nebraska at Omaha), assistant professor of economics, 1939-43; Central YMCA Junior College, Chicago, Ill., assistant professor of economics, 1943-45; Roosevelt University, Chicago, 1950—, began as assistant professor of economics, currently professor emeritus, chairman of department, 1950-65. Visiting professor, Stanford University. *Member:* American Economic Association, Association of Humanistic Psychology, American Economic History Association, American Association of University Professors.

*WRITINGS: The Psychology of Economics,* University of Chicago Press, 1955; *Alienation and Economics,* Dutton, 1971.

Contributor: A. H. Maslow, editor, *New Knowledge in Human Values,* Harper, 1958; H. Riehl, editor, *Festschrift fuer Walter Heinrich,* Graz, 1963; C. C. Walton and R. Eells, editors, *The Business Systems: Ideas and Concepts,* Macmillan, 1966; C. McConell, editor, *Economic Issues: Readings and Cases,* McGraw, 1966; Arthur MacEwan and Thomas Weisskopf, editors, *Readings in Economics,* Prentice-Hall, 1970; R. C. Edwards and others, editors, *The Capitalist System,* Prentice-Hall, 1972. Contributor to *Modern Review, Journal of Political Economy, Common Cause, American Journal of Economics and Sociology, Ethics, Annals, Social Research, Journal of Economic Issues,* and other publications.

\* \* \*

## WELLISZ, Leopold T. 1882-1972

1882—November 20, 1972; Polish-born American industrialist, patron of the arts, and writer on Poland and Polish literature. Obituaries: *New York Times,* November 23, 1972.

\* \* \*

## WELLMAN, Carl (Pierce) 1926-

*PERSONAL:* Born September 3, 1926, in Lynn, Mass.; son of Frank and Carolyn (Heath) Wellman; married Farnell Parsons (a librarian), June 20, 1953; children: Timothy, Philip, Lesley, Christopher. *Education:* University of Arizona, B.A., 1949; Harvard University, M.A., 1951, Ph.D., 1954; also attended Cambridge University, 1951-52. *Home:* 439 Westgate Ave., St. Louis, Mo. 63130. *Office:* Department of Philosophy, Washington University, St. Louis, Mo. 63130.

*CAREER:* Lawrence University, Appleton, Wis., instructor, 1953-57, assistant professor, 1957-62, then associate professor and professor of philosophy; Washington University, St. Louis, Mo., professor of philosophy, 1968—. Member of panel on research grants, National Endowment for the Humanities, 1968-71. *Member:* International Association for Philosophy of Law and Social Philosophy (secretary general, 1975-79), American Philosophical Association (member of executive committee, Western Division, 1975-78), Mind Association, Phi Beta Kappa. *Awards, honors:* American Council of Learned Societies fellow, 1965-66; National Endowment for the Humanities fellow, 1972-73.

*WRITINGS: The Language of Ethics,* Harvard University Press, 1961; *Challenge and Response,* Southern Illinois University Press, 1971; *Morals and Ethics,* Scott, Foresman, 1975. Contributor to philosophy journals.

*WORK IN PROGRESS: Legal and Natural Rights,* a philosophical analysis.

* * *

**WELLMAN, Henry Q. 1945-**

*PERSONAL:* Born March 10, 1945, in Brattleboro, Vt.; son of Henry D. and Ellen (Weaver) Wellman; married M. Carol Ostwald (an artist), May 21, 1966; children: Jennifer Carolyn, Michael Diedrich. *Education:* University of Vermont, B.A., 1967; graduate study at Georgetown University and American University. *Home:* 4015 North 20th St., Arlington, Va. 22267.

*CAREER:* National Home Study Council, Washington, D.C., administrative assistant, beginning 1968.

*WRITINGS: The Teenager and Home Study,* Richards Rosen, 1970. Contributor to *American Peoples Encyclopedia* and to education journals.††

* * *

**WELLS, Ronald Vale 1913-**

*PERSONAL:* Born August 16, 1913, in Cleveland, Ohio; son or Earl Harold (an educator and lawyer) and Irene (Leffler) Wells; married Patricia Woodburne, June 20, 1938; children: David Woodburne, Robert Vale. *Education:* Attended Iowa State University, 1931-33;, Denison University, A.B., 1935; Crozer Theological Seminary, B.D., 1938; Columbia University, Ph.D., 1942. *Home:* Box 255 Kelly Rd., East Chatham, N.Y. 12060. *Office:* United Presbyterian Church U.S.A., 475 Riverside Dr., New York, N.Y. 10027.

*CAREER:* Minister of American Baptist churches in Somerville, N.J., 1938-42, Bridgeport, Conn., 1942-47, and Ames, Iowa, 1947-52; American Baptist Convention, Board of Education, New York City, N.Y., associate executive secretary, 1952-62; Crozer Theological Seminary, Chester, Pa., president, 1962-70; Sioux Falls College, Sioux Falls, S.D., president, 1970-74; vice-president for educational affairs, Crozer-Chester Medical Center, 1974-76; United Presbyterian Church, Major Mission Fund, New York City, director and fund counselor, 1976—. *Awards, honors:* D.D., Denison University, 1959, Colby College, 1961, Brown University, 1962, Bucknell University, 1969; L.L.D., Franklin College, 1960; H.H.D., Widener College, 1970.

*WRITINGS: Three Christian Transcendentalists,* Columbia University Press, 1943, revised edition, Octagon, 1972. Contributor to *Journal of Pastoral Care* and *Christian Ministry.*

*WORK IN PROGRESS:* Further research on New England transcendentalism.

* * *

**WELSH, John R(ushing) 1916-1974**

*PERSONAL:* Born May 19, 1916, in Monroe, N.C.; son of John Rushing II (a pharmacist) and Hallie Hamilton (Benton) Welsh; married Ruth Elizabeth Davis, August 9, 1941 (divorced, 1962); married Sevena Wragg Molair, December 20, 1963; children: (first marriage) Nancy Benton, John R. IV; (stepson) William L. *Education:* University of the South, A.B., 1939; Syracuse University, M.A., 1941; Vanderbilt University, Ph.D., 1951. *Politics:* "Strictly independent." *Religion:* Episcopalian. *Home:* 6058 Robinwood Rd., Columbia, S.C. 29206. *Office:* Humanities Building 417-18, University of South Carolina, Columbia, S.C. 29208.

*CAREER:* University of South Carolina, Columbia, assistant professor, 1946-47, 1949-51, associate professor, 1951-60, professor of English, 1960-74, head of department, 1973-74, vice-president for instruction, 1974. Director of the University of South Carolina Educational Foundation, 1958-74. *Military service:* U.S. Army, 1943-46; became captain. *Member:* Modern Language Association of America, American Association of University Professors (president, 1954-55), South Atlantic Modern Language Association, Southeastern College English Association, Society for the Study of Southern Literature, South Caroliniana Society, Phi Beta Kappa, Pi Gamma Mu, Kappa Sigma, Blue Key. *Awards, honors:* Distinguished Teaching Award, University of South Carolina, 1958; Achievement Award, Wingate College, 1963.

*WRITINGS: The Mind of William Gilmore Simms: His Social and Political Thought,* Joint University Libraries, 1952; (contributor) Walker and Welker, editors, *Reality and Myth: Essays in American Literature,* Vanderbilt University Press, 1964; (editor and author of introduction) *John Esten Cooke's Autobiographical Memo,* Department of English, University of South Carolina, 1969. Associate editor, *South Atlantic Bulletin;* member of editorial board, *Centennial Edition of the Writings of William Gilmore Simms.* Contributor of articles to *Southern Literary Journal, Georgia Review, Journal of Southern History, South Atlantic Bulletin, Journal of American Studies, Notes on Mississippi Writers, South Carolina Historical Magazine,* and *Tennessee Historical Quarterly.*

*WORK IN PROGRESS:* Editing *The Essays of William Gilmore Simms,* Volume IV of the Centennial edition of Writings of William Gilmore Simms, for University of South Carolina Press; research on Washington Allston and John Esten Cooke; a book on the ante-bellum Charleston writers.†

(Died October 4, 1974)

* * *

**WENSINGER, Arthur S(tevens) 1926-**

*PERSONAL:* Born March 9, 1926, in Grosse Pointe, Mich.; son of Carl Franklin (a businessman) and Suzanne (Stevens) Wensinger. *Education:* Dartmouth College, B.A. (with honors), 1948; University of Michigan, M.A., 1951, Ph.D., 1958; additional graduate study at University of Munich, 1948, 1950-51, and University of Innsbruck, 1953-54. *Politics:* Independent. *Religion:* Episcopalian. *Home:* Candlewood Hill, Higganum, Conn. 16441. *Office:* Department of German Language and Literature, Wesleyan University, Middletown, Conn. 06457.

*CAREER:* Wesleyan University, Middletown, Conn., instructor, 1955-58, assistant professor, 1959-63, associate professor, 1963-69, professor, 1969-77, Marcus Taft Professor of German and Humanities, 1977—, chairman of department of German language and literature, senior tutor in College of Letters, 1963—. *Member:* International Brecht

Society, American Association of University Professors, American Translators Association, Modern Language Association of America, American Association of Teachers of German, Heinrich-von-Kleist Gesellschaft, Connecticut Academy of Arts and Sciences, Phi Beta Kappa, Phi Kappa Phi. *Awards, honors:* Fulbright fellow at University of Innsbruck, 1953-54; Danforth Foundation grant, 1959.

*WRITINGS:* (Translator; Walter Gropius, editor) Oskar Schlemmer and others, *The Theatre of the Bauhaus,* Wesleyan University Press, 1961; (editor with T. C. Dunham) Herman Hesse, *Siddhartha: Eine indische Dichtung,* Macmillan, 1962; (editor of German section) Wills Barnstone, general editor, *Modern European Poetry,* Bantam, 1963; (translator and contributor to German section) *The Langauge of Love* (short story anthology), Bantam, 1964; (contributor of translation) *Plays for a New Theater,* illustrated by George Grosz, New Directions, 1966; (editor and translator with W. B. Coley) *Hogarth on High Life: The Marriage a la Mode Series from Georg Christoph Lichtenberg's Commentaries,* Wesleyan University Press, 1970; (editor and contributor) P. Boynton, *Stone Island,* Harcourt, 1973. Translator of short stories, articles, and dramatic writings.

*WORK IN PROGRESS: Letters and Diaries of Paula Modersohn-Becker;* articles on T. H. Mann and Franz Kafka; translating works of R. M. Rilke.

*BIOGRAPHICAL/CRITICAL SOURCES: New York Review of Books,* August 13, 1970; *New York Times,* August 14, 1970; *Harper's,* October, 1970; *New Yorker,* December 12, 1970; *Newsweek,* December 14, 1970; *Nation,* June 21, 1971.

*  *  *

## WERBLOW, Dorothy N. 1908-1972

1908—August 8, 1972; American author of educational books for children. Obituaries: *New York Times,* August 9, 1972.

*  *  *

## WERTHEIM, Bill 1944-

*PERSONAL:* Born December 7, 1944, in Brooklyn, N.Y.; son of Elias and Celia (Kaplan) Wertheim. *Education:* Columbia University, B.A., 1965; State University of New York at Stony Brook, M.A., 1972.

*CAREER: New York Herald,* New York, N.Y., columnist. *Member:* Modern Language Association of America, Coordinating Council of Literary Magazines, Committee of Small Magazine Editors and Publishers.

*WRITINGS:* (Editor with Irma Gonzalez) *Talkin' About Us,* Appleton, 1970.

*WORK IN PROGRESS:* Studying American, Canadian, and British folklore at the State University of New York at Stony Brook; a proposed thesis on contemporary playwrights.††

*  *  *

## WERTHEIMER, Roger 1942-

*PERSONAL:* Born April 10, 1942, in Buffalo, N.Y.; son of Louis (a salesman and real estate broker) and Dorothea (Bennett) Wertheimer; married Patricia Anne (Scott) Olson (a high school principal), July 1, 1967; children: Christopher Olson. *Education:* Brandeis University, B.A., 1963; Harvard University, M.A., 1967, Ph.D., 1969. *Politics:* Independent. *Religion:* "None (was Jewish)." *Home:* 3210 Ni-

agara St., Pittsburgh, Pa. 15213. *Office:* Department of Philosophy, Carnegie-Mellon University, Pittsburgh, Pa. 15213.

*CAREER:* Portland State University, Portland, Ore., lecturer in philosophy, 1968-69; Sheriff's Office, Department of Public Safety, Multnomah County, Ore., deputy sheriff, 1969-70; University of Oregon, Eugene, assistant professor of philosophy, 1971; Graduate Center, City University of New York, New York, N.Y., assistant professor of philosophy, 1971-73; Guggenheim fellow, 1973-74; Boston State Hospital, Boston, Mass., researcher/therapist, 1975-77; Carnegie-Mellon University, Pittsburgh, Pa., associate professor of philosophy and head of philosophy program, 1977—. Lecturer in medical ethics, Downstate Medical Center, 1972; visiting assistant professor, Tufts University, 1974-75; visiting associate professor, University of Cincinnati, 1976, and University of Houston, 1977.

*WRITINGS: The Significance of Sense,* Cornell University Press, 1972. Contributor to *Journal of Philosophy* and *Philosophy and Public Affairs.*

*WORK IN PROGRESS:* A book which attempts to explain what people are asking when they ask whether life has meaning.

*SIDELIGHTS:* Roger Wertheimer told *CA,* "Writing is (a) mother."

*  *  *

## WEST, Bill G. 1930-

*PERSONAL:* Born May 24, 1930, in Paducah, Tex.; son of Kade and Ruth (Grayum) West; married Ann Radnor, June 12, 1976. *Education:* Baylor University, B.A., 1951; Southwestern Baptist Seminary, B.D., 1954, Th.D., 1957. *Home:* 21318 Park Willow, Katy, Tex. 77450. *Office:* 3221 Fondreau, Houston, Tex. 77042.

*CAREER:* Ordained Southern Baptist minister, 1951; student pastor, 1954-57; First Baptist Church, Okmulgee, Okla., 1957-65; River Oaks Baptist Church, Houston, Tex., pastor, beginning 1965; professional speaker and president of West & Associates, Houston, Tex. Former trustee, Houston Baptist College.

*WRITINGS: Free to Be Me,* Word Books, 1971.

*WORK IN PROGRESS: Effective Oral Communication and Stress Management.*

*AVOCATIONAL INTERESTS:* Cycling, photography, canoeing, hiking.

*  *  *

## WEST, Robert H(unter) 1907-

*PERSONAL:* Born May 20, 1907, in Nashville, Tenn.; son of Olin and Susie (Hunter) West; married Conn Harris, June 23, 1934; children: Susan McConnel. *Education:* Vanderbilt University, A.B., 1929, M.A., 1930, Ph.D., 1939. *Religion:* Episcopalian. *Home:* 133 West View Dr., Athens, Ga. 30606. *Office:* Department of English, University of Georgia, Athens, Ga. 30602.

*CAREER: Nashville Banner,* Nashville, Tenn., sports writer, 1930-32; University of Georgia, Athens, assistant professor, 1936-47, associate professor, 1947-52, professor of English, 1952-75, professor emeritus, 1975—. *Military service:* U.S. Army Air Forces, 1942-46; became captain; received three battle stars. *Member:* Modern Language Association of America, Milton Society of America, Shakespeare Association, South Atlantic Modern Language Association (president, 1971), Southeastern Renaissance Conference (president, 1966). *Awards, honors:* University of Georgia, Michael award for research, 1950; SAMLA University of Kentucky Press publication prize, 1967.

*WRITINGS: The Invisible World,* University of Georgia Press, 1939; *Milton and the Angels,* University of Georgia Press, 1955; *Shakespeare and the Outer Mystery,* University Press of Kentucky, 1968. Contributor to *Milton Encyclopedia,* Tufts University Press. Contributor of about seventy-five articles to learned journals.

*WORK IN PROGRESS:* Research on *Dr. Faustus.*

*BIOGRAPHICAL/CRITICAL SOURCES: Criticism,* fall, 1969.

\* \* \*

## WESTBROOK, Max (Roger) 1927-

*PERSONAL:* Born April 6, 1927, in Malvern, Ark.; son of Robert L. (a businessman) and Bessie (Rogers) Westbrook; married Frankie Wilson (a teacher), April 4, 1953; children: Lynn, Brett, Max, Jr. *Education:* Baylor University, B.A., 1949; University of Oklahoma, M.A., 1953; University of Wisconsin, graduate study, 1954-55; University of Texas, Ph.D., 1960. *Home:* 3206 Pickwick Lane, Austin, Tex. 78746. *Office:* Department of English, University of Texas, Austin, Tex. 78712.

*CAREER:* University of Kentucky, Lexington, instructor, 1960-61, assistant professor of English, 1961-62; University of Texas at Austin, assistant professor, 1962-68, associate professor, 1968-72, professor of English, 1972—. *Military service:* U.S. Navy, 1945-46. U.S. Army, 1951-52; became sergeant. *Member:* American Studies Association, American Association of University Professors, Western Literature Association (president, 1972-73).

*WRITINGS: The Modern American Novel: Essays in Criticism,* Random House, 1966; *Walter Van Tilburg Clark,* Twayne, 1969. Contributor to literature journals.

*WORK IN PROGRESS:* Literary criticism; a study of the American character; the University of Texas Hemingway collection.

*AVOCATIONAL INTERESTS:* Tennis, fishing, camping, writing poetry.

\* \* \*

## WESTLEY, William A. 1920-

*PERSONAL:* Born May 14, 1920, in Chester, Pa.; son of William and Grace (Merklejohn) Westley; married Margaret F. Weaver, February 13, 1943; children: Neil, Frances, Margaret. *Education:* Attended Cornell University, 1938-40; University of Chicago, B.A., 1947, M.A., 1949, Ph.D., 1951. *Office:* Industrial Relations Center, McGill University, 762 Sherbrooke St. W., Montreal, Quebec, Canada.

*CAREER:* Indiana University at Bloomington, lecturer in sociology, 1948-50; McGill University, Montreal, Quebec, associate professor, 1951-60, professor of sociology and anthropology, 1960—, chairman of department, 1955-65, director of Industrial Relations Center, 1965—. Speaker and moderator on Canadian television programs dealing with social problems. Research consultant, Defence Research Board on Crowd Control. *Military service:* U.S. Army, 1942-46; intelligence officer, serving in India and Burma, 1942-45; became first lieutenant. *Member:* Royal Society of Arts (London: fellow), Canadian Corrections Association, John Howard Society of Montreal (former director).

*WRITINGS: Nature and Control of Crowds,* Directorate of Scientific Affairs, Government of Canada, 1955; (with Nathan Epstein) *The Silent Majority,* Jossey-Bass, 1969; *Studies in Education and Work,* Queen's Printer, 1969; *Violence and the Police,* M.I.T. Press, 1970; (with wife, Margaret Westley) *The Emerging Worker,* McGill-Queens University Press, 1971.

Contributor: Iago Galdston, editor, *The Family in Contemporary Society,* International Universities Press, 1958; H. S. Becker, editor, *Institutions and the Person,* Aldine, 1968; D. Willner, editor, *Decisions, Values, and Groups,* Pergamon, 1969; E. W. Burgess and D. Bogue, editors, *Research Contributions to Urban Sociology,* University of Chicago Press, 1969. Contributor of articles to technical journals.

*WORK IN PROGRESS:* Studies of worker self-management in schools and factories in Canada, Norway, England, and Yugoslavia.

*AVOCATIONAL INTERESTS:* Tennis, badminton, swimming, reading.

\* \* \*

## WHEATCROFT, John 1925-

*PERSONAL:* Born July 24, 1925, in Philadelphia, Pa.; son of Allen Stewart (a clergyman) and Laura (Daniel) Wheatcroft; married Joan Osborne, November 10, 1950; children: Allen, David. Rachel. *Education:* Attended Temple University, 1942, 1946-48; Bucknell University, B.A., 1949; Rutgers University, M.A., 1950, Ph.D., 1960. *Home:* 135 South 11th St., Lewisburg, Pa. 17837. *Office:* Department of English, Bucknell University, Lewisburg, Pa. 17837.

*CAREER:* University of Kansas, Lawrence, instructor in English, 1950-52; Bucknell University, Lewisburg, Pa., instructor, 1952-57, assistant professor, 1957-62, associate professor, 1962-66, professor of English, 1966—. Distinguished visiting professor, University of Montana, Missoula, 1969. *Military service:* U.S. Navy, 1943-46. *Member:* Modern Language Association of America, American Association of University Professors. *Awards, honors:* Lindback award for distinguished teaching, 1964; Alcoa Playwriting Award and National Educational Television Award, 1967, for "Ofoti"; Yaddo resident fellow, 1972; MacDowell Colony resident fellow, 1974.

*WRITINGS: Death of a Clown* (poems), Thomas Yoseloff, Inc., 1964; *Prodigal Son* (poems), Thomas Yoseloff, Inc., 1967; *Ofoti* (play; produced by National Educational Television, 1966), A. S. Barnes, 1970; *Edie Tells* (novel), A. S. Barnes, 1975; *A Voice from the Hump* (poems), A. S. Barnes, 1977. Contributor of poetry to *Harper's Bazaar, Ladies' Home Journal, Mademoiselle, New York Times, Chicago Tribune, New York Herald Tribune,* and other magazines and newspapers.

*WORK IN PROGRESS:* A new collection of poems.

\* \* \*

## WHEELER, David L. 1934-

*PERSONAL:* Born July 30, 1934, in Saginaw, Mich.; son of Clayton Final (a locomotive engineer) and Blanche (Hunt) Wheeler; married Jane Louise Manchester, September 6, 1958; children: Elizabeth Hunt, Anne Braford. *Education:* University of Michigan, A.B., 1956, A.M., 1958, Ph.D., 1962. *Politics:* Independent. *Home:* 1423 Creek Mere Dr., Canyon, Tex. 79015. *Office:* Graduate School, West Texas State University, Canyon, Tex. 79016.

*CAREER:* Illinois State University, Normal, assistant professor, 1961-64, associate professor of geography, 1964-67, assistant dean of student services, 1967-68, associate dean, 1968-69, associate dean of Graduate School, 1969-72; West Texas State University, Canyon, professor of geography and dean of Graduate School and Research, 1972—. Summer visiting professor, University of Manitoba, 1967; summer lecturer, National Defense Education Act Institute, University of Illinois, 1968. Consultant to Fielder Publishing Co., 1962, McGraw-Hill Book Co., 1969, 1970, McLean County Regional Planning Commission, 1971, and Van Nostrand Reinhold Co., 1972. *Member:* Association of American Geographers (council member, 1963-64; chairman of West Lakes Division, 1963-64), National Council of University Research Administrators, National Association for Foreign Student Affairs (Illinois vice-chairman, 1968-71). *Awards, honors:* Office of Naval Research grant for study in Italy, 1960; Woodrow Wilson summer fellowship, 1961; Illinois State University faculty research grant, 1964, 1970; Robert G. Bone Fund Distinguished Teacher Award, 1969.

*WRITINGS: The Human Habitat: Contemporary Readings,* Van Nostrand, 1971. Contributor of fifteen articles and reviews to geography and history journals.

*WORK IN PROGRESS:* Research on the cattle industry in the southern high plains.

*AVOCATIONAL INTERESTS:* Outdoor activities, especially swimming, jogging, camping, and fishing; reading history; investments.

\* \* \*

## WHITBREAD, Leslie George 1917-

*PERSONAL:* Born December 15, 1917, in Bromley, Kent, England; son of Albert Wentworth (a publisher) and Helen (Kelsey) Whitbread; married Marjorie Evelyn Grace Bradon, July 3, 1963. *Education:* King's College, London, B.A., 1938, M.A., 1952, Ph.D., 1957, D.Lit., 1965. *Politics:* Republican. *Religion:* Episcopalian. *Home:* 6196 Chatham Dr., Apt. 133, New Orleans, La. 70122. *Office:* Department of English, Louisiana State University in New Orleans, New Orleans, La. 70122.

*CAREER:* University of London, London, England, lecturer in English, 1938-40; Louisiana State University in New Orleans, professor of English, 1966—. News commentator, YWES-TV, 1968-69. *Military service:* British Army, Intelligence Corps, 1939-45; became major. *Member:* Modern Language Association of America, American Name Society, International Speakers' Platform.

*WRITINGS: Fulgentius the Mythographer,* Ohio State University Press, 1971; *Placenames of Jefferson Parish,* [Metairie, La.], 1978. Contributor to linguistics and literature journals. Contributor to *Westminster Dictionary of Church History.*

*WORK IN PROGRESS: Dictionary of Louisiana Placenames.*

\* \* \*

## WHITE, Cynthia L(eslie) 1940-

*PERSONAL:* Born July 13, 1940, in Eastbourne, Sussex, England; daughter of Leslie Percy (a company depot manager) and Vera Mabel (Laws) White. *Education:* Bedford College, London, B.A. (honors), 1962, Ph.D., 1968; University of Michigan, postdoctoral study, summers, 1967, 1969. *Religion:* Church of England. *Home:* 4 St. Brelades, Trinity Place, Eastbourne, East Sussex BN213BT, England. *Office:*

Sociology Unit, City of London Polytechnic, Calcutta House, Old Castle St., London E1 7NT, England.

*CAREER:* Fawcett Library, London, England, commissioned to condense and reorganize library's holdings, 1968-70, member of executive committee, 1978—; City of London Polytechnic, London, England, senior lecturer 1970-73, principal lecturer in sociology, 1973-75, principal lecturer-in-charge, sociology unit, 1975—, community liaison officer, 1976—. Academic advisor to Royal Commission on the Press, 1975-76. Member, University Entrance and School Examinations Council, University of London, 1975—. *Member:* Fawcett Society (member of executive committee, 1964-65, 1971-72, 1975-78), National Association of Teachers in Further and Higher Education, Organization of Sociologists in Polytechnics, London Association of University Women, University Women's Club.

*WRITINGS: Women's Magazines, 1693-1968: A Sociological Study,* M. Joseph, 1970, Humanities, 1971. Writer and narrator of "Writers of Wrongs," produced by British Broadcasting Corp. Radio 4, 1970.

*SIDELIGHTS:* Cynthia White writes she is "currently responsible for coordinating and diecting an inter-disciplinary study of various aspects of educational demand in the Inner City. . . . This research supports the City of London Polytechnic's developing policy of close involvement with the local community through which it is hoped to make a major contribution in remedying severe educational deprivation in the inner city."

*BIOGRAPHICAL/CRITICAL SOURCES: Times* (London), March 9, 1970, November 21, 1970, September 2, 1977; *Guardian,* March 12, 1970, March 5, 1972, September 2, 1977; *New Statesman,* March 13, 1970; *Books and Bookmen,* May 1, 1970; *Times Literary Supplement,* November 27, 1970; *Financial Times,* September 2, 1977.

\* \* \*

## WHITE, Dori 1919-

*PERSONAL:* Born July 13, 1919, in Portland, Ore.; daughter of Charles Elmer (an educator) and Jessie (Hyde) Cleveland; married first husband, 1940; married second husband, Irle E. White (a teacher), September 16, 1957; children: (first marriage) Elizabeth (Mrs. Dean Douglas), Ronald. *Education:* Attended Whitman College, 1938-40; University of Iowa, B.A., 1940; University of Oregon, M.A., 1956. *Agent:* Elizabeth Otis, McIntosh & Otis, Inc., 475 Fifth Ave., New York, N.Y. 10017.

*CAREER:* Marylhurst College, Oswego, Ore., drama teacher, 1956-57; Kresge Eye Institute, Detroit, Mich., research assistant, 1957-60. *Member:* California Writers Association (honorary member), Burlingame Writers Association (president, 1966).

*WRITINGS: Sarah and Katie* (juvenile), Harper, 1972. Contributor of short fiction to national magazines, including *McCalls, Redbook,* and *Good Housekeeping.*

*WORK IN PROGRESS:* A sequel to *Sarah and Katie;* research for short stories.

*SIDELIGHTS:* In 1971-72, Dori White cruised on a schooner with her husband along the Pacific coast from San Francisco to Mexico, and to Hawaii. In August, 1972, the Whites left Hawaii for the South Pacific on the second stage of their cruise.†

## WHITE, Edward M.   1933-

*PERSONAL:* Born August 16, 1933, in Brooklyn, N.Y.; son of Joseph (a postal clerk) and Ida (Eisen) White; married Carol V. Moore, June 2, 1956 (divorced, 1976); married Volney D. Sposito, December 11, 1976; children: Katherine, Elizabeth; stepchildren: Douglas, Geraldine, Frank. *Education:* New York University, B.A., 1955; Harvard University, M.A., 1956, Ph.D., 1960. *Politics:* Democrat. *Religion:* Presbyterian. *Home:* 933 West Edgehill Rd., San Bernardino, Calif. 92407. *Office:* Department of English, California State College, San Bernardino, Calif. 92407.

*CAREER:* Wellesley College, Wellesley, Mass., instructor, 1960-63, assistant professor of English, 1963-65; California State College, San Bernardino, associate professor, 1965-69, professor of English, 1969—, chairman of department, 1966-75; California State University and Colleges, coordinator of English testing programs and consultant in credit by evaluation, 1974—. Member of executive committee, Conference on College Composition and Communication, 1976-78; participant in many other conferences. English Council of the California State Colleges, secretary-treasurer, 1966-68, vice-president, 1968-70. Manuscript consultant to W. W. Norton & Co., Inc., Macmillan Publishing Co., and Winthrop Publishers. *Member:* Modern Language Association of America, National Council of Teachers of English, Society for Values in Higher Education, American Association of University Professors. *Awards, honors:* Danforth fellow, 1955-60; Woodrow Wilson fellow, 1955-56; Huber Foundation research grant, 1962.

*WRITINGS: The Writer's Control of Tone,* Norton, 1970; *The Pop Culture Tradition,* Norton, 1972; *Comparision and Contrast: The CSUC English Equivalency Examination,* five volumes, California State University and Colleges, 1973-77; (contributor) Forest Burt and Sylvia King, editors, *Equivalency Testing,* National Council of Teachers of English, 1974; (contributor) *The Continuing Challenge: The Program for Innovation and Improvement in the Instructional Process,* California State University and Colleges, 1977. Contributor to English studies journals. Regular book reviewer, *Los Angeles Times,* 1966—.

*WORK IN PROGRESS:* A third composition textbook, tentatively entitled *Metaphor, Myth, and Future Myth,* for Norton; a book on the novels of Jane Austen.

*SIDELIGHTS:* Edward M. White writes in *The Writer's Control of Tone:* "I have come to think that far too much college composition is corrupt enterprise, writing for nobody. The student has nothing to say, imagines no audience who could care about what he has to say, but turns out his words on paper nonetheless. I am convinced that the most important job before teachers of writing is to resist and protest against the dehumanizing effect of materials and essay assignments that turn writing into academic gamesmanship. Writing has to be hard because writing and thinking go together, and thinking is hard. But, even though writing is hard, it is still human and personal. It is my hope that those using this text will understand that writing for somebody, and as somebody, makes writing worth reading."

*AVOCATIONAL INTERESTS:* Chess, playing chamber music, tennis, and squash.

\*     \*     \*

## WHITE, Elizabeth H(erzog)   1901(?)-1972

1901(?)—August 5, 1972; American anthropologist, government consultant, and authority on race and poverty problems. Obituaries: *New York Times,* August 11, 1972.

## WHITE, John W.   1939-

*PERSONAL:* Born August 16, 1939, in New York, N.Y.; son of Robert Paul (chemical salesman) and Jeanette (Zobel) White; married Barbara Devin, June 17, 1961; children: Sandra, Thomas, Sharon, Timothy. *Education:* Dartmouth College, B.A., 1961; Southern Connecticut College, teaching certificate, 1966; Yale University, M.A.T., 1969. *Home and office:* 60 Pound Ridge Rd., Cheshire, Conn. 06410.

*CAREER:* High school teacher in Cheshire, Conn., 1965-69; Southern New England Telephone Co., New Haven, Conn., writer and editor, 1969-72; Institute of Noetic Sciences, Palo Alto, Calif., director of education, 1972-74; currently freelance writer and editorial consultant. Instructor in English, South Central Community College, New Haven, 1969-70; instructor in English, Quinipiac College, Hamden, Conn., 1969-72; instructor in journalism, Southern Connecticut State College, 1976-77. Lecturer and workshop leader at various U.S. and Canadian colleges and universities, and for many organizations, including Esalen Institute, Human Dimensions Institute, American Orthopsychiatric Association, and Spiritual Frontiers Fellowship. Director of communications, EDMA Corp., Houston, Tex., 1972—. Consultant on consciousness to many organizations, including National Broadcasting Co., Hartley Productions, Agape Productions, Dick Feldman Associates, and Center for Interdisciplinary Creativity. Member of advisory board, Research Institute for Kundalina. *Military service:* U.S. Navy, 1961-65; became lieutenant, junior grade. *Member:* Library Association (vice-president, 1976-77), Phenix Society (member of board of directors, 1975-77), International Institute of Integral Human Sciences (fellow). *Awards, honors:* Doctor Honoris Causa, Instituto de Ciencias Parapsicologicas Hispani Americano, for excellence on psychic research.

*WRITINGS:* (Editor) *The Highest State of Consciousness,* Doubleday, 1972; (editor) *What Is Meditation?,* Doubleday, 1974; (editor) *Frontiers of Consciousness,* Avon, 1974; (editor) *Psychic Exploration,* Putnam, 1974; (editor with Brad Steiger) *Other Worlds, Other Universes: Playing the Reality Game,* Doubleday, 1975; *Everything You Want To Know about TM,* Pocket Books, 1976; (editor with James Fadiman) *Relax—How You Can Feel Better,* Dell, 1976; (editor with Stanley Krippner) *Future Science: Life Energies and the Physics of Paranormal Phenomena,* Doubleday, 1977; (editor) *Kundalina, Evolution and Enlightenment,* Doubleday, 1978. Also author of script for documentary film entitled *New Age.*

Contributor of columns to Connecticut newspapers. Contributor of poetry to anthologies, and of over two hundred articles on a variety of topics to numerous periodicals, including *Reader's Digest, Psychic, Fate, Health Foods and Nutrition News, Changing Education, Modern Fiction Studies,* and *College Composition and Communication.* Contributing editor, *New England Review,* 1968-69; eastern editor, *Psychic,* 1972-73; member of editorial board, *Journal of Altered States of Consciousness.*

*SIDELIGHTS:* "My career as a writer and editor grew out of my long-standing interest in literature and education. As a very young boy—age 8 or so—I wrote poetry (rhymed verse, really) and later as a teenager, under the influence of fantasy and science fiction, I dreamed of being a great novelist and reaching for the stars. In college, where I majored in English, I wrote poetry and stories primarily for self-expression. But it soon became apparent that non-fiction was my proper mode.

"Content is just as important as genre and style, however, and in that regard, my interest in literature began to focus on the psychology of characters. From psychology I levitated (gravitated simply is incorrect in this context) to parapsychology as the mystery of mind called ever more strongly. Parapsychology, in turn, led to numerous related fields of science, metaphysics and the spiritual life.

"From self to the cosmos—that was how it turned out. Today I describe my area of interest as consciousness research and my occupation as a journalist. I feel that what I am concerned with has great importance for awakening humanity to its higher nature—a condition of expanded awareness and new mental faculties that can give renewed vision of our oneness with creation. In short, my field of service turned out to be—against all expectations—cosmological education and self-knowledge through the written word. For which I thank the Creator."

\* \* \*

## WHITE, Lawrence J. 1943-

*PERSONAL:* Born June 1, 1943, in New York, N.Y. *Education:* Harvard University, A.B. (summa cum laude), 1964, Ph.D., 1969; London School of Economics, M.Sc., 1965. *Home:* 110 Bleecker St., Apt. 21-B, New York, N.Y. 10012. *Office:* Graduate School of Business Administration, New York University, 90 Trinity Rd., New York, N.Y. 10006.

*CAREER:* Harvard University, Development Advisory Service, Cambridge, Mass., development adviser to governments of Pakistan and Indonesia, 1969-70; Princeton University, Princeton, N.J., assistant professor of economics, 1970-76; New York University, New York, N.Y., associate professor of economics, Graduate School of Business Administration, 1976—. *Member:* American Economic Association.

*WRITINGS: The Automobile Industry since 1945,* Harvard University Press, 1971; *Industrial Concentration and Economic Power in Pakistan,* Princeton University Press, 1974.

Contributor: (With E. E. Bailey) W. G. Shepherd and T. G. Gies, editors, *Regulation in Further Perspective,* Ballinger, 1974; R. E. Canes and M. J. Roberts, editors, *Regulating the Product,* Ballinger, 1975; S. M. Goldfeed and R. E. Quandt, editors, *Studies in Non-Linear Estimation,* Ballinger, 1976; Walter Adams, editor, *The Structure of American Industry,* Macmillan, 1977; (with E. S. Mills) A. F. Friedlaender, editor, *Approaches to Controlling Air Pollution,* M.I.T. Press, 1978.

*WORK IN PROGRESS:* Research on public libraries, the determinate of international trade flows, and the causes of technological progress.

\* \* \*

## WHITE, W. D. 1926-

*PERSONAL:* Born March 14, 1926, in Tenaha, Tex.; son of John A. (a farmer) and Mary Belle (Holt) White; married Nancy Joan Salk, May 20, 1956 (divorced May 30, 1970); married Grace McSpadden Overholser, May 28, 1971 (died July, 1972); children: (first marriage) Brenda Joyce, Jonathan Paul. *Education:* Baylor University, B.A., 1947, M.A., 1949; University of Texas, Ph.D., 1958; Princeton University, M.A., 1960, Ph.D., 1968. *Politics:* Liberal Democrat. *Religion:* Baptist. *Home:* 1003 East Scotsdale, Laurinburg, N.C. 28352. *Office:* Department of English, St. Andrews Presbyterian College, Laurinburg, N.C. 28352.

*CAREER:* Baylor University, Waco, Tex., assistant pro-

fessor of English, 1953-56; St. Olaf College, Northfield, Minn., assistant professor of English, 1957-59; Duke University, Durham, N.C., assistant professor of religion, 1961-65; St. Andrews Presbyterian College, Laurinburg, N.C., professor of English and religion, 1965—. Consultant to various educational organizations. *Military service:* U.S. Army, 1944-46; became first lieutenant; received Bronze Star. *Member:* American Academy of Religion, Society of Biblical Literature (president, Southern section, 1966-67), Modern Language Association of America. *Awards, honors:* Fulbright scholar in Marburg, Germany, 1955-56.

*WRITINGS: The Preaching of John Henry Newman,* Fortress, 1969; (editor with Ronald H. Bayes and Harry Harvin) *Humane Learning in a Changing Age,* St. Andrews College Press, 1971. Also author of *John Henry Newman, Anglican Preacher: A Study in Religion and Literature.* Contributor of scholarly articles and abstracts to *South Atlantic Quarterly, Portland Review, Southern Humanities Review, Mosaic,* and *Journal of Ecumenical Studies.* Prose editor, *St. Andrews Review.*

*WORK IN PROGRESS:* A book on John Stuart Mill—his notions of individual and social freedom; essays on ethical and human problems in American medicine.

\* \* \*

## WHITE, William, Jr. 1934-
### (Spinossimus)

*PERSONAL:* Born June 8, 1934, in Philadelphia, Pa.; son of William (an accountant and auditor) and Ruth (McCaughan) White; married Sara Jane Shute (a nurse), September 8, 1956; children: Rebecca, Sara, William III, James M., Elizabeth, Margaret. *Education:* Haverford College, B.S., 1956; Westminster Theological Seminary, B.D., 1961, Th.M., 1963; Dropsie College for Hebrew and Cognate Learning (now Dropsie University), Ph.D., 1968. *Politics:* Christian-Social democrat (pacifist). *Religion:* Presbyterian (Reformed). *Home:* 2272 Patty Lane, Warrington, Pa. 18976. *Office:* Box 638, Warrington, Pa. 18976.

*CAREER:* Employed during his early career as mailman, hospital orderly, gas pumper, and mill hand; clergyman of Reformed Presbyterian Church; in U.S. Civil Service in Glenside, Pa., 1956-63; Temple University, Philadelphia, Pa., instructor in ancient history, 1964-68; Ellen Cushing College, Bryn Mawr, Pa., assistant professor of biology and physics. 1966-68; East Carolina University, Greenville, N.C., assistant professor of history, 1968-70; Philadelphia College of Textiles and Science, Philadelphia, professor of history, 1970-71; North American Publishing Co., Philadelphia, editorial director, 1971-73; Old Testament editor, Thomas Nelson, Inc., 1976—; publisher, Franklin Institute Press, 1976—. Writer for radio and television. Publisher of *Cancer Therapy Abstracts, Carcinogenesis Abstracts, Nutrition and Cancer,* and *International Bulletin of Magnetic Resonance.* Consultant to Auerbach Corporation, Data Communications; consultant in life sciences writing and publishing. Senior medical writer, Emergency Care Research Institute, 1972-74. *Member:* American Association for the Advancement of Science, American Historical Association, Mensa, Intertel, Tyndale House (Oxford, England). *Awards, honors:* National Endowment for the Humanities grant for study in Israel, 1968; fellow of International Committee for Chemical Research (Japan), 1969-70.

*WRITINGS:* (Editor) *A Babylonian Anthology,* Morris Press, 1966; (contributor) Stephen Benko and John J. O'Rourke, *The Catacombs and the Colosseum,* Judson,

1970; (editor) *Reference Encyclopedia of Women's Liberation,* North American Publishing, 1972; (editor) *Reference Encyclopedia of Drugs and Drug Abuse,* North American Publishing, 1972; (editor) *Reference Encyclopedia of Ecology and Pollution,* North American Publishing, 1972.

All published by Sterling: *A Frog Is Born,* 1972; *A Turtle Is Born,* 1973; *The Guppy: Its Life Cycle,* 1974; *The Siamese Fighting Fish: Its Life Cycle,* 1975; *An Earthworm Is Born,* 1975; *The Angelfish: Its Life Cycle,* 1975; (with Sara Jane White) *A Terrarium in Your Home,* 1976; *The Edge of the Pond,* 1976; *Forest and Garden,* 1976; *The Cycle of the Seasons,* 1977; *The American Chameleon,* 1977; *Edge of the Ocean,* 1977; *The Mosquito: Its Life Cycle,* 1978; *The Housefly: Its Life Cycle,* 1978. Contributor of several hundred articles on Near Eastern linguistics to *The Zondervan Pictorial Encyclopedia of the Bible,* Zondervan, 1975-76. Contributor of more than one thousand articles to periodicals, including *Vanguard of Canada, Christian Scholar's Review, Westminster Theological Journal, Industrial Research, Photographic Applications in Science and Medicine,* and *Mikroskopion.* Associate editor, *Data Processing Magazine;* managing editor, *Health Devices.*

*WORK IN PROGRESS: The Spider: Its Life Cycle,* for Sterling; fifty articles to be included in *The Moody Old Testament Wordbook* (Hebrew-English) and fifty to be included in *The Zondervan Dictionary of Biblical Archaeology;* editing the Old Testament in *The New King James Version,* and editing *The Bible Almanac,* both for Thomas Nelson; *The Life of Cornelius Pan Til,* for Thomas Nelson; *Brightleaf,* a novel; *Secrets in Clay; Das Narrenschiff,* a twentieth-century version of Sebastian Brandt's poem; a history of contemporary exact science; a full commentary on the Book of Genesis.

*SIDELIGHTS:* "As an author with a radical-Christian philosophy of science," William White, Jr. writes, "I have tried to innovate the use of the latest tools and methods in the biomedical field for use in juvenile books on science. I have utilized the light microscope, micromanipulation, photomacroscopy and scanning electron microscopy in illustrating explanations of growth-edge scientific ideas for young readers. This is done by using familiar life forms—turtles, lizards, exotic fishes, as the vehicle for demonstrating basic ideas in physiology, biochemistry, ethology, biophysics and ecology." *Avocational interests:* Literature, particularly Japanese and Russian; microbiology of the cold-blooded vertebrates; photography; ichthyology and herpetology.

\*     \*     \*

## WHITEHEAD, Frank S. 1916-

*PERSONAL:* Born August 23, 1916, in Long Eaton, England; son of Thomas Charlton and Dora (Browne) Whitehead; married Agnes Mary Wishart, 1939; married second wife, Winifred Peart (a college lecturer), 1951; children: (first marriage) Laurence Andrew, Miriam; (second marriage) Stephen Graham, Katharine Ruth, Valerie Jean. *Education:* Fitzwilliam House, Cambridge, B.A. (honors), 1938; Institute of Education, London, T.D., 1939. *Home:* 26 Victoria Rd., Broomhall, Sheffield S10 2DL, England. *Office:* Department of Education, University of Sheffield, Sheffield, England.

*CAREER:* Teacher, 1939-41; teacher of English at grammar school in Scunthorpe, England, 1946-48; University of London, Institute of Education, London, England, lecturer in English, 1948-62; University of Sheffield, Division of Education, Sheffield, England, senior lecturer, 1962-73, reader

in English and education, 1973—. Associate director, Dartmouth Anglo-American Seminar on the Teaching of English, 1966. *Military service:* British Army, Royal Artillery, 1941-43, Educational Corps, 1943-46; became temporary captain.

*WRITINGS:* (Editor and author of introduction and notes) *George Crabbe: Selections from His Poetry,* Chatto & Windus, 1955; (editor) *Six Stories of Mark Twain,* Chatto & Windus, 1963; *The Disappearing Dais: A Study of the Principles and Practices of English Teaching,* Chatto & Windus, 1966; (compiler) *Mainstream: Modern Short Stories,* Chatto & Windus, 1967; *Creative Experiment: Writing and the Teacher,* Chatto & Windus, 1970; *Moments of Truth,* Hart-Davis, 1974; (with A. C. Capey and W. Maddren) *Children's Reading Interests,* Evans/Methuen Educational, 1974; (with Capey, Maddren, and A. Williams) *Children and Their Books,* Macmillan Education (London), 1977. Editor, *Use of English,* 1969-75.

*WORK IN PROGRESS:* A study of the background, development, and treatment of the verse tale in Crabbe's poetry.

*BIOGRAPHICAL/CRITICAL SOURCES: New Statesman,* April 10, 1970.

\*     \*     \*

## WHITEHEAD, Robert J(ohn) 1928-

*PERSONAL:* Born January 21, 1928, in Logansport, Ind.; son of William B. (a plumber) and Kathleen (O'Morrow) Whitehead; married Mary Ellen Leffert, November 23, 1950; children: Mark, Kevin. *Education:* Ball State University, B.S., 1951, M.A., 1954; Indiana University, Ed.D., 1960. *Politics:* Democrat. *Religion:* Roman Catholic. *Home:* 2239 University Ave., Sacramento, Calif. 95825. *Office:* Department of Education, California State University, Sacramento, 6000 J St., Sacramento, Calif. 95819.

*CAREER:* Public school teacher in Logansport, Ind., 1951-56; Burris Laboratory School, Ball State University, Muncie, Ind., teacher, 1956-58; Indiana University at Bloomington, instructor in elementary education, 1958-60; California State University, Sacramento, professor of education, 1960—. *Military service:* U.S. Navy, 1946-48.

*WRITINGS:* (With Henry A. Bamman and others) *The Oral Interpretation of Children's Literature,* W. C. Brown, 1964, 2nd edition, 1971; *The First Book of Bears,* Watts, 1966; *Children's Literature: Strategies of Teaching,* Prentice-Hall, 1968; *The First Book of Eagles,* Watts, 1968; *Rabbits and Hares: A First Book,* Watts, 1976; *Early School Years Read Aloud Program,* four books, ETC Publications, 1975.

"World of Adventure" series, all with Henry Bamman, published by Benefic: *Hunting Grizzly Bears,* 1963, *The Sacred Well of Sacrifice,* 1964, *Lost Uranium Mine,* 1964, *Fire on the Mountain,* 1964, *City Beneath the Sea,* 1964, *The Search for Piranha,* 1964, *Viking Treasure,* 1965, *Flight to the South Pole,* 1965, *Teacher's Guide,* 1965, *Activity Book,* 1965.

"Checkered Flag" series, published by Addison-Wesley: *Wheels,* 1967, *Bearcat,* 1967, *Smashup,* 1967, *Riddler,* 1967, *Flea,* 1969, *Scramble,* 1969.

"Mystery Adventure" series, published by Benefic: *Mystery Adventure of the Jeweled Bell,* 1969; *... of the Talking Statues,* 1969; *... at Cave Four,* 1969; *... of the Smuggled Treasures,* 1969.

"Space Science Fiction" series, published by Benefic: *Space Pirate,* 1970, *Milky Way,* 1970, *Bone People,* 1970,

*Planet of the Whistlers*, 1970, *Ice Men of Rime*, 1970, *Inviso Man*, 1970.

"Field Literature Program," published by Addison-Wesley: *Windowpanes*, 1971, *Fox Eyes*, 1971, *Seabirds*, 1971, *Northern Lights*, 1971, *Thunderbolts*, 1971.

"Top Flight Readers," published in 1977 by Addison-Wesley: *Chopper, Test Pilot, Hang Glider, Bush Pilot, Barnstormers, Balloon.*

*WORK IN PROGRESS: Don Woods, Forest Ranger,* eight books, for Benefic.

*AVOCATIONAL INTERESTS:* Collector of alphabet books for children.

\* \* \*

## WHITLOCK, Virginia Bennett   ?-1972

?—October 27, 1972; American author of books and games for children. Obituaries: *New York Times*, October 30, 1972.

\* \* \*

## WHITTINGHAM, Jack   1910-1972

1910—July 4, 1972; English screen and television writer. Obituaries: *New York Times*, July 6, 1972.

\* \* \*

## WHITTINGHAM, Richard   1939-

*PERSONAL:* Born January 1, 1939, in Chicago, Ill.; son of Charles A. and Virginia (Hartke) Whittingham; married H. Ellen McCrae, August 3, 1964; children: Paige Allison, David Andrew. *Education:* Loyola University, Chicago, Ill., B.S., 1967. *Residence:* Wilmette, Ill.

*CAREER:* Formerly editor-in-chief of Hubbard Press, Northbrook, Ill.; currently a full-time writer. *Military service:* U.S. Army, 1962-64.

*WRITINGS:* (With Barbara Brooks) *Holidays and Entertainments* (juvenile), Southwestern Co., 1968; (with Brooks) *The Earth and the Stars* (juvenile), Southwestern Co., 1968; *Astronomy*, Hubbard Press, 1971; *Martial Justice*, Regnery, 1971. Contributor of articles on the military to magazines and newspapers.

*WORK IN PROGRESS:* A novel.

\* \* \*

## WHITWORTH, William   1937-

*PERSONAL:* Born February 13, 1937, in Hot Springs, Ark.; son of William C. and Lois (McNabb) Whitworth. *Education:* University of Oklahoma, B.A., 1960. *Residence:* New York, N.Y. *Agent:* International Famous Agency, Inc., 1301 Avenue of the Americas, New York, N.Y. 10019. *Office:* 25 West 43rd St., New York, N.Y. 10036.

*CAREER: Arkansas Gazette*, Little Rock, reporter, 1960-63; *New York Herald Tribune*, New York City, reporter, 1963-65; *New Yorker*, New York City, staff writer, 1966-72, associate editor, 1973—.

*WRITINGS: Naive Questions about War and Peace*, Norton, 1970.

*AVOCATIONAL INTERESTS:* Music.

*BIOGRAPHICAL/CRITICAL SOURCES: Art International*, Volume XV, June 20, 1971; *Wall Street Journal*, July 14, 1970.

## WICKE, Charles R(obinson)   1928-

*PERSONAL:* Born April 13, 1928, in Roanoke, Va.; son of Reginald Julius (an engineer) and Mary (Robinson) Wicke; married Concepcion Sanchez, August 29, 1965; children: Charles Jr., Clara Maria. *Education:* University of Virginia, B.A., 1948; Mexico City College (now University of the Americas), M.A., 1954; further graduate study at Escuela Nacional de Anthropologia e Historia, Mexico, 1955-56, and Universidad Nacional Autonoma de Mexico, 1958-60; University of Arizona, Ph.D., 1965. *Politics:* Democrat. *Religion:* None. *Home:* 809 Haliburton Rd., Victoria, British Columbia, Canada V8Y 1J1. *Office:* Department of History in Art, University of Victoria, Victoria, British Columbia, Canada V8W 2Y2.

*CAREER:* Mexico City College (now University of the Americas), Mexico City, Mexico, instructor in athropology, 1955-60; University of the Americas, Mexico City, assistant professor of anthropology, 1964-66; Universidad Nacional de Asuncion, Asuncion, Paraguay, Fulbright lecturer in anthropology, 1966-67; Northern Illinois University, De-Kalb, associate professor of anthropology, 1968-69; University of Oklahoma, Health Sciences Center, Oklahoma City, associate professor of anthropology, 1969-77; University of Victoria, Victoria, British Columbia, visiting associate professor, 1977—. *Military service:* U.S. Army, 1951-53.

*MEMBER:* American Anthropological Association (fellow), American Association for the Advancement of Science (fellow), Society for American Archaeology, Universities Art Association of Canada, Royal Anthropological Institute of Great Britain and Ireland (fellow), Sociedad Mexicana de Anthropologia, Centro de Estudios Antropologicos del Ateneo Paraguayo, Sigma Xi. *Awards, honors:* Buenos Aires Convention grant to Peru, 1957; U.S. Steel Foundation grants, 1963, 1964; Northern Illinois University faculty research grant, 1969.

*WRITINGS:* (Contributor) Carmen Cook de Leonard, editor, *Esplendor del Mexico Antiguo* (means "The Splendor of Ancient Mexico"), Centro de Investigaciones Anthropologicas de Mexico (Mexico), 1959; (contributor) John Paddock, editor, *Ancient Oaxaca*, Stanford University Press, 1966; *Olmec: An Early Art Style of Precolumbian Mexico*, University of Arizona, 1971. Contributor to professional journals in the United States and Latin America.

*WORK IN PROGRESS:* Research on the social background of Aztec sculpture.

\* \* \*

## WIDELL, Helene   1912-

*PERSONAL:* Surname is pronounced Wee-*dell;* born April 14, 1912; daughter of Niord Johan Fredrik (an engineer) and Elena (De Makeef) Gustafson; married Ernest H. Widell (a rancher), April 29, 1933; children: Elaine (Mrs. John Loseth), Rigmor (Mrs. John Clarke), Ernest, Jr., Marie (Mrs. Justin Sellors), Cathrine (Mrs. Robert McClelland), Michael, Ursula. *Education:* Attended Paahlmans Handels Institut, 1932. *Home address:* River Bend Ranch, Box 307, Valemount, British Columbia, Canada V0E 2Z0. *Agent:* A. L. Fierst, 630 Ninth Ave., New York, N.Y. 10036.

*CAREER:* School trustee, 1960-64.

*WRITINGS: The Black Wolf of River Bend*, Farrar, Straus, 1971.

*WORK IN PROGRESS: The Sasquach Trail; Ten Hours.*

*AVOCATIONAL INTERESTS:* Conservation of wild animals and plants, pollution control.†

## WIDENER, Don(ald)   1930-

*PERSONAL:* Surname is pronounced *Wide*-ner; born March 13, 1930, in Holdenville, Okla.; son of Carl James and Lucile (Cole) Widener; married Veda Rose Pannell, June 13, 1953; children: Jeffrey Scott, Christopher Neil. *Education:* Compton Junior College, A.A., 1950. *Politics:* Independent. *Religion:* Protestant. *Home:* P.O. Box 247, Lake Arrowhead, Calif. 92352. *Agent:* Reece Halsey Agency, 8733 Sunset Blvd., Los Angeles, Calif. 90069.

*CAREER:* Herald Publishing Co., Los Angeles, Calif., newspaper reporter and editor, 1954-58; Bendix Corp. (aerospace), Los Angeles, Calif., proposal writer, 1958-60; Rocket Power, Inc., Mesa, Ariz., assistant to the president, 1960-63; National Broadcasting Co., Los Angeles, Calif., press relations officer and producer-writer, 1964-70. Founding member of advisory board, California Museum Foundation; member, Museum of the Sea Committee ("Queen Mary" conversion). *Military service:* U.S. Air Force, Strategic Air Command, 1950-53; became staff sergeant.

*MEMBER:* American Federation of Radio and Television Artists, Writers Guild of America, West. *Awards, honors:* "Tijuana Revolution: The New Brass" received a Hugo Award at Chicago International Film Festival, 1967; "The Slow Guillotine" received Emmy awards of National Academy of Television Arts and Sciences as the best single television program and the best documentary in public interest, 1969, and also the Alfred I. duPont—Columbia University Broadcast Journalism Award for investigative reporting, Silver Award at New York Film and TV Festival, and other awards, 1969; "Timetable for Disaster" won an Emmy Award as the best news documentary of 1970.

*WRITINGS: Timetable for Disaster,* Nash Publishing, 1970; *N.U.K.E.E.* (fiction), Hawthorn, 1974; *Lemmon: Biography of Jack Lemmon,* Macmillan, 1975.

Television documentaries, all produced by National Broadcasting Co., except as indicated: "Tijuana Revolution: The New Brass," 1967; "The Slow Guillotine," 1969; "Timetable for Disaster," 1970; "A Sea of Trouble," 1970; "Powers that Be," 1971; "Power and the People," Metromedia, 1972; "Who's There," Metromedia, 1972; "O Tahiti Teie" [French government], 1972; "That Certain Spirit," Texas A&M University, 1974; "Plutonium: Element of Risk," Public Broadcasting System, 1977.

*WORK IN PROGRESS:* Further research on environmental problems.

*SIDELIGHTS:* Don Widener did filming in Europe in 1970 and returned to Germany later as a guest of the West German Government to study pollution problems there. Four of his award-winning documentaries were narrated by Jack Lemmon.

Widener told *CA: "Plutonium: Element of Risk* for PBS may be my last television documentary. Documentaries on important issues (therefore controversial) are nearly impossible to get on TV. Enormous pressure is brought by corporate and government interests to block these. The networks largely ignore them as in interference with the primary goal: making a buck. Independent documentary producers are blocked from handling any important projects for the networks because of a house rule at CBS, NBC, ABC which limits such productions to staff newsmen. Therefore little is produced by the networks and independents are limited to PBS or to the narrow possibilities available through feature films. In depth exploration of important issues is now largely

the province of the print medium. It is one of the tragedies of the century, in my view, that the great power of television has been aimed largely at the hustling of oil companies and feminine deodorants. Programming exists mainly to fill the void between sales pitches—as innocuously as possible."

*BIOGRAPHICAL/CRITICAL SOURCES: Rocky Mountain News-Times,* September 13, 1970; *News Republic,* September 19, 1970.

*       *       *

## WIEBE, Rudy (H.)   1934-

*PERSONAL:* Born October 4, 1934, in Fairholme, Saskatchewan, Canada; son of Abram J. (a farmer) and Tena (Knelsen) Wiebe; married Tena F. Isaak, March 1958; children: Adrienne, Michael, Christopher. *Education:* University of Alberta, B.A., 1956, M.A., 1960; Mennonite Brethren Bible College, B.Th., 1961; additional study at University of Tuebingen, 1957-58, University of Manitoba, 1961, and University of Iowa, 1964. *Religion:* Mennonite. *Home:* 5315 143rd St., Edmonton, Alberta, Canada. *Office:* Department of English, University of Alberta, Edmonton, Alberta, Canada.

*CAREER:* Glenbow Foundation, Calgary, Alberta, research writer, 1956; Government of Canada, Ottawa, Ontario, foreign service officer, 1960; English teacher in high school in Selkirk, Manitoba, 1961; *Mennonite Brethren Herald,* Winnipeg, Manitoba, editor, 1962-63; Goshen College, Goshen, Ind., assistant professor of English, 1963-67; University of Alberta, Edmonton, assistant professor, 1967-70, associate professor, 1970-76, professor of English, 1976—. *Awards, honors:* Rotary International fellow, 1957-58; Canada council bursary, 1964, senior arts award, 1972; Governor General's Award for Fiction, 1973, for *The Temptations of Big Bear.*

*WRITINGS: Peace Shall Destroy Many* (novel), McClelland & Stewart, 1962, Eerdmans, 1964; *First and Vital Candle* (novel), Eerdmans, 1966; *The Blue Mountains of China* (novel), Eerdmans, 1970; (editor) *The Story Makers* (short stories), Macmillan of Canada, 1970; (editor) *Stories from Western Canada,* Macmillan of Canada, 1972; *The Temptations of Big Bear* (novel), McClelland & Stewart, 1973; *Where Is the Voice Coming From?* (stories), McClelland & Stewart, 1974; (editor) *Double Vision* (anthology), McClelland & Stewart, 1976; (editor) *Getting There* (anthology), Newest Press, 1977; *Riel and Gabriel* (novel), McClelland & Stewart, 1977; *The Scorched-Wood People* (novel), McClelland & Stewart, 1977; *Far as the Eye Can See* (play), Newest Press, 1977. Work is also represented in *Fourteen Stories High,* edited by David Helwig, Oberon Press, 1971, *The Narrative Voice,* edited by John Metcalf, McGraw, 1972, *Modern Stories in English,* edited by W. H. New and H. J. Rosengarten, Crowell, 1975, and *Personal Fictions,* edited by Michael Ondaatje, Oxford University Press, 1977. Contributor of stories to Canadian Broadcasting Corp. (CBC-TV), including "Someday Soon . . . ," televised January, 1977. Contributor of short stories to many publications, including *Fiddlehead, Tamarack Review, Canadian Literature, Maclean's, Saturday Night,* and *The Bote.*

*SIDELIGHTS:* Reviewing *The Temptations of Big Bear* in *Saturday Night,* Myrna Kostash observes, ". . . It is the People's point of view, their version of events and their commentary on the experience . . . which is the single most important accomplishment of the novel."

"Rudy Wiebe's first three novels were good, but *Big Bear*

represents a quantum jump beyond their achievement," writes Douglas Barbour in *Canadian Literature*. He continues, "Wiebe's achievement here is to convince us that the white man's view of things is strange and somehow wrong, and that the Indian's perception is the truer one.... This is an exciting and arresting narrative, gripping in its violence and passion.... I don't think we can ask much more of a novel than that it create for us a world which is so achingly real it becomes our world while we read."

*Canadian Literature* reviewer Donald Stephens was not as impressed with *The Temptations of Big Bear* as some of the other reviewers. He feels "that Wiebe is much better with the short story, as a form, than he is with the novel." Referring to *Where Is the Voice Coming From?*, he comments, "The writing is active, alive, unassuming, and infinitely touched with a growing and well-grounded lyricism.... [Wiebe depicts] the will to grow, to discover, and to build that really is the essence of survival."

Rudy Wiebe is quoted in *Canada Writes* as saying, '... In my fiction I try to explore the world that I know: the land and people of western Canada, from my particular world view: a radical Jesus-oriented Christianity.'

*AVOCATIONAL INTERESTS:* Photography, watching people, travel.

*BIOGRAPHICAL/CRITICAL SOURCES: Canadian Forum*, January, 1968, December 1977; Donald Cameron, *Conversations with Canadian Novelists*, Macmillan, 1973; *Saturday Night*, February, 1974; *Canadian Literature*, summer, 1974, winter, 1975; *Contemporary Literary Criticism*, Gale, Volume VI, 1976; Patricia Morley, *The Comedians, Hugh Hood and Rudy Wiebe*, Clarke, Irwin, 1976; John Moss, *Sex and Violence in the Canadian Novel*, McClelland & Stewart, 1977; Dick Harrison, *Unnamed Country*, University of Alberta Press, 1977.

*       *       *

## WIEBENSON, Dora (Louise)   1926-

*PERSONAL:* Born July 29, 1926, in Cleveland, Ohio; daughter of Edward Ralph (a contractor) and Jeannette (Rodier) Wiebenson. *Education:* Vassar College, A.B., 1946; Harvard University, B. of Arch., 1951; New York University, A.M., 1958, Ph.D., 1964. *Office:* School of Architecture, University of Virginia, Charlottesville, Va. 22901.

*CAREER:* Designer and draftsman in architectural offices in New York City, 1951-58; independent architectural consultant in New York City, 1958-66; Columbia University, New York City, lecturer in architecture, 1966-68; University of Maryland, College Park, associate professor, 1968-72, professor of architectural history, 1972-77; University of Virginia, Charlottesville, professor of architectural history and chairman of division, 1977—. *Member:* College Art Association, Society of Architectural Historians (director, 1974-77), Victorian Society in America, American Society for Eighteenth-Century Studies. *Awards, honors:* American Association of University Women fellowship, 1963-64; American Philosophical Society grants, 1964-65, 1969-70; Samuel H. Kress Foundation grant, 1966, combined grant with National Endowment for the Humanities, 1972-73; American Council of Learned Societies grant, 1976.

*WRITINGS:* (Editor) *Marsyas XI: 1962-1964*, New York University, 1965; *Essays in Honor of Walter Friedlaender*, New York University, 1965; *Sources of Greek Revival Architecture*, Zwemmer, 1969; *Tony Garnier: The Cite Industrielle*, Braziller, 1969; *The Picturesque Garden in France*,

Princeton University Press, 1978. Contributor to art and architecture journals.

*WORK IN PROGRESS:* Research on architectural history education in schools of architecture.

*SIDELIGHTS:* Dora Wiebenson has traveled extensively in Europe, concentrating her architectural research in London and Paris.

*       *       *

## WIECEK, William Michael   1938-

*PERSONAL:* Born January 31, 1938, in Cleveland, Ohio; son of Michael Frank (a dentist) and Mary (Kotecki) Wiecek; married Maryann Pickarski (a graduate student), June 17, 1961; children: Michael, Sophie, Kristen. *Education:* Catholic University of America, B.A., 1959; Harvard University, LL.B., 1962; University of Wisconsin, Ph.D., 1968. *Politics:* Democrat (independent). *Religion:* Roman Catholic. *Home:* 1949 Jackson, Columbia, Mo. 65201. *Office:* Department of History, University of Missouri, Columbia, Mo. 65201.

*CAREER:* Snierson & Chandler (law firm), Laconia, N.H., associate, 1962-64; University of Missouri—Columbia, assistant professor, 1968-71, associate professor, 1971-77, professor of history, 1977—. *Military service:* U.S. Naval Reserve, 1966-68. *Member:* American Society for Legal History, Organization of American Historians, Phi Beta Kappa. *Awards, honors:* Summer fellowships from Newberry Library, 1970, National Endowment for the Humanities, 1971, and John Carter Brown Library, 1971.

*WRITINGS: The Guarantee Clause of the U.S. Constitution*, Cornell University Press, 1972; *The Sources of Antislavery Constitutionalism in America, 1760-1848*, Cornell University Press, 1977. Contributor to *Journal of Southern History, American Journal of Legal History, American Jewish Historical Quarterly*, and *American West*.

*WORK IN PROGRESS: Pillar of Fire: Antislavery in America*.

*       *       *

## WIECZYNSKI, Joseph L.   1934-

*PERSONAL:* Born April 13, 1934, in Baltimore, Md.; son of Joseph John and Margaret (Baranowski) Wieczynski; married Muriel Josephine Englert, May 19, 1962; children: Geoffrey, Daniel, Mary Faith. *Education:* St. Mary's Seminary and University, Baltimore, Md., B.A., 1956; additional study, University of Louvain, 1956-57, and U.S. Army Language School, 1957-58; Georgetown University, Ph.D., 1966. *Religion:* Roman Catholic. *Home:* 803 Preston Ave., Blacksburg, Va. 24060. *Office:* Department of History, Virginia Polytechnic Institute, Blacksburg, Va. 24061.

*CAREER:* U.S. National Security Agency, Washington, D.C., research analyst for Soviet affairs and section chief, 1960-62; Library of Congress, Washington, D.C., Soviet specialist and analyst in arms control and disarmament section, 1965-66; Edgewood College, Madison, Wis., assistant professor of history, 1966-68; Virginia Polytechnic Institute, Blacksburg, assistant professor, 1968-70, associate professor, 1970-74, professor of history, 1974—. Visiting professor, Oxford University 1976-77. Director and chief announcer of "Opera Theater," WUVT-Radio, 1972-74. Participant at various Slavic studies conferences. Editorial consultant, Academic International Press. *Military service:* U.S. Army, 1957-60. *Member:* American Historical Association, American Association for the Advancement of

Slavic Studies (member of executive committee, Virginia chapter, 1970—), American Catholic Historical Association, Southern Conference on Slavic Studies. *Awards, honors:* American Philosophical Society grants, for research on the history of medieval Novgorod, 1969, and for research on the history of the Russian Church, 1970, for research on the history of Russia, 1971 and 1973; Virginia Polytechnic Institute travel and research grants, 1972, 1972, 1974, 1975, and 1976.

*WRITINGS:* (Translator and editor) S. F. Platonov, *Moscow and the West,* Academic International, 1972; (translator and editor) Platonov, *Ivan the Terrible,* Academic International, 1973; (editor and translator) Paul Miliukov, *Outlines of Russian Culture: The Origins of Ideology,* Academic International, 1974; (editor and translator) Miliukov, *Outlines of Russian Culture: Ideologies in Conflict,* Academic International, 1975; *The Russian Frontier: The Impact of Borderlands upon the Course of Early Russian History,* University Press of Virginia, 1976; (editor) *The Modern Encyclopedia of Russian Soviet History,* Academic International, Volume I, 1976, Volume II, 1976, Volume III, 1977, Volume IV, 1977, Volume V, 1977. Contributor to *Richmond Times Dispatch* and to academic journals.

*WORK IN PROGRESS:* Translating and editing major prose works of A. S. Khomiakov, founder of the Slavophile school; researching the history of the Russian Church.

\* \* \*

### WIENER, Daniel N(orman)   1921-

*PERSONAL:* Born February 6, 1921, in Duluth, Minn.; son of Joseph B. (an educator) and Fannie (Winer) Wiener; married Phyllis Zaeger (an artist); children: Jonathan M., Paul H., Sara R. (Mrs. Gerald Pearson). *Education:* University of Minnesota, B.A., 1941, M.A., 1942, Ph.D., 1950. *Home:* 1920 South First St., Apt. 1804, Minneapolis, Minn. 55454. *Office:* Department of Psychology, University of Minnesota, Minneapolis, Minn.

*CAREER:* University of Minnesota, Minneapolis, assistant to dean of students, 1941-42; State of Connecticut, Department of Mental Health, clinical psychologist, 1943-44; Veteran's Administration Rehabilitation Program, Minneapolis, Minn., chief of counseling section, 1944-51; Veterans Administration Mental Hygiene Clinic, St. Paul, Minn., chief psychologist, 1951-76; University of Minnesota, assistant professor, 1952-59, clinical professor of psychology, 1959—. Diplomate and member, Board of Examiners in Professional Psychology. Chairman, Board of Examiners of Psychologists, State of Minnesota; chairman of board of review, Anoka State Hospital; member of board of directors, Jewish Family and Children's Service; president of board of directors, Guild of Performing Arts (Minneapolis). *Military service:* U.S. Army Air Forces, psychologist, 1942-43. *Member:* American Psychological Association (fellow), Minnesota Psychological Association (member of executive council).

*WRITINGS:* (With E. L. Phillips) *Discipline, Achievement and Mental Health,* Prentice-Hall, 1960, 2nd edition, 1972; (with D. R. Stieper) *Dimensions of Psychotherapy,* Aldine, 1965; (with Phillips) *Short-term Psychotherapy and Structured Behavioral Change,* McGraw, 1966; *Practical Guide to Psychotherapy,* Harper, 1969; (with Phillips) *Training Children in Self-Discipline and Self-Control,* Prentice-Hall, 1972; *Classroom Management and Discipline,* F. E. Peacock, 1972; *A Consumer's Guide to Psychotherapy,* Hawthorn, 1976.

### WIENER, Joel H.   1937-

*PERSONAL:* Born August 23, 1937, in New York, N.Y.; son of Philip Wiener; married Suzanne Wolff (a reading teacher), September 4, 1961; children: Paul, Deborah, Jane. *Education:* New York University, B.A., 1959; University of Glasgow, further study, 1961-63; Cornell University, Ph.D., 1965. *Home:* 267 Glen Court, Teaneck, N.J. 07666. *Office:* Department of History, City College of the City University of New York, Convent Ave. and 133rd St., New York, N.Y. 10031.

*CAREER:* Skidmore College, Saratoga Springs, N.Y., assistant professor of history, 1964-66; City College of the City University of New York, New York, N.Y., associate professor of history, 1966—. Visiting lecturer, University of York, 1971-73. *Member:* Royal History Society (fellow), Research Society for Victorian Periodicals, American Historical Association.

*WRITINGS: The War of the Unstamped,* Cornell University Press, 1969; *A Descriptive Finding List of Unstamped British Periodicals: 1830-1836,* Oxford University Press, 1970; (editor) *Great Britain: Foreign Policy and the Span of Empire, 1689-1970,* four volumes, McGraw, 1972; *Great Britain: The Lion at Home,* four volumes, Bowker, 1974.

*WORK IN PROGRESS:* A biography of Richard Carlile; editing a multivolumed dictionary of Victorian journalists.

*AVOCATIONAL INTERESTS:* Films, theater, dance, British art and architecture.

\* \* \*

### WIGGINS, James B(ryan)   1935-

*PERSONAL:* Born August 24, 1935, in Mexia, Tex.; son of James Benjamin (an oil operator) and Parley (Lain) Wiggins; married Kay Moeckly (an assistant professor of nursing), August 15, 1956; children: Bryan Gregory, Karis Kay. *Education:* Texas Wesleyan College, B.A., 1957; Southern Methodist University, B.D., 1959; Drew University, Ph.D., 1963; post-doctoral study in Tuebingen, Germany, 1968-69. *Politics:* Democrat-Independent. *Home:* 953 Westmoreland Ave., Syracuse, N.Y. 13210. *Office:* Department of Religion, Syracuse University, 310 H.B.C., Syracuse, N.Y. 13210.

*CAREER:* Union Junior College, Cranford, N.J., part-time instructor in English, 1960-63; Syracuse University, Syracuse, N.Y., assistant professor, 1963-69, associate professor, 1969-75, professor of religion, 1975—, director of graduate studies in religion, 1975—. *Member:* American Academy of Religion, American Society of Church History, American Association of University Professors, Society for Values in Higher Education. *Awards, honors:* Postdoctoral fellow, Society for Values in Higher Education, 1969.

*WRITINGS: The Embattled Saint: Aspects of the Life and Work of John Fletcher,* Wesleyan College, 1966; (with others) *Christian Word Book,* Abingdon, 1968; (with J. Bruce Burke) *Foundations of Christianity,* Ronald, 1970; *Religion as Story,* Harper, 1975. Contributor to religious journals.

*WORK IN PROGRESS: History as Story.*

*BIOGRAPHICAL/CRITICAL SOURCES: Christian Century,* May 6, 1970.

\* \* \*

### WIKE, Edward L.   1922-

*PERSONAL:* Born February 19, 1922, in Ravenna, Ohio;

son of Harry M. and Irene (Canning) Wike; married Joyce M. Lennon, August 13, 1948; married second wife, Sharron S. Knowles, December 13, 1959; children: (first marriage) Erik; (second marriage) Cynthia, Robert. *Education:* Santa Monica City College, A.A., 1942; University of California, Los Angeles, B.A., 1947, M.A., 1949, Ph.D., 1952. *Home:* 927 Pamela Lane, Lawrence, Kan. 66044. *Office:* Department of Psychology, University of Kansas, Lawrence, Kan. 66044.

*CAREER:* University of Kansas, Lawrence, assistant professor, 1952-57, associate professor, 1957-62, professor of psychology, 1962—, director of experimental psychology training program, 1968-72. Visiting associate professor, University of California, Los Angeles, summer, 1958. *Military service:* U.S. Army Air Forces, 1943-46; became first lieutenant. *Member:* American Psychological Association (fellow), Psychonomic Society, Sigma Xi.

*WRITINGS: Secondary Reinforcement: Selected Experiments,* Harper, 1966; (contributor) W. J. Arnold and D. Levine, editors, *1969 Nebraska Symposium on Motivation,* University of Nebraska Press, 1970; *Data Analysis: A Statistical Primer for Psychology Students,* Aldine-Atherton, 1971.

*WORK IN PROGRESS:* Research on statistical methodology.

*AVOCATIONAL INTERESTS:* Collecting and listening to dixieland jazz.

\*      \*      \*

### WILBUR, James B(enjamin) III   1924-

*PERSONAL:* Born February 21, 1924, in Hartford, Conn.; son of James B. (an industrialist) and Martha (Shekosky) Wilbur; married Margie Ann Mattmiller (an educator), July 9, 1949; children: James B. IV, Ann Elizabeth. *Education:* University of Kentucky, A.B., 1948; Harvard University, additional study, 1948-49; Columbia University, M.A., 1951, Ph.D., 1954. *Home:* 22 West View Crescent, Geneseo, N.Y. 14454. *Office:* Department of Philosophy, State University of New York College, Geneseo, N.Y. 14454.

*CAREER:* Adelphi University, Long Island, N.Y., assistant professor, 1954-59, associate professor of philosophy, 1959-64, head of department, 1954-64; University of Akron, Akron, Ohio, professor of philosophy, 1964-68, head of department, 1964-68; State University of New York College at Geneseo, professor of philosophy, 1968—, head of department, 1968—. Visiting professor at University of Kent, Canterbury, England, 1971. Member of board of advisors, Empire State College of the State University of New York, Saratoga Springs, N.Y., 1971-75. Founder and director of Conferences on Value Inquiry, 1967—. *Military service:* U.S. Army, 1942-45. *Member:* American Philosophical Association, American Association of University Professors, American Society of Value-Inquiry (secretary-treasurer, 1970-72; president, 1973), Long Island Philosophy Society (founder, 1964), Creighton Club (president, 1970-72), Rochester Oratorio Society.

*WRITINGS:* (With Harold Allen) *The Worlds of Plato and Aristotle,* American Book Co., 1962; (with Allen) *The Worlds of Hume and Kant,* American Book Co., 1965; (editor and contributor with B. Magnus) *Cartesian Essays,* Martinus Nijhoff, 1969; (editor with Erwin Laszlo) *Value in Philosophy and Social Science,* Gordon & Breach, 1970; (editor with Laszlo) *Human Values and Natural Science,* Gordon & Breach, 1970; (editor with Laszlo) *Human Values*

*and the Mind of Man,* Gordon & Breach, 1971; (editor and contributor) *Spinoza's Metaphysics,* Van Gorcum, 1976. Executive editor of *The Journal of Value Inquiry,* Nijhoff, 1967—.

*WORK IN PROGRESS:* Studies in Kant's ethics; *The Foundations of Corporate Responsibility.*

*AVOCATIONAL INTERESTS:* Golf.

\*      \*      \*

### WILCOX, Dennis L.   1941-

*PERSONAL:* Born March 31, 1941, in Rapid City, S.D.; son of Herbert Dennis (a banker) and Star (Polhemus) Wilcox; married Marianne Milstead (a dietitian), May 24, 1969. *Education:* University of Denver, B.A., 1963; University of Iowa, M.A., 1966; University of Missouri, Ph.D., 1974. *Politics:* Liberal Republican. *Religion:* Episcopalian. *Home:* 1740 Marina Way, San Jose, Calif. 95125. *Office:* Department of Journalism, San Jose State University, San Jose, Calif. 95114.

*CAREER: Grand Junction Daily Sentinel,* Grand Junction, Colo., reporter, 1963-64; Ohio State University, Columbus, editor of university publications, 1965-67; Ketchum, Inc. (fund development counsel), Pittsburgh, Pa., public relations associate, 1968-71; Chapman College, World Campus Afloat, Orange, Calif., public information officer and instructor, 1971-74; San Jose State University, San Jose, Calif., associate professor of journalism and public relations, 1974—. Visiting associate professor of journalism, University of Colorado, 1978. *Member:* Sigma Delta Chi, Sierra Club.

*WRITINGS: English Language Dailies Abroad,* Gale, 1967; *Mass Media in Black Africa: Philosophy and Control,* Praeger, 1975. Contributor of various articles on the African press and public relations education to periodicals.

*WORK IN PROGRESS:* Continuing research on mass media in Africa.

\*      \*      \*

### WILCOX, Francis (Orlando)   1908-

*PERSONAL:* Born April 9, 1908, in Columbus Junction, Iowa; son of Francis Oliver (a pharmacist) and Verna (Gray) Wilcox; married Genevieve Byrnes, July 23, 1933 (died, 1946); married Virginia Summerlin, August 8, 1968; children: (first marriage) Carol Lenore (Mrs. John P. Millard); (second marriage) Francis Oliver. *Education:* University of Iowa, B.A., 1930, M.A., 1931, Ph.D., 1933; University of Geneva, Doctor es Sciences Politiques, 1935; Hague Academy of International Law, additional study, 1937; also studied at University of Chicago and University of Michigan. *Home:* 2811 McGill Ter. N.W., Washington, D.C. 20008. *Office:* Atlantic Council of the United States, 1616 H St. N.W., Washington, D.C. 20006.

*CAREER:* University of Louisville, Louisville, Ky., assistant professor, 1935-37, associate professor of political science, 1937-39, chairman, Division of Social Sciences, 1939-42; United States Government, Washington, D.C., associate chief, Division of Inter-American Activities in the United States, Office of the Coordinator of Inter-American Affairs, 1942, program services section chief, Office of Civilian Defense, 1943, international organization analyst, Bureau of the Budget, 1943-44, head international relations analyst, Library of Congress, 1945-47; U.S. Senate Foreign Relations Committee, Washington, D.C., chief of staff, 1947-55; U.S. Assistant Secretary of State, 1955-61; Johns

Hopkins University, School of Advanced International Studies, Washington, D.C., dean and professor of political science, 1961-73; executive director, Commission on the Organization of the Government for the Conduct of Foreign Policy, 1973-75; Atlantic Council of the United States, Washington, D.C., director general, 1975—. Member of U.S. Delegation to United Nations Conference in San Francisco, Calif., 1945, to first U.N. General Assembly, London, England, 1946, and to subsequent U.N. General Assemblies in New York, N.Y.; member of President Nixon's Commission on the U.N., 1970-71. Delegate to various international conferences. Visiting professor, University of Michigan, 1941-42; lecturer on American foreign policy and international organization, George Washington University, 1945-46, and School of Advanced International Studies, Johns Hopkins University, 1946-51. Member of board of directors, Metropolitan Memorial Methodist Church, 1950—, United Givers Fund, 1957-63, and Dreyfus Corporation; consultant, Atomic Energy Commission, U.S. Department of State. *Military service:* U.S. Army Reserve, 1930-35, became second lieutenant; U.S. Navy, 1944-45, became lieutenant junior grade.

*MEMBER:* American Society of International Law (executive council, 1946-49, 1951-54, 1961-64), American Political Science Association (president, Washington branch, 1946-47; executive council, 1948-50; vice-president, 1957-58), American Academy of Political and Social Science, Foreign Policy Association (board of directors), Council on Foreign Relations, Phi Beta Kappa, Omicron Delta Kappa, Phi Kappa Phi, Sigma Chi, Chevy Chase Club, Metropolitan Club. *Awards, honors:* Carnegie Endowment for International Peace fellowship, 1933-34; Institute of International Studies, Geneva, fellowship, 1934-35; LL.D., University of Louisville, 1960, Hamline University, 1960, Dakota Wesleyan University, 1961; D.Litt., Simpson College, 1964; Knight-Commander in the Order of Merit, Republic of Italy, 1965.

*WRITINGS: Some Aspects of the Financial Administration of Johnson County, Iowa,* Iowa State Historical Society, 1934; *The Ratification of International Conventions: A Study of the Relationship of the Ratification Process to the Development of International Legislation,* Allen & Unwin, 1935, Macmillan, 1936; (with Carl Milton Marcy) *Congress and the United Nations,* Foreign Policy Association, 1951; (editor with Thorsten V. Kalijarvi) *Recent American Foreign Policy: Basic Documents, 1941-51,* Appleton, 1952; (with Marcy) *Proposals for Changes in the United Nations,* Brookings Institution, 1955; (editor with H. Field Haviland, Jr.) *The United States and the United Nations,* Johns Hopkins Press, 1961; *The United Nations and the Nonaligned Nations,* Foreign Policy Association, 1962; (editor with Haviland) *The Atlantic Community: Progress and Prospects,* Praeger, 1963; *Congress: The Executive and Foreign Policy,* Harper, 1971; (editor) *China and the Great Powers,* Praeger, 1974; (editor with Richard A. Frank) *The Constitution and the Conduct of Foreign Policy,* Praeger, 1976.

Contributor: Blair Bolles, *The Armed Road to Peace: An Analysis of NATO,* Foreign Policy Association, 1952; (author of introduction) J. William Fulbright, *The Arrogance of Power,* Random House, 1967; (author of introduction) Barbara Ward, *The Lopsided World,* Norton, 1968; (author of introduction) Gunnar Myrdal, *The Challenge of World Poverty: A World Poverty Program in Outline,* Pantheon, 1970. Also author of approximately twenty booklets on the United Nations, American foreign policy, and world population and peace, for the U.S. Department of State and U.S. Congress.

Contributor of articles to *American Journal of International Law, Current History, American Political Science Review, Annals of the American Academy of Political and Social Science, Journal of High Education,* and other journals. Member of board of editors, *American Political Science Review,* 1952-56.

*SIDELIGHTS:* Francis Wilcox told *CA* he was prompted to write his book, *Congress: The Executive and Foreign Policy,* as a result of his long service on Capitol Hill and as Assistant Secretary of State.

\*     \*     \*

## WILCOX, Virginia Lee   1911-

*PERSONAL:* Born November 28, 1911, in Portsmouth, Ohio; daughter of Ira Lloyd (a businessman) and Sallye (Foley) Wilcox; married Paul G. Herold (a professor at the Colorado School of Mines), May 13, 1972. *Education:* Attended Averett College, 1930-31, 1933-34; University of Denver, A.B. and certificate in library science, 1937, M.A., 1953. *Politics:* Republican. *Religion:* Presbyterian. *Home:* 1780 Stringer Gap Rd., Grants Pass, Ore. 97526. *Office:* Colorado School of Mines Library, Golden, Colo. 80401.

*CAREER:* Colorado Fuel and Iron Corp., Pueblo, Colo., librarian, 1937-40; Colorado School of Mines, Golden, assistant librarian, 1940-42, 1946-55, head librarian, 1956-77, librarian emerita, 1977—. *Military service:* U.S. Army, librarian at U.S. Air Force base library, LaJunta, Colo., 1943-45, librarian at base library, Rheims, France, 1945, area librarian, 1945-46. *Member:* Special Libraries Association (president, Colorado chapter, 1956-57; chairman, petroleum division, 1965-66), American Society for Engineering Education (secretary of engineering school libraries division, 1969-71; chairman, 1971-72), Council of Librarians, State Institutions of Higher Education in Colorado (chairman, 1964-66), Colorado Library Association, Bibliographical Center for Research, Rocky Mountain Region (executive council chairman, 1959-60), Mountain-Plains Library Association, Colorado State Historical Society, The Westerners, Altrusa, PEO.

*WRITINGS: Colorado: A Selected Bibliography of Its Literature, 1858-1952,* Sage Books, 1954; (author of subject index) *Westerners Brand Books,* The Westerners, 1954; (author of comprehensive index) *Westerners Brand Books, 1944-61,* The Westerners, 1962; *Guide to Literature on Metals and Metallurgical Engineering,* American Society for Engineering Education, 1970; *Guide to Literature on Mining and Mineral Resources Engineering,* American Society for Engineering Education, 1972. Contributor to *Encyclopedia of Library and Information Science,* Dekker.

*AVOCATIONAL INTERESTS:* Travel, conservation, especially wildlife.

\*     \*     \*

## WILD, John D(aniel)   1902-1972

April 10, 1902—October 23, 1972; American educator and author of books on philosophy. Obituaries: *New York Times,* October 25, 1972.

\*     \*     \*

## WILD, Peter   1940-

*PERSONAL:* Born April 25, 1940, in Northampton, Mass.; son of Arnold Arthur and Edith (Meshivkovsky) Wild; married Silvia Cervantes Ortiz, December 17, 1967. *Education:* University of Arizona, B.A., 1962, M.A., 1967; University of California, Irvine, M.F.A., 1969. *Home:* 1405 East Lester, Tucson, Ariz. 85719. *Office:* Department of English, University of Arizona, Tucson, Ariz.

*CAREER:* University of Arizona, Tucson, associate professor of English, member of creative writing faculty, 1971—. *Member:* Sierra Club.

*WRITINGS*—Poems: *The Good Fox* (chapbook), Goodly Co., 1967; *Sonnets* (chapbook), Cranium Press, 1968; *Mica Mountain Poems* (chapbook), Lillabulero Press, 1968; *The Afternoon in Dismay*, Art Association of Cincinnati, 1968; *Fat Man Poems*, Hellric, 1970; *Terms and Renewals*, Two Windows Press, 1970; *Wild's Magical Book of Cranial Effusions*, New Rivers Press, 1971; *Grace*, Stone Press, 1971; *Peligros*, Ithaca House, 1972; *New and Selected Poems*, New Rivers Press, 1973; *Cochise*, Doubleday, 1973; *The Cloning*, Doubleday, 1974; *Chihuahua*, Doubleday, 1976; *Wilderness*, New Rivers Press, in press. Contributor of poetry to *Chicago Riveiw* and other literary periodicals.

*WORK IN PROGRESS: Pioneer Conservationists of Western America*, for Colorado Associated University Press.

* * *

## WILDEN, Anthony 1935-

*PERSONAL:* Born December 14, 1935, in London, England; son of Frank Clover (a watchmaker) and Lilian (Ballard) Wilden; married Patricia Rosalie Anderson, 1956 (divorced, 1971); children: Mark Andrew, Christopher Paul. *Education:* Attended University of Victoria, Victoria, British Columbia, 1960-61, 1963-65; Johns Hopkins University, Ph.D., 1968. *Home:* 4372 Oxford St., Burnaby, British Columbia, Canada V5C 1E4. *Office:* Department of Communication, Simon Fraser University, Burnaby, British Columbia, Canada V5A 1S6.

*CAREER:* Farmworker, factory worker, timber cruiser, stock-car driver, free-lance photographer, autoelectric mechanic, used-car salesman, and correspondence school instructor, 1952-61; teacher of classics and French, Shawnigan Lake School, British Columbia, 1962-65; Johns Hopkins University, Baltimore, Md., teaching assistant, 1965-67; University of California at San Diego, assistant professor of literature, 1968-74 (on leave, 1971-74); visiting professor at Faculty de Droit et des Sciences Economiques, Universite du Benin, Lome, Togo, 1971, and Center for the Study of Mass Communication, Ecole Pratique des Hautes Etudes, Sorbonne, University of Paris, 1971-72; Michigan State University, National Science Foundation Ecosystems Project, East Lansing, research associate in department of electrical engineering and systems science, 1973-74; Simon Fraser University, Burnaby, British Columbia, professor of communication, 1974—. Visiting professor at Fairhaven College, 1976, and University of British Columbia, 1977. Has lectured and done consultant work in a number of fields, including film theory, structuralism, cybernetics, psychiatry, anthropoligical theory, water control projects, urban ecosystems, resource conservation, and communications and social relations. *Member:* Society for General Systems Research.

*WRITINGS:* (With Jacques Lacan) *The Language of the Self,* Johns Hopkins University Press, 1968, revised edition, 1976; *System and Structure: Essays in Communication and Exchange,* Tavistock Publications, 1972, 2nd edition, 1978; (contributor) *The Legacy of the German Refugee Intellectuals,* Schocken, 1972; (contributor) D. E. Washburn and D. R. Smith, editors, *Coping with Increasing Complexity,* Gordon & Breach, 1974; (contributor) K. Riegel, editor, *Structure and Transformation,* Wiley, 1975; (contributor with Tim Wilson) Carlos Sluzki and Donald Ransom, editors, *Double Bind: The Foundation of the Communicational Approach to the Family,* Grune & Stratton, 1976; (contributor) M. Maruyama and A. Harkins, editors, *Cultures of the Future,* Mouton, in press; (contributor) K. Krippendorff, editor, *Communication and Control in Society,* Gordon & Breach, in press. Contributor of articles to other books and to *Enciclopedia Einaudi.* Contributor to *Semiotica, Modern Language Notes, Contemporary Psychoanalysis, Communications, Psychology Today,* and other periodicals.

*WORK IN PROGRESS: Lacan et le discours de l'Autre;* a collection of essays on the ecology of communication and context; a book on information and communication, tentatively entitled *Language, Communication, and Reality;* continuing research into the nature and history of socioeconomic development and revolution, with emphasis on the contributions of Marx and Engels to ecosystemic and economic theory; writing on Marx, Freud, and the modern world ecosystem.

*SIDELIGHTS:* Anthony Wilden's *System and Structure* approaches communicational theory and practice from a metadisciplinary perspective. The book employs and criticizes concepts drawn from such diverse fields as psychoanalysis, exchange theory, psychology, philosophy, linguistics, cybernetics, biology, anthropology, systems ecology, and semiotics. Wilden is especially critical of social and scientific discourse which are ethnocentric, logocentric, and phallocentric, which he considers symptoms of pathological communication.

Bob Scholte calls *System and Structure* "exceptional in scope, importance, and degree of complexity.... The integrative theme of Wilden's wide-ranging argument is the problem of knowledge—specifically, the genesis, structure, function, and critique of scientific discourse." Carlos Sluzki and Donald Ransom believe the book provides "a contribution to our 'knowledge about knowledge' at an abstract level, as well as supplying ammunition in the struggle with the concrete reality that information is power and the scientific discourse is a hidden weapon in the arsenal of social control." According to Gary Lee Stonum, *System and Structure* is "the first full-scale attempt to join the methods and assumptions of the Parisian *sciences humaines* with those of cybernetics and general systems theory. Wilden's subject is an immensely ambitious one, human communication in and between systems—social systems, person, psychic systems, and also texts and systems of discourse."

Wilden's writing has been translated into French, Spanish, Danish, and Italian.

*AVOCATIONAL INTERESTS:* Change; flying (Wilden has a private pilot's license).

*BIOGRAPHICAL/CRITICAL SOURCES: New Society,* October, 1972; *Times Literary Supplement,* December 8, 1972; *Erasmus,* April, 1973; *Psychology Today,* June, 1973; *Prisma,* September, 1973; *Journal of Industrial Relations,* March, 1974; *Educational Resources Information Center,* June, 1974; *Contemporary Psychology,* July, 1974; *Co-Evolution Quarterly,* summer, 1974; *Diacritics,* fall, 1974; *Australian Journal of Psychology,* December 1974; *Telos,* winter, 1974-75; Carlos Sluzki and Donald Ransom, editors, *Double Bind: The Foundation of the Communicational Approach to the Family,* Grune & Stratton, 1976; *American Anthropologist,* March, 1976; *American Political Science Review,* September, 1976; *Modern Language Notes,* October, 1976.

## WILDMAN, John Hazard 1911-

PERSONAL: Born January 22, 1911, in Mobile, Ala.; son of Alexander James (a banker) and Rachel (Whitaker) Wildman. Education: Brown University, Ph.B., 1933, M.A., 1934, Ph.D., 1937. Politics: Democrat. Religion: Roman Catholic. Home: 1809 Spring Hill Ave., Mobile, Ala. 36607. Office: Department of English, Louisiana State University, Baton Rouge, La. 70803.

CAREER: Brown University, Providence, R.I., instructor in English, 1937-40; Louisiana State University, Baton Rouge, instructor, 1940-46, assistant professor, 1946-51, associate professor, 1951-58, professor of English, 1958—. Military service: U.S. Army Air Forces, 1942-45. Member: Modern Language Association of America, American Association of University Professors, South Central Modern Language Association, Louisiana Folklore Society, Phi Beta Kappa.

WRITINGS: Anthony Trollope's England, Brown University Press, 1940; Peter Marvell, Humphries, 1952; Fever, Exposition, 1953; Sing No Sad Songs, Exposition Press, 1955; Sun on the Night, Sheed, 1962; (contributor) Sharon Osborne Brown, editor, Two Centuries of Brown Verse, 1764-1964, Brown University Press, 1965; Forgotten Land: Another Look, Dorrance, 1966; Old Louisville, Urban Renewal and Community Development Agency of Louisville, 1967. Contributor to short story and poetry anthologies, and to Collier's Encyclopedia. Contributor of short stories, poems, and articles and reviews to New York Times, Catholic World, Commonweal, Sewanee Review, South Atlantic Quarterly, Southern Review, Georgia Review, Studies in the Literary Imagination, and other publications.

WORK IN PROGRESS: Several novels.

SIDELIGHTS: John Hazard Wildman told CA: "My writing is not so much the response to a compulsion as it is the fulfillment of an opportunity. Involvement in a university for five days of the week with books, ideas, and people leaves my mind and imagination with an embarrassment of unassorted riches. In the calm of a weekend office, I can discover a way in which, not to summarize the past week or to fictionalize my friends, but rather to bring out into consciousness something rare, not at all I emphasize, an account of the preceding week, but something other, mysteriously triggered by it. The undisturbed weekend is also an opportunity for giving this thing form—during recent times, novels. Teaching and writing complement each other."

* * *

## WILEY, Raymond A(loysius) 1923-

PERSONAL: Born October 30, 1923, in New York, N.Y.; son of Samuel Romaine (a lawyer) and Mary A. (Brown) Wiley; married Elizabeth M. Schneider, September 4, 1948; children: Anne, Joseph, Maureen, Edward, Madeline, Jeanne, John, Therese. Education: Fordham University, A.B. (magna cum laude), 1946, M.A., 1948; Goethe Institut, Munich, Germany, German certificate, 1956; Syracuse University, Ph.D., 1966. Home: 101 North Highland Ave., East Syracuse, N.Y. 13057. Office: Department of German, Le Moyne College, Le Moyne Heights, Syracuse, N.Y. 13214.

CAREER: Boston College, Chestnut Hill, Mass., instructor in English and German, 1947-48; Le Moyne College, Syracuse, N.Y., instructor, 1948-51, assistant professor, 1953-66, associate professor of English and German, 1966-71, professor of German, 1971—, acting chairman of classics,

1976—. Public information officer, Onondaga County Office of Civil Defense, 1951-52; editorial counsel, New York State Commission of Civil Defense, 1951; public relations director and executive secretary of Onondaga County Chapter, Association for Retarded Children, 1953-55; volunteer teacher of religious education, East Syracuse, N.Y., 1966—. Wartime service: U.S. Air Force, civilian education officer, 1952-53. Member: American Association of Teachers of German (central New York chapter, secretary, 1956-59; vice-president, 1965-67; president, 1967-69; member of executive board, 1969-72), New York State Association of Foreign Language Teachers. Awards, honors: Fulbright summer study grant to Germany, 1956; Encaenia award of Fordham University, 1956.

WRITINGS: John Mitchell Kemble and Jakob Grimm, A Correspondence: 1832-1852, Brill, 1971. Editor, Austausch, 1970-74. Contributor of articles to German Quarterly, Journal of English and Germanic Philology, German American Studies, and Pennsylvania Gazette.

WORK IN PROGRESS: Further work on Jakob Grimm; a biography of J. M. Kemble.

* * *

## WILGUS, D. K. 1918-

PERSONAL: Born December 1, 1918, in West Mansfield, Ohio; son of Robert Nathaniel and Cora (Knight) Wilgus; married Evelyn Hastings (a researcher), November 23, 1940; children: Karen Wilgus Abbott, Liscinda (Mrs. Willard Fox III). Education: Ohio State University, B.A. and B.Sc., 1941, M.A., 1947, Ph.D., 1954. Home: 1064 Stanford St., Santa Monica, Calif. 90403. Office: Center for the Study of Comparative Folklore and Mythology, University of California, Los Angeles, Calif. 90024.

CAREER: Purdue University, Lafayette, Ind., director of education, 1941-42; Ohio State University, Columbus, instructor in English, 1946-50; Western Kentucky State College (now Western Kentucky University), Bowling Green, associate professor, 1950-60, professor of English and folklore, 1960-62; University of California, Los Angeles, associate professor, 1962-66, professor of English and Anglo-American folksong, 1966—, head of folksong program, Center for the Study of Comparative Folklore and Mythology, 1962—, chairman, folklore and mythology program, 1965—. Military service: U.S. Army, 1942-45; became sergeant. Member: American Folklore Society (fellow; president, 1971-72), Modern Language Association of America, Folklore Society (England), Folklife Society (England), Folksong Society of Ireland, Northeast Folkore Society, California Folklore Society, Kentucky Folklore Society (president, 1962-63; director, 1963—), North Carolina Folklore Society, Indiana Folklore Society, Oregon Folklore Society. Awards, honors: Chicago Folklore Prize, 1956; Guggenheim fellow, 1957-58.

WRITINGS: Anglo-American Folksong Scholarship since 1898, Rutgers University Press, 1959; (editor with Carol Sommer) Folklore International: Essays in Traditional Literature, Belief, and Custom in Honor of Wayland Debs Hand, Folklore Associates, 1967; (editor) Josiah Henry Combs, Folk-Songs of the Southern United States, University of Texas, 1967. Contributor of articles to music and folklore journals and to Archivist. Editor, Kentucky Folklore Record, 1955-61, and Western Folklore, 1970-75.

WORK IN PROGRESS: Catalogue of Irish Narrative Folksongs in English, completion expected in 1978; Ballads on the Sinking of the Titanic, 1979; The Blues Ballad, 1980; Type-Index of Anglo-American Traditional Narrative Song.

## WILHELM, Kate   1928-

*PERSONAL:* Born June 8, 1928, in Toledo, Ohio; daughter of Jesse Thomas and Ann (McDowell) Meredith; married Joseph B. Wilhelm, May 24, 1947 (divorced, 1962); married Damon Knight (a writer and editor), February 23, 1963; children: (first marriage) Douglas, Richard; (second marriage) Jonathan. *Home:* 1645 Horn Lane, Eugene, Ore. 97404. *Agent:* Brandt & Brandt, 101 Park Ave., New York, N.Y. 10017.

*CAREER:* Author. Co-director, Milford Science Fiction Writers Conference, 1963-76; lecturer at Clarion Fantasy Workshop, Michigan State University, 1968-78. *Member:* Science Fiction Writers of America, Authors Guild, P.E.N. *Awards, honors:* Nebula Award of Science Fiction Writers of America, 1968, for best short story, "The Planners"; Hugo Award of World Science Fiction Convention, 1977, and Jupiter Award, 1977, both for *Where Late the Sweet Birds Sang.*

*WRITINGS: More Bitter Than Death,* Simon & Schuster, 1962; *The Mile-Long Spaceship* (short stories), Berkley Publishing, 1963 (published in England as *Andover and the Android,* Dobson, 1966); (with Theodore L. Thomas) *The Clone,* Berkley, 1965; *The Nevermore Affair,* Doubleday, 1966; *The Killer Thing,* Doubleday, 1967; *The Downstairs Room* (short stories), Doubleday, 1968; *Let the Fire Fall,* Doubleday, 1969; (with Thomas) *The Year of the Cloud,* Doubleday, 1970; *Abyss,* Doubleday, 1971; *Margaret and I,* Little, Brown, 1971; *City of Cain,* Little, Brown, 1973; (editor) *Nebula Award Stories,* Number 9, Gollancz, 1974, Harper, 1975; *The Clewiston Test,* Farrar, Straus, 1976; *Where Late the Sweet Birds Sang,* Harper, 1976; *The Infinity Box* (short stories), Harper, 1976; *Fault Lines,* Harper, 1976; (editor) *Clarion Four,* Berkley Publishing, 1976; *Somerset Dreams and Other Fictions,* Harper, 1978.

*SIDELIGHTS:* Kate Wilhelm writes: "If I could sum up my philosophies and compulsions in a few paragraphs, there would be no need to write books, and there is a need. I believe we are living in an age of cataclysmic changes; we are living in an age that is the end of an era. My work is my attempt to understand how we got here, why we stay, and what lies ahead if anything does."

Joanna Russ calls Wilhelm "an escapee from the feminine mystique.... Until recently we have had of the female experience only versions sentimentalized and distorted in the service of self-glorification and the status quo.... Like Kipling, Kate Wilhelm manages to be both an artist and the voice of an experience *that is defined by its not having a voice.* To find a voice one must move out of this culture and yet stay in it; Wilhelm almost does this." Gerald Jonas, reviewing *Where Late the Sweet Birds Sang,* comments: "The clones' dream is to build a new society, free of any taint of individuality, competition, or selfishness. But the clones have a fatal flaw—growing up surrounded by 8 or 10 identical twins, they never experience the terrors, or the benefits, of being alone. As a result, they have no art, no imagination, no creativity. Wilhelm traces the rise and fall of the clone 'utopia' through the eyes of several well-drawn characters. At times, her prose strains for 'poetic effects,' but her cautionary message comes through loud and clear: Giving up our humanity to save our skins is a bad bargain no matter how you look at it."

*BIOGRAPHICAL/CRITICAL SOURCES: Magazine of Fantasy and Science Fiction,* November 1971; *Detroit News,* November 14, 1971; *New Yorker,* November 29, 1971; *New York Times Book Review,* March 10, 1974, January 18, 1976, February 22, 1976; *Psychology Today,* October, 1975; *Newsweek,* February 9, 1976; *Contemporary Literary Criticism,* Volume VII, Gale, 1977.

\* \* \*

## WILKINSON, Norman Beaumont   1910-

*PERSONAL:* Born November 6, 1910, in Philadelphia, Pa.; son of Frederick (a mechanic) and Mary Elizabeth (Clough) Wilkinson; married Marian A. Lambert (a librarian), December 30, 1933; children: David Lambert. *Education:* Muhlenberg College, B.A., 1938; University of Pennsylvania, M.A., 1942, Ph.D., 1958. *Politics:* Independent. *Religion:* Presbyterian. *Address:* P.O. Box 3942, Greenville, Del. 19807. *Office:* Eleutherian Mills-Hagley Foundation, Inc., Greenville, Del. 19807.

*CAREER:* Muhlenberg College, Allentown, Pa., instructor in history, 1942-47; Pennsylvania History and Museum Commission, Harrisburg, assistant state historian, 1947-54; Hagley Museum, Greenville, Del., director of research, 1954—. *Member:* Society for the History of Technology, Pennsylvania Historical Association, Historical Society of Delaware, Historical Society of Pennsylvania, Archaeological Society of Delaware. *Awards, honors:* Award of merit from American Association for State and Local History, 1957, for *Bibliography of Pennsylvania History;* Abbott Payson Usher Award from Society for History of Technology, 1963, for "Brandywine Borrowings from European Technology."

*WRITINGS:* (With E. G. Alderfer) *Northampton Heritage,* Northampton County Historical Society, 1953; (editor with R. L. Brunhouse) *Writings in Pennsylvania,* Pennsylvania Historical Association, 1946; *Bibliography of Pennsylvania History,* Pennsylvania History and Museum Commission, 1957; *Explosives in History* (booklet), Rand McNally, 1966; *The Brandywine Home Front during the Civil War,* Kaumagraph Co., 1966; *E. I. Du Pont, Botaniste: The Beginning of a Tradition,* University Press of Virginia, 1972; *Papermaking in America* (booklet), Hagley Museum, 1975. Contributor to history journals in England and the United States. Book review editor, *Pennsylvania History,* 1956—.

*WORK IN PROGRESS: Lammot du Pont (1831-1884): A Biography;* research for restoration of an early nineteenth-century garden.

*AVOCATIONAL INTERESTS:* Gardening, reading.†

\* \* \*

## WILLETT, T(erence) C(harles)   1918-

*PERSONAL:* Born December 23, 1918, in Birmingham, England; son of Charles Joseph (a merchant) and Elsie Jane (Allport) Willett; married Winifred Small (a bacteriologist), December 12, 1942; children: Mark, Susan. *Education:* Graduate of Army Staff College, Camberley, 1951; University of London, B.Sc., 1957, London School of Economics and Political Science, Ph.D., 1962. *Religion:* Anglican. *Home:* 136 Bagot St., Kingston, Ontario, Canada K7L 3E5. *Office:* Department of Sociology, Queen's University, Kingston, Ontario, Canada.

*CAREER:* In business in England, 1934-39; British Army, Royal Regiment of Artillery, 1939-58, retiring as lieutenant colonel; Royal Military Academy, Sandhurst, Camberley, England, senior lecturer, 1958-64; University of Reading, Reading, England, lecturer in sociology, and warden of Windsor Hall, 1964-70; Queen's University, Kingston, Ontario, 1970—, began as associate professor, currently professor of sociology and chairman of department. Part-time lecturer, Police College, Bramshill, England; lecturer at magistrates' training courses in England. Justice of the Peace, Berkshire, England, 1968-70. Member, Civil Service Selection Board; fellow, Inter-Universities Seminar on Armed Forces and Society. *Member:* British Sociological Association, Canadian Sociology Association, Canadian Anthropology Association, Canadian Association for the Prevention of Crime, American Sociological Association, American Society of Criminology. *Awards, honors:* Research grants from British Home Office, 1964, Ministry of Transport, 1965, Nuffield Foundation, 1967, Canadian Penitentiary Service, 1972, Canada Council, 1977; runner-up, Denis Carrol Memorial Prize, International Society of Criminology, 1964, for *Criminal on the Road.*

*WRITINGS: Criminal on the Road,* Tavistock Publications, 1964; *Drivers after Sentence,* Heinemann, 1973; (contributor) *Annual Review of Research on Armed Forces and Society,* Sage Publications, 1978. Contributor to *British Army Review, Twentieth Century, Medico-Legal Journal, World Medicine, Observer, Canadian Journal of Criminology and Corrections, Queens' Law Review,* and other publications.

*WORK IN PROGRESS: The World View of the Prison Guard in Canada; The Citizen and Social Control in Canada: The Case of the Canadian Militia.*

\* \* \*

## WILLIAMS, Benjamin H(arrison) 1889-1974

*PERSONAL:* Born March 23, 1889, in Eugene, Ore.; son of John Monroe (an attorney) and Jennie (Gwin) Williams; married Helene Ogsbury, June 17, 1917 (died, 1948); married Evelyn Allemong, August 25, 1951; children: (first marriage) Patricia Gwynne (Mrs. Robert Case McMann), Stanton Monroe. *Education:* University of Oregon, B.A., 1910, M.A., 1912; Harvard University, graduate study, 1912-13; University of California, Berkeley, Ph.D., 1921. *Politics:* Independent Democrat. *Religion:* Unitarian-Universalist. *Home:* 3 Forestdale Dr., Asheville, N.C. 28803.

*CAREER:* State Industrial Accident Commission, Salem, Ore., statistician, 1914-16, Extension Division, secretary of social welfare, 1916-17; University of Pennsylvania, Philadelphia, instructor in political science, 1921-23; University of Pittsburgh, Pittsburgh, Pa., assistant professor, 1923-27, associate professor, 1927-30, professor of political science, 1930-43; analyst in Military Intelligence Division, U.S. Department of War, 1943; division assistant, U.S. Department of State, 1943-44; Industrial College of the Armed Forces, member of staff in political economy, 1944-59, specialist in education, 1950-59. Visiting summer professor, University of Oregon, 1921, 1923, 1925, 1927; lecturer, Bryn Mawr College, 1923. Consultant to U.S. Information Agency, 1960. *Military service:* U.S. Army, 1917-19; became first lieutenant. *Member:* American Association for the Advancement of Science (fellow), National Academy of Economics and Political Science (chairman, 1948-59). *Awards, honors:* Decoration for exceptional civilian service, U.S. Department of the Army.

*WRITINGS: Economic Foreign Policy of the United States,* McGraw, 1929, reprinted, Fertig, 1967; *The United States and Disarmament,* McGraw, 1931, reprinted, Kennikat, 1973; *American Diplomacy: Policies and Practice,* McGraw, 1936; *Retrospect and Prospect,* [Washington, D.C.], 1963; (with Harold J. Clem) *United States Foreign Economic Policy,* Industrial College of the Armed Forces,

1965; *The United States in the Nuclear Age.* Sadna Prakashan, 1970; *Humbug, Brainwash, and Other Verse,* Carlton, 1972. General editor, "Economics of National Security," twenty-two volumes, Industrial College of the Armed Forces, 1952-58. Associate editor, *Scholastic,* 1927-28, and *Social Science,* 1955.

*WORK IN PROGRESS:* Research on current foreign policy of the United States.

*SIDELIGHTS:* Benjamin Williams traveled and studied in Europe.†

(Died September 11, 1974)

\* \* \*

## WILLIAMS, C(harles) K(enneth) 1936-

*PERSONAL:* Born November 4, 1936, in Newark, N.J.; son of Paul B. and Dossie (Kasdin) Williams; married Catherine Mauger (an editor), April 13, 1975; children: (previous marriage) Jessica Anne; (present marriage) Jed Mauger. *Education:* University of Pennsylvania, B.A., 1959. *Home:* 634 Rodman St., Philadelphia, Pa. 19147.

*CAREER:* Poet; teacher at Beaver College, Drexel University, Franklin and Marshall College, Poetry Center Workshop, and Young Men's and Young Women's Hebrew Association of Philadelphia.

*WRITINGS: A Day for Anne Frank,* Falcon Press, 1968; *Lies* (poems), Houghton, 1969; *I Am the Bitter Name* (poems), Houghton, 1972; *With Ignorance* (poems), Houghton, 1977; (translator with Gregory Dickerson) Sophocles, *Women of Trachis,* Oxford University Press, 1978. Contributing editor, *American Poetry Review.*

*WORK IN PROGRESS:* Poetry; a translation of Euripedes' *Bacchae.*

*BIOGRAPHICAL/CRITICAL SOURCES: Shenandoah,* summer, 1970; *American Poetry Review,* fall, 1972, winter, 1977; *New York Times,* July 10, 1977.

\* \* \*

## WILLIAMS, Catharine M(elissa) 1903-

*PERSONAL:* Born February 17, 1903, in West Mansfield, Ohio; daughter of Horton Blake (a farmer and salesman) and Frances (Roling) Williams. *Education:* Ohio State University, B.S. 1924, M.A., 1927, Ph.D., 1947. *Politics:* Democrat. *Religion:* Protestant. *Home:* 1889 Andover Rd., Columbus, Ohio 43212. *Office:* Department of Education, Ohio State University, Columbus, Ohio 43210.

*CAREER:* Assistant director, Darke County Normal School, Ohio, 1924-25; director at Madison County Normal School, 1925-26, and Noble County Normal School, 1926-28; Bowling Green University, Bowling Green, Ohio, demonstration teacher, 1928-30; Ohio State University, Columbus, instructor in education, 1930-44, assistant professor, 1955-62, associate professor of education, 1962-73, associate professor emeritus, 1973—, supervisor of Curriculum Materials Center, 1944-54. Visiting professor of summer sessions at University of Cincinnati, 1932, 1933, University of Michigan, 1935, 1936, Central State Teachers College (now Central Michigan University), 1938, and University of Florida, 1956. *Member:* American Association of University Women, Association for Better Broadcasts, Association for Supervision and Curriculum Development, Common Cause, Delta Kappa Gamma (president of Ohio Gamma chapter, 1954-56), Pi Lambda Theta.

*WRITINGS: Teaching Arithmetic in the Elementary*

*Schools,* Hinds Hayden & Eldridge, 1946; *Sources of Teaching Materials,* Ohio State University, 1949, 5th edition, 1972; *How to Make and Use the Feltboard* (pamphlet and filmstrip), Teaching Aids Laboratory, Ohio State University, 1956; *The Diorama as a Teaching Aid* (pamphlet and filmstrip), Teaching Aids Laboratory, Ohio State University, 1957; *Study Pictures and Learning,* (pamphlet and filmstrip), Teaching Aids Laboratory, Ohio State University, 1960; *Learning from Pictures,* Department of Audiovisual Instruction, National Education Association, 1963, revised edition, 1968; (with Collins W. Burnett) *The Teen Tutor and Learning,* E.S.E.A. Title III Publication, 1970; (with I. Keith Tyler) *Educational Communication in a Revolutionary Age,* Charles A. Jones Publishing, 1973; *The Community As Textbook,* Phi Delta Kappa Educational Foundation, 1975.

*WORK IN PROGRESS:* A book for adults concerned with communication; an animal story for children.

\* \* \*

## WILLIAMS, Cyril Glyndwr 1921-

*PERSONAL:* Born June 1, 1921, in Carmarthenshire, Wales; son of David and Hannah (Davies) Williams; married Irene Daniels, August 9, 1945; children: Martyn Huw, Eirian John. *Education:* University of Wales, B.A. (honors), 1941, B.D., 1944, M.A., 1955. *Office:* Department of Religious Studies, University College of Wales, University of Wales, Aberystwyth, Wales.

*CAREER:* Ordained minister of Congregational Church, 1944; Congregational minister in London and Wales, 1944-58; University of Wales, Cardiff, Wales, lecturer in history of religions, 1958-68; Carleton University, Ottawa, Ontario, associate professor, 1968-69, professor of religion, 1969-73; University of Wales, University College of Wales, Aberystwyth, senior lecturer, 1973-75, reader in religious studies, 1975—. *Member:* International Association for the History of Religions, Society for Old Testament Studies, Canadian Society for the Study of Religion, American Academy of Religion.

*WRITINGS: Clywsoch Yr Enw,* Welsh Modern Publications, 1966; *Crist Ein Cenhadaeth,* John Penry, 1967; (contributor) D. Z. Phillips, *Saith Ysgrif Ar Grefydd,* Gee (Denbigh), 1967; *Crefyddau'r Dwyrain,* University of Wales, 1968; (translator) *Cod: Pontydd,* Tregaron, 1978. Also author of *Nadolig yn Calcutta,* Gomer. Contributor of articles to *Religious Studies, Numen, Journal of Religion and Religions,* and Welsh journals.

*WORK IN PROGRESS:* Research in history of religions; research in glossolalia and related phenomena.

*AVOCATIONAL INTERESTS:* Preservation of Welsh culture, poetry, travel.

\* \* \*

## WILLIAMS, Ethel L.

*PERSONAL:* Born in Baltimore, Md.; daughter of William Herbert (a produce broker) and Carrie (Sampson) Langley; married Louis J. Williams (a counselor in District of Columbia public schools); children: Carole Juanita (Mrs. George Jones). *Education:* Howard University, A.B., 1930, M.S., 1945; Columbia University, B.S., 1933. *Politics:* Democrat. *Religion:* Protestant Episcopal Church. *Home:* 1625 Primrose Rd. N.W., Washington, D.C. 20012. *Office:* School of Religion Library, Howard University, Washington, D.C. 20001.

*CAREER:* District of Columbia Board of Public Welfare, Washington, caseworker, 1933-36; Library of Congress, Washington, D.C., searcher, 1936-40; Howard University, School of Religion, Washington, D.C., librarian, 1940—. *Member:* Association for the Study of Negro Life and History, American Theological Library Association, District of Columbia Library Association, Washington Urban League.

*WRITINGS:* (Editor) *Biographical Directory of Negro Ministers,* Scarecrow, 1965, 3rd edition, G. K. Hall, 1975; *Afro-American Religious Studies: A Cumulative Bibliography,* Scarecrow, 1972; *The Howard University Bibliography of African and Afro-American Religious Studies,* Scholarly Resources, 1977.

\* \* \*

## WILLIAMS, Francis Stewart 1921-1974

*PERSONAL:* Born November 10, 1921, in Portsmouth, England; son of Stewart Gordon and Fanny (Leat) Williams; married Violet Sanderson (a school secretary), November 10, 1944; children: Lawrence Bouquet, Timothy Anthony. *Education:* Kingston College of Art, Diploma in Intermediate Craft and Design and National Diploma in Design (honors), 1954. *Politics:* Liberal. *Home:* 25 Locke King Rd., Weybridge, Surrey KT13 0SY, England.

*CAREER:* Heathside County Secondary School, Weybridge, Surrey, England, head of art department, 1955-74. Examiner in art, Cambridge University Syndicate, 1956-74. Teacher of summer courses in art for Field Study Council. Artist; has had three one-man exhibitions in London, England. Chairman, Willesden Arts Council, 1945-47. Adviser in art, Young Women's Christian Association.

*WRITINGS: Painting in Mantua, Padua, Siena, and Urbino,* Pergamon, 1970, text edition, British Book Center, 1976.

*WORK IN PROGRESS: Painting in England, 1500-1700,* and *Painting in England, 1700-1900.*†

(Died October 24, 1974)

\* \* \*

## WILLIAMS, Harold A(nthony) 1916-

*PERSONAL:* Born April 22, 1916, in Milwaukee, Wis.; son of Harold Ambrose (a railroad executive) and Helen (Schmitt) Williams; married Ruth Edna Smith, October 17, 1942; children: Anne (Mrs. Lee Hartman), Mary Helen, Sara Brooke, Julie Cary. *Education:* University of Notre Dame, A.B. (cum laude), 1938. *Residence:* Baltimore, Md. *Office:* Sunpapers, 501 North Calvert St., Baltimore, Md. 21203.

*CAREER: Baltimore Sun,* Baltimore, Md., 1940—, began as reporter, special writer, 1946-49, European correspondent, 1949-50, then assistant city editor and assistant to executive editor, editor of *Sunday Sun,* 1954—. *Military service:* U.S. Army, Counter-Intelligence Corps, 1942-46. *Member:* American Association of Sunday and Feature Editors (secretary, 1958-59; president, 1959-60; member of executive committee, 1960—), Maryland Historical Society, Baltimore Bibliophiles (president, 1977—), Baltimore Wine and Food Society (member of board of directors, 1971—), Newspaper Comics Council (chairman, 1970-72; member of executive committee, 1972—).

*WRITINGS: A History of the Western Maryland Railway,* Schneidereith, 1952; *Baltimore Afire,* Schneidereith, 1954; *Guide to Baltimore and Annapolis,* Bodine, 1957; *History of the Hibernian Society of Baltimore,* Schneidereith, 1957; *A History of Eudowood,* Schneidereith, 1964; *Robert Garrett & Sons,* Schneidereith, 1965; *Bodine: A Legend in His Time,* Bodine, 1971.

\*     \*     \*

## WILLIAMS, John R(yan)   1919-

*PERSONAL:* Born November 21, 1919, in Detroit, Mich.; son of Ralph Hill (a chemical engineer) and Myrtle Anna Williams; married Madeleine Louise Josephine Cremilliac (a painter), August 28, 1952; children: Jacques Ralph Andre, Mark Thinh Tien. *Education:* Lawrence College, B.A. (summa cum laude), 1944; University of Chicago, graduate study, 1946; Johns Hopkins University, M.A., 1947; Duke University, Ph.D., 1951; London School of Economics and Political Science, postdoctoral study, 1951-52. *Politics:* "Conservative and Unionist." *Religion:* Church of England. *Home:* 1498 Eastern Ave., Morgantown, W.Va. 26505. *Office:* Department of Political Science, West Virginia University, Morgantown, W.Va. 26505.

*CAREER:* Wellesley College, Wellesley, Mass., instructor in political science, spring, 1947, 1948-49; West Virginia University, Morgantown, assistant professor, 1949-56, associate professor, 1956-61, professor of political science, 1961—, chairman of department, 1961-72, coordinator of Honors Program, 1972—, member of University Senate, 1974-80, chairman of committee on faculty welfare, 1975-77. Fellow in political science, Australian National University, 1958-60; visiting professor at Waynesburg College, 1962-63, and Pennsylvania State University, Fayette Campus, 1967-68; academic visitor, London School of Economics and Political Science, 1972. Vice-president, Suncrest Lake Association, 1961-67. *Member:* American Political Science Association, Canadian Political Science Association, Australasian Political Studies Association, Australian Institute of Political Science, International Platform Association, American Association of University Professors, University Professors for Political Academic Order, Monongalia United Nations Association, West Virginia Political Science Association (vice-president, 1967-68; president, 1968-69), Phi Beta Kappa, Pi Sigma Alpha. *Awards, honors:* Haynes Foundation fellow, 1951-52; Fulbright fellow, National University of Australia, 1958-60.

*WRITINGS: The Conservative Party of Canada,* Duke University Press, 1956; *John Latham and the Conservative Recovery from Defeat,* Australasian Political Studies Monograph, 1969. Author of weekly column, "Past, Present and Future," in *Dominion Post* (Morgantown, W.Va.). Contributor of about a dozen articles to political science journals.

*WORK IN PROGRESS: The Impact of the European Common Market on British Political Parties.*

\*     \*     \*

## WILLIAMS, Juanita da Lomba Jones   1925-

*PERSONAL:* Born December 7, 1925, in Boston, Mass.; daughter of John Querino (a railroad clerk) and Vivian (a finishing school dean; maiden name Hunt) da Lomba; married William Wilfred Jones (a real estate broker); married second husband, Earl DeWitt Williams (a teacher), June 25, 1966; children: (first marriage) William Wilfred, II, Cherie Diedre. *Education:* St. Augustine's College, A.B., 1942; Agricultural and Technical College of North Carolina (now North Carolina Agricultural and Technical State University), M.S., 1952; additional study at University of Texas, New York University, and Loyola College, Baltimore, Md. *Poli-*

*tics:* Democrat. *Religion:* Episcopal. *Home:* 6120 Talles Rd., Baltimore, Md. 21207.

*CAREER:* Prairie View Agricultural and Mechanical College, Prairie View, Tex., instructor in English, 1958-60; Virginia Union University, Richmond, Va., assistant professor of reading, 1960-61; Coppin State College, Baltimore, Md., assistant professor of English, 1962-63, assistant to registrar, 1970-71; Alabama State University, Montgomery, Ala., associate professor of literature, 1963-65; St. Augustine's College, Raleigh, N.C., associate professor of English, 1965-67. Visiting professor, Baltimore Junior College, Baltimore, Md., 1967-69. *Member:* National Council of English Teachers, National Association of Dramatic Directors, Women's Business and Professional Clubs.

*WRITINGS: He Who Perpetrates,* Phylon, 1963; *My Day for Freedom,* Mainstream, 1965; *Freedom House Girds for Campaign,* Afro-Am Publishing, 1970. Assistant editor, *Modern Youth,* 1968. Author of column, "From My Point of View," in *The Daily Texan,* Austin, Tex.

*WORK IN PROGRESS: The Life and Times of Mrs. Eleanor Frances Roosevelt.*†

\*     \*     \*

## WILLIAMS, Oliver P(erry)   1925-

*PERSONAL:* Born March 14, 1925, in McPherson, Kan.; son of Oliver Perry (a minister) and Lucy (Sell) Williams; married Marion Malakoff, September 9, 1953; children: Ruth L., Jessica S. *Education:* Reed College, B.A., 1951; University of Chicago, M.A., 1954, Ph.D., 1955. *Residence:* Philadelphia, Pa. *Office:* Department of Political Science, University of Pennsylvania, Philadelphia, Pa. 19104.

*CAREER:* Wesleyan University, Middletown, Conn., assistant professor of political science, 1955-57; Michigan State University, East Lansing, assistant professor of political science, 1957-60; University of Pennsylvania, Philadelphia, assistant professor, 1960-65, associate professor, 1965-68, professor of political science, 1968—, chairman of department, 1967-75, director of masters of public administration program at Wharton School of Finance and Commerce, 1971-73. *Wartime service:* Civilian public service as conscientious objector to military duty, 1943-46. *Member:* American Political Science Association.

*WRITINGS:* (Editor with Charles Press) *Democracy in Urban America,* Rand McNally, 1961; (with Charles Adrian) *Four Cities,* University of Pennsylvania Press, 1963; (with Harold Herman, Charles Liebman, and Thomas R. Dye) *Suburban Differences and Metropolitan Policies,* University of Pennsylvania Press, 1965; *Metropolitan Political Analysis,* Free Press, 1971. Contributor to political science, social science, and urban affairs journals.

\*     \*     \*

## WILLIAMS, Robert C.   1938-

*PERSONAL:* Born October 14, 1938, in Boston, Mass.; son of Charles Regan (a public health official) and Dorothy (Chadwell) Williams; married Ann Kingman (a biology assistant), August 27, 1960; children: Peter, Margaret. *Education:* Wesleyan University, Middletown, Conn., B.A., 1960; Harvard University, A.M., 1962, Ph.D., 1966. *Home:* 428 Melville Ave., University City, Mo. 63130. *Office:* History Department, Washington University, St. Louis, Mo. 63130.

*CAREER:* Williams College, Williamstown, Mass., assistant professor of history, 1965-70, assistant to the provost,

1968-70; Washington University, St. Louis, Mo., 1970—, began as associate professor, currently professor of history. *Member:* American Association for the Advancement of Slavic Studies (president, Central Slavic Conference, 1970-71), Phi Beta Kappa, Sigma Xi. *Awards, honors:* Woodrow Wilson fellowship, 1960; Kennan fellow, 1976-77.

*WRITINGS: Culture in Exile: Russian Emigres in Germany, 1881-1941,* Cornell University Press, 1972; *Artists in Revolution: Portraits of the Russian Avant-garde, 1905-1925,* Indiana University Press, 1977. Contributor of articles to *Yale Review, Slavic Review, Journal of History of Ideas.* Editor of *Berkshire Review,* 1967-70, and *Kritika,* 1968.

*WORK IN PROGRESS:* A book, *The Culture Exchange: Russian Art and American Money, 1900-1940.*

\* \* \*

## WILLIAMS, Roger M(iller) 1934-

*PERSONAL:* Born February 21, 1934, in New York, N.Y.; son of Arden C. (a salesman) and Margaret (Vervaet) Williams; married second wife, Connie Louise Young, April 20, 1974; children: (first marriage) Christopher D., Diana M.; (second marriage) Christina B. *Education:* Amherst College, B.A., 1956. *Politics:* Independent Democrat. *Home:* 171 West 71st St., New York, N.Y. 10023. *Agent:* Rhoda Wey, William Morris Agency, 1350 Ave. of the Americas, New York, N.Y. 10019. *Office: Saturday Review,* 1290 Ave. of the Americas, New York, N.Y. 10019.

*CAREER:* Macy Westchester Newspapers, Westchester County, N.Y., reporter, 1958; *Sports Illustrated* (magazine), New York City, reporter and staff writer, 1959-62; *Time* (magazine), New York City, correspondent in Los Angeles, Calif., Miami, Fla., and Atlanta, Ga., 1962-71; *World* (magazine), New York City, senior editor, 1972-74; *Saturday Review* (magazine), New York City, contributing editor, 1974-77, senior editor, 1977—. Contributing writer, *Signature* (magazine), 1977—. *Military service:* U.S. Army, 1956-58. *Awards, honors:* American Political Science Association fellowship, 1970-71.

*WRITINGS: Sing a Sad Song: The Life of Hank Williams,* Doubleday, 1970; *The Bonds: An American Family,* Atheneum, 1971. Contributor of articles to *Fortune, American Heritage, True, Playboy, Americana, Columbia Journalism Review, Nation, New Republic,* and other publications.

*SIDELIGHTS:* Roger Williams' favorite author is George Orwell, "whose independence of judgment and clarity of style," Williams says, "I have always admired." *Avocational interests:* Folk guitar, tennis.

*BIOGRAPHICAL/CRITICAL SOURCES: New York Times,* April 27, 1970; *Washington Post,* July 3, 1970.

\* \* \*

## WILLIAMS, Roger Neville 1943-

*PERSONAL:* Born March 28, 1943, in Muncie, Ind.; son of Donald Charles (a metallurgist) and Eileen (Boughton) Williams; married Judith Dome (a teacher and writer), March 15, 1969. *Education:* Attended University of Colorado and University of Neuchatel, Switzerland.

*CAREER:* Worked as ordinary seaman on the Great Lakes, 1962, a travel lecturer, Cleveland, Ohio, 1963, a bosun's mate on a schooner in the West Indies, 1964, a tour manager for a travel agency, Chicago, Ill., 1965-68, and as a freelance correspondent in Vietnam, 1968. Investigative reporter, NBC News; reporter, *National Enquirer;* assistant

editor, *Midnight.* Has worked politically and socially with an American exile community in Montreal, Quebec. *Awards, honors:* U.S. College Editors Conference award, 1965, for best piece of commentary on international affairs in a university newspaper.

*WRITINGS: The New Exiles: American War Resisters in Canada,* Liveright, 1971. Contributor to national magazines, including *Ramparts, New Republic,* and *Evergreen Review,* and newspapers, including *Denver Post, Boston Globe,* and *Los Angeles Free Press.*

*WORK IN PROGRESS:* Research for a book on American emigration abroad; a novel.

*SIDELIGHTS:* Roger Williams has travelled through sixty countries; he made a motorcycle trip from Cairo to Capetown in 1963.†

\* \* \*

## WILLIAMSON, Juanita V. 1917-

*PERSONAL:* Born January 18, 1917, in Shelby, Miss.; daughter of John M. (a minister and teacher) and Alice (McAllister) Williamson. *Education:* LeMoyne College, B.A., 1938; Atlanta University, M.A., 1940; University of Michigan, Ph.D., 1961. *Religion:* Congregational United Church of Christ. *Home:* 1217 Cannon St., Memphis, Tenn. 38106. *Office:* Department of English, LeMoyne College, Memphis, Tenn. 38126.

*CAREER:* LeMoyne College, Memphis, Tenn., 1946—, began as assistant professor, currently professor of English, and director of freshman composition. Visiting professor at Ball State University, 1962-63, University of Wisconsin—Milwaukee, summer, 1970. Linguist at NDEA Summer Institutes at Southern University, 1961, Atlanta University, 1963, Hampton Institute, 1965, University of Wisconsin—Milwaukee, 1966, 1967, Memphis State University, 1969. *Member:* American Association of University Professors, College Language Association, American Dialect Society, Linguistic Society of America, Modern Language Association of America, National Council of Teachers of English, Conference on College Composition and Communication.

*WRITINGS: A Phonological and Morphological Study of the Speech of the Negro of Memphis, Tennessee,* American Dialect Society, 1970; (editor with Virginia Burke) *A Various Language: Perspectives on American Dialects,* Holt, 1971. Contributor of articles to *College Language Association, Word Study, Crisis.*

*WORK IN PROGRESS:* Research in speech of the South; research in speech of Black Americans.†

\* \* \*

## WILLIAMSON, Richard 1930-

*PERSONAL:* Born October 16, 1930, in San Francisco, Calif.; son of Arthur Louis (a mechanic) and Edith (Partridge) Williamson. *Education:* San Francisco State College (now University), A.B., 1953, M.A., 1958; attended Center for Advanced Film Studies, Beverly Hills, Calif., 1971. *Home:* 50 Collingwood St., San Francisco, Calif. 94114. *Office:* Language Arts Division, College of San Mateo, San Mateo, Calif. 94402.

*CAREER:* Santa Barbara City College, Santa Barbara, Calif., instructor in English, 1958-63, head of department, 1961-63; College of San Mateo, San Mateo, Calif., instructor in English and filmmaking, 1963—, assistant chairman of

English department, 1964. Lecturer in higher education, San Francisco State College (now University), 1966; writer and consultant, Aspen Institute for Humanistic Studies, 1976—. *Military service:* U.S. Navy, 1953-55. *Member:* Conference on College Composition and Communication (member of executive committee, 1969-76; chairman of National Junior College committee, 1972-74), Pacific Coast Regional Conference on English in the Two-Year College (treasurer, 1967-69; member of executive committee, 1967-76; national representative, 1969-76).

*WRITINGS:* (With Laura Hackett) *Anatomy of Reading,* McGraw, 1965, 2nd edition, 1970; (with Hackett) *Design for a Composition,* Harcourt, 1966. Contributor of articles to *College Composition and Communication* and Association of Departments of English *Bulletin.*

*WORK IN PROGRESS:* Screenplay and script for feature film to be made in Canada, tentatively entitled "Thunder Bay."

\*    \*    \*

**WILLING, Martha Kent   1920-**

*PERSONAL:* Born February 8, 1920, in Philadelphia, Pa.; daughter of S. Leonard (a hydroelectric engineer) and Elizabeth (Cryer) Kent; married E. Shippen Willing, Jr., 1942; children: Peter, Matthew Cryer, Thomas Shippen, Stephen Lee. *Education:* Bryn Mawr College, B.A. (cum laude), 1941; University of Washington, Seattle, M.A., 1965. *Politics:* Independent. *Religion:* "Unaffiliated." *Office:* Population Dynamics, 3829 Aurora Ave. N., Seattle, Wash. 98103.

*CAREER:* Bryn Mawr College, Bryn Mawr, Pa., research assistant in biology, 1941-43; University of Washington, Seattle, research assistant in biology, 1957-58; Population Dynamics, Seattle, treasurer, 1967—, administrator, 1971—. Free-lance script writer and film producer, 1967—. *Member:* Sigma Xi.

*WRITINGS: Beyond Conception,* Gambit, 1971. Film scripts: "Insertion and Removal of an I.U.D."; "Beyond Conception"; "His Majesty's Wish: Nepal Family Planning"; "Vasectomy Technique"; "The Missed Period."

*WORK IN PROGRESS:* A second book; research on a philosophy of ecology and human behavior in a closed system.

*AVOCATIONAL INTERESTS:* Botany, bird study.

\*    \*    \*

**WILLINGHAM, John J.   1935-**

*PERSONAL:* Born March 29, 1935, in Charleston, Ill.; son of Russell T. and Edna (Kingery) Willingham; married Carol Lanehart, 1972; children: (previous marriage) John J., Scott R., Andrew M., Lynna M. *Education:* Eastern Illinois University, B.S., 1957; Pennsylvania State University, M.S., 1959; Ohio State University, Ph.D., 1963. *Office:* Department of Accounting, University of Houston, Houston, Tex. 77004.

*CAREER:* Dill and Rowland, Certified Public Accountants, State College, Pa., staff accountant, 1958-59; Murphey, Jenney & Jones, Certified Public Accountants, Decatur, Ill., staff accountant, 1959-60; Ohio State University, Columbus, instructor in accounting, 1960-63, instructor in sociology, 1963; Pennsylvania State University, University Park, assistant professor, 1963-66, associate professor of accounting, 1966-67; University of Texas at Austin, visiting associate professor, 1966-67, associate professor of accounting, 1967-70; University of Texas at Arlington, professor of

accounting and chairman of department, 1970-72; University of Houston, Houston, Tex., professor of accounting, 1972—. Certified public accountant in Illinois, 1960, Ohio, 1961. Consultant, U.S. Department of Commerce, 1965-67; information systems consultant to industry.

*MEMBER:* American Accounting Association, American Institute of Certified Public Accountants, American Institute of Decision Sciences, Institute of Internal Auditors, Texas Society of Certified Public Accountants, Beta Alpha Psi, Pi Omego Pi, Alpha Kappa Psi, Alpha Kappa Delta.

*WRITINGS:* (With J. C. Gray, K. S. Johnston, and R. Gene Brown) *Accounting Information and Business Decisions: A Simulation,* McGraw, 1964; (with R. E. Malcom) *Accounting in Action: A Simulation,* McGraw, 1965; (with W. J. Schrader and Malcom) *Financial Accounting: An Input-Output Approach,* Irwin, 1970; (with D. R. Carmichael) *Auditing Concepts and Methods,* McGraw, 1971, 2nd edition, 1975; (with Carmichael) *Perspectives in Auditing: Readings and Analysis Situations,* McGraw, 1971, 2nd edition, 1975. Contributor of over thirty articles and reviews to accounting journals in the United States and abroad.

\*    \*    \*

**WILLIS, E(dward) David   1932-**

*PERSONAL:* Born May 29, 1932, in Sterling, Colo.; son of Edward Shields (an agronomist) and Alice (O'Brian) Willis; married Florence Irene Siebens, December 28, 1955; children: Elizabeth, Benjamin, Matthew, Catherine. *Education:* Northwestern University, B.A., 1954; Princeton University, B.D., 1957; University of Geneva, graduate study, 1957-58; Harvard University, Th.D., 1963; Free University of Berlin, graduate study, 1967. *Home:* 134 Bolinas Ave., San Anselmo, Calif. 94960. *Office:* Graduate Theological Union, 2465 LeConte, Berkeley, Calif.; and San Francisco Theological Seminary, 2 Kensington Rd., San Anselmo, Calif.

*CAREER:* Ordained minister of Presbyterian Church, 1957; assistant minister, Cambridge, Mass., 1960-61; Congregational minister in South Merrimack, N.H., 1961-62 and Amherst, N.H., 1962-63; Harvard University Divinity School, Cambridge, Mass., teaching fellow, 1961-63; Princeton Theological Seminary, Princeton, N.J., instructor, 1963-65, assistant professor of systematic theology, 1965-66; San Francisco Theological Seminary, San Anselmo, Calif., associate professor, 1966-70, professor of historical theology, 1970-74, California Professor of Church History and Historical Theology, 1974—; Graduate Theological Union, Berkeley, Calif., associate professor, 1966-70, professor of historical theology, 1970—. Presbyterian minister in Silver Lake, Pa., summer, 1957. Visiting lecturer at University of California, Berkeley, springs, 1969 and 1971, Pacific School of Religion, winter, 1969, San Francisco College for Women (now Lone Mountain College), spring, 1969. Member of summer faculty at Princeton Theological Seminary, 1965, San Francisco Theological Seminary, 1968, and Union Theological Seminary, Richmond, Va., 1969. Member of theological commission, World Alliance of Reformed Churches, 1969—; chairman of committee on interchurch affairs, Commission on Ecumenical Mission and Relations, 1971—; member of executive committee, United Presbyterian Church of the United States of America, 1971—. *Member:* Renaissance Society of America, American Society for Reformation Research, Association d'Humanisme et Renaissance, American Academy of Religion, American Society of Church History, American Historical Association. *Awards, honors:* Newberry Prize, 1957; American Association of Theological Schools faculty fellowship, 1969-70.

*WRITINGS:* (Contributor) F. N. Magill and I. B. McGreal, editors, *Masterpieces of Christian Literature,* Harper, 1963; (contributor) John A. Tedeschi, editor, *Italian Reformation Studies in Honor of Laelius Socinus,* Le Monnier, 1965; *Calvin's Catholic Christology,* Brill, 1966; (contributor) Allen O. Miller, editor, *Reconciliation in Today's World,* Eerdmans, 1969; (editor and contributor) *Baptism: Decision and Growth,* Office of the General Assembly, United Presbyterian Church of the United States of America, 1972; (editor with A. J. McKelway, and contributor) *The Context of Comtemporary Theology,* John Knox, 1974; *Daring Prayer,* John Knox, 1977. Contributor of articles to *Archiv fuer Reformationsgeschichte, Reformed World, Harvard Divinity Bulletin, Theology Today.* Editor, *Pacific Theological Review,* 1973—.†

\* \* \*

## WILLIS, John H(oward), Jr. 1929-

*PERSONAL:* Born November 15, 1929, in Brooklyn, N.Y.; son of John H. and Geraldine (Henning) Willis; married Anne Romberg, July 16, 1960; children: John, Tom, Susan. *Education:* University of Virginia, B.A., 1951; Columbia University, M.A., 1959, Ph.D., 1967. *Home:* 135 Ridings Cove, Williamsburg, Va. 23185. *Office:* Department of English, College of William and Mary, Williamsburg, Va. 23185.

*CAREER:* College of William and Mary, Williamsburg, Va., instructor, 1959-64, assistant professor, 1962-65, associate professor, 1967-77, professor of English, 1977—, administrative assistant to president, 1962-65, associate dean, 1967-68, acting dean of graduate studies, 1967-68, branch college liaison officer, 1968-70, assistant vice-president for academic affairs, 1968-71. *Military service:* U.S. Navy, 1951-54; became lieutenant junior grade.

*WRITINGS: William Empson,* Columbia University Press, 1969. Contributor to *Encyclopedia Americana.*

\* \* \*

## WILLIS, Sharon O(zell) 1938-

*PERSONAL:* Born June 11, 1938, in West Frankfort, Ill.; daughter of George L. (a miner) and Eugenia (Seibel) Farmer; married Carl G. Willis (a counseling psychologist), November 25, 1960; children: Christopher Joseph, Shari Lorraine. *Education:* Southern Illinois University, B.S., 1960; University of Illinois, M.S., 1963. *Home:* 606 Westridge, Columbia, Mo. 65201. *Office:* School of Library and Informational Science, University of Missouri, Columbia, Mo. 65201.

*CAREER:* Teacher in public schools in Illinois, 1960-62; Wisconsin State University—River Falls (now University of Wisconsin—River Falls), laboratory school librarian and instructor in library science, 1962-64; Oklahoma State University, Stillwater, cataloger in library and instructor in library science, 1964-66; University of Missouri—Columbia, School of Library and Informational Science, information librarian, 1966-67, library science librarian, 1967-68, instructor in library science, 1966—. *Member:* Missouri Library Association, Missouri Association of School Librarians, University of Illinois Library Science Association, Epsilon Beta (adviser).

*WRITINGS:* (With Margaret L. Brewer) *The Elementary*

*School Library,* Shoe String, 1970. Editor of Missouri University Library Staff Association *Newsletter,* 1969-71, and Missouri Association of School Librarians *Newsletter,* 1970—.

*WORK IN PROGRESS:* Preparing a series of slides depicting different types of libraries, including those in the British Isles, Newfoundland, and Nova Scotia.

*AVOCATIONAL INTERESTS:* Collecting antiques, sewing.

\* \* \*

## WILLISON, George F(indlay) 1896-1972

July 24, 1896—July 30, 1972; American educator, historian, public relations consultant, and government employee. Obituaries: *New York Times,* August 1, 1972. (See index for *CA* sketch)

\* \* \*

## WILLOUGHBY, David P(atrick) 1901-

*PERSONAL:* Born March 17, 1901, in New Orleans, La.; son of David (an engineer) and Mary Ann (Small) Willoughby; married Jeannete Norine Murray, 1936 (divorced, 1943); married Carol Harwood Kelley, September 6, 1946; children: David F. Kelley (stepson). *Education:* Attended public schools in Minneapolis, Minn., and Los Angeles, Calif., 1909-1914; mainly self-educated. *Religion:* Agnostic. *Home:* 820 Wilson St., Laguna Beach, Calif. 92651.

*CAREER:* Mechanical draftsman, physical instructor, and medical illustrator, 1915-38; California Institute of Technology, Pasadena, Calif., research assistant and scientific illustrator in vertebrate paleontology, Division of the Geological Sciences, 1938-53, engineering draftsman and technical artist in Jet Propulsion Laboratory, 1953-69.

*WRITINGS*—Published by A. S. Barnes: *The Super-Athletes,* 1970; *The Empire of Equus,* 1974; *Growth and Nutrition in the Horse,* 1974; *All about Gorillas,* 1978; *Elephants and Mammoths,* in press. Contributor of articles and essays on morphology of man, and on the anthropoid apes and other mammals, to *Human Biology, Natural History, Scientific Monthly,* and other periodicals.

*AVOCATIONAL INTERESTS:* Literary research, chiefly on athletics and natural history.

\* \* \*

## WILSON, Douglas L. 1935-

*PERSONAL:* Born November 10, 1935, in St. James, Minn.; son of Charles E. (a railroad clerk) and Mae (Lawson) Wilson; married Sharon Sheldon, June 8, 1957; children: Cynthia Ann, Timothy Charles. *Education:* Doane College, A.B., 1957; University of Pennsylvania, M.A., 1959, Ph.D., 1964. *Home:* 844 North Academy, Galesburg, Ill. 61401. *Office:* Library, Knox College, Galesburg, Ill. 61401.

*CAREER:* Knox College, Galesburg, Ill., instructor, 1961-64, assistant professor, 1964-69, associate professor of English, 1969—, director of library, 1972—. *Member:* American Association of University Professors.

*WRITINGS:* (Editor) George Santayana, *The Genteel Tradition,* Harvard University Press, 1967. Contributor to *New England Quarterly, Western Humanities Review,* and *Illinois State Historical Journal.*

*WORK IN PROGRESS:* A book on American agrarian traditions.

*AVOCATIONAL INTERESTS:* Country life, wild plants.

*       *       *

## WILSON, Edmund   1895-1972

May 8, 1895—June 12, 1972; American poet, social and literary critic, essayist, lecturer, editor, playwright, and man of letters. Obituaries: *New York Times,* June 13, 1972; *Washington Post,* June 13, 1972; *L'Express,* June 20-July 2, 1972; *Antiquarian Bookman,* June 26, 1972; *Time,* June 26, 1972; *Current Biography,* July, 1972. (See index for *CA* sketch)

*       *       *

## WILSON, Fred   1937-

*PERSONAL:* Born December 27, 1937, in Hamilton, Ontario, Canada; son of Fred Forster (a printer) and Mary (Carroll) Wilson; married Gail C. Colburn (a librarian), August 5, 1965 (divorced, 1976); married Linda Rothman (an office manager), March 13, 1976. *Education:* McMaster University, B.Sc., 1960; University of Iowa, Ph.D., 1965. *Politics:* Socialist. *Religion:* Atheist. *Home:* 440 Wellesley St. E., Toronto, Ontario, Canada. *Office:* Department of Philosophy, University of Toronto, Toronto 181, Ontario, Canada.

*CAREER:* University of Toronto, Toronto, Ontario, assistant professor, 1965-69, associate professor of philosophy, 1969—, graduate secretary and associate chairman of department, 1971-74, program director of University College, 1975—. *Member:* American Philosophical Association, Western Division, Philosophy of Science Association, Canadian Philosophical Association.

*WRITINGS:* (With Alan Housman) *Carnap and Goodman: Two Formalists,* Nijhoff, 1967. Contributor of articles to *Philosophy of Science, British Journal for the Philosophy of Science, Synthese, Dialogue, New Scholasticism, Modern Schoolman,* and *Australasian Journal of Philosophy.*

*WORK IN PROGRESS:* Manuscripts—*An Empiricist Critique of Oxford Philosophy and Hegel, Philosophy and Ontology of Logic, In Defence of an Operationist Philosophy of Science;* research in philosophy of psychology; research in history of early modern philosophy.

*       *       *

## WILSON, L(eland) Craig   1925-

*PERSONAL:* Born May 31, 1925, in Gastonia, N.C.; son of Maurice Clement (a teacher) and Mae Irene (Card) Wilson; married Helen Theresa Nunez, June 22, 1945; children: Craig Robert, Karen Theresa. *Education:* East Tennessee State College (now University), B.S., 1947; University of Tennessee, M.S., 1949; George Peabody College for Teachers, Ph.D., 1952. *Home:* Unami Trail, R.D.2, Newark, Del. 19711. *Office:* College of Education, University of Delaware, Newark, Del. 19711.

*CAREER:* Teacher in Johnson City, Tenn., 1947, and Oak Ridge, Tenn., 1947-50; George Peabody College for Teachers, Nashville, Tenn., research assistant of Southern States Cooperative Program in Educational Administration, 1950-57, regional coordinator of program in local school administration, 1952-55; Alabama Polytechnic Institute (now Auburn University), Auburn, Ala., graduate professor of school administration, 1955-57; West Virginia Department of Education, Charleston, assistant state superintendent of schools and director of Division of Research and Planning, 1957-61; research and planning assistant to Governor of

West Virginia, 1961-62; University of Delaware, Newark, professor of education, 1962—. Regional research director, Southern Education Foundation, 1955-57. *Military service:* U.S. Army Air Forces, 1943-47. *Member:* American Association of School Administrators, National Association of Secondary School Principals, Delaware Association of School Administrators, Phi Delta Kappa, Pi Gamma Mu.

*WRITINGS:* (With Truman Pierce, E. C. Merrill, and Ralph Kimbrough) *Community Leadership for Public Education,* Prentice-Hall, 1955; (with John Montgomery, Ralph Purdy, and D. D. Harrah) *School-Community Improvement,* World Book Co., 1959; (with T. Madison Byar, Arthur Shapiro, and Shirley Schell) *Sociology of Supervision,* Allyn & Bacon, 1969; *The Open Access Curriculum,* Allyn & Bacon, 1971; *Survival Behavior for Schools: Strategies for the Educator,* Allyn & Bacon, 1978. Writer of about forty-five research and special reports; contributor to education journals.

*       *       *

## WILSON, Larman C.   1930-

*PERSONAL:* Born April 20, 1930, in Lincoln, Neb.; son of Curtis M. and Naomi J. (a professor; maiden name, Gilbert) Wilson; married Olga Jurevitch, September 5, 1959; children: Natalia Ann, Katherine Teresa. *Education:* Attended University of Minnesota, 1950; Chadron State College, B.A., 1952; University of Florida, graduate study, 1954; University of Maryland, M.A., 1957, Ph.D., 1964. *Religion:* Protestant. *Home:* 4843 Chevy Chase Blvd., Chevy Chase, Md. 20015. *Office:* School of International Service, American University, Washington, D.C. 20016.

*CAREER:* University of Maryland, College Park, lecturer in political science and economics in Atlantic Division of Overseas Program in Bermuda, Labrador, Newfoundland, Iceland, and Greenland, 1957-59, lecturer in political science, 1961-64; U.S. Naval Academy, Annapolis, Md., assistant professor of political science, 1964-68; American University, Washington, D.C., associate professor, 1968-74, professor of international relations, 1974—. President, Inter-American Council, 1973-74. Consultant on international law, development in developing countries, the Dominican Republic, the Caribbean, Central America, and Mexico. *Member:* American Political Science Association, American Society of International Law, International Studies Association, Latin American Studies Association, American Association of University Professors. *Awards, honors:* Organization of American States fellowship to Tercer Curso de Derecho Internacional (Brazil), 1976.

*WRITINGS:* (With D. S. Hitt) *A Selected Bibliography of the Dominican Republic: A Century after the Restoration of Independence,* Center for Research in Social Systems, 1968; (with Eugenio Chang-Rodriguez and others) *The Lingering Crisis: A Case Study of the Dominican Republic,* Las Americas Publishing, 1969; (with G. Pope Atkins) *The United States and the Trujillo Regime,* Rutgers University Press, 1972; (with Harold E. Davis and others) *Latin American Foreign Policies,* Johns Hopkins University Press, 1975. Also author of *The Teaching of International Law,* 1973. Contributor to journals of international affairs and Latin American studies.

*WORK IN PROGRESS:* A book on the Inter-American system.

## WILSON, Theodore A(llen) 1940-

*PERSONAL:* Born September 27, 1940, in Evansville, Ind.; son of Benjamin H. (a trainman) and Anna L. (Basham) Wilson; married Judith Kay Juncker, September 5, 1962; children: Laura Marie, Andrew Allen. *Education:* Indiana University at Bloomington, B.A., 1962, M.A., 1963, Ph.D., 1966. *Politics:* Democrat. *Home:* 2925 Topeka Lane, Lawrence, Kan. 66044. *Office:* Department of History, University of Kansas, Lawrence, Kan. 66044.

*CAREER:* University of Kansas, Lawrence, assistant professor, 1965-69, associate professor, 1969-73, professor of history, 1973—, associate dean, College of Liberal Arts, 1976—. Senior research associate, Harry S Truman Library Institute, Independence, Mo., 1969-72. Visiting professor, University College, University of Dublin, 1975-76. *Member:* Society of American Historians, American Historical Association, Society for Historians of American Foreign Relations, Organization of American Historians, Common Cause, Phi Beta Kappa. *Awards, honors:* Francis Parkman Prize, Society of American Historians, 1970, for *The First Summit;* Guggenheim fellowship, 1972-73.

*WRITINGS: The First Summit: Roosevelt and Churchill at Placentia Bay, 1941,* Houghton, 1969; (editor) *World War II: Critical Issues,* Scribner, 1974; (co-editor) *Makers of American Diplomacy,* Scribner, 1974; (co-author) *Three Generations in Twentieth Century America,* Dorsey, 1976. Contributor of articles to *Maryland Historical Magazine, Prologue,* and *American History Illustrated.*

*WORK IN PROGRESS: Origins and Evolution of Foreign Aid, 1943-53;* a biography of Henry A. Wallace.

\* \* \*

## WILSON, W(illiam) Harmon 1905-

*PERSONAL:* Born January 2, 1905, in Lebanon, Ohio; son of William Harmon and Minnie Louise (Munger) Wilson; married Helen Gertrude Fahrney, June 21, 1930; children: Janet Sue Wilson Jones, Marcia Helen Wilson Hendricks. *Education:* University of Cincinnati, Comml. Engr., 1929. *Home:* 6511 Mariemont Ave., Cincinnati, Ohio 45227. *Office:* South-Western Publishing Co., 5101 Madison Rd., Cincinnati, Ohio 45227.

*CAREER:* South-Western Publishing Co., Cincinnati, Ohio, assistant sales manager, 1929-37, sales manager, 1937-40, vice-president, 1940-50, executive vice-president, 1950-60, president and treasurer, 1960-68, chairman of board of directors, 1968—. Member of board of directors of Scott, Foresman & Co., Glenview, Ill., and Gage Educational Publishing, Toronto, Ontario. Lecturer at University of Cincinnati, 1931-47; lecturer at colleges and universities throughout the country and at educational programs and workshops. Member of board of Ohio Institute for Certifying Secretaries, 1958-61, and of Ohio Council on Economic Education, 1963-71; trustee of Cincinnati Better Business Bureau, 1970-72.

*MEMBER:* American Educational Publishers (member of board of directors, 1956-59; vice-president, 1958-59), American Management Association, Beta Gamma Sigma, Delta Sigma Pi, Delta Pi Epsilon. *Awards, honors:* Distinguished Alumnus Award, University of Cincinnati, 1969; LL.D. from Rider College, 1969, and Eastern Michigan University, 1970.

*WRITINGS:* (With Harald G. Shields) *Business-Economic Problems,* South-Western Publishing, 1935, 2nd edition, 1944; (with Bernard A. Shilt) *Business Principles and Man-* *agement,* South-Western Publishing, 1940, 5th edition, 1967; (with Shields) *Consumer Economic Problems,* South-Western Publishing, 1940, 7th edition (5th through 7th editions revised by Wilson and Elvin S. Eyster), 1966, 8th edition (revised with Roman F. Warmke and others), 1971; (contributor) James E. Mendenhall and Henry Harap, editors, *Consumer Education,* Appleton, 1943; (with Shilt) *The Small Business,* South-Western Publishing, 1943; (with Warmke) *Life on Paradise Island: Economic Life on an Imaginary Island,* Scott, Foresman, 1970. Contributor to *Dictionary of Education,* McGraw, *American Business Education Yearbook,* and to other business education yearbooks and journals. Editor, *Balance Sheet,* 1930-60; member of advisory board, *Deltasig.*†

\* \* \*

## WING, Donald G(oddard) 1904-1972

1904—October 8, 1972; American librarian and bibliographer. Obituaries: *New York Times,* October 11, 1972; *Antiquarian Bookman,* October 16, 1972.

\* \* \*

## WINGO, E(lvis) Otha 1934-

*PERSONAL:* Born September 17, 1934, in Booneville, Miss.; son of Elijah and Edna (Goodin) Wingo; married Ann Hardy, June 11, 1961; children: Deborah Lynn, Eric Otha, James Vincent. *Education:* Attended Northeast Mississippi Junior College, 1951-52; Mississippi College, B.A., 1955; University of Illinois, Urbana, M.A., 1956, Ph.D., 1963. *Home:* 126 Camellia Dr., Cape Girardeau, Mo. 63701. *Office:* Department of Classical Languages, Southeast Missouri State University, Cape Girardeau, Mo. 63701.

*CAREER:* University of Missouri, Columbia, instructor in classics, 1957-58; William Jewell College, Liberty, Mo., assistant professor of Latin, 1958-60; Southeast Missouri State University, Cape Girardeau, associate professor, 1962-75, professor of classical languages, 1975—. Visiting lecturer at St. Mary's Seminary, Perryville, Mo., 1963-65. Special probation officer of juvenile court, 32nd Judicial Circuit, Cape Girardeau, Mo., 1970-74. *Member:* American Philological Association, American Federation of Astrologers, International Society for Astrological Research, Huna Research Associates (research director, 1971—), Missouri Federation of Astrologers (vice-president, 1973—). *Awards, honors:* Woodrow Wilson fellow, 1955.

*WRITINGS: Latin Punctuation in the Classical Age,* Mouton, 1972; (editor) Max Freedom Long, *Tarot Card Symbology,* Huna Research Associates, 1972; *Letters on Huna: The Fundamentals of Huna Psychology,* Huna Research Associates, 1973. Research editor for *Bulletin of Huna Research Associates,* 1972—; editor, Huna Research Publications, 1972—.

*WORK IN PROGRESS:* Research in correlation between astrology and mythology; research in Huna, psycho-religious system of the Polynesians; text materials for college courses in astrology.

*SIDELIGHTS:* E. Otha Wingo told *CA:* "As a classicist, I am interested in antiquities. But my emphasis, both in teaching and in writing, is on the practical use of the ancient wisdom in modern living." *Letters on Huna* has been translated into German.

\* \* \*

## WINK, Walter Philip 1935-

*PERSONAL:* Born May 21, 1935, in Dallas, Tex.; son of N.

Edwin and Florence (Gidinghagen) Wink; married Virginia Moore Conerly, March 24, 1956; children: Stephen Philip, Christopher Warren, Rebecca Marie. *Education:* Southern Methodist University, B.A. (magna cum laude), 1956; Union Theological Seminary, New York, B.D., 1959; Th.D., 1963. *Office:* Auburn Theological Seminary, 3041 Broadway, New York, N.Y. 10027.

*CAREER:* Ordained to the Methodist ministry, Texas Conference, 1961; East Harlem Protestant Parish and Broadway Temple Methodist Church, New York City, youth worker, 1956-59; First Methodist Chruch, Hitchcock, Tex., pastor, 1962-67; Methodist Ministry at University of Texas Medical Branch, Galveston, chaplain and director, 1967; Union Theological Seminary, New York City, assistant professor, 1967-70, associate professor of New Testament, 1970-76; Auburn Theological Seminary, New York City, professor of Biblical interpretation, 1976—. Visiting lecturer at Drew University, spring, 1969 and Columbia University, spring, 1970, 1973; staff associate, Hartford Seminary Foundation. *Member:* Society of Biblical Literature, American Academy of Religion, Studiorum Novi Testamenti Societas, Clergy and Laymen Concerned (member of steering committee), Phi Beta Kappa.

*WRITINGS: John the Baptist in the Gospel Tradition,* Cambridge University Press, 1968; *The Bible in Human Transformation,* Fortress Press, 1973.

*WORK IN PROGRESS: The Powers.*

\* \* \*

## WINNER, Thomas G(ustav)   1917-

*PERSONAL:* Surname legally changed in 1951; born May 4, 1917, in Prague, Czechoslovakia; son of Julius Gustav (a businessman) and Franziska (Gruenhutova) Wiener; married Irene Portis (an anthropologist), September 25, 1942; children: Ellen, Lucy Franziska. *Education:* Attended Charles University, Prague, 1936-38; Harvard University, B.A., 1942, M.A., 1943; Columbia University, Ph.D., 1950. *Home:* 19 Garden St., Cambridge, Mass. 02138. *Office:* Box E, Brown University, Providence, R.I. 02912.

*CAREER:* Johns Hopkins University, Walter Hines Page School for International Studies, Baltimore, Md., visiting fellow, 1947-48; Duke University, Durham, N.C., instructor, 1948-50, assistant professor, 1950-57, associate professor of Russian language and literature, 1957-58; University of Michigan, Ann Arbor, associate professor, 1958-60, professor of Slavic languages and literature, 1960-66; Brown University, Providence, R.I., professor of Slavic languages, 1966—, professor of Slavic languages and comparative literature, 1977—, chairman of department, 1968-72, director, Center for Research on Semiotics, 1977—. Fulbright lecturer in Russian, Sorbonne, University of Paris, 1956-57. Fulbright scholar at University of Zagreb, spring, 1972-73, and University of Warsaw, 1972-73. *Member:* Modern Language Association of America, International Association for Semiotic Studies, International Comparative Literature Association, Semiotic Society of America (vice-president, 1976-77; president, 1977-78), Federation Internationale des langues et litteratures modernes, American Association of Teachers of Slavic and East European Languages, American Association for the Advancement of Slavic Studies, Czechoslovak Society of Arts and Sciences. *Awards, honors:* Ford Foundation faculty fellow, 1951-52; M.A., Brown University, 1967; National Endowment for the Humanities senior fellow, 1972; Rockefeller Foundation humanities senior fellow, 1977.

*WRITINGS: The Oral Art and Literature of the Kazakhs of Russian Central Asia,* Duke University Press, 1958; *Chekhov and His Prose,* Holt, 1966; (editor and author of foreword) Iu. M. Lotman, *Lektsii po struktural 'noi poetike,* Brown University, 1967; (editor and author of foreword) Roman Jakobsen, *O cheshskom stikhe,* Brown University, 1968; (editor and author of foreword) Lotman, *Struktura khudozhest-vennogu teksta,* Brown University, 1971; (editor and author of foreword) *Raboty uchennikov Tolstogo u Yasnoi Poliane,* Brown University, 1974; (editor) *Semiotic Theories, East and West,* Peter de Ridder Press, in press. Also editor, *Czech Literature and Poetics.* Also editor and author of foreword, Mikhail Gershenzon, *Meehta i mysl' Turgeneva,* Brown University, and Mark Aldanov, *Zagadka Tostogo,* Brown University.

*WORK IN PROGRESS: The Theories of the Prague Linguistic Circle and Modern Semiotics.*

*BIOGRAPHICAL/CRITICAL SOURCES: Books Abroad,* winter, 1968.

\* \* \*

## WINNETT, Fred Victor   1903-

*PERSONAL:* Born May 25, 1903, in Oil Springs, Ontario, Canada; son of Frederick Walter (a boilermaker) and Jennie (Blain) Winnett; married Margaret J. Taylor, September 15, 1928; children: William, Jane Marilyn. *Education:* University of Toronto, B.A., 1923, M.A., 1924, Ph.D., 1928; additional study at Knox Theological College, 1923-27, and Hartford Theological Seminary, 1928-29. *Home:* 56 Otter Crescent, Toronto, Ontario, Canada M5N 2W5.

*CAREER:* University of Toronto, University College, Toronto, Ontario, lecturer in Department of Oriental Languages, 1929-35, assistant professor, 1935-44, associate professor, 1944-52, professor and chairman of Department of Near Eastern Studies, 1952-67, vice-principal of University College, 1966-69. Director, American School of Oriental Research, Jerusalem, 1950-51, 1958-59. With W. L. Reed and F. S. Vidal, carried out an archaeological and epigraphical survey in northern Saudi Arabia, 1962; with Reed, carried out a similar survey of the Ha'il area of north Arabia, 1967. *Military service:* Canadian Army, 1942-44; became first lieutenant. *Member:* Society of Biblical Literature (president, 1964), American Oriental Society, Toronto Oriental Club.

*WRITINGS: A Study of the Lihyanite and Thamudic Inscriptions,* University of Toronto Press, 1937; *The Mosaic Tradition,* University of Toronto Press, 1949; *Safaitic Inscriptions from Jordan,* University of Toronto Press, 1957; *The Excavations at Dibon (Dhiban) in Moab,* Part I: *The First Campaign, 1950-1951,* American Schools of Oriental Research, 1964; (with William L. Reed) *Ancient Records from North Arabia,* University of Toronto Press, 1970; (with G. L. Harding) *Inscriptions from Fifty Safaitic Cairns,* University of Toronto Press, 1978. Contributor to scholarly journals.

*BIOGRAPHICAL/CRITICAL SOURCES:* J. W. Wevers and D. B. Redford, editors, *Studies on the Ancient Palestinian World* (festschrift presented to Winnett on his retirement), University of Toronto Press, 1972.

\* \* \*

## WINSLOW, Dean Hendricks, Jr.   1934-1972
## (Pete Winslow)

*PERSONAL:* Born October 19, 1934, in Seattle, Wash.; son

of Dean Hendricks (a salesman) and Esther (Carlberg) Winslow; married Jane Jacobson (a teacher), June 23, 1963; children: Peter. *Education:* University of Washington, Seattle, B.A. (journalism), 1956, B.A. (English literature), 1958. *Politics:* "Surrealist." *Religion:* "Surrealist." *Home:* 396 Lombard St., San Francisco, Calif. 94133. *Office: The Livermore Independent,* 2219 First St., Livermore, Calif.

*CAREER: Seattle Post-Intelligencer,* Seattle, Wash., reporter, 1956-58; worked for several small newspapers in Washington and California, 1959-63; *Fremont News Register,* Fremont, Calif., reporter and editor, 1963-65; Parks Job Corps Center, Pleasanton, Calif., writer, editor, and teacher, 1965-67; *Livermore Independent,* Livermore, Calif., reporter and editor, beginning 1967. *Military service:* U.S. Army Reserve, 1956-64; became first lieutenant.

*WRITINGS*—All under name Pete Winslow: *Whatever Happened to Pete Winslow,* Tolle House, 1960; *The Rapist and Other Poems,* Golden Mountain, 1962; *Monster Cookies,* privately printed, 1967; *Mummy Tapes,* Medusa Press, 1971; *A Daisy in the Memory of a Shark,* City Lights, 1973. Writer of two unpublished books, "Mount Gogo" (novel), and "Woven Balloon" (poetry). Contributor of essays and poems to literary magazines and of an article to *Nation.*

*WORK IN PROGRESS: Unwinding the Stone: Essays on Contemporary American Poets;* continuing research on nuclear radiation safeguards.

*AVOCATIONAL INTERESTS:* Long-distance running.†

(Died September 17, 1972)

\*         \*         \*

## WINSLOW, John Hathaway 1932-

*PERSONAL:* Born April 16, 1932, in Trieste, Italy; son of Rollin R. (a diplomat and attorney) and Mary M. (Macgowan) Winslow; married Joan Leddick; children: Christopher, Ethan, Jonathan. *Education:* University of Michigan, B.A.; attended University of California, Berkeley; Cambridge University, Ph.D. *Home:* 2050 South Franklin St., Seaside, Ore. 97138.

*CAREER:* California State College (now University), Hayward, founder of department and assistant professor of geography and anthropology, 1960-64, 1968-71, acting chairman of department; University of Papua and New Guinea, Port Moresby, 1971-74, associate professor, and reader in geography. Visiting professor, Trinity College, University of Dublin, 1976-78. *Military service:* U.S. Marine Corps, 1954-56; became first lieutenant. *Member:* Institute of British Geographers. *Awards, honors:* National Science Foundation science faculty fellow, Cambridge University; Research Corp. fellow.

*WRITINGS: San Nicolas Island,* University of California, 1960; (with Richard Pierce) *H.M.S. Sulphur in California,* Book Club of California, 1969; *Darwin's Victorian Malady,* American Philosophical Society, 1971; (editor) *The Melanesian Environment,* Australian National University Press, 1977. Contributor to *Annals of American Georgraphers, Cambridge Geographical Articles, Journal of Historical Geography.*

*WORK IN PROGRESS: A Most Darkling Figure,* on the perpetrator of the Piltdown hoax and other acts; *The Expendables.*

*SIDELIGHTS:* John Winslow, in 1967, followed the land route of Charles Darwin through South America in a landrover. He is currently starting a campaign to save the almost one million blacks in Irian Jaya (western New Guinea), the world's last major colony, from their Indonesian overlords. He has already written briefly on the subject in his book, *The Melanesian Environment,* and intends to continue to do so until the world's statesmen begin to show the same kind of concern for the human rights of the blacks of the Western Pacific that they have shown for the blacks of South Africa.

\*         \*         \*

## WINTER, Roger 1931-

*PERSONAL:* Born June 14, 1931, in South Bend, Ind.; son of Ray G. (an entertainer) and Thelma (Andrews) Winter; married Theresa Drenth, October 2, 1954; children: Lori D. *Education:* Attended Kalamazoo College. *Politics:* Democrat. *Religion:* Church of God. *Home:* 815 East Chippewa Ave., South Bend, Ind. 46614.

*CAREER:* Magazine & Greeting Card Service, South Bend, Ind., owner , 1964—.

*WRITINGS:* (With Kenneth Hall) *Point after Touchdown,* Warner Press, 1964; *I'll Walk Tomorrow,* Warner Press, 1971. Also author, with Don Rice, of a play, "The Death of Polycarp," published in *Youth* and *The Hi-Way.* Contributor of articles and devotionals to religious periodicals.

*BIOGRAPHICAL/CRITICAL SOURCES:* E. Stanley Jones, *Conversion,* Abingdon, 1959; Ward Oury, *Power,* Scripture Press, 1957; Charles Ludwig, *Reach,* 1971.††

\*         \*         \*

## WINTER, Ruth (Nancy G.) 1930-

*PERSONAL:* Born May 29, 1930, in Newark, N.J.; daughter of Robert Delmas (a judge) and Rose (a physical education teacher; maiden name, Rich) Grosman; married Arthur Winter (a neurosurgeon), June 16, 1955; children: Robin, Craig, Grant. *Education:* Upsala College, B.A., 1951. *Home:* 44 Holly Dr., Short Hills, N.J. 07078. *Agent:* Toni Mendez, Inc., 140 East 56th St., New York, N.Y. 10022.

*CAREER:* General assignment reporter for *Newark Star Ledger,* Newark, N.J., 1951-55, and *Houston Press,* Houston, Tex., 1955-56; *Newark Star Ledger,* science editor, 1956-69; Los Angeles Times Syndicate, Los Angeles, Calif., columnist, 1974-78; currently editor of *Pulse of Sports* (newsletter of Sports Safety and Health Care Society). Instructor in Teach Prose Program, St. Peter's College, 1969. Director of Non-Fiction Writer's Conference, American Society of Journalists and Authors and Long Island University, 1975, 1976, 1978. Fellow of board of trustees, Upsala College. *Member:* Authors League of America, American Society of Journalists and Authors (president, 1977-78), Overseas Press Club, National Association of Science Writers, American Medical Writers, American Association for the Advancement of Science, New Jersey Presswomen's Association, New Jersey Daily Newspaperwomen. *Awards, honors:* New Jersey Daily Newspaperwomen, award for news, 1958, award for series, 1960, Woman of Achievement Award, 1971; Science Writer's Award, American Dental Association, 1966; New Jersey Dental Society Award, 1968; Cecil Award, Arthritis Foundation, 1968, for series on arthritis in *Newark Star Ledger,* 1977, for article, "Update on Arthritis," in *Ladies Home Journal;* Citizens Award, New Jersey Academy of General Practice, 1969; Essex County Heart Association Award, 1969; Upsala College Alumna of the Year, 1970; New Jersey Presswomen's Association Award for Books, 1975, for *Don't Panic;* National Association of Science Teachers Award, 1977, for *Scent Talk among Animals;* additional awards from American Academy of General Practice, 1971, American Osteopathic Association, and American Academy of Family Practice.

*WRITINGS: Poisons in Your Food,* Crown, 1969, revised edition published as *Beware of the Foods You Eat,* 1971; *How to Reduce Your Medical Bills,* Crown, 1971; *A Consumer's Dictionary of Food Additives,* Crown, 1972, revised edition, 1978; *Vitamin E: The Miracle Vitamin,* Arco Publishing, 1972; *Ageless Aging,* Crown, 1973; *A Consumer's Dictionary of Cosmetic Ingredients,* Crown, 1973, revised edition, 1976; *So You Have Sinus Trouble,* Grosset, 1973; *So You Have a Pain in the Neck,* Grosset, 1974; *Don't Panic,* Western Publishing, 1975; *The Fragile Bond,* Macmillan, 1976; *Triumph over Tension,* Grosset, 1976; *The Smell Book,* Lippincott, 1976; *Scent Talk among Animals* (juvenile), Lippincott, 1977; *A Consumer's Dictionary of Suspected Cancer Causing Agents,* Crown, in press. Contributor to *Ladies Home Journal, L' Officiel, Woman's Day, Family Circle, Family Weekly, Science Digest, Reader's Digest, Glamour, Town and Country,* and other periodicals.

*WORK IN PROGRESS: The Great Self-Improvement Sourcebook,* for Pocket Books.

\* \* \*

**WIRKUS, Tom E(dward) 1933-**

*PERSONAL:* Born May 31, 1933, in Marshfield, Wis.; son of Joseph Albert (a retail clerk) and Jamina (Hansen) Wirkus; married Lois Ann Langfeldt (a physical education teacher), July 28, 1956; children: Terry, Sheila, Mary, Timothy. *Education:* University of Wisconsin—Stevens Point, B.S., 1956; University of Wisconsin—Madison, M.S., 1959; Northwestern University, Ph.D., 1966. *Religion:* Roman Catholic. *Home:* 1620 State St., La Crosse, Wis. 54601. *Office:* Department of Speech and Theatre, University of Wisconsin, La Crosse, Wis. 54601.

*CAREER:* High school teacher in Iola, Wautoma, and Wausau, Wisconsin, 1956-58; University of Wisconsin—La Crosse, instructor, 1959-62, assistant professor, 1962-64, associate professor, 1964-66, professor of speech, 1966—, head of Department of Speech and Theatre, 1970—. *Member:* Speech Communication Association, Central States Speech Association, Wisconsin Communication Association, Association of University of Wisconsin Faculties, Phi Delta Kappa, La Crosse Concert Band.

*WRITINGS: Communication and the Technical Man,* Prentice-Hall, 1972. Contributor of articles to *The Catholic Educator.*

*WORK IN PROGRESS:* Research in speech programs in the secondary schools; effective listening.

*AVOCATIONAL INTERESTS:* Music (drumming).

\* \* \*

**WISER, William**

*PERSONAL:* Born in Cincinnati, Ohio; son of Clarence F. (a salesman) and Ethel (Francis) Wiser; married Micheline Vandenschrieck (a Belgian-born artist), April 19, 1962; children: Eric Paul, Anne Karin. *Education:* Attended high school in Covington, Ky. *Home:* Chemin de la Moliere, Speracedes 06530, Peymeinade, France.

*CAREER:* Worked as a bellboy, beachboy, and hotel clerk in Miami, Fla., 1950-55, and as a bookstore clerk, census-taker, and psychiatric aide in New York City, 1955-58; New York Public Library, New York City, clerk, 1958-60; writer, living in France, 1960—. Writer-in-residence, Drake University, 1974-75; lecturer in writing, University of Texas, 1977-78. *Military service:* U.S. Navy and U.S. Naval Reserve, 1949-54. *Awards, honors:* Centro Mexicano de Escritores fellowship, 1962; Mary Roberts Rinehart Foundation Award, 1964, to complete manuscript, "Short Sketches of Bohemia" (published as *K*); National Endowment for the Arts fellowship, 1978.

*WRITINGS: K* (novel), Doubleday, 1971; *The Wolf Is Not Native to the South of France,* Harcourt, 1978. Contributor to short story anthologies, including *Best American Short Stories 1967.* Short stories and articles have been published in *Playboy, Cosmopolitan, Redbook, Harper's Bazaar, Cavalier, Reporter, Escapade, Antioch Review, Kenyon Review, Carleton Miscellany, Nugget,* and other magazines.

*WORK IN PROGRESS:* A short story collection and a novel.

*SIDELIGHTS:* William Wiser does his writing in a small stone house near a lake in France, adjacent to his home, a converted olive mill. He and his family spend summers on the North Sea in Belgium.

*BIOGRAPHICAL/CRITICAL SOURCES: Best Sellers,* March 1, 1971.

\* \* \*

**WISHARD, Armin 1941-**

*PERSONAL:* Surname is accented on the first syllable; born June 7, 1941, in Gmunden, Austria; son of Lester L. and Irmgard (Nadolny) Wishard. *Education:* Pasadena City College, A.A., 1963; University of California, Riverside, B.A., 1965, M.A., 1967; University of Oregon, Ph.D., 1969. *Home:* 1105 South Cherry, Apt. 5-208, Denver, Colo. 80222. *Office:* Department of German, Colorado College, Colorado Springs, Colo. 80903.

*CAREER:* University of Oregon, Eugene, instructor in German, 1967-69; Washington State University, Pullman, assistant professor of German, 1969-70; Colorado College, Colorado Springs, assistant professor, 1970-77, associate professor of German, 1977—. *Military service:* U.S. Air Force, 1957-61. *Member:* Modern Language Association of America, American Association of University Professors, American Association of Teachers of German.

*WRITINGS*—All with Edward Diller; all published by Norton: *Spiel und Sprache,* 1971; *Noch Einmal Spiel und Sprache,* 1973; *Cuentos y juegos,* 1975. Contributor of articles on the German Democratic Republic, to *Papers on Language and Literature, Unterrichtspraxis, Bulletin of American Council of Teachers of Foreign Language.*

*WORK IN PROGRESS: Au fil des mots,* for Norton.

*SIDELIGHTS:* Armin Wishard's extensive research on the life and letters of the German Democratic Republic has included seven trips to Germany. He is fluent in German and French, and speaks some Russian, Swedish, and Spanish.

\* \* \*

**WISSE, Ruth R(oskies) 1936-**

*PERSONAL:* Surname rhymes with "ice"; born May 13, 1936, in Cernauti, Rumania; daughter of Leo and Masha (Welczer) Roskies; married Leonard Wisse (a lawyer), March 17, 1957; children: William, Jacob, Abigail. *Education:* McGill University, B.A., 1957, Ph.D., 1969; Columbia

University, M.A., 1961. *Religion:* Jewish. *Home:* 656 Roslyn Ave., Montreal, Quebec, Canada. *Office:* McGill University, Montreal, Quebec, Canada.

*CAREER:* McGill University, Montreal, Quebec, assistant professor of Yiddish literature, 1968-71; Tel Aviv University, and Hebrew University, Tel Aviv, Israel, senior lecturer, 1971-73; McGill University, associate professor, 1976—. Consultant for Y.I.V.O. Institute for Jewish Research, New York.

*WRITINGS:* (Translator) *The Well by Chaim Grade,* Jewish Publication Society, 1967; *The Schlemiel as Modern Hero,* University of Chicago Press, 1970; *A Shtetl and Other Yiddish Novellas,* Behrman, 1972. Contributor of essays to *Commentary,* and *Moment.*

*SIDELIGHTS:* Ruth Wisse is fluent in Yiddish, Hebrew, and French.

\* \* \*

## WITKIN, Erwin 1926-

*PERSONAL:* Born August 19, 1926, in Omaha, Neb.; son of Louis and Bessie (Burstein) Witkin; married Helen Silverman (a teacher and therapist), June 20, 1948; children: Robert, Karen, Gary. *Education:* Johns Hopkins University, B.A., 1947; University of Nebraska, M.D., 1951. *Politics:* Democrat. *Religion:* Jewish. *Home:* 6807 Maurleen Rd., Baltimore, Md. 21209. *Agent:* Annie Laurie Williams, Inc., 18 East 41st St., New York, N.Y. 10017.

*CAREER:* Licensed to practice medicine in Nebraska, 1951, in Maryland, 1955, and in California, 1969; Sinai Hospital, Baltimore, Md., internship and residency training in obstetrics and gynecology, 1951-55; private practice of medicine in Baltimore as specialist in gynecology, 1965—. Chief medical consultant, U.S. Social Security Administration, Bureau of Health Insurance (Medicare), 1966-69; president, Institute of Medical Programming, 1967-68; associate, Block, McGibony & Associates, Inc. (hospital and health consultants), Silver Spring, Md., 1970—. Lecturer at School of Public Health and Administrative Medicine, Columbia University, 1967, and at other universities. *Military service:* U.S. Army Air Forces, 1945-46.

*MEMBER:* American Medical Association, American College of Obstetrics and Gynecology (fellow), American Society of Abdominal Surgeons, American Fertility Society, Southern Medical Association, Medical and Chirugical Faculty of Maryland, Maryland Society of Obstetrics and Gynecology, Baltimore City Medical Society.

*WRITINGS: The Impact of Medicare,* C. C Thomas, 1971. Contributor to medical journals, including *Medical Economics.* Writer of regular column on medicine in *Montgomery County Sentinel,* 1966.

*WORK IN PROGRESS: For I Was a Son,* a novel.††

\* \* \*

## WITT, Reginald Eldred 1907-

*PERSONAL:* Born February 12, 1907, in Southampton, England; son of John Alexander (an officer in Mercantile Marine) and Edith Elizabeth (Wickens) Witt; married Mary Elizabeth Lean, March 30, 1940; children: Richard Clement Hartley, Elizabeth Clemency. *Education:* Attended University of Southampton; University of London, B.A. (external), 1927; University of Birmingham, M.A., 1929; Cambridge University, Ph.D., 1934. *Politics:* "A Liberal, as understood by Browning the Poet." *Religion:* "A blend of Protes-

tant Nonconformity and Greek Orthodoxy." *Home:* 1 Oakwood Park Rd., Southgate, London N14 6QB, England.

*CAREER:* Departmental head of English and classics at five grammar schools in England, 1929-67; headmaster of Calday Grange School, West Kirby, 1945-53, and of Totenham Grammar School, London, 1953-67; associated with John Lyon School, Harrow, England, 1968; University of London, Queen Mary College, London, England, member of faculty, 1968-72. Regular lecturer for National Tourist Office of Greece in Great Britain; lecturer for British Council in Thessalonica, Athens, and at Orthodox Academy, Crete. Justice of the Peace for county of Middlesex, 1957—; retired lay reader at St. Andrew's Church, Southgate, and preacher at St. Andrew's Church and at other churches.

*MEMBER:* Royal Society of Literature (fellow), Classical Association (life member), Royal Institute of Philosophy (life member), Hellenic Society (life member), Anglo-Hellenic League (life member), Magistrates Association (life member), Cambridge Philological Society (life member), Overseas Club (life member), Historical and Archaeological Society of Western Crete (honorary), London Motet and Madrigal Club.

*WRITINGS: Albinus and the History of Middle Platonism,* Cambridge University Press and Macmillan, 1937, Volume III: *Cambridge Classical Studies,* reprinted, 1971; *Greece the Beloved,* Institute for Balkan Studies (Salonica), 1965; *Isis in the Graeco-Roman World,* Cornell University Press, 1971. Has translated verses from Modern Greek into English for *Hellas,* and *Thorn,* Zeno Publishers, 1977. Contributor to *Vermaseren Festschrift,* 1978; contributor of articles to *Aktines, Syzitisis, Greek Gazette,* and other Greek periodicals, and reviews to professional journals in English. Former editor, *Eastern Churches News Letter.*

*WORK IN PROGRESS:* The cults of Mithras and Isis as forerunners of later systems, such as Christianity and Freemasonry; the origins and development of the Theotokos doctrine; a history of Cretan civilization; translation of a work by D. Tsakonas.

*SIDELIGHTS:* Reginald Witt travels regularly to Greece. He says that four visits to Mount Athos "opened my eyes to the importance of Isis for an understanding of Christianity." *Avocational interests:* Music (piano soloist at schools and churches), walking, Mediterranean swimming.

\* \* \*

## WITUCKE, Virginia 1937-

*PERSONAL:* Surname is pronounced wit-*tuck*-key; born May 7, 1937, in Oak Park, Ill.; daughter of Frank Joseph and Alice (Brown) Witucke. *Education:* Illinois State University, B.S. in Ed., 1957; Western Michigan University, M.A., 1961; Columbia University, D.L.S., 1974. *Home:* 1585 Ridge, Evanston, Ill. 60201.

*CAREER:* Bellwood Public Schools, Bellwood, Ill., teacher, 1957-60; Oak Ridge Public Schools, Oak Ridge, Tenn., librarian, 1961-63; Lansing Public Schools, Lansing, Mich., librarian, 1963-65; Decatur Public Schools, Decatur, Ill., librarian, 1965-66; Purdue University, Lafayette, Ind., assistant professor of education, 1966-70; University of Iowa, Iowa City, assistant professor, 1973-76; Pratt Institute, Brooklyn, N.Y., associate professor, 1976-78. *Member:* American Library Association, National Council of Teachers of English, Association for Educational Communications and Technology, Freedom to Read Foundation, New York Library Association.

WRITINGS: Poetry in the Elementary School, W. C. Brown, 1970. Member of selection panel, The Paperback Goes to School.

*    *    *

## WIZARD, Mariann G(arner)  1946-

PERSONAL: Born September 30, 1946, in Fort Worth, Tex.; daughter of Carl Douglas and Catherine (Cooper) Garner; married George J. Wizard IV, December 18, 1965 (died, 1967); married Larry Gene Waterhouse (a writer), October 9, 1970. Education: Attended University of Texas at Austin, 1965-72, and Free University of Austin, 1965-66; Antioch University/Juarez Lincoln Center, Austin, Tex., B.A., 1978. Residence: Austin, Tex. Agent: Waterwizards Productions, P.O. Box 13313, Austin, Tex. 78711.

CAREER: Journalist; social service and educational office and field worker; community and political organizer; Water-wizards Productions, Austin, Tex., director, 1973—. Researcher and writer, Collegiate Research Systems, 1973-75; production manager, Ag Trucking News, 1974. Former "underage illegal topless dancer." Awards, honors: National Merit Scholarship finalist, 1964; honorable mention in political criticism, Harper's College Criticism Contest, 1970, for article, "United Front against Fascism."

WRITINGS: (With husband, Larry G. Waterhouse) Turning the Guns Around: Notes on the G.I. Movement, Praeger, 1971; (contributor of poetry) Seems Southern to We, edited by Larry E. Evans, Office of Minority Student Affairs, University of Kentucky, 1977. Also contributor of poetry to Women and Their Work, 1977. Contributor to periodicals, including Monterey County Nose, Rag, NOLA Express, Worker (now Daily World), and "numerous alternative and 'underground' publications." Art director, Texas Ranger, 1969-70; assistant and associate editor, Free & Easy, 1974-76.

WORK IN PROGRESS: A collection of semi-autobiographical sketches and poems, tentatively entitled Narrow Escapes.

SIDELIGHTS: Mariann Wizard describes her "religiopolitics" as "Tight End Pantheism and Community Trust." A "former communist" and member of the Students for a Democratic Society, she was cited by the Senate Subcommittee on Internal Security as one of four people "responsible for student unrest in Texas and Oklahoma" in 1968. She told CA: "The political awareness and activity of the sixties led me to my first efforts with the underground and alternate media press, and eventually, to a Marxist-Leninist analysis of events. It is difficult at this point in my existence to determine whether writing is my vocation and socio/political activism my avocation, or vice-versa.

"I view most of my writing as a contribution to raising the consciousness of myself and my readers, and strive for perfection too much for my own good. I am most moved to write by the petty tyrannies and abuses of power which characterize life in America at this time. I feel an obligation to be objective, but as a Libra, am often confused. I believe in fairy tales despite losing streaks on three continents."

AVOCATIONAL INTERESTS: Reading (especially science fiction), "rapping, rock and roll, the pursuit of happiness, my weird, wonderful family and friends."

*    *    *

## WOESSNER, Warren (Dexter)  1944-

PERSONAL: Born May 31, 1944, in New Brunswick, N.J.; son of Warren Wendling (a chemist) and Flora (Dexter) Woessner; married Joyce Howe (a University of Wisconsin state employee), April 17, 1971. Education: Cornell University, A.B., 1966; University of Wisconsin—Madison, Ph.D., 1971. Home: 2322 Rugby Row, Madison, Wis. 53705. Office: Miles Laboratories, Kinsman Blvd., Madison, Wis. 53704.

CAREER: University of Wisconsin—Madison, research associate in School of Pharmacy, 1971-72; Miles Laboratories, Madison, Wis., senior research scientist, 1972—. Member: American Chemical Society. Awards, honors: Memorial Union Creative Writing Contest awards, University of Wisconsin—Madison, 1967, 1968, 1969, 1970; National Endowment for the Arts creative writing fellowship, 1974; Wisconsin Arts Board fellowships in creative writing, 1975, 1976.

WRITINGS—All poetry: The Forest and the Trees, Quixote Press, 1968; The Rivers Return, Gunrunner Press, 1969; Inroads, Modine Gunch Press, 1970; Landing, Ithaca House, 1974; Lost Highway, Poetry Texas, 1977. Contributor of poetry to Poetry, Poetry Northwest, Nation, Hanging Loose, Bones, and other periodicals. Editor, Abraxas (poetry magazine).

WORK IN PROGRESS: A collection of poetry, No Hiding Place; more poetry and criticism.

AVOCATIONAL INTERESTS: Ornithology, photography, community radio, travel.

*    *    *

## WOLD, Ruth  1923-

PERSONAL: Born August 31, 1923, in Gordon, Tex.; daughter of Vernon (a road commissioner and rancher) and Irene (Butler) Rexroat; married Ivor P. Wold, October 5, 1959 (divorced, 1964). Education: North Texas State Teachers College (now North Texas State University), B.A., 1945; University of Texas at Austin, M.A., 1948, Ph.D., 1956. Home: 9830 Reseda, Northridge, Calif. 91324. Office: Department of Spanish, California State University, Northridge, Calif. 91324.

CAREER: Arkansas Agricultural and Mechanical College (now University of Arkansas at Monticello), instructor in Spanish and English, 1948-50; University of Arizona, Tucson, instructor in Spanish, 1959-60; California State University, Northridge, 1960—, began as assistant professor, currently professor of Spanish. Consultant to Great Lakes College Association, summer, 1964. Member: Modern Language Association of America, American Association of Teachers of Spanish and Portuguese, American Association of University Professors, Philological Association of the Pacific Coast, Pacific Coast Council on Latin American Studies.

WRITINGS: El Diario de Mexico, Gredos (Madrid), 1970. Contributor of articles to Revista Interamericana de Bibliografia and Hispania.

WORK IN PROGRESS: Spanish word frequencies.

*    *    *

## WOLFE, Martin  1920-

PERSONAL: Born July 6, 1920, in Newark, N.J.; son of George Dichter (an accountant) and Mary (Reich) Wolfe; married Dorothy Wexler (a college mathematics teacher), June 7, 1942; children: Carolyn. Education: University of Illinois, B.A., 1941; Columbia University, M.A., 1946,

Ph. D., 1950. *Politics:* Democrat. *Religion:* Jewish. *Home:* 245 Hathaway Lane, Wynnewood, Pa. 19096. *Office:* Department of History, University of Pennsylvania, Philadelphia, Pa. 19174.

*CAREER:* Wayne University (now Wayne State University), Detroit, Mich., instructor, 1948-52, assistant professor of history, 1952-53; University of Pennsylvania, Philadelphia, assistant professor, 1953-63, associate professor, 1963-70, professor of history, 1970—. Fulbright lecturer, 1956-57. *Military service:* U.S. Army Air Forces, radio operator, 1942-45; became staff sergeant; received Air Medal with seven oak leaf clusters. *Member:* Economic History Association, Society of French Historical Studies.

*WRITINGS: The French Franc between the Wars: 1919-1939,* Columbia University Press, 1950; (with John Jensen and James Hardy) *The Maclure Collection of French Revolutionary Materials,* University of Pennsylvania Press, 1965; *The Economic Causes of Imperialism,* Wiley, 1972; *The Fiscal System of Renaissance France,* Yale University Press, 1972. Contributor of articles to economic history journals. Associate editor, *Journal of Economic History,* 1953-55.

*WORK IN PROGRESS:* Studies on the time table of fiscal absolutism in early modern Europe; the economic and social history of welfare in western Europe.

*BIOGRAPHICAL/CRITICAL SOURCES: Times Literary Supplement,* July 13, 1967.

\*      \*      \*

## WOLFF, Charlotte 1904-

*PERSONAL:* Born September 30, 1904, in Germany. *Education:* Attended Universities of Freiburg, Munich, and Berlin; University of Berlin, M.D., 1928. *Home:* 10 Redcliffe Pl., London SW10 9DD, England.

*CAREER:* Psychiatrist in private practice in London, England, 1951—. *Member:* Psychological Society (England; fellow), Royal College of Psychiatrists.

*WRITINGS: Studies in Hand-Reading,* translated from the original German manuscript by O. M. Cook, preface by Aldous Huxley, Chatto & Windus, 1936; *The Human Hand,* Methuen, 1942, Knopf, 1943, 3rd edition, Methuen, 1949; *A Psychology of Gesture,* translated from the original French manuscript by Anne Tennant, Methuen, 1942, 2nd edition, 1948; *The Hand in Psychological Diagnosis,* Methuen, 1951, Philosophical Library, 1952; *On the Way to Myself: Communications to a Friend* (autobiography), Methuen, 1969; *Love between Women,* St. Martin's, 1971; *An Older Love* (novel), Virago, 1976; *Bisexuality: A Study,* Quartet, 1977. Contributor to professional journals.

*WORK IN PROGRESS:* A new edition of *Love between Women;* psychological research.

*SIDELIGHTS:* Charlotte Wolff writes: "My interest in homosexual inclination and behaviour has two roots—the poetry of Sappho, which induced me to learn Greek—and my medico-psychological studies and practice. My latest book, *Love between Women,* originated from an essay I wrote many years ago. I had the most rare opportunity to collect a great number of non-clinical lesbians for my research which was statistically evaluated by the Medical Research Council."

Charlotte Wolff has appeared on British television and radio several times as an expert on the subject of female homosexuality. Many of her books have appeared in German, French, Italian, and Spanish editions.

*AVOCATIONAL INTERESTS:* Poetry, literature.

\*      \*      \*

## WOLFF, Konrad (Martin) 1907-

*PERSONAL:* Born March 11, 1907, in Berlin, Germany; son of Martin (a professor of law) and Marguerite (Jolowicz) Wolff; married Ilse Bing (an artist; former photographer), November 4, 1937. *Education:* Attended University of Heidelberg; University of Berlin, Dr. Jur., 1930; Faculte de Droit, Diplomes d'Etudes superieures, 1935; Columbia University, M.A., 1957. *Home:* 210 Riverside Dr., New York, N.Y. 10025. *Office:* Department of Music, Montclair State College, Upper Montclair, N.J. 07043.

*CAREER:* Law student and researcher, 1925-36; pianist; "New Friends of Music," New York, N.Y., assistant musical director, 1942-50; teacher of piano at Westchester Conservatory of Music, White Plains, N.Y., 1949-54, Drew University, Madison, N.J., 1956-62, Peabody Conservatory, Baltimore, Md., 1963-74, Rutgers State University, New Brunswick, N.J., 1974-75, and Smith College, Northampton, Mass., 1975-76; Montclair State College, Upper Montclair, N.J., professor, 1976—. *Member:* American Musicological Society, Music Teachers of America, American Association of University Professors.

*WRITINGS:* (Editor) Robert Schumann, *On Music and Musicians,* Pantheon, 1946; (with Rene Leibowitz) *Erich Itor Kahn* (in French), Buchet Chastel, 1958; *The Teaching of Artur Schnabel,* Praeger, 1972. Contributor to music journals, including *Piano Quarterly.*

*WORK IN PROGRESS: Introduction to the Piano Music of the Great Masters of the Past.*

\*      \*      \*

## WOLFF, Ruth 1909(?)-1972

1909(?)—June 13, 1972; American novelist and short story writer. Obituaries: *Publishers Weekly,* July 31, 1972.

\*      \*      \*

## WOLGENSINGER, Bernard 1935-

*PERSONAL:* Born December 25, 1935, in Nancy, France; son of Francois and Helene (Millet) Wolgensinger. *Education:* Ecole nationale superieure des beaux arts, D.P.L.G., 1962. *Religion:* None. *Home:* 36 Rue Boissonade, Paris 75014, France. *Office:* 67 Rue Vergniaud, Paris 75013, France.

*CAREER:* Architect, 1962—.

*WRITINGS:* (With Jacques Debaigts) *Maisons de vacances en Europe—Ferienhauser in Europa—Vacation Houses of Europe* (text in French, German, and English; German translation by Gerda Ringger-Anhegger, English translation by Gabriel Otvos), Tuttle, 1968; *Maisons de vacances au soleil—Ferienhauser in der Sonne—Vacation Houses in the Sun* (text in French, German, and English; German translation by Ingrid Debains and Jacques Debains, English translation by Douglas-J. Gillam), Office du Livre, 1971, published as *Villas in the Sun,* Tuttle, 1971; (with Jose Daidone) *Votre Jardin: Architecture et art floral—Personal Gardens: Architecture and Floral Design—Su Jardin: Arquitectura y arte floral* (text in French, English, and Spanish; English translation by J. A. Underwood, Spanish translation by Pedro Lahiguera), Office du Livre, 1975, published as *The Personal Garden: Its Architecture and Design,* Van Nostrand, 1975 (published in England as *Town*

*Gardens: Their Architecture and Design,* Studio Vista, 1975).

\*　\*　\*

## WOLKSTEIN, Diane 1942-

*PERSONAL:* Born November 11, 1942, in New York, N.Y.; daughter of Harry W. (a certified public accountant) and Ruth (Barenbaum) Wolkstein; married Benjamin Zucker (a gem merchant), September 7, 1969; children: Rachel Cloudstone. *Education:* Smith College, B.A., 1964; studied pantomime in Paris, 1964-65, Bank Street College of Education, M.A., 1967. *Religion:* Jewish. *Home:* 10 Patchin Pl., New York, N.Y. 10011. *Agent:* Marilyn Marlow, 60 East 56th St., New York, N.Y. 10022.

*CAREER:* Hostess of weekly radio show, "Stories from Many Lands with Diane Wolkstein," WNYC-Radio, New York City, 1967—. Instructor in storytelling and children's literature, Bank Street College, New York City, 1970—; leader of storytelling workshops for librarians and teachers. *Awards, honors:* Litho-Osborne fellowship, 1976.

*WRITINGS: 8,000 Stones,* Doubleday, 1972; *The Cool Ride in the Sky,* Knopf, 1973; *Squirrel's Song,* Knopf, 1976; *Lazy Stories,* Seabury, 1976; *The Visit,* Knopf, 1977; *The Red Lion,* Crowell, 1977; *The Magic Orange Tree and Other Maitian Folk Tales,* Knopf, 1978. Contributor of articles to *Wilson Library Bulletin, Children's Literature in Education,* and *School Library Journal.*

*SIDELIGHTS:* Diane Wolkstein was guest storyteller at the John Masefield Storytelling Festival in Toronto, 1972, and at the Fifth National Association for the Preservation of Storytelling Festival in Jonesboro, Tenn., in 1977. On two separate occasions, she has told stories to Queen Margareta of Denmark and Princess Benedikta.

Wolkstein has recorded stories for Canadian Broadcasting Corporation Radio and TV, and has told stories in various cities of Europe. She has recorded many of her short stories including: "Tales of the Hopi Indians," 1972, "California Fairy Tales," 1972, "Eskimo Stories Tales of Magic," 1974, and "The Cove Kids in the Sky," 1975.

*AVOCATIONAL INTERESTS:* Travel.

\*　\*　\*

## WOLMAN, Harold L. 1942-

*PERSONAL:* Born September 4, 1942, in Dayton, Ohio; son of Walter (a health administrator) and Margaret (Weltman) Wolman; married Dianne Miller (a government administrator), January 4, 1970; children: Andrew Miller. *Education:* Oberlin College, A.B., 1964; University of Michigan, M.A., 1965, Ph.D., 1968; Massachusetts Institute of Technology, M.C.P., 1976. *Home:* 5435 41st Pl. N.W., Washington, D.C. 20015.

*CAREER:* University of Pennsylvania, Philadelphia, assistant professor of political science, 1968-70; National Urban Coalition, Washington, D.C., assistant director of National Priorities Project, 1970-71; legislative assistant to Senator Adlai E. Stevenson III, Washington, D.C., 1971-73; University of Massachusetts—Boston, associate professor of politics, 1974-75; legislative assistant to Senator Stevenson, 1975-76; House of Representatives, Banking Committee, Washington, D.C., staff director of Subcommittee on City, 1977; White House Conference on Balanced National Growth and Economic Development, Washington, D.C., deputy director, 1977-78; Urban Institute, Washington, D.C., senior research associate, 1978—. *Member:* Phi Beta

Kappa. *Awards, honors:* Woodrow Wilson fellow, 1965—; National Endowment for the Humanities fellow, 1973-74.

*WRITINGS: Politics of Federal Housing,* Dodd, 1971; (with Robert Benson) *Counterbudget,* Praeger, 1971; *Goals and Strategies for Federal Income Support Programs,* National Urban Coalition, 1971; *Housing and Housing Policy in the U.S. and the U.K.,* Lexington Books, 1975.

\*　\*　\*

## WOLOZIN, Harold 1920-

*PERSONAL:* Born July 7, 1920, in Milford, Mass.; son of Morris and Elizabeth Wolozin; married Ruth Swartz, October 19, 1947 (deceased); children: Deborah, Benjamin, Sarah. *Education:* Tufts University, B.S., 1942; University of Cincinnati, graduate study, 1942-43; Columbia University, Ph.D., 1955. *Home:* 131 Hubbard St., Concord, Mass. 01742. *Office:* Department of Economics, University of Massachusetts, Boston, Mass. 02116.

*CAREER:* Rutgers University, Newark, N.J., instructor in economics, 1950-51; Hecht Co. (department stores), Washington, D.C., corporate economist, 1953-55; U.S. Department of Labor, Washington, D.C., chief of price research in Bureau of Labor Statistics, 1956-59; U.S. Department of Interior, Washington, D.C., economist, 1959-60; U.S. Department of Commerce, Washington, D.C., special assistant for economic research, 1960-61; American University, Washington, D.C., associate professor of economics, 1962-66; University of Massachusetts—Boston, professor of economics, 1966—, chairman of department, 1966-69. Lecturer at New York University, 1947-48, American Institute of Banking, 1947-52, and University of Virginia, 1953-61. Consultant to government and private groups.

*WRITINGS:* (Contributor) Ben B. Seligman, editor, *Poverty as a Public Issue,* Free Press, 1965; (contributor) *Goals, Priorities, and Dollars,* National Planning Association, 1965; (editor and contributor) *The Economics of Air Pollution,* Norton, 1966; (editor) *American Monetary and Fiscal Policy,* Quadrangle, 1970; (editor) *Introduction to Economics: An Interdisciplinary Approach,* Holbrook, 1973; (editor with Raymond Torto) *Domestic Economic Problems: A Reader,* Holbrook, 1973; (contributor) *The Economics of Pollution,* Lexington Books, 1974; *Energy and the Environment,* General Learning Press, 1974; *The Value of Volunteer Service in the United States,* ACTION, 1977. Author of monographs; contributor of about fifty articles to economics journals.

*WORK IN PROGRESS: Aging and Retirement; Volunteering in the United States; The Retirement Decision.*

\*　\*　\*

## WOLVERTON, Robert E(arl) 1925-

*PERSONAL:* Born August 4, 1925, in Indianapolis, Ind.; son of Robert Newton Wolverton and Vivian (Leffler) Wolverton Overton; married Margaret Jester, September 13, 1952; children: Robert, Jr., Laurie, Edwin, Gary. *Education:* Hanover College, A.B. (with honors), 1948; University of Michigan, A.M., 1949; University of North Carolina, Ph.D., 1954. *Politics:* Independent. *Religion:* Roman Catholic. *Home:* 108 Edinburgh Dr., Starkville, Miss. 39759. *Office:* 608 Allen Hall, Mississippi State University, Mississippi State, Miss. 39762.

*CAREER:* Florida State University, Tallahassee, instructor, 1951-52, assistant professor, 1962-65, associate professor of classics, 1965-67, director of honors program, 1966-

67; University of Georgia, Athens, assistant professor of classics, 1954-59; Tufts University, Medford, Mass., assistant professor of classics and history, 1959-62, assistant to dean of graduate studies, 1960-62, acting head, department of classics, 1961-62; University of Illinois at Urbana-Champaign, associate professor of classics and associate dean of graduate college, 1967-69; Miami University, Oxford, Ohio, professor of classics and dean of graduate school and research, 1969-72; College of Mount St. Joseph on the Ohio, Mount St. Joseph, Ohio, president, 1972-77; Mississippi State University, Mississippi State, vice-president, 1977—. Fellow, Academic Administration Internship Program, Mills College, 1965-66. Consultant, U.S. Office of Education and University Associates, Inc., both Washington, D.C.

*MEMBER:* American Association of University Professors (president, University of Georgia chapter, 1958-59, Tufts University chapter, 1961-62, and Florida State University chapter, 1963-64), American Classical League (member of executive committee, 1962-70; president, 1972-76), American Association of Higher Education, American Philological Association, Council of Graduate Schools (member of executive committee, 1971-73), Classical Association of Middle West and South, Midwestern Association of Graduate Schools (chairman, 1971-72), Phi Kappa Phi, Omicron Delta Kappa, Eta Sigma Phi, Oxford Federation of Clubs (president, 1972-74), Oxford Kiwanis (director, 1971-72), International Torch Club.

*WRITINGS:* (With M. Gordon Brown) *A Primer of Foreign Language Study,* Georgia Education Association, 1958; (contributor) Charles Henderson, editor, *Studies in Honor of B. L. Ullman,* Edizioni di Storia e Lettera (Rome), 1963; (contributor) Eugene Davis, editor, *Studies in Honor of W. E. Caldwell,* University of North Carolina Press, 1964; *Classical Elements in English Words,* Littlefield, 1965; *An Outline of Classical Mythology,* Littlefield, 1966. Contributor of articles, reviews, and translations to *Classical Journal, Classical Outlook, Eleusis,* and other journals.

*SIDELIGHTS:* Robert Wolverton told *CA:* "Much of my adult thinking and views flow from the classical authors I've studied and taught, especially Greek dramatists and historians and Roman poets and historians. Other authors who have influenced me are Robert Hutchins, Paul Goodman, and Rollo May. Moving from classroom to administration has presented very broadened horizons and challenges, suggesting that interpersonal relationships may differ, but they are still the key to success."

*AVOCATIONAL INTERESTS:* Coaching basketball and tennis, umpiring football and baseball, teaching bridge.

\* \* \*

## WOOD, Chauncey 1935-

*PERSONAL:* Born June 16, 1935, in Englewood, N.J.; son of Earl C. and Carol (Derby) Wood; married Sarah Bennett, September 9, 1961; children: Stephanie, Jennifer. *Education:* Union College and University, Schenectady, N.Y., A.B., 1957; Princeton University, M.A., 1960, Ph.D., 1963. *Home:* 231 Rosemary Lane, Ancaster, Ontario, Canada L9G 2K6. *Office:* Department of English, McMaster University, Hamilton, Ontario, Canada L8S 4L9.

*CAREER:* Hollins College, Hollins College, Va., instructor, 1960-63, assistant professor of English, 1963-64; University of Cincinnati, Cincinnati, Ohio, assistant professor of English, 1964-65; University of Wisconsin—Madison, assis-

tant professor of English, 1965-68; McMaster University, Hamilton, Ontario, associate professor, 1968-72, professor of English, 1972—. *Member:* Modern Language Association of America, Mediaeval Academy of America, Phi Beta Kappa. *Awards, honors:* Hollins College faculty research grants, 1962, 1963, 1964; University of Wisconsin summer research grant, 1966; National Endowment for the Humanities summer research grant, 1967; American Council of Learned Societies study fellowship, 1967-68; fellow, Institute for Research in the Humanities, University of Wisconsin, 1967-68; Canada Council leave fellowship, 1974-75.

*WRITINGS:* (Contributor) Beryl Rowland, editor, *Companion to Chaucer Studies,* Oxford University Press, 1968; (contributor) D. W. Robertson, Jr., editor, *The Literature of Medieval England,* McGraw, 1970; *Chaucer and the Country of the Stars: Poetic Uses of Astrological Imagery,* Princeton University Press, 1970. Contributor to *Modern Language Quarterly, Traditio, Philological Quarterly, English Language Notes,* and other publications.

*WORK IN PROGRESS: The Mood of Chaucer's Troilus; The Dimensions of Chaucer's General Prologue;* several articles on Chaucer.

\* \* \*

## WOOD, Leonard C(lair) 1923-

*PERSONAL:* Born January 1, 1923, in Utica, Pa.; son of John Barnard (a farmer) and Ethel (Boughner) Wood; married Tanya Bogoslovsky (a book store owner), July 19, 1953; children: Stephen Jeffrey, Anthony Christopher, John Michael, Sarah Elizabeth. *Education:* Slippery Rock State Teachers College (now Slippery Rock State College), B.S., 1943; University of Pennsylvania, M.A., 1948, Ph.D., 1960; University of London, additional study, 1950-51. *Politics:* Democrat. *Home:* R.R. 4, Charleston, Ill. 61920. *Office:* Department of History, Eastern Illinois University, Charleston, Ill. 61920.

*CAREER:* McGraw-Hill Book Co., New York City, editor-writer, 1952-54; Henry Holt and Co., New York City, chief social studies editor, 1954-57; Macmillan & Co., New York City, senior editor, 1957-60; Eastern Illinois University, Charleston, assistant professor, 1960-65, associate professor, 1965-71, professor of history, 1971—, director of cooperative education, 1975—. Visiting professor at Miami University, Miami, Ohio, 1969. *Military service:* U.S. Naval Reserve, 1943-45; became lieutenant junior grade. *Member:* American Historical Association, Society for French Historical Studies. *Awards, honors:* Harrison fellow, University of Pennsylvania, 1948-50; Fulbright scholar, University of London, 1950-51.

*WRITINGS: The Soviet Army,* U.S. Government Printing Office, 1953; *The Satellite Armies,* U.S. Government Printing Office, 1954; *Sir Edmund Monson: Ambassador to France,* Ann Arbor Publishers, 1960; (contributor) *American Civics,* Harcourt, 1967; *America: Its People and Values,* Harcourt, 1971, revised edition, 1975. Associate editor, Cooperative Education Association *Newsletter,* 1976—.

*WORK IN PROGRESS:* Preparing special feature articles to be printed in forthcoming (social sciences) texts; research in Anglo-American relations in late nineteenth century.

\* \* \*

## WOOD, Michael 1936-

*PERSONAL:* Born August 19, 1936, in Lincolnshire, England; son of George William (a cashier) and Winifred

(Horsefield) Wood; married Elena Uribe (an anthropologist), September 23, 1967; children: Gabriela, Patrick, Audrey. *Education:* Cambridge University, B.A., 1957, M.A. and Ph.D., 1961. *Home:* 90 Morningside Dr., New York, N.Y. 10027. *Agent:* Harold Matson Co., Inc., 22 East 40th St., New York, N.Y. 10016. *Office:* Columbia University, 412 Hamilton Hall, New York, N.Y. 10027.

*CAREER:* Cambridge University, St. John's College, Cambridge, England, fellow in French literature, 1961-64; Columbia University, New York, N.Y., instructor, 1964-66, assistant professor, 1968-71, associate professor, 1971-74, professor of comparative literature, 1974—. *Awards, honors:* Guggenheim fellow, 1973-74.

*WRITINGS: Stendhal,* Cornell University Press, 1971. Co-author of screenplays for "Scene Nun, Take One," 1966, and "Praise Marx and Pass the Ammunition," 1968. Author of a regular column in *New Society.* Contributor to periodicals and newspapers, including *New Statesman, New York Review of Books,* and *Observer.*

*WORK IN PROGRESS:* A book on the nineteenth-century novel in England and France; a book on Luis Bunuel.

*AVOCATIONAL INTERESTS:* Travel.

\* \* \*

### WOOD, Phyllis Anderson 1923-

*PERSONAL:* Born October 24, 1923, in Palo Alto, Calif.; daughter of Carl Arthur (a high school principal) and Beulah (Davidson) Anderson; married Roger Holmes Wood (an insurance underwriter), December 26, 1947; children: Stephen Holmes, David Anderson, Martha Helen. *Education:* University of California, Berkeley, A.B., 1944; Stanford University, teaching certificate, 1946; San Francisco State University, M.A., 1977. *Religion:* Presbyterian. *Home:* 65 Capay Circle, South San Francisco, Calif. 94080.

*CAREER:* Teacher of speech, drama, and English in high schools in California, 1944-49; teacher of reading courses for adults in Daly City, Calif., 1965-71; Thornton High School, Daly City, reading teacher and director of reading laboratory, 1966-76; Jefferson High School, Daly City, teacher of reading and basic writing skills, 1976—. *Member:* International Reading Association, San Mateo County Reading Council.

*WRITINGS*—For young adults; all published by Westminster: *Andy,* 1971; *Your Bird Is Here, Tom Thompson,* 1972; *I've Missed a Sunset or Three,* 1973; *Song of the Shaggy Canary,* 1974; *A Five Color Buick and a Blue-Eyed Cat,* 1975; *I Think This Is Where We Came In,* 1976; *Win Me and You Lose,* 1977; *Get a Little Lost, Tina,* 1978. Also author of *The Novels of Phyllis Anderson Wood,* New American Library, 1977.

*SIDELIGHTS:* Phyllis Anderson Wood told *CA:* "I began writing for young adults because as a teacher of high school reading classes I was continually hampered by the lack of books that appealed to students who hadn't yet formed a reading habit. For the past seven years, through the publication of eight novels, my students have been both my soundest critics and my warmest fans. Having had to decide, initially, whether I would write to please the students or the critics, and having opted for the students' enthusiasm, I now am pleased to be getting positive support from both groups."

\* \* \*

### WOOD, Ruth C.

*PERSONAL:* Born in Colorado; daughter of David (a stockman) and Fanny Wood. *Education:* Colorado College, B.A., 1914; University of Colorado, M.A., 1934. *Politics:* Independent. *Religion:* Protestant. *Home:* 1410 Cannell Ave., Grand Junction, Colo. 81501.

*CAREER:* Teacher in Gooding County, Idaho, 1916-17; high school English teacher in Shoshone, Idaho, 1918-19; high school English and Latin teacher in Glenns Ferry, Idaho, 1919-23; Grand Junction High School, Grand Junction, Colo., teacher of English and Latin, 1923-60.

*WRITINGS*—Juvenile: *Mystery of the Absent Neighbors,* Harvey House, 1968; *Mystery of Gold Hill,* Harvey House, 1972. Contributor of articles to magazines, including *American Rose Annual.*

*WORK IN PROGRESS:* Research on American Indians, American Revolutionary War period, and Elizabethan period.

*AVOCATIONAL INTERESTS:* Travel through the United States, growing roses, collecting Navajo rugs and other Indian products, reading.

\* \* \*

### WOODS, John David 1939-

*PERSONAL:* Born October 26, 1939, in Brighton, England; son of Ronald Ernest Goff and Marjorie (Wood) Woods; married Irina von Arnim (conference interpretor), June 19, 1971. *Education:* Imperial College, London, B.Sc., 1961, ARCS, 1961, DIC, 1965, Ph.D., 1965. *Politics:* European. *Religion:* Church of England. *Home:* 18A Caprivistr, Kiel, Germany. *Office:* Department of Oceanography, University of Kiel, Kiel, Germany.

*CAREER:* Meteorological Office, Bracknell, England, research fellow, 1966-72; University of Southampton, Southampton, England, professor of oceanography, 1972-77; University of Kiel, Kiel, Germany, professor of oceanography, 1977—. *Member:* Royal Geographical Society (expeditions committee, 1965—), Royal Meteorological Society, The Underwater Association (Malta). *Awards, honors:* Royal Geographical Society, Back Prize, 1968; Ministry of Defence, L. G. Groves Memorial Prize, 1968.

*WRITINGS:* (Editor with J. N. Lythgoe) *Underwater Science: An Introduction to Experiments by Divers,* Oxford University Press, 1971; (editor with Lythgoe) *Underwater Research,* Academic Press, 1975.

*WORK IN PROGRESS: The Seasonal Thermocline.*

\* \* \*

### WOODSON, Wesley E(dward) 1918-

*PERSONAL:* Born November 18, 1918, in El Cajon, Calif.; son of Wesley E. (a farmer) and Lois (Price) Woodson; married Dorothy Van Gundy (a legal secretary), December 25, 1941; children: Charles, Donald, Ronald, Shirley Woodson Wright. *Education:* Southwestern College, Winfield, Kan., B.A., 1941. *Politics:* Republican. *Religion:* Presbyterian. *Home:* 1300 Hacienda Dr., El Cajon, Calif. 92020. *Office:* Man Factors, Inc., 4433 Convoy, San Diego, Calif. 92111.

*CAREER:* U.S. Navy Electronics Laboratory, San Diego, Calif., psychologist, 1946-56; General Dynamics—Convair, San Diego, Calif., human factors engineer, 1956-66; Man Factors, Inc., San Diego, Calif., president, 1966—. Member of San Diego Symphony; member of president's advisory committee on consumer product safety. *Military service:* U.S. Army, 1941-45; became captain. *Member:* Human Factors Society (president), Institute of Electrical and Electronic Engineers, Society of Automotive Engineers, Illuminating Engineering Society, American Institute of Aeronautics and Astronautics, New York Academy of Sciences, Rotary, Masons.

*WRITINGS:* (Contributor) W. D. Cockrell, editor, *Industrial Electronics Handbook,* McGraw, 1948; (with Donald W. Conover) *Human Guide for Equipment Designers,* 2nd revised edition (Woodson was not associated with earlier editions), University of California Press, 1964. Also author of *Human Engineering Applications to Consumer Product Design,* Wiley. Contributor to *Encyclopaedia Britannica.*

*WORK IN PROGRESS:* Human factors studies in highway safety, underwater ergonomics, architectural design, and consumer product safety.

\*     \*     \*

## WOODWARD, Daniel Holt   1931-

*PERSONAL:* Born October 17, 1931, in Fort Worth, Tex.; son of Enos Paul (a businessman) and Jessie (Butts) Woodward; married Mary Jane Gerra, August 27, 1954; children: Jeffrey, Peter. *Education:* University of Colorado, B.A., 1951, M.A., 1955; Yale University, Ph.D., 1958; Catholic University of America, M.S.L.S., 1969. *Politics:* Democrat. *Home:* 1540 San Pasqual, Pasadena, Calif. 91106. *Office:* Henry E. Huntington Library and Art Gallery, 1151 Oxford Rd., San Marino, Calif. 91108.

*CAREER:* Mary Washington College, Fredericksburg, Va., assistant professor, 1957-61, associate professor, 1961-66, professor of English, 1966-72, librarian, 1969-72; Henry E. Huntington Library and Art Gallery, San Marino, Calif., librarian, 1972—. *Military service:* U.S. Army, 1952-54. *Member:* Renaissance Society of America, Bibliographical Society of America, Historical Society of Southern California, Zamorano Club, Grolier Club, Phi Beta Kappa.

*WRITINGS:* (Editor) *The Poems and Translations of Robert Fletcher,* University of Florida Press, 1970. Contributor of articles and reviews to literary and history journals.†

\*     \*     \*

## WOODWORTH, David (Perrin)   1932-

*PERSONAL:* Born October 5, 1932, in Crewe, Cheshire, England; son of Bertram (an electrical engineer) and Dorothy (Carr) Woodworth; married Joyce R. Allsop (a librarian), May 26, 1956; children: Stephen P., Martin N., Amanda J., Sara L. *Education:* College of Commerce, Associateship of the Library Association, 1953-54, B.A., 1976, M.I.Inf.Sc., 1977. *Religion:* Church of England. *Home:* "The Quintain," 12, Windmill Close, Ashby-de-la-Zouch, Leicestershire LE6 SEQ, England. *Office:* School of Librarianship, Loughborough, England.

*CAREER:* Dewsbury Public Library, Yorkshire, England, assistant, 1949-51, 1954-55; Northamptonshire Country Library, Corby, Northamptonshire, England, senior assistant, 1955-58; County Technical Library, Corby, deputy technical librarian, 1958-59; National Coal Board, Stoke Orchard, Gloucester, England, librarian and information officer, 1960-62; British Cast Iron Research Association, Birmingham, England, technical librarian, 1962-64; British Institute of Management, London, England, librarian, 1964-65; Port of London Authority, London, librarian, 1965-66; School of Librarianship, Loughborough, England, lecturer, 1966-76, senior lecturer, 1976—. *Military service:* Royal Air Force, 1951-53. *Member:* Library Association, Aslib (chairman of

East Midlands sub-section), British Standards Institution, Ashby/Coalville Lions Club (founder; president, 1976-77), Ashby Round Table (secretary, 1968-69; vice-chairman, 1971-72; chairman, 1972-73).

*WRITINGS:* (Editor) *Guide to Current British Journals,* two volumes, Library Association, 1970, Gale, 1971, 3rd edition, CBD Research, 1973; (compiler) *Directory of Publishers of British Journals,* Gale, 1971; (contributor) *The Administration of a Serials Collection,* Bingley, 1978. Indexer, *Library Association Record.*

\*     \*     \*

## WOOLF, James Dudley   1914-

*PERSONAL:* Born July 7, 1914, in Rector, Ark.; son of James Edgar (a highway engineer) and Erin (Mack) Woolf; married Carolyn Meiers, December 20, 1953; children: Elizabeth, James, Jr., Annelle. *Education:* College of the Ozarks, B.A., 1942; University of Michigan, M.A., 1949; Vanderbilt University, Ph.D., 1953. *Home:* 3810 Trier Rd., Fort Wayne, Ind. 46805. *Office:* Department of English, Indiana University, 2101 Coliseum Blvd., Fort Wayne, Ind. 46805.

*CAREER:* University of Kentucky, Lexington, instructor in English, 1948-49; Wayne University (now Wayne State University), Detroit, Mich., instructor in English, 1949-50; Arkansas State College (now University), Jonesboro, associate professor of English, 1953-59; Memphis State University, Memphis, Tenn., associate professor of English, 1959-66; Indiana University at Fort Wayne, associate professor, 1966-70, professor of English, 1970—. *Military service:* U.S. Navy, 1942-46; became lieutenant junior grade. *Member:* Modern Language Association of America, American Association of University Professors, Indiana College English Association.

*WRITINGS: Sir Edmund Gosse,* Twayne, 1972; (editor) E. Gosse, *An Unequal Yoke,* Scholar's Facsimiles & Reprints, 1976. Contributor of articles to *English Literature in Transition, 1880-1920.*

*WORK IN PROGRESS: The Poetry of Thomas Hardy.*

\*     \*     \*

## WORRELL, Albert C(adwallader)   1913-

*PERSONAL:* Born May 14, 1913, in Philadelphia, Pa.; son of Pratt Bishop (a clerk) and Bertha May (Cadwallader) Worrell; married Helen Haffner Diefendorf, July 31, 1937; children: Kathleen (Mrs. James E. Howard), Frederick Strayer, Nancy (Mrs. George A. Shumaker). *Education:* University of Michigan, B.S.F. and M.F., 1935, Ph.D., 1953. *Home:* 81 Hilltop Rd., Cheshire, Conn. 06410. *Office:* School of Forestry and Environmental Studies, Yale University, 205 Prospect St., New Haven, Conn. 06511.

*CAREER:* U.S. Department of Agriculture, Soil Conservation Service, assistant forester, 1936-40; State of Virginia Forest Service, district forester, 1944-47; University of Georgia, Athens, assistant professor, 1947-53, associate professor of forest economics, 1953-55; Yale University, New Haven, Conn., associate professor, 1955-63, professor of forest economics, 1963-67, Edwin W. Davis Professor of Forest Policy, 1967—. Forest economist, U.S. Economic Commission for Latin America, Santiago, Chile, 1960-61. Guest professor of forest economics, University of Freiburg, Freiburg, Germany, 1970.

*WRITINGS: Economics of American Forestry,* Wiley, 1959; *Forest Resources, Private Enterprise and the Future,*

Industrial Forestry Association, 1967; *Principles of Forest Policy,* McGraw, 1970; (with J. A. Sinden) *Unpriced Values for Environmental Policy,* Wiley-Interscience, 1978. Contributor to professional journals.

\*　　　\*　　　\*

### WORTHAM, John David 1941-

*PERSONAL:* Born December 22, 1941, in Beaumont, Tex.; son of C. L. and Lucile (McCaghn) Wortham; divorced; children: John D., Jr. *Education:* Lamar State College of Technology (now Lamar University), B.A., 1963; University of Houston, M.A., 1964; University of Texas at Austin, Ph.D., 1967. *Home:* 309 Le Jeune Way, Homewood, Ala. 35209. *Office:* Department of History, University of Alabama in Birmingham, Birmingham, Ala. 35294.

*CAREER:* Worked as a teacher in Houston, Tex., 1964-65; Georgia Southern College, Statesboro, Ga., assistant professor of history, 1967-69; University of Alabama in Birmingham, assistant professor of history, 1969—. *Member:* American Historical Association, Conference on British Studies.

*WRITINGS: The Genesis of British Egyptology: 1549-1906,* University of Oklahoma Press, 1971.

*WORK IN PROGRESS:* A book about the major naval battles of the War of the League of Augsburg, Bantry Bay, Beachy Head, and Cape Barfleur.

\*　　　\*　　　\*

### WREN, Melvin C(larence) 1910-

*PERSONAL:* Born June 18, 1910, in Iowa City, Iowa; son of Clarence W. (an engineer) and Dorothy (Kahler) Wren; married Ester Gwendolyn Schlunz, November 28, 1936; children: David, Nancy Wren Wilkenloh (deceased). *Education:* University of Iowa, B.A., 1936, M.A., 1938, Ph.D., 1939; University of California, postdoctoral study, 1945-46. *Politics:* Independent. *Religion:* None. *Home:* Losvar Condo, Mukilteo, Wash. 98275.

*CAREER:* University of Montana, Missoula, instructor in history, 1940-41; American University, Washington, D.C., instructor in economics, 1941-42; University of Montana, associate professor, 1942-50, professor of history, 1950-67, chairman of department, 1958-67; University of Toledo, Toledo, Ohio, professor of history, 1967-77, professor emeritus, 1977—. Visiting professor, University of Washington, 1958, and University of Nebraska, 1971; visiting lecturer, University of Maryland, 1962-63. *Member:* American Historical Association, American Political Science Association. *Awards, honors:* American Council of Learned Societies fellow, 1946.

*WRITINGS: The Course of Russian History,* Macmillan, 1958, 4th edition, 1978; *Ancient Russia,* Weidenfeld & Nicolson, 1965; *The Western Impact upon Tsarist Russia,* Holt, 1971. Contributor of articles to economics and history journals.

*WORK IN PROGRESS:* Research on the Western impact upon Soviet Russia.

*AVOCATIONAL INTERESTS:* European travel.

\*　　　\*　　　\*

### WRIGHT, H(ugh) Elliott 1937-

*PERSONAL:* Born November 20, 1937, in Athens, Ala.; son of Hugh E. (a clergyman) and Angeline (Shannon) Wright; married Juanita Bass (an editor), December 30, 1963. *Education:* Birmingham-Southern College, A.B., 1959; Vanderbilt University, B.D., 1962, M.Div., 1967; Harvard University, graduate study, 1962-63. *Politics:* Democrat. *Home:* 4761 Henry Hudson Pkwy., Bronx, N.Y. 10471.

*CAREER:* Ordained minister of United Methodist Church-Tennessee Annual Conference, 1962; youth director in Nashville, Tenn., 1961-62, and Belmont, Mass., 1962-63; pastor in Baxter, Tenn., 1963-64; Tennessee Heart Association, Nashville, field secretary, 1964-65; associate pastor in Nashville, 1965-66; pastor in Brentwood, Tenn., 1966-67; Religious News Service, New York City, Protestant-Orthodox editor, 1967-75; Riverdale Presbyterian Church, Bronx, N.Y., pastoral associate, 1974—. Editorial assistant, *Motive,* 1965-67; host, "Challenge to Faith" program, WOR-Radio, 1973-75. Research fellow, Auburn Theological Seminary, 1976—. Consultant, Hartford Seminary Foundation, 1972, 1976-78, United Methodist Board of Global Ministries, 1975-78. *Member:* Authors Guild, Religion Newswriters Association, United Presbyterian Men, Alpha Tau Omega, Alpha Psi Omega, Eta Sigma Phi, Phi Beta Kappa, Sigma Delta Chi. *Awards, honors:* Founders Medal, Vanderbilt University, 1962; Shepherd Prize, Vanderbilt University, 1962; Religious Heritage of America Award in Journalism, 1972.

*WRITINGS:* (With R. S. Lecky) *Can These Bones Live? The Failure of Church Renewal,* Sheed, 1969; (editor with Lecky) *Black Manifesto: Religion, Racism, and Reparation,* Sheed, 1969; (with R. W. Lynn) *The Big Little School: Two Hundred Years of the Sunday School,* Harper, 1971; *Go Free,* Friendship Press, 1973; (with wife, Juanita B. Wright) *The Challenge of Mission,* United Methodist Board of Global Ministries, 1973; (with Howard Butt) *At the Edge of Hope,* Seabury, 1978. Also author of a viewers' guide to "Six American Families" television series, 1977. Ghost writer, including one major autobiography. Contributor to *New York Times, Washington Post,* and to religious journals.

*WORK IN PROGRESS:* Study of World Council of Churches and the Third World; research on history of religion in American news media; research on U.S. churches and taxation.

\*　　　\*　　　\*

### WRIGHT, John S(hup) 1910-

*PERSONAL:* Born May 1, 1910, in Enid, Okla.; son of Thomas Clayton (a banker) and Ethel (Shup) Wright; married Lucille Wilson (a teacher), June 19, 1939; children: Thomas Clayton, Roy Wilson, John S., Jr. *Education:* University of Illinois, A.B., 1931, M.A., 1938; University of Chicago, Ph.D., 1946. *Politics:* Democrat. *Religion:* Presbyterian. *Home:* 2014 Peyton Dr., Las Vegas, Nev. 89104. *Office:* Department of History, University of Nevada, Las Vegas, Nev. 89109.

*CAREER:* High school history teacher in Newton, Ill., 1934-38; Illinois College, Jacksonville, instructor, 1938-41, professor of history, 1946-56; University of Nevada—Las Vegas, associate professor, 1956-60, professor of history and political science, 1960—, chairman of Social Science Division, 1960-66. *Military service:* U.S. Army, 1942-45; became captain; received Bronze Star. *Member:* American Historical Association, Organization of American Historians.

*WRITINGS: Lincoln and the Politics of Slavery,* University of Nevada Press, 1970.

*WORK IN PROGRESS:* Research on Gamiliel Bailey, the National Era, and political abolitionalism, possibly resulting in a book.

*AVOCATIONAL INTERESTS:* Travel.

*       *       *

# WRIGHT, Nathan, Jr. 1923-
## (Nathaniel Wright, Jr.)

*PERSONAL:* Born August 5, 1923, in Shreveport, La.; son of Nathan, Sr. (an insurance agent) and Parthenia (Hickman) Wright; married Carolyn May, July 18, 1969; children: two sons, three daughters. *Education:* Attended St. Augustine's College, Raleigh, N.C., 1941-42, West Virginia State College, 1943, and Temple University, 1943-44; University of Cincinnati, A.B., 1947; Episcopal Theological School, Cambridge, Mass., B.D., 1950; Harvard University, S.T.M., 1951, Ed.D., 1964; State College at Boston (now Boston State College), Ed.M., 1961. *Politics:* Republican. *Religion:* Episcopalian. *Home:* Wright Rd., Selkirk, N.Y. 12158. *Agent:* C. May Associates, 507 Fifth Ave., New York, N.Y. 10017. *Office:* Department of Afro-American Studies, State University of New York, Albany, N.Y.

*CAREER:* Ordained minister of Episcopal church, 1950; St. Cyprian's Church, Boston, Mass., rector, 1950-64; Children's Medical Center, Boston, chaplain, 1956-64; Lasell Junior College, Auburndale, Mass., instructor, 1964; Diocese of Newark, Department of Urban Work, 1964-69; State University of New York at Albany, professor of urban affairs and chairman, department of Afro-American studies, 1969—. Chairman, National Conference on Black Power, Newark, N.J., 1967, International Conference on Black Power, 1968, Seminar on the Education of Black Youth, Buffalo, N.Y., 1971. Lecturer on education, urban affairs, religion, and race to universities. Has served on several government committees, including Massachusetts Governor's Advisory Committee on Civil Rights and Boston Mayor's Committee on Housing. *Military service:* U.S. Army; became second lieutenant; received citation for promoting morale of military personnel. *Member:* Congress on Racial Equality (CORE). *Awards, honors:* First prize, Christian Research Foundation, 1960, for manuscript of *One Bread, One Body;* Urban League Service award; Media Workshop Award, for *Black Power and Urban Unrest;* nomination for Pulitizer Prize, for *Let's Work Together;* LL.D., Upsala College, 1969.

*WRITINGS: The Riddle of Life,* Bruce-Humphries, 1952; *The Song of Mary,* Bruce-Humphries, 1957; *One Bread, One Body,* Seabury, 1962; *Black Power and Urban Unrest: The Creative Possibilities,* Hawthorn, 1967; *Ready to Riot,* Holt, 1968; *Let's Work Together,* Hawthorn, 1968; *Let's Face Racism,* Thomas Nelson, 1970; *What Black Educators Are Saying,* Hawthorn, 1971; *What Black Politicans Are Saying,* Hawthorn, 1972. Also author of weekly column, Newark *Star–Ledger,* beginning 1968.

*WORK IN PROGRESS:* Two books, *The Politics of Truth* and *Programs for Power.*

*SIDELIGHTS:* A writer for *Publishers Weekly* once pointed out that "both Dr. Wright and his wife are fourth-generation college graduates. 'I don't think there are ten Negro families in the country that can make that claim,' [Wright] said." Listing his professional roles as educator, poet, and civil rights worker, a *New York Times* reporter wrote: "If Stokely Carmichael and H. Rapp Brown represent the abrasive side of Black Power, Dr. Nathan Wright Jr. represents sophistication, scholarship, and media-

tion.... Beneath the scholarly surface, Dr. Wright considers himself ideologically close to Mr. Carmichael, Mr. Brown, and even to the slain black nationalist leader, Malcolm X." This reporter goes on to say that Wright subscribes to Frederick Douglass's views on "the friendly troops of the oppressor." "People who are members of a majority group," Wright says, "however sympathetic they may be with those who are oppressed, can never fully identify themselves with the oppressed."

A self-styled pacifist, Wright puts forth what many, including Simon Lazarus of *New Republic,* call "a benign version of black power" in his books. August Meier of *Saturday Review* said of *Let's Work Together:* "[Although] thin in content, ... the volume does, however, lucidly summarize the major ideas of the reformist (as opposed to the revolutionary) version of the concepts of Black Consciousness and Black Power. Wright's vision is not the destruction of America but the fulfillment of its ideals under the leadership of its creative black minority." Unlike many of the accounts of the urban riots of 1967, *Ready to Riot* is a sociological analysis of the ghetto conditions leading to Newark's rebellions (Wright prefers "rebellion" to "riot"). The *Publishers Weekly* writer notes that Wright "thinks the only way for the Negro to achieve his rightful place in our society is through self-direction, even if that means separatism." He believes that, with white financial and moral support, the black man "has to overcome his monumental inferiority complex" and get "into the dynamics of American life."

*BIOGRAPHICAL/CRITICAL SOURCES: New York Times,* July 22, 1967; *New York Review of Books,* February 29, 1968; *Publishers Weekly,* March 18, 1968; *New Republic,* June 8, 1968; *New York Times Book Review,* June 16, 1968; *Saturday Review,* September 21, 1968, October 19, 1968; *Best Sellers,* October 1, 1968.†

*       *       *

# WRIGHT, Sarah E.

*PERSONAL:* Born in Wetipquin, Md.; married Joseph G. Kaye (a composer); children: Michael, Shelley. *Education:* Attended Howard University, 1945-49; and Cheyney State Teachers College (now Cheyney State College), 1950-52; also studied at University of Pennsylvania writers workshop and at New School for Social Research writers workshops. *Home:* 780 West End Ave., Apt. 1-D, New York, N.Y. 10025. *Agent:* Roberta Pryor, International Famous Agency, 1301 Avenue of the Americas, New York, N.Y. 10019.

*CAREER:* Writer; has worked as teacher, bookkeeper, and office manager. *Member:* Authors Guild, Authors League of America, International PEN, Harlem Writers Guild (past vice-president). *Awards, honors:* Baltimore Sun Readability Award, 1969, for *This Child's Gonna Live;* McDowell Colony fellow.

*WRITINGS:* (With Lucy Smith) *Give Me a Child* (poetry), Kraft Publishing, 1955; *This Child's Gonna Live* (novel), Delacorte, 1969. Contributor to anthologies including *The Poetry of Black America, The Poetry of the Negro, 1746-1970, Beyond the Blues,* and *Poets of Today;* contributor of essays, reviews, and poetry to journals.

*WORK IN PROGRESS:* A sequel to *This Child's Gonna Live;* a collection of verse tentatively entitled *Why Do I Have Corns on My Feet?*

*BIOGRAPHICAL/CRITICAL SOURCES: New York Times Book Review,* June 29, 1969; *Best Sellers,* August 1,

1969; *Negro Digest,* August, 1969; *Times Literary Supplement,* October 16, 1969; *Harper's,* December, 1969.†

\* \* \*

## WU, Silas H. L. 1929-

*PERSONAL:* Born March 10, 1929, in China; son of Lao-tsun and Tung-shih Wu; married Beatrix Lee, September 4, 1964; children: Christopher Yalun, Melinda. *Education:* National Taiwan University, B.A., 1954; University of California, Berkeley, B.A., 1961; Yale University, M.A., 1963; Columbia University, Ph.D., 1967. *Residence:* Newton Centre, Mass. *Office:* Department of History, Boston College, Chestnut Hill, Mass. 02167.

*CAREER:* Yale University, New Haven, Conn., instructor in Chinese, 1960-64; Boston College, Chestnut Hill, Mass., assistant professor, 1966-68, associate professor, 1968-71, professor of Asian history, 1971—. Associate in research, East Asian Research Center, Harvard University. *Member:* American Historical Association, Association for Asian Studies, Ch'ing Society. *Awards, honors:* Research grants from East Asian Research Center, 1967-70; American Council of Learned Societies travel research grant to Asia, 1970; Social Science Research grants, 1973, for research trip to Peoples Republic of China, 1974, for research on Chinese village life in Peoples Republic of China; Fulbright grant, 1978.

*WRITINGS: Communication and Imperial Control in China: Evolution of the Palace Memorial System, 1693-1735,* Harvard University Press, 1970; *Passions and Politics in Imperial China: K'ang-hsi and His Heir Apparent, 1661-1722,* Harvard University Press, 1979.

*WORK IN PROGRESS: Personality, Legend, History: The Yung-cheng Emperor and His Images in Twentieth Century Historiography, Fiction and Film;* a chapter for the book, *Cambridge History of China.*

\* \* \*

## WUNDERLICH, Ray C., Jr. 1929-

*PERSONAL:* Born August 11, 1929, in St. Petersburg, Fla.; son of Ray C. (a physician) and Myrtle Ruth (Parr) Wunderlich; married Elinor Howell (a registered nurse), 1954; children: Mary, Janet, Ray, David. *Education:* University of Florida, B.S. (with honors), 1951; Columbia University, M.D., 1955. *Religion:* Protestant. *Home:* 1620 Serpentine Dr. S., St. Petersburg, Fla. 33712. *Office:* 666 6th St., S., St. Petersburg, Fla. 33701.

*CAREER:* Interned and took pediatric residency at Strong Memorial Hospital, Rochester, N.Y.; pediatrician in private practice, specializing in learning disorders of children, St. Petersburg, Fla., 1961-75; currently "practicing preventive medicine for patients of all ages." Staff member of All Children's Hospital (and director of diagnostic and evaluation clinic, 1966-68), St. Anthony's Hospital, Bayfront Medical Center, and Suncoast Medical Clinic. Director, Learning and Maturation Study Center. Guest lecturer on early childhood development, St. Petersburg Junior College and

Eckerd College, 1968—. *Military service:* U.S. Air Force, 1957-59. *Member:* American Academy of Pediatrics (fellow), American Academy for Cerebral Palsy (fellow), American College of Allergists (fellow), American Academy of Orthopsychiatry (fellow), American Society for Photobiology, Florida Pediatric Society, Pinellas County Medical Society, Phi Beta Kappa, Alpha Omega Alpha.

*WRITINGS*—All published by Johnny Reads, except as indicated: *Kids, Brains, and Learning: What Goes Wrong—Prevention and Treatment,* 1970; *Allergy, Brains, and Children Coping,* 1973; *Fatigue: What Causes It, What It Does to You, What You Can Do About It,* 1976; *Improving Your Diet,* 1976; (contributor) R. C. Orem, *Developmental Vision in Lifelong Learning,* Mafex, 1977; *Sugar and Your Health,* 1978; (contributor) S. Paltobi Ramon, *Nutrition In Human Development,* Greylock Publishers, in press; (contributor) J. Leonard Hippchen, editor, *Ecologic-Biochemical Approaches to Treatment of Delinquents and Criminals,* Van Nostrand, in press.

*SIDELIGHTS:* Ray Wunderlich told *CA:* "I began writing to educate myself and educate others. In attempting to reach a closure in regard to the wealth of information that I had, I wrote to clarify the issues. Through writing, I have been able to gain overviews and insights that I did not previously have. If I can set out information in a way that is clear to others, then I can be sure that it is clear to myself."

\* \* \*

## WYATT, William F., Jr. 1932-

*PERSONAL:* Born July 14, 1932, in Medford, Mass.; son of William F. (a professor) and Natalie (Gifford) Wyatt; married Sandra Skellet, June 6, 1959; children: Nathaniel Gifford, Lydia Ann, John William. *Education:* Bowdoin College, B.A., 1953; Harvard University, M.A., 1957, Ph.D., 1962. *Home:* 642 Angell St., Providence, R.I. 02906. *Office:* Department of Classics, Brown University, Providence, R.I. 02912.

*CAREER:* University of Washington, Seattle, assistant professor of classics, 1960-67; Brown University, Providence, R.I., professor of classics, 1967—, chairman of department, 1972-76, associate dean, 1976—. Director of summer session, American School of Classical Studies, Athens, Greece, 1969, 1972, 1973, member of managing committee, 1971—, member of alumni council, 1972-75; Alumni Council of Bowdoin College, member, 1972-73, secretary, 1975—. Rhode Island Committee for the Humanities, member, 1973—, vice-chairman, 1977—. *Member:* Bowdoin Club of Rhode Island (president, 1971-72), Review Club of Providence, Narragansett Boat Club (president, 1977—).

*WRITINGS: Metrical Lengthening in Homer,* Ateneo, 1969; *Indo-European,* University of Pennsylvania Press, 1970; *Greek Prothetic Vowel,* Press of Case Western Reserve University, 1972; *Anthropology and the Classics,* American Philological Association, 1977.

*WORK IN PROGRESS: The Relation of Linguistics to Archaeology and History;* a book on anthropology and ancient society.

# Y

## YAARI, Ehud 1945-

*PERSONAL:* Born March 1, 1945, in Tel Aviv, Israel; son of Isaac Y. (a journalist) and Shulamit (Yahalom) Yaari; married Hava Rosenberg, December 26, 1967; children: Efrat. *Education:* Attended Hebrew University of Jerusalem and Tel Aviv University. *Religion:* Jewish. *Home:* 88 Bnei Dan, Tel Aviv, Israel. *Office:* Davar, 45 Sheinkin, Tel Aviv, Israel.

*CAREER: Davar* (daily newspaper), Tel Aviv, Israel, Arab affairs commentator, 1964—; Galei Zahal (radio station), Tel Aviv, Arab affairs commentator, 1968—. With Israeli Defense Ministry, 1968; Middle East correspondent for *Politikn,* Copenhagen, 1970—.

*WRITINGS: Strike Terror: The Story of Fatah,* Sabra Books, 1970. Also author of a monograph on Egypt and the Fedayeen, 1975. Contributor to *Midstream* and other journals.

*WORK IN PROGRESS: El-Ard: The History of an Arab Militant Group in Israel.*

*SIDELIGHTS:* Yaari speaks English, French, Arabic, and Persian, as well as Hebrew. *Avocational interests:* Chess, football, travel.†

\* \* \*

## YALMAN, Ahmet Emin 1888-1972

May 14, 1888—December 19, 1972; Turkish journalist and historian. Obituaries: *New York Times,* December 20, 1972.

\* \* \*

## YANDELL, Keith E. 1938-

*PERSONAL:* Born July 16, 1938, in Davenport, Iowa; son of Phil Ray and Velma Helena (Edleman) Yandell; married Sharon Dee Murphy, August 22, 1960; children: Karen Gail, Keith David, Eric Thomas, Merritt Katherine. *Education:* Wayne State University, B.A. (with honors), 1959, M.A., 1960; Ohio State University, Ph.D., 1966. *Home:* 414 South Segoe Rd., Madison, Wis. 53711. *Office:* 5163 Helen C. White Hall, University of Wisconsin, Madison, Wis. 53706.

*CAREER:* Kings College, Briarcliff Manor, N.Y., instructor in philosophy, 1961-63; Ohio State University, Columbus, instructor in philosophy, 1965-66; University of Wisconsin—Madison, assistant professor, 1966-70, associate professor, 1970-73, professor of philosophy, 1973—,

professor of South Asian studies, 1977—. *Member:* American Philosophical Association, Hume Society. *Awards, honors:* National Endowment for the Humanities Academic Year Younger Humanist fellow, 1972-73.

*WRITINGS: Basic Issues in the Philosophy of Religion,* Allyn & Bacon, 1971; (editor with Julius Weinberg) *Problems in Philosophical Inquiry,* Holt, 1971 (also published as *Theory of Knowledge, Metaphysics, Ethics, and Philosophy of Religion);* (editor) *God, Man and Religion,* McGraw, 1972; (editor) *Ockham, Descartes, and Hume,* University of Wisconsin Press, 1977. Contributor to *Sophia, Religious Studies, Christian Scholars Review, Thought, International Journal for Philosophy of Religion,* and other philosophy and theology journals.

*WORK IN PROGRESS:* Two books, *Ethics, Evils, and Theism: A Comprehensive Study of the Problem of Evil,* and *Escape from Mystery,* a study of David Hume's philosophy of religion; as well as papers on the evidential value of religious experience.

*AVOCATIONAL INTERESTS:* Reading mystery novels.

\* \* \*

## YANKER, Gary 1947-

*PERSONAL:* Born October 20, 1947, in New York, N.Y.; son of Peter N. (an engineer) and Elizabeth (Krauter) Yanker. *Education:* Leningrad University, certificate of Russian Language, 1967; University of Fribourg, diploma for Sovietology, 1968; Georgetown University, B.A. (magna cum laude), 1969; Columbia University, J.D. and M.B.A., 1973. *Agent:* Informagency, Inc., 211 East 51 St., New York, N.Y. 10022.

*CAREER:* San Jacinto Lawn and Garden Service, San Jacinto, Calif., founder and manager, 1963-65; Yankee Enterprises (a poster publishing and distributing firm), Bern, Switzerland, founder, 1967-69; World Political Parties and Groups Institute, New York City, director, 1969—; Enterprise, Research and Organization, Inc., New York City, president, 1971—. *Military service:* U.S. Army Reserve, Military Intelligence, 1969-75; became second lieutenant. *Member:* Phi Beta Kappa, Phi Sigma Alpha.

*WRITINGS: Prop Art* (introduction by John Chancellor; Book-of-the-Month selection), New York Graphic Society, 1972; (with Harry Steinberg and Jack White) *The Angry Buyer's Complaint Directory,* Peter H. Wyden, 1974; (with

White) *Improve Yourself,* Dodd, 1975. Contributor to national magazines, including *Saturday Review, World Affairs,* and *Politea.*

*WORK IN PROGRESS:* "Confidential."

\* \* \*

## YARMOLINSKY, Adam 1922-

*PERSONAL:* Born November 17, 1922, in New York, N.Y.; son of Avrahm (an author) and Babette (an author; maiden name Deutsch) Yarmolinsky; married Harriet Rypins (a consultant on early childhood), March 24, 1945; children: Sarah, Tobias, Benjamin, Matthew. *Education:* Harvard University, A.B., 1943; Yale University, LL.B., 1948. *Politics:* Democrat. *Home:* 2828 Wisconsin Ave. N.W., Washington, D.C. 20007. *Office:* U.S. Arms Control and Disarmament Agency, Washington, D.C. 20451.

*CAREER:* U.S. Second Circuit Court of Appeals, New York City, law clerk for Judge Charles E. Clark, 1948-49; Root, Ballantine, Harlan, Bushby & Palmer (law firm), New York City, associate, 1949-50; U.S. Supreme Court, Washington, D.C., law clerk for Justice Reed, 1949-51; Cleary, Gottlieb, Friendly & Ball (law firm), Washington, D.C., associate, 1951-55; Fund for the Republic, New York City, secretary, 1955-57; Doubleday & Co., New York City, public affairs editor, 1957-59; consultant to philanthropic foundations, 1959-61; U.S. Government, Department of Defense, Washington, D.C., special assistant to secretary of defense, 1961-64, deputy director of President's Task Force on the War Against Poverty, 1964, chief of U.S. Emergency Relief Mission to Dominican Republic, 1965, principal deputy assistant secretary of defense, International Security Affairs, 1965-66; Harvard University, Cambridge, Mass., professor of law, 1966-72, member of Institute of Politics, John Fitzgerald Kennedy School of Government, 1966-72; University of Massachusetts, Boston, Ralph Waldo Emerson Professor of the University, 1972—; U.S. Arms Control and Disarmament Agency, Washington, D.C. (on leave from University of Massachusetts), counselor of agency, 1977—. Lecturer at American University, 1951-56, and Yale University, 1958-59. Chief executive officer, Welfare Island Development Corp., 1970-72. Trustee, Robert F. Kennedy Memorial, and Vera Institute of Justice. *Military service:* U.S. Army Air Forces, 1943-46.

*MEMBER:* American Academy of Arts and Sciences (fellow), American Bar Association, American Law Institute, Center for Inter-American Relations, Council on Foreign Relations, Hudson Institute, International Institute for Strategic Studies, Institute of Medicine of the National Academy of Sciences, Association of the Bar of the City of New York, Century, Coffee House (New York City), Federal City (Washington, D.C.), St. Botolph Club (Boston). *Awards, honors:* Distinguished Public Service Medal, U.S. Department of Defense, 1966.

*WRITINGS:* (Editor) *Case Studies in Personnel Security,* Bureau of National Affairs, 1955; *The Pursuit of Excellence,* Free Press, 1960; *The Military Establishment,* Harper, 1971. Contributor of articles to various periodicals.

*BIOGRAPHICAL/CRITICAL SOURCES: Washington Post,* Februrary 8, 1970.

\* \* \*

## YAR-SHATER, Ehsan O(llah) 1920-
### (Rahsepar)

*PERSONAL:* Name sometimes appears as Yarshatir or Yarshater; born April 3, 1920, in Hamadan, Persia (now Iran); came to United States, 1958; son of Hashem (a businessman) and Rouhaniyeh Yar-Shater; married Latifeh Alvieh, October 30, 1961. *Education:* University of Teheran, License in Persian Literature, 1941, License in Law, 1944, D.Litt., 1947; University of London, M.A., 1951, Ph.D., 1960. *Home:* 450 Riverside Dr., New York, N.Y. 10027. *Office:* 604 Kent Hall, Columbia University, New York, N.Y. 10027.

*CAREER:* University of Teheran, Teheran, Iran, associate professor, later professor of old Persian and Avestan, 1953-60; Columbia University, New York, N.Y., visiting associate professor of Indo-Iranian, 1958-60, Hagop Kevorkian Professor of Iranian Studies, 1961—, chairman of department of Middle East languages and cultures, 1967-73, director of Iran Center, 1961—. Director of Royal Institute for Translation and Publication, Teheran, Iran, 1953-61; trustee of American Institute of Iranian Studies. *Member:* American Oriental Society, American Institute of Iranian Studies, Middle East Studies Association of North America, American Academy of Political Science, Royal Asiatic Society, Society for the study of Islamic Philosophy and Sciences (executive committee), Book Society of Persia (president, 1957—). *Awards, honors:* Iranian Royal Prize, 1959, for *Dastanha-ye Iran-e Bastan;* UNESCO Prize for best book for young readers, 1961, for *Dastanha-ye Shah-nameh.*

*WRITINGS:* (Editor) Avicenna, *Tarjomey-e farsi-e Esharat va tanbihat* (title means "The Persian Translation of the Theorems and Remarks"), Anjoman-e Athar-e Melli (Teheran), 1954; (editor) Avicenna, *Panj resaleh* (title means "Five Treaties"), Anjoman-e Athar-e Melli, 1954; *Dastanha-ye Iran-e Bastan* (title means "Myths of Ancient Iran"), Ministry of Education (Teheran), 1954; *She'r-e farsi dar nime-ye avval-e qarn-e nohom* (title means "Persian Poetry in the 15th Century"), The University Press (Teheran), 1955; (editor with W. B. Henning) *A Locust's Leg: Studies in Honor of S. H. Taqizadeh,* Lund & Humphries, 1962; *A Grammar of Southern Tati Dialects,* Humanities, 1969; (editor) *Iran Faces the Seventies,* Praeger, 1971. Also author of *Dastanha-ye Shah-nameh.* Contributor of articles on Iranian languages and Persian literature and culture to scholarly journals.

Under pseudonym, Rahsepar: *Naqqashi-ye Novin* (title means "Modern Painting") two volumes, Amire Kabir (Teheran), 1965-66.

Editor, "Persian Texts Series", 1954—, "Persian Heritage Series", 1963—, "Bibliotheque des Oeuvres Classiques Persanes," 1966—, *Encyclopaedia Iranica,* 1972—, and "Modern Persian Literature Series," 1977—; founding editor, *Rahnemay-e Ketab* (journal of Persian language and literature and book reviews), 1957—.

*WORK IN PROGRESS:* Editing *Cambridge History of Iran,* Volume III (on the Seleucid, Parthian, and Sasanian periods); studies on Iranian legendary history and on the Median dialects of Persia.

\* \* \*

## YATRON, Michael 1921-
### (Byron Sorel)

*PERSONAL:* Born July 20, 1921, in Reading, Pa.; son of Peter H. and Rallio (Papoutsis) Yatron; married Georgine Ortiz (a college instructor), January 8, 1954; children: Peter, Byron. *Education:* Kutztown State Teachers College (now Kutztown State College), B.S., 1942; Harvard University, graduate study, 1942-43; University of California, Berkeley, graduate study, 1943-44, 1944-45; Temple University, M.A., 1950, Ph.D., 1957. *Home:* 1533 Garfield Ave., Wyomissing, Pa. 19610. *Office:* Department of English, Kutztown State College, Kutztown, Pa. 19530.

*CAREER:* University of Puerto Rico, Mayaquez, P.R., instructor in English, 1953-55; Delaware State College, Dover, Del., assistant professor, 1957-59, associate professor, 1959-60, professor of English, 1960-63; Kutztown State College, Kutztown, Pa., professor of English, 1963—.

*WRITINGS: America's Literary Revolt,* Philosophical Library, 1959; (under pseudonym Byron Sorel) *Sappho's Island* (novel), Adelphi Press, 1964; (under pseudonym Byron Sorel) *In Pink Balloons* (novel), William-Frederick, 1967.

\* \* \*

## YEARWOOD, Richard M(eek) 1934-

*PERSONAL:* Born March 28, 1934, in Knoxville, Tenn.; son of Cecil Ralph and Marjorie (Query) Yearwood; married Betty Ann Lebow, November 26, 1954; children: Richard S., Guille R., Susan G. *Education:* Gardner-Webb College, A.A., 1954; University of Tennessee, B.A., 1958, M.A., 1959; University of Florida, Ph.D., 1966. *Politics:* Democrat. *Religion:* Protestant. *Home:* 1204 Gladewood Dr., Blacksburg, Va. 24060. *Office:* College of Architecture, Virginia Polytechnic Institute and State University, Blacksburg, Va. 24061.

*CAREER:* Millikin University, Decatur, Ill., assistant professor of history and political science, 1961-62; University of Tennessee, Knoxville, assistant professor of political science, 1962-64; Tennessee State Planning Commission, Knoxville, senior planner, 1964; Asheville Metropolitan Planning Board and Western North Carolina Regional Planning Commission, Asheville, N.C., executive director, 1964-67; Virginia Polytechnic Institute and State University, Blacksburg, associate professor of urban planning, 1967—, associate dean of graduate school, 1969-70. Director, Tennessee Citizens Planning Association, 1962-64; chairman, Board of Zoning Appeals of Montgomery County, Va., 1969, and Blacksburg Planning Commission, 1975-77. Consultant to local and state governments and to private enterprise. *Military service:* U.S. Army, 1954-56. *Member:* American Institute of Planners, American Political Science Association, American Society of Planning Officials, American Association of University Professors, Southern Political Science Association, Pi Sigma Alpha, Phi Alpha Theta, Tau Sigma Delta, Sigma Pi Alpha, Delta Psi Omega.

*WRITINGS: Population and Economy of Lake City,* Tennessee State Planning Commission, 1964; *Anderson County Subdivision Regulations,* Tennessee State Planning Commission, 1964; *Public Improvements and Capital Budget for Clinton,* Tennessee State Planning Commission, 1964; *Population and Economy of Sylva,* Western North Carolina Regional Planning Commission, 1965; *Sylva Zoning Ordinance,* Western North Carolina Regional Planning Commission, 1966; *Rutherfordton Zoning Ordinance,* Western North Carolina Regional Planning Commission, 1966; *Population and Economy of Jackson County,* Western North Carolina Regional Planning Commission, 1966; *Columbus Zoning Ordinance,* Western North Carolina Regional Planning Commission, 1966.

*Population and Economy of Bryson City,* Western North Carolina Regional Planning Commission, 1967; (with others) *The Comprehensive Planning Process,* Center for Urban and Regional Studies, 1968; (with Alan W. Steiss) *Planning Legislation for the Trust Territory of Micronesia,* Hawaii

Architects and Engineers, 1968; *A Law Enforcement Plan for the Roanoke Valley Region,* Roanoke Valley Regional Planning Commission, 1969; *Goals for the Region,* Roanoke Valley Regional Planning Commission, 1969.

*Land Use Controls in Urban Communities in Virginia,* Center for Urban and Regional Studies, 1970; *Pulaski Subdivision Regulations,* Center for Urban and Regional Studies, 1970; *Pulaski Zoning Ordinance,* Center for Urban and Regional Studies, 1970; (contributor) *Planning Commissioner's Handbook,* Virginia Citizen's Planning Association, 1971; *Land Subdivision Regulation,* Praeger, 1971. Contributor to *Journal of Urban Law, Plan, Current Municipal Problems, State Government, American Journal of Economics and Sociology,* and other publications.

*WORK IN PROGRESS:* Research in planning theory and public policy analysis.

\* \* \*

## YERBURY, Grace D. 1899-

*PERSONAL:* Born July 8, 1899, in Danbury, Conn.; daughter of John Hall (a businessman) and Jessie E. (Merritt) Davies; married Charles S. Yerbury (an organist), July 24, 1922 (deceased). *Education:* Hunter College (now Hunter College of the City University of New York), B.A., 1920; New York University, B.Mus., 1931; Columbia University, M.A., 1933; Indiana University, Ph.D., 1953. *Politics:* "Unsettled." *Religion:* "Anti-establishment." *Home and office:* 518 East Macomb, Belvidere, Ill. 61008.

*CAREER:* Teacher of mathematics in high school in Brooklyn, N.Y., 1920-22; music teacher and concert and church artist in New York City, 1922-40; music teacher at Braumiller Studios in Hoboken, N.J., 1940-42; *Eastern Underwriter,* New York City, editorial assistant, 1943-44; G. Schirmer, New York City, member of staff, orchestral division, 1944-46; New York University, New York City, instructor in music, 1946-48; Moravian Seminary and College for Women (now Moravian College), Bethlehem, Pa., associate professor of music, 1948-50; George Washington University, Washington, D.C., research assistant in psychological warfare, 1950-51; Northeast Louisiana State College (now University), Monroe, professor of music, 1954-56; Oakland City College, Oakland City, Ind., professor of English and music, 1957-58; Campbellsville College, Campbellsville, Ky., professor of English, 1958-60; Missouri Valley College, Marshall, Mo., professor of English and head of department, 1960-69. *Member:* World Poetry Society, Illinois State Poetry Society, Phi Beta Kappa, Mu Sigma, Pi Delta Epsilon, Pi Kappa Lambda, Sigma Tau Delta, Alpha Psi Omega. *Awards, honors:* Hamilton Smith Award of Corpus Christi Writers' Conference; Clara Thompson Wilkinson Award of Deep South Writers' Conference.

*WRITINGS: Refracted Light,* Pageant, 1956; *Reed Song,* Naylor, 1965; *Song in America from Beginnings to about 1850,* Scarecrow, 1971; *Vistas Unvisited,* Prairie Press, 1973. Contributor to *Walt Whitman Quarterly* and *Louisiana Quarterly;* contributor of poetry to anthologies and newspapers. Editor, *Rockford Review,* 1971.

*WORK IN PROGRESS: A Shovel of Stars for Keeps,* a novel; a religious book, *Timbrel Time.*

\* \* \*

## YGLESIAS, Helen 1915-

*PERSONAL:* Born March 29, 1915, in New York, N.Y.;

daughter of Solomon and Kate (Goldstein) Bassine; married Bernard Cole (a photographer), 1937; married second husband, Jose Yglesias (a writer), August 20, 1950; children: (first marriage) Tamar (Mrs. Richard Lear), Lewis Cole; (second marriage) Rafael. *Residence:* North Brooklin, Me. 04661. *Agent:* Hoffman-Sheedy, 145 West 86th St., New York, N.Y. 10024.

*CAREER: Nation,* New York City, literary editor, 1965-69; Columbia University, School of the Arts, New York City, adjunct professor of non-fiction, spring, 1973. *Member:* Brooklin Garden Club. *Awards, honors:* Houghton Mifflin Literary fellowship, 1971, for *How She Died.*

*WRITINGS: How She Died* (novel), Houghton, 1972; *Family Feeling* (novel; Literary Guild selection), Dial, 1976.

*WORK IN PROGRESS: Starting,* non-fiction, for Rawson Associates.

*SIDELIGHTS:* "In spite of the articulation of the Kate Milletts and Germaine Greers, no one had effectively described what it was like to be a woman in these times until Helen Yglesias wrote this brilliant Literary Fellowship Award first novel," *Detroit News* reviewer Shirley Duller writes in priase of *How She Died.* She continues, ". . . With warmth and wisdom and humor, Helen Yglesias examines human reaction, the death-life conflict and the rationalization for survival."

". . . My first impulse was to put *How She Died* aside and forget it as quickly as possible," Christopher Lehmann-Haupt writes in *New York Times.* "It had aroused any number of unpleasant feelings in me—revulsion at the dying heroine's cancer, exasperation with her friends' disorganized attempts to help her, frustration over everyone's inability to cope . . . —and my inclination was to dismiss the whole business as a bad piece of work. . . . [But] I end up feeling that while I dislike Mrs. Yglesias's people and the web of life they are caught in, both people and the life have worked a powerful effect on me."

In *Books and Bookmen,* Roger Baker describes the same book as ". . . a profound, painful, moving and superbly written novel. Rarely, in my experience, does a writer expose the nerve-endings of people, probe their interpersonal relationships and isolate the tensions operating upon them with such simplicity and directness. . . . The writing is excellent, the use of imagery deft and understated."

Yglesias's second novel, *Family Feeling,* "is an example of one kind of first-rate fiction: the reification and artful shaping of the obvious and overlooked," writes Ivan Gold in the *New York Times Book Review.* Hers is ". . . a style of deceptive simplicity, a language pared of all frills and distractions, and as fine an ear for the speech rhythms of the scores of complex characters as I've lately encountered." *Nation* reviewer Marjorie Pryse feels that the book "yokes the two elements of a contemporary paradox: family negates feelings at the same time that feeling creates family."

Helen Yglesias does her writing in a two hundred-year-old farmhouse, located down the road from noted author R. B. White, with her husband and two sons who are also writers.

*BIOGRAPHICAL/CRITICAL SOURCES: New York Times,* February 8, 1972, October 10, 1976; *New York Times Book Review,* February 13, 1972, February 1, 1976; *New Yorker,* February 26, 1972; *Detroit News,* March 5, 1972; *Newsweek,* March 6, 1972; *Saturday Review,* March 18, 1972; *New York Review of Books,* April 6, 1972; *Book World,* April 16, 1972; *Nation,* June 19, 1972, May 1, 1976; *Times Literary Supplement,* January 26, 1973; *Books and*

*Bookmen,* May, 1973; *Village Voice,* March 15, 1976; *Hudson Review,* Volume XXIX, number 2, summer, 1976; *Contemporary Literary Criticism,* Volume VII, Gale, 1977.

\*    \*    \*

## YGLESIAS, Rafael 1954-

*PERSONAL:* Born May 12, 1954, in New York, N.Y.; son of Jose (a writer) and Helen (a writer, maiden name Bassine) Yglesias. *Education:* Attended public schools in New York, N.Y. *Politics:* "Communist, though not the party." *Religion:* None. *Residence:* New York, N.Y.

*CAREER:* Writer. *Member:* United States Chess Federation.

*WRITINGS*—All novels: *Hide Fox, and All After,* Doubleday, 1972; *The Work Is Innocent,* Doubleday, 1976; *The Game Player,* Doubleday, 1978.

*SIDELIGHTS:* Rafael Yglesias was fifteen years old when he wrote his first novel, *Hide Fox, and All After.* The son of novelists Jose and Helen Yglesias, Rafael left school when in tenth grade to devote his time entirely to writing. "I felt I had just reached a point where I wanted to go out into the world," Rafael states in a *New York Times* article. "My brother and sister were eight and 10 years older than I. Dinner conversations were adult, about books and writing. There were no limitations intellectually. I felt there was nothing better, more influential to do, than write. . . ."

Referring to *Hide Fox, and All After,* Yglesias admits in a *Time* review, "It is so close to being autobiographical that at times it was hard to avoid writing my own name down or rather to stop calling myself 'Raul' when I was talking to people." The reviewer observes: "It is not often that a writer sees his main character as clearly and directly as Rafael Yglesias sees Raul, the precocious 14-year-old who bombs out of private school in this brief and crystalline first novel. The author avoids displays of virtuosity, the pleasures of romantic posturing, and all other possible uses of fiction except this one: to watch with great care the being who fascinates him. . . . Yglesias is still capable of childish sentences. But his is a superior novel, without regard to the age of the author."

*BIOGRAPHICAL/CRITICAL SOURCES: Time,* January 3, 1972; *Book World,* January 30, 1972; *New York Times,* February 2, 1972; *Best Sellers,* February 15, 1972; *Virginia Quarterly Review,* spring, 1972; *New York Times Book Review,* April 15, 1972; *New York Review of Books,* May 4, 1972; *Commonweal,* June 16, 1972.†

\*    \*    \*

## YOCHIM, Louise Dunn 1909-

*PERSONAL:* Born July 18, 1909, in Jitomir, Ukraine, Russia; daughter of Solomon (a clergyman) and Gitil (Milstein) Dunn; married Maurice Yochim (a professor of art), June 19, 1932; children: Jerome. *Education:* Attended Art Institute of Chicago, 1929-32, B.A.E., 1942, M.A.E., 1952; also attended University of Chicago, 1930, 1931, 1956. *Politics:* Democrat. *Religion:* Jewish. *Home:* 9545 North Drake Ave., Evanston, Ill. 60203. *Office:* Chicago Board of Education, 228 North LaSalle St., Chicago, Ill. 60601.

*CAREER:* Professional artist, Chicago, Ill., 1933—; Board of Education, Chicago, high school teacher of art, 1934-50, supervisor of art, District 6, 1950—. Has taught art at Chicago Academy of Fine Art, Chicago Teachers College, and Wright Junior College; lecturer on art education. Work exhibited at one-man shows in Chicago, and in group shows at

Art Institute of Chicago, Detroit Institute of Art, Des Moines Art Center, and other galleries in Kansas City, Washington, D.C., and elsewhere. Art consultant, Area C, Chicago Public Schools, 1972. *Member:* National Education Association, National Art Education Association, National Committee on Art Education, Chicago Society of Artists (president, 1972-78), Renaissance Society (University of Chicago), Delta Kappa Gamma. *Awards, honors:* Prizes for paintings and graphic work.

*WRITINGS: Building Human Relationships through Art,* Stein Publishing, 1954; *Perceptual Growth in Creativity,* International Textbook Co., 1967; (editor) *Art in Action,* District 6, Chicago Public Schools, 1969; *Role and Impact: The Chicago Society of Artists,* Publications Trade Press, 1978. Contributor to art journals.

*WORK IN PROGRESS:* Two books titled *The Technical Aspects of Art Education: Media, Processes and Methods* and *The Beauty and Wonderment of a Painter's Vision;* a biography of artist William S. Schwartz.

*SIDELIGHTS:* Louise Dunn Yochim told *CA:* "I write because I am impelled to write as I feel deeply moved by social iniquities—or by a desire to use the means at my command to help change the behaviour of the deviate learner, or the socially maladjusted. In a sense, my first volume, *Building Human Relationships through Art,* was an earnest attempt to guide teachers of art in the realization of these goals. Being an artist and art educator, [my] natural intent [in writing this book] was to share with others the knowledge that the creative realm embodies an inexaustible reservoir which can be instrumental in generating the noblest feelings of man. The books which followed, *Perceptual Growth in Creativity, Art in Action,* and others, provided the ways and means through which teachers of art may implement an art education program in their schools."

*Role and Impact: The Chicago Society of Artists,* which "chronicles the achievement of more than 400 Chicago artists since 1888," was written as a result of Yochim's more recent focus on art and artists.

\*   \*   \*

## YODER, J(ames) Willard 1902-

*PERSONAL:* Born May 19, 1902, in Shipshewana, Ind.; son of James Michael and Sarah Ellen (Large) Yoder; married Elsie Mae Loertz (an artist and teacher), October 2, 1932; children: John James W., James Willard I., Felicia (Mrs. William Pryor), Margaret (Mrs. Bruce Johnston), Sherida. *Education:* Tri-State College (now University), A.B. and A.B. in Ed., 1922; Indiana University, M.A., 1926; University of the South, M.Div., 1956; additional study at Indiana University, New York University, University of Chicago, and University of Pennsylvania. *Politics:* Independent Republican. *Home:* 137 Illinois Ave., Paterson, N.J. 07503. *Office:* Discovery House, Marlboro Psychiatric Hospital, Marlboro, N.J. 07746.

*CAREER:* Episcopal minister in Indiana, New York, and New Jersey, 1922—. Adjunct professor of clinical psychology at Indiana University, Purdue University, and other schools, 1930-48; associate professor of psychology, William Paterson College, 1958-64; clinical psychologist in narcotic addiction treatment, State of New Jersey, 1968—. *Military service:* U.S. Army, auxiliary chaplain, 1943-46. *Member:* American Psychological Association (life member), American Association of University Professors, National Education Association, Eastern Psychological Association (life member), Association of New Jersey State College Faculties (honorary life member).

*WRITINGS:* (With others) *A Guide to Human Development and Behavior,* William Paterson State College, 1963, revised edition, 1965. Contributor of articles on religion and mental health to *Living Church.* Press representative, *American Church News;* former press representative, *Living Church;* former editor, *Indianapolis Church News,* and newsletter of Indiana Association of Clinical Psychologists.

*WORK IN PROGRESS: Jesus as Psychologist; The Therapeutic Community for Narcotic Addicts.*

*SIDELIGHTS:* J. Willard Yoder told *CA* that his writing career began when he was asked to write a weekly essay during the period of Lent one year. He feels he writes best when under pressure and recommends setting a goal of a certain number of pages per day.

\*   \*   \*

## YOLTON, John W(illiam) 1921-

*PERSONAL:* Born November 10, 1921, in Birmingham, Ala.; son of Robert Elgene (an engineer) and Ella Maud (Holmes) Yolton; married Jean Mary Sebastian (a librarian), September 5, 1945; children: Karin Frances (Mrs. Bryant Griffith), Pamela Holmes (Mrs. Derek A. Smith). *Education:* University of Cincinnati, B.A., 1945, M.A., 1946; University of California, Berkeley, graduate study, 1946-50; Balliol College, Oxford, D.Phil., 1952. *Religion:* None. *Home:* 29 Lorraine Gardens, Islington, Ontario, Canada M9B 4Z5. *Office:* Department of Philosophy, York University, Downsview, Ontario, Canada.

*CAREER:* Johns Hopkins University, Baltimore, Md., visiting lecturer in philosophy, 1952-53; Princeton University, Princeton, N.J., assistant professor of philosophy and bicentennial preceptor, 1953-57; Kenyon College, Gambier, Ohio, associate professor of philosophy, 1957-61; University of Maryland, College Park, professor of philosophy, 1961-63; York University, Downsview, Ontario, professor of philosophy, 1963—, chairman of department, 1963-72, acting president, 1973-74. *Member:* American Philosophical Association, Canadian Philosophical Association, Mind Association, American Society for Eighteenth Century Studies. *Awards, honors:* Fulbright fellow at Oxford University, 1950-52; Leonard Nelson Foundation prize, 1959.

*WRITINGS: John Locke and the Way of Ideas,* Clarendon Press, 1956; *Philosophy of Science of A. S. Eddington,* Nijhoff, 1960; (editor) *Locke's Essay Concerning Human Understanding,* Dent, 1961, revised edition, 1965; *Thinking and Perceiving,* Open Court, 1962; *Theory of Knowledge,* Macmillan, 1965; *Metaphysical Analysis,* University of Toronto Press, 1967; *John Locke: Problems and Perspectives,* Cambridge University Press, 1969; *John Locke and the Compass of Human Understanding,* Cambridge University Press, 1970; *Locke and Education,* Random House, 1971; (author of introduction and commentary) John Locke, *The Locke Reader,* Cambridge University Press, 1977.

*WORK IN PROGRESS:* Research on philosophy of action and on seventeenth- and eighteenth-century philosophy.

\*   \*   \*

## YOUNG, Bernice Elizabeth 1931-

*PERSONAL:* Born October 7, 1931, in Cleveland, Ohio; daughter of James Anthony (a real estate broker) and Josephine (Page) Young. *Education:* Attended Vassar College, 1949-51, and Western Reserve University (now Case Western Reserve University), 1951-52. *Politics:* "I wish I knew!" *Religion:* Episcopalian. *Home and office:* 333 East 34th St., New York, N.Y. 10016.

*CAREER:* Writer and publicist; Trinity Cathedral, Cleveland, Ohio, public relations adviser, 1957-68; American Greeting Corp., Cleveland, writer and assistant to humor editor, 1959-61; Charles of the Ritz (cosmetics), New York City, assistant to director of advertising, 1961-64; American representative for "The Beatles," Cilla Black, "Gerry and the Pacemakers," and all other artists under the management of Brian Epstein, 1964-67; Girl Scouts of the U.S.A., New York City, Protestant adviser/media adviser, 1968; Addison, Goldstein & Walsh, New York City, account executive, 1969-1970.

*WRITINGS: Harlem: The Story of a Changing Community,* Messner, 1972; *The Picture Story of Hank Aaron,* Messner, 1974; *The Picture Story of Frank Robinson,* Messner, 1975. Also author of *Tribes of Africa,* 1975. Writer of daily radio series on consumer problems, 1970. Contributor to religious journals.

*SIDELIGHTS:* Bernice Young is competent in French, Spanish, Latin, Greek, Italian, and German. *Avocational interests:* Music, ballet, reading.†

\*    \*    \*

## YOUNG, Eleanor R.   1918-

*PERSONAL:* Born May 8, 1918, in Boston, Mass.; daughter of John (a florist) and Annie (Weinstein) Robbins; married Herbert Young (a manufacturer and importer), January 25, 1942; children: Martha Jean (Mrs. Peter Hasselbacher). *Education:* Radcliffe College, A.B., 1939; Boston University, M.Ed., 1960. *Home:* 405 Langley Rd., Newton Center, Mass. 02159; and Deerfield Beach, Fla. (winter residence).

*CAREER:* Elementary teacher in public schools of Newton, Mass., 1959-67; Ginn & Co., Boston, Mass., writer of social studies workbooks and teacher's guides, 1967-69; free-lance writer of children's books and educational materials, 1969—. Consultant to companies manufacturing educational materials and games. *Member:* Pi Lambda Theta.

*WRITINGS: Pearls,* F. Watts, 1970; *Mothers, Mothers, Mothers,* Denison, 1971; *Fathers, Fathers, Fathers,* Denison, 1971; *Rice,* F. Watts, 1971; *Guide to Buying Pearls,* Industrias Heusch Reunidas, S.A. (Barcelona), 1972; *Venereal Disease; the Questions, the Answers,* F. Watts, 1973; *Needlepoint,* F. Watts, 1976; *Crewel Embroidery,* F. Watts, 1976. Also author of *Babies, Babies, Babies* and *Grandmothers.*

Writer of teacher's guides: *Many Peoples, One Country,* with workbook, Ginn, 1971; *Culture Regions in the Eastern Hemisphere,* Heath, 1971; *We the People,* Heath, 1971. Also writer of teacher guide, *The Story of Man's Past,* with workbook, 1969. Writer of independent workbook (not linked to any text), *Skillsbooks for Everyone,* Cebco Standard Publishing, 1971, of teacher's guides for educational cassettes issued by C. E. Merrill, 1970, and of a ten-part "Basic Skills" series. Contributor to workbooks and teacher's guides published by Lyons & Carnahan and Heath.

*WORK IN PROGRESS: Come Along to Greece,* for Denison; *Learning the Metric System, Learning How to Fill Out Forms and Make Applications,* and *Learning about Income Taxes,* all part of the "Basic Skills" series.

*SIDELIGHTS:* With her husband, Eleanor Young made many trips to Europe and the Middle East, and visited the Philippines, Thailand, Japan, and Taiwan, gathering information for her books. Young told *CA:* "Since I am a free-lance writer, assignments come from many sources. . . . The

subject matter has run from pearls to venereal disease; . . . the research is interesting and the work is always challenging." Young is especially proud of her "Basic Skills" series. She comments: "Parents all over the country have been complaining that their children are graduating from high school without mastering certain basic skills. . . . My books are aimed at helping to remedy this situation."

*AVOCATIONAL INTERESTS:* Collecting antiques and art objects.

\*    \*    \*

## YOUNG, Kenneth T(odd)   1916-1972

June 22, 1916—August 29, 1972; Canadian-born American diplomat and U.S. State Department consultant on Asian affairs. Obituaries: *New York Times,* August 30, 1972; *Newsweek,* September 11, 1972.

\*    \*    \*

## YOUNG, Mary Elizabeth   1929-

*PERSONAL:* Born December 16, 1929, in Utica, N.Y.; daughter of Clarence Whitford (a professor) and Mary (Tippit) Young. *Education:* Oberlin College, B.A., 1950; Cornell University, Ph.D., 1955. *Politics:* Democrat. *Home:* 655 French Rd., Rochester, N.Y. 14618. *Office:* Department of History, University of Rochester, Rochester, N.Y. 14627.

*CAREER:* Ohio State University, Columbus, instructor, 1955-58, assistant professor, 1958-63, associate professor, 1963-69, professor of history, 1969-73; University of Rochester, Rochester, N.Y., professor of history, 1973—. *Member:* American Historical Association, Organization of American Historians, Social Science History Association. *Awards, honors:* Louis Pelzer Prize, Mississippi Valley Historical Association for article "The Creek Frauds: A Study of Conscience and Corruption," 1955.

*WRITINGS: Redskins, Ruffleshirts, and Rednecks: Indian Allotments in Alabama and Mississippi, 1830-1860,* University of Oklahoma Press, 1961; (editor with David M. Ellis) *The Frontier in American Development,* Cornell University Press, 1969. Contributor to report of American Indian Policy Review Commission, U.S. Congress, 1977. Contributor of articles to history journals.

*WORK IN PROGRESS: The Price of Progress: The Cherokee Nation and the American Republic;* research on history of public land administration in the nineteenth century.

\*    \*    \*

## YOUNG, Miriam   1913-1974

*PERSONAL:* Born February 26, 1913, in New York, N.Y.; daughter of Frank A. (an actor) and Myrtle (McKenley) Burt; married Walter Young (an artist), September 7, 1934 (deceased); children: Peter, Nancy, Barry. *Education:* Attended Erasmus Hall High School, Brooklyn, N.Y., and then Columbia University. *Home:* Lake Katonah, Katonah, N.Y. 10536. *Agent:* Diarmuid Russell, Russell & Volkening, Inc., 551 Fifth Ave., New York, N.Y. 10017.

*CAREER:* Writer, principally for children.

*WRITINGS—Adult: Mother Wore Tights* (nonfiction), McGraw, 1944; *Heaven Faces West* (fiction), Appleton, 1948.

Juvenile: *Prance, a Carousel Horse,* Crowell, 1950; *Georgie Finds a Grandpa,* Golden Press, 1954; *Five Pennies to Spend,* Golden Press, 1955; *Marco's Chance,* Harcourt,

1959; *Up and Away!*, Harcourt, 1960; *The Most Beautiful Kitten*, Parents' Magazine Press, 1961; *The Dollar Horse*, Harcourt, 1961; *Please Don't Feed Horace*, Dial, 1961; *The Secret of Stone House Farm*, Dial, 1963; *Miss Suzy*, Parents' Magazine Press, 1964; *Jellybeans for Breakfast*, Parents' Magazine Press, 1968; *Billy and Milly*, Lothrop, 1968; *A Bear Named George*, Crown, 1969; *The Witchmobile*, Lothrop, 1969; *If I Drove a Truck*, Lothrop, 1969; *If I Flew a Plane*, Lothrop, 1970; *Slow as a Snail, Quick as a Bird*, Lothrop, 1970; *Something Small*, Putnam, 1970; *Can't You Pretend?*, Putnam, 1970; *Beware the Polar Bear*, Lothrop, 1970; *Peas in a Pod*, Putnam, 1971; *If I Drove a Car*, Lothrop, 1971; *If I Sailed a Boat*, Lothrop, 1971; *If I Drove a Train*, Lothrop, 1972; *Christy and the Cat Jail*, Lothrop, 1972; *Miss Suzy's Easter Surprise*, Parents' Magazine Press, 1972; *King Basil's Birthday*, F. Watts, 1973; *Witch's Garden* (junior novel), Atheneum, 1973; *If I Drove a Tractor*, Lothrop, 1973; *If I Rode a Horse*, Lothrop, 1973; *If I Drove a Bus*, Lothrop, 1973; *If I Rode a Dinosaur*, Lothrop, 1974; *If I Rode an Elephant*, Lothrop, 1974; *Miss Suzy's Birthday*, Parents' Magazine Press, 1974; *Truth and Consequences*, Four Winds, 1975; *No Place for Mitty*, Four Winds, 1976; *So What If It's Raining!*, Parents' Magazine Press, 1976.

*SIDELIGHTS:* Although she wrote mainly for children, Miriam Young's most famous book was *Mother Wore Tights*, an adult bestseller about her life as a "backstage baby" with her parents, vaudevillians who performed for years as the team of Burt and Rosedale. The book was made into what *Time* magazine called "one of Hollywood's most extravagant movie musicals of the 1940s," starring Betty Grable and Dan Dailey. Young described *No Place for Mitty* as "a fictionalized account of my mother's childhood in San Francisco in 1895."

*BIOGRAPHICAL/CRITICAL SOURCES: Book World*, October 26, 1969; *New York Times Book Review*, November 9, 1969; *America*, December 1, 1973; *New York Times*, September 13, 1974; *Time*, September 23, 1974; *Times Literary Supplement*, December 6, 1974; *Childhood Education*, November, 1975; *Language Arts*, May, 1976; *New Republic*, November 27, 1976.†

(Died September 11, 1974)

\* \* \*

## YOUNG, Thomas Daniel 1919-

*PERSONAL:* Born October 22, 1919, in Louisville, Miss.; son of William A. (a physician) and Lula (Wright) Young; married Arlease Lewis, December 21, 1941; children: Thomas Daniel, Jr., Terry Lewis, Kyle David. *Education:* University of Southern Mississippi, B.A., 1941; University of Mississippi, M.A., 1948; Vanderbilt University, Ph.D., 1950. *Religion:* Methodist. *Home:* 857 Highland Crest, Nashville, Tenn. 37205. *Office:* Department of English, Vanderbilt University, Nashville, Tenn. 37203.

*CAREER:* University of Mississippi, University, instructor in English, 1946-48; Mississippi Southern College (now University of Southern Mississippi), Hattiesburg, assistant professor, 1950-51, professor of English and chairman of department, 1951-57, acting dean, Basic College, 1954-55; Delta State College, Cleveland, Miss., professor of English and dean, 1957-61; Vanderbilt University, Nashville, Tenn., dean of admissions, 1961-64, professor of English and chairman, 1964-72, Gertrude Conaway Vanderbilt Professor of English, 1972—. *Military service:* U.S. Army Air Forces, 1942-45. *Member:* Modern Language Association of Amer-

ica, South Atlantic Modern Language Association, (chairman of American literature section, 1970).

*WRITINGS:* (With F. C. Watkins) *The Literature of the South*, Scott, Foresman, 1952, revised edition, 1968; (with M. T. Inge) *Donald Davidson: An Essay and a Bibliography*, Vanderbilt University Press, 1965; (with Ronald Fine) *American Literature: A Critical Survey*, American Book Co., 1968; (editor) *John Crowe Ransom: Critical Essay and a Bibliography*, Louisiana State University, 1968; *John Crowe Ransom: An Introduction*, Steck, 1970; (with Inge) *Donald Davidson*, Twayne, 1971; (editor) *The Literary Correspondence of Allen Tate and Donald Davidson*, University of Georgia Press, 1975; *Gentleman in a Dustcoat: A Biography of John Crowe Ransom*, Louisiana State University, 1976; (author of introduction) Allen Tate, *The Fathers and Other Fiction*, Louisiana State University, 1977; (editor) *The New Criticism and After*, University Press of Virginia, 1977. Contributor of articles to *Modern Fiction Studies*, *Sewanee Review*, *Mississippi Quarterly*, *Southern Review*, *Georgia Review*, and other journals.

*WORK IN PROGRESS: Selected Letters of John Crowe Ransom*, for Louisiana State University; a contribution on Sidney Lanier for *American Writers*.

*SIDELIGHTS:* Thomas Daniel Young's book on John Crowe Ransom is called "the definitive biography" by a *Choice* reviewer. Critic L. D. Rubin writes, "This biography is neither eulogy nor expose, but the kind of intelligent, careful delineation that is appropriate to the subject."

*BIOGRAPHICAL/CRITICAL SOURCES: Books Abroad*, spring, 1967; *Georgia Review*, spring, 1967, spring, 1969; *South Atlantic Quarterly*, spring, 1969; *New Republic*, February 12, 1977; *Book World*, February 20, 1977; *Book Forum*, spring, 1977; *Antioch Review*, spring, 1977; *Christian Century*, April 27, 1977; *Choice*, June, 1977; *Sewanee Review*, July, 1977; *Virginia Quarterly Review*, autumn, 1977.

\* \* \*

## YOUNGBLOOD, Ronald F. 1931-

*PERSONAL:* Born August 10, 1931, in Chicago, Ill.; son of William C. (a banker) and Ethel (Arenz) Youngblood; married Carolyn Johnson, August 16, 1952; children: Glenn, Wendy. *Education:* Valparaiso University, B.A., 1952; Fuller Theological Seminary, B.D., 1955; Dropsie College for Hebrew and Cognate Learning (now Dropsie University), Ph.D., 1961. *Religion:* Baptist. *Office:* Bethel Theological Seminary, 3949 Bethel Dr., St. Paul, Minn. 55112.

*CAREER:* Bethel Theological Seminary, St. Paul, Minn., assistant professor, 1961-65, associate professor, 1965-70, professor of Old Testament, 1970—. Has spent four summers in Europe as translator-editor of the new international version of the *Old Testament*, sponsored by New York International Bible Society. *Member:* Society of Biblical Literature, Evangelical Theological Society, Near East Archaeological Society (member of board).

*WRITINGS: Great Themes of the Old Testament*, Harvest Publishing, 1968, revised and reissued as *The Heart of the Old Testament*, Baker Book, 1971; *Special Day Sermons*, Baker Book, 1973; *Faith of Our Fathers*, Regal Books (Colendale, Calif.), 1976. Contributor of articles to *Journal of Biblical Literature*, *Bulletin of American Schools of Oriental Research*, *Journal of the Evangelical Theological Society*, and *Jewish Quarterly Review*. Editor, *Journal of the Evangelical Theological Society*.

*WORK IN PROGRESS:* Commentaries on Judges, Samuel 1 and 2, Exodus, and Genesis 1 through 11.

*SIDELIGHTS:* Ronald F. Youngblood is fluent in Hebrew and has made seven trips to the Middle East.

\*          \*          \*

## YU, David C. 1918-

*PERSONAL:* Born July 3, 1918, in Foochow, China; son of Na-heng (a lawyer) and Ming-chien (Hu) Yu; married Ruth Elizabeth Crisman, June 22, 1958 (died, 1963); married second wife Ellen Frances Bolser, February 22, 1969; children: David Nathan, Nancy Ellen. *Education:* Soo Chow University, LL.B., 1941; University of Missouri, M.A., 1950; University of Chicago, Ph.D., 1959. *Home:* 5315 East 17th Ave., Denver, Colo. 80220. *Office:* Colorado Women's College, Montview and Quebec, Denver, Colo. 80220.

*CAREER:* Bluefield State College, Bluefield, W.Va., assistant professor of religion, 1959-61; University of Virginia, Charlottesville, Va., assistant professor of religion, 1961-67, chairman of department, 1962-67; Colorado Women's College, Denver, Colo., associate professor of Asian studies, 1967-70, professor of Asian studies, 1970-73, professor of history of religions, 1973—. Visiting professor of religion, Chinese University of Hong Kong, 1972-73; member of undergraduate curriculum project, State of New York Center of Foreign Area Materials, 1972—; board member of University of Chicago alumni fund, 1971-74. *Member:* American Association of University Professors, Association for Asian Studies, American Academy of Religion, Society for the Study of Chinese Religion, International Society for Chinese Philosophy.

*WRITINGS:* (With S. Vernon McCasland and Grace E. Cairns) *Religions of the World,* Random House, 1969; (with Laurence G. Thompson) *A Guide to Chinese Religion,* G. K. Hall, 1978; (contributor) Donald H. Bishop, editor, *Chinese Thought: An Introduction,* Philosophical Library, 1978. Contributor to *International Encyclopedia of Higher Education,* 1977. Contributor to *Journal of American Academy of Religions, History of Religions, Journal of Asian Studies, Journal of Scientific Study of Religion, Chinese Culture, Christian Century,* and other journals.

*WORK IN PROGRESS: The Religious Dimension of Maoism.*

\*          \*          \*

## YURCHENCO, Henrietta 1916-

*PERSONAL:* Born March 22, 1916, in New Haven, Conn.; daughter of Edward and Rebecca (Birnblum) Weiss; married Basil Yurchenco, 1936 (divorced, 1955); married Irving Levine (an architect), 1965; children: (first marriage) Peter. *Education:* Studied composition and piano, 1926-36; attended Yale University, 1935-37, and David Mannes College of Music, 1936-38. *Home:* 360 West 22nd St., New York, N.Y. 10011. *Office:* School of Music, City College of the City University of New York, New York, N.Y. 10031.

*CAREER:* WNYC-Radio, New York City, producer, 1939-41, 1960-69; WBAI-Radio, New York City, producer, 1959-61; teacher of folk music at New School for Social Research, New York City, 1961-68, at Queens College of the City University of New York, Flushing, N.Y., and Brooklyn College of the City University of New York, Brooklyn, N.Y., 1966-68; City College of the City University of New York, New York City, associate professor, 1963-78, professor of music, 1978—. Member of folk music panel, U.S. State Department of Performing Arts, 1967-72. Has recorded folk and primitive music for Library of Congress, U.S. State Department, Governments of Mexico and Guatemala, and others. *Member:* Society of Asian Music (member of executive board), Society of Ethnomusicology, International Folk Music Council. *Awards, honors:* Five grants from American Philosophical Society for research in Spain, North Africa, Balearic Islands, Mexico, South America, and Puerto Rico; similar grants from Library of Congress, U.S. State Department, Departments of Education of Mexico and Guatemala, City University of New York, and Instituto de Antropologia e Historia de Mexico.

*WRITINGS: A Fiesta of Folksongs from Spain and Latin America,* Putnam, 1967; *A Mighty Hard Road: The Woody Guthrie Story,* McGraw, 1970; *Hablamos!: Puerto Ricans Speak,* Praeger, 1971. Folk music editor for *American Record Guide, Sing Out!, Musical America,* and *Music Library Notes.*

*SIDELIGHTS:* Henrietta Yurchenco has recorded field material consisting of music from Mexico, Guatemala, Puerto Rico, and John's Island in South Carolina, which has been released under Library of Congress, Nonesuch, Folkways, and Asch labels. She told *CA:* "These recordings are the most important publications of my career as an ethnomusicologist. They include music from Indian, Afro-Caribbean, mestizo, and Spanish sources. I cannot at this moment calculate the exact number of songs and instrumental pieces but there are thousands. These include ritual songs (including peyote chants), songs celebrating the food gathering, hunting, and agricultural stages [of culture development], children's songs, cult music, traditional love songs, pre-hispanic chants, music for the dance, various instrumental ensembles, etc. I was the pioneer recorder of Indian music in Mexico and Guatemala."

# Z

## ZABLOCKI, Benjamin 1941-

*PERSONAL:* Born January 19, 1941, in Brooklyn, N.Y.; son of Henry Isaac (a pharmacist) and Ethel (Kuby) Zablocki; married Elaine Finkelstein, September 16, 1962 (divorced, 1966); married Lisa Rossman, September 1, 1971; children: (first marriage) Abraham; (second marriage) Daniel, Matthew. *Education:* Columbia University, B.A., 1962; Johns Hopkins University, Ph.D., 1967. *Residence:* Highland Park, N.J. 08904. *Office:* Department of Sociology, Rutgers University, New Brunswick, N.J. 08903.

*CAREER:* University of California, Berkeley, assistant professor of sociology, 1966-72; formerly affiliated with department of sociology, Columbia University, New York, N.Y.; currently associate professor of sociology, Rutgers University, New Brunswick, N.J. Research sociologist, Haight-Ashbury Project, Mt. Zion Hospital, San Francisco, Calif. *Member:* American Sociological Association.

*WRITINGS: The Joyful Community,* Penguin, 1971; *Alienation and Charisma,* Free Press, 1978.

*WORK IN PROGRESS:* Research on communes, simulations of social processes, collective behavior, and collective decision making.

*       *       *

## ZACEK, Joseph Frederick 1930-

*PERSONAL:* Surname is pronounced *Zah*-check; born December 18, 1930, in Berwyn, Ill.; son of Joseph (a machinist) and Emilie (Dvorakova) Zacek; married Judith Ellen Cohen (a historian), February 15, 1963 (divorced, 1975); children: Natalie Ann. *Education:* University of Illinois, B.A. (summa cum laude), 1952, M.A., 1953, Ph.D., 1962; Columbia University, certificate of Institute on East Central Europe, 1962. *Office:* Department of History, State University of New York, Albany, N.Y. 12222.

*CAREER:* Occidental College, Los Angeles, Calif., assistant professor of history, 1962-65; University of California, Los Angeles, assistant professor of history, 1965-68; State University of New York at Albany, associate professor, 1968-71, professor of history, 1971—, chairman of department, 1974-77. Visiting scholar, Institute on East Central Europe, Columbia University, 1977-78. Member of National Board of Consultants, National Endowment for the Humanities, 1975—. Consultant, Center for Global Perspectives, 1978—, State University of New York Press, *Choice: Books*

*for College Libraries,* and to various professional journals and publishers. *Military service:* U.S. Army, 1954-57; served in Intelligence Corps. *Member:* American Historical Association, American Association for the Advancement of Slavic Studies, Conference Group for Central European History, Conference on Slavic and East European History, Northeastern Slavic Conference, Far Western Slavic Conference (secretary-treasurer, 1965-68), Immigration Study Group, Group for the Study of Nationalism, Phi Beta Kappa, Phi Kappa Phi, Phi Alpha Theta. *Awards, honors:* Ford Foundation Foreign Area Training fellowships, 1960-62; research and travel grants for the study of the Soviet Union and Eastern Europe from Haynes Foundation, American Council of Learned Societies, American Philosophical Society, Duke Foundation, International Research and Exchanges Board, National Science Foundation, State University of New York Research Foundation, University of Minnesota Immigration History Research Center, and Rockefeller Foundation.

*WRITINGS: The Soviet Union* (history textbook), University of California Extension, Berkeley, 1966; *Palacky: The Historian as Scholar and Nationalist,* Mouton, 1970, Humanities, 1971.

Contributor: Joseph Dunner, editor, *Handbook of World History: Concepts and Issues,* Philosophical Library, 1967; Stephen Horak, compiler, *Junior Slavica: A Selected Annotated Bibliography of Books in English on Russia and Eastern Europe,* Libraries Unlimited, 1968; Miloslav Rechcigl, Jr., editor, *Czechoslovakia, Past and Present,* Volume I: *Political, International, Social and Economic Aspects,* Humanities, 1968; (author of introduction) Robert J. Kerner, *Bohemia in the Eighteenth Century: A Study in Political, Economic, and Social History, with Special Reference to the Reign of Leopold II, 1790-1792,* 2nd edition, Academic International, 1969; Charles Jelavich, editor, *Language and Area Studies, East Central and Southeastern Europe: A Survey,* University of Chicago Press, 1969; Peter F. Sugar and Ivo J. Lederer, editors, *Nationalism in Eastern Europe,* University of Washington Press, 1969.

Peter Brock and H. Gordon Skilling, editors, *The Czech Renascence of the Nineteenth Century: Essays in Honour of Otakar Odlozilik,* University of Toronto Press, 1970; Raymond Phineas Stearns, *Science in the British Colonies of America* (winner of National Book Award, 1970), University of Illinois Press, 1970; Peter F. Sugar, editor, *Native*

*Fascism in the Successor States, 1918-1945,* American Bibliographical Center-Clio Press, 1971; A. Vantuch and L. Holotik, editors, *Der oesterreichisch-ungarische Ausgleich, 1867,* Slovak Academy of Sciences, 1971; A. Cienciala, editor, *American Contributions to the Seventh International Congress of Slavists,* Volume III, Mouton, 1973; *Studies in Czechoslavak History,* Volume I, [Meerut, India], 1976.

Editor of "Central and East European Series," Academic International, 1970—. Contributor of articles on Eastern Europe, especially on Czech and Slovak affairs and peoples, to *American Philosophical Society Yearbook, Encyclopedia Americana, Encyclopedia Year Book,* and *Austrian History Yearbook,* and to various newspapers and journals, including *Journal of Central European Affairs, Occidental Impromptu, Slavic Review, Los Angeles Times, East European Quarterly, Vecernik* (Bratislava), *Canadian Slavic Studies,* and to *Proceedings* of the Institute of World Affairs.

Contributor of reviews to *American Historical Review, Historian, Polish Review, Journal of Modern History, Slavic Review, East European Quarterly, Austrian History Yearbook, International Migration Review,* and to other periodicals. Contributor of regular section to "Bibliographical Supplement" of *Canadian-American Slavic Studies* (formerly called *Canadian Slavic Studies*), 1968—; contributor of regular section on Czechoslovakia to *New Slavic Publications: A Guide to Selection and Acquisition in the Social Sciences and Humanities* (Association of Research Libraries publication), 1970-72; contributor of annual section on Czech and Slovak nationalism to annotated bibliography of *Canadian Review of Studies in Nationalism.* Corresponding editor, *Canadian-American Slavic Studies,* 1968—; associate editor, *East Central Europe* (University of Pittsburgh, Center for International Studies publication), 1972—; member of editorial advisory board, *Canadian Review of Studies in Nationalism.*

*WORK IN PROGRESS: Palacky and the Revival of the Czech Nation*; translating Edward Benes' *Munich Days* into English, for Cornell University Press; *The Czechs and Slovaks in America,* for Twayne's series, "The Immigration Heritage of America"; editing and contributing to *Frantisek Palacky (1798-1876): A Centennial Appreciation; A Modern History of the Czechs and Slovaks;* an article entitled "Czechs in America," for *Harvard Encyclopedia of American Ethnic Groups.*

*SIDELIGHTS:* Joseph Frederick Zacek has scholarly competence in French, German, Czech, Slovak, Russian, and Hungarian, and since 1954 has frequently lived and traveled throughout Europe, especially Central and Eastern Europe, except in the country of Albania. He told *CA:* "As an American scholar of Czech extraction, I am devoted to helping to arrange that 'white ethnics' are properly represented in U.S. history, and *East* European history properly represented in *general* European history."

\*      \*      \*

### ZANTS, Emily   1937-

*PERSONAL:* Born August 3, 1937, in Tulsa, Okla.; daughter of Emil (a cutler) and Edna Rebecca (Glenn) Zants. *Education:* Stanford University, B.A., 1958; Sorbonne, University of Paris, certificat, 1959; Columbia University, M.A., 1961, Ph.D., 1965. *Office:* Department of European Languages and Literature, University of Hawaii, Honolulu, Hawaii 96822.

*CAREER:* Columbia University, New York, N.Y., in-structor in general studies, 1960-62; Brooklyn College of the City University of New York, Brooklyn, N.Y., instructor in French literature, 1962-67; University of California, Davis, assistant professor of French literature, 1967-72; University of Hawaii, Honolulu, associate professor of French literature, 1972—. *Member:* Modern Language Association of America, American Association of Teachers of French, American Society for Eighteenth Century Studies, American Association of University Professors. *Awards, honors:* French Government scholarship, 1958-59; Mabelle McLeod Lewis Award from Stanford University, 1972.

*WRITINGS: The Aesthetics of the New Novel in France,* University of Colorado Press, 1968. Contributor to *Encyclopedia of World Literature;* contributor of articles and reviews to literature journals.

*WORK IN PROGRESS: The Structure of Flaubert's Novels; Literary Theories and Architecture.*

*SIDELIGHTS:* Emily Zants told *CA:* "Language perpetuates the social structure by its relatively permanent form. The visual arts provide a more dynamic means of change where needed than the linguistic medium. But since people perceive only what they are accustomed to seeing, verbal means are necessary to call attention to new forms."

\*      \*      \*

### ZATUCHNI, Gerald I.   1935-

*PERSONAL:* Surname is pronounced Za-touch-knee; born October 5, 1935, in Philadelphia, Pa.; son of Samuel and Minnie (Pollack) Zatuchni; married Bette R. Cohen (a designer), June 15, 1958; children: Cheryl Lee, Bettina, Mimi. *Education:* Temple University, A.B., 1954, M.D., 1958, M.Sc., 1965. *Home:* 38 Ch. des Tuileries, Geneva 1293, Switzerland.

*CAREER:* Temple University, Philadelphia, Pa., instructor in obstetrics and gynecology, 1965-66; Population Council, International Postpartum Family Planning Program, New York, N.Y., director, 1966-69; Government of India, New Delhi, consultant, 1969-71; World Health Organization, Geneva, Switzerland, consultant, 1971-73; Government of Iran, adviser, 1973—. Private practice as obstetrician and gynecologist, Philadelphia, 1965-66. *Military service:* U.S. Army, Medical Corps, 1957-62; became captain. *Member:* American College of Obstetricians and Gynecologists, American Association of Planned Parenthood Physicians, American Association for the Advancement of Science, Babcock Honor Surgical Society. *Awards, honors:* Temple University Mosby Award in surgery, 1958; Philipp Williams Award of Obstetrical Society of Philadelphia, 1964.

*WRITINGS: All India Hospital Postpartum Programme Manual,* Department of Family Planning, Government of India, 1969; (contributor) Bernard Berelson, editor, *Family Planning Programs: An International Survey,* Basic Books, 1969; (editor) *Postpartum Family Planning: A Report on the International Program,* McGraw, 1971; *Maternity-Centered Family Planning Programme Guidelines,* World Health Organization, 1971. Writer of monographs and research reports; contributor of about twenty articles to medical and population journals.

*AVOCATIONAL INTERESTS:* Photography, travel (has visited seventy-two countries).†

\*      \*      \*

### ZAX, Melvin   1928-

*PERSONAL:* Born April 14, 1928, in Cambridge, Mass.;

son of Joseph (a real estate manager) and Sadie (Kirshner) Zax; married Joanne Prives (a reading consultant), June 19, 1952 (divorced October, 1976); married Ruth V. Isaacson (an administrator), April 23, 1977; children: (first marriage) Jeffrey Stephen, David Bruce, Jonathan Barry. *Education:* Boston University, A.B., 1951, A.M., 1952; University of Tennessee, Ph.D., 1955. *Religion:* Jewish. *Home:* 575 Mt. Hope Ave., Rochester, N.Y. 14620. *Office:* Department of Psychology, University of Rochester, River Campus Station, Rochester, N.Y. 14627.

*CAREER:* St. Elizabeth's Hospital, Washington, D.C., staff psychologist, 1956-57; University of Rochester, Rochester, N.Y., assistant professor, 1952-62, associate professor, 1962-67, professor of psychology, 1967—. Member of National Institute of Mental Health Experimental and Special Training Committee, 1968-72. *Military service:* U.S. Army, 1946-47. *Member:* American Psychological Association, American Association of University Professors, Eastern Psychological Association.

*WRITINGS:* (With George Stricker) *Patterns of Psychotherapy,* Macmillan, 1963; (with Stricker) *The Study of Abnormal Behavior,* Macmillan, 1964, 2nd edition, 1969; (editor with E. L. Cowen and E. A. Gardner) *Emergent Approaches to Mental Health Problems,* Appleton, 1967; (with Cowen) *Abnormal Psychology: Changing Conceptions,* Holt, 1972; (with G. A. Specter) *An Introduction to Community Psychology,* Wiley, 1974; (with F. McKinney and R. P. Lorion) *Effective Behavior and Human Development,* Macmillan, 1976; (with M. P. Nichols) *Catharsis in Psychotherapy,* Gardiner Press, 1977. Advisory editor, *Journal of Consulting and Clinical Psychology.*

*WORK IN PROGRESS:* Research on neonatal factors in serious mental illness; a book on comparative approaches to child discipline.

\* \* \*

## ZELLERS, Parker 1927-

*PERSONAL:* Born March 25, 1927, in Worcester, Mass.; son of Lloyd P. and Ethel (Richardson) Zellers. *Education:* Emerson College, B.A., 1950; Indiana University, M.A., 1956; University of Iowa, Ph.D., 1964. *Home:* 777 Washtenaw, Ypsilanti, Mich. 48197. *Office:* Department of Speech and Dramatic Arts, Eastern Michigan University, Ypsilanti, Mich. 48197.

*CAREER:* Monmouth College, Monmouth, Ill., instructor, 1956-59, assistant professor of speech and drama, 1960-61; Eastern Michigan University, Ypsilanti, assistant professor, 1964-66, associate professor, 1967-70, professor of speech and dramatic arts, 1971—. *Military service:* U.S. Army, 1945-46; became sergeant. *Member:* Speech Communication Association, American Theatre Association, Michigan Speech Association.

*WRITINGS: Tony Pastor: Dean of the Vaudeville Stage,* Eastern Michigan University Press, 1971. Contributor to *Educational Theatre Journal.*

\* \* \*

## ZIEMKE, Earl F(rederick) 1922-

*PERSONAL:* Born December 16, 1922, in Wisconsin; married Ida Mae Saltenberger, June 12, 1949; children: Caroline. *Education:* University of Wisconsin, B.S.Ed., 1948, M.A., 1949, Ph.D., 1952; Catholic University of America, M.S.L.S., 1957. *Religion:* Episcopalian. *Home:* 400 Brookwood Dr., Athens, Ga. 30604. *Office:* Department of History, University of Georgia, Athens, Ga. 30601.

*CAREER:* Columbia University, Bureau of Applied Social Science Research, Alexandria, Va., researcher, 1951-56; Department of the Army, Office of the Chief of Military History, Washington, D.C., historian, 1956-67; University of Georgia, Athens, university research professor of history, 1967—. *Military service:* U.S. Marine Corps, 1943-46. *Member:* American Historical Association, Association of American University Professors, American Military Institute. *Awards, honors:* Meritorious Civilian Service Award, Department of the Army, 1967.

*WRITINGS: The German Northern Theater of Operations,* U.S. Government Printing Office, 1959; (contributor) K. K. Greenfield, editor, *Command Decisions,* Harcourt, 1962; (contributor) V. C. Esposito, editor, *A Concise History of World War II,* Praeger, 1964; *Stalingrad to Berlin,* U.S. Government Printing Office, 1968; *The Fall of Berlin,* Ballantine, 1969; *The Army in the Occupation of Germany,* U.S. Government Printing Office, 1976.

*WORK IN PROGRESS: Moscow to Stalingrad.*

\* \* \*

## ZIF, Jay Jehiel 1936-

*PERSONAL:* Surname legally changed; born December 10, 1936, in Israel; son of Isaac and Ester (Greenwald) Silberstein; married Yael Levy (a lecturer), March 21, 1961; children: Ronit, Dror Daniel. *Education:* Technion-Israel Institute of Technology, B.S., 1958, Dipl.Ing., 1959; New York University, M.B.A., 1962, Ph.D., 1966. *Religion:* Jewish.

*CAREER:* High school physics teacher in Haifa, Israel, 1957-58; Technion-Israel Institute of Technology, Tel-Aviv, Israel, lecturer on management and industrial engineering in Extension Division, 1959-61; Maidenform, Inc., New York, N.Y., industrial engineer, 1962-64; H. P. Hood & Sons, Inc., Boston, Mass., manager of marketing research, 1964-67; Abt Associates, Inc., Cambridge, Mass., area manager for marketing information systems, 1967-68; Creative Studies, Inc. (educational research and development), Boston, founder and president, beginning 1968. Part-time associate professor of management science, Northeastern University, 1966-71. *Military service:* Israel Defense Forces, 1958-60; became lieutenant. *Member:* Institute of Management Science, American Marketing Association.

*WRITINGS:* (With R. E. Otlewski) *Contract Negotiations,* Macmillan, 1970; (with Arthur H. Walker and William T. Archey) *Managing the Worker,* Macmillan, 1970; (with Walker and Eliezer Orbach) *The Personnel Department,* Macmillan, 1970; (with Walker, Orbach, and Howard Schwartz) *Reorganization,* Macmillan, 1970; (with Iqal Ayal and Orbach) *Marketing a New Product,* Macmillan, 1971; (with W. J. Jenkins) *Planning the Advertising Campaign,* Macmillan, 1971; (with Ayal and Orbach) *Supermarket Strategy,* Macmillan, 1971; (with Orbach, Archey, and Ayal) *Sales Strategy and Management,* Macmillan, 1971; (with Raymond A. Montgomery and Stephen J. Fischer) *Inner City Planning,* Macmillan, 1971; (with Montgomery and Fischer) *Yes But Not Here,* Macmillan, 1971; (with Dov Izraeli) *Societal Marketing Boards,* Halsted, 1977.†

\* \* \*

## ZIMMERMAN, Ed 1933(?)-1972

1933(?)—July 6, 1972; American actor and novelist. Obituaries: *New York Times,* July 8, 1972.

## ZIMMERMAN, Irene 1907-

*PERSONAL:* Born February 23, 1907, in Idana, Kan.; daughter of Harvey A. (a Presbyterian minister) and Mary Catherine (Mechlin) Zimmerman. *Education:* College of Emporia, B.A., 1927; University of Chicago, M.A. (Spanish), 1937; Columbia University, M.A. (history), 1938; University of Michigan, A.M.L.S., 1951, Ph.D., 1956; summer study at University of Mexico, 1931, University of Hawaii, 1933, Middlebury College, 1943, University of Havana, 1946, and University of Southern California, 1950. *Politics:* Democrat. *Religion:* Protestant. *Home:* 1126 Northwest 33rd Ave., Gainesville, Fla. 32601.

*CAREER:* High school teacher of Spanish and history in Ray, Ariz., 1928-37, in Spokane, Wash., 1939-41, in Teaneck, N.J., 1941-43; Colby Junior College, New London, N.H., instructor in Spanish and Latin American literature and history, 1943-48; Bucknell University, Lewisburg, Pa., instructor in Spanish language and literature, 1948-50; University of Florida Libraries, Gainesville, assistant librarian, 1951-62, associate librarian, 1962-69, librarian, 1969-77, librarian of Latin American collection, 1967-77. Visiting summer professor, University of Michigan, 1966. *Member:* Association of College and Research Libraries, American Library Association (life member), Seminars on Acquisition of Latin American Library Materials (chairman of committee on bibliography, 1964-67), Latin American Studies Association, American Association of University Professors, Southeastern Library Association, Southeastern Conference on Latin American Studies, Pi Kappa Delta, Pi Gamma Mu, Sigma Delta Pi, Phi Alpha Theta, Beta Phi Mu.

*WRITINGS: Guide to Current Latin American Periodicals: Humanities and Social Sciences,* Kallman, 1961; *Current National Bibliographies of Latin America: A State of the Art Study,* Center for Latin American Studies, University of Florida, 1971. Contributor to library journals.

*AVOCATIONAL INTERESTS:* Politics, international relations, race relations, travel, swimming.

\*          \*          \*

## ZIMPEL, Lloyd 1929-

*PERSONAL:* Born September 2, 1929, in Princeton, Minn.; son of George and Erna (Kuether) Zimpel; married Nina Youkelson (a teacher), June 16, 1956; children: Benjamin, Jason, Aaron. *Education:* University of Minnesota, B.A., 1954; graduate study at University of Iowa, 1956-57, and San Francisco State College (now University), 1960-61. *Home:* 38 Liberty St., San Francisco, Calif. 94110. *Agent:* Ruth Cantor, 156 Fifth Ave., New York, N.Y. 10010.

*CAREER:* West Coast Life Insurance Co., San Francisco, Calif., advertising director, 1959-63; California Fair Employment Practice Commission, San Francisco, education officer, 1963—. *Military service:* U.S. Army, 1951-53; served in Korea. *Awards, honors:* Quill Awards from University of Massachusetts, 1961, 1968, for best short story of the year in *Massachusetts Review.*

*WRITINGS:* (With Daniel Panger) *Business and the Hardcore Unemployed,* Fell, 1970; (editor) *The Disadvantaged Worker,* Addison-Wesley, 1971; *Meeting the Bear: Journal of the Black Wars,* Macmillan, 1971. Contributor to literary and national magazines, including *Nation, New Republic, Carleton Miscellany, Transatlantic Review,* and *Commonweal.*

*WORK IN PROGRESS: City Notes,* a novel; *The New Worker,* a collection of essahs on the bluecollar worker of the 1970's; *Workingmen,* a collection of short stories.

\*          \*          \*

## ZOBER, Martin 1918-

*PERSONAL:* Born June 12, 1918, in Pittsburgh, Pa.; son of Morris (a merchant) and Fanny (Chasinoff) Zober; married Edith Swartz (a research consultant), December 21, 1940; children: Norman Alan, Janet Ruth (deceased). *Education:* University of Pittsburgh, B.A., 1940, M.Litt., 1943, Ph.D., 1950. *Politics:* Democrat. *Religion:* Jewish. *Home:* 615 Carr Dr., Ames, Iowa 50010. *Office:* Department of Industrial Administration, Iowa State University of Science and Technology, Ames, Iowa 50010.

*CAREER:* Upper Iowa University, assistant professor of marketing, 1947-51; Drake University, Des Moines, Iowa, associate professor of marketing, 1951-57; Iowa State University of Science and Technology, Ames, professor of marketing, 1957—. Consultant to Meredith Press, Maytag Co., and to other companies and advertising agencies. *Military service:* U.S. Army, paratrooper, 82nd Airborne Division, 1943-45; received Purple Heart. *Member:* American Marketing Association (president of Iowa chapter, 1957-58), National Association of Purchasing Management.

*WRITINGS: Marketing Management,* Wiley, 1964; *Principles of Marketing,* Allyn & Bacon, 1971.

*WORK IN PROGRESS:* A book on sales forecasting and one on a holistic approach to the social responsibility of business.

\*          \*          \*

## ZODIKOFF, David H(yman) 1933-

*PERSONAL:* Born March 31, 1933, in Binghamton, N.Y.; son of Jacob and Ellen (Rothschild-Meier) Zodikoff; married Christina Goloshevski (a teacher), June 9, 1957; children: Michele. *Education:* Cortland State Teachers College (now State University of New York College at Cortland), B.S., 1957; Columbia University, M.A., 1960; Syracuse University, Ed.D., 1967. *Religion:* Jewish. *Home:* 6 Henry St., Homer, N.Y. 13077. *Office:* Department of Education, State University of New York College, Cortland, N.Y. 13045.

*CAREER:* Elementary and junior high school teacher in Islip, N.Y., 1957-65; State University of New York College at Cortland, assistant professor, 1967-69, associate professor of social studies education, 1969—. Consultant for Jerome Bruner's "Man: A Course of Study." *Military service:* U.S. Navy, 1950-54. *Member:* American Association of Colleges for Teacher Education, American Federation of Teachers, National Council for Social Studies, New York State Council for Social Studies, B'nai B'rith (president of local chapter, 1973-74).

*WRITINGS:* (Editor) *Readings in Social Studies Education,* MSS Educational Publishing Co., 1971; *Comprehensive Teaching Models in Social Studies Education,* Kendall/Hunt, 1973, revised edition published as *Alternative Teaching Models in Social Studies Education,* 1976. Social studies consultant and book reviewer for *Choice.* Contributor of articles to education journals.

*WORK IN PROGRESS:* A text dealing with personal reflections of public school and college teaching.

## ZONIS, Marvin 1936-

*PERSONAL:* Born September 18, 1936, in Boston, Mass. *Education:* Attended Harvard University, 1957, graduate study, 1958-59; Yale University, B.A., 1958; Massachusetts Institute of Technology, Ph.D., 1968. *Home:* 4938 South Ellis Ave., Chicago, Ill. 60615. *Office:* Pick 213, University of Chicago, 5828 South University, Chicago, Ill. 60637.

*CAREER:* Massachusetts Institute of Technology, Cambridge, instructor in political science, 1965-66; University of Chicago, Chicago, Ill., assistant professor of political and social science, 1966-71, associate professor of behavioral sciences, 1971—, director, Center for Middle Eastern Studies, 1975—. *Member:* American Council of Learned Societies-Social Science Research Council Joint Committee on the Middle East (chairman, 1970-76), American Institute of Iranian Studies (president, 1969-71). *Awards, honors:* Research training fellowship of Social Science Research Council, 1963-65.

*WRITINGS: Education and Development: Selecting a Sample of Iranian Secondary Schools,* National Teachers' College Press (Tehran), 1965; *A Study of the Future "Technocrats" of Iran: The Formation of a Development Cadre,* National Teachers' College Press, 1965; *The Political Elite of Iran,* Princeton University Press, 1971; (co-author) *An Analysis of U.S.–Iranian Cooperation in Higher Education,* American Council of Education, 1976.

Contributor: Tareq Y. Ismael, *Comparative Politics of the Middle East,* Dorsey, 1970; Michael Adams, editor, *The Middle East,* Anthony Blond, 1971; E. Yar Shater, editor, *Iran Faces the 1970's,* Praeger, 1971; F. Tachau, editor, *Comparative Politics of the Middle East,* Schenkman, 1974. Contributor of articles to *Comparative Political Studies, Iranian Studies, Technology Review, Middle East Journal, American Journal of Sociology, American Political Science Review,* and *Journal of Psychohistory.*

*WORK IN PROGRESS: Political Socialization and Political Development,* a book based on a survey of a national sample of 5500 Iranian students; *The Role of the Individual in Social and Political Development.*

\* \* \*

## ZOPF, Paul E(dward), Jr. 1931-

*PERSONAL:* Born July 9, 1931, in Bridgeport, Conn.; son of Paul E. (a cabinetmaker) and Hilda E. (Russell) Zopf; married Evelyn L. Montgomery, August 5, 1956; children: Eric Paul. *Education:* University of Connecticut, B.S., 1953; University of Florida, M.S., 1955, Ph.D., 1966; post-doctoral study, Tulane University, 1956-57. *Politics:* Independent. *Religion:* Quaker. *Home:* 815 George White Rd., Greensboro, N.C. 27410. *Office:* Department of Sociology, Guilford College, Greensboro, N.C. 27410.

*CAREER:* Guilford College, Greensboro, N.C., assistant professor, 1959-66, associate professor, 1966-68, professor, 1968-71, Dana Professor of Sociology, 1971—. Laboratory technician, University of Connecticut, summers, 1953-57; University of Florida, laboratory technician, 1957-59, research assistant, 1965-66. *Member:* American Sociological Association, Rural Sociological Society, International Union for Scientific Study of Population, American Academy of Political and Social Science, Southern Sociological Society, North Carolina Sociological Society.

*WRITINGS: North Carolina: A Demographic Profile,* Carolina Population Center, 1967; (with T. Lynn Smith) *Demography: Principles and Methods,* F. A. Davis, 1970, 2nd edition, Alfred Publishing, 1976; (with Smith) *Principles of Inductive Rural Sociology,* F. A. Davis, 1970; *The People of Guilford County,* Greensboro Chamber of Commerce, 1972; *A Demographic and Occupational Profile of State Planning Region G,* Carolina Population Center, 1974; *Profile of Women in Greensboro: 1990,* City of Greensboro, 1977; *Sociocultural Systems,* University Press of America, 1978. Contributor of articles and reviews to professional journals.

*WORK IN PROGRESS: Cultural Accumulation in Latin America; The Demography of Death.*

*SIDELIGHTS:* Paul Zopf told *CA:* "Several of my books and other writings are closely related to the college courses I teach. Therefore, they are designed chiefly to help students, to expand my own depth and breadth of study, and to enhance my academic career. I attempt to transform some of the more abstract and difficult areas of social science into intelligible forms and to broaden the acquaintanceship with sociological knowledge and insight. Another substantial share of my work is done in a community-service context to analyze local demographic and occupational conditions [for planning agencies and various local governments] and to point up such problems as I can identify."

*AVOCATIONAL INTERESTS:* Woodworking, gardening, clockmaking, mineral hunting, archaeology.

\* \* \*

## ZSOLDOS, Laszlo 1925-

*PERSONAL:* Born January 29, 1925, in Szentes, Hungary; naturalized American citizen in 1956; son of Laszlo (an executive) and Adrienne (Hainrickffy) Zsoldos; married Silvia Tammisto, December 21, 1952; children: Peter, Diane, Carolyn. *Education:* Attended University of Kolozsvar, 1942-44, and Jozsef Nador University of Technology, 1944-48; University of Cincinnati, A.B., 1952, M.A., 1955; Ohio State University, Ph.D., 1961. *Home:* 22 North Wynwyd Dr., Newark, Del. 19711. *Office:* Department of Economics, University of Delaware, Newark, Del. 19711.

*CAREER:* Palmer Thermometers, Inc., Cincinnati, Ohio, cost analyst, 1952-54; Ohio State University, Columbus, instructor in economics, 1957-60; University of Kentucky, Lexington, assistant professor of economics, 1960-64; University of Delaware, Newark, assistant professor, 1960-64, associate professor, 1964-69, professor of economics, 1969—, chairman of department, 1967-70, acting dean, College of Business and Economics, 1970-72. Participated in Ford Foundation Workshop in International Business, Workshop of Joint Council for Economic Education, and in Voice of America round table interviews. *Member:* American Economic Association, Association for the Study of Soviet-type Economies, American Business History Conference, Southern Conference on Slavic Studies, Omicron Delta Epsilon, Beta Gamma Sigma. *Awards, honors:* William Howard Taft Memorial fellowship, 1955; Earhart fellowship, 1957.

*WRITINGS: The Economic Integration of Hungary into the Soviet Bloc,* Ohio State University Press, 1963; (with Max J. Wasserman and Charles W. Hultman) *International Finance,* Heath, 1967; (contributor) Paul Horecky, editor, *Eastern Europe: An Annotated Bibliography,* University of Chicago Press, 1969; (contributor) Zbigniew M. Fallenbuchl, editor, *Economic Development in the Soviet Union and Eastern Europe,* Volume II, Praeger, 1976. Contributor to economics journals.

## ZUBEK, John P(eter) 1925-

*PERSONAL:* Born March 10, 1925, in Trnovec, Czechoslovakia; son of John Joseph and Mary (Hrubos) Zubek; married Mary Sparling (a high school teacher), July 1, 1961; children: Elizabeth. *Education:* University of British Columbia, B.A., 1946; University of Toronto, M.A., 1948; Johns Hopkins University, Ph.D., 1950. *Politics:* "No political affiliation." *Religion:* Roman Catholic. *Office:* Department of Psychology, University of Manitoba, Winnipeg, Manitoba, Canada.

*CAREER:* McGill University, Montreal, Quebec, assistant professor of psychology, 1950-53; University of Manitoba, Winnipeg, professor of psychology, 1953-61, research professor of psychology, 1961—, head of department, 1953-61, director of Sensory Deprivation Laboratory, 1959—. *Member:* American Association for the Advancement of Science, American Psychological Association, Canadian Psychological Association (fellow), Manitoba Psychological Society, New York Academy of Sciences, Phi Beta Kappa. *Awards, honors:* Defense Research Board of Canada grant, 1959-72; U.S. Public Health Service grant, 1964-67.

*WRITINGS:* (With P. A. Solberg) *Doukhobors at War,* Ryerson, 1952; (with Solberg) *Human Development,* McGraw, 1954; (editor) *Sensory Deprivation,* Appleton, 1969; (editor with A. W. Pressey) *Readings in General Psychology: Canadian Contributions,* McClelland & Stewart, 1970; (editor with Lois M. Brockman and J. H. Whiteley) *Child Development: Selected Readings,* McClelland & Stewart, 1973. Contributor of about eighty articles to scientific journals.

*WORK IN PROGRESS:* Research on physiological and behavioral effects of prolonged isolation and confinement.

*AVOCATIONAL INTERESTS:* Military history (Napoleonic period), world travel.†

\*    \*    \*

## ZUCKER, David Hard 1938-

*PERSONAL:* Born May 27, 1938, in Cleveland, Ohio; son of Lester and Louise (Hard) Zucker; married Susan Shapiro, March 11, 1962; children: Erika Abby, Amy Isabel. *Education:* Oberlin College, B.A., 1960; Syracuse University, M.A., 1964, Ph.D., 1968. *Politics:* Liberal Democrat. *Religion:* Jewish. *Home:* 34 Gordon St., Hamden, Conn. 06517. *Office:* Department of English, Quinnipiac College, Hamden, Conn. 06518.

*CAREER:* Columbia University Press, New York, N.Y., assistant editor, 1960-62; Syracuse University, Syracuse, N.Y., instructor in English, 1962-68; Washington and Lee University, Lexington, Va., assistant professor of English, 1968-71; Quinnipiac College, Hamden, Conn., assistant professor, 1971-73, associate professor of English, 1973—. *Military service:* U.S. Army Reserve, 1961-62. *Awards, honors:* National Endowment for the Humanities fellow, 1974, 1977; Yale University summer faculty fellowship, 1975.

*WRITINGS:* (Editor with Donald A. Dike) *Selected Essays of Delmore Schwartz,* University of Chicago Press, 1970; *Stage and Image in Plays of Marlowe,* [Salzburg, Austria], 1972. Contributor to literary journals.

*WORK IN PROGRESS:* Writing poetry, fiction, and criticism.

*BIOGRAPHICAL/CRITICAL SOURCES: New York Times,* January 14, 1971.

## ZUCKERMAN, Michael 1939-

*PERSONAL:* Born April 24, 1939, in Philadelphia, Pa.; son of Hyman (a lawyer) and Henrietta (Wolodin) Zuckerman; married Diane Weitzman, June 12, 1966; children: Adam, Harmon, Maria. *Education:* University of Pennsylvania, B.A., 1961; Harvard University, Ph.D., 1967. *Religion:* Jewish. *Home:* 336 South 24th St., Philadelphia, Pa. 19103. *Office:* Department of History, University of Pennsylvania, Philadelphia, Pa. 19104.

*CAREER:* University of Pennsylvania, Philadelphia, instructor, 1965-67, assistant professor, 1967-70, associate professor of history, 1970—. Visiting professor, Johns Hopkins University, University of Oregon, 1970, and Hebrew University (Jerusalem), 1977-78. *Member:* Phi Beta Kappa. *Awards, honors:* Social Science Research Council fellowship, 1968; National Endowment for the Humanities senior fellowship, 1972-73; Guggenheim fellowship, 1977-78 (declined); American Council of Learned Societies fellowship, 1977-78 (declined); Rockefeller fellowship, 1978-79.

*WRITINGS: Peaceable Kingdoms: New England Towns in the Eighteenth Century,* Knopf, 1970; (contributor) Charles Rosenberg, editor, *The Family in History,* University of Pennsylvania Press, 1975; (contributor) John Kushma and Mark Levine, editors, *The New Political History,* University of Pennsylvania Press, 1978. Contributor of articles and reviews to *William and Mary Quarterly, American Quarterly, New England Quarterly,* and other journals.

*BIOGRAPHICAL/CRITICAL SOURCES: New York Times,* April 18, 1970; *Newsweek,* April 20, 1970; *Nation,* August 3, 1970; *Virginia Quarterly Review,* autumn, 1970.

\*    \*    \*

## ZULLI, Floyd 1922-

*PERSONAL:* Born September 22, 1922, in Westbury, N.Y.; married, 1966. *Education:* Lafayette College, B.A., 1943; Columbia University, M.A., 1946; New York University, Ph.D., 1955. *Home:* 8 Monfort Dr., Huntington, N.Y. 11743. *Office:* Department of French-Italian Languages, New York University, Washington Sq., New York, N.Y. 10003.

*CAREER:* Severn School, Severna Park, Md., teacher, 1943-45; New York University, New York, N.Y., instructor, 1946-55, assistant professor, 1956-57, associate professor, 1958-63, professor of Romance languages and comparative literature, 1964—, acting chairman of department, 1962. Television and radio lecturer on books and literature, 1957-68. *Awards, honors:* Four television awards, 1958; Knight of L'Ordre des Palmes Academiques, 1959.

*WRITINGS:* (Editor) Honore de Balzac, *Cousin Bette,* Modern Library, 1958; (editor) Gustave Flaubert, *Madame Bovary,* Modern Library, 1959; (editor) Nathaniel Hawthorne, *The Scarlet Letter,* F. Watts, 1966; (editor) Edgar Allan Poe, *Selected Stories and Poems,* F. Watts, 1967; *Invitation to Great Reading,* Grolier, 1970; *The Joy of Reading,* F. Watts, 1972. Contributor to *Medallion Encyclopedia* and to professional journals. General editor, "Masterworks Program," Doubleday, 1962; member of editorial board, *World's Great Classics,* Grolier, 1969-70.

*WORK IN PROGRESS:* A study of Edmond de Goncourt.

\*    \*    \*

## ZUPKO, Ronald Edward 1938-

*PERSONAL:* Born August 5, 1938, in Youngstown, Ohio;

son of Michael Edward (a teacher) and Frances (Bartek) Zupko; married Kathleen Monroe (a teacher), July 27, 1974; children: (previous marriage) Sarah Josefina. *Education:* Youngstown State University, B.A., 1960; University of Chicago, M.A., 1963; University of Wisconsin, Ph.D., 1966. *Home:* 526 North 77th St., Wauwatosa, Wis. 53213. *Office:* Department of History, Marquette University, Charles L. Coughlin Hall, Milwaukee, Wis. 53233.

*CAREER:* Marquette University, Milwaukee, Wis., assistant professor, 1966-69, associate professor, 1969-75, professor of medieval economic and social history, 1976—. Assistant chairman of department of history, 1971-75. Member of faculty, School of Historical Studies, Institute for Advanced Study, Princeton, N.J., 1975. *Member:* Mediaeval Academy of America, Economic History Association, Midwest Medieval Association, Economic Historians of Wisconsin, Pi Gamma Mu, Phi Alpha Theta.

*WRITINGS: A Dictionary of English Weights and Measures from Anglo-Saxon Times to the Nineteenth Century,* University of Wisconsin Press, 1968; *British Weights and Measures: A History from Antiquity to the Seventeenth Century,* University of Wisconsin Press, 1977; *French Weights and Measures before the Revolution: A Dictionary of Provincial and Local Units,* Indiana University Press, 1978. Contributor of many articles to economics, history of science, and medieval studies journals.

*WORK IN PROGRESS: A Dictionary of Weights and Measures for the British Isles from Anglo-Saxon Times to the Twentieth Century,* for University of Wisconsin Press; *Italian Weights and Measures from the Middle Ages to the Nineteenth Century,* for Indiana University Press; *German Weights and Measures: The Sixteenth to the Nineteenth Century,* for Indiana University Press; *British Weights and Measures since the Seventeenth Century: The Impact of Science and Technology.*

\*     \*     \*

## ZYLBERCWEIG, Zalman   1894-1972

1894—July 25, 1972; Polish-born historian of the Yiddish theatre. Obituaries: *New York Times,* July 27, 1972.